THE UNIVERSAL DICTIONARY OF THE ENGLISH LANGUAGE

COPYRIGHT

1938

STANDARD AMERICAN CORPORATION

PRINTED AND BOUND IN THE UNITED STATES
OF AMERICA BY THE CUNEO PRESS, INC.

THE UNIVERSAL DICTIONARY OF THE ENGLISH LANGUAGE

A new and original compilation giving all pronunciations in simplified and in more exact phonetic notations, extensive etymologies, definitions, the latest accepted words in scientific, technical, and general use, with copious illustrative phrases, and colloquialisms

•

Edited by
HENRY CECIL WYLD
B.Litt., M.A., Hon. Ph.D. Upsala, Honorary Member of the Linguistic Society, and of the Modern Language Association of America; Merton Professor of English Language and Literature in the University of Oxford
Author of A HISTORY OF MODERN COLLOQUIAL ENGLISH; A SHORT HISTORY OF ENGLISH; STUDIES IN ENGLISH RHYMES FROM SURREY TO POPE, etc., etc., etc.

With Preface to the American Edition by
ALLEN WALKER READ
B.Litt. (Oxon.), M.A., Research Associate in English, University of Chicago, and
Assistant Editor, *Dictionary of American English on Historical Principles*

•

Published by
STANDARD AMERICAN CORPORATION
CHICAGO, 1938

American Preface

WHERE are the headquarters of the English language? We can point to Washington as the headquarters of the United States government, to Hollywood as the headquarters of the motion picture industry, and to Wall Street as the headquarters of American finance; but with language we have a much more complicated problem. Everyone is free to speak as he chooses, and no man or group of men has the right to dictate to others in this matter. As free citizens of the English-speaking world, we do not acknowledge that the language has any headquarters or that we are bound by any authority. Nevertheless it is a comfort to be able to refer to dictionaries. These works are based on a wider experience with the usage of words than any one person can ever have in his own life. A great body of information about words has been built up over many years, and certain men have made it their business to collect it and to organize it in dictionary form.

This book by Professor Wyld has the highest possible claim as a useful and trustworthy dictionary. Professor Wyld has spent a lifetime in studying English and holds the most important position in all England for the teaching of the English language—the leading professorship in the subject at Oxford University. For several generations a great tradition in dictionary-making has been carried on at Oxford, and Professor Wyld's work represents this tradition at its best. Furthermore, this book is recommended by its universal usefulness as well as by the scholarly reputation of its author.

Inasmuch as the English language is not uniform over all parts of the English-speaking world, the dictionary-maker has a difficult problem to decide what type of English he will record. In the British Isles alone there are, in addition to the numerous dialects, four kinds of "standard" English, and the use of each kind, if the speaker has been brought up in it, is beyond criticism. There is the Scottish standard (used by cultivated Scotsmen), the Irish standard (used by the best people of Dublin), Northern English (spoken over the greater part of England), and Southern English (developed by well-spoken people around London). Many observers believe that Irish speech preserves in best form the features of historic English. Then each of the great British dominions has a speech with a character of its own, and the United States has, since 1776, been rightfully going its own way. The great body of the language, however, is the same in all these parts, and the differences seem important only when one focuses one's attention on details.

Professor Wyld comes from a Scottish family, but his early training and his studies have led him to champion the type of speech found in the south of England. His term for it, "Received Standard," has become widely current. In general it is the kind of English used on the stage in both England and America. Sometimes it is called "Oxford English," particularly when it is overdone by affected people; but on the whole it has achieved greater prestige than any other form of English. Americans will find it of special value to have an accurate record of this variety of English, and Professor Wyld's work has not been altered in these pages.

Since, however, most of our writing and speaking is done in order to communicate with the people round about us, it is the wisest policy for Americans to follow the usage that is generally accepted in the American branch of the language. The differences consist chiefly in intonation, voice quality, and speech tune, and these cannot in any case be recorded in a dictionary; but in addition there are a few special American spellings and pronunciations.

It is amusing to an American to find how

bitterly many Englishmen feel about the so-called American spellings. One would gather from them that the *-or* ending in words like *honor* and the *-er* in words like *center* are corruptions that mark the downfall of the language. It is this class of Englishmen who were up in arms when Noah Webster in 1807 left off the final *k* in *musick, physick, logick,* etc., although later Englishmen have followed him in this. Since our American variations are in the direction of simplicity, they may be regarded as improvements and will no doubt eventually carry the day. In many cases Professor Wyld has given both forms, and Americans may take their choice in such pairs as the following:

BRITISH	AMERICAN
connexion	connection
gaol	jail
omelette	omelet
plough	plow
programme	program
pyjamas	pajamas
storey	story

In other cases well-known American spellings can be substituted without inconvenience. The *-or* ending is to be preferred to the *-our* in words like *behavior, color, honor,* and *labor*. The ending *-er* is preferable in words like *center, sepulcher,* and *theater;* the *l* need not be doubled in *councilor, counselor, traveler;* and an *s* is usual rather than a *c* in *defense* and *pretense*. Other American forms are *curb* rather than *kerb, mold* rather than *mould,* and *cozy* rather than *cosy*.

When a choice between two pronunciations is given, both of them may be regarded as correct, and the second one may represent the better choice for an American. Choices are given, for instance, under *dynasty, garage, neither, patriotic,* and *schedule*. Americans will have no trouble in inserting the *r* in the right places, and the broad *a* rather than the Italian *a* can be substituted in such words as *grass, half,* and *path*. In *docile, fragile, futile, hostile,* etc., the English give the *-ile* its long value, while the Americans pronounce it as a short syllable. In certain words, Professor Wyld has recorded only the usage of his "Received Standard" type of English, and Americans are well-advised to follow the pronunciations that seem normal to them. Examples of these are *again, been, clerk, evolution, lieutenant,* and *quinine*.

A comparison of the various dictionaries produced at Oxford will show beyond a doubt that this one is not only the result of profound and thorough learning but at the same time the easiest for the ordinary user to understand. It is a pleasure to present this monument of scholarship to the American public.

ALLEN WALKER READ, B.LITT. (Oxon.), M.A.
Research Associate in English, University of Chicago, and
Assistant Editor, DICTIONARY OF AMERICAN ENGLISH ON HISTORICAL PRINCIPLES

CHICAGO, 1938

Rules for Pronunciation
(1) Key to the Popular Phonetic Spelling for the use of the General Reader
(2) The System of Phonetic Notation summarized for Advanced Students

THE accepted spelling of English is by no means always a reliable guide to pronunciation. Owing to various historical circumstances English spelling has come to be considerably divorced from the pronunciation. It is *inconsistent*—the same letter does not always stand for the same sound; it is *redundant*—the spelling of many words contains letters which represent no sound at all; it is *incomplete*—some words contain sounds of which the spelling takes no account and for which no letter is written. The important element of accentuation is entirely disregarded.

Under these circumstances, if we wish to indicate the actual pronunciation of English words, we must employ what is called a *phonetic notation*. This is a means of remedying the defects of ordinary spelling. The general characteristics of a phonetic system of spelling are (1) that it is consistent—the same letter, or combination of letters, always stands for the same sound; (2) letters are not written where no sound is pronounced (e.g. *gh* are not wanted in *right*); (3) differences of quantity, or length, are distinguished; (4) accented syllables are marked; the acute accent ´ implies the chief or strongest stress, or accent, the grave accent ` implies secondary or weaker accent; unstressed syllables are unmarked.

Throughout this Dictionary two systems of phonetic notation are employed, numbered respectively 1. and 2., these phonetic spellings being enclosed in square brackets [ ]. The following are examples of their use :

advocacy, n. [1. ádvokasi ; 2. ǽdvəkəsi].
afford, vb. trans. [1. afórd ; 2. əfɔ́d].
affranchise, vb. trans. [1. afránchīz ; 2. əfrǽntʃaiz].
agitation, n. [1. àjitáshun ; 2. ædžitéiʃən].

System No. 1 may be preferred by the general reader because it contains no unfamiliar letters or symbols. By this system a very fairly accurate idea of the pronunciation can be conveyed.

System No. 2 is more precise, and distinguishes more minutely the various sounds and shades of sound which occur in English speech. It contains, however, a number of letters or symbols which are unfamiliar to the general reader, and on this account he may prefer to disregard it, and to trust to system No. 1. This more elaborate system (No. 2) is, however, in accordance with the principles demanded by exact notation, and such systems are commonly employed by philologists today in scientific descriptions of pronunciation, and in the discussion of linguistic facts.

The keys provided below should make clear the phonetic values of the symbols of both systems.

It must be borne in mind that no system of this kind, whether popular in character or of a more exact kind, can be self-explanatory, but demands that the reader should make himself familiar, by constant reference to the key, with the sound values attached to the various symbols.

Key to System No. 1

a as in h*a*t	e as in b*e*ll	i as in b*i*t	ō as in n*o*te	ūr as in l*ure*	th as in *th*ink
ah as in f*a*ther	ē as in b*e*	ī as in b*i*te	ōr as in m*ore*	oo as in p*u*t	dh as in *th*ere
ā as in h*a*te	ēr as in d*ee*r	īr as in f*i*re	u as in b*u*t	ōō as in b*oo*n	gh as in lo*ch*
ār as in h*a*re	ë as in h*e*rd, b*i*rd	o as in n*o*t	ū as in t*u*ne	ou as in n*ow*, *ou*t	zh as in plea*s*ure

Key to System No. 2

SIMPLE VOWELS

(Symbols) (Phonetic Values)
ā   as in h*a*! f*a*ther, h*a*rd.
æ   as in Standard Southern English h*a*t, str*a*p.
a   as in b*u*t, r*u*st, bl*oo*d, M*o*nday.
ɛ   as in h*e*n, g*e*t.
i   as in p*i*n, h*i*d, pr*i*vate.
ī   as in s*ea*t, h*ee*d, mach*i*ne.
ɔ   as in h*o*t, w*a*nt.
ɔ̄   as in *aw*e, c*au*ght, t*o*rn, h*a*ll.
Ā   as in b*i*rd, t*u*rn, l*ea*rn, w*o*rd.
ə   only in unstressed or unaccented syllables, as butt*er*, tog*e*ther, the dog, p*er*haps.
ū   as in h*oo*t, br*oo*d, r*u*de, r*ue*.
u   as in p*u*t, p*u*ll, f*oo*t, c*ou*ld.

In French words, &c.
a   as in Fr. p*a*tte.
y   as in Fr. p*u*re.
e   as in Fr. d*é*.
ē   as in Ital. cr*e*dere.
i   as in Fr. s*i*.
ø   as in Fr. p*eu*.

(Symbols) (Phonetic Values)
o   as in Fr. b*eau*.
ã   as in Fr. *an*, *an*ge, p*en*ser.
õ   as in Fr. s*on*.
æ̃   as in Fr. v*in*, s*in*ge.
ø̃   as in Fr. *un*.

DIPHTHONGS
(i.e. combinations of two vowel sounds of which only the first is accented and syllabic)
au   as in h*ou*se, c*ow*, pl*ough*.
ou   as in st*o*ne, gr*ow*.
ai   as in wh*i*te, n*igh*t, *I*, fl*y*.
ɔi   as in t*oy*, b*oi*l.
ɛə   as in *air*, b*are*, th*eir*.
ei   as in m*a*de, t*a*ke, ag*ai*n, v*ei*n.
iə   as in h*ear*, qu*eer*, b*ier*, imper*ia*l.
īə   as in f*ie*ld, kn*ee*l, s*ea*led.
uə   as in one pronunciation of s*ure*, p*oor*.

CONSONANTS
b   as in *b*at.
p   as in *p*ot.
v   as in *v*ain, o*f*.
f   as in *f*at, enou*gh*.

(Symbols) (Phonetic Values)
d   as in *d*ark.
t   as in *t*ake, dance*d*, min*t*.
ð   as in *th*is, bo*th*er.
þ   as in *th*ink, brea*th*.
l   as in *l*ook.
ḷ   as in Fr. souff*le*.
j   as in *y*acht, *y*ear, few [fjū].
ž   as in Fr. *j*our; Engl. plea*s*ure [plɛžə], bri*dge* [bridž].
ʃ   as in *sh*ip, wi*sh*, cheap [tʃīp], na*ti*on [neiʃən].
z   as in la*z*y, cau*s*e, dog*s*, i*s*.
s   as in *s*ip, cat*s*, pie*ce*.
g   as in *g*ood, be*g*.
k   as in *k*ite, *c*at, lo*ck*.
n   as in *n*o, *kn*ow, *gn*aw.
m   as in *m*ill, li*m*b, hy*mn*.
ŋ   as in si*ng*, lo*ng*, thi*nk* [piŋk].
r   as in *r*ing, *wr*ite, ve*r*y.
ř   as in Fr. rencont*r*e.
h   as in *h*ome.
w   as in *w*ill, d*w*ell, *qu*een.
ʒ   as in Germ. ta*g*.
χ   as in Scots lo*ch*.
ç   as in Germ. Rei*ch*.

Principles of Strict Phonetic Notation Explained

By using a phonetic notation we attempt to convey, as accurately as this can be done by graphic symbols, some of the actual facts concerning pronunciation. In order to accomplish this, it is necessary (*a*) that there should be a separate symbol for every sound which occurs in the language, and (*b*) that every time a given sound occurs it should be represented by the same symbol. The first two essentials, then, are completeness in the set of symbols employed, and consistency in using them.

A third condition which must be observed is that no symbol be written uselessly, that is, a letter is not written where no sound is pronounced. Thus there is no sound corresponding to *l* in *talk*; it has long since disappeared from English pronunciation. Therefore when this or similar words are expressed by phonetic notation, no symbol is written between the vowel and the final consonant. We think of the word simply as it appeals to the ear, as a combination of sounds, every one of which must be expressed by a symbol. Where no sound is heard, no symbol is written.

Quantity. Long vowels are marked by placing the ordinary mark of length over them, as [ā, ī] &c. Short vowels are left unmarked [æ, i] &c.

Some vowels popularly called 'long' are in reality diphthongs, that is, they consist of two distinct vowel sounds; they are therefore written with two symbols. Thus 'long *i*' as in *white* consists of the two short vowels [a] as in German *mann*, and [i] as in Engl. *bit*. This diphthong is therefore written [ai]. The vowels in *take* and *stone* are often referred to respectively as 'long *a*' and 'long *o*'. In reality, in educated English speech, they also are diphthongs, and are therefore written [ei, ou].

Stress or Accent. The stressed or accented syllable of a word is indicated by placing an acute accent over the vowel, thus [fáðə]. If a word, such as certain compounds, has a strong stress on two syllables, both are marked, as [háihǽndid] 'high-handed'.

Where a word of several syllables has, in addition to the chief stress and the unstressed or weak syllables, also one which has a secondary or weaker stress than that of the syllable which has the chief or strongest stress, this secondary stress is marked by placing the grave accent over it, as [ìndifǽtigəbl] 'indefatigable.'

It must be remembered that what a phonetic notation as used in a dictionary can accomplish is to show in which words and syllables certain sounds are used. It cannot, without entering into long discussions which would be almost useless to those who had not received a special training in Phonetics, inform the reader what is the precise nature and character of *the sounds themselves*. Thus the vowel sound in *hand* may be pronounced in a dozen different ways in different English dialects; that is to say, that all over England perhaps a dozen different vowel sounds may be heard in this word. When therefore, in this Dictionary, the pronunciation of *hand* is indicated as [hænd] the reader is not informed which of the exact varieties is intended. All he can discover is that the writer of the Dictionary states that the same vowel is pronounced here as in all other words in which the symbol [æ] is written.

When it is said, then, that a Dictionary tells us how to pronounce, the claim as a rule is, in reality, too wide. All it does is to show the *distribution of sounds*, to indicate in which words the same sounds occur. It also tells us where the accent is placed, and whether the vowels are short or long. But it does not give what a phonetician would call an exact analysis of the sounds themselves. Key words are given as a guide to what is called 'the values' of the symbols, but since different people may have different pronunciations of the words given, none can be certain that his sound in a given word is exactly that intended by the person who drew up the tables. All that can be said is that the sounds which the writer of this Dictionary had in mind are those in use among the majority of persons who speak Southern *Standard*, or better, *Received Standard English*. If this description is considered too vague, it must suffice here to say that *Received Standard* is that type of English which is spoken by those who have been educated at one of the older Public Schools. It is by no means the exclusive property of these, but from them at any rate we may be pretty sure of hearing it.

Note on Method of Arrangement

As the plan of this Dictionary differs in some details from that of others of its size, a short exposition of this is given here.

Each entry appears in black type, followed immediately by the part of speech, noun, verb, preposition etc. Homonyms, i.e. words having the same form but different sense (e.g. *bear*, the verb, and *bear*, the animal), are given separate entries, followed by Roman figures enclosed in brackets: **bear (I.)**, vb.; **bear (II.)**, n. This plan is also usually followed for words used as two or more different parts of speech: **account (I.)**, n.; **account (II.)**, vb.

Next comes the pronunciation in the two forms of phonetic notation, enclosed in square brackets.

Following the pronunciation, and preceding the definition of the word, its origin is indicated. This may consist merely in a reference to another entry (e.g. See prec.; See next word &c.) or in a reference in black type to one or more other entries (e.g. under *aeroplane*, See **aero-** & **plane**) where the various parts of the word are fully dealt with. Under the main etymology is given the history of the word as far as it can be traced, working back, for example, from the modern form to Old English, Germanic, and finally to the most primitive Aryan form, or through Middle English to French, Latin, and possibly Greek. The relation of the word to words in other languages is indicated, and references are given in black type to other entries in the Dictionary which should be looked up in order to trace the interesting connexion which often exists between words apparently unrelated. See under **abstruse, affray, agglomerate, air (I.)**.

It may happen occasionally that the etymology of a simple word is so long and interesting as completely to overshadow the short definition which appears at the end of the entry. An instance of this occurs under **albatross**.

After the history of the word comes its use in present-day English. For greater clarity this is usually subdivided. In the case of a verb which is used transitively and intransitively, the main divisions are headed, e.g. **A.** trans., **B.** intrans. (see **act (II.)**). Each of these divisions is divided into minor divisions, numbered **1, 2, 3**, and so on, and each of these subdivisions may be further divided into **a, b, c** &c. Occasionally one of these small subdivisions is again divided into (i.), (ii.), (iii.).

In addition to defining the meaning of a word in all its developments and applications, short sentences illustrating its various uses are given in *italics*. Special idiomatic uses, including colloquialisms and slang expressions are given, preceded by Phr., e.g. Phr. *that cock won't fight*, q.v. under **cock (I.)**.

Note on the Marking of Pronunciation

American readers will find that Professor Wyld has marked the pronunciation with unusual care. Two systems are used here, and each word has its pronunciation recorded according to both systems. The first system is designed for the general reader and is much like the marking that will be remembered from school text-books. It will suffice for most purposes. Following the numeral 2, within the square brackets, is the same pronunciation according to the second system, which is much more scientific than the first. This plan of marking will be understood after paying careful attention to the key on the preceding page.

It is important to observe, therefore, that the pronunciations marked 1 and 2 are the same thing under a different dress. In a few cases Professor Wyld has set down two possible pronunciations after the numeral 1 and after the numeral 2, and the reader can choose whichever seems the most natural to him. Some remarks for American users of the work concerning the type of pronunciation recorded here will be found in the "American Preface" in Part I.

Abbreviations used in this Dictionary

abbr.	abbreviated, abbreviation	corrupt.	corruption	illit.	illiterate	Nthn.	northern	R.C.	Roman Catholic
abl.	ablative	cp.	compare	imit.	imitative	numis.	numismatics	redupl.	reduplicated
absol.	absolute(ly)	crystal.	crystallography	imperat.	imperative			ref.	reference
acc.	accusative			imperf.	imperfect	O.	Old	reflex.	reflexive
A.D.	Anno Domini	Dan.	Danish	impers.	impersonal	obs.	obsolete	reg.	regular
ad.	adapted	dat.	dative	indef.	indefinite	obsolesc.	obsolescent	rel.	relative
adj.	adjective	def.	definite	indic.	indicative	O.D.	Old Dutch	relig.	religion
adv.	adverb	demons.	demonstrative	infin.	infinitive	O.E.	Old English	rhet.	rhetorical
advbl.	adverbial	dial.	dialect	intens.	intensive	O. Fr.	Old French	Rom.	Roman
aeron.	aeronautics	dimin.	diminutive	interj.	interjection	O. Fris.	Old Frisian	Russ.	Russian
A.-Fr.	Anglo-French	dist.	distinguished	internat.	international	O.H.G.	Old High German	R.V.	Revised Version
Afr.	African	Du.	Dutch	interrog.	interrogative	O.L.G.	Old Low German		
agric.	agriculture			intrans.	intransitive	O.N.	Old Norse	S.	South
alchem.	alchemy	E.	East	Ir.	Irish	opt.	optics	sc.	scilicet (namely)
alg.	algebra	eccles.	ecclesiastical	iron.	ironical(ly)	orig.	original(ly)	Scand.	Scandinavian
Am.	American	econ.	economics	irreg.	irregular	ornith.	ornithology	Scrt.	Sanscrit
anal.	analogy	educ.	education	Ital.	Italian	O.S.	Old Saxon	sculp.	sculpture
anat.	anatomy	e.g.	exempli gratia (for example)			O.T.	Old Testament	shd.	should
anct.	ancient			Jap.	Japanese			sing.	singular
anthropol.	anthropology	Egyptol.	Egyptology	Jav.	Javanese	paint.	painting	Slav.	Slavonic
antiq.	antiquities	elect.	electricity			palaeont.	palaeontology	Span.	Spanish
Arab.	Arabic	engin.	engineering	L.	Late	parl.	parliamentary	specif.	specific(ally)
archaeol.	archaeology	Engl.	English	Lat.	Latin	pass.	passive	spirit.	spiritualism
archit.	architecture	entom.	entomology	Lett.	Lettish	pathol.	pathology	Sthn.	southern
arith.	arithmetic	equiv.	equivalent	L.G.	Low German	perf.	perfect	subj.	subjunctive
art.	article	esp.	especially	lit.	literal(ly)	perh.	perhaps	suff.	suffix
astrol.	astrology	ethnol.	ethnology	liter.	literature, literary	Pers.	Persian	superl.	superlative
astron.	astronomy	etymol.	etymology	Lith.	Lithuanian	pers.	person	surg.	surgery
attrib.	attributive(ly)			log.	logic	Peruv.	Peruvian	surv.	surveying
auxil.	auxiliary	facet.	facetious			pharm.	pharmacology	Swed.	Swedish
A.V.	Authorized Version	fem.	feminine	mach.	machinery	philol.	philology	syll.	syllable
		feud.	feudal(ism)	Malay.	Malayan	philos.	philosophy		
bacter.	bacteriology	fig.	figurative	manuf.	manufacturing	phon.	phonetic(s)	techn.	technical, technology
Balto-Slav.	Balto-Slavic	Finn.	Finnish	masc.	masculine	photog.	photography		
B.C.	Before Christ	Flem.	Flemish	math.	mathematics	Phr.	phrase	teleg.	telegraphy
Bib.	Biblical	foll.	following	M. Du.	Middle Dutch	phren.	phrenology	teleph.	telephony
bibliog.	bibliography	fort.	fortification	M.E.	Middle English	phys.	physics	theatr.	theatrical
biog.	biography	Fr.	French	mechan.	mechanics	physiol.	physiology	theol.	theology
biol.	biology	fr.	from	Med.	Mediaeval	pl.	plural	theos.	theosophy
bot.	botany	freq.	frequentative	med.	medical, medicine	Pl.-N.	Place-Name	trans.	transitive
Brazil.	Brazilian	Fris.	Frisian	metal.	metallurgy	poet.	poetry, poetical	transf.	transference, transferred
Bret.	Breton	fut.	future	metaph.	metaphysics	Pol.	Polish		
B.V.M.	Blessed Virgin Mary			meteor.	meteorology	polit.	political	transl.	translated, translation
		Gael.	Gaelic	M. Fr.	Middle French	Port.	Portuguese		
		Gaul.	Gaulish	M.H.G.	Middle High German	possess.	possessive	trig.	trigonometry
c.	circa (about)	gen.	generally			P.P.	past participle	Turk.	Turkish
cap.	capital	geneal.	genealogy	mil.	military	Pr.	Primitive	typog.	typography
Carib.	Caribbean	genit.	genitive	min.	mining	prec.	preceding		
cd.	could	geog.	geography	mineral.	mineralogy	pred.	predicate, predicatively	univ.	university
Celt.	Celtic	geol.	geology	M.L.G.	Middle Low German			U.S.A.	United States of America
cent.	century	geom.	geometry			pref.	prefix		
Ch.	church	Germ.	German (modern)	Mod.	Modern	prep.	preposition	usu.	usually
chem.	chemistry	Gk.	Greek	mus.	music	Pres. Part.	present participle		
Chin.	Chinese	Gmc.	Germanic	mythol.	mythology	pret.	preterite	vb.	verb
class.	classical	Goth.	Gothic			print.	printing	vbl. n.	verbal noun
cogn.	cognate	gram.	grammar	N.	North	priv.	privative	veter.	veterinary
coll.	collective(ly)			n.	noun	prob.	probably	vulg.	vulgar
colloq.	colloquial	Heb.	Hebrew	nat. hist.	natural history	pron.	pronoun		
commerc.	commercial	her.	heraldry	nat. sc.	natural science	Prot.	Protestant	W.	Welsh
compar.	comparative	Hind.	Hindustani, Hindi	naut.	nautical	Provenç.	Provençal	w.	with
conj.	conjunction	hist.	history	nav.	naval	provinc.	provincial	wd.	would
conn.	connected	horol.	horology	neg.	negative	psychol.	psychology	W. Gmc.	West Germanic
Copt.	Coptic	hort.	horticulture	neut.	neuter	punct.	punctuation	wh.	which
Corn.	Cornish	ibid.	ibidem (the same)	nom.	nominative			wk.	weak
correl.	correlative	Icel.	Icelandic	Norm.	Norman	q.v.	quod vide (which see)	W.S.	West Saxon
		i.e.	id est (that is)	Norw.	Norwegian			zool.	zoology
				N.T.	New Testament				

An asterisk (*) preceding a word indicates a form of which there is no actual record, but which is reconstructed in accordance with known rules of development.

Bibliographical Note

In the etymologies reference is frequently made to authorities on philology, whose opinions are quoted, e.g. 'According to Skeat . . .', 'Walde says that . . .' &c. We give below the titles of the works from which such quotations are made and others that have been consulted.

Berneker, E. Slavisches etymologisches Wörterbuch, vol. I. Heidelberg, 1908-13.
Boisacq, Émile. Dictionnaire étymologique de la langue grecque. 2nd ed. Heidelberg and Paris, 1923.
Bosworth-Toller. Anglo-Saxon Dictionary. Oxford. Supplement (Toller). Oxford, 1921.
(Stratmann-)Bradley. Middle English Dictionary. Oxford, 1891.
Concise Oxford Dictionary of Current English. (H. W. and F. G. Fowler.) Oxford, 1929.
Hellquist, E. Svensk Etymologisk Ordbok. Lund, 1921.
Kluge, F. Etymologisches Wörterbuch der deutschen Sprache. 9th ed. Berlin and Leipzig, 1921.
Lewis and Short. A Latin Dictionary. Oxford, 1927.
Liddell and Scott. A Greek-English Lexicon. Oxford, 1929.
Meyer-Lübke, W. Romanisches etymologisches Wörterbuch. 2nd ed. Heidelberg, 1924.
New Standard Dictionary of the English Language. Funk & Wagnalls Company, New York, 1930.

Oxford English Dictionary. A New English Dictionary on Historical Principles. Edited by Sir James Murray, Henry Bradley, W. A. Craigie, and C. T. Onions. Oxford, 1884-1928. (Abbr. O.E.D.)
Roget, Peter. Thesaurus of English Words. New ed. 1920.
Skeat, W. W. An Etymological Dictionary of the English Language. New ed. Oxford, Clarendon Press, 1910.
Uhlenbeck, C. Kurz gefasstes etymologisches Wörterbuch der gotischen Sprache. 1896.
Walde, Alois. Lateinisches etymologisches Wörterbuch. 2nd ed. Heidelberg, 1910.
Webster's New International Dictionary of the English Language. G. Bell & Sons, London, 1924.
Weekley, E. An Etymological Dictionary of the English Language. London, 1921.
Yule, Henry, and Burnell, A. C. Hobson-Jobson, A Glossary of Colloquial Anglo-Indian Words and Phrases. New ed. by W. Crooke. London, Murray, 1903.

soupçon, n. [1. sōōpson; 2. sŭpsɔ̄]. Fr., 'suspicion; slight trace', see **suspicion**. A suspicion, suggestion, mere trace, or taste, of anything, material or non-material: *a soupçon of garlic is the making of a salad*; *a soupçon of humour will enliven the driest of lectures*.

soup-kitchen, n. Public charitable institution where soup and other food is supplied free among the poor in times of distress.

soup-plate, n. Plate with deep centre for serving soup.

soup-ticket, n. Ticket entitling a person to obtain soup &c. from a soup-kitchen.

sour (I.), adj. [1. sour; 2. sauə]. O.E. *sūr*, M.E. *soure*; O.H.G. *sūr*, Mod. Germ. *sauer*; Du. *zuur*; O.N. *sūrr* &c.; cogn. w. Lith. *súrus*, 'salt to the taste', O. Slav. *syrŭ*, 'rough, raw'; possibly cogn. w. Lat. *rūta*, 'a bitter herb', & *rumex*, 'sorrel', if fr. **srū-*, & Gk. *rhutē*, 'a bitter herb'; cp. also **sorrel** (II.). **1.** (of taste or smell) a Acid, acrid, sharp, tart to the taste, as vinegar, lemon juice, unripe fruit &c.; **b** (of milk) rancid, turned. **2.** (of the temper &c.) Morose, cross, crabbed, disagreeable, bitter, acrimonious: *sour looks*; *a sour temper* &c.; also of persons, *a sour old maid*. **3.** (of soil) Poor, cold, and damp; impoverished, unproductive.

sour (II.), n., fr. prec. That which is sour; esp. fig. that which is unpleasant or bitter, in Phr. *to take the sweet with the sour*, accept all the changes and chances of life as they come.

sour (III.), vb. trans. & intrans. See **sour** (I.). **1.** trans. **a** To turn, make sour, acid, or rancid: *thunder will sour beer, milk* &c.; **b** (fig.) to make morose and gloomy; to render unhappy: *a temper soured by disappointments*. **2.** intrans. To become sour or rancid: *milk sours quickly in heat* (also fig.).

source, n. [1. sors; 2. sōs]. M.E. *sours*, fr. O. Fr. *sorse, surse* (later & Mod. Fr. *source*), fem. of *sors*, P.P. of *sordre*, 'to rise', fr. Lat. *surgere*, see **surge**. **1. a** The point at which a river or stream rises; the fount; a spring at its rising point; **b** (poet.) a stream, a rill, generally. **2.** The starting-point, place of origin of anything, esp. when regarded as the cause: *literature is a source of endless pleasure to many thousands*; *the sources of political unrest are often obscure*. **3. a** Documents or other means of knowledge from which information, esp. historical, is directly derived: *sources of knowledge*; *historical sources*; **b** literary works which have supplied later poets with inspiration, models, plots &c.: *many of Chaucer's sources are to be sought in France and Italy*.

source-book, n. Collection of historical documents of primary authority as sources of our knowledge of certain events, transactions &c.

sourdine, n. See **sordine**.

sourish, adj. [1. sóurish; 2. sáuəriʃ]. **sour** (I.) & **-ish**. Somewhat, tending to become, sour.

sourly, adv. [1. sóurli; 2. sáuəli]. See prec. & **-ly**. In a sour manner; chiefly (fig.) with ill-temper, morosely: *he looked sourly on the merriment of others*.

sourness, n. [1. sóurnes; 2. sáuənis]. See prec. & **-ness**. Condition, quality, of being sour.

souse (I.), n. [1. sous; 2. saus]. In M.E. fr. O. Fr. *sause*. See **sauce**. **1. a** Salt pickle; **b** something steeped in such pickle, as herrings, pigs' trotters &c. **2. a** A soaking, drenching with water or other liquid: *to get a thorough souse in a thunderstorm*; **b** a plunge, dip into water &c.; a ducking: *pitch him into the pond and give him a souse*.

souse (II.), vb. trans., fr. prec. **1.** To pickle, steep in souse: *soused herring* &c. **2. a** To soak, drench with water &c.: *we were soused to the skin*; **b** to plunge, duck in water: *souse him thoroughly in the pond*.

souse (III.), vb. intrans., fr. O. Fr. *sorse*, 'swoop, spring', fr. *sordre*, 'to rise'. See **source**. (obs. or archaic) Of bird &c., to swoop, spring upwards or downwards.

souse (IV.), adv., fr. prec. but confused w. **souse** (I.). Down with a plunge, with a splash: *to fall souse into the water*.

soused, adj. [1. soust; 2. saust], fr. P.P. of **souse** (II.). (slang) Drunk, half-seas over, pickled.

soutane, n. [1. sōōtáhn; 2. sùtɑ̃n]. Fr., in O. Fr. *sotane*, fr. Med. L. Lat. *subtāneus*, also L. Lat. *subtāna*, 'under garment', fr. *sub*, 'beneath', see **sub-**. Long black outer garment resembling a cassock, worn as walking dress by Roman Catholic priests in France and other foreign countries.

souteneur, n. [1. sōōtenër; 2. sùtənɑ̄]. Fr., 'supporter, protector'; also specif. in sense below. Man who lives on the immoral earnings of a woman; a bully.

south (I.), n. [1. south; 2. sauþ]. O.E. *sūð*, adj. for **sunð, sūða*, n., *sūðan*, adv.; M.E. *sūþ, south*; O.N. *sunnr, sūðr*; O.H.G. *sund*, adj., *sundan*, n. & adv; Germ. *süd*; Du. *zuid*; prob. fr. same base as **sun**. **1.** One of the four cardinal points of the compass; the point facing one, N. of the equator, when turned towards the sun at midday; the point opposite to the north. **2.** The southern hemisphere; the Antarctic regions; southern parts of the earth generally; also people living in southern regions of the globe: *the tropical south*; '*bright and fierce and fickle is the south*' (Tennyson). **3.** That part of a country, town, district &c. which lies south of a specified line or towards the south: *the south of England, of France* &c.; *the Solid South*, the Southern States of U.S.A., which seceded in 1862 at Civil War, usually voting for Democratic party.

south (II.), adj., fr. prec. **1. a** Situated at, lying in or towards, the south; southern: *the south country*, southern part of England &c.; so *south countryman*; *south latitudes*; *the South Pole*; **b** directed towards the south, facing south: *a south aspect, window* &c.; *south side*, of church, that side which is on the right hand of one looking towards the altar; the Epistle side: **c** coming from the south: *a south wind*. **2.** In combination (cap.), as part of the name of the southern part of a sea, country, district &c., or of peoples living in the South: *South Atlantic*; *South America*; *South Africans*; *to live in South London*; *the South Seas*, Pacific Ocean; *the South Downs*, the chalk hills of Sussex; also applied to the Hampshire downs.

south (III.), adv., see **south** (I.). Towards the south, in a southerly direction: *to sail, go south*.

south (IV.), vb. intrans., fr. prec. **1.** To move, go, towards the south or in a southerly direction, esp. of ships. **2.** (of the moon) To cross the meridian.

Southdown, adj. & n. [1. sóuthdoun; sáupdaun]. See **south** (II.), **2**. **1.** adj. Pertaining to a breed of sheep of the South Downs of Sussex and Hampshire: *Southdown mutton*. **2.** n. A Southdown sheep: *flock of Southdowns*.

south-east, southeast, also **sou'east**, n., adj., & adv. [1. sóu(th) ést; 2. sáu(þ) íst]. **1.** n. Point of the compass half-way between due south and east; region, district &c. towards this point: *the south-east of London*; *south-east by east* or *by south*, one point east or south of due south-east. **2.** adj. **a** Situated in or towards the south-east, facing, directed towards the south-east: *south-east London, aspect* &c.; **b** coming from the south-east: *a south-east wind*. **3.** adv. Towards the southeast: *to sail south-east*.

south-easter, n. [1. sòuth éster; 2. sàuþ ístə]. Prec. & **-er**. A strong wind blowing from the south-east.

south-easterly, adj. & adv. Prec. & **-ly**. **1.** adj. **a** Situated in or towards, pertaining to the south-east; **b** coming from the south-east: *south-easterly wind*. **2.** In a south-easterly direction, towards the south-east.

south-eastern, adj. **south & eastern**. Situated in, pertaining to, the south-east.

south-eastward, adj., adv., & n. **south & eastward**. **a** adj. Situated in or towards the south-east; **b** adv., in a south-east direction; **c** n., the south-east.

south-eastwardly, adv. South-eastward.

southerly, adj. & adv. [1. súdherli; 2. sáðəli]. See next word & **-ly**. **1.** adj. **a** Toward the south: *a southerly course*; **b** coming from the south: *a southerly breeze*. **2.** adv. **a** Towards the south: *sail southerly*; **b** from the south: *wind blows southerly*.

southern, adj. [1. súdhern; 2. sáðən]. O.E. *sūðerne*, see **south** (I.), & **-ern**. Pertaining to, situated in, characteristic of, the south: *Southern railway*; *Southern States of U.S.A.*; *Southern Cross*, bright constellation of the Southern hemisphere; *southern habits, customs*.

southerner, n. [1. súdherner; 2. sáðənə]. Prec. & **-er**. Person belonging to the south; specif., inhabitant of the Southern States of U.S.A.

southernmost, adj. [1. súdhernmōst; 2. sáðənmoust]. **southern & -most**. Most southern; farthest south.

southernwood, n. [1. súdhernwood; 2. sáðənwud]. O.E. *sūðerne wudu*; it first came from S. Europe. A shrubby plant, *Artemisia*, with scented leaves, allied to wormwood.

southing, n. [1. sóudhing; 2. sáuðiŋ]. **south** (I.) & **-ing**. (of ships) Difference in latitude south from last point of reckoning.

south-polar, adj. **south & polar**. Antarctic: *south-polar regions, exploration* &c.

southron, n. [1. súdhrun; 2. sáðrən]. Variant of **southern**. (archaic) Inhabitant of a southern part of a country, one who lives south of one, a southerner, esp. applied by the Scots to the English.

south-south-east, n., adj., & adv. [1. sóu(th) sou(th) ést; 2. sáu(þ) sau(þ) íst]. (In or towards) direction, point, midway between south and south-east.

south-south-west, n., adj., & adv. [1. sóu(th) sou(th) wést; 2. sáu(þ) sau(þ) wést]. (In or towards) direction, point, midway between south and south-west.

southward, southwards, adv., adj., & n. [1. sóuthward(z); 2. sáuþwəd(z)]. O.E. *sūðweard*; **south** (I.) & **-ward**; **-s** is advbl. Toward the south; southerly: *sailing southward(s)*; *take a southward direction*; *to the southward*.

southwardly, adv. [1. súdherdli; 2. sáðədli]. Prec. & **-ly**. Southward, southerly.

southwards, adv. Variant of **southward**.

south-west, southwest, also **sou'west**, n., adj., & adv. [1. sòu(th) wést; 2. sàu(þ) wést]. **1.** n. Point of the compass half-way between due south and west; region, district, towards this point: *in the south-west of London*; *south-west by west* or *by south*, one point west or south of due south-west. **2.** adj. Situated in or towards the south-west, facing or coming from the south-west: *the south-west district*; *a south-west aspect, wind* &c. **3.** adv. Towards the south-west.

southwester, sou'wester, n. [1. sóu(th)wéster; 2. sáu(þ)wéstə]. Prec. & **-er**. **1.** A strong south-west wind. **2.** (always *sou'wester*) A waterproof hat with broad flap behind to protect the neck, worn by sailors &c. in stormy and wet weather.

south-westerly, sou'westerly, adv. & adj. Prec. & **-ly**. Towards or from the south-west.

south-western, adj. [1. sòu(th) wéstern; 2. sàu(þ) wéstən]. **south & western**. Situated in, pertaining to, the south-west.

south-westward(s), adv., adj., & n. [1. sóu(th) wéstward(z); 2. sáu(þ) wéstwəd(z)]. **a** adv. In a south-west direction; **b** adj., situated in or toward the south-west; **c** n., the south-west.

souvenir, n. [1. sōōvenër; 2. sùvənɪə]. Fr., fr. vb. *souvenir*, 'to remember', fr. Lat. *subvenire*, 'to come up in, recur to, the mind'; see **sub- & venue**. An object preserved, or serving, as a reminder or memento of a place, event &c., keepsake.

sovereign (I.), adj. [1. sóvrin; 2. sóvrin], fr. O. Fr. & M.E. *soverain*; later spelling influenced by **reign**; fr. L. Lat. *superānus*, 'chief, principal', fr. Lat. *super*, 'above', see **super-**. 1. Supreme, superior to others, paramount, chief: *sovereign authority, power, rights*. 2. Possessing, wielding, supreme power and dominion; royal, reigning: *a sovereign prince; a sovereign state*, one exercising supreme, independent, unlimited power and jurisdiction within its own territories. 3. Excellent; efficacious, effectual to a high degree: *a sovereign remedy*.

sovereign (II.), n., fr. prec. 1. a One who exercises supreme rule; a monarch, king, emperor; b (in political science or jurisprudence) a sovereign State; the body or person in whom sovereign power is vested and by whom it is exercised. 2. A gold coin of Great Britain, value 20 shillings, £1 sterling; *half-sovereign*, smaller gold coin, value 10s.; both so called from the sovereign's head on the obverse.

sovereignty, n. [1. sóvrinti; 2. sóvrinti], fr. O. Fr. *soveraineté*. See prec. & **-ty**. 1. State, position, of holding and exercising sovereign power; state of being a sovereign. 2. a Supreme, sovereign power in a State; b power exercised over other States.

soviet, n., Engl. pronunc. [1. sóviet; 2. sóviɛt], Russ. [1. suvyét; 2. savjét], 'council'. A council of workers and soldiers, the political unit of the Communist, proletarian (Bolshevik) federated republic of Russia, the official title of which is *the Union of Soviet Socialist Republics*, U.S.S.R.

sovietism, n. [1. sóvietizm; 2. sóviɛtizəm]. Prec. & **-ism**. Principles, system, of government by Soviets or workers' councils; Bolshevism.

sovietist, n. [1. sóvietist; 2. sóviɛtist]. See prec. & **-ist**. Supporter, adherent, of Sovietism.

sovietize, vb. trans. [1. sóvietīz; 2. sóviɛtaiz]. soviet & **-ize**. To give the form of a soviet to a government.

sovran, adj. [1. sóvran; 2. sóvrən]. Archaic form and spelling of **sovereign (I.)**. Sovereign, esp. in sense of effectual, efficacious: *sovran remedies*.

sow (I.), n. [1. sou; 2. sau]. O.E. *sugu*, *sū*, M.E. *sūwe, sowe*; O.H.G. *sū*; O.N. *sȳr*; cogn. w. Lat. *sūs*; Gk. *hûs* or *sûs*; Ir. *suig*; fr. Aryan base *su-*, 'to bring forth, produce'. See also **son** & **swine**. 1. A fully grown female pig. Proverb. Phrs. *to take, get, the wrong sow by the ear*, (i.) to attribute an action, mistake &c. to the wrong person; (ii.) to settle on the wrong thing as the cause; *you cannot make a silk purse out of a sow's ear*, it is impossible to make a good thing, or get a good result, from bad or poor materials; esp., impossible to make a rough, ill-bred person into a polished gentleman. 2. a One of the large or main channels or moulds into which molten metal, as iron, is run, the smaller branches being styled 'pigs'; b large bar of iron cast in such channel or mould; any bar of cast iron larger than a 'pig'. 3. A movable covering for besiegers in attacking a wall in ancient warfare.

sow (II.), vb. trans. & intrans. [1. sō; 2. sou]. O.E. *sāwan*, M.E. *sōwen*; O.H.G. *sāwen*, O.N. *sā*; Goth. *saian*; cogn. w. Lat. *sēmen*, 'seed', see **semen**; cp. also **seed** & cognates there referred to. A. trans. 1. a To scatter, cast (seed or specific kind of seed) on the ground so that it shall grow and produce: *to sow seed in autumn and spring; sow wheat, oats* &c. Phrs. *to sow one's wild oats*, indulge in youthful follies before settling down in life; *to sow the wind and reap the whirlwind*, to find that one's actions produce a greater and more violent result than one anticipated or desired; b (fig.) *to sow the seeds of* (hatred, revolution &c.), to spread abroad, disseminate, inculcate &c. 2. To scatter, cast, seed upon; to plant with seed: *to sow a field with wheat; sow a garden with annuals*. 3. Only in P.P.: *sown with pearls*, thickly studded or embroidered with; *a sky sown with stars*, densely bespangled. B. intrans. To perform the act of sowing seed: *not yet time to sow*. Phr. *as a man sows, so he shall reap*, our own actions determine the future course of our lives for good or ill.

sowar, n. [1. sowár; 2. sɔwā́]. Pers. & Hind. *sāwar*, 'rider'. A trooper of native Indian cavalry; a mounted orderly; member of a mounted escort.

sow-bread, n. sow (I.) & bread. Popular name of the wild cyclamen.

sower, n. [1. sōer; 2. sóuə]. sow (II.) & **-er**. a One who sows seed: '*a sower went forth to sow his seed*'; b (fig.) one who spreads, disseminates: *a sower of discord*.

sowing, n. [1. sōing; 2. sóuiŋ]. sow (II.) & **-ing**. a Act, process, of scattering seed in the ground; b that which is sown; seed.

sown, vb. [1. sōn; 2. soun]. O.E. (*ge*)*sāwen*; M.E. *sōwe*(*n*); P.P. of sow (II.).

sow-thistle, n. sow (I.) & thistle. Popular name for various species of a perennial or annual wild herb or plant, genus *Sonchus*, with spiked leaves, yellow flowers, and milky juice.

soy, n. [1. soi; 2. sɔi]. Jap. *shōyū*, 'sauce from soya-bean', fr. Chin. *shi*, 'beans', & *yin*, 'oil'. A Chinese and Japanese sauce for fish made from fermented soya-beans pickled in brine.

soya-, soy-bean, n. [1. sóia, sói, bēn; 2. sóiə, sói, bīn], fr. prec. An Asiatic leguminous plant, the beans of which yield a rich oil, which is used in making margarine, and also an oil-cake for feeding cattle.

spa, n. [1. spah, spaw; 2. spā, spɔ], fr. Spa, town in Belgium. 1. Health resort having a mineral spring. 2. Mineral spring.

space (I.), n. [1. spās; 2. speis], fr. O. Fr. *espace*, fr. Lat. *spatium*, 'space, room, extent, distance'; cp. Scrt. *sphā́yati*, 'increases'; O. Slav. *spĕja*, 'to be successful'; *spĕšiti*, 'to hasten'; Lett. *spĕt*, 'to be able'; *spēks*, 'power'; O.H.G. *spuot*; O.S. *spōd*; O.E. *spēd*, 'success', see **speed**; cp. also Gk. *spáein*, 'to draw, draw out', see **spasm**; *spádion*, 'racecourse'; fr. Aryan base **spē(i)-*, **spə(i)-*, **sphē-* &c., 'to stretch out, extend in time or space'. See **spadix, span, spathe**. 1. One of the conditions of material existence, characterized by dimension; limitless extension considered with or without reference to what it contains: *our existence is governed by conditions of time and space*. 2. A portion of extension; interval between two or more objects; distance: *a space of 100 yards; not enough space between the houses; an open space; an enclosed space*. 3. Specif. (print.) a blank interval between words; b the type which effects this. 4. (mus.) Interval between the lines on a score. 5. Portion, interval, duration, of time: *to live in London for a space; the space of a month* &c.

space (II.), vb. trans. & intrans., fr. prec. 1. trans. To set, place, arrange, with space(s) between: *to space men in a line, lines of type, words in line of type* &c. 2. intrans. *Space out*, (print.) to arrange with specially large spaces between: *to space out words, head-lines* &c.

space-bar, n. Flat bar in typewriter &c. pressed down to make a space between words &c.

space-key, n. Key taking place of space-bar in typewriter &c.

spaceless, adj. [1. spásles; 2. spéislis]. space (I.) & **-less**. Having no space, deficient in space.

spacer, n. [1. spáser; 2. spéisə]. space (II.) & **-er**. One who, that which, spaces; specif. a space-bar; b instrument for reversing telegraphic current.

space-time, n. (phys.) An amalgamation of space and time into one system or continuum of four dimensions.

space-writer, n. Journalist &c. paid for articles according to the space they occupy in print.

space-writing, n. Journalistic articles paid for in proportion to the space they occupy.

spacial, adj. [1. spáshal; 2. spéiʃəl]. Variant of spatial.

spacing, n. [1. spásing; 2. spéisiŋ]. space (II.) & **-ing**. 1. Act, method, of placing or arranging with fixed or suitable spaces between, arrangement at intervals. 2. Space between words, lines &c. in printing &c.

spacious, adj. [1. spáshus; 2. spéiʃəs], fr. Fr., fr. Lat. *spatiōs-*(*us*), 'roomy, ample, extensive', fr. *spati-*(*um*), 'space', see space (I.), & **-ous**. 1. Of large or considerable extent, affording ample space; extensive, roomy: *a spacious plain, hall, realm* &c. 2. (fig.) Of great capacity, breadth; ample; not narrow, limited, or restricted: *of spacious intellect*.

spaciously, adv. Prec. & **-ly**. In a spacious manner.

spaciousness, n. See prec. & **-ness**. State or quality of being spacious; ample room.

spadassin, n. [1. spádasin; 2. spǽdəsin], fr. Fr., fr. Ital. *spadacchino*, fr. Lat. *spatha*, 'spade', see **spathe**. Man expert in swordsmanship, esp. one making use of his skill in acts of violence; bravo.

spade (I.), n. [1. spād; 2. speid]. O.E. *spadu*= M.E. *spāde*; cogn. w. O.S. *spado*; cogn. w. Gk. *spáthē*, 'flat wooden instrument', see **spathe**. Cp. also Gk. *spidés*, 'long, extensive'; fr. Aryan base **spēi-*, **spəi-*, **spī-*, 'to press or stretch out, extend'; see **space (I.)**. 1. Tool, used for digging, with broad, nearly flat blade of metal with sharpish edge, attached to long handle; similarly shaped implement of wood, esp. one of small size used by children at the seaside. Phr. *to call a spade a spade*, speak plainly and unambiguously; to call things by their right names. 2. Flat-bladed tool resembling a spade; specif. a spade-like tool for breaking ice; b tool used in cutting cameos; c instrument for cutting whale's blubber.

spade (II.), vb. trans., fr. prec. To dig or cut with a spade.

spade (III.), n., fr. Span. *espada*, 'sword', fr. Lat. *spatha*, 'spade; broad two-edged sword', see **spathe**. (cards) 1. a Conventional representation of a spade, consisting of a black heart-shaped figure with projection below, as distinctive mark on playing-card; b card bearing one or more of these marks: *to lead a spade*. 2. (usually pl.) Suit of cards marked with spade(s): *spades are trumps*.

spade (IV.), n., fr. spado. Castrated animal, gelding.

spade-bayonet, n. Broad-bladed bayonet used as tool and weapon.

spade-bone, n. Shoulder-blade, scapula.

spade-foot, n. Kind of toad with spade-like projection on hind feet used for burrowing.

spadeful, n. [1. spádfool; 2. spéidful]. spade (I.) & **-ful**. Amount taken up by, and contained in, a spade.

spade-guinea, n. Guinea issued 1787-99, having on the reverse a shield shaped like spade on a playing-card.

spade-husbandry, n. Method of cultivation in which deep digging is substituted for subsoil ploughing.

spade-work, n. (fig.) Laborious, detailed work, drudgery, necessary as the basis of higher, constructive work.

spadger, n. [1. spájer; 2. spǽdʒə], fr. sparrow. (slang) Sparrow.

spadiceous, adj. [1. spādíshus; 2. speidíʃəs], fr. Lat. *spādic-*, stem of *spādix*, 'broken branch'. See **spadix** & **-eous**. (bot.) Of, having, of the nature of, a spadix.

spadicose, adj. [1. spádikōs; 2. spéidikous], fr. Lat. *spādic-*, stem of **spadix**, & **-ose**. Spadiceous.

spadille, n. [1. spadíl; 2. spədíl], fr. Fr., fr. Span. *espadilla*, dimin. of *espada*, 'spade', see **spade (III.)**. Ace of spades in ombre or quadrille.

spadix, n. [1. spádiks; 2. spéidiks]. Lat. *spādix*, 'broken palm-branch with its fruit', fr. Gk. *spádix*; cp. Gk. *spáein*, 'to tear away, rend'; *spásma*, 'spasm, convulsion', see **spasm**; *spadṓn*, 'eunuch'; *spádion*, 'racecourse'; fr. Aryan base **spē(i)-*, **spə(i)-* &c., 'to spread or stretch out', see **space**, **spade (I.)**, **speed, span**. Spike of flowers round a fleshy axis, usually wholly or partially surrounded by a spathe.

spado, n. [1. spǎdō; 2. spéidou], fr. Lat. *spado*, fr. Gk. *spadṓn*, 'eunuch', fr. *spá-(ein)*, 'to tear, destroy'. See **spadix**. Person incapable of procreation.

spaghetti, n. [1. spagéti; 2. spagéti]. Ital., pl. of *spaghetto*, dimin. of *spago*, 'cord', fr. its appearance. Kind of thin macaroni.

spahi, spahee, n. [1. spáhhē; 2. spǎhī], fr. Fr. *spahi*, fr. Turk., fr. Pers. *sipahi*, 'soldier', see **sepoy**. 1. Member of Turkish irregular cavalry corps founded in 14th cent. and disbanded in 1835. 2. Member of native Algerian cavalry corps in French army.

spake, vb. [1. spǎk; 2. speik]. Archaic or obs. Pret. of **speak**. M.E. *spǎk(e)*, earlier *spak*, O.E. *sp(r)æc*, w. vowel lengthened through the influence of the infin., Pret. pl., & P.P., all of wh. had long vowels in M.E.

spalder, n. [1. spáwlder; 2. spǒldə]. M.E. *spald-(en)*, 'to split', see **spall (II.)** & **-er**. Man employed in spalling stone or ore.

spall (I.), n. [1. spawl; 2. spǒl], fr. next word. Flake, chip, splinter, esp. of stone.

spall (II.), vb. trans. & intrans. M.E. *spalden*, 'to chip, split'; cp. Germ. *spalten*, 'to split'; M. Du. *spalden*; O.N. *spjald*, 'plank'; Goth. *spilda*, 'writing-tablet'; Scrt. *sphatáti*, 'tears'; Gk. *sphélas*, 'block of wood'; prob. cogn. w. Lat. *pellis*, 'skin', orig. 'flayed skin'. See **pellicle**. A. trans. 1. To break up roughly in preparation for sorting: *to spall ore*. 2. To give preliminary dressing to: *to spall stone*. B. intrans. 1. To spall ore. 2. (of stone) To splinter, chip.

spalpeen, n. [1. spáwlpēn; 2. spǒlpīn]. Ir. *spailpín*, 'rascal', fr. *spailp*, 'dandy'; pride, conceit'; cp. *spailp*, 'to strut'. Rascal, ne'er-do-well.

spalt, n. [1. spawlt; 2. spǒlt], fr. Germ., fr. *spalten*, 'to split', q.v. under **spall (II.)** Scaly mineral used in fusing metals.

span (I.), vb. trans. & intrans. [1. span; 2. spæn]. O.E. *spannan*, 'to clasp, enfold, fasten, stretch'; M.E. *spannen*; cp. O.H.G. *spannan*; O.H.G. *spanna*; cp. O.E. *spann*, 'span, measure'; O.N. *spǫnn*; Du. *spannen*, 'to span; fasten'; fr. same base as **space**. A. trans. 1. To stretch thumb and finger(s) around or across for measurement &c.; to encircle: *to span one's wrist*. 2. To measure, determine, breadth of: *his eye spanned the intervening space*. 3. a To cross, extend over, stretch across: *the bridge spans the river*; hence, b (fig.) to extend over, cover: *imagination will span the gap in our knowledge*. 4. (naut.) To fasten with ropes; esp. *to span a boom*. B. intrans. (of span-worm &c.) To advance by a series of contractions and extensions.

span (II.), n. O.E. *spann*, 'span'. See prec. 1. a Distance between tip of thumb and tip of little finger when hand is fully extended; b average span as measure, 9 inches; c (fig.) short period or distance: *how brief is the span of human life*. 2. a Extreme measurement, full extent, length from end to end: *the span of one's arms, of a bridge, girder* &c.; b extreme, extreme lateral measurement of an aeroplane from tip to tip; c (fig.) the whole extent of a period of time: *his life had wellnigh completed its span*. 3. Space between bases or supports of arch, abutments of bridge &c. 4. (naut.) Rope fastened at both ends, leaving loop in centre free to take a purchase on. 5. (U.S.A., S. Afr.) Pair or team of horses, mules, oxen &c.

spancel, vb. trans. [1. spánsl; 2. spǽnsl], fr. M. Du. *spansel*, fr. *spannen*, 'to stretch', see **span (I.)**. To tether, hobble, hindlegs of, to prevent kicking while milking: *to spancel a cow*.

span-dogs, n. Pair of hooked bars used in hauling timber.

spandrel, n. [1. spándrel; 2. spǽndrəl], fr. O. Fr. *espandre*, q.v. under **expand**, & **-el**. 1. Triangular space between shoulder of arch and right angle of frame surrounding it. 2. Triangular space between the curves of adjoining arches and a straight cornice &c. above them.

spandrel-wall, n. Wall built above arches and filling in spandrels between them.

spangle (I.), n. [1. spánggl; 2. spǽŋgl]. M.E. *spangel*, fr. O.E. *spang*, 'clasp, buckle'; cp. Germ. *spange*; perh. cogn. w. Gk. *sphíggein*, 'to bind'; *sphigktḗr*, 'band, bond', see **sphincter**; Lett. *spaiglis*, 'fork for catching crabs'; O.N. *spīkr*, 'nail'. See further **spica, spike, spile, spire**. 1. Very small, thin disc of brilliant metal, usually with hole in centre, attached to dress &c. for ornament. 2. Hence, any small, esp. round, glistening object. 3. (bot.) Small, spongy excrescence on oak-leaf.

spangle (II.), vb. trans., fr. prec. To adorn with, as with, spangles; to cover, sprinkle, with a number of shining objects: *a spangled scarf*; *grass spangled with dewdrops*; *the heavens spangled with stars*.

spangly, adj. [1. spánggli; 2. spǽŋgli]. **spangle (I.)** & **-y**. Of, like, adorned with, spangles.

Spaniard, n. [1. spányerd; 2. spǽnjəd], fr. M.E. *Spa(y)gn-(el)*, 'Spanish', w. change of suff.; cp. O. Fr. *espaignard*. See next word & **-ard**. Native of Spain.

spaniel, n. [1. spányel; 2. spǽnjəl]. M.E. *spa(i)gnel*, 'Spanish; spaniel', fr. O. Fr. *espagneul*; fr. Span. *español*, 'Spanish', fr. *España*, 'Spain', fr. Lat. *Hispānia*. Any of many closely related breeds of dogs, with long, silky hair and large, drooping ears. Phr. *a tame spaniel*, person who is at another's beck and call; a fawning flatterer.

Spanish, adj. & n. [1. spánish; 2. spǽniʃ]. M.E. *Spainisch*; fr. *Spain*, fr. Lat. *Hispānia*, & **-ish**. 1. adj. Of, pertaining to, coming from, Spain; *Spanish Armada*, see **Armada**; *Spanish bayonet*, kind of yucca; *Spanish broom*, Mediterranean shrub with showy yellow flowers; *Spanish black*, pigment obtained from charred cork; *Spanish brown*, dark reddish-brown earth used as pigment; *Spanish chalk*, kind of talc; *Spanish chestnut*, see **chestnut**; *Spanish fly*, kind of beetle from which cantharides, used for blistering, is obtained; *Spanish fowl*, breed of greenish-black domestic fowl; *Spanish grass*, esparto grass; *Spanish main*, see **main (I.)**. 2. n. Language of Spain.

Spanish American, adj. & n. 1. adj. Of, pertaining to, a part of America in which Spanish or a form of Spanish is spoken. 2. n. Person of Spanish descent inhabiting Spanish America.

spank (I.), vb. trans. & intrans. [1. spangk; 2. spæŋk]. Cp. Dan. *spanke*, 'to strut'. A. trans. 1. To strike, slap, smack, with open hand or other flat object, as punishment. 2. To urge on, drive forward, esp. by slapping, striking, with flat object. B. intrans. *Spank along*, to move along swiftly; (of horses) to move with a brisk, spirited action.

spank (II.), n., fr. prec. Single slap with flat of hand &c.

spanker, n. [1. spángker; 2. spǽŋkə]. **spank (I.)** & **-er**. 1. One who, that which, spanks; specif. a a horse that moves with a fast, spirited, showy action; b (slang) a brilliant, spirited, striking person. 2. (naut.) Fore-and-aft sail extended by spars from after side of mizzen-mast.

spanking (I.), n. [1. spángking; 2. spǽŋkiŋ]. **spank (I.)** & **-ing**. Series of slaps administered as punishment.

spanking (II.), adj., fr. Pres. Part. of **spank (I.)**. 1. Brisk, rapid: *a spanking trot*. 2. (slang) Fine, strong, striking; esp. *a spanking breeze*.

spanless, adj. [1. spánles; 2. spǽnlis]. **span (II.)** & **-less**. (poet.) Not capable of being spanned; measureless.

spanner, n. [1. spáner; 2. spǽnə]. **span (I.)** & **-er**. One of various tools for tightening or loosening nuts and bolts; a wrench.

span-roof, n. Roof with two slopes inclining towards a common ridge.

span-worm, n. Larva of geometer moth.

spar (I.), n. & vb. intrans. [1. spar; 2. spā]. M.E. *sparre*, 'spar, beam, rafter'; cp. O.E. *spearrian*, 'to shut, bar'; O.N. *sparri*; O.H.G. *sparro*; M. Du. *sparre*. 1. n. (naut.) Pole for supporting or extending sail(s); mast, yard, gaff &c. 2. vb. a To furnish with, support on, a spar; b to take (a ship) over bar, through shallows &c., by means of spars and tackle.

spar (II.), n. O.E. *spær(stān)*, 'gypsum'; cp. O.E. *spæren*, 'chalky'; M.H.G. *spār*, 'gypsum'. One of various kinds of crystalline mineral; esp. *fluor-spar*, calcium fluoride; *Greenland spar*, cryolite; *Iceland spar*, transparent calcite used in making optical instruments.

spar (III.), vb. intrans., fr. O. Fr. *esparer* (of cock), 'to strike with spurs', prob. of Gmc. origin. See **spur**. 1. To fight with the fists; to box; *spar at*, to make motions with the fists towards (a person) as though about to strike. 2. (fig.) To engage in dispute; to wrangle. 3. (of cocks) To fight, esp. with protected spurs.

spar (IV.), n., fr. prec. a Act of sparring; boxing-match; b wordy dispute, quarrel, wrangling; c a cock-fight.

sparable, n. [1. spárabl; 2. spǽrəbl], fr. earlier *sparrow-bill*, fr. shape of nail. Small, headless nail used in shoemaking.

spar-buoy, n. Buoy consisting of, or supporting, vertical spar to indicate channel &c.

spar-deck, n. Upper deck of ship, including quarter-deck and forecastle.

spare (I.), adj. [1. spār; 2. speə]. O.E. *spær*, 'sparing, frugal'; M.E. *spāre*; cp. O.N. *sparr*; O.H.G. *spar*, 'frugal' &c.; O.E. *sparian*, 'to abstain from; to show mercy to'; formed fr. base **spa-*, **spō-*, meaning 'to prosper, succeed, promote advance' &c. See further under **speed**. 1. Not plentiful; scanty, meagre: *spare diet*. 2. Lean, thin, having little flesh: *a spare form, frame*. 3. In excess of absolute necessity, additional to what is in ordinary use; available at will, after usual requirements are fulfilled; *spare time*, leisure time, left over after discharge of duties or completion of other work; *spare cash*, that left after supplying one's needs, paying one's legal debts &c.; *spare wheel* (on motor-car), an extra, additional, wheel carried to take the place of one of those in use, in case of emergency; *spare parts*, extra parts of machine, esp. of a motor-car, kept in stock or reserve for replacement; *spare room, spare bed-room*, specif., room in a house unoccupied under ordinary circumstances and reserved for visitors; a guest-room.

spare (II.), vb. trans. & intrans. O.E. *sparian*, 'to show mercy to; abstain from; preserve'. See prec. A. trans. 1. To refrain from using, to withhold use or expenditure of; to grudge: *to spare neither trouble nor expense*. Phr. *spare the rod and spoil the child*, discipline and punishment are necessary in the training of the young. 2. To dispense with, do without; to lose use or services of; to afford: *could you spare a poor man a copper, sir?*; *a public servant of a kind that can ill be spared*; *I have no time to spare today*. Phr. *enough and to spare*, sufficient for all needs and something over. 3. a To show mercy, leniency, consideration, to; to refrain from killing, injuring, destroying &c.: *the victorious enemy spared neither young nor old*; *he doesn't spare his dearest friends when he is roused*; Phrs. *spare my life*, don't kill me; *if we are spared* (i.e. by Providence), if we are still alive; b (i.) to spare oneself, to economize one's strength, reserve oneself for a later effort; to take things easily, not to exert oneself; (ii.) *not to spare oneself*, to be severe or exacting with oneself; to put forth all one's efforts, show great zeal in performance of a task; c to secure, preserve (a person) against, or from, some specified misfortune; to save from, protect from undergoing: *I want to spare you all the suffering I can*; *I will spare you the humiliation of a public exposure*; *pray spare me the tedium of hearing your story all over again*. B. intrans. 1. To be frugal, practise economy. 2. To exercise mercy, refrain from inflicting injury &c.

sparely, adv. [1. spǎrli; 2. spéəli]. **spare (I.)** & **-ly**. In a spare manner; scantily, meagrely.

spareness, n. [1. spǎrnes; 2. spéənis]. See prec. & **-ness**. State, quality, of being spare; leanness; scantiness.

sparerib, n. [1. spǎrrib, spárib; 2. spéərib, spéərib]. Part of ribs of pork so trimmed that very little meat is left on the bones.

sparger, n. [1. spárjer; 2. spǎdʒə], fr. rare or obs. *sparge*, 'to sprinkle', fr. Lat. *sparg-(ere)*, 'to scatter, sprinkle'; cogn. w. O.E. *spearca*, 'spark', see **spark (I.)**; O. Ir. *arg*, 'drop'; Scrt. *parjányaš*, 'rain'; Lith. *sproga*, 'spark'; Gk. *spargáein*, 'to swell'. See **asperges**, **asparagus**. Apparatus for sprinkling; specif. (brewing) machine for sprinkling hot water in mash-tub.

spar-hawk, n. [1. spár hawk; 2. spǎ hɔ̄k], fr. **sparrow-hawk**. Sparrow-hawk.

sparing, adj. [1. spǎring; 2. spéəriŋ], fr. Pres. Part. of **spare (II.)**. Moderate, frugal, restricted; not copious or excessive: *a sparing use of alcohol*; *be sparing of your epithets in writing*.

sparingly, adv. Prec. & **-ly**. In a sparing manner, with restraint and moderation.

spark (I.), n. [1. spark; 2. spǎk]. O.E. *spearca*; M.E. *sparke*; cp. M. Du., M.L.G. *sparke*; cp. also M. Du. *spranken*, 'to sparkle'; Lith. *sproga*, 'spark'; Lat. *spargere*, 'to scatter, sprinkle', see **sparger**; further cogn. w. O.E. *spræc*, 'shoot, twig'; O.E. *spræc*, O.N. *sprakr*, 'lively'; cp. Gk. *aspháragos*, see **asparagus**; perh. also O.E. *sprecan*, 'to speak, give forth utterance', see **speak**. 1. Small glowing particle thrown off by a body in combustion or in a state of incandescence: *sparks fly out of the fire*; *to strike a spark from flint*. Phrs. *as the sparks fly upward*, in accordance with an irresistible tendency; *the vital spark*, life. 2. (in various fig. senses) a Animating, kindling principle, germ: *the spark of life, of learning, religious zeal* &c.; b slight vestige, trace: *he showed not a spark of interest, intelligence* &c. 3. a Light, brief flash accompanying an electric discharge; b (pl., naut. slang) wireless operator on a ship.

spark (II.), vb. intrans. O.E. *spearcian*, fr. *spearc-(a)*, 'spark'. See prec. a To give out sparks; b specif., to produce electric sparks and secure ignition.

spark (III.), n. & vb. intrans., fr. O.N. *sparkr*, 'lively'; cogn. w. **spark (I.)**. 1. n. Gay, dashing fellow; a gallant, a beau: *a gay young spark*. 2. vb. To play the spark.

spark-arrester, n. [1. spárk aréster; 2. spǎk ərɛ́stə]. Device to prevent sparking in part of electric circuit when this is not desired.

sparking-plug, n. [1. spárking plùg; 2. spǎkiŋ plàg]. Device for securing electric ignition in an internal-combustion engine.

sparkish, adj. [1. spárkish; 2. spǎkiʃ]. **spark (III.)** & **-ish**. Like, having the character of, a spark; lively, gay; apt to make love.

sparkle (I.), vb. intrans. [1. spárkl; 2. spǎkl]. M.E. *sp(e)arclen*, freq. fr. **spark (I.)** & **-le**. 1. To give forth shifting sparks of light; to flash, scintillate, coruscate: *a thousand gems, bright eyes, sparkled*; (of intellectual brilliance) *his wit, he, sparkles in society*. 2. To give out bubbles of gas; to effervesce (of champagne &c.).

sparkle (II.), n. M.E. *sparcle*, fr. prec. Physical or intellectual scintillation, coruscation, shifting flash, glitter.

sparkler, n. [1. spárkler; 2. spǎklə]. **sparkle (I.)** & **-er**. That which sparkles; a (thieves' slang) a diamond; b a brilliant, beautiful, showy person.

sparkless, adj. [1. spárkles; 2. spǎklis]. **spark** & **-less**. Emitting no sparks.

sparklet, n. [1. spárklet; 2. spǎklit]. **spark (I.)** & **-let**. a Small spark; b trade or proprietary name for small metal capsule filled with carbonic acid gas, used in conjunction with a special type of syphon for aerating water.

sparkling, adj. [1. spárkling; 2. spǎkliŋ]. **sparkle (I.)** & **-ing**. 1. a Giving off sparks, flashing, glittering, scintillating; b intellectually brilliant. 2. (of wines &c.) Giving out continuously small bubbles of gas; effervescing; contrasted with *still*.

sparklingly, adv. Prec. & **-ly**. In a sparkling manner.

sparring-match, n. [1. spáhring màch; 2. spǎriŋ mætʃ]. Pres. Part. of **spar (III.)** & **match (I.)**. Boxing-match, esp. for exhibition or exercise.

sparring-partner, n. See prec. & **partner**. Boxer with whom professional boxer spars as part of training.

sparrow, n. [1. spárō; 2. spǽrou]. O.E. *spearwa*; M.E. *sparewe*; cp. Goth. *sparwa*; O.H.G. *sparo*; O.N. *spörr*, 'sparrow'; O.S. *sprā*, 'starling'; Lat. *parra*, 'a bird of ill omen'; Gk. *sporgílos*, 'sparrow'; *spardsion*, 'sparrow'; O. Prussian *spurglis*, 'sparrow'; cp. **spavin**. One of various small passerine birds, allied to the finches, with dull-coloured, plain, streaked, or speckled plumage; esp. *house-sparrow (Passer domesticus)*, small brown kind found frequently in neighbourhood of human habitations; the *hedge-sparrow*, *Accentor modularis*, is not of the same family, but is allied to the thrushes.

sparrow-bill, n. Sparable.

sparrow-grass, n. By popular etymol. fr. **asparagus**. (vulg.) Asparagus.

sparrow-hawk, n. O.E. *spear-hafoc*. **sparrow** & **hawk**. Small species of hawk, *Accipiter nisus*, which hunts sparrows and other small birds as prey; it has shortish wings and a light grey barred breast.

sparry, adj. [1. spáhri; 2. spǎri]. **spar (II.)** & **-y**. Of, like, containing, abounding in, spar.

sparse, adj. [1. spars; 2. spǎs], fr. Lat. *spars-(um)*, P.P. type of *spargere*, 'to scatter', q.v. under **sparger**; prob. cogn. w. many words beginning w. *sp(r)-*. See also **asperges**, **spark**. Occurring here and there, singly, or in scattered groups; planted, growing, thinly; reverse of *dense, close*: *a sparse population*; *a sparse vegetation*; *a sparse beard*.

sparsely, adv. Prec. & **-ly**. In a sparse manner.

sparseness, n. See prec. & **-ness**. State of being sparse.

sparsity, n. [1. spársiti; 2. spǎsiti]. See prec. & **-ity**. Sparseness; scarcity, lack.

Spartacist (I.), n. [1. spártasist; 2. spǎtəsist], fr. *Spartac-(us)*, leader of army of slaves who rebelled against Rome in 73-71 B.C., & **-ist**. Adherent of Liebknecht, who adopted the penname of Spartacus, and was leader of the extreme revolutionary Socialist party organized in Germany in 1918.

Spartacist (II.), adj., fr. prec. Connected with, pertaining to, the Spartacists.

Spartan (I.), adj. [1. spártan; 2. spǎtən], fr. Lat. *Spartān-(us)*, 'of Sparta', fr. Lat. *Sparta*, fr. Gk. *Spártē*, capital of Laconia, the people of wh. were noted for their hardihood, endurance, & the simplicity of their lives. 1. Of, pertaining to, Sparta or Laconia. 2. Characteristic of, resembling, the Spartans: *Spartan courage, simplicity*; hence, austere, hardy; the reverse of luxurious: *a Spartan diet*.

Spartan (II.), n., fr. prec. 1. Native, inhabitant, of Sparta, characterized by courage, severe discipline &c. 2. (fig.) A hardy, robust, courageous person; one who lives a rigorous, austere, simple life.

spartein, sparteine, n. [1. spártiin, -iēn; 2. spǎtiin, -iīn], fr. Mod. Lat. *sparta*, 'broom'; fr. Gk. *spártos*, 'esparto grass'; cp. Gk. *speíra*, 'net, cordage'; cogn. w. Lith. *spartas*, 'thong'. See **spire (III.)**. Colourless, oily liquid obtained from the broom and used as a narcotic.

sparterie, n. [1. spárteri; 2. spǎtəri], fr. Fr., fr. Span. *esparteria*. **esparto** & **-ery**. a Fabric woven from esparto grass; b mats, ropes &c. made from this fabric.

spasm, n. [1. spázm; 2. spǽzəm], fr. Fr. *spasme*, fr. Lat. *spasmus*, fr. Gk. *spasmós*, 'spasm, convulsion'; fr. *spá-(ein)*, 'to draw, drag, tear; to contract violently; to tear out', fr. base **spě(i)-, *spə(i)-* &c., 'to stretch or press out, extend, prolong'. See also **space, span, speed** &c. 1. Sudden, violent, involuntary contraction of the muscles. 2. Sudden, violent, convulsive mental or physical reaction to shock, powerful emotion &c.: *a spasm of fear, pain* &c.

spasmodic, adj. [1. spazmódik; 2. spæzmódik], fr. Gk. *spasmōd-(és)*, 'of the nature of a spasm', fr. *spasm-(ós)*, 'spasm', see prec., **-oid**, & **-ic**. 1. Characteristic of, characterized by, of the nature of, a spasm; convulsive: *spasmodic twitching of the limbs*; *spasmodic sobs* &c. 2. Taking place, carried out, from time to time, at no fixed period, and by fits and starts; intermittent: *spasmodic attempts*.

spasmodical, adj. [1. spazmódikl; 2. spæzmódikl]. Prec. & **-al**. (rare) Spasmodic.

spasmodically, adv. Prec. & **-ly**. In a spasmodic manner.

spasmology, n. [1. spazmóloji; 2. spæzmólədʒi]. **spasm** & **-o-** & **-logy**. Branch of pathology dealing with spasms.

spastic, adj. [1. spástik; 2. spǽstik], fr. Gk. *spastik-(ós)*, 'afflicted with a spasm', fr. *spá-(ein)*, 'to tear, draw; to contract, convulse', see **spasm**. (med.) Spasmodic.

spasticity, n. [1. spastísiti; 2. spæstísiti]. Prec. & **-ity**. Tendency to spasms or to spasmodic action.

spat (I.), n., vb. intrans. & trans. [1. spat; 2. spæt]. Prob. cogn. w. **spit (III.)**. 1. n. a Spawn of shellfish, esp. of oyster; b young oyster before it becomes fixed in position. 2. vb. a intrans. (of oyster &c.) To spawn; b trans., to deposit (spawn).

spat (II.), n., abbr. of **spatterdashes**. Short gaiter of cloth &c. covering upper part of boot or shoe, buttoned a short way up the ankle, and strapped under the instep.

spat (III.), vb. O.E. *spætte*, fr. *spætan*, 'to spit', Pret. of **spit (III.)**.

spatchcock, n. & vb. trans. [1. spáchkok; 2. spǽtʃkɔk]. Either *dispatch-cock* or variant of **spitchcock**. 1. n. (rare) Bird killed and cooked immediately in an emergency &c. 2. vb. (colloq.) To interpolate, put in, as an afterthought, between or amongst other things &c.: *to spatchcock a sentence into a letter*.

spate, n. [1. spāt; 2. speit], fr. O. Fr. *espoit*, fr. Du. *spuiten*, 'to flow, flood, spout', cogn. w. **spout**. Flood, esp. sudden flood of river after rain, when it is said to be *in spate*.

spathaceous, adj. [1. spathāshus; 2. spæpéiʃəs]. Next word & **-aceous**. a Having a spathe; b of the nature of, resembling, a spathe.

spathe, n. [1. spādh; 2. speið], fr. Lat. *spatha*, fr. Gk. *spáthē*, 'broad, flat wooden instrument for stirring &c.; broad, flat sword; spathe of palm tree'; cogn. w. O.E. *spadu*, see **spade**, & cognates given under **space**. Large leaf-like, single or double sheath surrounding flower-cluster, bract enfolding spadix.

spathic, adj. [1. spáthik; 2. spǽþik], fr. Mod. Germ. *spat(h)*, 'spar', M.H.G. *spāt*, possibly cogn. w. **spar (II.)**, & **-ic**. Of, resembling, of the nature of, spar.

spathiform, adj. [1. spáthiförm; 2. spǽþifɔ̄m], fr. Germ. *spat(h)*, 'spar', see prec., & **-i-** & **-form**. Having the character or appearance of spar.

spathose (I.), adj. [1. spáthōs; 2. spéipous]. **spathe** & **-ose**. Of, pertaining to, of the nature of, a spathe.

spathose (II.), adj. [1. spáthōs; 2. spǽpous], fr. Mod. Germ. *spat(h)*, 'spar', see **spathic**, & **-ose**. Spathic.

spathous, adj. [1. spáthus; 2. spéipəs]. **spathe** & **-ous**. Spathose (I.).

spatial, adj. [1. spáshal; 2. spéiʃəl], fr. Lat. *spati-(um)*, 'space , see **space**, & **-al**. Pertaining to, connected with, involving, space, or relations in space.

spatiality, n. [1. spàshiáliti; 2. spèiʃiǽliti]. Prec. & **-ity**. State of being spatial.

spatially, adv. [1. spáshali; 2. spéiʃəli]. See prec. & **-ly**. In relation to space.

spatter (I.), vb. trans. & intrans. [1. spáter; 2. spǽtə]. Perh. fr. Du. *spatten*, 'to sprinkle'. A. trans. 1. To sprinkle, splash, drops of liquid upon : *spattered with mud* &c. 2. To splash, scatter, in drops : *to spatter water on a surface*. 3. (fig.) To smirch, defame, reputation of. B. intrans. To fall, splash, in form of intermittent drops.

spatter (II.), n., fr. prec. Light splash, sprinkling; slight shower.

spatterdashes, n. pl. [1. spáterdàshez; 2. spǽtədæ̀ʃiz]. Prec. & **dash**. (obs.) Leggings worn as protection from rain, mud &c. (cp. **spat** (II.)).

spatula, n. [1. spátula; 2. spǽtjulə]. Lat. *spat(h)ula*, dimin. of *spatha*, 'broad, flat instrument or weapon', see **spathe**, & **-ule**. Knife-like instrument with broad, usually flat, blade and often rounded end, used for mixing or spreading plaster, enamel, artist's pigments &c.

spatular, adj. [1. spátūlar; 2. spǽtjulə]. Prec. & **-ar**. Connected with, resembling, a spatula.

spatulate, adj. [1. spátūlàt; 2. spǽtjulèit]. Next word & **-ate**. Having the form of a spatula; specif. (bot., of leaf) having a narrow base and broad, rounded end.

spatule, n. [1. spátūl; 2. spǽtjūl], fr. Fr., Lat. *spatula*. See **spatula**. (zool.) Spatulate formation.

spatuliform, adj. [1. spátūlifòrm; 2. spǽtjulifòm]. See **spatula** & **-i-** & **-form**. Having the shape of a spatula.

spavin, n. [1. spávin; 2. spǽvin]. M.E. *spaveine*, fr. O. Fr. *esparvin*, fr. Med. Lat. **sparvānus*, fr. O.H.G. *sparw-*, nom. *sparo*, 'sparrow', see **sparrow**, fr. jerky movement of spavined horse. Disease of hock-joint of horse; **a** *blood-, bog-spavin*, distension of joint with lymph &c. ; **b** *bone-spavin*, stiffening of the joint through a morbid bony deposit.

spavined, adj. [1. spávind ; 2. spǽvind]. Prec. & **-ed**. Affected with spavin.

spawn (I.), vb. trans. & intrans. [1. spawn ; 2. spɔ̄n]. M.E. *spaunen*, fr. A.-Fr. *espaundre*, O. Fr. *espandre*, 'to expand', see **expand**. A. trans. 1. (of fish, crustaceans, amphibians &c.) To produce, lay, deposit (eggs &c.). 2. (contemptuously) To generate, bring forth as offspring : *the lowest types of humanity spawned in some reeking slum*. B. intrans. 1. To produce spawn. 2. (of young fish &c.) To be produced in the form of spawn.

spawn (II.), n., fr. prec. 1. Eggs of fish, amphibians, crustaceans &c. 2. (contemptuously) Offspring : *the spawn of the ghetto*. 3. Thread-like substance from which mushrooms or other fungi are developed.

spawner, n. [1. spáwner; 2. spɔ̄nə]. **spawn**(I.) & **-er**. Female fish at spawning time.

spay, vb. trans. [1. spā ; 2. spei], fr. Romance, fr. L. Lat. *spadāre*, 'to castrate ', fr. *spado*, 'castrated person or animal', see **spado**. To remove ovaries of (female animal).

speak, vb. intrans. & trans. [1. spēk ; 2. spīk]. O.E. *sp(r)ecan* ; M.E. *spēken* ; cp. O.H.G. *sprechan* ; Du. *spreken*, 'to speak '. Gmc. is the only branch of Aryan speech wh. uses this word in the specialized sense of uttering language ; the orig. & more general sense of the base was ' to start, spring, burst forth '; many cognates occur w. varying meanings ; cp. further O.E. *spræc*, 'shoot of a plant '. See the words cited under **spark**. A. intrans. 1. To make use of vocal language ; to utter intelligible words and sentences without musical modulation of the voice ; contrasted with *sing* : *the baby hasn't yet learnt to speak* ; *to speak clearly* ; *to speak in a whisper* ; *he refused to speak* ; *to teach a parrot to speak*. Phrs. *so to speak, as one might say* ; *strictly, properly, speaking*, in the exact, true, sense of the words; *roughly speaking*, without strict accuracy as to detail ; *to speak (a person) fair*, speak politely, or flatteringly, and reassuringly, to ; *to speak for oneself*, (i.) to express one's own sentiments &c. in one's own way ; (ii.) to express one's personal views which are different from those of others ; *I will now let Mr X speak for himself*, I won't anticipate what he is going to say ; *speak for yourself*, don't include others in, or associate them with, what you have said ; don't attribute such sentiments as you have uttered to them ; *that speaks for itself*, is so clear, or so excellent, that it carries its own explanation, or justification &c. 2. To address an audience, pronounce a discourse, harangue : *to speak in public* ; *the president will now speak*. 3. To express, convey, an idea, emotion, &c. be expressive, significant : *actions speak louder than words*. 4. (of musical instrument) To produce sounds : *the trumpets spoke*. B. trans. 1. To utter with the vocal organs : *to speak words of wisdom*. Phr. *to speak volumes (for)*, be very significant (of). 2. To convey, express, make known, in words : *to speak the truth*. Phr. *to speak one's mind*, say exactly what one thinks. 3. To express oneself in, use as medium of oral expression: *to speak French, Standard English* ; *to speak several languages*. 4. (archaic) To bespeak, show, indicate, proclaim, be significant, afford evidence of the fact : *his action speaks him a rogue*. 5. (naut.) To hail for the purpose of communicating with : *to speak a ship*. C. Followed by adverb or preposition. *Speak for*, to speak, give evidence on behalf of : *to speak well for*, witness favourably to. *Speak of*, to mention in speaking, talk about ; Phr. *nothing to speak of, nothing worth mentioning*. *Speak out*, **a** to speak, produce the voice, clearly and distinctly ; **b** to speak freely, without fear of consequences &c. *Speak to*, **a** to address or converse with ; **b** to witness, testify to, to attest. *Speak up*, to speak loudly and distinctly.

speak-easy, n. [1. spěk ězi ; 2. spīk īzi]. (U.S.A. slang) Illicit drinking-place.

speaker, n. [1. spěker ; 2. spīkə]. **speak** & **-er**. One who speaks ; **a** a person actually engaged in speaking : *the voices of (the) speakers in the next room could be faintly heard* ; **b** (i.) one who speaks in public ; a maker of speeches : *a poor, a timid, speaker* &c. ; (ii.) a good speaker, an orator : *he is a good administrator but no speaker* ; specif. **c** (cap.) *the Speaker*, presiding officer in British House of Commons, addressed in the House as *Mr. Speaker* ; similar officer in U.S. House of Representatives and other legislative assemblies.

speakership, n. [1. spěkership ; 2. spīkəʃip]. Prec. & **-ship**. Office, tenure of office, of Speaker.

speaking, adj. [1. spěking ; 2. spīkiŋ], fr. Pres. Part. of **speak**. 1. Used in, adapted for, ordinary speech, as distinct from singing : *a good speaking voice*. 2. Various special uses : *a speaking acquaintance*, formal acquaintance, sufficient to admit of conversation ; **b** *not on speaking terms*, (i.) not having a speaking acquaintance with ; (ii.) having quarrelled with, renounced acquaintance of ; **c** *a speaking knowledge of a language*, one enabling one to speak it. 3. Very expressive : *a speaking look* ; *a speaking likeness*, lifelike portrait.

speaking-trumpet, n. Instrument for collecting and intensifying the tones of the voice : **a** for enabling a deaf person to hear ; **b** for enabling the voice to carry to a distance.

speaking-tube, n. Tube through which the voice can be heard, carried along or through walls and floors, from one part of a building to another ; short tube passing from the inside to the outside of a closed carriage or motor-car, enabling the occupants to speak with the driver.

spear (I.), n. [1. spēr ; 2. spiə]. O.E. *spere* ; M.E. *spēre* ; cp. M. Du. *spere* ; O.H.G. *sper* ; cogn. w. Lat. *sparus*, 'short hunting-spear ' ; perh. orig. 'something thrown or tossed forward ' ; cp. Lat. *spernere*, 'to push away, reject '; O.E. *spurnan*, 'to strike with the foot, kick away', see **spurn**. 1. Weapon with sharply pointed, usually metal, head and wooden shaft, used in hunting or fighting, for throwing or stabbing. Phr. (archaic) *spear side*, male branch of family, contrasted with *distaff* or *spindle side*. 2. Man armed with spear.

spear (II.), vb. trans. & intrans., fr. prec. 1. trans. **a** To pierce, stab, with spear ; **b** to catch with spear : *to spear fish*. 2. intrans. (of plant) To develop a long tapering shoot.

speargrass, n. [1. spěrgrahs ; 2. spíəgrās]. One of various kinds of meadow grass.

spearhead, n. [1. spěrhed ; 2. spíəhed]. Pointed metal or flint head for spear.

spearman, n. [1. spěrman ; 2. spíəmən]. Man armed with spear.

spearmint, n. [1. spěrmint ; 2. spíəmint]. Aromatic herb of Europe &c., common garden mint.

spear-thistle, n. Purple-flowered thistle.

spear-thrower, n. Instrument used by primitive races for hurling a spear ; throwing-stick.

spearwort, n. [1. spěrwèrt ; 2. spíəwʌ̀t]. One of several varieties of crow's-foot with long tapering leaves.

spec, n. [1. spek ; 2. spek]. Abbr. fr. **speculation**. Phr. *on spec*, as a speculation, on the chance of a successful result.

special (I.), adj. [1. spéshl ; 2. spéʃl], fr. O. Fr. *(e)special*, fr. Lat. *speciāl-(is)*, 'individual, particular ', fr. *speci-(ēs)*, 'sight, view ; shape, appearance ; kind, sort ', see **species**. 1. **a** Of particular, individual character or importance ; having distinctive character ; particular, exceptional : *a day of special thanksgiving* ; *as a special favour* ; *for a special purpose* ; *to receive special care* ; **b** devoted to a particular purpose ; specialized ; particular, minute, detailed, intensive ; contrasted with *general* : *special study, work* ; *one's special subject*, that to which one has devoted special study and attention ; *a special subject* (in an examination), one selected for special, intensive, study. Phr. *special jury*, one drawn from particular social class. 2. Peculiar, individual, private, not for public or general use or attention : *my special chair* ; *one's special work, duty* &c. 3. Designed for, applied to, special use or purpose ; appointed, prepared, for specific purpose, duty &c. ; limited in scope, duty, application &c. : *special agent, correspondent, train* &c. ; *special anatomy*, of specific part of body ; *special case*, (legal) agreed written statement presented jointly by contesting parties to a court for decision ; *special constable*, civilian enrolled in police force in time of civil emergency ; *special edition*, of newspaper, published later than ordinary edition, usually to include special news ; *special hospital*, treating particular class of cases ; *special licence*, sanctioning marriage of specified persons at any place or time, and without publication of banns ; *special logic*, rules of thinking to be applied to particular subject ; *special pleader*, counsel employed to give an opinion on special points submitted to him, and to prepare papers dealing with proceedings out of the usual course ; *special pleading*, (i.) new evidence brought up in law court to oppose evidence offered by other side ; (ii.) (colloq.) specious, unfair, biassed, argument ; *special verdict*, one stating facts proved in evidence, but leaving the court to draw conclusions from them. 4. Definite, specific : *do you want to come on any special day ?*

special (II.), n., fr. prec. Person or thing appointed or prepared for a special purpose ; specif. **a** special constable ; **b** special edition of newspaper ; **c** special train.

specialism, n. [1. spéshalizm; 2. spéʃəlizəm]. special & -ism. Devotion of effort to a special line of study, research &c., or to some special branch of a profession.

specialist, n. [1. spéshalist; 2. spéʃəlist]. special & -ist. Person engaging in special line of study, research &c., or in special branch of a profession; one who has special knowledge in some field of learning or science: *a specialist in geology, diseases of the heart* &c.

specialistic, adj. [1. speshalístik; 2. spɛʃəlístik]. Prec. & -ic. Characteristic of, pertaining to, a specialist, or specialism.

speciality, n. [1. spèshiáliti; 2. spèʃiǽliti], fr. O. Fr. *specialite*, fr. Lat. *specialitāt-(em)*, 'peculiarity', fr. *special-(is)*, 'peculiar, individual'. See **special** (I.) & -ity. 1. Distinctive feature, characteristic, peculiarity. 2. Object, occupation, branch of study, to which special attention is given. 3. Article of commerce in selection or manufacture of which the vendor takes special care and pride.

specialization, n. [1. spèshalizáshun; 2. spèʃəlaizéiʃən]. Next word & -ation. Act of specializing, state of being specialized.

specialize, vb. trans. & intrans. [1. spéshalīz; 2. spéʃəlaiz]. **special** (I.) & -ize. A. trans. 1. a To give a special definition to, make special or specific, to qualify, limit: *to specialize a statement, application* &c.; **b** to direct, and limit, to a particular object: *to specialize a course of study* &c. 2. (biol.) To develop, evolve (an organ or part), in particular direction, or adapt to specific function. 3. To limit to a particular purpose or function; reverse of *generalize*: *the word 'shroud' has a specialized meaning in Modern English*. B. intrans. 1. To particularize. 2. To engage in special study, occupation &c. 3. (biol.) To assume, develop, a special character or function.

specially, adv. [1. spéshali; 2. spéʃəli]. **special** (I.) & -ly. 1. In a special manner; particularly, individually: *he was specially mentioned*. 2. For specific purpose: *specially selected, appointed* &c.

specialty, n. [1. spéshalti; 2. spéʃəlti], fr. O. Fr. *specialite*. See **speciality**. 1. Speciality. 2. (law) A contract embodied in a document bearing a seal.

specie, n. [1. spésh(i)ē; 2. spíʃ(i)ī], fr. Lat. *specie*, abl. of **species**. Money in metal form, coin, as distinct from paper money.

species, n. [1. spésh(i)ēz; 2. spíʃ(i)īz]. Lat. *speciēs*, 'sight, look; appearance, shape, form; kind, class; ornament, beauty'; cp. Lat. *specere*, 'to see, look at'; Gk. *sképtomai*, 'to look closely at', for *spek-*, see **sceptic**; *skopós* for *spok-*, 'one who sees', see **scope**; Scrt. *spáçati*, 'sees'; O.H.G. *spehōn*, 'to watch', cp. **spy**. 1. (theol.) The appearance as presented to the senses of either of the consecrated elements in the Eucharist. 2. (log.) A group of individuals possessing common attributes, and designated by a common name. 3. (biol.) A term of classification used to denote a group of animals or plants, larger than a *variety* and smaller than a *genus*, possessing certain distinctive characters in common, capable of interbreeding and of transmitting their distinctive characters to their offspring. 4. Sort, kind: *a species of fierce egotism which one hopes is rare*.

specifiable, adj. [1. spésifīabl; 2. spésifàiəbl]. specify & -able. Capable of being specified.

specific (I.), adj. [1. spesífik; 2. spisífik]. Med. Lat. *specificus*; Lat. *speci-(ēs)*, see **species**, & -fic. 1. Characteristic of a species; possessing the distinguishing features of a species: *specific forms, variations, characters, in animals or plants*; *specific difference*, one constituting a species. 2. Characteristic of a particular, distinct, class, sort, kind: *there is no specific distinction between a language and a dialect*; *specific gravity*, see **gravity**. 3. a (of drugs) Acting upon some particular organ or part of the body; **b** (of disease) produced by a particular micro-organism. 4. a Clearly defined or formulated; precise, explicit, definite: *a specific statement*; *to have a specific aim and object in view*; *specific performance*, carrying out of strict terms of contract, esp. at the order of court of equity; **b** definitely limited in force and application: *the word 'whisper' is used by phoneticians with a perfectly specific meaning*.

specific (II.), n., fr. prec. A specific drug or medicine.

specifically, adv. [1. spesífikali; 2. spisífikəli]. **specific** (I.) & -al & -ly. In a specific manner; precisely, definitely.

specification, n. [1. spèsifikáshun; 2. spèsifikéiʃən]. See **specify** & -fication. 1. Act of specifying. 2. A detailed descriptive statement; esp. **a** one made in reference to the design and particulars of a building, piece of machinery, or other constructive work; **b** a statement embodying a definition of specific charges brought against a person; a specific enumeration of the terms of a contract &c. 3. (law) Working up of material into a different form, character, product, adjudged not to be the property of the owner of the material.

specificity, n. [1. spèsifísiti; 2. spèsifísiti]. **specific** (I.) & -ity. Specificness.

specificness, n. [1. spesífiknes; 2. spisífiknis]. **specific** (I.) & -ness. State or quality of being specific.

specify, vb. trans. [1. spésifī; 2. spésifai], fr. O. Fr. *specifier*, fr. Med. Lat. *specificāre*, 'to specify'. See **species** & -fy. 1. To make specific; to make definite and particular mention of, state, indicate, precisely, enumerate: *to specify the grounds of complaint*; *to specify those to whom invitations are to be sent*. 2. To include, insert, in a specification.

specimen, n. [1. spésimen; 2. spésimin]. Lat. *specimen*, 'indication, distinctive mark, sign', fr. *spec-(ere)*, 'to look at', see **species**, & -i- & -men. 1. **a** One of a class, taken and regarded as possessing the characteristic features, qualities &c. of the whole class, and serving as a representative example: *a fine specimen of English manhood*; *a specimen of the first issue of English postage stamps*; **b** specif., an example of any kind of natural object preserved, classified, and exhibited as a sample of its kind: *a museum specimen*; *his house was full of stuffed specimens, and specimens in spirits*. 2. **a** A part of anything, taken as an example or pattern of the whole: *a specimen of fourteenth-century handwriting*; **b** isolated characteristic instance: *a specimen of a person's manners, of English weather*; *specimen page, of book or other publication*, one showing style, size of type &c., esp. one printed in publisher's prospectus. 3. (colloq.) An eccentric, unusual person; one exhibiting some marked characteristic; a remarkable type: (usually in unfavourable sense) *a queer, a rum, specimen*.

speciological, adj. [1. spèshiolójikl; 2. spìʃiəlódʒikl]. Next word & -ic & -al. Of, pertaining to, speciology.

speciology, n. [1. spèshióloji; 2. spìʃíɔlədʒi]. **species** & -o- & -logy. The science of the origin and development of species.

speciosity, n. [1. spèshiósiti; 2. spìʃiósiti], fr. Lat. *speciōsitāt-(em)*, 'beauty', fr. *speciōs-(us)*, 'beautiful', see next word, & -ity. State or quality of being specious; speciousness.

specious, adj. [1. spéshus; 2. spíʃəs], fr. Lat. *speciōs-(us)*, 'beautiful, showy; plausible', fr. *speci-(ēs)*, 'appearance', see **species**, & -ose. Having superficial beauty or excellence; seeming good on the surface, but deceptive and lacking genuineness; plausible, meretricious: *a specious appearance of prosperity*; *a specious excuse, plea* &c.; *a specious refinement*.

speciously, adv. Prec. & -ly. In a specious manner.

speciousness, n. See prec. & -ness. Speciosity.

speck (I.), n. [1. spek; 2. spɛk]. O.E. *specca*, 'speck, spot', M.E. *specke*. 1. **a** Small spot, stain, dot, mark; **b** specif., a small spot in fruit caused by disease &c. 2. **a** Minute object; a small grain, a particle: *a speck of dust*; **b** something which appears like a speck from being remote; *the ship became a mere speck in the distance*.

speck (II.), vb. trans., fr. prec. To mark with small spots or specks.

speck (III.), n. O.E. *spic*, 'bacon'; cp. O.N. *spik*; O.H.G. *spec*; Du. *spek*. Blubber of whales or seals; also (U.S.A. and S. Afr.) fat meat, esp. bacon.

speckle, n. & vb. trans. [1. spékl; 2. spékl]. **speck** (I.) & -le. 1. n. Small spot or mark distinct in colour from surrounding surface. 2. vb. (chiefly in P.P.) To mark, cover, with speckles; to dot, variegate with spots.

speckless, adj. [1. spékles; 2. spéklis]. **speck** (I.) & -less. Without a speck; spotless; also fig.

specktioneer, specksioneer, n. [1. spekshunēr; 2. spekʃəníə], fr. Du. *speksnijer*, fr. *spek*, 'blubber', see **speck** (III.), & *snij-(den)*, 'to cut', & -er. The Gmc. stem **snīþ*-, 'cut', appears in O.E. *snīðan*, Mod. Germ. *schneiden*, 'to cut' &c., but apparently has no cognates outside Gmc. Chief harpooner in whaler.

specky, adj. [1. spéki; 2. spéki]. **speck** (I.) & -y. Marked with specks, esp. of fruit with spots of rottenness.

specs, n. [1. speks; 2. spɛks]. Abbr. fr. *spectacles*, see next word. (colloq.) Pair of spectacles.

spectacle, n. [1. spéktakl; 2. spéktəkl], fr. Fr., fr. Lat. *spectāculum*, 'show, sight; public spectacle', fr. *spect-(āre)*, 'to see, watch', fr. *spect-(um)*, P.P. type of *specere*, 'to look', see **species**. 1. Something looked at; specif., something exhibited to public view; a show, a remarkable display. 2. Something unusual, esp. that which arouses pity, contempt, reprobation &c. when seen: *he is a sad spectacle in his infirm old age*. 3. (pl.) (*Pair of*) *spectacles*, pair of optical lenses for correcting the sight, fitted into a frame, supported by the nose, and held in place by thin bars of metal or tortoiseshell passing behind the ears; (colloq., cricket slang) a failure to score in both innings; a duck in both innings.

spectacled, adj. [1. spéktakld; 2. spéktəkld]. Prec. & -ed. **a** Wearing spectacles; **b** having markings resembling a pair of spectacles: *spectacled bear, cobra* &c.

spectacular, adj. [1. spektákūlar; 2. spɛktǽkjulə], fr. Lat. *spectācul-(um)*, 'show', see **spectacle**, & -ar. Of, pertaining to, of the nature of, characteristic of, a spectacle: *a spectacular display*.

spectacularism, n. [1. spektákūlarizm; 2. spɛktǽkjulərizəm]. Prec. & -ism. State or quality of being spectacular.

spectacularly, adv. [1 spektákūlarli; 2. spɛktǽkjuləli]. See prec. & -ly. In a spectacular manner.

spectator, n. [1. spektátur; 2. spɛktéitə], fr. Lat. *spectātor*, 'observer, spectator', fr. *spectāt-(um)*, P.P. type of *spectāre*, 'to see, watch', see **spectacle**, & -or. 1. Person who watches, sees, looks on at, a performance, an action, an event; an observer, an onlooker: *a crowd of spectators at a football match*; *he remained a mere spectator of the great occurrences of his time*. 2. (cap.) Title of periodical.

spectatorial, adj. [1 spektatóriali; 2. spɛktatóriəl]. Prec. & -ial. Of, pertaining to, a spectator.

spectatorship, n. [1. spektáturship; 2. spɛktéitəʃip]. See prec. & -ship. State of being a spectator.

spectatress, n. [1. spektátres; 2. spɛktéitris]. See prec. & -ess. Female spectator.

spectra, pl. of **spectrum**.

spectral, adj. [1. spéktral; 2. spéktrəl]. See **spectre, spectrum**, & -al. 1. Pertaining to, resembling, of the nature of, a spectre; ghostly. 2. Pertaining to the spectrum: *spectral analysis, colours*.

spectrally, adv. Prec. & -ly. Like, after the manner of, a spectre.

spectre, n. [1. spékter; 2. spéktə], fr. O. Fr. *spectre*, fr. Lat. *spectrum*, 'appearance, form; apparition'. See **spectrum**. 1. Disembodied spirit in visible form; apparition, ghost.

2. *Spectre of the Brocken*, huge, ghost-like image of spectator projected on mist at the summit of mountain, as on the Brocken in the Harz Mountains.

spectre-bat, n. S. American leaf-nosed bat.

spectre-crab, n. The transparent larva of certain crustaceans.

spectre-insect, n. Walking-stick insect.

spectre-lemur, n. The tarsier.

spectre-shrimp, n. Shrimp with long, slender body.

spectro-, pref. Form of **spectrum**, used in compounds.

spectrogram, n. [1. spèktrogràm; 2. spéktrəgræm]. Prec. & -gram. Reproduction of a spectrum by means of a spectrograph.

spectrograph, n. [1. spéktrogràhf; 2. spéktrəgràf]. See prec. & -graph. Instrument for representing or reproducing a spectrum photographically &c.

spectrographic, adj. [1. spèktrográfik; 2. spèktrəgræfik]. Prec. & -ic. Of, pertaining to, by means of, a spectrograph.

spectrography, n. [1. spèktrógrafi; 2. spèktrógrəfi]. See prec. & -y. Art of reproducing spectra by means of a spectrograph.

spectrological, adj. [1. spèktrolójikl; 2. spèktrəlódžikl]. See spectrology & -ic & -al. Pertaining to spectrology.

spectrologically, adv. Prec. & -ly. By means of spectrology.

spectrology, n. [1. spèktróloji; 2. spèktrólədži]. **spectro-** & **-logy**. Science of spectral analysis.

spectrometer, n. [1. spèktrómeter; 2. spèktrómitə]. See prec. & -meter. Instrument for measuring angular deviation of ray of light passing through prism.

spectrophone, n. [1. spéktrofòn; 2. spéktrəfòun]. See prec. & -phone. Form of spectroscope in which the different light-rays are made to produce distinctive sounds.

spectroscope, n. [1. spéktroskòp; 2. spéktrəskoup]. See prec. & -scope. Instrument for analysing the spectra of rays emitted by luminous bodies.

spectroscopic(al), adj. [1. spèktroskópik(l); 2. spèktrəskópik(l)]. Prec. & -ic & -al. Of, pertaining to, formed by, a spectroscope.

spectroscopically, adv. Prec. & -ly. By means of a spectroscope.

spectroscopist, n. [1. spektróskopist; 2. spektróskəpist]. **spectroscope** & -ist. Student of, one learned in, spectroscopy.

spectroscopy, n. [1. spektróskopi; 2. spektróskəpi]. See prec. & -y. 1. Use of the spectroscope. 2. Science of spectral phenomena and analysis.

spectrum, n., pl. **spectra** [1. spéktrum, -a; 2. spéktrə(m)]. Lat. *spectrum*, 'form, image'; formed fr. *spect-(um)*, P.P. type of *specere*, 'to look', see **species**. 1. Image presented by a ray of light which has passed through, and been broken up by, a prism, consisting of a series of bands of the different colours forming the constituents of the ray; *spectrum analysis*, chemical analysis carried out by examination of the spectrum of a compound; also *spectral analysis*. 2. Image retained by the retina of the eye, after the object which caused the stimulus to the optic nerve is removed; after-image.

specular, adj. [1. spékular; 2. spékjulə], fr. Lat. *specular-(is)*, 'of, of the nature of, a mirror'. See **speculum** & -ar. Of, pertaining to, having the property of, a speculum; *specular iron*, lustrous variety of haematite.

speculate, vb. intrans. [1. spékulàt; 2. spékjuleit], fr. Lat. *speculāt-(um)*, P.P. type of *speculāri*, 'to observe, examine', fr. *specula*, 'watch-tower', fr. base **spec-*, 'to look at', see **species**. 1. To consider, form theory about, ruminate, ponder, meditate : *to speculate concerning the future life*. 2. To invest money in uncertain security, under circumstances involving risk of loss or possibility of gain : *to speculate in mining shares*.

speculation, n. [1. spèkuláshun; 2. spèkjuléiʃən], fr. Lat. *speculātiōn-(em)*, 'observation, contemplation'. **speculate** & -ion. 1. Act or process of speculating mentally. 2. a Theory, opinion, arrived at by speculation; b conjecture. unconfirmed hypothesis. 3. Investment of money in hope of gain but with risk of loss : *to engage in speculation*; *to buy land* &c., *as a speculation*. 4. Kind of card game.

speculative, adj. [1. spékulativ; 2. spékjulətiv]. **speculate** & -ive. 1. Pertaining to, derived from, given to, mental speculation. 2. Of the nature of, given to, financial speculation; hence, risky, uncertain.

speculatively, adv. Prec. & -ly. In a speculative manner.

speculativeness, n. See prec. & -ness. State or quality of being speculative.

speculator, n. [1. spékulàtur; 2. spékjuléitə]. **speculate** & -or. Person engaging in speculation, esp. in finance.

speculum, n. [1. spékulum; 2. spékjuləm]. Lat. *speculum*, 'mirror', fr. *spec-(ere)*, 'to look at', see **species**, & -ule. 1. (med.) Instrument for dilating a cavity &c., of the body, to facilitate the inspection of the interior. 2. Mirror, usually of polished metal, used as reflector in telescope &c. 3. (ornith.) Patch of distinct colour on bird's wing.

speculum-metal, n. Hard alloy of copper and tin, capable of taking a brilliant polish, used for making the speculum of a telescope.

sped, vb. [1. sped; 2. spɛd]. O.E. *spedde*, M.E. *spedde*. Pret. & P.P. of **speed (II.)**.

speech, n. [1. spēch; 2. spītʃ]. O.E. *sp(r)ǣc*, M.E. *spēche*; cp. O.H.G. *sprāhha*; O.S. *sprāka*; O. Fris. *sprēke*; in gradational relation to O.E. *sprecan*, 'to speak'; wh. has also the type *sprǣc-* in Pret. pl. See **speak**. 1. a The expression of ideas and thoughts by means of articulate sounds produced by vocal organs; language; Phr. *figure of speech*, see **figure**; b the faculty of thus expressing ideas and thoughts. 2. a Particular form of language used by the people of a given country; a tongue, a language : *English speech*; *the native speech of Ireland*; b manner of speaking, dialect, jargon, in vogue among a limited section of the community : *the speech of the proletariat*; c mode of utterance, articulation, enunciation : *his speech was very indistinct*. 3. Act of speaking : *speech is silver, silence is golden*. Phr. *to have speech of (a person)*, to converse with. 4. A formal public utterance, an address, harangue. 5. Sound produced by musical instrument, esp. organ or organ-pipe.

speech basis, n. (philol.) The group of mental and physical habits, esp. habits of using the vocal organs, peculiar to an individual speaker, or to the speakers of a given language or dialect.

speech-day, n. Annual school celebration at which prizes are presented &c.

speechification, n. [1. spēchifikáshun; 2. spītʃifikéiʃən]. See **speechify** & **-fication**. Act of speechifying.

speechifier, n. [1. spéchifier; 2. spītʃifaiə]. Next word & -er. Person given to speechifying.

speechify, vb. intrans. [1. spéchifi; 2. spītʃifai]. **speech** & -i- & -fy. (contemptuous or facet.). To make (public) speeches : esp. to make long, or frequent, speeches.

speechifying, n. [1. spéchifìing; 2. spītʃifaiiŋ]. Prec. & -ing. Act of making speeches; the making of long or frequent speeches : *do not let us have too much speechifying after dinner*.

speechless, adj. [1. spéchles; 2. spītʃlis]. **speech** & -less. 1. Lacking the faculty of speech, dumb. 2. Not actually speaking at a given moment; temporarily unable to speak : *he remained speechless the whole evening*; *speechless with indignation*; (slang) dead drunk. 3. Not expressed, not expressible in speech : *speechless fear, grief* &c.

speechlessly, adv. Prec. & -ly. In a speechless manner; without speaking.

speechlessness, n. See prec. & -ness. State of being speechless.

speech-maker, n. Person who makes a speech; one given to making speeches.

speech-reading, n. Interpretation of speaker's words by observation of movements of mouth &c., as practised by the deaf &c.; lip-reading.

speech-sound, n. Single articulate sound produced by the vocal organs and forming an element of language.

speed (I.), n. [1. spēd; 2. spīd]. O.E. *spēd*, fr. **spōdi-*, 'success, prosperity'; M.E. *spēd*, 'speed'; cp. O.S. *spōd*; O.H.G. *spuot*, 'success'; cogn. w. O.E. *spōwan*; O.H.G. *spuon*, 'to prosper, succeed'; cp. further O. Slav. *spěja*, 'to be successful'; *spěšiti*, 'to hasten'; Lith. *spēt*, 'to be able'; Scrt. *sphāyati*, 'increases'; *sphārás*, 'spread out, broad'; Lat. *spatium*, 'extent'. See **space**. 1. (obs., except in archaic Phr.) To wish good speed (to); *God send you, give you, good speed*, prosperity, luck, success. 2. Quick motion, swiftness, rapidity : *to move with incredible speed*; *at full speed*. 3. Rate of motion; velocity : *with gradually increasing speed*; *at a reasonable speed*.

speed (II.), vb. trans. & intrans., fr. O.E. *spēdan*, 'to succeed, make successful', fr. *spēd*, 'success'. See prec. A. trans. 1. a To wish good luck, or success to : *to speed the parting guest*; b to help forward, be propitious to, give, grant, success to : *God speed you*; '*What recks it them? What need they? They are sped*' = they have succeeded, have got what they want (Milton, 'Lycidas', 122). 2. To accelerate, increase speed of; also *speed up*. B. intrans. 1. To go with speed, to move swiftly forward, to hasten, hurry : *a boat speeds across the waves*; *the arrow sped forth on its flight*. 2. To make progress, fare, get on : to prosper : *how have you sped?*

speeder, n. [1. spéder; 2. spīdə]. **speed** & -er. Attachment to machine for regulating or increasing its speed.

speedily, adv. [1. spédili; 2. spīdili]. **speedy** & -ly. In a speedy manner; rapidly, promptly.

speediness, n. [1. spédines; 2. spīdinis]. See prec. & -ness. Haste, rapidity; promptitude.

speed-limit, n. Legal limit of speed at which a vehicle, esp. a motor, may travel.

speedometer, n. [1. spèdómeter; 2. spīdómitə]. **speed** & -o- & -meter. Instrument which registers the speed at which a vehicle, esp. a motor, is travelling.

speedway, n. [1. spédwà; 2. spīdwei]. Public track for motor-cycle racing; dirt-track.

speedwell, n. [1. spédwel; 2. spīdwɛl]. Genus, *Veronica*, of low-growing herbs, with small, blue, pink, or white flowers.

speedy, adj. [1. spédi; 2. spīdi]. O.E. *spēdiġ*, 'prosperous'; M.E. *spēdi*. **speed** & -y. 1. Characterized by swiftness of motion; rapid, quick : *a speedy flight*. 2. Undelayed, prompt; made or occurring soon : *a speedy recovery, return, retribution* &c.

speiss, n. [1. spis; 2. spais], fr. Germ. *speise*, 'food, meal; amalgam of metal', fr. Med. Lat. *spēsa*, 'food, provisions', fr. Lat. *expensa*, 'disbursement'. See **expense**. Arsenical compound of copper, iron, nickel, &c. produced in smelting certain ores.

spelaean, adj. [1. spēlèan; 2. spīlīən], fr. Lat. *spēlae-(um)*, fr. Gk. *spēlaion*, 'cave'; cp. Gk. *spēlugx*, *spēos*, 'cave'; etymol. doubtful. Of, pertaining to, inhabiting, a cave.

spelaeology, n. [1. spēlēóloji; 2. spīlióledži]. See prec. & -logy. The science or study of caves.

spelican, n. [1. spélikan; 2. spélikən]. See **spillikin**.

spell (I.), n. [1. spel; 2. spɛl]. O.E. *spell*, 'saying, narrative, discourse'; cp. O.H.G. *spel*; O.N. *spjall*; Goth. *spill*, 'tale, saying'; Goth. *spillōn*; O.H.G. *spellōn*, 'to tell'; possibly cogn. w. Lat. *appellāre*, 'to speak to', see **appeal**; Gk. *apeilé*, 'threat'; cp. second element of **gospel**. 1. Magical formula, incantation, charm. 2. Irresistible fascination, sway, overpowering attraction : *under the spell of beauty, eloquence* &c.

spell (II.), vb. trans. & intrans., fr. O. Fr. *espeler*, fr. L.G. *spellen*, 'to say'; cogn. w. O.E. *spellian*, 'to tell, narrate'; *spell*, 'tale'. See prec. **A.** trans. **1.** To name, or write, in succession, the letters used to express (a word) in writing: *to spell a word*; *how do you spell your name?*; *is 'harass' spelt with one r or two?*; *spell out*, (i.) to decipher slowly and with difficulty; (ii.) (as direction to printer) spell in full, not in contracted form. **2.** (of letters) To form a word when arranged in specific order: O-N-E, *spells 'one'*. **3.** To involve, result in, have as consequence; signify: *such an error spells the ruin of our hopes*. **B.** intrans. To put down, or mention the right letters of a word in the right order; to express words in writing, in the correct, recognized, conventional manner: *learn to spell*; *we do not pronounce as we spell*.

spell (III.), n., fr. next word. **1.** Single period, bout, turn, of activity, esp. as coming in rotation: *to take a spell at the oars*; *a spell of work*. **2.** Short period, interval, brief space; *a season*: *to sleep for a spell*; *a spell of fine weather*.

spell (IV.), vb. trans. O.E. *spelian*, 'to act, deputize, for another'; prob. related to *spilian*, 'to play'; cogn. w. O.H.G. *spilôn* O.N. *spila*, 'to play'; O. Fris. *spil, spel*, 'sport, game'. (rare) To take turns with in working, give temporary relief from duty to.

spell-binder, n. (U.S. slang) Speaker able to hold an audience spell-bound.

spell-bound, adj. a Overcome by, or as by, a spell; fascinated, entranced; hence **b** amazed, dumbfounded.

speller, n. [1. spélér; 2. spélə]. **spell (II.)** & **-er**. **1.** One who spells; (usually qualified): *a good, careless, speller &c*. **2.** Spelling-book.

spelling, n. [1. spéling; 2. spéliŋ]. **spell (II.)** & **-ing**. **1.** Act of naming or writing down in order the letters which express a word graphically. **2.** Way in which a word is spelt: *an incorrect spelling*; *variant spellings*.

spelling-bee, n. Competitive exercise in spelling.

spelling-book, n. Book of exercises for teaching children to spell.

spelt, n. [1. spelt; 2. spɛlt]. O.E. *spelt*; cp. O.H.G. *spelza*; Lat. *spelta* is prob. a loan-word fr. Gmc. Kind of wheat, resembling both wheat and barley, grown in the mountains of Switzerland, Germany, and Spain; German wheat.

spelter, n. [1. spéltér; 2. spéltə], fr. L.G. *spialter*, 'pewter'; cp. Du. *spiauter*; perh. cogn. w. **pewter**. Zinc.

spence, spense, n. [1. spens; 2. spɛns]. M.E. *spens, spence*, fr. O. Fr. *spense*, abbr. fr. *despense*. See **dispense**. (archaic) Larder, pantry.

spencer (I.), n. [1. spénsér; 2. spénsə]. Named after Earl Spencer, d. 1845. **1.** Short overcoat, esp. of early 19th cent. **2.** Short woollen jacket.

spencer (II.), n. Etymol. unknown. (naut.) Trysail.

Spencerian, adj. & n. [1. spensérian; 2. spensíəriən], fr. Herbert Spencer (1820–1903), & **-ian**. **a** adj. Pertaining to, connected with, Herbert Spencer or his synthetic philosophy; **b** n., a follower of Herbert Spencer.

Spencerianism, n. [1. spensérianizm; 2. spensíəriənizəm]. Prec. & **-ism**. Philosophic doctrines and system of Herbert Spencer.

Spencerism, n. [1. spénserizm; 2. spénsərizəm]. See prec. & **-ism**. Spencerianism.

spend, vb. trans. & intrans. [1. spend; 2. spɛnd]. O.E. *spendan*, fr. Lat. *dispend-(ere)*, 'to weigh out', fr. *dis-* & *pendere*, 'to weigh, pay out; to ponder'. See **pendant**. **A.** trans. **1.** To give out in payment, pay out, for a thing(s) bought: *to spend a penny on sweets*; *how much have you spent?* **2.** To use up gradually, consume, expend: *to spend one's efforts, strength, to no purpose*; **b** to pass: *to spend one's life, the time*; *to spend a sleepless night*. **3.** To wear out, exhaust, consume,

work itself out: *to spend one's strength*; *the storm has spent itself*; also (archaic) *the night is far spent*, far advanced. **4.** (naut.) To lose: *to spend a mast*. **B.** intrans. **1.** To pay out, disburse, money: '*Getting, and spending, we lay waste our powers*' (Wordsworth). **2.** (of fish &c.) To emit spawn.

spendable, adj. [1. spéndabl; 2. spéndəbl]. Prec. & **-able**. Capable of being spent; available for spending.

spender, n. [1. spéndér; 2. spéndə]. **spend & -er**. One who spends money: *a lavish spender*.

spendthrift, n. & adj. [1. spén(d)thrift; 2. spén(d)θrift]. **1.** n. One who spends lavishly, and extravagantly; a wastrel, a prodigal, a squanderer. **2.** adj. Characteristic of a spendthrift; extravagant, prodigal, thriftless: *spendthrift lavishness*.

spense, n. See **spence**.

Spenserian, adj. [1. spensérian; 2. spensíəriən], fr. Edmund Spenser (1552–99) & **-ian**. Pertaining to, characteristic of, Edmund Spenser; esp. *Spenserian stanza*, that used in the *Faerie Queene*, consisting of nine lines, the first eight having ten syllables, the last being an alexandrine.

spent, adj. [1. spent; 2. spɛnt], fr. P.P. of **spend**. **1.** Worn out by effort, exhausted; *spent bullet* &c., with speed reduced after traversing distance. **2.** (of fish &c.) Having deposited spawn.

sperm (I.), n. [1. spérm; 2. spɑ̄m], fr. Fr. *sperme*, fr. Lat. *sperma*, fr. Gk. *spérma*, 'seed; germ; sperm'; cogn. w. Gk. *speirein*, 'to sow'; *sporá*, 'sowing'; *sporás*, 'scattered, sparse'. See also **spray** & words there referred to. Male generative substance.

sperm (II.), n. Abbr. of **spermaceti**. **1.** Also *sperm-whale*, whale yielding spermaceti. **2.** Spermaceti.

spermaceti, n. [1. spérmaséti; 2. spɑ̄məséti], fr. Lat. *sperma*, 'sperm', see **sperm (I.)**, & *cēti*, gen. of *cētus*, 'whale', see **cetacean**. White, waxy substance obtained from the oil in the head of the sperm-whale, used as basis for ointments, and in making candles &c.

spermary, n. [1. spérmari; 2. spɑ̄məri]. **sperm & -ary**. Male generative gland.

spermatic, adj. [1. spermátik; 2. spɑ̄mætik], fr. Gk. *spérmat-*, stem of *spérma*, 'sperm'. See **sperm (I.)** & **-ic**. **1.** Pertaining to, containing, sperm. **2.** Pertaining to the spermary.

spermatism, n. [1. spérmatizm; 2. spɑ̄mətizəm]. See **spermatic** & **-ism**. **1.** Discharge of seminal fluid. **2.** Spermism.

spermatist, n. [1. spérmatist; 2. spɑ̄mətist]. See prec. & **-ist**. Spermist.

spermatize, vb. intrans. [1. spérmatīz; 2. spɑ̄mətaiz]. See **spermatic** & **-ize**. To emit seminal fluid.

spermato-, pref. representing Gk. *spérmat-*, stem of *spérma*, 'seed, sperm'. See **sperm (I.)**.

spermatoblast, n. [1. spérmatōblàhst; 2. spɑ̄mətoublàst]. Prec. & Gk. *blastós*, 'bud, sprout', see **blastoderm**. Cell from which spermatozoon develops.

spermatogenesis, n. [1. spérmatōjénesis; 2. spɑ̄mətoudʒénisis]. See prec. & **genesis**. Development of spermatozoa.

spermatogenous, adj. [1. spérmatójenus; 2. spɑ̄mətódʒinəs], fr. **spermato-** & base **gen-*, 'produce', see **genesis**, & **-ous**. Producing sperm.

spermatogeny, n. [1. spérmatójeni; 2. spɑ̄mətódʒini]. See prec. & **-y**. Formation of sperm.

spermatological, adj. [1. spérmatōlójikl; 2. spɑ̄mətoulódʒikl]. See next word & **-ic** & **-al**. Pertaining to spermatology.

spermatologist, n. [1. spérmatólojist; 2. spɑ̄mətólədʒist]. Next word & **-ist**. Student of spermatology.

spermatology, n. [1. spérmatóloji; 2. spɑ̄mətólədʒi]. **spermato- & -logy**. Branch of biology treating of the properties and character of the male generative principle.

spermatophore, n. [1. spérmatōfōr; 2. spɑ̄mətoufɔ̄]. **spermato- & -phore**. Case containing spermatozoa in some invertebrates.

spermatorrhoea, n. [1. spérmatōrēa; 2. spɑ̄mətouríə]. **spermato- & rheo-**. Involuntary emission or flow of sperm.

spermatozoal, adj. [1. spérmatōzōal; 2. spɑ̄mətouzóuəl]. See **spermatozoon** & **-al**. Of, pertaining to, a spermatozoon.

spermatozoan, adj. [1. spérmatōzōan; 2. spɑ̄mətouzóuən]. See next word & **-an**. Spermatozoal.

spermatozoon, n., pl. **spermatozoa** [1. spérmatōzóon, -a; 2. spɑ̄mətouzóuən, -ə]. **spermato- & Gk. *zôon*, 'animal'.** See **zoo-**. One of the germ-cells forming the fertilizing elements in the semen of male animals.

spermism, n. [1. spérmizm; 2. spɑ̄mizəm]. **sperm (I.) & -ism**. Theory that the spermatozoon contains the complete germ of the future animal.

spermist, n. [1. spérmist; 2. spɑ̄mist]. **sperm (I.) & -ist**. Adherent of the theory of spermism.

spermo-, pref. representing Gk. *spérm-(a)*, 'seed'. See **sperm (I.)**. Seed; sperm.

spermoblast, n. [1. spérmoblàhst; 2. spɑ̄məblàst]. Prec. & Gk. *blastós*, 'bud'. See **blastoderm**. Spermatoblast.

spermological, adj. [1. spérmolójikl; 2. spɑ̄məlódʒikl]. **spermology & -ic & -al**. Pertaining to spermology.

spermologist, n. [1. spérmólojist; 2. spɑ̄mólədʒist]. Next word & **-ist**. Student of spermology.

spermology, n. [1. spérmóloji; 2. spɑ̄mólədʒi]. **spermo- & -logy**. **1.** Spermatology. **2.** Branch of botany treating of seeds.

sperm-whale, n. Large whale or cachalot, the head of which contains spermaceti.

spew, spue, vb. intrans. & trans. [1. spū; 2. spjū]. O.E. *spēowan*; M.E. *spēwen*, 'to vomit, to spit'; cp. Germ. *speien*; O.N. *spýja*; Gk. *ptúein*; Lat. *spuere*; Lith. *spiáuju*, 'to spit'. Prob. imitative. **A.** intrans. **1.** To vomit. **2.** (of gun) To sink at the muzzle after too quick firing. **B.** trans. To vomit up, eject.

sphacelate, vb. trans. & adj. [1. sfáselāt; 2. sfǽsileit], fr. Gk. *sphákel-(os)*, 'gangrene; convulsive movement, spasm'; prob. fr. Aryan base **sphē-*, **sphə-*, 'to stretch, draw out'; cp. parallel base **spē(i)-* &c. See **space**. **1.** vb. (of flesh or bone) To be affected with necrosis; to mortify, become gangrenous. **2.** adj. Mortified, gangrenous.

sphacelation, n. [1. sfáselāshun; 2. sfǽsileiʃən]. Prec. & **-ion**. Mortification, necrosis.

sphaer(o)-, pref. representing Gk. *sphair-(a)*, 'ball; sphere'; cp. Gk. *sphurón*, 'ankle'; *spairein*, 'to move convulsively, gasp'; Lith. *spiriù*, 'I kick'; Scrt. *sphuráti*, 'to kick, trample'; Lat. *spernere*, 'to reject, spurn'; O.E. *spurnan*, 'to spurn', see **spurn**; fr. base **sp(h)er-*, **sp(h)erē-*, 'muscular contraction, tension, spasmodic movement', fr. **sp(h)ē-* &c., 'to stretch or spread out'. See **space, spasm**. Spherical shape; esp. in botanical terms, e.g. *sphaerella*, a genus of fungi.

sphagnum, n. [1. sfágnum; 2. sfǽgnəm], fr. Gk. *sphágn-(os)*, *spháklos*, 'kind of fragrant moss'; also, 'sage'; prob. named fr. the astringent properties of the latter; cp. Gk. *sphákelos*, 'convulsive movement; gangrene'. See **sphacelate**. Gen. *sphagnum moss*, genus of mosses; peat-moss.

sphen(o)-, pref. representing Gk. *sphēn*, 'wedge'; cogn. w. Scrt. *sphyáś*, 'splinter of wood'; O.N. *spānn*; O.H.G. *spān*, 'splinter', O.E. *spōn*, 'chip, shaving'; M.H.G. *spāt*, 'splinter'; cogn. w. **spathe**. **1.** Wedge-shaped. **2.** Of the sphenoid bone.

sphenoccipital, adj. [1. sfénoksípitl; 2. sfīnəksípitl]. Prec. & **occipital**. Of the sphenoid and occipital bones.

sphenocephalous, adj. [1. sfénōséfalus; 2. sfīnouséfələs]. **sphen(o)- & -cephalous**. Having a wedge-shaped head.

sphenogram, n. [1. sfēnŏgrăm; 2. sfīnougræm]. **sphen(o)-** & **-gram**. Cuneiform character.

sphenographic, adj. [1. sfēnŏgrăfik; 2. sfīnougrăfik]. See prec. & **-graphic**. Of, pertaining to, written in, cuneiform characters.

sphenography, n. [1. sfēnŏgrafi; 2. sfīnŏgrafi]. See prec. & **-graphy**. Cuneiform writing.

sphenoid, adj. & n. [1. sfēnoid; 2. sfīnɔid], fr. Gk. *sphēn*, 'wedge', see **sphen(o)-**, & **-oid**. 1. adj. **a** Wedge-shaped, esp. *sphenoid bone*, large bone at base of skull; **b** of the sphenoid bone. 2. n. (anat.) Sphenoid bone.

sphenoidal, adj. [1. sfēnóidl; 2. sfīnóidl]. Prec. & **-al**. Of, pertaining to, the sphenoid bone.

sphenoido-, pref. representing **sphenoid** & *-o-*. Of the sphenoid bone, e.g. *sphenoidoparietal*, of the sphenoidal and parietal diameters of the skull.

sphere (I.), n. [1. sfēr; 2. sfiə], fr. Lat. *sphaera*, fr. Gk. *sphaira*, 'ball, globe, sphere'. See **sphaero-**. 1. Solid figure of such a form that every point on its surface is equidistant from a fixed point (the centre) within; *doctrine of the sphere*, spherical geometry and trigonometry. 2. Any completely or approximately spherical solid; ball, globe; specif. **a** one of the heavenly bodies; **b** globe representing the earth or the apparent surface of the heavens; **c** one of the spherical, hollow bodies, revolving round the earth, in which ancient astronomers believed the heavenly bodies to be enclosed; esp. *music of the spheres*, produced by movements of the spheres. 3. **a** *Celestial sphere*, spherical surface on which the heavenly bodies appear to be set; **b** (poet.) sky, heavens. 4. **a** Scope, range, compass, province; field of action, knowledge, or influence; **b** normal circumstances, condition of life, social circle: *to remain in one's proper sphere*.

sphere (II.), vb. trans., fr. prec. To enclose in, form into, a sphere.

spheric, adj. & n. [1. sfĕrik; 2. sfĕrik], fr. Gk. *sphairik-(ós)*, 'spherical'. **sphere (I.)** & **-ic**. 1. adj. **a** (poet.) Connected with, pertaining to, the heavenly bodies; celestial; **b** spherical. 2. n. (pl.) Spherical geometry and trigonometry.

spherical, adj. [1. sfĕrikl; 2. sfĕrikl]. Prec. & **-al**. 1. Shaped like a sphere; round, globular. 2. Pertaining to spheres: *spherical geometry, spherical triangle, polygon* &c., on the surface of a sphere and bounded by arcs of great circles.

spherically, adv. Prec. & **-ly**. In spherical form.

sphericity, n. [1. sfĕrísiti; 2. sfĕrísiti]. **spheric** & **-ity**. State of being a sphere.

spheriform, adj. [1. sfĕrifòrm; 2. sfĕrifòm]. **sphere (I.)** & *-i-* & **-form**. Shaped like a sphere.

spherograph, n. [1. sfĕrografh; 2. sfiərəgrăf]. **sphere (I.)** & *-o-* & **-graph**. Device for finding spherical triangles.

spheroid, n. [1. sfĕroid; 2. sfiərɔid], fr. Gk. *sphairoeidés*, 'spherical'. **sphere (I.)** & **-oid**. Solid generated by revolution of an ellipse about either of its axes; body which is nearly but not quite spherical; *prolate, oblate, spheroid*, slightly lengthened, slightly flattened, sphere.

spheroidal, adj. [1. sfĕróidl; 2. sfiərɔidl]. Prec. & **-al**. Of, pertaining to, shaped like, a spheroid.

spheroidally, adv. See prec. & **-ly**. In a spheroidal manner.

spheroidic(al), adj. [1. sfĕróidik(l); 2. sfiərɔidik(l)]. **spheroid** & **-ic** (& **-al**). Spheroidal.

spheroidicity, n. [1. sfĕroidísiti; 2. sfiərɔidísiti]. Prec. & **-ity**. State of being a spheroid.

spherometer, n. [1. sfĕrómeter; 2. sfiərómitə]. **sphere (I.)** & *-o-* & **-meter**. Instrument for measuring curvature or radius of spherical surface or body.

spherular, adj. [1. sfĕroolar; 2. sfĕrulə]. **spherule** & **-ar**. Of, pertaining to, shaped like, a sphere.

spherulate, adj. [1. sfĕroolat; 2. sfĕrulət]. Next word & **-ate**. Of, pertaining to, bearing spherules.

spherule, n. [1. sfĕrool; 2. sfĕrul], fr. Lat. *sphaerula*, 'small ball'. **sphere (I.)** & **-ule**. Minute sphere.

spherulite, n. [1. sfĕroolit; 2. sfĕrulait]. Prec. & **-ite**. Spherical group of minute crystals found in siliceous rock.

spherulitic, adj. [1. sfĕroolítik; 2. sfĕrulítik]. Prec. & **-ic**. Of, pertaining to, containing, spherulites.

spherulitize, vb. trans. [1. sfĕroolitīz; 2. sfĕrulitaiz]. **spherulite** & **-ize**. To form into spherulites.

sphery, adj. [1. sfĕri; 2. sfiəri]. **sphere (I.)** & **-y**. 1. Pertaining to, resembling, a sphere. 2. (poet.) Belonging to the heavens; celestial.

sphincter, n. [1. sfīngkter; 2. sfíŋktə]. Lat. *sphincter*, fr. Gk. *sphigktér*, 'band'; cp. Gk. *sphíggein*, 'to bind tightly'; *sphigma*, 'knot'; *sphigx*, 'sphinx'; prob. a nasalized form of base *sp(h)eig-* &c., expanded fr. *sp(h)ei(*-&c., 'to stretch'. See **spasm**, **space**, **speed**. Muscular ring surrounding an orifice of the body and serving to close it.

sphincteral, adj. [1. sfīngkteral; 2. sfíŋktərəl]. Prec. & **-al**. Of, pertaining to, a sphincter.

sphincterial, adj. [1. sfingktĕrial; 2. sfiŋktíəriəl]. **sphincter** & **-ial**. Sphincteral.

sphincteric, adj. [1. sfingktĕrik; 2. sfiŋktĕrik]. **sphincter** & **-ic**. Sphincteral.

sphinx, n. [1. sfingks; 2. sfiŋks]. Lat. *sphinx*, fr. Gk. *sphígx*, 'sphinx', q.v. under **sphincter**. 1. (cap., Gk. mythol.) Monster, usually represented with a woman's head and the body of a winged lion, who sat on a rock near Thebes and strangled all passers-by who could not solve the riddle which she put to them. 2. (cap.) Egyptian sculptured figure of wingless lion with head of man, ram, or hawk; esp. *the Sphinx*, colossal, human-headed sphinx of Gizeh. 3. (fig.) Person of mysterious or enigmatic character; inscrutable person. 4. (zool.) **a** Hawk-moth; **b** Guinea baboon.

sphinx-like, adj. Resembling a sphinx.

sphinx-moth, n. Hawk-moth.

sphragistics, n. [1. sfrajístiks; 2. sfrədzístiks], fr. Gk. *sphrāgistik-(ós)*, 'of seals', fr. *sphrāgízō*, 'I seal', fr. *sphrāgís*, 'seal, signet-ring, engraved stone'. Etymol. unknown. Study of engraved seals.

sphygmic, adj. [1. sfígmik; 2. sfígmik]. See **sphygmo-** & **-ic**. Pertaining to, resembling, the action of the pulse.

sphygmo-, pref. representing **sphygmus** & *-o-*. Pulse.

sphygmogram, n. [1. sfígmogrăm; 2. sfígməgræm]. Prec. & **-gram**. Graphic record of pulse-beats made by a sphygmograph.

sphygmograph, n. [1. sfígmografh; 2. sfígməgrăf]. **sphygmo-** & **-graph**. Instrument recording the force and rate of the pulse and its variations.

sphygmographic, adj. [1. sfigmográfik; 2. sfigmægrǽfik]. **sphygmo-** & **-graphic**. Pertaining to, recorded by, sphygmography.

sphygmography, n. [1. sfigmógrafi; 2. sfigmógrafi]. **sphygmo-** & **-graphy**. **a** Use, art of using, the sphygmograph; **b** study of sphygmograms.

sphygmology, n. [1. sfigmóloji; 2. sfigmólədʒi]. **sphygmo-** & **-logy**. The study of the pulse.

sphygmometer, n. [1. sfigmómeter; 2. sfigmómitə]. **sphygmo-** & **-meter**. Instrument for measuring blood-pressure in the arteries.

sphygmophone, n. [1. sfigmofŏn; 2. sfigməfoun]. **sphygmo-** & **-phone**. Instrument for making the pulse-beat audible.

sphygmoscope, n. [1. sfigmoskŏp; 2. sfigməskoup]. **sphygmo-** & **-scope**. Instrument representing the pulse-beat in visible form.

sphygmus, n. [1. sfígmus; 2. sfígməs]. Mod. Latinized form of Gk. *sphugmós*, 'pulsation'; cp. Gk. *sphúzein*, 'to beat, pulsate'; *ásphuktos*, 'pulseless, lifeless'; prob. fr. a variant *sphuk-*, of the base *sphək-* &c. seen in Gk. *sphákelos*, 'convulsive movement'. See **sphacelate**. Pulse.

spica, n. [1. spíka; 2. spáikə]. Lat. *spīca*, 'ear of corn'; cp. Lat. *spīna*, 'thorn'; cogn. w. Lett. *spīle*, 'wooden fork'; M. Du. *spīcher*, 'nail'; O.N. *spīkr*, 'spike, nail', see **spike**; O.H.G. *spēnala*, 'needle'; O.E. *spinl*, 'spindle', see **spindle**. Cp. further O.E. *spitu*, 'spit', see **spit (I.)**; Lith. *spitnà*, 'tongue of buckle'; Lat. *pinna*, 'pinnacle', see **pinna**; fr. base *(s)pi-, *spei-*, 'point'. 1. (bot.) Spike, flower-spike. 2. (surg.) Spiral bandage with turns arranged in herring-bone pattern.

spicate(d), adj. [1. spíkăt, spíkāted; 2. spáikeit, spaikéitid]. Prec. & **-ate** & **-ed**. (bot.) Arranged in form of, forming, consisting of, a spike.

spice (I.), n. [1. spis; 2. spais], fr. O. Fr. *espice*, *espece*, fr. Lat. *speciēs*, 'kind, sort'. See **species**. 1. **a** Pungent, aromatic preparation, usually dried, of vegetable root, seed, &c., used for flavouring; **b** spices collectively. 2. (fig.) Quality, feature, giving a characteristic touch or flavour: *a spice of malice in one's words*; *a spice of the devil in one's character*.

spice (II.), vb. trans., fr. prec. 1. To flavour with spice. 2. (fig.) To give a characteristic tinge or piquancy to.

spice-box, n. Box in which spices are kept; esp. ornamental box of china &c.

spicebush, n. [1. spísboosh; 2. spáisbuʃ]. Aromatic American shrub, *Lindera Benzoin*, of the laurel family.

spicery, n. [1. spíseri; 2. spáisəri]. **spice** & **-ery**. Spices generally.

spicewood, n. [1. spíswood; 2. spáiswud]. Spicebush.

spicily, adv. [1. spísili; 2. spáisili]. **spicy** & **-ly**. In a spicy manner.

spiciness, n. [1. spísines; 2. spáisinis]. **spicy** & **-ness**. State or quality of being spicy; pungency.

spick and span, adj. [1. spík an(d) spán; 2. spík ən(d) spæn]. Formerly *spick-and-span-new*; perh. variant of **spike** & **spoon**= new and fresh as a chip or spike just made. Very smart, fresh, and spruce; bright, clean, and tidy: *he looked very spick and span*; *the whole place is thoroughly spick and span*.

spicular, adj. [1. spíkular; 2. spíkjulə]. **spicule** & **-ar**. Having the shape of, covered with, spicules.

spiculate, adj. [1. spíkŭlăt; 2. spíkjuleit]. Next word & **-ate**. Having, covered with, divided into, spicules.

spicule, n. [1. spíkul; 2. spáikjul], fr. Lat. *spīcul-(um)*, 'small, sharp point; dart, arrow'; dimin. of *spica*, 'ear of corn', see **spica**, & **-ule**. Any small, sharply pointed object; specif. **a** (bot.) small, secondary spike; **b** (zool.) small, hard, often needle-shaped, granule found in invertebrates, esp. as forming skeleton of sponge.

spicy, adj. [1. spísi; 2. spáisi]. **spice (I.)** & **-y**. 1. Flavoured or perfumed with spice; pungent, aromatic. 2. (fig.) Piquant, racy: *spicy conversation*; *spicy bits of scandal*.

spider, n. [1. spíder; 2. spáidə]. M.E. *spīðre*, prob. fr. earlier *spinþer*, fr. base of *spinnan*, 'to spin', & agent suff.; cp. Dan. *spinder* & see **spin**. 1. A member of the order *Araneida*, with eight legs in four pairs and body of two segments, furnished with silk glands and spinnerets with which they spin webs for catching insects, thus distinguished from other arachnids, to which class they belong. 2. Utensil, framework &c. resembling a spider in having long slender legs; specif. **a** trivet; **b** long-handled frying pan with feet to support it above a fire.

spider-catcher, n. [1. spíder kácher; 2. spáidə kætʃə]. Kind of East Indian bird.

spider-crab, n. Sea-crab with long, slender legs.

spider-like, adj. Resembling a spider, esp. in having long, thin legs.

spider-line, n. Thread of spider's web used in delicate weighing instruments or to form reticle of telescope.

spider-monkey, n. Thin, long-legged, long-tailed monkey of S. and Central America.

spider-wasp, n. Wasp that provides in its nest a store of spiders &c. for its young.

spider-web, n. Web spun by spider to catch flies &c.; also *spider's web*.

spiderwort, n. [1. spíderwĕrt; 2. spáidəwǎt]. Plant of the genus *Tradescantia*, esp. American perennial, deep-blue variety.

spidery, adj. [1. spíderi; 2. spáidəri]. **spider** & -y. 1. Connected with, pertaining to, a spider; resembling a spider in shape; *spidery handwriting*, with thin, sprawling strokes. 2. Infested with spiders.

spied, vb. [1. spīd; 2. spaid]. Pret. & P.P. of **spy**.

spiegeleisen, n. [1. spḗgl-īzen; 2. spígl-àizn], fr. Germ. *spiegel*, 'mirror', fr. O.H.G. *spiagal*, fr. Lat. *speculum*, 'mirror', see **speculum**, & *eisen*, 'iron', cogn. w. **iron**. Hard, brittle, white cast iron, containing manganese, used in making steel by Bessemer process.

spif(f)licate, vb. trans. [1. spíflikāt; 2. spíflikeit]. Etymol. unknown. (slang) **a** To squash, scotch; **b** to confound, disconcert.

spif(f)lication, n. [1. spìflikắshun; 2. spìflikéiʃən]. Prec. & -ion. Act of spifflicating; state of being spifflicated.

spigot, n. [1. spígut; 2. spígət]. In M.E. perh. fr. Provenç. *espigot*, 'ear of corn', fr. Lat. *spica*, 'ear', see **spica**, & dimin. suff. Small plug for stopping air-hole in a cask; vent-peg.

spike (I.), n. [1. spīk; 2. spaik]. Partly fr. Lat. *spica*, 'ear of corn,' see **spica**, chiefly fr. O.N. *spík*, 'nail'; cp. O.H.G. *speihha*; O.E. *spáca*, 'spoke', see **spoke (I.)**; Lett. *spikis*, 'bayonet'; M. Du. *spícher*, 'nail'. See also **spire, spindle**. 1. Any tapering, sharp-pointed rod, bar, projection; specif. **a** a sharp - pointed metal projection on top of wall, railing &c.; **b** on soles of shoes &c. to prevent slipping. 2. Strong, stout metal nail, esp. as used in fixing railway lines. 3. Steel pin or stopper used for plugging vent of cannon. 4. Ear of corn. 5. (bot.) Inflorescence consisting of small sessile flowers arranged about an axis. 6. (slang) A High-Churchman, a ritualist.

spike (II.), vb. trans., fr. prec. 1. To provide, furnish, set, with spike(s): *spiked shoes*; *a spiked pole*. 2. To stop up vent of (cannon) with spike. Phr. (fig.) *to spike a person's guns*, to upset, frustrate, his plans, bring his devices to naught. 3. To pierce, fix, impale, with spike.

spike-lavender, n. French lavender, from which spike-oil is obtained.

spikelet, n. [1. spíklet; 2. spáiklit]. **spike (I.)** & -let. Small spike; esp. (bot.) secondary spike of inflorescence.

spike-nail, n. Large nail used for fastening thick planks together.

spikenard, n. [1. spíknàrd; 2. spáiknǎd]. M.E. *spíkenard*, fr. O. Fr. *spiquenard*, fr. Lat. *spica nardi*, 'spike of nard'. See **spica, nard**. 1. Perennial aromatic herb resembling valerian. 2. Fragrant, costly ointment anciently prepared from this herb. 3. Kind of aromatic, vegetable oil.

spike-oil, n. Oil obtained from a species of lavender.

spike-plank, n. Platform before mizzen-mast of ship in polar regions.

spikewise, adv. [1. spíkwīz; 2. spáikwaiz]. **spike (I.)** & -wise. In the form of a spike.

spiky, adj. [1. spíki; 2. spáiki]. **spike (I.)** & -y. 1. **a** Set, bristling, with spikes; **b** (fig., of persons) difficult to deal with, cantankerous, touchy. 2. Resembling a spike in form.

spile (I.), n. [1. spīl; 2. spail]. Cp. Du. *spijl*, 'bar'; Germ. *speiler*, 'skewer'; cp. M.H.G. *spille*, 'peg'; O.N. *spila*, 'narrow piece of wood'. Cp. further Lat. *spīna*, 'thorn', see **spine**; *spica*, 'ear of corn', see **spica**. See also **spoke (I.), spire, spindle (II.)**. 1. Timber driven into ground as foundation for building or other erection; pile. 2. Wooden spigot, a vent-peg.

spile (II.), vb. trans., fr. prec. To pierce hole in (a cask) for spile; to vent: *to spile a cask*.

spiling, n. [1. spīling; 2. spáiliŋ]. Prec. & -ing. 1. Set of piles for building; spiles collectively. 2. (naut.) Curve of plank in ship's hull.

spill (I.), vb. trans. & intrans. [1. spil; 2. spil]. L.O.E. *spillan*, 'to destroy', fr. O.N. *spilla*; cp. O.E. *spildan*, 'to kill'; M. Du. *spillen*, *spilden*; O.H.G. *spaltan*, 'to split'; O.N. *spjald*, 'plank'; M.H.G. *spĕlte*, 'splinter'; M.E. *spalden*, 'to split, chip'. See **spall (II.)**. **A**. trans. 1. To allow (liquid &c.) to splash or run out of vessel, esp. unintentionally, permit to escape or be wasted: *to spill gravy, salt, a glass of milk, on the tablecloth*; Phr. (slang) *to spill the beans*, divulge a secret, blow the gaff. 2. (colloq.) To throw out or off, upset: *to be spilt from vehicle, horse* &c. 3. (naut.) To empty of wind before reefing &c.: *to spill a sail*. **B**. intrans. (of liquid &c.) To flow, splash, be upset, out of a vessel.

spill (II.), n., fr. prec. (colloq.) A fall, esp. from a horse or vehicle; a toss, a tumble.

spill (III.), n. Cp. O.E. *speld*, 'a splinter of wood; a torch'; Goth. *spilda*, 'writing-tablet'; O.N. *spjald*, 'plank', q.v. under **spall (II.)**. A thin, narrow shaving or strip of wood, or paper, used for lighting pipes &c.

spiller, n. [1. spíler; 2. spílə]. Etymol. doubtful. Small mackerel-seine let down into larger one to remove the fish.

spillikin, n. [1. spílikin; 2. spílikin], fr. M.E. *spelleken*, fr. M. Du., dimin. of *spelle*, 'pin, peg', prob. cogn. w. O.E. *speld*, 'splinter of wood', q.v. under **spall (II.)**. **a** Slender strip of wood, ivory &c. used in the game of spillikins; **b** (pl.) the game itself.

spilling-line, n. [1. spíling lìn; 2. spíliŋ làin]. (naut.) Rope used for spilling a square-sail.

spillway, n. [1. spílwā; 2. spílwei]. **spill (I.)** & -way. Passage in a dam to carry off overflow of water.

spilth, n. [1. spilth; 2. spilþ]. **spill (I.)** & -th. (archaic) Surplus, overflow, excess.

spin (I.), vb. trans. & intrans. [1. spin; 2. spin]. O.E. *spinnan*; M.E. *spinnen*; cp. O.H.G. *spinnan*; O.N. *spinna*; Goth. *spinnan*, 'to spin'; cogn. w. Lith. *pinù*, 'to stretch, draw, tie'; O. Slav. *pąto*, 'fetter'; cp. further O.E. *spannan*, 'to clasp, enfold', see **span (I.)** &, further, **space**, & cp. **spindle**. **A**. trans. 1. To draw out and twist (yarn, wool, fibre) into threads. 2. **a** To make (thread) by spinning; Phrs. *to spin a yarn*, tell a story; *to spin out*, protract unduly; **b** (of silkworm &c.) *to spin a cocoon*, to form by exuding silk. 3. **a** To cause to revolve rapidly, to twirl, twist, rotate: *to spin a ball, a top*; specif., *to spin a coin*, to toss up; **b** (slang) to reject, plough (examination candidate). **B**. intrans. 1. To practise the art, engage in occupation of, spinning thread: '*the lilies of the field . . . toil not, neither do they spin*'. 2. To revolve rapidly, rotate, turn, on axis. Phr. *to send (person or thing) spinning*, to strike forcibly and cause to fall, roll, stagger.

spin (II.), n., fr. prec. 1. Act of spinning, rapid rotation, whirl; twist given to a ball. 2. Short spell of rapid, brisk exercise or movement: *to go for a spin in a car, on a horse* &c.

spinaceous, adj. [1. spinā́shus; 2. spinéiʃəs]. **spinach** & -aceous. Pertaining to, resembling, spinach.

spinach, spinage, n. [1. spínij; 2. spínidʒ], fr. O. Fr. *espinache*; fr. Span., fr. Arab. *aspanakh*, fr. Pers. Annual garden herb, *Spinacia oleracea*, with hollow stems, and edible, bitter, fleshy leaves, used as a vegetable.

spinach beet, n. Vegetable resembling and cooked to look like spinach, but having a different flavour.

spinal, adj. [1. spīnl; 2. spáinl], fr. L. Lat. *spīnāl-(is)*, 'spinal'. **spine & -al**. Pertaining to, connected with, the spine: *spinal injury, curvature* &c.; *spinal column*, spine, backbone; *spinal cord*, structure of nerve-fibres and cells passing down the spinal column and forming an important part of the nervous system.

spindle (I.), n. [1. spíndl; 2. spíndl]. O.E. *spinl*; M.E. *spindle*; cp. O.H.G. *spinala*, 'spindle'; *spĕnala*, 'needle'; fr. base seen in **spine, spike**; possibly having orig. connexion w. **spin (I.)**, but in any case associated w. it. 1. Slender rod on which the thread from the distaff is wound in hand-spinning; Phr. *spindle side*, maternal side, female line. 2. Rod holding the bobbin of a spinning-machine. 3. Rod, pin, shaft, axis, on which anything rotates; e.g. *the spindle of a lathe*.

spindle (II.), vb. intrans., fr. prec. To grow into, assume, a long slender shape.

spindle-legged, adj. Having long, slender legs.

spindle-shanked, adj. [1. spíndl shàngkt; 2. spíndl ʃæŋkt]. Spindle-legged.

spindle-shanks, n. [1. spíndl shàngks; 2. spíndl ʃæŋks]. Spindle-shanked person.

spindle-shaped, adj. Shaped like a spindle; in the form of a slender cylinder tapering at both ends.

spindle-tree, n. Shrub, *Euonymus*, with close-grained wood used for spindles, skewers &c.

spindle-whorl, n. Perforated disk of stone, pottery &c. used to weight a spindle.

spindly, adj. [1. spíndli; 2. spíndli]. **spindle (I.)** & -ly. Spindle-shaped; long and thin.

spindrift, n. [1. spíndrift; 2. spíndrift]. Variant of *spoon-drift*, earlier *spoom-drift*, fr. Lat. *spūma*, 'foam', see **spume**, & **drift**. Spray blown over water from crests of waves; (attrib.) *spindrift clouds*, light, feathery clouds.

spine, n. [1. spīn; 2. spain], fr. O. Fr. *espine*, fr. Lat. *spīna*, 'thorn', spine, prickle; backbone', fr. base *(s)pī-, *(s)pei-, 'point', as in **spica, spike** &c. 1. Bony column composed of series of small bones or vertebrae, jointed together, running from the back of the head to the hips in vertebrates, and in animals other than man, being continued to form the tail. 2. Any stiff, pointed, spiky structure on the surface of an animal's body: *the spines of a porcupine*. 3. (bot.) Sharply pointed, slender projection resulting from modification of a leaf or other organ; thorn: *the spines of a fir tree*.

spineback, n. [1. spínbak; 2. spáinbæk]. Fish with spines on ridge of back.

spined, adj. [1. spīnd; 2. spaind]. **spine** & -ed. Having a spine or spines.

spinel (I.), n. [1. spinél; 2. spinél], fr. O. Fr. *espinelle*, dimin. of *espine*, 'spine', see **spine**. Kind of vitreous, crystalline mineral, red, blue, green, or brown; *spinel ruby*, red variety.

spinel (II.), n. [1. spínel; 2. spínəl]. Origin unknown. Linen yarn used for making tape.

spineless, adj. [1. spínles; 2. spáinlis]. **spine** & -less. 1. Having no backbone; invertebrate. 2. (fig.) Lacking moral backbone; irresolute, lacking in force of character. 3. (bot.) Without spines: *spineless cactus*.

spinet, n. [1. spínet, spinét; 2. spínɛt, spinét], fr. M. Fr. *espinette*, fr. Ital. *spinetta*, dimin. of *spina*, 'thorn, spine', see **spine**, named fr. the quills w. wh. the strings were plucked; or fr. the name of the alleged inventor, G. Spinetti, of Venice (c. 1500). Small keyboard instrument of 16th, 17th, and 18th cents., ancestor of the harpsichord and piano.

spini-, pref. representing Lat. *spīna*, 'thorn; spine; backbone', see **spine**. 1. Backbone. 2. Thorn, spine.

spinicerebrate, adj. [1. spìnisérebrāt; 2. spàiniséribreit]. Prec. & **cerebro- & -ate**. Having a brain and spinal cord.

spiniferous, adj. [1. spiníferus; 2. spainífərəs]. **spini- & -ferous**. Producing spines, thorns.

spinifex, n. [1. spínifeks; 2. spínifɛks]. Kind of Australian grass with stiff, sharply pointed leaves.

spiniform, adj. [1. spíniform; 2. spáinifɔ̀m]. **spini- & -form**. Having the shape of a spine, or thorn.

spininess, n. [1. spínines; 2. spáininis]. **spiny & -ness**. State or quality of being spiny.

spinitis, n. [1. spīnītis; 2. spaindáitis]. spini- & -itis. Inflammation of the spinal cord.

spinnaker, n. [1. spínaker; 2. spínəkə]. Possibly connected w. **spin**. Large triangular sail carried on the side opposite the mainsail by racing-cutters &c. when running before the wind.

spinner, n. [1. spíner; 2. spínə]. **spin** (I.) & **-er**. 1. One who, that which, spins; specif. **a** one who shapes cups &c. on a revolving lathe; **b** spinning-machine. 2. Spinneret.

spinneret, n. [1. spíneret; 2. spínərət]. Prec. & **-et**. Silk or thread-spinning organ of silkworm, spider &c.

spinney, n. [1. spíni; 2. spíni], fr. O. Fr. *espinoye*, fr. Lat. *spinētum*, ' thorn-hedge, thicket ', fr. *spīna*, ' thorn ', see **spine**, & cp. suff. in **arboretum**. Copse, thicket.

spinning-house, n. [1. spíning hous; 2. spíniŋ haus]. (hist.) Women's house of correction, the inmates of which were made to spin.

spinning-jenny, n. Machine for spinning several threads at the same time.

spinning-wheel, n. Instrument used for household spinning, with spindle rotated by fly-wheel usually worked by a treadle.

spinose, adj. [1. spīnōs; 2. spáinous], fr. Lat. *spinōsus*, ' thorny, prickly '. **spine** & **-ose**. Full of, covered with, spines; spiny, prickly.

spinosity, n. [1. spīnósiti; 2. spainósiti], fr. L. Lat. *spinōsitātem*, ' thorniness '. Prec. & **-ity**. State of being spinose.

spinous, adj. [1. spīnus; 2. spáinəs]. **spine** & **-ous**. 1. Having, producing, spines; spinose. 2. Having the shape of a spine; spiniform; *spinous process*, part of vertebra projecting backwards.

Spinozism, n. [1. spī-, spīnózizm; 2. spai-, spinóuzizəm], fr. Benedict de Spinoza, d. 1677, & **-ism**. Philosophical system of Spinoza.

Spinozist, n. [1. spīn-, spīnózist; 2. sp(ə)inóuzist]. See prec. & **-ist**. Adherent of Spinoza.

Spinozistic, adj. [1. spīn-, spīnózistik; 2. sp(ə)inouzístik]. Prec. & **-ic**. Pertaining to, resembling, Spinozism.

spinster, n. [1. spínster; 2. spínstə]. M.E. *spinnester*, ' woman who spins '. **spin** (I.) & **-ster**. Unmarried woman; (popularly) esp. elderly unmarried woman.

spinsterhood, n. [1. spínsterhood; 2. spínstəhud]. Prec. & **-hood**. State of being a spinster.

spinthariscope, n. [1. spinthárískōp; 2. spinþǽriskoup], fr. Gk. *spinthárís*, ' spark '; cp. Gk. *spinthḗr*, ' spark '; Lith *spistu*, ' to shine, sparkle '; Lett. *spídu*, ' to shine '; *spudrs*, ' brilliant '; & **-scope**. Instrument for exhibiting the scintillations caused by the impact of products of radium disintegration against a screen.

spinule, n. [1. spínūl; 2. spáinjūl], fr. Lat. *spinula*, ' little thorn '. **spine** & **-ule**. Small spine, prickle.

spinuliferous, adj. [1. spīnūlíferus; 2. spàinjulíferəs]. Prec. & **-i-** & **-ferous**. Bearing spinules.

spinulose, adj. [1. spínulōs; 2. spáinjulous]. **spinule** & **-ose**. Having, covered with, spinules.

spinulous, adj. [1. spínulus; 2. spáinjuləs]. **spinule** & **-ous**. Of, like, covered with, small spines.

spiny, adj. [1. spíni; 2. spáini]. **spine** & **-y**. 1. Having, covered with, full of, spines; *spiny ant-eater*, echidna; *spiny rat*, genus of rats of Central and South America, with spines among the hair. 2. (fig.) Difficult, perplexing, harassing: *a spiny subject to discuss*.

spiracle, n. [1. spírakl; 2. spáiərəkl], fr. Lat. *spīrāculum*, ' breathing-hole ', fr. *spīrāre*, ' to breathe ', see **spirant**, & **-cule**. External orifice used in respiration; breathing-hole, air-hole; specif. **a** external opening of trachea of insect; **b** blow-hole of cetacean.

spiracular, adj. [1. spīrákular; 2. spairǽkjulə], fr. Lat. *spīrāculum*, see prec., & **-ar**. Pertaining to, of the nature of, a spiracle.

spiraculate, adj. [1. spīrákūlāt; 2. spairǽkjuleit], fr. Lat. *spīrāculum*, see **spiracle**, & **-ate**. Having a spiracle or spiracles.

spiraea, n. [1. spīrḗa; 2. spairḯə]. Lat. *spīraea*, fr. Gk. *speiraiā*, ' meadow-sweet '; cp. Gk. *speira*, ' spiral; net; tissue ', see **spire** (III.). Genus of small rosaceous shrubs or herbs with feathery clusters of small white or pink flowers.

spiral (I.), adj. [1. spíral; 2. spáiərəl], fr. Lat. *spīrālis*, ' spiral ', fr. *spīra*, ' coil ', see **spire** (III.), & **-al**. 1. Forming a curve that winds continually about a centre from which it constantly recedes. 2. Winding constantly about a centre while undergoing continual change of plane, as on surface of cylinder or cone: *spiral staircase, spring, thread of screw* &c.; *spiral balance*, instrument measuring weight by the torsion of a spiral spring.

spiral (II.), n., fr. prec. 1. **a** Spiral curve remaining in one plane; **b** spiral curve that changes its plane continuously, forming a cone or cylinder. 2. Object or series of objects arranged to form a spiral; specif. **a** spiral spring; **b** spiral or whorled shell.

spiral (III.), vb. trans. & intrans., fr. prec. 1. trans. To form into, arrange as, a spiral; to make spiral. 2. intrans. To move in, form, a spiral.

spirality, n. [1. spīráliti; 2. spaiərǽliti]. **spiral** (I.) & **-ity**. State of being spiral.

spirally, adv. [1. spírali; 2. spáiərəli]. See prec. & **-ly**. In a spiral manner, so as to form a spiral.

spirant, n. & adj. [1. spírant; 2. spáiərənt], fr. Lat. *spīrantem*, Pres. Part. of *spīrāre*, ' to breathe, blow '; cp. Lat. *spīritus*, ' breath; spirit '; prob. fr. base *(s)peis-, ' to blow ', as in O. Slav. *pislą*, ' to pipe '; see **spirit** (I.) & cp. **despair**. 1. n. (phon.) A consonantal sound formed by a constriction, but not a total closure, of the air-passage, so that the airstream passes continuously, and the sound can be prolonged indefinitely; called also *open consonant*; contrasted with *stop*. 2. adj. Of the nature of a spirant.

spirated, adj. [1. spírāted; 2. spáiəreitid]. **spire** (III.) & **-ate** & **-ed**. Twisted into spiral form.

spire (I.), n. [1. spīr; 2. spaiə]. O.E., M.E. *spīr*, ' sprout; spire '; cp. M.L.G. *spīr*; O.N. *spīra*, ' point, ear of corn '; fr. base *spī-, *spei-, ' point '. Seen also in **spike, spine** &c. 1. Tall, slender prolongation of a tower, which tapers to a point. 2. Any of various objects tapering to a point, e.g. flower-cluster of this shape; an ear of corn; the upper part of a tapering tree such as a poplar.

spire (II.), vb. intrans. & trans., fr. prec. (rare) 1. intrans. To taper upwards, shoot up, in a spire. 2. trans. To furnish with, build with, a spire.

spire (III.), n., fr. Fr., fr. Lat. *spīra*, fr. Gk. *speira*, ' coil, twist; braid; net '; cp. Gk. *speirāma*, ' fold of a serpent '; *speiron*, ' web, tissue '; *speiraiā*, ' spiraea '; cp. further Gk. *spártos*, ' esparto grass '; *spurís*, ' woven basket '; Lith. *spartas*, ' bond '. **a** Spiral coil, esp. rising spiral; **b** single coil or twist of a spiral; whorl.

Spirillum, n., pl. **Spirilla** [1. spīrílum, -a; 2. spairílə(m)]. Mod. Lat., dimin. of Lat. *spīra*, ' coil, twist ', see **spire** (III.). A genus of bacteria, of spiral or twisted thread-like shape; one species is the cause of cholera.

spirit (I.), n. [1. spírit; 2. spírit]. M.E. *spirit, sprit*, fr. O. Fr. *espirit*, fr. Lat. *spīritus*, ' breath; breeze; breath of life; life; soul, mind, spirit; energy, courage; pride, arrogance ', fr. *spīrāre*, ' to breathe ', see **spirant**. 1. The life-giving principle; breath of life, conceived of as animating the body. 2. **a** The immortal, non-material part of, or element in, man, which wills, thinks, and feels; thought of as a gift of God; contrasted with *body*; intelligence, soul; (translating Gk. *pneūma*, or Lat. *spiritus*, and *anima*): *the spirit shall return to God who gave it*; *to lead the life of the spirit*; **b** this element or principle thought of as separated from the body; disembodied intelligence: *the spirits and souls of the righteous; the abode of spirits*. 3. Life, will, and consciousness thought of as existing apart from matter, and as never being associated with a body, and yet as pervading all things; contrasted with *matter*: *God is pure spirit*; (specif.) *the Holy Spirit*, the third Person of the Trinity; Holy Ghost. 4. A materialized, sometimes visible, disembodied spirit; an apparition, spectre, ghost: *are the phenomena of the séance room really the work of spirits?* 5. Individual human being, a person, thought of as exhibiting certain qualities of mind, character, disposition: *Dr. Johnson is recognized as one of the greatest spirits of his day*. 6. Temper, mood, disposition; mental attitude, frame of mind: ' *His spirits do not seem to have been high, but they were singularly equable* ' (Macaulay, on Milton); *a noble spirit animates all Burke's speeches*; *to show a mean, a proper, the right, spirit*; *high spirits*, cheerfulness, elation; *low spirits*, dejection, depression, of mind. 7. Vigour, energy of mind and character; liveliness, vivacity, fire; noble pride and courage; contempt for what is mean and base: *a young man of spirit*; *a cowardly wretch who shows no spirit*; *the king faced his accusers with spirit*. 8. Real meaning, true intention, underlying principle; contrasted with *letter*: *he obeyed the true spirit of the law*; *you must understand this in the spirit in which it was written*. 9. **a** A volatile distilled essence, alcohol: *to burn spirit in a lamp*; **b** *spirits*, (i.) powerful alcoholic drink; (ii.) any powerful distilled alcoholic liquor: *anatomical specimens are often preserved in spirits*. 10. (obs.) An aspirate, a rough breathing; translating Lat. *spiritus asper*.

spirit (II.), vb. trans., fr. prec. 1. Usually *spirit away, off*, to carry off, remove, secretly, swiftly, and mysteriously. 2. To give spirit to, animate, cheer.

spirit-blue, n. Kind of aniline dye soluble in alcohol.

spirit-duck, n. Kind of wild duck with unusually rapid dive.

spirited, adj. [1. spírited; 2. spíritid]. **spirit** & **-ed**. 1. Vigorous, animated, full of life, spirit, or courage: *spirited dialogue*; *a spirited attack, defence*; *a spirited horse*. 2. (in compounds) **a** Having specified character or disposition: *poor-, high-spirited*; *public-spirited*; **b** showing specified mood: *low-spirited*.

spiritedly, adv. Prec. & **-ly**. 1. In a spirited manner. 2. (in compounds) In a manner showing specified kind of spirit(s): *high-spiritedly*.

spiritedness, n. See prec. & **-ness**. 1. State or quality of being spirited. 2. (in compounds) State of having specified spirit(s).

spirit-gum, n. Gum dissolved in alcohol, used by actors &c. to affix false beard &c.

spiritism, n. [1. spíritizm; 2. spíritizəm]. **spirit** & **-ism**. 1. Spiritualism. 2. Animism.

spiritist, n. [1. spíritist; 2. spíritist]. **spirit** & **-ist**. Believer in spiritism, spiritualist.

spirit-lamp, n. One in which alcohol is burnt.

spiritless, adj. [1. spíritles; 2. spíritlis]. **spirit** & **-less**. Lacking spirit, animation, energy, vigour, or courage; listless, apathetic.

spiritlessly, adv. Prec. & **-ly**. In a spiritless manner.

spiritlessness, n. Prec. & **-ness**. State or quality of being spiritless; listlessness.

spirit-level, n. Glass tube almost completely filled with spirit, and used in surveying &c. to show any deviation from the level.

spiritoso, adv. [1. spīritóso; 2. spìritóusou]. Ital. **spirit** & **-ose**. (mus.) With spirit, with animation.

spirit-rapping, n. [1. spírit ráping; 2. spírit rǽpiŋ]. **a** Raps on table &c., made at spiritualist séances, as it is alleged, by disembodied spirits; **b** (loosely) the physical phenomena generally, said to be produced by spirits.

spirit-room, n. Paymaster's storeroom.

spirit(s) of wine, n. [1. spírit(s) uv wīn; 2. spírit(s) əv wáin]. Pure alcohol.

spirit-stove, n. Stove for cooking &c., heated by burning spirit.

spiritual (I.), adj. [1. spírichooal; 2. spíritʃuəl], fr. O. Fr., fr. Lat. *spīrituālis*, 'of breathing; of the spirit', fr. *spīritus*, 'breath, spirit'. See **spirit** (I.), & **-al**; see also **spirant**. **1.** Pertaining to, of the nature of, spirit; contrasted with *material*; incorporeal: *spiritual beings*. **2. a** Pertaining to the soul or spirit; connected with the inner life and being; contrasted with *physical, carnal*, or *bodily*: *the spiritual life*; *spiritual concerns, ideals*; *spiritual growth*; **b** preoccupied with the things of the spirit; expressing, animated by, thoughts and interests connected with the spirit; not centred in material, or worldly things: *a spiritual mind*; *a spiritual face, expression* &c. **3.** Proceeding from, inspired by, the Holy Spirit: *spiritual gifts*; *psalms and hymns and spiritual songs*. **4.** Of, pertaining to, the Church or to religion; ecclesiastical as opposed to secular or temporal: *a spiritual court*; *Lords Spiritual*, peers of Parliament who are bishops.

spiritual (II.), n., fr. prec. Also *negro spiritual*, a sacred song or hymn as sung by the negroes in the U.S.A.

spiritualism, n. [1. spírichooalizm; 2. spíritʃuəlizəm]. **spiritual** (I.) & **-ism**. **1.** Philosophical theory that spirit is the ultimate reality; idealism. **2. a** Belief that the spirits of the dead can and do communicate with the living by means of material manifestations; **b** the system of belief, beliefs collectively, of spiritualists; practices based on these beliefs.

spiritualist, n. [1. spírichooalist; 2. spíritʃuəlist]. **spiritual** (I.) & **-ist**. Believer in spiritualism; **a** in sense **1**; **b** in sense **2**.

spiritualistic, adj. [1. spìrichooalístik; 2. spìritʃuəlístik]. Prec. & **-ic**. Of, pertaining to, a spiritualist or to spiritualism.

spirituality, n. [1. spirichooáliti; 2. spìritʃuǽliti], fr. O. Fr., fr. L. Lat. *spīrituālitātem*, 'spirituality'. **spiritual** (I.) & **-ity**. **1.** Quality of being spiritual; spiritual character or nature; contrasted with *materiality, sensuality* &c. **2. a** The spiritual jurisdiction belonging to the Church or to an ecclesiastical office; **b** fees and revenues due to the holder, as such, of an ecclesiastical benefice.

spiritualization, n. [1. spìrichooalīzáshun; 2. spìritʃuəlaizéiʃən]. Next word & **-ation**. Act of spiritualizing; state of being spiritualized.

spiritualize, vb. trans. [1. spírichooalīz; 2. spíritʃuəlaiz]. **spiritual** (I.) & **-ize**. **1.** To render spiritual; to purify; to give a spiritual, elevated, non-material character to (a person, belief &c.). **2.** To give a spiritual meaning to; contrasted with *literalize*.

spiritually, adv. [1. spírichooali; 2. spíritʃuəli]. **spiritual** (I.) & **-ly**. In a spiritual manner.

spiritualness, n. [1. spírichualnes; 2. spíritʃuəlnis]. See prec. & **-ness**. State or quality of being spiritual.

spirituelle, adj. [1. spìritūél; 2. spìritjuél]. Fr. *spirituelle*, fem. form of *spirituel*, fr. Lat. *spīrituālis*, 'of a spirit', see **spiritual**. **1.** Delicate, graceful, ethereal. **2.** Delicately and gracefully witty.

spirituous, adj. [1. spíritūus; 2. spíritjuəs], fr. O. Fr. *spiritueux*, fr. Lat. *spīritus*, 'breath; spirit', see **spirit** (I.) & **-ous**. Containing a large percentage of alcohol; esp. of distilled liquor as distinct from fermented.

spirituousness, n. Prec. & **-ness**. State or quality of being spirituous.

spiritus, n. [1. spíritus; 2. spáiəritəs]. Lat. *spīritus*, 'breath; (gram.) breathing, aspiration', see **spirit**. (Gk. gram.) *Spiritus asper*, rough breathing, aspiration; *spiritus lenis*, smooth breathing.

spirivalve, adj. [1. spírivàlv; 2. spáiərivǽlv], fr. Lat. *spīra*, 'coil, spiral', see **spire** (III.), & *-i-* & **valve**. **1.** Having a spiral shell. **2.** (of shell) Spiral, whorled.

spirket, n. [1. spérket; 2. spʌ́kit]. Etymol. unknown. Space between floor-timbers of a ship, forward and aft.

spirketing, n. [1. spérketing; 2. spʌ́kitiŋ]. Prec. & **-ing**. Part of inside planking of a ship.

spiro- (I.), pref. representing Lat. *spīra*, 'coil', see **spire** (III.). Spiral, whorled; e.g. *Spirochaete*, a thread-like bacterium of the genus *Spirochaeta*, of the *Spirillum* type, one species, *S. pallida*, is the cause of syphilis; *Spirodela*, genus of aquatic plants including the great duckweed.

spiro- (II.), pref. representing Lat. *spīr-(āre)*, 'to breathe'. See **spirant**. Breath, breathing.

spirograph, n. [1. spírōgràhf; 2. spáiərougrɑ̀f]. **spiro-** (II.) & **-graph**. Instrument recording movements made in breathing.

spirometer, n. [1. spīrómeter; 2. spairómitə]. **spiro-** (II.) & **-meter**. Instrument for measuring the capacity of the lungs.

spirometric, adj. [1. spírōmétrik; 2. spáiəroumétrik]. Prec. & **-ic**. Pertaining to, recorded by, a spirometer.

spirometry, n. [1. spìrómetri; 2. spàirómitri]. **spiro-** (II.) & **-metry**. The measurement of the breathing capacity of the lungs.

spirophore, n. [1. spírōfòr; 2. spáiəroufɔ̀]. **spiro-** (II.) & **-phore**. Instrument for inducing artificial respiration.

spirt (I.), **spurt**, vb. intrans. & trans. [1. spërt; 2. spʌt]. Metathesized form of O.E. *spryttan*, 'to shoot forth, sprout'; cp. O.E. *sprūtan*, 'to sprout', see **sprout**. **1.** intrans. (of liquid) To shoot out, gush out, in a small, sudden jet or stream. **2.** trans. To squirt out, pour out in a sudden jet.

spirt (II.), **spurt**, n., fr. prec. See also **spurt** (I.) w. special sense. Sudden, small, but strong jet or stream of liquid.

spiry (I.), adj. [1. spíri; 2. spáiəri]. **spire** (I.) & **-y**. **a** Of, pertaining to, having the form of, having, a spire; **b** abounding in spires.

spiry (II.), adj. **spire** (III.) & **-y**. Spiral, coiled.

spit (I.), n. [1. spit; 2. spit]. O.E. *spitu*; M.E. *spite*; cp. O.H.G. *spiz*; M. Du. *spit, spet*; cp. also O.H.G. *spizzi*; Mod. Germ. *spitz*, 'point'; cogn. w. Lith. *spitnà*, 'tongue of a buckle'; Lat. *pinna*, 'pinnacle'; *bipinnis*, 'two-edged'; fr. base **(s)pi(d)-*, **(s)pi(t)-*, 'point', expanded fr. **(s)pei-*, **spī-*, 'point', see **spine, spike**. **1.** Long, thin pointed bar of iron thrust through and supporting meat to be roasted before a fire. **2.** Long, narrow point of land or sandbank extending into the sea, separating lagoon from sea &c.

spit (II.), vb. trans., fr. prec. To pierce, penetrate, transfix, with, or as with, a spit.

spit (III.), vb. intrans. & trans. O.E. *spittan*; M.E. *spitten*; fr. *spit-*, gradational variant of base in O.E. *spǣtan*, 'to spit', wh. is for **spāt-jan*, earlier **spait-*; ultimately related to **spew** & **sputum**. **A.** intrans. **1. a** To eject saliva from the mouth; Phr. *spit upon* (fig.), to treat, regard, with contempt; **b** (of an angry cat) to make a noise like that of spitting, or hissing. **2.** (of boiling liquid, fat &c.) To sputter, hiss, spirt out in minute drops. **3.** To rain intermittently and lightly. **B.** trans. **1. a** Often *spit out*, to eject from the mouth; *to spit blood*, cough it up from the lungs or throat; **b** (vulg.) to utter, say, tell; esp. in Phr. *spit it out*, out with it. **2.** To utter violently, as in anger, contempt, malice: *he spat his words at his hearers*.

spit (IV.), n., fr. prec. **1.** Act of spitting. **2.** Saliva, spittle; Phr. *the dead spit of* (a person), another who resembles him exactly, living image. **3.** Frothy secretion of certain insects. **4.** A sprinkle of rain.

spit (V.), n. Prob. fr. Du. *spit*, 'a spit'; cp. O.E. *spittan*, 'to dig'. Depth of earth equal to blade of spade.

spitchcock, n. & vb. trans. [1. spíchkok; 2. spítʃkɔk]. Etymol. doubtful. **1.** n. Eel split and broiled. **2.** vb. To split and broil (eel, bird &c.).

spite (I.), n. [1. spīt; 2. spait]. Abbr. of **despite**. **1.** Malice, malevolence, mean or petty hatred: *the victim of another's spite*; *to do something out of spite*; Phr. *spite of, in spite of*, notwithstanding, in defiance of. **2.** Cause of dislike or desire to injure; grudge: *to have a spite against one*.

spite (II.), vb. trans., fr. prec. To injure, annoy, through malevolence; to act maliciously towards: *it is only done to spite me*.

spiteful, adj. [1. spítfool; 2. spáitful]. **spite** (I.) & **-ful**. Full of, caused by, spite; malicious, malevolent, meanly hostile.

spitefully, adv. Prec. & **-ly**. In a spiteful manner.

spitefulness, n. See prec. & **-ness**. Quality of being spiteful.

spitfire, n. [1. spítfīr; 2. spítfaiə]. **spit** (III.) & **fire** (I.). Sharp-tongued person; one given to hasty, biting speech.

spittle, n. [1. spítl; 2. spítl]. O.E. *spātl*; M.E. *spōtel*; remodelled on **spit** (III.). Secretions of the glands of the mouth, saliva, esp. when ejected.

spittoon, n. [1. spitóon; 2. spitún]. **spit** (III.) & **-oon**. Receptacle for saliva ejected by smokers.

spitz, n. [1. spits; 2. spits], fr. Germ. *spitzhund*, fr. *spitz*, 'point', q.v. under **spit** (I.). Also *spitz-dog*, breed of small dog, with narrow, tapering muzzle and long, silky hair; Pomeranian.

splanchnic, adj. [1. splángknik; 2. splǽŋknik], fr. Gk. *splágkhna*, 'viscera'. See next word & **-ic**. Of, pertaining to, the abdominal viscera, esp. the intestines.

splanchno-, pref. representing Gk. *splágkhnon*, 'viscera'; prob. cogn. w. *splḗn*, 'spleen', see **spleen**, cogn. w. Scrt. *plīhán-*; Lat. *liēn*; O. Slav. *slezena*, 'spleen'. The abdominal viscera.

splanchnology, n. [1. splàngknóloji; 2. splæ̀ŋknɔ́lədʒi]. Prec. & **-logy**. The science or study of the viscera.

splanchnoskeleton, n. [1. splángknōskéletun; 2. splæŋknouskélitən]. **splanchno-** & **skeleton**. Part of the skeleton surrounding the viscera.

splanchnotomy, n. [1. splàngknótumi; 2. splæŋknɔ́təmi]. **splanchno-** & **-tomy**. Dissection of the viscera.

splash (I.), vb. trans. & intrans. [1. splash; 2. splæʃ]. Of imitative origin. **A.** trans. **1.** (of liquid) To scatter, fly about, and fall in drops upon: *the mud has splashed my dress*. **2.** To cause (liquid) to fly or scatter in drops or small streams: *to splash ink on to one's fingers*. **3.** To cause liquid to scatter or fall in drops upon: *to splash a page with ink*. **4.** To achieve, effect, by splashing: *to splash one's way through the mud*. **5.** To adorn with scattered ornament irregularly placed. **B.** intrans. **1.** (of liquid) To fly about, scatter, in drops or small streams, esp. as result of sudden pressure of falling body: *the mud splashed up at every step*. **2.** To strike liquid so as to cause it to fly or scatter in drops. **3.** To pass, go, so as to cause splashing: *to splash through the stream*.

splash (II.), n., fr. prec. **1.** Act of splashing: *to fall into water with a splash*. Phr. *to make a splash*, to create a sensation by display &c. **2.** Sound produced by splashing. **3. a** Spot, streak, or patch of liquid splashed on to a surface: *a splash of ink on the carpet*; **b** patch or streak of colour on a surface. **4.** Kind of white face-powder.

splash-board, n. Screen or guard protecting passengers in a vehicle from splashes caused by wheels &c.

splasher, n. [1. splásher; 2. splǽʃə]. **splash** (I.) & **-er**. **1.** One who, that which, splashes. **2.** Screen &c. giving protection from splashes; specif. **a** splash-board; **b** mudguard over wheel of locomotive; **c** curtain &c. protecting wall behind wash-stand.

splashy, adj. [1. spláshi; 2. splǽʃi]. **splash** & **-y**. Liable to splash; wet, muddy.

splatter, vb. intrans. & trans. [1. spláter; 2. splǽtə]. Variant of **spatter**. **A.** intrans.

splay, *vb. trans., -n., & adj.* [1. splā; 2. splei]. M.E. *splayen*, 'to turn outwards, spread out', abbr. fr. **display**. 1. *vb.* **a** (archit.) To slope, slant, bevel, form with oblique surface: *to splay the sides of a window outwards*; **b** (veter. surg.) to dislocate: *a splayed shoulder-bone*. 2. *n.* Sloping or bevelled edge, angle, or surface; esp. sloping side of splayed window, embrasure. 3. *adj.* Sloping, oblique, forming an angle, spreading out.

splay-foot(ed), *adj.* Having flat feet turned outwards to an abnormal degree.

splay-mouth, *n.* Wide, or widely opened, mouth.

spleen, *n.* [1. splēn; 2. splīn]. Lat. *splēn*, fr. Gk. *splḗn*, earlier **splegkh*; prob. cogn. w. *splágkhnon*, 'entrails', see **splanchno-**, cogn. w. Lat. *liēn*; Scrt. *plīhán-*; O. Slav. *slezena*, 'spleen'. 1. Small, soft, vascular ductless gland situated near the stomach, which modifies the character of the blood; formerly supposed to be the seat of certain emotions. 2. **a** Ill-humour, spite; **b** dejection, melancholy.

spleenful, *adj.* [1. splēnfool; 2. splīnful]. spleen & -ful. Characterized by, showing, ill-temper; peevish, fretful, irascible.

spleenfully, *adv.* Prec. & -ly. In a spleenful manner.

spleenish, *adj.* [1. splēnish; 2. splīniʃ]. spleen & -ish. Peevish, ill-tempered.

spleenishly, *adv.* Prec. & -ly. In a spleenish manner.

spleenless, *adj.* [1. splēnles; 2. splīnlis]. spleen & -less. Having no spleen; (chiefly fig.) lacking malice, good-tempered.

spleenwort, *n.* [1. splēnwĕrt; 2. splīnwāt]. Genus, *Asplenium*, of ferns with pinnate leaves, formerly used medicinally.

spleeny, *adj.* [1. splēni; 2. splīni]. spleen & -y. Spleenful.

splen-, pref. representing Lat. *splēn*, 'spleen', see **spleen**. Spleen.

splenalgia, *n.* [1. splenáljia; 2. splīnǽldʒə]. Prec. & Gk. *álgos*, 'pain', & -ia; cp. Gk. *alégein*, 'to suffer', q.v. under **neglect**. Pain in the spleen.

splenalgic, *adj.* [1. splenáljik; 2. splīnǽldʒik]. Prec. & -ic. Pertaining to, of the nature of, splenalgia.

splendent, *adj.* [1. splĕndent; 2. splĕndənt], fr. Lat. *splendent-(em)*, Pres. Part. of *splendēre*, 'to shine, gleam, glisten', cogn. w. Lith. *spléndžiu*, 'I shine'; M. Ir. *lainn*, 'bright'; more remotely connected w. Scrt. *sphulingaś*, 'spark'; Germ. *flinken*, 'to glitter', fr. **(s)pleŋk-*. Lustrous, glossy; brilliant, gleaming.

splendid, *adj.* [1. splĕndid; 2. splĕndid], fr. Fr., fr. Lat. *splendidus*, 'bright, brilliant; gorgeous, magnificent; eminent, illustrious', fr. *splend-(ēre)*, 'to shine', see **splendent**, & -id. 1. Magnificent, gorgeous, making a striking impression on the senses: *a splendid scene*. 2. Worthy of honour or fame; eminent, illustrious, admirable: *splendid heroism*. 3. (colloq.) Very satisfactory, excellent: *a splendid idea*; *fir-cones make splendid fuel*.

splendidly, *adv.* Prec. & -ly. 1. In a splendid manner. 2. (colloq.) Excellently, very well.

splendiferous, *adj.* [1. splĕndíferus; 2. splĕndífərəs]. As though fr. **splendour** & -ferous. (slang or facet.) Gorgeous, magnificent.

splendour, *n.* [1. splĕndur; 2. splĕndə], fr. O. Fr., fr. Lat. *splendōr-(em)*, 'brilliance, magnificence; grandeur', fr. *splendēre*, 'to shine', see **splendent**, & -our. 1. Brilliance, radiance, dazzling lustre, brightness. 2. Magnificence, gorgeousness, sumptuousness. 3. Intellectual or moral magnificence; impressiveness, pre-eminence, greatness: *the splendour of his achievements, exploits*.

splenectomy, *n.* [1. splenéktumi; 2. splīnék-təmi]. **splen-** & Gk. *ek*, 'out of', q.v. under **ecto-**, & -**tomy**. Removal of the spleen.

splenetic (I.), *adj.* [1. splenétik; 2. splīnétik], fr. O. Fr. *splenetique*, fr. L. Lat. *splēnēticus*, 'affected with spleen', w. Gk. suff., fr. *splēn*, 'spleen', see **spleen**, & -ic. 1. Of, pertaining to, the spleen; splenic. 2. Ill-tempered, fretful or sulky.

splenetic (II.), *n.*, fr. prec. 1. Person affected with spleen; one who is peevish, ill-humoured. 2. Person suffering from a splenic disorder. 3. Medicine for disorder of the spleen.

splenetically, *adv.* [1. splenétikali; 2. splīnétik-əli]. Prec. & -al & -ly. In a splenetic manner, ill-humouredly.

splenial, *adj.* [1. splēniəl; 2. splīniəl]. **splenius** & -al. 1. Of, pertaining to, the splenius. 2. Of, shaped like, serving as, a splint.

splenic, *adj.* [1. splēnik; 2. splīnik], fr. O. Fr. *splenique*, fr. Lat. *splēnicus*, fr. Gk. *splēnikós*, 'splenetic', fr. *splēn*, 'spleen', see **spleen**, & -ic. Pertaining to, situated near, the spleen.

splenitic, *adj.* [1. splenítik; 2. splīnítik]. See next word & -ic. Pertaining to, of the nature of, splenitis.

splenitis, *n.* [1. splenítis; 2. splīnáitis]. **splen-** & -itis. Inflammation of the spleen.

splenius, *n.* [1. splēnius; 2. splīniəs]. Mod. Lat., fr. Gk. *splēnion*, 'bandage', dimin. of *splēn*, 'spleen; absorbent bandage', see **spleen**. Large, strong muscle on either side of back of the neck.

splenization, *n.* [1. splēnizáshun; 2. splīnaizéi-ʃən], fr. Lat. *splēn*, 'spleen', see **spleen**, & -ize & -ation. (pathol.) Morbid development of organ into tissue resembling that of the spleen, esp. of the lung in certain pulmonary diseases.

splenoid, *adj.* [1. splēnoid; 2. splīnoid], fr. Lat. *splēn*, 'spleen', see **spleen**, & -oid. Resembling spleen in character and appearance.

splenological, *adj.* [1. splēnolójikl; 2. splīnə-lódʒikl]. Next word & -ic & -al. Pertaining to splenology.

splenology, *n.* [1. splēnóloji; 2. splīnólədʒi]. **splen-** & -o- & -logy. The study of the spleen.

splenotomy, *n.* [1. splēnótumi; 2. splīnótəmi]. **splen-** & -o- & -tomy. **a** Removal of the spleen; **b** dissection of the spleen.

splice (I.), *vb. trans.* [1. splīs; 2. splais], fr. M. Du. *splissen*, 'to splice'; fr. *splijten*, 'to split; to unravel'; cogn. w. **split (I.)**. 1. To join (two ropes or ends of rope) end to end, by unlaying and then interweaving the strands; Phr. *to splice the main-brace*; **a** to drink; **b** to serve out an allowance of spirits. 2. To join up, connect, timbers &c., by overlapping the ends, or fitting one end into the other, and binding. 3. (slang) To perform marriage ceremony for, join in marriage.

splice (II.), *n.*, fr. prec. 1. Join made in two ropes or two parts of rope by interweaving the strands. 2. Joining of timbers &c. by overlapping, or fitting the ends, and binding.

spline, *n.* [1. splīn; 2. splain]. Etymol. unknown. 1. Square end of a wheel shaft which fits into a similarly shaped opening in hub of a wheel, and ensures that the shaft revolves with the wheel. 2. Long, flexible strip of wood or solid rubber used by mechanical draughtsmen for drawing large curves, esp. in shipbuilding &c.

splint (I.), *n.* [1. splint; 2. splint], fr. Sw. *splint*, 'spike, pointed rod'; cp. Swed. *splinta*, 'to split'; Dan. *splint*, 'splinter'; Mod. Germ. *splint*, 'steel strip'; nasalized form of stem **split*, 'to tear asunder', see **split (I.)**. 1. Padded strip of wood or other appliance for keeping the two ends of a fractured bone in position. 2. Flexible strip of split wood used for basket-making or other wickerwork. 3. Also *splint-bone*, **a** (anat.) fibula; **b** (of horse) one of two bones lying near cannon-bone. 4. (veter. surg.) Bony tumour on horse's splint-bone caused by disease.

splint (II.), *vb. trans.*, fr. prec. To furnish with, hold in place by means of, splint(s).

splint-coal, *n.* Bituminous coal found in slaty masses.

splinter (I.), *vb. trans. & intrans.* [1. splínter; 2. splíntə], fr. Swed. *splinta*, 'to split', see **splint (I.)**, & -er. 1. *trans.* To break into long, thin pieces, split, shiver, divide into slivers, as by a violent blow &c. 2. *intrans.* To break, split up, into splinters.

splinter (II.), *n.*, fr. prec. Thin, sharp, irregularly shaped fragment of wood or other harder substance, torn or split from a larger mass.

splinter-bar, *n.* 1. Crossbar supporting springs of vehicle. 2. Rigid bar of gun-carriage &c., to which traces are attached.

splinter-bone, *n.* Splint-bone (see **splint (I.)**).

splinter-proof, *adj.* Proof against flying shell-splinters.

splintery, *adj.* [1. splínteri; 2. splíntəri]. **splinter (II.)** & -y. 1. Of the nature of, like, splinters. 2. Liable to splinter.

split (I.), *vb. intrans. & trans.* [1. split; 2. split], fr. M. Du. *splitten*; cp. Dan. *splitta*; Mod. Germ. *spleissen*; Du. *splijten*, 'to split'; fr. base **split-*, 'to tear asunder', not known outside Gmc. **A**. *intrans.* 1. **a** (of hard substances) To be ruptured, cloven, shivered; to divide, into two or more parts with long narrow crack or cracks between, as a result of pressure, a sudden impact or blow, the insertion of a wedge, changes of temperature &c.; Phr. *the rock on which we split*, (i.) the subject of disagreement between us; (ii.) the cause of our misfortunes; **b** (of soft, thin substance) to burst, gape, open suddenly, as result of excessive lateral strain: *gloves often split the first time they are worn*. 2. **a** To become disunited, to undergo division, become alienated, in sympathies, opinions &c.: *the old Liberal party split over the question of Irish Home Rule*; **b** to undergo differentiation, divide up into two or more different entities: *a primitive language splits into several dialects; the crowd is splitting into small groups*. **B**. *trans.* 1. To cause to split; to shiver, rupture, crack suddenly; to cleave, burst, apart: *to split wood, to split one's skull open*. Phrs. *to split hairs*, to make subtle distinctions; *to split one's sides*, to laugh uncontrollably; *a splitting headache*, one that is very severe. 2. To divide into parts; to share: *to split a bottle of wine with a person; to split the profits*. Phr. *to split the difference*, to take the mean between two amounts &c. in dispute. 3. To cause dissension, disunion, disagreement, between; to provoke differences of opinion among or between: *the Church is split by parties and factions*. **C**. Followed by adverb or preposition with special meanings. *Split off*, **a** *trans.*, to break off by splitting; **b** *intrans.*, to become separated, to divide off by fission; (in material and non-material senses). *Split on*, *intrans.* (slang) to inform against a person. *Split up*, (in material and non-material senses) 1. *trans.*, to divide, break up, into parts, to disunite; 2. *intrans.*, to be broken up, forcibly divided.

split (II.), *n.*, fr. prec. 1. **a** Process of splitting; **b** result of splitting; a narrow fissure, a crack, a cleft, a tear (in fabric). 2. Moral or physical separation, disunion. 3. **a** Flexible strip of wood for basket-making &c.; **b** wooden strip forming part of reed of loom. 4. Single thickness of hide split horizontally. 5. (slang) **a** A half-glass or portion of brandy, whisky &c.; **b** a small bottle of soda water. 6. (colloq.) *The splits*, acrobatic feat in which the legs are opened until both lie almost flat, upon the ground, the trunk being kept upright. 7. (Corn.) Small soft roll or scone, split and spread with cream and jam.

split cloth, *n.* Surgical bandage with four, six, or more tails, used for head or face.

split infinitive, *n.* Construction in which an adverb is inserted between the particle *to* and the infinitive; e.g. *I wish to highly recommend him for the post.*

split-moss, n. Family of mosses whose seed-capsules split open when ripe.

split peas(e), n. Peas shelled, dried, and split in halves for cooking.

split shot, stroke, n. (croquet) Stroke by which two balls are driven in different directions.

splitter, n. [1. splíter; 2. splítə]. **split** (I.) & **-er**. One who, that which, splits; sometimes in compounds, e.g. *side-splitter*.

splodge, n. [1. sploj; 2. splɔdž]. Variant of next word. Irregular patch, smear, blotch, splash.

splotch, n. [1. sploch; 2. splɔtʃ]. Cp. O.E., M.E. *splot*, 'spot'; but perh. a blend of **spot** & **splash**. Splodge.

splotchy, adj. [1. splóchi; 2. splɔ́tʃi]. Prec. & -y. Marked with splotches.

splurge, n. & vb. intrans. [1. splérj; 2. splʌdž]. Prob. imitative. (colloq., slang) **1.** n. Ostentation, obtrusive display. **2.** vb. To show off, make a splurge.

splutter (I.), vb. intrans. & trans. [1. splúter; 2. splátə]. Variant of **sputter**. **1.** intrans. **a** To eject, throw off, liquid, saliva &c. with succession of spitting sounds; to sputter; **b** to speak hastily and indistinctly, as from anger or other form of excitement. **2.** trans. To utter in a sputtering manner.

splutter (II.), n., fr. prec. Spluttering noise.

splutterer, n. [1. splúterer; 2. splátərə]. See prec. & -er. One who splutters.

Spode, n. [1. spōd; 2. spoud]. Name of maker, Josiah Spode (1754–1827), of Stoke-on-Trent, Staffordshire. Also *Spode ware*, a highly decorated form of chinaware.

spoil (I.), n. [1. spoil; 2. spoil]. M.E. *spoile*, fr. O. Fr. *espoille*, fr. Lat. *spolium*, 'skin or hide stripped from animal; arms taken from defeated enemy; prey, booty'; cogn. w. Gk. *spolás*, 'flayed skin; leather jerkin'; Scrt. *phálaš*, 'ploughshare'; O. Slav. *plévą*, 'to weed out'. **1.** Property, goods, taken by violence; loot, plunder, booty: *the thieves escaped with their spoil*; (also in pl.) *the spoils of war*. **2.** (fig.) Profit, benefit, arising from contest with, or effort against, another; (specif. U.S.A.) public offices and their emoluments given by political party as rewards to their adherents; *spoils system*, political service given in hope of reward.

spoil (II.), vb. trans. & intrans., fr. M.E. *spoilen*, fr. O. Fr. *espoillier*, fr. Lat. *spoliāre*, 'to strip, rob, plunder', fr. *spolium*, 'spoil', see prec. **A.** trans. **1.** (archaic) To take spoils from; plunder, rob with violence: *to spoil the Egyptians*. **2. a** (of physical effect) To injure, impair, do harm to; to injure the appearance of; to detract from the beauty, value, or usefulness of: *the fresh paint has been spoilt by the rain*; *the picture is spoilt by too much detail*; *the damp has spoilt my watch*; *don't spoil your new clothes by wearing them too much*; Phrs. *to spoil one's appetite*, reduce desire for a meal by eating beforehand; *to spoil one's dinner*, lessen appetite for, enjoyment of, by eating beforehand; **b** (in non-material sense) to detract from extent or merit of, lessen enjoyment of: *to spoil one's pleasure*; *he spoilt the effect of his genuine kindness of heart by his rudeness and moroseness*; **c** to cause to deteriorate, to make bad: *his temper had been spoilt by petty worries*. **3.** Specif., to injure character of; to cause character of to develop badly, to encourage growth of selfishness and unruliness in, by wrong modes of training, by lack of discipline, over-indulgence &c.; esp. *to spoil a child*; *she had been thoroughly spoilt by adulation and flattery*. **B.** intrans. To deteriorate, to become impaired, lose quality, value, usefulness: *delicate fabric soon spoils if exposed to the sun*. Phr. *to be spoiling for* (*a fight* &c.), be eager for.

spoilage, n. [1. spóilij; 2. spóilidž]. **spoil** & -age. Paper spoilt or wasted in printing.

spoiler, n. [1. spóiler; 2. spóilə]. **spoil** & -er. Person who takes spoils; plunderer.

spoil-five, n. Card game for three or more persons, to each of whom five cards are dealt.

spoilsman, n. [1. spóilzman; 2. spóilzmən]. Person engaging in political career in the hope of financial gain.

spoil-sport, n. A dismal, disagreeable person who objects to, and tries to prevent, other people enjoying themselves; the skeleton at the feast.

spoke (I.), n. [1. spōk; 2. spouk]. O.E. *spāca*, M.E. *spōke*, 'spoke'; cp. M.L.G. *spēke*, O.H.G. *speicha*; cogn. w. **spike**. **1.** Any one of the bars radiating from the hub of a wheel and joining this to the outer rim or felly. **2.** Rung of ladder. **3.** Bar of wood used to prevent the wheels of a cart &c. from turning, acting as a drag downhill. Phr. *to put a spoke in a person's wheel*, to upset or delay his plans. **4.** (naut.) One of the handles projecting from the rim of the steering-wheel.

spoke (II.), vb. trans., fr. prec. **1.** To supply, fit, with spokes. **2.** To hinder movement of (wheel &c.) with spoke.

spoke (III.), vb. Pret. of **speak**, fr. P.P. spoken.

spoke-bone, n. Bone extending from elbow to wrist; radius.

spoken, vb. [1. spóken; 2. spóukən]. P.P. of **speak**; M.E. *spōken*, formed on the anal. of **broken**; cp. O.E. *sp(r)ecen*, P.P.

-spoken, adj., fr. prec. (in compounds) Characterized by specific manner of speech: *ill-, fair-, soft-spoken* &c.

spoke-shave, n. Small blade set in the middle of a piece of wood which, grasped by a hand at either end, is used for planing and smoothing curved wood articles.

spokesman, n. [1. spóksman; 2. spóuksmən], fr. *spoke*, Pret. of **speak**, & -es & -**man**. Person who speaks as representative of others.

spokewise, adv. [1. spókwīz; 2. spóukwaiz]. **spoke** (I.) & -**wise**. Arranged as spokes; in the position of a spoke; radiating.

spolia opima, n. pl. [1. spólia opíma; 2. spóuliə əpáimə]. Lat., fr. pl. of *spolium*, 'booty', see **spoil** (I.), & *optimus*, 'rich; fat'; prob. cogn. w. Gk. *pīmelé*, 'fat', Lat. *pinguis*, 'rich, fat', see **pinguid**. Arms taken by Roman general from enemy's commander in single combat; hence, rewards, honours, received as result of contest.

spoliation, n. [1. spōliáshun; 2. spòuliéiʃən], fr. Lat. *spoliātiōnem*, fr. *spoliātum*, P.P. type of *spoliāre*, 'to pillage', see **spoil** (II.), & -**ion**. **1.** Robbery with violence, plunder, esp. plunder of neutral trading-vessel by nation at war. **2.** (eccles.) Illegal appropriation of tithes &c. **3.** (legal) Wilful destruction, mutilation &c., of document liable to be put in evidence.

spoliator, n. [1. spóliātur; 2. spóulieitə], fr. Lat. *spoliātum*, P.P. type of *spoliāre*, 'to pillage', see **spoil** (I.), & -**or**. Plunderer, spoiler.

spoliatory, adj. [1. spóliaturi; 2. spóuliətəri], fr. Lat. *spoliātum*, see prec., & -**ory**. Of the nature of, causing, spoliation.

spondaic, adj. [1. spondáik; 2. spɔndéiik], fr. O. Fr. *spondaique*, fr. L. Lat. *spondaicus*, *spondīacus*, fr. Gk. *spondeiakós*, 'spondaic', fr. *spondeios*, 'spondee', see next word. Pertaining to, composed in, spondees; *spondaic hexameter*, one that has a spondee in fifth foot.

spondee, n. [1. spóndē; 2. spɔ́ndī], fr. Lat. *spondēus*, fr. Gk. *spondeios (poús)*, 'metrical foot used at a libation, esp. in making a treaty'; cp. *spéndein*, 'to pour forth as a libation'; *spondḗ*, 'libation; treaty, alliance'; Lat. *spondēre*, 'to promise', see **sponsion**. Metrical foot consisting of two long syllables.

spondulics, n. pl. [1. spondúliks; 2. spɔndjúliks]. Origin doubtful; Weekley suggests that first element may be fr. Du. *spaan*, 'a chip', see **spoon** (I.), used also in sense of 'money'. (Am. slang) Money; equivalent to **dibs**.

spondyl(e), n. [1. spóndil; 2. spɔ́ndil], fr. Fr., fr. Lat. *spondylus*, fr. Gk. *spónd-*, *sphóndulos*, 'vertebra'; cp. Gk. *sphendónē*, 'sling'; prob. related to Gk. *sphaddzein*, 'to move convulsively'; Scrt. *spandatē*, 'to start up'. One of the bones of the spinal column; vertebra.

spondyl(o)-, pref. representing prec. & -**o-**. Vertebra; e.g. *spondylitis*, inflammation of the vertebrae.

sponge (I.), n. [1. spunj; 2. spandž], fr. O. Fr. *esponge*, fr. Lat. *spongia*, fr. Gk. *spoggiá*, 'sponge'; etymol. doubtful. **1.** Marine animal, belonging to the phylum *Porifera*, with tough, fibrous skeleton and without tentacles, usually found fixed to a rock. **2.** Elastic, absorbent, fibrous network left after removal of living matter from a sponge, used for applying water to the body or other surface for cleansing &c. Phr. *to throw up the sponge*, (of boxer and fig.) to admit defeat; to give up a struggle of any kind. **3.** Object or substance resembling a sponge in structure, appearance, or use; specif. **a** light, porous mass of fermented dough before kneading; **b** sweet cake of light, soft, elastic consistency; **c** soft pad &c. used for cleaning bore of cannon. **4.** Person living at another's expense; hanger-on, parasite, a cadger.

sponge (II.), vb. intrans. & trans., fr. O. Fr. *espongier*, fr. L. Lat. *spongiāre*, 'to sponge', fr. *spongia*, 'sponge'; see prec. **A.** intrans. **1.** To collect, gather, sponges. **2.** To play the part of a social sponge; to live at the expense of others. **B.** trans. To apply water to, wash, wipe, cleanse, by means of a sponge. **C.** Followed by adverb or preposition, with special meanings. *Sponge down*, trans., to wash, pour water over, with a sponge. *Sponge on*, intrans., to live in dependence on, as parasite of. *Sponge out*, trans. (lit. and fig.), to erase, efface, wipe out, with or as with a sponge. *Sponge up*, trans., To absorb, take up, with a sponge.

sponge (III.), n., fr. prec. Act of sponging; process of being sponged: *to have a sponge (down)*.

sponge-cake, n. Soft, light, sweet cake made of eggs, sugar, and flour.

sponge-cucumber, n. Tropical plant producing a large gourd, the fibrous network of which is dried and used as a rubber in Turkish baths.

sponge-gourd, n. Sponge-cucumber.

spongelet, n. [1. spúnjlet; 2. spándžlit]. **sponge** (I.) & -**let**. Spongiole, q.v.

sponger, n. [1. spúnjer; 2. spándžə]. **sponge** (II.) & -**er**. **1.** One who sponges; apparatus for sponging. **2.** Parasite, hanger-on.

sponge tree, n. Tropical tree with round clusters of sweet-scented yellow flowers.

spongiform, adj. [1. spúnjiform; 2. spándžifōm]. **sponge** (I.) & -**i**- & -**form**. Resembling a sponge in form, structure, or texture.

sponginess, n. [1. spúnjines; 2. spándžinis]. **spongy** & -**ness**. State of being spongy.

sponging-house, n. [1. spúnjing hòus; 2. spándžiŋ hɑus]. Bailiff's house where debtors were formerly detained in custody before being committed to prison.

spongiole, n. [1. spúnjiōl; 2. spándžioul]. **sponge** (I.) & -**i**- & dimin. -**ole**, as in **aureole**, **foliole**. Protective tissue covering the tip of the root of a plant.

spongiopiline, n. [1. spùnjiopílīn; 2. spàndžiopáil(ə)in], fr. Lat. *spongia*, 'sponge', see **sponge**, & -**o**- & Gk. *pilos*, 'felt'; cp. Lat. *pilleus*, 'felt cap', & see **pile** (VII.). Material made of small pieces of sponge and vegetable fibre, waterproofed on one side; used wet as a poultice.

spongo-, pref. representing Gk. *spóggos*, *spoggiá*, 'sponge', see **sponge** (I.). Sponge.

spongoid, adj. [1. spónggoid; 2. spɔ́ŋgɔid]. See prec. & -**oid**. Like, of the nature of, a sponge.

spongologist, n. [1. spònggólojist; 2. spɔ̀ŋgɔ́lədžist]. Next word & -**ist**. Student of, one versed in, spongology.

spongology, n. [1. spònggóloji; 2. spɔ̀ŋgɔ́lədži]. **spongo-** & -**logy**. Study of sponges.

spongy, adj. [1. spúnjer; 2. spándži]. **sponge** (I.) & -**y**. **1.** Like a sponge in structure; elastic and porous. **2.** (of land) Wet, marshy, absorbent. **3.** (of metal) Of open texture, loosely coherent.

sponsion, n. [1. spónshun; 2. spónʃən], fr. Lat. *spōnsiōnem*, 'engagement, covenant', fr. *spōnsum*, P.P. type of *spondēre*, 'to warrant, give, assurance, promise'; cp. Lat. *respondēre*, 'to promise in return; to reply', see **respond**; cogn. w. Gk. *spéndein*, 'to pour out a libation; to promise'; *spondḗ*, 'libation; treaty'. **1.** Act of becoming surety for another, of entering into an engagement on another's behalf. **2.** (legal) International agreement made on behalf of a state by an official not fully empowered to enter into it.

sponson, n. [1. spónsun; 2. spónsən]. Possibly a popular modification of **expansion**. Curved projection from side of vessel; specif. **a** outward curve of planking before and behind each wheel of paddle-steamer; **b** projection on side of warship to enable gun to be swung round to a different angle.

sponsor, n. [1. spónsur; 2. spónsə], fr. Lat. *spōnsor*, 'surety', fr. *spōnsum*, P.P. type of *spondēre*, 'to bind oneself', see **sponsion**, & **-or**. **a** Person who enters into an agreement on another's behalf; one who makes himself responsible for another's obligations, or who vouches for his character; specif. **b** godfather or godmother.

sponsorial, adj. [1. sponsórial; 2. spɒnsɔ́riəl]. Prec. & **-ial**. Pertaining to a sponsor.

sponsorship, n. [1. spónsurship; 2. spónsəʃip]. sponsor & **-ship**. State of being a sponsor.

spontaneity, n. [1. spòntanéiti; 2. spɒ̀ntəníiti]. See next word & **-ity**. State or quality of being spontaneous; spontaneous action.

spontaneous, adj. [1. spontáneus; 2. spɒntéiniəs], fr. Lat. *spontāneus*, 'of one's free will, voluntary', fr. *sponte*, 'of one's own accord', fr. **spons*, 'free will, desire'; cp. O.H.G. *spanst*, 'charm, allurement'; *spanan*, 'to entice'; O.E. *spanan*, 'to entice'). **1.** Arising from one's own internal tendency, disposition, inclination, without external influence, constraint, compulsion; voluntary: *a spontaneous expression of admiration; spontaneous generosity*. **2.** Self-acting; produced by internal, natural impulse or energy; not due to external agency or stimulus: *spontaneous movement, action, growth*.

spontaneous combustion, n. See **combustion**.

spontaneous generation, n. Process, the existence of which is no longer believed in, whereby life, as it was held, originated spontaneously, in non-living matter, under certain conditions, without the presence of pre-existing living organisms.

spontaneously, adv. [1. spontáneusli; 2. spɒntéiniəsli]. **spontaneous** & **-ly**. In a spontaneous manner.

spontaneousness, n. [1. spontáneusnes; 2. spɒntéiniəsnis]. See prec. & **-ness**. State or quality of being spontaneous.

spontoon, n. [1. spontóōn; 2. spɒntúːn], fr. Fr. *sponton*, fr. Ital. *spontone*, fr. *spontāre*, fr. Lat. **expunctāre*, 'to blunt the point', fr. **ex-** & *punctum*, 'point', see **point**. (hist.) Kind of halberd, usually with hook, sometimes carried by infantry officers.

spoof, vb. trans. & n. [1. spoōf; 2. spūf]. Invented by Arthur Roberts, the comedian, b. 1852. (slang) **1.** vb. To deceive, hoax, swindle. **2.** n. Hoax, swindle.

spook, n. [1. spoōk; 2. spūk], fr. Du. *spook*; cp. Germ. (dial.) *spuk*; Dan. *spog*. Ghost, apparition, wraith.

spookish, adj. [1. spoōkish; 2. spūkiʃ]. Prec. & **-ish**. Of, like, a ghost.

spooky, adj. [1. spoōki; 2. spūki]. **spook** & **-y**. Pertaining to, resembling, a ghost; suggesting the presence of ghosts; haunted.

spool (I.), n. [1. spoōl; 2. spūl], fr. M. Du. *spoele*; cp. Germ. *spule*; etymol. doubtful. Bar, cylinder &c., on which thread &c. is wound; a reel for cotton &c.; specif., bar of reel on fishing-rod, on which line is wound.

spool (II.), vb. trans., fr. prec. To wind on a spool.

spoon (I.), n. [1. spoōn; 2. spūn]. O.E. *spōn*, 'a shaving, chip of wood'; cp. Du. *spaan*; O.H.G. *spān*; O.Fris. *spōn*; O.N. *spānn, spǫnn*, 'chip, splinter'; cogn. w. Gk. *sphḗn*, 'wedge'; Scrt. *sphyáś*, 'splinter of wood'; fr. base **sp(h)ei-, *sp(h)i-* &c., 'to spread out, stretch', seen in **spathe, spade (I.)** &c. **1.** Implement made of wood, iron, nickel &c., or (esp. for table use) of silver, with long handle ending in a shallow oval or round bowl, used for measuring or stirring liquid &c., in cooking &c., and for conveying food to the mouth; often in compounds, named according to use &c.: *egg-, tea-, dessert-, table-, mustard-spoon* &c.; Phr. *wooden spoon*, specif. **a** that formerly given to candidate placed lowest in Cambridge mathematical tripos; **b** man attaining this distinction. **2.** Instrument somewhat resembling a spoon in form; specif. **a** kind of oar with curved blade; **b** (golf) kind of wooden-headed club; **c** spoon-bait.

spoon (II.), vb. trans. & intrans., fr. prec. **A.** trans. **1.** To use a spoon for; to lift, convey, with a spoon: *to spoon up liquid; to spoon liquid out of a vessel*. **2.** To lift, move, as with a spoon; (specif. croquet) to push or scoop with mallet. **B.** intrans. To fish with spoon-bait.

spoon (III.), n. Prob. same as **spoon (I.)**, cp. use of **stick** or **pump** as terms for a stupid, empty-headed person. **1.** Foolish fellow, simpleton. **2.** One who makes love in a foolish and demonstrative manner.

spoon (IV.), vb. intrans. & trans., fr. prec. (vulg. slang) **1.** intrans. To make love. **2.** trans. To make love to, to court.

spoon-bait, n. Bright piece of metal, shaped like bowl of spoon with hook at one end, attached by swivel to fishing-line and drawn through the water.

spoonbill, n. [1. spoōnbil; 2. spúnbil]. Family of wading birds resembling ibises, having a broad, flat bill expanded at the end in the shape of a spoon.

spoondrift, n. [1. spoōndrift; 2. spúndrift]. Spindrift, q.v.

Spoonerism, n. [1. spoōnerizm; 2. spúnərizəm], fr. name of the Rev. W. A. Spooner, D.D., formerly Warden of New College, Oxford. Involuntary transposition of sounds in successive words; e.g. *bilging buns*, for *bulging bins*; *queer dean*, for *dear queen* &c.

spoon-fed, adj. **a** Fed (as infant, invalid &c.) with a spoon; **b** (fig., of industries &c.) encouraged, aided, by artificial financial support; **c** (of pupils) taught by the repeated administration of small doses of information, cut and dried, and carefully adapted to the comprehension of the recipients.

spoon-food, n. Food taken with a spoon, esp. by infants or invalids.

spoonful, n. [1. spoōnfool; 2. spúnful]. **spoon (I.)** & **-ful**. Amount contained in a spoon.

spoonily, adv. [1. spoōnili; 2. spúnili]. **spoony** & **-ly**. In a spoony manner.

spooniness, n. [1. spoōnines; 2. spúninis]. See prec. & **-ness**. State of being spoony.

spoon-meat, n. Soft or liquid food, esp. infant's food.

spoon-net, n. Fisherman's landing-net.

spoony, adj. [1. spoōni; 2. spúni]. **spoon (III.)** & **-y**. Amorous; inclined for lovemaking.

spoor (I.), n. [1. spōr, spoor; 2. spō, spuə]. Du. *spoor*; cp. Germ. *spur*, 'track'; O.N. *spor*; O.E. *spor*; perh. cogn. w. O.E. *spora*, 'spur'; see **spur (I.)**. **1.** Trail, track, succession of footprints, of wild animals. **2.** Animal's scent.

spoor (II.), vb. trans. & intrans., fr. prec. **1.** trans. To follow the track or scent of. **2.** intrans. To follow a spoor.

sporadic(al), adj. [1. sporádik(l); 2. spərǽdik(l)], fr. Gk. *sporadikós*, fr. *sporád-*, stem of *sporás*, 'scattered'; cp. Gk. *spóros*, 'sowing'; *speirein*, 'to sow, scatter'; *spérma*, 'seed, germ', see **sperm**. Occurring at irregular intervals; scattered; (esp. of disease) not epidemic or widely prevalent, occurring in single cases.

sporadically, adv. [1. sporádikali; 2. spərǽdikəli]. Prec. & **-ly**. In a sporadic way.

sporadicalness, n. [1. sporádiklnes; 2. spərǽdikəlnis]. See prec. & **-ness**. State of being sporadic.

sporange, n. [1. spóranj; 2. spórændʒ], fr. next word. Sporangium.

sporangium, n. [1. sporánjium; 2. spərǽndʒiəm], fr. **spore** & Gk. *aggeion*, dimin. of *ággos*, 'vessel, receptacle'. Sac within which spores are developed.

sporation, n. [1. spŏráshun; 2. spŏréiʃən]. Next word & **-ation**. Production of spores.

spore, n. [1. spōr; 2. spō], fr. Gk. *sporá*, 'sowing, seed'; cp. Gk. *spóros*, 'sowing', & see **sporadic, sperm (I.)**. (biol.) **a** Minute reproductive organism of flowerless plant, capable of developing into a new individual; **b** minute animal organism as in bacteria &c. developing into a new individual.

sporo-, pref. representing **spore** & **-o-**. Spore.

sporogenesis, n. [1. spŏrojénesis; 2. spŏrədʒénisis]. Prec. & **genesis**. Reproduction by means of spores.

sporogenous, adj. [1. spŏrójenus; 2. spŏrɔ́dʒinəs]. **sporo-** & **-genous**. Reproducing by means of spores.

sporran, n. [1. spóran; 2. spórən], fr. Gael. *sporan*. Leather pouch, usually having the fur left on, worn by Scottish Highlanders with the kilt, slung round the waist by a leather thong and hanging down in front.

sport (I.), n. [1. sport; 2. spōt]. Abbr. of **disport**. **1.** Any of various forms of activity, engaged in as recreation; **a** hunting, shooting, fishing; sailing a boat; **b** outdoor games; **c** athletics, swimming, boxing, fencing, wrestling &c.; **d** (vulg.) a sporting person. **2.** Sports, meeting for athletic contests: *school sports; sports day* &c. **3. a** Jest, raillery, fun: *to say a thing in sport*; **b** plaything; object, victim, of caprice: *to become the sport of fortune*; (fig.) *the sport of the waves*. **4.** A diverting action, occurrence, or experience: *children think it great sport to dress up, and pretend to be grown up*. **5.** (biol.) Plant or animal varying spontaneously from the normal type; a freak.

sport (II.), vb. intrans. & trans., fr. prec. **1.** intrans. To frolic, disport oneself; to dally: '*To sport with Amaryllis in the shade*' (Milton, 'Lycidas', 68). **2.** trans. To wear or carry, esp. ostentatiously, for display: *to sport a rose in one's buttonhole*; (Phr., university) *to sport one's oak*, shut the outer (oaken) door of college rooms, as indication that one must not be disturbed.

sporting, adj. [1. spórting; 2. spótiŋ]. Pres. Part. of **sport (II.)**. **1.** Of, pertaining to, engaging in, addicted to, sport. **2.** Characteristic of a sportsman; sportsmanlike; enterprising, willing to take risks; Phr. *a sporting chance*, one involving risk, but offering possibility of success.

sportingly, adv. Prec. & **-ly**. In a sporting manner.

sportive, adj. [1. spórtiv; 2. spótiv]. **sport** & **-ive**. Inclined to sport, playful, frolicsome.

sportively, adv. Prec. & **-ly**. In a sportive manner.

sportiveness, n. See prec. & **-ness**. State or quality of being sportive.

sportless, adj. [1. spórtles; 2. spótlis]. **sport (I.)** & **-less**. (of country, region &c.) Giving no opportunity for sport.

sportsman, n. [1. spórtsman; 2. spótsmən]. **1.** Person engaged in, or addicted to, sport. **2.** (fig.) Person possessing the qualities attributed to a sportsman; a chivalrous, fair-minded person; one willing to incur risks, and prepared to suffer defeat in fair competition without complaining.

sportsmanlike, adj. [1. spórtsmanlīk; 2. spótsmənlaik]. Prec. & **-like**. Of the nature of, characteristic of, suitable for, a sportsman.

sportsmanship, n. [1. spórtsmanship; 2. spótsmənʃip]. **sportsman** & **-ship**. Skill in, devotion to, sport; sportsmanlike quality or character.

sporular, adj. [1. spórūlar; 2. spɔ́rjulə]. Next word & **-ar**. Of, pertaining to, a sporule.

sporule, n. [1. spórūl; 2. spɔ́rjūl]. **spore** & **-ule**. Small spore.

spot (**I.**), n. [1. spot; 2. spɔt]. M.E.; also in O. Du. Origin unknown. **1. a** A patch, speck, fleck on a surface, differing in colour from the rest: *a black dog with white spots*; **b** a stain, discolouration: *a spot of ink, blood* &c.; **c** (specif.) a pimple, pustule on the skin: *his face was covered with spots.* **2.** A moral stain, flaw, blemish; defect of character, matter of reproach: *a character without spot or stain.* **3.** A definite part of space; a specific place, locality, region: *a lovely spot on which to build a house.* Phr. *on the spot*, at a given place: *the doctor was on the spot a few minutes after the accident*; *the people on the spot*, those who live in a given place, and who know the facts &c. connected with it; *a tender spot*, (fig.) subject on which one's feelings are easily aroused. **4.** (specif., billiards) **a** One of the black spots on the table upon which balls are placed on opening and on other occasions during the game; *spot barred*, game in which players are not allowed to place the red ball on the spot and continue to hole it indefinitely; Phr. *to be on the spot*, (fig.) alert, wide-awake, equal to the situation; *to act on the spot*, there and then without delay; **b** small black spot on one of the white balls to distinguish it from the other; *the spot ball*, that bearing the spot; *spot* (contrasted with *plain*) the spot ball. **5.** (colloq.) **a** Small quantity of liquor; a splash: *won't you have a spot of whisky?* **b** small quantity of food: *how about a spot of lunch?* **6.** (commerc.) *Spot cash*, paid on delivery; *spot price*, price for spot cash; *spot goods, wheat, cotton* &c., sold for immediate delivery; *spots*, spot goods.

spot (**II.**), vb. trans. & intrans., fr. prec. **A.** trans. **1.** To mark, stain, with spots: *to spot one's fingers with ink.* **2.** To mar, impart moral blemish to. **3.** (colloq.) **a** To identify, pick out, recognize, at sight: *it is difficult to spot people in a crowd*; **b** to detect, find out, perceive true character of: *I spotted his roguery as soon as I met him.* **B.** intrans. To become discoloured or injured by spots: *a delicate fabric which spots very easily.*

spotless, adj. [1. spótles; 2. spɔ́tlis]. **spot** (**I.**) & **-less**. **1.** Without spot or stain; hence, scrupulously clean: *the room was absolutely spotless*; *a spotless white shirt-front.* **2.** Free from moral stain; immaculate, irreproachable.

spotlessly, adv. Prec. & **-ly**. To the degree of being spotless: *spotlessly clean.*

spotlessness, n. See prec. & **-ness**. State or quality of being spotless.

spotlight, n. [1. spótlīt; 2. spɔ́tlait]. **1.** Strong beam of light thrown on to a performer on the stage &c. **2.** Electric searchlight used in theatre &c. to project such a beam.

spotted, adj. [1. spóted; 2. spɔ́tid]. **spot** (**II.**) & **-ed**. Marked with, characterized by, spots, esp. in names of birds, fishes, and other animals, plants &c.: *spotted bass, flycatcher* &c.; *spotted dog*, (slang) plain, boiled suet pudding with currants &c.

spotted fever, n. Cerebro-spinal meningitis.

spottedness, n. [1. spótednes; 2. spɔ́tidnis]. **spotted** & **-ness**. State of being spotted.

spottiness, n. [1. spótines; 2. spɔ́tinis]. Next word & **-ness**. State of being spotty.

spotty, adj. [1. spóti; 2. spɔ́ti]. **spot** (**I.**) & **-y**. Marked, covered, with spots (in various senses); **a** patchy, diversified by patches of different colours: *seen from a distance the different uniforms produced a spotty effect*; **b** pimply: *a spotty complexion.*

spousal, n. [1. spóuzl; 2. spáuzl]. Variant of **espousal**. (archaic) Marriage, nuptials; also *spousals.*

spouse, n. [1. spouz; 2. spauz], fr. O. Fr. *espous(e)*, 'spouse', fr. Lat. *spōns(um), spōns(a)*, 'bride(groom)', fr. P.P. type of *spondēre*, 'to engage oneself, promise', see **sponsion**; cp. Lat. *sponsāre*, 'to marry', *sponsālia*, 'marriage'. Either of two persons joined by marriage; a husband or a wife.

spouseless, adj. [1. spóuzles; 2. spáuzlis]. Prec. & **-less**. Without a spouse.

spout (**I.**), vb. intrans. & trans. [1. spout; 2. spaut]. M.E. *spouten*; cp. M. Du. *spuiten*; O.N. *spȳta*; O.H.G. *spiutzen*, 'to spout'; perh. remotely connected w. **spit** (**III.**). **A.** intrans. **1.** To burst, gush, spurt, pour forth, be discharged, in a copious stream: *blood spouted from the wound.* **2.** To discharge liquid forcibly: *the whale spouts.* **3.** To make speeches, harangue, copiously and often: *a good fellow but too fond of spouting.* **B.** trans. **1.** To pour out in a stream, discharge forcibly, cause to gush forth in a jet: *the volcano spouts lava*; *the whale spouts water*; *the chimney spouted smoke and flame.* **2.** (colloq.) To utter, recite, esp. in a fluent and declamatory manner: *to spout one's own verses.* **3.** (slang) To pawn, pledge.

spout (**II.**), n., fr. prec. **1. a** Narrow, specially shaped, projecting part, orifice, mouth of a receptacle, through which the liquid contents are poured out; piece of projecting pipe discharging water: *the spout of a tea-pot, jug*; *spout of a pump*; **b** (archit.) carved or moulded projection of stone or lead for conveying water from a roof. **2.** Shoot, or small lift, in pawnbroker's shop, by means of which pledged articles are conveyed to place of storage; (hence vulgar) *up the spout*, in pawn. **3.** Blow-hole of whale &c. **4.** Stream, jet, gush, of water or other liquid, esp. one discharged or escaping with considerable force and volume; (specif.) **a** column of water shot into the air by whale &c., in breathing; **b** water-spout. **5.** A copious, sudden discharge, burst, gust, of vapour, steam, smoke, dust.

spout-hole, n. Blow-hole of cetacean; spiracle.

spoutless, adj. [1. spóutles; 2. spáutlis]. **spout** (**I.**) & **-less**. Without a spout.

sprag, n. [1. sprag; 2. spræg]. Dan. *sprag*, 'twig, sprig'; cogn. w. **spray** (**I.**). Billet or block of wood, bar of steel &c., used to check movement of wheel &c., as prop in mining &c.

sprain, vb. trans. & n. [1. sprān; 2. sprein], fr. O. Fr. *esprein-*, stem of *espreindre*, 'to press out', fr. Lat. *exprimere*, 'press out; to squeeze, wring', fr. **ex-** & *premere*, 'to press', see **press**. **1.** vb. To strain excessively, but without dislocation, by a sudden twist or wrench, the tendons and muscles connected with a joint; esp. those of the ankle or wrist. **2.** n. **a** Violent wrench or twist given to the muscles, ligaments, or tendons of a joint, without dislocation; **b** inflammation and swelling resulting from such a wrench.

spraints, n. [1. sprānts; 2. spreints], fr. O. Fr. *espraintes*, fr. P.P. of *espreindre*, 'to press out', see **sprain**. Otter's dung.

sprang, vb. [1. sprang; 2. spræŋ]. O.E., M.E. *sprang*, Pret. of **spring** (**I.**).

sprat, n. [1. sprat; 2. spræt]. O.E., M.E. *sprott*; cp. L.G. *sprotte*, 'sprat'; prob. a gradational form of base in **sprout**. The present-day form shows unrounding of M.E. *ŏ*, as in **gad** (**I.**) & **strap**. Small, edible fish of the herring family, found off W. Europe.

sprat-day, n. November 9th, on which sprat season begins.

spratter, n. [1. spráter; 2. sprǽtə]. **sprat** & **-er**. Man or vessel engaged in fishing for sprats.

sprawl (**I.**), vb. intrans. & trans. [1. sprawl; 2. sprɔl]. Connected w. O.E. *sprēawlian*, 'to move convulsively', M.E. *spraulen*; cp. Norw. *sprala*; origin unknown. **A.** intrans. **1. a** (of person) To lie or sit with limbs relaxed and spread out in careless ungainly manner; to loll; **b** (of limbs) to be stretched out in an ungainly manner. **2.** To be spread out irregularly, so as to cover considerable space; to straggle: *handwriting in which a single word sprawls half across a page*; *sprawling shoots of roses.* **B.** trans. To cause to sprawl.

sprawl (**II.**), n., fr. prec. Sprawling position or movement.

spray (**I.**), n. [1. sprā; 2. sprei]. M.E. *sprai*; cp. Dan. *sprag*; O.E. *spræc*, 'twig, shoot'; O.N. *sprek*; cogn. w. Gk. *spargâein*, 'to be swollen, be ripe', Lith. *sprógti*, 'to bud'; *spùrgas*, 'sprout'; Scrt. *sphúrjati*, 'breaks forth'; cp. also Lat. *spargere*, 'to scatter', & see **sparse** & **spark**. See also next word. **1.** Small branch or stem of tree or plant, sprig, twig, with flowers or smaller branches spreading from it. **2. a** Design, pattern, ornament, representing spray of flowers &c.; **b** similar design representing other objects.

spray (**II.**), n., fr. L.G. *sprei*, 'spray, drizzle'; cp. O.H.G. *spriu*, 'spray'; M.H.G. *spraewen*; M. Du. *spraeien*, 'to spray, scatter'; cogn. w. O.E. *sprūtan*, 'to sprout', see **sprout** (**I.**); fr. base **sper-*, **sprē-* &c., 'to scatter, sow; to grow up, sprout'; see **sparger, spring, spark**. **1.** Fine particles of water, larger than those of vapour, carried in a cloud from a breaking wave, or from a waterfall. **2. a** Liquid disinfectant, chemical disease-killer, or perfume &c., driven in fine particles resembling spray by an atomizer; **b** mechanical device for producing such a spray.

spray (**III.**), vb. intrans. & trans., fr. prec. **1.** intrans. To form spray. **2.** trans. To treat with liquid in the form of spray: *to spray one's throat, an apple tree* &c.

spray-board, n. Board on gunwale of boat to throw off spray.

spray-drain, n. Trench filled with branches and covered in with earth, to serve as drain.

sprayer, n. [1. spráer; 2. spréiə]. **spray** (**III.**) & **-er**. One who, that which, sprays; device for spraying.

sprayey (**I.**), adj. [1. sprái; 2. spréii]. **spray** (**I.**) & **-y**. In the form of, consisting of, sprays.

sprayey (**II.**), adj. **spray** (**II.**) & **-y**. Resembling, in the form of, full of, spray.

spread (**I.**), vb. trans. & intrans. [1. spred; 2. spred]. O.E. *sprǣdan*, M.E. *sprēden*; evidently fr. **spraidjan*, cp. O.H.G. *spreiten*, 'to extend' &c. Origin of base unknown. **A.** trans. **1.** To cause (a substance) to cover a larger surface, **a** by pressing and smearing: *to spread butter on bread*; **b** by laying or scattering on, and scraping it out thin: *to spread mortar on a stone, manure over a field*; **c** to cover a surface by unfolding, and stretching: *to spread a carpet on a floor, a cloth on a table.* **2.** To cover (surface) with a substance or material: *to spread bread with honey, butter* &c.; *to spread a table with a cloth, with a meal.* **3.** To extend, stretch out, reach out: *to spread one's hands to the fire*; *a bird spreads its wings*; *a tree spreads its branches to the light.* **4.** To diffuse, disseminate, hand on, extend, cause to be widely circulated; **a** (of material things) *to spread disease*; **b** (of non-material things) *to spread news, learning, knowledge, a love of virtue*; *to spread one's interests over too many subjects*; also *to spread oneself*, engage in variety of activities; (slang) **a** to talk, write, at length, or self-assertively; **b** be profuse in hospitality. **B.** intrans. **1.** To extend, cover larger surface: *the floods have spread over the valley.* **2.** To extend in time, be prolonged during: *the course of study spreads over three years.* **3.** To open out, be extended or displayed: *a broad plain spread before us.* **4.** (of material and non-material things) To be diffused, disseminated, circulated, handed on: *measles has spread to the school*; *the bad news, rumour, spread like wildfire.* **C.** Followed by adverb with special meanings. *Spread out*, **1.** trans., **a** to unfold: *to spread out a carpet*; **b** to stretch out, extend: *to spread out one's hands, arms, legs*; **c** to scatter, sprinkle, here and there over a surface: *to spread out manure over a field* &c.; **2.** intrans., to be extended, unfolded, displayed: *the branches spread out like a fan.*

spread (**II.**), n., fr. prec. **1.** Process of extending over wider area; extension, expansion, increase: *the alarming spread of the floods.* **2.** Process of circulation, diffusion, dissemina-

tion; increased prevalence: **a** (material) *the spread of disease*; **b** (non-material) *the spread of religion, scientific knowledge*. **3.** Extent, amount, of expansion: *the spread of a bird's wings*. **4.** (colloq.) A copious repast; a feast, banquet: *he gave us a regular spread*.

spread eagle (I.), n. **1.** (her.) Figure of an eagle with wings raised and legs spread out; an eagle displayed. **2.** Bird split open lengthwise and broiled.

spread-eagle (II.), vb. trans. To tie up (person) with arms and legs spread out; specif., to tie up thus for punishment by flogging.

spread-eagle (III.), adj. (Am., not Engl.) Extravagant, bombastic.

spreader, n. [1. spréder; 2. sprédə]. **spread (I.) & -er**. One who, that which, spreads; specif., one of various mechanical devices for spreading flame of lamp, scattering water from hose-pipe for spraying lawn &c.

spread over, n. In industry, esp. mining, an arrangement by which the workers can spread the allotted number of working hours per week over a longer period, e.g. instead of working 45 hours in each of two successive weeks, they can work 60 hours in one and 30 in the other.

spree, n. & vb. intrans. [1. sprē; 2. sprī]. Cp. Ir. *spre*, Gael. *spraig*, 'spark; spirit'; perh. fr. O.N. *sprakr*; cp. **spark**. **1.** n. **a** A bout of dissipation, a drunken frolic; Phrs. *on the spree*, engaged in a drinking bout; *to go on the spree*, give oneself up temporarily to drinking and dissipation; **b** a spell of innocent amusement; an amusing experience; a lark: *it would be rather a spree to run up to town for a few theatres*. **2.** vb. To indulge in a spree.

sprent, adj. [1. sprent; 2. sprent], also **besprent**. M.E. *spre(i)nt*, P.P., fr. O.E. *sprengan*, 'to sprinkle'; cp. O.H.G. *sprengan*; O.N. *sprengja*; fr. *sprang*-, Pret. stem of *spring*-, 'to spring, jump', see **spring (I.)**. (archaic) Sprinkled, scattered, over: *sprent with dew*.

sprig, n. [1. sprig; 2. sprig]. M.E. *sprigge*, precise origin not clear; prob. related to **spray (I.)**. **1.** Small branching twig, spray, cluster. **2.** Small spray-like design, branching pattern, e.g. on a fabric, wall-paper &c. **3.** Small headless nail, brad. **4.** a Scion, offshoot of a family: *a sprig of nobility*; **b** a young man, young spark: *a lively young sprig*.

sprigged, adj. [1. sprigd; 2. sprigd]. Prec. & **-ed**. Covered, beset, with sprigs.

spriggy, adj. [1. sprigi; 2. sprigi]. **sprig & -y**. Full of, covered with, consisting of, sprigs.

sprightliness, n. [1. sprítlinəs; 2. spráitlinis]. Next word & **-ness**. State or quality of being sprightly; liveliness, animation.

sprightly, adj. [1. sprítli; 2. spráitli]. **sprite & -ly**. Gay, vivacious, lively, lightly animated.

sprigtail, n. [1. sprígtāl; 2. sprígteil]. Kind of sharp-tailed duck or grouse.

spring (I.), vb. intrans. & trans. [1. spring; 2. sprinj]. O.E. *springan*; M.E. *springen*; cp. O.H.G. *springan*, 'to spring, rise'; O.N. *springa*, 'to burst'; fr. base *sprē*-, *sper*- &c., 'to scatter, sow; to shoot forth, grow up'; see **sparger, spark, spray, & words** there referred to. **A.** intrans. **1. a** To jump, leap, bound; move upwards or forwards &c. by sudden contraction of the muscles: *to spring up into the air, over a gate, out of bed* &c.; *to spring to one's feet*, rise rapidly and suddenly from sitting posture; *to spring at, upon, a person*, attack suddenly; **b** hence, to move swiftly, rush, dart: *his hand sprang to his sword-hilt*. **2.** To come, pass, suddenly and rapidly into a different condition, set of circumstances &c.: *to spring into fame, notoriety* &c. **3.** To move suddenly and rapidly by, as if by, the action of a spring, as result of reaction, recoil: *the doors spring open*. **4. a** (of water, stream &c.) To rise from, or as from, a source, to bubble up, gush, flow forth; to well; (also of tears) to gather suddenly; **b** (also *spring up*; of plants) to grow from root or seed; to show above ground, sprout up: *daisies spring on every side*; *weeds spring up as fast as one exterminates them*; **c** (fig.; also *spring up*) to come into existence, arise, emerge suddenly, become apparent: *new factions sprang up in the state*; *dangers and difficulties spring up on every side*; **d** (sometimes *spring up*) to grow, rise, in the mind: *strange thoughts spring from lonely contemplation*; '*Hope springs eternal in the human breast*' (Pope, 'Ess. on Man', i. 95). **5.** To arise from, have as cause, motive &c.: *all our errors have sprung from carelessness*; *his actions spring from malice and fear*. **6.** (of arch) To start from the impost. **7.** (of timber) To become warped or bent. **B.** trans. **1.** To cause to act, move, close, open &c. by reaction, recoil of spring &c.: *to spring a trap*. **2. a** To discharge, explode: *to spring a mine* (often fig.); **b** (fig.) to reveal, disclose, bring to notice, unexpectedly and suddenly: *to spring a surprise, a new proposal, on one*. **3.** To overstrain, cause to split or warp. Naut. Phrs. *to spring a butt*, loosen end of timber through heavy seas; *to spring a leak*, begin leaking.

spring (II.), n., fr. prec. **1.** Act of springing; a leap, jump, bound. **2.** Elastic body or appliance, often a curve or spiral of metal, tending to return to its original shape or position on release from pressure; used a to supply motive power: *spring of a watch*; **b** to reduce effects of concussion: *spring of a carriage*; **c** to ascertain weight of object, by the amount of resistance offered to pressure or pulling. **3.** Elastic movement, recoil, rebound. **4. a** Elastic quality, resilience: *the spring of a bow*; *a spring in one's step*; **b** mental resilience; spirit; initiative: *his mind had lost its spring*. **5. a** Source, well, fount, in the ground, from which water rises naturally; **b** small stream, flow of water from its source. **6.** (fig.) Motive, cause of action; impelling power: *springs of action*. **7.** (fig.) Source, origin: *the springs of affection*. **8.** Time of year between winter and summer, when the new growth of vegetation begins. **9.** (naut. &c.) **a** Warp, split, crack, in timber; **b** leak caused by warping or cracking. **10.** (archit.) Lower part, starting-point, of curve of arch, vault &c.

springal(d), n. [1. spríngal(d); 2. sprínəl(d)]. M.E. *springal(d)*; connected w. **spring (I.)**. (archaic or obs.) Young man, youth, stripling.

spring-balance, n. Balance measuring weight by action on spring.

spring-beam, n. Beam spanning considerable space without intermediate support.

spring-bed, n. Spring-mattress.

spring-board, n. Elastic board having one end off the ground and the other firmly fastened; used to give impetus for leap, dive &c.

springbok, n. [1. spríngbòk; 2. spríŋbòk]. S. Afr. Du. See **spring (I.) & buck**. Small S. African gazelle, named from its habit of springing vertically into the air when alarmed.

spring-carriage, n. Carriage with body mounted on springs.

spring-cart, n. Cart with body mounted on springs.

springe, n. [1. sprinj; 2. sprindž]. Variant of **spring (II.)**. Snare, noose, attached to branch &c. for catching small game.

springer, n. [1. springer; 2. sprínə]. **spring (I.) & -er**. **1.** One who, that which, springs. **2.** Small variety of spaniel used in pheasant-shooting &c. **3.** Springbok. **4.** Grampus. **5.** (archit.) **a** Lowest part of curve of arch; **b** rib in vaulted roof &c.; **c** lowest stone in coping of gable.

spring-gun, n. Gun set to go off when struck accidentally by trespasser, animal &c.

spring-halt, n. Involuntary jerk of horse's hind leg in walking.

springiness, n. [1. springinəs; 2. sprínjinis]. **springy & -ness**. State or quality of being springy.

springless, adj. [1. springles; 2. sprínlis]. **spring (II.) & -less**. **1.** Without springs. **2.** Having no natural fountains of water.

springlet, n. [1. springlet; 2. sprínlit]. **spring (II.) & -let**. Small spring of water.

springlike, adj. [1. springlík; 2. sprínlaik]. **spring (II.) & -like**. Resembling, characteristic of, the season of spring.

spring-mattress, n. Mattress made of a series of spiral springs set in a rigid frame.

spring-tail, n. Small wingless insect with two stiff, elastic bristles on the tail, which by bending and extending impart a springing movement.

springtide, n. [1. springtíd; 2. sprínjtaid]. Springtime.

spring-tide, n. [1. spring tíd; 2. sprín tàid]. The tide occurring at new and full moon, when the distance between high- and low-water marks is greatest, cp. neap.

springtime, n. [1. springtím; 2. sprínjtaim]. Season of spring.

spring-water, n. Water obtained from spring.

springy, adj. [1. springi; 2. sprínji]. **spring (II.) & -y**. Having spring; elastic, resilient.

sprinkle (I.), vb. trans. & intrans. [1. springkl; 2. sprínkl]. M.E. *sprenkelen*, fr. *sprengan*, 'to scatter'; freq. of *springan*, see **spring (I.)**, **& -le**. **A.** trans. **1.** To cause to fall in small drops or particles; to scatter, strew: *to sprinkle salt, water &c. on an object*. **2.** To cause small drops or particles to fall upon, besprinkle: *to sprinkle a dish with flour*. **B.** intrans. To fall in small, scattered particles or drops.

sprinkle (II.), n., fr. prec. Light, scattered shower of liquid or particles of dry matter: *a sprinkle of snow*.

sprinkler, n. [1. springkler; 2. sprínklə]. **sprinkle (I.) & -er**. One who, that which, sprinkles; object, vessel, device, for sprinkling liquid &c.

sprinkling, n. [1. springkling; 2. sprínkliŋ]. **sprinkle (I.) & -ing**. **1.** Small quantity of liquid or dry substance falling in scattered drops or particles; a sprinkle: *a sprinkling of snow*. **2.** Small number of persons, or objects, scattered here and there: *a sprinkling of visitors among the usual inhabitants*.

sprint (I.), vb. intrans. & trans. [1. sprint; 2. sprint]. Cp. O.N. *spretta*. **1.** intrans. To run at full speed for short distance. **2.** trans. To run (distance) at top of one's speed.

sprint (II.), n., fr. prec. Short run performed at full speed throughout.

sprinter, n. [1. sprinter; 2. sprintə]. **sprint (I.) & -er**. One who sprints; specif., athlete specializing in sprinting.

sprint-race, n. Foot-race run at top speed, usually up to or under 440 yards.

sprit, n. [1. sprit; 2. sprit]. O.E. *sprēot*; M.E. *sprēte*; cp. M.L.G. *sprēt*; M. Du. *spriet*, 'sprit, pole'; cogn. w. **sprout (I.)**. Spar extending diagonally upwards from mast.

sprite, n. [1. sprīt; 2. sprait]. M.E. *sprīte*, variant of **spirit**. Small supernatural being: fairy, elf.

spritsail, n. [1. sprítsl; 2. sprítsl]. Triangular sail extended by sprit.

sprocket, n. [1. spróket; 2. sprókit]. Etymol. unknown. Projecting tooth on rim of wheel, engaging with links of chain &c.; *sprocket-wheel*, one fitted with sprockets.

sprout (I.), vb. intrans. & trans. [1. sprout; 2. spraut]. O.E. *sprūtan*; M.E. *sprūten*, 'to sprout'; cp. O. Fris. *sprūta*; M. Du. *spruiten*; M.H.G. *spriuzen*; cp. also O.E. *spryttan*; M.H.G. *sprützen*, 'to sprout'; fr. base *spreu*-, *spru*- &c., 'to sprout', expanded fr. *sper*-, *sprē*- &c., 'to scatter, sow; to sprout, germinate', see **spark, sparger, sperm, &** words there referred to. **1.** intrans. (of plant, bud, seed &c.) To put forth shoots, develop, begin to grow. **2.** trans. To put forth, develop, as, or in the manner of, a sprout.

sprout (II.), n., fr. prec. **1.** Young shoot, new growth from bud, seed &c. **2.** *Sprouts*, for *Brussels sprouts* see **Brussels**.

spruce (I.), adj. [1. sprōōs; 2. sprūs]. Prob. as **spruce (III.)**, w. special reference to Prussian leather, fashionable in 16th cent. Neat, smart, trim, dapper.

spruce (II.), vb. trans., fr. prec. Usually *spruce up*, to make spruce, tidy, smarten.

spruce (III.), n. Abbr. fr. *spruce-fir*, for Prussian fir, fr. M.E. (*s*)*pruce*, O. Fr. *Pruce*, 'Prussia'; see **Prussian**. 1. (also *spruce-fir*) Coniferous tree of the pine family, genus *Picea*, indigenous to northern hemisphere, of many kinds, as the *black* and *white spruce*, *Norway spruce*, *Douglas fir* &c. 2. Timber of this tree.

spruce-beer, n. Beer made from leaves and twigs of spruce-fir.

sprue (I.), n. [1. sprōō; 2. sprū]. Etymol. unknown. **a** Aperture through which molten metal is poured into a mould; **b** piece of metal remaining in this.

sprue (II.), n., fr. Du. *spruw*, 'thrush' (the disease). Tropical disease characterized by inflammation and ulceration of the mouth and throat, and by enteritis.

sprung, adj. [1. sprung; 2. spraŋ]. P.P. of **spring (I.)**; O.E. (*ge*)*sprungen*. 1. (of bat, racquet) Split, cracked. 2. (slang) Slightly intoxicated, tipsy.

spry, adj. [1. sprī; 2. sprai]. Cp. Swed. *sprygg*; O.N. *sprakr*; O.E. *spræc*, 'lively', q.v. under **spark**. Active, nimble, and alert in movement, agile; also alert in mind; smart. Phr. *look spry*, hurry up, look sharp.

spud (I.), n. [1. spud; 2. spad]. M.E. *spudde*; cp. Dan. *spyd*; O.N. *spjot*, 'spear'. 1. Small spade or chisel-shaped tool for digging up weeds &c. 2. (colloq.) Potato.

spud (II.), vb. trans., fr. prec. To remove, dig up, with a spud.

spuddle, vb. intrans. [1. spúdl; 2. spádl]. Prob. freq. of prec. (dial.) To use a spud; esp. to dig carelessly or desultorily, potter about with a spade.

spuddy, adj. [1. spúdi; 2. spádi]. **spud (I.)** & -y. Short, plump, thickset.

spue, vb. See **spew**.

spume, n. [1. spūm; 2. spjūm], fr. Lat. *spūma*, 'foam, froth'; perh. cogn. w. Lat. *pūmex*, 'pumice-stone', see **pumice**; cogn. w. Scrt. *phénaš*, 'foam'; O.H.G. *feim*; O.E. *fām*, 'foam', see **foam**; cp. Lith. *spáine*, 'foam'. Foam, froth, scum.

spumescence, n. [1. spūmésens; 2. spjūmésəns]. See next word & -**ence**. State or quality of being frothy, foaming.

spumescent, adj. [1. spūmésent; 2. spjūmésənt], fr. Lat. *spūmescent-(em)*, Pres. Part. of *spūmescere*, 'to grow frothy', fr. *spūma*, 'foam', see **spume**. Producing or resembling foam; frothy.

spuminess, n. [1. spúmines; 2. spjúminis]. **spumy** & -ness. State or quality of being spumy.

spumous, adj. [1. spúmus; 2. spjúməs], fr. Lat. *spūmōsus*, 'full of foam'; **spume** & -ous. Of, pertaining to, resembling, covered with, foam.

spumy, adj. [1. spúmi; 2. spjúmi]. **spume** & -y. Spumous.

spun, adj. [1. spun; 2. span]. P.P. of **spin (I.)**; O.E. (*ge*)*spunnen*. *Spun glass*, stretched into threads while hot; *spun gold*, thread of gold-covered fibre for weaving &c.; *spun silk*, material woven of thread spun from short fibres of silk; *spun yarn*, (naut.) rope made of two or four loosely twisted strands.

spunge. Archaic spelling variant of **sponge**.

spunk, n. [1. spungk; 2. spaŋk], fr. Ir. *sponc*, 'tinder', fr. Lat. *spongia*, 'sponge', see **sponge**. 1. Touchwood, tinder made from dried fungus impregnated with inflammable substance. 2. (Scots) **a** Courage, spirit; **b** hot temper, irascibility.

spunky, adj. [1. spúngki; 2. spáŋki]. Prec. & -y. 1. Resembling, of the nature of, spunk or tinder. 2. **a** Courageous, mettlesome; **b** angry, ill-tempered.

spur (I.), n. [1. spër; 2. spə̄]. O.E. *spura*, *spora*; M.E. *spur*, *spore*; cp. O.H.G. *sporo*;
O.N. *spori*; Du. *spoor*; Germ. *sporn*, 'spur'; cogn. w. Gk. *sphurón*, 'ankle'; cp. also O.H.G. *spornōn*, 'to strike with the heels'; O.E. *spurnan*, 'to drive away, reject', see **spurn**. 1. **a** Instrument fitted to rider's heel, with sharp point, or series of points on revolving wheel or rowel, for pricking horse's flanks; **b** (hist.) specif., spur, esp. of gold, as emblem of knighthood. Phr. *to win one's spurs*, (i.) attain the rank of knight; (ii.) (fig.) achieve honour and reputation. 2. Sharply pointed, spur-like object; specif. **a** stiff, pointed projection on wing of bird or leg of bird or insect, esp. horny projection on leg of cock; **b** projection from, or elongated part of, flower; **c** projecting cliff, ridge, or part of mountain range &c.; **d** wall connecting part of rampart with interior work. 3. (fig.) Keen impulse, instigation, stimulus, incitement: *ambition is an excellent spur for the young*. Phr. *on the spur of the moment*, without previous intention or preparation.

spur (II.), vb. trans. & intrans., fr. prec. **A.** trans. 1. To strike, prick, urge on, with spurs. 2. To provide, equip, with spurs: *booted and spurred*. 3. (fig.) To stimulate, incite, urge on: *to spur a person into action*. **B.** intrans. **a** To use spurs to urge on a horse; hence, **b** to ride fast and urgently.

spurge, n. [1. spërj; 2. spādž], fr. O. Fr. *espurge*, fr. *espurger*, 'to purge', fr. Lat. *expurgāre*, 'to cleanse, purge'; see **expurgate**. Genus of plants, *Euphorbia*, usually having fleshy stems containing a highly acrid, milky juice.

spurge-laurel, n. Evergreen shrub, *Daphne laureola*, with yellow flowers and poisonous berries.

spurious, adj. [1. spúrius; 2. spjóriəs], fr. Lat. *spurius*, 'of illegitimate birth; false, spurious'; prob. fr. Gk. *sporá*, 'sowing; seed; generation; birth'; see **sperm (I.)**. 1. Of origin different from that claimed, not genuine, false, counterfeit, sham: *spurious bank-notes*; *spurious sentiment*. 2. (biol.) Having superficial resemblance to some organ, limb &c., but differing in function or origin.

spuriously, adv. Prec. & -ly. In a spurious manner.

spuriousness, n. See prec. & -ness. State or quality of being spurious.

spurless, adj. [1. spërles; 2. spāˊlis]. **spur (I.)** & -less. Without spurs.

spurling-line, n. [1. spërling lı̆n; 2. spāˊliŋ lāin]. Etymol. unknown. (naut.) Cord attached to helm and serving to show position of the latter on an indicator.

spurn, vb. trans. & intrans. [1. spërn; 2. spān]. O.E. *spurnan*, *spornan*, 'to kick, thrust at with foot; to drive away, reject'; cp. O.N. *spyrna*, 'to drive away'; O.H.G. *spornōn*, 'to kick'; cogn. w. **spur (I.)**, & further w. Scrt. *sphurati*, 'to push with the foot', Lat. *spernere*, 'to repulse'; Gk. *spaírein*, 'to palpitate'; see also **sphaero-**. **A.** trans. 1. (archaic) To thrust at with the foot; chiefly now in Phr. *to spurn the ground*, to leap. 2. To drive away roughly or rudely, repel: *to spurn a poor relation from one's door*. 3. To reject scornfully, refuse with disdain, show contempt for: *to spurn one's offers, affection* &c. **B.** intrans. *Spurn at*, (rare) to reject with scorn.

spurrier, n. [1. spërier, spúrier; 2. spāˊriə, spáriə]. **spur (I.)** & -ier. Maker of spurs.

spur-royal, n. Gold coin of James I., worth about 15s., having on the reverse side a star resembling a rowel.

spurry, spurrey, n. [1. spúri; 2. spári], fr. O. Fr. *spurrie*; cp. Med. Lat. *spergula*. Genus, *Spergula*, of small, slender, annual, herbaceous plants with small white or pink flowers.

spurt (I.), vb. intrans. & n. [1. spërt; 2. spāt]. See also **spirt**. 1. vb. To make a sudden violent effort, put forward all one's strength for a short spell, in racing &c. 2. n. Sudden, short spell of violent exertion, esp. at the end of a race &c.

spurt (II.), vb. intrans. & trans. & n. O.E. *spryttan*; M.E. *sprutten*, *spritten*, 'to shoot forth', see **spirt (I.)**. Same as **spirt (I.)** and (II.).

spur-wheel, n. Gear-wheel with toothed rim.

spurwort, n. [1. spërwërt; 2. spāˊwāt]. Madder, from the whorls of leaves encircling the stem.

sputter (I.), vb. intrans. & trans. [1. spúter; 2. spáta], fr. M.E. *spouten*, 'to spout', see **spout** & -er. **A.** intrans. 1. To make a series of spitting sounds or light explosive noises; to splutter. 2. To speak rapidly, jerkily, and indistinctly. **B.** trans. To utter rapidly and indistinctly, jabber.

sputter (II.), n., fr. prec. Sputtering noise or speech.

sputteringly, adv. [1. spúteriŋli; 2. spátəriŋli], fr. Pres. Part. of **sputter (I.)** & -ly. In a sputtering manner, with a sputter.

sputum, n. [1. spútum; 2. spjútəm]. Lat. *spūtum*, 'spittle', fr. neut. P.P. of *spuere*, 'to spit'; cogn. w. Gk. *ptíō*, Goth. *speiwan*; O.N. *spýja*; Lith. *spiáuju*, 'to spit', see **spew**. 1. Saliva. 2. (often pl., *sputa*) Matter that has been expectorated, esp. when considered as characteristic of specific disease.

spy (I.), vb. trans. & intrans. [1. spī; 2. spai]. M.E. *spien*, fr. O. Fr. *espier*, fr. O.H.G. *spehōn*, 'to see, spy'; cp. O.H.G., O.S. *spāhi*, 'wise, discriminating, prudent'; Scrt. *spáçati*, 'sees'; Lat. *specere*, 'to see'; *species*, 'appearance'; see **species**. 1. trans. To see, discern, perceive, make out, espy. Phr. *I spy strangers*, used in British House of Commons by a Member who wishes to have the galleries cleared. 2. intrans. To act as a spy: *he spies for the enemy*. 3. Followed by adverbs and prepositions in special senses. *Spy into*, to examine, investigate, carefully and secretly: *to spy into one's actions*. *Spy out*, to make clandestine investigations in, explore secretly: *to spy out the land*. *Spy upon*, to keep a secret watch upon, examine closely and secretly: *to spy upon a person*.

spy (II.), n. M.E. *spie*, fr. O. Fr. *espie*, fr. *espier*, 'to spy', see prec. **a** Person keeping secret watch on another's speech, conduct, actions; specif. **b** person employed to obtain secret information about another country, its social conditions, military preparations, political intentions &c.

spy-glass, n. Small hand telescope.

spy-hole, n. Hole through which one can see without being seen; peep-hole.

squab, adj. & n. [1. skwob; 2. skwɔb]. Cp. Swed. *sqvabb*, 'loose flesh'. 1. adj. Short, plump and thick; stumpy. 2. n. Short, fat, round object; specif. **a** young, unfledged pigeon or rook; **b** short, stout person; **c** small, stuffed cushion.

squabble (I.), n. [1. skwóbl; 2. skwóbl]. Cp. Swed. *skvabbel*, 'a dispute'. Undignified quarrel, a petty wrangle; a bicker.

squabble (II.), vb. intrans. & trans., fr. prec. 1. intrans. To engage in squabbles; to quarrel, to bicker. 2. trans. (print.) To disarrange, upset, disturb position of (composed type).

squabby, adj. [1. skwóbi; 2. skwóbi]. **squab** & -y. Short, plump, and stumpy.

squab-chick, n. Young bird, fledgeling.

squab-pie, n. 1. Pigeon-pie; rook-pie. 2. Pasty made of mutton, apples, and onions.

squacco, n. [1. skwákō; 2. skwǽkou]. Imitative. Small crested heron of Southern Europe, Africa, and Asia.

squad, n. [1. skwod; 2. skwɔd], fr. M. Fr. *esquadre*, fr. Ital. *squadra*, 'square', fr. L. Lat. *exquadrāre*, 'to form into a square'; see **square (I.)**. 1. Small detachment of troops &c. for drill. Phr. *awkward squad*, body of new, and still raw, recruits; (chiefly fig.) of inefficient group of people &c. 2. Small group of persons acting together.

squadron (I.), n. [1. skwódrun; 2. skwɔ́drən], fr. M. Fr. *esquadron*, fr. Ital. *squadrone*, fr. *squadra*, 'square', see **squad**, & -oon. 1. Body of cavalry, consisting of 120 to 200

squadron (I.) men; two troops. 2. a Group or detachment of ships of war detached for special service; b group of twelve military aeroplanes. 3. Organized group of persons; squad.

squadron (II.), vb. trans., fr. prec. To form into squadrons, organize as squadron.

squadron-leader, n. Officer in Royal Air Force commanding a squadron of twelve aeroplanes, ranking with a major in the army.

squail, n. [1. skwāl; 2. skweil]. Etymol. unknown; cp. dial. *squail*, 'to strike, pelt'; see **squailer**. 1. Small wooden counter used in the game of squails. 2. (pl.) Table game played by snapping small discs from the edge to centre of a board.

squail-board, n. Round board used in the game of squails.

squailer, n. [1. skwāler; 2. skwéilə], fr. dial. *squail*, 'to strike, pelt', of doubtful origin. Stick with weighted knob used as missile in hunting animal &c.

squalid, adj. [1. skwólid; 2. skwólid], fr. Lat. *squālidus*, 'rough, neglected; filthy', fr. *squālēre*, 'to be stiff with dirt or dryness'; cogn. w. Gk. *pēlós*, 'clay', fr. *skwēlos*; O. Slav. *kalŭ*, 'mud, loam, clay'. a Filthy and degraded; foul, unclean, dingy: *a squalid slum*; *squalid surroundings*; b (in moral sense) base, sordid, mean: *a squalid quarrel*.

squalidity, n. [1. skwolíditi; 2. skwɔlíditi]. Prec. & **-ity**. State or quality of being squalid.

squalidly, adv. [1. skwólidli; 2. skwólidli]. See prec. & **-ly**. In a squalid manner.

squalidness, n. [1. skwólidnes; 2. skwólidnis]. See prec. & **-ness**. Squalor.

squall (I.), vb. intrans. & trans. [1. skwawl; 2. skwɔl], fr. O.N. *skvala*, 'to squeal'; cp. Swed. *sqvala*, 'to gush out'; prob. imitative in origin. 1. intrans. a To cry out loudly and shrilly; to bawl; b To sing loudly, unmelodiously. 2. trans. To utter with a squall.

squall (II.), n., fr. prec. 1. Loud, discordant cry; harsh, shrill shriek; a squawk. 2. Sudden, violent brief storm of wind, whether accompanied or not with rain or snow. Phr. *look out for squalls*, be on your guard against trouble, esp. that due to another's temper.

squally, adj. [1. skwáwli; 2. skwɔ́li]. Prec. & **-y**. Liable to, abounding in, characterized by, squalls.

squaloid, adj. [1. skwáloid; 2. skwéilɔid], fr. Mod. Lat. *squalus*, 'shark', fr. Lat. *squalus*, 'kind of large fish'; cp. O.N. *hvalr*; O.E. *hwæl*, 'whale', see **whale**; perh. cogn. w. Gk. *skúlion*, 'kind of shark'; & **-oid**. Of, pertaining to, resembling, a shark.

squalor, n. [1. skwóler; 2. skwólə]. Lat. *squālor*, 'stiffness, roughness, filth', fr. *squālēre*, 'to be stiff with dirt', see **squalid**, & **-or**. State or quality of being squalid; physical or moral uncleanness, filth, sordidness.

squama, n. [1. skwāma; 2. skwéimə]. Lat. *squāma*, 'scale'; etymol. doubtful. Scale, or scale-like structure or object.

squami-, squamo-, prefs. representing Lat. *squāma*, 'scale'; see prec. Scale.

squamiferous, adj. [1. skwāmíferus; 2. skweimífərəs]. Prec. & **-ferous**. Bearing scales.

squamiform, adj. [1. skwámiform; 2. skwéimifɔ̄m]. squami- & -form. In the form of a scale.

squamoid, adj. [1. skwámoid; 2. skwéimɔid]. squama & -oid. Like, having the form of, a squama.

squamose, adj. [1. skwāmōs; 2. skwéiməus], fr. Lat. *squāmōsus*, 'scaly'; squama & -ose. Of the nature of, resembling, covered with, scales.

squamo-temporal, adj. [1. skwámō témpural; 2. skwéimou témpərəl]. Of the squamous part of the temporal bone.

squamous, adj. [1. skwámus; 2. skwéiməs]. squama & -ous. Squamose.

squamule, n. [1. skwámūl; 2. skwéimjūl]. Lat. *squāmula*, 'little scale'; squama & -ule. Small scale.

squander, vb. trans. [1. skwónder; 2. skwóndə]. Etymol. dubious. To spend wastefully and extravagantly; to dissipate; to disperse, expend foolishly and to no purpose: *to squander money, time, talents* &c.

squanderer, n. [1. skwónderer; 2. skwóndərə]. Prec. & **-er**. Person given to squandering.

squanderingly, adv. [1. skwónderingli; 2. skwóndəriŋli]. Pres. Part. of squander & -ly. Extravagantly.

squandermania, n. [1. skwóndermánia; 2. skwóndəméiniə]. A journalistic invention. Mania for spending money, esp. applied to any government expenditure on objects of which the user of the word disapproves.

square (I.), n. [1. skwār; 2. skweə], fr. O. Fr. *esquarre*, fr. Low Lat. *exquadrāre*, 'to form into a square', fr. ex- & *quadra*, 'square'; cp. Lat. *quadru-, quadri-*, 'four' (in compounds), & see **quadri-**. 1. a Plane rectangular figure enclosed by four equal sides; b four equal lines, at right angles to each other, enclosing such a figure. 2. a Object having the shape of a square: *a square of glass, linen* &c.; b specif., division of chessboard &c. 3. a Square or oblong open space in town usually laid out as a garden, fenced in and bounded by a street of houses on at least two sides; b large open space, or place in a town, bounded by streets, and usually with several important buildings looking into it, used for fairs, markets &c. 4. Body of troops &c. drawn up to form a square. 5. Measure for flooring &c. = 100 square feet. 6. Instrument for measuring or determining right angles, consisting of two wooden or metal bars at right angles to each other, in form of L or T. Phr. *on the square*, honest, sincere, genuine. 7. (arith.) Product of quantity multiplied by itself.

square (II.), adj., fr. prec. 1. Having, bounded by, four equal sides and four right angles; rectangular. 2. Forming, having, a right angle; placed at right angles: *square corners*. Phr. *a square meal*, a solid, substantial one. 3. (of shape) a Having a firm outline suggestive of a square: *square shoulders*; *a square chin* &c.; b broad in proportion to height, square-built. 4. (lit. and fig.) On equal terms, with debit and credit balanced; even: *to get one's accounts square*. Phrs. *to get square with*, get even with, retaliate upon; *all square*, (golf) with neither side leading; even. 5. Honest, genuine, straightforward, just: *square dealing*; *he is absolutely square*. 6. Unequivocal, unambiguous, clear: *a square refusal*. 7. (arith.) a Of, pertaining to, quantity multiplied by itself; having two equal factors: *square number*; *square inch, foot* &c., surface area equal to square each of whose sides measures one inch, foot &c.; b *square measure*, giving table of measurement of superficial area; c *square root*, see **root**.

square (III.), vb. trans. & intrans., fr. square (I.). A. trans. 1. To make square, give square shape to. Phr. *to square the circle*, (i.) to construct a square equal in area to a given circle; (ii.) to express or determine the exact area of a circle in terms of its radius; (iii.) (fig.) to perform an impossibility. 2. a To make square, form into a right angle: *to square the edge of a board*; b to raise, place, so as to form a horizontal line: *to square one's shoulders, elbows*, esp. in preparation for fighting. 3. To settle, make even, balance: *to square accounts with*. 4. a To induce, persuade, by illicit means, to act in a certain way, or to abstain from hostile action; to bribe: *it was said that the police had been squared*; b to persuade by legitimate means; to satisfy, convince; to settle with: *to square one's creditors by paying them*. 5. To adapt, reconcile, bring into line: *to square one's theories with ascertained facts*. 6. (arith.) To multiply (quantity) by itself. 7. (naut.) a To get (dead-eyes &c.) in line with each other; b to lay (yards &c.) parallel to deck and at right angles to ship's length. B. intrans. 1. To be at right angles, form a right angle. 2. To assume an attitude with squared elbows &c., assume boxer's preliminary position: *to square up to a person*. 3. To harmonize, be in agreement with: *statement does not square with the facts*.

square (IV.), adv., fr. square (II.). 1. At right angles, so as to form a right angle; squarely: *to stand square*. 2. Honestly, fairly: *fair and square*.

square-built, adj. Broad in proportion to height, and with straight outlines.

square-head, n. (U.S. slang) Scandinavian immigrant in America.

square-leg, n. (cricket) Fielder standing at right angles to wicket on the on-side.

squarely, adv. [1. skwárli; 2. skweáli]. square (II.) & **-ly**. 1. So as to form a right angle. 2. Directly opposite: *to face a person squarely*. 3. Unambiguously, without equivocation. 4. Honestly, equitably, on the square.

squareness, n. [1. skwárnes; 2. skweánis]. See prec. & **-ness**. 1. State of being square. 2. Honesty, sincerity, square dealing.

square-rigged, adj. (of ship) Having the yards horizontal and at right angles to keel; opposed to *fore-and-aft*.

square-rigger, n. [1. skwār riger; 2. skweə rigə]. Square-rigged vessel.

squaresail, n. [1. skwársl; 2. skweásl]. Four-cornered sail extended by yard lying across mast, esp. on fore-and-aft rigged ship.

square-shouldered, adj. Having shoulders which give the impression of being approximately at right angles to the neck; contrasted with sloping.

square-toed, adj. 1. (of shoes &c.) Having square toes. 2. (fig.) Puritanical, over-rigid, and scrupulous.

square-toes, n. [1. skwār tōz; 2. skweə touz]. Exact, punctilious, conventional, puritanical person.

squarish, adj. [1. skwárish; 2. skweárif]. square (II.) & -ish. Nearly square.

squarrose, adj. [1. skwárōs; 2. skweárous], fr. L. Lat. *squarrōsus*, 'scaly, scurfy', prob. w. assimilation to squama, fr. Gk. *eskhára*, 'scab'. With rough, scale-like projections.

squarrous, adj. [1. skwárus; 2. skweárəs]. See prec. & -ous. Squarrose.

squarson, n. [1. skwársun; 2. skwásən]. Coinage fr. a blend of **squire** & **parson**. Clergyman who is also a landowner, esp. one who is both the squire and the incumbent of his parish.

squash (I.), vb. trans. & intrans. [1. skwosh; 2. skwɔʃ]. M.E. *squacchen*, fr. O. Fr. *esquacher*, fr. ex- & Low Lat. *coacticāre*, 'to press together', fr. Lat. *coactus*, P.P. of *cōgere*, 'to drive together; to compel'. See **cogent**. A. trans. 1. a To crush, press, to a shapeless mass or pulp; b to compress, crush, jam, press or squeeze flat. 2. (fig., colloq.) To disconcert, crush, abash, by sarcastic speech &c. B. intrans. 1. To become crushed, squeezed, compressed to a soft or pulpy mass: *the fruit will squash if it is badly packed*. 2. To squeeze, force one's way by pressure.

squash (II.), n., fr. prec. 1. Condition of being closely packed and crushed; a jam. 2. Mass of soft, moist substance which has been crushed and bruised: *the strawberries have all gone to squash*. 3. a Closely packed crowd of persons &c.; b process, or sensation, of being squeezed in a crowd. 4. Drink made of the juice of crushed fruit; chiefly in the compounds, *lemon-squash, orange-squash*. 5. Squash rackets.

squash (III.), n., fr. Am. Indian *askutasquash*. Thick fleshy fruit of various kinds of trailing plant, eaten as vegetable &c.

squash-hat, n. Soft felt hat with broadish brim.

squashiness, n. [1. skwóshines; 2. skwóʃinis]. squashy & **-ness**. State or quality of being squashy.

squash-rackets, n. Game resembling rackets, but played in a smaller court, by two persons, with a soft india-rubber ball.

squashy, adj. [1. skwóshi; 2. skwóʃi]. **squash** (II.) & **-y**. Tending, liable, to become squashed; soft and pulpy; reduced to a soft moist mass.

squat (I.), vb. intrans. [1. skwot; 2. skwɔt]. M.E. *squatten*, fr. O. Fr. *esquatir*, fr. **ex-** & *quatir*, 'to flatten', fr. Lat. *coactus*, P.P. of *cōgere*, 'to drive together; to compel'. See **cogent**. **1.** (of person) To sit back, resting on the heels, or, generally, to crouch on the ground with the feet drawn up to the body. **2.** (of animal) To crouch with legs close to body. **3. a** To settle down on land without permission of owner, or on common land without authorization; **b** to occupy land as a settler in a wild, thinly populated country; esp. a settler on Government land in Australia.

squat (II.), adj., fr. prec. Short and thick, stumpy and square.

squatter, n. [1. skwóter; 2. skwɔ́tə]. **squat** (I.) & **-er**. **1.** Person or animal that squats. **2.** Person who settles on common land, on outlying portion of an estate, without right or permission. **3.** (in Australia) Person who settles on Government land with a view to eventual ownership.

squaw, n. [1. skwaw; 2. skwō], fr. N. Am. Ind. *squa*, 'woman'. North American Indian woman.

squawk, vb. intrans. & n. [1. skwawk; 2. skwɔ̄k]. Imitative. **1.** vb. To utter a short, shrill, harsh cry. **2.** n. Short, harsh cry.

squaw-man, n. White man married to American Indian woman.

squeak (I.), vb. intrans. & trans. [1. skwēk; 2. skwīk]. In Shakespeare; of Scand. origin; cp. M. Swed. *sqvæka* in same sense. **A.** intrans. **1.** To utter a squeak. **2.** (slang) To betray secrets, inform on a person &c. **B.** trans. To utter, pronounce, in a squeak.

squeak (II.), n., fr. prec. Weak, thin, high-pitched cry of fright or excitement, as made by small animals such as rats, mice, bats, or by young children; high piercing, grating sound, such as that made by a pencil on a slate, an unoiled hinge or wheel &c. Phr. *a narrow squeak*, narrow margin of success, performance, escape from danger &c.

squeaker, n. [1. skwēker; 2. skwīkə]. **squeak** (I.) & **-er**. **1.** One who, that which, squeaks; specif., young pigeon. **2.** (slang) An informer, esp. a criminal who betrays his companions to the police.

squeakily, adv. [1. skwēkili; 2. skwīkili]. Next word & **-ly**. With a squeaky sound.

squeaky, adj. [1. skwēki; 2. skwīki]. **squeak** (II.) & **-y**. Producing, of the nature of, a squeak; liable to squeak.

squeal (I.), vb. intrans. & trans. [1. skwēl; 2. skwīəl]. M.E. *squēlen*; of Scand. origin, cp. M. Swed. *sqvæla*; prob. connected w. **squeak** & **squall**. **1.** intrans. **a** To utter a high, shrill, but ringing, prolonged cry; **b** to complain. **2.** (slang) To act as informer, betray confederates &c. **3.** trans. To utter with a squeal.

squeal (II.), n., fr. prec. High, shrill, prolonged cry, louder and stronger than a squeak.

squealer, n. [1. skwēler; 2. skwīlə]. **squeal** & **-er**. One who, that which, squeals; specif. **a** young bird, esp. pigeon; **b** a person who is always complaining.

squeamish, adj. [1. skwēmish; 2. skwīmiʃ]. M.E. *squeimous*, fr. A.-Fr. *escoimous*, 'squeamish, disdainful', etymol. doubtful, & **-ish**. **1.** Easily affected by nausea; slightly nauseated. **2.** Highly fastidious or scrupulous; easily offended or disgusted; very sensitive.

squeamishly, adv. Prec. & **-ly**. In a squeamish manner.

squeamishness, n. See prec. & **-ness**. State or quality of being squeamish.

squeegee (I.), n. [1. skwējē; 2. skwídʒī], fr. popular form of **squeeze** & **-ee**. **1.** Long-handled wooden instrument with rubber blade for clearing water, mud &c. from smooth surface of a road, deck &c. **2.** Small implement in form of a rubber roller for drying photographic prints &c.

squeegee (II.), vb. trans., fr. prec. To treat, dry, sweep, with a squeegee.

squeezability, n. [1. skwēzabíliti; 2. skwīzəbíliti]. See next word & **-bility**. State or quality of being squeezable.

squeezable, adj. [1. skwēzabl; 2. skwīzəbl]. Next word & **-able**. **a** Capable of being squeezed; yielding to pressure; **b** capable of being persuaded or coerced.

squeeze (I.), vb. trans. & intrans. [1. skwēz; 2. skwīz]. Prob. fr. O.E. (non-W.S.) *cwēsan*, 'to bruise, dash against; to squeeze', w. O. Fr. pref. *es-*, fr. Lat. **ex-**, as intens.; further connexions of *cwēsan* are doubtful. **A.** trans. **1.** To compress (esp. a soft substance) between two or more surfaces or between the fingers; to press firmly; to mould, knead: *to squeeze moist clay*; *to squeeze a person's hand*. **2. a** To exert pressure upon for the purpose of extracting moisture: *to squeeze a sponge*; *to squeeze a lemon dry*; **b** to extract (moisture) by squeezing: *to squeeze juice from a lemon*. **3.** (fig.) **a** To bring moral pressure of persuasion or fear to bear upon, constrain; to practise extortion upon: *a usurer squeezes his victims*; **b** to extort, extract, by moral pressure, threats &c.: *to squeeze money, a confession, from a person*. **4.** To pack tightly, cram, compress; jam in, by pressing: *to squeeze things into a box*; *to squeeze oneself into a room* &c. **5.** To gain, force, by pushing and pressing: *to squeeze one's way through a crowd*. **6.** To take an impression of (moulded, engraved, inscribed object &c.) on a plastic surface. **B.** intrans. To go, move, pass, force one's way by squeezing and compressing: *to squeeze through a narrow opening*.

squeeze (II.), n., fr. prec. **1.** Act of squeezing: *to give one's hand a squeeze*. **2.** Crowding, compression, state of being packed closely together: *it was a tight squeeze to get everything in*. **3.** Impression of inscription, coin &c., taken by pressure on soft surface, such as on damp paper.

squeezer, n. [1. skwēzer; 2. skwīzə]. **squeeze** (I.) & **-er**. **1.** One who, that which, squeezes; specif. **a** device for extracting juice from fruit &c.; **b** machine for removing air-bubbles from puddled iron. **2.** *Squeezers*, playing-cards with value indicated in top right-hand corner.

squelch (I.), vb. intrans. [1. skwelch; 2. skwel(t)ʃ]. Imitative. **1.** To produce a splashing, gurgling sound, or a sound of suction, as by walking in wet boots through adhesive mud &c. **2. a** To crush, annihilate, as by treading upon; **b** (fig.) to disconcert, reduce to silence by rebuke or irony.

squelch (II.), n. See prec. **1.** Sound of suction made in walking through wet, thick mud &c. **2.** Act of squelching; **a** a crushing extermination; **b** rebuke or retort which silences opposition, disconcerts, and abashes &c.

squib (I.), n. [1. skwib; 2. skwib], fr. next word. **1.** Small firework which, when lighted, gives off a series of sparks, ending with a loud but harmless explosion. **2.** Tube of gunpowder used to fire a charge. **3.** Short satirical composition, a lampoon.

squib (II.), vb. trans. Perh. a dialectal variant fr. M.E. *swippen*, 'to move quickly, vibrate', fr. O.N. *svipa*, 'quick movement'; sharp blow; flash'; cp. O.H.G. *sweifan*, 'to swing, give turning movement to'; O.E. *swāpan*, 'to move, sweep'; see **sweep**. To attack with squibs.

squid (I.), n. [1. skwid; 2. skwid]. Origin uncertain; perh. related to O.N. *skvetta*, 'squirt'. **1.** Kind of cuttle-fish with a slender body and long arms and tentacles; esp. the common squid, used as bait. **2.** Kind of artificial bait, sometimes made of metal in imitation of a squid.

squid (II.), vb. intrans., fr. prec. To fish with squid as bait.

squiffer, n. [1. skwifer; 2. skwifə]. Etymol. unknown. (slang) Concertina.

squiffy, adj. [1. skwifi; 2. skwifi]. Etymol. unknown. Slightly intoxicated, tipsy.

squilgee, n. & vb. trans. [1. skwiljē; 2. skwíldʒī]. See **squeegee**; origin of variant unknown.

squill, n. [1. skwil; 2. skwil]. M.E., fr. M. F. *squille*, fr. Lat. *squilla*, fr. Gk. *skilla*, 'squill, sea-onion'. **1.** Genus, *Scilla*, of plants of the lily family with blue or purplish, bell-shaped flowers; the bulb of some species is used medicinally. **2.** Dried and sliced bulb of the squill, used as purgative and emetic drug. **3.** Genus of crustaceans, esp. kind of shrimp.

squinancy, n. [1. skwínansi; 2. skwínənsi]. The quinsy-wort; see **quinsy**.

squinch, n. [1. skwinch; 2. skwintʃ]. Variant of **sconce**. Arch or series of arches across interior right angle, esp. of square tower, to support octagonal spire &c.

squint (I.), n. [1. skwint; 2. skwint]. Occurs in Early M.E. in adv. *asquint*; cp. O. Fris. *schūn*, 'oblique', & *schūnte*, 'obliquity'; also Dan. *paa skōns*, 'aslant'. Prob. connected w. **askance**. **1.** Condition in which both eyes cannot look, at the same time, straight at an object; condition in which the eyes tend to converge or to diverge, caused by an affection of the eye-muscles or nerves; strabismus: *to have a bad squint*. **2.** (colloq.) Look, peep, glance: *let me have a squint at it*. **3.** Small tunnel open at either end, made through the thickness of the wall of church to enable the high altar to be seen from transepts, side-chapels &c.

squint (II.), vb. intrans. & trans., fr. prec. **A.** intrans. **1.** To be affected with strabismus or squint; to look in different directions with the two eyes. **2.** *Squint at*, **a** to look hastily and sideways at; **b** (colloq.) to glance, look, at. **B.** trans. (rare) To cause (eyes) to squint: *to squint the eyes*.

squint (III.), adj., fr. **squint** (I.). (rare) Affected with strabismus, squinting.

squint-eyed, adj. **1.** Affected with squint. **2.** Having an evil, malicious look; malevolent, evil, spiteful.

squinting, adj. [1. skwinting; 2. skwíntiŋ], fr. Pres. Part. of **squint** (II.). **a** Affected with squint, with distorted vision; **b** awry, out of the straight.

squintingly, adv. [1. skwíntingli; 2. skwíntiŋli]. Prec. & **-ly**. In a squinting manner.

squire (I.), n. [1. skwīr; 2. skwaiə], fr. **esquire**. **1.** (hist.) Man of gentle or noble birth in attendance on knight. **2.** Member of landed gentry, owner of country estate, esp. *the squire*, chief landowner of particular village &c. **3.** Man escorting or attentive to woman: *squire of dames*, man often in attendance on women.

squire (II.), vb. trans., fr. prec. To act as squire, escort, be attentive to: *to squire a lady*.

squirearch, n. [1. skwírark; 2. skwáiərāk], fr. **squire** & Gk. *arkhós*, 'leader, chief', see **arch-**. Member of squirearchy.

squirearchal, -archical, adj. [1. skwírārk(ik)l; 2. skwáiərāk(ik)l]. **squirearchy** & **-ic** & **-al**. Pertaining to, of the nature of, a squirearchy.

squirearchy, n. [1. skwírarki; 2. skwáiərāki]. **squire** & **-archy**. **1.** Landed gentry, country landowners, collectively. **2.** Government by landed classes.

squireen, n. [1. skwirēn; 2. skwaiərín]. **squire** & Ir. dimin. suff. *-een, -ín*. Small landowner in Ireland; esp. a rough country gentleman with little education or experience of the world.

squirehood, n. [1. skwírhood; 2. skwáiəhud]. **squire** & **-hood**. Rank of squire.

squirelet, n. [1. skwírlet; 2. skwáiəlit]. **squire** & **-let**. Petty squire.

squireling, n. [1. skwírling; 2. skwáiəliŋ]. **squire** & **-ling**. Squirelet.

squirely, adj. [1. skwírli; 2. skwáiəli]. **squire** (I.) & **-ly**. Pertaining to a squire.

squireship, n. [1. skwírship; 2. skwáiəʃip]. **squire** (I.) & **-ship**. State of being a squire, rank of squire.

squirm (I.), vb. intrans. [1. skwerm; 2. skwə̄m]. Etymol. doubtful; perh. imitative. **1.** To

squirm (II.), n., fr. prec. 1. Squirming, writhing motion; wriggle. 2. (naut.) Kink in rope.

squirrel, n. [1. skwírel; 2. skwírǝl]. M.E. *squirel*, fr. O. Fr. *escurel*, fr. L. Lat. *scurellus*, fr. *sciūrus*, 'squirrel', fr. Gk. *skiouros*, fr. *skiá*, 'shadow', see **sciagraphy**, & *ourá*, 'tail'; cp. Gk. *ourakhós*, 'point'; cogn. w. Lat. *urruncum*, 'lowest part of ear of corn'; see also **uro-**. Small, arboreal, bushy-tailed, hibernating rodent, genus *Sciurus*, with reddish, dark-brown, or grey fur; *barking squirrel*, prairie-dog; *flying squirrel*, species with extensible, lateral membranes serving as parachutes.

squirrel-fish, n. Reddish fish of West Indies.

squirrel-grass, n. Wild barley.

squirrel monkey, n. **a** Small, long-tailed monkey of S. America; **b** marmoset.

squirrel-tail, n. Kind of grass resembling barley.

squirt (I.), vb. trans. & intrans. [1. skwërt; 2. skwᾱt]. Cp. L.G. *swirtjen*. 1. trans. To eject (liquid) in a thin but fairly powerful stream, or jet. 2. intrans. To spurt out, be forced out, in a jet.

squirt (II.), n., fr. prec. 1. Jet, stream, of liquid &c. 2. Instrument for ejecting liquid in a jet; syringe. 3. (colloq. and vulg.) Conceited, bumptious, insignificant upstart; pert, self-satisfied person.

squish, n. [1. skwish; 2. skwiʃ]. Prob. variant of **squash (II.)**. (colloq.) Marmalade.

stab (I.), vb. trans. & intrans. [1. stab; 2. stæb]. Etymol. doubtful; perh. fr. Swed. *stabbe*, 'a stub, stump'. **A.** trans. 1. To pierce, wound, penetrate flesh or substance of, with stick, or pointed weapon (esp. with a knife or dagger): *to stab one in the arm*. Phr. *to stab in the back*, to disparage, injure, in underhand way, to backbite. 2. To cause to pierce; to stick, jab: *to stab a weapon into*. 3. (fig.) To attack, assail, injure maliciously: *to stab one's reputation*. 4. To roughen surface of (wall &c.) by blows from a pick, to enable it to hold a coat of plaster. **B.** intrans. 1. To aim a blow, to make a thrust, with pointed weapon: *to stab at a person*. 2. (of wound, pain) To produce sensation of stabbing, to shoot, throb suddenly and painfully.

stab (II.), n., fr. prec. **a** Sharp, sudden, violent blow, thrust, with pointed weapon: *a stab in the breast*; Phr. (fig.) *a stab in the back*, a malicious, treacherous attempt to injure; **b** a sudden sharp shoot, or throb, of pain.

Stabat Mater, n. [1. stáhbat máhter; 2. stǽbət mātə]. Lat. *stabat māter (dolorōsa)*, 'the mother stood', first words of hymn. 1. Mediaeval Latin sequence on the Crucifixion. 2. Musical setting of this.

stabber, n. [1. stáber; 2. stǽbə]. **stab (I.)** & -**er**. 1. One who stabs; an assassin, one who kills by stabbing. 2. That which stabs, esp. instrument for stabbing or piercing.

stability, n. [1. stabíliti; 2. stəbíliti]. Lat. *stabilitāt-(em)*, 'firmness', fr. *stabilis*, 'firm, stable', see **stable (I.)**, & -**ity**. State or quality of being stable; steadiness, firmness.

stabilization, n. [1. stàbilīzāshun; 2. stæ̀bəlaizéiʃən]. Next word & -**ation**. Act of stabilizing; state of being stabilized; esp. of a country's currency, by fixing a definite gold value for it.

stabilize, vb. trans. [1. stáb-, stǽbiliz; 2. stǽb-, stéibilaiz], fr. Lat. *stabilis*, 'firm', see **stable (I.)**, & -**ize**. To make stable, bring into a state of stability or equilibrium, specif., *to stabilize a currency*.

stabilizer, n. [1. stábilizer; 2. stǽbilaizə]. Prec. & -**er**. One who, that which, stabilizes; specif., an additional plane or fin attached to aeroplane &c. to maintain stability in flight.

stable (I.), adj. [1. stábl; 2. stéibl], fr. Lat. *stabilis*, 'firm, steady, constant', fr. *sta-*, fr. base *sta-*, *stə-*, 'to stand', see **stand**, **state**, & -**ble**. 1. (of material and non-material things) Fixed, firmly established, steady; not easily moved or upset: *stable foundations*; *a stable government*; *stable currency*; reverse of shifting, uncertain, fluctuating. 2. Resolute, unwavering, steadfast, tenacious of purpose. 3. (mechan.) *Stable equilibrium*, tendency of body to return to position of rest when moved or disturbed.

stable (II.), n., fr. O. Fr. *estable*, fr. Lat. *stabulum*, 'stable, stall, lair, hive; hut, hovel', fr. *stə-dhlo-*, expanded fr. *stā-*, *stə-*, 'to stand'; cogn. w. **stall (I.)**. See also **stand**, **state**, & prec. 1. Building fitted and used as shelter for cattle or, more usually, for horses. 2. Group of horses kept in any particular stable, and belonging to a given owner.

stable (III.), vb. trans. & intrans., fr. prec. 1. trans. To put into a stable. 2. intrans. To be kept in, occupy, a stable.

stable-boy, n. Boy employed in stable.

stable-call, n. Signal in cavalry regiment for watering and grooming horses.

stableman, n. [1. stáblmen; 2. stéiblmǝn]. Man employed in or about a stable.

stableness, n. [1. stáblnes; 2. stéiblnis]. **stable (I.)** & -**ness**. Quality of being stable; stability.

stabling, n. [1. stábling; 2. stéibliŋ]. **stable (II.)** & -**ing**. Set of stables, accommodation for horses &c.

stablish, vb. trans. [1. stáblish; 2. stǽbliʃ]. Abbr. fr. **establish**. (archaic) To make firm, set stably; to found, establish.

stably, adv. [1. stábli; 2. stéibli]. **stable (I.)** & -**ly**. In a stable manner, firmly.

staccato, adv. & adj. [1. stakáhtō; 2. stəkátou]. Ital., P.P. of *staccare*, fr. *distaccare*, 'to detach'; cp. **detach** & see **tack (I.)**. (mus.) 1. adv. With each note played in a sharply detached, abrupt manner. 2. adj. (of passage, note &c.) To be played staccato: *staccato mark*, dot above or below musical note to show that it is to be played staccato.

stack (I.), n. [1. stak; 2. stæk]. M.E. *stac*, fr. O.N. *stakkr*, 'stack'; cogn. w. Lith. *stókas*, 'pillar'; O. Prussian *staklan*, 'support'; fr. base *stə-k-* &c., expanded fr. *stə-*, *stā-* &c., 'to stand'; see **stand**, & words there referred to. 1. Large, symmetrical pile of hay, straw, or unthrashed corn, usually round or rectangular, with top sloping to a peak or ridge; rick. 2. Any orderly heap, pile, or group: *a stack of wood* &c.; specif. **a** pyramidal pile of rifles &c., with muzzles upwards; **b** cluster of chimneys projecting above a roof. 3. Also, *smoke-stack*, chief chimney or funnel of locomotive engine, furnace &c. 4. (esp. Scots) Tall, detached shaft of rock. 5. (as measure of firewood &c.) One hundred and eight cubic feet. 6. (colloq.) Any large pile, heap: *a stack of papers*, *books*.

stack (II.), vb. trans., fr. prec. To place, arrange, pile up, in a stack. Phr. *stack arms!*, (mil.) command to pile rifles &c. in a stack.

stack-funnel, n. Vertical, cylindrical opening down centre of haystack &c., to prevent overheating.

stack-stand, n. Rough platform on short stone or wooden posts, faggots &c., to raise stack above ground to prevent injury from damp, rats &c.

stack-yard, n. Enclosure in farm &c., within which stacks are erected.

stacte, n. [1. stáktē; 2. stǽktī]. Lat. *stactē*, 'oil of myrrh', fr. Gk. *staktḗ*, fr. *stázein*, 'to drop, drip'; cp. Gk. *stagṓn*, 'flowing drop'; cogn. w. Lat. *stagnum*, 'pond', see **stagnant**. Spice used by ancient Jews in making incense (cp. Exodus xxx. 34).

stactometer, n. [1. staktómeter; 2. stæktómitə], fr. Gk. *staktós*, 'flowing in drops', fr. *stázein*, 'to flow', see prec., & -**meter**. Tubular instrument pierced with minute hole for measuring liquid in drops.

stadium, n. [1. stádium; 2. stéidiəm]. Lat. *stadium*, fr. Gk. *stádion*, 'racecourse, stadium', apparently through the influence of *stádion*, 'firm', fr. base *stə-*, 'to stand', q.v. under **stand (I.)**, for earlier *spádion*, 'racecourse', fr. *spáein*, 'to draw out, stretch', q.v. under **spathe**, **spasm**, **span**, **speed**. 1. (Gk. antiq.) Foot racecourse at Olympia &c., where games were held. 2. Course specially prepared for foot-races, consisting of a large open space enclosed by walls and tiers of seats for spectators. 3. Length of Olympic stadium from end to end, as ancient Greek measure of length, equal to nearly 203 yards. 4. (med.) Specific phase or stage of disease.

stad(t)holder, n. [1. stáhd-, stád-, stáht-hōlder; 2. stád-, stǽd-, státhouldə], fr. Du. *stadhouder*, but influenced by **holder**, & partly by Germ. *stadt*, 'town', q.v. under **stead**. (Du. hist.) 1. Governor or lieutenant of town or province. 2. Chief magistrate of the seven United Provinces.

stad(t)holderate, n. [1. stáhd-hōlderit; 2. stǽd-houldərit]. Prec. & -**ate**. Office of stadtholder.

stad(t)holdership, n. [1. stáhd-hòldership; 2. stǽdhòuldəʃip]. See prec. & -**ship**. Stadholderate.

staff (I.), n. [1. stahf; 2. stãf]. O.E. *stæf*; M.E. *staf*, 'stick, staff; letter, verse', cp. O. Fris. *stef*; O.N. *stafr*; O.H.G. *stab*; cogn. w. Scrt. *stabhnáti*, 'supports'; *stambhaḥ*, 'post'; Lith. *stếbas*, 'staff, pole', & further w. **stem (I.)**. 1. **a** (archaic) Strong, relatively slender stick, rod, pole, esp. for aid in walking &c., or as weapon; **b** staff or wand in various forms as a badge of office, or authority &c.: *pastoral staff* (of a bishop). 2. Tall pole serving as a support: *flagstaff*. 3. Instrument used **a** in surveying; **b** (naut.) for taking altitudes. 4. (surg.) Curved steel instrument for guiding knife into bladder. 5. (fig.) Support, prop, stay: *bread is the staff of life*; *a son should be the staff of his father's old age*. 6. Organized group of persons working under central direction; esp. in a factory, an educational or other institution &c.: *the nursing*, *medical*, *staff of a hospital*; *the staff of a college*; *teaching staff* &c. 7. (mil.) Group of officers of various ranks, not themselves in command, serving at the headquarters of a military unit larger than a regiment, under the commander of the unit, and engaged in administrative or executive duties connected with the various branches of military operations and organization; *General Staff*, that for the army as a whole. 8. (mus.) Group of five parallel horizontal lines and intermediate spaces used for indicating pitch of notes.

staff (II.), n. Etymol. unknown. Plastic compound of plaster-of-Paris, glycerine, cement &c., used as material for building, architectural ornament &c.; esp. for temporary structures.

staff captain, n. Junior staff officer of a military unit higher than a regiment.

staff college, n. Establishment for instruction and training of officers for the General Staff.

staffed, adj. [1. stahft; 2. stãft]. **staff (I.)** & -**ed**. Having, provided with, a staff: *a well-staffed institution*.

staff notation, n. Musical notation in which the pitch of the notes is indicated by position on the staff.

staff officer, n. Officer serving on the General Staff.

staff sergeant, n. Non-commissioned officer serving on regimental staff.

staff tree, n. Genus, *Celastrus*, of small trees and climbing shrubs with brightly coloured fruit.

staff work, n. **a** Work of organization and direction carried out by military staff; hence **b** organization and management of any undertaking.

stag, n. [1. stag; 2. stæg]. Scand., cp. O.N. *steggr*, 'male bird; male cat'. 1. Male of red deer, esp. in and after fifth year. 2. Male of other varieties of large deer. 3. Bull castrated when full-grown. 4. (Stock Exchange)

stag-beetle, n. Genus of beetles with large, strong, branched mandibles.

stage (I.), n. [1. stāj; 2. steidž], fr. O. Fr. *estage*, fr. Low Lat. **staticum*, fr. *statum*, P.P. type of *stāre*, 'to stand', see **state** (I.). 1. Platform for raising, supporting or displaying any object, person &c.; specif. **a** platform supported by scaffolding, slung by ropes, &c., for workmen at work; **b** small adjustable shelf of microscope, supporting object to be examined; **c** usually *landing-stage*, part of dock or wharf, on which passengers disembark from vessel. 2. **a** Raised platform in theatre on which dramatic performance &c. takes place; Phr. *to go on the stage*, take up acting as profession; **b** any space, surface, enclosure &c. for dramatic performance. 3. Dramatic literature; the drama: *the mediaeval stage*. 4. Acting as a profession; occupation of an actor: *to give up the law for the stage* &c. 5. (fig.) Scene of action, place where plans are carried out, events happen &c. 6. Period of development; specific point of progress &c.: *at an early stage in his career*; *different stages of education*; *negotiations had reached their final stage*. 7. **a** One of a series of stopping-places in a journey, of a public vehicle on a regular course &c.: *to travel to the last stage*; **b** distance between two successive stopping-places: *to travel by short stages*. 8. Stage-coach.

stage (II.), vb. trans., fr. prec. 1. To arrange, prepare (play &c.) for public performance on the stage, put on the stage. 2. To arrange the sequence of events in a pageant or other public show so as to produce the greatest dramatic effect.

stage-coach, n. Large, public conveyance plying regularly by stages, as means of communication between two places.

stage-coachman, n. Driver of stage-coach.

stage-craft, n. Skill in writing plays for performance on the stage; skill and experience in everything connected with the production of plays in public.

stage-direction, n. Instruction to the actors of a play regarding their entrances, exits, their relative positions on the stage, and the like, written or printed on the copies of a play.

stage-door, n. Door leading to back of theatre for the use of actors, workmen &c.

stage-effect, n. Effect produced on, characteristic of, or suitable for, the stage.

stage-fever, n. Infatuation for everything connected with the theatre; esp. a strong desire to embark on an actor's career.

stage-fright, n. Nervousness experienced by actor or speaker on facing an audience.

stage-manager, n. Person superintending the acting of a play.

stager, n. [1. stájer; 2. stéidžə]. **stage** (I.) & -er. In Phr. *old stager*, person of long experience.

stage-right, n. Right of producing a play.

stage-struck, adj. Infatuated with the theatre; desirous of embracing a theatrical career.

stag-evil, n. Lock-jaw in horses.

stage whisper, n. Loud whisper as of actor on stage, intended to be heard by audience.

staggard, n. [1. stágard; 2. stǽgəd]. **stag**-**ard**. Stag of the fourth year.

stagger (I.), vb. intrans. & trans. [1. stáger; 2. stǽgə]. M.E. *stakkeren*, fr. O.N. *stakra*, 'to cause to reel'; cp. O.N. *staka*, 'to push'; M. Du. *staggeren*. **A.** intrans. 1. To move with an unsteady, uneven, uncertain gait, as from weakness, shock, intoxication &c.; to reel, walk stumblingly. 2. (fig.) To become irresolute, vacillating, hesitant. **B.** trans. 1. (fig.) To disconcert, overwhelm, as by amazement, horror &c., by the shock of something unexpected &c.: *I was positively staggered by the news*; *the size of the bill staggered him*. 2. (mechan.) To set (wheel spokes) inclined alternately to right and left.

stagger (II.), n., fr. prec. 1. Staggering, tottering, unsteady, jerky movement. 2. *The staggers*, a feeling of giddiness; vertigo; **b** often *blind staggers*, nervous disease of cattle and horses, characterized by staggering movements in walking.

staggerer, n. [1. stágerer; 2. stǽgərə]. **stagger** (I.) & -er. **a** One who, that which, staggers or disconcerts; specif. **b** disconcerting or difficult question &c.; poser.

staggering, adj. [1. stágering; 2. stǽgəriŋ], fr. Pres. Part. of **stagger** (I.). 1. Tottering, reeling, unsteady: *staggering gait*. 2. Causing one to stagger: *a staggering blow*. 3. Of a kind, size, amount, to produce a shock of amazement; overwhelming, gravely disconcerting: *a staggering piece of news, sum, misfortune*.

staggeringly, adv. Prec. & -ly. To an extent which staggers one.

stag-horn, n. 1. Kind of branching moss or fern. 2. Kind of large coral.

staghound, n. [1. stág-hound; 2. stǽghaund]. One of a large, swift breed of dogs used for stag-hunting.

stag-hunting, n. The chase of the stag on horseback, with pack of hounds.

staginess, n. [1. stájines; 2. stéidžinis]. **stagy** & -ness. State or quality of being stagy; theatricality.

staging, n. [1. stájing; 2. stéidžiŋ]. **stage** (I.) & -ing. 1. Temporary platform or scaffolding for use of men at work on the face of a building. 2. Method or process of presenting a play on the stage.

Stagirite, n. [1. stájirīt; 2. stǽdžirait], fr. Lat. *Stagirītes*, fr. Gk. *Stageirítēs*, fr. *Stágeira*, town in Macedonia, & **-ite**. Native of Stageira; esp. *the Stagirite*, Aristotle.

stagnancy, n. [1. stágnansi; 2. stǽgnənsi]. **stagnant** & -cy. Condition of being stagnant.

stagnant, adj. [1. stágnant; 2. stǽgnənt], fr. Lat. *stagnantem*, Pres. Part. of *stagnāre*, 'to become a pool', fr. *stagnum*, 'pool'; cogn. w. Gk. *stagón*, 'drop'; *stázein*, 'to drip'; cp. **stacte**. 1. (of water) **a** Not moving or flowing; having no current, remaining stationary as in a pond, ditch &c.; **b** esp. stale, foul, unhealthy, through lack of motion. 2. Inactive, remaining in a dull, inefficient state; torpid, sluggish; reverse of *brisk, lively*: *trade is stagnant*; *a stagnant brain*.

stagnantly, adv. Prec. & -ly. In a stagnant manner.

stagnate, vb. intrans. [1. stágnāt; 2. stǽgneit], fr. Lat. *stagnāt-(um)*, P.P. type of *stagnāre*, 'to become a pool', fr. *stagnum*, 'pool', see **stagnant**. 1. (of water) To remain stationary, without current or flowing motion; esp. to become foul through remaining in a pond, ditch, barrel &c. without inlet or outlet. 2. (fig.) To be and remain inactive; to become dull and lifeless through lack of use; to lack variety and movement.

stagnation, n. [1. stagnáshun; 2. stǽgnéiʃən]. Prec. & **-ion**. (lit. and fig.) Act or process of stagnating; condition of being stagnant.

stagnicolous, adj. [1. stagníkulus; 2. stǽgníkələs], fr. Lat. *stagnum*, 'pond, swamp', see **stagnant**, & *-i-*, & *colere*, 'to inhabit', see **colony**, & **-ous**. Living in or near stagnant water, marsh &c.

stag's-horn fern, n. Genus, *Platycerium*, of evergreen ferns, with broad, antler-like fronds.

stagy, adj. [1. stáji; 2. stéidži]. **stage** (I.) & -y. Characteristic of the stage; (usually in unfavourable sense) over-emphatic in manner or mode of speech; producing an effect of unreality and insincerity; artificial, theatrical.

staid, adj. [1. stād; 2. steid]. Variant of *stayed*, P.P. of **stay** (I.). Steady, sober, sedate; reverse of frivolous or flighty.

staidly, adv. Prec. & -ly. In a staid manner.

staidness, n. See prec. & -ness. Quality of being staid.

stain (I.), vb. trans. & intrans. [1. stān; 2. stein]. M.E. *steinen*, abbr. fr. *disteinen*, fr. O. Fr. *disteindre*, 'to colour', fr. *dis-* & Lat. *tingere*, 'to dye, stain', see **tinct**. **A.** trans. 1. To make a stain on surface of; to discolour: *to stain one's fingers with ink*, *one's coat with blackberry juice*. 2. To impart colour, esp. by a deliberate process, to the surface of (substance): *to stain wood, glass* &c. 3. To colour (part of tissue &c.) for greater distinctness in examination under a microscope, by staining with a substance whose chemical reaction affects some cells &c. but not others. 4. To mar, impart moral blemish to: *his character was stained by cruelty and rapacity*. **B.** intrans. 1. To be affected by, susceptible of, discolouration; to be liable to staining: *the cloth will not stain*. 2. To be liable to cause a stain, or produce discolouration: *ink stains worse than almost anything*.

stain (II.), n., fr. prec. 1. Discolouration; dirty mark; patch, streak, spot, of distinct colour, or foreign substance, esp. upon the surface of some other substance or material: *a stain on the cloth*; *petrol will remove stains of grease*; *ink-stains*; *blood-stains* &c. 2. Colour given to wood, glass, wall-paper &c. by staining or dyeing. 3. Pigment, colouring-matter, used for staining. 4. Moral defect, blemish, spot: *without a stain on one's character*.

stainable, adj. [1. stánabl; 2. stéinəbl]. **stain** (I.) & **-able**. Capable of being stained.

stainer, n. [1. stáner; 2. stéinə]. **stain** (II.) & -er. One who, that which, stains; specif., colouring-matter used in staining.

stainless, adj. [1. stánles; 2. stéinlis]. **stain** (I.) & **-less**. 1. Without a stain; (esp. in moral sense) spotless, immaculate, unstained. 2. Not liable to become stained: *stainless steel*.

stainlessly, adv. Prec. & -ly. In a stainless manner, without causing stains or becoming stained.

stainlessness, n. See prec. & -ness. State or quality of being stainless.

stair, n. [1. stār; 2. stɛə]. O.E. *stǣger*, 'stair, ladder'; M.E. *steire*; fr. **staig-ir-*, earlier **staig-*, cp. M. Du. *stēger*; cp. same base in Goth. *staiga*; O.H.G. *steiga*, 'path'; in gradational relation w. O.E. *stīgan*; O.H.G. *stīgan*, 'to climb, go up', cp. **stile** (I.); cogn. w. Scrt. *stighnóti*, 'to ascend'; Lett. *staigát*, 'to go, walk'; *stiga*, 'path'; O. Slav. *stĭgna*, 'street'; Gk. *steikhein*, 'to go'; *stíkhos*, 'rank, line'; see **stichic**. 1. One of a series of steps leading from one floor to another in a building: *a short passage and then three stairs*. 2. **a** (in sing.) A flight, series, of steps forming part of the structure of house or other building, leading from one floor to another: *a winding stair*; *a short stair leads to the first floor*; *the stair is very steep*; more commonly, **b** (pl.) *stairs*: *the stairs are steep*; *a flight of stairs*; Phr. *below stairs*, in the lower floor of a house; specif., the kitchen and servants' quarters in a house with a basement.

stair-carpet, n. Carpet woven in narrow strip for laying on stairs.

staircase, n. [1. stárkās; 2. stéəkeis]. 1. The part of a building in which the stairs are constructed. 2. The stairs themselves, including the banisters; flight of stairs in any one part of a house, forming a continuous series: *a narrow staircase*; *the principal staircase*; *large houses often have several staircases*; *corkscrew staircase*, flight of stairs winding spirally round central pillar; also *spiral staircase*.

stair-rod, n. Metal or wooden bar for holding stair-carpet in position at bottom of each riser.

stairway, n. [1. stárwā; 2. stéəwei]. Staircase, flight of steps.

staith, n. [1. stāth; 2. steiþ]. O.E. *stæþ*; M.E. *stǣpe, staþ*, 'bank, shore'; cp. O.N. *stöth*, 'landing-stage'; cogn. w. O.E. *stede*, 'place'; see **stead** & **stand**. Wharf with apparatus for loading coal &c.

staithe, n. [1. stādh; 2. steið]. Variant of prec.

stake (I.), n. [1. stāk; 2. steik]. O.E. *staca*; M.E. *stāke*, 'stake'; cp. O. Fris. *stake*; O.N. *stjaki*; O.H.G. *stehho*, 'pillar, stake'; cogn. w. Lett. *stēga*, 'stake'; prob. also w. Lat. *tignum*, 'beam'; gradational variant of **stick (II.)**. **1.** Bar of wood, strong but slender relatively to its length, pointed for driving into the ground: *to tether an animal to a stake*; *to tie a plant to a stake*; *to fix a row of stakes*. **2. a** Stout post to which person was tied when being burnt alive: *burnt at the stake*; hence, **b** *the stake*, death by burning: *some died by the axe, some perished at the stake*. **3.** Small anvil used by tinsmith &c. **4.** Money &c. risked on a bet &c.; amount or object wagered; esp. (pl.), money &c. deposited with third person until wager is decided. Phr. *at stake*, risked, depending, on the outcome of an event &c. **5.** (pl.) **a** Money offered as prize for horse-race &c.; **b** race run for such a prize. **6.** Interest, share in chances of profit or loss; concern: *a stake in an undertaking, in the country*.

stake (II.), vb. trans., fr. prec. **1. a** To fasten, support, secure, with stake(s): *dahlias and Michaelmas daisies should be staked long before they attain their full growth*; **b** to pierce, impale, with a stake: *my horse got staked in trying to jump a very big fence*. **2.** Usually *stake off, out*, to mark (boundary &c.) by driving in stakes: *to stake out a boundary* &c. Phr. *to stake out a claim*, (i.) (lit.) mark out the piece of land which one claims as one's own (in a new settlement, minefield &c.); (ii.) (fig.) to set up, make, a claim, generally. **3.** To put on as a stake, to wager, hazard, risk, as a bet: *to stake a fortune on a single race*; (also fig.) *to stake one's future on a single chance*; *I stake my reputation on his honesty*, will forfeit my reputation if he be not honest.

stake-boat, n. Boat anchored or moored to post at starting point or as winning post in boat race.

stakeholder, n. [1. stákhōlder; 2. stéikhōuldə]. Person appointed to hold the stakes for a wager &c.

stake-net, n. Fishing-net stretched on stakes in shallow water near shore of river or estuary.

stalactic, adj. [1. staláktik; 2. stælǽktik], fr. Gk. *stalaktós*, fr. *stalássein*, 'to drop, drip'; cp. Gk. *télma*, 'stagnant water, marsh'; cogn. w. M.L.G. *stal*, 'urine of horses', see **stale (II.)**. Of, pertaining to, in the form of, containing, stalactites.

stalactiform, adj. [1. staláktiform; 2. stælǽktifōm]. See prec. & *-i-* & **-form.** Having the structure or appearance of a stalactite.

stalactite, n. [1. stálaktīt, staláktīt; 2. stǽləktait, stælǽktait], fr. Gk. *stalaktós*, 'dripping', see **stalactic**, & **-ite.** Long, tapering or cylindrical, calcareous formation, resembling an icicle in form, hanging from roof of cavern, produced by continuous deposits of limy matter dissolved in the water which percolates through; distinguished from *stalagmite*.

stalactitic, adj. [1. stàlaktítik; 2. stæ̀ləktítik]. Prec. & **-ic.** Same as **stalactic**; *stalactitic column*, formed by the uniting of a stalactite with a stalagmite.

stalagmite, n. [1. stalágmīt, stálagmīt; 2. stælǽgmait, stǽləgmait], fr. Gk. *stalagmós*, 'dripping', fr. *stalássein*, 'to drip', see **stalactic**, & **-ite.** Formation analogous to stalactite, but formed from below, by limy matter deposited on the floor of a cavern by water dropping from roof; a stalagmite often becomes united into a continuous column with the stalactite forming from above.

stalagmitic, adj. [1. stàlagmítik; 2. stæ̀ləgmítik]. Prec. & **-ic.** Of, pertaining to, of the nature of, a stalagmite.

stalagmitically, adv. [1. stàlagmítikali; 2. stæ̀ləgmítikəli]. Prec. & **-al** & **-ly.** In the manner of a stalagmite, as a stalagmite.

stale (I.), adj. [1. stāl; 2. steil]. M.E. *stāle*, 'stale'; prob. fr. next word. **1.** Not fresh, having lost some original, vital quality; specif. **a** (of air) heavy, close, stagnant, vitiated; **b** (of food &c.) beginning to decay, or grow sour &c.; *stale bread*, dry, not freshly baked; **c** (of wine) flat, insipid. **2.** Having lost bodily or mental freshness, vigour, spring; grown out of condition; fatigued by prolonged strain or monotony: *one's mind gets stale with too much teaching*; *an athlete becomes stale through overtraining*. **3.** (fig.) Lacking in interest or originality; no longer new and fresh; grown tedious from frequent repetition or long familiarity: *a stale joke*; *stale news*.

stale (II.), n. Cp. M.L.G. *stal*, 'urine of horses'; L.G. *stallen*; Lith. *telžu*, 'to make water'; cogn. w. Gk. *télma*, 'stagnant water'; *stalássein*, 'to drip'; cp. **stalactic.** Urine of cattle and horses.

stale (III.), vb. trans., fr. **stale (I.)**. (rare) To make stale; (chiefly in spiritual sense).

stale (IV.), vb. intrans. Cp. **stale (II.)**. (of horses and cattle) To discharge urine.

stale (V.), n. O.E. *stalu*; M.E. *stāle*, 'theft'; cp. O.H.G. *stala*, 'theft'; gradational variant of **steal.** (rare or archaic) Victim of deception; dupe, gull; laughing-stock, butt.

stalely, adv. [1. stálli; 2. stéilli]. **stale (I.)** & **-ly.** In a stale manner.

stalemate, n. & vb. trans. [1. stálmāt; 2. stéilmeit]. **stale (I.)** & **mate (I.)**, in chess. **1.** n. **a** (chess) Position in which one player can make no move without bringing his king into check; **b** (fig.) a deadlock, an impasse in negotiations. **2.** vb. To put (opponent) into this position.

staleness, n. [1. stálnes; 2. stéilnis]. **stale (I.)** & **-ness.** State or quality of being stale.

stalk (I.), n. [1. stawk; 2. stōk]. M.E. *stalke*, 'stalk, reed'; formed w. dimin. suff. *-oc, -uc*, cp. **bullock**, fr. O.E. *stela*, *stæla*, 'stalk, support'; cp. O.H.G. *stil*, Mod. Germ. *stiel*, 'stem, stalk'; poss. cogn. w. Lat. *stilus*, 'a stake' (but see alternative explanation of this under **style (I.)**); perh. also Gk. *steleós*, 'handle of an axe', & *stélekhos*, 'trunk, log'; cp. further the gradational variant Lat. *stolō*, 'shoot from a root, sucker'. The last is connected by Walde w. Lat. *lātus*, 'broad, expansive', fr. **stlātos*, q.v. under **latitude.** **1.** (bot.) **a** Central support, stem, axis, of a plant, esp. of herbaceous plant; **b** any secondary stem, petiole &c. supporting a leaf, flower, fruit, or other part of a plant. **2.** (zool.) Slender part supporting an organ; stem; peduncle. **3.** Object or part of object resembling a stalk in appearance or function; specif. a stem of a glass, goblet &c.; **b** shaft of feather; **c** tall, slender chimney. **4.** (archit.) Moulding, fluting &c., resembling a stalk.

stalk (II.), vb. intrans. & trans. O.E. *stealcan*, M.E. *stalken*, 'to walk carefully'; perh. orig. 'to walk lifting the feet high at each step'; the word has been connected w. O.E. *stealc*, 'steep, lofty'. **A.** intrans. **1. a** To walk with a lofty, stately, dignified stride; to move with a certain pride and arrogance; **b** (fig. of disease, death, misfortune) to sweep silently but irresistibly along: *pestilence and famine stalked unchecked through the land*. **2.** To practise the stalking of game. **B.** trans. **1.** To pursue, approach, get close to (game &c.) cautiously and noiselessly, without being seen, heard, or winded. **2.** To stride through, across, along: *to stalk the land, the streets*.

stalk (III.), n., fr. prec. **1.** Stiff, imposing gait. **2.** Act of stalking game; stealthy pursuit.

stalked, adj. [1. stawkt; 2. stōkt]. **stalk (I.)** & **-ed.** Having, supported by, a stalk.

stalker, n. [1. stáwker; 2. stṓkə]. **stalk (II.)** & **-er.** One who stalks; esp. one who pursues game by stalking; esp. *deer-stalker* &c.

stalk-eyed, adj. (of crustacean &c.) Having the eyes supported on stalk-like structures.

stalking-horse, n. [1. stáwking hòrs; 2. stṓkiŋ hȍs]. **1.** Horse used as cover by hunter in stalking game. **2.** (fig.) Alleged motive, pretext concealing real intention.

stalkless, adj. [1. stáwkles; 2. stṓklis]. **stalk (I.)** & **-less.** Without, unsupported by, a stalk.

stalklet, n. [1. stáwklet; 2. stṓklit]. **stalk (I.)** & **-let.** Small stalk.

stalky, adj. [1. stáwki; 2. stṓki]. **stalk (I.)** & **-y.** **1.** Like a stalk. **2.** (of plant) Having a long stalk with few or no leaves; leggy.

stall (I.), n. [1. stawl; 2. stōl]. O.E. *steall*, *stall*, 'stable', M.E. *stall*; O.H.G. *stall*; O.N. *stallr*; all fr. Gmc. **staðla-*; cp. also O.E. *staðol*, O.H.G. *stadal*, 'foundation, base'; fr. Aryan type **stədhlo-*, whence also Lat. *stabulum*, see **stable (II.)**. The word is extended fr. the base **stā-*, **stə-* &c., q.v. under **stand (I.)**; **state (I.)** &c. **1.** Division, compartment, in stable, cow-house &c., in which horse or beast is kept, fed &c. **2. a** Small recess with seat, in choir of cathedral, church, chapel &c., sometimes assigned by right of office to specific church dignitary: *canons' stalls* &c.; hence, **b** ecclesiastical office, dignity, entitling holder to a stall in a cathedral &c.: *to hold a prebendal stall*. **3. a** Small shelter or enclosed space, compartment, booth, in market, fair, or other public place, for sale of goods: *a stall at a bazaar*; also in compounds; *book-stall* &c.; **b** table, counter &c. in a booth on which goods for sale are displayed. **4.** Theatre seat forming one of a series, usually with arms, on ground floor of auditorium and nearest the stage; *orchestra stalls*, those in front; *pit stalls*, those in rear. **5.** Covering, sheath, for injured finger &c.; usually compounded: *finger-*, *thumb-stall* &c. **6.** Recess for single workman in coal-mine &c.

stall (II.), vb. trans. & intrans., fr. prec. **A.** trans. **1. a** To place, keep, in a stall; specif. **b** to fatten (cattle) in a stall. **2.** To furnish (stable &c.) with, divide into, stalls. **B.** intrans. **a** (of horse, vehicle, train &c.) To be brought to a standstill, stuck, obstructed, by snow, mud &c.; **b** (of engine, esp. of motor) to stop working; **c** (of aeroplane) to lose speed to such an extent that the machine becomes out of control.

stall (III.), n. Variant of **stale (V.)**. Thief's accomplice, who distracts victim's attention during perpetration of theft &c.

stallage, n. [1. stáwlij; 2. stṓlidž]. **stall (I.)** & **-age.** **1. a** Space for stall in market &c.; **b** rent paid for such space. **2.** Right of erecting stalls in market-place &c.

stall-fed, adj. (of cattle) Fed, fattened, in a stall instead of in the open fields.

stall-feed, vb. trans. To keep and feed (cattle) in a stall, esp. for fattening.

stallion, n. [1. stáliun; 2. stǽliən]. M.E. *stalun*, fr. O. Fr. *estalon*, lit. 'horse kept in a stall', fr. O.H.G. *stal*, 'stall', see **stall (I.)**, & **-oon.** Uncastrated male horse; an entire horse, esp. a sire for breeding.

stalwart (I.), adj. [1. stáwlwart; 2. stṓlwət]. O.E. *stǣlwierðe*, 'able to stand one in good stead; serviceable', M.E. *stǣlewurþe*, *stalwurþe* &c., also once *staðelwurþe*, 'firm'; the O.E. form may be for **staðolwierþe*, 'firm on its base', or may simply be fr. a Gmc. **stǣl-*, cp. O.E. *stǣl*, 'place, relation; assistance', wh. is a gradational variant of **stall-* as in Mod. Germ. *stellen* (fr. **stalljan*), 'to place'; cp. also Gk. *stéllein*, 'to arrange, set in order' &c. (with orig. *e*). The base is an extension of **stə-* &c., 'stand'; see **stall (I.)** & **stand (I.)**; see second element under **worth.** **1.** Tall and muscular; robust, strong. **2.** Staunch, reliable, unflinchingly loyal to a person or cause: *stalwart defenders*.

stalwart (II.) n., fr. prec. A staunch, reliable person, who is unshakable in defence and support of a cause, of a party in politics &c.

stalwartly, adv. Prec. & **-ly.** In a stalwart manner.

stalwartness, n. See prec. & **-ness.** State or quality of being stalwart.

stamen, n. [1. stāmen; 2. stéimən]. Lat. *stāmen*, 'warp in upright loom'; cp. Gk. *stḗmōn*, 'warp'; fr. base **stā-*, 'to stand', see **stand (I.)**. Cp. further Scrt. *sthāman-*, 'station'; Goth. *stōma*, 'material'; Lith. *stomũ*, 'stature'. (bot.) Pollen-bearing organ of flower.

stamened, adj. [1. stámend; 2. stéimend]. Prec. & -ed. Having stamens.

stamina, n. [1. stámina; 2. stǽminə]. Lat. *stāmina*, pl. of *stāmen*, 'warp of upright loom', see **stamen**. Vigour of constitution, vitality, staying power.

staminal, adj. [1. stá-, stáminal; 2. stéi-, stǽmin əl], fr. Lat. *stāmin-*, stem of **stamen**, & **-al**. 1. (bot.) Of, pertaining to, stamens. 2. Of, pertaining to, giving, stamina.

staminate, adj. [1. stámināt; 2. stǽmineit], fr. Lat. *stāmin-*, stem of **stamen**, & **-ate**. (bot.) Having stamens; esp. having stamens but no pistils.

stamineal, adj. [1. stáminēal; 2. stéiminiəl]. See next word & **-al**. Staminal.

stamineous, adj. [1. stámíneus; 2. stéimíniəs], fr. Lat. *stāmin-*, stem of **stamen**, & **-eous**. Of, pertaining to, stamens.

staminiferous, adj. [1. stàminíferus; 2. stèiminífərəs], fr. Lat. *stāmin-*, stem of **stamen**, & *-i-* & **-ferous**. Producing stamens.

stammer (I.), vb. intrans. & trans. [1. stámer; 2. stǽmə]. M.E. *stameren*; cp. M. Du. *stameren*; O.H.G. *stammalōn*; in gradational relation w. O.S. & O.H.G. *stum*, 'dumb'. 1. intrans. a Specif., to speak with a nervous impediment or hesitation, esp., to utter certain sounds repeatedly, pause on certain sounds, through inability to complete the articulation; to stutter; b to speak incoherently, jerkily, and brokenly through nervousness; to hesitate, hum and haw in speaking. 2. trans. To utter, pronounce, with a stammer: *to stammer, stammer out, a few words*.

stammer (II.), n., fr. prec. Nervous defect in articulation arising from a kind of partial paralysis in, and lack of control of, the tongue and lips, resulting in the speaker dwelling unduly on the beginning or end of a sound through inability, sometimes to begin, sometimes to complete it, and pass on to the next sound of a series; a stutter.

stammerer, n. [1. stámerer; 2. stǽmərə]. **stammer (I.) & -er**. Person afflicted with a stammer.

stammering, adj. [1. stámering; 2. stǽməriŋ], fr. Pres. Part. of **stammer (I.)**. 1. Specif., afflicted with, speaking with, a stammer. 2. a (of speaker) Halting, hesitating; b uttered with hesitation: *a stammering speech*.

stammeringly, adv. Prec. & **-ly**. In a stammering manner.

stamp (I.), vb. trans. & intrans. [1. stamp; 2. stæmp]. M.E. *stampen*; cp. O.E. *stempan*; M.L.G., M. Du. *stampen*; O.H.G. *stamfōn*; 'to pound'; O.N. *stappa*, 'to stamp'; cogn. w. Gk. *stémbein*, 'to crush with the feet', nasalized variant of base in **step (II.)**. A. trans. 1. a To imprint (inscription, pattern, mark &c. on) by means of a die &c.: *to stamp a document with the address and date*; *metal stamped with a design*; *goods stamped with the maker's name*; b to imprint on a surface by means of a die &c.: *to stamp one's name on a title-page*. 2. To affix a postage-stamp to (letter, document &c.). 3. To crush, pulverize (ore &c.), by pressure, esp. in a stamp-mill. 4. Usually *stamp out*, to cut out, give shape to (piece of metal, dough &c.), by means of die, cutter &c. 5. To imprint, impress, upon the mind: *the scene is stamped on my memory*. 6. (fig.) To distinguish, characterize, mark, give specific character to; reveal true nature of: *his manners stamp him as a cad*. 7. To bring down (one's foot) heavily to the ground, strike ground violently with (foot), esp. as indication of anger, impatience &c. 8. *Stamp down, flat &c.*, to crush, flatten &c. by stamping heavily upon with the foot: *to stamp the grass flat*. Phr. *to stamp out*, (i.) to destroy, extinguish, by crushing with foot: *to stamp a fire out*; (ii.) (fig.) to suppress, extirpate, by drastic measures: *to stamp out disease, a rebellion &c*. B. intrans. To strike the ground violently with the foot: *to stamp with rage*; 'the wild ass Stamps o'er his head, but cannot break his sleep' (Fitzgerald, 'Omar Khayyam', xviii.

stamp (II.), n., fr. prec. 1. Act of stamping, heavy blow of foot on ground &c. 2. a Design, mark, signature &c. impressed or printed upon the surface of something by means of a die &c.; b specific mark &c. stamped on goods &c. by maker, owner &c. as sign of genuineness, ownership &c.: *every article bears the stamp of the maker*. 3. Object used for stamping, having a design incised or in relief upon it. 4. a Official device imprinted on certain documents, goods &c. to indicate that the necessary duty, fee &c. has been paid; b paper label, often adhesive, bearing such a device to be affixed to documents &c. in proof of payment of fee &c.; specif., stamped piece of paper bearing value engraved on it attached to letters for the post; also *postage-stamp*. 5. Machine, part of machine, implement, for stamping, crushing &c. 6. Characteristic indication, sign or mark, evidence, of specific quality, kind, nature: *to bear the stamp of breeding, learning &c*. 7. Kind, class, character: *men of the same stamp*.

stamp act, n. Act of Parliament &c., imposing stamp-duty; specif. (cap.) act of 1765, imposing stamp-duty on colonists in N. America.

stamp-album, n. Book in which stamp-collector preserves his specimens.

stamp-collector, n. Person who collects postage-stamps &c. as hobby; philatelist.

stamp-duty, n. Tax levied upon certain legal instruments, payment of which is indicated by an official stamp impressed upon, or affixed to, the document.

stampede (I.), n. [1. stampéd; 2. stæmpíd], fr. Span. *estampido*, fr. *estampar*, 'to stamp', of Gmc. origin; see **stamp (I.)**. 1. Sudden, combined, headlong rush of horses, cattle &c. caused by fright. 2. a Panic-stricken rush or scattering of crowd of people, soldiers &c.; b any confused, unreasoning rush on the part of a crowd of people &c.

stampede (II.), vb. intrans. & trans., fr. prec. 1. intrans. To take part in a stampede. 2. trans. To cause to stampede.

stamper, n. [1. stámper; 2. stæmpə]. **stamp (I.) & -er**. One who, that which, stamps; esp. machine for pulverizing stone, ore &c.

stamp-machine, n. Machine for stamping or crushing material; esp. machine for reducing rags to pulp in the manufacture of paper.

stamp-mill, n. Machine for crushing ore &c.

stamp-office, n. Office where government stamps are issued and the revenue from stamp-duties received.

stance, n. [1. stans; 2. stæns], fr. O. Fr. *estance*, fr. L. Lat. *stantia*, 'place, abode', fr. *stāre*, 'to stand'; variant of **stanza**. Position, attitude, assumed by player when making a stroke, at such games as golf, cricket &c.

stanch (I.), **staunch**, vb. trans. [1. stahnch, stawnch; 2. stän(t)ʃ, stōn(t)ʃ]. M.E. *sta(u)nch en*, fr. O. Fr. *estanchier*, fr. Low Lat. *stagnicāre*, 'to stop the flow', fr. *stagnāre*, 'to be or cause to become stagnant', see **stagnant**. a To stop or retard flow of (blood) from wound &c., esp. by use of absorbents, pads &c.; b to plug, bandage, or otherwise treat (a wound), so as to arrest bleeding.

stanch (II.), adj. See **staunch (I.)**.

stanchion (I.), n. [1. stánshun, stáhnshun; 2. stánʃən, stǎnʃən], fr. Norm. Fr. *estanchon*, fr. O. Fr. *estance*, 'place, situation', see **stance & stanza**. Upright post or bar acting as support &c.; specif. a iron rod fixed in masonry &c. for support; b bar or pair of bars, usually removable, for fastening cattle &c. in a stall; c (naut.) post supporting deck-beam &c.

stanchion (II.), vb. trans., fr. prec. 1. To furnish, support, with stanchions. 2. To fasten (cattle) in a stall with stanchions.

stand (I.), vb. intrans. & trans. [1. stand; 2. stænd]. O.E. *standan*; M.E. *standen*; cp. O.L.G., Goth. *standan*; O.N. *standa*; O.H.G. *stantan*, 'to stand'; cogn. w. Lat. *stāre*; Gk. *hístēmi*, 'I stand'; Lith. *stójûs*; O. Slav. *stajǫ*, 'I place myself'; fr. base *stā-, *sta-, 'to stand', wh. appears in many words in all the Aryan languages; see **stable (I.), state, station, stead, stolid, locus, stool &c**. A. intrans. 1. a (of men and quadrupeds) To place the body and limbs in such a position that the weight of the body rests, and is balanced, upon the feet, the legs being more or less straightened and braced; contrasted with *sit, kneel, lie*: *very young children cannot stand without support*; *so giddy that one cannot stand*; *no one may sit down as long as the king is standing*; *the cow is so weak that she can't stand*; b specif. (of human beings) to support weight of body on the feet, the back being relatively straight and the head erect; contrasted with *crouch, squat &c.*: *stand straight, don't stoop*. 2. To assume a standing position, to rise to the feet from a sitting or recumbent posture: *everyone stood as the king entered*; *the congregation shall now stand*. 3. To remain standing, without moving from one place to another; contrasted with *go, walk, run, trot &c*.: *it is more tiring to stand for long periods than to walk a long distance*; *a horse that won't stand is a great nuisance*. 4. (of inanimate objects) To be upright, remain vertical: *the glass stands on a stem*; *the table will not stand without support*; *one's hair stands on end*. 5. (archaic) To halt, cease motion, stop: *stand and deliver!* 6. To move into particular position: *to stand aside, back, clear, down, out &c*. 7. To be in a specific place, position, situation; to be placed or situated: *the stuffed parrot stands on the table*; *the house stands by the river*; *the chairs stand by the wall*; *a Roman camp once stood on the hill-top*; *the stones stand in a circle*. 8. To remain in, maintain, be left in, original position, be undisturbed: *the walls of the keep still stand*; *not a stone was left standing*; *to stand fast*; Phr. *to stand pat*, in poker, to play the hand dealt without drawing cards; also Am. polit. slang, to stick firmly to one's party's politics and platform, esp. on tariff matters. Phr. *it stands to reason*, is a logical deduction, can be proved logically. 9. a To be in specified state or condition: *to stand in awe of*; *to stand ready for anything*; *to stand accused of murder, convicted of treason*; Phrs. *to stand alone*, (i.) to be unequalled, pre-eminent; (ii.) to be without supporters &c.; *to stand corrected*, accept correction; *to stand well with*, be on good terms with, esteemed by; *to stand one in good stead*, be of use, come in handy; b to be at, reach, particular price, measure, degree &c.: *the thermometer stands at 90°*; *he stands six feet*. 10. To remain valid, hold good, be in force: *the order will still stand*; *his resolution still stands*; *that translation may stand*. 11. (of dog) To point. 12. (naut.) To steer, lay, a course: *to stand in, off &c*. B. trans. 1. To put into a more or less upright position, cause to remain vertical, or nearly so: *to stand a ladder against a wall*. 2. To remain firmly at, or on, resist attempts to remove from; esp. in Phr. *to stand one's ground*. 3. (of physical action or process) a To tolerate, endure, be able to bear: *I cannot stand great heat*; *she will not stand another winter in England*; b to remain uninjured by, to resist, be proof against: *your coat won't stand much rain*; *these boots have stood a good deal of wear*. 4. (of moral attitude) To tolerate, bear, with patience, to suffer willingly: *I can stand a good deal, but I won't have insolence*; *I will not stand any nonsense*. Phr. *I can't stand (such and such a person or thing)*, I detest, dislike extremely. 5. To undergo, be subjected to: *to stand one's trial*. 6. To treat (person) to, pay for on behalf of: *to stand one's friend a dinner*. C. Followed by adverbs and prepositions with special meanings. *Stand by*, a to remain as an onlooker, refrain from interfering; b to support, aid, be loyal to: *to stand by one's friends*, c to adhere to, refrain from breaking or abandoning: *to stand by one's promise, faith &c.*; d (naut.) to remain near in order to help: *to* *stand by a sinking ship* (of another ship), also absol. *Stand for*, **a** to support, be adherent of, strive for: *I stand for liberty*; **b** to symbolize, be typical of: *the olive branch stands for peace*; **c** to represent, be significant of: *what do the initials stand for?*; **d** to be a candidate for, aim at election to: *to stand for Parliament*; **e** to tolerate, put up with: *I won't stand for that*. *Stand in*, (colloq.) **a** to cost, cause expense of: *it stood me in a lot of money*; **b** to participate in, take a share, give help: *if you are starting a movement for brighter streets, I'll stand in*. *Stand in with*, **a** to be in agreement with, to support, ally oneself to: *to stand in with the progressive party*; **b** to take a share in along with: *I'll stand in with you in this expense*. *Stand off*, (lit. and fig.) to be aloof, withdraw, keep one's distance. *Stand off and on*, (naut.) to tack along a coast. *Stand on*, (naut.) to follow a specific course. *Stand out*, **a** to be in clear relief, be distinctly outlined: *to stand out against a background*; **b** to remain firm, be obstinate in objecting, refuse to yield. *Stand to*, to adhere to, abide by: *to stand to one's word*; Phr. (fig.) *to stand to one's guns*, to stick to one's principles, decision &c. *Stand up*, **a** to be on one's feet, be standing; **b** to assume an erect position, rise to one's feet; **c** to hold oneself erect, refrain from stooping. *Stand up for*, to defend, maintain: *to stand up for oneself, for the truth*. *Stand up to*, to face boldly, meet courageously. *Stand upon*, to take one's stand on, rely upon, insist upon: *to stand upon one's rights*.

stand (II.), n., fr. prec. **1.** Halt, stoppage, arrest, cessation of progress: *to come to, be at, a stand*. Phr. *to make a stand (against)*, offer determined resistance. **2. a** Position, situation: *to take one's stand on the platform*; **b** moral position, that on which one relies for support: *my stand is on the strict interpretation of the law*. **3.** Place appointed for vehicles to stand; parking-place; also in compounds: *cab-stand* &c. **4. a** Any structure, framework &c. on which objects are kept, supported, displayed &c.; also in many compounds: *hat-stand, music-stand, wash-stand* &c.; specif. **b** stall, table &c. for display of goods for sale: *a stand for fruit in a market-place*. **5.** Raised platform or enclosure on which persons may sit or stand: *bandstand*; *grand stand*. **6.** Growing crop in specific area, year's growth &c.: *a stand of clover*.

standard (I.), n. [1. stándard; 2. stǽndəd], fr. O. Fr. *estandard*, 'banner', of Gmc. origin, cp. **stand** (I.); or connected w. **extend**; also in some senses fr. Engl. *stand*. **1.** A flag, banner; *royal standard*, that bearing the royal, national arms, flown only by the Sovereign; specif., flag of cavalry regiment, contrasted with *colours* of infantry. Phrs. *raise the standard of revolt* &c., initiate revolt; *to march under the standard of*, to be a follower, adherent, of. **2.** That which is constituted by authority as a fixed basis of comparison by which weights, measures, values (of gold and silver) are tested and tried; fixed rule, official gauge, criterion. Hence, **3.** Style, mode, type, accepted and recognized by convention, within a community, at a given time, as the criterion of what is best in speech, behaviour, conduct, action, taste, morality &c.; test, criterion, pattern, approved model: *to sin against, fall short of, accepted standards*; *up to, below, standard*; *society punishes those who will not conform to its standards*. **4.** Any of various upright shafts, poles, columns serving as supports &c.; e.g. upright stand supporting a lamp; perpendicular pole used in scaffolding &c. **5.** (hort.) A shrub or other plant growing with an upright, tree-like stem or growing from a bud grafted upon an upright stem; contrasted with a *bush, tree, climber* &c.

standard (II.), adj., fr. prec. **1.** In accordance with, serving as, a recognized standard: *standard weights, measures*; *standard English*. **2.** Having permanent, undisputed value: *a standard writer*; *the standard books on history* &c. **3. a** Supported by a standard, standing on but raised above the ground: *a standard lamp*; **b** (hort.) growing, grown, in form of a standard: *a standard tree, rose, apple* &c.

standard-bearer, n. **1.** a Member of regiment, army &c., who carries the standard; hence, **b** leader of party, movement, cause &c. **2.** (cap.) Hereditary officer who bears the king's standard on great ceremonial occasions, esp. at a coronation.

standard bread, n. Bread containing at least four-fifths of whole meal.

standardization, n. [1. stàndərdīzǎshun; 2. stændədaizéiʃən]. Next word & **-ation**. Act of standardizing; state of being standardized.

standardize, vb. trans. [1. stándərdīz; 2. stændədaiz]. **standard** (II.) & **-ize**. **a** To reduce to an unvarying standard: *to standardize English speech*; **b** to regard as standard, recognize as the standard type, measure, value &c.: *one type of English has been standardized as the proper form for literature*.

stand-by, n. [1. stánd bī; 2. stǽnd bai]. Person, object, line of action &c., to which one has recourse in an emergency &c.; trustworthy, reliable, person or thing.

standing (I.), adj. [1. stánding; 2. stǽndiŋ], fr. Pres. Part. of **stand** (I.). **1.** Remaining in an erect position: *standing corn*. Phr. *standing jump*, one made without preliminary run. **2.** Permanent, lasting, perennial, remaining always in being; contrasted with *temporary*: *a standing joke, menace*; *standing orders*; *a standing army*. **3.** (print.) Remaining set up, not distributed: *standing type*.

standing (II.), n. **stand** (I.) & **-ing**. **1.** Position, rank, reputation: *a person of high standing*. **2.** Duration, period, of existence: *a custom of long standing*.

standing gear, rigging, n. (naut.) The shrouds and stays which are more or less permanent, and support the masts, bowsprit &c.

standing part, n. (naut.) That part of a rope &c. which is made fast; fixed end.

standing room, n. Room, space, for person(s) to stand.

standing stone, n. Vertical monolith of unhewn stone.

standish, n. [1. stándish; 2. stǽndiʃ]. **stand** (II.) & **dish**. (archaic) Inkstand.

stand-offish, adj. [1. stánd áwfish; 2. stǽnd ɔ́fiʃ]. Aloof, distant, reserved, repellent, in manner, character &c.; haughty.

stand-offishly, adv. Prec. & **-ly**. In a stand-offish manner.

stand-offishness, n. See prec. & **-ness**. Quality of being stand-offish.

standpatter, n. [1. stándpàter; 2. stǽndpætə]. (Am. polit. slang) One who stands pat, i.e. sticks firmly to his party platform, esp. in tariff matters.

stand-pipe, n. Vertical pipe for water, steam, gas &c.

standpoint, n. [1. stándpoint; 2. stǽndpɔint]. **a** Position from which a thing is seen, point of view; **b** mental attitude; point of view.

stand-rest, n. Sloping seat supporting person in half-standing position.

standstill, n. [1. stándstil; 2. stǽndstil]. Complete cessation of progress; halt: *to come to a standstill*; *work was at a standstill*.

stand-up, adj. [1. stánd up; 2. stǽnd ap]. **1.** Erect, upright: *a stand-up collar*. **2.** Done, taken, while standing: *a stand-up meal*. Phr. *stand-up fight*, serious fight or scuffle in which blows are exchanged.

stanhope, n. [1. stánup; 2. stǽnəp], fr. name of inventor. Light, open, two- or four-wheeled carriage, usually with single seat.

Stanhope-lens, n. Lens with differently curved, convex faces, invented by the Earl of Stanhope (1753–1816).

Stanhope-press, n. Iron printing press invented by Lord Stanhope, as prec.

staniel, n. [1. stányel; 2. stǽnjəl]. O.E. *stăngella*, fr. *stăn*, 'stone', see **stone**, & *gella*, 'screamer', fr. *ģellan*, 'to yell', see **yell**. Kind of small falcon; kestrel.

stank, vb. [1. stangk; 2. stæŋk]. Pret. of **stink**; O.E. *stanc*.

stannary, n. & adj. [1. stánari; 2. stǽnəri]. Med. Lat. *stannărius*, fr. Lat. *stagnum, stannum*, 'an alloy of silver and lead; tin'; possibly cogn. w. Gk. *staphúlē*, 'plummet'; but perh. of Celt. origin, cp. W. *ystaen*, 'tin'. **1.** n. **a** Tin-mine; **b** district in which tin-mines are situated. **2.** adj. Of, pertaining to, tin-mines; *stannary courts*, tin-miners' courts held in Cornwall.

stannate, n. [1. stánat; 2. stǽnət], fr. Lat. *stannum*, 'tin', see prec., & **-ate**. (chem.) Salt of stannic acid.

stannic, adj. [1. stánik; 2. stǽnik], fr. Lat. *stannum*, 'tin', see **stannary**, & **-ic**. Of, derived from, tin.

stanniferous, adj. [1. staníferus; 2. stæníferəs], fr. Lat. *stannum*, 'tin', see **stannary**, & **-i-** & **-ferous**. Containing, producing, tin.

stannite, n. [1. stánīt; 2. stǽnait], fr. Lat. *stannum*, 'tin', see **stannary**, & **-ite** (I.). Grey or black mineral compound of tin, copper, iron, and sulphur.

stannous, adj. [1. stánus; 2. stǽnəs], fr. Lat. *stannum*, 'tin', see **stannary**, & **-ous**. Of, pertaining to, containing, tin.

stanza, n. [1. stánza; 2. stǽnzə], fr. Ital. *stanza*, fr. L. Lat. *stantia*, 'place, situation', see **stance**. Group of four or more rhymed verse-lines arranged according to a specific metrical scheme; esp. one of series of such groups: *Spenserian stanza*.

stanzaed, adj. [1. stánzad; 2. stǽnzəd]. Prec. & **-ed**. Arranged in, consisting of, stanzas; (in compounds) consisting of stanzas of a specific type.

stanzaic, adj. [1. stanzáik; 2. stænzéiik]. **stanza** & **-ic**. Of, pertaining to, consisting of, arranged in, stanzas.

stapes, n. [1. stápēz; 2. stéipīz]. Med. Lat. *stapes*, 'stirrup'. Du Cange has *stapes, stapedium, stapeda, straphes* (once each); possibly fr. a form of Lat. *stăre*, 'to stand', see **state**, & Lat. *ped-(em)*, 'foot', see **pedal**. Stirrup-shaped bone of the middle ear; stirrup-bone.

staple (I.), n. [1. stápl; 2. stéipl]. O.E. *stapul*; M.E. *stapel*, 'pillar, prop; step'; cp. O. Fris. *stapul*; M. Du. *stapel*; O.H.G. *stafol*, 'rung'; cogn. w. O.E. *stōpol*, 'footprint', & O.H.G. *stuofa*, 'threshold'; cp. Mod. Germ. *stufe*, 'degree, stage in development'; fr. same base as **step** (II.). One of various objects used for fastening; specif. **a** metal bar, wire &c., pointed at both ends and bent into U-shape, used as fastening for holding end of bolt &c.; **b** metal tube holding ends of reeds in oboe and similar musical instruments; **c** bent wire used in bookbinding for stitching with wire.

staple (II.), vb. trans., fr. prec. To fasten, hold, with a staple.

staple (III.), n., fr. O. Fr. *estapel*, 'market, staple'; fr. L.G. *stapel*, 'step; pile; market', cogn. w. **staple** (I.). **1.** (hist.) Centre of trade, principal market of district &c. **2.** Leading article of commerce, principal commodity, of country, district, town &c. **3.** Leading factor, element, chief material: *the staple of diet, conversation* &c. **4.** Raw material; stuff, matter, ready for manufacture. **5.** Thread, fibre, of wool or cotton: *wool of fine staple*.

staple (IV.), adj., fr. prec. Of the nature of a staple; forming an important factor or part; leading, principal: *staple products of a country*; *the staple topic of conversation*.

staple (V.), vb. trans., fr. **staple** (III.). To sort, classify, grade (wool &c.) according to quality of fibre.

stapler, n. [1. stápler; 2. stéiplə]. Prec. & **-er**. Person who grades wool &c., esp. *wool-stapler*.

stapling-machine, n. [1. stápling mashēn; 2. stéipliŋ məʃīn]. (bookbinding) Machine for wire-stitching.

star (I.), n. [1. star; 2. stā]. O.E. *steorra*; M.E. *sterre*; cp. O.H.G. *sterro, sterno*; O.N. *stjarna*; Goth. *stairnō*; cogn. w. Lat. *stēlla*, 'star', see **stellar**; Gk. *astḗr, ástron*, 'star', see **astral**; Scrt. *star-*, 'star'. **1. a** One of the distant, luminous, heavenly bodies, appearing to be of small size as compared with sun and moon; Phr. *to see stars*, to have the sensation of seeing luminous flashes, as after a severe blow on the eye, back of the head &c.; **b** specif., a fixed heavenly body, contrasted with a planet. **2.** Any of various objects or figures resembling a star in shape or appearance; specif. **a** five- or six-pointed device formed by producing sides of pentagon or hexagon, used as ornament, emblem &c.; Phr. *stars and stripes*, flag of U.S.A., bearing a pattern of stars and stripes; **b** jewel or personal ornament in the shape of a star; object of this shape in precious metal, and highly decorated, forming the regalia, or part of it, of an order of knighthood; also the order itself: *the Star of India* &c.; **c** an asterisk used in printing; **d** white mark on a horse's forehead. **3.** Heavenly body considered as influencing person's character, fortunes &c.: *to be born under a lucky star*; *one's star is in the ascendant*; *to thank one's stars*, to be thankful, consider oneself lucky. **4.** Person who excels, is eminent, in particular field, profession &c.: *a literary, operatic, film, star* &c.; specif., leading actor or actress in theatrical production.

star (II.), vb. trans. & intrans., fr. prec. **A.** trans. **1.** To mark, adorn, set, with design of stars. **2.** To mark, distinguish, with an asterisk. **3.** To present as a star or theatrical celebrity in a play. Phr. *to star it*, to play the part of theatrical star. **B.** intrans. To appear as leading actor on the stage or in a film play: *to star in the provinces*.

star-apple, n. **1.** Evergreen tree of tropical America producing an apple-like fruit whose carpels exhibit a star-shaped figure when the fruit is cut open. **2.** The fruit of this tree.

starblind, adj. [1. stárblīnd; 2. stáblaind]. O.E. *stær-, stareblind*, 'quite blind'; cp. O. Fris. *stareblind*; O.H.G. *starablind*; cp. O.E. *stær*, 'stiff'; *starian*, 'to gaze fixedly', see **stare (I.)**. Half blind; having dim sight.

starboard, n., adj., & vb. trans. [1. stárbord; 2. stábəd]. O.E. *stēorbord*; M.E. *sterbord*; fr. O.E. *stēor*, 'rudder', q.v. under **steer (I.)**, & **board**. **1.** n. Right-hand side of ship, from point of view of observer standing on ship and looking towards bow. **2.** adj. Situated on, pertaining to, the starboard. **3.** vb. To turn (helm) to starboard.

starch (I.), n. [1. starch; 2. stātʃ]. M.E. *starche*, O.E. **sterċe*, 'stiff'; cp. *sterċed-*, 'resolute'; fr. *stearc*, 'strong, stiff'; see **stark**. **1. a** White, tasteless substance found in all vegetables except fungi, esp. in grain, beans, potatoes &c., and forming a valuable constituent of food; **b** starch in granular or powdered form as extracted from vegetable matter. **2.** Sticky, thick, jelly-like preparation of starch with boiling or cold water, used for stiffening clothes in washing &c. **3.** (fig.) Stiffness, formality, rigidity, of manner, mind, or character.

starch (II.), adj. See prec. (archaic, lit. and fig.) Stiff, rigid.

starch (III.), vb. trans., fr. prec. To make (linen &c.) stiff with starch.

Star-chamber, n. So called fr. decoration of ceiling. (cap.) Civil and criminal court abolished in 1641, characterized by arbitrary methods of procedure.

starched, adj. [1. starcht; 2. stātʃt], fr. P.P. of **starch (III.)**. (fig.) Stiff, formal, rigid, precise, in manner.

starchedly, adv. [1. stárchedli; 2. státʃidli]. Prec. & **-ly**. In a starched manner.

starchedness, n. [1. stárchednes; 2. státʃidnis]. See prec. & **-ness**. Quality of being starched.

starchily, adv. [1. stárchili; 2. státʃili]. **starchy** & **-ly**. In a starchy manner.

starchiness, n. [1. stárchines; 2. státʃinis]. Next word & **-ness**. State or quality of being starchy.

starchy, adj. [1. stárchi; 2. státʃi]. **starch (I.)** & **-y (IV.)**. **1.** Containing, composed of, starch: *starchy food*. **2.** Stiffened with starch. **3.** (fig.) Prim, precise, formal, stiff, in manner &c.

star-drift, n. United motion in the same direction by a group of fixed stars in a particular region of the heavens.

stare (I.), vb. intrans. & trans. [1. stār; 2. stεə]. O.E. *starian*, 'to look, gaze, upon'; M.E. *stāren*, 'to look fixedly; to gleam, shine'; cp. O.H.G. *storrēn*, 'to stand out, project'; M.H.G. *starren*, 'to be stiff'; Mod. Germ. *starr*, 'stiff'; Goth. *andstaúrran*, 'to be opposed to, murmur at'; O.N. *stōrr*, 'proud'; cogn. w. Gk. *stereós*, 'stiff, firm'; *strēnés*, 'hard, rough'; Lat. *strēnuus*, 'vigorous', see **strenuous**; Scrt. *sthirás*, 'hard, firm'; Lith. *stóras*, 'thick'; *styru*, 'to be stiff'; O. Slav. *starŭ*, 'old'. See also **stern (I.)**, **sterile**, **stark**. **1. a** (i.) To look or gaze intently, fixedly, as though with curiosity: *it is very rude to stare*; (ii.) to gaze abstractedly: *to stare straight in front of one*; **b** *stare at*, to contemplate, gaze at intently, as with surprise or curiosity. Phr. (*the fact, thing &c.*) *stares you, is staring you, in the face*, it is perfectly plain and obvious; *to make people stare*, surprise, shock, them; '*And paid a tradesman once to make him stare*' (Pope, Moral Essays, Epist. ii. 56); *to stare a person out of countenance*, stare at him until he becomes confused. **2.** (of colour &c., rare except as adj. in Pres. Part.) See **staring**.

stare (II.), n., fr. prec. **1.** A prolonged, fixed, intent, look, or gaze, expressive of curiosity, surprise, contempt &c. **2.** Peculiar fixed expression of the eyes when the lids are widely opened and the eyes immovable; a glare: *the eyes of the dead man were fixed in a terrifying stare*.

starfinch, n. [1. stárfinch; 2. stáfin(t)ʃ]. Bird of the warbler family, redstart.

starfish, n. [1. stárfish; 2. stáfiʃ]. Kind of echinoderm, esp. one with a central body from which five or more rays or arms project in the form of a star.

star-gazer, n. [1. stár gāzer; 2. stá gèizə]. (facet.) **a** Astronomer; **b** an absent-minded, dreamy person.

star-gazing, n. [1. stár gāzing; 2. stá gèiziŋ]. **a** Practice of observing the stars; **b** absent-mindedness, abstraction.

staring, adj. & adv. [1. stāring; 2. stέəriŋ], fr. Pres. Part. of **stare (I.)**. **1.** (of the eyes) Fixed as in a stare; wide open and glaring. Phr. *stark, staring mad*, completely mad. **2.** (of colours) Presenting too violent a contrast to surroundings; brilliant to excess. **3.** (of animal's coat) Bristling, rough, esp. in illness.

staringly, adv. Prec. & **-ly**. In a staring manner, with a fixed gaze.

stark (I.), adj. [1. stark; 2. stāk]. O.E. *stearc*; M.E. *stark*, 'strong'; cp. O. Fris. *sterk*; O.H.G. *starch*; O.N. *starkr*, 'strong'; Goth. *gastaúrknan*, 'to stiffen'; cogn. w. Lith. *stregti*, 'to stiffen, freeze'. Cp. further O.E. *stær*; Mod. Germ. *starr*, 'stiff'; & see **stare (I.)**, **stern (I.)**, **sterile**. **1.** Stiff, rigid, esp. in, or as in, death: *stark and cold*. **2.** (archaic and poet.) **a** Strong, powerful, firm; **b** resolute, unyielding. **3.** Absolute, utter, downright: *stark madness*.

stark (II.), adv., fr. prec. Absolutely, thoroughly: *stark mad*.

stark (III.), adj., for *stark-naked*.

stark-naked, adj. M.E. *stert-nāked*, fr. O.E. *steort*, 'tail'; cp. O. Fris. *stert*; O.H.G. *sterz*, 'tail; plough handle'; M.H.G. *sterzen*, 'to stick out stiffly'; fr. base **ster-* &c., 'stiff'; see **stare (I.)**, **stern (I.)**, & cp. **redstart**. Completely naked.

starless, adj. [1. stárles; 2. stális]. **star (I.)** & **-less**. Without stars.

starlet, n. [1. stárlet; 2. stálit]. **star (I.)** & **-let**. Small star.

starlight, n. & adj. [1. stárlīt; 2. stálait]. **1.** n. Light given by stars. **2.** adj. Lighted by stars: *a starlight night*.

star-like, adj. Resembling a star in shape, appearance, brilliance &c.

starling (I.), n. [1. stárling; 2. stáliŋ]. O.E. *stær(ling)*; M.E. *stare(ling)*; cp. O.H.G. *stāra*, O.N. *stari*; cogn. w. Lat. *sturnus*, 'starling'. Genus, *Sturnus*, of birds with glossy iridescent black plumage, of gregarious habits and often nesting near human dwellings.

starling (II.), n. Cp. Swed. *stör*, 'stake'; but perh. fr. earlier *staddling*, fr. O.E. *staðolung*, 'foundation', fr. *staðol*, 'support, foundation', q.v. under **stall (I.)**. Ring of piles surrounding and protecting the pier of a bridge &c.

starlit, adj. [1. stárlit; 2. stálit]. **star (I.)** & **lit**. Lit up, illuminated, by stars: *a starlit landscape*.

star of Bethlehem, n. [1. stár uv béthlēem; 2. stár əv béþliəm]. Herbaceous plant, *Ornithogalum umbellatum*, of lily family, with long narrow leaves and six-petalled white flowers having green stripes on the back.

starred, adj. [1. stard; 2. stād], fr. P.P. of **star (II.)**. **1.** Marked, set, adorned, with a star or stars; specif., to mark with an asterisk. **2.** Affected by influence of stars; esp. in compounds: *ill-starred*, unlucky, unfortunate.

starriness, n. [1. stáhrines; 2. stárinis]. Next word & **-ness**. State of being starry.

starry, adj. [1. stáhri; 2. stári]. **star (I.)** & **-y (IV.)**. **1.** Pertaining to, covered with, stars: *the starry sky*. **2.** Bright, shining like stars: *starry eyes*.

star-shell, n. (mil.) Metal cylinder filled with illuminating explosives, fired so as to burst in the air and light up enemy's lines.

star-spangled, adj. Studded, adorned, with stars; esp. *star-spangled banner*, U.S.A. flag, the Stars and Stripes.

star-stone, n. Variety of corundum, esp. kind of sapphire, showing starlike markings when cut.

start (I.), vb. intrans. & trans. [1. start; 2. stāt]. M.E. *sterten*, 'to start, leap'; fr. O.N. *sterta*; cp. Du. *storten*; O.H.G. *sturzen*, 'to overthrow'; perh. fr. same base as O.E. *steort*, 'tail', see under **stark-naked**; for meaning cp. Fr. *culbuter*, 'to upset'. **A.** intrans. **1.** To make a sudden, involuntary movement as from fear, shock, surprise &c.: *to start at the sound of a rifle-shot*. **2.** To move, jump, suddenly, in specified direction: *to start back, forward* &c. **3. a** To begin a journey &c., set out: *we must start early, as we have a long way to go*; *to start for the continent*; **b** to begin to move forward: *the train has just started*; to begin to work: *I can't get the engine* (of motor-car) *to start*; **c** specif., to begin to run, be among those who come up to scratch, in a race. **4.** To begin, embark on, a course of action, begin to do something: *to start on a course of study*; *he started to whistle a tune*. **5.** To come into existence, begin to exist, to have origin: *the fire started in the cellar*. **6.** To get out of position, be displaced, or warped: *the timbers have started*. **B.** trans. **1.** To begin (an action), set out on (a journey): *to start work, a meal*; *to start crying*; *start one's travels*. **2.** To cause to start, put in motion, set going: *to start an engine, car* &c. **3.** To give signal for starting to: *to start runners in a race*. **4.** To give a start to, enable to start: *to start a person in life*. **5.** To arouse, put up: *to start a hare*; (also fig.) *to start another hare*, to raise a fresh, irrelevant, subject for discussion. **6. a** To be the cause of, cause to begin, bring into existence: *to start a fire*; **b** to originate, initiate: *to start an idea, a discussion* &c. **7.** To displace, cause to move suddenly from position: *the damp has started the timbers*. **8.** To tap, cause contents to flow from. **C.** Followed by adverbs and prepositions with special meanings. *Start in*, intrans. (colloq.), to begin, set to work: *just start in and clean out the stables*. *Start out*, intrans. (colloq.), to have the intention, propose to oneself (to do something): *he* *started out to reform the society.* *Start up,* **1.** intrans., **a** to spring suddenly to one's feet, jump up; **b** to come suddenly into existence, appear abruptly: *a new leader, idea &c. has started up*; **2.** trans., to cause to begin working, put into motion: *to start up an engine.*

start (**II.**), n., fr. prec. **1.** Slight shock, caused by some sudden, unexpected occurrence, a fright &c.; involuntary jerky muscular movement resulting from this: *your sudden, silent appearance gave me quite a start*; Phr. *by fits and starts,* irregularly, intermittently. **2. a** Act of setting out on journey &c.: *to make an early start*; *to prepare for the start*; Phrs. *a start in life,* beginning of one's career; *to give one a start in life,* help one, afford one an opportunity for making a good beginning; **b** beginning of race &c.: *to line up for the start.* **3.** Commencement of action, work &c.: *the workmen looked on for several hours before making a start on the job.* **4.** Place at which a start is made, esp. starting-point of race &c. Phr. *from start to finish,* from beginning to end. **5.** Advantageous position, distance in advance, allowed or obtained at beginning of race, pursuit &c.: *to have a few yards' start*; *you must give me a start if I'm to race you.*

starter, n. [1. stárter; 2. stắtə]. **start** (**I.**) & **-er.** **1.** Person who gives signal for a race to start. **2.** Person, or horse, who starts in a race as a competitor. **3. a** Device for causing an engine to start working; esp. *self-starter*; **b** motor-car provided with such a device.

starting-gate, n. [1. stárting gắt; 2. stắtiŋ gèit]. Movable barrier at starting-post in horse-race, for ensuring a fair start.

starting-point, n. Place or point at which a start or beginning is made; **a** of a journey or a race; **b** of a course of action, line of thought, argument &c.

starting-post, n. Post or mark from which a race is begun.

starting price, n. Odds offered immediately before start of race.

startle, vb. trans. [1. stártl; 2. stắtl]. O.E. *steartlian,* 'to stumble', M.E. *stertlen,* 'to rush along'; mod. vb. prob. a new formation fr. **start** (**I.**) & freq. **-le.** **1. a** (i.) To cause to start; to scare, frighten, alarm suddenly: *to startle a herd of deer*; (ii.) to cause slight shock to, by a sudden, and unexpected appearance, noise, movement, action &c.: *you startled me by bursting in so suddenly*; **b** to cause shock of surprise to (usually in bad sense) as by an unexpected occurrence, piece of news &c.: *I was startled by the news of his death, by the magnitude of the demands made* &c. **2.** To rouse, stimulate, goad (into action) by startling: *to startle a person out of his apathy, into doing some hard work.*

startling, adj. [1. stártling; 2. stắtliŋ], fr. Pres. Part. of prec. Causing alarm or astonishment: *startling events, developments* &c.

startlingly, adv. Prec. & **-ly.** In a startling manner; to a startling degree.

starvation, n. [1. starvắshun; 2. stāvéiʃən]. Next word & **-ation**; a hybrid word dating fr. late 18th cent. Act or process of starving; state of being starved.

starve, vb. intrans. & trans. [1. starv; 2. stāv]. O.E. *steorfan,* 'to die', M.E. *sterven*; cp. O. Fris. *sterva*; O.H.G. *sterban*; 'to die'; cp. O.N. *starf,* 'toil; effort', *stjarfe,* 'tetanus', *stirfenn,* 'stubborn'; cogn. w. Gk. *stérphos,* 'thick, hard skin; leather'; fr. an expansion of base ***ster-**, 'stiff', see **stare, stark**; possibly also remotely cogn. w. O. Slav. *tirpstŭ,* 'to stiffen'; Lat. *torpēre,* 'to be numb, torpid, sluggish'; see **torpid.** **A.** intrans. **1.** Original, general sense of to die preserved only in Phr. *starving with cold.* **2.** To die from insufficient food: *he bolted to America and left his family to starve.* **3.** To suffer from lack of food; to be reduced to extreme weakness and emaciation by hunger: *many live in luxury while others are starving*; Phr., (colloq.) *I'm simply starving, you must be starving* = to be very hungry. **4.** To abstain from food temporarily: *when one is ill it is very good to starve for a bit.* **5.** *To starve for,* long for, hunger after; to feel the lack of: *to be starving for companionship*; *a mind starving for knowledge.* **B.** trans. **1.** To cause to suffer greatly; to kill; only in Phr. *starved with cold.* **2.** To kill by depriving of food. **3.** To supply with insufficient food, to nourish inadequately; Phr. *to starve into submission, surrender,* induce, compel, to submit, surrender, by starvation.

starveling, n. & adj. [1. stárvling; 2. stắvliŋ]. **starve** & **-ling** (**I.**). **1.** n. Thin, weak, underfed person or animal. **2.** adj. Hungry, emaciated, ill-fed.

stasis, n. [1. stắsis; 2. stéisis], fr. Gk. *stásis,* 'a standing still', see **state** (**I.**). Stoppage of the circulation of any of the fluids of the body.

statable, adj. [1. stắtabl; 2. stéitəbl]. **state** (**III.**) & **-able.** Capable of being stated.

state (**I.**), n. [1. stāt; 2. steit], fr. O. Fr. *estat,* see **estate,** fr. Lat. *status,* 'posture, attitude; place, position; condition, circumstances; public affairs; constitution; form of government', fr. P.P. type of *stāre,* 'to stand'; cp. Lat. *stō,* 'I stand', earlier **stājō*; cogn. w. O. Slav. *stają,* 'I stand'; Lith. *stójůs,* 'I put myself'; Lith. *stataũ,* 'to place'; Scrt. *sthitáš,* 'standing'; Gk. *statós,* 'placed'; Scrt. *sthítiš,* 'act of standing'; Gk. *stásis,* 'standing'; O.E. *stede,* 'place', see **stead.** All fr. base **stə-*, **stā-* &c., 'to stand', seen also in **stall** (**I.**), **still** (**I.**), **stamen, status, stool, stand, locus** &c. **1. a** Temporary or permanent set of circumstances: *a building in an unfinished state*; *affairs in a state of confusion*; physical or mental condition: *a wonderful state of preservation*; *in a state of coma*; *a poor state of health*; *an unhappy state of mind*; (colloq.) **b** bad condition of body or mind: *to get oneself into such a state that one is unfit to be seen*; **c** agitation, anxiety: *in a terrible state.* **2. a** Rank, position, social circumstances: *persons in every state of life*; **b** specif., high station, dignity: *to live in a style befitting one's state.* **3.** Elaborate style of living, pomp, ceremony: *to keep up considerable state*; *the state with which he is surrounded.* Phr. *in state,* with great pomp and circumstance, ceremony. **4.** (often cap.) Body of persons inhabiting an area, or country, with defined limits or frontiers, organized as political unity under one supreme ruler or government: *to fight for the State*; *the State declared war*; *to be a menace to the State.* Phr. *States of the Church, Papal States,* parts of Italy formerly under the temporal authority of the Pope. **5.** Partially autonomous division of federal republic; specif., one of the states forming the United States of America; *free states,* part of U.S.A. in which slavery did not exist, as opposed to *slave states.* **6. a** Government, political authority, of state: *schools provided by the State*; **b** specif., civil, as distinct from ecclesiastical, government: *Church and State.* **7.** (pl.) **a** Legislative body in islands of Jersey and Guernsey; **b** *States General,* legislative body of the Netherlands, and of France before 1879. **8.** (biol.) Organized community of insects, organisms &c. **9.** (archaic) **a** Dais or throne; **b** canopy above throne. **10.** (engraving) Any one of the stages through which a plate passes in the process of engraving.

state (**II.**), adj., fr. prec. **1.** Pertaining to the State: *state papers, state prisoner,* person arrested for or convicted of felony, esp. for political crime; *state trial,* that of person prosecuted by the State, esp. on political charge. **2. a** Performed upon, used for, intended for, occasions of special ceremony: *state coach*; **b** intended, reserved for persons of exalted rank: *state apartments.*

state (**III.**), vb. trans., fr. **state** (**I.**). **1.** To express in words, affirm, relate, say: *the witness stated that he was struck on the head*; *it is sometimes stated that English weather is uncertain*; *travellers state that the wild boar is more ferocious than the tiger.* **2.** To put down clearly in words, to expound, give a reasoned exposition of: *to state one's case*; *he stated Verner's Law with great lucidity.* **3.** (math.) To express (problem &c.) in algebraic symbols.

state bank, n. Bank under the control of the state.

statecraft, n. [1. stắtkrahft; 2. stéitkrāft]. **state** (**I.**) & **craft.** The art of government; statesmanship.

stated, adj. [1. stắted; 2. stéitid], fr. P.P. of **state** (**III.**). Appointed, established, definitely fixed: *at a stated time*; *at stated intervals*; *a stated meeting.*

statedly, adv. Prec. & **-ly.** In a stated manner.

stateliness, n. [1. stắtlines; 2. stéitlinis]. Next word & **-ness.** Quality of being stately.

stately, adj. [1. stắtli; 2. stéitli]. **state** (**I.**) & **-ly.** Grand, impressive and dignified; imposing; nobly proportioned; well balanced: *a stately manner, walk*; *stately dances*; *stately buildings*; *stately rhythm, phraseology* &c.

statement, n. [1. stắtment; 2. stéitmənt]. **state** (**III.**) & **-ment.** **1.** Act of stating; utterance; verbal expression: *belief and statement are two different things.* **2.** That which is stated; **a** expression of a judgement, belief, opinion, in words; assertion, affirmation: *to make a statement*; *an astonishing statement*; **b** a reasoned exposition, a setting forth; mode of stating: *a new statement of old truths is often necessary*; *an admirable statement of the case.* **3.** Official report or summary of financial position issued by commercial firm &c.

stater, n. [1. stắter; 2. stéitə]. Lat. *statēr,* fr. Gk. *statḗr,* 'stater'; orig. 'a weight'; cp. Scrt. *sthātṛ,* 'upright object'; fr. base **stā-*, **stə-*, 'to stand', see **state** (**I.**). Ancient Greek coin of different values, esp. **a** Persian gold coin worth about 22s.; **b** later silver coin worth four drachmas.

stateroom, n. [1. stắtroom; 2. stéitrum]. Private cabin on ship.

statesman, n. [1. stắtsman; 2. stéitsmən]. **state** (**I.**), & genit. *-es* & **-man.** **1.** Person taking part in state government; specif., who has constructive ability and foresight in the management of public affairs; often contrasted with *politician,* which is used in sense of one interested merely in party politics. **2.** Small landowner, farming his own land, in the North of England.

statesmanlike, adj. [1. stắtsmanlīk; 2. stéitsmənlaik]. Prec. & **-like.** Characteristic of, befitting, a statesman.

statesmanly, adj. [1. stắtsmanli; 2. stéitsmənli]. See prec. & **-ly.** Statesmanlike.

statesmanship, n. [1. stắtsmanship; 2. stéitsmənʃip]. **statesman** & **-ship.** Art of a statesman; statecraft.

state trial, n. Trial in which the state is the prosecuting party, esp. for a political offence.

static(al), adj. [1. státik(l); 2. stǽtik(l)], fr. Gk. *statikós,* 'causing to stand', fr. stem **stat-*, in Gk. *statós,* 'placed; standing', fr. base **stə-*, 'to stand', see **state** (**I.**) & **-ic** & **-al.** **1.** At rest, not in motion; stationary. **2.** Pertaining to, connected with, bodies in a state of rest; contrasted with *dynamic,* or *kinetic*; *static pressure,* that caused solely by weight without motion. **3.** (elect.) Shortened form of electro-static.

statically, adv. Prec. & **-ly.** In a static manner; by means of pressure.

statice, n. [1. státisē; 2. stǽtisī], fr. Gk. *statikós,* 'stanching blood', see **static.** (bot.) Genus of plants, including the sea-lavender, a shore plant with lilac flowers.

statics, n. [1. státiks; 2. stǽtiks], fr. **static.** **a** Branch of mechanics dealing with bodies remaining at rest, and the equilibrium of forces; contrasted with *dynamics*; **b** (wireless) name given to naturally produced ether waves, causing irregular disturbances in reception, cp. *atmospherics.*

station (**I.**), n. [1. stắshun; 2. stéiʃən], fr. Lat. *statiōn-(em),* 'act of standing; place, posi-

station (II.), vb. trans., fr. prec. a To place in a specific spot, assign a station to: *to station a guard at the gate*; *to station oneself at a window*; b specif. (mil.) *a regiment stationed at Quetta.*

stational, adj. [1. stáshunal; 2. stéiʃənəl]. station (I.) & -al. Relating to a station.

stationariness, n. [1. stáshunarines; 2. stéiʃənərinis]. Next word & -ness. State of being stationary.

stationary (I.), adj. [1. stáshunari; 2. stéiʃənəri], fr. Lat. *stationārius*, 'pertaining to a post or station'; station (I.) & -ary. 1. At rest, remaining in one place or position, not in motion, not moving from one place to another: *to remain stationary*; *a row of stationary vehicles*; *stationary air*, that remaining in lungs during normal respiration; *stationary diseases*, local ailments appearing and disappearing in accordance with specific atmospheric conditions. 2. Remaining at the same degree, amount, value, size &c.; neither increasing nor diminishing: *the population has remained stationary since the last census*; *the glass is stationary for the moment*. 3. Acting, or intended to act, in one fixed position; not capable of being, or liable to be, moved: *a stationary crane*; *stationary troops.*

stationary (II.), n., fr. prec. Stationary object or person, esp. member of stationary force.

station-bill, n. (naut.) Document showing post allotted to each member of the crew in specific operations.

stationer, n. [1. stáshuner; 2. stéiʃənə]. M.E. *stacyonere*, 'a bookseller', fr. Med. Lat. *stationārius*, 'bookseller', so called fr. his station or stall. 1. Old meaning survives only in *Stationers' Hall*, the headquarters of the guild of stationers or booksellers, at which, until 1911, every book published in England had to be 'entered' or registered for purposes of copyright. 2. (present use) A dealer in all kinds of writing materials.

stationery, n. [1. stáshuneri; 2. stéiʃənəri]. Prec. & -ery. All those classes of goods, collectively or separately, in which a stationer deals; specif., writing paper; in Phr. *stationery and envelopes.*

station-house, n. Building used as station, esp. police-station.

station-master, n. Official of railway staff in charge of railway station.

station-pointer, n. Three-armed protractor used in determining point on chart from given data.

statist, n. [1. státist; 2. stéitist]. state (I.) & -ist. 1. (obs.) Politician. 2. Statistician.

statistic(al), adj. [1. statístik(l); 2. stətístik(l)]. Prec. & -ic & -al. Pertaining to, consisting of, based on, statistics.

statistically, adv. Prec. & -ly. According to, by means of, statistics.

statistician, n. [1. stàtistíshan; 2. stætistíʃən]. statistic & -ian. Person skilled in collecting, dealing with, interpreting, statistics.

statistics, n. [1. statístiks; 2. stətístiks]. statist & -ics. 1. Systematic collection and arrangement of numerical facts: *statistics of crime, disease, births and deaths* &c. 2. Science of collecting and tabulating numerical facts, esp. such as bear upon social conditions.

statistology, n. [1. stàtistóloji; 2. stætistólədži]. See prec. & -logy. Science of collecting and classifying statistics.

statoscope, n. [1. státoskōp; 2. stætəskoup], fr. Gk. *statós*, 'placed, fixed', q.v. under state (I.), & -scope. Instrument showing minute variations in atmospheric pressure.

statuary (I.), adj. [1. státuari; 2. stætjuəri], fr. Lat. *statuārius*, 'of statues'; statue & -ary. Connected with, pertaining to, suitable for, statues: *statuary marble.*

statuary (II.), n., fr. Lat. *statuārius*, 'maker of statues'; *statuāria*, 'art of making statues'; statue & -ary. 1. Art of making or carving statues. 2. Statues collectively; sculpture; group of sculptured figures. 3. Maker of statues; a sculptor.

statue, n. [1. státū; 2. stætjū, stætʃū]. M.E., fr. O. Fr. *statue*, fr. Lat. *statua*, 'image, statue', fr. *statum*, P.P. type of *stāre*, 'to stand', see state (I.). Human or animal figure, approaching or exceeding life-size, carved or modelled, in the round.

statued, adj. [1. státūd; 2. stætjūd]. Prec. & -ed. Having, adorned with, statues.

statuesque, adj. [1. statūésk; 2. stætjuésk]. statue & -esque. Resembling, having the dignity, noble proportions or serenity, of a statue: *a lady of statuesque beauty.*

statuesquely, adv. Prec. & -ly. In a statuesque manner.

statuesqueness, n. See prec. & -ness. State or quality of being statuesque.

statuette, n. [1. statūét; 2. stætjuét]. statue & -ette. A small statue.

statu quo. See status quo.

stature, n. [1. státūr; 2. stætʃə], fr. Fr., fr. Lat. *statūra*, 'statue', fr. *stat-(um)*, P.P. type of *stāre*, 'to stand', see state (I.) & -ure. a Bodily proportion, height, size: *of imposing stature*; *to grow in stature*; b intellectual proportions, mental or moral calibre.

statured, adj. [1. státurd; 2. stætʃəd]. Prec. & -ed. Having specified stature, chiefly in compounds, *small-statured* &c.

status, n. [1. státus; 2. stéitəs]. Lat. *status*, 'mode of standing, posture; position, circumstances; civil standing; rank', fr. P.P. type of *stāre*, 'to stand', see state (I.). 1. a Standing, rank, social position; b relative position in regard to others in attainments, professional reputation and the like: *a man's status as a scholar*. 2. (law) Legal position of a person; a in relation to the state; b in relation to other persons.

status lymphaticus, n. [1. státus limfátikus; 2. stéitəs limfǽtikəs]. Lat.; see prec. & lymphatic. A pathological condition of the lymphatic vessels, associated with an enlargement of the thymus gland.

status quo, in quo, n. [1. státus (in) kwō; 2. stéitəs (in) kwou]. Lat.; see status. (lit.) Position, condition in which; state, condition in which things were before certain date or event; unaltered condition; esp. in such Phrs. as *to preserve the status quo*; *in statu quo*; also in full *in statu quo ante (bellum)*, in state as before the war.

statutable, adj. [1. státūtabl; 2. stætjutəbl]. statute & -able. Statutory.

statutably, adv. Prec. & -ly. According to, by means of, statutes.

statute, n. [1. státūt; 2. stætjūt], fr. O. Fr. *statūt*, fr. L. Lat. *statūtum*, 'law, decree', fr. P.P. type of *statuere*, 'to cause to stand, set up, erect; to establish, constitute; to determine', fr. *statum*, P.P. type of *stāre*, 'to stand', see state (I.). 1. Enactment of a legislative body, expressly stated and fully authorized; act of parliament: *declaratory statute*, giving authoritative explanation of previous statute; *private statute*, applying to individuals only; *statutes at large*, statutes of legislative body, in full as originally enacted, and not abridged. 2. Decree, ordinance, rule, of corporation, founder of institution &c., made as permanent rule.

statute-book, n. Register of statutes.

statute-law, n. Law expressed in statutes; contrasted with *common law.*

statutory, adj. [1. státūturi; 2. stætjutəri]. statute & -ory. Pertaining to, in the form of, depending on, enacted by, a statute.

staunch (I.), stanch, adj. [1. stawnch, stahnch; 2. stōn(t)ʃ, stān(t)ʃ], fr. O. Fr. *estanche*, 'seaworthy, watertight; staunch, reliable'; cp. O. Fr. *estanchier*, 'to stop the flow', & see stanch (I.). Reliable, dependable, trustworthy, loyal.

staunch (II.), vb., variant of stanch (I.).

staunchly, adv. staunch (I.) & -ly. In a staunch manner; loyally.

staunchness, n. See prec. & -ness. Quality of being staunch.

stauroscope, n. [1. stóroskōp; 2. stórəskòup], fr. Gk. *staurós*, 'stake, pile; cross'; cogn. w. Lat. *staurāre*, 'to stand', see restore; cp. O.N. *staurr*, 'post', see steer (I.), fr. base *stā-*, *stǎ-*, 'to be upright', parallel to *stā-*, *stə-*, 'to stand', see stand, state, & -scope. Instrument for determining the direction of polarized light in crystals.

stauroscopic, adj. [1. stóroskópik; 2. stórəskópik]. Prec. & -ic. Pertaining to, carried out by, a stauroscope.

stave (I.), n. [1. stāv; 2. steiv]. M.E. *stāve*, fr. inflected form of O.E. *stæf*, 'bar, staff', see staff (I.). 1. Curved and shaped strip of wood forming part of wall of cask, pail &c. 2. Rung of ladder. 3. Stanza, verse, section, of poem or song. 4. (mus.) Group of lines and intermediate spaces used for showing relative pitch of notes; staff.

stave (II.), vb. trans., fr. prec. 1. To furnish with staves. 2. *Stave in*, to break, strike a hole in, break through: *to stave in a cask, side of boat* &c. 3. *Stave off*, to keep off, defer, delay progress or performance of: *to stave off bankruptcy, arrest, starvation* &c.

stave-rhyme, n. After Germ. *stabreim*. Alliteration, esp. as prominent feature of verse.

stavesacre, n. [1. stávzăker; 2. stéivzèikə], fr. O. Fr. *stavesaigre*, fr. Med. Lat. *staphisagria*, fr. Gk. *(a)staphís*, 'raisins'; cp. Gk. *staphulé*, 'bunch of grapes'; prob. cogn. w. Scrt. *stambhaṣ̌*, 'pillar'; *stabhnāti*, 'to lean'; Lith. *stébas*, 'rod'; O.E. *stæf*, 'rod, staff', see staff (I.). The second element is Gk. *agria*, 'wild', cogn. w. *agrós*, 'field', q.v. under agronomy. Kind of Southern European larkspur, the seeds of which have emetic properties.

stay (I.), vb. trans. & intrans. [1. stā; 2. stei], fr. O. Fr. *estayer*, fr. M. Du. *stade*, 'support, prop'; cogn. w. O.H.G. *stat*; Goth. *staþs*; O.E. *stede*, 'place'; see stead. A. trans. 1. a To check, restrain, hold back, stop or hinder progress of: *to stay the spread of a disease*; Phr. *to stay one's hand*, refrain from action; b specif. (law) to delay, defer, suspend, postpone: *to stay judgement, proceedings*. 2. To retain one's energy, continue, last out, during: *to stay the course*. B. intrans. 1. To remain, stop, refrain, from departure; be continuously in specified place or condition: *to* *have no time to stay; to stay where one is; to stay in bed; to stay still; the fine weather has come to stay.* **2.** To have a temporary abode, reside for a time, be a guest, visitor: *to stay at the seaside; to stay with friends, at a hotel &c.*; (colloq.) *I don't live here, I'm only staying.* **3.** (in imperat., archaic) To stop, halt, cease motion, speech &c.: *stay! not so fast!* **4.** To be capable of prolonged effort, endure, last out: *to be unable to stay to the end of a race; staying power.*

stay (II.), n., fr. prec. **1.** Act of staying, period of continuance in one place &c.: *to make a long stay.* **2.** Restraint, controlling influence: *to put a stay on one's thoughts.* **3.** (legal) Postponement, suspension, of proceedings &c.: *stay of execution,* of writ &c. **4.** (fig.) Endurance, persistence, power of sustained effort.

stay (III.), n. In specif. naut. sense, fr. O.E. *stæġ,* 'rope for supporting mast'; but cp. also O. Fr. *estai,* 'prop', borrowed fr. Gmc. word, e.g. O. Du. *stag,* cogn. w. the O.E. Largely confused w. **stay (I.).** **1.** (naut.) Rope supporting mast or spar. Phr. *in stays,* going about. **2.** a A prop, support, strut; **b** a moral support; a stand-by: *religion is the stay of thousands in times of trouble.* **3.** (pl.) *Stays,* tightly fitting garment, stiffened with whalebone, worn by women on the upper portion of the body to give support to the figure; corset.

stay (IV.), vb. trans., fr. prec., influenced by **stay (I.).** **1.** To support, prop, by means of a stay or stays. **2.** To support, sustain; to satisfy: *to stay one's stomach; to stay one's appetite.* **3.** *Stay up,* to support by means of a stay or prop.

stay-at-home, adj. & n. [1. stá at hōm; 2. stéi ət houm]. **1.** adj. Addicted to staying at home. **2.** n. Stay-at-home person.

stay-bar, n. Bar used as support in building, machinery &c.

stayer, n. [1. stáer; 2. stéiə]. **stay (I.)** & **-er.** One who stays; specif. (colloq.) person, horse &c. capable of prolonged effort.

stay-lace, n. Cord for lacing stays.

stayless, adj. [1. stáles; 2. stéilis]. **stay (II.)** & **-less.** **1.** Without support. **2.** Not wearing stays.

stay-maker, n. Manufacturer of stays or corsets.

stay-rod, n. Stay-bar.

staysail, n. [1. stásl; 2. stéisl]. Sail extended on a stay.

stead, n. [1. sted; 2. stɛd]. O.E., M.E. *stede,* 'place'; O.H.G. *stat;* cp. Goth. *staþs;* O.N. *staðr,* 'place'; cogn. w. Lat. *status,* 'position', see **status** &c. **1.** Place, in Phr. *I am come in his stead, in the stead of,* as substitute for; cp. **instead.** **2.** Service, advantage; in Phr. *it will stand, has stood, me in good stead.*

-stead, fr. prec.; in compounds *farmstead, homestead* &c.

steadfast, adj. [1. stédfəst; 2. stédfəst]. O.E. *stedefæst;* **stead** & **fast (I.). 1. a** (archaic) Firmly fixed, unshakable: '*the stedfast ground*' (Spenser, 'F. Q.'); **b** intent, steady, unwavering: *a steadfast gaze.* **2.** (in moral sense) Firm, constant, steady; enduring, unwavering: *a steadfast faith &c.*

steadfastly, adv. Prec. & **-ly.** In a steadfast manner.

steadfastness, n. See prec. & **-ness.** Quality of being steadfast.

steadily, adv. [1. stédili; 2. stédili]. **steady (I.)** & **-ly.** In a steady manner.

steadiness, n. [1. stédines; 2. stédinis]. See prec. & **-ness.** State or quality of being steady.

steading, n. [1. stéding; 2. stédiŋ]. **stead** & **-ing.** Farmstead.

steady (I.), adj. [1. stédi; 2. stédi]. M.E. *stēdi,* 'stable, steady'; **stead** & **-y (IV.). 1.** Firmly supported, not liable to fall, shake, or totter: *hold the ladder steady; a steady hand,* (i.) one which does not tremble; (ii.) (fig.) resolute leadership, guidance, command. **2.** Uniform, regular, constant, not fluctuating; uninterrupted: *a steady light, improvement, flow of talk &c.* **3.** Firm, unwavering, constant: *a steady look, faith &c.* **4.** Sober and regular in conduct &c.; not erratic or dissipated: *a very steady young man.* **5.** (naut.) In Phr. *keep her steady,* order to keep ship on her course. **6.** *Steady!,* command to slacken speed, to be cautious, prepare for careful action &c.

steady (II.), vb. trans. & intrans., fr. prec. **1.** trans. (lit. and fig.) To make, cause to become, steady (in various senses of adj.). **2.** intrans. To become steady.

steady (III.), n., fr. **steady (I.).** Rest for supporting hand, tool &c., when at work.

steak, n. [1. stāk; 2. steik]. M.E. *stēke,* fr. O.N. *steik,* lit. 'something stuck on a spit'; cp. O.N. *steikja,* 'to roast on a spit'; cogn. w. O.E. *stician,* 'to stab, pierce'; see **stick (I.). 1.** a Thick slice of meat or fish for grilling or frying; often preceded by specifying word: *beef-steak, cod-steak, rump-steak* &c.; **b** specif., beef-steak.

steal, vb. trans. & intrans. [1. stēl; 2. stīl]. O.E. *stelan;* M.E. *stēlen,* 'to steal; hide; move stealthily'; cp. Goth. *stilan;* O.H.G. *stelan;* O.N. *stela,* 'to steal, hide'; origin uncertain. **A.** trans. **1.** To seize (the property of another) unlawfully, and appropriate it to one's own use or purpose. Phr. *to steal a march on,* gain an advantage over another by anticipating a move of his. **2. a** To gain by stealth or art, obtain without permission: *to steal a kiss, a glance at &c.;* **b** to win subtly by art or cunning: *to steal a person's heart.* **B.** intrans. **1.** To practise stealing; to thieve: '*Too proud to beg but not ashamed to steal*'. **2. a** To pass, glide, move, furtively, silently: *he stole cautiously round to the back-door; clouds stole across the face of the moon;* **b** to invade, overwhelm gradually: *a sense of peace and happiness stole over him.* **3.** *Steal away,* to slip, go, away, furtively and silently; *steal out,* slip out silently &c.

stealth, n. [1. stelth; 2. stɛlþ]. Prec. & **-th (I.).** Secret, concealed, furtive action or movement: '*Do good by stealth and blush to find it fame*' (Pope, Epilogue to Satires).

stealthily, adv. [1. stélthili; 2. stélþili]. **stealthy** & **-ly.** In a stealthy manner; secretly, furtively.

stealthiness, n. [1. stélthines; 2. stélþinis]. Next word & **-ness.** State or quality of being stealthy.

stealthy, adj. [1. stélthi; 2. stélþi]. **stealth** & **-y (IV.).** Characterized by, performed with, stealth; furtive, secret; cautious: *a stealthy tread, glance, whisper &c.*

steam (I.), n. [1. stēm; 2. stīm]. O.E. *stēam,* 'exhalation, vapour, steam'; M.E. *stēm,* 'steam, flame'; cp. M. Du. *stoom,* further connexions unknown. **1.** Water in the form of vapour; transparent elastic gas produced from water by boiling; used for heating, cooking, and under pressure as motive power &c.; *dry, wet, steam,* steam without or with a mixture of suspended particles of water; *saturated steam,* in contact with water at the same temperature; *superheated steam,* not in contact with water but with addition of heat, thus increasing volume and temperature. Phr. *to get up steam,* (colloq., fig.) to prepare oneself for special effort. **2.** Cloudy mass or film, mist, formed by partially condensed vapour: *windows covered with steam.*

steam (II.), vb. intrans. & trans. O.E. *stēman,* 'to give out an odour'; see prec. **A.** intrans. **1. a** To give out steam: *the kettle was steaming on the hob;* **b** to give out vapour: *the fields are steaming in the frosty air; a horse steams after a hard gallop; he wiped his steaming forehead; steam away,* (of water) to become exhausted, dissipated, in the form of steam or vapour. **2.** To move along by means of steam: *the train steamed into the station.* **B.** trans. To subject to the influence of, bring into contact with, steam; specif., to cook (food) by this means.

steamboat, n. [1. stémbōt; 2. stímbout]. Vessel driven by steam.

steam-boiler, n. Boiler in which steam is generated for engine &c.

steam-box, n. Chamber through which steam passes from boiler to cylinder of engine.

steam-brake, n. Brake worked by steam.

steam-chest, n. Steam-box.

steam-colour, n. Colour printed on material &c. by action of steam.

steam-engine, n. Engine worked by action of steam.

steamer, n. [1. stémer; 2. stímə]. **steam** & **-er.** One who, that which, steams; specif. **a** a steamship; **b** domestic utensil for cooking food by steam.

steam-gas, n. Gas produced by superheating steam.

steam-gauge, n. Device for indicating the pressure of steam.

steam-hammer, n. Powerful machine hammer worked by steam.

steam-heat, n. **1.** Heat required to convert water at freezing-point into steam. **2.** Heat given off by steam.

steaminess, n. [1. stémines; 2. stíminis]. **steamy** & **-ness.** State or quality of being steamy.

steam-jacket, n. Chamber filled with steam, enclosing a cylinder in machinery.

steam-navvy, n. Excavating machine worked by steam.

steam-port, n. Opening for the passage of steam, esp. between steam-chest and cylinder.

steam-power, n. Steam employed as motive power &c.

steam-roller, n. Heavy roller, propelled by steam, for levelling roads.

steamship, n. [1. stémship; 2. stímʃip]. Large vessel driven by steam.

steam-tight, adj. Capable of resisting passage or pressure of steam.

steam-whistle, n. Powerful whistle worked by a jet of steam.

steamy, adj. [1. stémi; 2. stími]. **steam (I.)** & **-y. a** Of the nature of, resembling, steam; vaporous; **b** covered with, enveloped in, steam; teeming with, giving off, vapour; misty, hazy.

stearate, n. [1. stéarāt; 2. stíəreit]. See **stearin** & **-ate.** A salt of stearic acid.

stearic, adj. [1. stéarik; 2. stíərik]. See next word & **-ic.** Of, derived from, stearin; *stearic acid,* fatty acid obtained from stearin and used for making candles &c.

stearin, n. [1. stéarin; 2. stíərin], fr. Gk. *stéar,* 'fat'; see under **steat(o)-,** & **-in. 1.** White, fatty, crystalline compound contained in many animal and vegetable fats. **2.** Stearic acid.

stearinery, n. [1. stéarineri; 2. stíərinəri]. Prec. & **-ery.** Manufacture of stearin.

steatite, n. [1. stéatīt; 2. stíətait]. **steat(o)-** & **-ite.** Massive variety of talc, usually white or yellow; soapstone.

steatitic, adj. [1. stéatitik; 2. stíətítik]. Prec. & **-ic.** Of, pertaining to, resembling, containing, composed of, steatite.

steat(o)-, pref. representing Gk. *stéat-,* stem of *stéar,* 'fat'; cp. Gk. *staïs,* 'dough'; *stiā,* 'pebble'; *stiphrós,* 'hard, firm'; cogn. w. Lat. *stipāre,* 'to press together, cram', see **stipate**; Scrt. *styáyatē,* 'to congeal, coagulate, harden'; fr. base **stī-, *st(e)jā-,* 'to condense, congeal', seen also in Goth. *stains*; see under **stone**; cp. also **stiff**; perh. ultimately allied to the base **stā-* &c., 'to stand'; see **stand (I.).** Fat, fatty.

steatopygia, n. [1. stéatōpíjia; 2. stíətoupáidʒiə]. Prec. & Gk. *pūgé,* 'buttocks'; prob. w. orig. sense 'swelling', & cogn. w. Scrt. *pūgaś,* 'heap, crowd'. Abnormal accumulation of fat on the buttocks, esp. as in some primitive African races.

steatopygous, adj. [1. stéatōpígus; 2. stíətoupáigəs]. Prec. & **-ous.** Affected by, exhibiting, steatopygia.

steatosis, n. [1. stéatósis; 2. stíətóusis]. **steato-** & **-osis.** Fatty degeneration of an organ.

steed, n. [1. stēd; 2. stīd]. O.E. *stēda*, 'horse, stallion'; M.E. *stēde*; cp. O.E. *stōd*, 'stud', see **stud**; cp. O.N. *stōð*, 'stud'; O.E. *stōd*, Pret. sing. of *standan*, 'to stand', see **stand (I.)**. (poet. or facet.) Horse.

steedless, adj. [1. stédles; 2. stídlis]. Prec. & **-less**. Without a steed.

steel (I.), n. [1. stēl; 2. stīl]. O.E. *stēle*, (W.S. *stīele*); O.H.G. *stahal*; M. Du. *stael*; O.N. *stāl*, 'steel'; O. Prussian *stakla*, 'steel'; Kluge connects w. Zend *stuχra*, 'firm, strong'. **1.** Form of iron, containing a certain proportion of carbon alloy, hardened and toughened by heating to a very high temperature and cooling suddenly. **2.** Any of several objects made of steel; specif. **a** sword, cutting weapon; Phrs. *cold steel*, weapons of steel &c., as distinct from fire-arms; *a foeman worthy of one's steel*, (chiefly fig.) a redoubtable opponent; **b** bar of steel with roughened or fluted surface for sharpening knives; **c** thin, flexible strip of steel for stiffening dress, corsets &c.; **d** piece of steel for striking fire from flint.

steel (II.), adj., fr. prec. Made of, resembling, containing, steel.

steel (III.), vb. trans., fr. prec. **1.** To cover, strengthen, edge, with steel. **2.** (fig.) To harden, make obdurate, firm, unyielding; esp. *to steel one's heart*.

steel-clad, adj. Covered with steel; clad in armour.

steel-engraving, n. Engraving by means of a steel plate.

steelify, vb. trans. [1. stélifī; 2. stílifai]. **steel (I.)** & *-i-* & **-fy**. To convert into steel.

steeliness, n. [1. stélines; 2. stílinis]. **steely** & **-ness**. State or quality of being steely.

steel-plated, adj. [1. stél plāted; 2. stíl pleitid]. Covered with steel plates, armoured: *a steel-plated ship* &c.

steel-points, n. Small steel studs or nails fixed in soles of shoes to prevent slipping.

steelwork, n. [1. stélwërk; 2. stílwʌ̄k]. Tools and other goods made of steel.

steely, adj. [1. stéli; 2. stíli]. **steel (I.)** & **-y (IV.)**. **a** Of, pertaining to, like, made of, steel; **b** (fig.) obdurate, relentless, unyielding.

steelyard, n. [1. stélyard; 2. stíljād], fr. the Steelyard, London meeting-place of German traders; fr. Germ. *stahlhof*, 'sample yard', misunderstood as 'steel yard'. Instrument with a short arm for supporting object to be weighed, and a weight moving on long, graduated arm.

steen, vb. trans. [1. stēn; 2. stīn]. Cp. O.E. *stǣnan*, 'to pelt with stones; to set with stones; to bejewel'; fr. **stān-jan*, fr. O.E. *stān*, see **stone (I.)**. To line a (well) with stone or brick.

steenbok, n. [1. sténbok; 2. stínbɔk]. Du. *steenbok*, fr. *steen*, 'stone', q.v. under **stone (I.)**, & *bok*, 'buck', see **buck**. Small S. African rock-dwelling antelope.

steening, n. [1. sténing; 2. stíniŋ]. **steen** & **-ing**. Material used for lining a well.

steenkirk, n. [1. sténkërk; 2. stínkʌ̄k]. Named after battle of Steenkerke, in Belgium, 1692. (hist.) Kind of lace cravat, wig, buckle &c. of late 17th cent.

steep (I.), adj. [1. stēp; 2. stīp]. O.E. *stēap*, 'lofty, tall; prominent'; M.E. *stēp(e)*, 'steep, difficult'; cp. O. Fris. *stāp*, & see **stoop (I.)**. **1.** Having a pronounced slope, making a considerable angle with the level, ascending or descending sharply: *a steep hill, roof* &c.; *steep stairs*. **2.** (colloq.) Exorbitant, excessive, considerably above what is normal or expected: *steep prices, demands* &c.; hence, preposterous, intolerable: *I thought his conduct a bit steep*.

steep (II.), n., fr. prec. (chiefly poet.) Precipitous slope, hill; steep ascent or descent: *the rugged steeps of the mountains*.

steep (III.), vb. trans. M.E. *stēpen*, 'to steep', fr. O.N. *steypa*, 'to pour; to rush down; to overthrow'; cogn. w. **stoop (I.)**. **1.** To soak in liquid. **2.** To bathe, wet thoroughly, saturate, with liquid. **3.** (fig.) To soak, immerse, imbue, impregnate: *steeped in crime, blood, sorrow* &c.; *to steep oneself in a subject, a language* &c.

steep (IV.), n., fr. prec. **1.** Act of steeping; state of being steeped. **2.** Liquid in which anything is steeped.

steepen, vb. trans. & intrans. [1. stépen; 2. stípən]. **steep (I.)** & **-en (V.)**. **1.** trans. To make steep. **2.** intrans. To become, grow, steep or steeper.

steeper, n. [1. stéper; 2. stípə]. **steep (III.)** & **-er**. Vessel containing articles in steep.

steeple, n. [1. stépl; 2. stípl]. O.E., M.E. *stēpel*, 'steeple', fr. **stēapil*, cp. O.E. *stēap*, 'lofty', see **steep (I.)**. Tall, tapering structure, usually surmounted by a spire, rising above roof of a building, esp. a church, and often containing a belfry.

steeplechase, n. [1. stéplchās; 2. stípltʃèis]. Horse-race across country, over hedges, walls, &c., or on a fixed track with built-up obstacles; so called because the first race of the kind was across country in a bee-line for a distant steeple.

steeplechaser, n. [1. stéplchāser; 2. stípltʃèisə]. Horse running, man riding, in steeplechase.

steeplechasing, n. [1. stéplchāsing; 2. stípltʃèisiŋ]. Steeplechases as a form of sport.

steeple-crowned, adj. [1. stépl kròund; 2. stípl kràund]. (of hat) Having a tall, tapering crown.

steepled, adj. [1. stépld; 2. stípld]. **steeple** & **-ed**. Having, surmounted by, a steeple.

steeplejack, n. [1. stēpljăk; 2. stīpldʒæk]. Man employed to scale steeples, chimneys, and other tall structures for purposes of repair &c.

steeple-top, n. Bowhead whale.

steeplewise, adv. [1. stéplwīz; 2. stíplwàiz]. Like a steeple.

steeply, adv. [1. stépli; 2. stípli]. **steep (I.)** & **-ly**. In a steep manner; with a steep slope.

steepness, n. [1. stépnes; 2. stípnis]. See prec. & **-ness**. State or quality of being steep.

steepy, adj. [1. stépi; 2. stípi]. **steep (I.)** & **-y (IV.)**. (poet.) Steep, sheer.

steer (I.), vb. trans. & intrans. [1. stēr; 2. stiə]. O.E. *stēoran*, 'to steer, guide'; M.E. *stēren*; cp. O.H.G. *stiuran*; O. Fris. *stiura*; O.N. *stȳra*, 'to steer'; Goth. *stiurjan*, 'to confirm, maintain'; cp. O.E. *stēor*, 'rudder'; O.N. *staurr*, 'post'; O.H.G. *stiura*, 'pillar'; Gk. *staurós*, 'pole'; see **stauroscope**; fr. base **st(h)ēu-r-*, **st(h)əu-r-*, &c., 'firm', parallel to base **stā-* &c., 'to stand', see **stand (I.)**, **state (I.)**; see further **stow, style (III.)**. **A.** trans. **1.** To direct movements and direction of (vessel) by means of rudder or instrument used as rudder. **2. a** To guide movements of (oneself, motor-car &c.), keep on a definite course; **b** (fig.) to direct, bring, guide, to specified position or condition: *to steer one's country to peace and prosperity*. **3.** To pursue, pick out, find, by steering: *to steer one's way*; *to steer a steady course* (lit. and fig.). **B.** intrans. To direct course of vessel &c. by means of a rudder or other instrument; Phr. *to steer clear of*, (chiefly in fig. sense) to avoid; (colloq.) *where are you steering for?*, where are you going, heading?

steer (II.), n. O.E. *stēor*; M.E. *steer*; cp. Goth. *stiur*; O.H.G. *stior*; cp. further O.H.G. *stūri*, 'strong, heavy'; L.G. *stūr*, 'large'; cogn. w. Scrt. *sthūrás*, 'thick, dense, heavy'; Gk. *stúrax*, 'butt of lance'; *staurós*, 'pole, pillar'; see **stauroscope, steer (I.)**. The connexion with Lat. *taurus*, 'bull', see **Taurus**, is improbable. Young ox, bullock.

steerable, adj. [1. stérabl; 2. stíərəbl]. **steer (I.)** & **-able**. Capable of being steered.

steerage, n. [1. stérij; 2. stíəridž]. **steer (I.)** & **-age**. **1. a** Act or process of steering; **b** the manner in which a vessel answers to the helm. **2. a** The end of a vessel from which she is steered; the stern; hence, **b** that part of a vessel in which are the quarters of passengers paying the lowest rates; **c** part of berth-deck of warship used as quarters for junior officers &c.

steerage-way, n. Movement of vessel sufficient to enable it to answer to the helm.

steerer, n. [1. stérer; 2. stíərə]. **steer (I.)** & **-er**. One who steers.

steering-gear, n. [1. stéring gēr; 2. stíəriŋ gìə]. Mechanism controlling the steering of a vessel, the rudder &c.

steering-wheel, n. Wheel controlling the rudder of ship, motor-car &c.

steersman, n. [1. stérzman; 2. stíəzmən]. Person steering a vessel.

steersmanship, n. [1. stérzmanship; 2. stíəzmənʃip]. Skill in steering.

steeve (I.), vb. intrans. & trans. [1. stēv; 2. stīv]. Scots variant of **stiff**. (naut.) **1.** intrans. (of bowsprit) To form an angle with the plane of the horizon. **2.** trans. To cause (bowsprit) to steeve.

steeve (II.), n., fr. prec. (naut.) Angle made by bowsprit with plane of horizon.

steeve (III.), vb. trans., fr. O. Fr. *estiver*, 'to cram', fr. Lat. *stīpāre*, 'to press closely; to cram', see **stipate**; cp. also **stevedore**. To pack, stow (cargo), with a steeve.

steeve (IV.), n., fr. prec. Spar with block at one end used in stowing cargo.

steganography, n. [1. stèganógrafi; 2. stègənɔ́grəfi], fr. Gk. *steganós*, 'covered', fr. *stégein*, 'to cover closely; to conceal'; cp. Gk. *stégos*, 'roof, house'; cogn. w. Lat. *tegere*, 'to cover', see **tegument**; O.E. *þæċ*, 'roof', see **thatch**; for the second element, see **-graphy**. Art, science or practice of writing in cipher.

Steinberger, n. [1. stínbërger; 2. stáinbʌ̄gə], fr. Steinberg, near Wiesbaden. Kind of white, Rhenish wine produced on the estate of Steinberg.

steinbock, n. [1. stínbok; 2. stáinbɔk]. Germ., fr. *stein*, 'stone, rock', q.v. under **stone (I.)**, & *bock*, 'buck', see **buck**. Steenbok.

stelar, adj. [1. stélar; 2. stílə]. Next word & **-ar**. Pertaining to, executed on, a stele.

stele, n. [1. stélē; 2. stílī]. Gk. *stḗlē*, 'block of stone, as gravestone, buttress, for inscription &c.'; cp. Gk. *stéllein*, 'to arrange, set in order'; *stolḗ*, 'adjustment, equipment; clothing', cp. **stole (I.)**; *steleón*, 'handle'; cogn. w. O.E. *stela*, 'handle', *still*, 'quiet', see **still (I.)**; Scrt. *sthálati*, 'stands'; Lat. *stolidus*, 'stupid', see **stolid**. Ancient Greek inscribed or sculptured upright stone slab, as monument, gravestone &c.

stelene, adj. [1. stélēn; 2. stílīn]. Prec. & **-ene**. Stelar.

stellar, adj. [1. stélar; 2. stélə], fr. L. Lat. *stēllāris*, 'of a star', fr. Lat. *stēlla*, 'star', fr. **stēr-lā*; cogn. w. Gk. *astḗr*, 'star', see **astral**, & w. O.E. *steorra*, 'star', see **star**. Connected with, pertaining to, the stars: *stellar light* &c.

stellate(d), adj. [1. stélāt(ed); 2. stéleit(id)], fr. Lat. *stēllāt-(um)*, P.P. type of *stēllāre*, 'to set with stars', fr. *stēlla*, 'star', see **stellar**, & **-ed**. Star-shaped, radiating from a centre.

stellately, adv. [1. stélātli; 2. stéleitli]. Prec. & **-ly**. In a stellate manner.

stelliferous, adj. [1. stelíferus; 2. stəlífərəs], fr. Lat. *stēlla*, 'star', see **stellar**, & *-i-* & **-ferous**. Set with many stars.

stelliform, adj. [1. stéliform; 2. stélifɔ̄m], fr. Lat. *stēlla*, 'star', see prec., & *-i-* & **-form**. Star-shaped.

stellular, adj. [1. stélūlar; 2. stéljulə], fr. Lat. *stēllula*, 'little star', fr. *stēlla*, 'star', see **stellar**, & **-ule** & **-ar**. **a** Shaped like a small star; **b** set with small stars.

stellulate, adj. [1. stélūlāt; 2. stéljuleit], fr. Lat. *stēllula*, 'little star', see prec., & **-ate**. Stellular.

stem (I.), n. [1. stem; 2. stəm]. O.E. *stæfn*, *stefn*, *stemn*, 'stem of tree; prow of ship; family'; M.E. *stam*, *stem*; cp. O.N. *stafn*; O.L.G. *stamn*; O.H.G. *stam*, 'stem, prow'; Du. *stam*, 'trunk'; cogn. w. O.E. *stæf*, see **staff (I.)**. **1.** Main part, body, support; trunk or stalk of tree, plant &c., as distinct from branches &c., usually ascending and aerial, but sometimes prostrate and subterranean.

STEM (II.)   1185   **STEPSON**

2. Slender branch from main stem of plant, supporting flower, fruit, or leaf; secondary stalk. **3.** Slender, stem-like part or growth; anything resembling a stem in form or function; specif. **a** slender part between foot and bowl of wineglass, egg-cup &c.; **b** short perpendicular line projecting above or below certain notes in written or printed music; **c** rod projecting from top of watch, by means of which the watch is wound; **d** (zool.) slender stalk supporting organ &c.; **e** (print.) vertical stroke forming part of letter. **4.** (archaic) Family, stock, ancestry, lineage: *the stem of Jesse*. **5.** Part of word to which inflexional endings are added. **6.** (naut.) Upright, usually curved, timber or metal bar, to which timbers of both sides of ship are joined at the bow; *false stem*, sharp-edged timber in front of stem, serving as cutwater. Phr. *from stem to stern*, throughout whole length of ship.

stem (II.), vb. trans., fr. prec. To remove stem(s) of.

stem (III.), vb. trans. M.E. *stemmen*, 'to stop'; cp. M.H.G. *stemmen*; O.N. *stemma*, 'to stop'; prob. cogn. w. **stammer (I.)**. **1.** To check, hold back, dam up: *to stem a torrent, flood, the flow of water, of blood* &c.; (also fig.) *to stem the flood of a person's eloquence*. **2.** To make progress, headway, against; chiefly in Phr. *to stem the tide*; often indistinguishable from No. **1** in fig. uses: *to stem the tide of opposition* &c.

stemless, adj. [1. stémles; 2. stémlis]. **stem (I.) & -less**. Without a stem.

stemlet, n. [1. stémlet; 2. stémlit]. **stem (I.) & -let**. Small stem or stalk.

stemma, n. [1. stéma; 2. stémə]. Lat. *stemma*, 'garland; pedigree; nobility', fr. Gk. *stémma*, 'wreath', fr. *stéphein*, 'to surround, wreathe, crown'; cp. Gk. *stéphanos*, 'crown'; cognates in other languages doubtful. **1. a** Pedigree, genealogical tree; **b** hence family, descent, lineage. **2.** (zool.) Simple eye or single facet of compound eye.

stemmed, adj. [1. stemd; 2. stɛmd]. **stem (I.) & -ed**. Having a stem; usually of specified character: *short-, rough-stemmed* &c.

stemmer, n. [1. stémer; 2. stémə]. **stem (II.) & -er**. Person employed in removing stems from tobacco-plants in making tobacco.

stemple, n. [1. stémpl; 2. stémpl]. Mod. Germ. *stempel*, 'a prop'; connected w. **stamp (I.)**. **1.** One of a series of cross-timbers forming steps in a shaft. **2.** Timber supporting platform &c.

stem-winder, n. Keyless watch.

stench, n. [1. stench; 2. stɛn(t)ʃ]. O.E. *stenč*, 'smell, odour'; M.E. *stench*; fr. **stanki-*, gradational variant of O.E. *stincan*, 'to smell', see **stink (I.)**. Strong, offensive smell. (Politer word than *stink*, n.)

stench-trap, n. Trap in sewer to prevent noxious smells from rising.

stencil (I.), n. [1. sténsil; 2. sténsil, sténsl]. Prob. fr. O. Fr. *estenceler*, 'to spangle', fr. *estencele*, 'spark', fr. Lat. *scintilla*, 'spark', see **scintillate**. **1.** Thin metal plate perforated with series of holes forming a design through which colouring-matter is applied to a surface. **2.** Pattern, design, produced by stencilling.

stencil (II.), vb. trans., fr. prec. **1.** To apply, produce (design &c.), by means of a stencil. **2.** To apply design to, produce pattern on, by means of a stencil.

stencil-plate, n. Stencil.

steno-, pref. representing Gk. *stenós*, 'narrow'; cp. Gk. *steînos*, 'confined space'; no certain cognates. Narrow; e.g. *stenosis*, constriction of the pores or other orifice.

stenochrome, n. [1. sténokrōm; 2. sténəkroum]. **steno- & chrome**. Print produced by stenochromy.

stenochromy, n. [1. stenókrumi; 2. stɛnókrəmi]. Prec. & **-y (I.)**. Art of printing in several colours at one impression by means of a group of pigment-blocks.

stenograph, n. [1. sténograhf; 2. sténəgrɑ̄f]. **steno- & -graph**. **1.** Character used in shorthand. **2.** Script in shorthand. **3.** Machine for writing in a form of shorthand.

stenographer, n. [1. stenógrafer; 2. stɛnógrəfə]. Prec. & **-er**. Shorthand writer.

stenographic, adj. [1. stènográfik; 2. stɛnəgráfik]. **stenograph & -ic**. Connected with, written in, shorthand.

stenographically, adv. [1. stènográfikali; 2. stɛnəgráfikəli]. Prec. & **-al & -ly**. By means of shorthand.

stenographist, n. [1. stenógrafist; 2. stɛnógrafist]. Next word & **-ist**. Stenographer.

stenography, n. [1. stenógrafi; 2. stɛnógrəfi]. **steno- & -graphy**. Shorthand; art of writing shorthand.

stenolalism, n. [1. stenólalizm; 2. stɛnóləlizəm], fr. **steno-** & Gk. *lálein*, 'to speak, chatter', see **alalia**, & **-ism**. Formation of a name or term from the initial letters or syllables of full title; e.g. *Anzac* (Australian and New Zealand Army Corps), *Cheka* (Chrezvychainaya Komisiya).

stenotype, n. [1. sténotīp; 2. sténətaip]. **steno- & type**. Letter, group of letters, representing in shorthand a word or phrase.

Stentor, n. [1. sténtōr; 2. sténtɔ]. Lat. *Stentor*, fr. Gk. *Sténtōr*. Person with unusually powerful voice; so called from the Greek herald of this name in Trojan war.

stentorian, adj. [1. stentórian; 2. stɛntóriən]. Prec. & **-ian**. Very loud or powerful: *a stentorian voice; stentorian tones*.

step (I.), n. [1. step; 2. stɛp]. O.E. *stæpe*, 'a step; a tread in stairs; degree'. See next word. **1.** Movement in walking, involving lifting the foot and putting it down further forward. Phrs. *step by step*, gradually; *to turn one's steps* (towards &c.), to go; *to retrace one's steps*, go back, return; *to watch one's steps*, act cautiously and prudently. **2. a** Space covered by a step; a pace; **b** a short distance: *it is only a step to the inn*. Phr. *unable to walk a step*, not able to walk at all. **3.** Sound of a footfall: *steps were heard approaching*. **4.** Mark made by a foot on the ground; footprint; (chiefly fig.) *to tread in the steps of*, follow example of, adopt same career &c. as. **5.** Mode of walking, tread: *a light, heavy, ponderous* &c. *step*. **6.** One of a series of characteristic movements executed by the feet in a dance. **7.** Regular, rhythmical pace made in marching or walking; esp. one made simultaneously by each of two or of more persons walking or marching together, so timed that each person advances the left or right leg at the same moment as all the others: *in step, out of step; to keep step* (with). **8.** An act performed with a view to securing some object; means, mode of procedure, measures. Phrs. *to take steps*, adopt means, measures &c.; *to take steps to avoid the repetition of an offence, to abolish a nuisance* &c.; *a false step*, wrong, foolish, measure. **9.** (fig.) A degree, stage, in progress, advance, or retrogression: *we have made a great step forward in our negotiations; a few steps nearer the grave*. **10.** An object designed as, or serving for, a support for the feet in moving from one level to another; one of rising or falling series of shelves, ledges, spars &c., upon which the foot is placed in ascending or descending; specif. **a** one of the treads in a set of stairs: *a flight of steps*, a staircase; **b** ledges cut on face of a rock, bank &c. for placing the feet upon; **c** small projecting metal or wooden ledge, some few inches from the ground, to facilitate entering or leaving a vehicle; **d** (i.) one of the rungs of a ladder; (ii.) *steps, pair of steps*, light short ladder, with hinged prop which keeps it upright when opened; step-ladder; **e** object in nature resembling a step, e.g. a plateau, esp. one of a series of plateaux, on the side of a hill &c. **11.** Higher or lower grade in rank: *a step in the peerage, in army rank* &c. Phr. *to get one's step*, be promoted to superior rank; *to rise a step in one's opinion, estimation* &c., be more highly thought of. **12.** (mus.) Degree, interval, between notes of a scale. **13.** (naut.) Socket in which lower end of mast rests. **14.** (mechan.) Socket or support for shaft &c.

step (II.), vb. intrans. & trans. O.E. *stæppan, steppan*; M.E. *steppen*; cp. O.H.G. *steffan*; O. Fris. *steppa*; cp. O.E. *stæpe*, 'a step'; & further w. nasal, O.H.G. *stampfōn*, O.E. *stempan*, 'to stamp with the feet', see **stamp (I.)**. **A**. intrans. **1.** To take a step or series of steps: *to step forward, back, over an obstacle, into a carriage, on a person's toe* &c. Phrs. *to step high*, raise foot high in taking a step; *to step out*, take long step, increase length of step; *to step short*, take too short a step. **2.** To move forward, walk, esp. a short distance, or in specified manner: *to step lightly; to step out briskly*. In various colloq. Phrs.: *will you step inside*, come in (to the house or room); *step outside*, go out; *step upstairs*; (also fig.) *to step aside*, withdraw in favour of another; *step in*, intervene. **B**. trans. **1.** To perform, execute, steps of (dance). Phr. *to step it*, to go on foot, to walk. **2.** Also *step out*, to measure by stepping: *to step* (out) *the length of a room* &c. **3.** To insert (mast) in socket &c., fix in position.

step-, pref. representing O.E. *stēop-*; M.E. *stēp-*; cp. O.N. *stiūp-*; O.H.G. *stiuf-, stiof-*; O. Fris. *stiap-, stiep-*, 'step'; cp. further O.H.G. *stiufan*, 'to bereave of parents, orphan'. Related by remarriage of one parent, e.g. *stepson, stepbrother, stepfather* &c.

stepbrother, n. [1. stépbrudher; 2. stépbradə]. Son of one's stepfather or stepmother.

stepchild, n. [1. stépchīld; 2. stéptʃaild]. Child of a husband or wife by a previous marriage.

stepdame, n. [1. stépdām; 2. stépdeim]. (archaic) Stepmother.

step-dance, n. Dance in which characteristic steps are executed.

stepdaughter, n. [1. stépdàwter; 2. stépdɔ̀tə]. Daughter of a husband or wife by a previous marriage.

stepfather, n. [1. stépfàhdher; 2. stépfɑ̀ðə]. Second or subsequent husband of one's mother.

stephanotis, n. [1. stèfanótis; 2. stèfənóutis], fr. Gk. *stéphanos*, 'wreath, crown', q.v. under **stemma**, & *ōt-*, stem of *oûs*, 'ear', see **otalgia**. Genus of tropical, twining shrubs with very fragrant, waxy flowers.

step-ladder, n. Ladder with flat steps which is not leant up against a wall &c., but has a folding support opening at an angle.

stepmother, n. [1. stépmudher; 2. stépmaðə]. One's father's second or subsequent wife; sometimes with implication of being unfeeling or negligent; also fig.: '*Oxford Street, stony-hearted stepmother*' (De Quincey).

stepmotherly, adj. [1. stépmudherli; 2. stépmaðəli]. Prec. & **-ly**. Pertaining to, befitting, like, a stepmother, often in bad sense, unfeeling, neglectful.

stepney, n. [1. stépni; 2. stépni], fr. name of inventor. Also *stepney-wheel*, spare wheel carried on motor-car.

step-parent, n. Stepfather or stepmother.

steppe, n. [1. step; 2. stɛp]. Fr. or Germ., fr. Russ. *step*. Broad, open, treeless, uncultivated plain, esp. of Russia and Siberia.

stepped, adj. [1. stept; 2. stɛpt]. **step (I.) & -ed**. Having, furnished with, forming, a series of steps: *stepped gables*.

stepper, n. [1. stéper; 2. stépə]. **step (II.) & -er**. One who, that which, steps, esp. in specified manner: *a high stepper*.

stepping-stone, n. [1. stéping stōn; 2. stépiŋ stoun]. **1.** One of a series of stones placed in stream so as to rise above water and form means of crossing. **2.** (fig.) Means or instrument to an end; position which leads to further advancement: *a stepping-stone to promotion, fame* &c.

stepsister, n. [1. stépsister; 2. stépsistə]. Daughter of one's stepfather or stepmother.

stepson, n. [1. stépsun; 2. stépsan]. Son of a person's husband or wife by a previous marriage.

stepwise, adv. [1. stépwīz; 2. stépwaiz]. step (I.) & -wise. In steps, so as to form steps.

-ster, suff. representing O.E. *-estre*, agent suff.; in O.E. restricted to fem. ns. (cp. **spinster**), but in M.E. & Mod. Engl. used to form ns. of either gender; denoting a trade, occupations, e.g. *brewster*, but esp. **a** in surnames, *Webster*, *Baxter* &c., derived from these, & **b** (in depreciatory sense) *punster*, *rhymester*, *youngster* &c.

stercoraceous, adj. [1. stẽrkuráshus; 2. stẫkəréiʃəs], fr. Lat. *stercor*-, stem of *stercus*, 'dung', perh. cogn. w. Lith. *trisziu*, 'to manure the ground'; Gk. *tárganon*, 'sour wine'; O.N. *þrekkr*, 'excrement'; for the second element see **-aceous**. Connected with, pertaining to, dung or excrement.

stercoral, adj. [1. stẽrkural; 2. stẫkərəl], fr. Lat. *stercor*-, stem of *stercus*, 'dung', see prec., & **-al**. Stercoraceous.

stereo, n. [1. stéreō, stěreō; 2. stériou, stiəriou]. Abbr. fr. **stereotype** (I.). Stereotype.

stereo-, pref. representing Gk. *stereós*, 'firm, stiff, solid'; cogn. w. O.H.G. *storren*, 'to rise stiffly'; cp. Goth. *(and)staurran*, 'to complain'; O.E. *stierne*, 'stiff, stern', see **stern** (I.). See also **stare**, & words there referred to. Solid.

stereobate, n. [1. stéreobāt; 2. stériəbeit]. **stereo-** & Gk. *bátēs*, 'that which treads, steps', cogn. w. **base** (I.). Solid or continuous substructure of building.

stereochemistry, n. [1. stéreōkémistri; 2. stérioukémistri]. **stereo-** & **chemistry**. Branch of chemistry dealing with the arrangement of atoms in the molecule.

stereochromy, n. [1. stéreōkrōmi; 2. stérioukroumi]. **stereo-** & **chrome** & **-y** (I.). Process of painting with colours fixed by waterglass.

stereogram, n. [1. stéreogram; 2. stériəgræm]. **stereo-** & **-gram**. Drawing made by stereographic means.

stereographic(al), adj. [1. stèreográfik(l); 2. stèriəgræfik(l)]. **stereo-** & **-graphic** & **-al**. Relating to, executed by means of, stereography.

stereographically, adv. Prec. & **-ly**. By stereographic means.

stereography, n. [1. stèreógrafi; 2. stèriógrafi]. **stereo-** & **-graphy**. The art of representing solids on a plane surface.

stereome, n. [1. stéreōm; 2. stérioum], fr. Gk. *stereōma*, 'a solid body'; see **stereo-**. Strengthening or supporting tissue of the cells of plants.

stereometer, n. [1. stèreómeter; 2. stèriómitə]. **stereo-** & **-meter**. **1**. Instrument measuring volume of a body, capacity of a vessel &c. **2**. Instrument for determining specific gravity of liquids &c.

stereometric(al), adj. [1. stèreométrik(l); 2. stèriəmétrik(l)]. **stereo-** & **-metric** & **-al**. Relating to, done by means of, stereometry.

stereometry, n. [1. stèreómetri; 2. stèriómitri]. **stereo-** & **-metry**. The art of determining the dimensions of solid bodies.

stereopticon, n. [1. stèreóptikun; 2. stèrióptikən]. See **stereo-** & **optic**. Double magic-lantern for exhibiting dissolving views.

stereoscope, n. [1. stéreoskōp; 2. stériəskòup]. **stereo-** & **-scope**. Optical instrument for representing to the eye as single object in relief two views of the object taken from slightly different angles.

stereoscopic, adj. [1. stèreoskópik; 2. stèriəskópik]. Prec. & **-ic**. Pertaining to, suitable for, of the nature of, a stereoscope.

stereoscopically, adv. [1. stèreoskópikali; 2. stèriəskópikəli]. Prec. & **-al** & **-ly**. By stereoscopic means.

stereoscopy, n. [1. stèreóskopi; 2. stèrióskəpi]. **stereoscope** & **-y**. Art of making or using a stereoscope.

stereotype (I.) n. [1. stéreotīp; 2. stériətàip]. **stereo-** & **-type**. (print.) Metal plate cast in mould taken from page &c., set up in ordinary type.

stereotype (II.), vb. trans., fr. prec. **1**. **a** To cast (printing-plate) from a mould; **b** to print (book &c.) from stereotypes. **2**. (fig.) To fix once for all; reproduce always according to one and the same fixed pattern; to repeat unalterably as though always from the same mould: *stereotyped features, ideas, phrases, lectures* &c.

stereotyper, n. [1. stéreotīper; 2. stériətàipə]. Prec. & **-er**. Person engaged in printing from or making stereotypes.

stereotypist, n. [1. stéreotīpist; 2. stériətàipist]. **stereotype** & **-ist**. Stereotyper.

stereotypography, n. [1. stéreōtipógrafi; 2. stérioutaipógrəfi]. **stereotype** & **-o-** & **-graphy**. Art or practice of printing from stereotypes.

stereotypy, n. [1. stéreōtīpi; 2. stérioutàipi]. **stereotype** & **-y** (I.). Art of making stereotypes.

sterile, adj. [1. stéril; 2. stérail], fr. Lat. *sterilis*, 'unfruitful'; cogn. w. Scrt. *stariš*, 'barren cow'; Gk. *steira*; Goth. *stairō*, 'sterile'; perh. fr. base **ster-*, 'to be stiff, rigid', q.v. under **stare**, **stereo-**, **stern** &c. **1**. (of animal, plant &c.) Incapable of reproducing itself in offspring; barren. **2**. (of soil, country &c.) Unproductive, infertile, unfruitful. **3**. (of food, liquid &c.) Containing no living bacteria, microbes &c. **4**. (of action, work &c.) Producing no result; ineffective. **5**. (of literary style &c.) Without life or interest; not stimulating; barren of suggestive ideas.

sterility, n. [1. steríliti; 2. steríliti], fr. Lat. *sterilitāt-(em)*, 'sterility'; **sterile** & **-ity**. State or quality of being sterile.

sterilization, n. [1. stèrilizáshun; 2. stèrilaizéiʃən]. Next word & **-ation**. Act of sterilizing; state of being sterilized.

sterilize, vb. trans. [1. stérilīz; 2. stérilaiz]. **sterile** & **-ize**. To make sterile; specif. **a** to deprive (animal) of reproductive power; **b** to render free of living organisms, esp. of bacteria: *to sterilize milk, surgical instruments* &c.

sterilizer, n. [1. stérilīzer; 2. stérilàizə]. Prec. & **-er**. One who, that which, sterilizes; esp. instrument, device, for sterilizing.

sterlet, n. [1. stérlet; 2. stə́ːlit], fr. Fr., fr. Russ. *sterlyadi*, apparently borrowed fr. a Fr. or Germ. form; cp. **sturgeon**. Kind of small sturgeon, yielding a superior variety of caviare.

sterling, adj. [1. stérling; 2. stə́ːliŋ]. In M.E. formerly supposed to be fr. *Easterling*, name given to traders of the Hanseatic League; in M.H.G. *sterlinc* was the name of a coin. Origin uncertain. **1**. (of British money, coinage, and of gold or silver) Of standard value, of quality fixed by Government: *sterling silver*; *five pounds sterling*. **2**. (fig.) Genuine, true, dependable, not sham or counterfeit: *sterling worth, qualities, sense* &c.

stern (I.), adj. [1. stërn; 2. stə́ːn]. O.E. *steorne*, W.S. *styrne*, M.E. *sterne*, 'stern, severe'; cp. O.H.G. *storren*, 'to rise stiffly'; M.H.G. *starren*, 'to stiffen'; Goth. *andstaurran*, 'to complain of'; cogn. w. Gk. *stereós*, 'firm, stiff'; see **stereo-**, **stare**, **stark**. Austere, rigid, unyielding, relentless, severe: *stern parents, discipline, necessity, resolve* &c.; *a stern look, command* &c.

stern (II.), n. [1. stërn, starn; 2. stə́ːn, stɑ̄n]. M.E. *stern*, fr. O.N. *stjorn*; cp. O. Fris. *stiorne*, 'rudder'; cogn. w. O.E. *stēoran*, 'to steer', see **steer** (I.); O.N. *stýra*; O.H.G. *stiurjan*, 'to steer, guide'. **1**. Back part of ship, part farthest from bow or stem. Phrs. *a stern chase*, in which pursuing ship follows in wake of pursued; *stern foremost*, backwards; *stern on*, with stern turned to observer &c. **2**. **a** Rump of animal; **b** tail of animal, esp. of foxhounds.

sternal, adj. [1. stérnl; 2. stə́ːnəl]. **stern(o)-** & **-al**. Of, pertaining to, situated near, the sternum.

sternalgia, n. [1. stèrnáljia; 2. stə̀ːnǽldʒiə], fr. **stern(o)-** & **-algia**; cp. Gk. *algein*, 'to suffer', q.v. under **neglect**. Pain near the breast-bone.

stern-chase(r), n. Gun mounted in stern of vessel for defence against pursuing ship.

sterned, adj. [1. stërnd; 2. stə́ːnd]. **stern** (II.) & **-ed**. (chiefly in compounds) Having a stern of specified kind.

stern-fast, n. Rope, chain &c. for mooring vessel by the stern.

sternly, adv. [1. stë́rnli; 2. stə́ːnli]. **stern** (I.) & **-ly**. In a stern manner.

sternmost, adj. [1. stë́rnmōst; 2. stə́ːnmoust]. **stern** (II.) & **-most**. Nearest to the stern.

sternness, n. [1. stë́rnnes; 2. stə́ːnnis]. **stern** (I.) & **-ness**. State or quality of being stern.

stern(o)-, pref. representing **sternum**. Sternum; near the sternum.

sternoclavicular, adj. [1. stèrnōklavíkular; 2. stə̀ːnouklǝvíkjulǝ]. **stern(o)-** & **clavicular**. Of the sternum and clavicle.

sternocostal, adj. [1. stèrnōkóstal; 2. stə̀ːnoukóstǝl]. **stern(o)-** & **costal**. Of the sternum and ribs.

sternoscapular, adj. [1. stèrnōskápular; 2. stə̀ːnouskǽpjulǝ]. **stern(o)-** & **scapular**. Of the sternum and scapula.

sternothyroid, adj. [1. stèrnōthroid; 2. stə̀ːnoupáiəroid]. **stern(o)-** & **thyroid**. Of the sternum and thyroid cartilage.

stern-post, n. Upright timber at vessel's stern, attached to keel, and usually supporting rudder.

stern-sheets, n. Part of boat between stern and rowers' thwarts.

sternum, n. [1. stérnum; 2. stə́ːnəm]. Lat. *sternum*, fr. Gk. *stérnon*, 'chest'; cp. Scrt. *stírnāš*, 'spread out'; O.H.G. *stirna*, 'forehead'; O.E. *steornede*, 'having a forehead'; Gaul. *sarn*, 'paved way'; O. Slav. *strand*, 'side, place'; fr. base **st(e)rē-*, **stor-*, **str-* &c., 'to spread out, extend', seen also in **stratum**, **strath**, **strand** (I.), **strew** &c. Breast-bone, vertical bone in front of thorax, to which the upper ribs are joined.

sternutation, n. [1. stèrnūtáshun; 2. stə̀ːnjutéiʃən], fr. Lat. *sternūtātiōn-(em)*, 'act of sneezing', fr. *sternūtāt-(um)*, P.P. type of *sternūtāre*, 'to sneeze', fr. *sternuere*, 'to sneeze'; cogn. w. Gk. *ptárnumi*; W. *ystrewi*, 'to sneeze'; O. Ir. *sren(n)im*, 'to snore'. Act of sneezing.

sternutative, adj. [1. stèrnútativ; 2. stə̀ːnjútǝtiv], fr. Lat. *sternūtāt-(um)*, P.P. type of *sternūtāre*, 'to sneeze', see prec., & **-ive**. Causing, tending to cause, sneezing.

sternutatory, adj. & n. [1. stèrnútaturi; 2. stə̀ːnjútǝtəri], fr. Lat. *sternūtāt-(um)*, see prec. & **-ory**. **1**. adj. Sternutative. **2**. n. Substance causing, or intended to cause, sneezing.

sternward, adj. & adv. [1. stë́rnward; 2. stə́ːnwǝd]. **stern** (II.) & **-ward**. **1**. adj. Situated near or towards the stern. **2**. adv. Towards the stern.

sternwards, adv. [1. stë́rnwardz; 2. stə́ːnwǝdz]. **stern** (II.) & **-wards**. Towards the stern.

stern-way, n. Backward motion of ship.

stern-wheeler, n. (U.S.A.) Steamboat with single paddle-wheel at stern.

stertorous, adj. [1. stë́rtorus; 2. stə́ːtǝrǝs], fr. Lat. *stertere*, 'to snore', & **-or** & **-ous**; etymol. doubtful; possibly fr. the same base as Lat. *sternuere*, 'to sneeze'; cp. O. Ir. *sren(n)im*, 'to snore', & see **sternutation**. (of breathing or person breathing) Characterized, accompanied by, producing sound like, snoring.

stertorously, adv. Prec. & **-ly**. In a stertorous manner.

stertorousness, n. See prec. & **-ness**. Quality of being stertorous.

stet, imperat. (intrans.) & vb. trans. [1. stet; 2. stet]. Lat. *stet*, 'let it stand', 3rd sing. pres. subj. of *stāre*, 'to stand', see **state**. **1**. imperat. Direction to printer &c., written in margin of a proof to cancel correction made in text, the letters thus replaced being dotted under. **2**. vb. trans. To cancel (correction in text) by placing dot(s) beneath and writing 'stet' in margin.

stethoscope, n. & vb. trans. [1. stéthoskōp; 2. stéþəskōup], fr. Gk. *stêthos*, 'breast'; cogn. w. Scrt. *stánaš*, 'breast'; for the second element see **-scope**. **1.** n. Slender tube with one flat and one bell-shaped end for auscultation of heart, lungs &c.; also more elaborate apparatus for same purpose. **2.** vb. To examine with a stethoscope.

stethoscopic, adj. [1. stèthoskópik; 2. stèþəskópik]. Prec. & **-ic**. Of, pertaining to, a stethoscope or stethoscopy.

stethoscopically, adv. [1. stèthoskópikali; 2. stèþəskópikəli]. Prec. & **-al** & **-ly**. In a stethoscopic manner; by means of the stethoscope.

stethoscopist, n. [1. stèthóskopist; 2. stèþóskəpist]. **stethoscope** & **-ist**. Person using or skilled in use of a stethoscope.

stethoscopy, n. [1. stèthóskopi; 2. stèþóskəpi]. **stethoscope** & **-y (I.)**. Art or practice of using a stethoscope.

stevedore, n. [1. stḗvedōr; 2. stívidō], fr. Span. *estivador*, fr. *estivar*, 'to pack, stow', fr. Lat. *stīpāre*, 'to pack tightly', see **steeve (III.)** & **stipate**; the Span. suff. *-dor*, corresponds to Lat. **-tor**, expressing the agent. Person employed at docks to stow and unload cargoes.

stew (I.), n. [1. stū; 2. stjū]. M.E. *stuve, stue*, fr. O. Fr. *estuve*, 'hot bath, bath-room; stew', of Gmc. origin; cp. Germ. *stube*, 'room'; M. Du. *stove*; O.E. *stofa*, 'heated room; bath-room'; see **stove (I.)**. Public baths were formerly, in many countries, the resort of persons of ill-fame. (archaic, usually pl. *stews*). A brothel.

stew (II.), vb. trans. & intrans. M.E. *stu(w)en*, 'to stew', fr. *stue*, 'hot bath', see prec. **1.** trans. To cook slowly by simmering in a small proportion of liquid, esp. in covered vessel: *to stew beef*; *stewed fruit*. **2.** intrans. (of food) To be cooked, be in process of cooking, by this method. Phr. *to let a person stew in his own juice*, abandon him to his fate, withhold help.

stew (III.), n., fr. prec. **1.** Dish of meat, fish, vegetables &c. cooked by stewing, usually with considerable number of ingredients; *Irish stew*, thick stew of mutton, onions, and potatoes. **2.** (slang) State of restless anxiety and excitement: *in a regular stew*.

stew (IV.), n. M.E. *stēwe*; cp. M.L.G. *stouwe*, 'fish-pond'; *stauen*, 'to dam'; O.H.G. *stowan, stūan*, 'to accuse, blame, take into custody'; Goth. *stōjan*, 'to judge', & see **stow**. Fish-pond serving as store for fish for the table.

steward, n. [1. stúard; 2. stjúəd]. O.E. *stiġweard*; M.E. *stīward*, 'steward'; fr. O.E. *stiġ*, 'sty, hall', see **sty**, & **ward**. **1. a** (hist.) An officer on the estate of a feudal lord having charge and management of the cattle; **b** generally, manager and administrator of a large estate and of all the business connected with it, agricultural, legal, and financial. **2.** Salaried manager of a large household and estate belonging to another. **3.** Person whose business it is to arrange for the supply of provisions in a college, club, or similar institution. **4.** Servant on a ship who waits on and attends to the passengers. **5.** One of a body of officials employed on various public occasions, e.g. at race meetings, at public balls. **6.** One of various high officers of State: *Lord High Steward of England*; *Lord Steward of the Household*.

stewardess, n. [1. stúardes; 2. stjúədis]. Prec. & **-ess**. Female steward, esp. on passenger-ship.

stewardship, n. [1. stúardship; 2. stjúədʃip]. **steward** & **-ship**. **a** Rank, office, functions of a steward; Phr. *to give an account of one's stewardship*, make a statement relative to the way in which one has discharged one's duties and responsibilities; **b** tenure of office of steward.

stew-pan, n. Covered vessel for stewing food.

stew-pot, n. Stew-pan.

sthenic, adj. [1. sthénik; 2. sþénik], fr. Gk. *sthénos*, 'strength'; etymol. doubtful. (pathol.) Abnormally active; applied to a state of morbid activity of some vital process.

stibial, adj. [1. stíbial; 2. stíbiəl], fr. Lat. *stibi, stibium*, fr. Gk. *stíbi*, 'a sulphuret of antimony', fr. Egyptian, & **-al**. Of, containing, consisting of, like, antimony.

stibialism, n. [1. stíbializm; 2. stíbiəlizəm]. Prec. & **-ism**. Poisoning by antimony.

stibium, n. [1. stíbium; 2. stíbiəm]. Lat., see **stibial**. (chem.) Antimony.

stichic, adj. [1. stíkik; 2. stíkik]. Gk. *stikhikós*, fr. *stíkhos*, 'file of soldiers; line of verse'; cp. Gk. *stoîkhos*, 'row, rank'; *steíkhein*, 'to advance'; cogn. w. Scrt. *stighnōti*, 'ascend'; Goth. *steigan*; O.N. *stīga*; O.E. *stīgan*, 'to ascend'; O.E. *stǣger*, 'stair', see **stair**. Connected with, consisting of, lines as metrical units.

stichomyth, n. [1. stíkomith; 2. stíkəmiþ], also **stichomythia** [1. stìkomíthia; 2. stìkəmíþiə]. Gk. *stikhomūthía*, 'conversation in alternate lines', fr. *stíkhos*, 'line of verse', see **stichic**, & *mûthos*, 'word, speech', see **myth**. Verse dialogue as in Greek plays.

stick (I.), vb. trans. & intrans. [1. stik; 2. stik], fr. two M.E. vbs., w. forms & meanings confused; (1) M.E. *steken* (str. vb.), 'to prick, fix, fasten'; cp. O.S. *stecan*; O.H.G. *stechan*, 'to prick'; (2) M.E. *stikien* (wk. vb.), 'to be infixed, to prick'; fr. O.E. *stician*, 'to prick, goad, stab'; to remain fixed, be infixed'; both cogn. w. Goth *stiks*; O.H.G. *stih*, 'prick, point'; cp. O.E. *sticca*, 'stick, peg, point'; see **stick (II.)**, L.G. *stikke*, 'to stick on', cp. **etiquette**; further, Gk. *stízein*, 'to prick, puncture'; *stiktós*, 'embroidered; variegated'; *stígma*, 'mark made by pointed instrument; scar; brand', see **stigma**; Lat. *instīgāre*, 'to goad', see **instigate**; Scrt. *tījatē*, 'is sharp'; *tigmáš*, 'pointed'; O. Pers. *tigra-*, 'sharp', see **tiger**. Cp. also **stake (I.)**. **A.** trans. **1. a** To pierce, thrust pointed object or instrument into or through: *to stick a pincushion full of pins*; **b** specif., *to stick a pig*, to kill it by sticking knife into its throat. Phr. *to stick pigs* (as sport), to hunt wild pigs on horseback with spear. **2.** To cause to penetrate, thrust into: *to stick a fork into a potato, a needle into one's finger* &c. **3.** (colloq.) To place, put, set, thrust: *stick it on the shelf*; *to stick one's hands into one's pockets*; *to stick one's tongue out*; *to stick a rose in one's buttonhole*; *to stick one's head round the door*. **4. a** To cause to adhere, cause to cling or cleave, fix in position, attach: *to stick a stamp on a letter*; *to stick bills, a notice, on a wall* &c.; **b** to mend, fasten together; *stick a thing, broken pieces &c., together with glue*. **5.** (slang) To tolerate, endure, stand: *I simply can't stick a whole summer in a town*. Phr. *to stick it*, to bear patiently (circumstances &c.), go through with, see it through. **B.** intrans. **1.** To remain fixed in, be held in position by point penetrating an object: *pins sticking in a pincushion*; *a dagger sticking in the corpse*. **2. a** To remain attached to, adhere, cleave, cling closely: *stamps stick together, to one's fingers* &c.; *burrs stick to one's clothes*; *to stick fast, like a limpet* &c.; (colloq.) *to stick on a horse*, be firmly seated on, not to fall off; **b** (fig.) to cling, cleave, remain in close association, avoid estrangement: *friends stick together*; **c** to remain, stop: *to stick at home, in the house* &c.; **d** to remain attached, become permanent, always used: *the nickname stuck*. **3. a** To become embedded, held fast, fixed; to be caught, entangled, attached: *to stick in the mud*; *the key has stuck in the lock*; *the door sticks*; *a fish-bone stuck in my throat*; Phr. *to stick in one's throat*, (fig.) be difficult to accept, acknowledge, utter &c.; **b** (fig.) to come to, be forced to, a standstill, be unable to proceed: *he tried to repeat Gray's 'Elegy', but stuck after the first few verses*. **C.** Followed by adverbs or prepositions with special meanings. *Stick at*, intrans., **1.** to remain at, persist in: *to stick at a piece of work*; **2.** to be checked, daunted by; to hesitate about, have scruples concerning: *he will stick at nothing to gain his ends*; *to stick at trifles*. *Stick out*, **1.** intrans., to project, stand out: *his ears stick out*; *buried in the sand with only his head sticking out*; **2.** trans., to cause to project, thrust out, force into prominence: *to stick out one's chest*. *Stick out for*, intrans., to persist in demanding, insist on having: *to stick out for higher wages*. *Stick to*, intrans., **a** to persevere in, continue at, refrain from abandoning: *to stick to one's work, post* &c.; Phr. *to stick to one's guns*, (fig.) adhere to one's opinions, refuse to be deflected from one's purpose, in spite of opposition; **b** (fig.) to be loyal, faithful, constant, to: *to stick to one's friends, one's word* &c. *Stick up*, **1.** intrans., to project upwards, stand upright: *hair sticking up on end*; *a head sticking up out of the water*; **2.** trans., **a** to cause to project upwards, put into upright position: *to stick up a post*; **b** (slang) to hold up, stop, or threaten for the purpose of robbing; **c** (slang) to puzzle, perplex. *Stick up for*, intrans., to defend, uphold; speak, or act in defence of: *to stick up for a friend, oneself, one's rights* &c.

stick (II.), n. O.E. *sticca*, 'stick, peg'; M.E. *sticke*; see prec. **1.** Slender, stiff shoot or twig of tree or shrub, light enough to be lifted or carried in the hand: *to collect dry sticks for the fire*; *to put a stick in the ground to mark a point*. Phrs. *to cut one's stick*, (colloq.) take one's departure; *in a cleft stick*, (fig.) dilemma, position from which one cannot extricate oneself; *to give one the stick*, cane him; *to get hold of the wrong end of the stick*, to misunderstand a situation, form a wrong idea concerning a matter; specif. **a** a stick seasoned, shaped &c. for support or defence, as symbol of office &c.; rod, staff: *to walk with, lean on, a stick*; **b** (usually in compounds) stick prepared or adapted for specific purpose: *fiddlestick, singlestick, broomstick, drumstick, hockey-stick* &c. **2.** Slender, usually cylindrical, bar or piece of some plastic substance: *a stick of sealing-wax, barley-sugar* &c. **3.** (print.) Composing-stick. **4.** (mus.) Conductor's baton. **5.** Stick-insect. **6.** (fig., colloq.) Dull, stiff, starched, unresponsive person: *he's a regular stick*; *a dry old stick*.

stick (III.), vb. trans., fr. prec. **1.** To support with a stick; to fasten to, supply with, sticks as support: *to stick peas*. **2.** (print.) To set up (type) in composing-stick.

sticker, n. [1. stíker; 2. stíkə]. **stick (I.)** & **-er**. **1.** One who, that which, sticks (in various senses); specif. **a** butcher &c. who sticks pigs; **b** one who fastens objects with adhesive compound: *bill-sticker* &c.; **c** (cricket) batsman who stays in for a long period but makes few runs. **2.** Person who sticks to, persists in, a piece of work, line of conduct &c.; a persistent, assiduous, persevering person. **3.** Wooden rod connecting two reciprocating levers in an organ &c.

stickful, n. [1. stíkfool; 2. stíkful]. **stick (II.)** & **-ful**. (print.) Amount of type that fills a composing-stick.

stickily, adv. [1. stíkili; 2. stíkili]. **sticky** & **-ly**. In a sticky manner.

stickiness, n. [1. stíkines; 2. stíkinis]. See prec. & **-ness**. State or quality of being sticky.

sticking-place, -point, n. [1. stíking plās, point; 2. stíkiŋ pleis, pɔint]. (chiefly fig.) Point at which something sticks, holds fast, remains fixed; esp. in Phr. *to screw one's courage to the sticking-point*.

sticking-plaster, n. Adhesive plaster for covering cuts &c. on the face &c.

stick-insect, n. Any of several kinds of insect resembling a twig or small stick.

stick-in-the-mud, adj. & n. [1. stík in dhe mud; 2. stík in ðə mad]. **1.** adj. Unprogressive, dull, without imagination, initiative &c. **2.** n. Stick-in-the-mud person, place &c.

stickjaw, n. [1. stíkjaw; 2. stíkdʒɔ̄]. (slang) Sweetmeat, pudding, which is sticky and difficult to masticate.

stickleback, n. [1. stíklbàk; 2. stíklbæ̀k], fr. O.E. *sticel*, 'sting', fr. *stician*, 'to prick', see **stick (I.)**, & **-le** & **back**. Small, fresh- and salt-water fish with a ridge of sharp dorsal spines.

stickler, n. [1. stíkler; 2. stíklə]. Obs. sense, 'umpire'; fr. M.E. *stihtlen*, 'to rule, dispose, set in order', fr. *stihten*, O.E. *stihtan*, 'to arrange, dispose', fr. **stik-tan*; cp. M. Du. *stichten*; O.H.G. *stiftan*, 'to arrange'. Only in Phr. *stickler for*, person who insists on, is punctilious about: *a stickler for ceremony, etiquette* &c.

sticky, adj. [1. stíki; 2. stíki]. **stick (I.)** & **-y (IV.)**. **a** Adhesive, glutinous, tending to cling to surfaces; **b** (in moral sense) difficult to move or influence; given to making objections, having scruples and hesitations: *rather sticky about giving his consent* &c.

stiff (I.), adj. [1. stif; 2. stif]. O.E. *stīf*; M.E. *stif*, 'stiff, strong'; cp. M.L.G. *stīf*; Du. *stijf*; O.N. *stīfr*, 'stiff'; cogn. w. Lat. *stīpāre*, 'to pack closely, cram', see **stipate**; *stīpes*, 'pillar'; Lith. *stiprùs*, 'strong'; cp. further Gk. *stiphrós*, 'thick, firm'; *steíbein*, 'to thicken'; fr. base **sti-*, **stei-* &c., 'to press close together'; see also **steato-**, **stone (I.)**. **1.** Rigid, firm, not easily bent; not flexible or pliant: *a stiff bar of iron*; *standing straight and stiff*; *stiff and cold in death*; *a stiff piece of cardboard*; *a stiff collar*. **2.** Dense in texture, only slightly plastic; thick: *stiff dough, paste, clay* &c. **3. a** Not moving freely, working with difficulty, owing to excessive friction &c.: *stiff joints, hinges* &c.; *a stiff neck*, rheumatism of muscles of neck; Phr. *to keep a stiff face, lip*, remain grave; (fig.) remain unmoved; *to keep a stiff upper lip*, remain firm in trouble or difficulty; **b** (of part of body) painful when moved through over-exertion; **c** (of person) suffering from stiffness of limb, muscle &c. through over-exertion: *feeling rather stiff*. **4. a** Formal, constrained, distant; reverse of natural, cordial, or easy in manner or character: *a stiff bow, greeting* &c.; *a stiff manner, style* &c.; **b** morally unyielding, not easily persuaded or influenced; severe. **5.** Requiring physical or mental effort; difficult: *a stiff climb, examination*. **6.** Of considerable strength, volume, amount &c.; specif. **a** *a stiff gale, breeze* &c., strong and steady; **b** *a stiff drink* &c., containing large proportion of spirit, drug &c.; **c** excessive: *a stiff demand, price* &c.; **d** (colloq.) startling, difficult to acquiesce in; preposterous; thick, steep (in colloq. senses).

stiff (II.), n., fr. prec. (slang) **1.** Paper money &c. **2.** A corpse.

stiff-bit, n. Horse's bit consisting of a single, rigid bar.

stiffen, vb. trans. & intrans. [1. stífen; 2. stífən]. **stiff (I.)** & **-en (V.)**. **A.** trans. **1.** To make stiff; specif. **a** to make rigid, difficult to bend: *to stiffen linen with starch*; **b** to increase density of, make less plastic: *to stiffen paste* &c. **2.** To render more resolute and unyielding; to inspire with power or will to resist: *the king tried to stiffen his wavering generals*. **B.** intrans. **1.** To become stiff; specif. **a** to grow rigid, lose flexibility; **b** to become less plastic; hard. **2.** To become colder in manner, more formal, distant, constrained. **3. a** To increase in intensity, force, volume: *the breeze stiffened*; **b** (fig.) to become firmer, more determined and unyielding: *one's resolution stiffens*.

stiffener, n. [1. stífener; 2. stífənə]. Prec. & **-er**. Something which causes stiffening; **a** (in material sense) specif. (slang) a stimulant, a tonic; **b** (in moral sense) circumstance which stiffens the courage, resolution &c.

stiffening, n. [1. stífening; 2. stífəniŋ]. See prec. & **-ing**. Material used to stiffen substance or object.

stiffish, adj. [1. stífish; 2. stífiʃ]. **stiff (I.)** & **-ish (I.)**. Fairly stiff.

stiffly, adv. [1. stífli; 2. stífli]. **stiff (I.)** & **-ly**. In a stiff manner.

stiff-necked, adj. [1. stíf nekt; 2. stíf nekt]. (fig.) Stubborn, unyielding, obstinate.

stiffness, n. [1. stífnes; 2. stífnis]. **stiff (I.)** & **-ness**. State or quality of being stiff.

stifle (I.), vb. trans. & intrans. [1. stīfl; 2. stáifl], fr. O.N. *stīfla*, 'to choke', fr. *stīva*, 'to stiffen'; cogn. w. M.L.G. *stīven*; M. Du. *stijven*, 'to stiffen'; cp. O.N. *stīfr*; O.E. *stīf*, 'stiff'; see **stiff (I.)**. **A.** trans. **1. a** To choke, suffocate; kill, destroy, by stopping air supply; **b** to render breathing difficult, deprive of adequate supply of fresh air. **2. a** To suppress, damp down, cause to die down, to extinguish, to quench: *to stifle fire, flames*; **b** (fig.) to quell, put down: *to stifle complaints, rebellion* &c. **3. a** To repress (feelings &c.), to crush down, keep in check, control, refrain from giving vent to or expressing: *to stifle one's hopes, fears, affection* &c.; **b** *to stifle a noise, laughter, sobs* &c. **B.** intrans. To experience sensation of stifling.

stifle (II.), n. Prob. fr. O.N. *stīva*, 'stiffen', see prec. **1.** Joint in hind leg of horse or dog, above the hock; also *stifle-joint*. **2.** Disease of stifle-joint or stifle-bone.

stifle-bone, n. Horse's knee-pan.

stifled, adj. [1. stīfld; 2. stáifld]. **stifle (II.)** & **-ed**. Affected with stifle.

stifle-joint, n. See **stifle (II.)**.

stifle-shoe, n. Horseshoe designed to correct a stifled joint.

stifling, adj. [1. stīfling; 2. stáifliŋ]. **stifle (I.)** & **-ing**. Tending to stifle; suffocating; stuffy, airless; also in moral sense.

stiflingly, adv. Prec. & **-ly**. So as to stifle.

stigma, n. [1. stígma; 2. stígmə], pl. *stigmas*; (eccles., anat.) *stigmata* [1. stígmata; 2. stígmətə]. Lat., fr. Gk. *stígma*, 'puncture; brand', fr. stem of *stízein*, 'to prick, brand, tattoo'; cogn. w. Lat. *instīgāre*, 'to goad', see **instigate**; also w. O.E. *stician*, 'to prick', see **stick (I.)**. **1.** (archaic) Mark made with branding-iron on slave or criminal; brand. **2.** Moral reproach, brand of disgrace or infamy: *the stigma of illegitimacy*. **3.** (eccles., commonly in pl., *stigmata*) Marks, or periodically bleeding wounds, corresponding to the five wounds of the Saviour, appearing miraculously on the bodies of some saints and other persons. **4.** (anat.) Any small mark or scar on the body; specif., small spot that bleeds periodically or under certain mental or physical stimuli. **5.** (bot.) That part of a pistil which receives the pollen.

stigmatic, adj. [1. stigmátik; 2. stigmǽtik], fr. Lat., fr. Gk. *stígmat-*, stem of *stígma*, 'brand', see **stigma**, & **-ic**. Of the nature of a stigma.

stigmatiferous, adj. [1. stìgmatíferus; 2. stìgmətífərəs], fr. Gk. *stígmat-*, as in prec., & *-i-* & **-ferous**. Bearing stigmas.

stigmatism, n. [1. stígmatizm; 2. stígmətizəm], fr. Gk. *stígmat-*, as in prec., & **-ism**. **1.** Condition of bearing stigmata. **2.** Property of an optical lens, or of that of the eye, of focussing rays of light upon a single point.

stigmatist, n. [1. stígmatist; 2. stígmətist], fr. Gk. *stígmat-*, see prec., & **-ist**. (eccles.) Person supposed to bear the marks of the stigmata.

stigmatization, n. [1. stìgmatīzáshun; 2. stìgmətaizéiʃən]. Next word & **-ion**. Act of stigmatizing; state of being stigmatized.

stigmatize, vb. trans. [1. stígmatīz; 2. stígmətaiz], fr. Gk. *stígmat-*, see **stigmatic**, & **-ize**. **1.** (fig.) To designate, brand, as (something discreditable); to describe by an opprobrious name: *to stigmatize a person as a rogue*. **2.** (eccles.) To impress, mark, stigmata upon; to mark with stigmata.

stigmatose, adj. [1. stígmatōs; 2. stígmətous], fr. Gk. *stígmat-*, see prec., & **-ose**. Bearing, marked with, having, a stigma.

stilbite, n. [1. stílbīt; 2. stílbait]. Formed fr. Gk. *stílbein*, 'to glitter'; cp. Gk. *stilpnós*, 'shining'; perh. cogn. w. O. Ir. *sell*, 'eye'. A white, crystalline mineral.

stile (I.), n. [1. stīl; 2. stail]. O.E. *stiǵel*, 'place for climbing over fence; stile'; M.E. *stīle*; cp. M.H.G. *stigele*; M.L.G. *stegel*, 'stile'; cp. further O.E. *stīgan*, 'to climb'; P.P. *(ǵe)stigen*; & see **stair** & **sty (I.)**. Device for facilitating the climbing of a wall or fence, usually consisting of a bar or rail, and more or less rough steps of wood or stone placed permanently on either side.

stile (II.), n. Origin unknown. Upright piece in frame of door &c.

stiletto, n. & vb. trans. [1. stilétō; 2. stilétou], fr. Ital. *stiletto*, dimin. of *stilo*, fr. Lat. *stilus*, 'pointed instrument', see **style (I.)**. **1.** n. **a** Small, slender, continuously tapering dagger; **b** small pointed instrument of metal, ivory &c. for making eyelet-holes in textile fabric &c. **2.** vb. (rare) To pierce, make holes in, stab, with a stiletto.

still (I.), adj. [1. stil; 2. stil]. O.E. *stille*, 'at rest; silent; secret'; cp. M. Du. *stille*; O.H.G. *stilli*, 'still'; cogn. w. Gk. *stéllein*, 'to set in order'; *stḗlē*, 'pillar', see **stele**; *stélekhos*, 'stem'; Scrt. *sthálam*, 'place, position'; Lat. *locus*, O. Lat. *stlocus*, 'place', see **locus**; fr. base **stĕl-*, **stŏl-*, **stl̥-* &c., 'to place'; expansion of **stā-*, **stə-*, 'to stand'; see **stand**, **state**. **1. a** Devoid of motion: *still water*; *the air is perfectly still*; *a still evening*; **b** no longer moving, having come to rest: *keep your feet still*; *never still for a moment*. **2.** (of wine) Not sparkling or effervescent. **3.** Devoid of sound, no longer heard; silent: '*The trumpet's silver sound is still*' (Scott, Introd. to Canto I. of 'Marmion').

still (II.), n., fr. prec. Cp. O.H.G. *stillī*, 'stillness'. (rare and poet.) Stillness, quiet, calm.

still (III.), vb. trans. & intrans., fr. **still (I.)**. **1.** trans. To make still; **a** to cause to be quiet or silent; to calm, hush: *to still the clamours of envy*; **b** to soothe, assuage: *to still the pain of a wound*. **2.** intrans. (rare) To become still.

still (IV.), adv. O.E. *stille*, 'quietly', see **still (I.)**. **1.** (archaic or obs.) Continuously, constantly. **2.** Right up to specified time, even now or even then: *he is still asleep*; *will you still be here when I return?* **3.** Nevertheless, even, granting that, notwithstanding: *he is an awful bore—still we are bound to ask him*. **4.** (after or before a compar. adj.) Even, yet, more, to an increasing degree: *he is tall enough, but his brother is still taller*, or *taller still*.

still (V.), vb. trans. & intrans. Abbr. fr. **distil**; but cp. also Lat. *stillāre*, 'to fall in drops; to cause to fall in drops', fr. *stīlla*, 'a small drop', dimin. of *stīria*, 'small drop, icicle'; cogn. w. *stīpāre*, 'to press together', q.v. under **stiff**, & cp. **stipate**. **1.** trans. To distil; produce (spirit) from a still. **2.** intrans. (poet.) To fall drop by drop, trickle.

still (VI.), n. M.E. *stillatorie*, fr. *stillāt-(um)*, P.P. type of *stillāre*, see prec., & **-ory**. Apparatus for distilling; apparatus in which the more volatile parts of a liquid are separated from it by heat and subsequently condensed.

stillage, n. [1. stílij; 2. stílidž]. Formed fr. base of **stilling**, **stillion**, & **-age**. Framework, bench, stool &c. for raising things off the floor, e.g. yarn &c. while draining, goods ready for packing &c.

still-birth, n. Birth of a dead child.

still-born, adj. Dead when born.

still-fish, vb. intrans. To fish from an anchored boat.

stilling, n. [1. stíling; 2. stíliŋ], fr. L.G. *stelling*, fr. *stellen*, 'to place', cogn. w. **stall (I.)**, & **-ing (I.)**. Stand, framework, supporting cask &c.

stillion, n. [1. stílyun; 2. stíljən]. Variant of prec. Stilling.

still life, n. Pictorial representation of inanimate objects.

stillness, n. [1. stílnes; 2. stílnis]. **still (I.)** & **-ness**. State or quality of being still.

still-room, n. **1.** Room in which distilling is carried on. **2.** Housekeeper's store-room; one where home-made preserves &c. are kept.

stilly (I.), adv. [1. stílli; 2. stílli]. **still (I.)** & **-ly**. In a still manner, quietly.

stilly (II.), adj. [1. stíli; 2. stíli]. **still (I.)** & **-y (IV.)**. (poet.) Still, quiet, silent.

stilt, n. [1. stilt; 2. stĭlt], fr. Swed. *stylta*; cp. Germ. *stelze*, 'stilt'. 1. (usually pl.) *Stilts*, device used for raising a walker above the ground, consisting of a pair of long, light poles, with supports for the feet eighteen inches or so from the ground, the upper part of each resting in crook of elbow and grasped lower down by the hand. 2. Also *stilt-bird*, *stilt-plover*, genus of three-toed wading birds, with long, slender legs.

stilt-bird, n. See stilt, 2.

stilted, adj. [1. stĭlted; 2. stĭltid]. stilt & -ed. 1. Stiff, pretentious, bombastic (of style and manner); literally resembling gait of person on stilts. 2. (archit.) *Stilted arch*, one springing from a series of horizontal courses of masonry above the impost, and not from the impost itself.

stiltedly, adv. Prec. & -ly. In a stilted manner.

stiltedness, n. See prec. & -ness. State or quality of being stilted.

Stilton, n. [1. stĭltun; 2. stĭltən], fr. Stilton, Hunts. Kind of rich cheese.

stilt-petrel, n. Long-legged petrel.

stilt-plover, n. See stilt, 2.

stilt-sandpiper, n. Kind of North American sandpiper.

stimulant (I.), adj. [1. stĭmulant; 2. stĭmjulənt], fr. Lat. *stimulāre*, 'to prick with a goad; to stimulate', fr. *stimulus*, 'goad', see **stimulus**, & -ant. Serving to stimulate; acting as a stimulant.

stimulant (II.), n., fr. prec. Something which stimulates; specif. **a** a drug or other agent which increases the activity of some bodily organ or function, or which excites emotions; in Phr. *to take stimulants*, refers specifically to alcohol; **b** some motive or influence which incites (persons) to action: *ambition is often a stimulant of industry*.

stimulate, vb. trans. [1. stĭmulāt; 2. stĭmjuleit], fr. Lat. *stimulāt-(um)*, P.P. type of *stimulāre*, 'to prick with a goad; to rouse up, stimulate', fr. *stimulus*, 'goad', see **stimulus**. 1. To cause activity in, rouse up, excite, act as stimulus to; specif. **a** to excite a nerve: *light stimulates the optic nerve*; **b** to increase, arouse, provoke, an emotion: *to stimulate one's curiosity*; **c** to increase action of a bodily organ: *to stimulate (the action of) the heart*. 2. To provide a motive or incentive to human action; to urge, incite: *I couldn't stimulate him into a display of spirit or courage*.

stimulating, adj. [1. stĭmulāting; 2. stĭmjulèitiŋ]. Prec. & -ing. Acting as stimulus, exciting, provoking, increasing, bodily or mental activity; bracing.

stimulation, n. [1. stĭmulāshun; 2. stĭmjuléiʃən]. stimulate & -ion. Act of stimulating; state of being stimulated.

stimulative, adj. [1. stĭmulativ; 2. stĭmjulətiv]. stimulate & -ive. Tending to stimulate.

stimulator, n. [1. stĭmulāter; 2. stĭmjuleitə]. stimulate & -or. One who, that which, stimulates, esp. object or substance used for stimulating.

stimulose, adj. [1. stĭmulōs; 2. stĭmjulous], fr. Lat. *stimulōsus*, 'stimulative'; see **stimulus** & -ose. (bot.) Having a sting.

stimulus, n. [1. stĭmulus; 2. stĭmjuləs]. Lat. *stimulus*, 'goad, sting; pang; spur, incentive'; cp. Lat. *stilus*, 'pointed instrument'; fr. base *sti-, *stei-, *stoi- &c., 'sharp'; cp. Avest. *staēra*, 'peak'. From the same base w. addition of formative element -g-, cp. Lat. *(in)stīgāre*, 'to goad', see **instigate**; Gk. *stigma*, 'prick', see **stigma**; O.E. *sticca*, 'stick, peg', see **stick**(I.). 1. Anything which excites action or reaction in tissue, muscle, nerve &c. 2. (bot.) Plant's sting. 3. (eccles.) Point at end of ecclesiastical staff. 4. **a** Substance, drug &c. which increases and provokes activity of bodily function; a stimulant; **b** something which incites to mental or moral action; an incentive, a motive, an inducement: *interest and curiosity provide a sufficient stimulus to industry*; *without the stimulus of poverty and ambition he would never have reached success*.

stimy. See stymie.

sting (I.), vb. trans. & intrans. [1. sting; 2. stiŋ]. O.E. *stingan*; M.E. *stingen*; cp. O.N. *stinga*; Goth. *-stiggan*, 'to sting'; prob. a nasalized form of base in **stick**(I.). **A**. trans. 1. (of insect, plant &c.) To pierce, wound, with a sting: *to be stung by a bee*. 2. To cause a sharp, smarting, tingling sensation or pain to: *a stinging blow*; *the hail stings one's face*. 3. (fig.) **a** To give keen mental pain to, cause to suffer acutely: *to be stung by remorse, an insult* &c.; **b** to stimulate, provoke: *the insult stung him into a reply*. **B**. intrans. 1. (zool., bot.) **a** To have a sting; **b** to inflict a sting. 2. To feel a sharp, smarting sensation, to tingle: *the blow made his hand sting*. 3. (fig.) To give acute mental pain: *reproach stings*.

sting (II.), n. O.E. *sting*, see prec. 1. (zool.) Sharply pointed organ of offence or defence of an animal, as insect, reptile &c. 2. (bot.) Sharp, stiff hair, containing tube leading from poison-gland; as in a nettle. 3. **a** Act of stinging; **b** wound or puncture caused by sting. 4. Sharp pain caused by, or as by, a sting: *to feel a sharp sting*; *the sting of the wind*; *the stings of hunger*. 5. Property of, capacity for, inflicting keen mental or moral suffering: '*O Death, where is thy sting?*' 6. Stimulating force, keenness, power to rouse, excite; bite, tang: *the breeze has a sting in it*.

stingaree, n. [1. stĭnggarè; 2. stĭŋgəri], fr. sting-ray. Sting-ray.

sting-bull, n. Kind of sharp-spined fish; weever.

stinger, n. [1. stĭnger; 2. stĭŋə]. sting (I.) & -er. One who, that which, stings; esp. stinging blow.

sting-fish, n. Sting-bull.

stingily, adv. [1. stĭnjili; 2. stĭndʒili]. stingy & -ly. In a stingy manner.

stinginess, n. [1. stĭnjines; 2. stĭndʒinis]. See prec. & -ness. State or quality of being stingy.

stinging, adj. [1. stĭnging; 2. stĭŋiŋ], fr. Pres. Part. of sting (I.). 1. (of plant, insect &c.) Having a sting; able to sting. 2. Producing a sharp, smarting, painful sensation: *a stinging blow*. 3. (fig.) Causing acute exasperation, irritating like a sting: *stinging words*.

stingingly, adv. Prec. & -ly. So as to sting: *to retort briefly but stingingly*.

stinging-nettle, n. Species of nettle with stings on leaf.

stingless, adj. [1. stĭngles; 2. stĭŋlis]. sting (II.) & -less. Without a sting.

stingo, n. [1. stĭnggō; 2. stĭŋgou], fr. sting. (archaic) Strong beer.

sting-ray, n. Kind of ray with a sharp spine near the base of the long whip-like tail.

sting-winkle, n. Kind of shellfish that perforates the shells of other shellfish.

stingy, adj. [1. stĭnji; 2. stĭndʒi], fr. O.E. **stingiġ*, 'stinging'. See sting (II.) & -y (IV.). Disinclined to spend money; not in the habit of giving; penurious, mean, niggardly; reverse of *open-handed, generous, liberal*.

stink (I.), vb. intrans. & trans. [1. stingk; 2. stiŋk]. O.E. *stincan*, 'to emit vapour; to give forth odour (good or bad)'; M.E. *stinken*; cp. O.H.G. *stinchan*; M.L.G. *stinken*, 'to smell'; prob. cogn. w. Gk. *taggós*, 'rancid'; fr. a nasalized form of base seen in O.N. *stökr*, 'stinking'. See also **stench**. 1. intrans. To give out a strong, unpleasant smell, have an offensive odour. Phrs. (fig.) *to stink of money*, be conspicuously rich; *to stink in one's nostrils*, be highly offensive to one. 2. trans. Only in *stink out*, to drive out by stinking.

stink (II.), n., fr. prec. 1. (not a refined word) Strong, offensive, disgusting smell; a stench. 2. (slang) *Stinks*, chemistry; natural science.

stink-alive, n. Kind of fish, whiting pout.

stinkard, n. [1. stĭngkard; 2. stĭŋkəd]. stink (I.) & -ard. Stinking person, animal; esp. the stinking badger, teledu.

stink-ball, n. Ball or vessel filled with explosives or combustibles, designed to produce noxious fumes, formerly used to fling on to hostile ships in naval warfare.

stinker, n. [1. stĭngker; 2. stĭŋkə]. stink (I.) & -er. 1. One who, that which, stinks; stinkard. 2. Kind of petrel, esp. giant fulmar.

stink-horn, n. Kind of fungus growing on decayed vegetable matter.

stinking, adj. [1. stĭngking; 2. stĭŋkiŋ], fr. Pres. Part. of stink (I.). Emitting an offensive odour; e.g. *stinking badger*, E. Indian badger secreting a malodorous fluid, the teledu; *stinking cedar*; *stinking crane's-bill*, *night-shade* &c.; *stinking elder*, common elder; *stinking-weed*, kind of W. Indian cassia.

stinkingly, adv. Prec. & -ly. In a stinking manner.

stink-pot, n. 1. Stink-ball. 2. Term of abuse.

stink-stone, n. Kind of rock, esp. limestone, which emits a fetid odour when struck or split.

stink-trap, n. Contrivance to prevent escape of effluvia from drains.

stink-wood, n. Valuable, durable, but ill-smelling timber obtained from a South African tree.

stint (I.), vb. trans. [1. stint; 2. stint]. O.E. *styntan*, 'to stupefy'; M.E. *stinten*, 'to stop, stint'; fr. O.E. *stunt*, 'dull'; cp. O.N. *stuttr*, 'short'; cogn. w. Lat. *tundere*, 'to beat'. Cp. Scrt. *tundatē*, 'pricks, pushes', &, without the nasal, Lat. *tudēs*, 'hammer'; cp. the same base w. a different formative element in **type**; & cp. **toil** (II.). See also **stunt** (I.) & cp. **contuse**. 1. To be chary of bestowing, to limit, be too sparing in bestowal of: *he does not stint his praise*. 2. To grudge, be niggardly with, dole out inadequate quantities of (thing), to (person): *to stint one's children of food*; also *to stint oneself (of)*.

stint (II.), n., fr. prec. 1. Restriction, limitation; chiefly in Phr. *without stint*, unrestrictedly, ungrudgingly, lavishly. 2. (archaic) Limited, appointed, assigned proportion or task. 3. Small sandpiper, esp. the dunlin.

stinting, adj. [1. stĭnting; 2. stĭntiŋ], fr. Pres. Part. of stint (I.). Grudging, niggardly.

stintingly, adv. Prec. & -ly. Grudgingly, sparingly.

stintless, adj. [1. stĭntles; 2. stĭntlis]. stint (II.) & -less. Without stint, unlimited.

stipate, adj. [1. stĭpāt; 2. stáipeit], fr. Lat. *stīpāt-(um)*, P.P. type of *stīpāre*, 'to press together, compress'; cp. Lat. *stīpes*, 'pillar; stem'; cogn. w. **stiff** (I.). (bot.) Compressed, crowded.

stipe, n. [1. stīp; 2. staip]. Fr., fr. Lat. *stīpes*, 'stem', see prec. Stalk, stem, support; specif. (bot.) **a** a stalk of fern-frond; **b** stem-like part of mushroom or similar fungus.

stipel, n. [1. stĭpel; 2. stáipel]. Prec. & -el. Small, secondary stipule, esp. at base of leaflet in compound leaf.

stipellate, adj. [1. stĭpelāt; 2. stáipeleit]. Prec. & -ate. (bot.) Having a stipel.

stipend, n. [1. stĭpend; 2. stáipənd], fr. Lat. *stīpendium*, 'tax, impost; pay, stipend; income', earlier **stipipendium*, fr. *stips*, 'payment, donation'; the orig. sense may possibly have been 'stem, rod'; specif., bar of copper used as form of currency'; cp. Lat. *stipula*, 'stalk, straw', see **stipule** & **stipate**. Regular periodical payment made for services rendered in some permanent post or employment; salary.

stipendiary, adj. & n. [1. stĭpéndiari; 2. staipéndiəri], fr. Lat. *stīpendiārius*, 'of tribute; receiving pay', fr. *stīpendium*, 'tax; payment'. See prec. & -ary. 1. adj. Receiving periodical payment, serving for pay. 2. n. In full, *stipendiary magistrate*, one appointed by Home Secretary and paid by Government, presiding in certain metropolitan or other borough police courts.

stipes, n. [1. stípēz; 2. stáipīz]. Lat., 'stalk, stem'. See under **stipate**. Stipe.

stipiform, adj. [1. stípiform; 2. stáipifōm]. **stipe** & -i- & -**form**. Having the form of a stipe.

stipitate, adj. [1. stípitāt; 2. stáipitèit], fr. Lat. *stīpit-*, stem of *stipes*, 'stem', see **stipe** & -**ate**. Having, supported by, a stipe.

stipitiform, adj. [1. stípitiform; 2. stáipitifōm], fr. Lat. *stīpit-*, stem of *stipes*, 'stalk', see **stipes** & -i- & -**form**. Stipiform.

stipple (I.), vb. trans. & intrans. [1. stípl; 2. stípl], fr. Du. *stippelen*, fr. *stippel*, dimin. of *stip*, 'point, dot'; cp. M. Du. *stippen*, 'to prick'; fr. base **sti-*, **stoi-* &c., 'sharp, pointed', seen in **stimulus, stigma, stick** &c. **1.** trans. To execute, draw, engrave &c. in stipple. **2.** intrans. To work in stipple.

stipple (II.), n., fr. prec. Method of painting or engraving in which dots are used in place of lines.

stipple-graver, n. Instrument for making dots in stippling.

stippler, n. [1. stípler; 2. stíplə]. **stipple** (I.) & -**er**. **1.** Painter, engraver, using stipple. **2.** Paint-brush used in stippling.

stippling, n. [1. stípling; 2. stíplíŋ]. **stipple** (I.) & -**ing**. Etching or engraving in which effect is produced by dots and points; work done in stipple.

stipulaceous, adj. [1. stìpuláshus; 2. stìpjuléiʃəs]. **stipule** & -**aceous**. Stipular.

stipular, adj. [1. stípular; 2. stípjulə]. **stipule** & -**ar**. Pertaining to, of the nature of, a stipule.

stipulary, adj. [1. stípulari; 2. stípjulərí]. **stipule** & -**ary**. Stipular.

stipulate (I.), vb. intrans. & trans. [1. stípulāt; 2. stípjuleit], fr. Lat. *stipulāt-(um)*, P.P. type of *stipulāri*, 'to demand a formal promise; to bargain, stipulate', fr. O. Lat. *stipulus*, 'firm'; cp. Lat. *stīpes*, 'trunk, stem'; *stīpāre*, 'to press together, make compact'. See **stipate**. **1.** intrans. To make stipulations, esp. in Phr. *to stipulate for*, make a necessary condition of an agreement &c., insist expressly on : *the contract stipulates for the use of seasoned timber; the witness, before telling his story, stipulated that his name should be kept secret*. **2.** trans. To demand as essential part of agreement or contract : *an increase in the working hours was not stipulated; to use the stipulated material*.

stipulate (II.), adj. **stipule** & -**ate**. (bot.) Having a stipule.

stipulation (I.), n. [1. stìpūláshun; 2. stìpjuléiʃən]. **stipulate** (I.) & -**ion**. **1.** Act of stipulating. **2.** That which is stipulated; point, condition, undertaking, insisted on in a contract, agreement, bargain &c.

stipulation (II.), n. **stipule** & -**ation**. (bot.) Character, formation, arrangement, of stipules.

stipulator, n. [1. stípūlāter; 2. stípjuleítə]. **stipulate** & -**or**. Person who makes a stipulation.

stipule, n. [1. stípūl; 2. stípjūl], fr. Lat. *stipula*, 'stalk, stem, blade, straw', dimin. of *stīpes*, 'stem, trunk'. See **stipes** & -**ule**. Appendage at the base of a leaf-stalk, usually in the form of a small leaf, or of a scale, or tendril.

stipuliform, adj. [1. stípūlifōrm; 2. stípjulifōm]. Prec. & -i- & -**form**. Having the shape of a stipule.

stir (I.), vb. trans. & intrans. [1. stēr; 2. stā]. O.E. *styrian*, 'to set in action; to agitate'; M.E. *stiren*; cp. O.H.G. -*stōren*, 'to disturb'; Germ. *stören*, 'to disturb'; *sturz*, 'plunge, overthrow'; cp. also **storm**; cogn. w. Lat. *trua*, 'scoop, ladle, spoon for stirring', see **trowel**. **A**. trans. **1.** To set in motion, cause to move, alter position of : *the wind stirs the leaves*. Phr. *to stir one's stumps* (lit. and fig.), move or act briskly, energetically ; *to stir the fire*, poke it, move pieces of burning fuel &c.; *not to stir an eyelid*, remain perfectly motionless ; *not to stir a finger*, make no effort. **2.** To give circular motion to (fluid, semi-fluid, or dry particles) in a vessel with a spoon, cause to move round and round, to mix thoroughly, make or keep smooth : *to stir one's tea, soup, porridge, mincemeat*. **3.** To affect the emotions (of) ; to move, rouse : *he was deeply stirred by the news ; to stir the imagination, enthusiasm* &c. Phr. *to stir the blood*, rouse to excitement, enthusiasm &c. **B**. intrans. **1.** To move, be in motion : *not a wind was stirring ; something stirred in the wood*. **2.** To shift from one position to another : *don't stir for a moment ; the cat lay the whole day on the chair without stirring*. **C**. Followed by adverbs or prepositions, with special meanings. *Stir up*, trans., **1.** to mix, stir thoroughly, cause particles of to intermingle ; **2.** to disturb, cause to rise, by stirring : *don't stir up the dregs*; **3.** to rouse, excite, bring into existence or action : *to stir up interest in a subject ; to stir up strife*.

stir (II.), n., fr. prec. **1.** Act of stirring ; stirring movement or action : *to give the fire, porridge &c. a stir*. **2.** Mental excitement, disturbance, commotion ; esp. public excitement, sensation : *the news created a tremendous stir in the country*.

stirabout, n. & adj. [1. stêrabòut; 2. stā́rəbàut]. **1.** n. Kind of porridge. **2.** adj. Active, busy, bustling.

stirless, adj. [1. stêrles; 2. stā́lis]. **stir** (II.) & -**less**. (rare) Without a stir, motionless.

stirpiculture, n. [1. stêrpikùlchur; 2. stā́pikàltʃə], fr. Lat. *stirp-*, stem of *stirps*, 'stock', see next word, & -i- & **culture**. Breeding of animals &c. from special strains or with special characteristics.

stirps, n. [1. stêrps; 2. stā́ps]. Lat. *stirps*, 'roots and stem of tree, stock ; stem ; branch of family, race ; foundation' ; etymol. unknown. (law) Person from whom a family descends; common ancestor of a group of persons.

stirrer, n. [1. stêrer; 2. stā́rə]. **stir** (I.) & -**er**. One who, that which, stirs ; (specif.) instrument for stirring food &c.

stirring, adj. [1. stêring; 2. stā́riŋ], fr. Pres. Part. of **stir** (I.). **1.** Having the property of affecting, rousing the emotions ; exciting, moving : *a stirring incident, speech, song* &c. **2. a** Active, brisk, busy : *a stirring person, a stirring body*, **b** characterized by, filled with, incident, activity, business &c. : *stirring times*.

stirringly, adv. Prec. & -**ly**. In a stirring manner.

stirrup, n. [1. stírup; 2. stírəp]. O.E. *stiġrāp*, 'stirrup' ; M.E. *stirop, stirep* ; cp. O.N. *stigreip* ; O.H.G. *stegereif*, 'stirrup' ; cp. O.E. *stīgan*, 'to climb' ; *stigel*, 'stile', see **stair, stile** (I.). For the second element see **rope**. **1. a** One of two metal hoops or rings, with flat base, hung by straps, one either side, from a saddle to support foot of rider ; also *stirrup iron* : *to have one's feet in the stirrups* ; **b** strap from which stirrup-iron is suspended : *to shorten, lengthen, one's stirrups* ; called also *stirrup-leather*. **2.** (naut.) Rope which supports the foot-rope below a ship's yard.

stirrup-bar, n. Short, horizontal iron bar, let into rider's saddle, to which stirrup-leather is attached.

stirrup-bone, n. Stirrup-shaped bone of the middle ear; stapes.

stirrup-cup, n. Parting cup of wine &c. drunk by rider mounted for departure.

stirrup-iron, n. The metal ring in which the foot of a rider is placed ; stirrup ; contrasted with *stirrup-leather*.

stirrup-leather, n. Strap attaching stirrup to saddle.

stirrupless, adj. [1. stíruples; 2. stírəplis]. **stirrup** & -**less**. Without stirrups.

stirrup-piece, n. (mechan., carpentry &c.) Hanging, metal loop supporting bar, beam &c.

stirrup-strap, n. Stirrup-leather.

stitch (I.), n. [1. stich; 2. stitʃ]. O.E. *stiċe*, 'stab, prick, puncture' ; M.E. *stiche* ; cp. O.E. *slician*, 'to prick' ; fr. **stiki*, see **stick** (I.). **1.** Single, complete in-and-out action of needle in sewing ; act of passing needle through material from above and bringing point out to upper surface again by a forward movement. **2. a** Piece of thread &c. drawn through material by needle, and left to cover part of material, used for ornamentation, for joining two pieces or parts of material together &c. : *to make small, long, neat, stitches ; to put a stitch in a garment* &c., make slight repair in ; Phr. *without a stitch of clothing, not a stitch on*, completely naked ; **b** specif., stitch made by surgeon to close wound &c. : *to put in several stitches ; to take out the stitches* &c. **3.** Single, complete loop or knot made by needle or hook in knitting, crochet &c. Phr. *to drop a stitch*, allow it to slip off needle. **4. a** Method of forming, character, structure, of stitch in sewing, knitting, crochet &c. : *to learn a new stitch* ; esp. in compounds, *buttonhole-, feather-, slip-, satin-stitch* &c. ; **b** style of work produced by characteristic stitch, chiefly in compounds, *cross-, stocking-stitch* &c. **5.** (bookbinding) Loop of thread, wire &c., securing sheets of book &c. **6.** Sudden, sharp, stabbing pain in the side.

stitch (II.), vb. trans. & intrans., fr. prec. **1.** trans. **a** To secure, fasten together, with stitch(es), sew ; **b** to ornament with stitches, embroider. **2.** intrans. To make stitches, sew.

stitching-horse, n. [1. stíching hòrs ; 2. stítʃiŋ hòs]. Saddler's clamp for holding harness steady during stitching.

stitch-wheel, n. Saddler's toothed wheel for marking position for series of holes in leather &c.

stitchwort, n. [1. stíchwêrt ; 2. stítʃwāt]. O.E. *stiċwyrt* ; **stitch** (I.) & **wort** (I.), so called from its supposed efficacy for a stitch in the side. Genus of herbaceous plants, *Stellaria*, esp. *greater stitchwort*, with white star-like flowers and grass-like leaves.

stithy, n. [1. stídhi ; 2. stíði], fr. M.E. *stithe, stethe*, 'anvil', fr. O.N. *steði*, 'anvil' ; cogn. w. **stead**. (archaic) Smith's workshop, smithy, forge.

stiver, n. [1. stíver ; 2. stáivə], fr. Du. *stuiver*, small coin formerly current in the Netherlands. A trifling amount ; worthless object : *not worth a stiver ; to lose every stiver one possesses*.

stoa, n. [1. stóa ; 2. stóuə]. Gk. *sto(i)á*, 'colonnade, cloister, portico', prob. fr. the base **sthă-, *sthau-* &c., 'to be upright', seen in Gk. *stûlos*, 'column', see **style**(III.) ; cogn. w. Scrt. *sthănă*, 'pillar' ; O.E. *stōw*, 'place' ; see **stow** & words there referred to. Cp. also **stoic**. (Gk. archit.) Cloister; colonnade walled at the back, with the front opening upon a public place.

stoat, n. [1. stōt ; 2. stout]. M.E. *stōte*, inflected form of *stot*, 'stoat ; bullock ; male animal'; cp. Swed. *stut* ; Dan. *stud*, 'bullock' ; cogn. w. Goth. *stautan* ; O.H.G. *stōzan*, 'to push' ; Lat. *tundere*, 'to beat' ; cp. further O.E. *stunt*, 'dull' ; *styntan*, 'to stupefy', see **stint**. **1.** Small animal, *Mustela erminea*, resembling weasel, esp. in russet summer coat ; also called ermine in white winter coat. **2.** Any animal of weasel family.

stock (I.), n. [1. stok ; 2. stɔk]. O.E. *stocc*, 'trunk, log, stock'; M.E. *stoc(k)* ; cp. O. Fris. *stok* ; O.N. *stokkr* ; O.H.G. *stoc*, 'trunk, stock', orig. 'hewn stump ; log chopped off' ; cp. Norw. *stauka*, 'to strike, push'; O.N. *stūka*, 'to push'; cogn. w. Scrt. *tuñjati*, 'strikes, pushes'; Lith. *tūzgénti*, 'to knock at'. Cp. further, w. different formative element, Gk. *stúpos*, 'stock'; *túptein*, 'to strike'; *túpos*, 'stamp, impression', see **type**; O.N. *stufr*, 'stump'; O. Slav. *tŭpati*, 'to beat, palpitate'. See also **stint, stub, stump, stupid**. **1. a** Main stem of tree or plant ; esp. lower part of trunk ; bole, stem ; Phr. *stocks and stones*, inanimate, insensible, objects ; **b** (fig.) only in *laughing-stock*, butt, target, object, of attack, ridicule &c. **2.** Main body, base, solid part, serving as support, handle &c., of an object, piece of mechanism &c.: *stock of a rifle, plough, plane* &c.; specif. **a** *stock of an anvil*, support, heavy block, on which it stands; **b** *stock of an anchor*, wooden crosspiece into which the shank is fastened. **3.** (pl.) Framework of solid timbers supporting ship in course of construction. Phr. *on the stocks*, in process of making, undergoing construction. **4.** (pl., hist.) Heavy wooden framework to which offenders were fastened by having their feet passed through holes in the timbers. **5. a** Stem into which a graft is inserted; **b** plant from which cuttings are taken. **6. a** Descent, ancestry, lineage: *to come of good, noble, talented, stock* &c.; **b** (biol.) colony, related group, of organisms. **7.** (of material and non-material things) **a** Supply on which one may draw, material ready for use; equipment, store, effects: *to lay in a stock of flour; a contribution to the common stock; the general stock of human knowledge;* Phrs. *live stock*, domestic animals kept on farm &c.; *dead stock*, agricultural implements &c. as part of equipment of farm; *to take stock,* (lit. and fig.) to make an inventory of, review, one's stock, assets; *to take stock of,* (fig.) estimate character &c. of, by observation; specif. **b** supply of articles of commerce kept in reserve at a given moment, by a shopkeeper, from which to supply his customers. Phr. *to have, keep, in stock,* have in store, on hand, and available for sale. **8.** Raw or partially prepared material for manufacture &c.; specif. **a** also *paper-stock,* rags, pulp &c., for making paper; **b** also *soup-stock,* broth, liquor, in which bones, vegetables &c. have been boiled, used in cooking for making soup, gravy &c. **9. a** Broad band of leather or stiffened silk &c., formerly worn by men round neck; now largely superseded by a collar and tie, though still worn in modified forms; **b** woman's upright collar. **10.** Genus, *Matthiola,* of half-shrubby garden plants, usually having brightly coloured, scented flowers. **11.** (finance) **a** Originally a wooden tally representing a sum of money lent to the king; hence, **b** money lent at specified rate of interest to a government, usually divided into shares or units of £100; *the stocks,* the total of the money lent to a State upon which interest is paid: *to have money in the stocks;* **c** capital of a company or corporation divided into units, often of £100, entitling holders to a proportion of the profits.

stock (II.), vb. trans. & intrans., fr. prec. **A.** trans. **1.** To supply with stock, equip, store: *to stock a shop with goods; to stock a farm; a mind well stocked with information.* **2.** To keep in stock, have as part of regular stock: *the shop only stocks cheap goods.* **3.** To fit, supply (gun &c.), with stock. **4.** To put in the stocks as punishment. **5.** To sow, plant (land). **B.** intrans. (of plant) To produce suckers.

stock (III.), adj., fr. **stock** (I.). **a** Constantly kept in stock: *stock sizes in boots;* hence, **b** (fig.) habitually produced, stereotyped, commonplace, hackneyed: *stock examples, jokes, arguments.*

stockade, n. & vb. trans. [1. stokád; 2. stɔ̀kéid]. Fr. *estacade, estocade,* cp. O. Fr. *estaque,* 'a stake', of Gmc. origin, see **stake**; cp. Ital. *steccata,* 'palisade'; Fr. form w. *o,* & present Engl. form influenced by **stock**(I.) or its continental cognates. **1.** n. Barrier, enclosure, wooden fence, for defence, consisting of a series of stakes or posts planted upright in the ground; a palisade. **2.** vb. To defend, supply, with a stockade, set up a stockade around.

stock-book, n. Commercial register of goods bought and sold.

stock-breeder, n. Person engaged in breeding live stock.

stock-broker, n. Member of Stock Exchange who buys and sells stocks and shares for clients.

stock-broking, n. Business, occupation, of a stock-broker.

stock-car, n. Railway truck for transporting cattle &c.

stockdove, n. [1. stókduv; 2. stɔ́kdav]. Small, dark, European wild pigeon, without the white markings of the ring-dove; so called as nesting in stocks of trees or as supposed to be of the original stock from which domestic pigeons were bred.

Stock Exchange, n. **a** Organized body or association of stock-brokers, the membership of which is limited and regulated by various conditions imposed by the governing body; **b** the building in which stock-brokers meet to discuss and transact their business.

stock-farm, n. Farm used for the raising of live-stock.

stock-farmer, n. Farmer engaged in the rearing of cattle, sheep &c.

stockfish, n. [1. stókfish; 2. stɔ́kfiʃ]. Cod, hake &c., prepared for keeping by being split and dried without salt.

stock-gang, n. Set of saws in saw-mill cutting log into series of planks by single simultaneous action.

stock-gillyflower, n. Genus of half-shrubby garden plants with scented flowers, now usually *stock;* see **stock** (I.), 10.

stock-holder, n. (finance) Owner of stock.

stockily, adv. [1. stókili; 2. stɔ́kili]. **stocky** & -ly. In a stocky manner.

stockiness, n. [1. stókines; 2. stɔ́kinis]. See prec. & -ness. Quality of being stocky.

stockinet, n. [1. stókinèt; 2. stɔ́kinèt]. Next word & -et. Elastic knitted or woven material for dresses, underclothing &c.

stocking, n. [1. stókiŋ; 2. stɔ́kiŋ]. **stock** (I.) & -ing (III.); cp. earlier (*nether*)-*stocks,* from knee downwards, regarded as cut off from original long hose, from waist downwards. **1.** Knitted or woven, elastic, close-fitting covering for leg and foot, made of wool, silk, cotton thread &c.; often *pair of stockings.* Phrs. *to stand six feet in one's stockings,* i.e. without additional height given by heel of shoe; *elastic stocking* &c., surgical device, shaped like a stocking or part of stocking, woven with rubber &c., for compressing part of leg. **2.** Lower part of leg of horse &c., when of distinct colour from upper part: *a horse with one white stocking.*

stockinged, adj. [1. stókingd; 2. stɔ́kiŋd]. Prec. & -ed. Wearing, covered with, stocking(s); chiefly in compounds, *silk-stockinged* &c.

stocking-feet, n. pl. *In* (*his*) *stocking-feet,* without boots or shoes.

stocking-frame, n. Machine for knitting stockings.

stockingless, adj. [1. stókingles; 2. stɔ́kiŋlis]. **stocking** & -less. Without stocking(s).

stocking-loom, n. Machine for knitting stockings.

stock-in-trade, n. **a** Stock goods, appliances, equipment, tools &c. required for the carrying on of particular trade, business, occupation: *books are a scholar's stock-in-trade;* **b** (fig.) any habitual, stereotyped trick, mannerism, trite utterance, set phrase &c., characteristic of a particular profession or individual: *grimaces and posturings are part of an actor's stock-in-trade; catchwords, and promises never to be fulfilled, are the stock-in-trade of the professional politician.*

stock-jobber, n. Member of the Stock Exchange from whom the broker buys and to whom he sells stocks and shares on behalf of his clients.

stockless, adj. [1. stókles; 2. stɔ́klis]. **stock** (I.) & -less. Without a stock, esp. of gun &c.

stock-list, n. Periodical list of current prices of stocks and shares.

stock-man, n. (chiefly Australian) Man in charge of stock on farm &c.

stock-market, n. **a** Stock Exchange; **b** business transacted on Stock Exchange.

stock-owl, n. Eagle-owl.

stock-pot, n. Vessel in which bones &c. are boiled to make stock.

stock-raising, n. [1. stók ràzing; 2. stɔ́k rèiziŋ]. The raising of live-stock on a farm &c.

stock-rider, n. (chiefly Australian) A mounted herdsman.

stock-still, adv. As still as a stock; absolutely motionless: *to stand stock-still.*

stock-taking, n. Periodical taking of inventory of stock in a shop &c.

stock-whip, n. Herdsman's short-handled, long-lashed whip.

stocky, adj. [1. stóki; 2. stɔ́ki]. **stock** (I.) & -y (IV.). Short and thickset, sturdy.

stock-yard, n. Enclosure fitted with pens &c., where cattle &c. are kept for market &c.

stodge, n. & vb. intrans. [1. stoj; 2. stɔdʒ]. Possibly imitative. **1.** n. **a** Heavy, solid food; **b** substantial, heavy meal; **c** (fig.) dull, heavy intellectual pabulum. **2.** vb. To eat heartily and greedily; to stuff and cram.

stodginess, n. [1. stójines; 2. stɔ́dʒinis]. Next word & -ness. State or quality of being stodgy.

stodgy, adj. [1. stóji; 2. stɔ́dʒi]. **stodge** & -y (IV.). **1.** (of food &c.) Heavy, solid, substantial. **2.** (of literary style &c.) Dull, heavy, uninteresting, difficult to read; verbose; lacking lightness of touch.

stoep, n. [1. stoop; 2. stūp]. S. Afr. Du., in European Du. = 'a threshold'; cogn. w. O.H.G. *stuopa,* 'threshold'; Mod. Germ. *stufe,* 'stage, degree'; cp. **step** (I.). Verandah in front of African Dutch house.

stoic (I.), n. [1. stóik; 2. stóuik], fr. Gk. *stōikós,* 'Stoic', fr. *stoá,* 'cloister, colonnade', specif., the *Stoā Poikílē,* 'Painted Porch', the colonnade at Athens where Zeno and his followers taught; see **stoa** & -ic. **1.** (cap.) Follower of the philosopher Zeno of Citium (c. 340–260 B.C.), who taught that virtue or conformation to the divine will was the highest good and insisted on complete submission to the divine will with indifference to external pleasure and pain. **2.** Person who does not feel, or controls, personal emotions; person of rigid calm, fortitude, or impassivity.

stoic (II.), adj., fr. prec. (often cap.) Of, pertaining to, characteristic of, a Stoic: *Stoic doctrines; stoic calm* &c.

stoical, adj. [1. stóikl; 2. stóuikl]. **stoic** (I.) & -al. Pertaining to, characteristic of, resembling, a Stoic; hence, impassive, indifferent to external conditions and circumstances.

stoically, adv. Prec. & -ly. In a stoical manner; like a Stoic.

stoichiometry, n. [1. stòikiómetri; 2. stɔ̀ikiɔ́mitri], fr. Gk. *stoikheîon,* 'base, element', fr. same as *stoikhos,* 'row', see **stichic** &-metry. That branch of chemistry which deals with determination of atomic and molecular weights of elements &c.

stoicism, n. [1. stóisizm; 2. stóuisìzəm]. **stoic** (I.) & -ism. **1.** (cap.) Doctrine, philosophy, of the Stoics. **2.** Stoical impassivity, calm fortitude, rigid indifference.

stoke, vb. trans. & intrans. [1. stōk; 2. stouk], fr. **stoker**. **1.** trans. **a** To feed (furnace, fire &c.) with fuel; **b** to feed furnace of (engine &c.). **2.** intrans. **a** To tend a furnace, act as stoker; **b** (slang, also *stoke up*) to eat, take, a meal.

stokehold, n. [1. stókhōld; 2. stóukhould]. Space, compartment, from which ship's boilers are fed.

stoke-hole, n. Small room or enclosure near a furnace in which a stoker works.

stoker, n. [1. stóker; 2. stóukə], fr. Du., fr. *stoken,* 'to light a fire', fr. *stok,* 'stick', cogn. w. **stock** (I.). **1.** Person employed in feeding a furnace, esp. of boiler on ship, steam-engine &c.; a fireman. **2.** Mechanical device for supplying a furnace with fuel.

Stokes mortar, n. [1. stóks mórtar; 2. stóuks mɔ̀tə], fr. inventor, Sir Wilfrid Stokes (1860–1927). Light, easily transported, trench mortar; also *Stokes gun.*

stole (I.), n. [1. stōl; 2. stoul], fr. Lat. *stola*, fr. Gk. *stolé*, 'equipment; apparel; garment'; cp. Gk. *stéllein*, 'to put in position; to arrange, equip, prepare; to array, dress'; *stélē*, 'column'; see **stele**, & words there referred to. **1.** (also in Lat. form, *stola*) Long outer garment of Roman matron. **2.** Long strip of coloured cloth or silk, usually embroidered and having fringed ends, part of the Eucharistic vestments, worn over the neck so that the ends hang down in front on either side, and reach to just above the knee. **3.** Woman's long, narrow wrap of fur &c. worn round the neck with the ends hanging down.

stole (II.), n., fr. **stolon**. Stolon.

stole (III.), vb. Pret. of **steal**; fr. P.P.

stoled, adj. [1. stōld; 2. stould]. **stole** (I.) & -ed. Wearing a stole.

stolen, vb. [1. stōlen; 2. stóulən]. P.P. of **steal**; O.E. (*ge*)*stolen*; M.E. *stōlen*.

stolid, adj. [1. stólid; 2. stólid], fr. Lat. *stolidus*, 'slow, dull, obtuse'; cp. Lat. *stultus*, 'foolish', see **stultify**; cogn. w. O.E. *still*, 'motionless', see **still** (I.); cp. further Lat. *locus*, O. Lat. *stlocus*, 'place', see **locus**; Gk. *stéllein*, 'to place', see **stele**. Dull and impassive, not betraying emotion; lifeless, lacking animation or agitation.

stolidity, n. [1. stolíditi; 2. stolíditi], fr. Lat. *stoliditātem*, 'obtuseness'; prec. & -ity. State or quality of being stolid.

stolidly, adv. [1. stólidli; 2. stólidli]. **stolid** & -ly. In a stolid manner.

stolidness, n. [1. stólidnes; 2. stólidnis]. See prec. & -ness. Quality of being stolid; stolidity.

stolon, n. [1. stólon; 2. stóulən]. Lat. *stolōn*-, nom. *stolō*, 'shoot; sucker'; possibly, according to Walde, fr. base *(s)telā-, *stolā- &c., 'broad, extended', whence Lat. *lātus*, earlier *stlātus, 'broad', see **latitude**. Prostrate shoot, or sucker from a plant, which roots; a runner, an offset.

stolonate, adj. [1. stólonāt; 2. stóulənèit]. Prec. & -ate. Having, producing, a stolon.

stoloniferous, adj. [1. stoloníferus; 2. stòulənífərəs]. **stolon** & -i- & -**ferous**. Producing a stolon.

stoma, n. [1. stóma; 2. stóumə]. Gk. *stóma*, 'mouth'; see **stomach** (I.). Minute mouth-like orifice in one of the lower animals, or in a plant cell.

stomach (I.), n. [1. stúmak; 2. stámək]. M.E. *stomak*, fr. O. Fr. *estomac*, fr. Lat. *stomachus*, 'gullet; stomach; taste' (lit. and fig.), fr. Gk. *stómakhos*, 'gullet', fr. *stóma*, 'mouth'; cogn. w. Goth. *stibna*; O. Fris. *stifne*; O.E. *stefn*, 'voice'. **1.** Internal sac in the animal body within which the chief part of the process of digestion is carried on, formed by an enlargement of the alimentary canal, connected with the mouth by the gullet, and passing on the digested food into the intestine. **2.** The lower external front part of the body below the diaphragm; the belly, abdomen : *to get a kick in the stomach*; *a pain in the stomach*. **3. a** Desire for food; appetite; **b** desire, inclination, generally : *no stomach for fighting*. **4.** (archaic) Disposition, character; bearing and deportment as expressive of these : *a man of a proud and haughty stomach*.

stomach (II.), vb. trans., fr. prec. **1.** To deal with in the stomach, to digest; hence to relish, manage to eat (food). **2.** (fig.) To tolerate, put up with, accept without protest : *to stomach an insult*; *insolence from an insignificant scoundrel is more than I will stomach*.

stomach-ache, n. Pain in stomach or bowels.

stomachal, adj. [1. stúmakl; 2. stáməkl]. **stomach** (I.) & -al. Of, pertaining to, the stomach.

stomach-cough, n. Cough caused by irritation in digestive organs.

stomacher, n. [1. stúmaker; 2. stámәkә]. **stomach** (I.) & -er. Part of woman's dress in 15th-17th cents., consisting of a piece of material, triangular in shape, often embroidered or otherwise ornamented, covering breast and upper part of abdomen.

stomachful (I.), n. [1. stúmakfool; 2. stáməkful]. **stomach** (I.) & -ful. Amount sufficient to fill the stomach.

stomachful (II.), adj. (archaic or obs.) Proud, haughty.

stomachic, adj. & n. [1. stomákik; 2. stomǽkik]. **stomach** (I.) & -ic. **1.** adj. **a** Pertaining to, connected with, arising from, the stomach; **b** promoting action of the stomach; digestive. **2.** n. Medicinal substance with stomachic properties.

stomachless, adj. [1. stúmakles; 2. stáməklis]. **stomach** (I.) & -less. **a** Without a stomach; **b** without appetite.

stomach-pump, n. Apparatus with indiarubber tube attached used for washing out the stomach.

stomach-staggers, n. Apoplexy in horses, caused by paralysis of the stomach.

stomach-tooth, n. Infant's lower canine tooth.

stomach-tube, n. One of the tubes of a stomach-pump.

stomatitis, n. [1. stomatítis; 2. stòumətáitis]. See next word & -itis. Inflammation of the mucous membrane of mouth, as in thrush &c.

stomato-, pref. representing Gk. *stómat*-, stem of *stóma*, 'mouth', q.v. under **stomach** (I.). Mouth; e.g. *stomatogastric*, of mouth and stomach.

stomatology, n. [1. stomatóloji; 2. stóumətólədži]. **stomato-** & -**logy**. The study of the diseases of the mouth.

stomatoscope, n. [1. stomátoskŏp; 2. stóumətəskòup]. **stomato-** & -**scope**. Instrument for inspecting the mouth.

stone (I.), n. [1. stōn; 2. stoun], O.E. *stān*; M.E. *stōn*; cp. O.H.G. *stein*; O. Fris. *stēn*; Du. *steen*; O.N. *steinn*; Goth. *stains*, 'stone'; cp. further O. Slav. *stěna*, 'wall'; fr. base *stei(ā)-, *sti-, &c., 'to stiffen, become thick, compressed'; seen also in Lat. *stīpāre*, 'to pack closely', see **stipate**; Gk. *stía*, 'pebble'; Lith. *stings*, 'stiff'; Lat. *stīpes*, 'stem, pillar'; see **stipes**; O.E. *stif*, see **stiff** (I.). **1.** Single lump or piece of rock of comparatively small size : *to throw stones*; *to trip over a stone*; *the horse has a stone in its hoof*; *a heap of stones*. Phrs. *rolling stone*, person of restless temperament and habits; esp. one who is constantly changing his occupation, situation, and place of abode; *to leave no stone unturned*, use every effort; *to throw a stone at*, (fig.) make an imputation against, to censure; *to mark* (*a day*) *with a white stone*, record as exceptionally happy or fortunate; *stone of Sisyphus*, task involving constant, but unsuccessful effort; *a stone's throw*, short distance; *as cold, as hard, as a stone*, very cold, or hard; *precious stone*, a gem of high value, such as a diamond, ruby, sapphire &c. **2.** Solid mineral matter, rock, esp. as material for building &c.: *a wall of stone*; *a floor paved with stone*; *blocks of stone*; also in compounds: *sandstone, limestone* &c. Phr. *a heart of stone*, an unfeeling, callous nature. **3.** Block or slab of stone cut or shaped for some specific purpose; usually in compounds, e.g. *paving-, stepping-stone, millstone, oilstone, keystone* &c.; specif. **a** for sharpening tools &c.: *whetstone, grindstone* &c.; **b** as memorial, often inscribed : *tombstone, gravestone, headstone* &c.; **c** *curling-stone*; **d** stone used for lithographing. **4.** Specif., a precious stone of any kind, a gem: *a ring set with five stones*. **5.** A hailstone. **6.** (bot.) **a** Hard shell enclosing the kernel of certain fruits; e.g. *peach-, plum-, cherry-stone* &c.; **b** hard, grain-like seed of the grape. **7.** (med.) **a** Hard concretion formed in an organ of the body, calculus, esp. *gallstone*; **b** disease characterized by such a concretion : *an operation for stone*. **8.** (archaic) A testicle. **9.** (with invariable pl., 10 stone &c.) Measure of weight differing in different substances : avoirdupois weight, 14 lb.; in weighing meat, 8 lb.; cheese, 16 lb.; hay, 22 lb.; wool, 24 lb.

stone (II.), vb. trans., fr. prec. **1.** To throw stones at, pelt with stones : *to stone a man to death*. **2.** To supply with stone paving, lining, facing &c.: *to stone a wall, well* &c. **3.** To remove stone from (cherries, raisins &c.).

stone (III.), adj., fr. **stone** (I.). Connected with, pertaining to, made of, stone(s) : *a stone wall*; *stone implements*.

Stone Age, n. Prehistoric period in which stone was used for weapons, cutting-tools &c.

stone-axe, n. Heavy axe with short handle at right angles, having one blunt edge for breaking and one sharper edge for shaping stone.

stone-blind, adj. Quite blind.

stone-blue, n. Mixture of indigo and whiting.

stone-boiling, n. Primitive method of heating water for cooking by placing hot stones in it.

stone-borer, n. Kind of bivalve.

stone brash, n. Limy subsoil containing detached pieces of stone of varying size.

stone-break, n. Saxifrage.

stone-breaker, n. **a** One who breaks stones, esp. for road-making &c.; **b** machine for crushing stones.

stone-buck, n. Steenbok.

stone-butter, n. Variety of alum.

stone-cast, n. As far as one can fling a stone, short distance, stone's cast.

stonechat, n. Small European bird, *Pratincola rubicola*, black above, with reddish breast and white collar, allied to the wheatear.

stone-circle, n. Prehistoric ring of upright megaliths.

stone-coal, n. **a** Mineral coal, as opposed to *charcoal*; **b** hard coal, anthracite.

stone-cold, adj. Very cold, quite cold.

stonecrop, n. [1. stónkrop; 2. stóunkrɔp]. Sedum; esp. *common stonecrop*, small creeping plant with fleshy leaves and yellow flowers.

stone-curlew, n. Large species of plover, the thick-kneed curlew or plover, *Oedicnemus*.

stone-cutter, n. Person employed in shaping stone for architectural purposes &c.

stoned, adj. [1. stōnd; 2. stound]. **stone** (I.) & -ed. (of fruit) With stone(s) removed: *stoned raisins*.

stone-dead, adj. Quite dead.

stone-deaf, adj. Completely deaf.

stone-dresser, n. Person employed in dressing stone for building &c.

stone-eater, n. Stone-borer.

stone fence, n. (U.S. slang) Mixed alcoholic drink, esp. whisky and cider.

stone-fern, n. Kind of fern growing on stone walls.

stone-fly, n. Kind of insect used as fishing-fly.

stone-fruit, n. Fruit containing a stone; drupe, e.g. plum, damson &c., as opposed to *soft fruit*.

stone-gall, n. Clayey mass sometimes found in sandstone.

stone-horse, n. (archaic) Stallion.

stoneless, adj. [1. stónles; 2. stóunlis]. **stone** (I.) & -less. (esp. of fruit) Without a stone.

stone-lily, n. Fossil crinoid.

stone-man, n. Cairn.

stone-mason, n. Man employed in hewing, dressing, and laying building-stone.

stone-parsley, n. Tall herb of parsley family, with clusters of creamy flowers.

stone-pine, n. Umbrella-shaped pine of Mediterranean coast, with edible seeds.

stone-pit, n. Pit from which stone is quarried.

stone-pitch, n. Hard pitch.

stone-plover, n. Stone-curlew.

stone-rag, n. Kind of lichen.

stone-rue, n. Kind of fern.

stone-saw, n. Instrument for cutting stone.

stone-snipe, n. North American bird, yellow-legs.

stone-still, adj. As still as a stone, very still.

stone-walling, n. [1. stōn wáwling; 2. stóun wɔ́liŋ]. **1.** (cricket) Batting with little effort to make runs. **2.** (politics) Opposition by obstruction.

stone-ware, n. Kind of coarse, glazed pottery, made of siliceous clay.

stone-weed, n. Kind of plant with stony seeds, lithospermum, gromwell.

stone-work, n. Masonry.

stonewort, n. [1. stṓnwërt; 2. stóunwʌ̄t]. Kind of wild parsley.

stonily, adv. [1. stṓnili; 2. stóunili]. **stony** & **-ly**. In a stony manner.

stoniness, n. [1. stṓnines; 2. stóuninis]. Next word & **-ness**. State or quality of being stony.

stony, adj. [1. stṓni; 2. stóuni]. **stone (I.)** & **-y (IV.)**. **1.** Of, containing, full of, stones: *stony ground*; *a stony path.* Phr. (slang) *stony broke,* financially ruined. **2.** (fig.) **a** Like stone, hard, unfeeling: *a stony heart*; **b** fixed, unmoving: *a stony stare.*

stony-hearted, adj. Unfeeling, pitiless.

stood, vb. [1. stood; 2. stud]. O.E. *stōd*, M.E. *stood*, Pret. & P.P. of **stand (I.)**.

stook, n. & vb. trans. [1. stook; 2. stuk]. M.E. *stouke*, 'pile of sheaves'; cp. L.G. *stūke*, 'bundle'. **1.** n. Group of sheaves of corn set up in field; shock. **2.** vb. To set up, arrange (sheaves, corn &c.), in stooks.

stool (I.), n. [1. stōōl; 2. stūl]. O.E., M.E. *stōl*; cp. Goth. *stōls*; O.N. *stōll*; O.H.G. *stuol*, 'stool, seat'; cogn. w. O. Slav. *stolŭ*, 'throne, seat'; Lith. *pastólas*, 'stand'; fr. base **stā-*, **stə-* &c., 'to stand', as in **stand**; **state (I.)** &c. **1.** Seat for one person, consisting of a flat top supported by one, three, or four legs, and without a back. Phr. *to fall between two stools*, lose an opportunity by hesitating between two courses. **2.** Low stool or bench for resting feet or kneeling on; also *footstool.* **3.** **a** Seat used for evacuation of the bowels; Phr. *to go to stool*, evacuate the bowels; **b** act of evacuating bowels; **c** faeces discharged. **4.** Portable framework to which a wooden pigeon is attached to serve as decoy. **5.** Root from which a sprout or sucker springs.

stool (II.), vb. intrans., fr. prec. **1.** (of plant) To produce shoots or suckers. **2.** (archaic or obs.) To evacuate the bowels.

stool-ball, n. Game resembling cricket, popular in 17th cent., and now played in Sussex and elsewhere, chiefly by women.

stool-pigeon, n. Wooden pigeon used as decoy; also fig., chiefly U.S.A., of persons.

stoop (I.), vb. intrans. & trans. [1. stōōp; 2. stūp]. O.E. *stūpian*; M.E. *stūpen*; cp. O.N. *stūpa*; M. Du. *stuipen*; cogn. w. **steep (I.)**. **A.** intrans. **1.** To curve, bend, the upper part of the body forwards and downwards towards the ground: *to stoop to pick a flower*; *the doorway is so low that you must stoop.* **2.** (fig.) To demean oneself by unworthy conduct; lower oneself by an action below one's dignity and character; to condescend: *to stoop to meanness and duplicity*; rarely absol., but cp. title of Goldsmith's play, '*She Stoops to Conquer*'. **3.** To hold, carry, oneself with the back and shoulders curved and bent forward: *sit up straight and don't stoop*; *to stoop over one's books.* **4.** **a** (of hawk &c.) To swoop; **b** hence (fig.) to pounce, make swooping attack. **B.** trans. To bend (head and neck) forward and downwards.

stoop (II.), n., fr. prec. Act, position, of stooping; curved, hunched attitude of the back and shoulders: *he has a shocking stoop.*

stoop (III.), n. See **stoup**.

stoop (IV.), n. Variant spelling of **stoep**. (U.S.A.) Uncovered verandah, porch, platform &c. at door of house.

stooping, adj. [1. stōōping; 2. stūpiŋ], fr. Pres. Part. of **stoop (I.)**. Bent forward and downward; bowed, humped: *stooping shoulders.*

stoopingly, adv. Prec. & **-ly**. In a stooping manner.

stop (I.), vb. trans. & intrans. [1. stop; 2. stɔp]. O.E. (*for*)*stoppian*, 'to stop up, close'; M.E. *stoppen*; cp. O.N. *stoppa*; M. Du. *stoppen*; M.H.G. *stopfen*; fr. L. Lat. *stuppāre*, 'to stuff, stop up', fr. Lat. *stuppa*, 'tow', fr. Gk. *stúppē*, 'tow'; possibly cogn. w. Scrt. *stupáš*, 'tuft of hair'. **A.** trans. **1.** **a** To stuff up, close, place obstruction in, so as to check egress or ingress: *to stop a hole, leak, crack* &c.; Phrs. *to stop one's ears*, (i.) place hands &c. over them to prevent hearing; (ii.) (fig.) refuse to listen; *to stop a gap*, (fig.) act as substitute in emergency &c.; take someone's place; *to stop a person's mouth*, (colloq.) prevent his speaking; *to stop the way*, (lit. and fig.) hinder progress or passage; **b** specif., to stanch, check: *to stop the flow of blood*; **c** to fill up, pack tightly with cement &c.: *to stop a tooth.* **2.** **a** To cause (moving object) to cease motion; to arrest motion of, cause to come to rest, bring to a standstill: *to stop the traffic, a runaway horse*; *stop the train!*; *he was running too fast to stop himself*; *the fielder stopped the ball*; **b** to cause to cease operation, put out of action: *to stop an engine, watch* &c. **3.** To arrest progress or course of, cause cessation of, hold up (action or process): *to stop a fight*; *the rain stopped further play*; *frost has stopped the growth of plants.* Phr. *to stop a cheque*, order bank not to pay it. **4.** To prevent, hinder (person &c.) from action: *nothing will stop his, him from, interfering*; *what is to stop me from coming?* **5.** (of agent) To discontinue, leave off, cease from (an action which one is in course of performing): *to stop work*; *to stop talking*; *stop that chatter!* **6.** To discontinue supply of, cut off, deprive of: *to stop one's allowance, wages* &c. Phr. *to stop payment*, (i.) to stop a cheque &c., (ii.) (of bank), be unable to continue financial operations. **7.** (mus.) To alter pitch of musical note by pressing down string, closing hole &c., to change rate of vibration: *to stop a string* &c. **8.** (naut.) To make fast, lash firmly. **B.** intrans. **1.** **a** To cease movement or advance, come to rest, halt: *the train stops at all stations*; *to stop short, stop dead*; *it's time we stopped to rest*; **b** (of mechanism, organ &c.) to cease operation, cease to function: *the clock has stopped*; *his heart had stopped.* **2.** **a** To break off, discontinue, make an end of action; to pause: *he began to speak, but suddenly stopped*; *we will work for an hour and then stop*; **b** to be discontinued, come to an end: *the music, rain, rush of visitors &c., has stopped.* **3.** (colloq.) To stay, remain for a time: *to stop at home, in bed* &c.; *don't stop out too long*; *to stop with friends, at a hotel* &c., be a guest, visitor. **C.** Followed by adverbs or prepositions, with special meanings. *Stop down*, trans., (photog.) to reduce exposed part of (lens) by partially covering with a diaphragm. *Stop off*, intrans., (founding) to fill up part of mould with sand. *Stop out*, trans., (etching) to cover part of (plate &c.), with some substance which prevents action of acid upon that part. *Stop up*, trans., to obstruct, choke, close, fill up: *to stop up a hole*; *the drain is stopped up.*

stop (II.), n., fr. prec. **1.** Act of stopping; state of being stopped; cessation of movement or action: *to come to a sudden stop*; *the train goes through without a stop*; *Oxford is the first stop*, i.e. place of first stop. Phr. *to put a stop to*, cause to cease, bring to an end. **2.** (mus.) **a** Key or other device for depressing string, closing hole, &c. to alter pitch of note; **b** lever, movable knob &c., for opening or closing particular set of organ pipes, and producing specific quality or volume of tone; **c** (fig.) quality, character, of speech; style, tone &c. designed to produce specific effect: *to pull out the sympathetic stop.* **3.** Punctuation mark; *full stop*, dot indicating end of sentence, an abbreviation &c.; a period. Phr. *to come to a full stop*, (fig.) be obstructed or checked in action, be unable to continue. **4.** (joinery) Peg, block &c., checking movement of drawer, window-sash, door &c., at specific point. **5.** (phon.) Also *stop consonant*, consonant formed by complete stoppage of air-stream at some point, followed by its sudden release. **6.** (photog.) Diaphragm reducing aperture of lens. **7.** (naut.) Line used for lashing.

stop (III.), vb. trans., fr. prec. To put in the stops (in a piece of writing); to punctuate.

stop-cock, n. Tap for opening or closing pipe, cask &c.

stop-collar, n. Ring limiting motion of shaft &c.

stop-cylinder, n. Kind of mechanical printing press.

stop-drill, n. Drill with collar stopping its operation at specific depth.

stope, n. [1. stōp; 2. stoup]. Perh. connected w. **step**. (min.) Space cut through seam, usually roughly in the form of steps, between two galleries in a mine.

stopgap, n. [1. stópgap; 2. stɔ́pgæp]. Person or object supplying the place of another in an emergency.

stop-knob, n. Knob controlling organ-stop.

stopless, adj. [1. stóples; 2. stɔ́plis]. **stop (II.)** & **-less**. Without stops.

stop-motion, n. Mechanical device for arresting motion of machine automatically at certain point(s).

stop-order, n. Order fixing the prices above or below which stock is to be bought or sold, in order to limit losses.

stoppage, n. [1. stópij; 2. stɔ́pidž]. **stop (I.)** & **-age**. Act of stopping, state of being stopped; cessation of action, movement, or progress.

stopper (I.), n. [1. stóper; 2. stɔ́pə]. **stop (I.)** & **-er**. **1.** One who, that which, stops; specif. **a** object designed to fit into and close an opening, esp. the mouth of bottle &c.; **b** *tobacco-stopper*, instrument for packing tobacco into pipe. **2.** (naut.) Line for lashing, checking motion of, or shortening a cable &c.

stopper (II.), vb. trans., fr. prec. To fit, close, with a stopper: *to stopper a bottle.*

stopping (I.), adj. [1. stóping; 2. stɔ́piŋ], fr. Pres. Part. of **stop (I.)**. Specif. (of train &c.) calling at intermediate stations; contrasted with *non-stop, fast, express, train.*

stopping (II.), n. **stop (I.)** & **-ing**. **1.** Act of one who, that which, stops; specif. (mus.) act of pressing a string or closing hole &c.; *double-stopping*, simultaneous stopping of two strings. **2.** Material used for stopping; specif., cement, gold &c. used to stop a tooth.

stop-plate, n. Plate fixed to the end of an axle to prevent too great lateral play of the wheel.

stopple, n. & vb. trans. [1. stópl; 2. stɔ́pl]. **stop (I.)** & **-le**. **1.** n. Object for closing mouth of bottle &c.; stopper. **2.** vb. To close with a stopple.

stop-press, n. Late news inserted in special column of a newspaper after printing has begun.

stop-valve, n. Valve for controlling volume of water or steam passing through a pipe.

stop-watch, n. Watch, the hands of which can be instantaneously stopped or started by pressing a knob in the rim, in order to measure the exact duration of an action or event.

storable, adj. [1. stṓrabl; 2. stɔ́rəbl]. **store (II.)** & **-able**. Capable of being stored, suitable for storing.

storage, n. [1. stṓrij; 2. stɔ́ridž]. **store (II.)** & **-age**. **1.** Act of storing, state of being stored: *in cold storage*, in refrigerator. **2.** Space devoted to, available for, storing goods. **3.** Charge made for storing of goods.

storage battery, n. (elect.) Accumulator.

storax, n. [1. stṓraks; 2. stɔ́ræks]. Lat. *storax*, fr. Gk. *stúrax*, 'kind of resin'; Semitic loan-word. **1.** Resin with scent like vanilla, formerly used in medicine; *liquid storax*, kind of balsam. **2.** Tree from which this resin is obtained.

store (I.), n. [1. stōr; 2. stɔ̄]. M.E. *stōr*, fr. O. Fr. *estōr*, fr. L. Lat. (*in*)*staurum*, fr. Lat. *instaurāre*, 'to renew, restore, repair', q.v. under **restore**, **steer (I.)**, **stauroscope**. **1.** **a** Reserve supply, stock, accumulation of goods, material, provisions, kept for use when needed: *a store of food, fuel &c.*; *to lay in stores for the winter*; Phrs. *to set store by*, consider valuable; *to set no (great) store by*, regard as unimportant; **b** (pl.) supply of goods of specific kind, or needed for specific purpose: *naval, military, ship's stores* &c.; *marine stores*, old ship materials, cables &c., offered for sale; **c** accumulation of knowledge in the mind: *a store of learning, information* &c.

2. Place in which goods are stored ; **a depôt, warehouse, magazine** &c. Phr. *in store,* (i.) reserved for future use ; (ii.) (fig.) reserved by fate ; destined to come or happen in the future : *to have a disappointment in store for one ; who knows what the future may hold in store?* **3.** Place in which goods are sold ; specif. **a** *stores,* large general shop containing a number of departments for sale of goods of various kinds ; **b** (Am.) *a store,* a shop ; *to buy candy and crackers at the store,* to buy sweets and biscuits at the shop. **4.** (usually pl.) Store-cattle.

store (II.), vb. trans. M.E. *stōren,* fr. O. Fr. *estorer,* fr. *estor,* ' store ', see prec. **1.** To fill, furnish, stock, with supplies, reserves ; **a** (in material sense) *to store one's cupboards with food ;* **b** *to store the mind with knowledge, with pleasant memories* &c. **2. a** Often *store up* (in material and non-material sense), to put away, lay up, set aside carefully, reserve, for future use, consideration &c. : *to store up fuel for the winter ; to store up a fact in one's mind ;* specif., **b** to place, deposit (furniture &c.), temporarily in warehouse &c., for safe-keeping ; **c** (of elect.) to accumulate. **3.** To hold, provide storage room for : *the shed will store 20 ton of coal.*

store-cattle, n. Cattle kept for future fattening for killing.

storehouse, n. [1. stórhous ; 2. stŏ́haus]. **a** Building in which goods &c. are stored ; warehouse, repository ; also **b** (fig., of person, mind &c.), *he is a storehouse of information.*

store-keeper, n. **1.** Official in charge of stores, esp. naval and military stores. **2.** (Am.) Shopkeeper.

store-room, n. Room in which supplies are kept, esp. for household use.

store-ship, n. Vessel carrying supplies for fleet &c.

storey, story, n. [1. stóri ; 2. stóri]. Earlier, ' building ', fr. O. Fr. *estorée,* P.P. of *estorer,* ' to build, construct ; to repair, renew ', fr. Lat. *(in)staurāre,* ' to renew ', see **store (II.)** ; or perh. fr. Med. Anglo-Lat. *(h)istoria* (as **history**) in the sense of storey marked by paintings, painted windows, carving &c. Single horizontal section of house or other building, the whole set of rooms, passages &c. on the same level. Phr. *the upper storey,* (slang) the brain, mind.

storeyed, storied, adj. [1. stórid ; 2. stó́rid]. Prec. & **-ed.** (of building) Having specified number of storeys : *three-storeyed* &c.

storey-post, n. Upright post supporting floor-beam &c.

storiated, adj. [1. stŏriāted ; 2. stŏ́rieitid], fr. **historiated.** (of letter, page, of book or manuscript) Decorated with elaborate design.

storied (I.), adj. [1. stórid ; 2. stó́rid]. **story (I.)** & **-ed. 1.** Celebrated, made famous, in story. **2.** Ornamented with, bearing, significant design or inscription, adorned with scene(s) from history &c. : ' *Storied windows richly dight* ' (Milton, ' Il Penseroso ', 158) ; ' *Can storied urn, or animated bust, Back to its mansion call the fleeting breath?* ' (Gray's ' Elegy ').

storied (II.), adj. See **storeyed.**

storiette, n. [1. stŏriét ; 2. stŏ́riét]. **story (I.)** & **-ette.** Story in miniature, very short tale.

storiology, n. [1. stŏriŏ́loji ; 2. stŏ́riŏlədȝi]. **story (I.)** & **-o-** & **-logy.** The study of folktales.

stork, n. [1. stork ; 2. stŏk]. O.E., M.E. *storc* ; cp. O.N. *storkr* ; M.L.G. *störk* ; O.H.G. *storch,* ' stork ' ; cogn. w. Gk. *tórgos,* ' vulture ' ; prob. fr. base **ster-g-,* ' strong ', expanded fr. **ster-* &c., ' stiff, firm, strong ', q.v. under **stare (I.), stark (I.).** Large, long-legged, long-necked, long-billed, wading bird resembling heron, ibis &c. ; esp. *common or white stork, Ciconia alba,* migratory European stork, often frequenting human habitations, nesting on housetops &c.

stork's bill, n. Plant of genus *Erodium* or *Pelargonium.*

storm (I.), n. [1. storm ; 2. stŏm]. O.E., M.E. *storm ;* cp. M.L.G., M. Du. *storm ;* O.H.G.

sturm ; O.N. *stormr,* ' storm, tumult ' ; fr. base seen in O.E. *styrian,* ' to stir up, put in motion, whirl round ', see **stir** &c. **1.** Violent atmospheric disturbance involving strong wind, with or without rain, sleet &c., and sometimes accompanied by thunder and lightning ; sometimes in compounds, indicating specific character of storm, e.g. *thunder-storm ; sand-, dust-storm,* clouds of sand, dust, carried and whirled round, by the wind ; *cyclonic storm,* cyclone ; *magnetic storm,* disturbance of magnetic field, indicated by oscillation of magnetic needle. Phr. *a storm in a tea-cup,* a fuss about trifles. **2.** Violent atmospheric precipitation, with or without wind : *a storm of rain, hail ;* also in compounds, *hail-, rain-, snow-storm* &c. **3.** (naut. and meteorol.) Wind of specific velocity, usually 70-80 miles per hour, between gale and hurricane. **4.** Dense shower or volley of objects flying through the air : *a storm of arrows, missiles* &c. **5.** Loud, repeated, tumultuous expression of emotion by persons, voices &c., in unison : *a storm of cheers, applause, hisses* &c. **6. a** Violent mental or emotional agitation, disturbance, commotion, gust of passion ; esp. one affecting a large number of people : *a storm of indignation swept over the country ;* cp. *brain-storm ;* Phr. *storm and stress,* period of restlessness, agitation, or revolutionary change, in intellectual development &c. ; **b** violent upheaval in social or political conditions : *the storm of revolution.* **7.** (mil.) Sudden violent assault on fortified post &c. Phr. *to take by storm,* (i.) capture by sudden attack ; hence (ii.) (fig.) captivate instantaneously and completely : *he took her, her affections, by storm.*

storm (II.), vb. trans. & intrans., fr. prec. **A.** trans. (mil.) To take by storm, capture by sudden assault. **B.** intrans. **1.** (of wind &c.) To be boisterous, violent, tempestuous. **2.** (fig.) To give violent expression to anger, agitation &c., to rage ; also, *storm at,* to upbraid loudly and violently ; to scold, vituperate.

storm-beaten, adj. Injured by storms.

storm-belt, n. Area in which storms are specially frequent.

storm-bird, n. Bird supposed to presage approach of storm, esp. stormy petrel.

storm-bound, adj. Delayed by storms.

storm-card, n. Chart indicating position of ship in relation to storm-centre.

storm-centre, n. **a** Point of lowest atmospheric pressure in a storm area ; **b** (fig.) person or group of persons who form a centre and starting-point of unrest and disturbance.

storm-cloud, n. **a** Cloud portending or accompanying storm ; hence, **b** (fig.) signs of approaching danger or disturbance.

storm-cock, n. Kind of bird, esp. fieldfare or missel-thrush.

storm-cone, n. Large canvas cone hoisted as storm-signal.

storm-door, n. Supplementary outer door to protect entrance to building &c. in a storm.

storm-drum, n. Canvas-covered cylinder used, in conjunction with storm-cone, as storm-signal.

stormer, n. [1. stórmer ; 2. stŏ́mə]. **storm (II.)** & **-er.** One who, that which, storms, esp. member of storming-party.

storm-finch, n. Stormy petrel.

stormful, adj. [1. stórmfool ; 2. stŏ́mful]. **storm (I)** & **-ful.** (rare) Abounding in storms.

storm-glass, n. Glass-tube containing a chemical solution, the precipitate of which changes in appearance in varying atmospheric conditions.

stormily, adv. [1. stórmili ; 2. stŏ́mili]. **stormy** & **-ly.** In a stormy manner.

storminess, n. [1. stórmines ; 2. stŏ́minis]. See prec. & **-ness.** State or quality of being stormy.

storming-party, n. [1. stórming pàrti ; 2. stŏ́miŋ pàti]. Member of military party detailed to storm fortified post &c.

stormless, adj. [1. stórmles ; 2. stŏ́mlis]. **storm (I.)** & **-less.** Without, free from, storms.

storm-petrel, n. Stormy petrel.

storm-proof, adj. Not liable to be injured, affected, or penetrated by storm.

storm-sail, n. Heavy canvas sail used in rough weather.

storm-signal, n. Signal displayed on coast &c. to give warning of storm.

storm-tossed, adj. [1. stórm tost ; 2. stŏ́m tost]. (lit. and fig.) Suffering from effects of storm.

storm-wind, n. Violent wind, constituting or accompanying a storm.

storm-window, n. Extra, external window for protection in a storm.

stormy, adj. [1. stórmi ; 2. stŏ́mi]. **storm (I.)** & **-y (IV.). 1.** Of, pertaining to, characteristic of, agitated by, storms : *stormy weather, winds, sea.* **2.** Indicating presence or approach of storm : *a stormy sunset, sky* &c. ; *stormy petrel,* kind of petrel thought to portend a storm, called by sailors ' Mother Carey's chicken '. **3.** Characterized by violent emotion ; passionate, agitated by strong contending feeling, opinions &c. : *a stormy discussion ; the meeting was rather stormy.*

storm-zone, n. Storm-belt.

stort(h)ing, n. [1. stórting ; 2. stó́tiŋ]. Norw., lit. ' the great meeting or place of discussion ' ; fr. O.N. *storr,* ' great ', ' proud ', see under **stare (I.),** & O.N. *þing,* ' meeting ', see under **thing.** Norwegian parliament.

story (I.), n. [1. stóri ; 2. stó́ri]. M.E., fr. A.-Fr. *storie ;* O. Fr. *estoire,* fr. Lat. *historia,* see **history. 1. a** History ; account and description of a series of past events and actions: *the story of the rise of England's sea-power ;* ' *In this harsh world draw thy breath in pain, To tell my story* ' (' Hamlet ') ; **b** what is told in the form of traditional, often legendary, recital, concerning the lives and adventures of heroes and other great personages of the past : *a name famous in story ; the story goes that.* **2. a** Piece of imaginative writing, whether in prose or verse, shorter than a novel, describing adventures and episodes in the lives of a group of personages ; esp. an account of a complete action or adventure with a rounded-off conclusion ; also *short story ;* **b** a recital by word of mouth of such an action or adventure ; a tale : *please tell us a story ; children like to listen to a story.* Phr. *a very different story,* something quite different. **3.** An interesting series of events, adventures, actions, associated with a person or object : *there is often a story connected with a famous jewel.* **4.** A brief, pointed, narrative, relating a single saying, adventure, or action of a specific person ; an anecdote : *he told some good stories of Oxford dons.* **5.** The plot, intrigue, dénouement of a work of fiction or of a drama : *a novel with very little story.* **6.** Childish word for lie ; untrue statement, fib.

story (II.), n. See **storey.**

story-book, n. Collection of short stories ; book containing a single story ; a novel, a romance.

story-teller, n. **1.** One who relates a story ; writer or reciter of stories. **2.** (childish) Liar, fibber.

story-writer, n. Writer of stories.

stoup, n. [1. stoōp ; 2. stūp]. Cp. O.N. *staup ;* Du. *stoop ;* O.E. *stēap,* ' flagon '. **1.** Drinking-vessel, flagon, goblet. **2.** Vessel or basin for holy water.

stout (I.), adj. [1. stout ; 2. staut]. M.E. *stout,* fr. O. Fr. *estout,* fr. M. Du. *stolt,* ' stout, strong, bold ' ; cp. O.N. *stoltr ;* O.H.G. *stolz,* ' proud ' ; the Gmc. words are possibly for Lat. *stultus,* ' foolish ' ; see **stultify. 1.** Strong, tough, durable, able to stand strain or pressure : *stout cords ; a stout staff ; a stout ship.* **2.** Brave, resolute ; capable of, characterized by, endurance : *a stout fellow ; a stout fighter ; a stout heart ; stout resistance.* **3.** Full-bodied ; fat, plump, corpulent, obese.

stout (**II.**), n., fr. prec. A dark, strong, superior kind of porter.
stout-hearted, adj. Having a stout heart; courageous, resolute.
stout-heartedly, adv. Prec. & **-ly**. In a stout-hearted manner.
stout-heartedness, n. See prec. & **-ness**. State or quality of being stout-hearted.
stoutish, adj. [1. stóutish; 2. stáutiʃ]. **stout** (**I.**) & **-ish** (**I.**). Fairly stout.
stoutly, adv. [1. stóutli; 2. stáutli]. **stout** (**I.**) & **-ly**. In a stout manner; resolutely.
stoutness, n. [1. stóutnes; 2. stáutnis]. See prec. & **-ness**. State or quality of being stout; **a** obesity; **b** toughness; **c** resoluteness.
stove (**I.**), n. [1. stōv; 2. stouv]. O.E. *stofa*; M.E. *stōve*, 'bathroom, heated room'; O.H.G. *stuba*, 'heated chamber; bath', Mod. Germ. *stube*, 'room'; cp. further Ital. *stufa*, Fr. *étuve*, 'heated chamber; stove'; fr. Low Lat. **stūba*, prob. fr. *extufāre*, whence Fr. *étouffer*, 'suffocate', & Ital. *tufo*, 'vapour'. Ultimately fr. Gk. *tûphos*, 'mist, vapour, cloud'. This is fr. base **dhŭ-*, q.v. also under **dust** & **fume**. Apparatus, burning different kinds of fuel, as coke, gas, oil, electricity, of various shapes and sizes, for heating and cooking.
stove (**II.**), vb. trans., fr. prec. To raise (plants) in a stove.
stove (**III.**), vb. Pret. & P.P. of **stave** (**II.**).
stove-pipe, n. Metal pipe carrying off smoke &c. from stove; *stove-pipe hat*, (U.S.A.) top-hat.
stow, vb. trans. [1. stō; 2. stou]. O.E. *stōwian*; M.E. *stōwen*, 'to place, stow away'; fr. O.E. *stōw*, 'place'; cp. O.N. *stō*, 'place'; Goth. *stōjan*, 'to direct'; cogn. w. Lith. *stovà*, 'position'; Lett. *stāwēt*, 'to stand'; Scrt. *sthīnā*, 'pillar'; Gk. *stoā*, 'colonnade', see **stoa**; fr. base **st(h)ĕu-*, **st(h)ŏu-* &c., 'to stand firm', seen also in **steer** (**I.**), **restore**. **a** To pack carefully, closely, and compactly in a receptacle: *to stow clothes into a box* &c.; Phr. (vulg. slang) *stow it!*, shut up!; **b** to fill (receptacle) with goods: *to stow the hold with cargo*.
stowage, n. [1. stóij; 2. stóuidž]. **stow** & **-age**. **a** Method of stowing; **b** space for stowing; **c** charge for stowing.
stowaway, n. [1. stóawā; 2. stóuəwei]. Person who conceals himself in outward-bound ship in order to obtain a free passage.
stow-wood, n. Wooden blocks for wedging and steadying casks in ship's hold &c.
strabismal, adj. [1. strabízmal; 2. strəbízməl]. See **strabismus** & **-al**. Of, pertaining to, affected with, strabismus; cross-eyed.
strabismic, adj. [1. strabízmik; 2. strəbízmik]. See next word & **-ic**. Strabismal.
strabismus, n. [1. strabízmus; 2. strəbízməs]. Mod. Lat. fr. Gk., fr. *strabós*, 'crooked, squinting'; cp. Gk. *stróbīlos*, 'spinning, whirling', see **strobile**; *stróbos*, 'whirlpool'; *streblós*, 'twisted; squinting'. Cp. further Gk. *stréphein*, 'to turn, twist'; *strophḗ*, 'action of turning'. See **strophe**. Affection of eye-muscles which makes it impossible for both eyes to look straight at an object at the same time; squint, cast, in the eye.
strabotomy, n. [1. strabótumi; 2. strəbɔ́təmi], fr. Gk. *strabós*, 'squinting', see prec., & **-tomy**. Surgical operation of cutting contracted muscle of eyeball to cure squint.
Strad, n. [1. strad; 2. stræd]. Abbr. fr. **Stradivarius**.
straddle (**I.**), vb. intrans. & trans. [1. strádl; 2. strǽdl]. Perh. a freq. fr. **stride**; vowel unexplained. **A.** intrans. **1.** To sit, stand, or walk with feet far apart, to stretch the legs out widely. **2.** (fig.) To assume a doubtful or hesitating position; to hedge, vacillate. **3.** (naut.) To drop shots of known range beyond and short of an object in order to determine the range of the latter. **B.** trans. **1.** To sit or stand with a leg on either side of: *to straddle a fence*. **2.** To double (the opening stakes), at poker, before examining one's cards.
straddle (**II.**), n., fr. prec. **1.** Act of straddling; straddling position. **2. a** (poker) A doubling of opening stakes before looking at one's cards; **b** (Stock Exchange) a form of contract which gives right of calling for or delivering stock at an agreed price.
straddle-legged, adj. Having the legs wide apart.
Stradivarius, n. [1. stràdivárius, -váhrius; 2. strædivέəriəs, -vāriəs], fr. name of Antonio Stradivari, violin-maker of Cremona, d. 1737. Violin, viola, or violoncello made by this maker.
strafe, vb. trans. & n. [1. strahf; 2. strāf], fr. Germ. Phr. *Gott strafe England*, 'God punish England', used in Great War. (slang) **1.** vb. **a** To shell, bombard, heavily; hence, **b** (i.) to damage, punish; (ii.) to scold severely. **2.** n. **a** Heavy gunfire, bombardment; hence, **b** punishment, injury.
straggle, vb. intrans. [1. strágl; 2. strǽgl]. Origin uncertain. **1. a** To loiter, stray, wander in the rear of a group; to loiter along in isolated, irregular groups: *children straggling home from school*; **b** to stray irregularly from the rest of a mass, bunch, bundle, plait &c.: *a wisp of hair straggled across her ear*. **2.** To extend, in isolated, scattered, groups: *the town straggles out into the country*; *a few houses straggling along the road*.
straggler, n. [1. strágler; 2. strǽglə]. Prec. & **-er**. One who, that which, straggles.
straggling, adj. [1. strágling; 2. strǽgliŋ]. Pres. Part. of **straggle**. **1.** Detached from the main body, forming an irregular, outlying portion; scattered: *a straggling line of soldiers, of houses, of bushes*. **2.** Drooping, projecting, untidily from its place: *a straggling wisp of hair*; *a shrub with straggling shoots*.
stragglingly, adv. Prec. & **-ly**. In a straggling manner.
straggly, adj. [1. strágli; 2. strǽgli]. **straggle** & **-y** (**IV.**). Straggling.
straight (**I.**), adj. [1. strāt; 2. streit]. M.E. *streiht*, fr. O.E. *streht*, P.P. of *streććan*, 'to extend'. See **stretch** (**I.**). **1.** Extending constantly, throughout its length, in one direction; lying evenly between its extreme points; contrasted with *crooked, bent*, or *curved*: *a straight line, road, stick, hedge* &c.; *straight arch*, having sides without curve; *straight hair*, without curl or wave. **2.** Upright; not bent, stooping, or inclined; vertical: *a straight back, tree-trunk* &c. **3.** Level, not crooked, esp. parallel to a given line or surface: *to put a picture, mat, one's hat, straight*. **4.** In order, properly arranged, worked out, balanced &c.: *to put a room straight*; *to get one's affairs straight*. **5.** Direct, frank, not ambiguous or equivocal, without concealment: *a straight question, answer, look* &c. **6.** Morally upright; honest, sincere; equitable: *a thoroughly straight fellow*; *a person who is not quite straight*; *straight dealing*; *to keep straight*. **7.** (slang) Authoritative, reliable: *a straight tip for a race*.
straight (**II.**), n., fr. prec. **1.** State, quality, of being straight; esp. *out of the straight*, crooked. **2.** Straight stretch of road, river &c.; specif., final straight part of racecourse. **3.** A sequence, in card games, esp. poker.
straight (**III.**), adv., fr. **straight** (**I.**). **1.** In a straight line; directly; without forming or following a curve or angle: *the smoke rises straight upwards*; *to fly straight as an arrow*; *to look straight ahead*; *he can't walk straight*. Phrs. *to hit, shoot, straight*, take accurate aim; *to ride straight*, ride across country after hounds, taking all fences &c. and not stopping to go through gates; *to run straight*, (fig.) behave as an honest man. **2.** Upright, not crouching or stooping: *to stand straight*. **3. a** Directly, by direct route, without making a detour; without intermediate stages, without breaking the journey: *I shall go straight to Paris without stopping at Dover*; **b** directly in thought or speech, without circumlocution, digression, or ambiguity: *to come straight to the point*; *tell me straight what you think*; also *to say, tell, something straight out*. **4. a** (archaic) At once, immediately, straightway; **b** (*I will do it*) *straight off*, straight away, immediately, without delay, hesitation, or reflection; at once.
straight-cut, adj. (of tobacco) Made from leaf cut lengthwise.
straight-edge, n. Wooden or metal bar or strip with one straight edge for testing straightness of line, level surface &c.
straighten, vb. trans. & intrans. [1. strātn; 2. stréitn]. **straight** (**I.**) & **-en** (**V.**). **1.** trans. To make, put, straight. **2.** intrans. To become straight.
straightforward, adj. [1. strātfórward; 2. stréitfɔ̄wəd]. **1.** Acting, speaking, openly, without concealment or ambiguity; made, done, in this way; frank, candid, honest: *a straightforward person, answer*; *straightforward behaviour*. **2.** Not elaborate or complicated; simple: *a straightforward piece of work*.
straightforwardly, adv. Prec. & **-ly**. In a straightforward manner.
straightforwardness, n. See prec. & **-ness**. State or quality of being straightforward.
straightness, n. [1. strātnes; 2. stréitnis]. **straight** (**I.**) & **-ness**. State or quality of being straight (in material and moral sense).
straightway, adv. [1. strātwā; 2. stréitwei]. (archaic) Immediately, at once.
strain (**I.**), vb. trans. & intrans. [1. strān; 2. strein]. M.E. *streinen*, 'to strain, stretch; to constrain', fr. O. Fr. *estreign-*, Pres. stem of *estreindre*, 'to strain', fr. Lat. *stringere*, 'to draw tightly'. See **stringent**. **A.** trans. **1.** To stretch tightly, make taut: *to strain a wire in a fence*. **2.** To exert (bodily faculty) to the utmost, use, tax, to the utmost capacity: *to strain one's ears to catch a sound*. Phr. *to strain every nerve*, use every effort, employ every means. **3.** To over-exert, over-tax, put too great a strain or tax upon (bodily faculty); to fatigue by excessive use: *to strain one's eyes by reading small print*. **4. a** To wrench, tear, sprain, cause injury to, by sudden or too violent effort or movement: *to strain a tendon*; **b** to twist, pull awry, cause to warp (part of a structure): *to strain the timbers of a ship*. **5.** To presume too much upon; to exact too much from, try too far: *to strain a person's patience, good temper, politeness* &c. **6.** To wrest, pervert (meaning) of; to put an interpretation upon, read a meaning into (words), different from, or wider than, what appears to be the natural implication; Phr. *to strain a point* (esp. *in a person's favour*), to interpret a statement, rule, as liberally as possible. **7.** To embrace tightly, clasp, press closely: *to strain a person to one's heart*. **8. a** To filter by passing through perforated object or porous substance: *to strain wine, soup* &c.; **b** to remove by straining, also *strain out*. **B.** intrans. **1.** To make a violent effort, exert all one's forces, strive with difficulty: *a swimmer straining to reach the shore*; *eyes straining through the mist*. **2.** To become strained or clarified; to percolate slowly through filtering object or substance. **C.** Followed by adverbs or prepositions in special senses. *Strain after*, intrans., to strive laboriously for, make utmost efforts to obtain or produce: *a writer who strains after effect*. *Strain at*, intrans., **a** to apply exertion to, push or pull at: *to strain at a rope*; *the horse strains at his collar*; **b** (with reference to Matt. xxiii. 24) to make a fuss about tolerating or accepting: *one shouldn't strain at a few tactless words*. *Strain off*, trans., to remove (impurities &c.) from liquid by passing through strainer &c.
strain (**II.**), n., fr. prec. **1. a** Condition of tension; tautness, tightness: *to keep a strain on a rope*; **b** amount of force exerted on an object by tension: *the rope broke under the strain*. **2.** Severe bodily or mental effort: *it was a hard strain to reach the top of the mountain*; *the constant strain of anxiety*. **3.** Effect on body or mind of an excessive strain; **a** bodily injury, lesion, sprain;

b nervous fatigue resulting from prolonged and severe tension. **4.** (mechan.) Effect exerted upon, alteration caused in shape of, material, by pressure, stress, thrust.

strain (III.), n. Neither spelling nor pronunciation can be derived fr. O.E. *strēon*, 'treasure; propagation, offspring, progeny', as many dictionaries appear to suggest, & as there is no connexion in sense w. **strain (I.)** there is no ground for assuming that this word could have influenced the form, wh. remains a puzzle. The old word in its normal modern form is used by Spenser: '*yborne of heauenly strene*', race, lineage ('F. Q.' v. 9. 32). **1. a** Breed, stock, ancestry: *he comes of a noble strain*; **b** inherited characteristics, line of descent from a particular stock: *Alsatian dogs seem to have a wolf strain in their ancestry*. **2. a** Cast of mind, disposition, tendency; characteristic quality; tinge, streak: *a strain of melancholy, cruelty &c. in a man's character*; **b** characteristic mode of expression; style, manner, tenor: *he spoke in a dismal strain*; *he said he had been grossly betrayed, and much more in the same strain*. **3. a** (often pl.) A song, melody, musical air, note: *the strains of the human voice, of a harp*; *the melancholy strains of the bagpipe*; *strains of mirth &c.*; **b** (poet.) poetry, minstrelsy, song: '*Soul-animating strains, alas, too few!*' (Wordsworth, of Milton's Sonnets).

strainable, adj. [1. stránabl; 2. stréinəbl]. **strain (I.)** & **-able**. Capable of being strained.

strained, adj. [1. stránd; 2. streind], fr. P.P. of **strain (I.)**. **1.** (in moral sense) Warped, distorted, awry; awkward, constrained: *relations between us have become strained*. **2.** Produced with effort; forced, unnatural: *strained merriment*; *his jokes were rather strained*.

strainer, n. [1. stráner; 2. stréinə]. **strain (I.)** & **-er**. One who, that which, strains; specif., device with a mesh for removing solids or impurities from liquid.

strait (I.), adj. [1. strǎt; 2. streit]. M.E. *streit*, fr. A.-Fr. *estreit*, 'narrow', fr. Lat. *strictum*, P.P. type of *stringere*, 'to draw together'; see **strict, stringent**. **1.** (archaic) Narrow, restricted; in Phr. *the strait gate* (Matt. vii. 13). **2.** (archaic) Strict, scrupulous, rigorous.

strait (II.), n., fr. prec. **1.** Narrow channel of water connecting two larger bodies of water: *Menai Strait*; (also pl.) *the Straits of Dover*. **2.** Position, circumstances, of difficulty and perplexity; an awkward fix, situation of stringency; (often pl.) *to be in a strait*; *in great straits*.

straiten, vb. trans. [1. strátn; 2. stréitn]. **strait (I.)** & **-en (I.)**. **1.** (archaic) To make narrow, confine, limit. **2.** (chiefly in P.P. as adj.) To restrict, make difficult, put into difficulties, embarrass: *in straitened circumstances*.

strait jacket, n. Strait waistcoat.

strait-laced, adj. (fig.) Rigid, severe, strict, austere in morals or opinions.

straitly, adv. [1. strátli; 2. stréitli]. **strait (I.)** & **-ly**. (archaic) Strictly, narrowly.

straitness, n. [1. strátnes; 2. stréitnis]. See prec. & **-ness**. (archaic) Strictness.

strait waistcoat, n. Kind of coat made to confine arms and used to restrict movements of dangerous lunatic or criminal.

strake, n. [1. strǎk; 2. streik]. Variant of **streak**. Single breadth of plank or plating running continuously from stem to stern of ship, and forming a section of her side.

stramineous, adj. [1. stramíneus; 2. stramín-iəs], fr. Lat. *strāmineus*, 'like, made of, straw', fr. *strāmin-*, stem of *strāmen*, 'straw, litter'; cp. Gk. *strōma*, 'straw, litter, cover'; see **stroma**. Scrt. *stárīman*, 'spreading out'; cp. further Lat. *strātum*, 'something spread out, layer'; see **stratum**, & words there referred to. (archaic) Of, like, straw; esp. of the colour of straw.

stramonium, n. [1. stramónium; 2. stramóu-niəm]. Etymol. doubtful. Poisonous narcotic drug obtained from the *Datura* or thornapple, used medicinally for asthma &c.

strand (I.), n. [1. strand; 2. strænd]. O.E., M.E. *strand*; cp. M.H.G. *strant*; prob. cogn. w. Lat. *sternere*, P.P. *strātum*, 'to spread, scatter', see **stratum**; O. Slav. *strana*, 'region'; Scrt. *str̥ṇāti*, 'strews'; see also **straw, strew**. (chiefly poet.) Shore, beach, of sea, lake, or river.

strand (II.), vb. trans. & intrans., fr. prec. **1.** trans. To run (ship) aground, cause to run aground. **2.** intrans. (of ship &c.) To run aground.

strand (III.), n., fr. O. Fr. *estran*, fr. O.H.G. *streno*, 'skein'; cp. Du. *streen*, 'skein'; prob. cogn. w. Lat. *stria*, 'furrow, channel, fluting'; see **stria**; cp. also O.H.G. *strīmo*, 'stripe, streak'. Single thread, fibre, or part twisted with another or others to form yarn, rope &c.

strand (IV.), vb. trans., fr. prec. **1.** To break a strand of (rope &c.). **2.** To make (rope, yarn &c.) by twisting strands together.

stranded, adj. [1. strǎnded; 2. strǽndid], fr. P.P. of **strand (II.)**, fr. idea of ship & crew left on a rock, barren shore &c. Left destitute or helpless, without means of escape or extrication from difficulty; left without resources.

strange, adj. [1. stránj; 2. streindž]. M.E. *strǎnge*, fr. O. Fr. *estrange*, fr. Lat. *extrāneus*, 'strange, foreign', see **extraneous**. **1.** Not known, unfamiliar, not recognizable, not previously seen, heard, experienced &c.: *a strange man, face, voice, handwriting &c.*; *to wake in a strange place*; *the language is quite strange to me*. **2.** Foreign, alien, exotic, not one's own: *to visit strange lands*; *to follow strange gods*. **3.** Remarkable from its newness or unexpectedness; unusual, uncommon, singular; difficult to explain: *what a strange thing!*; *to see strange sights*; *it's very strange that you haven't heard from him*; *a strange expression on one's face*; *a strange thing to say*; *to speak with a strange reluctance*. Phr. *strange to say*, it is surprising that. **4.** (of persons) Inexperienced, raw; unfamiliar, unaccustomed, out of one's element: *he is still strange to the job, place &c.*; *to feel strange*.

strangely, adv. Prec. & **-ly**. In a strange manner; esp. remarkably, unusually; to a remarkable degree: *strangely silent about it*.

strangeness, n. See prec. & **-ness**. State or quality of being strange; esp. **a** unfamiliarity; **b** remarkableness, queerness.

stranger, n. [1. stránjer; 2. stréindžə]. M.E. *stranger*, fr. O. Fr. *estrangier*; **strange** & **-er**. **1.** Person unknown to one; one who is unfamiliar, not an acquaintance: *a stranger came to the door*; *he is a stranger to me*; *to be shy in the presence of strangers*. Phrs. *to see, spy, strangers*, said in House of Commons in order to have House cleared of all but members; *you are quite a stranger, you have not been here, or to see us, for a long time*. **2.** Person coming from another place or country; foreigner, alien: *I'm a stranger in these parts*; *a stranger in a strange land*. **3.** Person unfamiliar with, not experienced in, unaccustomed to, some particular condition, circumstances, occupation: *no stranger to sorrow*; *a stranger to your way of thinking*.

strangle, vb. trans. [1. stránggl; 2. strǽŋgl], fr. O. Fr. *estrangler*, fr. Lat. *strangulāre*, 'to strangle, choke'; to check, constrain', see **strangulate**. **1. a** To kill by suffocation caused by constriction of windpipe; hence, **b** of anything placed or worn round neck, to be uncomfortably tight for, choke. **2.** (fig.) To suppress, keep back, stifle: *to strangle a sob, oath, sigh &c*.

strangle-hold, n. Hold in wrestling involving the temporary choking of one's opponent (also fig.).

strangles, n. [1. stránggls; 2. strǽŋglz], fr. **strangle**. Infectious catarrhal disease in horses.

strangulate, vb. trans. [1. stránggūlàt; 2. strǽŋgjulèit], fr. Lat. *strangulātum*, P.P. type of *strangulāre*, 'to strangle; to stifle, suppress', fr. Gk. *straggaloûn*, 'to twist, strangle'; cp. Gk. *straggálē*, 'cord, lace'; *strágx*, 'drop squeezed out'; cogn. w. Lett. *stringt*, 'to dry up, stiffen'; Ir. *sreang*, 'cord'; cp. further O.E. *streng*, 'cord', see **string**; O.N. *strangr*, 'rough, strong', see **strong**. See also **stringent**. To strangle; hence, (specif. med. and surg.) to compress, constrict (vein, duct, intestine &c.), so as to obstruct passage.

strangulation, n. [1. strànggūláshun; 2. strǽŋ-gjuléiʃən]. Prec. & **-ion**. (med.) Compression, constriction, of some channel or tube in the body, which prevents passage of air, liquid &c.

strangurious, adj. [1. strànggúrius; 2. strǽŋ-gjóriəs]. Next word & **-ous**. Of, pertaining to, characteristic of, strangury.

strangury, n. [1. stránggùri; 2. strǽŋgjuri], fr. Lat. *strangūria*, fr. Gk. *straggouría*, 'strangury', fr. Gk. *stragg-*, stem of *strágx*, 'drop', q.v. under **strangle**, & *oûron*, 'urine', q.v. under **urine**, & **-ia**. Difficult and painful urination.

strap (I.), n. [1. strap; 2. stræp]. O.E. *stropp*, 'thong'; M.E. *strop*; fr. Lat. *struppus*, 'thong, strap', fr. Gk. *stróphos*, 'cord, band'; see **strophe**. **1.** Strip of flexible material, usually of leather; esp. such a strip furnished with a buckle, used for fastening and securing; (fig.) *the strap*, corporal punishment, from use of strap in castigation. **2.** Flat piece of metal for holding timbers, or parts of a machine, together. **3.** Blade of grass-leaf.

strap (II.), vb. trans., fr. prec. **1.** To fasten, secure, bind, with a strap. **2.** To fasten with strips of adhesive plaster; esp. to fasten (edges of wound) together in this way; also, *strap up (a wound)*. **3.** To chastise with a strap. **4.** To sharpen on a strap; to strop.

strap-hanger, n. Passenger in train, bus, or tram who cannot obtain a seat and has to hold on to a strap.

strap-laid, adj. *Strap-laid rope*, flat band made of several ropes laid side by side and fastened in position.

strappado, n. & vb. trans. [1. strapádò; 2. stræ-péidou], fr. Ital. *strappata*, fr. *strappare*, 'to pull'. **1.** n. Punishment or torture in which the victim is raised above the ground by a rope fastened to his wrists, and then allowed to fall to the length of the rope. **2.** vb. To torture by this method.

strapped, adj. [1. strapt; 2. stræpt], fr. P.P. of **strap (II.)**. Fastened, secured, with a strap; *strapped trousers*, fastened down by straps passing under insteps; ornamented by straps or flat bands of material.

strapper, n. [1. stráper; 2. strǽpə]. **strap (I.)** & **-er**. **1. a** One who fastens or fixes straps; specif. **b** one who harnesses horses; stableman. **2.** (colloq.) Large, robust, strapping person.

strapping (I.), adj. [1. stráping; 2. strǽpiŋ]. **strap (II.)** & **-ing (II.)**. (colloq.) Tall, robust, largely made and well-proportioned; bouncing: *a fine strapping wench, girl*.

strapping (II.), n. **strap (II.)** & **-ing (I.)**. **a** Material used for straps, **b** specif. (surg.) strips of adhesive plaster used to bring edges of a wound together, to hold bandages in place &c.

strap-work, n. (archit.) Ornamentation representing a series of narrow, interlacing bands.

strapwort, n. [1. strápwèrt; 2. strǽpwāt]. Maritime plant with white flowers, *Corrigiola littoralis*.

strata, pl. of **stratum**.

stratagem, n. [1. strátajem; 2. strǽtədžem], fr. O. Fr. *stratageme*, fr. Lat. *stratēgēma*, fr. Gk. *stratēgēma*, 'piece of generalship; device, stratagem', fr. *stratēgein*, 'to lead as general', fr. *stratēgós*, 'general'; see **strategus**. Cunning device intended to deceive; artifice, clever trick.

stratal, adj. [1. strátl; 2. stréitl]. See **stratum** & **-al**. Pertaining to, arranged in, characteristic of, strata.

strategic(al), adj. [1. stratḗjik(l); 2. strətídžik(l)], fr. Gk. *stratēgikós*, 'of a general', fr. *stratēgós*, 'general', see **strategus**, & **-ic** (& **-al**). Of, pertaining to, carried out by, characterized by, strategy : *a strategic retreat*.

strategically, adv. Prec. & **-ly**. In a strategic manner.

strategics, n. [1. stratḗjiks; 2. strətídžiks], fr. Gk. *stratēgós*, 'general', see **strategus**, & **-ics**. Science of strategy.

strategist, n. [1. strátejist; 2. strǽtidžist]. **strategy** & **-ist**. Person skilled in strategy.

strategus, n. [1. stratḗgus; 2. strətígəs]. Lat. *stratēgus*, fr. Gk. *stratēgós*, 'strategus', fr. *stratós*, 'army; crowd; division of people'; cp. Scrt. *strtáš*, 'spread out'; cogn. w. Lat. *strātum*, 'layer'; see **stratum**, & *ágein* 'to lead': see **act (I.)**. General commanding ancient Greek army; esp. one of the ten Athenian officers elected yearly to commands in army and navy.

strategy, n. [1. strátēji; 2. strǽtidži], fr. Gk. *stratēgía*, 'office of general; skill of general', fr. *stratēgós*, 'general', see prec., & **-ia**. The art of conducting a military campaign; specif., the art of preparing, moving, and using armed forces in a war so as to secure the initiative and ultimately to win the war; distinguished from *tactics*; also fig.

strath, n. [1. strath; 2. stræþ]. Gael. *srath*, 'valley'; cp. M. Ir. *srath*, 'shore; valley'; W. (*y*)*strad*, 'plain'; cogn. w. Lat. *strātum*, 'layer', see **stratum**; Gk. *strōma*, 'layer, carpet', see **stroma**; O.E. *strēawian*, 'to spread', see **strew**. (Scots) A broad, open valley through which a river runs.

strathspey, n. [1. strathspā; 2. stræþspei], fr. name of district in Eastern Scotland. **a** Kind of Scottish dance, rather slower than reel; **b** music for this dance.

strati-, pref. representing **stratum**. Stratum or strata.

straticulate, adj. [1. stratíkūlāt; 2. strætíkjuleit]. Prec. & **-cule** & **-ate**. (geol.) Having, arranged in, deposited as, a series of thin layers.

stratification, n. [1. stràtifikāshun; 2. strætifikéiʃən]. See **stratify** & **-fication**. Process of stratifying; state of being stratified; specif., deposition of sediment in distinct layers by the action of water, wind, or other agency; relative position or arrangement of such layers in specific type of rock.

stratiform, adj. [1. strátiform; 2. strǽtifōm]. **strati-** & **-form**. Having the character of, forming, a stratum.

stratify, vb. trans. [1. strátifī; 2. strǽtifai]. **strati-** & **-fy**. To arrange, deposit, in layers; specif., *stratified rock*, deposited in the form of layers of sediment by the action of water &c.

stratigraphic, adj. [1. stràtigráfik; 2. strætigrǽfik]. **strati-** & **-graphic**. Of, pertaining to, stratigraphy.

stratigraphically, adv. [1. stràtigráfikali; 2. strætigrǽfikəli]. Prec. & **-al** & **-ly**. According to the methods of stratigraphy.

stratigraphy, n. [1. stratígrafi; 2. strætígrəfi]. **strati-** & **-graphy**. Science or description of relative position of strata of rock.

strato-, pref. representing **stratus** & **-o-**. Stratus; e.g. *strato-cirrus*, *-cumulus*, cloud formations resembling cirrus or cumulus and stratus.

stratocracy, n. [1. stratókrasi; 2. strətókrəsi], fr. Gk. *stratós*, 'army; division of people', q.v. under **strategus**, & **-cracy**. Government by the army; military domination in a state.

stratum, n., pl. **strata** [1. strátum, -a; 2. stréitəm, -ə]. Lat. *strātum*, 'covering; blanket; bed'; orig. 'thing spread out', fr. P.P. type of *sternere*, 'to spread out, stretch out; to scatter, strew; to cover'; fr. base **ster-*, **stor-*, **stṛ-* &c., 'to spread out, extend'; cp. Lat. *strāmen*, 'straw', see **stramineous**; Gk. *stórnūmi*, 'to spread out'; *strōma*, 'layer, carpet', see **stroma**; Scrt. *stṛṇāti*, 'scatters'; Goth. *straujan*; O.E. *strēawian*, 'to scatter', see **strew**; Gk. *stérnon*, 'surface; breast', see **sternum**; O. Slav. *stĭrą*, 'to spread out'; *strana*, 'region'; see also **street**. Layer, bed, horizontal division of distinct character; specif. **a** (geol.) layer of deposited rock distinguished from layers above and below; **b** (fig.) anything thought of as resembling a stratum or layer : *a stratum of society*, social division, class; *the various strata of Latin loan-words in English*, groups of words of Latin origin, each containing a number of words borrowed from the same source at the same period.

stratus, n., pl. **strati** [1. strátus, -ī; 2. stréitəs, -ai]. Lat. *strātus*, masc. sing. of P.P. of *sternere*, see prec. Low, horizontal, uniform layer of cloud.

straw (I.), n. [1. straw; 2. strō]. O.E. *strēaw*; M.E. *strau*, 'straw'; cp. O.N. *strā*; O. Fris. *strē*; O.L.G. *strō*; O.H.G. *strō*, *strou*; cp. further O.E. *strēawian*, 'to scatter', see **strew**; cogn. w. Lat. *strāmen*, 'straw', see **stramineous**; see also **stratum**, & words there referred to. **1**. Hollow stem, stalk, or portion of stalk, of grain, esp. that of wheat, oats, barley, rye &c.; Phrs. *to catch at a straw*, resort desperately to any expedient available; *the last straw*, (fig.) final addition to a burden, hardship &c., which renders it unendurable; *not worth a straw*, worth nothing; *not to care a straw*, to be indifferent; *straws which show the way the wind blows*, slight indications of the trend of events, of public opinion &c. **2**. Stalks of grain collectively, esp. after drying and threshing, used for thatching, bedding, for making textile fabric for mats, hats &c. : *stuffed*, *thatched &c.*, *with straw*. Phr. *man of straw*, effigy made of or stuffed with straw; hence (i.) imaginary person regarded as opponent in controversy &c.; (ii.) an unreliable person, with no solidity or strength of character; (iii.) person of no financial substance. **3**. Straw hat.

straw (II.), vb. trans. M.E. *strāwen*, 'to scatter', variant of *strēwen*, see **strew**. (archaic) To scatter, strew.

strawberry, n. [1. stráwberi; 2. strɔ́bəri]. O.E. *strēawberige*; perh. so called because the runners were supposed to resemble straw, or because straw was used to keep the fruit off the ground; this name may, however, be due to an anct. popular etymol., & it has been suggested that the first syll. is fr. Aryan **sragʷo-*, whence Gmc. **straʒʷ-*; cp. Lat. *frāgum* for *srāghom, 'strawberry'; Gk. *hrāgós*, fr. *srāgos, 'a grape'; Scrt. *sraj-*, 'wreath, crown'. **a** Fruit of any plant of genus *Fragaria*, consisting of a pulpy, sweet, juicy, red or yellowish body bearing seeds on the surface; *crushed strawberry*, dull crimson colour; **b** plant bearing these berries.

strawberry-leaf, n. **a** Triple leaf of strawberry; **b** representation of this forming part of ornamentation of the coronet of a duke, marquess, or earl; hence specif., *strawberry leaves*, ducal rank.

strawberry-mark, n. Dull reddish birthmark.

strawberry-pear, n. Red pear-shaped fruit of a tropical American cactus.

strawberry-roan, adj. & n. Reddish roan.

strawberry-tree, n. Small S. European, evergreen tree, *Arbutus unedo*, with edible fruit which resembles a strawberry in appearance.

straw-board, n. Kind of coarse cardboard made of straw pulp.

straw-colour, n. Clear, pale yellow; the colour of straw.

straw-coloured, adj. Of the colour of straw.

straw-stem, n. Wineglass stem made in one piece with the bowl, by drawing out part of the material of the latter.

straw-worm, n. Caddis.

strawy, adj. [1. stráw-i; 2. strɔ́i]. **straw (I.)** & **-y (IV.)**. Connected with, resembling, full of, covered with, straw.

stray (I.), vb. intrans. [1. strā; 2. strei]. M.E. *straien*, 'to stray, wander', fr. O. Fr. *estraier*, prob. fr. Lat. *strāta*, 'way, road', see **street**. **1. a** To go or wander beyond appointed limits, leave enclosure or recognized path : *don't stray too far from the path*; *the sheep have strayed (from a field &c.)*; *a child that has strayed from home*; **b** (poet.) to wander, roam, rove : *to stray aimlessly through the woods*. **2**. To wander from the path of virtue and rectitude; to fall into sin. **3**. (of thoughts, affections &c.) To wander; not to be concentrated on a single object, or the subject of study or discussion.

stray (II.), n., fr. prec. **1**. Domestic animal that has strayed. **2**. Person or child who is lost, has wandered from its home, or is without a proper home, esp. in Phr. *waifs and strays*. **3**. (law, in pl. *strays*) Property passing to Crown in default of heirs to deceased owner. **4**. (wireless, in pl. *strays*) Atmospherics.

stray (III.), adj., fr. prec. **1**. Having strayed; wandering, lost : *stray cattle*; *a stray dog*. **2**. Occurring here and there, at irregular and infrequent intervals; scattered, sporadic.

strayed, adj. [1. strād; 2. streid], fr. P.P. of **stray (I.)**. Having strayed, wandering, astray : *a strayed horse*.

streak (I.), n. [1. strēk; 2. strīk]. Cannot be derived fr. O.E. *strica*, 'mark, stroke of the pen', though it may come fr. a cogn. of this, & of **strike (I.)** & **stroke (I.)**; we may assume an O.E. **strǣc-*, fr. *strāki, wh. wd. normally give M.E. *strēch*; the final -*k* may be due to anal. w. *strike*, *stroke* &c. **1**. Long, narrow, usually irregular, mark, line, stripe on a surface, distinct in colour : *an apple with a red streak*; *streaks of light in the east*; *streak of lightning*, a flash. Phr. *off like a streak (of lightning)*, very swiftly. **2**. (fig.) Tendency, strain : *he hasn't a streak of humour in him*.

streak (II.), vb. trans., fr. prec. To mark with streaks.

streakily, adv. [1. strḗkili; 2. strī́kili]. See next word & **-ly**. In a streaky manner.

streakiness, n. [1. strḗkines; 2. strī́kinis]. Next word & **-ness**. State or quality of being streaky.

streaky, adj. [1. strḗki; 2. strī́ki]. **streak** & **-y (IV.)**. Arranged in, marked with, showing, streaks : *streaky bacon*, with alternate layers of fat and lean.

stream (I.), n. [1. strēm; 2. strīm]. O.E. *strēam*, 'current; river'; M.E. *strēme*; cp. O.H.G. *stroum*; O. Fris. *strām*; O.N. *straumr*; fr. Gmc. **straum-*; cogn. w. Scrt. *srávati*, 'flows'; *srótaš*, 'stream'; Gk. *rhóos*, 'stream'; *rhéein*, 'to flow', fr. Aryan **srow-*, *srew-*, see **rheo-**. **1**. Body of running water, flowing naturally from its source, in a bed or channel; rivulet, brook; river : *the Thames is a noble stream*. Phr. *the stream of time*. **2. a** A flow of water or other liquid; a jet, gush : *water flowing from the burst main in a great stream*; *a stream of blood*; **b** flow of molten matter : *a stream of lava*. **3. a** Direction in which a stream or river moves; current : *with*, *against*, *the stream*; **b** (fig.) trend, drift, of events, of popular feeling or opinion &c.; direction in which events, feelings &c. tend, are moving : *the stream of popular prejudice is against what is new*. **4**. Continuous series of moving objects : *a stream of people*, *motor-cars*; *the stream of traffic*.

stream (II.), vb. intrans. & trans., fr. prec. **A**. intrans. **1**. (of fluid) To flow in, or as in, a stream, to flow freely, form a continuous line of moving matter, pour forth : *tears streamed down her cheeks*; *people streamed out of the building*; *light streamed through the window*. **2**. To pour forth liquid in a stream, be suffused with, run with, liquid : *eyes that streamed with tears*; *a streaming cold*, one accompanied by copious discharge from eyes and nose. **3**. To fly out, be extended; float (on the air); to trail : *hair streaming in the wind*; *the comet's tail streams behind it*. **B**. trans. To pour out, cause to issue, emit, in a stream : *wounds streaming blood &c.*

stream-anchor, n. Anchor of medium size.

streamer, n. [1. strḗmer; 2. strímə]. **stream (II.)** & **-er**. **1.** Strip of material designed to hang down, be extended, float, in the air &c., esp. flag, ribbon &c., attached at one end. **2.** Ray of light seen shooting up or across the sky in the aurora borealis.

streamless, adj. [1. strḗmles; 2. strímlis]. **stream (I.)** & **-less**. Without, lacking in, streams.

streamlet, n. [1. strḗmlet; 2. strímlit]. **stream (I.)** & **-let**. Small stream, brook.

stream-line, n., adj., & vb. trans. **1.** n. Natural flow of current in air or water without eddying. **2.** adj. (of shape of fish, aircraft, motor-car &c.) Such as to offer the least resistance to currents in air or water. **3.** vb. To give a stream-line form to (submarine, body of car &c.).

streamy, adj. [1. strḗmi; 2. strími]. **stream (I.)** & **-y (IV.)**. Of, like, flowing in, a stream; abounding in streams.

street, n. [1. strēt; 2. strīt]. O.E. *strǣt*; M.E. *strēte*, 'paved road'; cp. O.L.G. *strāta*; O.H.G. *strāza*; Du. *straat*; borrowed in continental period, fr. Lat. *strāta (via)*, 'paved way', fr. P.P. of *sternere*, 'to spread, scatter; to cover, pave', see **stratum**. **1.** Formerly applied to the old Roman roads in England; cp. *Watling Street, Akeman Street*. **2.** Properly constructed, metalled road in a town or large village, with buildings on one or both sides: *the chief street of the town*; *to live in a quiet street*; *the village street*; *to run out into the street*; *High Street*. Phrs. *street arab*, homeless waif; *street cries*, of hawkers calling their wares; *on the streets*, earning a living as a prostitute; *not in the same street with*, not to be compared with, not nearly as good as.

street-door, n. That door of a house which opens on to a street.

street-orderly, n. Street scavenger.

street-sweeper, n. **a** Person occupied in sweeping streets; **b** machine with revolving brushes for sweeping streets.

street-walker, n. Prostitute.

streetward, adj. & adv. [1. strḗtward; 2. strítwəd]. **street** & **-ward**. **1.** adj. Situated in or near the street. **2.** adv. Towards the street.

strength, n. [1. strength; 2. streŋþ]. O.E. *strengþ(o)*, 'strength; severity; efficacy'; M.E. *strengþ*; fr. **strang-iþu*; **strong** & **-th (I.)**. **1. a** Quality, condition, of being strong; bodily or intellectual vigour, power; capacity for exertion or endurance: *a man of enormous strength*; *the strength of his mind was such that he overcame all obstacles*; **b** special quality, aptitude, talent, that in which one excels; forte: *his strength lay in lucid exposition rather than in original discovery*. **2.** Quality in materials which enables them to resist strains, bear weights &c.; toughness, durability; opposite of *fragility*: *the strength of a beam, bridge* &c. **3.** Power of resisting attack; impregnability: *the strength of a fortified place*. **4.** Large numbers; power, efficiency, completeness considered as depending on numbers: *the enemy were in great strength*. Phrs. *up to, below, strength*, of a regiment, or other body of fixed size, having full complement, or less than full complement, of men; (mil.) *on the strength*, on the muster-roll. **5.** Source of power, efficiency &c.; that which makes one strong in some specified way: *high courage and cheerfulness are a great strength to a general*; *he was a strength and support to his father in old age*. **6.** Intensity, potency; degree of capacity for producing characteristic effects: *the strength of a poison*; *the strength of colour*; *the strength of one's affections*. **7.** Power to effect an intellectual or moral result; compelling power, cogency: *the strength of an argument*. Phr. *on the strength of* (*what was said, of a promise* &c.), having regard to, relying on, influenced, persuaded, by.

strengthen, vb. trans. & intrans. [1. stréngthen; 2. stréŋþən]. Prec. & **-en (I.)**. **1.** trans. To make strong, increase strength of, reinforce. **2.** intrans. To grow strong, increase in strength.

strengthening, adj. [1. stréngthening; 2. stréŋþəniŋ]. Prec. & **-ing**. Tending, serving, to strengthen; invigorating: *strengthening food*.

strengthless, adj. [1. stréngthles; 2. stréŋþlis]. **strength** & **-less**. (rare) Devoid of strength; weak.

strenuous, adj. [1. strénūus; 2. strénjuəs], fr. Lat. *strēnuus*, 'brisk, active, vigorous'; cp. Gk. *strēnés*, 'keen, strong'; *strênos*, 'haughtiness'; cp. O.E. *styrne*, 'hard, keen, severe', see **stern (I.)**; O. Slav. *strada*, 'labour'; the base **st(e)rē-* &c., 'vigorous, powerful', is prob. expanded fr. **ster-*, **stṛ-* &c., 'stiff, strong', see **stare**, **stark**, **sterile**. Characterized by, putting forth, continuous, intense, unremitting effort; unrelaxing and vigorous: *strenuous supporters of a cause*; *a strenuous worker*; *strenuous efforts*; *the strenuous life*.

strenuously, adv. Prec. & **-ly**. In a strenuous manner.

strenuousness, n. See prec. & **-ness**. Quality of being strenuous.

Strephon, n. [1. stréfun; 2. stréfən]. Shepherd lover in Sidney's *Arcadia*. Lover; counterpart of Chloe.

strepitoso, adv. [1. strèpitṓsō; 2. strèpitóusou]. Ital., fr. Lat. *strepit-(us)*, 'confused noise', fr. P.P. type of *strepere*, 'to make a noise; to clatter, rattle, roar'; perh. related to *strīdēre*, 'to hiss, creak, buzz' &c., see **strident**, fr. base **stre(i)-*, 'to make a harsh noise'. (mus.) Boisterously, loudly, vigorously.

strepto-coccus, n. [1. stréptō kókus; 2. stréptou kɔ́kəs]. Coined fr. Gk. *streptós*, 'easy to bend, pliant', fr. base **strebh-* in Gk. *stréphein*, 'to twist, turn'; cp. gradational form *strophḗ*, 'a turn, twist', see **strophe**; *coccus* is Neo-Lat. fr. Gk. *kókkos*, 'a kernel, a berry'; see **coccus** & **cochineal**. One of a genus of bacteria of virulent character found in the blood in several diseases, such as pneumonia, septicaemia &c.

stress (I.), n. [1. stres; 2. stres]. M.E. *stresse*, 'force', fr. O. Fr. *estrecier*, fr. Low Lat. **strictiāre*, 'to constrain', fr. Lat. *strict-(um)*, P.P. type of *stringere*, 'to draw tight', see **stringent**. **1.** Strain, tension, intense effort: *in times of stress*. **2.** Impelling force, pressure, power or influence exercising constraint or compulsion: *under stress of weather, circumstances* &c. **3.** Importance, weight, emphasis; esp. in Phr. *to lay stress on*, indicate importance of, bring into prominence. **4. a** Relative force with which a word or syllable is uttered; accent: *strong, secondary, weak, stress*; esp. **b** highest degree of force used in uttering a group of syllables or words; strong stress: *the stress is on the first syllable*; *to put special stress on a word*; *there are two stresses in each half-line*. **5.** (mechan.) Force(s) exerted on a solid body and tending to alter its shape.

stress (II.), vb. trans., fr. prec. **1.** To lay stress on, emphasize, indicate importance or prominence of: *St. Paul specially stresses charity as the greatest of the virtues*. **2.** To utter (word or syllable) with stress, esp. with strong stress; to accentuate: *stressed syllables*. **3.** (mechan.) To subject to stress.

stressless, adj. [1. strésles; 2. stréslis]. **stress** & **-less**. Without stress.

stretch (I.), vb. trans. & intrans. [1. strech; 2. stretʃ]. O.E. *streċċean*, M.E. *stre(t)chen*; O.H.G. *strecchan*; perh. fr. base **srak-*, a parallel form of **rak-* in **reach**; or connected w. **stark**, &, more remotely, w. **strong**; cp. also O.E. *strec*, 'strong, vehement, violent'. **A.** trans. **1. a** To cause to increase in length or breadth by forcibly pulling longitudinally or laterally: *to stretch a pair of gloves to make them fit*; also **b** (fig.) *to stretch the law, a rule*, to strain it, so as to make it more inclusive. Phr. *to stretch a point (in a person's favour)*, to go beyond what is strictly and literally legal or legitimate. **2. a** To pull or spread (object or material) tightly to its fullest extent, without attempting to increase this: *to stretch a rope between two posts*; *to stretch a carpet upon the floor*; *to stretch one's neck in order to see over the heads of a crowd*, to crane it, extend it fully; *to stretch (out) one's arm, hand*, reach it out, extend it; *to stretch oneself*, extend one's muscles fully by stretching out one's limbs. Phr. *to stretch one's legs*, exercise them; to go for a walk after a period of inactivity; **b** (reflex.) *stretch oneself*, to extend the limbs forcibly as far as muscles and tendons will allow, as on waking from sleep. **3.** To knock down, cause to lie at full length on the ground: *a blow behind the ear stretched him unconscious on the floor*. **4.** (slang) **a** To hang by the neck; **b** to lay out for burial. **B.** intrans. **1.** To be capable of extension, to have elastic properties; to become larger by being stretched: *my gloves are too tight, but no doubt they'll stretch*; *iron may stretch slightly, but not stone*. **2. a** To extend, reach, lie spread out: *the plain stretches for miles*; *the range of mountain stretches across the frontier*; also, **b** (of time) to last; to extend: *the Middle English Period stretches (down) roughly to the early years of the 15th century*; *a dreary life stretches before prisoners*. **3.** To stretch oneself, extend one's limbs to the utmost, as after sleep or prolonged inactivity, to stretch oneself: *he sat up in bed, yawned, and stretched*.

stretch (II.), n., fr. prec. **1. a** Act of stretching: *to give, make, a stretch of the arm*; *a stretch of the imagination*; **b** state of being stretched, strained, tightened; specif., bodily or mental tension or strain: *nerves on the stretch*. **2. a** Unbroken period or spell of time: *to work for six hours at a stretch*; **b** (slang) period, term of imprisonment, esp. of penal servitude. **3. a** Uninterrupted tract of space; a reach, extent, expanse: *a fine stretch of country, of water*; **b** (sailing) distance traversed on a single tack.

stretcher, n. [1. strécher; 2. strétʃə]. **stretch (I.)** & **-er**. **1.** One who, that which, stretches; esp. **a** apparatus for stretching something, also in compounds, *glove-stretcher, boot-stretcher*; **b** wooden frame for stretching and tautening artist's canvas. **2.** Apparatus, consisting of a light wooden framework covered with canvas &c., for carrying injured or wounded person, hence *stretcher-bearer*. **3.** Crosspiece in boat, against which the rower braces his feet. **4.** (masonry) Brick or stone laid longitudinally along line of wall. **5.** (slang) Exaggerated or untrue statement.

stretcher-bond, n. (masonry) Method of building in which bricks or stones are laid lengthwise in successive courses.

stretchiness, n. [1. stréchines; 2. strétʃinis]. Next word & **-ness**. State or quality of being stretchy.

stretchy, adj. [1. stréchi; 2. strétʃi]. **stretch** & **-y (IV.)**. Capable of being stretched, liable to stretch; pliant, elastic.

strew, vb. trans. [1. stroo; 2. strū]. O.E. *strēawian*; M.E. *strēwen*, 'to scatter'; cp. Goth. *straujan*, 'to scatter'; see **straw**, **stratum**. **1.** To scatter, drop, or fling hither and thither in small quantities; to sprinkle, spread irregularly: *to strew rushes on the floor*. **2.** To cover lightly and irregularly, scatter, bestrew: *to strew a grave with flowers*; *the road was strewn with stones*.

stria, n., pl. **striae** [1. stría, strīē; 2. stráiə, stráiī]. Lat. *stria*, 'furrow, channel, fluting'; cogn. w. O.H.G. *strīmo*, 'stripe'; *streno*, 'skein', see **strand (III.)**; cp. also Lat. *striga*, 'stroke, stripe, swath', see **strigil**; see also **stringent**. (zool., bot., geol. &c.) Narrow, lengthwise mark, stripe, channel, groove &c.; thread-like or flute-like marking.

striate (I.), adj. [1. stríat; 2. stráiət], fr. Lat. *striāt-(um)*, P.P. type of *striāre*, 'to groove, flute', fr. *stria*, 'furrow', see prec. **1.** Marked with striae; striped, fluted, variegated. **2.** Of, resembling, forming, striae.

striate (II.), vb. trans. [1. stríāt; 2. stráieit], fr. Lat. *striātum*, see prec. To mark with striae.

striated, adj. [1. strīā́ted; 2. straiéitid], fr. P.P. of **striate (II.)**. Striate.

striately, adv. [1. stríatli; 2. stráiətli]. **striate (I.)** & **-ly**. In striae.

striation, n. [1. strīā́shun; 2. straiéiʃən]. **striate (II.)** & **-ion**. **1.** Act of striating; state of being striated; variegation; arrangement of striae. **2.** Stria.

striature, n. [1. stríachur; 2. stráiətʃə]. **striate (I.)** & **-ure**. Arrangement of striae; striation.

stricken, adj. [1. stríken; 2. stríkən]. Archaic P.P. of **strike**. **1.** (archaic) Wounded, injured by missile &c.; struck down: *a stricken deer.* **2.** Smitten, affected by grief, illness &c.; *stricken with disease* &c.; sometimes in compounds, *terror-stricken*; *stricken field*, pitched battle, or the place where it was fought. **3.** *Stricken in years*, of advanced age, old.

strickle, n. [1. stríkl; 2. stríkl]. O.E. *stricel*, 'rod', cogn. w. **strike**. Rod used for levelling grain in a heaped vessel to ensure accurate measure; see **strike-measure**.

strict, adj. [1. strikt; 2. strikt]. Lat. *strictus*, 'drawn together, tight; close-knit, narrow'; fr. P.P. of *stringere*, 'to draw tight', see **stringent**, & cp. **strait (I.)**. **1. a** Precise, accurate, exact; reverse of lax, loose, equivocal: *the strict truth*; *take the words in their strict sense*; *a strict interpretation*; *in strict accuracy, law* &c.; **b** punctilious, nice, rigidly conscientious; admitting no deviation from what is correct: *a strict observer of rules, of the truth*; *a strict Protestant.* **2. a** Admitting no infringement; inflexible, exacting: *a strict system of government*; *the game laws are very strict*; *a school must have strict rules*; **b** rigorous in preserving law and order, insistent on discipline; stern, severe, austere: *schoolmasters should be strict but just*; *it doesn't do to be too strict with very young children.*

strictly, adv. Prec. & **-ly**. **1. a** Precisely, exactly, with rigid accuracy: *strictly (speaking) you ought not to leave*; **b** punctiliously: *he stuck strictly to his own business.* **2.** Severely, sternly, rigidly: *he preserved discipline strictly, but with fairness.*

strictness, n. See prec. & **-ness**. Quality of being strict in all senses.

stricture, n. [1. stríkchur; 2. stríktʃə], fr. Lat. *strictūra*, 'contraction, compression; suffering', fr. *stric-(tum)*, P.P. type of *stringere*, 'to draw together, bind tightly', see **stringent**, & **-ure**. **1.** (med.) Constriction, contraction, of a duct or vessel of the body, esp. of the urethra. **2.** (fig., often pl.) Severe criticism, reflection, censure: *strictures were passed on his conduct.*

strictured, adj. [1. stríkchurd; 2. stríktʃəd]. Prec. & **-ed**. Affected by stricture.

stridden, vb. [1. strídn; 2. strídn]. P.P. of **stride (I.)**. O.E. *(ġe)striden.*

stride (I.), vb. intrans. & trans. [1. strīd; 2. straid]. O.E. *strīdan*; M.E. *strīden*, 'to stride, step'; cp. M. Du. *strīden*; cogn. w. O.H.G. *strītan*, 'to fight'; O.S. *strīd*, 'eagerness'; O.N. *strīðr*, 'strong, firm, obstinate'; fr. base **ster-*, **str-*, 'to stiffen, become strong'; see **stare**, **stark**, & words there referred to. **A.** intrans. **1.** To walk with long, swinging, or measured steps. **2.** To take a single long step in crossing a space, obstacle &c.: *to stride over an obstacle, across a brook* &c. **B.** trans. **1.** To cross, pass over, with a single long step. **2.** To bestride, stand or sit with a leg on either side of.

stride (II.), n., fr. prec. **1.** Long step in walking: *to walk with rapid strides*; Phr. *to make great, rapid, strides* (in learning &c.), to progress rapidly; *to take something in one's stride*, to do something easily, without special effort, without going out of one's way. **2. a** Distance between feet when standing astride; **b** greatest length of pace.

strident, adj. [1. strīdent; 2. stráidənt], fr. Lat. *strīdent-(em)*, Pres. Part. of *strīdēre*, 'to make a shrill, harsh, or creaking sound'; cogn. w. Gk. *trízein*, 'to utter a shrill sound'; cp. also Gk. *strix*, 'owl'; Lat. *strix*, 'screech owl'. (of sound, voice &c.) Loud, harsh, jarring.

stridently, adv. Prec. & **-ly**. In a strident manner.

stridulant, adj. [1. strídūlant; 2. strídjulənt]. Lat. *strīdulus*, 'creaking', see next word & **-ant**. (of insect) Producing stridulations.

stridulate, vb. intrans. [1. strídūlāt; 2. strídjuleit], fr. Lat. *strīdulus*, 'creaking, grating', fr. *strīdēre*, 'to make a shrill, harsh sound', see **strident**, & **-ule**, & **-ate**. (Of crickets, locusts, grasshoppers &c.) To produce a shrill chirping or creaking noise by rubbing parts of the hard integument together.

stridulation, n. [1. strìdūlā́shun; 2. strìdjuléiʃən]. Prec. & **-ion**. **1.** Act of stridulating. **2.** Noise produced by stridulating.

stridulator, n. [1. strídūlātur; 2. strídjulèitə]. **stridulate** & **-or**. Insect that stridulates.

stridulous, adj. [1. strídūlus; 2. strídjuləs]. See **stridulant** & **-ous**. Resembling, characterized by, stridulation.

strife, n. [1. strīf; 2. straif]. M.E. *strīf*, fr. O. Fr. *estrīf*, fr. O.N. *strīþ*, 'oppression, pain'; cp. O.N. *strīðr*, 'strong, obstinate'; see **stride (I.)**. Conflict, struggle, combat, controversy; reciprocal hostile action; quarrelling, war.

striga, n. [1. strīga; 2. stráigə]. Lat. *striga*, 'furrow, stroke, stripe'; see **strigil**. (bot.) Short bristle or hair-like scale.

strigil, n. [1. stríjil; 2. strídžil], fr. Lat. *strigilis*, 'scraper'; cp. Lat. *striga*, 'swath, furrow, stroke, stripe'; cogn. w. O. Slav. *strigą*, 'to shear'; O.E. *strīcan*, 'to rub'; see **strike (I.)**, **stringent**. (Rom. antiq.) Instrument of metal, bone, or horn used for scraping the skin after the bath.

strigose, adj. [1. strígōs; 2. stráigous], fr. Lat. *striga*, 'swath, furrow', q.v. under **strigil**, & **-ose**. (bot.) Covered with short, stiff bristles or hair-like scales.

strigous, adj. [1. strígus; 2. stráigəs], fr. Lat. *striga*, 'swath', see prec., & **-ous**. (bot.) Strigose.

strike (I.), vb. trans. & intrans. [1. strīk; 2. straik]. O.E. *strīcan*, 'to rub; to move, go'; M.E. *strīken*, 'to strike, stroke, rub'; cp. M.L.G. *strīken*, M. Du. *strȳken*; O.H.G. *strīhhan*; O.N. *strȳkna*, 'to rub, stroke'; cp. further Goth. *striks*; O.E. *strica*, 'stroke of pen'; cogn. w. O. Slav. *strigą*, 'stripe, stroke, swath'; Lat. *strigilis*, 'scraper', see **strigil**; cp. w. infixed nasal Lat. *stringere*, 'to touch, graze; to draw out; to draw together', see **stringent**; Gk. *strígx*, 'line, ray, channel'. Cp. further Lat. *stria*, 'channel, furrow', see **stria**; O.H.G. *strīmo*, 'stripe'; *streno*, 'skein', see **strand (III.)**; see also **stroke (I.)**. The word expresses generally violent, or sudden, & rapid action or movement. **A.** trans. **1.** To hit, smite, give a blow to; bring (an object) violently into contact with (another): *to strike the table with one's fist*; *to strike a person a violent blow*; *to strike a ball with a racket*; *the wall sounds hollow when struck*; Phr. *to strike hands*, (archaic) make a bargain or agreement. **2.** To cause to hit or impinge upon, bring (object) violently into contact with another: *to strike one's head against the lintel.* **3.** To pierce, penetrate, by a blow: *to strike a person to the heart with a dagger.* **4.** To give, deal, aim, deliver: *to strike a blow*; *to strike the first blow*; Phr. *to strike a blow for*, make an effort in support of. **5.** To come suddenly in contact with, impinge upon: *the ship struck a rock*; *a falling rock struck his head*; *the ball struck him in the eye.* **6. a** To come upon, to reach, to find: *we shall strike the main road beyond the wood*; **b** to come across, happen upon, to discover as by chance: *I struck a good place for a holiday*; *to strike a bad hotel, an amusing book*; Phr. *to strike oil*, (i.) to discover a gusher; (ii.) (fig.) to make a lucky hit, make one's fortune. **7.** To produce by striking: *to strike a light*; *to strike sparks from flint.* **8.** To produce by striking musical instrument; cause to sound: *to strike a chord, note*; Phr. *to strike a note*, to convey a specific impression, emotion &c. **9.** To make by stamping, to coin: *to strike a medal.* **10.** To pull down, take down, lower: *to strike a sail, tent* &c.; *to strike camp*, remove, break up, encampment; *to strike one's flag*, esp. in token of surrender &c. **11.** To bring suddenly into a specific condition, affect suddenly and violently: *to be struck dumb, blind, with disease* &c.; Phr. *to strike dumb*, (fig.) make speechless with amazement, terror &c.; *to strike one all of a heap*, (colloq.) to astound. **12.** To inspire, instil, with (some violent emotion): *to strike terror and dismay into every heart.* **13. a** To affect the judgement, produce an impression on the mind of; to impress: *how does his playing strike you?*; *the idea strikes me as a good one*; *the humorous side of it struck me very forcibly*; specif. **b** to make a favourable, deep, lasting, impression upon: *to be struck by a person's beauty, ability* &c.; **c** (of ideas &c.) to come into the mind of, occur to: *an idea has just struck me*; *it strikes me that ...* **14.** To assume, put oneself into (esp. by a sudden, rapid movement): *to strike an attitude.* **15.** (of clock) To sound, announce by striking: *the clock strikes the hours and quarters*; *it has just struck four.* **16.** To make (measure) level, by smoothing of piled-up grain &c. from the top by means of a rod &c. **17.** To come to, make, arrive at, by reckoning, agreement &c.: *to strike a balance, a bargain, an average* &c. **18.** (fishing) To fix hook in mouth of (fish), by quick, upward stroke of the rod: *to strike a fish.* **19. a** To cause to take root; set, plant: *to strike cuttings*; **b** (of plant) *to strike root*, to form roots. **20.** To tap, broach (cask). **21.** *To strike work*, **a** to cease work; specif. **b** to go on strike. **B.** intrans. **1.** To hit, smite, deliver blow(s): '*Willing to wound, and yet afraid to strike*' (Pope, Epistle to Dr. Arbuthnot, 203). Phr. *to strike while the iron's hot*, act promptly, and at appropriate moment. **2.** To come sharply into contact with an object or surface: *the ship struck (on a rock* &c.*)*; *his foot struck against a stone.* **3.** To be kindled by striking: *the match wouldn't strike.* **4.** To direct one's course, turn; to penetrate, pass: *to strike to the left*; *the disease struck inwards*; *the light strikes through the darkness, the clouds* &c.; *the damp strikes through the walls.* **5. a** (of plant) To take root; **b** (of oyster &c.) to become fixed, adhere to rock &c. **6.** To strike one's flag as sign of surrender or respect. **7. a** (of clock) To announce hour &c. by specific number of strokes: *I didn't hear the clock strike*; **b** (of hour) be recorded by striking of clock: *the hour has struck*; Phr. *his hour has struck*, he is about to die. **C.** Followed by adverbs or prepositions, with special meanings. *Strike at*, intrans., to aim at, aim blow or attack at, direct blow towards; Phr. *to strike at the root of*, try to destroy or exterminate utterly. *Strike down*, trans., **a** to fell with a blow; **b** to attack, prostrate by illness &c. *Strike in*, intrans., **1.** (of disease) to affect internal organs instead of surface of body or extremities; **2.** to interrupt, interpose: *here someone struck in with a question.* *Strike into*, **1.** intrans., **a** to turn off abruptly into: *to strike into the fields*; **b** to break into, start off suddenly into: *to strike into a gallop*; **2.** trans., to cause to penetrate, drive: *to strike spurs into a horse.* *Strike off*, trans., **1.** to remove by striking: *to strike off a person's head*; **2.** to cancel, remove by drawing stroke through &c.: *to strike a name off a list*; **3.** to print: *to strike off a hundred copies.* *Strike out*, **1.** intrans., to aim a blow, hit out; **2. a** (of swimmer, skater) to make a stroke, esp. in specific direction: *to strike out for the shore*; **b** (fig.) to begin action, make a start: *to strike out in a line of one's own*; **3.** trans., **a** to cancel, erase, cross out (word &c.); **b** to produce, originate: *to strike out a new idea, a line of one's own.* *Strike through*, trans., to cross out, cancel, by stroke of pen &c. *Strike up*, trans., **1.** to begin to play or sing: *to strike up a song*; **2.** to begin, bring into being: *to strike up a friendship*; **3.** intrans., to begin to play or sing: *now then, strike up*; *the band struck up as the King entered.*

strike (II.), n. & vb. intrans. Noun fr. prec., in specialized sense, as in Phr. *to strike work*; vb., a new formation fr. n. **1.** n. Legalized method for workers of dealing, and bargaining for terms, with employers, by an organized general stoppage of work among all workers in a given trade or industry, or in a branch of a trade &c., until agreement is reached regarding wages, hours of work, or other matters in dispute. **2.** vb. To engage, take part, in a strike.

strike-a-light, n. [1. strík a līt; 2. stráik ə lait]. Apparatus for producing spark from flint and steel &c.

strike-breaker, n. Worker brought in from outside to replace striker.

strike-measure, n. Method of measuring grain &c., in which the surplus is levelled off from a heaped vessel with a rod.

strike-pay, n. Allowance made by trade union to workmen during a strike.

striker (I.), n. [1. stríker; 2. stráikə]. **strike** (I.) & -er. **1.** One who strikes; specif. (tennis &c.), player to whom ball is served. **2.** Instrument, device, mechanism, for striking.

striker (II.), n., fr. strike (II.) & -er. Workman, employee, who takes part in a strike.

striking, adj. [1. stríking; 2. stráikiŋ], fr. Pres. Part. of strike (I.). Producing an effect on, impressing, appealing to, the mind, or imagination; hence, arresting, remarkable; provoking wonder, admiration &c.: *a striking face, portrait, likeness &c.; a striking example of folly &c.*

strikingly, adv. Prec. & -ly. In such a manner as to impress; remarkably.

strikingness, n. See prec. & -ness. Quality of being striking.

striking-plate, n. Metal plate securing latch when door is closed.

string (I.), n. [1. string; 2. striŋ]. O.E. *streng*, 'string of bow, of harp; rope, cable; sinew'; M.E. *streng, string*; cp. O.N. *strengr*; M.L.G. *streng*; fr. *strangi-*, see **strong** (I.). **1.** a Slender, tough line of twisted fibre &c. used for tying; cord, twine: *a piece, ball, of string; to tie a parcel up with string; to pull a toy along by a string*; Phrs. *to pull strings*, use one's influence to bring about some result; specif. **b** cord of bow, bow-string. Phr. *to have two strings to one's bow*, have more than one expedient or means for attaining one's end; *first, second, string,* person or thing that main, alternative, reliance is placed upon. **2.** Slender cord of stretched gut or wire, in certain musical instruments, tightened until it gives forth a specific musical note when made to vibrate: *the strings of a harp, violin &c.* Phrs. *to touch the strings*, to play (harp &c.); *to be for ever harping on the same string*, dwelling on the same subject, idea &c. **3.** Narrow strip of ribbon or other textile fabric used for tying parts of wearing apparel &c. together &c.: *the strings of a bonnet, apron &c.* **4.** Strong, slender, string-like object or substance; specif. **a** tendon: *the string of the tongue, eyes &c.*; **b** fibre connecting the two halves of a pod. **5.** Series of objects threaded on a string; a chain: *a string of beads, pearls &c.* **6.** Long succession of persons, objects &c.: *a string of people, horses*; also *a string of oaths*, series uttered in rapid succession. **7.** (mus., in pl.) *The strings*, group of stringed instruments in an orchestra &c.

string (II.), vb. trans. & intrans., fr. prec. **A.** trans. **1. a** To supply, furnish, with a string or strings: *to string a bow*; **b** (fig.) usually *string up*, to tune; key up, brace: *to string oneself up to a high pitch of expectancy &c.; nerves strung up to the highest pitch*. **2.** To join, link, by a string; to thread, suspend, on a string &c.: *to string beads; beads strung on wire*. Phr. *to string up*, to hang. **3.** To remove string or fibre from (beans &c.). **B.** intrans. (of glue) To become stringy. **C.** Followed by adverb with special meaning. *String out*, to extend in a long line, form into a series: *to string out scouts along the road.*

string-alphabet, n. Alphabet in which each letter is represented by a specific knot or group of knots tied in a cord.

string-band, n. Orchestra of stringed instruments.

string-bark, n. Kind of eucalyptus tree with fibrous bark.

string-board, n. Board running up side of staircase, at right angles to and receiving ends of steps.

string-course, n. Projecting moulding running horizontally along the wall of a building.

stringed, adj. [1. stringd; 2. striŋd]. **string** (I.) & -ed. Having a string or strings: *stringed instruments*; also *four-stringed &c.*

stringency, n. [1. strínjensi; 2. stríndžənsi]. See **stringent** & -ency. State or quality of being stringent; specif. **a** severity; **b** scarcity of money.

stringendo, adv. [1. strinjéndō; 2. strindžéndou]. Ital., fr. Lat. *stringent-(em)*, see next word. (musical direction) Increasing the tempo, accelerating.

stringent, adj. [1. strínjent; 2. stríndžənt], fr. Lat. *stringent-(em)*, Pres. Part. of *stringere*, 'to draw or bind tightly; to touch lightly, graze; to pull or cut off; to draw from the sheath; to check, restrain'; according to Walde, fr. two orig. distinct vbs.: (1) earlier *strengere*, 'to draw tightly'; cogn. w. Gk. *straggaloūn*, 'to twist, strangle', see **strangle**; O.N. *strangr*, 'violent', see **strong** (I.) & **string** (I.); (2) fr. base *streig-*, *stri-g- &c.*, 'to rub, scrape', seen also in Lat. *strigilis*, 'scraper', see **strigil**; O. Slav. *strigǫ*, 'to shear'; O.E. *strīcan*, 'to rub', see **strike**; cp. base *streu-*, 'to rub', seen in **strip** (I.), **stripe** (I.). **1.** Requiring exact obedience or fulfilment, binding, not to be evaded; rigid, rigorous, severe: *stringent regulations*. **2.** (finance) Marked by shortage or scarcity of money; tight: *a stringent money-market.*

stringently, adv. Prec. & -ly. In a stringent manner.

stringer, n. [1. stríngər; 2. strínŋə]. **string** (II.) & -er. **1.** One who, that which, strings. **2.** Timber forming part of framework and supporting other parts of the same structure.

string-halt, n. Disease of muscles in horse's hind leg causing a jerky action; spring-halt.

stringiness, n. [1. stríngines; 2. stríŋinis]. **stringy** & -ness. State or quality of being stringy.

stringless, adj. [1. stríngles; 2. stríŋlis]. **string** (I.) & -less. Without a string or strings.

string-orchestra, n. Orchestra composed of stringed instruments.

string-piece, n. String-board.

string quartet, n. **1.** Quartet of players on stringed instruments, usually two violins, a viola, and a violoncello. **2.** Piece of music composed for such a combination of players.

stringy, adj. [1. stríngi; 2. stríŋi]. **string** (I.) & -y (IV.). **1.** Resembling string; consisting of, containing, tough fibres: *stringy meat; a stringy throat*, one in which the tendons are very apparent. **2.** (of glue &c.) Forming thick, viscous strings; ropy.

stringy-bark, n. String-bark.

strip (I.), vb. trans. & intrans. [1. strip; 2. strip]. O.E. *strȳpan*; M.E. *strīpan*, 'to strip'; cp. O.H.G. *stroufen*, 'to flay'; M. Du. *stroopen*; etymol. obscure; perh. ultimately connected w. base seen in **strike**. **A.** trans. **1. a** To tear off (skin, outer covering &c.): *to strip the bark from a tree, paper off a wall, the hide from a carcass &c.*; **b** to deprive (object) of outer covering, skin, or some external appendage: *to strip a tree of its bark, leaves &c.; the birds have completely stripped the currant bushes*. **2.** Strip (person or thing) of, to deprive of, remove, take away from, bereave, despoil; *to strip a man of his honours, wealth, possessions, pretensions &c.; to strip a house of its furniture*. **3.** Phr. *to strip a cow*, milk her dry, remove all the milk from her. **B.** intrans. **1.** To take one's clothes off; to undress. **2.** Specif. (of a screw) to have the thread torn off.

strip (II.), n., fr. prec., perh. partially influenced in meaning by **stripe** (I.). **1.** Long, narrow, flat piece of thin material; **a** an irregular piece torn, or partially torn, from something; a tatter, a shred: *paper hanging in strips from the wall*; **b** narrow piece of anything, cut or shaped into more or less regular breadth: *a strip of wood nailed over a crack; a strip of paper as a book-mark; a dress trimmed with strips of velvet*. **2.** Long narrow piece of land or vegetation &c. distinct from surroundings: *a strip of garden, woodland, turf, gravel &c.*

stripe (I.), n. [1. strīp; 2. straip]. M.E. *strīpe*, fr. M. Du. *strijpe*; cp. O.H.G. *strīf*; Germ. *streifen*, 'to touch lightly, graze; to strip off; to mark with stripes'; Du. *strippen*, 'to strip off leaves'; prob. related to **strip**. **1. a** Long, narrow mark, line, band, division visibly distinct in colour or character from the surface on which it appears; a streak, stria, variegation: *the stripes of a tiger, zebra; the material is blue with yellow stripes*; specif. **b** stripe or chevron worn on sleeve of uniform as symbol of military rank: *a sergeant's stripes*. Phr. *to get, lose, one's stripes*, be promoted from, degraded to, the ranks. **2.** Blow, stroke, delivered by a rod, lash.

stripe (II.), vb. trans., fr. prec. To impose stripes upon, to mark with a stripe.

striped, adj. [1. strīpt; 2. straipt]. **stripe** (I.) & -ed. Having, marked with, stripes: *striped cloth &c.*; also specif. of animals, e.g. *striped squirrel*.

stripiness, n. [1. strípines; 2. stráipinis]. **stripy** & -ness. State or quality of being stripy.

strip-leaf, n. Tobacco with stalks removed.

stripling, n. [1. strípling; 2. strípliŋ]. **strip** (II.) & -ling (I.). Young man, youth, lad.

stripper, n. [1. strípər; 2. strípə]. **strip** (I.) & -er. One who, that which, strips; esp. a mechanical device for stripping off bark &c.

stripy, adj. [1. strípi; 2. stráipi]. **stripe** (I.) & -y (IV.). Having, marked with, stripes.

strive, vb. intrans. [1. strīv; 2. straiv]. M.E. *strīven*, fr. O. Fr. *estriver*, fr. O. Fr. *estrif*, 'strife, effort'; see **strife**. **1.** To make great efforts, try earnestly, exert oneself: *the swimmer strives to reach the shore; to strive to understand; to strive for victory*. **2.** To fight, struggle, engage in combat: *to strive with, against, an enemy, temptation &c.*

strobile, n. [1. stróbil, stróbīl, -il; 2. stróbil, stróub(a)il], fr. L. Lat. *strobilus*, 'pine-cone', fr. Gk. *stróbīlos*, 'anything twisted or whirling; whirlwind; pirouette; pine-cone'; cp. *stróbos*, 'a twisting round'; *streblós*, 'twisted'; *strabós*, 'crooked', see **strabismus**. (bot.) Pine-cone, fir-cone.

strode, vb. [1. strōd; 2. stroud]. O.E. *strād*, M.E. *strōd*. Pret. of **stride** (I.).

stroke (I.), n. [1. strōk; 2. strouk]. O.E. *strāc*; M.E. *strōk*, 'stroke'; cp. M.H.G. *streich*; cp. also O.E. *strīcan*, 'to rub, stroke', Pret. sing. *strāc*; & see **strike** (I.). **1.** Action of one who strikes; a blow: *with one stroke of the axe*; '*How bowed the woods beneath their sturdy stroke*' (Gray's 'Elegy'). Phrs. *a stroke of genius*, action inspired by genius; *a stroke of luck*, fortunate event or experience; piece of good fortune. **2. a** Single movement of the hand(s), or of an instrument guided by hand, in performing some operation, esp. in games: *a stroke in cricket, tennis, golf, billiards &c.; a backhand stroke; to do a hole in three strokes*; **b** single movement forming part of rhythmical series: *the stroke of a bird's wing, of person swimming, of an oar in rowing &c.* **3. a** Movement of the striking mechanism or hammer in a clock in sounding the hour, blow &c.; **b** sound made by such a blow. Phr. *on the stroke of (five &c.)*, as the hour is being struck or is about to strike. **4.** Line produced by single movement of pen, pencil, brush &c.: *straight, thick,* *fine, strokes* &c. **5.** Sudden attack or access of illness; esp. *paralytic, apoplectic, stroke*; also without qualifying word: *to have a stroke.* **6.** Oarsman nearest stern of boat, and setting time of stroke: *to row stroke.*

stroke (II.), vb. trans., fr. prec., **6.** *To stroke a boat*, row stroke in it.

stroke (III.), vb. trans. O.E. *strācian*; M.E. *strōken*, 'to stroke'; fr. O.E. *strāc*, 'stroke', see **stroke (I.)**. **1.** To draw one's hand with gentle pressure over surface of, to caress: *to stroke one's hair, a cat.* Phrs. *to stroke one (up) the wrong way*, irritate him; *to stroke one down*, soothe him, allay irritation. **2.** To smooth, set in order (gathers in needlework &c.), by drawing point of needle &c. down each.

stroke (IV.), n., fr. prec. Act of stroking.

strokingly, adv. [1. strṓkingli; 2. stróukiŋli], fr. Pres. Part. of **stroke (III.)** & **-ly.** In the manner of one who strokes; caressingly.

stroll (I.), vb. intrans. [1. strōl; 2. stroul]. Origin unknown. To take a short, leisurely walk; to saunter, walk quietly and without hurry.

stroll (II.), n., fr. prec. A quiet, leisurely walk; a saunter.

stroller, n. [1. strṓler; 2. stróulə]. **stroll (I.)** & **-er.** One who strolls; specif. (rare) strolling player.

strolling, adj. [1. strṓling; 2. stróuliŋ], fr. Pres. Part. of **stroll (I.)**. Going from place to place, itinerant: *a strolling player, minstrel* &c.

stroma, n. [1. strṓma; 2. stróumə]. Gk. *strôma*, 'covering'; cp. Gk. *strōtós*, 'spread out'; *stórnūmi*, 'I extend, spread out; spread a covering over'; Lat. *strātus*, 'layer, covering'; see **stratum**, & words there referred to. (biol.) Fine network of connective tissue forming the framework of an organ or cell.

stromatic, adj. [1. strōmátik; 2. stroumǽtik], fr. Gk. *strômat-*, stem of *strôma*, 'covering', see prec., & **-ic.** Of, pertaining to, forming, of the nature of, a stroma.

strong (I.), adj. [1. strong; 2. strɔŋ]. O.E., M.E. *strang, strong*; cp. O.N. *strangr*; O.H.G. *strang, streng*, 'strong, severe, powerful'; prob. cogn. w. M. Ir. *srengim*, 'I draw, drag'; Gk. *straggaloûn*, 'twist, strangle', see **strangle**; Lett. *stringt*, 'to stiffen'; see also **string (I.)**. **1. a** Physically powerful, capable of exerting great force; muscular: *strong arms*; *he is enormously strong*; Phr. *with a strong hand*, forcibly; **b** morally powerful, possessing great force of character, tenacity of purpose: *the strong man of the government*; *a strong, silent man*; **c** intellectually powerful, capable of vigorous, clear thinking: *a strong brain, intelligence, imagination.* **2. a** Tough, firm, stout, durable; not easily broken; resisting strains: *a strong chain, branch*; *strong cord, wall* &c.; **b** difficult to capture, capable of resistance, well protected, easy to defend: *a strong fortress, position* &c. Phr. *one's strong point*, something in which one excels; a good quality &c. **3.** Producing considerable effect, rigorous, drastic, acting powerfully: *strong remedies*; *to take strong measures.* **4.** Robust, vigorous, hale; in good health and physical condition; sound: *he is far from strong, quite strong again*; *a strong constitution.* **5.** Not weak or diluted; containing a large proportion of essential quality: *strong tea, coffee, whisky* &c.; *strong drink*, alcoholic liquor. **6.** Affecting the senses powerfully and keenly: *a strong smell, taste* &c.; specif. **b** rank, ill-smelling. **7. a** Deeply felt, vigorously held; pronounced, decided, intense; *strong opinions, suspicions*; *a strong sense of disappointment*; *strong feeling*; **b** appealing powerfully to the mind; cogent, conclusive: *strong reasons, arguments.* **8.** Expressing ideas and emotions vigorously and unambiguously: *a strong expression.* Phr. *strong language*, swearing, blasphemy. **9.** Possessing a stated strength; amounting to, reckoned at, a specified number or figure: *an army 10,000 strong.* **10.** (of wind) Moving rapidly, of considerable velocity. **11.** (gram.) **a** *Strong verb*, in Germanic languages, one which exhibits gradational changes in conjugation; **b** *strong noun*, in Germanic and Aryan, one which had originally a vowel stem. **12.** (commerc.) *Markets, prices, are strong*, tending to rise.

strong (II.), adv., fr. prec. (slang) Strongly, vigorously; esp. in Phr. (*he is*) *going strong*, continues to be vigorous, healthy &c.; still in action; *that is coming it rather strong*, making an extravagant claim, proposal &c.; *going it rather strong*, behaving in an extravagant manner.

strong-box, n. Strong chest of iron for storing deeds and other important documents.

stronghold, n. [1. stróng-hōld; 2. strɔ́ŋhould]. Place of defence or refuge, fortified or defensible position: *a robber's stronghold in the mountains*; (also fig.) *a stronghold of superstition* &c., place where it flourishes.

strongish, adj. [1. stróngish; 2. strɔ́ŋiʃ]. **strong (I.)** & **-ish (I.)**. Fairly strong.

strongly, adv. [1. stróngli; 2. strɔ́ŋli]. **strong (I.)** & **-ly.** In a strong manner, vigorously.

strong-minded, adj. **a** Having capable, vigorous, resolute mind; **b** specif., *strong-minded woman*, one who is free, or supposed to be free, from ordinary feminine weaknesses.

strong-room, n. Fire-proof or burglar-proof room, usually built in thickness of a wall, and provided with heavy iron door, for storing valuables.

strontia, n. [1. strónsha; 2. strɔ́nʃə]. See **strontium** & **-ia.** Oxide of strontium.

strontian, n. & adj. [1. strónshan; 2. strɔ́nʃən]. See **strontium** & **-an.** **1.** n. Oxide of strontium. **2.** adj. Pertaining to, consisting of, strontia or strontium.

strontium, n. [1. strónshum; 2. strɔ́nʃəm], fr. Strontian, in Argyllshire, where the metal was first found, & **-ium.** Yellowish, ductile, metallic element, whose salts burn with a red flame.

strop, n. & vb. trans. [1. strop; 2. strɔp]. O.E., M.E. *stropp*; see **strap (I.)**. **1.** n. **a** Leather strap, or a piece of wood covered with leather &c., for putting an edge on razors; **b** (naut.) band of leather, rope, or iron round pulley. **2.** vb. To put an edge on to (a razor) by applying it to a strop.

strophanthus, n. [1. strofánthus; 2. strɔfǽnþəs], fr. Gk. *strophḗ*, see **strophe**, & *ánthos*, 'flower', see **anther**. **a** A genus of tropical African plants; **b** a poisonous drug made from the seeds of this, used in heart disease, also called *strophanthin.*

strophe, n. [1. strṓfi; 2. stróufi], more rarely [1. strófi; 2. strɔ́fi]. Gk. *strophḗ*, 'a turning, twisting'; cp. Gk. *stróphos*, 'cord'; *stréphein*, 'to turn'; fr. base **strebh-*; cp. the parallel form **streb-*, 'to turn, twist', in Gk. *streblós*, 'twisted'; *stróbos*, 'whirlpool'; *strabós*, 'squinting'; see **strobile, strabismus,** & **strepto-coccus.** **1.** (Gk. theatre) **a** Specif., the dancing of chorus in Greek play towards one side of scene; **b** song sung during this evolution. **2.** A regular arrangement or group of metrical lines in a poem; **a** loosely, a verse, a stanza; **b** strictly, former of two corresponding stanzas, in an ode, of which the second is the antistrophe.

strophic, adj. [1. strṓfik, strófik; 2. stróufik, strɔ́fik]. Prec. & **-ic.** Pertaining to, characteristic of, written in, strophes.

strove, vb. [1. strōv; 2. strouv]. Pret. of **strive**, formed on the anal. of the Engl. strong vb. *drive, drove* &c.

strow, vb. trans. [1. strō; 2. strou]. O.E. *strāwian, strēawian*; M.E. *strōwian*, variant of **strew.** (archaic) To strew, scatter.

struck, vb. [1. struk; 2. strak]. Pret. & P.P. of **strike.** The form *struck* occurs fr. the early 17th cent., perh. on the anal. of **stuck.** Cp. O.E. *strāk*, M.E. *strook.*

structural, adj. [1. strúkchural; 2. strákt∫ərəl]. **structure** & **-al.** Pertaining to, connected, associated, with, structure: *the structural beauties of a building, a play* &c.

structurally, adv. Prec. & **-ly.** From the point of view of structure, as regards structure.

structure, n. [1. strúkchur; 2. strákt∫ə]. Lat. *structūra*, 'mode of building, construction; edifice, erection; arrangement, order', fr. *struct-(um)*, P.P. type of *struere*, 'to put together, construct, erect, build'; cp. Lat. *struēs*, 'heap, pile; series of layers'; Lat. *strātum*, 'layer'; cogn. w. O.E. *strēawian*, 'to scatter', see **strew, straw (I.)**. **1.** Way in which a body is built up; arrangement and mode of connexion of the parts of an organic whole; formation, construction, organization of component parts: *the structure of a building, cell, organ* &c.; *the structure of rocks*; *the structure of a sentence, of a language.* **2.** Something that is constructed; specif., a building: *a tall, top-heavy structure*; *the earthquake shook the structure to its foundations.*

structured, adj. [1. strúkchurd; 2. strákt∫əd]. Prec. & **-ed.** Having a structure of specific kind; having carefully designed mode of arrangement.

structureless, adj. [1. strúkchurles; 2. strákt∫əlis]. **structure** & **-less.** Without structure; lacking any specific arrangement of parts.

struggle (I.), vb. intrans. [1. strúgl; 2. strágl]. M.E. *strogelen*, 'to struggle'; origin uncertain; perh. connected w. **strike (I.)** & **stroke (I.)**. **1. a** To fight, offer resistance; to attempt to free oneself from physical constraint by violent bodily movements: *the prisoner struggled fiercely with the police before being arrested*; *the rabbit struggled to escape from the snare*; **b** to grapple with, attempt to solve or overcome, intellectual difficulty: *to struggle with mathematical problems* &c. **2.** To move the limbs and body violently and convulsively: *he struggled for a moment and then died*; *to struggle to one's feet.* **3.** To make a strenuous effort, attempt vigorously, to accomplish something: *to struggle to get a position in society*; *to struggle to make oneself heard.*

struggle (II.), n., fr. prec. **1.** Act of struggling; **a** violent movement, effort to free oneself from constraint, or against odds, or to reach a position in spite of opposition; a fight, a rough-and-tumble: *a violent struggle to escape*; *a sharp struggle with the police*; **b** convulsive movement of limbs: *the wounded animal made a short struggle, and then lay still.* **2.** Effort of any kind, strenuous attempt to overcome difficulties: *a desperate struggle to make both ends meet*; *the struggle for existence*; *a hard struggle to get one's work done in time.*

struggling, adj. [1. strúgling; 2. strágliŋ], fr. Pres. Part. of **struggle (I.)**. Engaged in a struggle; esp. striving with difficulty to overcome poverty or obscurity &c.: *a struggling painter, genius* &c.

strugglingly, adv. Prec. & **-ly.** With, by means of, a struggle.

struldbrug, n. [1. strúldbrug; 2. stráldbrag]. Arbitrary coinage. One of a class of human beings in Luggnagg, described in Swift's *Gulliver's Travels* (Vge. to Laputa, ch. x.), who were unable to die, but who, after the age of eighty, exhibited all the signs of senility, gradually lost both physical and mental vigour, and were unable to remember the words of their own language, or to understand that spoken by the younger generation.

strum (I.), vb. intrans. & trans. [1. strum; 2. stram]. Prob. fr. **thrum (II.)**. **1.** intrans. To play musical instrument by thumping heavily, or plucking the strings violently; to play noisily and carelessly: *to strum on a piano, on a banjo*; *he strums from morning to night.* **2.** trans. To strum on: *to sit for hours strumming the piano.*

strum (II.), n., fr. prec. Act of strumming; noisy, careless playing on a piano or plucking instrument.

struma, n. [1. strōōma; 2. strū́mə]. Lat. *strūma*, 'scrofulous tumour; swollen neck'; prob. cogn. w. Gk. *strūphnós*, 'hard, firm'; O.N. *str(j)ūpi*, 'throat'; O.H.G. *strūbēn*, 'to stand stiffly'. **1.** Scrofula. **2.** Morbid enlargement of the thyroid gland; goitre. **3.** (bot.) Small, soft swelling at the base of an organ.

strumose, adj. [1. strōōmōs; 2. strŭmous], fr. Lat. *strŭmōsus*, 'scrofulous'; prec. & **-ose**. Strumous.

strumous, adj. [1. strōōmus; 2. strŭməs]. **struma** & **-ous**. a Resembling, of the nature of, struma; **b** afflicted with struma.

strumpet, n. [1. strúmpet; 2. strámpit]. M.E. *strumpet*, possibly fr. O. Fr. *strupe*, *stupre*, fr. Lat. *stuprum*, 'dishonour, violation'; orig. 'punishment, banishment', cogn. w. Gk. *túptein*, 'to strike'; *túpos*, 'blow, imprint', see **type** (I.); O. Fris. *stŭpa*, 'chastisement'. A prostitute.

strung, vb. [1. strung; 2. straŋ]. Pret. & P.P. of **string**, vb.

strut (I.), vb. intrans. & n. [1. strut; 2. strat]. O.E. *strŭtian*, 'to stand stiffly'; M.E. *strouten*, 'to swell out, strut'; cp. M.H.G. *strŭz*, 'swelling, contention'; cogn. w. Lat. *trŭdere*, 'to push, press', see **intrude**; O. Slav. *truditi*, 'to trouble'; cp. also without initial *s*-, O.E. *prēatian*, 'to threaten', see **threat** & **thrust** (I.); O.H.G. *drīozan*, 'to oppress'. **1.** vb. To walk with stiff, pompous, affected, self-conscious gait. **2.** n. Act of strutting; self-satisfied, swaggering, pompous gait.

strut (II.), n. & vb. trans. Cp. L.G. *strutt*, 'stiff, rigid'; cogn. w. prec. **1.** n. A prop, stay, or support, esp. for a wooden structure, consisting of a piece of timber placed at an angle and pressing in the contrary direction from the strain or thrust. **2.** vb. To support, keep in position by a strut.

struthious, adj. [1. strōōthius; 2. strŭpiəs], fr. Lat. *strŭthio*, fr. Gk. *strouthós*, 'sparrow', ostrich'; prob. earlier **strousthos* & cogn. w. O.H.G. *drōsca*; O.E. *þrysce*, 'thrush', see **throstle**; Lat. *turdus*, 'thrush', see **turdine**; O. Prussian *tresde*, 'thrush'. Pertaining to, connected with, the ostrich.

strutting, adj. [1. strúting; 2. strátiŋ], fr. Pres. Part. of **strut** (I.). Performed with, characterized by, a strut: *a strutting walk*.

struttingly, adv. Prec. & **-ly**. In a strutting manner.

strychnia, n. [1. stríknia; 2. strikniə], fr. Lat. *strychnos*, fr. Gk. *strúchnos*, 'kind of nightshade', etymol. unknown, & **-ia**. (archaic) Strychnine.

strychnic, adj. [1. stríknik; 2. stríknik], fr. Lat. *strychnos*, 'nightshade', see prec., & **-ic**. Pertaining to, caused by, strychnine.

strychnin(e), n. [1. stríknin, -ēn; 2. stríknin, -īn], fr. Lat. *strychnos*, 'nightshade', see **strychnia**, & **-ine**. White, crystalline, highly poisonous alkaloid, obtained from tropical plants of the genus *Strychnos*, especially *S. Nux vomica*; used medicinally in minute quantities as a stimulant for the nerves.

strychn(in)ism, n. [1. stríkn(in)izm, -ēnizm; 2. strĭkn(in)izəm, -īnizəm]. Prec. & **-ism**. Strychnine poisoning, characterized by spasm and violent contraction of the muscles.

stub (I.), n. [1. stub; 2. stab]. O.E. *stybb*; M.E. *stubbe*, 'stock of tree'; cp. M.L.G. *stubbe*; O.N. *stubbi*; cogn. w. O.N. *stŭfr*, 'stump'; Gk. *stúpos*, 'stump, stick'; Lett. *stups*, 'stump'; cp. further Gk. *túptein*, 'to strike'; *túpos*, 'blow'; imprint'; & see **type** (I.), **stump** (I.). **1.** Lower part of trunk or stalk of a tree left when upper part is cut off; a stump. **2.** Short, thick, portion, or stump, of such an object as a pencil, cigar, &c., the main part of which has been worn down, used, or consumed.

stub (II.), vb. trans., fr. prec. **1.** To clear (land) of stumps, roots &c. **2.** (usually, *stub up*) To remove (stumps &c.) from ground. **3. a** To strike (foot) accidentally against a hard object, esp. *to stub one's toe*; **b** to thrust, poke, with, or as with, a stub.

stubble, n. [1. stúbl; 2. stábl]. M.E. *stuble*, *stobul*; fr. O. Fr. *estouble*, fr. Lat. *stipula*, 'stalk, stem'; straw; stubble', see **stipule**. **1.** Short, stiff stalks of grain left standing in the field after reaping. **2.** Anything resembling stubble, esp. short, stiff, bristling growth of hair on the chin.

stubbly, adj. [1. stúbli; 2. stábli]. Prec. & **-y** (IV.). **1.** Of, covered with, full of, stubble. **2.** Like stubble, short and bristling.

stubborn, adj. [1. stúbern; 2. stábən]. M.E. *stoburn*, *stiborn*, prob. fr. O.E. *stybb*, 'stump of tree', see **stub** (I.). **1.** Resolute, determined, inflexible; not easily overcome, staunch: *stubborn courage*; *a stubborn resistance*. **2.** (of persons) Not accessible to reason; obstinate, intractable, pig-headed.

stubbornly, adv. Prec. & **-ly**. In a stubborn manner.

stubbornness, n. See prec. & **-ness**. Quality of being stubborn.

stubby, adj. [1. stúbi; 2. stábi]. **stub** (I.) & **-y** (IV.). Like a stub; short, thick, stumpy, squat: *a stubby bit of pencil*; *a short stubby figure*.

stub-iron, n. Iron refashioned from old horseshoe nails and used for gun-barrels.

stucco, n. & vb. trans. [1. stúkō; 2. stákou]. Ital., fr. O.H.G. *stucchi*, 'crust; piece, fragment'; cp. O.E. *stock*, 'stump, piece', see **stock** (I.). **1.** n. Fine white plaster used as external coating for walls, for architectural ornaments in relief &c. **2.** vb. To cover (wall, house &c.) with stucco.

stuck, vb. [1. stuk; 2. stak]. Pret. & P.P. of **stick**, perh. on the anal. of **stung**, Pret. of **sting**.

stuck-up, adj. [1. stúk up; 2. sták ap], fr. P.P. of **stick**. (colloq.) Vain, conceited, haughty.

stud (I.), n. [1. stud; 2. stad]. O.E., M.E. *stōd*, 'stud, herd of horses'; cp. O.N. *stōð*, O.H.G. *stuot*, 'stud', Mod. Germ. *stute*, 'mare'; cp. also O.E. *stēda*, 'a stallion', see **steed**; the word is fr. base **stā-* &c., 'to stand', & the orig. sense was prob. 'standing-place (for horses)'; cp. similar transference of sense in **stable** (II.) **a** Number of horses and mares kept for breeding; **b** collection of horses for hunting, racing &c.

stud (II.), n. O.E. *studu*, 'post, buttress'; M.E. *stude*, 'stud, button'; cp. O.H.G. *(unter)stuzzen*, 'to prop, support'; O.N. *styðja*, 'to establish, support'; fr. base **stā-* as Gk. *stúlos*, 'pillar', see **style** (III.). **1.** One of a series of supporting posts in a framework &c. **2.** Large-headed, projecting nail or peg used to strengthen or ornament a surface. **3.** Kind of button consisting of a short neck, with a flattened base and a smaller round or flat head, used to fasten collar, shirt-front &c.; similar object used for buttoning two edges of leather &c. together. **4.** Cross-bar strengthening a link in a chain cable.

stud (III.), vb. trans., fr. prec. (chiefly in P.P.) **1.** To cover, ornament with short, projecting studs: *an iron-studded door*. **2. a** To set thickly, encrust: *a box studded with gems*; **b** to sprinkle, bespangle: *sky studded with stars*; *a plain studded with trees*.

stud-book, n. Register of pedigrees of thoroughbred horses.

studding-sail, n. [1. stúnsl; 2. stánsl]. Etymol. unknown. Narrow, auxiliary sail set beyond outer edge of square sail in light wind.

student, n. [1. stúdnt; 2. stjúdnt], fr. Lat. *student-(em)*, Pres. Part. of *studēre*, 'to apply oneself to, engage in, occupy oneself with'; either cogn. w. Goth. *stiwiti*, 'patience, endurance', fr. **stewedjo-*, cp. Lat. *studium*, 'zeal, eagerness', see **study**, or, w. orig. sense, 'to strive after, aim at something', connected w. Lat. *tundere*, 'to strike', & *tudes*, 'hammer', see **stint** (I.). **1.** Specif., person engaged in the acquisition of knowledge, esp. one not yet a graduate, at a university, college &c.; person engaged in a course of study at a learned institution: *a medical student*; *a hostel for students*. **2.** One who studies; **a** a person who is devoted to learning, who pursues study or investigation in any special branch of knowledge or human experience: *a profound student of theology, archaeology &c.*; **b** a person of studious habits: *he is a man of action rather than a student*. **3.** (cap.) At Christ Church, Oxford, senior member of the foundation, and of the governing body of the college; equivalent to a Fellow at other colleges.

studentship, n. [1. stúdntship; 2. stjúdntʃip]. Prec. & **-ship**. **1.** Endowment for scholarship at certain colleges. **2.** Position of a student at Christ Church, Oxford.

stud-farm, n. Farm where horses are bred.

stud-groom, n. Groom employed in looking after a stud; esp. head-groom.

stud-horse, n. Horse kept for breeding, a stallion.

studied, adj. [1. stúdid; 2. stádid], fr. P.P. of **study** (II.). Carefully planned, deliberate, intentional, premeditated: *studied indifference*; *a studied insult*; *a style which is too studied*, mannered, over-careful, lacking spontaneity.

studiedly, adv. Prec. & **-ly**. In a studied manner; deliberately.

studio, n. [1. stúdiō; 2. stjúdiou]. Ital., fr. Lat. *studium*, 'zeal, eagerness, exertion, study'; see **study** (I.), **student**. Workroom of painter, sculptor, photographer &c.

studious, adj. [1. stúdius; 2. stjúdiəs], fr. Lat. *studiōsus*, 'zealous, assiduous; devoted to study', fr. *studium*, 'zeal, application, study', see **study** (I.), & **-ous**. **1.** Devoted to, occupied with, engaged in, study. **2.** Deliberate, careful, studied: *studious politeness*. **3.** Eager, careful, zealous: *studious to obey*.

studiously, adv. Prec. & **-ly**. In a studious manner.

studiousness, n. Prec. & **-ness**. State or quality of being studious.

study (I.), n. [1. stúdi; 2. stádi]. M.E. *studie*, 'thought, study'; fr. O. Fr. *estudie*, fr. Lat. *studium*, 'zeal, eagerness; assiduity, application; application to learning, study'. Cp. **student**. **1.** Object of solicitude; earnest endeavour, deliberate intention: *his constant study is to please*. **2.** Act of applying the mind to the acquisition of erudition and knowledge; systematic cultivation and pursuit of science and learning: *fonder of sport than of study*. **3. a** Systematic attention to, and pursuit of, knowledge in some specific branch of learning or science: *the study of history, ancient languages, electricity, politics &c.*; *to begin, interrupt, one's studies*; **b** careful examination, scrutiny, critical consideration, concentration of the attention: *the study of a document*; *the study of human nature*; Phr. *in a brown study*, in an abstracted state of mind, distrait. **4.** Subject studied; branch of learning, department of knowledge: *philology and archaeology are comparatively modern studies*; *humane studies*. **5.** Something deserving or attracting attention, interest, or observation: *his face was a perfect study*. **6.** An excursus, dissertation, essay, embodying the results of a special investigation: Froude's '*Short Studies in Great Subjects*'. **7.** A drawing, painting, sketch, **a** exhibiting an experimental treatment of an object, as part of a training; or **b** an experimental, tentative, essay to portray some particular aspect or part of a subject. **8.** Musical composition designed as an exercise in technique. **9.** Actor considered from the point of view of his faculty for memorizing a part in a play: *a quick study &c.* **10.** Room in which studies are carried on; specif., a room in a private house devoted to one person, generally containing a library, in which reading, writing, and the transaction of private business is carried out.

study (II.), vb. trans. & intrans. M.E. *studien*, fr. O. Fr. *estudier*, fr. *estudie*, 'study', see prec. **A.** trans. **1. a** To pay great attention to, be concerned with or for, act in regard to: *to study one's own interests, another's comfort &c.*; **b** to show deference, solicitude, regard, respect, consideration, for: *he studies his parents in every possible way*. **2.** To seek to acquire knowledge of, apply oneself to learning: *to study history, medicine &c.* **3. a** To examine, investigate, make a

study of: *to study social conditions at first hand*; **b** specif., to scrutinize, gaze carefully at, examine in detail: *to study a map, a person's face* &c. **4.** To learn by heart, memorize (part in play &c.). **B.** intrans. **1.** To endeavour, direct one's efforts, apply one's mind to: '*May he ever study to preserve thy people committed to his charge*'; *study to be wise*. **2.** To engage in study; be a student; **a** to carry out the process of acquiring knowledge, to receive one's intellectual training and education: *to study at a university*; **b** to work at, endeavour to increase one's knowledge by study: *he never studied after he left the university*. **3.** (archaic) To reflect, contemplate, meditate. **C.** Followed by adverbs or prepositions with special meanings. *Study for*, to undertake special course of instruction or training for: *to study for the Bar, the Church* &c. *Study out*, to elucidate by study; to puzzle out: *to study out a plan, a problem* &c.

stuff (I.), n. [1. stuf; 2. staf]. M.E. *stuffe, stoffe*, fr. O. Fr. *estoffe*, fr. Lat. *stuppa*, 'coarse part of flax, tow', q.v. under **stop (I.)**. **1. a** Substance, matter of all sorts: *dynamite is queer stuff to play with*; *rhubarb is nasty stuff to take*; (also of non-material things) *his poems are poor stuff*. Phrs. (colloq.) *the sort of stuff, the stuff, to give them*, the proper treatment, the right way to deal with, the right thing to say; *green stuff*, vegetables; *doctor's stuff*, medicine; **b** (disparaging or contempt.) (i.) rubbish, worthless, heterogeneous material or objects: *what shall I do with all this stuff from the cupboard?*; (ii.) silly, fantastic nonsense: *all stuff! I don't believe a word of it*; *stuff and nonsense!* **2. a** That from which anything, material or non-material, is constructed or made: *tallow is the stuff of which candles are made*; *to collect the stuff for a book*; (fig.) *he is made of sterner stuff than his father*, has a more resolute character; *not the stuff of which poets are made*, not possessing the mental qualities, temperament &c.; **b** essential quality, character, content, constituent elements: *a man with plenty of good stuff in him*. **3.** Textile fabric: *I don't like the stuff that your dress is made of*; specif., woollen fabric: *a dress made of stuff*.

stuff (II.), adj., fr. prec. Made of woollen fabric: *stuff gown*, specif., gown worn by barrister before becoming a king's counsel and adopting a silk gown.

stuff (III.), vb. trans. & intrans., fr. **stuff (I.)**. **A.** trans. **1. a** (i.) To fill tightly, pack, cram, with: *to stuff a box with old clothes, a sack with leaves* &c.; (ii.) (fig.) *to stuff one's mind, head, with facts* &c., fill full, overload; (colloq.) *to stuff a person*, tell him what is untrue, hoax him, play on his credulity; specif. **b** to fill (a pillow, mattress, seat of a chair &c.) as an upholsterer does: *this cushion ought to be freshly stuffed*; *a mattress stuffed with horsehair*; **c** to fill with food: *to stuff oneself*, overeat. **2.** To preserve (a dead animal, bird &c.) by packing the skin with tow &c., treating with preservatives, placing limbs in a lifelike attitude, and mounting. **3.** To put spices, condiments &c. into: *to stuff a duck with sage and onions* &c. **4.** To thrust, crowd, cram, ram, press (objects), with force into a receptacle or into a narrow space: *to stuff one's clothes into a trunk*; *just stuff a cushion behind my head, please*. **B.** intrans. To eat to excess; to eat voraciously, overeat; to cram, guzzle, eat like a pig.

stuffiness, n. [1. stúfines; 2. stáfinis]. **stuffy** & **-ness**. State of being stuffy.

stuffing, n. [1. stúfing; 2. stáfiŋ]. **stuff (III.)** & **-ing**. Material with which something is stuffed or packed: *a the stuffing of a cushion, doll* &c.; Phr. (colloq.) *to knock the stuffing out of*, (i.) take self-confidence or conceit out of, disconcert, discompose (a person); (ii.) to unnerve, render weak & shaky, as by a shock, illness &c.; (iii.) show (argument &c.) to be worthless; (iii.) render ineffective; **b** compressed mass of pungent, savoury spices, herbs, chopped meat &c., inserted and cooked in a bird or joint of meat to impart flavour.

stuffing-box, n. Chamber filled with packing to reduce leakage of steam, water &c. from the hole in which a piston-rod moves.

stuffy, adj. [1. stúfi; 2. stáfi]. **stuff (I.)** & **-y (IV.)**. **1. a** (of room) Ill-ventilated, imperfectly supplied with fresh air; close, airless, fusty, frowsty; **b** (of air) exhausted, reverse of fresh, used-up, musty; **c** (of weather) close, steamy, reverse of bracing. **2.** (of persons, mind) Not easily accessible to new ideas; dull, stodgy; sticky.

stuggy, adj. [1. stúgi; 2. stági]. Prob. a variant of **stocky**. Stocky.

stultification, n. [1. stùltifikáshun; 2. stàltifikéiʃən]. See next word & **-fication**. Act of stultifying; state of being stultified.

stultify, vb. trans. [1. stúltifi; 2. stáltifai], fr. L. Lat. *stultificāre*, 'to make foolish', fr. *stultus*, 'foolish', & **-fy**; cp. Lat. *stolō*, 'useless sucker'; *stolidus*, 'dull, stupid', see **stolid**; cogn. w. Scrt. *sthūláš*, 'thick, coarse, stupid'; O.E. *stille*, 'motionless, silent', see **still (I.)**. To make of no effect, cause to appear in a foolish light; make inconsistent, destroy value or weight of, spoil effect of: *to go back on one's word now would be to stultify oneself hopelessly*; *this clause is stultified by what follows*.

stum, n. & vb. trans. [1. stum; 2. stam], fr. Du. *stom*, 'stum', fr. adj. *stom*, 'silent, still'; cp. Mod. Germ. *stumm*, 'dumb'; cp. **stammer** & **stem (III.)**. **1.** n. Wholly or partially unfermented grape-juice. **2.** vb. To prevent or hinder fermentation of (grape-juice) by adding sodium sulphite &c.

stumble (I.), vb. intrans. & trans. [1. stúmbl; 2. stámbl]. M.E. *stom(b)len*; cp. M. Du. *stomelen*; cp. M.E., M. Du. *stameren*; O.H.G. *stammalōn*, 'to stammer', see **stammer** & prec. **A.** intrans. **1. a** To trip up, miss one's footing, lose balance, in walking, running &c., esp. by catching foot in, or striking foot against, an object, or from weakness &c.: *to stumble and fall*; *to stumble over a stone*; **b** (fig.) to err, make a mistake, to be guilty of a moral or intellectual lapse. **2.** To speak, read, recite &c. haltingly, with frequent mistakes, hesitations &c.; to falter, blunder: *to stumble over one's words*; *to stumble through a speech, lesson* &c. **B.** trans. (archaic) To disconcert, perplex, trouble. **C.** Followed by adverbs or prepositions with special meanings. *Stumble across*, intrans., to come upon, discover, by chance. *Stumble along*, intrans., to walk or run with a stumbling gait. *Stumble at*, intrans., to hesitate over, be disconcerted, perplexed, embarrassed by. *Stumble (up)on*, stumble across.

stumble (II.), n., fr. prec. Act of stumbling; sudden loss of foothold, halt in progress due to catching one's foot &c.

stumbling, adj. [1. stúmbling; 2. stámbliŋ], fr. Pres. Part. of **stumble (I.)**. Hesitating, unsteady, faltering: *a stumbling gait*; *a stumbling speech*.

stumbling-block, n. (fig.) Something that hinders progress; impediment, obstacle: *a stumbling-block to faith*.

stumblingly, adv. [1. stúmblingli; 2. stámbliŋli]. **stumbling** & **-ly**. In a stumbling manner.

stumer, n. [1. stúmer; 2. stjúmə]. Etymol. unknown. (slang) Worthless, forged, counterfeit, coin, note, or cheque.

stump (I.), n. [1. stump; 2. stamp]. M.E. *stumpe, stompe*, fr. O.N. *stumpr*; cp. M. Du. *stomp*; M.L.G. *stump*; M.H.G. *stumpf*; cogn. w. Scrt. *tu(m)páti*, 'strikes, pushes'; cp. further, without m, O.N. *stúfr*, 'stump'; Gk. *stúpos*, 'stick'; *túptein*, 'to strike'; *túpos*, 'blow', see **type (I.)**; cp. Lett. *stupe*, 'broomstick'. **1. a** Lower part of trunk of tree left in ground when upper part has fallen or been felled; stock, stub; specif. **b** tree-stump or similar object from which speaker addresses crowd &c. Phr. *stump oratory, speeches* &c., bombastic, ranting speeches, esp. on political affairs, such as are made from a stump; Phr. *to go, be, on the stump*, engage in a campaign of stump oratory. **2.** Any short, thick, more or less cylindrical body left when the remainder has been removed, worn off &c.: *the stump of a tooth, amputated limb, mast, pencil, candle* &c. Phr. *to stir one's stumps*, move the legs, walk, hurry. **3.** (cricket) One of three upright sticks forming the wicket. **4.** Pointed, rubber stick, or stiff cylinder of paper, used to apply or soften charcoal &c. in drawing.

stump (II.), vb. trans. & intrans., fr. prec. **A.** trans. **1. a** (cricket) To put batsman out by striking the bails from the wicket while he is outside his ground; **b** (fig., colloq.) to puzzle, disconcert, defeat, esp. by asking questions which cannot be answered, or presenting difficulties which cannot be resolved: *to be stumped by an examination question*; *I was completely stumped when the car began to slide backwards down the hill*. **2.** (drawing &c.) To apply (pigment), tone down, soften, with a stump. **3.** (See prec. **1. b**.) In Phr. *to stump the country*, a constituency, to travel about addressing meetings in support of a political or other cause: *to stump the country on Tariff Reform* &c. **B.** intrans. To walk with stiff, heavy steps; esp. *stump along*. **C.** Followed by adverb. *Stump up*, trans., (slang) to pay out.

stumper, n. [1. stúmper; 2. stámpə]. **stump (II.)** & **-er**. One who, that which, stumps; specif. (colloq.) puzzling problem, question &c.; a poser.

stumpily, adv. [1. stúmpili; 2. stámpili]. **stumpy** & **-ly**. In a stumpy manner.

stumpiness, n. [1. stúmpines; 2. stámpinis]. Next word & **-ness**. Quality of being stumpy.

stumpy, adj. [1. stúmpi; 2. stámpi]. **stump (I.)** & **-y (IV.)**. Short and thickset, stubby, stocky, cobby.

stun, vb. trans. [1. stun; 2. stan]. M.E. *stonien* &c., 'to stun, astonish', fr. O. Fr. *estoner*, 'to stun, resound', fr. L. Lat. *extonāre*, 'to resound'; cp. also O.E. *stunian*, 'to resound, dash against'; O.N. *stynia*, 'to groan'; cogn. w. Gk. *sténein*, 'to groan'; Scrt. *stánati*, 'thunders'; *tányati*, 'rustles, roars'; Lat. *tonāre*, 'to thunder'; O.E. *þunor*, 'thunder', see **thunder**. **1.** To inflict a severe physical shock to, as by a heavy blow or impact, which temporarily destroys consciousness and power of movement. **2.** To cause a shock to the nerves; to amaze, astound, by unexpected news &c., to the point of producing momentary confusion of mind: *completely stunned by the (news of the) disaster*.

Stundism, n. [1. stóondizm; 2. stúndizəm], fr. Germ. *stunde*, 'hour; lesson'; cp. O.E., O.N. *stund*; O. Fris. *stunde*, 'moment, time, hour'. Doctrine of the Stundists.

Stundist, n. [1. stóondist; 2. stúndist]. See prec. & **-ist**. Member of a body of dissenters from the Russian Orthodox Church, rejecting all forms and ceremonies, and basing their doctrines entirely on the Modern Russian translation of the Bible (1861).

stung, vb. [1. stung; 2. staŋ]. Pret. & P.P. of **sting**; O.E. *(ge)stungen*, P.P.

stunk, vb. [1. stungk; 2. staŋk]. Pret. & P.P. of **stink**; O.E. *(ge)stuncen*, P.P.

stunner, n. [1. stúner; 2. stánə]. **stun** & **-er**. (slang) Person or object that surprises and delights by his or its qualities of beauty or excellence.

stunning, adj. [1. stúning; 2. stániŋ]. Pres. Part. of **stun**. **1.** Producing physical or mental shock; causing loss or partial loss of consciousness: *a stunning blow on the head*; (also fig.) *stunning blow*, terrible, paralysing shock. **2.** (slang) Producing a pleasant surprise; hence highly delightful, splendid; topping.

stunningly, adv. Prec. & **-ly**. In a stunning manner.

stunsail, n. [1. stúnsl; 2. stánsl]. Contracted fr. studding-sail. Studding-sail.

stunt (I.), vb. trans. [1. stunt; 2. stant], fr. M.E., O.E. *stunt*, 'dull, foolish'; cp. O.N. *stuttr*; M.H.G. *stunz*, 'short'; see **stint** (I.). To check growth, development, of; to dwarf: *stunted trees, intelligence* &c.

stunt (II.), n. Introduced fr. America; orig. athletic slang; fr. Germ. *stunde*, 'lesson'; see **Stundism**. (slang) A showy, striking performance; feat, display, of skill.

stuntedness, n. [1. stúntednes; 2. stántidnis], fr. P.P. of **stunt** (I.) & -ness. Condition, state, of being stunted or dwarfed.

stupa, n. [1. stōōpa; 2. stúpə]. Scrt. *stūpa*, 'mound'; cp. Hind. *top*. A round, domed tumulus in India, containing a Buddhist shrine; a tope.

stupe, n. & vb. trans. [1. stūp; 2. stjūp], fr. Lat. *stūpa*, variant of *stuppa*, 'tow', see **stop** (I.). 1. n. Compress, cloth wrung out in hot water &c., as fomentation for wound &c. 2. vb. To apply a stupe to; to poultice, foment.

stupefacient, adj. & n. [1. stūpefāshent; 2. stjūpiféiʃənt]. See **stupefy** & -**facient**. 1. adj. Tending to stupefy. 2. n. (med.) Stupefacient substance; a narcotic.

stupefaction, n. [1. stūpefákshun; 2. stjūpifækʃən]. See **stupefy** & -**faction**. a Act of stupefying; state of being stupefied; b specif., amazement; cause of amazement.

stupefactive, adj. [1. stūpefáktiv; 2. stjūpifæktiv]. See prec. & -**ive**. Having the power of stupefying; stupefacient.

stupefy, vb. trans. [1. stūpefī; 2. stjūpifai], fr. Lat. *stupefacere*, 'to make senseless, benumb, deaden', fr. *stupēre*, 'to be stunned, stupefied; to be amazed', q.v. under **stupid**. a To deaden the faculties or senses of, make stupid, dull, deprive of perceptive power; **b** to stun with astonishment, to amaze.

stupendous, adj. [1. stūpéndus; 2. stjūpéndəs], fr. Lat. *stupendus*, 'amazing', gerundive of *stupēre*, 'to be benumbed, amazed', see **stupid**, & -**ous**. Possessing some quality in an extraordinary degree; astonishing by virtue of size, volume, force &c.: *stupendous height*; *a stupendous mistake*.

stupendously, adv. Prec. & -**ly**. In a stupendous manner.

stupendousness, n. See prec. & -**ness**. Quality of being stupendous.

stupeous, adj. [1. stúpeus; 2. stjūpiəs], fr. Lat. *stūpeus*, 'of tow', fr. *stūpa*, 'tow', see **stupe**, &-**eous**. Having, bearing, long, loose, threadlike hairs or scales.

stupid (I.), adj. [1. stūpid; 2. stjūpid, stjúpid], fr. Lat. *stupidus*, 'struck senseless, amazed; dull, stupid', fr. *stupēre*, 'to be stunned, senseless; to be amazed'; cogn. w. Scrt. *tu(m)pāti*, 'strikes, pushes'; Gk. *túpos*, 'blow; imprint', see **type** (I.); see **stub** (I.) **stump** (I.), & words there referred to. **1**. With senses or faculties deadened, dull, benumbed; stupefied; in a state of stupor: *to be stupid with sleep*. **2**. Characterized by, evincing, lack of intelligence, wisdom, prudence &c.; dull, foolish, slow-witted: *a stupid person, action, book*; *a stupid thing to do*.

stupid (II.), n., fr. prec. (colloq.) Stupid person.

stupidity, n. [1. stūpíditi; 2. stjupíditi], fr. Lat. *stupiditātem*, 'dullness, stupidity', fr. *stupidus*, 'dull', see prec., & -**ity**. Quality of being stupid; mental dullness, lack of intelligence, slowness of wit.

stupidly, adv. [1. stūpidli; 2. stjūpidli]. Prec. & -**ly**. In a stupid manner.

stupor, n. [1. stúper; 2. stjūpə], fr. Lat. *stupor*, 'numbness, insensibility; dullness', fr. *stupēre*, 'to be senseless; to be amazed', see **stupid**, & -**or**. **1**. Partial insensibility, torpor, deadened condition of faculties and senses; state of coma. **2**. Mental dullness or helplessness caused by intense astonishment, shock &c.

stuporous, adj. [1. stúporus; 2. stjūpərəs]. Prec. & -**ous**. Of, characteristic of, affected with, stupor.

stupose, adj. [1. stúpōs; 2. stjúpous], fr. Lat. *stūpa*, 'tow', see **stupe**, & -**ose**. Having tufts of tow-like filaments.

sturdied, adj. [1. stérdid; 2. stádid]. **sturdy** (II.) & -**ed**. Affected with sturdy.

sturdily, adv. [1. stérdili; 2. stádili]. **sturdy** (I.) & -**ly**. In a sturdy manner.

sturdiness, n. [1. stérdines; 2. stádinis]. See prec. & -**ness**. State or quality of being sturdy.

sturdy (I.), adj. [1. stérdi; 2. stádi]. M.E. *stourdi*, 'sturdy, stubborn', fr. O. Fr. *estourdi*, 'astounded'; etymol. uncertain. **1**. Strong, vigorous, robust, well developed, stout: *a sturdy youngster*; *a sturdy oak*; *sturdy beggar*, specif., one able, but unwilling, to work. **2**. Characterized by, evincing, strength, vigour, robustness: *a sturdy common sense, resistance, faith*.

sturdy (II.), n., fr. O. Fr. *estourdie*, 'giddiness', fr. *estourdi*, 'amazed', see prec. Disease of sheep characterized by giddiness and stupor.

sturgeon, n. [1. stérjun; 2. stádʒən]. M.E. *sturgiun*, fr. O. Fr. *esturgeon*, fr. Med. Lat. *sturiōnem*, fr. O.H.G. *sturjo*, 'sturgeon'; cp. O.E. *styria*, 'sturgeon'; origin obscure. Large fish, genus *Acipenser*, of N. Atlantic coasts and N. American and N. European rivers, from which caviare and isinglass are obtained.

sturnoid, adj. [1. stérnoid; 2. stánoid], fr. Lat. *sturnus*, 'starling', see **starling** (I.), & -**oid**. Pertaining to, like, the starlings.

stutter (I.), vb. intrans. & trans. [1. stúter; 2. státə], fr. M.E. *stutten*, 'to hesitate, stammer'; cp. O.N. *stauta*; Du. *stotteren*, 'to stutter'; Goth. *stautan*; O.H.G. *stōzzan*, 'to strike'; cp. further O.E. *styntan*, 'to stupefy', see **stint** (I.); O.N. *stuttr*, 'short'. **1**. intrans. To speak with involuntary, spasmodic hesitations and repetitions; to stammer. **2**. trans. To pronounce, utter, with hesitation: *to stutter (out) an apology*.

stutter (II.), n., fr. prec. Speech-defect characterized by spasmodic repetition of initial sounds; a stammer.

stuttering, adj. [1. stútering; 2. státəriŋ], fr. Pres. Part. of **stutter** (I.). Characterized by a stutter.

stutteringly, adv. Prec. & -**ly**. In a stuttering manner.

sty (I.), n. [1. stī; 2. stai]. O.E. *stig*, M.E. *sti*, 'sty'; fr. the base in O.E. *stīgan*, 'to rise, mount'; also in O.S. & O.H.G.; Goth. *steigan*; cogn. w. Gk. *steikhein*, 'to walk, go'; Scrt. *stighnati*, 'he climbs'. See also **stair**, **steward**, & **stile** (I.). Enclosure, pen, for pig.

sty (II.), vb. trans., fr. prec. (rare) To enclose, keep, in a sty.

sty (III.), **stye**, n. [1. stī; 2. stai]. M.E. *stī(en)*, 'sty'; O.E. *stīgend*, 'sty in the eye'; prob. fr. O.E. *stīgan*, 'to rise', q.v. under **sty** (I.). Small, inflamed swelling on the eyelid.

Stygian, adj. [1. stíjian; 2. stídʒiən], fr. Lat. *Stygius*, fr. Gk. *Stúgios*, 'Stygian', fr. *stug*-, stem of *Stúx*, 'Styx, river of the nether regions'; cp. Gk. *stugein*, 'to hate'; *stugnós*, 'hateful'. Of, pertaining to, characteristic of, the Styx or the infernal regions, esp. in Phr. *Stygian gloom, darkness* &c.

style (I.), n. [1. stīl; 2. stail]. M.E. *stīle*, 'style, pen'; fr. O. Fr. *stile*, *style*, fr. Lat. *stilus*, 'pointed instrument, spike, pale; instrument for writing on waxed tablets; writing; composition; mode of expression, style'; cogn. w. Lat. *stimulus*, 'point, goad'; fr. base **sti-*, **stoi-*, 'sharp, pointed', whence also Lat. *instigāre*, 'to goad, prick', see **instigate**; O.E. *sticca*, 'stick, peg', see **stick** (I.) &c. **1**. a Small, slender, pointed instrument anciently used for inscribing letters on waxed tablets; hence, **b** (archaic) pen, pencil. **2**. Object or formation resembling a style in shape; specif. **a** engraving tool; **b** etching needle; **c** (zool.) small, pointed projection or process. **3**. a Mode of verbal expression, way of putting ideas into words in speech or writing; manner: a concise, rhetorical, turgid, style; a style of one's own; **b** distinguished, good, clear, graceful, style &c.: *a writer without style*; **c** specific mode of expression characteristic of an individual, a period, a school &c.: *in the Elizabethan, eighteenth-century, style*; *in the style of Pope*. **4**. Mode, method, of execution, expression, in any of the fine arts; esp. method characteristic of specific person, country, period &c.: *the Byzantine, Romanesque, style*; *in the style of Rubens*; *classical styles of architecture*; *furnished in Mid-Victorian style*. **5**. Way of moving in carrying out some skilled action or series of actions, e.g. in games &c.: *the style of a cricketer, fencer, lawn-tennis player* &c. **6**. Fashion in dress, mode: *all the latest styles from Paris*. **7**. a Way of carrying and behaving oneself; general bearing, manner, deportment, in relation to the usages of good society: *ladies tell me that the new Mayoress is shocking bad style*; **b** specif., good style; distinction of bearing and manner; good breeding: *a woman who naturally has style can afford to be plain*. **8**. Sort, kind, particular variety: *just the style of dinner I detest*; *he called me a fool, and more in the same style*. Phrs. *style of thing*, way of behaving, speaking; the way things happen, particular kind of event &c.: *I've had quite enough of that style of thing*. **9**. Mode of address, proper title, designation: *what is the proper style of a bishop?* **10**. Mode of reckoning date: *Old Style*, with reference to date reckoned according to Julian calendar; *New Style*, according to Gregorian calendar.

style (II.), vb. trans., fr. prec. To call, name, designate, address, speak of, by title of: *the heads of several Oxford Colleges are styled Warden*; *an impostor styling himself a baronet*.

style (III.), n., fr. Gk. *stûlos*, 'pillar'; cp. Gk. *stûō*, 'I set upright'; *staurós*, 'stake', see **stauroscope**; O.N. *staurr*, 'post'; O.E. *stow*, 'place'; see **stow**, **steer** (I.), & words there referred to. **1**. Gnomon, pointer, of sun-dial. **2**. (bot.) Slender part of pistil, between ovary and stigma.

style (IV.). See **stile**.

stylet, n. [1. stílet; 2. stáilet], fr. O. Fr. *stilet*, fr. Ital. *stiletto*. **1**. Small, slender, pointed instrument or weapon. **2**. (med.) Wire extending and stiffening catheter.

styliform, adj. [1. stíliform; 2. stáilifɔːm]. **style** (I.) & -**i**- & -**form**. Having the shape of a style.

stylish, adj. [1. stílish; 2. stáiliʃ]. **style** (I.) & -**ish** (I.). (often vulg.) a Having social style: *a stylish woman*; **b** fashionable, smart: *a stylish hat*; *a coat of stylish cut*.

stylishly, adv. Prec. & -**ly**. In a stylish manner.

stylishness, n. See prec. & -**ness**. Quality of being stylish.

stylist, n. [1. stílist; 2. stáilist]. **style** (I.) & -**ist**. Writer or other artist who has a good, or a characteristic, style; one who pays great attention to style.

stylistic, adj. [1. stīlístik; 2. stailístik]. Prec. & -**ic**. Of, pertaining to, literary style.

stylistically, adv. [1. stīlístikali; 2. stailístikəli]. Prec. & -**al** & -**ly**. From a stylistic point of view.

stylite, n. [1. stílīt; 2. stáilait], fr. L. Gk. *stūlítēs*, 'stylite', fr. *stûlos*, 'pillar', see **style** (III.), & -**ite** (I.). One of a class of religious ascetics of the early Middle Ages, who lived without shelter on the tops of pillars.

stylize, vb. trans. [1. stílīz; 2. stáilaiz]. **style** (I.) & -**ize**. To conventionalize.

stylo, n. [1. stílō; 2. stáilou]. Abbr. form of stylograph.

stylo-, pref. representing **style** (I.) & -**o**-. Styloid process; e.g. *stylohyoid*, (muscle &c.) of the styloid process and the hyoid bone.

stylobate, n. [1. stílobāt; 2. stáilobeit], fr. L. Lat. *stylobates*, fr. Gk. *stūlobátēs*, 'pedestal of a row of columns', fr. **style** (III.) & -**o**- & -*batēs*, fr. *bainein*, 'to go', see **basis**. Continuous foundation, base, for two or more columns.

stylograph, n. [1. stílogràhf; 2. stáilə-, stáiləgràf]. **style (I.)** & -o- & -**graph**. Kind of fountain-pen with needle-like point.

stylographic, adj. [1. stilográfik; 2. stàilográefik]. Prec. & -**ic**. Of, pertaining to, of the nature of, a stylograph: *stylographic pen*.

stylographically, adv. [1. stilográfikali; 2. stàilográfikəli]. Prec. & -**al** & -**ly**. By means of a stylograph.

styloid, adj. & n. [1. stíloid; 2. stáiloid]. **style (I.)** & -**oid**. **1.** adj. (anat.) *Styloid process*, spiny projection at the base of the temporal bone. **2.** n. Styloid process.

stymie, stimy, n. & vb. trans. [1. stími; 2. stáimi]. Etymol. unknown. (golf) **1.** n. Position in which the opponent's ball lies between that of player and the hole. **2.** vb. trans. **a** (of opponent's ball) To lie between (ball of player) and the hole; **b** (of player) to leave ball between that of (opponent) and the hole.

styptic, adj. & n. [1. stíptik; 2. stíptik], fr. Fr., fr. Lat. *stypticus*, fr. Gk. *stūptikós*, ' astringent; styptic '; cp. Gk. *stúphein*, ' to contract ; to be astringent '; *stúpsis*, ' contraction '; fr. base *stāu-, *stū- &c., ' to condense ', parallel w. *st(h)ā- &c., ' to stand ', see under **stand (I.)**, **state (I.)**. **1.** adj. Tending to check bleeding, esp. by contraction of blood-vessels. **2.** n. Styptic substance.

styrax, n. [1. stíraks; 2. stáiræks], fr. Lat. *styrax*, fr. Gk. *stúrax*, ' styrax '; Semitic loanword. **1.** Genus of trees and shrubs yielding a fragrant resin. **2.** Gum obtained from this plant.

Styx, n. [1. stiks; 2. stiks]. Lat. *Styx*, fr. Gk. *Stúx*, ' Styx ', see **Stygian**. (Gk. mythol.) River of the infernal regions, across which the shades of the departed had to pass. Phr. *to cross the Styx*, to die.

Suabian. See **Swabian**.

suability, n. [1. sùəbíliti; 2. sjùəbíliti]. See next word & -**bility**. State of being suable.

suable, adj. [1. súəbl; 2. sjúəbl]. **sue** & -**able**. Capable of being, liable to be, sued.

suasion, n. [1. swázhun; 2. swéizən]. Lat. *suāsiōnem*, ' advice, persuasion ', fr. *suāsum*, P.P. type of *suādēre*, ' to advise, recommend, persuade ', q.v. under **suave**. Act of persuading; persuasion; now chiefly in Phr. *moral suasion*, as opposed to force.

suasive, adj. [1. swásiv; 2. swéisiv]. See prec. & -**ive**. Persuasive, tending to persuade.

suave, adj. [1. swāv; 2. sweiv], fr. Fr., fr. Lat. *suāvis*, ' sweet, pleasant, agreeable ', earlier *swādwis*; cp. Lat. *suādēre*, ' to recommend, persuade '; Scrt. *svādúš*, ' pleasant to the taste '; Gk. *hēdús*, see **hedonic**; O.E. *swēte*, ' sweet ', see **sweet (I.)**. **1.** Possessing, exhibiting, a smooth, ingratiating courtesy; bland, urbane, gracious, affable: *suave manners, smile* &c. **2.** (of wine &c.) Smooth, reverse of acid or astringent.

suavely, adv. Prec. & -**ly**. In a suave manner.

suavity, n. [1. swáviti; 2. swæviti], fr. Lat. *suāvitātem*, ' sweetness '; **suave** & -**ity**. Quality of being suave; urbanity.

sub (I.), n. [1. sub; 2. sab]. Abbr. fr. **subaltern**. (colloq.) Subaltern. Not in military usage.

sub (II.), prep. Lat. *sub, subs*, ' under '; cp. Lat. *super*, ' above ', prob orig., ' from below, upwards ', see **super**. According to Walde, fr. base *upo- &c., ' to, towards, up to ' &c., see **up**, w. pref. *ks-; see **sub-**. In Latin Phrs., e.g. *sub judice*, under consideration, awaiting decision; *sub rosa*, in secret; in confidence, privately; *sub voce*, under the word specified.

sub-, pref. Lat. *sub, (subs)*, (1) expressing spatial relations: below, under, beneath; near, at the foot of; (2) expressing relations of time: towards, about; just after. **A.** In compounds derived fr. Lat., *sub-* has the following senses: **1. a** Under, as in *submergere*, ' to dip under '; hence, **b** inferiority, as in *subcenturio*; **c** diminution, *subrīdēre*, ' to laugh slightly, smile '; **d** secrecy, as in *subornare*, ' to instigate secretly, suborn '; **e** substitution, *succēdere*, ' to come into another's place '. **2. a** From below, up, *suscipere*, ' to take up '; **b** assistance, *succurrere*, ' to run up (in order to help), to succour '. **3.** Propinquity, immediate succession, *subsequi*, ' to follow closely '. *Sub-* remains unaltered in form before vowels, & *b, d, j, l, n, s, t, v*; before *c, f, g, p, r*, the *b* is usually assimilated, thus *sub-* appears as *suc-, suf-, sug-* &c.; before *m* it appears sometimes as *sum-*, sometimes as *sub-*. It is assumed by Brugmann that the orig. form was *sup*, & the meaning, in Aryan, was ' from below, upwards, towards ', hence he connects Lat. *super*, ' above ', see **super-**; cp. also Gk. *hupó*, ' under ', & *hupér*, ' over ', see **hypo-** & **hyper-**. The Lat. *sup* is assumed to be formed fr. *(e)ks-*, ' from ', see **ex- (I.)**, & *upo*, for wh. cp. Scrt. *úpa*, ' towards; on '; & the group of Gmc. words wh. includes Goth. *iup*, ' upwards ', & O.E. *upp*, see **up**. **B.** *Sub-*, as living pref. in Engl. same as prec. in origin, having the following senses: **1.** Below, lower in degree or intensity: *subconscious, subnormal, subhuman*, less than human &c. **2.** Situated below, underneath: *subsoil, substratum*. **3.** Inferior in size, importance, rank &c.: *subdivision, subarea, subcommittee*. **4.** Approaching, bordering on; partly, to some extent, slightly (on anal. of genuine Lat. *subacidus*): *subtropical; subfebrile* &c.

subabdominal, adj. [1. sùbabdóminal; 2. sàbæbdóminəl]. Situated beneath the abdomen.

subacid, adj. [1. sùbásid; 2. sàbæsid]. Lat. *subacidus*, ' sourish '; **sub-** & **acid (I.)**. **1.** Moderately acid, tending to sourness. **2.** (fig.) Somewhat acid or biting.

subacidity, n. [1. sùbasíditi; 2. sàbəsíditi]. Prec. & -**ity**. Quality of being subacid.

subacute, adj. [1. sùbakūt; 2. sàbəkjūt]. Moderately acute, less acute than normal.

subadar, soubadar, n. [1. sōōbadar; 2. súbədā]. Hind., fr. Pers. *sūbadār*, ' one holding a province ', fr. *subah*, ' province ', & *dār*, ' master '. Native officer commanding a company in a native regiment in India.

subaerial, adj. [1. sùbárial; 2. sàbéəriəl]. Existing, formed, on the surface of the earth, contrasted with *subterranean, aerial*.

subaerialist, n. [1. subárialist; 2. sàbéəriəlist]. Prec. & -**ist**. One who attributes geological formations to changes produced subaerially.

subaerially, adv. [1. sùbáriali; 2. sàbéəriəli]. See prec. & -**ly**. On the surface of the ground.

subagency, n. [1. sùbájensi; 2. sàbéidʒənsi]. Office or position of a subagent.

subagent, n. [1. sùbájent; 2. sàbéidʒənt]. Person acting as representative of or employed by an agent.

subalpine, adj. [1. sùbálpin; 2. sàbælpain]. (bot., zool.) Of, pertaining to, part of mountainous district between Alpine region and timber-line.

subaltern, n. & adj. [1. súbaltern; 2. sábəltən], fr. Fr. *subalterne*, fr. Med. Lat. *subalternus*, **sub-** & *alternus*, ' one after the other ', see **alternate (I.)**. **1.** n. Any commissioned officer in the army, below rank of captain. **2.** adj. Of less importance, subordinate, of lesser rank, inferior; (esp. log.) specific, individual, particular, opposed to *universal, general*.

subandean, adj. [1. sùbandéan; 2. sàbændíən]. Pertaining to, characteristic of, the lower slopes of the Andes mountains.

subapennine, adj. [1. sùbápenīn; 2. sàbǽpinain]. Pertaining to, characteristic of, the lower slopes of the Apennines.

subapostolic, adj. [1. sùbàpostólik; 2. sàbæpəstólik]. Of, pertaining to, the period immediately following that of the Apostles.

subaquatic, adj. [1. sùbakwátik; 2. sàbəkwǽtik]. Partially aquatic.

subaqueous, adj. [1. sùbákweus; 2. sàbéikwiəs]. Existing, formed, intended for use, under water.

subarctic, adj. [1. sùbárktik; 2. sàbáktik]. Of, pertaining to, a region bordering on the Arctic.

subastral, adj. [1. sùbástral; 2. sàbæstrəl]. Situated, existing, below the stars; terrestrial.

subaudition, n. [1. sùbawdíshun; 2. sàbōdíʃən], fr. L. Lat. *subaudīt-(um)*, P.P. type of *subaudīre*, ' to understand, supply, a word omitted '; **sub-** & **audition**. Mental process of supplying, understanding, something implied, but not expressed in words.

subaural, adj. [1. sùbóral; 2. sàbórəl]. Situated below the ear.

subaxillary, adj. [1. sùbaksílari; 2. sàbæksíləri]. **a** Situated below the armpit; **b** (bot.) growing beneath the axil.

sub-base, n. [1. súb bàs; 2. sáb béis]. (archit.) Lowest division of a base divided horizontally.

subcaudal, adj. [1. sùbkáwdl; 2. sàbkódl]. Situated beneath or near the tail.

subcentral, adj. [1. sùbséntral; 2. sàbséntrəl]. Situated near or beneath the centre.

subcerebral, adj. [1. sùbséerebral; 2. sàbsérìbrəl]. Of, pertaining to, originating in, part of the body or nervous system below the brain.

subclass, n. [1. súbklahs; 2. sábklās]. (biol.) Subdivision of a class.

subclavian, adj. [1. sùbklávian; 2. sàbkléivìən]. Situated beneath the clavicle.

subclavicular, adj. [1. sùbklavíkular; 2. sàbkləvíkjulə]. Subclavian.

subcommittee, n. [1. súbkumìti; 2. sábkəmìti]. Committee formed as adjunct to general committee for specific purpose.

subconcave, adj. [1. sùbkónkāv; 2. sàbkónkeiv]. Slightly concave.

subconical, adj. [1. subkónikl; 2. sabkónikl]. Nearly conical; tapering slightly.

subconscious, adj. [1. sùbkónshus; 2. sàbkónʃəs]. Present in the consciousness, and capable of being the subject of, or involving, mental activity, but not fully perceived and recognized by the mind, or completely and clearly present to the attention: *subconscious ideas, reasoning*.

subconsciously, adv. Prec. & -**ly**. In a subconscious manner.

subconsciousness, n. See prec. & -**ness**. That region of the mind, the margin of consciousness, which lies outside attention and introspection.

subcontiguous, adj. [1. súbkontígūus; 2. sàbkontígjuəs]. Nearly, but not quite, touching.

subcontinent, n. [1. sùbkóntinent; 2. sàbkóntinənt]. Mass of land, large enough to be regarded as a separate continent, but not usually so called.

subcontract, n. [1. sùbkóntrakt; 2. sàbkóntrækt]. Contract subordinate to or forming part of a larger contract.

subcontrariety, n. [1. sùbkòntrarìeti; 2. sàbkòntrəráiiti]. (log.) Relation of subcontraries.

subcontrary, adj. & n. [1. sùbkóntrari; 2. sàbkóntrəri]. **1.** adj. Contrary in some, though not all, respects (esp. in log. and geom.). **2.** n. (log.) A subcontrary proposition; e.g. *some Englishmen are fair—some Englishmen are dark*, are subcontraries; but *all Englishmen are dark—no Englishmen are dark*, are contraries.

subconvex, adj. [1. sùbkónveks; 2. sàbkónveks]. Slightly convex.

subcorneous, adj. [1. sùbkórneus; 2. sàbkónìəs]. **1.** Somewhat horny. **2.** Situated beneath horn or horny growth, nail &c.

subcostal, adj. [1. sùbkóstl; 2. sàbkóstl]. Situated behind or between the ribs.

subcranial, adj. [1. sùbkránial; 2. sàbkréinìəl]. Situated beneath the cranium.

subcrystalline, adj. [1. sùbkrístalīn; 2. sàbkrístəlain]. Only partially crystallized.

subcutaneous, adj. [1. sùbkūtáneus; 2. sàbkjūtéinìəs]. Existing, applied, beneath the skin.

subcutaneously, adv. Prec. & -**ly**. Beneath the skin.

subcuticular, adj. [1. sùbkūtíkūlar; 2. sàbkjūtíkjulə]. Situated beneath the cuticle.

subcylindrical, adj. [1. sùbsilíndrikl; 2. sàbsilíndrikl]. Nearly cylindrical.

subdeacon, n. [1. súbdēkun; 2. sábdīkən]. Minister next below deacon in rank, in Roman Catholic and Eastern Churches.

subdean, n. [1. súbdēn; 2. sábdīn]. Assistant or deputy of a dean.

subdecuple, adj. [1. sùbdékŭpl; 2. sàbdékjupl]. In the ratio of 1 to 10.

subdelirium, n. [1. súbdelírium; 2. sábdilíriəm]. Condition bordering on delirium; intermittent delirium.

subdermal, adj. [1. sùbdérmal; 2. sàbdə́məl]. Beneath the skin.

subdiaconate, n. [1. sùbdiákunat; 2. sàbdaiǽkənit]. Rank or office, tenure of the office, of subdeacon.

subditítious, adj. [1. sùbditíshus; 2. sàbditíʃəs], fr. Lat. *subdiīcius*, 'substituted, spurious', fr. P.P. type of *subdere*, 'to place under; to substitute', fr. **sub-** & *dāre*, 'to give', q.v. under **date** (I.). Secretly substituted, insinuated, foisted on in place of something else.

subdivide, vb. trans. & intrans. [1. sùbdivíd; 2. sàbdiváid], fr. L. Lat. *subdividere*, 'to subdivide'. **sub-** & **divide** (I.). **1.** trans. To divide still further a part resulting from a previous division. **2.** intrans. To become subdivided, separated into lesser or subordinate parts.

subdivisible, adj. [1. sùbdivízibl; 2. sàbdivízibl]. Capable of being subdivided.

subdivision, n. [1. súbdivizhun; 2. sábdivìʒən]. **1.** Act of subdividing; state of being subdivided. **2.** Part, section, area, produced by subdividing.

subdominant, n. [1. sùbdóminant; 2. sàbdóminənt]. (mus.) Fourth note of the scale.

subdorsal, adj. [1. sùbdórsl; 2. sàbdósl]. Situated nearly on or near the back.

subdouble, adj. [1. sùbdúbl; 2. sàbdábl]. In the ratio of 1 to 2.

subduable, adj. [1. sùbdúabl; 2. səbdjúəbl]. **subdue** & **-able**. Capable of being subdued.

subdual, n. [1. sùbdúal; 2. səbdjúəl]. **subdue** & **-al**. Act of subduing; state of being subdued.

subduce, vb. trans. [1. sùbdús; 2. səbdjús], fr. Lat. *subdūcere*, 'to draw away; to withdraw', fr. **sub-** & *dūcere*, 'to lead', see **duke**. To take away, remove, withdraw, draw off.

subduct, vb. trans. [1. sùbdúkt; 2. səbdákt], fr. Lat. *subductum*, P.P. type of *subdūcere*, 'to draw away', see prec. To subduce.

subdue, vb. trans. [1. sùbdú; 2. səbdjú]. M.E. *sodewe*, 'to subdue', later *subdewe*, through influence of **sub-**; fr. O. Fr. *soduire*, 'to seduce', fr. Lat. *subdūcere*, 'to draw up, draw away', see **subduce**; the Engl. word has the sense of Lat. *subdere*, 'to place under', see **subditítious**. **1.** To conquer, repress, bring into subjection, gain authority over by force or effort: *to subdue one's enemies, one's passions* &c. **2.** To reduce, lessen, force, intensity, vigour of, diminish effect of, limit power of: *subdued light, voices, spirits*.

subduedness, n. [1. sùbdúdnes; 2. səbdjúdnis], fr. P.P. of prec. & **-ness**. State or quality of being subdued.

subduple, adj. [1. sùbdúpl; 2. sabdjúpl]. In the ratio of 1 to 2; subdouble.

subduplicate, adj. [1. sùbdúplikat; 2. sàbdjúplikit]. (math., of ratio) Expressed by the square root.

sub-edit, vb. trans. [1. sùb édit; 2. sàb édit]. To act as sub-editor of, prepare (copy &c.), for the press as assistant of editor.

sub-editor, n. [1. sùb éditor; 2. sàb éditə]. Assistant editor.

subepidermal, adj. [1. sùbepidérml; 2. sàbɛpidǽməl]. Situated beneath the epidermis.

subequal, adj. [1. sùbékwal; 2. sàbíkwəl]. **1.** Nearly equal, approximating in value &c. **2.** (of numbers in a group) Of such value that no one number equals the sum of the rest.

subequilateral, adj. [1. sùbekwilátəral; 2. sàbíkwilǽtərəl]. Nearly equilateral.

suberect, adj. [1. sùberékt; 2. sàbirékt]. Nearly upright; tending to become erect.

subereous, adj. [1. sūbéreus; 2. s(j)ūbíəriəs], fr. Lat. *sūbereus*, 'of cork, of the cork tree', fr. *sūber*, 'cork, cork tree', etymol. doubtful, & **-ous**. Of, pertaining to, like, cork.

suberic, adj. [1. sūbérik; 2. s(j)ūbérik], fr. Lat. *sūber*, 'cork', see prec. & **-ic**. Of, pertaining to, obtained from, cork.

suberin, n. [1. súberin; 2. s(j)úbərin], see prec. & **-in**. Waxy substance contained in cork tissue.

suberose, adj. [1. súberōs; 2. s(j)úbərous], fr. Lat. *sūber*, 'cork', see **subereous**, & **-ose**. Subereous.

subfamily, n. [1. súbfámili; 2. sábfæmili]. (bot., zool. &c.) Division of a family, consisting of a genus or group of genera.

subfebrile, adj. [1. súbfébril; 2. sábfíbrail]. Slightly or intermittently febrile.

subflavour, n. [1. súbflávur; 2. sábflèivə]. Secondary or underlying flavour.

subfusc, adj. [1. sùbfúsk; 2. sàbfásk], fr. next word. Subfuscous.

subfuscous, adj. [1. sùbfúskus; 2. sàbfáskəs], fr. Lat. *sub-, suffuscus*, 'brownish, dusky', fr. **sub-** & *fuscus*, 'dusky, tawny', see **fuscous**. Dull or dark in colour.

subgelatinous, adj. [1. sùbjelátinus; 2. sàbdʒilǽtinəs]. Somewhat gelatinous in character.

subgeneric, adj. [1. sùbjenérik; 2. sàbdʒinérik]. Pertaining to a subgenus.

subgenus, n. [1. súbjénus; 2. sábdʒìnəs]. (bot., zool. &c.) Division of a genus, consisting of one or more species.

subglacial, adj. [1. sùbglásial; 2. sàbgléisiəl]. **1.** Existing, formed, under a glacier. **2.** (of climate &c.) Partially glacial, verging on glacial conditions.

subglobular, adj. [1. sùbglóbūlar; 2. sàbglóbjulə]. Nearly globular.

subheading, n. [1. súbhèding; 2. sábhèdiŋ]. Heading of minor division of newspaper article &c.

subhepatic, adj. [1. sùbhepátik; 2. sàbhipǽtik]. Situated under the liver.

subhuman, adj. [1. sùbhúman; 2. sàbhjúmən]. Less than, inferior to, human.

sub-imago, n. [1. sùb imágō; 2. sàb iméigou]. (zool.) Stage between pupa and imago in the development of some insects.

subinfeudation, n. [1. sùbinfūdáshun; 2. sàbinfjūdéiʃən]. Grant of land by a vassal to a dependent.

subintestinal, adj. [1. sùbintestínal; 2. sàbintestáinəl]. Situated beneath or near the intestines.

subjacent, adj. [1. sùbjásent; 2. sàbdʒéisənt], fr. Lat. *subjacent-(em)*, Pres. Part. of *subjacēre*, 'to lie under or near', fr. **sub-** & *jacēre*, 'to lie', see **adjacent**. **1.** Situated, lying, directly below; underlying. **2.** Situated below, at the foot.

subject (I.), adj. [1. súbjekt; 2. sábdʒikt], fr. Lat. *subjectum*, P.P. type of *sub(j)icere*, 'to place or throw under; to submit, subject; to include, comprise; to subjoin, append', fr. **sub-** & *jacere*, 'to throw', see **jactitation** & **jet**. **1.** Under authority, not a free agent, owing or giving obedience: *subject nations, States; a State subject to another; subject to the law*. **2.** Having a tendency to; exposed, liable, to: *subject to sudden changes of temperature, fits of depression* &c. **3.** *Subject to*, conditional upon some other action or event: *a proposal subject to the approval of a higher authority*.

subject (II.), adv., fr. prec. *Subject to*, conditionally upon: *this can only be done subject to the consent of the king*.

subject (III.), n., fr. Lat. *subjectus*, 'an inferior, dependent', *subjectum*, 'grammatical subject', fr. P.P. type of *sub(j)icere*, see prec. **1.** Person owing, or giving, allegiance to a sovereign, or a sovereign State: *we in England are all the subjects of His Majesty King George*. **2. a** That which is treated or dealt with in specific way; person or object submitted to treatment, or process: *a hypnotic subject; to make a person the subject of an experiment*; specif. **b** dead body for anatomical dissection &c.; **c** person liable to specific disease, condition &c.: *a hysterical, gouty, subject*. **3. a** That which is dealt with in writing, painting &c.; matter written or spoken of; theme; leading figure, idea &c., in literary or artistic composition: *the subject of a story, play; to choose the subject of a dissertation; a painter with a leaning to mythological subjects; a subject for discussion*; **b** (mus.) short musical phrase, sentence, theme upon which a composition is founded. **4.** Cause, occasion, originating circumstance: *a subject for rejoicing* &c. **5.** (gram.) The nominative of a sentence; word or group of words in a sentence representing the person or thing about which something is predicated. **6.** (log.) That part of a proposition corresponding to the subject of a grammatical sentence, the person or thing concerning which a statement is made, or judgement expressed. **7.** (philos.) **a** The substance of anything, the thing in itself; substantive reality, as opposed to its qualities and attributes; that of which an attribute is affirmed, or in which it inheres; **b** the Ego, the self, the mind which thinks.

subject (IV.), vb. trans. [1. subjékt; 2. səbdʒékt], fr. **subject** (I.). **1.** To bring under authority, make subject, subordinate, subdue: *to subject a nation to one's rule*. **2. a** To cause to undergo, submit; to cause to be affected by some action, treatment, process: *to subject a person to cross-examination; to subject an object to extreme pressure; to subject a statement to criticism*; **b** to render liable: *to subject oneself to ridicule, insult* &c. **3.** To present, submit, place before: *to subject one's plans to another's consideration*.

subject-heading, n. Reference heading to a subject in a catalogue, index &c.

subjection, n. [1. subjékshun; 2. səbdʒékʃən]. **subject** (IV.) & **-ion**. Act of subjecting; state of being subjected; dependence, subordination: *she was in a state of complete subjection to her husband's authority*.

subjective (I.), adj. [1. subjéktiv; 2. səbdʒéktiv], fr. Lat. *subjectivus*, 'pertaining to the subject of a proposition'; **subject** (I.) & **-ive**. **1.** (philos.) Arising from, originating in, the mind itself; not produced by something external to one's own mind; opposed to *objective*: *subjective impressions; many believe the phenomena of spiritualism to be purely subjective*. **2.** (gram.) Pertaining to the grammatical subject; *subjective case*, the nominative.

subjective (II.), n., fr. prec. Subjective case, nominative.

subjectively, adv. **subjective** (I.) & **-ly**. (philos.) In a subjective manner, from a subjective point of view.

subjectiveness, n. See prec. & **-ness**. State, quality, of being subjective.

subjectivism, n. [1. subjéktivizm; 2. səbdʒéktivizəm]. **subjective** (I.) & **-ism**. Doctrine that all knowledge is the result of subjective experience, and that there is no objective test of truth.

subjectivist, n. [1. subjéktivist; 2. səbdʒéktivist]. **subjective** (I.) & **-ist**. Adherent of subjectivism.

subjectivity, n. [1. subjektíviti; 2. sàbdʒiktíviti]. **subjective** (I.) & **-ity**. **1.** Subjective quality or state. **2.** Doctrine that religious belief should be based upon subjective experience rather than upon external revelation.

subjectless, adj. [1. súbjektles; 2. sábdʒiktlis]. **subject** (III.) & **-less**. Without a subject.

subject-matter, n. Theme, that which is discussed or treated of.

subjoin, vb. trans. [1. sùbjóin; 2. sàbdʒóin], fr. O. Fr. *subjoindre*, fr. Lat. *subjungere*, 'to append, affix', fr. **sub-** & *jungere*, 'to join', see **join**. To add (statement) to what has already been stated.

subjoint, n. [1. súbjoint; 2. sábdʒoint]. Secondary joint, division of limb of animal &c.

subjugable, adj. [1. súbjoogabl; 2. sábdʒugəbl], fr. Lat. *subjugāre*, 'to subjugate', see next word, & **-able**. Capable of being subjugated.

subjugate, vb. trans. [1. súbjoogāt; 2. sábdʒugeit], fr. Lat. *subjugātum*, P.P. type of *subjugāre*, 'to subjugate', fr. **sub-** & *jugum*, 'yoke', see **jugate**. To bring under a yoke; force under control, subdue, bring into subjection.

subjugation, n. [1. sùbjoogáshun; 2. sàbdʒugéiʃən]. Prec. & **-ion**. Act of subjugating; state of being subjugated.

subjugator, n. [1. súbjoogātur; 2. sábdʒugeitə]. See prec. & **-or**. One who subjugates; conqueror.

subjunctive, adj. & n. [1. subjúngktiv; 2. səbdʒáŋktiv], fr. Lat. *subjunctīvus*, 'connecting; subjunctive', fr. *subjunct-(um)*, P.P. type of *subjungere*, 'to append, subjoin, subordinate', see **subjoin**, & **-ive**. 1. adj. (gram.) *Subjunctive mood*, that mood of a verb expressing an action or state of existence as hypothetical, contingent on something else, conditional; virtually obs. in English. 2. n. Subjunctive mood.

subjunctively, adv. Prec. & **-ly**. By means of, as, a subjunctive.

subkingdom, n. [1. súbkíngdom; 2. sábkiŋdəm]. (biol.) Subdivision of a kingdom.

sublanceolate, adj. [1. sùbláhnseolāt; 2. sàblǽnsiəleit]. (bot.) Somewhat lanceolate.

sublapsarian, adj. & n. [1. sùblapsárian; 2. sàblæpséəriən], fr. **sub-** & Lat. *lapsus*, 'act of falling', see **lapse (I.)**, & **-arian**. 1. adj. Pertaining to the Calvinist doctrine that the Fall of man was permitted, but not foredetermined, by God. 2. n. Person believing in this doctrine.

sublapsarianism, n. [1. sùblapsárianizm; 2. sàblæpséəriənizəm]. Prec. & **-ism**. The doctrine of the sublapsarians.

sublate, vb. trans. [1. sublát; 2. sabléit], fr. **sub-** & Lat. *lāt-(um)*, P.P. type of *tollere*, 'to carry'; see **ablation** & **tolerate**. (log.) To deny, refuse to regard as fact, opposed to *posit*.

sublation, n. [1. sùbláshun; 2. sàbléiʃən]. Prec. & **-ion**. (log.) Act of sublating.

sublease (I.), n. [1. súblēs; 2. sáblīs]. Lease granted by tenant or lessee to another person.

sublease (II.), vb. trans. [1. sublés; 2. sablīs]. To grant a sublease of.

sublessee, n. [1. sublesé; 2. sàblesī]. Person holding a sublease.

sublessor, n. [1. sublésor; 2. sáblesə]. Person granting a sublease.

sublet, vb. trans. & intrans. [1. súblét; 2. sáblét]. To let to another, a house, land &c., of which one is oneself a tenant.

sublibrarian, n. [1. sùblībrárian; 2. sàblaibréəriən]. Person acting as assistant to a librarian.

sublieutenant, n. [1. sùbleftēnant; 2. sàbleftēnənt]. Junior officer in the Navy holding rank next below that of a lieutenant.

sublimate (I.), vb. trans. [1. súblimāt; 2. sáblimeit], fr. Lat. *sublimātum*, P.P. of *sublimāre*, 'to lift up', fr. *sublīmis*, 'high, lofty, elevated', see **sublime (I.)**, **limen**. 1. (fig.) To refine, etherealize, elevate. 2. (chem.) To purify by heating from solid to vaporous state and subsequently restoring solidity.

sublimate (II.), adj. & n. [1. súblimat; 2. sáblimət], fr. Lat. *sublimātum*, see prec. 1. adj. (chem.) Refined by sublimation. 2. n. Sublimated substance.

sublimation, n. [1. sùblimáshun; 2. sàblimēiʃən]. **sublimate (I.)** & **-ion**. Act of sublimating, state of being sublimated.

sublime (I.), adj. [1. sublīm; 2. səbláim], fr. Lat. *sublīmis*, 'high, lofty, elevated, exalted', prob. fr. **sub-** & *limen*, 'threshold, lintel', see **limen**. 1. Characterized by extreme nobility and grandeur; majestic, grandiose, impressive, exalted, awe-inspiring: *sublime beauty, strength, valour, self-sacrifice*. 2. a Lofty, haughty, Olympian, supercilious; as though raised above ordinary human qualities: *sublime insolence, contempt*; **b** hence, showing, evincing, an indifference arising from a sense of superiority: *sublime ignorance, self-conceit*. 3. (anat.) Situated near the surface: *sublime nerves*.

sublime (II.), n., fr. prec. *The sublime*, a sublime thing or quality; that which inspires a sense of awe and reverence and impresses by virtue of its vastness, nobility, majesty.

sublime (III.), vb. trans. & intrans., fr. Med. Lat. *sublīmāre*, 'to sublimate', fr. Lat. *sublīmāre*, 'to exalt', see **sublimate (I.)**. 1. trans. (lit. and fig.) To sublimate. 2. intrans. (lit. and fig.) To refine, purify, by, or as by, sublimation.

sublimely, adv. [1. sublímli; 2. səbláimli]. **sublime (I.)** & **-ly**. In a sublime manner; to a sublime degree.

Sublime Porte, n. [1. sublím pórt; 2. səbláim pōt]. Fr., translating Turkish name of the Government central office. See **Porte**.

subliminal, adj. [1. sublíminal; 2. sablíminəl], fr. **sub-** & *liminal*, fr. Lat. *līmin-*, stem of *limen*, 'threshold', see **limen**, & **-al**. (psychol.) Present in the consciousness, but not consciously apprehended; *subliminal self*, the subconscious mind, regarded as a domain of the individual's personality distinct from, and unrecognized by, the ordinary waking consciousness.

sublimity, n. [1. sublímiti; 2. səblímiti], fr. Lat. *sublīmitātem*, 'loftiness, elevation'; **sublime (I.)** & **-ity**. State or quality of being sublime; sublime character.

sublingual, adj. [1. sùblíŋgwal; 2. sàblíŋgwəl]. Situated, existing, below the tongue.

sublittoral, adj. [1. sùblíteral; 2. sàblítərəl]. (zool.) Existing near the shore-line.

sublunar(y), adj. [1. sublōōnar(i); 2. sablūnə(ri)]. (poet.) Beneath the moon; belonging to this world; terrestrial, mundane.

submammary, adj. [1. sùbmámari; 2. sàbmǽməri]. Situated below the mammae.

submarine, adj. & n. [1. sùbmarēn; 2. sàbmərīn]. 1. adj. Existing, living, designed for use, below the surface of the sea: *submarine plants*; *submarine vessel* &c., one capable of being sunk and moved about below the surface of the sea, used esp. in war, for firing torpedoes &c. 2. n. Submarine vessel.

submaster, n. [1. súbmàhster; 2. sábmàstə]. Second master in certain schools.

submaxillary, adj. [1. sùbmaksílari; 2. sàbmæksíləri]. Situated under the lower jaw.

submembranous, adj. [1. sùbmémbranus; 2. sàbmémbrənəs]. Somewhat membranous in character.

submental, adj. [1. sùbméntl; 2. sàbméntl]. Situated below the chin.

submerge, vb. trans. & intrans. [1. submérj; 2. sabmə́dʒ], fr. Lat. *sub-*, *summergere*, 'to plunge under, sink, overwhelm', fr. **sub-** & *mergere*, to dip, plunge', see **merge**. 1. trans. To cause to plunge, dip, below surface of water; to cover with water or other liquid: *rocks submerged at high tide*. Phr. *the submerged tenth*, completely destitute, hopelessly poor class. 2. intrans. To go, sink, beneath the surface of water; esp. of submarines.

submergence, n. [1. submérjens; 2. səbmə́dʒəns]. Prec. & **-ence**. Act or process of submerging; state of being submerged.

submergible, adj. [1. submérjibl; 2. səbmə́dʒibl]. (rare) Capable of being submerged.

submerse (I.), vb. trans. [1. submérs; 2. sabmə́s], fr. Lat. *submersum*, P.P. type of *submergere*, 'to plunge under, sink', see **submerge**. To cause to sink under water; rare except in P.P., (bot.) see next word.

submerse (II.), adj., fr. Lat. *submersum*, see prec. Also *submersed*, (bot.) growing under water.

submersible, adj. [1. submérsibl; 2. sabmə́sibl]. Prec. & **-ible**. Capable of being submersed or submerged.

submersion, n. [1. submérshun; 2. sabmə́ʃən]. **submerse (I.)** & **-ion**. Act or process of submerging; state of being submerged.

submetallic, adj. [1. sùbmetálik; 2. sàbmitǽlik]. Somewhat metallic in character.

submission, n. [1. submíshun; 2. səbmíʃən], fr. Lat. *submiss-(um)*, P.P. type of *submittere*, 'to put or place below; to furnish, provide; to transfer, resign', see **submit**. 1. Act or process of submitting; state of being submitted. 2. Spirit of readiness to submit; resignation, surrender, acquiescence. Phr. *with all due submission*, with respect and humility.

submissive, adj. [1. submísiv; 2. səbmísiv], fr. Lat. *submissum*, see prec., & **-ive**. Ready to submit, expressing submission, acquiescing, resigned, docile.

submissively, adv. Prec. & **-ly**. In a submissive manner.

submissiveness, n. See prec. & **-ness**. State or quality of being submissive.

submit, vb. trans. & intrans. [1. submít; 2. səbmít], fr. Lat. *sub-*, *summittere*, 'to place, set, below; to furnish, provide; to transfer, resign; to reduce, moderate', fr. **sub-** & *mittere*, 'to send, place', see **missile**. A. trans. 1. (reflex.) To yield, surrender, resign: *to submit oneself to another's authority*. 2. To present, place before person, tribunal &c. for consideration, judgement &c.: *to submit a scheme, case* &c. 3. To suggest, put forward, urge: *I submit, with all respect, that what you propose is contrary to the statutes*. B. intrans. To give in to authority, superior force &c.; to yield, surrender, resign oneself, be submissive: *to refuse to submit tamely*; *to submit to control*; specif., *to submit to the Pope, the Church*, to acknowledge the absolute supremacy of.

submontane, adj. [1. sùbmóntān; 2. sàbmóntein]. Situated, formed, at the foot of a mountain or mountain-range.

submucous, adj. [1. sùbmúkus; 2. sàbmjúkəs]. Somewhat mucous in character.

submultiple, n. [1. sùbmúltipl; 2. sàbmáltipl]. Number contained in another an exact number of times; factor.

subnarcotic, adj. [1. sùbnarkótik; 2. sàbnākótik]. Slightly narcotic.

subnasal, adj. [1. sùbnázl; 2. sàbnéizl]. Situated beneath the nose.

subnatural, adj. [1. sùbnáchural; 2. sàbnǽtʃərəl]. Less than natural, opposed to *supernatural*.

subnormal, adj. [1. sùbnórml; 2. sàbnóməl]. Below normal.

suboccipital, adj. [1. sùboksípitl; 2. sàboksípitl]. Situated below the occiput.

suboceanic, adj. [1. sùbōshiánik; 2. sàbouʃiǽnik]. Situated beneath the surface of the ocean.

subocellate, adj. [1. sùbosélāt; 2. sàbosséleit]. Somewhat ocellate in appearance.

suboctuple, adj. [1. sùbóktūpl; 2. sàbóktjupl]. In the ratio of 1 to 8.

subocular, adj. [1. sùbókūlar; 2. sàbókjulə]. Situated beneath the eye.

suborbital, adj. [1. sùbórbitl; 2. sàbóbitl]. Situated beneath the orbit of the eye.

suborder, n. [1. súbórder; 2. sábódə]. (biol.) Subdivision of an order.

subordinal, adj. [1. sùbórdinal; 2. sàbódinəl]. Pertaining to, ranking as, a suborder.

subordinate (I.), adj. [1. subórdinat; 2. səbódinit], fr. **sub-** & Lat. *ordinātum*, P.P. type of *ordināre*, 'to ordain, appoint', see **ordain**. 1. Placed below, inferior in rank and importance, subject to the authority of another: *subordinate rank, position* &c. 2. Inferior in importance, dependent upon, subject to: *pleasure should be subordinate to duty*. 3. (gram.) *Subordinate clause*, part of a sentence introduced by a subordinative conjunction; dependent clause.

subordinate (II.), n., fr. prec. Person in a subordinate position; an inferior.

subordinate (III.), vb. trans. [1. subórdināt; 2. səbódineit], fr. prec. **a** To bring under

SUBORDINATELY

control of, make subservient to : *to subordinate one's own interest to the public good* ; **b** to place in inferior, less important, position ; regard as inferior : *it is sometimes necessary to subordinate an elderly official to one who is his junior in service*.

subordinately, adv. [1. subórdinatli ; 2. səbŏ́dinitli]. **subordinate** (I.) & -**ly**. In a subordinate manner.

subordination, n. [1. subòrdináshun ; 2. səbŏ̀dinéiʃən]. **subordinate** (III.) & -**ion**. Act of subordinating ; state of being subordinated.

subordinationism, n. [1. subòrdináshunizm ; 2. səbŏ̀dinéiʃənizəm]. Prec. & -**ism**. Doctrine of the superiority of the first Person of the Trinity over the second and third.

subordinative, adj. [1. subórdinativ ; 2. səbŏ́dinitiv]. **subordinate** (I.) & -**ive**. Tending to, expressing, subordination : *a subordinative conjunction*, one introducing a subordinate clause.

suborn, vb. trans. [1. subórn ; 2. səbŏ́n], fr. Fr. *suborner*, fr. Lat. *subornāre*, 'to provide, furnish ; to instigate, incite secretly ', fr. **sub-**, & *ornāre*, 'to equip', see **ornate**. To procure (a person) by bribery or other illicit means, to commit a crime, esp. that of perjury.

subornation, n. [1. subòrnáshun ; 2. səbŏ̀néiʃən], fr. Lat. *subornātum*, P.P. type of *subornāre*, 'to incite secretly ', see prec., & -**ion**. Act of suborning ; state of being suborned.

suboval, adj. [1. subŏ́vl ; 2. səbŏ́uvəl]. Nearly oval, somewhat egg-shaped.

subovate, adj. [1. subŏ́vat ; 2. səbŏ́uvət]. Suboval.

subparietal, adj. [1. subpariétl ; 2. sàbpəráiitl]. Situated beneath the parietal bones.

subphrenic, adj. [1. subfrénik ; 2. sàbfrénik]. Situated beneath the diaphragm.

subpilose, adj. [1. subpílōs ; 2. sàbpáilous]. Somewhat hairy.

subpleural, adj. [1. subplōóral ; 2. sàbplúərəl]. Situated beneath the pleura.

subpoena, n. & vb. trans. [1. subpéna ; 2. səbpíṇə], fr. first words of the document ; Lat. *sub poena*, 'under the penalty'; see **sub-**, **penal**. **1**. n. Writ summoning person to attend in court of justice. **2**. vb. To summon by subpoena.

subpolar, adj. [1. subpṓlar ; 2. sàbpóulə]. **1**. Near the North or the South Pole. **2**. (astron.) Situated directly beneath the celestial pole.

subprefect, n. [1. subpréfekt ; 2. sàbprífekt]. Official acting as assistant to prefect.

subprior, n. [1. subprior ; 2. sàbpráiə]. Official in religious house ranking next to prior.

subpyramidal, adj. [1. subpirámidl ; 2. sàbpirámidl]. Nearly pyramidal in shape.

subquadrate, adj. [1. subkwódrat ; 2. sàbkwódrət]. Nearly square.

subquadruple, adj. [1. subkwódroopl ; 2. sàbkwódrupl]. In the ratio of 1 to 4.

subquintuple, adj. [1. subkwíntupl ; 2. sàbkwíntjupl]. In the ratio of 1 to 5.

subramose, adj. [1. subrámōs ; 2. sàbréimous]. Slightly branching.

subrational, adj. [1. subráshunal ; 2. sàbrǽʃən(ə)l]. Nearly rational.

subrectangular, adj. [1. subrektánggūlar ; 2. sàbrektǽŋgjulə]. Almost rectangular.

subrector, n. [1. subréktor ; 2. sàbréktə]. Rector's assistant or deputy.

subregion, n. [1. súbrējun ; 2. sábridʒən]. Subdivision of a region, esp. with reference to distribution of fauna or flora.

subreption, n. [1. subrépshun ; 2. sabrépʃən], fr. Lat. *sub-*, *surreptiōn-(em)*, 'theft ', fr. *subreptum*, P.P. type of *subripere*, 'to steal or snatch away', & -**ion**; fr. **sub-** & *rapere*, 'to seize, snatch', see **rape** (I.). Obtaining of favour, property &c. by fraudulent concealment, misrepresentation of fact.

subretinal, adj. [1. subrétinal ; 2. sàbrétin(ə)l]. Situated beneath the retina.

subrhomboidal, adj. [1. subrombóidl ; 2. sàbrəmbóidl]. Nearly rhomboidal in shape.

subrogation, n. [1. subrogáshun ; 2. sàbrəgéi-ʃən]. (law) Substitution of one creditor for another.

subsacral, adj. [1. subsǻkral ; 2. sàbséikrəl]. Situated beneath the sacrum.

subscapular, adj. [1. subskápūlar ; 2. sàbskǽpjulə]. Situated beneath the scapula.

subscribe, vb. trans. & intrans. [1. subskríb ; 2. səbskráib], fr. Lat. *subscribere*, 'to write below ; to sign ; to agree to, approve of', fr. **sub-** & *scribere*, 'to write ', see **scribe** (I.). **A**. trans. **1**. To write (one's name &c.) at end of document, as attestation &c. **2**. To sign one's name at end of (document &c.), esp. to indicate consent, attestation &c. **3**. To pay, guarantee to pay, contribute (sum of money) to fund &c. : *to subscribe money to charities*. **B**. intrans. **1**. To signify one's agreement, approval, assent : *to subscribe to a proposal, opinion* &c. **2**. To contribute, pay or engage to pay sum of money, as one of a group of contributors, to fund, for publication of book &c., for regular receipt of periodical &c. : *to subscribe to a fund, journal* &c. ; *to subscribe for a book*.

subscriber, n. [1. subskríber ; 2. səbskráibə]. Prec. & -**er**. One who subscribes ; specif. **a** person who contributes, or undertakes to contribute, periodically, a specific sum for a specified purpose ; **b** a person who undertakes to receive and pay for a publication appearing at stated intervals.

subscript, adj. [1. súbskript ; 2. sábskript], fr. Lat. *subscript-(um)*, P.P. type of *subscribere*, 'to write below', see **subscribe**. *Iota subscript*, (in Gk.) a small iota written below ā, ē, ō, expressing originally the second element of a diphthong.

subscription, n. [1. subskrípshun ; 2. səbskrípʃən], fr. Lat. *subscriptiōn-(em)*, 'something written below; signature' &c. ; see prec. & -**ion**. **1**. Act of subscribing ; state of being subscribed. **2**. Signature to a document. **3**. **a** Sum paid or subscribed at regular intervals for a particular cause or purpose ; a contribution ; **b** sum charged or paid for a periodical publication.

subsection, n. [1. súbsekshun ; 2. sábsekʃən]. Division of a section.

subsellium, n. [1. subsélium ; 2. sabséliəm]. Lat. *subsellium*, 'bench, seat', fr. **sub-** & *sella*, 'seat', fr. earlier *sedlā*, cp. *sedēre*, 'to sit', & see **sedate**; cp. further O.E. *setl*, 'seat', see **settle** (I.). Low bench ; ledge below a hinged seat ; a misericord.

subsensible, adj. [1. subsénsibl ; 2. sàbsénsibl]. Beyond the range of, not capable of being perceived by, the senses.

subseptuple, adj. [1. subséptupl ; 2. sàbséptjupl]. In the ratio of 1 to 7.

subsequence, n. [1. súbsekwens ; 2. sábsikwəns]. See next word & -**ence**. Condition of being subsequent.

subsequent, adj. [1. súbsekwent ; 2. sábsikwənt], fr. Lat. *subsequentem*, Pres. Part. of *subsequor*, 'I follow, succeed', fr. **sub-** & *sequor*, 'I follow', see **sequela**. **1**. Following ; occurring, appearing, at a later time, coming after : *subsequent events showed that I was right* ; *subsequent to his death*. **2**. *Subsequent upon*, following as a result, consequent upon. **3**. (geol., of stream) Forming a primary tributary to main stream of river-system, and flowing in hollow formed by denudation.

subsequently, adv. Prec. & -**ly**. At a subsequent time ; later on, later.

subserous, adj. [1. subsérus ; 2. sàbsíərəs]. Somewhat serous in character.

subserve, vb. trans. [1. subsérv ; 2. səbsə́v], fr. Lat. *subservīre*, 'to be subject to, serve' ; **sub-** & **serve**. To promote, help on, be a useful adjunct to ; to fulfil : *to subserve a useful purpose*.

subservience, -**cy**, n. [1. subsérviens(i) ; 2. səbsə́viəns(i)]. See **subservient** & -**ence** & -**cy**. State of being subservient.

subservient, adj. [1. subsérvient ; 2. səbsə́viənt], fr. Lat. *subservient-(em)*, Pres. Part. of *subservīre*, 'to be subject to', see **subserve**. **1**. Obsequious, servile. **2**. Adapted to promote or forward, serving as means to an end ; acting in subordination to, as ancillary to.

subserviently, adv. Prec. & -**ly**. In a subservient manner.

subsessile, adj. [1. subsésīl ; 2. sàbsésail]. Nearly sessile.

subsextuple, adj. [1. subsékstūpl ; 2. sàbsékstjupl]. In the ratio of 1 to 6.

subside, vb. intrans. [1. subsíd ; 2. səbsáid], fr. Lat. *subsīdere*, 'to sit, sink, or settle down', fr. **sub-** & *sīdere*, 'to sit down' ; cp. Scrt. *sīdati*, 'sits'; fr. base **si-zd-*, redupl. fr. **sed-* &c., 'to sit' ; see **sit**, **sedate**. **1**. **a** To fall, pass, sink, to a lower level ; to settle or sink down : *the floods have subsided* ; **b** (of ground) to collapse, cave in, sink, esp. as result of undermining &c. **2**. To allow oneself to sink gradually : *to subside into a chair*. **3**. To decrease in volume, intensity, vigour &c., abate, slacken, diminish : *the gale, one's fury, fever &c. subsides*.

subsidence, n. [1. súbsidens ; 2. sábsidəns]. Prec. & -**ence**. Process of subsiding.

subsidiarily, adv. [1. subsídiarili ; 2. səbsídiərili]. Next word & -**ly**. In a subsidiary manner.

subsidiary (I.), adj. [1. subsídiari ; 2. səbsídiəri], fr. Lat. *subsidiārius*, 'forming a reserve', fr. *subsidium*, 'line of reserve, auxiliary troops ; help, succour', see **subsidy**, & -**ary**. **1**. Serving as support or supplement, additional, auxiliary, esp. in an inferior or subordinate position ; secondary. **2**. Pertaining to, of the nature of, a subsidy.

subsidiary (II.), n., fr. prec. (often pl.) Persons or things serving as or giving supplementary aid or support ; auxiliaries.

subsidize, vb. trans. [1. súbsidīz ; 2. sábsidaiz]. See **subsidy** & -**ize**. To give subsidy to, support by subsidy.

subsidy, n. [1. súbsidi ; 2. sábsidi], fr. Lat. *subsidium*, 'reserve troops ; support, help', fr. *subsidēre*, 'to be in reserve', fr. **sub-** & *sedēre*, 'to sit', see **sedate**, **sit**. **1**. Grant of public money to support or assist private industry or enterprise. **2**. (hist.) Grant of money by Parliament to Sovereign for State needs.

subsist, vb. intrans. & trans. [1. subsíst ; 2. səbsíst], fr. Lat. *subsistere*, 'to stand still ; to stop, halt; to remain', fr. **sub-** & *sistere*, 'to stand', redupl. form of base **stā-* &c., 'to stand', see **state** & **stand** (I.). **1**. intrans. **a** To remain in existence, be extant, continue in being : *a country where superstition still subsists* ; **b** to remain alive, sustain life : *we are unable to subsist without air and water*. **2**. trans. (rare) To provide food for, give sustenance to.

subsistence, n. [1. subsistens ; 2. səbsístəns]. Prec. & -**ence**. **1**. Act of subsisting ; state of being subsisted. **2**. Means of supporting life, that on which one subsists.

subsoil, n. [1. súbsoil ; 2. sábsoil]. Layer, stratum, of earth immediately below the top layer of the ground.

subspecies, n. [1. súbspēshēz ; 2. sábspīʃīz]. A division of a species.

subspecific, adj. [1. subspesífik ; 2. sàbspisífik]. Characteristic of a subspecies.

subspherical, adj. [1. subsférikl ; 2. sàbsférikl]. Nearly spherical.

subspinous, adj. [1. subspínus ; 2. sàbspáinəs]. Somewhat spinous.

substage, n. [1. súbstāj ; 2. sábsteidʒ]. Attachment below the stage of a microscope to hold diaphragm, mirror, condenser &c.

substance, n. [1. súbstans ; 2. sábstəns]. Lat. *substantia*, 'that of which a thing consists, material ; property, fortune' ; fr. *substant-(em)*, Pres. Part. of *substāre*, 'to stand firm' &c., see **sub-**, **state** (I.), & -**ce**. **1**. (philos.) The underlying permanent reality and cause of all outward phenomena ; the subject, essence, reality of anything in which properties, accidents, attributes inhere. **2**. The essential, most important elements or components of anything ; the true meaning, purport : *give me briefly the substance of his speech* ; *though differently expressed, the two* statements *agree in substance.* **3. a** The material of which a thing consists; a portion of solid matter; stuff: *soils consist of various chemical substances*; **b** (i.) solid character, firm consistency, body: *this fabric lacks substance*; also (ii.) (in non-material sense) intellectual or moral worth and value or content: *a piece of writing which lacks substance.* **4.** Material possessions, means, resources, property: *a man of substance*; *to waste one's substance.*

substantial, adj. [1. substánshal; 2. səbstǽnʃəl], fr. Lat. *substantiālis*, 'of the essence or substance', fr. *substantia*, 'substance', see prec., & -al. **1. a** Pertaining to, of the nature of, possessing, substance; material: *no mere apparition, but a substantial being*; **b** solid, firm, stout: *a substantial building*; *a substantial meal*, one that is solid, ample, satisfying. **2.** Considerable, weighty, important, valuable: *a substantial improvement, contribution*; *substantial additions.* **3.** Pertaining to, expressing, containing, agreeable to, the pith, essential meaning, true import: *in substantial agreement*; *substantial compliance with the law.* **4.** Possessing property, commanding resources; wealthy, well-to-do: *a substantial farmer.*

substantialism, n. [1. substánshalizm; 2. səbstǽnʃəlizəm]. Prec. & -ism. Doctrine that a permanent substratum of reality, or substance, underlies all phenomena.

substantialist, n. [1. substánshalist; 2. səbstǽnʃəlist]. substantial & -ist. Adherent of substantialism.

substantiality, n. [1. substànshiáliti; 2. səbstænʃiǽliti]. substantial & -ity. State or quality of being substantial.

substantialize, vb. trans. [1. substánshalīz; 2. səbstǽnʃəlaiz]. substantial & -ize. To make substantial, give substance or reality to.

substantially, adv. [1. substánshali; 2. səbstǽnʃəli]. substantial & -ly. In a substantial manner; to a substantial degree.

substantiate, vb. trans. [1. substánshiāt; 2. səbstǽnʃieit], fr. Lat. *substantia*, 'substance', see substance, & -ate. To give substance or reality to; to prove, confirm, establish; to show to be true or genuine, give evidence of the truth of: *to substantiate a statement, claim* &c.

substantiation, n. [1. substànshiáshun; 2. səbstænʃiéiʃən]. Prec. & -ion. Act of substantiating; state of being substantiated.

substantival, adj. [1. substantívl; 2. sàbstəntáivəl]. substantive (II.) & -al. (gram.) Pertaining to, of the nature of, a substantive.

substantivally, adv. Prec. & -ly. As a substantive.

substantive (I.), adj. [1. sústantiv; 2. sǽbstəntiv], fr. Lat. *substantīvus*, 'self-existent', fr. *substantia*, 'substance', see substance, & -ive. **1.** Existing independently, of individual importance, having distinct or real existence: *a substantive being*; (mil.) *substantive rank*, one which entitles the holder to full pay, or pension of that rank; contrasted with honorary or brevet rank: *a substantive major* &c. **2.** (gram.) **a** Expressing existence: *the verb 'to be' is the substantive verb*; **b** *noun substantive*, one which is the name of a specific object, idea &c.

substantive (II.), n., fr. prec. Noun substantive.

substantively, adv. substantive (I.) & -ly. Substantivally.

substation, n. [1. súbstāshun; 2. sǽbsteiʃən]. Subsidiary or subordinate station.

substernal, adj. [1. sùbstérnal; 2. sàbstə́n(ə)l]. Situated below the sternum.

substitute (I.), n. [1. súbstitūt; 2. sǽbstitjūt], fr. Lat. *substitūt-(um)*, P.P. type of *substituere*, 'to put instead of', fr. sub- & *statuere*, 'to place, put', see statute. **a** Something put in the place of, used instead of, something else; **b** person taking the place of, acting instead of, acting as deputy for, another.

substitute (II.), vb. trans., fr. Lat., see prec. To put, use, in place of another person or thing: *to erase a word and substitute another.*

substitution, n. [1. sùbstitúshun; 2. sàbstitjúʃən], fr. Lat. *substitūtiōnem*, 'a putting in the place of another'; prec. & -ion. Act of substituting; state of being substituted.

substitutional, adj. [1. sùbstitúshunal; 2. sàbstitjúʃənəl]. Prec. & -al. Of, pertaining to, substitution; serving as substitute.

substitutionally, adv. Prec. & -ly. As a substitute, by means of substitution.

substitutionary, adj. [1. sùbstitúshunari; 2. sàbstitjúʃənəri]. substitution & -ary. Substitutional.

substitutive, adj. [1. súbstitūtiv; 2. sǽbstitjūtiv]. substitute (II.) & -ive. Capable of being substituted; liable to substitution.

substratum, n. [1. súbstrátum; 2. sǽbstréitəm]. **a** Lower stratum, underlying layer: *a substratum of rock*; **b** (also in non-material sense) underlying basis, foundation: *a substratum of fact, truth.*

substructural, adj. [1. sùbstrúkchural; 2. sàbstrʌ́ktʃərəl]. Next word & -al. Pertaining to a substructure.

substructure, n. [1. súbstrŭkchur; 2. sǽbstrʌ́ktʃə]. Lower or basic structure, foundation; lowest part of structure.

subsume, vb. trans. [1. sùbsúm; 2. sàbsjúm], fr. sub- & Lat. *sūmere*, 'to take, lay hold of', see assume & sumption. To classify, include, under, regard as belonging to, a specific category; to include in a specific class.

subsumption, n. [1. sùbsúmpshun; 2. sàbsámpʃən]. sub- & sumption. **1.** Act of subsuming; state of being subsumed. **2.** That which is subsumed, special instance &c. classified under a general category.

subsumptive, adj. [1. sùbsúmptiv; 2. sàbsámptiv]. See prec. & -ive. Pertaining to, of the nature of, a subsumption.

subtemperate, adj. [1. sùbtémperat; 2. sàbtémpərit]. (of region, climate &c.) Of, approaching, bordering on, the temperate zone; slightly colder than the temperate zone.

subtenancy, n. [1. súbtènansi; 2. sǽbtènənsi]. Next word & -cy. **1. a** Act of holding property as a subtenant; **b** period, duration, of such holding.

subtenant, n. [1. súbtènant; 2. sǽbtènənt]. Person who holds a lease from one who is himself a tenant.

subtend, vb. trans. [1. sùbténd; 2. sàbténd], fr. Lat. *subtendere*, 'to stretch underneath', fr. sub- & *tendere*, 'to stretch', see tense (II.). (geom., of side of triangle) To extend under, be opposite to.

subtense, n. [1. sùbténs; 2. sàbténs]. sub- & tense (II.). (geom.) Line subtending an arc or angle.

subter-, pref. representing Lat. *subter*, 'below, beneath', fr. sub- & compar. suff. -ter, cp. inter-. Lower, beneath, less than; e.g. *subterhuman* &c., contrasted with *superhuman* &c.

subterfuge, n. [1. súbterfūj; 2. sǽbtəfjùdʒ], fr. L. Lat. *subterfugium*, 'subterfuge', fr. *subterfugere*, 'to depart secretly; to evade, avoid', fr. subter- & *fugere*, 'to flee', see fugitive. An artifice, means of evasion, disingenuous pretext; prevarication, sophistry, equivocation.

subterminal, adj. [1. sùbtérminal; 2. sàbtə́minəl]. Approaching, near, the end.

subterposition, n. [1. sùbterpozíshun; 2. sàbtəpəzíʃən]. State of being below, underneath, some substance or thing.

subterranean, subterraneous, adj. [1. sùbteránean, -eus; 2. sàbtiréiniən, -iəs], fr. Lat. *subterrāneus*, 'underground', fr. sub- & *terra* & -aneous & -an. Situated, existing, underground: *a subterranean dwelling*; *subterranean fire.*

subterraneously, adv. [1. sùbterráneusli; 2. sàbtiréinəsli]. See prec. & -ly. Beneath the surface of the earth, underground.

subterrestrial, adj. [1. sùbteréstrial; 2. sàbtiréstriəl]. Subterranean, underground.

subthoracic, adj. [1. sùbthorásik; 2. sàbθɔrǽsik]. Situated under the thorax.

subtil(e), adj. [1. sútl; 2. sátl]. Archaic spelling of subtle.

subtilization, n. [1. sùtilizáshun; 2. sàtilaizéiʃən]. Next word & -ation. Act of subtilizing; state of being subtilized.

subtilize, vb. trans. & intrans. [1. sútiliz; 2. sátilaiz]. subtil(e) & -ize. **1.** trans. **a** To make subtle, refined, ethereal; **b** to make subtle distinctions in (thought &c.). **2.** intrans. To make subtle distinctions.

subtilty, n. [1. sútlti; 2. sátlti], fr. Lat. *subtīlitātem*, 'fineness, acuteness, simplicity'; subtil(e) & -ity. Archaic for subtlety.

subtitle, n. [1. súbtitl; 2. sǽbtàitl]. Secondary, additional, title of book &c.

subtle, also (archaic) **subtil(e)**, adj. [1. sútl; 2. sátl], fr. Lat. *subtīlis*, 'fine, thin; delicate, subtle; clear, simple', earlier *subtexlis, 'finely woven', fr. sub- & *tex-*, stem of *texere*, 'to weave', see textile; cp. Lat. *tēla*, 'web', fr.* texlā; see tela. **1.** Rarefied, highly refined, delicate; elusive, indefinable: *a subtle delight.* **2. a** (of the mind and its operations) Keen, penetrating, nicely critical and discriminating; **b** (in bad sense) crafty, designing, underhand. **3.** Possessing, exhibiting, delicacy of touch and exquisite skill in craftsmanship; deft, highly accomplished: *a subtle artist*; *a subtle bit of work.*

subtlety, n. [1. sútlti; 2. sátlti]. Prec. & -ty (I.). **1.** State or quality of being subtle (in various senses of the adj.). **2.** Something that is subtle; esp. nice distinction, over-refined point or argument; a quibble, a splitting of hairs.

subtly, adv. [1. sútli; 2. sátli]. subtle & -ly. In a subtle manner.

subtonic, n. [1. súbtónik; 2. sábtónik]. (mus.) Seventh note of the scale.

subtract, vb. trans. [1. subtrákt; 2. səbtrǽkt], fr. Lat. *subtractum*, P.P. type of *subtrahere*, 'to draw off, carry away, withdraw', fr. sub- & *trahere*, 'to carry, draw', see tract (I.). To take away (a part, amount, quantity) from another amount or number; to lessen an amount or number by: *to subtract 2 from 4.*

subtraction, n. [1. subtrákshun; 2. səbtrǽkʃən]. Prec. & -ion. Act of subtracting; specif., (math.) process of taking away a number from another number.

subtractive, adj. [1. subtráktiv; 2. səbtrǽktiv]. subtract & -ive. Tending, having the power, to subtract.

subtrahend, n. [1. subtrahend; 2. sábtrəhend], fr. Lat. *subtrahendum*, gerundive of *subtrahere*, 'to remove', see subtract. (arith. &c.) Amount, number, to be subtracted.

subtransparent, adj. [1. sùbtrahnspárent; 2. sàbtrænspéərənt]. Almost transparent.

subtriangular, adj. [1. sùbtríanggŭlar; 2. sàbtraiǽŋɡjulə]. Nearly triangular in shape.

subtribe, n. [1. súbtrīb; 2. sǽbtraib]. A subdivision of a tribe.

subtriple, adj. [1. súbtripl; 2. sǽbtripl]. In the ratio of 1 to 3.

subtriplicate, adj. [1. sùbtríplikat; 2. sàbtríplikit]. (of ratio) Expressed by cube roots.

subtropical, adj. [1. sùbtrópikl; 2. sàbtrópikl]. Verging on the tropical, slightly colder than tropical region &c.; intermediate between temperate and tropical.

subulate, adj. [1. súbulat; 2. sjúbjulət], fr. Lat. *sūbula*, 'awl'; cp. O. Slav. *šilo*, 'awl'; O.H.G. *siula*, 'awl, needle'; cp. further Lat. *suere*, 'to sew', & see suture (I.). (zool., bot.) Slender and pointed, awl-shaped.

subuliform, adj. [1. súbuliform; 2. sjúbjulifɔm], fr. Lat. *sūbula*, 'awl', see prec., & -i- & -form. Awl-shaped.

subungulate, adj. [1. sùbúngulat; 2. sàbáŋɡjulət]. (zool.) With hoof divided into digits.

suburb, n. [1. súberb; 2. sǽbāb], fr. Lat. *suburbium*, 'suburb', fr. sub- & *urb-*, stem of *urbs*, 'city', see urban. Part of town lying on its outskirts; residential area outside boundaries of a town; (often pl.) *to live in the suburbs* &c.

suburban, adj. [1. subérban; 2. səbā́bən], fr. Lat. *suburbānus*, 'near the city'; prec. &

-an. Pertaining to, situated in, living in, a suburb; characteristic of a suburb or of the inhabitants of a suburb; often (in derogatory sense), prejudiced, limited in intellectual outlook; having the good qualities neither of the town, nor of the country.

subursine, adj. [1. sŭbḗrsīn; 2. sàbás(a)in]. Somewhat ursine in character or appearance.

subvention, n. [1. subvénshun; 2. səbvénʃən], fr. Lat. *subventiōn-(em)*, 'assistance', fr. *subvent-(um)*, P.P. type of *subvenīre*, 'to come to the aid of', fr. **sub-** & *venīre*, 'to come', see **venue,** & **-ion.** Grant of money, esp. one made by a government, or public body, in support of industry, institution, enterprise &c.; a subsidy.

subversion, n. [1. subvḗrshun; 2. sabvā́ʃən], fr. Lat. *subversiōn-(em)*, 'overthrow', fr. *subversum*, P.P. type of *subvertere*, 'to overthrow', see **subvert,** & **-ion.** Act of subverting; state of being subverted.

subversive, adj. [1. subvḗrsiv; 2. səbvā́siv], fr. Lat. *subvers-(um)*, see prec. & **-ive.** Tending to subvert; destructive.

subvert, vb. trans. [1. subvḗrt; 2. səbvā́t], fr. Lat. *subvertere*, 'to overthrow, destroy, ruin', fr. **sub-** & *vertere*, 'to turn', see **version.** To destroy, overthrow, bring to ruin.

subvertebral, adj. [1. sùbvḗrtebral; 2. sàbvā́tibral]. Situated under the vertebrae.

subvertical, adj. [1. sùbvḗrtikl; 2. sàbvā́tikl]. Nearly vertical.

subvitreous, adj. [1. sùbvítreus; 2. sàbvítriəs]. Somewhat glassy.

subway, n. [1. súbwā; 2. sábweɪ]. A road, path, passage, under another road, or under railway lines &c.

suc-, pref. Form of **sub-** used in compounds before *-c-*.

succades, n. pl. [1. sukắdz; 2. sakéɪdz], fr. Lat. *succus, sūcus*, 'juice, sap'; cp. Lat. *sūgere*, O.E. *sūcan*, 'to suck'; see **suck (I.),** & **-ade.** (commerc.) Candied fruits.

succedaneous, adj. [1. sùksedā́neus; 2. sàksidéɪnɪəs], fr. Lat. *succēdāneus*, 'following, supplying place of, substituted for, something', fr. *succēdere*, 'to follow', see **succeed,** & **-aneous.** Of, pertaining to, serving as, a succedaneum.

succedaneum, n. [1. sùksedā́neum; 2. sàksidéɪnɪəm]. Lat. *succēdāneum*, neut. form of *succēdāneus*, see prec. Something used, serving, acting, in place of another; substitute.

succeed, vb. trans. & intrans. [1. suksḗd; 2. səksī́d], fr. Lat. *succēdere*, 'to go under or from under; to follow in space or time; to be successful, prosper', fr. **suc-** & *cēdere*, 'to go', see **cede** & **cease (I.). A.** trans. **1.** To follow, come, occur, appear after; contrasted with *precede*: *night succeeds day; the storm was succeeded by calm; one exciting event succeeded another; as fast as one man was shot down he was succeeded by another.* **2. a** To follow (a person) in an office, rank, employment &c.: *Asquith succeeded Campbell-Bannerman as Premier*; **b** specif., to follow as heir, obtain property, honours, rank, office of, as lawful hereditary successor to: *the late peer left none to succeed him; King George V. succeeded his father King Edward.* **3.** (rare, poet.) to grant success to, cause to succeed or prosper: '*Pallas from the skies Accords their vow, succeeds their enterprise*' (Pope, 'Iliad'). **B.** intrans. **1.** To follow, come immediately after, another (person, thing, event &c.): *the storm died down, and a great calm succeeded; often succeed to: a long period of peace succeeded to the stormy days of the Napoleonic wars.* **2. a** To take up another's office, duties &c., after him: *to succeed to the Archiepiscopal throne, to the office of Lord Chancellor &c.*; **b** specif., to acquire property, office, rank, as hereditary successor or heir: *when a peer dies his eldest son succeeds; to succeed to one's father's estate; no woman could succeed to the throne of Hanover.* **3. a** To attain one's object, be successful, have success; to accomplish, complete, one's purpose: *if you try often enough you'll succeed at last; succeed in (doing &c.), contrive to do*; **b** (of action, attempt &c.) to be satisfactorily accomplished, attain object for which it was undertaken, be crowned with success: *the attack succeeded beyond all expectations; half-hearted attempts rarely succeed.* **4.** To become prosperous, be fortunate in one's career; to acquire wealth: *to succeed in life, as a doctor, politician &c.*

succentor, n. [1. suksḗntor; 2. səksḗntə], fr. L. Lat. *succentor*, 'one who accompanies in singing', **suc-** & Lat. *cantor*, 'singer', see **cantoris** & **cant (I.). 1.** Leading bass, bass soloist, in a choir. **2.** Sub-precentor, precentor's deputy.

succès d'estime, n. [1. sóoksā destḗm; 2. sykse dsstī́m]. Fr. Applause accorded to a work, performance &c., on account of the respect in which the performer is held, rather than on account of the merits of the work itself.

success, n. [1. suksḗs; 2. saksés], fr. O. Fr. *succes*, fr. Lat. *successus*, 'advance, approach; good result', fr. *success-(um)*, P.P. type of *succēdere*, 'to go under, from under; to march up to; to follow; to prosper'; see **succeed. 1.** Fortunate accomplishment of an aim, or attempt; attainment of desired object, or result: *my efforts were crowned with success.* **2.** Prosperity, good fortune: *he has had great success in life.* **3. a** Person who, that which, attains success: *he was not a success as a speaker; my holiday in Switzerland was a great success*; **b** action in which one has been successful; a triumph, lucky hit: *I count that speech, book, among my successes; Marlborough's battles were a series of successes.*

successful, adj. [1. suksésfool; 2. səksésful, -fəl]. Prec. & **-ful. 1. a** Having attained one's object, having succeeded in an attempt: *I tried to persuade him but was not successful*; **b** (of action, effort &c.) producing, resulting in, a desired effect. **2.** Fortunate, happy in one's career, prosperous: *he had all the appearance of a successful man.*

successfully, adv. Prec. & **-ly.** In a successful manner.

successfulness, n. See prec. & **-ness.** Quality of being successful.

succession, n. [1. sukséshun; 2. səkséʃən]. Lat. *successiōn-(em)*, 'a coming into the place of; a succession in office &c.', fr. *success-(um)*, P.P. type of *succēdere*, see **succeed,** & **-ion. 1.** Act or process of succeeding, or following; **a** in office, employment &c.: *a man's succession to another as editor &c.*; *Apostolic Succession,* continuous transmission of the spiritual authority of the Apostles through bishops; **b** act, or right of succeeding as heir, lawful descendant, hereditary successor: *the succession of King Charles II. to the throne of his ancestors; War of the Spanish Succession; law of succession,* that which defines and regulates conditions for the inheritance of property; *succession duties,* those payable by an heir on succeeding to property. **2.** Number of persons, objects, events, actions which follow one another in time or space; a series, sequence: *a succession of remarkable victories; famous personages rode past in rapid succession.*

successional, adj. [1. suksḗshunal; 2. səkséʃənəl]. Prec. & **-al.** Pertaining to a succession; coming, occurring, in regular sequence.

successionist, n. [1. suksḗshunist; 2. səkséʃənist]. See prec. & **-ist.** One who attaches great importance to lawful and regular succession; specif. one who holds Apostolic Succession to be essential to the validity of the Christian Ministry.

successive, adj. [1. suksḗsiv; 2. səksḗsiv]. See **success** & **-ive.** Coming in immediate succession, occurring consecutively: *on three successive occasions*; *in successive reigns.*

successively, adv. Prec. & **-ly.** In a successive manner; in succession.

successiveness, n. See prec. & **-ness.** State of being successive.

successor, n. [1. suksésur; 2. səksésə]. See **success** & **-or. 1. a** Person who follows another in an office, employment &c.: *when a great public servant dies or retires, it is not always easy to find a worthy successor*; **b** one who succeeds another as lawful heir, by descent, according to fixed rule &c.: *King George is the regular successor of William the Conqueror.* **2.** Object, event, which comes after another as part of a sequence, which takes the place of another as representing a stage in regular progress &c.: *the tank and the aeroplane are to a great extent the successors of cavalry in warfare; the summer before last was dryer than its successor.*

succinct, adj. [1. suksíngkt; 2. səksíŋkt], fr. L. Lat. *succinct-us*, 'prepared, ready; concise', fr. P.P. type of *succingere*, 'to gird; to prepare, equip', fr. **suc-** & *cingere*, 'to gird'; see **cincture (I.). 1.** Concisely expressed, terse. **2.** (archaic and poet.) Girded, tucked up: '*with garbs succinct*', with clothes tucked up (Pope, translating Homer).

succinctly, adv. Prec. & **-ly.** In a succinct manner.

succinctness, n. See prec. & **-ness.** Quality of being succinct.

succory, n. [1. súkuri; 2. sákəri]. Variant of **chicory.** Chicory plant.

succose, adj. [1. sukṓs; 2. sákous], fr. Lat. *succus*, 'juice, sap', see **succades,** & **-ose.** Full of juice, sappy.

succotash, n. [1. súkotash; 2. sákətæʃ], fr. Amer. Ind. *msiquatash*. (U.S.A.) Dish of green corn and beans boiled together, usually with pieces of salt pork.

succour (I.), vb. trans. [1. súkur; 2. sákə]. M.E. *socouren*, fr. O. Fr. *succurre,* fr. Lat. *succurrere*, 'to run under; to run to the aid of; to help, assist', fr. **suc-** & *currere*, 'to run'. See **courier.** To help, aid, assist, relieve.

succour (II.), n. M.E. *socour*, fr. O. Fr. *socors*, fr. Lat. *succursus*, 'help', fr. P.P. type of *succurrere*, 'to help'. See prec. **1.** Help, relief, support, given to one in difficulty or danger. **2.** (pl., archaic) Auxiliary troops, reinforcements.

succourless, adj. [1. súkurles; 2. sákəlis]. Prec. & **-less.** Without succour, helpless.

succuba, succubus, n. [1. súkūba, -us; 2. sákjubə, -əs]. Lat. *succuba, succubus,* 'succuba', fr. *succu(m)bere*, 'to lie down, lie under'. See **succumb.** A lascivious spirit supposed to have the power of acquiring a material body, and of having sexual intercourse with human beings; *succuba,* a female spirit of this kind; *succubus,* used either of male or female. See **incubus.**

succulence, n. [1. súkulens; 2. sákjuləns]. Next word & **-ce.** State or quality of being succulent.

succulent, adj. [1. súkulent; 2. sákjulənt], fr. Lat. *succulentus*, 'juicy', fr. *succus*, 'juice, sap', see **succades.** Juicy, full of juice or sap.

succulently, adv. Prec. & **-ly.** In a succulent manner, with succulent material, food &c.: *to feed succulently.*

succumb, vb. intrans. [1. sukúm; 2. səkám], fr. Lat. *succumbere*, 'to lie down, sink down; to submit, surrender', fr. **suc-** & *-cumbere,* 'to lie down', q.v. under **cubicle. a** To yield, submit, be overcome (by), give way (to), cease to resist: *to succumb to superior force; to be forced to succumb; to succumb to temptation*; **b** specif., to die.

succursal, adj. [1. sukḗrsl; 2. sakā́səl], fr. Fr. *succursale,* fr. L. Lat. *succursus,* 'help', see **succour (I.)** & **course (I.)** & **-al.** (of church, chapel of ease &c.). Subsidiary, ancillary.

such (I.), adj. [1. such; 2. satʃ]. O.E. *swylc, swilc; swelce;* M.E. *such, swu(l)ch,* 'such'; earlier **swilic, *swalic;* cp. O.H.G. *solich,* Goth. *swāleiks;* so & **-like. 1. a** Of that or similar kind; of the same nature, quality, degree &c.; of kind, like that, specified, or implied: *I never saw such a sight before; I know of no such place; there are few such towns*

such (II.), pron., fr. prec. 1. Such person(s) or thing(s): '*All such as have erred and are deceived*'; '*Peace to all such, but were there one whose fires*' &c. (Pope). 2. (commerc. or vulg.) It, them, those: *we note your remarks, and in reply to such* . . .

such-and-such, adj. [1. súch an(d) sùch; 2. sátʃən(d) sàtʃ]. Certain, particular but not expressly stated: *the payment of such-and-such sums to such-and-such persons*.

suchlike, adj. [1. súchlik; 2. sátʃlaik]. Similar, of the same kind: *avoid pork and suchlike indigestible food*.

suck (I.), vb. trans. & intrans. [1. suk; 2. sak]. O.E. *sūcan*; M.E. *souken*; cp. O.E. *sūgan*; O.N. *sūga*; O.H.G. *sūgan*, 'to suck'; cogn. w. Lat. *sūgere*, 'to suck'; *sūcus, succus*, 'juice, sap'; Lett. *sūkt*, 'to suck'; cp. further, w. different formative element, Scrt. *sūpaś*, 'broth'; O.E. *sūpan*, 'to sup', see **sup (I.)**. A. trans. 1. a To draw (liquid) into the mouth by an inward rush of air following a partial vacuum formed by action of lips: *to suck lemonade through a straw*; *to suck the juice from an orange*; *vampires that suck one's blood*; **b** to absorb, take up (liquid &c.) by action resembling sucking: *bees suck honey*. 2. To draw liquid into the mouth from, by means of action of lips &c.: *to suck oranges*; *to suck the breast*. 3. To dissolve in the mouth or hold in the mouth and lick repeatedly with tongue: *to suck a lozenge*; *to suck one's thumb*. 4. (fig.) **a** To take into the mind, absorb, imbibe: *to suck knowledge into one's mind*; **b** to draw, absorb (profit, advantage &c.). B. intrans. 1. **a** To perform the action of sucking liquid &c. into the mouth; specif. **b** (of child, young animal) to draw milk into the mouth from breast, udder &c. 2. To make sound as of person, &c. sucking, draw in air with this sound: *a pump that sucks*. C. Followed by adverbs or prepositions with special meanings. *Suck at*, intrans., to apply lips to, and carry out action of sucking: *to suck at a pipe* &c. *Suck in*, trans., **a** to draw (liquid, air &c.) into mouth; **b** to draw in and down, to engulf, by suction: *to be sucked in by a quicksand*; **c** (of porous substance) to absorb. *Suck out*, trans., to draw out by suction. *Suck up*, trans., **a** to draw up by, or as by suction: *the sun sucks up the mist*; **b** (of porous substance) to absorb, draw into itself: *blotting-paper sucks up ink*; (Phr., colloq.) intrans., *suck up to* (person), try to propitiate by flattery, cajolery &c.

suck (II.), n., fr. prec. 1. Act of sucking; state of being sucked; sucking action: *the suck of the whirlpool*. Phr. *to give suck* (to), suckle. 2. (slang) **a** Small drink, mouthful of liquid; **b** a sell, hoax.

sucker (I.), n. [1. súker; 2. sákə]. **suck (I.)** & -er. 1. One who, that which, sucks; specif. **a** sucking-pig; **b** newly born whale; **c** (Am. slang) a person easily duped or swindled; a greenhorn. 2. A Genus of freshwater, edible fish with thick, protractile lips; **b** one of several other varieties of fish. 3. **a** Flexible, usually concave disk, which is made to adhere to a surface by atmospheric pressure; specif., **b** organ by which shellfish &c. adhere to a surface; acetabulum; sucking-disk. 4. Piston of suction-pump. 5. (bot.) **a** Shoot from subterranean stem; **b** abnormal shoot from axis of branch &c.

sucker (II.), vb. trans. & intrans., fr. prec. (bot.) 1. trans. To remove suckers from. 2. intrans. To produce suckers.

sucking, adj. [1. súking; 2. sákiŋ], fr. Pres. Part. of **suck (I.)**. **a** (of child, young animal) Being suckled, not yet weaned; **b** (fig.) incipient, inexperienced.

sucking-disk, n. Same as **sucker (I.)** 3.

sucking-pig, n. Young pig, sucker.

suckle, vb. trans. [1. súkl; 2. sákl]. M.E. *sokelen*; **suck (I.)** & -le. To give suck to; to feed with milk from the breast.

suckling, n. [1. súkling; 2. sákliŋ]. M.E. *sokelinge*; **suck (I.)** & -ling (I.). **a** Unweaned child or other young mammal; hence (fig.) **b** inexperienced, unsophisticated person; esp. in Phr. *babes and sucklings*.

sucrose, n. [1. súkrōs; 2. sjúkrous], fr. Fr. *sucre*, q.v. under **sugar (I.)**, & -ose. (chem.) White, sweet, crystalline compound obtained from various plants but identical in composition; sugar.

suction, n. [1. súkshun; 2. sákʃən], fr. Lat. *suctum*, P.P. type of *sūgere*, 'to suck', q.v. under **suck (I.)**, & -ion. **a** Act or process of sucking; **b** specif., act or process of causing fluid to pass in a given direction by exhausting the air behind it over a small surface, so that it is driven by atmospheric pressure.

suction-fan, n. Rotating fan which separates chaff from grain by a process of suction.

suction-pipe, n. Pipe through which fluid is drawn by suction.

suction-plate, n. Plate holding artificial teeth in place by suction.

suction-pump, n. Pump raising water by suction.

suctorial, adj. [1. suktōrial; 2. saktōriəl], fr. Lat. *suct-(um)*, P.P. type of *sūgere*, 'to suck', q.v. under **suck (I.)**, & -ory & -al. 1. Of, pertaining to, adapted for, sucking. 2. (zool.) Having, adhering by means of, a sucker.

Sudanese, adj. & n. [1. sōōdanḗz; 2. sùdəníz]. 1. adj. Of, belonging to, the Sudan, Africa. 2. n. Native of the Sudan.

sudarium, n. [1. sūdárium; 2. sjūdéəriəm]. Lat. *sūdārium*, 'a cloth for wiping off perspiration, a handkerchief', fr. *sūd-(or)*, 'sweat', see next word, & -ary. 1. **a** St. Veronica's handkerchief which received a miraculous impression of the face of Christ on His way to Calvary; hence, **b** portrait of Christ produced by miraculous means. 2. Napkin wrapped about the head of Christ in the sepulchre.

sudation, n. [1. sūdáshun; 2. sjūdéiʃən], fr. Lat. *sūdātiōn-(em)*, 'sweating', fr. *sūdāt-(um)*, P.P. type of *sūdāre*, 'to sweat'; cp. Lat. *sūdor*, 'sweat'; fr. base **swoid-*, **sweid-*, **swīd-*, 'sweat', whence also Scrt. *svídyati*, 'sweats'; Lett. *swēdri*; Gk. *hĩdrós*, 'sweat', fr. **swīd-*; O.S. *swēt*; O.E. *swāt*, 'sweat', see **sweat (I.)**. **a** Process of sweating; **b** sweat, perspiration.

sudatorium, n. [1. sūdatōrium; 2. sjùdətōriəm]. Lat. *sūdātōrium*, 'sweating-bath', fr. *sūdātum*, see prec., & -ory. Hot room for inducing perspiration in Roman bath.

sudatory, adj. & n. [1. súdaturi; 2. sjúdətəri], fr. Lat. *sūdātōrius*, 'sudatory', see prec. 1. adj. Connected with, promoting, perspiration. 2. n. (med.) Sudatory substance, sudorific.

sudd, n. [1. sud; 2. sad]. Arab. *sudd*, 'barrier'. Floating mass of water-weeds, reeds &c., forming obstruction on White Nile.

sudden, adj. & n. [1. súdn; 2. sádn]. M.E. *sodein*, fr. O. Fr. *soudain*, fr. Lat. *subitāneus*, 'sudden', fr. *subitus*, 'sudden, happening unexpectedly', fr. P.P. type of *subīre*, 'to go under, up to; to advance secretly; to occur', fr. *sub-* & *ire*, 'to go', see **itinerant**. 1. adj. **a** Happening, occurring, done unexpectedly, without previous indication or warning: *a sudden shout, shock, idea*; *sudden death*; **b** acting unexpectedly, abrupt: *to be sudden in one's actions*. 2. n. State of being sudden, sudden happening; only in Phr. *(all) of, on, a sudden*, suddenly.

suddenly, adv. Prec. & -ly. In a sudden manner, with suddenness.

suddenness, n. See prec. & -ness. State or quality of being sudden.

sudoriferous, adj. [1. sùduríferus; 2. sjùdəríferəs], fr. Lat. *sūdorifer*, stem of *sūdor*, 'sweat', see **sudation**, & -ferous. (of gland) Secreting sweat.

sudorific, adj. & n. [1. sùdurífik; 2. sjùdərífik], fr. Lat. *sūdōri-*, 'sweat', see prec. & **sudation**, & -fic. 1. adj. Promoting perspiration. 2. n. Sudorific medicine, drug &c.

Sudra, n. [1. sōōdra; 2. súdrə]. Hind., fr. Scrt. *śūdra-*. Member of lowest Hindu caste, originally non-Aryan.

suds, n. pl. [1. sudz; 2. sadz]. Cp. O.E. *sēoðan*, 'to boil', P.P. *soden*; see **seethe**, **sodden (I.)**. Frothy substance from dissolved soap, which floats on surface of water.

sue, vb. trans. & intrans. [1. sū; 2. sjū], fr. O. Fr. *suir*, 'to follow', fr. L. Lat. *sequere*, variant of *sequi*, 'to follow', see **sequela**, & cp. second element in **ensue, pursue**. A. trans. 1. To bring a legal action against, prosecute: *to sue a person for libel*. 2. To beseech, entreat. B. intrans. 1. To take legal action, prosecute claim &c. by legal proceedings. 2. To make entreaties, beg, plead: *to sue for peace*.

suède, n. [1. swād; 2. sweid]. Fr. *Suède*, 'Sweden'. Soft, undressed leather made of kid-skin, used for gloves &c.

suet, n. [1. sŭet; 2. sjúit], fr. O. Fr. *seu*, fr. Lat. *sēbum, sēvum*, 'tallow, suet', see **sebaceous**, & -et. Cogn. w. O.H.G. *seifa*; O.E. *sāpe*, 'soap', see **soap (I.)**. Solid fatty tissue formed around kidneys &c. of oxen, sheep &c.

suety, adj. [1. sŭeti; 2. sjúiti]. Prec. & -y (IV.). Like, abounding in, greasy with, suet.

suf-, pref. Form of **sub-**, w. assimilation of *b* when compounded w. words beginning w. *f-*.

suffer, vb. trans. & intrans. [1. súfer; 2. sáfə]. M.E. *suffren*, fr. O. Fr. *sufrir*, fr. Lat. *sufferre*, 'to submit to; to undergo, endure'; fr. **suf-** & *ferre*, 'to carry, bear, endure', see **-ferous**. A. trans. 1. To experience (something painful or unpleasant), undergo, be subjected to: *to suffer pain, torture, hardship, wrong, death, punishment, loss*. 2. To allow, permit, tolerate: *if I suffer you to be present, you must remain silent*; chiefly with negative: *I will not suffer such conduct*; *one cannot easily suffer ingratitude and treachery in a friend*. Phr. *not to suffer fools gladly*, to be impatient and intolerant of folly and stupidity in others. B. intrans. 1. **a** To experience mental or physical pain: *men are born to suffer*; *learn to suffer without complaining*; **b** suffer from, to be liable to, be afflicted by: *to suffer from gout*; *he is now suffering from measles*; *I do not suffer from shyness*. 2. To be the worse, be injured, harmed, impaired: *neither car nor passengers suffered much in the accident*; *his reputation suffered greatly by his failure at a critical moment*. 3. **a** To be punished: *we must all suffer sooner or later for our sins and follies*; **b** to be executed, esp. to undergo martyrdom: *King Charles I. suffered on Jan. 30th, 1649*.

sufferable, adj. [1. súferabl; 2. sáfərəbl]. Prec. & -able. Capable of being tolerated.

sufferance, n. [1. súferans; 2. sáfərəns], fr. Lat. *sufferentia*, 'suffering, toleration'; **suffer** & -ence. 1. (archaic) Submission, endurance, passive resignation. 2. Tacit consent, acceptance, permission, implied by failure to forbid or object; esp. in Phr. *on sufferance*, without explicit consent, merely tolerated or acquiesced in.

sufferer, n. [1. súferer; 2. sáfərə]. **suffer** & -er. One who suffers; **a** one suffering from disease, pain &c.: *sufferers in hospitals*; *a great sufferer from rheumatism*; **b** one who has been injured, one who has suffered loss or other injury in some way specified or implied: *the poor are the greatest sufferers in times of famine*; *he tried to injure others, but was himself the sufferer*.

suffering, n. [1. súfering; 2. sáfəriŋ]. **suffer** & -ing. Experience of, process of undergoing, physical or mental pain; anguish, agony, of

SUFFETE — **SUGGESTIVENESS**

body or mind; tribulation: *the sufferings of Napoleon's army in Russia were indescribable*; *it is hard to be patient under severe suffering*.

suffete, n. [1. súfĕt; 2. sáfĭt], fr. Lat. *sūfet-*, stem of *sūfes*, 'suffete', fr. Carthaginian. (antiq.) Chief Carthaginian magistrate.

suffice, vb. intrans. & trans. [1. sufís; 2. səfáis]. M.E. *suffīsen*, fr. stem of O. Fr. *suffire*, 'to suffice', fr. Lat. *sufficere*, 'to put, supply, as a substitute; to give, supply; to satisfy, be enough'; fr. suf- & -*facere*, 'to make', see fact. 1. intrans. To be sufficient, be enough, be adequate; to satisfy demand or requirements: *a small amount of food suffices for old people*; *a brief statement will suffice*. 2. trans. To be enough for, satisfy, be adequate for needs or purpose of: *nothing would suffice him but the whole story*.

sufficiency, n. [1. sufíshensi; 2. səfíʃənsi], fr. L. Lat. *sufficientia*; see **sufficient (I.)** & -cy. 1. a That which suffices; sufficient quantity, adequate amount, ample supply; specif. b adequate pecuniary resources, competency. 2. (archaic) Efficiency, capability.

sufficient (I.), adj. [1. sufíshent; 2. səfíʃənt], fr.Lat. *sufficient-(em)*, Pres. Part. of *sufficere*, 'to suffice', see **suffice**. 1. Adequate in size or quantity, enough; capable of meeting demands; as much as is requisite for particular purpose: *to lack sufficient food*; *the rain was not sufficient to do any harm*; *I have not sufficient room for my family*. 2. (archaic) Capable, efficient, well qualified, for specific task.

sufficient (II.), n., fr. prec. (colloq.) A sufficient quantity: *thank you, I have quite sufficient*.

sufficiently, adv. **sufficient (I.)** & -ly. To a sufficient degree, in sufficient amount: *sufficiently provided with means* &c.

sufficingly, adv. [1. sufísingli; 2. səfáisĭŋli], fr. Pres. Part. of **suffice** & -ly. Sufficiently, so as to suffice.

suffix (I.), n. [1. súfiks; 2. sáfiks], fr. Lat. *suffixum*, P.P. of *suffigere*, 'to attach, affix', fr. suf- & *fīgere*, 'to fasten, fix', see fix (I.). Syllable or group of syllables appended as formative element to end of word or stem.

suffix (II.), vb. trans. [1. sufíks; 2. safíks], fr. prec. To add as a suffix, add to end of word or stem.

suffocate, vb. trans. & intrans. [1. súfokăt; 2. sáfəkèit], fr. Lat. *suffōcātum*, P.P. type of *suffōcāre*, 'to choke, stifle, strangle', fr. suf- & dial. form of *fauc-*, stem of *faux*, 'throat', see faucal. A. trans. 1. To deprive of fresh air, cause difficulty in breathing to: *to be suffocated by close atmosphere*. 2. To kill by depriving of air; to choke: *to be suffocated by poisonous fumes, by a pillow pressed over one's mouth and nose*. B. intrans. To have difficulty in breathing, choke, stifle.

suffocating, adj. [1. súfokăting; 2. sáfəkèitĭŋ], fr. Pres. Part. of **suffocate**. Liable to cause, causing, suffocation; stifling, very close: *a suffocating atmosphere*; *suffocating heat*.

suffocatingly, adv. Prec. & -ly. So as to suffocate; to the point of suffocation.

suffocation, n. [1. sùfokáshun; 2. sàfəkéiʃən]. **suffocate** & -ion. a Act or process of suffocating; b state of being suffocated.

suffragan, adj. & n. [1. súfragan; 2. sáfrəgən], fr. Med. Lat. *suffrāgāneus*, 'assistant', fr. Lat. *suffrāgor*, 'I vote for, support', fr. *suffrāgium*, 'vote', see **suffrage**, & -an. 1. adj. a *Suffragan bishop*, or *bishop suffragan*, one appointed as assistant to a diocesan, esp. for work in specific part of diocese; b of any bishop considered in relation to his archbishop; c (of see) under suffragan bishop. 2. n. Suffragan bishop.

suffraganship, n. [1. súfraganship; 2. sáfrəgənʃĭp]. Prec. & -ship. Rank, office of, period of work as, suffragan.

suffrage, n. [1. súfrij; 2. sáfridʒ], fr. Fr., fr. Lat. *suffrāgium*, 'voting-tablet; vote; right of voting; assent, support', prob. orig. 'concerted cheer or shout of agreement or approval', fr. suf- & stem *frăg-, seen in *frăgor*, 'noise, din, crash', *frangere*, 'to break' &c.; see **fragment, fragile**. 1. a Vote given on a question of controversy; b approval, assent, support, signified by vote or otherwise: *I hope to secure your suffrages in my candidature*. 2. The right to express an opinion by voting on political questions; esp. the right to vote at parliamentary elections: *manhood suffrage*.

suffragette, n. [1. sùfrajét; 2. sàfrədʒét]. Prec. & -ette. (derisive) Woman who insisted on the right of women to have a parliamentary vote, and to be elected to Parliament, in the days before this right was secured by law; esp. a woman who emphasized her claims by violent words and acts.

suffragist, n. [1. súfrajìst; 2. sáfrədʒìst]. **suffrage** & -ist. Person advocating some extension of the right of voting.

suffuse, vb. trans. [1. sufúz; 2. səfjúz], fr. Lat. *suffūsum*, P.P. type of *suffundere*, 'to pour into, overspread; to mingle, blur', fr. suf- & *fundere*, 'to pour', see fuse (I.). (of fluid, light, colour) To spread over surface of, flood, cover: *sky suffused with light*; *eyes suffused with tears*; *blushes suffused her face*.

suffusion, n. [1. sufúzhun; 2. səfjúʒən], fr. Lat. *suffūsiōnem*, 'a pouring or spreading over', prec. & -ion. Act of suffusing; state of being suffused.

sufi, sofi, n. [1. sōōfi, sōfi; 2. súfi, sóufi], fr. Arab. Member of a class of Mohammedan mystics, philosophic and pantheistic.

sufic, sofic, adj. [1. sōō-, sōfik; 2. sú-, sóufik]. Prec. & -ic. Of, pertaining to, a sufi.

sufism, sofism, n. [1. sōō-, sōfizm; 2. sú-, sóufizəm]. **sufi** & -ism. Doctrines, practices, of a sufi.

sug-, pref. Form of sub- w. assimilation of *b* when compounded w. words beginning w. *g-*.

sugar (I.), n. [1. shōōgar; 2. ʃúgə]. M.E. *sugre, suger*, fr. O. Fr. *sucre*, fr. Arab. *sukkar*; cp. Scrt. *čarkarā*; Pers. *shakar*. Cp. **saccharo-** & **crocodile**. 1. A sweet, white, or pale brown, crystalline substance extracted from the juice of various plants, esp. from the sugar-cane or from beetroot; often with qualifying noun or adjective, indicating a source, e.g. *cane-, beet-, maple-sugar*; b place of origin, e.g. *Demerara sugar*; c appearance, character &c., e.g. *white, lump, granulated, castor sugar* &c.; d use or purpose, e.g. *icing, preserving, sugar*. 2. (chem.) One of many varieties of sweet, soluble carbohydrates found esp. in plants, including glucose, lactose, saccharose &c. 3. Substance resembling sugar in appearance or taste; esp. *sugar of lead, of milk*. 4. (fig.) Flattery, smooth-speaking, words designed to please.

sugar (II.), vb. trans., fr. prec. 1. a To sweeten with sugar; b to cover, coat, sprinkle, with sugar. 2. (fig.) a To flatter, speak honeyed words to; b to disguise nature of, make alluring, by flattery &c.

sugar-basin, n. Small basin of metal or china for holding sugar at table.

sugar-bean, n. Kind of kidney-bean.

sugar-beet, n. Kind of beetroot from the juice of which sugar is obtained.

sugar-bird, n. Bird that sucks honey from flowers.

sugar-candy, n. Sugar crystallized in large, hard lumps.

sugar-cane, n. Tall, perennial grass, with strong, jointed stalk, from 6 to 20 ft. in height, from the juice of which sugar is extracted.

sugar-gum, n. Large Australian eucalyptus with sweet leaves.

sugar-house, n. Factory for manufacture of sugar.

sugariness, n. [1. shōōgarines; 2. ʃúgərinis]. **sugary** & -ness. State or quality of being sugary.

sugarless, adj. [1. shōōgarles; 2. ʃúgəlis]. **sugar (I.)** & -less. Without, containing no, sugar.

sugar-loaf, n. 1. Hard, conical mass of sugar. 2. Anything resembling sugar-loaf in shape, e.g. conical hill; sometimes in compounds, *sugar-loaf hat* &c.

sugar-maple, n. Kind of maple from which sugar is obtained.

sugar-mill, n. Establishment in which juice is extracted from sugar-cane &c.

sugar-mite, n. Mite sometimes infesting unrefined sugar.

sugar-orchard, n. Plantation of sugar-maples.

sugar-planter, n. Owner of a plantation of sugar-cane.

sugar-plum, n. A small hard ball or cylinder of sugar, sometimes enclosing a caraway seed.

sugar-refiner, n. Person engaged in refining sugar.

sugar-refinery, n. Establishment in which raw sugar is refined.

sugar-tongs, n. pl. Small metal tongs for lifting lump sugar from sugar-basin.

sugary, adj. [1. shōōgari; 2. ʃúgəri]. **sugar (I.)** & -y (IV.). 1. Containing, abounding in, covered with, tasting of, sugar. 2. (fig.) Flattering, honeyed, excessively sweet: *a sugary voice, compliments* &c.

suggest, vb. trans. [1. sujést; 2. sədʒést], fr. Lat. *suggestum*, P.P. type of *suggerere*, 'to lay beneath; to furnish, supply; to suggest, prompt', fr. sug- & *gerere*, 'to carry, bring', see **gest, gesture (I.)**. 1. a To bring into the mind, call up idea of; to imply: *his skill suggests long training*; *his appearance suggests an open-air life*; specif. b to arouse in the mind by association &c.: *does the name suggest anything to you?*; c (reflex.) to come into the mind, present itself: *an idea suggests itself to me*. 2. To put forward, lay before a person, as hypothesis, possible course of action &c.; to introduce, present for consideration: *to suggest a plan*; *to suggest a walk*; *what do you suggest we should do?*; *have you nothing further to suggest?* 3. To imply, intimate, state, as completed action, motive, fact, &c.: *I suggest that you are not speaking the truth*.

suggestibility, n. [1. sujèstibíliti; 2. sədʒèstibíliti]. See next word & -ity. State or quality of being suggestible.

suggestible, adj. [1. sujéstibl; 2. sədʒéstibl]. **suggest** & -ible. 1. Capable of being suggested. 2. Capable of being acted upon by suggestion.

suggestio falsi, n. [1. sujéstiō fálsī; 2. sədʒéstiou fǽlsai]. Lat., see next word & **false (I.)**. Suggestion of falsehood; statement which, without actually being false, nevertheless conveys a false impression, and allows the hearer to believe what is untrue.

suggestion, n. [1. sujéschun; 2. sədʒéstʃən], fr. Lat. *suggestiōnem*, 'suggestion'; **suggest** & -ion. 1. a Act of suggesting; specif. b act or process of conveying an idea or impulse to the mind by hypnotic influence. 2. a Something suggested, implied, hinted, intimated, called up in the mind by association &c.: *a suggestion of a nautical roll in his gait*; *there is no suggestion of provincial accent in his speech*; *a building calling up suggestions of the past*; *to make a suggestion*; *his suggestion was approved*; b specif., something, idea, impulse of action, conveyed to the mind by hypnotic influence. 3. A suggesting of, or tendency to suggest, what is indecent or improper.

suggestionization, n. [1. sujèschunīzáshun; 2. sədʒèstʃənaizéiʃən]. Prec. & -ation. a Act or process of suggestionizing; b state of being suggestionized.

suggestionize, vb. trans. [1. sujéschunīz; 2. sədʒéstʃənaiz]. Prec. & -ize. To subject to, influence by, suggestion; esp. to incite to action by hypnotic suggestion.

suggestive, adj. [1. sujéstiv; 2. sədʒéstiv]. **suggest** & -ive. 1. Tending to suggest, arousing mental associations: *a melody suggestive of the rolling of waves*. 2. Full of suggestion; a stimulating to the mind, provoking thought and ideas: *a suggestive article on educational method*; b specif., tending to suggest what is evil; smacking of impropriety.

suggestively, adv. Prec. & -ly. In a suggestive manner.

suggestiveness, n. See prec. & -ness. Quality of being suggestive (in good and bad senses).

sui, pron. [1. sŭī; 2. sjúai]. Lat. *suī*, genit. of *suus*, 'his', fr. Aryan pronominal form *s(e)wo-, *swe-, *se- &c.; cp. Gk. *heós*, 'his'; Scrt. *svayám*, 'self'; O.H.G. *swās*; O.E. *swǣs*, 'own, familiar'; O.E. *sīn*, 'his'; O. Prussian *se*, 'self' &c. Cp. **custom**. In Latin Phrs. *sui generis*, of his, its &c. own special kind; unique, highly characteristic; *sui juris*, in his &c. own law or right; legally independent, of age to act for oneself.

suicidal, adj. [1. sŭisĭdl; 2. sjúisàidl]. **suicide** & **-al**. 1. Of, pertaining to, inclining to, suicide. 2. (fig.) Tending to one's own ruin, destruction, downfall: *his life of debauchery and extravagance was utterly suicidal*.

suicidally, adv. Prec. & **-ly**. In a suicidal manner, by means of suicide.

suicide, n. [1. sŭisīd; 2. sjúisaid], fr. Lat. *suī*, genit. of *suus*, 'his; himself', see **sui**, & **-cide**, on anal. of **matricide** &c. 1. Person who deliberately takes his own life. 2. Crime of self-murder: *to commit suicide*. 3. (fig.) Act tending to one's own downfall and ruin, moral, political, or social.

suilline, adj. [1. sŭilīn; 2. s(j)úilain], fr. Lat. *suillus*, 'of swine', fr. stem seen in *sūs*, 'swine'; cp. Scrt. *sūkaraś*, 'boar'; Gk. *hûs*; O.E. *sū*, *sugu*, 'sow', see **sow** (I.); cp. further Lat. *suīnus*, 'of a pig'; O. Slav. *svinŭ*, 'of swine'; O.H.G., O.E. *swīn*, 'swine', see **swine**. Of, pertaining to, like, the pig family; pig-like.

suint, n. [1. sŭint, swint; 2. sjúint, swint], fr. Fr., fr. O. Fr. *suint*, fr. *suer*, 'to sweat', fr. Lat. *sūdāre*, 'to sweat', see **sudation**. The natural grease of sheep's wool, containing potassium salts and used as a source of potash.

suit (I.), n. [1. sūt; 2. sjūt], fr. O. Fr. *suite*, 'following', fr. Lat. *secūta*, fem. P.P. of *sequi*, 'to follow', see **sequela**. 1. a Act of suing; request, prayer, solicitation: *to grant one's suit*; **b** specif., act of seeking woman's hand in marriage: *to press one's suit*; *to fail, prosper, in one's suit*. 2. (law) Judicial action to enforce claim or redress grievance, often *law-suit*. 3. **a** Set of clothes to be worn together, esp. man's outer garments, including coat, waistcoat, and trousers or breeches &c., made of same material: *a suit of clothes, a new suit*; **b** complete set of harness for a horse: *a suit of harness*; **c** complete set of armour. 4. (naut.) Set of sails to be used simultaneously. 5. (cards) **a** One of the four distinctive sets of cards, hearts, diamonds, clubs, and spades, composing a pack; Phr. *to follow suit*, (i.) to play a card of same suit as that led; hence, (ii.) to follow another's example, do as he does; **b** number of cards of one suit held by one player; *long suit*, consisting of four or more cards; *short suit*, less than four cards.

suit (II.), vb. trans. & intrans., fr. prec. A. trans. 1. To be satisfactory, or convenient to; to meet requirements or wishes of: *the plan, date, arrangement &c. suits me well*; *when will it suit you to start?*; *to try to suit everybody, all tastes &c.*; *to suit oneself*, act in accordance with one's own wishes or convenience. 2. To be appropriate to, befit, be in accordance with character of: *buffoonery does not suit an old man*. 3. To be adapted to temperament or abilities &c. of: *the rôle does not suit him*. 4. To be becoming to, be in harmony with, improve, appearance of: *this hat, colour &c. suits me*. 5. To conduce to health of, agree with: *climate, food, that suits one*. 6. To cause to conform to, make appropriate, adapt: *to suit one's matter to one's hearers*; *suiting the action to the word*. B. intrans. To be convenient, satisfactory: *will that time suit?*

suitability, n. [1. sūtabiliti; 2. sjùtəbíliti]. See **suitable** & **-ity**. State, quality, of being suitable.

suitable, adj. [1. sūtabl; 2. sjūtəbl]. **suit** (II.) & **-able**. Appropriate to character, position, or circumstances; fitting, proper; adapted for specific purpose: *to say a few suitable words*; *clothes suitable for the country*.

suitableness, n. Prec. & **-ness**. Suitability.

suitably, adv. See prec. & **-ly**. In a suitable manner.

suit-case, n. Portable, flat, shallow, oblong case of leather, fibre &c., for carrying clothes &c. for travelling.

suite, n. [1. swēt; 2. swīt], fr. O. Fr. *suite*, 'following'; see **suit** (I.). 1. Band of retainers; group of attendants and servants in the train of a person of rank &c.; train. 2. Group or set of things standing in proximity to each other, or of similar design, and forming a unity of some kind; specif. a set of rooms connecting, or intended for the use of one person or party: *a suite of apartments*; **b** set of furniture made to match. 3. (mus., orig.) Musical composition consisting of a series of dances in one key; (now often) series of movements of which some at least are in dance rhythm, and the first and last are in the same key.

suited, adj. [1. sūted; 2. sjútid], fr. P.P. of **suit** (II.). *Suited to, for*, adapted to, having qualifications for, fitted for: *not suited to the teaching profession*; *hardly suited for such a post*.

suiting, n. [1. sūting; 2. sjútiŋ]. **suit** (I.) & **-ing**. (tailor's word) Material for making suits of clothes.

suitor, n. [1. sūter; 2. sjútə]. **suit** (I.) & **-or**. 1. Person instituting a lawsuit. 2. **a** One who presents a petition, asks a favour, proffers a request; specif. **b** person seeking woman's hand in marriage.

suivez, vb. [1. swēvā; 2. swívei]. Fr. *suivez*, 'follow', imperat. of *suivre*, 'to follow', fr. L. Lat. *sequere*, 'to follow', see **sue**. (mus.) Direction to accompanist to follow soloist in tempo &c.

sulcate, adj. [1. súlkāt; 2. sálkeit], fr. Lat. *sulcus*, 'furrow, trench'; cp. Gk. *holkós*, 'furrow'; *hélkein*, 'to draw'; O.E. *sulh*, 'plough'. (anat. and bot.) Marked with long, narrow grooves; fluted.

sulk, vb. intrans. & n. [1. sulk; 2. salk]. Back-formation, fr. **sulky** (I.). 1. vb. To be sulky. 2. n. (usually pl.) Sulky mood: *in the sulks*; *a fit of the sulks*.

sulkily, adv. [1. súlkili; 2. sálkili]. **sulky** (I.) & **-ly**. In a sulky manner.

sulkiness, n. [1. súlkines; 2. sálkinis]. Next word & **-ness**. State of being sulky; sulky behaviour.

sulky (I.), adj. [1. súlki; 2. sálki], fr. a base seen in O.E. *āseolcan*, 'to be slothful or remiss', P.P. *asolcen*; cp. N. Fris. *sulke*, 'to sulk'. Sullen; showing ill-temper and resentment by silent, gloomy, moroseness, and by shunning conversation and society.

sulky (II.), n., fr. prec. Light, two-wheeled vehicle for one horse and one person.

sullen, adj. & n. [1. súlen; 2. sálin]. M.E. *solein*, fr. O. Fr. *solain*, 'lonely', fr. Lat. *sōlus*, 'alone', see **sole** (IV.) & **-an**. 1. adj. **a** Obstinately gloomy and ill-tempered, morose, surly; persistently sulky; **b** making, conveying, a gloomy, depressing, sombre impression; lowering; *a sullen landscape*; **c** expressing sullenness: *a sullen face, expression &c*. 2. n. (pl.) *The sullens*, sulks, gloomy ill-temper.

sullenly, adv. Prec. & **-ly**. In a sullen manner.

sullenness, n. See prec. & **-ness**. State or quality of being sullen.

sully, vb. trans. [1. súli; 2. sáli]. O.E. *sylian*; M.E. *sulien*, 'to soil'; cp. O.L.G. *sulian*, 'to defile'; cp. O.E. *sol*, 'dirty'; O.E. *sol*, 'muddy pool'; Lith. *sulà*, 'flowing sap'. To impair, mar, tarnish, the purity or freshness of; to stain, soil, defile: (chiefly in non-material or fig. sense) *to sully one's hands by an infamous action*; *a reputation sullied by many crimes*.

sulph(o)-, pref. representing **sulphur** (I.). Sulphur; e.g. *sulphacid*, acid of sulphur; *sulphocyanic*, derived from sulphur and cyanogen.

sulphate, n. [1. súlfāt, -it; 2. sálfeit, -it]. Prec. & **-ate**. Salt of sulphuric acid; *calcium sulphate*, gypsum; *magnesium sulphate*, Epsom salts; *sodium sulphate*, Glauber's salts; *sulphate of copper, iron, zinc*, varieties of vitriol.

sulphide, n. [1. súlfīd; 2. sálfaid]. **sulph(o)-** & **-ide**. Compound of sulphur with another element; *sulphide of iron*, pyrites; *sulphide of mercury*, cinnabar.

sulphite, n. [1. súlfīt; 2. sálfait]. **sulph(o)-** & **-ite** (I.). Salt of sulphurous acid.

sulphonal, n. [1. súlfonal; 2. sálfənəl], fr. **sulph(o)-**. Crystalline compound used as anaesthetic and hypnotic.

sulphur (I.), n. [1. súlfur; 2. sálfə]. Lat. *sulphur, sulfur, sulpur*, 'sulphur'; prob. fr. earlier *sulkʷ-*; cp. Goth. *swibls*; O.H.G. *swebal*; O.E. *swefel*, 'sulphur'. 1. Non-metallic, light-yellow, inflammable, fusible, crystalline or amorphous element, burning with a blue flame, and used for making sulphuric acid, for matches, gunpowder, vulcanized rubber, and medicinally: *flowers of sulphur*, sulphur in the form of fine powder, condensed from sulphur vapour; *roll, stick, sulphur*, purified sulphur moulded in the form of rolls or sticks; *sulphur dioxide*, suffocating gas produced by burning sulphur. 2. Kind of yellow butterfly.

sulphur (II.), adj., fr. prec. Of the colour of sulphur, pale lemon yellow.

sulphur (III.), vb. trans., fr. prec. To fumigate with burning sulphur.

sulphurate, vb. trans. [1. súlfūrāt; 2. sálfjurèit]. **sulphur** (I.) & **-ate**. 1. To combine, mix, impregnate, with sulphur. 2. To bleach by means of sulphurous acid, or by fumes of burning sulphur.

sulphuration, n. [1. sùlfūrāshun; 2. sàlfjuréiʃən]. Prec. & **-ion**. Process of sulphurating; state of being sulphurated.

sulphurator, n. [1. súlfūrātur; 2. sálfjurèitə]. **sulphurate** & **-or**. Apparatus for bleaching by sulphur fumes.

sulphureous, adj. [1. sùlfūreus; 2. sàlfjóriəs], fr. Lat. *sulphureus*; **sulphur** (I.) & **-eous**. 1. Of, pertaining to, like, sulphur; having the colour or smell of burning sulphur. 2. (bot.) Pale yellow, sulphur-coloured.

sulphuretted, adj. [1. súlfūrèted; 2. sálfjurètid], fr. obs. *sulphuret*, 'sulphide'; **sulphur** (I.) & **-et** & **-ed**. Combined with sulphur; *sulphuretted hydrogen*, hydrogen sulphide.

sulphuric, adj. [1. sulfúrik; 2. salfjórik]. **sulphur** (I.) & **-ic**. Of, pertaining to, containing, derived from, sulphur; *sulphuric acid*, colourless, corrosive, oily, liquid compound, used extensively as basis of chemical operations and manufactures; oil of vitriol: *sulphuric ether*, liquid derived from alcohol by the action of sulphuric or other acid, used as anaesthetic.

sulphurization, n. [1. sùlfūrīzāshun; 2. sàlfjuraizéiʃən]. Next word & **-ation**. Act of sulphurizing; state of being sulphurized.

sulphurize, vb. trans. [1. súlfūrīz, sulfúrīz; 2. sálfjuraiz, sálfəraiz]. **sulphur** (I.) & **-ize**. To sulphurate.

sulphur-ore, n. Sulphide of iron, pyrites.

sulphurous, adj. [1. súlfūrus, sulfúrus; 2. sálfjurəs, sálfərəs]. **sulphur** (I.) & **-ous**. 1. Of, derived from, impregnated with, sulphur. 2. (fig.) Heated, inflammable, pervaded by intense passion: *the atmosphere of the meeting became rather sulphurous towards the close*.

sulphur-spring, n. Natural spring impregnated with sulphur.

sulphur-wort, n. Herb with sulphur-coloured flowers.

sulphury, adj. [1. súlfuri; 2. sálfəri]. **sulphur** (I.) & **-y** (IV.). Resembling, pertaining to, sulphur.

sultan, n. [1. súltan; 2. sáltən], fr. Fr., fr. Arab. *sultān*, 'victorious; ruler'. 1. Mohammedan prince or king; specif., *the Sultan*, former sovereign of the Turkish Empire. 2. Kind of purple gallinule. 3. Breed of small domestic hen, originally from Turkey. 4. Kind of garden annual, *Centaurea*, with yellow (*yellow sultan*) or purple (*sweet sultan*) flowers.

sultana, n. [1. sultáhna; 2. saltǎnə]. Ital., fr. Arab.; see prec. 1. Sultan's wife, daughter, or sister. 2. Mistress of king or prince. 3. Kind of small, seedless raisin from Smyrna.

sultanate, n. [1. súltanāt; 2. sáltəneit]. **sultan & -ate.** 1. Rank, authority, of a sultan. 2. Jurisdiction, dominion, of a sultan.

sultaness, n. [1. súltanes; 2. sáltənis]. **sultan & -ess.** Sultana.

sultriness, n. [1. súltrines; 2. sáltrinis]. Next word & -ness. State of being sultry.

sultry, adj. [1. súltri; 2. sáltri], fr. obs. *sweltry*; **swelter (I.) & -y (IV.).** a (of weather, climate, atmosphere &c.) Hot and damp, moist and stuffy, close, oppressive; also b (fig.) of temper, language &c.; violent, hectic, lurid.

sum (I.), n. [1. sum; 2. sam], fr. Fr. *somme*, fr. Lat. *summa*, 'top, summit; chief place, highest rank, chief point, essence; amount, quantity; total', fr. fem. form of *summus*, 'highest', assimilated fr. *sup-mo-; cp. Lat. *super*, 'above'; *sub*, 'below', see **sub-**; Scrt. *upamáś*, 'the highest'; Gk. *húpatos*, 'the first'; O.E. *ufema*, 'highest'. 1. Amount produced by adding two or more numbers, magnitudes, quantities, together; the total, also *sum total*. 2. Group of related ideas, facts, points, considered together, total result, compendium of such points &c.; the essence: *the sum of the whole matter*. 3. A quantity, or amount, of money: *to spend large sums*. 4. a A problem in arithmetic; b (pl.) *sums*, arithmetical calculation: *to do sums*; *good at sums*.

sum (II.), vb. trans. & intrans., fr. Fr. *sommer*, fr. *somme*, 'sum', see prec. A. trans. 1. Often *sum up*, to add up, give total of, give result of addition of, reckon up: *to sum up one's takings*. 2. Also *sum up*, to present in the form of a brief review, summarize, recapitulate shortly: *to sum up facts, statements, evidence, arguments* &c. B. intrans. *Sum up*, specif. (of a judge) to review and comment upon facts proved in evidence, &c.

sumac(h), n. [1. shoōmak; 2. ʃúmæk], fr. Fr., fr. Span. *zumaque*, fr. Arab. *summāq*. 1. Shrub or small tree of the genus *Rhus*, with pinnate or trifoliate leaves and clusters of small flowers. 2. Dried leaves of some species of sumac, used in dyeing and tanning.

Sumerian, adj. & n. [1. sūmérian; 2. sjūmíəriən], fr. *Sumer*, ancient district of Babylonia, & -ian. 1. adj. Pertaining to, characteristic of, the civilization of Sumer. 2. n. a The language of the Sumerian inscriptions &c.; b an inhabitant of Sumer.

summarily, adv. [1. súmarili; 2. sáməriĺi]. **summary (I.) & -ly.** In a summary manner.

summarist, n. [1. súmarist; 2. sáməriĺist]. **summary (I.) & -ist.** Person who prepares a summary.

summarize, vb. trans. [1. súmarīz; 2. sáməraiz]. **summary (I.) & -ize.** To make, present, a summary of, present in a brief review; to epitomize.

summary (I.), adj. [1. súmari; 2. sáməri], fr. Lat. *summārium*, 'summary, abstract'; **sum (I.) & -ary.** 1. Condensed, brief, giving the substance or gist: *summary reports*. 2. Carried out without many formalities, effected without delay or debate: *summary justice, punishment*; specif. *summary jurisdiction*, that of petty sessions, exercised by justices of the peace, in cases of trivial, more or less light, offences &c.

summary (II.), n., fr. prec. Brief statement of leading points of argument, book &c.; epitome, digest, concise review.

summation, n. [1. sumáshun; 2. saméiʃən], fr. Fr. *sommation*; **sum (II.) & -ation.** Act of summing, of reckoning a total; summing up, computation.

summer (I.), n. [1. súmer; 2. sámə]. O.E. *sumor*; M.E. *somer*; cp. O.H.G. *sumar*; O. Fris. *sumur*; O.N. *sumarr*, 'summer'; cogn. w. Scrt. *sámā*, 'year, season'; O. Ir. *sam*, 'summer'. 1. Season in which the sun has the greatest power, usually (in Northern Hemisphere) considered to include June, July, and August; astronomically, June 21 to Sept. 22; Phr. *Indian summer*, short spell of warm, dry weather in the autumn, with hazy atmosphere; *St. Luke's, St. Martin's, summer*, short periods of mild, dry weather sometimes occurring about October 18th (St. Luke's Day) and November 11th (St. Martin's Day). 2. (fig.) Prime, best part, most flourishing period of life. 3. (pl.) Years of age: *a young woman of some twenty summers*.

summer (II.), vb. intrans. & trans., fr. prec. 1. intrans. To spend the summer: *to summer in Scotland*. 2. trans. To feed, graze (cattle) during the summer.

summer (III.), adj., fr. **summer (I.).** Of, pertaining to, suitable for, occurring in, the summer: *summer holidays*.

summer (IV.), n., fr. Fr. *sommier*, 'beam'; see **breastsummer**. a Large, horizontal beam or girder supporting a superstructure; b stone resting on a column, and supporting an arch &c.

summer-house, n. Small, ornamental building used in a garden as a place to sit in.

summerless, adj. [1. súmerles; 2. sáməlis]. **summer (I.) & -less.** Without a summer, having no summer.

summer lightning, n. Sheet lightning without audible thunder.

summerlike, adj. [1. súmerlĭk; 2. sáməlaik]. **summer (I.) & -like.** Like summer.

summerly, adj. [1. súmerli; 2. sáməli]. **summer (I.) & -ly.** Like, characteristic of, summer.

summersault, -set, n. See **somersault**.

summer school, n. Organized course of lectures &c. at a university during long vacation.

summer-time, n. 1. Season of summer. 2. Time as reckoned during spring and summer, one hour in advance of Greenwich mean time, adopted for daylight-saving (q.v.) purposes.

summery, adj. [1. súmeri; 2. sáməri]. **summer (I.) & -y (IV.).** Of, like, characteristic of, suitable for, summer.

summing-up, n. [1. súming úp; 2. sámiŋ áp]. Review, recapitulation, of, comments upon, the chief points of evidence, made by a judge at the conclusion of a trial, before the jury retire to consider their verdict.

summit, n. [1. súmit; 2. sámit], fr. Fr. *sommet*, 'summit', fr. *som*, 'top', fr. Lat. *summum*, 'top', neut. form of *summus*, 'highest', see **sum (I.), & -et.** 1. Highest part of hill or mountain &c., top, peak: *to climb to the summit*. 2. (in non-material sense) Highest point, acme, maximum: *to reach the summit of fame*.

summitless, adj. [1. súmitles; 2. sámitlis]. Prec. & -less. Without a summit.

summit-level, n. Highest point (of railway, road &c.).

summon, vb. trans. [1. súmun; 2. sámən], fr. O. Fr. *somoner*, fr. Lat. *sub-*, *summonēre*, 'to remind, hint', fr. **sub-** & *monēre*, 'to warn', see **monition** & **mental (I.).** 1. a To call authoritatively for, demand presence of, send for: *to summon a servant*; b specif. to require attendance of, in court of law as witness, defendant, or juror. 2. To call upon with insistence and authority, require, to carry out some action: *to summon a garrison to surrender*. 3. To bring into play; to collect, gather together: *to summon all one's energy*; also, *to summon up (one's courage* &c.).

summons, n. & vb. trans. [1. súmunz; 2. sámənz], fr. A.-Fr. *somonse*, fr. O. Fr. *semonse*, fr. P.P. of *somoner*, see prec. 1. n. a Call to appear or attend, demand for presence at specific time or place: *to receive a summons*; *to answer one's summons*; specif. b notice, citation, to appear before a judge or magistrate. 2. vb. To issue a summons to, cite.

summum bonum, n. [1. súmum bŏnum; 2. sámam bóunam], fr. Lat. *summum bonum*, 'highest good'; see **sum (I.) & bonus**. Supreme good, chief end of being.

sump, n. [1. sump; 2. samp]. Cp. Dan. *somp*, 'swamp'; Germ. *sumpf*, 'bog', & see **swamp.** 1. Lowest part of mine, pool at the bottom of a mine from which water is pumped. 2. Reservoir for superfluous lubricating oil in a motor-car.

sumpitan, n. [1. súmpitan; 2. sámpitən]. Malay. Blow-pipe used by natives of Borneo for shooting arrows.

sumpter, n. [1. súmpter; 2. sámptə], fr. O. Fr. *sommetier*, fr. Low Lat. *sagmatarius, fr. Lat. *sagmārius*, fr. *sagma*, 'pack-saddle', fr. Gk. *ságma*, 'equipment; pack-saddle'; cp. Gk. *sáttein*, 'to pack, press, equip'; *saktós*, 'crammed'; cp. **summer (IV.) & breastsummer**. (archaic) Beast of burden, packhorse; usually *sumpter-horse, -mule* &c.

sumption, n. [1. súmpshun; 2. sámpʃən], fr. Lat. *sumptiōn-(em)*, 'major premise', fr. *sumpt-(um)*, P.P. type of *sūmere*, 'to take hold of; to select; to assume', earlier *subs-emere, fr. **sub-** & *emere*, 'to take, buy', see second element of **exempt (I.).** (log.) Major premise.

sumptuary, adj. [1. súmptūari; 2. sámptjuəri], fr. Lat. *sūmptuārius*, 'of expense', fr. *sūmpt-(um)*, P.P. type of *sūmere*, 'to take hold of; to select; to acquire; to spend', see prec., & -ary. Of, pertaining to, regulating, expense; esp. *sumptuary laws* &c., regulating expenditure and intended to check extravagance.

sumptuous, adj. [1. súmptūus, súmpchoous; 2. sámptjuəs, sámptʃuəs], fr. Lat. *sūmptuōsus*, 'costly', fr. *sūmptus*, 'expense', fr. P.P. type of *sūmere*, 'to take; to spend', see **sumption**, & -ous. Luxurious, rich, costly; involving or indicating expenditure on a lavish scale: *sumptuous clothes, food* &c.

sumptuously, adv. Prec. & -ly. In a sumptuous manner.

sumptuousness, n. See prec. & -ness. Quality of being sumptuous.

sun (I.), n. [1. sun; 2. san]. O.E. *sunne*, M.E. *sonne*; cp. O.L.G., O.H.G., O.N. *sunna*, Goth. *sunnō*, 'sun'; fr. stem **su-n-*, **swe-n-*; fr. same base, but having formative -*l*-, are Goth. *sauil*; O.E. *sōl*; Lat. *sōl*, 'sun', see **sol (I.)**; O.E. *swegle*, 'shining'; O.E. *swelan*, 'to glow'; cp. also Gk. *selénē*, 'moon', see **selenium**. 1. Heavenly body forming the centre of, and chief source of light and heat in, the solar system. Phrs. *midnight sun*, as seen from polar regions; *mock-sun, sun-dog, parhelion; sun's backstays, eyelashes, sun drawing water*, (naut.) appearance in sky of parallel lines of dust particles lit up by sun shining through rifts in clouds; *the sun rises*, is brought into view above the horizon by the earth's rotation; *the sun sets*, disappears from view below horizon through earth's motion; *one's sun is set*, one's day is over; one's reputation has declined; *the Sun of Righteousness*, Christ; *against the sun*, counter-clockwise; *with the sun*, in direction of sun's apparent course; *to hold a candle to the sun*, perform useless or superfluous action; *a place in the sun*, prominent position; *to rise with the sun*, get up at daybreak; *to see the sun*, be born; *to take, shoot, the sun*, (naut.) to determine sun's altitude by means of a sextant; *to determine latitude from sun's altitude*; (*everything* &c.) *under the sun*, in the world, on earth. 2. Direct rays of sun; sunlight: *to sit in the sun*; *to have the sun in one's eyes*; *no sun ever gets into this room.* 3. (poet.) Period of earth's revolution about the sun; year: '*A thousand suns will stream on thee, A thousand moons will quiver*' (Tennyson, 'A Farewell'). 4. Any star forming the centre of a system, with planets revolving about it. 5. (her.) Disk, or representation of human face, with rays radiating from it. 6. Circular group of gas-jets &c., arranged to reflect downwards.

sun (II.), vb. trans. & intrans., fr. prec. 1. trans. a To expose to rays of sun, place in the sun; b (reflex.) *sun oneself*, go into, remain in the sunlight. 2. intrans. To be exposed to sun's rays, bask in the sun.

sun-and-planet, n. [1. sún an(d) plánet; 2. sán ən(d) plǽnit]. Combination of two toothed wheels, so adjusted that one on a central axis (sun-wheel) imparts its motion to the other or planet wheel.

sun-bath, n. Exposure of body to direct rays of the sun.

sun-bathing, n. Act, habit, or cult of the sun-bath.

sunbeam, n. [1. súnbēm; 2. sánbīm]. Single distinct ray of sunlight becoming visible through its shining on dust-particles through aperture.

sun-bird, n. Brightly coloured bird of Asia, Africa, and Australia, with long, slender beak and protractile tongue.

sun-bittern, n. Bird of Central and South America, resembling the crane and heron, and elaborately striped or mottled with brown, black, and white.

sun-blind, n. Movable, outside shade or awning, protecting window &c. from direct rays of sun.

sun-bonnet, n. Linen bonnet, with a projecting brim to shade the face and eyes, and flap to protect back of neck.

sun-bow, n. Rainbow produced by sun shining on spray of waterfall &c.

sunburn, n. [1. súnbĕrn; 2. sánbăn]. Darkening of skin through exposure to sun.

sunburned, sunburnt, adjs. [1. súnbĕrnd, -bĕrnt; 2. sánbănd, -bănt], fr. prec. Affected, tanned, by exposure to sun.

sun-burner, n. Circular group of gas jets or electric lights.

sun-burst, n. Sudden flood of light caused by sun coming out suddenly from behind clouds.

sundae, n. [1. súndi, -ē; 2. sándi, -ī]. Etymol. unknown. An ice-cream with crushed fruit, fruit-juice &c.

sun-dance, n. N. American Indian religious dance.

Sunday, n. [1. súndi; 2. sándi]. O.E. sunnan dæg, 'sun's day'; M.E. sonnedai; **sun(I.) & day.** 1. First day of the week, kept as day of special worship and of rest from business &c.; Low Sunday, Sunday after Easter; Mid-Lent, Refreshment, Mothering, Sunday, fourth Sunday of Lent; Palm Sunday, Sunday before Easter; Show Sunday, (Oxford University) Sunday before Commemoration; a month of Sundays, long time. Phr. (colloq.) to look two ways to find Sunday, to squint. 2. (attrib.) Of, pertaining to, suitable for, characteristic of, Sunday: Sunday clothes, dinner &c. Phr. one's Sunday best, (colloq. or facet.) best clothes worn on Sunday.

Sunday school, n. School for religious instruction held for children on Sundays, under direction of authorities of church, chapel &c.

sunder, vb. trans. & intrans. [1. súndĕr; 2. sándə]. O.E. syndrian, 'to separate', M.E. sundren, fr. sunder, 'apart'; cp. O.H.G. suntar; O.S. sundor; O.N. sundr, 'apart', either **a** fr. base *sem-, *sṃ-, 'alone', see **simple (I.), single (I.);** or **b** cogn. w. Lat. sine, 'without'; Scrt. san-utár, 'away'. **1.** trans. To put apart, separate, prevent union of, sever. **2.** intrans. To separate, keep apart.

sunderance, n. [1. súnderans; 2. sándərəns]. Prec. & **-ance.** Act of sundering, state of being sundered.

sundew, n. [1. súndū; 2. sándjū]. Low-growing herb, genus *Drosera*, found in bogs &c., with clusters of small flowers, and hairy leaves exuding a viscous liquid which serves to catch insects on which the plant feeds.

sundial, n. [1. súndı̆al; 2. sándáiəl]. Instrument for indicating the hour by means of the shadow of a pointer or gnomon, cast by the sun on to a numbered plate.

sun-dog, n. Mock-sun, parhelion.

sundown, n. [1. súndoun; 2. sándaun]. Sunset, evening.

sundowner, n. [1. súndŏuner; 2. sándàunə]. Prec. & **-er.** (Australia) A tramp arriving at a station after sundown, to secure food and lodging for the night.

sun-dried, adj. [1. sún drīd; 2. sán draid]. (of fruit &c.) Dried by natural, as distinct from artificial heat.

sundry, adj. & n. [1. súndri; 2. sándri]. O.E. syndriġ, 'separate, several', fr. sundor, 'apart', see **sunder,** & **-y (IV.).** **1.** adj. Several, various, of indefinite number: to talk of sundry matters. **2.** n. **a** (pl.) Unspecified items, odds and ends: hotels charge considerable sums for what they call sundries; **b** Phr. all and sundry, everyone, collectively and individually: to extend a welcome to all and sundry.

sunfish, n. [1. súnfish; 2. sánfiʃ]. Large, N. Atlantic fish with nearly spherical body flattened at the back.

sunflower, n. [1. súnflòur; 2. sánflàuə]. Plant of the genus *Helianthus*, with large flowers having bright yellow petals radiating from a centre.

sung, vb. [1. sung; 2. saŋ]. O.E., M.E. sungen, P.P. of **sing.**

sun-glow, n. Corona of sun.

sun-god, n. Personification of the sun worshipped as a god.

sun-hat, n. Large, shady, broad-brimmed hat.

sun-helmet, n. Helmet of pith, with brim to give protection to the head and neck from sun.

sunk, adj. [1. sungk; 2. saŋk]. P.P. of **sink,** O.E. (ġe)suncen; M.E. sunke(n). Placed, existing, below normal level of surface: sunk fence, placed along bottom of ditch.

sunken, adj. [1. súngken; 2. sáŋkən]. P.P. of **sink,** see prec. (of cheeks, eyes &c.) Abnormally depressed, fallen in, hollow.

sunless, adj. [1. súnles; 2. sánlĭs]. **sun(I.) & -less.** Receiving little or no light and heat from the sun.

sunlessness, n. Prec. & **-ness.** State of being sunless.

sunlight, n. [1. súnlīt; 2. sánlait]. Light radiated by the sun.

sunlike, adj. [1. súnlīk; 2. sánlaik]. **sun(I.) & -like.** Like the sun; bright, glowing.

sunlit, adj. [1. súnlit; 2. sánlit]. Illuminated by the sun.

sun-myth, n. Solar myth.

sunn, n. [1. sun; 2. san], fr. Hind. *san*. Also *sunn hemp*, fibre obtained from inner bark of a leguminous Indian plant.

Sunna(h), n. [1. súna; 2. sánə]. Arab. *sunna*, 'tradition'. Part of Mohammedan law based on tradition of Mohammed's actions and teaching, accepted by orthodox as equal in authority to the Koran and rejected by the Shiites. See **Shiah.**

Sunni, n. [1. súnē; 2. sánī]. See prec. Orthodox Mohammedan, accepting the authority of the Sunnah.

sunnily, adv. [1. súnili; 2. sánı̆li]. **sunny & -ly.** In a sunny manner.

sunniness, n. [1. súnines; 2. sánı̆nı̆s]. **sunny & -ness.** State or quality of being sunny.

Sunnite, n. [1. súnīt; 2. sánait]. **Sunna(h) & -ite (I.).** Sunni.

sunny, adj. [1. súni; 2. sání]. **sun(I.) & -y(IV.).** **1.** Illuminated, made bright, by the light of the sun; pervaded by, bathed in, sunlight: sunny days, weather; a sunny room, hill-side &c. Phr. to look on the sunny side of things, take a cheerful view of life &c. **2.** (fig.) Cheerful, genial, bright: a sunny disposition, smile &c.

sun-picture, n. Photograph.

sun-power, n. Power obtained by concentrating the heat of the sun.

sunproof, adj. [1. súnprōōf; 2. sánprūf]. Impervious to, unaffected by, rays of sun.

sun-recorder, n. Instrument for recording duration and intensity of sunlight.

sunrise, n. [1. súnrīz; 2. sánraiz]. **a** Appearance of sun above the horizon at daybreak; **b** time at which this takes place.

sun-rose, n. Kind of rock-rose, *Helianthemum*.

sunset, n. [1. súnset; 2. sánset]. **a** Disappearance of sun below horizon in the evening; **b** time at which this takes place; **c** appearance, colour(s), of sky at sunset; **d** (fig.) decline, end, final period: the sunset of life.

sunshade, n. [1. súnshād; 2. sánʃeid]. Light umbrella carried as protection against sun; parasol.

sunshine, n. [1. súnshīn; 2. sánʃain]. **1. a** Rays of sun, bright light of sun; **b** fine, bright weather. **2.** Cheerfulness, brightness; enlivening or animating influence: the sunshine of her smile, presence.

sunshiny, adj. [1. súnshīni; 2. sánʃàini]. Prec. & **-y(IV.).** Of, pertaining to, like, sunshine.

sun-snake, n. Ornament typical of early N. European art, snake curved in form of letter S with small circle at the centre.

sun-spot, n. **1.** Dark, irregular, fluctuating spot, the origin of which is uncertain, sometimes visible on surface of sun. **2.** Freckle.

sun-star, n. Kind of starfish.

sun-stone, n. Kind of feldspar.

sunstroke, n. [1. súnstrōk; 2. sánstrouk]. Illness characterized by severe fever, headache, and nervous prostration, caused by prolonged exposure to the fierce heat of the sun.

sun-up, n. [1. sún up; 2. sán ap]. (U.S.A.) Sunrise.

sunward, adj. & adv. [1. súnward; 2. sánwəd]. **sun(I.) & -ward.** **1.** adj. Facing, toward, the sun. **2.** adv. Sunwards.

sunwards, adv. [1. súnwardz; 2. sánwədz]. **sun(I.) & -wards.** Towards, in the direction of, the sun.

sunwise, adv. [1. súnwīz; 2. sánwaiz]. **sun & -wise.** In the direction of the sun's apparent course through the sky.

sun-worship, n. Adoration of the sun as a deity, or as the symbol of a god.

sun-worshipper, n. One practising sun-worship.

sup (I.), vb. trans. & intrans. [1. sup; 2. sap]. O.E. *sūpan*, M.E. *sūpen*, 'to sup, drink'; cp. O.N. *sūpa*; O.H.G. *sūfan*, 'to sup'; cogn. w. Scrt. *sūpaš*, 'broth'; cp. w. different formative element Lat. *sūcus*, 'sap'; Lat. *sūgere*, O.E. *sūcan*, 'to suck'; see **suck (I.).** **1.** trans. To eat or drink in small mouthfuls; to sip. **2.** intrans. To take drink or liquid food in small mouthfuls.

sup (II.), n., fr. prec. Small amount, mouthful, taste, of liquid or semi-liquid food: a sup of broth; neither bite nor sup.

sup (III.), vb. intrans. & trans., fr. Fr. *souper*, O. Fr. *soper*, 'to sup'; see **supper.** **1.** intrans. To take supper. **2.** trans. To furnish, supply, supper for.

sup-, pref. Form of **sub-** in compounds where the second element begins w. *p-*.

super, n. [1. sŭper; 2. sjŭpə]. Abbr. fr. **supernumerary.** (slang) Supernumerary actor.

super-, pref. representing Lat. *super*, 'above', prob. w. earlier sense 'from below upwards'; cogn. w. **sub-;** cp. **hyper-.** In words derived fr. Lat. or formed on analogy of Lat. words, in following senses: **a** implying action of placing above or outside: *superimpose, superscribe, supersede*; **b** position above, something placed above: *superaltar, supercolumniation, superstructure*; **c** situated above or at top of specified part or level: *superaqueous, supercilious, supercretaceous, superficial*; **d** being, moving, acting, at higher level: *superincumbent, supernatant*; **e** from above: *superintend, supervise*; **f** at top as distinct from bottom, affecting surface only: *superembattled, superdentate, supercarbonize*; **g** transcending, superior to, more than: *superhuman, supernatural, supersubstantial, superman, super-Dreadnought*; **h** exceeding the normal in quality or degree: *superfine, superacute, supersensible*; **i** excessive, beyond normal limit: *superabundance, supererogation, superheat, supernumerary, supersaturate*; **j** addition: *superadd, superinduce*, **k** in secondary degree: *superfeudation, superparasite, superreflexion*; **l** including subordinate classes &c.: *superclass, superfamily*; **m** higher in pitch: *supertonic, superdominant*; **n** (math.) indicating some ratio, e.g. *superbipartient*, in the ratio 5:3; *superbiquintal*, 7:5.

superable, adj. [1. sŭperabl; 2. sjŭpərəbl], fr. Lat. *superābilis*, 'superable', fr. *superāre*, 'to

surmount', fr. *super*, 'over', see **super-**, & **-able**. (rare) Capable of being overcome, not insurmountable.

superably, adv. Prec. & **-ly**. To a superable degree; so as to be superable.

superabound, vb. intrans. [1. sŭperabóund; 2. sjŭpərəbáund]. To have an abundance, abound greatly.

superabundance, n. [1. sŭperabúndans; 2. sjŭpərəbándəns]. Next word & **-ce**. State of being superabundant; excessive amount, excess, superfluity.

superabundant, adj. [1. sŭperabúndant; 2. sjŭpərəbándənt], fr. L. Lat. *superabundant-(em)*, 'superabundant'; **super-** & **abundant**. In excess of requirements or of normal amount; abounding, copious.

superabundantly, adv. Prec. & **-ly**. In a superabundant manner.

superadd, vb. trans. [1. sŭperád; 2. sjŭpəræd], fr. Lat. *superaddere*, 'to add besides'; **super-** & **add**. To add to something already added, make a further addition.

superaddition, n. [1. sŭperadíshun; 2. sjŭpərədíʃən]. Prec. & **-ition**. Act of superadding; state of being superadded.

superaltar, n. [1. sŭperàwltar; 2. sjŭpərɔ́ltə]. Consecrated stone slab used as portable altar, and placed upon unconsecrated altar.

superangelic, adj. [1. sŭperanjélik; 2. sjŭpərændʒélik]. More than, transcending, above, the angels.

superannuate, vb. trans. [1. sŭperánŭāt; 2. sjŭpəránjueit], fr. **super-** & Lat. *annus*, 'year', see **annual** (I.), & **-ate**. **a** To put on retired list, pension off, require retirement of, on account of age; **b** to request, or insist on, the withdrawal of (a boy) from school because he has not reached the required standard of his age.

superannuated, adj. [1. sŭperánŭāted; 2. sjŭpəránjueitid], fr. P.P. of prec. **a** Incapacitated by age, past work; **b** out-of-date, no longer current.

superannuation, n. [1. sŭperànŭáshun; 2. sjŭpəránjueiʃən]. Prec. & **-ion**. 1. Act of superannuating; state of being superannuated. 2. Pension given to official &c. retiring on account of age.

superaqueous, adj. [1. sŭperákweus; 2. sjŭpəréikwiəs]. Situated, existing, above water.

superb, adj. [1. sŭpérb; 2. sjŭpə́b], fr. Lat. *superbus*, 'haughty, proud'; prob. fr. **super-**, & stem **bhwe-*, **bhū-* &c., 'to be'; cp. Gk. *huperphuḗs*, 'overgrown', & see **be, future** (I.). Of the finest quality, magnificent; of highest excellence, value, beauty.

superbipartient, adj. [1. sŭperbípárshent; 2. sjŭpəbáipáʃənt]. (of number or quantity) Standing to another in the ratio of 5 to 3.

superbiquintal, adj. [1. sŭperbíkwintl; 2. sjŭpəbáikwintl]. In the ratio of 7 to 5.

superbitertial, adj. [1. sŭperbítérshal; 2. sjŭpəbáitə́ʃəl]. In the ratio of 5 to 3.

superbly, adv. superb & **-ly**. In a superb manner.

superbness, n. See prec. & **-ness**. Quality of being superb.

supercalendered, adj. [1. sŭperkálenderd; 2. sjŭpəkǽləndəd]. (of paper) Finished with a high polish by means of repeated rollings.

supercanopy, n. [1. sŭperkánopi; 2. sjŭpəkǽnəpi]. Arch or gable placed above another.

supercapital, n. [1. sŭperkápitl; 2. sjŭpəkǽpitl]. Capital placed above another to support a superstructure &c.

supercargo, n. [1. sŭperkárgō; 2. sjŭpəkǽgou], fr. Span. *sobrecarga*; **super-** & **cargo**. Agent in merchant ship travelling in charge of cargo and superintending its sale &c.

supercelestial, adj. [1. sŭperseléstial; 2. sjŭpəsiléstiəl]. 1. Existing, situated, above the sky or firmament. 2. Above, transcending, the angels.

supercharger, n. [1. sŭperchàrjer; 2. sjŭpətʃɑ́dʒə]. Blowing apparatus, in motor-car &c., for forcing extra amount of petrol vapour into the cylinders.

superciliary, adj. [1. sŭpersíliari; 2. sjŭpəsíliəri], fr. Lat. *supercilium*, 'eyebrow', fr. **super-** & *cilium*, 'eyelid, eyelash', see **cilia**, & **-ary**. Situated above the eyebrow; *superciliary ridge*, projecting curve of frontal bone above the eye.

supercilious, adj. [1. sŭpersílius; 2. sjŭpəsíliəs], fr. Lat. *superciliōsus*, see prec. & **-ous**. Showing haughtiness and contempt for others, their capacity, belongings &c., as though looking down on them from the height of one's own superiority; loftily arrogant and superior.

superciliously, adv. Prec. & **-ly**. In a supercilious manner.

superciliousness, n. See prec. & **-ness**. Quality of being supercilious.

supercivilized, adj. [1. sŭpersívilizd; 2. sjŭpəsívilaizd]. Over-civilized.

superclass, n. [1. sŭperklàhs; 2. sjŭpəklɑ́s]. Group or class comprising more than one class.

supercolumnar, adj. [1. sŭperkolúmnar; 2. sjŭpəkəlámnə]. Characterized by, built with, supercolumniation.

supercolumniation, n. [1. sŭperkolùmniáshun; 2. sjŭpəkəlàmniéiʃən]. Arrangement of one architectural order above another.

supercooled, adj. [1. sŭperkōōld; 2. sjŭpəkúld]. (chem.) Having temperature brought to a point below freezing-point without freezing.

supercretaceous, adj. [1. sŭperkretáshus; 2. sjŭpəkritéiʃəs]. **super-** & **cretaceous**. (geol.) Lying above the chalk.

superdentate, adj. [1. sŭperdéntāt; 2. sjŭpədénteit]. Having teeth in upper jaw only.

superdominant, n. [1. sŭperdóminant; 2. sjŭpədómɪnənt]. (mus.) Note immediately above dominant.

super-Dreadnought, n. [1. sŭper drédnawt; 2. sjŭpə drédnōt]. Large and powerful type of battleship, superior to the Dreadnought class.

supereminence, n. [1. sŭperéminens; 2. sjŭpəréminəns]. Supreme eminence.

supereminent, adj. [1. sŭperéminent; 2. sjŭpərémɪnənt]. Supremely, conspicuously, eminent.

supereminently, adv. Prec. & **-ly**. Eminently to a supreme degree.

supererogation, n. [1. sŭperèrogáshun; 2. sjŭpərèrɔgéiʃən], fr. Lat. *supererogāt-(um)*, P.P. type of Lat. *supererogāre*, 'to spend in addition', fr. **super-** & *erogāre*, 'to pay out', fr. **e-** & *rogāre*, 'to ask, demand, beg, borrow', see **rogation**. (theol.) *Work(s) of supererogation*, pious works performed by good men over and above what is necessary for their own salvation; these are held to constitute a fund in the general treasury of the Church, which is available for the benefit of others who have need of it.

supererogatory, adj. [1. sŭperérogāturi; 2. sjŭpərírɔgətəri], fr. Lat. *supererogāt-(um)*, see prec. & **-ory**. Of, pertaining to, of the nature of, supererogation.

super-ethical, adj. [1. sŭper éthikl; 2. sjŭpər épikl]. Transcending, above the scope of, ethics.

superexcellence, n. [1. sŭperékselens; 2. sjŭpərékseləns]. Next word & **-ce**. Extreme, unusual, excellence.

superexcellent, adj. [1. sŭperékselent; 2. sjŭpərékseleənt]. Of more than normal excellence.

superexcitation, n. [1. sŭperèksitáshun; 2. sjŭpəréksitéiʃən]. Excitation to an abnormally high degree.

superfamily, n. [1. sŭperfàmili; 2. sjŭpəfǽmili]. (zool. and bot.) Category of classification larger than a family; a suborder.

superfatted, adj. [1. sŭperfáted; 2. sjŭpəfǽtid]. (of soap) Containing a large proportion of fat.

superfecundation, n. [1. sŭperfèkundáshun; 2. sjŭpəfèkəndéiʃən]. Superfetation.

superfetation, n. [1. sŭperfētáshun; 2. sjŭpəfitéiʃən]. Second conception by female already pregnant.

superficial, adj. [1. sŭperfíshl; 2. sjŭpəfíʃl], fr. Lat. *superficiālis*, 'of the surface', fr. *super-*

ficiēs, 'surface', see **superficies**, & **-al**. 1. Of, pertaining to, affecting, existing on, the surface: *superficial colour, wounds, appearance* &c. 2. (of non-material things) Slight, shallow, not deep or thorough: *superficial knowledge, character*; *a superficial writer*.

superficiality, n. [1. sŭperfishiáliti; 2. sjŭpəfíʃiǽliti]. Prec. & **-ity**. State or quality of being superficial.

superficially, adv. [1. sŭperfíshali; 2. sjŭpəfíʃli]. See prec. & **-ly**. In a superficial manner.

superficies, n. [1. sŭperfíshiēz; 2. sjŭpəfíʃīz]. Lat. *superficiēs*, 'surface', fr. **super-** & *faciēs*, 'face', see **face** (I.). Surface, outer or upper face.

superfine, adj. [1. sŭperfīn; 2. sjŭpəfáin]. 1. Over-subtle, refined to excess. 2. (commerc.) Of the finest quality, extra fine.

superfineness, n. Prec. & **-ness**. State or quality of being superfine.

superfluity, n. [1. sŭperflōōiti; 2. sjŭpəflúiti]. See next word & **-ity**. 1. State or quality of being superfluous. 2. **a** Something which is superfluous: *to keep a carriage as well as a motor-car is a superfluity*; specif. **b** pecuniary surplus, wealth beyond one's needs: *to give of one's superfluity*.

superfluous, adj. [1. sŭperflóous; 2. sjŭpǽfluəs], fr. Lat. *superfluus*, 'unnecessary', fr. **super-** & *fluere*, 'to flow', see **fluent** (I.), & **-ous**. Beyond requirements, forming a surplus or unnecessary adjunct; more than is necessary; redundant.

superfluously, adv. Prec. & **-ly**. In a superfluous manner.

superfluousness, n. See prec. & **-ness**. State of being superfluous; superfluity.

superheat, vb. trans. [1. sŭperhét; 2. sjŭpəhít]. To raise (vapour) to a temperature above that of boiling-point of water.

superheater, n. [1. sŭperhéter; 2. sjŭpəhítə]. Prec. & **-er**. Apparatus in a steam-engine for raising temperature of steam after leaving the boiler or when no longer in contact with the water.

superhive, n. [1. sŭperhìv; 2. sjŭpəhàiv]. Hive placed above or fitting on to top of another.

superhuman, adj. [1. sŭperhúman; 2. sjŭpəhjúmən]. Exceeding normal human power, wisdom, size &c.; possessing more than human capacity.

superhumanly, adv. Prec. & **-ly**. In a superhuman manner.

superhumeral, n. [1. sŭperhúmeral; 2. s(j)ŭpəhjúmərəl], fr. **super-** & Lat. *humerus*, 'shoulder', see **humerus**, & **-al**. Vestment worn on the shoulders; specif. **a** priest's amice; **b** bishop's pallium; **c** Jewish ephod.

superimpose, vb. trans. [1. sŭperimpóz; 2. sjŭpərimpóuz]. To lay, place, establish, on top of something else: *to superimpōse a building on the remains of another*; *a superimposed mass*.

superimpregnation, n. [1. sŭperìmpregnáshun; 2. sjŭpərìmpregnéiʃən]. Superfetation.

superincumbent, adj. [1. sŭperinkúmbent; 2. sjŭpərìnkámbənt]. Lying, resting, on top of something else: *a superincumbent weight*.

superinduce, vb. trans. [1. sŭperindús; 2. sjŭpərindjús]. To induce, develop, give rise to, as an addition to something else.

superinduction, n. [1. sŭperindúkshun; 2. sjŭpərindákʃən]. Act of superinducing; state of being superinduced.

superinstitution, n. [1. sŭperinstitúshun; 2. sjŭpərìnstitjúʃən]. The institution of a priest in a benefice already in the possession of an incumbent.

superintend, vb. trans. & intrans. [1. sŭperinténd; 2. sjŭpərinténd], fr. **super-** & Lat. *intendere*, 'to stretch out; to pay attention to', see **intend**. To direct, guide, control, working of; to supervise functioning or organization of, regulate progress of.

superintendence, n. [1. sŭperinténdens; 2. sjŭpərinténdəns]. Next word & **-ce**. Act or quality of superintending; state of being superintended.

superintendent, n. [1. sŭperinténdent; 2. sjŭ-pərinténdənt]. **super-** & Pres. Part. of Lat. *intendere*, see **intend**. a Person who superintends, esp. some specific official organization, institution, department &c.; manager, overseer, director; specif. b police officer above the rank of inspector.

superior (I.), adj. [1. sŭpérier; 2. sjŭpíəriə], fr. Lat. *superior*, compar. of *superus*, 'higher', see **super-**. 1. Higher in physical position, above, more elevated; specif. a (bot., anat., zool. &c.) situated nearer the head or upper side; growing above another organ &c.: *superior wings, calyx* &c.; b (print., of letter or figure) printed above the line. 2. Of higher rank or grade; of more authoritative position: *superior officer, court* &c.; *superior genus*, including more categories; *superior planets*, those revolving beyond the earth's orbit. 3. a Of better quality, of greater skill, power, capability, excellence &c., surpassing in quantity or degree: *superior strength, skill, knowledge* &c.; b of great excellence, eminently satisfactory, reliable &c.; of excellent quality or attainments; above the average: *made of superior cloth*; *a very superior man*. 4. Larger in number or amount: *the enemy attacked with superior forces*; *a superior volume of fire*. 5. *Superior to*, rising above influence of, not affected, swayed or biassed by: *superior to temptation*; *to rise superior to hardship, obstacles* &c.; *to be superior to prejudice*.

superior (II.), n., fr. prec. 1. a Person placed over another; person of greater rank, position, authority &c.: *to look up to one's superiors*; b person surpassing another in merit, in intellectual or spiritual qualities, skill &c.: *he was his brother's superior in every way*. 2. (cap.) Person presiding over religious house; director of monastery, convent &c.: *Father, Mother, Superior*.

superioress, n. [1. sŭpérieres; 2. sjŭpíəriərəs]. Prec. & **-ess**. Mother Superior.

superiority, n. [1. sŭpèrióriti; 2. sjŭpìəriórìti]. **superior** (I.) & **-ity**. State or quality of being superior.

superiorly, adv. [1. sŭpérierli; 2. sjŭpíəriəli]. **superior** (I.) & **-ly**. (bot. &c.) In a superior position.

superjacent, adj. [1. sŭperjásent; 2. sjŭpə-dźéisnt], fr. **super-** & Lat. *jacent-(em)*, Pres. Part. of *jacēre*, 'to lie', see **adjacent**. Lying above, resting upon, something else.

superlative (I.), adj. [1. sŭpérlativ; 2. sjŭpá-lətiv], fr. Lat. *superlatīvus*, 'exaggerated'; in the superlative degree', fr. **super-** & *latum*, P.P. type of Lat. *ferre*, 'to carry', fr. *tlāt-, fr. base *tel-, *tol- &c.; see **tolerate** & **-ive**. 1. Of the highest degree of excellence; of supreme quality or merit: *superlative beauty, goodness, virtue* &c. 2. (gram.) *Superlative degree*, highest degree of comparison of adjective or adverb, expressing the existence of a quality in the highest degree.

superlative (II.), n., fr. prec. a (gram.) Superlative degree, form indicating this degree; b word in the superlative: *to speak in superlatives*, implying exaggeration, over-enthusiasm &c.

superlatively, adv. Prec. & **-ly**. To a superlative degree.

superlativeness, n. See prec. & **-ness**. State or quality of being superlative.

superlunar(y), adj. [1. sŭperlŭnər(i); 2. sjŭpə-ljŭnər(i)]. **super-** & **lunar**. a Beyond the moon, celestial; specif. b not earthly, transcending things of this world.

superman, n. [1. sŭpermàn; 2. sjŭpəmǽn]. Hypothetical being possessing supreme physical and mental powers; the overman, q.v.

supermedial, adj. [1. sŭpermédial; 2. sjŭpə-mídiəl]. Situated above the middle.

supermolecule, n. [1. sŭpermólekūl; 2. sjŭpə-mólikjūl]. Group of molecules regarded as a unit.

supermundane, adj. [1. sŭpermúndān; 2. sjŭpə-mándein]. Above, superior to, transcending mundane things.

supernacular, adj. [1. sŭpernákūlar; 2. sjŭpə-nækjulə]. See next word & **-ar**. (of wine) Worthy to be drunk supernaculum; first-rate.

supernaculum, adv. & n. [1. sŭpernákūlum; 2. sjŭpənækjuləm], fr. **super-** & Latinized form of Germ. *nagel*, 'nail', q.v. under **nail** (I.), w. reference to custom of reversing emptied wine-glass &c. & pouring last drop on finger-nail. 1. adv. To the last drop, so as to finish completely. 2. n. Wine of fine quality, worthy of being drunk supernaculum.

supernal, adj. [1. sŭpérnal; 2. sjŭpə́nəl], fr. Lat. *supernus*, 'celestial', fr. *super*, 'above', see **super-**, **-al**. (poet.) Heavenly, celestial.

supernatant, adj. [1. sŭpernátant; 2. sjŭpə-néitənt], fr. **super-** & *natant-(em)*, Pres. Part. of Lat. *natāre*, 'to swim, float', see **natation**. Floating on the surface.

supernatural, adj. [1. sŭpernáchural; 2. sjŭpə-nætʃərəl]. Existing outside of, transcending, effected by, a force above the normal laws of nature; miraculous.

supernaturalism, n. [1. sŭpernáchuralizm; 2. sjŭpənætʃərəlizəm]. Prec. & **-ism**. Belief in the supernatural.

supernaturalist, n. [1. sŭpernáchuralist; 2. sjŭpənætʃərəlist]. **supernatural** & **-ist**. Believer in the supernatural.

supernaturalistic, adj. [1. sŭpernáchuralístik; 2. sjŭpənætʃərəlístik]. Prec. & **-ic**. Characteristic of a supernaturalist.

supernaturalize, vb. trans. [1. sŭpernáchuraliz; 2. sjŭpənætʃərəlaiz]. **supernatural** & **-ize**. To make, regard as, supernatural, bring into the domain of the supernatural.

supernaturally, adv. [1. sŭpernáchurali; 2. sjŭpənætʃərəli]. See prec. & **-ly**. In a supernatural manner.

supernaturalness, n. [1. sŭpernáchuralnes; 2. sjŭpənætʃərəlnis]. See prec. & **-ness**. State or quality of being supernatural.

supernormal, adj. [1. sŭpernórmal; 2. sjŭpə-nóməl]. Above the normal.

supernumerary, adj. & n. [1. sŭpernŭmerari; 2. sjŭpənjŭmərəri], fr. L. Lat. *super-numerārius*, 'supernumerary', fr. **super-** & *numerus*, 'number', see **number** (I.), & **-ary**. 1. adj. Exceeding, beyond, the normal or necessary number; extra. 2. n. Person or thing in excess of the normal, necessary, or appointed number.

supernutrition, n. [1. sŭpernŭtrishun; 2. sjŭ-pənjutríʃən]. Extra or excessive feeding.

superoctave, n. [1. sŭperóktāv; 2. sjŭpər-ókteiv]. Organ-stop coupling any note with its octave.

superorder, n. [1. sŭperòrder; 2. sjŭpərɔ̀də]. Group comprising more than one order.

superordinal, adj. [1. sŭperórdinal; 2. sjŭpər-ódinəl]. Of, pertaining to, a superorder.

superordinary, adj. [1. sŭperórdinari; 2. sjŭpər-ódinəri]. Above the ordinary.

superorganic, adj. [1. sŭperorgánik; 2. sjŭpər-ɔ̀gǽnik]. Above, superior to, not dependent upon, a physical organism; psychical.

superparasite, n. [1. sŭperpárasit; 2. sjŭpə-pǽrəsait]. The parasite of a parasite.

superparasitic, adj. [1. sŭperpárasitik; 2. sjŭ-pəpærəsítik]. Prec. & **-ic**. Characteristic of, pertaining to, a superparasite.

superphosphate, n. [1. sŭperfósfāt; 2. sjŭpə-fósfeit]. (chem.) a An acid phosphate; b a fertiliser consisting of soluble phosphates.

superphysical, adj. [1. sŭperfízikl; 2. sjŭpə-fízikl]. Not to be explained by known physical laws.

superpose, vb. trans. [1. sŭperpóz; 2. sjŭpə-póuz]. To lay, deposit, place (one thing) above another.

superposition, n. [1. sŭperpozíshun; 2. sjŭpə-pəzíʃən]. Act of superposing; state of being superposed; (geol.) *law of superposition*, principle that in stratified rock underlying beds are older than those which are above them.

superquadripartient, adj. [1. sŭperkwòdri-párshent; 2. sjŭpəkwɔ̀dripáʃənt]. In the ratio of 9 to 5.

superquadriquintal, adj. [1. sŭperkwòdri-kwíntl; 2. sjŭpəkwɔ̀drikwíntl]. In the ratio of 9 to 5.

superroyal, adj. [1. sŭperóial; 2. sjŭpəróiəl]. (of paper) Of a size larger than *royal*.

supersacral, adj. [1. sŭpersákral; 2. sjŭpə-séikrəl]. Situated above the sacrum.

supersaturate, vb. trans. [1. sŭpersáchurāt; 2. sjŭpəsǽtʃəreit]. (chem.) To saturate beyond the normal degree.

supersaturation, n. [1. sŭpersàchuráshun; 2. sjŭpəsætʃəréiʃən]. Prec. & **-ion**. State of being supersaturated.

superscribe, vb. trans. [1. sŭperskrìb; 2. sjŭpə-skràib], fr. Lat. *superscribere*, 'to write above'; see **super-** & **scribe** (I.). To write, engrave &c. (name, inscription &c.), on the outer or upper side of anything.

superscript, adj. [1. sŭperskrìpt; 2. sjŭpə-skrìpt], fr. Lat. *superscriptum*, see **super-** & **script**. (of letter, figure &c.) Written above, over the top.

superscription, n. [1. sŭperskrípshun; 2. sjŭpə-skrípʃən]. Prec. & **-ion**. 1. Act of superscribing. 2. Something superscribed.

supersede, vb. trans. [1. sŭperséd; 2. sjŭpəsíd], fr. Fr. *supersèder*, 'to desist'; fr. Lat. *super-sedēre*, 'to forbear, refrain, desist', fr. **super-** & *sedēre*, 'to sit, remain', see **sedentary** (I.). 1. To put or use in the place of; replace by some other person, thing, method &c.: *to supersede a general*. 2. To take the place of, supplant, be adopted instead of: *the use of machinery has largely superseded manual labour*.

supersedeas, n. [1. sŭpersédeas; 2. sjŭpə-sídiæs], fr. Lat. *supersedeas*, 2nd sing. subj. Pres. of *supersedēre*, 'to desist, refrain', see **supersede**. (legal) Writ issued to stay proceedings or stop execution of another writ.

supersedence, n. [1. sŭpersédens; 2. sjŭpə-sídəns]. **supersede** & **-ence**. (rare) Act of superseding; state of being superseded.

supersensible, adj. [1. sŭpersénsibl; 2. sjŭpə-sénsibl]. Above, beyond the range of, the senses.

supersensitive, adj. [1. sŭpersénsitiv; 2. sjŭpə-sénsitiv]. Highly, abnormally, sensitive.

supersensual, adj. [1. sŭpersénsual, -sénshooal; 2. sjŭpəsénsjuəl, -sénʃuəl]. Supersensible.

supersensuous, adj. [1. sŭpersénsūus; 2. sjŭpə-sénsjuəs]. Supersensual.

supersesquialteral, adj. [1. sŭpersèskwiál-teral; 2. sjŭpəsèskwiæltərəl]. In the ratio of 5 to 2.

supersesquitertial, adj. [1. sŭpersèskwitér-shal; 2. sjŭpəsèskwitáʃəl]. In the ratio of 7 to 3.

supersession, n. [1. sŭperséshun; 2. sjŭpə-séʃən], fr. Lat. *supersess-(um)*, P.P. type of *supersedēre*, 'to refrain', see **supersede**, & **-ion**. Act of superseding; state of being superseded.

supersolar, adj. [1. sŭpersólar; 2. sjŭpəsóulə]. Situated above the sun.

supersolid, n. [1. sŭpersòlid; 2. sjŭpəsɔ́lid]. A solid body of more than three dimensions.

superspiritual, adj. [1. sŭperspírichooal; 2. sjŭpəspíritʃuəl]. More than normally spiritual.

superspirituality, n. [1. sŭperspìrichoóaliti; 2. sjŭpəspìritʃuǽliti]. Prec. & **-ity**. Quality of being superspiritual.

superstition, n. [1. sŭperstíshun; 2. sjŭpəstí-ʃən], fr. Lat. *superstitiōn-(em)*, 'superstition', orig. 'prophesy, soothsaying'; fr. *superstāre*, 'to stand over', see **super-**, & **station** (I.). 1. Irrational dread of the supernatural; excessive credulity with regard to what is mysterious and unexplained; belief in magic and in the influence of inanimate objects on human life and destiny. 2. Opinion, act, practice, based on superstition: *heathen superstitions*.

superstitious, adj. [1. sŭperstíshus; 2. sjŭpə-stíʃəs], fr. Lat. *superstitiōsus*, 'full of superstition; prophetical', fr. *superstitio*, see prec., & **-ous**. Pertaining to, influenced by, involving, based on, superstition: *superstitious people, beliefs, customs* &c.

superstitiously, adv. Prec. & -ly. In a superstitious manner.

superstitiousness, n. See prec. & -ness. Quality of being superstitious.

superstratum, n. [1. sùperstrátum; 2. sjūpəstréitəm]. Stratum imposed upon, overlying, another.

superstructural, adj. [1. sùperstrúkchural; 2. sjūpəstráktʃərəl]. Of, pertaining to, a superstructure.

superstructure, n. [1. sùperstrúkchur; 2. sjūpəstráktʃə]. Any structure built upon another.

supersubstantial, adj. [1. sùpersubstánshal; 2. sjūpəsəbstǽnʃəl]. Above, transcending, outside the sphere of, mere substance or matter.

supersubtle, adj. [1. sùpersútl; 2. sjūpəsátl]. Over-subtle.

supersubtlety, n. [1. sùpersútlti; 2. sjūpəsátlti]. Prec. & -ty (I.). Quality of being supersubtle.

supertax, n. [1. sùpertáks; 2. sjūpətǽks]. A tax paid on incomes in excess of a certain figure, paid in addition to, but separate from, the ordinary income-tax.

supertelluric, adj. [1. sùpertelúrik; 2. sjūpətèljŏrik], fr. **super-** & Lat. tellūr-, stem of tellūs, 'earth', see **tellurium**. Above, beyond, the earth's atmosphere.

supertemporal, adj. [1. sùpertémporal; 2. sjūpətémpərəl]. 1. Beyond the limits of time. 2. Situated above the temporal bone.

superterrene, adj. [1. sùpertérēn; 2. sjūpətérīn]. Above the earth, celestial; supermundane.

superterrestrial, adj. [1. sùperteréstrial; 2. sjūpətəréstriəl]. Superterrene.

supertonic, n. [1. sùpertònik; 2. sjūpətònik]. (mus.) Note immediately above the tonic of the scale.

supertripartient, adj. [1. sùpertripárshent; 2. sjūpətràipá(ʃənt]. In the ratio of 7 to 4.

supertriquartal, adj. [1. sùpertrikwórtl; 2. sjūpətràikwɔ́tl]. Supertripartient.

supertuberation, n. [1. sùpertùberǎ́shun; 2. sjūpətjùbəréiʃən]. Development of young tubers from one still growing.

supervacaneous, adj. [1. sùpervakǎ́neus; 2. sjūpəvəkéiniəs], fr. Lat. supervacāneus, 'superfluous', fr. **super-** & vacāre, 'to be empty', see **vacant**, & **-aneous**. Superfluous, redundant.

supervene, vb. intrans. [1. sùpervēn; 2. sjūpəvīn], fr. Lat. supervenīre, 'to follow, come after, follow upon', fr. **super-** & venīre, 'to come', see **venue**. To come directly after, to come into existence, occur, as an addition to, or in consequence of, some other condition, event &c.; to be introduced as something additional or extraneous.

supervention, n. [1. sùpervénshun; 2. sjūpəvénʃən], fr. Lat. superventum, P.P. type of supervenīre, 'to follow', see prec., & **-ion**. Act or process of supervening.

supervise, vb. trans. [1. sùpervīz; 2. sjūpəváiz], fr. **super-** & Lat. vīsum, P.P. type of vidēre, 'to see', see **vision (I.)**. To superintend, give oversight to, direct, the work or progress of.

supervision, n. [1. sùpervízhun; 2. sjūpəvíʒən]. Prec. & **-ion**. Act of supervising; state of being supervised.

supervisor, n. [1. sùpervīzer; 2. sjūpəváizə]. **supervise** & **-or**. Person who supervises.

supervisory, adj. [1. sùpervízeri; 2. sjūpəváizəri]. Prec. & **-y**. Pertaining to, characteristic of, a supervisor, or of supervision: supervisory duties.

supinate, vb. trans. [1. súpināt; 2. sjūpineit], fr. Lat. supīnātum, P.P. type of supīnāre, 'to bend back, turn over', fr. supīnus, 'on the back', see **supine (I.)**. To place (hand) with palm upwards; reverse of pronate.

supination, n. [1. sùpinǎ́shun; 2. sjūpinéiʃən]. Prec. & **-ion**. Act of supinating; state of being supinated; rotation of the hand at the wrist so that the palm is turned upwards; reverse of pronation.

supinator, n. [1. súpinǎter; 2. sjūpineitə]. **supinate** & **-or**. Muscle of the fore-arm by means of which supination is produced.

supine (I.), adj. [1. sūpīn, sūpín; 2. sjūpain, sjūpáin], fr. Lat. supīnus, 'thrown backwards; on the back, backwards, indolent, negligent', fr. stem *sup-, 'beneath', seen in **sub-, super-**. 1. Lying on the back, with face upwards, opposed to prone. 2. Averse to, not taking, action; inactive.

supine (II.), n., fr. Lat. (verbum) supīnum. See prec. Latin verbal noun formed from P.P. stem.

supinely, adv. **supine (I.)** & **-ly**. In a supine manner or position.

supineness, n. See prec. & **-ness**. State or quality of being supine.

supper, n. [1. súper; 2. sápə], fr. O. Fr. soper, fr. vb. soper, 'to sup', fr. L.G. sūpen, 'to sup', cogn. w. **sup (I.)**. Last meal of the day, substituted for, or following, dinner. Phrs. the Last Supper, the last meal of Christ with His disciples before the Crucifixion; the Lord's Supper, the Holy Eucharist.

supperless, adj. [1. súperles; 2. sápəlis]. Prec. & **-less**. Without supper.

supplant, vb. trans. [1. supláhnt; 2. səplánt], fr. O. Fr. supplanter, fr. Lat. supplantāre, 'to trip up', fr. **sup-** & planta, 'sole of the foot', see **plantar**. To take the place of, oust, usurp position or function of, esp. by art or fraud.

supple (I.), adj. [1. súpl; 2. sápl], fr. O. Fr. souple, fr. Lat. supplex, 'submissive, supplicating', fr. **sup-** & plic-, stem of plicāre, 'to bend, fold', see **plicate**; & cp. ending of double, triple. 1. Pliant, flexible, easily bent: supple leather; a supple cane, bow &c.; supple limbs. 2. **a** Docile, amenable, easily led or influenced; **b** cunningly compliant; sly, adroit.

supple (II.), vb. trans. & intrans., fr. prec. 1. trans. **a** To make supple: 'Their joints they supple with dissolving oil' (Pope, 'Homer'); **b** to train (horse) to be docile, quickly obedient. 2. intrans. To grow supple.

supple-jack, n. **a** One of several varieties of climbing plant with tough, woody, pliant stems; **b** walking-stick cut from the wood of this plant.

supplement (I.), n. [1. súplement; 2. sáplimənt], fr. Fr., fr. Lat. supplēmentum, 'that which supplies, fills up', fr. supplēre, 'to fill out, make good', fr. **sup-** & plēre, 'to fill', q.v. under **plenum**, & **-ment**. 1. **a** Something added to supply a deficiency; that which is added to fulfil requirements, ensure adequacy &c.; specif. **b** (i.) additional matter included at the end of a book giving fuller or later details on subjects dealt with in the body of the work; (ii.) special additional number or part of a periodical devoted to a particular range of subjects. 2. (math.) Angle that must be added to another to make two right angles.

supplement (II.), vb. trans. [1. sùplemént; 2. sàplimént], fr. prec. To add something to in order to make up deficiencies in, to provide something additional for.

supplemental, adj. [1. sùpleméntl; 2. sàpliméntl]. **supplement (I.)** & **-al**. Supplementary.

supplementary, adj. [1. sùpleméntari; 2. sàpliméntəri]. **supplement (I.)** & **-ary**. Of the nature of a supplement; supplying deficiencies, adding something that was lacking.

supplementation, n. [1. sùplementǎ́shun; 2. sàpliméntéiʃən]. **supplement (II.)** & **-ation**. Act of supplementing; state of being supplemented.

suppleness, n. [1. súplnes; 2. sáplnis]. **supple (I.)** & **-ness**. State or quality of being supple.

suppliance, n. [1. súplians; 2. sápliəns]. See next word & **-ce**. (rare) Act of supplicating; state of being suppliant.

suppliant, adj. & n. [1. súpliant; 2. sápliənt], fr. Fr., fr. supplier, 'to beg', fr. Lat. supplicāre, 'to kneel down, beg, beseech', see **supplicate**. 1. adj. Entreating, beseeching, making, uttering, supplication. 2. n. One who supplicates; person making humble entreaty.

suppliantly, adv. Prec. & **-ly**. In a suppliant manner; as a supplicant.

supplicate, vb. trans. & intrans. [1. súplikàt; 2. sáplikèit], fr. Lat. supplicāt-(um), P.P. type of supplicāre, 'to kneel down, humble oneself, beg, beseech', fr. supplic-, stem of supplex, 'kneeling, entreating, suppliant', see **supple (I.)**. 1. trans. **a** To ask humbly and earnestly for; to pray, beg, entreat for: to supplicate pardon; **b** to address entreaty to, pray, petition: to supplicate a person. 2. intrans. To make supplication, proffer humble entreaties, beg earnestly: to supplicate for mercy.

supplicating, adj. [1. súplikàting; 2. sáplikèitiŋ]. Prec. & **-ing**. Of, consisting of, expressing, supplication.

supplicatingly, adv. Prec. & **-ly**. In a supplicating manner; with supplication.

supplication, n. [1. sùplikǎ́shun; 2. sàplikéiʃən]. **supplicate** & **-ion**. Act of supplicating; humble request, prayer, petition.

supplicatory, adj. [1. súplikaturi; 2. sáplikətəri]. **supplicate** & **-ory**. Of the nature of, expressing, supplication.

supply (I.), vb. trans. [1. suplí; 2. səplái], fr. O. Fr. supploier, 'to fill up', fr. Lat. supplēre, 'to fill out, make good', see **supplement (I.)**. 1. To equip with, provide, furnish, satisfy needs and requirements of: cows supply us with milk; the butcher supplies us with meat. 2. To provide, produce, yield, afford for use: the cow supplies milk; trees supply shade in summer. 3. To make good, make up for, compensate for: to supply a need, deficiency &c.; Phr. to supply the place of, to replace, act as substitute for.

supply (II.), n., fr. prec. 1. Something which is supplied; amount, store, stock: a supply of food, water &c. 2. (pl.) Supplies, specif., the whole of the necessities of life supplied to a large body of men, esp. an army, the inhabitants of a country. 3. (econ.) Total quantity of an article or commodity, available at a given price; contrasted with demand. 4. Person who takes the place of another, a (temporary) substitute; esp. a teacher temporarily in charge of a school, or of a class in a school, in an emergency.

supply (III.), adv. [1. súpli; 2. sápli]. **supple (I.)** & **-ly**. In a supple manner.

support (I.), vb. trans. [1. supórt; 2. səpɔ́t], fr. Fr. supporter, 'to bear, endure', fr. Lat. supportāre, 'to convey', fr. **sup-** & portāre, 'to carry', see **port (IV.)**. 1. To bear weight of, prevent from falling or sinking, hold up from below: a roof supported by pillars; to support one's chin on one's hand; to support oneself with a stick. 2. **a** To sustain, maintain, keep vigorous: air is necessary to support life; **b** to maintain mental or spiritual vigour of, uphold: to be supported by courage, vigour &c. 3. **a** To have dependent on one, provide subsistence for, maintain: to support a family; **b** to subscribe to, give financial help to: to support hospitals by voluntary subscriptions. 4. To bear, endure, submit to, put up with: to support fatigue &c. 5. **a** To give help, sanction, approval to, assist, further, promote progress of: to support a cause, leader, motion &c.; **b** to show approval of, aid, by one's presence: the speaker was supported on the platform by the mayor. 6. To confirm, corroborate, show proof of, vindicate: to support an argument, claim &c. 7. To assume and carry out (part, rôle &c.); to represent successfully.

support (II.), n., fr. prec. 1. Act of supporting, state of being supported: to walk, stand, without support; Phr. in support of, in order to uphold, promote, advocate &c. 2. **a** One who, that which, supports: the neck orms a support for the head; to provide a structure with supports; **b** means of maintenance or sustenance: the sole support of an aged mother. 3. **a** Spiritual or moral help, prop, stay; sustaining power: the support of a good conscience;

supportable, adj. [1. supórtabl; 2. səpṓtəbl]. **support** (I.) & **-able**. Capable of being endured; tolerable, endurable.

supportably, adv. Prec. & **-ly**. In a supportable manner.

supporter, n. [1. supórter; 2. səpṓtə]. **support** (I.) & **-er**. 1. Person who supports another person, or a cause; an adherent, a partisan. 2. (her.) One of two human or animal figures represented on either side of a shield.

supportless, adj. [1. supórtles; 2. səpṓtlis]. **support** (II.) & **-less**. Without support.

supposable, adj. [1. supṓzabl; 2. səpóuzəbl]. **suppose** & **-able**. Capable of being supposed; conceivable.

supposably, adv. Prec. & **-ly**. As is to be supposed; presumably.

suppose, vb. trans. [1. supṓz; 2. səpóuz], fr. Fr. *supposer*, fr. **sup-** & *poser*, 'to place', see **pose** (I.); corresponding to Lat. *supponere* in meaning. 1. To assume tentatively, as a hypothesis, for the sake of argument: *let us suppose for a moment that what you say is true*. 2. To imagine, conjecture, fancy, believe, to be: *I should suppose him to be about fifty; I never supposed him (to be) a hero; I suppose you like London; I don't suppose I shall be very long*. 3. To require as a natural or logical result or concomitant, to presuppose, to involve as a necessary presumption: *success in any walk of life supposes both ability and careful training*. 4. **a** In imperat., introducing a proposal or suggestion: *suppose we take a holiday next week*; **b** in Pres. Part., having force of *if*: *supposing you miss your tiger, he is not likely to miss you*; Phr. *always supposing*, provided that.

supposed, adj. [1. supṓzd; 2. səpóuzd]. Prec. & **-ed**. Accepted as, believed to be, genuine; assumed: *the supposed prince turned out to be a draper's assistant*.

supposedly, adv. [1. supṓzedli; 2. səpóuzidli]. Prec. & **-ly**. According to what is, or may be, supposed; as may be assumed: *he was supposedly grateful for your kindness*.

supposition, n. [1. supozíshun; 2. sàpəzíʃən]. **suppose** & **-ition**. 1. Act of supposing. 2. That which is supposed, hypothetical conjecture; assumption: *the whole story is based on mere supposition; on the supposition, on the assumption, assuming, in the expectation*.

suppositional, adj. [1. supozíshunal; 2. sàpəzíʃənəl]. Prec. & **-al**. Based on, of the nature of, supposition.

suppositionally, adv. Prec. & **-ly**. As a supposition, by way of supposition.

supposititious, adj. [1. supozitíshus; 2. səpòzitíʃəs], fr. Lat. *supposītīcius*, 'substituted', fr. *supposit-(um)*, P.P. type of *suppōnere*, 'to put in place of another', fr. **sup-** & *pōnere*, 'to place'; see **pose** (I.) & **-ious**. 1. Substituted for genuine object or person with intent to defraud; spurious: *supposititious writings*. 2. (rare) Suppositional.

supposititiously, adv. Prec. & **-ly**. In a supposititious manner.

supposititiousness, n. See prec. & **-ness**. Quality of being supposititious.

suppositive, adj. [1. supózitiv; 2. səpózitiv], fr. Lat. *supposit-(um)*, see **supposititious** & **-ive**. Of the nature of, implying, based on, supposition.

suppository, n. [1. supózituri; 2. səpózitəri], fr. L. Lat. *suppositōrius*, 'something placed underneath', fr. *supposit-(um)*, P.P. type of *suppōnere*, 'to place under or instead of another', see **supposition**, & **-ory**. Stick or lump of solid medicinal, or nutritive substance, inserted and allowed to dissolve and be absorbed, in a canal or organ of the body.

suppress, vb. trans. [1. suprés; 2. səprés], fr. Lat. *suppress-(um)*, P.P. type of *supprimere*, 'to keep back, restrain'; to check, repress', fr. **sup-** & *premere*, 'to press', see **press** (I.).

1. **a** To restrain, check, keep back, prevent, the development or occurrence of: *to suppress a smile, a yawn, an involuntary movement*; **b** to keep back, repress, stifle, smother, silence, the expression or manifestation of (an emotion &c.): *to suppress an inclination to laugh, a sob, a sigh, an exclamation of astonishment* &c. 2. To put down by force, to quell, subdue, crush: *to suppress a heresy, a popular rising, a rebellion, mutiny* &c. 3. **a** To disallow the publication of: *to suppress a newspaper, a book*; **b** to cut out, eliminate: *to suppress a phrase, a passage, in a book, article* &c. 4. To conceal, refuse to reveal or divulge, to keep back, prevent statement of: *to suppress important facts, the truth*.

suppressed, adj. [1. suprést; 2. səprést], fr. P.P. of prec. 1. (of disease) Arrested in development, checked in its normal development, not manifesting usual external symptoms: *suppressed scarlet fever* &c. 2. Checked in process of utterance; muffled: *sounds of suppressed laughter*.

suppressible, adj. [1. suprésibl; 2. səprésibl]. Prec. & **-ible**. Capable of being suppressed.

suppression, n. [1. supréshun; 2. səpréʃən], fr. Lat. *suppressiōn-(em)*, 'restraint'; **suppress** & **-ion**. Act of suppressing; state of being suppressed.

suppressio veri, n. [1. suprésio vḗri; 2. səprésiou víərai]. Lat. *suppressio veri*, 'suppression of the truth'; see prec., & **veracious**. Concealment of the truth; esp. the withholding of facts, a knowledge of which is essential to the formation of a correct judgement.

suppressive, adj. [1. suprésiv; 2. səprésiv]. **suppress** & **-ive**. Tending to suppress.

suppurate, vb. intrans. [1. súpūrāt; 2. sápjurèit], fr. Lat. *suppūrātum*, P.P. type of *suppūrāre*, 'to form pus', fr. **sup-** & *pūr-*, stem of *pūs*, 'pus, matter', see **pus**. (of wounds, sores &c.) To produce pus.

suppuration, n. [1. supūráshun; 2. sàpjuréiʃən]. Prec. & **-ion**. Process of suppurating.

suppurative, adj. [1. súpūrativ; 2. sápjurətiv]. **suppurate** & **-ive**. Tending to suppurate; causing, characterized by, suppuration.

supra-, pref. representing Lat. *suprā*, 'on the top, above'; cp. Lat. *super*, 'above', apparently orig. 'from below upwards'; Lat. *sub*, 'below', see **sub-**. In its modern use, the pref. is usually interchangeable w., but rarer than, **super-**. 1. Forming scientific terms denoting position above part, structure, or organ specified; e.g. *supraciliary*, above the eyebrow; *supraclavicular*, situated above the clavicle; *supracretaceous*, (geol.) lying above the chalk; *supradorsal*, situated on the back; *supra-orbital*, above the orbit of the eye; *suprarenal*, situated above the kidneys. 2. Before, at a prior time; e.g. *supralapsarian*, member of a group of Calvinists who regard predestination as preceding the Creation and the Fall. 3. Above, transcending, superior; e.g. *supramortal*, beyond the power or attributes of mortals; *supramundane*, above the world or worldly things; *suprasensible*, beyond the range of the senses.

supremacy, n. [1. suprémasi; 2. s(j)uprémasi], fr. O. Fr. *suprematie*, fr. Lat. *suprēmus*, 'supreme', see next word, & **-acy**. State or quality of being supreme; supreme power or authority, domination. Phr. *Act of Supremacy*, Parliamentary Act of 1534, declaring the Sovereign of England to be supreme head on earth of the Church of England.

supreme, adj. [1. suprḗm; 2. s(j)uprī́m], fr. Lat. *suprēmus*, 'highest', superl. form of *superus*, 'above', see **superior** (I.); *-mo-* is an old superl. suff., seen also in **-most**. 1. Above, superior to, all others, in rank, power, jurisdiction &c.: *supreme head, ruler, tribunal* &c. Phr. *the Supreme Being, God*; *the Supreme Court of Judicature*, High Court of Justice; *supreme good*, highest possible good. 2. Exceeding all others in degree, quality, intensity &c.; utmost: *supreme sacrifice, devotion, goodness* &c.

supremely, adv. Prec. & **-ly**. In a supreme manner; to a supreme degree or extent.

sur- (I.), form of **sub-**, w. assimilation of *-b* in compounds where the second element begins w. *r-*.

sur- (II.), pref. representing O. Fr. *sur-*, 'above, over, beyond', fr. Lat. **super-**; a in loan-words fr. O. Fr., e.g. *surcoat*, *surface*, *surprise* &c.; **b** in some scientific or technical terms &c., in place of **supra-**, **super-**, e.g. *surangular*, *surbase* &c.

sura(h), n. [1. sōōra; 2. súrə], fr. Arab. *sūra*, 'step'. Chapter, section, of the Koran.

surah, n. [1. súra; 2. sjúərə]. Prob. fr. Surat, in Western India, see **surat**. Also *surah silk*, soft twilled silk fabric.

sural, adj. [1. súral; 2. sjúərəl], fr. Lat. *sūra*, 'calf of the leg'; cp. Gk. (Ionic) (h)ṓrē, 'calf of the leg'. Pertaining to, connected with, the calf of the leg.

surat, n. [1. soorát; 2. surǽt], fr. Surat, town in Western India, north of Bombay. 1. Kind of cotton grown in Bombay Presidency. 2. Coarse cotton fabric made in Surat district.

surbase, n. [1. sérbās; 2. sá́bèis]. **sur-** (II.) & **base** (I.). (archit.) Moulding, cornice, above base of pedestal &c.

surcease, n. & vb. intrans. [1. sérsḗs; 2. sāsī́s], w. assimilation of **cease** (I.), fr. A.-Fr. *sursise*, P.P. of *surseer*, 'to delay, restrain', fr. O. Fr. *surseoir*, fr. Lat. *supersedēre*, 'to refrain from, forbear', see **supersede**. (archaic) 1. n. Complete cessation, end. 2. vb. To stop, cease finally.

surcharge (I.), n. [1. surchárj; 2. sətʃáʤ], fr. O. Fr., **sur-** (II.) & **charge** (I.). 1. Excessive, additional, extra, load, burden, charge; specif. a sum added to price &c.; extra charge. **a** Additional charge made on property by assessors of taxes, as penalty for inaccurate return; **b** extra charge on letter or parcel for understamping; **c** special charge made on the individual members of a local authority by the auditor on account of expenditure wrongly incurred. 3. Additional imprint, superimposed upon original design &c., showing change of value &c. on postage-stamp &c.

surcharge (II.), vb. trans., fr. prec. 1. To overcharge, charge to excess or beyond requirements. 2. To demand additional payment or surcharge from. 3. To print a surcharge upon.

surcingle (I.), n. [1. sérsìnggl; 2. sá́sìngl], fr. O. Fr. *surcengle*, fr. **sur-** (II.) & *cengle*, 'girth', fr. Lat. *cingula*, *-um*, 'girdle, girth', see **cinch**, **cingulum**. 1. Belt or strap round body of horse &c. to hold saddle, blanket &c. in position. 2. A priest's girdle.

surcingle (II.), vb. trans., fr. prec. **a** To gird, surround; **b** to fasten with a surcingle.

surcoat, n. [1. sérkōt; 2. sá́kout]. M.E., O. Fr. *surcote*; **sur-** (II.) & **coat**. 1. Loose gown worn over armour in Middle Ages. 2. Short coat worn by women in 14th-15th centuries.

surculose, adj. [1. sérkulōs; 2. sá́kjulous], fr. Lat. *surculus*, 'shoot, sprout', dimin. of *surus*, 'twig, branch', & **-ose**; cogn. w. Scrt. *sváruš*, 'pole'; O.E. *swēr*, M.H.G. *swir*, 'pillar'. (bot.) Producing suckers.

surculous, adj. [1. sérkulus; 2. sá́kjuləs], fr. Lat. *surculus*, 'shoot, sprout', see prec., & **-ous**. Surculose.

surd (I.), adj. [1. sérd; 2. sā́d], fr. Lat. *surdus*, 'deaf, dull-sounding', earlier 'dull, dark, in colour'; cp. Lat. *sordēre*, 'to be soiled, become dull, dirty', see **sordid**. 1. (math., of number, quantity) Irrational. 2. In antiquated phonetic terminology, (of consonants) voiceless; uttered without accompanying vibration of vocal chords.

surd (II.), n., fr. prec. 1. (math.) Irrational number. 2. Voiceless consonant.

sure (I.), adj. [1. shōr, shōōr; 2. ʃō, ʃuə]. M.E. *sur*, fr. O. Fr. *seur*, fr. Lat. *sēcūrus*, 'free from care, untroubled'; heedless, careless; free from danger, safe', see **secure** (I.).

SURE (II.)

1. a Certain to produce a particular result; unfailing in action, effectiveness &c.: *a sure way to injure oneself*; *a sure method*; *a sure shot*; *slow and sure*; '*our defence is sure*'; **b** reliable, dependable: *to send a letter by a sure hand*; *sure grounds for belief*; **c** safe, secure, trustworthy: *a sure footing*. **2.** Certain to do some specific thing, action, or to undergo specific experience, be in specific condition: *he is sure to come*; *it's sure to be wet*. Phrs. *be sure to*, take care to, be certain to: *be sure to tell me*. **3.** Positively true, well authenticated as a fact, undoubted: *a sure and certain hope*. Phrs. *to make sure*, (i.) to feel sure, be convinced, persuaded: *I made sure it would rain today*: (ii.) to ascertain beyond doubt, satisfy oneself: *I believe the line is from 'Lycidas', but you had better make sure*; *to make sure of*, (i.) to secure evidence of reliability of: *to make sure of one's facts*; (ii.) to secure possession of, make certain of obtaining: *I must make sure of a house for the winter*; (iii.) to ascertain that one can count on support &c. of: *I fancy X will vote for us, but we must make sure of him*; *to be sure*, **a** (implying concession) indeed; it is granted, admitted; **b** (as exclamation) denoting surprise, *well, to be sure!*, just fancy that! **4.** Having reasonable grounds for belief, basing one's opinion on positive or apparent fact; confident, free from doubt or uncertainty: *to be sure of one's facts*; *I am sure he is honest*; *I am not sure if I can do it*; Phrs. *to feel sure (that)*, be convinced, be confident that; *I'm not so sure, I don't feel absolute confidence*; *sure of*, having good reasons for expecting or depending on: *to be sure of a living, a welcome &c.*; *sure of oneself*, having self-confidence.

sure (II.), adv., fr. prec. Surely, certainly; archaic, except in colloq. Phr. *as sure as*, as certainly, truly, as; *sure enough*, certainly, in fact.

sure-footed, adj. Not liable to stumble or slip: *mountain ponies are very sure-footed*.

surely, adv. [1. shórli, shōōrli; 2. ʃǒli, ʃúəli]. **sure (I.)** & **-ly**. **1.** Without danger, safely, securely. **2.** Without doubt, inevitably: *he must surely fail*. **3.** Expressing strong hope or belief in the probability, though not absolute certainty, that something is so, that it will happen or be done: *you surely don't mean to be cruel*; *surely something can be done to help him*; *surely this drought can't last much longer*.

sureness, n. [1. shórnes, shōōrnes; 2. ʃǒnis, ʃúənis]. See prec. & **-ness**. State or quality of being sure.

surety, n. [1. shórti, shōōrti; 2. ʃǒti, ʃúəti]. Doublet of **security**; M.E. *seurtee*, fr. O. Fr. *seurte*, fr. Lat. *sēcūritāt-(em)*, 'safety, security'; see **sure (I.)** & **-ty**. **1.** State of being sure; certainty, sureness. Phr. (archaic) *of a surety*, certainly. **2.** Person who makes himself responsible for the good conduct of another, for his appearance in court, payment of a debt &c.

suretyship, n. [1. shórti-, shōōrtiship; 2. ʃǒti-, ʃúətiʃip]. Prec. & **-ship**. Position, obligation, of person acting as surety.

surf, n. [1. sėrf; 2. sǎf]. Earlier *suffe*, perh. a variant of **sough**. Foamy spray produced by waves breaking on the shore or on a reef of rocks.

surface (I.), n. [1. sėrfis; 2. sǎfis], fr. O. Fr. *surface*; **sur- (II.)** & **face**; cp. **superficies**. **1.** Outer part of anything having length and breadth; any two-dimensional limit of a solid object; outside, exterior: *the surface of the earth, ocean*; *wood with a polished surface*; *beneath the surface*. **2.** (geom.) Part of space existing in two dimensions, having length and breadth but not depth; *plane surface*, plane. **3.** (in material and non-material sense) Outward appearance, outward part, exterior, that part or aspect of anything which meets the eye, which is obvious, or apparent on a cursory inspection, or to the inner perception from a brief experience or contemplation: *his cleverness is only on the surface*; *to look below the surface of things*; Phr. *on the surface*, so far as appearances go.

surface (II.), adj., fr. prec. Existing only on, affecting only, pertaining only to, the surface; superficial: *surface appearance, politeness* &c.

surface (III.), vb. trans., fr. **surface (I.)**. To produce a specific kind of surface on; to finish off, dress, surface of.

surface-current, n. Current of little depth at surface of water.

surfaced, adj. [1. sėrfist; 2. sǎfist], fr. P.P. of **surface (III.)**. Having, provided with, finished with, a specific kind of surface.

surface-flow, n. (geol.) Flow of lava &c. over a land-surface.

surfaceman, n. [1. sėrfisman; 2. sǎfismən]. Workman employed on railway to keep permanent way in repair.

surface-printing, n. Printing on textile fabric from a plate with design in relief.

surface-tension, n. Property of liquids, due to molecular action, which causes the outer, exposed surface to contract to a minimum area, thus forming a very thin film of appreciable toughness.

surface-water, n. Water lying on or drained from surface of ground.

surf-bird, n. Bird resembling plover, found on west coast of America.

surf-board, n. Oblong board used for surf-riding.

surf-boat, n. Boat specially constructed for use in surf.

surf-duck, n. Kind of sea-duck of northern regions.

surfeit (I.), n. [1. sėrfit; 2. sǎfit]. M.E. *surfēt*, fr. O. Fr. *sorfait*, fr. P.P. of *sorfaire*, 'to increase, cause to exceed', fr. **sur- (II.)** & Lat. *facere*, 'to do', see **fact**. **1.** Excess, esp. in feeding; overeating or overdrinking. **2.** Result of over-indulgence in food or drink; satiety, repletion. **3.** Excess of intellectual or spiritual experience: *a surfeit of concerts, of detective novels*.

surfeit (II.), vb. trans. & intrans., fr. prec. **1.** trans. To over-indulge, overfeed; to satiate, cloy, with excessive indulgence. **2.** intrans. To indulge (oneself) to excess; to become satiated, experience satiety.

surf-man, n. Man engaged or skilled in management of surf-boat.

surf-riding, n. A form of sport in which one endeavours to balance oneself on an oblong board while being swept along by heavy surf.

surfy, adj. [1. sėrfi; 2. sǎfi]. **surf** & **-y**. Abounding in, resembling, of the nature of, surf.

surge (I.), vb. intrans. [1. sėrj; 2. sǎdž], fr. O. Fr. *surgir*, fr. Lat. *surgere*, 'to raise; to rise', fr. **sur- (I.)** & *-rigere*, fr. *regere*, 'to guide, direct', see **regent, rex**. **1.** (of water, waves &c.) To swell, rise, with violent, tumultuous motion. **2. a** To move to and fro, billow, like waves: *surging crowds*; **b** (fig., of emotion &c.) to rise tumultuously.

surge (II.), n., fr. prec. **1.** Act, process, of surging. **2. a** Mass of heaving, billowing water, tumultuous waves; **b** (poet.) the sea.

surgeon, n. [1. sėrjun; 2. sǎdžən]. M.E. *surgien*, contracted fr. *cirurgien*, fr. O. Fr. *cirurgien*, see **chirurgeon**. **1.** Medical practitioner in that branch of the profession which treats diseases and injuries by operation and manipulation; contrasted with *physician*. **2.** General term for a doctor in the army and navy; also a doctor on a merchant-ship.

surgeon-dentist, n. Dentist holding diploma of Royal College of Surgeons.

surgeon-fish, n. Brightly coloured fish of West Indies &c., with sharp spines at either side of the tail.

Surgeon-General, n. (cap.) Military surgeon holding the rank of a general in the army.

surgery, n. [1. sėrjeri; 2. sǎdžəri]. M.E. *surgerie*, fr. O. Fr. *cirurgie*, fr. L. Lat. *chirurgia*, 'surgery', see **surgeon**. **1.** The art and science of treating diseases and injuries by operation and manipulative means. **2.** Doctor's office or consulting-room and dispensary.

surgical, adj. [1. sėrjikl; 2. sǎdžikl]. See **surgeon** & **-ic** & **-al**. Connected with, pertaining to, characteristic of, surgery or surgeons: *surgical treatment, training, knowledge* &c.; *surgical instruments*, those used in surgical operations.

surgically, adv. Prec. & **-ly**. By means of, according to the methods of, surgery.

suricate, n. [1. súrikāt; 2. sjúərikeit], fr. native name. South African four-toed burrowing mammal allied to the mongoose; the meerkat.

Surinam toad, n. [1. súrinam tŏd; 2. sjúərinæm tòud], fr. Surinam, Dutch Guiana. Large aquatic toad of Brazil and Guiana, the eggs of which develop in the back of the female.

surlily, adv. [1. sėrlili; 2. sǎlili]. **surly** & **-ly**. In a surly manner.

surliness, n. [1. sėrlines; 2. sǎlinis]. See prec. & **-ness**. State or quality of being surly.

surloin. Variant of **sirloin**.

surly, adj. [1. sėrli; 2. sǎli]. Not found before 16th cent.; used by Spenser & Shakespeare. Origin doubtful; derivations fr. *sir-like*, in sense of haughty, & *sour* & *-ly* have been suggested. Sullen, morose, gloomy, gruff and churlish.

surmaster, n. [1. sėrmahster; 2. sǎmāstə]. **sur- (II.)** & **master (I.)**. (rare) The second master in some schools.

surmisable, adj. [1. sėrmízabl; 2. sǎmáizəbl]. **surmise (II.)** & **-able**. Capable of being surmised; conjecturable.

surmise (I.), n. [1. sėrmíz; 2. sǎmáiz], fr. O. Fr. *surmise*, fr. P.P. of *surmettre*, 'to lay to one's charge, accuse', fr. **sur- (II.)**, & *mettre*, 'to put', fr. Lat. *mittere*, 'to send', see **mission**. Conclusion, inference, formed from data which do not amount to absolute proof; a conjecture, a guess.

surmise (II.), vb. intrans. & trans., fr. prec. **1.** intrans. To form a surmise, to conjecture. **2.** trans. To guess, reach by a surmise: *to surmise the truth*.

surmount, vb. trans. [1. sėrmóunt; 2. sǎmáunt], fr. O. Fr. *surmonter*; **sur- (II.)** & **mount (II.)**. **1.** To overcome, get the better of, rise superior to (difficulties, obstacles &c.). **2.** To rise, stand, be placed over the top of, be above: *elaborate carving surmounts the entrance*; (chiefly used in P.P.) *his head was surmounted by a tuft of feathers*.

surmountable, adj. [1. sėrmóuntabl; 2. sǎmáuntəbl]. Prec. & **-able**. Capable of being surmounted, overcome.

surmullet, n. [1. sėrmúlet; 2. sǎmálit], fr. O. Fr. *surmulet*, fr. *sor*, 'reddish-brown', see **sorrel (II.)**, & **mullet (I.)**. European edible fish with two barbels below the mouth; red mullet.

surname, n. & vb. trans. [1. sėrnām; 2. sǎneim]. **sur- (II.)** & **name (I.)**, on anal. of Fr. *surnom*, fr. **sur- (II.)** & Lat. *nōmen*, 'name', see **nominal**. **1.** n. **a** (formerly) A distinctive personal appellation, often a nickname, bestowed upon an individual in addition to his baptismal name; **b** permanent, hereditary name borne by all the members of a family, and usually transmitted through direct male ancestors from father to son. **2.** vb. To give a surname (in sense a) to, call (person) by surname: *they surnamed King Edward VII. 'the Peace-maker'*; *King John was surnamed Lackland*.

surpass, vb. trans. [1. sėrpáhs; 2. sǎpǎs, səpǎs], fr. O. Fr. *surpasser*, 'to excel'; **sur- (II.)** & **pass (I.)**. To rise above, go beyond, excel, in degree, quality, intensity &c.: *the reality surpassed all their expectations*; *he surpassed all his brothers in strength and comeliness*.

surpassing, adj. [1. sėrpáhsing; 2. səpǎsiŋ], fr. Pres. Part. of prec. Exceeding or excelling others, pre-eminent, matchless: *surpassing beauty*.

surpassingly, adv. Prec. & **-ly**. To a surpassing degree.

surplice, n. [1. sẽrplis; 2. sʌ́plis, -əs]. M.E. *surplis*, fr. O. Fr. *surplis, surpliz*, fr. Med. Lat. *superpelliceum*, fr. **super-** & Lat. *pelliceum*, 'tunic of skins'; see **pelisse** & **pellicle.** Loose, white vestment of varying length, with wide sleeves, worn by clergy, and usually by a choir, at divine service.

surpliced, adj. [1. sẽrplist; 2. sʌ́plist]. **surplice** & **-ed.** Wearing a surplice.

surplice-fee, n. Clergyman's fee for marriage, baptism &c.

surplus, n. & adj. [1. sẽrplus; 2. sʌ́pləs], fr. O. Fr. *surplus*, fr. Med. Lat. *superplus*, 'excess'; **super-** & **plus. 1.** n. Amount over and above what is required; quantity or sum left over; excess, residue. **2.** adj. Remaining as residue; forming a redundant amount or supply: *surplus food* &c.

surplusage, n. [1. sẽrplusij; 2. sʌ́pləsidž]. Prec. & **-age.** Surplus, overplus.

surprisal, n. [1. surprízl; 2. səpráizl]. **surprise (II.)** & **-al.** (rare) Act of surprising.

surprise (I.), n. [1. surpríz; 2. səpráiz], fr. O. Fr. *surprise*, fr. P.P. of *surprendre*, 'to surprise'; see **sur- (II.)** & **prize (III.). 1.** Emotion aroused by sudden, unexpected action, circumstance, or event; wonder, astonishment. **2.** That which arouses surprise; unexpected action, circumstance, or event: *his arrival was a great surprise.* **3.** Act of seizing, overcoming, taking (person &c.) unawares; unexpected attack: *to capture a force by surprise.* Phr. *to take one by surprise*, take unawares, surprise.

surprise (II.), vb. trans., fr. prec. **1.** To come upon, attack, capture, or overcome unexpectedly; to take, overcome by surprise: *to surprise the enemy's camp.* **2. a** To cause surprise to, excite surprise in; to astonish: *it takes a good deal to surprise an experienced man of the world; nothing he can do would surprise me;* **b** to shock, startle: *I am surprised at you*, am shocked by your conduct &c. Phr. *I shouldn't be surprised if*, I rather expect that . . . **3.** *Surprise into*, to cause (person) to do something, by startling him, taking him unawares, by making a sudden unexpected challenge &c.: *to surprise a person into a confession.*

surprise (III.), adj., fr. **surprise (I.).** Occurring as a surprise, unexpected; done without previous warning: *a surprise visit* &c.

surprisedly, adv. [1. surprízedli; 2. səpráizidli], fr. P.P. of **surprise (II.)** & **-ly.** In a manner expressing surprise.

surprising, adj. [1. surprízing; 2. səpráiziŋ], fr. Pres. Part. of **surprise (II.).** Causing, exciting, surprise; astonishing.

surprisingly, adv. Prec. & **-ly.** In a surprising manner; to a surprising degree.

surra, n. [1. sōōra; 2. súrə], fr. Marathi *sūra.* A disease of horses, cattle, and camels in India and Burma; a form of pernicious anaemia, caused by a parasitic trypanosome.

surrebut, vb. intrans. [1. sùrebút; 2. sàribát]. **sur- (II.)** & **rebut.** To make a surrebutter.

surrebutter, n. [1. sùrebúter; 2. sàribátə]. **sur- (II.)** & **rebutter.** (law) Plaintiff's reply to defendant's rebutter.

surrejoin, vb. intrans. [1. sùrejóin; 2. sàridžóin]. **sur- (II.)** & **rejoin.** To make a surrejoinder.

surrejoinder, n. [1. sùrejóinder; 2. sàridžóində]. **sur- (II.)** & **rejoinder.** (law) Plaintiff's reply to defendant's rejoinder.

surrender (I.), vb. trans. & intrans. [1. surénder; 2. səréndə], fr. O. Fr. *surrendre*, fr. **sur- (II.)** & *rendre*, 'to give', see **render. A.** trans. **1. a** To give up, yield possession of, relinquish, under pressure or compulsion: *to surrender a fort to the enemy; to surrender one's sword;* **b** to give up voluntarily, relinquish, resign, cease claim to: *to surrender one's freedom, rights, position, a lease* &c.; specif., to give up a claim under an insurance policy, on repayment of proportion of premiums paid, i.e. the *surrender value.* **2.** (reflex.) To give oneself over, abandon oneself, to a specified mood, state of mind: *to surrender oneself to despair.* **B.** intrans. To yield oneself, or something in one's possession or keeping, to superior force &c.; to submit, cease to resist: *the fort, ship &c. surrendered; to surrender to the enemy.*

surrender (II.), n., fr. prec. Act of surrendering: *there must be no surrender.*

surreptitious, adj. [1. sùreptíshus; 2. sàreptíʃəs], fr. Lat. *surrepticius*, 'secret, surreptitious', fr. *surreptum*, P.P. type of *surripere*, 'to creep, steal, along', fr. **sur- (I.)** & *rapere*, 'to seize, snatch', see **rapid (I.).** Done, formed, in a secret, underhand manner, with intent to avoid observation; clandestine, stealthy, furtive.

surreptitiously, adv. Prec. & **-ly.** In a surreptitious manner.

surrogate, n. [1. súrogit, -gāt; 2. sárəgit, -geit], fr. Lat. *surrogāt-(um)*, P.P. type of *surrogāre*, 'to elect in another's place, substitute', fr. **sur- (I.)** & *rogāre*, 'to ask, demand', see **rogation.** Substitute, deputy; specif., an ecclesiastical officer acting as deputy for the bishop, or his chancellor, in granting marriage licences.

surrogateship, n. [1. súrogātship; 2. sárəgeitʃip]. Prec. & **-ship.** Office, rank, period of tenure of office, of surrogate.

surround (I.), vb. trans. [1. suróund; 2. səráund], fr. obs. *surround*, 'to overflow', fr. O. Fr. *surrunder*, fr. **sur- (II.)** & Lat. *undāre*, 'to rise in waves, surge, swell', fr. *unda*, 'wave'; see **undulate (I.)**; cp. **abound**; the present meaning is influenced by **round (I.). 1. a** To extend round about on all or nearly all sides; to circumscribe, enclose, encircle, encompass: *a wall surrounds the garden; hills surround the plain; a crowd surrounded him;* **b** specif. (mil.) to invest, beset (fortress, body of troops &c.); **c** to stand round, be present in numbers at: *all his family surrounded his death-bed.* **2.** To cause to be surrounded; to fence round, place a boundary round: *to surround a park with a wall.* **3.** (fig.) **a** To bring into contact with, subject to influence of, encompass; to lap in: *to surround a person with every comfort, with luxury, affection* &c.; **b** (i.) to beset, press in upon, be ready to assail: *many dangers surround us;* (ii.) to be close at hand, be readily available: *surrounded with, by, hosts of friends* &c.

surround (II.) n., fr. prec. Floor-covering between carpet and walls.

surrounding, adj. [1. suróunding; 2. səráundiŋ], fr. Pres. Part. of prec. Lying adjacent to, extending in proximity on all sides: *surrounding country* &c.

surroundings, n. pl. [1. suróundingz; 2. səráundiŋz]. **surround** & **-ing. 1.** Things, objects, persons, area, lying, existing, in immediate proximity or relation; surrounding country &c.: *a fine house in ugly surroundings; pleasant social surroundings.* **2. a** External circumstances and conditions of existence; material environment: *unhealthy surroundings; surroundings favourable to work;* **b** moral and intellectual environment, surrounding influences: *the stimulating surroundings of college life; to live amid religious surroundings.*

surtax, n. & vb. trans. [1. sẽrtàks; 2. sʌ́tæ̀ks]. **sur- (II.)** & **tax (I.). 1.** n. A term used, since 1929–30, for the tax previously called 'super-tax'; unlike the latter, it is assessed not separately, but for the same year and on the same return as the ordinary income-tax. **2.** vb. To impose an extra tax on.

surtout, n. [1. sẽrtōō; 2. sʌ̄tú], fr. Fr. *surtout*, 'long coat', lit. 'an overall', fr. **sur- (II.)** & *tout*, 'all', fr. Lat. *tōtus*, 'all', see **total.** (archaic or obs.) Man's overcoat; an old-fashioned style of frock-coat.

surveillance, n. [1. sẽrvályens; 2. sʌ̄véiljəns], fr. Fr. *surveillance*, fr. *surveiller*, 'to watch over', fr. **sur- (II.)** & *veillant*, Pres. Part. of *veiller*, 'to watch', fr. Lat. *vigilāre*, 'to be watchful', see **vigilant**, & **-ce.** Constant supervision, watch, observation, kept over person's movements: *under surveillance.*

survey (I.), vb. trans. [1. servā́; 2. səvéi], fr. A.-Fr. *surveier*, fr. O. Fr. *surveeir*, 'to look over', fr. **sur- (II.)** & *veeir*, 'to see', fr. Lat. *vidēre*, 'to see', see **vision (I.)**, & words there referred to. **1.** To look over, view full extent of, take comprehensive view of: *to survey the scene, a landscape* &c. **2.** To take a general view of, consider at large, review (circumstances, facts &c.): *to survey the situation.* **3.** specif. **a** To inspect carefully, measure by geometrical and trigonometrical methods (a tract of country, coast, a piece of land &c.), and record the exact extent, shape, contours, natural features &c.; **b** to inspect (house, piece of property) in order to ascertain its condition and to estimate its value.

survey (II.), n. [1. sẽrvā; 2. sʌ́vei], fr. prec. **1.** General view, comprehensive examination, of a scene, group of objects &c.: *to make a rapid survey of a house and grounds.* **2.** General review, consideration, of facts, circumstances, situation &c.: *a survey of our present position.* **3.** Specif. **a** (i.) act, process, of surveying a country, tract of land &c. from the point of view of its size and physical features; (ii.) department of government &c. carrying out a series of surveying operations; (iii.) record of result of such survey; **b** (i.) inspection, examination, of condition, extent &c. of buildings, esp. for purposes of valuation; (ii.) record of result of such examination.

surveying, n. [1. servā́ing; 2. sʌ̄-, səvéiiŋ]. **survey (I.)** & **-ing.** Science or practice of determining extent, physical features &c. of a part of the earth's surface by means of measurements and mathematical calculations.

surveyor, n. [1. servā́er; 2. sʌ̄-, səvéiə]. **survey (I.)** & **-or. a** Person employed in land-surveying; specif. **b** official inspector or superintendent.

surveyorship, n. [1. servā́ership; 2. sʌ̄-, səvéiəʃip]. Prec. & **-ship.** Position, office, of a surveyor.

survival, n. [1. servívl; 2. sʌ̄-, səváivl]. **survive** & **-al. 1.** Act of surviving; state of being alive after specific event or after period of existence of another person, animal &c. Phr. *survival of the fittest*, (biol.) theory that as a result of natural selection only those organisms which can adapt themselves to their environment can survive, the others being eliminated. **2.** That which survives, something continuing in existence after specific event or period: *survivals of mediaeval customs.*

survive, vb. trans. & intrans. [1. servív; 2. sʌ̄-, səváiv], fr. Fr. *survivre*, fr. Lat. *supervīvere*, 'to outlive', fr. **super-** & *vīvere*, 'to live', see **vital. A.** trans. **1.** To live longer than, outlive; live, exist, beyond term of existence of: *he survived his wife for many years; his mental faculties survived his physical powers.* **2.** To continue to live or exist after, and in spite of, a specified event or experience: *to survive a shipwreck* &c. **B.** intrans. To continue to exist, be still in existence or operation: *not one of the family survives; the custom still survives.*

survivor, n. [1. servíver; 2. sʌ̄-, səváivə]. **survive** & **-or.** One who survives; **a** one who outlives another or others; **b** one who survives an event: *the survivors of the earthquake.*

survivorship, n. [1. servívership; 2. sʌ̄-, səváivəʃip]. Prec. & **-ship. 1.** State of being a survivor. **2.** (law) Right of surviving tenant of jointly held property to claim entire estate.

sus-, pref. Form of **sub-**, perh. fr. the earlier form *subs*, w. loss of *-b-*, used in Lat. compounds where the second element begins w. *c-*, *p-*, *t-*.

susceptibility, n. [1. susèptibíliti; 2. səsèptibíliti]. See **susceptible** & **-ity. 1.** State or quality of being susceptible. **2.** (pl.) *Susceptibilities*, responsiveness to, capacity for reacting to, emotional stimulus; sensibility.

susceptible, adj. [1. suséptibl; 2. səséptibl], fr. Lat. *suscept-(um)*, P.P. type of *suscipere*, 'to take up, receive, hold up', fr. sus- & capere, 'to take', see **captive**, & -ible. **1. a** Easily accessible, keenly responsive to, emotional appeal; readily influenced by feelings and emotions; highly sensitive: *he is a susceptible fellow where the ladies are concerned*; *a too susceptible heart is often troublesome*; **b** *susceptible to*, capable of feeling, readily influenced by, accessible to: *susceptible to flattery, to kind treatment*. **2.** (pred. only, followed by *of*) Patient of, admitting, allowing: *to be susceptible of proof, of several interpretations*.

susceptibly, adv. Prec. & -ly. In a susceptible manner.

susceptive, adj. [1. suséptiv; 2. saséptiv], Lat. *susceptum*, P.P. type of *suscipere*, 'to receive', see **susceptible**, & -ive. Connected with, pertaining to, the reception of emotional impressions or influences.

susceptiveness, n. Prec. & -ness. Quality of being susceptive.

susceptivity, n. [1. sùseptíviti; 2. sàseptíviti]. See prec. & -ity. Quality of being susceptive.

susi, n. [1. sŏōsi; 2. sǔsi]. Hind. E. Indian striped fabric of cotton and silk.

suslik, n. [1. sŏŏslik; 2. súslik]. Russ. Greyish-brown ground squirrel of Northern Europe and Asia.

suspect (I.), adj. & n. [1. súspekt; 2. sáspekt], fr. Fr., fr. Lat. *suspectum*, P.P. type of *suspicere*, 'to look upwards, to look secretly at; to mistrust, suspect', fr. **sub-** & *specere*, 'to look', see **species**. **1.** adj. Open to suspicion; liable to be mistrusted, of doubtful character. **2.** n. Suspected person.

suspect (II.), vb. trans. & intrans. [1. suspékt; 2. səspékt]. Lat. *suspectāre*, 'to look at secretly', fr. *mistrust*, freq. of *suspicere*, see prec. **A.** trans. **1.** To have a vague idea or inkling of the existence of; to feel persuaded of existence of, or of the future occurrence of: *I suspected the presence of fire from the odour*; *from the symptoms one might suspect measles*; *I strongly suspect an underhand plot*. **2.** To have misgivings regarding, to doubt, mistrust, be inclined to disbelieve in: *I strongly suspect the truth of the story, the genuineness of his professions, the authenticity of the document*. **3.** To believe guilty, to attribute guilt to; to consider the guilt of (a person) probable: *to suspect a person of murder, of lying*; *to suspect an innocent man*; *suspect* in such connexion may involve various degrees of moral certainty short of absolute conviction based upon proof. **4.** To suppose, presume, expect; to think it probable, to feel persuaded (that): *I suspect that we shall have rain before night*; *I suspect he was only too glad not to be asked to sing*; also absol. *you are pretty tired after your journey, I suspect*. **B.** intrans. To entertain suspicions, to be suspicious.

suspectable, adj. [1. suspéktabl; 2. səspéktəbl]. Prec. & -able. Capable of being suspected; liable to suspicion.

suspend, vb. trans. [1. suspénd; 2. saspénd], fr. Lat. *suspendere*, 'to hang up; to check, interrupt, suspend', fr. **sus-** & *pendere*, 'to hang', see **pendant**. **1.** To hang up, cause to hang from above: *to suspend a birdcage from the ceiling*. **2.** To postpone, defer, arrest, delay (a physical or mental action): *to suspend judgement, proceedings, business &c.* Phrs. *to suspend payment* (of a bank &c.), fail to meet financial obligations; *to suspend one's judgement*, delay coming to a decision pending further information and consideration. **3.** (i.) To debar, prohibit, temporarily, from exercise of privileges or functions; (ii.) remove from position: *to suspend a clergyman for misconduct*; *to suspend a clergyman from preaching*.

suspended, adj. [1. suspénded; 2. səspéndid], fr. P.P. of prec. **1.** Held in fixed position within the atmosphere, or in a fluid, without either rising or sinking: *dust suspended in the air*; *salt suspended in water*. **2.** Temporarily inactive, in state of abeyance: *suspended animation*, unconsciousness.

suspender, n. [1. suspénder; 2. səspéndə]. Prec. & -er. That which suspends; specif. a device for holding a sock or stocking in position on the leg; **b** (Am. usage, pl.) braces.

suspense, n. [1. suspéns; 2. səspéns], fr. Fr., fr. P.P. of *suspendre*, 'to hang', fr. Lat. *suspendere*, 'to hang', see **suspend**. **1.** State of mental uncertainty and anxiety as to the result of some action or event; anxious expectation: *to keep a person in suspense*; *to be unable to endure the suspense*. **2.** (law) Temporary cessation of a right. **3.** (bookkeeping) *suspense account*, account in which items are entered temporarily until their proper place is settled.

suspensibility, n. [1. suspènsibíliti; 2. səspènsibíliti]. See next word & -ity. State or quality of being suspensible.

suspensible, adj. [1. suspénsibl; 2. səspénsibl], fr. Lat. *suspens-(um)*, P.P. type of *suspendere*, 'to hang', see **suspense**, & -ible. Capable of being suspended.

suspension, n. [1. suspénshun; 2. səspénʃən]. suspense & -ion. Act of suspending; state of being suspended (in various senses of vb.).

suspension-bridge, n. Bridge suspended from chains or cables which are supported by towers at either end, or by a series of piers.

suspensio per collum, n. [1. suspénsiō pèr kólum; 2. səspénsiou pā kóləm]. Lat., 'hanging by the neck'. (law) Hanging as capital punishment; usually abbr. *sus. per coll.*

suspensive, adj. [1. suspénsiv; 2. səspénsiv], fr. Lat. *suspensum*, P.P. type of *suspendere*, 'to hang', see **suspend**, & -ive. **a** Tending, having the power, to suspend temporarily; **b** pertaining to, resulting from, characterized by, mental suspense.

suspensively, adv. Prec. & -ly. In a suspensive manner.

suspensory, adj. [1. suspénsuri; 2. səspénsəri], fr. Lat. *suspensum*, P.P. type of *suspendere*, 'to hang', see **suspend**, & -ory. **1.** Of, pertaining to, forming a means of, suspension: *suspensory bandage*. **2.** Tending to delay, suspend, arrest, operation.

suspicion, n. [1. suspíshun; 2. səspíʃən]. fr. O. Fr., fr. Lat. *suspiciōn-(em)*, 'mistrust, suspicion', earlier *suspēcio-, fr. **sub-** & stem *spĕc-, seen in Lat. *specere*, 'to see', see **species**; cp. **suspect** (I.). **1.** Feeling of vague belief in, inkling, glimmering, of, the existence or occurrence of something: *I had a suspicion of the truth though I was not certain*; *the disguise was so good that I had no suspicions of his real identity*. **2.** Act of suspecting; **a** feeling of doubt, mistrust; impression that something is probably not true, not genuine &c.: *I have grave suspicions of the man's integrity*; **b** belief in a person's guilt, tendency to suspect a person. **3.** State of being suspected: *to be under suspicion*, *above suspicion*. **4.** Slight trace, touch, hint, flavour, small portion: *just a suspicion of brandy in the pudding*; *a suspicion of arrogance in his manner*.

suspicionless, adj. [1. suspíshunles; 2. səspíʃənlis]. Prec. & -less. Without suspicion; unsuspecting.

suspicious, adj. [1. suspíshus; 2. səspíʃəs], fr. Lat. *suspiciōsus*, 'feeling or exciting suspicion', fr. *suspicio*, 'mistrust', see **suspicion**, & -ous. **1.** Inclined to, feeling, expressing, suspicion: *a suspicious nature* &c. **2.** Arousing, tending to excite, suspicion: *a suspicious character*; *suspicious actions*; *under suspicious circumstances*.

suspiciously, adv. Prec. & -ly. In a suspicious manner; a so as to express suspicion: *to glance suspiciously at a person*; **b** so as to excite suspicion: *to behave suspiciously*.

suspiciousness, n. See prec. & -ness. State or quality of being suspicious.

suspiration, n. [1. sùspiráshun; 2. sàspiréiʃən], fr. Lat. *suspirātiōn-(em)*, 'a sighing'; next word & -ation. Act or process of suspiring; a sigh.

suspire, vb. intrans. [1. suspír; 2. səspáiə], fr. O. Fr. *souspirer*, fr. Lat. *suspīrāre*, 'to draw a deep breath, to sigh', fr. **sub-** & *spīrāre*, 'to breathe', see **spirant**. (poet.) To draw a deep breath; to sigh.

sustain, vb. trans. [1. sustán; 2. səstéin]. M.E. *susteinen*, fr. O. Fr. *sustein-*, Pres. stem. of *sustener*, 'to hold up', fr. Lat. *sustinēre*, 'to hold up; to check, restrain; to uphold, maintain; to undergo, endure', fr. **sus-** & *tenēre*, 'to hold', see **tenable**. **1.** To support, carry weight of, hold up: *pillars sustain the arch*. **2. a** To undergo, endure, suffer (physical or mental experience): *to sustain injuries*, *a shock* &c.; specif. **b** to be able to endure without giving way or collapsing; to bear: *to be unable to sustain a shock*. **3.** To enable to endure, give physical, moral, or mental strength or support to: *food sufficient to sustain life*; *hope alone sustained him*. **4.** To uphold, support, approve as right or just: *the court sustained his claim*. **5.** To support, confirm, corroborate, help to prove: *the recently discovered facts sustain the contention*. **6. a** To keep up, maintain: *to sustain one's rôle*; *sustained efforts*; **b** to prolong, keep going: *to sustain a note*.

sustainable, adj. [1. sustánabl; 2. səstéinəbl]. Prec. & -able. Capable of being sustained.

sustainment, n. [1. sustánment; 2. səstéinmənt]. sustain & -ment. Act of sustaining; state of being sustained.

sustenance, n. [1. sústenans; 2. sástinəns], fr. O. Fr., fr. L. Lat. *sustinentia*, 'endurance', fr. *sustinent-(em)*, Pres. Part. of *sustinēre*, 'to hold up; to uphold, maintain; to endure', see **sustain**, & -ce, w. spelling altered on anal. of words in -ance, e.g. *governance* &c. **1.** (rare) Act of sustaining by nourishment, maintenance of strength. **2.** That which sustains or supports life or strength; nourishment.

sustentation, n. [1. sùstentáshun; 2. sàstintéiʃən], fr. O. Fr., fr. Lat. *sustentātiōnem*, 'maintenance', fr. *sustent-(um)*, P.P. of *sustinēre*, 'to uphold, support', see **sustain**, & -ation. Act or process of sustaining life; subsistence; *sustentation fund*, fund for supplying sustenance, or more generally for supporting, maintaining, an institution and the group of persons connected with it.

susurrant, adj. [1. sùsúrant; 2. sjusárənt], fr. Lat. *susurrant-(em)*, Pres. Part. of *susurrāre*, 'to buzz', see next word. Whispering, murmurous.

susurration, n. [1. sùsuráshun; 2. sjùsəréiʃən], fr. Lat. *susurrāt-(um)*, P.P. type of *susurrāre*, 'to buzz, murmur, whisper', fr. *susurrus*, 'hum, whisper'; a reduplicated base cogn. w. Scrt. *svárati*, 'sounds, resounds'; O. Slav. *svirati*, 'to pipe'; Mod. Germ. *schwirren*, 'to buzz'; see also **swarm** (I.). Soft murmur, whisper, or rustle.

susurrus, adj. [1. sùsúrus; 2. sjusárəs], fr. Lat. *susurrus*, 'whispering', fr. *susurrus*, 'a whisper', see prec., & -ous. Producing a soft murmuring or rustling sound.

sutler, n. [1. sútler; 2. sátlə], fr. Du. *zoetelaar*, 'sutler; camp cook; scullion'; cp. Mod. Germ. *sudeln*, 'to daub, sully'; according to Kluge, orig. 'to cook badly', cogn. w. **seethe**, **suds**. Camp-follower who sells goods, esp. food, to troops.

Sutra, n. [1. sŏōtra; 2. sŭtrə], fr. Scrt.; cp. Scrt. *sūtram*, 'thread'; cogn. w. Lat. *suere*, 'to sew'; *sūtor*, 'cobbler'; *sūtūra*, 'seam', see **suture** (I.). Series of aphoristic formulae, collection of precepts, in Sanscrit.

suttee, sati, n. [1. suté, súté; 2. satí, sátí], fr. Scrt. *satī*, 'faithful wife'. **1.** Custom of self-immolation formerly practised by high-caste Hindu widows on their husbands' funeral pyre. **2.** Hindu widow who sacrifices herself in this way.

sutteeism, n. [1. sutéizm; 2. satíizəm]. Prec. & -ism. Practice of suttee.

sutural, adj. [1. súchural; 2. sjútʃərəl] suture (I.) & -al. Of, pertaining to, situated near, a suture.

suturally, adv. Prec. & -ly. In the manner of a suture.

suturation, n. [1. sŭchurắshun; 2. sjūtʃəréiʃən]. **suture** (I.) & -ation. Joining by means of, formation of, a suture.

suture (I.), n. [1. sŭchur; 2. sjūtʃə], fr. Lat. *sūtūra*, 'a sewing together, seam', fr. *sūt-(um)*, P.P. type of *suere*, 'to sew', cogn. w. Scrt. *syūtắš*, 'stitched'; Gk. *(kas)súein*, 'to patch'; Goth. *siujan*; O.E. *sēowan*, 'to sew', see **sew**; O.N. *saumr*, O.E. *sēam*, 'seam', see **seam** (I.); & -**ure**. 1. (anat.) Interlocking joint of two bones along their edges; esp. articulation of bones of skull. 2. (bot., zool.) Line of junction between two adjacent parts. 3. **a** Act or process of joining edges of incised wound &c. by stitching; **b** stitch of thread, wire &c., used in surgical suture.

suture (II.), vb. trans., fr. prec. To join with a suture.

sutured, adj. [1. sŭchurd; 2. sjūtʃəd]. **suture** (I.) & -ed. Having, united by, a suture.

suzerain, n. [1. sŭzerăn; 2. s(j)ūzərein), fr. O. Fr. *suzerain*, formed on the anal. of *suverain*, see **sovereign** (I.), fr. *sus-*, 'over', fr. Lat. *su(r)sum*, 'from below, upwards, over, above', fr. *subs-*, see **sub-**, & *-vorsum*, 'turned'; cp. Lat. *vertere*, 'to turn', see **version, vertex, vortex**. 1. One who has supreme power, dominant authority, esp. in feudal system. 2. State exercising general, nominal, or limited control over another.

suzerainty, n. [1. sŭzerănti; 2. s(j)ūzəreinti]. Prec. & -**ty**. Rank, authority, of, or exercised by, a suzerain.

svelte, adj. [1. svelt; 2. svelt]. Fr. *svelte*, 'slim, slender', fr. *ex-* & L. Lat. *vellit-(um)*, used as P.P. of *vellere*, 'to pull, pluck, stretch', see **vellicate**. (of a woman's figure) Slender and graceful, lissom, willowy.

swab (I.), vb. trans. [1. swob; 2. swɔb], fr. **swabber**. 1. To clean, wash out, with a swab: *to swab (down) the decks*. 2. *To swab up*, to mop up, take up (liquid) with a swab.

swab (II.), n., fr. prec. 1. Mop or pad of absorbent substance for cleaning. 2. (naut.) Naval officer's epaulet. 3. (naut. slang) Awkward, clumsy, unskilful fellow.

swabber, n. [1. swóber; 2. swɔ́bə], fr. Du. *zwabber*, 'one who does dirty work'. 1. One who uses a swab. 2. Awkward, clumsy fellow.

Swabian, Suabian, adj. & n. [1. swábian; 2. swéibiən], fr. Swabia, Germ. *Schwaben*, cp. Lat. *Suevi*, & -**an**. 1. adj. Of, pertaining to, Swabia. 2. n. **a** Inhabitant of Swabia; **b** Swabian dialect.

swaddle, vb. trans. [1. swódl; 2. swɔ́dl]. M.E. *swathlen*, 'to swaddle, bind', fr. O.E. *swæðel*, 'bandage', fr. *swaðu*, 'band, track'. Cp. **swath**. To wrap up in long bandages or garments, bind, swathe, bundle up.

swaddling-bands, -clothes, n. [1. swódling băndz, klódhz; 2. swɔ́dliŋ băndz, klóuðz]. Long strip of material formerly used for wrapping round very young infants. Phr. (fig.) *still in, hardly, just, out of swaddling clothes*, very young and inexperienced; still under, just escaping from, strict parental supervision and control.

swadeshi, n. [1. swadáshi; 2. swadéiʃi]. Bengali, 'native country'. Indian nationalists' boycott of foreign, esp. British, goods, for the purpose of furthering their political aims.

swag (I.), n. [1. swag; 2. swæg], fr. obs. or provinc. *swag*, 'to sway'; prob. of Scand. origin; cp. Norw. *svaga*, 'to sway'; cogn. w. **sway** (I.). (slang) Plunder, booty, anything acquired by robbery or fraud.

swag (II.), n. See prec. A hanging wreath or festoon as an architectural or other ornament.

swage, n. & vb. trans. [1. swāj; 2. sweidʒ]. Origin uncertain. 1. n. Kind of die or tool for shaping wrought-iron &c. 2. vb. To shape (metal) with a swage.

swage-block, n. Kind of anvil with hollows or perforations for shaping wrought-iron &c.

swagger (I.), vb. intrans. & trans. [1. swáger; 2. swǽgə], fr. obs. *swag*, 'to sway', see **swag** (I.), & -**er**. A. intrans. 1. To walk, bear oneself, with a jaunty, self-satisfied air, strut about with an air of insolent superiority. 2. **a** To show off, give oneself airs; to affect superiority in bearing and speech; **b** *swagger about (one's) exploits, possessions* &c., to boast of. B. trans. (rare) To influence, affect, bluff, by boastful talk or bluster.

swagger (II.), n., fr. prec. 1. Swaggering gait. 2. Boastful, self-important manner, talk &c.

swagger (III.), adj., fr. prec. Smart, swell, ultra-fashionable or splendid: *swagger clothes*.

swagger-cane, n. Cane carried by soldier in uniform when not on parade.

swaggering, adj. [1. swágering; 2. swǽgəriŋ], fr. Pres. Part. of **swagger** (I.). Inclined to swagger, boastful.

swaggeringly, adv. Prec. & -**ly**. With (a) swagger.

Swahili, n. [1. swahhéli; 2. swahíli]. Arab., 'of the coast'. **a** Bantu inhabitants of Zanzibar and the neighbouring coasts; **b** dialect of these tribes.

swain, n. [1. swān; 2. swein]. M.E. *swein*, fr. O.N. *sveinn*, 'young man', cp. O.E. *swān*, 'herdsman', also as second element in **boatswain** & **coxswain**, etymol. doubtful. **a** (chiefly poet.) Country lad, young yokel; **b** rustic lover; hence, **c** lover, admirer: *a lady surrounded by adoring swains*.

swallet, n. [1. swólet; 2. swɔ́lit]. Prob. fr. next word. (provinc.) Underground rock-fissure through which a stream flows.

swallow (I.), vb. trans. & intrans. [1. swólō; 2. swɔ́lou]. M.E. *swolwen, swolgen, swelwen*, fr. O.E. *swelgan*, 'to swallow, engulf'; cp. O.H.G. *swelgan*; O.N. *svelga*, 'to swallow'; apparently has no cognates outside Gmc. A. trans. 1. To receive (food, drink &c.) into the mouth, and pass into the stomach, through the gullet, by the action of the muscles of the throat. Phrs. *to swallow one's words*, withdraw what one has said, recant; *to swallow the bait*, (fig.) to fall into the trap, to allow oneself to be deceived by a specious hope of advantage. 2. *Swallow up*, of the sea, mist, the earth (in an earthquake), to cover over, overwhelm, engulf; to conceal from sight, envelop, enshroud. 3. *Swallow up*, to use up, exhaust, absorb: *the expenses swallowed up most of the profits*. 4. To tolerate, put up with, receive patiently: *to swallow an insult*. 5. To believe, receive with credulity, accept as true: *he is so credulous that he swallows everything that is told him; such stories are rather hard to swallow*. B. intrans. To carry out the muscular action of swallowing.

swallow (II.), n., fr. prec. 1. Act of swallowing. 2. Amount swallowed at one time; mouthful: *to take a swallow of water*. 3. **a** Food passage in throat; gullet; **b** capacity of this in respect of size to allow a mouthful to pass: *to have a small swallow*. 4. Swallow-hole.

swallow (III.), n. O.E. *swalwe*; M.E. *swaluwe, swolwe*; cp. O.H.G. *swalawa*; M.Du. *swaluwe*; O.N. *svala*, 'swallow'; perh. fr. **swalgwō-*, in wh. case cogn. w. Gk. *alkuón*, 'kingfisher', for **swalkwōn*, see **halcyon**. Insectivorous, migratory bird, genus *Hirundo*, with long, pointed wings, forked tail, and short, broad beak.

swallowable, adj. [1. swólōabl; 2. swɔ́louəbl]. **swallow** (I.) & -**able**. Capable of being swallowed.

swallow-fish, n. Kind of gurnard, with much elongated pectoral fins.

swallow-hawk, n. Swallow-tailed hawk.

swallow-hole, n. Funnel-shaped, water-worn hole in limestone rock; rock-fissure through which stream flows underground.

swallow-plover, n. Pratincole.

swallow-shrike, n. Swallow-tailed bird of Australia and E. Indies.

swallow-tail, n. 1. Object, projection &c., with deep fork as in swallow's tail; specif. **a** *swallow-tails*, swallow-tailed coat; **b** small pennant with forked end. 2. Kind of humming bird. 3. Kind of butterfly with long projection from each lower wing.

swallow-tailed, adj. Prec. & -**ed**. Having a forked, pointed tail like that of a swallow; *swallow-tailed coat*, evening dress coat.

swallow-wort, n. 1. Herb of milkweed family. 2. Celandine.

swam, vb. [1. swam; 2. swæm]. O.E. *swam*, Pret. of **swim**.

Swami, n. [1. swáhmē; 2. swámī]. Hind. Title given to, form of address to, Brahmin.

swamp (I.), n. [1. swomp; 2. swɔmp], cp. Du. *zwamp*; Mod. Engl. *sump*; Mod. Germ. *sumpf*, 'pond'; O.N. *svoppr*, 'sponge'; cp. also Goth. *swamm*; O.H.G. *swamp*, 'sponge'; Gk. *somphós*, 'spongy, porous'. Level tract of land saturated with moisture; marsh, bog.

swamp (II.), vb. trans., fr. prec. 1. To fill, overwhelm, cover, with water: *a wave swamped the boat*. 2. (chiefly in P.P.) To overwhelm, inundate; bestow upon to excess: *to be swamped with invitations*.

swampy, adj. [1. swómpi; 2. swɔ́mpi]. **swamp** (I.) & -**y**. Resembling, of the nature of, a swamp; boggy, marshy.

swan, n. [1. swon; 2. swɔn]. O.E., M.E. *swan*, cp. Mod. Germ. *schwan*; O.S. *swan*; Du. *zwaan*; cogn. w. Scrt. *svánati*, 'it sounds'; *svanás*, 'tone'; Lat. *sonāre*, 'to sound'; *sonus*, 'sound'; see **sonant**; cp. also O.E. *swinsian*, 'to sing'. 1. Large, web-footed, long-necked bird, genus *Cygnus*, usually white in Northern Hemisphere; *black swan*, Australian black genus; according to an ancient tradition the swan is supposed to sing very melodiously just before its death. Phr. *the swan of Avon*, Shakespeare. 2. The constellation Cygnus.

swan-flower, n. Variety of tropical American orchid.

swan-goose, n. Chinese goose.

swan-herd, n. Official in charge of swan-marks of royal swans.

swank, vb. intrans. & n. [1. swangk; 2. swæŋk]. Etymol. unknown. (slang) 1. vb. To swagger, to show off; to behave or speak in a manner adopted to show one's superiority and importance. 2. n. Behaviour, mode of speech, of one who swanks; swagger, side.

swan-like, adj. **swan** & -**like**. Resembling a swan, specif., in whiteness, grace of form, neck &c.

swan-maiden, n. (in folk-tales) Maiden capable of becoming a swan by assuming a magic robe of feathers.

swan-mark, n. Mark of ownership, usually on swan's upper mandible.

swan-neck, n. Curved end of pipe &c. resembling in outline the curve of a swan's neck.

swannery, n. [1. swóneri; 2. swɔ́nəri]. **swan** & -**ery**. Place where swans are kept or bred.

swan's-down, n. 1. Down of swan, esp. as trimming for dress &c. 2. Fine, thick, woollen cloth.

swan-shot, n. Large size of shot.

swan-skin, n. Soft, fine flannel.

swan-song, n. 1. Fabled song of dying swan. 2. Last work, pronouncement, or utterances, esp. of a poet or orator, before his death or retirement from productiveness or activity.

swan-upping, n. [1. swón ùping; 2. swɔ́n ʌ̀piŋ]. Annual marking of swans in royal herd by a notch cut in the skin of the upper mandible.

swap. See **swop**.

Swaraj, n. [1. swaráhj; 2. swarádʒ], fr. Scrt. *svaraj*, 'self-ruling', fr. *svá-*, 'own', cogn. w. Lat. *suus*, 'one's own', see **sui**, & **raj**. Self-government for India, as aim of Indian Nationalists.

sward, n. [1. sword; 2. swɔd]. O.E. *sweard*, 'skin, rind'; M.E. *sward*; cp. O. Fris. *swarde*. M.H.G. *swarte*; O.N. *svǫrðr*, 'skin, scalp'; Du. *zwoord*, 'rind of bacon'. Grass-covered surface of ground, expanse of turf.

swarded, adj. [1. swórded; 2. swɔ́did]. Prec. & -**ed**. Covered with sward.

sware, vb. [1. swār; 2. swεə]. (archaic) Pret. of swear.

swarm (I.), n. [1. sworm; 2. swōm]. O.E. *swearm*; M.E. *swarm*; cp. M.H.G. *swarm*; O.N. *svarmr*, 'swarm, tumult'; Mod. Germ. *schwarm*, 'swarm of bees'; prob. cogn. w. Scrt. *svárati*, 'sounds, rings'; Lat. *susurrus*, 'hum, buzz', see **susurration**; O. Slav. *svirati*, 'to whistle'. **1. a** Large number or mass of insects, esp. with continuous, irregular movement within the group; specif. **b** cluster of bees, including a queen, leaving the parent hive to seek a new home. **2. a** Large body, throng, of moving persons, animals &c. ; large irregular cluster : *a swarm of sightseers*; *a swarm of children*; **b** large group, multitude, of inanimate objects : *a swarm of letters*.

swarm (II.), vb. intrans., fr. prec. **1. a** To come, cluster, throng, together in great numbers, as in a swarm; to crowd in an irregular mass : *a crowd of people swarmed to the spot, all over the ground*; *children came swarming round*; **b** (specif. of bees) to cluster together round queen in preparation for leaving parent hive. **2. a** To be present, frequent a place, exist, in swarms, or large numbers; to abound : *brigands simply swarm in the mountains*; **b** *swarm with*, to abound in, be much frequented by, thronged : *the place is swarming with strangers*; *a garden swarming with pests*.

swarm (III.), vb. trans. & intrans. Etymol. unknown. **a** trans. To climb by clasping with hands and legs : *to swarm a rope, a pole*; also *swarm up*; **b** intrans., to perform the act of swarming.

swarm-cell, n. Spore having power of independent motion; zoospore.

swarm-spore, n. Zoospore.

swart, adj. [1. swort; 2. swōt]. O.E. *sweart*; M.E. *swart*, 'dark'; cp. O.H.G. *swarz*; Goth. *swarts*; O.N. *svartr*; Du. *zwart*, 'dark'; cp. also O.N. *sorta*, 'dark colour'; prob. cogn. w. Lat. *sordēre*, 'to be soiled', see **sordid**; *surdus*, 'dark; dull; deaf', see **surd** (I.). Dark in colour, swarthy.

swarthily, adv. [1. swórdhili; 2. swɔ́ðili]. **swarthy** & **-ly**. In a swarthy manner.

swarthiness, n. [1. swórdhines; 2. swɔ́ðinis]. Next word & **-ness**. State or quality of being swarthy.

swarthy, adj. [1. swórdhi; 2. swɔ́ði], fr. obs. *swarth*, variant of **swart**, & **-y**. Dark-skinned, of brown, black, or sunburnt complexion.

swash (I.), vb. trans. & intrans. [1. swosh; 2. swɔʃ]. Imitative. (of liquid) **a** trans. To dash, splash, against; **b** intrans., to make a splash in, or as in, striking solid object, dash, wash.

swash (II.), n., fr. prec. Noise of dashing or splashing water.

swashbuckler, n. [1. swóshbùkler; 2. swɔ́ʃ-bàklə]. See next word. A bold, dashing, adventurous, rather unscrupulous fighting man.

swashing, adj. [1. swóshing; 2. swɔ́ʃiŋ], fr. **swash** (I.), in obs. or archaic sense, 'to strike violently'. (of blow) Violent, crushing.

swash-plate, n. Revolving disk set at an oblique angle to its shaft, used for communicating an up and down motion to a rod parallel to its shaft.

swastika, n. [1. swástika; 2. swǽstikə]. Scrt., lit. 'fortunate', fr. *svastiš*, 'welfare', fr. *su-*, 'well', & *asti*, 'being', cogn. w. Gk. *esti*, Lat. *est*, 'is' &c. ; see **esse**. Very primitive and widespread symbol consisting of cross with arms of equal length, each arm having a prolongation at right angles; said to have been primitively a sun-symbol, but it is also used in Christian decoration; also called a fylfot.

swat, vb. trans. [1. swot; 2. swɔt]. Imitative. (colloq.) To crush, squash (a wasp, fly &c.).

swath, n. [1. swawth, swath; 2. swɔ̄þ, swæþ]. O.E. *swaðu*, 'track, band'; M.E. *swāðe*; cp. M. Du. *swade*; cogn. w. **swaddle**. **1. a** The amount of grass cut with a single sweep of a scythe, and removed to one side by the blade; **b** the mark left by the scythe at each stroke. **2.** The space cleared by a mower in the whole course in a given direction.

swathe, vb. trans. & n. [1. swādh; 2. sweið]. M.E. *swāðen*, 'to bind', fr. O.E. *swaðu*, 'band, track', see prec. **1.** vb. To wrap, bind up, wind round, with long bandages or drapery. **2.** n. Bandage, wrapping.

sway (I.), vb. intrans.'& trans. [1. swā; 2. swei]. M.E. *sweien*; cp. O.N. *sveigja*, 'to bend, swing'. Cp. **swag** (I.). **A.** intrans. To swing unsteadily, lean to either side alternately with irregular motion, oscillate : *branches sway in the wind*; *the bridge swayed as the train passed over it*. **B.** trans. **1.** To cause to sway, give irregular swinging motion to : *the wind sways the branches*. **2. a** To move, incline, influence, by moral power : *to sway the minds of men*; *he is not to be swayed by argument or entreaty*; **b** (poet.) to have dominion over; to rule, govern, by authority : *to sway the realm*; *to sway the sceptre*.

sway (II.), n., fr. prec. **1.** Swaying movement, oscillation. **2.** Influence, power to move or direct; rule, dominion, jurisdiction; royal or other authority : *King Alfred held sway over all England*; *to own love's sway*.

sway-backed, adj. Of horses and cattle, having the back abnormally hollowed.

swayed, adj. [1. swād; 2. sweid], fr. P.P. of **sway** (I.). Sway-backed.

swear (I.), vb. trans. & intrans. [1. swār; 2. swεə]. O.E. *swerian*; M.E. *swēren*; cp. O.H.G. *swer(i)en*; O.N. *sverja*; Goth. *swaran*, 'to swear'; earlier sense, 'to speak'; cp. O.E. & O.S. *andswearian*, 'to address, answer', see **answer** (I.); O.N. *svara*, 'to answer (for); to stand surety'; cogn. w. Lat. *sermo*, 'conversation', see **sermon**; O. Slav. *svara*, 'dispute'. **A.** trans. **1. a** To assert, vow, promise solemnly, on one's oath : *I believe it to be true, but I can't swear it*; *to swear allegiance, eternal friendship*; **b** specif., *swear an oath*, (i.) to make a solemn vow, take one's oath, (ii.) to utter a profane oath, curse, imprecation; Phr. *to swear a charge, accusation, against*, accuse on oath. **2. a** To make a solemn promise, pledge, bind, oneself by an oath (that something is, or to do something) : *to swear to speak the truth, that what one says is true*; *to swear to be faithful*; **b** (colloq.) to assert emphatically, express a strong conviction that : *I swear I'll never go near the place again*; *I'd swear that picture was never painted by Turner*. **3. a** To obtain a solemn promise from under oath, cause to take an oath : *to swear a person to secrecy*; specif. **b** to administer a legal oath to : *to swear a jury, a witness* &c.; also *swear in*. **B.** intrans. To utter profane or blasphemous oaths or imprecations; to curse; to vent one's rage by uttering blasphemies : *he began to curse and swear*; *it is enough to make one swear*. **C.** Followed by adverbs and prepositions with special meanings. *Swear at*, intrans., to address oaths or imprecations to; to curse at, vituperate. *Swear by*, intrans., **a** to invoke as witness of oath : *to swear by all that's holy*; **b** to have entire confidence in, recommend highly : *he swears by quinine for preventing colds*; Phr. *not enough to swear by*, a very small amount. *Swear in*, trans., to administer oath of office to : *the members of the jury were sworn in*. *Swear off*, intrans., to promise or swear to renounce : *to swear off smoking* &c. *Swear to*, intrans., to affirm on oath : *I believe that is true, but I could not swear to it*.

swear (II.), n., fr. prec. (colloq., rare) An oath, blasphemy, imprecation.

swear-word, n. (colloq.) A profane oath.

sweat (I.), n. [1. swet; 2. swεt]. O.E. *swāt*, fr. *swāti*, variant of *swāt*, 'sweat'; M.E. *swēt*; cp. O.H.G. *sweiz*; O.S. *swēt*, 'sweat'; cogn. w. Lat. *sūdor*, 'sweat', see **sudation**; Gk. *idos*; Scrt. *svéda-*, 'sweat'; *svidyati*, 'he sweats'; Lett. *swēdri*, 'sweat'. The word in a physiological sense is often avoided in polite conversation, *perspiration* being commonly used instead in sense **1. 1. a** Moisture exuded by pores of skin; perspiration; Phr. *by the sweat of one's brow*, by hard work; **b** moisture resembling sweat exuded from any substance, and condensing on the surface. **2. a** Process of sweating : *a good sweat often cures a cold*; **b** state characterized by pronounced sweating : *to be in a sweat*; *a cold sweat*, accompanied by chilly feeling, induced by fear &c. **3.** (colloq.) Something that promotes sweat; work, toil, heavy labour; troublesome, tedious work; a grind : *compiling a dictionary is an awful sweat*.

sweat (II.), vb. intrans. & trans. O.E. *swǣtan*, 'to sweat', fr. *swāt*, 'sweat', see prec. The word is often avoided, esp. in physiological sense, *perspire* being substituted. **A.** intrans. **1. a** (of animals) To exude sweat, to perspire; Phr. *to sweat with fear, emotion* &c., to be strongly moved or affected; **b** (of other objects and substances) to give out moisture from a surface in drops like sweat : *apples sweat after they are gathered*; *a new house is apt to be damp till the stone has sweated thoroughly*. **2.** To work hard, toil : *to sweat (away) at one's job*. **B.** trans. **1.** To give out, exude, in form of, or as, sweat : *to sweat blood*. Phr. *to sweat out (a cold* &c.), get rid of it by sweating. **2.** To cause to sweat, cause to perspire freely, by drugs or physical exercise: *doctors sweat their patients*; *to sweat a horse*. **3.** To remove, scrape, sweat from (horse &c.). **4.** To force hard work from (workmen &c.) at insufficient wages. **5.** To wear down edges or surface of (coins &c.) by friction.

sweat-band, n. Strip of leather &c. forming lining for hat.

sweat-cloth, n. Cloth placed under horse's collar or saddle.

sweat-duct, n. Duct carrying sweat from sweat-gland to surface of skin.

sweated, adj. [1. swéted; 2. swétid], fr. P.P. of **sweat** (II.). **a** (of persons) Forced to work at inadequate wage; **b** (of labour) inadequately paid; **c** (of commodities) made, produced, by workers who are inadequately paid.

sweater, n. [1. swéter; 2. swétə]. **sweat** (II.) & **-er**. **1.** One who sweats excessively. **2.** Employer who sweats his workpeople. **3.** Heavy jersey worn by athletes after severe exercise &c.

sweat-gland, n. Small subcutaneous gland which secretes sweat.

sweatily, adv. [1. swétili; 2. swétili]. **sweaty** & **-ly**. In a sweaty manner.

sweatiness, n. [1. swétines; 2. swétinis]. See prec. & **-ness**. Sweaty condition.

sweating-bath, n. [1. swéting bàhth; 2. swét-iŋ bɑ̀þ]. Bath intended to increase perspiration.

sweating-iron, n. Metal scraper for removing sweat from horse.

sweating room, n. Hot room in Turkish bath.

sweating-sickness, n. Fatal, inflammatory fever, epidemic in Europe in 15th and 16th cents.

sweatless, adj. [1. swétles; 2. swétlis]. **sweat** (I.) & **-less**. Without, producing no, sweat.

sweaty, adj. [1. swéti; 2. swéti]. **sweat** (I.) & **-y**. **a** Covered with sweat; inclined to sweat; **b** resembling sweat.

Swede, n. [1. swēd; 2. swīd]. **1.** Native of Sweden. **2.** (without cap.) The Swedish turnip, with yellow, edible root.

Swedenborgian, adj. & n. [1. swèdenbórjian; 2. swìdənbɔ́ʤiən], fr. Swedish philosopher Swedenborg, d. 1772. **1.** adj. Pertaining to the system of philosophy and religious mysticism established by Swedenborg, or to the church founded by him. **2.** n. Adherent of Swedenborg or the Swedenborgian church.

Swedenborgianism, n. [1. swèdenbórjianizm; 2. swìdənbɔ́ʤiənizəm]. Prec. & **-ism**. Doctrine, philosophy, of Swedenborg.

Swedish, adj. & n. [1. swédish; 2. swídiʃ]. **Swede** & **-ish**. **1.** adj. Pertaining to Sweden or the Swedes. **2.** n. Language of Sweden.

sweeny, n. [1. swéni; 2. swíni]. Origin doubtful. Muscular atrophy in horses.

sweep (I.), vb. intrans. & trans. [1. swēp; 2. swīp]. M.E. *swēpan*, 'to sweep, move rapidly', wh. presupposes an O.E. **swǣpan*, (unrecorded) fr. base **swāp-* w. *i*-mutation, cp. O.E. *swāpan*, 'to sweep with a broom; to brandish (sword); to rush, dash (of wind)'; cp. also O.E. *swipu*, 'a whip'; O.H.G. *sweifan*; see further under **swift** (I.), **swipe** (I.), & **swoop** (I.). **A.** intrans. **1. a** (i.) To move along, pass, with a swift, impetuous rush; to rush, dash, drive: *a pestilence swept over the land*; '*Your manly hearts shall glow, As ye sweep through the deep, While the stormy winds do blow*' (Campbell); *the cavalry swept down the valley*; (ii.) to be driven with irresistible force: *snow, rain, wind, sweeps across the country*; **b** (of non-material process) *a wave of indignation swept through the country*; *a deadly fear swept over him.* **2.** To walk with vigorous motion, and a stately, proud, important bearing, to sail along, sail in: *the archbishop swept up the aisle in his flowing robes.* **3.** To extend, be shaped, in a wide, bold, curve: *the coast-line sweeps away to the east in a deep bay.* **4.** Specif., to perform the action of sweeping, brushing, with a broom: *I can't sweep without a broom.* Phr. *a new broom sweeps clean*, new men, new measures. **B.** trans. **1.** To descend upon, traverse, pass along, through, over, impetuously, with violence, irresistibly: *the waves swept the deck*; *the storm swept the whole countryside.* **2. a** To execute a rapid, abrupt gesture with; to brush: *to sweep one's hand over one's face, across the strings of a harp* &c.; **b** to touch, brush, with a rapid gesture: *to sweep the notes of a piano, the strings of a harp* &c. **3.** To pass searchingly over or through; to traverse in all directions: *our ships swept the sea for weeks but could not find the enemy*; *to sweep the horizon with a telescope*; *to sweep the faces of an audience with a hasty glance.* **4.** Specif. **a** to clean, remove dirt, dust, rubbish &c. from with a broom: *to sweep (out) a room, the pavements, a chimney* &c.; Phr. *to sweep the board*, win all stakes on gaming-table; hence, (fig.) to win all the prizes, be victorious in all contests &c.; **b** to collect together and remove by sweeping with a broom: *to sweep away, up, dust, snow, rubbish* &c. **5.** (gen.) **a** To remove, drive, brush, away, eliminate, cause to disappear, by violent or drastic action: *death sweeps away great and small*; *the waves swept away the breakwater*; *our troops swept the enemy before them*; *to be swept along in the crowd*; *the wind swept his hat off his head*; *to be swept off one's feet (by a wave* &c.); (also fig.) to be carried away, overcome, by emotion &c.; **b** to obliterate, wipe out, destroy, abolish: *to sweep away slum areas, trees which obstruct the view* &c.

sweep (II.), n. See prec. **1.** Act of sweeping with a broom: *to give a room a good sweep.* Phr. *to make a clean sweep of*, to get rid of, do away with utterly. **2. a** Person who sweeps a chimney; Phr. *as black as a sweep*, very black, grubby; **b** a dirty, grubby person, esp. *a regular little sweep*, a grubby child; **c** (slang) a mean, ill-mannered, ill-conditioned, disagreeable person. **3. a** A steady, irresistible movement, flux, flow: *the sweep of the tide*; **b** a steady, spacious, movement, esp. of progress, in affairs, events, intellectual development &c.: *the onward sweep of civilization.* **4. a** A wide sweeping movement, swing, stroke, made or delivered by a weapon, implement &c.: *the sweep of a sword, scythe*; **b** large, vigorous bodily gesture: *a sweep of the arm*; **c** a wide searching inspection with a telescope &c. of the heavens. **5. a** The extent of a sweeping movement; range, reach: *a two-handed sword had a wide sweep*; **b** intellectual range, scope, grasp, comprehensiveness: *a mind of wonderful sweep.* **6.** A long, heavy oar, moved with a sweeping action, used for propelling or steering heavy barges, sailing-boats &c. **7.** A long, flowing curve: *the graceful sweep of draperies.* **8.** (colloq.) Abbr. of *sweepstake.*

sweeper, n. [1. swēper; 2. swīpə]. **sweep** (I.) & **-er**. **a** Mechanical device for sweeping (floors, streets); **b** person employed in sweeping; esp. in compound *crossing-sweeper.*

sweeping, adj. [1. swēping; 2. swīpiŋ], fr. Pres. Part. of **sweep** (I.). **a** Comprehensive, of wide range; unqualified; of too great inclusiveness: *a sweeping statement*; **b** complete, thorough-going, radical: *sweeping changes.*

sweepingly, adv. Prec. & **-ly**. In a sweeping manner.

sweepingness, n. See prec. & **-ness**. Quality of being sweeping.

sweepings, n. pl. [1. swēpingz; 2. swīpiŋz]. **sweep** (I.) & **-ing**. **a** Matter such as rubbish or refuse swept up from floor, ground &c; **b** (fig.) *the sweepings of the gutter*, the lowest dregs of the population.

sweep-net, n. **1.** Large fishing-net paid out in an arc of a circle and drawn ashore. **2.** Net with handle, swept to and fro above bushes &c., for catching insects.

sweep-seine, n. Sweep-net, **1.**

sweepstake(s), n. [1. swēpstāk(s); 2. swīpsteɪk(s)]. Form of gambling on horse-race &c. in which those taking part pay money into a common fund which is afterwards divided between those who have drawn numbered tickets representing winning or placed horses.

sweet (I.), adj. [1. swēt; 2. swīt]. O.E., M.E. *swēte*, fr. **swōti-*, 'sweet, pleasant'; cp. O.S. *swōti*; O.H.G. *suozi*; O.N. *sǿtr*; Goth. *sūts*; cogn. w. Lat. *suāvis*, fr. **swādwi-*, 'sweet, pleasant', see **suave**; Gk. *hēdús*, fr. **swādu-*, 'sweet', see **hedonic**; Scrt. *svādúś*, 'pleasant in taste'. **1.** Having the taste of sugar; reverse of *bitter* or *sour*: *sweet cakes, apples*; *to be fond of sweet things*; *the pudding is too sweet*; *sweet wine*, reverse of *dry.* Phr. *to have a sweet tooth*, like sweet things. **2.** Pleasing to sense of smell or taste; fresh, pure; reverse of *tainted, stale, stinking, rancid*: *the milk, water, meat, air &c. is quite sweet.* **3.** Pleasing to sense of smell; fragrant, agreeably scented: *sweet flowers*; *a sweet smell*; *the rose smells sweet*; *sweet herbs*, culinary herbs. **4. a** Pleasing to sense of hearing, gentle, soothing, melodious: *a sweet voice*; *sweet melodies*; **b** having a sweet, pleasant voice: *a sweet singer.* **5.** Agreeable, pleasant, gratifying, to body or mind; delightful or restful: *sweet sleep*; *sweet words*; *praise was sweet to him.* **6. a** Kind, tender, gentle: *a sweet temper, disposition* &c.; Phr. *sweet on* (a person), in love with; **b** having or revealing a sweet disposition: *a sweet woman*; *a sweet face.* **7.** (colloq.) Pretty, charming, delightful: *a sweet frock*; *a sweet little dog*; *he was perfectly sweet to her.*

sweet (II.), n., fr. prec. **1.** Anything with sweet taste, esp. **a** small sweetmeat; **b** sweet dish as course at dinner &c. **2.** Something sweet, delightful &c.: *the sweet of the year*, i.e. sweet season. **3.** (usually pl.) Enjoyment, delight, pleasure, joy: *the sweets of life, victory, success.* **4.** Sweet, beloved, person, darling: **a** '*She is coming, my own, my sweet*' (Tennyson, 'Maud'); **b** (as form of address) '*Sweet, be not proud of those two eyes Which starlike sparkle in their skies*' (Herrick).

sweetbread, n. [1. swētbred; 2. swītbrɛd]. Pancreas or thymus, esp. of calf, used as food.

sweet-brier, -briar, n. Species of brier-rose with aromatic leaves.

sweeten, vb. trans. & intrans. [1. swētn; 2. swītn]. **sweet** (I.) & **-en**. **A.** trans. **1.** To make sweet, impart sweetness (in any sense) to: *to sweeten sauce* &c.; *a temper sweetened by sympathy.* **2.** To render pleasant, make more endurable: *to sweeten toil.* **B.** intrans. To become sweet.

sweetening, n. [1. swētn-ing; 2. swītn-iŋ]. Prec. & **-ing**. That which sweetens; sweet substance added to food &c.

sweet-flag, n. A plant of the Arum family, with sword-shaped leaves and aromatic root, growing in marshy ground.

sweet-gale, n. A plant of the myrtle family, with aromatic leaves, growing in marshy ground; bog-myrtle.

sweetheart, n. & vb. intrans. [1. swēt-hart; 2. swīthāt]. The suff. orig. **-ard**, cp. **drunkard**, but associated w. **heart** (I.). **1.** n. **a** Lover; **b** (as form of affectionate address) beloved, darling. **2.** vb. Esp. in Phr. *to go sweethearting*, to go courting, love-making.

sweeting, n. [1. swēting; 2. swītiŋ]. **sweet** (I.) & **-ing**. **1.** A sweet apple. **2.** (archaic) Sweetheart, darling.

sweetish, adj. [1. swētish; 2. swītiʃ]. **sweet** (I.) & **-ish**. Fairly sweet.

sweet-john, n. Narrow-leaved variety of sweet-william.

sweetly, adv. [1. swētli; 2. swītli]. **sweet** (I.) & **-ly**. **1. a** In a sweet manner: *to speak, sing, sweetly*; **b** to the extent of being sweet; in Phr. *sweetly pretty.* **2.** (of machines) Smoothly, easily: *the engine runs sweetly.*

sweetmeat, n. [1. swētmēt; 2. swītmīt]. Small piece of sweet confection made of or containing sugar, chocolate &c.

sweetness, n. [1. swētnes; 2. swītnis]. **sweet** (I.) & **-ness**. Quality of being sweet.

sweet-oil, n. Olive oil.

sweet-pea, n. Cultivated annual of pea family with white or brightly coloured, very fragrant flowers.

sweet-potato, n. Creeping plant, *Ipomaea*, of warm climates, with sweetish, farinaceous, edible root.

sweet-root, n. Liquorice.

sweet-rush, n. Sweet-flag.

sweet-scented, adj. Having sweet odour, fragrant.

sweet-sop, n. Sweet, pulpy, egg-shaped fruit of tropical American tree.

sweet-sultan, n. Garden annual, variety of the plant sultan, with purple flowers.

sweet-tempered, adj. Amiable, gracious, gentle in disposition.

sweet-water, n. Kind of white grape.

sweet-william, n. [1. swēt wílyum; 2. swīt wíljəm]. A perennial pink, *Dianthus*, with clusters of small, white, red, pink, or particoloured flowers.

sweet-willow, n. Sweet-gale.

sweetwood, n. [1. swētwood; 2. swītwud]. The bay, the wood of which is fragrant when crushed.

sweety, n. [1. swēti; 2. swīti]. **sweet** (I.) & **-y**. Sweetmeat.

swell (I.), vb. intrans. & trans. [1. swel; 2. swel]. O.E. *swellan*, M.E. *swellen*; O.H.G. *swellan*; cp. O.E. *swyle*, fr. **swuli-*, 'tumour'; cogn. w. Lat. *(in)solens*, 'immoderate, haughty', see **insolent**. **A.** intrans. **1. a** To expand, dilate, become larger by pressure exerted from within, as by inflation; to be blown out, puffed out: *a tire swells as it is filled with air*; **b** specif., to become tumefied and puffy from inflammation, accumulation of purulent matter &c.: *his legs swelled with dropsy.* Phr. *to have, suffer from, swelled head*, to have an exaggerated idea of one's own importance. **2.** To be increased in size, volume, number, by external addition: *the book has now swelled to an inordinate size*; *all the streams have swelled since the thaw*; *population in many places has swelled beyond the limits of actual housing accommodation.* **3. a** (of surface of the ground or of water) To rise into a curved protuberance above surrounding level; to billow; **b** (of sails &c.) to be filled with wind; to belly; **c** (of a contour) to bulge out, become larger at a given point: *the vase swells into a beautiful curve in the middle*; (often in Pres. Part. as adj.) *the swelling sides of a ship.* **4.** (of sound) To increase in volume and intensity: *the first occasional twitter of birds at dawn soon swells into a full-voiced chorus.* **5.** To have a sense of elation, of mental or moral excitement under the stress of powerful emotion: *to swell with pride, with indignation.* **B.** trans. **1.** To cause to swell (in various senses); **a** to add to amount of: *to swell the national debt*; **b** to augment numbers of: *to swell the popu-*

lation; **c** to increase volume of: *the melting snow swells the rivers*; **d** to increase size or bulk of: *new notes and additions of all kinds have swelled the book out to monstrous size*; **e** to render arrogant, puff up morally; (chiefly in P.P.) *swollen with pride* &c. **2.** (mus.) To increase the loudness, volume, intensity of (a note &c.): '*The pealing anthem swells the note of praise*' (Gray's 'Elegy'). Phr. *to swell the chorus* (*of admiration* &c.), join one's voice, add one's opinion, to that of others (perhaps also under **1. b** above).

swell (II.), n., fr. prec. **1.** (rare) Process of swelling, increase in magnitude or volume. **2.** Slow, steady, continuous, undulation of the sea unbroken by waves after a storm. **3. a** (mus.) Gradual increase in volume of sound; **b** gradual increase and diminution of volume and loudness of a note. **4.** Mechanical device in an organ producing alternate increase and diminution of loudness at the will of the player. **5.** (colloq. slang) **a** A person who is smartly, richly, fashionably, dressed; a dandy, a buck, a blood; **b** a person of eminence, position, and distinction: *the Bishop and the other swells sat on the platform*; **c** person who excels in some particular bodily or mental accomplishment: *a swell at tennis, at polo*; *a swell at Latin prose*.

swell (III.), adj., fr. prec. (colloq.) **a** Specif., smart, dandified, extremely fashionable: *swell clothes*; *a swell walking-stick*; **b** (gen.) of excellent quality; first-rate; admirable, meritorious: *a swell tennis-player*; *a swell speech, book*.

swell-blind, n. One of the shutters of a swell-box.

swell-box, n. Chamber enclosing organ-box and fitted with movable slats or shutters to release or muffle the sound.

swelldom, n. [1. swéldum; 2. swéldəm]. **swell** (II.) & **-dom**. (colloq.) Fashionable society.

swell-fish, n. Fish capable of inflating itself.

swelling (I.), n. [1. swéling; 2. swéliŋ]. **swell** (I.) & **-ing**. **1.** Something which is swollen; specif., swelled part of the body; a tumour. **2.** That which swells; specif. **a** an undulation of the ground, a hillock; **b** an increase in size of one part of an object, part that is more prominent than the rest: *the swelling of a cask*.

swelling (II.), adj., fr. Pres. Part. of **swell** (I.). **1.** Rising in an undulation, sloping, curving, into a mound: *the swelling turf*. **2.** Formed so as to curve outwards, having a bulge: *the swelling sides of a ship*.

swellish, adj. [1. swélish; 2. swéliʃ]. **swell** (II.) & **-ish**. (colloq.) Of, pertaining to, a swell; ultra-fashionable.

swell-mob, n. (coll.) Well-dressed criminals.

swell-organ, n. Organ fitted with swell-box.

swell-pedal, n. Pedal controlling shutter of swell-box.

swell-rule, n. (print.) Diamond-shaped rule with elongated ends.

swelter (I.), vb. intrans. [1. swélter; 2. swéltə]. O.E. *sweltan*; M.E. *swelten*, 'to grow faint, die', & **-er**; cp. O.N. *svelta*; Goth. *swiltan*, 'to die'; see also **sultry**. To be, feel, extremely hot.

swelter (II.), n., fr. prec. Sweltering state or condition.

swept, vb. [1. swept; 2. swept]. Pret. & P.P. of **sweep** (I.).

swerve (I.), vb. intrans. & trans. [1. swërv; 2. swɑ̄v]. O.E. *sweorfan*, 'to scrub, file'; M.E. *swerven*, 'to swerve'; cp. O.N. *sverfa*, 'to scour'; Goth. (*af*)*svairban*, 'to wipe out'; O.H.G. *swerban*, 'to wipe, rub, dry'; M. Du. *swerven*, 'to wander'. **A.** intrans. **1.** To deviate from a straight line of progress; to start aside from one's course: *the runner swerved suddenly*; *some bowlers can make the ball swerve in the air*. **2.** To depart, deviate, from a straight line of conduct: *to swerve from the path of duty*. **B.** trans. (rare) To cause (esp. a ball) to swerve.

swerve (II.), n., fr. prec. Act of swerving; turning aside, divergence from straight course; specif., turn or twist of cricket-ball in the air.

swerveless, adj. [1. swërvles; 2. swʌ́vlis]. **swerve** (II.) & **-less**. Not liable to swerve.

swift (I.), adj. [1. swift; 2. swift]. O.E., M.E. *swift*, 'swift', fr. Gmc. **swip-ta-*; cp. O.E. *swipa*, O.N. *svipa*, 'whip'; O.H.G. *sweif*, 'rotation'; O.N. *svifa*, 'to sweep'; O.E. *swifan*, 'to move, sweep'; *swāpan*, 'to sweep, rush', see **sweep** (I.). **1. a** Moving or capable of moving quickly; rapid, fleet: *a swift runner, horse*; *as swift as thought*; *swift feet*; **b** (of time) *swift years*. **2.** (of motion) Rapid, quick: *a swift movement, glance* &c.; *birds of swiftest flight*. **3.** Acting or happening promptly; not delayed, speedy: *swift revenge*; *a swift response*. **4.** Acting readily and promptly: *swift to take offence*.

swift (II.), adv. O.E. *swifte*, fr. prec. Swiftly; chiefly in compounds: *swift-passing* &c.

swift (III.), n., fr. prec. (**swift** (I.). Swift-moving bird, insect, object &c.; specif. **a** genus, *Cypselus*, of swallow-like birds with long, pointed wings, capable of rapid and prolonged flight; **b** breed of pigeons; **c** common European newt; **d** ghost-moth or other species of the *Hepialidae*; **e** reel for winding yarn.

swift-footed, adj. Moving on rapid feet, walking or running quickly; also fig. of time &c.

swift-handed, adj. **a** Quick and deft in action; **b** (fig., of justice, vengeance &c.) coming promptly, not delayed.

swiftlet, n. [1. swíftlet; 2. swíftlit]. **swift** (III.) & **-let**. Small kind of swift (*Cypselus*).

swiftly, adv. [1. swíftli; 2. swíftli]. **swift** (I.) & **-ly**. Rapidly, quickly.

swiftness, n. [1. swíftnes; 2. swíftnis]. See prec. & **-ness**. Quality of being swift; speed, rapidity, quickness.

swift-winged, adj. Flying on swift wings.

swig, vb. trans. & intrans. & n. [1. swig; 2. swig]. Etymol. unknown. (now, vulg. slang) **1.** vb. **a** trans. (i.) To drink, esp. in large quantities; (ii.) cp. Dryden's usage: '*but the bleating lambs Securely swig the dug, beneath the Dams*' ('Æneid', ix. 72-3); **b** intrans., to imbibe drink. **2.** n. Draught of liquor; a pull: *to take a swig at*.

swill (I.), vb. trans. & intrans. [1. swil; 2. swil]. O.E. *swilian*; M.E. *swilen*, 'to swill, wash'. **A.** trans. **1.** To rinse, wash out, drench, with water; also *swill out*. **2.** (vulg.) To drink large quantities of: *to swill beer*. **B.** intrans. To absorb liquor in large quantities, greedily.

swill (II.), n., fr. prec. **1.** Act of swilling; rinse, wash. **2.** Liquid mixture of kitchen refuse &c., as food for pigs &c.; wash. **3.** Draught of liquor, esp. of poor quality.

swim (I.), vb. intrans. & trans. [1. swim; 2. swim]. O.E. *swimman*, 'to swim, float'; cp. O.H.G. *swimman*; O.N. *svimma*, 'to swim'; O.N. *svamla*, 'to swim'; cp. further Goth. *swumfsl*, 'pool'; *swamms*, 'sponge'; O.E. *sund*, 'swimming; sea'; see **sound** (V.). **A.** intrans. **1.** (of living creatures) To proceed through water by movements of the limbs, tail, fins, or other parts of the body: *to swim across the river*; *to swim about in the sea*; *to swim on one's back*; *to swim under water*. Phrs. *to swim like a stone*, sink; *to swim with the tide, stream*, follow popular custom or convention; *sink or swim*, fail, be ruined, or succeed, prosper. **2. a** To be supported upon surface of water, float: *the leaf swims down the river*; **b** to be supported, held in suspension: *specks of dust that swim in sunbeams*. **3.** To move with or as with smooth, gliding, buoyant motion: '*like some watcher of the skies When a new planet swims into his ken*' (Keats, 'Chapman's Homer'). **4.** To be deluged in, saturated with: *food swimming in butter*. **5.** To overflow, be flooded, with: *eyes that swam with tears*; see **swim** (III.). **B.** trans. **1.** To cause, compel, to swim: *to swim a horse across a river*. **2.** To traverse by swimming: *to swim the Channel*. **3.** To swim for (specified distance): *to swim a mile*. **4. a** To engage in (swimming-race); **b** to oppose (person) in swimming-race.

swim (II.), n., fr. prec. **1. a** Act of swimming: *to enjoy a swim*; **b** spell of swimming: *to go for a long swim*. Phr. *in the swim*, familiar with current events, tendencies, activities. **2.** Deep pool in river, abounding in fish.

swim (III.), vb. intrans. Now felt as belonging to **swim** (I.), but partly influenced in meaning by obs. O.E. *swīma*, M.E. *swīme*, 'giddiness'; cp. **swindler**. **1.** To feel giddy; to reel, spin: *his head swam*. **2.** To produce a visual impression of revolving, rocking, oscillating; to be seen hazily, as through a mist by one who is giddy: *everything swam before his eyes*.

swimmer, n. [1. swímer; 2. swímə]. **swim** (I.) & **-er**. One who swims: *a poor, strong, swimmer*.

swimmeret, n. [1. swímeret; 2. swímərət]. Prec. & **-et**. Abdominal appendage used by crustacean for swimming.

swimming-bath, n. [1. swíming bàth; 2. swímiŋ bɑ̄þ]. Large tank filled with water, usually under cover, used for swimming.

swimming-bell, n. Bell-like swimming organ of jelly-fish &c.

swimming-belt, n. Pneumatic belt for supporting a person in the water.

swimming-bladder, n. Fish's air-bladder; sound.

swimming-foot, n. Swimmeret.

swimmingly, adv. [1. swímingli; 2. swímiŋli]. fr. Pres. Part. of **swim** (I.) & **-ly**. With easy, unhindered, progress; successfully, prosperously: *everything went swimmingly*; *to get on swimmingly*.

swimming-stone, n. Light, porous variety of quartz.

swindle (I.), vb. trans. & intrans. [1. swindl; 2. swindl]. Back-formation fr. **swindler**. **1.** trans. **a** To cheat, defraud: *you've been swindled*; **b** to obtain (money, &c.) by swindling: *to swindle money out of a person*. **2.** intrans. To practise swindling; to cheat.

swindle (II.), n., fr. prec. **1.** Act of swindling; a fraudulent transaction: *he carried out a series of gigantic swindles*. **2.** Something which is different from, and inferior to, what it is represented to be; something of which the nature and qualities have been deliberately misrepresented with intent to defraud; a take-in: *a cheap watch advertised as made of gold is usually a swindle*.

swindler, n. [1. swíndler; 2. swíndlə], fr. Germ. *schwindler*, 'one who plans extravagant schemes; swindler, cheat', fr. *schwindeln*, 'to be giddy', O.H.G. *swintilōn*, 'to be giddy'; cp. O.H.G. *swintan*, 'to be faint; to vanish'; cogn. w. O.E. *swīma*, 'dizziness', see **swim** (III.); O.N. *svīmi*, 'giddiness'. Person who swindles; a cheat, a sharper.

swindlingly, adv. [1. swíndlingli; 2. swíndliŋli], fr. Pres. Part. of **swindle** (I.) & **-ly**. By means of a swindle, fraudulently.

swine, n. [1. swīn; 2. swain]. O.E., M.E. *swīn*; cp. Germ. *schwein*; Goth. *swein*; cogn. w. Lat. *suīnus*, 'of swine', see **suilline**; O. Slav. *svinija*, 'swine'; Gk. *huēnós*, 'of swine'. **1.** (archaic in sing.) **a** Hoofed, omnivorous mammal, wild or domesticated, of subfamily *Suinae*, esp. of genus *Sus scrofa*; a pig; **b** (as pl.) pigs collectively: *a herd of swine*; *some sheep and several swine*. **2.** Term of violent abuse; a detestable, disgusting person; one guilty of low, mean, or dishonourable conduct.

swine-bread, n. Truffle.

swine-fever, n. Contagious disease which attacks the lungs and intestines of domestic swine.

swineherd, n. [1. swínhërd; 2. swáinhɜ̄d]. Man in charge of swine.

swine-plague, n. Swine-fever.

swine-pox, n. Form of chicken-pox.

swinery, n. [1. swíneri; 2. swáinəri]. **swine** & **-ery**. Place in which swine are kept.

swine's-snout, n. Dandelion.

swing (I.), vb. intrans. & trans. [1. swing; 2. swiŋ]. O.E. *swingan*; M.E. *swingen*, 'to swing'; cp. O.S., O.H.G. *swingen*; Du. *zwenken*, 'to swing'; Goth. *(af)swaggwjan*, 'to cause to waver'. A. intrans. 1. a To carry out the movement characteristic of a hanging object; to move backwards and forwards; to sway to and fro, oscillate: *to let one's legs swing*; *to swing by one hand from a branch*; *a lamp swung from a hook*; Phr. (slang) *to swing for* (a person), be hanged for murdering him; b specif. (as form of recreation) to move rhythmically backwards and forwards on a seat suspended by ropes &c. 2. a To turn, move, on or as on a pivot or hinge: *the door swung open, back* &c.; *to swing to*, close; *he swung round on his heel*; *the ship swung slowly round*; b to move freely, as with the movements of water, about a fixed point: *the boat swings at her moorings*. 3. To walk, run &c. with smooth, steady, easy, swaying motion: *the troops went swinging past*. B. trans. 1. a To cause, allow, to swing; to impart swinging motion to; to wave to and fro: *to swing a cane, one's arms*; b to hold suspended and allow to dangle: *to swing a parcel from one's finger*; *to swing a lamp from the ceiling*; Phr. *no room, not large enough, to swing a cat (in)*, (of room, enclosed space) very small and confined; *to swing the lead*, soldiers' and sailors' slang, to pretend to work hard, to malinger; c to cause to swing to and fro, in regular curves &c., as a form of exercise: *to swing Indian clubs*; d to give a rhythmic motion to (person &c.) on a swing, in a hammock &c., by pushing or pulling. 2. To sling, hoist, up, with a rapid swinging motion: *to swing a child on to one's shoulder*. 3. To cause to wheel from a fixed point, to cause to move on or as on a pivot: *to swing a battalion into line*; *the tide swung the boat round on its moorings*.

swing (II.), n., fr. prec. 1. Act, process, of swinging; swinging movement, motion to and fro; a *the swing of a pendulum*; Phr. *the swing of the pendulum*, inevitable ebb and flow, action and reaction, in human affairs, opinions &c.; *in full swing*, at the height of activity or operation; b mode of swinging, e.g. in playing golf, tennis &c. 2. Free, easy, swaying gait: *to walk with a swing*. 3. Rhythm, rhythmic movement: *the swing of music, verse, a dance*; Phr. *to go with a swing*, (i.) (of a tune, verse &c.) run with easy, rapid movement; (ii.) (fig., of an event, organized action, entertainment &c.) to pass off satisfactorily, cheerfully, with zest &c. 4. Freedom to swing without obstruction or hindrance. 5. Specif. a apparatus consisting of a seat &c. suspended by ropes &c., on which one may sit and swing backwards and forwards as recreation; b act of swinging in such an apparatus; c spell of such swinging. 6. Distance swung, compass of swing; sweep.

swing-boat, n. Boat-shaped swing with seats for two or more persons.

swing-bridge, n. Bridge moving on a pivot to allow passage of boats &c.

swinge, vb. trans. [1. swinj; 2. swindž]. O.E. *swengan*, fr. **swang-jan*, 'to strike, fling aside'; cp. Goth. *(af)swaggwjan*, 'to cause to waver'; see **swing (I.)**. (archaic) To strike, give heavy blow to.

swingeing, adj. [1. swínjing; 2. swíndžiŋ]. fr. Pres. Part. of prec. 1. (of blow &c.) Heavy, forcible. 2. (colloq.) Large, huge, very considerable.

swinging, adj. [1. swínging; 2. swíŋiŋ], fr. Pres. Part. of **swing (I.)**. Having, performed with, a swing; a rapid, vigorous; active, buoyant: *a swinging stride*; b lilting, leaping, swiftly moving: *a swinging rhythm*.

swingingly, adv. Prec. & -ly. With a swing.

swingle, n. & vb. trans. [1. swínggl; 2. swíŋgl]. **swing (I.)** & -le. 1. n. Wooden instrument used for beating flax to separate woody part from fibre. 2. vb. To dress flax by beating with a swingle.

swingle-tree, n. Horizontal bar to which traces, chains &c. of cart, plough &c. are attached; whipple-tree.

swingling-tow, n. [1. swíngglingtō; 2. swíŋ-gliŋ tòu]. Coarse, woody part of flax.

swing-plough, n. Plough without wheels.

swinish, adj. [1. swínish; 2. swáiniʃ]. **swine** & -ish. Resembling, befitting, swine.

swinishly, adv. Prec. & -ly. In a swinish manner.

swinishness, n. See prec. & -ness. State or quality of being swinish; disgusting, mean, or dishonourable conduct.

swink, vb. intrans. & n. [1. swingk; 2. swiŋk]. O.E. *swincan*, 'to work'; M.E. *swinken*. (obs. or deliberately archaic) 1. vb. To toil, labour. 2. n. Toil, drudgery.

swipe (I.), vb. intrans. & trans. [1. swīp; 2. swaip]. O.E. *swīpian*, 'to beat, vibrate'; cp. O.E. *swipe*, 'whip; stroke'; O.N. *svipa*, 'whip'; see **swift (I.)**; **sweep (I.)**. 1. intrans. a To hit hard, deliver a powerful blow, esp. at cricket; b *swipe at*, to aim a powerful blow at, hit out wildly at. 2. trans. To strike (ball) hard with a bat.

swipe (II.), n., fr. prec. Strong, violent blow, given with full swing of arm.

swipes, n. [1. swīps; 2. swaips]. Prob. fr. prec. in obs. sense, 'drink off'. Weak, muddy, inferior beer.

swirl (I.), vb. intrans. & trans. [1. swērl; 2. swā̇l], fr. O.N. *svirla*, 'to whirl', fr. *sverra*, 'to whirl; to hum'; cp. Germ. *schwirren*, 'to buzz', cogn. w. **swarm (I.)**. 1. intrans. (of spray, water, dust, snow) To be whirled, or whisked, into an eddy; to eddy; to revolve rapidly and in spirals. 2. (rare) trans. To cause to swirl; to whirl.

swirl (II.), n., fr. prec. 1. Eddying motion of water, snow &c. 2. Swift, darting movement of fish through water.

swish (I.), vb. trans. & intrans. [1. swish; 2. swiʃ]. Imitative. A. trans. 1. To whirl, flirt, flick, quickly through the air with an audible, whistling sound: *the cow swished her tail*. 2. a To thrash, strike, flog; b *swish off*, to strike, cut, off, with a swishing blow. B. intrans. To pass, cut, through the air with sweeping movement and whistling, hissing, sound: *the sword-blade swished past my ear*.

swish (II.), n., fr. prec. 1. Sharp, whistling, hissing sound produced by slender, flexible body moving quickly through the air. 2. Quick movement producing swishing sound: *a swish of a cow's tail*.

Swiss (I.), adj. [1. swis; 2. swis], fr. Fr. *suisse*, fr. M.H.G. *swiz*. Pertaining to Switzerland, its inhabitants or dialects.

Swiss (II.), n., fr. prec. 1. a Native of Switzerland; b one of the German, French, or Italian dialects spoken in Switzerland. 2. Specif. a a Swiss porter, or guard, formerly employed by the French kings, now only by the Pope; b a porter or guard generally.

swiss-roll, n. Thin layer of light, spongy cake spread with jam and rolled up while hot.

switch (I.), n. [1. swich; 2. switʃ]. Perh. partly imitative of sound; cp. also M. Du. *swick*, 'whip'. 1. a Small, slender, flexible shoot, twig, rod; b specif., such a rod used as a riding-whip. 2. Tress of false hair, fastened at one end. 3. Device for making or breaking electric circuit or transferring current. 4. Device for moving short section of railway-line, to allow train &c. to pass from one track to another.

switch (II.), vb. trans. & intrans., fr. prec. A. trans. 1. To strike, lash with switch or other slender, flexible object. 2. To move, swing, with a quick jerk or flick; to whisk: *the horse switched its tail*. 3. a To transfer, shift, (train) to another track; b to make or break electric or other similar circuit: *to switch electric light on, off*; *to switch* (person) *on, off*, make, break, telephone connexion for. B. intrans. a To transfer, be transferred to another track; b to turn (electric current) by means of a switch; (also fig.) *to switch off to another line of thought*. Phr. *to switch off*, cut off telephone connexion.

switchback, n. [1. swíchbak; 2. swítʃbæk]. 1. Railway laid in zigzags to facilitate ascension by trains of very steep slope. 2. Steeply undulating track up and down which a car moves on runners or rollers, at great speed, by its own impetus; form of amusement at fairs &c.

switchboard, n. [1. swíchbord; 2. swítʃbōd]. Set of switches, at a telephone exchange, for connecting a series of electric circuits.

switch-lever, n. Lever for operating a switch.

switch-man, n. Man working railway switches.

switch-signal, n. Device, usually automatic, for indicating position of railway switch.

Switzer, n. [1. swítser; 2. swítsə], fr. Swiss-Germ. form corresponding to Germ. *Schweizer*, fr. *Schweiz*, 'Switzerland', & -er. (archaic) Swiss native.

swivel (I.), n. [1. swívl; 2. swívl], fr. next word. Part of an attachment made to turn round, such as the shank of a hook which turns in a ring, being secured by a nut or bolt from slipping through.

swivel (II.), vb. intrans. & trans., fr. O.E. *swīfan*, 'to move, turn', see **swift (I.)**, **sweep (I.)**, & -le. To turn on or as on a swivel.

swivel-eye, n. (colloq.) An eye which looks in a different direction when the other is directed on an object; an eye with a strong cast.

swivel-gun, n. Gun mounted on a pivot.

swob, n. [1. swob; 2. swɔb]. Variant of **swab**.

swollen, vb. [1. swólen; 2. swóulən]. O.E. *(ge)swollen*; M.E. *swollen*; P.P. of **swell**.

swoon (I.), vb. intrans. [1. swōōn; 2. swūn]. M.E. *swōghnen*, *swownen*, 'to swoon', fr. O.E. *swōgan*, 'to sigh, sough', see **sough**. 1. To faint, be overcome by syncope. 2. (poet., of sound) To fade gradually, die away.

swoon (II.), n., fr. prec. Fainting-fit.

swooningly, adv. [1. swōōningli; 2. swūniŋli]. Pres. Part. of **swoon (I.)** & -ly. As though swooning; in a die-away manner.

swoop (I.), vb. intrans. & trans. [1. swōōp; 2. swūp]. O.E. *swāpan*, q.v. under **sweep (I.)**, M.E. *swōpen*, w. alteration of ō due to the influence of *w-*. 1. intrans. To sweep, pounce down suddenly and impetuously, descend in sudden attack (esp. of bird of prey): *the eagle was about to swoop*, *swooped*, (*down*) *upon its prey*; *the robbers swooped down on the unsuspecting travellers*. 2. trans. (colloq.) Usually *swoop up*, to snatch up, seize with sweeping motion.

swoop (II.), n., fr. prec. Act of swooping; sudden, swift, sweeping descent of, or as of, bird of prey.

swop, swap (I.), vb. trans. & intrans. [1. swop; 2. swɔp]. Prob. fr. M.E. *swappen*, 'to strike', fr. *swap*, O.E. *swāp*, 'blow'; cp. O.N. *svipa*, 'whip'; see **sweep (I.)**, **swift (I.)**. 1. trans. To give as reciprocal equivalents; to exchange: *to swop hats*; *to swop yarns*; *to swop a penknife for a guinea-pig*. Now colloquial, but formerly in literary use in this sense, cp. Dryden, 'Cleomenes': '*I would have swopped Youth for old age*'. 2. intrans. To carry out an exchange.

swop, swap (II.), n., fr. prec. Act of swopping; exchange.

sword, n. [1. sord; 2. sōd]. O.E. *sweord, sword*; M.E. *swerd*; cp. O. Fris. *swerd*; O.H.G. *swert*; O.N. *sverðr*; Du. *zwaard*. 1. Cutting and thrusting weapon of attack and defence, with a long blade, sharpened on one or both edges, fixed in a hilt; *cavalry sword, sabre*; *duelling-, small-sword*, light, straight, triangular-bladed sword; *sword of state*, sword carried before sovereign on state occasions. Phrs. *sword of Damocles*, a danger which is constantly threatening; *fire and sword*, general destruction by invading army; *at the point of the sword*, under compulsion, under threat of death; *to cross, measure, swords with*, to oppose; *to draw, sheathe, the sword*, to begin, end, hostilities; '*to put to the sword*, kill, massacre. 2. *The sword*, military methods or power; warfare.

sword-arm, n. That used in wielding a sword, the right arm.

sword-bayonet, n. Bayonet with a handle and a sword-like blade, capable of being used as sword.

sword-bearer, n. Official carrying a sword before the sovereign at ceremonies.

sword-belt, n. Belt to which sword-sheath is attached.

sword-bill, n. South American humming-bird with long, slender beak.

sword-cane, n. Sword-stick.

sword-cut, n. **a** Cut delivered by sword-blade; **b** scar left by this.

sword-dance, n. Dance in which swords are used, esp. one with elaborate steps performed in and out between the blades of two crossed swords laid on the ground.

sword-dollar, n. Scottish silver coin of James VI., with a sword on the reverse.

sworded, adj. [1. sórded ; 2. sǒdid]. **sword & -ed.** Having, equipped with, a sword.

sword-fish, n. Large ocean fish, *Xiphias*, allied to the mackerel, with upper jaw elongated to form a long sword-like projection.

sword-flag, n. Water-flag, yellow iris.

sword-flighted, adj. [1. sórd flīted ; 2. sǒd flàitid]. (of bird) Having wing-feathers of distinct colour, producing effect of a sword at the side when folded.

sword-grass, n. Kind of sedge.

sword-guard, n. Part of a sword-hilt which protects the hand.

sword-hand, n. Hand used in wielding sword; the right hand.

sword-knot, n. Loop of leather attached to the hilt of a sword, through which the hand is passed when grasping the sword for use, so that if the grasp be relaxed the sword is not dropped, but can be seized again ; a sword-knot may also be purely ornamental and made of gold wire.

sword-law, n. Military rule.

swordless, adj. [1. sórdles ; 2. sǒdlis]. **sword & -less.** Without, not relying upon, a sword.

sword-like, adj. **sword & -like.** Resembling a sword in shape, keenness &c.

sword-lily, n. Gladiolus.

sword-play, n. Fencing.

sword-proof, adj. Not liable to be pierced by sword.

swordsman, n. [1. sórdzman ; 2. sǒdzmən]. Man skilled in use of sword ; skilful fencer.

swordsmanship, n. [1. sórdzmanshìp ; 2. sǒdzmənʃìp]. Prec. & **-ship.** Skill in the use of the sword.

sword-stick, n. Hollow walking-stick containing a thin sword-blade.

swore, vb. [1. swōr ; 2. swō]. O.E. *swōr*, M.E. *swōr*, Pret. of **swear**.

sworn, adj. [1. sworn ; 2. swǒn], fr. P.P. of **swear** ; O.E., M.E. *sworen*. Under a vow, pledged: *sworn brothers, friends* ; *sworn enemies*, bitter, irreconcilable.

swot, vb. intrans. & n. [1. swot ; 2. swɔt]. Prob. a variant of **sweat**. (slang) **1.** vb. To work hard, toil. **2.** n. Hard mental work, drudgery.

swum, vb. [1. swum ; 2. swam]. P.P. of **swim** ; O.E. (*ge*)*swummen* ; M.E. *swumme*(*n*).

swung, vb. [1. swung ; 2. swaŋ]. Pret. & P.P. of **swing** ; O.E. (*ge*)*swungen*, P.P. ; M.E. *swunge*(*n*).

sy-, pref. representing Gk. **syn-** before *s* & consonant, or *z* ; e.g. *system*, *systole*, *syzygy*.

sybarite, n. & adj. [1. síbarīt ; 2. síbərait], fr. Lat. *Sybarīta*, fr. Gk. *Subarítēs*, inhabitant of Sybaris, in Italy, near the Gulf of Tarentum, noted for the luxury of the inhabitants. **1.** n. Person given up to luxury and effeminacy. **2.** adj. Luxurious and effeminate.

sybaritic, adj. [1. sibarítik ; 2. sibərítik]. Prec. & **-ic.** Pertaining to, characteristic of, a sybarite.

sybaritically, adv. [1. sibarítikali ; 2. sibərítikəli]. Prec. & **-al** & **-ly.** In a sybaritic manner.

sybaritism, n. [1. síbarītìzm ; 2. síbəraitìzəm]. sybarite & **-ism.** Sybaritic life or habits.

sybil, n. See **sibyl**.

sycamine, n. [1. síkamīn, -mìn ; 2. síkəmin, -main], fr. Lat. *sỹcamīnus*, fr. Gk. *sūkámīnos*, Semitic loan-word, influenced by Gk. *sūkon*, 'fig', see **syconium** ; cp. Heb. *šiqmā*, 'mulberry'. Black mulberry.

sycamore, n. [1. síkamōr ; 2. síkəmō], fr. Lat. *sỹcomorus*, fr. Gk. *sūkómoros*, 'mulberry tree', prob. of Semitic origin, see prec., influenced by Gk. *sūkon*, 'fig', see **syconium**, *móron*, 'mulberry', see under **mulberry**. **1.** Also *sycamore fig*, Egyptian and Syrian tree of fig family. **2.** Also *sycamore maple*, broad-leaved maple of Northern Europe.

syce, sice, n. [1. sīs ; 2. sais]. Hind., fr. Arab. An Indian groom.

sycee, n. [1. sīsē ; 2. saisī], fr. Chinese *si szĕ*, 'fine silk'. Ingots of silver, varying in size, used in China as medium of exchange ; also *sycee silver*.

sychnocarpus, adj. [1. sìknōkárpus ; 2. sìknoukápəs], fr. Gk. *sukhnós*, 'many ; frequent ; dense, compact', earlier **tuk-sno-*, fr. stem **twek^w-, *tuk^w-,* seen in Gk. *sáttein*, 'to pack, press ; to equip' ; & Gk. *karpós*, 'fruit', see **carpel**. (bot.) Producing fruit for several seasons ; perennial.

syconium, n. [1. sī-, sikónium ; 2. sai-, sikóuniəm]. Mod. Lat., fr. Gk. *sūkon*, 'fig', prob. borrowed fr. a Mediterranean language. Fleshy fruit with seeds borne in a hollow receptacle, as in the fig.

sycophancy, n. [1. síkofansi ; 2. síkəfənsi]. Next word & **-cy.** Character, method, practice, of a sycophant.

sycophant, n. [1. síkofant ; 2. síkəfənt], fr. Lat. *sỹcophanta*, fr. Gk. *sūkophántēs*, 'informer', perh. orig. 'one who informed against persons exporting figs', fr. *sūkon*, 'fig', see **syconium**, & *-phant-*, fr. stem of *phainein*, 'to show', see **phantasm**. Servile flatterer, toady.

sycophantic, adj. [1. sìkofántik ; 2. sìkəfántik]. Prec. & **-ic.** Of, pertaining to, characteristic of, a sycophant.

sycosis, n. [1. sī-, sikōsis ; 2. sai-, sikóusis], fr. Lat., fr. Gk. *sukôsis*, 'fig-shaped ulcer', fr. *sūkon*, 'fig', see **syconium**, & *-osis*. Eruption on scalp or bearded part of face ; barber's itch.

syenite, n. [1. sīenìt ; 2. sáiindit], fr. Lat. *Syēnītēs* (*lapis*), a kind of red granite, fr. *Syēnē*, in Upper Egypt. Crystalline, igneous, alkaline rock containing little or no quartz.

syenitic, adj. [1. sīenítik ; 2. sáiinítik]. Prec. & **-ic.** Pertaining to, resembling, syenite.

syl-, pref. representing Gk. **syn-** before *-l* ; e.g. *syllable*, *syllogism*.

syllabary, n. [1. sílabari ; 2. síləbəri], fr. Lat. *syllaba*, 'syllable', see **syllable (I.)**, & **-ary.** List of syllabic characters used in some languages in place of an alphabet.

syllabic, adj. [1. silábik ; 2. siláébik], fr. Lat. *syllaba*, 'syllable', see **syllable (I.)**, & **-ic.** **1.** Connected with, pertaining to, a syllable. **2.** Representing a syllable : *syllabic character, symbol*. **3.** Forming, constituting, a separate syllable : *the sound l is syllabic in 'bottle'*.

syllabically, adv. [1. silábikali ; 2. siláébikəli]. Prec. & **-al** & **-ly.** In a syllabic manner ; according to syllables ; syllable by syllable.

syllabicate, vb. trans. [1. silábikāt ; 2. siláébikeit]. syllabic & **-ate.** **1.** To divide into syllables. **2.** To articulate syllable by syllable.

syllabication, n. [1. silàbikāshun ; 2. siláèbikéiʃən]. Prec. & **-ion.** Act of syllabicating ; state of being syllabicated.

syllabification, n. [1. silàbifikāshun ; 2. siláèbifikéiʃən]. See next word & **-fication.** Syllabication.

syllabify, vb. trans. [1. silábifī ; 2. siláébifai], fr. Lat. *syllaba*, 'syllable', see **syllable (I.)** & *-i-* & **-fy.** To treat, pronounce, as a syllable.

syllabize, vb. trans. [1. sílabīz ; 2. síləbaiz], fr. Lat. *syllaba*, 'syllable', see **syllable (I.)**, & **-ize.** To syllabify.

syllable (I.), n. [1. sílabl ; 2. síləbl]. M.E., fr. O. Fr. *sillabe*, fr. Lat. *syllaba*, fr. Gk. *sullabē*, 'that which holds together ; syllable', fr. **syl-** & *lab-*, stem of *lambánein*, 'to take, seize', cogn. w. Scrt. *lábhatē*, *rábhatē*, 'seizes' ; *rábhaš*, 'vehemence' ; Lat. *rabiēs*, 'rage, madness' ; see **rabid, catalepsy,** & **-le.** **1. a** Any sound or combination of sounds, the utterance of which produces upon the ear the impression of an unbroken unity, the principal condition of which is that the sonority shall be either gradually reduced or gradually increased during the utterance, but not reduced and then increased again ; such a new increase would constitute a fresh syllable ; **b** graphic representation of a syllable. **2.** Verbal utterance ; in such Phr. as : *he never uttered a syllable*, did not speak at all ; *I don't understand a syllable of what you say*, I understand nothing.

syllable (II.), vb. trans., fr. prec. **1.** To pronounce syllable by syllable. **2.** To utter, pronounce : '*Airy tongues that syllable men's names*' (Milton, 'Comus', 208).

syllabled, adj. [1. sílabld ; 2. síləbld]. **syllable (I.)** & **-ed.** Having specified number of syllables : *a three-syllabled word*.

syllabub, n. See **sillabub**.

syllabus, n. [1. sílabus ; 2. síləbəs], fr. L. Lat. *syllabus*, fr. Gk. *súllabos*, 'list, syllabus', fr. *sullambánein*, 'to gather together', fr. **syl-** & *lambánein*, 'to take', see **syllable (I.)**. **1. a** An outline, summary, containing the principal subjects to be dealt with in a course of lectures or other form of instruction ; programme of studies ; **b** such course of instruction &c. itself. **2.** (R.C. Ch.) Summary of decrees of Roman Curia ; specif. (cap.) list of eighty heretical doctrines &c. given in the encyclical letter of Pius IX., 1864.

syllepsis, n. [1. silépsis, siléʹpsis ; 2. silépsis, sílipsis]. Lat. *syllepsis*, fr. Gk. *súllēpsis*, 'a taking together, comprehension', fr. **syl-** & **lēp-*, a form of the base of *lambánein*, 'to take, seize', see **syllable (I.)**. Figure of rhetoric in which a word is used in two different senses at the same time, esp. in both a literal and a metaphorical sense ; e.g. *his temper was as short as his coat-tails*.

sylleptic, adj. [1. siléptik ; 2. siléptik], fr. Gk. *sullēpt-*, see prec., & **-ic.** Pertaining to, forming, of the nature of, a syllepsis.

sylleptically, adv. [1. siléptikali ; 2. siléptikəli]. Prec. & **-al** & **-ly.** By means of syllepsis.

syllogism, n. [1. sílojìzm ; 2. sílədʒìzəm], fr. Lat. *syllogismus*, fr. Gk. *sullogismós*, 'conclusion, inference from premises', fr. *sullogizomai*, 'to collect, bring before the mind, sum up, draw conclusions', fr. **syl-** & *logizomai*, 'to reckon, compute ; to conclude, infer', fr. *lógos*, 'word, speech, thought', see **logos**. (log.) Formal statement of an argument, consisting of three propositions, called respectively the major and minor premises and the conclusion ; e.g. *water is wet ; rain is water ; therefore rain is wet*.

syllogistic, adj. [1. sìlojístik ; 2. sìlədʒístik], fr. adj. stem of Gk. *sullogizomai*, 'to infer', see prec., & **-ic.** Pertaining to, of the nature of, in form of, a syllogism.

syllogistically, adv. [1. sìlojístikali ; 2. sìlədʒístikəli]. Prec. & **-al** & **-ly.** In a syllogistic manner or form.

syllogize, vb. intrans. & trans. [1. sílojīz ; 2. sílədʒaiz], fr. Gk. *sullogízomai*, 'to infer', see **syllogism**. **1.** intrans. To reason by syllogisms. **2.** trans. To put into syllogistic form.

sylph, n. [1. silf ; 2. silf], fr. Fr. *sylphe*, perh. fr. Gk. *sílphē*, 'insect, beetle, bookworm' ; etymol. doubtful. **1.** Air - spirit, elemental spirit existing in the air. **2.** Slender, graceful woman. **3.** Humming-bird with long, brightly coloured tail.

sylph-like, adj. Prec. & **-like.** Resembling a sylph ; slender and graceful.

sylvan, adj. See **silvan**.

sym-, pref. representing Gk. **sum-** ; form of **syn-**, before *b-, p-, m-* ; e.g. *symbol*, *symmetry*.

symbion(t), n. [1. símbion(t); 2. símbiən(t)], fr. Gk. *sumbion*, stem *sumbiont*-, Pres. Part. of *sumbioein*, 'to live together', fr. **sym-** & *bios*, 'life', see **bio-**. Organism living in symbiosis.

symbiosis, n. [1. sìmbióusis; 2. sìmbaióusis], fr. Gk. *sumbion*, see prec., & **-osis**. (biol.) A living together, in intimate relation, for purposes of nutrition, of two dissimilar organisms; a form of parasitism.

symbiotic, adj. [1. sìmbiótik; 2. sìmbiótik]. See prec. & **-otic**. Pertaining to, characterized by, symbiosis.

symbiotically, adv. [1. sìmbiótikali; 2. sìmbiótikəli]. Prec. & **-al** & **-ly**. By means of symbiosis.

symbol, n. [1. símbl; 2. símbl], fr. Fr. *symbole*, fr. Lat. *symbola*, fr. Gk. *súmbolon*, 'token; pledge; covenant', fr. *sumbállein*, 'to throw together, unite; to compare; to correspond', fr. **sym-** & *bállein*, 'to throw', see **ballistic**. 1. Something which represents or typifies another thing, quality &c.; outward sign, emblem of a person, cause, quality, principle, ideal &c.: *the owl was the symbol of Minerva; a circle is the symbol of eternity; a cross is the symbol of Christianity*. 2. Specif., a graphic character, letter, figure, sign, used to express a sound, a mathematical quantity &c.

symbolic(al), adj. [1. sìmbólik(l); 2. sìmbólik(l)]. Prec. & **-ic** & **-al**. Of, pertaining to, serving as, a symbol.

symbolically, adv. Prec. & **-ly**. In a symbolic manner; by means of a symbol.

symbolics, n. [1. sìmbóliks; 2. sìmbóliks]. symbol & **-ics**. Study of symbols.

symbolism, n. [1. símbolizm; 2. símbəlizəm]. symbol & **-ism**. 1. Representation by symbols. 2. System or group of symbols representing specific group of ideas &c.: *religious symbolism* &c. 3. Doctrines of a certain 19th cent. school of French poets and painters, denoting revulsion from the realistic or naturalistic school.

symbolist, n. [1. símbolist; 2. símbəlist]. symbol & **-ist**. a Person who is versed in the use of symbols; b person who makes use of symbols; c member of the French school of symbolism in art and literature.

symbolization, n. [1. sìmbolizáshun; 2. sìmbəlaizéiʃən]. Next word & **-ation**. Act of symbolizing; state of being symbolized.

symbolize, vb. trans. [1. símboliz; 2. símbəlaiz]. symbol & **-ize**. 1. To be a symbol of, typify, represent symbolically: *the peacock symbolizes pride*. 2. To represent by a symbol: *how shall we symbolize cunning?*

symbology, n. [1. simbóloji; 2. simbólədʒi]. symbol & **-logy**. Study of symbols; art of symbolic representation.

symbololatry, n. [1. símbólólatri; 2. símbəlólətri]. symbol & -o- & **-latry**. Worship of symbols; excessive reverence given to symbols.

symbolology, n. [1. símbolóloji; 2. símbəlólədʒi]. symbol & -o- & **-logy**. Symbology.

symmetrian, n. [1. simétrian; 2. simétriən]. symmetry & **-an**. Symmetrist.

symmetric(al), adj. [1. simétrik(l); 2. simétrik(l)]. symmetry & **-ic** & **-al**. Having, exhibiting, the quality of symmetry; duly proportioned, harmonious; conforming exactly in opposite parts.

symmetrically, adv. Prec. & **-ly**. In a symmetrical manner.

symmetrician, n. [1. sìmetríshan; 2. sìmitríʃən]. symmetry & **-ician**. Symmetrist.

symmetrist, n. [1. símetrist; 2. símitrist]. symmetry & **-ist**. Person who is careful of, insistent on, symmetry.

symmetrization, n. [1. símetrizáshun; 2. sìmitraizéiʃən]. Next word & **-ation**. Act of symmetrizing; symmetrical construction or arrangement.

symmetrize, vb. trans. [1. símetriz; 2. símitraiz]. symmetry & **-ize**. To make symmetrical; construct, arrange, symmetrically.

symmetrophobia, n. [1. simétrofóbia; 2. simétrəfóubiə]. symmetry & -o- & **-phobia**. Fear, dislike, or avoidance of symmetry, esp. in architecture.

symmetry, n. [1. símetri; 2. símitri], fr. O. Fr. *symmetrie*, fr. Lat. *symmetria*, fr. Gk. *summetria*, 'symmetry, due proportion', fr. *súmmetros*, 'commensurate; in due proportion; symmetrical', fr. **sym-** & *métron*, 'measure', see **metre**. 1. Such due proportion of the parts of a body or structure in relation to each other as conveys an impression of fitness and beauty, and produces a sense of pleasure. 2. Correspondence, similarity in or between the opposing sides of an object, considered as halves on either side of a central line, in form and dimensions: *the symmetry of a face is marred by a bulge in one cheek*.

sympalmograph, n. [1. simpálmograhf; 2. simpǽlməgrɑ̄f], fr. **sym-** & Gk. *palm-(ós)*, 'vibration', fr. *pállein*, 'to shake, throw', cogn. w. Gk. *pelemízein*, 'to shake, move violently', *pólemos*, 'fight, struggle' (see **polemic**); & -o- & **-graph**. Instrument recording sound-vibrations.

sympathetic (I.), adj. [1. sìmpathétik; 2. sìmpəpétik], fr. Gk. *sumpathētikós*, 'sympathetic'; **sym-** & **pathetic**. 1. Pertaining to sympathy; feeling, expressing, sympathy; arising from sympathy: *a sympathetic person, look, nature, understanding* &c.; *sympathetic words*. 2. In accordance with one's sympathies; consonant with one's tastes, feelings, opinions &c.; hence, congenial: *to live in sympathetic surroundings*. 3. *Sympathetic vibrations*, such as are set up indirectly by those occurring in another vibrating body, and transmitted by the air or other medium. 4. *Sympathetic sensation*, one due to an indirect stimulus applied at a different point from that at which it is felt; *sympathetic nerve*, one of the smaller nervous ganglia which connect the main nerves of the cerebro-spinal system. 5. *Sympathetic ink*, one which is invisible until exposed to heat, or treated with a chemical reagent.

sympathetic (II.), n., fr. prec. 1. Sympathetic nerve. 2. Person yielding easily to hypnotic influence.

sympathetically, adv. [1. sìmpathétikali; 2. sìmpəpétikəli]. Prec. & **-al** & **-ly**. In a sympathetic manner.

sympathize, vb. intrans. [1. símpathīz; 2. símpəpaiz]. sympathy & **-ize**. 1. To feel sympathy; to be affected by similar or corresponding ideas or emotions: *to sympathize with a person in his grief or in his joy*; *I can quite sympathize with your delight at your success; my father never sympathized with my desire to see the world*. 2. To express sympathy; to speak sympathetically; to condole.

sympathizer, n. [1. símpathīzer; 2. símpəpaizə]. Prec. & **-er**. 1. One who sympathizes; a person who shares another's opinions &c.; an adherent, supporter; b one who supports a cause, movement &c. 2. Person who shares the afflictions &c. of another, who expresses sympathy, who gives consolation.

sympathy, n. [1. símpathi; 2. símpəpi], fr. Lat. *sympathīa*, fr. Gk. *sumpátheia*, 'fellow-feeling, sympathy', fr. *sumpathḗs*, 'sympathizing with', fr. **sym-** & *páthos*, 'suffering', see **pathos**. 1. Community, identity, of feeling; fellow-feeling; a agreement with another in tastes, opinions, aspirations, or with the tastes and opinions, aspirations, of another: *I have every sympathy with you in your love of country life, or with your love* &c.; *he had small sympathy with the idle and frivolous*, or *with idleness and frivolity*. Phr. *in, out, of sympathy with*, in, out, of, agreement with; b conformity of temperament, spiritual harmony, and understanding: *perfect sympathy should exist between husband and wife*. 2. Specif. a the sharing of another's grief, sorrow, misery, misfortune &c.; feeling of compassion and pity, tenderness, aroused by the sufferings of others: *his infirmities and poverty could but excite sympathy in those who knew him*; *one should feel sympathy for* (or *with*) *misfortune even when it arises from misconduct*; *a man of ready sympathies*; b expression of sympathy; condolence, commiseration, consolation: *letters and messages of sympathy*. 3. (physiol.) Increase or diminution of activity in an organ as a result of a similar condition in another organ. 4. (phys.) a Correlation existing between vibrating bodies whereby the vibrations of one are transmitted indirectly to the other through a medium; b tendency of certain substances to act one upon the other, or to unite, e.g. the attraction of a magnet for steel.

sympelmous, adj. [1. simpélmus; 2. simpélməs], fr. **sym-** & Gk. *pélma*, 'sole of foot', see under **film (I.)**, & **-ous**. (of bird) Having the flexor tendons united.

sympetalous, adj. [1. simpétalus; 2. simpétələs]. **sym-** & **petal** & **-ous**. (bot.) With petals united.

symphonic, adj. [1. simfónik; 2. simfónik]. symphony & **-ic**. Pertaining to, resembling, in the form of, a symphony.

symphonious, adj. [1. simfónius; 2. simfóuniəs]. Next word & **-ous**. Characterized by harmony of sound; harmonious.

symphony, n. [1. símfuni; 2. símfəni], fr. O. Fr. *symphonie*, fr. Lat. *symphōnia*, fr. Gk. *sumphōnia*, 'concord of sound; harmony', fr. *súmphōnos*, 'agreeing in sound', fr. **sym-** & *phōné*, 'sound', see **phone (I.)**. 1. (archaic) Harmony of sounds, harmonious blending of sound. 2. (mus.) Sonata for an orchestra; orchestral composition in two or more contrasted movements.

symphoricarpous, adj. [1. sìmforikárpus; 2. sìmforikǽpəs], fr. **sym-** & Gk. *phorós*, 'bearing', see **-phore**, & Gk. *karpós*, 'fruit', see **carpel**, & **-ous**. Bearing fruit in clusters.

symphyllous, adj. [1. simfílus; 2. simfíləs], fr. **sym-** & Gk. *phúll-(on)*, 'leaf', see **phyllo-**, & **-ous**. Having leaves united.

symphyseal, adj. [1. simfízeal; 2. simfíziəl]. See next word & **-al**. Pertaining to a symphysis.

symphysis, n. [1. símfisis; 2. símfisis]. Gk. *súmphusis*, 'a growing together', fr. **sym-** & Gk. *phúsis*, 'nature, form, development', fr. *phúein*, 'to grow', see **physic (I.)**. Union, line of junction, between two parts of the skeleton, directly or by means of connecting cartilage &c.

sympiesometer, n. [1. sìmpiezómeter; 2. sìmpaizómitə], fr. Gk. *sympíes-(is)*, 'compression', fr. *sumpiézein*, 'to compress', fr. **sym-** & *piézein*, 'to compress', see **piezometer**; & -o- & **-meter**. a Instrument measuring velocity or force of current of water; b barometer indicating atmospheric pressure by compression of gas in a tube.

sympodium, n. [1. simpódium; 2. simpóudiəm]. Mod. Lat., fr. **sym-** & Gk. *pódion*, dimin. of *poùs*, stem *pod-*, 'a foot', see **pedal (I.)**. (bot.) Apparent main stem composed of a succession of branches.

symposiac, adj. [1. simpózìak; 2. simpóuziæk]. See **symposium** & **-ac**. Symposial.

symposial, adj. [1. simpózial; 2. simpóuziəl]. See **symposium** & **-al**. Of, pertaining to, a symposium.

symposiarch, n. [1. simpóziàrk, simpóziàrk; 2. simpóuziɑ̀k, simpóziɑ̀k], fr. Gk. *sumposiarkh-(os)*, 'symposiarch', fr. *sumpósion*, see next word, & *arkhós*, 'leader', see **arch-**. Director of a symposium; toast-master.

symposium, n. [1. simpózium, simpózium; 2. simpóuziəm, simpóziəm]. Lat., fr. Gk. *sumpósion*, 'drinking-party', fr. **sym-** & *pósis*, 'drinking', cogn. w. Lat. *pōtio*, see under **potion**. 1. a Drinking-feast, often with music &c., following dinner in ancient Greece; b drinking-party. 2. Meeting for philosophical discussion. 3. Collection of essays or comments by different writers upon a given subject.

symptom, n. [1. símptum; 2. símptəm], fr. O. Fr. *symptome*, fr. Gk. *súmptōma*, 'chance,

symptomatic, **casualty**', fr. *sumpiptein*, 'to fall in with; to happen', fr. **sym-** & *píptein*, 'to fall'; see **ptosis** & **ptero-**. **1.** Perceptible change in an organ, or organic function, due to, and indicating, presence or development of disease: *the symptoms point to poisoning* ; *to develop alarming symptoms* ; *he has all the symptoms of malaria*. **2.** Outward, recognizable, sign, indication, of the presence or existence of something else : *to show symptoms of fear, joy* ; *hesitation is not infrequently a symptom of cowardice*.

symptomatic, adj. [1. sìmptomátik ; 2. sìmptəmǽtik], fr. Gk. *sumptōmat-*, stem of *súmptōma*, 'chance', see prec., & **-ic**. Pertaining to, of the nature of, a symptom ; forming, to be regarded as, a symptom ; indicative.

symptomatically, adv. [1. sìmptomátikali ; 2. sìmptəmǽtikəli]. Prec. & **-al** & **-ly**. According to symptoms.

symptomatology, n. [1. símptomatóloji ; 2. sìmptəmætólədži], fr. Gk. *sumptōmat-*, stem of *súmptōma*, 'chance', see **symptom**, & **-o-** & **-logy**. Study of symptoms; investigation and classification of symptoms and their relation to disease.

syn-, pref. representing Gk. *sún*, 'with'; etymol. unknown. Found in compounds, usually representing or derived fr. Gk. words w. the sense of 'with, together'.

syn(a)eresis, n. [1. sinéresis ; 2. siníərisis]. Gk. *sunaíresis*, 'a taking, drawing, together', see **syn-** & **heresy**. Coalescence, contraction, of two vowels or syllables.

synagogic(al), adj. [1. sìnagógik(l), -gójik(l) ; 2. sìnəgógik(l), -gódžik(l)]. **synagogue** & **-ic** & **-al**. Pertaining to a synagogue.

synagog(u)al, adj. [1. sínagōgal ; 2. sínəgòugəl]. Next word & **-al**. Synagogical.

synagogue, n. [1. sínagòg ; 2. sínəgòg], fr. Fr., Lat. *synagōga*, 'congregation of Jews ', fr. Gk. *sunagōgḗ*, 'a bringing together ; place of assembly, synagogue ', fr. *sunágein*, 'to bring together', fr. **syn-** & *ágein*, 'to bring', see **agonistic**. **a** A Congregation or assembly of Jews organized for religious observances and instruction ; **b** meeting - place, place of worship, of Jewish congregation.

synallagmatic, adj. [1. sìnalagmátik ; 2. sìnælagmǽtik], fr. **syn-** & Gk. *allagmat-*, stem of *állagma*, 'thing taken in exchange', fr. stem of *allássein*, 'to exchange, barter', fr. *állos*, 'other', see under **alias**. Expressing, setting out, mutual obligations.

synal(o)epha, n. [1. sìnoléfa ; 2. sìnəlífə]. Lat. *synaloepha*, fr. Gk. *sunaloiphḗ*, 'contraction of two syllables', fr. **syn-** & *aleiphein*, 'to anoint, smear over'; cp. Gk. *lípos*, 'fat', & see **adipose**. Elision of final vowel before following initial vowel.

synantherous, adj. [1. sinántherus ; 2. sinǽnþərəs], fr. **syn-** & **anther** & **-ous**. (bot.) Having the anthers united.

synanthous, adj. [1. sinánthus ; 2. sinǽnþəs], fr. **syn-** & Gk. *ánth-(os)*, 'flower', see under **anther**, & **-ous**. (bot.) Producing flowers and leaves at the same time.

synaphe(i)a, n. [1. sinaféa ; 2. sìnəfíə], fr. **syn-** & Gk. *haphḗ*, 'touch', fr. *háptein*, 'to touch, fasten'; no cognates outside Gk. Metrical continuity between lines or halflines of verse.

synarthrosis, n. [1. sìnarthrōsis ; 2. sìnāprōusis]. Gk. *sunárthrosis*, fr. **syn-** & *árthr-(on)*, 'a joint', see **arthritis**, & **-osis**. Joint permitting of no movement between articulating bones.

syncarp, n. [1. sínkarp ; 2. sínkāp], fr. **syn-** & Gk. *karp-(ós)*, 'fruit', see **carpel**. Multiple or aggregate fruit, e.g. blackberry, mulberry.

syncarpous, adj. [1. sinkárpus ; 2. sinkǽpəs]. Prec. & **-ous**. Pertaining to, characterized by, syncarps.

synchondrosis, n. [1. sìnkondrōsis ; 2. sìnkondróusis]. Gk. *sugkhóndrōsis*, 'a growing together into one cartilage', fr. **syn-** & *khóndr-(os)*, 'cartilage', see **chondri-**, & **-osis**. Articulation of bones by means of a layer of cartilage, forming an almost immovable joint.

synchronism, n. [1. sínkronizm ; 2. sínkronìzəm]. See **synchronize** & **-ism**. State of being synchronous ; simultaneous occurrence or existence.

synchronistic, adj. [1. sìnkronístik ; 2. sìnkronístik]. See prec. & **-ist** & **-ic**. Synchronous.

synchronistically, adv. [1. sìnkronístikali ; 2. sìnkrənístikəli]. Prec. & **-al** & **-ly**. So as to synchronize ; synchronously.

synchronization, n. [1. sìnkronīzáshun ; 2. sìnkrənaizéiʃən]. Next word & **-ation**. Act of synchronizing; state, condition, of being synchronized.

synchronize, vb. intrans. & trans. [1. sínkroniz ; 2. sínkronàiz], fr. Gk. *súgkhronos*, 'contemporary', fr. **syn-** & *khrónos*, 'time', see **chronic**, & **-ize**. **A.** intrans. **1.** To agree in date or time, occur or exist at same period or point of time, be coincident. **2.** (of clocks &c.) To keep the same time. **B.** trans. **1.** To show (events &c.) to coincide in date, prove simultaneous existence or occurrence of. **2.** To regulate (a number of clocks), esp. by electric or other mechanical device, so that they all keep the same time.

synchronous, adj. [1. sínkrunus ; 2. sínkrənəs], fr. Lat. *synchronus*, fr. Gk. *súgkhronos*, 'contemporary', see **synchronize**, & **-ous**. Occurring, existing, at the same time ; simultaneous, coincident, contemporary.

synchronously, adv. Prec. & **-ly**. At the same point of time.

synchrony, n. [1. sínkruni ; 2. sínkrəni]. See **synchronous** & **-y**. (rare) Agreement in point of time ; synchronism.

synclastic, adj. [1. sinklástik ; 2. sinklǽstik], fr. **syn-** & Gk. *klastós*, 'broken', fr. *kláein*, 'to break'; see **cataclasm**. Curving similarly in all directions, convex or concave on all sides.

synclinal, adj. [1. sinklínal ; 2. sinkláinəl]. Next word & **-al**. (geol.) Forming a syncline.

syncline, n. [1. sínklīn ; 2. sínklain], fr. **syn-** & Gk. *klínein*, 'to slope; to lie'; see **clinical**. Geological formation with beds dipping down to the axis of a fold.

syncopate, vb. trans. [1. síngkopàt ; 2. síŋkəpèit], fr. Lat. *syncopāre*, 'to faint away', fr. *syncopē*, 'a swoon', see **syncope**, & **-ate**. **1.** (gram.) To shorten (a word) by omitting medial sound or syllable. **2.** (mus.) **a** To alter musical rhythm by beginning (a note) on a normally unaccented beat and holding it into next accented beat ; **b** to disturb rhythm of (musical composition) by syncopation.

syncopation, n. [1. sìngkopáshun ; 2. sìŋkəpéiʃən]. Prec. & **-ation**. Act of syncopating ; state of being syncopated.

syncope, n. [1. síngkopi ; 2. síŋkəpi]. Lat. *syncopē*, 'swoon'; syncope'; fr. Gk. *sugkopḗ*, 'a cutting short ; syncope', fr. **syn-** & *kopḗ*, 'act of cutting'; cp. Gk. *kóptein*, 'to strike, cut'; *kópos*, 'blow'; *kómma*, 'piece cut off', see **comma**. **1.** Fainting-fit, sudden loss of consciousness. **2.** (gram.) Contraction of a word by loss of medial sound or syllable. **3.** (mus.) **a** Syncopation ; **b** correspondence of two or more notes in one voice-part &c. to one note in another part.

syncopic, adj. [1. sinkópik ; 2. sinkópik]. Prec. & **-ic**. Of, pertaining to, of the nature of, affected by, syncope.

syncoptic, adj. [1. sinkóptik ; 2. sinkóptik], fr. Gk. *sugkóptein*, 'to cut up', fr. **syn-** & *kóptein*, 'to strike, cut', see **syncope**, & **-ic**. Syncopic.

syncotyledonous, adj. [1. sìnkotilédunus ; 2. sìnkɔtilídənəs]. **syn-** & **cotyledon** & **-ous**. (bot.) Having the cotyledons united.

syncretic, adj. [1. sinkrétik ; 2. sinkrítik]. See next word & **-ic**. Syncretistic.

syncretism, n. [1. sínkretizm ; 2. sínkritìzəm]. Gk. *sugkrētismós*, fr. *sugkrētízein*, 'to combine against a common enemy', fr. **syn-**, & the base seen in Gk. *keránnūmi*, 'to mix, blend', *krâsis*, 'mixture', q.v. under **crasis**. Attempt to reconcile or unite varying religious or philosophic systems (often in disparaging sense).

syncretistic, adj. [1. sìnkretístik ; 2. sìnkritístik]. See prec. & **-ist** & **-ic**. Pertaining to syncretism.

syncretize, vb. trans. & intrans. [1. sínkretīz ; 2. sínkritaiz], fr. Gk. *sugkrētízein*, see **syncretism**. **1.** trans. To carry out syncretism of ; to attempt to harmonize. **2.** intrans. (of conflicting religious or philosophic systems &c.) To come into harmony, be reconciled.

syncytium, n. [1. sinsíshium, -sítium ; 2. sinsíʃiəm, -sítiəm], fr. **syn-** & Gk. *kút-(os)*, 'hollow ; urn, vessel', see under **cutis**. (biol.) Mass of tissue containing many nuclei but not divided into separate cells.

syndactyl, adj. [1. sìndáktil ; 2. sìndǽktil], fr. **syn-** & Gk. *dáktulos*, 'finger', see **dactyl**. Having two or more digits united.

syndactylism, n. [1. sìndáktilizm ; 2. sìndǽktilìzəm]. Prec. & **-ism**. State of being syndactyl.

syndactylous, adj. [1. sìndáktilus ; 2. sìndǽktiləs]. See prec. & **-ous**. Syndactyl.

syndesmosis, n. [1. sìndezmōsis ; 2. sìndezmóusis], fr. **syn-** & Gk. *desmós*, 'band', fr. *déein*, 'to bind', see **diadem**, & **-osis**. Union of two parts of the skeleton by means of ligaments.

syndetic, adj. [1. sindétik ; 2. sindétik], fr. **syn-** & Gk. *detós*, 'bound', fr. *déein*, 'to bind', see prec., & **-ic**. (gram.) Connecting, being connected, by means of conjunctions.

syndic, n. [1. síndik ; 2. síndik], fr. Fr., fr. Lat. *syndicus*, 'representative of a corporation', fr. Gk. *súndikos*, 'public advocate', fr. **syn-** & *díkē*, 'judgement, justice', see **dicast**. **1.** An officer having magisterial functions in some European countries. **2.** (Cambridge University) Member of a special committee of the senate ; corresponding to a *delegate* in Oxford.

syndicalism, n. [1. síndikalizm ; 2. síndikəlìzəm]. Prec. & **-al** & **-ism**. **1.** Government, management of business, by a syndicate. **2.** Specif., system advocated by some tradeunionists whereby the ownership and management of an industry would be in the hands of the trade unions, the capitalist owner being abolished ; the term is derived from French *syndicat*, 'trade union'.

syndicate (I.), n. [1. síndikat ; 2. síndikət], fr. Med. Lat. *syndicātus* ; **syndic** & **-ate**. **1.** Body of syndics, council. **2.** Group of financiers, merchants &c. combining to carry out a commercial enterprise, esp. in the preliminary stages of forming a limited liability company prior to the issue of shares to the public ; group of persons &c. that buy up news &c. for simultaneous publication in different periodicals.

syndicate (II.), vb. trans. [1. síndikāt ; 2. síndikeit], fr. prec. **a** To combine into a syndicate ; **b** to publish (news &c.) in several papers at the same time.

syndication, n. [1. sìndikáshun ; 2. sìndikéiʃən]. Prec. & **-ion**. Act of syndicating ; state of being syndicated.

syne, n. [1. sīn ; 2. sain]. Scots for **since**. *Auld lang syne*, the days of long ago.

synecdoche, n. [1. sinékdoki ; 2. sinékdəki], fr. Lat. *synecdochē*, fr. Gk. *sunekdochḗ*, 'synecdoche', fr. **syn-** & Gk. *ek*, 'out of', see under **ex-**, & Gk. *dokhḗ*, 'reception' fr. *dék(h)omai*, 'I receive', fr. base **dek-*, see **dogma**. Figure of speech in which a part is used to imply a whole ; e.g. *blade* for *sword* ; *sail*, *keel*, *bottom*, for *ship* ; *hand* for *workman*.

synedrium, n. [1. sinédrium ; 2. sinédriəm], Lat., fr. Gk. *sunédrion*, 'assembly, council', fr. **syn-** & *hédra*, 'a seat ; a sitting', see under **cathedral** & **seat (I.)**. Council, assembly ; specif., the Jewish sanhedrim.

synesis, n. [1. sínesis ; 2. sínisis], fr. Gk. *súnesis*, 'coming together, union ; comprehension, undertaking', fr. *suniēmi*, 'I bring together', fr. **syn-** & *hiēmi*, 'I move forward, throw, send'; cogn. w. Lat. *jacere*, 'to throw', see **jactitation**. Construction in which there is a departure from strict syntax owing to the attraction exercised by some conception expressed in the sentence, e.g. *these sort of things*, *these* being affected by the plural *things*.

syngenesis, n. [1. sìnjénesis; 2. sìndžénisis]. **syn-** & **genesis**. Development of embryo from union of male and female elements.

syngnathous, adj. [1. singnăthus, síngnathus; 2. siŋnéipəs, síŋnəpəs], fr. **syn-** & Gk. *gnăth-(os)*, 'jaw', see **gnathic**, & **-ous**. (of fish) With mouth forming a tube.

synizesis, n. [1. sìnizēsis; 2. sìnizísis]. Gk. *synizēsis*, fr. **syn-** & *hizein*, 'to seat', cogn. w. Gk. *hézomai*, 'to sit', see under **sedentary** (I.). Contraction of two vowels, each originally forming a separate syllable, into one syllable.

synod, n. [1. sínod; 2. sínəd], fr. Fr., fr. Lat. *synodus*, 'ecclesiastical assembly', fr. Gk. *súnodos*, 'meeting, junction, assembly', fr. **syn-** & *hodós*, 'way', see **hodometer**. 1. Ecclesiastical council, whether local or general. 2. Council in Presbyterian Church, intermediate between General Assembly and presbyteries. 3. Deliberative assembly, council. 4. (astron., archaic) Conjunction.

synodal, adj. [1. sínodl; 2. sínədl]. Prec. & **-al**. Pertaining to a synod.

synodic(al), adj. [1. sinódik(l); 2. sinódik(l)]. **synod** & **-ic** & **-al**. Synodal.

synodically, adv. Prec. & **-ly**. After the manner of, by means of, a synod.

synoecious, adj. [1. sinēsius; 2. sinísiəs], fr. **syn-** & Gk. *oîkos*, 'house', see **economy**. (bot.) Having male and female elements in the same flower-head, or within the same receptacle.

synonym, n. [1. sínonim; 2. sínənim], fr. Lat. *synōnyma*, fr. Gk. *sunōnumos*, 'synonymous', fr. **syn-** & *ónoma*, 'name', see **onomatopeia**, & **name** (I.). 1. Word identical in meaning with another, or only slightly differentiated in sense or usage. 2. Word identical in meaning with another in one or more of its senses, but not all.

synonymatic, adj. [1. sinònimátik; 2. sinònimǽtik], fr. **syn-** & Gk. *onomat-*, stem of *ónoma*, 'name', see prec., & **-ic**. Of, pertaining to, making use of, constituting, a synonym.

synonymic, adj. [1. sìnonímik; 2. sìnənímik]. **synonym** & **-ic**. Synonymatic.

synonymity, n. [1. sìnonímiti; 2. sìnənímiti]. **synonym** & **-ity**. State of being synonymous; similarity or identity in meaning.

synonymous, adj. [1. sinónimus; 2. sinóniməs]. **synonym** & **-ous**. Of the nature of, constituting, a synonym; expressing the same or almost the same meaning, conveying the same or a similar idea: *the two terms are synonymous*; *high is synonymous with lofty*; *his name is synonymous with cowardice*.

synonymously, adv. Prec. & **-ly**. By means of, in the manner of, synonyms.

synonymy, n. [1. sinónimi; 2. sinónimi], fr. Gk. *sunōnumia*, fr. *sunōnumos*, 'synonymous'; **synonym** & **-y**. Synonymity.

synopsis, n. [1. sinópsis; 2. sinópsis], fr. Gk. *súnopsis*, 'general view', fr. **syn-** & *ópsis*, 'sight, view', see under **optic**. Comprehensive summary, general view, outline.

synoptic, adj. & n. [1. sinóptik; 2. sinóptik], fr. Gk. *sunoptikós*, 'taking a general view'; **syn-** & **optic**. 1. adj. **a** Pertaining to, of the nature of, giving, a synopsis; *the Synoptic Gospels*, those of St. Matthew, St. Mark, and St. Luke, which present similarity of treatment, as opposed to that of St. John; hence, **b** of, pertaining to, the Synoptic Gospels. 2. n. Writer of one of the Synoptic Gospels.

synoptical, adj. [1. sinóptikl; 2. sinóptikl]. Prec. & **-al**. Synoptic.

synoptically, adv. Prec. & **-ly**. In a synoptic manner, in outline, as a summary.

synoptist, n. [1. sinóptist; 2. sinóptist]. See **synoptic** & **-ist**. Writer of one of the Synoptic Gospels.

synosteology, n. [1. sìnosteóloji; 2. sìnəstióləǰi]. **syn-** & **osteology**. Study of the joints of the body.

synost(e)osis, n. [1. sìnost(e)ósis; 2. sìnəst(i)óusis], fr. **syn-** & Gk. *ostē-(on)*, 'bone', see **osteo-** & **os**, & **-osis**. Anchylosis.

synostotic, adj. [1. sìnostótik; 2. sìnəstótik]. See prec. & **-otic**. Pertaining to anchylosis.

synovia, n. [1. sinóvia; 2. sinóuviə], fr. **syn-** & perh. Lat. *ōv-(um)*, 'egg', see **ovum**, & **-ia**. Albuminous fluid secreted by glands between joints and acting as lubricator.

synovial, adj. [1. sinóvial; 2. sinóuviəl]. Prec. & **-al**. Of, pertaining to, secreting, synovia: *synovial membrane, fluid*.

synovitis, n. [1. sìnovītis; 2. sìnəváitis]. See **synovia** & **-itis**. Inflammation of the synovial membrane.

syntactic(al), adj. [1. sintáktik(l); 2. sintǽktik(l)], fr. Gk. *suntaktikós*, fr. **syn-** & *tássein*, 'to arrange, put together'; see **tactics**. Pertaining to syntax.

syntactically, adv. Prec. & **-ly**. From the point of view of, as regards, syntax.

syntactics, n. [1. sintáktiks; 2. sintǽktiks]. See **syntactic** & **-ics**. Branch of mathematics treating of the number of ways of putting things together, e.g. permutations and combinations.

syntax, n. [1. síntaks; 2. síntæks], fr. Fr. *syntaxe*, fr. Lat. *syntaxis*, fr. Gk. *súntaxis*, 'arrangement; grammatical construction', fr. **syn-** & *táxis*, 'arranging', see **taxis**. Arrangement and grammatical relation of words as members of a sentence; sentence construction.

synthesis, n. [1. sínthesis; 2. sínþisis], fr. Lat. *synthesis*, 'compound, mixture', fr. Gk. *súnthesis*, 'a putting together'; **syn-** & **thesis** (I.). 1. **a** The act or process of putting together, of combining; **b** the result of such a process; combination; the reverse of *analysis*. 2. (chem.) The process of building up a substance by combining the elements of which it is formed, or of forming compounds by bringing together a number of simpler compounds. 3. (philos.) The mental process of uniting the separate elements of thought or sensation into a complex conception. 4. (philol.) The process of combining into an inflected word various elements supposed to have been originally distinct, e.g. a base, secondary formative elements including the stem, and the suffix or inflexion.

synthesist, n. [1. sínthesist; 2. sínþisist]. Prec. & **-ist**. One who makes a synthesis.

synthesize, vb. trans. [1. sínthesīz; 2. sínþisaiz]. See **synthesis** & **-ize**. To synthetize.

synthetic(al), adj. [1. sinthétik(l); 2. sinþétik(l)], fr. Gk. *sunthetikós*, 'constructive', fr. *súnthetos*, 'compound', fr. **syn-** & *thetós*, 'placed', see **thesis**. 1. Pertaining to, of the nature of, a synthesis. 2. **a** Produced by, resulting from, a synthesis; specif. **b** (chem.) produced by artificial process of synthesis in a laboratory, and not by the ordinary process of nature: *synthetic wine, silk, rubber* &c.

synthetically, adv. Prec. & **-ly**. In a synthetic manner; by means of synthesis.

synthetist, n. [1. sínthetist; 2. sínþitist], fr. Gk. *súnthetos*, 'compound', see **synthetic**, & **-ist**. One who makes a synthesis.

synthetize, vb. trans. & intrans. [1. sínthetīz; 2. sínþitaiz], fr. Gk. *súnthetos*, 'compound', see **synthetic**, & **-ize**. **a** trans. To combine (things or ideas) by a process of synthesis; **b** intrans., to make a synthesis.

syntonic, adj. [1. sintónik; 2. sintónik]. **syntony** & **-ic**. (of wireless transmitter and receiver) Tuned to the same wave-length.

syntonization, n. [1. sìntonizéishun; 2. sìntənaizéiʃən]. Next word & **-ation**. Process of syntonizing, tuning of wireless receiver and transmitter to a certain wave-length.

syntonize, vb. trans. [1. síntonīz; 2. síntənaiz]. **syntony** & **-ize**. (wireless) To adjust (transmitter and receiver) to the same wave-length.

syntonizer, n. [1. síntonizer; 2. síntənaizə]. Prec. & **-er**. Device for syntonizing wireless apparatus.

syntony, n. [1. síntoni; 2. síntəni], fr. Gk. *suntonía*, 'agreement'; see **syn-** & **tone** (I.). State of being syntonized; specif., in wireless, the adjustment or tuning of one circuit to another so that their time-periods or frequencies are similar, see **resonance**.

sypher, vb. trans. [1. sífer; 2. sáifə]. Etymol. unknown. To join (planks) by overlapping the edges so as to produce a smooth surface.

sypher-joint, n. Joint made by syphering.

syphilis, n. [1. sífilis; 2. sífilis], fr. Fr., fr. *Syphilus*, name of a character in the 16th cent. Lat. poem of Frascatorius. Highly infectious venereal disease which starts with local symptoms and gradually, unless promptly treated, affects the whole system; caused by the micro-organism *Spirochaeta pallida*.

syphilitic, adj. [1. sìfilítik; 2. sìfilítik]. See prec. & **-itic**. Connected with, pertaining to, of the nature of, affected with, due to, syphilis.

syphilize, vb. trans. [1. sífilīz; 2. sífilaiz]. See **syphilis** & **-ize**. To inoculate with the virus of syphilis.

syphiloid, adj. [1. sífiloid; 2. sífiloid]. See **syphilis** & **-oid**. Resembling syphilis.

syphilology, n. [1. sìfilóloji; 2. sìfilóləǰi]. See **syphilis** & **-o-** & **-logy**. Study of syphilis and its treatment.

syphilous, adj. [1. sífilus; 2. sífiləs]. See **syphilis** & **-ous**. Syphilitic.

syphon, n. See **siphon**.

syren, n. See **siren**.

Syriac, n. & adj. [1. síriak; 2. síriæk], fr. Lat. *Syriacus*, fr. Gk. *Suriakós*, fr. *Suría*, 'Syria'. 1. n. Ancient Syrian dialect, western Aramaic. 2. adj. Of, pertaining to, written in, Syriac.

Syriacism, n. [1. síriasìzm; 2. síriəsìzəm]. Prec. & **-ism**. Syriac idiom or characteristic in Hebrew.

Syrian, adj. & n. [1. sírian; 2. síriən]. **Syria** & **-an**. 1. adj. Of, pertaining to, Syria. 2. n. Native of Syria.

syringa, n. [1. siríngga; 2. siríŋgə]. Mod. Lat., fr. *syring-*, stem of Lat. *syrinx*, 'pipe', see **syrinx**. Ornamental shrub, *Philadelphus*, with clusters of sweet-scented white flowers; mock orange.

syringe, n. & vb. trans. [1. sírinj; 2. sírindž], fr. Lat. *syring-*, stem of *syrinx*, 'pipe', fr. Gk. *súrigx*, 'pipe', see **syrinx**. 1. n. Tube into which liquid is drawn by suction, and ejected in a jet by pressure; *hypodermic syringe*, small, needle-pointed syringe used by surgeons &c. for subcutaneous injections. 2. vb. To apply a jet or spray of liquid to by means of a syringe.

syringeal, adj. [1. sirínjeal; 2. sirínǰiəl], fr. Lat. *syring-*, stem of *syrinx*, 'pipe', see **syrinx** & **-al**. Of, pertaining to, the syrinx.

syringeful, n. [1. sírinjfool; 2. sírindžfəl]. **syringe** & **-ful**. Amount of liquid contained in a syringe.

syringitis, n. [1. sirinjītis; 2. sìrindžáitis], fr. Lat. *syring-*, stem of *syrinx*, 'pipe', see **syrinx** & **-itis**. Inflammation of Eustachian tube.

syringotomy, n. [1. siringótomi; 2. siriŋgótəmi], fr. Lat. *syring-*, stem of *syrinx*, 'pipe', see **syrinx**, & **-o-** & **-tomy**. Operation on fistula.

syrinx, n. [1. síringks; 2. síriŋks]. Lat. *syrinx*, fr. Gk. *súrigx*, 'shepherd's pipe'; cp. Gk. *sōlēn*, 'channel, pipe', see **Solen**. 1. Ancient wind-instrument consisting of a set of hollow tubes of varying lengths; Pan-pipes. 2. Song-organ of birds, at the base of the windpipe. 3. Eustachian tube. 4. (surg.) Fistula. 5. (archaeol.) Narrow, horizontal, rock-hewn gallery in ancient Egyptian tomb.

Syro-, pref. representing Gk. *Súros*, 'Syrian', fr. *Suria*, 'Syria'. Syrian; Syriac; e.g. *Syro-arabian*, including Syriac and Arabic.

syrtis, n. [1. sĕrtis; 2. sʌ́tis]. Lat. *Syrtis*, fr. Gk. *Súrtis*, sand-bank on Libyan coast; cp. Gk. *súrtēs*, 'drag-rope'; *súrein*, 'to draw'. Quicksand.

syrup, sirup, n. [1. sírup; 2. sírəp], fr. O. Fr. *syrop*, fr. Arab. *sharāb*, 'drink', see **sherbet** & **shrub** (II.). 1. a Water saturated with sugar; b solution of sugar and water flavoured or mixed with fruit juice, medicinal substance &c. 2. a Condensed juice of sugar-cane &c. before separation of crystallizable sugar; b uncrystallizable part of juice of sugar-cane &c., separated from crystals by the process of refining; treacle; *golden syrup*, pale yellow syrup obtained from sugar-cane; *maple-syrup*, obtained from sap of sugar-maple.

syrupy, adj. [1. sírupi; 2. sírəpi]. Prec. & **-y**. Resembling syrup in consistency, stickiness, sweetness &c.

sys-, pref. representing Gk. **syn-** before s- followed by vowel.

syssarcosis, n. [1. sìsarkōsis; 2. sìsākóusis], fr. Gk. *sussárkōsis*, fr. **sys-** & *sarkóein*, 'to make like flesh', fr. *sark-*, stem of *sárx*, 'flesh', see **sarco-**, & **-osis**. Union of two adjoining parts of the skeleton by means of intervening muscle.

syssitia, n. [1. sisítia, sisítia; 2. sisítiə, sisáitiə], fr. Gk. *sussítia*, 'public mess', fr. **sys-** & *sítia*, pl. of *sítion*, 'food'; cp. Gk. *sitos*, 'grain; food', & see **sitology**. Communal meals in ancient Sparta, intended to promote discipline, economy, patriotism &c.

systaltic, adj. [1. sistʌ́ltik; 2. sistǽltik], fr. L. Lat. *systalticus*, fr. Gk. *sustaltikós*, 'drawing together', fr. *sustéllein*, 'to draw in', fr. **sy-** & *stéllein*, 'to place', see under **stole** (I.). Alternately contracting and dilating.

system, n. [1. sístem; 2. sístim], fr. Lat. *systēma*, fr. Gk. *sústēma*, 'whole compounded of parts; organized government', fr. **sy-** & *histēmi*, 'I place, stand', see **static**, & **-m**. 1. Group, association, aggregation, of things or objects, between which there exists connexion, relation, interaction, and which together form a unity: *solar system, nervous system, tramway system*. 2. A collection of related facts, principles, ideas, exhibited and arranged so as to show the relations and bearings of each in respect of others and of the whole: *a system of philosophy, of grammar* &c. 3. A plan, scheme, for arranging and classifying objects, facts, ideas, according to general principles determined by the mutual relations of the objects &c. so arranged: *a system of botanical, zoological, classification*. 4. Method, orderly mode of procedure, regularity of action: *system is necessary to success in business and affairs of every kind; studies conducted without a proper system are apt to lead to confusion of mind*. 5. Specif., the body as a whole considered in relation to efficient performance of all its functions: *too much tea is bad for the system; burgundy is highly recommended for the system; his system was much impaired by excesses*.

systematic, adj. [1. sistemátik; 2. sìstimǽtik], fr. Gk. *sustēmat-*, stem of *sústēma*, 'compound, organized whole', see **system**, & **-ic**. Made, carried on, performed in accordance with system, or a system; based on a system.

systematically, adv. [1. sistemátikali; 2. sìstimǽtikəli]. Prec. & **-al** & **-ly**. In a systematic manner.

systematism, n. [1. sístematìzm; 2. sístimətìzəm], fr. Gk. *sustēmat-*, see **systematic** & **-ism**. a Systematic arrangement or method; b exaggerated, blind, adherence to a system.

systematist, n. [1. sístematìst; 2. sístimətìst]. See prec. & **-ist**. a Person working according to system; b person who pursues a system too blindly and rigidly.

systematization, n. [1. sìstematìzáshun; 2. sìstimətàizéiʃən]. Next word & **-ation**. Act of systematizing; state of systematizing.

systematize, vb. trans. [1. sístematìz; 2. sístimətàiz], fr. Gk. *sustēmat-*, see **systematic**, & **-ize**. To arrange in accordance with a system, reduce to a system.

systemic, adj. [1. sistémik; 2. sistémik]. **system** & **-ic**. Pertaining to the human system, or body as a whole.

systemically, adv. [1. sistémikali; 2. sistémikəli]. Prec. & **-al** & **-ly**. In respect of the human system.

systemless, adj. [1. sístemles; 2. sístimlis]. **system** & **-less**. Without system.

systole, n. [1. sístoli; 2. sístəli], fr. Gk. *sustolé*, 'contraction', fr. *sustéllein*, 'to draw together', see **systaltic**. Periodic contraction of heart and arteries, alternating with diastole, q.v.

systolic, adj. [1. sistólik; 2. sistólik]. Prec. & **-ic**. Of, pertaining to, the contraction of the heart &c.

systyle, adj. [1. sístīl; 2. sístail], fr. Lat. *systylos*, fr. Gk. *sústulos*, 'systyle', fr. **sy-** & *stúlos*, 'pillar', see **style** (III.). (archit., of columns) Placed two diameters apart.

systylous, adj. [1. sístilus; 2. sístiləs]. Prec. & **-ous**. (bot.) Having the styles united.

syzygy, n. [1. síziji; 2. sízidʒi], fr. Lat. *sȳzigia*, fr. Gk. *súzugia*, 'yoke, pair', fr. *súzugos*, 'yoked', fr. **sy-** & *zugón*, 'yoke', see **zygo-**. (astron.) Point in an orbit at which a heavenly body is in conjunction with or opposition to, the sun, or, in the case of the moon, to the earth.

T

T, t [1. tē; 2. tī]. The twentieth letter of the English alphabet; for use in abbreviations &c. see list at end of Dictionary. In Phrs. (*it suits me*) *to a T*, as well as possible, exactly; *to cross one's t's*, pay careful attention to very minute points.

T-. Used before names of various objects shaped like the letter T; *T-bandage, -bar, bolt* &c.

ta, vb. [1. tah; 2. tā]. Imitative of *thank (you)*. (baby language) Thank you; (also in anticipation) please; a vulgarism when used by adults to each other.

taal, n. [1. tahl; 2. tāl]. Du. *taal*, 'language', see under **tale**. Dutch dialect spoken in S. Africa, esp. at the Cape; Cape Dutch.

tab, n. [1. tab; 2. tæb]. Etymol. unknown. Small flap, strip of cloth &c. attached to surface or edge of larger piece, to part of a garment &c.

tabard, n. [1. tábard; 2. tǽbəd], fr. O. Fr. *tabard*; etymol. doubtful. a (hist.) Cloak worn by lower classes in 15th cent. &c.; b short sleeveless garment worn by knights in Middle Ages over their armour, often emblazoned with arms of wearer; c similar garment worn by heralds, emblazoned with royal arms.

tabarder, n. See **taberdar**.

tabaret, n. [1. tábaret; 2. tǽbərɛt]. Possibly connected w. **tabby**. Fabric of satin and watered silk in alternate stripes, used in upholstery.

tabasheer, tabashir, n. [1. tàbashḗr; 2. tæbəʃíə]. Hind. & Pers. *tabāshīr*, 'sugar of bamboo'. Siliceous substance found in joints of the bamboo, formerly used in medicine.

tabby, n. [1. tábi; 2. tǽbi], fr. Fr. *tabis*, fr. Span. *tabi*, fr. Arab. 1. Kind of coarse, watered silk. 2. Also *tabby cat*, a brownish or brindled cat; cat with dark stripes on brown or grey; b hence, cat, esp. female cat. 3. Gossiping and spiteful old woman. 4. Kind of concrete made of lime, gravel &c.

tabby-moth, n. Kind of moth with streaked or mottled wings.

tabefaction, n. [1. tàbefákshun; 2. tæbifǽkʃən], fr. Lat. *tābefact-(um)*, P.P. type of *tābefacere*, 'to melt, dissolve'; fr. *tābē-(s)*, 'a wasting away'. See **tabes** & **-faction**. Emaciation caused by disease.

tabellion, n. [1. tabéliun; 2. təbéliən], fr. Fr., fr. Lat. *tabelliōn-(em)*, 'notary, scrivener', fr. *tabell-(a)*, 'tablet; deed, document', dimin. of *tabula*, 'tablet', see **table**. Official scrivener in ancient Rome; also, until 18th cent. in France.

taberdar, -er, n. [1. táberdar; 2. tǽbədə]. **tabard** & **-er**, fr. tabard formerly worn by taberdar. Name given to certain foundation scholars of Queen's College, Oxford.

tabernacle (I.), n. [1. tábernàkl; 2. tǽbənækl], fr. Fr., fr. Lat. *tabernāculum*, 'tent', fr. *taberna*, 'hut, booth, dwelling, shop', see **tavern**, & **-cule**. 1. a Temporary shelter, habitation; specif., light, portable temple used by the Israelites during their wanderings; *feast of tabernacles*, Jewish annual feast held in commemoration of the wanderings through the wilderness; b dissenting chapel or place of worship; c (fig.) human body thought of as temporary dwelling-place of the soul. 2. a (eccles.) Receptacle in which the Host is reserved in churches; b (archit.) canopied niche for the image of a saint &c. 3. (naut.) Socket in deck of vessel for a mast.

tabernacle (II.), vb. trans. & intrans., fr. prec. 1. trans. To furnish, provide with, a temporary dwelling or shelter. 2. intrans. To take up a temporary abode.

tabernacle-work, n. (archit.) Series of carved and ornamented canopies over stalls &c.

tabernacular, adj. [1. tàbernákūlar; 2. tæbənǽkjulə], fr. Lat. *tabernācul-(um)*, 'tent', see **tabernacle**, & **-ar**. Of, pertaining to, of the nature of, characteristic of, a tabernacle.

tabes, n. [1. tábez; 2. téibīz], fr. Lat. *tābēs*, 'a wasting away, dwindling; moisture of decaying matter'; cp. Lat. *tābēre*, 'to waste, be consumed'; supposed to be an extension w. *-bh* of base **tāw-*, 'to melt away'; cp. O. Slav. *tajati*, 'to melt'; also O.E. *þwīnan*, 'to dwindle', & cp. **thaw**. (med.) Wasting, emaciation; specif. *tabes dorsalis*, locomotor ataxia.

tabescence, n. [1. tabésens; 2. təbésəns]. See next word & **-ce**. State of emaciation.

tabescent, adj. [1. tabésent; 2. təbésənt], fr. Lat. *tābescent-(em)*, Pres. Part. of *tābescere*, 'to waste away', inchoative of *tābēre*, see **tabes**. Wasting away, tending to become emaciated.

tabetic, adj. & n. [1. tabétik; 2. təbétik], fr. **tabes**, on anal. of adjs. in **-etic**. 1. adj. Pertaining to, of the nature of, suffering from, tabes. 2. n. Person suffering from tabes.

tabic, adj. [1. tábik; 2. téibik], fr. **tabes** & **-ic**. Tabetic.

tabid, adj. [1. tábid; 2. téibid], fr. Lat. *tābid-(us)*, 'wasting'; see **tabes** & **-id**. Tabetic.

tabidly, adv. Prec. & **-ly**. In a tabid manner.

tabinet, n. [1. tábinet; 2. tǽbinɛt], fr. Fr.; etymol. doubtful. Watered fabric of silk and wool, used in upholstery.

tabitude, n. [1. tábitūd; 2. tǽbitjūd], fr. Lat. *tābitūd-(o)*, 'wasting away, consumption', see **tabes**, & **-i-** & **-tude**. State of being tabescent; emaciation.

tablature, n. [1. táblachur; 2. tǽblətʃə], fr. Fr., fr. Lat. *tabula*, 'plank; writing-tablet; painted panel', see **table**, & **-ate** & **-ure**. Ancient name for instrumental musical notation.

table (I.), n. [1. tábl; 2. téibl]. Fr., fr. Lat. *tabula*, 'board, plank; writing tablet';

etymol. uncertain; the suggested relations seem purely speculative. **1. a** Piece of household furniture consisting of a flat surface of wood supported on legs, used for eating and working at when sitting; **b** (in compounds) such piece of furniture used for a specified purpose, e.g. *billiard-, card-, dressing-table* &c. **2. a** A table considered primarily as a piece of furniture at which people sit at meals; Phrs. *at table*, (i.) in the act of partaking of a meal; (ii.) at, or for, meals; *the Lord's Table*, (chiefly Evangelical) (i.) the altar; (ii.) the Eucharist; **b** hence, the food itself consumed at table: *a liberal, good, table*, plentiful, good, food; **c** the persons seated at a table at a given time for a meal: *to set the table in a roar*. **3.** Inscribed flat slab of stone, wood, metal &c.; hence, **a** the inscription on such a slab: *the tables of the law*, the Ten Commandments, originally delivered to Moses on tables of stone; **b** a systematic list of figures, facts &c. arranged according to some definite plan: *a table of births and deaths*; *table of contents* (of a book &c.); *tables of weights and measures*; *mathematical tables*, of logarithms &c.; *multiplication table*, list of results of multiplying numbers, usually 1 to 12, by a given number: *twice two are four* &c. Phr. *to learn one's tables*, learn multiplication table, tables of weights and measures, by heart. **4.** A flat surface; in various specific and technical senses; e.g. **a** a flat elevated tract of land, a plateau; **b** the cut, flat surface of a gem; **c** either of two flat bony surfaces in the skull &c.

table (**II.**), vb. trans., fr. prec. **1.** To place upon a table; specif. **a** *to table a motion*, submit it for future discussion; **b** to inscribe upon a writing tablet; enter as a note &c.

tableau, n. [1. táblō; 2. tǽblou], fr. Fr. *tableau*, 'picture', dimin. of O. Fr. *table*, 'plank, table, panel, picture' &c., see **table** (**I.**). **a** Representation of some well-known picture, a striking historical scene &c., by living persons suitably dressed and posed in fixed attitudes; called also *tableau vivant*: **b** (fig.) dramatic situation.

table-clamp, n. Clamp for fastening object to table.

table-cloth, n. Piece of material for covering table; esp. one of white linen for use at meals.

table-cut, adj. (of diamond &c.) Cut with flat top and usually bevelled border.

table-d'hôte, n. [1. táhbl dōt; 2. tábl dóut]. Fr., lit. 'table of the host'. **1.** Public table for guests at hotel &c. **2.** Also *table-d'hôte breakfast, dinner* &c., meal in a hotel for which a fixed price is charged, consisting of a series of courses chosen and ordered by the management.

table-flap, n. Leaf of a table, on a hinge, which can be raised or lowered.

tableful, n. [1. tāblfool; 2. téiblful]. **table** (**I.**) & **-ful**. **a** Amount, number of objects, required to cover a table; **b** number of persons that may be seated round a table.

table-knife, n. Knife for use at meals.

table-land, n. Elevated plain, plateau.

table-leg, n. One of the vertical supports of a table.

table-linen, n. Table-cloths, napkins &c., used at table.

table-money, n. Allowance made to general officers in the Army, and flag-officers in the Navy for expenses of official hospitality.

table-spoon, n. Large spoon used for eating soup, and for helping vegetables &c.

tablespoonful, n. [1. tāblspōōnfool; 2. téiblspūnful]. As much as can be contained in a table-spoon.

tablet, n. [1. táblet; 2. tǽblit], fr. O. Fr. *tablette*, fr. Med. Lat. *tabulēta*; **table** (**I.**) & **-et**. **1.** Small flat slab of stone or metal inscribed with a design, inscription &c. **2.** Thin sheet of wood, ivory, metal &c., covered with wax or otherwise prepared, formerly used for writing upon; esp. one of a set of two or more sheets hinged or tied together at top or side. **3.** Small flat, compressed cake, usually round, containing medicinal drug.

table-talk, n. **a** Informal conversation at meals; **b** book containing record of such conversation.

table-tomb, n. Flat-topped burial-chest found in catacombs at Rome.

tablette, n. [1. táblet; 2. tǽblɛt], fr. Fr. *tablette*, see **tablet**. (archit.) Flat coping-stone of wall &c., projecting at either side.

table-turning, n. Act or process of causing a table to move by the unconscious action of a number of persons who place their hands lightly upon it.

tablier, n. [1. tábliā; 2. tǽbliei], fr. Fr. *tablier*, 'apron', fr. Lat. *tabulāri-(us)*, fr. *tabula*, see **table** (**I.**) & **-ary**. Small apron used as part of the trimming of a woman's dress.

tabling, n. [1. tābling; 2. téibliŋ]. **table** (**II.**) & **-ing**. **1.** (carpentry) Projection on piece of timber, designed to fit into corresponding groove or mortice in another piece. **2.** (naut.) Broad hem on sail.

tabloid, n. [1. tábloid; 2. tǽblɔid]. **table** & **-oid**. Copyright trade-name. Small, round, flat, compressed cake, containing a drug &c.; tablet. Phr. *in tabloid form*, (fig.) in concentrated, compressed form.

taboo (**I.**), n. [1. tabōō; 2. təbū́], fr. Polynesian *tapu*. **1.** (in Polynesian tribes) Custom of setting apart certain persons or objects as either sacred or accursed; this usually implies that such persons or things may not be touched, and that their names may not be uttered. **2.** Religious or social system characterized by taboo. **3.** Prohibition, ban, restraint.

taboo (**II.**), adj., fr. prec. (only predic.) **1. a** Set apart as sacred or accursed under taboo; **b** forbidden to be touched or spoken of. **2.** Prohibited, ruled out by convention, proscribed: *such things are taboo in decent society*.

taboo (**III.**), vb. trans., fr. **taboo** (**I.**). To prohibit, interdict; to avoid (a word, practice &c.) as taboo.

tabor, n. [1. tābor; 2. téibə, -ɔ̄], fr. O. Fr. *tabour*, fr. Arab., see **tambour**. Small drum resembling a tambourine or timbrel; used to accompany pipe.

tabouret, n. [1. táboret, táboorā; 2. tǽbɔrɛt, tǽburei], fr. O. Fr., 'stool', dimin. of O. Fr. *tabour*, 'drum', see **tabor**. **1.** Small stool. **2.** Embroidery frame. **3.** Needle-case. **4.** Small tabor; tabret.

tabret, n. [1. tábret; 2. tǽbrɛt]. Variant of prec. Small tabor; tabouret.

tabula, n. [1. tábūla; 2. tǽbjulə]. Lat. *tabula*, 'board, plank, writing-table; panel', see **table** (**I.**). (zool.) Flat plate of bone &c.; esp. horizontal plate in some corals.

tabula rasa, n. [1. tábūla ráhza; 2. tǽbjulə rázə]. Lat., 'erased tablet'. **a** Used of the mind before any impressions or ideas have been received; **b** complete obliteration, a blank; **a** clean sweep of what already exists.

tabular, adj. [1. tábūlar; 2. tǽbjulə], fr. Lat. *tabulār-(is)*, 'of boards or plates', fr. *tabula*, 'board, tablet', see **table** (**I.**), & **-ar**. **1. a** Having a flat table-like surface; **b** consisting of thin plates, laminated. **2. a** Arranged, set out, in tables: *in tabular form*; **b** stated, exhibited, by means of tables: *tabular results*.

tabularly, adv. Prec. & **-ly**. (rare) In tabular form; by means of a table.

tabulate (**I.**), vb. trans. [1. tábūlāt; 2. tǽbjuleit]. **tabula** & **-ate**. **1.** To arrange, display, in tabular form; to set out in systematic grouping: *to tabulate data, results* &c. **2.** To give a flat surface to.

tabulate (**II.**), adj. **tabula** & **-ate**. **1.** Having a broad flat surface. **2.** Arranged in series of thin plates; laminated.

tabulation, n. [1. tàbūláshun; 2. tæ̀bjuléiʃən]. **tabulate** (**I.**) & **-ion**. Act of tabulating; state of being put into tabular form.

tabulator, n. [1. tábūlātur; 2. tǽbjuleitə]. **tabulate** (**I.**) & **-or**. **a** Person who tabulates; **b** typewriter attachment for tabulating figures.

tacamahac, n. [1. tákama-hak; 2. tǽkəməhæk]. S. American Indian. **1.** Yellowish, bitter, aromatic gum-resin yielded by certain tropical trees; used in incense, ointment &c. **2.** Balsam poplar of N. America.

tac-au-tac, n. [1. ták ō ták; 2. tǽk ou tǽk], fr. Fr., imitative. (fencing) **a** Parry followed immediately by riposte; **b** series of swift attacks and parries.

tace, vb. intrans., imperat. [1. tāsi; 2. téisi]. Lat. *tacē*, imperat. of *tacēre*, 'to be silent'; cogn. w. Goth. *þahan*; O.N. *þegja*; O.S. *thagian*; O.H.G. *dagēn*, 'to be silent'. Be silent.

tacet, vb. intrans. [1. tāset, táset; 2. téisɛt, tǽsɛt]. Lat. *tacet*, 3rd sing. pres. of *tacēre*, 'to be silent', see prec. (in musical score) Direction for instrument to remain silent.

tache, n. [1. tahsh, tash; 2. tāʃ, tæʃ], fr. O. Fr. *tache*, 'spot', of Gmc. origin, see **tack** (**I.**). Coloured spot or blemish on the skin; a freckle.

tachometer, n. [1. takómeter; 2. tækɔ́mitə], fr. Gk. *tákho-(s)*, 'speed', etymol. doubtful, & **-meter**. Instrument for measuring speed.

tachometry, n. [1. takómetri; 2. tækɔ́mitri], fr. Gk. *tákho-(s)*, 'speed', see prec., & **-metry**. Art or practice of measuring speed.

tachycardia, n. [1. tàkikárdia; 2. tæ̀kikádiə], fr. Gk. *takhú-(s)*, 'swift', see **tachometer**, & *kardía*, 'heart', see **cardiac**. (med.) Abnormally rapid action of the heart.

tachygraphic(**al**), adj. [1. tàkigráfik(l); 2. tæ̀kigrǽfik(l)]. **tachygraphy** & **-ic** & **-al**. Of, pertaining to, written in, tachygraphy.

tachygraphy, n. [1. takígrafi; 2. tækígrəfi], fr. Gk. *takhú-(s)*, 'swift', q.v. under **tachometer**, & **-graphy**. System or use of shorthand; specif., one of the systems of notation used by ancient Greeks and Romans.

tachylyte, n. [1. tákilīt; 2. tǽkilait], fr. Gk. *takhú-(s)*, 'swift', see **tachometer**, & *lut-(ós)*, fr. *lúein*, 'to loosen, dissolve', q.v. under second element of **analysis**; so called because easily decomposed by acids. Kind of black, opaque, basaltic glass.

tachylytic, adj. [1. tàkilítik; 2. tæ̀kilítik]. Prec. & **-ic**. Of, of the nature of, consisting of, tachylyte.

tachymeter, n. [1. takímeter; 2. tækímitə], fr. Gk. *takhú-(s)*, 'swift', see **tachometer**, & **-meter**. Instrument used in surveying for the speedy measuring of distances, fixing of points &c.

tachymetry, n. [1. takímetri; 2. tækímitri]. See prec. & **-metry**. The use of a tachymeter.

tacit, adj. [1. tásit; 2. tǽsit], fr. Lat. *tacit-(um)*, P.P. type of *tacēre*, 'to be silent', see **tace**. Unspoken; understood without being expressed, implied by silence: *tacit approval*; *a tacit understanding*.

tacitly, adv. Prec. & **-ly**. In a tacit manner.

taciturn, adj. [1. tásitĕrn; 2. tǽsitʌn], fr. Lat. *taciturn-(us)*, 'quiet, taciturn', fr. *tacit-(um)*, see **tacit**. Habitually silent, speaking little, of few words, reserved in speech.

taciturnity, n. [1. tàsitérniti; 2. tæ̀sitʌ́niti], fr. Lat. *taciturnitāt-(em)*, 'taciturnity'; prec. & **-ity**. Quality of being taciturn.

taciturnly, adv. [1. tásitĕrnli; 2. tǽsitʌnli]. **taciturn** & **-ly**. In a taciturn manner.

tack (**I.**), n. [1. tak; 2. tæk], fr. A.-Fr. *taque*, 'nail'; cp. O. Fr. *tache*, 'point, spot'; of Gmc. origin; cp. Germ. *zacken*, 'tooth, prong'; Du. *tak*, 'twig'; cp. **attach**. **1.** Short, sharp, broad-headed, weakish nail; *tin-tack*, one made of iron coated with tin; Phr. (vulg.) (*come down to*) *brass tacks*, facts. **2.** (needlework) Long stitch used in making temporary seam or fastening. **3.** (naut.) **a** Rope for fastening corner of sail; **b** corner of sail to which this is attached; **c** ship's course in relation to position of sails; Phr. *on the port, starboard, tack*, with wind on port, starboard, side; **d** change of course produced by shifting sails to take advantage of wind. Phr. *tack and tack*, by a succession of tacks. **4.** (fig.) Course of action; policy: *on the wrong, right, tack*. **5.** (of varnish, printing-ink &c.) Viscous condition, stickiness.

tack (II.), vb. trans. & intrans., fr. prec. A. trans. **1.** To fasten with tack(s): *to tack the carpet down; to tack a notice to the wall.* **2.** To make a temporary seam or fastening in a garment or fabric, stitch together with long stitches: *to tack two pieces of silk together.* **3.** (fig.) To attach, link on, as a supplementary part; to append: *to tack a moral on to the end of a story.* B. intrans. **1.** To change ship's direction by bringing a different side to the wind. **2.** (fig.) To change one's line of action, one's opinions &c.; to adopt a new policy.

tack (III.), n. Etymol. unknown. Food, fare, provisions; esp. *hard tack*, ship's biscuits; *soft tack*, bread, as distinct from biscuit &c.; good food.

tackiness, n. [1. tákines; 2. tǽkinis]. **tacky & -ness.** State of being tacky; stickiness.

tackle (I.), n. [1. tákl; 2. tǽkl]. M.E. *takel*, fr. L.G. *takel*, fr. O.N. *taka*, 'to seize, grasp', & **-le**; see **take** (I.). **1.** Mechanical contrivance for moving, esp. for raising, heavy weights; specif., system of ropes, pulleys &c.; **a** for raising weights; **b** for handling ship's sails, spars &c. **2.** Gear, equipment, used in specific occupation; often in compounds, *fishing-tackle* &c. **3.** (fr. vb.) Act of tackling opposing player in football.

tackle (II.), vb. trans. & intrans., fr. prec. A. trans. **1.** To fasten, hoist, with tackle. **2.** (lit. and fig.) **a** To seize, grapple, come to grips with, attack; specif. (football) to seize and try to stop (opponent); **b** (fig.) To approach, deal with, confront, engage in argument with: *I tackled him on the question of free trade.* **3.** To turn one's attention to (a piece of work, a problem) with a view to completion, or solution; to undertake, start dealing with. B. intrans. To carry out the operation of tackling.

tackle-block, n. Pulley forming part of tackle.
tackle-fall, n. Rope connecting blocks.
tackling, n. [1. táklin̄; 2. tǽklin̄]. **tackle & -ing.** Apparatus for hoisting &c.; tackle.
tacky, adj. [1. táki; 2. tǽki]. **tack** (I.) & **-y.** (of varnish &c.) Thick, sticky, viscous.
tact, n. [1. takt; 2. tækt], fr. Lat. *tact-(us)*, 'touch'; sense of touch; effect, influence', fr. P.P. type of *tangere*, 'to touch', see **tangent. 1.** Keen, natural perception of what is right and fitting; quick apprehension of the right thing to say or do; instinctive skill, adroitness, discretion, in dealing with persons or difficult situations. **2.** (mus.) Most emphatic beat in a bar.
tactful, adj. [1. táktfool; 2. tǽktful]. Prec. & **-ful.** Possessing, exhibiting, tact.
tactfully, adv. Prec. & **-ly.** In a tactful manner.
tactical, adj. [1. táktikl; 2. tǽktikl]. See **tactics** & **-al.** Concerned with, pertaining to, tactics.
tactically, adv. Prec. & **-ly.** By means of, from the point of view of, according to the methods of, tactics.
tactician, n. [1. taktíshan; 2. tæktíʃən]. **tactics** & **-ian.** Student of, one skilled in, tactics.
tactics, n. [1. táktiks; 2. tǽktiks], fr. Gk. *taktik-(á)*, 'tactics', cp. *tássein*, fr. *tak-jo-*, 'to arrange'; cp. also *tagé*, 'order of battle'; *táxis*, 'arrangement; ordinance; post, rank; levy'; see **taxis** & **-ic. 1.** Art of handling troops in the field, in presence of enemy; also art of handling ships in a naval action; contrasted with *strategy*. **2.** Art of handling a political situation; adroit method of dealing with persons and circumstances so that a desired end may be gained as easily and smoothly as possible.
tactile, adj. [1. táktīl, -il; 2. tǽktail, -il], fr. Lat. *tactil-(is)*, 'tangible', fr. *tact-(um)*, P.P. type of *tangere*, 'to touch', see **tangent**, & **-ile. 1.** Concerned with, pertaining to, affected by, the organs, or the sense, of touch. **2.** Capable of being touched; tangible.

tactility, n. [1. taktíliti; 2. tæktíliti]. Prec. & **-ity. 1.** State or quality of being tactile. **2.** Tangibility.
tactless, adj. [1. táktles; 2. tǽktlis]. **tact & -less.** Lacking in tact.
tactlessly, adv. Prec. & **-ly.** In a tactless manner.
tactlessness, n. See prec. & **-ness.** Lack of tact.
tactual, adj. [1. táktūal; 2. tǽktjuəl], fr. Lat. *tactu-(s)*, 'touching', see **tact**, & **-al.** Pertaining to, derived from, the sense of touch.
tactually, adv. Prec. & **-ly.** By means of touch.
tadpole, n. [1. tádpōl; 2. tǽdpoul]. M.E. *tadpolle*, fr. O.E. *tād*, 'toad', see **toad**, & **poll** (I.). Larva of frog, toad &c., having a tail and external gills, later absorbed into the body.
tadpole-fish, n. Fish with broad, flat head.
taedium vitae, n. [1. tédium vítē; 2. tídiəm váitī]. Lat. *taedium vītae*, 'weariness of life'; see **tedium, vital.** (med.) Suicidal tendency caused by depression or weariness.
tael, n. [1. tāl; 2. teil]. Port., fr. Malay *tahil*, 'weight'. **a** Chinese ounce, 1½ oz. avoirdupois; **b** this weight in pure silver, as monetary unit.
ta'en, vb. [1. tān; 2. tein]. Contracted fr. **taken.** (poet.)
taenia, n. [1. ténia; 2. tíniə]. Lat. *taenia*, 'ribbon, band, fillet; ribbon-fish; tapeworm'; fr. Gk. *tainía*, 'band, fillet, bandage', fr. a form *tain-(ós)*, 'narrow', earlier *tan-jo-*; cp. Gk. *teínein, tanúein*, 'to stretch'; *tónos*, 'cord'; see **tone** & **thin. 1.** (Gk. and Rom. archaeol.) Hair-band, fillet. **2.** (archit.) Fillet above architrave on Doric column. **3.** (anat.) Ribbon-like organ, arrangement of muscle &c. **4.** Tape-worm.
taenioid, adj. [1. ténioid; 2. tíniɔid]. Prec. & **-oid. 1.** Ribbon-shaped. **2.** Connected with a tapeworm.
tafferel, n., usually **taffrail** [1. táfril; 2. tǽfril], fr. Du. *tafereel*, dimin. of *tafel*, 'table', fr. Lat. *tabula*, 'tablet, slab', see **tabula, table** (I.). Upper part of ship's stern.
taffeta, n. [1. táfeta; 2. tǽfitə], fr. Fr. *taffetas*, fr. Ital. *taffettà*, fr. Pers. *taftah*. Fabric of silk, or silk and linen.
taffrail, n. [1. táfril; 2. tǽfril], fr. Du. *tafereel*, 'tafferel', see **tafferel**, assimilated to *rail*. Rail round ship's stern.
Taffy (I.), n. [1. táfi; 2. tǽfi]. Welsh form of Davy, fr. David. (colloq.) Welshman.
taffy (II.), n. See **toffee.** American for toffee.
tafia, n. [1. táfia; 2. tǽfiə]. W. Indian. Kind of rum distilled from refuse of sugar manufacture &c.
tag (I.), n. [1. tag; 2. tæg]. Prob. Scand.; cp. Swed. *tagg*, 'spike, prickle, tooth'; Norw. *tagge*, 'tooth'. **1.** Appendage, something forming an end, point, or projecting flap, point &c.; specif. **a** metal point of lace; **b** tip of animal's tail; **c** loop or flap at back of boot to give purchase in drawing it on; **d** label tied by string &c.; **e** loose, hanging end, flap or torn edge; **f** ragged or matted lock of wool on sheep. **2.** Refrain of song or poem. **3.** Epilogue of play. **4.** Hackneyed phrase or quotation.
tag (II.), vb. trans., fr. prec. **1.** To furnish with a tag, add a tag to: *a tagged lace*. **2.** To join on, add, as an appendage, tack on; esp. to add something on to a literary composition. **3.** To cut tags from wool of: *to tag sheep.* **4.** (colloq.) To pursue closely, dog.
tag (III.), n. & vb. trans. Prob. fr. prec. **1.** n. Children's game in which one pursues and tries to touch others. **2.** vb. To overtake and touch another player in this game.
Tagetes, n. [1. tajétēz; 2. tædʒítiz]. Mod. Lat., origin doubtful; the name of an Etruscan deity *Tages* is suggested as possible source. Genus of plants of the aster family, with bright yellow or orange flowers; e.g. French marigold.
tagger, n. [1. táger; 2. tægə]. **tag & -er.** (pl.) Thin sheet-iron, esp. one without coating of tin.

Taic, adj. & n. [1. táh-ik; 2. tǎik], fr. *Tai*, a race of the Indo-Chinese peninsula, including Siamese &c., & **-ic. 1.** adj. Of, pertaining to, the Tai. **2.** n. Language of the Tai.
taiga, n. [1. tíga; 2. táigə]. Siberian. Belt of coniferous forest lying to the south of the tundra in N. Europe and Asia.
tail (I.), n. [1. tāl; 2. teil]. O.E. *tæg(e)l*; M.E. *teil*; cp. O.N., Goth. *tagl*; O.H.G. *zagel*, 'tail'. **1.** Prolongation of the spine in vertebrates, which extends beyond the body and constitutes a separate and distinctive part. Phrs. *to turn tail*, to show cowardice, run away from danger, a fight &c.; *with his tail between his legs*, (of dog, or fig. of person) cowed; dispirited, discouraged, as having suffered a rebuff; *to be unable to make head or tail of*, find unintelligible; *to twist the tail of*, to subject to annoyance, to torment; *close on a person's tail*, close behind him, as in pursuit. **2.** Any of several objects supposed to resemble a tail; **a** *a tail of hair*, a plait, a wisp; **b** *tail of kite*, length of string with series of twisted strips of paper knotted to it, attached to lowest point of kite; **c** *tail of comet*, luminous train extending behind the nucleus; **d** *tail of a letter*, line or loop extending below the line; **e** *tail of a note*, stroke extending above or below the line as part of a symbol of a musical note; **f** *tail of a wing*, slender point of a butterfly's lower wing. **3.** Lowest, hindmost, or subordinate part of object or group; specif. **a** *tail of a coat*, part below waist, skirt; half of skirt when divided; **b** *tail of a procession*, rear portion; **c** *tail of a cart*, back of cart; **d** *tail of one's eye*, outer corner; **e** *tail of a storm, gale*, comparative calm when gale has slackened; **f** *tail of a stream*, comparatively calm water after current or rough water; **g** exposed end of roofing-tile, slate &c.; **h** concealed end of brick &c. in wall; **i** (of coin) reverse side. **4.** Retinue, train, band of followers. **5.** (mil.) *Tail of the trenches*, part first dug by advance party. **6.** Horse-tail, formerly an emblem of rank in Turkey: *a Pasha with three tails.*
tail (II.), vb. trans. & intrans., fr. prec. A. trans. **1.** To provide with a tail. **2.** To follow (a person) closely, to track, esp. for the purpose of watching, and preventing escape of. **3.** To cut or pull stalk or lower end off: *to tail fruit.* B. intrans. (naut.) *To tail to the tide, tail up and down stream* (of anchored ship), to take up position according to direction of tide or current. C. Followed by adverbs and prepositions with special meanings. *Tail after*, intrans., to follow closely, esp. in line or procession. *Tail away*, intrans., to diminish gradually, fade away, grow sparser and sparser; straggle. *Tail in*, trans., to fix (timbers &c.) into wall or other structure by one end. *Tail off*, same as *tail away*. *Tail on*, trans., to join on as appendage or supplement.
tail (III.), n. & adj., fr. O. Fr. *taille*, 'notch, cutting', see **tailor** & **entail. 1.** n. Limitation of inheritance of an estate to descendants in particular line, of a particular person: *an estate in tail; in tail male.* **2.** adj. Limited, in respect of inheritance, in a particular way.
tail-bay, n. Part of lock between tail-gate and lower pond.
tail-board, n. Movable board forming back of cart.
tail-coat, n. Coat with tails, with division between them, and a button at the top of each, just below the waist.
-tailed, adj. [1. tāld; 2. teild]. **tail** (I.) & **-ed.** Having a particular kind of tail: *long-tailed; bob-tailed* &c.
tail-end, n. Last part, fag-end: *tail-end of a procession, of a speech* &c.
tail-feather, n. Longest or most conspicuous feather in a bird's tail.
tail-gate, n. Lower gate of canal lock.
tailing, n. [1. táling; 2. téiliŋ]. **tail** (II.) & **-ing.** In various senses; **a** concealed end of brick &c. in wall; **b** fault in calico-printing; **c** refuse separated from grain in threshing &c.; **d** inferior, useless part of ore.

tailless, adj. [1. tálles; 2. téillis]. **tail (I.)** & **-less.** Without a tail.

tail-margin, n. Margin at foot of page of book &c.

tailor (I.), n. [1. táler; 2. téilə], fr. M.E. *tailleur* &c., fr. O. Fr. *tailleor*, lit. 'cutter', fr. Low Lat. *tāliāre*, fr. Lat. *tālea*, 'rod; cutting for planting'; orig. 'sprout, fresh growth'; cogn. w. Gk. *têlis*, 'fenugreek'; Lith. (*at*)*tólas*, 'aftermath'. **a** Person who cuts out and makes clothes, esp. outer garments made from cloth; **b** tradesman who sells coats, and suits, esp. for men, which he employs others to make.

tailor (II.), vb. trans. & intrans. **1.** trans. **a** To work upon (clothes) as a tailor; to sew, press, and otherwise get ready, cloth garments; **b** to make clothes for. **2.** intrans. To ply the trade of tailor.

tailor-bird, n. Oriental bird that stitches leaves together to form a receptacle for its nest.

tailoress, n. [1. tálores; 2. téilərεs]. **tailor** & **-ess.** Female tailor.

tailoring, n. [1. táloring; 2. téilərin]. **tailor** & **-ing.** **a** Occupation, business, of a tailor; **b** the work of a tailor as exhibited in a particular garment.

tailor-made, adj. **a** (of woman's dress) Made by tailor; hence, cut like a man's suit, plain, well-fitting, and without trimmings, flounces &c.; **b** (of a woman) dressed in tailor-made clothes.

tail-piece, n. **1.** Longish, narrow piece of ebony on instruments of the violin class, to which the lower ends of the strings are fastened after passing over the bridge. **2.** Ornamental design on the lower half of the page of a book, at the end of a chapter or of the book itself.

tail-pipe, n. Suction-pipe in a pump.

tail-race, n. Part of mill-stream below water-wheel.

tain, n. [1. tān; 2. tein]. Origin doubtful; M.E. *tein*, fr. O.N. *teinn*, 'twig', relationship w. O.E. *tān*, Goth. *tains*, 'rod, twig', the origin of wh. is also unknown, is suggested by some dictionaries, but connexion in sense appears to be lacking; Lat. *taenia*, 'ribbon', see **taenia**, is hardly more convincing. Thin sheet of tin-foil used for the backing of mirrors.

taint (I.), n. [1. tānt; 2. teint], fr. Fr. *teinte*, fem. P.P. of *teindre*, 'to tinge, dye', fr. Lat. *tingere*, 'to stain, colour', see **tinge** & **tint.** Trace of physical corruption or decay; moral degeneration, imperfection; contamination, pollution.

taint (II.), vb. trans. & intrans., fr. prec. **1.** trans. To impart a taint to; to infect with physical or moral deterioration and corruption; to render unwholesome or noxious: *air tainted by smoke*; *character tainted by self-seeking*; *tainted meat*, incipiently putrescent. **2.** intrans. To become infected, corrupted, by something noxious, by decay &c.

taintless, adj. [1. tántles; 2. téintlis]. Prec. & **-less.** Without taint; uncorrupted, pure.

taintlessly, adv. Prec. & **-ly.** In a taintless manner.

Tai-ping, Tae-ping, n. [1. tí píng; 2. tái píŋ], fr. Chinese *t'ai p'ing*, 'great peace'. One taking part in Chinese Rebellion of 1850, finally crushed by Gordon in 1864.

taj, n. [1. tahj; 2. tādž]. Pers. *tāj*, 'crown'. Tall, conical cap worn by Mohammedan dervishes.

take (I.), vb. trans. & intrans. [1. tāk; 2. teik]. M.E. *tāken*; L.O.E. *tacan*, fr. O.N. *taka*, 'to touch, seize'; prob. cogn. w. Goth. *tēkan*, 'to touch', w. different grade; perh. remotely connected w. same base as Lat. *digitus*, 'finger', see **digit.** **A.** trans. **1.** (of bodily action) **a** To seize, lay hold of, grasp, esp. with the hand: *to take a person's head between one's hands*; *to take a person by the hand, by the nose*; Phrs. *to take one's arm*, lay hand on person's arm for guidance, support &c.; *to take arms*, arm oneself, prepare to fight; *to take in hand*, undertake; **b** to grasp, catch hold of, grip, otherwise than with the hand: *to take something between one's knees*; *to take (a person) to one's arms, to one's heart, breast*, (i.) to embrace him; (ii.) to admit, receive, him into one's affections. **2.** To receive, accept, have given, handed, transferred to one, receive into one's grasp or possession: *to take presents, what is offered*; *I can't take money from you*; Phrs. *to take things as they come*; *to take people as they are*; *to take the rough with the smooth*; *to take one's chance.* **3. a** To remove; pick up, and convey away: *some one has taken my pen*; *take the knife from the baby*; **b** (math.) to deduct, subtract: *to take 4 from 10.* **4.** To convey with one, **a** to convey in one's grasp or keeping, to carry: *to take a letter to the post*; *to take one's umbrella in case of rain*; **b** to conduct, cause to accompany one: *take me with you*; *to take the dog for a walk.* **5. a** To gain, obtain, possession of, power over, (i.) by one's efforts or skill in a transaction; to win, earn: *he took £100 at Ascot*; *large sums were taken at the gate*; (ii.) to obtain by force, to capture: *to take a fort, ship, a prisoner*; **b** to catch in trap, snare, with bait &c.: *to take fish*; **c** to gain, win, as result of contest: *to take a prize*; **d** (games, cards, chess, cricket &c.) to win: *to take a trick, a pawn, a wicket* &c.; **e** to affect, strike, make impression upon, (i.) bodily, to affect, hit: *the blow took him on the nose*; *the cold takes me in the chest*; (ii.) mentally: *to take one by surprise*; **f** to attract, charm: *to take one's fancy*; *to be much taken by something.* **6.** To draw, absorb, receive, into the system; **a** to inhale: *to take a deep breath*; *to take breath*; *to take the air*; *to take a pinch of snuff*; **b** to eat, drink, swallow, consume: *to take one's medicine*; *I never take wine*; *he can take no food*; *do you take sugar?* **7. a** To make use of, employ, procure, or select for use: *take a larger spoon*; *take a dozen eggs and a pound of flour*; **b** to select and associate oneself with: *take your partners*; **c** to select and acquire by marriage: *to take a wife.* **8.** To enter and avail oneself of for conveyance: *to take a train, car* &c.; *to take ship*, embark. **9. a** To make use of, occupy, spend, avail oneself of (time and amount): *he took an hour over his dinner*; *take as long as you like*; Phr. *to take one's time (over)*, to act, work, slowly and deliberately, be slow and unhurried; **b** (impers.) to require, demand, call for: *it takes too long*; *it only takes five minutes to walk there*; *it takes patience and industry to learn a language*; *it takes many men to build a house*; Phr. *it takes two to make a quarrel*, both parties are usually responsible. **10. a** To acquire, gain possession of, by payment; to purchase: *I will take as many eggs as you can supply*; **b** to reserve, engage, gain right to, by payment &c.; to hire: *to take seats at a theatre, tickets*; *to take a house, rooms* &c.; **c** to subscribe to, receive regularly: *to take a newspaper.* **11.** To be infected by, catch, have communicated to one: *to take cold*; *to take fire.* **12. a** To select, adopt, accept, for one's own use: *to take a seat*, sit down; *please take my seat*; Phrs. *to take the chair*, preside at meeting &c.; *to take a back seat*, occupy inferior or obscure position, play a less important part; **b** to assume, place oneself in, undertake, occupy oneself with: *to take one's proper position*; *to take command, charge, the lead, precedence*; *to take sides*; *to take part*; *the army takes the field*; **c** to adopt, transfer to oneself: *to take an assumed name.* **13.** To assume, gain attribute of, come into possession of as part of one's mental condition: *to take courage, heart, fright, offence, comfort, a dislike to, exception to* &c.; *to take care*, be careful; *take care of*, attend carefully to. **14.** To enjoy, use: *to take a rest, a holiday.* **15.** To perform a given action, act in specified way: *to take a leap, a look round, a step, flight*; *to take steps, measures, precautions*; *to take vengeance*; *to take one's leave, one's choice*; *to take account of, no notice of*; *a disease takes its course*; *the river takes its rise.* **16.** To adopt specified attitude towards: *to take it easy, calmly*; *to take something ill, amiss.* **17. a** To receive into the mind, have communicated to one; to grasp mentally and act upon: *to take a thing to heart*; *to take a hint, advice*; **b** to understand, comprehend: *to take one's meaning*; *do you take me?* **18.** To accept mentally, assume, presume: *I take him to be an honest man*; *I take it that you are fully acquainted with the facts of the case*; Phr. *you may take it from me*, you may assume it to be a fact. **19.** To observe as an example, point of argument &c.; to consider, turn one's attention to: *take the case of your brother, for instance*; *let us take the facts in order.* **20.** To ascertain, find out, determine: *to take measurements*; Phr. *to take a person's measure*, make an estimate of his character &c. **21.** To set down, record on, transfer to, paper or other surface: *to take notes, photographs* &c. **22.** To jump over, pass across: *the horse took the hedge*; *to take a stream in one's stride.* **23.** (gram.) **a** To have as inflexion: *most nouns take -s in the plural*; **b** to be followed by: *in O.E. verbs expressing deprivation take a genitive of the thing, and a dative of the person.* **B.** intrans. **1.** To have required effect, work effectively: *the vaccine did not take.* **2.** To become popular, capture general fancy: *the play did not take.* **3.** To make photographic impression of specified kind, give specific result when photographed: *to take well* &c. **C.** Followed by adverbs and prepositions, with special meanings. *Take aback*, trans., to disconcert, throw into confusion, surprise, startle. *Take after*, intrans., to resemble in features, character &c., have hereditary resemblance to: *to take after one's father.* *Take away*, trans., **a** to remove, cause to depart, convey away; **b** to deduct, subtract. *Take back*, trans., to retract, withdraw: *to take back one's words.* *Take down*, trans., **a** to lower, remove by lifting down: *to take down a picture from the wall*; **b** to take apart, pull down: *to take down a building*; *take down one's hair*, to undo fastenings of, and allow to flow down the back; **c** to swallow, gulp down; **d** to humble, reduce conceit of; esp. *to take a person down a peg*; **e** to record in writing, set down on paper &c.: *to take down a speech in shorthand.* *Take for*, trans., **a** to believe, consider to be: *what do you take me for?*; *do you take me for a fool?*; **b** to consider erroneously, mistake: *to be taken for one's sister.* *Take from*, intrans., to reduce, diminish, lessen amount or quality of: *the size of her hat takes from her height*; *his fortunate circumstances take from the merit of his achievements.* *Take in*, trans., **1.** to admit, receive, give entrance or welcome to: *to take in a homeless traveller, lodgers*; **2.** to receive, undertake, to do at home: *to take in washing*; **3.** to receive into the mind, grasp, comprehend: *he listens to the lectures without taking them in*; **4.** to reduce to smaller size, compass, extent: *to take in a dress*; *to take in a sail*, furl it; **5.** to deceive, impose upon, swindle: *he took me in over the purchase of a horse*; **6.** to subscribe to, receive regularly: *to take in a journal.* *Take into*, trans., *to take it into one's head, mind*, be seized with a sudden idea, notion, intention. *Take off*, **A.** trans. **1. a** to remove, lead, conduct, convey away: *to take oneself off*; *he took me off to the garden*; **b** to remove, lift or draw off, esp. from the body: *to take off one's hat*, esp. as salute; *to take off one's shoes*; **c** to lift, and move to another position: *please take your hand off me*; *take your foot off my toe*; to deduct, reduce by specified amount: *to take a penny off the price*; **2.** to swallow, take down; **3.** to mimic, burlesque. **B.** intrans., to leave ground in jumping, begin a leap. *Take on*, **1.** trans., **a** to engage in, undertake: *to take on a piece of work*; **b** to accept as opponent in a contest: *to take a man on at golf*; **2.** intrans., (colloq.)

to give way to emotion, be greatly agitated: *keep calm, don't take on so*. *Take out*, trans., 1. to remove from within, extract, take away: *to take a stain out*; *hot water will take out the stiffness*; Phr. *to take the nonsense out of a person*; *to take it out of one*, weary, exhaust; 2. to obtain, procure, have issued for one: *to take out a licence, insurance policy* &c. *Take over*, 1. trans., to have transferred to one, assume control of: *to take over the business, duties, responsibilities*; 2. intrans., to assume, have transferred to one, duties and responsibilities: *the new general will take over immediately from the retiring one*. *Take to*, intrans., 1. to feel attracted by, form a liking for: *to take to a person*; 2. to engage in, form a habit: *to take to drink, gardening*. *Take up*, trans., 1. to raise, lift up, pick up: *to take up a book*; Phr. *to take up arms, the gauntlet, the cudgels* &c. (see **arm, cudgel** &c.); 2. to catch end of and make secure: *to take up an artery, a dropped stitch*; 3. to receive, admit, into a vehicle: *to take up a passenger*; 4. a to absorb: *the blotting-paper takes up ink*; b to fill, occupy: *it takes up a lot of room, time*; 5. to take into custody, arrest; 6. a to engage in, adopt as occupation &c.: *to take up gardening*; b to turn one's attention to, pursue, deal with: *to take up a matter*; c to resume, return to: *to take up one's story*. *Take up with*, intrans., to adopt as companion &c., associate with. *Take upon*, trans., *to take (it) upon oneself to*, to assume responsibility of, presume to.

take (II.), n., fr. prec. 1. Amount of fish, game &c. taken at one time or in specific period. 2. Amount of money received at theatrical performance &c. 3. (print.) Portion of copy allotted to a compositor to set up.

take-in, n. [1. tǎk ín; 2. téik ín]. A deception, fraud, imposition, swindle.

taken, vb. [1. tǎken; 2. téikən]. P.P. of **take (I.)**; L.O.E. *(ġe)tacen*, M.E. *tāke(n)*.

take-off, n. [1. tǎk awf; 2. téik ŏf]. 1. Caricature, mimicry, burlesque imitation. 2. Place at which the feet leave the ground in jumping, often *a good, bad, take-off*, suitable, unsuitable, place for beginning a jump.

taker, n. [1. tǎker; 2. téikə]. **take (I.)** & -er. One who, that which, takes, specif., person who accepts a bet.

take-up, n. [1. tǎk up; 2. téik ap]. One of various mechanical devices for tightening thread in machine, taking in slack of rope &c.

takin, n. [1. táhkin; 2. tǎkin]. Assam. Large, heavy, reddish-brown, horned ruminant of Tibet, allied to the antelope.

taking (I.), n. [1. táking; 2. téikiŋ]. **take (I.)** & -ing. 1. (pl. *takings*) That which is taken, something received as payment; earnings, receipts, gains. 2. (colloq.) State of mental agitation, fuss, perplexity: *in a terrible taking*.

taking (II.), adj., fr. Pres. Part. of **take (I.)**. 1. Attractive, charming, captivating: *a taking manner*. 2. (of disease) Infectious, catching.

takingly, adv. Prec. & -ly. In a taking manner; attractively.

takingness, n. See prec. & -ness. State of being taking; attractiveness.

talapoin, n. [1. tálapoin; 2. tǽləpoin], fr. E. Indian. 1. Buddhist priest or monk in Siam, Burma &c. 2. Small W. African monkey.

talaria, n. pl. [1. taláría; 2. təlέəriə]. Lat. *tālāria*, 'ankles; winged shoes', neut. pl. form of adj. *tālārius*, 'of the ankle', fr. *tāl-(us)*, 'ankle', see **talus**, & -ary. Winged sandals represented in classical art as attributes of Hermes, and also of Iris, Perseus, Eros &c.

talbot, n. [1. táwlbot; 2. tŏlbət]. Origin unknown; perh. fr. name of family in whose arms talbots figure. Extinct breed of hound, with pendulous ears, somewhat resembling a bloodhound.

Talbot House, n. Society with branches all over the world for mutual help and service on Christian lines in memory of the Great War, founded in memory of Gilbert Talbot, killed 1915; usually styled Toc H., the signaller's pronunciation of T. H.

talc, n. [1. talk; 2. tælk], fr. Fr., fr. Arab. *talq*. Mineral, magnesium silicate, capable of being split into thin, transparent sheets, which are elastic and do not fracture, and are used for protecting the light in lanterns, for windscreens of motors &c.

talcky, adj. [1. tálki; 2. tǽlki]. **talc** & -y. Talcous.

talcoid, adj. [1. tálkoid; 2. tǽlkoid]. **talc** & -oid. Of, pertaining to, having the appearance of, talc.

talcose, adj. [1. tálkōs; 2. tǽlkous]. **talc** & -ose. Talcoid.

talcous, adj. [1. tálkus; 2. tǽlkəs]. **talc** & -ous. Of, composed of, containing, talc.

tale, n. [1. tāl; 2. teil]. O.E. *talu*, 'story, tale', *tæl*, 'number'; cp. O.N. *tal*, 'talk', *tala*, 'number'; Germ. *zahl*, 'number'; Du. *taal*, 'speech', cp. **taal**; O. Fris. *tale*, see **tell**. 1. (chiefly archaic) Number, total, amount : *the tale of dead and wounded* ; *the tale is complete*. 2. Connected oral or written narrative of any length ; account, record, of true or fictitious events &c. : *to tell the tale of one's adventures* ; *a stirring tale* ; *a fairytale*. Phrs. *old wives' tale*, incredible legend &c. ; *tells its own tale*, is self-explanatory, is obvious record of events &c. 3. Rumour, report (esp. of malicious reports). Phr. *to tell tales (out of school)*, (i.) reveal, esp. with malicious intent, something which should be kept secret or private; (ii.) to inform concerning another's faults and peccadilloes.

talebearer, n. [1. tǎlbārer; 2. téilbèərə]. Person who tells tales of others with malicious or mischievous intent; informer.

talebearing, n. [1. tǎlbāring; 2. téilbèəriŋ]. Prec. & -ing. Act of telling tales; the spreading of malicious reports.

talent, n. [1. tálent; 2. tǽlənt], fr. Fr., fr. Latin *talent-(um)*, fr. Gk. *tálanton*, 'pair of scales, balance; a weight; sum of money representing a talent of silver'; cp. Gk. *tálanta*, 'scales of balance', fr. *tálant-*, neut. stem of *tálās*, 'suffering, enduring, unhappy', fr. stem seen in archaic form *talássai*, 'to take upon oneself, support, undergo'; cogn. w. Scrt. *tulā*, 'balance'; Lat. *tollere*, 'to lift up'; *tolerāre*, 'to support, endure'; see **tolerate**; O.E. *polian*, 'to endure'; see **thole**. See also **atlas, tantalus**. 1. Ancient weight and sum of money, varying in different places and periods, e.g. *the Attic, Roman, Egyptian, talent*. 2. a Special gift or faculty, marked aptitude in a specific direction: *a talent for languages, for drawing*; to develop one's talents; Phr. *to hide one's talents in a napkin*, allow one's gifts and abilities to lie idle (cp. Matt. xxv. 15); b persons possessing talent: *the best talent in the country*; *to encourage local talent*.

talented, adj. [1. tálented; 2. tǽləntid]. Prec. & -ed. Possessing talent, naturally gifted.

talentless, adj. [1. tálentles; 2. tǽləntlis]. **talent** & -less. Without talent, having no special gifts or aptitude.

tales, n. [1. tālēz; 2. téilīz], fr. Lat. *tālēs*, 'such', first word of writ, pl. form of *tālis*, 'such', fr. pronominal stem **to-*, whence also **the, that** &c. (law) 1. Writ summoning additional jurors to make up deficiency. 2. List of persons who may thus be called upon to serve on a jury.

talesman, n. [1. tǎl(ē)zman; 2. téil(ī)zmən]. Prec. & **man**. Person summoned by a tales to serve on a jury.

taleteller, n. [1. tǎlteler; 2. téiltɛlə]. 1. One who relates true or fictitious stories; narrator. 2. One who makes malicious reports; talebearer.

taliacotian, adj. [1. tàliakóshan; 2. tǽliəkóuʃən], fr. the Italian surgeon Tagliacozzi (d. 1599) & -an. *Taliacotian operation*, formation of a new nose by grafting skin from the arm or forehead, the grafted skin being severed only when it has begun to grow in its new position.

talion, n. [1. tálion; 2. tǽliən], fr. Fr., fr. Lat. *tāliōn-(em)*, 'retaliation in kind', fr. *tāl-(is)*, 'such', see **tales** & cp. **retaliate**. Also called *lex taliōnis*; law of punishment by inflicting the same kind of injury as that suffered, on the principle of Levitical law, an eye for an eye, a tooth for a tooth &c.

talionic, adj. [1. tàliónik; 2. tǽliónik]. Prec. & -ic. Of, pertaining to, the law of talion.

taliped, adj. & n. [1. táliped; 2. tǽliped]. Mod. Lat., fr. *tālus*, 'ankle', see **talus**, & -i- & Lat. *ped-*, stem of *pēs*, 'foot', see **pedal**. 1. adj. a Suffering from talipes; club-footed; b (zool.) having the feet placed at peculiar angle &c., as the sloth. 2. n. a Taliped person; b taliped animal; the sloth.

talipes, n. [1. tálipēz; 2. tǽlipīz]. See prec. 1. a Club-foot; b state of having a clubfoot. 2. Peculiar position, formation, or distortion of foot.

talipot, n. [1. tálipot; 2. tǽlipət], fr. Hind. *talpat*, fr. Scrt. *tala*, 'palm', & *patra*, 'leaf'. East-Indian palm with large fan-shaped leaves.

talisman, n. [1. tálizman; 2. tǽlizmən], fr. Span., fr. Arab. *ṭilsaman* (pl.), fr. Gk. *télesma*, 'payment'; Late Gk. 'consecration, sacred rite, mystery', fr. *teléein*, 'to pay; to fulfil, perform; to initiate into mysteries', fr. *tél-os*, 'fulfilment, completion, end', see **tele-**. Object regarded as possessing supernatural power of influencing, protecting &c., the wearer; charm, amulet.

talismanic, adj. [1. tàlizmánik; 2. tǽlizmǽnik]. Prec. & -ic. Pertaining to, of the nature of, having the power of, a talisman.

talk (I.), vb. intrans. & trans. [1. tawk; 2. tŏk]. M.E. *talken*, cp. E. Fris. *talken*; connected w. O.E. *talian*, 'to reckon'; see **tale** & **tell**. A. intrans. a To express ideas &c. by means of language; to speak: *to learn to talk*; *to talk to a friend*; *stop talking*; *to talk too much*; Phrs. *to talk big*, boast; *to talk at*, refer pointedly to, direct remarks at (person), without addressing him directly; b specif. to gossip, comment on other people's affairs in a malicious spirit: *people are beginning to talk*. B. trans. 1. To give expression to in words, utter in speech: *to talk scandal, treason, nonsense, business*. 2. To use (a language) as means of expression; to speak: *to talk French* &c. 3. To bring into specified condition by talking: *to talk oneself hoarse*. Phr. *to talk a donkey's hind leg off*, talk incessantly, with great volubility. C. Followed by adverbs and prepositions with special meanings. *Talk about*, intrans., to talk upon the subject of, discuss, debate. *Talk down*, trans., to silence by louder or more effective talking. *Talk of*, intrans., a to discuss, talk about; Phr. *talking of*, à propos of, with reference to; b to put forward as a suggestion or intention: *they are talking of going abroad*. *Talk over*, trans. a to discuss, debate, hold council upon; b to persuade, win over, by talking. *Talk round*, a intrans., to discuss (subject) at some length without coming to the real point; b trans., to bring (person) over to one's own view by talking. *Talk to*, intrans., a to address in speech, converse with; b specif., to address reproaches to, reprove. *Talk up*, intrans., to speak loudly or clearly.

talk (II.), n., fr. prec. 1. a Act of talking, mutual communication of ideas in speech; conversation: *fond of good talk*; b a conversation, a chat: *to have a long, friendly talk*; c an informal lecture or address. 2. Specif. frivolous, idle, futile talk or discussion which leads to nothing: *he is all talk*; *we've had enough talk, it is time to act*. 3. Subject of conversation; gossip: *the talk of the town*.

talkative, adj. [1. táwkativ; 2. tŏkətiv]. **talk** & -ative. Given to, fond of, talking; loquacious; reverse of *taciturn*.

talkatively, adv. Prec. & -ly. In a talkative manner.
talkativeness, n. See prec. & -ness. Loquacity.
talkee-talkee, n. [1. táwki táwki ; 2. tŏki tŏki]. talk, & -ee, to suggest broken English. 1. Broken English, esp. of negroes &c. 2. Incessant, futile, idle chatter; useless, empty loquacity.
talker, n. [1. táwker ; 2. tŏkə]. talk (I.) & -er. 1. One who talks, esp. of specified kind : *a good talker*. 2. One who talks too much ; one who talks but does not act.
talkies, n. pl. [1. táwkiz ; 2. tŏkiz], fr. talk (I.) on the anal. of movies. (vulg. slang) Sound-films.
talking, adj. [1. táwking ; 2. tŏkiŋ], fr. Pres. Part. of talk (I.). 1. Having, using, the power of speech or of imitating speech : *a talking parrot* &c.; *talking doll*, one emitting squeaks when pressed &c. 2. Speaking, expressive.
talking-film, n. Sound-film.
talking-to, n. [1. táwking tōō ; 2. tŏkiŋ tū]. A reprimand, a reproof, a scolding : *I'll give him a good talking-to*.
tall (I.), adj. [1. tawl ; 2. tŏl]. Origin uncertain ; no cognates in other languages. 1. Above the average in stature ; high in relation to the average, or to surroundings : *a tall man* ; *a tall house, tower, tree, chimney, ship* &c. 2. Of a specified height: *six feet tall*. 3. (slang) Excessive, extravagant, inordinate, difficult to believe : *a tall story* ; Phr. *a tall order*, task, undertaking, difficult of fulfilment.
tall (II.), adv., fr. prec. (slang) Extravagantly, boastfully : *to talk tall*.
tallage, talliage, n. [1. tálij, táliij ; 2. tǽlidž, tǽliidž]. M.E. *tall(i)age*, fr. O. Fr. *taillage*, fr. *tailler*, ' to cut ', see tail (III.), & -age. Form of taxation, including customs and subsidies, established by Parliament in 1340.
tallboy, n. [1. táwlboi ; 2. tŏlbɔi]. tall & boy. Chest of drawers about double the usual height.
tallith, n. [1. tálith ; 2. tǽliþ]. Heb., ' covering '. Scarf, originally fringed mantle, worn by Jews round the neck, or on the head, while at prayer.
tallness, n. [1. táwlnes ; 2. tŏlnis]. tall (I.) & -ness. Quality of being tall; height.
tallow (I.), n. [1. tálō ; 2. tǽlou]. M.E. *tal(u)gh*; cp. Du. *talgh* ; M.L.G., Germ., Swed. *talg* ; O.N. *tólgr*. The coarser and harder animal fats melted down for making common kind of candles, for lubricating machinery &c.; *vegetable tallow*, similar substance made from vegetable fats.
tallow (II.), vb. trans., fr. prec. 1. To grease with tallow. 2. To fatten : *to tallow sheep*.
tallow-chandler, n. One who makes and sells tallow candles.
tallow-drop, n. Method of cutting precious stones so that one, or both sides are dome-shaped.
tallow-faced, adj. [1. tálō făst ; 2. tǽlou feist]. Having a pale, unhealthy complexion.
tallowish, adj. [1. tálōish ; 2. tǽlouiʃ]. tallow (I.) & -ish. Somewhat tallowy.
tallow-tree, n. One of various trees yielding vegetable tallow.
tallowy, adj. [1. tálōi ; 2. tǽloui]. tallow (I.) & -y. Pertaining to, like, containing, smeared with, tallow.
tally (I.), n. [1. táli ; 2. tǽli]. M.E. *tail*, fr. O. Fr. *taille*, ' notch, cut ', see tail (III.). 1. a Piece of wood with notches cut to indicate numbers, amount owing &c.; hence, b one of two accounts kept in duplicate. 2. A label, tag of identification.
tally (II.), vb. trans. & intrans., fr. prec. A. trans. 1. To reckon, register, keep account of, by tally. 2. (naut.) To put aft : *to tally a sheet* &c. B. intrans. To correspond, conform exactly, agree : *his statement does not tally with the facts*.
tally-ho, n. & vb. intrans. [1. tàli hŏ ; 2. tæ̀li hóu], fr. Fr. *taïaut*. 1. n. Huntsman's cry to hounds. 2. vb. To utter this cry.

tallyman, n. [1. táliman ; 2. tǽlimən]. tally & man. One who keeps a tally-shop.
tally-sheet, n. Paper on which tally is kept.
tally-shop, n. Shop where accounts are kept by tally and goods are paid by instalment.
talma, n. [1. tálma ; 2. tǽlmə], fr. François Talma, French actor, d. 1826. Long, sometimes hooded, man's or woman's cloak, worn in early part of 19th cent.
talmi-gold, n. [1. tálmi gŏld ; 2. tǽlmi gòuld]. Origin unknown. Kind of thinly gilt brass.
Talmud, n. [1. tálmud ; 2. tǽlmad]. Heb. *talmūd*, ' instruction '. Whole body of Jewish civil and canonical law and commentary thereupon, apart from that in the Pentateuch.
Talmudic(al), adj. [1. talmúdik(l), talmúdik(l); 2. tælmjúdik(l), tælmádik(l)]. Prec. & -ic & -al. Of, pertaining to, contained in, the Talmud.
Talmudist, n. [1. tálmudist ; 2. tǽlmədist]. Talmud & -ist. a One of the compilers of the Talmud ; b student of, one versed in, the Talmud.
Talmudistic, adj. [1. tàlmudístik ; 2. tælmədístik]. Prec. & -ic. Of, pertaining to, the Talmud or a Talmudist.
talon, n. [1. tálun ; 2. tǽlən], fr. Fr., fr. Lat. *tālōn-(em)*, ' ankle ; heel ' ; see talus. 1. a Claw of bird of prey ; b human finger nails when long and supposed to resemble a bird's claws. 2. Heel of sword-blade. 3. (archit.) Ogee moulding. 4. (cards) Part of pack left after dealing. 5. Certificate attached to a bond exchangeable for a further sheet of coupons.
taloned, adj. [1. tálund ; 2. tǽlənd]. Prec. & -ed. Having, furnished with, talon(s).
taluk, talook, n. [1. talōōk ; 2. təlúk]. Hind. *taluk*, fr. Arab. 1. Government district in southern and western India, paying fixed revenue in lieu of taxes. 2. Proprietary landed estate on special tenure, esp. in Oudh.
talukdar, n. [1. talōōkdar ; 2. təlúkdä]. Hind. Administrator of, owner of, a taluk.
talus, n. [1. tálus ; 2. téilas]. Lat. *tālus*, ' ankle, ankle-bone, heel ' ; etymol. doubtful. 1. a Ankle-bone, bone of tarsus which articulates with leg-bones ; b ankle. 2. Slope of wall or fortification. 3. (geol.) Sloping mass of fallen fragments at foot of cliff.
tamability, n. [1. tàmabíliti ; 2. tèimabíliti]. Next word & -ity. State of being tamable.
tamable, adj. [1. támabl ; 2. téiməbl]. tame & -able. Capable of being tamed.
tamableness, n. Prec. & -ness. Tamability.
tamale, n. [1. tamáhlä ; 2. təmále]. Span., fr. Mexican. Dish made of crushed Indian corn, meat, red peppers &c.
tamandua, n. [1. tamándūa ; 2. təmǽndjuə]. Brazilian. Small, arboreal ant-eater with prehensile tail.
tamanoir, n. [1. támanwar ; 2. tǽmənwǎ], fr. Fr., fr. prec. Great ant-eater of S. America, with long hair and snout.
tamanu, n. [1. támanōō ; 2. tǽmənū]. East Indian. Gamboge tree of East Indies and Pacific islands, yielding tacamahac.
tamarack, n. [1. támarak ; 2. tǽmərǽk]. Am. Indian. 1. N. American black larch. 2. Kind of N. American pine.
tamarin, n. [1. támarin ; 2. tǽmərin]. S. Am. Indian. S. American marmoset.
tamarind, n. [1. támarind ; 2. tǽmərind], fr. Span. *tamarindo*, fr. Arab. *tamr Hindi*, fr. *tamr*, ' date ', & *Hind*, ' India '. 1. Tropical tree with pinnate leaves and yellow flowers. 2. Pod of this tree, containing a brownish pulp used in cookery, medicine, for making cooling drinks &c.
tamarisk, n. [1. támarisk ; 2. tǽmərisk], fr. Lat. *tamarisc-(us)*, *tamarix*, ' tamarisk '. Genus of shrubs, esp. evergreen variety with minute leaves and pink and white flowers arranged in spikes.
tamasha, n. [1. tamáhsha ; 2. təmáʃə]. Arab. (Anglo-Indian) Elaborate function, entertainment.
tambour (I.), n. [1. tambōōr ; 2. tǽmbuə], fr. Fr., fr. Arab. *ṭambūr*, ' drum, lute '. 1. Drum, esp. bass-drum. 2. One of various objects resembling drum in shape ; specif. a wooden frame for stretching material for embroidery ; b (archit.) cylindrical stone forming part of column ; drum ; c kind of fish. 3. (archit.) Vestibule in church porch designed to prevent draughts. 4. Palisade defending gate &c. 5. Material embroidered in tambour.
tambour (II.), vb. trans., fr. prec. To embroider in a tambour.
tambourin, n. [1. támborin ; 2. tǽmbərin], fr. Fr., dimin. of prec. 1. Kind of Provençal drum. 2. a Dance accompanied by tambourin ; b music for this dance.
tambourine, n. [1. tàmborén ; 2. tæ̀mbərín], fr. Fr., prob. fr. prec. 1. Light instrument played by shaking and rapping, consisting of a round shallow frame with skin stretched over one side, and having jingling metal disks attached. 2. a Provençal dance ; b music for this dance. 3. S. African wild pigeon, white, with black-tipped wings and tail.
tambour-work, n. Embroidery done in frame.
tame (I.), adj. [1. tām ; 2. teim]. O.E. *tam*, M.E. *tāme*; cp. Du. *tam*; Germ. *zahm*, ' tame '; cogn. w. Lat. *domāre* ; Gk. *damáein*, ' to tame, subdue ' ; cp. Lat. *domus*, ' house ' ; see dome & words there referred to. 1. (of animal, bird) Brought under human authority, made friendly and tractable ; reverse of *fierce, wild*. 2. a Subdued, spiritless, passive ; b dull, flat, uninspiring : *a tame affair, retort, surrender* &c.
tame (II.), vb. trans. New formation fr. prec. ; cp. O.E. *temian*, ' to tame ' ; this stem has been lost. 1. To make tame ; reduce to domesticated state ; bring under human influence ; make docile and tractable : *to tame a wild animal, bird* &c. 2. To bring into subjection, gain authority over ; curb, subdue : *to tame one's spirit, tongue, ardour* &c.
tameless, adj. [1. támles ; 2. téimlis]. tame (II.) & -less. (poet.) Incapable of being tamed.
tamely, adv. [1. támli ; 2. téimli]. tame (I.) & -ly. In a tame manner ; without offering resistance : *to submit tamely to discipline* &c.
tameness, n. [1. támnes ; 2. téimnis]. See prec. & -ness. State or quality of being tame.
tamer, n. [1. támer ; 2. téimə]. tame (II.) & -er. One who tames : *a tamer of wild animals* ; (often in compounds) *lion-tamer* &c.
Tamil, n. [1. támil ; 2. tǽmil]. Native. 1. One of the Dravidian dialects of Ceylon and S. India. 2. Inhabitant of S. India or Ceylon.
Tamilian, n. [1. tamílian ; 2. tæmílian]. Prec. & -ian. Of, pertaining to, the Tamils or their language.
tamis, n. [1. támi(s) ; 2. tǽmi(s)]. Fr. *tamis*, ' sieve ' ; etymol. doubtful. Bag, cloth, for straining liquids, fruit-pulp &c.
Tammany, n. [1. támani ; 2. tǽməni], fr. Tammany Hall, in New York, headquarters of Tammany Society ; name is supposed to be that of an Indian chief. Also *Tammany Society*, organized Democratic party in New York City.
Tammanyism, n. [1. támaniizm ; 2. tǽmənizm]. Prec. & -ism. Tammany policy and principles.
tam-o'-shanter, n. [1. tám o shánter ; 2. tǽm ə ʃǽntə], fr. hero of Burns's poem of this name. Round woollen cap fitting closely round the head and having a flat, baggy top.
tamp, vb. trans. [1. tamp ; 2. tæmp]. Perh. fr. tampon. To pound, stamp, ram down ; specif., to ram down clay &c. on top of charge so as to plug the hole in blasting.
tampan, n. [1. támpan ; 2. tǽmpən]. Native. Poisonous S. African tick, biting flesh between fingers and toes.
tamper, vb. intrans. [1. támper ; 2. tǽmpə]. Variant of temper. Usually *tamper with*, to interfere, meddle, with ; specif. a to make changes in (a document) with fraudulent intent ; b to attempt to corrupt, to suborn (a witness).

tamping, n. [1. támping; 2. tæmpiŋ]. **tamp & -ing**. Material used to ram down a charge of explosive, to fill blast-hole &c.

tampion, n. [1. támpiun; 2. tæmpiən]. Variant of **tampon**. Disk or plug; **a** one for stopping the mouth of a gun; **b** a stopper for the end of an organ-pipe &c.

tampon, n. & vb. trans. [1. támpun; 2. tæmpən], fr. O. Fr., variant of *tapon*, 'bung, plug', fr. Du. *tap*, & **-oon**. **1.** n. Plug of lint &c. to stop haemorrhage. **2.** vb. To plug with a tampon.

tamponade, n. [1. tampunăd; 2. tæmpənéid]. Prec. & **-ade**. Use of a tampon to arrest haemorrhage.

tamponage, n. [1. támponij; 2. tæmpənidʒ]. tampon & **-age**. Use of, method of applying, tampons.

tamponment, n. [1. támponment; 2. tæmpənmənt]. tampon & **-ment**. Tamponade.

tamtam. See tomtom.

tan (I.), n. [1. tan; 2. tæn], fr. Fr., either fr. Germ. *tanne*, 'fir-tree', or fr. Celt., cp. Bret. *tann*, 'oak'. **1.** Bark of oak &c. bruised to extract tannic acid for use in tanning. **2.** Bark from which tannic acid has been extracted; also called *spent tan*. **3.** The colour of tan, i.e. yellowish brown.

tan (II.), vb. trans. & intrans., fr. prec. **A.** trans. **1.** To make (hides) into leather by steeping in a solution of tannic acid. **2.** To make brown: *complexion tanned by the sun*. **3.** To toughen with tannic acid: *to tan fish-nets* &c. **4.** (slang) To beat, flog. **B.** intrans. (of complexion &c.) To become brown through exposure to sun.

tan (III.), adj., fr. **tan (I.)**. Having the colour of tan; yellowish brown.

tan (IV.). Abbr. of **tangent (II.)**, 2.

tana, tanna, n. [1. táhna; 2. táʔnə], fr. Hind. *thāna*. (in India) **a** Military post; **b** police station.

tanager, n. [1. tánajer; 2. tænədʒə], fr. Brazilian *tangara*. Group of American birds of finch family, usually brilliantly coloured.

Tanagra, adj. [1. tánagra; 2. tænəgrə], fr. Tanagra in Boeotia, Greece, where many statuettes of this type have been found. Made at, coming from, Tanagra, esp. applied to a type of small coloured terra-cotta figurines or statuettes, usually of maidens &c., found in ancient graves and temples at Tanagra and elsewhere in Greece and Italy.

tanagrine, adj. [1. tánagrin; 2. tænəgrin]. Prec. & **-ine**. Of, pertaining to, the tanagers.

tanagroid, adj. [1. tánagroid; 2. tænəgrɔid]. tanager & **-oid**. Of, pertaining to, resembling, a tanager.

tan-ball, n. Compressed lump of spent tan used as fuel.

tandem, adv. & n. [1. tándem; 2. tændəm]. Orig. as pun, fr. Lat. *tandem*, 'at length', earlier **tamdem*, fr. *tam*, 'so', fr. pronominal stem **to-* &c., see under **the**, & pronominal stem **dě*, see **de-**. **1.** adv. (of two horses) Harnessed one behind another: *to drive tandem*, with horses so harnessed. **2.** n. **a** Pair of horses harnessed tandem; **b** carriage drawn by horses placed tandem; **c** bicycle with seats for two persons, one behind another. **3.** (attrib., of bicycle) Having seats for two persons, one behind another.

tändstickor, n. [1. téndstiker; 2. tændstikə], fr. Swed. *tändstickor*, 'matches', fr. *tända*, 'to kindle', cp. **tinder**, & *sticka*, 'slip of wood'; cp. **stick (II.)**. Wooden match.

tang (I.), n. [1. tang; 2. tæŋ]. M.E. *tange*, fr. O.N. *tange*, 'dagger'; cp. O.E. *tange*, 'pair of tongs', see **tongs**. **1.** Spike, pointed shank, projecting from upper end of blade of tool, knife, dagger &c., to fit into handle. **2.** Strong, penetrating, pungent taste or smell; (also in non-material sense).

tang (II.), vb. trans., fr. prec. To furnish with a tang or spike.

tang (III.), n., fr. Dan. *tang*, 'seaweed'; cp. O.N. *pang*, 'seaweed'. Kind of seaweed.

tang (IV.), vb. intrans. & trans. Imitative. **1.** intrans. To make a harsh, ringing sound, clang. **2.** trans. **a** To clash (metal) together; **b** *to tang bees*, cause them to settle when swarming by clanging metal, beating cans &c.

tang (V.), n., fr. prec. Harsh, ringing sound.

tangency, n. [1. tánjensi; 2. tændʒənsi].

tangent (I.) & **-cy**. State of being tangent.

tangent (I.), adj. [1. tánjent; 2. tændʒənt], fr. Lat. *tangent-(em)*, Pres. Part. of *tangere*, 'to touch'; cp. Lat. *integer*, 'whole, untouched'; *tagax*, 'thievish'; cogn. w. Gk. *tetagón*, 'grasping'; cogn. w. Goth. *tēkan*, 'to touch', see also **tact**. Meeting at a point without intersecting: *a line tangent to a curve, sphere* &c.

tangent (II.), n., fr. prec. **1.** Straight line touching a curve at one point only. Phr. *to go off, fly off, at a tangent*, to pass suddenly to an entirely different line of thought. **2.** (trig.) Tangent line subtending angle, expressed as ratio to radius of circle.

tangent-balance, n. Balance in which the weight is indicated by a pointer on a graduated arc.

tangential, adj. [1. tanjénshal; 2. tændʒénʃəl]. **tangent (II.)** & **-ial**. Of, pertaining to, forming, a tangent.

tangentially, adv. Prec. & **-ly**. In a tangential manner; as, in the direction of, a tangent.

Tangerine (I.), adj. [1. tánjerĕn; 2. tændʒəriːn], fr. Fr., fr. *Tanger*, 'Tangiers', & **-ine**. Of, pertaining to, coming from, Tangiers.

Tangerine (II.), n., fr. prec. **1.** Native, inhabitant, of Tangiers. **2.** (without cap.) A Tangerine orange; small thin-skinned, flattish orange from Tangiers; cp. *mandarine*.

tanghin, n. [1. tánggin; 2. tæŋgin], fr. Fr. native *tangena*. Evergreen tree of Madagascar, bearing poisonous fruit.

tangibility, n. [1. tanjibíliti; 2. tændʒibíliti]. **tangible** & **-ity**. State or quality of being tangible.

tangible, adj. [1. tánjibl; 2. tændʒibl], fr. L. Lat. *tangibilis*, 'that may be touched', fr. *tang-(ere)*, 'to touch', see **tangent (I.)**, & **-ible**. **1. a** Capable of being touched, perceptible by sense of touch; having material substance; specif. **b** (law, of property &c.) material, corporeal. **2.** (fig.) Clearly defined in the mind; definite, practical; not vague, illusory, or visionary: *a tangible reason, ground of complaint*.

tangibleness, n. Prec. & **-ness**. Tangibility.

tangibly, adv. See prec. & **-ly**. In a tangible manner.

tangle (I.), n. [1. tánggl; 2. tæŋgl]. Perh. fr. Dan. *tang*, 'seaweed', see **tang (III.)**, & **-le**; but cp. M.E. *tagle*, Swed. dial. *taggla*, 'to entangle'. **1.** Confused knot or mass of interwoven threads; intricate, disorderly, irregular interweaving of flexible materials: *a tangle of wool, briars* &c.; *to get one's hair in a tangle*. **2.** (in non-material sense) State of confusion, disorder, perplexity: *his affairs, thoughts, were in a tangle*. **3.** Device, consisting of iron frame with lines, hooks &c. attached, for drawing up seaweeds &c. from sea-bottom. **4.** Kind of seaweed.

tangle (II.), vb. trans. & intrans., fr. prec. **A.** trans. **1.** To form into an intricate, confused mass, to intertwine confusedly: *tangled threads*. **2.** (fig.) To complicate, confuse, make perplexing. **3.** To ensnare, catch, entangle. **B.** intrans. To become tangled, be inextricably twisted together.

tanglesome, adj. [1. tánggls*u*m; 2. tæŋglsəm]. **tangle (I.)** & **-some**. Intricately interwoven.

tangly, adj. [1. tánggli; 2. tæŋgli]. **tangle (I.)** & **-y**. Tangled, full of tangles.

tango, n. [1. tánggō; 2. tæŋgou]. Span.-American. **a** S. American dance of Spanish origin; **b** dance for two persons, derived from this, and introduced into Europe at the beginning of the 20th cent.

tangram, n. [1. tángram; 2. tæŋgræm]. Etymol. unknown. Chinese puzzle consisting of a square cut into seven specific shapes to be put together to form different figures.

tangy, adj. [1. tángi; 2. tæŋi]. **tang (I.)** & **-y**. Having a tang; producing a sharp, distinct flavour or odour.

tanist, n. [1. tánist; 2. tænist], fr. Ir. *tanaiste*, 'prince's heir', fr. *tan*, 'territory'. Heir elect to Celtic chief.

tanistry, n. [1. tánistri; 2. tænistri]. Prec. & **-ry**. System under the Brehon laws of ancient Ireland whereby the chieftaincy of a clan, although hereditary in a particular family, was fixed by the election of an individual from the members of the family.

tank, n. [1. tangk; 2. tæŋk], fr. Port. *tanque* for *estanque*, 'pond'; cp. Fr. *étang*, fr. earlier *estang*, fr. Lat. *stagnum*, 'pool, pond'; see **stagnant**. **1. a** Vessel, receptacle, cistern, for holding or storing water, oil, or gas; **b** specif., part of tender holding water-supply for locomotive engine; **c** artificial reservoir for water in India &c. **2.** (mil.) Heavy, armoured car carrying guns and moving on caterpillar wheels.

tankage, n. [1. tángkij; 2. tæŋkidʒ]. **tank & -age**. **1.** Storage of water, oil, gas &c. in tanks. **2.** Price charged for this. **3.** Cubic capacity of tank. **4.** Substance, used as fertilizer, obtained by rendering down refuse fat &c.

tankard, n. [1. tángkard; 2. tæŋkəd]. Cp. Du. *tanckaert*; O. Fr. *tancquard*; origin uncertain; perh. connected w. **tank**. **1.** Large drinking-vessel of metal, porcelain, or wood, sometimes with cover attached. **2.** Amount contained in tankard.

tank engine, n. Locomotive engine carrying its own supplies of water and coal instead of drawing a tender.

tanker, n. [1. tángker; 2. tæŋkə]. **tank & -er**. Vessel used for carrying and distributing oil as fuel to ships driven by oil, thus serving as a reservoir.

tan-liquor, n. Infusion of bark used for steeping hides in tanning.

tannable, adj. [1. tánabl; 2. tænəbl]. **tan (II.)** & **-able**. Capable of being tanned.

tan(n)adar, n. [1. tánadar; 2. tænədā]. Hind. Officer in charge of a tana.

tannage, n. [1. tánij; 2. tænidʒ]. **tan (II.)** & **-age**. Action, process, of tanning.

tannate, n. [1. tánāt; 2. tæneit]. **tan (I.)** & **-ate**. (chem.) A salt of tannic acid.

tanner (I.), n. [1. táner; 2. tænə]. **tan (II.)** & **-er**. Person engaged in the business of tanning.

tanner (II.), n. Etymol. unknown. (slang) A sixpence.

tannery, n. [1. táneri; 2. tænəri]. **tan (II.)** & **-ery**. Establishment for tanning.

tannic, adj. [1. tánik; 2. tænik]. **tan (I.)** & **-ic**. Of, pertaining to, obtained from, tan; esp. *tannic acid*, astringent substance obtained from oak-bark, gall-nuts &c., and used in preparation of leather, in medicine, and in making ink.

tanniferous, adj. [1. taníferus; 2. tæníferəs]. **tan (I.)** & **-i-** & **-ferous**. Yielding tannic acid.

tannin, n. [1. tánin; 2. tænin]. **tan (I.)** & **-in**. Tannic acid.

tanning, n. [1. táning; 2. tæniŋ]. **tan (II.)** & **-ing**. Art or process of preparing leather from hides.

tan-ooze, n. Tan-liquor.

tan-pickle, n. Tan-liquor.

tanrec, tenrec, n. [1. tánrek; 2. tænrɛk], fr. Fr., fr. Malagasy *tandraka*. Small insectivorous mammal of Madagascar, with a tailless body covered with spines.

tansy, n. [1. tánzi; 2. tænzi], fr. O. Fr. *tanasie*, fr. L. Lat., fr. Gk. *athanasía*, 'immortality', fr. neg. pref. **a-** & *thána-(tos)*, 'death', see **thanato-**. Bitter, aromatic, perennial herb, *Tanacetum*, with fine, deeply indented leaves and large heads of small, closely set yellow flowers.

tantalization, n. [1. tantalizáshun; 2. tæntəlaizéiʃən]. Next word & **-ation**. Act of tantalizing; state of being tantalized.

tantalize, vb. trans. [1. tántaliz; 2. tæntəlaiz]. See **tantalus** & **-ize**. To torment by constant, alternate renewal of hope and disap-

tantalizing, adj. [1. tántalizing ; 2. tǽntəlaiziŋ], fr. Pres. Part. of prec. Having the power to tantalize ; inspiring hope which is repeatedly renewed and disappointed.

tantalizingly, adv. Prec. & **-ly**. In a tantalizing manner.

tantalum, n. [1. tántalum ; 2. tǽntələm], fr. **tantalus**. Rare, silvery, hard, ductile metallic element used in making filaments for electric lamps.

tantalus, n. [1. tántalus ; 2. tǽntələs]. Lat. *Tantalus*, fr. Gk. *Tántalos*, son of Zeus, condemned to stand up to his chin in water with fruit suspended above his head, both food and drink receding when he tried to reach them ; formed by reduplication fr. stem *tal-, fr. *tl̥-, *tel-, ' to endure ', seen in Gk. *tálās*, ' suffering ', *tálanta*, ' scales of a balance ', see **talent**. **1.** Stand containing spirit decanters, open at the sides, with a bar which prevents removal of the bottles unless it is unlocked. **2.** Wood-ibis.

tantamount, adj. [1. tántamount ; 2. tǽntəmaunt], fr. A.-Fr. *tant amunter*, 'to amount to so much ', fr. O. Fr. *tant*, fr. Lat. *tant-(us)*, ' so much ', fr. pronominal stem *to-, seen in Lat. *tam*, 'so', see **tandem**, & **amount**. Of equal value or effect ; equivalent : *an invitation which is tantamount to a command*.

tantara, n. [1. tantáhra ; 2. tǽntdrə]. Imitative ; cp. **tarantara**. Blast or series of notes on trumpet, horn &c.

tantivy, n., vb. intrans., adj., adv. [1. tantívi ; 2. tæntívi]. Prob. imitative of hunting-horn. (all archaic or obs.) **1.** n. **a** Hunting cry ; **b** swift gallop or rush. **2.** vb. To gallop at full speed. **3.** adj. Swift, rushing. **4.** adv. Swiftly, headlong.

tantra, n. [1. tántra ; 2. tǽntrə]. Scrt. *tantra(m)*, ' thread ; rule ' ; cp. *tantrā́*, ' relaxation ' ; cogn. w. Lat. *tendere*, ' to strain, stretch ', see **tend** (II.). See further **tone**, **thin**, & words there referred to. One of the later Sanskrit religious text-books, chiefly on magic.

tantrism, n. [1. tántrizm ; 2. tǽntrizəm]. Prec. & **-ism**. Doctrines enunciated in the tantras.

tantrist, n. [1. tántrist ; 2. tǽntrist]. **tantra** & **-ist**. Student, adherent, of tantrism.

tantrum, n. [1. tántrum ; 2. tǽntrəm]. Etymol. unknown. (colloq.) Fit, outburst, of violent temper; exhibition of petulance: *to fly, go, into a tantrum*.

tan-yard, n. Establishment for conversion of hides into leather.

Taoism, n. [1. táh-ōizm, tóuizm ; 2. tǎouizəm, tǎuizəm], fr. Chinese *tao*, ' way ', & **-ism**. Chinese religious system founded upon the teaching of Lao-tsze (c. 500 B.C.).

tap (I.), n. [1. tap ; 2. tæp]. O.E. *tæppa*, M.E. *tappe*, cp. O.N. *tappi*. **1.** Device with turning valve or screw for controlling flow of liquid from pipe, cask &c. ; cock. Phr. *on tap*, (of liquor) kept in a cask fitted with tap and ready to be drawn off. **2.** Liquor obtained from particular cask ; special brew of liquor. **3.** Tap-room. **4.** Instrument for cutting internal screw-threads, in a nut &c.

tap (II.), vb. trans. O.E. *tæppan*, M.E. *tappen*, fr. O.E. *tæppa*, ' tap ', see prec. **1. a** To supply with a tap ; to fit a tap into (a cask &c.) and draw liquor from it ; **b** to pierce and draw liquid from a swelling in the body : *to tap a person for dropsy* ; **c** (slang) to extract, borrow, money from : *he tried to tap me for a fiver yesterday*. **2.** (by extension, in various senses) To obtain access to, to make available : *to tap new sources of information* ; *to tap a telephone wire*, to fix receiver to and listen to messages passing over it.

tap (III.), vb. trans. & intrans. M.E. *tappen*, fr. O. Fr. *taper*, prob. of Gmc. origin. **A**. trans. **1. a** To strike lightly, with slight, rapid blow : *to tap the floor with one's toe* ; *to tap a person on the shoulder* ; **b** to make use of (an object) in tapping : *to tap one's crutch on the floor*. **2.** To fix a piece of leather on to, in repairing : *to tap the heel of a shoe*. **B**. intrans. To knock lightly with a quick blow or series of blows ; to rap : *to tap on the door*.

tap (IV.), n., fr. prec. **1. a** Light, quick blow ; **b** sound made by such a blow. **2.** (pl. *taps*, mil.) Signal for extinguishing of lights in soldiers' quarters. **3.** Small piece of leather used to repair sole or heel of boot &c.

tapa, n. [1. táhpa ; 2. tǎpa]. Polynesian. Paper-like fabric made by Pacific Islanders from the bark of a kind of mulberry and used for mats, hangings &c.

tape (I.), n. [1. tāp ; 2. teip]. O.E. *tæppe* ; M.E. *tappe*, *tape*, ' tape, fillet ' ; cp. O.E. *tæppet*, ' cloth ', fr. Lat. *tapēte*, ' cloth, carpet, hangings ', fr. Gk. *tápēt-*, ' hangings, carpet ' ; prob. fr. Pers. or Armenian ; cp. Med. Pers. *tāftan*, ' to spin ' ; ultimately fr. base *ten-, ' to stretch ', cp. **tend** (II.) & **thin**. **1.** Linen or cotton thread woven into a strong narrow strip, used for tying things into bundles, binding edges of material, fastening garments &c. ; *red tape*, that formerly used for tying up legal documents, hence, (fig.) pedantic formality and insistence on routine in legal and other business. **2.** Length of tape &c. stretched between winning-posts on race-track. Phr. *to breast the tape*, reach winning post in foot-race. **3.** Narrow strip of paper on which message is printed in self-recording telegraph instrument.

tape (II.), vb. trans., fr. prec. **a** To join, fasten, bind, supply, with tape ; **b** specif. (bookbinding) to fasten together with bands of tape : *to tape the sections of a book*.

tape-line, n. Tape-measure.

tape-machine, n. (colloq.) Self-recording telegraph instrument.

tape-measure, n. Length of tape or strip of flexible metal, marked in inches, feet, yards &c., and used for measuring.

taper (I.), n. [1. táper ; 2. teipə]. O.E. *tapur* ; perh. Celt. ; cp. Ir. *tapar*. **a** Wick thinly coated with wax or tallow, used for lighting lamps &c. ; **b** a thin candle.

taper (II.), adj., fr. prec. (chiefly poet.) Tapering.

taper (III.), vb. intrans. & trans., fr. **taper** (I.) **1.** intrans. To narrow, contract, diminish, gradually to a point in one direction ; also *taper off*. **2.** trans. To cause to taper, give tapering shape to ; also *taper off*.

tapering, adj. [1. tápering ; 2. teipəriŋ]. Prec. & **-ing**. Growing gradually thinner, narrower, more contracted, towards one end, in one direction ; narrowing to a point.

taperingly, adv. Prec. & **-ly**. In a tapering manner.

taperness, n. [1. tápernes ; 2. teipənis]. **taper** (II.) & **-ness**. (rare) State of being tapering.

taperwise, adv. [1. tápərwīz ; 2. teipəwaiz]. **taper** (I.) & **-wise**. In a tapering manner, so as to taper.

tapestried, adj. [1. tápestrid ; 2. tǽpistrid]. Next word & **-ed**. Adorned, hung, covered, with tapestry.

tapestry, n. [1. tápestri ; 2. tǽpistri]. M.E. *tapicerie*, fr. O. Fr. *tapisserie*, fr. *tapiss-(er)*, ' to hang with tapestry ', fr. *tapis*, ' tapestry, carpet ', see **tapis**, & **tape** (I.). **a** Fabric of linen or some such material, upon which designs are wrought in wool by hand ; **b** fabric with designs woven upon it in imitation of tapestry.

tapeworm, n. [1. tápwėrm ; 2. teipwɪ̄m]. Kind of ribbon-shaped worm, genus *Taenia*, infesting alimentary canal of vertebrates.

tapioca, n. [1. tàpiōka ; 2. tǽpióukə], fr. Port., fr. Brazil. *tipioca*, ' cassava juice '. Starchy substance, in the form of rough, white grains obtained by drying manioc, boiled and used as food.

tapir, n. [1. táper, tápēr ; 2. teipə, teipiə], fr. Brazil. *tapira*. Herbivorous, pig-like mammal with short flexible proboscis, found in S. and C. America and E. Indies.

tapiroid, adj. [1. tápiroid ; 2. teipirɔid]. Prec. & **-oid**. Like, related to, the tapirs.

tapis, n. [1. táhpē ; 2. tǎpī], fr. Fr. *tapis*, ' carpet, tapestry ', fr. Lat. *tapēte*, ' carpet ' &c., see **tape** (I.). Only in Phr. *on the tapis*, under consideration and discussion.

tapotement, n. [1. tapōtment ; 2. təpóutmənt], fr. Fr., fr. *tapoter*, ' to tap ', freq. fr. *taper*, ' to tap ', see **tap** (III.), & **-ment**. (med.) Light manual percussion as form of massage.

tappet, n. [1. tápet ; 2. tǽpit]. Prob. **tap** (III.) & **-et**. (mechan.) Projecting arm &c. transmitting intermittent motion from moving part of machine to another part.

tappet-loom, n. Loom in which hammers are worked by tappets.

tap-room, n. **tap** (I.) & **room**. Place in public-house &c. where liquor is sold and drunk.

tap-root, n. Principal descending root of a plant.

tapster, n. [1. tápster ; 2. tǽpstə]. O.E. *tæppestre* ; **tap** (I.) & **-ster**. Man employed in tap-room to serve beer from cask &c.

tapu. Variant of **taboo**.

tar (I.), n. [1. tar ; 2. tā]. O.E. *te(o)ru* ; M. *terre* ; cp. O.N. *tjara* ; Dan. *tjære*, ' tar ' ; perh. ultimately cogn. w. **tree**. Thick, black, strong-smelling, viscous liquid obtained by distillation from wood and bituminous minerals such as coal &c. ; used as preservative and antiseptic, and in manufacture of aniline dyes. Phr. *a touch of the tar brush*, a dash of negro blood in one's veins.

tar (II.), vb. trans., fr. prec. To coat, smear, treat, with tar. Phrs. *tarred with the same brush*, having the same defects of character as someone else ; *to tar and feather*, smear (person) with tar, and then roll in feathers, as an unofficial punishment.

tar (III.), n. Abbr. fr. **tarpaulin**. (colloq.) A sailor ; chiefly in Phrs. *a jolly tar*, *an old tar* ; also *Jack tar*.

tara, n. [1. táhra ; 2. tǎrə]. Native. See **tara-fern**.

taradiddle. See **ta(r)radiddle**.

tara-fern, n. [1. táhra fėrn ; 2. tǎrə fɪ̄n]. Native. Kind of New Zealand bracken with edible rhizome.

tarantara, n. [1. tárentáhra ; 2. tǽrəntǎrə]. Lat. ; imitative in origin ; cp. **tantara**. Blast on horn or trumpet.

tarantass, n. [1. tárantas ; 2. tǽrəntæs], fr. Russ. *tarantas*. Large four-wheeled vehicle hung on bars instead of springs.

tarantella, **tarantelle**, n. [1. tàrentél(a) ; 2. tǽrəntél(ə)], fr. Ital. *tarantella*, fr. Taranto in S. Italy. **1.** Lively Italian dance for two persons, formerly considered a cure for tarantism. **2.** Music for this dance, usually in 6-8 time.

tarantism, n. [1. tárantizm ; 2. tǽrəntizəm], fr. Taranto, town in S. Italy, & **-ism**. Nervous disease ending in dancing mania, formerly supposed to be caused by the bite of the tarantula, common in Italy in 15th to 17th centuries.

tarantula, n. [1. tarántūla ; 2. tərǽntjulə], fr. Ital. *tarantola*, fr. *Taranto*. See prec. Large, black, hairy, venomous spider found in Southern Europe ; also a similar spider found in America.

tarantular, adj. [1. tarántūlar ; 2. tərǽntjulə]. Prec. & **-ar**. Of, resembling, produced by, the tarantula.

taratantara, n. [1. táratantáhra ; 2. tǽrətæntǎrə]. Lat. ; imitative. Trumpet or bugle call.

taraxacum, n. [1. tarákusakum ; 2. tərǽksəkəm]. Prob. fr. Pers. **a** Genus of plants, including dandelion, with toothed leaves, and yellow composite flowers supported on hollow scapes ; **b** laxative drug obtained from this.

tar-board, n. Strong millboard made from tarred rope &c.

tarboosh, n. [1. tárboōsh ; 2. tǎbúʃ]. Arab. *ṭarbūsh*. Brimless, tasselled, felt cap worn by Turks and Egyptians ; fez.

tardamente, adv. [1. tardamén'te ; 2. tǎdəménte]. Ital., fr. Lat. *tard-(us)*, ' slow '. See **tardo**. (mus.) Slowly.

Tardenoisean, adj. [1. tardenóizean ; 2. tǎdənóiziən]. (archæol.) Pertaining to the late palaeolithic culture represented by the finds at Tardenois, Aisne, France.

tardigrade, adj. & n. [1. tárdigrād; 2. tádigreid], fr. Lat. *tardigrad-(us)*, 'slow-paced', fr. *tard-(us)*, 'slow', see **tardo**, & *grad-(i)*, 'to walk', see **gradus**. (zool.) **1.** adj. Moving slowly, sluggish. **2.** n. Tardigrade animal; including the sloths.

tardily, adv. [1. tárdili; 2. tádili]. **tardy** & **-ly**. In a tardy manner, so as to be behindhand; dilatorily.

tardiness, n. [1. tárdines; 2. tádinis]. **tardy** & **-ness**. Quality of being tardy; lateness; dilatoriness.

tardo, adj. & adv. [1. tárdō; 2. tádou]. Ital., fr. Lat. *tard-(us)*, 'slow; late; dull'; prob. cogn. w. Lat. *terere*, 'to rub', see **teredo** & **trite**. (mus.) **1.** adj. Slow. **2.** adv. Slowly, slackening speed.

tardy, adj. [1. tárdi; 2. tádi], fr. O. Fr. *tardif*, fr. Lat. *tard-(us)*, 'slow; dull; late', see prec., & **-ive**. **1.** **a** Slow in action, sluggish; **b** reluctant to act, dilatory. **2.** Coming, arriving, performed, late; late in the day, behind the time, belated: *a tardy repentance*; *to make a tardy appearance.*

tare (I.), n. [1. tār; 2. tɛə]. M.E. *tāre*; etymol. unknown. **1.** Kind of vetch, esp. common vetch. **2.** (in Matt. xiii. 25 &c.) Unidentified weed, possibly the darnel.

tare (II.), n., fr. Fr., fr. Span. *tara*, fr. Arab. *ṭarḥah*, 'what is rejected'. **1.** Allowance made for weight of box, crate, sacks &c., in which goods are packed, in reckoning customs duties &c.; *tare and tret*, rules for calculating tare. **2.** Weight of a vehicle, after deducting that of the load, fuel &c. **3.** (chem.) Weight of vessel in which substance is weighed.

tare (III.), vb. trans., fr. prec. To reckon or determine weight for tare.

targe, n. [1. tarj; 2. tādž], fr. O. Fr. *targe*, *targue*, fr. O.N. *targe*, 'shield'; cp. O.E. *targe*, 'shield'; Germ. *zarge*, 'frame, rim'; O. Slav. *(po)dragŭ*, 'border'; cogn. w. Gk. *drássomai*, 'I take in the hand', orig. 'I enclose'; *drágma*, 'sheaf'; *drakhmḗ*, 'drachma', orig. 'handful', see **drachma**. Small round shield, buckler, target.

target, n. [1. tárget; 2. tágit], fr. O. Fr. *targuete*, dimin. of *targue*, see prec. **1.** Shield, buckler, targe. **2.** **a** Object to be aimed at in shooting-practice; esp. a flat circular board, or sheet of iron, painted with circles, the central and smallest one of which is known as the bull's eye; **b** any object at which one aims in shooting. **3.** (fig.) Person who, theory, action &c. which, is the object of attack: *to be a target for criticism.* **4.** Small, usually circular, railway-signal placed near switches &c. **5.** Neck and breast of lamb, cut in one piece as a joint for cooking.

target-card, n. Card marked like shooting target for recording score.

targeted, adj. [1. tárgeted; 2. tágitid]. **target** & **-ed**. Armed with a buckler.

targeteer, n. [1. tàrgetḗr; 2. tàgitíə]. **target** & **-eer**. Soldier armed with a shield.

target-ship, n. Ship used as target for naval gunnery practice.

Targum, n. [1. tárgum; 2. tágəm]. Chaldean *targum*, 'interpretation'; cp. **dragoman**. Any of several ancient Aramaic translations or paraphrases of Hebrew Old Testament.

Targumic, adj. [1. targū́mik; 2. tāgjū́mik]. Prec. & **-ic**. Of, pertaining to, the Targums.

Targumist, n. [1. tárgumist; 2. tágəmist]. See prec. & **-ist**. **1.** Composer, writer, of a Targum. **2.** Student of the Targums.

Targumistic, adj. [1. tàrgūmístik; 2. tàgjumístik]. Prec. & **-ic**. Of, pertaining to, the Targums or Targumists.

tariff (I.), n. [1. tárif; 2. tǽrif], fr. O. Fr. *tariffe*, 'arithmetic', fr. Span., fr. Arab. *ta'rīf*, fr. *'irf*, 'knowledge'. **1.** **a** List of articles upon which duties are charged by government when exported or imported; **b** the rate of duty charged according to tariff. **2.** List of prices and charges made for food, accommodation &c., together with the articles, rooms &c. for which the charges are made, esp. by a hotel; statement of terms, price-list.

tariff (II.), vb. trans., fr. prec. **1.** To include in a tariff, make list of duties payable on: *to tariff goods.* **2.** To put a price on; to value.

tarlatan, n. [1. tárlatan; 2. tálətən], fr. Fr. *tarlatane*, etymol. doubtful. Kind of open, transparent muslin.

tar-macadam, n. **tar** (I.) & **macadam.** (usually abbr. *tar-mac.*) Layer of broken stone mixed with tar &c. as road-surface.

tarn (I.), n. [1. tarn; 2. tān], fr. O.N. *tjörn*, 'small lake'; cp. Swed. dial. *tjärn*. Small lake high among mountains or on a moor.

tarn (II.). See **tern.**

tarnish (I.), vb. trans. & intrans. [1. tárnish; 2. tániʃ], fr. Fr. *tern-(ir)*, 'to tarnish', fr. M.H.G. *ternen*, 'to darken', fr. O.H.G. *tarni*, 'dark'; cp. O.E. *derne*, 'hidden, secret'; O.N. *dāra*, 'to deceive'; O.H.G. *terren*, 'to harm'; see **darn** (I.). **A.** trans. **1.** To spoil, dull, the brightness or lustre of by exposure to air, damp &c. **2.** (fig.) To diminish lustre of, to sully (reputation &c.): *to tarnish one's name, honour, fair fame* &c. **B.** intrans. To become tarnished; to be liable to become tarnished.

tarnish (II.), n., fr. prec. **1.** (lit. and fig.) Loss of brightness; blemish. **2.** Characteristic film of colour forming on face of mineral when exposed to the air.

tarnishable, adj. [1. tárnishabl; 2. tániʃəbl]. Prec. & **-able**. Liable to tarnish.

taro, n. [1. táhrō; 2. tárou]. Polynesian. **a** Tropical plant of arum family, with edible root and leaves; **b** root of this plant boiled and used as food in Pacific Islands.

taroc, n. [1. tárok; 2. tǽrək], fr. Ital. *tarocchi*; etymol. unknown. Tarot.

tarot, n. [1. tárō; 2. tǽrou], fr. Fr. *tarots*, fr. Ital. *tarocchi*, see prec. **1.** Each card of a pack of 78 painted playing-cards, used in Italy from 14th century onwards. **2.** Game played with such a pack.

tarpan, n. [1. tárpan; 2. tápæn]. Tartar. Small wild horse of Russian steppes.

tarpaulin, n. [1. tarpáwlin; 2. tāpṓlin]. **tar** (I.) & *palling*, 'covering', fr. obs. *pall*, 'to cover', fr. **pall** (I.). **1.** Waterproofed cloth or canvas, esp. canvas coated with tar. **2.** Sheet of this material as protection against rain &c. **3.** Sailor's oilskin or tarpaulin hat, coat &c. **4.** (obs.) Sailor, tar.

Tarpeian, adj. [1. tarpḗan; 2. tāpíən], fr. Lat. *Tarpēi-(us) (mons)*, '(rock) of Tarpeia', who was said to have been buried at its foot, & **-an.** *Tarpeian Rock*, cliff on Capitoline Hill at Rome from which state criminals were thrown.

tarpon, n. [1. tárpon; 2. tápən]. Prob. Am. Indian. Large game fish, *Tarpon*, or *Megalops atlanticus*, belonging to the herring family, with broad, silvery scales, of West Indies and Southern U.S.A.

tar(r)adiddle, n. [1. tàradídl; 2. tæ̀rədídl]. A modern invention. Prevarication, lie.

tarragon, n. [1. táragon; 2. tǽrəgən], fr. Span. *taragona*, fr. Arab. *tarkhūn*, fr. Gk. *drákōn*, 'dragon, large serpent', see **dragon.** **a** Perennial herb with aromatic leaves used in flavouring salads &c., and in making tarragon oil and vinegar; **b** vinegar made from this.

tarragona, n. [1. taragṓna; 2. tærəgóunə]. Province of N.E. Spain. Spanish wine resembling port.

tarras. See **trass.**

tarrock, n. [1. tárok; 2. tǽrək]. Supposed to be of Greenlandish origin. One of several kinds of sea-bird; **a** young kittiwake; **b** guillemot; **c** tern.

tarry (I.), adj. [1. táhri; 2. tári]. **tar** (I.) & **-y.** Resembling, covered with, of the nature of, tar.

tarry (II.), vb. intrans. & trans. [1. tári; 2. tǽri]. M.E. *tarien*, 'to vex, irritate; to hinder, delay', fr. O.E. *tergan*, 'to vex', confused in meaning with M.E. *targen*, 'to delay', fr. O. Fr. *targer*, fr. L. Lat. *tardicāre*, fr. Lat. *tardāre*, 'to delay', see **tardo.** (chiefly archaic) **A.** intrans. **1.** To linger, be slow in coming, delay: '*Why tarry the wheels of his chariots?*' (Judg. v. 28). **2.** To remain, stay, stop, in a place: *to tarry at home.* **3.** (rare) To wait, expect, be in expectation. **B.** trans. (rare) To await, wait for: *I will tarry his arrival.*

tarsal, adj. [1. társal; 2. tásəl]. **tarsus** & **-al.** Of, pertaining to, near, the tarsus.

tarsi-, pref. representing **tarsus.** Tarsus; e.g. *tarsitis*, inflammation of tarsus of eyelid.

tarsia, n. [1. társia; 2. tásiə]. Ital. See **tarsus.** Mosaic of coloured wood.

tarsier, n. [1. társier; 2. tásiə], fr. Fr., fr. **tarsus**, fr. peculiar structure of foot. Small, arboreal lemur of the East Indies, with large eyes and long tail, and with one of the tarsal bones much elongated.

tarso-, pref. representing **tarsus** in various anatomical terms.

tarsus, n. [1. társus; 2. tásəs]. Mod. Lat., fr. Gk. *tars-(ós)*, 'wicker-work; reed-mat; any flat surface'; cp. Gk. *trasiá*, 'crate for drying figs'; O.H.G. *darra*, 'drying oven', fr. stem **ters-*, 'to dry', seen in Gk. *térsomai*, 'to dry'; O.E. *þyrst*, 'thirst', see **torrid** & **thirst.** **1.** That part of the skeleton which lies between the leg and the metatarsus; the ankle. **2.** (ornith.) Shank of bird's leg. **3.** (zool.) Final segment of leg of insect or crustacean. **4.** Sheet of connective tissue in eyelid.

tart (I.), adj. [1. tart; 2. tāt]. O.E. *teart*, 'acid', perh. related to O.E. *teran*, see **tear** (I.). **1.** Acid, sour. **2.** (fig., of the temper, manner, mode of expression) Caustic, biting; sour, crabbed: *a tart reply.*

tart (II.), n., fr. O. Fr. *tarte*, but Mod. Fr. *tourte*; perh. variant of *torte*, fr. Lat. *tort-(um)*, P.P. type of *torquere*, 'to twist'; see **torque.** **a** Fruit cooked in a dish with top covering of pastry: *apple tart, damson tart* &c.; **b** fruit or jam cooked in flattish dish, with pastry below it but not covering it; called *an open tart.*

tartan (I.), n. [1. tártn; 2. tátən]. Etymol. unknown. **1.** Woollen fabric of various colours, with stripes of different widths and colours intersecting at right angles; esp. used for making kilts and plaids worn in Highland dress. **2.** Tartan of distinctive pattern peculiar to specific Highland clan. **3.** (attrib.) Made of tartan: *a tartan plaid* &c.

tartan (II.), n., fr. Fr. *tartane*, prob. fr. Arab. *tarīdah*, 'small ship'. Single-masted Mediterranean vessel carrying lateen sail.

tartar (I.), n. [1. tártar; 2. tátə], fr. Fr. *tartre*, fr. L. Lat. *tartarum*, fr. Arab. *durd*, 'dregs'. **1.** Compound of potash and lime deposited in the form of a crust by fermented wine; *cream of tartar*, purified form of this used medicinally and in cooking. **2.** *Tartar emetic*, compound of tartrate of potassium and antimony, used as emetic, in dyeing &c. **3.** Incrustation forming on the teeth, composed chiefly of calcium phosphate.

Tartar (II.), **Tatar**, adj. & n. [1. tártar; 2. tátə], fr. Pers. *Tatar*; the common spelling *Tartar* is influenced by **Tartarus.** **1.** adj. Of, pertaining to, the Tartars or Tatars. **2.** n. **a** Member of a branch of the Ural-Altaic family, including Turks, Cossacks &c., originally from Eastern Asia; **b** a savage, violent, intractable person; an awkward customer; Phr. *to catch a Tartar*, to have to do with an intractable, unmanageable person.

Tartarean, adj. [1. tartárean; 2. tātéəriən], fr. Lat. *Tartare-(us)*, 'of the infernal regions', see **Tartarus,** & **-an.** Of, pertaining to, characteristic of, Tartarus.

Tartarian, adj. [1. tartárian; 2. tātéəriən]. **Tartar** (II.) & **-ian.** Of, pertaining to, characteristic of, the Tartars.

tartaric, adj. [1. tartárik; 2. tātǽrik]. **tartar** (I.) & **-ic.** Of, pertaining to, derived from, containing, tartar.

tartarization, n. [1. tàrtarīzā́shun; 2. tàtəraizéiʃən]. Next word & **-ation.** **1.** Act of tartarizing, state of being tartarized. **2.** Formation of tartar.

tartarize, vb. trans. [1. tártarīz; 2. tátəraiz]. **tartar** (I.) & **-ize.** To treat with tartar.

tartarous, adj. [1. tártarus; 2. tátərəs]. **tartar** (I.) & **-ous.** Of, pertaining to, containing, tartar.

Tartarus, n. [1. tártarus; 2. tátərəs]. Lat. *Tartarus*, fr. Gk. *Tártaros*. (Gk. mythol.) 1. Dark abyss below Hades to which the Titans were consigned as a punishment. 2. Place of punishment for the wicked; hell.

tartlet, n. [1. tártlet; 2. tátlit]. **tart (II.)** & **-let**. Small open tart.

tartly, adv. [1. tártli; 2. tátli]. **tart (I.)** & **-ly**. In a tart manner; rudely, abruptly, crabbedly.

tartness, n. [1. tártnes; 2. tátnis]. See prec. & **-ness**. 1. Sourness, acidity. 2. Tart manner; abruptness, crabbedness, of speech or manner.

tartrate, n. [1. tártrāt; 2. tátreit]. **tartar (I.)** & **-ate**. Salt of tartaric acid.

Tartuf(f)e, n. [1. tartóof; 2. tātýf]. Fr. [tartyf], fr. name of character in Molière's comedy of same name. One who conceals a base nature under the guise of meekness and sanctity; a hypocrite.

Tartuf(f)ism, n. [1. tartóofizm; 2. tātýfizəm]. Prec. & **-ism**. Character of a Tartuffe; hypocrisy.

tar-water, n. Infusion of tar used as antiseptic.

taseometer, n. [1. tàseómetər; 2. tæsiómitə], fr. Gk. *tase-*, stem of *tásis*, 'stretching, tension'. See next word & *-o-* & **-meter**. Device for determining strains in buildings.

tasimeter, n. [1. tasímetər; 2. tæsímitə], fr. Gk. *tási-(s)*, 'stretching, tension', fr. stem of *teinein*, 'to stretch'; see **tend (II.)**, **tone**, & **-meter**. Electrical apparatus for measuring changes in pressure caused by changes in moisture or temperature.

tasimetric, adj. [1. tàsimétrik; 2. tæsimétrik]. Prec. & **-ic**; see **metric**. Of, pertaining to, tasimetry.

tasimetry, n. [1. tasímetri; 2. tæsímitri]. **tasimeter** & **-y**. Measurement of pressure.

task (I.), n. [1. tahsk; 2. tásk], fr. O. Nthn. Fr. *tasque*, Fr. *tasche*, fr. L. Lat. *tasca*, fr. Lat. *taxāre*, 'to censure; to touch'; see **tax (I.)**. 1. Specific piece or amount of work of any kind imposed by authority; specif., a piece of work, or 'lesson', prescribed for pupils by teachers at school. Phr. *to take a person to task*, find fault with him. 2. Any piece of work, whether imposed or undertaken voluntarily, which has to be accomplished.

task (II.), vb. trans., fr. prec. 1. To assign a piece of work to, set to a task. 2. (rare) To try, put a strain on, tax, mental or physical powers; to overtax: *to task one's memory, powers of endurance* &c.

taskmaster, n. [1. táhskmàhster; 2. táskmàstə]. An exacting master, teacher, or other person having authority to prescribe the work of others; esp. *a severe taskmaster*.

taskmistress, n. [1. táhskmìstres; 2. táskmìstris]. Feminine of prec.

taskwork, n. [1. táhskwërk; 2. táskwāk]. Piecework.

Tasmanian, adj. & n. [1. tazmănian; 2. tæzméiniən], fr. Tasmania, named after the Dutch navigator Tasman, d. 1659. 1. adj. Pertaining to Tasmania; specif., *Tasmanian devil*, a fierce, nocturnal, carnivorous marsupial, *Dasyurus ursinus*. 2. n. Inhabitant of Tasmania.

tass, n. [1. tas; 2. tæs], fr. O. Fr. *tasse*, 'cup', perh. fr. Arab. *tass*. Small draught, dram, esp. of spirits.

tassel (I.), n. [1. tásl; 2. tæsl]. M.E. & O. Fr. *tassel*, prob. fr. Lat. *taxillus*, 'small die', dimin. of *tālus*, 'ankle, knuckle-bone, heel'; see **talus**. The dimin. is prob. formed on the anal. of **axilla**, fr. *āla*, see **alar**, **aileron**. 1. Bunch of silk or other threads knotted or bound together at one end, used as ornament for dress, cap, banner &c. 2. Any of various objects resembling a tassel, e.g. the arrangement of inflorescence in some plants, such as Indian corn. 3. Narrow ribbon fastened to top of book to serve as marker. 4. Thin gold plate on back of bishop's glove.

tassel (II.), vb. trans., fr. prec. 1. To provide, adorn, with tassel(s). 2. To cut off tassels from (Indian corn) to strengthen the plant.

tastable, adj. [1. tástabl; 2. téistəbl]. **taste** & **-able**. Capable of being tasted.

taste (I.), vb. trans. & intrans. [1. tāst; 2. teist]. M.E. *tasten*, fr. O. Fr. *taster*, 'to handle, feel, taste', prob. fr. Low Lat. *taxitāre*, fr. Lat. *taxāre*, 'to appraise, value; to handle, touch', see **tax (I.)**. A. trans. 1. a To test, judge, appraise, flavour of by taking some into the mouth: *taste this coffee to see if you like it*; b specif., to act as professional taster of. 2. To perceive, distinguish, detect, the specific flavour of with the organs of taste: *I can taste pepper in this pudding*. 3. To partake of, eat or drink a small quantity of: *he hadn't tasted food for many hours*. 4. To experience, try: *to taste the joys of freedom*. B. intrans. 1. To experience the sensation of taste, be able to distinguish flavours: *I am quite unable to taste on account of my cold*. 2. (archaic) To eat or drink a small portion, partake: *to taste of strange dishes*. 3. (archaic) To experience, undergo: *to taste of danger, of death*. 4. To have particular flavour, convey specific sensation of taste to, have specific effect upon, the organs of taste: *the milk tastes sour; this sauce tastes of nothing at all*.

taste (II.), n. M.E. *tāst*, fr. O. Fr. *tast*, fr. *taster*, 'to taste'; see prec. 1. One of the five senses; the faculty of experiencing, perceiving, and discriminating different flavours on the tongue and palate: *a fine taste in wines*. 2. The characteristic sensation, other than that of texture, or of differences of temperature, produced upon the tongue by something coming into contact with it; flavour, gust, sapidity: *an unpleasant taste*. Phr. (fig.) *to leave a bad taste in the mouth*, to produce a bad impression, a feeling of disgust and repulsion. 3. Something which is tasted; specif. a a small portion of food or drink: *I'll have just a (small) taste of ham*; hence, b a slight suggestion; a touch, a tinge, a trace, a faint smack: *just a taste of sadness in his remarks*. 4. Intellectual, aesthetic, moral, discrimination; discernment, sensibility, trained judgement, critical appreciation: *a man of taste; a house furnished in the best taste; a cultivated taste in poetry, painting* &c. 5. Manner and expression as evincing sensibility and refinement; tact, delicacy of feeling; sense of what is fitting: *his speech was in excellent taste; his conduct was in the worst taste*. 6. Tendency, bias, towards; preference, predilection for; fondness, liking: *a taste for low company, for dissipation; a taste for the theatre, for horse-racing* &c. Phrs. *not at all to my taste*, not what I like; *very much to my taste*, just what I like. 7. An experience of anything; a sample, evidence: *he gave me a taste of his skill, of his bad manners* &c.

tasteful, adj. [1. tástfool; 2. téistful]. **taste (II.)** & **-ful**. Having, showing, good taste.

tastefully, adv. Prec. & **-ly**. In a tasteful manner.

tastefulness, n. See prec. & **-ness**. Quality of being tasteful.

tasteless, adj. [1. tástles; 2. téistlis]. **taste (II.)** & **-less**. 1. Without distinctive flavour; insipid, flat. 2. (rare) Lacking, having lost, the sense of taste. 3. Having bad taste; possessing, evincing, exhibiting, no discernment or discrimination; tactless.

tastelessly, adv. Prec. & **-ly**. In a tasteless manner.

tastelessness, n. See prec. & **-ness**. Quality of being tasteless.

taster, n. [1. táster; 2. téistə]. **taste (I.)** & **-er**. 1. One who tastes; specif. a (hist.) servant employed to taste his master's food and drink before it was served; b person employed professionally to test quality of articles of food and drink by tasting; esp. *tea-*, *wine-taster*. 2. (fig., colloq.) Publisher's reader. 3. Vessel or other device used in tasting or sampling; specif. a small metal cup for wine; b long-handled scoop for extracting sample from cheese &c.

tastily, adv. [1. tástili; 2. téistili]. Next word & **-ly**. (vulg. or colloq.) In a tasty manner.

tasty, adj. [1. tásti; 2. téisti]. **taste (II.)** & **-y**. 1. Having a distinctive, usually agreeable, flavour; savoury, pungent. 2. (vulg.) Tasteful, smart, attractive.

tat (I.), vb. intrans. & trans. [1. tat; 2. tæt]. Prob. back-formation fr. **tatting**. 1. intrans. To do tatting. 2. trans. To make by tatting.

tat (II.), n. Hind. Coarse Indian canvas.

tata, interj. [1. tatáh; 2. tætá, tàtá]. (child's word) Good-bye.

Tatar. See **Tartar (II.)**.

tatter, n. [1. táter; 2. tétə]. Cp. O.N. *töturr*; L.G. *tater*, 'rag'. Rag, shred, torn fragment (usually in pl.): *his coat was in tatters, hanging in tatters*. Phr. *to tear (an argument, statement* &c.) *to tatters*, demolish, disprove, refute it.

tatterdemalion, n. [1. tàterdemáliun; 2. tætədiméiliən]. Etymol. doubtful. A ragged, disreputable person.

tattered, adj. [1. táterd; 2. tætəd]. **tatter** & **-ed**. 1. Ragged, hanging in tatters. 2. Clothed in ragged garments.

Tattersall's, n. [1. tátersalz; 2. tætəsælz], fr. name of founder, Richard Tattersall, d. 1795. 1. London market for sale of hunters, racehorses &c. 2. This market regarded as the headquarters of racing and betting.

tattery, adj. [1. táteri; 2. tætəri]. **tatter** & **-y**. Tattered, ragged.

tatting, n. [1. táting; 2. tætiŋ]. Etymol. doubtful. Lace-like trimming of knotted and looped threads.

tattle, vb. intrans. & trans. [1. tátl; 2. tætl]. Imitative; cp. L.G. *tateln*, 'to gabble'. 1. intrans. To chatter idly, to gossip. 2. trans. To utter in idle chatter, gossip about.

tattle, n., fr. prec. Idle or indiscreet talk, chatter, gossip; more often *tittle-tattle*.

tattler, n. [1. tátler; 2. tætlə]. Earlier *tatler*; **tattle** & **-er**. 1. One who gossips or tattles. 2. Kind of sand-piper.

tattling, adj. [1. tátling; 2. tætliŋ]. **tattle** & **-ing**. Given to idle chatter, gossiping.

tattoo (I.), n. [1. tatóō; 2. tætú], fr. Du. *taptoe*, 'tattoo'; orig., of public-house, 'the tap is closed', fr. *tap*, 'tap-room'; see **tap (I.)**, **to**. 1. a Drum-beat or bugle-call summoning soldiers &c. to quarters at nightfall; Phr. *to beat the devil's tattoo*, drum with fingers on table &c.; b the hour at which tattoo is sounded. 2. Loud and prolonged knocking: *a loud tattoo on the door*. 3. Military display or pageant, performed, usually at night, to musical accompaniment.

tattoo (II.), vb. intrans., fr. prec. To sound a tattoo.

tattoo (III.), vb. trans. [1. tatóō; 2. tætú], fr. Tahitian *tatau*. 1. To mark (the skin) indelibly with pigments introduced into punctures arranged in a desired pattern. 2. To produce (designs) on the skin by tattooing: *to tattoo a butterfly on one's arm*.

tattoo (IV.), n., fr. prec. Design on skin produced by tattooing.

tatty, n. [1. táti; 2. tæti], fr. Hind. *ṭaṭṭi*, 'wicker frame'. Matting of cuscus-grass hung in doorway, window &c. and kept wet to cool the air.

tau, n. [1. taw; 2. tō]. Gk. *taû*, loan-word fr. Semitic; cp. Heb. *tāw*. 1. Greek letter corresponding to T; *tau cross*, T-shaped cross. 2. Fish with T-shaped markings; esp. toad-fish.

taube, n. [1. tóube; 2. táubə]. Germ., 'dove'; cogn. w. **dove**. German military monoplane.

taught, vb. [1. tawt; 2. tōt]. O.E. *tāht(e)*, *getǣht*, M.E. *taught(e)*; Pret. & P.P. of **teach**.

taunt (I.), vb. trans. & n. [1. tawnt; 2. tōnt]. fr. O. Fr. *tanter*, variant of *tenter*, 'to provoke, tempt', see **tempt**. 1. vb. To reproach contemptuously; to twit, gibe at; *taunt with*, reproach with. 2. n. A spiteful, sarcastic, sneering remark levelled at another; a jeer, a gibe; b object of taunts.

taunt (II.), adj. & adv., fr. adv. *ataunt*, (naut.) 'fully rigged', fr. Fr. *autant*, 'so much', fr. Lat. *tant-(us)*, 'so much'; see **tantamount**. (naut.) **a** adj. (of mast) Tall; **b** adv., fully rigged.

taunting, adj. [1. táwnting; 2. tɔ̄ntiŋ]. Pres. Part. of **taunt** (I.). Provoking by spiteful criticism and insult; mocking, gibing.

tauntingly, adv. Prec. & **-ly**. In a taunting manner.

tauriform, adj. [1. tŏriform; 2. tɔ̄rifɔ̄m]. See **Taurus** & **-form**. Having the form or appearance of a bull.

taurine, adj. [1. tŏrīn, tŏrīn; 2. tɔ̄rīn, tɔ̄rain], fr. Lat. *taurīn-(us)*, 'taurine', fr. *taur-(us)*, 'bull', see **Taurus**, & **-ine**. 1. Pertaining to, resembling, a bull; bovine. 2. Of, pertaining to, Taurus as a sign of the zodiac.

tauromachy, n. [1. tŏrómaki; 2. tɔ̄rómǝki], fr. Gk. *taûros*, 'bull'; cp. Lat. *taurus*, see **Taurus**, & **-machy**. **a** Bull-fighting; **b** a bull fight.

Taurus, n. [1. tŏrus; 2. tɔ̄rǝs]. Lat. *taurus*, 'bull'; cp. Gk. *taûros*, 'bull'; Lith. *tauras*, 'aurochs'; O.N. *þiorr*, 'bull'; prob. fr. base **tou-*, **tu-*, 'to swell'; see **tumid** & words there referred to. (cap.) 1. A constellation, containing the Pleiades. 2. One of the signs of the zodiac.

taut, adj. [1. tawt; 2. tɔ̄t]. M.E. *togt, toht*, 'firm, tight', fr. P.P. of *tōgen, tōwen*, O.E. *togian*, 'to draw, pull', see **tow** (I.), & **-t**, suff. of a weak P.P. 1. (of rope, sail &c.) Stretched tightly, tense. 2. In good condition, trim.

tauten, vb. trans. & intrans. [1. táwtn; 2. tɔ̄tn]. Prec. & **-en**. 1. trans. To stretch tightly, make taut. 2. intrans. To become taut.

tautly, adv. [1. táwtli; 2. tɔ̄tli]. **taut** & **-ly**. In a taut manner; **a** tightly, tensely; **b** trimly.

tautness, n. [1. táwtnes; 2. tɔ̄tnis]. See prec. & **-ness**. State of being taut.

tauto-, pref. representing Gk. *tautó*, contracted fr. *tò autó*, 'the same'; see under **the** & **auto-**. The same.

tautochrone, n. [1. táwtokrōn; 2. tɔ̄tǝkroun]. Prec. & Gk. *khrónos*, 'time', see **chronic**. Curve on which a body, moving from any point thereon by the force of gravity, will always reach the lowest point in the same space of time.

tautochronism, n. [1. tawtókronizm; 2. tɔ̄tókrǝnizǝm]. Prec. & **-ism**. Property of being tautochronous.

tautochronous, adj. [1. tawtókronus; 2. tɔ̄tókrǝnǝs]. See prec. & **-ous**. Having the nature of, pertaining to, a tautochrone.

tautog, n. [1. tawtóg; 2. tɔ̄tóg]. N. Am. Indian *tautaúog*. Edible fish of Atlantic coast of N. America.

tautologic(al), adj. [1. tàwtolójik(l); 2. tɔ̄tǝlódžik(l)]. **tautology** & **-ic** & **-al**. Connected with, of the nature of, tautology.

tautologically, adv. Prec. & **-ly**. In a tautological manner.

tautologist, n. [1. tawtólojist; 2. tɔ̄tólǝdžist]. **tautology** & **-ist**. Person given to tautology.

tautologize, vb. intrans. [1. tawtólojīz; 2. tɔ̄tólǝdžaiz]. **tautology** & **-ize**. To express oneself tautologically.

tautology, n. [1. tawtóloji; 2. tɔ̄tólǝdži], fr. Gk. *tautologia*; **tauto-** & **-logy**. Pleonastic repetition of the same idea in a sentence; e.g. *to speak all at once together*.

tautophony, n. [1. tawtófuni; 2. tɔ̄tófǝni]. **tauto-** & **-phone** & **-y**. Constant repetition of the same sound.

tavern, n. [1. távern; 2. tǽvǝn], fr. Fr. *taverne*, fr. Lat. *taberna*, 'hut; shop, booth; tavern'; prob. fr. earlier **traberna*, fr. stem of *trabs*, 'beam, timber'; cogn. w. O.W. *treb*, 'dwelling'; cp. *Tre-* in Corn. Pl.-Ns.; see also **tabernacle** & **trabeated**. Public house for retail of food and drink; an inn, hostelry.

taw (I.), vb. trans. [1. taw; 2. tɔ̄]. O.E. *tāwian, tēawian*; M.E. *tāwen, tēwen*, 'to prepare, dress' (leather, hemp &c.); cp. O.H.G. *zawan, zouwan*; Goth. *(ga)tēwjan*, 'appoint, arrange', & *tēwa*, 'order'; cp. **tool**. To prepare, dress (skins), make them into leather.

taw (II.), n. Etymol. unknown. 1. Line from which players shoot in game of marbles. 2. Game of marbles. 3. A marble.

tawdrily, adv. [1. táwdrili; 2. tɔ̄drili]. See **tawdry** & **-ly**. In a tawdry, flashy, manner.

tawdriness, n. [1. táwdrines; 2. tɔ̄drinis]. Next word & **-ness**. State or quality of being tawdry.

tawdry, adj. [1. táwdri; 2. tɔ̄dri], fr. St. Audry (pronounced [sǝn tɔ̄dri]), O.E. *Æðelðrýð*, on whose day, Oct. 17th, a fair was held, where gay finery was sold. Showy but of inferior quality; flashy, gaudy: *tawdry garments, decorations* &c.

tawer, n. [1. táw-er; 2. tɔ̄ǝ]. **taw** (I.) & **-er**. One who taws skins.

tawery, n. [1. táw-eri; 2. tɔ̄ǝri]. **taw** (I.) & **-ery**. Place where skins are tawed.

tawniness, n. [1. táwnines; 2. tɔ̄ninis]. Next word & **-ness**. State of being tawny; tawny colour.

tawny, adj. [1. táwni; 2. tɔ̄ni]. M.E. *tauni, tanni*, fr. O. Fr. *tanné*, P.P. of *tanner*, 'to tan', see **tan** (I.). Light brownish yellow, tan, or sand-coloured; *tawny port*, one that has been matured in the cask and has become pale.

taws(e), n. [1. tawz; 2. tɔ̄z]. Perh. cogn. w. **taw**(I.). (Scots) Strap for chastising children.

tax (I.), vb. trans. [1. taks; 2. tæks], fr. Fr. *taxer*, fr. Lat. *taxāre*, 'to estimate, compute; to censure, reproach; to touch'; prob. fr. Gk. *tássein*, 'to arrange, put in order; to appoint; to impose; to fix as payment'; cp. **taxis**. 1. **a** To impose tax upon (persons), compel to pay a tax; **b** to put a tax upon (articles of commerce). 2. To subject to a strain, make heavy demands upon: *to tax one's resources, memory, energies* &c. 3. *Tax with*, to accuse of, charge with, impute to: *to tax a person with rudeness, trickery*.

tax (II.), n., fr. prec. 1. Compulsory duty or impost levied by the State upon property, income, certain business transactions, articles of commerce, the right to use certain things &c. 2. Strain, serious burden, heavy demand: *a tax on one's endurance, strength, resources* &c.

taxability, n. [1. taksabíliti; 2. tæksǝbíliti]. See next word & **-bility**. State of being taxable.

taxable, adj. [1. táksabl; 2. tæksǝbl]. **tax** (I.) & **-able**. Capable of being taxed; subject to taxation.

taxableness, n. Prec. & **-ness**. Taxability.

taxation, n. [1. taksáshun; 2. tækséišǝn]. **tax** (I.) & **-ation**. Act of taxing; system of raising revenue by means of taxes; whole body of taxes payable at a given time.

tax-cart, n. Light, tradesman's or farm cart exempt from taxation.

tax-collector, n. Official whose business it is to collect taxes.

tax-farmer, n. Person who buys from the government the right to collect taxes in a specific district.

tax-free, adj. **a** Exempt from taxation; **b** (of dividends or interest) having the income-tax paid by the company and not deducted when dividend or interest is paid to the shareholders; as some British war loans.

tax-gatherer, n. [1. táks gàdherer; 2. tæks gǽðǝrǝ]. (archaic) Tax-collector.

taxi, n. [1. táksi; 2. tæksi]. Abbr. of **taximeter** (cab). Also *taxi-cab*, motor-cab for public hire, fitted with taximeter; by extension, any motor-car plying for hire.

taxi (II.), vb. intrans., fr. prec. 1. To travel in a taxi. 2. (of aeroplane) To move on surface of land or water under its own power.

taxidermal, adj. [1. tàksidérmal; 2. tæksidǽ́ml]. **taxidermy** & **-al**. Of, pertaining to, taxidermy.

taxidermic, adj. [1. tàksidérmik; 2. tæksidǽ́mik]. **taxidermy** & **-ic**. Taxidermal.

taxidermist, n. [1. táksidérmist; 2. tæksidǽ́mist]. **taxidermy** & **-ist**. Person who cures, stuffs, and mounts the skins of animals and birds so as to represent them as in life.

taxidermy, n. [1. táksidérmi; 2. tæksidǽ́mi], fr. Gk. *táxi-(s)*, 'arrangement', see **taxis**, & **-derm** & **-y**. Art of preparing, stuffing, and mounting skins of dead animals, birds &c. so as to represent them as they appeared when alive.

taximeter, n. [1. táksimèter; 2. tæksimītǝ]. Fr. *taximètre*, fr. *taxe*, 'charge, tariff, tax', see **tax** (II.), & **-meter**. Instrument fixed to a motor-car plying for hire, having a dial indicating automatically the distance travelled and the corresponding fare.

taxin, n. [1. táksin; 2. tæksin], fr. Lat. *tax-(us)*, 'yew', & **-in**. Etymol. uncertain. See under **toxic**. Poisonous, resinous compound obtained from leaves and berries of yew.

taxis, n. [1. táksis; 2. tæksis]. Gk. *táxis*, 'arrangement; battle array; order, relative position'; cp. Gk. *tássein*, 'to arrange'; no further cognates known certainly. 1. (Gk. antiq.) Division of Greek army, varying in size in different states. 2. (zool.) System of classification. 3. (surg.) Application of manual pressure to restore displaced organs &c. to their positions. 4. (gram.) Order, arrangement.

taxless, adj. [1. táksles; 2. tæksli̇s]. **tax** (II.) & **-less**. Without taxes, not liable to taxation.

taxology, n. [1. taksóloji; 2. tæksólǝdži], fr. Gk. *táx-(is)*, 'arrangement', see **taxis**, & **-o-** & **-logy**. Science of classification.

taxonomic(al), adj. [1. taksonómik(l); 2. tæksǝnómik(l)]. **taxonomy** & **-ic** & **-al**. Of, pertaining to, taxonomy.

taxonomist, n. [1. taksónomist; 2. tæksónǝmist]. Next word & **-ist**. Student of, one skilled in, taxonomy.

taxonomy, n. [1. taksónomi; 2. tæksónǝmi], fr. Fr., fr. Gk. *táx-(is)*, 'arrangement', see **taxis**, & *nóm-(os)*, 'law, ordinance &c.', see **Nemesis**. Science of classification.

taxpayer, n. [1. táksspàer; 2. tæksspèiǝ]. Person liable for payment of tax.

tazza, n. [1. tátsa, táhtsa; 2. tǽtsǝ, tátsǝ]. Ital., 'cup'; cp. Fr. *tasse*, see **tass**. Ornamental, decorated, flattish, shallow bowl mounted on a pedestal which forms a part of the vessel.

tea, n. [1. tē; 2. tī], fr. Fr. *thé*, fr. Chinese *chai*. 1. **a** Also *tea-plant*, evergreen shrub or small tree grown in China, Ceylon, Assam &c.; **b** leaves of tea-plant dried and used in infusion as a beverage. 2. The drink made by steeping the leaves of the tea-plant in boiling water. 3. Light meal, taken esp. in afternoon or evening, at which tea is drunk. 4. **a** Strong broth made by stewing down meat in a closed vessel: *chicken-, beef-tea*; **b** *black-currant tea*, drink made by soaking black-currant jam in boiling water.

tea-caddy, n. Air-tight box in which small supply of tea is kept for daily use.

tea-cake, n. Flat, slightly sweetened cake, toasted, buttered, and eaten at tea.

teach, vb. trans. [1. tēch; 2. titʃ]. O.E. *tǣcan*, fr. **tāhjan*; M.E. *tēchen*; cp. O.E. *tāc(e)n*, 'sign', see **token**; cogn. w. Gk. *deîgma*, 'proof, example', fr. base **deig-, *doig̑-*, 'to show', parallel to **deik̑-* &c., 'to show', seen in Goth. *gateihan*, 'to announce', &c.; cp. Lat. *dīcere*, 'to show, tell', see **diction**. 1. **a** (i.) To give instruction to, guide studies of, impart knowledge, experience, skill, to: *to teach children, apprentices* &c.; (ii.) (with two objects) to give instruction to (person &c.) in (a subject &c.): *to teach a child to read; to teach a class singing; to teach one French;* **b** to accustom, train, habituate: *to teach a child to obey, to tell the truth; to teach the ear to distinguish sounds;* **c** to train: *to teach a dog to beg*. 2. To give instruction in, to bring one to a knowledge of or skill in (a subject): *to teach music, riding* &c.

teachability, n. [1. tēchabíliti; 2. tītʃǝbíliti]. See next word & **-ity**. State of being teachable.

teachable, adj. [1. téchabl ; 2. tít∫əbl]. **teach & -able**. Capable of being taught, susceptible to training.

teachableness, n. Prec. & **-ness**. State of being teachable.

teacher, n. [1. téchər ; 2. tít∫ə]. **teach & -er**. **a** One who teaches ; trainer of the mind, instructor : *a child's first teacher is usually his mother* ; specif. **b** one who does this as a profession : *a teacher of drawing* ; *a schoolteacher*.

teachership, n. [1. téchership ; 2. tít∫ə∫ip]. Prec. & **-ship**. Office of a teacher.

tea-chest, n. Light wooden, metal-lined box in which tea is imported from the country in which it is grown.

teaching, n. [1. téching ; 2. tít∫iŋ]. **teach & -ing**. **1.** Act, occupation, of a teacher : *to take up teaching*. **2.** That which is taught, specific doctrine : *the teaching of the apostles*.

tea-cloth, n. **1.** Small cloth for tea-table. **2.** Cloth for drying tea-things &c. when washed.

tea-cup, n. **1.** Small cup used, as used, at tea. **2.** Tea-cupful.

tea-cupful, n. Amount contained in a tea-cup.

tea-fight, n. (slang) Tea-party.

tea-garden, n. Garden containing an open-air restaurant where tea and other light refreshments are obtainable.

tea-gown, n. Woman's loose gown worn for tea &c.

Teague, n. [1. tēg ; 2. tīg]. Ir. name. (contemptuously) Irishman.

tea-house, n. Restaurant in China or Japan where tea &c. is consumed.

teak, n. [1. tēk ; 2. tīk], fr. Port. *teca*, fr. Malayalam *tekka*. **1.** Large East Indian tree, *Tectona grandis*. **2.** The wood of this tree, a valuable kind of timber, used in shipbuilding &c.

tea-kettle, n. Smallish kettle as used to boil water for tea.

teal, n. [1. tēl ; 2. tīəl]. M.E. *tēle* ; etymol. doubtful. Kind of small wild-duck, genus *Nettion*, frequenting rivers and lakes.

tea-leaf, n. **1.** Leaf of tea-plant ; specif., the same dried and prepared for infusing and making into the beverage. **2.** (pl.) *Tea-leaves*, a collection of leaves of the tea-plant left after infusion.

team (I.), n. [1. tēm ; 2. tīm]. O.E. *tēam*, 'progeny, family ; team of oxen' ; M.E. *tēme* ; prob. connected (in Mod. sense) w. **tow (I.)**, **tug**, & w. Lat. *dūcere*, 'to draw', see **duct**, **duke** ; cp. also **teem (I.)**. **1.** Two or more beasts of burden or draught harnessed together : *a team of horses* ; *a sledge drawn by a dog-team*. **2.** Group of persons acting together in specific work, game &c. ; players forming one side.

team (II.), vb. trans., fr. prec. **1.** To harness together to form a team. **2.** (colloq.) To let out (work, job &c.) to contractor employing team of horses, men &c.

teaming, n. [1. téming ; 2. tímiŋ]. Prec. & **-ing**. (colloq.) System, method, of hiring out work to contractors employing gangs of workmen.

teamster, n. [1. témster ; 2. tímstə]. **team (I.) & -ster**. **a** Driver of team of animals ; **b** an animal in a team.

teamwise, n. [1. témwīz ; 2. tímwaiz]. **team (I.) & -wise**. In the form or manner of a team.

team-work, n. Organized joint effort, co-operation.

tea-party, n. Social gathering at afternoon tea.

tea-pot, n. Earthenware or metal vessel, with a lid, handle, and spout, in which tea is infused before being poured into cups.

teapoy, n. [1. tépoi ; 2. típɔi], fr. Hind. *tipāi*, fr. Pers. *sipai* ; associated popularly w. **tea**. Small three- or four-legged table, esp. one used as tea-table.

tear (I.), vb. trans. & intrans. [1. tār ; 2. tɛə]. O.E. *teran* ; M.E. *tēren* ; cp. Goth. *gatairan*, 'to break' ; O.N. *tæra* ; Germ. *zehren*, 'to consume' ; Goth. *-taúrnan*, 'to tear' ; cogn. w. Scrt. *dṛṇāti*, 'splits' ; Lith. *dirù* ; Gk. *dérein*, 'to flay' ; Gk. *dérma*, 'skin' ; see **derm(a)**. **A**. trans. **1. a** To pull apart, cause to divide along a gradually lengthening, straight or irregular line ; to rend, rip ; contrasted with *cut* : *to tear one's coat* ; *to tear a thing to pieces* ; Phrs. *to tear up*, destroy by tearing to pieces ; *to tear one's hair*, pull it violently ; (fig.) to show signs of despair, rage, or distress &c. ; *to tear a hole*, make one by tearing ; **b** to wound by tearing ; lacerate : *to tear one's hands on barbed wire*. **2.** To pull violently away, remove by violent effort, drag off or up : *to tear (plants) up by the roots* ; *to tear open an envelope* ; *to tear one's clothes off*. Phr. *to tear oneself away*, depart reluctantly. **3.** (fig.) **a** To make divisions or discord in, set at variance, destroy peace of : *a country torn by civil war, rival parties* &c. ; **b** to agitate, disturb : *a heart torn by anxiety*. **4.** *Torn between*, divided in mind between, attracted equally by, two alternative choices, lines of action &c. **B**. intrans. **1.** To be torn, undergo tearing : *paper tears easily*. **2.** To pull violently, attempt to rend : *he tore at the covering of the parcel*. **3.** To run quickly and impetuously ; to rush : *to tear about in excitement* ; *to tear down, along, the road*.

tear (II.), n., fr. prec. Rent, division, caused by tearing : *a tear in fabric, a garment* &c.

tear (III.), n. [1. tēr ; 2. tiə]. O.E. *tēar*, M.E. *tēre* ; O.H.G. *zahar* ; Goth. *tagr* ; cogn. w. Gk. *dákru* ; Lat. *lacrima*, 'tear', fr. *dacruma* ; see **lachrymal**. **1.** Single drop of the saline secretion of the lachrymal gland, which normally serves to moisten the eye-ball, but whose flow is increased by emotion or by violent contraction of the eye-muscles in coughing &c. : *to shed tears* ; *to wipe away one's tears* ; *eyes filled with tears*. Phr. *in tears*, weeping ; *crocodile tears*, sham, hypocritical grief. **2.** Drop or drop-like particle of liquid or transparent solid, e.g. drop of dew, resin, amber &c. ; *tears of strong wine*, drops forming on side of glass partly filled with port &c.

tear-drop, n. Single tear falling from the eye.

tear-duct, n. Duct passing from lachrymal gland to nose-passage.

tearful, adj. [1. tḗrfool ; 2. tíəful]. **tear (III.) & -ful**. **1.** Shedding tears ; given to weeping, lachrymose. **2.** Causing tears ; sad, lamentable.

tearfully, adv. Prec. & **-ly**. In a tearful manner, with tears.

tearfulness, n. See prec. & **-ness**. State of being tearful.

tear-gas, n. Poison gas, contained in shells or otherwise discharged, causing violent watering of the eyes and temporary blindness.

tearing, adj. [1. táring ; 2. téəriŋ]. **tear (I.) & -ing**. (colloq.) Violent, raging, furious : *a tearing rage* ; *a tearing hurry* ; *a tearing gale*.

tearless, adj. [1. tḗrles ; 2. tíəlis]. **tear (III.) & -less**. Not weeping ; not causing the shedding of tears.

tea-room, n. Restaurant in which tea, coffee, and light refreshments are obtainable ; room in hotel &c., set apart for tea.

tea-rose, n. Variety of China rose with scent supposed to resemble that of tea.

tear-shell, n. Explosive shell containing tear-gas that causes the eyes to water painfully.

tear-stained, adj. [1. tēr stānd ; 2. tíə steind]. Showing signs of recent tears.

tease (I.), vb. trans. [1. tēz ; 2. tīz]. O.E. *tǣsan*, 'to pluck, pull apart' ; M.E. *tēsen* ; cp. Dan. *tæse* ; M. Du. *teesen*. **1.** To tear apart fibres of, separate into parts : *to tease flax* &c. **2.** To raise a nap on (cloth), by scratching with teasels. **3. a** To worry, annoy, harass, bait, twit, make a mockery of ; **b** to subject to good-natured chaff ; to poke fun at, banter. **4.** To pester, importune, with persistent demands to do something : *he was always teasing her to marry him*.

tease (II.), n., fr. prec. Person given to teasing ; one indulging in arch banter.

teasel, teazel, teazle (I.), n. [1. tḗzl ; 2. tízl]. O.E. *tǣsel*, 'teasel', fr. base of *tǣsan*, 'to tease, pluck', see **tease (I.) & -el**. **1. a** Plant, genus *Dipsacus*, with large burrs, or heads covered with hooked prickles ; **b** one of these heads used in raising nap on cloth &c. **2.** Machine, brush &c., used in place of teasel.

teasel (II.), vb. trans., fr. prec. To dress, raise nap on (cloth), with teasel.

teaseler, teazler, n. [1. tḗz(e)ler ; 2. tíz(ə)lə]. Prec. & **-er**. Person employed in, machine used in, teaseling.

teaser, n. [1. tḗser ; 2. tízə]. **tease (I.) & -er**. **1.** Person given to teasing. **2.** (colloq.) Puzzling problem or task.

tea-service, n. Tea-set.

tea-set, n. Set of cups, plates &c., for use at tea.

teasing, adj. [1. tḗzing ; 2. tíziŋ], fr. Pres. Part. of **tease (I.)**. Harassing, tormenting, causing petty annoyance.

teasingly, adv. Prec. & **-ly**. So as to tease.

teaspoon, n. [1. tḗspoon ; 2. típun]. Small spoon, of size used for stirring tea &c.

teaspoonful, n. [1. tḗspoonfool ; 2. típunful]. Amount contained in a teaspoon, one-fourth of tablespoon.

teat, n. [1. tēt ; 2. tīt]. M.E. & O. Fr. *tete*, fr. L.G. *titte* ; cp. O.E. *titt* ; Germ. *zitze* ; cogn. w. Gk. *titthē*, 'nurse' ; fr. base *dhē-*, 'suck', & ultimately cogn. w. *thēlē*, 'teat' ; *thêsthai*, 'to milk' ; Scrt. *dhātri*, 'nurse' ; Lat. *fēlāre*, 'to suck' ; *fēmina*, 'woman' ; see **feminine & filial**. Pointed projection on the breast of a mammal through which milk passes ; nipple.

tea-table, n. Small table used for tea.

tea-things, n. Utensils prepared for use at tea.

teatlike, adj. [1. tḗtlik ; 2. títlaik]. **teat & -like**. Resembling a teat.

tea-tray, n. Small tray on which tea-things are set out, and carried.

tea-urn, n. Urn in which water is boiled for making tea.

teazel. See **teasel**.

tec, n. [1. tek ; 2. tɛk]. Abbr. of **detective**. (slang) Detective.

techily, adv. See **tetchily**.

techiness, n. See **tetchiness**.

technic, adj. & n. [1. téknik ; 2. téknik], fr. Gk. *tekhnik-(ós)*, 'made by art', fr. *tékhn-(ē)*, 'art, skill', & *-ic* ; cp. Gk. *téktōn*, 'carpenter, workman' ; Scrt. *tákṣan*, 'carpenter' ; O. Slav. *tesla* ; O.H.G. *dehsala*, 'axe'. Perh. cogn. w. Lat. *texere*, 'to weave, construct' ; see **text**. **1.** adj. Technical. **2. n. a** Technique ; **b** (pl. *technics*) the arts in general, branches of knowledge dealing with the mechanical arts ; **c** (pl.) vocabulary or rules of the arts.

technical, adj. [1. téknikl ; 2. téknikl]. Prec. & **-al**. **1.** Connected with, pertaining to, based on, the industrial or mechanical arts : *technical education*. **2.** Pertaining to, occurring, specially used in, some specific art, industry, branch of knowledge &c. : *technical knowledge, difficulty, terms* ; *the technical use of a word*.

technicality, n. [1. tèknikáliti ; 2. tèknikǽliti]. Prec. & **-ity**. **1.** State of being technical. **2.** Something, a term, method, procedure &c., connected with, and peculiar to, some specific art, science, branch of knowledge, occupation &c.

technically, adv. [1. téknikali ; 2. téknikəli]. See prec. & **-ly**. In a technical manner ; in a technical sense ; from a technical point of view.

technician, n. [1. tekníshan ; 2. tɛkní∫ən]. **technic & -ian**. Technicist.

technicist, n. [1. téknisist ; 2. téknisist]. **technic & -ist**. Student of, one skilled in, technics.

technicon, n. [1. téknikon ; 2. téknikɔn], fr. Gk. *tekhnikón*, neut. form of *tekhnikós*, see **technic**. Device or apparatus for exercising fingers of pianist.

techniphone, n. [1. téknifōn ; 2. téknifoun], fr. Gk. *tékhn-(ē)*, 'art, skill', see **technic**, & *-i-* & Gk. *phōnē*, 'sound' ; see **-phone**. Instrument with keyboard producing no sound, for exercising pianist's fingers ; dumb piano.

technique, n. [1. teknḗk ; 2. tɛknı́k]. Fr., fr. Gk. *tekhnik-(ós)*, 'of art', see **technic**. 1. Systematic and special method employed in carrying out some particular operation. 2. Skill in, practical acquaintance with, the methods of some particular art, specialized procedure, operation, and the like.

technologic(al), adj. [1. tèknolójik(l) ; 2. tèknɔlódžik(l)]. **technology** & **-ic** & **-al**. Of, pertaining to, technology.

technologist, n. [1. teknólojist ; 2. tɛknólədžist]. **technology** & **-ist**. Student of, one versed in, technology.

technology, n. [1. teknóloji ; 2. tɛknólədži], fr. Gk. *tékhn-(ē)*, 'art', see **technic**, & **-logy**. Science and history of the mechanical and industrial arts, contrasted with the fine arts.

techy. See **tetchy**.

tecnology, n. [1. teknóloji ; 2. tɛknólədži], fr. Gk. *tékno-(n)*, 'child', see under **teknonymy**, & **-logy**. The study of the development of the child.

tectological, adj. [1. tektolójikl ; 2. tɛktəlódžikl]. Next word & **-ic** & **-al**. Of, pertaining to, tectology.

tectology, n. [1. tektóloji ; 2. tɛktólədži], fr. Gk. *téktōn*, 'carpenter, builder', see **technic** & **-o-** & **-logy**. (biol.) Structural morphology.

tectonic, adj. & n. [1. tektónik ; 2. tɛktónik], fr. Lat., fr. Gk. *tektonik-(ós)*, 'skilled in building', fr. *téktōn*, 'carpenter', see **technic** & **-ic**. 1. adj. **a** Of, pertaining to, the art of building ; **b** (geol.) of, relating to, depending on, the structure of the earth. 2. n. (pl. *tectonics*) The art of designing and constructing implements, vessels, furniture, weapons &c., that combine usefulness with artistic merit.

tectorial, adj. [1. tektóriəl ; 2. tɛktóriəl], fr. Lat. *tectōri-(us)*, 'of, forming, a cover', fr. *tect-(um)*, P.P. type of *tegere*, 'to cover', see **tegument**, & **-ory** & **-al**. Of, forming, a covering ; esp. *tectorial membrane*, covering part of inner ear.

tectrices, n. [1. téktrisēz ; 2. téktrisīz]. Mod. Lat., pl. of *tectrix*, 'that which covers' ; fr. *tect-*, P.P. type of *tegere*, 'to cover' ; see **tegument**. (ornith.) Feathers covering base of tail-feathers ; tail coverts.

ted, vb. trans. [1. ted ; 2. tɛd], fr. O.N. *teðja*, 'to spread manure' ; fr. *tað*, 'manure' ; cogn. w. Gk. *datéomai*, 'to distribute, scatter', fr. base *dā-, *də-, 'to share', seen in Gk. *daiomai*, 'to share', & in **demon**. To toss, spread out and turn over (hay), in order to dry it.

tedder, n. [1. téder ; 2. tédə]. Prec. & **-er**. Machine for tedding hay &c.

teddy bear, n. [1. tédi bǎr ; 2. tédi béə]. Named after Theodore Roosevelt, President of U.S.A., and big-game hunter (1858–1919). Child's furry toy bear.

Te Deum, n. [1. tḗ dḗum ; 2. tī́ dı́əm]. Lat. *Tē Deum (laudāmus)*, '(we praise) Thee, O God', opening words of hymn. **a** Hymn ascribed to St. Ambrose, sung at Matins, or as a special thanksgiving hymn ; **b** musical setting for this.

tedious, adj. [1. tédius ; 2. tídiəs], fr. O. Fr. *tedieux*, fr. Lat. *taediōs-(us)*, 'tedious', fr. *taedium*, 'weariness', see **tedium**, & **-ous**. Wearying by length or monotony ; dull, tiresome, boring : *a tedious discourse, journey*.

tediously, adv. Prec. & **-ly**. In a tedious manner.

tediousness, n. See prec. & **-ness**. Quality of being tedious.

tedium, n. [1. tédium ; 2. tídiəm]. Lat. *taedium*, 'weariness, tediousness', fr. *taed-(et)*, 'it wearies, irks' ; cp. Lith. *tingùs* ; O. Slav. *težą*, 'dull, slow', *težíti*, 'to be unhappy'. Weariness, irksomeness, monotony.

tee (I.), n. [1. tē ; 2. tī], from letter T. 1. Letter T. 2. Anything in the shape of a T.

tee (II.), n., fr. Burmese *h'ti*, 'umbrella'. Umbrella-shaped finial on top of pagoda, usually gilded and hung with bells.

tee (III.), n. Prob. fr. mark **T** used to mark the place. 1. Mark aimed at in playing quoits, curling &c. 2. (golf) Small cone of sand, or of rubber &c., on which ball is placed for driving off at start and after each hole.

tee (IV.), vb. trans. & intrans., fr. prec. 1. trans. To place on a tee. 2. intrans. *Tee off*, to play ball from tee.

teem (I.), vb. trans. & intrans. [1. tēm ; 2. tīm]. O.E. *tēman*, 'to breed' ; M.E. *tēmen* ; fr. O.E. *tēam*, 'family, progeny', see **team**. A. trans. (archaic) To bear, bring forth, produce. B. intrans. 1. To bring forth young : '*A teeming mistress, but a barren bride*' (Pope, 'To a Lady', 72). 2. To be highly productive of, full to overflowing with, to abound in : *rivers teeming with fish*. 3. To be abundant, prolific : *wild life teems in the forest; the teeming population of the slums*.

teem (II.), vb. trans. M.E. *tēmen*, fr. O.N. *tœma*, 'to pour out', fr. *tōmr*, 'empty' ; cp. O.E. *tōm* ; L.G. *tōm*, 'free from'. (in steel-making) To pour from the crucible : *to teem molten steel*.

teen, n. [1. tēn ; 2. tīn]. O.E. *tēona*, 'accusation, injustice, injury, grief' ; M.E. *tēne* ; cp. O.L.G. *tiona*, 'injury' ; O.E. *tēon*, O.H.G. *zīhan*, 'to accuse' ; Goth. *gateihan*, 'to announce' ; cogn. w. Gk. *deiknūmi*, 'I show' ; Lat. *dīcere*, 'to say', see **diction**. (archaic) Misfortune, sorrow, grief.

-teen, suff. representing O.E. *tēne*, 'ten', see **ten**, forming cardinal numbers fr. 13 to 19 inclusive, indicating 10+3, 4 &c.

teens, n. [1. tēnz ; 2. tīnz], fr. prec. (pl.) Those years of human life counted in numbers ending in *-teen* ; age between 12 and 20 : *to be in, just out of, one's teens*.

teeny, adj. [1. téni ; 2. tíni]. Variant of **tiny**. Often used as intensive form of *tiny*, very tiny, minute ; also (colloq.) *teeny weeny*.

teepee, n. See **tepee**.

teeth, n. [1. tēth ; 2. tīþ]. Pl. of **tooth** ; O.E. *tēþ*, fr. *tōþ-i*.

teethe, vb. intrans. [1. tēdh ; 2. tīð]. As though fr. O.E. *tēðan*, fr. *tōþjan*, formed fr. *tōþ*, see **tooth**. To develop or cut teeth.

teething, n. [1. tédhing ; 2. tíðiŋ]. Prec. & **-ing**. Process or period of cutting of teeth ; dentition.

teetotal, adj. [1. tētótal ; 2. tītóutl]. Popular, reduplicated form of **total**. 1. Of, pertaining to, advocating, devoted to the cause of, total abstinence from intoxicants. 2. (colloq.) complete, absolute.

teetotalism, n. [1. tētótalizm ; 2. tītóutəlizəm]. Prec. & **-ism**. Adherence to, support of, doctrine of, total abstinence.

teetotaller, n. [1. tētótaler ; 2. tītóutələ]. **teetotal** & **-er**. Advocate of, one who practises, total abstinence from intoxicants.

teetotally, adv. [1. tētótali ; 2. tītóutəli]. See prec. & **-ly**. **a** After the manner of a teetotaller ; **b** (colloq.) totally, completely.

teetotum, n. [1. tētótum ; 2. tītóutəm], fr. letter T (for Lat. *tōtum*) marked on one side of toy, & *tōtum*, neut. form of Lat. *tōtus*, 'all' ; see **total**. Small, four-sided toy top, lettered on each side to indicate player's score.

teg(g), n. [1. teg ; 2. tɛg]. Etymol. unknown. Sheep in its second year.

tegular, adj. [1. tégular ; 2. tégjulə], fr. Lat. *tēgul-(a)*, 'tile', see **tegument** & **tile**, & **-ar**. Of, shaped like, used as, placed like, a tile.

tegularly, adv. Prec. & **-ly**. In a tegular manner, as a tile.

tegulated, adj. [1. tégulāted ; 2. tégjulèitid], fr. Lat. *tēgul-(a)*, 'tile'. See **tegular** & **-ate** & **-ed**. (zool.) Having scales or plates overlapping like tiles.

tegument, n. [1. tégument ; 2. tégjumənt], fr. Lat. *tegument-(um)*, 'covering', fr. *teg-(ere)*, 'to cover', & **-ment**. Cp. Lat. *tegulum*, 'roof' ; *tēgula*, 'tile' ; *toga*, 'robe', see **toga**. Cogn. w. Gk. *stégein*, 'to cover' ; Scrt. *sthágati*, 'conceals' ; O.H.G. *dah* ; O.N. *þak* ; O.E. *þæc*, 'roof', see **thatch**. Envelope of membrane enclosing animal body or organ ; integument.

tegumental, adj. [1. tèguméntl ; 2. tègjuméntl]. Prec. & **-al**. Of, forming, a tegument.

tegumentary, adj. [1. tèguméntari ; 2. tègjuméntəri]. **tegument** & **-ary**. Of, pertaining to, of the nature of, a tegument.

tehee, n. & vb. intrans. [1. tēhḗ ; 2. tīhí] ; in Chaucer as interj. : '*Tehee, quod she, and clapt the window to*' ('Miller's Tale', 554). Imitative. 1. n. A shrill, foolish, cackling laugh. 2. vb. To utter a high, shrill laugh.

Teian, Tean, adj. [1. téan ; 2. tí(i)ən], fr. Lat. *Tēi-(us)*, fr. Gk. *Tḗ-(ōs)*, in Ionia, & **-an**. **a** Of Teos ; **b** of Anacreon, born at Teos, c. 550 B.C.

teil, n. [1. tēl ; 2. tīl], fr. O. Fr., fr. Lat. *tilia*, 'lime-tree' ; cogn. w. M. Ir. *teile*, 'lime-tree'. Lime-tree.

teind, n. [1. tēnd ; 2. tīnd], fr. O.N. *tíund*, cogn. w. **tithe**. (Scots) Tithe.

teknonymous, adj. [1. teknónimus ; 2. tɛknónimǝs]. Next word & **-ous**. Of, pertaining to, teknonymy.

teknonymy, n. [1. teknónimi ; 2. tɛknónimi], fr. Gk. *téknon*, 'child', cogn. w. Scrt. *tákma*, 'descendant' ; O.E. *þegen* ; O.N. *þegn*, O.H.G. *degan*, 'warrior', see **thane** ; & Gk. *ónuma*, 'name', see **onomatopoeia**. Custom of certain savage races of naming the parent from the child.

tela, n. [1. téla ; 2. tílə]. Lat., 'web, tissue', earlier *texlā*, cogn. w. *texere*, 'to weave'. See **text**. (anat.) Web-like membrane.

telaesthesia, n. [1. tèlēsthḗzia ; 2. tèlisþízia], fr. **tele-**, & Gk. *aisthēsis*, 'perception', fr. *aisthánomai*, 'perceive', see **aesthete**, & **-ia**. (psychol.) Perception of objects, events &c., at a distance, not perceptible to the physical senses.

telaesthetic, adj. [1. tèlēsthḗtik ; 2. tèlisþétik]. See prec. & **-etic**. Of the nature of, pertaining to, telaesthesia.

telamon, n. [1. télamon ; 2. téləmən]. Lat. *telamon*, fr. Gk. *telamón*, 'strap, leather band ; male figure supporting entablature' ; fr. Aryan base ***telā-, *telə-** &c., 'to carry, support', seen in archaic Gk. *talássai*, 'to undertake' ; *tálanta*, 'balance' ; see **talent** ; *tlḗmōn*, 'one who endures' ; see base under **tolerate** ; cogn. w. **thole (I.)**. (archit.) Male figure supporting entablature ; cp. *caryatid*.

telary, adj. [1. télari ; 2. tíləri]. Lat. *telāris*, fr. *tēla*, 'web', see **tela**, & **-ary**. 1. Pertaining to, of the nature of, a web. 2. Spinning webs ; e.g. of spiders.

telautogram, n. [1. telǻwtogram ; 2. tɛlɔ́tǝgræm]. **tele-** & **auto-** & **-gram**. Writing, message, transmitted by telautography.

telautograph, n. [1. telǻwtograff ; 2. tɛlɔ́tǝgrɑ̀f]. See prec. & **-graph**. Electric instrument reproducing writing &c. at a distance.

telautographic, adj. [1. tèlawtográfik ; 2. tèlɔ̀tǝgrǽfik]. See prec. & **-graphic**. Pertaining to, effected by means of, telautography.

telautography, n. [1. tèlawtógrafi ; 2. tɛlɔ̀tógrafi]. See prec. & **-graphy**. The use of a telautograph.

tele-, pref. representing Gk. *tḗle*, 'far off, at a distance' ; cp. Gk. *télos*, 'end, result', prob. orig. in the sense of 'place where one stops and turns back', fr. base ***kʷel-, *kʷol-**, 'to turn', whence also **cycle**, **pole (III.)**, **wheel**. At a distance, from far off.

telebarograph, n. [1. tèlebárograff ; 2. tèlibǽrǝgrɑ̀f]. **tele-** & **barograph**. Self-recording telebarometer.

telebarometer, n. [1. tèlebárómeter ; 2. tèlibǝrómitǝ]. **tele-** & **barometer**. Barometer that transmits its readings to a distant point by means of electricity.

teledu, n. [1. téledōō ; 2. télidū̆]. E. Indian. Small, burrowing animal of Java and Sumatra ; the stinking badger.

telegonic, adj. [1. tèlegónik ; 2. tèligónik]. Next word & **-ic**. Pertaining to, characterized by, telegony.

telegony, n. [1. telégoni ; 2. tɛlégǝni], fr. **tele-** & Gk. *gónos*, 'procreation', cogn. w. *génos*, 'birth', q.v. under **genus**. Theory of the supposed transmission of characteristics from a previous male to offspring of the same mother by a later sire.

telegram, n. [1. télegram; 2. téligræm]. **tele-** & **-gram**. Message sent by telegraph.

telegraph (I.), n. [1. télegrahf; 2. téligrāf]. **tele-** & **-graph**. 1. Electrical apparatus for transmitting messages to a distance either with or without a wire. 2. Any of various devices for signalling or announcing something so as to be seen from a distance.

telegraph (II.), vb. intrans. & trans., fr. prec. A. intrans. 1. To send a message by electric telegraph. 2. (fig.) To make signals, communicate by signs with person without speaking. B. trans. 1. To send (message &c.) by means of electric telegraph: *to telegraph the news* &c. 2. To convey (one's wishes &c.) to a person by signs, without speaking.

telegrapher, n. [1. telégrafer; 2. təlégrəfə]. Prec. & **-er**. Person skilled in telegraphy; person employed in transmitting telegrams.

telegraphese, n. [1. tèlegrahféz; 2. tèligrǣfíz]. **telegraph** & **-ese**. Compressed style commonly used in telegrams.

telegraphic, adj. [1. tèlegráfik; 2. tèligrǣfik]. **telegraph** & **-ic**. Of, pertaining to, sent as, suitable for, telegram: *telegraphic message, code*; *telegraphic brevity*; *telegraphic address*, registered short form of address used in sending telegrams to a firm &c.

telegraphically, adv. [1. tèlegráfikali; 2. tèligrǣfikəli]. Prec. & **-al** & **-ly**. 1. a By means of the telegraph; b by means of signs. 2. In a manner suitable to, usual in, telegraphic messages; briefly, concisely.

telegraphist, n. [1. telégrafist; 2. təlégrəfist]. **telegraph** & **-ist**. Telegrapher.

telegraph-line, n. Telegraphic connexion.

telegraphone, n. [1. telégrafòn; 2. telégrəfoun]. See **telegraph** & **-phone**. Instrument which records telephone messages and afterwards reproduces these phonographically.

telegraph-plant, n. East Indian plant of the bean family, the leaves of which jerk spontaneously.

telegraph-pole, n. Pole supporting telegraph wires.

telegraph-post, n. Telegraph-pole.

telegraph-wire, n. Wire along which telegraphic messages are transmitted.

telegraphy, n. [1. telégrafi; 2. telégrəfi]. **tele-** & **-graphy**. Art, process, of communicating by telegraph; art of constructing telegraphic apparatus.

telekinesis, n. [1. tèlekinésis; 2. tèlikainísis]. **tele-** & Gk. *kinēsis*, 'movement', fr. *kinein*, 'to move', see **kinesis**. Motion produced in, movement of, an object without apparent physical connexion with any possible physical agent, esp. as a spiritualistic phenomenon.

telemark, n. [1. télemark; 2. télimāk]. Norw. Place-Name. A swinging turn in ski-ing.

telemechanics, n. [1. tèlemekániks; 2. tèlimikǣniks]. **tele-** & **mechanic** & **-s**. Mechanical control from a distance by rays.

telemeter, n. [1. telémeter; 2. telémitə]. **tele-** & **-meter**. Apparatus for determining distances; range-finder.

telemetric, adj. [1. tèlemétrik; 2. tèlimétrik]. See prec. & **-metric**. Pertaining to, determined by means of, telemetry.

telemetry, n. [1. telémetri; 2. təlémitri]. See prec. & **-metry**. Art of using a telemeter.

teleologic(al), adj. [1. tèleolójik(l); 2. tèliəlódžik(l)]. **teleology** & **-ic** (& **-al**). Of, pertaining to, teleology.

teleologically, adv. Prec. & **-ly**. From a teleological point of view.

teleologism, n. [1. tèleólojizm; 2. tèliólədžizəm]. **teleology** & **-ism**. Belief in final causes.

teleologist, n. [1. tèleólojist; 2. tèliólədžist]. See prec. & **-ist**. Student of, believer in, final causes.

teleology, n. [1. tèleóloji; 2. tèliólədži], fr. Gk. *télos*, genit. *téleos*, 'end'; result', see **tele-** & **-logy**. a Doctrine that all things in nature were created to fulfil a specific purpose; b systematic study of the evidences of this.

teleosaurus, n. [1. tèleosōrus; 2. tèliəsōrəs], fr. Gk. *téle-(os)*, 'complete', fr. *tél-(os)*, 'end',

see **tele-**, *-o-* & *saûros*, 'lizard', see **sauro-**. Genus of fossil mesozoic crocodiles.

teleostean, n. [1. tèleóstean; 2. tèlióstiən], fr. Gk. *téleos*, 'complete', see **tele-**, & Gk. *osté-(on)*, 'bone', see **osteo-** & **os** & **-an**. Pertaining to the order of fishes which have true bony skeletons.

telepathic, adj. [1. tèlepáthik; 2. tèlipǣþik]. **telepathy** & **-ic**. Of, pertaining to, acting by, telepathy.

telepathically, adv. [1. tèlepáthikali; 2. tèlipǣþikəli]. Prec. & **-al** & **-ly**. By means of telepathy.

telepathist, n. [1. telépathist; 2. telépəþist]. **telepathy** & **-ist**. Student of, one who believes in, or who practises, telepathy.

telepathize, vb. trans. & intrans. [1. telépathīz; 2. telépəþaiz]. Next word & **-ize**. 1. trans. To influence by telepathy. 2. intrans. To communicate by telepathy.

telepathy, n. [1. telépathi; 2. telépəþi]. **tele-** & **-pathy**. Communication between mind and mind, influence of one mind upon another, without the physical medium of the senses; thought transference.

telephone (I.), n. [1. télefòn; 2. télifoun]. **tele-** & **-phone**. Instrument by means of which the vibrations caused by sound are converted into an electric current which passes along a wire and is re-converted into sound-vibrations at the other end.

telephone (II.), vb. intrans. & trans., fr. prec. 1. intrans. To communicate by, make use of, a telephone. 2. trans. a To send, convey (a message), by telephone: *to telephone a message*; b to communicate with by telephone: *telephone me tomorrow*.

telephonic, adj. [1. tèlefónik; 2. tèlifónik]. **telephone** (I.) & **-ic**. Of, pertaining to, conveyed by, telephone.

telephonically, adv. [1. tèlefónikali; 2. tèlifónikəli]. Prec. & **-al** & **-ly**. By telephone, by means of a telephone.

telephonist, n. [1. teléfunist; 2. teléfənist]. **telephone** (I.) & **-ist**. Person operating telephone.

telephony, n. [1. teléfuni; 2. teléfəni]. **telephone** (I.) & **-y**. Process, method, of transmitting sounds, and communicating, by telephone.

telephote, n. [1. télefōt; 2. télifout], fr. **tele-** & Gk. *phōt-*, stem of *phôs*, 'light', see **phosphorus**. Apparatus for electrical reproduction of photographs at a distance.

telephoto, adj. [1. télefōtō; 2. télifoutou]. Telephotographic.

telephotograph, n. [1. tèlefótografh; 2. tèlifóutəgrāf]. **tele-** & **photograph**. Photograph a made with a telephoto lens; b reproduced by means of a telephote.

telephotographic, adj. [1. tèlefótográfik; 2. tèlifóutəgrǣfik]. Prec. & **-ic**. Pertaining to, effected by, telephotography.

telephotography, n. [1. tèlefotógrafi; 2. tèlifətógrəfi]. **tele-** & **photography**. a Method of photographing distant objects with a telephoto or telescopic lens; b the use of a telephote.

telergy, n. [1. télerji; 2. télədži]. Invented fr. **tele-** & **energy**. Force effecting telepathy.

telescope (I.), n. [1. téleskōp; 2. téliskoup]. **tele-** & **-scope**. Instrument consisting in its simplest, typical form of an arrangement of lenses in a tube, for enabling the observer to see objects or details at a distance.

telescope (II.), vb. trans. & intrans., fr. the form of construction of smaller, portable, telescopes. 1. trans. To press, drive, together, so that various sections slide one into the other, as into a series of sockets. 2. intrans. To close, slide together, like the sections of a portable telescope; to be forced one into the other: *the trains telescoped*.

telescopic, adj. [1. tèleskópik; 2. tèliskópik]. **telescope** & **-ic**. 1. Of, pertaining to, obtained by means of, a telescope: *telescopic investigation, knowledge*. 2. Visible only with a telescope. 3. Having, consisting of, sections sliding one into the other.

telescopically, adv. [1. tèleskópikali; 2. tèliskópikəli]. Prec. & **-al** & **-ly**. By means of a telescope: in a manner resembling that made possible by a telescope.

telescopiform, adj. [1. tèleskópiform; 2. tèliskópifōm]. **telescope** & *-i-* & **-form**. Having the form or construction of a telescope.

telescopist, n. [1. teléskopist; 2. teléskəpist]. **telescope** & **-ist**. Person skilled in the use of a telescope.

telescopy, n. [1. teléskopi, téleskopi; 2. teléskəpi, téliskəpi]. **telescope** & **-y**. Science of the use or construction of telescopes.

telescriptor, n. [1. téleskrìpter; 2. téliskrìptə]. **tele-** & **script** & **-or**. Telegraphic instrument worked by a lettered keyboard.

teleseme, n. [1. télesēm; 2. télisīm], fr. **tele-** & Gk. *sêma*, 'sign', see first element in **semantics**. System of transmitting signals by electricity, used in hotels &c.

telespectroscope, n. [1. tèlespéktroskōp; 2. tèlispéktrəskoup]. **tele-** & **spectroscope**. Combined telescope and spectroscope.

telethermometer, n. [1. tèleth̃ẽrmómeter; 2. tèlipāmómitə]. **tele-** & **thermometer**. Thermometer which transmits its readings to a distance by electricity.

television, n. [1. tèlevízhun; 2. tèlivížən]. **tele-** & **vision**. The act or process of seeing objects or events at a distance by means of electricity transmitted over a wire or by wireless waves.

tell, vb. trans. & intrans. [1. tel; 2. tel]. O.E. *tellan*, 'to reckon, calculate; consider (a thing to be so and so); to impute; to enumerate; later, to narrate, say'; M.E. *tellen*; fr. **tælljan*, cp. *tæl*, 'number', & *talu*, 'series; statement; discussion; claim; excuse; action at law'; see **tale**. A. trans. 1. (archaic) To count, reckon, compute: '*He telleth the number of the stars*' (Ps. cxlvii. 4). Phrs. *to tell one's beads*, say one's prayers (with rosary); see **bead**; *all told*, in all, altogether. 2. a To narrate, recount: *to tell a tale, story*; b to utter, express, in form of words: *to tell a lie, the truth*. Phr. *to tell fortunes*. 3. a To divulge, proclaim, reveal, express; impart information concerning: *tell me all you know*; *I can't tell you how sorry I am*; '*she never told her love*'; *to tell a secret*; *a man's face may tell a great deal about his character*; Phrs. *this tells its own tale*, explains itself, makes things clear; *to tell tales*, act as informer; b to point out, indicate, instruct as to: *tell me the best thing to do*; *to tell one the shortest way*; *clocks tell the time*; c to state positively, to affirm: *I tell you I'm sick of the whole thing*; *people are very angry let me tell you*. 4. a To make out, reckon out, find explanation of, account for, elucidate: *to tell the cause, the reason, of*; *difficult to tell how it is done*; *I can't tell what's the matter with him*; b to distinguish, discriminate: *to tell the true from the false*; *I can't tell one from the other*. 5. To order, give command to: *tell him to do as he's bid*; *I told you to be home by ten*. B. intrans. 1. *Tell of*, to make a report concerning, give an account: '*I will tell of all thy wondrous works*'. 2. To act as tale-bearer, to publish, divulge (secrets, news &c.): *I promise not to tell*; also (childish, colloq.) *tell on*, inform against. 3. a To produce an appreciable effect, to have a definite result: *blood tells in the long run*; *his unselfish work is at last beginning to tell*; b (of visual and auditive impressions) to have a value in contrast with other sounds, colours &c.; to show up, stand out, be distinctive compared with others: *a painter knows how to make every mass of colour tell*; *the tenor part in a part-song tells remarkably*. 4. *Tell on, upon*, to affect for the worse, to exhaust, wear out: *a youth of poverty and hardship told upon him in middle age*; *his age is beginning to tell upon him*.

tellable, adj. [1. télabl; 2. télabl]. Prec. & **-able**. Capable of being told.

teller, n. [1. téler; 2. télə]. **tell** & **-er**. One who tells; specif. a any one of four officials counting votes in House of Commons; b bank official whose duty it is to pay out money.

tellership, n. [1. télership; 2. téləʃip]. Prec. & -ship. Office of teller.

telling, adj. [1. téling; 2. téliŋ], fr. Pres. Part. of **tell**. Producing a marked effect; impressive, striking.

tellingly, adv. Prec. & -ly. In a telling manner.

telltale (I.), n. [1. téltāl; 2. télteil]. 1. a Person inclined to divulge the private affairs of others; a gossip; b one who tells things to another's discredit; a sneak, an informer. 2. (fig.) Thing conveying information; a token, sign, evidence.

telltale (II.), adj., fr. prec. Acting as telltale; tending to betray or reveal a secret, hidden feelings &c. : *a telltale blush*.

tellural, adj. [1. telúral; 2. tɛljɔ́rəl], fr. Lat. *tellūr-*, stem of *tellus*, 'earth', see **tellurium**, & -al. Of, pertaining to, the earth or its inhabitants.

tellurate, n. [1. télūrāt; 2. téljureit]. See **tellurium** & -ate. A salt of telluric acid.

telluret, n. [1. télūret; 2. téljurit]. See **tellurium** & -et. Compound of tellurium.

telluretted, adj. [1. télūrèted; 2. téljurètid]. Prec. & -ed. Containing tellurium.

tellurian, adj. & n. [1. telúriən; 2. tɛljɔ́riən], fr. Lat. *tellūr-*, stem of *tellūs*, 'earth', see **tellurium**, & -ian. 1. adj. Of, pertaining to, the earth. 2. n. Inhabitant of the earth.

telluric, adj. [1. telúrik; 2. tɛljɔ́rik]. See **tellurium** & -ic. Of, derived from, tellurium.

telluride, n. [1. télūrīd; 2. téljuraid]. See **tellurium** & -ide. Telluret.

tellurion, n. [1. telúrion; 2. tɛljɔ́riən], fr. Lat. *tellūr-*, stem of *tellūs*, 'earth', see **tellurium**. Apparatus illustrating motions of earth.

tellurium, n. [1. telúrium; 2. tɛljɔ́riəm], fr. Lat. *tellūr-*, stem of *tellūs*, 'earth', & -ium; cp. Scrt. *talam*, 'surface'; O. Slav. *tilo*, 'ground'. (chem.) Rare, brittle, lustrous, crystalline element resembling sulphur and selenium.

tellurous, adj. [1. télūrus; 2. téljurəs]. See **tellurium** & -ous. Containing tellurium.

telotype, n. [1. télotīp; 2. télotaip]. See **tele-** & **type**. 1. Electric telegraphic instrument which prints automatically. 2. Telegram printed by this instrument.

telpher, adj. & n. [1. télfer; 2. télfə]. Contracted fr. **tele-** & **-phore**. 1. adj. Conveying, transporting, by electricity: *telpher line, road* &c. 2. n. An electrically driven truck or carrier for conveying goods &c.

telpherage, n. [1. télferij; 2. télfəridž]. Prec. & -age. Transportation by electricity.

telson, n. [1. télsun; 2. télsən]. Gk. *télson*, 'limit'; prob. like *télos*, 'end', see **tele-**, fr. base *kʷel-*, 'to turn'; see **cycle** & **wheel**. Last abdominal section of some crustaceans.

Telugu, n. [1. téloogōō; 2. télugū]. Native. A Dravidian language of Southern India.

temenos, n. [1. témenos; 2. téminɔs]. Gk. *témenos*, 'sacred enclosure'; cp. *témnein*, 'to cut'; *tómos*, 'part, portion; volume'; see **tome** & cp. also **temple (I.)**. (Gk. archaeol.) Sacred enclosure round temple &c.

temerarious, adj. [1. tèmerārius; 2. tèməréəriəs]. Lat. *temerārius*, 'rash', see **temerity** & -ary & -ous. Foolishly venturesome, rash, reckless.

temerariously, adv. Prec. & -ly. In a temerarious manner.

temerariousness, n. See prec. & -ness. Quality of being temerarious; rashness, foolhardiness.

temerity, n. [1. teméritī; 2. timériti], fr. Lat. *temeritāt-(em)*, 'rashness', fr. *temere*, 'rashly, headlong', fr. **temes-*, 'dark'; cp. Lat. *tenebrae*, 'darkness'; Scrt. *támisrā*, 'darkness'; O.H.G. *dinstar*, 'dark'; Lith. *tamsà*, 'darkness'; cp. **tenebrae**. a Rashness, daring; b audacity, presumptuousness.

temp., adv. [1. temp; 2. tɛmp], abbr. of Lat. *tempore*, abl. of *tempus*, 'time', see **temporal (I.)**. In the time of : *temp. Edw. I*

Tempean, adj. [1. tempéan; 2. tɛmpíən], fr. Gk. *Témpē*, valley in Thessaly, & -an. Of, pertaining to, as beautiful as, the valley of Tempe.

temper (I.), vb. trans. & intrans. [1. témper; 2. témpə]. O.E. *temprian*, fr. Lat. *temperāre*, 'to combine in due proportion; to rule, regulate; to be moderate', fr. *tempor-*, stem of *tempus*, 'portion of time; due season; time'; see **tempus**. A. trans. 1. a (archaic) To blend, compound; b to moderate, regulate; to diminish, mitigate, potency of, by mingling with another ingredient : *to temper strong drink with water*; (also in non-material sense) *to temper justice with mercy*. Phr. *to temper the wind to the shorn lamb*, to make allowances, show consideration, for weakness, poverty, misfortune. 2. To reduce (clay) to desired consistency, by moistening and kneading. 3. To toughen and harden (metal or glass) by heating, sudden cooling, and reheating. (*N.B.*—Meanings 2 and 3 are probably influenced by Fr. *tremper*, 'to soak, temper steel' &c.). B. intrans. To have, attain, a desired quality or state; esp. to become soft and pliable.

temper (II.), n., fr. prec. 1. Consistency of clay, mortar &c. obtained by tempering. 2. Condition and degree of hardness and toughness in metal produced by tempering. 3. Disposition, cast, attitude, of mind; character, nature : *a stubborn, fiery, equable, uncertain, temper*. Phr. *to lose one's temper*, become suddenly angry; *recover, regain, one's temper*, become calm and equable again. 4. Particular mood, transient humour : *to be in a good, bad, temper*. 5. State of irritation of mind; anger, passion : *to get into a temper*; *to show signs of temper*. 6. Calmness, equable state of mind : '*To fall with dignity, with temper rise*' (Pope, 'Essay on Man', 378).

tempera, n. [1. témpera; 2. témpərə]. Ital. Distemper, esp. as used in fresco painting.

temperable, adj. [1. témperabl; 2. témpərəbl]. **temper** & -able. Capable of being tempered.

temperament, n. [1. témperament; 2. témpərəmənt], fr. Lat. *temperāment-(um)*, 'mixing in due proportion; disposition, constitution', fr. *temperā-(re)*, 'to mix, mingle, temper', see **temper (I.)**, & -ment. 1. a Characteristic combination of bodily, mental, and moral qualities, which together constitute the character and disposition of an individual, and predispose him to act and behave in a particular manner : *excitable, placid, easy-going &c., by temperament*; *the artistic temperament*; b specif., an intense, passionate nature and character : *a woman lacking temperament*. 2. Adjustment of the tones of the scale in instruments of fixed tone (e.g. piano &c.), so as to adapt the scale for use in all keys.

temperamental, adj. [1. tèmperaméntl; 2. tèmpərəméntəl]. Prec. & -al. Pertaining to, depending on, arising from, the temperament, esp. in sense 1, b.

temperamentally, adv. Prec. & -ly. By reason of temperament : *temperamentally disinclined for work*.

temperance, n. [1. témperans; 2. témpərəns], fr. O. Fr., fr. Lat. *temperantia*, 'temperance'; **temper (I.)** & -ance. 1. State or quality of being temperate; moderation, self-restraint, self-control, in action, conduct, speech, and, esp., in eating and drinking. 2. Specif. a Moderation in use of alcoholic liquor; b total abstinence from intoxicants; *temperance movement, society* &c., aiming at restriction or prohibition of intoxicating drinks; *temperance hotel*, one in which alcoholic liquors are not sold.

temperate, adj. [1. témperat; 2. témpərit]. **temper** & -ate. 1. (of persons) a Exercising self-restraint in pleasures; abstemious, not self-indulgent; b moderate in opinions; restrained in action, and expression &c. 2. (of ideas, opinions &c.) Not violent or excessive, not extreme. 3. (of climate) Not exhibiting extremes either of heat or cold; moderate, fairly equable.

temperately, adv. Prec. & -ly. In a temperate manner.

temperateness, n. See prec. & -ness. State of being temperate.

temperative, adj. [1. témperativ; 2. témpərətiv]. **temper (I.)** & -ative. Having the power of tempering.

temperature, n. [1. témperachur; 2. témp(ə)rətʃə], fr. L. Lat. *temperātūra*, 'temperature', see **temper** & -ure. 1. Degree of heat or cold : *the temperature of the room was intolerably hot*. 2. Degree of heat possessed by a living body. Phrs. *to take one's temperature*, measure and ascertain this by means of a clinical thermometer; *to have a temperature*, (colloq.) have a temperature above normal; to be feverish.

-tempered, adj. [1. témperd; 2. témpəd]. **temper (II.)** & -ed. Having a temper of specified kind : *good-, bad-, hot-tempered* &c.

-temperedly, adv. Prec. & -ly. In a manner characteristic of specific temper : *ill-temperedly* &c.

temperer, n. [1. témperer; 2. témpərə]. **temper (I.)** & -er. One who, that which, tempers; specif., machine for blending potter's clay.

tempest (I.), n. [1. témpest; 2. témpist]. M.E. fr. O. Fr. *tempeste*, fr. Low Lat. **tempesta*, Lat. *tempestas*, 'portion, space, of time, season, period; a storm'; see **tempus**, **temporal (I.)**. 1. Violent agitation of the elements; rough, tumultuous state of the weather; violent storm of wind, rain &c. 2. (fig.) Something resembling a tempest in violence; violent disturbance of the emotions; uncontrolled, tumultuous, expression of such disturbance : *a tempest of sobs, weeping* &c.

tempest (II.), vb. intrans. & trans., fr. prec. a intrans. To move violently and tumultuously, like a tempest : *to tempest through the house*; b trans., to cause a tempest in; raise to the fury of a tempest : '*Tempest the ocean*' (Milton).

tempestuous, adj. [1. tempéstūus; 2. tɛmpéstjuəs]. O. Fr. *tempestueux*, w. substitution of **-ous**; see **tempest (I.)**. a Resembling a tempest in violence; of the nature of a tempest; stormy : *a tempestuous wind*; b (fig., of the emotions, or behaviour) violent, turbulent, powerfully excited, agitated : *a tempestuous sitting of Parliament* &c.

tempestuously, adv. Prec. & -ly. After the manner of a tempest; violently, agitatedly.

tempestuousness, n. See prec. & -ness. State, quality, of being tempestuous.

Templar, n. [1. témplar; 2. témplə]. M.E. *templere*, L. Lat. *templarius*. see **temple (I.)** & -ar. 1. Member of the military religious Order, founded 1119 for the protection of the Holy Sepulchre; so called from headquarters of the Order, known as Solomon's Temple in Jerusalem; also called *Knight Templar*. 2. Law student; esp. one having chambers in the Temple in London, which formerly belonged to the Knights Templars : '*And wits and templars every sentence raise*' (Pope, 'To Arbuthnot', 211). 3. a Member of an order in modern Freemasonry styled *Knights Templars*; b member of a temperance society known as *Good Templars*.

template. See **templet**.

temple (I.), n. [1. témpl; 2. témpl]. Fr., fr. Lat. *templum*, 'place or space of observation, marked off by the Augur with his staff; any open space (poet.); place set apart for public functions; consecrated, sacred, place; place of refuge; place devoted to a particular deity; a fane'. Walde sees as the kernel of meaning, 'stretched, expectant', & connects the word w. Lat. *lendere*, 'to stretch', see **tend (II.)** & **tense (II.)**; other authorities regard the central meaning as 'place set apart, cut off, from surroundings', & connect w. Gk. *témenos*, 'sacred enclosure', see **temenos**, fr. Gk. *témnein*, 'to cut', connected w. *tomé*, 'slice', see **tome**. 1. A building set apart for worship; a a heathen fane; b place of Christian worship; a church; esp. a Protestant church (in France); c a Mormon place of worship. 2. Specif., *the Temple*, the chief place of worship of Jehovah, built in Jerusalem by the ancient Jews. 3. *The Temple*, **a** the Inns of Court, Inner and Middle Temple, in London, the site of which formerly belonged to the Knights Templars; **b** the Temple Church in London; **c** former headquarters of Templars in Paris. 4. Place or object sanctified by the Divine Presence; the body thought of as *the temple of the Holy Ghost*.

temple (II.), n. O. Fr. *temple*, fr. Lat. *tempora*, pl., 'the fatal spot', fr. *tempus*, 'period of time; the fitting time'; in pl. 'the fatal spot; the temples of the head'; see **tempus**. One of the sides of the head on either side of the forehead in front of the ear.

temple (III.), n. See **templet**. Device for keeping cloth taut on a loom.

templed, adj. [1. témpld; 2. témpld]. **temple** (I.) & **-ed**. Supplied with, abounding in, temples.

templet, n. [1. témplet; 2. témplit]. Fr. dimin. of *temple*; prob. fr. Lat. *templum*, in sense of 'small rafter, purlin', see **temple** (I.). 1. Thin plate of wood or metal used as a pattern or guide in cutting wood or stone. 2. Timber used under end of a girder or beam, to distribute weight. 3. Wedge under block on keel of a ship in process of construction.

tempo, n. [1. témpō; 2. témpou]. Ital. 'time', see **tempus**. (mus.) Degree of speed at which a passage is to be played.

temporal (I.), adj. [1. témporal; 2. témpərəl]. Lat. *temporālis*, 'belonging to time; lasting only for a time, temporary'; fr. *tempor-*, stem of **tempus**, & **-al**. 1. Belonging to, existing under, the limitation of time; contrasted with *spatial*. 2. Pertaining to, limited by, time; lasting only during the lifetime of humanity upon the earth; earthly, transient; contrasted with *eternal*. 3. Pertaining to civil affairs as distinguished from ecclesiastical: *the temporal power of the Pope*. 4. (gram.) Pertaining to tense.

temporal (II.), adj. & n. Cp. **temple** (II.). 1. adj. (anat.) Connected with, lying near, forming part of, the temples. 2. n. A temporal bone.

temporality, n. [1. tèmporáliti; 2. tèmpərǽliti]. **temporal** (I.) & **-ity**. Material rights and possessions; esp. those pertaining to an ecclesiastical authority; generally pl., *temporalities of the Church*.

temporalty, n. [1. témporalti; 2. témpərəlti]. See prec. (rare) Temporality.

temporarily, adv. [1. témporarili; 2. témpərərili]. **temporary** & **-ly**. For a time only.

temporariness, n. [1. témporarines; 2. témpərərinis]. See prec. & **-ness**. State of being temporary.

temporary, adj. [1. témporari; 2. témpərəri]. Lat. *temporārius*, 'belonging to time; lasting only for a time'; *tempor-*, stem of *tempus*, see **tempus**. **a** Lasting only for a time; transient, fleeting: *temporary pleasures, good fortune &c.*; contrasted with *lasting*; **b** held, occupied, during a limited time only; not permanent: *a temporary job, employment, post, appointment; temporary possession*.

temporization, n. [1. temporizáshun; 2. tèmpəraizéiʃən]. Next word & **-ation**. Act of temporizing.

temporize, vb. intrans. [1. témporiz; 2. témpəraiz], fr. *tempor-*, stem of Lat. *tempus*, see **tempus**, & **-ize**. 1. To pursue a non-committal line of conduct or action, give evasive, indecisive reply, so as to gain time before coming to irrevocable decision. 2. To play the part of time-server; comply, or appear to comply, with the requirements of the time and occasion.

temporizer, n. [1. témporizer; 2. témpəraizə]. Prec. & **-er**. Person given to temporizing.

temporizing, n. [1. témporīzing; 2. témpəraiziŋ]. **temporize** & **-ing**. Act of temporizing; temporization.

temporizingly, adv. Pres. Part. of **temporize** & **-ly**. In a temporizing manner.

temporo-, pref. Lat. *tempora*, see **temple** (II.). Connected with the head or facial areas, e.g. *temporo-maxillary*, pertaining to the temple and upper jaw.

tempt, vb. trans. [1. tempt; 2. tɛmpt]. M.E. *tempten, tenten*, fr. O. Fr. *tempter, tenter*, 'to try, attempt; to tempt'; Lat. *tentāre*, 'to handle, touch, feel; to prove, put to the test, try; to essay, attempt; to urge, incite'; the base is said by Walde to be an intens. of *tendere*, 'to stretch, stretch out; to aim, strive, direct one's course towards'; see **tend** (II.). 1. **a** (archaic, Bib.) To test, try, prove; **b** (poet.) to attempt. 2. (of human action) **a** To persuade, or endeavour to persuade, to do something, esp. something wrong, by holding out certain inducements; to seduce, incite, urge on, to evil: '*the woman tempted me*'; *to tempt a man to steal*; **b** (in innocent sense) to persuade, induce: *can't I tempt you to have another helping*; *I am almost tempted to accept*. Phr. *nothing would tempt me to (leave England), I am determined not to*. 3. (of effect of inanimate things, of circumstances &c.) To attract, allure, entice, excite desire in: *your offer doesn't tempt me at all*; *everything to tempt the appetite*.

temptation, n. [1. temptáshun; 2. temptéiʃən]. Prec. & **-ation**. 1. **a** Act of tempting. **b** state of being tempted. 2. That which tempts; an attraction, allurement, inducement; **a** (in bad sense) *one should not put temptation in the way of others*; *many temptations beset the young*; **b** (in innocent sense) *I am so comfortable here, that there is no temptation to leave*.

tempter, n. [1. témpter; 2. témptə]. **tempt** & **-er**. Person who tempts; specif., *the Tempter*, the Devil, Satan.

tempting, adj. [1. témpting; 2. témptiŋ], fr. Pres. Part. of **tempt**. Attractive, alluring, seductive: *a tempting offer*; *this peach looks very tempting*.

temptress, n. [1. témptres; 2. témptris]. **tempter** & **-ess**. Woman who tempts (chiefly in bad sense).

tempus, n. [1. témpus; 2. témpəs]. Lat. 'time; a period of time', stem *tempor-*, see **temporal** (I.) &c.; the etymol., like the orig. conception, whence the meaning springs, is doubtful. Some regard this as being 'a particular region of the sky', & connect w. **temple** (I.); others believe the basal idea to be 'that which lasts', & connect w. *tendere*, 'to stretch out, extend', & Scrt. *tanōti*, 'it lasts', & w. Goth. *þeihs*, fr. *þeŋx-*, 'time, season'; others again believe the orig. sense to have been 'particular, specific, period or point of time', still connecting w. *tendere*, & *þeihs*, & also w. O.N. *þing*, 'meeting held at fixed times', see **thing**. Time as thought of in connexion with music and prosody.

tempus fugit, phr. [1. témpus fújit; 2. témpəs fjúdʒit]. Lat. Time flies.

ten, numeral adj. & n. [1. ten; 2. tɛn]. O.E. *tíen, tēn*, O.H.G. *zehan*, Mod. Germ. *zehn*; O.S. *tehan*; Goth. *taihun*; all fr. Aryan **dek̑m̥*, whence also Gk. *déka*; Scrt. *dáśa*, Lat. *decem*, cp. **decimal**. 1. adj. One more than nine; twice five. Phrs. *ten times the man you are*, a much better man; *ten times as big*, a great deal bigger; *I'd ten times rather*, much rather. 2. n. **a** The number one more than nine; **b** the figure 10, or X, expressing this; **c** a collection of ten objects: *to arrange things in tens*. Phr. *the upper ten*, for *ten thousand*, the aristocracy.

tenable, adj. [1. ténabl, ténabl; 2. tínəbl, ténəbl]. Fr., fr. Lat. stem *ten-*, 'to hold', & **-able**. Lat. *tenēre*, 'to hold, grasp; have in one's power, have, keep, possession of; to hinder, restrain; to hold in the mind, to know; to take in, understand', is ultimately fr. same base as *tendere*, 'to stretch', q.v. under **tend** (II.) & cp. **tendon** & **tense** (II.). 1. (of a fortress, position &c.) Capable of being defended, maintained, held in possession. 2. (of opinions, ideas &c.) Capable of being reasonably held by the mind; in accordance with facts or with common sense; logical.

tenace, n. [1. tenás; 2. tɛnéis]. Fr., see next word. (whist) Combination of first and third best, or second and fourth best cards of the suit which has been led, held by the same hand.

tenacious, adj. [1. tenáshus; 2. tɛnéiʃəs]. Lat. *tenāci-*, stem of *tenax*, 'holding fast; sticky; stubborn', see base under **tenable**, & **-ous**. 1. Holding, grasping, firmly: *a tenacious grip*. 2. Holding together firmly; a tough, cohesive; **b** adhesive, sticky. 3. (of the mind and mental condition) **a** Grasping and keeping firmly; retentive: *a tenacious memory*; **b** adhering firmly to a purpose; unyielding, stubborn: *a tenacious foe*; *to be tenacious of one's rights*.

tenaciously, adv. Prec. & **-ly**. In a tenacious manner.

tenaciousness, n. See prec. & **-ness**. Quality, fact, of being tenacious (in physical and moral sense).

tenacity, n. [1. tenásiti; 2. tɛnǽsiti]. Lat. *tenācitāt-(em)*, 'a holding fast', fr. *tenāc-*, see **tenacious**, & **-ity**. **a** Resolution, fixity of purpose, stubbornness; **b** power of retaining; retentiveness.

tenaculum, n. [1. tenákūlum; 2. tɛnǽkjuləm]. Lat., 'a holder', formed fr. *tenāc-*, see **tenacious**. Sharp, slender hook used by surgeons.

tenail(le), n. [1. tenál; 2. tɛnéil]. Fr., fr. prec. (fort.) Outwork in main ditch between two bastions.

tenancy, n. [1. ténansi; 2. ténənsi]. Next word & **-cy**. 1. **a** Act of holding property as a tenant; **b** period, duration, of such holding. 2. Property, land, or house, held by a tenant.

tenant (I.), n. [1. ténant; 2. ténənt]. Fr., fr. Pres. Part. of *tenir*, 'to hold', fr. Lat. *tenēre*, see **tenable**. 1. (law) Person possessing real estate by any kind of right, whether for life, or for a term of years, or at the will of another. 2. Person who holds house or land belonging to another on payment of rent; contrasted with *landlord*. 3. Inhabitant, dweller, denizen: *tenants of the woods, trees &c.*, birds.

tenant (II.), vb. trans., fr. prec. To occupy, hold, possess, as a tenant; chiefly used in P.P.

tenantable, adj. [1. ténantabl; 2. ténəntəbl]. **tenant** (II.) & **-able**. Capable of being, fit to be, occupied by a tenant.

tenantless, adj. [1. ténantles; 2. ténəntlis]. **tenant** (I.) & **-less**. Empty, unoccupied, devoid of tenants or inhabitants.

tenantry, n. [1. ténantri; 2. ténəntri]. **tenant** (I.) & **-ry**. Body of tenants collectively.

tench, n. [1. tensh; 2. tɛnʃ]. O. Fr. *tenche*, L. Lat. *tinca*. A freshwater, cyprinid fish, *Tinca vulgaris*.

tend (I.), vb. trans. [1. tend; 2. tɛnd]. Form of **attend**. 1. To watch over, guard, look after, provide for the wants of: *to tend the sick and wounded*; *to tend sheep*. 2. (naut.) To stand by, in readiness to attend to (a rope &c.).

tend (II.), vb. intrans. Fr. *tendre*, fr. Lat. *tendere*, 'to stretch, extend; to direct oneself, or one's course'; cogn. w. *teinein*, fr. **tenjō-*, 'stretch'; Scrt. *tanōti*, 'he stretches' &c.; also w. Gk. *tónos*, see **tone**; Lat. *tenuis*, 'thin'; Scrt. *tamiš*, 'thin, tender'; cp. also **tantra, tender** (IV.), **thin** &c. 1. To move, be directed, in a certain direction. 2. To have an inclination, tendency, bias, in a certain direction; **a** (of human action) *he tends to become tedious and long-winded*; *I naturally tend towards conservatism*; **b** (of other processes) *it tends to become very cold at night now*; *the lowest rabble tend to get the upper hand in revolutions*. 3. To have the effect of, have a tendency to: *too much smoking tends to injure the voice*.

tendance, n. [1. téndans; 2. téndəns]. Form of **attendance**; see **tend** (I.). **a** Act of tending, caring for; **b** care, attention.

tendencious, tendentious, adj. [1. tendénshus; 2. tɛndénʃəs], fr. Germ. *tendenziös*, see next

word & -ous. (of writings, utterances) Having a distinct aim or purpose, or tendency; biassed, not impartial.

tendency, n. [1. téndensi; 2. téndənsi]. Fr. *tendance*; **tend (II.) & -ance & -cy.** Process of tending towards; inclination, bent; drift, trend : *a tendency to corpulence, to insomnia, to drink too much; the tendency of events is towards war.*

tender (I.), n. [1. ténder; 2. téndə]. **tend (I.) & -er.** 1. Person who tends (in various senses); specif., person who looks after the sick or young children. 2. Small ship in attendance upon a larger vessel for supplying stores, conveying messages &c. 3. Truck carrying fuel attached to locomotive.

tender (II.), vb. trans. & intrans. [1. ténder; 2. téndə], formed fr. next word. **A.** trans. 1. To offer in payment of amount due : *to tender a sum in satisfaction of a claim.* 2. To offer, present for acceptance : *to tender one's apologies, thanks* &c. **B.** intrans. To make a tender; to offer to carry out work at a specified price.

tender (III.), n., fr. Fr. infin. *tendre*, 'to reach out ; offer', used as n., fr. Lat. *tendere*, 'to stretch', see **tend (II.).** 1. Offer made by a contractor, to carry out work according to specification at a fixed price. 2. Money tendered or offered in payment of a debt, satisfaction of a claim &c. Phr. *legal tender*, any form of currency recognized by law in a given country as acceptable in payment of debt : *Russian roubles are not legal tender in England.*

tender (IV.), adj. M.E., fr. Fr. *tendre*, fr. Lat. *tener*, 'soft, delicate; susceptible; weak'; either fr. base *ten-* &c., 'to stretch', see **tend (II.);** or for **teren-*, influenced by *tenuis*, 'thin', cogn. w. Gk. *térēn*, 'delicate, tender'; Scrt. *tárunaš*, 'young, tender'; connected w. Lat. *terere*, 'to rub, wear down', see **trite** & cp. **teredo.** 1. **a** (of food, esp. meat) Soft, easily broken up by chewing; reverse of *tough*; **b** easily injured, broken, or torn, by rough handling; flimsy; not firm, strong, or resistent : *a tender structure, fabric* &c.; *a tender skin*; **c** (of colour) soft, delicate. 2. **a** Constitutionally delicate; not able to resist severe cold; feeble, liable to injury; reverse of *strong* or *hardy* : *a tender shoot, plant, blossom* &c.; also **b** immature, young : *of tender age; tender buds* &c. 3. Susceptible to pain, sensitive to pressure &c., as after an injury &c. : *a tender place on one's head; my bruise is still tender.* 4. **a** Morally susceptible, full of compunction; scrupulous : *a tender conscience;* **b** sensitive to, easily moved by, the suffering of others; pitiful, compassionate : *a tender heart.* 5. **a** Kind, loving, solicitous; feeling, expressing, affection : *a tender glance, touch* &c.; *tender care;* **b** careful not to wound; considerate : *be tender of his conscientious scruples; tender of hurting his feelings* &c.

tenderfoot, n. [1. ténderfoot; 2. téndəfut]. (Colonial slang) A new-comer, esp. in a newly formed, rough, settlement, camp &c.; an inexperienced novice, a greenhorn.

tender-hearted, adj. Having a tender heart; susceptible to, easily moved by, pity; kindly, compassionate.

tenderloin, n. [1. ténderloin; 2. téndəlɔin]. **tender (IV.) & loin.** (U.S.A.) 1. Undercut of sirloin. 2. District of New York or other city regarded as the centre of amusement.

tenderly, adv. [1. ténderli; 2. téndəli]. **tender (IV.) & -ly.** In a tender manner; with tenderness.

tenderness, n. [1. ténderness; 2. téndənis]. See prec. & **-ness.** State, quality, of being tender (in various senses). 1. Delicacy, softness, of texture. 2. Sensitiveness to pain. 3. **a** Sensitiveness to suffering of others, compassionateness : *tenderness of heart;* **b** moral scruple : *tenderness of conscience.* 4. **a** Affection, love, solicitude; **b** expression of these in action and behaviour; kindness, gentleness.

tendinous, adj. [1. téndinus; 2. téndinəs], fr. Mod. Lat. *tendin-*, stem of *tendo*, see next word, & **-ous.** Pertaining to, connected with, resembling, a tendon.

tendon, n. [1. téndun; 2. téndən]. Lat. *tendo*, fr. base in *tendere*, 'stretch, extend'; see **tend (II.).** (anat.) Tough, fibrous connective tissue which joins a muscle to some other part; a sinew. *Achilles tendon*, or *tendo Achillis*, that which connects the heel with the calf (so called because the heel was the one vulnerable spot of Achilles).

tendril, n. [1. téndril; 2. téndril, téndrəl], cp. Fr. *tendrille*, fr. **tender (IV.).** A slender organ in climbing plants, which coils in a spiral round neighbouring objects, parts of other plants &c., and serves to anchor and support the plant whence it grows.

tendrillar, adj. [1. téndrilar; 2. téndrilə]. Prec. & **-ar.** Pertaining to, playing part of, a tendril.

tenebrae, n. pl. [1. ténebrē; 2. ténibrī]. Lat., 'darkness'; for **temefrā*, fr. **temesrā;* cogn. w. Scrt. *támisrā*, 'darkness'; cp. O.H.G. *dinstar*, 'dark'; O.S. *thima*, 'dark'; cp. **temerity,** see also **dust.** Matins and lauds for the last three days of Holy Week, commemorating the passion and death of Christ, at which the candles are extinguished.

tenebrous, adj. [1. ténebrus; 2. ténibrəs]. Prec. & **-ous.** Dark, gloomy, dusky, shady.

tenement, n. [1. ténement; 2. ténimənt]. L. Lat. *tenementum*, fr. *tenēre*, 'to hold', see **tenant (I.).** 1. (law) That which is held by tenure, the possessor of which is a tenant; hence land, houses, and forms of incorporeal property held of another, whether for life or for a term of years; houses, rents, an office, a peerage &c. 2. **a** A dwelling-house; **b** one of a set of apartments in a building, each occupied by a separate family; also *tenement house*, one so occupied. 3. (fig., poet.) A dwelling-place : *the soul's tenement*, the body.

tenemental, adj. [1. téneméntl; 2. tènimént̩l]. Prec. & **-al.** Pertaining to a tenement; held by tenants.

tenementary, adj. [1. tèneméntari; 2. tèniméntəri]. See prec. & **-ary.** Tenemental; to be leased to tenants.

tenet, n. [1. ténet, ténet; 2. tínit, ténit]. Lat. 3rd pers. sing. indic. pres. of *tenēre*, 'to hold' &c.; see **tenable & tenant.** A principle, opinion, dogma, held and taught as true.

tenfold, adj. & adv. [1. ténfōld; 2. ténfould]. **ten & -fold.** Ten times repeated; ten times as many.

tenner, n. [1. téner; 2. ténə]. (colloq.) A ten-pound note; ten pounds.

tennis, n. [1. ténis; 2. ténis]. M.E. *teneis*; in one 15th cent. MS. *tenetz*; origin obscure; possibly fr. A.-Fr. *tenetz*, imper., 'hold, receive', i.e. 'play'. 1. Ancient ball game for two or four players, played in a specially made covered court, divided by a net, the ball being originally struck by the hand, later with racquets. 2. Somewhat similar game played on an open court : *lawn tennis.*

tennis ball, n. Ball used in playing tennis or lawn tennis.

tennis court, n. Court in or on which tennis or lawn tennis is played.

tennis elbow, n. Inflammatory condition of the elbow joint, caused by strain in playing tennis.

tenon, n. & vb. trans. [1. ténun; 2. ténən]. M.E., fr. O. Fr. *tenoun*, fr. *tenir*, 'to hold', fr. Lat. *tenēre*; see **tenable, -oon.** 1. n. Projection formed at the end of a piece of timber by cutting away wood around it, made to fit into a mortice cut in another timber. 2. vb. To shape (end of a timber) for insertion in a mortice.

tenor (I.), n. [1. téner; 2. ténə]. Lat., 'a holding on; uninterrupted course or career'; fr. base *ten-*, 'to hold'; see **tenable, tenant.** 1. Course, general direction followed, career : '*the noiseless tenor of their way*' (Gray). 2. General bearing, meaning, drift, of a statement, speech, document.

tenor (II.), n. Fr., fr. Ital. *tenore*, fr. Lat. *tenor*, see prec.; so called because this voice sang and kept the principal part. 1. The higher of the two adult types of male singing voice. 2. The part in a song sung in harmony, taken by this voice. 3. **a** The person who sings the tenor part; **b** an instrument which plays this part; the viola.

tenor (III.), adj., fr. prec. Pertaining to the tenor part, or to the quality of voice possessed by tenors.

tenorino, n. [1. tènorĕnō; 2. tènorínou]. Ital. dimin. of *tenore*, see **tenor (II.).** Falsetto; sham soprano produced by a male voice.

tenotomy, n. [1. tenótumi; 2. tənótəmi]. Gk. *ténōn*, 'tendon', & **-tomy**, 'a cutting'. Operation of cutting a tendon.

tense (I.), n. [1. tens; 2. tɛns]. O. Fr. *tens*, 'time', fr. Lat. *tempus*, see **tempus.** (gram.) That form in verbs which expresses the time—past, present, future—in which the action takes place.

tense (II.), adj., fr. Lat. *tensum*, P.P. of *tendere*, 'to stretch'; see **tend (II.).** 1. (of material object or substance) Tightly stretched, strained; braced up. 2. Specif. (phon.) *tense vowel*, one uttered with the tongue braced up, in a tense condition; contrasted with *slack.* 3. **a** (of the mind and emotions) Strained, keyed up; on the qui vive, alert; **b** (of the manner) expressing such a state of mind; strained, stiff, unnatural.

tense (III.), vb. trans., fr. prec. To brace, make tense (esp. the muscles); specif., to make a vowel sound tense by bracing up the tongue.

tensely, adv. [1. ténsli; 2. ténsli]. **tense (II.) & -ly.** In a tense manner.

tenseness, n. [1. ténsnes; 2. ténsnis]. See prec. & **-ness.** Condition of being tense.

tensibility, n. [1. tènsibíliti; 2. tènsibíliti]. Next word & **-ity.** Quality of being tensible; capacity for extension.

tensible, adj. [1. ténsibl; 2. ténsibl]. **tense (II.) & -ible.** Capable of being stretched out or extended.

tensile, adj. [1. ténsīl; 2. ténsail]. **tense (II.) & -ile.** 1. **a** Pertaining to tension; **b** (of musical instrument) producing notes from tightened strings. 2. Capable of being stretched; tensible.

tension, n. [1. ténshun; 2. ténʃən]. Lat. *tensiōn-(em)*, fr. *tens-*, P.P. type of *tendere*, 'to stretch', see **tense (II.),** & **-ion.** 1. **a** Act or process of straining, stretching, tightening; **b** state of being tightly stretched : *the tension of a fiddle-string.* 2. **a** Mental or emotional stress and strain; suppressed excitement; **b** social atmosphere of uneasiness, stiffness, in which those present exhibit emotional strain; **c** (elect.) only in compounds, *high-, low-tension.*

tensional, adj. [1. ténshunal; 2. ténʃənəl]. Prec. & **-al.** Pertaining to, of the nature of, tension.

tensive, adj. [1. ténsiv; 2. ténsiv]. See **tense (II.) & -ive.** Producing a feeling of tension or stiffness.

tenson, tenzon, n. [1. ténsn, -zn; 2. ténsn, -zn]. Ital. *tensione;* see **tension.** Contest of verse-making between troubadours.

tensor, n. [1. ténser; 2. ténsə]. See **tense (II.) & -or.** Muscle which stretches a part or renders it tense.

tent (I.), n. & vb. trans. & intrans. [1. tent; 2. tent]. Fr. *tente;* Med. Lat. *tenta*, prob. orig. 'something stretched'; see **tend (II.).** 1. n. Protection, shelter, covering, formed of canvas stretched over poles and kept tight by ropes pegged to the ground. 2. vb. (rare) **a** trans. To cover with or as with a tent; (in P.P.) *tented field*, having tents pitched in it; **b** intrans., to lodge in a tent, to encamp.

tent (II.), vb. trans. & n., fr. O. Fr. *tenter*, 'to try, probe', see **tempt.** 1. vb. To dilate (orifice of a wound or natural opening) by inserting a plug of lint, sponge &c. 2. n. Plug of lint, linen &c. used for keeping open a wound or dilating natural orifice.

tent (III.), n. Span. *tinto*, fr. Lat. *tinctum*, P.P. of *tingere*, 'to dye', see **tinge** & **tincture**. A sweet, dark-red Spanish wine, chiefly used for ecclesiastical purposes.

tentacle, n. [1. téntakl; 2. téntəkl]. Lat. *tentāculum*, fr. *tentāre*, 'to feel, handle'; see **tempt**. Any long, slender, flexible organ, or feeler, often prehensile, and used also for aiding movement, borne by many lower forms of animals.

tentacled, adj. [1. téntakld; 2. téntəkld]. Prec. & **-ed**. Possessing, bearing, tentacles.

tentacular, adj. [1. tentákūlar; 2. tentǽkjulə]. See **tentacle** & **-ar**. Resembling, of the nature of, a tentacle.

tentaculate(d), adj. [1. tentákūlāt(ed); 2. tentǽkjuleit(id)]. See **tentacle** & **-ate** (& **-ed**). Furnished with tentacles.

tentative, adj. & n. [1. téntativ; 2. téntətiv], fr. *tentāt-*, P.P. type of *tentāre*, 'to try' &c., see **tempt**, & **-ive**. 1. adj. Of the nature of a trial; experimental; done, made, as an experiment. 2. n. Something done, opinion, theory, put forward as a test or experiment.

tentatively, adv. Prec. & **-ly**. In a tentative manner; experimentally, by way of a test or trial.

tent-bed, n. Bed with a canopy.

tenter (I.), n. [1. téntər; 2. téntə], fr. Scots *tent*, form of **tend (I.)**. Person in charge of machinery.

tenter (II.), n. M.E. *tenture, tentoure*, fr. Fr. *tenture*, 'hangings, tapestry'; fr. Lat. *tentum*, P.P. of *tendere*, 'to stretch', see **tend (II.)**. Frame for stretching cloth so that it may dry square.

tenter-hook, n. One of the hooks that hold cloth on a tenter; Phr. *on tenter-hooks*, in a state of excitement, expectation, anxiety &c.

tenth, adj. & n. [1. tenth; 2. tenþ]. New formation fr. **ten** & **-th**, the O.E. being *tēoða*; see **tithe**. 1. adj. a Next after the ninth; b referring to one of ten equal parts of a whole : *tenth part*. 2. n. a A tenth part; b the object in a series next in order to, and immediately following, the ninth.

tent-pegging, n. [1. ténˈpèging; 2. ténˈpègiŋ]. Act, practised as part of cavalry exercise, of approaching at a gallop, lifting, and carrying off on the point of a lance a peg firmly fixed in the ground.

tenuis, n., pl., **tenues** [1. ténūis, -ēz; 2. ténjuis, -īz]. Lat., 'thin, fine'; used by grammarians to translate Gk. *psīlós*, 'bare; unaspirated'; the word is cogn. w. Gk. *tanu-*, 'slender, thin'; Scrt. *tanúš*, 'long, stretched out'; O.E. *pynn*, see **thin**; the orig. base is **ten-*, as seen in extended form in *tendere*, 'to stretch', see **tend (II.)**. Antiquated grammatical or phonetic term applied to any one of the sounds expressed respectively by *p, t, k*; now usually called *voiceless stops*.

tenuity, n. [1. tenúiti; 2. tɛnjúiti]. Fr. *tenuité*, Lat. *tenuitāt-(em)*, 'thinness, slenderness, fineness'; see prec. & **-ity**. Quality, state, of being tenuous; a rarity, thinness (of air, gas, liquid); b fineness, slenderness (of hair &c.); c thinness, lack of substance (in something flat); d simplicity, thinness, lack of grandeur (of style).

tenuous, adj. [1. ténūus; 2. ténjuəs]. Stem of **tenuis** & **-ous**. a (of material things) Fine, slender, thin; b (of distinctions) too subtle, over-refined.

tenure, n. [1. ténūr; 2. ténjə]. O. Fr. *teneure*, fr. *tenir*, 'to hold'; see **tenable** & **tenant**. 1. a Act of holding, right to hold, property; esp. holding of real estate, formerly from a superior or over-lord; b act, fact, of holding an office, dignity &c. 2. Manner in which, condition on which, property, a right, an office, is held.

tenurial, adj. [1. tenúrial; 2. tɛnjúəriəl]. Prec. & **-al**. Connected with, dependent on, tenure.

tenuto, adj. [1. tenōōtō; 2. tɛnúto]. Ital., 'held', P.P. of *tenēre*. (mus. direction) Sustained, given its full duration; contrasted with *staccato*.

teocalli, n. [1. tĕōkáli; 2. tɪoukǽli]. Aztec (Mexican), lit. 'house (*calli*) of the God (*teotl*)'. An ancient Aztec temple.

tepee, n. [1. tēpē; 2. típī], fr. N. Am. Indian *tipi*. A tent, hut, or wigwam of the N. American Indians.

tepefy, vb. trans. & intrans. [1. tépifī; 2. tépifai]. Lat. *tepēre*, 'to be lukewarm', see **tepid**, & **-fy**. a trans. To make tepid; b intrans., to become tepid.

tephrite, n. [1. téfrīt; 2. téfrait]. Gk. *téphrā*, 'ashes', & **-ite**; *téphrā* stands for **théphrā*, fr. earlier **dhegʷhrā*, cp. Scrt. *dáhati*, 'it burns'; fr. same base come Lat. *fovēre*, 'to warm; to foster', see **foment**, Lat. *febris*, 'fever', see **febrile**; see also **day**. Ashcoloured volcanic rock.

tepid, adj. [1. tépid; 2. tépid]. Lat. *tepidus*, 'warm', w. Scrt. *tápati*, 'it warms, burns'; O. Slav. *topitĭ*, 'to warm', *teplǔ*, 'warm'. Slightly warm, lukewarm : *tepid water*; also of the feelings.

tepidarium, n. [1. tèpidárium; 2. tèpidéəriəm]. Lat., see prec. & **-ary**. Intermediate room of moderate temperature in a Roman bath.

tepidity, n. [1. tepíditi; 2. tɛpíditi]. **tepid** & **-ity**. Quality, state, of being tepid.

ter, adv. [1. tĕr; 2. tā]. Lat., 'thrice'; see **tri-** & **three**. (mus.) Three times; indicating that a passage is to be played three times successively.

teraphim, n. pl., as coll. sing. [1. térafīm; 2. térəfīm]. Heb. Small idol or idols used in divination as a kind of household oracle among the ancient Jews.

terato-, pref. Gk., stem of *téras*, 'a monster', fr. **(s)kʷer-*; cp. O.N. *skars*, 'monster', *skyrse*, 'bad omen'; phantom, dreadful apparition'; cp. **scare**.

teratoid, adj. [1. tératoid; 2. tératɔid]. Prec. & **-oid**. Of the nature of a monster; of abnormal, pathological, growth.

teratologist, n. [1. tèratólojist; 2. tèrətólədʒist]. Next word & **-ist**. Student of teratology.

teratology, n. [1. tèratóloji; 2. tèrətólədʒi]. **terato-** & **-logy**. The scientific study of animal and vegetable freaks and monstrosities and malformations.

terbium, n. [1. tērbium; 2. tā́biəm]. Mod. Lat., fr. Ytterby, Sweden. A metallic element, one of the rare earths.

terce. See **tierce**.

tercel, n. [1. tĕrsl; 2. tā́sl]. Fr., fr. Lat. *tertiolus*, dimin. of *tertius*, 'third'; see **tertian**; fr. belief that the third egg of a hawk produced a small male bird. Male falcon.

tercentenary, adj. & n. [1. tĕrsentĕnari; 2. tàsentínəri]. **ter** & **centenary**. 1. adj. Pertaining to a period of three hundred years. 2. n. a Three hundredth anniversary of an event; b celebration of, commemorative festivity in connexion with, such an anniversary.

tercet, n., also **tiercet** [1. tĕrset, tĕrset; 2. tā́set, tíəset]. Fr., fr. Ital. *terzetto*, dimin. of *terzo*, fr. Lat. *tertium*, 'third'. (mus. or pros.) A triplet.

terebene, n. [1. térebēn; 2. tɛrɛbīn]. See next word & **-ene**. Disinfecting substance made from turpentine treated with sulphuric acid.

terebinth, n. [1. térebinth; 2. tɛrɛbinþ]. Gk. *terébinthos*. European balsamic tree which yields Chian turpentine.

terebra, n. [1. térebra; 2. tɛrɛbrə]. Lat., 'instrument for boring, a gimlet'; fr. *terere*, 'to rub, wear, away; to bore'; see **toreutic** & cp. **trite** & **triturate**. (zool.) A boring, egg-depositing organ of certain insects.

teredo, n. [1. terĕdō; 2. tɛrídou]. Gk. *terēdón*, 'wood-worm', fr. base **ter-*, 'to bore'; cogn. w. Lat. *terere*, see prec. Worm-like mollusc which bores into the timbers of ships; the ship-worm.

tergal, adj. [1. tĕrgal; 2. tā́gəl], fr. Lat. *tergum*, 'back'; covering of the back; skin, hide, leather'; cp. Gk. *térphos*, 'skin, hide, esp. that on hind quarters of beasts'. Belonging to the back; dorsal.

tergiversate, vb. intrans. [1. tĕrjivĕrsāt; 2. tā́dʒivā́seit]. Lat. *tergiversāri, tergiversāt-(um)*, P.P. type of 'to turn the back; to practise evasion', fr. *tergum*, 'back', see prec., & *versāri*, 'to turn oneself about', freq. of *vertere*, 'to turn', see **version**. To shuffle, behave in an evasive manner; to vacillate in one's opinions and intentions.

tergiversation, n. [1. tĕrjivĕrsā́shun; 2. tàdʒivāséiʃən]. Prec. & **-ion**. Act of tergiversating; vacillation; shifty conduct.

term (I.), n. [1. tĕrm; 2. tā́m]. M.E., fr. O. Fr. *terme*, fr. Lat. *termen*, also *terminus*, 'boundary, limit, end'; cogn. w. Gk. *térma, térmōn*, 'boundary, end'; fr. base **ter-*, 'to pass beyond, reach a point on the other side'; cp. Scrt. *tárati*, 'wins through'; ultimately connected w. **through**. 1. A limit, esp. of time : *to set a term to the existence of*. 2. (geom.) A limiting point, line, or surface. 3. a A fixed, limited period of time : *during one's term of office*; specif. b continuous period, officially fixed, during which instruction is given at a university or at a school; c continuous, specified period during which cases are heard in the courts of law. 4. (law) a Continuous, limited period of time during which, by agreement, certain rights are to be enjoyed : *to let a house for a term of years*; b day fixed for payment of rents &c. : quarter-day. 5. (med.) Menses. 6. (log.) One of the three parts of a syllogism : *major term*, predicate of the conclusion; *minor term*, subject of conclusion; *middle term*, the part common to both premises. 7. a Word expressing a definite object or conception; one in use in a particular branch of study, in a specific profession &c. : *hero is hardly the term to apply to him*; *terms of law*; *botanical terms &c.*; b (pl.) mode of expression, style of language : *he spoke in terms of approval, in flattering terms*. Phrs. *in set terms*, definitely; *contradiction in terms*, self-contradictory statement. 8. a Conditions of a contract : *the terms of an agreement*; Phrs. *terms cash*, conditions of business are payment on delivery; *to come to terms with*, reach an agreement, an understanding, with; b financial payment demanded for services &c. rendered : *the terms asked for lodgings are too high*; *terms for private lessons are so much an hour*. 9. a Personal relations : *on good or bad terms with*; *not on speaking terms*; b good, friendly, relations : *we are not on terms*; *to come to terms with*; see also 8, a. 10. (Rom. antiq.) A boundary post, usually taking the form of a tapering, square, or rectangular pillar supporting the head and shoulders of the god *Terminus*; cp. the corresponding Greek *herm*.

term (II.), vb. trans., fr. prec. To apply a term to; to designate, call : *his life might be termed happy*.

termagant, n. [1. tĕrmagant; 2. tā́məgənt]. M.E. *termagant, tervagant*, fr. O. Fr. *tervagant*; cp. Ital. *trivigante*; fr. Lat. *ter* or *tri-*, 'thrice', & Pres. Part. of *vagāri*, 'to roam about, wander'; see **vagrant**. *Termagant* was a fictitious personage, supposed by Christians to be a Mohammedan deity, and was represented as a boisterous, turbulent character. A noisy, quarrelsome, scolding woman.

termer, -or, n. [1. tĕrmer; 2. tā́mə]. 1. (law) *Termor*, person holding an estate for a term of years or for life. 2. *Termer*, person serving a term of imprisonment : *second, third, termer*.

terminability, n. [1. tĕrminabíliti; 2. tā̀minəbíliti]. See next word & **-ity**. Quality of being terminable.

terminable, adj. [1. tĕrminabl; 2. tā́minəbl]. See **terminate** & **-able**. Capable of being, liable to be, terminated; capable of being terminated after a specified time.

terminableness, n. [1. tĕrminablnes; 2. tā́minəblnis]. See prec. & **-ness**. State of being terminable.

40

terminal (I.), adj. [1. tĕrminal; 2. tǎminəl]. Lat. *terminālis*, see **term (I.)** & **-al**. 1. Connected with, pertaining to, situated at or near, a term, limit, end: *a terminal ornament, leaf &c.*; *terminal figure*, a term, see **term (I.), 10**. 2. Connected with a term or fixed period of time: *a terminal rent*; specif., connected with, occurring in or at end of, a university or school term: *terminal fees, examinations* &c.

terminal (II.), n., fr. prec. 1. Something forming the end or extremity of anything; specif. **a** (archit. &c.) an ornamental termination of a feature; a terminal figure; **b** the end of a wire conducting an electric current; **c** the end or terminus of a railway line. 2. Examination occurring in or at end of a term at a school or university.

terminally, adv. [1. tĕrmináli; 2. tǎminəli]. **terminal (I.)** & **-ly**. 1. At the end or extremity; finally. 2. At fixed intervals; every school or university term.

terminate, vb. trans. & intrans. [1. tĕrminăt; 2. tǎmineit], fr. Lat. *termināt-(um)*, P.P. of *termināre*, 'to set bounds to; to bring to an end'; fr. *termen*, see **term (I.)**. 1. trans. **a** To put a bound or limit to; **b** to bring to an end, finish, conclude. 2. intrans. To come to an end, reach a close; *terminate in*, **a** to have as a final phase or feature; to have as a terminal; **b** (gram.) to have as a final sound, syllable &c.

termination, n. [1. tĕrmináshun; 2. tǎminéiʃən]. Prec. & **-ion**. 1. Act or process of terminating; of bringing or coming to a close: *the termination of an agreement, of an enterprise, of a lease* &c. 2. That which forms the end or close; conclusion, completion; **a** in space: *the termination of a journey*; **b** in time: *the termination of one's life*; **c** of a series of events or actions: *the termination of an adventure, a quarrel, of a game* &c. 3. (of material objects) The end, extremity, final portion: *the termination of a line, a pillar*. 4. (gram.) Ending of a word; final sound or syllable; inflexion, final suffix.

terminational, adj. [1. tĕrmináshunal; 2. tǎminéiʃənəl]. Prec. & **-al**. Connected with, relating to, of the nature of, a termination, esp. in grammatical sense.

terminative, adj. [1. tĕrminativ; 2. tǎminətiv]. **terminate** & **-ive**. **a** Serving to terminate; **b** (gram., of verbal forms) distinguishing between beginning or end of action.

terminator, n. [1. tĕrminătər; 2. tǎmineitə]. See prec. & **-or**. Person who, or thing which, terminates; specif. (astron.) line dividing illuminated and unilluminated portion of disk of a heavenly body.

terminatory, adj. [1. tĕrminaturi; 2. tǎminətəri]. **terminate** & **-ory**. Terminative.

terminer, n. [1. tĕrminər; 2. tǎminə]. Fr. infin., 'to end', fr. Lat. *termināre*, see **terminate**. (law) A determining; for the writ of *oyer and terminer* see under **oyer**.

terminism, n. [1. tĕrminizm; 2. tǎminizəm]. Lat. *termin-*, stem of *termen*, 'limit' &c., q.v. under **term (I.)**, & **-ism**. Doctrine that the period during which a human being has the opportunity and offer of divine grace is limited.

terminist, n. [1. tĕrminist; 2. tǎminist]. Stem of prec. & **-ist**. Adherent of the doctrine of terminism.

terminological, adj. [1. tĕrminolójikl; 2. tǎminəlódʒikl]. **terminology** & **-ic** & **-al**. Connected with terminology, or the use of terms.

terminologically, adv. Prec. & **-ly**. From the point of view of terminology.

terminology, n. [1. tĕrminóloji; 2. tǎminóləʤi]. Lat. *termino-*, stem of *terminus*, 'limit'; term', see **terminus**, & **-logy**. System of special or technical terms used in some particular branch of learning, art, science, or in a specialized occupation, in a form of sport &c.

terminus, n. [1. tĕrminus; 2. tǎminəs]. Lat., 'boundary-line, boundary, limit'; see **term (I.)**. 1. (rare) Goal, final point reached or aimed at. 2. Station at the end of a line of railway: *Paddington is the London terminus of the G.W.R.* Lat. Phrs. *terminus ad quem*, goal of a line of action or argument; *terminus a quo*, starting-point of these. 3. **a** (cap.) The Roman God of boundaries; **b** a terminal figure or term.

termitary, n. [1. tĕrmitari; 2. tǎmitəri]. See next word & **-ary**. A nest, mound, of termites.

termite, n. [1. tĕrmīt; 2. tǎmait]. Lat. *termes*, 'wood worm', see base under **teredo**, & **-ite**. One of a family of insects, popularly and wrongly called 'white ants', living in communities and often, in tropical countries, building large mounds for nests; they are extremely destructive to wood, textiles, paper &c.

termless, adj. [1. tĕrmles; 2. tǎmlis]. **term (I.)** & **-less**. Having no term or boundary; limitless; unending.

tern (I.), n. [1. tĕrn; 2. tān]. O.N. *þerna*. One of various sea-birds of the gull family, often living in colonies; the common tern, *Sterna hirundo*, or sea-swallow, has forked tail and black head.

tern (II.), n. & adj., fr. Lat. *terni*, 'three each'; see **ter** & **tri-**. 1. n. Group of three; specif., group of three numbers in a lottery which win special prize if drawn together. 2. adj. Ternate.

ternal, ternary, adj. [1. tĕrnal, tĕrnari; 2. tǎnəl, tǎnəri]. Prec. & **-al**, or **-ary**. 1. adj. Threefold; (of numbers) consisting of, proceeding by, threes. 2. n., Ternary, the number three; a triad.

ternate, adj. [1. tĕrnăt; 2. tǎneit]. See **tern (II.)** & **-ate**. (bot., of leaves) Arranged in groups of three.

terne, n. [1. tĕrn; 2. tān], fr. Fr. *terne*, 'dull, lustreless', see **tarnish**. Alloy of tin and lead; *terne-plate*, sheet of iron coated with terne.

ternery, n. [1. tĕrneri; 2. tǎnəri]. **tern (I.)** & **-ery**. Breeding-place of terns.

terpene, n. [1. tĕrpĕn; 2. tǎpīn]. A combination of **terebinth** & **turpentine**. (chem.) One of a group of hydrocarbons, found in the volatile oils obtained by distillation from coniferous and other plants.

Terpsichorean, adj. [1. tĕrpsikorĕan; 2. tǎpsikəríən]. Lat., fr. Gk. *Terpsikhórē*, the muse of dancing, & **-an**. Pertaining to dancing: *the Terpsichorean art*.

terra, n. [1. tĕra; 2. tĕrə]. Lat. (or Ital.) *terra*, 'land, ground, soil; the earth'; fr. *tersa-*, 'dry'; cogn. w. Lat. *terrēre*, 'to burn, parch', fr. *tors-*, see **torrid** & **toast**; see also **thirst**. In various Latin words and phrases: *Terrae filius* [1. tĕrē fīlius; 2. tĕrī fáiliəs], lit. 'son of the soil'; person of humble origin. *Terra firma* [1. tĕra fĕrma; 2. tĕrə fǎmə], lit. 'firm earth'; dry land, contrasted with water. *Terra incognita* [1. tĕra inkógnita; 2. tĕrə inkógnitə], lit. 'unknown country'; unexplored country; (also fig.) an unfamiliar, uninvestigated, region of thought or knowledge.

terrace (I.), n. [1. tĕras; 2. tĕrəs]. O. Fr. *terrace*, fr. Ital. *terrazza*; see **terra**, 'earth'. 1. A long, raised, flat platform of earth, either built up and levelled, or cut in sloping ground; often forming a feature in gardens and pleasure-grounds. 2. (geol.) A flat, raised surface with steep side, bordering a river or lake, marking the ancient water-level. 3. A row of houses, properly one built on high level ground which slopes away immediately from the houses; often applied to any row of high houses standing back from a thoroughfare.

terrace (II.), vb. trans., fr. prec. To build up, or cut, into the form of a terrace: *a terraced walk*.

terra-cotta, n. [1. tĕra kóta; 2. tĕrə kótə]. Ital., 'baked earth'; see **terra**, & *cotta* fr. Lat. *cocta*, P.P. fem. of *coquere*, 'to boil' &c., see **cook**. Reddish or pale brown hard but porous pottery.

terrain, n. [1. tĕrān; 2. tĕrein]. Fr., fr. Lat. *terrēnus*, 'made of earth'; see **terrene**. A tract of land; specif. (mil.) a tract of ground considered in relation to its uses for a battle, or for fortifications.

terramara, n. [1. tĕramára; 2. tĕrəmɛ́ərə]. Ital., fr. Lat. *terra amara*, 'bitter land'. **a** Earthy deposit, especially from prehistoric mounds, suitable for use as a fertilizer; **b** (cap.) an early type of bronze age culture, found in lake dwellings &c. in Northern Italy.

terraneous, adj. [1. tĕraneus; 2. tɛreiniəs]. **terra** & **-aneous**. Growing on, belonging to, the earth.

terrapin, n. [1. tĕrapin; 2. tĕrəpin], fr. Am. Indian word for 'turtle'. Edible turtle, found in fresh or tidal water of the North Atlantic American coast.

terraqueous, adj. [1. tĕrákweus; 2. tĕreikwiəs]. See **terra** & **aqueous**. (of the earth) Consisting of, comprising, both land and water.

terrene, adj. [1. tĕrēn; 2. tĕrīn]. Lat. *terrēnus*, fr. *terra*, 'earth'; see **terra**. Connected with the earth; earthly, mundane.

terrestrial (I.), adj. [1. tĕrestrial; 2. tɛrĕstriəl]. O. Fr. *terrestriel*, fr. Lat. *terrestri-*, see **terra**, & **-al**. 1. Belonging to the earth; earthly, earthy; contrasted with *celestial*: *a terrestrial body*; *terrestrial preoccupations*. 2. **a** Consisting of this earth: *this terrestrial ball*; **b** made to represent the earth: *a terrestrial globe*. 3. Inhabiting, living upon, the dry land; contrasted with *aquatic*, *arboreal* &c.

terrestrial (II.), n., fr. prec. An inhabitant of the earth.

terret, n. [1. tĕret; 2. tĕrit]. M.E. *teret*, also *toret*; etymol. doubtful; prob. fr. O. Fr. *toret*, *touret*, 'ring for falcon's leash', cf. **tour (I.)**. One of the rings on a (driven) horse's harness-pad, or saddle, through which the reins pass.

terrible, adj. [1. tĕribl; 2. tĕrəbl, tĕribl]. Fr., fr. Lat. *terribilis*, 'frightful, dreadful'; fr. base of *terrēre*, 'to frighten'; for **ters-*, **teres-*; cogn. w. Gk. *tréein*, 'to tremble'; Scrt. *trásati*, 'trembles'; Goth. *þrasa(balþei)*, 'audacity'; the base is an extension of **ter-*, 'to tremble', as in Lat. *tremere*, 'to tremble'; see **tremble**, & *trepidus*, 'agitated, alarmed', see **trepidation**. 1. Inspiring, calculated to inspire, terror, dread, awe; fearful, frightful: *the terrible sufferings caused by war*; *terrible in anger*. 2. (colloq.) Excessive, tremendous: *a terrible heat, frost*; *a terrible man to drink*.

terribleness, n. Prec. & **-ness**. Quality, state, of being terrible.

terribly, adv. See prec. & **-ly**. In a terrible manner; horribly; to a terrible extent: *terribly injured, shocked*; (colloq.) excessively: *terribly afraid of dogs*; *terribly hungry*.

terrier (I.), n. [1. tĕrier; 2. tĕriə]. Fr. (*chien*) *terrier*, 'a burrowing dog', fr. L. Lat. *terrārium*, 'a burrow, hillock'; see **terra** & **-ier**. One of several breeds of small or medium-sized dogs kept as pets, very lively, courageous, and affectionate, and good at killing rabbits and rats.

terrier (II.), n. Fr. (*papier*) *terrier*, Lat. (*liber*) *terrārius*, 'book relating to land', fr. **terra**. Document or book setting forth extent, boundaries, rents, and rights in land.

terrific, adj. [1. tĕrifik; 2. tɛrífik]. Lat. *terrificus*, 'causing terror, frightful'; see **terrify**. Striking terror, of a nature to terrify; appalling, dreadful, awe-inspiring, esp. by reason of size or violence.

terrifically, adv. [1. tĕrifikali; 2. tɛrífikəli]. Prec. & **-al** & **-ly**. To a terrific extent.

terrify, vb. trans. [1. tĕrifi; 2. tĕrifai]. Fr. *terrifier*, fr. Lat. *terrificāre*, 'to frighten'; see **terror** & **-fy**. To strike terror in, to fill with fright, cause great alarm to.

terrigenous, adj. [1. tĕrijenus; 2. tɛrídʒinəs]. Lat. *terrigena*, 'born of the earth'; see **terra** & **-genous**. Earth-born; produced by the earth; native of the soil.

terrine, n. [1. térēn; 2. térīn]. Fr., fr. L. Lat. *terrineus*, 'made of earth', see **terra**. Vessel, dish, jar, of earthenware, esp. one used for containing and preserving some delicacy such as foie-gras, and sold with this.

territorial (I.), adj. [1. tèritŏrial; 2. tèritŏriəl]. **territory** & **-al**. 1. Connected with, consisting of, territory: *territorial owner, property* &c. 2. Pertaining, limited, to some particular region or country under control of a state: *territorial rights, waters, boundaries* &c. 3. (mil., cap.) Relating to a force of soldiers raised, by voluntary enlistment, in a particular area or county and serving as a second line to the Regular Army: *Territorial Army*.

territorial (II.), n., fr. prec. Member of the Territorial Army.

territorialism, n. [1. tèritŏrializm; 2. tèritŏriəlizəm]. Prec. & **-ism**. System of Church government, under which the ruler of a territory has religious jurisdiction over his subjects.

territorialize, vb. trans. [1. tèritŏrializ; 2. tèritŏriəlaiz]. **territorial** (I.) & **-ize**. 1. To extend (domains) by addition of fresh territory. 2. To reduce to condition of a territory.

territorially, adv. [1. tèritŏriali; 2. tèritŏriəli]. See prec. & **-ly**. From the point of view of, according to, territory.

territory, n. [1. térituri; 2. téritəri]. Lat. *territōrium*, 'land round a town; domain'; see **terra**. 1. Large tract of land; region, district. 2. Amount of land, country, under jurisdiction of a single ruler or government. 3. Part of a state ruled as a dependency and not having yet attained full rights as an independent state.

terror, n. [1. térŏr; 2. térə]. Lat., 'great fear, dread, alarm'; see under **terrible**. 1. Extreme, overwhelming, fear. 2. Person or thing which inspires terror: *Cromwell was a terror to his country's foes*. Phrs. *the king of terrors*, death; *the Reign of Terror, the Terror*, the period from May 1793 to July 1794 of the French Revolution, characterized by countless executions &c. 3. (colloq.) A troublesome, unmanageable person; a pest, a nuisance: *a perfect terror, a holy terror*.

terrorism, n. [1. térorizm; 2. térərizəm]. Prec. & **-ism**. Method of government by inspiring terror by acts of brutality and savagery.

terrorist, n. [1. térorist; 2. térərist]. **terror** & **-ist**. One who practises, or believes in, terrorism.

terrorization, n. [1. tèrorīzáshun; 2. tèrəraizéiʃən]. See next word & **-ation**. Act of terrorizing; state of being terrorized.

terrorize, vb. trans. [1. téroriz; 2. térəraiz]. **terror** & **-ize**. To reduce to state of terror by threats or acts of cruelty; to intimidate.

terry, n. [1. téri; 2. téri]. Connected w. Fr. *tirer*, 'to pull'? Loop left uncut from nap of velvet or other fabric.

terse, adj. [1. tèrs; 2. tɜːs]. Lat. *tersum*, P.P. of *tergēre*, 'to rub, wipe, off'; prob. connected w. *terere*, 'to rub'; see **trite**. **a** (of mode of expression) Concise, succinct, and polished; free from redundancy; **b** (of a speaker or writer) employing terse style.

tersely, adv. Prec. & **-ly**. In a terse, succinct manner.

terseness, n. See prec. & **-ness**. Quality of being terse.

tertial, adj. [1. tèrshial; 2. tɜːʃiəl]. Lat. *tertius*, see next word, & **-al**. (zool.) Referring to flight feathers of third row in a bird's wing.

tertian, adj. & n. [1. tèrshan; 2. tɜːʃən]. Fr., fr. Lat. *tertiānus*, fr. *tertius*, 'third', cogn. w. Goth. *þridja*, see **third**, & cp. **tri-** & **three**. 1. adj. (med.) Recurring every other day: *tertian fever*. 2. n. An intermittent disease; a tertian fever.

tertiary (I.), adj. [1. tèrshari; 2. tɜːʃəri]. Lat. *tertius*, 'third', see prec. & **-ary**. 1. Third in order, rank, occurrence, importance. 2. (geol., cap.) Pertaining to the era immediately following the Mesozoic, which was formerly called *Secondary*.

tertiary (II.), n., fr. prec. Member of third order in a monastic system.

tertium quid, n. [1. tèrshium kwíd; 2. tɜːʃiəm kwíd]. Lat., 'a third something'. Something intermediate between two other alternative, incompatible things, positions, possibilities.

tertius, adj. [1. tèrshus; 2. tɜːʃəs]. Lat. 'third'. See **tertian** & words there referred to. Used in some schools, after surname, to distinguish the youngest of three boys of the same name or family: *Smith tertius*.

terza rima, n. [1. tártsa rĕma; 2. téətsə rímə]. Ital., 'third, triple, rhyme'; fr. Lat. *tertia*, 'third', see **tertian**, & **rhyme**. System of verse in which the rhymes are arranged thus: *aba*; *bcb*; *cdc*.

terzetto, n. [1. tàrtsétō; 2. tɜːtsétou]. Ital. dimin. of *terzo*, 'third'. Part-song for three voices.

tessellar, adj. [1. téselar; 2. tésilə]. Lat. *tessella*, 'little cube', see **tessellate**, & **-ar**. Composed of tesserae.

tessellate, vb. trans. [1. téselāt; 2. tésileit]. Lat. *tessellātus*, 'composed of small stones or tesserae'; fr. *tessella*, 'small piece of stone, little cube', dimin. of *tessera*, & **-ate**. To pave by inlaying small blocks of stone in mosaic work.

tessellated, adj. [1. téselātĕd; 2. tésileitid], fr. P.P. of prec. Paved with small blocks of stone in form of a mosaic.

tessellation, n. [1. tèseláshun; 2. tèsiléiʃən]. **tessellate** & **-ion**. Work, esp. pavement, composed of tesserae; mosaic work.

tessera, n., pl. **tesserae** [1. tésera, -rē; 2. tésərə, -rī]. Lat., 'a square piece of stone, a die', fr. Gk. *téssares*, 'four', wh. is for *k^wetwar-*, cp. Scrt. *čatur*; Lat. *quātuor*, see **quater-**, & **four**. Small, approximately square piece of marble, glass &c. used in mosaic work.

tessitura, tessiture, n. [1. tèsitōōra, tésitūr; 2. tèsitúrə, tésitjuə]. Ital.; Fr., see **texture**. (mus.) Compass, range, within which the characteristics of a voice lie; compass of a voice part.

test (I.), n. [1. test; 2. test]. O. Fr., fr. Lat. *testum*, 'pot', cp. *testa*, 'piece of burnt clay, potsherd, shell, covering'; cogn. w. Scrt. *tašta*, 'shell, cup'. The starting-point of the Mod. meanings is a cup for refining metal. 1. **a** Movable bottom of furnace, also called *cupel*, in which precious metals are refined; **b** portion of refined metal isolated for weighing. 2. Process designed to try, or prove; a critical, searching examination; Phr. *put to the test*, prove quality of. 3. **a** (chem.) Process adopted to discover and distinguish the various substances of which anything is composed; an analysis; **b** (hist.) the oath taken under the *Test Act*, q.v.; **c** (colloq.) a test match, q.v. 4. Any method adopted to try and prove the extent of knowledge: *written examinations are the main test applied to candidates for degrees*. 5. Circumstances, experiences, trials, which when undergone by an individual, serve to show his real character, degree of moral worth, intelligence &c.; touchstone: *poverty is often a severe test of a man's integrity*.

test (II.), vb. trans., fr. prec. 1. (chem.) To analyse by application of reagents. 2. To put to the test; **a** to ascertain by searching scrutiny the truth, validity, soundness (of a statement, argument, theory &c.); **b** to prove the quality, extent (of knowledge &c.), or the moral worth, reliability &c. (of a person); **c** to ascertain the value, genuineness, quality (of a thing); *to test*, implies in all cases the application of a fixed principle to the person or thing tested, and the consideration of how far he, or it, conforms to a chosen standard.

test (III.), n. Lat. *testa*, 'shell', see **test** (I.). The hard shell or covering of molluscs, crustaceans, and many other invertebrates.

testable (I.), adj. [1. téstabl; 2. téstəbl]. **test** (II.) & **-able**. Capable of being tested.

testable (II.), adj. See **testament** & **-able**. (law) Capable of being disposed of by will.

testaceous, adj. [1. testáshus; 2. testéiʃəs]. Lat. *testaceus*, see **test** (III.), & **-aceous**. 1. Connected with, of the nature of, a shell; formerly applied to molluscs and brachiopods; in distinction to *crustaceous*. 2. (zool. and bot.) Brick red, brownish yellow; from original meaning of Latin *testa*, 'piece of burnt clay'.

Test Act, n. A statute of 1672, repealed 1828, requiring persons, before holding an office, to take the oaths of allegiance and supremacy, receive Communion according to the rites of the Church of England, and abjure transubstantiation.

testacy, n. [1. téstasi; 2. téstəsi]. See **testate** & **-cy**. State of being testate.

testament, n. [1. téstament; 2. téstəmənt]. Lat. *testāmentum*, 'declaration of one's will'; formed fr. Lat. *testāri*, 'to witness, testify', fr. *testis*, 'a witness'; according to Walde formed fr. *tristo-*, 'the third', cp. Lat. *trēs*, 'three', see **tri-**. The orig. sense was 'third party present at a transaction', as distinct fr. those actually engaged in it. 1. Translating Gk. *diathḗkē*, 'last will; covenant'; cp. Fr. use in this case, & **testamentary**; (obs. except Bib.) a either of the two covenants of God known respectively as the *Old* and *New Testament*; **b** (colloq.) the New Testament. 2. (law) Only in Phr. *last will and testament*, document in which a person sets forth his wishes for the disposal of his property after his death.

testamental, adj. [1. tèstaméntal; 2. tèstəméntəl]. Prec. & **-al**. Pertaining to a testament; testamentary.

testamentary, adj. [1. tèstaméntari; 2. tèstəméntəri]. **testament** & **-ary**. Pertaining to, bequeathed in, appointed by, a will or testament.

testamur, n. [1. testámur; 2. testéiməː]. Lat., 'we attest, testify', fr. *testāri*, see **testament**. University certificate stating officially that a person has passed a specified examination.

testate, adj. & n. [1. téstāt; 2. tésteit]. Lat. *testātus*, P.P. of *testāri*, see **testament**. (law) **a** adj. Having died leaving a valid will; **b** n., person in this position.

testator, n. [1. testáter; 2. testéitə]. Lat., 'one who makes a will', fr. *testāt-(um)*, P.P. type of *testāri*, see **testament**, & **-or**. Male person who makes a will; the maker of a particular will: *the testator*.

testatrix, n., fem. of prec. [1. testátriks; 2. testéitriks]. Lat., fem. of prec. Female who makes a will.

tester (I.), n. [1. téster; 2. téstə]. **test** (II.) & **-er**. **a** Person who tests (in various specific senses); **b** one of various mechanical devices for testing quality &c. of substances.

tester (II.), n. M.E. *testere*, 'headpiece, helmet', fr. O. Fr. *testiere* &c., fr. Lat. *testa*, 'potsherd; shell, skull'; whence O. Fr. *teste*, 'head'; see **test** (I.). Canopy for a bed, supported on posts.

tester (III.), n.; also *teston*, fr. O. Fr., fr. *teste*, Mod. Fr. *tête*, 'head', see prec. The name of the shilling of Henry VIII., which was later reduced to sixpence.

testicle, n. [1. téstikl; 2. téstikl]. Lat. *testiculus*, dimin. of *testis*, 'testicle'; etymol. uncertain. Male gland secreting spermatozoa.

testiculate, adj. [1. testíkūlāt; 2. testíkjuleit]. Lat. *testiculus*, see prec., & **-ate**. **a** Having testicles, or (of plants) organs corresponding to these; **b** shaped like a testicle.

testification, n. [1. tèstifikáshun; 2. tèstifikéiʃən]. See **testify** & **-fication**. **a** Act of testifying; **b** testified statement, evidence.

testify, vb. intrans. & trans. [1. téstifī; 2. téstifai]. Fr. *testifier*, fr. Lat. *testificāri*, 'to bear witness', fr. *testis*, 'witness', see **testament**, & **-fy**. 1. To make a solemn declaration, to bear witness that something has happened, to give evidence: *to testify that one has seen so-and-so*; also *to testify to the fact that* &c.; *testify against*, give, provide, evidence

testily, adv. [1. téstili ; 2. téstili]. **testy & -ly.** In a testy manner.

testimonial, n. [1. tèstimónial ; 2. tèstimóuniəl]. Lat. (literae) testimōniālēs, '(letters, document) containing testimony'; see **testimony & -al**. 1. Uttered or written statement setting forth a person's merits and qualities of character, his capacities and abilities, esp. a document stating a person's qualifications for an appointment. 2. A tribute in the form of a written expression, of respect and admiration, or of appreciation and gratitude for services rendered, often accompanied by a public presentation of a gift and a list of names of subscribers.

testimonialize, vb. trans. [1. tèstimŏnializ ; 2. tèstimóuniəlaiz]. Prec. & **-ize.** To write a testimonial for ; to present a testimonial to.

testimony, n. [1. téstimuni ; 2. téstiməni]. Lat. testimōnium, 'evidence, attestation', fr. testis, 'a witness', see **testament.** 1. Solemn statement made to establish a fact ; evidence given by a witness under oath in a court of law ; to bear testimony (to), to affirm (truth of), state as a fact. 2. a Series of statements ; general bearing, tenor, drift of such a series of statements : the testimony of the Fathers of the Church ; b the conclusion to which a series of actions, events, facts, points ; evidence, indication, afforded by such a series of events &c. : the testimony of the rocks is sometimes held to refute the Mosaic account of the Creation ; to bear testimony, to indicate, point to truth of, help to establish, certain facts. 3. Tables of the law ; divine revelation ; the Scriptures : the testimonies of the Lord.

testiness, n. [1. téstines ; 2. téstinis]. **testy & -ness.** Condition of being testy.

testis, n., usually pl. **testes** [1. téstis, -ēz ; 2. téstis, -īz]. Lat., see **testicle.** Testicle.

test match, n. A cricket match played between representative elevens of two countries.

test-tube, n. Slender tube of thinnish glass, usually closed at one end, used in chemical experiments.

testudinarious, adj. [1. tèstūdinárius ; 2. tèstjūdinéəriəs]. Lat. testūdin-, stem of testūdō, 'tortoise', see **testudo, & -arious.** Mottled with the colours seen in tortoise-shell.

testudinate, adj. [1. testúdināt ; 2. testjúdineit]. Lat. testūdin-, see prec., & **-ate.** Vaulted, arched, like the shell of a tortoise.

testudineous, adj. [1. testudíneus ; 2. testjūdíniəs]. Lat. testūdin-, see prec., & **-eous.** Resembling the shell of a tortoise.

testudo, n. [1. testúdō ; 2. testjúdou]. Lat., 'tortoise', formed fr. Lat. testa, 'shell', see under **test (I.) & (III.).** 1. (Rom. antiq.) Shed, covering, of wood used to protect besieging troops. 2. (Rom. archit.) An arched, vaulted, roof. 3. Land tortoise.

testy, adj. [1. tésti ; 2. tésti]. M.E. testif, fr. O. Fr. testu, 'headstrong', fr. teste, 'head', fr. Lat. testa, 'shell ; skull, head', see **test (I.) & (III.).** Easily angered ; irascible, irritable.

tetanic, adj. & n. [1. tetánik ; 2. tetǽnik]. See **tetanus & -ic. a** adj. Connected with, arising from, of the nature of, tetanus ; **b** n., a substance, such as strychnine, which produces muscular spasms similar to those of tetanus.

tetanization, n. [1. tètanīzáshun ; 2. tètənaizéiʃən]. See **tetanus, & -ize, & -ation. a** Process of causing tetanic contractions in a muscle ; **b** state of being affected by, or as by, tetanus.

tetanus, n. [1. tétanus ; 2. tétənəs]. Gk. tétanos, 'a stretching, straining', redupl. form fr. base *ten-, 'to stretch' &c., see **tend (II.).** a Disease caused by a specific bacillus, in which the muscles are violently contracted and affected with spasmodic movements ; when tetanus affects the muscles of the jaw, it is popularly called lockjaw ; **b** violent muscular contraction caused by drugs such as strychnine.

tetchily, adv. [1. téchili ; 2. tétʃili]. **tetchy & -ly.** In a tetchy manner.

tetchiness, n. [1. téchines ; 2. tétʃinis]. See next word & **-ness.** Condition of being tetchy.

tetchy, techy, adj. [1. téchi ; 2. tétʃi]. O. Fr. tache, 'speck, blemish', & **-y.** Touchy, thin-skinned ; irritable, testy, petulant.

tête-à-tête, adv., adj., n., Anglice [1. tát ah tát ; 2. téit à téit]. Fr., lit. 'head to head', cp. cheek by jowl. 1. adv. Privately, with no other person : to see a person tête-à-tête. 2. adj. Private, alone with one other person ; confidential. 3. n. A private meeting or conversation with one other person ; a confidential talk, private confab.

tether, n. & vb. trans. [1. tédher ; 2. téðə]. M.E. tedir, fr. O.N. tjōðr. 1 n. A long rope or chain by which a grazing animal is made fast to a peg fixed in the ground, to prevent it from straying ; Phr. at the end of one's tether, **a** at the end of one's physical and mental resources, on the verge of a break-down ; **b** at the end of one's financial resources ; **c** having done the utmost of what can be tolerated ; having reached the limits of another's indulgence. 2. vb. To fasten with a tether.

tetra-, pref. Gk., form used in compounds, fr. téttares, variant téssares, 'four'; see this numeral under **tessera, four, quater-.**

tetrachord, n. [1. tétrakord ; 2. tétrəkōd]. See prec. & **chord**, cp. Gk. tetrákhordos, 'four-stringed'. Series of four tones with interval of a fourth between first and last.

tetrad, n. [1. tétrad ; 2. tétræd]. Lat. tetrad-(em), fr. Gk. tetrad-, see **tetra-. a** The number four ; **b** group, set, of four things.

tetragon, n. [1. tétragon ; 2. tétrəgən]. **tetra- & -gon.** (geom.) Plane figure with four angles.

tetragonal, adj. [1. tetrágonal ; 2. tetrǽgənəl]. Prec. & **-al.** Pertaining to a tetragon ; having four angles.

tetragram, n. [1. tétragram ; 2. tétrəgræm]. **tetra- & -gram.** Word of four letters.

tetragrammaton, n. [1. tètragrámaton ; 2. tètrəgrǽmətən]. Gk., see prec. The four consonants forming the Hebrew name for God, the original pronunciation of which was lost as the word was only pronounced with vowels taken from other names for the Deity, no vowel symbols being written ; the word was variously reconstructed as Jahaveh, Jahveh &c.

tetragynous, adj. [1. tetrájinus ; 2. tetrǽdʒinəs]. **tetra- & -gynous.** (bot.) Having four pistils.

tetrahedral, adj. [1. tètra-hédral ; 2. tètrəhídrəl]. See next word & **-al.** Connected with, belonging to, of the form of, a tetrahedron.

tetrahedron, n. [1. tètra-hédron ; 2. tètrəhídrɔn]. Gk., fr. **tetra-**, 'four', & hédra, 'seat, base', wh. is cogn. w. Lat. sedēre, 'to sit', see **sedentary, & w. seat & sit.** Solid, four-sided figure ; a triangular pyramid.

tetralogy, n. [1. tetráloji ; 2. tetrǽlədʒi]. Gk. tetralogia, 'series of four dramas'; see **tetra- & -logy.** Series of four connected dramas, as found in Greek theatre, or in Wagner's 'Ring'.

tetrameter, n. [1. tetrámeter ; 2. tetrǽmitə]. See **tetra- & -meter.** Verse, line, of four measures or feet.

tetrandrous, adj. [1. tetrándrus ; 2. tetrǽndrəs]. **tetra- & -androus.** (bot.) Having four stamens.

tetrarch, n. [1. tétrark, tétrark ; 2. títrāk, tétrāk]. Gk. tetrárkhes, -arkhos, see **tetra- & -arch.** (Rom. antiq.) The governor of a part, orig. the fourth part, of a province.

tetrarchy, n. [1. tétrarki ; 2. tétrəki]. Gk. tetrarkhia, see prec. **a** The district ruled by a tetrarch ; **b** office of a tetrarch.

tetrastich, n. [1. tétrastik ; 2. tétrəstik]. Gk. tetrástikhon ; cp. **distich.** Poem of four lines.

tetter, n. [1. téter ; 2. tétə]. O.E. & M.E. teter, 'ringworm, skin disease'; cogn. w. Scrt. dadru, 'skin disease'. A disease of the skin such as ringworm, eczema &c.

Teucrian, adj. [1. tūkrian ; 2. tjúkriən], fr. Teucer, Gk. Teûkros, the first King of Troy. **a** Pertaining to Teucer ; **b** pertaining to the ancient Trojans.

Teuton, n. [1. tútun ; 2. tjútən]. Lat. Teutones, the name of an anct. Gmc. people ; fr. Gmc. þeuda-, 'people, race', cp. Goth. þiuda, O.E. þēod ; O.S. thioda ; O.H.G. diota ; fr. this word comes deutsch (= þiudisk-, 'belonging to the people'), & **Dutch.** **a** Member of the Germanic race ; **b** specif. (colloq.) a German.

Teutonic, adj. & n. [1. tūtónik ; 2. tjūtónik]. Prec. & **-ic.** 1. adj. **a** Pertaining to the Germanic race ; **b** to the primitive Germanic language ; **c** to a or any Germanic language. 2. n. Germanic speech, esp. primitive Germanic.

tew, vb. See **taw (I.).**

tewel, n. [1. túel ; 2. tjúɛl]. M.E. tuel, 'funnel, chimney', fr. O. Fr. tuiel, tuel, 'pipe', Mod. Fr. tuyau ; prob. fr. Gmc. source ; cp. Mod. Germ. tüte, düte, & see **Solen.** The pipe or chimney which carries away the smoke ; tuyère.

text, n. [1. tekst ; 2. tɛkst]. M.E., fr. O. Fr. texte, fr. Lat. textus, 'texture, structure ; grammatical construction ; context'; formed fr. text-(um), P.P. of texere, 'to weave, to plait, to fit together, contrive'; cogn. w. Scrt. takṣati, 'he fashions, constructs'; taṣtar, 'carpenter'; Gk. tékhnē, 'handicraft, art', cp. **technic.** The Lat. shows a specialization of meaning fr. an elementary sense 'construct, fashion'. 1. The original words of an author ; contrasted with paraphrase, commentary &c. : innumerable scholars have laboured to restore the text of Beowulf. 2. **a** A verse or short passage of Scripture : 'And many a holy text around she strews' (Gray's 'Elegy'); specif. **b** a verse of Scripture taken as the heading and general theme of a sermon ; hence, **c** the theme, subject, topic, of any discourse, argument, dissertation. 3. The principal part of a literary composition, as distinct from preface, notes &c. 4. Large type of handwriting ; also text-hand, in which the main part of a book was formerly written, the notes being in smaller writing.

text-book, n. A manual for instruction ; a compendious general treatise on a branch of learning ; applied both to elementary, introductory treatises, and to advanced, standard works.

text-hand, n. Large style of handwriting formerly used for the body or main part of a book.

textile, adj. & n. [1. tékstīl ; 2. tékstail]. Lat. textilis, 'woven, wrought', also as n., 'a fabric'; see **text & -ile.** 1. adj. Connected with weaving, or with woven material : textile industries. 2. n. A woven fabric.

textual, adj. [1. tékstūal ; 2. tékstjuəl]. M.E., fr. Fr. textuel, see **text. a** Pertaining to, concerned with, based on, derived from, the text of an author : textual criticism, emendation &c. ; hence **b** literal, word for word : a textual quotation.

textualism, n. [1. tékstūalizm ; 2. tékstjuəlizəm]. Prec. & **-ism.** Insistence upon a strict adherence to an author's text.

textualist, n. [1. tékstūalist ; 2. tékstjuəlist]. See prec. & **-ist.** 1. A student of an author's text ; a textual critic. 2. One who insists on rigid adherence to an author's text.

textural, adj. [1. tékschural ; 2. tékstʃərəl]. Next word & **-al.** Connected with texture.

texture, n. [1. tékschur ; 2. tékstʃə]. Lat. textūra, 'a web, texture ; fabric ; structure'; see **text & -ure.** 1. That which is woven ; a woven fabric. 2. **a** (i.) Way in which the threads of a fabric or constituent elements of a substance are arranged and put together ; a coarse, fine, harsh, texture (of cloth &c., also of wood, rock &c.) ; (ii.) sensation produced by this upon the sense of touch ; **b** (of the

-th (I.), Engl. suff. of Gmc. origin, forming abstract ns.; **a** fr. adj., as *health*, O.E. *hǣlu* (*-th* being a M.E. addition), fr. **hāli*, fr. *hāl*, see **whole**; *breadth*, fr. O.E. *brǣdu*, fr. *brād*, 'broad'; *youth*, O.E. *geoguþ*, fr. **juŋgunþ-*, cp. O.E. *geong*, 'young'; cp. Lat. suff. *-tūt-* in *juven-tūt-(em)*, 'youth'; **b** fr. vbs., expressing result of action, as *tilth*, *growth* &c. The suff. appears as *-t-* in *height*, earlier *heighth*, *highth*, O.E. *hēhþu*.

-th (II.), suff. O.E. *-þa*, forming ordinal numbers, as *fourth*, O.E. *feorþa*; the later ordinals in *-th* are new formations; cp. Gk. *-tos*, Lat. *-tus*.

thalamus, n. [1. thálamus; 2. þæləməs]. Lat., 'chamber', fr. Gk. *thálamos*, 'inner chamber, women's apartment', bride-chamber'; cogn. w. Gk. *thólos*, 'vault, vaulted building, a round chamber'; also cogn. w. O.E. *dæl*, 'valley', see **dale**. (anat.) Generally *optic thalamus*, that part of the brain from which the optic nerve springs.

thaler, n. [1. táhler; 2. tāˑlə]. Du. *daler*, whence **dollar**. Obsolete German coin formerly worth about three shillings.

Thalia, n. [1. thalía; 2. þəláiə]. Gk. *Tháleia*, one of the Muses, Muse of comedy and bucolic poetry; the word means 'the blooming, luxuriant one'; cp. Gk. *thaleîn*, 'to bloom, to flourish'; *thalía*, 'abundance, wealth; good cheer'; *thallós*, 'a young shoot'; perh. cogn. w. O.E. *deall*, 'proud, resplendent'.

thallic, adj. [1. thálik; 2. þæˑlik]. See next word & -ic. Pertaining to thallium, esp. of compounds containing the element with less proportion of oxygen than thallous compounds.

thallium, n. [1. thálium; 2. þæˑliəm], fr. Gk. *thallós*, 'young shoot', see **Thalia**; so called fr. the bright green line in its spectrum. Rare element connected with aluminium, resembling lead in its properties.

thallophyte, n. [1. thálofīt; 2. þæˑləfait]. See **thallus** & **-phyte**. (bot.) A plant belonging to the class *Thallophyta*, which includes the algae, lichens, fungi &c.

thallous, adj. [1. thálus; 2. þæˑləs]. See prec. & **-ous**. Pertaining to thallium, of compounds; contrasted with *thallic*.

thallus, n. [1. thálus; 2. þæˑləs]. Gk. *thallós*, 'young shoot', q.v. under **Thalia**. (bot.) Mass of undifferentiated vegetable tissue; the plant body found in algae, lichens, fungi.

than, conj. [1. dhan; 2. ðæn], when stressed; more usual in unstressed form [ðən]; O.E. *þonne*, *þon*, *þænne*; M.E. *thonne*, *thon*, *thenne*, *then*; prob. connected w. **the**, **then**, **there**. Particle used in the comparison of inequality, after the comparative adjective before the noun or pronoun representing the second of two things compared: *this is bigger than that*; *children are smaller than grown-up people* &c.; *you have more money than I have*.

thanage, n. [1. thánij; 2. þéinidʒ]. **thane** & **-age**. **1.** Rank, status, of a thane. **2.** Land held by a thane from the king.

thanato-, pref. Form used in compounds, fr. Gk. *thánatos*, 'death'; cogn. w. Scrt. *ádhvanīt*, 'becomes, is, extinguished', *dhvāntaś*, shrouded, dark'; prob. also W. *dyn*, 'man', i.e. 'mortal': *thanatophobia*, morbid fear of death.

thanatoid, adj. [1. thánatoid; 2. þæˑnətɔid]. Prec. & **-oid**. **a** Death-like; **b** deadly.

thane, n. [1. thān; 2. þein]. O.E. *þegn*, *þeġen*; M.E. *thein*; O.S. *thegan*, 'follower'; O.H.G. *degan*; O.N. *þegn*; cogn. w. Gk. *téknon*, 'child'; connected w. Gk. *tíktein*, aorist *étek-on*, 'to beget, produce, offspring'; cp. also Gk. *tókos*, 'birth; child, offspring'. Member of a class of nobles among the Anglo-Saxons and ancient Scandinavians who were members of the king's household and in attendance upon his person, esp. in war; in O.E. poetry the word is used to designate the faithful follower and companion-in-arms of a prince or superior lord.

thank (I.), n. [1. thangk; 2. þæŋk]. O.E. *þanc*, 'thought; favour, grace; pleasure, satisfaction; delight, thanks'; in gradational relation to O.E. *þynċan*, 'to seem', see under **think**. Now only in pl. *thanks*: **1.** Gratitude, grateful feeling: *thanks be to God*; *to express one's thanks*. Phr. *thanks to*, owing to, on account of, through the agency of: *thanks to his obstinacy he was landed in disaster*; *thanks to your help I was able to do it*; Phr. *we succeeded, small thanks to him*, it was not through his help that we succeeded; *no, thanks*, polite formula for declining an offer. **2.** Expression of gratitude, grateful acknowledgment of obligation: *please accept my best thanks*; (also in colloq. construction) *thanks very much*.

thank (II.), vb. trans. O.E. *þancian*, M.E. *thankie(n)*, *thanke(n)*, see prec. To express one's thanks or gratitude to, acknowledge gratefully the services, help, kindness &c. of: *to thank a person for what he has done*; *thank you*, common form of *I thank you*; *no, thank you*, form of declining an offer; *thank you for nothing*, ironical formula acknowledging refusal to help &c.; *I will thank you to be a little more polite*, urbane but peremptory request, almost amounting to a command; *you have only yourself to thank* (for the mess you are in &c.), it is no one's fault but your own.

thankful, adj. [1. tháŋkfool; 2. þæŋkful]. **thank (I.)** & **-ful**. Grateful, having a due sense of kindness received, and being eager to express it: *a thankful heart*. Phr. *I'm thankful (that it is no worse, that I saw him before he died* &c.), expressing satisfaction, relief &c.

thankfully, adv. Prec. & **-ly**. Gratefully; with gratitude.

thankfulness, n. See prec. & **-ness**. Gratitude; feeling of satisfaction, relief.

thankless, adj. [1. tháŋkles; 2. þæŋklis]. **thank (I.)** & **-less**. **1.** (of persons) Devoid of gratitude; not feeling or expressing gratitude. **2.** (of actions) Not arousing gratitude; not appreciated by others: *it is a thankless job, task, to tell people of their faults*.

thanklessly, adv. Prec. & **-ly**. In a thankless manner.

thanklessness, n. See prec. & **-ness**. Quality, state, of being thankless.

thank-offering, n. Offering made as an expression of gratitude.

thanksgiver, n. [1. tháŋksgiver; 2. þæŋksgivə]. Person who gives thanks.

thanksgiving, n. [1. tháŋksgiving; 2. þæŋksgiviŋ]. **1.** Act of expressing gratitude. **2.** Formula expressing gratitude, esp. for divine goodness. **3.** (cap.) Thanksgiving Day.

Thanksgiving Day, n. Day appointed for public thanksgiving for mercies vouchsafed by Providence; esp. annual thanksgiving in U.S.A., usually the last Thursday in November.

that (I.), demonstr. pron. [1. dhat; 2. ðæt]. O.E. *þæt*, neut. sing. nom. & acc. of the def. art. *se*, *sēo*, *þæt*, wh. already in O.E. has a certain demonstr. force; see **the**. **1.** The object, or idea, just referred to, or evidently to be understood from the context or circumstances: *that is what I want to know*, *what you, we, have just mentioned*; *that's no way to behave*; *his manner was that of a gentleman*, i.e. the manner of; *I can't agree to that*, to what you have just proposed. In colloq. speech also used contemptuously and disparagingly of persons: *do you call that an officer and a gentleman?* (prob. for *that thing*). **2.** The thing, object, over there, or more remote; contrasted with *this*, the one here: *which will you have, this or that?* Phrs. *to talk of this, that, and the other*, various things, all sorts of matters; *none of that, now, don't talk or behave in such a manner*.

that (II.), demonstr. adj.; same as prec. **1.** The one over there, the one we formerly saw, referred to &c.; contrasted with *this one here*: *I don't like that room you showed me first, I prefer this one*. **2.** Indicating something familiar and generally recognized: *that stately bearing, that benevolent expression, that sonorous voice which we knew so well*.

that (III.), rel. pron.; chiefly unstressed & pronounced [ðət]. **1.** The person or persons who, the thing or things which: *the man that I want to see*; *the woman that he loved*; *we have done those things that we ought not to have done*. **2.** (adverbially) On which, in which: *the last time that I saw you*; *the year that King Edward died*.

that (IV.), conj.; chiefly unstressed [ðət]; derived fr. rel., **that (III.)**. **1.** Introducing a subordinate clause: *I fear that I cannot come*; *I am sorry that you should attribute such motives to me*; *it seems that you have forgotten me*; *he said that he disliked exercise*; *he knew that it was impossible*; *there is no doubt that we were wrong from the start*. **2.** Expressing purpose: '*So run that ye may attain*'; *he only rested that he might engage in more arduous labours*; *he only fled that he might fight another day*; *also so that*; *to the end that*; *in order that*. **3.** Expressing cause: because: *if I find fault it is that I want you to improve*. **4.** Expressing result, effect: *I am so tired that I can hardly stand*; *he had lived so long abroad that he had got out of English ways*. **5.** Introducing a sentence expressing surprise, indignation, a strong wish: *I never knew you were here all this time!*; *O that, would that, I had never been born!*; *O that I might see him once more!*

that (V.), adv. (colloq. and illit. or facet.) To such an extent, so much: *I can't walk that far*; *he was that drunk he could scarcely stand*; *I'm that sleepy I can't keep my eyes open*.

thatch (I.), n. [1. thach; 2. þætʃ]. O.E. *þæc*, 'roof, thatch'; O.N. *þak*; O.H.G. *dah*, 'cover, roof'; cogn. w. Lat. *tegere*, 'to cover', see **tegument**; *tēgula*, 'tile', see **tile**, **toga**; cp. further under **deck (I.)**. **a** Roofing for a house, protective covering for a rick, composed of straw, reeds &c., arranged in rows of bundles and pegged and tied down; **b** (colloq.) thick covering of hair on the head.

thatch (II.), vb. trans. A new formation fr. prec. The O.E. vb. is *þeċċan*, 'to cover', fr. **þæċċ-jan*. To cover with thatch, fix thatch on to (roof of a house or top of a rick).

thatching, n. [1. tháching; 2. þætʃiŋ]. Straw, reeds &c. used as thatch for a roof &c.

thauma(to)-, pref. Gk. *thaúmat-*, fr. *thaûma*, 'a wonder, marvel, wondrous thing; a juggler's trick'; see further **theatre**.

thaumatrope, n. [1. tháwmatrōp; 2. þɔˑmətroup]. Prec. & *trópos*, 'a turning', see **trope**. Optical instrument, consisting either of a disk with two different pictures one on either side, which when the disk is rapidly spun round, appear to merge into a single picture, e.g. if a fish is on one side of the disk, and a bowl on the other, the fish appears to be inside the bowl; or a series of pictures on a flat disk, of the same object in slightly different positions, which when the disk is revolved, appear to be moving.

thaumaturge, n. [1. tháwmatėrj; 2. þɔˑmətɜdʒ]. Fr., fr. Gk. *thaumatourgós*, 'wonder-working', fr. **thauma(to)-** & *érgon*, 'work', see **erg**. A worker of miracles; a magician.

thaumaturgic(al), adj. [1. tháwmatėrjik(l); 2. þɔmətɜdʒik(l)]. Prec. & **-ic** (& **-al**). Pertaining to, of the nature of, magic.

thaumaturgist, n. [1. tháwmatėrjist; 2. þɔmətɜdʒist]. Next word & **-ist**. One who practises thaumaturgy; a magician.

thaumaturgy, n. [1. tháwmatėrji; 2. þɔmətɜdʒi]. Gk. *thaumatourgía*, 'magic'; **thaumaturge** & **-y**. Magic, conjuring, wonder-working.

thaw (I.), vb. intrans. & trans. [1. thaw; 2. þɔ]. O.E. *þāwian*, cp. O.N. *þeyja*, 'to melt'; connected w. Germ. (*ver*)*dauen*, 'to digest'; possibly also w. Lat. *tābēre*, 'to melt', see **tabes**; no connexion w. **dew** or Germ. *tau*, 'dew'. **A.** intrans. **1. a** (of the weather) *It is thawing*, passing to a degree of temperature sufficiently high for frost to disperse and ice to turn to water; **b** (of frozen matter, objects) to turn to water; to become liquid, to melt: *the ice is thawing*; *the snow on Scottish mountains thaws in summer*; **c** (colloq., of persons) to become warm, pass from state of extreme chill to normal temperature: *I was half frozen after my drive, but I'm gradually thawing.* **2.** (fig., of persons, manner, mental attitude &c.) To become genial, cordial, frank; to pass from frigidity, embarrassment, and stiffness to ease and naturalness. **B.** trans. To cause to thaw, to increase temperature of (frozen object) till liquefaction is produced.

thaw (II.), n., fr. prec. Process of becoming warmer, of passing from freezing-point to open, mild weather; change from frozen condition to liquefaction: *a thaw has set in and the snow is melting.*

the (I.), def. art. [1. dhē; 2. ðī] when stressed; normally, when unstressed [1. dhi; 2. ði], before words beginning w. a vowel; [1. dhe; 2. ðə] before words beginning w. a cons. Already in early M.E. *ðĕ* is used as indeclinable art. This is a new formation fr. the O.E. nom. masc. *se*, w. þ (*th*-) introduced fr. the other O.E. cases, all of wh., in all numbers & genders, begin w. þ- (*th*-), except nom. sing. masc. (*sĕ*), & nom. sing. fem. (*sēo*). Orig. a demonstr. pron. Cp. Lat. *is-te*, *is-tum* &c., 'that'; Gk. *tó*, neut. sing. of def. art., also other cases *tón*, *tḗn* &c.; Scrt. *ta*, *tam*, *tad* &c. See also **that** (I.), **their**, **them**. **1.** Indicating some particular person or thing; contrasted with the indef. art. *a*: *the man I loved*; *the King of England*; *the author of 'Hamlet'*; *the man for my money*; *the day that first we met* &c. **2.** Before a noun expressing some well-known object, thing, or personage: *the Thames*; *now they bring in the Boar's Head*; *the Wrekin*; *the Devil*; *the Pope*; *the King*, indicating either the Sovereign of one's own country, or of some other country about which one is speaking, or in which one is. **3. a** Used before titles: *the Lord Bishop of Oxford*; *the Venerable the Archdeacon of London*; *the Mayor of Yarmouth*; *the Duke of Wellington*; *the Earl of Oxford*; **b** used before the family name of the head of certain ancient families or clans, esp. in Scotland and Ireland: *the Mackintosh*; *the Chisholm*; *the Macgillicuddy.* **4.** Before a noun used to designate a whole class or genus: *the wild boar*; *the laughing jackass*; *the horse and the dog are faithful servants of mankind.* **5. a** Before adjectives referring to a person or to persons possessing the qualities which it denotes: '*The young, the beautiful, the brave*' (Byron, 'Bride of Abydos', ii. 1); *the living and the dead*; *a book much prized by the learned*; **b** before adjectives expressing an abstract idea: '*We needs must love the highest when we see it*' (Tennyson, 'Guinevere'); *the sublime and the beautiful*; *the public loves the sensational*; *the picturesque* &c. **6.** With stress [ðī] before a noun, denoting some unique object or person: *thé specialist on liver complaints*; *thé poet of the day*; *cider is thé drink for hot weather.*

the (II.), adv. [1. dhe; 2. ðə]. O.E. *þȳ*. Instrumental of def. art. By so much, by that amount: *the more the merrier*; *the more I practise, the worse I sing.*

theandric, adj. [1. thēándrik; 2. þīǽndrik]. Gk. *theós*, 'God', see **theo-**, & *andr-*, stem of *anḗr*, 'man', see first element of **androgynous**, & **-ic.** Pertaining to, based on, the combination of divine and human nature, as in Jesus Christ.

theanthropic(al), adj. [1. thèanthrópik(l); 2. þiænþrɔ́pik(l)]. Gk. *theós*, 'God', see **theo-**, & *ánthrōpos*, 'man', see **anthropo-**, & **-ic** (& **-al**). Divine and human; embodying God in human form.

theanthropism, n. [1. thèánthropizm; 2. þīǽnþrəpizəm]. **a** Anthropomorphism; **b** belief in the embodiment of God in human form.

theanthropist, n. [1. thèánthropist; 2. þīǽnþrəpist]. Believer in theanthropism.

thearchic, adj. [1. thēárkik; 2. þīɑ́kik]. Next word & **-ic.** Pertaining to, based on, of the nature of, thearchy.

thearchy, n. [1. thḗarki; 2. þīɑ̄ki]. See **theo-** & **-archy**. **a** Divine rulership; **b** government claiming direct divine authority and guidance, claiming to act as God's vicegerent; theocracy.

theatre, n. [1. thḗater; 2. þíətə]. Fr., fr. Lat. *theātrum*, fr. Gk. *théatron*, fr. *theā́*, 'sight, a spectacle'; cp. also *theáomai*, 'I gaze at, behold', & *theātós*, 'to be seen'; prob. related to Gk. *thaûma*, 'object of wonder' &c., see **thauma(to)-**. **1.** A building containing a large chamber, with a stage for the performance of dramatic pieces, and seats for spectators. **2.** A hall arranged like a theatre, with a dais, and rows of seats rising towards the back, for lectures, scientific demonstrations, surgical operations &c., or for public ceremonies: *operating, lecture, theatre*; *the Sheldonian Theatre* (at Oxford). **3.** The scene of important events or actions, region where these take place: *the theatre of war*; *the theatre of his early triumphs.* **4.** Dramatic literature collectively; esp. the dramatic writings of a particular author or period: *Goethe's theatre*; *the Elizabethan theatre.*

theatric, adj. [1. theátrik; 2. þiǽtrik]. Prec. & **-ic.** (rare, chiefly poet.) Showy; see next word.

theatrical, adj. [1. theátrikl; 2. þiǽtrikl]. Prec. & **-al.** **1.** Pertaining to, connected with, the theatre, or with dramatic representation. **2. a** (of manner) Affected, studied, not natural; adopted for the purpose of impressing; not restrained; **b** (of appearance) showy, unreal, artificial, meretricious.

theatricality, n. [1. theàtrikáliti; 2. þiætrikǽliti]. Prec. & **-ity.** Quality of being theatrical; affectation of manner &c.

theatrically, adv. [1. theátrikali; 2. þiǽtrikəli]. See prec. & **-ly.** In a theatrical manner; as though performing on the stage; affectedly, unnaturally.

theatricals, n. pl. [1. theátriklz; 2. þiǽtriklz]. Dramatic performances, esp. those executed by amateurs.

Thebaid, n. [1. thḗbāid; 2. þíbei-id]. Gk. *Thêbai*, 'Thebes'. **a** District round or near Thebes in Egypt; **b** poem (esp. that by Statius) upon the siege of Thebes in Boeotia.

theca, n., pl. **thecae** [1. thḗka, -kē; 2. þíkə, -kī]. Lat., fr. Gk. *thḗkē*, 'case in which to put anything'; fr. *títhēmi*, 'I place', see **theme.** (bot. and zool.) Sheath, case, capsule, as of mosses &c.; the case of the pupa of an insect &c.

thee, pron. Objective case of **thou.**

theft, n. [1. theft; 2. þeft]. O.E. *þīefþe*, *þēofþe*, see **thief** & **-th** (I.). **a** Act of stealing; **b** object stolen.

thegn, n. [1. thān; 2. þein]. O.E. See **thane.**

theine, n. [1. thḗin; 2. þíin], fr. *thea*, Latinized form of Gk. *theā́*, 'goddess', invented by Linnaeus, as scientific name for **tea**, & **-ine.** Caffeine as it occurs in tea.

their, pron. [1. dhār; 2. ðɛə]. O.N. *þeirra*, poss. pl. of 3rd pers. pron. See **they.**

theirs, pron., fr. prec., *-s* added on anal. of *his.* Form of *their* used absolutely: *this is yours and that is theirs*; also when preceded by *of*: *a favourite habit of theirs.*

theism (I.), n. [1. thḗizm; 2. þíizəm]. *Thea*, see **theine**, & **-ism.** Pathological condition due to excessive use of tea.

theism (II.), n. [1. thḗizm; 2. þíizəm]. Gk. *theós*, 'God', see **theo-** & **-ism.** Belief in a personal God capable of making Himself known by supernatural revelation.

theist, n. [1. thḗist; 2. þíist]. See **theo-** & **-ist.** Adherent of theism.

theistic, adj., rarer **theistical** [1. thēístik(l); 2. þiístik(l)]. Prec. & **-ic** (& **-al**). Connected with theism or theists.

them, pron. [1. dhem; 2. ðem, ðəm]. M.E. *þeim*, *þem*, fr. O.N. *þeim*, cogn. w. O.E. *þǣm*, dat. pl. of def. art. See **the, they.** Form of pron. of 3rd pers. used both as dat. & acc. pl.

thematic, adj. [1. thematik; 2. þimǽtik], fr. Gk. *themat-*, see **theme**, & **-ic.** **1.** (gram.) Pertaining to the stem or theme of a word. **2.** (mus.) Pertaining to the theme or melodic subject; *thematic catalogue*, one which gives, in addition to the title and full reference, also the opening measures of musical compositions. **3.** (rare) Relating to a theme or topic.

theme, n. [1. thēm; 2. þim]. M.E., fr. O. Fr. *teme*, Mod. Fr. *thème*, fr. Lat. *thema*, fr. Gk. *théma*, fr. *títhēmi*, 'I place', fr. base **dhē-* &c., whence also **deed, do** (I.), & Lat. *facere*, see **fact**; cp. also **thesis. 1.** Subject of thought, writing, discourse. **2.** (gram.) That part of a word to which the inflexions are suffixed; a stem. **3.** (mus.) A brief melody occurring and recurring in a composition, subsequently elaborated in variations.

Themis, n. [1. thḗmis; 2. þémis]. Gk., name of the goddess of law and order, 'Justice'; fr. the same word meaning 'that which is fixed, settled, agreed upon'; hence 'law, right' &c., fr. base **dhē-* &c., 'to place, set', see prec. Personification of law and justice.

themselves, pron. [1. dhemsélvz; 2. ðəmsélvz]. **1.** Emphatic form of pron. of 3rd pers. pl.: *they had often done the same thing themselves*, or *they themselves had* &c. **2.** Reflex. pron. pl.: *they were ashamed of themselves*; *they felt themselves to be in the wrong.*

then (I.), adv. & conjunc. [1. dhen; 2. ðen]. Same in origin as **than**; O.E. *þonne*. **A.** adv. **1. a** At that (specified) time in the future: '*now I know in part; but then shall I know even as also I am known*' (1 Cor. xiii. 12); *when I know what the price is, then I shall be able to decide*; *I shall see you on Monday, and will then tell you the facts*; **b** at some former time, in the past; in the old days; contrasted with *now*, *at present*: *ah, we were still young then*; Phrs. *there and then*, at that very moment; *now and then*, from time to time, occasionally. **2.** Next in order of time; immediately afterwards: *Queen Anne died in 1702, and then the first Hanoverian sovereign succeeded to the throne of England*; *he made a few convulsive movements and then died*; *take a hot drink and then go to bed.* **3.** At another, subsequent, time; later on: *he used to behave like a lunatic when he was in a rage, then, when the fit had passed, he would be full of contrition.* **4.** In that case, that being so: *if you are tired, then you had better stay at home*; *well then, please yourself about it*; *if you didn't understand, then you should have told me*; expressing rather unwilling acquiescence: *oh, all right then, do what you like.* **5.** Expressing condition; under the circumstances, from what you say: *you don't want to go after all, then*; *then you didn't expect me today.* **6.** *Now then*, expressing protest, warning &c.: *now then, what are you doing?*; *now then, don't hit me in the eye!*; *now then, a little less noise there.* **B.** conj. Moreover, in addition, also, further: *then there's the General still to be invited*; *then what about French, can you speak that language?*

then (II.), adj., fr. prec. Existing, acting, at a specified time: *the then governor was a man of probity and honour.*

then (III.), n. See prec. That (specified) time: *by then, till then, up to then, from then onwards.*

thenar, n. [1. thḗnar; 2. þínə]. Gk. *thénar*, 'palm of the hand', cogn. w. O.H.G. *tenar*, 'palm'. The palm of the hand; the protuberance in the palm at the base of the thumb.

thence, adv. [1. dhens; 2. ðens]. O.E. *þanon*, O.H.G. *danān* &c.; M.E. *þennes*, w. suff. of genit. used adverbially. **1.** From that place: *we went to Geneva, and thence to the Rhone Valley.* **2.** (rare) From that time, thenceforth: *a year thence*; contrasted with *a year hence.* **3.** On that account, for that reason; from what has been said; therefore: *thence it follows that we were wrong*; *he was very old, and thence very feeble.*

thenceforth, adv. [1. dhènsfórth; 2. ðènsfɔ́þ]. From that time or place, onwards; often *from thenceforth*.

thenceforward, adv. [1. dhènsfórward; 2. ðènsfɔ́wəd]. Thenceforth.

theo-, pref. Form used in compounds, fr. Gk. *theós*, 'god', later of the God of the Jews or of the Christians. The etymol. is disputed; some authorities derive the word fr. the base *dhwes-*, 'to breathe; breath, spirit, life', & connect w. Lat. *bēstia*, see **beast**, & w. **deer**; also w. Lat. *fūmus*, 'smoke', see **fume** & **dust**; others derive fr. *dhēs-* &c., 'religious act', & connect w. Lat. *fēriae*, 'religious festivals', see **ferial** & **fair** (I.), & w. Lat. *festus*, 'connected with holidays; solemn, festal' &c., & *festum*, 'festival, feast', see **feast**, **festive** &c.; also Lat. *fānum*, 'place consecrated to a deity', see **fane**.

theocentric, adj. [1. thēōséntrik; 2. þïouséntrik]. Prec. & **centric**. Considering God as the centre of the universe.

theocracy, n. [1. theókrasi; 2. þïókrəsi]. **theo-** & **-cracy**. **a** System of state government by direct guidance of God; **b** government by priests as purporting to represent God, and interpret His will.

theocrasy, n. [1. theókrasi, theokrási; 2. þïókrəsi, þïokréisi], fr. **theo-** & *krāsis*, 'a mixing', see **crasis**. Union of the soul with God in mystical contemplation.

theocrat, n. [1. thēókrat; 2. þïoukræt]. **theo-** & **-crat**. A ruler under a system of theocracy.

theocratic, adj. [1. thēōkrátik; 2. þïoukrǽtik]. Prec. & **-ic**. Pertaining to, based on, theocracy.

theodicy, n. [1. theódisi; 2. þïódisi]. **theo-** & Gk. *dikē*, 'justice', see **dicast**. Vindication of divine justice in permitting existence of evil.

theodolite, n. [1. theódolīt; 2. þïódəlait]. Origin unknown. Instrument used by surveyors for measuring angles.

theogony, n. [1. theóguni; 2. þïógəni]. Gk. *theogonia*, 'genealogy of the gods'; fr. **theo-** & *gónos*, 'race, offspring; begetting'; see under **genus**. Branch of ancient heathen theology, dealing with the origin and descent of the various gods.

theologian, n. [1. thēolójian; 2. þïəlóudʒ(i)ən]. Gk. word is *theológos*; our word fr. Fr. *théologien*; fr. *théologie*, see **theology** & **-an**. Student of, authority on, theology.

theological, adj. [1. thēolójikl; 2. þïəlódʒikl]. **theology** & **-ic** & **-al**. Connected with, based upon, of the nature of, theology.

theologically, adv. Prec. & **-ly**. From the point of view of theology, or of theologians.

theologico-, pref. Form of **theological** used in compounds: *theologico-philosophical*.

theologue, n. [1. theólŏg; 2. þïəlóug]. Fr., Lat. *theologus*, fr. Gk., see **theologian**. (archaic or obs.) Theologian.

theology, n. [1. theóloji; 2. þïóləẓi]. Gk. *theologia*, see **theo-** & **-logy**. Systematic study and inquiry into the nature and attributes of God; also the systematic study of religion and the foundations of belief.

theomachy, n. [1. theómaki; 2. þïóməki], fr. Gk. *theomakhia*, see **theo-** & **-machy**. A battle with or among the gods.

theomorphic, adj. [1. thēōmórfik; 2. þïoumɔ́fik], fr. Gk. *theómorph-(os)* & **-ic**, see **theo-** & first element in **morphology**. Having the form or appearance of a god; in the form of a god.

theophany, n. [1. theófani; 2. þïófəni], fr. Gk. *theopháneia*, fr. **theo-** & base discussed under **phantasm**. An appearance, manifestation of God in human or divine form to men.

theorbo, n. [1. theórbō; 2. þïɔ́bou]. Fr. *théorbe*, fr. Ital. *tiorba*. Origin unknown. Obsolete kind of lute, of large size, and having two necks, and sets of pegs and strings.

theorem, n. [1. theórem; 2. þïərem]. Gk. *theórēma*, 'a sight, speculation', see **theory**. **1**. Something established as a law or general principle; a speculative truth. **2**. (math.) A general statement; a proposition to be established by reasoning.

theorematic(al), adj. [1. thēōremátik(l); 2. þïərematik(l)], fr. *theoremat-*, stem of prec., & **-ic** (& **-al**). Pertaining to theorems.

theoretic(al), adj. [1. thēōrétik(l); 2. þïərétik(l)]. Gk. *theōrētikós*; see **theory**. **a** Pertaining to, based upon, theory; **b** speculative, not based on actual experience; contrasted with *practical*.

theoretically, adv. Prec. & **-y**. In theory, as a theory; from the point of view of theory.

theorist, n. [1. theórist; 2. þïərist]. **theory** & **-ist**. One given to forming theories; an unpractical person.

theorize, vb. intrans. [1. theórīz; 2. þïəraiz]. **theory** & **-ize**. To form, put forward, theories.

theory, n. [1. theóri; 2. þïəri]. Fr. *théorie*, Lat. *theōria*, fr. Gk. *theōría*, 'a spectacle, contemplation, speculation'; cp. *theōrós*, 'spectator', & *theâsthai*, 'to see'; see also **theatre**. **1**. A general principle, a supposition, advanced to explain a group of phenomena; esp. one which has been tested, and is regarded as supplying an acceptable explanation; distinct from *hypothesis*, which is an assumption not yet verified. **2**. General principles underlying a body of facts; contrasted with *practice*: *a theory of education, government; the theory of music*. **3**. Contemplation, speculation, as distinct from actual experience: *foreign travel is all very well in theory*. **4**. (popular usage) Opinion, fanciful belief; fad, whimsy: *I have a theory that a hot bath at night makes one sleepless*.

theosophic(al), adj. [1. thēōsófik(l); 2. þïəsófik(l)]. **theosophy** & **-ic** (& **-al**). Connected with, relating to, theosophy.

theosophist, n. [1. theósofist; 2. þïósəfist]. **theosophy** & **-ist**. Believer in theosophy.

theosophy, n. [1. theósofi; 2. þïósəfi]. Gk. *theosophía*, 'knowledge of divine things'; *theós*, 'God', see **theo-** & *sophía*, 'skill, wisdom', fr. *sophós*, 'skilled, clever, wise', see **sophist**. Mystic form of religious thought which aims at establishing a direct relation between the individual soul and the divine principle by contemplation and ecstasy, and thereby gaining superior spiritual insight and knowledge.

-ther, compar. suff., fr. base *ter-*, *tr-*, seen in Gk. *-teros*, Lat. *-ter(us)*, see **inter-**; found in prons. & advbs. implying comparison, alternative possibility, distinction &c., e.g. *either, other, whether, hither, nether*.

therapeutic(al), adj. [1. thèrapútik(l); 2. þèrapjútik(l)]. Gk. *therapeutikós*, 'attentive, obedient; able to cure', *therapeutiké*, 'the healing art'; cp. *therapeúein*, 'to serve, attend upon', fr. *therápōn*, 'an attendant, servant'; the orig. sense is perh. 'prop, support', cp. Gk. *thrânos*, 'a bench, form', & Lat. *firmus*, 'strong, firm', see **firm** (I.), & *frētus*, 'trusting to, relying on'. Connected with the art of healing, with the cure of disease.

therapeutics, n. pl. [1. thèrapútiks; 2. þèrapjútiks]. That side of medicine which is concerned with the treatment and cure of disease.

-therapy, suff. [1. thérapi; 2. þérəpi]. Gk. *therapeía*, 'service, attendance; medical attendance'; see **therapeutic**. Curative treatment, e.g. *radio-therapy*, cure by radium.

there, adv. & interj. [1. dhār; 2. ðɛə]. O.E. *ðǣr*; belongs to the group of demonstrative words including **the, that, then**. **1. a** In that place, referring to one other than that in which the speaker actually is; contrasted with *here*: *when we reached London my brother remained there, while I came on here*; **b** to, towards, that place: *I've never been to Rome, but I'm going there at Easter*. Phrs. *look there, look at that*, in that direction &c.; *there it is!* = what you are looking for &c. **2. a** At that point, stage (in action, discourse, argument &c.): *don't stop there, go on and tell us all about it*; **b** towards a certain point (in action &c.): *I have not yet reached your intellectual position, but I may get there in time*. Phrs. (slang) *to get there*, attain one's object, do what one is trying to do; *there it is*, that is the situation. **3**. Pronominally and impersonally, as subject of a verb, introducing a sentence: *there was once a great king*, at beginning of a narrative; *there was a sudden drop in the temperature*; *there was no excuse for his rudeness*; *what is there to do here?*; *there are plenty of foxes to be killed*; also archaic or poet., *a king there was* &c. **4**. (as interj.) *There, there!*, in soothing a child &c.; *there now, I told you it would land you in a mess!*; *there now, it has turned out all right after all!*

thereabouts, adv. [1. dhārabóuts; 2. ðɛərəbáuts]. **1**. Near that (specified) place: *he lives in Wantage or thereabouts*. **2**. Near to that amount, extent, degree, position &c.: *a thousand a year, or thereabouts*; *top of his school or thereabouts*.

thereafter, adv. [1. dhāráhfter; 2. ðɛərɑ́ftə]. O.E. *þǣræfter*. **1**. After that time. **2**. (rare) According to, in accordance with, that: *listen to his advice, and behave yourself thereafter*.

thereat, adv. [1. dhārát; 2. ðɛərǽt]. (archaic) At, on account of, by means of, that.

thereby, adv. [1. dhārbí; 2. ðɛəbái]. **1**. Near to that place. **2**. By that means: *I have learnt my lesson, and hope to profit thereby*.

therefor, adv. [1. dhārfór; 2. ðɛəfɔ́]. (archaic) For it, for that, or this; in exchange for that.

therefore, adv. [1. dhárfor; 2. ðɛ́əfɔ]. On this, or that, account; for this, or that, reason.

therefrom, adv. [1. dhārfróm; 2. ðɛəfróm]. From, away from, that; by means of that.

therein, adv. [1. dhārín; 2. ðɛərín]. **a** In that thing, or place; **b** in this, that, particular.

thereinafter, adv. [1. dhārináhfter; 2. ðɛərinɑ́ftə]. In that part which follows (in a speech, or document).

thereof, adv. [1. dhārόv, -óf; 2. ðɛəróv, -óf]. (archaic) Of it, of that: *thou shalt not eat thereof*.

thereon, adv. [1. dhārón; 2. ðɛərón]. (archaic) On this, on that.

thereto, adv. [1. dhārtōō; 2. ðɛətú]. (archaic) **1**. To it, to that, to that place. **2**. Moreover, in addition to that.

theretofore, adv. [1. dhārtoofór; 2. ðɛətufɔ́]. (archaic) Until then, up to that time.

thereunder, adv. [1. dhārúnder; 2. ðɛərándə]. (archaic) Under that.

thereunto, adv. [1. dhārúntōō; 2. ðɛərantú]. (archaic, or obs.) To that, to it.

thereupon, adv. [1. dhārupón; 2. ðɛərəpón]. **1**. Upon that. **2**. In consequence, as result, of that. **3**. At that point (of time); immediately after that.

therewith, adv. [1. dhārwídh, -wíth; 2. ðɛəwið, -wíþ]. (archaic) **1**. With that. **2**. Forthwith, at that moment, thereupon.

therewithal, adv. [1. dhārwidháwl; 2. ðɛəwiðɔ́l]. Besides, moreover; therewith.

theriac, n. [1. thériak; 2. þíəriæk]. Lat. *Theriaca (Andromachi)*, fr. Gk. *thēriaké*, 'antidote'; formed fr. *thērion*, 'wild beast', dimin. of *thér*, 'wild beast'; fr. *ghʷēr-*, & cogn. w. Lat. *ferus*, 'wild', see **feral**, & **ferocious**; cp. **treacle**. Ancient antidote for poison, composed of certain drugs mixed with honey.

therianthropic, adj. [1. thèrianthrópik; 2. þïəriænþrópik]. Gk. *thér*, 'animal, beast', see **therio-** & *ánthrōpos*, 'man', see **anthropo-**. Combining human and animal form, as the centaur.

therio-, pref., fr. Gk. *thērion*, 'beast, animal', fr. *thér*, 'wild beast', see **theriac**.

theriomorphic, theriomorphous, adj. [1. thèriōmórfik, -mórfus; 2. þïəriouμόfik, -mɔ́fəs]. Prec. & Gk. *morphé*, 'form', see first element in **morphology**. Having the form of an animal.

-therium, suff. Mod. Lat., fr. Gk. *thērion*, 'animal', see **theriac**: *megatherium* &c.

therm, n. [1. thĕrm; 2. þɜːm]. Gk. *thérmē*, 'heat', cp. *thermós*, 'hot, warm'; fr. base *ghʷerm-, *ghʷorm-, & cogn. w. Lat. *formus*, 'warm', also w. **warm**. Term for British thermal unit, or unit of heat, being the amount of heat required to raise a pound of water at maximum density, 1° Fahrenheit; abbreviated B.T.U.

thermae, n. pl. [1. thĕrmē; 2. þʎmī]. Lat., 'hot springs', fr. Gk. *thérmai*, pl. of *thérmē*, 'heat', see prec. Hot springs, or baths; specif., the springs connected with ancient Roman public baths, also the baths themselves.

thermaesthesia, n. [1. thĕrmesthēzia; 2. þʎmɛsþízɪə], fr. **thermo-** & Gk. *aisthēsis*, 'sensation', see **aesthete**, & **-ia**. (physiol.) Sensitiveness to heat.

thermal, adj. [1. thĕrmal; 2. þʎm(ə)l]. See **therm** & **-al**. **a** Pertaining to thermae; **b** pertaining to heat; hot: *thermal waters, springs* &c.

thermantidote, n. [1. thĕrmántidōt; 2. þʎmǽntɪdout]. See **therm** & **antidote**. Apparatus used in hot countries for cooling the air.

thermic, adj. [1. thĕrmik; 2. þʎmɪk]. See **therm** & **-ic**. Connected with, caused by, heat.

Thermidor, n. [1. thĕrmidōr; 2. þʎmɪdō]. Fr., fr. Gk. *thérmē*, 'heat', see **therm**, & *dôron*, 'gift', base of wh. see under **donate**. Name given in French Revolution to the eleventh month of their calendar, from July 19th to August 17th.

Thermidorian, n. [1. thĕrmidórian; 2. þʎmɪdóriən]. Prec. & **-an**. One of those who took part in, or favoured, the overthrow of Robespierre on 9th Thermidor (July 27th), 1794.

thermionic, adj. [1. thĕrmiónik; 2. þʎmɪónɪk], fr. **therm** & **-ion** & **-ic**. Term applied to a vacuum tube, *thermionic valve*, used in wireless, in which electrons given off by a heated filament carry current in one direction, thus converting the alternating current of the radio waves into wire-directional current which can be made to work a telephone and produce sound.

thermit(e), n. [1. thĕrmit, -īt; 2. þʎmɪt, -aɪt]. **thermo-** & **-ite**. A mixture of finely granulated aluminium with an iron oxide, used in welding.

thermo-, pref. Form used in compounds, fr. Gk. *thermós*, 'hot', or *thérmē*, 'heat', see **therm**.

thermobarometer, n. [1. thĕrmobarómeter; 2. þʎmoubərómɪtə]. Apparatus for measuring a height by determining the boiling-point of water at that altitude.

thermochemistry, n. [1. thĕrmōkémistri; 2. þʎmoukémistri]. Branch of chemistry treating of relation between heat and chemical action.

thermo-couple, n. [1. thĕrmō kùpl; 2. þʎmou kʌpl]. Thermopile.

thermodynamics, n. [1. thĕrmōdinámiks; 2. þʎmoudaɪnǽmiks]. Branch of science dealing with the relation between thermal and mechanical energy.

thermoelectric(al), adj. [1. thĕrmōeléktrik(l); 2. þʎmouɪléktrɪk(l)]. Pertaining to thermoelectricity.

thermoelectricity, n. [1. thĕrmōelektrísiti; 2. þʎmouɛlɪktrísɪti]. Electricity produced by the action of heat, by differences in temperature &c.

thermoelectrometer, n. [1. thĕrmōelektrómeter; 2. þʎmouɛlɪktrómɪtə]. Instrument for determining the power of an electric current by measuring the heat which it produces.

thermogenesis, n. [1. thĕrmōjénesis; 2. þʎmoudʒénisɪs]. The production of heat in the human body &c.

thermogenetic, adj. [1. thĕrmōjenétik; 2. þʎmoudʒɪnétik]. **thermo-** & **-genetic**. Pertaining to thermogenesis.

thermogenic, adj. [1. thĕrmōjénik; 2. þʎmoudʒénik]. **thermo-** & **-gene** & **-ic**. Relating to the production of heat.

thermogenous, adj. [1. thĕrmójenus; 2. þʎmódʒɪnəs]. See prec. & **-ous**. Producing heat.

thermogram, n. [1. thĕrmōgràm; 2. þʎmougrǽm]. **thermo-** & **-gram**. Record produced by a thermograph.

thermograph, n. [1. thĕrmōgràhf; 2. þʎmougrɑ̀f]. **thermo-** & **-graph**. Self-registering thermometer.

thermology, n. [1. thĕrmóloji; 2. þʎmólədʒi]. **thermo-** & **-logy**. The science of heat.

thermometer, n. [1. thĕrmómeter; 2. þʎmómɪtə]. **thermo-** & **-meter**. Instrument for measuring degrees of temperature.

thermometric(al), adj. [1. thĕrmōmétrik(l); 2. þʎmoumétrik(l)]. Prec. & **-ic** & **(-al)**. Pertaining to, measured by, a thermometer.

thermometrically, adv. [1. thĕrmōmétrikali; 2. þʎmoumétrikəli]. Prec. & **-ly**. By means of a thermometer.

thermometry, n. [1. thĕrmómetri; 2. þʎmómɪtri]. **thermo-** & **-metry**. The measurement of heat.

thermomotive, adj. [1. thĕrmōmōtiv; 2. þʎmoumóutɪv]. Pertaining to motion produced by heat.

thermomotor, n. [1. thĕrmōmōtor; 2. þʎmoumóutə]. An engine worked by heat, usually by hot air.

thermophilic, adj. [1. thĕrmófilik; 2. þʎmófilik]. **thermo-** & **-phil** & **-ic**. (of bacteria) Heat-loving; developing best at a comparatively high temperature.

thermophore, n. [1. thĕrmófōr; 2. þʎmoufɔ̀]. **thermo-** & **-phore**. Apparatus for conveying warmth; heating appliance.

thermopile, n. [1. thĕrmōpīl; 2. þʎmoupàɪl]. **thermo-** & **pile (III.)**. Thermoelectric battery, used as delicate form of thermometer, consisting of junctions of dissimilar metals which produce an electric current on the application of heat.

thermoplegia, n. [1. thĕrmōpléjia; 2. þʎmouplídʒiə]. **thermo-** & Gk. *plēgē*, 'blow, stroke', see under **plectrum** & **-ia**. A heat-stroke.

thermoscope, n. [1. thĕrmōskŏp; 2. þʎmouskòup]. **thermo-** & **-scope**. Instrument for indicating differences of temperature without exact measurement.

thermoscopic(al), adj. [1. thĕrmōskópik(l); 2. þʎmouskópik(l)]. Prec. & **-ic** & **(-al)**. Pertaining to, shown by, a thermoscope.

thermos flask, n. [1. thĕrmos flàhsk; 2. þʎmos flɑ̀sk]. Proprietary trade name, fr. Gk. *thermós*, 'hot', see **therm**. A kind of vacuum flask or bottle used for keeping liquids contained in it hot or cold; also *thermos*.

thermostat, n. [1. thĕrmōstàt; 2. þʎmoustǽt]. See **thermo-** & **static**. Device for regulating temperature automatically.

thermostatic, adj. [1. thĕrmōstátik; 2. þʎmoustǽtik]. Prec. & **-ic**. Pertaining to, carried out by, a thermostat.

thermostatics, n. [1. thĕrmōstátiks; 2. þʎmoustǽtiks]. See prec. & **-ics**. Branch of the science of heat dealing with the equilibrium of heat.

thermotaxic, adj. [1. thĕrmōtáksik; 2. þʎmoutǽksik]. **thermo-** & **taxis** & **-ic**. Pertaining to the regulation of bodily heat.

thermotensile, adj. [1. thĕrmōténsil; 2. þʎmouténsɪl]. Pertaining to variation in tensile force when affected by temperature.

thermotherapy, n. [1. thĕrmōthérapi; 2. þʎmouþérəpi]. The treatment of disease by heat.

thermotype, n. [1. thĕrmōtīp; 2. þʎmoutaɪp]. Impression of an object, e.g. a section of wood &c., produced by damping the object with dilute acid, taking a print from it, and developing this print by the application of heat.

theroid, adj. [1. thĕroid; 2. þíərɔɪd]. Gk. *thēr*, 'wild beast', see **theriac**, & **-oid**. Resembling a beast; like an animal in appearance and habits: *theroid idiot*.

therology, n. [1. thĕróloji; 2. þɪərólədʒi]. Gk. *thēr*, '(wild) beast', as in prec., & **-logy**. Study of mammals.

thesaurus, n. [1. thĕsórus; 2. þɪsɔ́rəs]. Lat., fr. Gk. *thēsaurós*, 'treasure; treasure house'; origin unexplained; prob. a primitive compound. A treasury; esp. a treasury or collection of words, phrases, literary extracts or the like; a lexicon.

these, demonstr. pron. [1. dhēz; 2. ðiz]. Pl. of **this**.

thesis (I.), n. [1. thésis; 2. þésis]. Gk. *thésis*, 'a setting, placing, arranging', fr. base in *títhēmi*, 'I set, place'; cogn. w. Engl. **do (I.)** & Lat. *facere*, 'do, make', see **fact**, & cp. **theme**. (pros.) The accented part of a metrical foot; contrasted with *arsis*, the unaccented part.

thesis (II.), n. [1. thésis; 2. þísis]; more rarely [1. thésis; 2. þésis]. Same as prec. **1**. Something advanced, maintained, laid down; a proposition. **2**. Specif., formerly, a proposition advanced and publicly disputed, defended, or maintained by a candidate for a university degree; hence, a dissertation, essay, treatise, written for purposes of a degree examination, embodying the candidate's research.

Thespian, adj. & n. [1. théspian; 2. þéspiən], fr. Gk. *Théspis*, supposed founder of Gk. drama, & **-an**. **1**. adj. Connected with the drama, or with acting. **2**. n. An actor.

theurgic(al), adj. [1. theĕrjik(l); 2. þɪǽdʒik(l)]. **theurgy** & **-ic** (& **-al**). Magical.

theurgist, n. [1. theĕrjist; 2. þíǽdʒist]. **theurgy** & **-ist**. A magician.

theurgy, n. [1. theĕrji; 2. þíǽdʒi]. Gk. *theourgía*, 'miracle', see **theo-**, 'God', & *érgon*, 'work', see **erg**. **a** A Divine work, miracle; **b** sorcery, magic.

thewed, adj. [1. thūd; 2. þjūd]. See **thews**. Having thews of specified kind.

thewless, adj. [1. thūles; 2. þjúlɪs]. **thew(s)** & **-less**. Lacking physical strength; lacking mental or moral fibre.

thews, n. pl. [1. thūz; 2. þjūz]. O.E. *þeaw*, 'custom, habit'; later, 'strength'; still used by Spenser in sense of 'manners, behaviour': *three daughters, well upbrought In goodly thewes, and godly exercise* ('F.Q.' I. x. 4); cogn. w. O.S. *thau*, 'habit, custom'; O.H.G. *thau*, 'discipline'; etymol. doubtful. **1**. Sinews, muscles; esp. *thews and sinews*. **2**. Moral or mental fibre, robustness, vigour.

thewy, adj. [1. thūi; 2. þjúi]. See prec. & **-y**. Muscular, sinewy.

they, pers. pron. of 3rd pers. pl. nom. [1. dhā; 2. ðeɪ]. M.E. *þei, thei* &c., fr. O.N. *þeirr*, wh. gradually takes the place of M.E. *hii* &c., fr. O.E. *hīe*; cogn. w. **the**.

thiasus, n. [1. thíasus; 2. þáɪəsəs]. Lat., fr. Gk. *thíasos*, etymol. doubtful. (Gk. antiq.) **a** Religious brotherhood formed in honour of a god; **b** the sacrifice, festival, of such a brotherhood.

thick (I.), adj. [1. thik; 2. þik]. M.E. *thikke* &c., prob. fr. O.N. *þykkr*; the O.E. cogn. *þicce* wd. result in **thitch*; O.S. *thikki* &c. O.H.G. *dicchi*; relations outside Gmc. doubtful. **1. a** (i.) Of great circumference relatively to length: *a thick bough, trunk*; *thick neck, legs, fingers*; (ii.) of great, or relatively great, depth laterally, from one surface to that opposite; reverse of *thin*: *a thick slice of meat, sheet of paper*; *thick cloth*; Phrs. (colloq.) *a bit thick*, of conduct, demands &c., hardly tolerable, too much of a good thing; of circumstances, fortune &c., hard to bear, exigent; **b** having, of, a specified thickness: *five-foot thick* &c. **2. a** (of fluids, vapours &c.) Having considerable density; of semi-solid consistency; inspissated; having component particles closely packed together; **b** (of a group of objects) placed close together, having small space between; dense: *a thick wood*; *corn standing thick*. **3**. (of water &c.) Muddy; turbid; reverse of *clear, limpid*: *the river looks thick after the rain*. **4. a** Frequent, occurring rapidly one after another, repeated; crowded, numerous: *with honours thick upon him*; *a thick shower of blows*; **b** full of, abounding in: *the air thick with rain, snow* &c. **5**. (of the voice, of sound) Dull; not distinct, resonant or ringing; reverse of *clear*. **6**. Dull of intellect, slow-witted, obtuse, dense. **7**. Intimate, much together, closely associated: *he and I are very thick*; Phr. *as thick as thieves*.

thick (**II.**), n., fr. prec. **1.** *The thick*, thickest, densest, part; place where most is taking place: *to plunge into the thick of the fight, of politics* &c. Phrs. *in the thick of it*, in the midst of, taking active part in, events, or affairs &c.; *to go through thick and thin*, face and overcome great difficulties, hardships &c. **2.** A person of thick wits, a blockhead.

thick (**III.**), adv., fr. **thick** (**I.**). Thickly: *the snow fell thick.*

thicken, vb. trans. & intrans. [1. thíken; 2. þíkən]. **thick** (**I.**) & **-en**. **a** trans. To make thick (in various senses); **b** intrans., to become thick.

thickening, n. [1. thíkening; 2. þík(ə)niŋ]. Prec. & **-ing**. **1.** Process of becoming thick, or thicker: *a thickening of the tissues.* **2.** Some thing or part which has become thick. **3.** Something which serves to thicken a liquid &c.

thicket, n. [1. thíket; 2. þíkit]. O.E. *þiccet*; Mod. form recast on type of **thick** (**I.**). Thickly wooded area, esp. one with dense undergrowth of low-growing shrubs and trees.

thicketed, adj. [1. thíketed; 2. þíkitid]. Prec. & **-ed**. Rich in thickets; covered with thicket.

thickhead, n. [1. thíkhed; 2. þíkhed]. A stupid person; a blockhead.

thickish, adj. [1. thíkish; 2. þíkiʃ]. **thick** (**I.**) & **-ish**. Rather thick.

thick-knee, n. Popular name of the stone-curlew.

thickly, adv. [1. thíkli; 2. þíkli]. **thick** (**I.**) & **-ly**. In a thick manner; **a** densely, closely; in such a way as to be, lie, thick: *thickly covered with snow*; **b** indistinctly: *to speak thickly*; **c** frequently, in rapid succession.

thickness, n. [1. thíknes; 2. þíknis]. See prec. & **-ness**. **1.** Quality of being thick (in various senses): *the thickness of his arms showed great muscular development*; *thickness of speech*; *thickness of intellect.* **2.** Amount by which, extent to which, a thing is thick; measurement other than in length and breadth: *a thickness of ten feet*; *three inches in thickness.* **3.** Thickest part of anything: *wounded in the thickness of the back.* **4.** Layer, fold, ply: *three thicknesses of felt.*

thickset, adj. **1.** [1. thíkset; 2. þíkset] Closely, densely, planted: *a thickset hedge.* **2.** [1. thíksét; 2. þíksét] Stumpy, stocky, short, and broadly, solidly, built; reverse of *slim, tall*: *a man who is sturdy and thickset.*

thick-skinned, adj. (chiefly fig.) Insensitive, having obtuse, blunted, sensibilities; slow to perceive or recognize subtle shades of feeling; not sensitive to the opinion of others.

thick-skulled, adj. Dense, stupid, mentally obtuse.

thief, n. [1. thēf; 2. þīf]. O.E. *þēof*, M.E. *þēf*, *thēf* &c.; O.S. *thiof*; O.H.G. *diob*; Goth. *þiufs*; etymol. unknown. **1.** Person who steals. **2.** (colloq.) Flaw in wick of a candle which causes this to gutter, thus wasting the wax.

thieve, vb. intrans. & trans. [1. thēv; 2. þīv]. O.E. *þēofian*. See prec. **a** intrans. To play the thief, be guilty of theft; **b** trans., to steal (a thing).

thievery, n. [1. thḗveri; 2. þívəri]. **thief** & **-ry**. The act of stealing; theft.

thievish, adj. [1. thḗvish; 2. þíviʃ]. **thief** & **-ish**. **1.** Addicted to thieving. **2.** Of the nature of theft: *thievish habits.*

thievishly, adv. Prec. & **-ly**. In a thievish manner; like a thief, dishonestly.

thievishness, n. See prec. & **-ness**. **a** Habit of stealing; **b** fact of being a thief.

thigh, n. [1. thī; 2. þai]. O.E. *þēoh*; M.E. *þēh*, *þīh*; O. Fris. *thiah*; O.H.G. *dioh*; cp. Lith. *táukas*, 'animal fat'; fr. base **teu-*, 'to swell', as in Lat. *tumēre*, 'to swell', see **tumid, tumour.** **a** The thick part of the leg in man, apes, and birds, and of the hind leg in quadrupeds, between the hip and the knee; **b** the bone of the thigh, the femur: *to break one's thigh.*

thigh-bone, n. Bone of the thigh; the femur.

thighed, adj. [1. thīd; 2. þaid]. Having specified kind of thigh: '*ostrich-thighed*' (Browning); *large thighed.*

thill, thiller, n. [1. thil(er); 2. þil(ə)]. O.E. *þille*, 'structure of planks, flooring' (fr. **þeli*); M.E. *thille*; cogn. w. O.E. *þel*, 'plank'; O.H.G. *dili*; O.N. *þilja*, 'plank'; cp. Mod. Germ. *diele*, & **deal** (**IV.**) (plank). Shaft of a cart.

thimble, n. [1. thímbl; 2. þímbl]. O.E. *þȳmel*, 'thumbstall', fr. *þūma*, see **thumb**, w. dimin. suff., see **-le**. **1.** Small cap of metal, bone &c. used to protect the finger when sewing. **2.** (naut.) Metal ring having the outer edge or surface grooved, fitted into a rope or sail, to prevent chafing.

thimbleful, n. [1. thímblfool; 2. þímblful]. Prec. & **-ful**. As much (liquid) as could be contained in a thimble; hence, a very small quantity of liquid.

thimblerig, n. & vb. intrans. [1. thímblrig; 2. þímblrig]. See prec. & **rig** (**III.**). **1.** n. Usually *thimblerigging*, swindling game at fairs &c., in which a player bets that he will detect under which of three small thimble-shaped cups a small pea or ball of pith is concealed, after the operator has rapidly and dexterously shifted it from one to the other many times; the swindle consists in the fact that there is often no ball under any of the cups. **2.** vb. To play this game; to swindle.

thimblerigger, n. [1. thímblrìger; 2. þímblrìgə]. Practitioner of thimblerigging.

thimblerigging, n. [1. thímblrìging; 2. þímblrìgiŋ]. **a** The game described under **thimblerig**; **b** (fig.) dishonest, unscrupulous practice.

thin (**I.**), adj. [1. thin; 2. þin]. O.E. *þynne*, M.E. *thinne*; O.H.G. *dunni*; O.N. *þunnr*; cogn. w. Lat. *tenuis*, 'thin, slender', see **tenuis**; Gk. *tanúein*, 'to stretch', & *tanu-* as in *tanú-glōssos*, 'long-tongued'; fr. base **ten-*, 'stretch', see **tend** (**II.**), **tense** (**II.**), & cp. **tone.** **1.** (of flat objects) Having small depth in relation to extent of surface; reverse of *thick*: *thin paper*; *a thin layer of butter*; *a thin blanket*; *a thin slice*; *thin clothes.* **2.** (of long objects) Having small circumference in relation to length; slender slim, tenuous: *a thin rope, chain*; *thin branch*; *thin fingers.* **3.** (of the animal body) Not thickly covered with fat or soft tissue; lean, gaunt, emaciated; reverse of *plump, stout, fat*: *arms too thin for beauty*; *thin in face*; *to look thin after an illness.* **4.** Widely spaced; not placed close together; sparse, scattered; reverse of *thick*, or *dense*: *hair rather thin on the top*; *thin growth of herbage*; also, *a thin audience, congregation* &c. **5.** **a** (of liquids, and gases) Rarefied, having small specific density; **b** (fig.) easily penetrated, refuted, or unmasked; transparent, flimsy: *a thin excuse, disguise, deception* &c. **6.** **a** Lacking in body, substance, richness: *thin ale, soup, porridge*; **b** (in non-material sense) lacking weightiness, solidity, intellectual substance and force: *the style of the book is elegant, but the matter is rather thin.*

thin (**II.**), vb. trans. & intrans., fr. prec. **1.** trans. To make thin (in various senses); **a** to reduce thickness of, make fine; **b** to weaken, make less dense; **c** to make sparser, by removing some: *to thin the branches of a tree*; *to thin out the shoots on a tree* &c. **2.** intrans. To become thinner (in various senses); also *thin down*, (of the body) to become thinner; *thin out*, (of an audience) to become sparser.

thine, possess. pron. of 2nd pers. sing. [1. dhīn; 2. ðain]. O.E. *þīn*, orig. genit. of **thou**; also declined as an adj. In M.E. *-n* is lost before words beginning with a consonant. See **thy.** (archaic, Bib., and liturgical) **1.** Possessive pronoun before vowel. **2.** Used absolutely: '*all that is in the heaven and in the earth is thine*' (1 Chron. xxix. 11).

thing, n. [1. thing; 2. þiŋ]. O.E., M.E. *þing*, also O.S. & O.N.; O.H.G. *ding*; the old meanings included those of 'object; action; event; condition; meeting'; cogn. w. O.E. *þingian*, 'to determine; settle, arrange; perh. connected w. Goth. *þeihs*, 'time, season', & *þeihan*, 'to advance, thrive', fr. Gmc. base **þiŋχ-*, Aryan **tenkkʷ-*, & further to be related to Lat. *tempus*, 'time', see **temporary** & **tempus.** At this rate the orig. meaning of *thing* wd. be 'something occurring at a given or fixed time, or under certain conditions', hence, 'event, circumstance, condition' &c., cp. Germ. *bedingen*, 'to make conditions, determine'. This is one of the words most highly generalized in meaning. **1.** **a** Any object that exists or is thought of as existing; whatever is conceived of as a separate object of thought; fact, idea; in the most general sense: *things of the intellect*; *the good things of life*; **b** a subject, topic, matter: *there's another thing I should like to speak to you about*; *he spoke of many things.* **2.** An inanimate object or what appears to be such: *to lose one's mind is to become a mere thing, devoid of life*; *what are those black things in the field?*; *not a thing to be seen anywhere.* **3.** (in pl.) **a** Personal property, belongings, baggage &c.: *I must collect my things at the station*; *take your things and go*; **b** specif., wearing apparel, clothes: *put on your things and come out for a walk.* **4.** (usually in pl.) **a** Circumstances, events, conditions of life &c.: *things are looking rather black for me*; *I want to think things over*; *I fear things are going wrong*; *I have many things to worry me*; Phrs. *that's a nice thing!*, ironic, expressing indignation; *it's a strange thing* (*that he doesn't write*); **b** (in sing.) action, aim: *the best thing* (*to do*); *the thing is* (*to say nothing for the moment*). **5.** **a** What is fitting or seemly: *it is not at all the thing to stare at people*; **b** what one wants, what is adapted to one's purpose: *a nice trout stream is the very thing for a holiday*; *a good thrashing would be the thing for him*; *just the thing*, exactly what is wanted. Phr. *not to look, feel, quite the thing*, to look, feel, unwell, out of sorts. **6.** (applied to persons) Expressing: **a** mild contempt, or indignation: *he's rather a stupid old thing*; *you're a horrid, mean, thing*; **b** affection, admiration (of women or children): *a dear little thing*; *a pretty little thing*; *a dear old thing*; **c** pity: *oh, poor thing!*; *the poor thing lost her husband in the War.*

thingamy, thingummy, n. [1. thíngumi; 2. þíŋəmi], also **thingumajig** [1. thíngumijig; 2. þíŋəmidʒig], **thingumbob** [1. thíngumbòb; 2. þíŋəmbɔ̀b]. Used for name of person or thing, when these escape the memory momentarily; equivalent to *what's-his-name, what-d'you-call-it.*

think, vb. intrans. & trans. [1. thingk; 2. þiŋk]. The form is derived fr. O.E. *þynćan*, 'to seem', see **methinks**, but the meanings come fr. the O.E. cogn. *þenćan*, 'to think' &c.; O.S. *thunkian, thenkian*; O.H.G. *denkan*; Goth. *þugkjan, þagkjan*, w. sense of corresponding O.E. vbs.; **thank** is also cogn. Outside Gmc. cp. Lat. *tongēre*, 'to know' (rare), wh. must be cogn., but other suggested connexions are purely speculative. **A.** intrans. **1.** To exercise the mental faculties, esp. to judge, draw inferences; to reason, ponder, reflect: *take time to think*; *learn to think clearly*; *unfortunately, he never thinks.* **2.** *Think about* (a person or thing): **a** to allow the mind to dwell upon: *to think about one's home and friends*; **b** to turn over in the mind, reflect upon: *I must think about it and let you know my decision.* **3.** To hold an opinion, to surmise, believe, expect; often contrasted with *know*: *I'm not sure, but I rather think so*; *I don't think, I know.* **4.** *Think of*, **a** to reflect upon: *think of what I told you*; **b** to allow to enter the mind, have in mind, contemplate: *it is so dreadful that I don't want to think of it*; Phr. *I shouldn't think of* (*doing such a thing*), emphatic for *I would not do*; **c** to dwell upon, have vividly before one: *to think of old times*; **d** to hit upon, invent, discover: *to think of a way out of a difficulty*; *what genius first thought of cooking?*; **e** to have an opinion concerning: (followed by qualifying adv.) *to think highly of a man*; *I don't think much of him.* Phrs. *to* *think better of*, reverse one's opinions, alter one's intentions ; *to think nothing of*, to disregard, attach no importance to. 5. *Think on, upon*, (archaic) same as *think of*. B. trans. 1. To conceive, imagine, have in mind : *to think evil* ; *to think no harm*. 2. To hold, esteem, consider, regard as : *I thought him a charming person* ; *to think oneself all-important*. Phr. (archaic) *to think scorn of*, to despise. 3. To surmise, believe, expect, that : *I don't think it will be very hot today* ; *are you coming with us? I don't think I will*. 4. To reduce to specified condition by thinking : *to think oneself into a fever*.

thinkable, adj. [1. thíŋkəbl ; 2. þíŋkəbl]. Prec. & **-able**. That can be thought of ; conceivable.

thinker, n. [1. thíŋkər ; 2. þíŋkə]. See prec. & **-er**. One who thinks ; a rational being ; a philosopher.

thinking, vbl. n. & adj. [1. thíŋking ; 2. þíŋkiŋ]. 1. n. The act of one who thinks ; thought, reflection : *you had better do a little hard thinking* 2. adj. Capable of thought, rational : *man is a thinking animal*.

thinly, adv. [1. thínli ; 2. þínli]. **thin (I.)** & **-ly**. In a thin manner ; sparingly ; flimsily.

thinness, n. [1. thínnes ; 2. þínnis]. See prec. & **-ness**. Quality, condition, of being thin.

thin-skinned, adj. (chiefly fig.) Sensitive ; easily offended, touchy.

thio-, pref. Form used in compounds, representing Gk. *theîon*, ' fumes of sulphur ', earlier *thweseion*, fr. base *dhwes-, *dhwos-, &c., ' spirit, breath ', see **theo-**. Containing sulphur ; e.g. *thio-acid*, an acid produced by substituting sulphur for oxygen in an oxygen acid ; *thionin*, the dark blue solution of a sulphur compound, used as a stain in microscopy.

third (I.), adj. [1. thërd ; 2. þə̄d]. O.E. *pridda*, M.E. *pridde* ; cp. Du. *derde* ; Goth. *pridja* ; Lat. *tertius* ; Gk. *trítos* ; see **three**. 1. Coming after the second ; specif. in *third person*, that expressed by pronouns *he, she, it, they*. 2. Forming one of three equal parts or divisions : *the third part of a ton*.

third (II.), n., fr. prec. 1. The person or thing coming next after the second in a series. 2. Third part ; one of three equal parts into which a thing or amount may be divided. 3. (mus.) Interval of four semitones.

third degree, n. (chiefly U.S.A.) Severe examination or treatment of prisoner by police to extort an admission.

thirdly, adv. [1. thërdli ; 2. þə̄dli]. **third (I.)** & **-ly**. In the third place.

third man, n. (cricket) Fielder placed rather deep on the offside between point and slip.

third party, n. (law) A party in a case other than the two principals ; *third party risks*, (insurance) of damage to persons not mentioned in policy.

third-rate, adj. Third in order of merit or quality ; hence, inferior, mediocre.

thirst (I.), n. [1. thërst ; 2. þə̄st]. O.E. *pyrst*, M.E. *thurst, thirst* ; O.S. *thurst* ; O.H.G *darst*, Goth. *paurstei* ; cp. also Goth. *paursus*, ' parched, dry ' ; cogn. w. Lat. *torrēre* for *tors-*, ' to parch, dry up ', see **torrid** ; Gk. *térsomai*, ' I become dry '. 1. a (in living animals) Sensation caused by prolonged abstinence from drinking ; natural craving for liquid ; b (fig., of ground, plant life &c.) condition of extreme dryness caused by prolonged lack of moisture, condition in which the earth &c. rapidly absorbs moisture. 2. a Craving for spiritual or intellectual nourishment : *a thirst for knowledge, for ghostly comfort* &c. ; hence, b powerful desire, yearning, craving in general : *a thirst for pleasure, excitement* &c.

thirst (II.), vb. intrans., fr. prec. 1. (absol., archaic) To experience thirst, to have a need of liquid in the system, to crave for something to drink : *I thirst*, now replaced by *I am thirsty*. 2. *Thirst for* : a to experience a powerful craving for liquid refreshment : *to be thirsting for a drink* ; b to crave, desire strongly and eagerly : *to thirst for information, for new sensations, for amusement* &c. ; also (rarer, except in fig. sense) *thirst after* ; *to thirst after new experiences*.

thirsty, adj. [1. thërsti ; 2. þə̄sti]. O.E. *pyrstig* ; see **thirst (I.)** & **-y**. 1. a Experiencing thirst, desiring to drink ; b causing thirst : *haymaking is thirsty work*. 2. Lacking moisture ; parched, dried up : *thirsty soil*.

thirteen, adj. & n. [1. thërtén ; 2. þə̄tín]. O.E. *préotēne* ; see **three & ten**. 1. adj. Cardinal numeral, one more than twelve. 2. n. a The number greater by one than twelve, or by three than ten ; b symbol representing this number.

thirteenth, adj. & n. [1. thërtẹnth ; 2. þə̄tínþ]. New formation fr. prec. & **-th** ; O.E. *prēotēopa*. 1. adj. a Next in order after the twelfth ; b being one of 13 equal parts. 2. n. One of thirteen equal parts.

thirtieth, adj. & n. [1. thërtieth ; 2. þə̄ti-iþ]. See next word & **-th**. 1. adj. a Next in order to twenty-ninth ; b being, making, one of thirty equal parts. 2. n. One of thirty equal parts.

thirty, adj. & n. [1. thërti ; 2. þə̄ti]. O.E. *prittig*, M.E. *pritty, thritty, therty* &c. ; see **three** & **-ty**. 1. adj. Being the amount of three times ten. 2. n. a A cardinal number, the sum of three tens ; b symbol expressing this ; c *the thirties*, (i.) that part of a century covering the time from the years thirty to thirty-nine of the century ; (ii.) period of a person's life from the ages of thirty to thirty-nine : *just out of one's thirties*.

this, demons. adj. & pron. [1. dhis ; 2. ðis]. O.E. *pis*, neut. sing. ; cp. **the** & **that**. 1. adj. a Referring to, indicating, person or thing actually present, or near to, the speaker ; often to something pointed to or touched when referred to in uttered speech ; contrasted with *that* ; b (i.) referring to present time or a current period : *this very moment* ; *this week, year* &c. ; (ii.) referring to a specified time, or if several periods or points of time are mentioned, to the last of these : *by this time (that which I have just referred to) the king was past all earthly help*. 2. pron. a In senses corresponding to above ; for *this one*, the thing here, near me, which I now point out to you : *the last house you had was charming, but this is not nearly so nice* ; b often referring to facts, actions, circumstances, situations &c., just mentioned, and assumed to be uppermost in the minds of hearers, and immediate to them : *what's all this?* = this confusion &c. ; *this will never do* ; *you mustn't behave like this* (as you are behaving) ; *I don't like this at all*, what has just happened, is happening, or of which you have just told me.

thisness, n. [1. dhísnes ; 2. ðísnis]. Prec. & **-ness**. (philosophical term) Quality of being this ; feeling of present reality.

thistle, n. [1. thísl ; 2. þísl]. O.E. *pistel* ; cp. O.H.G. *distila* ; O.N. *pistell*. One of various plants with purple flowers and prickly leaves and stalks. Phrs. *to grasp the thistle firmly*, to face, and deal with, difficulties, awkward situations &c. resolutely ; *Order of the Thistle*, the Scottish order of knighthood.

thistle-down, n. Light substance from ripe seed-vessel of the thistle which floats in the air and carries the seeds far and wide.

thistly, adj. [1. thísli ; 2. þísli]. **thistle** & **-ly**. a Resembling a thistle ; prickly ; b abounding in thistles.

thither, adv. & adj. [1. dhídher ; 2. ðíðə]. O.E. *pider* ; fr. demonstr. base as in *that, the, this*, & adv. suff. *-pra, -ō*, cp. Goth. *paprō*, ' thence ', & see **hither**. 1. adv. a To that specified place ; b to, towards, that direction, place, point, stage, result : *he has not yet joined the Church of Rome, but is tending thither*. 2. adj. (rare) a Lying beyond, on the other side (from the speaker) : *the thither side o the stream* ; b being beyond, farther from a specified point of time : *on the thither side of 40*.

thlipsis, n. [1. thlípsis ; 2. þlípsis]. Gk. *thlîpsis*, ' pressure ; oppression, affliction ' ; cp. *thlíbein*, ' to press, crush ', also *phlíbein*, the *th-* being prob. due to the influence of *thláō*, ' crush ' &c. ; the orig. form of *phlíb-* is *bhligʷ-*, whence also Lat. *flīgere*, ' strike ', see **afflict, inflict** ; Goth *bliggwan*, ' to strike, kill ', is prob. not connected. (med.) External compression of blood-vessels.

tho'. See **though**.

thole (I.), vb. trans. [1. thōl ; 2. poul]. O.E. *polian*, ' to endure, suffer ', M.E. *tholien, thōlen* ; O.S. *tholōn*, O.H.G. *dulēn* ; Goth. *pulan* ; fr. base *tel-, *tol- &c., ' to bear ' ; see further under **tolerate**. (archaic or provinc.) 1. To endure, bear, sustain, undergo. 2. To tolerate, suffer, permit, to stand.

thole (II.), thole-pin, n. O.E. *pol*, ' rowlock ' ; cp. Dan. *tol*, ' a stopple, thole, pin ' ; Swed. *tull*, ' thole ' ; *tall*, ' pine tree ' ; O.N. *pollr*, ' fir tree ' ; prob. fr. the base *tu-*, ' to swell ' ; see **tumid**. Peg in the gunwale of a rowing-boat, serving as fulcrum for the oar ; generally *thole-pin*.

Thomism, n. [1. tōmizm ; 2. tóumizəm]. After St. Thomas Aquinas (1225–74). Doctrines of Thomas Aquinas and his followers in philosophy and theology.

Thomist, adj. & n. [1. tōmist ; 2. tóumist]. See prec. & **-ist**. 1. adj. Also *Thomistic(al)* ; pertaining to the doctrines or followers of Thomism. 2. n. Adherent of Thomism.

thong, n. [1. thong ; 2. þoŋ]. O.E. *pwāng*, M.E. *pwōng* ; cp. O.N. *pvengr*, ' thong, latchet ' ; perh. cogn. w. **twinge**. Narrow strip of leather, a strap, as used for a rein, or for fastening harness &c. together, as a lash to a whip &c.

thoracic, adj. [1. thōrásik ; 2. þōrǽsik]. thorac- stem of **thorax**, & **-ic**. Connected with, situated on or in, the thorax.

thoraco-, pref. Form of **thorax** used in compounds, e.g. *thoracotomy*, (surg.) opening of the chest cavity.

thorax, n. [1. thōraks ; 2. þóræks]. Gk. *thōrax*, ' breastplate ; the chest ' ; Boisacq connects w. Scrt. *dhārayati*, ' he holds, supports '. a That part of the body of vertebrates between the neck and the abdomen, consisting of the ribs and breast-bone and the cavity enclosed by these ; b the second or middle segment of the body of an insect.

thorite, n. [1. thōrīt ; 2. þóraīt], fr. name of *Thor*, anct. Scand. god, see **Thursday**, & **-ite**. Mineral of blackish-brown colour found in Norway, a silicate of thorium.

thorium, n. [1. thōrium ; 2. þóriəm]. Mod. Lat., formed fr. prec. A rare metallic element, occurring in combination in thorite &c. ; it is highly radio-active, and the oxide is used in making incandescent gas-mantles.

thorn, n. [1. thorn ; 2. þōn]. O.E. *porn*, ' a thorn, prickle ; thorn tree ', also *pyrne*, ' thorn tree ' ; O.S. *thorn* ; Goth. *paurnus* ; cogn. w. O. Slav. *trŭnŭ*, ' Scrt. *tṛna-*, ' grass blade '. 1. A spiky excrescence, spine, prickle, growing from the stems and boughs of certain trees ; specif., one growing on a thorn tree, a rose, a bramble &c. Phrs. *no rose without a thorn*, all beautiful and pleasant things are liable to possess other, less desirable, qualities ; pleasure is often attended with pain ; *a thorn in one's side*, person or thing which is a constant source of annoyance ; *thorn in the, one's, flesh*, a secret but disabling infirmity. 2. The typical thorn-bearing tree, the hawthorn, or may tree. 3. The Old English name for the letter þ.

thornbill, n. [1. thórnbil ; 2. þōnbil]. S. American humming-bird with long, pointed bill.

thornless, adj. [1. thórnles ; 2. þónlis]. **thorn** & **-less**. Having no thorns.

thorny, adj. [1. thórni ; 2. þóni]. See prec. & **-y**. 1. Plentifully furnished with thorns. 2. (fig.) Difficult, arduous, painful : *a thorny subject*, one giving rise to differences of opinion and controversy. Phr. (*to tread*) *a thorny path*, pursue a difficult, arduous course of action.

thorough, adj. [1. thúro; 2. þárə]. O.E. *þuruh*, variant of *þurh*, see **through**. Complete, absolute, out-and-out, to the core, through and through: *a thorough blackguard; a thorough rest, holiday* &c.

thorough-bass, n. 1. System of musical notation in which chords are expressed by figures placed beneath the bass part. 2. Theory of harmony.

thorough-bred, adj. & n. 1. adj. **a** (of animals) Pure-bred; specif., sprung entirely from ancestors who are in the official pedigrees of the particular species, e.g. in the Stud Book in case of horses; **b** (of human beings) having the characteristics of aristocratic lineage; hence high-spirited, of lofty and dauntless character and distinguished bearing. 2. n. A thoroughbred animal or person.

thoroughfare, n. [1. thúrofār; 2. þárəfɛə]. A street or road through which traffic, on foot or wheels, may pass uninterruptedly, as contrasted with a cul-de-sac or a private road.

thorough-going, adj. Carried out completely, uncompromising, out-and-out: *thorough-going reforms; a thorough-going disciplinarian*.

thoroughly, adv. [1. thúroli; 2. þárəli]. **thorough** & **-ly**. In a thorough manner; completely: *a thoroughly bad man; to do a thing thoroughly*.

thoroughness, n. [1. thúrones; 2. þárənis]. See prec. & **-ness**. Quality of being thorough; completeness.

thorough-paced, adj. Originally of a horse, thoroughly trained in all its paces; hence thorough, out-and-out: *a thorough-paced rascal*.

thorp(e), n. [1. thorp; 2. þɔp]. O.E. *þorp*, 'village'; O.S. *thorp*; O.N. *þorp*; cogn. w. Germ. *dorf*, 'village'; Goth. *þaurp*; cogn. w. Lith. *trobà*, 'house, building'; W. *tref*, 'hamlet'; some authorities regard this group of words as cogn. w. Lat. *trabs*, 'beam', see **trabeated**; others deny this, & connect *thorp* w. Lat. *turba*, 'crowd, mob', see **turbulent**. Obs. except in Place-Names, orig. in sense of 'village'; occurring also in forms *-thrup, -trup; -threp, -trip*; cp. O.E. variants *þrop, -þrep*.

those, demons. pron. [1. dhōz; 2. ðouz]. O.E. *þās*, nom. & acc. pl. of *þes* &c., 'this'. Pl. of **that**.

thou, pron. of 2nd pers. sing. [1. dhou; 2. ðau]. O.E. *þū*, M.E. *thū, thou*; O.S. *thu*; Goth. *þu*; cogn. w. Lat. *tū*; Gk. (Doric) *tu*, (Attic) *su*; O. Slav. *toi*. Now entirely replaced by *you*, & obs. except in dial., poet., Bib., & Liturgical Engl., or in prayers to God; formerly used by the Quakers, who, however, now use *thee* as nom. in addressing a single person.

though, tho', conj. & adv. [1. dhō; 2. ðou]. M.E. *þogh, though* &c., fr. O.N. *þō*; cp. O.S. *thōh*; Goth. *þauh*; O.H.G. *doh*; the O.E. cogn. *þēah, þēh* &c. wd. produce *they or *thy in Mod. Engl., & survives as *thei* &c. in M.E. **1.** Although, notwithstanding that: *he seems perfectly healthy, though his heart is said to be weak; he made a number of debts though he had a large income*. **2.** *As though*, as if: *I felt as though I should die of hunger; it looks as though he wasn't coming after all*. **3.** (archaic) Even if, notwithstanding that: *though I were starving, I would not ask a favour of him*. **4.** (introducing a statement) All the same, nevertheless, in spite of this: *I will come, though I don't expect to enjoy myself; (also absol.) I'll come and see you tomorrow—I can only stay a few minutes, though*.

thought (I.), n. [1. thawt; 2. þɔt]. O.E. n. is *(ge)peaht*; M.E. *þought* is due to association w. P.P. type of **think**. **1. a** Act or process of thinking; reflection, cogitation: *to spend whole hours in thought; absorbed in thought*; **b** chain of reasoning, series of consecutive reasonings and reflections: *a pity he does not put more thought into his books*; **c** body of ideas and opinions based on consecutive reasoning which are current at a given time, esp. about a given subject: *modern thought rejects many of the old theological dogmas; scientific thought in the 19th century*. **2.** Solicitude, care, as resulting from reflection: *to take thought for, be anxious about; I am grateful for your kind thought of me in sending back my umbrella*. **3. a** The result of thinking and reflection; an idea, conception: *a great and noble thought; a striking and original thought; my mind is full of dismal thoughts*; **b** an opinion, belief: *I have very few thoughts on the subject*. Phrs. *on second thoughts*, after thinking it over; *second thoughts are best*. **4.** A slight, trifling, amount: *he looked a thought more serious than when I saw him last*.

thought (II.), vb. O.E. *þōht(e)*, M.E. *þought(e)*; Pret. & P.P. of **think**.

thoughtful, adj. [1. tháwtfool; 2. þɔtful]. **thought** (I.) & **-ful**. **1.** (of persons and the mind) **a** Given to thought; reflective, contemplative; **b** serious, sad, pensive. **2. a** Expressing thought; full of thoughts: *a thoughtful lecture, book*; **b** characterized by thought: *a thoughtful ramble*. **3.** Solicitous, anxious, considerate (for others): *it was kind and thoughtful of you to call*.

thoughtfully, adv. Prec. & **-ly**. In a thoughtful manner.

thoughtfulness, n. See prec. & **-ness**. Quality, fact, of being thoughtful; solicitude.

thoughtless, adj. [1. tháwtles; 2. þɔtlis]. **thought** (I.) & **-less**. **1.** Not given to thought; heedless, careless. **2.** Lacking consideration for others; inconsiderate.

thoughtlessly, adv. Prec. & **-ly**. In a thoughtless manner.

thoughtlessness, n. See prec. & **-ness**. Quality of being thoughtless.

thought-reader, n. One who reads a person's thoughts; esp. one who practises thought-reading.

thought-reading, n. The power or practice of reading people's thoughts by telepathy or thought-transference.

thought-transference, n. Telepathy.

thought-wave, n. Supposed telepathic vibration.

thousand, n. & adj. [1. thóuzand; 2. þáuzənd]. O.E. *þūsend*, M.E. *thūsend*; O.S. *thusind*; O.H.G. *tūsunt*; Goth. *þūsundi*; origin unexplained. **1.** n. **a** The number of 100 multiplied by 10: *many thousands of times*; Phr. *one in a thousand*, unique, extremely good, person or thing; **b** symbol for this number. **2.** adj. **a** Consisting of ten times one hundred; **b** used to express an indefinite number: *I have told you a thousand times not to do that*.

thousand-fold, adj. & adv. [1. thóuzan(d) fōld; 2. þáuzən(d) fould]. **1.** adj. A thousand times as much or as many. **2.** adv. A thousand times; to a thousand-fold degree.

thousandth, adj. & n. [1. thóuzanth; 2. þáuzənþ]. **1.** adj. **a** Next in order to the nine hundred and ninety-ninth in a series; **b** occurring after a large number: *I told him for the thousandth time*; **c** consisting of, being, one of a thousand equal parts. **2.** n. One of a thousand equal parts.

thraldom, n. [1. thráwldum; 2. þrɔldəm]. Next word & **-dom**. State of being a thrall; servitude, bondage.

thrall, n. [1. thrawl; 2. þrɔl]. L.O.E. *þræl*, fr. O.N. *þræll*, 'bondsman'; M.E. *þrall*; fr. *prahil*, cp. O.E. *prægan*; & Goth. *þragjan*, 'to run'; cogn. w. Gk. *trékhein*, 'to run', & perh., remotely, w. Lat. *trahere*, 'to draw'. **1. a** A slave, bondman; **b** (fig.) intellectual, moral, emotional, slave. **2.** Servitude, thraldom.

thrapple. See **thropple**.

thrash, see also **thresh**, vb. trans. & intrans. [1. thrash; 2. þræʃ]. O.E. *þerscan*, 'to beat, batter'; thrash corn', M.E. *threschen*, O.H.G. *dreskan*; O.N. *þreskja*; Goth. *þriskan*. A. trans. **1. a** To beat, flog; **b** (colloq.) to surpass, outdo, win victory over in a contest. **2.** To beat the grain out of (wheat and other cereals), either with a flail or mechanically; also **thresh**. **3.** (fig.) *Thrash out*, to discuss thoroughly and elucidate; to clear up (a problem, difficulty &c.) by discussion. B. intrans. **1.** To thrash wheat &c. **2.** To move, toss, about violently.

thrasher, n. [1. thrásher; 2. þræʃə]. Prec. & **-er**. **1.** Person who, thing &c. which, thrashes; specif. **a** person who thrashes wheat &c.; **b** one who flogs (boys &c.); **c** agricultural implement for thrashing grain. **2.** A kind of large shark with long, whip-like tail; also called *fox-shark*.

thrasonical, adj. [1. thrăsónikl; 2. þreisɔnikl], fr. Gk. *Thrásōn*, name of a braggart, fr. *thrasús*, 'over-bold', & **-ic** & **-al**; *thrasús* is cogn. w. Gk. *thársos, thrásos*, 'courage, rashness'; cp. Scrt. *dhársati*, 'to dare'; & Goth. *(ga-)dars*, 'dared', Pret. of *daursan*, q.v. under **dare**. Boastful.

thread (I.), n. [1. thred; 2. þred]. O.E. *þræd*, M.E. *thrēd(e)*; O.H.G. *drāt*; fr. same base as O.E. *þrāwan*, 'to twist'; see **throw** (I.). **1.** A very fine cord of twisted fibres of flax, cotton, silk &c., used for sewing. **2.** A very fine line or filament of any substance; a fibre: *gold thread; a thread of light*. Phrs. *the thread of life; to hang by a thread*, to be in a precarious, dangerous, state or position. **3.** Spiral groove with sharp edges; cut in a screw. **4.** Consecutive, connected, series of thoughts, train of reasoning; sequence of ideas, statements: *the thread of a narrative, discourse* &c.

thread (II.), vb. trans., fr. prec. **1.** To put (a thread) through the eye of: *to thread a needle*. **2.** To put upon a thread; to string: *to thread beads*. **3. a** To make one's way along, cautiously, deliberately, or through difficulties and intricacies: *to thread the paths of a wood*; **b** to pick out, select, and traverse with care: *to thread one's way*.

threadbare, adj. [1. thrédbār; 2. þredbɛə]. **1. a** (of fabric, clothes &c.) Worn down, rubbed by wear, so that the nap or upper surface is worn off and the thread of woof becomes visible; **b** (of persons) wearing threadbare garments; shabby. **2.** (fig.) Well worn, lacking novelty; hackneyed: *threadbare arguments, jokes* &c.

threader, n. [1. thréder; 2. þredə]. **thread** (II.) & **-er**. Specif., machine for putting thread on screws.

threadlike, adj. [1. thrédlik; 2. þredlaik]. **thread** (I.) & **-like**. Filamentous; resembling a fine thread.

threadworm, n. [1. thrédwerm; 2. þredwām]. Minute, threadlike, intestinal worm.

thready, adj. [1. thrédi; 2. þredi]. **thread** (I.) & **-y**. **a** Composed of, covered with, thread; **b** resembling a thread in fineness.

threat, n. [1. thret; 2. þret]. O.E. *þrēat*, 'crowd, troop; violence, punishment; threat'; cp. also O.E. *prēatian*, 'to afflict, threaten, compel by threats'; O.H.G. *(ir)driozan*; Goth. *(us)priutan*, 'to vex'; cogn. w. Lat. *trūdere*, 'to thrust'; O. Slav. *truditi*, 'to afflict', & *trudŭ*, 'oppression'; see also words ending in *-trude*, as **intrude, extrude** &c., & see **thrust**. **1.** Statement of intention to injure, punish, cause pain to &c.; menace: *to utter threats of violence, revenge* &c. **2.** Situation, circumstance, set of conditions, which seems to make probable the occurrence of something undesired; menace: *a threat of rain, drought* &c.

threaten, vb. trans. & intrans. [1. thrétn; 2. þretn]. O.E. *þrēatnian*, 'to urge, compel'; see prec. A. trans. **1.** To utter a threat to (a person), state intention of injuring, punishing &c.; also *threaten with*, to express intention of hurting, punishing &c. in a specified way: *he was threatened with imprisonment if he should ever transgress in the same way again*. **2.** To state intention to inflict: *to threaten immediate retribution upon evil-doers*. **3.** To present appearance, manifest a probability, of immanent occurrence, approach &c.; to menace: *the look of the sky threatens rain; danger and disaster threaten us on every side*. B. intrans. **1.** To utter threats: *Sir, do you mean to threaten?* **2.** To appear likely to occur, approach &c.: *if danger threatens, it* *is all the more important to keep an unmoved mind.*

threatening, adj. [1. thrétning; 2. þrétniŋ]. **a** Menacing, expressing threats; **b** portending, indicating, disaster or some unwished-for occurrence: *a threatening sky.*

three, adj. & n. [1. thrē; 2. þrī]. O.E. *þrēo*, fem., *þrī*, masc., O.S. *thria*, *threa*; O.H.G. *drī*; Goth. *þreis*; Lat. *trēs*, *tria*; Gk. *treis*, *tría*; Scrt. *tri*. **1.** adj. One more than two. Phr. *the three R's*, reading, writing, and arithmetic. **2.** n. **a** The number greater by one than two; **b** symbol representing this number. Phr. *rule of three*, in arithmetic, a sum in simple proportion.

three-colour process, n. Method or process of printing in colours, by use of three blocks, yellow, red, and blue, produced by photography.

three-cornered, adj. Having three corners or angles; triangular.

three-decker, n. **1.** Old-fashioned ship with three decks one above another. **2.** Obsolete form of pulpit having three floors.

threefold, adj. & adv. [1. thrēfōld; 2. þrīfould]. **a** adj. Thrice repeated; triple; **b** adv., triply.

three-halfpence, n. [1. thrē hăpens; 2. þrī héipəns]. **a** The sum of a penny halfpenny; **b** obsolete coin worth this amount.

three-legged race, n. [1. thrē légd, léged, rās; 2. þrī légd, légid, reis]. Race in which those taking part are linked together in pairs, in such a way that the right leg of one person is tied to the left leg of another, so that they must move at one and the same time.

three-master, n. Sailing-ship with three masts.

threepence, n. [1. thrépens, thrípens; 2. þrépəns, þrípəns]. The sum of three pennies considered as a monetary unit.

threepenny-bit, n. [1. thrépeni, thrípeni, bĭt; 2. þrépəni, þrípəni, bit]. The smallest English silver coin, of the value of three pence.

three-per-cents, n. British Government bonds yielding 3% interest.

three-ply, adj. Having, woven with, three strands (of thread, yarn &c.); also *three-ply wood*, of three thin plates or layers of wood glued together with grain arranged transversely.

three-quarter, n. One of the four backs in Rugby football, playing between the half-backs and the full-back.

threescore, n. [1. thrēskŏr; 2. þrīskō̌]. Three times twenty; sixty; *threescore years*, 60 years.

threesome, n. [1. thrēsum; 2. þrīsəm]. Game of golf played by three persons.

thremmatology, n. [1. thrèmatóloji; 2. þrèmətólədži], fr. Gk. *thremmat-*, stem of *thrémma*, 'nursling', & *-logy*; *thrémma* is connected w. vb. *tréphein*, 'to fatten, nourish', for *dhrebh-*, see **trophic** & cp. **thrombosis**. The science and art of breeding domestic animals.

threnetic(al), adj. [1. thrēnētik(l); 2. þrīnētik(l)]. Gk. *thrēnētikós*, fr. *thrēnos*, 'a dirge', fr. a variant of base *dhrew-* as in *thréomai*, 'I shout'; cp. Goth. *drunjus*, 'droning sound'; connected w. O.E. *drān*, see **drone (I.)**; cp. also O.E. *drēam*, 'revelry, joy', q.v. under **dream (I.)**. Mournful; of the nature of a dirge or lamentation.

threnode, also **threnody**, n. [1. thrēnōd, thrēnōdi; 2. þrénoud, þrínoudi]. Gk. *thrēnōidía*, fr. *thrēnos*, 'dirge', see prec. & **ode**. Funeral song, dirge, chant of lamentation.

threnodial, adj. [1. thrēnōdial; 2. þrīnóudiəl]. Prec. & -al. Threnodic.

threnodic, adj. [1. thrēnōdik; 2. þrīnóudik]. threnode & -ic. Pertaining to a threnody.

threnodist, n. [1. thrēnōdist; 2. þrénoudist]. threnode & -ist. One who sings or composes a threnody.

threnody, n. [1. thrēnōdi; 2. þrénoudi]. Threnode.

threpsology, n. [1. threpsóloji; 2. þrepsó-lədži]. Gk. *thrépsis*, 'nourishment', see **thremmatology** & **trophic**, & **-logy**. (med.) Theory of diet; treatise on this.

thresh, vb. trans. & intrans. [1. thresh; 2. þreʃ]. See **thrash**. Same as **thrash**; more commonly used of beating grain; (also fig.) *thresh out*, see *thrash out.*

thresher, n. [1. thrésher; 2. þréʃə]. Prec. & -er. Thrasher.

threshold, n. [1. thréshōld; 2. þréʃould]. O.E. *þerscold, -wold*, M.E. *threshwold*; cp. O.N. *þreskjǫldr*; fr. base *þersc-*, see **thrash**. **1.** Stone or plank immediately below a door; hence, entrance, to a building, house, room. **2.** (fig.) The entrance to, starting-point of something: *on the threshold of life*; *the threshold of new experiences, of a new order*. **3.** (psychol.) Usually *threshold of consciousness*, translating German *schwelle*, the lowest stage at which sensation becomes noticeable, the limen; cp. **subliminal**.

threw, vb. [1. throō; 2. þrū]. O.E. *þrēow*; M.E. *þrēw*; Pret. of **throw**.

thrice, adv. [1. thrīs; 2. þrais]. M.E. *thrīes*, fr. O.E. *þriga*, *þriwa*, 'three times', & genit. suff., used adverbially. See **three**. **1.** Three times. **2.** To a threefold degree; hence, merely as intensive, very much, thoroughly, fully: *thrice blessed, thrice happy.*

thrift, n. [1. thrift; 2. þrift], fr. O.N. *þrift*, 'prosperity'; connected w. **thrive**. **1.** Frugality; good, economical management; reverse of *extravagance, waste*. **2.** Genus of plant, *Statice*, esp. the sea-pink.

thriftily, adv. [1. thríftili; 2. þríftili]. **thrifty** & **-ly**. In a thrifty, careful manner; economically.

thriftiness, n. [1. thríftines; 2. þríftinis]. See prec. & -ness. Quality of being thrifty.

thriftless, adj. [1. thríftles; 2. þríftlis]. Wasteful, extravagant.

thrifty, adj. [1. thrífti; 2. þrífti]. **thrift** & **-y**. **a** Practising thrift; **b** exhibiting, betokening, thrift.

thrill (I.), vb. trans. & intrans. [1. thril; 2. þril]. O.E. *þyr(e)lian*, 'to pierce, perforate', M.E. *thirlen, thrillen*; still used in sense of 'pierce' by Spenser; cp. *þyrel*, 'hole', fr. *þurh*, 'through'; see **through (I.)**. **1.** trans. To cause profound emotional excitement in; to touch, cause glow of excitement in, stir, excite, penetrate deeply: *great actors thrill an audience to the point of pain*; *our hearts were thrilled by tales of heroism*. **2.** intrans. **a** To feel great emotional excitement; to be deeply stirred; to glow with enthusiasm, joy, indignation or the like; **b** to vibrate, tremble, tingle: *his voice thrilled through the hall.*

thrill (II.), n., fr. prec. Sensation of being thrilled; intense emotional stirring; a throb, glow: *a thrill of anticipation, of disgust, of terror* &c.

thriller, n. [1. thríler; 2. þrílə]. **thrill (I.)** & -er. One who, that which, thrills; specif., a highly sensational and exciting novel or play.

thrilling, adj. [1. thríling; 2. þríliŋ], fr. Pres. Part. of **thrill (I.)**. **a** Causing a thrill; stirring, exciting: *thrilling news*; **b** vibrant, penetrating: *a thrilling voice.*

thrips, n. [1. thrips; 2. þrips]. Gk., 'woodworm'; perh. having as fundamental meaning 'the borer', & fr. same base as O.E. *drīfan*, q.v. under **drive (I.)**. Name of various small insects which injure plants by sucking the vital juices.

thrive, vb. intrans. [1. thrīv; 2. þraiv]. M.E. *thriven*, fr. O.N. *þrīfa*, 'to grasp', prob. fr. reflex. *þrīfask*, 'to grasp oneself', hence 'to have oneself well in hand'. See also **thrift**. **1.** (of persons and businesses) To prosper, flourish, do well, be successful; specif., as a result of industry and thrift; (also in gen. sense) to flourish, grow strong: *wickedness of all kinds thrives in big cities*. **2.** (of living organisms) To prosper in health, grow fat and strong; to develop healthily and luxuriantly: *children thrive in good air*; *roses thrive in a heavy soil.*

thriven, vb. [1. thríven; 2. þriv(ə)n]. M.E. *þriven*; P.P. of **thrive**.

thriving, adj. [1. thríving; 2. þráiviŋ], fr. Pres. Part. of **thrive**. Prosperous, flourishing, successful.

throat (I.), n. [1. thrōt; 2. þrout]. O.E. *þrote*, M.E. *throte*; cp. O.H.G. *drozza*, 'throat', Mod. Germ. *drossel*; prob. cogn. w. Du. *strot(e)*, 'throat'. **1. a** The passage from the back of the mouth to the stomach and the lungs; gullet, windpipe: *sore throat*, inflamed condition of the lining of the throat; Phrs. *to stick in one's throat*, of words &c., (i.) to be difficult of utterance; (ii.) to be uttered with reluctance;(iii.) (of circumstances, actions &c.) to be repugnant to; *to ram, thrust, down another's throat*, force to accept against his will; **b** the external, front part of the neck, which covers the jugular vein: *to cut one's throat*, to commit suicide by severing the jugular vein, (also fig.) to adopt a dangerous or destructive course of action; *to take, seize, by the throat*, to strangle, throttle. **2.** A constricted passage, neck, as the narrowed part of a river, valley, pass &c.; the orifice of a vase &c.; specif. (archit.) a groove, channel, in or under the surface of a projection.

throat (II.), vb. trans., fr. prec. (archit., rare) To provide with a throat or groove.

-throated, adj. [1. thrōted; 2. þroutid]. Having a throat of specified kind: *red-throated*; *brazen-throated* &c.

throatiness, n. [1. thrōtines; 2. þroutinis]. See next word & -ness. Quality of being throaty.

throaty, adj. [1. thrōti; 2. þrouti]. **throat (I.)** & **-y**. **1.** (of the voice) Sounding as though produced in the back of the throat; muffled, not clear. **2.** (of persons) Having a sore, or sensitive throat; having a throaty voice.

throb, vb. intrans. & n. [1. throb; 2. þrob]. M.E. *throbben*; origin doubtful; possibly cogn. w. Lat. *trepidus*, 'agitated, anxious', & *trepidāre*, 'to bustle anxiously about; to move noisily and irregularly'; see **trepidation**. **1.** vb. **a** To beat, pulsate (as the heart, or a pulse): *his heart had ceased to throb*, i.e. he was dead; **b** to beat, palpitate, with abnormal rapidity or violence, as the heart &c., under stress of strong exertion or emotion: *his temples throbbed*. **2.** n. **a** A beat, pulsation, palpitation (of the heart &c.); **b** (fig.) a thrill, qualm.

throe, n. [1. thrō; 2. þrou]. O.E. *þrawu*, 'pain, punishment, affliction'; M.E. *throwe*, perh. influenced by the gradational variants O.E., M.E. *prowung*, 'affliction', *prōwian*, 'to suffer'; cp. O.N. *þrā*, 'pain, throe'. Great pain, anguish, access of pain, pang: *the throes of toothache, childbirth*. Phrs. *in the throes of*, in very general sense, struggling with, having come to grips with &c.: *in the throes of a spring-cleaning, a move* &c.

thrombosis, n. [1. thrombósis; 2. þrombóusis]. Gk. *thrómbōsis*, 'clot, coagulation'; cp. Gk. *tróphis*, 'fat, well-nourished'; see **trophic** & cp. **thremmatology**. Stoppage of a blood-vessel by a clot.

throne (I.), n. [1. thrōn; 2. þroun]. Lat. *thronus*, fr. Gk. *thrónos*, 'seat, chair; chair of state, throne; teacher's chair'; cp. also *thrânos*, 'a bench', *thrênus*, 'footstool'; cogn. w. Scrt. *dhārayati*, 'to support'; *dhárman-*, 'prop'; Lat. *firmus*, 'fast, firm', see **firm (I.)**. **1.** Chair, seat of state; specif. **a** official seat with canopy, occupied on ceremonial occasions by a king or other sovereign ruler; **b** official seat of archbishop or bishop, in a cathedral. **2. a** Royal power and authority: *loyalty to the king's throne and person*; **b** the king, or other sovereign ruler of a State: *it is rare in England that the throne is publicly attacked*. **3.** Superior order in the hierarchy of angels: '*Thrones, dominations, princedoms, virtues, powers*' (Milton, 'P. L.' v. 601).

throne (II.), vb. trans. & intrans., fr. prec. **1.** trans. **a** To place upon a throne, to enthrone; **b** (fig.) to accord a position of honour and dignity to; to esteem, venerate. **2.** intrans. (rare, lit. and fig.) To occupy a throne or position of honour.

throneless, adj. [1. thrṓnles; 2. þróunlis]. **throne (I.)** & **-less.** Without a throne; used of a deposed monarch.

throng, n. & vb. intrans. & trans. [1. throng; 2. þrɔŋ]. O.E. (*ge*)*þrang*, 'crowd, tumult'; cp. *þringan*, 'to press on, crowd; to afflict; to throng'; O.S. *thringan*; Goth. *þreihan*, fr. **þriŋχan*, 'to crowd round, press upon'. Etymol. doubtful; prob. not connected w. Lat. *truncus*, 'mutilated', see **truncate.** **1.** n. A crowd, a press of people; a multitude, host. **2.** vb. **a** intrans. To form, gather, into a throng; to crowd: *multitudes thronged to hear the new preacher*; **b** trans., to press, crowd into; to fill with a throng: *to throng the churches* &c.; (rarely) to crowd upon, press.

thropple, thrapple, n. [1. thrópl, thrápl; 2. þrɔ́pl, prǽpl], fr. O.E. *þrotbolla*, 'gullet, windpipe'; see **throat** & **boll.** (provinc. or rare) The throat.

throstle, n. [1. thrósl; 2. þrɔ́sl]. O.E. *þrostle*, M.E. *þrostel*; cp. Germ. *drossel* & O.N. *þröstr*; cogn. w. Lat. *turdus, turda*, 'thrush', for *(*s*)*tr̥zdos*; cp. Lith. *strãzdas*, 'thrush'; Gk. *strouthós*, 'sparrow'; **-le** is dimin.; see also **thrush (I.). 1.** The common song-thrush, mavis, *Turdus musicus.* **2.** Machine for spinning wool, cotton &c.; so called from the noise it makes.

throttle (I.), n. [1. thrótl; 2. þrɔ́tl]. Dimin. of **throat (I.). 1.** (colloq.) The throat. **2.** Valve in a machine which regulates flow of steam, gas &c.

throttle (II.), vb. trans., fr. prec. **1.** To impede breathing of, choke, by compressing the wind-pipe; to strangle. **2.** (fig.) To suppress, check: *to throttle discussion*; *to throttle trade* &c. **3.** (mechan.) To reduce flow of steam &c. in an engine or other machine; to lessen the speed in this way.

through (I.), prep. [1. throo͞; 2. þrū]. O.E. *þurh*, M.E. *thurgh, thurugh* &c.; O.S. *thurh*; O.H.G. *durh*; Goth. *þairh*; see **thorough, & thrill (I.)**, also *-tril* in **nostril. 1.** From one end to the other; traversing entire length, breadth, or depth; entering at one side or surface and coming out at opposite side &c.; penetrating the outer surface: *to get a bullet through the head*; *a wound passing through the cheek*; *to hammer a nail through the lid of a box.* **2.** Across; passing over the whole surface or extent of: *to travel through a country, continent* &c. **3. a** Along, surrounded by, moving in the midst of: *flying through the air*; *sailing through the water*; *walking through a wood*; **b** (also in non-material sense) *to pass, come, through dangers, tribulations, anxieties* &c. **4.** By way of; expressing penetration, traversing, of an intervening medium, opening, channel &c.: *to look through a window, through the keyhole* &c.; *hear sounds through a thin wall*; *to look through a telescope, listen through an ear-trumpet.* Phrs. *one can't see through a brick wall*, can't do what is impossible; (also fig.) *to see through a man, his character, a plot, scheme* &c., to detect faults and flaws in; not to be deceived by. **5.** Indicating channel, medium: '*But looks through Nature up to Nature's God*' (Pope, 'Ess. on Man', iv. 332). **6.** Expressing duration of time; during the whole of a specified period: *he won't last through the night*; *to stay through the autumn*; *to sit through a long sermon.* **7.** By agency of, by means of; by reason of; on account of: *I succeeded chiefly through your help*; *all his sorrows arose through the conduct of his son.*

through (II.), adv. See prec. **1.** From end to end, from side to side, so as to traverse entire extent from one end to the other: *to shoot, pierce, something through.* **2. a** From beginning to end: *to sing a song through*; *to read a book through*; **b** (of time) for the whole extent or duration of: *to sleep the whole night through.* **3.** Expressing completion; to the very end: *to carry one's plans through*; *to see a thing through*; *through and through*, in the whole substance, in all its parts, completely: *good sound material through and through*; *an honest man through and through.* Phr. *to be through with*, to have done with; to have completed, be quit of.

through (III.), adj. See prec. **1.** Going, passing, extending, through: *a through passage, way, channel.* **2.** Travelling direct from one place, station, or port, to another: *a through train, carriage, coach, boat.*

throughly, adv. [1. throo͞li; 2. þrū́li]. Prec. & **-ly.** (obs. and liturg. and Bib.) Completely, thoroughly: '*Wash me throughly from my wickedness*' (Psalm li. 2).

throughout, prep. & adv. [1. throo͞óut; 2. þrūáut]. **1.** prep. **a** Through every part of: *throughout the house*; **b** for whole duration of: *throughout one's life, the night, the war* &c. **2.** adv. **a** In, through, every part of; right through; in every particular: *this peach is ripe throughout*; *an honest man throughout*; **b** during the whole time: *it was a tedious discourse, but he sat perfectly still throughout.*

throve, vb. [1. thrōv; 2. þrouv]. Pret. of **thrive**, fr. O.N. *þrīfa*; M.E. *þrōf*, on the anal. of **drove (I.)** &c. Cp. the O.N. Pret. *þreif*, wh. is etymologically equiv. to the unrecorded O.E. **þrāf*, wh. wd. have become M.E. *þrōf*.

throw (I.), vb. trans. & intrans. [1. thrō; 2. þrou]. O.E. *þrāwan*, trans., 'to twist'; intrans., 'to revolve'; M.E. *þrōwen*; cogn. w. Lat. *terere*, 'to rub, wear away', see **termite** & **trite**; Gk. *tereîn*, 'to bore, turn', & *teírein*, 'to rub, wear, away', see **teredo. A.** trans. **1. a** To cause to fly through the air by a forcible movement, or jerk of the arm; to hurl, cast, fling, chuck: *to throw stones*; *to throw a ball*; *to throw a bone to a dog*; Phrs. (fig.) *to throw stones at*, to asperse, make imputations against; *to throw dust in the eyes of*, to hoodwink, deceive; *to throw a fly* (in fishing), make a cast; *to throw dice*, to fling them out upon the table; *to throw cold water on* (*a plan* &c.), to discourage (a person) in, make little of; **b** of other rapid movements, to cast &c.: *to throw a cloak round one*; **c** to upset (an opponent) in wrestling. **2.** To cast, propel, by mechanical means: *a big gun throws a heavy shell*; *a pump throws water.* **3. a** To direct, concentrate; to cause to appear: *to throw an angry, hasty, glance at*; *to throw a light on the scene*; *to throw a gloom on the proceedings*; **b** to cast: *to throw a veil of mystery over*; *the trees throw long shadows in the moonlight.* **4.** (of a horse) To dislodge from the saddle: *a horse that throws its rider.* **5.** To cast off, cast, slough: *a snake throws its old skin.* **6.** (of animals) To bring forth, give birth to: *a cow throws its calf, a mare its foal.* **7.** To bring into a specified condition, esp. suddenly, and by violent means: *to throw into confusion, into a state of agitation, into a fever* &c. **8.** To wind, twist (silk). **B.** intrans. To execute, carry out the act or process of throwing: *a long field must be able to throw*; *the fast bowler was thought by some to throw* (not bowl fairly). **C.** Followed by prepositions or adverbs. *Throw about*, trans., to fling in various directions, to scatter; also in special uses: *to throw one's arms about*, wave them; *to throw money about*, squander it. *Throw away*, trans., to waste, part with unwisely, sacrifice, lose through one's own act: *to throw money away*; *to throw away one's advantages.* *Throw back*, intrans., to reproduce, revert to the type of, a remote ancestor. *Throw down*, trans., **a** to overthrow, upset, overturn, cast down on the ground; pull down; Phr. *to throw down the gauntlet, glove*, to utter a challenge, to defy; **b** *throw oneself down*, to lie down with a sudden, forcible movement. *Throw in*, trans., to give over and above, in addition to what is bargained for, in return for an agreed price. *Throw off*, **1.** trans., **a** to fling aside, cast off, remove hastily: *to throw off one's clothes*; *to throw off one's disguise*; **b** to discard, repudiate, get rid of: *to throw off an acquaintance*; **c** to shake off, get rid of, recover from: *to throw off a cold, an illness* &c.; **d** to compose, utter, easily, without effort: *to throw off brilliant sayings, an epigram* &c.; **2.** intrans., to make a start with hounds at a hunt. *Throw* (*oneself*) *on, upon*, to trust to, commit oneself to; in Phr. *to throw oneself* (*up*)*on the mercy of.* *Throw open*, trans., **a** to open widely and suddenly: *to throw open a door*; Phr. *to throw open the door to* (*abuses* &c.), run the risk of, render possible; **b** to make widely accessible, permit entrance to: *to throw open the public parks on Sundays*; *to throw open one's house to all and sundry.* *Throw out*, trans., **a** to fling, cast out; specif., to eject, turn out: *to throw a rowdy out of a meeting*; **b** to reject, refuse to pass: *to throw out a bill in Parliament*; **c** to utter lightly and casually in passing: *to throw out a suggestion, a hint* &c.; **d** to build on; extend (a building) into: *to throw out a new wing, a bay window* &c. *Throw over*, trans., to abandon, give up: *to throw over a friend, a plan*; also *throw overboard.* *Throw up*, trans., **a** to toss into the air; Phrs. *to throw up the sponge*, acknowledge defeat, abandon the struggle; *to throw up a window*, lift the lower sash vigorously; **b** to pitch (a ball) in to a particular point, e.g. in cricket: *to throw the ball up to the wicket-keeper*; **c** to vomit, eject from the stomach.

throw (II.), n., fr. prec. Act or process of throwing something (in various special senses); **a** *a good, a straight, throw* (at cricket); *a throw of the hammer*; Phr. *a stone's throw*, a very short distance; **b** act of casting a fishing line; **c** act of casting dice: *it's your throw*; **d** act, manner, of throwing an opponent in wrestling.

throw-back, n. An individual of any species which reverts physically or mentally to an ancestral type.

thrower, n. [1. thrṓer; 2. þróuə]. **throw (I.)** & **-er.** One that throws; specific uses: **a** one who twists silk; a throwster; **b** person who shapes vessels on a potter's wheel.

thrown, vb. [1. thrōn; 2. þroun]. P.P. of **throw (I.)**; O.E. (*ge*)*þrāwen*; M.E. *þrōwen*.

throw-off, n. The start of a hunt.

throwster, n. [1. thrṓster; 2. þróustə]. **throw (I.)** & **-ster.** One who twists silk.

thrum (I.), n. & vb. trans. [1. thrum; 2. þram]. M.E., fr. O.N. *þrömr*, 'edge, brim'; cogn. w. Lat. **terminus. 1.** n. **a** The end of threads of warp on a loom after the web is cut; **b** any loose thread or yarn. **2.** vb. To cover with, provide with, thrums or fringe.

thrum (II.), vb. intrans. & trans. O.N. *þrumma*, 'to rattle'; prob. imitative in origin. **1.** intrans. To play carelessly, idly, noisily, or incorrectly (on a musical instrument); to strum; also *thrum on.* **2.** trans. To play (an instrument) badly, carelessly, incorrectly.

thrum-eyed, adj. (bot.) Having the anthers exserted, and visible at the throat of the corolla; contrasted with *pin-eyed.*

thrumming, n. [1. thrúming; 2. þrámiŋ]. **thrum (I.)** & **-ing. a** Act of, noise made by, one who thrums; **b** recurring beat, and accompanying sound, made by an engine when run.

thrush (I.), n. [1. thrush; 2. þraʃ]. O.E. *þrysće*; see **throstle.** One of several varieties of medium-sized singing birds, genus *Turdus*, with darkish plumage save on throat and belly, which are pale with dark spots; esp. the song thrush, *T. musicus*, and the missel-thrush, *T. viscivorus.*

thrush (II.), n. Cp. Dan. *tröske*; cogn. w. O.E. *þyrre*, 'dry', & *þyrst*; see **thirst (I.)** & **torrid.** (med.) Inflammatory affection of mouth and throat, occurring most frequently in young children.

thrust (I.), vb. trans. & intrans. [1. thrust; 2. þrast]. M.E. *thrusten*, fr. O.N. *þrýsta*; cogn. w. Lat. *trūdere*, 'to push, thrust'; see *-trude* in **extrude, intrude** &c., & cp. **threat. A.** trans. **1.** To push, shove, with a sudden, violent action: *to thrust a sword, a bayonet, a knife* &c., *into, or through, a body*; *to thrust one's fist in a person's face*; *he thrust his face into, close to, mine*; *to thrust a chair forward*; *to thrust one's hands into one's pockets, one's feet into a pair of slippers*; *thrust on*, put on with sudden, impulsive movement. Phrs. *to thrust one's way* (*through a crowd* &c.), to advance by pushing, and thrusting obstacles

aside; *thrust one's nose into* (*other people's affairs* &c.), interfere in, or with, uninvited. **2.** (reflex.) *Thrust oneself*, in various Phrs.: *to thrust oneself into* (*a good place* &c.), force one's way there; *thrust oneself forward*, (fig.) deliberately make oneself conspicuous, obtrude oneself; *thrust oneself into the society of*, obtrude oneself, force oneself into, intrude. **B. intrans. 1.** To make a thrust *at* (person &c.). **2.** To force oneself *through, past* &c.

thrust (II.), n., fr. prec. **1.** Act of thrusting; a sudden, violent push: *a thrust with the elbow*: **b** onset with a pointed weapon; a lunge: *a thrust with a sword*; blow delivered in this way: *a sword thrust*. **2.** (archit.) Outward pressure (e.g. against a wall) exerted by a weight from above. **3.** (min.) Breakdown of the roof of a gallery under weight from above.

thruster, n. [1. thrúster; 2. þrástə]. **thrust** (I.) & **-er**. Person who rides too close to, or over, hounds when hunting.

thud, n. & vb. intrans. [1. thud; 2. þad]. Cp. O.E. *þyddan*, ' to strike, thrust '. **1.** n. Dull sound, as of a heavy, solid, but not very hard, body falling from a height upon the ground. **2.** vb. **a** To make the sound of a thud; **b** to fall with a thud; also *thud down*.

thug, n. [1. thug; 2. þag]. Hind. *thag*, ' a deceiver, a robber '; Scrt. *sthaga*, ' a swindler '. **1.** Member of a fraternity of assassins and robbers in Northern India, suppressed in the late thirties of the 19th cent., whose method was to strangle their victims with a bow-string or a strip of linen, to plunder, and then bury the body. **2.** An assassin, a ruffian.

thuggee, n. [1. thúgē; 2. þágī]. Hind. *thagī*, ' the act of a thug '. System of murder by strangling as carried out by thugs.

thuggery, thuggism, n. [1. thúgeri, thúgizm; 2. þágəri, þágizəm]. **thug -ery**, or **-ism**. Thuggee; ruffianism.

thuja, n. [1. thúya; 2. þjújə]. Gk. *thuía*, Afr. tree with scented wood. The arbor vitae.

Thule, n. [1. thúlē; 2. þjúlī]. Name given by ancient geographers to the most northern of known lands, now only in Phr. *ultima Thule*, q.v. under **ultima**.

thumb, n. & vb. trans. [1. thum; 2. þam]. O.E. *þūma*, M.E. *þūme, thoumbe* &c.; O.H.G. *dūmo*, Mod. Germ. *daumen*; O.N. *þūmall*; fr. base *tūm-*, ' to swell '; see **tumid**; cp. also **thimble**. **1.** n. **a** The short, thick digit of the hand, opposable to the fingers; Phrs. *his fingers are all thumbs*, said of a clumsy person lacking manual dexterity; *rule of thumb*, any rough-and-ready, practical way of doing anything, a method not based on principles; *under the thumb of*, in power of; ruled, influenced, by; **b** the corresponding digit of animals; **c** the division of a glove which covers the thumb. **2.** vb. To wear, make dirty (the pages of a book &c.), by constant handling; to make thumb-marks upon.

thumb-mark, n. Dirty mark made by a person's thumb.

thumb-nut, n. One with a flattened top so that it can be turned by the thumb.

thumb-screw, n. Ancient instrument of torture, the functions of which are indicated by its name.

thumb-stall, n. Covering of leather &c. for protecting the thumb.

thummim. See under **urim and thummim**.

thump, n. & vb. trans. & intrans. [1. thump; 2. þamp]. Of imitative origin. **1.** n. Heavy blow inflicted with the fist or with a cudgel &c. **2.** vb. To inflict a thump or thumps upon, to pound with the fist.

thumping, adj. [1. thúmping; 2. þámpiŋ]. (colloq.) Very large, possessing to a marked degree some characteristic quality: *a thumping lie*; as adv., *a thumping* (*good, great*) *dinner*.

thunder (I.), n. [1. thúnder; 2. þándə]. O.E. *þunor*, M.E. *þuner, thunder* &c.; O.H.G. *donar*; cogn. w. Lat. *tonitrus*, ' thunder ', *tonāre*, ' to thunder ', & cp. **Thursday**. See also **astound**. **1.** Loud, crashing, or rumbling sound caused by electrical disturbance in the air. **2.** Loud sound bearing some resemblance to thunder: *thunders of applause*; *the thunder of the cataract*.

thunder (II.), vb. intrans. & trans. O.E. *þunrian*, see prec. **1.** intrans. **a** To emit thunder: *it is thundering*; *it thunders*; **b** to give forth a sound like that of thunder: *the waves thunder upon the shore*; *to thunder at the door*, knock loudly; **c** to speak in a loud voice, with powerful resonance; to roar: *preachers thunder weekly from a thousand pulpits*. **2.** trans. To utter with a loud, powerful voice: *to thunder words of warning in a person's ears*.

thunderbolt, n. [1. thúnderbōlt; 2. þándəboult]. **1.** Discharge of lightning and accompanying clap of thunder; so called from belief that the noise was caused by a bolt hurled by a god. Phrs. *it came upon me like a thunderbolt, was a regular thunderbolt*, a matter of overwhelming surprise, something entirely unexpected. **2.** Any of certain kinds of stone or fossils, supposed to have fallen from the clouds as a result of discharges of lightning. **3.** (her.) Representation of supposed thunderbolt, consisting of a bar with blazing ends, and four darts issuing from the centre.

thunder-clap, n. Clap of thunder.

thunderer, n. [1. thúnderer; 2. þándərə]. One who thunders; specif., *the thunderer*, one of the names of Jove.

thundering, adj. [1. thúndering; 2. þándəriŋ]. **1.** Making a sound like, as loud as, thunder. **2.** (colloq.) Very large, excessive; same as *thumping*, q.v.: *a thundering mistake*; *a thundering ass* &c.

thunderous, adj. [1. thúnderus; 2. þándərəs]. **thunder** (I.) & **-ous**. **1.** Thundery. **2.** As loud as, loud like, thunder.

thunder-storm, n. Storm of thunder and lightning.

thunder-struck, adj. Struck by lightning; (usually fig.) amazed, astonished, astounded.

thundery, adj. [1. thúnderi; 2. þándəri]. **thunder** (I.) & **-y**. (of weather) Tending to thunder, oppressive with thunder.

thurible, n. [1. thúribl; 2. þjúəribl]. Lat. *thūribulum*, formed fr. *thūri-*, stem of *thūs*, ' frankincense ', fr. Gk. *thúos*, ' sacrifice '; cp. *thúein*, ' to sacrifice '; orig. ' to cause to smoke ', fr. base *dhu-*, as in Gk. *thūmós*, ' passion, courage '; Lat. *fūmus*, ' smoke '; see **fume** (I.) & cp. **thyme**. A censer.

thurifer, n. [1. thúrifer; 2. þjúərifə], fr. *thuri-*, as in prec., & **-fer**. Person who carries a censer; an acolyte.

Thursday, n. [1. thérzdi; 2. þázdi]. O.E. *Þūres dæg*, fr. O.N. *Þōrr*, ' the god of thunder '; contracted fr. earlier *þonraz*, see **thunder** (I.). Day of the week following Wednesday and preceding Friday.

thus, adv. [1. dhus; 2. ðas]. O.E. *þus*, cp. **this, the, & that. 1.** In this (specified) way: *he spoke thus*. **2.** To this extent: *thus far shalt thou go*.

thwack, vb. trans. & n. [1. thwak; 2. þwæk]. Prob. a dialectal variant of **whack** (I.). **1.** vb. To thrash, flog, beat, belabour. **2.** n. A blow, a slap or thump.

thwaite, n. [1. thwāt; 2. þweit]. O.N. *þveit*, ' piece of enclosed land, i.e. land set apart or cut off from surrounding area '; cogn. w. O.E. *þwītan*, ' to cut ', q.v. under **whittle** (I.). (northern provinces and in northern Place-Names and surnames) Piece of wild or forest land cleared and cultivated.

thwart (I.), adv., prep., & adj. [1. thwort; 2. þwōt]. M.E. as adv., fr. O.N. *þvert*, neut. of *þverr*, ' across '; cogn. w. O.E. *þweorh*, ' across, crosswise '; perverse, angry '; Goth. *þwairhs*, ' angry '; prob. connected w. Lat. *torquēre*, ' to twist ' &c.; see **torque**. (obs. or archaic) Passing, lying, across. See **athwart**.

thwart (II.), n. See prec. Seat for oarsman in a boat.

thwart (III.), vb. trans. See **thwart** (I.). **a** To oppose will of; **b** to hinder, obstruct, prevent, fulfilment of (wishes, designs, intentions).

thy, possess. pron. of 2nd pers. sing. [1. dhī; 2. ðai]. See **thine & thou**. Of thee, belonging to thee.

thylacine, n. [1. thílasin; 2. þáiləsin], fr. Gk. *thúlax*, ' sack, pouch ', & *kun-*, stem of *kúōn*, ' dog '. Tasmanian marsupial, resembling a dog in appearance; greyish brown with darker stripes across back and hind quarters.

thyme, n. [1. tīm; 2. taim]. M.E. *tyme*, fr. O. Fr., fr. Lat. *thymus*, fr. Gk. *thúmos*; connected w. *thúein*, ' to sacrifice '; see **thurible**. Pungent, aromatic plant, *Thymus*, common in English gardens, with palish purple flowers; the leaves are used for flavouring in cookery; also the wild thyme growing on chalk downs &c.

thymol, n. [1. tímol; 2. táiməl]. Prec. & **-ol**. An aromatic substance obtained from the essential oil of thyme and other plants, also made synthetically, used medicinally as an antiseptic &c.

thymus, n. [1. thímus; 2. þáiməs], fr. Gk. *thúmos*, ' thyme ', q.v., fr. resemblance to shape of a bud of thyme. A small ductless gland, in upper part of the chest; it is one of the so-called sweetbreads of calves or lambs; its functions are obscure, but its enlargement is associated with ' status lymphaticus ', q.v.

thymy, adj. [1. tími; 2. táimi]. **thyme & -y**. Scented with, covered with, thyme.

thyroid, adj. & n. [1. thíroid; 2. þáiərɔid]. Gk. *thureoeidḗs*, ' shield-shaped '; fr. *thureós*, ' a large, oblong shield '; cogn. w. Gk. *thúrā*, ' a door '; see under **door & forum**; for ending see **-oid**. **1.** adj. Indicating a the ductless gland in the neck of vertebrates, which has an important effect on growth and metabolism: *thyroid gland*; *thyroid extract*, of sheep, used for metabolic diseases, such as goitre &c.; **b** the Adam's apple: *thyroid cartilage*. **2.** n. The thyroid gland or cartilage.

thyrsus, n. [1. thérsus; 2. þásəs]. Gk. *thúrsos*, ' a light wand '; etymol. unknown. A wand or staff; specif., a rod surmounted by a pine cone, and twined round with ivy or vine leaves and berries; the attribute of Bacchus.

thyself, pers. pron. [1. dhīsélf; 2. ðaisélf]. Reflex. & emphatic of **thou**.

tiara, n. [1. tiáhra, tiáhra; 2. taiɑ́rə, tiɑ́rə]. Lat., fr. Gk. *tiārā*; of Pers. origin. **1.** Ancient Persian head-dress. **2. a** Official head-dress of the Pope, consisting of a high conical cap, surmounted by three crowns, emblematical of the threefold sovereignty claimed by the Papacy, temporal, spiritual, purgatorial; **b** (fig.) the dignity and power of the Papacy. **3.** Jewelled head ornament or kind of coronet worn by women.

tibia, n. [1. tíbia; 2. tíbiə]. Lat. *tibia*, ' shin-bone; a flute '; Walde derives it fr. *twibh-*, whence also Gk. *siphōn*, see **siphon** (I.). (anat.) The larger of the two bones between the knee and the foot.

tibial, adj. [1. tíbial; 2. tíbiəl]. Prec. & **-al**. Pertaining to, connected with, the tibia.

tibio-, pref. Form of *tibia* used in compound words, e.g. *tibio*femoral, pertaining to the tibia and femur.

tic, n. [1. tik; 2. tik]. Fr., origin doubtful. Often *tic douloureux* [dūlūrā], a convulsive twitching of the facial muscles, associated with neuralgic pains.

tick (I.), n. [1. tik; 2. tik]. For **ticket** (I.). (slang) Credit: *to buy on tick*; *to get tick*.

tick (II.), n. Low Lat. *tēca*, Lat. *thēca*, fr. Gk. *thḗkē*, ' a case, cover '; fr. base of *títhēmi*, ' I put ', cogn. w. **do** (I.) & Lat. *facere*, ' to do, make ', see **fact**. **a** Outside cover of mattresses, bolsters, pillows; **b** coarse striped material of which this is made.

tick (III.), n. M.E. *tike, tēke*; cp. L.G. *teke*; Germ. *zecke*, origin unknown. Any of various parasitic arachnids, order *Acari*, which attach themselves to the skin of men or other animals and suck the blood of their hosts. Phr. *as full as a tick*.

tick (IV.), vb. intrans. & trans. & n. Imitative of sound. **1.** vb. **a** intrans. To make a slight, sharp, reiterated clicking, or tapping noise; specif. of a clock or watch, also of tape machine, to make the sound characteristic of the movements of the works; **b** trans., (i.) to mark with a small stroke of the pen or pencil placed against a word, name, letter &c.; Phr. (slang) *to tick off*, to reprimand; (ii.) also *tick out*, of tape machine, to give out the news on the roll of tape. **2.** n. **a** Sound made by clock or watch in ticking; **b** small mark or scratch of a pen &c.

ticker, n. [1. tíker; 2. tíkə]. Prec. & **-er.** (slang) **a** A watch; **b** a tape-machine.

ticket (I.), n. [1. tíket; 2. tíkit], fr. O. Fr. *estiquet*, see **etiquette**. **1.** Small piece of cardboard bearing necessary printed inscription, showing **a** that owner has paid the price charged for entrance to, and seat at, a concert, theatre, or other entertainment, or that he is for any reason entitled to go in; **b** that possessor has paid his fare for a railway or tram journey &c. Phrs. *to take tickets for the opera*; *to take one's ticket to Edinburgh* &c. **2.** Any of various short notices, announcements, printed on small cards or sheets of paper; e.g. a label indicating price of goods exhibited for sale: *price ticket*; brief document issued by pawnbroker when advancing money on an article left as a pledge: *pawn ticket*; or issued as certificate of share in a lottery &c.: *take a ticket in a sweepstake.* **3. a** List of political candidates for election, belonging to a particular party; **b** (fig.) the principles of a political party: *the Tory ticket.* Phrs. *the proper ticket*, orthodox ideas, behaviour &c.; *not quite the ticket*, not quite the right thing.

ticket (II.), vb. trans., fr. prec. To mark with a ticket, to affix a ticket to.

ticket-of-leave, n. [1. tíket uv lēv; 2. tíkit əv līv]. Permission granted to a convict to be at liberty, with certain restrictions, before expiry of his sentence. Phrs. *out (of prison) on ticket-of-leave*; *ticket-of-leave man*, prisoner released with such a ticket.

tickle (I.), vb. trans. & intrans. [1. tíkl; 2. tíkl]. Possibly freq. of **tick (IV.)**. **A.** trans. **1.** To excite, irritate, the superficial nerves and cause peculiar sensation, involuntary laughter, or slight spasm, by touching lightly and repeatedly some part of the skin; to titillate. **2. a** To please, gratify: *to tickle one's palate*; **b** to amuse, cause laughter, excite risibility in: *I was immensely tickled by his good stories.* **B.** intrans. **a** To experience a sensation of tickling, or irritation, on some part of the surface of the body; to itch, tingle: *my throat, nose &c. tickles*; **b** to cause, provoke, sensation of tickling: *nothing tickles so intolerably as a hair in the throat.*

tickle (II.), n., fr. prec. Sensation of tickling; tingling, irritation of superficial nerves: *a tickle in the throat.*

tickler, n. [1. tíkler; 2. tíklə]. **tickle (I.)** & **-er.** A puzzle, a difficult problem.

tickling, n. [1. tíkling; 2. tíkliŋ]. See prec. & **-ing.** A tickle.

ticklish, adj. [1. tíklish; 2. tíkliʃ]. **tickle (I.)** & **-ish. 1.** Sensitive to tickling, easily excited to laughter or irritation by tickling. **2. a** (of persons) Touchy, difficult to deal with; **b** (of affairs) delicate, hazardous, requiring skilful handling.

tick-tack, -tock, n. [1. tík tak, -tok; 2. tík tæk, -tɔk]. Reduplication of **tick (IV.)**. **1.** Childish name for a watch or clock. **2.** (slang, usually *tick-tack man*) A bookmaker's assistant who signals the change of odds and other news of a race from different parts of the course.

tidal, adj. [1. tídl; 2. táidl]. **tide (I.)** & **-al.** Connected with the tide or tides; specif. **a** experiencing alterations of tide: *a tidal river*; **b** caused by the tide: *tidal waves*; **c** sailing at times determined by the tide: *tidal steamer.*

tiddly-winks, n. [1. tídli wingks; 2. tídli wiŋks]. Child's game played on a table, in which counters are flipped from the edge into a receptacle in the centre.

tide (I.), n. [1. tīd; 2. taid]. O.E. *tīd*, 'time'; also O.S. & O. Fris.; O.H.G. *zīt*; see base under **time (I.)**. **1.** Period, season; obsolete except in *eventide, Christmastide, Whitsuntide, yule-tide*, and in proverb '*Time and tide wait for no man*'. **2.** Alternate rise and fall, ebb and flow, of the surface of the sea: *high, low, half, tide*; cp. also **neap- (I.)** and **spring-tide (II.)**. **3.** Trend, flow, tendency, **a** (in feeling and emotion) *the full tide of pleasure, passion* &c.; **b** (of circumstances and affairs) *the high tide of fortune.* Phr. *the turn of the tide*, reversal of fortune.

tide (II.), vb. intrans., fr. prec. **1.** (rare) To drift with the tide. **2.** Chiefly *tide over* (a difficulty &c.), to surmount, manage to overcome.

tideless, adj. [1. tídles; 2. táidlis]. **tide (I.)** & **-less.** Having no tide: *the Mediterranean is a tideless sea.*

tide-waiter, n. Custom-house official who boards vessels and watches landing of cargoes, to secure payment of duties.

tidewater, n. [1. tídwawter; 2. táidwōtə]. **tide (I.)** & **water.** (U.S.A.) **1. a** Water on sea-coast or in estuary &c., affected by tides; hence, **b** sea-coast. **2.** (attrib.) On, belonging to, the sea-coast.

tide-way, n. **a** Channel through which tide ebbs and flows; **b** ebb and flow of tide through such channel.

tidily, adv. [1. tídili; 2. táidili], fr. **tidy (I.)** & **-ly.** In a tidy manner.

tidiness, n. [1. tídines; 2. táidinis]. See prec. & **-ness.** State, quality, of being tidy.

tidings, n. pl. [1. tídingz; 2. táidiŋz]. Takes vb. either in pl. or sing. M.E. *tidinge, tīthinge, tīthinde*; prob. fr. O.N. *tiðindi*, cp., however, O.E. *tīdung*, fr. O.E. *tīdan*, 'to happen'; see **betide.** Piece of news, intelligence: *the good tidings*; *evil tidings.*

tidy (I.), adj. & n. [1. tídi; 2. táidi], fr. **tide (I.)** & **-y**, in sense of 'timely'; cp. Mod. Germ. *zeitig.* **1.** adj. **a** Orderly, neat, well-arranged; **b** (colloq.) considerable, of some size, amount &c.: *a tidy income*; *to leave a tidy sum to one's heirs.* **2.** n. **a** A small anti-macassar or chair cover; **b** small receptacle in which odds and ends of the dressing-table may be placed.

tidy (II.), vb. trans., fr. prec. To make tidy, to put in order: *to tidy a room, a garden*; *to tidy oneself*; also *tidy up* (*a room, myself* &c.); intrans., *I must just tidy up a bit*, put things in order.

tie (I.), n. [1. tī; 2. tai]. O.E. *tēah, tēh*, 'bond, chain; enclosure', M.E. *tēh, tēʒ(e), tīe*; cogn. w. O.N. *taug*, 'a string, a tie'; fr. Gmc. base **teuh-*, **tauh-* &c., 'to pull, draw'; cp. O.E. *tēon* (fr. **tēoh-*), 'to draw, pull', Goth. *tiuhan*, see **tow (I.)**, cogn. w. Lat. *dūcere*, 'to pull; to lead', see **duke**, & **duct. 1.** A knot, ligature, bond; rope, chain, string &c. used to fasten something. **2.** Specif., a strip of white lawn, or black silk, tied in a bow (evening tie), or folded piece of silk or other ornamental coloured material worn knotted round the neck; necktie. **3.** A bond, connecting piece, of wood, iron &c., used to hold together and make firm, or give support to, different parts of a structure; e.g. a wooden rod or spar fastened between two legs of a table or chair; a piece of timber, or an iron rod, used to hold together larger timbers in a building &c. **4.** A spiritual bond, connecting link of feeling between persons; a moral obligation: *the ties of parenthood, patriotism, friendship* &c. **5.** Object or circumstance the existence of which imposes certain duties and obligations that restrict one's actions, curb one's freedom &c.; a burden: *I find my large establishment rather a tie*; *a dog is a considerable tie if one has sole charge of it.* **6.** Equality of scores between two competitors in a sporting contest, or of votes between candidates in an election &c. **7.** Match or game played between pairs of opponents or teams, the loser or losing side being eliminated from the contest, the winner subsequently being matched against another winner, until all are eliminated but the winner in the final bout. **8.** (mus.) A curved line joining two notes of same pitch, indicating that the note is sustained for a period equivalent to the duration of both.

tie (II.), vb. trans. & intrans. O.E. *tēgan*, M.E. *tēʒen, tīʒen*; see prec. **A.** trans. **1.** To fasten, bind, attach, by means of a string, cord, rope: *to tie a branch of a rose to a trellis*; *to tie a horse to a tree* &c. Phrs. (fig.) *to tie the hands of*, to hamper, curtail freedom of; *to be tied hand and foot*, be completely hampered and hindered in freedom of action. **2. a** To form (a cord, string, strip of material &c.) into some kind of knot: *to tie one's tie*; *to tie a piece of ribbon into a knot or bow* &c.; **b** to form knot, twist &c.: *to tie a knot, a bow, a loop* &c. **3.** To make firm by connecting with a tie: *to tie the legs of a table.* **4. a** To bind, impose an obligation upon, force to act in a certain way: *I won't tie you too rigidly, but I expect you to do what I wish*; **b** to keep occupied, to engage; to hinder complete liberty of action: *my professional duties tie me for the greater part of each day.* **5.** To unite, bind: *to be tied to a wife.* **B.** intrans. **1.** To be capable of being tied or formed into a knot: *this rope won't tie.* **2.** (of two competitors in a contest) To make an equal score, obtain same number of votes &c. **C.** Followed by preposition or adverb. *Tie down*, trans., **1.** to fasten by tying so as to prevent from rising; **2.** to bind, restrain (a person), by conditions, obligations, to exact an undertaking from. *Tie up*, trans., **1.** to fasten securely together: *to tie up a truss of hay, a parcel* &c.; **2.** to bind up, swathe round, wrap up: *to tie up a person's head*; **3.** to take such measures as will restrict (a person's) freedom of action, to impose conditions, obligations, restrictions upon; **4.** to secure (property) by will &c. in such a way that it cannot be alienated or squandered, or so that it must pass to a certain line of heirs, or can only be enjoyed under certain conditions.

tied house, n. [1. tíd hóus; 2. táid háus]. Public-house the liquor for which must, by contract, be purchased from a single, specified, firm of brewers.

tier, n. [1. tēr; 2. tiə]. O. Fr. *tiere*, 'row, rank, series'; origin uncertain. **a** Originally, a row of guns (in a ship); **b** a row, series, of objects, forming one of several rows, also one of several shelves &c., placed one above another.

tierce, n. [1. tērs; 2. tiəs]. Fr. *tiers*, 'third', fr. Lat., see **tertius. 1.** Wine cask containing 42 gallons; one-third of a pipe. **2.** The third of the canonical hours; service said at that hour (9 A.M.). **3.** Position in fencing, both in attacking and parrying, in which the point of the weapon is on a level with the eye; the third position.

tiercel, tiercet. See **tercel, tercet.**

tiers état, n. [1. tyārz ātáh; 2. tjéər(z) eitá]. Fr., 'third estate'. The common people; the class coming after, and inferior to, the nobility and the clergy.

tiff, n. & vb. intrans. [1. tif; 2. tif]. Supposed to be fr. O.N. *þēfr*, 'a smell', with vb. *þēfa*, 'to sniff'; Mod. Norw. *teft*, 'a scent'. **1.** n. **a** A slight, passing, quarrel, trifling dispute; **b** (obs. or provinc.) a small draught or taste of liquor. **2.** vb. (rare or obs.) To be peevish, pettish.

tiffany, n. [1. tífani; 2. tífəni]. O. Fr. *tiffanie*, fr. L. Lat. *theophania*, 'manifesting of God'; fr. Gk., see **theophany** & cp. **epiphany.** Thin silk gauze; originally a dress for wearing on Twelfth Night.

tiffin, n. [1. tífin; 2. tífin]. Said to be for *tiffing*, fr. **tiff, 1, b.** Luncheon; word current among the English in India and the Far East.

tige, n. [1. tēzh; 2. tīž]. Fr., 'a stalk', fr. Lat.; see **tibia. 1.** (archit.) The shaft of a column. **2.** (bot.) Stalk, stem, of a plant.

tiger, n. [1. tíger; 2. táigə]. M.E., fr. O. Fr. *tigre*, fr. Lat. *tigris*, Gk. *tígris*; said to be fr.

an old Pers. word *tigra*, meaning 'an arrow'. **1.** Large, fierce, Asiatic carnivorous animal of the cat tribe, *Felis tigris*, measuring from 9 to 10 ft. to tip of tail, having a white throat and belly, and tawny yellow back and sides, with narrow black stripes; *American tiger*, the jaguar. **2.** (fig.) A violent, cruel, ruthless man. **3.** A small groom or pageboy in livery; probably so called because formerly these boys wore yellow waistcoats with black stripes. **4.** A yell, or supplementary cheer, at the end of a round of cheering: *three cheers and a tiger*.

tiger-beetle, n. One of several kinds of carnivorous beetles with stripes on the back.

tiger-cat, n. Large kind of wild cat, partly striped, such as the ocelot or the margay.

tiger-flower, n. Plant of iris family, *Tigridia*, the flowers of which are streaked with darker colour.

tig(e)rish, adj. [1. tíg(e)rish; 2. táig(ə)riʃ]. **tiger** & **-ish**. Like a tiger in character; fierce, rapacious, cruel, bloodthirsty.

tig(e)rishly, adv. Prec. & **-ly**. In a tigerish manner.

tiger-lily, n. Lily of Chinese origin, *Lilium tigrinum*, cultivated in English gardens, with orange-coloured flowers spotted with black.

tiger-moth, n. One of several varieties of large moths, found in England, with variegated wings, mottled with dark reddish-brown, yellow, and buff spots.

tiger('s)-eye, n. A chatoyant stone, yellowish brown in colour; polished and used as an ornament.

tiger-wood, n. Tree from British Guiana used in cabinet-making.

tight (I.), adj. [1. tīt; 2. tait]. M.E. *ti(g)ht* & *thiht*; prob. of Scand. origin, cp. O.N. *pēttr*, '(water-)tight'; cp. Mod. Germ. *dicht*, 'thick'; related to **thick (I.)**; orig. sense 'thickly set, dense, firm' & **1.** Drawn close, firm, compact: *a tight knot*. **2.** So compactly and closely put together as not to allow the passage of liquid; not leaky; esp. *a tight ship, cask*; cp. *water-tight*. **3.** Having all loose parts arranged to lie close and compact; hence trim, snug, neat: *a tight little vessel*; '*A right little, tight little island*'. **4.** (of a cord, line, chain &c.) Firmly held, pulled, and strained from either end; kept fully stretched; taut; reverse of *slack, loose*: *a tight rein*, one drawn so as to put a strain on the bit. Phr. (fig.) *to keep a tight rein, hand, on (a person)*, treat with severity. **5. a** Entirely filled with the contents, so as to be stretched from within; specif., clinging so close as to compress what is within or underneath; scanty, too small; reverse of *loose, easy*: *a tight boot, hat, coat*; *my coat is tight across the chest*; *a tight squeeze*; **b** (fig., of external conditions) cramped, making action difficult, hard to deal with; dangerous, oppressive; specif., *a tight corner*, difficult, dangerous, situation. **6. a** (of money) Scarce, difficult to obtain; **b** (of persons) close-fisted, stingy, niggardly. **7.** (slang) Drunk, intoxicated, tipsy. **8.** (of artistic method, treatment &c.) Lacking largeness and breadth; petty, finicky.

tight (II.), adv., fr. prec. Tightly, firmly: *a coat made to fit tight round the waist*; *to keep one's mouth tight shut*; *to sit tight (on a horse) over a fence*. Phr. *to sit tight*, to stick tenaciously to one's rights, position, opinions &c.

tighten, vb. trans. & intrans. [1. títn; 2. táitn]. **1.** trans. To draw, make, tight or tighter: *to tighten one's grip, the reins, a strap* &c. **2.** intrans. To become tight or tighter: *a tent-rope tightens when it gets wet*; *the grip of the enemy upon the small force of defenders tightened daily*.

tightly, adv. [1. títli; 2. táitli]. **tight (I.)** & **-ly**. In a tight manner; so as to constrict; compactly; firmly.

tightness, n. [1. títnes; 2. táitnis]. See **tight (I.)** & **-ness**. Quality, state, fact, of being tight; constriction.

tight-rope, n. Rope or wire tightly stretched some distance above the ground, upon which acrobats walk; *tight-rope dancer*, performer upon such a rope.

tights, n. pl. [1. tīts; 2. taits]. Garments made to fit tight to the skin; specif., garments fitting tight to the trunk and legs, worn by professional dancers, gymnasts &c.

tigress, n. [1. tígres; 2. táigris]. **tiger** & **-ess**. **1.** Female tiger. **2.** A fierce, cruel, violent woman.

tike, tyke, n. [1. tīk; 2. taik]. M.E. *tīke*, 'dog'; rustic; fr. O.N. **1.** A rough dog of no particular breed; a cur. **2.** A rough, uncultivated, ill-bred, mannerless, boorish fellow. Phr. *Yorkshire tike*, a rough, loutish Yorkshireman.

tilbury, n. [1. tílburi; 2. tílbəri], fr. name of inventor. A kind of high two-wheeled carriage with a hood.

tilde, n. [1. tíldā; 2. tíldɛ]. Span., fr. Lat. *titulo*, see **title**. **a** Mediaeval mark (~) placed over a letter to indicate that *n* follows; **b** mark (~) placed over *n* in Spanish writing indicating that this expresses a front nasal consonant, i.e. the sound written *gn(e)* in French and Italian.

tile, n. & vb. trans. [1. tīl; 2. tail]. O.E. *tiġele*, fr. Lat. *tēgula*, formed fr. base *teg-, 'to cover', as in *tegere*, 'to cover'; see **tegument** & cp. **thatch (I.)**. **1. n.** **a** A flat, generally rectangular, cake of baked clay or earthenware, used for roofing; or one made of finer clay or porcelain, and glazed, used for covering inside walls &c.; **b** (colloq.) a top hat. **2. vb.** **a** To cover with tiles; **b** to guard the entrance door of a masonic lodge.

tiler, n. [1. tíler; 2. táilə]. Prec. & **-er**. **1.** Man who makes tiles; one who lays tiles on roofs &c. **2.** External guard of the door of a masonic lodge while in session.

tilery, n. [1. tíleri; 2. táiləri]. Prec., sense **1**, & **-y**. Place where tiles are made and baked in a kiln.

tilestone, n. [1. tílstōn; 2. táilstoun]. A flat stone used for roofing.

tiliaceous, adj. [1. tiliáshus; 2. tiliéiʃəs], fr. Lat. *tilia*, 'linden tree', & **-aceous**. (bot.) Belonging to the family *Tiliaceae*, which includes the linden tree, bass-wood &c.

till (I.), prep & conj. [1. til; 2. til]. O.E. (Nthn. dial.) & M.E. 'to, up to'; perh. fr. O.N. *til* in same sense; cogn. w. O.H.G. *zil*, 'limit, end, aim'; cp. Goth. (*ga*)*tilon*, 'to obtain, reach', & (*ga*)*tils*, 'convenient, fit'; O.E. *til*, 'good', is the same word. **a** prep. To, up to, down to, up to the time when: *till tomorrow*; *till next week*; *till then*; *till now*; *true till death*; **b** conj., in same sense as the prep.: *wait till I come*; *till the day breaks*; '*till death us do part*'.

till (II.), vb. trans. O.E. *tilian*, 'to strive after; to provide for; to treat medically; to cultivate (land)'; fr. same base as prec. To cultivate (the land); to prepare (land) for sowing by ploughing &c.

till (III.), n. Connected w. M.E. *tillen*, 'to pull'; cp. O.E. (*for-*)*tyllan*, 'to draw, lead astray'; see also **tiller (II.)**. Small drawer in a shop counter where money is kept.

tillable, adj. [1. tílabl; 2. tíləbl]. **till (II.)** & **-able**. Capable of being tilled.

tillage, n. [1. tílij; 2. tílidʒ]. **till (II.)** & **-age**. **a** Act, process, of tilling or cultivating the ground; **b** tilled land.

tiller (I.), n. [1. tíler; 2. tílə], fr. **till (II.)** & **-er**. One who tills (the soil).

tiller (II.), n. Connected w. **till (III.)**. Bar, lever, fixed to head of rudder, worked by hand in a small vessel; or by tiller-chains or ropes fixed to steering wheel in larger vessels.

tiller (III.), n. & vb. intrans. O.E. *telgor*, 'shoot, twig'; cp. *telga*, 'branch'. **1. n.** A shoot, sucker, from a plant. **2. vb.** To shoot, put forth young shoots from root.

tilt (I.), vb. trans. & intrans., & n. [1. tilt; 2. tilt]. Cp. O.E. *tealtian*, 'to be unsteady'; O.E. *tealt*, 'unsteady, heaving', M.E. *tilten*, 'to totter, fall'. **1. vb.** **a** trans. To cause to slope, to tip; also *tilt up*; **b** intrans., to assume a sloping position, stand or lie at an angle, to slope; to heel over. **2. n.** A sloping position: *to give a tilt to a barrel*.

tilt (II.), vb. intrans. & n. Apparently same word as prec. **1. vb.** To take part in a tournament; specif., to make a charge on horseback with a lance; also *tilt at*, (chiefly fig.) to attack, protest, inveigh, against: *to tilt at abuses*. **2. n. a** Exercise of tilting; **b** thrust, charge, in tilting. Phr. *to run full tilt into, at, anything*, at full speed.

tilt (III.), n. M.E. *telt*, 'tent', loan-word fr. some other Gmc. tongue, the O.E. word being *teld*; O.H.G. *zelt*; the etymol. is obscure; perh. connected w. **tent (I.)**. A light canopy or covering, esp. one of canvas on a wooden frame, placed over a cart, a boat, or a street stall.

tilth, n. [1. tilth; 2. tilþ]. In O.E., see **till (II.)** & **-th**. **a** Act of tilling; **b** tilled land; tillage.

tilt-hammer, n. fr. **tilt (I.)**. A large heavy hammer used in iron-forging, raised or tilted and let fall by a wheel.

tilt-yard, n., fr. **tilt (II.)**. Place, courtyard, in which tilting was practised.

timbal, n. [1. tímbl; 2. tímbl]. See next word. A kettle-drum.

timbale, n. [1. tambáhl; 2. tæbál]. Fr., fr. Span. *timbal*, 'kettle-drum', fr. Arab. *atabal*; perh. influenced by Fr. *timbre*, see **timbre**. A highly flavoured dish of chicken, fish, lobster &c., cooked in a mould of rounded shape.

timber (I.), n. [1. tímber; 2. tímbə]. O.E. *timber*, 'timber; a building'; cp. also O.E. *timbrian*, 'to build'; O.H.G. *zimbar*, 'wooden building'; Mod. Germ. *zimmer*, 'room, chamber', cogn. w. Lat. *domus*, 'house' &c., see **dome (I.)**; also **tame (I.)**. **1. a** Wood cut up and prepared for building; **b** growing trees thought of as wood with commercial value for building. **2.** A shaped, fitted piece of wood designed to form, or actually forming, a structural element in a building, specif. in a house &c., or a ship.

timber (II.), vb. trans. O.E. *timbrian*, 'to build', see prec. To build up with timber; to furnish with timbers; to prop, support, pin, with timber.

timbered, adj. [1. tímberd; 2. tímbəd]. **a** Built of or with timber; **b** supplied with growing timber: *well-timbered land*.

timbering, n. [1. tímbering; 2. tímbəriŋ]. Timbers of a building collectively; timber work.

timber-toes, n. [1. tímber tōz; 2. tímbə touz]. (colloq. and facet.) Person with a wooden leg.

timbre, n. [1. támbr; 2. tæmbr]. Fr., 'bell sounded by being struck with a hammer; quality of sound, voice &c.'; see **tympanum** & next word. (mus.) The characteristic quality of the sound of an instrument, or of a human voice.

timbrel, n. [1. tímbrel; 2. tímbrəl]. See prec. & **tympanum**. Kind of small drum played by being struck by the hand; a tambourine.

time (I.), n. [1. tīm; 2. taim]. O.E. *tima*, 'time, date; proper time; period of time; lifetime; season of the year'; M.E. *time*; O.N. *tími*; fr. Gmc. base *tī-, & cogn. w. **tide (I.)**, q.v., w. different suff. The fundamental sense of the orig. base *dā(i)-, *dī- &c., is 'to divide; division'; cp. Lat. *daps*, 'religious feast'; Gk. *dêmos*, 'district; people', see **demos**; Scrt. *dāpayati*, 'he divides'; see also **damn (I.)**. **1.** A fundamental conception, involving recognition of the ideas of before and after, past, present, and future, in the sequence of events: *space and time are sometimes called 'categories of sense'*. Phr. *time and tide wait for no man*. **2.** Time regarded theoretically, as having a beginning and an end, as something limited by the duration of the external universe, or of man and human existence; contrasted with *eternity*: '*A rose-red city half as old as time*' (Burgon). Phrs.

from time immemorial, time out of mind, from the remotest period; (of legal memory) '*from time whereof the memory of man runneth not to the contrary*'. **3.** Duration of time; a length, portion, of time; a period: *I've only been here a short time; that will take a long time.* Phrs. *in no time*, very soon, in a brief space; *take your time*, don't hurry; *in one's own time*, in one's leisure moments, during time for which one is not paid; *there is no time to lose*, a the matter is urgent; **b** there is need of hurry; *to have no time to spare, to be pressed for time*, to have no leisure, to be very busy, to be compelled to hurry to get something done; *have I time (to catch the train &c.)?*, i.e. enough time; *to do time*, (colloq.) undergo period of imprisonment; *to serve one's time*, the agreed period of apprenticeship; *what time*, (archaic and poet.) at the moment when; while: '*What time the laboured ox In his loose traces from the furrow came*' (Milton, 'Comus', 291-2). **4.** (often pl.) Period distinguished by the occurrence of specific, memorable, historical events, by the activities of historical characters &c.; age, epoch: '*The spacious times of great Elizabeth*' (Tennyson, 'Dr. of Fair W.', v. 2); *life and times of Queen Victoria*. Phr. *the good old times*, the past. **5.** A portion of time characterized by specified conditions, or considered in relation to the kind of events that occur: *hard times; to pass through a terrible time; what wonderful times we live in.* Phrs. *to have a good time*, to enjoy oneself; *to have the time of one's life*, a period of extreme and exceptional happiness and enjoyment; *time was when…*, it used formerly to be that… **6. a** Lifetime, duration of one's life: *the house will last my time; such things never happened in the old squire's time;* **b** period in which one was associated with particular persons, places &c., or was engaged in some particular activities &c.: *he was no longer head of the college in my time*, that is, not while I was there; *all these things happened in my time.* **7.** Particular point or moment of time: esp. the customary, normal moment for something to happen; a time fixed for something to be done or to happen; season; the proper time: *I was ill at the time; he arrived in due time; the time has come when …; will you kindly fix a time to call?* Phrs. *there are times when …,* sometimes, at certain moments; *your, my, time has come,* you are, I am, going to die; *time of life,* age; (of a woman) *near her time*, shortly to be delivered; (*glad to see you*) *at all times*, always; *to do something in one's own good time*, when one chooses; *to be in (good) time (for)*, early enough, punctual; *all in good time*, soon enough, there's no hurry!; *time!*, (at contests &c. where a given time is allowed for performance) time is up!; stop! **8. a** Mode of computing, of reckoning, lapse of time: *Greenwich time; Summer time;* **b** specif., some particular hour in the day, or fraction of it, as reckoned in a given latitude: *what's the time?; the right time; the time of day.* Phrs. *to pass (him) the time of day*, to greet, salute, exchange formal greetings with; *at this time of day*, (fig.) so late, after all that has happened; (of a timepiece) *to keep good time*, show the hour correctly. **9.** a Portion of time in which an action is repeated, or an event recurs; occasion: *each time I see him I dislike him more and more; many a time, many times*, often, on many occasions; *time after time*, again and again, repeatedly; **b** (in pl.) as a sign of multiplication: *three times four is twelve.* Phr. *many times as large*, much larger. **10. a** (mus.) Measurement based on the periodicity of accents, and classified according to the subdivision of the beats; Phr. *to beat time*, indicate proper time by motions made with a baton; **b** (prosody) duration of utterance, including pause, as an element of metre.
time (II.), vb. trans., fr. prec. **1.** To calculate time that an action will take to perform, and adjust one's movements accordingly; to do something at, or within, the right, or a suitable, time: *to time one's arrival opportunely; to time one's start so as just to catch a train; to time one's blows skilfully.* **2.** To observe and note length of time taken in performing an action; esp. time taken in a race to run a given distance.
time-ball, n. Ball which falls at a given hour, usually at noon, as an indication of the time.
time-bargain, n. Contract to sell stocks, shares &c. at an agreed price at a fixed future time.
time-expired, adj. [1. tím ekspīrd; 2. táim ikspáiəd]. Having completed the term of service (of soldiers and sailors).
time-honoured, adj. [1. tím ònurd; 2. táim ònəd]. Long respected or observed; respected on account of its antiquity: *a time-honoured custom.*
time-keeper, n. **a** Person who keeps, observes, notes, measures, time, esp. that spent by men at their work; **b** a timepiece.
timeless, adj. [1. tímles; 2. táimlis]. **time (I.)** & **-less.** **1.** (poet.) **a** Not to be measured by time; unending, interminable; **b** (archaic) unseasonable. **2.** Pertaining to no fixed time.
timelessly, adv. Prec. & -**ly.** Unendingly.
timelessness, n. See prec. & **-ness.** State, quality, of being timeless.
timely, adj. & adv. [1. tímli; 2. táimli]. **time (I.)** & **-ly.** **1.** adj. Occurring at a suitable time; opportune: *timely help.* **2.** adv. (rare) In good, at a suitable, time; opportunely.
timenoguy, n. [1. tíménogī; 2. táimənəgai]. Origin unknown; cp. **guy rope** &c. (naut.) Taut rope over which running rigging slides, used to prevent fouling.
timeous, adj. [1. tímus; 2. táiməs]. **time (I.)** & **-ous.** (rare, or Scots, esp. Scots law) In good time; opportune; seasonable.
timeously, adv. Prec. & -**ly.** Seasonably, opportunely.
timepiece, n. [1. tímpēs; 2. táimpīs]. A watch or clock.
time-saving, adj. Serving to save time.
time-server, n. Person who in his behaviour and actions subordinates duty and principle to self-interest and expediency; an obsequious unprincipled toady who readily adapts his opinions and conduct to those which are popular at the time at which he lives, and among the more powerful people with whom he is brought in contact.
time-serving, adj. Practising the behaviour of a time-server; obsequious, pliant.
time-sheet, n. Record of time spent on a job of work or at work by a workman.
time-table, n. **1. a** List, in tabular form, showing the days and hours at which particular duties and work of any kind have to be done, or for which engagements, appointments &c. have been fixed; **b** the whole series of duties, engagements &c. assigned to particular days and hours. **2.** Specif. **a** table, book containing a list, showing hours of the arrival and departure of trains, boats, trams &c.; **b** the total number of departures and arrivals, at fixed hours, of trains, boats &c. running under direction of a particular company.
time-work, n. Work, esp. manual labour, which is paid at certain rates by the hour or day; contrasted with *piece-work.*
timid, adj. [1. tímid; 2. tímid]. Fr. *timide*, fr. Lat. *timidus*, 'faint-hearted, cowardly'; cp. also *timēre*, 'to be afraid'; the origin is uncertain; connexion w. Lat. *tenebrae*, 'darkness', see **tenebrae,** has been suggested. Easily frightened, lacking in courage, nerve, or spirit; lacking self-confidence and enterprise; diffident, shy. Phr. *as timid as a hare.*
timidity, n. [1. tímíditi; 2. timíditi]. Lat. *timiditāt-(em).* Prec. & -**ity.** Lack of courage and self-confidence; nervousness; shyness, diffidence.
timidly, adv. See prec. & -**ly.** In a timid manner; shyly, hesitatingly.
timidness, n. See prec. & -**ness.** Condition of being timid; shyness, timidity.
timist, n. [1. tímist; 2. táimist]. **time (I.)** & -**ist.** **1.** Musical performer considered according to the manner in which he observes the time of the piece which he is playing: *a good, poor, timist.* **2.** (prosody) One who emphasizes the importance of time as an element in metre.
timocracy, n. [1. tīmókrasi; 2. taimókrəsi]. Gk. *tīmokratía*, fr. *tīmḗ*, 'price, worth; moral worth, honour in which one is held; esteem, respect', & base **krat-*, 'strength; government, rule', see **-cracy;** *tīmḗ* contains the same base **tī-* as in Gk. *tíein*, 'to place a value on; to honour, esteem' &c., wh. is fr. **kʷei-*, **kʷi-* &c., 'to respect', whence also Scrt. *cāyati*, 'he worships, has high respect for'; it is possible that the first syllable of Lat. *caerimōnia*, 'religious awe, reverence; religious usage', is fr. the same source; see **ceremony.** **1.** A state in which the love of honour and glory is the ruling principle. **2.** A state in which political power is in proportion to the amount of property possessed.
timocratic, adj. [1. tīmokrátik; 2. taimokrátik]. See prec., w. substitution of suff. **-crat** & **-ic.** Pertaining to, based on, timocracy.
timorous, adj. [1. tímorus; 2. tímərəs], fr. Lat. *timor*, 'fear', see **timid,** & **-ous.** Exceedingly timid, easily startled, prone to take fright; apprehensive, faint-hearted.
timorously, adv. Prec. & -**ly.** In a timorous manner.
timorousness, n. See prec. & -**ness.** State, quality, of being timorous.
timothy (grass), n. [1. tímuthi (grahs); 2. tíməþi (grās)]. fr. name of introducer, Timothy Hanson. A grass with long spikes grown for hay in America and Europe.
timous, adj. See **timeous.**
timpano, n. [1. tímpanō; 2. tímpənou]. Ital., see **tympanum.** A kettle-drum.
tin (I.), n. [1. tin; 2. tin]. O.E. *tin*; in most Gmc. languages, e.g. O.N. *tin*; O.H.G. *zin* &c.; origin unknown; not related to Lat. *stagnum, stannum*, 'tin'. **1.** A white, malleable metal, taking a high polish, and almost unaffected by atmosphere. **2. a** Thin iron plate or sheet coated with tin, used for making vessels, cases &c. of various kinds: *a box made of tin*, made of tin plates: (also attrib.) *a tin box, saucepan* &c. Phr. *a little tin god*, an insignificant person who on the strength of his position or other accidental circumstances is regarded by others, or by himself, as being very important; *tin hat*, (slang) a soldier's steel helmet; **b** a receptacle made of such plates: *a tin for biscuits;* **c** the contents of a tin box or other receptacle; so much as such a box &c. will hold: *to eat a whole tin of sardines, of biscuits* &c. **3.** (slang) Money; wealth.
tin (II.), vb. trans., fr. prec. **1.** To coat with tin. **2.** To pack, preserve, in a box or case, made of tin-covered plates: *to tin fruit, fish* &c.
tinamou, n. [1. tínamōō; 2. tínəmū]. S. Am. word. S. American bird, member of the family *Tinamidae*, resembling a quail.
tincal, tinkal, n. [1. tíngkl; 2. tíŋkl]. Malay. word. Crude borax.
tin-clad, n. (facet.) An ironclad vessel; an ironclad.
tinct, adj. & n. [1. tingkt; 2. tiŋkt], fr. Lat. *tinctus*, P.P. of *tingere*, 'to wet, moisten; to soak, steep; to soak in colour, to dye'; earlier **tengere*, cp. Gk. *téngein*, 'to moisten', cogn. w. O.H.G. *dunkōn*, 'to steep, immerse'. (poet. and archaic) **1.** adj. Coloured, tinged. **2.** n. A colour, hue, shade of colour.
tinction, n. [1. tíngkshun; 2. tíŋkʃən]. Prec. & **-ion.** Act or process of staining or dyeing.
tinctorial, adj. [1. tiṅgktōrial; 2. tiŋktɔ́riəl]. Lat. *tinctōrius*, fr. *tinctor*, 'dyer', see **tinct,** & **-al.** **a** Connected with, pertaining to, dyeing; **b** pertaining to colour or colours; **c** tending to impart a colour.
tincture (I.), n. [1. tíŋkchur; 2. tíŋktʃə]. Lat. *tinctūra*, 'dyeing', see **tinct** & **-ure.** **1.** A tinge, shade of colour, a tint. **2.** (her.)

The word used for colour on shields and bearings, but including, beside the heraldic colours, also *metals* and *furs*. **3.** (med.) A solution of some substance, esp. of vegetable character, used as a drug. **4.** (fig.) **a** (material sense) A slight trace, faint taste, or colour; smack: *a faint tincture of tobacco, vanilla, of red* &c.; **b** (in moral sense) a superadded quality or characteristic; a veneer: *some tincture of education, civilization, of good breeding*.

tincture (**II.**), vb. trans., fr. prec. **1.** To impart a tincture to; to communicate a slight taste, shade of colour, to. **2.** (in moral sense) To affect slightly, imbue faintly; to impart a quality to in a small degree: *his character is but slightly tinctured with humanity*.

tindal, n. [1. tíndal; 2. tíndəl], fr. Malay. *tandal.* A petty officer of a lascar crew, subordinate to the serang.

tinder, n. [1. tínder; 2. tíndə]. O.E. *tynder, tyndre*, M.E. *tinder* &c.; O.H.G. *zuntara*; O.N. *tundr*; cp. O.E. (*on-*)*tendan*, fr. **tandjan*, 'to kindle; to inflame'; O.H.G. *zunten*, 'to burn, glow'; Goth. *tandjan*, 'to kindle'; cp. Swed. *tända*, see **tändstickor**, & Goth. *tunnan*, 'to become kindled, enflamed'. Inflammable material, esp. such as was formerly used for obtaining a light from a spark, consisting of scorched linen &c., impregnated with saltpetre. Phr. *to burn like tinder*, to blaze up and burn furiously.

tinder-box, n. Case used before the invention of modern matches, for obtaining a light, containing tinder, flint, and steel.

tindery, adj. [1. tínderi; 2. tíndəri]. **tinder** & **-y.** Like tinder; very dry and inflammable.

tine, n. [1. tīn; 2. tain]. O.E. *tind*, 'prong, spike'; O.N. *tindr*; cogn. w. O.E. *tōþ*, 'tooth', fr. **tanþ-*, of wh. base it is a gradational variant, w. *-d* instead of *-þ*, on account of the conditions of accent formulated under Verner's Law; see **tooth. a** One of the prongs of a fork; **b** one of the projecting spikes of a harrow; **c** a prong of a stag's antler.

tinea, n. [1. tínea; 2. tíniə]. Lat., 'worm, moth'. Prob. fr. **twinea*, & cogn. w. Gk. *sínomai*, 'to injure, damage'; & w. O.E. *þwīnan*, 'to dwindle', also w. O.E. *þwǣnan*, 'to moisten, soften'. The base, according to Walde, meant 'moisture, injury caused by damp' &c., & *tinea* meant 'a worm produced from damp mould'. See also **tabes. 1.** (entom.) The genus of clothes-moths. **2.** (med.) One of various skin diseases, esp. ringworm.

tin-foil, n. & vb. trans. **1.** n. Very thin sheet of tin, used for wrapping and packing. **2.** vb. To wrap up in, coat with, tin-foil.

ting, n. & vb. intrans. & trans. [1. ting; 2. tiŋ]. Imitative word. **1.** n. A tinkle, sound, made by a bell. **2.** vb. **a** intrans. To tinkle, sound as a bell; **b** trans., to ring, tinkle (a bell).

tinge (**I.**), vb. trans. & intrans. [1. tinj; 2. tin(d)ž], fr. Lat. *tingere*, 'to dye' &c., see **tinct. A.** trans. **1.** To colour slightly, to tint, imbue: *the setting sun tinges the sky with a rosy flush*. **2.** (fig., chiefly in P.P.) To affect faintly but perceptibly, to cast a shadow, shed a brightness upon, to colour: *memories of past events tinged with melancholy*; *present sorrow tinged with brighter hopes for the future*. **B.** intrans. (rare) To become tinged.

tinge (**II.**), n., fr. prec. **1.** Some degree of colour, usually a faint amount; a tincture. **2.** Admixture, addition, of some extraneous feeling, passion &c., to a prevailing state of mind; a spice, a touch: *his piety had no tinge of hypocrisy*; *his banter contained a tinge of malice*.

tingle (**I.**), vb. intrans. [1. tínggl; 2. tíŋgl]. Prob. freq. of **ting. 1.** To experience a sensation as of slight pricking, smarting, tickling, or stinging: *ears tingling with the cold*; *the blow made my cheek tingle*. **2.** To thrill, be excited, stirred, roused; to throb, flutter: *we were all tingling with eagerness and excitement*. **3.** To produce a sensation comparable to pricking or tingling; **a** to tremble, shimmer: *the tingling heat and sunlight of an August noon*; **b** to vibrate, throb: *the air still tingled with the sound of distant bells*.

tingle (**II.**), n., fr. prec. **a** The physical sensation of tingling; **b** the emotional condition of tingling.

tinker (**I.**), n. [1. tíngker; 2. tíŋkə]. In M.E.; lit. 'one who tinks', i.e. who makes a tinkling sound, as by striking a metal vessel with another piece of metal, as itinerant menders of pots and pans used formerly to do, to announce their coming. *Tink* was an imitative word; see **tinkle. 1.** A mender of metal articles such as kettles, pots, and pans, esp. an itinerant mender of these. **2.** A clumsy botcher, an unskilful workman. **3.** (re-formed from **tinker** (**II.**)) Act of tinkering; clumsy, unskilful attempt to mend or fix: *to have a tinker at the electric light*.

tinker (**II.**), vb. trans. & intrans., fr. prec. **1.** trans. **a** To apply the craft of a tinker to; **b** to mend roughly, unskilfully; to botch: *I've merely tinkered the pipe anyhow for the time being*. **2.** intrans. To ply the trade of a tinker: (fig.) *to tinker with* (*anything*), try to improve by hesitating, unskilful means; also *tinker away* (*at*), to make prolonged, clumsy, ineffectual efforts at repairing; to fiddle with; *tinker up*, to get, or try to get, into working order, at least temporarily, by hasty, insufficient means: *to tinker up a broken-down car*; *his doctor tinkered him up so that he could make his promised speech*.

tinkle, vb. intrans. & trans. & n. [1. tíngkl; 2. tíŋkl]; freq. of imitative *tink*. **1.** vb. **a** intrans. To give out a series of clear, light, metallic sounds as of a bell, or of a succession of light pieces of metal falling one upon another; to fall with a tinkling sound; **b** trans., to cause to tinkle: *to tinkle a bell*. **2.** n. The sound of a small bell; sound of pieces of metal &c. falling with ringing noise; a jingle.

tinkling, vbl. n. [1. tíngkling; 2. tíŋkliŋ], fr. prec. Sound of that which tinkles; succession of tinkles: '*Drowsy tinklings lull the distant folds*' (Gray's 'Elegy').

tinman, n. [1. tínman; 2. tínmən]. Craftsman who works in tin-plate; one who repairs articles made of this; manufacturer of tin-plate goods.

tinned, adj. [1. tind; 2. tind], fr. P.P. of **tin** (**II.**). **1.** Preserved in tins: *tinned salmon*. **2.** Coated with tin.

tinning, n. [1. tíning; 2. tíniŋ]. **1.** Act, trade, **a** of covering (iron plates &c.) with tin; **b** of enclosing and preserving (food) in tins. **2.** Lining of tin.

tinnitus, n. [1. tinítus; 2. tináitəs]. Lat., formed fr. *tinnītum*, P.P. of *tinnīre*, 'to ring, jingle, tinkle'; imitative. (med.) Affection of the organs of audition, which causes a sensation of a continuous ringing in the ears.

tin-plate, n. Thin sheet of iron coated with tin.

tinsel (**I.**), n. [1. tínsl; 2. tínsl], fr. O. Fr. *estencele*, 'spark', fr. Lat. **scintilla. 1. a** Glittering material composed of thin strips or shreds of metal, used for trimming, esp. of theatrical costumes &c.; **b** a thin textile material interwoven with metal threads. **2.** (fig.) Anything gaudy, outwardly and superficially showy, but really cheap and meretricious; sham splendour; hollow pretence.

tinsel (**II.**), adj., fr. prec. **1.** Made of tinsel. **2.** (fig.) Resembling tinsel; gaudy, cheaply showy; flashy.

tinsel (**III.**), vb. trans., fr. **tinsel** (**I.**). To cover, trick out, with tinsel.

tinsmith, n. [1. tínsmith; 2. tínsmiþ]. Worker in tin or tin-plate.

tint (**I.**), n. [1. tint; 2. tint], fr. earlier **tinct**; see also **taint** (**I.**). **1. a** A colour, a dye; **b** a particular shade, variety of a colour. **2.** A faint shade of colour, a slight tinge.

tint (**II.**), vb. trans., fr. prec. To impart (a slight) colour to; to stain, dye; to tinge.

tinter, n. [1. tínter; 2. tíntə]. Prec. & **-er. a** Person who, thing which, tints; specif. **b** coloured slide used with another in a magic lantern, to impart a particular tint.

tintinnabular(**y**), adj. [1. tintinábūlar(i); 2. tintinǽbjulə(ri)]; see **tintinnabulum** & **-ary. a** Connected with bells, with the sound of bells; **b** producing a sound of ringing.

tintinnabulation, n. [1. tintinabūláshun; 2. tintinæbjuléiʃən]. Lat. *tintinnāt-*, P.P. type of *tintinnāre*, 'to ring, jingle' &c., fr. *tinnīre*, q.v. under **tinnitus**, & **-ion.** Ringing sound of bells.

tintinnabulum, n. [1. tintinábūlum; 2. tintinǽbjuləm]. Lat., 'a door bell, a cattle bell'; formed fr. *tintinnāre*, 'to ring' &c. See prec. The ringing, clanging sound, of bells.

tintometer, n. [1. tintómeter; 2. tintómitə]. See **tint** (**I.**) & **-meter.** Instrument for testing and determining tints.

tiny, adj. [1. tíni; 2. táini]. Origin unknown. See also **teeny.** Minute, very small, diminutive; often *tiny little* (*piece* &c.).

-tion, suff. [1. shn; 2. ʃən]. Lat. suff. expressing action or state; used to form ns. fr. vbl. stems; *-t-* is the termination of the stem of the P.P. See also **-ion** & **-ation.**

tip (**I.**), n. [1. tip; 2. tip]. In M.E.; cp. M.H.G. *zippel*, 'point, peak'; origin doubtful. **1.** Pointed or tapering upper part of anything: *the tips of the ears*; *a mountain tip*. **2.** The pointed lower or outer end, extremity of anything: *the tips of one's fingers, toes, tongue*; *the tip of an animal's tail, of a wing* &c.; *the tip of a spear*; *the tip of one's stick* &c. Phrs. *to touch with the tips of one's fingers*, touch very lightly; barely touch; *to have something at the tips of one's fingers* (or *finger-tips*), handy, ready for use; *to the tips of one's fingers* (or *finger-tips*), through and through, completely; *at, on, the tip of one's tongue*, just about to be uttered. **3.** Various technical uses: e.g. a ferule for a stick or umbrella; upper section of a fishing-rod &c.

tip (**II.**), vb. trans., fr. prec. **1. a** To put a special tip or end to: *to have one's rod &c. tipped*; **b** (poet.) to affect, touch, adorn, the tip of: '*And tipped with silver every mountain-head*' (Pope, 'Il.', viii.). **2.** To cut off the tip(s) of: *to tip a bush* (in pruning); *to have one's hair tipped*. **3.** To touch very lightly, tap, as though with the tip of something. [Possibly should go under **tip** (**IV.**).]

tip (**III.**), n., fr. prec. in sense **3.** A slight, light touch, tap, or pat; *tip and run*, a form of primitive cricket, in which the batsman must run if the bat touches the ball.

tip (**IV.**), vb. trans. & intrans. M.E. *tipen*, 'to overthrow'; origin doubtful, perh. ultimately fr. **tip** (**I.**) & w. sense of 'to bend, press, the tip over', hence 'to upset'. **A.** trans. **1.** To cause to lean away from the vertical, to make to slant; to tilt, cant: *to tip a barrel*; *to tip a cart*. Phr. *to tip the scale*, to cause one scale to be lower than the other, to be heavier than something else; (fig.) to outweigh, preponderate over, have the advantage of. **2.** To cause to shoot out of a receptacle by tipping; to upset, empty out (a load) in this way: *to tip rubbish*. **B.** intrans. To lean out of the straight, to tilt, slant. **C.** Followed by prepositions or adverbs. *Tip off*, trans., to pour out (liquor) by tilting the vessel. *Tip out*, **a** trans., to cause to fall out by tilting; to upset: *to be tipped out of a cart*; **b** intrans., to fall out through being tilted; to be tipped out. *Tip over*, **a** trans., to upset, overturn; **b** intrans., to be upset, to capsize. *Tip up*, **1.** trans., **a** to cause to fall over, to upset; **b** to tilt backwards so that the lighter end rises: *to tip up a cart*; hence, *tip-up seat*, that allows free passage; **2.** intrans., to lose one's balance when leaning backwards; to fall over through being top-heavy; to topple over.

tip (**V.**), n. Place where rubbish &c. is tipped.

tip (**VI.**), n. & vb. trans. & intrans. Origin doubtful. **1.** n. **a** A present, voluntary gift of money, a gratuity; esp. a payment not legally enforce-

able, made to an inferior for some slight extra service; **b** a useful hint, piece of advice, supposed to be based upon private information, recommending a certain line of action; esp. regarding the probable winner of a horse race or concerning a financial speculation: *to get a good tip for the Derby*; *to get the tip to buy copper*. Phrs. *take my tip*, do what I advise; *to give a man the tip* (*to do something*), recommend him (to); *the straight tip*, a definite, unambiguous hint; sound advice. **2.** vb. **a** trans. (i.) To give a tip or present to: *to tip a waiter, a schoolboy*; (ii.) (colloq.) to give, bestow, communicate; (in restricted usage) *to tip the company a song*. Phrs. *to tip the wink*, give a hint, make a sign to; *to tip a winner*, indicate beforehand the horse which will win a race; **b** intrans., to give tips: *travelling is made easy if one tips freely*.

tip-cart, n. One made to tip backwards from the shafts.

tip-cat, n. Boys' game in which a small piece of wood is struck with a bat or stick, so as to cause it to fly into the air, and is then struck again so that it flies several yards.

tippet, n. [1. típet; 2. típit]. O.E. *tæppet*, fr. Lat. *tapēte*, 'tapestry, coverlet'; see **tapestry**. **a** Short cape covering shoulders and chest worn by women; **b** specif., cape or scarf worn officially by judges and by the clergy.

tipple (I.), vb. intrans. & trans. [1. típl; 2. típl]. Freq., fr. **tip** (IV.). **1.** intrans. To drink frequently; specif., to drink alcoholic liquor to excess. **2.** trans. To drink; implying excess in strong liquor: *to tipple brandy all day long*.

tipple (II.), n., fr. prec. **a** Strong drink; **b** (facet.) any kind of drink.

tippler, n. [1. típler; 2. típlə]. **tipple** (I.) & **-er**. One who tipples; person who partakes, frequently, and to excess, of strong drink; a drunkard, a bibber.

tipsily, adv. [1. típsili; 2. típsili]. **tipsy** & **-ly**. In a tipsy, drunken manner; as though tipsy.

tipsiness, n. [1. típsines; 2. típsinis]. **tipsy** & **-ness**. State of being tipsy; tipsy habits.

tipstaff, n. [1. típstahf; 2. típstáf]. **a** Rod tipped with metal, used as the badge of a sheriff's officer; **b** official who carries such a rod.

tipster, n. [1. típster; 2. típstə]. **tip** (VI.) & **-ster**. One who lives by selling tips on likely winners (of horse-races).

tipsy, adj. [1. típsi; 2. típsi]. **tip** (IV.) & **-sy**. (refined and slightly old-fashioned; lady's word) Drunk, intoxicated; the politest and mildest term, often implying only an early stage of intoxication.

tipsy-cake, n. Sponge cake soaked in wine, covered with jam, over which whipped cream is spread, the whole garnished with small macaroons or almonds.

tiptoe, adv. & vb. intrans. [1. típtō; 2. típtou]. Used by Chaucer. **1.** adv. Usually *on tiptoe*: **a** on the points, tips, of the toes; *to stand on tiptoe*, as though trying to see over something; **b** (fig.) nervously wrought up, stirred, eagerly expectant, agog: (*to be*) *on tiptoe with curiosity, excitement*. **2.** vb. To walk on tiptoe: *to tiptoe into the room, tiptoe about*, to walk gingerly as though to avoid making a noise or arousing attention.

tiptop, n. & adj. [1. típtop; 2. típtɔp]. **1.** n. **a** The highest point; esp. **b** (fig.) the highest point of excellence: *at the tiptop of his profession*. **2.** adj. (colloq.) First-rate, most excellent: *a tiptop lecture, dinner, rider &c.*

tirade, n. [1. tirád; 2. tiréid]. Fr., fr. Ital. *tirata*, 'a pulling; a lengthening; a long speech'; fr. *tirāre*, 'to draw'; see second element in **retire**, & cp. **tier**. Long, impassioned, or intemperate speech, esp. one in denunciation of a person or policy &c.

tirailleur, n. Compromise for Fr. pronunciation [1. tirī(l)yēr; 2. tirai(l)já]. Fr., 'skirmisher, sharp-shooter', fr. *tirailler*, 'to skirmish', fr. *tirer*, 'to draw (trigger), to shoot'. In French army, sharpshooter, an infantry skirmisher, esp. of the native, or colonial infantry.

tire (I.), vb. trans. & intrans. [1. tīr; 2. táiə]. Origin doubtful; the vowel in M.E. *tiren*, & in the present form, is difficult to explain if we derive them fr. O.E. *teorian*, 'to fail; not to be up to the mark; to be tired; to make tired'. Even if we suppose that the word was partly influenced by O.E. *tergan*, 'to irritate, annoy, afflict', it does not help us much for the present form. See **tarry** (II.). **A.** trans. **1.** To render weary, to fatigue, exhaust: *walking tires me*; *tire out*, render very weary, to exhaust completely. **2.** To render weary, sick of; to bore: *he tired me with his long speeches*. **B.** intrans. **1.** To become weary, grow fatigued; to become exhausted: *he tires very soon if he exerts himself*. **2.** *Tire of*, to become sick of, bored by, to lose patience over, and interest in: *I soon tire of listening to classical music*.

tire (II.), n. In sense **3** often **tyre**. Form of **attire** (II.). **1.** (archaic) Raiment, apparel. **2.** (archaic) Apparatus, equipment, furnishing, trapping. **3. a** Circular iron band surrounding the outside of the wheel of a vehicle, and forming the tread; **b** thick solid band of rubber on outside of carriage wheels; relatively thick, cushion-like inflated tube fixed to the outside of wheels of bicycles and motor vehicles.

tire (III.), vb. trans., fr. prec. **1.** (archaic) To attire, adorn, dress: '*she painted her face, and tired her head*' (II. Kings, 9. 30). **2.** To put a tire on (a wheel).

tire (IV.), n. See **tiara**. (archaic and poet.) A tiara.

tired, adj. [1. tīrd; 2. táiəd], fr. P.P. of **tire** (I.). **1.** Fatigued, exhausted, weary, in mind or body, as from exertion. **2.** *Tired of*, uninterested in, out of patience with, sick of, bored with: *tired of life, of doing, hearing, the same thing so often*; *to get very tired of constant complaints &c.*; (also absol.) *you can shout till you are tired*, i.e. tired of shouting &c. Also frequently, *sick and tired of*, thoroughly disgusted with and bored by.

tiredness, n. [1. tírdnes; 2. táiədnis]. Prec. & **-ness**. Fatigue, weariness.

tireless, adj. [1. tírles; 2. táiəlis]. **tire** (I.) & **-less**. **1.** (of persons) Unwearied, not easily fatigued; hence, very energetic, active, industrious. **2.** (of actions and activities) Showing no weariness on the part of performer; unwearying, ceaseless, unabated: *tireless energy, zeal, solicitude, industry &c.*

tirelessly, adv. Prec. & **-ly**. In a tireless manner.

tirelessness, n. See prec. & **-ness**. Quality of being tireless.

tiresome, adj. [1. tírsum; 2. táiəsəm]. **tire** (I.) & **-some**. **1.** Annoying, worrying, provoking, irritating, plaguy: *a tiresome child, illness, piece of work*. **2.** Tedious, devoid of interest, dull: *a tiresome lecture, sermon*.

tiresomely, adv. Prec. & **-ly**. In a tiresome way.

tiresomeness, n. See prec. & **-ness**. Quality of being tiresome.

tire-woman, n., fr. **tire**(III.). (archaic) Female attendant, lady's maid; esp. a dresser in a theatre.

tiring, adj. [1. tíring; 2. táiəriŋ], fr. Pres. Part. of **tire** (I.). **1.** Tending to produce fatigue, exhausting: *a very tiring job*. **2.** (more rarely) Tedious, boring.

tiring-room, n., fr. **tire** (III.). (archaic) Dressing-room in a theatre.

tiro, tyro, n. [1. tírō; 2. táiərou], fr. Lat. *tīro*, 'young, newly enlisted soldier; recruit; hence, beginner', etymol. doubtful. A beginner, a new, unskilled hand, one who is inexperienced in some particular occupation, craft, exercise &c.

tirocinium, n. [1. tīrōsíniŭm; 2. táirousíniəm]. Lat., 'the first military service or campaign of a young soldier; military inexperience'; fr. *tīro*, see prec. Apprenticeship; first steps in, elements of, an art or accomplishment.

tirra-lirra, n. [1. tíra líra; 2. tírə lírə]. Imitative of a bird's note. Used to designate a gay, light-hearted carolling; equivalent to *tralala* and such combinations, substituted for words in a song: '*Tirra-lirra by the river Sang Sir Lancelot*' (Tennyson, 'Lady of Shalott', iii. 4).

tir-wit, n. [1. tér wit; 2. tíə wit]. Imitative. Peewit, lapwing.

tisane, n. [1. tizán; 2. tizǽn]. See **ptisan**. A medicinal tea, herbal decoction.

tissue (I.), n. [1. tíshū, tísū, tíshōō; 2. tíʃju, tísju, tíʃū]. Fr. *tissu*, 'woven fabric', formed fr. *tisser*, 'to weave', fr. Lat. *texere*, 'to weave', q.v. under **text**. **1. a** A woven fabric; generally used only of finely woven material; specif. **b** light, gauzy silken material, esp. one interwoven with gold or silver threads. **2.** (biol.) The structural material of the body of plants or animals, consisting of groups of cells and the intercellular substance. **3.** Complicated, interwoven, series; web: esp. *a tissue of lies, falsehoods, absurdities*. **4.** Tissue-paper.

tissue (II.), vb. trans., fr. prec. (rare) To form into a tissue.

tissued, adj. [1. tísūd, tíshūd; 2. tísjud, tíʃjud], fr. P.P. of prec. **a** Clothed, covered, with tissue; **b** variegated like tissue.

tissue-paper, n. Kind of very thin, soft paper, used to wrap or protect delicate, fragile articles.

tit (I.), n. [1. tit; 2. tit]. Variant of **teat**.

tit (II.), n., in M.E. cp. O.N. *tittr*, 'a bird; a small thing'. **1.** Any of various kinds of small, bright-coloured birds. **2.** (archaic, rare) **a** A poor, small horse; **b** a child, girl.

tit (III.). Origin unknown. Cp. Fr. *tant pour tant*. Only in Phr. (to give, pay) *tit-for-tat*, blow for blow; an equivalent for something received; retaliation.

Titan, n. [1. títan; 2. táitən]. Gk. mythol. *Tītán*, name of one of the primitive deities, the gigantic children of Uranus & Gaea; fr. two of these, Cronos & Rhea, Zeus & the Olympians descended. The name is cogn. w. Lat. *titio*, 'a burning brand'; see **entice**. A person of heroic size and strength, or of surpassing genius and intellect; (also attrib.) gigantic, enormous: *Titan strength &c.*; specif., *Titan crane*, a large crane for hoisting and moving very heavy weights, travelling on rails under its own motive power.

Titanesque, adj. [1. títanésk; 2. táitənésk]. Prec. & **-esque**. Resembling, characteristic of, a Titan, or the Titans.

Titaness, n. [1. títanes; 2. táitənes]. **Titan** & **-ess**. Female Titan.

titanic, adj. [1. tītánik; 2. taitǽnik]. **Titan** & **-ic**. **1.** Huge, gigantic, colossal. **2.** (chem.) Connected with, derived from, titanium: *titanic acid*.

titanite, n. [1. títanīt; 2. táitənait]. See prec. & **-ite**. A mineral containing titanic acid, found in igneous rocks.

titanium, n. [1. tītánium; 2. taitéiniəm]. See prec. & **-ium**. A grey-coloured metallic element, somewhat resembling silicon, found only in combination.

titbit, n. [1. títbit; 2. títbit]. See **tit** (II.) = 'small', & **bit** (I.). A choice morsel, extra delicate or tender piece of food; (fig.) a spicy item of news &c.

tithable, adj. [1. tíðhabl; 2. táiðəbl]. **tithe** & **-able**. (of land) Subject to tithes.

tithe (I.), n. [1. tīdh; 2. taið]. O.E. *teogoþa, teóþa*, 'tenth part', M.E. *tithe, tithe*; fr. primitive **tigunþa*, cp. Goth. *taihunda*; O.N. *tíund*, formed fr. numeral **tegun*, '10', see **ten** & **-th**; **tenth** is a later formation. **1.** A tenth part; specif., a portion of the supposed yearly profit derived from a given piece of land, from stock &c., anciently set apart for the support of the Church. **2.** (popular usage) A small portion or proportion of anything, a fraction; in Phr. *not a tithe of*, only a very small part.

tithe (**II.**), vb. trans., fr. prec. To impose a tithe upon.

tithe-barn, n. One in which the grain representing the tithe payable by a parish was anciently stored.

tithe-pig, n. Pig set apart as tithe.

tithing, n. [1. tídhing; 2. táiðiŋ]. O.E. *tēoþung*, 'a group of ten (men)'; see **tithe** (**I.**) & **-ing**. Ancient administrative unit, consisting formerly of ten households living near together.

titillate, vb. trans. [1. títilāt; 2. títileit]. Lat. *tītillāt-(um)*, P.P. of *tītillāre*, 'to tickle'; prob. imitative of rapid movement. To tickle; usually in non-physical sense, to stimulate the mind, excite pleasurably; to exhilarate.

titillation, n. [1. titiláshun; 2. titiléiʃən]. Prec. & **-ion**. **1.** Act, process, of titillating. **2. a** Sensation of tickling; **b** sense of being stimulated, exhilarated.

titillative, adj. [1. títilativ; 2. títilətiv]. **titillate** & **-ive**. Serving to titillate, producing titillation.

titivate, tittivate, vb. trans. & intrans. [1. títivāt; 2. títiveit]. Origin unknown. **1.** trans. To smarten up, to make clean and tidy, and adorn. **2.** intrans. To smarten oneself up, put finishing touches to one's toilet.

titivation, n. [1. titiváshun; 2. titivéiʃən]. Prec. & **-ion**. **a** Act of titivating; **b** results of this process; smartness, extra adornment.

titlark, n. [1. títlark; 2. títlāk]. See **tit** (**II.**). Name of a bird; the meadow pipit.

title, n. [1. títl; 2. táitl]. M.E., fr. O. Fr. *title*, fr. Lat. *titulus*, 'inscription, superscription, label, title; honourable appellation'; the etymol. is entirely uncertain, & none of the various suggestions appears even at all plausible. **1.** Distinguishing, descriptive designation, or inscription, placed on the front page &c. of a book, pamphlet, or other literary work, at the head of a chapter of a book &c.; also, such a distinctive appellation given to a musical composition, to a picture, sculpture &c.; appellation, name by which any of these things is known and identified. **2.** Appellation of honour and distinction, whether inherited, or conferred upon an individual, borne by him, and used in addressing, and referring to him, in addition to, or instead of, his name; in specific sense, *a title* means either an hereditary dignity, e.g. that of *duke, earl, baron* &c., that of *baronet*, or one specifically conferred by the sovereign or his representative, e.g. that of *knight*; more generally, the term is used in reference to appellations indicating rank, status, such as *General, Admiral* &c., to those indicating some particular office such as *Professor, Judge* &c., and to others designating a degree conferred by a university, such as *Doctor*. **3.** (law) The heading forming the name of an act or statute. **4. a** An admitted, recognized claim or right; the ground, reason, of such a claim: *the Odes of Keats would alone be a sufficient title to a place among the greatest poets*; specif. **b** (law) the elements as a whole which constitute right of ownership of property, esp. in land; also the document whereby such rights are established; title-deed. **5.** (eccles.) Usually defined as sphere of work and source of maintenance, evidence of which is required by a bishop before he admits a candidate to Holy Orders, that is, evidence that such a candidate has been nominated to a curacy, College Fellowship, chaplaincy &c. **6.** (bookbinding) Panel on back of book which bears the name.

titled, adj. [1. títld; 2. táitld]. Prec. & **-ed**. Possessing a title; specif., possessing a title of nobility, a baronetcy, or a knighthood.

title-deed, n. Document which establishes ownership, esp. of land.

title page, n. Front page of a book, which bears the title.

title-rôle, n. That part or character in a play from which it takes its name; e.g. the part of Hamlet in the play of that name.

titling, n. [1. títling; 2. táitliŋ]. **title** & **-ing**. Act, process, of stamping the title on the back of a book.

titmouse, n. [1. títmous; 2. títmaus]. M.E. *titemōse*, fr. **tit** (**II.**) & O.E. *māse*, 'titmouse'; cp. O.H.G. *meisa*; the modern form has been influenced by *mouse*. Any one of the small birds belonging to the family *Paridae*, allied to the nuthatch.

titrate, vb. trans. [1. títrāt; 2. táitreit]. Fr. *titre*, see **title**, & **-ate**. To subject to titration.

titration, n. [1. titráshun; 2. taitréiʃən]. Prec. & **-ion**. Process of ascertaining the strength of a chemical solution by noting the amount of a standardized solution which requires to be added to it in order to produce a definite chemical reaction.

titter, vb. intrans. & n. [1. títer; 2. títə]. Imitative of sound made. **1.** vb. To utter a partially smothered laugh, to giggle. **2.** n. A shrill, smothered laugh.

tittle, n. [1. títl; 2. títl]. M.E. *titel*, 'superscription' &c., see **title**. **1.** (obs.) Diacritical mark over a letter or word to indicate contraction &c. **2.** A minute amount, particle: *not a tittle of evidence against him.*

tittle-tattle, n. & vb. intrans. Redupl. of **tattle** (**I.**). **1.** n. Gossip, idle talk; chatter, rumour. **2.** vb. To gossip, to put rumours about.

tittup, vb. intrans. & n. [1. títup; 2. títəp]. Perh. popular form of **titubate**. **1.** vb. To behave in a gay, frolicsome manner; to prance gaily about. **2.** n. Light-hearted frolic; lively, frisky movement.

tittuppy, adj. [1. títupi; 2. títəpi]. Prec. & **-y**. **1.** Gay, frolicsome, cheerful, and lively. **2.** Shaky, tottery, rocky, groggy.

titubate, vb. intrans. [1. títūbāt; 2. títjubeit]. Lat. *titubāt-(um)*, P.P. of *titubāre*, 'to stagger, totter; to stammer'; according to Walde, fr. base **steub-* &c.; cogn. w. **stumble**. (obs. or rare) **a** To reel in one's walk; to totter; **b** to stammer.

titubation, n. [1. titūbáshun; 2. titjubéiʃən]. Prec. & **-ion**. **a** Act of reeling, staggering &c.; specif. **b** (med.) unsteadiness in the gait due to some nervous disorder.

titular, adj. & n. [1. títūlar; 2. títjulə]. Lat. *titulus*, see **title**, & **-ar**. **1.** adj. **a** Connected with, of the nature of, a title: *a titular distinction*; **b** existing in name only, nominal; holding a title without in fact enjoying the dignity it connotes, or performing the functions of the office: *Charles Stuart, the Young Pretender, was titular Prince of Wales*; *titular bishop*, bishop who holds the title of an extinct see, esp. one the seat of which is now in Mohammedan possession. **2.** n. The nominal holder of a title of an office, who does not perform the functions of the office: *titular prince, professor, bishop.*

titulary, adj. & n. [1. títūlari; 2. títjuləri]. Prec. & **-y**. Titular.

tityre-tu, n. [1. títirā tū; 2. táitirei tjū], fr. the opening words of Virgil's 1st Eclogue, 'O Tityrus, thou &c.'. Name of a class or gang of young, noisy, and ruffianly men of fashion, infesting the streets of London during the late 17th cent., esp. during reign of Charles II.

tizzy, n. [1. tízi; 2. tízi]. Familiar form of **tester** (**III.**). (obsolesc. slang) A sixpence.

tmesis, n. [1. tmḗsis; 2. tmísis]. Gk. *tmēsis*, 'a cutting'; *tm-* is the 'vanishing' grade of Gk. base *tem-, tom-*, cp. *témnein*, 'to cut', & *tomé*, 'a cutting'; see under **tome**. (gram.) The interpolation of one or more words between the parts of a compound, thus dividing the word; e.g. *what name soever*; or (vulg.) *abso-blooming-lutely.*

to (**I.**), prep. [1. tōō; 2. tū] when stressed; the unstressed forms are [tə] before cons., & [tu] before vowels. O.E., O.S., & O. Fris. *tō*; O.H.G. *za, zuo* &c.; Germ. *zu*; outside Gmc. cp. Lat. *dē*, 'from; concerning' &c., see **de-**; O. Slav. *do*, 'up to, to, till'. **1.** Expressing movement towards, in the direction of; **a** (not implying arrival): *turn, keep, to the right*; *go to the south*; *on the way to London*; **b** (implying arrival) as far as: *I am going to London tomorrow, and leaving next day*; *you can't possibly get to Oxford tonight*; *to fall to the ground*; *to go to sea*; Phr. *to and fro*, backwards and forwards, there and back; see **fro**. **2.** Expressing **a** progress, change, trend, in direction of particular state, set of conditions or circumstances: *from bad to worse*; *brought to poverty*; *to sink to the worst depths of misery*; *to put to death*; **b** movement into and retention of certain position; starting and continuance of an action: *stand to attention*; *to horse!*; *to arms!* **3.** Expressing **a** some precise stage, phase, point, reached; just as far as: *done to a turn*; *expressed to a nicety, shade*; *frozen to the marrow*; *wet to the skin*; **b** extent, intensity, of some quality or action: *an Englishman to the core*; *sick to death*; *cut to the heart.* **4.** Expressing a final point of duration in time; until: *from Saturday to Monday*; *stay to the end of June*; *conscious to the last*; *to the end of his life he refused to see his brother.* **5.** Indicating the dative case relation; denoting the indirect object of an action, that to which the action is directed; person or thing affected by the action expressed by the verb; indicating the recipient, possessor, one to whom something is imparted &c.: *to do harm to a person*; *listen to me*; *I look to you for help*; *attend to what is said*; *hand round the wine to the company*; *to give money to the poor*; *it belongs to me*; *I wouldn't tell this to everybody*; *I put it to you.* **6.** Expressing comparison; compared with: *nothing to what it might have been*; *all former wars were mere child's play to the Great War*; *he's quite rich to what he once was.* **7.** In numerous phrases and constructions expressing various relations and conditions; **a** effect, consequence: *to my great distress*; *to my delight, horror*; *to his cost*; *to his credit be it said* &c.; **b** opposition: *hand to hand*; *face to face*; **c** amount, extent; *it comes to ten pounds*; *the park extends to several thousand acres*; **d** agreement: *quite to my taste*; *to the best of my belief*; *to my way of thinking*; **e** adaptation, suitability: *boots made to any foot*; *drawn to scale*; **f** addition, advantage: *put this to what you already have*; *to have a handle to one's name*; *five pounds to one's credit*; *all to the good*; **g** intention, purpose: *to that end*; *to the end that.* **8.** Followed by unaltered form of verb to form infinitive; **a** expressing purpose: *I said that to test you*; *everything was done to please her*; *he fights to win*; *have come to see you*; *I bought this house to live in*; *this was made to be used*; (archaic or provinc.) *for to do, see* &c.; **b** used before the second of two verbs: *I want to see*; *to refuse to stay*; *begin to talk* &c.; also elliptically at end of sentence, with verb omitted when it has been previously mentioned: *he asked me to go to dinner, but I don't want to, haven't time to* &c. (*go to dinner* understood); **c** forming with following verb the equivalent of a noun: '*To err is human, to forgive divine*' (Pope, 'Ess. on Crit.', ii. 526), =error, forgiveness; *to defy the law is a crime*, =defiance of; *it is foolish to speak of what one does not understand* &c.

to (**II.**), adv. Same as prec. **1.** Towards, into, the normal, desired, position, condition &c., esp. condition of repose: *push the door to*; *shut the window to*; *I can't get the lid of my trunk quite to.* **2.** After certain verbs: *bring to, come to, go to, fall to, heave to* &c.; see these verbs.

toad, n. [1. tōd; 2. toud]. O.E. *tādde*; usually *tādiġe*; etymol. unknown. Cp. **tadpole**. **1.** Amphibian, genus *Bufo*, shaped like a frog, but terrestrial in habits except at breeding season, more squat in shape, and having a rough skin, and less apt to leap. **2. a** A disgusting, loathsome person; **b** (archaic) applied playfully and affectionately to a person, esp. a child, without intention of disparagement: *the poor toad was delighted to see his mother again.*

toad-eater, n. **1.** Originally, a mountebank's assistant who pretended to swallow toads in order to show his master's skill at curing him of the poisonous effects. **2.** A flatterer, an obsequious sycophant.

toad-eating, n. Sycophancy, servility, obsequiousness.

toad-flax, n. Common European plant, *Linaria*, one species of which has flowers of two shades of yellow; called also *butter-and-eggs*.

toad-in-the-hole, n. [1. tŏd in dhe hōl; 2. tòud in ðə hóul]. Beef-steak cooked in batter.

toadstone, n. [1. tŏdstōn; 2. tóudstoun]. Stone formerly supposed to be formed in body of a toad, and to possess powers as a charm.

toadstool, n. [1. tŏdstōōl; 2. tóudstūl]. Any of various fungi other than mushrooms, esp. those of supposedly poisonous species.

toady, n. & vb. trans. [1. tŏdi; 2. tóudi]. Prob. fr. **toad-eater**. **1.** n. A servile flatterer, a truckling sycophant of the rich and powerful. **2.** vb. To truckle to, and flatter grossly, with ulterior motives of self-interest.

toast (I.), vb. trans. & intrans. [1. tōst; 2. toust]. O. Fr. *toster*, fr. Lat. *tostum*, P.P. of *torrere*, 'to parch, roast'; see **torrid**. **A.** trans. **1.** To render brown and dry by direct exposure to fire. **2.** To warm thoroughly: *to toast oneself, one's feet, before the fire*. **B.** intrans. **1.** To become toasted, become brown by exposure to the fire. **2.** To toast oneself.

toast (II.), n. O. Fr. *tostée*, 'toasted bread', P.P. See prec. **1. a** Slices of bread made brown and crisp on the outside by exposure to fire; **b** specif., such a slice soaked in hot wine; the wine together with the toast. **2. a** A person's health, a patriotic or other sentiment proposed, and honoured by the company raising their glasses and drinking in agreement: *to propose the toast of the King*; **b** person whose health is drunk; specif., a woman whose beauty and charm are frequently celebrated in toasts: *Mary Lepel was a favourite toast in the mid 18th century*; **c** act of proposing or honouring a toast.

toast (III.), vb. trans. & intrans., fr. prec. **1.** trans. To propose and drink the health of. **2.** intrans. To drink toasts.

toaster, n. [1. tōster; 2. tóustə]. Any of various devices for toasting bread &c.

toasting-fork, n. [1. tōsting fork; 2. tóustiŋ fōk]. Fork with a long handle with which bread is held before the fire to be toasted.

toast-master, n. Official who announces the toasts about to be proposed at a public dinner &c.

toast-rack, n. Small rack for holding slices of toast in vertical position on the table.

toast-water, n. Drink made by steeping well-browned toast in boiling water.

tobacco, n. [1. tobákō; 2. təbǽkou]. Span. *tabaco*; fr. a Carib. (Haiti) native word. **1.** A solanaceous plant, genus *Nicotiana*, grown for its leaves, which are smoked in a pipe; grown also in gardens for its flowers. **2.** The leaves of this plant, dried and variously treated, used for chewing, for smoking in pipes and cigarettes, rolled into cigars, and reduced to a fine powder and used as snuff.

tobacco heart, n. Affection of the heart due to excessive tobacco smoking.

tobacconist, n. [1. tobákunist; 2. təbǽkənist]. An irregular formation. **1.** Person who sells tobacco in all forms retail. **2.** (obs.) In 17th and 18th cents., one who smoked tobacco.

tobacco-pipe, n. Small tube of wood, meerschaum, clay &c., with mouth-piece at one end, and a receptacle or bowl at the other, in which tobacco is smoked.

tobacco-pouch, n. Bag or case of indiarubber, leather, or other air-tight material, in which tobacco is carried in the pocket.

toboggan, n. & vb. intrans. [1. tobógan; 2. təbógən], fr. Am. Indian name. **1.** n. Kind of sledge with flat bottom, without runners, having the forward end curved upward, much used in Switzerland for coasting down snow-covered slopes. **2.** vb. To use, travel, coast on, a toboggan.

toby jug, n. [1. tōbi jug; 2. tóubi dʒag]. Jug or tankard of porcelain, used for ale, in form of a fat squat man gaily dressed in 18th century style, wearing a three-cornered hat which forms the brim of the vessel.

toccata, n. [1. tokáhta; 2. təkǽta]. Ital. P.P. fem. of *toccāre*, see **touch (I.)**. Old musical composition for organ or piano, formerly intended as an exercise for the touch.

toccatella, n. [1. tòkatéla; 2. tòkətélə]. Ital. dimin. of prec. Short or simple toccata.

tocology. See **tokology**.

tocsin, n. [1. tŏksin; 2. tŏksin]. Fr., 'alarm-bell'; earlier *toquesing*, cp. Fr. *touquer*, 'to strike', see **touch (I.)**, & **sign (I.)**. **a** Bell sounded to give an alarm; **b** the sound of, alarm sounded by, such a bell.

tod, n. [1. tod; 2. tǒd]. O.N. *toddi*, 'mass, tuft'. **1.** (archaic) Bush, thick foliage. **2.** (provinc., from its bushy tail) A fox. **3.** (archaic) Weight of wool; usually 28 lbs.

Toda, n. [1. tŏda; 2. tóudə]. Member of a tribe in the Nilgiri Hills of Hindustan, speaking a Dravidian language, and characterized by a fair complexion and regular features.

today, adv. & n. [1. tudá; 2. tədéi]. O.E. *tō dæge*, also uninflected *tōdæg*; see **to (I.)** & **day**. **1.** adv. On this day; **b** at this present time, in the age in which we live: *our ideas today differ much from those prevalent in the 18th century*. **2.** n. This present time: *the writers of today*.

toddle (I.), vb. intrans. [1. tódl; 2. tŏdl]. Freq. of **totter**. **1.** To walk with short, hesitating, uncertain steps, as a child does; to walk like a very young child. **2.** (colloq.) **a** To walk, stroll, in a quiet unhurried manner: *do you feel inclined to toddle down to the club?*; **b** to take one's departure: *it's getting late, we must be toddling*.

toddle (II.), n., fr. prec. **a** Act of toddling; **b** a quiet, leisurely walk, stroll.

toddler, n. [1. tódler; 2. tŏdlə]. **toddle (I.)** & **-er**. Person who toddles; specif., a young child just learning, or having just learnt, to walk.

toddy, n. [1. tódi; 2. tŏdi]. Hind. *tārī*, 'juice of palmyra tree'. A drink composed of spirits, sugar, lemon, and hot water; punch.

to-do, n. [1. tu dōō; 2. tə dú]. See **to (I.)** & **do (I.)**. An ado, a fuss, commotion: *to make a terrible to-do about losing one's luggage*.

tody, n. [1. tódi; 2. tóudi], fr. Fr. *todier*, fr. Lat. *todus*, 'kind of small bird'. A small brightcoloured W. Indian bird allied to the king-fishers, living on insects and nesting in the banks of streams and rivers.

toe (I.), n. [1. tō; 2. tou]. O.E. *tā, tāhe*, M.E. *tō*; O.H.G. *zēha*; orig., 'the pointer'; cogn. w. Lat. *digitus* (fr. **dicitus*), 'finger, toe', see **digit**; fr. base **doikʷ-*, **dikʷ-* &c.; see also **diction, teach, token**. **1. a** (in man and monkey) One of the digits of the feet, corresponding to the fingers of the hand; Phrs. *to tread on a person's toes*, wound his susceptibilities; *to turn up one's toes*, to die; *from top to toe*, from head to foot; *big, great, toe*, largest of the toes on a human foot, corresponding to the thumb of the hand; *little toe*, smallest, outside, toe of human foot; **b** (in other animals) one of the digits on fore or hind feet. **2. a** That part of a boot, shoe, stocking &c. which covers the toes; **b** projecting point on under side of a horse-shoe, designed to prevent slipping. **3.** The fore part of the foot, contrasted with *heel*. **4.** (colloq.) The foot of man as a whole: *to toast one's toes*, warm one's feet. **5.** The outer end of the head of a golf-club.

toe (II.), vb. trans., fr. prec. **1.** To put a toe (cap) on to: *boots to be toed and heeled*. **2.** To bring the toes level with: *to toe the line*, originally of line marked at starting-point of a race; (fig.) to submit to discipline, conform to orders, custom &c. **3.** (slang) To kick with the toes: *to toe a person out of the room &c.* **4.** (golf) To strike (a ball) with part of club too near the toe.

toe-cap, n. That part of a boot or shoe which covers the toes, usually made separate from the rest of the boot.

-toed, suff. [1. tōd; 2. toud]. **toe (I.)** & **-ed**. As second element of compounds, having a particular kind of toe or certain number of toes: *square-toed; three-toed* &c.

toe-drop, n. Paralysis of foot muscles which causes inability to raise the toes.

toe-nail, n. Nail growing upon a toe.

toff, n. [1. tof, tawf; 2. tɒf, tɔ́f]. Origin unknown. (lower class slang) **a** A swell, a dandy; **b** a person of the better classes; a gentleman.

toffee, toffy, n. [1. tófi; 2. tɔ́fi]. Also Scots & U.S.A. *taffy*; origin doubtful. Compound of sugar and butter, boiled till it becomes thick, then poured into a dish and allowed to cool and harden.

toft, n. [1. toft; 2. tɒft]. In O.E., 'piece of ground; hillock', fr. O.N. *topt*, 'a green knoll; site marked out for a house'. (only provinc., and in place-names) **a** A knoll, hillock; **b** a homestead.

tog, vb. trans. [1. tog; 2. tɒg], fr. **togs**. (slang) Chiefly *tog out*, to dress, esp. carefully and elaborately: *togged out in full uniform*.

toga, n. [1. tōga; 2. tóugə]. Lat. *toga*, 'garment; esp. the outer garment of a Roman citizen in peace, assumed at age of 14 as sign of manhood'; connected w. *tegere*, 'to cover'; see this base under **tegument**; cp. **thatch (I.)**.

togaed, adj. [1. tōgad; 2. tóugəd]. Clad in, wearing, a toga.

together, adv. [1. togédher; 2. təgéðə]. O.E. *tōgædere*; see **to (I.)** & **gather (I.)**. **1.** In company, associated one with another: *to go about together*; *to live together*, specif. of persons of opposite sex, to live as man and wife. **2.** Against each other, in mutually hostile conjunction: *I can't have you two boys always fighting together*. **3.** Towards each other, into conjunction, so as to form a contact: *the opposing forces rushed together*; *to bring the blades of a pair of scissors together*. **4.** (of time) **a** (of divisions of time) In continuous succession, uninterruptedly, on end: *to ponder for hours together*; **b** (of events happening in time) at one and the same time or moment; synchronously: *all my troubles seem to come upon me together*. **5.** Together with, in combination with; also, as well as, in addition to: *I am sending you a dozen new-laid eggs, together with some fresh butter*.

togger, n. [1. tóger; 2. tɒ́gə]. Oxford University slang for **torpid (II.)**, college boat in the Lent Term races. Pl. **toggers**, inter-collegiate boat-races in Lent Term.

toggery, n. [1. tógeri; 2. tɒ́gəri]. See **togs** & **-ery**. (colloq.) Clothes collectively; esp. some special kind of dress, uniform &c.: *an actor's, a bishop's, general's, toggery*.

toggle, n. & vb. trans. [1. tógl; 2. tɒ́gl]. Etymol. uncertain; perh. connected w. **tug (I.)**. **1.** n. A metal pin fixed at right angles in the strands of a rope and projecting at either side, to serve as a means for holding another rope hitched over it. **2.** vb. To fasten by means of a toggle.

toggle-joint, n. Device for applying pressure sideways, consisting of two bars crossing each other near the ends, and pivoted or jointed together, so that force directed to straighten the joint is transmitted to the other end of each bar.

togs, n. pl. [1. togz; 2. tɒgz], fr. **toga**? (slang, esp. naut.) Clothes, dress: *fine new togs*.

toil (I.), n. [1. toil; 2. toil]. Fr. *toile*, 'cloth', fr. Lat. *tēla*, 'woven stuff, web'; fr. **texla*, cp. Lat. *texere*, 'to weave'; see **text**. Only used in pl. **toils**; net, meshes, snare; *in the toils*, lit. netted, caught; (fig.) deeply fascinated, charmed, under a spell &c.

toil (II.), vb. intrans. M.E. *toilen*, fr. O. Fr. *toillier*, 'to pull, drag about; cause to roll' &c., Lat. *tudiculāre*, 'to stir', fr. *tuditāre*, 'to thrust, push'; fr. *tudit-* stem of *tudēs*, 'hammer', connected w. the nasalized *tundere*, 'to strike'. Both nasalized & unnasalized forms of this base occur in other languages, cp. Scrt. *tundatē*, & *tudáti*, 'he pushes, strikes, pricks'.

See also **contuse**. 1. To exert strength, to work hard, labour; also *toil at*, to work at laboriously. 2. To go along, walk, painfully and with effort: *to toil up hill*; *to toil along the road* &c.
toil (III.), n., fr. prec. Severe, tedious labour, exacting, fatiguing work, drudgery.
toiler, n. [1. tóiler; 2. tóilə]. **toil** (I.) & **-er**. One who toils; a hard worker.
toilet, n. [1. tóilet; 2. tóilit], fr. *toilette*, dimin. of *toile*, 'cloth', see **toil** (I.). 1. (formerly, now obs.) A cloth for covering something; **a** one put over the shoulders while the hair was being dressed; **b** bag for night clothes. 2. **a** Process of dressing: *to spend time on one's toilet*; **b** mode of dressing; a female costume: *colour was given by the brilliant toilets of the ladies*.
toilet-cover, n. Cloth or sheet placed over dressing-table.
toilet-paper, n. Thin sheets used in the privy.
toilet-powder, n. Soothing powder applied to the skin after shaving &c.
toilet-set, n. Set of articles and utensils used in the toilet.
toilet-table, n. Dressing-table.
toilful, adj. [1. tóifool; 2. tóilful]. **toil** (III.) & **-ful**. Involving toil; toilsome.
toilfully, adv. Prec. & **-ly**. With toil; laboriously.
toilsome, adj. [1. tóilsum; 2. tóilsəm]. **toil** (III.) & **-some**. Laborious, wearying; involving toil.
toilsomely, adv. Prec. & **-ly**. Laboriously.
toilsomeness, n. See prec. & **-ness**. Quality of being toilsome; laboriousness.
toison d'or, n. [1. twahzon dốr; 2. twazɔ̃ dɔ́r]. Fr. The Golden Fleece.
Tokay, n. [1. tōkā́; 2. toukéi], fr. place in Hungary. 1. A rich, scarce, Hungarian wine coming from Tokay. 2. A kind of grape used in the making of this wine.
token, n. [1. tōken; 2. tóukən]. O.E. *tācn*, 'sign, token, emblem' &c.; M.E. *tōken*; O.S. *tēkan*; O.H.G. *zeihhan*; Goth. *taikns*; all fr. Gmc. **taikn-*, see also **teach**, fr. base **deik̑-*, **dik̑-* &c., 'to show, tell, point out' &c.; cp. Gk. *deiknŭmi*, 'I show' &c.; Lat. *dīcere*, 'to show, say, tell'; see **diction**. 1. A symbol, evidence: *a token of respect, regard, affection* &c.; *in token of*, as a sign, as evidence of. Phr. *by the same token*, to introduce additional or amplifying statement. 2. Object used, or given, as a symbol and sign of some quality, feeling, value &c.; specif., a piece of metal formerly used by tradesmen and others instead of, but representing, money; (also attrib.) *token-money*, see preceding sense; *token vote*, money vote taken in Parliament for specific purpose, with nominal sum stated, the full amount being afterwards voted under a supplementary estimate.
tokenless, adj. [1. tōkenles; 2. tóukənlis]. Prec. & **-less**. Without, lacking, a token.
tokology, tocology, n. [1. tokóloji; 2. tɔkóləʤi], fr. Gk. *tókos*, 'birth, offspring, child', fr. base **tek-*, cp. *tiktein*, 'to produce, beget offspring', *téknon*, 'child'; cp. **thane** & see **-logy**. The science of obstetrics; midwifery.
tola, n. [1. tōla; 2. tóulə]. Hind., fr. Scrt. *tulā*, 'weight'. An Indian weight, 180 grains troy.
tolbooth, n. See **tol(l)booth**.
told, vb. [1. tōld; 2. tould]. O.E. *talde*, *(ġe)tald* (cp. W.S. *tealde*); M.E. *tōld(e)*; Pret. & P.P. of **tell**.
Toledo, Toledo blade, n. [1. tōlédō (blād); 2. toulídou (bleid)]. Sword-blade of finely tempered steel made at Toledo in Spain.
tolerability, n. [1. tòlerabíliti; 2. tɔ̀lərəbíliti]. See next word & **-ity**. Quality, state, of being tolerable.
tolerable, adj. [1. tólerabl; 2. tɔ́lərəbl]. Lat. *tolerābilis*, see **tolerate** & **-able**. 1. Endurable, capable of being borne: *the pain was severe but tolerable*. 2. **a** Fairly good, neither of the highest excellence nor such as to merit severe condemnation: *the food was good and the company tolerable*; **b** (colloq.) in fairly good health, pretty well.
tolerably, adv. Prec. & **-ly**. Moderately, fairly; to a moderate degree or extent; (usually in favourable sense) *tolerably well*; *tolerably satisfied*.
tolerance, n. [1. tólerans; 2. tɔ́lərəns]. Lat. *tolerantia*, see **tolerant** & **-ce**. Disposition of mind which is inclined to tolerate, and show forbearance to, opinions, beliefs, which one does not share, or a line of action which one does not approve of; toleration; reverse of *bigotry*.
tolerant, adj. [1. tólerant; 2. tɔ́lərənt], fr. Lat. *tolerant-(em)*, Pres. Part. of *tolerāre*, 'to bear, endure', see **tolerate**. 1. Disposed to tolerate; forbearing, indulgent; esp. to opinions and lines of conduct which are not one's own. 2. (med.) Capable of bearing the action of a drug; inured by habit to considerable doses of poisonous drugs without suffering injury.
tolerate, vb. trans. [1. tólerāt; 2. tɔ́lereit], fr. Lat. *tolerāt-(um)*, P.P. of *tolerāre*, 'to bear, sustain, endure' &c.; fr. same base as *tollere*, 'to lift up; to accept'; cogn. w. Gk. *tálanton*, 'weight', see **talent**; also w. Lat. *lātus* for **tlātus*, 'borne', & Gk. *tlḗmōn*, 'enduring'; O.E. *polian*, 'to endure', see **thole** (I.). 1. **a** To endure, show forbearance to, bear with, put up with: *to tolerate a person's presence*; **b** to show toleration of the opinions, beliefs &c. of others. 2. To be able to resist or endure: *his delicate constitution could not tolerate the severities of a northern climate*. 3. To permit, suffer to be done without attempting to prevent: *I will not tolerate interference in my affairs*; *no responsible government can tolerate disregard of the law*.
toleration, n. [1. tòleráshun; 2. tɔ̀lərɛ́iʃən]. Prec. & **-ion**. Act of tolerating; mental disposition to allow freedom of opinion and belief &c. to others; tolerance; practice of allowing such freedom, esp. in religious beliefs.
tolerationist, n. [1. tòleráshunist; 2. tɔ̀lərɛ́iʃənist]. Prec. & **-ist**. One who advocates toleration, esp. in religion.
toll (I.), vb. trans. & intrans. [1. tōl; 2. toul]. In M.E.; etymol. uncertain; partly imitative. 1. trans. To cause to sound or ring in a series of strokes repeated at regular intervals: *to toll a bell*; *to toll a funeral knell*. 2. intrans. To sound, ring, clang, with a series of regularly repeated strokes (of a bell).
toll (II.), n., fr. prec. The sound made by the tolling of a bell.
toll (III.), n. O.E. *toll*, 'a tax; money due for rent' &c.; O.S. *tol*, O.H.G. *zol*; all fr. L. Lat. *tolōnium*, Lat. *telōneum*, 'toll-house', fr. Gk. *telṓnion*, cp. *telṓnēs*, 'tax-collector', & *télos*, 'tax'. 1. **a** Tax, duty, paid for some privilege; specif., one paid for the right to pass along a road, or over a bridge, for use of a market &c.; **b** the right to exact a toll. 2. Portion of grain kept by miller in payment for grinding; hence Phr. *to take toll of*, to exact something from.
tollable, adj. [1. tólabl; 2. tóuləbl]. Prec. & **-able**. Subject to toll.
tollage, n. [1. tólij; 2. tóuliʤ]. See prec. & **-age**. Payment, exaction, of toll.
toll-bar, n. Toll-gate.
tol(l)booth, n. [1. tólbōōth; 2. tɔ́lbúp]. Scots. 1. Formerly, temporary shed erected at a market &c. for payment of tolls. 2. (Scots) Town prison.
toll-gate, n. Gate placed across high road, kept closed to prevent persons and vehicles from passing until the toll is paid.
toll-house, n. House at a toll-gate, where the keeper of this lives.
Toltec, n. [1. tóltek; 2. tɔ́ltɛk]. Race possessing considerable civilization, who preceded the Aztecs in Mexico.
tolu, n. [1. tōlōō; 2. toulú], fr. Santiago de Tolu. Also *tolu balsam*, an aromatic resin obtained from a S. American tree, used medicinally and in perfumery.
toluene, toluol, n. [1. tólooēn, tóluol; 2. tólu̇ìn, tóljuəl], fr. prec. & second element of **benzene, benzol**. An aromatic hydrocarbon obtained by distillation of tolu balsam, and from coal tar; used in dyeing and manufacture of explosives.
tom, n. [1. tom; 2. tɔm]. Abbr. of *Thomas*. 1. (cap.) *Tom, Dick, and Harry*, all sorts and conditions, people in general without selection, anybody and everybody. 2. Denotes the male of certain animals, esp. of the cat.
tomahawk, n. & vb. trans. [1. tóma-hawk; 2. tɔ́məhɔ̄k]. Am. Indian. 1. n. A light axe or hatchet used by American Indians, often made with a hollow handle, the passage in which communicates with a bowl on reverse side of handle to the blade, so that the weapon can also be used as a tobacco pipe. 2. vb. To strike, kill, with a tomahawk.
tomalley, n. [1. tomáli; 2. tɔmǽli], fr. **tourmalin**, on account of colour. Liver of a lobster, which turns green when boiled.
toman, n. [1. tomáhn; 2. tɔmǽn]. Pers., 'heap; ten thousand'. Persian gold coin worth about 7s.
tomato, n., pl. *tomatoes* [1. tomáhtō; 2. təmǽtou]. Span. *tomate*, fr. Mex. *tomatl*. **a** A trailing plant, *Lycopersicum esculentum*, native of S. America, bearing juicy, acid fruit, red or yellow when ripe; **b** fruit of this, much used for salads.
tomb, n. [1. tōōm; 2. tūm]. M.E., fr. O. Fr. *tombe*, fr. Lat. *tumba*, fr. Gk. *túmbos*, cogn. w. **tumulus**. 1. **a** A grave in which the dead are buried; **b** a cavity in the earth, vault, in which the dead are deposited; **c** a monument erected over a grave or vault. 2. (fig.) *The tomb*, death; cp. *the grave*.
tomb (II.), vb. trans. (rare) To place in a tomb; to entomb.
tombac, n. [1. tómbak; 2. tɔ́mbæk]. Port. *tambaca*, fr. Malay. *tambāga*, 'copper'. Alloy of copper and zinc, used in making cheap jewellery.
tombola, n. [1. tómbōla; 2. tɔ́mboulə]. Ital., fr. *tombolare*, see **tumble** (I.). Kind of lottery.
tomboy, n. [1. tómboi; 2. tɔ́mbɔi]. A noisy, romping girl; (not in derogatory sense).
tombstone, n. [1. tōōmstōn; 2. tǘmstoun]. Stone placed over a grave recording the name, dates of birth and death &c. of the deceased.
tomcat, n. [1. tómkát; 2. tɔ́mkǽt]. Male cat.
tome, n. [1. tōm; 2. toum]. Fr., fr. Lat. *tomus*, fr. Gk. *tómos*, 'piece cut off, section'; cogn. w. Gk. *témnein*, 'to cut'; cp. **tmesis**; O. Russ. *timeti*, 'he strikes'; cp. also **-tomy**. 1. A volume, a book, esp. a large, ponderous volume. 2. A part, a volume, of a large work, usually bound separately.
-tome, suff. See prec. Form used in compounds, in sense of **a** a section, part; **b** instrument for cutting.
tomentose, adj. [1. tóments; 2. tóuməntous]. See next word & **-ose**. Covered with long or matted hairs.
tomentum, n. [1. toméntum; 2. touméntəm]. Lat., 'stuffing for cushions' (of wool, hair &c.); for **tovementum*, fr. same base as in *tōtus*, 'all', see **total** (I.), & *tumēre*, 'to swell', see **tumid**. (bot.) Covering of dense, matted, woolly hairs.
tomfool, n. [1. tómfōōl; 2. tɔ́mfúl]. A great fool, perfect fool; a silly buffoon.
tomfoolery, n. [1. tómfōōleri; 2. tɔ́mfúləri]. Prec. & **-ery**. Buffoonery; stupid, senseless behaviour, nonsense.
tommy, n. [1. tómi; 2. tɔ́mi]. Familiar form of *Thomas*. 1. (cap.) A private soldier; also *Tommy Atkins*. 2. Provisions given to workmen in lieu of wages; *tommy shop*, one where practice of providing tommy prevails. 3. (slang) *tommy rot*, rank foolishness, absurd nonsense.
tomorrow, n. & adv. [1. tumórō; 2. təmɔ́rou]. **to** (I.) & **morrow**. 1. n. The day which follows today: *let us hope tomorrow will be fine*. 2. adv. On the day following today: *we shall meet tomorrow*.
tompion, n. [1. tómpiun; 2. tɔ́mpiən]. Variant of **tampion**. Pad for inking, used in lithography.

tomtit, n. [1. tómtít; 2. tɔ́mtít]. Name of a bird; also called blue *titmouse*.

tomtom, n. [1. tómtom; 2. tɔ́mtɔm]. Hind. *tamtam*; imitative. Primitive kind of drum used in India.

-tomy, suff. fr. Gk. *-tomía*, fr. *tomḗ*, 'a cutting, section'; see **tome**. Indicates 'cutting', e.g. *anatomy, ovariotomy* &c.

ton (I.), n. [1. tun; 2. tan]. Variant spelling of **tun**. **1. a** A weight consisting of 20 hundredweights; *the long* or *gross ton*, of 2240 lb. avoirdupois; the *short, American, ton*, of 2000 lb.; *metric ton*, 1000 kilograms, 2204·6 lb.; **b** (colloq. and loosely) (i.) a very heavy weight: *this box of yours weighs a ton*, i.e. is very heavy; (ii.) a large quantity: *tons of money*; *you have tons of time*, plenty of time; *with tons of love* &c. **2.** A measure of amount, volume, or capacity, varying with the article, as of timber, gravel, coke, wheat &c. **3.** (naut.) **a** *Displacement ton*, 35 cubic feet of water; **b** *freight ton*, 40 cubic feet; **c** *register ton*, 100 cubic feet.

ton (II.), n. [1. ton; 2. tɔ̃]. Fr., see **tone (I.)**. Style; fashion, vogue.

tonal, adj. [1. tṓnal; 2. tóun(ə)l]. **tone (I.)** & **-al**. Connected with, pertaining to, tone or tonality.

tonality, n. [1. tōnáliti; 2. tounǽliti]. **tonal** & **-ity**. **1.** (mus.) Quality of a composition derived from its key or from its system of tones. **2.** (paint.) Quality, scheme, of colour.

tondo, n. [1. tóndō; 2. tɔ́ndou]. Ital., 'round plate', fr. Lat. *rotundus*, see **rotund**. **a** A circular painted panel or canvas; **b** a sculptured relief in circular form.

tone (I.), n. [1. tōn; 2. toun]. Fr. *ton*, fr. Lat. *tonus*, 'sound, tone, of an instrument', fr. Gk. *tónos*, 'that which tightens, or which can itself be strained or tightened; a cord, rope; a tightening, strain; a pitching of the voice; hence, a musical note'; cp. Gk. *teinein*, 'to stretch, strain, extend', fr. **ten-jo-*; base **ten-*, **ton-*, whence also **thin**; also Lat. *tenuis*, 'slight', see **tenuis**, & **tenuity**; & cp. **tend (II.)** &c. **1.** Sound, esp. conceived of as possessing a certain quality, resonance, pitch &c.; a musical sound: *the tones of the voice, of a harp* &c.; *sweet, silvery, harsh, gentle, tones*. **2.** Pitch of the voice; modulation of this in speaking, as expressing varying emotion: *angry, loving, tones*; *a tone of entreaty, apology* &c. **3.** (mus.) The larger interval between the notes of the diatonic scale, as distinguished from *semitone*. **4.** (phon.) One kind of accent; an intonation, degree of pitch in the voice in speaking; the note on which a given word or syllable is uttered; contrasted with *stress*. **5.** (med.) State of body or mind in which the organs and functions are vigorous. **6.** Prevailing spirit, mental attitude, moral atmosphere: *a school with a good, healthy, tone*; *the tone of a letter*; *the general tone of the speech was gloomy, frivolous, solemn* &c. **7.** Shade, degree of intensity of colour, hue.

tone (II.), vb. trans. & intrans., fr. prec. **A.** trans. **1.** To impart tone to: **a** of sound; **b** of colour. **2.** Specif. (photog.) to modify colour of by treating chemically. **B.** Followed by adverb or preposition. *Tone down*, **1.** trans., **a** to reduce intensity of colouring of; **b** (fig.) to mitigate, diminish violence, intensity, of (passions, opinions &c., or their expression); to subdue, render less marked and noticeable; **2.** intrans., to become softened, less intense, less marked; *tone in with*, **a** trans., to cause to blend; **b** intrans., to blend, become mingled, harmonize with; *tone up*, **1.** trans., to intensify, emphasize a colour of; **b** form of expression; **2.** intrans., to become intensified.

toned, adj. [1. tōnd; 2. tound], fr. P.P. of prec. Slightly tinted.

-toned, adj. Having a particular kind of tone: *loud-toned*; *sweet-toned* &c.

toneless, adj. [1. tṓnles; 2. tóunlis]. **tone (I.)** & **-less**. **1.** Giving forth no tone or sound; silent; lacking resonance. **2.** Lacking colour, character; spiritless.

tonelessly, adv. Prec. & **-ly**. In a toneless manner.

tonelessness, n. See prec. & **-ness**. Quality of being toneless.

tong, n. [1. tong; 2. tɔŋ]. Chinese *t'ang*, 'hall'. A Chinese secret society or club.

tonga, n. [1. tóngga; 2. tɔ́ŋgə]. Hind. *tānga*. Light two-wheeled carriage.

tongs, n. pl. [1. tongz; 2. tɔŋz]. O.E. *tange*, 'tongs, forceps'; O.H.G. *zanga*; O.N. *tǫng*; cogn. w. Gk. *dáknein*, 'to bite'. See **tang (I.)**. One of various kinds of objects, mostly consisting of two legs of metal joined by a pivot or by a spring, used for gripping, lifting, twisting &c.: *tongs for lifting pieces of coal*; *sugar tongs* &c. Phr. *I wouldn't touch him, it, with a pair of tongs*, he, it, is too disgusting to handle; (also fig.) it is the kind of business to avoid as much as possible.

tongue, n. [1. tung; 2. taŋ]. O.E. *tunge*, M.E. *tunge, tonge* &c.; O.S. *tunga*; O.H.G. *zunga*; Goth. *tungō*; cogn. w. Lat. *lingua*, 'tongue', fr. *dingua*, see **lingual**. **1.** Long, narrow, muscular, highly sensitive, and mobile organ in the mouth by means of which the act of licking is performed, and which plays a part in swallowing; the chief organ of taste, and, in man, of speech. Phrs. *to give tongue*, (i.) to shout, speak loud or vehemently; (ii.) to bark, as hounds on the scent; *to have a ready tongue*, be an easy, fluent speaker. **2.** (fig.) **a** Mode of speech, way of speaking: *a gentle tongue*; **b** mode of verbal expression: *the silver tongue of the orator*. **3.** A human language: *the ancient tongues*. **4.** The tongue of an animal, thought of as, and prepared for, food. **5.** Any of various things shaped, approximately, like a tongue; **a** thin leather flap fixed by lower end, under the laces of a boot or shoe, lying between them and the foot; **b** hinged or otherwise movable pin in a buckle, which passes through a hole in the strap; **c** thin, movable strip of metal occurring in various wind instruments; **d** clapper of a bell; **e** a narrow strip of land, esp. one that juts out into the water; **f** a thin, long, narrow flame; **g** thin projecting portion of a piece of wood, fitting into a corresponding groove or hollow in another piece.

tongue (II.), vb. trans. & intrans., fr. prec. **1.** trans. **a** To use the tongue in playing (a flute); **b** to execute (piece of music) by using the tongue. **2.** intrans. To produce staccato notes with the tongue (on a flute).

-tongued, adj. [1. tungd; 2. taŋd]. **tongue (I.)** & **-ed**. Having a particular kind of tongue, voice, sound &c.: *silver-tongued*; *dry-tongued*.

tongueless, adj. [1. túngles; 2. táŋlis]. **tongue (I.)** & **-less**. **1.** Lacking a tongue. **2.** Not using the tongue to speak; silent.

tongue-tied, adj. [1. túng tīd; 2. táŋ taid]. **a** Having an impediment in one's speech; **b** unable to speak, esp. through embarrassment; **c** not inclined to speak, taciturn, silent.

tonguing, n. [1. túnging; 2. táŋiŋ]. Staccato effect produced by tip of the tongue in playing a wind instrument.

tonic (I.), adj. [1. tónik; 2. tɔ́nik]. Fr. *tonique*, fr. Gk. *tonikós*; **tone (I.)** & **-ic**. **1.** (phon.) Pertaining to tones; *tonic accent*, one depending on alterations of pitch; contrasted with *stress accent*. **2.** (med.) **a** Distinguished by muscular contraction: *tonic spasms, convulsions*; **b** having an invigorating, stimulating effect upon the system: *a tonic drug* &c.; also, stimulating to the mind. **3.** Pertaining to colour tone, to light and shade, in a picture or landscape.

tonic (II.), n., fr. prec. **1.** The syllable in a word distinguished by the chief tonic accent. **2.** (mus.) The keynote. **3. a** An invigorating medicine; **b** something which stimulates the mind or character.

tonically, adv. [1. tónikali; 2. tɔ́nikəli]. **tonic (I.)** & **-al** & **-ly**. **1.** In respect of tone or pitch. **2.** As a tonic, so as to stimulate or invigorate.

tonicity, n. [1. tonísiti; 2. tənísiti]. **tonic (I.)** & **-ity**. Property of possessing tone; **a** condition of normal healthy muscular tension and elasticity; vigour; **b** musical tone.

tonic sol-fa, n. [1. tónik sòl fáh; 2. tɔ́nik sɔ̀l fā́]. System of musical notation based on tonality, consisting of a series of syllables, *do, re, mi* &c.

tonight, adv. & n. [1. tunít; 2. tənáit]. **to (I.)** & **night**. **1.** adv. On this night; on the night of today. **2.** n. This night; the night coming after this day.

tonite, n. [1. tṓnīt; 2. tóunait], fr. base of Lat. *tonāre*, 'to thunder', see **thunder (I.)**, & **-ite**. Explosive used for blasting.

tonka bean, n. [1. tóngka bēn; 2. tɔ́ŋkə bīn]. Native word. Aromatic seed of a plant growing in Guiana, used in perfumery.

tonnage, n. [1. túnij; 2. tánidž]. **ton (I.)** & **-age**. **a** Freight-carrying capacity of a ship, in tons; **b** total amount of a country's shipping calculated in tons; **c** duty payable on ships according to their tonnage.

tonneau, n. [1. tónō; 2. tɔ́nou]. Fr., 'cask', see **tun**. Rear part, containing back seats, of a motor-car.

-tonner, n. [1. túner; 2. tánə]. Having capacity of so many tons: *300-tonner* (of ships); weighing so many tons.

tonometer, n. [1. tōnómeter; 2. tounɔ́mitə]. See **tone (I.)** & **-meter**. Device for measuring tone or pitch.

tonsil, n. [1. tónsl, -il; 2. tɔ́nsl, -il]. Fr. *tonsille*, fr. Lat. *tonsillae* (pl.); connected w. Lat. *tōlēs*, 'goitre'; perh. ultimately fr. base **twen-*, 'to swell', see **tumid**. One of a pair of masses of lymphoid tissue on either side of the back of the throat.

tonsillar, adj. [1. tónsilar; 2. tɔ́nsilə]. Prec. & **-ar**. Connected with, pertaining to, the tonsils.

tonsillitic, adj. [1. tònsilítik; 2. tɔ̀nsilítik]. See next word & **-ic**. Pertaining to, of the nature of, tonsillitis.

tonsillitis, n. [1. tònsilítis; 2. tɔ̀nsiláitis]. See **tonsil** & **-itis**. Inflammation of the tonsils; quinsy.

tonsorial, adj. [1. tonsṓrial; 2. tɔnsɔ́riəl]. Lat. *tonsōrius*, 'pertaining to shearing', fr. *tonsor*, 'shearer, shaver, barber', & **-al**; fr. *tons-(um)*, P.P. type of *tondēre*, 'to shear, clip; to act as barber'; connected w. Gk. *téndein*, 'to gnaw, nibble'; the base **tend-*, **tond-*, is an extension of **tem-* &c., 'to cut', q.v. under **tmesis** & **tome**. Pertaining to a barber or his craft; (facet.) *tonsorial artist*, a barber, hairdresser.

tonsure, n. & vb. trans. [1. tónshur; 2. tɔ́nʃə]. Lat. *tonsūra*, 'a shearing, clipping'; fr. *tons-*, see prec., & **-ure**. **1.** n. **a** Act of shaving the crown of the head or part of it; a rite administered in Roman Church, to a person on admission to priest's orders, and to a monastic order; **b** that part of the head from which the hair has been removed. **2.** vb. To shave part of the head of; to administer the tonsure to; to make a tonsure on.

tonsured, adj. [1. tónshurd; 2. tɔ́nʃəd]. Prec. & **-ed**. **a** Having a tonsure; **b** shaven and shorn.

tontine, n. [1. tóntēn; 2. tɔ́ntīn]. Ital. *tontina*, fr. Tonti, the inventor (17th cent.). Arrangement whereby a number of persons share an annuity or other financial benefit, the share of each increasing as the number is diminished by death, until the last survivor obtains the whole sum.

too, adv. [1. tōō; 2. tū]. Stressed form of **to (I.)**. **1. a** Denoting superfluity; excessively; more than enough, in excess of what is required: *a hat far too big for him*; *too good to last*; *too good for him*; *too fat for beauty*; *too much*; *too little*, not enough; **b** (as intens.) equivalent to very: *you are really too kind*; *I shall be only too pleased to help you*. **2.** In addition, as well, moreover: *I had some food, and some wine too*; *to play, and sing too*; *won't you come too?* Phr. *very nice too*, strongly affirmative.

took, vb. [1. took ; 2. tuk]. L.O.E. *tōc* ; M.E. *tōk* ; Pret. of **take**.

tool (I.), n. [1. tōōl ; 2. tūl]. O.E. *tōl*, not found in other Gmc. languages ; prob. formed fr. the base seen in O.E. *tāwian*, 'to prepare land for sowing' ; *ġetǣwe*, 'apparatus', see **taw** (I.) ; cp. Goth. *taujan*, 'to make, do, effect' ; *tēwa*, 'order, arrangement' ; *tawi*, 'work'. **1. a** Any of a large variety of implements, instruments, utensils, used in making things, in shaping, working, preparing material &c. ; esp. an implement held in, and worked by the hand, as distinguished from one moved by machinery : *carpenter's, gardener's, blacksmith's tools* &c. ; **b** that part of a machine or mechanical contrivance which actually does the cutting, shaping &c. ; usually *machine tool*; **c** specif., a tool used by a bookbinder in decorating the cover of a book. **2.** The means whereby an occupation is pursued ; aid in, equipment for, intellectual work : *books are the tools of a scholar ; the tools of one's trade*. **3.** (usually derogatory) A person used by another to perform actions, esp. of a discreditable character, on his behalf, without the real mover appearing ; a cat's-paw, a servile confederate who acts as the instrument of another's will ; person who acts entirely at the instigation of another ; a puppet.

tool (II.), vb. trans. & intrans., fr. prec. **A.** trans. **1.** To use a tool upon ; specif., to decorate back or edges of a book-cover with a tool. **2.** (colloq.) To drive a person in a leisurely manner in a vehicle : *let me tool you down to the station*. **B.** intrans. (colloq.) To ride or drive oneself in an easy, leisurely way ; also *tool along*, to bowl along : *tooling along the road in fine style*.

tool-box, -chest, n. Box specially designed, and used, for keeping tools.

tooler, n. [1. tōōler ; 2. tūlə]. **tool** (II.) & **er**. Broad chisel for dressing stone.

tooling, n. [1. tōōling ; 2. tūliŋ]. See prec. & **-ing**. **1.** Mode of dressing stone, so that the marks of the chisel are left. **2.** Ornamentation, often gilt, made by pressing with a tool, on book bindings.

toon, n. [1. tōōn ; 2. tūn]. Hind. *tun, tuna*. An East Indian tree with fine-grained reddish wood, used for furniture-making ; sometimes known as Indian mahogany.

toot, vb. intrans. & n. [1. tōōt ; 2. tūt]. Prob. imitative ; the same word in very similar form exists in Du. & Scand. languages. **1.** vb. To blow a horn ; to sound like the note of a horn, to hoot. **2.** n. The sound of tooting or hooting.

tooth (I.), n. [1. tōōth ; 2. tūþ]. O.E. *tōþ*, M.E. *tōth* &c., fr. earlier **tanþ-*; cogn. w. O.S. *tand*; O.H.G. *zand*, Germ. *zahn*; Goth. *tunþus*; fr. participial base **(e)dent-, *(o)dont-* &c., fr. **ed-*, whence also *eat*; cogn. w. Scrt. *danta*; Gk. *odóntos*, see **odont-**; Lat. *dent-*, see **dental**; cp. also **tusk**. **1.** One of the hard, ivory-like objects in the gums of human beings and the lower animals, which serve to masticate food, and, for the latter, as weapons of attack and defence. Phrs. *to cast something in a person's teeth*, to reproach him with it ; *in the teeth of*, in opposition to ; in spite of ; *to draw a person's teeth*, (i.) to deprive him of his chief ground of complaint ; (ii.) to render him harmless, mollify him ; *to fight, oppose, tooth and nail*, with the utmost fierceness or energy ; *armed to the teeth*, very completely armed ; *(to escape) by* (properly *with*) *the skin of one's teeth*, by very slight margin, very narrowly ; *to have a sweet tooth*, to be fond of sweet things ; *to set one's teeth on edge*, disgust, cause to shudder ; *to show one's teeth*, to exhibit anger, resentment &c. **2.** Any of various objects resembling, or supposed to resemble, a tooth ; e.g. one of the separate divisions of a comb or saw ; one of the projecting points or cogs on a wheel &c.

tooth (II.), vb. trans. & intrans., fr. prec. **1.** trans. To furnish (a wheel &c.) with teeth. **2.** intrans. To interlock, as the teeth or cogs on two engaged wheels.

toothache, n. [1. tōōthāk ; 2. tūþeik]. Pain in the nerves of the teeth.

tooth-billed, adj. [1. tōōth bild ; 2. tūþ bild]. Having a bill the edges of which have projections or notches.

tooth-brush, n. Small brush for washing the teeth.

toothful, n. [1. tōōthfool ; 2. tūþful]. (of brandy &c.) A small draught.

tooth-paste, n. Cleansing, antiseptic paste used in brushing the teeth.

toothpick, n. [1. tōōthpik ; 2. tūþpik]. Small instrument with pliable point and end, of quill, gold &c., for dislodging portions of food from between the teeth.

tooth-powder, n. Medicated, gritty powder, used on tooth-brush, for cleaning the teeth.

toothsome, adj. [1. tōōthsum ; 2. tūþsəm]. **tooth** (I.) & **-some**. Dainty, choice, agreeable to the taste.

tootle, vb. intrans. & n. [1. tōōtl ; 2. tūtl]. Freq. of **toot**. **1.** vb. To toot, or hoot, repeatedly but not loudly, on a flute, horn &c. **2.** n. The sound made by one who tootles.

top (I.), n. [1. top ; 2. tɔp]. O.E. *topp*, 'summit' ; O.H.G. *zopf*, 'tuft of hair ; top of a tree' ; O.N. *toppr*, 'tuft of hair ; crest, summit'. **1. a** The highest part of anything ; summit : *the top of the head, of a hill, house, tree* ; Phrs. *the top of the tree, ladder*, highest point of success, excellence ; highest rank ; *from top to toe*, from head to foot ; *to come out on top*, to beat others in a contest, be successful in life ; *on top of everything else* &c., in addition to, as a last straw ; **b** the upper portion of a flat surface : *the top of the page*. **2.** Specif., kind of platform near the head of a ship's mast, to which part of rigging is fastened, and upon which men stand in taking in sail &c. ; also (pl.) *the tops*. **3.** A tuft springing from the top of anything. **4.** Upper surface, outer side of anything : *on the top of the ground*. **5.** That part of a plant above the ground ; contrasted with the root. **6.** The greatest degree of intensity, fullest extent : *at the top of one's voice*, very loud ; *the top of one's speed*. Phr. *to the top of one's bent*, as much as one could desire. **7.** The highest, most honourable, position, rank ; the highest place attainable : *the top of one's profession* ; *the top of a class*. **8.** Specif., a long fibre of wool after combing, fashioned into a continuous sliver for spinning, contrasted with *noil*, the short fibre.

top (II.), adj., fr. prec. **1.** Nearest to, or at the top ; highest : *the top shelf, layer, step* ; *top right-hand corner* (of a page &c.) ; *top rung of a ladder* &c. Phr. (fig.) *top rung*, highest point of success, chief position. **2.** Having the greatest degree of intensity : *top speed* ; *top price(s)*, highest price reached. **3.** Chief, foremost, highest in rank &c. : *the top place in a class*.

top (III.), vb. trans., fr. **top** (I.). **1.** To furnish with a top, cover top of. **2.** To cut off top of : *to top a tree*. **3.** To touch, strike, on upper part, above the centre : *to top a golf-ball*. **4.** To reach to the top of, come level with : *the wood just tops the rising ground*. **5.** To surpass in height, reach beyond top of : *he tops his father by half a head* ; (also fig.) be superior to : *his performance tops all previous records*.

top (IV.), n. O.E. *top*; fr. M.H.G. *topf*; etymol. doubtful. Child's toy of wood or metal, usually pear-shaped and tapering to a point, or round, having a central metal point upon which it is made to spin either by whipping, or by means of a string wound round it and unwound by a sudden jerk.

topaz, n. [1. tōpaz ; 2. tóupæz]. Lat., fr. Gk. *tópazos*; etymol. uncertain. Semi-precious stone, usually yellow, but sometimes white, or bluish.

top-boot, n. Riding boot reaching to just below the knee, having a band of light-coloured leather round the top.

topcoat, n. [1. tópkōt ; 2. tópkóut]. Coat worn above another coat ; overcoat.

top-dress, vb. trans. To apply top-dressing to.

top-dressing, n. Manure applied on the surface of the ground.

tope (I.), vb. intrans. & trans. [1. tōp ; 2. toup]. Fr. *toper*; etymol. doubtful. **1.** intrans. To drink alcoholic liquor frequently and to excess. **2.** trans. To drink (strong liquor) frequently and excessively.

tope (II.), n. Etymol. unknown. A small kind of shark ; dogfish.

tope (III.), n. Hind. *tōp*. Cylindrical tower surmounted by a cupola, containing a Buddhist shrine.

topee. See **topi**.

topek, n. [1. tōpek ; 2. tóupek]. Eskimo *tupek*. Eskimo hut of wood or some substance other than snow.

toper, n. [1. tōper ; 2. tóupə]. **tope** (I.) & **-er**. One who topes ; a drunkard.

topgallant, adj. [1. tópgálant ; 2. tópgælənt]. (naut.) Designating a position above top-mast and below royal-mast.

top-hamper, n. **1.** The upper rigging of a ship. **2.** The upper, smaller boughs or the thinner upper part of the stem of a large tree.

top-hat, n. Tall hat, silk hat.

top-heavy, adj. Ill-balanced through having the upper part too heavy for the base ; inclined to topple over.

Tophet, n. [1. tōfet ; 2. tóufet]. Heb. *topheth*, 'place to be spat upon'. Place in valley of Hinnom, near Jerusalem, where rubbish was perpetually being burnt, and where sacrifices to Moloch were performed.

top-hole, adj. (slang) Excellent, first-rate, tip-top.

tophus, n. [1. tōfus ; 2. tóufəs], fr. Fr., in Engl. sense ; cp. **tufa**. Calcareous deposit round the teeth ; gouty concretion in, or on, a joint.

topi, topee, n. [1. tōpē ; 2. tóupī]. Hind. *tōpi*. A pith hat or helmet, usually *sola topi*.

topiary, n. [1. tōpiari ; 2. tóupiəri]. Lat. *topiārius*, 'landscape gardener', fr. *topia*, 'mural decoration depicting landscapes of fanciful character', fr. Gk. *tópos*, 'place', see next word. The art of cutting living trees, esp. yews and boxes, into shapes of animals, birds, and other objects.

topic, n. [1. tópik ; 2. tópik]. Gk. *topikós*, 'belonging to a place ; concerning *tópoi*, i.e. commonplaces', fr. *tópos*, 'a place' ; prob. cogn. w. Lith. *tàpti*, 'to become' ; possibly also w. O.E. *þafian*, 'to consent', assuming that the orig. meaning was 'to yield place to', cp. **allow** for similar development. **1.** Theme, subject, of thought ; also, subject of discourse, conversation, discussion &c. **2.** One of the forms of argument employed in probable, as distinct from demonstrative, reasoning ; source from which arguments may be drawn.

topical, adj. [1. tópikl ; 2. tópikl]. Prec. & **-al**. **1.** Connected with a subject of current or local interest. **2.** Of the nature of a topic or general principle. **3.** (med.) Affecting a particular area of the body only.

topically, adv. Prec. & **-ly**. In a topical manner.

topknot, n. [1. tópnot ; 2. tópnɔt]. **1.** A tuft or bunch, projecting from the top of anything ; specif. **a** a tuft of hair or curl on the top of the head ; **b** (colloq.) the head itself. **2.** Species of flounder.

topless, adj. [1. tóples ; 2. tóplis]. **top** (I.) & **-less**. Having the top so high as to be invisible ; hence very lofty, of a height so great that it cannot be estimated : '*the topless towers of Ilium*' (Marlowe's 'Faustus').

top-light, n. Lantern in a ship's tops.

topmast, n. [1. tópmahst ; 2. tópmāst]. Mast between the lower and the topgallant mast.

topmost, adj. [1. tópmōst ; 2. tópmoust]. Highest ; chief, highest in importance or position.

topo-, pref., fr. Gk. *tópos*, 'place', see **topic**.

topographer, n. [1. topógrafer ; 2. təpógrəfə]. **topo-** & **-grapher**. One who describes a place or area ; student of, one skilled in, topography.

topographic(al), adj. [1. tòpográfik(l); 2. tòpəgræfik(l)]. topo- & graphic(al). Connected with topography; descriptive of an area or locality.

topographist, n. [1. topógrafist; 2. təpógrafist]. topography & -ist. Topographer.

topography, n. [1. topógrafi; 2. təpógrafi]. topo- & -graphy. 1. Systematic, detailed, description of a place, city &c., or of an area of country. 2. General characteristics and relative disposition of geographical and other features of a region.

topology, n. [1. topóloji; 2. təpólədži]. topo- & -logy. Study of topography.

toponomy, n. [1. topónomi; 2. təpónəmi], fr. topo- & Gk. *ónoma*, 'name', see **onomatopoeia**. Nomenclature, **a** of places; **b** of regions of the body.

topper, n. [1. tóper; 2. tópə]. **top (II.)** & **-er**. 1. Something which lies or is placed on the top; **a** large stone used as top course of a wall, often set edgewise; **b** (slang) a top-hat. 2. (colloq.) Person who, thing which, tops or surpasses others; specif., term of praise of persons, a good fellow, good sort; a thoroughly admirable and likable person.

topping (I.), vbl. n. [1. tóping; 2. tópiŋ]. **top (II.)** & **-ing**. 1. Act of one who tops or removes top. 2. Part removed from, cut off, the top of anything. 3. That which forms the top of anything.

topping (II.), adj., fr. Pres. Part. of **top (II.)**. Higher than, superior to; hence (colloq.) term of indiscriminate praise; excellent, very good, first-rate; agreeable, delightful: *a topping fellow*; *a topping dinner* &c.

toppingly, adv. Prec. & -ly. (colloq.) In a topping manner, excellently: *the car ran simply toppingly*.

topple, vb. intrans. & trans. [1. tópl; 2. tópl]. Freq. formed fr. **top (II.)**, lit. 'to fall because top-heavy'. 1. intrans. **a** To totter, rock; to overbalance, to be on the point of falling; **b** *topple over*, to lose balance and fall over; **c** *topple down*, (of an edifice, pile, single object) to tumble down; tip over. 2. trans. **a** To cause to totter or to be unsteady; **b** *topple over*, push over; **c** *topple down*, to send tumbling down.

topsail, n. [1. tópsl; 2. tópsl]. Square sail next above lowest.

top-sawyer, n. 1. Man who occupies upper place in sawing in a pit. 2. (archaic) Person occupying prominent, important position in life.

top-shaped, adj. **top (III.)**. Shaped like a top; pear-shaped.

topsides, n. pl. [1. tópsídz; 2. tópsáidz]. Upper part of ship's sides, above water.

topsyturvy, adv., adj., n. [1. tópsitĕrvi; 2. tópsitǎvi]. topsy-=top so; for -turvy cp. O.E. *tearflian*, 'to roll'. 1. adv. & adj. Upside-down, in confusion; upset, confused, the wrong way about. 2. n. State of confusion, a muddle.

topsyturvydom, n. [1. tópsitĕrvidum; 2. tópsitǎvidəm]. Prec. & -dom. Condition of upset and confusion, whether in material objects or in ideas, affairs &c.; an inversion of natural order and conditions.

toque, n. [1. tōk; 2. touk]. Fr., fr. Celt. 1. Small, close-fitting, round hat, esp. as worn by women. 2. Monkey found in Ceylon, *Macaca pileata*, the hair on the head of which gives it the appearance of wearing a cap.

tor, n. [1. tōr; 2. tō]. O.E. *torr*; a Celt. loanword; cp. O.W. *torr*; W. *tor*, 'a boss'. A high rocky pointed hill; now chiefly of such hills on Dartmoor.

torah, n. [1. tóra; 2. tórə]. Heb. **a** A law, precept; **b** divine revelation of law; specif., the Pentateuch.

toran, n. [1. tŏran; 2. tŏrən]. Scrt. *tōrana*, 'archway, gate'. The ceremonial gateway to a Buddhist temple.

torch, n. [1. torch; 2. tōtʃ]. M.E., fr. O. Fr. *torche*, 'rag, wisp', fr. L. Lat. *torca*, fr. Lat. **torqua*, variant of *torquis*, *torques*, 'twisted neck-chain, collar' &c., see **torque**, fr. base *torquēre*, 'to turn, twist, wind' &c.; see also **tort**. 1. **a** Piece of inflammable wood or wood soaked in inflammable substance, such as resin, pitch &c., which flares when kindled and is used to give light; a flambeau, a link; **b** (fig.) something which produces spiritual enlightenment or enthusiasm for worthy things: *the torch of learning* &c. Phr. *to hand on the torch*, to transmit a tradition of culture and spiritual enlightenment. 2. One of various devices for giving light, esp. *electric torch*, small electric lamp carried in the hand.

torchlight, n. [1. tórchlīt; 2. tótʃlait]. Light shed by torches; (attrib.) *torchlight procession*, one in which those taking part carry torches.

torchon, n. used attrib. [1. tórshon; 2. tóʃɔ̃, -ɔn]. Fr., 'a crumpled rag, wisp of cloth' &c.; see **torch**. *Torchon lace*, strong, coarse lace, made on a pillow; *torchon paper*, strong, hard paper with a rough surface, used for water-colour painting.

torcular, n. [1. tórkūlar; 2. tókjulə]. Lat., 'that which twists; a wine-press'; see **torque**. Tourniquet used by surgeons.

toreador, n. [1. tóreadōr; 2. tóriədɔ]. Span. Cp. Lat. *taurus*, 'bull'. See **taurus**. Mounted bull-fighter, cp. *torero*.

tore, vb. [1. tōr; 2. tō]. Pret. of **tear (I.)**; fr. M.E. P.P. type *tore*(n), see **torn**. Cp. O.E. Pret. *tær*; M.E. *tar*.

torero, n. [1. torǎro; 2. torɛərou]. Span. See **toreador**. A bull-fighter on foot.

toreutic, adj. & n. [1. torūtik; 2. torjútik]. Gk., fr. *toreutós*, 'worked in relief', fr. *toreúein*, 'to bore through; to work in relief'; cp. also *toreús*, 'graving tool of a sculptor'; connected w. Gk. *teírō*, fr. *ter-jō*, 'rub away, wear away'; cp. further Lat. *terere*, 'to rub to pieces, bruise, grind', *terebra*, 'instrument for boring', cp. **terebra**, **teredo**, & **triturate**; cogn. w. O.E. *þrawan*, 'to twist, turn round', see **throw (I.)**, & O.E. *þræd*, see **thread (I.)**. 1. adj. Pertaining to chased, embossed, wrought work, esp. in metal. 2. n. (pl.) Toreutics, carved, embossed work.

torfaceous, adj. [1. torfáshus; 2. tɔfɛ́iʃəs]. O.N. *torf*, see **turf**, & -aceous. Pertaining to, growing in, bogs or mosses.

torii, n. sing. & pl. [1. tŏriē; 2. tɔ́riː]. Jap. A structure of wood of two posts with lintel, forming an entrance-way to a Shinto temple.

torment (I.), n. [1. tórment; 2. tómənt]. Fr., fr. Lat. *tormentum*, 'instrument with which anything is turned, a windlass; an instrument of torture; torture, pain, anguish'; for **tor-quementum*, fr. *torquēre*, 'to twist' &c.; see **torque**. 1. **a** Severe suffering, anguish, pain, of mind or body; **b** pain deliberately inflicted on another; torture. 2. That which gives rise to mental irritation, worry, annoyance, anxiety: *his undutiful sons are the torment of his life*.

torment (II.), vb. trans. [1. tormént; 2. tó-mént], fr. prec. 1. To inflict extreme pain and suffering upon; to torture. 2. To cause severe suffering to: *to be tormented by tooth-ache*. 3. To annoy, tease, worry, harass: *to torment a person with perpetual questions, with one's complaints, with constant demands for money* &c.

tormentil, n. [1. tórmentil; 2. tóməntil]. Fr. *tormentille*, a woodland plant, supposed to relieve toothache &c., see **torment (I.)**. Rosaceous plant, genus *Potentilla*, with four-petalled yellow flowers, and an astringent root, used in medicine and in tanning.

tormenting, adj. [1. tormÉnting; 2. tómentiŋ], fr. Pres. Part. of **torment (II.)**. Causing torment, bodily pain, anxiety, annoyance &c.

tormentingly, adv. Prec. & -ly. So as to cause torment.

tormentingness, n. See prec. & -ness. Quality of being tormenting; annoyance.

tormentor, n. [1. torméntər; 2. tómɛ́ntə]. **torment (II.)** & -or. 1. Person who inflicts bodily or mental suffering upon another. 2. Kind of harrow. 3. Long meat-fork used on board ship by the cooks.

tormentress, n. [1. torméntres; 2. tómɛ́ntris]. See prec. & -ess. Woman who torments.

tormina, n. pl. [1. tórmina; 2. tómina]. Lat., 'pains in the bowels, gripes'; fr. base *torq-*, 'to twist' &c., see **torque**. (med.) Griping pains in the bowels.

torn, vb. [1. torn; 2. tōn]. O.E. (*ge*)*toren*; M.E. *tōren*; P.P. of **tear (I.)**.

tornado, n. [1. tornádō; 2. tōnéidou]. Span. *tronada*, 'thunderstorm', fr. *tronar*, 'to thunder', fr. Lat. *tonāre*; influenced by Lat. *tornāre*, 'to turn'. Violent, narrowly localized storm; hurricane; specif., rotary storm of extreme violence accompanied by a whirlwind and a cloud resembling a water-spout in appearance, occurring in West Africa, at beginning and end of rainy season, and in America during the summer months.

tornadic, adj. [1. tornádik; 2. tōnǽdik]. Prec. & -ic. Pertaining to, having the character of, a tornado.

torose, torous, adj. [1. tōrós, tórus; 2. tōróus, tórəs]. Lat. *torōsus*, 'brawny'; see **torus** & -ous. (zool. and bot.) Knobbed as with muscle; having surface covered with rounded projections.

torosity, n. [1. toróstí; 2. tōrósiti]. Prec. & -ity. Quality of being torose.

torpedo (I.), n. [1. torpédō; 2. tōpídou]. Lat. *torpēdo*, 'numbness', fr. *torpēre*, 'to be numb, inactive; to be stupefied'; prob. fr. base **(s)terep-* &c., 'numb, stiff', whence, w. *s-*, O.E. *steorfan*, 'to die', see **starve**; & fr. **terp-*, O.E. (*ge*)*deorf*, 'hardship', cp. also O.E. *þearfian*, 'to be indigent', & *þearf*, Pret. Pres., 'require; be compelled'. See **torpid**. 1. Also *torpedo fish*, the electric ray, which kills its prey with an electric shock. 2. **a** A cigar-shaped apparatus filled with explosive discharged on impact, propelled and steered by mechanism, used for destroying or injuring enemy ships at sea; **b** similarly shaped heavy bomb discharged from an aeroplane or airship. 3. Any of various kinds of explosive or detonating cartridge.

torpedo (II.), vb. trans., fr. prec. **a** To attack with a torpedo; **b** to strike or destroy with a torpedo.

torpedo-boat, n. Small, fast vessel, used for firing torpedoes.

torpedo-boat destroyer, n. Vessel of larger size, and still faster than a torpedo-boat, the purpose of which is to overtake and destroy one of these belonging to the enemy and to attack other vessels by launching torpedoes.

torpedo-netting, n. Heavy steel netting hung from booms used as a protection against attack by torpedoes.

torpedo station, n. Naval base for torpedo-boats and their supplies.

torpedo-tube, n. Steel tube through which torpedoes are discharged by compressed air.

torpid (I.), adj. [1. tórpid; 2. tópid]. Lat. *torpidus*, 'benumbed, stupefied'; fr. *torpēre*, 'to be numb' &c.; see **torpedo (I.)**. 1. (in physical sense) Inactive, sluggish. 2. (of the mind) Dull, lethargic, apathetic.

torpid (II.), n., fr. prec., facetiously in reference to their supposed inactivity. 1. Usually *torpids*, boat-races rowed at Oxford in Lent term between the second crews of colleges. 2. Boat with eight oars in which these races are rowed.

torpidity, n. [1. torpíditi; 2. tópíditi]. **torpid (I.)** & -ity. State or quality of being torpid.

torpidness, n. [1. tórpidnes; 2. tópidnis]. See prec. & -ness. Torpidity.

torpor, n. [1. tórper; 2. tópə]. Lat., 'numbness, stupefaction'; fr. same base as **torpid (I.)**. 1. Loss of power of motion; state of inactivity accompanied by partial insensibility. 2. Dullness, inactivity, of the mind.

torporific, adj. [1. torpórifik; 2. tópərifik]. *torpori-*, stem of prec., & -fic. Tending to produce torpor.

torquate, torquated, adjs. [1. tórkwat, tor-kwáted; 2. tókweit, tókwéitid]. Lat. *torquātus*, 'wearing a collar or neck-chain', fr.

torquis &c., 'collar', see **torque**, & **-ate.** (zool.) Having a ring round the neck distinct in colour from the rest of the feathers or fur.

torque, n. [1. tork; 2. tōk]. Lat. *torques*, 'necklace' &c.; fr. *torquēre*, 'to twist, bend' &c.; fr. same base also Scrt. *tarkúš*, 'spindle'; cp. also Goth. *þwairhs*, 'angry', O.E. *þweorh*, 'crosswise; perverse', O.N. *þverr*, 'across', see **thwart (I.)**; cp. also **torment**. **1.** A twisted ring, or chain, worn round the neck by the ancient Teutons, Gauls &c. **2.** (mechan.) A twisting force or movement.

torrefaction, n. [1. tòrefákshun; 2. tòrifǽkʃən]. Lat. *torrefact-*, P.P. type of *torrefacere*, see next word, & **-ion**. Act, process, of torrefying; state of being torrefied.

torrefy, vb. trans. [1. tórefī; 2. tɔ́rifai]. Fr. *torréfier*, Lat. *torrefacere*, fr. *torrēre*, 'to parch, roast, scorch', see **torrid**, & **-fy.** To dry by exposure to heat; to scorch, roast.

torrent, n. [1. tórent; 2. tɔ́rənt]. Lat. *torrent-(em)*, Pres. Part. of *torrēre*, 'to parch, scorch, burn, boil, rage', see **torrid**. **a** A violent rush; a pouring, rapidly flowing stream, of water, or other liquid, or of lava; a stream of water flowing down a steep incline; **b** (fig.) also applied to (i.) a rush of rapidly uttered words; (ii.) violent outburst of abuse, grief &c.

torrential, adj. [1. torénshal; 2. tərénʃəl]. Prec. & **-ial**. Like a torrent, flowing, falling, with great violence.

torrentially, adv. Prec. & **-ly.** After the manner of a torrent; flowing violently.

Torricellian, adj. [1. tòrisélian; 2. tɔ̀riséliən], fr. Torricelli, Italian physicist, 1608–47, & **-an.** Relating to, discovered by, Torricelli, esp. *Torricellian tube, vacuum* &c., in which mercury was first employed in measuring the pressure of the atmosphere, thus originating the mercury barometer.

torrid, adj. [1. tórid; 2. tɔ́rid]. Lat. *torridus*, 'parched, dried up'; fr. base **tors-*, **ters-*, whence also Scrt. *taršáyati*, 'makes thirsty, starves'; *taršaš*, 'thirst'; *tṛšyati*, 'thirsts'; Gk. *térsomai*, 'become dry'; *tarsiá*, 'drying frame'; Goth. *(ga)þairsan*, 'to dry' (fr. **ters-*), *þaursus*, 'dry', *þaurstei*, 'thirst'; O.E. *þyrst*, see **thirst (I.)**. **a** Parched, dried up, by the sun; **b** very hot: *torrid zone*, that between the tropics of Cancer and Capricorn.

torsel, n. [1. tórsl; 2. tɔ̄sl]. O. Fr., 'bundle', dimin. of *torce*, 'something twisted, bunch', fr. Lat. *torqu-*, 'to twist' &c., see **torque.** Piece of wood, or iron, let into a stone or brick wall, to support the end of a beam.

torsion, n. [1. tórshun; 2. tɔ̄ʃən]. L. Lat., fr. *tort-*, P.P. type of *torquēre*, 'to twist', see **torque** & **tort** & **-ion. 1.** Act of twisting, e.g. young shoots in early summer, to check growth; or the end of an artery which has been severed, to prevent haemorrhage. **2.** State of being twisted. **3.** (mechan.) Force with which a twisted wire, spring &c. tends to return to its untwisted state or form; *torsion balance*, apparatus used for measuring minute differences of electric and other forces, by the twisting and untwisting of a wire, spring &c.

torsional, adj. [1. tórshunal; 2. tɔ̄ʃənəl]. Prec. & **-al.** Pertaining to, causing, due to, torsion.

torsive, adj. [1. tórsiv; 2. tɔ̄siv]. Stem *tors-*, as in prec., & **-ive.** (bot.) Twisted spirally.

torsk, n. [1. torsk; 2. tɔ̄sk]. Scand.; O.N. *thorskr*, cp. Germ. *dorsch*. A valuable food fish, of the cod family, found in N. Atlantic.

torso, n. [1. tórsō; 2. tɔ̄sou]. Ital., fr. Lat. *thyrsos*, 'stalk, stem', fr. Gk. *thúrsos*, see **thyrsus. 1.** The upper part of the human body; trunk. **2.** Piece of sculpture which has been mutilated by removal of head and limbs. **3.** Any piece of work which is unfinished, incomplete.

tort, n. [1. tort; 2. tɔ̄t]. Fr., 'injury', fr. Lat. *tortum*, P.P. of *torquēre*, 'to twist' &c., see **torque.** (law) An injurious, harmful action, not involving a breach of contract, for which a civil action can be brought.

torticollis, n. [1. tòrtikólis; 2. tɔ̄tikɔ́lis]. Prec. & Lat. *collum*, 'neck', see **collar (I.)**. Twisted or stiff neck due to rheumatism.

tortile, adj. [1. tórtīl, -il; 2. tɔ̄tail, -il]. Lat. *tortilis*, 'twisted', fr. *tort-*, P.P. type of *torquēre*, see **tort**, & **-ile.** Twisted, coiled, wreathed.

tortility, n. [1. tortíliti; 2. tɔ̄tíliti]. Prec. & **-ity.** State of being twisted.

tortilla, n. [1. tortíla; 2. tɔ̄tílə]. Span. dimin. of *torta*, 'cake', fr. Lat. *torta*, 'twisted roll', fr. *tort-*, P.P. type of *torquēre*, see **tort.** Thin flat cake of maize flour, baked on iron plates, the typical bread of Mexicans &c.

tortious, adj. [1. tórshus; 2. tɔ̄ʃəs]. **tort** & **-ious.** Of the nature of, implying, a tort.

tortiously, adv. Prec. & **-ly.** In a tortious manner.

tortoise, n. [1. tórtus; 2. tɔ̄təs]; affected & artificial [1. tórtoiz; 2. tɔ̄tɔiz]. M.E. *tortuce*, Fr. *tortues*, pl. of *tortue*, fr. Lat. *tortus*, 'crooked, twisted', P.P. of *torquēre*, 'to twist', see **torque** & **tort.** Kind of reptile with complete scaly covering for the upper and under surfaces of the body, the head and legs being capable of protrusion beyond, or retraction within, the shell; a land turtle.

tortoise-shell, n. [1. tórtushèl; 2. tɔ̄təʃèl]. **1.** The material forming the hard external covering of the tortoise, esp. when polished and used for manufacture of various ornamental and useful objects. **2.** Tortoise-shell butterfly.

tortoise-shell butterfly, n. Common black and brownish-yellow butterfly with markings resembling those on polished tortoise-shell.

tortoise-shell cat, n. Female cat with dark brown, yellow, and black markings.

tortuosity, n. [1. tòrtūósiti; 2. tɔ̀tjuɔ́siti]. Next word & **-ity.** State of being tortuous; a winding, a twist, turn &c. (in physical and moral sense).

tortuous, adj. [1. tórchoous, tórtūus; 2. tɔ̄tʃuəs, tɔ̄tjuəs]. Lat. *tortuōsus*, 'twisting', fr. *tortus*, 'a twist', fr. P.P. of *torquēre*, 'to twist', see **tort, torque. 1.** Full of twists, turns, and windings. **2.** (in non-material sense, of the mind, methods, aims &c.) Not straightforward; devious, disingenuous.

tortuously, adv. Prec. & **-ly.** In a tortuous manner; with turns and twists.

tortuousness, n. See prec. & **-ness.** Condition of being tortuous; a tortuosity.

torturable, adj. [1. tórchurabl; 2. tɔ̄tʃərəbl]. **torture** & **-able.** Capable of being tortured.

torturableness, n. Prec. & **-ness.** Quality of being torturable.

torture (I.), n. [1. tórchur; 2. tɔ̄tʃə]. Fr., fr. Lat. *tortūra*, 'a twisting; torment', fr. base *torq-* as in *torquēre*, 'to twist' &c., see **torque, tort,** & **-ure. 1.** Act of deliberately inflicting severe bodily pain upon, of causing extreme physical suffering to, another, as a punishment, from revenge, or from love of cruelty &c.: *to put to the torture*. **2.** Extreme, intolerable, pain; anguish, agony, of body or mind: *to suffer the tortures of the damned*.

torture (II.), vb. trans., fr. prec. **1.** To inflict physical torture upon as a punishment, or in order to extract a confession. **2.** To cause extreme agony to, of body or mind: *tortured by gout, by doubt and anxiety*; *don't torture me by keeping me in suspense.*

torturer, n. [1. tórchurer; 2. tɔ̄tʃərə]. Prec. & **-er.** One who inflicts torture.

torturing, adj. [1. tórchuring; 2. tɔ̄tʃəriŋ], fr. Pres. Part. of **torture (II.)**. Causing torture of mind or body; tormenting, agonizing.

torturous, adj. [1. tórchurus; 2. tɔ̄tʃərəs]. **torture (I.)** & **-ous.** (rare) Connected with, of the nature of, causing, torture.

torula, n. [1. tórūla; 2. tɔ́rjulə]. Mod. Lat., Lat. *torulus*, 'little mound; a tuft' &c.; dimin. of *torus*, 'a prominence; a knot, bulge' &c.; see **torus. 1.** A genus of fungus. **2.** Chain of bacteria. **3.** (bot.) Small torus.

toruliform, adj. [1. tórūliform; 2. tɔ́rjulifɔ̄m]. Prec. & **-form.** Shaped like a torula.

torus, n. [1. tṓrus; 2. tɔ́rəs]. Lat., 'a prominence; a boss, knot, or bulge; a knoll, mound'; etymol. obscure. **1.** A round convex moulding used in the bases of columns. **2.** (bot.) Modified end of flower-stalk forming receptacle for the floral leaves. **3.** (anat.) A rounded muscular protuberance.

Tory, n. [1. tṓri; 2. tɔ́ri]. Perh. fr. Ir. *toiridhe*, 'pursuer', orig. applied to one of a class of outlaws in 16th & 17th cents., who professed to be royalists. **1.** Originally applied to a member of the party who were loyal to King James II. in 1688, opposed the Revolution, and who later favoured the Stuarts and opposed the accession of George I. on the death of Anne; a Jacobite; contrasted with *Whig*. **2.** Term at present time denoting a strong Conservative, esp. of the old-fashioned kind, who upholds the constitution, the Church, and the landed interest; contrasted with so-called Liberal Unionists, or Unionists; also attributively: *Tory party, principles* &c.

Toryism, n. [1. tṓriizm; 2. tɔ́riizəm]. Prec. & **-ism.** Political principles and practice of Tories.

tosh, n. [1. tosh; 2. tɔʃ]. Origin unknown. (slang) Rubbish, rot, nonsense.

tosher, n. [1. tósher; 2. tɔ́ʃə]. Corrupt. of **unattached.** (colloq., slang) Unattached student at a university.

toss (I.), vb. trans. & intrans. [1. taws, tos; 2. tɔ̄s, tɔs]. Etymol. doubtful. **A.** trans. **1. a** To fling, throw, with the hand: *to toss a ball*; also **b** (of a horse) to fling his rider from his back; also *toss off*. **2.** To fling, jerk, with a sudden swift upward movement: *to toss the head*, esp. as expressive of spirited protest, contempt &c., or (of horses) of vigour and fire. **3.** Specif. **a** (of a bull) to lift with the horns and fling into the air; **b** (of the sea in agitation) to fling (ships &c.) violently up and down, to cause to rise and fall with violence. **4.** (fig.) To cause agitation of mind to; to cast from one set of circumstances to another: *tossed about in the storms of life*. **5.** To give a fillip to and cause to spin into the air; in Phr. *to toss a coin*, specif., to decide for or against something according as head or tail comes uppermost. **B.** intrans. **1.** To fling oneself about from restlessness &c.: *to toss on a bed of pain*; also *toss about*: *to toss about on one's bed all night*. **2. a** (of the waves &c.) To be agitated, to leap up; **b** (of plumes or other floating, wavering objects) to sway in the air, float, tremble, rise and fall, be alternately raised and lowered with the movements of the wearer: *tossing plumes, crests, banners* &c. **3.** To be tossed in a ship &c.: *tossing for days on the ocean*. **4.** To spin a coin and allow the result to determine action; to bet upon result of a spun coin: *to toss for*. Phr. *I'll toss you for it*; also *toss up*: *let's toss up who has first choice*, or *for first choice*.

toss (II.), n., fr. prec. Act of tossing (in various senses); **a** *a toss from a bull*; **b** fact of being thrown by a horse; Phr. *to take a toss*, to be thrown, have a fall; **c** act of tossing, jerking, flinging up, the head: *a knowing, pert, proud, toss of the head*; **d** act of tossing, of spinning, a coin; result of this: *to win the toss*.

toss-up, n. [1. táws úp; 2. tɔ̄s ʌ́p]. **a** Act of tossing, spinning, a coin; hence, **b** an even chance: *it's a toss-up whether he succeeds or not.*

tot (I.), n. [1. tot; 2. tɔt]. Origin doubtful. A small, young child: *a tiny tot*.

tot (II.), n. & vb. trans. Lat., 'so many'; prob. also influenced by, or associated w., **total. 1.** n. **a** Aggregate, amount resulting from the addition of a row of figures; **b** an allotted portion, small glass, of drink. [By many included under **tot (I.)**.] **2.** vb. Usually *tot up*, to add up.

total (I.), adj. [1. tṓtl; 2. tóutl]. Lat. *tōtālis*, fr. *tōtus*, 'all, the whole of, entire'; for **towetos*, connected w. Lat. *tumēre*, 'to swell', see **tumid, tumour, tumulus. 1.** Entire; including, constituting, the whole; omitting nothing: *the total amount owed was . . .* **2.** Complete, utter, absolute; unqualified: *total absurdity*; *total eclipse*; *total loss*; *total* *abstinence*, complete abstention from alcoholic drink.

total (**II.**), n., fr. prec. Whole, complete amount or number: *the total of his gains amounted to millions.*

total (**III.**), vb. trans. & intrans., fr. **total** (**I.**). **1.** trans. To add up the whole of and ascertain total amount or number. **2.** intrans. To amount to as a whole, when every item is added.

totality, n. [1. tōtáliti; 2. toutǽliti]. **total** (**I.**) & **-ity.** The whole sum, quantity, number; entirety.

totalization, n. [1. tòtalīzáshun; 2. tòutəlaizéiʃən]. **totalize** & **-ation.** Act of totalizing; state of being totalized.

totalizator, totalizer, n. [1. tṓtalīzàter, tṓtalīzer; 2. tóutəlaizèitə, tóutəlaizə]. Machine for registering and indicating bets on the pari-mutuel system, in which the odds are calculated on the basis that the total amount of money staked is divided among those who have backed the winning horse, with a percentage deducted for expenses &c.

totalize, vb. trans. & intrans. [1. tṓtalīz; 2. tóutəlaiz]. **a** trans. To ascertain total of; **b** intrans., to make use of a totalizator.

totally, adv. [1. tṓtali; 2. tóutəli]. **total** (**II.**) & **-ly.** Entirely, completely, wholly.

tote (**I.**), n. [1. tōt; 2. tout]. Abbr. of **totalizator.**

tote (**II.**), vb. trans. Origin obscure. (chiefly U.S.A.) To carry, convey, lift.

totem, n. [1. tṓtem; 2. tóutɛm]. Prob. fr. Am. Ind. (anthrop.) **1.** Class of natural phenomena, or objects, esp. a species of animal or plant, between which and himself, or his family or tribe, the savage believes that an intimate and mysterious tie exists. **2.** A representation of the totem.

totemic, adj. [1. tōtémik; 2. toutémik]. Prec. & **-ic.** Connected with a totem, or with totemism.

totemism, n. [1. tṓtemizm; 2. tóutɛmizəm]. See prec. & **-ism.** Belief in totems; system of social custom based on this.

totemist, n. [1. tṓtemist; 2. tóutɛmist]. **totem** & **-ist.** Member of a community or tribe possessing a totem.

totemistic, adj. [1. tòtemístik; 2. tòutɛmístik]. Prec. & **-ic.** Connected with totems, or totemism; totemic.

tother, t'other, adj. & pron. [1. túdher; 2. táðə], fr. M.E. *þet ōþer*, pronounced & written *þe toþer*; now interpreted as equiv. to 'the other'. (obs., provinc., or colloq. slang) The other; **1.** adj., as in: *tother day*; **2.** pron., as in: *not to know one from tother.*

totidem verbis, adv. [1. tótidem vẽrbis; 2. tɔ́tidɛm vʌ́bis]. Lat., 'in as many words'.

toties quoties, adv. [1. tótiēz kwótiēz; 2. tɔ́tiiz kwɔ́tiiz]. Lat., 'as often . . ., so often'. Every time.

toto caelo, adv. [1. tṓtō sḗlō; 2. tóutou síilou]. Lat., 'by the whole heaven'. By an enormous amount; entirely: *to disagree toto caelo.*

totter, vb. intrans. [1. tóter; 2. tɔ́tə]. M.E. *toteren*; cp. Du. *touteren*, 'to swing'; Norw. dial. *totra*, 'to quiver'. **1.** To walk with shaky, uncertain, faltering steps. **2.** **a** (of a building &c.) To be shaky, insecure; to be, or appear to be, about to tumble down; **b** (fig.) to be ruined, to come to an end, be overtaken by destruction: *the great empire was tottering to its fall.*

tottery, adj. [1. tóteri; 2. tɔ́təri]. Prec. & **-y.** Shaky, insecure, faltering.

toucan, n. [1. tóokán; 2. túkǽn], fr. Braz. Port. *tucana*, fr. native name. One of several species of bird from tropical S. America, having an enormous, coloured beak and bright-coloured plumage.

touch (**I.**), vb. trans. & intrans. [1. tuch; 2. tatʃ], fr. O. Fr. *touchier* &c.; cp. Ital. *toccare*; Span. *tocar*; borrowed by Romance fr. Gmc., cp. O.E. *tucian*, 'to ill-treat, afflict'; orig. meaning 'to twitch, tug, pluck'; cogn. w. O.H.G. *zucchen*, 'to twitch, pluck'; an intensive formed fr. Gmc. base *tug-, *teuχ- &c., as in O.E. *tēon*, fr. **teuhan*, 'to draw', see **tow** (**I.**), & **tug** (**I.**); cogn. w. Lat. *dūcere*, 'to draw, lead' &c., see **duct**, & words ending in *-duce*. **A.** trans. **1.** To be, stand, lie, up against, in contact with: *the creeper is touching the window*; *the overhanging bough touches the water.* **2.** **a** To feel with the hand or fingers; to lay the hand upon; to handle, finger, lightly; to bring some part of the body into contact with: *to touch every lamp-post in passing*; *visitors are requested not to touch the exhibits*; *to touch a dog with one's foot*; Phrs. *to touch one's hat*, make a sign of greeting; *touch one's hat to*, to greet, express respect for, in this way; *to touch a person on the arm, shoulder*, call his attention in this way; **b** specif., to lay the hand on with a view to healing: *Dr. Johnson, as a child, was touched by Queen Anne for scrofula.* **3.** In various special senses implying physical contact; (usually in neg. sentences) **a** to taste, partake of (food or drink): *I haven't touched food all day*; *he couldn't touch his dinner*; *I couldn't touch anything*, I am not hungry; *I daren't touch lobster*; **b** to play (musical instrument): *I haven't touched the piano for months*; **c** to misappropriate, take to one's own use unlawfully: *to touch money that doesn't belong to one*; **d** to mishandle; ill-treat, molest: *what is the child crying for? I never touched him*; **e** to molest, affect injuriously: *the law can't touch him*; **f** to disturb, interfere with, move out of place: *nothing must be touched until the police have been*; **g** to concern, occupy, oneself with; to set about: *I haven't been able to touch my work all day.* **4.** To reach (to), come up to, go as far as, attain: *his head nearly touches the ceiling*; *the glass just touched 90 yesterday*; Phr. *to touch bottom*, (fig.) to reach lowest point of demerit, depravity &c. **5.** To deal with, affect, involve, include, be related to: *what you say does not touch the point at issue*; *the new law doesn't touch my case at all.* **6.** **a** To affect emotionally, stir feelings and emotions of; to move: *to touch the heart*; *his generosity touched me profoundly*; *he was greatly touched by the universal sympathy*; **b** to arouse, excite, irritate (passions &c.): *his vanity and self-esteem were touched no less than his sense of duty.* **7.** To equal, rival in merit, be as good as, come up to: *there is nothing to touch a hot bath when you are tired*; *there are few things to touch sea air for bracing you up.* **8.** (colloq. slang) To extract money from, esp. as a loan; attempt to borrow from: *to touch a man for a fiver.* **9.** To treat of, deal with, lightly and casually: *we touched many topics in our talk*; see also *touch on*, below. **10.** To receive, esp. as a stipend or salary: *to touch 1000 rupees a month.* **B.** intrans. **1.** To be in contact: *his nose and chin appear almost to touch.* **2.** To practise touching, or laying the hand upon, as formerly the kings of England and France, for king's evil: *James II. used to touch regularly and is said to have wrought many cures.* **C.** Followed by adverb or preposition. *Touch at*, intrans., (of a ship) *to touch at a port*, to visit for a brief time in the course of a voyage. *Touch on*, intrans., to refer to: *there are many other points which I have no time to touch on now.* *Touch up*, trans., **1.** to excite, stimulate; **2.** to put touches to in order to repair, improve appearance of. *Touch upon*, intrans., same as *touch on.*

touch (**II.**), n. See prec. **1.** Sense or sensation of feeling communicated by the nerves in the skin: *the sense of touch*; *soft to the touch.* **2.** Act, fact, of touching, or bringing the hand &c. into contact with, something; contact thus formed: '*O for the touch of a vanished hand*' (Tennyson). Phr. *in touch with*, in social or intellectual relation. **3.** **a** A light, slight, passing contact; faint stroke or impulse: *so fragile that the slightest touch will break it*; **b** (fig.) a slight degree of persuasion, moral pressure, suggestion: '*Ask me no more . . . for at a touch I yield*' (Tennyson). **4.** Something resembling a slight stroke; a mild attack of disease &c.: *a touch of gout, fever, lumbago*; *a touch of the sun*, slight sunstroke. **5.** Characteristic movement of keys of a piano, mode in which these respond to the fingers of the player. **6.** Characteristic, individual, mode of touching **a** a musical instrument, such as piano: *a light, firm, good, heavy, touch*; **b** particular mode of applying a brush in painting, or a chisel in sculpture &c.: *easy to recognize the touches of the master*; **c** particular mode of verbal expression: *a happy touch, a characteristic touch* (in a speech &c.). **7.** Characteristic mode of behaviour, individual manner of doing something, or of dealing with a situation: *the Nelson touch.* **8.** A stroke given, action performed, in the execution of a piece of work: *to put the finishing touches*; *a few deft, last touches.* **9.** Test, trial, proof; only in Phrs. *to put, bring, something to the touch*; *a near touch*, (colloq.) a close shave. **10.** A slight but perceptible amount; slight appearance, trace; a tinge, suggestion, dash, smack: *a touch of colour*; *a touch of bitterness in the voice*; *a touch of acidity to the taste*; *a touch of genius, of vulgarity*; *one touch of Nature.* **11.** (slang) A thing for which a certain price is asked: *a shilling touch.* **12.** (football) Part of the field beyond the flags. **13.** A child's game in which one player pursues and attempts to catch, or touch, any of the others, putting person so touched temporarily out of action.

touchable, adj. [1. túchabl; 2. tátʃəbl]. **touch** (**I.**) & **-able.** That can or may be touched; capable of being touched; tangible.

touchableness, n. Prec. & **-ness.** Capacity of being touched.

touch-and-go, adj. & n. [1. túch an(d) gṓ; 2. tátʃ ən(d) góu]. **1.** adj. Uncertain, risky, chancy: *a touch-and-go business.* **2.** n. A risky, dangerous, situation or affair.

touch body, corpuscle, n. One concerned in sense of touch; tactile body.

touch down, n. Placing of hand by player on ball when in touch-in-goal, behind his own goal-line, in Rugby football, which renders the ball dead.

touched, adj. [1. tucht; 2. tatʃt]. P.P. of **touch** (**I.**). Various specific uses: **1.** Emotionally moved, stirred, affected. **2.** Slightly mad, crazy; also *touched in the upper storey.* **3.** Phr. *touched in the wind*, broken-winded, short-winded, short of breath.

toucher, n. [1. túcher; 2. tátʃə]. **touch** (**I.**) & **-er.** That which touches; specif. **1.** (slang) a close shave; in Phr. *as near as a toucher*, very nearly. **2.** (bowls) Bowl that touches the jack before coming to rest.

touch-hole, n. Vent in old-fashioned guns through which the gunpowder was fired.

touchily, adv. [1. túchili; 2. tátʃili]. **touchy** & **-ly.** In a touchy manner.

touchiness, n. [1. túchines; 2. tátʃinis]. See prec. & **-ness.** Quality of being touchy.

touching (**I.**), adj. [1. túching; 2. tátʃiŋ], fr. Pres. Part. of **touch** (**I.**). Pathetic, moving.

touching (**II.**), prep. Regarding, concerning, with regard to, in reference to: *touching the subject of our conversation . . .*

touchingly, adv. **touching** (**I.**) & **-ly.** In a touching manner; pathetically.

touch-in-goal, n. (Rugby football) Each of the four corners between the touch-lines and goal-lines, if respectively produced.

touch-line, n. Side line bounding the field of play in Association and Rugby football.

touch-me-not, n. [1. túch mi nòt; 2. tátʃ mi nɔ̀t]. Garden balsam, or noli-me-tangere, whose ripe seed-pods explode at a touch.

touch-paper, n. Paper impregnated with nitre, used formerly for firing gunpowder.

touch-piece, n. Gold coin formerly presented by English sovereigns to the persons whom they touched for king's evil.

touchstone, n. [1. túchstōn; 2. tátʃstoun]. **1.** Black siliceous stone formerly used to test purity of gold and silver, which left a streak on the stone when rubbed upon it. **2.** Anything taken as a test, standard, or criterion.

touchwood, n. [1. túchwood; 2. tátʃwud]. Decayed wood, dried and used as tinder; also dried fungus used for same purpose.

touchy, adj. [1. túchi; 2. tátʃi]. Cp. provinc. **tetchy**. Easily offended, irritable; morbidly sensitive.

tough, adj. [1. tuf; 2. taf]. O.E. tōh, M.E. tough; fr. earlier *tanχ, cp. O.H.G. zāhi, Mod. Germ. zäh, 'tough'; the nasal, lost before -h, still remains in the O.E. cogn. (ġe-)tenġe, 'near by, close to; occupying the mind; pressing', fr. *(ga)tangi; O.S. (bi)tengi, 'oppressive'; cp. also O.E. (ġe)tang, 'in contact with'. The primitive sense of the base is 'closely pressed together, dense, tenacious'; cognates outside Gmc. have not been identified. **1.** (of material things) **a** Firm, resistant, of close, dense, consistency, resembling gristle or rubber; capable of being bent, but not liable to break or tear; difficult to cut or bite: *tough meat, leather, fibre* &c.; **b** (of human beings and animals) very strong and vigorous; resistant; having a powerful constitution and well-knit frame; robust, hardy; Phr. *a tough customer*, strong, robust person, one difficult to overcome and subdue; one likely to become violent if attacked; **c** also as noun (slang, U.S.A.) *a tough*, a criminal, ruffianly person, cp. *rough*. **2.** (in non-material sense) **a** (of mind, character &c.) Firm, possessing or evincing fortitude; tenacious, stubborn; **b** (of a task &c.) difficult, laborious, to carry out; uphill work: *a tough job, proposition* &c.; cp. such Phrs. as *a tough nut to crack*; *tough row to hoe* &c.

toughen, vb. trans. & intrans. [1. túfn; 2. táfən]. Prec. & **-en**. **1.** trans. **a** To make tough; **b** to render hardy and vigorous. **2.** intrans. To become tough.

toughish, adj. [1. túfish; 2. táfiʃ]. **tough & -ish**. Rather tough.

toughly, adv. [1. túfli; 2. táfli]. **tough & -ly**. In a tough manner; strenuously, with vigour.

toughness, n. [1. túfnes; 2. táfnis]. See prec. & **-ness**. Quality of being tough (in all senses).

toupee, n. [1. tōōpā; 2. túpei]. Fr. *toupet*, dimin., fr. Gmc.; connected w. **top** (I.). A tuft, esp. a tuft of hair on the front of the head; usually, a false front of hair.

tour (I.), n. [1. toor; 2. tuə]. Fr., see **turn**. **1.** A prolonged journey consisting of successive visits to different places; a series of short journeys from place to place; a round of visits: *a foreign tour; a tour of inspection; the grand tour*, journey through France and other European countries, formerly considered as necessary to put final touches on the education of a young man of the world. **2.** (mil.) A turn of duty.

tour (II.), vb. intrans. & trans., fr. prec. **1.** intrans. To undertake, make, a tour; to travel; also *tour about; tour through*. **2.** trans. To journey through, visit, as part of a tour: *to tour France and Italy*.

tourbillion, n. [1. toorbílyun; 2. tuəbíljən]. Fr. *tourbillon*, 'whirlwind'. Kind of firework which spins in the air, producing the effect of a spiral column of fire.

tour de force, n. [1. tóor de fórs; 2. túə də fɔ́s]. Fr. Action requiring special skill or effort.

touring, adj. [1. tōōring; 2. túəriŋ, tɔ́riŋ]. Pres. Part. of **tour** (II.). *Touring car*, large motor-car designed for touring.

tourist, n. [1. tōōrist; 2. túərist]. **tour** (I.) & **-ist**. Person who goes on a tour; one who travels about from place to place as a visitor, without having a fixed abode in any of the places he visits.

tourmalin(e), n. [1. tōōrmalēn, -in; 2. túəmalin, -in]. Fr., fr. Singhalese *tōramalli*, 'the carnelian'. A composite mineral of various colours, often transparent, used as a gem; the mineral has special optical properties and is used for making certain optical instruments, e.g. the *tourmaline tongs*.

tournament, n. [1. tóor-, tórnament; 2. túə-, tɔ́nəmənt]. M.E. *turnement*, fr. O. Fr. *tornoiement*, 'a turning, wheeling', fr. *tornoier*, 'to wheel, turn repeatedly'. See **turn** (I.). **1.** a Mediaeval assembly to witness the knightly sport of jousting; **b** series of contests between mounted men in armour, armed with the lance, with which weapon each combatant tried to unhorse his opponent; also series of tilting matches and similar sports. **2.** (modern usage) A series of sports, or a series of matches between groups of players, in the same game, lawn-tennis, croquet &c.; usually a competition for a championship; also applied to a series of contests in chess.

tourney, n. & vb. intrans. [1. tórni, tōōrni; 2. tɔ́ni, túəni]. O. Fr. *tornei, tornoi*, 'a turning'; see **tournament**. **1.** n. A tournament in mediaeval sense. **2.** vb. To take part in a tournament, to joust.

tourniquet, n. [1. tóor-, tórniket, -kā; 2. túə-, tɔ́niket, -kei]. Fr., 'turnstile', also in Engl. sense. See prec. Device used by surgeons for applying pressure by means of a screw to arteries to stop bleeding during operations or from accident.

tousle, vb. trans. [1. tóuzl; 2. táuzl]. Connected w. **tussle**. To make untidy and dishevelled; to tumble, ruffle: *tousled hair*.

tous-les-mois, n. [1. tōō lā mwah; 2. tū lei mwä]. Fr., 'every month'; origin uncertain. Kind of starch made from the tubers of canna, used for adulterating arrowroot and cocoa.

tout, vb. intrans. & n. [1. tout; 2. taut]. Origin doubtful; O.E. *tōtian*, 'to peep, pry', sometimes cited in connexion w. this word, wd. have become *toot [tūt]. **1.** vb. **a** To endeavour to obtain customers or clients by persistent and importunate offers of goods or services to persons who want neither; to pester persons to give their custom; to cadge; **b** *tout round*, to go about furtively in the hope of picking up scraps of private information, esp. concerning condition and chances of horses entered for a race. **2.** n. **a** Person who importunes and pesters those whom he hopes to have as customers; **b** one who professes to have, and endeavours to sell, information concerning likely winners of horse-races; a tipster.

tout court, adv. [1. tōō kōōr; 2. tu kúə]. Fr., 'quite briefly'. Without further formality, addition, explanation: *they addressed him as 'Bishop' tout court; I told him tout court that his services were not required*.

tout ensemble, n. [1. tōōt onsómbl; 2. tūt āsābl]. Fr., 'all together, the whole'. General effect, taken as a whole, without reference to single parts or details.

touter, n. [1. tóuter; 2. táutə]. **tout & -er**. More usually *tout*. One who touts.

tow (I.), vb. trans. & n. [1. tō; 2. tou]. O.E. *togian*, 'to pull, draw', M.E. *towen*; formed fr. Gmc. type *tug-*, of base *teug-, *teuh- &c., 'to draw, drag, pull'; cp. O.E. *tēon*, 'to draw' &c.; cogn. w. Lat. *dūcere*, 'to lead, draw' &c., see **duct, duke**, & cp. **tug** (I.). **1.** vb. **a** To draw (a barge &c.) along in the water by a rope, by power exerted by a horse or person moving along on the land, esp. in a canal or narrow river, the horse &c. walking along a path by the side of the water; **b** (of a ship) to draw along in the water another vessel which has broken down, or one wishing to enter or leave a port or an estuary where navigation is difficult; **c** to pull a motor-car or other vehicle along a road by means of a cable attached to a horse or to another motor-car &c. **2.** n. **a** Act of towing; chiefly in Phrs. *to take in tow; to have (person) in tow*, (fig.) (i.) have him under one's care, guidance; (ii.) to have a person in attendance upon one, at one's disposal: *the cinema star had a number of admirers in tow*. **b** vessel &c. which is being towed.

tow (II.), n. O.E. *tow-*, only in compounds, 'a spinning, weaving'; cogn. w. **taw** (I.) & **tool** (I.). Coarse fibre of hemp, from which ropes are made.

towage, n. [1. tóij; 2. tóuidž]. **tow** (I.) & **-age**. **a** Act of towing; **b** fee charged for towing a vessel &c.

toward (I.), adj. [1. tōard; 2. tóuəd]. O.E. *tōweard*, 'facing; imminent; future'; see **to** (I.); the second element is a form of the O.E. base *weorþ-*, as in *weorþan*, 'to become, happen' &c.; cogn. w. Lat. *vertere*, 'to turn', see **vertigo & verse** (I.), **version** &c. (obs. or archaic) **1.** Imminent, about to happen, at hand. **2.** Reverse of *froward*; docile, tractable, compliant.

toward (II.), prep., also **towards** [1. tuwórd(z); 2. təwód(z)], more rarely [1. tord(z); 2. tɔ́d(z)]. Same as **toward** (I.). O.E. *tōweard, tōweardes. Towards* gen. used in prose writing & in speaking. **1.** a (of relation in space) In the direction of: *towards the sun, the south, the sky* &c.; Phr. (now facet.) *I look(s) towards you*, formula used in drinking a person's health; **b** expressing direction of a tendency, result of an action: *moving towards better things; drifting towards war; striving towards a better understanding*. **2.** (of time) Approaching, round about, just before, specified hour or period: *he died towards six o'clock, towards dawn*; the present tense plural in *-en* died out of common use towards the end of the 15th century. **3.** With regard to, in respect of: *to feel kindly, well-disposed, towards a person*.

towardly, adj. [1. tóardli; 2. tóuədli]. **toward** (I.) & **-ly**. (archaic) Kindly, well-disposed, gentle.

towardness, n. [1. tóardnes; 2. tóuədnis]. See prec. & **-ness**. (archaic) Quality of being toward.

towel, n. & vb. trans. [1. tóuel, -il; 2. táuel, -il], vulg. [tauəl]. M.E. *towaille* &c., fr. O. Fr. *touaille*, fr. Low Lat. *toacula*; fr. Gmc. source, fr. some such form as *þwahila-*, cp. O.H.G. *dwahila*, M.H.G. *twāhele, dwāhele*, Mod. Germ. *zwehle*, 'towel'; fr. Gmc. base *þwah-*, 'to wash', cp. O.S. *thwahan*, Goth. *þwahan*, O.E. *þwēan*, 'to wash'; cp. also Goth. *þwahl*, 'bath', O.H.G. *dwahal*, O.E. *þwēal*, 'a washing, an ointment'. **1.** n. Cloth used for drying the person after washing; *oaken towel*, (archaic slang) a cudgel for administering a beating. **2.** vb. **a** To dry or rub with a towel; **b** (slang) to thrash.

towel-horse, n. A wooden frame on which towels may be hung.

towelling, n. [1. tóueling; 2. táueliŋ]. **a** Strips of cloth, specially woven, from which towels are cut; **b** (slang) a thrashing.

tower (I.), n. [1. tour; 2. táuə]. M.E., fr. O. Fr. *tour*; fr. Lat. *turris*, 'a tower for defence; a castle, high building'; prob. fr. Gk. *túrrhis, túrsis*, 'a tower'; origin & connexions doubtful. A lofty building, high in proportion to its diameter; a tower may be either round or square, and either isolated from other buildings, or forming a lofty part of a building, though distinct from the rest structurally and to the eye. Phr. *a tower of strength*, person who can be relied upon for help and support.

tower (II.), vb. intrans., fr. prec. **a** (of any tall object) To rise, rear itself: *the mountains seemed to tower to the clouds*; also *tower up*; **b** *tower above*, to be much taller, higher, than, rise far above: *he towered above the crowd*; (also fig.) to exceed in power of mind, genius, character &c.: *to tower above one's fellow-workers*.

towering, adj. [1. tóuering; 2. táuəriŋ]. Pres. Part. of prec. **1.** Lofty, rising to a great height. **2.** (fig.) In Phr. *towering rage, passion*, excessive, violent.

town, n. [1. toun; 2. taun]. O.E. *tūn*, 'enclosure, yard; estate, farm; village, town'; cogn. w. Mod. Germ. *zaun*, 'hedge, fence', O.H.G. *zūn*; cogn. w. O. Celt. *-dūnum*, 'fortress, city'; O. Ir. *dūn*, 'fortress'. Orig. meaning 'hedge, fence, that which encloses'; then, 'that which is enclosed or fenced in'. **1.** (gen. sense) **a** Large group of houses and other buildings with fixed, distinguishing name; larger than a *village*, but

town-clerk, n. Official, usually a lawyer, under a municipality, who keeps records of its proceedings and advises on legal questions.

town council, n. Governing body of a town or city.

town councillor, n. Member of a town council.

town crier, n. [1. tóun kríer; 2. táun kráiə]. Person employed by a municipality to make public announcements.

townee, n. [1. tòunē; 2. tàunī]. **town & -ee**. (univ. slang; disparaging and derogatory term) Person, esp. a tradesman, living in Oxford or Cambridge, who is not a member of the university.

town hall, n. Building in which a town council holds its meetings, and where the business of a municipality is transacted.

town house, n. Private residence in a town; esp. as contrasted with the *country house* of the same person.

townified, adj. [1. tóunifīd; 2. táunifaid]. See **town & -fy & -ed**. Pertaining to a town, or to a person living in and accustomed to a town; contrasted with *countrified*.

townsfolk, n. pl. [1. tóunzfōk; 2. táunzfouk]. **a** Inhabitants of towns; contrasted with those who live in the country; **b** the inhabitants of a particular town.

township, n. [1. tóunship; 2. táunʃip]. **1.** Ancient administrative unit, co-extensive with a parish. **2.** (U.S.A.) A unit of local administration in a county.

townsman, n. [1. tóunzman; 2. táunzmən]. **a** Man who lives in a town, as distinct from a country dweller; **b** inhabitant of a particular town; *fellow-townsman*, person belonging to the same town as another.

townspeople, n. pl. [1. tóunzpēpl; 2. táunzpīpl]. Townsfolk.

tow-path, n. Path running along the bank of a river or canal, used by horses towing barges.

tow-rope, n. Rope used in towing vessels.

toxaemia, n. [1. toksḗmia; 2. tɔksímiə]. See **toxic & haema-**. Blood-poisoning.

toxic, adj. [1. tóksik; 2. tɔ́ksik]. Lat. *toxicum*, 'poison in which arrows were dipped; a poison generally'; fr. Gk. *toxikón*, neut. of *toxikós*, 'connected with a bow', fr. *tóxon*, 'a bow'. The common view of a relationship between this word & Lat. *taxus*, 'yew', is not absolutely well authenticated since the latter never means 'bow' in Lat. nor the former 'yew' in Gk. Pertaining to, of the nature of, caused by, poison.

toxicant, adj. & n. [1. tóksikant; 2. tɔ́ksikənt]. Prec. & **-ant**. **1.** adj. Producing toxic results. **2.** n. Toxic drug or agent.

toxico-, pref. Form fr. Gk. *toxikós*, see **toxic**, used in compounds. Poison.

toxicological, adj. [1. tòksikolójikl; 2. tɔ̀ksikəlɔ́dʒikl]. Prec. & **-logy & -ic & -al**. Connected with poisons or with toxicology.

toxicologist, n. [1. tòksikólojist; 2. tɔ̀ksikɔ́lədʒist]. Next word & **-ist**. Student of poisons, their nature, and their effects on the living organism.

toxicology, n. [1. tòksikóloji; 2. tɔ̀ksikɔ́lədʒi]. **toxico- & -logy**. Systematic study of the nature and effects of poisons.

toxin, n. [1. tóksin; 2. tɔ́ksin]. Gk. *tóxon*, 'bow'; for mod. sense see **toxic**, & **-in**. A poisonous organic substance.

toxophilite, n. [1. toksófilīt; 2. tɔksɔ́filait]. Gk. *tóxon*, see **toxic**, & *philos*, 'loving', see **philo-**, & **-ite**. A lover, a practitioner, of archery; one skilled in shooting with the bow.

toxophilitic, adj. [1. tòksofilítik; 2. tɔ̀ksɔfilítik]. Prec. & **-ic**. Pertaining to archers or to archery.

toy, n. & vb. intrans. [1. toi; 2. tɔi]. Cp. Du. *tuig*, 'tool, implement; stuff'; cogn. w. Germ. *zeug*; cp. Du. *speeltuig*, Germ. *spielzeug*, 'plaything'; ultimately fr. same base as O.E. *tēon*, 'to draw, lead'; see **tow (I.)**. **1.** n. **a** A child's plaything; **b** any object which serves to amuse and distract; hence, **c** a trifle, bauble, thing of no value or importance. **2.** vb. **a** To indulge in dalliance; *toy with*, to caress amorously, sport with; **b** to trifle with, linger over carelessly: *to toy with the wing of a pheasant*; **c** to let the mind dwell on lightly, to consider casually and superficially: *to toy with an idea*.

toy dog, n. Very small lap-dog; *toy terrier*, very small breed of terrier.

toyshop, n. [1. tóishop; 2. tɔ́iʃɔp]. Shop where children's playthings &c. are sold.

tra-, pref. for **trans-**, in certain words derived fr. Lat. as *tradition* &c.

trabeated, adj. [1. trábeāted; 2. trǽbiéitid]. Lat. *trabs*, 'beam'; prob. cogn. w. Gk. *téremnon*, fr. **terebnon*, 'anything closed; room, chamber'; O.W. *treb*, 'dwelling'; Lith. *trobà*, 'building', & perh. O.E. *porp*, 'village', q.v. under **thorp**, & **-ate & -ed**. (archit.) Built with horizontal beams or lintels; not arcuate.

trabeation, n. [1. tràbeáshun; 2. træbiéiʃən]. See prec. & **-ion**. (archit.) Straight, distinguished from arched, construction; an entablature.

trabecula, n. [1. trabékula; 2. træbékjulə]. Lat., 'little beam', dimin. of *trabs*, see **trabeated**. (anat.) Small rod, or bundle, esp. bundle of fibres or connective tissue in framework of an organ.

trabecular, adj. [1. trabékular; 2. træbékjulə]. Prec. & **-ar**. Pertaining to, consisting of, trabeculae.

trabeculate, adj. [1. trabékulāt; 2. træbékjuleit]. **trabecula & -ate**. Trabecular.

trace (I.), n. [1. trās; 2. treis]. M.E. *trays*, pl., fr. O. Fr., *trais*, *traits*; see **trait**. Part of harness, consisting of two straps or chains, one end of which is fastened on either side, to the hames on the collar, of a draft animal, and connected at the other end with the vehicle or other object to be drawn. Phr. (fig.) *to kick over the traces*, to break loose from discipline, be guilty of unruly conduct.

trace (II.), vb. trans. M.E. *trācen*, fr. O. Fr. *tracier*, L. Lat. *tractiāre*, formed fr. *tract-(um)*, P.P. of *trahere*, 'to draw'; see **tract (I.)**. **1.** To draw, delineate, mark out with lines &c.; often *trace out*: **a** (on paper &c.) to *trace (out) a map, plan* &c.; **b** to lay out, mark out (plans of buildings &c.), on the ground. **2.** To follow exactly, with a pen or pencil, on thin, transparent paper &c., the lines of writing, or of a drawing placed below, and appearing through, the paper &c., on which one is working. **3.** To write, esp. deliberately, carefully, laboriously: *as I trace these words to you I am deeply moved* &c. **4. a** To perceive and follow a visible track: *to trace a person's footsteps in the snow* &c.; **b** to make out, discern: *I scarce could trace her features in the gloom*; **c** to find, reach, by following a series of clues: *to trace one's long-lost relations*; *to trace a criminal*; **d** to find, come upon, put one's hand on: *I am unable to trace the document to which you refer*; **e** to reason out, discover the various stages of, follow from point to point; work out the links of a chain of facts: *to trace the etymology of a word*; *the history, origin, of a family* &c. **5.** To follow, proceed along (a particular path or route); to walk, traverse; tread: *we traced the winding mazes of the wood*.

trace (III.), n. See prec. **1.** Mark made by something which has passed; track, trail, footstep, furrow &c.: *we could plainly see the traces of big game along the river-bank*. Phrs. *on the traces of*, *hot on the traces of* &c., on the trail, following keenly, about to come up with. **2. a** Visible marks, signs, evidence, left by some earlier event; vestige: *war had left its traces on the countryside*; *every trace of the crime had been removed*; **b** (in non-material sense) recognizable evidence, result, of earlier experience, circumstances &c.: *sorrow and disappointment had left their trace(s) upon his character*. **3.** A very small amount; a slight but perceptible smack, tinge, touch; **a** (of material things) *just a trace of onion in the salad*; *no trace of scent on the handkerchief*; **b** (of non-material things) *he betrayed not a trace of fear, emotion* &c.

traceability, n. [1. tràsabíliti; 2. trèisəbíliti]. **traceable & -ity**. Quality of being traceable.

traceable, adj. [1. trásabl; 2. tréisəbl]. **trace (II.) & -able**. Capable of being traced.

traceableness, n. Prec. & **-ness**. Quality, fact, of being traceable; traceability.

tracer, n. [1. trásér; 2. tréisə]. **trace (II.) & -er**. Person who, thing which, traces (in various senses); specif. **a** a device for tracing patterns on cloth &c.; **b** a person employed to trace out and find missing articles &c.; cp. also *tracer shell*, shell fired from a gun leaving a trail of smoke through the air, so that error in aim or trajectory &c. may be corrected.

tracery, n. [1. tráseri; 2. tréisəri]. **trace (III.) & -ery**. **1.** A series, system, group, of lines forming a kind of pattern, as though deliberately traced: *the delicate tracery of light and shade*. **2.** Specif. (archit.) system of decorative ramifications of open stonework in the upper part of windows.

trachea, n. [1. trakḗa; 2. trəkíə]. Mod. Lat., fr. Lat. *trachia*, fr. Gk. *trākheia* (*artēría*), lit. 'rough artery', fr. *trākhús*, 'harsh, rough, rugged'; cogn. w. Gk. *thrássein*, 'to disturb'; O.N. *dreggjar*, 'dregs' (see **dreg**); O. Prussian *dragios*, 'lees'. The wind-pipe; that part of the air-passage in vertebrates between the lungs and the back of the mouth.

tracheal, adj. [1. trakḗal; 2. trəkíəl]. Prec. & **-al**. Pertaining to, connected with, the trachea.

trachelo-, pref., fr. Gk. *trákhēlos*, 'neck, throat'; etymol. doubtful.

trachelotomy, n. [1. tràkēlótumi; 2. træˌkīlɔ́təmi]. Prec. & **-tomy**. (surg.) Incision in the neck of the uterus.

tracheo-, pref. See **trachea**. Concerned with, involving, the trachea.

tracheocele, n. [1. trákeōsèl; 2. tréikiousèl]. Prec. & **-cele**. Goitre.

tracheotomy, n. [1. tràkeótumi; 2. trèiːkiɔ́təmi]. **tracheo- & -tomy**. Operation consisting in making an incision in the trachea.

trachoma, n. [1. trakṓma; 2. trəkóumə]. Gk. *trákhōma*, 'roughness'; see **trachea & -oma**. (med.) Disease characterized by roughness on inner surface of eyelids.

trachyte, n. [1. trákit; 2. trǽkait]. Gk. *trākhús*, 'rough', see **trachea**, & **-ite**. Light-coloured volcanic rock with very rough surface when fractured.

tracing, n. [1. trásing; 2. tréisiŋ]. **trace (II.) & -ing**. Writing or drawing traced; reproduction of pattern, writing &c., made by following lines of the original which are visible through superimposed paper &c.

tracing-paper, n. Tough semi-transparent paper upon which tracings are made.

track (I.), n. [1. trak; 2. træk]. O. Fr. *trac*, 'track of horses &c.; trace'; origin doubtful; perh. fr. Gmc. source; cp. Du. *trek*, 'act of drawing'. **1. a** Mark left on the ground, or on surface of water, by something which has passed over it: *the track of a wagon, wheel* &c.; *the track of a vessel*; by extension also: *the track of a meteor*. **b** specif., a footprint, trace, vestige, made on the ground by man or beast. Phrs. *on the track of*, in pursuit; *to make tracks* (slang), to depart hurriedly; *to make tracks for*, go, run, towards; *to cover up one's tracks*, conceal one's plans, actions, designs &c.; *off the track* (fig.), on wrong path, following wrong line; *to lose track of* (fig.), lose sight of, be no longer in touch with (a person or thing). **2.** (in non-material sense) Signs, evidence, of a person's work, actions, designs &c.: *he has left his tracks everywhere in the affairs and organization of the office*; (often in bad sense) signs of intrigue &c. **3. a** A path, rough road, worn by use rather than properly made; Phrs. (fig.) *the beaten track*, the ordinary routine of action; the commonplace and conventional; *he never leaves the beaten track*, never launches out, never shows initiative, never does anything original; **b** a line of railway, including both rails; **c** a course, path, on which races are run.

track (II.), vb. trans., fr. prec. **1.** To follow the track of; trail, pursue by following tracks; *track down*, to run down, pursue to lair or hiding-place and capture. **2.** To make out, trace, by means of visible remains &c. **3.** To tow a vessel by a rope from the bank.

trackage, n. [1. trákij; 2. trǽkidʒ]. **track (I.) & -age. a** Railway tracks collectively; **b** extent of these.

tracker, n. [1. trákər; 2. trǽkə]. **track (II.) & -er. 1.** One who traces or tracks out a person or thing. **2.** One who tows a vessel from the bank.

trackless, adj. [1. trákles; 2. trǽklis]. **track (I.) & -less. 1. a** Not crossed by a path or track; untrodden: *a trackless waste*; **b** not having tracks or rails: *trackless trams*. **2.** Leaving no track, footprint, or other mark of passage.

tracklessly, adv. Prec. & **-ly**. Without leaving a track.

tracklessness, n. See prec. & **-ness**. Fact, quality, of being trackless.

tract (I.), n. [1. trakt; 2. trækt]. Lat. *tractus*, 'a drawing, draught; extent, distance; district, region; a space of time'; fr. *tract-(um)*, P.P. type of *trahere*, 'to draw'; the group of words to wh. this is related is disputed; Walde gives two possibilities: (1) fr. **dhragho-* & cogn. w. O.E. *dragan*, see **draw (I.)**; (2) fr. **trāgh-* & cogn. w. O. Ir. *traig*, 'fast'. **1. a** A continuous stretch, or expanse, of country; a region, area, district: *a tract of land*; also *tract of forest, woodland* &c., unbroken stretch; **b** expanse of water; **c** expanse of sky. **2.** (of time) Continuous period, unbroken duration; lapse, extent. **3.** (anat.) System of organs or parts of the body which fulfil a specific function or set of functions: *digestive tract*.

tract (II.), n. For **tractate**. A brief written dissertation or treatise; a pamphlet; esp. one designed to enforce some specific religious or political doctrine or theory.

tractability, n. [1. tràktəbíliti; 2. trǽktəbíliti]. **tractable & -ity**. Quality, condition, of being tractable; docile.

tractable, adj. [1. tráktəbl; 2. trǽktəbl]. Lat. *tractābilis*, 'manageable; yielding'; fr. base of *tractāre*, 'to drag about; to touch; to manage'; formed fr. *tract-(um)*, P.P. type of *trahere*, 'to draw' &c. See **tract (I.)** & cp. **trace (II.)**. **1.** Capable of being easily wrought. **2.** Capable of being easily managed; open to persuasion and influence; controllable.

Tractarian, n. [1. traktáriən; 2. træktéəriən]. **tract (II.) & -arian**. **a** One of the founders of Tractarianism; **b** a believer in the principles of Tractarianism.

Tractarianism, n. [1. traktáriənizəm; 2. træktéəriənizəm]. Prec. & **-ism**. Movement, in the Church of England, called also the *Oxford Movement*, started by the writers of the 'Tracts for the Times', Keble, Newman, Pusey, Hurrell Froude, and others, published in Oxford in the thirties and forties of the 19th cent. The main points of these teachings were a revolt against the extreme Protestantism which had become characteristic of the Church of England as a whole, an appeal in matters of faith and practice to the early fathers, and to the Anglican High Church divines of the 17th cent., such as Andrewes, Laud &c., and the insistence upon sacramental doctrine.

tractate, n. [1. tráktāt; 2. trǽkteit]. Lat. *tractātus*, 'a touching, handling; a treatment'; see **treat & treatise** & cp. **tract (II.)**. A treatise, an excursus, essay.

traction, n. [1. trákshun; 2. trǽkʃən], fr. Lat. *tract-(um)*, P.P. type of *trahere*, 'to draw', see **trace (II.)**, & **tract (I.) & -ion**. **1.** Act, process, of drawing; process of causing to move along by drawing. **2.** Method by which locomotive power is obtained; transport, esp. along roads: *motor, steam, traction*.

tractional, adj. [1. trákshunal; 2. trǽkʃənəl]. Prec. & **-al**. Pertaining to traction.

traction-engine, n. Locomotive engine generally driven by steam, used for drawing heavy trucks along roads.

tractive, adj. [1. tráktiv; 2. trǽktiv]. See **tract (I.) & -ive**. Having the function or property of drawing; tractional.

tractor, n. [1. tráktər; 2. trǽktə]. **tract (I.) & -or**. That which draws; specif. **a** a traction-engine; **b** motor vehicle used for drawing agricultural machines, other vehicles &c.

trade (I.), n. [1. trād; 2. treid]. M.E., 'a path'; connected w. **tread**. **1.** A handicraft, a skilled employment: *the trade of a saddler, of a blacksmith, a wheelwright* &c. **2. a** Business, commercial transactions, esp. those of buying and selling commodities; traffic, barter: *engaged in trade*, contrasted with one of the liberal professions; *Board of Trade*, (i.) one of the great Government departments, dealing with commerce and industry &c., strictly a committee of the Privy Council, its ministerial chief, *President of the Board of Trade* is usually a Cabinet Minister; (ii.) in U.S.A., a Chamber of Commerce; **b** often specif., retail business, shopkeeping, contrasted with *commerce*: *his father was in trade*, i.e. kept a shop. **3.** Occupation, employment of any kind; a calling: *the trade of war*. **4.** Group of persons engaged in some particular trade; specif., *the trade*, the brewers and distillers; sellers of liquor. **5.** (in pl.) *The trades*, trade-winds.

trade (II.), vb. intrans. & trans., fr. prec. **1.** intrans. To engage in, carry on trade, or a trade: *to trade with Russia*; *to trade in furs* &c. Phr. *to trade (up)on*, to presume upon, attempt to derive advantage from, esp. to exploit in an unscrupulous manner: *to trade (up)on one's father's reputation*; *to trade upon a person's tender heart*. **2.** trans. To barter, exchange: *to trade knives and beads with natives for skins*.

trade board, n. A board composed of equal numbers of representatives of employers and employed with a few nominated neutral members, appointed in certain industries by the Board of Trade, to fix minimum rates of wages &c.

trade-mark, n. Registered name, symbol, device, used by a manufacturer to distinguish the goods made by him from others.

trade-name, n. **1.** Name by which an article or commodity is known among those who trade in it. **2.** Name by which an individual or a firm of traders is known in the commercial world.

trade price, n. Price charged by manufacturers for their goods to those who deal in them.

trader, n. [1. trádər; 2. tréidə]. **trade (II.) & -er. 1.** One engaged in trade or commerce; a merchant: *an African trader*. **2.** A trading vessel.

tradesfolk, n. pl. [1. trádzfōk; 2. tréidzfouk]. Tradespeople.

tradesman, n. [1. trádzman; 2. tréidzmən]. **1.** Person engaged in trade, esp. in retail trade; a shopkeeper. **2.** A handicraftsman, a skilled worker.

tradespeople, n. pl. [1. trádzpēpl; 2. tréidzpīpl]. Persons engaged in retail trade, shopkeepers; the families of tradesmen; tradesmen as a class.

tradeswoman, n. [1. trádzwooman; 2. tréidzwumən]. Woman engaged in retail trade.

trade union, n. Legalized association of workers, clerks, or other employees in a particular trade, formed to protect the rights of the members by means of collective bargaining with the employers.

trade-unionism, n. Principles and methods followed by trade unions; system of having trade unions.

trade-unionist, n. Member of a trade union; supporter of the principles of trade-unionism.

trade-wind, n. Wind which blows continuously from N.E. on north side of equator, and from S.E. on south side.

trading, adj. [1. tráding; 2. tréidiŋ]. Engaged in, carrying on, trade or commerce: *a trading concern*.

tradition, n. [1. tradíshun; 2. trədíʃən]. Lat. *trāditiōn-(em)*, fr. *trādit-(um)*, P.P. of *trādere*, 'to give over, deliver, surrender; to betray', & **-ion**; *trādere* is for *trans*, 'over, beyond' &c., see **trans-**, & *dare*, 'to give', see **dower (I.) & donation**, & cp. **traitor & treason**. **1.** (legal) Act of handing over to, of delivering into the hands of, another; delivery. **2.** Belief, habit, practice, principle, handed down verbally from one generation to another, or acquired by each successive generation from the example of that preceding it: *the great traditions of the British Army*; *to keep up the family traditions*; *it is a misfortune to inherit no traditions*. **3. a** Doctrine, based on divine revelation, statement of alleged occurrence &c., transmitted orally though not recorded in documents, concerning matters of religious belief, or great religious teachers; **b** belief in occurrence of events in the remote past of the history of a race, tribe, family, based upon oral transmission from generation to generation. **4.** Group of principles in art or letters based on the accumulated practice and experience of a series of generations: *the Dryden tradition*.

traditional, adj. [1. tradíshunal; 2. trədíʃənəl]. Prec. & **-al**. **a** Based on, arising from, tradition; hence, **b** in accordance with, adhering to tradition; old-fashioned.

traditionalism, n. [1. tradíshunalizm; 2. trədíʃənəlizəm]. Prec. & **-ism**. **a** Adherence, exaggerated tendency to adhere, to tradition; **b** doctrine that religious belief must be based upon tradition of divinely revealed truth, and traditional interpretation of the Scriptures.

traditionalist, n. [1. tradíshunalist; 2. trədíʃənəlist]. See prec. & **-ist**. One firmly attached to tradition; believer in traditionalism.

traditionalistic, adj. [1. tradishunalístik; 2. trədiʃənəlístik]. Prec. & **-ic**. Pertaining to, characterized by, traditionalism.

traditionally, adv. [1. tradíshunali; 2. trədíʃənəli]. **traditional & -ly**. By, in accordance with, tradition.

traditionary, adj. [1. tradíshunari; 2. trədíʃənəri]. **tradition & -ary**. Traditional.

traditor, n. [1. tráditer; 2. trǽditə]. Lat., see **tradition & -or**, & see **traitor**. Early Christian who betrayed his fellow-Christians under persecution, or who handed over the Scriptures or sacred vessels to the Roman authorities.

traduce, vb. trans. [1. tradús; 2. trədjús]. Lat. *trādūcere*, 'to lead, bring, across'; see **trans- & duke & duct**. To hold up to contempt; to disparage, run down, defame, blacken the character of; to calumniate.

traducer, n. [1. tradúser; 2. trədjúsə]. Prec. & **-er**. One who traduces; a calumniator.

traducian, adj. [1. tradúsian; 2. trədjúsiən]. **traduce** (see Lat. sense) & **-ian**. Connected with, pertaining to, traducianism or traducianists.

traducianism, n. [1. tradúsianizm; 2. trədjúsiənizəm]. Prec. & **-ism**. Doctrine that the human soul is procreated along with the body in the act of generation.

traducianist, n. [1. tradúsianist; 2. trədjúsiənist]. See prec. & **-ist**. Adherent of traducianism.

traduction, n. [1. tradúkshun; 2. trədákʃən]. Fr., 'translation from one language to another', fr. Lat. *trāductiōn-(em)*, 'a transferring', fr. *traduct-(um)*, P.P. type of *trādūcere*, see **traduce** & **-ion**. (rare) 1. Act of transferring from one to another. Specif. 2. process of procreating the soul along with the body. 3. Translation.

traffic (I.), n. [1. tráfik; 2. trǽfik]. Fr. *trafic*, Ital. *traffico*, L. Lat. *trafficum*; origin unknown. 1. Act, or process, of buying and selling goods; barter, trade, commerce. 2. Passage to and fro; coming and going of pedestrians, vehicles, goods, over roads, or railways; also, movement of vessels, passengers, and cargoes between ports.

traffic (II.), vb. intrans. Fr. *trafiquer*; see prec. To trade, carry on the business of bartering, buying and selling goods; to deal in merchandise.

tragacanth, n. [1. trágakanth; 2. trǽgəkænþ]. Lat. *tragacanthum*, fr. Gk. *tragákantha*, lit. 'goat thorn', fr. *trágos*, 'he-goat', wh. is perh. fr. same orig. base as Lat. *turgere*, 'to swell', see **turgid**, & *ákantha*, 'thorn, thorn tree'; see **acanthus**. Kind of gum obtained from an Asiatic plant, *Astragalus*, used in pharmacy.

tragedian, n. [1. trajédian; 2. trədžídiən]. M.E. & O. Fr. *tragedien*, 'writer of tragedies'; see **tragedy**. 1. Writer of tragedies. 2. Actor of tragedy.

tragedienne, n. [1. trazhèdièn; 2. træžèdièn]. Fr., fem.; see prec. Tragic actress.

tragedy, n. [1. trájedi; 2. trǽdžidi]. M.E. & O. Fr. *tragedie*, fr. Lat. *tragoedia*, fr. Gk. *tragōidía*, cp. *tragōidós*, 'tragic poet and singer', orig. prob. 'goat singer', so called because the singers were clothed in goatskins, or because a he-goat was the prize; cp. *trágos*, 'he-goat', under **tragacanth**, & *ōidós*, 'singer', cp. *ōidé*, 'song' &c., q.v. under **ode**. 1. A form of dramatic composition; **a** in ancient tragedy the principal personages were conceived of, and represented, as being by force of circumstances, the natural trend of events, or by some peculiarity of character, inevitably driven, as by fate, to the final catastrophe; **b** in modern usage, a tragedy is simply a solemn play in which the principal personages pass through a series of misfortunes, and end unhappily. 2. The act of composing or representing tragedies. 3. (popular usage) A sad, lamentable, event; one causing or involving death and unhappiness.

tragic, more rarely **tragical**, adj. [1. trájik(l); 2. trǽdžik(l)]. Fr. *tragique*, fr. *tragicus*, fr. Gk. *tragikós*, 'pertaining to a tragedy; stately, majestic'; fr. *trágos*, see prec. 1. Pertaining to, connected with, dramatic tragedy: *the tragic art*; *a tragic actor*. 2. **a** (of events and actions) Involving calamity, death, destruction; calamitous; **b** (of persons, expression &c.) evincing, exhibiting, great unhappiness; mournful.

tragically, adv. Prec. & **-ly**. In a tragic manner; calamitously.

tragicalness, n. See prec. & **-ness**. Quality, fact, of being tragic.

tragi-comedy, n. [1. tráji kómedi; 2. trǽdži kómidi]. See **tragedy** & **comedy**. Play, series of events, in which tragic and comic elements intermingle.

tragi-comic, adj. [1. tráji kómik; 2. trǽdži kómik]. Exhibiting both tragic and comic scenes or elements.

tragopan, n. [1. trágōpan; 2. trǽgoupæn]. Gk., name of a fabulous bird, fr. *trágos*, 'he-goat', see **tragacanth**, & **Pan** (III.) (name of the god). Asiatic pheasant with fleshy erectile horns and bright-coloured wattles.

trail (I.), vb. trans. & intrans. [1. trāl; 2. treil]. O. Fr. *traillier*, 'to tow a boat; to follow a deer by trailing'; prob. fr. Lat. *trāgula*, 'a drag-net; a small sledge'; fr. *trahere*, 'to draw'. see **tract** (I.) & **trace** (II.). A. trans. 1. **a** To drag along the ground: *to trail one's skirt through the dust* &c.; Phr. (fig.) *to trail one's coat* (as though daring people to tread on it), to give provocation, invite attack; (mil.) *to trail arms*, to carry a rifle or pike with the butt-end near the ground, and the muzzle or point sloping forward; **b** to drag through the water: *to trail an oar*, allow the blade to drag over the surface of the water; *to trail a fishing line*, draw it along in the water after a boat. 2. To follow the track of, to track: *to trail a deer*. B. intrans. 1. To hang down loosely, so as to sweep the ground: *her long train trailed in the mud*. 2. To straggle, grow, or be placed, in an extended line from some fixed point; to stream out: *creepers trailing over the roofs and walls*; *seaweed trailing over the rocks*.

trail (II.), n. See prec. 1. Visible mark, track, wake, left by anything that has passed; also any other evidence of its passage left by an animal or thing, such as scent: *on the trail of*. 2. Path, track, esp. through bush or wild country, worn by those who have passed; course, line of route followed through wild country. 3. That extended part of a gun-carriage which rests upon the ground.

trailer, n. [1. trāler; 2. tréilə]. **trail** (I.) & **-er**. 1. One following the trail of another person or of an animal. 2. Straggling growth of a plant, a long runner of a creeping plant. 3. A vehicle of any kind drawn or trailed by another.

train (I.), vb. trans. & intrans. [1. trān; 2. trein]. O. Fr. *trahiner*, cp. Mod. Fr. *trainer*, 'to drag, draw along'; L. Lat. *trahinare*, formed fr. *trahere*, 'to draw', see **tract** (I.) & **trace** (II.). A. trans. 1. **a** To submit (a person) to discipline and instruction, to educate; to bring up, rear, in habits of good behaviour and conduct: *to train a child, a horse* &c.; **b** to exercise in some specific mental, moral, or bodily discipline; to accustom to specific bodily exercises, or particular mode of reasoning; to cause to acquire skill, deftness, facility; to bring to a certain standard, by systematic practice: *to train a child to obey*, *to read music at sight*, *to be a good gymnast* &c.; **c** to produce, form, by training: *to train a cricketer*; *to train hospital nurses, airmen, botanists* &c.; *to train racehorses* &c. 2. To cause (plants) to grow in a desired direction by bending, tying &c.: *to train roses against a wall*. 3. To direct upon, towards, a given point: *to train guns on a fort* &c. B. intrans. 1. To carry out the process of training, educating, instructing, either generally, or for some specific purpose and along special lines. 2. To bring oneself to required pitch of physical condition by dieting &c., and of skill and precision in movement, by steady practice, for a specific contest or form of sport: *to train for a boat race, for a boxing match, for mountain-climbing*.

train (II.), n. See prec. 1. A body of attendants, a retinue: *the prince and his train*. 2. A procession, cortège; a number of persons, vehicles &c. forming a continuous line, series, file: *a funeral train*. 3. Part of a dress, robe, cloak, cope &c., made long so as to extend along the ground behind the wearer. 4. Series of railway coaches or trucks, coupled together, and drawn as a unit by one or more locomotives: *when does the train start for London?* Phr. *by train*, by the railway, as contrasted with *by road, sea, air* &c.; also, *railway train*. 5. A series, sequence, of connected ideas &c.: *a train of thought, of reasoning*; (more rarely) *a train of words*. 6. Course of action; process of movement, preparation, development; esp. in such Phr. as *to put things in train*, to start, prepare for, action &c.; *everything is now in train for the attack*. 7. A continuous line, esp. of gunpowder, extending from a given point up to some explosive object or substance which it is desired to blow up.

train (III.), vb. intrans., fr. prec. 4. To travel by railway train.

train-band, n., for *trained band*. A company of trained citizens capable of being used for defence, started in London in 14th cent., which in the 18th cent. developed into the more highly organized militia.

train-bearer, n. Page or other attendant who holds up the train of the robe of a high personage on a ceremonial occasion, of bride at wedding &c.

trainer, n. [1. trāner; 2. tréinə]. **train** (I.) & **-er**. One who trains; specif., person who trains men for athletic competitions or horses for racing.

train-ferry, n. **a** A vessel specially built to carry a railway train and transport it and its passengers and freight across water; **b** service of such vessels.

training, n. [1. tráning; 2. tréiniŋ]. **train** (I.) & **-ing**. 1. **a** Act or process of forming, educating, instructing, disciplining: *training of mind and body*; *the training of teachers*, instruction given them in methods and practice of their profession; **b** state of being trained, practised, disciplined, in some branch of mental or physical proficiency: *in first-rate training for a race* &c.

training-college, n. Institution for instructing young teachers in the theory and art of their profession; a normal school.

training-ship, n. Vessel, usually moored in an estuary, in which the art and practice of seamanship is taught to boys.

training-stable, n. Stables, exercising ground &c. where racehorses are trained.

train-oil, n., fr. Du. *traen*, 'tear from the eye; train-oil'; cp. Germ. *träne*, 'tear'. Thick kind of lubricating oil made from whale blubber.

traipse, see **trapse**.

trait, n. [1. trā; 2. trei]. Fr., 'a stroke; a feature', orig. P.P. of *traire*, 'to draw', fr. Lat. *tract-(um)*, P.P. of *trahere*, see **tract** (I.) & **trace** (II.). 1. (rare) A stroke, touch: *a trait of humour*. 2. A characteristic feature, distinguishing mark: *the chief traits of a person's character*.

traitor, n. [1. trāter; 2. tréitə]. M.E. *traitour* &c., fr. O. Fr. *traïteur*, fr. Lat. *trāditor*, 'betrayer'; fr. *trādit-(um)*, P.P. type of *trādere*, 'to deliver, surrender'; see **traditor**. One who betrays a person or a cause to whom he owes allegiance; specif., one who is disloyal to his king and country, and who consorts with, and betrays secrets to, his country's enemies to the detriment of his native land.

traitorous, adj. [1. trāturus; 2. tréitərəs]. Prec. & **-ous**. **a** Pertaining to, of the nature of, a traitor or of treachery; **b** guilty of treachery, disloyal.

traitorously, adv. Prec. & **-ly**. In a traitorous manner.

traitorousness, n. See prec. & **-ness**. **a** Quality of being traitorous; **b** traitorous conduct.

traitress, n. [1. trātres; 2. tréitris]. **traitor** & **-ess**. A female traitor.

trajectory, n. [1. trajékturi; 2. trədžéktəri]. Lat. *trăject-(um)*, P.P. type of *trājicere*, 'to throw across', & **-ory**; see **trans-** & **jet** (III.). Path followed by a projectile fired at a given incline, and passing through the air at a given speed.

tram (I.), n. [1. tram; 2. træm]. Fr. *trame*, Lat. *trāma*, 'woof, weft', perh. for *tragh-sma*, cp. *trahere*, 'to draw' &c., see **tract** (I.) & **trace** (II.); another suggestion is that first element is *trans*, 'across', see **trans-**. Double twisted thread, spun. such forming weft of velvet or other silk fabrics.

tram (II.), n. & vb. intrans. Perh. Scand.; etymologists compare Swed. dial. *tromm*, 'a log'; Norw. *tram*, 'wooden doorstep'; but connexion in sense w. Engl. word is very vague. 1. n. **a** Large, heavy, public vehicle plying for hire, carrying passengers, and running on rails laid on a road; **b** truck used in coal-mines for conveying coal to entrance of mine. 2. vb. To travel by tram.

tram-car, n. Vehicle running on a rail laid upon a road; a tram.

tram-line, n. **a** One of the rails, these taken together, upon which a tram runs; **b** the whole route upon which rails for trams are laid.

trammel (I.), n. [1. tráml; 2. træml]. Fr. *tramail*, earlier *trémail*, 'net', fr. L. Lat.

tremaculum fr. *trēs*, 'three, triple', see **tri-**, & *macula*, 'a spot; mesh of a net', see **macula**, & **mail (I.)**. 1. (archaic) A net for catching birds. 2. A shackle for controlling motions of a horse. 3. Something which acts as a check or means of restraint; something which hampers and impedes movement and action; (esp. in fig. or non-material sense) *the trammels of the flesh*; *the trammels imposed by poverty* &c. 4. Hook for hanging a pot over a fire; a pot-hook; a figure (ʔ) in form of this. 5. Instrument for drawing ellipses. 6. One of various devices for adjusting and aligning parts of a machine. 7. (pl.) A beam-compass: *pair of trammels*.

trammel (II.), vb. trans., fr. prec. To impose trammels upon; (chiefly fig.) to hamper, impede, restrain.

tramontana, n. [1. tràmontáhna; 2. træmɔntǟna]. Ital.; see next word. Dry, strong, cold wind from the Adriatic.

tramontane, adj. & n. [1. tramóntän, trámontän; 2. træmóntein, træmɔntein]. Fr., fr. Ital. *tramontano*, fr. Lat. *trans*, 'across', see **trans-**, & *montānus*, 'of the mountains', see **mountain**. 1. adj. Coming from, lying, beyond the mountains; (from Ital. standpoint) foreign, barbarous. 2. n. A stranger, a foreigner.

tramp (I.), vb. intrans. & trans. [1. tramp; 2. træmp]. M.E. *trampen*; L.G. *trampen*, 'to trample'; cp. Goth. *(ana)trimpan*, 'to press down'; cp. **trample (I.)** & **trapse**. 1. intrans. **a** To walk, tread, heavily: *heavy footsteps tramping overhead*; **b** to plod along; to go on foot, in distinction to riding or going in a vehicle: *we shall have to tramp as there is no means of conveyance*; **c** (from n.) to travel on foot for long distances, after the manner of a tramp. 2. trans. To traverse by tramping: *to tramp the streets all night*. Phr. *to tramp it*, to walk, go on foot.

tramp (II.), n., fr. prec. 1. A homeless vagrant who wanders along the roads from place to place, sleeping out, and living by mendicancy, and by doing occasional short jobs of work. Phr. *to look like a tramp*, present a dirty, disreputable, shabby appearance. 2. A long, esp. a tedious and laborious, journey on foot. 3. Sound of a heavy tread, as of a regiment &c. marching past. 4. Cargo steamer making short journeys to any port as occasion arises, not always between the same ports, and not going on regular voyages. 5. Flat plate of iron on upper edge of blade of a spade to protect boot when pressing the spade into the ground.

trample (I.), vb. trans. & intrans. [1. trámpl; 2. træmpl]. M.E. *trampelen*; freq. of **tramp (I.)**. 1. trans. To tread heavily and repeatedly upon so as to crush: *to trample grapes*; *to trample grass down*; also *trample down (growing corn* &c.); (also fig.) to suppress: *to trample down one's feelings*; *to trample upon a person*, to oppress, domineer over. 2. intrans. To perform the act of trampling: *to hear a person trampling about overhead*.

trample (II.), n., fr. prec. **a** The act of trampling; **b** sound of trampling.

tram-rail, n. **a** Rail upon which trams run; **b** (pl.) whole system of such rails at given place.

tramway, n. [1. trámwä; 2. træmwei]. Road laid with rails for trams; (also loosely) a tram.

tran-, pref. Form of **trans-** used before words beginning w. *s-*.

trance, n. [1. trahns; 2. träns]. M.E., 'fright, access of fear', fr. O. Fr. *transe*, 'a swoon', fr. *transir*, 'to chill, penetrate deeply with cold, to benumb', fr. Lat. *transīre*, 'to pass over'; see **transire**. 1. (med.) Bodily condition attended with unconsciousness, in which complete insensibility occurs, and the vital functions are reduced to a very low ebb, the general appearance being that of profound and prolonged slumber. 2. Condition in which mystics believe that the soul leaves the body and passes into other spheres of being, seeing visions, and receiving enlightenment concerning spiritual mysteries.

tranquil, adj. [1. trángkwil; 2. træŋkwil]. Cp. Fr. *tranquille*, fr. Lat. *tranquillus*, 'quiet, calm, still'; prob. fr. *trans*, 'over' &c., w. intens. sense, see **trans-**, & **-quil-nos*, fr. same base as *quiēs*, 'rest, repose', see **quiet**. **a** (of material things) Calm, serene; not disturbed or agitated: *the tranquil air*; *tranquil waters of a lake* &c.; **b** (of non-material things) not excited; unruffled; not disturbed by violent emotions; peaceful: *a tranquil life*; *a tranquil heart*; **c** expressing no agitation or excitement; exhibiting serenity and calm: *a tranquil gaze, face, voice*.

tranquillity, n. [1. trangkwíliti; 2. træŋkwíliti]. **tranquil** & **-ity**. State of being tranquil; **a** material calm, peacefulness, quietness; **b** calmness, serenity, of mind; composure.

tranquillization, n. [1. tràngkwilizáshun; 2. træŋkwilaizéiʃən]. See **tranquillize** & **-ation**. Act of tranquillizing; state of being tranquillized.

tranquillize, vb. trans. & intrans. [1. trángkwilīz; 2. træŋkwilaiz]. **tranquil** & **-ize**. 1. trans. To cause to become tranquil; to quieten, appease, calm down. 2. intrans. To become tranquil; to die down, abate, become quiet.

trans-, pref. Lat. *trans*, 'across, over, beyond, on farther side of'. In most Engl. words this pref. is pronounced indifferently w. either [ah, ä] or [a, æ], even by the same speaker. In compounds, *trans-* has the senses: **a** 'over, across': *transīre*, 'to go over, across'; **b** 'through, through and through': *transfīgere*, 'to pierce through'; **c** 'beyond': *transalpīnus*, 'lying beyond the Alps'. In Lat. compounds, *trans* remains unchanged before vowels, & often before cons. other than *s-*. Before the latter, *tran-* is the form used; before cons. it sometimes appears as *trā-*, as in *trādo*, 'to give over, deliver' &c., see **tradition**, also *transdo*. In most Engl. words where *trans-* occurs the compound comes direct fr. Lat. As a living suff. it usually has sense of 'beyond, on farther side of', as in *trans-Caucasian*.

transact, vb. trans. & intrans. [1. trahnzákt; 2. tränzækt]. Lat. *transact-(um)*, P.P. type of *transigere* for *-agere*, 'to carry through, settle, dispatch'; see **trans-** & **act (I.)**. 1. trans. To carry through, perform, conduct (business, negotiations &c.). 2. intrans. To settle, put through, a piece of business.

transaction, n. [1. trahnzákshun; 2. tränzǽkʃən]. Prec. & **-ion**. 1. Act or process of conducting, settling (a piece of business): *the transaction of affairs* &c. 2. Something transacted, carried out, negotiated; a piece of business: *engaged in various transactions*. 3. (in pl.) Account, record, of business transacted; specif., record of papers read before a learned society; Proceedings: *Transactions of the Philological Society*. 4. (law) Compromise of a dispute by mutual concession and agreement.

transalpine, adj. & n. [1. trahnzálpīn; 2. tränzǽlpain], fr. Lat. *transalpīnus*, see **trans-** & **Alpine**. 1. adj. Situated, living, from Italian point of view, beyond the Alps. 2. n. Person living beyond the Alps.

transatlantic, adj. [1. trahnzatlántik; 2. tränzətlǽntik]. **a** Situated, living, across the Atlantic; **b** going, making a voyage, across the Atlantic: *transatlantic liner*.

transcend, vb. trans. & intrans. [1. trahnsénd; 2. tränsénd]. Lat. *transcendere*, 'to step over, surmount; to surpass'; **trans-** & *scandere*, 'to climb, ascend'; see **scan** & **scandal** & second element in **ascend** & **descend**. 1. To go beyond, overstep: *to transcend the limits of decency*. 2. To be superior to, to surpass, excel: *the genius of Shakespeare transcends that of all other human beings*.

transcendence, -ency, n. [1. trahnséndens(i); 2. tränséndəns(i)]. Lat. *transcendentia*, see next word & **-ce, -cy**. 1. Quality of being transcendent. 2. Specif. (theol.) essential attribute of God in being superior to, apart from, and not subject to, the conditions and limitations of the material universe.

transcendent (I.), adj. [1. trahnséndent; 2. tränséndənt]. Lat. *transcendent-(em)*, Pres. Part. of *transcendere*, see **transcend**. 1. Surpassing, excelling, superior to, others in quality or extent: *transcendent merit, beauty*; also *transcendent folly* &c. 2. Transcendental. 3. (theol., of God) Possessing transcendency; see **transcendence, 2**.

transcendent (II.), n., fr. prec. Person or thing which is transcendent.

transcendental, adj. [1. tràhnsendéntl; 2. tränsendéntl]. **transcendent (I.)** & **-al**. 1. (philos., of human experience and knowledge) Of a character which is a priori, intuitive, gained by intuition; contrasted with *empirical*. 2. (popular) Vague, fanciful, visionary; abstruse: *transcendental style (of writing)*.

transcendentalism, n. [1. tràhnsendéntalizm; 2. tränsendéntəlizəm]. Prec. & **-ism**. System of philosophy which emphasizes the intuitive rather than the empirical elements in thought and knowledge.

transcendentalist, n. [1. tràhnsendéntalist; 2. tränsendéntəlist]. See prec. & **-ist**. Believer in transcendentalism.

transcendentalize, vb. trans. [1. tràhnsendéntalīz; 2. tränsendéntəlaiz]. **transcendental** & **-ize**. To make, regard as, transcendental.

transcendentally, adv. [1. tràhnsendéntali; 2. tränsendéntəli]. See prec. & **-ly**. In a transcendental manner.

transcontinental, adj. [1. tráhnzkontinéntal; 2. tränzkɔntinéntəl]. Passing across, traversing, the Continent, or a continent.

transcribe, vb. trans. [1. trahnskrīb; 2. tränskráib]. Lat. *transcrībere*, 'to write, copy, from one document to another'; 'to copy off'; see **trans-** & **scribe (I.)**. To copy; to write out, write down.

transcript, n. [1. trahnskript; 2. tránskript]. Lat. *transcript-(um)*, P.P. type of *transcrībere*, see prec., & **trans-** & **script**. Something transcribed; a copy written from another document.

transcription, n. [1. trahnskrípshun; 2. tränskrípʃən]. Prec. & **-ion**. 1. Act, process, of transcribing. 2. A transcript, copy.

transcurrent, adj. [1. trahnzkúrent; 2. tränzkárənt]. Lat. See **trans-** & **current (I.)**, adj. Extending, running, across.

transect, vb. trans. [1. trahnsékt; 2. tränsékt], fr. Lat. *transect-(um)*, P.P. type of *transecāre*, 'to put across'; see **trans-** & **sect**. To cut across.

transection, n. [1. trahnsékshun; 2. tränsékʃən]. Prec. & **-ion**. **a** Act, process, of cutting across; **b** a transverse section.

transenna, n. [1. trahnséna; 2. tränséna]. Lat., 'a grating, lattice; fowler's net'. Etymol. entirely obscure. Screen of stone or metal lattice-work enclosing a shrine.

transept, n. [1. trán-, tráhnsept; 2. træn-, tränsept], fr. **trans-** & Lat. *septum*, 'a hedge; an enclosure'; see **septum**. That extension on either side of the nave of a church which crosses at right angles before the apse or choir.

transfer (I.), vb. trans. & intrans. [1. trahnsfér; 2. tränzfə́]. Lat. *transferre*, 'to carry over, transport' &c.; see **trans-** & **-ferous**. A. trans. 1. **a** To move, shift (person or thing) from one place to another, remove from one place or position and place in another: *to transfer a book from a table to a shelf*; *to transfer a boy to another school*; also *to transfer a name to a different list*; **b** (of non-material action) to transfer one's affections, allegiance &c. to a new object. 2. Specif., to convey, deliver over (property, shares &c.), into possession of, vest in, another. 3. (lithography &c.) To print, take an impression, from one surface to another. B. intrans. Specif., to change one's place from one tram, train, boat, to another.

transfer (II.), n. [1. tráhnzfer; 2. trănzfā́]. See prec. 1. Act of transferring, state of being transferred; specif. **a** conveyance, transference, of any kind of property or the right in it, by any means, to another person; **b** legal instrument by which such conveyance is effected. 2. Picture, device, design, made so that it can be transferred from one surface to another, esp. a highly coloured picture on very thin paper, fixed to a thicker paper, which on being immersed in water becomes detached from this, and can be transferred, and made to adhere to, another sheet or object.

transferability, n. [1. tràhnzferabíliti; 2. trănzfərəbíliti]. See next word & **-ity**. Condition, property, of being transferable.

transferable, adj. [1. trahnzférabl, tráhnzferabl; 2. trănzfā́rəbl, trănzfərəbl]. **transfer (I.) & -able**. Capable of being transferred; (specif. of rights, or documents attesting these) capable of being legally conveyed to, or vested in, another person: *transferable vote*, method of electing parliamentary and other candidates, in which the voter signifies on the ballot-paper the name of the candidate to whom his vote should be transferred if no candidate obtains an absolute majority.

transferee, n. [1. tràhnzferé; 2. trănzfərí]. **transfer (I.) & -ee**. Person to whom anything, esp. a legal right or interest, is transferred.

transference, n. [1. tráhnzferens; 2. trănzfərəns]. **transfer (I.) & -ence**. Act of transferring; **a** conveyance; **b** passage from one place &c. to another.

transferential, adj. [1. tràhnzferénshal; 2. trănzfərénʃəl]. Prec. & **-ial**. Pertaining to, of the nature of, a transfer or transference.

transferor, n. [1. tràhnzferór; 2. trănzfərṓ]. **transfer (II.) & -or**. One who transfers, esp. a legal right or interest.

transferrer, n. [1. trahnzférer; 2. trănzfā́rə]. See prec. & **-er**. Transferor (in gen. sense).

transfiguration, n. [1. trahnzfigūrā́shun; 2. trănzfigjəréiʃən, trănsfigəréiʃən]. See **transfigure & -ation**. A marked change of form or of appearance; specif. (cap.) **a** the miraculous change in the form and face of the Saviour, described in Matt. xvii.; **b** feast held by the Church in commemoration of this, on Aug. 6th.

transfigure, vb. trans. [1. trahnzfíger; 2. trănzfígə]. Fr. *transfigurer*, fr. Lat. *transfigūrāre*, 'to change in shape, to transform'; see **trans- & figure (I.)**. To alter the shape and appearance of; to transform; esp. to make more beautiful and glorious.

transfix, vb. trans. [1. trahnzfíks; 2. trănzfíks], fr. Lat. *transfix-(um)*, P.P. type of *transfigere*, 'to pierce through'; fr. **trans- &** *figere*, 'to fasten, fix, attach', see **fix (I.)**. To pierce through, penetrate; to impale: *to transfix a bird with an arrow* (also fig.) to affect profoundly: *to be transfixed with terror*.

transfixion, n. [1. trahnzfíkshun; 2. trănzfíkʃən]. Prec. & **-ion**. **a** Act of transfixing; **b** state of being transfixed.

transform, vb. trans. [1. trahnzfórm; 2. trănzfṓm]. Fr. *transformer*, fr. Lat. *transformāre*, 'to change shape of'; see **trans- & form (I.)**. 1. To alter the outward shape and appearance of to such an extent as to cause to appear something different: *he was quite transformed by the removal of his beard*. 2. **a** To change into a different substance, alter the nature of, transmute: *attempts to transform one metal into another are no longer considered practicable*; **b** to alter the essential character, functions, uses, of: *to transform a cottage into a mansion, a conventicle into a church*. 3. To change the spiritual nature and character of: *to transform a criminal into a decent member of society*.

transformable, adj. [1.trahnzfórmabl; 2. trănzfṓməbl]. Prec. & **-able**. Capable of being transformed.

transformation, n. [1. tràhnzformā́shun; 2. trănzfəméiʃən]. Lat.; see prec. & **-ation**. **a** Act of transforming; **b** condition of being transformed (in various senses both material and non-material).

transformation scene, n. Theatrical scene which gradually changes before the eyes of the audience; specif., one at the end of a pantomime, in which the characters in this change into those of the harlequinade.

transformative, adj. [1. trahnzfórmativ; 2. trănzfṓmətiv]. Fr. *transformatif*; **trans- & formative (I.)**. Tending, serving, to transform.

transformator, n. [1. trahnzfórmāter; 2. trănzfəméitə]. See prec. & **-or**. Mechanical device for altering strength of an electric current; transformer.

transformer, n. [1. trahnzfórmer; 2. trănzfṓmə]. **transform & -er**. Person who, thing which, transforms; esp. one of various mechanical devices in electricity or wireless for altering continuous into alternating current or the voltage of a continuous current.

transformism, n. [1. trahnzfórmizm; 2. trănzfṓmizəm]. **transform & -ism**. Biological doctrine, now obsolete, also called *mutability of species*, that entirely new species may arise from others already existing, chiefly through the modifying influence of environment.

transfuse, vb. trans. [1. trahnzfūz; 2. trănzfjúz], fr. Lat. *transfūs-(um)*, P.P. of *transfundere*, 'to pour from one (vessel) into another, to pour off'; see **trans- & fuse (I.)**. 1. To pour (liquid) from one receptacle into another. 2. To transfer (blood) from veins of one person or animal into those of another. 3. (in non-material sense) To instil into, penetrate deeply with, imbue: *to transfuse one's own enthusiasm into one's audience*.

transfusion, n. [1. trahnzfűzhun; 2. trănzfjúʒən]. Lat. *transfūsiōn-(em)*, 'a pouring from one vessel into another'; **trans- & fusion**. 1. Act, process, of transfusing in all senses; esp. *transfusion of blood*. 2. An intermingling, interpenetration, of different elements, properties, qualities.

transfusive, adj. [1. trahnzfúsiv; 2. trănzfjúsiv]. **transfuse & -ive**. Tending to transfuse, serving to bring about transfusion.

transgress, vb. trans. & intrans. [1. trahnzgrés; 2. trănzgrés]. Fr. *transgresser*, fr. Lat. *transgress-(um)*, P.P. of *transgredi*, 'to step across'; fr. **trans- &** *gradi*, 'to step, walk', fr. *gradus*, 'a step', see **grade (I.) & gradus**. A. trans. 1. To overstep, go beyond, exceed: *to transgress the bounds of decency, the limitations of an agreement &c*. 2. To violate, infringe, break: *to transgress the law, the Divine commands &c*. B. intrans. To commit a breach of the law; to violate a moral principle; to sin.

transgression, n. [1. trahnzgréshun; 2. trănzgréʃən]. Lat. *transgressiōn-(em)*, 'a going across, a passage', fr. *transgress-(um)*, see prec. & **-ion**. Act of transgressing; the overstepping of a moral bound or limit, a violation of a moral principle or rule of conduct; a misdeed, a sin.

transgressional, adj. [1. trahnzgréshunal; 2. trănzgréʃənəl]. Prec. & **-al**. Pertaining to transgression.

transgressive, adj. [1. trahnzgrésiv; 2. trănzgrésiv]. Fr. *transgressif*, fr. Lat. *transgressivus*; **transgress & -ive**. Prone, tending, to transgress.

transgressor, n. [1. trahnzgrésur; 2. trănzgrésə]. Lat.; **transgress & -or**. One who transgresses; **a** a breaker of laws or rules; **b** a violator of moral principles; a sinner.

tranship, vb. See **trans-ship**.

transience, transiency, n. [1. tráhnsiens(i); 2. trănsiəns(i)]. **transient & -ce, -cy**. Quality, fact, of being transient.

transient, adj. [1. tráhnsient; 2. trănsiənt]. As though fr. Lat. *transient-(em), Pres. Part. of *transīre*, 'to pass through, to pass'; on anal. of **ambient**; see **transire**. Passing, tending to pass away; lasting but a short time; fleeting, brief, momentary; contrasted with *lasting, permanent*; **a** (of material things) *a transient smile*; *a transient flush in the sky*; **b** (of non-material things) *transient pleasures, joys, success &c*.

transiently, adv. Prec. & **-ly**. For a moment; in a brief space of time; not permanently.

transilient, adj. [1. trahnsílient; 2. trănsíliənt]. Lat. *transilient-(em)*, Pres. Part. of *transilīre*, 'to spring over, or across'; fr. **trans- &** *salīre*, 'to leap'; see **salient (I.)**. (anat., of nerve-fibres) Passing from one convolution of the brain to another; not adjacent.

transilluminate, vb. trans. [1. tràhnzilū́māt; 2. trănziljúmineit]. **trans- & illuminate**. To cause light to pass through; esp. to pass light through some part of the body for purposes of examination, as by X-rays.

transillumination, n. [1. tràhnzilūmināshun; 2. trănziljúminéiʃən]. Prec. & **-ion**. Act, process, of transilluminating.

transire, n. [1. tràhnzíre; 2. trănzáiəri]. Lat. infin., 'to go through'; see **trans- &** base **i-*, 'to go', discussed under **itinerate**. Document issued by Custom-house officials describing cargo of a ship, enabling it to be cleared, and setting forth names of consignors and consignees.

trans-isthmian, adj. [1. tràhnz ísmian; 2. trănz ísmiən]. **trans- & isthmus & -an**. Across an isthmus or through a ship-canal through an isthmus, as through the Panama or Suez Canal: *a trans-isthmian canal*; *trans-isthmian traffic*.

transit (I.), n. [1. tráhnzit; 2. trănzit]. Lat. *transitus*, 'a going over, a passage', fr. *transit-(um)*, P.P. type of *transīre*, 'to pass over', see **transire**. 1. Passage through. 2. Act, process, of conveying, sending, transmitting, causing to pass: *the transit of goods*; Phr. *in transit*, said of goods during time which elapses between the moment of their being sent off and that of the receipt by the person to whom they are consigned. 3. Passage of a heavenly body, esp. of Venus or Mercury, across sun's disk, or across field of vision of a telescope, or apparent passage of a star across meridian.

transit (II.), vb. trans., fr. prec. (of a heavenly body) To pass across the sun's disk.

transit-circle, instrument, n. Instrument for observing the transit of heavenly bodies.

transition, n. [1. trahnzíshun; 2. trănzíʃən]. Lat. *transitiōn-(em)*, 'a passing over, passage'; see **transit (I.) & -ion**. 1. Change, passage, **a** from one place, or kind of place, to another: *a sudden transition from the plain to hilly country*; **b** passage, alteration, from one set of conditions, mode of existence, state &c. to another: *a gradual transition from a tropical to a cold climate*; *a rapid transition from poverty to wealth*; *a natural transition from grave to gay*; *a period of transition &c*. 2. (used attrib.) Indicating a process of gradual change and modification: *transition period*, one occurring between two well-marked, characteristic periods; *Transition English*; *Early Transition*, phase of English between Old and Middle English; *Late Transition*, that between Middle and Modern English.

transitional, adj. [1. trahnzíshunal; 2. trănzíʃənəl]. Prec. & **-al**. Pertaining to, occurring, existing, under conditions of transition; marked by, characterized by, change from one state of things to another.

transitionally, adv. See prec. & **-ly**. In a transitional manner.

transitionary, adj. [1. trahnzíshunari; 2. trănzíʃənəri]. **transition & -ary**. Transitional.

transitive, adj. [1. tráhnzitiv; 2. trănzitiv], fr. L. Lat. *transitīvus*; see **transit (I.) & -ive**. 1. (gram., of vbs.) Governing a direct object; *transitive verb*, one expressing an action which passes directly on to, and affects, the object, as *to strike the iron while it is hot*, contrasted with *intransitive*, as *to strike while the iron is hot*. 2. Having the property of passing or making a transit from one person or thing to another: *transitive heat*.

transitively, adv. Prec. & -ly. In a transitive manner; by use of a transitive verb.

transitiveness, n. See prec. & -ness. Quality of being transitive.

transitivity, n. [1. tràhnzitíviti; 2. trănzitíviti]. transitive & -ity. Property of being transitive; capacity of passing from one person or thing to another.

transitorily, adv. [1. tráhnziturili; 2. trănzitərili]. transitory & -ly. In a transitory manner; for a time only.

transitoriness, n. [1. tràhnziturines; 2. trănzitərinis]. Next word & -ness. Quality, state, of being transitory.

transitory, adj. [1. tráhnzituri; 2. trănzitəri]. Lat. *transitōrius*, 'adapted for passing through'; see **transit** (I.) & -ory. Not lasting, tending to pass away, enduring but for a time; fleeting, evanescent: *this transitory life*.

translatable, adj. [1. trahnzlátabl; 2. trănzléitəbl]. See next word & -able. Capable of being translated.

translate, vb. trans. & intrans. [1. trahnzlát; 2. trănzléit], fr. L. Lat. *translatāre*, formed fr. *translāt-(um)*, P.P. type of *transferre*, 'to carry over', see **transfer** (I.); trans-, & lāt-, wh. stands for *tlāt-; see base *tl- under **tolerate** & **thole**. A. trans. 1. a (archaic) To remove, transfer, from one place to another; specif. b to remove, transfer, (a bishop) from one see to another; c to remove the body or relics of a saint, confessor, or martyr from one place to another. 2. Specif., to remove, carry away, bodily, direct to heaven without death of the body: *Enoch is said to have been translated to heaven*. 3. To turn from one language into another; to render in one language what has been written or spoken in another. 4. To render what is expressed or conceived in one medium into another: *to translate promises, schemes &c. into actions*; *to translate phonetic symbols into sounds*. B. intrans. 1. To translate what is uttered or written in one language into another: *I can read Danish but can't translate into it*. 2. To be capable of translation: *poetry does not translate easily*.

translation, n. [1. trahnzláshun; 2. trănzléiʃən]. Lat. *translātiōn-(em)*, 'a removing, transferring, from one place to another'; also of language, 'a version, translation', see **translate** & -ion. 1. Act, process, of translating, a the transference of a bishop from one see to another; b removal to heaven without bodily death; c removal of body or relics of a saint &c. from one place to another. Specif. 2. a act of translating from one language into another; b something which is translated; esp. a version in a particular language of something originally written or uttered in a different language.

translational, adj. [1. trahnzláshunal; 2. trănzléiʃənəl]. Prec. & -al. Pertaining to, connected with, translation.

translative, adj. [1. trahnzlativ; 2. trănzlətiv]. Lat. *translātīvus*, 'belonging to transference; capable of being transferred'; see **translate** & -ive. a Connected with, denoting, a transfer of property; b indicating, expressing, a transference of meaning, state &c.

translator, n. [1. trahnzláter; 2. trănzléitə]. Lat. See **translate** & -or. One who translates; esp. one who translates from one language into another.

transliterate, vb. trans. [1. trahnzlíterat; 2. trănzlítəreit], fr. **trans-** & Lat. *lit(t)era*, 'letter', see **letter** (I.) & **literal** & -ate. To write what is actually or commonly written with the symbols of a given alphabet in the corresponding symbols of another: *in this Dictionary, Greek is always transliterated with Roman letters*.

transliteration, n. [1. tràhnzliteráshun; 2. trănzlítəréiʃən]. Prec. & -ion. a Act of transliterating; b written word &c. which has been transliterated.

translucence, translucency, n. [1. trahnzlúsens(i); 2. trănzljúsəns(i)]. Next word & -ce, -cy. Property, condition, of being translucent.

translucent, adj. [1. trahnzlúsent; 2. trănzljúsənt]. Lat., 'shining through'; see **trans-** & **lucent**. Allowing rays of light to pass through; transparent or semi-transparent.

transmarine, adj. [1. trahnzmarén; 2. trănzmərín]. trans- & marine (I.). adj. Situated, living, coming from, beyond, on the other side of, the sea.

transmigrant, adj. [1. trahnzmígrant; 2. trănzmáigrənt]. trans- & migrant. Migrating from one place or condition to another.

transmigrate, vb. intrans. [1. trahnzmígrāt; 2. trănzmáigreit]. trans- & migrate. 1. To migrate, go, from one place or country to another. 2. (of the soul) To pass at death into another body.

transmigration, n. [1. tràhnzmigráshun; 2. trănzmaigréiʃən]. trans- & migration. 1. Act of migrating from one place or country to another. 2. (specif. Hinduism &c.) The passage of the soul at death into another body, human or animal; metempsychosis; usually, *the transmigration of souls*.

transmigrator, n. [1. tràhnzmigráter; 2. trănzmaigréitə]. transmigrate & -or. One who transmigrates.

transmigratory, adj. [1. trahnzmígraturi; 2. trănzmáigrətəri]. transmigrate & -ory. Given to, liable to, transmigration.

transmissibility, n. [1. tràhnzmisibíliti; 2. trănzmisibíliti]. Next word & -ity. Condition, quality, of being transmissible; capacity of being transmitted.

transmissible, adj. [1. trahnzmísibl; 2. trănzmísibl]. transmiss- as in **transmission** & -ible. Capable of being transmitted.

transmission, n. [1. trahnzmíshun; 2. trănzmíʃən]. trans- & mission. a Act of transmitting; b condition of being transmitted.

transmit, vb. trans. & intrans. [1. trahnzmít; 2. trănzmít]. Lat. *transmittere*, 'to send, convey, across; to allow to pass through; to hand over'; trans-, & see **missile** & **mission** for base of second element. A. trans. 1. To hand over, cause to be received, pass on (by a physical action): *to transmit a package by rail, a letter by hand*. 2. To pass on, convey, hand on, or down, a by heredity: *parents transmit their characters and features to their offspring*; b by inheritance and descent: *to transmit property, a title, to one's heirs*. 3. To permit passage of, allow to pass along, serve as medium for: *wires transmit an electric current*. 4. To communicate, pass on, tell: *to transmit news*; *to transmit a tradition to the younger generation*. B. intrans. (law) To descend by transmission.

transmitter, n. [1. trahnzmíter; 2. trănzmítə]. Prec. & -er. a One who transmits: '*No tenth transmitter of a foolish face*' (Savage, 'The Bastard'); b that which transmits; part of a telephone or telegraphic apparatus which sends on the message; specif., apparatus by means of which wireless waves are sent out.

transmogrification, n. [1. tràhnzmogrifikáshun; 2. trănzmɔgrifikéiʃən]. See next word & -fication. Act of transmogrifying; a complete change or transformation.

transmogrify, vb. trans. [1. trahnzmógrifī; 2. trănzmɔ́grifai]. Mod. coinage. To cause to change completely in appearance or character; to transform, transmute.

transmutability, n. [1. trahnzmutabíliti; 2. trănzmjūtəbíliti]. Next word & -ity. Quality, fact, of being transmutable.

transmutable, adj. [1. trahnzmútabl; 2. trănzmjútəbl]. transmute & -able. Capable of being transmuted.

transmutably, adv. Prec. & -ly. So as to be transmutable.

transmutation, n. [1. tràhnzmūtáshun; 2. trănzmjūtéiʃən]. Lat. *transmūtātiōn-(em)*. trans- mute & -ation. 1. a Act or process of transmuting; complete change in nature, form, or conditions; transformation; *transmutations of fortune*, ups and downs, fluctuations; b state of being transmuted. 2. Specif. a (biol.) change of one species into another (a process now called *mutation*); b (alchem.) *transmutation of metals*, supposed conversion of base metals into gold.

transmutationist, n. [1. tràhnzmūtáshunist; 2. trănzmjūtéiʃənist]. Prec. & -ist. Believer in the transmutation of species or of metals.

transmutative, adj. [1. trahnzmútativ; 2. trănzmjútətiv]. Lat. *transmūtāt-(um)*, P.P. type of *transmūtāre*, 'to change over', see **transmute**, & -ive. Connected with, resulting from, transmutation.

transmute, vb. trans. [1. trahnzmút; 2. trănzmjút]. Lat. *transmūtāre*, 'to change, shift'; see **trans-** & **mutable**. To change from one form, character, set of conditions, into another; to transform.

transoceanic, adj. [1. tráhnzōsheánik; 2. trănzouʃiǽnik]. Across the ocean; a situated on the other side of, beyond, an ocean; b crossing an ocean.

transom, n. [1. tránsum; 2. trǽnsəm]. Lat. *transtrum*, 'a cross-timber, beam running from side to side in a vessel'; formed fr. **trans-**, w. formative -tr-, expressing an agent or instrument. a Horizontal stone or wooden beam or bar across the top of a doorway or of a window, or across the middle of a window; b beam or timber fixed across the stern-post of a vessel; c any cross-timber or strut used in building and engineering.

transom-window, n. Window over the transom of a door.

transpadane, adj. [1. trahnzpádan; 2. trănzpéidein], fr. Lat. *transpadānus*, fr. *trans*, 'across', see **trans-**, & *Padus*, the river Po, & -an(e). Situated, lying beyond, i.e. north of, the river Po.

transparence, n. [1. trahnspárens; 2. trănspɛ́ərəns]. transparent & -ce. Transparency 1.

transparency, n. [1. trahnspárensi; 2. trănspɛ́ərənsi]. transparent & -cy. 1. Quality of being transparent. 2. Something which is transparent; specif., a picture or device, concealed externally between thin sheets of paper, cloth &c., but becoming visible if looked at against a light.

transparent, adj. [1. trahnspárent; 2. trănspɛ́ərənt]. Lat. *transpārent-(em)*, Pres. Part. of *transpārēre*, fr. **trans-** & *pārēre*, 'to appear'; see **appear** & **pare**. 1. (of matter) a Permeable to light; having the property of letting rays of light pass through, and therefore of allowing objects and images behind or beneath, to be clearly seen; reverse of *opaque*; b (of fabric) open, having an open texture or mesh, so that what lies beneath is scarcely concealed: *transparent muslin* &c. 2. (of style) Clear, limpid, lucid, easy to be understood. 3. (of the character and spiritual qualities) Candid, frank, not attempting to hide or dissemble: *transparent honesty, sincerity* &c.

transparently, adv. Prec. & -ly. In a transparent manner (lit. and fig.).

transparentness, n. See prec. & -ness. Quality of being transparent.

transpierce, vb. trans. [1. trahnspérs; 2. trănspíəs]. trans- & pierce. To pierce through; to transfix.

transpirable, adj. [1. trahnspírabl; 2. trănspáiərəbl]. transpire & -able. Capable of being given off in vapour.

transpiration, n. [1. tràhnspiráshun; 2. trănspiréiʃən]. transpire & -ation. a Process of transpiring, of exhaling vapour; b moisture given off in form of vapour.

transpiratory, adj. [1. trahnspíraturi; 2. trănspáiərətəri]. Lat. *transpīrāt-(um)*, P.P. type of *transpīrāre*, see **transpire**, & -ory. Pertaining to, connected with, transpiration.

transpire, vb. intrans. & trans. [1. trahnspír; 2. trănspáiə]. Fr. *transpirer*, 'perspire' &c., fr. Lat. *transpīrāre*; tran- & *spīrāre*, 'to breathe, blow; to exhale'; see **spirant**. A. intrans. 1. To exhale, give off, watery vapour. 2. To pass off, be exhaled, in form of watery vapour. 3. (of events, or news concerning them) To become known, leak out : *nothing transpired of all that happened*; *what occurred did not transpire*; *it transpired that the Emperor was dead.* 4. (incorrect and vulg. usage) To take place, happen, occur : *grave events transpired which did not become known for many hours.* B. trans. To excrete, exhale through the pores, give off in form of vapour.

transplant, vb. trans. & intrans. [1. tràhnspláhnt ; 2. trănsplắnt]. See **trans-** & **plant** (I.). 1. trans. a To dig up, remove (plant &c.) from where it is growing, and re-plant in another place ; b to remove (persons) from one place of abode, and re-settle them elsewhere. 2. intrans. a (of persons) To perform the act of transplanting; b (of plants) to be capable of being transplanted, to bear transplantation.

transplantation, n. [1. tràhnsplahntáshun ; 2. trănsplăntéiʃən]. Prec. & **-ation**. a Act of transplanting (growing trees &c.); b removal of skin &c. by a surgeon, from one part of the body or from body of a given person, and the setting of it in another part, or in the body of another person &c. ; c removal of persons settled in one place, and resettling of them elsewhere.

transplanter, n. [1. trahnspláhnter ; 2. trănsplắntə]. **transplant** & **-er**. a Person who transplants ; b mechanical device for transplanting trees &c.

transpontine, adj. [1. trahnzpóntīn ; 2. trănzpóntain]. **trans-** & Lat. *pont-*, 'a bridge', see **pons**, & **-ine**. Lying on the other side of a bridge ; (specif. usage) referring to a type of melodrama formerly popular in theatres on the south side of London Bridge : *a transpontine drama, hero* &c.

transport (I.), vb. trans. [1. trahnzpórt ; 2. trănzpōt]. Lat. *transportāre*, 'to carry across', see **trans-** & **port** (IV.). 1. To carry, transfer, from one place to another : *to transport passengers and luggage* &c. 2. Specif., to convey criminals to a penal settlement, to banish as punishment for crime : *transported for sheep-stealing.* 3. (fig.) To take out of oneself, to ravish, charm, by powerful emotion : *transported with delight, grief* &c.

transport (II.), n. [1. tráhnzport ; 2. trănzpōt], fr. prec. 1. Act or process of transporting ; carriage, conveyance : *the transport of goods* &c. 2. a Vessel engaged in transporting goods and passengers: specif. b ship carrying troops. 3. Violent, overwhelming emotion ; gust of feeling, ecstasy : *a transport of joy, horror, rage* &c.

transportability, n. [1. tràhnzportabíliti ; 2. trănzpōtəbíliti]. Next word & **-ity**. Quality, state, of being transportable.

transportable, adj. [1. trahnzpórtabl ; 2. trănzpōtəbl]. **transport** (I.) & **-able**. Capable of being transported, carried, conveyed.

transportation, n. [1. tràhnzportăshun ; 2. trănzpōtéiʃən]. **transport** (I.) & **-ation**. 1. Act of transporting; conveyance, transport. 2. Fact of being sent to penal settlement ; punitive banishment: *transportation for life.*

transporter, n. [1. trahnzpórter ; 2. trănzpōtə]. **transport** (I.) & **-er**. a One who transports ; (in various senses) *transporter of goods* &c.; b machine, apparatus, for carrying goods from one place to another, a conveyor.

transposal, n. [1. trahnzpŏzl ; 2. trănzpóuzl]. See next word & **-al**. a Act of transposing ; b something transposed.

transpose, vb. trans. & intrans. [1. trahnzpŏz ; 2. trănzpóuz]. Fr. *transposer*; see **trans-** & **pose** (I.). A. trans. 1. a To change the respective places or order of things ; to put one thing in the place or order formerly occupied by another, and the latter in that place where, or order in which, the former stood; b to alter relative position and order (of words) in a sentence. 2. (mus.) To put into a different key. B. intrans. 1. Specif., to put piece of music into a different key. 2. To be capable of, lend itself to, transposition: *the sentence is ambiguous as it stands—won't it transpose?*

transposition, n. [1. tràhnzpozíshun ; 2. trănzpəzíʃən]. **trans-** & **position** (I.). Act of transposing ; result of this.

transpositive, adj. [1. trahnzpózitiv ; 2. trănzpózitiv]. See prec. & **-ive**. Consisting in transposition.

trans-ship, vb. trans. [1. trahnz shíp ; 2. trănz ʃíp]. **trans-** & **ship**. To remove, transfer (goods or passengers) from one ship to another, the voyage being continued in the latter.

trans-shipment, n. [1. trahnz shípment ; 2. trănz ʃípmənt]. Prec. & **-ment**. Act of trans-shipping.

transubstantiate, vb. trans. [1. tràhnsubstánshiāt ; 2. trănsəbstắnʃieit]. Med. Lat. *transubstantiāt-(um),* P.P. of *transubstantiāre*; see **trans-** & **substantiate**. To change into another substance, to transmute.

transubstantiation, n. [1. tràhnsubstànshiáshun ; 2. trănsəbstănʃiéiʃən]. Med. Lat. *transubstantiātiōn-(em).* See prec. & **-ion**. Doctrine that in the Eucharist a change is wrought in the elements at consecration, whereby the whole substance of these is transmuted into the very Body and Blood of Christ, nothing of the bread and wine remaining except the appearance.

transudation, n. [1. tràhnsūdăshun ; 2. trănsjūdéiʃən]. See **transude** & **-ation**. a Process of transuding ; b moisture which transudes.

transudatory, adj. [1. trahnsūdaturi ; 2. trănsjūdətəri]. See next word & **-ory**. Pertaining to, of the nature of, transudation.

transude, vb. intrans. [1. trahnsūd ; 2. trănsjūd]. **tran-** & Lat. *sūdāre*, 'to sweat, perspire'; see **sudation** & **sweat** (I.). To pass out through, or as through, the pores, in form of perspiration.

transversal, adj. & n. [1. trahnzvérsl ; 2. trănzvə́səl]. **transverse** & **-al**. 1. adj. Transverse. 2. n. Line that intersects other lines.

transversality, n. [1. trahnzvərsáliti ; 2. trănzvāsắliti]. Prec. & **-ity**. Quality of being transversal.

transversally, adv. [1. trahnzvérsali ; 2. trănzvə́səli]. See **transversal** & **-ly**. Transversely.

transverse, adj. & n. [1. trahnzvérs, tráhnzvērs ; 2. trănzvə́s, trắnzvəs]. Lat. *transversus,* also *trāversus,* 'going, lying, across, or athwart', fr. **trans-** & *vers-(um),* P.P. type of *vertere,* 'to turn', see **version**; cp. also **traverse** (I.). 1. adj. Passing, lying, placed, so as to cross ; cross-wise. 2. n. Something which lies in a transverse direction.

transversely, adv. [1. trahnzvérsli ; 2. trănzvə́sli]. Prec. & **-ly**. In a transverse direction.

tranter, n. [1. tránter ; 2. trắntə]. Etymol. doubtful ; Med. Lat. has *travetārius.* (provinc.) Hawker, carrier.

trap (I.), n. [1. trap ; 2. trắp]. Swed. *trappa,* 'stair'. Any of various kinds of darkcoloured, igneous rocks ; also *trap-rock*; so called because they occur in masses rising one above another somewhat in the form of flights of stairs.

trap (II.), n. M.E. has *trappen,* 'to clothe, furnish with trappings &c.'; origin doubtful, cp. Span. *trapo,* 'cloth'. Connexion w. Fr. *drap,* 'cloth', see **drape**, is doubtful. (colloq., usually pl. *traps*) Personal possessions, clothes &c., luggage.

trap (III.), n. O.E. *træppe,* M.E. *trappe,* origin unknown. 1. A mechanical or other material device for catching or snaring animals, birds &c. ; a pitfall ; a snare, a gin. 2. (fig.) a A stratagem, an artful scheme, device, or plan to ensnare and deceive, or to lead (persons) into an awkward dilemma ; b anything having a deceptive, misleading appearance ; a take-in, a pitfall. 3. Instrument used in trap-ball, consisting of a wooden arm with a pivot in the middle, raised from the ground below the pivot ; one end retains a ball and the other is struck downwards, causing the ball to fly up ; the ball is then struck and driven in desired direction. 4. Apparatus from which live or clay pigeons are released for shooting at. 5. Bend in the upper end of a drain-pipe, just below the opening, which holds a certain amount of water, and thus prevents noxious gases from escaping from the sewer. 6. A horse carriage, esp. one with only two wheels. 7. A trap-door.

trap (IV.), vb. trans. & intrans., fr. prec. A. trans. 1. a To catch in, or as in, a trap ; to snare ; also b (fig.) to catch by artifice and stratagems ; to cozen, deceive. 2. To supply (drain &c.) with a trap or traps. B. intrans. To set traps ; practise occupation of a trapper.

trapan, vb. trans. See **trepan** (II.).

trap-ball, n. Old game played with trap and ball.

trap-door, n. Hinged flap, opening upwards from a ceiling or roof, giving entrance to a loft &c. ; one giving access from below the stage of a theatre, for sudden appearance of demons, ghosts &c. ; *trap-door spider,* a kind of spider which nests in a cylindrical hole in the ground which it closes by a hinged door.

trapes, vb. See **trapse**.

trapeze, n. [1. trapḗz ; 2. trəpī́z]. Fr. *trapèze,* fr. Gk. *trapézion,* see **trapezium**. Short, swinging horizontal bar, suspended from two ropes, used by gymnasts and acrobats.

trapeziform, adj. [1. trapḗziform ; 2. trəpī́zifōm]. Prec. & **-form**. Having the form of a trapezium.

trapezium, n. [1. trapḗzium ; 2. trəpī́ziəm]. Lat., fr. Gk. *trapézion,* 'a little table' ; dimin. fr. *trápeza,* 'a table', fr. *tétra-,* 'four', see **tetra-**, & *péza,* 'a foot', q.v. under **pedal** (I.). (geom.) Four-sided plane figure, no two lines of which, or according to another definition, only two, are parallel.

trapezoid, adj. & n. [1. trápezoid ; 2. trắpezoid]. Prec. & **-oid**. 1. adj. Having the form of a trapezium ; also *trapezoidal.* 2. n. Trapezium.

trapper, n. [1. tráper ; 2. trắpə]. **trap** (IV.) & **-er**. Person who traps animals ; specif., one who traps animals for their skins.

trappings, n. pl. [1. trápingz ; 2. trắpiŋz]. See **trap** (II.). 1. Harness, accoutrements, caparison, of a horse ; esp. elaborately ornamented harness and adjuncts used on ceremonial occasions. 2. Ceremonial or official dress ; elaborate uniform with decorations.

Trappist, n. [1. trápist ; 2. trắpist], fr. monastery of La Trappe in Normandy. Member of a branch of Cistercian order of monks who observe strict silence among themselves.

trappy, adj. [1. trápi ; 2. trắpi]. **trap** (III.) & **-y**. Full of snares or traps ; tricky.

trapse, trapes, traipse, vb. intrans. [1. trăps ; 2. treips]. Perhaps related to, or the same as, obs. or dial. *trape, trappe,* & cogn. w. M. Du. *trappen,* Norw. dial. *trappa,* 'to tread, stamp'; cp. w. infixed nasal, **trample**. To ramble or gad about aimlessly.

trap-shooting, n. Shooting at live or clay pigeons released from a trap.

trash, n. [1. trash ; 2. trắʃ]. Cp. O.N. *tros,* 'rubbish, twigs &c. collected for fuel'. Origin doubtful. a Worthless stuff, rubbish ; shoddy, cheap material ; b literary or artistic work of very poor quality.

trashily, adv. [1. tráshili ; 2. trắʃili]. **trashy** & **-ly**. In a trashy manner or style.

trashiness, n. [1. tráshines ; 2. trắʃinis]. See next word & **-ness**. Quality of being trashy ; esp. in non-material sense : *the trashiness of much modern writing.*

trashy, adj. [1. tráshi ; 2. trắʃi]. **trash** & **-y**. Worthless, rubbishy (of material and non-material things).

trass, n. [1. tras ; 2. trắs]. Du. *tras,* perh. fr. Ital. *terrazza,* see **terrace**. A volcanic earth, used as a hydraulic cement.

trattoria, n. [1. tràtorḗa ; 2. trắtoría]. Ital. An Italian eating-house.

trauma, n. [1. tráwma; 2. trɔ́mə]. Gk. *traûma*, 'a wound; damage'; perh. fr. same base as Gk. *trṓein*, 'to wear down, or out'; cp. Lat. *terere*, 'to rub, wear away', see **teredo**, **termite** & words there referred to. (med.) A bodily injury, a wound.

traumatic, adj. [1. trawmátik; 2. trɔ̄mǽtik], fr. Gk. *traumat-*, stem of *traûma*, see prec., & **-ic**. Pertaining to, caused by, following after or in consequence of, a wound or other bodily injury: *traumatic neurasthenia* &c.

traumatism, n. [1. tráwmatizm; 2. trɔ́mətizəm]. See prec. & **-ism**. General pathological condition produced by severe wounds or injuries.

travail, n. & vb. intrans. [1. trávāl; 2. trǽveil]. O. Fr. *travail*, 'toil'; *travailler*, 'to labour, work'; perh. fr. L. Lat. *trepalium*, 'an instrument of torture'; fr. *trēs*, 'three', see **tri-**, & *pālus*, 'a stake', see **pale (I.)**. **1.** n. Pains of childbirth; labour. **2.** vb. **a** To feel the pains of childbirth, be in labour; **b** to toil painfully and laboriously.

travel (I.), vb. intrans. & trans. [1. trávl; 2. trǽvl]. Same word as prec.; derived fr. type accentuated on first syll. fr. early period. **A.** intrans. **1.** To move along, go, proceed: *a tram travels along a rail.* **2.** To make a journey; to go from place to place, esp. to journey for long distances, in remote places: *to travel on the Continent.* **3.** Specif., to journey from place to place with a view to selling goods or to obtaining orders for goods from customers; to ply the business of a commercial traveller. **B.** trans. To pass through or over (tract of country) in travelling; to traverse, journey through: *to travel the whole world in search of novelty.*

travel (II.), n., fr. prec. **1.** (rare) Process of travelling; movement; mode, rate, of movement or progress (of parts of machine &c.). **2.** (chiefly pl.) **a** Journeys, journeyings, wanderings; esp. long journeys, in foreign and remote parts: *travels abroad*; *back from one's travels*; **b** narrative, book containing this, of travels, and adventures occurring during these: *a book of travels.*

travelled, adj. [1. trávld; 2. trǽvld], fr. P.P. of **travel (I.)**. Having experience of travelling; having travelled widely.

traveller, n. [1. tráv(e)ler; 2. trǽv(ə)lə]. **travel (I.)** & **-er**. **a** One who travels; specif. **b** one who travels to obtain orders for a trading firm: *a commercial traveller.*

traveller's cheque, n. Cheque, usually for relatively small amount, issued by a banker to a client travelling abroad, payable by any agent of the bank which issues it.

traveller's-joy, n. Species of clematis, *Clematis vitalba.*

traveller's tale, n. A fantastic, exaggerated, highly coloured narrative; a tall story, story of fictitious adventures and exploits.

traversable, adj. [1. tráversabl; 2. trǽvəsəbl]. **traverse (I.)** & **-able**. Capable of being traversed; passable.

traverse (I.), vb. trans. & intrans. [1. trávers; 2. trǽvəs]. Fr. *traverser*, fr. O. Fr. *travers*, 'across'; see **transverse**. **A.** trans. **1.** To pass, run, lie, be placed, across: *the railway line traverses the road at this point.* **2. a** To cross, pass over, travel across: *to traverse the desert, the ocean* &c.; **b** (fig.) to go over, treat of, deal with, in discussion, argument, exposition: *I need not traverse that ground in my present lecture.* **3. a** To oppose, call in question, take exception to: *I must traverse several points in your statement*; **b** (law) to deny (allegation of other party). **4. a** (artillery) To move, turn sideways or laterally, in aiming: *to traverse a gun*; **b** (carpentry) to plane (wood) across the grain; **c** (mach.) to swivel, turn (lathe &c.) laterally. **B.** intrans. To execute a traverse, **a** in fencing; **b** in riding.

traverse (II.), adj. & adv.; see prec. **1.** adj. Lying across; formed, cut, crosswise: *traverse trench.* **2.** adv. Crosswise.

traverse (III.), n., fr. prec. **1.** Something which traverses, which lies across; **a** a dividing bar or partition; **b** a structural part, a beam, transom &c., crossing a ceiling, lying across top of a door &c.; **c** a path made across face of a cliff, glacier &c. in mountaineering; **d** earthwork placed at right angles to the front of a trench or covered way, dividing it into bays, thus giving protection against enfilade fire and localizing effect of shell-bursts. **2.** (fig.) Circumstance, event, which thwarts, hinders, a purpose or action; specif. (law) a formal denial of fact alleged by opposite party in a suit. **3.** A cross movement; **a** (fencing) movement made in opposing or counteracting an attack; **b** oblique, crosswise, forward movement of a horse.

traverser, n. [1. tráverser; 2. trǽvəsə]. **traverse (I.)** & **-er**. One who, that which, traverses; specif., device in form of platform on wheels moving laterally, used in shifting railway carriages from one line of rails to another; also *traverse-table.*

travertin(e), n. [1. trávertin; 2. trǽvətin]. Ital. *travertino*, Lat. *Tiburtīnus* (*lapis*), 'Tibur (stone)', now Tivoli. Hard, calcareous deposit of limy springs, used in Italy for building.

travesty, vb. trans. & n. [1. trávesti; 2. trǽvəsti], fr. Fr. *travesti*, P.P. of *travestir*, 'to disguise; make ridiculous', fr. **trans-** & Lat. *vestīre*, 'to clothe', see **vest (I.)**. **1.** vb. **a** To cause to appear ridiculous; to caricature, to burlesque, mimic; to imitate (deliberately) in such a manner as to bring ridicule upon: *to travesty a person's manner, mode of speech, style* &c.; **b** to render absurd, represent, perform badly, misinterpret, through incompetence or lack of skill: *to travesty the part of Hamlet, the position of chairman.* **2.** n. **a** A deliberate burlesque, parody, comical imitation or mimicry; **b** an incompetent performance; a distortion, perversion, misconception: *a travesty of justice, of discipline* &c.

trawl, vb. trans. & intrans. & n. [1. trawl; 2. trɔ̄l]. O. Fr. *troller*, 'to move about, go to and fro, in a desultory fashion'; see **troll (I.)**. **1.** vb. **a** trans. To drag along after a vessel: *to trawl a net, a fishing-line*; **b** intrans., to practise trawling: *first we tried throwing a fly, and then we trawled.* **2.** n. **a** A fishing-net with a wide mouth, held open by a frame, and dragged along the bottom of the sea; also *trawl-net*; **b** a long line having short lines coming at intervals from it, with baited hooks attached, stretched out, and buoyed, and anchored at both ends; also *trawl-line.*

trawler, n. [1. tráwler; 2. trɔ́lə]. Prec. & **-er**. **a** Person who trawls; **b** vessel used in trawling.

trawling, n. [1. tráwling; 2. trɔ́liŋ]. See prec. & **-ing**. Act or process of using a trawl-net or trawl-line for catching fish.

tray, n. [1. trā; 2. trei]. M.E. *treie* &c.; origin doubtful; possibly fr. an O.E. **trǣġ*, or **treġ*, & connected by gradation w. O.E. *trōg*, see **trough**. A flat, round, oval, or oblong board, plate, slab, of wood, metal, papier mâché &c., with edges slightly raised, used for holding, or carrying, light articles such as glass, china, crockery, silver &c., or for handing such articles or letters &c.

treacherous, adj. [1. trécherus; 2. trétʃərəs]. See **treachery** & **-ous**. **1. a** (of persons) Disloyal, false, apt to betray; unreliable; liable to break a pledge or a promise; perfidious; **b** (of actions, and bodily movements) expressing, involving, treachery and deceit, betrayal, disloyalty &c.: *a treacherous glance, smile, move* &c.; **c** (of mental functions) unreliable, uncertain, apt to fail: *a treacherous memory.* **2. a** (of animals) Not to be depended upon, liable to turn on their masters; **b** (of inanimate things) not as good as they appear, liable to disappoint expectation, not justifying hopes which they arouse: *treacherous ice, branch*, liable to break, though seeming sound; *treacherous weather*, bright but cold, or likely to turn to rain &c.

treacherously, adv. Prec. & **-ly**. In a treacherous manner.

treacherousness, n. See prec. & **-ness**. **a** Treacherous action, treachery; **b** disloyalty, falseness of heart and character.

treachery, n. [1. trécheri; 2. trétʃəri]. M.E., fr. O. Fr. *trech-*, *tricherie*, cp. *trechier*, 'to deceive'; cp. **trickery** & see **trick (I.)**. Disloyal action, betrayal; breach of trust, allegiance, or of plighted word; perfidy.

treacle, n. [1. trékl; 2. tríkl]. O. Fr. *triacle*; cp. Provenç. *triacla*, *tiriaca*; fr. Lat. *thēriaca*, 'antidote against poisonous beasts'; fr. Gk. *thēriakḗ*; see **theriac**. **1.** (obs.) **a** A sovran remedy, cure against poison, esp. of venomous reptiles &c. or disease; **b** remedy, balm, for spiritual ills. **2.** Thick, syrupy substance which drains out of sugar in the process of refining; molasses.

treacly, adj. [1. trékli; 2. trίkli]. Prec. & **-ly**. **a** Having a thick, sticky consistency, like that of treacle; **b** covered with treacle; **c** (fig.) unctuous: *a treacly smile.*

tread (I.), vb. intrans. & trans. [1. tred; 2. tred]. O.E. & O.S. *tredan*; M.E. *trēden*; O.H.G. *tretan*; Goth. *trudan* (*u* is difficult to equate w. the other forms); O.N. *troða*; not found outside Gmc., unless the base may be connected remotely w. that in Gk. *drómos*, a 'running', q.v. under **dromedary**. **A.** intrans. To walk, step, go; specif. (poet.) to go on foot, contrasted with *creep*; *tread on, upon*, to put one's foot upon; **a** to crush with the foot: *to tread (up)on a black beetle*; **b** to step, walk, upon (by mistake): *to tread upon a slide and fall down*; *tread down*, **a** to crush down, by treading: *to tread down flowers*; **b** to suppress, oppress, overpower: '*No hungry generations tread thee down*' (Keats, 'Nightingale'); also *to tread down one's feelings*; *tread under*, crush down; oppress; *tread out*, crush, cause to flow or come out, by treading: *to tread out the juice of the grape*; *to tread out the corn*; *tread in*, press into the earth by treading. **B.** trans. **1.** To beat, press down, by treading: *to tread a path through the grass.* **2.** To traverse, walk, pass, over; (often fig.) *to tread the paths of exile.* Phr. *to tread the boards*, be an actor. **3.** To execute on foot, by walking, dancing: '"*Now tread we a measure," said young Lochinvar*' (Scott). **4.** (of male birds) To have connexion with (the female).

tread (II.), n., fr. prec. **1. a** Act of treading, footstep: *the tread of armed men*; **b** mode of treading, or walking, stepping: *a sprightly, airy tread.* **2.** Thing, or part of something, designed for treading on; specif. **a** the flat, upper surface of a stair or step; **b** part of a boot or shoe which presses on the ground; **c** part of tire of a wheel which rests, presses, upon the ground. **3.** Copulation of male bird.

treadle, n. [1. trédl; 2. trédl]. O.E. *tredel*, fr. **tread (I.)**. Part of a machine on which the foot rests in working a crank which turns a wheel; e.g. in a bicycle, sewing-machine &c.

treadmill, n. [1. trédmil; 2. trédmil]. Mill worked by persons who tread upon steps made on the periphery; formerly used as a punishment, and also as a means of exercise, for convicts.

treason, n. [1. trézn; 2. trízn]. M.E. *tresun*, *traisoun* &c., fr. O. Fr. *traïson*, fr. Lat. *trāditiōn-(em)*, 'delivering up'; see **tradition**. **1.** Betrayal of trust, treachery, perfidy. **2.** Specif., disloyalty, treachery, to one's king and country; any attempt to overthrow government or well-being of a state to which one owes allegiance; the crime of giving comfort to the king's enemies; *high treason*, outrage offered to the king's person, to that of his consort, or that of his heir; attempt to depose the king or to levy war against him.

treasonable, adj. [1. trézunabl; 2. tríznəbl]. Prec. & **-able**. Pertaining to, involving, of the nature of, treason; treacherous, disloyal, perfidious.

treasonableness, n. See prec. & **-ness**. Quality of being treasonable.

treasonably, adv. Prec. & **-ly**. In a treasonable manner.

treason-felony, n. An act of high treason.

treasure (I.), n. [1. trézhur; 2. tréžə]. M.E. *tresor, tresour*; fr. O. Fr., fr. Lat. *thēsaurus*, fr. Gk. *thēsaurós*, 'a store laid up, treasure; a treasure-house; receptacle for treasure, a casket'; prob. an old, obscured compound; origin unexplained. **1.** Valuables stored up and carefully kept; esp. money, plate, jewels. **2.** Money: *the War cost the country great sacrifices in blood and treasure.* **3.** Something of great value, beauty, or rarity; object to which great importance is attached: *treasures of art in museums and picture galleries; the unique MS. of Beowulf is among the priceless treasures of the British Museum Library.* **4. a** A person (child or young woman) to whom one is devotedly attached; esp. as affectionate mode of address: *my treasure!*; **b** a person who is invaluable by reason of competence in his business, reliability of character, serviceableness &c.: *my new butler is a perfect treasure.*

treasure (II.), vb. trans., fr. prec. **1. a** To store, hoard up, keep as, treasure; also *treasure up*: *to treasure up money and jewels*; **b** to retain in the mind and memory, dwell on with affection, cherish fondly: *to treasure a person's memory; to treasure up in one's heart the recollection of former days* &c. **2. a** (of objects &c.) To set store by, regard as valuable, attach value and importance to: *that is not a book that I treasure very highly*; **b** (of persons) to feel warm affection for: *we cannot treasure our friends too much.*

treasure-house, n. Place, building, where treasure is kept; a treasury.

treasurer, n. [1. trézhurer; 2. tréžərə]. O. Fr. *tresorier*; **treasure** (II.) & **-er**. **a** An officer in charge of the funds, and who manages the finances, of a society, institution &c.; **b** title of various officers of state, or of Royal household; *Lord High Treasurer*, now obsolete; *Treasurer of the Household.*

treasure trove, n. [1. trézhur trṓv; 2. tréžə tróuv]. See **treasure** (I.) & **trover**. Gold or silver articles, bullion or coin, found hidden in the earth, for which no owner can be traced, the right to which lies in the Crown.

treasury, n. [1. trézhuri; 2. tréžəri], fr. O. Fr. *tresorie*; **treasure** (I.) & **-y**. **1. a** Place for storing of treasure; treasure-house; **b** (cap.) place where public revenues are stored; **c** department of state which collects public revenue, and controls taxation and the expenditure of public moneys; this department is controlled by the *Lords of the Treasury*, the nominal head of which is the First Lord of the Treasury, usually the Prime Minister or Leader of the House; the Chancellor of the Exchequer, and Junior Lords, the chief of which are the *Patronage Secretary*, who acts as chief whip, and the *Financial Secretary*, acting as assistant to the Chancellor of Exchequer. **2.** A literary collection or anthology: *the 'Golden Treasury'.*

Treasury bench, n. The front bench on the right-hand side of the Speaker in the House of Commons, on which sit the principal members of His Majesty's Government.

Treasury bill, n. A form of bill of exchange for raising short-term loans, offered for tender and issued to the highest bidder.

Treasury note, n. A form of currency note for £1 and 10s. respectively, issued by the Treasury from 1914 to 1928.

Treasury solicitor, n. A legal official, who acts in all cases taken to secure payments due to the Treasury, as King's Proctor and formerly as Public Prosecutor.

treat (I.), vb. trans. & intrans. [1. trēt; 2. trīt]. O. Fr. *traitier*, fr. Lat. *tractāre*, 'to drag, draw; to handle, manage; to perform, transact; to use, conduct oneself towards; to discuss, reflect upon'. See **tract** (I.) & **trace** (II.). **A.** trans. **1. a** To conduct, demean, oneself, behave, towards, to use: *to treat one's servants with consideration; to treat a dog kindly*; **b** to have a certain mental attitude towards; to consider, regard; to hold a certain view concerning, and express it in words and behaviour: *to treat the whole thing as a joke; to treat one's position as a means of securing one's own ends.* **2.** To cause to undergo, submit (objects) to, some special process, for a particular purpose; specif. **a** to deal with chemically: *to treat (a substance) with sulphuric acid*; **b** to apply to, cover with &c.: *to treat dry leather with grease; to treat fruit trees with chemical mixtures*; **c** to give medical or surgical care to, prescribe for: *to treat a man for gout.* **3.** To deal with, take as a theme for consideration, discussion, exposition &c.: *many aspects of the subject are not treated at all by the author.* **4.** To pay expenses of, or for, to bear the cost of entertaining (another), esp. to pay for some exceptional pleasure: *to treat a person to a new suit, to a good dinner, to a box at the opera.* Phr. *to treat oneself to (a bottle of champagne)*, to have as an exceptional indulgence. **B.** intrans. **1.** *Treat of*, to deal with, take as subject of discourse, discussion &c.: *the sermon treated of sin and death.* **2.** *Treat with*, to negotiate, discuss terms with, transact business with: *it is humiliating to have to treat with a rogue.* **3.** To stand expenses, bear the costs of entertainment: *whose turn is it to treat next?*

treat (II.), n., fr. prec. **1.** Event, circumstance, condition, which affords satisfaction and pleasure; esp. something unusual and therefore the more enjoyed: *it was a treat to hear a good sermon again; a great treat to me to be in the country; a fine day is a rare treat; if you are a good boy you shall come down to dessert as a treat.* **2.** Entertainment planned to give pleasure: *a Sunday School treat.* **3.** (colloq. and rare) **a** Act of treating, or bearing cost of entertainment &c.; chiefly in Phr. *to stand treat*, bear expenses of amusement &c. for another; **b** turn (of person) to treat.

treating, n. [1. trḗting; 2. trítiŋ]. Act of bearing another's expenses of eating and drinking; ordering and paying for food and drink for another: *treating in restaurants was forbidden during the war.*

treatise, n. [1. trḗtiz; 2. trítiz]. A.-Fr. *tretiz*, prob. connected w. **treat** (I.), Lat. *tract-*, in sense of something drawn up, or something treated of; cp. **tractate**. Systematic written account of something; an excursus, a monograph.

treatment, n. [1. trḗtment; 2. trítmənt]. **treat** (I.) & **-ment**. **1.** Way of behaving to, of using, treating; usage: *hard, rough, unkind, favourable, treatment.* **2.** Act, mode, of treating, managing, caring for, attempting to cure; act of subjecting to particular process: *a new treatment for black spot in roses, for consumption; medical, surgical, treatment.*

treaty, n. [1. trḗti; 2. tríti]. O. Fr. *traitie*, fr. Lat. *tractāt-(um)*, P.P. of *tractāre*,'to handle' &c.; see **treat** (I.). **1.** Negotiation, act of bargaining, discussion of terms and conditions; in Phr. *in treaty for (a house &c.)*, in process of making arrangements, of coming to terms. **2.** Specif., an agreement, engagement, covenant, contract, agreed upon, and entered into, between different states or rulers.

treble (I.), adj. [1. trébl; 2. trébl]. M.E., fr. O. Fr.; fr. Lat. *triplus*, 'threefold'; see **triple**. **1.** Threefold, triple. **2.** (mus.) Pertaining to what was formerly the third part, that is, the higher notes, sung by boys' voices; hence high, shrill.

treble (II.), n., fr. prec. **a** The treble part or notes; **b** a treble voice.

treble (III.), vb. trans. & intrans. **a** trans. To make threefold: *to treble one's income*; **b** intrans., to become, increase, threefold: *expenses have trebled.*

trebuchet, n. [1. trébūshā; 2. trébjuʃei]. O. Fr., 'a trap, gin'; cp. Fr. *trébucher*, 'to stumble'; fr. Fr. *tré*, fr. **trans-**, & Gmc. word for *belly*, cp. O.H.G. *būh*, Mod. Germ. *bauch*, 'belly'. Obsolete military apparatus for hurling stones.

trecentist, n. [1. trāchéntist; 2. treitʃéntist]. Next word & **-ist**. Writer or painter of the trecento; imitator of these.

trecento, n. & adj. [1. trāchéntō; 2. treitʃéntou]. Ital., 'three hundred'; for 'thirteen hundred'. The fourteenth century as expressed in the great poets and painters of this period in Italy.

trechometer, n. [1. trekómeter; 2. trekómitə], fr. base of Gk. *trékhein*, 'to run', see **troche**, & **-meter**. Device for range-finding; a hodometer.

tree (I.), n. [1. trē; 2. trī]. O.E. *trēo*, M.E. *trē*; O.S. *treo*; Goth. *triu*; cogn. w. Gk. *drûs*, 'tree, oak', see **dryad**, & *dóru*, 'beam, shaft, spear'; see also **trim** (I.). **1.** A perennial plant with a woody stem, or trunk, and boughs; often employed in distinction to *bush*, or *shrub*, of a plant which has considerable height of trunk in proportion to the reach of its boughs, and one whose stem is devoid of boughs for some considerable distance from the ground; roses are called indifferently *bushes* or *trees*. Phr. *up a tree*, in a fix. **2. a** Any of several objects made of timber (for which the word *tree* was formerly used), esp. in compounds: *axle-tree, boot-tree, saddle-tree, whipple-tree* (see these words); also **b** (archaic or obs., except Bib.) the Cross of Christ. **3.** Usually, *family tree*, **a** a diagram showing descent or development from a common ancestor or source, formerly drawn in form of a tree with stem and branches: *tree of Jesse*; hence, **b** a pedigree; lineage, descent.

tree (II.), vb. trans. & intrans., fr. prec. **1.** trans. **a** To drive up or into a tree; **b** (fig. and colloq.) to place in a dilemma, put in a difficult or awkward position. **2.** intrans. To form, grow into, a tree.

tree calf, n. Leather of fine calfskin, highly polished and grained to resemble polished wood; used for binding books.

tree-creeper, n. Small bird, *Certhia familiaris*, which creeps about the trunks and branches of trees in search of insects.

tree-fern, n. Large, tree-like fern of warm countries, with woody stem and branching leaves.

tree-frog, n. Small frog, genus *Hyla*, that climbs trees by means of small suckers on its toes.

tree-kangaroo, n. Small arboreal marsupial of Australia.

treeless, adj. [1. trḗles; 2. trílis]. **tree** (I.) & **-less**. Bare of trees.

tree-nail, trenail, n. [1. trḗnāl, trénl; 2. tríneil, trénl]. A long pin or nail of hard wood for fastening planks to a ship's timbers.

tree-peony, n. Chinese peony, *Paeonia Moutan*, growing in form of a shrub, with woody stem and branches.

trefoil, n. [1. trḗfoil; 2. trífɔil]. O. Fr. *trefueil*, fr. Lat. **trifolium**. **1.** Clover. **2.** (archit.) Conventionalized, carved, representation of clover leaf.

trek, vb. intrans. & n. [1. trek; 2. trek], fr. Cape Du.; cogn. w. **track** (I.). **1.** vb. **a** To travel, make a journey, in an ox-waggon; **b** to wander far afield in search of a fresh place of abode; to migrate. **2.** n. **a** Journey performed in an ox-waggon; **b** migration.

trellis, n. & vb. trans. [1. trélis; 2. trélis]. M.E. *trelis*, O. Fr. *treliz*; cp. Mod. Fr. *treillis*, formerly 'sackcloth', then 'trellis', fr. resemblance of lattice-work to the coarse mesh; fr. Low Lat. *trilīcius*, fr. Lat. *trilīx*, 'woven with three sets of leashes; triple-twilled'; **tri-** & *līcium*, 'thrum, or ends of a weaver's thread', see second element of **oblique** (I.). **1.** n. Light wooden structure formed of laths crossing each other and nailed together; similar structure of wire &c.; used as a screen and for training climbing plants. **2.** vb. To supply with a trellis; to screen off with a trellis.

trellis-work, n. Structure in form of a trellis; lattice-work.

tremble (I.), vb. intrans. [1. trémbl; 2. trémbl]. Fr. *trembler*, fr. L. Lat. *tremulāre*, formed **fr.** Lat. *tremulus*, 'quivering'; see **tremulous**. **1. a** To be shaken, agitated, with rapid, brief, intermittent, involuntary movements of the muscles, esp. such as are caused by fear, cold, excessive weakness; to shiver, to quake; **b** (fig.) to quail, be dismayed, terrified, seized with fear: *the stoutest hearts trembled at the sound.* **2.** (fig.) To experience great anxiety, perturbation of mind; to have grave misgivings or apprehensions: *I tremble for your safety; I tremble to think what might have happened.* **3.** (of the earth) To be shaken, as with earthquake; to quiver, as from the shock of a heavy body falling. **4.** (of light, fluttering or swaying objects) To be agitated with a rapid vibratory movement, to oscillate, be stirred, as by the wind, to flutter: *leaves of the poplars tremble; flags tremble in the gale;* Phr. (*his fate &c.*) *is trembling in the balance*, has reached the critical moment in which it will be decided one way or the other. **5.** To be tremulous, shaky, to give the impression of trembling or vibrating: *his voice trembled.*

tremble (**II.**), n., fr. prec. Involuntary act of trembling, shivering, shaking; a tremor, quiver &c. Phr. (colloq.) *all of a tremble*, shaking, trembling; greatly agitated and perturbed.

trembler, n. [1. trémbler; 2. trémblə]. See prec. & **-er**. One who, thing which, trembles.

trembling, n. [1. trémbling; 2. trémbliŋ]. **tremble** (**I.**) & **-ing**. State of one who trembles; **a** bodily shivering; **b** mental agitation. Phr. *in fear and trembling*, with great misgiving, diffidently.

tremblingly, adv., fr. Pres. Part. of **tremble** (**I.**) & **-ly**. **a** With physical, material trembling; **b** with fear and mental agitation; fearfully.

tremendous, adj. [1. treméndus; 2. triméndəs]. Lat. *tremendus*, 'causing quaking and shivering; dreadful, terrible', & **-ous**; fr. *tremere*, 'to quake, shiver'; see **tremble** (**I.**) & **tremulous**. **1. a** Awe-inspiring, overpowering, possessing great importance; momentous: *the tremendous events of the war*; hence, **b** (popularly) (i.) considerable in size, very large, huge, immense, enormous: *a tremendous house; tremendous applause*; (ii.) as adverb *a tremendous long way*; (also colloq.) *tremendous great* (*horse, book, jump, shout* &c.). **2.** (colloq.) In various rather vague senses, implying importance, magnitude &c.: *to get a tremendous fright; it is a tremendous thing for me*, a great advantage; *it means a tremendous lot to him*, is of vital importance.

tremendously, adv. Prec. & **-ly**. In a tremendous manner, to a tremendous extent; (colloq., as emphatic) very much, very: *tremendously improved; tremendously pleased to see you; I'm tremendously obliged to you.*

tremendousness, n. See prec. & **-ness**. (rare) State, quality, of being tremendous.

tremolo, n. [1. trémolō; 2. tréməlou]. Ital., fr. Lat. *tremulus*, see **tremulous**. Tremulous, vibratory, quivering, effect deliberately produced in the tones of the singing voice, or in those of a wind or string instrument, e.g. in the organ or the violin &c.

tremor, n. [1. trémur; 2. trémə]. Lat., 'a shaking, quivering', fr. *tremere*, 'to quiver' &c., see **tremulous**. A shaking, quivering, trembling, palsy; **a** of the limbs, voice, of leaves &c.; **b** (of the mind) (i.) a quailing of the spirit or courage, a qualm &c.: *he faced death without a tremor*; also, (ii.) a thrill: *a tremor of excitement.*

tremulous, adj. [1. trémūlus; 2. trémjuləs]. Lat. *tremulus*, 'shaking, quivering', & **-ous**; fr. base of *tremere*, 'to shiver, tremble' &c., cp. Gk. *trémein*, 'to shiver', & *trómos*, 'a trembling, quaking'; cogn. w. O.S. *thrimman*, 'to leap'; & Goth. *þramstei*, 'grasshopper'; ultimately prob. an extension of base seen in *terrēre*, 'to frighten'; see **terror**, **terrible**. **1.** Shaky; quivering, trembling; fluttering: *a tremulous hand; tremulous eyelids; tremulous plumes* &c. **2.** Timid, fearful: *tremulous maidens*; nervous, hesitating, vacillating.

tremulously, adv. Prec. & **-ly**. In a tremulous manner.

tremulousness, n. See prec. & **-ness**. State, quality, of being tremulous.

trench (**I.**), vb. trans. & intrans. [1. trench; 2. trentʃ]. O. Fr. *trenchier*, 'to cut', cp. Ital. *trinciare*; prob. connected w. **truncate**, cp. **trunk**. **A.** trans. **1. a** To cut furrows or trenches in; **b** to cultivate, dig (land) thoroughly, by making series of parallel trenches, each one of which is filled with the soil taken from the one dug immediately after it. **2.** (mil.) To cut entrenchments in; to protect with trenches. **B.** intrans. *Trench upon*, to encroach, infringe, upon: *to trench upon the sphere, rights, time &c., of another.*

trench (**II.**), n. M.E. & O. Fr. *trenche*, fr. prec. Long, narrow opening, ditch, furrow, cut or dug in the earth; specif., one made for soldiers to stand in, with the excavated earth thrown up in front, as protection from enemy's fire.

trenchancy, n. [1. trénshansi; 2. trénʃənsi]. Next word & **-cy**. Quality of being trenchant.

trenchant, adj. [1. trénshant; 2. trénʃənt]. In M.E., fr. O. Fr.; Pres. Part. of *trenchier*, 'to cut'; see **trench** (**I.**). **a** (chiefly poet.) Having a cutting edge, cutting, sharp: *a trenchant blade*; **b** (in non-material sense) keen, incisive, biting, penetrating: *a trenchant humour, wit, style.*

trench-coat, n. Short waterproof coat worn by a soldier in the trenches in war.

trencher (**I.**), n. [1. tréncher; 2. tréntʃə]. **trench** (**I.**) & **-er**. One who cuts or digs trenches.

trencher (**II.**), n. O. Fr. *trencheor*, 'platter (for cutting on)'. **trench** (**I.**). **1.** Wooden platter formerly used for cutting food, and as a plate from which food was eaten, now chiefly for cutting bread. **2.** (fig.) What is on a trencher; food.

trencher-man, n. One who eats from a trencher; esp. *a good, a poor, trencher-man*, a hearty, a small, eater.

trench-fever, n. A form of low, intermittent, infectious fever, transmitted by lice, suffered by troops after serving in the trenches during the War.

trench-foot, n. An affection of the feet and legs suffered by troops during the War after service in the trenches, due to long soddening in cold and muddy water; in severe cases ending in moist gangrene, as distinct from the dry gangrene of frost-bite.

trench mortar, n. A small, easily portable kind of mortar used for throwing bombs &c. short distances, from trench to trench.

trend, vb. intrans. & n. [1. trend; 2. trɛnd]. Origin doubtful, but connected w. O.E. *trendel* & *tryndel*, 'a wheel'; *trendlian*, 'to make round', & *trinde*, 'round lump'; cp. **trundle** **1.** vb. (rarish) **a** To bend, be bent, inclined, slope, go, in a particular direction; **b** (fig.) to have a particular tendency. **2.** n. **a** Inclination, course, direction: *trend of a coastline*; **b** (fig.) general tendency, line, course, drift: *the trend of public feeling; the trend of events.*

trental, n. [1. tréntl; 2. tréntl]. Low Lat. *trentale*, fr. Lat. *trīginta*, 'thirty', cp. Fr. *trente*, & see **tri-**. Series of thirty Masses for the dead.

trente-et-quarante, n. [1. trónt ā karónt; 2. trɑ̃t ei kærɑ̃t]. Fr., 'thirty and forty'. Gambling card-game played on a specially marked table.

trepan (**I.**), also **trephine**, vb. trans. & n. [1. trepán, trefín; 2. tripǽn, trifáin]. Fr. *trépan*, fr. L. Lat. *trepanum*, fr. Gk. *trúpanon*, 'a borer'; cp. *trūpân*, 'to bore', fr. *trûpa*, 'a hole'; ultimately connected w. base **ter-*, 'to bore, rub away'; see **toreutic** & words there referred to. **1.** vb. (surg.) To remove, by cutting, (a portion of bone from the skull) to relieve pressure on the brain. **2.** n. Saw for performing this operation.

trepan (**II.**), vb. trans., fr. O. Fr. *trappan*, n., perh. a loan-word connected w. **trap** (**III.**). (archaic) To ensnare, lure, delude.

trepang, n. [1. trepáng; 2. tripǽŋ]. Malay. Sea-slug, bêche-de-mer, used by Chinese for making soup.

trephine, vb. trans. & n. [1. trefín; 2. trifáin]. Fr. *tréfine*; see **trepan** (**I.**). **1.** vb. To trepan. **2.** n. A trepan.

trepidation, n. [1. trèpidáshun; 2. trèpidéiʃən]. Lat. *trepidātiōn-(em)*, formed fr. P.P. of *trepidāre*, 'to bustle about anxiously, be in a state of alarm'; fr. *trepidus*, 'agitated, disturbed, alarmed'; cogn. w. Gk. *trépein*, 'to burn'; cp. also **trope**. **1.** State of alarm; quaking, nervous fluster. **2.** Involuntary trembling or twitching of the limbs, as in paralysis &c.

trespass (**I.**), vb. intrans. [1. tréspas; 2. tréspəs]. O. Fr. *trespasser*, 'to go beyond; to die'; see **trans-** & **pass** (**I.**). **1.** (obs.) To die. **2.** To go unlawfully upon another's land: *to trespass in search of game.* **3.** To encroach, infringe, upon: *to trespass upon a person's leisure, time* &c. **4.** To go beyond, exceed, what is morally right and lawful; to offend, sin, commit an offence: *to trespass against the moral law*; '*as we forgive them that trespass against us*'.

trespass (**II.**), n. O. Fr. *trespas*, see prec. **1.** Act of trespassing upon another's land. **2. a** Act of sin, an offence against God; **b** an injury inflicted upon another person.

trespasser, n. [1. tréspaser; 2. tréspəsə]. **trespass** (**I.**) & **-er**. One who trespasses upon the land of another.

tress, n. & vb. trans. [1. tres; 2. trɛs]. M.E. *tresse*, 'lock of hair', fr. Fr. *tresse*; vb. fr. Fr. *tresser*, 'to plait, twist'; fr. Low Lat. *tricia*, fr. Lat. *trīcae*, pl., 'trifles, toys; subterfuges, tricks'; connected w. *torquēre*, 'to twist', see **torque**. **1.** n. **a** Lock of hair, ringlet, plait; esp. of long hair on a woman's head; (poet. or facet.) hair of the head generally: *golden, scanty, tresses*; **b** (rare) spray, cluster, of flowers. **2.** vb. To fasten, bind up, arrange (the hair).

tressed, adj. [1. trest; 2. trɛst]. Prec. & **-ed**. **a** Having tresses; **b** bound, twisted up.

tressure, n. [1. tréshur; 2. tréʃə]. **tress** & **-ure**. **1.** Fillet, band for the hair; head-dress. **2.** (her.) A double fillet round the shield, some distance from edge, ornamented with fleurs-de-lis.

tressy, adj. [1. trési; 2. trési]. **tress** & **-y**. Adorned with tresses.

trestle, n. [1. trésl; 2. trésl]. M.E., fr. O. Fr. *trestel*, Low Lat. **transtellum*, dimin. of *transtrum*, 'cross-beam' &c., see **transom**. **1.** Wooden structure consisting of a piece of timber lying horizontally, and supported by braced legs; used to support planks forming a table, platform &c. **2.** A large framework of braced open timber or steel work, used as the support of a *trestle-bridge.*

trestle-table, n. Table of movable planks resting upon trestles.

tret, n. [1. tret; 2. trɛt]. Fr. *traite*, 'transport', see **trait**, **tract** (**I.**). Allowance made to buyers of certain goods for wastage during transit.

trews, n. pl. [1. trōōz; 2. trūz]. See **trousers**. Trousers made of tartan cloth worn by Highlanders, esp. in Scottish non-kilted regiments.

trey, n. [1. trā; 2. trei], fr. O. Fr. *treis*, 'three', fr. Lat. *trēs*, see **three**. The three at dice or cards.

tri-, pref. Lat., or Gk. *tri-*, 'three, threefold, thrice'; form of Lat. *trēs*, *tria*, Gk. *treîs*, *tria*; Scrt. *tráyaś*, 'three'; see **three**, **thrice**. Three, threefold.

triable, adj. [1. tríabl; 2. tráiəbl]. **try** (**I.**) & **-able**. Capable of being, worthy to be, tried.

triad, n. [1. tríad; 2. tráiæd]. Lat. *triad-(is)*, genit., fr. Gk. *triád-(os)*; see **tri-**. Group of three persons or things; specif. **a** (chem.) trivalent element or radical, one with valency or combining power of three; **b** (mus.) chord of three tones; **c** form of Celtic poetical composition, in which the subjects are grouped in threes: '*Three things that ruin wisdom: ignorance, inaccurate knowledge, forgetfulness*'.

trial, n. [1. tríal; 2. tráiəl]. **try (I.) & -al.** 1. Act of trying, testing, proving (in various senses); **a** a test of strength, speed, skill &c. in comparison with that of another; a match to decide relative proficiency; **b** act of testing the qualities, merits &c. of anything by using it: *to give a thing a trial*; Phr. *to have something on trial*, in order to test it; **c** test of a person's character, temper, courage, patience, fortitude, honour, &c. 2. **a** Something which afflicts or grieves; a trying experience; adversity, ill-fortune, trouble: *the loss of friends is among the most frequent trials of life*; **b** an annoyance, source of irritation; a nuisance: *a dog that barks all night is rather a trial*. 3. A judicial inquiry in a court of law; **a** examination of evidence to establish the guilt or innocence of a prisoner charged with a crime: *a criminal trial*; *a trial for theft*; *the trial of a man for murder*; **b** legal proceedings to determine the rights and wrongs of a civil case, to substantiate or negative a claim &c.

triangle, n. [1. tríanggl; 2. tráiæŋgl]. **tri- & angle (I.).** 1. **a** Geometrical figure bounded by three lines forming three angles; **b** piece of ground, object, having approximately this form; Phr. *the eternal triangle*, three persons, consisting of a married pair and the lover of either. 2. Musical instrument consisting of a thin steel rod bent into the form of a triangle with one open end, suspended from a cord and sounded by being struck with another steel rod. 3. **a** Framework of three poles fixed in the ground at suitable distances, the tops being fastened together, to which military offenders were formerly bound, to receive corporal punishment; **b** structure of similar form, with pulley hanging from the top, used for hoisting weights.

triangular, adj. [1. triánggūlar; 2. traiæŋgjulə]. **tri- & angular.** 1. Having the form of a triangle; three-cornered. 2. Involving three persons or parties: *triangular fight, pact* &c.

triangularity, n. [1. triànggūláriti; 2. traiæŋgjulǽriti]. Prec. & **-ity.** Property of being triangular.

triangularly, adv. [1. triánggūlarli; 2. traiǽŋgjuləli]. See prec. & **-ly.** In triangular shape or form.

triangulate, vb. trans. & adj. [1. triánggūlāt; 2. traiǽŋgjuleit]. **triangle & -ate.** 1. vb. To divide into triangles for purpose of surveying, measuring heights, distances &c. 2. adj. Consisting of triangles, having form of a triangle.

triangulation, n. [1. triànggūláshun; 2. traiæŋgjuléiʃən]. Prec. & **-ion.** Process of surveying by triangulating the area.

Trias, n. [1. trías; 2. tráiəs]. See **triad.** (geol.) **a** Period preceding the Jurassic; **b** system of rocks formed during this period; so called by the Germans from their threefold division of the period.

Triassic, adj. [1. triásik; 2. traiǽsik]. Prec. & **-ic.** Pertaining to the Trias.

tribal, adj. [1. tríbl; 2. tráibl]. **tribe & -al.** Connected with, belonging to, a tribe: *tribal legends, feeling* &c.

tribalism, n. [1. tríbalizm; 2. tráibəlizəm]. Prec. & **-ism.** System of tribal organization, tribal sentiment, customs &c.; characteristic features of a tribe or of its organization &c.

tribasic, adj. [1. tribásik; 2. tràibéisik]. **tri- & basic.** (chem.) Having three hydrogen atoms in the molecule.

tribe, n. [1. tríb; 2. traib]. In M.E., fr. Lat. *tribus*, 'one of the three divisions of the Roman people'; orig. 'village'; cogn. w. O. Ir. *treb*; perh. fr. *tri-*, 'third', used in gen. sense of 'division', & base *bhu-*, 'to become, grow' &c.; see this further under **future (I.),** **folio (I.);** cp. also **physic (I.)** & **be.** 1. Social unit, a community, consisting of groups of families, or clans, descended, or originally supposed to be descended, from a common ancestor, together with their slaves and others living with the community; later, the bond between the families of a tribe consists more in common customs and institutions than in actual consanguinity. 2. Class, group, of persons having, or assumed to have, the same characteristics, occupation, habits, ideals &c.: *lawyers and all their tribe*; *the whole tribe of politicians*. 3. (biol., often loosely) Group: *the dog tribe*.

tribesman, n. [1. tríbzman; 2. tráibzmən]. **tribe & man.** Member of a tribe.

tribesmanship, n. [1. tríbzmanship; 2. tráibzmənʃip]. Prec. & **-ship.** Membership of a tribe.

triblet, triboulet, n. [1. tríblet, tríbolet; 2. tríblit, tríbəlet]. Fr. *triboulet*; Lat. *tribulus*, fr. Gk. *tríbolos*, 'instrument with three prongs, a caltrop'; **tri- & bólos,** 'a throw', connected w. *bállein*, 'to throw', see **ballistics,** & dimin. **-et.** Instrument for making rings, nuts &c.

tribrach, n. [1. trí-, tríbrak; 2. trái-, tríbræk]. Gk. *tríbrakhus*, 'consisting of three shorts'; **tri- & brakhús,** 'short', see **brachi-.** (prosody) Foot of three short syllables.

tribrachic, adj. [1. tribrákik; 2. traibrǽkik]. Prec. & **-ic.** Pertaining to, formed of, a tribrach.

tribulation, n. [1. tribūláshun; 2. trìbjuléiʃən]. L. Lat. *tribulátiōn-(em)*, fr. P.P. of *tribuláre*, 'to afflict', fr. *tríbulum*, 'instrument for thrashing', fr. *tri-*, cp. perf. *tri-vi*, of *terere*, 'to rub' &c., see **teredo & triturate,** & **-ion.** 1. State of mental suffering; grief, distress: *in great tribulation*. 2. Anything which causes suffering; an affliction, a trial: *beset by tribulations of all kinds*.

tribunal, n. [1. tribūnl; 2. traibjúnl]. Lat., 'raised platform where magistrates sat; judgement seat'; see **tribune (I.).** 1. Seat, bench, upon which judges and magistrates sit when hearing cases. 2. Court of justice; any court empowered to inquire into and decide an issue.

tribunary, adj. [1. tríbūnari; 2. tríbjūnəri]. **tribune & -ary.** Connected with, pertaining to, a tribune or tribunes.

tribunate, n. [1. tríbūnāt; 2. tríbjūneit]. **tribune & -ate.** **a** Office, status, of tribune; **b** tenure of this office.

tribune (I.), n. [1. tríbūn; 2. tríbjūn]. Lat. *tribūnus*, 'chieftain, headman of a tribe; a military officer with consular power; a civil magistrate'; cp. Fr. *tribun*; see **tribe.** 1. (Rom. hist.) Military or civil officer elected by the people to safeguard their liberties. 2. **a** A popular champion; **b** title of a newspaper.

tribune (II.), n. Fr., fr. Ital. or Med. Lat. *tribúna*, prob. fr. Lat. *tribúnal*, see **tribunal.** 1. **a** Raised dais for magistrate's chair in Roman basilica; **b** bishop's throne, and part of church containing this, in basilican church. 2. Raised dais for speakers addressing an assembly; specif., such a platform in the French Chamber of Deputies.

tribunicial, -itial, adj. [1. tribūnishl; 2. tribjunífl]. See **tribune (I.).** Pertaining to, befitting, a tribune.

tributary (I.), adj. [1. tríbūtari; 2. tríbjutəri]. Lat. *tribūtārius*, see **tribute & -ary.** 1. Paying tribute to a higher authority, as acknowledgement of the other's superiority or overlordship: *tributary kings.* 2. Bringing, contributing, supplies, additions, to; esp. a *tributary stream*, one flowing into a larger one.

tributary (II.), n., fr. prec. 1. State or head of state paying tribute to another. 2. A river or stream which discharges its waters into a larger river or stream.

tribute, n. [1. tríbūt; 2. tríbjūt]. Lat. *tribūtum*, 'stated payment, contribution, tax levied on citizens'; fr. P.P. of *tribuere*, 'to divide, distribute; to assign, allot'; see **tribe.** 1. Enforced payment of an annual sum imposed by a conqueror, or made in order to secure some benefit, such as immunity from attack &c. 2. Payment made by an individual to a sovereign or other overlord; a tax. 3. Act performed, words uttered, testifying approbation of, esteem, respect, affection for, a person, quality, action: *a tribute of admiration*; *a tribute to the bravery of the dead*; *to pay a tribute to*, express approbation of, admiration &c. for, utter words of praise &c.

tricar, n. [1. tríkar; 2. tráikā]. **tri- & car.** A small kind of motor-car with two front wheels and driving wheel behind.

trice (I.), vb. trans. [1. trīs; 2. trais]. M.E. *trisen*; cp. Swed. *trissa*, 'a pulley'. To haul up (a sail) and make fast.

trice (II.), n. Origin obscure. A brief space of time, an instant; chiefly in Phr. *in a trice*, in an instant, in the twinkling of an eye.

triceps, n. [1. tríseps; 2. tráisɛps]. Lat. adj., 'having three heads', fr. **tri-** & **-ceps,** fr. *caput*, 'head', as in **biceps.** Extensor muscle at the back of the upper arm.

tricerium, tricerion, n. [1. trisérium, -ion; 2. traisíəriəm, -ion]. Lat., fr. Gk. *trikérion*, **tri-** & *kērós*, 'wax', see **cere-.** (Gk. Ch.) Three-branched candlestick used by the bishop in blessing.

trichiasis, n. [1. trikíasis; 2. trikáiəsis]. Gk. *trikhíasis*, fr. *thríx*, genit. *trikhós*, 'hair', see **trich(o)-.** **a** Affection of the eyelashes in which these turn inwards and cause irritation; **b** occurrence of hairlike filaments in the urine.

trichina, n. [1. trikína; 2. trikáinə]. Mod. Lat. coinage, fr. Gk. *trikhinos*, 'hairy'; see prec. Minute, very fine, parasitic worm occurring in the flesh of diseased pigs, and sometimes introduced into the human body by means of imperfectly cooked pork.

trichinosis, n. [1. trikinósis; 2. trìkinóusis]. Prec. & **-osis.** Disease produced by the presence of trichinae in the system.

trich(o)-, pref. fr. Gk. *trikho-*, stem of *thrix*, 'a hair'; origin obscure.

trichoma, trichome, n. [1. tríkōma, tríkōm; 2. traikóumə, tráikoum]. Gk. *tríkhōma*, 'growth of hair', see prec. Any outgrowth, such as hair, nail &c., from the epidermis.

trichord, n. & adj. [1. tríkord; 2. tráikōd]. **tri- & chord (I.).** **a** n. A three-stringed musical instrument, as lyre or lute; **b** adj., having three strings.

trichosis, n. [1. trikósis; traikóusis]. **tricho- & -osis.** Disease of the hair.

trichotomous, adj. [1. trikótumus; 2. traikótəməs]. Next word & **-ous.** Connected with, of the nature of, trichotomy.

trichotomy, n. [1. trikótumi; 2. traikótəmi]. Gk. *trikha*, 'threefold', see **tri-** & **-tomy.** Threefold division; esp. division of human nature into body, soul, and spirit.

trichromatic, adj. [1. trìkrōmátik; 2. tràikroumǽtik]. **tri- & chromatic.** Three coloured.

trick (I.), n. [1. trik; 2. trik]. In M.E., 'an artifice; a trifle'; in pl. 'odds and ends, knickknacks'. Origin doubtful; perh. connected w. **treachery;** cp. Du. *trek*, 'trick', wh. may or may not be same word as *trek*, 'a pull, drawing' (cp. *trekken*, 'to draw'); & O. Fr. *triche*, n., & *trikier*, variant of *trichier*, 'to cheat' &c. The relations & origins of all these words are obscure. 1. **a** An artifice, dodge, deception, deliberate contrivance to deceive and hoodwink; a swindle, a piece of imposture: *to obtain money by a trick*; *none of your tricks with me*; Phr. *the tricks of the trade*, devices practised by the dishonest in any given trade or business to deceive and outwit customers; **b** an illusion: *a trick of the senses, of the imagination*; *tricks of the memory*, unreliability, temporary failure. 2. **a** A mischievous action; a playful, roguish prank, a whimsical practical joke; a harmless deception perpetrated without evil intent: *to play a trick upon*; *full of merry tricks*; also **b** (in bad sense) a mean, underhand prank: *that was a dirty trick*; *a nasty trick to play*. 3. **a** A personal habit, an unconscious idiosyncrasy, or oddity, of manner, behaviour, speech &c.; a mannerism: *queer little tricks of gesture and pronunciation*; a

2 A*

trick of scratching his head; **b** an affectation, a foppish mannerism, deliberate eccentricity; esp. *tricks of style*. **4.** A conjurer's artifice in imitation of magic, an act of sleight-of-hand, a piece of jugglery; Phr. *that just does, will just do, the trick*, just accomplishes its purpose. **5.** (card games) A unit of scoring; the cards played in one round. **6.** (see second M.E. sense of pl. cited in etymol.) In Phr. *the whole bag of tricks*, the whole matter and everything connected with it.

trick (II.), vb. trans. & intrans. See prec. **A.** trans. **1.** To swindle, cheat, impose upon: *he found the coin was false and that he had been tricked*; *to trick a person out of his money*, to obtain money by fraud; *to trick a person into doing something*, to induce him to do it by false representations, to lure, inveigle, him into doing it. **2.** *Trick out*, more rarely *trick up*, (fr. earlier sense of n., 'trifle, bauble, trinket' &c.) to deck, adorn, bedizen: *tricked out in jewels and finery*. **B.** intrans. To practise trickery.

trickery, n. [1. tríkeri; 2. tríkəri]. O. Fr. *triquerie*, dial. variant of *tricherie*, see **trick** (I.) & **-ery**. Act of tricking; fraud, knavery.

trickish, adj. [1. tríkish; 2. tríkiʃ]. **trick** (I.) & **-ish**. Inclined to trickery; undependable, rascally.

trickishly, adv. Prec. & **-ly**. In a trickish manner.

trickishness, n. See prec. & **-ness**. Quality of being trickish.

trickle, vb. intrans. & trans. & n. [1. tríkl; 2. tríkl]. Origin dubious. **1.** vb. **a** intrans. To flow slowly or in a thin stream: *the pipe was so small that the water could only trickle*; *tears trickled down her face*; *blood was trickling from the wound*; **b** trans., to cause to trickle. **2.** n. A thin flow: *the stream had shrunk to a mere trickle*.

trickster, n. [1. tríkster; 2. tríkstə]. **trick** (II.) & **-ster**. A cheat, a dishonest rogue, a swindler.

tricksy, adj. [1. tríksi; 2. tríksi]. **trick** (I.) & **-s-** (cp. *tipsy*) & **-y**. Artful, crafty; deceptive.

tricky, adj. [1. tríki; 2. tríki]. See prec. & **-y**. **1.** (of persons) Inclined to play tricks; unreliable, shifty. **2.** (of things) **a** Intricate, complicated, catchy; ingenious: *a tricky lock*; *a tricky brake, lamp* &c.; **b** difficult to follow, involved: *a tricky argument, problem* &c.

triclinic, adj. [1. tríklínik; 2. traiklínik]. **tri-** & **clinic**. (of crystals) Having three axes inclined at oblique angles to each other.

triclinium, n. [1. tríklínium; 2. traiklániəm]. Lat., fr. Gk. *tríklīnion*; fr. **tri-** & *klínē*, 'couch', see **clinic**. (class. antiq.) **a** A set of three couches set on three sides of a table for dining; **b** dining-room arranged with such tables.

tricolo(u)r, n. [1. tríkolòr, tríkulur; 2. tráikolɔ̀, tráikələ]. Fr. *(drapeau) tricolore*, 'flag of three colours', as n. See **tri-** & **colour** (I.). A national flag composed of three colours, arranged in equal stripes, esp. the French national flag consisting of red, white, and blue stripes of equal width.

tricot, n. [1. tríkō; 2. tríkou]. Fr., 'knitting'. **a** A coarse, large-stitched knitting; fabric of this; **b** garment, jersey, made of this.

tric-trac, n. [1. trík trak; 2. trík træk]. Fr. An early, difficult, and complicated form of backgammon.

tricuspid, adj. [1. tríkúspid; 2. traikáspid]. **tri-** & **cusp** (*-id-* is part of stem of latter). Having three cusps or points.

tricycle, n. [1. trísikl; 2. tráisikl]. **tri-** & **cycle** (I.). Cycle with three wheels; practically obsolete, except as tradesman's carrier.

tricyclist, n. [1. trísiklist; 2. tráisiklist]. Prec. & **-ist**. Rider of a tricycle.

trident, n. [1. trídent; 2. tráidənt]. Lat. *trident-(em)*, 'three-pronged spear', fr. **tri-** & **dent-**, 'tooth; prong', see **dental**. A three-pronged spear; esp. one represented as the characteristic symbol of Neptune and of naval power.

tridentate, adj. [1. trídentāt; 2. traidénteit]. Prec. & **-ate**. Having three prongs or divisions.

Tridentine, adj. & n. [1. trídentīn; 2. traidéntain]. Med. Lat. *Tridentum*, 'Trent'. **1.** adj. Belonging to, connected with, Trent, or the Council of Trent (1545–63). **2.** n. One who accepts the doctrines defined as *de fide* by the Council of Trent.

tried, adj. [1. trīd; 2. traid], fr. P.P. of **try** (I.). Proved, tested, reliable, well established: *a tried friend, friendship*; *a book of tried excellence*. Phr. *old and tried*.

triennial, adj. & n. [1. triénial; 2. traiéniəl], fr. Lat. *triennium*, 'space of three years', fr. **tri-** & *annus*, 'year', see **annual** (I.), & **-al**. **1.** adj. **a** Lasting for three years; **b** occurring, appearing, once in every three years. **2.** n. **a** Something that lasts for, or occurs once in, three years; **b** specif., a Mass said every day for three years for the repose of the soul of a deceased person.

trier, n. [1. tríer; 2. tráiə]. **try** (I.) & **-er**. **a** One who tries, attempts; **b** one who tests, esp. one who tests judicially.

trierarch, n. [1. tríerark; 2. tráiərāk]. Lat. *trierarchus*, fr. Gk. *triērarkhos*, 'commander of a trireme'; see **trireme** & **arch-**. **1.** Commander of a trireme. **2.** (in anct. Athens) Person who built and fitted out a trireme for the service of the state.

trierarchy, n. [1. tríerárki; 2. tráiərāki]. Prec. & **-y**. Office, functions, of a trierarch.

trifid, adj. [1. trífid; 2. tráifid]. Lat. *trifidus*, 'cleft in three parts; three-forked'; **tri-** & *fid-*, form of base occurring in perf. of *findere*, 'to split'; see this under **fissile**, & cp. **bite**. (zool. and bot.) Divided into three lobes or sinuses; tridentate.

trifle (I.), n. [1. trífl; 2. tráifl]. M.E. *trifle*, *trufle*, O. Fr. *trufle*, *trufe*, 'mockery, trickery'. Origin unknown; prob. same word as **truffle**. **1. a** Thing of no value; small, insignificant object: *a few trifles for your birthday*; **b** unimportant subject, a paltry matter; a worthless, trivial idea: *a mind occupied with, interested in, trifles*. Phrs. *he doesn't stick at trifles, not the man to stick at trifles*, he is entirely without scruples. **2.** A sweet dish made of cake soaked in wine, filled with jam, stuck over with almonds, and covered thickly with whipped cream. **3. a** (colloq.) A very small amount: *just the merest, a mere, trifle of sugar in my tea*; **b** (adverbially) slightly, somewhat: *a trifle sad, dull, annoyed* &c.

trifle (II.), vb. intrans. & trans. M.E. *trifelen*; see prec. **A.** intrans. **1. a** To speak jestingly, lightly, idly; **b** to speak and act without seriousness, speak insincerely; to play fast and loose, to promise without intending to fulfil: *I beg you not to trifle with me*; *in no mood for trifling*; *not a man to trifle with*; *I did but trifle*, didn't mean what I said. **2. a** To spend one's time idly; to lounge, dawdle, potter about, engage in frivolous pursuits: *he trifled through the best years of his life*; **b** to linger over, toy with, play with: *to trifle with, over, a light meal*. **B.** trans. To waste in trifling; chiefly *trifle away*: *to trifle away one's time, one's time away*.

trifler, n. [1. trífler; 2. tráiflə]. Prec. & **-er**. One who trifles; a frivolous, superficial person.

trifling, adj. [1. trífling; 2. tráifliŋ], fr. Pres. Part. of **trifle** (II.). Slight, unimportant, trivial; of small account, inconsiderable: *a trifling error, remark, jest* &c.; *a trifling ailment*.

triflingly, adv. Prec. & **-ly**. In a trifling manner; to a slight, trifling, extent.

trifoliate, adj. [1. trífóliāt; 2. traifóulieit]. See next word & **-ate**. Having three leaves or leaflets.

trifolium, n. [1. trífólium; 2. traifóuliəm]. Lat., 'trefoil', lit. 'three-leaved plant'; see **tri-** & **folio** (I.). Large genus of plants; the clovers.

triforium, n. [1. trífórium; 2. traifóriəm]. L. Lat., formed fr. **tri-**, & *foris*, 'door', q.v. under **forum**. Gallery with arched openings running along the nave and transepts of a church, above the main arches.

triform, adj. [1. tríform; 2. tráifɔm]. Lat. *triformis*, see **tri-** & **-form**. **a** Having three parts; **b** having a triple character or nature.

triformity, n. [1. trífórmiti; 2. traifɔ́miti]. Prec. & **-ity**. Quality, state, of being triform.

trifurcate, adj. & vb. intrans. and trans. [1. tríférkāt; 2. tráifəkeit]. **tri-** & Lat. *furca*, see **fork** (I.), & **-ate**. **1.** adj., also *trifurcated*. Having three branches; forking in three. **2.** vb. To branch out, divide, into three.

trifurcation, n. [1. tríférkāshun; 2. tráifākéi-ʃən]. Prec. & **-ion**. **a** Process of branching into three; **b** place where a road, stream, bough &c. trifurcates.

trig, adj. [1. trig; 2. trig]. O.N. *tryggr*, cogn. w. **true**. Smart, trim, in good order and condition.

trigamist, n. [1. trígamist; 2. trígəmist]. **trigamy** & **-ist**. One who has three wives or husbands at the same time.

trigamous, adj. [1. trígamus; 2. trígəməs]. See next word & **-ous**. **1.** Thrice married; having three wives or three husbands at same time. **2.** (bot.) Having male, female, and hermaphrodite flowers on same stem.

trigamy, n. [1. trígami; 2. trígəmi]. Gk. *trigamía*, see **tri-** & **-gamy**. Triple marriage; state of having three wives or husbands at the same time.

trigeminous, adj. [1. tríjéminus; 2. traidʒé-minəs]. Lat. *trigeminus*, 'three at a birth'; **tri-** & *geminus*, 'a twin', see **Gemini**, & **-ous**. Being one of three born at one birth.

trigger, n. [1. tríger; 2. trígə]. Earlier *tricker*; cp. Du. *trekker*, fr. *trekken*, 'to pull'; cp. **trek**. Lever which releases a spring; specif., one releasing the hammer of a firearm.

triglot, adj. [1. tríglot; 2. tráiglɔt]. **tri-** & Gk. *glôtta*, 'tongue, language', variant of *glôssa*, see **gloss** (III.), **glossary**. Written in, speaking, three languages.

triglyph, n. [1. tríglif; 2. tráiglif]. Gk. *trigluphos*, 'thrice-carved ornament', see **tri-** & **glyph**. Three-grooved tablet repeated at equal distances along the frieze in Doric architecture.

triglyphic, adj. [1. tríglífik; 2. traiglífik]. Prec. & **-ic**. Connected with, consisting of, triglyphs.

trigon, n. [1. trígon; 2. tráigɔn]. Gk. *trígonon*, 'triangle; musical instrument in this form'; see **tri-** & under **-gon**. **1. a** A triangle; **b** (anct. Gk.) triangular lyre. **2.** (astrol.) Division, group, of three signs of the zodiac.

trigonal, adj. [1. trí-, trígonal; 2. trái-, trí-gənəl]. Prec. & **-al**. (of a cross-section) Triangular.

trigonometric(al), adj. [1. trigonométrik(l); 2. trigənəmétrik(l)]. **trigonometry** & **-ic** (& **-al**). Pertaining to, based on, trigonometry.

trigonometry, n. [1. trigonómetri; 2. trigənɔ́mitri]. **trigon** & **-o-** of stem & **-metry**. Branch of mathematics dealing with the relations of the sides and angles of triangles.

trigonous, adj. [1. trí-, trígunus; 2. trái-, trí-gənəs]. **trigon** & **-ous**. Three-cornered, having three angles.

trigraph, n. [1. trígrahf; 2. tráigrāf]. **tri-** & **graph**. Group of three graphic symbols used to express a single sound; e.g. *sch*=[s], in *schism*.

trilateral, adj. & n. [1. trílateral; 2. trailǽt-ərəl]. **tri-** & **lateral** (I.). **a** adj. Having three sides; **b** n., three-sided figure or enclosed space.

trilby, n. [1. trílbi; 2. trílbi], fr. name of novel by George du Maurier. A soft felt hat.

trilemma, n. [1. tríléma; 2. trailémə]. Gk., see **tri-** & **lemma**, & cp. **dilemma**. Choice between three things or three courses of action.

trilinear, adj. [1. trĭlínear; 2. trəilíniə]. tri- & linear. Pertaining to, enclosed by, three lines.
trilingual, adj. [1. trĭlíŋgwal; 2. trəilíŋgwəl]. tri- & lingual. Speaking, written in, three languages.
triliteral, adj. & n. [1. trĭlíterəl; 2. trəilíterəl]. tri- & literal. A adj. Spelt with three letters; b n., word so spelt.
triliteralism, n. [1. trĭlíterəlizm; 2. trəilíterəlizəm]. See prec. & -ism. Property, condition, of being triliteral; specif. of Semitic languages, fact of having words consisting of 'roots' which have three fixed consonant sounds, the vowels varying in cognate words according to the sense.
trilith, trilithon, n. [1. trĭlith, trĭlithon; 2. trάilip, trάiliþon]. tri- & Gk. *lithos*, 'stone', see litho-. A prehistoric stone monument, consisting of two upright stones supporting a third stone as lintel.
trill (I.), vb. intrans. & trans. [1. tril; 2. tril]. Cp. Fr. *triller*; Ital. *trillare*; prob. imitative of sound. a intrans. To make a vibrating sound with the tongue, utter such a note with the voice, or produce such a note on an instrument; b trans., to pronounce (a sound), sing, or play (a note) with vibratory effect.
trill (II.), n. Fr. *trille*; Ital. *trilla*; see prec. 1. (singing &c.) a A rapid alternation of the voice between two notes, producing a vibratory effect; a shake; b a similar effect in a bird's song; a warble; c similar alternation of tone, and same effect, produced on a musical instrument. 2. (phon.) Consonantal sound produced by a rapid vibratory movement, a of the point of the tongue—[r] in Scots; b of the uvula—[r] in French.
trilling, n. [1. tríliŋ; 2. tríliŋ]. tri- & -ling; cp. Germ. *drilling*, fr. form of *drei*, 'three'. One of three children born at one birth.
trillion, n. [1. tríliun; 2. tríliən], fr. Fr.; tri- w. ending on anal. of million. a A million million million; expressed by a unit and 18 zeros; b (Fr. & Am. usage) a million million; expressed by a unit and 12 zeros.
trilobate, adj. [1. trĭlóbāt; 2. trəilóubeit]. tri- & lobate. (bot. &c.) Having three lobes.
trilobite, n. [1. trĭlobīt; 2. trάiləbait]. See prec. & -ite. An extinct marine arachnid with trilobate body, found as fossils in Cambrian and Silurian strata.
trilogy, n. [1. tríloji; 2. tríládži]. Gk. *trilogia*; see tri- & -logy. a A Series of three Greek dramas performed consecutively on the same day; b any connected series of three literary or musical compositions.
trim (I.), vb. trans. & intrans. [1. trim; 2. trim]. O.E. *trymman*, 'to make strong, fortify; to arrange, array', fr. O.E. *trum*, 'firm, strong, healthy'; cogn. w. Lat. *dūrus*, 'hard, strong', wh. is for *drūros, see durable; cp. further Gk. *drūmós*, 'oak-coppice', & *drūs*, 'oak', q.v. under dryad. The base **derewo-* meant orig. 'tree-trunk', & the adj. derived fr. this had the sense 'hard, firm, as a tree' &c. See also tree (I.). General sense, to set in order, bring to a desired shape, condition &c.; various specialized uses. A. trans. 1. To clean up, smooth (wick of a lamp), so that it will burn; to arrange (a fire), make compact, put in condition favourable to combustion. 2. To make tidy, shapely; cut into desired shape and size: *to trim a hedge*; *to trim one's moustache, one's nails* &c.; *trim oneself up*, make oneself clean and neat. 3. (naut.) a To adjust balance of, distribute weight in (a boat), so that she floats level in the water; b to arrange (sails) in position suitable for sailing. 4. To ornament, attach edging, fringe, lace &c. to: *to trim a jacket with fur*; to adorn with ribbons, flowers &c.: *to trim a (woman's) hat*. B. intrans. To perform act of trimming (in various senses); specif. (fig.) to waver in one's principles, adjust one's sentiments, or the expression of them, to modify one's policy &c. to suit circumstances, public opinion &c.
trim (II.), n. See prec. a Condition, mode of adjustment or arrangement; order: *to put a home, garden &c. in good, proper, trim*;

b bodily condition; c frame of mind, state of intellectual balance, mental disposition.
trim (III.), adj., fr. trim (I.). Neat, trig, spruce; in good order; in condition suited for a particular purpose or function.
trimester, n. [1. triméster; 2. triméstə]. Fr. *trimestre*, fr. *trimestris*, 'of three months'; tri- & *mensis*, 'month', see meno-. Period of three months; school or university term of this length.
trimeter, n. [1. trímeter; 2. trímitə]. See tri- & metre (I.). (prosody) A verse of three measures.
trimetric(al), adj. [1. trimétrik(l); 2. trimétrik(l)]. Prec. & -ic (& -al). Pertaining to, of the nature of, a trimeter.
trimly, adv. [1. trímli; 2. trímli], fr. trim (III.) & -ly. In trim, neat, condition or manner.
trimmer, n. [1. trímer; 2. trímə]. trim (I.) & -er. 1. a Person who trims (in various senses); b instrument for trimming or clipping &c. 2. Specif., person who sacrifices principle to expediency; a time-server.
trimming, n. [1. tríming; 2. trímiŋ]. See prec. & -ing. 1. Action of one who trims. 2. a Material, ornamental edging, border, frill &c. used to trim a garment; ornamental edging to a table dish; b (fig.) flowers of speech, ornamental redundancies of speech. 3. Adjuncts, accessories: *boiled beef and trimmings*.
trimness, n. [1. trímnes; 2. trímnis], fr. trim (III.) & -ness. Condition of being trim; tidiness, order, neatness.
trine, adj. & n. [1. trīn; 2. train]. Lat. *trinus*, 'threefold'; see tri-. 1. adj. Threefold, triple. 2. n. a A group of three; b (astrol.) aspect of planets 120° apart; Phr. *in trine*.
tringle, n. [1. tríŋgl; 2. tríŋgl]. Fr.; origin doubtful. 1. Rod for curtain, or for bed canopy. 2. a (archit.) Narrow, square moulding; b (artillery) bar on gun platform which takes up the recoil of the gun on discharge.
Trinitarian, adj. & n. [1. trinitárian; 2. trinitéəriən]. trinity & -arian. 1. adj. Pertaining to the Trinity, or to the doctrine of the Trinity. 2. n. Believer in the doctrine of the Trinity.
Trinitarianism, n. [1. trinitárianizm; 2. trinitéəriənizəm]. Prec. & -ism. The doctrine of the Trinity; faith in this.
trinitrotoluene, n. [1. trĭnītrōtólūēn; 2. trainάitroutóljuīn]. tri-, nitro-, & toluene. Abbr. T.N.T., a high explosive obtained by action of nitric and sulphuric acids on toluene.
trinity, n. [1. tríniti; 2. tríniti]. M.E. *trinitee*, L. Lat. *trinitāt-(em)*, see trine & -ity. 1. Combination of three (objects or persons) considered as forming a unity. 2. Specif. (theol., cap.) the union of the three divine persons, Father, Son, Holy Ghost, in the Godhead.
Trinity House, n. A corporate body which licenses pilots, erects and maintains lighthouses, buoys &c.
Trinity Sunday, n. The Sunday next after Whitsunday; the day on which the feast of the Blessed Trinity is kept.
trinket, n. [1. tríŋket; 2. tríŋkit]. M.E. *trenket*, 'small ornamental knife'; O. Fr. *trenquet*, cp. *tranchier*, 'to cut'; see trench (I.). a Small ornament, a jewel, a bauble; b small, insignificant, trivial object; a worthless trifle.
trinomial, adj. & n. [1. trĭnómial; 2. trainóumiəl], cp. Lat. *trinominis*, adj., 'having three names'. See tri- & nominal. The above word is formed as though fr. *trinomius & -ālis; see -al. 1. adj. a (alg.) Having, consisting of, three terms; b (bot. and zool.) composed of three names or words; more usually **trinominal**, q.v. 2. n. (alg.) Expression, equation, consisting of three terms.
trinominal, adj. [1. trĭnóminal; 2. trainóminəl]. Lat., see prec. Having three names; esp. (bot. and zool.) *trinominal system*, of describing animals or plants by genus, species, and subspecies.
trio, n. [1. trēō; 2. tríou]. Ital., fr. Lat. *tri-*, 'three'; see tri-. 1. Musical composition

a for three voices, b for three instruments. 2. Group of three persons or things.
triolet, n. [1. trēólā, trēólet; 2. tríoulei, tríoulet]. Fr. Prec. & -let. Poem of eight lines with rhymes in the order *abaaabab*.
trior, n. See trier.
trip (I.), vb. intrans. & trans. [1. trip; 2. trip]. M.E. *trippen*; cp. Swed. *trippa*; prob. connected w. Germ. *treppe*, 'flight of steps', & w. trap (III.), a snare. A. intrans. 1. To move nimbly along with light, rapid, graceful steps. 2. a To stumble, catch one's foot in an obstacle in walking or running and lose one's balance so as to fall, or nearly to fall; also *trip up*; b to perform the act of tripping another: *it is not legitimate to trip in football*. 3. (fig.) a To commit an error, be guilty of an offence, or indiscretion in behaviour: *he was caught tripping several times and at last was dismissed*; b to make an error in statement of fact, be inaccurate; c to halt, hesitate, stumble, over a word &c. in speaking; to make a slip of the tongue. B. trans. 1. (rare) To dance lightly and nimbly: '*Come and trip it as ye go, On the light fantastic toe*' (Milton, 'L'Allegro', 33-34); *to trip a measure*. 2. a To cause to stumble or fall, e.g. by putting an obstacle in the way of the feet and suddenly checking forward progress, or (in wrestling) by catching and pulling away a leg; also *trip up*; b *trip up*, to detect in an error of statement, or in conduct in another; to catch (person) in a lapse from truth or honesty. 3. To upset plans of, to outwit, cause to fail in enterprise. 4. To loose (an anchor) from bottom of sea by means of cable.
trip (II.), n., fr. prec. 1. A journey, tour; an excursion; esp. one of short duration for purposes of pleasure; a jaunt, an outing: *a trip to the Continent, to the seaside*. 2. A light, nimble, rapid motion forward on the feet. 3. a Act of tripping or stumbling; a false step, a slip, lurch forward; b act of causing another to stumble or fall; wrestler's device for causing opponent to lose his footing. 4. (fig.) A slip, a faux pas, an offence, in conduct; a slip of the tongue, an error in statement &c.
tripartite, adj. [1. trĭpártīt; 2. traipάtait]. tri- & part (I.) & -ite. 1. Divided into, consisting of, three parts. 2. Existing, arranged between, three parties.
tripartition, n. [1. trĭpartíshun; 2. trəipātíʃən]. tri- & partition. Division into three parts.
tripe, n. [1. trīp; 2. traip]. Fr., origin unknown. 1. (obs. or vulg.) The entrails, the guts. 2. Part of the stomach of an animal of the ox kind, used as food. 3. (slang) Worthless stuff, rubbish; applied to inferior literary work.
tripedal, adj. [1. trĭpédl; 2. trάipídl]. tri- & pedal (I.). Having three feet.
trip-hammer, n. A tilt-hammer.
triphthong, n. [1. trífthoŋ; 2. trífθɔŋ]. tri- & second element as in diphthong. A combination, or series, of three vowel sounds, of which only one is stressed; e.g. [áiə] as in *fire*.
triplane, n. [1. trĭplān; 2. trάiplein]. tri- & plane (V.). Aeroplane with three supporting planes.
triple, adj. & vb. trans. & intrans. [1. trípl; 2. trípl]. Fr., fr. Lat. *triplus*; see tri- & cp. formation of *duplus* under double (I.). 1. adj. Threefold. 2. vb. a trans. To multiply, increase, threefold; b intrans., to become three times as great, to treble (?).
triplet, n. [1. tríplet; 2. tríplit]. Prec. & -et. Group, series, of three; a three lines rhyming together; b three notes played or sung in time of two; c any one of three children born at one birth.
triplex, adj. & n. [1. trípleks; 2. trípleks]. Lat., 'triple'; fr. tri- & base *plic-*, 'fold', see plicate. 1. adj. a Threefold b producing threefold effect. 2. n. (mus.) Triple time.

triplicate, adj., n., & vb. trans. [1. tríplikāt; 2. tríplikeit]. Lat.; see **tri-** & **plicate**. **1.** adj. Threefold; esp. reproduced in three identical copies. **2.** n. One of three identical things or copies. **3.** vb. To make three copies of; to treble.

triplication, n. [1. trìplikáshun; 2. trìplikéiʃən]. Prec. & **-ion**. **a** Act of triplicating; **b** that which is triplicated.

triplicity, n. [1. trī-, triplísiti; 2. trai-, triplísiti]. Lat. *triplic-*, stem of **triplex**, & **-ity**. State of being threefold.

tripod, n. [1. trípod; 2. tráipəd]. Gk. *tripod-*, 'three-legged'; see **tri-** & **pedal (I.)**. **1.** A stand, table, stool &c. standing on three legs. **2.** Specif., three-legged stool, or altar, of bronze, on which the priestess sat in the temple of Apollo at Delphi when giving the answers of the oracle.

tripoli, n. [1. trípoli; 2. trípəli], fr. name of place in Africa. Friable, siliceous deposit; also called *rotten-stone*.

tripos, n. [1. trípos; 2. tráipəs]. Gk. *trípous*, nom., of wh. the stem is seen in **tripod**. Honours examination at University of Cambridge; formerly the list of successful candidates in the examination; from the three-legged stool upon which the M.A. sat who delivered the satirical Latin speech at the degree-giving on Ash Wednesday.

tripper, n. [1. tríper; 2. trípə]. **trip (I.)** & **-er**. One who takes trips; a tourist, an excursionist.

tripping, adj. [1. tríping; 2. trípiŋ], fr. Pres. Part. of **trip (I.)**. Walking with light, rapid, nimble steps.

trippingly, adv. Prec. & **-ly**. **a** As though tripping; nimbly; **b** (of speech, utterance) flowingly, fluently, readily.

triptych, n. [1. tríptik; 2. tríptik]. Gk. *tríptukhos*, 'consisting of three layers, or plates', fr. **tri-** & *ptúx*, genit. *ptukhós*, 'layer, fold'; the origin of latter is doubtful. Cp. **diptych**. Picture or carving upon three panels placed side by side; esp. one as altar-piece with large central panel and a smaller one on either side.

triquetra, n. [1. trīkwétra; 2. traikwétrə]. Lat., fem. of *triquetrus*, 'having three corners'; fr. **tri-** & second element orig. **quadros*, 'sharp, pointed', cogn. w. O.E. *hwæt*, 'sharp; bold' &c., q.v. under **whet (I.)**. Ornament consisting of three arcs interlaced.

triquetrous, adj. [1. trīkwétrus; 2. traikwétrəs]. Prec. & **-ous**. Having three acute angles or edges.

trireme, n. [1. trírēm; 2. tráiərīm]. Lat. *trirēmis*, 'having three banks of oars'; fr. **tri-** & *rēmus*, 'oar', fr. **retsmos*, cogn. w. O.E. *rōðor*, 'oar', see **rudder**, & **row (II.)**. Ancient galley, esp. a Greek galley, with three benches for rowers.

Trisagion, n. [1. triságion; 2. triságiən]. Gk. *trís*, 'three times', see under **tri-**, & *hágion*, neut., 'holy', q.v. under **hagiology**. Greek hymn which invokes God three times as holy.

trisect, vb. trans. [1. trīsékt; 2. traisékt], fr. Lat. **tri-** & *sect-(um)*, P.P. of *secāre*, 'to cut'; see **sect**. To divide, cut, into three, esp. three equal parts (specif. geom.).

triskelion, n. [1. triskélion; 2. triskéliən], fr. Gk. *triskelés*, 'three-legged', fr. **tri-** & *skélos*, 'leg', see **isosceles**. Name given to a device of three curves or branches joined at a centre, developing into the three legs of the coins of ancient Sicily, and of the arms of the Isle of Man.

trismus, n. [1. trízmus; 2. trízməs]. Latinized fr. Gk. *trismós*, 'a squeaking, creaking', cp. *trízein*, 'to squeak, creak', fr. base **streid-*, **strid-*, cp. Lat. *strīdēre*, 'to creak, rattle' &c., see **strident**. (med.) Lockjaw.

trisyllabic, adj. [1. trìsilábik; 2. trìsilǽbik]. **tri-** & **syllabic**. Having three syllables.

trisyllable, n. [1. trisílabl; 2. trisíləbl]. **tri-** & **syllable (I.)**. Word of three syllables.

tritagonist, n. [1. trītágunist; 2. traitǽgənist]. Gk. *tritagōnistḗs*, fr. *trítos*, 'third', cp. **third (I.)**, & *agōnistḗs*, 'actor'; see **agonistic**. Cp. **protagonist**. Character third in importance in a Greek play.

trite, adj. [1. trīt; 2. trait]. Lat. *trīt-(um)*, P.P. of *terere*, 'to rub, wear away'; see also **teredo** & **toreutic**; prob. cogn. w. **throw (I.)**. Lacking novelty and freshness; commonplace, hackneyed, banal: *a trite remark, expression.*

tritely, adv. Prec. & **-ly**. In a trite manner.

triteness, n. See prec. & **-ness**. Condition, quality, of being trite.

tritheism, n. [1. trítheizm; 2. tráiþiizəm]. **tri-** & **theism (II.)**. Heretical opinion that as each of the Persons of the Trinity is God, there are therefore three Gods.

tritheist, n. [1. tríthēist; 2. tráiþiist]. **tri-** & **theist**. Believer in tritheism.

Triton, n. [1. trítun; 2. tráit(ə)n]. Gk. *Trītōn*. **a** (Gk. mythol.) A minor sea-god, son of Poseidon and Amphitrite, depicted with a fish's tail, and holding a conch shell as a trumpet; also, one of a number of demi-gods resembling Triton. Phr. *a Triton among minnows*, of important personage among people of little or no consequence; **b** a genus of marine gastropod molluscs with large spiral shells.

triturable, adj. [1. trítūrabl; 2. trítjurəbl]. L. Lat. *tritur-*, as in next word, & **-able**. Capable of being triturated.

triturate, vb. trans. [1. trítūrāt; 2. trítjəreit]. L. Lat. *trītūrāt-(um)*, P.P. of *trītūrāre*, 'to grind, pulverize', formed fr. Lat. *trīt-(um)*, P.P. of Lat. *terere*, see **trite**. To rub, grind down, pulverize, reduce to a fine powder.

trituration, n. [1. trìtūráshun; 2. trìtjəréiʃən]. Prec. & **-ion**. Act or process of triturating.

triumph (I.), n. [1. tríumf; 2. tráiəmf]. Lat. *triumphus*, earlier *triumpus*, 'solemn procession attending entrance of a general into Rome after an important victory'; fr. Gk. *thríambos*, 'procession in honour of Bacchus'; the etymol. is doubtful; some authorities interpret as 'a dance in three-time', & derive fr. Gk. *trís*, 'thrice', & a hypothetical **ambos*, 'a dance', supposed to be cogn. w. Scrt. *ángam*, 'a limb', O.H.G. *ancha*, 'leg'; others believe that *thríambos* & *dīthúrambos*, see **dithyramb**, are borrowed fr. Asia Minor, the source being unidentifiable. **1.** Victory, ascendancy: *the triumph of good over evil*; achievement, success: *the triumphs of modern science*. Phr. *in triumph*, with victory, having achieved success. **2. a** Sense of, feeling of, exultation over, success achieved, victory gained &c.: *he could hardly conceal his triumph at the result of the election*; *a note of triumph in his voice*; **b** outward expression of sense of success &c.: *there was triumph in the eye of the conqueror*. **3.** Something which constitutes a victory, which is the expression of achievement and success: *Pope's life was a triumph over weakness and ill-health.*

triumph (II.), vb. intrans. Fr. *triompher*, Lat. *triumphāre*; see prec. **1.** To win the victory, achieve success: *we hope that in the end righteousness will triumph*; *triumph over*, to defeat, obtain ascendancy over: *good sense has triumphed over unreasoning impetuosity*. **2.** To feel and express joy and satisfaction at success; to exult; commonly *triumph over*: *it is ungenerous to triumph over a defeated enemy.*

triumphal, adj. [1. trīúmfl; 2. traiámfl]. Lat. *triumphālis*, 'belonging to a triumph'; see **triumph (I.)** & **-al**. Pertaining to a triumph; expressing triumph: *a triumphal procession, arch* &c.

triumphant, adj. [1. trīúmfant; 2. traiámfənt]. Lat. *triumphant-(em)*, Pres. Part. of *triumphāre*, see **triumph (II.)**. **1.** Victorious, successful: *triumphant generals*; *the triumphant progress of knowledge*. **2. a** Feeling exultation; **b** expressing exultation, manifesting a sense of successful achievement or of victory: *a triumphant shout*; *triumphant bearing.*

triumphantly, adv. Prec. & **-ly**. **1.** Successfully, victoriously: *to return triumphantly from the wars*. **2.** Exultingly, so as to express joy in, assurance of, success: *to smile triumphantly.*

triumvir, n. [1. trīúmvēr; 2. traiámviə]. Lat., fr. *trium*, genit. pl. of *trēs*, 'three', see **tri-**, & *vir*, 'a man', see **virile**. The *triumviri* were three men holding a public office conjointly, a board of three joint commissioners. A *triumvir* was one of these.

triumvirate, n. [1. trīúmvirāt, -it; 2. traiámvireit, -it]. Lat. *triumvirātus*, 'office, dignity, of a triumvir; a group of triumvirs'; see prec. & **-ate**. **a** A group of three having conjoint authority; specif. **b** (Rom. hist.) one of two such associations formed in Rome in 60 B.C. and 43 B.C.

triune, adj. [1. tríūn; 2. tráijūn]. **tri-** & Lat. *ūnus*, 'one', see **union**. Three in one.

triunity, n. [1. trīūniti; 2. traijūniti]. Prec. & **-ity**. **a** Fact, condition, of being triune; **b** a trinity.

trivet, n. [1. trívet; 2. trívit]. O.E. *trefet*, fr. Low Lat. form of Lat. *triped-*, 'three-footed'; see **tri-** & **pedal (I.)**. Iron stand with three legs for holding a pot or kettle; iron utensil with three projections on lower surface, made to hook over bars of a grate and support a kettle &c. Phr. *right as a trivet*, all right.

trivial, adj. [1. trívial; 2. tríviəl]. Lat. *triviālis*, 'belonging to the cross-roads or public streets'; hence 'commonplace, vulgar, ordinary'; fr. **tri-** & *via*, 'a way', see **trivium**. **1.** (archaic) Commonplace, ordinary: '*The trivial round*'. **2. a** Unimportant, of small value, not weighty; insignificant, trifling, negligible: *a trivial remark*; *a trivial mind*; **b** inconsiderable, slight, not severe: *a trivial injury*; *trivial expenses.*

triviality, n. [1. trìviáliti; 2. trìviǽliti]. Prec. & **-ity**. **1.** Quality, condition, of being trivial. **2.** A trivial thing; a trifling, trite, unimportant idea, piece of work &c.

trivially, adv. [1. tríviali; 2. tríviəli]. **trivial** & **-ly**. In a trivial, trifling, manner.

trivialness, n. [1. trívialnes; 2. tríviəlnis]. See prec. & **-ness**. Quality of being trivial; triviality.

trivium, n. [1. trívium; 2. tríviəm]. Lat., 'place where three roads meet; public square; highway', fr. **tri-** & *via*, 'a way, road', see **via**. The initial course of study in mediaeval schools, consisting of the three liberal arts, grammar, rhetoric, and logic; corresponding to the B.A. course of later universities; cp. *quadrivium.*

-trix. Lat. suff. expressing a female agent; corresponding to masc. *-tor*.

trocar, trochar, n. [1. trṓkar; 2. tróukā]. Fr. *trocart*, fr. *trois*, 'three', & *carre*, 'side of a square', fr. Lat. *quadra*, see **quadrate (I.)**. Surgical piercing instrument with triangular point used for drawing off fluid from the body.

trochaic, adj. & n. [1. trōkáik; 2. troukéiik]. See **trochee** & **-ic**. **1.** adj. Pertaining to, composed in, trochees. **2.** n. A trochaic verse or line.

troche, n. [1. trṓkē; 2. tróuki]. Gk. *trokhós*, 'something which runs round; a round wheel; a round ball or cake'; connected w. *trékhein*, 'to run'; this base is seen in O.E. *prǣgan*, 'to run', see **thrall**. Small, round, flat lozenge of medicinal drugs.

trochee, n. [1. trṓkē; 2. tróukī]. Lat. *trochaeus*, fr. Gk. *trokhaîos*, 'tripping, running', see prec. A metrical foot consisting (in Greek and Latin) of a long syllable followed by a short; or (in English and other languages where stress metre prevails) of a stressed syllable followed by an unstressed.

trochilus, n. [1. trókilus; 2. trókiləs]. Lat., fr. Gk. *trokhílos*, lit. 'a runner'; applied to several small birds; connected w. base **trekh-*, 'to run'; see **troche**. **1.** A small bird, a variety of sandpiper, said to accompany the crocodile and clear it of leeches and other parasites. **2.** (ornith., cap.) A genus of humming-birds.

trochlea, n. [1. tróklea; 2. trókliə]. Lat., 'a block containing a pulley', fr. Gk. *trokhilia*,

trochlear, adj. [1. tróklear; 2. tróklǐə]. Prec. & -ar. (anat.) Pertaining to a trochlea: *trochlear muscle.*

trocho-, pref. Gk. *trokhós*, 'wheel'; see **troche**.

trochoid, adj. [1. trókoid; 2. tróukɔid]. Prec. & -oid. **a** Working like a wheel, i.e. rotating on own axis; **b** wheel-shaped.

trochometer, n. [1. trŏkómeter; 2. troukómǐtə]. trocho- & -meter. Hodometer or trechometer.

troco, n. [1. trókō; 2. tróukou]. Span. *truco*; origin doubtful. Obsolete game played on a lawn with wooden balls and spoon-shaped cues.

trod, vb. [1. trod; 2. trɔd]. Pret. of **tread** (I.), fr. M.E., P.P. type *trode(n)*, see **trodden**. Cp. O.E. Pret. *træd*; M.E. *trad*.

trodden, vb. [1. tródn; 2. trɔ́dn]. P.P. of **tread**; O.E. (*ǵe*)*troden*; M.E. *troden*.

troglodyte, n. [1. tróglodīt; 2. tróglədait]. Gk. *trōglodútēs*, 'one who creeps into holes'; fr. *trôglē*, 'a hole', cp. *trôgein*, 'to gnaw', fr. base **trōg-*, **terg-* &c., cogn. w. Goth. *þairkō*, 'hole', & O.E. *þyrel*, 'hole', see **nostril** & **through** (I.). The second element is formed fr. *dúein*, 'to enter', the origin of wh. is uncertain. 1. Primitive cave-dweller, cave-man; (fig.) recluse. 2. *Troglodytes parvulus*, the common wren.

troglodytic, adj. [1. tròglodítik; 2. trɔ̀glɔdítik]. Prec. & -ic. Pertaining to a troglodyte.

trogon, n. [1. trógon; 2. tróugɔn]. Invented word, fr. Gk. *trôgōn*, Pres. Part. of *trôgein*, 'to gnaw', see prec. Typical genus of a family of brilliantly coloured birds, chiefly of S. America.

troika, n. [1. tróika; 2. tróikə]. Russ., cp. *tri*, 'three'; cogn. w. **tri-**. Carriage sledge, drawn by three horses harnessed abreast.

trois-temps, n. [1. trwáh tom; 2. trwɑ̃ tɑ̃]. Fr., 'three time'. The musical time or rhythm of a waltz.

Trojan, adj. & n. [1. trójan; 2. tróudžən]. Lat. *Trojānus*, fr. *Troia*, 'Troy'. 1. adj. Belonging to, connected with, Troy. 2. n. Inhabitant of Troy. Phr. *to work like a Trojan*, work industriously and laboriously.

troll (I.), vb. intrans. & trans. [1. trōl; 2. troul], fr. O. Fr. *troller*, prob. fr. Gmc. origin; cp. Germ. *trollen*, 'to roll, troll'; M.H.G. sense, 'to run with short steps'; etymol. doubtful. **A**. intrans. 1. To fish by trailing or spinning a revolving bait or lure, esp. behind a boat. 2. (archaic or obs.) To pass the bottle round. **B**. trans. 1. (rare) To fish (area of water) by trolling. 2. To sing in a careless, light-hearted manner : *to troll a stave.*

troll (II.), n. O.N. & Swed. Fabulous creature, either a giant or a mischievous dwarf.

trolley, n. [1. tróli; 2. trɔ́li]. Perh. fr. **troll** (I.), see **trawl**. 1. Any of various vehicles; **a** a light cart usually on two wheels, pushed by hand; **b** a strong low truck on four wheels, running on rails, for moving stones and other heavy objects. 2. Steel arm with pulley projecting from electric tram-car, running along overhead wire and conveying current to the car; (also attrib.) *trolley-car, -pole* &c.

trolley-lace, n. Origin doubtful. Coarse lace the pattern on which is outlined in thick threads.

trollius, n. [1. trólius; 2. trɔ́liəs]. Mod. Lat. fr. Hung. *torolya*, the name of the plant. Genus of ranunculaceous plants, with globe-shaped yellow or orange flowers.

trollop, n. [1. trólop; 2. trɔ́ləp], fr. **troll** (I.) in old sense 'roll'; cp. Fr. *rouleuse* for meaning. A slatternly, disreputable woman.

trombone, n. [1. trómbōn; 2. trɔ́mboun]. Ital., fr. *tromba*, 'trumpet', see **trump** (I.), & **-oon**. Powerful brass wind instrument consisting of a tube bent and rebent on itself, with a bell-shaped end, and a sliding section, by moving which the various notes are made.

trommel, n. [1. trómel; 2. trɔ́məl]. Germ., 'a drum', q.v. Revolving sieve used in cleansing ores.

tromometer, n. [1. tromómeter; 2. trɔmómǐtə], fr. Gk. *trómos*, 'a trembling', cogn. w. **tremor**, & **-meter**. Instrument for measuring earth tremors.

trompe, n. [1. tromp; 2. trɔmp]. Fr., see **trump** (I.). Apparatus for making powerful draught in a blast furnace, by means of falling water; water-bellows.

troop (I.), n. [1. trōop; 2. trūp]. Fr., see **troupe**. 1. A number of people. 2. (specif. mil.) A division of a cavalry squadron, commanded by a captain, and corresponding to a company in an infantry regiment. 3. Specif. (pl.) military forces.

troop (II.), vb. intrans. & trans., fr. prec. 1. intrans. To move forward in large numbers; to flock : *people came trooping out of the theatre.* 2. trans. In Phr. (mil.) *to troop the colour*, to perform ceremony of escorting the colour through the regiment on parade.

trooper, n. [1. trōoper; 2. trūpə]. troop & -er. Private soldier in a cavalry regiment. Phr. *to swear like a trooper*, to swear fluently and forcibly.

troop-ship, n. Vessel carrying soldiers; a transport.

Tropaeolum, n. [1. tropéolum; 2. trɔpíələm]. Latinized dimin. of Gk. *trópaion*, 'trophy', see **trophy**; so called fr. the shield-shaped leaves & scarlet flowers of the plant. Genus of slender S. American climbing plants with masses of scarlet or orange flowers, including the nasturtium and canary creeper.

trope, n. [1. trōp; 2. troup]. Gk. *trópos*, 'turn, direction, way', fr. same base as *trépein*, 'to turn'; cogn. w. O. Lat. *trepit*, 'turns'; see under **trepidation**. Figure of speech; figurative, metaphorical, use of a word.

-trope, suff. Gk. *tropé*, 'a turning'; cogn. w. prec. Used in compounds, e.g. *heliotrope, zoetrope* &c., in sense of 'that which turns'.

trophic, adj. [1. trófik; 2. trɔ́fik]. Gk. *trophikós*, fr. *trophḗ*, 'food, nourishment'; fr. same base **dh(e)rebh-*, &c., as *tréphein*, 'to make firm; to feed, nourish, to cherish'; cp. further Gk. *trophālis*, 'curdled milk'; *thrómbos*, 'clot, lump', fr. **dhro(m)bh-*, see **thrombosis**. Cp. also Lith. *drabnús*, 'thick, fat'; & see **draff**. Connected with nutrition.

trophy, n. [1. trófi; 2. tróuti]. Fr. *trophée*, Ital. *trofeo*, Lat. *trophaeum, tropaeum*, fr. Gk. *trópaion*, fr. neut. of *tropaîos*, 'connected with turning, or with a change; connected with defeat'; hence token of an enemy's defeat, consisting of shields, helmets &c., hung on trees or posts. See **trope**. 1. Memorial, token, of victory; something taken from a defeated enemy; spoils of victory. 2. **a** Something preserved in memory of victory, success, achievement; **b** specif., group of such objects, such as weapons, heads or antlers of stags &c., arranged in picturesque design, and fixed on wall as an ornament : *trophies of the chase* &c.

-trophy, suff. Gk. *-trophia*, fr. *trophḗ*, 'nourishment'; see **trophic**. Form used in compounds, *atrophy, hypertrophy*, with sense of 'nutrition'.

tropic, n. & adj. [1. trópik; 2. trɔ́pik]. In M.E., fr. Lat. *tropicus*, fr. Gk. *tropikós (kúklos)* 'pertaining to a turn'; see **trope**. 1. n. **a** Each of the parallels of latitude about 23½ degrees N. (*tropic of Cancer*) and S. (*tropic of Capricorn*) of the Equator, bounding zone where sun reaches zenith; **b** region of the earth lying between the two parallels of latitude; usually *the tropics*. 2. adj. Belonging to the tropics.

tropical, adj. [1. trópikl; 2. trɔ́pikl]. tropic & -al. 1. Occurring in, characteristic of, the tropics : *tropical vegetation, diseases* &c. 2. (of weather, temperature &c.) Resembling that of the tropics; very hot, sultry. 3. Pertaining to, of the nature of, a trope; figurative.

tropically, adv. Prec. & -ly. **a** In a tropical state &c.; **b** figuratively.

tropic bird, n. One of several kinds of bird resembling a tern, found in the tropics.

tropist, n. [1. trópist; 2. tróupist]. **trope** & -ist. One who indulges in figures of speech or tropes.

tropological, adj. [1. tròpolójikl; 2. trɔ̀pɔlɔ́džikl]. See next word & -ic & -al. Characterized by tropes.

tropology, n. [1. tropóloji; 2. trɔpɔ́lədži]. **trope** & **-logy**. 1. Figurative, metaphorical, mode of speech; use of tropes. 2. Specif. method of interpreting Scripture so as to make words bear a figurative meaning.

troppo, adv. [1. trópō; 2. trɔ́ppou]. Ital. Cp. Fr. *trop*, 'too much'. (mus.) Too much; esp. *non troppo*, not to excess.

trot (I.), vb. intrans. & trans. [1. trot; 2. trɔt]. M.E. *trotten*, fr. O. Fr. *trotter*; prob. of Gmc. origin; cp. O.H.G. *trottōn*, wh. is cogn. w. **tread** (I.). **A**. intrans. 1. Specif. **a** (of horse, mule &c.) to move along at a trot; **b** (of persons) to ride at a trot. 2. (of human beings) To move along with short, rapid steps; used **a** to express the motion of a jerky, irregular run; and **b** that of a hurried walking pace in which short steps are taken; contrasted with *stride*. 3. *Trot along*, (colloq.) **a** to move off rapidly to perform some specific task : *you had better trot along and feed the dogs*; **b** to take one's departure : *good-bye, I must trot along now*. **B**. trans. 1. To cause to move at a trot : *to trot a horse*. 2. *Trot round*, (colloq.) to conduct (a person) from one place to another in succession : *I'll trot you round Oxford and show you the colleges*. 3. *Trot out*, **a** to put (a horse) through its paces so as to show it off, produce, exhibit, show off for another's inspection; (colloq.) **b** to bring out, and submit (a thing) for another's approval or acceptance : *to trot out one's best wines*; **c** to submit, bring forward (a proposal, suggestion &c.) for consideration; to bring to another's notice : *he trotted out all the old arguments*.

trot (II.), n., fr. prec. 1. **a** The rapid pace of a horse &c., between pacing and galloping, in which the fore and hind legs on the same side move forward at once, in regular succession; **b** a ride on a horse &c., at this pace. 2. (colloq.) **a** The movement of a rapid walk or run of human beings; **b** a spell of rapid exercise on foot; a quick walk, a jog. Phrs. (*always*) *on the trot*, to be kept on the trot, continuously moving, constantly busy. 3. (colloq.) A small child, a toddler.

troth, n. [1. trōth; 2. trouþ]. Variant of **truth**; M.E. *trowthe*. (archaic) Faith, fidelity, word of honour; chiefly in Phr. *to plight one's troth*, to pledge one's word; specif. in marriage.

trotter, n. [1. tróter; 2. trɔ́tə]. trot (I.) & -er. One who, that which, trots (in various specif. senses) : 1. A horse specially bred and used for trotting. 2. **a** The foot of a sheep or pig, esp. thought of as food; **b** (colloq. and facet.) the foot of a person, esp. of a child or young girl.

trottoir, n. [1. trótwar; 2. trɔ́twɑ̄]. Fr., fr. **trot** (I.). Pavement, side-walk, for pedestrians, at the side of a road.

troubadour, n. [1. trōobadōr; 2. trū́bədɔ̄]. Fr., fr. Provenç. *trobador*; either formed fr. *trobar*, 'to find, invent, compose poetry'; cp. Fr. *trouver*, q.v. under **trove, trover**, & **trouvère**; or fr. a Low Lat. **tropāre*, 'to make tropes, to sing'; cp. Lat. *tropus*, 'a trope; a song', fr. Gk., see **trope**. A mediaeval lyric and amatory poet of a school that flourished in Provence and the south of France, during late 11th and down to end of 13th centuries.

trouble (I.), vb. trans. & intrans. [1. trúbl; 2. trábl]. O. Fr. *trobler, troubler*, fr. L. Lat. *turbulāre*, 'to disturb, agitate', fr. *turbula*, dimin. of *turba*, 'a crowd'; see **turbulent**. **A**. trans. 1. (of physical action) To agitate, cause to become ruffled, put into violent motion : *to trouble the waters.* Phr. *troubled waters*, disturbed, confused state of affairs. 2. To cause agitation of mind to, to vex, render anxious, to perturb, to harass: *he was greatly troubled about his son's misconduct*; *what troubles me is the thought of her sufferings.* **3. a** To cause annoyance to, to pester, inconvenience, importune, worry, esp. with demands to do something, complaints &c.; to disturb: *he is always troubling me about his private affairs*; *I'm sorry to trouble you about such trivial matters*; also **b** in polite requests: *I fear I must trouble you to come upstairs*; *may I trouble you to pass the salt*; (also ironical) *I'll trouble you to hold your tongue.* **4.** To cause physical pain or discomfort to: *his wound troubles him a good deal*; *much troubled by gout.* **5.** To be a source of difficulty to, to compel to make an effort: *the learning of languages never troubled him much.* **B.** intrans. **1.** To take pains, give oneself trouble; to make an effort: *he never even troubled to answer*; *don't trouble to write*; *if it is inconvenient to come, don't trouble.* **2.** To feel anxious, to be in a state of mental agitation; to worry: *I shall not trouble if I never see him again.*

trouble (**II.**), n., fr. prec. **1.** Mental agitation, grief, care, affliction: *one could read trouble on his face*; *a heart full of trouble*; Phr. *in trouble,* (i.) sad, afflicted; (ii.) in danger of being punished for an offence; *to get into trouble,* render oneself liable to punishment; *to ask for trouble,* to behave in such a way as to court danger, disaster; to lay oneself open to opposition and attack; to create difficulties for oneself. **2. a** Difficulty, necessity for special effort or exertion: *I had some trouble in reading his handwriting*; *he opened the safe without any trouble*; **b** effort, labour, pains: *to take trouble*; *thank you for all your trouble on my behalf.* **3.** Cause, source, of trouble; something which afflicts, which causes grief or annoyance: *life is full of petty troubles*; *tell me all your troubles.* **4.** State of political or social unrest, disturbance, confusion. **5. a** An ailment; physical or mental ill-health: *heart trouble, mental trouble*; **b** specif. (popular) childbirth, confinement: *Mrs. Jones is over her trouble.*

troublesome, adj. [1. trúblsum; 2. tráblsəm]. Prec. & **-some.** Causing trouble (in various senses); **a** difficult, wearisome, laborious: *a troublesome job*; **b** persistently harassing; *a troublesome cough*; **c** unruly, undisciplined, obstreperous: *a troublesome child.*

troublesomely, adv., fr. prec. Prec. & **-ly.** In a troublesome manner.

troublous, adj. [1. trúblus; 2. trábləs]. **trouble** (**II.**) & **-ous.** (archaic) Characterized by troubles; disturbed, unsettled; esp. *troublous times.*

trough, n. [1. trawf, trof, truf; 2. trɔ̄f, trɔf, traf]. O.E. *trōg, trōh,* 'a hollowed wooden vessel'; O.N. *trōg*; possibly connected w. **tree** (**I.**). **1. a** A wooden vessel, or receptacle; esp. a long, narrow, open one used for holding water or food for animals; **b** a similar vessel of iron or stone; **c** wooden vessel in which dough is kneaded. **2.** A hollow, narrow channel between two waves: *the trough of the sea.* **3.** (meteor.) Line in a cyclonic area in which barometric pressure reaches the lowest point.

trounce, vb. trans. [1. trouns; 2. trauns]. Fr. *tronce,* 'a stump, thick piece of wood', variant of *tronche*; see **truncheon. a** To beat severely, castigate thoroughly; **b** (fig.) to castigate verbally; to criticize, censure, severely.

troupe, n. [1. tro͞op; 2. trūp]. Fr., 'band, troop'; see also **troop**; origin uncertain. Derivation has been suggested fr. L.G. *dorp,* 'a village', cogn. w. Engl. **thorp.** A band of actors or of other performers on the stage.

trousered, adj. [1. tróuzerd; 2. tráuzəd]. See **trousers** & **-ed.** Wearing, clothed in, trousers.

trousering, n. [1. tróuzering; 2. tráuzəriŋ]. **trousers** & **-ing.** (tailor's word) Material from which trousers are made.

trousers, n. pl. [1. tróuzerz; 2. tráuzəz]. Formerly *trouses,* fr. Fr. *trousse,* 'bundle'; see **trousse** & **truss** (**I.**) & cp. **trews. a** Male outer garment extending from the waist to the ankle, covering the lower part of the body and having a separate tubular covering for each leg; also *pair of trousers*; **b** long frilled drawers reaching to the foot worn by women in early 19th cent. Rarely used in sing., & chiefly in such Phrs. as *the leg of my trouser*; also in compounds *trouser-button, trouser-leg, trouser-stretcher.*

trousse, n. [1. tro͞os; 2. trūs]. Fr., 'a bundle'; see **truss** (**I.**). Case for holding a surgeon's smaller instruments.

trousseau, n. [1. tro͞osō; 2. trúsou]. Fr., 'bundle; clothes given to a bride', fr. O. Fr. *trossel,* dimin. of **trousse.** Outfit of clothes, jewellery, and other personal belongings provided for a woman on her marriage.

trout, n. [1. trout; 2. traut]. O.E. *truht,* fr. Lat. *tructa,* fr. Gk. *trṓktēs,* 'a nibbler, gnawer', fr. *trṓgein,* 'to gnaw'; see **troglodyte.** Any of various species of small or moderate-sized edible fish of genus *Salmo,* found in rivers and lakes, whose flesh resembles somewhat that of the salmon, but is more delicate in taste and texture, and of a lighter pink in colour; the colour of the skin varies from silvery white to brown, and is in many species sprinkled with pink spots.

trouvère, n. [1. tro͞ovār; 2. trúvɛə]. O. Fr. & Mod. Fr.; see **troubadour.** One of a school of poets belonging to Northern France, who flourished from 11th to 14th cent., and composed chiefly narrative poems—the so-called 'Chansons de geste'.

trove, adj. [1. trōv; 2. trouv]. O. Fr. *trové,* 'found'. See next word. Only in Phr. *treasure trove,* q.v.

trover, n. [1. trṓver; 2. tróuvə]. O. Fr., 'to find', cp. Mod. Fr. *trouver,* Ital. *trovare,* 'to find'; according to Meyer-Lübke, orig. 'to disturb, frighten, start, stir up (fish), fr. Lat. *turbāre,* 'to disturb', fr. *turba,* 'uproar, disorder, confusion', see **turbid, turbulent.** (law) **1.** Acquisition of personal property by finding or otherwise than by purchase. **2.** Action at law to recover goods, or the value of goods (assumed by a legal fiction to have been found), wrongfully detained.

trow, vb. intrans. [1. trou; 2. trau]. O.E. *trūwian,* 'to trust, believe'; connected w. **true.** (obs. or deliberately archaic) To suppose, believe; generally, *I trow.*

trowel, n. [1. tróuel; 2. tráuil]. Fr. *truelle,* 'mason's trowel', fr. L. Lat. *truella,* dimin. of Lat. *trua,* 'ladle', cp. also Lat. *trulla*; cogn. w. Gk. *torúnē,* 'implement for stirring'; prob. fr. base **twer-,* 'to stir', whence also O.E. *þweran,* 'to stir'; cp. also O.E. *þwirel,* 'a whisk for whipping cream' &c. Connexion w. words in *st-,* e.g. **stir** (**I.**), **storm** (**I.**), is purely speculative. One of various small hand implements, of which the chief are **a** one with a flat blade, usually pointed, for spreading mortar (*mason's trowel*); Phr. *to lay it on with a trowel,* to flatter grossly; **b** one with a hollowed-out blade and sharpened edge for lifting small plants, stirring and scooping out the earth in planting &c. (*gardener's trowel*).

troy, adj. & n. [1. troi; 2. trɔi], fr. Troyes in France. Only in *troy weight*; *so many ounces troy* &c.; indicating method of weighing, standard of weight used for gold and silver, in pounds, ounces, pennyweights, grains; one pound troy consists of 12 oz.

truancy, n. [1. tro͞oansi; 2. trúənsi]. Next word & **-cy. a** Act of playing truant; **b** state of being a truant.

truant, n. & adj. [1. tro͞oant; 2. trúənt]. O. Fr., 'a vagrant'; prob. fr. Celt., cp. W. *truan,* 'wretched'. **1.** n. **a** Person who absents himself from his duties for his own pleasure and without just cause; **b** specif., boy or girl who stays away from school. Phr. *to play truant,* remain away from one's duties, esp. to shirk school. **2.** adj. Shirking duty; staying away from school.

truce, n. [1. tro͞os; 2. trūs]. Apparently fr. M.E. *trēwes,* pl. of *trēwe,* 'fidelity, pledge; truce', fr. *trēwe,* 'true, faithful', see **true** (**I.**). **1.** Cessation of hostilities, generally for a considerable period, by arrangement between the commanders of opposing forces, upon terms agreed upon by both parties; *flag of truce,* a white flag borne by party sent to ask for a truce; *truce of God,* suspension of all warfare, enforced by the Mediaeval Church at stated holy seasons. **2.** Cessation, intermittence; esp. in such Phr. as *a truce to jesting* &c.

truck (**I.**), n. & vb. trans. [1. truk; 2. trak]. M.E. *truken,* 'to exchange'; cp. O. Fr. *troque,* 'exchange, sale, bargain', fr. Flem. *trok,* 'pay; sale'; cp. also A.-Fr. *troquier,* 'to barter'; perh. connected w. Du. *trekken,* 'to draw'; see **trek. 1.** n. **a** Barter, exchange; hence, commerce, intercourse: *to have no truck with a person,* have nothing to do with him; **b** small wares; hence, objects of small value; rubbish, nonsense; *truck system* (of wages), payment in kind instead of in cash; *Truck Acts,* various statutes abolishing the truck system. **2.** vb. (rare) To exchange, barter.

truck (**II.**), n. & vb. trans., fr. Lat. *trochus,* 'an iron hoop', fr. Gk. *trokhós,* 'a wheel', q.v. under **trochee. 1.** n. **a** Any of various strongly built, low vehicles, running on small, strong wheels, used for conveying heavy weights; e.g. (i.) two-wheeled barrow used by railway porters for moving luggage; (ii.) an open waggon on a railway for transporting heavy goods, coal, iron &c.; **b** the framework and wheels upon which a railway carriage is built. **2.** vb. To place (goods) in or on a truck.

truckage, n. [1. trúkij; 2. trákidž]. Prec. & **-age. a** Conveyance of goods by truck; **b** charge made for this.

truckle (**I.**), n. [1. trúkl; 2. trákl]. Dimin. of **truck** (**II.**). **1.** (obs.) A small wheel. **2.** A small cylindrical cheese; also *truckle cheese.* **3.** A truckle-bed.

truckle (**II.**), vb. intrans., fr. prec. Orig., to sleep on a truckle-bed, hence to behave as befits one who sleeps on a truckle-bed, i.e. as one in a servile relation to another. To cringe, behave in a servile, obsequious manner; also *truckle to,* cringe to, submit to (a person) as a servant to his master.

truckle-bed, n. See **truckle** (**I.**). A small, low bed, esp. one on wheels; formerly one occupied by a servant, which could be pushed under that of his master in the daytime.

truckler, n. [1. trúkler; 2. tráklə]. **truckle** (**II.**) & **-er.** One who truckles; a servile, obsequious person.

truculence, -cy, n. [1. trúkūlens(i), tro͞ok-; 2. trákjuləns(i), trúk-]. Lat. *truculentia,* 'savageness, harshness'; next word & **-ce, -cy.** Quality of being truculent.

truculent, adj. [1. trúkūlent, tro͞okūlent; 2. trákjulənt, trúkjulənt], fr. Lat. *truculentus,* 'savage, cruel, harsh, grim, stern', fr. *truc-,* base of *trux,* w. same meaning; the etymol. is uncertain. Fierce, harsh, overbearing, arrogant, haughtily defiant.

truculently, adv. Prec. & **-ly.** In a truculent manner.

trudge, vb. intrans. & n. [1. truj; 2. tradž]. Origin uncertain; the various forms commonly adduced fr. O.N. or Mod. Scand. dial. appear to agree neither in form nor meaning w. the Engl. word. **1.** vb. To walk along laboriously and wearily; to pursue a tedious and tiring course on foot. **2.** n. **a** A long, tedious, laborious walk; **b** a long walk undertaken for the sake of exercise rather than for pleasure: *let's go for a good trudge.*

trudgen, n. [1. trújen; 2. trádžən], fr. J. Trudgen, swimmer who popularized the stroke. Also *trudgen stroke* (erroneously *trudgeon*), swimming stroke in which the arms are brought over the head alternately and the head kept well down.

true (**I.**), adj. [1. tro͞o; 2. trū]. O.E. (*ġe*)*trēowe, -trīewe,* 'faithful, trusty, honest', M.E. *trēwe*;

O.S. *triuwi*; Germ. *trau*; Goth. *triggws*; O.N. *tryggr*. **1.** Faithful, loyal, constant, staunch; reverse of *perfidious*: *good men and true*; *true to one's king, principles*; *a man should remain true to his wife*. Phr. *true as steel*. **2. a** In accordance with fact, veracious; contrasted with *false*: *a true story*; *what you say is not true*; Phrs. *to come true*, to happen as was foretold, be realized in fact; *true as gospel*; **b** (more rarely of persons) adhering to, telling, the truth, truthful; **c** *the true*, something which is true, truth: '*Who battled for the True, the Just*' (Tennyson, 'In Mem.' lv. 5). **3.** Genuine, actual, authentic; not a sham, not counterfeited: '*I am the true vine*'; *a true son of his race*; in accordance with a standard, pattern, ideal; exact, accurate: *a true copy, version, reproduction*; *a true Christian*; *true to type*; *weights and measures ought to be strictly true*; *the true time*.

true (**II.**), adv., fr. prec. **1.** Truly: *tell me true*. **2.** In accordance with ancestral type; of animals, *to breed true*; of plants from seed, *to come true*.

true (**III.**), vb. trans., fr. **true** (**I.**). To make true, accurate; to adjust accurately, make straight &c.: *to true (up) a machine* &c.

true bill, n. A bill of indictment found to be based on prima-facie evidence and endorsed as such by a grand jury.

true-blue, adj. & n. **1.** adj. **a** Of a fast and lasting blue colour; **b** (fig., of persons) adhering rigidly and uncompromisingly to a principle, party &c. **2.** n. **a** True-blue colour; **b** (fig.) true-blue person.

true-bred, adj. **1.** Of pure and genuine breed: *a true-bred West Highland terrier*. **2.** (of persons) Well bred; possessing real breeding in manner, character &c.

true-hearted, adj. Faithful, loyal.

true-love, n. O.E. *trēowlufu*, 'faithful love', M.E. *truelove* &c. Beloved being, sweetheart.

true-love, or **true-lover's**, **knot**, n. Intricate knot of two interlaced bows, hard to untie, symbolical of the lasting nature of love.

trueness, n. [1. tro͞ones; 2. trūnis]. **true** (**I.**) & **-ness**. Quality of being true; **a** truth, veracity; **b** fidelity; **c** accuracy, exactness.

truffle, n. [1. trúfl, tro͞ofl; 2. tráfl, trūfl]. O. Fr. *truffle, truffe*; origin doubtful; perh. connected w. **tuber**. Round, edible fungus, with pungent flavour, growing below the ground, used for flavouring, esp. in pâté de foie gras.

truism, n. [1. tro͞oizm; 2. trūizəm]. **true** (**I.**) & **-ism**. A statement the truth of which is self-evident; a trite saying the truth of which no one disputes, and which it is unnecessary to utter.

trull, n. [1. trul; 2. tral]. Cp. Mod. Germ. *trolle*; variant of **troll** (**II.**). A slatternly, disreputable woman; a low strumpet.

truly, adv. [1. tro͞oli; 2. trūli]. **true** (**I.**) & **-ly**. In a true manner (in various senses); **a** faithfully, loyally: *to serve a person truly*; formula concluding letters: *yours (very) truly*; **b** veraciously: *tell me truly what you think*; **c** genuinely, actually, essentially: *a truly good man*; *to be truly happy*; in Phr. *truly I am puzzled* &c., really, speaking honestly.

trumeau, n. [1. tro͞omō; 2. trūmou]. Fr.; etymol. doubtful; possibly of Gmc. origin. (archit.) Piece of wall or pillar between two windows or other openings in a wall.

trump (**I.**), n. [1. trump; 2. tramp]. M.E. *trumpe, trompe*, Fr. *trompe*; perh. fr. Lat. *triumphus*, see **triumph**. The sound made by a trumpet or a sound resembling this: *the last trump*, that of the day of judgement.

trump (**II.**), n. & vb. trans. & intrans. Ultimately same word as prec. **1.** n. **a** The last card dealt by the dealer, dealt to himself and left face upwards on the table; this and any card of same suit takes any card of other suits; also any card of a suit declared by bidding &c. to be trumps, as at bridge; **b** a card belonging to the trump suit; **c** (fig.) a good-natured, obliging person: *he behaved like a regular trump*. **2.** vb. To take (a trick) with a trump-card.

trump (**III.**), vb. trans. Fr. *tromper*, 'to deceive'; orig. 'to blow a trumpet'. (gen.) *Trump up*, to fabricate, concoct, deliberately and with intent to deceive: *to trump up an accusation, a charge, against*.

trump-card, n. **a** Last card in a pack, dealt to himself by the dealer and turned up; see **trump** (**II.**); **b** (fig.) the chief and most effective means in one's possession of obtaining one's purpose, gaining one's point &c. Phr. *to play one's trump-card*, to make use of one's best weapon for gaining one's end.

trumpery, n. & adj. [1. trúmperi; 2. trámpəri]. Fr. *tromperie*, 'deceit', fr. *tromper*, 'to deceive', same word as that meaning 'to blow a trumpet'. **1.** n. Showy, meretricious object or material, of small value; rubbish; nonsense. **2.** adj. Showy but worthless; rubbishy; weak and ineffective: *trumpery ornaments*; *trumpery arguments*.

trumpet (**I.**), n. [1. trúmpet; 2. trámpit]. M.E. *trompete*, Fr. *trompette*, dimin. of *trompe*, see **trump** (**I.**). **1.** Musical wind instrument consisting of a long metal tube, usually bent several times upon itself, having a mouthpiece, a wide end where the air passes out, and stops worked by the fingers which form the different notes. Phr. *to blow one's own trumpet*, praise oneself. **2.** Instrument shaped like a trumpet, esp. an instrument for intensifying sounds, e.g. an *ear-trumpet*, used for speaking to deaf persons; kind of horn for intensifying sounds produced by a phonograph, gramophone &c., or transmitted by wireless. **3.** Sound produced by a trumpet.

trumpet (**II.**), vb. trans. & intrans., fr. prec. **1.** trans. **a** To proclaim by, or as by, a trumpet; **b** (fig.) to announce widely and loudly: *to trumpet a person's fame abroad*. **2.** intrans. (of elephant) To utter characteristic cry through the trunk.

trumpet-call, n. **a** Call made by sounding a trumpet; **b** (fig.) imperative call or summons to action.

trumpeter, n. [1. trúmpeter; 2. trámpitə]. **trumpet** (**II.**) & **-er**. **1.** One who plays on a trumpet. **2.** One of several kinds of birds with long neck and legs, found in S. America.

trumpet-flower, n. Name applied to various plants with trumpet-shaped flowers, e.g. honeysuckle, datura &c.

trumpeting, n. [1. trúmpeting; 2. trámpitiŋ]. **trumpet** (**II.**) & **-ing**. **a** Sound made by blowing a trumpet; **b** cry made by elephants.

trumpet-shaped, adj. Shaped like a trumpet, i.e. hollow, and broadening gradually from a narrow end towards a broad bell, or cup-shaped mouth.

truncal, adj. [1. trúngkl; 2. tráŋkl]. **trunk** & **-al**. Belonging to the trunk or to the body.

truncate, vb. trans. & adj. [1. trungkāt; 2. traŋkéit]. Lat. *truncātum*, P.P. of *truncāre*, 'to cut off'. See **trunk**. **1.** vb. To cut off, shorten, lop. **2.** adj. Shortened as by lopping; e.g. of spiral shells the point of which is broken or worn off.

truncated, adj. [1. trungkāted; 2. traŋkéitid]. Prec. & **-ed**. **a** Shortened by, or as though by, lopping; maimed; **b** (of writings, speeches &c.) abbreviated, drastically reduced in length, esp. in such a way as to produce effect of incompleteness; mutilated.

truncation, n. [1. trungkāshun; 2. traŋkéiʃən]. **truncate** & **-ion**. Act of truncating.

truncheon, n. [1. trúnshun; 2. tránʃən]. M.E. *tronchoun*, 'broken shaft', O. Fr. *tronchon*, variant of Fr. *tronçon*, fr. L. Lat. formation fr. Lat. *truncus*, 'stem, stock, trunk of a tree' &c.; see **trunk**. A short thick staff or cudgel, esp. one used by policeman; the baton of office of the Earl Marshal.

trundle, n. & vb. trans. & intrans. [1. trúndl; 2. trándl]. O.E. *tryndel, trendel*, 'a ring, a circle, a wheel', cp. *trind(e)*, 'a round lump', & *trendlian*, 'to make round'; cp. **trend** (**I.**). **1.** n. A small broad, strong wheel. **2.** vb. **a** trans. To cause to roll along, to bowl: *to trundle a hoop, a cask* &c.; **b** intrans., to roll, be capable of being rolled.

trundle-bed, n. A low bed on wheels, capable of being easily wheeled about; a truckle-bed.

trunk, n. [1. trungk; 2. traŋk]. Fr. *tronc*, Lat. *truncus*, (1) adj., 'maimed, mutilated'; hence, (2) 'stem or bole of a tree', orig. 'the stem with the boughs lopped off'; etymol. doubtful; possibly fr. same base as O.E. *þringan*, 'to press, crowd', see **throng**. **1.** The main stem of a tree. **2.** The body of a man or an animal, not including the head or limbs. **3.** The main body or line (of railways, telephones; also of an artery) as distinct from side-lines and branches; cp. *trunk call* (on telephone). **4.** Receptacle, with lid on hinges, made of hide, leather, or other materials; esp. as used by travellers for transporting their clothes &c. **5.** (for **trump** (**I.**), cp. Fr. *trompe*) The proboscis, or long tube-like prehensile organ, formed by extension of the nose of an elephant. **6.** (pl.) *Trunks*, trunk-hose.

trunk-hose, n. Short full breeches covering the lower part of the trunk and part of the thighs, as worn in 16th and 17th cents.

trunk-line, n. Main line of a railway, telegraph, or telephone system.

trunnel, n. [1. trúnl; 2. tránəl]. Corrupt variant of tree-nail.

trunnion, n. [1. trúniun; 2. tránjən], fr. Fr. *trognon*, 'core of a fruit'; according to Meyer-Lübke, formed fr. Lat. *truncus*, see **trunk**. One of two parts, or gudgeons, projecting horizontally from either side of a cannon, or other heavy cylindrical apparatus, serving as pivots upon which it rests and by means of which its angle can be altered.

truss (**I.**), n. [1. trus; 2. tras]. Fr. *trousse*, 'bundle', O. Fr. *tros, tourse*, fr. Lat. *thyrsus*, 'stalk, stem', fr. Gk. *thúrsos*, see **thyrsus**. **1.** A bundle, package; esp. *a truss of hay, straw*, oblong package of compressed hay or straw tightly tied with bands of coarse string which pass round it a short distance from either end; *a truss of hay* or *straw* is a specific measure, the former being 60 lb. (new), the latter 36 lb. **2.** A cluster of blossom growing on a single stem. **3.** Combination of timbers or of iron rods forming a rigid framework, used in building and engineering. **4.** Apparatus used to give support by applying continuous pressure in cases of rupture.

truss (**II.**), vb. trans.; see prec. **1.** To bind up into a truss or bundle. **2. a** To tie tightly and secure wings of (a fowl) close to the body before cooking; **b** *truss up*, to tie up limbs close to the body and hang up. **3.** To support (part of building) by a truss, framework, girder &c.

trust (**I.**), n. [1. trust; 2. trast]. M.E. *trust, trist*; prob. Scand., cp. O.N. *traust*, 'confidence'; Swed. *tröst*, 'consolation'; cogn. w. Goth. *trausti*, 'a covenant', & **true** (**I.**). **1.** Firm conviction in another's reliability, integrity, honour; implicit confidence, faith, reliance: '*Put not your trust in princes*'. Phr. *to take something on trust*, to believe that it is what it appears or is asserted to be, without looking closely into the evidence for oneself. **2.** Duty or task, responsibility, committed to, imposed upon, one, which one is morally bound to undertake: *I regard it as a sacred trust to fulfil my father's last wishes*. **3.** Something committed to one's charge and care, to be used for the benefit of another; specif. (law) **a** the vesting of the legal ownership of property in a person or persons, *trustees*, for the benefit of another or others, the *cestui que trust*; **b** property so vested. **4.** A combination of several commercial firms or businesses, effected for the purpose of regulating conditions of business and the price of commodities; or, less justifiably, for the purpose of obtaining control of a particular branch of business activity, and a monopoly of certain articles of commerce.

trust (**II.**), vb. trans. & intrans. M.E. *trusten* &c.; see prec. **A.** trans. **1.** To place reliance, confidence, in; to rely upon; have faith in integrity of: *I trust him as I would myself*; *not a man to be trusted.* **2.** To allow to do something, or go somewhere, with full assurance that one's confidence will not be abused: *he may be trusted to do the work well*; *I wouldn't trust that man round the corner.* **3. a** To entrust (a person) with something: *I should not like to trust him with large sums of money*; **b** to entrust (a thing) to the care of: *I wouldn't trust my watch to him.* **4.** To have a confident expectation that something will happen, or does exist, or is in the condition that one desires; to hope: *I trust (that) nothing will prevent our meeting*; *I do trust you will be successful*; *I trust this is the book you wanted*; also absol., *you are feeling better, I trust.* **5.** To have a firm conviction that, to believe: '*The knight's bones are dust, And his good sword rust, His soul is with the saints, I trust*' (Coleridge, 'Knight's Tomb'). **B.** intrans. To perform the mental act of trusting: *it is hard to trust where respect is lacking.*

trustee, n. [1. trustḗ; 2. trastí]. **trust** (I.) & **-ee.** **1.** One to whom a trust is committed: *we are trustees of our country's honour.* **2.** One holding property in trust for another.

trustful, adj. [1. trústfool; 2. trástful]. **trust** (I.) & **-ful.** Disposed to trust, confiding.

trustfully, adv. Prec. & **-ly.** In a trustful manner.

trustiness, n. [1. trústines; 2. trástinis]. **trusty** & **-ness.** Quality of being trusty.

trustless, adj. [1. trústles; 2. trástlis]. **trust** (I.) & **-less.** Not to be trusted; unreliable, disloyal.

trustworthiness, n. [1. trústwërdhines; 2. trástwə̄ðinis]. See next word & **-ness.** Reliability, dependability.

trustworthy, adj. [1. trústwërdhi; 2. trástwə̄ði]. **trust** (I.) & **worthy** (I.). **a** (of persons) Worthy of trust; reliable, dependable, honourable; **b** (of statements) worthy of credence, consonant with fact, accurate.

trusty, adj. [1. trústi; 2. trásti]. **trust** (I.) & **-y.** **a** (of persons) Deserving to be trusted; faithful, loyal, staunch: *a trusty servant*; **b** (archaic, of things) reliable, to be counted on to serve their purpose: *my trusty sword, steed.*

truth, n. [1. trōōth; 2. trūþ]. O.E. *trēoþ*, *trīewþ*, 'good faith, fidelity', M.E. *treuþe*; see **true** (I.) & **-th.** **1.** Moral quality of being true and honest; sincerity, loyalty, trustiness: *to doubt a person's truth.* **2.** Conformity to fact and reality to the utmost extent that these are discoverable by the human mind; verity. **3.** Conformity to fact in statement; veracity; the reverse of *a lie*: *to tell, speak, the truth*; *the truth is, you ought never to have come.* **4. a** Ascertained fact in science; sound, reliable doctrine in religion, esp. as known by revelation: *biological truth*; *Gospel, Christian, truth*; **b** an established principle or law: *the great truths of morals, science, philosophy* &c. **5.** Accuracy, exactness, in formation and adjustment in mechanism; esp. in Phr. *out of truth.*

truthful, adj. [1. trōōthfool; 2. trūþful]. Prec. & **-ful.** **a** (of persons) Habitually speaking the truth, veracious; **b** (of statements) in accordance with the truth, true.

truthfully, adv. Prec. & **-ly.** In a truthful manner; in accordance with truth; with truth, veraciously.

truthfulness, n. See prec. & **-ness.** Quality of being true; veracity.

try (I.), vb. trans. & intrans. [1. trī; 2. trai]. M.E. *trīen*, 'to select'; cp. Fr. *trier*, 'to set apart, select', fr. L. Lat. *trītāre*, 'to rub down, separate the grain from the husk'; formed fr. *trīt-*, P.P. type of *terere*, 'to rub, grind, thresh', q.v. under **trite.** **A.** trans. **1.** (obs.) To pick out (the best) from the rest; to separate one sort from another. **2.** Also *try out*, to separate the dross from the ore, impure matter from the pure substance; to refine; to assay, test purity of (metals); also of whale blubber, so as to extract the oil. **3. a** To test (qualities), put to the test or proof: *to try one's skill, strength*; **b** to put a strain upon; make demands upon: *his patience, courage, was severely tried*; *it tries the eyes to read in a bad light*; **c** to afflict, cause suffering to: *he has been very sorely tried*; *rheumatism tries me a good deal.* **4. a** To make use of in order to test properties of, to find out by using how far something will serve one's purpose, prove a remedy, be to one's taste &c.: *I have tried all the makes of safety razor blades*; *try our pills for dyspepsia*; *have you tried tea with a slice of lemon in it?*; **b** *try on*, (i.) to test fit of (clothes) by putting them on: *to try a coat on*; *to try on a new coat*; (ii.) *to try it on*, to do something audacious, to test how far one will be allowed to go. **5.** To make an effort to do, to attempt: *he tried an impossible feat*; *don't try more than you can do.* **6.** To test by means of experiment, to carry out an experiment in order to discover: *try which is the highest note you can sing*; *try how far you can jump.* **7. a** To conduct judicial inquiry into, hear arguments concerning, in a court of law: *to try a case*; **b** to conduct trial of, inquire into innocence or guilt of: *to try a criminal.* **B.** intrans. To endeavour, exert oneself, make an attempt or effort (to do something): *I doubt if I can do it, but I'll try*; *I have never tried to ski*; *he makes very little progress though he tries hard*; *try to please your employers, to do your duty*; frequently *try and* (in colloq. speech): *try and be punctual*; *now try and repeat it correctly*; *do try and behave better*; Phr. *to try one's best, one's hardest*, do as well as one can; use one's utmost efforts.

try (II.), n. See prec. **1.** (colloq.) An attempt: *have a try at.* **2.** (Rugby football) Touch down behind opponent's goal and within the touch-in-goal, on which the ball is brought out and a place kick is taken aimed between the goal-posts, above the cross-bar; a try, if not thus converted, counts 3 points, as opposed to 5 for a goal.

trying, adj. [1. trīing; 2. tráiiŋ], fr. Pres. Part. of **try** (I.). **1.** Tending to try, test, put a strain upon; (i.) provoking, exasperating: *trying to the temper*; *a trying person to deal with*; (ii.) exacting: *a trying bit of work.* **2. a** Fatiguing, irksome, wearisome: *a trying journey*; **b** afflicting, grievous, painful: *a trying time, situation, experience.*

trypanosome, n. [1. trípanosōm; 2. trípənəsoum], fr. Gk. *trúpanon*, 'borer, piercer', see **trepan** (I.), & *sôma*, 'body', see **somatic.** A minute whip-like parasite, belonging to the genus *Trypanosoma*, transmitted to the blood of man and animals by the bite of the tsetse-fly, q.v., and causing disease (see below).

trypanosomiasis, n. [1. trìpanōsōmíasis; 2. trìpənousoumáiəsis]. Prec. & **-iasis.** Disease caused by presence of a trypanosome in the blood, specif., sleeping sickness in man, nagana in cattle.

trypsin, n. [1. trípsin; 2. trípsin]. Invented Germ. word fr. Gk. *trīein*, 'to rub, consume', cogn. w. Lat. *terere*, see **trite**, & **pepsin.** (physiol.) A digestive ferment or enzyme formed in the pancreatic juice.

trysail, n. [1. trísl; 2. tráisl]. **try** (I.) & **sail** (I.). A small fore-and-aft sail attached to a gaff.

tryst, n. & vb. trans. & intrans. [1. trīst, trist; 2. traist, trist]. M.E., fr. O. Fr. *triste, tristre*, 'waiting or watching place'; prob. of Scand. origin, see **trust** (I.). **1.** n. **a** Engagement to meet; **b** agreed upon, appointed, meeting-place. **2.** vb. To promise to meet at agreed time and place.

tsar. See **czar.**

tsetse-fly, n. [1. tsétsi flī; 2. tsétsi flai]. Cape Du. fr. Native Afr. An African fly, *Glossina*, which acts as intermediate host of the parasitic trypanosome, q.v., and thus infects the blood of man and animals, one species being the carrier of sleeping sickness, to man, another of nagana, q.v., or tsetse-fly disease, to cattle.

tuatara, n. [1. tooatáhra; 2. tuətā́rə]. Maori. A large lizard-like reptile, genus *Sphenodon*, once common in New Zealand.

tub, n. & vb. intrans. [1. tub; 2. tab]. M.E. *tubbe*, cp. Du. *tobbe*; perh. fr. Lat. *tubus*, see **tube.** **1.** n. **a** Wooden vessel made in various shapes, often in form of a cask; used for various purposes, e.g. *wash-tub, butter-tub, rain-water tub* &c.; **b** (colloq.) a bath: *to take one's tub, a cold tub, every morning*; **c** boat used in practising rowing; **d** a kind of bucket or box used for conveying coal or ore in mines from the workings to the shaft. **2.** vb. (colloq.) To take a bath.

tuba, n. [1. tū́ba; 2. tjū́bə]. Lat., 'trumpet'; see **tube.** **a** A type of brass wind musical instrument with deep tone, including the bombardon and euphonium; **b** a reed stop in an organ.

tubal, adj. [1. tū́bl; 2. tjū́bl]. **tube** & **-al.** Pertaining to, connected with, a tube.

tubby, adj. [1. túbi; 2. tábi]. **tub** & **-y.** **1.** Shaped like a tub; fat, squat, and round. **2.** (of musical instruments) Lacking resonance, giving out a dull sound.

tube, n. [1. tūb; 2. tjūb]. Lat. *tubus*, 'a pipe, tube'; cogn. w. *tuba*, 'trumpet'; etymol. uncertain. **1. a** Long hollow cylinder, or pipe, of any size, of various materials, and used for many purposes: *glass tube, metal tube*; *a tube of paint*; *vacuum tube* &c.; **b** an organ of the body in form of a tube; esp. *bronchial tubes.* **2.** Underground electric railway system in London, the lines of which are laid in enormous steel tubes.

tuber, n. [1. tū́ber; 2. tjū́bə]. Lat., 'a bump, swelling, protuberance'; contains the same base ***tu-** as **tumid, tumour**, w. different formative elements. Modified part of stem of certain plants, such as the potato and Jerusalem artichoke, containing buds whence new plants are formed.

tubercle, n. [1. tū́berkl; 2. tjū́bəkl]. Lat. *tuberculum*, dimin. of **tuber.** **1.** Small rounded protuberance on part of an animal or plant. **2.** (pathol.) Small granular morbid growth in the substance of an organ of the body, such as the lungs, causing the disease known as *tuberculosis.*

tubercular, adj. [1. tūbërkūlar; 2. tjubə́kjulə]. Prec. & **-ar.** **a** Connected with, of the nature of, a tubercle; **b** affected by tuberculosis; tuberculous.

tubercularize, vb. trans. [1. tūbërkūlarīz; 2. tjubə́kjuləraiz]. Prec. & **-ize.** To infect with tubercle or tuberculosis.

tuberculosis, n. [1. tūbërkūlṓsis; 2. tjubə̀kjulóusis]. Formed fr. Lat. *tubercul-*, see **tubercle**, & **-osis.** Infectious disease of the tissues of an organ of the body caused by the tubercle bacillus, which produces disintegration of the organ or part affected, as *pulmonary tuberculosis*, phthisis &c.

tuberculous, adj. [1. tūbërkūlus; 2. tjubə́kjuləs]. See prec. & **-ous.** **a** Having tubercles; **b** affected by tuberculosis.

tuberose, n. [1. tū́berōz; 2. tjū́bərouz]. Orig., an adj., fr. **tuber** & **-ose.** See also **tuberous.** Bulbous plant, *Polianthes tuberosa*, resembling a lily, cultivated in gardens for its spikes of blossom.

tuberosity, n. [1. tūberósiti; 2. tjūbərɔ́siti]. See prec., **tuberous**, & **-ity.** Quality of being tuberous.

tuberous, adj. [1. tū́berus; 2. tjū́bərəs]. **tuber** & **-ous.** **a** Producing, growing from, tubers; **b** covered with rounded excrescences; knobby.

tubing, n. [1. tū́bing; 2. tjū́biŋ]. **tube** & **-ing.** **1.** A series, collection, system, of tubes. **2.** A length, portion, piece, of tube: *india-rubber tubing.*

tubular, adj. [1. tū́būlar; 2. tjū́bjulə]. Lat. *tubulus*, dimin. of *tubus*, 'tube', & **-ar.** **a** Having the form of a tube or pipe; **b** provided with tubes.

tubule, n. [1. tū́būl; 2. tjū́bjūl]. Lat. *tubulus*, see prec. A small tube.

tuck (I.), vb. trans. & intrans. [1. tuk; 2. tak]. M.E. *tucken*, 'to pull, draw'; usually derived

tuck (II.) by dictionary makers fr. Continental Gmc.; but it is possibly fr. O.E. *tūcian*, ' to afflict ', the primary meaning of wh. may well have been ' to pluck, tug, pull ' ; cp. provinc. Engl. ' to tuck peas, beans, fruit &c.', i.e. to pluck, gather. The word is prob. an anct. doublet fr. base **tug-*, ' pull, draw ' &c. See **tow (I.)** & **tug (I.). A.** trans. **1.** To gather (loose folds of cloth or garments, loose ends of cord, line &c.) together tightly, and push away out of sight behind other folds, or under something firmly fixed ; also *tuck in* : to tuck one's *handkerchief into one's pocket* ; *tuck up*, to fold back and fasten firmly, as to *tuck up one's shirt-sleeves* ; *to tuck a child up in bed*, pull the sheets and blankets well over him and push the ends under mattress ; *tuck away*, to place securely and neatly ; also to hide away where discovery is difficult : *a great deal of learning is tucked away in the notes (of the book)*. **2.** (new formation from n.) To put a tuck or tucks in (a sleeve &c.). **B.** intrans. **1.** To make tucks. **2.** (colloq.) *a Tuck in*, to eat hungrily and copiously ; **b** *tuck into*, trans.

tuck (II.), n., fr. prec. **1.** Permanent fold or hem, made and sewed, in a skirt, in the sleeve of a shirt &c. **2.** (schoolboy slang) Food, esp. food of an attractive character, eaten rather from greed than hunger ; sweetmeats, cakes ; tasty meats, delicacies.

tuck (III.), n. Fr. *toquer*, Nthn. form of *toucher*, see **touch (I.)**, & cp. **tocsin**. The sound, roll, of a drum.

tucker, n. [1. túkər ; 2. tákə]. **tuck (I.)** & **-er. 1.** Piece of linen formerly worn by women, folded across the breast ; now only in Phr. *one's best bib and tucker*, best, smartest, clothes. **2.** Device for making tucks in clothes.

tucket, n. [1. túket ; 2. tákit]. Cp. Ital. *toccata*, ' a prelude ', P.P. fem. of *toccare* ; see **touch**. A flourish of trumpets, a fanfare.

tuck-shop, n. Shop at a school where ' tuck ' is sold ; a confectioner's, a sweet shop.

-tude, suff. Lat. *-tūdō*, genit. *-tūdinis* ; suff. used to form abstract ns. fr. Lat. adjs. or P.P.'s : *plenitude*, fr. Lat. *plēnum*, ' full ', &c.

Tudor, adj. [1. túdor ; 2. tjúdə], fr. name of a family descended fr. Owen Tudor, members of wh. occupied the throne of England & included all monarchs fr. Henry VII. to Elizabeth inclusive. Pertaining to, made in, characteristic of, the age of the Tudors : *Tudor architecture*, *style* &c. ; *Tudor rose*, one combining the red rose of Lancaster and the white rose of York, used as royal badge of England after marriage of Henry VII. (of Lancaster) with Elizabeth, heiress of York.

Tuesday, n. [1. túzdi ; 2. tjúzdi]. O.E. *Tīwesdæg*, M.E. *Tēwesday*, fr. *Tīw*, the name of an anct. Gmc. war god ; the name is cogn. w. Gk. *Zeús*, Lat. *Jū-piter* ; see **jovial** & **Jupiter** & **deity**. Third day of the week, between Monday and Wednesday.

tufa, n. [1. túfa ; 2. tjúfə]. Cp. Ital. *tufo*, ' soft ', fr. Lat. *tōfus, tōphus*, ' volcanic rock ' ; Oscan-Umbrian loan-word ; origin unknown. Porous rock of volcanic origin, also called ' tuff '.

tufaceous, adj. [1. tūfáshus ; 2. tjūféiʃəs]. Prec. & **-aceous**. Connected with, resembling, tufa.

tuff. See **tufa**.

tuft (I.), n. [1. tuft ; 2. taft]. M.E. *tuft* ; origin doubtful ; perh. connected w. **top (I.)**. **1.** A bunch, bundle, cluster, of anything resembling threads, fastened together at the base or growing thickly from a common point : *a tuft of feathers, grass, hair*. **2.** (obs. slang) A person of importance, a swell ; from the *tuft* or gold tassel formerly worn in their college caps by noblemen at English universities.

tuft (II.), vb. trans. & intrans., fr. prec. *a* trans. **1.** To furnish with tufts ; **b** intrans., to form, grow, into tufts.

tufted, adj. [1. túfted ; 2. táftid], fr. P.P. of prec. *a* Having, provided with, a tuft or tufts ; **b** growing thickly in tufts.

tuft-hunter, n. See **tuft (I.)**, **2.** (archaic) One who seeks the acquaintance of, and behaves obsequiously to, persons of importance, wealth, or distinguished birth, formerly called ' tufts ' ; a toady, a sycophant.

tufty, adj. [1. túfti ; 2. táfti]. **tuft (I.)** & **-y**. Growing in, forming, tufts.

tug (I.), vb. trans. & intrans. [1. tug ; 2. tag]. M.E. *tuggen* ; Scand., cp. O.N. *toga*, ' to pull ' ; cogn. w. **tow (I.)**. **1.** trans. *a* To pull violently ; to exert effort, to strain, in pulling ; to haul ; **b** to pull suddenly and jerkily. **2.** intrans. To exert effort in pulling ; often *tug at*.

tug (II.), n., fr. prec. **1.** The act of tugging ; a sudden, violent pull. **2.** Small steamer with powerful engines, used to tow large vessels into, or out of, a harbour &c.

tug of war, n. [1. tùg uv wŏr ; 2. tág əv wɔ́]. Contest of strength in which each of two parties, pulling in different directions on the same rope, attempts to pull the other across a line marked on the ground.

tuition, n. [1. tūíshun ; 2. tjuíʃən]. Lat. *tuitiōn-(em)*, ' a looking after, guardianship, defence ' ; fr. *tuit-(um)*, P.P. of *tuēri*, ' to look after, guard, protect ' ; see **tutor (I.)**. **1.** (archaic or obs.) Guardianship, care of a pupil or ward. **2. a** Act of teaching ; **b** instruction given by a tutor or teacher.

tulip, n. [1. túlip ; 2. tjúlip]. Fr. *tulipe*, O. Fr. *tulipan*, cp. Ital. *tulipano*, fr. Turk. *tulbend*, ' turban ', fr. supposed resemblance of flower to this ; see **turban**. Liliaceous plant with many species, genus *Tulipa*, growing from bulbs, and having bright-coloured bell-shaped flowers, supported on stiff stalks.

tulip root, n. Disease in oats characterized by a swelling in the stem resembling the bulb of a tulip.

tulip tree, n. N. American tree, *Liriodendron tulipiferum*, allied to the magnolia, with red or yellow flowers resembling those of the tulip.

tulip wood, n. Wood of tulip tree, used in cabinet-making.

tulle, n. [1. tool ; 2. tul], fr. name of a town in France. Soft, silky material, used for making women's garments.

tulwar, n. [1. túlwar ; 2. tálwə]. Hindi. Kind of curved sabre used among N. Indian tribes.

tumble (I.), vb. intrans. & trans. [1. túmbl ; 2. támbl]. Apparently a freq. form fr. O.E. *tumbian*, ' to dance, tumble ' ; cp. also Du. *tuimelen*, ' to fall ', & Swed. *tumla*. **A.** intrans. **1. a** To fall heavily and clumsily ; also *tumble down* ; *tumble over*, (i.) to fall down, be upset ; (ii.) to stumble, trip up over (an obstacle) : *to tumble over a hassock* ; **b** to move forward in a disorderly, violent manner, to rush helter-skelter : *to tumble into a room anyhow*. **2.** To toss about, roll over, as with restlessness and discomfort : often *to tumble and toss*. **3.** To turn somersaults, as an acrobat. **4.** (slang) *Tumble to* (a suggestion &c.), to take in, grasp, understand. **B.** trans. **1.** To cause to tumble ; to overturn, upset, throw down ; frequently, *tumble over (something)* : *his horse tumbled him over a bank* ; also *tumble out* : *to tumble passengers out of a carriage*. **2.** To put into confusion, disturb, rumple, ruffle : *to tumble a bed*, *one's clothes, hair* &c.

tumble (II.), n., fr. prec. Act of tumbling ; *a* a fall, a toss ; **b** an acrobat's somersault &c.

tumble-down, adj. [1. túmbl doun ; 2. támbl daun]. Dilapidated, ruinous, shabby : *a tumble-down house*.

tumbler, n. [1. túmbler ; 2. támblə]. **tumble (I.)** & **-er**. **1.** An acrobat who throws somersaults. **2.** Kind of domestic pigeon which makes movements resembling somersaults while in flight. **3.** One of several movable portions of the internal mechanism of a lock, which has to be made to occupy a certain position by the working of the key before the bolt can be shot. **4.** Drinking-glass without a foot, standing flat on its own bottom.

tumbrel, -il, n. [1. túmbril ; 2. támbril]. Connected w. Fr. *tomber*, ' to fall ', of Gmc. origin ; cp. O.E. *tumbian*, ' to dance, tumble ', & see **tumble (I.)**. *a* A heavy cart, made to tip backwards from the shafts, for carting and shooting dung and refuse &c. ; **b** name given by historians to the carts in which the victims of the French Revolution were taken to the guillotine ; **c** light two-wheeled military cart for carrying ammunition, tools &c.

tumefacient, adj. [1. tūmefásient ; 2. tjūmiféisiənt]. Lat., Pres. Part. of *tumefacere*, ' to cause to swell, to inflate ' ; see **tumid** & **fact**. Causing swelling.

tumefaction, n. [1. tūmefákshun ; 2. tjūmifǽkʃən]. Lat., fr. *tumefact-(um)*, P.P. type of *tumefacere*, see prec., & **-ion**. **1.** The process of swelling. **2.** A swelling, a tumour.

tumefy, vb. trans. & intrans. [1. túmefī ; 2. tjūmifai]. Fr. *tuméfier* ; see under **tumid** & **-fy**. *a* trans. To cause to swell ; **b** intrans., to swell up.

tumescent, adj. [1. tūmésent ; 2. tjūmésənt]. Lat., Pres. Part. of *tumescere*, ' to begin to swell, swell up ', inchoat. of *tumēre*, ' to swell ' ; see **tumid**. Inclined to swell up ; slightly swollen.

tumid, adj. [1. túmid ; 2. tjúmid]. Lat. *tumidus*, ' swollen, protuberant ' ; cp. Lat. *tumēre*, ' to swell ' ; *tumor*, ' swelling, protuberance ', see **tumour** ; *tumulus*, ' raised heap of earth ' ; w. this base etymologists connect a large number of words ; O.E. *þūma*, see **thumb** ; O.E. *þēoh*, see **thigh** ; see further **thousand** & **taurus**. Puffed up, swollen, inflated (in material and non-material senses).

tumidity, n. [1. tūmíditi ; 2. tjūmíditi]. Prec. & **-ity**. State of being tumid.

tumour, n. [1. túmor ; 2. tjúmə]. Lat. *tumor*, ' a swelling ; protuberance ' ; see under **tumid**. A swelling in some part of the body ; an abnormal growth and increase of size in some of the tissues, whether benign or malignant.

tumult, n. [1. túmult ; 2. tjúmalt]. Lat. *tumultus*, ' an uproar, violent commotion, disturbance ' ; fr. base **tum-*, ' to swell ', see **tumid**. **1. a** Uproar, confused noise, as that made by the voices and movements of large crowds ; hence, **b** the noise of a disturbance ; a disturbance, commotion, turbulence. **2.** Profound and violent disturbance, agitation, commotion, *a* of the forces of nature ; **b** of the mind ; great mental excitement and confusion.

tumultuary, adj. [1. tūmúltūari ; 2. tjumáltjuəri]. Lat. *tumultuārius*, see prec. & **-ary**. Of the nature of a tumult ; confused ; agitated.

tumultuous, adj. [1. tūmúltūus ; 2. tjumáltjuəs]. Lat. *tumultuōsus*, ' full of bustle and confusion ; turbulent, restless ' ; see **tumult** & **-ous**. **1.** Characterized by tumult and disturbance ; uproarious, noisy : *a tumultuous meeting, assembly*. **2.** Greatly agitated, deeply stirred : *tumultuous passions*.

tumultuously, adv. Prec. & **-ly**. In a tumultuous manner.

tumultuousness, n. See prec. & **-ness**. State, quality, of being tumultuous.

tumulus, n., pl. **tumuli** [1. túmŭlus, -ī ; 2. tjúmjuləs, -ai]. Lat., ' heap of earth, a mound ' ; fr. base ' to swell ', as in **tumid** &c. An artificially raised mound, esp. an ancient burial mound or barrow.

tun, n. & vb. trans. [1. tun ; 2. tan]. O.E. *tunne*, ' a cask ' ; also in O.H.G. &c. ; origin doubtful. **1.** n. A large cask or vat for storing, also for fermenting, beer and wine ; formerly a specific measure of 252 gallons. **2.** vb. To enclose and store in a tun.

tuna, n. [1. túna ; 2. tjúnə]. Span. form of **tunny**. The great tunny, esp. of the Pacific, Californian, coast of N. America.

tunable, adj. [1. túnabl ; 2. tjúnəbl]. **tune (II.)** & **-able**. *a* Capable of being tuned ; **b** capable of yielding a tune ; hence, melodious : *a tunable voice*.

tunableness, n. Prec. & -ness. Quality of being tunable.

tunably, adv. See prec. & -ly. Harmoniously, melodiously.

tundra, n. [1. túndra; 2. tándrə]. Russ. Barren plain in N. Russia or other arctic region, constituting a frozen, or partially frozen, desert, which produces only mosses and lichens in the way of vegetation.

tundun, n. [1. túndun; 2. tándan]. Native. The bull-roarer, q.v., of Australian aborigines.

tune (I.), n. [1. tūn; 2. tjūn]. M.E., fr. A.-Fr. *tune*, fr. O. Fr. *ton*; variant of **tone** (I.). **1. a** Air, melody, with or without harmony : *a good, a poor, a catchy, popular, tune* ; *a difficult tune to remember* ; **b** quality of having a well-marked air : *the piece has very little tune about it*. **2.** Harmony, agreement in tone, pitch &c., with a definite standard : *to sing in, out of, tune* ; *your fiddle isn't in tune*. Phrs. (fig.) *in tune, out of tune, with* (one's surroundings &c.), congenial, uncongenial ; *to be charged to the tune of* (such an amount), implying extortionate charge ; *to sing another tune, change one's tune*, change one's way of talking ; as from respectful to insolent or vice versa &c.

tune (II.), vb. trans. & intrans., fr. prec. **A.** trans. **1. a** To bring (musical instrument) into tune, adjust the pitch of the strings &c. to the required degree ; **b** *tune up*, to bring to a desired degree, or standard, of efficiency, excellence, health &c. **2.** To bring (wireless apparatus) into relation with waves of a certain length. **B.** intrans. **1.** *Tune in*, to tune wireless apparatus (see **resonance**). **2.** *Tune up*, **a** (of instruments in orchestra) to start tuning ; **b** to begin to play or to sing.

tuneful, adj. [1. túnfool; 2. tjūnful]. **tune** (I.) & -ful. **a** Exhibiting a well-marked air ; **b** melodious, harmonious ; producing song and melody : *the tuneful choir of birds* &c.

tunefully, adv., fr. prec. Prec. & -ly. In a tuneful manner.

tunefulness, n. See prec. & -ness. Quality of being tuneful.

tuneless, adj. [1. túnles; 2. tjūnlis]. **tune** (I.) & -less. **a** Lacking an air ; harsh, unmelodious ; **b** not producing melody, unmusical.

tuner, n. [1. túner; 2. tjūnə]. **tune** (II.) & -er. **1.** One who tunes musical instruments : *piano tuner* &c. **2. a** Device attached to pipe for tuning an organ ; **b** device for tuning electrical current &c.

tungsten, n. [1. túngsten; 2. táŋstən]. Swed., fr. *tung*, 'heavy', & *sten*, 'stone'. A rare metallic element, found in combination with other minerals, grey in colour and very hard, and only fusible at very high temperatures, used in an alloy of steel and for making the filaments of incandescent electric lamps.

tungstic, tungstous, adj. [1. túngstik, túngstus; 2. táŋstik, táŋstəs], fr. prec. & -ic, -ous. (chem.) Of, pertaining to, tungsten.

tunic, n. [1. túnik; 2. tjūnik]. Lat. *tunica*, 'thin undergarment with sleeves' (worn by both sexes); also 'coating, membrane, husk'; fr. early form *ktun-ica, Heb. loan-word ; cp. also Gk. *khitōn*, fr. Heb. *kithonet*, 'garment worn next skin', cp. **chiton**. **1.** Any of various loose garments, esp. as worn by the ancients or modern Orientals. **2.** Regimental coat worn by British officers and private soldiers ; the name is properly restricted to one particular kind of coat, namely, that worn for full dress, made of scarlet cloth. **3.** Natural covering, integument, husk.

Tunicata, n. pl. [1. tùnikātā; 2. tjūnikéitə]. Lat., 'covered by a tunic, coated'; see prec. Group of marine animals with thick outer covering, membrane, or tunic.

tunicate, adj. & n. [1. túnikāt; 2. tjūnikeit]. See prec. **1.** adj. (bot. and zool.) Having several coats or layers of covering. **2.** n. Member of the group of Tunicata.

tunicle, n. [1. túnikl; 2. tjūnikl]. Lat. *tunicula*, dimin. of *tunica*, see **tunic**. **1.** Closefitting vestment, smaller than the dalmatic, worn by deacons at Eucharist, and by bishops under the dalmatic when pontificating. **2.** Thin, natural, outer covering.

tuning-fork, n. [1. túning fork; 2. tjūniŋ fɔ̄k]. Instrument of steel with two prongs, which, on being struck, gives out a particular note ; used as a standard in tuning musical instruments.

tunnel, n. & vb. trans. & intrans. [1. túnl; 2. tánl]. O. Fr. *tonnel*, dimin. of *tonne*, see **tun**. **1.** n. A passage, usually cylindrical in form, cut underground ; e.g. one cut through a hill or mountain for the laying of a railway line &c. **2.** vb. **a** trans. To cut a tunnel through : *to tunnel a hill* &c. ; **b** intrans., to cut a tunnel.

tunny, n., also **tunny fish** [1. túni (fish) ; 2. táni (fiʃ)]. Ital. *tonno*, Lat. *thunnus*, fr. Gk. *thúnnos*, also *thûnos* ; origin obscure ; prob., according to Boisacq, a pre-Hellenic loan-word. Large, edible fish of the mackerel family, with somewhat oily flesh, found in Mediterranean, also, as the great tunny, *Thunnus thynnus*, in the Atlantic, where it is known as 'horse-mackerel', and in the N. Pacific, the tuna.

tup, n. [1. tup ; 2. tap]. M.E. *tuppe* ; origin doubtful. A ram.

tu quoque, n. [1. tū kwókwe; 2. tjū kwóukwi]. Lat., 'thou also'. A retort of 'you are, or did, the same as I', so you can't blame me.

Turanian, adj. [1. tūrănian; 2. tjuréiniən]. Of race and language, Ural-Altaic, q.v.

turban, n. [1. térban; 2. tə́bən]. Earlier *turbant, turband* ; cp. Ital. *turbante*, fr. Turk. *tulbend*. See also **tulip**. **1.** Head-dress worn by men in the East consisting of a long strip of silk, or cotton cloth, wound round and round the head. **2.** Woman's head-dress, resembling the Oriental turban, worn at end of 18th and beginning of 19th cent.

turbary, n. [1. térbəri ; 2. tə́bəri]. Low Lat. *turbāria*, 'place where peat is dug', fr. *turba*, 'turf, peat'; see **turf**. **a** Right to dig turf or peat on the land of another ; **b** place where peat is dug.

turbid, adj. [1. térbid ; 2. tə́bid]. Lat. *turbidus*, 'confused, disordered ; thick, muddy'; cp. *turbāre*, 'to confuse, bewilder', also *turba*, 'uproar, confusion, tumult ; a crowd'. See **turbinal, turbulent**, & cp. **thorp**. **a** (of liquids) Having the sediment disturbed ; hence thick, muddy ; **b** (fig.) confused, disturbed ; lacking clarity.

turbidity, n. [1. térbidĭti; 2. tə́bíditi]. Prec. & -ity. Condition, quality, of being turbid.

turbidly, adv. [1. térbidli ; 2. tə́bidli]. **turbid** & -ly. In a turbid manner.

turbidness, n. [1. térbidnes ; 2. tə́bidnis]. See prec. & -ness. Turbidity.

turbinal, adj. [1. térbinal; 2. tə́binəl]. Lat. *turbin-*, stem of *turbō*, 'violent, circular motion ; something that spins, a top ; something spiral and twisted, a whorl', & -al ; perh. fr. same base as *turba*, 'uproar' &c. See **turbid**. (anat. and zool.) Having the form of a spiral or scroll.

turbinate, adj. [1. térbināt ; 2. tə́bineit]. *turbin-*, as in prec., & -ate. **1.** Whirling like a top. **2.** Shaped like a top or like an inverted cone. **3.** (anat.) Of some bones, scroll-shaped.

turbination, n. [1. térbināshun ; 2. tə̀binéiʃən]. Prec. & -ion. **1.** Act or movement of spinning like a top. **2.** Something turbinate in shape.

turbine, n. [1. térbīn ; 2. tə́bain]. Lat. *turbin-*, see **turbinal**. Wheel, serving as a motor, which is rotated by means of a stream of water or steam, under pressure over rotating vanes on the shaft, and thus used to generate electric power or to drive a steamship &c.

turbit, n. [1. térbit ; 2. tə́bit]. Origin doubtful. Kind of fancy pigeon with short head and beak and a frill.

turbot, n. [1. térbot ; 2. tə́bət]. Fr., O. Fr. *torbout*; perh. fr. Lat. *turbō*, 'top', see **turbinal**, fr. shape of the fish, & obscure suff. ; cp. **halibut**. Large flat sea-fish, with firm, white flesh much sought after as food.

turbulence, n. [1. térbūlens ; 2. tə́bjuləns]. Lat. *turbulentia*, see next word & -ce. **a** Turbulent conduct ; unruliness, commotion ; **b** unsettled social or civic condition ; lack of order, discipline, and quiet ; disturbance, lawlessness.

turbulent, adj. [1. térbūlent ; 2. tə́bjulənt]. Fr., fr. Lat. *turbulentus*, fr. *turba*, 'disorder, confusion' &c., see **turbinal** & cp. **turbid**. **a** In commotion, in violent movement, fiercely agitated : *turbulent waves* ; **b** unruly, vehement, boisterous, ill-controlled : *a turbulent character* ; *turbulent passions* &c. ; **c** uproarious, insubordinate, disorderly : *a turbulent mob*.

Turcophil(e), adj. & n. [1. térkōfil ; 2. tə́koufil]. **Turk** & -phil(e). **1.** adj. Admiring the Turks and their political and social qualities. **2.** n. A Turcophil person.

Turcophobe, adj. & n. [1. térkōfōb ; 2. tə́koufoub]. See prec. & -phobe. **1.** adj. Hating and fearing the Turks, their civilization, political influence &c. **2.** n. A Turcophobe person.

turdine, adj. [1. térdīn ; 2. tə́dain]. Lat. *turdus*, 'a thrush', for *tṛzdos* ; cp. Lith. *strāsdas* ; O.N. *þröstr*; O.E. *prostle*, see **throstle** & **thrush**, & cp. **struthious**. Connected with the thrush genus, *Turdus*, or family, *Turdidae*, of birds including the thrush, ousel, blackbird &c.

tureen, n. [1. tūrḗn ; 2. tjurī́n]. Fr. *terrine*, 'earthen vessel', fr. Lat. *terra*, 'earth', see **terra**. Boat-shaped dish for holding soup.

turf, n. [1. térf ; 2. tə̄f]. O.E. & M.E. *turf* ; cp. O.N. *torf* ; cogn. w. Scrt. *darbha*, 'tuft of grass'. **1. a** Thin upper stratum of the earth covered with grass ; lawn, sward ; **b** a sod. **2.** Mass of compressed ancient vegetable fibre, dead grass &c., peat ; esp. as used for fuel. **3.** Horse-racing : *on the turf*, engaged in racing.

turfy, adj. [1. térfi ; 2. tə́fi]. Prec. & -y. **a** Abounding in, covered with, turf ; **b** having character or appearance of turf.

turgescence, n. [1. térjésens ; 2. tādʒésəns]. Next word & -ce. **a** Process of swelling ; **b** condition of being turgescent ; **c** bombast.

turgescent, adj. [1. térjésent ; 2. tādʒésənt]. Lat. *turgescent-(em)*, Pres. Part. of *turgescere*, inchoative of *turgēre*, 'to swell' ; see **turgid**. **a** Swelling, inflated ; **b** (fig., of style &c.) pompous, bombastic.

turgid, adj. [1. térjid ; 2. tā́dʒid]. Lat. *turgidus*, 'inflated, distended'; cp. *turgēre*, 'to swell'; contains the base *tu-, 'to swell', see **tumid**. **1.** Swollen, puffed up. **2.** (of style &c.) Inflated, bombastic, pompous.

turgidity, n. [1. terjíditi ; 2. tādʒíditi]. Prec. & -ity. State, quality, of being turgid.

turgidly, adv. [1. térjidli ; 2. tə́dʒidli]. See prec. & -ly. In a turgid manner.

turion, n. [1. tū́rion ; 2. tjúəriən]. Lat. *turiōn-(em)*, 'shoot, sprout'; connected w. base *tu-, 'to swell' &c. ; see **turgid** & **tumid**. (bot.) Scaly shoot developed from a subterranean bud.

Turk, n. [1. térk ; 2. tə̄k]. Fr. *Turc*, Ital. *Turco* ; prob. of Tatar origin. **1.** Member of the Turkish race ; specif. of Osmanli or Ottoman branch. **2.** (facet.) An unruly, unmanageable, mischievous boy ; esp. *a regular young Turk*.

turkey (I.), n. [1. térki ; 2. tə́ki]. So called fr. belief that the birds came orig. fr. Turkey. Large domestic gallinaceous bird introduced from America, whose flesh is prized as food, and largely eaten in England at Christmas time.

Turkey (II.), country of Ottoman Turks. Used attributively in various combinations. *Turkey carpet*, one made of wool, with a thick pile, usually with pattern of bold design in red, blue, and green ; *Turkey red*, a scarlet pigment obtained from madder or synthetically from coal-tar ; *Turkey towel*, rough kind of bath towel.

turkey buzzard, n. A kind of vulture, *Cathartes aura*, common in South and Central America.

turkey-cock, n. **a** A male turkey; **b** (fig.) a strutting, pompous person.

Turki, adj. & n. [1. to͝orkē; 2. túəkī]. Pers., 'Turk'. **1.** adj. Of, belonging to, a group of Ural-Altaic languages and races, which includes Turkish. **2.** n. This language, group, or race.

Turkish, adj. & n. [1. tẽrkish; 2. tə́kiʃ]. **Turk** & **-ish**. **1.** adj. Belonging to, connected with, Turkey, the Turks, or their language, which is Turki much mixed with Arabic and Persian. **2.** n. The language of the Turks.

Turkish bath, n. A hot-air or steam bath, inducing extreme perspiration, followed by shampooing and massage &c.

Turkish delight, n. A sweetmeat made of gelatine flavoured and coated with powdered sugar.

Turkish pound, n. 100 piastres, value about 18s. 2d., usually written £T.

Turk's head, n. A long-handled broom or brush with head of feathers, used for dusting ceilings &c.

turmalin(e), n. See **tourmalin**.

turmeric, n. [1. tẽrmerik; 2. tə́mərik]. Supposed to be fr. Fr. *terre-mérite*, itself perh. a corrupt. of Arab. *kurkum*, 'curcuma', q.v. An aromatic plant of the ginger family, the root of which is ground to a powder, and used as a condiment, a medicine, and a dye.

turmeric paper, n. Paper impregnated with turmeric, used as a test for alkali, in contact with which it turns brown, and for boric acid, which turns it reddish brown.

turmoil, n. [1. tẽrmoil; 2. tə́mɔil]. Origin doubtful. Perh. fr. intens. *tur-* for **tra-** & **moil**. Agitation, uproar, unrest, confusion, tumult.

turn (**I.**), vb. trans. & intrans. [1. tẽrn; 2. tə̄n]. M.E. *turnen, tournen* &c., fr. O.E. *tyrnan*, & *turnian*, 'to revolve', intrans., also combined w. O. Fr. *torner, tourner*; O.E. & Fr. both fr. Lat. *tornāre*, 'to polish, round off, fashion', fr. *tornus*, 'a lathe; a graver's tool'; borrowed fr. Gk. *tórnos*, 'turner's wheel; graver's chisel'; prob. cogn. w. Lat. *teres*, 'rubbed, rounded off, well turned, smooth', cp. *terere*, 'to rub, wear down' &c., & Gk. *teírein*, 'to rub', fr. **ter-j-*; see **teredo, toreutic, trite, triturate**. **A.** trans. **1. a** To shape, cut out, on a lathe: *to turn brass*; *to turn a candlestick out of brass*; **b** (fig.) to polish, shape, execute, in an elegant manner; give a graceful form to: *to turn a compliment, an epigram*; *to turn a couplet* &c. **2.** To give a circular motion to, cause to revolve, spin round; to wind: *to turn a handle, a wheel*; also *to turn the leaves of a book*. Phr. *to turn* (*a person*) *round one's little finger*, to influence him as one chooses. **3. a** (of physical act or process) To cause to assume a particular, often a different, position; to move, cause to face, or be inclined in particular direction; to direct: *to turn one's head*; *turn your eyes this way*; *turn the camera more to the right*; Phrs. *to turn one's back on* (various fig. senses), to refuse to recognize or to associate with; to have nothing more to do with; to express disapproval of, or contempt for &c.; *to turn a deaf ear to*, refuse to listen or to attend to; *to turn one's steps*, to go; *turn tail*, to run away; *not to turn a hair*, to be quite unaffected, unperturbed; *to turn the edge of* (*a knife* &c.), to blunt; **b** (of intellectual action) in Phr. *turn one's thoughts, attention, efforts* &c. to direct, concentrate (thoughts &c.). **4. a** To guide, cause to go in particular direction, alter course of: *to turn one's horse to the hills*; *to turn a beast into a field*; **b** to deflect, persuade to pursue different course of action: *when once he has made up his mind, nothing will turn him.* **5. a** To reverse position of, so that the upper surface lies underneath, and the lower surface upwards: *to turn things upside-down*; *to turn a chop on a gridiron*; Phr. *to turn an honest penny*, to earn a profit; **b** to cause outer surface of anything to be on the inside, and vice versa: *to turn something inside out*; *to have a suit turned.* Phr. *to turn one's coat*, change one's opinions and principles; to give up one's old allegiance and accept a new one. **6. a** To bring, cause to pass, into a specified condition: *his behaviour turns me sick*; *the success of others turns him green with envy*; *thundery weather turns milk sour*; **b** specif., to render (food) curdled, sour, tainted, corrupt &c.: *the heat has turned the milk.* **7. a** To change, transmute (things, feelings &c.) into something different: *to turn water into wine*; *to turn love to hate*; **b** to translate: *to turn a passage into Latin.* **8.** To disturb, upset, derange: *the mere sight of food turns my stomach.* Phrs. *to turn a person's head*, upset mental balance; render conceited: *flattery has turned his head*; *to turn* (*person's*) *brain*, make him mad. **9. a** To reach, and pass, a certain point in time, period of life &c.: *it has just turned four*; *he has not yet turned sixty*; **b** *to turn a* (or *the*) *corner*; (i.) to go up a street branching off that in which one is; (ii.) (fig.) *turn the corner*, to reach and pass successfully, a crisis in illness, or in one's affairs. **10.** (mil.) *To turn an enemy's flank*, pass round, take up position behind or across; to outflank. **11.** To use, employ, for particular purpose: *to turn one's hand to useful work*; *turn to account*, make use of. **B.** intrans. **1. a** To use a lathe; **b** (of material) to be capable of being shaped or turned on a lathe. **2. a** To perform revolutions, to rotate, as on a pivot or axis; **b** (fig.) to depend, hinge, upon, be involved in: *the whole dispute turns on a single point.* **3. a** To direct one's course towards, pursue, a particular direction: *to turn to the right*; *to turn west*; Phr. *not to know where, which way, to turn*, to be at end of one's resources, be hard pressed, desperate &c.; **b** to direct one's thought, attention, glance &c., towards: *to turn to the last page.* **4. a** To reverse one's course or direction, and pursue an opposite one; to retrace one's steps: *he turned and went away in a rage*; *it is time to turn now if we wish to get home in time for dinner*; **b** (fig.) to reverse one's course of action. **5.** To alter one's position, move from the side on which one is lying, on to the other: *to turn in bed, in one's sleep.* Phrs. *enough to make* (someone who is dead) *turn in his grave*, would shock and distress him, very much; *the worm turns*, even the patient and humble show resentment after a certain point; *to turn turtle*, to capsize. **6.** (of tide) To change from ebb to flow, or vice versa; (also fig.) *the tide has turned*, the course of affairs has altered, events are beginning to develop favourably or unfavourably. **7. a** To alter in specified way, in physical character, appearance, composition, general condition &c.; to pass into a specified state, to become: *the weather is turning colder*; *the milk has turned sour*; *water turns to ice*; *he turned very red*; *to turn sick*; **b** to change one's opinions, principles, profession &c.: *to turn Tory*; *to turn soldier, cook, schoolmaster* &c.; *to turn traitor*; *to turn Christian.* **8.** Specif. (of food &c.) to pass into first stage of decay, sourness, acidity &c.: *the milk has turned.* **C.** Followed by adverbs or prepositions. *Turn aside*, **1.** trans., to divert, put on a different course; **2.** intrans., to pursue a new course, deviate. *Turn away*, **1.** trans., to reject, refuse entrance to, dismiss: *to turn crowds away from the door* &c.; **2.** intrans., to turn in different direction; direct one's attention, refuse to look; show contempt or disapproval. *Turn back*, **1.** trans., to refuse to allow to proceed, cause to return; **2.** intrans., to return, retrace one's steps; (fig.) to discontinue course of action. *Turn against*, **1.** trans., to make (person) hostile to; **2.** intrans., to become hostile to, oppose. *Turn down*, **1.** trans., **a** to fold down: *to turn down one's collar*; **b** to diminish intensity of by lowering: *to turn down the light*; **c** (fig.) to reject, refuse to consider: *to turn down a proposal* &c.; **2.** intrans., **a** to be folded down; **b** to be capable of being lowered. *Turn in*, **1.** trans., to cause to point or incline inwards: *to turn in one's toes*; **2.** intrans., **a** to be inclined inwards: *his toes turned in*; **b** (colloq.) to go to bed. *Turn off*, **1.** trans., **a** to check, shut off, supply or flow of, by turning a tap &c.: *to turn off water, gas*; **b** to dismiss from service: *to turn off workmen* (*from one's employ*); **2.** intrans., **a** (of persons &c.) to leave road on which one is walking &c., and go up another leading from it; **b** (of roads &c.) to branch off, bifurcate. *Turn out*, **1.** trans., **a** to dismiss, eject, expel: *to turn a person out of the room, of his office, situation, a club* &c.; **b** to put horses, cattle &c. out to grass, as contrasted with keeping them in a stable; **c** to produce as result of labour and skill: *to turn out beautiful fabrics from the looms*; **d** to furnish with equipment, clothing &c., to fit out, dress: *an exquisitely turned out young woman*; **e** to turn off, to extinguish: *to turn out the light, the gas*; **2.** intrans., **a** to point, be inclined, outwards: *his toes turn out too much*; **b** to go out, esp. as result of expulsion: *to turn out of one's house*; **c** to get up from bed; **d** to come out in order to perform some duty: *the fire brigade turned out as soon as the alarm was given*; **e** to prove, be shown to be: *he turned out an excellent administrator*; *the day is turning out fine*; Phr. *to turn out well*, to be satisfactory, a success &c.; *as it turned out*, as it chanced, happened. *Turn over*, **1.** trans., **a** to reverse position of, cause to roll over: *to turn over the pages of a book*, to look through while turning; Phr. *to turn over a new leaf*, make amends for past, behave better; **b** to hand over, transfer, to: *to turn one's business over to one's son*; **c** to ponder, consider, dwell upon: *to turn* (*the matter*) *over in one's mind*; **d** to handle, take in, in the course of business: *the business turns over several thousands a year*; **2.** intrans., to alter one's position by rolling over: *to turn over in bed.* *Turn to*, intrans., **a** to rely upon, trust to, apply to: *to turn to a friend for help*; **b** (absol.) to set to, set to work, act with vigour. *Turn up*, **1.** trans., to bend up, cause to incline upwards, bring lower side, or end, uppermost: *to turn up the ends of one's trousers*; *to turn up the soil*, plough or dig it. Various special uses: **a** *to turn a child up*, put face downwards over one's knee to whip him; *to turn up a decanter*, empty the last drops it contains into one's glass; *to turn up one's nose at*, to feel and show contempt for, to despise; *to turn up one's toes*, (colloq.) to die; *his conduct, the sight, turned me up*, disgusted, nauseated me. **2.** intrans. **a** To incline, be inclined, bend, slope, upwards: *the bough turns up at the end*; *her nose turns up*; **b** (i.) (of persons) to appear, come on the scene, visit one, esp. casually and unexpectedly: *my brother has just turned up from India*; *he turned up in London the other day*; *I shouldn't think he'll turn up tonight*; (ii.) (of objects) to come to light, be found, esp. by accident: *the book I lost hasn't turned up yet*; *I wouldn't waste time looking for your knife, it will turn up some day*; Phr. *to wait for something to turn up*, await the course of events passively, in the hope that some favourable opportunity, or some piece of good fortune, will come to one. *Turn upon*, trans., **a** to attack; **b** to depend upon.

turn (**II.**), n., fr. O. Fr. *torn*, later *tour*; see prec. **1.** Act or process of turning; rotation, revolution: *the turn of a wheel*; a turning movement: *a turn of the wrist*; movement made in a particular direction: *a turn to the right.* **2.** Something which turns or winds; a bend, curve: *a turn in a road, in a river.* **3. a** Change in direction, reverse movement: *the turn of the tide*; Phr. *the turn of the tide*, (fig.) reversal of fortune; **b** change, new departure, vicissitude, in affairs, fortune, health &c.: *matters, affairs, have taken a bad turn*; *the patient has taken a turn for the better, for the worse.* **4. a** A spell of action, bout of activity: *to take a turn at the oars*; **b** a form of activity, an action, regarded as affecting another in some particular way : *to do one a good turn*, render him a service ; *a bad turn*, a disservice. Phr. *one good turn deserves another*. **5.** A short spell of exercise, a walk, ride &c. : *let us take a turn along the sea-front*. **6.** Opportunity which recurs at regular intervals ; right, or obligation to do, or enjoy something at certain recurring periods, which alternate with periods during which others are liable to the obligation or enjoy the right : *everyone must take his turn to keep watch ; it is your turn to have dinner next ; my turn will come*. Phrs. *by turns, turn and turn about*, alternately. **7.** Special need, requirement, exigency : *this stick will serve my turn to beat him with*. **8.** Special aptitude, bent, predisposition : *a distinct turn for music*. **9.** A short performance on the stage, display of agility, skill &c. lasting for a brief period, forming a definite part of an entertainment : *a variety entertainment with several good and some poor turns*. **10.** Special form, shape, cast ; characteristic style : *a peculiar turn of mind*. **11.** (colloq.) Physical or moral shock, a qualm, a jar ; esp. *it gave me quite a turn*. **12.** Phr. (food) *done to a turn*, cooked with absolute perfection, neither underdone, nor over-cooked.

turncoat, n. [1. těrnkōt ; 2. tǎnkout]. (contemptuous) Person who changes his political or religious opinions and principles, esp. one who does so from interested motives.

turncock, n. [1. těrnkok ; 2. tǎnkok]. Man employed by water company to regulate the water from the mains &c.

turned, adj. [1. těrnd ; 2. tǎnd]. P.P. of **turn** (I.). (print.) *A turned letter*, one inverted or reversed.

turner, n. [1. těrner ; 2. tǎnə], fr. **turn** (I.) & -**er**. One who practises turning with a lathe as a skilled trade.

turnery, n. [1. těrneri ; 2. tǎnəri]. Fr. *tournerie*. **1.** Art of turning with a lathe. **2. a** (coll.) Objects turned with a lathe ; **b** ornamentation wrought with a lathe.

turning, n. [1. těrniŋ ; 2. tǎniŋ]. **turn** (I.) & -**ing**. **1.** A winding, twisting, bend : *turnings and twistings of a road, river* &c. **2.** Place where one road branches off from another : *first turning to the right*. **3.** Act, art, of turning with a lathe ; turnery.

turning-point, n. Point or place of turning ; (usually in non-material sense) point at which a new departure is made ; crisis : *the turning-point of an illness, of a career*.

turnip, n. [1. těrnip ; 2. tǎnip]. First element of doubtful origin ; the second is O.E. *nǣp*, M.E. *nēpe*, ' turnip ', early loan-word fr. Lat. *nāpus*, ' turnip ' ; cp. Gk. *nâpu*, later form of *sināpi*, ' mustard ' ; prob. of Egyptian origin. See **sinapism** & cp. second element in **parsnip**. **1. a** Plant, *Brassica campestris*, var. *rapa*, with globular or long root, with a sweetish or, when old, hot taste ; used as a vegetable and for feeding sheep and cattle ; **b** specif., the edible root of this plant. **2.** (slang) A large, clumsy, common silver watch.

turnip fly, n. **a** A hymenopterous insect, *Athalia spinarum*, whose larva feeds on turnip-leaves ; **b** small beetle (also *turnip-flea*), *Phyllotreta nemorum*, which feeds on young turnip-leaves.

turnip-tops, n. pl. Leaves and stems of the turnip, esp. the young sprouts from previous season's root, considered as a vegetable.

turnkey, n. [1. těrnkē ; 2. tǎnkī]. Person who keeps the keys of the cells in a prison.

turn-out, n. [1. těrnóut ; 2. tǎn áut]. **1.** Gathering, assembly, of persons who have come together for a particular purpose : *quite a good turn-out at the lecture*. **2.** (colloq.) A carriage, horses, and servants, considered as a whole or ensemble : *a smart turn-out*.

turnover, n. [1. těrnōver ; 2. tǎnouvə]. **1.** Something bent or folded over ; specif., a kind of pie made by doubling or folding over a piece of dough. **2.** Amount of money handled, taken in, and paid out in a business within a given time. **3.** Article in a newspaper extending from one page on to another.

turnpike, n. [1. těrnpīk ; 2. tǎnpaik]. Gate kept closed across a road and not opened to passengers until they have paid toll ; a tollgate, originally a pointed bar turning on a pivot, worked by the keeper.

turnpike road, n. One which has a turnpike across it.

turnsole, n. [1. těrnsōl ; 2. tǎnsoul]. Fr. *tournesol* ; **turn** (I.) & Lat. *sol*, ' sun ', see **sol** (I.). Plant whose flowers are supposed always to face the sun ; sunflower.

turnspit, n. [1. těrnspit ; 2. tǎnspit]. One of a small breed of dog used formerly for turning a spit upon which meat was cooked.

turnstile, n. [1. těrnstīl ; 2. tǎnstail]. Mechanical device consisting of a heavy revolving gate so constructed that only one person can pass at a time ; used at the entrance of theatres, on piers &c., to regulate speed of entrance while tickets are collected.

turnstone, n. [1. těrnstōn ; 2. tǎnstoun]. Popular name for a shore bird, allied to the plover, which turns over the pebbles on a beach in search of food.

turn-table, n. Circular revolving platform upon which rails are laid corresponding with those of a railway line, used for reversing locomotives.

turn-up, n. [1. těrn úp ; 2. tǎn áp]. **1.** Something turned up, as *the turn-up of one's trousers*. **2.** (colloq.) A commotion, a row ; a fight or noisy wrangle.

turpentine, n. [1. těrpentīn ; 2. tǎpəntain]. O. Fr. *terbentine*, Lat. *terebinthinus*, ' turpentine tree ', fr. Gk. *terébinthos*, see **terebinth**. **1.** Oily, fluid or semi-fluid, sticky substance secreted by pine trees. **2.** Popular name for *spirits of turpentine*, distilled from turpentine ; used for mixing with paints and varnishes.

turpentine tree, n. Terebinth tree.

turpeth, n. [1. těrpeth ; 2. tǎpeþ]. O. Fr. *turbith*, fr. Pers. *turbid*, ' a purge '. The root of an Asiatic plant, used as a purgative.

turpitude, n. [1. těrpitūd ; 2. tǎpitjūd]. Fr., fr. Lat. *turpitūdo*, ' ugliness, foulness ', fr. *turpis*, ' ugly, foul, filthy ; shameful, base ' ; cogn. w. O. Lat. *trepit*, ' turns away ', see **trepidation** ; fundamental sense of adj. is ' revolting, causing one to turn away '. Wickedness, depravity, infamy.

turps, n. [1. těrps ; 2. tǎps]. Popular abbreviation of spirits of turpentine.

turquoise, n. [1. těrkwoiz, těrkwahz ; 2. tǎkwɔiz, tǎkwǎz], formerly [1. těrkis ; 2. tǎkis]. Fr. fem. adj., ' Turkish '. **a** Semiprecious stone, opaque, and bright blue or greenish blue in colour ; **b** bright blue or greenish colour, like that of the turquoise, (also attrib.) *turquoise blue, green*.

turret, n. [1. túret ; 2. tárit]. Fr. *tourette*, ' little tower ' ; see **tower** (I.) & -**et**. **1.** A small tower, esp. one built out and projecting from a larger building. **2.** (nav.) Revolving, tower-like, armoured structure upon which a ship's guns are mounted.

turreted, adj. [1. túreted ; 2. táritid]. Provided with a turret or turrets.

turret-gun, n. Ship's gun mounted upon a turret.

turriculate(d), adj. [1. turíkūlāt(ed) ; 2. tarikjuleit(id)]. Lat. *turricula*, ' little tower ', dimin. of *turris*, ' tower ', see **tower** (I.), & -**ate**. **a** Provided with small turrets ; **b** (of shells) resembling a turret in shape.

turtle (I.), n. [1. těrtl ; 2. tǎtl]. Lat. *turtur*, ' dove ', imitative of bird's note ; usually *turtle-dove*. Any of various kinds of wild dove with soft cooing note ; supposed to show great affection for, and fidelity to, its mate ; hence (fig.) *a pair of turtle-doves*, lovers.

turtle (II.), n. Form perh. suggested by prec., fr. Span. *tortuga*, ' tortoise ' ; see **tortoise**. A marine tortoise ; reptile of various species, having the body enclosed in a hard bony shell ; several kinds have edible flesh, especially used for soup. Phr. *to turn turtle*, (chiefly of a ship) to capsize.

Tuscan, adj. & n. [1. túskan ; 2. táskən]. Lat. *Tuscānus*. **1.** adj. **a** Pertaining to Tuscany ; **b** (archit.) of, pertaining to, the Tuscan order, of late Roman origin, plain in style, with unfluted columns. **2.** n. **a** Inhabitant of Tuscany ; **b** language of Tuscany.

tush (I.), interj. & vb. intrans. [1. tush ; 2. taʃ]. Imitative. (archaic) **a** interj. Exclamation expressive of contempt or impatience ; **b** vb., to utter this exclamation.

tush (II.), n. O.E. *tūsć*, for earlier *tunsk-, cp. Goth. *tunþ-us*, ' tooth ', gradational variant of Gmc. *tanþ-, whence O.E. *tōþ*, see **tooth** ; the form presupposes an orig. *dnt-ko-, the suff. being adjectival. Cp. **tusk**. One of the long prominent side teeth of a horse.

tushery, n. [1. túsheri ; 2. táʃəri]. **tush** (I.) & -**ery**. Term applied by R. L. Stevenson to affected literary archaisms.

tusk, n. & vb. trans. [1. tusk ; 2. task]. In M.E., fr. O.E. *tūx*, metathesized form of O.E. *tūsć*, see **tush** (II.) ; *tūx* undergoes a later metathesis to *tŭsk*. **1.** n. **a** An enormously long prominent tooth which always projects outside the mouth, found esp. in the elephant, in the walrus, and similar marine animals, and on a smaller scale in the wild boar ; **b** (facet.) a human tooth, esp. when exceptionally long and prominent. **2.** vb. To strike at, wound, gore, with the tusks.

tusked, adj. [1. tuskt ; 2. taskt]. Prec. & -**ed**. Having tusks.

tusker, n. [1. túsker ; 2. táskə]. An elephant or boar with large tusks.

tussal, adj. [1. túsal ; 2. tásəl], fr. Lat. *tussis*, ' cough ', origin doubtful, & -**al**. (med.) Pertaining to, connected with, a cough.

tussicular, adj. [1. tusíkūlar ; 2. tasíkjulə]. Lat. *tussicula*, ' slight cough ', dimin. of *tussis*, see prec., & -**ar**. Having the character of a slight cough.

tussive, adj. [1. túsiv ; 2. tásiv]. Lat. *tussis*, ' cough ', see **tussal**, & -**ive**. Connected with, due to, a cough.

tussle, n. & vb. intrans. [1. túsl ; 2. tásl]. Etymol. doubtful ; possibly connected w. **tousle**. **1.** n. A fight ; a rough struggle ; a strenuous effort. **2.** vb. To engage in a rough, violent struggle.

tussock, n. [1. túsuk ; 2. tásək]. Etymol. obscure. A tuft, thick bunch, of grass &c.

tussock grass, n. Grass which grows in tufts on damp, marshy soil ; specif., species of tall tufted grass of the Falkland Islands and Patagonia.

tussock moth, n. Kind of moth whose caterpillar has tufts of hair on its back.

tussocky, adj. [1. túsuki ; 2. tásəki]. Prec. & -**y**. Full of tussocks ; tufty.

tussore, n. [1. túsōr ; 2. tásō], **tussah, tussar, tusseh, tusser, tussur**, fr. Hind. *tassar*, ' shuttle '. **1.** Indian undomesticated silkworm that feeds on oak leaves. **2.** a Coarse, fawn-coloured fibre produced by these silkworms ; **b** fabric woven from this.

tut, interj. & vb. & n. [1. tut ; 2. tat]. Conventionalized spelling attempting to express sound. **a** interj. Exclamation of impatience, annoyance &c. ; **b** vb., to give utterance to such an exclamation.

tutelage, n. [1. tútelij ; 2. tjútilidʒ]. Lat. *tūtēla*, ' charge, guardianship ', fr. *tūtus*, ' safe, secure ', see **tuition** & **tutor**, & -**age**. **1.** Act of protecting, of acting as guardian. **2.** State of being under guardianship, in the protection of a tutor.

tutelar, tutelary, adj. [1. tútelar(i) ; 2. tjútilə(ri)]. Lat. *tūtēla*, see prec., & -**ar** (& -**y**). Having guardianship ; acting as a guardian or protector ; protective : *tutelar(y) power, deities*.

tutor (I.), n. [1. tútur ; 2. tjútə]. Lat., ' protector, defender, legal guardian ', fr. base *tūt-*, P.P. type of *tuēri*, ' to guard, protect ' ; cogn. w. Goth. *þiuþ*, ' good ', n. ; perh. ultimately connected w. base of *tumēre*, ' to swell ', see **tumid** ; see further **tuition, tute-**

lage, tutelar. Less probable is Brugmann's derivation of this group fr. the base *$tug^wh\bar{o}$-&c., seen in Gk. *sophós*, ' wise ', see **sophism**. **1.** (Rom. law) One having charge of a person below the age of puberty, and of his property; a guardian. **2.** A teacher, instructor; **a** college official, usually a specialist in some branch of learning, who directs the studies of undergraduates at Oxford and Cambridge; contrasted with a university professor; **b** a private instructor; often a person living with the family of his pupil; **c** a coach, a teacher who prepares young men for some particular examination.

tutor (II.), vb. trans. & intrans., fr. prec. **a** trans. To act as tutor to; **b** intrans., to engage in tutorial work, perform the duties of a tutor.

tutoress, n. [1. tútores; 2. tjútərɛs]. **tutor (I.)** & **-ess**. Woman tutor.

tutorial, adj. & n. [1. tūtórial; 2. tjūtŏ́riəl]. **tutor (I.)** & **-ial. 1.** adj. **a** Pertaining to a tutor or to his duties; **b** pertaining to, of the nature of, tuition. **2.** n. (Oxford slang) A spell of instruction given by a college tutor.

tutorially, adv. Prec. & **-ly.** After the manner of a tutor.

tutorship, n. [1. tútership; 2. tjútəʃip]. **tutor (I.)** & **-ship. a** Office, functions, of a tutor; **b** an engagement, appointment, as tutor.

tutsan, n. [1. tútsan; 2. tátsən]. Fr. *toute-saine*, lit. ' entirely wholesome or healthy '. Cp. **total (I.)** & **sane.** The plant St.-John's-wort, *Hypericum Androsaemum*, from which a healing ointment was formerly made.

tutti, adj. [1. tóoti; 2. túlti]. Ital., ' all '. (mus. direction) All players, instruments, or voices.

tutti-frutti, n. [1. tóoti fróoti; 2. túlti frúlti]. Ital., ' all fruits '. Sweetmeat made of a mixture of various kinds of preserved fruits.

tutty, n. [1. túti; 2. táti]. Fr. *tutie*, fr. Arab. *tūtiyā*, ' vitriol '. Brown substance obtained from flues of furnaces in which zinc is smelted; a crude oxide of zinc.

tuum, pron. [1. túum; 2. tjúəm]. Lat. neut. sing. of possessive pron. of 2nd pers., cogn. w. thou. Thine; in Phr. *meum and tuum*, see **meum.**

tu-whitt, tu-whitt tu-whoo, n. [1. tōō wít tōō wōō; 2. tū wít tū wū̃]. Imitative of the cry of the owl.

tuxedo, n. [1. tuksédō; 2. taksídou], fr. name of a country club, Tuxedo Park, New York. (U.S.A.) Dinner jacket.

tuyère, n. [1. twéyār; 2. twíjeə]. Fr., ' pipe ', connected w. *tuyau*, q.v. under **tewel.** Pipe through which air is pumped into a furnace.

twaddell, n. [1. twódl; 2. twódl]. After name of inventor. Kind of hydrometer.

twaddle, n. & vb. intrans. [1. twódl; 2. twódl]. Prob. variant of **tattle. 1.** n. Empty, foolish, trite talk; nonsense: *to talk mere twaddle.* **2.** vb. To talk twaddle.

twain, adj. & n. [1. twān; 2. twein]. O.E. *twēġen,* masc., ' two ', M.E. *twēine, twēyen* &c. See **two.** (archaic or poet.) Two: (*to cut*) *in twain,* asunder, in two parts; ' *and never the twain shall meet* '.

twang, n. & vb. trans. & intrans. [1. twaŋ; 2. twæŋ]. Imitative. **1.** n. **a** A sharp sound, as of the string of a fiddle &c. suddenly and sharply plucked; **b** nasalized speech utterance; effect produced by speaking through the nose: *an American twang.* **2.** vb. **a** To pluck the string of a musical instrument sharply so that it gives forth a twang; **b** (rarely) to speak with a nasal twang.

twayblade, n. [1. twáblād; 2. twéibleid], fr. O.E. *twēġe(n),* ' two ', see **twain,** & **blade.** A plant of the orchidaceous family, genus *Listera,* with two broad leaves, opposite each other, on the stem; also N. American species of the genus *Liparis.*

tweak, vb. trans. & n. [1. twēk; 2. twīk]. Variant of **twitch (I.);** the formal relation to M.E. *twikken* is not clear. **1.** vb. To pluck, nip, or pinch with a sharp, sudden, jerky action. **2.** n. A sharp, sudden nip, pinch, or plucking.

tweed, n. [1. twēd; 2. twīd]. Hardly fr. **twill,** as sometimes suggested, as the two kinds of cloth have no resemblance; prob. fr. name of Scottish river. A soft woollen cloth, usually woven from yarns of several colours or shades, but without a regular pattern; primarily used of cloth woven in Scotland.

tweedle-dum and tweedle-dee, ns. [1. twēdl dúm an(d) twēdl dḗ; 2. twídl dám ən twídl dí]. Imit. of high-pitched note; first quoted in O.E.D. in Phr. *tweedle-dum and tweedle-dee* of two musicians (1725). Designation of two persons who are considered very alike in appearance, character, opinion, or behaviour &c.; more rarely of things, modes of conduct &c. which are very much alike and differ chiefly in name.

'tween, prep. [1. twēn; 2. twīn]. Abbr. for **between.**

tweeny, n. [1. twēni; 2. twíni]. Prec. & **-y.** (colloq.) A young servant girl who helps two other maids with their work; also **tweeny-maid.**

tweezers, n. pl. [1. twḗzerz; 2. twízəz], fr. obs. *tweeze,* ' a small pocket-case ', fr. Fr. *étui,* ' case '; fr. such a phr. as *a pair of twees,* ' a folding case '; hence *tweezers,* primarily instrument carried in a case. Small pair of pincers used for grasping a small blood-vessel, plucking out thorns from the flesh &c.

twelfth, adj. & n. [1. twelfth; 2. twɛlfþ]. O.E. *twelfta,* M.E. *twelfte*; see **twelve. 1.** adj. Next in order after eleventh; ordinal adj. of *twelve.* **2.** n. **a** The twelfth thing; **b** a twelfth part.

Twelfth-night, n. Evening of twelfth day after Christmas, that is, of the Feast of the Epiphany.

twelve, adj. & n. [1. twelv; 2. twɛlv]. O.E. *twelf,* M.E. *twelf, twelve*; cp. O.S. *twelif*; O.H.G. *zwelif,* Goth. *twalif.* The word is compounded of the elements in **two** & **leave (II.)**; cp. also **eleven**; & the primitive sense is ' two over ' or ' two in addition ' (to ten). **1.** adj. One more than eleven, two more than ten; a dozen. **2.** n. **a** The number one more than eleven; Phr. *the twelve,* the twelve Apostles; **b** symbol for this: *put down a twelve*; **c** colloquial abbreviation for 12 o'clock.

twelvemo, n. [1. twélvmō; 2. twélvmou]. A duodecimo, written 12mo.

twelvemonth, n. [1. twélvmunth; 2. twélv-manþ]. A year: *this day twelvemonth*; *it will take a twelvemonth to finish.*

twentieth, adj. & n. [1. twéntieth; 2. twénti-iþ]. O.E. *twentigoða*; see **twenty** & **-th. 1.** adj. Ordinal of twenty. **2.** n. **a** Thing next in order after the nineteenth; **b** one of twenty equal parts.

twenty, adj. & n. [1. twénti; 2. twénti]. O.E. *twēntiġ,* M.E. *twenti*; O.S. *twēntig*; O.H.G. *zweinzug*; cp. Goth. *twai tigjus,* ' two tens '; see **twain** & **-ty** & **ten. 1.** adj. One more than nineteen. **2.** n. **a** The number following nineteen; **b** symbol for this; **c** collection of twenty things; a score.

twi-, pref. O.E. *twi,* ' two, double '; see **twice, twain,** & **two.**

twibill, n. [1. twíbil; 2. twáibil]. Prec. & **bill (I.). 1.** (obs.) Sword, battle-axe, with two blades. **2.** Mattock with two cutting edges.

twice, adv. [1. twīs; 2. twais]. M.E. *twīes,* formed fr. O.E. *twiwa, twiga,* ' twice ', w. the addition of genit. suff. *-es,* used adverbially; cp. O.H.G. *zwi-*; O.N. *tvi-*; cogn. w. Scrt. *dvi-*; Gk. *di-*; Lat. *bi-* for **dwi-*, see **bi-** & **two.** Two times: *to do something twice.* Phrs. *to think twice* (before doing &c.), to ponder well, hesitate; *not to think twice about,* (i.) not to think of again, to forget, disregard; (ii.) to do (something) without hesitation, reluctance, or misgiving; *I shouldn't think twice about refusing his offer*; *twice as good as*; *twice as much,* in double quantity, to a double degree.

twicer, n. [1. twíser; 2. twáisə]. See prec. & **-er.** One who does something twice; specif. **a** Presbyterian who goes to church twice a year; **b** printer who is both compositor and pressman.

twice-told, adj. Told, narrated, constantly; hence, hackneyed, commonplace.

twiddle, vb. trans. & intrans. & n. [1. twídl; 2. twídl]. O.N. *tvidla,* ' to stir '. **1.** vb. **a** trans. To twist, twirl; Phr. *to twiddle one's thumbs,* spend one's time idly, to have no serious occupation; **b** intrans., to shake, tremble, vibrate. **2.** n. **a** The action or motion of twiddling; **b** a vibration, shake, flourish, of the voice or of a musical instrument; **c** a twisting, wavy line.

twig (I.), vb. trans. & intrans. [1. twig; 2. twig]. Cp. Ir. *tuigaim,* ' I understand '. (slang) **a** intrans. To have understanding of, follow, catch on to (a proposal, explanation &c.): *I don't quite twig, will you tell me again?*; **b** trans., to understand, apprehend shrewdly: *to twig a person's meaning.*

twig (II.), n. O.E. *twig,* ' branch, stalk ' cp. O.H.G. *zwig*; prob. connected w. **twi-** & **two.** Thin slender branch, or end of branch, of a tree. Phr. (slang) *to hop the twig,* to die.

twiggy, adj. [1. twígi; 2. twígi]. Prec. & **-y.** Covered with, abounding in, twigs.

twilight, n. [1. twílīt; 2. twáilait]. 15th cent.; see **twi-** & **light (I.). 1. a** Half-light, subdued light just before and after sundown; **b** the time when such light prevails; period between late afternoon or evening and night. Phr. *twilight of the gods* (anct. Gmc. mythol.), the great struggle in which the gods and giants will destroy each other; also (attrib.) *twilight sleep,* condition of semi-unconsciousness induced by narcotics for relieving the pains of childbirth. **2.** (fig.) Obscurity of meaning; imperfect comprehension.

twill, n. & vb. trans. [1. twil; 2. twil]. Cp. O.E. *twilic,* ' woven double ', see **twi-**; cp. M.H.G. *zwilich,* ' of two threads '; perh. formed on anal. of Lat. *bilix,* ' two-threaded ', fr. *bi-,* ' double ', & the base of *licium,* ' thread, something worn '. The Mod. Engl. word is prob. borrowed fr. a L.G. dial., *tvillen,* ' to make double '. **1.** n. **a** Fine diagonal rib in fabric, formed by the mode of weaving; **b** cloth so woven. **2.** vb. To weave (cloth) with a twill.

twin, adj., n., & vb. [1. twin; 2. twin]. O.N. *tvinnr,* ' double ', O.E. *ġetwinnas,* ' twins '; see **twi-. 1.** adj. Specif. **a** being one of two children born at one birth: *twin brothers, sisters*; **b** double, twofold: *twin blades in a knife*; **c** closely connected or related, nearly resembling each other: *twin houses, projects* &c.; **d** closely connected in affection, mode of thought; having spiritual affinity: *twin souls.* **2.** n. **a** Either of two persons or animals born at one birth; **b** (pl.) two persons, animals, things, which closely resemble each other in appearance, character, activities, function &c.; specif., compound crystal, with pair of crystals in exactly reversed position on opposite side of axis; **c** (cap.) *the Twins,* constellation and sign of the zodiac, also called *Gemini,* i.e. Castor and Pollux. **3.** vb. To form (into) twin crystals.

twin-born, adj. Born at one birth.

twine, n. & vb. trans. & intrans. [1. twīn; 2. twain]. O.E. *twīn,* ' linen ', implying fabric made of double or twisted thread; later in present sense of n. From base in **twi-** & **two. 1.** n. **a** Twisted threads of jute, hemp &c., formed into a strong line, used for tying parcels &c.; string; **b** act or process of twining; **c** a twist, convolution. **2.** vb. **a** trans. To twist, wind, form into (wreaths): *to twine garlands for the feast*; *to twine one's arms round,* to embrace; **b** intrans., to twist, wreathe, encircle, form into winding folds: *in the woodland the ivy twines*; *ivy twines round the trunks of trees.*

twiner, n. [1. twíner; 2. twáinə]. Prec. & **-er.** That which twines; esp. a rambling, twisting plant.

twinge, n. & vb. intrans. [1. twinj; 2. twin(d)ž]. The n. is fr. the vb., but is now far more frequently used than the latter; O.E. *twengan*, 'to press, pinch', M.E. *twingen*, 'to afflict'; origin doubtful. **1.** n. **a** A sudden, sharp, shooting pain, a pang, a qualm: *a twinge of toothache, of lumbago* &c.; **b** a sudden mental qualm, sharp stab of remorse: *a twinge of conscience, compunction.* **2.** vb. To throb, shoot, with sudden pain.

twinkle, vb. intrans. & n. [1. twíngkl; 2. twíŋkl]. O.E. *twinclian*, 'to twinkle', M.E. *twinclien*, cp. M.H.G. *zwinken, zwingen*, 'to blink, wink'. **1.** vb. **a** (of lights, stars &c.) To produce effect of winking, to flash, sparkle, intermittently; to scintillate; **b** (of the eyes) to wink, blink (rare); to light up with sudden gleam of mirth &c.; **c** to move rapidly in different directions, to flash into sight and disappear by turns: *feet twinkling in the dance* &c. **2.** n. **a** (i.) An intermittent gleam, flash, sparkle; a scintillation; (ii.) a fleeting expression of mirth or humour in the eye; **b** a rapid, flashing movement, a twinkling.

twinkling, n. [1. twíngkling; 2. twíŋkliŋ]. Prec. & **-ing. 1.** A rapid, flickering movement; a momentary glimpse caught of this: *the twinkling of a rabbit's tail.* Phr. *the twinkling of an eye*, a brief instant of time. **2.** Intermittent flashing or sparkling of light: *the twinkling of the stars.*

twinning, n. [1. twíning; 2. twíniŋ]. **twin**, vb., & **-ing.** Formation of twin crystals.

twirl, vb. trans. & intrans. & n. [1. twĕrl; 2. twə̄l]. Freq. of O.E. *þweran*, 'to stir, churn', cogn. w. *þwære*, 'a churn'; cogn. w. Lat. *trua*, 'a ladle', & *trulla*, 'a dipper, scoop', q.v. under **trowel. 1.** vb. **a** trans. To cause to revolve, whirl, or spin round: *to twirl one's moustache*; to twist so as to impart a rotatory movement to, to flourish: *to twirl a cane*; **b** intrans., to whirl, spin round. **2.** n. **a** Act of twirling; a whirling, a rotatory movement; **b** something twirled; a twist, coil; **c** a flourish, a twisting line, a twiddle.

twist (I.), n. [1. twist; 2. twist]. O.E. *twist* in the compound *mæst-twist*, 'mast-rope, stay'; formed fr. base in **twi-** & **two. 1.** Mass, bundle, formed by winding, twining, plaiting, flexible strands or some soft substance; **a** a hank of thread or yarn; **b** particular kind of yarn; **c** kind of coarse tobacco twisted into a tight roll; **d** loaf made of dough twisted into spiral form. **2.** A spinning, twisting, motion imparted to an object in throwing or striking it, which causes it to deviate suddenly from the original direction it follows: *to give a twist to a ball.* **3.** Act of twisting, bending; torsion, flexure: *to give a twist to a rope, to a person's arm.* **4.** A bend, coil, kink, turn, convolution: *a twist in a rope.* **5. a** Deviation, departure, from a straight line; curve, tortuosity: *a twist in a road, stream*; **b** (fig., in moral sense) (i.) departure from probity and uprightness in character or conduct; disingenuousness, lack of straightforwardness, candour, honesty: *a twist in one's nature*; also (ii.) abnormality, peculiar warped tendency of mind.

twist (II.), vb. trans. & intrans. M.E. *twisten*, see prec. **A.** trans. **1.** To plait, twine, interweave: *to twist threads into yarn, strands of jute &c. into a rope; to twist flowers into a wreath.* **2.** To wreathe, encircle with, wind round: *to twist wreaths round a column.* **3.** To impart spiral form to by torsion, that is by holding ends of and turning hands in opposite directions; to wring: *to twist a stick, a cloth* &c. **4.** (fig.) To distort, wrest, interpret in a sense at variance with true meaning: *to twist what is said so as to give a wrong impression.* **B.** intrans. **1. a** To assume spiral form; to wind, coil; to be distorted, to curve; **b** to writhe. **2.** To deviate suddenly from a straight line and move in different direction: *a cricket ball twists on the wicket.* **3. a** To move forward in a curving, winding path; to pursue a tortuous course: *the road, stream, turns and twists a good deal*; **b** (fig.) to be guilty of duplicity, to pursue a disingenuous line of conduct with a view to deceive.

twister, n. [1. twíster; 2. twístə]. Prec. & **-er. 1.** Person who twists (in various senses); specif. (fig.) one who speaks or acts insincerely, an unreliable, dishonest person, a dodger. **2.** Thing that twists; **a** a ball which turns suddenly in different direction, which breaks or screws; **b** machine for twisting threads; **c** (i.) a difficult task or problem; (ii.) word or combination of sounds difficult to pronounce; also *tongue-twister.*

twisty, adj. [1. twísti; 2. twísti]. **twist (I.)** & **-y. a** Abounding in twists and turns, curving, winding; **b** (fig., of persons) fond of and practising deception and intrigues; disingenuous, tortuous, dishonest, unreliable.

twit, vb. trans. [1. twit; 2. twit]. O.E. *ætwītan*, 'to reproach, blame', w. loss of the unstressed initial vowel; the first element is **at**; the second is the base *wīt*, *wit-* &c., 'to see, to know', wh. also expresses blame, hostility &c., cp. O.E. *witan*, 'to reproach with', *wīte*, 'torture, misery', Goth. *fraweitan*, 'to avenge', *fraweit*, 'punishment, vengeance'; see under **wit (I.)** & cp. **vision (I.)**, & **idea, idol.** To reproach (a person) with (a fault, weakness, defect &c.); to bring such up against him; to remind (person) of (fault &c.) and taunt him with it: *to twit a person with*, or (more rarely) *about, his timidity, conceit, humble origin* &c.

twitch (I.), vb. trans. & intrans. [1. twich; 2. twitʃ]. M.E. *twicchen*; cp. O.E. *twiċċian*, 'to pluck (fruit)', see **tweak**; connected w. O.E. *tucian*, 'pluck; oppress', see **tuck (I.). 1.** trans. **a** To pluck, pull, with a sudden, jerking movement: *to twitch a cloth off a table*; *his cup was suddenly twitched from his hand*; **b** to move (something) with sudden jerky or tremulous motion: *a horse twitches his ears, tail* &c.; *to twitch one's eyelids.* **2.** intrans. To be seized, agitated, by a spasmodic, convulsive (usually involuntary), muscular movement: *his face twitched with pain, emotion* &c.; *a horse's ears twitch.*

twitch (II.), n. See prec. **1.** Act of twitching; process of being twitched; **a** a sharp, sudden pull, tweak or jerk; **b** a convulsive movement of part of the body. **2.** Something used for twitching; specif., a device consisting of a short handle with a cord attached which is twisted tightly round the upper lip of a horse, and held, to make him stand still while being clipped, shod, or subjected to some operation.

twitter, vb. intrans. & n. [1. twíter; 2. twítə]. M.E. *twiteren*; prob. imitative. **1.** vb. **a** (of birds) To utter a running series of shrill, intermittent notes, as at dawn or nightfall: '*And gathering swallows twitter in the skies*' (Keats, 'To Autumn'); **b** (of persons) to talk with a rapid, unresonant utterance, expressive of feebleness, timidity, and futility. **2.** n. **a** Sound made by birds that twitter; **b** rapidly uttered, feeble, futile speech or chatter. Phr. *in a twitter*, in an excited, nervous condition which tends to evoke shrill, rapid chatter.

twittering, n. [1. twítering; 2. twítəriŋ]. Prec. & **-ing.** Sounds, collectively, as uttered by birds or persons that twitter.

'twixt, prep. [1. twikst; 2. twikst]. Abbr. for **betwixt.**

two, adj. & n. [1. tōō; 2. tū]. O.E. *twā* (fem. & neut.), see also **twain**; M.E. *twō*; O.S. *twā* (fem.); O.H.G. *zwei*; Goth. *twai*; O.N. *tveir*; cogn. w. Lat. *duo*; Gk. *dúo*, see **dual**; Scrt. *dvā(u)*; O. Slav. *duva, dva*; see also **bi-, dis-. 1.** adj. One more than one; twice one. Phrs. *to cut in two*, divide into two parts; *to put two and two together*, to draw the obvious conclusion; *one or two*, a few. **2.** n. **a** A pair, group of two persons or things; *in two's and three's*, in small groups or batches; **b** symbol representing the number two—2, II., ii.

two-edged, adj. Having two cutting edges: *a two-edged sword*; also fig., *a two-edged compliment*, one that is ambiguous, and may be interpreted as an insult.

two-faced, adj. **a** Having two faces; **b** (fig.) double-faced, false.

twofold, adj. & adv. [1. tōōfōld; 2. tūfould]. **a** adj. Double; **b** adv., doubly.

two-handed, adj. **1.** Having two hands. **2.** Requiring two hands to lift, move, use &c.: *a two-handed sword.* **3.** (of games) Played by two persons.

two-headed, adj. Having two heads.

two-legged, adj. Having two legs; contrasted with *four-legged.*

two-line, adj. (typog., of a letter on page) Occupying the space, having the height, of two lines of specified type: *two-line brevier.*

twopence, n. [1. túpens; 2. tápəns]. The sum, value, of two pennies considered as a unity; formerly a coin of this value.

twopenny, adj. & n. [1. túpeni; 2. tápəni]. **1.** adj. Of the value or price of twopence: *a twopenny bun.* **2.** n. (slang) Head, in Phr. *tuck in your twopenny.*

twopenny-halfpenny, adj. [1. túpeni hápeni; 2. tápəni héipəni]. Insignificant, contemptible, trivial: *twopenny-halfpenny squabbles.*

two-ply, adj. **a** Having double thickness; **b** woven double; **c** having two strands.

two-power standard, n. Principle of naval construction based on having a navy equal to a combination of the navies of the two next strongest powers.

two-seater, n. Motor-car designed to seat two people.

two-sided, adj. Having two sides; having two aspects; having a double bearing.

twosome, n., orig. adj. [1. tōōsum; 2. tūsəm]. Game played by two players only.

two-speed, adj. Adaptable to two different speeds: *two-speed gear.*

two-step, n. **a** A dance in polka time; **b** music composed for such a dance.

-ty (I.), suff. forming abstract ns. fr. adj.; fr. Fr. *-té*, fr. Lat. *-tāt-*; *piety*, Fr. *piété*, Lat. *pietāt-(em)*, fr. *pius* &c.

-ty (II.), suff. O.E. *-tiġ*, 'ten', cp. O.E. *tīen*, '10', Goth. *tigus*, 'group of ten', *taihun*, '10'; see **ten.** Suffix used to denote so many times ten: *twenty, thirty* &c.

Tyburn, n. [1. tíburn; 2. táibən]. Former place of execution in London, close to present Marble Arch. *Tyburn tippet*, halter for hanging a criminal; *Tyburn tree*, the gallows.

tycoon, n. [1. tīkōōn; 2. tàikūn]. Jap. *taikun*, 'great ruler'. Title applied formerly to the hereditary commander-in-chief, the shogun, in Japan; office and title now abolished.

tyke. See **tike.**

tyler. See **tiler.**

Tylopod, n. [1. tílopod; 2. táiləpɔd], fr. Gk. *túlos*, 'lump, knot', fr. base **tu-*, 'to swell', see **tumid, tumour** &c., & *pod-*, stem of *poús*, 'foot', see **pedal (I.).** Member of a division of ruminant mammals, including the camels, llamas &c.

tylosis, n. [1. tīlṓsis; 2. tailóusis]. Gk. *túlos*, 'lump, knot', see prec. & **-osis. 1.** (med.) A thickening, hardening, of tissue. **2.** (bot.) Irregular mass of cells formed by growth of one plant cell into another.

tymp, n. [1. timp; 2. timp]. See next word. Covering of opening in a blast-furnace, through which molten metal and slag pass.

tympan, n. [1. tímpan; 2. tímpən]. Shortened form of **tympanum.** Thin sheet of paper, parchment &c., in a printing press, placed between the platen and the upper surface of the paper which is being printed.

tympanic, adj. [1. timpánik; 2. timpǽnik]. **tympanum** & **-ic. 1.** Pertaining to, resembling, a tympanum or drum. **2.** Specif., pertaining to the tympanum of the ear.

tympanites, n. [1. tìmpanítēz; 2. tìmpənáitīz]. Gk., see **tympanum** & **-ite.** Tightening, distension, of the abdomen, due to accumulation of gas in the intestines.

tympanitis, n. [1. tìmpanítis; 2. tìmpənáitis]. **tympanum** & **-itis.** Inflammation of the membrane of the middle ear.

tympano-, pref. Form of **tympanum** used in compounds.

tympanum, n. [1. tímpanum; 2. tímpənəm]. Lat., fr. Gk. *túmpanon*, 'a kettle-drum', also *túpanon*, fr. base *tup-*, as in Gk. *túptein*, 'to strike'; cogn. w. Scrt. *túmpati, tupáti*, 'he strikes'; O. Slav. *tŭpati*, 'to palpitate'; see also **type** (I.). **1.** (anat.) The drum or membrane of the ear. **2.** (archit.) Flat triangular space enclosed by the sides of a pediment or gable at the end of buildings; similar space over a door, between the lintel and the arch.

Tynewald, n. [1. tínwold; 2. táinwəld]. O.N. *ping-völlr*, lit. 'assembly field ', the first element is cogn. w. Engl. **thing**, the second pref. w. Engl. **weald**. The legislative assembly or parliament of the Isle of Man.

type (I.), n. [1. tîp; 2. taip]. Fr., fr. Lat. *typus*, 'figure, image', fr. Gk. *túpos*, 'a blow; mark of a blow; impress of a seal; stamp on a coin; original pattern, model, mould'; fr. base *tup-*, 'to strike'; see **tympanum**. **1.** (rare) Characteristic mark; sign, stamp, impress. **2.** Person, thing, action, event, which is a symbol, or prefiguration of some other person, thing, action &c.: *the king's sceptre is a type of royal authority; the slaying of the lamb at the Passover is a type of Christ's death*. **3. a** Mode of form or structure, combination of physical features, characteristic of all the members of a group: *each of the great races of mankind exhibits a definite type*; **b** class or group, which is recognizable as such by the possession of certain characteristic features and peculiarities of structure &c.: *Australia has many types of animal and plant life not found in other continents; it is now disputed whether there is such a thing as a criminal type; true to type*, exhibiting the distinguishing features of a class. **4.** Class or group, also a member or example of such, distinguished by having certain material or moral qualities common to the whole class: *this is just the type of house I require*; *men of his type are not to be trusted*. **5.** A member of a class or group regarded as exhibiting the characteristics and qualities of the class in a very complete manner, and as constituting a standard; pattern, model: *a perfect type of English country gentleman*. **6. a** Block of metal, more rarely of wood, upon the upper surface of which a letter or other symbol is cast or cut, from which an impression is taken in printing; **b** (collectively) a set, collection, of types: *books are stereotyped to avoid keeping large quantities of type lying idle*; Phr. *in type*, set up in the press all ready for printing; **c** style, shape, kind, of type: *the type of the book is admirable*.

type (II.), vb. trans. & intrans., fr. prec. **1.** trans. (rarely) To typify, be a type of. **2. a** trans. To print (words) with a typewriter, to typewrite; **b** intrans., to use a typewriter.

-type, suff., fr. **type** (I.). **1.** Representative, exemplar: *prototype*. **2.** Print, mode of printing, of reproduction: *autotype, stereotype*.

type-founder, n. One who casts type for printing.

type-foundry, n. Place where metal is cast into type.

type-setter, n. Compositor in printing works.

typewrite, vb. trans. & intrans. [1. típrīt; 2. táiprait]. **a** trans. To print, copy, with a typewriter; **b** intrans., to make use of a typewriter.

typewriter, n. [1. típrītər; 2. táipràitə]. Machine worked by the fingers, which transmits printed characters to paper, used instead of handwriting.

typewritten, adj. [1. típritn; 2. táipritn], fr. P.P. of **typewrite**. Copied, written, on a typewriter.

typhlitis, n. [1. tifflítis; 2. tifláitis]. Coined fr. Gk. *tuphlós*, 'blind, closed' (for cognates see **deaf**), on anal. of med. Lat. *caecum*, & *-itis*. Inflammation of the caecum.

typhoid, adj. & n. [1. tífoid; 2. táifɔid]. See **typhus** & **-oid**. **a** adj. Resembling, of the nature of, typhus; *typhoid fever*, an infectious fever, originally thought to be a form of typhus, but now known to be due to a bacillus, *typhoid bacillus*, conveyed by infected drinking water, milk, or food; the disease is now usually styled *enteric fever*; **b** n., typhoid fever.

typhoidal, adj. [1. tifóidl; 2. taifɔ́idl]. Prec. & **-al**. Pertaining to, resembling, typhoid fever.

typhomania, n. [1. tifōmánia; 2. tàifouméiniə]. **typhus** & **mania**. Delirium characteristic of typhus fever.

typhonic, adj. [1. tifónik; 2. taifɔ́nik]. See next word & **-ic**. Pertaining to, of the nature of, a typhoon.

typhoon, n. [1. tifōōn; 2. taifún]. Earlier *tuffoon*, Port. *tufão*; prob. fr. Gk. *tuphôn*, 'furious storm, hurricane'; fr. base **dhū-* &c.; see **typhus** & words there referred to. The Chinese *tai fêng*, 'great wind', may possibly have been the starting-point, but the above quite unrelated Gk. word is responsible for the form of the word we use. Violent whirlwind, a hurricane; specif., one occurring in China seas.

typhous, adj. [1. tífus; 2. táifəs]. **typhus** & **-ous**. Connected with, of the nature of, typhus.

typhus, n. [1. tífus; 2. táifəs], fr. Gk. *tûphos*, 'smoke, mist, cloud'; cp. *túphein*, 'to smoke', for **thūph-*, cogn. w. Scrt. *dhūpa*, 'smoke'; fr. base **dhū-* &c., q.v. under **dust** (I.) & **fume** (I.). Contagious fever due to a bacillus conveyed by lice, fleas, and other parasites, causing great weakness, and accompanied by red spots on the body; formerly called *jail fever* and *putrid fever*.

typic, adj. [1. típik; 2. típik]. Fr. *typique*, Lat. *typicus*, fr. Gk. *tupikós*; **type** (I.) & **-ic**. Typical.

typical, adj. [1. típikl; 2. típikl]. Prec. & **-al**. **1.** Possessing, exhibiting, so fully the characteristics of a type as to serve as an example, specimen, or representative of this: *a typical Oxford don*; *a typical British officer* &c. **2.** Symbolical, emblematic: *the Passover was typical of Christ's death*.

typically, adv. [1. típik(a)li; 2. típik(ə)li]. Prec. & **-ly**. In a typical manner.

typify, vb. trans. [1. típifī; 2. típifai]. See **type** (I.) & **-fy**. **1.** To be a type, symbol, of, to prefigure. **2.** To exhibit essential characteristic features of; to exemplify.

typist, n. [1. típist; 2. táipist]. **type** (II.) & **-ist**. Person who works a typewriting machine.

typo-, form of Gk. *túpos* used in compounds; see **type** (I.).

typographer, n. [1. típógrafer; 2. taipɔ́grəfə]. **typo-** & **-graph** & **-er**. One who has to do with type and printing; a printer.

typographic(al), adj. [1. típográfik(l); 2. tàipəgræfik(l)]. See prec. & **-ic** & (**-al**). Connected with, pertaining to, the art of printing.

typographically, adv. Prec. & **-ly**. As regards printing.

typography, n. [1. típógrafi; 2. taipɔ́grəfi]. **typo-** & **-graphy**. **a** The art of printing from type; **b** style of printing, mode of arrangement of type.

typology, n. [1. típóloji; 2. taipɔ́lədži]. **typo-** & **-logy**. **a** Doctrine that events &c. recorded in the New Testament are prefigured in the Old; **b** treatise on the types of Scripture.

tyrannical, adj. [1. ti-, tiránikl; 2. ti-, tairǽnikl]. Lat. *tyrannicus*, fr. Gk. *turannikós*; see **tyrant** & **-ic** & **-al**. Characteristic of, natural to, befitting, resembling, a tyrant; hence, oppressive, arbitrarily harsh, despotic.

tyrannically, adv. Prec. & **-ly**. In a tyrannical, oppressive manner; harshly and unjustly.

tyrannicidal, adj. [1. tirànisídl; 2. tirænisáidl]. Next word & **-al**. Pertaining to the killing of a tyrant, or of tyrants.

tyrannicide, n. [1. ti-, tiránisīd; 2. ti-, tairǽnisaid]. Lat. (i.) *tyrannicīdium*, 'killing of a tyrant'; (ii.) *tyrannicīda*, 'killer of a tyrant'; see **tyrant** & **-cide**. **1.** Act of killing a tyrant. **2.** One who kills a tyrant.

tyrannize, vb. intrans. [1. tíraniz; 2. tírənaiz]. Fr. *tyranniser*, fr. Gk. *turannízein*, 'to play the part of a tyrant'; see **tyrant** & **-ize**. To play the tyrant; to rule, exert authority harshly, arbitrarily, and unjustly; *tyrannize over*.

tyrannous, adj. [1. tíranus; 2. tírənəs]. O. Fr. *tiran-*, see **tyrant**, & **-ous**. Like a tyrant, tyrannical.

tyrannously, adv. Prec. & **-ly**. In a tyrannous manner.

tyrannousness, n. See prec. & **-ness**. **a** Quality of being tyrannous; **b** tyrannous conduct.

tyranny, n. [1. tírani; 2. tírəni]. M.E., fr. O. Fr. *tirannie*, fr. Gk. *turannía*, 'rule of a tyrant'; see **tyrant** & **-y**. **1.** (Gk. hist.) Government, jurisdiction, of a tyrant in old sense (see **tyrant**, 1). **2.** Harsh, arbitrary, unjust exercise of authority; despotism, oppressive rule. **3.** A tyrannical action; an example of the exercise of despotic power, or of an unduly rigorous discipline.

tyrant, n. [1. tírant; 2. táiərənt]. M.E. *tirant*, fr. O. Fr. *tirant*, earlier *tiran*; fr. Lat. *tyrannus*, fr. Gk. *túrannos*, 'an absolute prince or ruler; a cruel, unjust ruler'. According to some authorities the word is of Phrygian origin; others connect w. the base in Lith. *tverti*, 'to seize'; others again w. Scrt. *tūrvati*, 'to subjugate'. **1.** (anct. Gk. hist.) An absolute ruler; applied to one who had seized the supreme power, as contrasted with a hereditary king. **2. a** A despotic, harsh, unjust, arbitrary, ruler; one who oppresses his people; **b** any masterful person who exerts his authority in a cruel, oppressive manner.

tyre. See **tire** (II.), 3.

tyro. See **tiro**.

tyro-, pref., fr. Gk. *tūrós*, 'cheese'; prob. fr. same base as Lat. *turgēre*, 'to swell'; see **turgid**, & second element of **butter** (I.). Occurs as prefix in a few scientific words, e.g. *tyrotoxicon*, poisonous substance occurring in putrid cheese, milk, or butter.

tzar, **tzarina** &c. See **czar** &c.

tzetze-fly. See **tsetse-fly**.

Tzigany, adj. & n. [1. tsigáhni; 2. tsigɑ́ni]. Fr. *tzigane*, fr. Magyar c(z)*igány*. **a** adj. Pertaining to a (Hungarian) gipsy; **b** n., a Hungarian gipsy.

U

U, u, [1. ū; 2. jū]. The twenty-first letter of the English alphabet; for use in abbreviations &c. see list at end of Dictionary.

uberous, adj. [1. úberus; 2. júbərəs]. Lat. *ūber*, 'a teat, breast, udder'; also as adj., 'rich, full, fertile'; for suff. see **-ous**. *Uber* is cogn. w. Gk. *oûthar*; Scrt. *ū́har*, 'udder', also w. O.E. *ūder*, see **udder**. (rare) Plentiful, copious; fertile.

uberrima fides, n. [1. ūbérima fídēz; 2. jūbérimə fáidīz]. Lat. superl. of *ūber*, 'fruitful' &c., see prec.; for *fidēs*, 'faith', see **fidelity**. (law) The most complete good faith, esp. applied to contracts entered into by parties standing in a particular relation of mutual

trust, as guardian and ward, solicitor and client &c.

ubiety, n. [1. ŭbíeti ; 2. jūbáiiti]. Neo-Lat. *ubietāt-*, stem of *ubietas*, 'wheresoever', formed fr. Lat. *ubi*, 'where', for **cubi*, as in *alicubi*, 'elsewhere'; Aryan **k^wu-* &c. (orig. a pronominal stem) appears also in Scrt. *kvà*, 'where, whither'; Gk. *póteron*, 'whether' &c.; see also under **how** & **where** (I.). (philos.) Whereness; quality or state of being in a place in relation to another thing; abstract, relative position.

Ubiquitarian, n. [1. ŭbikwitárian ; 2. jūbikwitéəriən]. Formed fr. **ubiquity** & **-arian**. (theol.) One who believes in the ubiquity or omnipresence of the body of Christ in all things, not only in heaven and the Eucharist, a doctrine held by certain Lutheran theologians.

Ubiquitarianism, n. [1. ŭbikwitárianizm ; 2. jūbikwitéəriənizm]. Prec. & **-ism**. (theol.) Doctrine of the Ubiquitarians.

ubiquitous, adj. [1. ŭbíkwitus ; 2. jūbíkwitəs]. **ubiquity** & **-ous**. Being, existing, found, present, everywhere, omnipresent.

ubiquitously, adv. Prec. & **-ly**. In a ubiquitous manner; as if present everywhere.

ubiquitousness, n. See prec. & **-ness**. State of being ubiquitous or present everywhere.

ubiquity, n. [1. ŭbíkwiti ; 2. jūbíkwiti], fr. O. Fr. *ubiquite*, as if fr. Lat. **ubīquitas*, fr. *ubīque*, 'everywhere', see **ubiety**, & **-ity**. State, quality, of being ubiquitous; presence, existence, in every place or an indefinite number of places at the same time; omnipresence. Phr. *the ubiquity of the king*, (law) the assumed presence of the sovereign in all his courts of justice in the person of his judges.

ubi supra, adv. [1. ŭbi sŭprə ; 2. jūbi sjūprə]. Lat., 'where above'. In the place above mentioned; as reference in book to a work, passage &c. cited previously.

U-boat, n. [1. ŭ bŏt ; 2. jū bòut]. A German submarine; these in the German navy were lettered U followed by a numeral, as abbreviation of *Unter-see boot*, lit. 'under-sea boat, submarine'.

udal, n. [1. údal ; 2. jūdəl], also *odal*, fr. O.N. *ōðal*, Dan. *odel*, cogn. w. O.H.G. *uodil*, 'farm'. (legal hist.) A form of land tenure, *udal tenure*, existing in Scotland prior to the establishment of the feudal system, and still existing in Orkney and Shetland, in which land is held by right of uninterrupted possession and descends to all the children equally; *udal man, woman*, male, female, owner by udal; udaller.

udaller, n. [1. údaler ; 2. jūdələ]. Prec. & **-er**. Owner of land by udal tenure.

udder, n. [1. úder ; 2. ádə]. O.E. *ūder*, M.E. *uddir* &c.; O.H.G. *ūtar*, Mod. Germ. *euter*, cogn. w. Lat. *ūber*, see **uberous**. The large, pendulous external milk gland with more than one teat or nipple, esp. of cows, sheep, goats &c.

-uddered, adj. [1. úderd ; 2. ádəd]. Prec. & **-ed**. Having so many or such udders : *double-, two-uddered* &c.; *large-, small-uddered*.

udderless, adj. [1. úderles ; 2. ádəlis]. **udder** & **-less**. Deprived of udders or nourishment from the mother; hence, motherless: *udderless lambs*.

-ude, suff. [1. ūd ; 2. jūd], fr. Lat. *-ūdo*, forming abstract ns. fr. adjs. & P.P.'s w. stems ending in *-t*; see **-tude**.

udograph, n. [1. údōgrahf ; 2. jūdougráf]. See first element of **udometer** & **-graph**. An automatic, self-registering rain-gauge.

udometer, n. [1. údōmeter ; 2. jūdómitə], fr. Lat. *ūdus*, 'wet', contracted fr. **uoidus*, 'wet, damp, moist', cogn. w. Gk. *hugrós*, 'wet, moist'; further related to Scrt. *uksáti*, 'he sprinkles'; prob. also to Scrt. *ukśan-*, 'ox'; see also **ox**; for suff. see **-meter**. A rain-gauge.

udometric, adj. [1. ŭdōmétrik ; 2. jūdoumétrik]. Prec. & **-ic**. Pertaining to a rain-gauge or measurement of rainfall by such instrument.

udometry, n. [1. ŭdómetri ; 2. jūdómitri]. Measurement of rainfall by a udometer or rain-gauge.

ugh, interj. [1. ugh ; 2. aχ]. Imitative. An expression of disgust, contempt, disapproval, and dislike.

uglify, vb. trans. [1. úglifī ; 2. áglifai]. **ugly** (I.) & **-fy**. To make ugly; to spoil the beauty or attractiveness of.

uglily, adv. [1. úglili ; 2. áglili]. **ugly** (I.) & **-ly**. In an ugly manner.

ugliness, n. [1. úglines ; 2. áglinis]. **ugly** (I.) & **-ness**. Condition, quality, of being ugly.

ugly (I.), adj. [1. úgli ; 2. ágli]. Scand., fr. O.N. *uggligr*, 'fearful, horrible, awful', fr. *uggr*, 'fear', cogn. w. **awe** (I.); the suff. is O.N. *-ligr*, see **-ly**. 1. Repulsive, unpleasing to the sight : hideous, unbecoming, the opposite of *beautiful, handsome*, or *pleasing* or *becoming* : *an ugly face* ; *ugly building* ; *ugly clothes* ; *ugly way of doing the hair*. 2. Offensive to the moral sense, repulsive, vile, unpleasantly suggestive, disreputable: *ugly customs and habits* ; *an ugly crime* ; *there are ugly rumours about his past*. 3. Threatening, menacing; foreboding danger or unpleasantness: *ugly weather* ; *the sky has an ugly look* ; *the crowd made an ugly rush* ; *the situation becomes more ugly every day* ; *an ugly wound*. Phr. *an ugly customer* (colloq.), a dangerous, rough, violent, person.

ugly (II.), n., fr. prec. 1. (colloq.) An ugly person or thing. 2. A shade attached to the front part of a bonnet, worn during the middle part of the 19th cent.

Ugrian, adj. & n. [1. ūgrian ; 2. jūgriən], fr. Ugra, name of the country on both sides of the Ural Mountains & **-ian**. 1. adj. Of, belonging to, the Eastern division of the races and their languages, known as the Finno-Ugrian or Finnic peoples, including the Ostyaks and Voguls of Asiatic Russia, and specif., the Hungarians and Magyars. 2. n. a A member of these races; b one of the languages spoken by them.

Ugric, adj. [1. ūgrik ; 2. jūgrik]. See prec. & **-ic**. Ugrian.

uhlan, n. [1. ōōláhn ; 2. ūlán]. Germ., fr. Pol. *ulan*, 'lancer', fr. Turk. and Tatar *oglān*, 'son, child'; also as title of a chief. A light cavalry soldier, armed with a lance, of the pre-War German or Austrian armies.

ukase, n. [1. ūkáz ; 2. jukéiz]. Fr., fr. Russ. *ukaz*, 'edict; order, decree', fr. *ukazat*, 'to order'. An edict or decree having the force of law on proclamation, as in Tsarist Russia.

ukulele, n. [1. ūkuláli ; 2. jūkəléili]. Hawaiian, lit. 'jumping insect, flea'. A Hawaiian musical stringed instrument, shaped like a guitar or banjo and twanged with the fingers or plectrum.

ulcer, n. [1. úlser ; 2. álsə], fr. Fr. *ulcère*, fr. Lat. *ulcer-(em)*, stem of *ulcus*, 'a sore'; cogn. w. Gk. *hélkos*, 'wound, abscess', cp. Scrt. *arçás*, 'haemorrhoids'. See **helcosis**. 1. An open sore, discharging pus, whether on the external surface of the skin or on an internal mucous membrane : *a varicose ulcer* ; *gastric ulcer* &c. 2. (fig.) A source of moral contagion, corruption; corrupting, festering influence, a moral sore : *the ulcer of discontent, envy* &c.

ulcerate, vb. trans. & intrans. [1. úlserāt ; 2. álsəreit], fr. Lat. *ulcerāt-(um)*, P.P. type of *ulcerāre*, 'to make sore'; see prec. & **-ate**. 1. trans. a To cause the formation of an ulcer in; to infect with an ulcer or ulceration; rare except in P.P. as adj. : *ulcerated sore throat, gums, leg* &c.; b to corrupt morally. 2. intrans. To become ulcerated; to form ulcers.

ulceration, n. [1. ŭlseráshun ; 2. àlsəréiʃən]. Prec. & **-ion**. a Ulcerated condition; b process of becoming ulcerated.

ulcerative, adj. [1. úlserativ ; 2. álsərətiv]. **ulcerate** & **-ive**. 1. Tending to cause or produce ulcers; ulcerating. 2. Infected with ulcers; ulcerous.

ulcered, adj. [1. úlserd ; 2. álsəd]. **ulcer** & **-ed**. Affected by an ulcer; ulcerated; festered.

ulcerous, adj. [1. úlserus ; 2. álsərəs], fr. Lat. *ulcerōsus*; **ulcer** & **-ous**. 1. a Of the nature of an ulcer; sore and discharging pus: *an ulcerous wound*, b (fig.) corrupting, festering: *an ulcerous hatred*. 2. Affected by an ulcer or ulcers; ulcerated: *an ulcerous leg, gums* &c.

ulcerously, adv. Prec. & **-ly**. In an ulcerous manner.

ulcerousness, n. See prec. & **-ness**. State of being ulcerous or ulcerated.

-ule, dimin. suff., fr. Lat. words ending in *-ulus, -a, -um*; as *globule*, or in mod. formations on anal. of Lat., as *pillule*.

ulema, n. [1. óolema ; 2. úlimə], fr. Arab. *'ulamā*, 'learned men', pl. of *'alim*, 'wise, learned', fr. *'alama*, 'to know, be wise'. Men learned in Moslem theology and law, specif., the college of doctors of sacred law, presided over by the Sheikh-ul Islam of Turkey.

uliginose, uliginous, adj. [1. ūlíjinōs, -us ; 2. jūlídʒinous, -əs], fr. Lat. *ūlīginōsus*, 'damp, wet, marshy', fr. *ūlīgin-(em)*, stem of *ūligo*, 'moisture, dampness, marshiness'; for **ūviligo*, w. dial. *l* for earlier *d* ; cp. *ūvidus, ūdus*, 'moist, damp'; see first element of **udometer**. 1. Oozy, muddy, slimy. 2. (bot.) Growing in swampy, muddy places.

ullage, n. [1. úlij ; 2. álidʒ], fr. Provenç. *ulhage*, in O. Fr. *eullage, ouillage*, fr. Provenç. *ulha*, 'to fill up (cask) to the bung or eye'; ultimately fr. Lat. *oculus*, 'eye', see **ocular**, & **-age**. The amount by which a cask or bottle of liquor is short of being full.

ulmaceous, adj. [1. ulmáseus ; 2. alméisiəs], Mod. formation fr. Lat. *ulmus*, 'the elm', see **elm**, & **-aceous**. (bot.) Of, belonging to, the family of trees, *Ulmaceae*, which includes the elms.

ulmic, adj. [1. úlmik ; 2. álmik]. **ulmin** & **-ic**. (chem.) Of, pertaining to, obtained from, ulmin: *ulmic acid*, an acid found in humus.

ulmin, n. [1. úlmin ; 2. álmin]. New formation, fr. Lat. *ulmus*, 'elm', see **elm**, & **-in**. (chem.) A brown, sticky substance found on elms and other trees, and also in decaying vegetable mould or humus; one of the chemical constituents of humus.

ulna, n., pl. **ulnae**, [1. úlna, -nē ; 2. álnə, -nī]. Lat., 'elbow'; fr. **ŏlenā*, fr. Gk. *ōlénē*, 'elbow'; cogn. w. Goth. *aleina*; O.E. *eln*; see **ell** & **elbow**. (anat.) The inner of the two bones of the forearm, or of the two similar bones of the fore-limb of vertebrate animals.

ulnar, adj. [1. úlnar ; 2. álnə]. Prec. & **-ar**. (anat.) Pertaining to, situated on, the same side as the ulna: *ulnar artery, nerve, vein*.

ulno-, pref. Form of **ulna** used in compounds; *ulnocarpal*, pertaining to the ulna and carpus.

ulotrichous, adj. [1. ūlótrikus ; 2. jūlótrikəs], fr. Gk. *oulóthrix*, genit. *oulótrikhos*, 'woolly haired', fr. *oũlos*, 'curly, woolly', & *thríx, trikhós*, 'hair'. The first element is for **wolnos*, & is cogn. w. Lat. *lāna*, 'wool', fr. **wlāna*, see **lanate**; & O.E. *wull*, see **wool**; for second element see **tricho-**. (ethnol.) Having woolly hair; esp. of the woolly-haired or negroid races.

ulster, n. [1. úlster ; 2. álstə], fr. Ulster, the N.E. province of Ireland. A long heavy loose overcoat, usually furnished with a belt, and sometimes with a small hood which hangs down the back when not used for protecting the head.

ulterior, adj. [1. ultérior ; 2. altíəriə]. Lat., 'farther, beyond', compar. of an old adj. **ulter*, the base of wh. is seen in *ultrā* & *ultro*, & in O. Lat. *uls, ols*, 'beyond', cp. also O. Lat. *ollus*, 'that one', later *ille*. 1. (of position) Lying on the farther side of or beyond a specified boundary line: *on the ulterior side of the river*. 2. (of time) Following, succeeding in the future; later in time; prospective: *ulterior steps will be taken to secure this object*; *the ulterior consequences of his act*. 3. (of motives, aims, intentions &c.) More remote; not plainly avowed; undisclosed: *ulterior*

motives; *ulterior objects, plans* &c.; *for the sake of ulterior ends.*

ulteriorly, adv. Prec. & **-ly**. In an ulterior manner; more remotely.

ultima, adj. & n. [1. última; 2. áltimə]. Lat., fem. sing. of *ultimus*, 'last, latest', superl. of **ulter*, see **ulterior**. 1. adj. Last, final; in Phrs. *ultima ratio*, the last, final reason or argument or sanction, force or violence; *ultima ratio regum*, 'the final argument of kings', war and its instruments; *ultima Thule*, furthest Thule, an island placed by ancient geographers north of the British Isles; hence, any far-distant, unknown land. 2. n. The final syllable of a word.

ultimate, adj. [1. últimat; 2. áltimit], fr. Lat. *ultimāt-(um)*, P.P. type of *ultimāre*, 'to be at the last, to come to an end', fr. *ultimus*, 'last', see prec. word. 1. (of place) Farthest, most distant, beyond which one cannot go: *to the ultimate ends of the earth*; *the ultimate regions of space*. 2. (of time) Last, latest, final: *man's ultimate end, destiny*; *to look forward to an ultimate peace.* 3. Last in a series, chain of succession, or consequences: *the ultimate results of one's action.* 4. Final, fundamental; beyond further analysis, primary: *ultimate causes, principles*; *the ultimate sources of belief.*

ultimately, adv. Prec. & **-ly**. In an ultimate manner; finally, in the end, at last.

ultimateness, n. See prec. & **-ness**. State, quality, of being ultimate; finality.

ultimatum, n. [1. ùltimátum; 2. àltiméitəm], pl. *ultimata*, or *ultimatums*. Lat., neut. sing. of P.P. of *ultimāre*, 'to come to an end'. Formed fr. *ultimus*, 'last', see **ultimate**. The last word, final expression of intentions &c.; specif., the final terms, admitting of no further discussion, proposed by a government or other administrative or executive body, or by an individual, in negotiating with another; the rejection of an ultimatum by the party to whom it is presented implies the end of friendly negotiations and a resort to methods designed to compel compliance with the will of the party presenting it.

ultimo, adv., abbr. *ult.* [1. últimō; 2. áltimou], fr. Lat. *ultimō*, sc. *mense*, 'in the last month'; see **ultima**. In the month preceding the present or current month: *in answer to your letter of the 16th ultimo*; cp. *instant* and *proximo.*

ultimogeniture, n. [1. últimōjénichur; 2. áltimoudžénitʃə]. Prec. & **-geniture**. (law) A system of inheritance by which landed property descends to the youngest son, as in Borough-English, contrasted with *primogeniture.*

ultra, adj. & n. [1. últra; 2. áltrə]. Lat. adv. & prep., 'beyond, on the other, far side of', see **ulterior**. 1. adj. Extreme in views, opinions &c.; favouring extreme principles: *an ultra Conservative, Protestant* &c. 2. n. One who holds extreme opinions &c.; an extremist: *a thorough-paced ultra.*

ultra-, pref., fr. prec., quite freely used w. adjs. & derivative ns., indicating, to an excessive degree or extent, beyond what is customary, ordinary, natural, proper, or reasonable; *ultra-conservative*; *ultra-fashionable*; *an ultra-Protestant* &c.; only words with a special meaning are given separate entries.

ultraism, n. [1. últraìzm; 2. áltrəìzəm]. **ultra-** & **-ism**. The holding of extreme, esp. political, opinions.

ultraist, n. [1. últraist; 2. áltrəist]. As prec. & **-ist**. One who holds extreme opinions.

ultramarine (I.), adj. [1. últramarén; 2. áltrəmərín]. **ultra-** & **marine** (I.). Situated beyond the sea or seas; overseas: *ultramarine dominions*; *ultramarine trade.*

ultramarine (II.), n. & adj., fr. Ital. *oltramarino*, 'beyond the seas', w. first syll. Latinized; applied to lapis lazuli, wh. had to be imported. 1. n. A brilliant pure blue pigment, originally obtained from powdered lapis lazuli, now artificially produced from kaolin, silica, sulphate and carbonate of soda &c. 2. adj. Of blue colour, as in this pigment.

ultra-microscopic, adj. **ultra-** & **microscopic**. Beyond the range of the microscope; too small to be visible under the microscope.

ultramontane, adj. & n. [1. últramóntān; 2. áltrəmóntein]. See **ultra-** & **montane**; cp. Fr. *ultramontain*, Ital. *oltramontano*, fr. L. Lat. *ultramontānus*, in Class. Lat. *trāmontānus*, see **tramontane**. 1. adj. a Beyond, on the other side of, the mountains, i.e. the Alps; applied to Italians by northern peoples as living on the south side, and vice versa; b specif., pertaining to, supporting, the extreme claims of the Papacy to absolute authority in all matters of faith and discipline, over-riding general Councils, together with refusal to allow any independence to national Roman Catholic Churches outside Italy; a term used by opponents of the full enforcement of the decrees of the Vatican Council of 1870. 2. n. a One who lives beyond the Alps; b (cap.) a supporter of the ultramontane policy in the Roman Catholic Church.

ultramontanism, n. [1. últramóntinizm; 2. áltrəmóntinizəm]. Prec. & **-ism**. Principles, policy, of the ultramontanes.

ultramontanist, n. [1. últramóntinist; 2. áltrəmóntinist]. **ultramontane** & **-ist**. An ultramontane.

ultramundane, adj. [1. últramúndān; 2. áltrəmándein]. **ultra-** & **mundane**. (rare) Beyond, outside, the world, or the limits of the solar system.

ultra-red, adj. **ultra-** & **red**. (phys.) Of those rays of the spectrum which are below the red, the lowest visible rays; infra-red.

ultra-violet, adj. **ultra-** & **violet**. (phys.) Of those electro-magnetic waves which in the spectrum fall between the visible violet and the X-rays.

ultra vires, adv. or adj. [1. últra vírēz; 2. áltrə váiəriz]. Lat., 'beyond powers or strength'; **ultra** & *vīrēs*, pl. of *vis*, 'force, strength', see **virile**. (law) Beyond, transcending, power or authority; exceeding the powers granted by law; used esp. of actions taken by the directors of a company or by municipal or local authorities in excess of their powers.

ululant, adj. [1. ūlulant; 2. júljulənt], fr. Lat. *ululant-(em)*, Pres. Part. of *ululāre*, see next word. Howling, hooting.

ululate, vb. intrans. [1. ūlulāt; 2. júljuleit], fr. Lat. *ululāt-(um)*, P.P. type of *ululāre*, 'to howl'; imitative. To howl, hoot, as wolves, owls &c.

ululation, n. [1. ùlūláshun; 2. jùljuléiʃən]. Prec. & **-ion**. a The sound of lamentation; howling, wailing; b the act of howling &c.; used of the cries of owls, wolves &c., also of human wailing.

umbel, n. [1. úmbl; 2. ámbl], fr. Lat. *umbella*, 'a little shade, a sunshade, parasol', dimin. of *umbra*, 'shade, shadow', q.v. under **umbra**. (bot.) A type of flower cluster or inflorescence in which the stalks radiate from a single point forming a flat or convex head of flowers.

umbellal, adj. [1. úmbelal; 2. ámbələl]. **umbel** & **-al**. (bot.) Umbellate.

umbellar, adj. [1. úmbelar; 2. ámbələ]. As prec. & **-ar**. (bot.) Umbellate.

umbellate, adj. [1. úmbelāt; 2. ámbεleit]. **umbel** & **-ate**. (bot.) Having umbels; arranged in umbels.

umbellet, n. [1. úmbelet; 2. ámbεlεt]. **umbel** & **-et**. (bot.) An umbellule.

umbelliferous, adj. [1. ùmbelíferus; 2. àmbεlífərəs]. **umbel** & **-ferous**. (bot.) a Bearing, having, umbels; b belonging to the Umbelliferae, a large order of plants chiefly characterized by the umbels of their inflorescence.

umbelliform, adj. [1. umbéliform; 2. ambélifɔm]. **umbel** & **-form**. (bot.) Having the form or shape of an umbel.

umbellule, n. [1. úmbelūl; 2. ámbεljul]. **umbel** & **-ule**. (bot.) One of the secondary umbels in a compound umbelliferous plant; umbellet.

umber (I.), n. [1. úmber; 2. ámbə], fr. O. Fr. *ombre*, in this sense short for *terre d'ombre*, 'earth for giving shadow' to pictures, fr. Lat. *umbra*, 'shade, shadow'; see **umbra**. 1. An earthy, mineral pigment of a yellowish-brown colour, in raw or natural state, and with a reddish tint when burnt or calcined. 2. a The grayling (fish); b umber-bird or umbrette.

umber (II.), adj., fr. prec. Of dark-brown colour.

umber (III.), vb. trans. To colour, paint, with umber.

umber-bird, n. An African wading-bird, *Seopus umbretta*, allied to the herons, of dark-brown plumage, large bill and crested head; the umbrette.

umbilical, adj. [1. umbílikl; 2. ambílikl]. See **umbilicus** & **-al**. 1. Of, pertaining to, situated in the region of, the umbilicus or navel: *umbilical cord*, the navel cord, the rope-like structure joining the foetus of a mammal to the placenta and containing the *umbilical veins and arteries*, through which blood passes to and from the placenta; *umbilical hernia*, hernia of the bowels at or near the umbilicus. 2. In the position of, shaped like, an umbilicus or navel: *an umbilical pillar* of a dome or vault; *umbilical opening*, in a dome. 3. (rare) Descended from the mother's side.

umbilicate, adj. [1. umbílikāt; 2. ambílikeit]. **umbilicus** & **-ate**. 1. a Having an umbilicus or navel; b having a depression in the centre like an umbilicus. 2. Shaped like an umbilicus.

umbilication, n. [1. ùmbilikáshun; 2. àmbilikéiʃən]. Prec. & **-ion**. A navel-like depression.

umbilicular, adj. [1. ùmbilíkūlar; 2. àmbilíkjulə]. **umbilicus** & **-ule** & **-ar**. Of, pertaining to, the umbilicus; umbilical.

umbilicus, n. [1. ùmbilíkus; 2. àmbiláikəs]. Lat. *umbilicus*, cogn. w. Gk. *omphalós*, & **navel**; cp. **umbo**. 1. The anatomical name for the navel, q.v. 2. a A circular navel-like central depression, as in certain shells; b the hilum or 'eye' of beans and other seeds. 3. (Rom. antiq.) The boss at each end of the wooden staff on which manuscripts were rolled. 4. (geom.) a (obs.) Focus; b point on a surface through which all lines of curvature pass.

umbiliform, adj. [1. umbíliform; 2. ambílifɔm]. Prec. & **-form**. Shaped like an umbilicus.

umble pie, n. [1. úmbl pí; 2. ámbl pái]. See **humble pie**, & for etymol. see next word.

umbles, n. [1. úmblz; 2. ámblz]. Also *numbles*, M.E. *noumbles*, fr. O. Fr. *nombles*, properly *lombles*, fr. L. Lat. *lumbulus*, dimin. of *lumbus*, 'loin', see **lumbar**. (obs.) The entrails of a deer.

umbo, n. [1. úmbō; 2. ámbou]. Lat., 'a convex elevation; the boss of a shield', cogn. w. **umbilicus**. 1. The boss of a shield, usually in the centre and having a corresponding depression on the other or internal side. 2. Any round, elevated protuberance, usually with corresponding depression; a (anat.) part of the drum of the ear where it joins the malleus; b (bot.) protuberance on the top surface of various fungi; c (zool.) similar protuberance forming the first stage in the development of a valve in the shells of various molluscs.

umbonal, adj. [1. úmbonal; 2. ámbənəl], fr. Lat. *umbōn-(em)* & **-al**. Pertaining to, situated near, the umbo.

umbonate, adj. [1. úmbonāt; 2. ámbənèit]. As prec. & **-ate**. Shaped like an umbo or boss.

umbra, n., learned pl. **umbrae** [1. úmbra, úmbrē; 2. ámbrə, ámbri]. Lat., 'shade, shadow'; said by Walde to be fr. **unkʷs-ra*, 'shadow, shade', & cogn. w. Lith. *unks-na*, 'shade', & *úkanas*, 'cloudy'. 1. (astron.) a The complete or perfect shadow thrown in an eclipse by the moon, earth &c., leaving

UMBRACULIFEROUS

none of the sun's light visible, opposed to *penumbra*; **b** the central, darkest part of a sun-spot. **2.** (Rom. antiq.) An uninvited guest who comes as the shadow of an invited guest.

umbraculiferous, adj. [1. úmbrakūlíferus; 2. ámbrəkjulíferəs]. **umbraculum & -ferous.** (bot.) Bearing umbracula.

umbraculiform, adj. [1. umbrákūliform; 2. ambrǽkjulifōm]. As prec. & **-form.** (bot.) Shaped like an umbraculum.

umbraculum, n., pl. **umbracula** [1. umbrákūlum, -la; 2. ambrǽkjuləm, -lə]. Lat., 'umbrella', dimin. of **umbra**. (bot.) An umbrella-shaped appendage, as in such plants as the liverwort.

umbrage, n. [1. úmbrij; 2. ámbridž], fr. Fr. *ombrage*, 'shadow, suspicion', fr. Lat. *umbra*, 'shade, shadow', see **umbra & -age**. **1.** (poet.) a Shadow, shade: '*In the deep umbrage of a green hill's shade*' (Byron, 'Childe Harold'); **b** a shadow, reflection: '*His semblable is his mirror*; . . . *his umbrage, nothing more*' (Shakespeare, 'Hamlet'). **2.** Suspicion of slight or injury; feeling of offence or resentment: *to give, take, umbrage*.

umbrageous, adj. [1. umbrájus; 2. ambréidžəs]. Prec. & **-ous. 1.** Shady; giving, affording, shade; shaded, enjoying shade. **2.** (rare) Disposed to take umbrage; suspicious, resentful.

umbrageously, adv. Prec. & **-ly.** In an umbrageous manner.

umbrageousness, n. See prec. & **-ness.** Condition, quality, of being umbrageous.

umbral, adj. [1. úmbral; 2. ámbrəl]. **umbra & -al.** (astron.) Connected with, pertaining to, an umbra or complete shadow; contrasted with *penumbral*.

umbrella, n. [1. umbréla; 2. ambrélə]. Ital., also more commonly *ombrella*, dimin. of *ombra*, 'shade', fr. Lat. **umbra. 1. a** A light, folding framework of flexible ribs of steel &c., radiating from, and sliding up and down on, a stick, covered with silk, gingham, or other material; carried above the head as a protection against rain or against the sun, though in the latter case usually termed 'parasol' or 'sunshade'; **b** a similar device of elaborate and decorative character borne by attendants above the head of Eastern and African potentates as a symbol of dignity. **2.** (zool.) The umbrella-shaped disk forming the upper part of the body of a jelly-fish, by the expansion and contraction of which it swims.

umbrella ant, n. A South American ant which devours leaves, which it carries to its nest over its back; also called the *parasol ant*.

umbrella bird, n. A Central and S. American bird, of black plumage, with a large umbrella-shaped, erectile crest.

umbrella pine, n. A Japanese pine tree with an umbrella-shaped crown, and pine-needles clustered like umbrellas to the twigs.

umbrella shell, n. A marine gastropod mollusc, forming a genus, *Umbrella*, with thick foot and small shell partially covering the body.

umbrella tree, n. A North American dwarf magnolia, *Magnolia tripetala*, with leaves arranged in an umbrella-like cluster at the end of the branches.

umbrette, n. [1. umbrét; 2. ambrét], fr. Fr. *ombrette*, dimin. of *ombre*, 'umber'. The umber-bird.

Umbrian, adj. & n. [1. úmbrian; 2. ámbriən]. Lat. & Ital. *Umbria* & **-an. 1.** adj. Pertaining to the ancient or modern Umbria, Central Italy, its people, language &c.; *Umbrian school* of painting, of Perugino and his pupil Raphael. **2.** n. **a** A native of Umbria; **b** the language of ancient Umbria.

umbriferous, adj. [1. umbríferus; 2. ambríferəs]. Lat. *umbrifer*, see **umbra & -ferous.** Casting, giving, a shade; shady.

umiak, n. [1. ōōmiak; 2. úmiæk]. Eskimo. An Eskimo boat of skins stretched over a wooden framework, used by women; cp. *kayak*.

umlaut, n. & vb. trans. [1. óomlout; 2. úmlaut]. Germ. *um*, 'round, about', & *laut*, 'sound'. **1.** n. (philol.) Term invented by Grimm, and adopted by all German, and formerly by most English grammarians, to denote the change of a vowel in Germanic languages through the influence of another vowel, chiefly *i* (or *j*) or *u*, in the following syllable; the process is now often called *i*-, *j*-, or *u*- mutation in English; example O.E. *mȳs* from *mūsi-, 'mice'. **2.** vb. (rare) To change or mutate a vowel by this process.

umpirage, n. [1. úmpīrij; 2. ámpaiəridž]. **umpire & -age.** (rare, archaic) **a** Position, authority, of an umpire; **b** decision, ruling, of an umpire.

umpire (I.), n. [1. úmpīr; 2. ámpaiə]. M.E. *numpere*; the mod. form is due to *a numpire* being taken for *an umpire*; cp. **apron, adder** &c.; fr. O. Fr. *nomper*, 'not equal, peerless; odd'; hence, 'the odd man, third man with a casting vote', (cp. O.N. *oddemaðr*, 'odd man', in sense of arbitrator), fr. *non*, 'not', & *par*, 'equal', see **par (I.)** & **peer (I.).** A person chosen to judge, decide, arbitrate upon a question in dispute; specif. **a** person chosen to enforce the rules of, and see fair play in, a game, and to decide doubtful points in favour of one side or other; **b** (law) a third person called in to decide when arbitrators have failed to agree.

umpire (II.), vb. intrans. & trans., fr. prec. **1.** intrans. To act as umpire: *will you umpire for our side, for us?; he umpired in the last test match*. **2.** trans. To act as umpire in: *to umpire a championship game at Wimbledon*.

umpteen, adj. [1. úmptēn; 2. ámptīn]. Invented on analogy of *thirteen* &c. See **-teen.** (slang) Many, a large number of.

un- (I.), pref. O.E. *un-*, O.H.G. & Goth. *un-*; O.N. *ū-*; M.E. *un-*; cogn. w. Scrt. *an-*, *a-*, Gk. *an-*, *a-*, see *a-* & **an-**; Lat. *in-*, see **in- (II.)**; Ir. & W. *an*; this pref. is cogn. w. the negatives Lat. *nē*, Scrt. *nā*, Gk. *nē-*; O.E. *ne*, Goth. *ni*, 'not'; see also **no (I.), not, nor (I.).** The force of the pref. *un-* is purely neg., & usually expresses simply 'not' when used before adj. or adv., & 'lack of, reverse of', before ns. It is used: **a** before adjs., whether primary, as *unhappy*, or derived fr. Pres. Part., *unwilling, unbecoming*, or fr. P.P., *unwanted, unsought, undone*='not done', *unforgotten* &c.; **b** before advs., as *unhappily, unchastely* &c.; **c** before abstract ns. derived fr. adjs., such as *unhappiness, unsuitability, unimportance* &c.; **d** before a certain number of primary ns., as in *unrest, unfaith, untruth* &c. The pref. even when unstressed retains the character of the vowel sound, being always [an] & never [ən]. As regards mode of stressing, the following principles cover most cases. **1.** Words compounded w. *un-* usually retain the same conditions of stress as when uncompounded, e.g. *háppy, unháppy; abáshed, unabáshed; relìabílity, unrelìabílity*. In the two last the pref. itself may receive slight secondary stress, *ùnabáshed* &c. **2. a** The pref. itself is completely unstressed when the chief stress falls on the syll. immediately following it, e.g. *unháppy, uncháste*; **b** the pref. is strongly stressed in sentences where positive & neg. forms are contrasted, as in *some men are háppy, some are únhàppy*; **c** (i.) when the pref. is strongly stressed in this way, the following syll., if normally bearing the chief stress, receives only secondary stress. (ii.) In words where the chief stress does not normally fall immediately after the pref. as in *ùnreliable*, this strong syll. receives only the secondary stress when the pref. bears the chief (contrasting) stress, e.g. *réliable and únrèliable*. **3. a** When used before long words wh. when uncompounded have both a strong & a secondary stress, such as *relìabílity*, the pref. itself also receives a secondary stress, as *ùnrelìabílity*; **b** when in such words the pref. is emphasized (in contrast), & receives the principal stress, that syll. wh. has normally the principal stress now has secondary stress,

UNACCOMPLISHED

& that wh. normally has the secondary stress receives a still weaker degree of stress, sufficient, however, to distinguish it fr. the completely unstressed sylls., e.g. *únrèlìabìlity*. The numbers above the sylls. refer to the relative degree of stress wh. each receives.

un- (II.), pref. O.E. *on-* & *un-*, M.E. *un-*; the fuller form is preserved in O.E. *ondswarian*, see **answer**; cp. Du. *ont-*, O.H.G. *ant-* & *int-*, Mod. Germ. *ant-*, *ent-*; cogn. w. Gk. *anti-*; see **anti-**. A pref. used before vbs., expressing **a** the reversal of the action of the vb. to wh. it is attached, as *undo, unlace, unlock* &c.; **b** deprivation, separation; removal, as *unfrock, undress, unsex, unearth, unhorse*. The remarks on stressing & pronunciation under **un- (I.)** apply also to **un- (II.).**

unabashed, adj. [1. ùnabásht; 2. ənəbǽʃt, ànəbǽʃt]. **un- (I.)** & **abash(ed).** Not abashed; **a** unashamed, shameless; **b** not intimidated, preserving composure of mind and bearing.

unabated, adj. [1. ùnabéted; 2. ənəbéitid]. **un- (I.)** & **abate(d).** Not abated, undiminished; preserving full intensity.

unabating, adj. [1. ùnabéting; 2. ənəbéitiŋ]. Not abating; continuing with full intensity.

unabbreviated, adj. [1. ùnabrévīāted; 2. ànəbrívièitid]. **un- (I.)** & **abbreviate(d).** Not abbreviated, preserving full length; unshortened.

unabetted, adj. [1. ùnabéted; 2. ànəbétid]. **un- (I.)** & **abet(ted).** Not abetted.

unabiding, adj. [1. ùnabíding; 2. ànəbáidiŋ]. **un- (I.)** & **abiding.** Not abiding; not lasting; transient, transitory.

unable, adj. [1. ùnábl; 2. anéibl]. **un- (I.)** & **able. 1.** Not able; incapable: *unable to do anything*. **2.** (rare, poet.) Feeble, weak, impotent.

unabolished, adj. [1. ùnabólisht; 2. ànəbóliʃt]. **un- (I.)** & **abolish(ed).** Not abolished; still in force or current; not repealed.

unabridged, adj. [1. ùnabrídj; 2. ànəbrídžd]. **un- (I.)** & **abridge(d).** Not abridged, unshortened; given in full.

unabsorbable, adj. [1. ùnabsórbabl; 2. ànəbsóbəbl]. **un- (I.)** & **absorb & -able.** Not absorbable; incapable of being absorbed.

unabsorbed, adj. [1. ùnabsórbd; 2. ànəbsóbd]. **un- (I.)** & **absorb(ed).** Not absorbed.

unabsorbent, adj. [1. ùnabsórbent; 2. ànəbsóbənt]. **un- (I.)** & **absorbent.** Not absorbent.

unaccented, adj. [1. ùnaksénted; 2. ànəksénted]. **un- (I.)** & **accent(ed).** Not accented, having no accent; specif., of syllables, unstressed.

unaccentuated, adj. [1. ùnakséntūāted; 2. ànəkséntjuèitid]. **un- (I.)** & **accentuate(d).** Not accentuated; not emphasized or brought into prominence.

unacceptability, n. [1. ùnaksèptabíliti; 2. ànəksèptəbíliti]. **un- (I.)** & **acceptability. a** Condition of being unacceptable or unwelcome; **b** lack of welcome or pleasing qualities.

unacceptable, adj. [1. ùnakséptabl; 2. ànəkséptəbl]. **un- (I.)** & **acceptable.** Not acceptable; unwelcome; not giving satisfaction.

unacceptably, adv. Prec. & **-ly.** In an unacceptable manner.

unaccommodating, adj. [1. ùnakómadāting; 2. ànəkómədèitiŋ]. **un- (I.)** & **accommodating.** Not accommodating, not disposed to be compliant or obliging.

unaccompanied, adj. [1. ùnakúmpanid; 2. ànəkámpənid]. **un- (I.)** & **accompany & -ed.** Not accompanied; **a** without a companion; **b** (mus.) without an accompaniment.

unaccomplished, adj. [1. ùnakómplisht; 2. ànəkómpliʃt]. **un- (I.)** & **accomplish(ed).** Not accomplished. **1.** Not completed or brought to a conclusion; not achieved. **2.** Having no accomplishments, not clever or skilful.

unaccountability, n. [1. ùnakòuntəbíliti; 2. ᴧnəkàuntəbíliti]. See next word & -ity. State, quality, of being unaccountable.

unaccountable, adj. [1. ùnakóuntəbl; 2. ᴧnəkáuntəbl]. un- (I.) & accountable. 1. Not to be accounted for; inexplicable. 2. Not responsible.

unaccountably, adv. Prec. & -ly. In an unaccountable manner; inexplicably, strangely.

unaccredited, adj. [1. ùnakrédited; 2. ᴧnəkréditid]. un- (I.) & accredit(ed). Not accredited.

unaccustomed, adj. [1. ùnakústumd; 2. ᴧnəkástəmd]. un-(I.)&accustomed. 1.(with *to*) Not accustomed; unused, not habituated, unfamiliar with: *unaccustomed to hot climates, public speaking*. 2. Not customary; unusual, strange: *with unaccustomed rudeness*; *his unaccustomed absence*.

unachievable, adj. [1. ùnachévabl; 2. ᴧnətʃívəbl]. un- (I.) & achieve & -able. Not to be achieved; incapable of achievement.

unachieved, adj. [1. ùnachévd; 2. ᴧnətʃívd]. un- (I.) & achieve(d). Not achieved.

unacknowledged, adj. [1. ùnaknólejd; 2. ᴧnəknólidžd]. un- (I.) & acknowledge(d). Not acknowledged; a (i.) not recognized, or admitted: *an unacknowledged branch of the family*; (ii.) not returned: *an unacknowledged greeting*; (iii.) (of letters &c.) not answered; b not confessed, owned: *unacknowledged crimes, faults* &c.

unacquainted, adj. [1. ùnakwǎnted; 2. ᴧnəkwéintid]. un- (I.) & acquaint(ed). Not acquainted; having no acquaintance with, or knowledge of.

unacquirable, adj. [1. ùnakwírabl; 2. ᴧnəkwáiərəbl]. un- (I.) & acquire & -able. Not acquirable, not to be acquired; unprocurable.

unacquired, adj. [1. ùnakwírd; 2. ᴧnəkwáiəd]. un- (I.) & acquire(d). Not acquired.

unactable, adj. [1. unáktabl; 2. ᴧnǽktəbl]. un- (I.) & act & -able. Not actable; not fit or suitable for acting.

unacted, adj. [1. unákted; 2. ᴧnǽktid]. un- (I.) & act(ed). 1. Not acted, not done, accomplished, or performed. 2. Not produced, performed, on the stage.

unadaptable, adj. [1. ùnadáptabl; 2. ᴧnədǽptəbl]. un- (I.) & adaptable. Not adaptable.

unadapted, adj. [1. ùnadápted; 2. ᴧnədǽptid]. un- (I.) & adapt(ed). Not adapted; unsuitable for specified purpose.

unaddicted, adj. [1. ùnadíkted; 2. ᴧnədíktid]. un- (I.) & addicted. Not addicted (*to*).

unaddressed, adj. [1. ùnadrést; 2. ᴧnədrést]. un- (I.) & address(ed). Not addressed; (of letter &c.) having no address written upon it.

unadjusted, adj. [1. ùnajústed; 2. ᴧnədžástid]. un- (I.) & adjust(ed). Not adjusted, not settled; unregulated.

unadministered, adj. [1. ùnadmínisterd; 2. ᴧnədmínistəd]. un- (I.) & administer(ed). Not administered.

unadmired, adj. [1. ùnadmírd; 2. ᴧnədmáiəd]. un- (I.) & admire(d). Not admired.

unadmitted, adj. [1. ùnadmíted; 2. ᴧnədmítid]. un- (I.) & admit(ted). Not admitted.

unadmonished, adj. [1. ùnadmónisht; 2. ᴧnədmónɪʃt]. un- (I.) & admonish(ed). Not admonished; uncorrected; not warned or cautioned.

unadorned, adj. [1. ùnadórnd; 2. ᴧnədónd]. un- (I.) & adorn(ed). Not adorned, without adornment; simple, plain.

unadulterated, adj. [1. ùnadúlterăted; 2. ᴧnədáltərèitid]. un- (I.) & adulterate(d). 1. Not adulterated; free from adulteration. 2. Free from sophistication; genuine, pure, unmixed: *unadulterated praise, nonsense*.

unadventurous, adj. [1. ùnadvénchurus; 2. ᴧnədvéntʃərəs]. un- (I.) & adventurous. 1. Lacking a spirit of adventure; not venturesome or enterprising. 2. Not attended by adventures; safe, uneventful: *an unadventurous journey*.

unadvisability, n. [1. ùnadvìzabíliti; 2. ᴧnədvàizəbíliti]. un- (I.) & advisability. State, quality, of being unadvisable.

unadvisable, adj. [1. ùnadvízabl; 2. ᴧnədváizəbl]. un- (I.) & advisable. Not advisable; not to be recommended; inexpedient.

unadvised, adj. [1. ùnadvízd; 2. ᴧnədváizd]. un- (I.) & advise(d). Not advised; a not having received advice; b imprudent, rash.

unadvisedly, adv. [1. ùnadvízedli; 2. ᴧnədváizidli]. Prec. & -ly. Without proper advice; without due consideration; imprudently, rashly.

unaffected, adj. [1. ùnafékted; 2. ᴧnəféktid]. un- (I.) & affected. Not affected. 1. *Unaffected by*, a not moved, changed, or altered: *the ground was unaffected by the recent wet weather*; b unmoved, uninfluenced: *he was quite unaffected by the appeal*. 2. Free from affectation; a not marked by affectation or mannerisms; plain, simple: *unaffected manners; an unaffected, direct style*; b not assumed out of affectation; genuine, sincere, not pretended; not put on or hypocritical: *unaffected grief; he expressed unaffected delight; unaffected kindness of heart*.

unaffectedly, adv. Prec. & -ly. In an unaffected manner.

unaffiliated, adj. [1. ùnafíliăted; 2. ᴧnəfílièitid]. un- (I.) & affiliate(d). Not affiliated (*to*).

unafflicted, adj. [1. ùnaflíkted; 2. ᴧnəflíktid]. un- (I.) & afflict(ed). Not afflicted.

unafraid, adj. [1. ùnafrád; 2. ᴧnəfréid]. un- (I.) & afraid. Not afraid; undismayed.

unaggressive, adj. [1. ùnagrésiv; 2. ᴧnəgrésiv]. un- (I.) & aggressive. Not aggressive; pacific.

unaided, adj. [1. ùnáded; 2. ᴧnéidid]. un- (I.) & aid(ed). Not aided; unassisted; without aid, help, or assistance: *he did it unaided; by his unaided efforts*.

unaired, adj. [1. ùnárd; 2. ᴧnéəd]. un- (I.) & air(ed). Not aired; a not ventilated, deprived of air: *an unaired room*; b not dried by airing; damp: *unaired bed, sheets*.

unalarmed, adj. [1. ùnalármd; 2. ᴧnəlámd]. un- (I.) & alarm(ed). Not alarmed, undismayed; not startled.

unalarming, adj. [1. ùnalárming; 2. ᴧnəláming]. un- (I.) & alarming. Not alarming; not causing or tending to cause alarm.

unalleviated, adj. [1. ùnaléviăted; 2. ᴧnəlívièitid]. un- (I.) & alleviate(d). Not alleviated, not lessened, mitigated, or relieved.

unallied, adj. [1. ùnalíd; 2. ᴧnəláid]. un- (I.) & allied. Not allied, having no relation or connexion: *unallied species, genera* &c.

unallotted, adj. [1. ùnalóted; 2. ᴧnəlótid]. un- (I.) & allot(ted). Not allotted.

unallowable, adj. [1. ùnalóuabl; 2. ᴧnəláuəbl]. un- (I.) & allowable. Not allowable, not permissible.

unallowed, adj. [1. ùnalóud; 2. ᴧnəláud]. un- (I.) & allow(ed). Not allowed; not permitted; forbidden.

unalloyed, adj. [1. ùnalóid; 2. ᴧnəlóid]. un- (I.) & alloy(ed). Not alloyed. 1. (of metals) Free from alloy; pure. 2. (of feelings &c.) Unmixed, unqualified: *unalloyed happiness*.

unalluring, adj. [1. ùnalúring; 2. ᴧnəljúriŋ]. un- (I.) & alluring. Not alluring.

unalterability, n. [1. ùnawlterabíliti; 2. ᴧnòltərəbíliti]. un- (I.) & alterability. Condition, quality, of being unalterable; unalterableness.

unalterable, adj. [1. ùnáwlterabl; 2. ᴧnóltərəbl]. un- (I.) & alterable. Not alterable; incapable of being altered; fixed, unchangeable.

unalterableness, n. Prec. & -ness. Unalterability.

unalterably, adv. See prec. & -ly. In an unalterable manner.

unaltered, adj. [1. ùnáwlterd; 2. ᴧnóltəd]. un- (I.) & alter(ed). Not altered, unchanged.

unaltering, adj. [1. ùnáwltering; 2. ᴧnóltəriŋ]. un- (I.) & alter & -ing. Not altering, constant, unchanging.

unamazed, adj. [1. ùnamázd; 2. ᴧnəméizd]. un- (I.) & amaze(d). Not amazed.

unambiguous, adj. [1. ùnambígūus; 2. ᴧnæmbígjuəs]. un- (I.) & ambiguous. Not ambiguous; clear, plain; not having a doubtful meaning; leaving no room for doubt.

unambiguously, adv. Prec. & -ly. Not ambiguously; plainly, clearly.

unambiguousness, n. See prec. & -ness. Condition, quality, of being unambiguous.

unambitious, adj. [1. ùnambíshus; 2. ᴧnæmbíʃəs]. un- (I.) & ambitious. Not ambitious; modest, unpretentious.

unambitiously, adv. Prec. & -ly. In an unambitious manner; modestly, unpretendingly.

unambitiousness, n. See prec. & -ness. Condition, quality, of being unambitious.

unamenable, adj. [1. ùnaménabl; 2. ᴧnəmínəbl]. un- (I.) & amenable. Not amenable: *unamenable to treatment, discipline* &c.

unamendable, adj. [1. ùnaméndabl; 2. ᴧnəméndəbl]. un- (I.) & amend & -able. Not amendable, incapable of being amended.

unamended, adj. [1. ùnaménded; 2. ᴧnəméndid]. un- (I.) & amend(ed). Not amended.

un-American, adj. [1. ùn amérikan; 2. ᴧn əmérikən]. un- (I.) & American. Not American; not in accordance with American (United States) customs, principles &c.

unamiability, n. [1. ùnàmiabíliti; 2. ᴧnèimiəbíliti]. un- (I.) & amiability. Condition, quality, of being unamiable; moroseness, surliness; disobligingness.

unamiable, adj. [1. ùnǎmiabl; 2. ᴧnéimiəbl]. un- (I.) & amiable. Not amiable; disagreeable, disobliging.

unamiably, adv. Prec. & -ly. In an unamiable manner.

unamusing, adj. [1. ùnamúzing; 2. ᴧnəmjúziŋ]. un- (I.) & amusing. Not amusing.

unanalysable, adj. [1. ùnanalízabl; 2. ᴧnænəláizəbl]. un- (I.) & analyse & -able. Not analysable; not capable of analysis or being analysed.

unanalysed, adj. [1. ùnanalízd; 2. ᴧnænəláizd]. un- (I.) & analyse(d). Not analysed.

unanchor, vb. trans. & intrans. [1. unángkur; 2. ᴧnǽŋkə]. un- (II.) & anchor. 1. trans. To loosen, set free (ship), from an anchor or anchorage. 2. intrans. To be set free from an anchor &c.; to weigh anchor.

unaneled, adj. [1. ùnanéld; 2. ᴧnənéld]. un- (I.) & anele(d). (archaic) Not aneled, unanointed; without having the sacrament of extreme unction administered: '*unhousel'd, disappointed, unaneled*' (Shakespeare, 'Hamlet').

unanimated, adj. [1. unánimăted; 2. ᴧnǽnimèitid]. un- (I.) & animate(d). Not animated.

unanimiter, adv. [1. ùnanímiter; 2. jùnənímitə]. Lat., see next word. (law) Unanimously.

unanimity, n. [1. ùnanímiti; 2. jùnənímiti], fr. Fr. *unanimité*, fr. Lat. *ūnanimitāt-(em)*; see unanimous & -ity. State, quality, of being unanimous: *the unanimity of the Cabinet; the unanimity of the applause*.

unanimous, adj. [1. ūnánimus; 2. junǽniməs], fr. Lat. *ūnanimus*, 'of one mind', fr. *ūnus*, 'one', & *animus*, 'mind', see unity, one, & animus. 1. (of persons) Being of one mind; agreeing in opinion and decision: *the Cabinet was unanimous; the meeting was unanimous in refusing to listen to the speaker*. 2. Held, formed, passed, given with the agreement of all: *a unanimous vote of thanks; greeted with unanimous applause*.

unanimously, adv. Prec. & -ly. In a unanimous manner; with unanimity.

unannealed, adj. [1. ùnanéld; 2. ᴧnəníld]. un- (I.) & anneal(ed). (of glass, metals) Not annealed; not heated first and then cooled slowly.

unannounced, adj. [1. ùnanóunst; 2. ᴧnənáunst]. un- (I.) & announce(d). Not announced; without previous announcement.

Phr. *to enter unannounced*, without one's name being first called out.

unanointed, adj. [1. ùnanóinted; 2. ănənóintid]. un- (I.) & anoint(ed). Not anointed.

unanswerability, n. [1. unȧhnserabíliti; 2. anȧnsərəbíliti]. un- (I.) & answerable & -ity. Condition, state, of being unanswerable.

unanswerable, adj. [1. unȧhnserabl; 2. anȧnsərəbl]. un- (I.) & answerable. Not answerable; incapable of being answered or refuted; conclusive.

unanswerableness, n. Prec. & -ness. Unanswerability.

unanswerably, adv. See prec. & -ly. In an unanswerable manner; conclusively.

unanswered, adj. [1. unȧhnserd; 2. anȧnsəd]. un- (I.) & answer(ed). Not answered; a left without an answer, unreplied to: *an unanswered letter, question, appeal*; **b** not refuted: *the criticism remains unanswered*; *unanswered accusations*; **c** not returned or requited: *unanswered affection*.

unanticipated, adj. [1. unȧntísipăted; 2. ănæntísipèitid]. un- (I.) & anticipate(d). Not anticipated or expected; unexpected.

unapocryphal, adj. [1. ùnapókrifl; 2. ănəpókrifl]. un- (I.) & apocryphal. Not apocryphal, genuine; canonical.

unapostolic, adj. [1. unȧpostólik; 2. anæpəstólik]. un- (I.) & apostolic. Not apostolic; having no apostolic authority; contrary to apostolic usage.

unappalled, adj. [1. ùnapáwld; 2. ănəpóld]. un- (I.) & appal(led). Not appalled; undaunted, unafraid.

unapparel, vb. trans. [1. ùnapárel; 2. ănəpǽr(ə)l]. un- (II.) & apparel. (archaic) To remove the apparel of; to undress, unclothe.

unapparelled, adj. [1. ùnapáreld; 2. ănəpǽr(ə)ld]. un- (I.) & apparel(led). Not apparelled; unclothed, without apparel.

unapparent, adj. [1. ùnapárent; 2. ănəpéərənt]. un- (I.) & apparent. Not apparent, not visible, not manifest.

unappealable, adj. [1. ùnapélabl; 2. ănəpíləbl]. un- (I.) & appealable. Not appealable; **a** incapable of being taken to a higher court: *an unappealable case*; **b** incapable of being appealed from: *an unappealable decision, judge*.

unappeasable, adj. [1. ùnapézabl; 2. ănəpízəbl]. un- (I.) & appeasable. Not appeasable; incapable of being appeased, satisfied, placated, or satiated: *unappeasable hunger, anger*.

unappeased, adj. [1. ùnapézd; 2. ănəpízd]. un- (I.) & appease(d). Not appeased; unsatisfied.

unappetizing, adj. [1. unȧpetìzing; 2. anǽpitàiziŋ]. un- (I.) & appetizing. Not appetizing; not appealing favourably to the taste; repellent, causing disgust.

unappetizingly, adv. Prec. & -ly. In an unappetizing manner.

unapplied, adj. [1. ùnaplíd; 2. ănəpláid]. un- (I.) & apply & -ed. Not applied; not used for a specific purpose or object.

unappreciated, adj. [1. ùnapréshiàted; 2. ănəprí∫ièitid]. un- (I.) & appreciate(d). Not appreciated; not valued.

unappreciative, adj. [1. ùnapréshiativ; 2. ănəprí∫iətiv]. un- (I.) & appreciative. Not appreciative.

unapprehended, adj. [1. ùnapreprehénded; 2. ănæprihénded]. un- (I.) & apprehend(ed). Not apprehended; **a** not taken into custody; still at large: *the criminal remains unapprehended*; **b** not understood, not clearly perceived: *such theories are unapprehended by ordinary people*.

unapprehensive, adj. [1. ùnaprehénsiv; 2. ănæprihénsiv]. un- (I.) & apprehensive. Not apprehensive; **a** not feeling apprehension, not suspicious or suspecting; not fearful; **b** not quick or ready at apprehension or understanding.

unapprehensiveness, n. Prec. & -ness. Condition, quality, of being unapprehensive.

unapprised, adj. [1. ùnaprízd; 2. ănəpráizd]. un- (I.) & apprise(d). Not apprised, not informed or told of beforehand.

unapproachability, n. [1. ùnaprȯchabíliti; 2. ănəpròut∫əbíliti]. un- (I.) & approachability. Condition, quality, of being unapproachable; inaccessibility, unapproachableness.

unapproachable, adj. [1. ùnaprȯchabl; 2. ănəpróut∫əbl]. un- (I.) & approachable. Not approachable; inaccessible; exhibiting a frigid aloofness of manner or character.

unapproachableness, n. Prec. & -ness. Unapproachability.

unapproachably, adv. See prec. & -ly. In an unapproachable manner; inaccessibly.

unappropriated, adj. [1. ùnaprȯpriated; 2. ănəpróuprieitid]. un- (I.) & appropriate(d). Not appropriated; specif. **a** (of funds, money &c.) not granted for, not applied to, or used for, a specific purpose; **b** (of land &c.) not granted to, or taken by, a person, company &c., to the exclusion of others.

unapproved, adj. [1. ùnaprōóvd; 2. ănəprúvd]. un- (I.) & approve(d). Not approved; not having received approval.

unapproving, adj. [1. ùnaprōóving; 2. ănəprúviŋ]. un- (I.) & approve & -ing. Not approving; disapproving.

unapprovingly, adv. Prec. & -ly. In an unapproving manner.

unapt, adj. [1. unȧpt; 2. anǽpt]. un- (I.) & apt; cp. inept. Not apt; **a** not ready, quick; slow, unskilful: *unapt to learn*; *unapt at games*; **b** not accustomed to, not inclined to: '*unapt to weep*' (Shakespeare, '1 Henry VI.'); **c** not fit, not suitable, not appropriate: *an unapt quotation*.

unaptly, adv. Prec. & -ly. In an unapt manner; not aptly; inappropriately.

unaptness, n. See prec. & -ness. State, quality, of being unapt.

unargued, adj. [1. unȧrgūd; 2. anǻgjūd]. un- (I.) & argue(d). Not argued; not disputed; not debated.

unarm, vb. trans. & intrans. [1. unȧrm; 2. anǻm]. un- (II.) & arm (III.). 1. trans. **a** To deprive of arms, armour, or other means of offence or defence; to disarm; **b** (by transf., poet.) to deprive of means of inflicting injury. 2. intrans. To lay down one's arms; to render oneself incapable of offence or defence.

unarmed, adj. [1. unȧrmd; 2. anǻmd]. Prec. & -ed. 1. **a** Lacking arms, armour &c.; **b** not wearing, unprovided with, weapons or other means of attack or defence. 2. (zool. and bot.) Not having points, prickles, spines, or other defensive protection.

unarmoured, adj. [1. unȧrmurd; 2. anǻməd]. un- (I.) & armour(ed). Not armoured; not protected by armour, esp. of cruisers and other war-vessels.

unarraigned, adj. [1. ùnarȧnd; 2. ănəréind]. un- (I.) & arraign(ed). Not arraigned, not brought to trial.

unarranged, adj. [1. ùnarȧnjd; 2. ănəréin(d)ʒd]. un- (I.) & arrange(d). 1. Not arranged, not placed in order; not classified. 2. Not planned, prepared beforehand: *our meeting was fortuitous and quite unarranged*.

unarrayed, adj. [1. ùnarȧd; 2. ănəréid]. un- (I.) & array(ed). Not arrayed; **a** not drawn up in array or line of battle; not arranged in order; **b** not dressed in array, not decked out for display; unadorned.

unarrested, adj. [1. ùnaréstəd; 2. ănəréstid]. un- (I.) & arrest(ed). Not arrested.

unartful, adj. [1. unȧrtfl; 2. anǻtfl]. un- (I.) & artful. Not artful; **a** not cunning; **b** artless, frank, genuine; **c** without art or skill; unskilful.

unartificial, adj. [1. unȧrtifíshl; 2. anǻtifí∫l]. un- (I.) & artificial. Not artificial; free from artifice, natural, simple.

unartistic, adj. [1. unȧrtístik; 2. anǻtístik]. un- (I.) & artistic. Not artistic; specif., not concerned with art or artists; contrasted with *inartistic*, contrary to the rules of art.

unascertainable, adj. [1. ùnasertȧnabl; 2. ănæsətéinəbl]. un- (I.) & ascertainable. Not ascertainable; not capable of being ascertained or known with certainty.

unascertained, adj. [1. ùnasertȧnd; 2. ănæsətéind]. un- (I.) & ascertain(ed). Not ascertained.

unashamed, adj. [1. ùnashȧmd; 2. ănə∫éimd]. un- (I.) & ashamed. Not ashamed; unabashed; shameless, exhibiting effrontery.

unasked, adj. [1. unȧhskt; 2. anǻskt]. un- (I.) & ask(ed). Not asked; unsolicited; unsought.

unaspirated, adj. [1. unȧspirǎted; 2. anǽspirèitid]. un- (I.) & aspirate(d). Not aspirated; not pronounced or written with an aspirate.

unaspiring, adj. [1. ùnaspíring; 2. ănəspáiəriŋ]. un- (I.) & aspire & -ing. Not aspiring; unambitious, modest.

unassailable, adj. [1. ùnasȧlabl; 2. ănəséiləbl]. un- (I.) & assailable. Not assailable; a proof against attack: *an unassailable fortress, position*; **b** irrefutable, incontestable: *unassailable arguments*.

unassayed, adj. [1. ùnasȧd; 2. ănəséid]. un- (I.) & assay(ed). Not assayed; a not tried or attempted; **b** not subjected to a metallurgical or other assay or test; untested.

unassignable, adj. [1. ùnasínabl; 2. ănəsáinəbl]. un- (I.) & assignable. **a** Not assignable; not capable of transference by assignment; **b** not attributable: *results unassignable to any known cause*.

unassimilated, adj. [1. ùnasímilàted; 2. ănəsímilèitid]. un- (I.) & assimilate(d). Not assimilated.

unassisted, adj. [1. ùnasísted; 2. ănəsístid]. un- (I.) & assist(ed). Not assisted.

unassuming, adj. [1. ùnasūmíng; 2. ănəsjúmiŋ]. un- (I.) & assuming. Not assuming; unpresuming, modest.

unassured, adj. [1. ùnashórd; 2. ănə∫ɔ́d]. un- (I.) & assure(d). Not assured; a having no assurance, not confident or bold; **b** not insured against loss; not holding a policy of assurance or insurance.

unatoned, adj. [1. ùnatȯnd; 2. ănətóund]. un- (I.) & atone(d). Not atoned; unexpiated.

unattached, adj. [1. ùnatácht; 2. ănətǽt∫t]. un- (I.) & attached. Not attached. Specif. 1. (law) not seized or attached for debt. 2. (mil., of officers) Not assigned to a particular regiment or other unit. 3. (univ.) Not attached to a particular college, though a member of the university; non-collegiate. 4. Not fastened.

unattainable, adj. [1. ùnatȧnabl; 2. ănətéinəbl]. un- (I.) & attainable. Not attainable; impossible of attainment; out of reach.

unattainableness, n. Prec. & -ness. Condition, quality, of being unattainable.

unattempted, adj. [1. ùnatémpted; 2. ănətémptid]. un- (I.) & attempt(ed). Not attempted.

unattended, adj. [1. ùnaténded; 2. ănəténdid]. un- (I.) & attend(ed). Not attended. 1. Having no attendants; not escorted or waited on. 2. Receiving no attention, not attended to; undressed: *unattended wounds*.

unattested, adj. [1. ùnatésted; 2. ănətéstid]. un- (I.) & attest(ed). Not attested; lacking attestation; not supported by evidence of a witness &c.

unattractive, adj. [1. ùnatráktiv; 2. ănətrǽktiv]. un- (I.) & attractive. Not attractive; unprepossessing, plain; repellent.

unattractively, adv. Prec. & -ly. In an unattractive manner; so as to fail to attract.

unattractiveness, n. See prec. & -ness. Condition, quality, of being unattractive.

unaugmented, adj. [1. ùnawgménted; 2. ănɔgméntid]. un- (I.) & augment(ed). Not augmented; specif. (Gk. gram.) having no augment prefixed.

unauthentic, adj. [1. ùnawthéntik; 2. ănɔþéntik]. un- (I.) & authentic. Not authentic; apocryphal; not genuine.

unauthenticated, adj. [1. ùnawthéntikāted; 2. ànōpéntìkèitid]. un- (I.) & authenticate(d). Not authenticated; not shown or proved to be true.

unauthorized, adj. [1. unáwthorĭzd; 2. anōpərdizd]. un- (I.) & authorize(d). Not authorized; having no proper authority or sanction.

unavailable, adj. [1. ùnaválabl; 2. ànəvéiləbl]. un- (I.) & available. Not available; not within one's reach, not at one's disposal.

unavailing, adj. [1. ùnaváling; 2. ànəvéiliŋ]. un- (I.) & avail & -ing. Not availing; not effectual or effective; fruitless, vain.

unavailingly, adv. Prec. & -ly. In an unavailing manner; without avail; fruitlessly.

unavenged, adj. [1. ùnavénjd; 2. ànəvéndžd]. un- (II.) & avenge(d). Not avenged.

unavoidable, adj. [1. ùnavóidabl; 2. ànəvóidəbl]. un- (I.) & avoidable. 1. Not avoidable; incapable of being avoided; not to be prevented or escaped; inevitable. 2. Not voidable; incapable of being rendered null and void.

unavoidably, adv. Prec. & -ly. In an unavoidable manner; in a way that cannot be avoided.

unavowed, adj. [1. ùnavóud; 2. ànəváud]. un- (I.) & avow(ed). Not avowed, not acknowledged; unconfessed.

unawakened, adj. [1. ùnawåkend; 2. ànəwéikənd]. un- (I.) & awaken(ed). 1. Not awakened; not roused from sleep. 2. Not yet aroused; dormant, quiescent: *unawakened passions, ambition* &c.

unaware, adj. [1. ùnawår; 2. ànəwéə]. un- (I.) & aware. (only used pred.) Not aware, not knowing or noticing; ignorant; not awake to or conscious of: *unaware of their danger*; *they remained unaware that war was near*.

unawares, adv. [1. ùnawårz; 2. ànəwéəz]. Prec. & advbl. suff. -s. 1. Without knowing or noticing; unintentionally, undesignedly: *to do something unawares*; *he slew his father unawares*. 2. Without warning, unexpectedly, by surprise: *to be taken unawares*, *to take a person unawares*, to be surprised, to surprise. Phr. *at unawares*, by surprise.

unbacked, adj. [1. unbákt; 2. anbækt]. un- (I.) & back(ed). Not backed. 1. (of horse) Not ridden before, not broken in. 2. a Without supporters or backers, unsupported, unaided; b (of horse in a race &c.) having no bets made upon it.

unbag, vb. trans. [1. unbág; 2. anbæg]. un- (II.) & bag (II.). To take out, let go, from a bag: *to unbag a ferret*.

unbagged, adj. [1. unbágd; 2. anbægd], fr. P.P. of prec. 1. Let loose, taken out of a bag. 2. Not placed or kept in a bag.

unbaked, adj. [1. unbákt; 2. anbéikt]. un- (I.) & bake(d). a Not baked; b (fig.) immature, crude.

unbalance, vb. trans. [1. unbáláns; 2. anbǽləns]. un- (II.) & balance (II.). To upset, destroy, the balance of; to throw off or out of balance or equipoise, physical or mental: *the water jump will unbalance several of the riders*; *his financial anxieties went far to unbalance him (his mind)*.

unbalanced (I.), adj. [1. unbálanst; 2. anbǽlənst], fr. P.P. of prec. Thrown out of balance or equipoise; thrown, put, off one's balance; upset, unsteady (of physical or mental states): *an unbalanced rider, seat on a horse*; *an unbalanced mind*.

unbalanced (II.), adj. un- (I.) & balance(d). Not balanced. 1. a Not fitted with a balance or counterweight, not counterpoised rightly: *a pair of unbalanced scales*; b (i.) lacking balance or equipoise; unsteady: *an unbalanced type of character*; (ii.) lacking restraint or poise: *an unbalanced style of writing*. 2. (commerc.) Not brought to a balance, not equal on debit and credit sides: *unbalanced books, accounts* &c.

unballast, vb. trans. [1. unbálast; 2. anbǽləst]. un- (II.) & ballast (II.). To discharge, remove, the ballast from: *to unballast a ship, balloon* &c.

unballasted (I.), adj. [1. unbálasted; 2. anbǽləstid]. P.P. of prec. Freed from, discharged of, ballast; having discharged its ballast: *the ship, balloon, was by this time unballasted*.

unballasted (II.), adj. un- (I.) & ballast(ed). Not ballasted; a not provided with ballast: *an unballasted ship* &c.; *an unballasted railway track*; b unsteady, lacking ballast or a steadying influence: *an unballasted character, type of mind* &c.

unbank, vb. trans. [1. unbángk; 2. anbæŋk]. un- (II.) & bank (II.). 1. (of fires, furnaces &c.) To loosen, take away, the ashes banked on the top of a fire, so as to cause it to burn brightly again: *unbanked fire, furnace*. 2. (of rivers &c.) To remove or damage the banks so as to cause an overflow.

unbanked, adj. [1. unbángkt; 2. anbæŋkt]. un- (I.) & bank(ed). Not banked: a having no banks or sides; b not placed in a bank: *unbanked cheques, money* &c.

unbaptized, adj. [1. unbaptízd; 2. anbæptáizd]. un- (I.) & baptize(d). Not baptized; not having received the sacrament of baptism.

unbar, vb. trans. [1. unbár; 2. anbǎ]. un- (II.) & bar (II.). To remove, take away, a bar or bars from; to unfasten, unbolt, to throw open: *to unbar a gate, door*; *unbar the prison*; (also fig.) *get rid of tariffs and unbar the channels of trade*; *the path to knowledge is now unbarred*.

unbarbed, adj. [1. unbárbd; 2. anbǎbd]. un- (I.) & barb(ed). Not barbed, not furnished with barbs or reversed points.

unbarbered, adj. [1. unbárberd; 2. anbǎbəd]. un- (I.) & barber(ed). Not barbered; unshaven, unkempt.

unbark, vb. trans. [1. unbárk; 2. anbǎk]. un- (II.) & bark (I.). To strip the bark from, to deprive of bark.

unbated, adj. [1. unbáted; 2. anbéitid]. un- (I.) & bate(d). (rare or poet.) Unabated; a not bated or abated, not diminished: '*unbated fire*' (Shakespeare, 'Merchant of Venice'); b (of weapon) not blunted, without a button on the point: '*You may choose A sword unbated*' (Shakespeare, 'Hamlet').

unbathed, adj. [1. unbádhd; 2. anbéiðd]. un- (I.) & bathe(d). a Not bathed; unwashed; b not wetted, dry.

unbear, vb. trans. [1. unbár; 2. anbéə]. un- (II.) & bear (I.). To remove or unloose the bearing-rein of a horse.

unbearable, adj. [1. unbárabl; 2. anbéərəbl]. un- (I.) & bearable. Not bearable, not to be borne; intolerable, insupportable.

unbearably, adv. Prec. & -ly. In an unbearable manner; to an unbearable extent.

unbearded, adj. [1. unbérded; 2. anbíədid]. un- (I.) & beard(ed). Not bearded; a having no beard; beardless: *an unbearded face, youth*; b not having beards or awns: *unbearded wheat, barley* &c.

unbeaten, adj. [1. unbětn; 2. anbítn]. un- (I.) & beaten. 1. Not flogged. 2. Not beaten by the feet; untrodden. Phr. *unbeaten track*: (i.) an unexplored region of the earth; (ii.) (fig.) unexplored region of thought, scientific investigation &c. 3. a Unconquered: *an unbeaten army*; b not surpassed or excelled in competition of any kind: *unbeaten as a tennis-player*; *an unbeaten steeple-chaser*; *an unbeaten record*.

unbeautiful, adj. [1. unbǔtifl; 2. anbjútifl]. un- (I.) & beautiful. Not beautiful; ugly, plain.

unbecoming, adj. [1. ùnbekúming; 2. ànbikámiŋ]. un- (I.) & becoming. Not becoming, not suitable; unsuitable. 1. Not befitting; unbefitting, not appropriate to, not suited for: *conduct unbecoming to a gentleman*; *expenditure, house* &c. *unbecoming in a person of his class*. 2. Improper, unseemly, indecent: *unbecoming conduct, language*. 3. Not suiting, not suited to, detracting from the attractiveness of: *unbecoming style of dress, fashions* &c.; *a pretty face spoiled by an unbecoming hat*.

unbecomingly, adv. Prec. & -ly. In an unbecoming manner; unsuitably, improperly.

unbecomingness, n. See prec. & -ness. Condition, quality, of being unbecoming.

unbed, vb. trans. [1. unbéd; 2. anbéd]. un- (II.) & bed (II.). To lift (plant), move from a bed.

unbedded, adj. [1. unbéded; 2. anbédid]. un- (I.) & bed(ded). Not bedded; a not placed or planted in a bed; b (archaic) not brought to bed; unwedded, virgin; c (of stone) not firmly fixed on its bed; loosened from, not laid upon, its bed.

unbefitting, adj. [1. unbefíting; 2. anbifítiŋ]. un- (I.) & befitting. Not befitting; unbecoming.

unbefriended, adj. [1. unbefrénded; 2. anbifréndid]. un- (I.) & befriend(ed). Not befriended; not aided or helped by friends; friendless.

unbegotten, adj. [1. unbegótn; 2. anbigótn]. un- (I.) & begotten. Not begotten; not generated; specif. (of God) self-existent, eternal.

unbeguiled, adj. [1. unbegíld; 2. anbigáild]. un- (I.) & beguile(d). Not beguiled; not deceived.

unbeknown, unbeknownst, adj. & adv. [1. unbenón(st); 2. anbinóun(st)]. un- (I.), be-, & know & -n. (illit. or colloq., with to). 1. adj. Unknown, not known. 2. adv. Without the knowledge of: *he did it unbeknownst to me*.

unbelief, n. [1. unbelěf; 2. anbilíf]. un- (I.) & belief, cp. O.E. *ungeléafa*. Withholding of belief or faith; refusal to believe; want of faith; disbelief, scepticism, esp. in matters of religion or divine revelation: '*He upbraided them with their unbelief*' (Mark xvi. 14).

unbelievability, n. [1. unbelěvabíliti; 2. anbilìvəbíliti]. un- (I.) & believable & -ity. Condition of being unbelievable.

unbelievable, adj. [1. unbelěvabl; 2. anbilívəbl]. un- (I.) & believable. Not believable, not to be believed, incredible.

unbelievably, adv. Prec. & -ly. In an unbelievable manner; to an unbelievable degree or extent; incredibly.

unbeliever, n. [1. unbelěver; 2. anbilívə]. un- (I.) & believer. One who does not or who refuses to believe, esp. in religion or in a divine revelation; an infidel, pagan; a sceptic.

unbelieving, adj. [1. unbelěving; 2. anbilíviŋ]. un- (I.) & believing. Refusing to believe; not believing; incredulous, sceptical.

unbelievingly, adv. Prec. & -ly. In an unbelieving manner.

unbeloved, adj. [1. unbelúvd; 2. anbilávd]. un- (I.) & beloved. Not beloved.

unbelt, vb. trans. [1. unbélt; 2. anbélt]. un- (II.) & belt (II.). 1. To remove, loosen, the belt of; to ungird. 2. To take off by loosening or removing a belt: *to unbelt a sword*.

unbend, vb. trans. & intrans. [1. unbénd; 2. anbénd]. un- (II.) & bend (I.). A. trans. 1. a (in physical senses) To free, change, release, from a bent position; to straighten, flatten out: *to unbend a bow*, by unstringing it; *to unbend a link, staple* &c., by hammering it flat; b (in non-physical senses) to relax, relieve from effort, strain, or constraint: *to unbend the mind*; *to unbend oneself in congenial company*. 2. (naut.) a To unfasten from yards and stays: *to unbend the sails*; b to cast off or loose: *to unbend a cable*, from the anchor; c to untie: *to unbend a rope*. B. intrans. 1. To become unbent, to cease to be bent; to become straght or flat: *the bow unbends when the string is loosened*. 2. To relax one's rigidity of bearing, to abandon coldness and constraint; to get rid of, behave without, stiffness of manner; to be affable: *he only unbends in the family circle*.

unbending, adj. [1. unbénding; 2. anbéndiŋ]. Pres. Part. of prec. 1. a Not pliant or easily bent; stiff, rigid; b (fig., of character &c.) not easily moved from one's intentions, principles, line of conduct &c.; inflexible, resolute, determined; unyielding, obstinate: *'the stern unbending Tories'*. 2. Becoming relaxed from effort or constraint, becoming free from constraint or stiffness in manner; given, yielding, to relaxation or amusement: *a few unbending hours of ease; found him in a gay, unbending mood.*

unbendingly, adv. Prec. & -ly. In an unbending manner.

unbeneficed, adj. [1. unbénefist; 2. anbénifist]. un- (I.) & benefice(d). Not beneficed; not holding an ecclesiastical benefice or incumbency: *the unbeneficed clergy.*

unberufen, adj. [1. óonberōōfen; 2. únbiruˈfən]. Mod. Germ., 'not called, summoned'. Phrase used to deprecate the intervention of fate, after boasting, making a too-confident statement as to the future &c.; a form of verbal warding off the unlucky, corresponding to touching wood in the same circumstances.

unbeseem, vb. trans. [1. ùnbesém; 2. ànbisíˈm]. un-(II.) & beseem. (rare) To do anything unbecoming or unworthy of; to be unbecoming or unworthy of.

unbeseeming, adj. [1. ùnbesēˈming; 2. ànbisíˈmiŋ]. un- (I.) & beseem & -ing. Not beseeming; unbefitting, unbecoming.

unbeseemingly, adv. Prec. & -ly. In an unbeseeming manner.

unbesought, adj. [1. ùnbesáwt; 2. ànbisóˈt]. un- (I.) & besought, see beseech. Not besought; not entreated; not asked for.

unbespoken, adj. [1. ùnbespṓken; 2. ànbispóukən]. un- (I.) & bespoken. See bespeak. Not bespoken, not ordered or reserved in advance.

unbestowed, adj. [1. ùnbestṓd; 2. ànbistóud]. un- (I.) & bestow(ed). Not bestowed, not given.

unbias, vb. trans. [1. unbías; 2. anbáiəs]. un- (II.) & bias. (rare) To free from, get rid of, bias or prejudice.

unbiased, unbiassed, adj. [1. unbíast; 2. anbáiəst]. un-(I.) & bias & -ed. Not biased; without preconceived notions; unprejudiced.

unbiblical, adj. [1. unbíblikl; 2. anbíblikl]. un- (I.) & biblical. Not biblical, not contained in the Bible, not authorized by the Bible.

unbidden, adj. [1. unbídn; 2. anbídn]. un- (I.) & bid(den). Not bidden; **a** not commanded, not ordered; freely given; spontaneous; **b** not invited; uninvited.

unbigoted, adj. [1. unbígut̄ed; 2. anbígətid]. un- (I.) & bigoted. Not bigoted.

unbind, vb. trans. [1. unbíind; 2. anbáind]. un- (II.) & bind. 1. **a** To unfasten, untie what was bound or fastened; to loose: *to unbind the ropes;* **b** to release, free from bonds: *to unbind a prisoner;* to unfasten: *she unbound her hair.* 2. To remove the binding from: *to unbind a book.*

unbishop, vb. trans. [1. unbíshop; 2. anbíʃəp]. un- (II.) & bishop. 1. To deprive of, degrade from, the rank and dignity of a bishop; to take away a bishopric: *the Queen threatened to unbishop him.* 2. To deprive of the rank of an episcopal see or bishopric: *to unbishop a diocese, cathedral town.*

unbitt, vb. trans. [1. unbít; 2. anbít]. See un- (II.) & bitts. To uncoil, unfasten, as the turns of rope or cable, from a bitt.

unbitted, adj. [1. unbíted; 2. ənbítid]. un-(I.) & bit(ted). Not bitted, not restrained by a bit or bridle.

unbitten, adj. [1. unbítn; 2. anbítn]. un-(I.) & bitten. Not bitten.

unblamable, adj. [1. unblámabl; 2. anbléiməbl]. un- (I.) & blame & -able. Not blamable; blameless, innocent.

unbleached, adj. [1. unblécht; 2. anblítʃt]. un- (I.) & bleach(ed). Not bleached; left in its natural colour: *unbleached calico.*

unblemished, adj. [1. unblémisht; 2. anblémiʃt]. un- (I.) & blemish(ed). Not blemished; **a** not marked with physical blemishes or stains; **b** morally pure, without fault; spotless: *an unblemished reputation, character* &c.

unblended, adj. [1. unblénded; 2. anbléndid]. un- (I.) & blend(ed). Not blended, not mixed with other kinds; pure, unmixed.

unblessed, unblest, adj. [1. unblést; 2. anblést]. un- (I.) & blessed, blest. Not blessed or blest; accursed; unhappy.

unblock, vb. trans. [1. unblók; 2. anblók]. un- (II.) & block (II.). To remove a block from; to clear away an obstacle or that which blocks.

unblooded, adj. [1. unblúded; 2. anbládid]. un- (I.) & blood(ed). Not blooded; not having pure blood or descent; not thoroughbred: *an unblooded horse.*

unbloody, adj. [1. unblúdi; 2. anbládi]. un-(I.) & bloody. Not bloody; **a** not stained or marked with blood; **b** not accompanied by bloodshed; specif., *the unbloody sacrifice of the Eucharist*; **c** not bloodthirsty.

unblotted, adj. [1. unblóted; 2. anblótid]. un- (I.) & blot(ted). Not blotted; **a** not marked with blots or stains; **b** not blotted out, not erased or deleted.

unblown, adj. [1. unblṓn; 2. anblóun]. un-(I.) & blow(n). Not blown; **a** not sounded, as of trumpet, signal by trumpet &c.; **b** not in full bloom, not in flower, still in bud; **c** not exhausted by running, still having wind.

unblushing, adj. [1. unblúshing; 2. anbláʃiŋ]. un- (I.) & blushing. Not blushing; without a blush of shame; unashamed, shameless, barefaced.

unblushingly, adv. Prec. & -ly. In an unblushing manner; shamelessly.

unblushingness, n. See prec. & -ness. State, quality, of being unblushing; shamelessness.

unbodied, adj. [1. unbódid; 2. anbódid]. un- (I.) & (II.) & -bodied. Freed from the body, disembodied; incorporeal, spiritual.

unboiled, adj. [1. unbóild; 2. anbóild]. un-(I.) & boil(ed). Not boiled; not brought to the boiling-point.

unbolt, vb. trans. [1. unbólt; 2. anbóult]. un- (II.) & bolt (II.). To draw back the bolt or bolts of; to unfasten, open (a door &c.), by drawing back the bolt.

unbolted (I.), adj. [1. unbólted; 2. anbóultid]. un- (I.) & bolted (I.). Not bolted, not fastened by bolting.

unbolted (II.), adj. un- (I.) & bolted (II.). (of flour &c.) Not bolted, not sifted or strained; not having the bran removed.

unbone, vb. trans. [1. unbón; 2. anbóun]. un- (II.) & bone (I.). To rid of bone, to remove the bones from (meat).

unbonnet, vb. intrans. & trans. [1. unbónet; 2. anbónit]. un- (II.) & bonnet (II.). 1. intrans. To remove one's bonnet or cap; to take off the hat as a salutation: *to unbonnet to a person.* 2. trans. To remove the bonnet or hat from: esp. by knocking it off.

unbonneted, adj. [1. unbóneted; 2. anbónitid], fr. P.P. of prec. Not bonneted, without a bonnet or cap on; bareheaded, uncovered.

unbookish, adj. [1. unbóokish; 2. anbúkiʃ]. un- (I.) & bookish. Not bookish; **a** not devoted to books or reading; **b** not gaining knowledge from books alone, not depending merely on books.

unboot, vb. trans. & intrans. [1. unbōōt; 2. anbút]. un-(II.) & boot (II.). 1. trans. To remove, take off the boots of, esp. riding boots. 2. intrans. To take off one's boots.

unborn, adj. [1. unbórn; 2. anbón]. un- (I.) & born. Not yet born; still to be born; future: *unborn generations.*

unborrowed, adj. [1. unbóröd; 2. anbóroud]. un- (I.) & borrow(ed). Not borrowed; not copied or plagiarized; original.

unbosom, vb. trans. [1. unbóozum; 2. anbúzəm]. un- (II.) & bosom. 1. To disclose, display, confess: *to unbosom one's feelings, thoughts, secrets* &c. 2. (reflex.) *To unbosom oneself*, to open one's heart, to reveal one's intimate feelings, hopes, plans; to confess.

unbought, adj. [1. unbáwt; 2. anbót]. un-(I.) & bought. Not bought; **a** not acquired by payment; given freely and without price; **b** not sold, left unsold; **c** not bought over or gained by money or bribes.

unbound (I.), adj. [1. unbóund; 2. anbáund]. P.P. of **unbind**. Freed from bonds or shackles: *the prisoner was left unbound.*

unbound (II.), adj. un- (I.) & bound (VI.). Not bound, not in binding, loose (of books, papers &c.).

unbounded, adj. [1. unbóunded; 2. anbáundid]. un- (I.) & bound (II.) & -ed. Not bounded; **a** not bounded by material confines or limits; limitless: *unbounded space;* **b** unrestricted, unlimited; boundless: *unbounded pride, ambition, joy* &c.

unboundedly, adv. Prec. & -ly. In an unbounded manner.

unboundedness, n. See prec. & -ness. State, quality, of being unbounded.

unbowed, adj. [1. unbóud; 2. anbáud]. un-(I.) & bow(ed). 1. Not bowed, not bent or curved. 2. Not conquered, undefeated, unsubdued.

unbox, vb. trans. [1. unbóks; 2. anbóks]. un-(II.) & box (III.). To take out of, remove from, a box.

unbrace, vb. trans. [1. unbrás; 2. anbréis]. un- (II.) & brace (II.). 1. To free from a brace or braces; to loosen: *to unbrace the yards of a ship, a drum* &c. 2. To relax, to free from tension: *to unbrace the muscles, nerves* &c.; *to unbrace the mind.*

unbraced (I.), adj. [1. unbrást; 2. anbréist]. P.P. of prec. Freed from a brace or braces.

unbraced (II.), adj. un- (I.) & brace(d). **a** Not braced, without braces; **b** relaxed.

unbraid, vb. trans. [1. unbrád; 2. anbréid]. un- (II.) & braid (I.). To separate the braids or strands of; to unfasten, unweave, the braids of, as of hair &c.

unbred, adj. [1. unbréd; 2. anbréd]. un- (I.) & bred. Not bred; **a** not begotten, not reared; unborn; **b** without breeding; ill-bred; **c** not bred up to, not trained or taught.

unbreech, vb. trans. [1. unbréch, -bríːch; 2. anbrítʃ, -brítʃ]. un- (II.) & breech. **a** To remove the breeches of: **b** to free the breech of a cannon from fastenings.

unbreeched, adj. [1. unbrícht; 2. anbrítʃt]. un- (I.) & breech(ed). Not breeched; (of boy) not yet put into breeches or trousers, still in short clothes.

unbribable, adj. [1. unbríbabl; 2. anbráibəbl]. un- (I.) & bribable. Not bribable; not open to bribes, incorruptible.

unbridle, vb. trans. [1. unbrídl; 2. anbráidl]. un- (II.) & bridle (II.). 1. To take off, loosen the bridle of: *to unbridle a horse.* 2. (fig.) To free from constraint or restraint: *to unbridle the tongue* &c.

unbridled, adj. [1. unbrídld; 2. anbráidld]. un- (I.) & bridle(d). Not bridled; not controlled, free from all restraint, esp. (fig.) violent: *unbridled passions, language* &c.

unbroken, adj. [1. unbróken; 2. anbróukən]. un- (I.) & broken. Not broken. 1. Not broken in two or up; not shattered, whole, intact: *an unbroken window, mast* &c. 2. Not subdued, not crushed or weakened: *unbroken spirit, morale.* 3. Not interrupted, continuous: *unbroken fine weather, sleep, peace.* 4. Not broken in, not trained to saddle or bridle: *an unbroken colt.* 5. (also *unbroke*) Not opened up by the plough, untilled, virgin: *unbroken soil, land.* 6. Not violated; kept: *unbroken promises, word, faith* &c. 7. Not surpassed, not beaten: *an unbroken record.*

unbrotherliness, n. [1. unbrúdherlines; 2. anbrádəlinis]. See next word & -ness. State, quality, of being unbrotherly.

unbrotherly, adj. [1. unbrúdherli; 2. anbrádəli]. un- (I.) & brotherly. Not brotherly; not showing normal feelings of, or acting as, one brother to another; unfriendly.

unbuckle, vb. trans. [1. unbúkl; 2. anbákl]. un- (II.) & buckle. To unfasten the buckle of; to release from a buckle: *to unbuckle a strap, belt, shoe &c.; to unbuckle a sword from its belt.*

unburden, vb. trans. [1. unbḗrdn; 2. anbádn]. un- (II.) & burden (II.). **1.** To take away, remove, relieve of, a burden or load. **2.** (fig.) To throw off, as a load, from the mind, by confession, disclosure: *to unburden one's heart, mind, conscience; to unburden one's heart to another.*

unburdened, adj. [1. unbḗrdnd; 2. anbádnd]. un- (I.) & burden(ed). Not burdened; not weighed down, loaded, with cares, sins, secrets &c.

unburied (I.), adj. [1. unbérid; 2. anbérid]. P.P. of **unbury**. Disinterred, exhumed, dug up from the grave.

unburied (II.), adj. un- (I.) & buried. Not buried, not interred.

unburned, unburnt, adj. [1. unbḗrnd, -t; 2. anbánd, -t]. un- (I.) & burn(ed), burn(t). Not burned; not burned up.

unbury, vb. trans. [1. unbéri; 2. anbéri]. un- (II.) & bury. To disinter, exhume.

unbusinesslike, adj. [1. unbízníslik; 2. anbíznislaik]. un- (I.) & business-like. Not businesslike; lacking, not evincing, business capacity.

unbutton, vb. trans. [1. unbútn; 2. anbátn]. un- (II.) & button. **a** To undo, unfasten, the buttons of, to open by disengaging the buttons from the buttonholes; **b** (fig.) to unbend.

uncage, vb. trans. [1. unkáj; 2. ankéidž]. un- (II.) & cage (II.). To release, set free, from a cage.

uncalled, adj. [1. unkáwld; 2. ankóld]. un- (I.) & call(ed). Not called, not summoned, not invited.

uncalled-for, adj. [1. unkáwld for; 2. ankóld fō]. Not demanded or required by the situation and circumstances; gratuitous, impertinent; brought forward without excuse or reason; obtruded: *an uncalled-for rebuke, insult, remark &c.; his exhibition of temper was quite uncalled for.*

uncandid, adj. [1. unkándid; 2. ankǽndid]. un- (I.) & candid. Not candid, not frank, open, or sincere; disingenuous.

uncandidly, adv. Prec. & -ly. In an uncandid manner; not candidly.

uncannily, adv. [1. unkánili; 2. ankǽnili]. uncanny & -ly. In an uncanny manner; weirdly, mysteriously.

uncanniness, n. [1. unkánines; 2. ankǽninis]. Next word & -ness. State, quality, of being uncanny.

uncanny, adj. [1. unkáni; 2. ankǽni]. un- (I.) & canny. Producing a sense of awe, mystery, dread; weird.

uncanonical, adj. [1. ùnkanónikl; 2. ànkənónikl]. un- (I.) & canonical. Not canonical; **a** not according to the canon law; *uncanonical hours*, hours during which it is not allowed to hold a marriage service; **b** not contained in the canon of the Bible: *uncanonical books*, the Apocrypha.

uncanonically, adv. Prec. & -ly. In an uncanonical manner.

uncanonized (I.), adj. [1. unkánonized; 2. ankǽnənaizd]. un- (I.) & as next word. Not canonized as a saint.

uncanonized (II.), adj. un- (II.) & canonize(d). Deprived of the status of a canonized saint.

uncap, vb. trans. & intrans. [1. unkáp; 2. ankǽp]. un- (II.) & cap. **1.** trans. To take off the cap or cover from. **2.** intrans. To take one's cap or hat off in salutation.

uncared-for, adj. [1. unkárd for; 2. ankéəd fō]. un- (I.) & care(d) (II.). Not cared for; neglected.

uncart, vb. trans. [1. unkárt; 2. ankát]. un- (II.) & cart. **1.** To discharge, unload, from a cart. **2.** (stag hunting) To set (deer) loose or free from the cart in which it is carried to the meet.

uncase, vb. trans. [1. unkás; 2. ankéis]. un- (II.) & case. To remove from a case or covering; specif., to remove from the case and display (the colours of a regiment).

uncatalogued, adj. [1. unkátalògd; 2. ankǽtəlògd]. un- (I.) & catalogue(d). Not catalogued; not appearing or found in any catalogue.

uncate, adj. [1. únkāt; 2. ánkeit], fr. Lat. *uncus*, 'hook', & -ate, see uncinate. Hooked, uncinate.

uncaught, adj. [1. unkáwt; 2. ankót]. un- (I.) & caught. Not caught, not captured or taken prisoner.

uncaused, adj. [1. unkáwzd; 2. ankózd]. un- (I.) & cause(d). Not caused; existing without an antecedent cause, self-existent, uncreated, eternal.

unceasing, adj. [1. unsésing; 2. ansísiŋ]. un- (I.) & cease & -ing. Not ceasing, without ceasing or stopping; incessant, continual.

unceasingly, adv. Prec. & -ly. In an unceasing manner; without ceasing, continually.

uncelebrated, adj. [1. unsélebrāted; 2. ansélibreitid]. un- (I.) & celebrate(d). **a** Not celebrated, not famous; **b** not observed or kept by celebrations.

uncensored, adj. [1. unsénsurd; 2. ansénsəd]. un- (I.) & censor(ed). Not censored; published, printed &c. without a censor's examination or permission.

uncensured, adj. [1. unsénshurd; 2. ansénʃəd]. un- (I.) & censure(d). Not censured, not blamed; exempt from censure or blame.

unceremonious, adj. [1. unsèremónius; 2. ansèrimóuniəs]. un- (I.) & ceremonious. Not ceremonious; **a** without ceremony or formality; informal, easy, familiar: *an unceremonious gathering, entertainment; an unceremonious farewell; talked to me in a quite unceremonious way;* **b** not expressing, observing, or practising ceremony; hence also abrupt, discourteous, in manner: *he is rather too unceremonious for my taste; unceremonious treatment; a sharp, unceremonious dismissal.*

unceremoniously, adv. Prec. & -ly. In an unceremonious manner; without ceremony; familiarly; abruptly, rudely.

unceremoniousness, n. See prec. & -ness. Quality of being unceremonious.

uncertain, adj. [1. unsértin; 2. ansə́tin]. un- (I.) & certain. Not certain. **1. a** Not certainly known; doubtful, problematical: *the date of their arrival is uncertain; the danger is plain, success is uncertain;* Phr. *a lady of uncertain age*, no longer young, yet not old; middle-aged; **b** not having certain knowledge, not assured or sure of: *I am quite uncertain as to my movements, as to when I shall leave &c.; he is uncertain of success.* **2. a** Not certain or sure in action or purpose; undecided, vacillating; unsteady: *a person of uncertain character; his aim was somewhat uncertain;* **b** liable to change; variable; not to be depended or relied on; capricious, unreliable: *an uncertain temper; uncertain weather; he is a good golfer, but very uncertain.*

uncertainly, adv. Prec. & -ly. In an uncertain manner; not certainly, without certainty.

uncertainty, n. [1. unsértinti; 2. ansə́tinti]. un- (I.) & certainty. Condition, quality, of being uncertain; absence, lack, of certainty; **a** want of certain knowledge, state of not being sure or assured of: *to be in a state of uncertainty; uncertainty as to one's fate, as to results &c.;* legal Phr. *void for uncertainty*, of bequests, documents &c., in which the intention is stated in terms too vague to be carried out with certainty; **b** state of not being certainly known or predictable; doubtful: *the uncertainty of life;* **c** undependableness, tendency to vary; esp. *uncertainty of temper.*

uncertificated, adj. [1. ùnsertífikèitid; 2. ànsətífikèitid]. un- (I.) & certificate(d). Not certificated, not having obtained a certificate.

uncertified, adj. [1. unsértifíd; 2. ansə́tifaid]. un- (I.) & certify & -ed. Not certified; not guaranteed.

unchain, vb. trans. [1. unchán; 2. antʃéin]. un- (II.) & chain. To free, loose, from a chain; to unfasten the chain of.

unchallengeable, adj. [1. uncháленjabl; 2. antʃǽlindžəbl]. un- (I.) & challengeable. Not challengeable; not to be challenged, called to account or question.

unchallenged, adj. [1. unchálenjd; 2. antʃǽlindžd]. un- (I.) & challenge(d). Not challenged; unquestioned, not disputed.

unchangeability, n. [1. unchànjabíliti; 2. antʃèin(d)žəbíliti]. un- (I.) & changeability. State, quality, of being unchangeable, unchangeableness.

unchangeable, adj. [1. unchánjabl; 2. antʃéin(d)žəbl]. un- (I.) & changeable. Not changeable; not liable to change; immutable.

unchangeableness, n. Prec. & -ness. Unchangeability.

unchangeably, adv. See prec. & -ly. In an unchangeable manner.

unchanged, adj. [1. unchánjd; 2. antʃéin(d)žd]. un- (I.) & change(d). Not changed; unaltered, remaining the same.

unchanging, adj. [1. unchánjing; 2. antʃéin(d)žiŋ]. un- (I.) & change & -ing. Not changing, not varying; not liable to undergo change; invariable.

unchangingly, adv. Prec. & -ly. In an unchanging manner; without changing.

uncharged, adj. [1. uncháanjd; 2. antʃádžd]. un- (I.) & charge(d). Not charged. **1.** Not loaded; not fitted with a charge. **2.** Not charged with a crime, not accused.

uncharitable, adj. [1. uncháritabl; 2. antʃǽritəbl]. un- (I.) & charitable. Not charitable. **1.** (rare) Not disposed to almsgiving, not giving generously to charitable objects. **2.** Not ruled by, or acting in accordance with, the virtue of charity; censorious, unforgiving, judging harshly of others.

uncharitableness, n. Prec. & -ness. Quality of being uncharitable.

uncharitably, adv. See prec. & -ly. In an uncharitable manner.

uncharted, adj. [1. uncháart; 2. antʃátid]. un- (I.) & chart(ed). **a** Not marked on a chart or map; **b** not mapped, not described or delineated on a chart or map.

unchartered, adj. [1. uncháarterd; 2. antʃátəd]. un- (I.) & chartered. Not chartered, not having a charter of incorporation; unlicensed.

unchary, adj. [1. uncháari; 2. antʃéəri]. un- (I.) & chary. Not chary; **a** not frugal or sparing; **b** not cautious, rash.

unchaste, adj. [1. uncháast; 2. antʃéist]. un- (I.) & chaste. Not chaste; incontinent.

unchastely, adv. Prec. & -ly. In an unchaste manner.

unchastened, adj. [1. uncháasend; 2. antʃéisnd]. un- (I.) & chasten(ed). Not chastened.

unchastised, adj. [1. ùnchastízd; 2. àntʃæstáizd]. un- (I.) & chastise(d). Not chastised; unpunished.

unchastity, n. [1. uncháastiti; 2. antʃǽstiti]. unchaste & -ity. Want of chastity; incontinence; state, quality, of being unchaste.

unchecked, adj. [1. unchékt; 2. antʃékt]. un- (I.) & check(ed). Not checked. **1. a** Not stopped or reduced (in motion); **b** not disciplined, restrained, or controlled. **2.** Not examined or tested.

unchivalrous, adj. [1. unshívlrus; 2. anʃívlrəs]. un- (I.) & chivalrous. Not chivalrous, wanting in chivalry.

unchristian, adj. [1. únkríschan; 2. ankrístʃən]. un- (I.) & Christian. Not Christian; **a** (rare) not belonging to the Christian religion; heathen; **b** not in accordance with the spirit of Christianity, uncharitable; unbecoming a Christian.

unchristianize, vb. trans. [1. unkríschaniz; 2. ankrístʃənaiz]. un- (II.) & christianize. To cause to abandon Christianity.

unchristianly, adj. & adv. [1. unkríschanli; 2. ankrístʃənli]. unchristian & -ly. **a** adj. Unchristian; **b** adv., in an unchristian way.

unchurch, vb. trans. [1. unchẽrch; 2. antʃʌtʃ]. un- (II.) & church. To deprive of the rights and privileges of the Church; to expel from the Church, to excommunicate.

uncia, n., pl. **unciae** [1. únsia, -ē; 2. ánsiə, -ī]. Lat., for *oincia, 'unity', fr. ūnus, O. Lat. oinos, 'one', see uni-, & cp. inch (I.) & ounce (I.). (Rom. antiq.) One twelfth part, a of the *libra* or pound, an ounce, esp. as coin, one-twelfth of the *as*; b of the *pes*, or foot, an inch.

uncial, adj. & n. [1. únshal, únsial; 2. ánʃəl, ánsiəl], fr. Lat. *unciālis*, 'pertaining to an ounce or inch'; prec. & -al. The term *litterae unciāles*, 'letters an inch high', was used by St. Jerome of very large letters, not necessarily an inch in height. 1. adj. Designating, pertaining to, consisting of, written in, a type of large MS. letter, used from the 4th to the 9th centuries A.D., differing from the capital 'majuscules' and the later cursive 'minuscules'. 2. n. a An uncial letter; b a MS. written in uncial letters.

unciferous, adj. [1. unsíferus; 2. ansíferəs], fr. Lat. *unc-(us)*, 'hook', see uncus, & -ferous. (zool.) Bearing a hook or hook-like structure.

unciform, adj. [1. únsiform; 2. ánsifōm]. See prec. & -form. (anat. and zool.) Shaped like a hook; hook-shaped.

uncinal, adj. [1. unsínl; 2. ansáinl], fr. L. Lat. *uncīn-(us)*, variant of Lat. *uncus*, 'hook', see uncus, & -al. Hook-like, uncinate.

uncinate, adj. [1. únsināt; 2. ánsineit], fr. Lat. *uncīnāt-(us)*, fr. *uncīnus*, see prec. (anat., bot., and zool.) Hooked, bent like a hook; uncate; bearing hooked spines or prickles.

uncircumcised, adj. [1. unsẽrkumsìzd; 2. ansäkəmsaìzd]. un- (I.) & circumcise(d). a Not having undergone the rite of circumcision; hence, non-Jewish or Hebraic; Gentile; b (fig.) unregenerate, heathen, pagan.

uncircumcision, n. [1. ùnsẽrkumsízhun; 2. ansākəmsízən]. un- (I.) & circumcision. a Non-circumcision; state of being uncircumcised; b (Bib.) *the uncircumcision*, the Gentiles.

uncircumstantial, adj. [1. ùnsẽrkumstánshl; 2. ànsākəmstǽnʃəl]. un- (I.) & circumstantial. Not circumstantial, not given in detail, not examined in detail or going into details.

uncivil, adj. [1. unsívl; 2. ansívl]. un- (I.) & civil. 1. Not civil or courteous; rude, impolite, ill-mannered: *uncivil language, manners, treatment* &c. 2. (rare) Not civilized; barbarian: *an uncivil state of society*.

uncivilized, adj. [1. unsívilizd; 2. ansívilaizd]. un- (I.) & civilize(d). Not civilized; barbarous, savage.

uncivilly, adv. [1. unsívili; 2. ansívili]. uncivil & -ly. In an uncivil manner; rudely.

unclad, adj. [1. unklád; 2. anklǽd]. un- (I.) & clad, P.P. of clothe. Not clad; unclothed.

unclaimed, adj. [1. unklǽmd; 2. ankléimd]. un- (I.) & claim(ed). Not claimed.

unclasp, vb. trans. [1. unkláhsp; 2. anklǽsp]. un- (II.) & clasp (I.). To loose, unfasten, the clasp of; to open something fastened by a clasp; to open something clasped: *to unclasp a brooch*; *to unclasp a box, case* &c.; *to unclasp one's hands*.

unclassed, adj. [1. unkláhst; 2. anklǽst]. un- (I.) & class(ed). 1. Not classed, not placed in a class. 2. Not placed first, second, or third in a competition.

unclassified, adj. [1. unklásifīd; 2. anklǽsifaid]. un- (I.) & classify & -ed. Not classified; not arranged according to a classification.

uncle, n. [1. úngkl; 2. áŋkl]. A.-Fr., Mod. Fr. *oncle*, fr. Lat. *avunculus*, 'one's mother's brother', lit. 'a little grandfather', fr. *avus*, 'grandfather', & suff. -*unculus*; see atavism & cp. avuncular. 1. a The brother of one's father or mother; b the husband of one's aunt. Phr. *Uncle Sam*, the United States of America, as personified in its government or a typical citizen. 2. (Southern U.S.A.) A term of friendly or familiar address to an old negro: *Uncle Tom's Cabin*: *Uncle Remus*

&c. 3. (slang) The pawnbroker: *he has left his watch with his uncle*; cp. French slang, *ma tante*.

-uncle, suff., fr. Lat. *-unculus*, a variant of suff. *-culus*, cp. carbuncle, furuncle &c.; also *-uncule*, as in *homuncule*, or as Lat., *ranunculus*.

unclean, adj. [1. unklẽn; 2. anklín]. un- (I.) & clean. Not clean: a dirty, filthy, unwashed; b not ceremonially or ritually clean; c impure, unchaste, obscene.

uncleanliness, n. [1. unklénlines; 2. anklénlinis]. See next word & -ness. State, quality, of being uncleanly.

uncleanly, adj. [1. unklénli, -klẽnli; 2. anklénli, -klínli]. un- (I.) & cleanly. Not cleanly; having dirty habits, not attentive to cleanliness.

uncleanness, n. [1. unklénnes; 2. anklínnis]. unclean & -ness. State, quality, of being unclean, esp. in a moral sense; impurity, unchastity.

uncleared, adj. [1. unklẽrd; 2. anklíəd]. un- (I.) & clear(ed). Not cleared. 1. Not removed, not taken away; not freed from what should be cleared or removed: *the table is still uncleared*; *land uncleared of weeds, timber* &c. 2. Not acquitted, not freed from a charge or accusation: *his character remains uncleared of a terrible suspicion*.

unclench, unclinch, vb. trans. [1. unklénch, -klínch; 2. anklén(t)ʃ, -klín(t)ʃ)]. un- (II.) & clench, clinch. To open, force open, what is clenched: *to unclench one's fist, teeth*.

unclerical, adj. [1. unklérikl; 2. anklérikl]. un- (I.) & clerical. Not clerical; a not characteristic of the clergy; lay: *unclerical dress*; b not befitting, unbecoming in, clerics: *very unclerical language*.

uncleship, n. [1. úngklship; 2. áŋklʃip]. uncle & -ship. (rare) Condition, relationship, of an uncle.

unclinch. See **unclench**.

uncloak, vb. trans. & intrans. [1. unklõk; 2. anklóuk]. un- (II.) & cloak. 1. trans. To remove the cloak from; to uncover. 2. intrans. To take off one's cloak.

unclog, vb. trans. [1. unklóg; 2. anklɔ́g]. un- (II.) & clog. To free from a clog or obstruction; to remove that which clogs.

unclose, vb. trans. & intrans. [1. unklõz; 2. anklóuz]. un- (II.) & close. To open, unfasten.

unclosed, adj. [1. unklõzd; 2. anklóuzd]. un- (I.) & close & -ed. Not closed or shut, a open: *an unclosed door*; b not enclosed or shut in: *an unclosed view*; c not finished or concluded: *an unclosed controversy, argument*.

unclosured, adj. [1. unklõzhurd; 2. anklóuʒəd]. un- (I.) & closure(d). Not closured; not ended by the use of the parliamentary closure.

unclothe, vb. trans. [1. unklódh; 2. anklóuð]. un- (II.) & clothe. To remove, strip off, the clothes of; to divest of clothing.

unclothed, adj. [1. unklódhd; 2. anklóuðd]. un- (I.) & clothe(d). Not clothed, naked.

unclouded, adj. [1. unklóuded; 2. anklάudid]. un- (I.) & cloud(ed). Not clouded, not obscured by mist or cloud; clear, bright: *unclouded skies*; (also fig.) bright, serene: *a life of unclouded happiness*.

unclutch, vb. trans. [1. unklúch; 2. anklát∫]. un- (II.) & clutch. To disengage a clutch; to free from a clutch.

unco', adj., adv., & n. [1. únkõ; 2. áŋkou]. Scots. variant of uncouth. 1. adj. Strange, wonderful, weird: *an unco' sicht*. 2. adv. Very, exceedingly, remarkably, excessively: *unco' quid*, exceedingly good; *the unco' quid*, excessively good people, usually with suggestion of hypocrisy. 3. n. An extraordinary, strange, remarkable person or thing.

uncock, vb. trans. [1. unkók; 2. ankɔ́k]. un- (II.) & cock (II.). To lower the hammer of a cocked gun without discharging it.

uncoffined, adj. [1. unkófind; 2. ankɔ́find]. un- (I.) & coffin(ed). Not enclosed in a coffin.

uncoil, vb. trans. & intrans. [1. unkóil; 2. ankóil]. un- (II.) & coil. 1. trans. To unwind, to unfasten the coils of: *to uncoil a rope*. 2. intrans. To unwind, to come out of coils: *the snake slowly uncoiled*.

uncoined, adj. [1. unkóind; 2. ankóind]. un- (I.) & coin(ed). Not coined; a not minted into coins: *uncoined silver*; b (fig.) not counterfeit; genuine, unfeigned: '*A fellow of plain, uncoined constancy*' (Shakespeare, '*Henry V.*').

uncollected, adj. [1. ùnkolékted; 2. ànkəléktid]. un- (I.) & collect(ed). Not collected; a not collected or gathered together, not brought to one place or point; scattered: *uncollected rays of light*; b not gathered in, not demanded and received: *uncollected taxes*; c not brought under control; disordered: *uncollected wits*.

uncoloured, adj. [1. unkúlurd; 2. ankáləd]. un- (I.) & colour(ed). Not coloured; a not painted in colours; left in natural colours; drawn in black and white; b (fig.) not exaggerated, not heightened by imagination; related with simplicity and truth; plain, unvarnished: *a plain uncoloured tale*.

uncombed, adj. [1. unkõmd; 2. ankóumd]. un- (I.) & comb(ed). Not combed; tangled, unkempt.

uncombined, adj. [1. ùnkombínd; 2. ànkəmbáind]. un- (I.) & combine(d). Not combined; not formed into a combination or compound.

un-come-at-able, adj. [1. ùn kum át abl; 2. àn kam ǽt əbl]. (colloq.) Not to be come at; not attainable, inaccessible.

uncomeliness, n. [1. unkúmlines; 2. ankámlinis]. uncomely & -ness. State, quality, of being uncomely; a want of beauty, plainness, ugliness; b lack of decency or seemliness; unseemliness.

uncomely, adj. [1. unkúmli; 2. ankámli]. un- (I.) & comely. Not comely; a not beautiful or graceful; plain, ugly; b not seemly or becoming; indecent.

uncomfortable, adj. [1. unkúmfortabl; 2. ankámfətəbl]. un- (I.) & comfortable. Not comfortable, physically or mentally; a feeling, experiencing, discomfort, disagreeably placed or situated; uneasy: *to be uncomfortable in tight boots*; *to feel uncomfortable with strangers, about the political situation* &c.; b causing discomfort or uneasiness; awkward: *an uncomfortable hat, seat*; *the country is in an uncomfortable predicament*; *an uncomfortable prospect of increased taxation*.

uncomfortableness, n. Prec. & -ness. State, quality, of being uncomfortable; discomfort.

uncomfortably, adv. See prec. & -ly. In an uncomfortable manner.

uncomforted, adj. [1. unkúmforted; 2. ankámfətid]. un- (I.) & comfort(ed). Not comforted; unconsoled.

uncommendable, adj. [1. ùnkoméndabl; 2. ànkəméndəbl]. un- (I.) & commendable. Not commendable; not to be commended, not worthy of commendation.

uncommercial, adj. [1. ùnkomẽrshl; 2. ànkəmǽʃəl]. un- (I.) & commercial. Not commercial, a not engaged in, not pertaining to, commerce or trade: *an uncommercial nation*; *uncommercial interests, undertaking* &c.; b not in accordance with commercial principles or usage: *an uncommercial system of taxation*; c not actuated by desire of financial profit: *very uncommercial in his aims*.

uncommissioned, adj. [1. ùnkomíshund; 2. ànkəmíʃənd]. un- (I.) & commission(ed). Not commissioned, not entrusted with a commission or duty; not authorized.

uncommitted, adj. [1. ùnkomíted; 2. ànkəmítid]. un- (I.) & commit(ted). Not committed. 1. Not done, not effected: *scarcely a crime left uncommitted*. 2. Not pledged or bound (to): *he is still uncommitted to any definite course of action*. 3. Not referred to a parliamentary committee, not yet in the committee stage: *the bill remains uncommitted*.

uncommon, adj. & adv. [1. unkómun; 2. ankómən]. **un-** (I.) & **common** (I.). **1.** adj. Not common; a not commonly found, or occurring; infrequent, rare: *an uncommon bird*; **b** not usual; strange, extraordinary, remarkable: *an uncommon act of courage, charity &c.* **2.** adv. (colloq., illit.) Uncommonly, remarkably: *I feel uncommon queer*; *uncommon good beer in this pub*.

uncommonly, adv. Prec. & -ly. **1.** In an uncommon manner; not commonly; infrequently, rarely: *a bird uncommonly found in England.* **2.** To an uncommon degree, remarkable; very: *it is uncommonly cold for the time of year*; *an uncommonly tall man*.

uncommonness, n. State, quality, of being uncommon; infrequency, rarity; strangeness.

uncommunicable, adj. [1. ùnkomúnikabl; 2. ànkəmjúnikəbl]. **un-** (I.) & **communicable**. Not communicable, not to be communicated; incapable of being imparted or shared.

uncommunicated, adj. [1. ùnkomúnikàted; 2. ànkəmjúnikeitid]. **un-** (I.) & **communicate**(d). Not communicated; a not disclosed or made known to others; **b** not imparted to, not shared with, others.

uncommunicative, adj. [1. ùnkomúnikativ; 2. ànkəmjúnikətiv]. **un-** (I.) & **communicative**. Not communicative; not disposed to communicate information; reserved, taciturn.

uncommunicativeness, n. Prec. & -ness. State, quality, of being uncommunicative.

uncompanionable, adj. [1. ùnkumpániunabl; 2.ànkəmpǽnjənəbl]. **un-**(I.)& **companionable**. Not companionable; unsociable.

uncomplaining, adj. [1. ùnkompláning; 2. ànkəmpléiniŋ]. **un-** (I.) & **complain** & -ing. Not complaining, making no complaints; patient, long-suffering.

uncomplainingly, adv. Prec. & -ly. In an uncomplaining manner, without complaint; resignedly.

uncomplaisant, adj. [1. ùnkumplásant; 2. ànkəmpléisənt]. **un-**(I.) & **complaisant**. Not complaisant; not obliging or courteous.

uncomplaisantly, adv. Prec. & -ly. In an uncomplaisant manner.

uncompleted, adj. [1. ùnkumplḗted; 2. ànkəmplítid]. **un-** (I.) & **complete**(d). Not completed; not finished, incomplete.

uncomplicated, adj. [1. ùnkómplikàted; 2. ankómplikèitid]. **un-** (I.) & **complicated**. Not complicated; not involved or intricate; simple.

uncomplimentary, adj. [1. ùnkompliméntari; 2. ànkompliméntəri]. **un-** (I.) & **complimentary**. Not complimentary; rude, discourteous.

uncompounded, adj. [1. ùnkompóunded; 2. ànkəmpáundid]. **un-** (I.) & **compound**(ed). Not compounded; not formed into a compound; unmixed; simple.

uncomprehensive, adj. [1. ùnkompreénsiv; 2. ànkəmprihénsiv]. **un-** (I.) & **comprehensive**. Not comprehensive. **1.** Not inclusive of a large number or quantity. **2.** (rare) Not able to comprehend or understand.

uncompromising, adj. [1. ùnkómpromìzing; 2. ankómprəmàiziŋ]. **un-** (I.) & **compromise** & -ing. Not compromising; **a** not given to making compromises; admitting of no compromise; **b** inflexible, determined, decided, unyielding; strict.

uncompromisingly, adv. Prec. & -ly. In an uncompromising manner; without compromise.

unconcealed, adj.[1.ùnkonséld; 2.ànkənsḗld]. **un-** (I.) & **conceal**(ed). Not concealed; shown, displayed, openly.

unconcern, n. [1. ùnkonsérn; 2. ànkənsə́n]. **un-** (I.) & **concern**. Absence of, freedom from, concern, anxiety, care; indifference, apathy: *he regards such matters with complete unconcern*.

unconcerned, adj. [1. ùnkonsérnd; 2. ànkənsə́nd]. **un-** (I.) & **concern**(ed). Not concerned. **1. a** *Unconcerned in*, not implicated, uninvolved, not taking part in: *he was unconcerned in the conspiracy*; **b** *unconcerned with*, not interested in, not affected by: *to be unconcerned with politics.* **2.** *Unconcerned about*, free from concern or anxiety; easy in mind: *to be unconcerned about the future.* **3.** (absol.) Unperturbed; unmoved, apathetic.

unconcernedly, adv. [1. ùnkunsérnedli; 2. ànkənsə́nidli]. Prec. & -ly. In an unconcerned manner; indifferently, without concern.

uncondemned, adj. [1. ùnkondémd; 2. ànkəndémd]. **un-** (I.) & **condemn**(ed). Not condemned; **a** not found guilty or sentenced to punishment; **b** not blamed or disapproved of.

uncondensed, adj. [1. ùnkondénst; 2. ànkəndénst]. **un-** (I.) & **condense**(d). Not condensed.

unconditional, adj. [1. ùnkondíshunal; 2. ànkəndíʃənəl]. **un-** (I.) & **conditional**. Not conditional, not subject to or limited by conditions or reservations; absolute, not dependent on terms: *demanded an unconditional surrender*; *gave an unconditional refusal*; *made an unconditional offer to purchase*.

unconditionality, n. [1. ùnkondishunáliti; 2. ànkəndiʃənǽliti]. Prec. & -ity. State, quality, of being unconditional.

unconditionally, adv. [1. ùnkondíshunali; 2. ànkəndíʃənəli]. See prec. & -ly. Without conditions or terms; absolutely: *to surrender, accept, unconditionally*.

unconditioned, adj. [1. ùnkondíshund; 2. ànkəndíʃənd]. **un-**(I.) & **condition**(ed). Not conditioned, not subject to conditions; unconditional; specif. (philos.) not subject to limitations or relations; absolute, infinite.

unconfessed, adj.[1. ùnkonfést; 2. ànkənfést]. **un-** (I.) & **confess**(ed). Not confessed; **a** not acknowledged or admitted: *an unconfessed crime*; **b** not having confessed one's sins and received absolution: *to die unconfessed*.

unconfined, adj. [1. ùnkonfínd; 2. ànkənfáind]. **un-** (I.) & **confine**(d). Not confined; **a** not fastened up; loose, free : *with tresses unconfined*; **b** unrestricted, not subject to restrictions and limitations; free, unchecked: *thoughts and speculations unconfined by prejudice or fear*.

unconfirmed, adj. [1. ùnkonférmd; 2. ànkənfə́md]. **un-** (I.) & **confirm**(ed). Not confirmed. **1.** Not corroborated, not established by authoritative statement: *unconfirmed rumours*. **2.** Not having received the rite of confirmation.

unconformability, n. [1. ùnkonfòrmabíliti; 2. ànkənfɔ̀məbíliti]. See next word & -ity. State, quality, of being unconformable.

unconformable, adj. [1. ùnkonfórmabl; 2. ànkənfɔ́məbl]. **un-** (I.) & **conformable**. Not conformable, not conforming, not consistent; specif. (geol.) exhibiting unconformity: *unconformable strata.*

unconformably, adv. Prec. & -ly. In an unconformable manner; without conformity.

unconformity, n. [1. ùnkonfórmiti; 2. ànkənfɔ́miti]. **un-** (I.) & **conformity**. Want, absence, of conformity; specif. (geol.) break in continuity in series of strata, due to interruption of the process of formation.

unconfused, adj. [1. ùnkonfúzd; 2. ànkənfjúzd]. **un-** (I.) & **confuse**(d). Not confused; **a** free from confusion or disorder; **b** not embarrassed.

unconfusedly, adv. [1. ùnkonfúzedli; 2. ànkənfjúzidli]. Prec. & -ly. Not in a confused manner; without confusion or embarrassment.

uncongenial, adj. [1. ùnkonjénial; 2. ànkəndʒíniəl]. **un-** (I.) & **congenial**. Not congenial; **a** not sympathetic, not agreeing with one's character, temperament &c.: *in uncongenial company*; **b** distasteful, repugnant: *an uncongenial task.*

uncongeniality, n. [1. ùnkonjèniáliti; 2. ànkəndʒìniǽliti]. Prec. & -ity. State, quality, of being uncongenial.

uncongenially, adv. [1. ùnkonjéniali; 2. ànkəndʒíniəli]. See prec. & -ly. In an uncongenial manner.

unconnected, adj. [1. ùnkonékted; 2. ànkənéktid]. **un-** (I.) & **connect**(ed). Not connected; **a** not joined or linked physically together; separated: *unconnected lines of railway*; **b** not joined by a chain of causation: *events seemingly unconnected*; **c** not allied by ties of relationship: *families bearing the same name but unconnected*; **d** not logically connected; incoherent; disconnected; disjointed, rambling: *an unconnected narrative*; *loose, unconnected arguments.*

unconnectedly, adv. Prec. & -ly. In an unconnected manner; without connexion.

unconquerable, adj. [1. ùnkóngkerabl; 2. ankɔ́ŋkərəbl]. **un-** (I.) & **conquerable**. Not conquerable, incapable of being conquered or subdued; indomitable, invincible.

unconquerably, adv. Prec. & -ly. So as to be unconquerable; invincibly.

unconquered, adj. [1. ùnkóngkerd; 2. ankɔ́ŋkəd]. **un-** (I.) & **conquer**(ed). Not conquered; unsubdued, undefeated.

unconscientious, adj. [1. únkònshiénshus; 2. ànkɔ̀nʃiénʃəs]. **un-** (I.) & **conscientious**. Not conscientious, unscrupulous.

unconscientiously, adv. Prec. & -ly. In an unconscientious manner; unscrupulously.

unconscientiousness, n. See prec. & -ness. State, quality, of being unconscientious.

unconscionable, adj. [1. ùnkónshunabl; 2. ankɔ́nʃənəbl]. **un-** (I.) & *conscionable*, 'governed by conscience, scrupulous; reasonable', formed irregularly fr. **conscience**. **1. a** Not governed or restrained by conscience; unscrupulous: *unconscionable usurers*; *unconscionable subterfuges*; **b** (law) unfair, exceeding the limits of conscientious dealing: *an unconscionable bargain*. **2.** Not reasonable; excessive, inordinate: '*an unconscionable time a-dying*' (Charles II.).

unconscionably, adv. Prec. & -ly. In an unconscionable manner; to an unconscionable degree.

unconscious, adj. [1. ùnkónshus; 2. ankɔ́nʃəs]. **un-** (I.) & **conscious**. Not conscious. **1.** (with *of*) Not knowing; not alive to, unaware: *they were unconscious of any danger*; *unconscious of one's mistake, of one's absurd appearance &c.* **2.** Deprived of consciousness; in a state when all power of perception is lost: *after the accident he was unconscious for several days*; *he still remains in an unconscious condition.* **3.** Not apprehended or realized by the consciousness; not the result of will, not deliberately intended: *unconscious humour.* **4.** Taking place, carried out, without the participation of conscious will; involuntary: *unconscious movements*; *unconscious cerebration*, working of the mind without conscious effort; *the unconscious*, as n., in psychology and psycho-analysis, the unconscious elements and working of the mind, as distinct from and in contrast with the conscious. **5.** Non-conscious, not possessed of self-consciousness or of perception: *unconscious nature.*

unconsciously, adv. Prec. & -ly. Not consciously; in an unconscious manner; without consciousness.

unconsciousness, n. See prec. & -ness. Condition of being unconscious; absence, lack, of consciousness.

unconsecrated, adj. [1. ùnkónsekràted; 2. ànkɔ́nsikrèitid]. **un-** (I.) & **consecrate**(d). Not consecrated.

unconsenting, adj. [1. ùnkonsénting; 2. ànkənséntiŋ]. **un-** (I.) & **consent** & -ing. Not consenting, withholding consent; non-acquiescent.

unconsidered, adj. [1. ùnkonsídərd; 2. ànkənsídəd]. **un-** (I.) & **consider**(ed). Not considered, disregarded, not taken into consideration; negligible.

unconstitutional, adj. [1. unkònstitûshunal; 2. ankònstitjúʃənəl]. un- (I.) & constitutional. Not constitutional; not in accordance with, opposed to, the principles of the constitution of a state.

unconstitutionality, n. [1. unkònstitûshunáliti; 2. ankònstitjúʃənǽliti]. Prec. & -ity. Quality of being unconstitutional.

unconstitutionally, adv. [1. unkònstitûshunali; 2. ankònstitjúʃənəli]. See prec. & -ly. In an unconstitutional manner; in breach of the constitution.

unconstrained, adj. [1. ùnkonstránd; 2. ànkənstréind]. un- (I.) & constrain(ed). Not constrained. 1. Free from restraint or compulsion; free to act or not. 2. Not done under compulsion; done voluntarily. 3. Free from constraint of manner, unembarrassed, not self-conscious; easy.

unconstrainedly, adv. [1. ùnkonstránedli; 2. ànkənstréinidli]. Prec. & -ly. In an unconstrained manner.

unconsumed, adj. [1. ùnkonsûmd; 2. ànkənsjûmd]. un- (I.) & consume(d). Not consumed.

unconsummated, adj. [1. unkónsumàted; 2. ankónsəmèitid]. un- (I.) & consummate(d). Specif. (of marriage) not consummated.

uncontainable, adj. [1. ùnkontánabl; 2. ànkəntéinəbl]. un- (I.) & contain & -able. Not containable; not to be contained or held in; irrepressible.

uncontaminated, adj. [1. ùnkontáminàted; 2. ànkəntǽminèitid]. un- (I.) & contaminate(d). Not contaminated; pure, unsullied (in material and spiritual sense).

uncontemplated, adj. [1. unkóntemplàted; 2. ankóntempleitid]. un- (I.) & contemplate(d). Not contemplated; not expected.

uncontested, adj. [1. ùnkontésted; 2. ànkəntéstid]. un- (I.) & contest(ed). Not contested; specif., *an uncontested election*, one without a rival candidate.

uncontracted, adj. [1. ùnkontrákted; 2. ànkəntrǽktid]. un- (I.) & contract(ed). Not contracted; not shrunk or made smaller.

uncontradicted, adj. [1. unkòntradíkted; 2. ankòntrədíktid]. un- (I.) & contradict(ed). Not contradicted; not denied, undisputed.

uncontrollability, n. [1. ùnkontròlabíliti; 2. ànkəntròulabíliti]. See next word & -ity. State of being uncontrollable.

uncontrollable, adj. [1. ùnkontrólabl; 2. ànkəntróuləbl]. un- (I.) & controllable. Not controllable, incapable of being controlled or restrained; ungovernable, unmanageable : *an uncontrollable temper; uncontrollable children* &c.

uncontrollably, adv. Prec. & -ly. In an uncontrollable manner; beyond control.

uncontrolled, adj. [1. ùnkontróld; 2. ànkəntróuld]. un- (I.) & control(led). Not controlled; free from control, unrestrained.

uncontrolledly, adv. [1. ùnkontróledli; 2. ànkəntróulidli]. Prec. & -ly. In an uncontrolled manner; without control or restraint; freely.

uncontroversial, adj. [1. unkòntrovérshl; 2. ankòntrəvə́ʃl]. un- (I.) & controversial. Not controversial; not a subject of, or giving rise to, controversy.

uncontroverted, adj. [1. unkòntrovérted; 2. ankòntrəvə́tid]. un- (I.) & controvert(ed). Not controverted; undisputed, indisputable.

unconventional, adj. [1. ùnkonvénshunal; 2. ànkənvénʃənəl]. un- (I.) & conventional. Not conventional; a not in strict accordance with established custom and usage; b free and easy in manner; not strictly observant of the accepted rules and customs in manners, dress &c.

unconventionality, n. [1. únkonvènshunáliti; 2. ánkənvènʃənǽliti]. Prec. & -ity. Condition of being unconventional; freedom from established custom or usage.

unconventionally, adv. [1. ùnkonvénshunali; 2. ànkənvénʃənəli]. See prec. & -ly. In an unconventional manner.

unconversable, adj. [1. ùnkonvérsabl; 2. ànkənvə́səbl]. un- (I.) & conversable. Not conversable; not free or easy in conversation; not easy to get on with; unsociable.

unconversant, adj. [1. unkónversant; 2. ankónvəsənt]. un- (I.) & conversant. Not conversant; not familiarly acquainted with.

unconverted, adj. [1. ùnkonvérted; 2. ànkənvǽtid]. un- (I.) & convert(ed). Not converted. 1. Not changed into or exchanged for another substance or body; not changed in substance or form. 2. Not changed or converted in mind or heart; a not brought into acquaintance with Christianity or other specified religion; still in a state of heathendom; specif. b not having undergone conversion in special sense; not having felt the workings of faith and religion in the heart, or realized the inward truth of these. 3. Not persuaded of, brought round to, some specified body of opinion.

unconvertible, adj. [1. ùnkonvértibl; 2. ànkənvǽtibl]. un- (I.) & convertible. Not capable of being converted or changed into something else; specific usages: a (of any form of money) not convertible into another form; b *unconvertible terms*, not capable of being used one for the other, not synonymous.

unconvinced, adj. [1. ùnkonvínst; 2. ànkənvínst]. un- (I.) & convince(d). Not convinced, unpersuaded.

unconvincing, adj. [1. ùnkonvínsing; 2. ànkənvínsiŋ]. un- (I.) & convincing. Not convincing; not bringing conviction.

unconvincingly, adv. Prec. & -ly. In an unconvincing manner.

uncooked, adj. [1. unkóokt; 2. ankúkt]. un- (I.) & cook(ed). Not cooked; raw.

uncord, vb. trans. [1. unkórd; 2. ankɔ́d]. un- (II.) & cord. To unfasten, undo knots, and remove cords from (a box, trunk &c.).

uncork, vb. trans. [1. unkórk; 2. ankɔ́k]. un- (II.) & cork. a To draw the cork from, take the cork out of : *to uncork a bottle of wine*; b (colloq.) to set loose what is bottled up, to give vent to : *to uncork one's feelings*.

uncorrected, adj. [1. ùnkorékted; 2. ànkərǽktid]. un- (I.) & correct(ed). Not corrected; not revised; not rebuked.

uncorroborated, adj. [1. unkoróborāted; 2. ànkəróbəreitid]. un- (I.) & corroborate(d). Not corroborated; unconfirmed.

uncorroded, adj.[1. ùnkoróded; 2. ànkəróudid]. un- (I.) & corrode(d). Not corroded, not impaired by rust; not acted on by acid.

uncorrupted, adj. [1. ùnkorúpted; 2. ànkərǽptid]. un- (I.) & corrupted. Not corrupted; a not putrefied; b not morally corrupted; not bought with bribes.

uncorruptible, adj. [1. ùnkorúptibl; 2. ànkərǽptibl]. un- (I.) & corruptible. Not corruptible, not liable to moral corruption; incorruptible.

uncountable, adj.[1. ùnkóuntabl; 2. ankáuntəbl]. un- (I.) & count & -able. Not countable, not to be counted; innumerable, countless.

uncounted, adj. [1. unkóunted; 2. ankáuntid]. un- (I.) & count(ed). Not counted, unnumbered.

uncountenanced, adj. [1. unkóuntenanst; 2. ankáuntinənst]. un- (I.) & countenance(d). Not countenanced; unsupported by others; not sanctioned.

uncouple, vb. trans. [1. unkúpl; 2. ankápl]. un- (II.) & couple (II.) a To loose from a couple or leash : *to uncouple greyhounds*; b to disconnect from couplings, to separate : *to uncouple railway trucks*.

uncoupled, adj. [1. unkúpld; 2. ankápld]. un- (I.) & couple(d). Not coupled, not joined together; disconnected.

uncourteous, adj. [1. unkórteus, -kérteus; 2. ankɔ́tiəs, -kǽtiəs]. un- (I.) & courteous. Not courteous; discourteous, rude.

uncourteously, adv. Prec. & -ly. In an uncourteous manner; discourteously, rudely.

uncourteousness, n. See prec. & -ness. Want of courtesy; discourtesy.

uncourtliness, n. [1. unkórtlines; 2. ankɔ́tlinis]. See next word & -ness. State of being uncourtly; want, absence, of courtliness.

uncourtly, adj. [1. unkórtli; 2. ankɔ́tli]. un- (I.) & courtly. Not courtly, not trained in, or used to, the manners of a court; unpolished, unrefined.

uncouth, adj. [1. unkóoth; 2. ankúp]. O.E. *uncūð*, 'unknown, strange', un- (I.) & *cúþ*, 'known', cp. O.S. *cūð*, O.H.G. *chund*, Goth. *kunþs*; fr. base seen in **cunning**, **can** (I.); cp. also **know**. 1. (archaic and obs.) Unknown, strange, unfamiliar, mysterious: '*Find out His uncouth way*' (Milton, 'P. L.' II. 407). 2. Awkward, unrefined, clumsy, boorish : *an uncouth rustic; of uncouth manners, appearance* &c.

uncouthly, adv. Prec. & -ly. In an uncouth manner.

uncouthness, n. See prec. & -ness. State, quality, of being uncouth.

uncovenanted, adj. [1. unkúvenanted; 2. ankávənəntid]. un- (I.) & covenant(ed). Not covenanted. 1. Not founded on, not promised by, a covenant; specif. (theol.) *uncovenanted mercies of God*, mercies of salvation extended by God to those outside the Covenant of Grace and Redemption through Christ. 2. Not bound by a covenant or agreement; specif., *Uncovenanted Civil Service*, a branch of the Indian Civil Service, members of which are appointed without examination, have no right to a pension, and may retire at will.

uncover, vb. trans. & intrans. [1. unkúver; 2. ankávə]. un- (II.) & cover (I.). A. trans. 1. a To remove a cover or covering from : *to uncover a dish of food*; *to uncover a protected cricket pitch* &c.; b to remove the covering from (any part of the body) : *to uncover the face, feet* &c., esp. *to uncover the head*, *uncover oneself*, to take off the hat or other head-covering as a sign of salutation or respect. 2. a (by transf. or fig.) To lay open to view, to disclose, lay bare : *to uncover one's position*; *to uncover one's heart to*; specif. b (mil.) to disclose position of troops by deploying to right and left the leading lines which cover them. 3. To remove cover or protection from; to leave unguarded, unprotected. B. intrans. To take off the hat or other head-covering as a salutation or in token of respect: *everyone uncovered when the signal sounded*.

uncovered, adj. [1. unkúverd; 2. ankávəd]. un- (I.) & cover(ed). Not covered; a devoid of cover; bare, unprotected : *the position lies quite uncovered and open to attack*; b with the hat off : *to stand uncovered*.

uncoveted, adj. [1. unkúveted; 2. ankávitid]. un- (I.) & covet(ed). Not coveted.

uncowl, vb. trans. [1. unkóul; 2. ankául]. un- (II.) & cowl. a To remove the cowl from : *to uncowl one's face, head*; b to take the cowl away from, to deprive of right to wear the cowl : *to uncowl a monk*.

uncreate (I.), vb. trans. [1. ùnkrēát; 2. ankriéit]. un- (II.) & create. (rare) To reverse the process of creation in respect of; wipe out of existence, annihilate : '*Who can uncreate thee thou shalt know*' (Milton, 'P. L.' v. 895).

uncreate (II.), adj. un- (I.) & (archaic) create(d). Not created; uncreated : '*The Father uncreate, the Son uncreate*' &c. (Athanasian Creed).

uncreated, adj. [1. ùnkrēáted; 2. ankriéitid]. un- (I.) & create(d). 1. Not yet created, not existing, non-existent. 2. Self-existing, existing eternally; existing, having its origin, independently of creation; uncreate.

uncredited, adj. [1. unkrédited; 2. ankréditid]. un- (I.) & credit(ed). Not credited, not believed.

uncrippled, adj. [1. unkrípld; 2. ankrípld]. un- (I.) & cripple(d). Not crippled; a not lamed; not injured in the limbs: *hands, feet, uncrippled by gout*; **b** not damaged or injured, not prevented by injury or loss from movement or activity: *the ships remained uncrippled by the heavy fire; the business is uncrippled in spite of the heavy loss incurred*.

uncritical, adj. [1. unkrítikl; 2. ankrítikl]. un- (I.) & critical. Not critical; a not disposed, unwilling, to criticize: *an enthusiastic and uncritical audience*; **b** not capable of criticism, wanting in powers of critical judgement, unable to criticize: *the uncritical applause of the uneducated*; **c** not according to the rules or principles of criticism: *an uncritical appreciation, estimate, review* &c.

uncritically, adv. Prec. & -ly. In an uncritical manner.

uncriticized, adj. [1. unkrítisīzd; 2. ankrítisaizd]. un- (I.) & criticize(d). Not criticized; not subjected to criticism.

uncropped, adj. [1. unkrópt; 2. ankrópt]. un- (I.) & crop(ped). Not cropped. 1. (of land) Not sown, planted, with crops. 2. (of crops) Not reaped, gathered in, or harvested. 3. (of hair, ears) Not trimmed, not lopped or cut short.

uncross, vb. trans. [1. unkráws; 2. ankrós]. un- (II.) & cross. To change from a crossed position; to put straight what is crossed: *to uncross one's legs*.

uncrossed, adj. [1. unkráwst; 2. ankróst]. un- (I.) & cross(ed). Not crossed. 1. Not placed across one another: *knives must lie uncrossed on the table*. 2. (of cheque) Not crossed so as to indicate that it must be paid through an account at a bank. 3. Not thwarted, not opposed: *a rapid rise to power uncrossed by any rivals*.

uncrown, vb. trans. [1. unkróun; 2. ankráun]. un- (II.) & crown. To deprive of a crown, to dethrone, depose from position as king (lit. and fig.).

uncrowned, adj. [1. unkróund; 2. ankráund]. un- (I.) & crown(ed). Not crowned; a not yet crowned; not having gone through the ceremony of coronation; **b** having the power but not the title of king: *some called Parnell the uncrowned king of Ireland*.

unction, n. [1. úngkshun. 2. áŋkʃən]. O. Fr., Mod. Fr. *onction*, fr. Lat. *unctiōn-(em)*, 'anointing'; fr. *unct-(um)*, P.P. type of *unguere*, 'to anoint', see **unguent**, & -ion. 1. Act of anointing with oil as a ceremony or rite or symbol of consecration; **a** in the sacrament given to the dying in the Roman Catholic and Orthodox Churches, the blessed oil being applied to the head, hands, feet, and chest: *Extreme Unction*; **b** in the coronation of the king. 2. Act of applying, by rubbing or smearing, oil, ointment, or unguent for medical purposes. 3. **a** That which is used in anointing; an oil, ointment, or unguent; **b** (fig.) anything which soothes or assuages: '*Lay not that flattering unction to your soul*' (Shakespeare, 'Hamlet'). 4. **a** A quality in language, voice, manner, or style which expresses or excites deep feeling or fervour, esp. religious fervour: *unction is no longer admired in a preacher; the sermons of to-day lack unction*; **b** exaggerated, affected, fervour; insincere emotion, sympathy, or suavity, gush, unctuousness: *the unction of a Pecksniff*; **c** relish, gusto, enjoyment: *an amusing story told with unction*.

unctuous, adj. [1. úngktūus; 2. áŋktjuəs], fr. O. Fr. *unctueus*, Mod. Fr. *onctueux*, fr. L. Lat. *unctuōsus*, fr. Lat. *unctus*, 'an anointing, unguent'; see prec. & -ous. 1. Of the nature of an unguent or ointment; **a** greasy, oily; **b** having a soapy, greasy feeling or touch, as some minerals, e.g. fuller's earth, soapstone &c. 2. Full of unction, esp. of simulated, exaggerated fervour or emotion; insincerely suave or gushing: *an unctuous person*; *an unctuous voice, manner* &c.

unctuously, adv. Prec. & -ly. In an unctuous manner; with affected, exaggerated, unction.

unctuousness, n. See prec. & -ness. Condition, quality, of being unctuous (lit. and fig.).

unculled, adj. [1. unkúld; 2. ankáld]. un- (I.) & cull(ed). Not culled, ungathered; not separated.

uncultivable, adj. [1. unkúltivabl; 2. ankáltivəbl]. un- (I.) & cultivable. Not cultivable; not capable of cultivation or tillage.

uncultivated, adj. [1. unkúltivāted; 2. ankáltivèitid]. un- (I.) & cultivate(d). Not cultivated. 1. Not tilled, not employed for agricultural purposes, production of food &c.: *uncultivated land*. 2. (fig.) **a** Not practised, not promoted, neglected: *uncultivated art, talents* &c.: *an uncultivated genius*. 3. Not civilized; barbarous, rude, uncultured: *uncultivated races*, not refined by instruction and education.

uncultured, adj. [1. unkúlchurd; 2. ankáltʃəd]. un- (I.) & culture(d). Not cultured; uneducated, uncultivated.

uncurb, vb. trans. [1. unkérb; 2. ankáb]. un- (II.) & curb. To free from a curb, to loosen the curb of, to ride on the snaffle only: *to uncurb a horse*; (also fig.) to unloose, let loose from control: *to uncurb one's passions*.

uncurbed, adj. [1. unkérbd; 2. ankábd]. un- (I.) & curb(ed). Not curbed; **a** not provided with a curb: *an uncurbed bridle*; **b** (fig.) not checked or controlled; unrestrained: *uncurbed passions, ambitions* &c.

uncurl, vb. trans. & intrans. [1. unkérl; 2. ankál]. un- (II.) & curl. 1. trans. To put, take, out of curl, to straighten out from curl. 2. intrans. **a** To come out of curl, come uncurled, to become straight; **b** to unroll, come out of a curled-up posture.

uncursed, adj. [1. unkérst; 2. ankást]. un- (I.) & curse(d). Not cursed; free from a curse.

uncurtailed, adj. [1. ùnkērtáld; 2. ànkātéild]. un- (I.) & curtail(ed). Not curtailed; not cut short, unabbreviated; existing, given, in full.

uncurtain, vb. trans. [1. unkértin; 2. ankátin]. un- (II.) & curtain. To remove a curtain from; to draw aside the curtains of; to disclose, reveal.

uncurtained, adj. [1. unkértind; 2. ankátind]. un- (I.) & curtain(ed). Not curtained; **a** having no curtains; **b** having the curtains drawn aside or back.

uncus, n., pl. **unci** [1. úngkus, únsī; 2. áŋkəs, ánsai]. Lat., 'hook', fr. Gk. *ógkos*; see also under **angle** (I.). (anat., zool.) A hook, barb; a hook-like appendage or process.

uncushioned, adj. [1. unkóoshund; 2. ankúʃənd]. un- (I.) & cushion(ed). Not cushioned; not provided with, not resting on, cushions; not padded.

uncustomary, adj. [1. unkústumari; 2. ankástəməri]. un- (I.) & customary. Not customary; not according to the usual custom.

uncustomed, adj. [1. unkústumd; 2. ankástəmd]. un- (I.) & custom(ed). 1. Not liable to, or charged with, customs duty. 2. Not having paid customs duty.

uncut, adj. [1. unkút; 2. ankát]. un- (I.) & cut (I.). Not cut; specif., of books, with margins of the pages not trimmed or cut down from the original width, as for binding.

undam, vb. trans. [1. undám; 2. andám]. un- (II.) & dam (II.). To remove a dam from, clear obstruction from: *to undam a river, reservoir* &c.

undamaged, adj. [1. undámijd; 2. andámidʒd]. un-(I.) & damage(d). Not damaged, having suffered no damage; uninjured, unspoilt; sound, whole.

undammed, adj. [1. undámd; 2. andámd]. un- (I.) & dam(med) (III.). Not dammed; not blocked, obstructed, or held back by a dam.

undamned, adj. [1. undámd; 2. andámd]. un- (I.) & damned. Not damned; uncondemned.

undamped, adj. [1. undámpt; 2. andámpt]. un- (I.) & damp(ed). Not damped; a not disheartened; **b** specif. (elect.) of oscillations, maintained with increasing amplitude.

undate, adj. [1. úndāt; 2. ándeit], fr. Lat. *unda*, 'a wave', & -ate; cogn. w. Scrt. *undati*, 'it springs; it moistens'; & *udán*, 'water'; Gk. *húdōr*, 'water', see **hydro**-; O.E. *wæter*, see **water** (I.). Wavy, undated.

undated (I.), adj. [1. úndāted; 2. ándeitid]. Prec. & -ed. (bot.) Wavy, undulate.

undated (II.), adj. [1. undāted; 2. andéitid]. un- (I.) & date(d). **a** Not dated; bearing no date, as a document, cheque &c.; **b** not having the time fixed or agreed upon.

undaunted, adj. [1. undáwnted; 2. andɔ́ntid]. un- (I.) & daunt(ed). Not daunted, not dismayed or cowed by fear; fearless, courageous.

undauntedly, adv. Prec. & -ly. In an undaunted manner; fearlessly.

undauntedness, n. See prec. & -ness. Condition, quality, of being undaunted.

undazzled, adj. [1. undázld; 2. andǽzld]. un- (I.) & dazzle(d). Not dazzled; not blinded, as by too much brightness.

undé, adj. [1. úndi; 2. ándi], fr. Fr. *ondé*, see **undate**. (her.) Wavy.

undebated, adj. [1. ùndebáted; 2. àndibéitid]. un- (I.) & debate(d). Not debated; undiscussed.

undebauched, adj. [1. ùndebáwcht; 2. àndibɔ́tʃt]. un- (I.) & debauch(ed). Not debauched; **a** not corrupted in morals; **b** not dissolute in behaviour.

undecagon, n. [1. undékagon; 2. andékəgɔn], fr. Lat. *undec-(im)*, 'eleven', *ūnus*, 'one', & *decem*, 'ten', & -gon. (geom.) A plane figure, having eleven angles and eleven sides.

undeceive, vb. trans. [1. ùndesév; 2. àndisív]. un- (II.) & deceive. To cause to be no longer deceived, to disillusion; to open the eyes of, to cause to see things as they really are: *he believes that he is certain to win, and I have not the heart to undeceive him*.

undeceived, adj. [1. ùndesévd; 2. àndisívd]. un- (I.) & deceive(d). Not deceived; not under the influence of illusion or self-deception: *undeceived by false hopes and promises, he prepared for the worst*.

undecennial, adj. [1. ùndesénial; 2. àndisénial]. Lat. *undecim*, 'eleven', see first element of **undecagon**, & for suff. see that of **decennial**. Occurring, observed, every eleventh year.

undecided, adj. [1. ùndesíded; 2. àndisáidid]. un- (I.) & decided. Not decided. 1. **a** Not yet settled or determined: *an undecided question*; **b** (of weather) unsettled; **c** not having made up one's mind: *I'm undecided whether to go or stay*. 2. Lacking decision of character; irresolute, incapable of coming to a decision: *an undecided character*. 3. Not clearly marked, not definite in form or outline; vague, unpronounced: *a person of undecided features*.

undecidedly, adv. Prec. & -ly. In an undecided manner; irresolutely, waveringly.

undecidedness, n. See prec. & -ness. State, quality, of being undecided.

undecipherable, adj. [1. ùndesífferabl; 2. àndisáifərəbl]. un- (I.) & decipherable. Not decipherable; incapable of being deciphered; illegible.

undeck, vb. trans. [1. undék; 2. andék]. un- (II.) & deck (I.). (poet.) To deprive, divest, of adornments: '*Undeck the pompous body of a king*' (Shakespeare, 'Richard II.').

undecked (I.), adj. [1. undékt; 2. andékt]. un- (I.) & deck(ed). Not decked out or adorned.

undecked (II.), adj. un- (I.) & deck (II.), & -ed. (of boats) Not furnished with a deck.

undeclared, adj. [1. ùndeklárd; 2. àndikléəd]. un- (I.) & declare(d). 1. Not declared, not made known, not disclosed. Specif. 2. (of goods subject to customs duty) Not exhibited to officials of the customs for assessment of duty.

undedicated, adj. [1. undédikăted; 2. andédikèitid]. un- (I.) & dedicate(d). Not dedicated. 1. a (of church) Not consecrated, not dedicated to a patron saint; b (of book) not dedicated to a patron; without a dedication. 2. (of a road) Not handed over to a public authority but maintained at private expense by the makers or the owners of property along it.

undeeded, adj. [1. undéded; 2. andídid]. un- (I.) & deed(ed). (law) Not transferred by deed.

undefended, adj. [1. undefénded; 2. andiféndid]. un- (I.) & defend(ed). Not defended. 1. a Not defended; unprotected, without defence or protection, defenceless: *an undefended town*; b not supported or maintained by argument, excuse &c.: *an undefended act, measure* &c. 2. a Not defended by counsel: *an undefended prisoner*; b without a defence being entered or put forward: *an undefended charge, action at law* &c.

undefiled, adj. [1. undefíld; 2. andifáild]. un- (I.) & defile(d) (I.). Not defiled, unpolluted; pure; unmixed with baser elements.

undefined, adj. [1. undefínd; 2. andifáind]. un- (I.) & define(d). Not defined. 1. Not clearly marked; indefinite, vague. 2. Not explained or described by a definition.

undeify, vb. trans. [1. undéifi; 2. andíifai]. un- (II.) & deify. To degrade from the position of a deity or god; to deprive of the sanctity of, rites and worship due to, a god.

undelayed, adj. [1. undeláid; 2. andiléid]. un- (I.) & delay(ed). Not delayed, not held back by delays.

undelegated, adj. [1. undélegăted; 2. andéligeitid]. un- (I.) & delegate(d). Not delegated, not transferred or committed to another: *undelegated powers or authority*.

undelivered, adj. [1. undelíverd; 2. andilívəd]. un- (I.) & deliver(ed). Not delivered; a not set free, released, liberated: *an undelivered prisoner*; b not handed over, not distributed: *undelivered message, letters, parcels* &c.; c not pronounced, uttered, recited: *an undelivered speech, address*.

undemanded, adj. [1. undemáhnded; 2. andimándid]. un- (I.) & demand(ed). Not demanded, not claimed or asked for.

undemonstrable, adj. [1. undemónstrabl; 2. andimónstrəbl]. un- (I.) & demonstrable. Not demonstrable, incapable of being demonstrated.

undemonstrated, adj. [1. undemónstrăted; 2. andémənstrèitid]. un- (I.) & demonstrate(d). Not demonstrated; not proved by demonstration.

undemonstrative, adj. [1. undemónstrativ; 2. andimónstrətiv]. un- (I.) & demonstrative. Not demonstrative, not effusive, not addicted to strong expression of feeling, opinion &c.; reserved.

undemonstratively, adv. Prec. & -ly. In an undemonstrative manner.

undeniable, adj. [1. undeníabl; 2. andináiəbl]. un- (I.) & deniable. Not deniable; a not capable of being denied or refuted; indisputable: *undeniable truth, evidence* &c.; b decidedly excellent: *of undeniable antecedents*; c unmistakable: *an undeniable Jew*.

undeniably, adv. Prec. & -ly. In an undeniable manner; indisputably, unmistakably.

undenominational, adj. [1. undenòminăshunal; 2. andinòminéiʃənəl]. un- (I.) & denominational. Not denominational; specif., not restricted to, not in accordance with the characteristic tenets of any particular religious denomination: *undenominational education*.

undenounced, adj. [1. undenóunst; 2. andináunst]. un- (I.) & denounce(d). Not denounced. 1. a Not openly charged with, not informed against: *the conspirators remain undenounced*; b not inveighed against, not repudiated. 2. Not formally terminated: *the treaty is still undenounced though obsolete*.

undependable, adj. [1. undepéndabl; 2. andipéndəbl]. un- (I.) & dependable. Not dependable, not to be depended on; untrustworthy.

undeplored, adj. [1. undeplórd; 2. andiplód]. un- (I.) & deplore(d). Not deplored, unlamented.

undeposed, adj. [1. undepózd; 2. andipóuzd]. un- (I.) & depose(d). Not deposed.

undepraved, adj. [1. undeprávd; 2. andipréivd]. un- (I.) & deprave(d). Not depraved, not corrupted in morals.

undepreciated, adj. [1. undepréshiăted; 2. andipríʃieitid]. un- (I.) & depreciate(d). Not depreciated; a not disparaged, not belittled: *an undepreciated reputation*; b not lowered or reduced in value: *undepreciated currency*.

undepressed, adj. [1. undeprést; 2. andiprést]. un- (I.) & depress(ed). Not depressed; esp. in mind, spirits; not dejected, not cast down: *undepressed by their losses*.

undeprived, adj. [1. undeprívd; 2. andipráivd]. un- (I.) & deprive(d). Not deprived; not dispossessed of.

under (I.), prep. [1. únder; 2. ándə]. O.E. & M.E. *under*; O.S. *undar*; O.H.G. *untar*, Du. *onder*, Germ. *unter*, O.N. *undir* &c.; cogn. w. Lat. *infrā*, ' below '. See infra, & cp. Scrt. *adhaś*, ' below '. 1. In, at, to a lower place or position than; below, the opposite of *over*; cp. *beneath* and *above*: *to lie down under a tree*; *you will find it under the seat*; *river flowing under a bridge*; a with sense of submersed in, covered by: *under the water*; *under the ground*; *hid his face under the bedclothes*; b inside, within: *under the skin*; *under the lee of*, to leeward of, sheltered from the wind by; c at the foot of: *village nestling under a hill*; *stand under the wall*; in various Phrs.: *under foot*, beneath one's feet, trodden; *under one's nose*, right in front of one, close to, so that one cannot help seeing it or noticing it; *under one's eye*, in sight; *under hatches*, with hatches closed down; safely secured; *under cover*, sheltered. 2. With sense of sustaining, being loaded with or oppressed by (lit. and fig.): *cannot march under such a load*; *broke down under the burden of sorrow, care, debts* &c. Phr. *under arms*, armed. 3. In sense of being in certain conditions or states (lit. and fig.) analogous to that of position under or beneath: a as subjected to, undergoing: *died under an operation*, *under the surgeon's knife*; *to be brave under trials and adversities*; *confessed under torture, the rack*; Phrs. *to be under a cloud*, be in disgrace, suspected, out of favour; *under fire*, fired upon; *under sail*, driven by wind; *under sentence of death, ten years' penal servitude* &c., sentenced to; b as in course of: *road under repair*; *bill now under discussion*; c as controlled or governed by: *England under the Stuarts*; *under the authority of the law*; d implying obligation, liability: *the terms under a contract*; *under a vow of secrecy*; *to give evidence under oath*; e as included in, in the same division or class as: *spiders, mites, ticks* &c. *are dealt with under (the head of) Arachnida*; f as indicating shelter, cover, or disguise &c.: *went under a false name*; *under the pretence of collecting for charity*; g as indicating a general state: *under such conditions, under the circumstances*; h during, in the time of: *under the later Roman Empire*, *under the Third French Republic*. 4. Less than, inferior to: a (of position) *no one under (rank of) a colonel*; b (of age) *all children under 10 years old*; Phr. *under age*, not 21 years old; c in less time than: *cannot reach the place under two hours*; *run a hundred yards under ten seconds*; d (of price, value &c.) *won't sell under £1000*; e (of number, quantity &c.): *under 50 people were there*; *under 100 acres in area*.

under (II.), adj., fr. prec. Lower, subordinate, inferior; usually compounded, with or without hyphen, as *under-tenant*, *an underlease* &c.; see under-.

under (III.), adv., see prec. In a lower, inferior position, usually in various verbal Phrs.: *to bring, go, keep, under*, bring to, descend to, keep in, a lower condition; *to knuckle under*, to submit to slavishly.

under-, pref., fr. prec., w. force of prep., adv., or adj. 1. Below, beneath: *underclothes*, *underfoot* &c.; *to underbid*, *to underline*. 2. From beneath: *undermine*, *underprop*. 3. Not completely, insufficient: *understaff*, *understatement*. 4. Inferior, subordinate: *underling* &c.

underact, vb. trans. & intrans. [1. únderákt; 2. andərákt]. under- & act. 1. trans. To act (stage play) without sufficient passion, vigour, spirit; to act in such a manner that a character or part is insufficiently emphasized: *to underact the character of Macbeth*; *the play was underacted throughout*. 2. intrans. To act in the above way.

underaction, n. [1. únderákshun; 2. andərákʃən]. under- & action. Subordinate action; action not essential to the main action; an episode.

under-agent, n. [1. únder ájent; 2. ándər éidʒənt]. under- & agent. A subordinate agent.

underarm, adj. & adv. [1. únderàrm; 2. ándəràm]. under- & arm (I.). (cricket, tennis) Bowled, served, with the fore-arm and hand, the elbow held downwards; underhand: *an underarm delivery, service*; *he bowls underarm*.

underbid, vb. trans. [1. únderbíd; 2. andəbíd]. under- & bid. To bid or offer less than; to offer a less price for a service or contract; to offer to sell goods, contract to perform some service, at a lower price than: *our commercial rivals can underbid us in foreign markets*.

underbidder, n. [1. únderbíder; 2. andəbídə]. Prec. & -er. One who underbids; a one who has successfully offered a lower price for supply of goods, for contract of service &c.: *our underbidders for coal in Europe*; b one who has failed to buy an object &c. at an auction, usually the person who has bid next highest price to the successful bidder: *the picture fell at £10,000 to Messrs. A*; *the underbidders were Messrs. B*.

underbitten, adj. [1. únderbítn; 2. andəbítn]. under- & bitten. (etching) Not bitten in on the copper sufficiently deep for printing.

underbrace, vb. trans. [1. únderbrás; 2. andəbréis]. under- & brace (II.). To brace, tie, fasten, together below or underneath: *to underbrace rafters, girders* &c.

underbraced, adj. [1. únderbrást; 2. andəbréist]. under- & brace(d). Insufficiently braced or supported.

underbred, adj. [1. únderbréd; 2. andəbréd]. under- & bred. Not well-bred, not thoroughbred; showing ignorance of the standards of manners, and the customs of polite society; not animated by the ideals and traditions of manners and conduct current among well-bred persons; ill-bred.

underbrush, n. [1. únderbrúsh; 2. andəbráʃ]. under- & brush (I.). Undergrowth, underwood.

underbuy, vb. trans. [1. únderbí; 2. andəbái]. under- & buy. To buy at a lower price than its real value or than the price at which it is offered; to buy cheaper than another.

undercharge (I.), vb. trans. [1. únderchárj; 2. andətʃádʒ]. under- & charge (I.). 1. To charge less than the true or fair price for; to charge too little for: *this account is undercharged*; *you have undercharged me for, on, this bill, for the books sent* &c. 2. To load with an insufficient charge: *to undercharge a gun*.

undercharge (II.), n. [1. úndercharj; 2. andətʃádʒ]. An insufficient charge.

under-clay, n. [1. únder klå; 2. ándə kléi]. under- & clay. A bed, stratum, of clay beneath a coal seam.

under-clerk, n. [1. únder klárk; 2. ándə klák]. under- & clerk. A subordinate clerk.

under-clerkship, n. [1. únder klárkship; 2. ándə klákʃip]. Prec. & -ship. Position, office, of an under-clerk.

undercliff, n. [1. únderklif; 2. ándəklif]. under- & cliff. A raised terrace or second-

underclothed, adj. [1. ùnderklṓdhd; 2. àndəklóuəd]. under- & clothe(d). Insufficiently clothed.

underclothes, n. pl. [1. úndərklò(dh)z; 2. ándəklòu(ð)z]. under- & clothes. Clothes worn under the outer clothes, esp. those worn next the skin; undergarments, underclothing.

underclothing, n. [1. úndərklṑdhing; 2. ándəklòuðiŋ]. under- & clothing. Underclothes.

undercoat, n. [1. úndərkòt; 2. ándəkòut]. under- & coat. a A coat worn under another; b the growth of short hair beneath the longer, outer hair of an animal's coat.

undercroft, n. [1. úndərkràwft; 2. ándəkrɔ̀ft]. under- & obs. croft, 'vault'; cp. Dut. krocht, O.H.G. chruft, ad. fr. Lat. crupta, crypta, see **crypt**. A vaulted chamber beneath a church or other building; a crypt.

undercurrent, n. [1. úndərkùrənt; 2. ándəkàrənt]. under- & current (II.). 1. A current of water, as in a river, sea &c., flowing beneath the surface and in a contrary direction to that of the main or upper current. 2. (fig.) A tendency, influence, as of opinion, feeling &c., not definitely expressed or apparent on the surface, sometimes running contrary to, or different from, the general or more obvious tendency: *amid the general acclamation an undercurrent of doubt and suspicion may be traced*. 3. Specif. (gold min.) a large shallow box at the side of a main sluice with a steeper fall.

undercut (I.), vb. trans. [1. ùndərkút; 2. àndəkát]. under- & cut. 1. To cut away a lower part of anything so as to leave a projecting edge; to cut away from underneath (a raised, curved, or sculptured design), so that it should stand out in high relief: *moulding deeply undercut*. 2. To cut, reduce, prices of goods, so as to sell cheaper than another: *to undercut prices*; *to undercut a commercial rival*. 3. (golf) To hit a ball so that it rises sharply and falls dead without much run.

undercut (II.), n. [1. úndərkùt; 2. ándəkàt]. a The tender meat on the lower or under side of the bone of a sirloin of beef; b (boxing) a blow delivered with an upward swing or punch of the arm.

under-develop, vb. trans. [1. ùndər devélop; 2. àndə divéləp]. under- & develop. (photog., of plate or film) To develop insufficiently.

under-developed, adj. [1. ùndər devélopt; 2. àndə divéləpt]. Not sufficiently developed; a not developed physically or mentally: *an under-developed child, mind*; b (photog., of plate or film) insufficiently developed.

underditch, vb. trans. [1. ùndərdích; 2. àndədít∫]. under- & ditch. To dig an underground or deep ditch to drain heavy soil: *to underditch a field*.

underdo, vb. trans. [1. ùndərdóō; 2. àndədú]. under- & do. To cook, as meat, insufficiently; usually in P.P. pass., *underdone*.

underdog, n. [1. úndərdóg, úndərdòg; 2. ándədóg, ándədòg]. under- & dog (I.). Also *the under dog*; a the dog which gets the worst of it in a fight with another dog; b (fig.) one who comes off badly in the struggle of life: *we naturally tend to sympathize with the underdogs*.

underdone, adj. [1. ùndərdún; 2. àndədán]. P.P. of underdo. a Insufficiently cooked, too raw: *the mutton's underdone again*; b not cooked too thoroughly; left slightly red or raw: *I like beef rather underdone*.

underdose (I.), vb. trans. [1. ùndərdós; 2. àndədóus]. under- & dose (II.). a To administer an insufficient dose to: *to underdose a patient*; b (reflex.) to take an insufficient dose: *to underdose oneself*.

underdose (II.), n. [1. úndərdòs; 2. ándədòus]. An insufficient dose.

underdrain (I.), vb. trans. [1. ùndərdrán; 2. àndədréin]. under- & drain. To drain, as land, by cutting drains or trenches below the surface.

underdrain (II.), n. [1. úndərdràn; 2. ándədrèin]. A drain or trench cut below the surface of the ground.

underdraw, vb. trans. [1. ùndərdráw; 2. àndədrɔ́]. under- & draw. To draw without enough definiteness or spirit.

underdress, vb. trans. & intrans. [1. ùndərdrés; 2. àndədrés]. under- & dress. a To dress inadequately or too scantily; to wear insufficient clothes; b to dress more simply and plainly than the occasion demands.

underestimate (I.), vb. trans. [1. ùndəréstimàt; 2. àndəréstimeit]. under- & estimate. To estimate at below the true figure; to undervalue, underrate, miscalculate: *to underestimate the cost of a holiday*; *to underestimate a person's abilities &c.*; *to underestimate a distance*.

underestimate (II.), n. [1. ùndəréstimat; 2. àndəréstimit]. An estimate below the true value or cost; an inadequate estimate.

underestimation, n. [1. úndərèstimā́shun; 2. ándərèstiméi∫ən]. underestimate (I.) & -ion. An underestimate.

under-expose, vb. trans. [1. ùndər ekspṓz; 2. àndər ɛkspóuz]. under- & expose. (photog.) To expose a plate or film for too short a time.

under-exposure, n. [1. ùndər ekspṓzhur; 2. àndər ɛkspóuʒə]. (photog.) Exposure of plate &c. for too short a time.

underfeed, vb. trans. & intrans. [1. ùndərféd; 2. àndəfíd]. under- & feed. a trans. To feed with too little or inadequate food; to supply with too little food: *never underfeed children*; b intrans., to eat less than normal amount of food: *the doctor advises me to underfeed for a bit*.

under-fired, adj. [1. ùndər fírd; 2. àndə fáiəd]. under- & fire(d). (of pottery &c.) Not sufficiently fired or baked.

underflow, n. [1. úndərflṓ; 2. ándəflòu]. under- & flow (II.). An undercurrent.

underfoot, adv. [1. ùndərfóot; 2. àndəfút]. under- & foot (I.). Under, beneath, one's feet; underneath; a *it is very damp underfoot*; b (fig.) in subordinate position, in subjection: *he kept his subjects underfoot*.

underframe, n. [1. úndərfràm; 2. ándəfrèim]. under- & frame (II.). A frame below another frame; a supporting frame for an upper part or body, as of the chassis of a motor-car &c.

underfur, n. [1. úndərfèr; 2. ándəfɔ̀]. under- & fur (I.). The short, thick, soft fur beneath the coarser and long hair of certain fur-bearing animals, as seals, beavers &c.

undergarment, n. [1. úndərgàrmənt; 2. ándəgàmənt]. under- & garment. A garment worn under outer garments, usually one worn next the skin; (pl.) underclothes.

undergird, vb. trans. [1. ùndərgĕ́rd; 2. àndəgə́d]. under- & gird (I.). a To gird below or round the bottom of: '*to undergird the ship*' (Acts xxvii. 17); b to place girders beneath or below: *to undergird a roof*.

undergo, vb. trans. [1. ùndərgṓ; 2. àndəgóu]. O.E. *undergān*; under- & go. To experience, endure, suffer; to be subjected to: *to undergo fatigue, a long journey &c.*; *he has undergone an operation*.

undergraduate, n. [1. ùndərgrádūit; 2. àndəgrǽdjuit]. under- & graduate (I.). 1. A member of a university who has not taken his or her first or bachelor's degree. 2. (attrib.) Of, pertaining to, an undergraduate or undergraduates.

undergraduateship, n. [1. ùndərgrádūitship; 2. àndəgrǽdjuit∫ip]. Prec. & -ship. Status, position, of an undergraduate.

underground (I.), adv. [1. ùndərgrównd; 2. àndəgráund]. under- & ground (I.). a (in physical sense) Under, beneath, the ground, below the surface of the earth: *miners who work underground*; b (fig.) secretly, surreptitiously, in an obscure, hidden manner: *schemes are being concocted underground*.

underground (II.), adj. & n. [1. úndərgrònd; 2. ándəgràund]. 1. adj. a (in physical sense) Situated, moving, beneath the surface of the ground: *an underground cellar, basement*;

an underground railway &c.; b (fig.) secret, surreptitious, obscure: *underground intrigues, influence &c.* 2. n. An underground railway: *to travel by the Underground*.

undergrown, adj. [1. ùndərgrṓn; 2. àndəgróun]. under- & grown. Not sufficiently or fully grown or developed; underdeveloped.

undergrowth, n. [1. úndərgrṑth; 2. ándəgròuþ]. under- & growth. That which grows below something else; small trees, bushes, shrubs, growing beneath the larger trees in a wood; underbrush.

underhand (I.), adv. [1. ùndərhánd; 2. àndəhǽnd]. under- & hand. 1. (cricket, tennis &c.) With the hand and arm below the elbow or shoulder; contrasted with *overarm* or *overhand*: *to bowl, serve, underhand*. 2. (fig.) Secretly, clandestinely, not openly; contrasted with *above-board*: *he worked underhand to discredit his political rivals*.

underhand (II.), adj. [1. úndərhànd; 2. ándəhǽnd]. 1. (cricket &c.) Delivered, served, with the hand and arm below the elbow or shoulder: *underhand bowling, service*. 2. (fig.) Secret, clandestine, not open and above-board: *underhand intrigues*.

underhanded, adj. [1. ùndərhánded; 2. àndəhǽndid]. Prec. & -ed. a Underhand, clandestine, secret; b insufficiently supplied with hands or assistants; short-handed.

underhandedly, adv. Prec. & -ly. In an underhanded manner; underhand.

underhew, vb. trans. [1. ùndərhū́; 2. àndəhjú]. under- & hew. To hew a log of timber by cutting away a portion below the surface so that it appears of larger cubic content than it really is.

underhung, adj. [1. ùndərhúng; 2. àndəháŋ]. under- & P.P. of hang. a (of lower jaw) Projecting beyond the upper jaw; b having the lower jaw so projecting: *an underhung face*; *she is slightly underhung*.

underived, adj. [1. ùndirívd; 2. àndiráivd]. un-(I.) & derive(d). Not derived. 1. Original, not dependent on anything else: *absolute, underived power or authority*. 2. Not traced to its original source; without derivation.

under-king, n. [1. únder kìng; 2. ándə kìŋ]. under- & king. A subordinate, inferior, vassal king.

underlaid, adj. [1. úndərlàd; 2. ándəlèid]. P.P. of underlay. Laid, placed, underneath; specif. (print.) having something laid underneath to raise the type or impression: *an underlaid plate*.

underlap, vb. trans. & intrans. [1. ùndərláp; 2. àndəlǽp]. under- & lap (II.). To extend, project, to be folded under, the edge of something above; contrasted with *overlap*: *one plank slightly underlaps the other*; *an underlapping plank*.

underlay (I.), vb. trans. & intrans. [1. ùndərlá; 2. àndəléi]. O.E. *underlecġan*, under- & lay (III.). 1. trans. To lay, place, something under or beneath something; specif. (print.) to support, raise, type &c. by laying something, as a sheet of paper or cardboard, beneath it, so as to throw the impression up: *to underlay a plate, block &c.* 2. intrans. (min., of veins, lodes &c.) To incline from a perpendicular direction, to hade.

underlay (II.), n. [1. úndərlà; 2. ándəlèi]. a Paper, cardboard, placed beneath type, block &c., to raise the impression; b (min.) dip, inclination, of a vein or lode, from the perpendicular; hade.

underlay (III.), Pret. of **underlie**.

underlease, n. [1. úndərlès; 2. ándəlìs]. under- & lease. The lease by a tenant or lessee of part of the term of his lease to another; a sublease.

underlet, vb. trans. [1. ùndərlét; 2. àndəlét]. under- & let (II.). a To let at a lower rent than its real or full value; b to sublet.

underletting, n. [1. ùndərléting; 2. àndəlétiŋ]. under- & let(ting). The letting of a house, land &c., a below its full value; b to a subtenant; subletting.

underlie, vb. trans. [1. ùnderlí; 2. àndəlái]. Pret. *underlay*, P.P. *underlain*; O.E. *underlicgan*, **under-** & **lie** (III.). **1.** To lie, be placed, under or beneath; (also absol., esp. in Pres. Part.) *the coal measures which underlie the English Channel; gravel underlain by clay; the underlying strata.* **2.** (in non-physical sense) To form the basis or foundation of: *the principles which underlie our foreign policy.*

underline (I.), vb. trans. [1. ùnderlín; 2. àndəláin]. **under-** & **line** (III.). **1.** To mark with a line underneath, as a sign of emphasis or to indicate to the printer that the words are to be printed in italics. **2.** To emphasise, lay stress upon: *the sudden summoning of the Cabinet underlines the seriousness of the situation.*

underline (II.), n. [1. úndərlìn; 2. ándəlàin]. **under-** & **line** (II.). **a** A line drawn under a word, phrase &c., as a sign of emphasis; **b** (theatr.) an announcement of a forthcoming play, printed at the foot of the announcement, bill &c., of a current play.

underlinen, n. [1. úndərlìnen; 2. ándəlìnin]. **under-** & **linen**. Underclothing of linen or other material; body-linen.

underling, n. [1. úndərling; 2. ándəlìŋ]. M.E. **under-** & **-ling**. (contemptuous) Person in a subordinate position, one occupying a humble office without authority or responsibility.

underlooker, n. [1. úndərlòoker; 2. ándəlùkə]. **under-** & **look** & **-er**. (coal min.) An official who inspects the condition of a mine below the surface; an underviewer.

underman, vb. trans. [1. ùndermán; 2. àndəmæn]. **under-** & **man** (II.). To supply, furnish, with too few men, esp. too small a crew for a ship: *to underman a ship*; *they set sail much undermanned*, i.e. short-handed.

undermasted, adj. [1. ùndermáhsted; 2. àndəmástid]. **under-** & **mast** & **-ed**. (of ship) Having too few or too small masts for the necessary or full spread of sail.

under-master, n. [1. únder máhster; 2. àndə mástə]. **under-** & **master**. A subordinate master at a school; any master other than the headmaster.

undermentioned, adj. [1. ùnderménshund; 2. àndəménʃənd]. **under-** & **mention(ed)**. Mentioned, alluded to, below or later.

undermine, vb. trans. [1. ùndermín; 2. àndəmáin]. **under-** & **mine** (III.). **1. a** To dig a mine, excavate ground under something in order to cause its fall or destruction by an explosion or collapse: *to undermine a fortress, line of trenches, wall* &c.; **b** to wear away the base or foundations of, by erosion: *the sea is undermining the cliffs of the south coast.* **2.** (fig.) **a** To weaken, to sap, by secret, under-hand means; to injure by insidious attacks: *to undermine a person's influence, reputation* &c.; **b** to wear away, impair: *dissipation has undermined his health.*

underminer, n. [1. ùndermíner; 2. àndəmáinə]. Prec. & **-er**. One who undermines.

undermost, adj. [1. úndermōst; 2. ándəmoust]. **under** (I.) & **-most**. Lowest in position, rank &c.

underneath, adv. & prep. [1. ùnderneéth; 2. àndəníp]. M.E. *undirnethe*; see **under-** & **(be)neath**. **1.** adv. In, at, to a lower place; beneath, below: *the river flowing underneath.* **2.** prep. Under, below: *the river flowing underneath the bridge.*

underogatory, adj. [1. ùndirógaturi; 2. àndirógətəri]. **un-** (I.) & **derogatory**. Not derogatory; not disparaging or detracting.

underpay, vb. trans. [1. ùnderpá; 2. àndəpéi]. **under-** & **pay** (I.). To pay inadequately or insufficiently: *underpaid workmen.*

underpayment, n. [1. ùnderpáment; 2. àndəpéimənt]. Prec. & **-ment**. Inadequate, insufficient, pay.

underpin, vb. trans. [1. ùnderpín; 2. àndəpín]. **under-** & **pin** (II.). To support (wall, bank &c.) by additional props of stone, brick, timber &c. introduced below, or so as to take the place of, existing foundations.

underpinning, n. [1. ùnderpíning; 2. àndəpíniŋ]. Prec. & **-ing**. **a** Act of supporting by props of stone &c. below foundations; **b** the props or other material used for this purpose.

underplay (I.), vb. intrans. & trans. [1. ùnderplá; 2. àndəpléi]. **under-** & **play** (I.) **1.** intrans. (cards) To lose a trick intentionally by playing a low card instead of a higher one in the hand, in view of later advantages; to finesse. **2.** trans. To play a part inadequately, to underact.

underplay (II.), n. [1. únderplà; 2. ándəplei]. Act of underplaying.

underplot, n. [1. únderplot; 2. ándəplɔt]. **under-** & **plot** (III.). A subordinate, secondary, plot in a novel or play.

under-populated, adj. [1. ùnder pópūlāted; 2. àndə pópjuleitid]. **under-** & **populate**(d). Insufficiently populated in relation to the extent and fruitfulness &c. (of an area).

underpraise, vb. trans. [1. ùnderpráz; 2. àndəpréiz]. **under-** & **praise**. To praise less than is deserved.

under-produce, vb. intrans. [1. ùnder prodús; 2. àndə prədjús]. **under-** & **produce**. To produce commodities below the general demand for such commodities, with the object of forcing up prices.

under-production, n. [1. ùnder prodúkshun; 2. àndə prədákʃən]. **under-** & **production**. Production of commodities below the demand, or below normal rate of production.

under-proof, adj. [1. ùnder prōōf; 2. àndə prúf]. **under-** & **proof** (II.). Containing less alcohol than proof spirit.

underprop, vb. trans. [1. ùnder próp; 2. àndə próp]. **under-** & **prop** (II.). To place a prop under; to support from below by props.

underquote, vb. trans. [1. ùnderkwōt; 2. àndəkwóut]. **under-** & **quote**. To quote, or offer goods for sale, at a lower price than others; to offer a lower price than.

underrate, vb. trans. [1. ùnderát; 2. àndəréit]. **under-** & **rate** (II.). To rate, value, too low, to place too low an estimate on; to underestimate: *one should not underrate the abilities of one's enemies.*

under-reckon, vb. trans. [1. ùnder rékun; 2. àndə rékən]. **under-** & **reckon**. To reckon too low; to underestimate.

under-ripe, adj. [1. ùnder ríp; 2. àndə ráip]. **under-** & **ripe**. Not fully ripe.

underrun, vb. trans. [1. ùnderún; 2. àndərán]. **under-** & **run**. **1.** (rare) To run, pass, under: *the boat underran the bridge.* **2.** (specif. naut.) To examine a cable, hose &c., by lifting it and passing it through the hands.

underscore, vb. trans. [1. ùnderskór; 2. àndəskɔ́]. **under-** & **score** (II.). To underline.

under-secretary, n. [1. ùnder sékretari; 2. àndə sékrit(ə)ri]. **under-** & **secretary**. An assistant, subordinate secretary, esp. of Government departments; *Parliamentary Under-Secretary*, a member of the Ministry, vacating office at change of Government; *Permanent Under-Secretary*, member of the Civil Service, the official head of a department.

under-secretaryship, n. [1. ùnder sékretariship; 2. àndə sékrit(ə)riʃip]. Prec. & **-ship**. Position, status, of an under-secretary.

undersell, vb. trans. [1. ùndersél; 2. àndəsél]. **under-** & **sell**. To sell commodities at a lower price than: *to undersell one's rivals in trade.*

underseller, n. [1. ùnderséler; 2. àndəsélə]. Prec. & **-er**. One who undersells.

under-servant, n. [1. ùndersérvant; 2. àndəsávənt]. **under-** & **servant**. A subordinate, inferior, servant.

underset (I.), vb. trans. [1. ùndersét; 2. àndəsét]. **under-** & **set** (I.). To support, prop (a wall, roof &c.), by masonry, brickwork &c.

underset (II.), n. [1. úndersèt; 2. ándəsèt]. **under-** & **set** (II.). (naut.) A set, current, beneath the surface of water, contrary to the general set of the water or to the wind.

under-sheriff, n. [1. únder shérif; 2. ándə ʃérif]. **under-** & **sheriff**. A deputy sheriff.

under-shirt, n. [1. únder shèrt; 2. ándə ʃɜ̀t]. **under-** & **shirt**. A shirt worn next the skin; a vest.

undershot, adj. **under-** & **shot** (II.). **1.** [1. úndershòt; 2. ándəʃɔt] (of water-wheel) Moved, driven, by water flowing under it, contrasted with *overshot*. **2.** [1. ùndershót; 2. àndəʃɔ́t] (of jaw) Underhung.

undershrub, n. [1. úndershrùb; 2. ándəʃràb]. **under-** & **shrub** (I.). A small shrubby plant.

undersign, vb. trans. [1. ùndersín; 2. àndəsáin]. **under-** & **sign** (II.). To sign a document &c. at the foot; to write one's name at the end of a letter or document.

undersigned, adj. [1. úndersìnd, ùndersínd; 2. ándəsàind, àndəsáind]. In *the undersigned members*, those members whose names are signed below (at end of a document); *we the undersigned*, we who have signed our names below.

undersized, adj. [1. úndersízd; 2. àndəsáizd]. **under-** & **-sized**. Of less than the normal or average size; dwarfish, stunted.

underskirt, n. [1. únderskèrt; 2. ándəskɜ̀t]. **under-** & **skirt**. A skirt worn under another or outer skirt; petticoat.

undersleeve, n. [1. úndersìèv; 2. ándəslìv]. **under-** & **sleeve**. A sleeve worn under an outer sleeve.

undersoil, n. [1. úndersòil; 2. ándəsɔ̀il]. **under-** & **soil**. Subsoil.

undersong, n. [1. úndersòng; 2. ándəsɔ̀ŋ]. **under-** & **song**. The burden, refrain, of a song.

understand, vb. trans. & intrans. [1. ùnderstánd; 2. àndəstǽnd]. O.E. *understandan*, lit. 'to stand under, beneath'; the sense-development is not clear; Skeat, giving *under* here the sense of 'among', compares Lat. *intelligere*, fr. *inter*, 'between', cp. **intelligence**; O.E. has *undergietan*, lit. 'to under get', in same sense, cp. also O.N. *undirstanda*. **A.** trans. **1.** To comprehend, perceive, the meaning of; to grasp the meaning, purport, of; to hear, read, and interpret to oneself: *I can hear your voice but cannot understand you; can you understand German? please understand me, I absolutely refuse.* Phr. *to make oneself understood*, to make one's language, meaning, clear. **2.** To apprehend by the mind, to grasp, take in the idea of; to perceive the full significance or force of: *we do not yet understand the nature of electricity; does the child understand the meaning of an oath?; try and understand my difficulties.* Phr. *to understand one another*, (i.) to come to an understanding or agreement with another; (ii.) to be clearly aware of, though not necessarily sharing, each other's opinions, intentions &c.; (iii.) to be on good terms through comprehending and sympathizing each with the other's aims &c. **3.** To learn, be informed of: *we understand from an unofficial source that the measure is to be dropped.* Phr. *to give to understand*, to tell, inform. **4. a** To assume, infer; to take as meant or implied, often indicating surprise, warning &c.: *I understood him to say that; what are we to understand from such contradictory statements?*; **b** to supply mentally though not expressed: *when we say X is a millionaire, are we to understand pounds or dollars?* **B.** intrans. **1.** To have understanding; to have the powers, faculties, of mental comprehension; to be an intelligent being: *do animals understand?; the people listen but will not understand.* **2.** To be informed, to learn, hear, be told: *the news is better, so I understand.*

understandable, adj. [1. ùnderstándabl; 2. àndəstǽndəbl]. Prec. & **-able**. Able to be understood; intelligible.

understanded, adj. [1. ùnderstánded; 2. àndəstǽndid]. P.P. of **understand**; used in 16th cent. (archaic) Understood: '*language understanded of the people*', plain, ordinary language or words (Art. of Relig. **xxiv.**).

understanding (I.), n. [1. ùnderstánding; 2. àndəstǽndiŋ]. understand & abstract suff. -ing. 1. Act of one who understands; mental grasp, comprehension, knowledge; discernment: *he tried to get some understanding of the question*. 2. Intelligence; power, faculty, of comprehension or thought; sense: *a person of understanding*; *God give us understanding*. 3. Agreement, unity of thought, feeling &c.; that which is mutually agreed upon or understood: *to have an understanding with another*; *to come to a definite understanding about*. Phr. *on the understanding that*, on such terms or conditions as are stated. 4. (pl., colloq., facet.) Legs: *he has a sound pair of understandings*.

understanding (II.), adj., fr. Pres. Part. of understand. Intelligent, discerning, sensible: *an understanding man*.

understandingly, adv. [1. ùnderstándingli; 2. àndəstǽndiŋlí]. Prec. & -ly. (rare or archaic) In an understanding manner; with understanding, intelligence, discernment.

understate, vb. trans. [1. ùnderstǽt; 2. àndəstéit]. under- & state (III.). Not to state fully or adequately, not to bring out all the points of; to minimize in statement, put forward with studied moderation; reverse of *exaggerate*: *to understate one's abilities, claims, case* &c.

understatement, n. [1. ùnderstǽtmənt; 2. àndəstéitmənt]. Prec. & -ment. 1. Act of understating. 2. A statement which errs on the side of moderation, which does not represent with completeness all the aspects of a case; reverse of *exaggeration*.

understock, vb. trans. [1. ùnderstók; 2. àndəstók]. under- & stock. 1. To put less stock on (land) than it will properly carry. 2. To furnish (shop, store &c.) with smaller supply of commodities or stock than the demand and requirements warrant.

understood, vb. [1. ùnderstóod; 2. àndəstúd]. Pret. & P.P. of understand.

understrapper, n. [1. ùnderstràper; 2. àndəstrǽpə]. under- & strap & -er. (colloq.) An underling, a subordinate; an inferior agent, official or employee.

under-stratum, n. [1. únder strátum; 2. ándə strétəm]. under- & stratum. A substratum; a layer or stratum of earth on which the soil rests.

understudy, n. & vb. trans. [1. ùnderstùdi; 2. ànderstǽdi]. under- & study. 1. n. One who studies or learns the part of the regular actor in order to be able to play it in his absence. 2. vb. a To study a theatrical part for this purpose: *to understudy Hamlet*; b to act as understudy to: *to understudy Irving in 'Hamlet'*.

undertake, vb. trans. & intrans. [1. ùndertǽk; 2. àndətéik]. M.E. undertaken. under- & take. A. trans. 1. To take upon oneself, to lay oneself under an obligation to do: *to undertake a responsible post*; *to undertake a task, responsibility* &c.; *he has undertaken too much*; *to undertake to do anything*; *to undertake that it is so*. 2. To engage in, take steps to perform, embark upon: *to undertake a journey*. 3. (archaic) To challenge, engage with another in a contest, an argument. B. intrans. 1. (archaic) To be guarantee for; to take on oneself a duty for another: *to undertake for another*. 2. (colloq.) To carry on the business of, to be, an undertaker.

undertaker, n. [1. úndertàker; 2. ándətèikə]. Prec. & -er. One who undertakes or engages to perform some task &c.; a contractor. 1. Specif., one whose business and trade it is to undertake all duties connected with the burial of the dead; one who manages funerals. 2. (hist., usually cap. and in pl., *the Undertakers*) a The settlers on the forfeited lands of the Earl of Desmond in Ireland, at the end of the 16th century; b a party of members of the Parliament of 1614 who undertook to manage elections, secure supplies and passage of bills &c. in the interest of James I.

undertaking, n. [1. ùndertǽkiŋ; 2. àndətéikiŋ]. undertake & -ing. 1. That which is undertaken; an enterprise, task: *a difficult, dangerous, undertaking*. 2. Promise, guarantee, obligation: *an undertaking to pay the debt within six months*. 3. The professional activities, the trade, of an undertaker.

under-tenancy, n. [1. únder tènansi; 2. ándə tènənsí]. under- & tenancy. A tenancy, lease, held from or under another tenant or lessee, and not directly from the landlord; a subtenancy.

under-tenant, n. [1. únder tènant; 2. ándə tènənt]. under- & tenant. A tenant under another tenant; a subtenant.

under-timed, adj. [1. ùnder tímd; 2. àndə táimd]. under- & time(d). (photog.) Underexposed.

undertint, n. [1. úndertìnt; 2. ándətìnt]. under- & tint (I.). A subdued, faint, tint or colour; undertone.

undertone, n. [1. úndertòn; 2. ándətòun]. under- & tone (I.). 1. A subdued tone or note; low, subdued voice: *to speak in undertones*. 2. A subdued, faint, colour; an undertint.

undertook, vb. [1. ùndertóok; 2. àndətúk]. Pret. of undertake.

undertow, n. [1. úndertò; 2. ándətòu]. under- & tow (I.). The backward flow, drag, or pull of a wave or the sea after it breaks on the shore; underset.

undervaluation, n. [1. ùndervàlùǽshun; 2. àndəvæljuéiʃən]. under- & valuation. Act of undervaluing; a valuation, estimate, of anything which is below its real value or worth.

undervalue, vb. trans. [1. ùndervǽlù; 2. àndəvælju]. under- & value. To value at less than the real worth; to set too low a value upon.

underwear, n. [1. úndervǽr; 2. ándəwèə]. under- & wear (II.). (shop term) Clothes worn below others; underclothing, undergarments.

underwent, vb. [1. ùnderwént; 2. àndəwént]. Pret. of undergo.

underwing, n. [1. úndervìng; 2. ándəwìŋ]. under- & wing. Any kind of various nocturnal moths with conspicuous, banded markings on the under or posterior wings.

underwood, n. [1. úndervood; 2. ándəwud]. under- & wood. Undergrowth, underbrush.

underwork (I.), vb. trans. & intrans. [1. ùnderwèrk; 2. àndəwǽk]. under- & work. 1. trans. a To exact too little work from; to put to work for too short a time: *to underwork a machine, horse* &c.; b to work for a lower price than: *one trader tries to underwork another*. 2. intrans. To work inadequately, to do less work than one should or is capable of: *a modern tendency to underwork*.

underwork (II.), n. [1. úndervèrk; 2. ándəwàk]. Inferior, subordinate, work; slack, inadequate, work.

underworld, n. [1. úndervèrld; 2. ándəwǽld]. under- & world. 1. The lower, nether, world; the infernal regions; place of departed spirits; hell: *spirits from the underworld*. 2. (poet. and rare) The world on the other side of the globe; the antipodes: '*the first light glimmering on a sail That brings our friends up from the underworld*' (Tennyson, '*Princess*', iv. 45). 3. That part of a community who live entirely by vice and crime: *gangster leaders or the kings of the underworld*.

underwrite, vb. trans. & intrans. [1. ùnderít; 2. ànderáit]. under- & write. A. trans. 1. To write below or underneath, to subscribe (rare, except in P.P.): *the underwritten signatures, names*, the undersigned. 2. Specif. a to execute, by the signature of one's name to the document, and deliver a policy of insurance, esp. of marine insurance, guaranteeing, on payment of a premium, to make good loss or damage to the property insured; to take a risk on a policy of (marine) insurance: *to underwrite a ship, cargo* &c.; *to underwrite any kind of risk*; b to undertake, guarantee, to buy such of the stock or shares to be issued by a company as are not subscribed for by the public, for a named consideration or commission of so much per cent. B. intrans. To be in business as an underwriter.

underwriter, n. [1. únderìter; 2. ándəràitə]. Prec. & -er. a One whose business it is to underwrite policies, esp. of marine insurance: *an underwriter at Lloyd's*; b one who underwrites the shares newly issued by a company.

underwriting, n. [1. úndertiting; 2. ándəràitiŋ]. underwrite & -ing. The business of an underwriter.

undescribed, adj. [1. ùndeskríbd; 2. àndiskráibd]. un- (I.) & describe(d). Not described.

undescried, adj. [1. ùndeskríd; 2. àndiskráid]. un- (I.) & *descried*, P.P. of descry. Not descried; undiscovered, unseen.

undeserved, adj. [1. ùndezǽrvd; 2. àndizǽvd]. un- (I.) & deserve(d). Not deserved; unmerited.

undeservedly, adv. [1. ùndezǽrvedli; 2. àndizǽvidli]. Prec. & -ly. In an undeserved manner; without deserving praise or blame.

undeserving, adj. [1. ùndezǽrving; 2. àndizǽviŋ]. un- (I.) & deserving. Not deserving; a not meritorious, having earned no claim (to help &c.) by personal virtue: *the undeserving poor*; b undeserving of, not meriting, unworthy of: *undeserving of pity*.

undesignated, adj. [1. ùndézignàted; 2. àndézigneitid]. un- (I.) & designate(d). Not designated; unspecified; undescribed; unappointed.

undesigned, adj. [1. ùndezínd; 2. àndizáind]. un- (I.) & design(ed). Not designed; not intended, unintentional.

undesignedly, adv. [1. ùndezínedli; 2. àndizáinidli]. Prec. & -ly. In an undesigned manner; unintentionally.

undesigning, adj. [1. ùndezíning; 2. àndizáiniŋ]. un- (I.) & designing. Not designing; not engaged in crafty schemes; not having ulterior motives; ingenuous.

undesirability, n. [1. ùndezírabíliti; 2. àndizàiərəbíliti]. See next word & -ity. Condition, quality, of being undesirable; undesirableness.

undesirable, adj. & n. [1. ùndezírabl; 2. àndizáiərəbl]. un- (I.) & desirable. 1. adj. Not desirable, not to be desired; having no qualities to recommend (him, it): a *an undesirable alien*; b *undesirable manners, language* &c.; c *he called at a most undesirable moment*. 2. n. An undesirable person.

undesirableness, n. Prec. & -ness. Undesirability.

undesirably, adv. See prec. & -ly. In an undesirable manner.

undesired, adj. [1. ùndezírd; 2. àndizáiəd]. un- (I.) & desire(d). Not desired; a unwished for, unwanted; b not asked for, unsolicited.

undesirous, adj. [1. ùndezírus; 2. àndizáiərəs]. un- (I.) & desirous. Not desirous of, not desiring: *undesirous of distinctions, rank* &c.

undestroyable, adj. [1. ùndestróiabl; 2. àndistróiəbl]. un- (I.) & destroyable. Not destroyable; indestructible.

undetected, adj. [1. ùndetékted; 2. àndiféktid]. un- (I.) & detect(ed). Not detected, undiscovered.

undetermined, adj. [1. ùndetérmind; 2. ànditǽmind]. un- (I.) & determine(d). 1. Not determined; not settled, fixed, or decided: *one question still remained undetermined*. 2. Irresolute, vacillating, vague: *an undetermined character*.

undeterred, adj. [1. ùndetérd; 2. ànditǽd]. un- (I.) & deter(red). Not deterred.

undeveloped, adj. [1. ùndevélopt; 2. àndivélopt]. un- (I.) & develop(ed). Not developed. 1. (of persons &c.) a (in physical sense) Not fully grown; not grown to normal size for its age: *an undeveloped child, muscles, body* &c.; b *an undeveloped mind, character*. 2. (of land) Not put to its fullest use, whether for cultivation or building.

undeviating, adj. [1. undḗviāting; 2. andívi-èitiŋ]. un- (I.) & Pres. Part. of **deviate**. Not deviating; **a** not departing from a straight course, not wandering into by-paths; **b** not turning aside from a fixed line in conduct, purpose, principle.

undeviatingly, adv. Prec. & -ly. In an undeviating manner.

undevout, adj. [1. ùndevóut; 2. àndiváut]. un- (I.) & **devout**. Not devout.

undevoutly, adv. Prec. & -ly. In an undevout manner.

undies, n. [1. úndiz; 2. ándiz]. Abbr. of **underclothes**, w. dimin. ending. (colloq.) Women's underclothes.

undifferentiated, adj. [1. ùndiferénshiāted; 2. àndifərénʃieitid]. un- (I.) & **differentiate(d)**. Not differentiated; homogeneous.

undiffused, adj. [1. ùndifúzd; 2. àndifjúzd]. un- (I.) & **diffuse(d)**. Not diffused.

undigested, adj. [1. ùndijésted; 2. àndidʒéstid]. un- (I.) & **digest(ed)**. Not digested; **a** not yet assimilated by the organs of digestion; not absorbed into the system; **b** not fully assimilated by the mind; not analysed, arranged, correlated: *undigested facts, theories &c.*

undignified, adj. [1. undígnifīd; 2. andígnifàid]. un- (I.) & **dignified**. Not dignified; inconsistent with, wanting in, dignity.

undiluted, adj. [1. ùndilúted; 2. àndailjútid]. un- (I.) & **dilute(d)**. Not diluted; not mixed with extraneous matter; at full strength, unweakened by admixture of other elements.

undiminished, adj. [1. ùndimínisht; 2. àndimíniʃt]. un- (I.) & **diminish(ed)**. Not diminished, not lessened; retaining full force, quality &c.

undimmed, adj. [1. undímd; 2. andímd]. un- (I.) & **dim(med)**. Not dimmed.

undine, n. [1. ooṇdēn; 2. undín], fr. Mod. Germ., taken fr. Fr. *ondine*, fr. Lat. *unda*, ' wave ', see **undulate** (I.). A female water-sprite, or elemental spirit, who, according to the system of Paracelsus, obtained a human soul by marrying, and bearing a child to, a mortal; cp. *salamander*, *gnome*, and *sylph*; whence (cap.) the name of the principal character in La Motte Fouqué's romance ' Undine '.

undiplomatic, adj. [1. ùndiplōmátik; 2. àndiploumǽtik]. un- (I.) & **diplomatic**. Not diplomatic; blunt, tactless.

undiplomatically, adv. [1. ùndiplōmátikali; 2. àndiploumǽtikəli]. Prec. & -al & -ly. Not diplomatically.

undirected, adj. [1. ùndirékted; 2. àndiréktid]. un- (I.) & **direct(ed)**. Not directed. **1**. Left without direction or guidance: *undirected zeal*. **2**. Not addressed; having no address affixed: *undirected letters*.

undiscerned, adj. [1. ùndizḗrnd; 2. àndizə́nd]. un- (I.) & **discern(ed)**. Not discerned; unperceived; not perceived clearly in the mind.

undiscernible, adj. [1. ùndizḗrnibl; 2. àndizə́nibl]. un- (I.) & **discernible**. (rare) Not discernible.

undiscerning, adj. [1. ùndizḗrning; 2. àndizə́niŋ]. un- (I.) & **discerning**. Not discerning; deficient in mental or moral discernment; dull of perception; obtuse.

undiscerningly, adv. Prec. & -ly. In an undiscerning manner; without discernment.

undischarged, adj. [1. ùndischárjd; 2. àndistʃɑ́dʒd]. un- (I.) & **discharge(d)**. Not discharged. **1**. Not fulfilled or carried out: *an undischarged duty*. **2**. Not freed from obligation; not having received a discharge: *undischarged bankrupt*. **3**. Not fired: *an undischarged gun*.

undisciplined, adj. [1. undísiplind; 2. andísiplind]. un- (I.) & **discipline(d)**. Not disciplined; a not subject, or having been subjected, to mental or moral training and control: *an undisciplined mind, character &c.*; **b** specif., not properly exercised in military discipline; not trained to obey orders; not observing due order and discipline: *not an army but an undisciplined mob*.

undisclosed, adj. [1. ùndisklōzd; 2. àndisklóuzd]. un- (I.) & **disclose(d)**. Not disclosed; kept secret, undivulged.

undiscomfited, adj. [1. ùndiskúmfited; 2. àndiskámfitid]. un- (I.) & **discomfit(ed)**. Not discomfited; undefeated.

undisconcerted, adj. [1. ùndiskunsḗrted; 2. andiskənsə́tid]. un- (I.) & **disconcert(ed)**. Not disconcerted.

undiscouraged, adj. [1. ùndiskúrijd; 2. àndiskáridʒd]. un- (I.) & **discourage(d)**. Not discouraged.

undiscoverable, adj. [1. ùndiskúverabl; 2. àndiskávərəbl]. un- (I.) & **discoverable**. Not discoverable; not to be discovered.

undiscoverably, adv. Prec. & -ly. So as not to be discovered.

undiscovered, adj. [1. ùndiskúverd; 2. àndiskávəd]. un- (I.) & **discover(ed)**. Not discovered, not found out; unknown.

undiscriminated, adj. [1. ùndiskrímināted; 2. àndiskrímineitid]. un- (I.) & **discriminate(d)**. Not discriminated; not separated or distinguished; indiscriminate.

undiscriminating, adj. [1. ùndiskríminātiŋg; 2. àndiskrímineitiŋ]. un- (I.) & **discriminating**. Not discriminating; not exhibiting discrimination; uncritical.

undiscriminatingly, adv. Prec. & -ly. In an undiscriminating manner; without discrimination.

undiscussed, adj. [1. ùndiskúst; 2. àndiskást]. un- (I.) & **discuss(ed)**. Not discussed; undebated; not argued.

undisfigured, adj. [1. ùndisfígurd; 2. àndisfígəd]. un- (I.) & **disfigure(d)**. Not disfigured.

undisguised, adj. [1. ùndisgízd; 2. àndisgáizd]. un- (I.) & **disguise(d)**. Not disguised. **1**. Not covered or veiled under a disguise, mask &c. **2**. Open, plain, avowed, unconcealed: *with undisguised pleasure, hatred; he made an undisguised attack*.

undisguisedly, adv. [1. ùndisgízedli; 2. àndisgáizidli]. Prec. & -ly. In an undisguised manner; without disguise; frankly.

undismayed, adj. [1. ùndismǽd; 2. àndisméid]. un- (I.) & **dismay(ed)**. Not dismayed; not terrified; not disheartened.

undisparaged, adj. [1. ùndispárijd; 2. àndispǽridʒd]. un- (I.) & **disparage(d)**. Not disparaged.

undispatched, adj. [1. ùndispácht; 2. àndispǽtʃt]. un- (I.) & **dispatch(ed)**. Not dispatched, not sent.

undispelled, adj. [1. ùndispéld; 2. àndispéld]. un- (I.) & **dispel(led)**. Not dispelled.

undispersed, adj. [1. ùndispḗrst; 2. àndispə́st]. un- (I.) & **disperse(d)**. Not dispersed; kept together.

undisplayed, adj. [1. ùndisplǽd; 2. àndispléid]. un- (I.) & **display(ed)**. Not displayed.

undisposed, adj. [1. ùndispōzd; 2. àndispóuzd]. un- (I.) & **dispose(d)**. Not disposed; **a** not inclined; unwilling, indisposed: *undisposed to do &c.*; **b** not disposed of, not set apart, not allocated to a specific use, not distributed: *undisposed property*; **c** (rare, archaic) unwell, indisposed.

undisputed, adj. [1. ùndispúted; 2. àndispjútid]. un- (I.) & **dispute(d)**. Not disputed; unquestioned.

undissected, adj. [1. ùndisékted; 2. àndiséktid]. un- (I.) & **dissect(ed)**. Not dissected.

undissembled, adj. [1. ùndisémbld; 2. àndisémbld]. un- (I.) & **dissemble(d)**. Not dissembled; undisguised, open, unfeigned.

undissembling, adj. [1. ùndisémbling; 2. àndisémbliŋ]. un- (I.) & Pres. Part. of **dissemble**. Not dissembling, free from dissimulation; frank, honest.

undissolved, adj. [1. ùndizólvd; 2. àndizólvd]. un- (I.) & **dissolve(d)**. Not dissolved.

undistinguishable, adj. [1. ùndistíŋggwishabl; 2. àndistíŋgwiʃəbl]. un- (I.) & **distinguishable**. Not distinguishable; not to be known apart; not clearly separable.

undistinguishably, adv. Prec. & -ly. In an undistinguishable manner.

undistinguished, adj. [1. ùndistíŋggwisht; 2. àndistíŋgwiʃt]. un- (I.) & **distinguished**. Not distinguished. **1**. Not regarded as distinct or separate. **2**. Having no distinction; commonplace, ordinary, mediocre.

undistressed, adj. [1. ùndistrést; 2. àndistrést]. un- (I.) & **distress(ed)**. Not distressed; not troubled, physically or mentally.

undistributed, adj. [1. ùndistríbuted; 2. àndistríbjutid]. un- (I.) & **distribute(d)**. Not distributed; specif. (log.) of a middle term used with different quantity in the major and minor premise, thus concealing a fallacy in the conclusion.

undisturbed, adj. [1. ùndistḗrbd; 2. àndistə́bd]. un- (I.) & **disturb(ed)**. Not disturbed; **a** not moved or placed in another position; **b** not worried or distressed in mind.

undiversified, adj. [1. ùndivḗrsifīd; 2. àndaivə́sifaid]. un- (I.) & **diversify & -ed**. Not diversified; uniform.

undivided, adj. [1. ùndivīded; 2. àndiváidid]. un- (I.) & **divide(d)**. Not divided; **a** not separated or broken into two or more parts; whole, continuous: *an undivided line, property &c.*; **b** not distracted; not directed or concentrated upon more than one object: *undivided attention*.

undivulged, adj. [1. ùndivúljd; 2. àndaivǽl(dʒ)d]. un- (I.) & **divulge(d)**. Not divulged.

undo, vb. trans. [1. undōō; 2. andú]. un- (II.) & **do**. **1**. To reverse what has been done; to annul: *what's done cannot be undone; attempt to undo the past, the mischief, an injury to others &c.* **2. a** To unfasten, unloose, untie: *to undo a button, one's clothes, collar &c.*; **b** to free from what encloses, fastens; to unbutton, unfasten, (person's clothes &c.) and free him &c.: *he is choking, undo him; undo a parcel*. **3**. (archaic) To bring to ruin, poverty &c.; to ruin, damage, the character, fortunes, of: *his extravagance will undo him some day*.

undock, vb. trans. [1. undók; 2. andók]. un- (II.) & **dock** (II.). To take (vessel) out of a dock.

undoer, n. [1. undōōer; 2. andúə]. **undo- & -er**. One who undoes; specif., one who brings another to ruin &c.: *this faithless friend was his undoer*.

undoing, n. [1. undōōing; 2. andúiŋ]. **undo & -ing**. **1**. Act of reversing what has been done; reversal, annulment of the past: *there can be no undoing of the injury done to him*. **2**. Act of untying, unfastening: *the undoing of a parcel &c.* **3. a** Act or process of bringing to ruin: *it is melancholy to see the gradual undoing of a great man*; **b** cause, source, of ruin, destruction, misfortune &c.: *his overweening self-confidence proved his undoing in the end*.

undomesticated, adj. [1. ùndōméstikāted; 2. àndouméstikèitid]. un- (I.) & **domesticate(d)**. **1**. (of animals) Not tamed, unaccustomed to live in contact with, or under care of man; wild. **2**. (of human beings) Not fond of home, unsuited for family life in the domestic circle.

undone (I.), adj. [1. undún; 2. andán], fr. P.P. of **undo**. **1**. Unfastened, unloosed, untied. **2**. Ruined; brought to misery.

undone (II.), adj. un- (I.) & P.P. of **do**. Not done; not carried out; uncompleted: '*left undone those things which we ought to have done*'; *half his work is undone*.

undoubted, adj. [1. undóuted; 2. andáutid]. un- (I.) & **doubt(ed)**. Not doubted or called in question; indisputable; genuine, indubitable: *undoubted evidence*; *an undoubted masterpiece*; *an undoubted Rembrandt*.

undoubtedly, adv. Prec. & -ly. Without doubt or question; indubitably.

undoubting, adj. [1. undóuting; 2. andáutiŋ]. un- (I.) & **doubting**. Not doubting; not suspecting.

undoubtingly, adv. Prec. & -ly. In an undoubting manner; unsuspectingly.

undrape, vb. trans. [1. undráp; 2. ʌndréip]. un- (II.) & drape. To remove drapery, covering, or clothing from; to uncover, unclothe.

undraped, adj. [1. undrápt; 2. ʌndréipt]. un- (I. & II.) & drape(d). Not draped; unclothed; with drapery removed.

undreamed, -dreamt, adj. [1. undrēmd, -drém(p)t; 2. ʌndrímd, -drém(p)t]. un- (I.) & dream(ed). (chiefly *undreamed-*, *undreamt-of*) Not dreamed or dreamt of; not conceived or thought of; unimagined, unexpected, unsuspected: *an undreamt-of success; wonders still undreamt of.*

undress (I.), vb. trans. & intrans. [1. undrés; 2. ʌndrés]. un- (II.) & dress. **1.** trans. To take clothes off, strip, divest of clothing. **2.** intrans. To take one's clothes off.

undress (II.), n. [1. úndrès; 2. ʌ́ndrès]. **a** Ordinary dress, as distinguished from 'full or parade dress', as of military and naval or other uniform; **b** loose, informal dress, déshabille.

undressed (I.), adj. [1. undrést; 2. ʌndrést]. P.P. of *undress* (I.). Having the clothing removed, without clothing; nude; specif., having one's day clothing removed, and in night attire.

undressed (II.), adj. un- (I.) & dress(ed). (of wounds, leather &c.) Not dressed.

undrilled, adj. [1. undríld; 2. ʌndríld]. un- (I.) & drill(ed). Not drilled.

undrinkable, adj. [1. undríŋkəbl; 2. ʌndríŋkəbl]. un- (I.) & drinkable. Not drinkable.

undue, adj. un- (I.) & due (I.). **1.** [1. úndū; 2. ʌ́ndjū] Not according to what is right or proper; **a** excessive, immoderate: *treated the matter with undue haste; had an undue fondness for whisky*; **b** improper: *undue influence*, influence improperly exercised over another, so as to induce him to do what he otherwise would not have done, as in making a will &c.; undue influence is sufficient to invalidate a will if established; **c** unbecoming, unsuitable, to the occasion: *undue levity*. **2.** [1. undū́; 2. ʌndjū́] Not yet due or owing (rare, except of a bill of exchange or other negotiable instrument).

undulate (I.), adj. [1. úndūlàt; 2. ʌ́ndjuleit], fr. Lat. *undulātus*, 'wavy, undulated', rare & post-class., fr. *undula*, dimin. of Lat. *unda*, 'wave, water'; cp. Lat. *ūdus*, 'wet'; cogn. w. Gk. *húdōr*, 'water', see **hydro-**, & Engl. **water & wet**; the Lat. *und-* is seen also in *abound, redundant, surround* &c. (rare, except bot., of leaves &c.) Wavy, having a wavy or undulating margin.

undulate (II.), vb. intrans. See prec. **1.** (of a moving surface) To rise and fall in a regular series of alternate ridges and furrows (of the surface of the sea, or other large sheet of water; of standing corn swept by the wind &c.). **2.** (of a firm surface) To be diversified by a series of gently rising and falling curved slopes: *the land undulates as far as the eye can see*. **3.** (of an edge) To be cut or shaped into a series of alternately concave and convex curves.

undulating, adj. [1. úndūlàtiŋ; 2. ʌ́ndjuleitiŋ]. Pres. Part. of prec. Undulated, wavy; having undulation; esp. of surface of ground.

undulatingly, adv. Prec. & -ly. In an undulating manner.

undulation, n. [1. ùndūláshun; 2. ʌ̀ndjuléiʃən]. undulate (II.) & -ion. **1. a** Undulating motion, like that of waves on surface of water, standing corn &c.; **b** a wavy, undulating contour; a gentle sloping rise or hollow on the surface of the ground. **2.** (phys.) Vibratory movement in the ether or other liquid or elastic substance, esp. of a wave of light or sound.

undulatory, adj. [1. úndūlaturi; 2. ʌ́ndjulətəri]. undulate (II.) & -ory. Pertaining to, caused by, of the nature of, undulations, on water, the surface of the ground, or in the ether; *undulatory theory* (of light &c.), wave theory.

unduly, adv. [1. undúli; 2. ʌndjúli]. undue & -ly. In an undue manner; **a** to an undue extent; immoderately, excessively: *unduly heated by the arguments*; **b** improperly: *unduly influenced by another*.

undutiful, adj. [1. undū́tifl; 2. ʌndjū́tifl]. un- (I.) & dutiful. Not dutiful; rebellious.

undutifully, adv. Prec. & -ly. In an undutiful manner.

undutifulness, n. See prec. & -ness. State of being undutiful.

undying, adj. [1. undī́iŋ; 2. ʌndái-iŋ]. un- (I.) & Pres. Part. of die. **a** Immortal, everlasting: *undying glory, fame*; **b** unceasing, never-ending: *with undying hatred*.

unearned, adj. [1. unérnd; 2. ʌnʌ́nd]. un- (I.) & earn(ed). Not earned, not gained by personal services or work; specif., *unearned income*, income derived from investments, as distinguished from salary, wages, fees for work done, and subject to a higher rate of income tax; *unearned increment*, increase in value of landed property due to causes other than expenditure of the owner in developing it, such as increased demand from growth of population, expenditure of public money &c.

unearth, vb. trans. [1. unérth; 2. ʌnʌ́þ]. un- (II.) & earth. **1. a** To dig out of, up from, the earth: *to unearth a buried treasure*; **b** to drive (fox &c.) from its earth or burrow, with a terrier &c. **2.** (fig.) To discover, bring to light, by diligent search: *to unearth hitherto unknown documents, a secret, a mystery &c.*

unearthliness, n. [1. unérthlines; 2. ʌnʌ́þlinis]. See next word & -ness. State, quality, of being unearthly.

unearthly, adj. [1. unérthli; 2. ʌnʌ́þli]. un- (I.) & earthly. **a** Not earthly, not of this world; supernatural: *unearthly light, appearance, beauty*; **b** mysterious, weird, ghastly: *an unearthly scream*.

uneasily, adv. [1. unézili; 2. ʌnízili]. uneasy & -ly. In an uneasy manner.

uneasiness, n. [1. unézines; 2. ʌnízinis]. See next word & -ness. State of being uneasy.

uneasy, adj. [1. unézi; 2. ʌnízi]. un- (I.) & easy. **1. a** Not enjoying bodily ease; uncomfortable, restless: *uneasy in tight clothes*; **b** not firmly settled: *uneasy in the saddle*; (fig.) *uneasy on the throne*. **2. a** Disturbed in mind, anxious, perturbed: *to feel uneasy about the future, the weather &c.*; **b** arising from, causing, anxiety or uneasiness of mind; disturbing: *uneasy dreams, fears &c.* **3.** (of manner &c.) Evincing lack of ease; constrained, awkward, embarrassed, self-conscious.

uneatable, adj. [1. unétabl; 2. ʌnítəbl]. un- (I.) & eatable. Not eatable.

uneaten, adj. [1. unétn; 2. ʌnítn]. un- (I.) & eat(en). Not eaten.

uneconomic(al), adj. [1. ùnèkonómik(l); 2. ʌ̀nīkənómik(l)]. un- (I.) & economic(al). Not economic; **a** not in accordance with the principles of economics: *uneconomic expenditure, prices, wages &c.*; **b** not economical; extravagant, wasteful: *an uneconomic manager*.

unedifying, adj. [1. unédifīiŋ; 2. ʌnédifái-iŋ]. un- (I.) & edifying. Not edifying; not tending to moral edification; degrading: *an unedifying spectacle*.

unedited, adj. [1. unédited; 2. ʌnéditid]. un- (I.) & edit(ed). Not edited; specif., not published before, of literary and other works.

uneducated, adj. [1. unédūkāted; 2. ʌnédjukèitid]. un- (I.) & educate(d). Not educated; illiterate.

unembarrassed, adj. [1. unembárast; 2. ʌnimbǽrəst]. un- (I.) & embarrass(ed). Not embarrassed; **a** free from mental or money troubles; **b** free from awkwardness of manner; easy.

unemotional, adj. [1. unemóshunl; 2. ʌnimóuʃənl]. un- (I.) & emotional. Not emotional; not readily feeling or showing strong emotion; not liable to having the emotions strongly roused.

unemployable, adj. [1. ùnemplóiabl; 2. ʌ̀nimplóiəbl]. un- (I.) & employable. Not employable; **a** not usable; **b** not capable of being employed for labour.

unemployed, adj. & n. [1. ùnemplóid; 2. ʌ̀nimplóid]. un- (I.) & employ(ed). **1.** adj. Not employed; **a** not used or put to use or profit: *unemployed talents, energies, capital &c.*; **b** not occupied: *to have a few hours a day unemployed*; **c** not employed or engaged in regular labour; out of work: *an unemployed labourer, craftsman*. **2.** n. (coll.) *The unemployed*, body of workmen out of work at a specified time or in a specified district.

unemployment, n. [1. ùnemplóiment; 2. ʌ̀nimplóimənt]. un- (I.) & employment. **a** State of being unemployed or out of work; **b** the fluctuating number of workers out of work at any specific moment or in any specific district: *statistics of unemployment; what is the unemployment of this area?*; also (attrib.) as *unemployment benefit*, payment made to unemployed workers under various insurance acts; *unemployment insurance*, insurance against unemployment by means of contributions from workers, employers, and the State, in a specific industry.

unencumbered, adj. [1. ùnenkúmberd; 2. ʌ̀ninkʌ́mbəd]. un- (I.) & encumber(ed). Not encumbered, without encumbrances; specif., of landed estates, not burdened with mortgages or other charges, such as life interests, annuities &c.

unending, adj. [1. unéndiŋ; 2. ʌnéndiŋ]. un- (I.) & end(ing). Not ending; **a** eternal, everlasting: *in unending bliss*; **b** never ceasing; ceaseless, continuous: *unending toil; unending chatter*.

unendingly, adv. Prec. & -ly. In an unending manner; **a** eternally; **b** ceaselessly.

unendowed, adj. [1. unendóud; 2. ʌnindáud]. un- (I.) & endow(ed). Not endowed; without endowments.

unendurable, adj. [1. unendū́rabl; 2. ʌnindjū́rəbl]. un- (I.) & endurable. Not endurable; not to be endured, intolerable.

un-English, adj. [1. unínggliʃ; 2. ʌníŋgliʃ]. un- (I.) & English. Not English; not like, not characteristic of, Englishmen or their ways &c.

unenlightened, adj. [1. ùnenlītnd; 2. ʌ̀ninláitnd]. un- (I.) & enlightened. Not enlightened; in state of intellectual darkness; benighted.

unenterprising, adj. [1. unénterprīziŋ; 2. ʌnéntəpráiziŋ]. un- (I.) & enterprising. Not enterprising; unwilling to embark on new enterprises; unadventurous.

unenviable, adj. [1. unénviabl; 2. ʌnénviəbl]. un- (I.) & enviable. Not enviable, not to be envied.

unequable, adj. [1. unékwabl; 2. ʌníkwəbl]. un- (I.) & equable. Not equable; **a** not even or uniform; **b** easily put out or troubled; uncertain in temper.

unequal, adj. [1. unékwal; 2. ʌníkwəl]. un- (I.) & equal. Not equal; **a** not of the same size, weight, length &c.; **b** not equally matched; uneven, ill-matched; **c** not of the same merit or quality throughout; **d** followed by *to*, not sufficient for, not up to: *unequal to the task*.

unequalled, adj. [1. unékwald; 2. ʌníkwəld]. un- (I.) & equal(led). Not equalled or to be equalled; unrivalled, unmatched, unparalleled.

unequally, adv. [1. unékwali; 2. ʌníkwəli]. unequal & -ly. In an unequal manner.

unequivocal, adj. [1. ùnekwívokl; 2. ʌ̀nikwívəkl]. un- (I.) & equivocal. Not equivocal; without equivocation; not ambiguous; clear, plain, straightforward.

unequivocally, adv. Prec. & -ly. In an unequivocal manner.

unerring, adj. [1. unériŋ; 2. ʌnʌ́riŋ]. un- (I.) & err(ing). Not erring; not making, incapable of making, any mistake; not missing; not failing; sure, certain: *unerring aim; unerring judgement, insight &c.*

unerringly, adv. Prec. & -ly. In an unerring manner.

unessential, adj. [1. ùnesénshl; 2. ànisénʃəl]. un- (I.) & essential. Not essential; not belonging to the essence; not indispensable; not necessary; unimportant.

uneven, adj. [1. unéven; 2. anívən]. un- (I.) & even (II.). Not even; a not level or smooth, rough : *uneven surfaces, road* ; b not uniform, unequal, not equable : *of uneven temper* ; c not of uniform or equal quality throughout : *an uneven performance* ; d not divisible by two without remainder ; odd : *uneven numbers*.

unevenly, adv. Prec. & -ly. In an uneven manner.

uneventful, adj. [1. ùnevéntfl; 2. àniventfl]. un- (I.) & eventful. Not eventful; not characterized by numerous noteworthy or important events : *an uneventful life, year* &c.

uneventfully, adv. Prec. & -ly. In an uneventful manner.

unexampled, adj. [1. ùnegzáhmpld; 2. ànigzámpld]. un- (I.) & example(d). Without example ; unprecedented, unparalleled ; exceptional.

unexceptionable, adj. [1. ùneksépshunabl; 2. àniksépʃənəbl]. un- (I.) & exceptionable. Not exceptionable ; not subject or liable to exceptions ; unobjectionable ; irreproachable ; perfect, excellent.

unexceptionably, adv. Prec. & -ly. In an unexceptionable manner.

unexecuted, adj. [1. unéksekûted; 2. anéksikjùtid]. un- (I.) & execute(d). Not executed; esp. of legal document, not finally signed and witnessed.

unexhausted, adj. [1. ùnegzáwsted; 2. ànigzóstid]. un- (I.) & exhaust(ed). Not exhausted; esp. not consumed, not entirely used up, still producing something ; *unexhausted improvements*, such as manure put on agricultural land of which the benefit has not ceased.

unexpected, adj. [1. ùnekspékted; 2. ànikspéktid]. un- (I.) & expect(ed). Not expected ; not provided for ; coming without warning ; unforeseen, sudden.

unexpectedly, adv. Prec. & -ly. In an unexpected manner.

unexpired, adj. [1. ùnekspírd; 2. ànikspáiəd]. un- (I.) & expire(d). Not expired, esp. of lease or tenancy, of which a portion of the term has still to run.

unexpressive, adj. [1. ùnekspresív; 2. ànikspresív]. un- (I.) & expressive. 1. Inexpressive. 2. (obs.) Inexpressible, ineffable: '*he . . . hears the unexpressive nuptial song, In the blest kingdoms meek of joy and love*' (Milton, 'Lycidas', 176-7).

unexpurgated, adj. [1. ùnékspurgàted; 2. anékspəgèitid]. un- (I.) & expurgate(d). Not expurgated, of book &c., with no passages suppressed ; published in full with no omissions.

unfading, adj. [1. ùnfáding; 2. anféidiŋ]. un- (I.) & Pres. Part. of fade. Not fading; not liable to fade or pass away ; imperishable : esp. *unfading glory* ; (in material sense chiefly poet.) *unfading flowers*.

unfailing, adj. [1. unfáling; 2. anféiliŋ]. un- (I.) & fail(ing). Not failing, not liable to fail ; a not running or falling short ; inexhaustible : *an unfailing supply of water, source of amusement* ; *unfailing courage* ; b not likely to mislead or disappoint ; staunch : *an unfailing champion, friend, defender* &c.

unfailingly, adv. Prec. & -ly. In an unfailing manner; without failing.

unfair, adj. [1. unfár; 2. anféə]. un- (I.) & fair (II.). Not fair ; a unjust, inequitable, showing, resulting from, a lack of impartiality: *an unfair judge, judgement* &c. ; b having recourse to tricks and shifts and mean devices; dishonest : *an unfair player, opponent* ; c based on, derived from, tricky, mean, dishonest methods: *an unfair advantage*; *unfair means* &c.

unfairly, adv. Prec. & -ly. In an unfair manner.

unfairness, n. See prec. & -ness. Quality of being unfair.

unfaith, n. [1. únfáth; 2. ánfèiþ]. un- (I.) & faith. (rare and poet.) Want of faith; lack of honour, untrustworthiness ; distrust : '*Faith and unfaith can ne'er be equal powers*' (Tennyson, 'Merlin and Vivien', 388).

unfaithful, adj. [1. unfáthfl; 2. anféiþfl]. un- (I.) & faithful. Not faithful. 1. a not observing vows, obligations, duty &c. : *an unfaithful servant* ; b disloyal : *an unfaithful friend, subject*. 2. Specif., not true to marriage vows ; guilty of adultery : *an unfaithful wife, husband*. 3. Not true to fact, inaccurate : *an unfaithful version, transcript*.

unfaithfully, adv. Prec. & -ly. In an unfaithful manner.

unfaithfulness, n. See prec. & -ness. State of being unfaithful.

unfaltering, adj. [1. unfáwltering; 2. anfólt(ə)riŋ]. un- (I.) & falter(ing). Not faltering. 1. a Steady, not stumbling : *with unfaltering steps* ; b not trembling : *unfaltering voice, tone* ; c not shifting ; intent : *unfaltering gaze*. 2. (fig.) Unhesitating, resolute, undeviating ; inflexible : *unfaltering courage, determination*.

unfamiliar, adj. [1. ùnfamíliar; 2. ànfəmíliə]. un- (I.) & familiar. Not familiar. 1. a Not well known, not recognized as being known before; strange : *unfamiliar faces* ; *an unfamiliar landscape* ; b unaccustomed, unknown: *an unfamiliar language*. 2. *Unfamiliar with*, unacquainted with, not accustomed to, inexperienced in : *quite unfamiliar with the habits of refined society*.

unfamiliarity, n. [1. ùnfamìliáriti; 2. ànfəmìliériti]. Prec. & -ity. Want of familiarity.

unfamiliarly, adv. [1. ùnfamíliarli; 2. ànfəmíliəli]. See prec. & -ly. In an unfamiliar manner.

unfashionable, adj. [1. unfáshunabl; 2. anfǽʃənəbl]. un- (I.) & fashionable. Not fashionable; behind, not in accordance with, the fashion.

unfashionably, adv. Prec. & -ly. In an unfashionable manner.

unfashionableness, n. See prec. & -ness. State, quality, of being unfashionable.

unfashioned, adj. [1. unfáshund; 2. anfǽʃənd]. un- (I.) & fashion(ed). Not fashioned, unshaped ; shapeless.

unfasten, vb. trans. [1. unfáhsn; 2. anfǽsn]. un- (II.) & fasten. To loose, free from, a fastening ; to unbind, untie, unfix, undo.

unfastened (I.), adj. [1. unfáhsnd; 2. anfǽsnd]. P.P. of prec. Loosed, freed, from a fastening.

unfastened (II.), adj. un- (I.) & fasten(ed). Not fastened.

unfathered, adj. [1. unfáhdherd; 2. anfǽðəd]. un- (I.) & father(ed). a Having no father ; fatherless ; b not acknowledged by his, its, father, begetter, or author.

unfatherly, adj. [1. unfáhdherli; 2. anfǽðəli]. un- (I.) & fatherly. Not fatherly; unbecoming a father ; harsh, cruel.

unfathomable, adj. [1. unfádhumabl; 2. anfǽðəməbl]. un- (I.) & fathom & -able. Not fathomable; a not to be fathomed or plumbed ; bottomless : *unfathomable sea, lake*; b not to be fully grasped by the mind ; inexplicable, insoluble : *an unfathomable mystery*.

unfathomed, adj. [1. unfádhumd; 2. anfǽðəmd]. un- (I.) & fathom(ed). Not fathomed ; unplumbed (lit. and fig.).

unfavourable, adj. [1. unfávurabl; 2. anféivərəbl]. un- (I.) & favourable. Not favourable ; unpropitious, adverse.

unfavourableness, n. Prec. & -ness. State of being unfavourable.

unfavourably, adv. See prec. & -ly. In an unfavourable manner.

unfeasible, adj. [1. unfézibl; 2. anfízibl]. un- (I.) & feasible. Not feasible ; not to be done ; impracticable.

unfeathered, adj. [1. unfédherd; 2. anféðəd]. un- (I.) & feather(ed). Not feathered ; having no feathers, unfledged.

unfed, adj. [1. unféd; 2. anféd]. un- (I.) & fed. Not fed.

unfeeling, adj. [1. unféling; 2. anffliŋ]. un- (I.) & feel(ing). Not feeling ; lacking feeling(s) ; callous, hard-hearted.

unfeelingly, adv. Prec. & -ly. In an unfeeling manner.

unfeigned, adj. [1. unfánd; 2. anféind]. un- (I.) & feign(ed). Not feigned ; real, sincere, genuine.

unfeignedly, adv. [1. unfánedli; 2. anféinidli]. Prec. & -ly. In an unfeigned manner; sincerely.

unfelt, adj. [1. unfélt; 2. anfélt]. un- (I.) & felt (II.). Not felt.

unfeminine, adj. [1. unféminin; 2. anféminin]. un- (I.) & feminine. Not feminine; unwomanly.

unfermented, adj. [1. ùnferménted; 2. ànfəméntid]. un- (I.) & ferment(ed). Not fermented.

unfertile, adj. [1. unfértil; 2. anfǽtail]. un- (I.) & fertile. Not fertile ; infertile (perhaps the more usual form).

unfertilized, adj. [1. unfértilizd; 2. anfǽtilaizd]. un- (I.) & fertilize(d). Not fertilized.

unfetter, vb. trans. [1. unféter; 2. anfétə]. un- (II.) & fetter (II.). To free, loose, from fetters or chains, to set at liberty (lit. and fig.).

unfettered (I.), adj. [1. unféterd; 2. anfétəd]. fr. P.P. of prec. Freed from fetters.

unfettered (II.), adj. un- (I.) & fetter(ed). Not hampered or restricted in thought or action ; independent, free.

unfigured, adj. [1. unfígurd; 2. anfígəd]. un- (I.) & figure(d). Not figured ; not decorated or marked with figures.

unfilial, adj. [1. unfílial; 2. anfíliəl]. un- (I.) & filial. Not filial ; not becoming a son or child ; undutiful.

unfilially, adv. Prec. & -ly. In an unfilial manner.

unfilterable, adj. [1. unfílterabl; 2. anfíltərəbl]. un- (I.) & filterable. Not filterable ; specif. (biol.) of certain micro-organisms that pass through all filtering media.

unfinished, adj. [1. unfínisht; 2. anfíniʃt]. un- (I.) & finish(ed). Not finished ; a not completed, not brought to completion : *an unfinished house, story* ; b not highly wrought ; rough, unpolished : *an unfinished style*.

unfirm, adj. [1. unférm; 2. anfǽm]. un- (I.) & firm. Not firm ; shaky, likely to fall down or apart, of structures &c. ; cp. different use of *infirm*.

unfit (I.), adj. [1. unfít; 2. anfít]. un- (I.) & fit (IV.). Not fit. 1. Not sound; diseased, defective, in body or mind : *unfit to plead* &c. ; *the unfit* (coll. pl.), those who are unfit in any sense. 2. Unsuited, unsuitable for, not adapted to, some specified purpose : *unfit for such a profession* ; *mind unfit for a philosopher* ; *unfit to conduct such delicate inquiries* ; *unfit for work* ; *houses unfit for human habitation*.

unfit (II.), vb. trans. un- (II.) & fit (III.). To deprive of fitness, physical or mental ; to make unsuitable ; disqualify : *drink unfits a man for work* ; *his age unfits him for such a position*.

unfitly, adv. [1. unfítli; 2. anfítli]. unfit (I.) & -ly. In an unfit manner or condition.

unfitness, n. [1. unfítnes; 2. anfítnis]. See prec. & -ness. Condition of being unfit.

unfitted (I.), adj. [1. unfíted; 2. anfítid]. P.P. of unfit (II.). Rendered unfit or unsuitable; deprived of fitness, disqualified : *unfitted for such a position* &c.

unfitted (II.), adj. un- (I.) & fit(ted). Not fitted, furnished, or supplied with : *houses unfitted with baths*.

unfitting, adj. [1. unfíting; 2. anfítiŋ]. un- (I.) & fitting (I.). Not fitting; unbecoming, unsuitable.

unfittingly, adv. Prec. & -ly. In an unfitting manner.

unfix, vb. trans. [1. unfíks; 2. anfíks]. un- (II.) & fix. To make not fixed ; to remove from a fixed position : *unfix bayonets !*

unfixed (I.), adj. [1. unfíkst; 2. anfíkst]. P.P. of prec. Removed from a fixed position.

unfixed (II.), adj. un- (I.) & fix(ed). Not fixed.
unflagging, adj. [1. unfláging; 2. anflǽgiŋ]. un- (I.) & flag(ging). Not flagging, not drooping; unremitting: *unflagging spirits, zeal, energy* &c.
unflaggingly, adv. Prec. & -ly. In an unflagging manner.
unflattering, adj. [1. unflátering; 2. anflǽtəriŋ]. un- (I.) & flattering. Not flattering.
unflatteringly, adv. Prec. & -ly. In an unflattering manner.
unfledged, adj. [1. unfléjd; 2. anflédžd]. un- (I.) & fledge(d). Not yet fully fledged or feathered; (fig.) not fully developed, immature.
unfleshed, adj. [1. unflésht; 2. anfléʃt]. un- (I.) & flesh(ed). Not fleshed; not yet dipped in blood; not yet used in fighting: *an unfleshed sword.*
unfleshly, adj. [1. unfléshli; 2. anfléʃli]. un- (I.) & fleshly. Not fleshly, not worldly; spiritual.
unflinching, adj. [1. unflínshing; 2. anflínʃiŋ]. un- (I.) & flinch(ing). Not flinching, not shrinking; steadfast, unyielding, resolute.
unflinchingly, adv. Prec. & -ly. In an unflinching manner.
unfold, vb. trans. & intrans. [1. unfóld; 2. anfóuld]. un- (II.) & fold. A. trans. 1. a To open the folds of; to unwrap and spread out what is folded: *to unfold a newspaper, a tablecloth* &c.; b to expand, spread open: *plant unfolds its leaves, flower its buds.* 2. (by transf. and fig.) To open, reveal, disclose, display: *to unfold one's plans*; 'I could a tale unfold'. B. intrans. (of leaves, buds &c.) To become open or expanded: *buds unfold in the sunshine.*
unforeseen, adj. [1. ùnforsén; 2. ànfōsín]. un- (I.) & foresee(n). Not foreseen; unexpected.
unforgettable, adj. [1. ùnforgétabl; 2. ànfəgétəbl]. un- (I.) & forgettable. Not forgettable; not to be forgotten, ever memorable.
unforgivable, adj. [1. ùnforgívabl; 2. ànfəgívəbl]. un- (I.) & forgivable. Not forgivable; not to be forgiven; unpardonable.
unforgiven, adj. [1. ùnforgívn; 2. ànfəgívən]. un- (I.) & forgive(n). Not forgiven, not pardoned.
unforgiving, adj. [1. ùnforgíving; 2. àrfəgíviŋ]. un- (I.) & forgiving. Not forgiving.
unforgotten, adj. [1. ùnforgótn; 2. ànfəgótn]. un- (I.) & forgot(ten). Not forgotten; remembered.
unformed, adj. [1. unfórmd; 2. anfómd]. un- (I.) & form(ed). Not yet formed; not fully developed; untrained.
unfortunate, adj. & n. [1. unfórchunit; 2. anfótʃənit]. un- (I.) & fortunate. 1. adj. a Not fortunate; unlucky, unhappy; unsuccessful; b not accompanied by good fortune: *an unfortunate day.* 2. n. An unfortunate person; specif., a prostitute.
unfortunately, adv. Prec. & -ly. In an unfortunate manner.
unfounded, adj. [1. unfóunded; 2. anfáundid]. un- (I.) & found(ed). Not founded on fact; without foundation, baseless: *unfounded accusations, reports, hopes* &c.
unframed, adj. [1. unfrámd; 2. anfréimd]. un- (I.) & frame(d). Not framed; not furnished with a frame, as a picture, drawing &c.
unfree, adj. [1. unfré; 2. anfrí]. un- (I.) & free. (rare) Not free; not enjoying liberty; in a state of slavery or subjection; specif. (legal hist.) of tenure of land in which the service to be performed was uncertain and fixed more or less at the will of the feudal lord.
unfrequented, adj. [1. ùnfrekwénted; 2. ànfrikwéntid]. un- (I.) & frequent(ed). Not frequented; seldom or rarely visited or used by people: *an unfrequented valley, road* &c.
unfriended, adj. [1. unfrénded; 2. anfréndid]. un- (I.) & friend & -ed. Having no friends; not befriended.

unfriendliness, n. [1. unfréndlines; 2. anfréndlinis]. See next word & -ness. Unfriendly feeling, conduct, manner; hostility.
unfriendly, adj. & adv. [1. unfréndli; 2. anfréndli]. un- (I.) & friendly. 1. adj. Not friendly; unkind; hostile: *an unfriendly act.* 2. adv. (rare and archaic) In an unfriendly manner: *I do not mean it unfriendly.*
unfrock, vb. trans. [1. unfrók; 2. anfrók]. un- (II.) & frock. To remove the frock from; specif., to deprive of the status of a priest, degrade from the priesthood; (in P.P. as adj.) *an unfrocked priest.*
unfruitful, adj. [1. unfróōtfl; 2. anfrútfl]. un- (I.) & fruitful. Not fruitful; a (rare or archaic) not yielding fruit; barren, unprolific, unproductive: *an unfruitful vine, tree, land*; b not yielding results; vain, fruitless: *our efforts at reform were at first unfruitful.*
unfruitfully, adv. Prec. & -ly. In an unfruitful manner; without result.
unfruitfulness, n. See prec. & -ness. Condition of being unfruitful.
unfulfilled, adj. [1. ùnfoolfíld; 2. ànfulfíld]. un- (I.) & fulfil(led). Not fulfilled; not achieved; unrealized, unaccomplished: '*Inheritors of unfulfilled renown*' (Shelley, '*Adonais*'); *our hopes remain unfulfilled.*
unfunded, adj. [1. unfúnded; 2. anfándid]. un- (I.) & fund & -ed. (of debt) Not funded; floating.
unfurl, vb. trans. & intrans. [1. unférl; 2. anfə́l]. un- (II.) & furl. 1. trans. To unroll, spread out: *to unfurl sails, a flag* &c. 2. intrans. To become unfurled.
unfurnished, adj. [1. unférnisht; 2. anfə́niʃt]. un- (I.) & furnish(ed). Not furnished; esp. of rooms &c. without furniture.
ungainliness, n. [1. ungánlines; 2. angéinlinis]. See next word & -ness. Condition of being ungainly.
ungainly, adj. [1. ungánli; 2. angéinli]. M.E. *ungeinliche*, as adv., w. suff. *-liche*, see -ly, added to *ungein*, 'awkward, inconvenient', fr. un- (I.) & O.N. *gegn*, 'ready, convenient, serviceable', cogn. w. *gegna*, 'to meet', *gegn*, 'against'; see further again & against. Awkward, clumsy.
ungallant, adj. un- (I.) & gallant. 1. [1. ungálant; 2. angǽlənt] Not gallant, not evincing gallantry. 2. [1. ùngalánt; 2. àngəlǽnt] Not polite, esp. not showing due deference and courtesy to women.
ungallantly, adv. Prec. & -ly. In an ungallant manner.
ungarbled, adj. [1. ungárbld; 2. angábld]. un- (I.) & garble(d). Not garbled; not mutilated or falsified for the purpose of misleading; accurate; plain, straightforward: *ungarbled report, statement, version* &c.
ungenerous, adj. [1. unjénerus; 2. andžénərəs]. un- (I.) & generous. Not generous; a not lavish or liberal; b mean; unfair.
ungenerously, adv. Prec. & -ly. In an ungenerous manner.
ungenial, adj. [1. unjénial; 2. andžíniəl]. un- (I.) & genial (I.). Not genial; not kindly; unsociable.
ungentle, adj. [1. unjéntl; 2. andžéntl]. un- (I.) & gentle. Not gentle; a not of gentle birth; b rude, rough.
ungentlemanlike, adj. [1. unjéntlmanlik; 2. andžéntlmənlàik]. un- (I.) & gentlemanlike. Unbefitting, unlike, a gentleman; unlike the manners or conduct of a gentleman; ill-bred, vulgar, caddish.
ungentlemanliness, n. [1. unjéntlmanlines; 2. andžéntlmənlinis]. See next word & -ness. State of being ungentlemanly.
ungentlemanly, adj. [1. unjéntlmanli; 2. andžéntlmənli]. un- (I.) & gentlemanly. Often used now for *ungentlemanlike*.
un-get-at-able, adj. [1. ùn get át abl; 2. àn gət ǽt əbl]. un- (I.) & get-at-able. Not get-at-able; not easily reached, inaccessible: *he lives in a remote, un-get-at-able village.*
ungird, vb. trans. [1. ungérd; 2. angə́d]. un- (II.) & gird. To remove the girdle from; to unloose one's girdle.

ungirt (I.), adj. [1. ungért; 2. angə́t]. P.P. of prec. With girdle loosed or removed.
ungirt (II.), adj. un- (I.) & P.P. of gird. Having no girdle on.
unglazed, adj. [1. unglázd; 2. angléizd]. un- (I.) & glaze(d). a Not glazed; b not covered by or fitted with glass.
ungodliness, n. [1. ungódlines; 2. angódlinis]. See next word & -ness. State of being ungodly.
ungodly, adj. [1. ungódli; 2. angódli]. un- (I.) & godly. Not godly; neglectful of God; not fearing or worshipping God; impious, wicked; *the ungodly*, wicked people.
ungovernable, adj. [1. ungúvernabl; 2. angávənəbl]. un- (I.) & governable. Not governable; incapable of restraint; wild, unruly: *ungovernable rage, passions* &c.
ungraceful, adj. [1. ungrásfl; 2. angréisfl]. un- (I.) & graceful. Not graceful; awkward, clumsy.
ungracefully, adv. Prec. & -ly. In an ungraceful manner.
ungracious, adj. [1. ungráshus; 2. angréiʃəs]. un- (I.) & gracious. Not gracious; not courteous, generous-minded, or kindly; churlish.
ungraciously, adv. Prec. & -ly. In an ungracious manner.
ungrammatical, adj. [1. ùngramátikl; 2. àngrəmǽtikl]. un- (I.) & grammatical. Not grammatical; not according to the rules of grammar.
ungrammatically, adv. Prec. & -ly. In an ungrammatical manner.
ungrateful, adj. [1. ungrátfl; 2. angréitfl]. un- (I.) & grateful. Not grateful. 1. Not feeling or expressing gratitude. 2. Not repaying one's labour; irksome, disagreeable; unpleasing: *an ungrateful task.*
ungratefully, adv. Prec. & -ly. In an ungrateful manner.
ungratefulness, n. See prec. & -ness. State of being ungrateful; ingratitude.
ungratified, adj. [1. ungrátifíd; 2. angrǽtifaid]. un- (I.) & P.P. of gratify. Not gratified; unsatisfied.
ungrounded, adj. [1. ungróunded; 2. angráundid]. un- (I.) & ground(ed). Not well grounded; lacking grounds or reasons; unfounded.
ungrudging, adj. [1. ungrújing; 2. angrádžiŋ]. un- (I.) & grudging. Not grudging; unstinted, unsparing: *ungrudging attention, praise* &c.
ungrudgingly, adv. Prec. & -ly. In an ungrudging manner; freely, generously.
ungual, adj. [1. únggwal; 2. áŋgwəl]. fr. Lat. *unguis*, 'nail, hoof, claw', cogn. w. Gk. *ónux*, 'nail', see onyx; O.E. *nægel*, 'nail', see nail (I.), & -al. Pertaining to, having a nail, claw, talon, hoof &c.
unguarded, adj. [1. ungárded; 2. angádid]. un- (I.) & guard(ed). Not guarded; showing a lack of circumspection or caution; careless, thoughtless, incautious: *an unguarded remark, expression* &c.; *in an unguarded moment*, when off one's guard.
unguardedly, adv. Prec. & -ly. In an unguarded manner.
unguent, n. [1. úngwent; 2. áŋgwənt]. fr. Lat. *unguent-(um)*, 'ointment', fr. *unguere, ungere*, 'to anoint', see unctuous & unction, & cp. ointment & anoint. An ointment.
unguided, adj. [1. ungíded; 2. angáidid]. un- (I.) & guide(d). Not guided; lacking a guide or guidance.
unguiform, adj. [1. únggwiform; 2. áŋgwifōm], fr. Lat. *unguis*, see ungual, & -form. Shaped like, in the form of, a nail, claw, or hoof.
ungulate, adj. & n. [1. únggūlāt; 2. áŋgjuleit], fr. Lat. *ungula*, 'hoof', also 'claw, talon'; dimin. form, without force, of *unguis*, 'nail, claw', see ungual, & -ate. 1. adj. (zool.) a Having hoofs; b belonging to the order or group, *Ungulata*, hoofed mammals, including the ruminants, swine, horses &c. 2. n. A hoofed mammal.

42 a

unhackneyed, adj. [1. unháknid; 2. anhǽknid]. un- (I.) & hackneyed. Not hackneyed; not trite or stale; fresh, original.

unhallowed, adj. [1. unhálōd; 2. anhǽloud]. un- (I.) & hallow(ed). Not hallowed or consecrated; unholy, profane, wicked.

unhampered, adj. [1. unhámperd; 2. anhǽmpəd]. un- (I.) & hamper(ed). Not hampered; free, untrammelled.

unhand, vb. trans. [1. unhánd; 2. anhǽnd]. un- (II.) & hand. To take the hands off or from; to release, let go, from one's grasp.

unhandsome, adj. [1. unhánsum; 2. anhǽnsəm]. un- (I.) & handsome. 1. Not handsome in appearance; ugly, plain. 2. Ungenerous, mean; ungracious.

unhandy, adj. [1. unhándi; 2. anhǽndi]. un- (I.) & handy. 1. Not near at, or ready to, hand; not convenient. 2. Not handy; awkward, clumsy.

unhang, vb. trans. [1. unháng; 2. anhǽŋ]. un- (II.) & hang. a To remove from a hanging position; b to clear (wall &c.) of hangings.

unhappily, adv. [1. unhápili; 2. anhǽpili]. unhappy & -ly. In an unhappy manner. 1. Unfortunately: *unhappily we unintentionally offended him*. 2. Without happiness, miserably: *they lived unhappily together*.

unhappiness, n. [1. unhápines; 2. anhǽpinis]. See prec. & -ness. State of being unhappy; misery.

unhappy, adj. [1. unhápi; 2. anhǽpi]. un- (I.) & happy. Not happy; unfortunate. 1. Miserable, wretched: *an unhappy life*. 2. Unlucky: *an unhappy meeting, ship*. 3. Unsuitable, out of place, not felicitous: *an unhappy remark*.

unharmed, adj. [1. unhármd; 2. anhɑ́md]. un- (I.) & harm(ed). Not harmed, uninjured, undamaged; safe and sound.

unharness, vb. trans. [1. unhárnes; 2. anhɑ́nis]. un- (II.) & harness. a To take (horse &c.) out of the shafts and remove harness from; b to strip armour or harness from.

unhasp, vb. trans. [1. unhásp; 2. anhǽsp]. un- (II.) & hasp. To loose, free, unfasten, from a hasp; as a chain, bracelet &c.

unhealthily, adv. [1. unhélthili; 2. anhélθili]. unhealthy & -ly. In an unhealthy manner.

unhealthiness, n. [1. unhélthines; 2. anhélθinis]. See prec. & -ness. State of being unhealthy.

unhealthy, adj. [1. unhélthi; 2. anhélθi]. un- (I.) & healthy. Not healthy; a wanting in health, not in sound health; diseased in body or mind; b not conducive to bodily or mental health; unwholesome: *an unhealthy occupation, district* &c.; c indicating want of health: *an unhealthy complexion*.

unheard, adj. [1. unhérd; 2. anhɑ́d]. un- (I.) & hear(d). Not heard; a not perceived by the ear; b not given a hearing; not listened to: *to be condemned unheard*.

unheard-of, adj. [1. unhérd ov; 2. anhɑ́d ɔv]. Not heard of before; unprecedented: *an unheard-of calamity*.

unheeded, adj. [1. unhéded; 2. anhídid]. un- (I.) & heed(ed). Not heeded; disregarded; unnoticed.

unheedful, adj. [1. unhédfl; 2. anhídfl]. un- (I.) & heedful. Not heedful; unheeding, not paying regard, careless.

unheeding, adj. [1. unhéding; 2. anhídiŋ]. un- (I.) & heed(ing). Not heeding; inattentive, unheedful, careless.

unhelm, vb. trans. & intrans. [1. unhélm; 2. anhélm]. un- (II.) & helm. a trans. To take off the helm or helmet of; b intrans., to take off one's helmet.

unhelpful, adj. [1. unhélpfl; 2. anhélpfl]. un- (I.) & helpful. Not helpful; affording no help.

unhelpfully, adv. Prec. & -ly. In an unhelpful manner.

unheralded, adj. [1. unhéralded; 2. anhérəldid]. un- (I.) & herald(ed). Not heralded; unannounced, unproclaimed; unforetold.

unheroic, adj. [1. ùnheróik; 2. ànhiróuik]. un- (I.) & heroic. Not heroic; lacking heroism.

unhesitating, adj. [1. unhézitàting; 2. anhéziteitiŋ]. un- (I.) & Pres. Part. of hesitate. Not hesitating; a acting without hesitation; prompt, ready: *unhesitating in his obedience*; b performed, given, without hesitation: *unhesitating reply, obedience* &c.

unhesitatingly, adv. Prec. & -ly. Without hesitation.

unhinge, vb. trans. [1. unhínj; 2. anhín(d)ž]. un- (II.) & hinge (II.). 1. To take off, remove from, the hinges: *to unhinge a door* &c. 2. (fig.) To throw (the mind) out of its normal course, to cause madness: *to unhinge the mind; a mind unhinged by troubles*.

unhistorical, adj. [1. ùnhistórikl; 2. ànhistórikl]. un- (I.) & historical. Not historical; not in accordance with the facts of history.

unhistorically, adv. Prec. & -ly. In an unhistorical manner.

unhitch, vb. trans. [1. unhích; 2. anhítʃ]. un- (II.) & hitch. To free from a hitch or from being hitched; to unfasten.

unholily, adv. [1. unhólili; 2. anhóulili]. un- holy & -ly. In an unholy manner.

unholiness, n. [1. unhólines; 2. anhóulinis]. See next word & -ness. State of being unholy.

unholy, adj. [1. unhóli; 2. anhóuli]. un- (I.) & holy. Not holy; a not sacred or consecrated, profane; b wicked, impious; c (colloq.) as mere intensive epithet: *an unholy row* &c.

unhonoured, adj. [1. unónord; 2. anónəd]. un- (I.) & honour(ed). Not honoured.

unhook, vb. trans. [1. unhóok; 2. anhúk]. un- (II.) & hook. a To remove from a hook; b to detach hooks, so as to unfasten: *to unhook a dress*.

unhoped, adj. [1. unhópt; 2. anhóupt]. un- (I.) & hope(d). Not hoped; unexpected: also, more usual, unhoped for, as *unhoped-for success* &c.

unhopeful, adj. [1. unhópfl; 2. anhóupfl]. un- (I.) & hopeful. Not hopeful.

unhorse, vb. trans. [1. unhórs; 2. anhɔ́s]. un- (II.) & horse. To throw, cause to fall, from a horse.

unhouse, vb. trans. [1. unhóuz; 2. anháuz]. un- (II.) & house. To deprive of, drive from, a house or shelter; to deprive of means of living in a house.

unhoused (I.), adj. [1. unhóuzd; 2. anháuzd]. P.P. of prec. Deprived of, expelled from, a house or houses.

unhoused (II.), adj. un- (I.) & house(d). Not provided with a house or houses.

unhouseled, adj. [1. unhóuzld; 2. anháuzld]. un- (I.) & housel(ed). (archaic) Not having received the Eucharist.

unhuman, adj. [1. unhúman; 2. anhjúmən]. un- (I.) & human. Not human, cp. *inhuman*.

unhurt, adj. [1. unhért; 2. anhɑ́t]. un- (I.) & hurt. Not hurt; undamaged, uninjured.

uni-, pref. Form of Lat. *ūnus*, 'one', used to form compounds. Lat. *ūnus*, O. Lat. *oinos*, is cogn. w. Gk. *oînos, oinē*, 'the one on a die'; Goth. *ains*, O.E. *ān*, see one (I.). Formed, consisting of, having, only one element; single-; freely used in scientific terminology, as *uni-articulate*, single-jointed, *unisexual* &c.

Uniat(e), n. [1. úniat; 2. júniət], fr. Russ. *uniyata*, 'united', fr. *uniya*, 'union', fr. Lat. *ūnus*, see one (I.). A member of various Eastern Christian Churches which, while retaining the Greek liturgy, rites, customs &c., acknowledge the supremacy of the Pope and are thus members of the Roman Church; (also attrib.) *the Uniate churches*.

uniaxial, adj. [1. ùniáksial; 2. jùniǽksiəl]. uni- & axial. Having one axis or single line of growth.

unibranchiate, adj. [1. ùnibrángkiāt; 2. jùnibrǽŋkieit]. uni- & branchiate. Having a single branchia or gill.

unicameral, adj. [1. ùnikámeral; 2. jùnikǽmərəl]. uni- & Lat. *camera*, 'chamber', see camera, & -al. (of legislative bodies) Having a single chamber.

unicapsular, adj. [1. ùnikápsūlar; 2. jùnikǽpsjulə]. uni- & capsule & -ar. (bot.) Having a single capsule.

unicellular, adj. [1. ùnisélūlar; 2. jùniséljulə]. uni- & cellular. (biol.) Composed of a single cell.

unicoloured, adj. [1. únikùlurd; 2. júnikʌləd]. uni- & colour(ed). Having only one colour, uniform in colour.

unicorn, n. [1. únikòrn; 2. júnikɔn], fr. Lat. *ūnicornis*, 'one-horned'; also in Vulgate 'the unicorn'; fr. uni- & *cornu*, 'horn'. See corn (III.) & horn (I.). 1. a A fabulous animal, usually described and depicted with the body and head of a horse, a lion's or horse's tail, the hind quarters of an antelope, and a single twisted horn; b as word used in A.V. (*unicornis* in Vulgate) to translate Heb. *r'ēm*, in R.V. 'wild ox'. 2. (her.) A figure of a unicorn as a supporter, formerly used for the Scottish royal arms, and since the Union the left-hand supporter facing the lion in the British royal arms. 3. A team of three horses driven two abreast and a third as leader in front between them. 4. Applied attributively a to the narwhal, *unicorn fish*; b to a moth, *unicorn moth*, the caterpillar of which has a single horny growth; c to a mollusc, *unicorn shell*, with a horny spike projecting from the forepart of the shell.

unicostate, adj. [1. ùnikóstāt; 2. jùnikósteit]. uni- & costate. (bot., of leaves) Having a single, primary rib.

unicuspid, adj. [1. ùnikúspid; 2. jùnikáspid]. uni- & cusp. (of teeth) Having a single cusp.

unidea'd, unideaed, adj. [1. ùnídēad; 2. ànaidíəd]. un- (I.) & idea'd. Having no ideas; without imagination, stupid, dull.

unideal, adj. [1. ùnidéal; 2. ànaidíəl]. un- (I.) & ideal. Not ideal; a materialistic, realistic; b dull, prosaic, ordinary.

unidentified, adj. [1. ùnidéntifid; 2. ànaidéntifaid]. un- (I.) & P.P. of identify. Not identified.

unidimensional, adj. [1. ùnidiménshunal; 2. jùnidaiménʃənəl]. uni- & dimensional. Having only one dimension, as a geometrical line.

unidiomatic, adj. [1. ùnidiōmátik; 2. ànidioumǽtik]. un- (I.) & idiomatic. Not idiomatic.

unidirectional, adj. [1. ùnidirékshunal; 2. jùnidirékʃənəl]. uni- & direction & -al. Having only one direction; esp. of electric currents, flowing in one direction only, continuous.

unifiable, adj. [1. únifīabl; 2. júnifəiəbl]. unify & -able. Capable of being unified.

unification, n. [1. ùnifikáshun; 2. jùnifikéiʃən]. uni- & -fication; see unify. a Act of unifying; b state of being unified.

unifier, n. [1. únifīer; 2. júnifəiə]. unify & -er. One who, that which, unifies.

uniflagellate, adj. [1. ùniflájelāt; 2. jùniflǽdʒileit]. uni- & flagellate (II.). (of bacteria &c.) Having only one flagellum or whip-like process.

unifoliate, adj. [1. ùnifóliāt; 2. jùnifóulieit]. uni- & foliate. (bot.) Having one leaf.

uniform (I.), adj. [1. úniform; 2. júnifɔm], fr. Fr. *uniforme*, fr. Lat. *ūniformis*, 'having one form', see uni- & form (I.). 1. (of various things) Having the same form, shape, or pattern; agreeing with each other in some particular; conforming to some common standard: *all must wear a dress of uniform pattern; articles of uniform weight* &c. 2. (of single object &c.) Not varying or changing from time to time or place to place: *keep the room at a uniform temperature*. 3. Homogeneous.

uniform (II.), n., fr. prec. A prescribed form of dress worn as an official costume to distinguish members of an organized body; esp. the official dress worn by soldiers, sailors, police,

uniformed, adj. [1. ùnífòrmd; 2. júnifŏmd]. Prec. & -ed. a Furnished with, habitually wearing, a uniform : *uniformed constabulary*; b actually wearing a uniform : *a uniformed constable guarded the door.*

uniformity, n. [1. ùnifórmiti; 2. jùnifŏmiti], fr. L. Lat. *ūniformitāt-(em)*, see **uniform** (I.) & **-ity**. Quality, state, of being uniform; sameness, consistency, homogeneity; conformity to one pattern, standard, or rule.

uniformly, adv. [1. úniformli; 2. júnifŏmli]. **uniform** (I.) & **-ly**. In a uniform manner; without change or variation.

unify, vb. trans. [1. únifi; 2. jùnifai], fr. L. or Med. Lat. *ūnificāre*, cp. Fr. *unifier*, see **uni-** & **-fy**. To cause to be one ; to reduce to unity or uniformity.

Unigenitus, n. [1. ùnijénitus; 2. jùnidženitəs]. Med. Lat., 'only begotten'. The name of a Papal Bull, issued in 1713, by Clement XI. against Jansenism, from the word with which it begins.

unilateral, adj. [1. ùniláteral; 2. jùnilǽtərəl]. **uni-** & **lateral**. a Having, arranged on, affecting, one side only; one-sided; specif. b (law) binding, obligatory, for one party only, as by a deed poll : *unilateral contract.*

unilaterally, adv. Prec. & **-ly**. In a unilateral manner.

uniliteral, adj. [1. ùnilíteral; 2. jùnilítərəl]. **uni-** & **literal**. Having, consisting of, one letter only.

unilluminated, adj. [1. ùnilúminàted; 2. àniljúmineitid]. **un-** (I.) & **illuminate(d)**. Not illuminated (lit. and fig.).

unillustrated, adj. [1. unilústràted; 2. aniləstreitid]. **un-** (I.) & **illustrate(d)**. Not illustrated; without illustrations.

unilocular, adj. [1. ùnilókūlar; 2. jùnilókjulə]. **uni-** & **locular**. (bot. and zool.) Having one cell or cavity.

unimaginable, adj. [1. ùnimájinabl; 2. ànimǽdžinəbl]. **un-** (I.) & **imaginable**. That cannot be imagined; inconceivable.

unimaginative, adj. [1. ùnimájinativ; 2. ànimǽdžinətiv]. **un-** (I.) & **imaginative**. Not imaginative; without imagination.

unimpaired, adj. [1. ùnimpárd; 2. ànimpéəd]. **un-** (I.) & **impair(ed)**. Not impaired; not weakened, diminished, or damaged.

unimpeachability, n. [1. ùnimpèchabíliti; 2. ànimpìtʃəbíliti]. See next word & **-ity**. State of being unimpeachable; exemption from being called in question or doubted; freedom from fault or blame.

unimpeachable, adj. [1. ùnimpéchabl; 2. ànimpítʃəbl]. **un-** (I.) & **impeachable**. Not impeachable; not liable to be called in question or doubted; irreproachable; blameless.

unimpeachably, adv. Prec. & **-ly**. In an unimpeachable manner.

unimpeded, adj. [1. ùnimpéded; 2. ànimpídid]. **un-** (I.) & **impede(d)**. Not impeded; unhindered.

unimportance, n. [1. ùnimpórtans; 2. ànimpótəns]. **un-** (I.) & **importance**. State of being unimportant; want, lack, of importance; insignificance, triviality.

unimportant, adj. [1. ùnimpórtant; 2. ànimpótənt]. **un-** (I.) & **important**. Not important; of no weight or value; insignificant, trivial.

unimposing, adj. [1. ùnimpózing; 2. ànimpóuziŋ]. **un-** (I.) & **imposing**. Not imposing, unimpressive, in appearance.

unimpressionable, adj. [1. ùnimpréshunabl; 2. ànimpréʃənəbl]. **un-** (I.) & **impressionable**. Not impressionable.

unimpressive, adj. [1. ùnimprésiv; 2. ànimprésiv]. **un-** (I.) & **impressive**. Not impressive.

unimproved, adj. [1. ùnimprõovd; 2. ànimprúvd]. **un-** (I.) & **improve(d)**. Not improved, esp. of land, not cultivated ; not developed for building &c.: *unimproved site value*, land value as divested of all improvements.

unincumbered. See **unencumbered**.

uninflammable, adj. [1. ùninflámabl; 2. àninflǽməbl]. **un-** (I.) & **inflammable**. Not inflammable.

uninflated, adj. [1. ùninflátəd; 2. àninfléitid]. **un-** (I.) & **inflate(d)**. Not inflated.

uninflected, adj. [1. ùninflékted; 2. àninfléktid]. **un-** (I.) & **inflect(ed)**. Not inflected; esp. of a language or a word, having no inflexions.

uninfluenced, adj. [1. uníinflooenst; 2. àninfluənst]. **un-** (I.) & **influence(d)**. Not influenced.

uninfluential, adj. [1. ùninflooénshl; 2. àninfluénʃ(ə)l]. **un-** (I.) & **influential**. Not influential; having no influence.

uninformed, adj. [1. ùninfórmd; 2. ànínfŏmd]. **un-** (I.) & **informed**. Not informed; a having no information concerning, not told of ; b lacking information or knowledge; untaught, ignorant.

uninhabitable, adj. [1. ùninhábitabl; 2. àninhǽbitəbl]. **un-** (I.) & **inhabitable**. Not inhabitable; not fit to be lived in.

uninhabited, adj. [1. ùninhábited; 2. àninhǽbitid]. **un-** (I.) & **inhabit(ed)**. Not inhabited; deserted, empty.

uninitiated, adj. [1. ùninínshiàted; 2. àniníʃieitid]. **un-** (I.) & **initiate(d)**. Not initiated.

uninjured, adj. [1. ùnínjurd; 2. anínd̩žəd]. **un-** (I.) & **injure(d)**. Not injured.

uninspired, adj. [1. ùninspírd; 2. àninspáiəd]. **un-** (I.) & **inspire(d)**. Not inspired; without, lacking, inspiration.

uninstructed, adj. [1. ùninstrúkted; 2. àninstráktid]. **un-** (I.) & **instruct(ed)**. Not instructed; untaught.

uninstructive, adj. [1. ùninstrúktiv; 2. àninstráktiv]. **un-** (I.) & **instructive**. Not instructive.

unintelligent, adj. [1. ùnintélijent; 2. ànintélidžənt]. **un-** (I.) & **intelligent**. Not intelligent; stupid.

unintelligently, adv. Prec. & **-ly**. In an unintelligent manner ; stupidly.

unintelligibility, n. [1. ùnintèlijibíliti; 2. ànintèlidžibíliti]. **un-** (I.) & **intelligibility**. State of being unintelligible; lack of intelligibility.

unintelligible, adj. [1. ùnintélijibl; 2. ànintélidžəbl]. **un-** (I.) & **intelligible**. Not intelligible.

unintelligibly, adv. Prec. & **-ly**. In an unintelligible manner.

unintentional, adj. [1. ùninténshunal; 2. àninténʃənəl]. **un-** (I.) & **intentional**. Not intentional; not deliberate; involuntary.

unintentionally, adv. Prec. & **-ly**. In an unintentional manner; involuntarily.

uninterested, adj. [1. ùnínteresed; 2. àníntrəstid]. **un-** (I.) & **interest(ed)**. Not interested.

uninteresting, adj. [1. ùnínteresting; 2. ànínt(ə)ristiŋ]. **un-** (I.) & **interesting**. Not interesting; dull.

uninterestingly, adv. Prec. & **-ly**. In an uninteresting manner.

unintermitted, adj. [1. ùnintermíted; 2. ànintəmítid]. **un-** (I.) & **intermit(ted)**. Not intermitted; uninterrupted.

unintermitting, adj. [1. ùnintermíting; 2. ànintəmítiŋ]. **un-** (I.) & **intermit(ting)**. Not intermitting; ceaseless, continuous.

unintermittingly, adv. Prec. & **-ly**. Without intermission; ceaselessly, continuously.

uninterrupted, adj. [1. ùninterúpted; 2. ànintəráptid]. **un-** (I.) & **interrupt(ed)**. Not interrupted.

uninterruptedly, adv. Prec. & **-ly**. Without interruption.

uninventive, adj. [1. ùninvéntiv; 2. àninvéntiv]. **un-** (I.) & **inventive**. Not inventive; without the faculty of invention.

uninvited, adj. [1. ùninvíted; 2. àninváitid]. **un-** (I.) & **invite(d)**. Not invited; having received no invitation.

uninviting, adj. [1. ùninvíting; 2. àninváitiŋ]. **un-** (I.) & **inviting**. Not inviting; unattractive; repellent.

uninvolved, adj. [1. ùninvólvd; 2. àninvólvd]. **un-** (I.) & **involve(d)**. Not involved; simple, direct.

Unio, n. [1. úniō; 2. júniou]. Lat., 'union, unity ; a single large pearl', see next word & cp. **onion**. (zool.) A genus of freshwater mussels, having a pearly shell, and producing pearls.

union, n. [1. úniun; 2. júniən]. Fr., fr. Lat. *ūniōn-(em)*, 'unity, union'; fr. *ūnus*, 'one', see **uni-**. **1. a** Act of uniting or joining two or more things into one : *to promote, accomplish, the union between two families, states &c.*; **b** state of being united in marriage; a marriage. **2.** State of being united : *a lasting union*; specif., a political combination or fusion of two countries under a single sovereign or government, as *the Union of England and Scotland, 1707* ; *of Great Britain and Ireland, 1801 &c.* **3.** A combination of various political or administrative bodies for a specific common purpose : *the Latin monetary union* ; *the postal union*. **4.** Specif. **a** a combination of parishes for administration of the Poor Law under a Public Assistance Authority ; **b** the workhouse administered by such body : *to go into the union* ; *tramping from one union to another*. **5.** That part of a national flag which symbolizes the political union of two or more states, occupying usually the upper canton next the staff : *to fly a flag union down*, as signal of distress ; hence a union flag or jack (see below). **6.** A trade union.

Union flag, n. [1. úniun flág; 2. júniən flǽg]. The national flag of Great Britain, signifying the union of England, Scotland, and Ireland, being a combination of the crosses of St. George, St. Andrew, and St. Patrick; commonly known as the *Union Jack*, whether flown as a jack or not.

unionism, n. [1. úniunìzm; 2. júniənìzəm]. **union** & **-ism**. Specif. **1. a** the political principle of uniting under a central government the various kingdoms, states, provinces, dominions, forming the British Empire; the principle of maintaining the unity of the Empire, as distinct from establishing 'Home Rule' or independent governments in each portion or province; **b** specif., these principles as applied to Ireland. **2.** Principles of trade-unionism.

unionist, n. [1. úniunist ; 2. júniənist]. **union** & **-ist**. **1. a** One who advocates the political principles of unionism within the Empire ; specif. **b** a member of the party which, basing itself on these principles, opposed Home Rule for Ireland ; **c** name often applied latterly, until the establishment of the Irish Free State, to the Conservative party in Great Britain. **2.** A member of a trade union; supporter of trade-union principles.

Union Jack, n. [1. úniun ják; 2. júniən džǽk]. The Union flag of Great Britain when flown as a jack, q.v.; (in common usage) the Union flag.

uniparous, adj. [1. ūníparus; 2. jùnípərəs]. **uni-** & **-parous**, fr. Lat. *parēre*, 'to bring forth, beget', & **-ous**; cp. **parent**. **a** (of animals) Producing, normally, only one at a birth; **b** (of plants) having a single axis or stem.

unipartite, adj. [1. únipártīt; 2. jùnipátait]. **uni-** & **part** & **-ite**. **1.** Not divided into parts. **2. a** (math.) Characterizing a single set of objects of the same kind ; **b** (of curves) having all its real points comprised in one series through infinity or finity.

unipersonal, adj. [1. ùnipérsunal; 2. jùnipə́sənəl]. **uni-** & **personal**. (theol., of the Godhead) Consisting of, existing as, a single person.

unipolar, adj. [1. ùnipólar; 2. jùnipóulə]. **uni-** & **polar**. Having only one pole or kind of polarity.

unique, adj. [1. ūnék; 2. jùnîk]. Fr., fr. Lat. *ūnicus*, 'one and no more, only, single', fr. *ūnus*, 'one'. Single in kind or excellence ; having no like or equal ; unmatched,

unequalled, unparalleled: *a unique event; perhaps a unique survival; this picture is thought to be unique*; (in illit. usage) remarkable, wonderful, singular, and hence used wrongly with comparatives: *we had rather a unique experience; she dresses in a most unique fashion*.

uniquely, adv. Prec. & -ly. In a unique manner.

uniqueness, n. See prec. & -ness. State, quality, of being unique.

uniradial, uniradiate, adj. [1. ŭnirádial, -iat; 2. jŭnirēidiəl, -iət]. uni- & radial, -ate. Having one radius, ray, or arm.

unirrigated, adj. [1. unírigated; 2. anírigèitid]. un- (I.) & irrigate(d). Not irrigated; not under irrigation.

unisexual, adj. [1. ŭnisékshooal; 2. jŭniséksjuəl]. uni- & sexual. (bot.) Having one sex only, male or female, with stamen or pistil; not hermaphroditic.

unisolated, adj. [1. unísəlāted; 2. anáisəlèitid]. un- (I.) & isolate(d). Not isolated.

unison, n. [1. únizun; 2. júnizən, fr. M.E. unis(s)on, Lat. únisonus, adj., ' having one sound ', fr. uni- & sonus, ' sound ', see sound (I.). a Harmony, concord, agreement, in sound; specif. b (mus.) identity of pitch: *to sing in unison*, to sing so that all the voices sing the same note, without producing harmony.

unisonance, n. [1. unisónans; 2. junisóunəns]. Next word & -ce. Accordance, agreement, of sounds.

unisonant, adj. [1. unisónant; 2. junisóunənt]. See prec. & -ant. Sounding together, agreeing in sound.

unissued, adj. [1. uníshŭd; 2. aníʃjud]. un- (I.) & issue(d). Not issued, esp. of shares of a company authorized but held in reserve and not issued to the public for subscription.

unit, n. [1. únit; 2. júnit]. A shortened form of unity. 1. A single individual object or person; a group of objects or persons regarded **a** as forming a unity or whole complete in itself; or **b** as forming that into which a whole may be divided most conveniently for a specific purpose: *a division is now regarded as the unit of an army; the parish, we may say, has almost ceased to be the unit of local government*. 2. (math.) The least whole number, one. 3. (phys.) Any determinate single quantity used as a standard by which other quantities are measured or expressed: *international electrical units, as the volt, ohm &c.; units of mass, energy &c.*

Unitarian, n. & adj. [1. ŭnitárian; 2. jŭnitéəriən], fr. unity & -arian, on anal. of Trinitarian. 1. n. Member of a religious body which rejects the doctrine of the Trinity and the Divinity of Christ, and asserts that God is unipersonal. 2. adj. Pertaining to this body and their beliefs; pertaining to any set of religious doctrines which deny the Divinity of Christ and the existence of the Trinity.

Unitarianism, n. [1. ŭnitárianizm; 2. jŭnitéəriənizəm]. Prec. & -ism. Religious doctrines and philosophy of Unitarians.

unitary, adj. [1. únitari; 2. júnitəri]. unit & -ary. 1. Pertaining to a unit or units: *unitary system, method &c.* 2. Single; not double or divided: *unitary government; a unitary state*.

unite, vb. trans. & intrans. [1. ŭnít; 2. jŭnáit], fr. Lat. (rare or post-class.) ūnīt-(um), P.P. type of ūnīre, ' to make one, join ', fr. ūnus, ' one ', see uni-. A. trans. 1. To join several things, objects, together, into one, bring into close contiguity, and form into a single whole; to combine, amalgamate: *to unite pieces of metal with solder; to unite two neighbouring portions of land*. 2. To join, bring, together into close social or family relationship: *to unite two families by marriage; to unite one's son to a suitable wife*. 3. To possess, exhibit, equally, as elements of character, mind, habit &c., several qualities, traits, accomplishments &c.: *he unites the best qualities of the gentleman and the Christian*. B. intrans. 1. (of physical process) To become joined together; become one or a whole; to combine, coalesce: *oil and water will not unite*. 2. To become associated, to join, become one, in opinions, principles &c.: *all parties can unite in patriotic sentiment in a national crisis*. 3. To become associated, join together, in action; to act as one: *let us unite in singing ' God save the King ', in resisting foreign aggression &c.*

united, adj. [1. ŭníted; 2. jŭnáitid], fr. P.P. of prec. 1. Joined together; **a** joined politically, as *United Kingdom of Great Britain and (Northern) Ireland; the United States of America &c.*; **b** joined in spirit, sympathy, affection; not divided by disagreements and quarrels: *a united family*. 2. **a** Associated together for purposes of common action: *the united forces of Christendom resisted Mohammedan aggression*; **b** arising from, based on, association for a common purpose: *united action*.

unitedly, adv. Prec. & -ly. In a united manner; harmoniously.

unitive, adj. [1. únitiv; 2. júnitiv], fr. L. Lat. ūnitīvus, see unity & -ive. Having the power of uniting; tending to unite.

unity, n. [1. úniti; 2. júniti], fr. O. Fr. unité, fr. Lat. ūnitāt-(em); fr. ūnus, ' one ', see uni-. 1. State of being one, single, individual; grouping, arrangement, of component elements or parts so as to form or produce the sense of a single coherent whole: *to find unity in diversity; the plan and underlying idea which give unity to a work of art; the dramatic unities,* those of time, place, and action which the perfect classical drama was supposed to observe. 2. Oneness of spirit; harmony, agreement, of aims, interests, feeling, thought &c.; amity, concord: *national unity; family unity; to live in unity with all men*; ' *Give to all nations unity, peace, and concord* ' (The Litany). 3. Specif. **a** (math.) any definite quantity taken as one; the number one; **b** (law) joint tenancy of a property by two or more persons.

univalence, -cy, n. [1. ŭnivalens(i); 2. jŭnivéiləns(i). uni- & valence, -cy. (chem.) State, quality, of being univalent.

univalent, adj. [1. ŭniválent; 2. jŭnivéilənt]. uni- & -valent. (chem.) Having a valency or combining power of one.

univalve, adj. & n. [1. únivalv; 2. júnivælv]. uni- & valve. **a** adj. (of molluscs) Having only one valve or shell, not bivalve; **b** n., mollusc with only one valve or shell.

universal (I.), adj. [1. ŭnivérsl; 2. jŭnivāsl]. universe & -al. 1. **a** Pertaining to the universe; referring to, embracing, the whole world or the whole of created things: *the universal Church*; **b** involving the whole world or universe; complete, absolute: ' *Universal ruin* '(Milton, ' P. L.' vi. 797); **c** affecting, held, done, used, by everybody; widespread: *the almost universal belief is that vaccination has nearly stamped out smallpox; superstition is universal among savages; a universal practice; a universal language*, one artificially and deliberately compiled with a view to its being learnt and spoken by people of all races; a real language that actually is spoken in all parts of the world: *English is fast becoming a universal language*. 2. **a** Applicable to every member of a genus; general; contrasted with *particular*; (esp. log.) affirmed or denied of a whole class: *a universal proposition; a universal negative; e.g. no man is infallible*; **b** true of, applying to, all cases: *universal rules*. 3. (mechan.) Capable of being used for objects of all shapes and sizes; adaptable for all purposes; moving in all directions: *a universal spanner, bevel, joint &c.* 4. (law) Pertaining to, applying to, including, the whole of a person's rights, advantages, duties, arising from a specified position, capacity, relation: *a universal successor, legacy, partnership, trustee &c.*

universal (II.), n. Med. Lat. *universale*; see prec. 1. (log.) **a** A universal proposition; **b** that which may be predicated of anything; any one of the five predicables. 2. (philos.) A general concept; an abstract, general term.

universalism, n. [1. ŭnivérsalizm; 2. jŭnivāsəlizəm]. universal (I.) & -ism. The theological belief that ultimately all mankind will be saved.

universalist, n. [1. ŭnivérsalist; 2. jŭnivāsəlist]. See prec. & -ist. Believer in universalism.

universalistic, adj. [1. ŭnivérsalístik; 2. jŭnivāsəlístik]. Prec. & -ic. Pertaining to universalism.

universalize, vb. trans. [1. ŭnivérsaliz; 2. jŭnivāsəlaiz]. universal (I.) & -ize. To make, treat as, universal.

universe, n. [1. únivěrs; 2. júnivās], fr. Fr. *univers*, fr. Lat. *ūniversum*, ' the whole world, the universe ', neut. sing. as n., of *universus*, adj., ' turned, combined into one, all collectively; whole, general, universal ', fr. uni-, ' one ', & vers-(um), P.P. of vertere, ' to turn ', see version. 1. The whole system of suns, planets &c. existing in space; the cosmos. 2. The whole system of created things viewed as a whole. Phr. *to behave as though one owned the universe*, to give oneself airs of inordinate importance and authority. 3. The world.

university, n. [1. ŭnivérsiti; 2. jŭnivāsiti]. M.E. *universite*, fr. Fr. *université*, fr. Lat. *ūniversitāt-(em), ūniversitas*, ' the whole; whole number of things; the universe, the world; (as a term of law) number of persons associated together as one body; community; a corporation '. The use of the term in Med. Lat. for a university in the present sense is prob. due to such a body being a *universitas facultatum*, or combination of all the Faculties, but there was also possibly an idea of the whole of learning being taught. See universe & -ity. 1. An institution for the purpose of educating students in the arts and sciences and all the higher branches of learning, with a body of professors and other teachers conducting examinations and conferring degrees. In the cases of Oxford, Cambridge, and London, the university consists of and includes a number of different individual colleges, separate foundations, having a very large degree of independence, and each providing courses of instruction in addition to those provided by the university in the narrower sense. 2. The members of a university collectively; the governing body or bodies of a university: *the opinion of the university is &c.; the university has elected X their Chancellor*. 3. Team, crew, athletes &c. representing a university: *the university was beaten by an innings*.

universology, n. [1. ŭnivěrsóloji; 2. jŭnivāsóladʒi]. See universal & -logy. Science which deals with everything pertaining to the universe or to the whole range of human activities.

univocal, adj. & n. [1. ŭnivókl; 2. jŭnivóukl]. uni- & vocal. 1. adj. **a** Speaking with a single voice; having only one meaning, not equivocal; **b** (mus.) having unison; played, sung, in unison. 2. n. **a** A word having only one meaning; **b** (log.) a generic term applied in one sense only to all the species it includes.

univocally, adv. Prec. & -ly. In a univocal manner.

unjaundiced, adj. [1. unjáhndist, -jáwndist; 2. andʒándist, -dʒóndist]. un- (I.) & jaundice(d). Not jaundiced; not affected by feelings of envy or jealousy; unprejudiced.

unjoin, vb. trans. [1. unjóin; 2. andʒóin]. un- (II.) & join. To separate that which is joined; to disjoin.

unjoint, vb. trans. [1. unjóint; 2. andʒóint]. un- (II.) & joint (III.). To separate the joints; to unfasten what is jointed; to disjoint.

unjust, adj. [1. unjúst; 2. andʒást]. un- (I.) & just. Not just; **a** not animated by justice; acting contrary to just principles: *an unjust judge; the unjust, unjust persons*; in Phr. *on the just and the unjust*, everybody; **b** contrary to justice, not conformable with just principles: *an unjust sentence*.

unjustifiable, adj. [1. ùnjustifīabl; 2. àndžastifáiəbl]. **un- (I.) & justifiable.** Not justifiable, without justification.
unjustifiably, adv. Prec. & **-ly.** In an unjustifiable manner; to an unjustifiable extent.
unjustly, adv. [1. unjústli; 2. andžástli]. **unjust & -ly.** In an unjust manner.
unkempt, adj. [1. unkém(p)t; 2. ankém(p)t]. fr. **un- (I.) & M.E.** *kempt, kembed*, P.P. of obs. O.E. *cemban*, 'to comb', see **comb**. **a** (obs.) Not combed; **b** untidy, shaggy; badly dressed, neglected: *unkempt appearance*.
unkennel, vb. trans. [1. unkénl; 2. ankénl]. **un- (II.) & kennel (II.).** To loose, drive (dogs &c.) from a kennel.
unkind, adj. [1. unkīnd; 2. ankáind]. **un- (I.) & kind (II.).** Not kind; harsh, cruel, inconsiderate.
unkindliness, n. [1. unkīndlines; 2. ankáindlinis]. **unkindly (I.) & -ness.** State of being unkindly; an unkindly action.
unkindly (I.), adj. [1. unkīndli; 2. ankáindli]. **un- (I.) & kindly (I.).** Not kindly; ungracious, unfriendly, harsh.
unkindly (II.), adv. **un- (I.) & kindly (II.).** In an unkind manner.
unkindness, n. [1. unkīndnes; 2. ankáindnis]. **unkind & -ness.** State of being unkind; an unkind action.
unking, vb. trans. [1. unkíng; 2. ankíŋ]. **un- (II.) & king.** (rare) To deprive of rank and status of king; to depose.
unkingly, -like, adj. [1. unkíngli, -līk; 2. ankíŋli, -laik]. **un- (I.) & kingly, -like.** Not kingly or kinglike; not royal; unworthy of a king.
unknightly, adj. [1. unnītli; 2. annáitli]. **un- (I.) & knightly.** Not knightly or chivalrous; unworthy of a knight.
unknit, vb. trans. [1. unnít; 2. annít]. **un- (II.) & knit.** (esp. fig.) To undo what has been knitted or fastened together.
unknot, vb. trans. [1. unnót; 2. annót]. **un- (II.) & knot (II.).** To untie that which is knotted; to unloose the knots from.
unknowable, adj. [1. unnōábl; 2. annóuəbl]. **un- (I.) & knowable.** Not knowable; not capable of being known; (esp. philos.) beyond the powers or limits of man's intelligence; also as noun: *the unknowable*, that which cannot be known, the absolute, the first cause, the ultimate reality of things.
unknowing, adj. [1. unnōing; 2. annóuiŋ]. **un- (I.) & Pres. Part. of know.** Not knowing; ignorant, unwitting.
unknowingly, adv. Prec. & **-ly.** Not knowingly; ignorantly.
unknown, adj. & n. [1. unnōn; 2. annóun]. **un- (I.) & know(n).** **1.** adj. Not known; **a** not within one's knowledge; unascertained: *address unknown*; *an unknown country*; **b** not within one's experience; not to be described or told; incalculable: *to experience unknown delights*; **c** (math.) to be ascertained or found out, as of quantities in equations, usually denoted by the later letters of alphabet: *x, y, z are the unknown quantities*; Phr. *an unknown quantity*, person, thing, whose influence, power &c. is not yet known or calculable. **2.** n. *The unknown*, that which is unknown; an unknown quantity: *to venture into the unknown*, into an unexplored, unknown region, country, or domain of thought or experience: *the unknown is always mysterious and attractive*; *the Great Unknown*, name given to the author of the Waverley Novels (Sir Walter Scott) before his identity had been revealed.
unlabelled, adj. [1. unlábld; 2. anléibld]. **un- (I.) & label(led).** Not labelled.
unlaboured, adj. [1. unlāburd; 2. anléibəd]. **un- (I.) & laboured.** Not laboured; done without great effort; (esp. of style) easy, spontaneous.
unlace, vb. trans. [1. unlās; 2. anléis]. **un- (II.) & lace (II.).** **1.** To undo the laces of, to unfasten that which is laced; to free from laces or being laced: *to unlace one's boots*, *stays* &c.; *unlace a woman*, unlace her stays. **2.** Old phr. of the chase, *to unlace a boar*, to cut it up when killed.
unlade, vb. trans. [1. unlād; 2. anléid]. **un- (II.) & lade.** To unload, **a** to take out the cargo or load from: *to unlade a ship*; **b** to take out, remove from: *to unlade the cargo from a ship*; *to unlade hay from cart* &c.; **c** to discharge: *ship will unlade cargo today*.
unladen, adj. [1. unlādn; 2. anléidn]. **un- (I.) & lade(n).** Not laden, not burdened (esp. fig.): *unladen with sorrow, anxieties* &c.
unladylike, adj. [1. unládilīk; 2. anléidilaik]. **un- (I.) & ladylike.** Not ladylike; not worthy of a lady; vulgar, common.
unlaid, adj. [1. unlād; 2. anléid]. **un- (I.) & P.P. of lay.** Not laid; **a** not placed, fixed, or arranged: *the table is still unlaid*; **b** not put at rest, not allayed: *an unlaid, restless spirit*; specif. **c** (of paper) without parallel watermark lines.
unlamented, adj. [1. ùnlaménted; 2. ànləméntid]. **un- (I.) & lament(ed).** Not lamented; not mourned; unregretted.
unlash, vb. trans. [1. unláṣh; 2. anléʃ]. **un- (II.) & lash.** To unfasten that which is lashed; to loose the lashings of.
unlatch, vb. trans. [1. unlách; 2. anlétʃ]. **un- (II.) & latch.** To undo, release, the latch of (as of a door).
unlawful, adj. [1. unláwfl; 2. anlófl]. **un- (I.) & lawful.** Not lawful; forbidden or not permitted by the law; illegal: *unlawful assembly*, a meeting of three or more persons for purposes forbidden by law or in such a manner as to endanger or be likely to endanger the public peace.
unlawfully, adv. Prec. & **-ly.** In an unlawful manner.
unlawfulness, n. See prec. & **-ness.** State of being unlawful.
unlay, vb. trans. [1. unlā; 2. anléi]. **un- (II.) & lay (III.).** (naut.) To untwist the strands of (a rope &c.).
unlearn, vb. trans. [1. unlérn; 2. anlán]. **un- (II.) & learn.** To forget what one has learnt; to lose the memory of; to learn the opposite of what one has been taught, esp. of erroneous teaching or methods.
unlearned (I.), adj. [1. unlérned, -lérnd; 2. anlắnid, -lắnd]. **un- (I.) & learned.** Not learned; ignorant, illiterate; also with definite article, as collective plural noun: *the unlearned*, the ignorant mob.
unlearned (II.), unlearnt, adj. [1. unlérnd, unlérnt; 2. anlắnd, anlắnt]. **un- (I.) & learn(ed).** Not learnt: *unlearned lessons*.
unlearnedly, adv. [1. unlérnedli; 2. anlắnidli]. **unlearned (I.) & -ly.** In an unlearned manner; illiterately, ignorantly.
unleash, vb. trans. [1. unléṣh; 2. anlíʃ]. **un- (II.) & leash.** To free from, let go from, a leash.
unleavened, adj. [1. unlévnd; 2. anlévnd]. **un- (I.) & leaven(ed).** Not leavened; made without leaven (of bread; also fig.).
unled, adj. [1. unléd; 2. anléd]. **un- (I.) & P.P. of lead (IV.).** Not led, not guided; without guidance or leaders.
unleisured, adj. [1. unlézhurd; 2. anléžəd]. **un- (I.) & leisured.** Not leisured; having little or no leisure; hard-worked, busy.
unleisurely, adj. [1. unlézhurli; 2. anléžəli]. **un- (I.) & leisurely.** Not leisurely; hurried.
unless, conj. [1. unlés; 2. anlés]. Earlier *onless(e)*, followed by a *that* clause, *on less(e) that ye wait* &c.; the orig. sense being, 'on the less supposition than, in a less case than'; fr. **on**, in earlier sense of 'in', & **less**. If not, supposing that not, except that: *I shall not go unless the weather is fine*; *unless you work harder you will never pass your examination*; *unless you are a perfect fool you will behave properly to your uncle.*
unlettered, adj. [1. unléterd; 2. anlétəd]. **un- (I.) & letter(ed).** Illiterate, uneducated; without knowledge or love of literature.
unlicensed, adj. [1. unlīsenst; 2. anláisənst]. **un- (I.) & license(d).** Not licensed.
unlicked, adj. [1. unlíkt; 2. anlíkt]. **un- (I.) & lick(ed).** Cp. Phr. *lick into shape*, q.v. under **lick**. (chiefly attrib.) Not licked into shape; in Phr. *an unlicked cub*, a crude, conceited, impudent, underbred young fool.
unlighted, adj. [1. unlīted; 2. anláitid]. **un- (I.) & light(ed).** Not lighted; unlit.
unlike, adj. & prep. [1. unlīk; 2. anláik]. **un- (I.) & like.** **1.** adj. Not like; dissimilar, different, having little or no resemblance: *the two cases are quite unlike*; *no two people could be more unlike in appearance or character*. **2.** prep. Not like, having no resemblance to, different from, in appearance, character &c.: *the picture is quite unlike him*; *how unlike you to forget your dinner*; *unlike his predecessor, he was more concerned with his own future than his duty.*
unlikelihood, n. [1. unlíklihood; 2. anláiklihud]. **unlikely & -hood.** State, fact, of being unlikely; improbability, unlikeliness: *the unlikelihood of the fine weather continuing*; *unlikelihood of success.*
unlikeliness, n. [1. unlíklines; 2. anláiklinis]. See next word & **-ness.** State of being unlikely; unlikelihood.
unlikely, adj. [1. unlíkli; 2. anláiklí]. **un- (I.) & likely.** Not likely; **a** improbable: *in the unlikely event of* &c.; *a victory is unlikely but not impossible*; **b** not likely to succeed; unpromising: *engaged on an unlikely adventure.*
unlimber, vb. trans. [1. unlímber; 2. anlímbə]. **un- (II.) & limber (I.).** To detach and take away the limber from (gun) so as to prepare for action.
unlimited, adj. [1. unlímited; 2. anlímitid]. **un- (I.) & limited.** Not limited; **a** having no limits; boundless: *the unlimited expanse of the sky, of ocean*; **b** unrestricted, not confined and narrow: *an unlimited field for talents, enterprise* &c.; **c** not restricted in amount or extent; unconditional: *unlimited liability*; *unlimited discretion, authority*; **d** unbounded; very great, excessive: *he has unlimited assurance, impudence.*
unlimitedly, adv. Prec. & **-ly.** In an unlimited manner.
unlimitedness, n. See prec. & **-ness.** State of being unlimited.
unline, vb. trans. [1. unlín; 2. anláin]. **un- (II.) & line (IV.).** To remove the lining from, take lining out of.
unlink, vb. trans. [1. unlíngk; 2. anlíŋk]. **un- (II.) & link (II.).** To undo, separate, unfasten the links of; separate that which is linked together.
unliquidated, adj. [1. unlíkwidāted; 2. anlíkwidèitid]. **un- (I.) & liquidate(d).** Not liquidated, (esp. law) of damages, not fixed or determined.
unlit, adj. [1. unlít; 2. anlít]. **un- (I.) & lit, P.P. of light.** Not lit; unlighted, dark.
unload, vb. trans. & intrans. [1. unlōd; 2. anlóud]. **un- (II.) & load.** **A. 1.** trans. **a** To remove the load, cargo &c. from: *to unload a ship, truck, cart* &c.; **b** also, to unload cargo from a ship, goods from a truck &c. **2.** To remove the charge from: *unload a gun*. **3.** (of stocks and shares) To get rid of one's holding, sell out. **B.** intrans. To discharge cargo, load: *the ships will unload tomorrow*.
unlocated, adj. [1. unlōkáted; 2. ànloukéitid]. **un- (I.) & locate(d).** Not located; unplaced; (U.S.A.) not surveyed.
unlock, vb. trans. [1. unlók; 2. anlók]. **un- (II.) & lock.** To undo, open, lock of (a locked door, box &c.); (fig.) *to unlock one's heart*, reveal one's feelings.
unlooked-for, adj. [1. unlóokt fôr; 2. anlúkt fō]. **un- (I.) & look(ed) & for.** Not looked-for; unexpected.
unloose, unloosen, vb. trans. [1. unlōōs(n); 2. anlús(n)]. **un- (II.) & loose(n).** To make loose; to loose; to set free.
unlovable, adj. [1. unlúvabl; 2. anlávəbl]. **un- (I.) & lovable.** Not lovable; not likely or worthy to be loved; not exciting love; disagreeable, repellent.

unloved, adj. [1. unlúvd; 2. anlávd]. un- (I.) & love(d). Not loved.

unloveliness, n. [1. unlúvlines; 2. anlávlinis]. unlovely & -ness. Ugliness.

unlovely, adj. [1. unlúvli; 2. anlávli]. un- (I.) & lovely. Not lovely; ugly, unpleasing, unattractive, in physical and moral senses.

unloverlike, adj. [1. unlúverlik; 2. anlávəlaik]. un- (I.) & loverlike. Not loverlike; not characteristic of, or like, (that of) a lover.

unloving, adj. [1. unlúving; 2. anláviŋ]. un- (I.) & loving. Not loving; not affectionate; cold, harsh.

unlovingly, adv. Prec. & -ly. In an unloving manner.

unluckily, adv. [1. unlúkili; 2. anlákili]. unlucky & -ly. In an unlucky manner; unfortunately.

unluckiness, n. [1. unlúkines; 2. anlákinis]. Next word & -ness. State of being unlucky.

unlucky, adj. [1. unlúki; 2. anláki]. un- (I.) & lucky. Not lucky; a unfortunate, unsuccessful; always meeting with bad luck: *an unlucky gambler*; *lucky at cards, unlucky in love*; **b** ill-omened, inauspicious, not bringing good luck; *Friday is an unlucky day*; *green is thought an unlucky colour*; **c** not happily chosen, ill-timed, inopportune: *an unlucky moment for their meeting*; *a most unlucky speech*.

unmade, adj. [1. unmád; 2. anméid]. un- (I.) & made, P.P. of make. Not made.

unmaidenly, adj. [1. unmádnli; 2. anméidnli]. un- (I.) & maidenly. Not maidenly, unbecoming a maiden; immodest.

unmaintainable, adj. [1. unmántánabl; 2. anmeintéinəbl]. un- (I.) & maintainable. Not maintainable.

unmake, vb. trans. [1. unmák; 2. anméik]. un- (II.) & make. To destroy what has been made; to change the form or qualities of; to annul.

unman, vb. trans. [1. unmán; 2. anmǽn]. un- (II.) & man. 1. To deprive of manly spirit, courage, fortitude &c.: *quite unmanned by the terrible news*, *by the sight* &c. 2. (rare) To deprive (a ship) of its crew.

unmanageable, adj. [1. unmánijabl; 2. anmǽnidžəbl]. un- (I.) & manageable. Not manageable; not easily controlled or regulated.

unmanlike, adj. [1. unmánlik; 2. anmǽnlaik]. un- (I.) & manlike. Not manlike; unlike mankind; not human.

unmanliness, n. [1. unmánlines; 2. anmǽnlinis]. unmanly & -ness. State of being unmanly.

unmanly, adj. [1. unmánli; 2. anmǽnli]. un- (I.) & manly. Not manly; cowardly; effeminate; womanly.

unmannerliness, n. [1. unmánerlines; 2. anmǽnəlinis]. See next word & -ness. State of being unmannerly.

unmannerly, adj. [1. unmánerli; 2. anmǽnəli]. un- (I.) & mannerly. Not mannerly; rude, ill-mannered, ill-bred.

unmarked, adj. [1. unmárkt; 2. anmǽkt]. un- (I.) & mark(ed). Not marked; a having no marks; **b** not noticed: *the mistake passed unmarked*.

unmarketable, adj. [1. unmárketabl; 2. anmǽkitəbl]. un- (I.) & marketable. Not marketable; not fit or suitable for market; unsalable.

unmarriageable, adj. [1. unmárijebl; 2. anmǽridžəbl]. un- (I.) & marriageable. Not marriageable; not fit or old enough for marriage.

unmarried, adj. [1. unmárid; 2. anmǽrid]. un- (I.) & married, P.P. of marry. Not married; single.

unmask, vb. trans. & intrans. [1. unmáhsk; 2. anmǽsk]. un- (II.) & mask. 1. trans. **a** To remove the mask from; to take a mask off; **b** to reveal true character of; to expose: *to unmask a traitor, his treachery*. 2. intrans. **a** To take off one's mask; **b** to reveal one's true character.

unmasked, adj. [1. unmáhskt; 2. anmǽskt]. P.P. of prec. **a** With mask removed; **b** revealed, exposed.

unmatchable, adj. [1. unmáchabl; 2. anmǽtʃəbl]. un- (I.) & match (II.) & -able. Not matchable; not to be matched.

unmatched, adj. [1. unmácht; 2. anmǽtʃt]. un- (I.) & match(ed). Not matched; matchless, without an equal.

unmated, adj. [1. unmáted; 2. anméitid]. un- (I.) & mate(d). Not mated; having no mate.

unmaterial, adj. [1. unmatérial; 2. anmətíəriəl]. un- (I.) & material. Not material; not composed of material, cp. *immaterial*.

unmaterialized, adj. [1. unmatérializd; 2. anmətíəriəlaizd]. un- (I.) & materialize(d). Not materialized; not in bodily shape or form; not fully developed.

unmatured, adj. [1. unmatúrd; 2. anmətjód]. un- (I.) & mature(d). (esp. of wine) Not matured; cp. *immature*.

unmeaning, adj. [1. unméning; 2. anmíniŋ]. un- (I.) & mean(ing). Empty of meaning or significance; senseless, meaningless.

unmeaningly, adv. Prec. & -ly. In an unmeaning manner.

unmeant, adj. [1. unmént; 2. anmént]. un- (I.) & mean(t). Not meant; unintended, unintentional.

unmeasured, adj. [1. unmézhurd; 2. anméžəd]. un- (I.) & measure(d). 1. Not measured. 2. **a** Boundless, limitless: *unmeasured tracts of desert*; **b** abundant, unstinted: *unmeasured liberality*. 3. Without due limits; immoderate, excessive: *unmeasured abuse*; *in unmeasured terms*.

unmechanical, adj. [1. unmekánikl; 2. anmikǽnikl]. un- (I.) & mechanical. Not mechanical.

unmeet, adj. [1. unmét; 2. anmít]. un- (I.) & meet (III.). Not meet or fit; unsuitable.

unmelodious, adj. [1. unmelódius; 2. anmilóudiəs]. un- (I.) & melodious. Not melodious; discordant, unmusical.

unmelodiously, adv. Prec. & -ly. In an unmelodious manner.

unmelodiousness, n. See prec. & -ness. Quality of being unmelodious.

unmentionable, adj. [1. unménshunabl; 2. anménʃənəbl]. un- (I.) & mentionable. Not mentionable; not fit to be mentioned; as n., (obs. or rare) *unmentionables*, facetious euphemism for 'trousers'.

unmerchantable, adj. [1. unmérchantabl; 2. anmǽtʃəntəbl]. un- (I.) & merchantable. Not merchantable; not fit for sale, through defect of quality, quantity &c.; unsalable, unmarketable.

unmerciful, adj. [1. unmérsifl; 2. anmǽsifl]. un- (I.) & merciful. Not merciful; showing no mercy; pitiless, cruel.

unmercifully, adv. Prec. & -ly. In an unmerciful manner; mercilessly.

unmerited, adj. [1. unmérited; 2. anméritid]. un- (I.) & merit(ed). Not merited; undeserved.

unmethodical, adj. [1. unmethódikl; 2. anmipódikl]. un- (I.) & methodical. Not methodical; lacking method; confused, muddled.

unmetrical, adj. [1. unmétrikl; 2. anmétrikl]. un- (I.) & metrical. Not metrical; not according to the rules of metre; not metrically arranged.

unmetrically, adv. Prec. & -ly. In an unmetrical manner.

unmilitary, adj. [1. unmílitari; 2. anmílitəri]. un- (I.) & military. Not military; not like or worthy of a soldier; unsoldierly.

unmindful, adj. [1. unmíndfl; 2. anmáindfl]. un- (I.) & mindful. Not mindful; forgetful; regardless.

unmindfully, adv. Prec. & -ly. In an unmindful manner.

unmistakable, adj. [1. unmistákabl; 2. anmistéikəbl]. un- (I.) & mistakable. Not mistakable; not to be mistaken; leaving no room for error or misunderstanding; clearly recognizable.

unmistakably, adv. Prec. & -ly. In an unmistakable manner.

unmitigated, adj. [1. unmítigáted; 2. anmítigèitid]. un- (I.) & mitigate(d). Not mitigated; unqualified, absolute: *an unmitigated nuisance*; *an unmitigated liar, blackguard* &c.

unmixed, adj. [1. unmíkst; 2. anmíkst]. un- (I.) & mix(ed). Not mixed; uniform in character throughout; pure, unqualified: *not an unmixed blessing*, a condition, situation, not entirely satisfactory.

unmodernized, adj. [1. unmódernizd; 2. anmódənaizd]. un- (I.) & modernize(d). Not modernized; not brought up to date, old-fashioned.

unmodified, adj. [1. unmódifíd; 2. anmódifaid]. un- (I.) & modified, P.P. of modify. Not modified; without modification.

unmolested, adj. [1. unmolésted; 2. anmouléstid]. un- (I.) & molest(ed). Not molested; left in peace.

unmoor, vb. trans. [1. unmór, móor; 2. anmó, -múə]. un- (I.) & moor (III.). To free (ship &c.) from moorings; to loose the moorings of; to weigh one of several anchors by which ship is moored.

unmoral, adj. [1. unmóral; 2. anmórəl]. un- (I.) & moral. Not moral; not concerned with, or related to, morals or morality; nonmoral; contrasted with *immoral*.

unmounted, adj. [1. unmóunted; 2. anmáuntid]. un- (I.) & mount & -ed. Not mounted. 1. Not on horseback; standing, going, on foot. 2. Not having a mount or setting, as a picture, jewellery &c.

unmourned, adj. [1. unmórnd; 2. anmónd]. un- (I.) & mourn(ed). Not mourned; unregretted.

unmoved, adj. [1. unmóovd; 2. anmúvd]. un- (I.) & move(d). Not moved (chiefly in moral sense); **a** not having feelings and emotions stirred; **b** not to be deflected or dissuaded from a purpose or determination.

unmoving, adj. [1. unmóoving; 2. anmúviŋ]. un- (I.) & moving. Not moving; a fixed, stationary, motionless; **b** not affecting, not arousing, feeling or emotion.

unmuffle, vb. trans. [1. unmúfl; 2. anmáfl]. un- (II.) & muffle. **a** To remove muffler, scarf, or other covering from the face, throat &c.; **b** to remove the muffling from a drum, bell, oars &c.

unmurmuring, adj. [1. unmérmering; 2. anmáməriŋ]. un- (I.) & Pres. Part. of murmur. Not murmuring; uncomplaining.

unmurmuringly, adv. Prec. & -ly. Without a murmur or complaint.

unmusical, adj. [1. unmúzikl; 2. anmjúzikl]. un- (I.) & musical. Not musical; a not pleasing, as music, to the ear; discordant (of sound, voice &c.); **b** not skilled or versed in, not caring for, indifferent to, music.

unmusically, adv. Prec. & -ly. In an unmusical manner.

unmutilated, adj. [1. unmútiláted; 2. anmjútilèitid]. un- (I.) & mutilate(d). Not mutilated.

unmuzzle, vb. trans. [1. unmúzl; 2. anmázl]. un- (II.) & muzzle. **a** To remove the muzzle from, to free (dog &c.) from a muzzle; **b** (fig.) to allow to speak freely, to remove restrictions on utterance or expression of opinions &c.: *the Press is unmuzzled at last*.

unnail, vb. trans. [1. unnál; 2. annéil]. un- (II.) & nail. To remove the nails from; to unfasten that which is nailed.

unnamable, adj. [1. unnámabl; 2. annéiməbl]. un- (I.) & namable. Not namable; not to be named or described.

unnamed, adj. [1. unnámd; 2. annéimd]. un- (I.) & name(d). Not named; having no name; not mentioned.

unnatural, adj. [1. unnáchural; 2. annǽtʃərəl]. un- (I.) & natural. 1. Not natural; **a** contrary to, violating, the laws or common order of nature; monstrous: *unnatural crimes* &c.; **b** not in accordance with what usually happens; not to be expected, out of the

ordinary course: *it is unnatural not to love one's children*. 2. Not exhibiting normal, natural feelings: *an unnatural parent, child* &c.

unnaturalized, adj. [1. unnáchurǎlĭzd; 2. annǽtʃərəlàizd]. un- (I.) & naturalize(d). Not naturalized.

unnaturally, adv. [1. unnáchurali; 2. annǽtʃərəli]. unnatural & -ly. In an unnatural manner.

unnaturalness, n. [1. unnáchuralnes; 2. annǽtʃərəlnis]. See prec. & -ness. State of being unnatural.

unnavigable, adj. [1. unnávigabl; 2. annǽvigəbl]. un- (I.) & navigable. Not navigable.

unnecessarily, adv. [1. unnésesarili; 2. annésisərili]. unnecessary & -ly. In an unnecessary manner.

unnecessariness, n. [1. unnésesarines; 2. annésisərinis]. See prec. & -ness. State of being unnecessary.

unnecessary, adj. & n. [1. unnésesari; 2. annésis(ə)ri]. un- (I.) & necessary. 1. adj. Not necessary; superfluous; not required by the circumstances of the case; needless, useless. 2. n. (rare, usually pl.) Things which are unnecessary.

unneeded, adj. [1. unnḗded; 2. annī́dĭd]. un- (I.) & need(ed). Not needed; needless; unwanted.

unneedful, adj. [1. unnḗdfl; 2. annī́dfl]. un- (I.) & needful. Not needful; not requisite; not indispensable.

unneedfully, adv. Prec. & -ly. In an unneedful manner.

unnegotiable, adj. [1. unnegṓshiabl; 2. annigóuʃiəbl]. un- (I.) & negotiable. Not negotiable; not to be negotiated, esp. of bills of exchange &c.

unneighbourliness, n. [1. unnáburlines; 2. annéibəlinis]. See next word & -ness. Quality of being unneighbourly.

unneighbourly, adj. [1. unnáburli; 2. annéibəli]. un- (I.) & neighbourly. Not neighbourly; unfriendly, unsociable.

unnerve, vb. trans. [1. unnḗrv; 2. annv̄́v]. un- (II.) & nerve. To deprive of, cause to lose, nerve; to unman.

unnerved, adj. [1. unnḗrvd; 2. annv̄́vd]. P.P. of prec. Deprived of nerve; having lost one's courage.

unnoted, adj. [1. unnṓted; 2. annṓutid]. un- (I.) & note(d). Not noted; unheeded; unmarked.

unnoticed, adj. [1. unnṓtist; 2. annṓutist]. un- (I.) & notice(d). Not noticed; unobserved.

unnourished, adj. [1. unnúrisht; 2. annáriʃt]. un- (I.) & nourish(ed). Not nourished, insufficiently nourished.

unnumbered, adj. [1. unnúmberd; 2. annámbəd]. un- (I.) & number(ed). Not numbered, uncounted; innumerable, countless.

unobjectionable, adj. [1. unobjékshunabl; 2. ànəbdʒékʃənəbl]. un- (I.) & objectionable. Not objectionable; not open to objection; inoffensive.

unobliging, adj. [1. unoblíjing; 2. ànəbláidʒiŋ]. un- (I.) & obliging. Not obliging; disobliging.

unobliterated, adj. [1. unóblíterāted; 2. ànoublítərèitid]. un- (I.) & obliterate(d). Not obliterated.

unobscured, adj. [1. unobskúrd; 2. ànəbskjṓd]. un- (I.) & obscure(d). Not obscured.

unobservant, adj. [1. unobzérvant; 2. ànəbzv̄́vənt]. un- (I.) & observant. Not observant; lacking powers of observation.

unobtainable, adj. [1. unobtánabl; 2. ànəbtéinəbl]. un- (I.) & obtainable. Not obtainable; out of one's reach.

unobtrusive, adj. [1. unobtrṓsiv; 2. ànəbtrū́siv]. un- (I.) & obtrusive. Not obtrusive; modest, retiring.

unobtrusively, adv. Prec. & -ly. In an unobtrusive manner.

unobtrusiveness, n. See prec. & -ness. State, quality, of being unobtrusive.

unoccupied, adj. [1. unókŭpīd; 2. anókjupaid]. un- (I.) & occupied, P.P. of occupy. Not occupied; a (of house, seat &c.) untenanted; b (of persons) disengaged.

unoffending, adj. [1. unoféndĭng; 2. ànəféndiŋ]. un- (I.) & offending. Not offending; harmless, inoffensive.

unofficial, adj. [1. unofíshl; 2. ànəfíʃl]. un- (I.) & official. Not official; not announced through official channels.

unofficially, adv. Prec. & -ly. In an unofficial manner; not officially.

unopened, adj. [1. unṓpend; 2. anṓupənd]. un- (I.) & open(ed). Not opened; closed, shut.

unoperated, adj. [1. unóperāted; 2. anópəreitid]. un- (I.) & operate(d). Not operated, not worked; not in operation or at work.

unopposed, adj. [1. unopṓzd; 2. anəpóuzd]. un- (I.) & oppose(d). Not opposed.

unorganized, adj. [1. unórganīzd; 2. anṓgənàizd]. un- (I.) & organize(d). Not organized; specif. (biol.) lacking organic structure.

unoriginal, adj. [1. unoríjinal; 2. ànərídʒinəl]. un- (I.) & original. Not original; having no originality; derived from other sources; derivative, imitative.

unornamental, adj. [1. unornaméntl; 2. ànōnəméntl]. un- (I.) & ornamental. Not ornamental; plain; ugly, unsightly.

unorthodox, adj. [1. unórthodoks; 2. anṓpədɔks]. un- (I.) & orthodox. Not orthodox.

unostentatious, adj. [1. unostentáshus; 2. ànɔstentéiʃəs]. un- (I.) & ostentatious. Not ostentatious; unassuming; not boastful; not showy or glaring.

unostentatiously, adv. Prec. & -ly. In an unostentatious manner.

unostentatiousness, n. See prec. & -ness. Quality of being unostentatious.

unowed, adj. [1. unṓd; 2. anṓud]. un- (I.) & owe(d). Not owed, not due.

unowned, adj. [1. unṓnd; 2. anṓund]. un- (I.) & own(ed). Not owned; without a master; unacknowledged.

unpacified, adj. [1. unpásifīd; 2. anpǽsifaid]. un- (I.) & pacified, P.P. of pacify. Not pacified; not subdued or at peace.

unpack, vb. trans. & intrans. [1. unpák; 2. anpǽk]. un- (II.) & pack. 1. trans. a To open and take out the contents of: *to unpack a trunk, box, package* &c.; b to take out from trunk or package: *to unpack one's clothes, the wedding presents* &c. 2. intrans. To carry out the process of unpacking trunks &c.: *I shan't unpack until tomorrow morning*.

unpacked, adj. [1. unpákt; 2. anpǽkt]. P.P. of prec. Removed from trunk &c.; emptied of contents.

unpaged, adj. [1. unpájd; 2. anpéidʒd]. un- (I.) & page(d). Not paged; not having the pages numbered.

unpaid, adj. [1. unpád; 2. anpéid]. un- (I.) & P.P. of pay. Not paid. 1. (of bills, debt &c.) Not discharged, not cancelled by payment. 2. (of persons, office &c.) a Not receiving payment; without salary or wages: *an unpaid secretary*; b not paid for, performed gratuitously: *unpaid work* &c.

unpaired, adj. [1. unpárd; 2. anpéəd]. un- (I.) & pair(ed). Not paired; specif., not having arranged for a parliamentary 'pair', or member voting in the opposite sense to oneself, in an approaching division.

unpalatable, adj. [1. unpálatabl; 2. anpǽlətəbl]. un- (I.) & palatable. Not palatable; a disagreeable, unpleasing, to the taste; nasty: *unpalatable medicine* &c.; b displeasing to the mind, offensive to the susceptibilities: *they must be told the truth, however unpalatable it may be*.

unpalatably, adv. Prec. & -ly. In an unpalatable manner.

unparalleled, adj. [1. unpárạlèld; 2. anpǽrəlèld]. un- (I.) & parallel(ed). Not to be paralleled; incomparable; unprecedented.

unpardonable, adj. [1. unpárdunabl; 2. anpā́d(ə)nəbl]. un- (I.) & pardonable. (of conduct, actions) Not pardonable; not deserving pardon; inexcusable.

unpardonably, adv. Prec. & -ly. In an unpardonable manner.

unparental, adj. [1. unparéntl; 2. ànpəréntl]. un- (I.) & parental. Not parental; unlike, unworthy of, a father or mother.

unparented, adj. [1. unpárented; 2. anpéərəntid]. un- (I.) & (II.) & parent(ed). Without a parent; orphaned; deserted by the parents.

unparliamentary, adj. [1. unparlaméntari; 2. ànpāləméntəri]. un- (I.) & parliamentary. Not parliamentary; not permissible in parliament; contrary to the usage, rules &c. of parliament; esp. *unparliamentary language*, abuse, strong language in general.

unpatriotic, adj. [1. unpatriótik; 2. ànpætriṓtik]. un- (I.) & patriotic. Not patriotic.

unpatriotically, adv. [1. unpatriótikali; 2. ànpætriótikəli]. Prec. & -al & -ly. In an unpatriotic manner.

unpatronized, adj. [1. unpátrunīzd; 2. anpǽtrənàizd]. un- (I.) & patronize(d). Not patronized.

unpaved, adj. [1. unpávd; 2. anpéivd]. un- (I.) & pave(d). Not paved; without paving or pavement.

unpeaceful, adj. [1. unpḗsfl; 2. anpī́sfl]. un- (I.) & peaceful. Not peaceful, not at peace or at rest; restless, unquiet.

unpedantic, adj. [1. unpedántik; 2. ànpidǽntik]. un- (I.) & pedantic. Not pedantic.

unpedigreed, adj. [1. unpédigrēd; 2. anpédigrīd]. un- (I.) & pedigree(d). Having no pedigree.

unpeg, vb. trans. [1. unpég; 2. anpég]. un- (II.) & peg (II.). To remove the pegs from; to unfasten what is pegged down or pegged together; specif. (of prices, currency &c.) to remove regulations fixing or pegging prices &c.

unpen, vb. trans. [1. unpén; 2. anpén]. un- (II.) & pen (I.). To release, as sheep &c., from a pen.

unpensioned, adj. [1. unpénshund; 2. anpénʃənd]. un- (I.) & pension(ed). Not pensioned; not eligible for a pension; not receiving a pension.

unpeople, vb. trans. [1. unpḗpl; 2. anpī́pl]. un- (II.) & people (II.). To remove the population from; to depopulate.

unpeopled, adj. [1. unpḗpld; 2. anpī́pld]. un- (I.) & people(d). Not populated.

unperceived, adj. [1. unpersévd; 2. ànpəsī́vd]. un- (I.) & perceive(d). Not perceived; unnoticed.

unperforated, adj. [1. unpérforāted; 2. anpā́fəreitid]. un- (I.) & perforate(d). Not perforated; specif., of older issues of postage-stamps, having no perforations to enable one stamp to be torn from those next it in the sheet.

unperformed, adj. [1. unperfórmd; 2. ànpəfṓmd]. un- (I.) & perform(ed). Not performed; not done or carried out.

unperjured, adj. [1. unpérjurd; 2. anpv̄́dʒəd]. un- (I.) & perjure(d). Not perjured.

unpersuadable, adj. [1. unpérswādabl; 2. ànpāswéidəbl]. un- (I.) & persuadable. Not persuadable; not to be persuaded; not open to persuasion.

unpersuaded, adj. [1. unpérswāded; 2. ànpāswéidid]. un- (I.) & persuade(d). Not persuaded.

unpersuasive, adj. [1. unpérswásiv; 2. ànpāswéisiv]. un- (I.) & persuasive. Not persuasive.

unperturbed, adj. [1. unpertérbd; 2. ànpətv̄́bd]. un- (I.) & perturb(ed). Not perturbed; unruffled, calm, undisturbed; not alarmed.

unperused, adj. [1. unperṓozd; 2. anpirū́zd]. un- (I.) & peruse(d). Not perused; not read through.

unphilosophical, adj. [1. unfilosófikl; 2. ànfiləsófikl]. un- (I.) & philosophical. Not philosophical; wanting in philosophy; contrary to philosophical principles.

unphilosophically, adv. Prec. & -ly. In an unphilosophical manner.

unphilosophicalness, n. See prec. & -ness. State of being unphilosophical.

unpick, vb. trans. [1. unpík; 2. anpík]. un- (II.) & pick (II.). To undo, loosen, unfasten, remove (stitches &c.) by picking.

unpicked (I.), adj. [1. unpíkt; 2. anpíkt]. P.P. of prec. Picked loose; unfastened by picking.

unpicked (II.), adj. un- (I.) & pick(ed). a Not picked out, not selected or chosen; b (of flowers) not picked, plucked, or gathered.

unpiloted, adj. [1. unpíloted; 2. anpáilətid]. un- (I.) & pilot(ed). Not piloted; not guided by a pilot; (also fig.) undirected, unguided.

unpin, vb. trans. [1. unpín; 2. anpín]. un- (II.) & pin (II.). To unfasten what is pinned together; to remove pins from.

unpitied, adj. [1. unpítid; 2. anpítid]. un- (I.) & P.P. of pity. Not pitied; having received no pity: 'Thy fate unpitied, and thy rites unpaid' (Pope, 'Unfortunate Lady', 48).

unpitying, adj. [1. unpíti-ing; 2. anpíti-iŋ]. un- (I.) & Pres. Part. of pity. Feeling no pity; callous, remorseless.

unpityingly, adv. Prec. & -ly. In an unpitying manner.

unplaced, adj. [1. unplást; 2. anpléist]. un- (I.) & place(d). Not placed; (esp. of horses) not placed among the first three in a race.

unplait, vb. trans. [1. unplát; 2. anplǽt]. un- (II.) & plait (II.). To unfasten the plaits of, as hair &c.

unplanned, adj. [1. unplánd; 2. anplǽnd]. un- (I.) & plan(ned). Not planned; not provided for in plans; not properly thought out.

unplanted, adj. [1. unpláhnted; 2. anplántid]. un- (I.) & plant(ed). Not planted.

unplausible, adj. [1. unpláwzibl; 2. anplózibl]. un- (I.) & plausible. Not plausible.

unplausibly, adv. Prec. & -ly. In an unplausible manner.

unplayable, adj. [1. unpláabl; 2. anpléiəbl]. un- (I.) & playable. Not playable; a of a ball at cricket or tennis, that cannot be played or effectively taken and dealt with by the player receiving it; b (of ground) not fit to play on.

unpleasant, adj. [1. unplézant; 2. anplézənt]. un- (I.) & pleasant. Not pleasant; a disagreeable, offensive, causing disgust, discomfort, or repulsion to any of the senses: *an unpleasant sight, smell, voice &c.*; b provoking moral disapproval or dislike; shocking the taste, the sense of propriety: *an unpleasant person; unpleasant manners; an unpleasant subject.*

unpleasantly, adv. Prec. & -ly. In an unpleasant manner.

unpleasantness, n. See prec. & -ness. State or quality of being unpleasant. 1. a Lack of positive or good qualities; sense of want of external beauty, comfort, charm &c.: *the unpleasantness of a neighbourhood, landscape*; b presence of repellent and disgusting physical qualities or properties: *the unpleasantness of a smell, sight &c.* 2. Qualities or conditions which shock, repel, disgust the mind, something which offends the taste, sense of propriety &c.: *the unpleasantness of a person's manners.* 3. Lack of agreement between persons; disagreement, misunderstanding, friction, quarrel: *we have had a slight unpleasantness with our landlady.*

unpleasing, adj. [1. unplézing; 2. anplíziŋ]. un- (I.) & pleasing. Not pleasing; not giving pleasure, disagreeable, unattractive.

unpledged, adj. [1. unpléjd; 2. anplédžd]. un- (I.) & pledge(d). a Not pledged; not promised; b not pawned.

unpliable, adj. [1. unplíabl; 2. anpláiəbl]. un- (I.) & pliable. Not pliable (in lit. and fig. senses).

unpliant, adj. [1. unplíant; 2. anpláiənt]. un- (I.) & pliant. Not pliant; stiff, stubborn.

unploughed, adj. [1. unplóud; 2. anpláud]. un- (I.) & plough(ed). Not ploughed; not tilled or cultivated.

unplug, vb. trans. [1. unplúg; 2. anplág]. un- (II.) & plug (II.). To remove the plug from.

unplugged, adj. [1. unplúgd; 2. anplágd]. un- (I.) & plug(ged). Not plugged.

unplumbed, adj. [1. unplúmd; 2. anplámd]. un- (I.) & plumb(ed). Not plumbed, unfathomed (lit. and fig.): *unplumbed depths of ignorance.*

unpoetical, adj. [1. unpóetikl; 2. anpouétikl]. un- (I.) & poetical. Not poetical; prosaic.

unpoetically, adv. Prec. & -ly. In an unpoetical manner.

unpointed, adj. [1. unpóinted; 2. anpóintid]. un- (I.) & pointed. Not pointed. 1. Without a point; blunt. 2. Without vowel points or diacritical marks. 3. (of joints between the stones or bricks in masonry) Not pointed by an external streak of mortar or cement.

unpolished, adj. [1. unpólisht; 2. anpólişt]. un- (I.) & polish(ed). Not polished; (in lit. and fig. senses): *unpolished stone, style, manners &c.*

unpolitical, adj. [1. unpólítikl; 2. anpoulítikl]. un- (I.) & political. Not political; not interested in or concerned with politics; cp. *impolitic.*

unpolled, adj. [1. unpóld; 2. anpóuld]. un- (I.) & poll(ed). Not polled; specif. (of voters) not having cast a vote; (of votes) not cast or registered at the polling station.

unpolluted, adj. [1. unpolúted; 2. anpɔljútid]. un- (I.) & pollute(d). Free from pollution; pure.

unpopular, adj. [1. unpópular; 2. anpópjulə]. un- (I.) & popular. Not popular; not a general favourite; out of popular favour or fashion.

unpopularity, n. [1. unpopuláriti; 2. anpɔpjuláriti]. Prec. & -ity. State of being unpopular; popular disfavour.

unpopularly, adv. [1. unpópularli; 2. anpópjuləli]. See prec. & -ly. In an unpopular manner.

unpossessed, adj. [1. unpozést; 2. anpəzést]. un- (I.) & possess(ed). a Not possessed; not owned, not held in possession; b *unpossessed of*, not in possession (of).

unposted, adj. [1. unpósted; 2. anpóustid]. un- (I.) & post(ed). Not posted. 1. Not placed in or delivered to the post. 2. Not posted up, not in possession of information; uninformed.

unpractical, adj. [1. unpráktikl; 2. anpræktikl]. un- (I.) & practical. Not practical; cp. *impracticable.*

unpracticality, n. [1. unpraktikáliti; 2. anpræktikæliti]. Prec. & -ity. State of being unpractical.

unpractically, adv. [1. unpráktikali; 2. anpræktikəli]. See prec. & -ly. In an unpractical manner.

unpractised, adj. [1. unpráktist; 2. anpræktist]. un- (I.) & practise(d). Not practised; a not put into practice; b unskilled, inexperienced.

unprecedented, adj. [1. unprésédentid; 2. anprésidèntid]. un- (I.) & precedented. Without a precedent; for which there is no prior example; unparalleled; novel.

unprecedentedly, adv. Prec. & -ly. In an unprecedented manner.

unpredicted, adj. [1. unprédíkted; 2. anpridíktid]. un- (I.) & predict & -ed. Not predicted.

unprefaced, adj. [1. unpréfast; 2. anpréfist]. un- (I.) & preface(d). Not prefaced; a without a preface; b without warning or introduction.

unprejudiced, adj. [1. unpréjudist; 2. anprédžudist]. un- (I.) & prejudice & -ed. Not prejudiced; free from, without, prejudice, or bias; impartial, fair.

unpremeditated, adj. [1. unprémédítèited; 2. anprímédiːtèitid]. un- (I.) & premeditate(d). Not premeditated; done &c. without premeditation; not deliberately planned or thought out previously; unprepared.

unprepared, adj. [1. unprepárd; 2. anpripéəd]. un- (I.) & prepare(d). Not prepared; a done without preparation; impromptu: *an unprepared retort, reception*; b not ready: *you caught me unprepared.*

unpreparedness, n. [1. unprepár(e)dnes; 2. anpripéə(r)dnis]. Prec. & -ness. State of being unprepared.

unprepossessing, adj. [1. unprèpozésing; 2. anprìpəzésiŋ]. un- (I.) & prepossessing. Not prepossessing; unattractive, unpleasing.

unpresentable, adj. [1. unprezéntabl; 2. anprizéntəbl]. un- (I.) & presentable. Not presentable; specif. a not suitable to present in refined and highly civilized society; ill-mannered, ill-bred, ungentlemanlike; b unattractive in appearance; plain, ill-favoured.

unpresuming, adj. [1. unprezúming; 2. anprizjúmiŋ]. un- (I.) & presuming. Not presuming; without presumption; unassuming; modest.

unpresumptuous, adj. [1. unprezúmptūus; 2. anprizámptjuəs]. un- (I.) & presumptuous. Not presumptuous.

unpretending, adj. [1. unpreténding; 2. anpriténdiŋ]. un- (I.) & pretend & -ing. Not making pretences; not pretending to be what one is not; unassuming; modest, humble.

unpretendingly, adv. Prec. & -ly. In an unpretending manner.

unpretentious, adj. [1. unpreténshus; 2. anpriténʃəs]. un- (I.) & pretentious. Not pretentious.

unpretentiously, adv. Prec. & -ly. In an unpretentious manner.

unpreventable, adj. [1. unprevéntabl; 2. anprivéntəbl]. un- (I.) & preventable. Not preventable; not to be prevented, inevitable.

unpriced, adj. [1. unpríst; 2. anpráist]. un- (I.) & price(d). Having no fixed price; without prices stated or marked.

unpriestly, adj. [1. unpréstli; 2. anprístli]. un- (I.) & priestly. Not priestly; a not like a priest; b not characteristic of, not befitting, a priest.

unprincely, adj. [1. unprínsli; 2. anprínsli]. un- (I.) & princely. Not princely; not worthy of, not befitting, a prince.

unprincipled, adj. [1. unprínsipld; 2. anprínsipld]. un- (I.) & principle(d). a Having no fixed moral principles; unscrupulous, dishonest: *an unprincipled rogue*; b not based on, governed, or dictated by, not in accordance with, moral principles: *unprincipled conduct.*

unprintable, adj. [1. unpríntabl; 2. anpríntəbl]. un- (I.) & printable. Not printable; too indecent or profane to be printed.

unprinted, adj. [1. unpríntéd; 2. anpríntid]. un- (I.) & print & -ed. Not printed; existing only in MS. form.

unprivileged, adj. [1. unprívilejd; 2. anprívilidžd]. un- (I.) & privilege(d). Not privileged; without special privileges.

unprized, adj. [1. unprízd; 2. anpráizd]. un- (I.) & prize(d). Not prized; not valued highly.

unprobed, adj. [1. unpróbd; 2. anpróubd]. un- (I.) & probe(d). Not probed; (chiefly fig.) not looked into, not examined, thoroughly.

unproclaimed, adj. [1. unproklámd; 2. anprokléimd]. un- (I.) & proclaim(ed). Not proclaimed; unannounced.

unprocurable, adj. [1. unprokŭrabl; 2. anprɔkjŏrəbl]. un- (I.) & procurable. Not procurable; not to be procured.

unproductive, adj. [1. unprodúktiv; 2. anprədáktiv]. un- (I.) & productive. Not productive; barren; unprofitable; ineffective.

unproductively, adv. Prec. & -ly. In an unproductive manner.

unproductiveness, n. See prec. & -ness. State of being unproductive.

unprofaned, adj. [1. unprofánd; 2. anproféind]. un- (I.) & profane(d). Not profaned: '*thy cheek unprofaned by a tear*' (T. Moore).

unprofessional, adj. [1. ŭnproféshunal ; 2. ănprəféʃənəl]. un- (I.) & **professional**. Not professional. **1.** Not having a profession ; not belonging to a specified, or to any, profession : *unprofessional people ; the unprofessional mind*. **2.** Contrary to the rules, etiquette &c. of a profession : *unprofessional conduct*.

unprofessionally, adv. Prec. & -ly. From an unprofessional point of view ; in an unprofessional manner.

unprofitable, adj. [1. unprófitabl ; 2. anprófitəbl]. un- (I.) & **profitable**. Not profitable ; **a** yielding no profit ; entailing loss ; **b** yielding no advantage or favourable results.

unprofitably, adv. Prec. & -ly. In an unprofitable manner.

unprogressive, adj. [1. ŭnprogrésiv ; 2. ănprəgrésiv]. un- (I.) & **progressive**. Not progressive ; not in favour of social or political progress ; reactionary.

unprolific, adj. [1. ŭnprolífik ; 2. ănprəlífik]. un- (I.) & **prolific**. Not prolific ; infertile.

unpromising, adj. [1. unprómising ; 2. ănprómisiŋ]. un- (I.) & **promising**. Not promising ; not likely to be successful ; not holding out good prospects.

unprompted, adj. [1. unprómpted ; 2. ănprómptid]. un- (I.) & **prompt(ed)**. Not prompted ; without prompting, spontaneous, on one's own initiative.

unpronounceable, adj. [1. ŭnpronóunsabl ; 2. ănprənáunsəbl]. un- (I.) & **pronounceable**. Not pronounceable ; difficult, or impossible, to pronounce.

unprop, vb. trans. [1. unpróp ; 2. anpróp]. un- (II.) & **prop**. To remove the props, or support, from ; to deprive of support.

unprophetic, adj. [1. ŭnprofétik ; 2. ănprəfétik]. un- (I.) & **prophetic**. Not prophetic.

unpropitious, adj. [1. unpropíshus ; 2. ănprəpíʃəs]. un- (I.) & **propitious**. Not propitious ; inauspicious ; ill-omened ; unlucky.

unpropitiously, adv. Prec. & -ly. In an unpropitious manner.

unpropitiousness, n. See prec. & -ness. State of being unpropitious.

unproportional, adj. [1. ŭnpropórshunal ; 2. ănprəpóʃənəl]. un- (I.) & **proportional**. Not proportional.

unprosperous, adj. [1. unprósperus ; 2. ănprósperəs]. un- (I.) & **prosperous**. Not prosperous.

unprotected, adj. [1. unprotékted ; 2. ănprətéktid]. un- (I.) & **protect(ed)**. **1.** Lacking protection or a protector ; liable to attack or molestation : *an unprotected female*. **2.** Not fortified, or armoured : *an unprotected town, cruiser*. **3.** Specif., not protected by a tariff : *unprotected industries*.

unprotested, adj. [1. unprotésted ; 2. ănprətéstid]. un- (I.) & **protest(ed)**. Not protested, esp. of bills of exchange.

unprovable, adj. [1. unproóvabl ; 2. anprúvəbl]. un- (I.) & **provable**. Not provable ; incapable of proof.

unproved, adj. [1. unproóvd ; 2. anprúvd]. un- (I.) & **prove(d)**. Not proved.

unprovided, adj. [1. ŭnprovíded ; 2. ănprəváidid]. un- (I.) & **provide(d)**. Not provided ; **a** not supplied, or furnished with ; **b** not ready, not prepared for.

unprovoked, adj. [1. ŭnprovókt ; 2. ănprəvóukt]. un- (I.) & **provoke(d)**. Not provoked ; done without provocation : *an unprovoked assault* &c.

unpublished, adj. [1. unpúblisht ; 2. anpábliʃt]. un- (I.) & **publish(ed)**. Not published ; **a** not made public or generally known ; **b** not printed and published.

unpucker, vb. trans. [1. unpúker ; 2. anpákə]. un- (II.) & **pucker**. To remove, get rid of, puckers or wrinkles from.

unpunctual, adj. [1. unpúngkchooal ; 2. anpáŋktʃuəl]. un- (I.) & **punctual**. Not punctual ; not up to time for appointments &c. ; arriving, doing something, happening, after the hour fixed.

unpunctuality, n. [1. ŭnpungkchooáliti ; 2. ănpáŋktʃuæliti]. Prec. & -ity. State, quality, of being unpunctual.

unpunctually, adv. [1. unpúngkchooali ; 2. anpáŋktʃuəli]. See prec. & -ly. So as to be unpunctual.

unpunctuated, adj. [1. unpúngkchooāted ; 2. anpáŋktʃuèitid]. un- (I.) & **punctuate** & -ed. Not punctuated ; without stops or marks of punctuation.

unpunishable, adj. [1. unpúnishabl ; 2. anpániʃəbl]. un- (I.) & **punishable**. Not punishable ; not entailing punishment.

unpunished, adj. [1. unpúnisht ; 2. anpániʃt]. un- (I.) & **punish(ed)**. Not punished ; having escaped punishment.

unpurchasable, adj. [1. unpérchasabl ; 2. anpə́tʃəsəbl]. un- (I.) & **purchasable**. Not purchasable, not to be bought at any price.

unpurged, adj. [1. unpérjd ; 2. anpə́dʒd]. un- (I.) & **purge(d)**. Not purged ; esp., of crimes or offences &c., not cleared or atoned for by confession, and submission to a sentence by a court of law.

unpurified, adj. [1. unpúrifīd ; 2. anpjórifaid]. un- (I.) & P.P. of **purify**. Not purified.

unpuzzle, vb. trans. [1. unpúzl ; 2. anpázl]. un- (II.) & **puzzle** (I.). To puzzle out, decipher, solve (a puzzle, problem &c.).

unquailing, adj. [1. unkwáling ; 2. ankwéiliŋ]. un- (I.) & **quail(ing)**. Not quailing, not shrinking from or before.

unqualified, adj. [1. unkwólifīd ; 2. ankwólifaid]. un- (I.) & P.P. of **qualify**. Not qualified. **1.** Without the necessary legal, or natural, qualifications for : *an unqualified medical practitioner* ; *to be unqualified to teach, preach, advise others*. **2.** Not modified, not restricted by qualifications, exceptions &c., absolute : *an unqualified assertion, denial, statement* ; (also colloq.) downright : *he is an unqualified liar*.

unquelled, adj. [1. unkwéld ; 2. ankwéld]. un- (I.) & **quell(ed)**. Not quelled ; not put down.

unquenchable, adj. [1. unkwénchabl ; 2. ankwéntʃəbl]. un- (I.) & **quenchable**. Not quenchable ; not to be quenched : *unquenchable thirst, enthusiasm* &c.

unquenchably, adv. Prec. & -ly. In an unquenchable manner.

unquestionable, adj. [1. unkwéschunabl ; 2. ankwéstʃənəbl]. un- (I.) & **questionable**. Not questionable, not to be questioned or doubted ; indisputable, certain.

unquestionably, adv. Prec. & -ly. In an unquestionable manner ; undoubtedly ; to a degree, in a manner, beyond all question.

unquestioned, adj. [1. unkwéschund ; 2. ankwéstʃənd]. un- (I.) & **question(ed)**. Not questioned ; not called in question ; undoubted ; not examined or disputed.

unquestioning, adj. [1. unkwéschuning ; 2. ankwéstʃəniŋ]. un- (I.) & **question(ing)**. Not questioning ; asking no questions, unhesitating ; without questions asked : *his unquestioning supporters* ; *their unquestioning loyalty*.

unquestioningly, adv. Prec. & -ly. In an unquestioning manner ; without question or hesitation.

unquiet, adj. [1. unkwíet ; 2. ankwáiət]. un- (II.) & **quiet**. Not quiet ; restless, disturbed, uneasy : *unquiet minds* ; *an unquiet age*.

unquietly, adv. Prec. & -ly. In an unquiet manner.

unquietness, n. See prec. & -ness. State, quality, of being unquiet.

unquotable, adj. [1. unkwótabl ; 2. ankwóutəbl]. un- (I.) & **quotable**. Not quotable ; not suitable for quotation ; unfit to be quoted or repeated.

unquoted, adj. [1. unkwóted ; 2. ankwóutid]. un- (I.) & **quote(d)**. Not quoted.

unransomed, adj. [1. unránsumd ; 2. anrǽnsəmd]. un- (I.) & **ransom(ed)**. Not ransomed.

unrated, adj. [1. unráted ; 2. anréitid]. un- (I.) & **rate(d)**. Not rated. **1.** Not subject to a local or other rate. **2.** Not included in a rate or class.

unravaged, adj. [1. unrávijd ; 2. anrǽvidʒd]. un- (I.) & **ravage(d)**. Not ravaged ; not plundered or devastated.

unravel, vb. trans. [1. unrávl ; 2. anrǽvl]. un- (II.) & **ravel**. **1.** To disentangle, separate (what is ravelled or tangled together) : *to unravel a skein of wool, the threads of a tangled skein* &c. **2.** (fig.) To clear up, to solve (a mystery &c.) : *to unravel a plot (of story* &c.).

unreachable, adj. [1. unréchabl ; 2. anrítʃəbl]. un- (I.) & **reachable**. Not reachable ; not to be reached ; unattainable.

unread, adj. [1. unréd ; 2. anréd]. un- (I.) & P.P. of **read**. Not read ; **a** (of books) not perused ; **b** (of persons) not well read ; not scholarly ; unlearned ; illiterate.

unreadable, adj. [1. unrédabl ; 2. anrídəbl]. un- (I.) & **readable**. Not readable. **1.** Illegible : *unreadable handwriting*. **2.** (of book, style &c.) Not attractive to read ; impossible, difficult, to read without boredom ; dull, uninteresting. **3.** Not fit to be read.

unreadily, adv. [1. unrédili ; 2. anrédili]. un**ready** & -ly. In an unready manner ; without readiness or promptitude.

unreadiness, n. [1. unrédines ; 2. anrédinis]. See next word & -ness. State, quality, of being unready.

unready, adj. [1. unrédi ; 2. anrédi]. un- (I.) & **ready**. Not ready. **1.** Not prepared. **2.** Not quick in mental reactions ; not prompt, slow, lacking alertness of mind.

unreal, adj. [1. unréal ; 2. anríəl]. un- (I.) & **real**. Not real ; not based on reality ; imagined, visionary, unsubstantial.

unreality, n. [1. unréaliti ; 2. anríæliti]. Prec. & -ity. State of being unreal ; want of reality.

unrealizable, adj. [1. unrealízabl, unrélizabl ; 2. anrí əláizəbl, anrí əlaizəbl]. un- (I.) & **realizable**. Incapable of being realized ; illusory.

unrealized, adj. [1. unréalīzd ; 2. anrí əlaizd]. un- (I.) & **realize(d)**. Not realized ; unfulfilled.

unreally, adv. [1. unréali ; 2. anríəli]. **unreal** & -ly. In an unreal manner.

unreason, n. [1. unrézn ; 2. anrízn]. un- (I.) & **reason**. Lack of reason ; stupidity, folly, absurdity.

unreasonable, adj. [1. unrézunabl ; 2. anríznəbl]. un- (I.) & **reasonable**. Not reasonable. **1.** Not animated by, amenable to, reason ; acting on impulse, without taking full account of circumstances and conditions ; making extravagant claims ; capricious ; expecting more than can reasonably be looked for : *an unreasonable person*. **2.** Not governed by reason : *unreasonable conduct*. **3.** Beyond, overstepping the bounds of, what is reasonable ; immoderate : *an unreasonable claim, demand* ; specif. (of price, charge &c.) too high, exorbitant.

unreasonableness, n. Prec. & -ness. Quality of being unreasonable.

unreasonably, adv. See prec. & -ly. In an unreasonable manner ; to an unreasonable extent.

unreasoning, adj. [1. unrézuning ; 2. anrízəniŋ]. un- (I.) & **reasoning**. Not reasoning, not using reason, not guided by reason ; irrational ; unreasonable : *the unreasoning multitude* ; *an unreasoning hatred*.

unreasoningly, adv. Prec. & -ly. In an unreasoning manner.

unrebuked, adj. [1. unrebúkt ; 2. anribjúkt]. un- (I.) & **rebuke(d)**. Not rebuked ; without incurring, or receiving, rebuke ; unchecked by rebuke.

unrecallable, adj. [1. unrekáwlabl ; 2. anrikólabl]. un- (I.) & **recallable**. Not recallable.

unrecalled, adj. [1. unrekáwld ; 2. anrikóld]. un- (I.) & **recall(ed)**. Not recalled.

unreceipted, adj. [1. ùnreséted ; 2. ănrisítid]. un- (I.) & receipt(ed). Not receipted.

unreceivable, adj. [1. ùnresévabl ; 2. ănrisívabl]. un- (I.) & receivable. Not receivable.

unreceived, adj. [1. ùnresévd ; 2. ănrisívd]. un- (I.) & receive(d). Not received.

unreciprocated, adj. [1. ùnresíprokăted ; 2. ănrisíprəkèitid]. un- (I.) & reciprocate(d). Not reciprocated.

unreckoned, adj. [1. ùnrékund ; 2. ănrékənd]. un- (I.) & reckon(ed). Not reckoned ; not included in a reckoning or estimate.

unreclaimed, adj. [1. ùnreklắmd ; 2. ănrikléimd]. un- (I.) & reclaim(ed). Not reclaimed (in material and moral senses), cp. *irreclaimable*.

unrecognizable, adj. [1. ùnrékognízabl ; 2. ănrékəgnàizəbl]. un- (I.) & recognizable. Not recognizable.

unrecognized, adj. [1. ùnrékognízd ; 2. ănrékəgnàizd]. un- (I.) & recognize(d). Not recognized ; not having received due recognition or reward : *humble, unrecognized merit*.

unrecompensed, adj. [1. ùnrékumpènst ; 2. ănrékəmpènst]. un- (I.) & recompense(d). Not recompensed ; without reward or recompense.

unreconciled, adj. [1. ùnrékunsìld ; 2. ănrékənsdìld]. un- (I.) & reconcile(d). Not reconciled ; not reunited to friendship ; not made to agree.

unrecorded, adj. [1. ùnrekórded ; 2. ănrikódid]. un- (I.) & record(ed). Not recorded ; not placed on record ; not found in records.

unrectified, adj. [1. ùnréktifíd ; 2. ănréktifaid]. un- (I.) & P.P. of rectify. Not rectified. **1.** Not put right or corrected. **2.** (chem.) Not purified or refined.

unredeemable, adj. [1. ùnredémabl ; 2. ănridímǝbl]. un- (I.) & redeemable. Not redeemable, cp. *irredeemable*.

unredeemed, adj. [1. ùnredémd ; 2. ănridímd]. un- (I.) & redeem(ed). Not redeemed. **1.** Not fulfilled or carried out : *unredeemed promises*. **2.** Not taken out of pawn, by payment of sum advanced, with interest : *sale of unredeemed pledges*. **3.** Having no redeeming quality ; unmitigated : *a stupid, pretentious play unredeemed by the saving quality of humour*. **4.** Not recovered, of areas of country lost to a foreign State : *unredeemed Italy*, cp. *irredentist*. **5.** Not recalled by payment of value : *an unredeemed bill of exchange*.

unredressed, adj. [1. ùnredrést ; 2. ănridrést]. un- (I.) & redress(ed). Not redressed.

unreel, vb. trans. & intrans. [1. unrél ; 2. anríəl]. un- (II.) & reel (II.). To unwind, become unwound, from a reel.

unrefined, adj. [1. ùnrefínd ; 2. ănrifáind]. un- (I.) & refine(d). Not refined. **1.** Not purified or clarified : *unrefined sugar* &c. **2.** Having no refinement ; unpolished, coarse, vulgar : *unrefined manners, society*.

unreflecting, adj. [1. ùnrefléktíng ; 2. ănriflĕktiŋ]. un- (I.) & reflect(ing). **1.** Not reflecting light. **2.** Not using the mind in reflection ; unthinking, thoughtless.

unreflectingly, adv. Prec. & -ly. In an unreflecting manner ; without reflection.

unreformable, adj. [1. ùnrefórmabl ; 2. ănrifómǝbl]. un- (I.) & reform & -able. Not reformable.

unreformed, adj. [1. ùnrefórmd ; 2. ănrifómd]. un- (I.) & reform(ed). Not reformed.

unrefuted, adj. [1. ùnrefúted ; 2. ănrifjútid]. un- (I.) & refute(d). Not refuted ; not disproved.

unregarded, adj. [1. ùnregárded ; 2. ănrigádid]. un- (I.) & regard(ed). Not regarded ; disregarded ; neglected.

unregeneracy, n. [1. ùnrejéneràsi ; 2. ănridźénǝrǝsi]. un- (I.) & regeneracy. State of being unregenerate.

unregenerate, adj. [1. ùnrejénerat ; 2. ănridźénǝrit]. un- (I.) & regenerate. Not regenerate ; esp. (theol.) not reconciled to God through regeneration.

unregistered, adj. [1. ùnréjisterd ; 2. ănrédžistəd]. un- (I.) & register(ed). Not registered.

unregretted, adj. [1. ùnregréted ; 2. ănrigrétid]. un- (I.) & regret(ted). Not regretted ; unlamented.

unregulate(d), adj. [1. ùnrégulăt(ed) ; 2. ănrégjuleit(id)]. un- (I.) & regulate(d). Not regulated ; undisciplined.

unrehearsed, adj. [1. ùnreherst ; 2. ănrihə́st]. un- (I.) & rehearse(d). Not rehearsed ; occurring spontaneously, and without design ; unpremeditated : *an unrehearsed effect*.

unrein, vb. trans. [1. unrắn ; 2. anréin]. un- (II.) & rein. To unloose the reins of ; to give the rein to, release (esp. fig.).

unreined, adj. [1. unránd ; 2. anréind]. un- (I.) & rein(ed). Not reined in ; unrestrained, unbridled : *unreined passions*.

unrelated, adj. [1. ùnrelắted ; 2. ănriléitid]. un- (I.) & relate(d). Not related.

unrelenting, adj. [1. ùnrelénting ; 2. ănriléntiŋ]. un- (I.) & relent & -ing. Not relenting ; relentless ; inflexible ; merciless.

unrelentingly, adv. Prec. & -ly. In an unrelenting manner.

unreliability, n. [1. ùnrelìabíliti ; 2. ănrilàiəbíliti]. un- (I.) & reliability. State of being unreliable.

unreliable, adj. [1. ùnrelíabl ; 2. ănriláiəbl]. un- (I.) & reliable. Not reliable, not to be relied on ; untrustworthy.

unreliably, adv. Prec. & -ly. In an unreliable manner.

unrelieved, adj. [1. ùnrelévd ; 2. ănrilívd]. un- (I.) & relieve(d). Not relieved.

unreligious, adj. [1. ùnrelíjus ; 2. ănrilídžəs]. un- (I.) & religious. Not concerned or connected with religion ; not involving, or involved in, religious ideas or questions ; nonreligious ; cp. *irreligious*.

unremembered, adj. [1. ùnremémberd ; 2. ănrimémbəd]. un- (I.) & remember(ed). Not remembered ; forgotten.

unremitting, adj. [1. ùnremíting ; 2. ănrimítiŋ]. un- (I.) & remit(ting). Without remission ; unceasing, incessant ; not relaxing effort ; persistent, persevering : *unremitting toil, energy*.

unremittingly, adv. Prec. & -ly. In an unremitting manner ; unceasingly.

unremunerative, adj. [1. ùnremúnerativ ; 2. ănrimjúnǝrǝtiv]. un- (I.) & remunerative. Not remunerative ; unprofitable.

unrenewed, adj. [1. ùnrenúd ; 2. ănrinjúd]. un- (I.) & renew(ed). Not renewed.

unrenounced, adj. [1. ùnrenóunst ; 2. ănrináunst]. un- (I.) & renounce(d). Not renounced.

unrenovated, adj. [1. ùnrénovăted ; 2. ănrénəveitid]. un- (I.) & renovate(d). Not renovated.

unrepair, n. [1. ùnrepár ; 2. ănripéǝ]. un- (I.) & repair. State of disrepair, dilapidation.

unrepealed, adj. [1. ùnrepĕld ; 2. ănripíǝld]. un- (I.) & repeal(ed). Not repealed.

unrepentance, n. [1. ùnrepéntans ; 2. ănripéntǝns]. un- (I.) & repentance. Lack of repentance ; state of being unrepentant ; impenitence.

unrepentant, adj. [1. ùnrepéntant ; 2. ănripéntǝnt]. un- (I.) & repentant. Not repentant ; showing no repentance ; impenitent.

unrepentantly, adv. Prec. & -ly. Without repentance ; impenitently.

unrepining, adj. [1. ùnrepíning ; 2. ănripáiniŋ]. un- (I.) & repine & -ing. Not repining ; uncomplaining.

unrepiningly, adv. Prec. & -ly. In an unrepining manner, without complaint.

unreported, adj. [1. ùnrepórted ; 2. ănripótid]. un- (I.) & report(ed). Not reported ; specif., not to be found in the legal or parliamentary reports.

unrepresentative, adj. [1. ùnreprézentativ ; 2. ănrèprizéntǝtiv]. un- (I.) & representative. Not representative.

unrepresented, adj. [1. ùnreprézénted ; 2. ănrèprizéntid]. un- (I.) & represent(ed). Not represented.

unreprieved, adj. [1. ùnreprévd ; 2. ănriprívd]. un- (I.) & reprieve(d). Not reprieved.

unreproachful, adj. [1. ùnreprŏchfl ; 2. ănriprŏutʃfl]. un- (I.) & reproachful. Not reproachful.

unreproved, adj. [1. ùnreprŏŏvd ; 2. ănriprúvd]. un- (I.) & reprove(d). Not reproved ; without incurring, unchecked by, reproof.

unrequisite, adj. [1. ùnrékwizit ; 2. ănrékwizit]. un- (I.) & requisite. Not requisite ; unnecessary.

unrequited, adj. [1. ùnrekwíted ; 2. ănrikwáitid]. un- (I.) & requite(d). Not requited ; **a** not returned or reciprocated : *unrequited affections* ; **b** not recompensed : *unrequited labours* ; **c** unavenged : *wickedness does not go altogether unrequited*.

unrescinded, adj. [1. ùnresínded ; 2. ănrisíndid]. un- (I.) & rescind(ed). Not rescinded ; not revoked or cancelled.

unresented, adj. [1. ùnrezénted ; 2. ănrizéntid]. un- (I.) & resent(ed). Not resented.

unresenting, adj. [1. ùnrezénting ; 2. ănrizéntiŋ]. un- (I.) & resenting. Not resenting ; not feeling or showing resentment.

unresentingly, adv. Prec. & -ly. In an unresenting manner ; without resentment.

unreserve, n. [1. ùnrezérv ; 2. ănrizə́v]. un- (I.) & reserve (II.). Want of reserve in speech or behaviour.

unreserved, adj. [1. ùnrezérvd ; 2. ănrizə́vd]. un- (I.) & reserve(d). Not reserved. **1.** Free from reserve in speech, manner, character ; **a** frank, open ; **b** not possessing or showing proper restraint and decorum. **2.** Free from reservations, restrictions, or qualifications ; unrestricted, unqualified : *in unreserved agreement*. **3.** Not allotted or booked in advance, not kept for specific persons or purposes : *unreserved seats*, at theatre &c.

unreservedly, adv. [1. ùnrezə́rvedli ; 2. ănrizə́vidli]. Prec. & -ly. In an unreserved manner ; without reserve or reservations.

unreservedness, n. [1. ùnrezə́rv(e)dnes ; 2. ănrizə́v(i)dnis]. See prec. & -ness. State, quality, of being unreserved in speech, manner &c.

unresisted, adj. [1. ùnrezísted ; 2. ănrizístid]. un- (I.) & resist(ed). Not resisted ; unopposed.

unresisting, adj. [1. ùnrezísting ; 2. ănrizístiŋ]. un- (I.) & resist(ing). Not resisting, not offering resistance ; yielding.

unresistingly, adv. Prec. & -ly. Without resistance.

unresolved, adj. [1. ùnrezólvd ; 2. ănrizólvd]. un- (I.) & resolve(d). Not resolved. **1. a** Lacking resolution ; irresolute, undecided ; **b** not having made a decision ; uncertain. **2. a** Not separated or analysed into its component (material) parts or elements ; **b** not analysed, disentangled, or made clear in, or to, the mind ; unsolved, not cleared up : *an unresolved mystery* ; *my doubts are still unresolved*.

unrespected, adj. [1. ùnrespékted ; 2. ănrispéktid]. un- (I.) & respect(ed). Not respected ; despised : *an unrespected old age*.

unresponsive, adj. [1. ùnrespónsiv ; 2. ănrispónsiv]. un- (I.) & responsive. Not responsive, not reacting easily or readily to a physical, intellectual, or emotional stimulus ; not impressionable ; not readily accessible to an emotional or intellectual appeal.

unresponsively, adv. Prec. & -ly. In an unresponsive manner.

unresponsiveness, n. See prec. & -ness. State of being unresponsive.

unrest, n. [1. unrést ; 2. anrést]. un- (I.) & rest (I.). Restlessness, disquiet ; a state of disturbance or agitation ; esp. *political, industrial, unrest* ; **b** anxious, disturbed state of mind.

unrestful, adj. [1. unréstfl ; 2. anréstfl]. un- (I.) & restful. Not restful ; **a** not conducive to peace of mind ; **b** restless, fidgety.

unrestfully, adv. Prec. & -ly. In an unrestful manner.
unrestfulness, n. See prec. & -ness. State of being unrestful.
unresting, adj. [1. unrésting; 2. anrέstiŋ]. **un-** (I.) & **rest(ing)**. Not resting, taking no rest; untiring: *unresting activity, energy*.
unrestingly, adv. Prec. & -ly. In an unresting manner.
unrestrained, adj. [1. ùnrestránd; 2. ànristréind]. **un-** (I.) & **restrain(ed)**. Not restrained; without restraint or control; uncontrolled; unreserved.
unrestrainedly, adv. [1. ùnrestráinedli; 2. ànristréinidli]. Prec. & -ly. In an unrestrained manner.
unrestraint, n. [1. ùnrestránt; 2. ànristréint]. **un-** (I.) & **restraint**. Lack of restraint, lack of self-control.
unrestricted, adj. [1. ùnrestríkted; 2. ànristríktid]. **un-** (I.) & **restrict(ed)**. Not restricted; free from restrictions, limitations &c.
unretarded, adj. [1. ùnretárded; 2. ànritάdid]. **un-** (I.) & **retard(ed)**. Not retarded; unhampered, undelayed.
unrevealed, adj. [1. ùnrevéld; 2. ànrivíəld]. **un-** (I.) & **reveal(ed)**. Not revealed; hidden, secret; not divulged.
unrevenged, adj. [1. ùnrevénjd; 2. ànrivéndžd]. **un-** (I.) & **revenge(d)**. Not revenged; unavenged.
unrevised, adj. [1. ùnrevízd; 2. ànriváizd]. **un-** (I.) & **revise(d)**. Not revised.
unrevoked, adj. [1. ùnrevókt; 2. ànrivóukt]. **un-** (I.) & **revoke(d)**. Not revoked.
unrewarded, adj. [1. ùnrewórded; 2. ànriwóəd]. **un-** (I.) & **reward(ed)**. Not rewarded.
unrhetorical, adj. [1. ùnretórikl; 2. ànritórikl]. **un-** (I.) & **rhetorical**. Not rhetorical; free from false rhetoric; simple, straightforward, in style and expression.
unrhymed, adj., pred. [1. unrímd; 2. anráimd]; attrib. [1. únrimd; 2. ánraimd]. **un-** (I.) & **rhyme(d)**. Not rhymed; written without rhymes.
unrhythmical, adj. [1. unríthmikl; 2. anrípmikl]. **un-** (I.) & **rhythmical**. Not rhythmical.
unrhythmically, adv. Prec. & -ly. Without rhythm.
unridable, adj. [1. unrídabl; 2. anráidəbl]. **un-** (I.) & **ridable**. Not ridable; incapable of being ridden.
unridden, adj. [1. unrídn; 2. anrídn]. **un-** (I.) & **ridden**. Not ridden.
unriddle, vb. trans. [1. unrídl; 2. anrídl]. **un-** (II.) & **riddle (II.)**. To solve the riddle of; to explain, interpret: *unriddle this mystery*.
unrifled, adj. [1. unrífld; 2. anráifld]. **un-** (I.) & **rifle(d)**. Not rifled; not plundered or robbed.
unrig, vb. trans. [1. unríg; 2. anríg]. **un-** (II.) & **rig (I.)**. To strip (ship &c.) of rig or rigging.
unrigged, adj. [1. unrígd; 2. anrígd]. **un-** (I.) & **rig(ged)**. (of ship) Not rigged; without rigging.
unrighteous, adj. [1. unríchus; 2. anráitʃəs]. **un-** (I.) & **righteous**. Reverse of *righteous*. 1. Not pious; wicked, ungodly; Phr. *the unrighteous*, wicked people. 2. Unjust, not in accordance with justice and equity: *an unrighteous judgement*.
unrighteously, adv. Prec. & -ly. In an unrighteous manner.
unrighteousness, n. See prec. & -ness. Wickedness, ungodliness.
unrip, vb. trans. [1. unríp; 2. anríp]. **un-** (II.) & **rip (I.)**. To rip open; to rip out stitches from.
unripe, adj. [1. unríp; 2. anráip]. **un-** (I.) & **ripe**. Not yet ripe; immature (lit. and fig.): *unripe fruit*; *an unripe mind*; *land unripe for development*.
unripeness, n. Prec. & -ness. State of being unripe; immaturity.

unrisen, adj. [1. unrízn; 2. anrízn]. **un-** (I.) & **rise(n)**. Not yet risen.
unrivalled, adj. [1. unrívld; 2. anráivld]. **un-** (I.) & **rival(led)**. Having no rival; unsurpassed, unequalled.
unrivet, vb. trans. [1. unrívet; 2. anrívit]. **un-** (II.) & **rivet**. To remove rivets from; to unfasten what is riveted.
unrobe, vb. trans. & intrans. [1. unrób; 2. anróub]. **un-** (II.) & **robe**. **a** trans. To take off (the), esp. official, robe(s) of; to disrobe, undress; **b** intrans., to take off one's own robes.
unroll, vb. trans. & intrans. [1. unról; 2. anróul]. **un-** (II.) & **roll**. **a** trans. To roll back, open, what is rolled up; **b** intrans., to become unrolled; to unfold.
unromantic, adj. [1. ùnrōmántik; 2. ànroumǽntik]. **un-** (I.) & **romantic**. Not romantic; lacking in romance; commonplace, matter-of-fact.
unromantically, adv. [1. ùnrōmántikali; 2. ànroumǽntikəli]. Prec. & -al & -ly. In an unromantic manner.
unroof, vb. trans. [1. unróof; 2. anrúf]. **un-** (II.) & **roof (II.)**. To take off, carry away, the roof of (house); to destroy the roof of.
unroofed, adj. [1. unróoft; 2. anrúft]. **un-** (I.) & **roof(ed)**. Not roofed; having lost its roof.
unroot, vb. trans. [1. unróot; 2. anrút]. **un-** (II.) & **root (II.)**. To pull, tear, up by the root; to uproot; to eradicate.
unround, vb. trans. [1. unróund; 2. anráund]. **un-** (II.) & **round**, vb. (phon.) To pronounce (vowel) with lips drawn back to natural position, instead of being protruded: *the sound* [y] *when unrounded becomes* [i].
unroyal, adj. [1. unróial; 2. anróiəl]. **un-** (I.) & **royal**. Not royal; not like or not worthy of, not befitting, a king.
unroyally, adv. Prec. & -ly. In an unroyal manner.
unruffled, adj. [1. unrúfld; 2. anráfld]. **un-** (I.) & **ruffle(d)**. Not ruffled; not agitated or disturbed; calm, serene (lit. and fig.).
unruled, adj. [1. unróold; 2. anrúld]. **un-** (I.) & **rule(d)**. Not ruled. 1. Not marked with lines or rulings. 2. Not governed; uncontrolled.
unruliness, n. [1. unróolines; 2. anrúlinis]. See next word & -ness. State of being unruly.
unruly, adj. [1. unróoli; 2. anrúli], fr. 15th cent.; fr. **un-** (I.), **rule (I.)**, & -ly. Not obedient, or subservient, to rule or restraint; disorderly, ungovernable, disobedient, refractory.
unsaddle, vb. trans. & intrans. [1. unsádl; 2. ansǽdl]. **un-** (II.) & **saddle (II.)**. **a** trans. To take the saddle off (horse &c.); **b** intrans., to unsaddle one's horse.
unsafe, adj. [1. unsáf; 2. anséif]. **un-** (I.) & **safe (I.)**. Not safe; dangerous.
unsafely, adv. Prec. & -ly. In an unsafe manner.
unsafeness, n. See prec. & -ness. State of being unsafe.
unsaid, adj. [1. unséd; 2. anséd]. **un-** (I.) & **said**. Not said; unspoken: *things better left unsaid*.
unsaintly, adj. [1. unsántli; 2. anséintli]. **un-** (I.) & **saintly**. Not saintly.
unsalability, n. [1. ùnsālabíliti; 2. ànseiləbíliti]. See next word & -ity. State of being unsalable.
unsalable, adj. [1. unsálabl; 2. anséiləbl]. **un-** (I.) & **salable**. Not salable; that cannot be sold; unmarketable.
unsalaried, adj. [1. unsálarid; 2. ansǽlərid]. **un-** (I.) & **salaried**. Not salaried, not receiving a salary; unpaid, honorary.
unsanctified, adj. [1. unsángktifid; 2. ansǽŋktifaid]. **un-** (I.) & **sanctified**. Not sanctified; unholy.
unsanctioned, adj. [1. unsángkshund; 2. ansǽŋkʃənd]. **un-** (I.) & **sanction(ed)**. Not sanctioned; unauthorized.
unsanitary, adj. [1. unsánitari; 2. ansǽni-

t(ə)ri]. **un-** (I.) & **sanitary**. Not sanitary; unhealthy; insanitary.
unsated, adj. [1. unsáted; 2. anséitid]. **un-** (I.) & **sate(d)**. Not sated; unsatisfied.
unsatisfactorily, adv. [1. unsàtisfáktorili; 2. ansǽtisfǽktərili]. **unsatisfactory** & -ly. In an unsatisfactory manner.
unsatisfactoriness, n. [1. unsàtisfáktorines; 2. ansǽtisfǽktərinis]. See prec. & -ness. State of being unsatisfactory.
unsatisfactory, adj. [1. unsàtisfáktori; 2. ansǽtisfǽktəri]. **un-** (I.) & **satisfactory**. Not satisfactory; giving no satisfaction.
unsatisfied, adj. [1. unsátisfid; 2. ansǽtisfaid]. **un-** (I.) & **satisfy** & -ed. Not satisfied; unappeased.
unsatisfying, adj. [1. unsátisfiing; 2. ansǽtisfaiiŋ]. **un-** (I.) & **satisfying**. Not satisfying.
unsatisfyingly, adv. Prec. & -ly. In an unsatisfying manner.
unsaturated, adj. [1. unsáchurāted; 2. ansǽtʃəreitid]. **un-** (I.) & **saturate(d)**. Not saturated.
unsavourily, adv. [1. unsávurili; 2. ansέivərili]. **unsavoury** & -ly. In an unsavoury manner.
unsavouriness, n. [1. unsávurines; 2. ansέivərinis]. See next word & -ness. State of being unsavoury.
unsavoury, adj. [1. unsávuri; 2. ansέivəri]. **un-** (I.) & **savoury**. Not savoury; uninviting, unattractive; unpleasant, disgusting.
unsay, vb. trans. [1. unsá, únsā; 2. anséi, ánsei]. **un-** (II.) & **say**. To recall, retract (what has been said).
unscalable, adj. [1. unskálabl; 2. anskέiləbl]. **un-** (I.) & **scalable**. Not scalable; not to be scaled; unclimbable.
unscale, vb. trans. [1. unskál; 2. anskέil]. **un-** (II.) & **scale**. To remove scales from (boilers &c.).
unscannable, adj. [1. unskánabl; 2. anskǽnəbl]. **un-** (I.) & **scannable**. (of verse) Not scannable; impossible to scan.
unscared, adj. [1. unskárd; 2. anskέəd]. **un-** (I.) & **scare(d)**. Not scared; not frightened.
unscarred, adj. [1. unskárd; 2. anskάd]. **un-** (I.) & **scar(red)**. Not scarred; without a scar or wound.
unscathed, adj. [1. unskádhd; 2. anskέiðd]. **un-** (I.) & **scathe(d)**. Not scathed; physically or morally uninjured.
unscented, adj. [1. unsénted; 2. anséntid]. **un-** (I.) & **scent(ed)**. Not scented; having, yielding, no perfume: *an unscented rose*.
unscholarly, adj. [1. unskólarli; 2. anskóləli]. **un-** (I.) & **scholarly**. Not scholarly; **a** devoid of scholarship; **b** not done after the manner of a scholar.
unschooled, adj. [1. unskóold; 2. anskúld]. **un-** (I.) & **school(ed)**. Not schooled; not taught, not trained or disciplined; not experienced: *unschooled in deceit, in vice*.
unscientific, adj. [1. unsìentífik; 2. ansɔiəntífik]. **un-** (I.) & **scientific**. Not scientific; not in accordance with scientific principles or methods.
unscientifically, adv. [1. unsìentífikali; 2. ansɔiəntífikəli]. Prec. & -al & -ly. In an unscientific manner.
unscreened, adj. [1. unskrénd; 2. anskrínd]. **un-** (I.) & **screen(ed)**. Not screened. 1. Not sheltered by a screen. 2. Not passed through a screen or riddle; unsifted.
unscrew, vb. trans. & intrans. [1. unskróo; 2. anskrú]. **un-** (II.) & **screw**. 1. trans. **a** To remove, draw out screw(s) from: *to unscrew the lid of a coffin*; **b** to loosen and withdraw (screw) by turning it reverse way. 2. intrans. **a** To become unscrewed; **b** to permit of being unscrewed: *the nut won't unscrew*.
unscriptural, adj. [1. unskrípchural; 2. anskríptʃərəl]. **un-** (I.) & **scriptural**. Not scriptural; not in conformity with or according to the Bible.
unscripturally, adv. Prec. & -ly. In an unscriptural manner.

unscrupulous, adj. [1. unskrōōpulus ; 2. anskrŭpjuləs]. un- (I.) & scrupulous. Not scrupulous; without scruples or moral principles ; unprincipled.

unscrupulously, adv. Prec. & -ly. In an unscrupulous manner.

unscrupulousness, n. See prec. & -ness. State of being unscrupulous.

unseal, vb. trans. [1. unsēl ; 2. ansīəl]. un- (II.) & seal (IV.). To break or remove the seal of, to open that which is sealed, as a letter &c.

unsealed, adj. [1. unsēld ; 2. ansīəld]. a un- (I.), b un- (II.), & see prec. a Not sealed up; not under seal ; b having the seal broken or removed.

unseam, vb. trans. [1. unsēm ; 2. ansīm]. un- (II.) & seam. To cut, rip open, the seams of.

unsearchable, adj. [1. unsĕrchabl ; 2. ansătʃəbl]. un- (I.) & searchable. Not to be discovered or found out by searching ; mysterious ; inscrutable.

unseasonable, adj. [1. unsēzonabl ; 2. ansīzənəbl]. un- (I.) & seasonable. Not seasonable ; a occurring out of its proper or normal season of the year, unusual for the season : *unseasonable weather, heat* &c. ; b done, said, at the wrong time, ill-timed, untimely ; inopportune : *unseasonable humour*.

unseasonableness, n. See prec. & -ness. State of being unseasonable.

unseasonably, adv. Prec. & -ly. In an unseasonable manner.

unseasoned, adj. [1. unsēznd ; 2. ansīznd]. un- (I.) & season(ed). Not seasoned. 1. Without seasoning or flavouring. 2. Not matured or ripened.

unseat, vb. trans. [1. unsēt ; 2. ansīt]. un- (II.) & seat. 1. To displace (rider) from his seat on horseback ; to throw. 2. To remove from, dispossess of, a seat in Parliament, either by votes at an election, or by a decision in court that election was invalid.

unseated, adj. [1. unsēted ; 2. ansītid]. un- (I.) & seat(ed). Not provided or furnished with a seat or seats.

unseaworthiness, n. [1. unsēwĕrdhines ; 2. ansīwāðinis]. See next word & -ness. State of being unseaworthy.

unseaworthy, adj. [1. unsēwĕrdhi ; 2. ansīwāði]. un- (I.) & seaworthy. Not seaworthy ; not in fit condition to undertake a sea voyage.

unseconded, adj. [1. unsĕkonded ; 2. ansĕkəndid]. un- (I.) & second(ed). 1. Not seconded, helped, assisted. 2. (of a motion) Not seconded when proposed. 3. Not provided with, supported by, a second at a duel.

unsectarian, adj. [1. unsektărian ; 2. ansɛktɛ́əriən]. un- (I.) & sectarian. Not sectarian ; a free from the prejudices and narrowness of religious sects ; b not in accordance with the tenets of any specific sect.

unsectarianism, n. [1. unsektărianizm ; 2. ansɛktɛ́əriənizəm]. Prec. & -ism. Freedom from sectarian prejudices.

unsecured, adj. [1. unsekūrd ; 2. ansikjŏd]. un- (I.) & secure(d). Not secured ; (esp. of debts and creditors) not covered by assets &c.

unseductive, adj. [1. unsedŭktiv ; 2. ansidáktiv]. un- (I.) & seductive. Not seductive.

unseeing, adj. [1. unsēing ; 2. ansī-iŋ]. un- (I.) & seeing. Not seeing ; unobservant ; blind ; unsuspecting.

unseemliness, n. [1. unsĕmlines ; 2. ansīmlinis]. See next word & -ness. State of being unseemly.

unseemly, adj. [1. unsĕmli ; 2. ansīmli]. un- (I.) & seemly. Not seemly ; not becoming or befitting ; improper, indecent.

unseen, adj. & n. [1. unsēn ; 2. ansīn]. un- (I.) & seen, see see (I.). 1. Not seen ; not visible : *unseen dangers ; the unseen*, what is unseen, the invisible, spiritual world. 2. a Only in *unseen translation, passage*, translation of unprepared passages in a foreign tongue, ancient or modern ; b *an unseen*, a passage set for translation in an examination, without previous preparation ; an unseen passage.

unseizable, adj. [1. unsēzabl ; 2. ansīzəbl]. un- (I.) & seizable. Not to be seized.

unseldom, adv. [1. unsĕldum ; 2. ansĕldəm]. un- (I.) & seldom. (rare) Not seldom ; often.

unselected, adj. [1. unselĕkted ; 2. ansilĕktid]. un- (I.) & select(ed). Not selected.

unselfish, adj. [1. unsĕlfish ; 2. ansĕlfiʃ]. un- (I.) & selfish. Not selfish ; thinking of others rather than of oneself ; altruistic.

unselfishly, adv. Prec. & -ly. In an unselfish manner.

unselfishness, n. See prec. & -ness. a State, quality, of being unselfish ; b unselfish actions.

unsensational, adj. [1. unsensăshunal ; 2. ansɛnsĕiʃənəl]. un- (I.) & sensational. Not sensational ; not causing or likely to cause a sensation.

unsensationally, adv. Prec. & -ly. In an unsensational manner.

unsent, adj. [1. unsĕnt ; 2. ansĕnt]. un- (I.) & sent. Not sent.

unsentimental, adj. [1. unsentimĕntl ; 2. ansɛntimĕntl]. un- (I.) & sentimental. Not sentimental.

unseparated, adj. [1. unsĕparăted ; 2. ansĕpərĕitid]. un- (I.) & separate(d). Not separated ; undivided.

unserviceable, adj. [1. unsĕrvisabl ; 2. ansə́visəbl]. un- (I.) & serviceable. Not serviceable ; unfit for use.

unserviceably, adv. Prec. & -ly. In an unserviceable manner.

unset (I.), vb. trans. [1. unsĕt ; 2. ansĕt]. un- (II.) & set (I.). To undo the setting of ; to remove (jewel &c.) from its setting.

unset (II.), adj., attrib. [1. unsĕt ; 2. ansɛt] ; pred. [1. unsĕt ; 2. ansĕt]. un- (I.) & P.P. of set (I.). Not set (in various senses of the verb) : *unset limb, jewel* &c.

unsettle, vb. trans. [1. unsĕtl ; 2. ansĕtl]. un- (II.) & settle (II.). 1. To change from a fixed or settled position or state. 2. To disturb in mind, feelings &c. ; to disarrange ; to throw into a state of unrest, agitation &c. ; to render unsettled : *to unsettle a person's opinions, affections* &c. ; *to unsettle a boy at school*.

unsettled, adj. [1. unsĕtld ; 2. ansĕtld]. un- (I.) & settle(d). Not settled (in various senses) ; a changeable, unstable : *unsettled weather* ; b unpaid : *unsettled claims, debts* ; c unallocated, not allotted ; not subject to a deed of settlement : *an unsettled estate ; unsettled lands* &c.

unsettling, adj. [1. unsĕtling ; 2. ansĕtliŋ]. unsettle & -ing. Disturbing : *unsettling news*.

unsevered, adj. [1. unsĕverd ; 2. ansĕvəd]. un- (I.) & sever(ed). Not severed.

unsex, vb. trans. [1. unsĕks ; 2. ansĕks]. un- (II.) & sex. To deprive of sex ; esp. to deprive (woman) of her feminine qualities ; commonly in P.P. as adj. *unsexed*.

unshackle, vb. trans. [1. unshăkl ; 2. anʃǽkl]. un- (II.) & shackle. To loose, unfasten, the shackles of ; to free from shackles.

unshackled, adj. [1. unshăkld ; 2. anʃǽkld]. un- (I.) & shackle(d). Not shackled (esp. in fig. sense) ; unrestrained : *unshackled by conventions, conscientious scruples* &c.

unshaded, adj. [1. unshăded ; 2. anʃĕidid]. un- (I.) & shade(d). Not shaded ; free from shade ; not showing differences of light and shade, esp. of a drawing &c.

unshadowed, adj. [1. unshădōd ; 2. anʃǽdoud]. un- (I.) & shadow(ed). Not shadowed, not overcast by shadow ; (esp. fig.) not darkened, not rendered sad and gloomy : *a life unshadowed by any calamity*.

unshakable, adj. [1. unshăkabl ; 2. anʃĕikəbl]. un- (I.) & shakable. (esp. fig.) Not shakable ; not to be shaken or upset ; firmly established : *unshakable loyalty*.

unshaken, adj. [1. unshāken ; 2. anʃĕik(ə)n]. un- (I.) & shake(n). Not shaken ; (esp. fig.) firm, steady, unwavering : *unshaken courage, resolution* &c.

unshapeliness, n. [1. unshāplines ; 2. anʃĕiplinis]. See next word & -ness. State of being unshapely.

unshapely, adj. [1. unshāpli ; 2. anʃĕipli]. un- (I.) & shapely. Not shapely ; ill-formed, ill-proportioned ; misshapen.

unshaven, adj. [1. unshāven ; 2. anʃĕivən]. un- (I.) & shave(n). Not shaven ; a not newly shaven ; b wearing a beard.

unsheathe, vb. trans. [1. unshēdh ; 2. anʃīð]. un- (II.) & sheathe. To take out, draw (sword &c.) ; (fig.) *to unsheathe the sword*, to declare or begin war.

unshed, adj. [1. unshĕd, ŭnshed ; 2. anʃĕd, ánʃed]. un- (I.) & shed (I.). Not shed ; esp. *unshed tears*.

unsheltered, adj. [1. unshĕlterd ; 2. anʃĕltəd]. un- (I.) & shelter(ed). Not sheltered ; exposed, unprotected ; specif., *unsheltered industries*, those which are subject to competition by imports of the same kind from foreign countries.

unship, vb. trans. [1. unshĭp ; 2. anʃíp]. un- (II.) & ship (II.). a To discharge, unload (cargo &c.), from a ship ; b to disembark (passengers) from a ship ; c to remove (oar) from rowlock, or (tiller) from place in a boat &c. where it is fixed or fitted.

unshod, adj. [1. unshŏd ; 2. anʃŏd]. un- (I.) & shod. Not shod ; barefoot.

unshoe, vb. trans. [1. unshōō ; 2. anʃū]. un- (II.) & shoe (I.). To remove shoes from (horse &c.).

unshorn, adj. [1. unshŏrn ; 2. anʃŏn]. un- (I.) & shorn. Not shorn ; having the hair long and needing to be cut.

unshrinkable, adj. [1. unshrĭngkabl ; 2. anʃríŋkəbl]. un- (I.) & shrink & -able. Not shrinkable ; made so as not to shrink from wet (of flannel, cloth).

unshrinking, adj. [1. unshrĭngking ; 2. anʃríŋkiŋ]. un- (I.) & shrinking. Not shrinking ; undaunted ; unhesitating, unflinching.

unshriven, adj. [1. unshrĭvn ; 2. anʃrívn]. un- (I.) & shrive(n). Not shriven ; not having confessed, done penance, and received absolution from a priest.

unshut, adj. [1. unshŭt, ŭnshut ; 2. anʃát, ánʃat]. un- (I.) & P.P. of shut. Not shut ; wide open ; not capable of shutting : 'great whales ... with unshut eye' (M. Arnold).

unshutter, vb. trans. [1. unshŭter ; 2. anʃátə]. un- (II.) & shutter. To remove, open, the shutters from windows of.

unsifted, adj. [1. unsĭfted ; 2. ansíftid]. un- (I.) & sift(ed). Not sifted (lit. and fig.).

unsighted, adj. [1. unsīted ; 2. ansáitid]. un- (I.) & sight(ed). Not sighted. 1. Not seen, not brought within view. 2. a (of gun &c.) Not provided with sights ; b (of shot) aimed without use of sights.

unsightliness, n. See next word & -ness. State, quality, of being unsightly.

unsightly, adj. [1. unsītli ; 2. ansáitli]. un- (I.) & sightly. Not sightly ; displeasing to the sight ; ugly.

unsigned, adj. [1. unsīnd ; 2. ansáind]. un- (I.) & sign(ed). Not signed ; not identified by the signature of author &c.

unsinged, adj. [1. unsĭnjd ; 2. ansíndžd]. un- (I.) & singe(d). Not singed.

unsisterly, adj. [1. unsĭsterli ; 2. ansístəli]. un- (I.) & sisterly. Not sisterly, not behaving like a sister ; unbecoming in, unworthy of, a sister.

unskilful, adj. [1. unskĭlfl ; 2. anskílfi]. un- (I.) & skilful. Not skilful ; wanting skill or dexterity ; clumsy, awkward.

unskilfully, adv. Prec. & -ly. In an unskilful manner.

unskilfulness, n. See prec. & -ness. State of being unskilful.

unskilled, adj. [1. unskĭld ; 2. anskíld]. un- (I.) & skill(ed). Not skilled ; not possessing or requiring special skill or training ; specif. *unskilled labour*, manual labour which it requires little or no special skill or training to perform.

unslaked, adj. [1. unslákt; 2. ansléikt]. un- (I.) & slake(d). Not slaked. 1. (of thirst) Not satisfied; unassuaged. 2. (of lime) Not mixed with water.

unsleeping, adj. [1. unslêping; 2. anslípiŋ]. un- (I.) & sleep(ing). Not sleeping, (usually fig.) tireless, alert, constantly watchful : *unsleeping vigilance.*

unsling, vb. trans. [1. unslíng; 2. anslíŋ]. un- (II.) & sling (I.). a To remove (an object, a rifle &c.) from the place where it has been slung; b (naut.) to release from slings, remove the slings from (cargo, yards &c.).

unsociability, n. [1. ùnsòshabíliti; 2. ànsouʃəbíliti]. See next word & -ity. State, quality, of being unsociable.

unsociable, adj. [1. unsóshabl; 2. ansóuʃəbl]. un- (I.) & sociable. Not sociable; disinclined, unsuited, to mix in society; reserved.

unsociably, adv. Prec. & -ly. In an unsociable manner.

unsocial, adj. [1. unsóshl; 2. ansóuʃl]. un- (I.) & social. Not social; not promoting, antagonistic to, the social relations of individuals or nations.

unsoiled, adj. [1. unsóild; 2. ansóild]. un- (I.) & soil(ed). Not soiled; clean.

unsolaced, adj. [1. unsólast; 2. ansólist]. un- (I.) & solace(d). Not solaced; not comforted or relieved.

unsold, adj. [1. unsóld; 2. ansóuld]. un- (I.) & sold. Not sold; still on the market and open for sale.

unsolder, vb. trans. [1. unsóder, -sólder; 2. ansódə, -sóldə]. un- (II.) & solder. To remove solder from; to divide, separate (what has been soldered).

unsoldierly, adj. [1. unsóljerli; 2. ansóuldʒəli]. un- (I.) & soldierly. Not soldierly; not like, not worthy of, unbecoming in, a soldier.

unsolicited, adj. [1. únsolísited; 2. ànsəlísitid]. un- (I.) & solicit(ed). Not solicited; not asked or requested; gratuitous.

unsolvable, adj. [1. unsólvabl; 2. ansólvəbl]. un- (I.) & solvable. Not solvable; not to be solved; cp. *insoluble.*

unsolved, adj. [1. unsólvd; 2. ansólvd]. un- (I.) & solve(d). Not solved.

unsophisticated, adj. [1. ùnsofístikāted; 2. ànsəfístikèitid]. un- (I.) & sophisticate(d). Not sophisticated; a simple-minded, ingenuous, inexperienced, innocent; b not adulterated; pure, genuine.

unsophisticatedly, adv. Prec. & -ly. In an unsophisticated manner.

unsophisticatedness, n. See prec. & -ness. State of being unsophisticated.

unsought, adj. [1. unsáwt; 2. ansót]. un- (I.) & P.P. of seek. Not sought; not looked for; unasked, unsolicited.

unsound, adj. [1. únsóund; 2. ánsáund]. un- (I.) & sound (III.). Not sound (in various senses of the word), as a not in sound or healthy condition : *an unsound horse; to have an unsound heart*; Phr. *of unsound mind*, insane; b decayed, rotten : *unsound fruit, fish, timber*; c not based on sound reasoning; ill-founded, fallacious : *unsound arguments; a thoroughly unsound scheme* &c.

unsounded, adj. [1. unsóunded; 2. ansáundid]. un- (I.) & sound(ed). Not sounded; unfathomed, unplumbed.

unsoundly, adv. [1. unsóundli; 2. ansáundli]. unsound & -ly. In an unsound manner.

unsoundness, n. [1. unsóundnes; 2. ansáundnis]. See prec. & -ness. State of being unsound.

unsown, adj. [1. unsón; 2. ansóun]. un- (I.) & sow(n). Not sown.

unsparing, adj. [1. unspáring; 2. anspéəriŋ]. un- (I.) & sparing. Not sparing. 1. Not showing mercy or forgiveness; hard, severe : *an unsparing taskmaster.* 2. Not parsimonious; liberal, profuse, lavish : *unsparing kindness, generosity; unsparing in his offers of help* &c.

unsparingly, adv. Prec. & -ly. In an unsparing manner.

unsparingness, n. See prec. & -ness. State of being unsparing.

unspeakable, adj. [1. unspékabl; 2. anspíkəbl]. un- (I.) & speak & -able. Not capable of being uttered, expressed in words; indescribable, ineffable; a (in good sense) *unspeakable blessing, delight* &c.; b (in bad sense) too bad, horrible &c., to mention or describe : *unspeakable torments, misery*; (colloq.) *his manners are unspeakable.*

unspeakableness, n. Prec. & -ness. State of being unspeakable (chiefly in bad sense).

unspeakably, adv. See prec. & -ly. In an unspeakable manner; to an unspeakable degree.

unspecialized, adj. [1. unspéshalīzd; 2. anspéʃəlaizd]. un- (I.) & specialize(d). Not specialized; specif. (biol.), of organism, organ &c.) not specially modified or adapted for particular functions.

unspecified, adj. [1. unspésifīd; 2. anspésifaid]. un- (I.) & P.P. of specify. Not specified; not particularly indicated or stated.

unspeculative, adj. [1. unspékūlativ; 2. anspékjulətiv]. un- (I.) & speculative. Not speculative; not given to (mental) speculation.

unspent, adj. [1. unspént; 2. anspént]. un- (I.) & spent. Not spent; not tired, unexhausted.

unspilt, adj. [1. unspílt; 2. anspílt]. un- (I.) & P.P. of spill (I.). Not spilt.

unspiritual, adj. [1. unspírichooal; 2. anspírítʃuəl]. un- (I.) & spiritual. Not spiritual; wanting in spirituality; worldly, material.

unspirituality, n. [1. ùnspìrichooáliti; 2. ànspìritʃuáliti]. Prec. & -ity. State, quality, of being unspiritual.

unspiritually, adv. [1. unspírichooali; 2. anspírítʃuəli]. See prec. & -ly. In an unspiritual manner.

unspoiled, unspoilt, adj. [1. unspóild, -spóilt; 2. anspóild, -spóilt]. un- (I.) & P.P. of spoil. Not spoiled; undamaged.

unspoken, adj. [1. unspóken; 2. anspóukən]. un- (I.) & P.P. of speak. Not spoken; unuttered.

unspontaneous, adj. [1. ùnspontáneus; 2. ànspontéiniəs]. un- (I.) & spontaneous. Not spontaneous; produced, or appearing to be produced, by deliberate effort; laboured, forced.

unspontaneously, adv. Prec. & -ly. In an unspontaneous manner.

unsporting, adj. [1. unspórting; 2. anspótiŋ]. un- (I.) & sporting. (colloq.) Not sporting; unsportsmanlike.

unsportsmanlike, adj. [1. unspórtsmanlīk; 2. anspótsmənlaik]. un- (I.) & sportsmanlike. Not sportsmanlike; not behaving according to, done in defiance of, the rules and principles of sportsmanship; unchivalrous.

unspotted, adj. [1. unspóted; 2. anspótid]. un- (I.) & spot(ted). Not spotted; (esp. fig.) untainted with guilt, uncontaminated : *unspotted from the world*; immaculate : *unspotted honour.*

unstable, adj. [1. unstábl; 2. anstéibl]. un- (I.) & stable (I.). Not stable; a unsteady, easily upset; liable to shift, or be shifted, in position or direction; changeable; not firmly fixed; b (in moral sense) wavering, unreliable; inconstant; unbalanced.

unstained, adj. [1. unstánd; 2. anstéind]. un- (I.) & stain(ed). Not stained; (esp. fig.) unblemished, untarnished, in character, reputation &c.

unstamped, adj. [1. unstámpt; 2. anstǽmpt]. un- (I.) & stamp(ed). Not stamped; (of letters, documents &c.) without a stamp affixed.

unstarched, adj. [1. unstárcht; 2. anstátʃt]. un- (I.) & starch(ed). Not starched; a not stiffened with starch; limp; b not stiff in manner and bearing &c.; easy, natural.

unstated, adj. [1. unstáted; 2. anstéitid]. un- (I.) & state(d). Not stated; not expressed in definite terms.

unstatesmanlike, adj. [1. unstátsmanlīk; 2. anstéitsmənlaik]. un- (I.) & statesmanlike. Not statesmanlike.

unstatutable, adj. [1. unstátūtabl; 2. anstǽtjutəbl]. un- (I.) & statutable. Not statutable; not warranted by statute.

unsteadfast, adj. [1. unstédfast; 2. anstédfəst]. un- (I.) & steadfast. Not steadfast; wavering in courage &c., irresolute.

unsteadfastly, adv. Prec. & -ly. In an unsteadfast manner.

unsteadfastness, n. See prec. & -ness. Quality of being unsteadfast.

unsteadily, adv. [1. unstédili; 2. anstédili]. unsteady & -ly. In an unsteady manner.

unsteadiness, n. [1. unstédines; 2. anstédinis]. See prec. & -ness. State of being unsteady.

unsteady, adj. [1. unstédi; 2. anstédi]. un- (I.) & steady. Not steady. 1. Shaky, unstable, not firm; easily upset or thrown down : *unsteady on one's feet; an unsteady post.* 2. (in moral sense) a Variable, changeable, wavering, unreliable, not constant in character : *unsteady of purpose*; b not irreproachable in conduct; dissipated, profligate.

unstep, vb. trans. [1. unstép; 2. anstép]. un- (II.) & step. (naut.) To remove (mast) from step or socket.

unstick, vb. trans. [1. unstík; 2. anstík]. un- (II.) & stick (I.). To separate what is stuck together.

unstimulated, adj. [1. unstímūlāted; 2. anstímjulèitid]. un- (I.) & stimulate(d). Not stimulated.

unstinted, adj. [1. unstínted; 2. anstíntid]. un- (I.) & stint(ed). Not stinted; lavish.

unstipulated, adj. [1. unstípūlāted; 2. anstípjulèitid]. un- (I.) & stipulate(d). Not stipulated.

unstitch, vb. trans. [1. unstích; 2. anstítʃ]. un- (II.) & stitch (II.). To undo what is stitched together; to remove stitches from.

unstocked, adj. [1. unstókt; 2. anstókt]. un- (I.) & stock(ed). Not stocked, not provided with supplies : *an unstocked larder.*

unstop, vb. trans. [1. unstóp; 2. anstóp]. un- (II.) & stop. a To remove, take out, a stopper from; b to clear away a stoppage.

unstopped, adj. [1. unstópt; 2. anstópt]. un- (I.) & stop(ped). Not stopped; specif. (phon.) a (of air-passage) not closed, partially open; b (of consonants) formed with the airpassage partially open.

unstrained, adj. [1. unstránd; 2. anstréind]. un- (I.) & strain(ed). Not strained. 1. Not passed through a strainer or filter. 2. Not subjected to strain; unforced, easy, natural.

unstrap, vb. trans. [1. unstráp; 2. anstrǽp]. un- (II.) & strap (II.). To loosen, undo, the straps of; to remove straps from.

unstratified, adj. [1. unstrátifīd; 2. anstrǽtifaid]. un- (I.) & P.P. of stratify. (geol.) Not stratified.

unstressed, adj. [1. unstrést; 2. anstrést]. un- (I.) & stress(ed). Not stressed; a not emphasized; b (of syllables or words in a sentence) not uttered with force or stress; not bearing the chief or any stress or accent.

unstring, vb. trans. [1. unstríng; 2. anstríŋ]. un- (II.) & string (II.). 1. To loosen or remove the string or strings from (any stringed instrument). 2. To remove from a string, to unthread : *to unstring a necklace of pearls.*

unstrung, adj. [1. unstrúng; 2. anstrǻŋ]. P.P. of prec. Relaxed, out of control, no longer subject to the will : *his nerves are all unstrung.*

unstudied, adj. [1. unstúdid; 2. anstádid]. un- (I.) & P.P. of study (II.). Not studied; attained without conscious art or effort; unpremeditated, spontaneous, easy, natural : *unstudied graces; an unstudied pose.*

unsubdued, adj. [1. ùnsubdúd; 2. ànsəbdjúd]. un- (I.) & subdue(d). Not subdued; unconquered, unrepressed.

unsubmissive, adj. [1. ùnsubmísiv; 2. ànsəbmísiv]. un- (I.) & submissive. Not submissive, not readily yielding obedience; not subservient.

unsubmissively, adv. Prec. & -ly. In an unsubmissive manner.

unsubmissiveness, n. See prec. & -ness. State of being unsubmissive.

unsubstantial, adj. [1. ùnsubstánshl; 2. ànsəbstǽnʃl]. un- (I.) & substantial. Not substantial. 1. (in physical sense) Lacking substance or solidity, not solid or heavy; light, flimsy: *an unsubstantial protection against the weather; an unsubstantial meal* &c. 2. (in non-physical sense) Lacking reality or substance; unreal, visionary: *unsubstantial hopes, dreams, arguments* &c.

unsubstantiality, n. [1. ùnsubstànshiáliti; 2. ànsəbstænʃiǽliti]. Prec. & -ity. State of being unsubstantial.

unsubstantially, adv. [1. ùnsubstánshali; 2. ànsəbstǽnʃəli]. See prec. & -ly. In an unsubstantial manner.

unsubstantiated, adj. [1. ùnsubstánshiàted; 2. ànsəbstænʃièitid]. un- (I.) & substantiate(d). Not substantiated, confirmed, or proved: *unsubstantiated evidence, report* &c.

unsuccess, n. [1. ùnsuksés; 2. ànsəksés]. un- (I.) & success. Want of success; failure.

unsuccessful, adj. [1. ùnsuksésfl; 2. ànsəksésfl]. un- (I.) & successful. Not successful; a meeting with failure, disappointment, or misfortune; missing success: *an unsuccessful man, business* &c.; b not producing the desired results: *unsuccessful efforts* &c.

unsuccessfully, adv. Prec. & -ly. In an unsuccessful manner; without success.

unsuitability, n. [1. ùnsūtabíliti; 2. ànsjūtəbíliti]. See next word & -ity. State of being unsuitable; unsuitableness.

unsuitable, adj. [1. ùnsūtabl; 2. ansjūtəbl]. un- (I.) & suitable. Not suitable, not fitting or adapted for; not fulfilling requirements; unbecoming.

unsuitableness, n. Prec. & -ness. Unsuitability.

unsuitably, adv. See prec. & -ly. In an unsuitable manner.

unsuited, adj. [1. ùnsūted; 2. ansjūtid]. un- (I.) & suit(ed). Not suited, not fit or adapted, for; ill-matched, incompatible.

unsullied, adj. [1. ùnsúlid; 2. ansálid]. un- (I.) & P.P. of sully. Not sullied; unblemished, untarnished: *unsullied glory, reputation* &c.

unsummed, adj. [1. ùnsúmd; 2. ansámd]. un- (I.) & sum(med). Not summed or counted.

unsummoned, adj. [1. ùnsúmund; 2. ansámənd]. un- (I.) & summon(ed). Not summoned, not called upon to appear; uninvited.

unsung, adj. [1. ùnsúng; 2. ansáŋ]. un- (I.) & sung. Not sung; not celebrated in poetry: '*Unwept, unhonoured, and unsung*' (Scott, 'Last Minstrel', vi. 1).

unsunned, adj. [1. ùnsúnd; 2. ansánd]. un- (I.) & sun(ned). Not warmed or lighted by the sun.

unsunny, adj. [1. ùnsúni; 2. ansáni]. un- (I.) & sunny. Not sunny; dark, gloomy.

unsupplied, adj. [1. ùnsuplíd; 2. ànsəpláid]. un- (I.) & P.P. of supply. Not supplied; not furnished (with).

unsupported, adj. [1. ùnsupórted; 2. ànsəpōtid]. un- (I.) & support(ed). Not supported.

unsuppressed, adj. [1. ùnsuprést; 2. ànsəprést]. un- (I.) & suppress(ed). Not suppressed.

unsure, adj. [1. unshōr; 2. anʃō]. un- (I.) & sure. Not sure; a unsafe; insecure; b uncertain.

unsurmountable, adj. [1. ùnsurmóuntabl; 2. ànsəmáuntəbl]. un- (I.) & surmountable. Not surmountable; not to be surmounted or overcome; insuperable.

unsurmounted, adj. [1. ùnsurmóunted; 2. ànsəmáuntid]. un- (I.) & surmount(ed). Not surmounted.

unsurpassable, adj. [1. ùnsurpáhsabl; 2. ànsəpásəbl]. un- (I.) & surpassable. Not surpassable, not to be surpassed.

unsurpassably, adv. Prec. & -ly. In an unsurpassable manner.

unsurpassed, adj. [1. ùnsurpáhst; 2. ànsəpást]. un- (I.) & surpass(ed). Not surpassed.

unsusceptible, adj. [1. ùnsuséptibl; 2. ànsəséptibl]. un- (I.) & susceptible. Not susceptible; insusceptible.

unsuspected, adj. [1. ùnsuspékted; 2. ànsəspéktid]. un- (I.) & suspect(ed). Not suspected; not supposed or known to exist.

unsuspectedly, adv. Prec. & -ly. In an unsuspected manner.

unsuspecting, adj. [1. ùnsuspékting; 2. ànsəspéktiŋ]. un- (I.) & suspect & -ing. Not suspecting; having no suspicion.

unsuspectingly, adv. Prec. & -ly. In an unsuspecting manner.

unsuspicious, adj. [1. ùnsuspíshus; 2. ànsəspíʃəs]. un- (I.) & suspicious. Not suspicious; a without suspicion; b not arousing suspicion.

unsuspiciously, adv. Prec. & -ly. In an unsuspicious manner.

unsuspiciousness, n. See prec. & -ness. State of being unsuspicious.

unsustainable, adj. [1. ùnsustánabl; 2. ànsəstéinəbl]. un- (I.) & sustainable. Not sustainable, not to be sustained; not to be encouraged or upheld: *an unsustainable position, opinion* &c.

unsustained, adj. [1. ùnsustánd; 2. ànsəstéind]. un- (I.) & sustain(ed). Not sustained; not upheld; unsupported.

unswathe, vb. trans. [1. unswádh; 2. answéið]. un- (II.) & swathe. To remove the swathings or bandages of.

unswayed, adj. [1. unswǎd; 2. answéid]. un- (I.) & sway(ed). Not swayed or influenced (by); unbiassed, unprejudiced.

unswear, vb. trans. [1. unswǎr; 2. answéə]. un- (II.) & swear. To recant, recall, on oath (that which has been sworn); to abjure.

unsweetened, adj. [1. unswétnd; 2. answítnd]. un- (I.) & sweeten(ed). Not sweetened.

unswerving, adj. [1. unswěrving; 2. answə́viŋ]. un- (I.) & swerve & -ing. Not swerving, (esp. fig.) firm, constant, undeviating: *unswerving loyalty*.

unswervingly, adv. Prec. & -ly. In an unswerving manner; undeviatingly.

unsworn, adj. [1. unswórn; 2. answɔ́n]. un- (I.) & sworn. Not sworn; not put on oath.

unsymbolical, adj. [1. ùnsimbólikl; 2. ànsimbɔ́likl]. un- (I.) & symbolical. Not symbolical.

unsymmetrical, adj. [1. ùnsimétrikl; 2. ànsimétrikl]. un- (I.) & symmetrical. Not symmetrical.

unsymmetrically, adv. Prec. & -ly. Without symmetry.

unsympathetic, adj. [1. ùnsimpəthétik; 2. ànsimpəpétik]. un- (I.) & sympathetic. Not sympathetic; a not showing sympathy with or to; hard, callous; b antipathetic.

unsympathetically, adv. [1. ùnsimpəthétikali; 2. ànsimpəpétikəli]. Prec. & -al & -ly. In an unsympathetic manner.

unsystematic, adj. [1. ùnsistemátik; 2. ànsistimǽtik]. un- (I.) & systematic. Not systematic.

unsystematically, adv. [1. ùnsistemátikali; 2. ànsistimǽtikəli]. Prec. & -al & -ly. In an unsystematic manner; without system.

untack, vb. trans. [1. untǽk; 2. antǽk]. un- (II.) & tack (II.). To undo, unfasten (what is tacked together); to remove tacks from.

untactful, adj. [1. untáktfl; 2. antǽktfl]. un- (I.) & tactful. Not tactful; lacking tact; tactless.

untactfully, adv. Prec. & -ly. In an untactful manner.

untactfulness, n. See prec. & -ness. State of being untactful; want of tact.

untainted, adj. [1. untánted; 2. antéintid]. un- (I.) & taint(ed). Not tainted; (esp. in fig. sense) without blemish or taint of guilt, shame &c.

untalented, adj. [1. untálented; 2. antǽləntid]. un- (I.) & talent(ed). Not talented; without talents or talent.

untamable, adj. [1. untámabl; 2. antéiməbl]. un- (I.) & tamable. Not tamable.

untamableness, n. Prec. & -ness. State of being untamable.

untamably, adv. See prec. & -ly. In an untamable manner.

untamed, adj. [1. untámd; 2. antéimd]. un- (I.) & tame(d). Not tamed; a wild, undomesticated; b not subdued, controlled, disciplined: *untamed passions*.

untangle, vb. trans. [1. untánggl; 2. antǽŋgl]. un- (II.) & tangle (II.). To loose, free from a tangle; to unravel, disentangle.

untanned, adj. [1. untánd; 2. antǽnd]. un- (I.) & tan(ned). Not tanned; a (of hides) not dressed; b (of human skin) not sunburnt.

untarnished, adj. [1. untárnisht; 2. antániʃt]. un- (I.) & tarnish(ed). Not tarnished (lit. and fig.).

untasted, adj. [1. untásted; 2. antéistid]. un- (I.) & taste(d). Not tasted; not yet enjoyed.

untaught, adj. [1. untáwt; 2. antɔ́t]. un- (I.) & taught. 1. Not taught; uninstructed; illiterate, ignorant. 2. Acquired without teaching: *those untaught graces of style*.

untaxed, adj. [1. untákst; 2. antǽkst]. un- (I.) & tax(ed). Not taxed; free from, not liable to, taxation.

unteach, vb. trans. [1. untéch; 2. antítʃ]. un- (II.) & teach. To cause to forget what has been taught; to teach the contrary of what has been learnt or a different method of learning.

unteachable, adj. [1. untéchabl; 2. antítʃəbl]. un- (I.) & teachable. Not teachable; incapable of being taught.

unteachableness, n. Prec. & -ness. State of being unteachable.

untearable, adj. [1. untárabl; 2. antéərəbl]. un- (I.) & tear & -able. Not tearable; incapable of being torn.

untechnical, adj. [1. unténkikl; 2. anténknikl]. un- (I.) & technical. Not technical.

untemper, vb. trans. [1. untémpər; 2. antémpə]. un- (II.) & temper (I.). To take away, remove, the temper of (metal).

untempered, adj. [1. untémpərd; 2. antémpəd]. un- (I.) & temper(ed). Not tempered; (esp. fig.) not modified or qualified: *untempered abuse, harshness; justice untempered with mercy*.

untenability, n. [1. ùntenabíliti; 2. àntinəbíliti]. See next word & -ity. State, quality, of being untenable.

untenable, adj. [1. unténabl; 2. antínəbl]. un- (I.) & tenable. Not tenable; not to be defended or maintained: *an untenable position* (lit. and fig.).

untenably, adv. Prec. & -ly. In an untenable state.

untenantable, adj. [1. unténantabl; 2. anténəntəbl]. un- (I.) & tenantable. Not tenantable; not fit to be let to or be occupied by a tenant.

untenanted, adj. [1. unténanted; 2. anténəntid]. un- (I.) & tenant(ed). Not tenanted; unoccupied by a tenant; vacant.

untended, adj. [1. unténded; 2. anténdid]. un- (I.) & tend(ed). Not tended; neglected, uncared for.

unterrified, adj. [1. untérifīd; 2. antérifaid]. un- (I.) & P.P. of terrify. Not terrified.

untested, adj. [1. untésted; 2. antéstid]. un- (I.) & test(ed). Not tested; untried.

untether, vb. trans. [1. untédher; 2. antéðə]. un- (II.) & tether. To loose from a tether; to set free (what has been tethered).

unthanked, adj. [1. unthángkt; 2. anpǽŋkt]. un- (I.) & thank(ed). Not thanked.

unthankful, adj. [1. unthángkfl; 2. anpǽŋkfl]. un- (I.) & thankful. Not thankful; ungrateful.

unthankfully, adv. Prec. & -ly. Without thanks or gratitude.

unthankfulness, n. See prec. & -ness. State of being unthankful; ingratitude.

unthink, vb. trans. [1. unthíngk; 2. anþíŋk]. un- (II.) & **think**. (rare) To dismiss from the thoughts; to change one's thoughts or mind about.

unthinkable, adj. [1. unthíngkabl; 2. anþíŋkəbl]. un- (I.) & **thinkable**. Not thinkable; not to be thought of; (colloq.) extremely improbable or unlikely.

unthinking, adj. [1. unthíngking; 2. anþíŋkiŋ]. un- (I.) & Pres. Part. of **think**. Not thinking; thoughtless, heedless, inconsiderate.

unthinkingly, adv. Prec. & -ly. In an unthinking manner; thoughtlessly.

unthought (of), adj. [1. unthóut (ov); 2. anþót (ov)]. un- (I.) & **thought** (II.). Not thought of, having never entered one's thoughts; unimagined; highly improbable, quite unexpected.

unthoughtful, adj. [1. unthóutfl; 2. anþótfl]. un- (I.) & **thoughtful**. Not thoughtful; inconsiderate, heedless.

unthoughtfully, adv. Prec. & -ly. In an unthoughtful manner.

unthoughtfulness, n. See prec. & -ness. Lack of thoughtfulness; thoughtlessness, inconsiderateness.

unthread, vb. trans. [1. unthréd; 2. anþréd]. un- (II.) & **thread** (II.). To remove, take out, the thread or threads from; (also fig.) to find one's way through, or out of, to disentangle (a mystery &c.).

unthrift, n. [1. únthrift; 2. ánþrift]. un- (I.) & **thrift**. (archaic) Want, lack, of thrift; thriftlessness.

unthriftily, adv. [1. unthríftili; 2. anþríftili]. **unthrifty** & -ly. In an unthrifty manner.

unthriftiness, n. [1. unthríftines; 2. anþríftinis]. See prec. & -ness. State of being unthrifty, lack of thrift; extravagance, wastefulness.

unthrifty, adj. [1. unthrífti; 2. anþrífti]. un- (I.) & **thrifty**. Not thrifty; thriftless, extravagant, wasteful.

unthrone, vb. trans. [1. unthrón; 2. anþróun]. un- (II.) & **throne**. To remove from a throne; to dethrone, to depose (a king).

unthwarted, adj. [1. unthwórted; 2. anþwótid]. un- (I.) & **thwart(ed)**. Not thwarted, not frustrated or crossed in purpose.

untidily, adv. [1. untídili; 2. antáidili]. **untidy** & -ly. In an untidy manner.

untidiness, n. [1. untídines; 2. antáidinis]. See prec. & -ness. State of being untidy.

untidy, adj. [1. untídi; 2. antáidi]. un- (I.) & **tidy**. Not tidy; lacking neatness and order; disarranged, in confusion.

untie, vb. trans. [1. untí; 2. antái]. un- (II.) & **tie** (II.). To undo, unfasten, what is tied, as a package &c.; to undo knot in.

untied, adj. [1. untíd; 2. antáid]. **a** fr. un- (I.); **b** fr. un- (II.) & **tie**(d). **a** Not tied; **b** unfastened, loosed from tie.

until, prep. & conj. [1. until]. In M.E., variant of **unto**; see un- (II.) & **till** (I.). (of time) **1**. prep. Till, so far as, as late as, up to: *until his death; wait until four o'clock*. **2**. conj. Up to the time when: *wait here until I come; until he returns, nothing can be done.*

untiled, adj. [1. untíld; 2. antáild]. un- (I.) & **tile**(d). Not tiled. **1**. (of roofs &c.) Not covered with tiles. **2**. (freemasonry, of lodge) Not closed or guarded by the tiler.

untilled, adj. [1. untíld; 2. antíld]. un- (I.) & **till**(ed). Not tilled; uncultivated.

untimeliness, n. [1. untímlines; 2. antáimlinis]. Next word & -ness. State of being untimely.

untimely (I.), adj. [1. untímli; 2. antáimli]. un- (I.) & **timely**. **1**. Not occurring at the normal time; unseasonable; specif., occurring, done, before its time; too early; premature: *an untimely death*. **2**. Done, said, occurring, at an unsuitable time; inopportune: *an untimely remark*.

untimely (II.), adv. **a** Prematurely; **b** inopportunely.

untinctured, adj. [1. untíngkchurd; 2. antíŋktʃəd]. un- (I.) & **tincture**(d). Not tinctured; (usually fig.) unmixed with, unaffected by (some quality), without a flavour or taste of: *cruelty untinctured by remorse*.

untinged, adj. [1. untínjd; 2. antíndžd]. un- (I.) & **tinge**(d). Not tinged; not coloured or modified with (some quality).

untiring, adj. [1. untíring; 2. antáiəriŋ]. un- (I.) & **tiring**. Not tiring; unwearying, unflagging: *with untiring energy*.

untiringly, adv. Prec. & -ly. In an untiring manner.

untithed, adj. [1. untíðd; 2. antáiðd]. un- (I.) & **tithe**(d). Not tithed, not subject to tithe.

untitled, adj. [1. untítld; 2. antáitld]. un- (I.) & **title**(d). Not titled; having no title.

unto, prep. [1. úntoo; 2. ántu]. In M.E., fr. *und to; und-, un-, 'as far as', as in **until**, cp. O. Fris. & O.S. *und*, 'until', & **to**. (archaic, Bib., and formal) To.

untold, adj. [1. úntóld; 2. ántóuld]. un- (I.) & P.P. of **tell**. Not told. **1**. Not recounted or related; not revealed or communicated: *left the story, secret, untold*. **2**. Not counted, beyond counting: *untold wealth*.

untormented, adj. [1. untórmented; 2. antōméntid]. un- (I.) & **torment**(ed). Not tormented.

untouchable, adj. [1. untúchabl; 2. antátʃəbl]. un- (I.) & **touchable**. Not touchable; not to be touched; specif., of the pariah or non-caste peoples of India; also as noun: *an untouchable*, a non-caste person.

untouched, adj. [1. untúcht; 2. antátʃt]. un- (I.) & **touch**(ed). Not touched.

untoward, adj. [1. untóward; 2. antóuəd]. un- (I.) & **toward** (I.). (archaic) **a** Perverse, froward: *'this untoward generation'* (Acts ii. 40); **b** unlucky, inconvenient, awkward: *a most untoward event*.

untowardly, adv. Prec. & -ly. In an untoward manner.

untraceable, adj. [1. untrásabl; 2. antréisəbl]. un- (I.) & **traceable**. Not traceable, not to be traced; not to be found.

untrained, adj. [1. untránd; 2. antréind]. un- (I.) & **train**(ed). Not trained. **1**. Not disciplined in mind; not having received a training in the methods of some particular kind of intellectual work. **2**. Not trained or exercised in some form of physical activity; specif. **a** not trained for some form of athletic exercise; **b** not trained as a soldier in military exercises.

untrammelled, adj. [1. untrámld; 2. antræmld]. un- (I.) & **trammel**(led). Not trammelled; free from impediments or restrictions; unhampered.

untransferable, adj. [1. untrahnsférabl; 2. antrænsfárəbl]. un- (I.) & **transferable**. Not transferable; not to be transferred.

untranslatability, n. [1. untrahnzlátabíliti; 2. antrænzleitəbíliti]. See next word & -ity. State, quality, of being untranslatable.

untranslatable, n. [1. untrahnzlátabl; 2. antrænzléitəbl]. un- (I.) & **translatable**. Not translatable; unadapted to, incapable of, translation.

untranslated, adj. [1. untrahnzláted; 2. antrænzléitid]. un- (I.) & **translate**(d). Not translated.

untravelled, adj. [1. untrávld; 2. antrǽvld]. un- (I.) & **travel**(led). Not travelled; **a** not having travelled; without experience of travel in foreign countries; **b** not traversed, untrodden, by travellers.

untraversed, adj. [1. untráverst; 2. antrǽvəst]. un- (I.) & **traverse**(d). Not traversed. **1**. Not passed over or crossed. **2**. Not denied or controverted.

untried, adj. [1. untríd; 2. antráid]. un- (I.) & P.P. of **try**. Not tried; not yet experienced; not having passed a preliminary trial.

untrodden, adj. [1. untródn; 2. antródn]. un- (I.) & P.P. of **tread**. Not trodden on; unfrequented.

untroubled, adj. [1. untrúbld; 2. antrábld]. un- (I.) & **trouble** & -ed. Not troubled; **a** undisturbed in mind, unperturbed, unperplexed; **b** (in material sense) calm, unruffled, not stirred into movement: *the untroubled surface of a lake*.

untrue, adj. [1. untróo; 2. antrú]. un- (I.) & **true**. Not true. **1**. **a** False, not in accordance with the truth or with facts; **b** unfaithful, disloyal. **2**. Not exactly conforming or corresponding to, not in agreement with, a particular standard, pattern, or measure: *untrue to type*; *the angles are untrue and out of the square*.

untruly, adv. [1. untróoli; 2. antrúli]. Prec. & -ly. In an untrue manner.

untrustworthiness, n. [1. untrústwěrdhines; 2. antrástwæðinis]. Next word & -ness. State, quality, of being untrustworthy.

untrustworthy, adj. [1. untrústwěrdhi; 2. antrástwæði]. un- (I.) & **trustworthy**. Not trustworthy; not to be relied and depended on; shifty, undependable.

untruth, n. [1. untróoth; 2. antrúþ]. un- (I.) & **truth**. **a** Quality of being untrue; falsity; lack of veracity: *marked by dissimulation and untruth*; *quick to discern the untruth in such rumours*; **b** an untrue statement, a falsehood, a lie: *never told an untruth in his life*.

untruthful, adj. [1. untróothfl; 2. antrúþfl]. un- (I.) & **truthful**. Not truthful; **a** given to saying what is untrue; not adhering to the truth in one's statements; apt to tell lies; **b** not in accordance with the truth; untrue, unveracious, lying: *an untruthful account, description*.

untruthfully, adv. Prec. & -ly. In an untruthful manner.

untruthfulness, n. See prec. & -ness. Quality of being untruthful; **a** habit, practice, of lying; **b** falsehood, absence of veracity (in a statement &c.).

untuck, vb. trans. [1. untúk; 2. anták]. un- (II.) & **tuck**. To undo, unfold, what is tucked up; to free, unfasten, tucks in.

untune, vb. trans. [1. untún; 2. antjún]. un- (II.) & **tune** (II.). To put out of tune, to make untuneful or discordant.

untuned, adj. [1. untúnd; 2. antjúnd]. un- (I.) & **tune**(d). Not tuned, not in tune.

untuneful, adj. [1. untúnfl; 2. antjúnfl]. un- (I.) & **tuneful**. Not tuneful; discordant.

untunefully, adv. Prec. & -ly. In an untuneful manner.

unturf, vb. trans. [1. untěrf; 2. antǽf]. un- (II.) & **turf**. To remove the turf from.

unturned, adj. [1. untěrnd; 2. antǽnd]. un- (I.) & **turn**(ed). Not turned (over); esp. in Phr. *leave no stone unturned*, use every effort, leave nothing undone or untried.

untutored, adj. [1. untútord; 2. antjútəd]. un- (I.) & **tutor**(ed). Not tutored; not taught; uninstructed; hence, rude, barbarous, uncultivated.

untwine, vb. trans. & intrans. [1. untwín; 2. antwáin]. un- (II.) & **twine**, vb. **1**. trans. To unwind, loosen, undo, what is twined; to untwist. **2**. intrans. To become untwined.

untwist, vb. trans. & intrans. [1. untwíst; 2. antwíst]. un- (II.) & **twist** (II.). **1**. trans. To undo, loosen, what is twisted; to unravel, disentangle. **2**. intrans. To become untwisted.

unurged, adj. [1. unérjd; 2. anǽdžd]. un- (I.) & **urge**(d). Not urged.

unused, adj. un- (I.) & **use**(d). **1**. [1. unúzd; 2. anjúzd] Not used; not made use of, not in use: *an unused room*. **2**. [1. unúst; 2. anjúst] Unaccustomed to; unfamiliar with, inexperienced in, not habituated to: *unused to society, to foreign travel*; *quite unused to public speaking*.

unusual, adj. [1. unúzhooal; 2. anjúžuəl]. un- (I.) & **usual**. Not usual; uncommon, rare; unfamiliar, strange; exceptional, odd.

unusually, adv. Prec. & -ly. In an unusual manner; (colloq.) to a high degree, extremely: *an unusually nice person*.

unutilized, adj. [1. unútilizd; 2. anjútilɑizd]. un- (I.) & **utilize**(d). Not utilized; not made use of, not turned to account.

unutterable, adj. [1. unúterabl; 2. anátərəbl]. un- (I.) & utterable. Not to be uttered; a unspeakable, inexpressible, indescribable: *unutterable despair*; *in unutterable confusion*; b so bad as to be beyond description; indescribable; hence out-and-out, thoroughgoing: *an unutterable scoundrel*.

unutterably, adv. Prec. & -ly. In an unutterable manner.

unuttered, adj. [1. unúterd; 2. anátəd]. un- (I.) & utter(ed). Not uttered; existing in the mind but unspoken: *unuttered prayers*.

unvaccinated, adj. [1. unváksinātəd; 2. anvǽksinèitid]. un- (I.) & vaccinate(d). Not vaccinated.

unvalued, adj. [1. unválūd; 2. anvǽljūd]. un- (I.) & value(d). Not valued; a not prized or esteemed; b not held in esteem; not considered valuable.

unvanquished, adj. [1. unvángkwisht; 2. anvǽŋkwiʃt]. un- (I.) & vanquish(ed). Not vanquished; unconquered.

unvaried, adj. [1. unvárid; 2. anvéərid]. un- (I.) & P.P. of vary. Not varied; a not varying, always the same; constant, enduring: *unvaried kindness*; *unvaried hostility*; b showing no variety; monotonous, tedious: *the unvaried routine of daily duties*.

unvarnished, adj. [1. unvárnisht; 2. anvániʃt]. un- (I.) & varnish(ed). Not varnished; a not covered with a coat of varnish; b (fig.) not embellished or tricked out; plain, simple: *an unvarnished tale*.

unvarying, adj. [1. unvárīiŋ; 2. anvéəri-iŋ]. un- (I.) & vary(ing). Not varying; not altering or changeable; constant; invariable.

unvaryingly, adv. Prec. & -ly. In an unvarying manner.

unveil, vb. trans. & intrans. [1. unvál; 2. anvéil]. un- (II.) & veil (II.). 1. trans. a To remove the veil or covering from: *to unveil one's face*, *oneself*; *to unveil a statue*, to perform the public ceremony of disclosing to view a newly erected statue; b (fig.) to disclose, reveal, make plain (what is secret): *to unveil a secret plan*, *one's purpose*. 2. intrans. a To take the veil off one's face or person; b to reveal oneself; to show one's true character.

unventilated, adj. [1. unvéntilātəd; 2. anvéntilèitid]. un- (I.) & ventilate(d). Not ventilated; a (of rooms &c.) not adequately supplied with fresh air; hence stuffy, airless; b not submitted to discussion: *unventilated grievances*.

unveracious, adj. [1. ùnverǽshus; 2. ànviréiʃəs]. un- (I.) & veracious. Not veracious; (chiefly applied to statements &c.) lacking veracity, untruthful.

unverifiable, adj. [1. unvérifiabl; 2. anvérifaiəbl]. un- (I.) & verifiable. Not verifiable; not capable of being verified.

unverified, adj. [1. unvérifid; 2. anvérifaid]. un- (I.) & P.P. of verify. Not verified, not proved or established as true.

unversed, adj. [1. unvérst; 2. anvə́st]. un- (I.) & versed. Not versed or skilled in.

unvexed, adj. [1. unvékst; 2. anvékst]. un- (I.) & vex(ed). Not vexed.

unvindicated, adj. [1. unvíndikātəd; 2. anvíndikeitid]. un- (I.) & vindicate(d). Not vindicated.

unviolated, adj. [1. unvíolātəd; 2. anváiəlèitid]. un- (I.) & violate(d). Not violated; (lit. and fig.) kept inviolate.

unvisited, adj. [1. unvízited; 2. anvízitid]. un- (I.) & visit(ed). Not visited; unfrequented.

unvitiated, adj. [1. unvíshiātəd; 2. anvíʃieitid]. un- (I.) & vitiate(d). Not vitiated; unspoiled; pure, not corrupted.

unvoiced, adj. [1. unvóist; 2. anvóist]. un- (I.) & voice(d). a Not expressed or uttered; b (phon.) not voiced; uttered without vibration of the vocal chords.

unvouched, adj. [1. unvóucht; 2. anváutʃt]. un- (I.) & vouch(ed). Not vouched (for); not attested.

unwaked, -wakened, adj. [1. unwākt, -wākend;

2. anwéikt, -wéikənd]. un- (I.) & wake(ne)d. Not waked or awakened.

unwalled, adj. [1. unwáwld; 2. anwɔ́ld]. un- (I.) & wall(ed). Not walled; without walls or fortifications.

unwanted, adj. [1. unwónted; 2. anwɔ́ntid]. un- (I.) & want(ed). Not wanted.

unwarily, adv. [1. unwárili; 2. anwéərili]. unwary & -ly. In an unwary manner; incautiously.

unwariness, n. [1. unwárines; 2. anwéərinis]. See prec. & -ness. State of being unwary.

unwarlike, adj. [1. unwórlik; 2. anwɔ́laik]. un- (I.) & warlike. Not warlike; unmilitary; pacific.

unwarned, adj. [1. unwórnd; 2. anwɔ́nd]. un- (I.) & warn(ed). Not warned.

unwarped, adj. [1. unwórpt; 2. anwɔ́pt]. un- (I.) & warp(ed). Not warped; not biassed; unprejudiced.

unwarrantable, adj. [1. unwórantabl; 2. anwɔ́rəntəbl]. un- (I.) & warrantable. Not warrantable; unjustifiable, indefensible; improper.

unwarrantably, adv. Prec. & -ly. In an unwarrantable manner.

unwarranted, adj. [1. unwóranted; 2. anwɔ́rəntid]. un- (I.) & warrant(ed). Not warranted; a without a warrant or guarantee; b unauthorized.

unwary, adj. [1. unwári; 2. anwéəri]. un- (I.) & wary. Not wary; incautious; unguarded; rash.

unwashed, adj. [1. unwósht; 2. anwóʃt]. un- (I.) & wash(ed). Not washed; a dirty: Phr. *the great unwashed*, the mob; b not touched or reached by the sea, river &c.

unwasted, adj. [1. unwásted; 2. anwéistid]. un- (I.) & waste(d). Not wasted.

unwatched, adj. [1. unwócht; 2. anwɔ́tʃt]. un- (I.) & watch(ed). Not watched; unguarded.

unwatchful, adj. [1. unwóchfl; 2. anwɔ́tʃfl]. un- (I.) & watchful. Not watchful; careless.

unwatchfully, adv. Prec. & -ly. In an unwatchful manner.

unwatchfulness, n. See prec. & -ness. Quality, state, of being unwatchful; lack of vigilance.

unwatered, adj. [1. unwáwterd; 2. anwɔ́təd]. un- (I.) & water(ed). Not watered; a not diluted; b not supplied with water; c not sprinkled, moistened, irrigated, with water.

unwavering, adj. [1. unwávering; 2. anwéivəriŋ]. un- (I.) & wavering. Not wavering; steadfast, firm.

unwaveringly, adv. Prec. & -ly. In an unwavering manner.

unweaned, adj. [1. unwénd; 2. anwínd]. un- (I.) & wean(ed). Not yet weaned; still at the breast.

unwearable, adj. [1. unwárabl; 2. anwéərəbl]. un- (I.) & wearable. Not wearable; a not fit to be put on and worn; b not to be worn out.

unwearied, adj. [1. unwérid; 2. anwíərid]. un- (I.) & wearied. Not wearied; not tired; unfatigued; indefatigable.

unweary, adj. [1. unwéri; 2. anwíəri]. un- (I.) & weary. Not weary.

unwearying, adj. [1. unwériiŋ; 2. anwíəri-iŋ]. Prec. & -ing. Not wearying; showing no weariness; untiring, indefatigable; persistent.

unwearyingly, adv. Prec. & -ly. In an unwearying manner.

unweave, vb. trans. [1. unwév; 2. anwív]. un- (II.) & weave. To undo what is woven; to separate the threads of.

unwed, -wedded, adj. [1. unwéd(ed); 2. anwéd(id)]. un- (I.) & wed(ded). Not wedded; unmarried, single.

unweighed, adj. [1. unwád; 2. anwéid]. un- (I.) & weigh(ed). Not weighed; not duly pondered or considered.

unwelcome, adj. [1. unwélkum; 2. anwélkəm]. un- (I.) & welcome. Not welcome.

unwell, adj. [1. unwél; 2. anwél]. un- (I.) &

well (IV.). Not well in health; ailing, indisposed; specif., sick, suffering from nausea.

unwept, adj. [1. unwépt; 2. anwépt]. un- (I.) & P.P. of weep. Not wept for; unmourned, unlamented.

unwhipped, adj. [1. unwípt; 2. anwípt]. un- (I.) & P.P. of whip. Not whipped, esp. of one needing a whipping: *an unwhipped cub*.

unwholesome, adj. [1. unhólsum; 2. anhóulsəm]. un- (I.) & wholesome. Not wholesome. 1. a Bad for the health; likely to cause disease; b suffering from bad health; unhealthy. 2. Morally unhealthy; tending to promote immorality: *an unwholesome book*.

unwholesomeness, n. Prec. & -ness. State, quality, of being unwholesome.

unwieldiness, n. [1. unwéldines; 2. anwíəldinis]. See next word & -ness. State of being unwieldy.

unwieldy, adj. [1. unwéldi; 2. anwíəldi]. un- (I.) & obs. *wieldy*, 'easy to wield or handle', see wield & -y. Not easy to handle or move; bulky, unmanageable; ponderous, clumsy.

unwifely, adj. [1. unwífli; 2. anwáifli]. un- (I.) & wifely. Not wifely; unlike a wife; not befitting or worthy of a wife.

unwill, vb. trans. [1. unwíl; 2. anwíl]. un- (II.) & will. To will the exact reverse of what one has willed, or has been willed to do.

unwilling, adj. [1. unwíliŋ; 2. anwíliŋ]. un- (I.) & willing. Not willing; reluctant, disinclined.

unwillingly, adv. Prec. & -ly. In an unwilling manner, against one's will.

unwillingness, n. See prec. & -ness. State of being unwilling.

unwind, vb. trans. & intrans. [1. unwínd; 2. anwáind]. un- (II.) & wind (IV.). 1. trans. To wind off what has been wound; to loose, separate, what has been wound. 2. intrans. To become unwound.

unwinking, adj. [1. unwíngking; 2. anwíŋkiŋ]. un- (I.) & wink(ing). Preserving a steady gaze without a tremor of an eyelid; openeyed, wide awake; (fig., rare) vigilant.

unwisdom, n. [1. unwízdum; 2. anwízdəm]. un- (I.) & wisdom. Reverse of wisdom; folly, unwise conduct.

unwise, adj. [1. unwíz; 2. anwáiz]. un- (I.) & wise. Not wise; foolish, imprudent.

unwisely, adv. [1. unwízli; 2. anwáizli]. Prec. & -ly. In an unwise manner; foolishly.

unwished, adj. [1. unwísht; 2. anwíʃt]. un- (I.) & wish(ed). Not wished (for), not desired.

unwitnessed, adj. [1. unwítnest; 2. anwítnist]. un- (I.) & witness(ed). Not witnessed; a not seen; b uncorroborated by a witness; c not signed by a witness.

unwitting, adj. [1. unwíting; 2. anwítiŋ]. un- (I.) & Pres. Part. of wit (II.). Not witting; unknowing, unconscious, unintentional.

unwittingly, adv. Prec. & -ly. In an unwitting manner; unconsciously, inadvertently.

unwomanly, adj. [1. unwóomanli; 2. anwúmənli]. un- (I.) & womanly. Not womanly; not characteristic of, unbefitting, a (good) woman.

unwon, adj. [1. unwún; 2. anwán]. un- (I.) & won. Not won; not gained.

unwonted, adj. [1. unwóunted; 2. anwóuntid]. un- (I.) & wonted. Not wonted; unaccustomed; unusual; infrequent, rare.

unwontedly, adv. Prec. & -ly. In an unwonted manner.

unwontedness, n. See prec. & -ness. State, quality, of being unwonted.

unwooded, adj. [1. unwóoded; 2. anwúdid]. un- (I.) & wood(ed). Not wooded, not covered with woods or forests.

unwooed, adj. [1. unwóod; 2. anwúd]. un- (I.) & woo(ed). Not wooed; uncourted.

unwork, vb. trans. [1. unwérk; 2. anwə́k]. un- (II.) & work (II.). To undo, destroy, what has been worked or done.

unworkable, adj. [1. unwĕrkabl; 2. anwǎkəbl]. un- (I.) & **workable**. Not workable; difficult or impossible to work, manage, or carry out : *an unworkable machine, plan &c.*

unworked, adj. [1. unwĕrkt; 2. anwǎkt]. un- (I.) & **work(ed)**. Not worked.

unworkmanlike, adj. [1. unwĕrkmanlīk; 2. anwǎkmənlaik]. un- (I.) & **workmanlike**. Not workmanlike; not like the work of a good and skilled craftsman; badly, unskilfully, done.

unworldliness, n. [1. unwĕrldlines; 2. anwǎldlinis]. See next word & -**ness**. An unworldly habit of mind; unworldly conduct.

unworldly, adj. [1. unwĕrldli; 2. anwǎldli]. un- (I.) & **worldly**. Not worldly; **a** not of this world; spiritual; **b** spiritually minded; not concerned with material or worldly things; specif., not seeking worldly advantage and gain.

unworn, adj. [1. unwórn; 2. anwǒn]. un- (I.) & **worn**. Not worn; **a** not showing signs of wear; **b** (of clothes) having never been worn; **c** not usually worn.

unworthily, adv. [1. unwĕrðhili; 2. anwǎðili]. unworthy & -**ly**. In an unworthy manner.

unworthiness, n. [1. unwĕrðhines; 2. anwǎðinis]. See next word & -**ness**. State, quality, of being unworthy.

unworthy, adj. [1. unwĕrðhi; 2. anwǎði]. un- (I.) & **worthy**. **1.** Not worthy; lacking moral worth, not having or deserving respect, worthless : *an unworthy person.* **2.** Not deserving some specified position, reward &c.; not possessing the moral or intellectual requirements for a specified position, rank, status : *an unworthy member of the Church ; a humble, but, I fear, an unworthy pupil of a great teacher.* **3.** *Unworthy of,* **a** not deserving : *unworthy of respect, of promotion ; reports unworthy of credence;* **b** below the dignity of, unbecoming in : *conduct unworthy of a gentleman.*

unwound, adj. [1. unwóund; 2. anwáund]. **a** un- (II.); **b** un- (I.) & **wound** (III.). **a** Wound off, freed from windings; unwrapped, untwisted, disentangled; **b** not wound.

unwounded, adj. [1. unwōōnded; 2. anwúndid]. un- (I.) & **wound(ed)**. Not wounded; without, not having received, a wound.

unwoven, adj. [1. unwóven; 2. anwóuvən]. un- (I.) & **woven**. Not woven.

unwrap, vb. trans. [1. unráp; 2. anrǎp]. un- (II.) & **wrap** (I.). To undo, unfold, or open what is wrapped; to take off the wrappings from (parcel &c.).

unwrapped, adj. [1. unrápt; 2. anrǎpt]. **a** un- (II.); **b** un- (I.) & P.P. of **wrap** (II.). **a** Unfolded; freed from wrappings; **b** not wrapped (up).

unwritten, adj. [1. unrítn; 2. anrítn]. un- (I.) & P.P. of **write**. Not written. Not embodied in or reduced to writing : *unwritten law,* a customary or common law, as opposed to *statute ;* **b** an assumed rule or custom by which a verdict of acquittal is given in cases of crime committed in defence of, or in revenge for seduction or attempt on the virtue of, a wife, daughter &c.

unwrought, adj. [1. unráwt; 2. anrǒt]. un- (I.) & **wrought**. Not wrought; not worked or manufactured; not elaborated or worked up.

unwrung, adj. [1. unrúng; 2. anráŋ]. un- (I.) & **wrung**. Not wrung, esp. in Phr. *my, his, withers are unwrung,* not touched by charge, accusation &c.

unyielding, adj. [1. unyélding; 2. anjíəldiŋ]. un- (I.) & **yield(ing)**. Not yielding; a incapable of being bent or moved; rigid; **b** refusing to alter a decision, opinion &c., inflexible, obstinate, determined.

unyieldingly, adv. Prec. & -**ly**. In an unyielding manner.

unyoke, vb. trans. [1. unyók; 2. anjóuk]. un- (II.) & **yoke** (II.). To loose, free from, the yoke; to disconnect, separate.

unyoked, adj. [1. unyókt; 2. anjóukt]. **a** un- (II.); **b** un- (I.) & **yoke(d)**. **a** Freed, loosed, from the yoke; **b** not yoked.

unzealous, adj. [1. unzélus; 2. anzéləs]. un- (I.) & **zealous**. Not zealous.

up (I.), adv. [1. up; 2. ap]. O.E. ŭpp, 'up', *uppe,* 'on high, up'; M.E. *up ;* cp. O.S. *uppa, uppe ;* O.H.G. ūf, ūfe : Goth. *iup,* 'up, upwards'; the orig. Gmc. form was **upp,* fr. Aryan **upnă;* the Gmc. type fr. Aryan **up-* has *f* as in Goth. *ufar,* O.E. *ofer,* see **over**. The following are a few cognates : Scrt. *úpa,* 'towards: on, upon'; & *upa-máś,* 'uppermost'; Gk. *hupér,* 'over', see **hyper-**, &, in spite of the difference of meaning, also *hupó,* 'under', see **hypo-**; further Lat. *sub,* 'under', orig. 'from below towards, from below upwards'; see also etymol. of **sub-** & discussion there of changes in meaning. Above, aloft, on high; reverse of *down.* **1. a** Expressing (i.) movement from a lower to a higher position : *to go up to the top of a hill ; come up here and look at the view ;* Phr. *to get up,* rise from bed ; *to go up to the University, up to Oxford, Cambridge ;* (ii.) movement from South to North : *to run up North, up to Scotland ;* **b** expressing (i.) rest at, or in, a higher place or position : *to stay up in the hills ; to sleep up at the top of the house ; to live several storeys up ;* Phrs. *to be up, stay up* (all night), not to be in bed, not to go to bed ; *to be up and doing,* alert and active ; *up at Oxford, up at the University,* in residence at Oxford &c.; *shall you be up during the Vac. ?,* residing in Oxford; (ii.) rest at or in, being at or in, a northerly part of the country : *to live up in Scotland ;* (iii.) motion to, rest at, the metropolis or nearest important centre; *up to, up in, London, in town, up in Glasgow* (from country); *up from the country.* **2.** After various verbs expressing movement, *fly up, pull up, throw up, jump up, stand up* &c.; and others expressing continuance in same position or state : *lie up, sit up* &c. See under the verbs severally. **3.** Expressing change, development, from an inferior or simpler, to a superior or more complex state : *to bring, train, up a child ; a plant grows up from a seed ; many large cities have sprung up from very humble beginnings.* **4.** Expressing the passage from an inferior to a superior social grade, official or other worldly position &c. : *to come up from poverty to affluence ; up from the ranks ;* Phr. *to come, move, up in the world,* rise in social scale. **5.** Expressing the coming into importance, under notice, consideration &c. : *the question came up for discussion, came up in conversation* &c.; *the case is up before the High Court ; up before the local Bench* &c. Phrs. *is anything up ?,* anything happening; *what's up* (with you)*?,* what's the matter?, what do you complain of ?, &c.; *it's up to me, you &c., to do* &c., it is my business, is incumbent on me &c. **6.** *Up to, up with,* **a** abreast of, alongside of, at the same distance from the starting-point, or from the objective : *I could not get, catch, up to him ; slow down a bit and let me come up with you ;* **b** (fig.) expressing equality, or approximation to, in merit, success, attainments &c. : *he is not up to his father as a scholar ;* Phr. *not up to his job &c.,* incompetent to carry it out. **7.** Expressing completeness, finality &c.; after various verbs: *to eat up everything on the table ; to finish up ; work up ; to tear up a letter ; to dry up ; burnt up to a cinder ; shrivelled up ; to boil up, heat up* &c. Phrs. *it's all up,* there is no more hope; *it's all up with him,* he is dying, is ruined, is done for &c.; *the game is up,* the thing is at an end, there's nothing more to be done, it's all over. **8.** Expressing **a** (physical) an increase in intensity, loudness, activity &c. : *to speak up, sing up, keep the voice up ; to play up, buck up ; to light up ; blow the fire up ; to flare up ; the hunt is up ; the temperature has gone up ; the cider is very much up,* highly charged with gas, effervescing; **b** increased intensity in mental activity, feeling, passion &c. : *his temper is up ; to fire up* (fig.), become suddenly angry ; *his spirits went up ;* **c** expressing various conceptions of increase, enhancement &c.; (i.) (of price, value &c.) : *consols are up this morning ; prices have gone up ;* (ii.) (of moral estimate): *he has gone up considerably in my opinion ;* **d** (rise in musical pitch) *I can't get up to that note ; the piano is up a tone.* **9.** Expressing condition of inactivity, being out of use, put by, or aside : *laid up with gout ; put up your swords into their sheaths ; to lay up treasure.* **10.** *Up to,* (colloq.) occupied with, engaged in : *what have you been up to ? ; he's up to no good,* engaged in some wickedness, mischief &c. **11.** *Up against,* (colloq.) faced, confronted with (difficulty &c.). **12.** *Up and down,* (i.) rising and falling : *to bob up and down ;* (ii.) backwards and forwards, to and fro : *to walk up and down.* (N.B.—For various idiomatic uses of *up* after vbs., other than those mentioned, see under the various vbs. themselves.)

up (II.), prep. See prec. **1. a** From a lower to, or at, a higher position, place, spot : *to walk, live, up a mountain ; to go up a ladder ; to climb up a tree ;* **b** to a position of greater importance, superiority &c. : *to work one's way up a form, a school* &c.; *he went steadily up the social scale.* **2.** From the direction of a river's mouth towards its source ; in the contrary direction to the current : *to row up the stream ; to walk up the river bank ;* also *to live, camp, further up the stream,* nearer the source than a spot specified or understood. **3.** Along a road, away from speaker, or farther in a given direction from a specified spot : *to walk up the road, street, lane.* **4.** Away from the sea towards the interior of a country : *to travel up (the) country.*

up (III.), adj., fr. **up** (I.). Tending towards, in direction of, a higher position ; only in a few expressions : *on the up grade,* tending to rise ; *the up train,* that which goes towards a big city, esp. to London ; *up line,* railway line on which the up trains run ; *the up side,* that side of a railway station on which is the up line ; *up platform,* that on the up line.

up (IV.), n., fr. prec. Only in Phr. *ups and downs,* rise and fall, fluctuation (in various senses) : *ups and downs of fortune, of health ;* also *a house full of ups and downs,* numerous small staircases, landings &c.

up (V.), vb. intrans. O.E. has *uppian,* 'to rise', fr. ŭp(p), see **up** (I.), but M.E. *uppen,* 'to bring up, disclose', is fr. O.E. *yppen,* fr. **ŭppjan.* The present word is almost certainly a new formation. (colloq. and vulg. or facet.) To rise, get up; to start into activity; only in such Phrs. as *he ups and says* &c.; *he up* (Past.) *and struck me, sauced me* &c.

up-, pref., fr. **up** (I.), (II.), or (III.), used in compounds in the varying senses of these. See the following words.

up-and-down, adj. [1. úp an(d) dòun ; 2. áp ən dàun]. Fluctuating, varying, alternately rising and falling (in material and non-material senses): *an up-and-down motion ; an up-and-down road, country* &c.; *an up-and-down life,* one distinguished by variations of fortune &c.

Upanishad, n. [1. ōōpáhnishahd ; 2. ŭpǎnifad]. Scrt. Lit. 'a sitting-down' (at another's feet to be taught by him). A class of metaphysical treatises, one of the divisions of the Vedas.

upas (tree), n. [1. úpas (trē) ; 2. júpəs (trī)]. Malay. (Jav.), 'poison', esp. *pūku ūpas,* 'the poison tree'. **a** The antiar, a large tree, *Antiaris toxicaria,* of Java and the adjacent islands, allied to the fig, which yields a very poisonous milky sap; from an unfounded traveller's tale, it was believed to destroy every living thing within a radius of many miles, whence *upas tree* is used of anything of poisonous or corrupting influence; **b** the poisonous juice, *antiar,* derived from this tree.

upbear, vb. trans. [1. upbár ; 2. apbéə]. **up-** & **bear** (I.). To hold up, to sustain, support; usually poet. & in P.P. : '*Upborne with indefatigable wings*' (Milton, 'P. L.', II. 408).

upbraid, vb. trans. [1. upbrā́d; 2. apbréid]. M.E. *upbreiden*, 'to reproach'; fr. **up-** & O.E. *breġdan*, 'to throw, brandish; to pluck'; cp. also the O.E. n. *bræġd*, *breġd*, *ġebreġd* &c., 'skill, cunning; trick, deceit'. For etymol. see **braid.** To censure, reproach, scold, chide: *he upbraided her fiercely*; also *upbraid with*, to charge, reproach with.

upbraiding, adj. & n. [1. upbrā́ding; 2. apbréidiŋ]. Prec. & **-ing. a** adj. (fr. Pres. Part.) Reproachful: *upbraiding looks* &c.; **b** n., reproach, reproof.

upbraidingly, adv. Prec. & **-ly.** In an upbraiding manner; reproachfully.

upbringing, n. [1. úpbringing, upbrínging; 2. ápbriŋiŋ, apbríŋiŋ]. **up-** & *bringing*, as vbl. n. of 'to bring up' children &c. A bringing up, education, mode of training, nurture: *the result of his good, bad, upbringing.*

upcast, adj. & n. [1. úpkahst; 2. ápkāst]. **up-** & **cast** (**I.**). **1.** adj. Cast, directed, upwards: *with upcast looks*; cp. *downcast.* **2.** n. **a** That which is cast or thrown up; **b** a casting or throwing upwards, specif., a shaft in a mine through which air passes up after ventilation.

upcountry, n. & adj. [1. úpkùntri; 2. ápkàntri]; adv. [1. upkúntri; 2. apkántri]. **up-** & **country.** (a colonial usage) **a** n. The interior, part of country, area, away from the coast, or up a river: *the upcountry is barren*; **b** adj., pertaining to the interior, away from the coast: *an upcountry farm*; **c** adv., (colloq.) in a direction towards the interior, away from the coast: *travelled upcountry for a hundred miles.*

upgrowth, n. [1. úpgrōth; 2. ápgrouþ]. **up-** & **growth. a** Process of growing up; **b** that which grows up.

upheaval, n. [1. uphḗvl; 2. aphívl]. **upheave** & **-al. a** Act, process, of heaving or lifting up, as by a natural cataclysm; **b** sudden change, disturbance, upset, in ideas, habits, social conditions, circumstances of life &c.

upheave, vb. trans. [1. uphḗv; 2. aphív]. **up-** & **heave.** To heave, or lift, up, to raise: said especially of a great cataclysm of nature such as volcanic action, earthquake &c.

uphill, attrib. adj. [1. úphil; 2. áphil]; pred. adj. & adv. [1. uphíl; 2. aphíl]. **up-** & **hill. 1.** adj. **a** Going, sloping, up; ascending; passing towards higher ground: *an uphill climb, road* &c.; *the road is uphill all the way*; **b** difficult, laborious: *an uphill task.* **2.** adv. Towards the top, or higher areas, of a hill, slope, or incline: *to go, run, uphill.*

uphold, vb. trans. [1. uphṓld; 2. aphóuld]. **up-** & **hold. 1.** To hold up, support, keep from falling: *slender columns uphold the great dome*; *strong arms upheld him while he hung in mid-air.* **2. a** To give moral support and encouragement to: *your praise and sympathy have upheld me greatly*; **b** to approve, give countenance to: *I cannot uphold such unscrupulous conduct*; **c** to confirm, maintain: *the Court of Appeal upheld Mr. Justice X's ruling.*

upholder, n. [1. uphṓlder; 2. aphóuldə]. Prec. & **-er.** One who upholds; supporter, defender.

upholster, vb. trans. [1. uphṓlster; 2. aphóulstə]. Back-formation fr. next word. **1.** To provide, furnish, with carpets, curtains, furniture &c.: *to upholster a house, room* &c. **2. a** To provide with stuffing, springs, coverings: *to upholster a sofa or chair*; **b** to cover (chair &c.) with some material.

upholsterer, n. [1. uphṓlsterer; 2. aphóulstərə]. Earlier *upholdster*, also *upholder*, orig. an auctioneer or broker, one who 'holds up' goods for inspection and sale. The suff. *-ster* is substituted on the anal. of *maltster*, & perh. influenced by association w. *holster*; the final (redundant) *-er* may be compared w. that in *fruiterer, poulterer* &c. **a** One who supplies upholstered furniture, carpets, curtains &c. for a house or room; **b** one who repairs and covers chairs, sofas &c. with **upholstery.**

upholstery, n. [1. uphṓlsteri; 2. aphóulstəri]. Prec. & **-y. 1.** The work and trade of an upholsterer: *to learn upholstery.* **2. a** Such goods, articles of household furniture, as are supplied by an upholsterer, including chairs, sofas, carpets, hangings; specif. **b** stuffing and coverings of chairs and sofas; **c** the way in which this work is carried out: *highly skilled upholstery.*

uphroe, n. [1. ū́frō; 2. júfrou]. Corrupt. of Du. *juffrouw*, 'young woman; pulley', fr. *jung*, 'young', & *frouw*, 'woman'. (naut.) A block of wood pierced with holes through which cords for an awning are passed.

upkeep, n. [1. úpkēp; 2. ápkīp]. **up-** & **keep** (**II.**). **a** Act of keeping up or maintaining; specif., maintenance of land, houses &c. in good condition and repair; **b** money spent on, the cost of, such maintenance.

upland, n. & adj. [1. úpland; 2. áplənd]. **up-** & **land. 1.** n. High land or ground; upper level of ground by a river, in a valley, or on foothills of a mountain; also in pl., *uplands*, upland country. **2.** adj. Pertaining to, situated in, the uplands, high in situation: *an upland road, farm*; *upland country* &c.

uplift (**I.**), vb. trans. [1. uplíft; 2. aplíft]. **up-** & **lift** (**II.**). (archaic) To lift up, raise, elevate: *with uplifted hands, eyes*; also in moral sense: *spirits uplifted by the news.*

uplift (**II.**), n. [1. úplift; 2. áplift], fr. prec. **a** Uplifting; upheaval: *an uplift of strata*; **b** (an Americanism) moral, spiritual elevation, emotional fervour: *preacher celebrated for his uplift.*

upmost, adj. & adv. [1. úpmōst; 2. ápmoust]. Archaic, for **uppermost.**

upon, prep. [1. upón; 2. əpón]. O.E. *úppon*, M.E. & Early Mod. *úppen*; **up** (**I.**) & **on** (**I.**). The distinction in usage between *on* and *upon* is very slight. It may be said that the two are almost always interchangeable, but that generally speaking, *upon* is less colloquial than *on. Upon* is often preferred when it follows a verb, esp. at end of a sentence: *nothing to go upon*; *not a chair to sit upon*; *very little to live upon.* On the other hand, while we could say either *her picture still hangs on*, or *upon, the wall*, we should probably not say *which wall did you hang it upon?*, but rather *on. Upon* is preferred in some Phr. such as *upon my word.* See idiomatic uses of *upon* after verbs under these.

upper (**I.**), adj. [1. úper; 2. ápə]. Compar. of **up. 1.** Higher in physical position; placed, situated above: *upper seats, the upper circle*, in theatre &c.; *shave the upper lip*; Phrs. *to have the upper hand of*, to be superior to, have authority or power over; *to get the upper hand of*, obtain advantage or power over; *upper storey*, (colloq.) the head, brains; specif., *upper case*, that holding capital letters &c. in printing; hence capital letters. **2.** Higher in rank, dignity &c.: *the Upper House*, House of Lords, Senate &c.; *upper servants*, butler, housekeeper &c. Phr. *the upper ten* (*thousand*), the highest ranks in society, the aristocracy.

upper (**II.**), n. (usually pl. *uppers*) Part of a shoe or boot above the sole: esp. in Phr. *down on one's uppers*, out at heel, with boots worn out, hence, desperately poor, in low water financially.

upper-cut, n. **upper** (**I.**) & **cut.** (boxing) A short-arm blow, delivered upwards at opponent's chin or jaw.

uppermost, adj. & adv. [1. úpermōst; 2. ápəmoust]. **upper** & **-most. 1.** adj. Highest in position, rank, influence; predominant. **2.** adv. In the highest position, at the top.

uppish, adj. [1. úpish; 2. ápiʃ]. **up** (**III.**) & **-ish.** Inclined to be presuming; impudent, cheeky.

uppishly, adv. Prec. & **-ly.** In an uppish manner.

uppishness, n. See prec. & **-ness.** State, quality, of being uppish; presumption, impudence.

upraise, vb. trans. [1. uprā́z; 2. apréiz]. **up-** & **raise.** (archaic) To raise, to lift up: (usually in P.P.) *with hands upraised to heaven*; *with voice upraised in anger.*

upright (**I.**), adj. & n. [1. úprīt; 2. ápráit]. O.E. *ūp(p)riht*, **up-** & **right. A.** adj. **1.** Erect, pointing directly upwards; vertical, perpendicular: *an upright tree, pillar*; *pattern with upright lines*; *take an upright position*; *has an upright, athletic figure*; specif., *upright piano*, one in which the strings are laid vertically, distinct from *a grand piano.* **2.** Possessing, showing, moral rectitude and integrity; honourable. **B.** n. Upright post, beam &c., esp. one used to support a structure.

upright (**II.**), adv. [1. uprī́t; 2. apráit]. In an upright position: *to stand, walk, upright.*

uprightly, adv. [1. uprī́tli; 2. apráitli]. **upright** (**I.**) & **-ly.** In an upright manner; chiefly in moral sense.

uprightness, n. [1. uprī́tnes; 2. apráitnis]. See prec. & **-ness.** State of being morally upright; integrity.

uprise, vb. intrans. [1. uprī́z; 2. apráiz]. **up-** & **rise.** (poet.) To rise, stand, get up.

uprising, n. [1. uprī́zing; 2. apráiziŋ]. Prec. & **-ing. a** Act of rising, esp. from bed: '*New every morning is the love Our wakening and uprising prove*' (Ken's Morning Hymn); **b** an insurrection, revolt; a rising: *the uprising was suppressed with great difficulty.*

uproar, n. [1. úprōr; 2. áprɔ̄]. Earlier *uprore*; borrowed fr. Du. *oproer*, 'commotion, tumult; sedition', fr. *op*, 'up' & *roeren*, 'to stir, move'; cogn. w. O.E. *hrēran*, 'to stir, agitate', O.S. *hrōrian*; O.H.G. *ruoren*, 'to move', cp. Mod. Germ. *aufruhr*, 'tumult'. Present spelling is due to association w. *roar.* Violent, excited, noisy tumult; clamour, rowdy disturbance: *the town, meeting, was in an uproar.*

uproarious, adj. [1. uprṓrius; 2. aprɔ́riəs]. Prec. & *-i-* & **-ous. a** Making an uproar; distinguished by disturbance and noise; violently rowdy: *an uproarious meeting*; *uproarious revellers*; **b** boisterous, noisy, tumultuous: *uproarious applause, laughter.*

uproariously, adv. Prec. & **-ly.** In an uproarious manner.

uproariousness, n. See prec. & **-ness.** State of uproar; noisy disturbance; noisy hilarity.

uproot, vb. trans. [1. uprṓot; 2. aprū́t]. **up-** & **root** (**II.**). **1. a** To root up, tear up by the roots: *to uproot a tree* &c.; **b** (fig.) to remove from established or natural abode or residence: *pathetic exiles uprooted from their homelands.* **2.** (in fig. sense) To destroy as from the root, to eradicate, extirpate: *long-established customs and habits are hard to uproot.*

uprouse, vb. trans. [1. upróuz; 2. apráuz]. **up-** & **rouse.** To rouse, stir up.

upset (**I.**), vb. trans. & intrans. [1. upsét; 2. apsét]. **up-** & **set. 1.** trans. **a** To turn upside-down, throw down; to overset, overturn, to capsize: *to upset a boat, motor-car* &c.; **b** to defeat, overthrow: *to upset a government* &c.; **c** to disturb, to put out of gear, frustrate: *you have upset all my plans*; also **d** (i.) to disturb mind of, distress: *the bad news completely upset him*; *much upset by his friend's coldness*; (ii.) to injure the health of, render ill: *I think it must have been the lobster last night that upset me.* **2.** intrans. To be overturned: *the car upset after a violent skid*; *if you don't sit still, the boat will upset.*

upset (**II.**), n. [1. úpsét; 2. ápsét], fr. prec. **a** A fall, overturning, tumble: *a bad upset from a dog-cart*; **b** disturbance of normal, quiet, orderly conditions; state of disorder and confusion: *the sudden departure of all our servants caused rather an upset*; **c** a disagreement, quarrel: *a bit of an upset with his father.*

upset (**III.**), adj. [1. úpset; 2. ápsɛt]. Set up, fixed; only in Phr. *upset price*, the lowest price at which property or an article will be sold, as at an auction; reserve price.

upshot, n. [1. úpshot; 2. ápʃɔt]. **up-** & **shot** (**IV.**), in sense of 'share, reckoning'. The final issue of anything; conclusion, end, general result or effect: *the upshot of the whole trouble.*

upside, also **up side**, n. [1. úpsīd; 2. ápsaid]. **up-** & **side**. a The top or upper side; b the side, as of a railway line or platform, on which an up train travels, as to London or nearest principal town or terminus.

upside-down, adv. [1. úpsīd dóun; 2. ápsaid dáun]. Changed for M.E. *up so down*, 'up and so down'; associated w. *up side*. a With the top or upper part or side underneath or inverted: *turn the box upside-down*; b in confusion or disorder; higgledy-piggledy, topsy-turvy: *turned the room upside-down to hunt for a lost collar-stud*.

upsides, adv. [1. upsídz; 2. apsáidz]. **up-** & **side(s)**. (provinc. in Phr.) *To be upsides with*, to be equal to, get the better of person, thing.

upstair(s), adj. [1. úpstār(z); 2. ápstɛə(z)]. **up-** & **stair**. Belonging to, situated on, an upper storey; above stairs: *an upstair(s) room*.

upstairs, adv. [1. upstárz; 2. apstéəz]. **up-** & **stair(s)**. Towards, in, an upper storey; at the top of a staircase, above stairs; to, in, a higher storey than that in which speaker is, or to which reference is made: *go upstairs and look at the view*; *upstairs in bed*; *my room is upstairs again after the third flight*.

upstanding, adj. [1. upstánding; 2. apsténdiŋ]. **up-** & **stand(ing)**. Standing upright, well set-up in figure: *a fine, upstanding young fellow*.

upstart, n. [1. úpstart; 2. ápstāt]. **up-** & **start**. a Person who has started or sprung up suddenly from a low position to wealth or importance; a parvenu: *the crowd of upstarts who pushed themselves into prominence after the war*; b an insolent and arrogant nobody: *he could snub an upstart with a look*; (also attrib.) *these upstart pushers into society*.

upstream, adv. & adj. [1. upstrém; 2. apstrím]. **up-** & **stream**. a adv. Against the stream or current; b adj., moving against the stream or current.

upstroke, n. [1. úpstrōk; 2. ápstrouk]. **up-** & **stroke**. An upward line or stroke, as in writing &c.

uptake, n. [1. úptāk; 2. ápteik]. **up-** & **take**. a (rare) Act of taking or lifting up; b (a Scots Phr.) understanding, power of apprehension, intellectual grasp: *quick, slow, in the uptake*.

upthrow, n. [1. úpthrō; 2. ápθrou]. **up-** & **throw**. A throwing up, upheaval; specif. (geol.) displacement upwards on one side of a fault.

upthrust, n. [1. úpthrust; 2. ápθrast]. **up-** & **thrust**. A thrusting upwards; specif. (geol.) elevation of part of the crust of the earth; upheaval.

upturn, vb. trans. [1. uptérn; 2. aptə́n]. **up-** & **turn**. To turn up, to throw up.

upward, adj. [1. úpward; 2. ápwəd]. **up-** & **-ward**. Directed, turned, moving, to a higher place or in a higher direction, ascending (lit. and fig.): *an upward course, glance*; *the constant upward move of prices, taxation &c.*; *an upward trend in social customs and manners*.

upwardly, adv. Prec. & **-ly**. In an upward direction; upwards.

upwards, (also poet. or liter.) **upward**, adv. [1. úpward(z); 2. ápwəd(z)]. In an upward direction, towards a higher position: *to move, look, upwards*. Phrs. *and upwards*, and more: *soldiers of ten years' service and upwards*; *upwards of*, more than: *upwards of a million unemployed*.

uraemia, n. [1. ūrḗmia; 2. jūrímiə]. Neo-Lat., fr. Gk. *oûron*, see **urine**, & *haîma*, 'blood', see **haemo-**. A morbid condition of the blood, due to the failure of the kidneys and bladder to carry away by natural secretion various toxic substances.

uraemic, adj. [1. ūrḗmik; 2. jūrímik]. Prec. & **-ic**. Affected by, characteristic of, uraemia.

uraeus, n. [1. ūrḗus; 2. jūríəs]. Neo-Lat.; fr. Gk. *ouraîos*, 'pertaining to a tail, tailed', fr. *ourá*, 'tail', see **uro-** (II.). A figure of the sacred or king cobra with head erect and hood expanded, worn, as a symbol of kingship, by the kings of Ancient Egypt.

Ural-Altaic, adj. & n. [1. ūral altáik; 2. júərəl æltéi-ik], fr. the Ural & Altaic Mountains of Asia. **1.** adj. Pertaining to, a a racial group of people lying between these ranges; b a group of agglutinative languages spoken in Eastern Europe and Central Asia, including Finnish, Turki, Mongol &c. **2.** n. Ural-Altaic language.

uralite, n. [1. ūralīt; 2. júərəlait]. As found first in the Ural Mountains. A kind of hornblende.

Urania, n. [1. ūránia; 2. ju(ə)réiniə]. Lat., fr. Gk. *ourania*, fem. of *ouránios*, 'heavenly', fr. *ouranós*, 'heaven', fr. *oworanos*; cogn. w. Scrt. *varunaś*, 'the god of the evening sky'. (class. mythol.) a The Muse of Astronomy; b epithet of Aphrodite (Venus); spiritual love, as opposed to *pándēmos*, sexual love.

uranic, adj. [1. ūránik; 2. juréinik]. **uranium** & **-ic**. (chem.) Pertaining to, containing, uranium, as *uranic acid*.

uranium, n. [1. ūrắnium; 2. ju(ə)réiniəm], fr. name of the planet *Uranus*, discovered by Herschel a few years before. (chem.) A white, malleable, metallic, radioactive element, found in pitchblende; used as an alloy in steel manufacture.

urano-, pref. Form used in compounds, fr. Gk. *ouranós*, 'heaven', see **Urania**; as *uranography*, description of the heavens and heavenly bodies; *uranometry*, measurement of stellar distances.

uranous, adj. [1. ūránus; 2. ju(ə)réinəs]. **uranium** & **-ous**. (chem.) Pertaining to, containing, uranium, esp. of compounds of lower valency than uranic compounds.

Uranus, n. [1. ūranus; 2. jú(ə)rənəs]. Lat., fr. Gk. *ouranós*, 'heaven', see **Urania**. a (Gk. mythol.) The husband of Gaia, the Earth, and father of Cronos (Saturn) and the Titans; b (astron.) the seventh of the major planets, farthest from the sun, except Neptune and Pluto, discovered 1781 by Sir W. Herschel.

urban, adj. [1. érban; 2. ə́bən], fr. Lat. *urbānus*, 'of the city', fr. *urbs*, 'a city'; prob. fr. **wrbhis*, 'place surrounded by a hedge'; cp. Lith. *virbas*, 'a twig, a rod'; fr. the same base w. a different gradational form comes the first syll. of **verbena**. Pertaining to, situated, living in, a city or town, as distinguished fr. *rural*: *urban population &c.*; *urban district council*, an administrative district and its council, for local government purposes.

urbane, adj. [1. erbán; 2. ə̄béin], fr. Lat. *urbānus*, see prec., in sense of 'polished, refined, well-bred'. Polished, refined, affable, courteous.

urbanely, adv. Prec. & **-ly**. In an urbane manner; courteously.

urbanity, n. [1. erbániti; 2. ə̄bǽniti], fr. Lat. *urbānitāt-(em)*, see **urbane** & **-ity**. Grace and affability of manner, bearing, character; gracious and polished courtesy.

urbanization, n. [1. erbanīzáshun; 2. ə̄bənaizéiʃən]. See next word & **-ation**. a Act, process, of urbanizing; b state of being urbanized.

urbanize, vb. trans. [1. érbanīz; 2. ə́bənaiz]. **urban** & **-ize**. To make urban; to change from a rural to an urban condition or character.

urceolate, adj. [1. érseolāt; 2. ə́siəleit], fr. Lat. *urceolus*, dimin. of *urceus*, 'an urn, pitcher', cogn. w. Gk. *úrkhā*, 'an earthen vessel for salted fish'; further Lith. *waršas*, 'basket used for catching fish'. The original *urceus* was perhaps a rude wicker-work frame plastered w. clay. See also **urn**. (bot.) Shaped like a pitcher or urn, as the flowers of various plants.

urchin, n. [1. érchin; 2. ə́tʃin]. M.E. *urchon*, also *irchon*, fr. O. Fr. *herichon*, variant of *ireçon*, whence Mod. Fr. *hérisson*, formed w. dimin. *-on* fr. Lat. *ēricius*, expanded form of *ēr* for **hēr*, 'hedgehog', cogn. w. Gk. *khḗr*, lit. 'the bristly, prickly creature'; fr. base **ǵher-*, **ǵhers-*, 'to become stiff, to bristle'; cp. Scrt. *hárṣatē*, 'becomes stiff, bristles, rises; shudders'; see further cogn. under **horror, hirsute, gorse**. **1.** (provinc.) A hedgehog. **2.** Sea-urchin, the echinus. **3.** a (archaic) Goblin, an imp, who was supposed to take the form of a hedgehog; b a mischievous, roguish boy.

Urdu, n. [1. óordōō; 2. úədū]. Hind., 'camp,' esp. in *urdū-zabān*, 'camp language'; cp. **horde**. A form of Hindustani, spoken chiefly by the Moslem races in India; it has a large admixture of Persian and Arabic words.

-ure, suff. Fr., fr. Lat. *-ūra*, suff. used to form ns. for P.P. type of vbs. Many words thus formed in Fr. are derived direct fr. Lat., e.g. *nature, literature &c.*; others are formed in Fr. itself, as *tournure, bordure, &c.* The force of the suff. is, a an act, process, existence, as *culture &c.*; b result of an act, *picture &c.*; c collective body of official persons, *legislature, judicature*.

urea, n. [1. ūrḗa; 2. juəríə]. Neo-Lat., formed fr. **urine**. A crystalline, soluble compound found in the urine of mammals, birds and some reptiles; also obtained synthetically from ammonium cyanate.

ureal, adj. [1. ūrḗal; 2. juəríəl]. Prec. & **-al**. Pertaining to, containing, urea.

uredo, n. [1. ūrḗdō; 2. juərídou]. Lat., 'a burning; a blight'; fr. *ūrere*, P.P. *us-tum*, 'to burn, scorch'; see second element of **combustion**. a A kind of rust-fungus, affecting plants; b a burning, itching sensation, as in nettle-rash &c.

ureter, n. [1. ūrḗter; 2. juərítə], fr. Gk. *ourētḗr*, fr. *ouréin*, 'to pass urine', see **urine**. An excretory duct of the kidney conveying urine to the bladder.

ureteritis, n. [1. ūrēterítis; 2. juərītəráitis]. Prec. & **-itis**. Inflammation of the ureter.

urethra, n. [1. ūréthra; 2. juəríθrə]. Lat., fr. Gk. *ourḗthra*, see **ureter**. The canal or passage through which urine is discharged from the bladder.

urethral, adj. [1. ūréthral; 2. juəríθrəl]. Prec. & **-al**. Pertaining to the urethra.

urethritis, n. [1. ūréthrītis; 2. jùərīθráitis]. **urethra** & **-itis**. Inflammation of the urethra.

urethroscope, n. [1. ūréthroskōp; 2. juəríθroskoup]. See prec. & **-scope**. Instrument for the examination of the interior of the urethra.

uretic, adj. [1. ūrétik; 2. ju(ə)rétik], fr. Gk. *ourētikós*, see **ureter** & **-ic**. Pertaining to the urine; diuretic.

urge (I.), vb. trans. [1. érj; 2. ə́dʒ]. A late word, fr. 16th cent., fr. Lat. *urgēre*, fr. **wr̥g-*, 'to drive, urge', cogn. w. Gk. *eírgein*, fr. **wergj-*, 'to repress, constrain'; further Goth. *wrikan*, 'to persecute'; O.E. *wrecan*, 'to drive, expel; to avenge', see **wreak**. **1.** To drive, press, impel, push forward, whether by blows, threats, or by persuasive words &c.: *to urge a horse on*; *he urged (on) the crew to greater efforts*. **2.** To press, persuade, encourage, exhort, insistently and vigorously: *to urge a person to do something*, *we are urged to economize in every way*. **3.** To bring forward, bring to notice, or to the attention, pressingly and insistently; to press, insist upon: *to urge the necessity for immediate action*; *let me urge upon you the importance of this measure*.

urge (II.), n., fr. prec. (mod. Americanism, to be avoided) Powerful, spiritual impulse; sense of being compelled to do something; strong impelling motive, incentive: *an urge to go and convert the heathen*; *to feel the urge of ambition*.

urgency, n. [1. érjensi; 2. ə́dʒənsi], fr. Fr. *urgence*. Next word & **-cy**. Quality of being urgent. **1.** Stress, exigency, pinch: *the urgency of poverty*. **2.** The need for haste, necessity for immediate action; pressing character: *a matter of great urgency*. **3.** Insistence, importunity: *the urgency of a claimant*.

urgent, adj. [1. ẽrjent; 2. ʌ́džənt]. Fr., fr. Lat. *urgent-(em)*, Pres. Part. of *urgēre*, 'to press, force, impel'. See **urge (I.)**. **1.** (of circumstances) Extremely pressing, demanding immediate attention or action; gravely important: *urgent necessity*; *in urgent need of help*. **2. a** (of persons) Using great insistence in demanding; pressing, plying, with persistence and importunity: *an urgent suitor*; **b** (of pleas, demands &c.) made, pressed, with insistence and importunity.

urgently, adv. Prec. & **-ly**. In an urgent manner; insistently; to an urgent degree.

-uria, form used as suff. in compounds, fr. Gk. suff.- *ouría*, fr. *oûron*, see **urine**; as *dysuria*, difficulty in passing urine; *pyuria*, urine containing pus &c.

uric, adj. [1. úrik; 2. júərik, jɔ́rik], fr. **urine** & **-ic**. Pertaining to, found in, urine; esp. *uric acid*, a white, almost insoluble acid, forming the chief constituent of the urine of birds and reptiles, and existing also, in small quantities, in normal mammalian urine, but in morbid conditions deposited as calculi or stone in the kidney and bladder, or as concretions in the joints of gouty subjects &c.

urim and thummim, ns. [1. úrim ən(d) thúmim; 2. júərim ən(d) þámim]. Heb. pls., lit. 'light' & 'perfection'. Two objects, mentioned in the Bible, first in connection with the casting of lots, secondly as kept in the breastplate of the High Priest.

urinal, n. [1. úrinal; 2. jɔ́rinəl]. O. Fr., fr. L. Med. Lat. *ūrīnāle*, 'a urinal', neut. sing. of Lat. *ūrīnālis*, adj., 'pertaining to urine', see **urine** & **-al**. **1.** Vessel into which urine may be discharged, esp. one of a special shape, easy of use by sick persons in bed. **2.** A fixed receptacle, or series of receptacles for urine, in a covered place, esp. one for the use of the public; a lavatory.

urinary, adj. [1. úrinari; 2. júərinəri]. See **urine** & **-ary**, cp. Med. Lat. *ūrīnārium*. Pertaining to urine: *urinary diseases, organs* &c.

urinate, vb. intrans. [1. úrināt; 2. júərineit], fr. Med. Lat. *ūrīnāt-(um)*, P.P. type of *ūrīnāre*; see **urine** & **-ate**. To pass urine, micturate.

urine, n. [1. úrin; 2. júərin, jɔ́rin]. O. Fr., fr. Lat. *ūrīna*, cogn. w. Gk. *oûron*, 'urine', & Scrt. *vāri*. A yellow-coloured fluid secreted by the kidneys, passed by the ureter into the bladder and thence discharged from the body through the urethra.

urino-, pref. Form used in compounds, fr. prec., as *urinogenital*, pertaining to the urinary and reproductive organs; *urinometer*, instrument for measuring the specific gravity of urine.

urn (I.), n. [1. ẽrn; 2. ʌ̄n], fr. Fr. *urne*, fr. Lat. *urna* for **urcna*, cogn. w. *urceus*, 'pitcher', see **urceolate**. **1.** A vase-shaped vessel, of pottery or metal, usually with a foot or pedestal and rounded in the centre with narrow neck, used to contain the ashes of the dead: *a cinerary, funeral, urn*; also, a sculptured representation of such on a tomb: '*storied urn or animated bust*' (Gray's 'Elegy'). **2.** A large metal vessel with tap, heated by a spirit lamp or other method, in which tea, coffee &c. can be kept hot and served to a large number of people.

urn (II.), vb. trans., fr. prec. (very rare) To place, preserve (as ashes of the dead), in an urn.

urnful, n. [1. ẽrnfool; 2. ʌ́nful]. **urn (I.)** & **-ful**. As much as an urn will hold.

uro- (I.), pref. Form used in compounds, fr. Gk. *oûron*, see **urine**, w. same force as *urino-*, as *urology*, science dealing with the urinary organs, their diseases &c.; *urosepsis*, septic condition due to disease of these organs.

uro- (II.), pref. Form used esp. in anatomical terminology, fr. Gk. *ourá*, 'tail', allied to *órros*, 'rump, base of the spine', fr. **órsos*, cogn. w. O.H.G. *ars*, O.E. *ærs*; as *urodaeum* (Neo-Lat. w. second element fr. Gk. *hodós*, 'way, passage'), the cloacal cavity of birds and reptiles.

Ursa, n. [1. ẽrsa; 2. ʌ́sə]. Lat., 'she-bear', fem. of *ursus*, 'bear', fr. **urcsos*, cogn. w. Gk. *árktos*, see **arctic**. Name of two northern constellations, *U. Major*, the Great Bear, Charles's Wain, the Plough; *U. Minor*, the Little Bear, which contains the Pole Star.

ursine, adj. [1. ẽrsīn; 2. ʌ́sain], fr. Lat. *ursīnus*, fr. *ursus*, 'bear', see prec., & **-ine**. Pertaining to, like, a bear.

urticaceous, adj. [1. ẽrtikáshus; 2. ʌtikéiʃəs], fr. Lat. *urtīca*, 'nettle', origin very doubtful, & **-aceous**. (bot.) Pertaining to the nettle family, *Urticaceae*, of plants and shrubs.

urticaria, n. [1. ẽrtikária; 2. ʌtikéəriə]. Neo-Lat., see prec. (med.) Nettle-rash.

urticate, vb. trans. [1. ẽrtikāt; 2. ʌ́tikeit], fr. Med. Lat. *urticāt-(um)*, *urticāre*, fr. Lat. *urtīca*, 'nettle', see **urticaceous**. To sting, as a nettle; to whip with nettles, in order to restore circulation &c.

urtication, n. [1. ẽrtikáshun; 2. ʌtikéiʃən]. See next word & **-ion**. Itching, tingling, burning, sensation on the skin, as from nettle stings, or in nettle-rash.

urubu, n. [1. ŏŏroobŏŏ; 2. úrubū]. Native name. The black vulture of the Amazon districts &c. of S. America.

urus, n. [1. úrus; 2. júərəs]. Lat., fr. Gmc., cp. O.H.G., O.E. *ūr*; cogn. w. Scrt. *usrá-*, 'ox'. See also **aurochs**. The wild ox of Europe, the aurochs.

us, pron. pl. [1. us; 2. as]. Objective case of **we**; O.E. *ūs*, dat., fr. **uns-*; M.E. *ous, ūs*; O.H.G. *uns*; Goth. *uns*; Aryan type **ṇs*, cogn. w. Lat. *nōs*; Gk. dual. *nṓ*, pl. *nemâs*; Scrt. *nās*; O. Slav. *nasŭ*.

usable, adj. [1. úzabl; 2. júzəbl]. **use (I.)** & **-able**. Capable of being, fit to be, used.

usage, n. [1. úzij; 2. júzidž]. M.E., fr. O. Fr.; fr. L. Med. Lat. *ūsagium, ūsaticum*, see **use (I.)** & **-age**. **1. a** Way, manner, of using, treating, handling; treatment: *such delicate instruments will not stand rough usage*; *good usage has preserved them*; **b** way of using a word to express a particular sense, shade of meaning &c. **2.** Habitual practice, long established use or custom, esp. as establishing a legal right, an acknowledged standard &c.: *to keep an old usage alive*; *some modern usages could be dispensed with*; *common usage has accustomed us to this*.

usance, n. [1. úzans; 2. júzəns]. O. Fr.; see **use** & **-ance**. (commerc.) Time allowed by custom for the payment of foreign bills of exchange.

use (I.), n. [1. ūs; 2. jūs]. M.E. *ūs*, O. Fr. *ūs*, fr. Lat. *ūs-us*, n., 'usage, custom, use'; also P.P. of *ūti*, 'to use'; the older Lat. form is *oisus, oiti*. Further connexions highly uncertain. In the legal sense (see **6** below), the word is strictly fr. O. Fr. *oes, ues*, 'profit, benefit', fr. Lat. *opus*, 'work, need, employment', see **opus**, but was levelled in pronunciation w. O. Fr. *us*, 'use'. **1.** Act of employing, or using anything; employment in, application to, some purpose or service: *to teach, learn, the use of tools, implements* &c.; *the proper use of one's faculties, limbs*; *the use of the telephone is growing very rapidly*; *the use of coal for domestic fires ought to be diminished*. Phrs. *to be in use*, be used, employed; *to be, fall, out of use*, cease to be used; *with use*, by using constantly; *to make use of, put to use*. **2. a** Capacity, power, of using: *to lose the use of one's legs, eyes* &c.; **b** liberty, right to use: *he put the use of his house, purse &c., at my disposal*; **c** need, opportunity, occasion, for using: *will there be any further use for big battleships in war?* **3. a** Usefulness, utility; advantage, purpose served: *to be of use, of no use*; *what's the use of so many officials?*; *is there any use in discussing the matter further?*; **b** purpose, end, object, for which something is used: *to find a use for old scrap iron*; *to have no further use for anything*; (colloq.) *to have no use for*, to dislike, see no merits in. **4.** Custom, usage, habit, continued practice, wont (slightly archaic): *it was his use to walk ten miles every day*; *according to an ancient use*. Specif. **5.** (eccles.) a special ritual or liturgy as observed by a church or diocese: *the Roman, Orthodox, Anglican use*; *the use of Sarum, Bangor* &c. **6.** (law) The profit or benefit from lands or tenements held in trust for another; the beneficial or equitable as contrasted with the legal ownership; profit or benefit from a trust.

use (II.), vb. trans. [1. ūz; 2. jūz], fr. O. Fr. *user*, fr. L. Lat. *ūsāre*, 'to use', formed fr. Lat. *ūs-(um)*, P.P. type of *ūti*, 'to use'; see prec. word. **A.** trans. **1.** To employ, to apply to a purpose, to put to a useful service; to handle usefully or properly; **a** in physical sense, of implements &c.: *to learn to use a saw*; **b** of mental action: *to use information to serve one's ends*; *to know how to use books*. **2.** (of one's faculties, body &c.) To exercise, employ actively, to put to use (in physical and mental sense): *to use one's legs*, to walk; *one's eyes*, to look; *one's ears*, to hear; *to use one's brains, wits*, to think. **3.** To consume, exhaust, expend: *to use a ton of coal in a month*; *how many eggs has the cook used for this omelette?*; *too little paint has been used on the gate*; *use up*, to consume completely, exhaust altogether: *the coal is all used up*; *to use up one's energy in fruitless efforts*; *to feel used up*, feel quite exhausted. **4.** To bring to bear, put into operation: *to use care, diligence*; *to use all one's skill*. **5.** To behave toward, treat, in some specified way: *to use a person well or ill*; *to ill-use*; (archaic, ending of letters) *yours as you shall use me*. **6.** To have the use of, avail oneself of: *use my house as if it were your own*; *may I use your telephone?* **B.** intrans. **a** (i.) (archaic except in pret.) To be accustomed, make a practice, have the habit, be wont: '*Were it not better done, as others use, To sport with Amaryllis in the shade?*' (Milton, 'Lycidas', 67-8); (ii.) pret. [jūst]: *I used to see him often*; *I used to smoke pipes when I was young*; (iii.) in neg. sentences, *use(d)n't* (to), (illit. or vulg.) *didn't use* (*to*), [jūsnt, dídnt jūs(tu)]; **b** impersonal constructions: *it used to be said*; *there used to be a house here*.

used, adj. [1. ūst; 2. jūst], fr. P.P. of **use (II.)**. Accustomed, habituated, inured to; experienced in: *you'll soon get used to our ways*; *quite used to one's new surroundings*; *I'm not used to being spoken to like that*; *used to hardship, to hard work*; *used to every comfort and luxury*; *he is not used to good society yet*.

useful, adj. [1. úsfl; 2. júsfl]. **use (I.)** & **-ful**. Of use; serviceable, advantageous, productive of good results, helpful (in material and non-material senses): *a stout stick is useful in emergencies as a weapon*; *a useful remedy to have by one*; *to give useful advice*; *a useful book for young students*.

usefully, adv. Prec. & **-ly**. In a useful manner; so as to serve a useful purpose: *I can't usefully intervene at this point*.

usefulness, n. See prec. & **-ness**. State, quality, of being useful.

useless, adj. [1. úsles; 2. júslis]. **use (I.)** & **-less**. Of no use, unserviceable; not producing or productive of good results; serving no useful purpose, ineffectual: *a well-advertised but quite useless remedy*; *material aid is now useless*; *good advice is useless for some people*.

uselessly, adv. Prec. & **-ly**. In a useless manner.

uselessness, n. See prec. & **-ness**. State, quality, of being useless.

user (I.), n. [1. úzer; 2. júzə]. **use (I.)** & **-er**. One who uses or employs anything: *users of this remedy will probably be disappointed*.

user (II.), n., fr. O. Fr., infin. as n., see **use (I.)**. (law) Use or enjoyment of property; presumptive right to such by prescription.

ushabti, n. [1. ŏŏshábti; 2. uʃǽbti]. Egyptian, lit. 'answerer'. A small figure, in the form of a mummy, made of stone or wood, and later, of glazed faience, representing a servant &c., and deposited in an ancient Egyptian tomb with the body in order to accompany and serve the dead person in the other world.

usher (I.), n. [1. úsher; 2. áʃə]. M.E. *uschere, huissher,* fr. A.-Fr. *usser,* O. Fr. *ussier, (h)uissier,* fr. Lat. *ōstiārius,* 'door-keeper, porter', fr. *ōstium,* 'door, entrance', fr. *ōs, ōris,* 'mouth', see **oral**. **1. a** Official in charge of the door or entrance to a court, hall &c., who admits or keeps out the public, shows people to their seats, keeps order and silence &c.: *an usher of the High Court of Justice* &c.; **b** one of several officials, *gentlemen ushers,* of the Royal Household, who precede ceremonial processions &c., specif., a high official of the principal orders of knighthood, as *Gentleman Usher of the Black Rod,* i.e. of the Garter &c. **2.** (obsolesc., except as term of contempt) An under-master at a school for boys.
usher (II.), vb. trans., fr. prec. **1.** To act as usher or introducer; to walk before and conduct; to show in, introduce, announce: *a footman ushered me to the drawing-room; I was ushered in with great ceremony.* **2.** (fig. or poet.) *Usher in,* to precede, to herald, to be the harbinger of: *the song of birds that ushers in the dawn; the passing of the first Reform Bill ushered in a new era in English politics.*
ushership, n. [1. úshership; 2. áʃəʃip]. **usher (I.)** & **-ship**. Post, situation, of an usher, esp. in a school; an under-mastership.
usquebaugh, n. [1. úskwibáw; 2. áskwibɔ́]. fr. Ir. *uisge beatha,* lit. 'water of life; whisky', The first element is fr. O. Ir. *usce, uisce,* 'water', fr. *wud-ko-; cogn. w. Scrt. *udán-,* 'water'; Gk. *húdōr,* see **hydro-**; Lat. *unda,* 'wave', see **undulate**; O. Slav. *voda,* 'water', see **vodka**; O.E. *wæter,* 'water', & *wæt,* see **water** & **wet**. The second element is fr. O. Ir. *bethu,* 'life', cogn. w. Gk. *bíos,* see **bio-**; Lat. *vīta,* 'life', see **vital**; O.E. *cwicu,* 'living', see **quick**. (archaic) Whisky.
ustulation, n. [1. ùstuláshun; 2. àstjuléiʃən]. fr. obs. *ustulate,* 'to burn, scorch', & **-ion**, fr. Lat. *ustulāt-(um), ustulāre,* in same sense, fr. *ūrere, ust-(um),* 'to burn', see second element in **combustion**. (rare and obs.) Scorching, burning, (esp. chem.) the drying by heat of moist substances as a preparatory stage of reducing them to powder.
usual, adj. [1. úzhooal; 2. júʒuəl], fr. Fr. *usuel,* fr. Lat. *usuālis,* fr. *ūsu-,* stem of *ūsus,* 'use', see **use (I.)**, & **-al**. In accordance with ordinary use, practice, custom, habit; such as is commonly met with in ordinary experience; such as is to be expected under given circumstances; habitual; commonplace, ordinary, familiar; the reverse of *strange, exceptional, extraordinary: the wedding was celebrated with the usual rites; the usual tale which such people tell; he said all the usual things; the usual people were there; it is usual for the king to open Parliament in person; it is not usual for shops to open on Sundays.* Phrs. *as usual,* in accordance with what is usual, in the ordinary way; *the usual (thing),* that which is usually done, said, received &c.
usually, adv. Prec. & **-ly**. As a matter of habit, custom &c.; generally, in the ordinary way: *one usually takes one's hat off in the house; he usually spent the morning at work, in bed.*
usualness, n. See prec. & **-ness**. (rare) State, quality, of being usual; commonplaceness.
usucaption, also **usucapion**, n. [1. ùzukápshun, -kápiun; 2. jùzukǽpʃən, -kéipiən], fr. Lat. *ūsucaptiōn-(em),* 'prescription', fr. *ūsucapt-,* P.P. type of *ūsucapere,* 'to obtain, possess, by long use or prescription'; fr. *ūsus,* 'use', see **use, user,** & **captive**. (Rom. and civil law) Acquisition of right or title to property by uninterrupted use or possession for specified period of time; prescription.
usufruct, n. [1. úzufrukt; 2. júzjufrakt], fr. Lat. *ūsusfructus,* in same sense, fr. *ūsus,* 'use', see prec., & *fructus,* 'fruit', see **fruit**. (Rom. and civil law) Right to the use and profits of property belonging to another without damage to it or waste.
usufructuary, n. [1. ùzufrúktuari; 2. jùzjufrǽktjuəri], fr. L. Lat. *ūsusfructuārius,* see prec. & **-ary**. One having the usufruct of property.
usurer, n. [1. úzhurer; 2. júʒərə]. In M.E., fr. O. Fr. *usurier,* fr. L. Lat. *ūsuārius,* see **usury** & **-er**. **a** (archaic and Bib.) One who lends money at interest; **b** one who lends money at exorbitant or illegal rates of interest; an extortionate money-lender.
usurious, adj. [1. uzhōōrius; 2. juʒɔ́riəs]. **usury** & **-ous**. **a** Of the nature of usury, involving usury: *a usurious rate of interest, loan, bond* &c.; **b** practising usury, extortionate.
usuriously, adv. Prec. & **-ly**. In a usurious manner; with usury.
usuriousness, n. See prec. & **-ness**. State, quality, of being usurious.
usurp, vb. trans. & intrans. [1. uzə́rp; 2. juzə́ːp]. M.E., fr. Fr. *usurper,* fr. Lat. *ūsurpāre,* 'to gain, acquire', in bad sense, 'to seize, usurp'; for *ūsu-rapere,* fr. *ūsu-,* see **use (I.),** & *rapere,* 'to seize'. See **rapid** & **rapt**. **1.** trans. To seize, take, assume, possession of, without right or by force: *to usurp the throne, office, power, the functions of a dictator* &c. **2.** intrans. (rare or archaic) *Usurp (up)on,* to encroach upon.
usurpation, n. [1. ùzerpáshun; 2. jùzəpéiʃən], fr. Lat. *ūsurpātiōn-(em),* fr. *ūsurpāt-(um),* P.P. type of *ūsurpāre,* see prec., & **-ion**. Act of usurping; wrongful or violent seizure of power, authority &c.: *the usurpation of a throne; a flagrant usurpation on the prerogatives of others.*
usurper, n. [1. uzə́rper; 2. juzə́ːpə]. **usurp** & **-er**. One who usurps; esp. one who wrongfully takes, accepts, holds, kingly status and authority in place of the rightful heir.
usurpingly, adv. [1. uzə́rpingli; 2. juzə́ːpiŋli]. Pres. Part. of **usurp** & **-ly**. By usurpation.
usury, n. [1. úzhuri; 2. júʒəri]. M.E. *usure, usurie, userie,* fr. Fr. *usure,* fr. Lat. *ūsūra,* 'use, enjoyment'; also 'interest, usury', fr. *ūsus,* see **use (I.),** & **-ure** & **-y**. **1 a** (archaic and Bib.) Practice of lending money at interest; **b** the lending of money at illegal or exorbitant rates of interest: *various statutes have been passed to check or limit usury.* **2.** Interest charged or received (often fig.): *she returned his love and devotion with usury.*
ut (I.), conj. [1. ut; 2. at]. Lat., 'as', fr. same base (w. different formative suff.) as *u-bi,* 'where', see **ubiety**. Chiefly in phr. *ut supra, infra,* as shown above, below.
ut (II.), n. [1. oot. 2. ut]. See **gamut**. The first or key note in the musical scale of Guido d' Arezzo, now, in solmization, replaced by *Do.*
utas, n. [1. útas; 2. jútæs]. M.E., fr. A.-Fr. *utaves,* fr. O. Fr. *oitauve,* fr. Lat. *octāva (diēs),* 'eighth day', see **octave**. (eccles., rare or archaic) The octave or eight days of a feast.
utensil, n. [1. uténsl; 2. juténsl], fr. M. Fr. *utensile,* Mod. Fr. *ustensile,* fr. Lat. *ūtensilis,* 'fit for use', esp. in neut. pl. *ūtensilia,* 'things for use', for *ūtentilis,* fr. *ūtent-,* Pres. Part. stem of *ūti,* 'to use', see **use (II.).** **a** Any object or implement, a tool, usually one of moderate size, used for a specified purpose: *writing utensils; farming utensils;* **b** specif., a vessel of any kind used in the household or the dairy.
uterine, adj. [1. úterin; 2. jútərain]. Fr., fr. L. Lat. *uterīnus,* see next word & **-ine**. **1.** (med.) Pertaining to the uterus or womb: *uterine artery, disease* &c. **2.** Born of the same mother but by a different father: *uterine brother(s);* so also *uterine descent* &c.
uterus, n., pl. **uteri** [1. úterus, -ī; 2. jútərəs, -ai]. Lat., 'womb', cogn. w. Scrt. *udára-,* 'belly'. The womb.
utilitarian (I.), adj. [1. ùtilitárian; 2. jùtilitɛ́əriən]. A mod. word coined fr. **utility** & **-arian** by Bentham. **1.** Conducing to, aiming at, utility; materially or practically useful; serving material or practical ends (often in derogatory sense): *from the merely utilitarian point of view; true education cannot be purely utilitarian or professional.* **2.** Pertaining to the Utilitarians, or to their school of thought.
Utilitarian (II.), n., fr. prec. A follower of the political philosophy of Jeremy Bentham and John Stuart Mill, which makes utility, in the widest sense, the test of the rightness of political and moral action, and virtue to consist in promoting the happiness of the greatest number.
Utilitarianism, n. [1. ùtilitárianizm; 2. jutìlitɛ́əriənizəm]. Prec. & **-ism**. (philos.) The political and ethical theory of the Utilitarians, namely, that the end and criterion of all individual and political action should be the greatest happiness of the greatest number.
utility, n. [1. útiliti; 2. jutíliti], fr. Fr. *utilité,* fr. Lat. *utilitāt-(em),* fr. *utilis,* 'useful', fr. *ūt-,* a form of the base seen in *ūsus,* see **use (I.)**; cp. also infin. *ūti,* Pres. *ūtor* &c. **1.** State, property, quality, of being useful; usefulness, advantageousness, the being profitable. Phr. *of no utility,* useless. **2.** Usually *utilities,* useful things; (theatr. slang) *utility man,* man capable of playing various kinds of minor parts; general handy-man.
utilizable, adj. [1. útilizabl; 2. jutílaizəbl]. **utilize** & **-able**. Capable of being utilized or used.
utilization, n. [1. ùtilizáshun; 2. jùtilaizéiʃən]. **utilize** & **-ation**. **a** Act of utilizing; **b** state of being utilized.
utilize, vb. trans. [1. útiliz; 2. jútilaiz]. Fr., fr. *utiliser,* a mod. word fr. Lat. *ūtilis,* 'useful', see **utility**, & **-ize**. To put to use, make use of; to turn to profitable use or account.
utmost (I.), adj. [1. útmost; 2. átmoust]. O.E. *ūtemest,* M.E. *ūtemest* &c., superl. of *ūt(e),* 'out', see **out**; the O.E. ending is an old double superl. suff.; this was later influenced in form by *most,* see **-most**. **1.** Outermost, situated at farthest extreme or limit; farthest, most extreme: *to the utmost ends of the earth; utmost limits; filled to its utmost capacity.* **2.** To, of, the greatest, highest, degree: *in the utmost danger and misery; ready to help with the utmost pleasure.*
utmost (II.), n., fr. prec. The most that can be done, the most possible; the greatest possible effort: *that is the utmost that I can do; try your utmost to succeed; to the utmost of one's power* &c.
Utopia, n. [1. utópia; 2. jutóupiə], lit. 'nowhere', coined by Sir Thomas More, fr. Gk. *ou,* 'not' (etymol. unknown), & *tópos,* 'place', see **topic**. **1.** (cap.) The name of the imaginary island governed on a perfect political and social system, giving the title to More's book, 'Utopia', published 1516. **2.** Any ideal community or state; an ideally perfect social and political system, usually with the implication that such is impossible of realization: *the foundation of Utopias in imagination will never cease; the new Utopia has failed.* **3.** Any literary work describing such an ideal state or system: *Samuel Butler's Utopia is styled 'Erewhon'.*
Utopian, adj. & n. [1. utópian; 2. jutóupiən]. Prec. & **-an**. **1.** adj. **a** Pertaining to, characteristic of, a Utopia, ideally perfect but impracticable; chimerical, visionary: *Utopian schemes;* **b** apt to form or imagine Utopias: *a Utopian dreamer.* **2.** n. Inhabitant of a Utopia.
utricle, n. [1. útrikl; 2. jútrikl]. Fr., fr. Lat. *utriculus,* 'a little bag', dimin. of *uter,* 'leather sack or bag', a collateral form of *uterus.* (physiol.) **a** A cell or sac in an animal or plant, esp. an air sac or vesicle in certain aquatic plants, as the bladderworts *(Utricularia)* &c.; **b** a cavity in the labyrinth of the inner ear.
utricular, adj. [1. utríkular; 2. jutríkjulə], fr. Lat. *utriculus,* see prec. & **-ar**. Pertaining to, resembling, a utricle.
utter (I.), adj. [1. úter; 2. átə]. O.E. *ūtera,*

2 C

UTTER (II.)

uttra, 'outer', M.E. *ŭt(t)ere*, an old compar. adj. formed fr. O.E. *ūt*, see **out**; shortening of the old long vowel takes place in M.E. in the first syll. of a three-syllabled word. **1.** Outer, situated on the outside; now obs. except in the rarely used *utter bar, barrister*, for those members of the bar who have not been called within the bar; the junior bar, those who are not King's Counsel or, formerly, serjeants-at-law. **2. a** Complete, total: *utter darkness, misery, ruin* &c.; **b** unconditional, final, peremptory: *an utter refusal, denial* &c.; **c** unqualified, absolute: *an utter scoundrel; the utter folly of such a policy*.

utter (II.), vb. trans. M.E. fr. *uttren*, formed fr. *uttere*, see prec., or formed again later fr. the adv. or adj. **1.** (orig. meaning) To put out, or forth, now only **a** *to utter a libel*, publish it; **b** *to utter false coin, notes* &c., to produce and put these into circulation: *charged with forging and uttering cheques* &c. **2. a** (i.) To produce audibly by means of the vocal organs; to pronounce: *to utter a vowel sound; not a sound was uttered; the last words to be uttered*; also (ii.) to breathe out, to emit through the mouth: *to utter a groan, a sigh*; **b** to express, make known, by word of mouth or in writing: *to utter one's thoughts, feelings* &c.

utterable, adj. [1. úterəbl; 2. átərəbl]. Prec. & **-able**. (rare) Capable of being uttered.

utterance (I.), n. [1. úterəns; 2. át(ə)rəns].

utter (II.) & **-ance**. **1.** Act of uttering or expressing in words &c.: *to give utterance to one's feelings*. **2.** Mode, style, manner, of speaking; pronunciation, delivery: *a thick, clear, slovenly, utterance* &c. **3.** That which is uttered; spoken or written expression of thoughts, opinions &c.; pronouncement: *the pompous utterances of the platform, the press* &c. **4.** (rare) Act of uttering or circulating; putting, passing, into circulation: *utterance of false coin*.

utterance (II.), n. M.E., fr. Fr. *outrance*, see **outrance**, & **ultra**; influenced in form by association w. **utter**, adj. (archaic, poet.) Extremity; the uttermost: *to the utterance*, (Shakespeare, 'Macbeth').

utterer, n. [1. úterer; 2. átərə]. **utter** (II.) & **-er**. One who utters (in various senses): *an utterer of slander, of false coins* &c.

uttering, n. [1. úteriŋ; 2. átəriŋ]. **utter** (II.) & **-ing**. **a** Act of expressing in words &c.; **b** act of circulating: *the forging and uttering of a cheque*.

utterly, adv. [1. úterli; 2. átəli]. **utter** (I.) & **-ly**. To the fullest extent; completely, totally: *utterly exhausted, ruined* &c.

uttermost, adj. & n. [1. úterməst; 2. átəməst]. **utter** (I.) & **-most**. **1.** adj. **a** Farthest away, farthest out: *to the uttermost ends of the earth*; **b** extreme, utmost; being of the highest, greatest, degree: *the uttermost limit of forbearance*. **2.** n. The utmost; highest degree or extremity: *to the uttermost of one's power, capacity* &c.

utterness, n. [1. úternes; 2. átənis]. **utter** (I.) & **-ness**. Quality of being extreme; completeness: *the utterness of his folly and wickedness*.

uvula, n., pl. **uvulae** [1. úvūla, -lē; 2. júvjulə, -lī], fr. *uvula*, fr. L. or Med. Lat. *ūvula*, dimin. of Lat. *ūva*, 'a grape, bunch of grapes, uvula'; fr. *oiwā*; cogn. w. Gk. *óā*, Ionic *óē, oiē* for *oiwā-, 'service-tree; a berry'. (anat.) **a** A fleshy, hanging protuberance in the centre of the posterior part of the soft palate; **b** similar protuberance in the cerebellum and the bladder.

uvular, adj. [1. úvūlar; 2. júvjulə]. Prec. & **-ar**. Pertaining to the uvula; specif. (phon.) velar.

uvulitis, n. [1. ûvūlítis; 2. jùvjuláitis]. See prec. & **-itis**. Inflammation of the uvula.

uxorious, adj. [1. ukzṓrius; 2. akzṓriəs], fr. Lat. *uxōrius*, 'pertaining to, excessively fond of, a wife', fr. *uxor*, 'wife'; perh. orig. 'she who is led home', fr. base seen in Lat. *vehere*, 'to draw' &c., see **vehicle**; cp. Lith. *vedú*, 'I lead, conduct', & Scrt. *vadhú-*, 'bride'. Excessively fond of or devoted to one's wife; too submissive to the will of one's wife.

uxoriously, adv. Prec. & **-ly**. In an uxorious manner.

uxoriousness, n. See prec. & **-ness**. State, quality, of being uxorious.

V

V, v [1. vē; 2. vī]. **a** The twenty-second letter of the alphabet; for use in abbreviations &c. see end of Dictionary; **b** the Roman symbol for the numeral 5; **c** a V-shaped object.

vac, n. [1. vak; 2. væk]. Colloq. abbr. of **vacation**.

vacancy, n. [1. vákansi; 2. véikənsi]. Through Fr. *vacance*, or directly fr. L. or Med. Lat. *vacantia*, fr. Lat. *vacant-(em)*, see **vacant**, & **-ancy**. **1.** (in physical senses) **a** Condition, state, of being vacant, unoccupied, or empty; emptiness: *to gaze on the vacancy of the polar ice-fields*; *look down from the precipice into vacancy*; **b** an empty, unoccupied, unfilled, space; a vacant space: *there is still a vacancy for another villa in the new road*. **2. a** State of being mentally vacant; absent-mindedness, lack of interest, listlessness; inanity, vacuity: *an expression of vacancy on his face*; *sudden periods of vacancy preceded his breakdown*; **b** state of being unoccupied or freed from work or business; inactivity, want of occupation: *an active, busy man dreads the vacancy of retirement*; **c** a gap, blank, deficiency: *it will fill a vacancy in our knowledge*. **3.** A vacant, unfilled, unoccupied, post, situation, or office; form of employment waiting to be filled: *there are still a few vacancies on the staff to be filled*; *his death has caused a vacancy in the Cabinet*.

vacant, adj. [1. vákant; 2. véikənt]. Through O. Fr. or directly fr. Lat. *vacant-(em)*, Pres. Part. type of *vacāre*, 'to be empty; to be unoccupied or without an owner; to lack or be without; to be free from toil, be at leisure'. The base is seen also in Lat. *vănus*, 'void, vacant; fruitless', see **vain**; cp. also **vacuous**. **1.** Empty, void, not filled by anything; having no material contents: *look down into vacant space; the vast and vacant regions of infinite space*. **2. a** Not occupied by man; uninhabited; not populated or developed: *the vacant regions of the North-West; vacant prairies clamouring for colonists*; **b** not held or occupied by owner or tenant; untenanted: *many vacant farms; increase of vacant houses in a town*; Phr. *vacant possession*, legal or auctioneer's term implying that immediate occupation and possession of house, farm &c. is offered; **c** not engaged or let; not already booked: *not a room vacant in the hotel; many vacant seats in the theatre*; **d** no longer occupied: *the vacant chair*. **3.** (of office, benefice &c.) Not held, filled, or occupied by anyone; left unoccupied by death, resignation &c.; waiting to be filled: *situations vacant; the resignation of Lord X leaves an important Cabinet post vacant*. **4.** (of periods of time) Not occupied by work or business; not engaged; leisured: *some occupation to fill the vacant hours; keep a day next week vacant if you can*. **5.** (of mental state, character &c.) **a** Not active or occupied with serious work or thought; empty, idle, vacuous: 'the loud laugh that spoke the vacant mind' (Goldsmith, 'Deserted Village', 122); *to lead a silly, vacant life*; **b** characteristic of, expressing, such an unoccupied, empty mind: *a vacant stare, look* &c.

vacantly, adv. Prec. & **-ly**. In a vacant manner: *to stare, laugh, vacantly*.

vacate, vb. trans. [1. vakát, vākát; 2. vəkéit, veikéit], fr. Lat. *vacāt-(um)*, P.P. type of *vacāre*, 'to be empty; to be free from' &c., see **vacant**. **1.** To make, leave, vacant; to go away, depart from and leave unoccupied: *to vacate a house, rooms* &c.; *the enemy vacated the town as we advanced*. **2.** To give up, to resign from; to leave unfilled or unoccupied: *to vacate the throne; one bishopric vacated by death and two by translation; to vacate a seat in parliament*. **3.** (mil.) To remove, order to leave position, camp &c.: *all troops must be vacated from the town before noon*. **4.** (law) To render void; to annul, cancel, invalidate: *to vacate a contract, deed, registration* &c.

vacation, n. [1. vakáshun; 2. vəkéiʃən]. Lat. *vacātiōn-(em)*, fr. *vacāt-*, see prec., & **-ion**. **1.** Act of vacating or leaving vacant, unfilled or unoccupied: *his sudden vacation of office is unexplained*. **2.** Period during which an office, benefice &c. is left vacant: *the vacation of the benefice was prolonged*. **3.** A fixed, stated, interval in a year during which the ordinary business, work, study &c. is suspended; used esp. of courts of law and of a university; period when the courts are 'up' or not sitting, or when the university is 'down' or not in residence: *the Christmas, Easter,* vacation; *the long vacation*, that which occupies the summer months.

vaccinal, adj. [1. váksinal; 2. væksinəl]. Fr., see **vaccine** & **-al**. Pertaining to vaccine or vaccination.

vaccinate, vb. trans. [1. váksinát; 2. væksinèit], fr. **vaccine** & **-ate**; it was ad. fr. Fr. *vacciner*, c. 1803, in place of the earlier *inoculate*. **1.** To inoculate (child, person) with the vaccine, i.e. the virus, of cowpox, in the form of calf-lymph, as a protection against smallpox. **2.** To inoculate with other kinds of vaccine.

vaccination, n. [1. vàksináshun; 2. væksinéiʃən]. Prec. & **-ion**. Inoculation with a vaccine, esp. that of cowpox or vaccinia, as a protection against smallpox.

vaccinationist, n. [1. vàksináshunist; 2. væksinéiʃənist]. Prec. & **-ist**. One who advocates vaccination, esp. compulsory vaccination as protection against smallpox.

vaccinator, n. [1. váksinàter; 2. væksineitə]. **vaccinate** & **-or**. **1.** Person, esp. public (medical) official, who performs compulsory vaccination on children and others. **2.** Instrument, scarifier, used in vaccination.

vaccine, n. [1. váksēn; 2. væksīn], fr. Fr. *vaccin*, fr. Lat. *vaccīnus*, 'pertaining to cows', fr. *vacca*, 'cow', cogn. w. Scrt. *vačā*, 'cow', prob. connected w. Scrt. *väčati*, 'cries, lows', & cogn. w. Lat. *vōx*, see **vocal**. **1.** n. **a** The virus of cowpox, 'vaccinia', obtained now from calves specially inoculated with the disease, in the form of lymph and used in vaccination for protection against smallpox; **b** the virus of other diseases, culture of the bacteria of such diseases as plague &c., used as inoculation against such diseases; cp. **serum**. **2.** (attrib.) Pertaining to a vaccine: *vaccine therapy*, treatment, prevention, of diseases by means of inoculation with a vaccine.

vaccinia, n. [1. vaksínia; 2. væksíniə]. Neo-Lat., fr. prec. Cowpox, a disease cognate with smallpox, now especially inoculated into calves for the purpose of obtaining a vaccine in form of lymph, used in vaccination against smallpox.

vaccinic, adj. [1. vaksínik; 2. væksínik]. **vaccine** & **-ic**. Pertaining to a vaccine or vaccines; vaccinal.

vacillate, vb. intrans. [1. vásilāt; 2. vǽsileit], fr. Lat. *vacillāt-(um)*, P.P. type of *vacillāre*, 'to sway, waver, vacillate', formed as if fr. an adj., *vacillus, fr. base *wak^w-, q.v. under **vehicle**. 1. (somewhat rare) To sway, oscillate; to stagger. 2. To waver in mind, intentions &c.; to hesitate, to change from one opinion to another; to alternate between two opinions or courses of action.

vacillating, adj. [1. vásilāting; 2. vǽsileitiŋ], fr. Pres. Part. of prec. Hesitating, wavering, in opinion or action.

vacillatingly, adv. Prec. & -ly. In a vacillating manner.

vacillation, n. [1. vàsilāshun; 2. vǽsiléiʃən], fr. Lat. *vacillātiōn-(em)*; see **vacillate** & -ion. Act of vacillating, wavering, or hesitating in opinions, intentions, action; hesitation, unsteadiness of opinion or character.

vacuity, n. [1. vakúiti; 2. vəkjúiti], fr. Lat. *vacuitāt-(em)*, *vacuitas*, fr. *vacuus*, 'empty', see **vacuous** & -ity. 1. (rare or obs.) Emptiness, empty space. 2. Emptiness of mind; lack of ideas, interest &c.: *vacuity of mind*; *vacuity of expression*.

vacuolar, vacuolate, adjs. [1. vákuolar, -āt; 2. vǽkju(ə)lə, -eit]. See next word & **-ar** & **-ate**. (biol.) Pertaining to, containing, a vacuole or vacuoles.

vacuole, n. [1. vákuōl; 2. vǽkjuoul]. Fr., a dimin. formed fr. Lat. **vacuum**. (biol.) A small vesicle or cavity, as in plant tissue, protoplasm &c., containing fluid or air.

vacuous, adj. [1. vákūus; 2. vǽkjuəs], fr. Lat. *vacuus*, 'empty, void; free from toil, care &c.', cogn. w. *vacāre*, see **vacant**, & -ous. 1. Empty (archaic or obs. in physical sense). 2. a Vacant in mind, empty-headed; stupid, unintelligent, meaningless: *an idle and vacuous young fellow*; *a vacuous stare*; **b** unoccupied, purposeless, idle; not profitably or usefully employed: *a selfish, vacuous life*.

vacuously, adv. Prec. & -ly. In a vacuous manner; vacantly, idly.

vacuousness, n. See prec. & **-ness**. State, quality, of being vacuous.

vacuum, n. [1. vákūum; 2. vǽkjuəm], pl. *vacuums*, learned pl. *vacua*. Lat.; neut. sing. of *vacuus*, 'empty', see **vacuous**. 1. Space empty or devoid of all matter or content: *nature abhors a vacuum*. 2. Specif., space or vessel from which the air has by various means been wholly or partially exhausted: *the vacuum of a barometer, in the atmosphere* &c. 3. (lit. or fig.) Any space unoccupied or unfilled; a void, blank: *to leave a vacuum difficult to fill*; (also facetiously) *feel a vacuum in the lower regions*, be hungry.

vacuum brake, n. A continuous brake, used on railway trains, worked by the action of compressed air on a vacuum.

vacuum cleaner, n. An apparatus used for removing dust and dirt from carpets, curtains, upholstery &c. by means of suction.

vacuum flask, n. A double-walled vessel, with the air exhausted in the space between the walls, thus forming a vacuum; flask in which liquids may be kept either hot or cold for a considerable period; cp. *thermos flask*.

vacuum gauge, n. Gauge for measuring pressure in a vacuum.

vacuum pump, n. a Pump for exhausting air from an enclosed space and creating a vacuum; air-pump; **b** pump by which water is raised by pressure of air and steam on a vacuum.

vacuum tube, n. A sealed glass tube or vessel containing exhausted or highly rarefied air or gas with electrodes at each end through which a current of electricity is passed exhibiting various electrical, radio-active, and other phenomena; a special type called 'thermionic valve' is used in wireless telephony.

vade-mecum, n. [1. vāde mēkum; 2. véidi mīkəm]. Lat., 'go with me'; fr. Lat. *vādere*, 'to go', is related by gradation to *vadum*, 'ford', & cogn. w. O.E. *wadan*, 'to go, wade', see **wade**; O.H.G. *watan*, O.N. *vaða* &c. A handbook or manual that one carries about with one for quick reference; often used as title for such a book.

vagabond (I.), adj. [1. vágabond; 2. vǽgəbənd, -bɔnd]. O. Fr., fr. Lat. *vagābundus*, 'wandering', formed as gerundive suff. *-bundus*, fr. *vagāri*, 'to wander, roam, about', see **vagary**. 1. a Wandering, roaming, from place to place without a fixed abode or settled mode of life: *vagabond family of beggars*; *the vagabond classes*; *a vagabond singer* &c.; **b** inclined to live a wandering life; not steady or settled in character; worthless: *a vagabond kind of fellow*. 2. Characteristic of wanderers; wandering, roving, irregular: *lead a vagabond life*; *vagabond habits*.

vagabond (II.) n., fr. prec. **a** One who wanders about without a fixed abode or regular means of livelihood; a tramp, vagrant: *actors were once classed with rogues and vagabonds*; (legal) an idle, disorderly person, as included under various *Vagrancy Acts* &c.; **b** (as term of abuse or reproach) an idle, worthless fellow: *she called her husband a lazy old vagabond*.

vagabond (III.), vb. intrans., fr. prec. (rare) To wander, roam, about, like a vagabond: *to go vagabonding all the world over*.

vagabondage, n. [1. vágabòndij; 2. vǽgəbɔndidʒ]. Fr.; see prec. words & **-age**. a State, character, of a vagabond; vagabond life or habits: *the charm of vagabondage which some people feel*; *to take to vagabondage*; **b** people living a vagabond life; the vagabond class; vagabonds collectively: *all the vagabondage of the countryside were there*.

vagabondism, n. [1. vágabondizm; 2. vǽgəbəndizəm, -bɔnd-]. **vagabond** & **-ism**. Habit of living a vagabond life; vagabondage.

vagabondize, vb. intrans. [1. vágabəndīz; 2. vǽgəbəndaiz]. See prec. & **-ize**. To live as a vagabond; to wander about.

vagal, adj. [1. vágal; 2. véig(ə)l]. See **vagus** & **-al**. (anat.) Pertaining to, affecting, the vagus or pneumogastric nerve.

vagarious, adj. [1. vágārius; 2. vəgéəriəs]. See **vagary** & **-ous**. Full of, characterized by, vagaries; erratic, capricious.

vagary, n. [1. vagári; 2. vəgéəri], fr. 17th cent., usually in verbal phrs., 'to make, lead &c. a vagary'; also in form *fegary, figary*; apparently borrowed as a n., fr. Lat. *vagāri*, 'to wander, roam, about', fr. *vagus*, 'wandering'; the base is prob. a variant form of that seen in **vacillate**; cp. **vague** & distinguish **vagrant**. 1. (orig. meaning, now obs.) A wandering, ramble, an aimless excursion: *they led us a pretty vagary*; (also fig.) *the vagaries of the mind*. 2. A prank, freak; whimsical, erratic, eccentric, fancy, act, conduct; caprice, whim: *the vagaries of a pampered film-star*; *the usual vagaries of fashion*; '*straight they changed their minds, . . . and into strange vagaries fell*' (Milton, 'P. L.', vi. 613-14).

vagina, n. [1. vajína; 2. vədʒáinə]. Lat. *vāgīna*, 'sheath, scabbard', fr. *vāsgīna*; cogn. w. *vās*, 'vessel', see **vase** & cp. **vest (I.)**. A sheath or sheath-like covering; specif. **a** (anat.) the canal leading from the female external organ of generation to the uterus; **b** (bot.) the sheath formed by a leaf round a stem, as in grasses.

vaginal, adj. [1. vajínal; 2. vədʒáinl]. Prec. & **-al**. 1. Pertaining to, connected with, the vagina. 2. Sheath-like, serving as a sheath: *vaginal process*, of the temporal bone.

vaginate(d), adj. [1. vájinăt(ed); 2. vǽdʒineit(id)]. See **vagina** & **-ate**. (bot.) Sheathed, closed in a vagina, as the leaf-stalk of grasses &c.

vaginitis, n. [1. vàjinítis; 2. vǽdʒináitis]. **vagina** & **-itis**. (med.) Inflammation of the vagina.

vago-, pref. Form, fr. **vagus**, used in anatomy & physiology, in compounds denoting connexion w. that nerve: *vago-accessory, -sympathetic* &c.

vagrancy, n. [1. vágransi; 2. véigrənsi]. See **vagrant** & **-ancy**. State of being vagrant; habit, act, of wandering from place to place without settled abode or means of livelihood; vagrants or tramps collectively: *vagrancy has increased since the war*; *statistics, suppression, of vagrancy*; *Vagrancy Acts*, various statutes, of wide application, dealing with rogues, vagabonds, idle and disorderly persons &c.

vagrant (I.), adj. [1. vǎgrant; 2. véigrənt]. M.E. *vagaraunt, vagraunt*, fr. A.-Fr. *wakerant*, O. Fr. *wan(l)erant*, Pres. Part. of *walerer*, 'to walk, wander about', also *wal-, waucrant*; of Gmc. origin, see **walk**, but confused w. & assimilated to Lat. *vagāri*, 'to wander', cp. **vagabond** & **vagary**. 1. Wandering, roaming, from place to place; nomadic, itinerant, living the life of a vagabond or tramp: *a band of vagrant minstrels, beggars* &c.; *the vagrant tribes of the desert*. 2. Characteristic of a wanderer or vagabond devoted to wandering or vagrancy: *a vagrant life*; *vagrant habits*. 3. (fig.) Flitting hither and thither, wayward, roving: *vagrant thoughts, fancies* &c.

vagrant (II.), n., see prec. One who wanders from place to place; a vagabond, a tramp; person with no settled abode or livelihood; an idle and disorderly person.

vagrantly, adv. [1. vǎgrantli; 2. véigrəntli]. **vagrant (I.)** & **-ly**. In a vagrant, wandering manner; as a vagrant or tramp.

vagrom, adj. [1. vágrom; 2. véigrəm]. Dogberry's corruption of **vagrant** in 'Much Ado about Nothing'.

vague, adj. [1. vāg; 2. veig]. Fr., 'wandering', fr. *vaguer*, 'to wander', fr. Lat. *vagāri*, see **vagary**, or fr. *vagus*, 'wandering'. 1. Perceived indistinctly by the senses; not clearly defined; blurred; indeterminate, shadowy, indefinable; difficult to recognize with certainty: *a vague and shadowy outline*; *a vague, subtle odour*; *a vague taste of bitter almonds*; *the rather vague quality of unstressed vowels in English*. 2. Not clearly perceived, grasped, conceived by the mind; indefinite, lacking precision: *vague hopes, ideas*; *his knowledge is rather vague*; *I haven't the vaguest notion what to do*, *where I left my umbrella*. 3. Not expressed or defined with clearness and precision; ambiguous, equivocal, conveying an uncertain meaning; loosely phrased: *vague answers, statements, promises*; *the powers of the Board are purposely left vague*. 4. (of persons) **a** Absent-minded, distrait, appearing not to be fully alive to what is taking place or being said; not having clear ideas &c.: *she is so vague that I never feel sure whether she realizes who one is*; **b** expressing oneself without precision, not given to clear-cut statements; not making wishes, opinions, intentions &c. absolutely clear and unambiguous: *he is very vague as to what he really wants*.

vaguely, adv. Prec. & **-ly**. In a vague way.

vagueness, n. See prec. & **-ness**. State, quality, of being vague.

vagus, n. [1. vǎgus; 2. véigəs], fr. Lat., 'wandering', see **vagary**. (anat.) The pneumogastric nerve.

vail (I.), n. [1. vāl; 2. veil]. Shortened form of **avail**, in sense of 'profit, aid'. (archaic) A gratuity, tip; servant's perquisites.

vail (II.), vb. trans. & intrans.; shortened form fr. *avale*, fr. Fr. *avaler*, 'to cast down, let fall', fr. *à val*, 'to the valley, downwards'; cp. **avalanche**. (obs., except as liter. or poet. archaism) **a** trans. (i.) To take off, doff (hat &c.): '*vailed was her lofty crest*' (Spenser, 'F. Q.', III. 9, 20); '*The bonnets . . . were now at once vailed in honour of the royal warrant*' (Scott); (ii.) to lower, allow to fall; '*He looked but once, and vail'd his eyes again*' (Tennyson) &c.; **b** intrans. to take off hat &c.; lower one's head &c. as sign of greeting or respect.

vain, adj. [1. vān; 2. vein]. M.E. *vayn, veyn, vain* &c., fr. O. Fr. *vein, vain*, fr. Lat. *vānus*, 'empty, vain'; cogn. w. Goth. *wans*, 'lacking'; O.H.G., O.S., O.E. *wan*, 'lacking, deficient'; O.N. *vanr*, see **want**; further Gk. *eûnis*, 'deficient', Scrt. *ūnás*, 'in-

VAINGLORIOUS   1344   **VALKYRIE**

complete'. **1. a** Without result; useless, idle, fruitless, futile, unavailing: *all our efforts were vain*; *in the vain hope of success*; *it is vain to try to escape*; Phr. *in vain* (adv.), (i.) to no end or purpose, uselessly, fruitlessly: *to try in vain to succeed*; *all our efforts were in vain*; *in vain did I point out how time was getting on*; *these men have laboured and died in vain*; (ii.) (fr. Low Lat.) *in vanum nomen Dei assumere*, ' take the name of God in vain ', to use it lightly, heedlessly, or profanely; also *take a person's name in vain*, speak of him slightingly, without due respect; **b** trivial; concerned with trifles; slight, petty, unsubstantial: *the vain day-dreams of youth*; *to waste one's life in vain pleasures*; *vain delights* &c. **2.** Having no real significance or foundation; unreal, baseless, empty: *vain threats, boasting, protestations of affection* &c. **3.** Ostentatious, concerned with outward show only; lacking real worth; hollow: *the vain pomps of a court*; *how vain are earthly splendours*. **4.** Having an exaggerated sense or opinion of one's own importance, personal appearance, one's possessions, talents, abilities &c.; conceited, self-satisfied, self-complacent: *a very vain man*; *adulation is apt to make men vain*; *vain of*, proud of, feeling self-satisfaction at: *little boys are naturally vain of their first long trousers*.

vainglorious, adj. [1. vănglŏ́rius; 2. vèinglŏ́riəs], fr. **vainglory** & **-ous**. Med. Lat. has *vănaglōriōsus*. **a** Given to, filled with, vainglory; inordinately, ostentatiously, vain or proud of one's actions, abilities &c.; boastful: *the defeat of these vainglorious athletes was popular*; **b** characteristic of, arising out of, exhibiting, vainglory: *vainglorious confidence.*

vaingloriously, adv. Prec. & **-ly**. In a vainglorious manner.

vaingloriousness, n. See prec. & **-ness**. Quality, condition, character, of being vainglorious.

vainglory, n. [1. vănglŏ́ri; 2. vèinglŏ́ri]. M.E. *vainglorie*; fr. O. Fr. *vaine gloire*, Med. Lat. *vāna glōria*, see **vain** & **glory**. Inordinate, ostentatious pride or vanity; boastfulness.

vainly, adv. [1. vănli; 2. véinli]. **vain** & **-ly**. **1.** Uselessly, in vain, futilely: *vainly tried to speak*. **2.** Conceitedly: *vainly proud of his appearance.*

vainness, n. [1. vănnes; 2. véinnis]. **vain** & **-ness**. Quality, state, of being vain, useless, or futile.

vair, n. [1. văr; 2. veə]. In M.E. & O. Fr., fr. Lat. *varius*, ' varied, parti-coloured ', see **various** & cp. **minever**. **1.** (hist. and archaic) A parti-coloured fur, bluish grey and white, esp. that of a kind of squirrel, used as a trimming or lining for robes of knights. **2.** (her.) One of the heraldic furs, represented by rows of small shields or bells, alternately azure and argent unless otherwise mentioned.

Vaisya, n. [1. víshia; 2. váiʃia]. Scrt. *vaiśya*, ' settler, peasant ', fr. base *viś*-, ' to dwell ', cogn. w. Lat. *vīcus*, ' village '; see **vicinity**. The third of the great Hindu castes, including agriculturists and merchants.

vaivode. See **voivode**.

vakeel, vakil, vakul, n. [1. vakél; 2. vækíəl]. Hind., fr. Arab. *wakīl*. **a** A deputy, representative; minister, ambassador; **b** a native attorney or pleader in the law courts.

valance, n. [1. válans; 2. vǽləns]. Of uncertain origin; fr. 15th cent.; usually supposed to be the name of a material made at Valence, in France, used for curtains; possibly fr. a hypothetical A.-Fr. *valance*, fr. *valer*, Fr. *avaler*, ' to let down, fall ', see **avalanche** & **vail** (II.). A hanging border of drapery for a window, shelf &c., esp. one that hangs from the framework of a bed to the floor.

vale (I.), n. [1. văl; 2. veil], fr. O. Fr. *val*, fr. Lat. *vallis*, ' valley ', cogn. w. Gk. *hélos*, ' low, marshy ground by a river '. Valley, esp. a low-lying wide tract of land between hills; a dale; now chiefly poet., but surviving in such Place-Names as *Vale of Evesham, of Aylesbury, of the White Horse*. Phr. *this vale of tears, woe, misery*; *earthly vale* &c., the world, this mortal life.

vale (II.), interj. & n. [1. văli; 2. véili]. Lat., 2nd pers. sing. imperat. of *valēre*, ' to be well, strong ', see **valiant**. **a** interj. Farewell, good-bye; **b** n., a farewell; a farewell greeting, letter &c.: *to say, take, write, one's vale.*

valediction, n. [1. vàledíkshun; 2. vælidíkʃən]. Formed fr. Lat. *valedict-(um)*, P.P. type of *valedīcere*, ' to say farewell ', & **-ion**, see **vale** (II.) & **diction**. **a** Act of saying farewell; bidding good-bye to; a farewell; **b** word(s) of farewell.

valedictory, adj. & n. [1. vàledíkturi; 2. vælidíktəri]. Lat. *valedict-*, see prec., & **-ory**. **1.** adj. Spoken, uttered, in saying farewell; of the nature of a valediction: *valedictory speech, letter* &c. **2.** n. (chiefly U.S.A.) A valedictory speech, address &c.

valence. See **valency**.

Valencia, n. [1. valénshia; 2. vəlénʃiə]. Name of town and province in Spain. (usually in pl.) A kind of cloth, of wool, with silk or cotton warp, usually with a fine stripe.

Valenciennes, n. [1. vàlensénz; 2. væ̀lənsénz], or as Fr. [1. válonsién; 2. valãsien]. Name of town in France, celebrated for its lace. A variety of bobbin lace made here or in Belgium.

valency, valence, n. [1. válens(i); 2. véiləns(i)], fr. L. Lat. *valentia*, ' power, strength ', fr. *valent-(em)*, Pres. Part. type of *valēre*, ' to be well, strong ', see **valiant**. (chem.) Term used in defining the combining powers of atoms in molecular compounds, hydrogen, as univalent and unvarying in its valency, being the standard of comparison.

-valent, suff., fr. Lat. *valent-(em)*, see prec. Having a specified valency or combining power; e.g. *univalent*.

valentine, n. [1. válentìn; 2. vǽləntàin], fr. O. Fr. *Valentin*, fr. Lat. *Valentīnus*, name of two early saints, whose feast day was Feb. 14th, *Valentine's day*, when birds were supposed to begin mating; hence the day when sweethearts were chosen. **1.** A sweetheart, lover: *will you be my valentine?* **2.** A card decorated with emblems and messages of love, and formerly sent to persons of the opposite sex on Valentine's day; also *mock-valentine*, a scurrilous, satirical picture sent to make fun of person of opposite sex on this day.

valerian, n. [1. valérian; 2. vəlíəriən], fr. O. Fr. *valeriane*, Med. Lat. *valeriāna*, fr. *valeriānus*, adj., formed fr. Lat. proper name *Valerius*, or fr. *Valeria*, a province in Pannonia. **a** A genus of perennial herbs, wild or cultivated, with small red or white flowers in clusters; **b** the root of *Valeriana officinalis*, which has a nauseous smell and is used medicinally in nervous diseases or hysteria.

valerianic, adj. [1. valèrianik; 2. vəlìəriæ̀nik]. Prec. & **-ic**. (chem.) Obtained, derived, from the root of valerian.

valeric, adj. [1. válerik; 2. vǽlərik]. See **valerian** & **-ic**. (chem.) Valerianic.

valet, n. & vb. trans. [1. válet; 2. vǽlit]; vulg. [1. válā; 2. vǽlei], fr. O. Fr. *valet*, earlier *vaslet*. See **varlet** & cp. **vassal**. **1.** n. A gentleman's personal servant, who looks after his clothes, helps him in dressing &c. **2.** vb. To act as valet to; to attend, wait, on as personal servant: *the butler valets me very well.*

valet de pied, n. [1. vàlă de pyắ; 2. vǽlei də pjéi]. Fr. A footman.

valetudinarian, adj. & n. [1. vàletùdinárian; 2. væ̀litjūdinǽriən]. See **valetudinary** & **-an**. **1.** adj. **a** Having constant poor health; perpetually ailing **b** engrossed in the state of one's health, and apprehensive of illness, often without cause; valetudinary. **2.** n. One who is in constant poor health; a chronic invalid; person unduly preoccupied with the state of his health.

valetudinarianism, n. [1. vàletùdinárianizm; 2. væ̀litjūdinǽriənizəm]. See prec. & **-ism**. The state of mind or body of a valetudinarian.

valetudinary, adj. & n. [1. vàletúdinari; 2. væ̀litjūdinəri], fr. Fr. *valetudinaire*, fr. Lat. *valētūdinārius*, ' sickly, infirm ', also as n. ' an invalid '; formed w. adj. suff. & *-ārius*, see **-ary**, fr. *valētūdin-(em)*, *valētūdo*, ' state of health, whether good or bad ', fr. *valēre*, ' to be well, strong '; see **valiant**. Valetudinarian, now the more usual word.

Valhalla, n. [1. vàlhála; 2. vælhǽlə]. Cp. Mod. Germ. & Fr. *walhalla*. Ad. fr. O.N. *Valhǫl*, ' the hall of the slain in battle ', fr. *valr*, ' the slain ' (cogn. w. O.E. *wæl*, ' slaughter, the slain; a dead body ', & prob. O.E. *wōl*, ' pestilence '), & *hǫll*, ' a royal hall ', cogn. w. **hall**. **1.** (Scand. mythol.) The hall of Odin in Asgard, where the souls of heroes slain in battle feast, attended by the Valkyries. **2.** A hall or other building in which a nation's illustrious dead are buried or commemorated, and where their statues or monuments are placed; a Pantheon.

vali, n. [1. valé; 2. vælí]. Turk. & Arab. *valī*. The civil governor of a Turkish *vilayet* or province.

valiance, n. [1. válians; 2. vǽliəns], fr. O. Fr. *vaillance*. See **valiant** & **-ance**. (obs. or archaistic) Bravery, courage; a brave, valiant deed.

valiant, adj. [1. váliant; 2. vǽliənt]. In M.E. in various forms, ' strong, brave, courageous ', fr. O. Fr. *valant, vailant, vailant*, Pres. Part. of *valoir*, ' to be worth, to be good for, to serve ', fr. Lat. *valēre*, ' to be strong and vigorous, to be healthy; to be strong enough to do some specific thing, to be able; to be powerful, have influence; to have a specific value, to be worth '. The base is cogn. w. that in O.E. *(ge)weald*, ' power, strength ', & *wealdan*, ' to have control over, to rule; to wield (weapon) '. See **wield**. **1.** (provinc.) Strong, sturdy, of body; stalwart. **2.** Courageous, brave, heroic (of persons and acts): *our valiant soldiers, their valiant deeds* &c.

valiantly, adv. Prec. & **-ly**. In a valiant manner; with valour; bravely.

valid, adj. [1. válid; 2. vǽlid], fr. Fr. *valide*, fr. Lat. *validus*, ' strong ', fr. *valēre*, ' to be strong &c.', see under **valiant**. **1.** (rare or archaistic) Sound, strong, in body or health; cp. *invalid*, n. **2.** Having legal force and authority, properly and formally executed; sound in law: *a valid contract, marriage* &c. **3.** Well founded, soundly based; capable of being supported and defended; not open to objection: *valid arguments*; *have you any valid reason against the proposal?*; *there is no valid objection to* &c.

validate, vb. trans. [1. válidāt; 2. vǽlideit], fr. Med. Lat. *validāt-(um)*, P.P. type of *validāre*, ' to make valid ', see prec., & **-ate**. To render, declare to be, valid: *to validate a treaty, election* &c.; but cp. the negative *invalidate.*

validity, n. [1. valíditi; 2. vəlíditi], fr. L. or Med. Lat. *validitāt-(em)*, *validitas*, see **valid** & **-ity**. State, quality, of being valid; a legal force or authority; quality of being legally binding and enforceable: *the validity of a marriage, of a contract* &c.; **b** soundness, strength, force, cogency (of an argument, objection &c.).

validly, adv. [1. válidli; 2. vǽlidli]. **valid** & **-ly**. In a valid manner; with validity.

valise, n. [1. valēz; 2. vəlíz]. Fr., fr. Ital. *valigia*, cp. Med. Lat. *valesia, valisia, valixia*; Span. *balija*; etymol. unknown, possibly of Arab. origin. A small portmanteau or travelling bag, formerly one carried strapped to a horse's saddle; now obsolescent, except as official term for a soldier's kitbag.

Valkyr, Valkyria, n. [1. vălkēr, valkíria; 2. vǽlkiə, vælkíriə]. Valkyrie.

Valkyrie, n. [1. valkíri; 2. vælkáiəri], more rarely [1. válkiri; 2. vǽlkiri]. O.N. *Valkyrja*, lit. ' chooser of the slain '; the exact equivalent

wælcyriġe is found in O.E.; for the first element see **Valhalla**; the second is formed fr. *kur-, a form of the O.N. *kjōsa*, O.E. *cēosan*, 'to choose', see **choose**, & cp. *kur- in Germ. *kurfürst*. (Scand. mythol.) One of the twelve war-goddesses, handmaids of Odin, who ride through the air over a battlefield, choose those who are to be slain, and guide them to, and serve them in, Valhalla.

vallation, n. [1. valáshun; 2. væléiʃən]. fr. L. Lat. *vallātiōn-(em)*, fr. *vallāt-(um)*, P.P. type of *vallāre*, 'to build a vallum or wall'. See **vallum**. A rampart, earthwork; more commonly *circumvallation*.

vallecula, n., pl. **valleculae** [1. valékula, -lē; 2. vælékjulə-, -lī]. L. Lat. dimin. of *vallis*, see **valley**. (anat. and bot.) A groove, channel, fossa, furrow, cleft.

valley, n., pl. **valleys** [1. váli; 2. væli], fr. O. Fr. *valee* (Mod. Fr. *vallée*), earlier form *vallede*, cp. Ital. *vallata*, fr. Lat. *vallis*, 'valley', see **vale** (I.). 1. A tract of land lying between mountains or hills, generally traversed by a stream or river, or containing a lake; usually narrower than a vale and lying between steeper slopes. Phr. *the valley of the shadow of death*, the dread hour of impending death, from Psalm xxiii. 2. (geog.) A large river basin or flat country drained by a river system: *the Thames valley; valley of the Euphrates and Tigris*. 3. (building and archit.) The internal angle formed by two sloping roofs or by a roof and a wall.

vallonia. See **valonia**.

vallum, n. [1. válum; 2. væləm]. Lat., 'a wall'; orig. 'a stockade, defence of stakes'; a coll. neut., fr. *vallus*, 'stake'; prob. cogn. w. Gk. *hēlos*, 'nail or stud'. See also **wall** (I.). (Roman antiq.) A defensive rampart set with stakes, a palisaded earthwork, formed of earth cast up from the ditch, also built of and strengthened with stone, sods of turf &c.

valonia, vallonia, n. [1. valónia; 2. vælóuniə]. Ital. *vallonia*, fr. Mod. Gk. *balaniá*, 'evergreen oak, ilex', fr. *baláni*, anct. Gk. *bálanos*, 'acorn', see **balaniferous**. The dried acorn cup of a species of ilex, or evergreen oak, *Quercus Aegilops*, or valonia oak, used in tanning, dyeing, and ink-making.

valorous, adj. [1. válorus; 2. vælərəs]. O. Fr. *valeureux*, Med. Lat. *valorōsus*, see **valour** & -ous. a (of persons) Possessing, exhibiting, valour; brave, intrepid, courageous; b (of actions) requiring valour from those who perform them; displaying, performed with, valour.

valorously, adv. Prec. & -ly. In a valorous manner; with valour.

valour, n. [1. válur; 2. vælə], fr. O. Fr. *valour*, Mod. Fr. *valeur*, 'value; bravery'; fr. L. Lat. *valōr-(em)*, stem of *valor*, 'worth, value, courage', fr. *valēre*, 'to be strong, worth' &c., see **valiant**. Courage of a noble and lofty quality; continuous, active, bravery exhibited in actions performed in the face of personal danger.

valse, n. & vb. [1. vahls; 2. vɑːls]. Fr. form of **waltz**.

valuable (I.), adj. [1. válūabl; 2. væljuəbl], fr. **value** (II.) & -able. 1. (rare) Capable of being valued or estimated: *rarities once in a public museum or library cease to be valuable in terms of money* (cp. the more common negative form, *invaluable*). 2. a Having monetary or exchange value; worth something which can be expressed in terms of money, exchange, or benefit; in legal Phr. *valuable consideration*. b having considerable or great value, worth a good deal of money or exchange value; precious, costly: *collection of valuable pictures*; *a valuable property for sale*; *catalogue of the valuable kinds of wood of the Empire*. 3. Having a use or value; capable of serving a useful and important purpose; possessing and exhibiting qualities which are prized and esteemed as necessary for the performance of specific duties and functions: *a valuable public servant*; *gave me valuable service, information*; *a book which will be very valuable for teachers*.

valuable (II.), n. See prec. (usually in pl.) Objects of value; valuable goods or possessions: *plate, jewels, and other valuables*; *lost all their valuables in the fire*.

valuableness, n. [1. válūablnes; 2. væljuəblnis]. **valuable** (I.) & -ness. Condition, quality, of being valuable.

valuably, adv. [1. válūabli; 2. væljuəbli]. See **valuable** (I.) & -ly. In a valuable manner; usefully: *his support has helped the cause most valuably*.

valuation, n. [1. vàlūáshun; 2. væljuéiʃən], fr. **value** (II.) & -ation. 1. a Act of valuing, of settling, or estimating, the value, or proper price, of anything: *engaged in the valuation of property for probate*; *the quinquennial valuation of ratable buildings*; b value or price so estimated and arrived at: *I was offered the fixtures at a moderate valuation*. 2. Estimation, degree of appreciation, in which a person, or his moral or intellectual qualities, are held: *to take a man at (on) his own valuation*; *they put his services at the highest valuation*.

value (I.), n. [1. válū; 2. væljū]. O. Fr., fem. sing. of *valu*, P.P. of *valoir*, 'to be worth', fr. Lat. *valēre*; see **valiant**. 1. a Worth, that quality or property of anything which renders it desirable or useful: *the value of sunlight, fresh air, exercise, for health*; *the value of good books, education*; b (i.) worth of anything as compared with that of other things; degree of such worth: *to be of great, little, no value*; *your help was of value to me*; (ii.) estimation, valuation: *to set a high value on one's abilities*. 2. Worth of anything as estimated in terms of something else for which it can be exchanged, either in other goods, labour, services, or, esp., in money or other standard medium of exchange; purchasing power, monetary price: *economic, exchange, value*; *to pay, give, get, full value for something*; *the value of this kind of picture has fallen greatly*. Phr. *for value received*, form used in promissory notes for stating valuable consideration. 3. (in various specific uses) a Precise import, meaning, bearing, force; *the value of a word in a given phrase* &c.; b relative proportion of light and shade in a picture or drawing, as distinct from that of colour; c length or duration of a note of music; d quantity denoted by an algebraic symbol or expression; e (pl.) relative ethical standards.

value (II.), vb. trans., fr. prec. 1. To estimate the value or worth of, to assign a price or value to; to put a price on, fix a price for, to appraise: *I value the house and contents at £10,000*; *to value an estate for probate*. 2. (in moral sense) a To rate at a specified degree of worth, to hold in specified degree of esteem: *to value one's life highly, not at all*; b (absol.) to attach a high degree of value to, rate highly: *I shall always value your friendship*; *we do not always value advice from others*.

valued, adj. [1. válūd; 2. væljūd]. P.P. of prec. Highly esteemed, greatly regarded; considered as being of great value to some specified person; precious: *one's most valued possession*; *a valued friend of the late king*.

valueless, adj. [1. válūles; 2. væljulis]. **value** (I.) & -less. Of no value or use; worthless, destitute of value (in material or non-material sense): *valueless pictures, stocks and shares*; *a book valueless for its purpose*; *valueless advice*.

valuelessness, n. [1. válūlesnes; 2. væljulisnis]. Prec. & -ness. State, quality, of being valueless.

valuer, n. [1. válūer; 2. væljuə]. **value** (II.) & -er. One who fixes or assesses the monetary or material value of anything; specif., person who estimates values and prices professionally as a matter of business: *a surveyor and valuer*; *valuer for probate* &c.

valuta, n. [1. valūta; 2. vəljūtə]. Ital., 'value', q.v. The value of a national currency as fixed in terms of a foreign currency, exchange value of a currency in relation to a specified foreign currency in distinction from its internal value; also attributively.

valval, valvar, adj. [1. válval, -ar; 2. vælvəl, -ə]. **valve** & -al, -ar. Valvular, chiefly in botanical terminology.

valvate, adj. [1. válvāt; 2. vælveit]. **valve** & -ate. (bot.) Meeting at the edges without overlapping (of leaves and sepals).

valve, n. [1. valv; 2. vælv]. Fr., fr. Lat. *valva*, 'leaf of a folding-door', usually in pl. *valvae*, 'a folding-door'; cogn. w. *volvere*, 'to roll', see **volute**. 1. One of the leaves of a folding door, now rare except as applied to lock-gates, sluices &c. 2. Any of various devices which open and shut, like the leaves of a folding door, thus regulating the passage of air, liquid, gas &c. through an opening, tube, pipe &c., often acting automatically, as *the safety-valve* of a steam-engine, *the slide* or *key valves* of musical wind instruments &c. 3. (in various specific uses) a (anat.) A membrane in a vein, artery or lymphatic which allows the passage one way only of the blood or lymph; b (bot.) one of the separable parts of a pod, pericarp, or capsule; c (zool.) one of the two shells of molluscs such as the oyster; or of the several parts of the shell of compound molluscs. 4. (wireless) A special form of vacuum tube used for the reception of messages, as *thermionic valve* &c.; (also attrib.) *valve set*, one fitted with such valves, distinct from *crystal set*.

valved, adj. [1. valvd; 2. vælvd]. **valve** & -ed. Furnished, fitted, with valves; also in compounds, having so many valves: *three-valved* &c.

valveless, adj. [1. válvles; 2. vælvlis]. **valve** & -less. Having no valves; not provided with a valve or valves.

valvular, adj. [1. válvūlar; 2. vælvjulə], fr. Lat. *valvulae*, dimin. of *valvae*, see **valve**, & -ar. 1. Pertaining to, affecting, a valve or valves, esp. those of the heart: *valvular disease*. 2. Consisting, made up, of valves or segments, esp. of plant formations.

valvulitis, n. [1. vàlvulítis; 2. vælvjuláitis]. See prec. & -itis. (med.) Inflammation of the valves of the heart.

vambrace, n. [1. vámbrās; 2. væmbreis]. Earlier *vantbrace* (cp. Milton, 'Samson', 1151), fr. A.-Fr. *vantbras* for *avant-bras*, fr. *avant*, 'before, in front', see **advance**, & *bras*, 'arm', see **brace** (I.). A piece of armour for the forearm.

vamoose, vamose, vb. intrans. [1. vamōoz, vamōz; 2. væmúz, væmóuz], fr. Span. *vamos*, 'let us go'. (slang, U.S.A., often as imperat.) To go away, decamp, get off.

vamp (I.), n. [1. vamp; 2. væmp]. M.E. *vaumpé*, fr. O. Fr. *avampié*, later *avant-pied*, 'forepart of the foot', fr. *avant*, 'before', see **advance** (I.), & *pied*, 'foot', see **pedal** (I.). 1. a That part of a boot or shoe which covers the front part of the foot; b a piece of leather used in repairing the front part of a boot or shoe; a patch to a boot or shoe. 2. (a back-formation from vb.) Something vamped or patched up; a patchwork, esp. a simple, improvised musical accompaniment to a song &c.

vamp (II.), vb. trans. & intrans., fr. prec. 1. trans. a To repair (boot &c.) by putting a new vamp on it; to repair, mend (worn boots and shoes); b *vamp up*, to patch up, renew, furbish up, (anything) so as to look like new: *to vamp up some old furniture* &c.; c (by transf.) to patch together, make something out of old or used material; to make a patchwork of: *to vamp up a farce, new business for a play* &c.; d specif. (mus.) to improvise (an accompaniment) in a simple, crude way, to a song, dance &c. 2. intrans. To improvise a simple accompaniment to a song &c., on the piano &c.

vamp (III.), n. & vb. trans. & intrans.; abbr. of **vampire**. (slang) 1. n. An adventuress, a woman who uses her physical charms to extort or extract money from her victims; a female blood-sucker. 2. vb. To fascinate (men) and extract money from them.

vampire, n. [1. vámpīr; 2. væmpaiə]. Fr., fr. Magyar or Serbian *vampir*, also found in

43

Russ., Bulgarian, Pol. & other Slav. languages in various forms as *vepir, upyr* &c. ; prob. fr. a Turk. *uber*, 'witch'; the word has been borrowed fr. Slav. sources in other European languages, as Germ. *vampyr*. **1.** An evil, malignant spirit with the power of entering and reviving a corpse; person whose dead body is thus revived, and renews its life at night by visiting and sucking the blood of sleepers. **2.** (by transf.) An unscrupulous, malignant extortioner, male or female; a blood-sucker, a ruthless blackmailer or money-lender. **3.** A vampire bat. **4.** (in a theatre) A kind of trap in the floor of the stage working by springs, allowing a demon &c. to appear or disappear suddenly.

vampire bat, n. Either of two small bloodsucking bats, *Desmodus* and *Diphylla*, of tropical S. America, which suck the blood of animals, esp. horses, and are said to attack human beings in their sleep.

vampirism, n. [1. vámpīrizm; 2. væmpaiərizəm]. **vampire** & -ism. **a** Habits, practices, of a vampire; **b** superstitious belief in vampires.

vamplate, n. [1. vámplāt; 2. væmpleit], fr. Fr. *avant-plat*, cp. **vambrace** & **plate (I.)**. (hist.) An iron guard-plate for the hand, fixed on a lance.

van (I.), n. & vb. trans. [1. van; 2. væn]. Shortened form of **caravan**. **1. a** A large covered vehicle for the conveyance of goods by road: *furniture van* &c.; **b** a covered truck or closed carriage on a railway: *guard's van*; *luggage, goods, van*; **c** closed vehicle for conveying prisoners by road: 'Black Maria'; **d** a caravan, in sense 2; (also attrib.) *van boy, van dwellers* &c. **2.** vb. To place (goods) in, convey (goods) by, a van.

van (II.), n. Shortened form of **vanguard**. **1.** The front of an army or fleet, when in battle formation or moving to battle; the leading division of an army or fleet. **2.** The leading part of any troop or concourse of people moving forward: *the van of a procession* &c. **3.** (fig.) Those who lead and are in the front of any forward intellectual, social, or political movement: Phrs. *in the van of, leading*; *to lead the van of* &c.

van (III.), n., fr. Lat. *vannus*, see **fan (I.)**. (archaic or dial.) **a** A winnowing fan or machine; **b** (poet.) the wing of a bird; **c** a shovel used for washing ore.

vanadate, n. [1. vánadāt; 2. vænədeit]. **vanadium** & -ate. (chem.) A salt of vanadic acid.

vanadic, adj. [1. vanádik, -ádik; 2. vænædik, -éidik]. See prec. & -ic. (chem.) Pertaining to, containing, vanadium: *vanadic acid*; esp. of compounds in which vanadium has a higher valence than in *vanadious* compounds.

vanadious, adj. [1. vanádius; 2. væneidiəs]. See prec. & -ous. (chem.) Of compounds of vanadium with lower valence than vanadic compounds.

vanadium, n. [1. vanádium; 2. væneidiəm]. Invented word, fr. *vanadis*, an Old Norse title for the Scand. goddess *Freyja*. (chem.) A rare metallic element, found in certain iron, lead, and uranium ores, used esp. in making alloys of steel.

Vandal (I.), n. [1. vándl; 2. vændl]. L. Lat. *Vandalus*, usually in pl. *Vandali*, also *Vandilii*; in O.E. *Wendlas*, pl. of *Wendil*, O.N. *Vendill*. **1.** One of the Germanic races, closely related to the Goths, which invaded Western Europe in 5th century A.D., sacking Rome under their leader Genseric in 455, settling in Gaul and Spain and finally in N. Africa; traditionally regarded as the great destroyers of Roman civilization, art, and literature. **2.** (by transf., with or without cap.) One who through ignorance and lack of taste and sensibility sweeps away or spoils beautiful things in art or nature: *the vandals who cover the countryside with cigarette tins and chocolate boxes*; *19th century vandals often pulled down mediaeval buildings to make room for new ones of churchwarden's Gothic*.

vandal (II.), adj., fr. prec. **1.** (hist., cap.) Pertaining to the Vandals: *the Vandal invasions, invaders* &c. **2. a** Barbarous; ruthlessly, ignorantly, destructive of beauty and culture: *the vandal despoilers of our churches*; **b** characterized by such destruction: *the vandal defacement of the countryside*.

Vandalic, adj. & n. [1. vandálik; 2. vændælik]. Prec. & -ic. **a** adj. Of, characteristic of, the Vandals or a vandal; **b** n., the language of the Vandals.

vandalism, n. [1. vándalizm; 2. vændəlizəm]. **Vandal (I.)** & -ism. **a** (cap.) The characteristic spirit or conduct of the Vandals; **b** (usually without cap.) hostility to things of art, beauty &c.; vandalization.

vandalization, n. [1. vàndalizáshun; 2. vændəlaizéiʃən]. **vandalize** & -ation. **a** Act of vandalizing; ignorant, tasteless, ruthless destruction of beautiful things; **b** state of being vandalized; barbarous destruction.

vandalize, vb. trans. [1. vándalīz; 2. vændəlaiz]. **Vandal (I.)** & -ize. To treat (objects of art, or the face of the countryside) like a vandal; to destroy, or make hideous, things of beauty in art or nature wilfully and ignorantly.

Vandyke (I.), n. [1. vandík; 2. vændáik], fr. Engl. spelling of A. Van Dyck, Flemish painter, 1599-1641, the Court painter of Charles I. **1.** (cap.) A portrait or painting by Vandyke. **2.** Specif. (with or without cap.) **a** a deep lace falling collar with deeply indented edge, as frequently seen in portraits of and by Vandyke; **b** any deeply indented or zigzag edge or border; one of the points or indentations of such an edge or border.

Vandyke (II.), adj., fr. prec. **1.** (cap.) **a** Of, by, Vandyke, the painter: *a Vandyke portrait*; **b** resembling a picture by, or in the style of, Vandyke: *a Vandyke beard*, a close-cut, pointed one; *Vandyke brown*, a deep brown. **2.** (usually cap.) Deeply indented, bordered with vandykes, zigzagged: *Vandyke collar* &c.

vandyke (III.), vb. trans., fr. **Vandyke (I.)**. To indent edge, border with vandykes.

vane, n. [1. vān; 2. vein]. O.E. *fana*, 'flag', cogn. w. Lat. *pannus*, see **pane (I.)**. The v- in present-day form is a survival of M.E. Southern dialect. See **gonfalon. 1.** A weathercock. **2. a** The sail of a windmill; **b** the blade of a ship's or aeroplane's propeller; **c** movable sight of a surveyor's levelling staff, quadrant &c.; **d** the web of a feather.

Vanessa, n. [1. vanésa; 2. vənésə]. Origin of name uncertain. (entom.) A genus of butterflies, including the peacock and red admiral &c.

vang, n. [1. vang; 2. væŋ]. Du., 'a catch', fr. *vangen*, 'to seize, catch', see **fang (I.)**. (naut.) One of two guys from the peak of a gaff to deck used to keep it steady.

vanguard, n. [1. vángàrd; 2. væŋgàd], fr. Fr. *avant-garde*, fr. *avant*, 'before', see **advance**, & *garde*, **guard. 1.** Advanced troops of an army or military force; the van; also the leading squadron of a fleet in battle formation. **2.** (fig.) The leaders of an intellectual, social, or political movement.

vanilla, n. [1. vaníla; 2. vənílə]. Ad. fr. Span. *vainilla*, dimin. of *vaina*, 'sheath, pod', see **vagina**, fr. the shape of the fruit of the plant. **a** A climbing orchidaceous plant, of genus *Vanilla*, esp. *Vanilla planifolia* of tropical America, with scented flowers and pods or beans which yield an aromatic substance used for flavouring ices, confectionery &c.; **b** the extract obtained from vanilla pods.

vanish, vb. intrans. [1. vánish; 2. væniʃ]. M.E. *vanissen*, fr. O. Fr. *e(s)vanniss-*, Pres. Part. stem of *e(s)vanir*, fr. Lat. *ēvānescere*, 'to fade, vanish away', fr. e- for ex- & *vānescere*, 'to fade, vanish, become empty', fr. *vānus*, 'empty', see **vain** & cp. **evanescent. 1.** To disappear, pass out of sight; to become invisible: *shadows vanish with the dawn*; *as we entered the figure vanished*. **2.** To fade away, to decay and disappear: *all the colour has vanished from the picture*. **3.** To cease to exist, to come to an end: *all our hopes of a speedy success vanished at the news*; *the fears of overnight vanish with the morning*. **4.** (math.) To become zero.

vanishing point, n. [1. vánishing pòint; 2. væniʃiŋ pòint]. **a** The converging point in a perspective drawing &c. at which receding parallel lines appear to meet; **b** (colloq.) point at which anything comes to an end, or tends to disappear: *our money, strength, has reached the vanishing point*.

vanity, n. [1. vániti; 2. væniti]. M.E. *vanite*, fr. Fr. *vanité*, fr. Lat. *vānitāt-(em)*, 'emptiness, worthlessness', fr. *vānus*, 'empty' &c., see **vain**, & -ity. **1.** Quality of being vain, empty or worthless; futility, unsubstantiality; worthlessness, emptiness: *the vanity of human wishes*, *of earthly greatness*. **2.** That which is vain, worthless; an unprofitable, futile thing, act &c.: '*to renounce the pomps and vanity of this wicked world*' (Catechism); '*all is vanity, saith the Preacher*'. **3.** Quality of being personally vain; exaggeratedly high opinion of, and pride in, one's own appearance, physical or mental capacities &c.; conceit: *a man's vanity is his tenderest spot*; *an injury to vanity will never be forgiven*.

vanity bag, n. A small ornamental hand-bag which women carry to hold a mirror, powderpuff, and cosmetics with which to make up their complexion.

Vanity Fair, n. The world of idle amusements and luxury; the fashionable world of society; fr. Bunyan's 'Pilgrim's Progress'.

vanquish, vb. trans. & intrans. [1. vángkwish; 2. væŋkwiʃ]. M.E. *venkisen, venkusen, venquisshen* &c., fr. A.-Fr. *venquiss-*, O. Fr. *veinquiss-*, Pres. Part. stem of *venquir, veinquir*, Mod. Fr. *vaincre*, 'to conquer', fr. Lat. *vincere*, *vict-(um)*, 'to conquer', see **vincible. 1.** trans. To conquer, defeat, overcome, reduce to subjection; to subdue, in physical and non-physical senses: *to vanquish the enemy in battle, one's opponents in argument, the temptations of the flesh* &c. **2.** intrans. To be victorious.

vanquishable, adj. [1. vángkwishabl; 2. væŋkwiʃəbl]. Prec. & -able. Capable of being vanquished, overcome, or subdued; cp. **invincible**.

vanquished, adj. & n. [1. vángkwisht; 2. væŋkwiʃt], fr. P.P. of **vanquish**. **a** adj. Conquered, defeated; subdued: *our vanquished enemy*; *vanquished temptations*; **b** n., *the vanquished*, defeated person or persons.

vanquisher, n. [1. vángkwisher; 2. væŋkwiʃə]. See prec. & -er. Conqueror, victor.

vantage, n. [1. váhntij; 2. vàntidʒ]. Variant of **advantage**. Advantage, gain, profit now archaic or obs. except as, **a** commonly used in calling score in lawn-tennis, and **b** Phrs. *vantage-ground, point of vantage*, superior, commanding position; favourable position (lit. and fig.) from which to attack an opponent or ward off his attack.

vanward, adj. & adv. [1. vánward; 2. vænwəd]. **van (II.)** & -ward. **a** adj. Placed, coming, in the van or front: '*The vanward clouds of evil days*' (Keats); **b** adv., towards the van; forward.

vapid, adj. [1. vápid; 2. væpid], fr. Lat. *vapidus*, 'that has lost its vapour or life'; flavourless, insipid'; cp. *vappa*, 'flat, stale wine', see **vapour (I.)**. **1.** (in material sense, rare) Tasteless, flavourless; insipid, flat. **2.** (non-material sense) Lifeless, uninteresting; lacking point, pungency, salt; insipid, dull: *vapid platitudes*; *the dialogue was vapid and commonplace*; *vapid compliments*.

vapidity, n. [1. vapíditi; 2. væpíditi]. Prec. & -ity. Quality, state, fact, of being vapid; insipidity, vapidness.

vapidly, adv. [1. vápidli; 2. væpidli]. See prec. & -ly. In a vapid manner.

vapidness, n. [1. vápidnes; 2. vǽpidnis]. See prec. & -ness. Vapidity.

vaporability, n. [1. vàporabíliti; 2. vèipərəbíliti]. **vaporable & -ity.** State, quality, of being vaporable.

vaporable, adj. [1. váporabl; 2. véipərəbl]. See **vapour & -able.** Capable of being vaporized or converted into vapour.

vaporific, adj. [1. vàporífik; 2. vèipərífik]. See **vapour & -fic.** Producing vaporization.

vaporimeter, n. [1. vàporímeter; 2. veipərímitə]. See prec. & **-meter.** Instrument for measuring the volume or pressure of vapour.

vaporization, n. [1. vàporizáshun; 2. vèipəraizéiʃən]. **vaporize & -ation.** Act, or process of vaporizing, of converting into vapour; process of becoming vapour.

vaporize, vb. trans. & intrans. [1. vápoŕiz; 2. véipəraiz]. **vapour & -ize. 1.** trans. To convert into vapour. **2.** intrans. To be converted into, to pass off as, vapour.

vaporizer, n. [1. vápoŕizer; 2. véipəraizə]. Prec. & **-er.** Apparatus for converting substances, such as oils, into vapour.

vaporous, adj. [1. váporus; 2. véipərəs], fr. Lat. *vapōrus* or *vapōrōsus*, see **vapour & -ous. a** Resembling, having the character or consistency of, vapour; **b** filled with vapour; foggy, steamy; **c** (archaic) having the vapours, fanciful.

vapour (I.), n. [1. váper; 2. véipə]. Through A.-Fr. *vapour*, O. Fr. *vapeur*, or direct fr. Lat. *vapōr*, 'steam, vapour', cogn. w. Gk. *kapnós*, 'smoke', *kapúein*, 'to breathe forth'; Sert. *kapis*, 'incense', Lith. *kvãpas*, 'breath, fragrance'; all fr. base *$k^w ap$-; related also to Goth. (*af-*)*hwapjan*, 'to choke', fr. Aryan variant *$k^w ab$-. Cp. **cupid. 1. a** A visible diffusion, exhalation, of moisture floating in the air, as fog, mist, steam &c., arising from the action of heat on water, damp ground &c.; **b** specif. (phys.) the gaseous state or form to which a solid or liquid may be reduced by the action of heat; a liquid or solid substance reduced by heat to a gaseous, elastic condition. **2.** (fig.) a Something unsubstantial, transitory, or fleeting; an idle fancy, freak of imagination: *his brain clouded by vapours and dreams*; *all his schemes were but the vapour of an excited imagination*; **b** (archaic) futile, empty boasting; vapouring. **3.** (in pl.) **a** (anct. med.) Morbid condition of body and mind due to supposed exhalations from the stomach; such exhalations; **b** *the vapours*, hysteria, mental depression, hypochondria: *a fit of the vapours once fashionable among young ladies*.

vapour (II.), vb. intrans., fr. prec. **1.** (rare) To pass off as vapour, to evaporate, be exhaled. **2.** To boast, brag; indulge in empty high-flown chatter.

vapour-bath, n. **a** A bath in hot vapour or steam; **b** closed place, apparatus, for such a bath. Phr. (of a place, part of the country) *like a vapour-bath*, very hot, steamy, relaxing.

vapourer, n. [1. váperer; 2. véipərə]. **vapour (II.) & -er. 1.** One who vapours or boasts; a flatulent, pretentious chatterer. **2.** (entom.) Moth of genus *Orgyia*, with wingless female, very destructive to vegetation.

vapouring (I.), n. [1. vápering; 2. véipəriŋ]. **vapour (II.) & -ing.** Often *vapourings*. Empty high-flown talk.

vapouring (II.), adj., fr. Pres. Part. of **vapour (II.)**. **a** Empty and pretentious; **b** full of vapours; hysterical, hypochondriacal.

vapoury, adj. [1. váperi; 2. véipəri]. **vapour (I.) & -y.** Full of vapour; misty, clouded with mist or vapour.

vapulation, n. [1. vàpuláshun; 2. væpjuléiʃən], fr. Lat. *vāpulāt*-(*um*), *vāpulāre*, 'to be flogged, whipped'; etymol. uncertain. (rare or facetiously archaistic) A beating, flogging.

vapulatory, adj. [1. vápulatuŕi; 2. væpjulətəri]. See prec. & **-ory.** Pertaining to flogging or beating.

vaquero, n. [1. vakáŕō; 2. vækéəŕou]. Span. 'cowherd', fr. *vaca*, 'cow', fr. Lat. *vacca*, see **vaccine.** (in Spanish America, Mexico &c.) A drover; a man in charge of cattle, horses, or mules; a herdsman; cowboy.

Varangian, n. & adj. [1. varánjian; 2. værǽndʒiən], fr. Med. Lat. *Varangus*, fr. Med. Gk. *Bára*(*n*)*ggos*, through Slav., fr. O.N. *Væringi*, pl. *Væringjar*, 'confederate, ally', fr. *vārar*, 'pledges, oaths'. **1.** n. **a** One of the Northman rovers who harried the Baltic and founded a dynasty in Russia in 9th and 10th centuries; **b** one of the 'Varangian Guard'. **2.** adj. **a** Pertaining to the Varangians; **b** composed of Varangians, esp. *Varangian Guard*, a bodyguard of the Byzantine emperors, recruited from Varangians and other Northern peoples of Europe.

varec, n. [1. várek; 2. vǽrɛk]. Fr., also *varech*, of Gmc. origin; see **wreck (I.).** Calcined ash of seaweed used in manufacture of iodine &c.; kelp.

variability, n. [1. vàriabíliti; 2. vèəriəbíliti]. See **variable & -ity.** Quality, condition, of being variable; liability, tendency, to variation.

variable (I.), adj. [1. váriabl; 2. véəriəbl]. Fr., fr. L. Lat. *variābilis*, see **vary & -able. 1.** Liable to vary; tending to vary; changeable, fluctuating, not constant or steady: *variable weather, temperature, wind &c.*; *a man of variable character, temper &c.* **2.** Capable of being varied or changed; admitting of variation in degree &c.: *prices are variable according to the exchanges.* **3.** Specific uses: **a** (astron.) periodically changing in apparent magnitude or brightness: *variable stars*; **b** (biol.) liable to variation; tending to deviate from type, aberrant: *variable species*; **c** (math.) increasing or decreasing, indeterminate: *variable quantities*.

variable (II.), n., fr. prec. **a** A variable quantity, an indeterminate quantity, one subject to increase or decrease; **b** a variable star.

variableness, n. [1. váriablnes; 2. véəriəblnis]. **variable (I.) & -ness.** State, quality, of being variable; liability to change or vary.

variably, adv. [1. váriabli; 2. véəriəbli]. See prec. & **-ly.** In a variable manner.

variance, n. [1. várians; 2. véəriəns]. O. Fr., fr. Lat. *variantia*; **variant & -ce. 1.** Act or fact of varying; variation; a change, alteration: *some variance of temperature is to be expected*; *such sudden variance of public taste is remarkable.* **2.** Active disagreement between persons in opinions, tastes, ideals &c.; strife, dissension, antagonism; esp. in Phr. *at variance (with)*, differing, in a state of estrangement (from); holding dissentient views (from), opposed to &c.: *old friends now at variance*; *he was at variance with his colleagues on one subject only*; *such opinions are quite at variance with those he formerly held.* **3.** (law) Discrepancy between two portions in legal proceedings, as between a statement in pleadings and evidence in proof of it.

variant, adj. & n. [1. váriant; 2. véəriənt]. O. Fr., fr. Lat. *variant*-(*em*), Pres. Part. of *variāre*, see **vary & -ant. 1.** adj. **a** Differing, varying, from one another or from some standard which is accepted as normal; esp. *variant reading* (Lat. *varia lectio*), a reading, as in a MS. &c., different from the accepted reading, or from that in another text; **b** varying, showing variation, varied: *to obtain variant results from what is apparently the same process.* **2.** n. A variant form, reading, version &c.; something which is appreciably different from something else with which it has a common origin or close connexion: *hame and home are dialectal variants of the same word*; *different MSS. of the same work often contain variants introduced by copyists.*

variation, n. [1. vàriáshun; 2. vèəriéiʃən]. O. Fr., fr. Lat. *variātiōn*-(*em*), fr. *variāt*-(*um*), P.P. type of *variāre*, see **vary & -ation. 1. a** Act, process, or fact of varying in form, state, degree, quality &c., from type, standard, the normal &c.; alteration, modification: *variation of temperature, colour, tone &c.*; *a principle without variation*; *subject, liable, to, capable of, variation*; **b** amount, extent, rate, of change: *slight, marked, great, variations in temperature, price &c.* **2.** Specif. **a** (astron.) deviation or change in the mean motion or orbit of a heavenly body; **b** (biol.) deviation or divergence of an organism in structure, or of a function in mode of operation, from that which is typical or usual in the group or species to which it belongs; **c** (magnetism) deviation of the magnetic needle from true North and South; declination; **d** (math.) relation between changes of quantities which vary as each other; permutation; **e** (mus.) repetition of a theme or melody with various, usually progressive, developments; any elaboration of a simple theme.

variational, adj. [1. vàriáshunal; 2. vèəriéiʃənəl]. Prec. & **-al.** Pertaining to, marked by, characteristic of, arising from, variation.

varicated, adj. [1. várikàted; 2. vǽrikeitid]. See **varix & -ate & -ed.** (of shells) Having varices or ridges.

varicella, n. [1. vàriséla; 2. vǽrisélə]. An irregular, mod. dimin. of **variola.** (med.) Chicken-pox.

varicocele, n. [1. várikòsèl; 2. vǽrikousiəl]. See **varicose & -cele.** A varicose condition or enlargement of the veins of the spermatic cord or of the scrotum.

varicoloured, adj. [1. várikùlurd; 2. véərikàləd]. See **various & colour(ed).** Of various colours; variegated, parti-coloured.

varicose, adj. [1. várikōs; 2. vǽrikous], fr. Lat. *varicōsus*, fr. *varic*-(*em*), *varix*, see **varix, & -ose. a** Suffering from, affected by, a varix or varices, or abnormally dilated veins: *a varicose leg, patient, symptom &c.*; **b** abnormally dilated; of veins, esp. those of the leg; hence *varicose ulcer*, such a vein when ulcerated; **c** designed for varicose veins: *varicose bandage &c.*

varicosis, n. [1. vàrikósis; 2. vǽrikóusis]. See prec. & **-osis.** (med.) State of having varicose veins or of being varicose; varicosity.

varicosity, n. [1. vàrikósiti; 2. vǽrikósiti]. See prec. & **-ity.** Varicosis.

varied, adj. [1. várid; 2. véərid], fr. P.P. of **vary. 1.** Exhibiting variety; various: *varied scenes*; *birds of the most varied kinds*; *indulge in varied pleasures, ideas.* **2.** Changing, differing, from time to time; characterized by variety: *live a varied life*; *delightfully varied scenery.*

variedly, adv. Prec. & **-ly.** In a varied manner; with many or constant changes.

variegate, vb. trans. [1. várigāt; 2. véərigeit], fr. L. Lat. *variegāt*-(*um*), P.P. type of *variegāre*, 'to make of various colours', fr. *varius*, see **various,** & *ag-*, stem of *agere*, 'to drive, do' &c., see **agent.** To diversify the colour of, to mark with different colours.

variegated, adj. [1. várigāted; 2. véərigèitid], fr. P.P. of prec. **1.** Diversified in colour; parti-coloured; streaked with various colours. **2.** (fig.) **a** Diversified by change, variety of experience &c.: *a variegated career*; **b** exhibiting different qualities intermingled: *a character strangely variegated with good and evil.*

variegation, n. [1. vàrigáshun; 2. vèərigéiʃən]. See prec. & **-ion.** Diversified colouration; intermingled streaks or patches of colour.

variety, n. [1. variéti; 2. vəráiəti], fr. O. Fr. *variete*, fr. Lat. *varietāt*-(*em*), fr. *varius*, see **various, & -ty. 1.** Quality of being various; reverse of *monotony*; absence of sameness; diversity in external objects or conditions, or of qualities &c.: *the variety of town life*; *the extraordinary variety of his character*; *variety is what the public wants.* **2.** A number or collection, group, of various or different things: *to have a great variety to choose from*; *a variety of excellent dishes*; *owing to a variety of causes.* **3. a** Something varying from others of the same kind; a different kind or form of something; a kind, sort: *a rare variety of old English glass*; *a collection of stamps with many*

VARIFORM 1348 VAST

varieties; *distinguish the varieties of strata, of Gothic architecture* &c.; specif. **b** (biol.) a group or member of a group of animals or plants, differing from related groups, but not so far as to allow them to be classified as a separate species or subspecies, esp. the various kinds or breeds of domesticated animals or cultivated plants; **c** any one of the types of speech, or dialects, into which one original dialect or language has been differentiated. **4.** That form of entertainment which is given at a *variety theatre* or music-hall, a mixed entertainment of individual singers, acrobats, comedians, dancers &c., each giving a separate, distinct turn; known in U.S.A. as *vaudeville*: *variety seemed to have been killed by the films and by revues*; also attrib.: *variety show, artist* &c.

variform, adj. [1. váriform; 2. véərifɔ̄m], fr. **various** & **-form.** Varied in form, having various forms.

variola, n. [1. varíola, vàrióla; 2. vəráiələ, vèərióulə]. Med. Lat., fr. Lat. *varius*, see **various.** (med.) Smallpox.

variolar, adj. [1. varíolar, vàriólar; 2. vəráiələ, vèərióulə]. Prec. & **-ar.** (med.) Pertaining to variola or smallpox; pitted like those attacked by smallpox.

variolite, n. [1. váriōlīt; 2. véəriouláit]. See prec. & **-ite.** A kind of diorite in which whitish spherules of other rock are embedded, giving a pitted appearance like that of smallpox.

varioloid, adj. & n. [1. váriōlòid; 2. véərioulòid], fr. **variola** & **-oid. a** adj. Resembling smallpox; **b** n., a mild form of smallpox, as modified by previous vaccination.

variolous, adj. [1. varíolus, vàriólus; 2. vəráiələs, vèərióuləs]. **variola** & **-ous.** Variolar.

variometer, n. [1. vàriómeter; 2. vèəriɔ́mitə]. fr. **various** & **-meter.** (elect.) **a** An instrument for the comparison of magnetic forces; **b** device for varying the magnetic inductance in a circuit, used in wireless receiving sets for adjustment of wave-lengths &c.

variorum, adj. [1. vàriórum; 2. vèəriɔ́rəm]. Lat., genit. pl. of *varius*, **various**, lit. 'of various persons'. *Variorum edition*, Lat. *editio cum notis variorum*, with notes of various commentators &c.

various, adj. [1. várius; 2. véəriəs]. fr. Lat. *varius*, 'changing, varying; varied'; etymol. dubious. **1.** Different, diverse; having, showing, many different characteristics; varied: *the effects of this disease are various in different cases*; '*Party leaders . . . maintaining . . . their various opinions*' ('The Gondoliers', Gilbert). **2. a** Possessing and exhibiting a variety of qualities, talents &c.; many-sided, versatile; rare or archaic, but familiar from Dryden's '*A man so various, that he seemed to be Not one, but all mankind's epitome*' ('Absalom and Achitophel', i. 545-6); **b** diversified by many and different experiences, adventures, occupations; reverse of monotonous: (The Muse) '*Eyes the calm sunset of thy various day*' (Pope, 'To Earl of Oxford', 38). **3. a** Several, many; also, of several different sorts or kinds: *various people declared they had seen the man*; *there are various reasons for believing*; **b** (colloq. and vulg. as pron. or elliptically as n.) *various of the speakers were inaudible*; *we were assured by various that . . .*

variously, adv. Prec. & **-ly.** In a various manner; in various ways.

variousness, n. See prec. & **-ness.** State, quality, of being various or diversified; variety.

varix, n., pl. **varices** [1. váriks, várisēz; 2. véəriks, vǽrisīz]. Lat., 'dilated vein'; etymol. doubtful; connected w. *varus*, 'a blotch, pimple'; Walde connects this word w. the base of Lat. *vermis*, 'worm', see **vermi-**. **1.** (med.) A varicose vein. **2.** (zool.) A projecting ridge or rib on surface of certain shells.

varlet, n. [1. várlet; 2. vάlit]. O. Fr., 'groom; a youth'; earlier *vaslet*, whence **valet**; *vaslet* is for **vasalet*, dimin. of *vas(s)al*, see **vassal. 1.** (hist.) A groom, attendant; personal servant of a knight or squire; a manservant. **2.** (archaic) A low fellow, rogue, rascal.

varmint, n. [1. vármint; 2. vάmint]. Variant of **vermin**; a pronunciation current in 17th and 18th cents., even among speakers of the higher class. (colloq., slang, or dial.) Rascal, mischievous boy, scamp; esp. *a young varmint.*

varnish (I.), n. [1. várnish; 2. vάniʃ]. M.E. *vernisshe* &c., fr. O. Fr. *vernis*, cp. Ital. *vernice*, Span. *barniz*; Med. Lat. has *vernicium* & Med. Gk. *berníkē*; etymol. unknown. **1.** A gum or resin dissolved in oil or spirit and forming a solution which after application to the surface of wood, leather, metal &c., dries and hardens into a glossy, translucent coating. **2.** (by transf.) A natural glossy surface, as on the leaves of holly, ivy &c.; artificial glaze on pottery. **3.** (fig.) Outward superficial brilliance or polish; gloss; specious appearance or show, serving as a covering for some deficiency &c.: *his occasional association with good society had imparted a certain varnish to his manners*; *even the apologists of the Borgias find it difficult to put a varnish on their characters.*

varnish (II.), vb. trans.; fr. O. Fr. *vernisser*, fr. *vernis*, see prec.; later form *vernir*. **1.** To cover, paint over, with varnish; give a coat of varnish to (a picture, piece of furniture &c.). **2.** (fig.) To cover over with a superficial attractiveness; to gloze over; to hide with a fair, outward appearance: *a hard, merciless character varnished with an attractive air of geniality*; *they hope to varnish their unpopular policy with some vague promises of social reform.*

varnishing day, n. [1. várnishing dā; 2. vάniʃiŋ dèi]. Day before the public opening of an exhibition of pictures, on which the artists are able to put the finishing touches to their exhibits.

'Varsity, adj. & n. [1. vársiti; 2. vάsiti]. Colloq. form of *university*: *at the 'Varsity*; *'Varsity match, team* &c.

varsovienne, n. [1. vàrsōvién; 2. vàsouvién]. Fr., fr. *Varsovie*, 'Warsaw'. A kind of dance, based, in rhythm &c., on Polish national dances.

varus, n. [1. várus; 2. véərəs], fr. Lat. *vārus*, adj., 'bent, crooked', prob. for **văkros*, fr. same base as in *vacillāre*, see **vacillate.** (med.) A form of clubfoot; in full, *talipes varus.*

vary, vb. intrans. & trans. [1. vári; 2. véəri], fr. Fr. *varier*, fr. Lat. *variāre*, 'to change, vary', fr. *varius*, see **various. 1.** intrans. To change, become different; to undergo a change from one condition to a different one: *colours varying with every change of light*; *the weather varies from hour to hour*; *his principles have never varied.* **2.** trans. To cause to change in form, substance, character &c.; to alter; to make different, to modify: *to vary one's plans*; *to vary a patient's treatment*; *to vary the rules, procedure of a court* &c.; *to vary one's meals, method of work* &c.

vas, n., pl. **vasa** [1. vas, vása; 2. væs, véisə]. Lat. *văs*, 'vessel, vase', etymol. uncertain. (anat.) A vessel or duct, as *vas deferens*, excretory, spermatic duct.

vasal, adj. [1. vásl; 2. véisl]. Prec. & **-al.** Pertaining to a vas.

vascular, adj. [1. váskūlar; 2. vǽskjulə], fr. Lat. *vāsculum*, dimin. of *vās*, see **vas**, & **-ar.** (physiol.) Of plants and animals, pertaining to, containing, consisting of, the vessels, ducts &c.: *vascular system*, the circulatory system of blood-vessels, lymphatics, ducts &c.: *vascular tissue*, containing, full of, blood and other vessels &c.

vascularity, n. [1. vàskūláriti; 2. væ̀skjulǽriti]. Prec. & **-ity.** State of being vascular; vascular form.

vascularization, n. [1. vàskularīzáshun; 2. væ̀skjuləraizéiʃən]. See next word & **-ation. a** Act, process, of vascularizing; **b** state of being vascularized.

vascularize, vb. trans. [1. váskūlarīz; 2. vǽskjuləraiz]. **vascular** & **-ize.** To render, cause to become, vascular.

vasculum, n., pl. **vascula** [1. váskūlum, -a; 2. vǽskjuləm, -ə]. Lat. dimin. of *vās*, cp. **vascular. 1.** A small vessel or vase-shaped organism; an ascidian. **2.** A small cylindrical metal case with opening on one side, used by collectors for carrying botanical specimens.

vase, n. [1. vahz; 2. vāz]; archaic [1. vawz; 2. vɔ̄z]; spelling pronunciation [1. vāz; 2. veiz]. Fr., fr. Lat. *vās*, 'vessel', see **vas. 1. a** A general term for a vessel, usually of a decorative kind, of many shapes and sizes, made of glass, pottery, porcelain, or metal, used chiefly as an ornament; **b** a vessel usually more or less tall and slender, but variously shaped, used to contain cut flowers. **2.** Specif., *Greek*, formerly *Etruscan*, *vase*, type of vessel of baked earthenware, made in many varying sizes and forms, and diversely decorated, used as cinerary urns, and for many other purposes, ceremonial and domestic, e.g. for holding wine, water &c. as drinking vessels: *black, red-figured vases* &c.; so *vase painting.* **3.** A sculptured representation of such a vessel in marble or other stone, used as an architectural feature or as a decorative object.

vaseline, n. [1. váselēn; 2. vǽsəlīn]. Modern concoction fr. Germ. *wasser*, 'water', & Gk. *élaion*, 'oil', & **-ine.** A trade and proprietary name of a soft petroleum jelly, without smell or taste, and usually of a yellow colour, used as the basis of ointments, as a lubricant &c.

vasi-, pref. Form fr. Lat. *văs*, 'vessel', see **vas** & **vascular**; used in compounds: *vasiform*, adj., **a** of the shape of a vas or blood-vessel; tubular; **b** shaped like a vase.

vaso-, pref. Form fr. same source as above, used in physiol. & anatomy, in sense of pertaining to, affecting, vascular system, esp. of nerves, drugs &c.; *vaso-constrictor*, constricting, *-dilator*, dilating, or *-motor*, controlling, the blood and other vessels.

vassal, n. [1. vásl; 2. vǽsl]. O. Fr.; represented in Low & Med. Lat. by *vassallus*, or in the more orig. form *vassus*, 'servant, retainer'; a Celt. word, cp. Bret. *goaz*, fr. W. *gwas*, 'youth, servant'; cp. **valet** & **varlet. 1.** (Med. hist., feudalism) One who has vowed fealty and done homage to a superior lord, and holds land from him by so doing; a feudal tenant, feudatory. **2.** (by transf. or fig.) One who is in a subordinate position to another; a dependant, devoted subject; bondman. **3.** (attrib.) Pertaining to, like, a vassal; subject; servile: *vassal homage, fealty*; *a vassal kingdom* &c.

vassalage, n. [1. vásalij; 2. vǽsəlidž]. O. Fr., Mod. Fr. *vasselage*, Med. Lat. *vassalāgium*; see **vassal** & **-age. a** State of being a vassal; allegiance, fealty due from a vassal to his superior; **b** dependence, subordinate position, servitude.

vast, adj. [1. vahst; 2. vāst], fr. Fr. *vaste*. Walde distinguishes two Lat. words, *văstus*, 'huge, immense; shapeless', & *vāstus*, 'barren, void, waste, empty'; Lewis & Short, who give only one word, include under it all the above meanings. The type *vāst-* is cogn. w. O.H.G. *wuosti*, 'barren, empty', O.S. *wōsti*, & O.E. *wēste*, w. same meaning; O. Ir. *fās*, 'empty'. See also **waste** (I.). The form *văst-* is fr. **wazdhos*, & cogn. w. O. Ir. *fot*, 'length'. **1.** Of great size, breadth &c.; very extensive, huge, enormous, immense: **a** (in physical sense) *vast expanse of desert, ocean* &c.; *the vast mountains of the Andes*; *buildings become ever vaster in London*; **b** (in non-physical sense) *vast plans of development*; *a scheme of vast scope.* **2.** Very great in number, amount, or quantity: *spent vast sums of money*; *drank vast quantities of beer*; *a vast crowd of people.* **3. a** Very great: *there is a vast difference between* &c.; *of vast importance*; *a vast improvement*; **b** (archaistic, as a colourless intens.): *it gives me vast pleasure.* **4.** (as n., with art.) *A vast, the vast, of ocean, water* &c., immense tract.

vastly, adv. Prec. & **-ly**. **1.** To a vast, enormous, extent: *the Empire that was so vastly enlarged in the 19th century*; *this book adds vastly to our knowledge*. **2.** Greatly, as mere intensive; very, to a very large extent: *vastly superior to*; (also archaic) *am vastly pleased, obliged* &c.: *vastly pleasant*, extremely amusing.

vastness, n. See prec. & **-ness**. Quality of being vast; immensity, hugeness; vast size.

vasty, adj. [1. váhsti; 2. vásti]. **vast** & **-y**. Vast, immense: Shakespeare, '1 Henry IV.' III. i. 52, '*I can call spirits from the vasty deep*'; '*The vasty hall of death*' (M. Arnold, 'Requiescat').

vat, n. & vb. trans. [1. vat; 2. væt]. Southern dial. variant of O.E. *fæt*, M.E. *vat*, *fat*, 'a vessel' (cp. **vane**, **vixen**), O.N. *fat*, Du. *vat*, Germ. *fass*, 'cask, tub', cogn. w. O.H.G. *fazzōn*, 'to hold; to catch, seize; contain', the orig. meaning of word being 'container'. Cp. *wine fat* in N.T., wh. shows the usual Midl. form of O.E. *f-*. **1.** n. A large vessel for containing liquids, esp. in process of fermentation, maturing, manufacture &c., as in brewing, tanning, dyeing &c. **2.** vb. To place, store, mature, in a vat: *old vatted whiskies* &c.

Vatican, n. [1. vátikan; 2. vætikən]. Fr., fr. Lat. *Vāticānus*, sc. *mons*, one of the hills of ancient Rome. **1.** **a** The palace, with its library, museum, chapels &c. of the Pope in Rome, built on the Vatican hill, the official residence of the Pope and centre of Papal government; hence **b** the Papacy, Papal authority and government; Phr. *thunders of the Vatican*, excommunication, anathemas, of the Roman Church. **2.** (attrib.) *Vatican library, gallery* &c.; *Vatican Council*, that of 1869–70, which established the doctrine of Papal Infallibility &c.

Vaticanism, n. [1. vátikanizm; 2. vætikənizəm]. Prec. & **-ism**. The principle, system, of Papal supremacy and infallibility; ultramontanism.

vaticinal, adj. [1. vatísinl; 2. vætísinl], fr. Lat. *vāticinus*, see **vaticinate** & **-al**. (rare) Pertaining to, of the nature of, vaticination or prophecy; prophetic.

vaticinate, vb. trans. & intrans. [1. vatísināt; 2. vætísineit], fr. Lat. *vāticināt-(um)*, P.P. type of *vāticinārī*, 'to prophesy, foretell', fr. *vātes*, 'prophet, seer'; cogn. w. Goth. *wōþs*, 'possessed, mad'; O.E. *wōd*, 'frenzied, mad'; O.H.G. *wuot*, 'mad; madness'; also O.E. *wōþ*, 'voice; melody, song'; O.N. *ōðr*, 'song, poetry', fr. **woð*. See also **Edda** & cp. **Wednesday**. **a** trans. To prophesy, foretell; **b** intrans., to utter prophecies.

vaticination, n. [1. vàtisináshun; 2. vætisinéiʃən], fr. Lat. *vāticinātiōn-(em)*; see prec. & **-ion**. **a** Act of prophesying or foretelling; **b** a prophecy.

vaticinator, n. [1. vatísināter; 2. vætísineitə]. Lat., see prec. & **-or**. Prophet, seer.

vaudeville, n. [1. vṓdvil; 2. vóudvil]. Fr., corrupt. of earlier (*chanson de*) *Vau de Vire*, i.e. of the valley, or gorge, of the Vire, in Normandy, where Basselin, the best-known composer of such songs, lived. **1.** (Fr. liter. hist.) **a** A light, convivial song such as those of Basselin, c. 1400–50; **b** a form of light, satirical, topical verse, often accompanied by songs, dances, and pantomime, popular in the 17th cent., written in couplets. **2.** **a** (Engl. usage) A form of light, musical comedy; **b** (U.S.A.) a variety or music-hall entertainment.

vault (**I.**), n. [1. vawlt; 2. vɔlt]. M.E. *voute*, *vowte*, fr. O. Fr. *voute*, *voulte*, *vaute* &c., Mod. Fr. *voûte*, fr. Low Lat. *vol(u)ta*, fr. P.P. of Lat. *volvere*, 'to roll', cp. **volute** & see **volume**. **1.** An arched roof or ceiling; the covering of an open space by stone or brick supported on a continuous series of arches, as in the 'barrel' vault, or on connected arched ribs meeting in a central point and depending on thrust and counter-thrust for stability, the intersecting or 'groined' vault. **2.** A vaulted chamber or space, specif. **a** an underground cellar or chamber with arched roof: *wine vaults*; **b** a strong room in which safes are kept: *safety vault*; **c** an underground brick or stone chamber in which coffins are laid in a cemetery and, formerly, beneath the flooring of a church, in a crypt &c.: *family vault*. **3.** **a** Any naturally formed subterranean cavern with arching roof; **b** an arched cavity in the body of an animal &c. **4.** (fig.) The arched canopy of the sky: *the blue vault of heaven*.

vault (**II.**), vb. trans., fr. prec. **a** To cover, roof over with a vault; to build a vault over; **b** (fig.) to cover as with a vault.

vault (**III.**), vb. intrans. & trans., fr. M. Fr. *volter*, 'to leap, gambol', cp. Ital. *volta*, 'the turn, swerve, bound, of a horse'; cp. **vault** (**I.**), wh. is the same word w. differentiation of meaning. **1.** intrans. To leap, spring, with a single movement, esp. with the support of the hand or hands or of a leaping-pole: *to vault over a gate, ditch*; *to vault on to a horse, into the saddle*. **2.** trans. To leap over, with support of the hand: *to vault a gate*.

vault (**IV.**), n., fr. prec. Leap, jump, with single movement with support of hand &c.

vaulted, adj. [1. váwlted; 2. vɔ́ltid]. P.P. of **vault** (**II.**). **a** Built with vaults, or as a vault; arched: *a vaulted roof*; **b** covered by a vault: *vaulted aisle, chamber* &c.

vaulter, n. [1. váwlter; 2. vɔ́ltə]. **vault** (**III.**) & **-er**. One who vaults or leaps.

vaulting (**I.**), n. [1. váwlting; 2. vɔ́ltiŋ], fr. **vault** (**II.**) & **-ing**. **a** The construction, building, of a vault or vaults; **b** a vaulted building; **c** the vaults, collectively, of a roof &c.

vaulting (**II.**), n. & adj., fr. **vault** (**III.**) & **-ing**; **2** is fr. Pres. Part. of same. **1.** n. Act of leaping with support of the hand &c. **2.** adj. Leaping with a vault; (also fig.) fr. *vaulting ambition* (Shakespeare, 'Macbeth'), that vaults over, surmounts, all obstacles.

vaunt (**I.**), vb. intrans. & trans. [1. vawnt; 2. vɔnt]. M.E. *avaunten* (cp. **avaunt**), also later without the intens. *a-*; fr. O. Fr. (*se*) *vanter*, 'to boast', fr. Low Lat. *vānitāre*, 'to flatter', fr. Lat. *vānitas*, see **vanity** & **vain**. **1.** intrans. **a** *Vaunt of*, to boast about, proclaim in boastful terms: *to vaunt of one's skill*; **b** *vaunt over*, to triumph over malevolently and boastfully: *to vaunt over another's failure*. **2.** trans. **a** To boast, brag about: *to vaunt one's skill*; (also as adj. fr. P.P.): *his vaunted courage*; **b** to proclaim the merits of, to praise highly, celebrate: *to vaunt the beauties of the Scottish lochs*.

vaunt (**II.**), n., fr. prec. Boasting; boastful language; a boast.

vaunter, n. [1. váwnter; 2. vɔ́ntə]. **vaunt** (**I.**) & **-er**. One who vaunts; a boaster, braggart.

vavasour, n. [1. vávasōr; 2. vævəsɔ]. O. Fr.; in Med. Lat. *vavassor*, *valvassor*, *vasvassor*, apparently a corrupt. of *vassus vassorum*, 'vassal of vassals', see **vassal**. (Med. hist.) A term, of varying applications, for a subordinate or mediate vassal; a person holding a fief from one who was himself the vassal to another; also a vassal who had subordinate vassals himself.

veal, n. [1. vēl; 2. vīl]. M.E. *veel*, 'calf; veal', fr. O. Fr. *veël*, later, as in Mod. Fr., *veau*, fr. Lat. *vitellus*, dimin. of *vitulus*, 'calf'; cogn. w. Gk. *italós*, fr. **witalos*; Scrt. *vatsa*, 'calf'; the orig. meaning is 'yearling', cp. Gk. *étos* for **wetos*, 'year'; wh. base is seen also in Lat. *vetus*, 'old', see **veteran**; further in O.E. *weþer*, see **wether**. The flesh of a calf, as used for food; the word was used occasionally for the living animal as late as 18th cent.

vector, n. [1. vékter; 2. véktə]. Lat., 'carrier, bearer, conveyer', fr. *vect-(um)*, P.P. type of *vehere*, 'to convey', see **vehicle**, & **-or**; see also **weight** (**I.**). (math.) A quantity involving direction as well as magnitude.

vectorial, adj. [1. vektṓrial; 2. vektɔ́riəl]. Prec. & **-i-** & **-al**. (math.) Pertaining to vectors.

Veda, n. [1. váda; 2. véidə]. Scrt. *vēda*, 'knowledge; sacred book of wisdom', fr. base **weid-*, **woid-*, **wid-*, q.v. also under **idol**, **idea**, **-oid**, **vision** (**I.**), **wit** (**I.**). One of the four ancient sacred books of the Hindus.

Vedanta, n. [1. vādánta; 2. veidæntə]. Scrt., fr. **Veda** & *anta*, 'end'. The system of Hindu pantheistic philosophy.

Veddah, n. [1. véda; 2. védə]. Cingalese, 'hunter'. Member of the primitive, aboriginal race inhabiting the jungles of Ceylon.

vedette, n. [1. vedét; 2. vedét]. Fr., fr. Ital. *vedetta*, fr. *vedere*, 'to see', fr. Lat. *vidēre*, see **vision**. A mounted sentry, placed in advance of an outpost.

Vedic, adj. [1. vádik; 2. véidik]. **Veda** & **-ic**. Pertaining to the Vedas: *Vedic literature* &c.

veer, vb. intrans. & trans. [1. vēr; 2. viə], fr. Fr. *virer*, 'to turn round, change direction', cp. Span. *virar*, *birar*, Ital. *virare*; of doubtful etymol.; L. Lat. has *virāre*, wh. has been referred to stem seen in Lat. *viriae*, pl., 'bracelets', dimin. form *viriola*, & second element in **environ**, the orig. meaning being 'to twist, wind round'; this base is also seen in **wire** (**I.**) & **withy**. **1.** intrans. **a** To shift, change, turn, in position or direction: *the wind, the vane, has veered round to the south*; specif. (of a ship) to change course as preparation for tacking; Phrs. *veer and haul*, to pay out and haul in (rope) alternately; *veer out*, pay out; **b** (fig.) to change about, shift, from one opinion, belief, set of feelings, intentions &c., to another; *to veer round to the opposite party* &c. **2.** trans. To alter, change, the course of, as a ship &c.

veeringly, adv. [1. vḗringli; 2. víəriŋli], fr. Pres. Part. of prec. & **-ly**. In a veering, shifting manner; with change of direction, esp. of mind or opinion.

Vega (**I.**), n. [1. vḗga; 2. vígə]. Med. Lat., fr. Arab. *wāqis*, adj., 'falling'. The brightest star in the constellation Lyra.

vega (**II.**), n. [1. vága; 2. véigə]. Span. A low-lying damp or grassy tract of ground, esp. in South America; also tobacco field, in Cuba.

vegetable (**I.**), adj. [1. véjetabl; 2. védžitəbl]. Fr., fr. L. Lat. *vegetābilis*, 'enlivening, animating', w. suff. *-bilis*, fr. Lat. *vegetāre*, 'to arouse, animate, invigorate', fr. *vegetus*, 'vigorous, active, lively', fr. *vegēre*, 'to be active, lively; to quicken, arouse'; the base is seen in the Lat. derivatives **vigil** & **vigour**; also in O.E. *wacor*, 'watchful, vigilant', cp. *wacan*, 'to awake, be born', see **wake** (**I.**). A fuller form of this base, **aweg-*, is seen in Lat. *augēre* for **awegēre*, 'to cause to grow, to increase', see **augment** (**I.**) & **eke** (**II.**), & cp. **hygiene**. Pertaining to, belonging to, composed of, comprising, including, affecting, of the nature of, plants, or plant life: *the vegetable kingdom*; *vegetable life* &c.; *vegetable tissue*; *vegetable as distinct from mineral drugs*; *vegetable diseases* &c.

vegetable (**II.**), n., fr. prec. **1.** Anything that grows in the ground; any form of plant life. Phr. *to become a mere vegetable*, said of a person who is thoroughly inactive in mind and body. **2.** Specif., the edible leaves, stalks, flowers, seeds, pods, or roots of certain plants specially cultivated for human food; greens, greenstuff; in common colloquial usage a distinction is made between *potatoes* and *vegetables*, the latter including peas, beans, cabbage of all kinds, asparagus, turnips, carrots &c.; *green vegetables*, (i.) those whose leaves &c. are eaten, as distinct from the roots; (ii.) vegetables cooked green and fresh, as distinct from dried peas &c.; *vegetable dish*, one in which vegetables are brought to table.

vegetable ivory, n. A hard white seed or nut of a South American palm, which is used as a substitute for ivory in manufacture of buttons &c.

vegetable marrow, n. A kind of edible gourd, *Cucurbita Pepo ovifera*.

vegetal, adj. [1. véjetal; 2. védžit(ə)l]. Fr., fr. Lat. *vegetus*, see **vegetable**, & **-al**. **1.** Pertaining to, of the nature of, a plant or vegetable; vegetable: *vegetal life, structure* &c. **2.** (physiol.) Pertaining to growth or the functions; especially concerned with growth or maintenance of life in living organisms, both animals and plants; vegetative.

vegetarian, n. & adj. [1. vèjetárian; 2. vèdžitéəriən]. A modern, coined word, fr. *veget-*, see **vegetable (II.)**, & **-arian**. **1.** n. One whose food consists solely or mainly of vegetables, fruit, nuts &c.; one who, on principle, abstains from all forms of animal food, esp. from such as involves the taking of animal life. **2.** adj. **a** Pertaining to vegetarians, their principles &c.: *vegetarian society, system, principles* &c.; **b** consisting solely of vegetables, providing vegetables only as food: *vegetarian diet, dishes, restaurant* &c.

vegetarianism, n. [1. vèjetárianizm; 2. vèdžitéəriənizəm]. See prec. & **-ism.** Principles, practice, of vegetarians; abstention from all animal foods.

vegetate, vb. intrans. [1. véjetāt; 2. védžiteit], fr. Lat. *vegetāt-(um)*, P.P. type of *vegetāre*, 'to give life and vigour to, to animate', fr. *vegetus*, see **vegetable (I.)**. **a** To grow, pass one's life, like a plant; live a purely physical life, devoid of all intellectual and spiritual activities; **b** to live a dull, monotonous, unvaried life with few social or other distractions.

vegetation, n. [1. vèjetáshun; 2. vèdžitéiʃən], fr. L. Lat. *vegetātiōn-(em)*, see prec. & **-ion.** **1.** Act, process, of growing or vegetating; plant growth and development: *vegetation is at its height in spring.* **2.** Plants collectively: *a tropical, luxuriant, vegetation*; *the vegetation is sparse.*

vegetative, adj. [1. véjetativ; 2. védžitətiv], fr. Med. Lat. *vegetātīvus*, see **vegetate** & **-ive.** **1.** Having the capacity of growth; growing: *the vegetative as opposed to the reproductive system of plants.* **2.** Pertaining to, connected with, growth: *vegetative functions*; *during the vegetative stage.* **3.** Productive of growth or vegetation: *vegetative soils.* **4.** (fig.) Living an inactive life; vegetating, passive; passed in mere sloth or idleness: *a placid, vegetative sort of character, existence.*

vegetatively, adv. Prec. & **-ly.** In a vegetative manner.

vegetativeness, n. See prec. & **-ness.** State, quality, of being vegetative.

vehemence, rarely **vehemency**, n. [1. vḗemens(i); 2. víəmǝns(i)], fr. L. Lat. *vehementia*, see **vehement** & **-ency.** State, quality, of being vehement; violence, intensity, impetuosity, force, eagerness; in material and non-material sense: *the vehemence of the storm, attack* &c.; *carried away by the vehemence of his own eloquence, passions* &c.

vehement, adj. [1. vḗement; 2. víəmənt]. O. Fr., fr. Lat. *vehement-(em), vehemens*, 'eager, violent, furious, vehement; forcible, vigorous', the first element is fr. the base *vehere*, 'to carry, convey', see under **vehicle.** Orig. sense, 'transported (as with strong emotion), carried out of oneself'. The form *vehemens* was probably orig. participial: **vehemenos.* **1.** Acting with great material force, strength or violence; furious: *vehement heat, wind*; *a vehement current* &c. **2.** (in non-material sense) Passionate, **a** (of actions, emotions &c.) impetuous, eager, ardent: *vehement opposition, strife*; *vehement desire, hatred* &c.; **b** (of persons) exhibiting vehemence of character, passion &c.: *a vehement partisan, opponent* &c.

vehemently, adv. Prec. & **-ly.** In a vehement manner; with vehemence; ardently, passionately.

vehicle, n. [1. vḗikl; 2. víikl, víəkl], fr. Lat. *vehiculum*, 'carriage, conveyance', formed w. dimin., see **-cule**, fr. base of *vehere*, 'to bear, carry, convey', this base **wegh-, *wogh-*, is seen in Scrt. *vahati*, 'he carries, conveys'; Gk. (Pamphylian) *ékhos* for **wekhos*, 'wagon', *(w)ekhétō*, 'let him bring'; *ókhos* for **wokhos*, 'wagon'; Goth. *(ga)wigan*, 'to shake, to move'; O.E. *wegan*, 'to carry', see **weigh (I.)**, also **way.** **1.** That in which anything can be carried; esp. a wheeled carriage, cart, car, or other conveyance by which persons or goods may be transported by land. **2.** A means of transmission; a medium, in various senses: *the ether is the vehicle of light and electric waves*; *a sweet syrup is a good vehicle for the administration of nauseous drugs*; *milk is often a vehicle of infection.* **3.** A means of communicating ideas: *English is a noble vehicle of human thought.*

vehicular, adj. [1. vēhíkūlar; 2. vihíkjulə], fr. L. Lat. *vehiculāris*, see prec. & **-ar.** Pertaining to, concerned with, consisting of, carried by, vehicles: *vehicular transport*; *vehicular traffic.*

vehmgericht, n. [1. vám-, fámgeright; 2. véim-, féimgərijt]. Germ., also *fehmgericht*, fr. *vehme, fehme*, 'judgement, punishment', origin doubtful, & *gericht*, 'jurisdiction, court, tribunal', cp. **right (I.)**. **a** A special form of criminal jurisdiction, prevalent in Germany, esp. in Westphalia, during the Middle Ages until the 16th cent., exercised by judges chosen from those pledged by oaths to secrecy, trying serious crimes with power of life and death, and usually though not necessarily sitting in secret; **b** a court of this kind.

vehmic, also **fehmic**, adj. [1. vámik, fámik; 2. véimik, féimik]. See prec. & **-ic.** Pertaining to the vehmgericht: *vehmic courts.*

veil (I.), n. [1. vāl; 2. veil], fr. O. Fr. *veile*, Mod. Fr. *voile*, fr. Lat. *vēlum*, 'sail; piece of cloth; curtain, veil'; see **velum.** **1.** A covering for the face or head, esp. as worn by women, either (i.) as by Moslem women, nuns &c., to conceal their features, or (ii.) as a protection against sun, wind &c., or (iii.) at the dictates of fashion; Phr. *to take the veil*, to become a nun. **2.** (eccles.) **a** A curtain or cloth hanging, esp. that dividing the Sanctuary from the main body of the Jewish Temple; **b** a piece of drapery of silk &c., used to cover a chalice, crucifix &c., esp. during Lent. **3.** **a** Something which covers and hides (an object) from the sight: *a veil of mist over the landscape*; **b** something which obscures the mental vision; something which renders complete and clear mental perception difficult: *the facts are hidden in a veil of mystery.* **4.** (bot. and zool.) Velum.

veil (II.), vb. trans., fr. O. Fr. *veiler*, fr. Lat. *vēlare*, 'to veil, conceal', see prec. **1.** To cover with, or as with, a veil; to throw a veil over: *to veil one's face, head* &c. **2.** **a** To conceal, hide from sight: *clouds veiled the sun*; **b** to conceal from another's mental perception; to render imperceptible to mental observation; to disguise, dissimulate: *to veil one's dislike, suspicion*; *his malevolence was veiled by an urbane manner.*

veiled, adj. [1. vāld; 2. veild], fr. P.P. of prec. **1.** Wearing a veil, with head and face &c. covered by a veil: *the veiled Tuaregs*; *veiled nun*; *with veiled eyes.* **2.** Concealed, disguised, masked: *veiled hatred* &c.

veiling, n. [1. váling; 2. véiliŋ]. **veil (II.)** & **-ing.** Soft, thin material suitable for veils &c.

veilless, adj. [1. vālles; 2. véillis]. **veil (I.)** & **-less.** Without a veil; unveiled.

vein (I.), n. [1. vān; 2. vein]. M.E. & Fr. *veine*, fr. Lat. *vēna*; possibly for **vexna*, & connected w. base seen in *vehere*, 'to carry, convey', see **vehicle.** **1.** One of the tubular vessels which convey the blood returned from the capillaries to the heart, cp. *artery*; (loosely) any blood-vessel. **2.** Something resembling a vein in appearance; as **a** one of the fine ribs or branches of the framework of a leaf, insect's wing &c.; **b** a coloured streak or mark, natural or artificial, in stone, wood &c. **3.** A fissure, cleft, in rock, earth &c., filled with a different rock, or mineral ore; a seam, lode. **4.** **a** Distinctive strain or tendency or characteristic quality which runs through a man's nature as a vein of ore &c. through rock &c.; a streak: *he had a strong vein of humour, of cruelty*; *his characteristic vein of sarcasm*; **b** mood, disposition: *to be in the vein for composing, writing* &c.

vein (II.), vb. trans., fr. prec. To mark, cover, with veins; usually in P.P. *veined.*

veininess, n. [1. vánines; 2. véininis]. **veiny** & **-ness.** State, quality, of being veiny.

veinless, adj. [1. vánles; 2. véinlis]. **vein (I.)** & **-less.** Lacking veins; unveined.

veiny, adj. [1. váni; 2. véini]. **vein (I.)** & **-y.** Covered with, full of, veins; showing the veins prominently, on face, hand &c.

velamen, n., pl. **velamina** [1. velámen, -ina; 2. veléimen, -inə]. Lat., 'covering', fr. *vēlāre*, see **velum.** (anat.) A membrane, velum.

velar, adj. & n. [1. vḗlar; 2. vílə], fr. Lat. *vēlāris*, see **velum** & **-ar.** **1.** adj. Connected with, related to, arising from, the velum or soft palate; *velar consonants*, those formed by the back of the tongue in proximity to the velum. **2.** n. A velar consonant, i.e. a back consonant.

velarium, n. [1. vēlárium; 2. viléəriəm]. Lat. See prec. **a** (Rom. antiq.) The large awning which could be stretched over the auditorium of an amphitheatre or theatre as protection against the sun; **b** (zool.) a membranous rim, in certain jelly-fish.

veld(t), n. [1. velt, felt; 2. velt, felt]. S.-Afr. Du., fr. Du. *veld*, cogn. w. **field (I.)**. The open grass-country, mostly treeless, of S. Africa.

veld(t)-schoen, n. [1. vélt, félt, shōōn; 2. vélt, félt, ʃūn]. S.-Afr. Du. See prec. & **shoe (I.)**. Shoe made of untanned hide, as used in S. Africa by natives and Boer farmers &c.

velite, n. [1. vḗlīt; 2. vílait], fr. Lat. *vēlīt-*, stem of *vēles*, cogn. w. *vēlox*, 'swift', see **velocity.** (Rom. antiq.) Light-armed soldier, skirmisher.

velleity, n. [1. veléiti; 2. veliiti], fr. Med. Lat. *velleitāt-(em), velleitas*, fr. Lat. *velle*, 'to will, wish', see **voluntary (I.)**; cp. also **will (I.)**. (philos.) Imperfect volition, the weakest form of desire.

vellicate, vb. trans. & intrans. [1. vélikāt; 2. vélikeit], fr. Lat. *vellicāt-(um)*, P.P. type of *vellicāre*, freq. of *vellere*, 'to pluck, twitch; to tear, pull off', earlier **vels-*; fr. base **vel-, *vol-* &c., 'to tear, break', seen also in **vulture, vulnerable**; & in Lat. *vellus*, 'sheepskin with wool left on', see **villus.** From another grade of the same base is Lat. *lāna* for **wlana*, 'wool', see **laniferous**; & further, O.E. *wull*, see **wool (I.)**. (rare) To twitch; to contract, move, convulsively or spasmodically.

vellication, n. [1. vèlikáshun; 2. vèlikéiʃən]. Prec. & **-ion.** (med.) A spasmodic, convulsive local twitching of muscular tissue, esp. of the face.

vellum, n. [1. vélum; 2. véləm]. Earlier *velym, velim*, fr. O. Fr. *velin*, w. change of final *n* to *m*, as in **venom**; Mod. Fr. *vélin*; fr. *vel*, 'veal', or fr. Lat. *vitulīnus*, 'belonging to a calf', *vitulus*, see **veal**; the L. Lat. name for 'vellum' was *pellis vitulīna.* A fine calf-skin parchment, used for MSS. or for binding.

velocipede, n. [1. velósipēd; 2. velósipīd]. Fr.; modern concoction fr. Lat. *vēlōci-, vēlox*, 'swift', see **velocity**, & *ped-(em), pēs*, 'foot', see **pedal (I.)**. Name formerly given to, **a** a kind of hobby-horse on wheels propelled by the rider's feet touching, and pushing off from, the ground; **b** the earliest form of bicycle; a bone-shaker.

velocity, n. [1. velósiti; 2. vilósiti], fr. Fr. *vélocité*, fr. Lat. *vēlōcitāt-(em), vēlōcitas*, 'swiftness', fr. *vēlōci-, vēlox*, 'swift', for **wegslo-*, fr. the base of *vehere*, 'to carry' &c., see **vehicle.** **1.** **a** Swiftness, speed, rapidity of motion: *darted off with the velocity of a bird*; *what limit is there to an aeroplane's velocity?*; **b** quickness, rapidity of action or of events: *the world was rushed into war with startling velocity.* **2.** Rate of motion, rapidity relative to time: *at a velocity of 100 miles per hour*; *muzzle velocity*, that of projectile on leaving the gun or rifle.

velours, n. [1. velóor; 2. velúə]. Fr.; O. Fr. *velour, velous*, fr. Lat. *villōsus*, 'shaggy', see **velvet.** **a** A material with a soft pile like that of velvet; **b** hat of this material.

velum, n., pl. **vela** [1. vélum, -a; 2. vīlə(m)]. Lat., 'sail; piece of cloth, curtain, veil'; etymol. disputed; prob. for *vecslom*; fr. base *weg-*, 'to weave'; cp. Ir. *figim*, 'I weave'; O.H.G. *wickilin*, 'woollen yarn for spinning'; see further under **wick** (of candle). **1.** (anat.) The soft palate. **2. a** (bot.) A membranous covering seen in certain fungi; **b** (zool.) a membranous organ in jelly-fish, molluscs &c.

velure, n. [1. velúr; 2. veljúə], fr. O. Fr. See **velours**. A variant of velours, q.v.

velvet (I.), n. [1. vélvet; 2. vélvit]. A.-Fr., fr. L. or Med. Lat. *ve(e)lvētum*, apparently for *velluētum*, a variant form of *vellūtum*, whence Ital. *velluto*; fr. Lat. *villus*, 'shaggy, rough hair', cogn. w. *vellus*, 'fleece of wool'; cp. Lat. *vellere*, 'to pluck'; see **vellicate**. The Lat. adj. *villōsus*, 'shaggy', gave O. Fr. *velous*, later *velours*, 'velvet', see **velours**. **1.** A textile, properly of silk or of silk on a cotton or linen backing, with a thick, close, soft pile or nap on one side. **2.** The soft, velvety covering of newly grown antlers of deer. **3.** Any soft surface resembling velvet in touch or appearance, as on a peach, cheek &c.; or of mossy stone, tree trunk &c.; Phr. *to be on velvet*, to be in a safe or advantageous position, esp. in money matters, specif. in betting or speculation, so that whatever happens one may win but cannot lose.

velvet (II.), adj., fr. prec. **1.** Made of velvet; Phr. *iron hand in the velvet glove*, sternness, force, ruthlessness, concealed by a suave, courteous manner. **2.** Like, resembling, velvet, to the touch or in appearance; soft, velvety, often in names of plants, animals &c.: *velvet ant, moss, sponge* &c.

velveteen, n. [1. vělvetén; 2. vělvitín], fr. Fr. *velvetine*. **velvet & -een**, variant of **-ine**, indicating an imitation or derivative. An imitation velvet made of cotton; *velveteens*, breeches made of this, often worn by gamekeepers; hence, a gamekeeper.

velvety, adj. [1. vélveti; 2. vélviti]. **velvet (I.) & -y**. Like velvet; having the texture of velvet to the touch; smooth and non-astringent to the taste: *a velvety wine*.

venal, adj. [1. věnl; 2. vīnl]. Through O. Fr. or directly fr. Lat. *vēnālis*, 'for sale, purchasable; that can be bought or bribed'; fr. *vēnum*, also *vēnus*, for *vesn-*, 'sale'; cp. Scrt. cogn. *vasnál*, 'purchase price', *vasnam*, 'reward'; further Gk. *ōnos* for *wōsnos*, 'price'. **1.** (of persons) Capable of being bought or bribed; influenced by hope of reward; mercenary, corrupt: *a venal judge, politician; a venal police force; the venal races of the Levant* &c. **2.** (of actions and motives) Controlled, influenced, by hope of gain or reward; springing from, instigated by, corrupt, mercenary, motives.

venality, n. [1. věnáliti; 2. vīnǽliti], fr. Fr. *vénalité*, fr. L. Lat. *vēnālitāt-(em)*, see **venal & -ity**. Quality of being venal; mercenary behaviour.

venally, adv. [1. věnali; 2. vīnəli]. **venal & -ly**. In a venal manner; corruptly.

venatic, adj. [1. venátik; 2. vinǽtik], fr. Lat. *vēnāticus*, fr. *vēnāri*, 'to hunt', see **venery (I.) & venison**. (rare, archaistic) Pertaining to the chase or hunting.

venation, n. [1. věnáshun; 2. vīnéiʃən], fr. Lat. *vēna*, see **vein & -ation**. The arrangement or system of veins in a leaf or insect's wing.

vend, vb. trans. [1. vend; 2. vɛnd], fr. O. Fr. *vendre*, fr. Lat. *vendere*, 'to sell', fr. *vēnum dāre*, 'to offer for sale', fr. *vēnum*, 'price, sale', see **venal**, & *dāre*, 'to give, offer', see **date (I.), donation**. To sell or offer for sale; chiefly a legal term, or used in sense of to peddle (small wares).

vendace, n. [1. věndás; 2. véndeis]. Apparently fr. O. Fr. *vendese*, Mod. Fr. *vandoise*, 'dace'; etymol. doubtful. A small freshwater fish, genus *Coregonus*, of some Scottish and English lakes.

Vendean, adj. & n. [1. věndéan; 2. vɛndíən], fr. Fr. *Vendéen*, fr. Vendée, department in N.W. France. **1.** adj. Of La Vendée, esp. in connexion with the struggle there against the Revolution in 1793. **2.** n. An inhabitant of La Vendée; participator in the struggle against the Revolution.

vendee, n. [1. vendé; 2. vɛndí]. **vend & -ee**. (legal) Person to whom anything is sold; purchaser.

Vendémiaire, n. [1. vàhndāmiǽr; 2. vǎdemiɛ̃r]. Fr., fr. Lat. *vindēmia*, 'vintage', see **vintage**. The first month, Sept. 22nd to Oct. 21st, of the French Revolutionary calendar.

vender, n. [1. vénder; 2. véndə]. **vend & -er**. One who vends, sells, or offers to sell; cp. *vendor*.

vendetta, n. [1. vendéta; 2. vɛndétə]. Ital., 'revenge', fr. Lat. *vindicta*, see **vindictive**. A blood feud; family vengeance, esp. as practised through generations, as in Corsica.

vendibility, n. [1. věndibíliti; 2. vɛndibíliti]. See next word & **-ity**. Quality of being vendible or salable.

vendible, adj. [1. véndibl; 2. véndibl], fr. Lat. *vendibilis*, see **vend & -ible**. Salable.

vendor, n. [1. véndŏr; 2. vɛndô]. **vend & -or**. One who sells or offers for sale; vender; esp. (legal) the seller of real property: *the law of vendor and purchaser*; contrasted with *vendee*.

veneer (I.), vb. trans. [1. venér; 2. vənə́]. Earlier *faneer, fineer*, fr. Germ. *furniren*, 'to inlay, veneer', lit. 'to furnish with pieces of inlay', fr. Fr. *fournir*, 'to furnish', itself fr. O.H.G., see **furnish**. **1.** To cover, overlay, (object of common wood) with a thin sheet of fine wood, or (a piece of fine wood) with a thin sheet of wood of same kind, but of better grain and texture; also, similarly, to overlay (wood, stone &c.) with a thin plate of ivory, marble, mother-of-pearl &c. **2.** (fig.) To attempt to conceal beneath a specious appearance of refinement and polish something which is essentially unrefined and coarse: *his innate vulgarity was veneered with an affectation of ease and geniality*.

veneer (II.), n., fr. prec. **1.** (cabinet-making) A thin plate or layer of wood of fine grain and texture, laid and glued over wood of inferior quality and appearance, so as to produce the impression that the wood so treated is of fine quality throughout. **2.** (fig.) A superficial appearance of some quality, mode of behaviour &c., assumed as being superior to that which it is designed to hide; a specious gloss: *a thin veneer of education, good breeding, respectability* &c.; *a Scotch accent with a veneer of cockney*.

veneering, n. [1. venéring; 2. vəníəriŋ]. **veneer (I.) & -ing**. **1.** Process of applying veneer to wood. **2.** Material used as veneer.

venenate, vb. trans. [1. vénenát; 2. véneneit], fr. Lat. *venēnāt-(um)*, P.P. type of *venēnāre*, 'to infect with poison', fr. *venēnum*, 'poison', see **venom**. (rare, med.) To poison, infect with poisonous substance.

venenation, n. [1. věnenáshun; 2. vɛnɛnéiʃən]. Prec. & **-ion**. Poisoning.

venerability, n. [1. věnerabíliti; 2. vɛnərəbíliti], fr. L. Med. Lat. *venerābilitāt-(em)*, see next word & **-ity**. Quality of being venerable.

venerable, adj. [1. vénerabl; 2. vénərəbl], fr. O. Fr., fr. Lat. *venerābilis*, fr. *venerāri*, see **venerate**, & **-able**. **1. a** (of persons) Worthy of being venerated; deserving honour and respect; esp. **b** (of persons and things) deserving respect and veneration as having lived long and honourably, or having lasted for a very long time: *the venerable commander, prelate* &c.; also *a venerable building, a venerable oak* &c. Thus venerable comes to mean 'old', but nearly always with the implication of 'deserving respect': *venerable age, antiquity*. **2.** Specif., an ecclesiastical title, **a** in the Anglican Church, for an archdeacon: *the Venble. Archdeacon Brown* &c.; **b** in Roman Catholic Church, for one who has passed the first stage of canonization, prior to beatification: *the Venerable Bede* (traditional title). **3.** (of things) Held in great honour and esteem for historical, religious associations &c.: *venerable ruins* &c.

venerableness, n. Prec. & **-ness**. Venerability.

venerably, adv. See prec. & **-ly**. In a venerable manner.

venerate, vb. trans. [1. vénerát; 2. vénəreit], fr. Lat. *venerāt-(um)*, P.P. type of *venerāri*, 'to reverence, worship, venerate'; fr. *vener-*, stem of *venus*, 'love, desire', see **Venus**. **1.** To reverence, revere; to regard with feelings of profound respect. **2.** To worship, adore.

veneration, n. [1. veneráshun; 2. venəréiʃən], fr. Lat. *venerātiōn-(em)*, see prec. & **-ion**. Act of venerating; deep respect and reverence accorded to persons, objects, qualities, or actions.

venerator, n. [1. venerátĕr; 2. vénəreitə]. Lat., see **venerate & -or**. One who venerates or reverences.

venereal, adj. [1. venéreal; 2. veníəriəl], fr. Lat. *venereus*, fr. *vener-*, stem of *venus*, 'sexual love, desire', see **Venus, & -al**. Pertaining, due, to sexual intercourse; esp. *venereal diseases*, as syphilis, gonorrhoea &c.

venery (I.), n. [1. véneri; 2. vénəri], fr. O. Fr. *venerie*, fr. *vener*, 'to hunt', fr. Lat. *vēnāri*, 'to hunt; to seek after, pursue'; cogn. w. Scrt. *vēti*, 'follows after'; more remotely w. O.H.G. *weida*, 'fodder, pasture, pasture-ground; the chase', fr. base *wēi-, *wai-*, & **-ery**. (archaic) Hunting, the chase: *learned in all the arts of venery*; '*a boke of venerie*'.

venery (II.), n., fr. Lat. *vener-*, stem of *venus*, 'sexual love, desire', see **Venus**. (archaic) Sexual love; indulgence in sexual gratification.

venesection, n. [1. věnesékshun; 2. vīnisékʃən], fr. Med. Lat. *vēnae sectio*, 'cutting of a vein', see **vein (I.) & section (I.)**. (med.) The opening of a vein to let blood; blood-letting, as formerly practised as a remedy; phlebotomy.

Venetian, adj. & n. [1. venéshan; 2. viníʃən], fr. Med. Lat. *Venetiānus*, fr. *Venetia*, Venice. **1.** adj. Pertaining to, made in, used in, Venice: *Venetian glass*, from Murano; *Venetian blind*, one made of movable slats of wood; *Venetian mast*, spirally painted pole used in street decorations. **2.** n. Inhabitant, native, of Venice.

vengeance, n. [1. vénjans; 2. véndʒəns]. M.E., fr. O. Fr., fr. *venger*, 'to avenge', & **-ance**, fr. Lat. *vindicāre*, see **vindicate**. **1.** The infliction of punishment or exaction of retribution for wrong done or received; often with sense of vindictive punishment: '*Vengeance is mine, I will repay*' (Rom. xii. 19). Phr. *to take vengeance upon*, exact retribution from. **2.** An instance of this: *a fearful vengeance*. Phr. (colloq.) *with a vengeance*, to a high degree, to an extreme extent, very thoroughly: *he laid about him with a vengeance*.

vengeful, adj. [1. vénjfl; 2. véndʒfl], fr. obs. *venge*, 'to avenge', see prec., & **-ful**. Vindictive, revengeful.

vengefully, adv. Prec. & **-ly**. Revengefully, vindictively.

vengefulness, n. See prec. & **-ness**. Revengefulness, vindictiveness.

venial, adj. [1. věnial; 2. víniəl]. O. Fr., fr. L. Lat. *veniālis*, 'gracious; pardonable, venial'; fr. Lat. *venia*, 'grace, kindness, pardon, mercy', fr. base seen in **venerate & Venus**. **a** Pardonable, excusable; trivial, unimportant: *a venial error; such childish, venial faults*; **b** (theol.) entitled to remission of punishment and to forgiveness: *venial sin*; contrasted with *mortal sin*.

veniality, n. [1. věniáliti; 2. vìniǽliti]. See prec. & **-ity**. Quality of being venial, pardonable, or excusable.

venially, adv. [1. věniali; 2. víniəli]. **venial & -ly**. In a venial manner.

venire facias, n. [1. venīre fásias; 2. vináiəri fǽsiæs]. Lat., 'cause, make, to come'. (legal hist.) Name of a judicial writ, now obsolete, issued to a sheriff ordering him to summon certain persons as jurors.

venison, n. [1. vénzun; 2. vénz(ə)n; vulgarly [vénizən], fr. O. Fr. veneson, veneison, Mod. Fr. venaison, fr. Lat. vēnātiōn-(em), 'hunting, the chase', fr. vēnāri, 'to hunt', see **venery** (I.). The flesh of deer, as food; formerly applied to the flesh of various other animals, such as the boar &c., killed in the chase.

Venite, n. [1. veníti; 2. vináiti]. Lat., 'come ye', 2nd pers. pl. imperat. of venīre, 'to come', see **venue**, & cp. **event** & **come**. a Name of the ninety-fifth psalm, 'O come, let us sing unto the Lord', in Lat. '*Venite, exultemus Domino*', esp. as the Canticle sung at Morning Prayer before the Psalms for the day; **b** a musical setting for this.

venom, n. [1. vénum; 2. vénəm]. M.E. venym, venim, fr. O. Fr. venim, venin, fr. Lat. venēnum, 'a drug, potion; a poisonous drug &c.; poison'; the suggestion that this is for *venesnom, & orig. meant 'a love potion', fr. **Venus**, is now considered improbable. No convincing etymol. is offered. **1. a** The poisonous fluid secreted from glands in certain reptiles, such as snakes, scorpions, and some insects, such as wasps, bees &c., injected by bite or sting; **b** (now rare) any poison or poisonous thing. **2.** (fig.) Malignity, spite, malice; venomous conduct, language &c.: *the venom of malignant tongues*; *she cast a look of venom at him* &c.

venomed, adj. [1. vénumd; 2. vénəmd]. Prec. &-ed. Poisoned; charged with, full of, venom; often in fig. sense : *a venomed tongue* &c.; more usually **envenomed**.

venomous, adj. [1. vénumus; 2. vénəməs]. M.E. venimous, fr. O. Fr. venimeux, fr. Lat. venēnōsus, see **venom** & **-ous**. **1.** Secreting poison, infecting with poison : *venomous snakes* &c. **2.** (fig.) Full of venom or malice; malignant, spiteful, maleficent : *a venomous opponent*; *she had a venomous tongue*; *these venomous attacks on his character*.

venomously, adv. Prec. & -ly. In a venomous manner; malignantly.

venomousness, n. See prec. & -ness. State, quality, of being venomous.

venose, adj. [1. vēnōs; 2. vínous], fr. Lat. vēnōsus, 'full of veins', fr. vēna, see **vein**, & -ose, -ous. (bot.) Full of veins, veined, veiny; cp. venous.

venosity, n. [1. vēnósiti; 2. vinósiti]. Prec. & -ity. **1.** Quality, state, of being venose or veined. **2.** Quality of being venous; **a** (of organs &c.) presence, excess, of venous, as opposed to arterial, blood; **b** (of arterial blood) admixture of venous blood.

venous, adj. [1. vĕnus; 2. vínəs], fr. Lat. vēnōsus, see **venose**. **1.** (physiol.) Pertaining to, contained in, the veins, distinguished from *arterial* : *venous blood*. **2.** (bot.) Venose, full of veins; veiny.

vent (I.), n. [1. vent; 2. vɛnt]. M.E. *fent*, fr. O. Fr. fente, 'cleft, slit, cranny', fr. fendre, 'to cleave, split', fr. Lat. findere, fiss-(um), see **fissile**; to this word many of the meanings of **vent (II.)** are often referred; the O.E.D. keeps them entirely separate. **1.** A slit or opening in a garment, common in the slashed garments of the 15th and 16th cents.; now only as a tailor's term for the slit at the back of a coat. **2.** (obs. or hist.) Opening or crenel in a battlemented wall.

vent (II.), n., fr. O. Fr. vent, fr. Lat. ventus, 'wind', see **ventilate** & **wind (I.)**; or fr. or influenced by O. Fr. esvent, Fr. event, 'a breaking, bursting forth', fr. e(s)venter, 'to break forth', fr. es-, e-, see **ex-**, & vent, 'wind', as above. **1.** Aperture, hole, outlet, passage, in anything, which allows air, liquid &c. to escape, or admits air, as *the vent of a cask, of a fire-arm* &c.; *a vent in the crater of volcano* &c.; specif., the anal or cloacal opening of birds, reptiles, and fishes. **2.** Means of exit; outlet; power, opportunity to escape, esp. in Phr. **a** *to find* (a) *vent for* (in material or non-material senses): *the enclosed steam must find a vent or burst the boiler*; *he found some vent for his emotion in violent exercise, bad language* &c.; **b** *to give vent to*, to give means of escape to, provide outlet for (usually in non-material sense), to express, give utterance to : *to give vent to one's anger* &c. **3.** Act of an otter in coming to the surface to breathe.

vent (III.), vb. trans. & intrans. In sense **1**, fr. O. Fr. venter; other senses fr. n., see **vent (II.)**. **A.** trans. **1.** To provide a vent for; to make a vent in; specif., *to vent a cask*, to bore through the wooden bung in the top so as to allow gas to escape. **2.** To give vent to, to discharge, allow to escape : *the chimneys vented their smoke in great clouds*; *to vent one's wrath, indignation, high spirits*. **B.** intrans. Specif. (of a hunted otter), to come to surface of water in order to breathe.

vent (IV.), n., fr. Fr. vente, 'sale', fr. vendre, 'to sell', see **vend**. (archaic or obs.) Market, opening, for sale of goods; in such Phr. as *to find a vent for* &c., it is difficult to distinguish from same phrase in **vent (II)**.

ventage, n. [1. véntij; 2. véntidž]. **vent (II.)** & -age. **1. a** Means of escape for air, gas, liquid &c.; **b** means of relief to the emotions. Phr. *to give ventage to anger, indignation, rage* &c. **2.** A finger-hole in a musical wind instrument.

ventail, n. [1. véntāl; 2. vénteil]. O. Fr. ventaile, fr. vent, 'wind', see **ventilate**. (hist.) The lower movable part of the visor of a helmet.

venter, n. [1. vénter; 2. véntə]. Lat., 'belly, womb'; for *vend-tro, fr. base *wened-, wh. is explained by some as a nasalized form of that seen in Scrt. utáram, 'belly', & Lat. uterus; see **uterus**. **1.** (anat.) The abdominal cavity in insects and other invertebrate animals. **2.** (law, O. Fr. in origin) Womb; hence (by transf.) mother, as in such Phr. as *born of a second venter* &c.

vent-hole, n. **vent (II.)** & **hole**. Hole, aperture, for passage of air, light, smoke, gas &c.

ventiduct, n. [1. véntidùkt; 2. véntidâkt], fr. Lat. venti-, ventus, 'wind', see **ventilate** & **duct**. (archit.) A pipe or other passage used for passage of air in ventilating a building, room &c.

ventilate, vb. trans. [1. véntilāt; 2. véntileit], fr. Lat. ventilāt-(um), P.P. type of ventilāre, 'to brandish in the air; to fan, winnow; to set in motion; to agitate', fr. ventus, 'wind'; cp. W. gwynt, Bret. gwent; Aryan type *awe-, 'to blow', cp. Gk. áēmi for *áwēmi, 'I blow', & see **air** & **wind (I.)**. **1.** To cause fresh air to circulate in (a room, building, mine &c.); to render (the air of a room &c.) fresh and cool by adopting various means for the withdrawal or escape of vitiated, and the continual supply of fresh, air. **2.** To expose (blood) to, and purify by, the free action of oxygen; to aerate. **3.** (fig.) To allow, cause, to become known, and to be freely and widely discussed; to submit for investigation : *to ventilate a grievance*; *the new policy has now been freely ventilated*.

ventilation, n. [1. vèntiláshun; 2. vèntiléiʃən], fr. Lat. ventilātiōn-(em), see prec. & -ion. **1. a** Admission, free circulation, of fresh air into an enclosed space or chamber; **b** state of room &c. in relation to the free circulation of fresh air : *the ventilation of the crowded room was appalling*; **c** means of ventilating; apparatus adopted for ventilating : *the ventilation of the mine broke down*. **2.** Free discussion of a subject; public examination and debate : *a full ventilation of grievances*.

ventilative, adj. [1. véntilativ; 2. véntilətiv]. ventilate & -ive. Pertaining to, tending to produce or facilitate, ventilation.

ventilator, n. [1. véntilāter; 2. véntiléitə]. ventilate & -or; Lat. ventilātor only in sense of 'one who winnows grain'. **1.** Apparatus used in drawing out exhausted or stagnant, and admitting fresh, cool, air to room, building, mine &c. **2.** One who ventilates or submits a subject &c. for examination and discussion : *he was a great ventilator of grievances by letters to the daily press*.

ventless, adj. [1. véntles; 2. véntlis]. **vent (II.)** & -less. Having no vent or outlet.

Ventôse, n. [1. vahntôz; 2. vătóuz], fr. Lat. ventōsus, 'windy', fr. ventus, 'wind', see **ventilate**. Sixth month of the French Revolutionary calendar, from Feb. 19th to Mar. 20th.

vent-peg, n. **vent (II.)** & **peg**. A small peg of wood driven into the vent-hole of a cask or barrel, used to allow escape of excess of gas from the liquor, and to permit enough air to enter for the liquor to be drawn off through the tap.

ventral, adj. [1. véntral; 2. véntrəl], Fr., fr. Lat. ventrālis, fr. venter, 'belly', see **venter**, & -al. Pertaining to the belly or abdominal region; esp. situated on the under side or that opposite the back; cp. *dorsal*; *ventral fin*, of fish, one situated on the under side of the body behind the pectoral fins.

ventrally, adv. Prec. & -ly. In a ventral position or direction.

ventri-, pref. Form of Lat. venter, 'belly', used in compounds; see **venter**.

ventricle, n. [1. véntrikl; 2. véntrikl], fr. Fr. ventricule, or directly fr. Lat. ventriculus, dimin. of venter. A cavity in an organ of the body, as in the brain or larynx; specif., one of the two chambers of the heart, receiving the blood from the auricles and discharging it into the arteries.

ventricular, adj. [1. ventríkūlar; 2. ventríkjulə]. Prec. & -ar. Pertaining to, affecting, a ventricle, as of the brain or heart.

ventriloquial, adj. [1. vèntrilókwial; 2. vèntrilóukwiəl], fr. Lat. ventriloquus, lit. 'one who speaks from his belly; ventriloquist'; ventriloquy & -al. Pertaining to, produced by, ventriloquism : *the ventriloquial art*; *ventriloquial effects*.

ventriloquially, adv. Prec. & -ly. By means of ventriloquism.

ventriloquism, n. [1. ventrílokwizm; 2. ventrílǝkwizəm]. ventriloquy & -ism. Art of, skill in, so modifying the voice in speaking, or producing sounds with the vocal organs, that the voice, or the sound made, appears to come from a place remote from, or a person other than, the actual speaker.

ventriloquist, n. [1. ventrílokwist; 2. ventríləkwist]. ventriloquy & -ist. One who is skilled in ventriloquism; esp. a professional entertainer in this art.

ventriloquize, vb. intrans. & trans. [1. ventrílokwīz; 2. ventríləkwàiz]. ventriloquy & -ize. **a** intrans. To practise ventriloquy; **b** trans., to utter, speak, ventriloquially.

ventriloquy, n. [1. ventrílokwi; 2. ventríləkwi], fr. Fr. ventriloquie, fr. Med. Lat. ventriloquium, see **ventri-**, & base loqui, 'to speak', see **loquacious**, & -y. Ventriloquism.

ventripotent, adj. [1. ventrípotent; 2. ventrípotənt]. Fr. See **ventri-** & **potent**. **a** Big-bellied; **b** having a large capacity or appetite for food.

ventro-, pref. Form of venter, 'belly', in compounds, as *ventro-dorsal*, pertaining to, extending from, the ventral and dorsal parts of the body; *ventro-lateral*, pertaining to the ventral and lateral parts of the body.

venture (I.), n. [1. vénchur; 2. véntʃə]. Aphetic form of earlier M.E. aventure, fr. O. Fr. fr. L. Lat. adventūra, 'adventure', q.v., formed as if fem. of adventūrus, Fut. Part. of Lat. advenīre, 'to come to, happen', fr. **ad-** & venīre, 'to come', see **venue**. **1.** Chance, fortune, luck, event, not to be calculated; contingency; rare or archaic, except in Phr. *at a venture*, at random, without foreseeing or calculating the results. **2. a** Enterprise, undertaking, of a hazardous nature; some course of action attended by risk or danger of loss; **b** specif., a financial or commercial speculation : *a bold venture is often successful*; *a lucky, profitable, disastrous, venture*.

venture (II.), vb. trans. & intrans. See prec. **A.** trans. **1.** To expose to risk or danger, to run the chance of losing; to risk, hazard : *to venture one's life, happiness, on a doubtful* *enterprise*; (also reflex.) *venture oneself*. **2.** To stake, risk, for monetary or other gain: *to venture £1000, all one's wealth* &c.; *to venture a fortune on a single chance.* Proverbial Phr. *nothing venture, nothing have*, no gain without some risk. **3.** To undertake the risk of, dare to go &c.: *will you venture a flight in an aeroplane, a climb down these rocks?; I won't venture a step farther.* **4.** To put forward, advance, express, in a tentative, diffident, undogmatic manner: *to venture an opinion, criticism* &c. **B.** intrans. **1.** Also *venture on, upon*, **a** to dare, be bold enough, to go; to risk oneself by going: *I should not venture too near the edge if I were you; to venture on a stormy sea*; **b** to take the risk of (doing something): *will you venture on another glass of wine?* **2.** To presume, to make so bold as, go so far as: *I venture to assert that* &c.; *I should not venture to offer an opinion*; in polite formulae expressing diffidence: *if I might venture to make a remark; may I venture to ask your opinion?*

venturer, n. [1. vénchurer; 2. véntʃərə]. Prec. & **-er**. One who ventures; an adventurer; used esp. of the old 16th and 17th trading companies: *the Merchant Venturers of Bristol.*

venturesome, adj. [1. vénchursum; 2. véntʃəsəm]. **venture (I.)** & **-some**. **a** (of persons) Daring, foolhardy, rash; **b** (of actions &c.) involving risk or danger; rash, hazardous, dangerous.

venturesomely, adv. Prec. & **-ly**. In a venturesome manner.

venturesomeness, n. See prec. & **-ness**. State, quality, of being venturesome.

venue, n. [1. vénū; 2. vénjū]. Fr., 'arrival, coming', fem. of *venu*, P.P. of *venir*, 'to come', fr. Lat. *venīre*, 'to come', fr. **gwenīre*, earlier **gwemīre*; Aryan base **gʷem-*, cp. Scrt. *gam-*, 'to come, go', Gk. *bainein*, see **basis**; Goth. *qiman*, O.E. *cuman*, earlier **cwiman*; see **come**. **a** (law) The locality or place to which a jury is summoned for the trial of a case, originally in the neighbourhood where the cause of action has arisen or a crime been committed. Phr. *to change the venue*, to alter the place of trial, remove it to another county, to Central Criminal Court &c.; **b** (popular) meeting-place.

Venus, n. [1. vḗnus; 2. vínəs]. Lat. *venus, veneris*, 'desire, sexual love; beauty'; (cap.) 'the goddess of beauty and love'; the same base is seen in **venerate**; also in O.E. *wynn*, 'joy, delight', see **winsome**; in O.E. *wȳscan*, 'to desire, wish', see **wish (I.)**. **1.** (mythol.) The Roman, Latin, goddess of beauty and growth, later identified with the Greek Aphrodite, goddess of sexual love; *Mount of Venus* (palmistry), protuberance on the palm, at base of the thumb. **2.** (astron.) The second of the major planets in order from the sun, appearing as the evening and morning star, Hesperus and Lucifer. **3. a** A statue, picture of the goddess: *the Venus di Milo*; **b** a beautiful woman. Phr. *pocket Venus*, a beautiful, petite woman, of exquisite form and features.

Venus's comb, n. **a** A kind of marine shellfish with spiny edges; **b** a plant, akin to the parsley, with fruit toothed like a comb.

Venus's flower-basket, n. A kind of sponge, shaped like a tube of delicate network, found in East Indian waters.

Venus's fly-trap, n. An insectivorous plant, *Dionaea muscipula*, of the Carolina coast, N. America, cultivated as a curiosity.

Venus's slipper, n. Lady's slipper; the wild orchid, *Cypripedium*; also the garden calceolaria.

veracious, adj. [1. veráshus; 2. veréiʃəs], fr. Lat. *vērāci-*, stem of *vērax*, 'truthful, speaking the truth', fr. *vērus*, 'true'; fr. **vesros*, 'that which is', fr. the Aryan base **wes-*, 'to be', see **was**; cogn. w. O.H.G. *wār*, 'true', for **wǣz*; see also **verify** & **very (I.)**. For similar development of meaning cp. **sooth**. **1.** (of person &c.) Truthful, observant of the truth, habitually speaking the truth; trustworthy: *a veracious witness* &c. **2.** (of statement &c.) Founded on the truth or on fact; true; to be believed: *a veracious narrative; veracious evidence.*

veraciously, adv. Prec. & **-ly**. In a veracious manner.

veraciousness, n. See prec. & **-ness**. Veracity.

veracity, n. [1. verásiti; 2. virǽsiti], fr. Fr. *véracité*. See **veracious** & **-ity**. **a** Quality of habitually speaking the truth; truthfulness: *his veracity is unquestioned*; **b** agreement with the facts or the truth; truth: *one doubts the veracity of such statements.*

veranda(h), n. [1. veránda; 2. vərǽndə]. Introduced in 18th cent. fr. India & taken to be a native word; it represents Port. & Span. *varanda*, 'railing, balustrade, balcony', prob. fr. *vara*, 'rod, pole', fr. Lat. *vāra*, 'forked pole on which fishing nets are spread'. Covered space with a roof and pavement, in immediate proximity to the wall of a house, some windows of which open on to it; the front and sides are open or partially glazed, and the roof is supported at the back by the house wall and in front by pillars.

veratria, veratrine, n. [1. verátria, -trin; 2. vɛréitriə, -trin], fr. Lat. *vērātrum*, 'hellebore'. A bitter, poisonous alkaloid obtained from the root of various kinds of hellebore, used externally in medicine, in an ointment for the relief of neuralgia and rheumatism.

verb, n. [1. vërb; 2. vāb], fr. Fr. *verbe*, fr. Lat. *verbum*, 'word', cogn. w. O.E. *word*, see **word**; fr. base **werēi-*, 'to speak'; whence also Gk. *eírō*, 'I say', fr. **werjō*, & *rhḗtōr*, 'orator', for **wrḗtōr*, see **rhetoric** & **word**; Scrt. *vratám*, 'order, command, law'. (gram.) The part of speech which expresses existence or action and affirms or predicates that a person or thing *is, does*, or *suffers* something.

verbal, adj. [1. vërbl; 2. vābl]. Fr., fr. L. Lat. *verbālis*, see prec. & **-al**. **1.** Pertaining to, concerned with, words; expressed in, or composed of, words: *verbal felicities, mistakes; verbal wit; a good verbal memory*, one retentive of the exact words, or wording of something heard or read; *verbal inspiration*, the direct influence of God assumed to have inspired every actual word of the Holy Scriptures. **2.** Dealing, concerned, with the words only, not with the substance: *a purely verbal criticism; a verbal pedantry; the difference between the two accounts is merely verbal.* **3.** Literal, word for word: *a verbal translation.* **4.** Oral, by word of mouth, spoken, not embodied in a written document: *a verbal contract; a verbal message will suffice.* **5.** (gram.) Pertaining to, derived from, a verb: *verbal inflexions; verbal nouns and adjectives.*

verbalism, n. [1. vërbalizm; 2. vābəlizəm]. Prec. & **-ism**. **1.** Expression in words; that which is expressed in words; use, choice, of words. **2.** Undue attention to the mere words; verbal criticism and pedantry.

verbalist, n. [1. vërbalist; 2. vābəlist]. **verbal** & **-ist**. One given too much to verbalism; a verbal critic.

verbalization, n. [1. vërbalīzáshun; 2. vābəlaizéiʃən]. See next word & **-ation**. **a** Act of verbalizing; **b** state of being verbalized.

verbalize, vb. trans. [1. vërbalīz; 2. vābəlaiz]. **verbal** & **-ize**. **a** To convert into a verb; **b** to put into words.

verbally, adv. [1. vërbali; 2. vābəli]. **verbal** & **-ly**. By word of mouth, by means of, in, uttered words; contrasted with *in writing.*

verbascum, n. [1. vërbáskum; 2. vābǽskəm]. Lat., 'mullein'. (bot.) A genus of herbaceous plants, the mulleins, with tall spikes of clustered yellow, white, or purple flowers.

verbatim, adv., adj., & n. [1. verbátim; 2. vābéitim]. Lat., fr. *verbum*, 'word', see **verb**. **1.** adv. Word for word, in exactly the same words; literally: *to report a speech, translate a book, verbatim.* **2.** adj. Following words exactly; reporting word for word: *a verbatim report, translation.* **3.** n. A verbatim report.

verbena, n. [1. verbḗna; 2. vəbínə]. Lat., usually in pl. *verbēnae*, 'leaves and branches of laurel, myrtle, olive' &c., used in sacred ceremonies'; allied to *verber*, usually in pl. *verbera*, 'rods', cp. **reverberate**, cogn. w. Gk. *rhábdos*, 'rod', for **wrábdos*, & *hráptein*, 'to sew, stitch'; cp. also **warp (I.)**, & see **vervain.** (bot.) A genus of herbaceous plants, the vervains, esp. several cultivated species with blue, white, crimson, purple, or striped flowers; *lemon-scented verbena* with fragrant leaves is not a true verbena but belongs to the genus *Lippia.*

verbiage, n. [1. vërbiij; 2. vābiidž]. Fr., fr. *verbe*, see **verb**, & **-age**. **a** The use of too many, of unnecessary, words; verbosity, prolixity, circumlocution; **b** (depreciatory) actual words used, choice of words.

verbose, adj. [1. vërbṓs; 2. vābóus], fr. Lat. *verbōsus*, fr. *verbum*, 'word'; see **verb** & **-ose**. **a** (of speakers, writers) Using a large, unnecessary, number of words; prolix, long-winded; **b** (of style, verbal expression) characterized by too many words, overloaded with words; wordy.

verbosely, adv. Prec. & **-ly**. In a verbose manner.

verboseness, n. See prec. & **-ness**. Verbosity.

verbosity, n. [1. vërbósiti; 2. vābósiti], fr. Fr. *verbosité*, see **verbose** & **-ity**. Quality of being verbose; prolixity, wordiness, verboseness.

verb. sap., Phr. [1. vërb sáp; 2. vāb sǽp], abbr. fr. Lat. phr. *verbum sat est sapienti.* A word is enough for the wise.

verdancy, n. [1. vërdansi; 2. vādənsi]. See **verdant** & **-ancy**. Quality, state, of being verdant; greenness; **a** (lit.) *the verdancy of the fields and woods*; **b** (fig.) greenness, rawness, crudity, immaturity of knowledge, character, judgement; innocence, simplicity, arising from inexperience: *with the rashness typical of his youthful verdancy.*

verdant, adj. [1. vërdant; 2. vādənt]. Not till 16th cent.; formed w. adjectival suff. **-ant**, fr. O. Fr. *verd*, Mod. Fr. *vert*, 'green', cp. **verdure**, used much earlier; O. Fr. had *verdissant, verdeant, verdoyant*, Pres. Part., fr. *verdir*, 'to become green'; ultimately fr. Lat. *viridis*, 'green; fresh, young', see **vert (I.)**. **1.** Green, of the colour of fresh, young grass or foliage; covered with green, growing herbage: *the verdant grass, trees, leaves; verdant lawns; a smiling, verdant landscape.* **2.** Youthful, inexperienced, unsophisticated, simply innocent: *in his verdant youth.*

verd-antique, n. [1. vārd antḗk; 2. vǽəd ãtík]. Fr., fr. earlier *verd*, now *vert*, 'green', see prec., & **antique**. **a** A kind of serpentine marble mottled or veined with green; also a green variety of porphyry; **b** the green incrustation or patina, the result of long exposure to the air, seen on ancient bronzes &c.

verdantly, adv. [1. vërdantli; 2. vādəntli]. **verdant** & **-ly**. In a verdant green; freshly, youthfully.

verderer, n. [1. vërderer; 2. vādərə]. A.-Fr., also *verder*, fr. Fr. *verd, vert*, 'green', see **vert (I.)**; the Med. Lat. word was *viridārius*, fr. Lat. *viridis*, 'green'. (legal hist.) An official of the king's forests who sees to the maintenance of the *vert*, i.e. the green wood, the protection of the venison or deer therein and punishment of all trespassers &c.

verdict, n. [1. vërdikt; 2. vādikt]. M.E. *verdit*, fr. A.-Fr. *verdit*, O. Fr. *voirdit*, fr. Lat. *vērē dictum*, 'truly said', in Med. Lat. *vērēdictum*, 'verdict', fr. *vērē*, 'truly', fr. *vērus*, 'true', see **veracious, very (I.)**, & *dictum*, P.P. of *dīcere*, 'to say', see **diction**. **1.** The finding or decision of a jury given to a judge on an issue of fact in any cause, civil or criminal, submitted to them: *a verdict for the plaintiff, defendant, of guilty or not guilty; open verdict* &c. **2.** A decision, judgement, opinion, pronounced on anything: *a popular verdict in* *favour of the government; my verdict differs from yours in this matter.*

verdigris, n. [1. vĕrdigrĕs; 2. vʌ́digrìs]. M.E. *verdegrece*, fr. O. Fr. *vert de Grece*, later *vert de gris*, lit. 'green of Greece', in Med. Lat. *viride grecum*, 'Greek green', fr. *vert* 'green', see **vert** (I.). The second element is popularly associated w. the word **grease**. **a** The green or greenish-blue deposit or incrustation, forming on copper or brass vessels &c. as a rust; **b** (chem.) a poisonous blue or green acetate of copper, obtained by the action of acetic acid on copper, employed as a pigment and mordant in dyeing &c.

verdigrised, adj. [1. vĕrdigrĕst; 2. vʌ́digrìst]. Prec. & **-ed**. Coated, covered, with verdigris.

verditer, n. [1. vĕrditer; 2. vʌ́ditə], fr. O. Fr. *verd de terre*, lit. 'green of earth', fr. *verd, vert*, 'green', see **vert** (I.), & *terre*, fr. Lat. *terra*, 'earth', see **terra**. A blue or green pigment obtained from azurite or malachite, both being chemically copper carbonates.

verdure, n. [1. vĕrjur, vĕrdūr; 2. vʌ́dʒə, vʌ́djə]. Fr., fr. O. Fr. *verd*, later *vert*, 'green', see **vert** (I.), fr. Lat. *viridis*, see **viridity**, & **-ure**. **1. a** Green vegetation; grass, herbage; **b** the fresh, green colour of growing herbage &c. **2.** (fig.) Freshness, vigour, as of youth.

verdured, adj. [1. vĕrjurd; 2. vʌ́dʒəd]. Prec. & **-ed**. Covered with verdure.

verdureless, adj. [1. vĕrjurles; 2. vʌ́dʒəlis]. See prec. & **-less**. Destitute, deprived, of verdure; barren, bare of grass &c.

verdurous, adj. [1. vĕrjurus; 2. vʌ́dʒərəs]. **verdure** & **-ous**. Abounding in, covered with, verdure; green and fresh.

verge (I.), n. [1. vĕrj; 2. vʌ̄dʒ]. O. Fr., 'wand, rod', fr. Lat. *virga*, 'twig, rod, wand'; see **virgate** (I.). **1.** A wand or staff of office, now only used of such as are borne before ecclesiastical dignitaries in processions &c. **2.** (hist.) **a** A rod or stick placed by the lord of the manor in the hand of a tenant on admission to his land, esp. in copyholds, whence Phr. *tenant by the verge*; **b** the jurisdiction of the Lord Steward of the Household and the area of this jurisdiction, within a certain distance of the royal palace: as *within the verge; coroner of the verge*, the King's Coroner, whose jurisdiction lies within the palace precincts. **3.** A small rod or spindle as in a watch or linotype machine. **4.** (now the chief usage) Border, edge, brink, margin; the horizon; **a** (in phys. sense) (i.) grass edge of road, garden bed or border; (ii.) (poet.) '*a sail That sinks with all we love below the verge*' (Tennyson, 'Princess', iv. 47); **b** (fig.) a state bordering on one which is specified: *on the verge of tears, of a collapse; on the verge of war.* **5.** The projecting edge or border of tiles or slates on a roof; hence, *verge-board*, now *barge-board*, q.v.

verge (II.), vb. intrans.; fr. Lat. *vergere*, 'to bend, turn, incline'; the meaning has prob. been influenced by prec. word. The base is *wereg- &c., 'to bend, turn, twist', & appears also in Scrt. *varjati*, 'turns', *vṛjinás*, 'crooked'; Lith. *veržiù*, 'to snare'; & further in many Gmc. words; cp. **wrench, wring, wrinkle, wrong**. Another form of the base *wer-, 'to twist', appears in **vermi-**, & **worm**. **1.** To bend, incline, descend, towards or in a certain direction: *the sun now verging toward the horizon; we were gradually verging nearer the cliff.* **2.** (fig.) To be on the verge of; to tend towards, approach, border on, some specified state or condition; chiefly *verge on*: *such a remark verges on impertinence; he appears to be verging on insanity, delirium*; also *verge towards*: *we seem to be verging towards a quarrel.*

verge-board. See **barge-board**.

verger, n. [1. vĕrjer; 2. vʌ́dʒə]. O. Fr., fr. *verge*, 'rod, wand', see **verge** (I.), & **-er**; the Med. Lat. word was *virgārius*. **a** One who bears a verge, or wand or staff of office, as before ecclesiastical dignitaries; **b** specif., an official attached to a church, who shows worshippers to their seats &c.

veridical, adj. [1. verídikl; 2. vərídikl], fr. Lat. *vēridicus*, fr. *vērus*, 'true', see **veracious** & **very** (I.), & *dīc-*, stem of *dīcere*, 'to speak, say', see **diction**. Veracious, truthful; corresponding with the facts or real things; esp. of various psychical phenomena, as dreams, hallucinations, mediumistic messages &c.

veridically, adv. Prec. & **-ly**. In a veridical manner; veraciously.

verifiability, n. [1. vèrifīabíliti; 2. vèrifàiəbíliti]. See next word & **-ity**. State, fact, of being verifiable.

verifiable, adj. [1. vérifīabl; 2. vérifàiəbl]. See **verify** & **-able**. Capable of being verified, or proved to be true.

verification, n. [1. vèrifikáshun; 2. vèrifikéiʃən], fr. O. Fr. *verificacion*, fr. Med. Lat. *vērificāt-(um), vērificāre*, see **verify**, & **-fication**. **a** Act of verifying; **b** state of being verified; confirmation of the truth of anything by examination of and comparison with the real facts.

verify, vb. trans. [1. vérifī; 2. vérifai], fr. O. Fr. *verifier*, fr. Med. Lat. *vērificāre*, fr. Lat. *vērus*, 'true', see **veracious**, & **-fy**. **1.** To prove, confirm the truth of; to check, ascertain, make sure of, by examination of and comparison with facts: *to verify one's references, statements, details* &c. **2.** To confirm, fulfil; to bear out; to prove to be true by result: *events have verified the prophecy; his suspicion was speedily verified.* **3.** (law) To authenticate, prove the authenticity of, by proofs, affidavit &c.: *to verify documents, claims, pleadings* &c.

verily, adv. [1. vérili; 2. vérili], fr. **very** (I.), in orig. sense of 'true', & **-ly**. In very truth; truly, really, without doubt, certainly (now archaic or liter.): *Verily I say unto you*; principally used as a mere emphatic: *verily this is a strange saying.*

verisimilar, adj. [1. vèrisímilar; 2. vèrisímilə], fr. Lat. *vērisimilis* & **-ar**. See next word. (rare) Having the appearance of truth; likely, probable.

verisimilitude, n. [1. vèrisimílitūd; 2. vèrisimílitjūd]. fr. Lat. *vēri-similitūdin-(em)*, fr. *vērus*, 'true', see **veracious**, & *similitūdo*, 'likeness, similitude', see **similitude**. The appearance of truth; apparent probability, likelihood.

veritable, adj. [1. véritabl; 2. véritəbl]. O. Fr. See **verity** & **-able**. True, real, genuine, actual.

veritably, adv. Prec. & **-ly**. In a veritable manner.

verity, n. [1. vériti; 2. vériti], fr. O. Fr. *verite*, Mod. Fr. *vérité*, fr. Lat. *vērităt-(em)*, fr. *vērus*, 'true', see **veracious**, & **-ity**. **1.** Quality of being true; truth; truthfulness: *a man of unquestioned verity; to doubt the verity of a statement.* **2.** Something which is stated, and is to be accepted as true; a fundamental and essential truth: *the verities of the Christian religion.* Phr. *of a verity*, in truth, as a truth.

verjuice, n. [1. vĕrjōōs; 2. vʌ́dʒūs], fr. O. Fr. *vertjus, verjus*, fr. *vert*, 'green', see **vert** (I.), & *jus*, see **juice**. The acid, sour juice of green, unripe grapes or apples; often fig., of sour looks, temper &c.

vermeil, n. & adj. [1. vĕrmāl; 2. vʌ́meil]. O. Fr., see **vermilion**. **1.** n. **a** (poet. and liter.) Vermilion colour, bright red, of lips &c. '*What need a vermeil-tinctured lip for that?*' (Milton, 'Comus', 751); **b** silver gilt, gilded bronze. **2.** adj. Bright, vermilion red in colour.

vermi-, pref. Form used in compounds, fr. Lat. *vermis*, 'worm'; orig. 'that which twists, writhes, turns', fr. base *wer-, 'twist, turn', whence a number of words w. this sense; cp. the nearest cogn. **worm**, also **wrench** & **wring**, & perh. also **work**.

vermicelli, n. [1. vĕrmiséli; 2. vʌ́miséli]. Ital., pl. of *vermicello*, 'little worm', fr. Lat. *vermiculus*, dimin. of *vermis*, 'worm', see prec. A paste of wheat-flour &c., of the same kind as macaroni, made into very slender, worm-like threads.

vermicide, n. [1. vĕrmisīd; 2. vʌ́misàid]. See **vermi-** & **-cide**. **a** A drug, used medicinally, for killing intestinal, parasitic worms; an anthelmintic; **b** a chemical substance used for killing earth-worms.

vermicular, adj. [1. vĕrmíkūlar; 2. vʌ̄míkjulə], fr. L. Lat. *vermiculāris*, fr. Lat. *vermiculus*, dimin. of *vermis*, see **vermi-**. **1.** Shaped like a worm; vermiform; having convolutions or wavy markings, as of a collection of worms. **2.** Moving like a worm, with sinuous, wavy motion; peristaltic.

vermiculated, adj. [1. vĕrmíkūlāted; 2. vʌ̄míkjulèitid], fr. Lat. *vermiculāt-(um)*, P.P. of *vermiculāri*, 'to be full of worms, worm-eaten'; See prec. **a** Worm-eaten; **b** (archit.) decorated with deeply cut convolutions, of stonework &c.; **c** decorated with, having a wavy pattern of, sinuous lines.

vermiculation, n. [1. vĕrmikuláshun; 2. vʌ̀mikjuléiʃən]. See prec. & **-ion**. **1.** A wavy, sinuous, peristaltic movement in the intestines. **2.** (archit.) Vermiculated work.

vermiform, adj. [1. vĕrmifòrm; 2. vʌ́mifɔ̀m]. **vermi-** & **-form**. Having the shape of a worm; specif. (anat.) *vermiform appendix*, a small blind tube issuing from the large intestine, the seat of appendicitis; *vermiform process*, a part of the median lobe of the cerebellum.

vermifuge, n. [1. vĕrmifūj; 2. vʌ́mifjūdʒ]. **vermi-** & **-fuge**. A medicinal drug which expels intestinal parasitic worms; an anthelmintic.

vermilion, n., adj., & vb. trans. [1. vermílion; 2. vəmíliən], fr. O. Fr. *vermeillon, vermillon*, fr. *vermeil*, 'vermilion', fr. Lat. *vermiculus*, dimin. of *vermis*, 'worm', i.e. 'the cochineal insect', see **vermi-** & cp. **crimson**. **1.** n. **a** A brilliant scarlet pigment, obtained from sulphide of mercury in its natural form (cinnabar) or artificially; (also loosely) lead oxide, minium or red lead; **b** the colour of this pigment, a brilliant scarlet. **2.** adj. Having the colour of vermilion. **3.** vb. To colour, dye, vermilion (chiefly poet.).

vermin, n. [1. vĕrmin; 2. vʌ́min], fr. O. Fr. *vermine*, fr. Low Lat. **vermina*, fr. Lat. *vermis*, 'worm', see **vermi-**. A collective name for, **1.** Animals, including some birds, usually small, which are noxious or harmful, esp. (i.) those which prey upon game, poultry &c., as weasels, hawks, owls &c.; also (ii.) applied to those which are generally destructive, as rats and mice &c. **2.** Insects, usually wingless or creeping, of disgusting look or habit, esp. those which infest dirty houses, clothes &c., or are parasites upon the person, as lice, bugs, fleas &c. **3.** Pestilent human beings; the criminal and predatory classes of society; low riff-raff, the scum or dregs of the population.

verminate, vb. intrans. [1. vĕrmināt; 2. vʌ́mineit], fr. Lat. *vermināt-(um)*, P.P. type of *vermināre*; fr. *vermis*, see **vermi-**. **1.** To be infested with parasitic worms. **2.** To breed parasitic vermin, such as lice.

verminous, adj. [1. vĕrminus; 2. vʌ́minəs], fr. **vermin** & **-ous**, cp. Fr. *vermineux*; Lat. *verminōsus*, means 'full of worms, wormy.' **1.** Infested with insect vermin, e.g. bugs, fleas, lice &c.: *verminous persons.* **2.** Caused by such parasitic vermin: *verminous diseases* &c. **3.** (as term of contempt &c.) Resembling vermin in character; base, degraded; noxious.

verminously, adv. Prec. & **-ly**. In a verminous state or manner.

vermouth, n. [1. vĕrmōōt; 2. vʌ́mūt], fr. Fr. *vermout*, fr. Germ. *wermuth*, O.H.G. *wermot*, 'wormwood' of wh. the exact equiv. *wermōd* occurs in O.E. The etymol. is quite obscure. See also **wormwood**. An alcoholic beverage made of white wine fortified with spirit and flavoured with various bitter tonic substances such as wormwood; used, often with gin added, as an *apéritif*, also as a basis for cocktails; it may be sweet, 'Italian', or dry, 'French vermouth'.

vernacular, adj. & n. [1. vernákūlar; 2. vənǽkjulə]. Formed w. suff. **-ar**, fr. Lat. *vernā-*

culus, 'born in one's house, of slaves; native'; fr. *verna*, 'slave born in his master's house'; the etymol. of this word is much disputed. Walde says the connexion w. the idea of a 'slave' is secondary, the essential idea being 'common life, community', thus *verna* was 'one born within the community, or the house; within doors'; it derives fr. base **wer-*, 'to shut'; see **vestibule**, Lat. *vestibulum*, for **versostibulum*; see also **aperient**. **1.** adj. Pertaining to the country in which one was born; native, indigenous; now only used of language, in following senses, **a** commonly spoken or used by the people of a country, district &c.: *the vernacular languages of India*; *a vernacular idiom*; **b** written in such language: *the vernacular poems of Burns*; *newspapers in vernacular Greek*; **c** using such language: *Barnes, the vernacular poet of Dorset* &c. **2.** n. A vernacular language, or dialect; specif. (i.) a regional, provincial dialect, as distinguished from the standard, literary language; (ii.) (facet.) type of language supposed to be popularly current, i.e. strong language, profanity: *he addressed me forcibly in the vernacular*, i.e. swore at me.

vernacularism, n. [1. vernákūlarizm; 2. vənǽkjulərizəm]. See prec. & **-ism**. A vernacular usage or idiom.

vernacularization, n. [1. vernákūlarīzáshun; 2. vənǽkjulərdizéiʃən]. See next word & **-ation**. Act of vernacularizing or making vernacular.

vernacularize, vb. trans. [1. vernákūlarīz; 2. vənǽkjuləraiz]. **vernacular** & **-ize**. To make vernacular, adapt to the usage of a vernacular language.

vernacularly, adv. [1. vernákūlarli; 2. vənǽkjuləli]. **vernacular** & **-ly**. In a vernacular manner, according to vernacular usage &c.; in popular language, profanely.

vernal, adj. [1. vẽrnl; 2. vʌ́nl], fr. Lat. *vernālis*, fr. *vernus*, 'pertaining to spring', for **vērinos*, formed fr. *vēr*, 'spring', fr. **vēsr*, *vesr*, cogn. w. Gk. *éar* for **wesar*, 'spring', *earinós*, 'springlike', for **wesarinos*; cp. Scrt. *vasantaš*; O. Slav. *vesna*, 'early part of the year, spring'; Lith. *vasarà*, 'summer'; O.N. *var*. Further attempted identifications of this base are very doubtful. **1.** Belonging to, occurring, coming, in the spring: '*Or sight of vernal bloom, or summer's rose*' (Milton, 'P. L.' iii. 43); *the vernal equinox*; *the vernal migration of birds*. **2.** Like, appropriate to, suggestive of, the spring: *vernal weather*; *the vernal aspect of the woods and fields*. **3.** (fig.) Having the freshness and strength natural and suited to the spring time of life: *the vernal spirits of youth*.

vernant, adj. [1. vẽrnant; 2. vʌ́nənt], fr. Lat. *vernant-*, Pres. Part. of *vērnāre*, 'to appear like spring', to flourish, see prec. Springlike, coming in spring: '*else had the spring Perpetual smiled on earth with vernant flowers*' (Milton, 'P. L.').

vernation, n. [1. vẽrnáshun; 2. vʌnéiʃən], fr. Lat. *vernātiōn-(em)*, 'a snake's sloughing of skin in spring', fr. *vernāt-(um)*, P.P. type of *vernāre*, 'to be like the spring, to be verdant, to bloom, to grow young', fr. *vēr*, 'spring', see prec. (bot.) The arrangement of the growing leaves within the bud.

Verner's Law, n. [1. vẽrnerz láw; 2. vʌ́nəz lɔ́]. Statement by Karl Verner in 1877 of the precise conditions under which the Aryan consonants *p, t, k*, appear in Gmc. as the voiced sounds *b, d, g*, instead of as the voiceless *f, þ, χ*, as is more common. The law may be briefly stated thus: When, in Aryan, the accent fell on any other syllable of the word than that immediately preceding the *p, t, k*, these sounds appear in Gmc. as voiced open consonants, usually written *b, d, g*, in the old languages. The law explains a large number of forms previously regarded as 'exceptions' to Grimm's Law, and may be considered as supplemental to this.

vernicle, n. [1. vẽrnikl; 2. vʌ́nikl]. O. Fr., for *veronicle*, *veronique*, fr. Med. Lat. *veronica*, fr. St. Veronica; & **-le**; in Gk. *Bereníkē*; a popular derivation of the name was fr. the hybrid form *vera ikonica*, fr. Gk. *eikon*, 'true image'. **a** The handkerchief or napkin, Lat. *sudarium*, of St. Veronica with which Christ wiped His face as He carried the Cross, and which was miraculously imprinted with His portrait; **b** a reproduction of the face of Christ, in various forms, esp. such as were carried as badges or signs by pilgrims in the Middle Ages.

vernier, n. [1. vẽrnier; 2. vʌ́niə], fr. the inventor, P. Vernier, a French mathematician (1580–1637). A small, movable, graduated slip of wood, ivory &c., fixed to scale of surveying instrument &c., and used to subdivide divisions of this.

vernis martin, n. [1. várnē mártan; 2. vɛrnī martæ̃]. Fr. *vernis*, see **varnish**. A fine green varnish with powdered gold, used in the reign of Louis XV. by the Martin family of cabinet-makers.

veronal, n. [1. véronal; 2. vérənəl]. Germ., invented as a trade-name. A powerful soporific drug, in the form of a white, slightly bitter powder.

Veronica, n. [1. verónika; 2. vərɔ́nikə]. Named after St. Veronica, in Gk. *Bereníkē*, cp. **vernicle**. (bot.) Genus of herbs or plants with spikes of blue, pink, or white flowers.

verricule, n. [1. vérikūl; 2. vérikjūl], fr. Lat. *verriculum*, 'net', fr. *verrere*, 'to sweep', & **-cule**; cogn. w. Gk. *érrhein*, 'to move with difficulty'; O.S. *werran*, 'to confuse'; & perh. w. Goth. *wairsiza*; O.E. *wyrsa*, 'worse', see **worse**. (entom.) Tuft of hairs.

verruca, n. [1. veróōka; 2. verūkə]. Lat. *verrūca*, 'excrescence, swelling; wart'; for **versūca*; cogn. w. Scrt. *váršman-*, 'height, point'; O. Slav. *vrŭhŭ*, 'point, peak'; O.E. *wearh*, *weart*, 'wart' (fr. **wars(u)h?*). **a** (med.) A wart on the hand or face; **b** (zool.) wart-like excrescence on the skin of animals.

verrucose, adj. [1. veróōkōs; 2. verūkous], fr. Lat. *verrūcōsus*, see prec. & **-ose**. Warty; covered with warts or wart-like excrescences.

versatile, adj. [1. vẽrsatīl; 2. vʌ́sətail], fr. Lat. *versātilis*, 'turning round, revolving; versatile'; fr. *vers-(um)*, P.P. type of *vertere*, 'to turn', see **version**. **1.** (in physical sense, rare, except in bot. and zool.) Capable of revolving, swinging, or turning freely in different directions, as an anther, joint, muscle &c. **2.** (of character, mental characteristics) **a** Changeable, inconstant, fickle, capricious: *versatile affection, disposition* &c.; **b** readily and easily applied, adaptable, to different subjects in turn; many-sided: *a versatile genius*; *a versatile but erratic mind*; (also of persons) having a versatile mind, talented in various ways: *a versatile writer, actor* &c.

versatilely, adv. Prec. & **-ly**. In a versatile manner.

versatility, n. [1. vẽrsatíliti; 2. vʌsətíliti]. Fr. *versatilité*, see **versatile** & **-ity**. Quality, character, of being versatile; capacity for doing many different things, varied ability; many-sidedness of character, interests, or abilities.

vers de société, n. [1. vār de sosiātā; 2. vɛr də sosīete]. Fr. Society verse; poetry of a light, easy, witty kind, dealing with familiar social events, habits &c.

verse (I.), n. [1. vẽrs; 2. vʌs]. M.E., fr. O. Fr. *vers*, 'division of a poem, stanza', fr. Lat. *versus*, 'a furrow; a line, row; a line of poetry, verse'; fr. *vers-(um)*, P.P. type of *vertere*, 'to turn'; see **version**. **1. a** A metrical line containing a certain number of feet or accented syllables, arranged according to a definite metrical rule; a line of poetry as metrically arranged: *a hexameter, iambic, Alexandrine &c. verse*; **b** (pl.) a set of such, as translated into Greek or Latin: *to set Latin, Greek, verses*. **2.** Metrical composition or structure: *Latin verse*; *his prose lapses into verse at moments of emotion*; *free verse*, such composition of an irregular nature, untrammelled by rules of prosody &c. **3.** A division of a poem consisting of several lines, forming in itself a unity, and having a definite structure as regards number of lines and rhymes and the arrangement of the latter. **4.** Poetry: *English lyrical verse*. **5.** One of the sections or short divisions into which a chapter of the Bible is divided. Phr. *to give chapter and verse for*, give the exact reference, authority &c., for any statement.

verse (II.), vb. trans. & intrans., fr. prec. **1.** trans. To express in verse, to make verses about: *to verse one's emotions*; *he versed the praises of the conqueror*. **2.** intrans. To compose, make, verses: *taught to verse*.

versed, adj. [1. vẽrst; 2. vʌst], fr. Lat. *versātus*, P.P. of *versāri*, 'to turn, move about in a place; to be circumstanced, situated, in; to be engaged, occupied, in', freq. form of *vertere*, 'to turn', formed fr. *vers-(um)*, P.P. type. See **version**. Skilled, practised, experienced, *in* some subject, art &c.

versed sine, n., fr. Mod. Lat. *versus sinus*, P.P. of *vertere*, 'to turn', see **version**, & **sine**. (math.) Reversed sine.

verset, n. [1. vẽrset; 2. vʌ́sɛt]. **verse** & **-et**. Short musical prelude, played on an organ before a church service.

versicle, n. [1. vẽrsikl; 2. vʌ́sikl], fr. Lat. *versiculus*, 'a little verse', dimin. of *versus*, see **verse**. A short verse; specif., one of the short, liturgical verses, often taken from the Psalms, intoned or read by the officiating minister and answered by the responses of the choir and congregation.

versicoloured, adj. [1. vẽrsikùlurd; 2. vʌ́sikàləd], fr. Lat. *versicolor*, fr. *vers-(um)*, *vertere*, 'to turn, change', see **version**, & *color*, **colour**, & **-ed**. Changing, varying, in colour; iridescent.

versification, n. [1. vẽrsifikáshun; 2. vʌ̀sifikéiʃən], fr. Lat. *versificātiōn-(em)*, see **versify** & **-ation**. **a** Art, practice, of versifying or of making verse; **b** mode, style, of metrical composition; metre, prosody.

versifier, n. [1. vẽrsifier; 2. vʌ́sifaiə]. Next word & **-er**. One who versifies; usually in deprecatory sense, verse-monger, poetaster.

versify, vb. trans. & intrans. [1. vẽrsifī; 2. vʌ́sifai], fr. Fr. *versifier*, fr. Lat. *versificāre*, see **verse** & **-fy**. **1.** trans. **a** To turn into verse from a prose form, to translate into verse; **b** to tell, recount, in verse. **2.** intrans. To compose verses.

versifying, n. [1. vẽrsifiing; 2. vʌ́sifaiiŋ]. See prec. & **-ing**. The making, composing, of verses; versification.

version, n. [1. vẽrshun; 2. vʌ́ʃən]. Fr., fr. Lat. *versiōn-(em)*, fr. *vers-(um)*, fr. **vert-tom*, P.P. of *vertere*, 'to turn', & **-ion**. The base **wert-* is found in Scrt. *vártatē*, 'he turns, rolls'; Gk. *rhatánē* for **wrat-*, fr. **wr̥t-*, 'a stirrer, ladle'; O. Slav. *vrŭtěti*, 'to turn, twist'; the base exists in all Gmc. languages, e.g. O.H.G. *werdan*, O.E. *weorþan*, 'to become, turn out, happen', see **worth** (III.) & **weird** (I.); cp. also *-vert* in **convert** &c.; also **vertex** & **vortex**. **1.** A translation or rendering of a book, passage &c., from one language into another: *the Authorized, Revised, Versions of the Bible*; *a neat version of some of Horace's Odes*; *a comparison of the French and English versions of the document shows some divergencies*. **2.** An account, statement, of something from a personal or particular point of view: *the police gave a different version of the incident from that of the prisoner*.

vers libre, n. [1. vār lébr; 2. vẽr líbr]. Fr. Free verse; verse with no regular metrical system but arranged in lines of irregular length and with certain rhythms or rhythmical structure.

vers librist(e), n. [1. vār lébrist; 2. vẽr líbrist]. Fr. Prec. & **-ist(e)**. Writer of free verse.

verso, n. [1. vẽrsō; 2. vʌ́sou]. Lat., sc. *folio*, 'leaf', abl. sing. of *versus*, 'turned', see **version**. **a** The left hand or reverse of a page of a book; used esp. of a folded sheet of vellum or paper, cp. *recto*; **b** the reverse of a coin, medal &c., cp. *obverse*.

verst, n. [1. vĕrst; 2. vʌ̄st], fr. Russ. *versta* for **vert-ta*, fr. *vertyet*, 'to turn', fr. base discussed under **version**. A Russian measure of length, 3500 Engl. ft., about ⅔ of a mile.

versus, prep. [1. vĕrsus; 2. vʌ́səs]. Lat., see **version**. Against (abbr. *v.* or *vs.*); esp. in describing a case at law: *Rex* v. *Jones*, *Smith* v. *Robinson* &c.; also in matches, *Lancashire* v. *Yorkshire*.

vert (**I.**), n. [1. vĕrt; 2. vʌ̄t]. O. Fr., Fr., earlier form *verd*, fr. Lat. *viridis*, 'green', see **viridity**. **1.** (forest law) **a** The green growth of a forest, esp. as cover for deer: *vert and venison*; **b** right to cut the greenwood in a forest; cp. *verderer*. **2.** (her.) The colour or tincture green.

vert (**II.**), vb. intrans. & n.; abbr. of *convert* or *pervert*. (colloq.) **1.** vb. To change one's religious faith; esp. to abandon Protestantism for Roman Catholicism, or vice versa. **2.** n. A convert or pervert to or from Roman Catholicism.

vertebra, n., pl. **vertebrae** [1. vĕrtebra, -ē; 2. vʌ́tibrə, -ī]. Lat., fr. base of *vertere*, 'to turn', see **version**. (anat.) One of the joints of the backbone or spinal column in vertebrate animals; (pl.) *the vertebrae*, the backbone or spinal column in vertebrate animals.

vertebral, adj. [1. vĕrtebral; 2. vʌ́tibrəl]. Prec. & **-al**. **a** Pertaining to, situated near, the vertebrae or joints of the spine; **b** composed of vertebrae: *vertebral column*, the spine.

vertebrally, adv. Prec. & **-ly**. By means of vertebrae.

vertebrate, adj. & n. [1. vĕrtibrat, -āt; 2. vʌ́tibrit, -eit], fr. Lat. *vertebrātus*, 'jointed, articulated', fr. *vertebra*, see **vertebra**, & **-ate**. **1.** adj. Having a spinal column or vertebrae; belonging to the Vertebrata or group of animals which have a spinal column, including mammals, birds, reptiles, fish, and batrachians. **2.** n. A vertebrate animal; member of the Vertebrata.

vertebration, n. [1. vĕrtebrā́shun; 2. vʌ̀tibréiʃən]. See prec. & **-ion**. Arrangement, division, into vertebrae.

vertex, n., pl. **vertices** [1. vĕrteks, -isēz; 2. vʌ́tɛks, -isīz]. Lat., variant of *vortex*, q.v. for differentiation of meaning; 'the top, crown, of the head; highest point, top, summit; the pole, zenith'; fr. base of *vertere*, 'to turn', the orig. sense being that wh. turns about itself; see **version** &c. The highest or principal point; top, summit; specif. **a** (anat.) crown of the head; **b** (astron.) the zenith; **c** (geom.) the point or angle of a figure opposite to the base.

vertical, adj. [1. vĕrtikl; 2. vʌ́tikl]. Fr., fr. Lat. *vertic-(em)*, *vertex*, see prec., & **-al**. **1.** Situated at the vertex or highest point; directly overhead, at the zenith: *the vertical point of the heavens*. **2.** Perpendicular, at right angles to the plane of the horizon; upright; opposed to *horizontal*: *a vertical line* &c. **3.** Directed downwards or upwards at right angles to the plane of the ground: *a vertical wall, fall* &c. **4.** (elliptically as n.) *The vertical*, vertical line, position; the perpendicular.

verticality, n. [1. vĕrtikáliti; 2. vʌ̀tikǽliti]. Prec. & **-ity**. Quality, condition, of being vertical.

vertically, adv. [1. vĕrtikali; 2. vʌ́tikəli]. See prec. & **-ly**. In a vertical manner, position, direction; directly overhead or below.

verticil, verticel, n. [1. vĕrtisil; 2. vʌ́tisil], fr. Lat. *verticillus*, dimin. of *vertex*, 'whorl of a spindle', see **vertex**. (bot.) A circle of leaves, florets &c., round a central axis; a whorl.

verticillate, adj. [1. vĕrtísilāt; 2. vʌ̄tísileit]. Prec. & **-ate**. (bot., of leaves &c.) Arranged in verticils or whorls.

vertiginous, adj. [1. vĕrtíjinus; 2. vʌ̄tídžinəs], fr. Lat. *vertiginōsus*, fr. *vertīgin-(em)*, *vertīgo*, see **vertigo**, & **-ous**. **1.** Turning, whirling, round and round: *vertiginous current, wind* &c. **2.** Dizzy, giddy, suffering from vertigo: *to feel, grow, vertiginous at great heights*. **3.** Causing, inducing, vertigo or giddiness: *a vertiginous height, precipice* &c.

vertiginously, adv. Prec. & **-ly**. In a vertiginous manner; dizzily, giddily.

vertigo, n. [1. vĕrtigō; 2. vʌ́tigou]. Lat. *vertīgo*, 'giddiness', fr. base in *vertere*, 'to turn', see **version**. The medical term for the sensation of giddiness, dizziness, or swimming in the head, often accompanied by faintness, experienced after turning rapidly round and round, or during an attack of sea-sickness, or when at a great height.

vertu. See **virtu**.

vervain, n. [1. vĕrvān; 2. vʌ́vein], fr. O. Fr. *verveine*, fr. Lat. *verbēna*. Popular name of various species of *Verbena*, esp. the common wild verbena, *V. officinalis*.

verve, n. [1. vĕrv; 2. vʌ̄v]. Fr., etymol. obscure; in O. Fr. it meant 'an odd humour, fancy'; perh. fr. a Low Lat. **verva*, fr. Lat. *verba*, 'words, talk', see **verb**. Display of vigour and liveliness of spirit and imagination; gusto, in the work of a poet, painter, or other artist.

vervet, n. [1. vĕrvet; 2. vʌ́vɛt]. Fr.; etymol. doubtful; usually supposed to be fr. a combination of *vert*, 'green', & *grivet*, a name of a small grey monkey, fr. *gris*, 'grey'. A small Central and S. African monkey, *Cercopithecus pygerythrus*, with greyish-green fur and black extremities and red patch at base of tail.

very (**I.**), adj. [1. véri; 2. véri]. M.E. *verai*, *verray* &c., fr. O. Fr. *verai*, later & Mod. Fr. *vrai*; fr. Low Lat. **vēracus*, fr. Lat. *vērāc-* 'true', stem of *vērax*, see **veracious**. **1.** **a** Having the true, proper character of a person or thing; truly and really that which the word implies; genuine, actual, real: '*Very God of very God*' (Nicene Creed); *this is my very son*; also in such Phrs. as: *in very truth, deed* &c.; **b** exactly that which is implied by the noun qualified, just the same as, neither more nor less than: *for very shame they must confess*; *for very pity's sake have mercy*. **2.** Used intensively or emphatically: **a** *the very*, actual, same, identical; *caught in the very act*; *the very fact of your hesitating proves* &c.; *the very question I wanted to ask*; *the very thing I was looking for*; **b** (with *this, that* &c.) *this very day, at that very moment*; **c** (with possessive) *did it under your very eyes*; *his very look betrayed him*. **3.** With *a* and comparative, or *the* and superlative: *a verier humbug would be hard to meet*; *the veriest scoundrel unhung*.

very (**II.**), adv., fr. prec. **1.** In a high degree, to a great extent, exceedingly, extremely; **a** (with adjs.) *very large, small*; *very hot, cold*; *very dangerous* &c.; Phrs. *very good*, as form of assent or agreement; also *very well*, often with sense of reluctance or compulsion: *oh, very well! if you insist*; **b** (with vbl. adjs.) *a very dazzling light*; *a very puzzling question*; *a very interesting book*; *substance very resistant to cold*; **c** (with P.Ps.) (i.) when used as adjs.: *a very valued friend*; *a very over-weighted car*; *a very harassed mind*; *wore a very worried look*; (ii.) otherwise, *very much*: *was very much pleased, annoyed*; *this road is very much used by travellers*; **d** (with neg.) usually in sense of moderately, rather: *not a very good bit of work*, rather bad; *I don't sing very well*, i.e. I sing pretty badly; *I am not very keen on going there*, I don't want to go. **2.** Before superlative, used intensively or emphatically: *the very last thing I should have expected*; *he came the very next day*; *the very best thing you can do*. **3.** Emphasising complete identity or difference: *he used the very same words as I had*; *said the very opposite of what I expected*. Phrs. *my, your, his &c. very own*, mine &c. absolutely, beyond dispute; with possession not shared by another: *the property is my very own*; *if you make good use of the book you shall have it for your very own*.

Very light, n. [1. véri līt; 2. véri láit], fr. S. W. Very, of U.S.A. navy, inventor, 1877. A form of signal in which coloured lights or flares are fired from a large-bore pistol, used with a code for signalling at night.

vesica, n. [1. vésika; 2. vésikə]. Lat. *vēsīca*, 'bladder; blister', cogn. w. Scrt. *vasti*, 'bladder'. **a** (anat.) Bladder, esp. the urinary bladder in animals or the swim-bladder of fish, whence *vesica piscis*, term used in Gothic architecture and painting, as design for seals &c., for a pointed oval, often forming an aureole or glory for a sacred figure; **b** (bot.) a small sac or cyst, vesicle.

vesical, adj. [1. vésikl; 2. vésikl]. Prec. & **-al**. Pertaining to a vesica or bladder.

vesicant, adj. & n. [1. vésikant; 2. vésikənt]. See next word & **-ant**. **a** adj. Causing, raising, blisters; blistering; **b** n., a blistering substance.

vesicate, vb. trans. & intrans. [1. vésikāt; 2. vésikeit], fr. Lat. *vēsīca*, in sense of 'blister', & **-ate**. (med.) **a** trans. To raise a blister on, to blister; **b** intrans., to become blistered.

vesicle, n. [1. vésikl; 2. vésikl], fr. Lat. *vēsīcula*, 'a small blister, sac' &c., dimin. of **vesica**. A small membranous cavity or sac; esp. one filled with air or fluid, as in the animal body, on a leaf &c.

vesico-, pref. Form fr. **vesica**, used to form compounds denoting connexion or relationship with the bladder.

vesicular, adj. [1. vesíkūlar; 2. vɛsíkjulə], fr. Lat. *vēsīcula*, see **vesicle**, & **-ar**. **a** Shaped like a vesicle or small cyst or sac; **b** having, composed of, vesicles.

vesiculate, adj. [1. vesíkūlāt; 2. vesíkjuleit]. See prec. & **-ate**. Vesicular.

vesper, n. [1. vésper; 2. véspə]. Lat., also *vespera*, 'evening, the even-tide; the evening star', cogn. w. Gk. *hésperos*, fr. **wesperos*, adj. & n., 'evening, evening star', *hesperā*, 'evening'; O. Slav. *večerŭ*, 'evening'. The specif. eccles. use is derived fr. O. Fr. *vespres*, Mod. Fr. *vêpres*, fr. Lat. *vesperae*, pl., cp. **matins**. **1.** (cap.) The evening star, Hesperus, the planet Venus appearing as the evening star in the west. **2.** (pl.) Evensong, the evening service, the sixth of the canonical hours of the Roman Catholic and Orthodox Greek Churches. *Sicilian Vespers*, (hist.) the massacre of the French in Sicily, which began at Palermo, at the hour of Vespers on Easter Monday, 1282.

vespertilionid, adj. & n. [1. vèspertílionid; 2. vèspətílionid]. Mod. Lat. *Vespertilionidae*, fr. Lat. *vespertilio*, 'a bat', fr. *vesper*, 'evening', see prec. (zool.) **a** adj. Belonging to the large group, *Vespertilionidae*, of insectivorous bats, which includes the common European bats; **b** n., one of this group of bats.

vespertine, adj. [1. véspertīn; 2. véspətain], fr. Lat. *vespertīnus*, 'belonging to the evening; western', see **vesper**. **a** Pertaining to, done, occurring, in the evening; **b** (of animals &c.) appearing in the evening; **c** (astron.) setting at evening or just after sunset.

vespiary, n. [1. véspiari; 2. véspiəri]. On anal. of **apiary**, fr. Lat. *vespa*, 'wasp'; fr. **vopsa*, fr. Aryan base **webh-*, 'to weave, spin'; cp. O. Prussian *wobse*, 'gadfly'; see **wasp** & **weave**. A wasp's nest.

Vespidae, n. pl. [1. véspidē; 2. véspidī]. Med. Lat., fr. Lat. *vespa*, 'wasp', see prec. & **-idae**. (zool.) One of the families of wasps, including the social wasps and hornets.

vespiform, adj. [1. véspifòrm; 2. véspifɔ̄m], fr. Lat. *vesp-(a)*, 'wasp', see prec., & **-form**. Formed like, resembling, a wasp; wasp-like.

vespine, adj. [1. véspīn; 2. véspain]. See prec. & **-ine**. Pertaining to wasps.

vessel, n. [1. vésl; 2. vésl]. O. Fr., also *vaissel*, Mod. Fr. *vaisseau*, esp. in sense of 'ship', fr. Lat. *vascellum*, rare variant of *vasculum*, dimin. of *vās*, see **vase**, & cp. **vascular**. **1.** **a** A general term for any hollow article or utensil serving as a receptacle for liquids, food, or other substance, usually round in shape, as a jug, pot, pan, dish &c., esp. as designed for domestic use; **b** (fig., from Bib. usage) person regarded as that which contains or receives some mental or spiritual quality: *a vessel of wrath*; *a chosen vessel*; *woman the weaker vessel* &c. **2.** A ship, usually of a larger kind than one styled 'boat'. **3. a** (anat.) Any one of the tubes, canals, or ducts which contain and circulate the blood or other fluid contents or secretions of the animal body: *blood-vessel*; *the lymphatic vessels* &c.; **b** (bot.) a cellular tube or duct containing and circulating the sap in plants.

vest (I.), n. [1. vest; 2. vɛst], fr. Lat. *vestis*, 'garment; covering for the body, clothes'; fr. Aryan base *wes-, 'to put on, clothe'; cogn. w. Scrt. *vas-*, 'to put on', *vastra*, 'garment', Gk. *esthḗs*, 'clothing', *hénnūmi*, fut. *hésō*, for **wésnumi*, 'I clothe, put on', Goth. *(ga)wasjan*, 'to clothe', O.E. *werian*, 'to wear (clothes)', see **wear (I.)**. **1.** (archaic or obs.) Robe, vestment, clothing. **2.** Undergarment of wool, silk &c. worn on the upper part of the body next the skin. **3.** (shop term) A waistcoat: *gent's black coat and vest with striped trousers*.

vest (II.), vb. trans. & intrans., fr. O. Fr. *vestir*, Mod. Fr. *vêtir*, fr. Lat. *vestīre*, 'to clothe', fr. *vestis*, see prec. **A.** trans. **1.** To clothe with, put on, a robe or garment, (chiefly in eccles. usage of liturgical vestments) *a priest vested with chasuble, alb, and stole*; *the celebrant vests himself in the sanctuary*. **2. a** To invest, endow with, to put in possession of, secure possession to: *to vest a person with rights in an estate, property* &c.; **b** to confer an immediate fixed right of present or future possession of: *to vest property, rights, authority, in a person*. **B.** intrans. **1.** (of rights, property &c.) To become fixed or vested in a person. **2.** To array oneself, esp. put on vestments of ceremony: *a chaplain assists the bishop to vest*.

Vesta, n. [1. vésta; 2. vɛ́stə]. Lat.; cogn. w. Gk. *hestía* for **westia*, 'hearth, home', also (cap.) 'the goddess of the home'; etymol. doubtful, but cp. **combustion**. **1.** (Roman mythol.) The goddess of flocks and herds and of the household, homestead; also goddess of fire and the household hearth, for whom a sacred communal fire was kept always burning in her temple. **2.** (astron.) The name of one of the earlier discovered minor planets or asteroids. **3.** (without cap.) A wax match.

vestal, adj. & n. [1. véstl; 2. vɛ́stl], fr. Lat. *Vestālis*, see prec. & **-al**. **1.** adj. **a** (Roman mythol.) Belonging to, dedicated to, the goddess Vesta, esp. *vestal virgin*, one of the virgins, vowed to perpetual chastity, whose duties included keeping the sacred *vestal fire* safe and perpetually burning in the temple at Rome; **b** (by transf.) chaste, pure, virgin. **2.** n. A vestal virgin; a virgin, a pure, chaste woman; a nun.

vested, adj. [1. vésted; 2. vɛ́stid], fr. P.P. of **vest** (II.). Fixed, settled, secured in the possession of a person; specif. (law) not contingent or in state of suspension: *vested rights, interests* &c.

vestibular, adj. [1. vestíbūlar; 2. vestíbjulə]. See next word & **-ar**. Pertaining to, serving as, a vestibule.

vestibule, n. [1. véstibūl; 2. vɛ́stibjūl], fr. Lat. *vestibulum*, 'entrance or fore-court to a house'; various explanations have been proposed, of wh. Walde favours the derivation fr. **ver(o)stabulum*, 'place before the door', fr. **vero*, 'door', lit. 'means of closure', q.v. under **vernacular** & **aperient**, & *stabulum*, 'standing-place; habitation; stable', see **stable** (II.). **1. a** A covered entrance to a house; ante-chamber, entrance hall, lobby; **b** (U.S.A.) enclosed platform at end of a railway train. **2.** (anat.) A communicating channel or chamber, esp. the central cavity in the ear.

vestige, n. [1. véstij; 2. vɛ́stidž]. Fr., fr. Lat. *vestigium*, 'footprint, step, track'; prob. for **verstigium*, derived fr. *verrere*, 'to sweep, brush along', w. suff. on anal. of *fastīgium*, 'gable', for **farstigium*, cp. Scrt. *bhṛ́ṣṭiš*, 'point, prong', & see **bristle** (I.). **1.** (rare or poet.) The mark of a foot left on the ground; footprint, track, spoor, of man or animal. **2. a** A visible trace, material sign, or mark left behind by something destroyed or vanished; any material evidence of something no longer existing: *only a few vestiges of the great building remain*; *the last vestiges of prehistoric life and culture*; **b** (biol.) a rudimentary, degenerate survival of a former organ or structure: *the vestige of a tail in the human body*; *the pineal gland may be the vestige of a third eye*. **3.** (in non-material sense) A perceptible trace, slight survival, or indication: *not a vestige left of former hatred or jealousy*; *soon there will hardly be left a vestige of our former rights and liberty*.

vestigial, adj. [1. vestíjial; 2. vestídžiəl]. See prec. & **-al**. Surviving as a vestige or indication of something which has passed away, disappeared; (esp. biol.) rudimentary, atrophied, degenerate: *vestigial organs, structure* &c.

vesting, n. [1. vésting; 2. vɛ́stiŋ]. **vest** (II.) & **-ing**. **1.** The act of putting on robes or vestments: *the vesting of a priest* &c. **2.** Act of confirming, settling, the legal possession: *vesting of property in trustees* &c.

vestment, n. [1. véstment; 2. vɛ́stmənt], fr. O. Fr. *vestement*, Mod. Fr. *vêtement*, fr. Lat. *vestīmentum*, 'clothing', fr. *vestis*, 'a garment', see **vest** (I.), & **-ment**. **a** A robe, dress; esp. one of the liturgical articles of dress worn by the officiating clergy during divine service, as *Mass vestments*, those ordered to be worn by priests and deacons at the celebration of the Eucharist, the essential or principal Mass vestment being the chasuble, q.v.; in general, the dress worn by the clergy and choir during divine service, as cassock, stole, and surplice; **b** specif., *the vestment*, the chasuble; used already in the 15th cent. in this special sense.

vestry, n. [1. véstri; 2. vɛ́stri], fr. O. Fr. *vestiarie, vestiaire*, fr. Lat. *vestiārium*, 'chest, cupboard for clothes, wardrobe', fr. *vestis*, 'garment', see **vest** (I.), & **-ry**. **1.** Building or chamber attached to a church in which the vestments, surplice, cassocks &c. of the clergy and choir, or the liturgical vestments, if any, are kept and put on before a service, and where the Communion vessels are stored when not in use; also used for such church business as signing of registers and other parochial matters; when attached to a cathedral or other large church it is usually styled *sacristy*. **2.** A similar building or chamber in a nonconformist chapel where chapel business is carried on, prayer-meetings are held &c. **3.** Body of ratepayers of parish which elects churchwarden and manages the business of the church, presided over by the rector or vicar, and meeting usually in the vestry; formerly having general administrative secular powers in the parish, but now superseded by the parish council when not embodied in a large local administrative unit such as a rural or urban district council &c.

vestry clerk, n. The clerk to a vestry; parish clerk.

vestrydom, n. [1. véstridum; 2. vɛ́stridəm]. See **vestry** & **-dom**. Government by a parish vestry; esp. referring to the formerly often inefficient and corrupt administration by the old vestries; cp. *bumbledom*.

vestryman, n. [1. véstriman; 2. vɛ́strimən]. Member of a parish vestry.

vesture, n. [1. véschur; 2. vɛ́stʃə]. O. Fr., Mod. Fr. *vêture*, fr. Lat. *vestis*, see **vest** (I.), & **-ure**. **a** Garments, clothing, raiment; a garment, robe &c.; now chiefly poetical or reminiscent of Biblical usage in '*They cast lots upon my vesture*'; '*the Queen in a vesture of gold*' (Ps. 45); **b** (poet.) covering in nature: *a vesture of mist, of verdure* &c.

vestured, adj. [1. véschurd; 2. vɛ́stʃəd]. Prec. & **-ed**. **a** Dressed, robed; **b** covered as with a vesture.

vesturer, n. [1. véschurer; 2. vɛ́stʃərə]. **vesture** & **-er**. An official of a cathedral or collegiate church in charge of ecclesiastical vestments.

Vesuvian, adj. & n. [1. vesū́vian; 2. vəsjū́viən], fr. Vesuvius & **-an**. **1.** adj. Of, pertaining to, resembling, the volcano Vesuvius, near Naples. **2.** n. (obsolesc., without cap.) A kind of fusee.

vet (I.), n. [1. vet; 2. vɛt]. Colloq. abbr. of **veterinary** (surgeon).

vet (II.), vb. trans., fr. prec. **a** (colloq.) To examine, treat (animal, human being) medically or surgically; **b** (colloq.) to examine (manuscripts &c.) critically; *he got a publisher's reader to vet his first novel*.

vetch, n. [1. vech; 2. vɛtʃ], fr. O. Fr. *veche*, fr. Lat. *vīcia*, 'vetch', cp. Germ. *wicke*; prob. fr. the base **wei-*, 'to bind', seen in Lat. *vītis*, 'the vine', *viēre*, 'to twine' &c., see **vine**. A climbing or trailing leguminous plant of many varieties, esp. *Vicia sativa* or tare, used as green fodder.

vetchy, adj. [1. véchi; 2. vɛ́tʃi]. Prec. & **-y**. Made of, full of, vetches.

veteran, n. & adj. [1. véteran; 2. vɛ́tərən], fr. Lat. *veterānus*, 'old, veteran', adj. & n.; fr. *veter-(is), vetus*, 'old'; cp. also Lat. *vitulus*, 'yearling, calf', see **veal**, cogn. w. Scrt. *vatsáš*, 'year'; Gk. *étos* for **wétos*, 'a year'; O. Slav. *vetŭχŭ*, 'old'; cp. also O.E. *weþer*, 'sheep' &c., see **wether**. **1.** n. One old and experienced in service, esp. an old tried soldier or sailor. **2.** adj. Old and experienced, tried in service: *a veteran soldier, member of Parliament* &c.

veterinarian, adj. & n. [1. vèterinā́rian; 2. vètərinɛ́əriən]. See next word & **-an**. **a** adj. Veterinary; **b** n., a veterinary surgeon.

veterinary, adj. & n. [1. véterinari; 2. vɛ́tərinəri], fr. Lat. *veterīnārius*, fr. *veterīnus*, 'belonging to beasts of burden, draught animals', esp. *veterīna*, sc. *bestia*, 'a draught animal'; fr. *vetus, veteris*, 'old', draught animals being those too old for other purposes; see **veteran**. **1.** adj. Pertaining to, concerned with, affecting, the diseases of animals, esp. cattle and other domestic animals: *veterinary science, surgeon* &c. **2.** n. A veterinary surgeon.

veto (I.), n. [1. vḗtō; 2. vītou]. Lat. *veto*, 'I forbid'; *vetāre*, 'to oppose, forbid', appears first in the form *votāre*, the etymol. of wh. is very doubtful; the Roman tribunes of the people used the word in the exercise of their power of blocking measures of the Senate or acts of other magistrates. **1. a** The constitutional right or power residing in various persons or bodies, as a sovereign, a legislative assembly &c., of forbidding or preventing the carrying out of an enactment or act of administration: *the veto of the Crown has not been exercised since the reign of Queen Anne*; **b** an exercise of this power or right: *the veto of the Lords has fortunately hung the bill up for the present*; specif., *local veto*, right of a locality by vote to prohibit the sale of alcoholic liquor within the area as a measure of temperance reform. **2.** (in gen. sense) Prohibition, refusal to allow anything to be done, said &c.: *to put, set, a veto on a proposal*; *a public veto on such performances was only to be expected*.

veto (II.), vb. trans., fr. prec. **a** Specif., disallow, prevent enaction of (a measure, proposal, bill), by exercising the veto: *the Crown may, but never does, veto a bill that has passed both Houses*; **b** to refuse to allow, prohibit absolutely (an action, conduct &c.): *in public schools smoking by the boys is vetoed*.

vetturino, n. [1. vètoorḗnō; 2. vèturīno]. Ital., fr. *vettura*, 'carriage', fr. L. Lat. *vectūra*, fr. *vect-(um)*, P.P. type of *vehere*, 'to draw, carry', see **vehicle**. Driver of a hackney or hired carriage in Italy.

vex, vb. trans. [1. veks; 2. vɛks], M.E. *vexen*, fr. O. Fr. *vexer*, fr. Lat. *vexāre*, 'to agitate, shake, toss; to harass, trouble, vex'; prob. fr. *vex-*, variant form of P.P. of *vehere*, 'to draw, carry', cp. *convex* & see **vehicle**. **a** To irritate, disturb, distress, cause worry to, by petty annoyances, esp. in mind; to cause grief to; **b** to render mildly angry, excite mild

vexation (cont.)

wrath of; esp. in P.P. as adjective: *I shall be seriously vexed if you speak to me like that*; also *vexed with* (a person), angry with.

vexation, n. [1. veksāshun; 2. vekséiʃən], fr. Lat. *vexātiōn-(em)*, fr. *vexāt-(um)*, P.P. type of *vexāre*, see **vex**, & **-ation**. 1. State of being vexed; esp. mental distress, irritation, feeling of annoyance or worry: '*vanity and vexation of spirit*'; *much to my vexation I just missed a chance of a good profit*. 2. Cause of distress or annoyance; worry: *all the trifling vexations one has to put up with*.

vexatious, adj. [1. veksāshus; 2. vekséiʃəs]. See prec. & **-ous**. 1. Causing vexation; troublesome, irritating, annoying: *moving house is a vexatious business*; *how vexatious to miss one's train!* 2. (law) Undertaken for trivial reasons, done for purpose of annoyance or irritation: *a vexatious suit or action*.

vexatiously, adv. Prec. & **-ly**. In a vexatious manner.

vexatiousness, n. See prec. & **-ness**. State of being vexatious.

vexillum, n., pl. **vexilla** [1. veksílum, -a; 2. veksíləm, -ə]. Lat., 'military ensign; standard'; for *vecslom*, variant of *vēlum*, 'veil' &c., see **velum** & **veil**. 1. a The military standard of a company of the Roman legion, being a small square cloth hung from a cross-bar borne on a pole; b a company of soldiers under such a standard. 2. (eccles.) A scarf wrapped round a bishop's pastoral staff. 3. a (zool.) The web of the feather of a bird; b (bot.) the larger upper petal in flowers such as the sweet-pea.

vexing, adj. [1. véksing; 2. véksiŋ], fr. Pres. Part. of **vex**. Causing vexation; annoying, irritating; troublesome.

vexingly, adv. Prec. & **-ly**. In a vexing manner, so as to cause vexation.

via (I.), n. [1. vía; 2. váiə]. Lat. *via*, 'path, street, highway; passage, channel; pipe'; fr. *weja-*, whence also Lat. *venor*, 'to hunt, follow after', see **venery** (I.); Scrt. *vēti*, 'he follows, pursues, strives after'; *vī-thī-*, 'row, street, way'; perh. also Gk. *oī-mos*, 'way, road', for *woi-*. Only in *via media* [1. vía média; 2. váiə mídiə]. Lat., 'middle path' (fig.) a moderate course between two extremes; esp. of Church of England as lying between the extremes of Roman Catholicism and Protestantism; *Via Lactea*, n. [1. vía láktea; 2. váiə lǽktiə]. Lat., 'Milky Way'.

via (II.), prep. Abl. of Lat. *via*, see prec. By way of, passing through, calling at: *to travel via London*; as indication on luggage: *Tunbridge Wells via Reading and Redhill* &c.

viability, n. [1. viəbíliti; 2. vàiəbíliti]. Next word & **-ity**. Condition of being viable; capacity for living.

viable, adj. [1. víabl; 2. váiəbl]. Fr., fr. *vie*, 'life', Lat. *vita*, see **vital**, & **-able**. Capable of living; a having all the organs &c. at such a state of development as to enable life to be carried on; said esp. of a newly born infant; b able to live in a particular climate and environment.

viableness, n. [1. víablnes; 2. váiəblnis]. Prec. & **-ness**. Viability.

viaduct, n. [1. víadukt; 2. váiədakt]. Lat. *via*, see **via** (I.), *ducta*, 'conducted', see **duct**. A long bridge, supported upon a series of arches and pillars, which carries a road or railway line across a valley or gorge.

vial, n. [1. víal; 2. váiəl]. M.E. *viole*, fr. variant of Fr. *fiole*, fr. Lat. *phiala*, fr. Gk. *phiálē*, 'cup, bowl, drinking-bowl'; etymol. doubtful. A small glass bottle for medicine &c. Phr. (Bib.) (*to pour out*) *the vials of one's wrath*.

viameter, n. [1. viámeter; 2. vaiǽmitə]. **via** (I.) & **-meter**. Instrument for measuring distances on roads; a hodometer.

viand, n. [1. víand; 2. váiənd]. Fr. *viande*, 'food, meat', fr. L. Lat. *vivenda*, Lat. *vivenda*, neut. pl. gerundive, fr. *vīvere*, 'to live'; see **vivid** & **vital**; cp. **vivandière**. Article of food; more often collectively *viands*.

viatic, adj. [1. viátik; 2. vaiǽtik]. Lat. *viāticus*, 'pertaining to a road or to a journey',

see **via** (I.) & **-atic**. Connected with a journey, with travels.

viaticum, n. [1. viátikum; 2. vaiǽtikəm]. Lat., neut. sing. of *viāticus* as n., see prec. 'provision for a journey; allowance of soldiers on service'. 1. (rare) Provisions for a journey. 2. The consecrated wafer, the Host, as administered to the dying.

vibracular, adj. [1. vibrákūlar; 2. vaibrǽkjulə]. See next word & **-ar**. Pertaining to, caused by, of the nature of, vibracula.

vibraculum, n., pl. **vibracula** [1. vibrákūlum, -a; 2. vaibrǽkjuləm, -ə]. Lat., formed fr. *vibra-*, see **vibrate**, w. dimin. suff., see **-cule**. Filamentous spine-like organ of certain polyzoans, by means of the vibratory movements of which food is brought within reach.

vibrancy, n. [1. víbransi; 2. váibrənsi]. **vibrant** & **-cy**. State or property of being vibrant; resonance.

vibrant, adj. [1. víbrant; 2. váibrənt]. Fr., fr. Lat. *vibrant-(em)*, Pres. Part. of *vibrāre*, see **vibrate**. a Vibrating, tremulous; b (of sound, the voice) setting up vibrations, resonant.

vibrate, vb. intrans. & trans. [1. vibrát, víbrāt; 2. vaibréit, váibreit], fr. Lat. *vibrāt-(um)*, P.P. type of *vibrāre*, 'to set in tremulous motion, cause to move rapidly to and fro; to shake, to agitate'; expanded fr. base *wei-*, 'to tremble' &c.; also fr. this base are O.H.G. *wipf*, 'swing, impetus', *wipfil*, 'top of a tree', *wimpal*, 'veil, headgear', see **wimple**. The base in its simpler form is seen in Lat. *viēre*, 'to twist, bend', *vītis*, 'grape vine'; see further under **viti-**, **vine**, & **withy**. A. intrans. 1. a To move rapidly to and fro, to oscillate; esp. to quiver, thrill, with incessant, tremulous, rapid movement, as of a thin, or tightly stretched, flexible or elastic body: *a fiddle string vibrates when touched with the bow*; *the atmosphere vibrates in response to the oscillations of a fiddle string*; b (fig.) to be deeply stirred emotionally, have the feelings profoundly moved; to thrill: *to vibrate with passion, at a person's touch* &c. 2. a To move, swing, steadily backwards and forwards between two points; e.g. of a pendulum; b (rare, fig.) to hesitate between two opinions, courses of action &c. B. trans. To cause to vibrate.

vibratile, adj. [1. víbratīl; 2. váibrətail]. **vibrate** & **-ile**. Capable of vibrating, tending to vibrate.

vibratility, n. [1. vibratíliti; 2. vàibrətíliti]. Prec. & **-ity**. Property of being vibratile.

vibration, n. [1. vibráshun; 2. vaibréiʃən]. **vibrate** & **-ion**. 1. a Rapid, tremulous, oscillating movement to and fro, as of a tense elastic, or fluid body; b (fig.) tremulous stirring, or thrilling, of the emotions. 2. (more rarely) Steady swinging movement to and fro. 3. Act or process of causing (a body) to vibrate.

vibrational, adj. [1. vibráshunal; 2. vaibréiʃənəl]. Prec. & **-al**. Pertaining to, connected with, of the nature of, vibration.

vibrative, adj. [1. víbrativ; 2. váibrətiv]. **vibrate** & **-ive**. Of the nature of, causing, vibration.

vibrato, n. [1. vibráhtō; 2. vibrátou]. Ital., P.P. of *vibrare*, see **vibrate**. Tremulous effect produced by variation of emphasis or loudness in the same note.

vibrator, n. [1. víbrátor; 2. vaibréitə]. **vibrate** & **-or**. That which vibrates.

vibratory, adj. [1. víbraturi; 2. váibrət(ə)ri]. **vibrate** & **-ory**. Vibrative.

vibrio, n. [1. víbriō; 2. víbriou]. Neo-Lat., formed fr. *vibrāre*, see **vibrate**. Kind of bacteria which are endowed with the power of vibratory or undulatory movement.

vibrioid, adj. & n. [1. víbrioid; 2. víbrioid]. Prec. & **-oid**. 1. adj. Like a vibrio. 2. n. A vibrioid body, or vibrio.

vibrissa, n., pl. **vibrissae** [1. vibrísa, -ē; 2. vaibrísə, -ī]. Lat., fr. base of **vibrate**. Stiff hair in the human nostril; hair round the muzzle of mammals, the whiskers of the cat &c.

vibrograph, n. [1. víbrograhf; 2. váibrəgraf]. Base of **vibrate** & **-graph**. Device for recording vibrations.

vibroscope, n. [1. víbroskōp; 2. váibrəskòup]. Base of **vibrate** & **-scope**. Instrument for observing and recording vibrations.

vibroscopic, adj. [1. vibroskópik; 2. vàibrəskópik]. Prec. & **-ic**. Pertaining to, observed by, the vibroscope.

viburnum, n. [1. vibérnum; 2. vaibə́nəm]. Lat., translated as 'the wayfaring tree'. The element *vi-* is fr. base in Lat. *viēre*, 'to twine' &c., see under **viti-** & **vibrate**, & refers to the habit of the tree; the second element is like that in **laburnum** & is unexplained. A genus of shrubs and trees, the guelder roses, wild and cultivated in gardens for their flowers and foliage.

vicar, n. [1. víkar; 2. víkə]. M.E. *vicair*, *vicar* &c., fr. O. Fr. *vicaire*, in eccles. sense, fr. Lat. *vicārius*, 'a deputy, substitute, proxy', see **vicarious**. 1. Deputy; rare except in Phr. *the Vicar of Christ*, title claimed by, and accorded to, the Pope; *Vicar-general*, deputy of the Pope or of an Archbishop. 2. The incumbent of an English parish who is not a rector, i.e. one who does not receive the great tithes, but is paid a stipend from other sources; formerly called a *perpetual curate*. The parish of a vicar is either a new one carved out of a larger, older parish, the rector retaining the old parish church and the great tithes, or one in which these tithes belong to a layman or a corporation.

vicarage, n. [1. víkarij; 2. víkəridʒ]. **vicar** & **-age**. 1. The residence of a vicar. 2. (more rarely) The office of a vicar.

vicar-apostolic, n. (R.C. Ch.) 1. Archbishop or bishop to whom the Pope delegated his authority. 2. An ecclesiastic exercising episcopal jurisdiction in a diocese during a vacancy, or on account of the illness of the bishop. 3. A titular bishop exercising his functions in a country where there are no episcopal sees.

vicar-capitular, n. (R.C. Ch.) Person elected by the Chapter (in England) to rule the diocese, after the death of a bishop, until the new bishop is appointed.

vicar-choral, n. Clergyman or layman whose duty it is to sing part of the service in a cathedral.

vicar-forane, n. [1. víkar fórin; 2. víkə fórin]. Lat. *forāneus*, see **foreign**. (R.C. Ch.) Priest appointed by the bishop to exercise certain limited jurisdiction in a particular town &c. within the diocese.

vicarial, adj. [1. vikárial; 2. vikéəriəl]. **vicar** & **-ial**. 1. Pertaining to, acting as, a vicar. 2. (rare) Vicarious.

vicariate, n. [1. vikáriat; 2. vikéəriət]. **vicar** & **-i-** & **-ate**. Office of a vicar; period of tenure of this.

vicarious, adj. [1. víkárius; 2. vaikéəriəs]. Lat. *vicārius*, 'substituted, delegated', fr. *vicis*, 'change, interchange, alternation', see **vice** (IV.), & **-ary**, & **-ous**. 1. Connected with, pertaining to, a vicar or deputy; deputed: *vicarious authority*. 2. Performing duties as the substitute or deputy of another: *a vicarious ruler*, *agent*. 3. Performed, undergone, by one person &c., on behalf of, in the place of, another: *the vicarious sufferings*, *sacrifice*, *of Christ*. 4. (med.) *Vicarious haemorrhage*, one taking place from an organ other than the normal one, the usual flow from the latter being suppressed.

vicariously, adv. Prec. & **-ly**. In a vicarious manner; as a deputy; by deputy.

vicariousness, n. See prec. & **-ness**. State, quality, of being vicarious.

vice (I.), n. [1. vīs; 2. vais]. In M.E., fr. O. Fr. fr. Lat. *vitium*, 'fault, defect, blemish; moral fault; crime'; perh. cogn. w. O.E. *wīdl*, 'defilement, impurity'; the etymol. is disputed; perh. fr. the base in Lat. *viēre*, 'to bend, twine' &c., see **viti-**, in the sense of 'bending aside, departure, from the normal or healthy condition'. 1. A grave moral fault;

ingrained defect in the character: *avarice and cruelty are among the most detestable vices*. **2. a** Immoral, degrading, conduct or habit; gross wickedness, depravity, lewdness: *vice of all kinds exists, unfortunately, in all big cities*; **b** *the Vice*, a character in English Morality plays, usually a buffoon, who represented some particular vice. **3.** Specif., *vice in a horse*, bad, incorrigible tricks and habits, such as bolting, shying, rearing &c., which make the animal difficult to ride or drive with comfort. **4. a** Physical defect or disability; diseased taint: *he has certain vices of constitution which render his life precarious*; **b** defect, blemish, imperfection in organization, social structure &c.: *the vices of our social system*; **c** a fault in, a bad form of, expression; esp. *a vice of literary style, oratory, drawing* &c.

vice (II.), n. & vb. trans. M.E., fr. O. Fr. *vis*, 'a screw; a winding stair', fr. Lat. *vītis*, 'a vine', fr. base *vī-* in *viēre*, 'to twist together, to weave', see **viti-**. **1. n.** A device, usually of iron, and screwed to a bench, consisting of two parts worked by a screw so as to be brought together and held immovable at the desired distance apart, used by smiths, and workers in wood or metal, for gripping, holding, an object in a given position while being carved, chiselled, hammered or otherwise worked on; Phrs. *as firm as a vice*; *a grip like a vice* &c. **2. vb.** (rare) To grip, hold firm, in a vice.

vice (III.), n. Colloq. abbr. for *vice-chancellor*, *vice-president* &c.

vice (IV.), prep. [1. vīsi; 2. váisi]. Lat., abl. of *vicis*, 'change, interchange, alternation, reciprocal succession'; cogn. w. Gk. *eikō* for *weikō*, 'I yield, draw back, give way' &c.; Scrt. *viṣṭi*, 'changeable'; further (Gmc. *k* fr. Aryan *kn-*), O.S. *wikan*, O.E. *wīcan*, 'to give way, collapse', O.H.G. *wīhhan*, O.E. *wāc*, 'weak', O.N. *veikr*, fr. *waik-*, see **weak**; & prob. O.E. *wicu*, see **week**. Instead of, in the place of: *an examiner in Greek will be appointed vice Mr. Jones, who retires*; *to be Brigade Major vice Captain X*.

vice-, pref. [1. vīs; 2. vais]. Fr., for etymol. see prec. Prefix placed before the names of offices and ranks to express: **a** persons entitled, qualified, appointed, to hold such offices as deputies for others and to perform certain delegated functions: *vice-agent, vice-sheriff, vice-warden* &c.; **b** expressing a rank next in order below that to which the prefix is attached: *vice-admiral*.

vice-admiral, n. Officer in the navy next in rank below an admiral.

vice-admiralty, n. Rank, office, of a vice-admiral; term of this office.

vice-chairman, n. Permanent officer of a company, corporation, deliberative body &c., who presides at the meetings in the absence of the chairman.

vice-chairmanship, n. Office of a vice-chairman; term of this.

vice-chamberlain, n. Deputy of a chamberlain or lord chamberlain.

vice-chancellor, n. **1.** Formerly (down to 1873) a judge appointed to the Chancery Court of England. **2.** The chief executive officer of a University acting also as deputy of the Chancellor.

vice-consul, n. The deputy of a consul; official appointed by a government to watch commercial interests of its subjects in a foreign country, in a town, when these subjects are not sufficiently numerous or the business sufficiently important for a consul.

vice-consulate, n. Residence, office, term of office, of a vice-consul.

vice-consulship, n. Status, office, of a vice-consul; term of this office.

vicegerent, n. [1. vīsjérent; 2. vaisdžíərənt]. vice & gerent. One who rules as the deputy of another; *God's vicegerent*, the Pope.

vice-governor, n. Deputy governor.

vice-governorship, n. Office, term of office, of vice-governor.

vicennial, adj. [1. vīsénial; 2. vaiséníəl]. Lat. *vicennium*, 'period of 20 years', *vicēni*, '20', & *annus*, 'year', see **annual**, & **-al**. The first element is cogn. w. Lat. *vīginti*, fr. *wīkṇtói*; Scrt. *viçati*; Gk. *eikosi*; O.W. *uceint*, 'twenty'. The meaning is 'two tens', fr. base *wī-*, *wei-*, &c., 'two', see **divide**; & *kṃt*, earlier *dkṃt-*, 'ten, a decade', see **hundred, deca-**. Lasting for, recurring every, twenty years.

vice-presidency, n. Office, term of office, of vice-president.

vice-president, n. Deputy of a president.

viceregal, adj. [1. vīsrégl; 2. vaisrígl]. **vice-** & **regal** (I.). Pertaining to, connected with, a viceroy or vicereine: *the viceregal palace, ball* &c.

vicereine, n. [1. vísrān; 2. váisrein]. **vice-** & Fr. *reine*, 'queen', fr. Lat., see **regina**. Wife of a viceroy.

viceroy, n. [1. vísroi; 2. váisrɔi]. **vice-** & Fr. *roi*, 'king', fr. Lat., see **rex**. One who rules a country, province, colony, in the name and with the authority of, and as representing, the sovereign.

viceroyal, adj. [1. vīsróial; 2. vaisrɔ́iəl]. Prec. & **-al**. (rare) Viceregal.

viceroyalty, n. [1. vīsróialti; 2. vaisrɔ́iəlti]. Prec. & **-ty**. The dignity and office of a viceroy; term of this office.

viceroyship, n. [1. vísroiship; 2. váisrɔiʃip]. Viceroyalty.

vice versa, adv. [1. vísi vérsa; 2. váisi və́sə]. Lat., **vice (IV.)** & abl. fem. of P.P. of *vertere*, 'to turn', see **version**. Conversely, the relations being reversed: *I dislike him, and vice versa*, i.e. and he dislikes me; *he's afraid of horses, and vice versa*, i.e. horses are nervous with him.

Vichy water, n. [1. véshi wàwter; 2. víʃi wɔ́tə]. Mineral medicinal water obtained from the springs of Vichy, France.

vicia, n. [1. vísia; 2. vísiə]. Lat., 'a vetch'; fr. base *vei-* &c. as in Lat. *viēre*, 'to twist, bend', see under **viti-**. The vetch family of plants.

vicilin, n. [1. vísilin; 2. vísilin], fr. prec. Chemical substance found in the broad bean, pea, and other fabaceous plants.

vicinage, n. [1. vísinij; 2. vísinidž], fr. Lat. *vīcīnus*, 'near, neighbouring', fr. *vīcus*, 'district, quarter, of a city; village, hamlet'; fr. *woikos*; cogn. w. Gk. *oîkos*, fr. *woikos*, 'house', see first element of **economy**; Scrt. *veçáś*, 'house', & *viç*, 'dwelling-place'; Goth. *weihs*, 'village'; cp. further, O.E. *wīc*, 'dwelling, village', either borrowed direct fr. Lat. *vīcus*, or fr. *wīkná*, cp. Pl.-Ns. in *-wich*, & **wick (II.)**; for suff. see **-age**. **1.** Area, tract of country, place, lying near by; neighbourhood, neighbouring country or place; vicinity. **2.** Common rights arising to neighbouring tenants of the same barony.

vicinal, adj. [1. vísinal; 2. vísinəl]. Lat. *vīcīnālis*, 'neighbouring', fr. *vīcīn-*, see prec. & **-al**. Neighbouring.

vicinism, n. [1. vísinizm; 2. vísinizəm]. Lat. *vīcīn-*, see vicinage, & **-ism**. (biol.) Tendency of forms to vary owing to the influence of related forms living in the same vicinity.

vicinity, n. [1. visíniti; 2. visíniti]. Fr. *vicinité*, fr. Lat. *vīcīnitāt-(em)*, 'neighbourhood', fr. *vīcīn-*, as in vicinage, & **-ity**. **1.** State of being near; nearness, propinquity. **2.** Neighbouring area, adjacent regions, neighbourhood.

vicious, adj. [1. víshus; 2. víʃəs]. O. Fr. *vicious*, fr. Lat. *vitiōsus*, fr. *vitium*, see **vice (I.)** & **-ous**. **1.** Affected by, characterized by, practising, vice; grossly immoral, lewd: *a vicious book*; *a vicious life*; *a vicious person*. **2.** Malignant, spiteful, malevolent: *a vicious look, speech, blow*. **3.** Faulty, imperfect, defective (in various senses): *a vicious text* (of an author), corrupt: *a vicious style*, pronunciation, full of faults and blemishes; vulgar; *a vicious argument*, one logically defective. Phr. *a vicious circle*, (i.) a set of undesirable circumstances which act and react detrimentally upon each other, so that one condition or circumstance leads to another, which in turn intensifies and aggravates the former, and so on; (ii.) (in reasoning) a conclusion based upon an unsound premise, and serving as the basis for establishing the former. **4.** (of a horse) Showing vice; having certain bad tricks and habits; badly trained, hard to manage.

viciously, adv. Prec. & **-ly**. In a vicious manner.

viciousness, n. See prec. & **-ness**. **1.** Quality of being vicious; **a** gross wickedness, immorality; vice; **b** malignity, ill nature, spite. **2.** Faultiness, defectiveness.

vicissitude, n. [1. vīsísitud; 2. vaisísitjūd]. Fr., fr. Lat. *vicissitūdo*, 'change, interchange, alternation'; formed fr. Lat. *vicis*, 'change', see **vice (IV.)** & **-tude**. **1.** Irregular alternation, change, mutation, esp. of circumstances, experience, worldly condition; ups-and-downs of life: *the vicissitudes of fate*. **2.** (obs. or poet.) Regular change and succession, orderly alternation: 'Where light and darkness . . . Lodge and dislodge by turns, which makes . . . Grateful vicissitude, like day and night' (Milton, 'P. L.' vi. 6-8).

vicissitudinary, adj. [1. vīsisitūdinari; 2. vaisisitjūdinəri]. Lat. *vicissitūdin-*, stem of *vicissitūdo*, see prec., & **-ary**. Characterized by, liable to, vicissitude.

vicissitudinous, adj. [1. vīsisitūdinus; 2. vaisisitjūdinəs]. Same stem as prec. & **-ous**. Vicissitudinary.

victim, n. [1. víktim; 2. víktim]. Fr. *victime*, fr. Lat. *victima*, 'beast of sacrifice, victim'; formed fr. *vict-*, 'something consecrated', fr. base *wĭk-*, 'sacred'; cogn. w. Goth. *weihs* (=*wīhs*), 'holy', *weihan*, 'to make holy, consecrate', *weiha*, 'priest'; O.H.G. *wīhan*, Mod. Germ. *weihen*, 'to consecrate, devote' &c. The orig. meaning seems to be 'to set apart', cp. Scrt. *viktár*, 'separated off, set apart'. **1.** Human being or animal devoted, consecrated, to a god, or to God, slain, and offered as a sacrifice. **2. a** Person or living creature that is the object of, and that suffers from, another's anger, ill-will, persecution, evil passions &c.: *the victim of malice, dislike, hatred* &c., *the victim of another's greed* &c.; **b** one who suffers through, is a prey to, some bad qualities, or defects, in his own character or behaviour: *the victim of his own folly, cowardice, extravagance* &c.; **c** one who suffers through the operation of external circumstances and conditions which he cannot control: *a victim of poverty, of the war, of disease* &c.; Phr. *the victim of circumstances*, a wrongdoer who sins owing to the stress of forces and conditions which overmaster him, so that he is not wholly responsible. **3.** A person who is brought under the sinister influence of another, and is deceived and injured by him: *the victim of a swindler*; (facet.) *fell a victim to the lady's charms*, was captivated by these.

victimizable, adj. [1. víktimìzəbl; 2. víktimàizəbl]. victimize & **-able**. Capable of being, liable to be, victimized.

victimization, n. [1. vìktimizǽshun; 2. vìktimaizéiʃən]. See prec. & **-ation**. Condition of being victimized; act, process, of victimizing.

victimize, vb. trans. [1. víktimīz; 2. víktimaiz]. victim & **-ize**. To make a, or the, victim of; to cause to suffer; **a** to deceive, cheat: *victimized by rogues*; **b** to cause to suffer, or endure: *I was victimized the whole evening by the worst bore in the room*.

victor, n. [1. víktor; 2. víktə]. Lat., 'conqueror', formed fr. *vict-(um)*, P.P. type of *vincere*, 'to vanquish', see **vincible**, & **-or**. One who is successful in battle or in a contest; a conqueror, vanquisher, winner; (also attrib.) 'See where the victor victim bleeds' (Shirley).

victoria, n. [1. viktória; 2. viktɔ́riə]. Lat., 'victory'; fr. *vict-* as in victor, & see **-ory**; used as proper name. Name of a light, low, four-wheeled carriage, drawn by one or two

Victoria Cross, n. Abbr. V.C., commonly called [1. vḗ sḗ; 2. ví sí]. Decoration, founded by Queen Victoria in 1856, awarded to soldiers and sailors for an act of remarkable bravery in the presence of the enemy; it consists of a bronze Maltese cross, suspended from a crimson ribbon, for the Army, or from a dark blue one for the Navy. V.C. is also applied to a holder of the decoration: *he is a V.C. and a D.S.O.*

victoria lily, n. Gigantic S. American water-lily, *Victoria regia*.

Victorian, adj. & n. [1. viktṓrian; 2. viktṓriən]. **victoria** & **-an**. 1. adj. Pertaining to, characteristic of, living, made, in the reign of Queen Victoria: *Victorian habits, dress, furniture; Victorian statesmen, writers* &c. 2. n. A person, esp. a writer or other public character, living during the reign of Queen Victoria.

Victorian Order, n. Order founded in 1896 by Queen Victoria, and awarded for personal service to the sovereign.

victorine, n. [1. víktorèn; 2. víktərìn], fr. woman's name. 1. Fur tippet with long narrow ends, formerly worn by women. 2. A kind of peach.

victorious, adj. [1. viktṓrius; 2. viktṓriəs]. Lat. *victōriōsus*; see **victory** & **-ous**. Having the victory in a battle, in war, or in a contest of any kind: *victorious troops; the victorious football team*.

victoriously, adv. Prec. & **-ly**. In a victorious manner; with victory; so as to win.

victoriousness, n. See prec. & **-ness**. (rare) Condition, quality, of being victorious.

victory, n. [1. víktori; 2. víktəri]. M.E., fr. O. Fr. *victorie*, fr. Lat. *victōria*, see **victoria**. 1. **a** Success in battle or in a contest of any kind; act or fact of defeating an enemy in the field, or an opponent in a dispute, competition, game &c.; conquest, act of winning; **b** success in any kind of effort or struggle: *a victory over every difficulty, over one's lower self* &c. 2. (cap.) Roman goddess of victory.

victress, n. [1. víktres; 2. víktris], fr. **victor** & **-ess**. Female victor.

victual, n. & vb. trans. & intrans. [1. vítl; 2. vítl]. M.E., fr. O. Fr. *vitaille*, fr. Lat. *victuālia*, neut. pl., 'provisions', formed fr. *victus*, 'nourishment, fr. *vict-(um)*, P.P. type of *vīvere*, 'to live', see **vital**. 1. n. Generally *victuals*, food, provisions. 2. vb. **a** trans. To supply, provide with, food or stores; **b** intrans. (i.) to procure, take in, stores (of a ship &c.); (ii.) to consume food.

victualler, n. [1. vítaler; 2. vítələ]. Prec. & **-er**. 1. One who provides victuals; (now chiefly) *licensed victualler*, one licensed to sell alcoholic liquor; an innkeeper, a publican. 2. A ship carrying provisions and stores for other ships, or supplying military forces; also *victualling ship*.

victualling, n. [1. vítaling; 2. vítəliŋ]. See **victual** & **-ing**. *Victualling bill*, list of stores to be used on a voyage, and held in bond, furnished to Customs authorities; *victualling house*, eating-house; *victualling note*, one issued by Naval Paymaster, authorizing a ship's steward to supply food to a seaman; *victualling office*, one supplying naval stores &c.; *victualling ship*, victualler; *victualling yard*, one in which naval supplies are stored.

vicuna, vicuña, n. [1. vīkúna, vīkṓōnya; 2. vaikjúnə, vaikúnjə]. Span. *vicuña*, fr. Peruv. 1. Ruminant animal of Peru, Bolivia, and Ecuador, closely related to the llama; hunted for its fine wool. 2. Fine, woolly cloth made from the wool of the vicuna, or from some wool resembling this; also *vicuna cloth*.

vide, vb. [1. vīdi; 2. váidi]. Imperat. sing. of Lat. *vidēre*, 'to see'; cogn. w. a series of Gk. words, meaning 'see' and 'know', q.v. under **-oid**; **idea**; **idol**; for Gmc. cognates see **wit (I.)**; cp. also **vision**. See; used in referring to a passage &c., quoted in a book &c.: *vide* (or *v.*) *p. 30* &c.; q.v., *quod vide*, which see.

videlicet, adv. [1. vi-, vīdḗliset; 2. vi-, vaidḗliset]. Lat., for *vidēre licet*, 'it is permitted to see'; abbr. *viz.*, wh. is commonly rendered *namely*. Generally used to introduce a fuller explanation, or expansion, of what has been stated so briefly as to demand a further elaboration: *the animal kingdom may be divided into three great groups, viz. the vertebrates, invertebrates, and protozoa*.

vidette. See **vedette**.

vidimus, n. [1. vīdimus; 2. váidiməs]. Lat. *vidimus*, 'we have seen', perf. pl. of *vidēre*, see **vide**. A formal inspection of documents.

vidual, adj. [1. vídūal; 2. vídjuəl]. Lat. *vidua*, 'widow' & **-al**; see **divide** & **widow**. Pertaining to, connected with, a widow, or widows.

viduate, n. [1. vídūāt; 2. vídjueit]. Lat. *vidua*, see prec., & **-ate**. Position or status of a widow; condition of being a widow.

vie, vb. intrans. [1. vī; 2. vai]. M.E. *vīen*, fr. *envīen*, see **envy**. *Vie with*, to strive with for superiority in any form; to contest place of superiority with; to rival: *to vie with another for power* &c.; *various kinds of vegetation vying with each other for supremacy; in my opinion few fruits can vie with the apple*.

Viennese, adj. & n. [1. vìenḗz; 2. vìenḯz]. Vienna & **-ese**. **a** adj. Belonging to, coming from, Vienna; **b** n., (sing. & pl.) inhabitant of Vienna.

vi et armis, adv. [1. vī̇ et ármis; 2. vái ɛt ā́mis]. Lat., 'by force and arms', see **vis**. (law) By force and with arms, as showing how damage to person or property was caused.

view (I.), n. [1. vū; 2. vjū]. M.E. *veue*, 'the sense of sight', fr. O. Fr., P.P. Fem. of *veoir*, 'to see', fr. Lat. *vidēre*, see **vide** & **vision**. 1. Act of seeing; inspection, examination, by eye; sight: *this ruin is well worth our view; the jury had a view of the body; a private view* (of pictures on exhibition). Phr. *to keep, have, something in view*, under observation, within range of vision, under one's eye; also (fig.) in one's mind or memory; *on view*, on exhibition; *in full view of*, so as to be visible to, or from. 2. **a** Something that is seen; impression presented to the eye; a prospect, a sight, a scene: *a fine view of the surrounding country, of the proceedings, of the Lord Mayor's show*; specif. **b** a prospect of nature, of a tract of country or natural scenery: *I want a house with a view*. 3. A representation in art, photography &c., of a scene, esp. of a landscape, a building &c.: *to do, take, some views of the Lakes, of a cathedral* &c. 4. **a** Mental impression; a critical survey based on a mental examination of anything; an estimate, sizing-up: *I have not yet formed a clear view of the situation; he presented quite a new view of the affair; I take a grave view of his conduct*; **b** an intellectual judgement, an opinion: *to hold extreme views; what are your views on Protection?; in my view it would be unwise to proceed further with the matter*; Phr. *in view of*, considering, seeing, having regard to. 5. Design, plan, intention; expectation: *I will try to meet your views in every way; I have quite other views for my son's future; I have views on a meal at the next town*. Phrs. *with a view to, with the view of*, with the intention of.

view (II.), vb. trans., fr. prec. 1. To inspect, look at: *to view the pictures, a house and grounds* &c.; specif., *to view the body* (of jury at an inquest). Phr. *an order to view*, authoritative permission to inspect (house, estate &c.) 2. (poet., obsolesc.) To see, look upon: *'that dear home she ne'er might view again'* (T. Haynes Bayly). 3. To contemplate, look forward to: *I can only view the future with misgiving*. 4. To have a specified view of, hold specified opinion concerning; to estimate: *I view his conduct in the gravest light*.

viewable, adj. [1. vū́abl; 2. vjū́əbl]. Prec. & **-able**. Capable of being viewed; visible.

view-finder, n. **view (I.)** & **finder**. The small aperture in a camera with a mirror in which is shown the view of that which is to be photographed.

view-hallo(o), n. [1. vū haló; 2. vjū həlóu]. The hallo(o) or call of huntsman when the fox is viewed on breaking cover.

viewless, adj. [1. vū́les; 2. vjū́lis]. **view (I.)** & **-less**. (poet.) **a** Invisible: *'Each stair ... drawn up to heaven sometimes Viewless'* (Milton, 'P. L.' iii. 516-18); **b** unseeing, blind.

viewy, adj. [1. vū́i; 2. vjū́i]. **view (I.)** & **-y**. Full of views and opinions, esp. of fantastic views; visionary; cranky.

vigil, n. [1. víjil; 2. vídžil]. Lat. *vigilia*, 'wakefulness, sleeplessness', fr. *vigil*, 'awake, wakeful, alert', fr. the base in *vigēre*, 'to be lively, to flourish'; this base is cogn. w. that in Lat. *vegēre*, 'to move, to excite' &c., see **vegetable**; cp. also **wake (I.)**. 1. The act of being awake; the act of watching, e.g. in a sick-room, or over the dead. 2. **a** Devotional waking and watching; *vigils*, nocturnal devotions; **b** specif., the night spent in prayer before a feast of the Church; the eve of a feast-day.

vigilance, n. [1. víjilans; 2. vídžiləns]. Lat. *vigilantia*; see **vigilant** & **-ce**. 1. Watchfulness, alertness. 2. (med.) Insomnia, sleeplessness.

vigilance committee, n. 1. (chiefly U.S.A.) Voluntary, self-chosen body of citizens who assume responsibility for the preservation of order, and the summary punishment of crime in a community which has no regular government, or in one in which the government is temporarily inadequate. 2. More usually *watch committee*, a similar voluntary local body in a town looking for breaches of morals, infringement of licensing laws &c. and reporting to the police, instigating prosecutions &c.

vigilant, adj. [1. víjilant; 2. vídžilənt], fr. Lat. *vigilant-(em)*, Pres. Part. of *vigilāre*, 'to watch, be wakeful', formed fr. *vigil*, 'wakeful' &c., see **vigil**. Watchful, alert; keenly alive to possible danger, and to the necessity of securing safety; attentive, wary.

vigilantly, adv. Prec. & **-ly**. In a vigilant manner; with vigilance.

vigilantness, n. See prec. & **-ness**. State, quality, of being vigilant; vigilance.

vignette (I.), n. [1. vinyét; 2. vinjét]. Fr., dimin. fr. *vigne*, 'vine', see **vine**, & **-ette**. 1. (obs.) Originally, a decoration consisting of conventionalized representation of vine leaves, tendrils, and bunches of grapes. 2. **a** A small ornamental design placed at the beginning or end of chapters or of books; **b** a picture or photograph which merges gradually in the surrounding background, without a definite boundary line. 3. **a** A small delicate illustration on the page of a book; **b** a short highly-wrought picture in words.

vignette (II.), vb. trans., fr. prec. To depict in the form of a vignette.

vignettist, n. [1. vinyétist; 2. vinjétist]. **vignette (I.)** & **-ist**. A maker of vignettes.

vigoroso, adv. [1. vìgorōsō; 2. vìgoróusou]. Ital., fr. L. Lat. *vigōrōsus*, see **vigorous**. (musical direction) With vigour.

vigorous, adj. [1. vígorus; 2. vígərəs]. L. Lat. *vigōrōsus*, see **vigour** & **-ous**. 1. Abounding in bodily or mental vigour, vitality; strong, potent; virile. 2. **a** Exhibiting vigour in bodily growth, activity, action; active, lively: *a vigorous plant; a vigorous player; a vigorous attack*; **b** showing, acting with, intellectual vigour and strength of character; forcible, forceful; animated: *a vigorous thinker; a vigorous writer, style* &c.; *a vigorous commander*.

vigorously, adv. Prec. & **-ly**. In a vigorous manner.

vigorousness, n. See prec. & **-ness**. Condition, quality, of being vigorous; vigour.

vigour, n. [1. vígor; 2. vígə]. M.E., fr. O. Fr. *vigóur*, Lat. *vigor*, 'liveliness, activity, force'; fr. base in *vigēre*, 'to be lively', q.v. under **vigil**, & cp. **vegetable**. 1. **a** Animal strength, force, potency, vitality; **b** powers of intellect, mental strength. 2. **a** Strength, force, as exhibited in power of growth or of movement or action; activity; strength of bodily constitution; **b** force of character; **c** forceful, powerful action.

viking, n. [1. víking; 2. váikiŋ]. Affectedly & erroneously [víkiŋ]. O.N. víkingr; prob. fr. víg, 'a fight, battle'; cp. O.E. wíg, 'war'; cogn. w. Lat. vic-, form of vincere, 'to conquer', see **victor** & **vincible**; popularly confused w. sea-king, as though the second element in both words were the same, although there is in reality no connexion. An ancient Scandinavian pirate; one of the northern adventurers who from the 8th to the 10th century ravaged and plundered nearly every coast in Europe.

vilayet, n. [1. vìlayét, viláhyet; 2. vìlajét, vìldjet]. Turk. viláyet; see **Blighty**. One of the chief provinces of the old Ottoman Empire.

vile, adj. [1. vīl; 2. vail]. M.E., fr. O. Fr. vil, fr. Lat. vīlis, 'of small price or value'; trifling, paltry, common'; etymol. unexplained; objections have been taken to each of the attempted solutions. **1.** (rare, archaic) Of no account, common, mean: *silver was held a vile thing in the days of Solomon*; '*our vile body*' (Phil. iii. 21). **2.** Morally degraded and debased; depraved; sinful. **3.** (colloq., as term of disapprobation) Highly objectionable; of bad, inferior, quality; atrocious, shocking: *a perfectly vile hat; a very vile phrase*.

vilely, adv. Prec. & **-ly**. In a vile manner; (colloq.) very badly: *the dinner is vilely cooked; a vilely written letter*.

vileness, n. See prec. & **-ness**. State, quality, of being vile.

vilify, vb. trans. [1. vílifī; 2. vílifai]. Lat. vilificāre, 'to esteem of small value', see **vile** & **-fy**. **1.** To speak ill of, to defame, traduce. **2.** (rare and archaic) To render vile; to degrade.

vilipend, vb. trans. [1. vílipend; 2. vílipend]. Lat. vilipendere, 'to hold in light esteem, to despise', fr. vīlis, see **vile**, & pendere, 'to weigh, estimate', see **pendant**. To speak slightingly of, to disparage.

villa, n. [1. víla; 2. vílə]. Lat. villa, 'a country house, seat, farm, villa', for *vīcsla, fr. vīcus, 'hamlet, village', see **vicinage**. **a** A house of some pretensions, or pretentiousness, detached, and with some ground round it, usually in a suburban area; also used **b** of a house, sometimes of considerable size in fairly large grounds, with a few acres of vineyard, olive-trees &c., used as a residence for part of the year, in Italy or the south of France: *a villa on the Riviera*.

villadom, n. [1. víladum; 2. vílədəm]. Prec. & **-dom**. Suburban society.

village, n. [1. vílij; 2. vílidž]. M.E., fr. O. Fr., fr. Lat. villāticus, 'connected with a villa, or country house', see **villa**. A collection of houses, larger than a hamlet, in a country district, usually an ancient settlement, containing a church and forming the residential nucleus of a parish.

village community, n. Term used by 19th century writers on early society, to designate a primitive organized agricultural community, concerning the precise structure of which some difference of opinion exists.

villager, n. [1. víliјеr; 2. vílidžə]. **village** & **-er**. One who lives in a village; a countryman; specif., one of the poorer, labouring inhabitants of a village.

villain, n. [1. vílan; 2. vílin, -ən]. M.E. villain, villein, fr. O. F., fr. L. Lat. villānus, 'pertaining to a villa, or farm', see **villa**. **1.** (hist.) Now usually spelt villein; **a** originally, a free-born peasant, one of an inferior class of landholders; **b** later (13th cent.) the term was applied to a class of serfs, adscript to the soil, and with no rights except to some degree of protection from their lord, by whom they could, however, be removed at will from such lands as they enjoyed. Later still the position of this class improved, so that they became free, and gradually, as regards tenure, developed into the class of copyholders. **2.** (obs. or archaic) A low-born person, a churl; a rustic boor. **3. a** A scoundrel; one likely to commit, or who has committed, grave crimes; an infamous knave; **b** used playfully and affectionately, as: *the young villain has finished the jam*; cp. similar use of rascal and rogue.

villa(i)nage, n. See **villeinage**.

villainous, adj. [1. vílanus; 2. vílənəs]. **villain** & **-ous**. **1.** Characteristic of a villain, **3 a**; infamous, exhibiting wickedness and rascality: *a villainous countenance*; *villainous conduct*. **2.** (colloq.) As general expression of disapproval; thoroughly bad in quality; badly done or made; ugly, nasty &c.: *a villainous piece of mutton, suit of clothes, dinner* &c.

villainously, adv. Prec. & **-ly**. **a** In a villainous manner; after the manner of a villain; **b** very badly: *a villainously delivered sermon* &c.

villainousness, n. See prec. & **-ness**. **a** State or quality of being villainous; **b** villainous conduct.

villainy, n. [1. vílani; 2. víləni]. M.E., fr. O. Fr. vile(i)nie; see **villain** & **-y**. **1.** (obs.) Boorishness, rudeness, discourtesy. **2.** Villainous conduct; great wickedness, rascality, blackguardism.

villanella, n. [1. vìlanéla; 2. vìlənélə]. Ital., see **villa**, **-an**, & **-elle**. Old Italian rustic dance accompanied by singing.

villanelle, n. [1. vìlanél; 2. vìlənél]. Fr. form of prec. A poem, esp. in French, usually of 19 lines, and with only two rhymes.

villatic, adj. [1. vilátik; 2. vilǽtik]. Lat. villāticus, 'pertaining to a farm', see **village**. **a** Pertaining to a country-house; **b** pertaining to a farm; rustic; **c** domestic: '*the perched roosts and nests in order rang'd Of tame villatic fowl*' (Milton, 'Samson', 1695; contrasted with *the eagle*).

villegiatura, n. [1. vilèjatoorá; 2. vilèdžatúrə]. Ital. villagio, see **village** & **-ture**. **a** Stay in the country; rustication; **b** a villa, house, in the country.

villein, n. [1. vílin; 2. vílin]. Spelling variant of **villain**, 1, with differentiation of meaning fr. **villain**, 2, 3.

villeinage, n. [1. vílinij; 2. vílinidž]. Prec. & **-age**. (feud. law) **a** Status of a villein, see **villain**, 1; **b** tenure by which a villein or villain held his land; copyhold.

villiform, adj. [1. vílifɔrm; 2. vílifɔ̄m]. See **villus** & **-form**. Resembling villi in form and appearance; resembling pile of velvet.

villosity, n. [1. vilósiti; 2. vilɔ́siti]. **villous** & **-ity**. Condition or quality of being villous.

villous, adj. [1. vílus; 2. víləs]. Lat. villōsus, 'hairy, shaggy', see **villus** & **-ous**. Covered with fine, woolly hairs; having a nap like velvet.

villus, n., pl. **villi** [1. vílus, -ī; 2. víləs, -ai]. Lat., 'shaggy hair, tuft of hair'; a dialectal variant of Lat. vellus, 'fleece'; pelt with wool left on it'; see **vellicate**. **1.** One of the minute processes resembling hairs which cover the mucous membrane of the intestines, giving a velvety appearance. **2.** One of the soft, woolly hairs found on some fruits and flowers.

vim, n. [1. vim; 2. vim]. Lat., acc. of vīs, 'force', see **vis**. (colloq.) Energy, vigour; spirit, abandon, go.

vimen, n. [1. vímen; 2. váimen]. Lat., 'a pliant twig, a switch'; an osier', fr. the base of viēre, 'to bend, twist, twine', see **vine** & **viti-**. A long, slender, pliant shoot or branch.

viminal, adj. [1. víminl; 2. váiminl]. Stem of prec. & **-al**. **a** Pertaining to, of the nature of, resembling, a shoot or osier; **b** tending to produce long, slender shoots.

vimineous, adj. [1. vimíneus; 2. vaimíniəs]. Stem of **vimen** & **-eous**. Viminal; consisting, made, of pliant stems.

vinaceous, adj. [1. vīnáshus; 2. vainéiʃəs]. See **vine** & **-aceous**. **a** Pertaining to, resembling, the vine, or grapes; **b** having the colour of red wine.

vinaigrette, n. [1. vìnāgrét; 2. vìneigrét]. Fr., fr. vinaigre, see **vinegar** & **-ette**. **a** A small gold or silver box with a perforated inner lid, for carrying on the person, containing a small portion of sponge soaked in aromatic vinegar; **b** a smelling-bottle.

vincibility, n. [1. vìnsibíliti; 2. vìnsibíliti]. Next word & **-ity**. Quality of being vincible.

vincible, adj. [1. vínsibl; 2. vínsɪbl]. Lat. vincibilis, 'that can be easily gained', fr. vincere, 'to conquer, defeat; to gain'; nasalized form of base *wic-, as in perf. vīci, 'I have conquered'; cogn. w. Goth. weihan; O.E. & O.H.G. wīgan, 'to fight'; see further **victor**. (rare) Conquerable; not invincible.

vincibleness, n. [1. vínsiblnes; 2. vínsɪblnis]. See prec. & **-ness**. Vincibility.

vinculum, n. [1. víngkūlum; 2. víŋkjuləm]. Lat., 'that with which anything is bound, a bond, a fetter', fr. base of vincīre, 'to bind, fetter'; an expansion of base *vi-, 'to bend, twist', as in viēre, cp. **viburnum** & **vimen** & see **vine** & **viti-**. **1.** A bond, a tie. **2.** (math.) A straight, horizontal line placed over two or more numbers of a compound quantity.

vindicability, n. [1. vìndikabíliti; 2. vìndikəbíliti]. Next word & **-ity**. Quality of being vindicable.

vindicable, adj. [1. víndikabl; 2. víndikəbl]. See next word & **-able**. Capable of being vindicated or justified.

vindicate, vb. trans. [1. víndikāt; 2. víndikeit], fr. Lat. vindicāt-(um), P.P. of vindicāre, 'to lay legal claim to anything'; to revenge, avenge, take vengeance on'; formed fr. vindic-, stem of vindex, 'one who lays legal claim to anything, a claimant; a protector, deliverer; an avenger'; the origin of vin- is disputed; the second element is the base *deik̑-, *dik̑-, 'to show, point out' &c., q.v. under **diction**. **1.** To establish the justice and validity of, to make good, to prove, obtain recognition of: *to vindicate one's claim, rights*. **2.** To disprove, dispose of, aspersions, accusations, imputations against; to establish integrity or soundness of: *to vindicate one's honour, character, honesty* &c.; *to vindicate one's judgement*; also, to defend (person) from imputations &c.

vindication, n. [1. vìndikáshun; 2. vìndikéiʃən]. Prec. & **-ion**. Act of vindicating; state of being vindicated; **a** establishment of claims &c.; **b** justification, defence, exculpation, from or against accusations, imputations &c.

vindicative, adj. [1. víndikativ; 2. víndikətiv]. **vindicate** & **-ive**. Tending to vindicate; of the nature of vindication.

vindicatively, adv. Prec. & **-ly**. So as to vindicate.

vindicativeness, n. See prec. & **-ness**. Quality of being vindicative.

vindicatory, adj. [1. víndikaturi; 2. víndikətəri]. **vindicate** & **-ory**. Vindicative.

vindictive, adj. [1. vindíktiv; 2. vindíktiv]. Lat. vindict-, 'punishment, vengeance, revenge', see **vindicate**, & **-ive**. **a** Animated by, arising from, characterized by, a desire for revenge; bearing a grudge, revengeful: *a vindictive character, spirit, action*; **b** punitive: *vindictive damages*, heavy damages awarded against a defendant with the intention of punishing him.

vindictively, adv. Prec. & **-ly**. In a vindictive manner.

vindictiveness, n. See prec. & **-ness**. **a** Quality of being vindictive; **b** a vindictive action or spirit.

vine, n. [1. vīn; 2. vain]. M.E., fr. O. Fr. vigne, fr. Lat. vīnea, 'a plantation of grapes, a vineyard', fr. vīnum, 'wine', for *woinom*; cogn. w. Gk. oínē, 'the vine', oînos, 'wine', for *woin-*; cp. further Lat. vītis, 'grape vine', vine-branch', wh. together w. vīnum, goes back to the base *vī- &c., 'to bend, to twist, to twine, ramble', as in Lat. viēre, 'to bend,

twist' &c.; see further under **viti-**, & cp. **vimen**. O.E. *win*, see **wine**, is borrowed direct fr. Lat. *vīnum*. 1. The plant, *Vitis*, esp. species *V. vinifera*, which bears grapes. 2. Any plant with long, slender, pliant stems and tendrils, which twists and climbs or rambles; esp. the trailing shoots and stems of such a plant: *a hop-vine; the vines of a melon, of a pea* &c.

vine-beetle, n. Kind of beetle that destroys the shoots and leaves of the vine.

vine-borer, n. Reddish-brown weevil which bores into the stems of the vine.

vine-dresser, n. One who tends and prunes grape-vines.

vinegar, n. [1. vínegar; 2. vínigə]. M.E. *vinegre*, Fr. *vinaigre*, lit. 'sour wine', see **vine** & **eager**. A liquid of extreme acidity, used as a preservative and a condiment, made by the fermentation of diluted wine, beer, or cider.

vinegar eel, n. Minute worm found in vinegar and in sour or fermenting vegetable substances.

vinegar plant, n. Microscopic fungus which produces vinegar by causing fermentation of wine &c.

vinegar tree, n. Kind of sumach the acid berries of which are sometimes used to flavour vinegar.

vinegary, adj. [1. vínegari; 2. vínigəri]. **vinegar** & **-y**. 1. a Saturated with, tasting of, vinegar; b very sour, or acid. 2. (fig.) Expressing ill-temper, bitterness, malignity &c.: *a vinegary smile*.

vine maple, n. Kind of American maple with recumbent stems which strike root and form a dense thicket.

vinery, n. [1. víneri; 2. váinəri]. **vine** & **-ry**. Heated glass-house in which grapes are grown.

vineyard, n. [1. vínyerd; 2. vínjəd]. **vine** & **yard**. An enclosed piece of ground in which grape-vines are grown.

vingt-et-un, n. [1. vánt ā ē; 2. vǣteŏ]. Fr., 'twenty-one'. Card game in which each player attempts to obtain from the dealer cards showing a total of 21 pips and no more.

vinic, adj. [1. vínik; 2. váinik]. Lat. *vīnum*, 'wine', see **vine**, & **-ic**. Pertaining to, occurring in, wine.

vinicultural, adj. [1. vìnikúlchural; 2. vìnikáltʃərəl]. **viniculture** & **-al**. Pertaining to viniculture.

viniculturalist, n. [1. vìnikúlchuralist; 2. vìnikáltʃərəlist]. Prec. & **-ist**. Person who engages in viniculture.

viniculture, n. [1. vínikulchur; 2. vínikaltʃə]. **vine-**, fr. Lat. *vīnum*, see **vine**, & **culture**. The cultivation of the vine; viticulture.

viniferous, adj. [1. vìníferus; 2. vainífərəs]. Lat. *vīnum*, 'wine', see **vine**, & **-ferous**. Producing wine.

vinification, n. [1. vìnifikắshun; 2. vìnifikéiʃən]. **vini-** as in prec. words, & **-fication**. Process whereby grape or other fruit juice becomes alcoholic by fermentation.

vinificator, n. [1. vínifikàtor; 2. vínifikèitə]. See prec. & **-or**. Apparatus for collecting alcoholic vapours in wine making.

vin ordinaire, n. [1. ván ordinǎr; 2. vǣn ōdinéə]. Fr., 'common wine'. The cheap wine most abundantly produced in a given district in France; commonly mixed with water.

vinosity, n. [1. vīnósiti; 2. vainósiti]. Lat. *vīnōsitāt-(em)*, see **vinous** & **-ity**. Quality of being vinous.

vinous, adj. [1. vínus; 2. váinəs]. Lat. *vīnōsus*, 'full of, drunk with, wine; tasting of wine', fr. *vīnum*, 'wine', see **vine**, & **-ous**. 1. Connected with wine; a having the properties, taste, smell, of wine; b wine-coloured. 2. a Inspired by wine: *vinous mirth*; b affected by wine: *in a somewhat vinous condition*.

vintage, n. [1. víntij; 2. víntidʒ]. M.E. *vindage*, *vendage*, fr. O. Fr. *vendenge*, cp. Mod. Fr. *vendange*, 'the gathering of grapes', fr. Lat. *vīndēmia*, 'grape-gathering', fr. *vīnum*, 'wine', see **vine**, & an abstract suff. formed fr. *dēmere*, 'to take away', formed fr. *dē*, 'away, from', see **de-**, & *emere*, 'to take, receive'; later, 'to purchase', see second element in **exempt**, **redeem**, & **pre-emption**; the Mod. Engl. word has been influenced in form by association w. **vintner**. 1. a Act of gathering and collecting grapes from the vines for wine-making; b the period in a season during which this takes place. 2. The yield of wine grapes in a given year: *a poor, an abundant, vintage this year; the great vintages of the seventies*. 3. Vintage wine: *he brought out his rare old vintages*.

vintager, n. [1. víntijer; 2. víntidʒə]. Prec. & **-er**. Grape-gatherer.

vintage wine, n. That made from the vintage of a specially good year, carefully set apart as the wine of that particular year.

vintner, n. [1. víntner; 2. víntnə]. M.E. *viniter*, *vintener*, fr. O. Fr. *vinetier*, fr. *vinet*, dimin. of *vin*, 'wine', fr. Lat. *vīnum*, see **vine**, & **-er**. 1. A wholesale seller of wine; a wine merchant. 2. *The Vintners*, *Vintners' Company*, one of the great, ancient City livery companies of London.

vinum, n. [1. vínum; 2. váinəm]. Lat., 'wine', see **vine**. (pharm.) Medicated wine; medicinal substance dissolved in wine.

viny, adj. [1. víni; 2. váini]. **vine** & **-y**. Pertaining to, resembling, abounding in, vines.

viol, n. [1. víol; 2. váiəl]. M.E., fr. Fr. *viole*, fr. Ital. or Span. *viola*, or Provenç. *viula*. Origin uncertain; the Provenç. may be fr. an earlier *viudla*, w. metathesis, fr. *vidula*, fr. L. Lat. *vītula*, 'a viol', see **fiddle**, but this is very doubtful. Musical instrument of the fiddle family; the size and the number of strings vary; varieties are bass-viol, or double bass; viol da braccio; see also next word.

viola (I.), n. [1. víola, viǒla; 2. váiələ, vióulə]. Ital. See prec. Specif., the *viol(a) da braccio*, or tenor violin, larger than the ordinary violin, and smaller than the 'cello; played held in the left hand; its strings are tuned c g d a; the strings are thicker than those of a violin, and the tone deeper; *viola da gamba*, a larger type, held between the legs, resembling the 'cello.

viola (II.), n. [1. víola; 2. váiələ]. Lat., according to Walde, a dimin. of *via-*, borrowed fr. Gk. *ion*, earlier *wion-*; perh. related to the base in Gk. *itus*, 'edge or rim', wh. is prob. cogn. w. Lat. *viēre*, 'to bend, twist', see **viti-** & **vine**, the viola or violet being used in weaving wreaths and crowns. Genus of flowering plants, of the family *Violaceae*, including the pansy; the flowers are predominatingly blue, purple, white, and yellow, in various shades.

violable, adj. [1. víolabl; 2. váiələbl]. See **violate** & **-able**. Capable of being violated.

Violaceae, n. pl. [1. vìolásiē; 2. vàiouléisi-ī]. See **viola (II.)** & **-aceae**. (bot.) Large family of flowering plants including violet and viola.

violaceous, adj. [1. vìoláshus; 2. vàiouléiʃəs]. See prec. & **-aceous**. a (bot.) Belonging to the family Violaceae; b having the colour of violets, of a blue purple.

violate, vb. trans. [1. víolāt; 2. váiəleit], fr. Lat. *violāt-(um)*, P.P. type of *violāre*, 'to treat with violence; to injure, dishonour', formed fr. *viol-*, as in Lat. *violent-(em)*, see **violent**, wh. is an expansion of *vīs*, 'strength, force', see **vis**. 1. (obs. or archaic) To treat with violence, mishandle, abuse. 2. To desecrate, profane, treat with indignity (that which is sacred): *to violate a tomb, a shrine, a church* &c. 3. a To infringe, break, disregard, act in contradiction to (*a promise, oath, treaty* &c.); b to touch, seize, possess, wrongfully: '*to violate The sacred fruit forbidden*' (Milton, 'P. L.', ix. 903-4). 4. To have carnal knowledge of, possess, (a woman) by force; to rape, to ravish.

violation, n. [1. vìoláshun; 2. vàiəléiʃən]. Lat. *violātiōn-(em)*, see prec. & **-ion**. Act of violating; state of being violated (in various senses); a desecration; b infringement, breaking (of an oath &c.); c interruption of, breaking into (a sleep, privacy &c.); d rape.

violence, n. [1. víolens; 2. váiələns]. Fr., fr. Lat. *violentia*, see **violent** & **-ce**. 1. a Energetic, forcible action; effort vigorously exerted; impetuosity, vehemence: *to attack an enemy with violence*; b powerful, impetuous, tumultuous movement: *the violence of the wind and waves*; also c of non-material effort or vigour: *violence of invective, of a person's passions, emotions* &c. 2. Force, strength, effort, exerted with undue, unnecessary, or unlawful vehemence and rigour; roughness; turbulence; (in material and non-material sense) *to handle a prisoner, a patient, with violence; the mob behaved with great violence; crimes of violence; the speech was uncompromising, but free from violence*. 3. Injury, insult, profanation offered to what is sacred: *you have done violence to my deepest convictions; to do violence to the holy things of God*. 4. Specif., rape.

violent, adj. [1. víolent; 2. váiələnt]. Fr., fr. Lat. *violent-(em)*, see **violate**. 1. Characterized by very forcible, vehement, rapid, often sudden, movement; boisterous, tumultuous, impetuous: *a violent storm, wind, earthquake*. 2. a Requiring, exhibiting, a powerful voluntary exertion of muscular strength: *violent efforts, exertion, struggle to escape; a violent blow*; b showing results of, caused by, some powerful stimulus independent of the will; severe, intense: *a violent cough, spasm* &c. 3. Due to a powerful external physical cause; caused by violence; unnatural: *a violent death*. 4. Characterized by, arising from, violence of the emotions and passions: *a violent rage, a violent speech* &c. 5. (as intens.) a Very great, of intense severity: *a violent toothache; a violent attack of the gout*; b exaggerated, extreme: *a violent contrast of colour*. Phr. (law) *a violent presumption*, one based on evidence that is practically conclusive.

violescent, adj. [1. vìolésent; 2. vàiəlésənt]. **viola** & **-escent**. Tending towards the colour of violets.

violet (I.), n. [1. víolet; 2. váiəlit]. Fr. *violette*, see **viola (I.)** & **-et(te)**. 1. Flower or plant of the viola species; specif., a common sort, wild or cultivated, with strongly scented flowers, purple, mauve, or white, also a rather similar flower found in woods &c. without a scent. 2. The colour resembling that of violets, a bluish-purple, found at the higher end of the spectrum.

violet (II.), adj., fr. prec. Having the colour of violets; bluish-purple.

violet-powder, n. Toilet-powder scented with the perfume of violets.

violet-root, n. Trade name for orris-root.

violin, n. [1. vìolín; 2. vàiəlín]. Ital. *violino*, dimin. of **viola (I.)**. A fiddle; smaller instrument of the viola family, having a treble tone and four strings, g, d, a, e, held in left hand and supported under the chin, the notes being formed by the fingers of left hand upon the strings, which are set in vibration with a bow.

violinist, n. [1. vìolínist; 2. vàiəlínist]. Prec. & **-ist**. A player of the violin.

violist, n. [1. víolist; 2. váiəlist]. **viol** or **viola (I.)** & **-ist**. Player of the viol or viola.

violoncellist, n. [1. vĕolonchélist; 2. vìələntʃélist]. Next word & **-ist**. Player of the violoncello.

violoncello, n. [1. vĕolonchélŏ; 2. vìələntʃélou]. Ital., dimin. of *violone*, 'a large viola'; see **viola (I.)**. A bass viol; stringed instrument similar in shape to a viola and a violin, but much larger than the former; played by being held between the knees and fingered like a violin. The strings are very thick and have a bass tone.

violone, n. [1. vĕolŏnā; 2. vìoulóunei]. Ital., see **violoncello**. 1. The largest instrument of the viola family; the contra-bass, or double bass. 2. An organ stop with similar quality of tone.

viper, n. [1. víper; 2. váipə]. Fr. *vipère*, fr. Lat. *vīpera*; fr. base **wei-p-*, **wei-b-*, 'to move rapidly, twist, coil', see discussion under **vibrate** & **vine**; the type **woip-* occurs in Goth. *(bi)-waibjan*, 'to weave round, wind about'. **1.** Any of several venomous snakes, of which the adder is the only one found in Britain. Phr. *to cherish a viper in one's bosom*, to show kindness to one who proves an unworthy and ungrateful traitor. **2.** A malignant, ungrateful, treacherous person.

viperiform, adj. [1. víperiform; 2. váipərifɔ̄m]. Prec. & **-form**. Shaped like, resembling, a viper.

viperine, adj. [1. víperin; 2. váipərin]. **viper** & **-ine**. Pertaining to, resembling, of the nature of, a viper.

viperish, adj. [1. víperish; 2. váipəriʃ]. **viper** & **-ish**. Like a viper in character; malignant, treacherous.

viperous, adj. [1. víperus; 2. váipərəs]. **viper** & **-ous**. Viperish.

viperously, adv. Prec. & **-ly**. In a viperous way.

viperousness, n. See prec. & **-ness**. Quality of being viperous; malignity, spite, treachery.

virago, n. [1. virágō; 2. viréigou]. Lat., 'a man-like, vigorous maiden; a female warrior', fr. *vir*, 'a man', see **virile**. A violent, brawling female; a loud-voiced, ill-tempered, scolding woman; a vixen, termagant, shrew.

virelai, n. [1. vírelā; 2. vírəlei]. O. Fr. *vireli*, perh. orig. a meaningless refrain, later *-lai*, through association w. **lay (I.)**. One of several kinds of Old French poems, having two rhymes and a refrain, or in stanza form, the stanzas being interlocked by recurrent rhymes.

virescence, n. [1. virésens; 2. virésəns]. **virescent** & **-ce**. **a** Process of becoming, state of being, green; greenness; **b** specif. (bot.) abnormal greenness in petals of flowers usually white or coloured.

virescent, adj. [1. virésent; 2. virésənt]. Lat. *virescent-(em)*, Pres. Part. of *virescere*, 'to grow green', freq. of *virēre*, 'to be green, to be fresh and vigorous; to flourish', cp. *viridis*, 'green'; prob. related to *vīvere*, 'to live'; see **viridity** & words there referred to. Becoming, turning, green; greenish.

virgate (I.), adj. [1. vérgāt; 2. vágeit]. Lat. *virgātus*, 'made of twigs or osiers', fr. *virga*, 'twig, sprout, switch, rod'; this is for earlier **vizgā-*, the basal meaning of wh. seems to be 'a pliant shoot or twig'; cogn. w. Scrt. *vēškáš*, 'a noose'; O.H.G. *wisk*, 'a whisk, switch', see **whist (II.)**, w. wh. cp. O.E. *wioxian*, fr. **wiscian*, 'to clean (a house &c.)', lit. 'to sweep it with a whisk or besom of twigs', for suff. see **-ate**. (bot.) Rod- or wand-shaped.

virgate (II.), n. L. Lat. *virgāta*, *virgāta terrae*, a land measure; cp. **rod** in sense of a measure. Same word as prec. Old English measure of land equal to a quarter of an acre.

Virgilian, adj. [1. vĕrjílian; 2. vādžílian], fr. name of Virgil, Latin poet, & **-an**. Connected with, in the style of, Virgil.

virgin (I.), n. [1. vĕrjin; 2. vádžin]. M.E., fr. O. Fr. *virgine*, fr. Lat. *virgin-(em)*, 'a virgin'; stem of **Virgo**. **1. a** A woman who has had no carnal knowledge of a man; **b** a member of a female religious or other order bound by vows of chastity. **2. a** *The Virgin*, the Mother of Christ, the Virgin Mary; **b** *a Virgin*, picture or statue of the Virgin Mary. **3.** (more rarely) A man who has had no carnal knowledge of women. **4.** Female insect that produces eggs without impregnation. **5.** The sign of the zodiac, *Virgo*.

virgin (II.), adj., fr. prec. **1.** Being a virgin, chaste: '*For I was ever virgin save for thee*' (Tennyson). Phr. *the Virgin Queen*, Queen Elizabeth. **2.** Characteristic of, befitting, a virgin; chaste, modest: *virgin blushes*; *virgin fancies*. **3.** Untouched, untrampled, undefiled, unsullied: *virgin snow*. **4.** Undisturbed, unapproached; unmixed; never yet used; never before cultivated; in various Phrs.: *virgin forest*, from which no timber has been cut; *virgin gold*, pure, unalloyed; *virgin honey*, that which flows from an unopened comb, without pressure; *virgin oil*, that produced from the first, light pressure of olives; *virgin parchment*, that made from the skins of new-born lambs; *a virgin peak*, one which has never yet been scaled; *virgin soil*, (i.) land which has never before been cultivated; (ii.) (fig.) said of a mind which is unsophisticated and untouched by prejudice, or which is new to a particular range of ideas.

virginal (I.), adj. [1. vĕrjinal; 2. vádžinəl]. Fr. *virginal*, fr. Lat. *virginālis*, see **virgin (I.)** & **-al**. Belonging to, befitting, becoming in, a virgin; unsullied, pure, innocent: *virginal bloom, modesty* &c.; *virginal generation*, parthenogenesis; *virginal membrane*, the hymen.

virginal (II.), n., fr. prec.; prob. so called fr. being commonly played by young men & girls. A kind of spinet, with one string to a note, square and without legs, popular in the 16th and 17th centuries; (also in pl.) *the virginals*.

virginhood, n. [1. vĕrjinhood; 2. vádžinhud]. **virgin** & **-hood**. State of being a virgin.

Virginia, n. [1. vĕrjínia; 2. vādžínia]. One of the States of N. America; named after the *Virgin Queen* (Elizabeth). *Virginia creeper*, Ampelopsis, ornamental rambling and climbing plant with large leaves, which turn red in autumn, grown on the walls of buildings; *Virginia tobacco*, also called simply *Virginia*, tobacco grown in Virginia and other Southern States of U.S.A.

Virginian, adj. & n. [1. vĕrjínian; 2. vādžínian]. Prec. & **-an**. **a** adj. Belonging to, coming from, the State of Virginia; **b** n., a native of Virginia.

virginity, n. [1. vĕrjíniti; 2. vādžíniti]. M.E., fr. Fr. *virginité*, fr. Lat. *virginitāt-(em)*, see **virgin** & **-ity**. State, quality, of being a virgin.

virgo, n. [1. vĕrgō; 2. vágou]. Lat., 'virgin'; etymol. doubtful, but most prob. connected w. Lat. *virga*, 'young, pliant shoot, twig', see **virgate (I.)**; cp. *young sprig*, for a youth. **1.** (cap.) The constellation, known also as *the Virgin*, the sixth sign of the zodiac. **2.** *Virgo intacta*, Lat., 'intact virgin', a woman or girl who is a complete virgin, never approached by a man.

virgulate, adj. [1. vĕrgūlāt; 2. vágjuleit]. Lat. *virgula*, dimin. of *virga*, 'a rod' &c., see **virgate**, & **-ate**. Rod-shaped.

virgule, n. [1. vĕrgūl; 2. vágjūl]. Fr., fr. Lat. *virgula*, see prec. A comma in punctuation.

viridescence, n. [1. viridésens; 2. viridésəns]. Next word & **-ce**. **1.** Greenness, verdancy, verdure; colour of grass or of young foliage. **2.** Freshness, vigour, youthful vitality.

viridescent, adj. [1. viridésent; 2. viridésənt]. Lat. *viridescent-(em)*, Pres. Part. of *viridescere*, 'to grow green', formed fr. *viridis*, 'green', see **viridity**, & freq. suff. See **-esce**. Greenish, verging on green in colour.

viridity, n. [1. viríditi; 2. viríditi]. Lat. *viriditāt-(em)*, fr. *viridis*, 'green', & **-ity**; *viridis* for **gʷir-* is connected w. Lat. *virēre*, 'to be green, to bloom, to flourish', see **virescent**; cp. the cognates, Gk. *dierós*, fr. **gʷieros*, 'moist, fresh, juicy; fresh, active'; Scrt. *jiráš*, 'lively, active, stirring', also for **gʷīr-*, & O. Slav. *žirŭ*, fr. *gʷiru-*, 'pasture'. The underlying base is **gʷī-*, 'to live, be lively' &c., whence Lat. *vīvere*, 'to live', see **vivacious**, & *vīta*, 'life', see **vital**; cp. also **verdant, verdure, vert (I.)**. **a** Greenness, esp. of grass or young foliage; **b** mental or bodily freshness, liveliness, springiness: *to show a healthy viridity in old age*.

virile, adj. [1. víril; 2. víril], more rarely [1. vírīl; 2. váiərail]. Lat. *virīlis*, 'belonging to a man, male, masculine; manly, firm, vigorous, spirited', fr. *vir*, 'a male person, a man'; cogn. w. Goth. *wair*, 'man'; O.H.G., O.S., & O.E. *wer*, see first element in **werewolf**; Scrt. *vīraš*, 'man, hero'; Lith. *výras*, 'man'. The word is ultimately fr. the base in Lat. *vīs*, 'strength, vigour', for *vīr-*, see **vis**; cp. also **virtue**. **1.** Having the physical attributes and qualities of fully grown, mature man; specif., capable of procreation, not impotent. **2.** Having the characteristics of a man in habits, mind, character; male, masculine, manly; contrasted with *womanly, feminine*: *virile strength, courage, voice, glance*; *a virile intelligence*. **3.** Hence, strong, vigorous, forceful, forcible, spirited, sturdy, robust: *a virile government*; *a virile mind*; *a virile literary style*.

virilescence, n. [1. virilésens; 2. virilésəns]. Next word & **-ce**. The acquiring of male characters by a female animal when old or sterile.

virilescent, adj. [1. virilésent; 2. virilésənt]. Lat. *virīl-*, see **virile**, & inchoative suff., see **-esce**. Tending to acquire male characters; of female animals in old age and sterility.

virility, n. [1. viríliti; 2. viríliti]. Lat. *virilitāt-(em)*. See **virile** & **-ity**. Quality of being virile; **a** potency, power of procreation; **b** masculinity of character &c., manliness; **c** vigour, force, robustness: *virility of style*.

virose, adj. [1. vírōs; 2. váiərous]. Lat. *vīrōsus*, 'poisonous', fr. *vīrus*, 'poison', see **virus**, & **-ose**. Poisonous; having a bad smell, fetid.

virous, adj. [1. vírus; 2. váiərəs]. Prec. w. suff. **-ous**. Virose.

virtu, n. [1. vertōō; 2. vātū]. Ital. *virtù*, 'excellence', see **virtue**. **1.** Esp. in Phr. *object, article, of virtu*, object &c. possessing qualities of artistic merit, and value, of rarity and exquisite workmanship. **2.** Love for, knowledge of, fine art and craftsmanship; fondness for antiquities and curios.

virtual, adj. [1. vĕrchooal, vĕrtūal; 2. vātʃuəl, vātjuəl]. Fr. *virtuel*; see **virtue** & **-al**. Being in effect and essence, though not in name, that specified; being for all practical purposes though not defined as such: *the Prime Minister is the virtual ruler of the country*.

virtuality, n. [1. vĕrchooáliti, vĕrtūáliti; 2. vātʃuǽliti, vātjuǽliti]. Prec. & **-ity**. State, quality, of being virtual.

virtually, adv. [1. vĕrchooali; 2. vātʃuəli]. **virtual** & **-ly**. In point of fact, to all intents and purposes: *the dialect of the City of London in the 12th and 13th centuries was virtually the same as that of Essex*.

virtue, n. [1. vĕrchōō; 2. vātʃu, -ū]. M.E., fr. O. Fr. *vertú*, Lat. *virtūt-(em)*, stem of *virtus*, 'manliness, manhood; excellence, virtue, merit; moral perfection, virtue; courage, valour; value', fr. *vir*, 'a man', see **virile**. **1.** Positive, active, quality or property; capacity to affect a definite, specific result; potency: '*When that Aprille with his shoures sote . . . had . . . bathéd every veyne in swich licóur, Of which vertú engendred is the flour*' (Chaucer, Prol. of 'C. T.', 1-4); *Jesus perceived that virtue had gone out of Him when a woman touched Him in the crowd*; *every quack extols the virtue of the nostrums which he sells*. Phrs. *by virtue of*, by means of, through the instrumentality of; *in virtue of*, on the strength of, on the ground of: *promoted in virtue of his high descent, rather than of his abilities*. **2.** Good quality, merit, value: *a place which lacks the virtue of beauty, but has at least that of being bracing*. **3. a** Moral excellence; the practice of goodness; integrity, uprightness of character, honourable conduct, rectitude: *we have all been taught to love virtue, but we too often forget it in our conduct*; **b** some specific moral excellence: *humility is a virtue difficult to attain to*. Phrs. *the cardinal virtues*, prudence, fortitude, temperance, justice; *theological, Christian, virtues*, faith, hope, charity; *to make a virtue of necessity*, affect to do from a sense of duty that which one is compelled to do. **4.** Chastity, esp. in a woman: *it is hard for a poor, unprotected girl to preserve her virtue in a dissolute city*. Phr. *a lady of easy virtue*, one who is unchaste. **5.** One of the orders of celestial beings: '*Thrones, dominations, princedoms, virtues, powers*' (Milton, 'P. L.', v. 601).

virtuosity, n. [1. vĕrtūósiti; 2. vǎtjuósiti]. virtuoso & -ity. 1. Quality, state, of being a virtuoso. 2. High degree of technical skill and dexterity in one of the fine arts, esp. in music. 3. Fondness for, knowledge of, articles of virtu.

virtuoso, n. [1. vĕrtūósō, vĕrtōō-; 2. vǎtjuóusou, virtū-], pl. **virtuosos**, **virtuosi** [1. vĕrtōōŏsē; 2. virtūóusī]. Ital., fr. Lat. virtuōsus, see **virtuous**. 1. A person with a high degree of technical skill as a performer in one of the fine arts, esp. in music. 2. Person with an intimate knowledge of curios, antiques &c.

virtuous, adj. [1. vĕrchoous; 2. vǎtʃuəs]. Lat. virtuōsus, see **virtue** & **-ous**. 1. Having, practising, moral virtue; morally good; honourable. 2. Specif. (of women) chaste.

virtuously, adv. Prec. & -ly. In a virtuous manner.

virtuousness, n. See prec. & -ness. Quality of being virtuous; the practice of virtue.

virulence, **-cy**, n. [1. vírūlens(i); 2. vírjuləns(i)]. Next word & -ce or -cy. Quality, state, of being virulent (in material and non-material senses).

virulent, adj. [1. vírulent; 2. vírjulənt]. Fr., fr. Lat. vīrulentus, 'poisonous', see **virus**. 1. Poisonous, venomous; deadly, noxious, extremely severe: *a virulent disease*; *measles of the most virulent kind*. 2. Malignant, bitter, spiteful: *virulent animosity*, *abuse* &c.

virulently, adv. Prec. & -ly. In a virulent manner, to a virulent degree; with virulence.

virus, n. [1. vírus; 2. váirəs]. Lat., 'a slimy liquid, slime; a poisonous liquid, poison; pungency'; for *vīzus, cogn. w. Gk. īós, 'poison', fr. *wīsos; Scrt. visám, 'poison'; connected w. Scrt. vešati, 'melts, liquefies'; also w. Lat. viscum, 'mistletoe', lit. 'the sticky berry', see **viscum**. 1. (med.) The active organic element or poison which infects with and produces contagious disease: *the virus of scarlet fever, of rabies, anthrax* &c. 2. Any influence which causes moral corruption, which affects adversely the mind or the spirit: *the virus of revolution, of sedition, heresy* &c.

vis, n. [1. vis; 2. vis]. Lat. vis, pl. vīres, 'physical or mental strength; force, vigour, power, energy; hostile force, strength, violence'; cogn. w. Gk. *is* for *wís, 'strength, force, nerve, thew, sinew'; Scrt. váyas, 'vital force'; connected w. Lat. vir, 'man', see **virile**. Used in various Phrs.: *vis animi*, 'force of soul', courage; *vis inertiae*, 'force of inertia', tendency of bodies to remain at rest if resting, or to move uniformly in a straight line if moving; *vis medicātrix nātūrae*, 'healing power of nature', natural power of recovery, tendency to throw off disease; *vis mortua*, 'dead force', tendency towards motion; *vis mōtīva*, power of producing mechanical effect; *vis vīva*, 'living force', measure of a body's mass multiplied by the measure of its velocity. In plural, see **ultra vires**.

visa, n. & vb. [1. véza; 2. vízə]. See **visé**.

visage, n. [1. vízij; 2. vízidʒ]. Fr., fr. O. Fr. vis, 'face', cp. **vis-à-vis**, fr. Lat. vīsus, 'sight, faculty of seeing; a look, a glance', see **vision**(I.), & **-age**. The face, countenance, of a human being; rarely applied to the face of an animal.

visaged, adj. [1. vízijd; 2. vízidʒd]. Prec. & -ed. Having a specified kind of visage; esp. in compounds: *dark-visaged*, *long-visaged* &c.

visard. See **visor**.

vis-à-vis, adv. & n. [1. víz a vē; 2. víz ə vī]. Fr., 'face to face', fr. vis, 'face', see **visage**. 1. adv. Opposite: *he and I sat vis-à-vis at meals during the voyage*. 2. n. a Person placed, sitting, opposite to another: *I haven't yet spoken to my vis-à-vis*; b a conveyance in which passengers sit facing one another; c S-shaped couch or seat in which persons sitting at the ends face each other.

viscacha, n. [1. viskácha; 2. viskǽtʃə]. Span., fr. S. American. S. American burrowing rodent, resembling, but larger than, a chinchilla, with valuable soft grey fur.

viscaria, n. [1. viskária; 2. viskéəriə]. fr. Lat. viscum, 'mistletoe; birdlime', see **viscum** & **viscous**. Alpine plant with upright viscous stems.

viscera, n. pl. [1. vísera; 2. vísərə]. Lat., pl. of viscus, 'internal organs of an animal'; according to Walde, most prob. fr. base *wei- &c., 'to twist, wind round', as in Lat. viēre, 'to twist, twine' &c., see **vine** & **viti-**. The internal organs of the animal body, esp. the heart, lungs, bowels, liver &c.

visceral, adj. [1. víseral; 2. vísərəl]. Prec. & -al. Pertaining to, connected with, of the nature of, viscera.

viscerate, vb. trans. [1. víserāt; 2. vísəreit]. viscera & -ate. (rare) To eviscerate, remove the viscera from.

visceri-, **viscero-**, pref. Forms of **viscera** used in compounds: *visceri-pericardial*, of the body cavity of molluscs, which is divided into two parts, the upper containing the heart, the lower the other viscera; *viscero-motor*, conducting motor impulses to the viscera.

viscid, adj. [1. vísid; 2. vísid]. Lat. viscidus, 'sticky', fr. viscum, 'mistletoe, birdlime', see **viscum**. Glutinous, sticky; having a syrupy consistency.

viscidity, n. [1. visíditi; 2. visíditi]. Prec. & -ity. Stickiness, adhesiveness.

viscin, n. [1. vísin; 2. vísin]. See **viscum** & **-in**. Sticky substance occurring in the berries of the mistletoe.

viscose, n. [1. vískōs; 2. vískous]. See prec. & **-ose**. Form of cellulose used in artificial silk manufacture.

viscosity, n. [1. viskósiti; 2. viskósiti]. **viscous** & **-ity**. Stickiness; property in viscous fluids whereby resistance is offered to rearrangement of the molecules.

viscount, n. [1. víkount; 2. váikaunt]. O. Fr. viscomte, see **vice** (IV.) & **count** (III.). Male person holding the rank of nobility immediately below that of earl; often as second title of an earl, and used as courtesy title by his eldest son before he succeeds.

viscountess, n. [1. víkountes; 2. váikauntis]. Prec. & -ess. Wife of a viscount; courtesy title often borne by wife of an earl's eldest son; lady holding this rank in her own right.

viscountship, n. [1. víkountship; 2. váikauntʃip]. See prec. & -ship. Viscounty.

viscount(c)y, n. [1. víkount(s)i; 2. váikaunt(s)i]. **viscount** & -y. Rank, status, of a viscount.

viscous, adj. [1. vískus; 2. vískəs]. Lat. viscōsus, 'sticky', fr. viscum, 'birdlime', see **viscum**, & **-ous**. Sticky, glutinous, adhesive; possessing viscosity.

viscum, n. [1. vískum; 2. vískəm]. Lat., 'mistletoe; birdlime'; cogn. w. Gk. *ixós* for *wiskos, 'mistletoe, birdlime'; O.H.G. & dimin. suff. wīhsela, Mod. Germ. weichsel, 'wild cherry'; fr. the Gmc. word, w. different suff., comes O. Fr. guisne for *wisn-, Mod. Fr. guigne, 'wild cherry'; the -n- suff. occurs also in the O. Slav. cogn. višnja; cp. also O. Fr. guis, Mod. Fr. gui, 'mistletoe', fr. a Gmc. *wisk-. Walde suggests that the base is ultimately connected w. **virus**. 1. The mistletoe, a parasitic plant bearing greenish-white berries filled with a sticky glutinous substance. 2. Birdlime, often made from the berries of the mistletoe.

visé, n. & vb. trans. [1. vēzā; 2. vízei]. Fr., P.P. of viser, 'to inspect', formed fr. vis, 'a look, glance', see **vis-à-vis**. 1. n. Also visa, official endorsement on a passport showing that it has been examined and authenticated. 2. vb. To put a visé upon (a passport).

visibility, n. [1. vìzibíliti; 2. vizibíliti]. **visible** & -ity. State, quality, of being visible; specif., state of the atmosphere and light in reference to the distance at which objects can be clearly seen.

visible, adj. [1. vízibl; 2. vízibl]. Fr., fr. Lat. vīsibilis, fr. vīs-, a form of base *vid- &c., 'to see', see **vision** (I.), & **-ible**. 1. To be seen; perceptible, apparent, to the eye; discoverable by the eye: *lights no longer visible*; *many stars are visible by the help of a telescope, but not visible to the naked eye*; *without visible means of support*; *the visible church*, the whole body of the faithful throughout the world; *visible horizon*, farthest distance that can be seen from a given spot; *visible speech*, a system of phonetic notation invented by Melville Bell (1819–1905), later known as the Organic Alphabet, by means of which each speech-sound is represented by a symbol indicating the actual positions of the vocal organs. 2. (as n.) *The visible*, the material, visible world, contrasted with the invisible or spiritual world.

visibleness, n. Prec. & -ness. Visibility.

visibly, adv. See prec. & -ly. In a visible manner, to a visible extent; so as to be visible; perceptibly, appreciably: *visibly excited, moved*; *not visibly larger than it was an hour ago*.

vision (I.), n. [1. vízhun; 2. vížən]. Lat. vīsiōn-(em), 'act or sense of seeing, sight'; apparition, appearance; a notion'; fr. vīs-, type seen in P.P. of vidēre, 'to see', see also **vide**; *vīs- arises fr. *vid-to, whence *visso-, whence *vīs-, w. simplification of -ss- after a long vowel. The Aryan base is *weid-, *woid-, *wid-, 'to know, to see'; for other cognates see -**oid**, **idea**, **idol** (Gk.), & **wit** (I.), **wise** (I.) (Gmc.). 1. a The sense by which light, colour, form, are perceived by the eye; power, faculty, of seeing; sight; b the act of sight, actual seeing. 2. a Faculty of forming mental images, pictures of objects and conditions, esp. the power of seeing things in the mind as they really are; imagination, insight, intuition: *vision is as indispensable to a statesman as to a poet*; b specific mental picture evoked by the power of the prophetic imagination; a poet's dream: 'Saw the vision of the world, and all the wonder that would be' (Tennyson, 'Locksley Hall'); '*The poet's vision of eternal fame*' (Pope, 'Dunciad', iii. 12). 3. a Something seen; a sight, a spectacle, a view: *the bride was a lovely vision*; *I had only a momentary vision of the sea*; b something seen or believed to be seen under conditions which are abnormal; a sight prophetically revealed to the bodily eyes by supernatural means; an appearance, supposed to be more substantial than a dream, of objects, scenes, or events which, though real, are not actually present in a material state to the eye of the beholder; an apparition, a phantasm.

vision (II.), vb. trans., fr. prec. (very rare) To perceive in the form of a vision.

visional, adj. [1. vízhunal; 2. vížənəl]. **vision** (I.) & -al. Pertaining to, of the nature of, a vision.

visionary (I.), adj. [1. vízhunari; 2. vížənəri]. **vision** (I.) & -ary. 1. Pertaining to, of the nature of, a vision; seen in a vision: *a visionary form beckoned me to follow*. 2. Existing only in visions; having no reality or substance; unsubstantial, imaginary, unreal, chimerical; impossible of realization; impracticable: *madmen often live amid visionary splendours*; *visionary schemes, projects* &c. 3. (of persons) Given to seeing visions; a dreamy, imaginative, idealistic; b given to forming impracticable, unworkable schemes; unpractical; flighty, viewy.

visionary (II.), n., fr. prec. 1. One who sees visions; a dreamer, an idealist; one having prophetic vision; a mystic. 2. One who dreams of hopes for, impossible things; one who lives in an unreal world of his own and forms impracticable, unsubstantial projects, and plans that are impossible to carry out.

visit (I.), vb. trans. & intrans. [1. vízit; 2. vízit]. Fr. visiter, fr. Lat. vīsitāre, 'to see frequently; to go to see'; freq. of visāre, 'to look at often or attentively; to behold, survey; to go to see, visit'; formed fr. vīs-, as in vīsum, P.P. of vidēre, 'to see', see **vide**, & **vision** (I.). A. trans. 1. To go to see, call upon, (a person) as a social duty, out of friendliness, friendship, or as an act of kindness: *to visit a new neighbour, an old friend, a sick person*. 2. To go to see, examine, inspect, as a matter of professional duty, or as an official: *a doctor visits his patients*; *a bishop cannot visit every parish in his diocese every year.* **3. a** To go to (a place): *to visit foreign countries, a picture gallery* &c.; **b** to be habitually or constantly at; to frequent: *to visit public-houses and low haunts.* **4.** To come to or upon with some definite object, or with some definite result; **a** (archaic) to come upon with blessing: '*He hath visited and redeemed his people*'; **b** to attack: *plague and famine often visit India.* **B.** intrans. To make, pay, visits: *to visit in the country*; *to visit at strange houses.*

visit (**II.**), n. Fr. *visite*, fr. prec. **1.** Act of visiting; **a** a journey to the house of another in order to see and converse with him; a friendly call; **b** a call made for professional, business, or official reasons: *my doctor charges half a guinea for each visit*; *a visit from a tax-collector, an inspector of drains, a policeman*; **c** journey to a specific object or place for the purpose of inspecting or becoming acquainted with it: *a visit to the Tower, to London* &c. **2.** A temporary sojourn or stay in a house, at a place, other than one's habitual place of residence: *I don't live here, I'm only on a visit*; *a brief visit to Ireland*; *to pay a round of visits in country houses.*

visitable, adj. [1. vízitabl; 2. vízitəbl]. **visit** (**I.**) & **-able**. **1.** To which a visit may be made; worth visiting: *hardly anything visitable in the place.* **2.** Desirable to visit; of such social standing as to warrant a visit: *a few visitable neighbours.*

visitant, adj. & n. [1. vízitant; 2. vízitənt]. Lat. *vīsitant-(em)*, Pres. Part. of *vīsitāre*, see **visit** (**I.**). **1.** adj. (rare) Visiting. **2.** n. **a** (poet. or rhet.) A passing visitor, a temporary guest; esp. an important, august, visitor: *a glorious visitant from some brighter sphere*; **b** specif., a migratory bird; **c** (cap.) a nun of the Order of Visitation in R.C. Church.

visitation, n. [1. vìzitáshun; 2. vìzitéiʃən]. Lat. *vīsitātiōn-(em)*, see **visit** (**II.**) & **-ation**. **1.** Act of visiting; state of being visited; a visit. **2.** Specif., an official, ceremonial, visit of a high official or dignitary for purposes of inspection, conference, giving of admonition and instruction &c.: *archdeacons hold periodical visitations in their archdeaconries*; *visitation of the sick*, (i.) visit of a clergyman to sick parishioners; (ii.) office for such occasions in Prayer Book. **3. a** Visit of a herald to inquire into the right to bear arms, or to hear claims for grants of arms, to persons within his province; **b** official document recording results of a herald's visitation. **4.** (colloq.) A protracted visit: *I fear we have paid you a regular visitation.* **5.** Special act (i.) of divine favour, or, (ii.) more commonly, of wrath; a calamity, an awe-inspiring event, thought of as directly retributive: *plague was formerly regarded as a visitation of God for the people's sins*; *the late gale was a disastrous visitation.* **6.** (zool.) An unusually large migration of birds or animals, or one taking place at an unusual season. **7.** (cap.) Festival commemorating the visit of St. Elizabeth to the B.V.M.

visitatorial, adj. [1. vìzitatórial; 2. vìzitətórial]. L.L. *vīsitātor*, 'visitor', & **-ial**. Pertaining to, connected with, an official visitor, superintendent &c., or his visitations: *visitatorial powers, functions* &c.; *Visitatorial Board*, (Oxford University) a permanent body having powers of supervision and control over the teachers and other officers of the University in the performance of their duties.

visiting, adj. [1. víziting; 2. vízitiŋ]. Pres. Part. of **visit** (**I.**). *Visiting card*, small strip of cardboard with name and address of caller engraved upon it, left at houses on the occasion of a visit. Phr. *on visiting terms*, having social relations sufficiently intimate for the exchange of visits.

visitor, n. [1. vízitor; 2. vízitə]. **visit** (**I.**) & **-or**, cp. Fr. *visiteur*. **1.** One who visits; a caller: *we had quite a number of visitors this afternoon.* **2.** Person making a temporary stay at a place, in a house, other than his own place of abode: *we had a succession of visitors all the summer*; *visitors' book*, one kept, according to law, in an hotel, in which the names and addresses of visitors are written; book kept in private house, in which guests inscribe their names and the dates of their arrival and departure. **3.** (usually cap.) Official specially appointed to make visits of inspection to a corporate body, institution &c. to hear statements of grievances, to give a ruling on the interpretation of statutes, and generally to act as superintendent and adviser.

visor, vizor, visard, vizard, n. [1. vízor(d); 2. váizə(d)]. M.E., fr. A.-Fr. *visere*, O. Fr. *visiere*, fr. O. Fr. *vis*, 'face', see **vis-à-vis**. **1.** Part of a helmet which could be raised or lowered to cover and protect the face. **2.** The peak of a cap.

vista, n. [1. vísta; 2. vístə]. Ital., 'sight, view', fem. of *visto*, P.P. of *vedere*, Lat. *vidēre*, see **view, vision** (**I.**), **vide**. **1.** A view, prospect, esp. one seen through a long narrow space enclosed on either side, as by rows of trees, sides of a mountain &c.; also the narrow space itself before it opens out. **2.** Mental view or prospect; long series of memories of past events and experiences &c. called up before the mind's eye; also a series of such mental pictures representing hopes and anticipations for the future: *to look back through the vistas of the past*; *I seem to see long vistas of future happiness.*

visual, adj. [1. vízhūal, vízūal; 2. víʒjuəl, vízjuəl]. O. Fr., fr. Lat. *vīsuālis*, fr. *vīsus*, 'sight', see **vision** (**I.**), & **-al**. **1.** Connected, concerned, with the sense of sight: *visual images, sensations*; used in sight: *the visual nerve.* **2.** Perceived by the eye, visible: *the apparition was visual, not a product of the imagination.*

visuality, n. [1. vìzhūáliti, vìzūáliti; 2. vìʒjuǽliti, vìzjuǽliti]. Prec. & **-ity**. Condition, quality, of being visual; visibility.

visualization, n. [1. vìzhū-, vìzūalīzáshun; 2. vìʒju-, vìzjuəlaizéiʃən]. **visualize** & **-ation**. **1.** Act, process, power, of visualizing. **2.** Mental image created by visualizing; that which is visualized. **3.** Faculty of producing vivid mental images in others by artistic description.

visualize, vb. trans. & intrans. [1. vízhū-, vízūalīz; 2. víʒju-, vízjuəlaiz]. **visual** & **-ize**. **1.** trans. To render visual; specif., to call up a clear image of in the mind, to see with the eye of the mind: *I find it difficult to visualize the garden as it will be after the alterations*; *if I shut my eyes I can visualize the scene and the actors, as I actually saw them.* **2.** intrans. To carry out the process, perform the act, of visualizing: *some people can recall a sound or a tune mentally, but are quite unable to visualize.*

visualizer, n. [1. vízhū- vízūalīzer; 2. víʒju-, vízjuəlàizə]. Prec. & **-er**. Person who visualizes, one who is able to visualize; specif., one whose mental images are mainly visual.

visually, adv. [1. vízhūali, vízūali; 2. víʒjuəli, vízjuəli]. **visual** & **-ly**. In a visual manner; so as to become visual.

vita glass, n. [1. víta glahs; 2. váitə glās]. Trade and proprietary name, fr. Lat. *vīta*, 'life'; see next word. A special kind of glass, for windows &c., which does not exclude the health-giving ultra-violet rays of the sunlight.

vital, adj. [1. vítl; 2. váitl]. Lat. *vītālis*, 'belonging to life', fr. *vīta*, 'life', & **-al**; *vīta*, 'life, livelihood, way of life', is for **vīvita*, fr. Lat. base in *vīvere*, 'to live, be alive; to lead a specified kind of life; to remain, endure'; the Aryan base is **gʷīw-*, **gʷei(w)-* &c., wh. has many derivatives in most Aryan languages; close cognates w. Lat. *vīta*, fr. **gʷīwita*, are Gk. *biótēs*, 'life, means of life', *bioteía*, 'way of life, livelihood', for **gʷīwot-*, cp. *bíos*, 'course of life', see **bio-**; O. Ir. *biad*, 'means of life'; *bethu*, 'life', fr. **gʷīwot-*; Goth. *qius*, 'living', see **quick** (**I.**); further cognates under this word & **bio-**; see also **zoo-**. **1.** Connected with, pertaining to, having to do with, essential to, arising from, animal life: *vital functions, power*; *vital part* (of the body); *vital movements*; *vital warmth*; *vital wound*, one in a vital part; mortal; *vital statistics*, those dealing with the duration of life, and conditions affecting this, in a given area. **2. a** Having life, living (rare or archaic in physical sense); **b** full of life, vitality, and spirit; lively, animated: *his style was always vital and interesting.* **3.** Essential to the existence of something, necessary, essential to some object or purpose; important, momentous: *vital to one's purpose, to a scheme*; *this paragraph is vital*; *of vital importance.*

vitalism, n. [1. vítalizm; 2. váitəlizəm]. Prec. & **-ism**. Doctrine that organic life is the result of a principle outside of, and distinct from, the operation of physical forces; contrasted with *mechanism.*

vitalist, n. [1. vítalist; 2. váitəlist]. **vital** & **-ist**. Adherent of vitalism.

vitalistic, adj. [1. vìtalístik; 2. vàitəlístik]. Prec. & **-ic**. Pertaining to vitalism or to vitalists; of the nature of vitalism.

vitality, n. [1. vītáliti; 2. vaitǽliti]. Lat. *vītālitāt-(em)*. See **vital** & **-ity**. **1.** Vital force, animal life; strength, bodily vigour; capacity to live: *vitality is greatly reduced in old age.* **2.** Vigour, liveliness, elasticity, of mind; spirit, animation; expression of this in literature and art. **3.** Capacity to last, quality of permanence, durability: *much of the poetry of every age is of merely transitory value and lacks vitality.*

vitalization, n. [1. vìtalīzáshun; 2. vàitəlaizéiʃən]. See next word & **-ation**. Act, process, of vitalizing; state of being vitalized.

vitalize, vb. trans. [1. vítalīz; 2. váitəlaiz]. **vital** & **-ize**. **a** To give, impart, vitality to, to make alive, endow with life: *good food vitalizes the blood*; **b** (more frequent in non-material sense) (i.) to give spirit, animation, to, make living: *to vitalize a dull subject of study*; (ii.) to revive, render active and vital: *to vitalize one's religion, the patriotic spirit* &c.

vitalizer, n. [1. vítalīzer; 2. váitəlàizə]. Prec. & **-er**. He who, that which, vitalizes.

vitals, n. pl. [1. vítlz; 2. váitlz]. **vital**, as n. **a** The vital organs; the parts of the body necessary to life and health, esp. the heart, lungs, liver, bowels &c.; **b** (fig.) that which is of the essence of anything; the inner kernel: *to tear the vitals out of a subject*, get at the real gist.

vitamin, n. [1. vítamin; 2. váitəmin]. Word coined fr. Lat. *vīta*, 'life'. See **vital** & **amine**. Any one of various substances, the chemical nature of which is imperfectly known, present in the food, in its natural state, of man and animals, derived originally from plants, and essential to health and life, deficiency or lack of which causes such diseases as beri-beri, rickets, scurvy &c.; vitamins are classified as being soluble in fat or in water, and are divided into classes A, B, C &c.; they are found in butter-fat, cod-liver oil, green leaves, yeast, some fresh fruits &c.

vitel-. See **vitello-**.

vitellarian, adj. [1. vìtelárian; 2. vìteléəriən]. **vitellarium** & **-an**. Connected with the vitellarium.

vitellarium, n. [1. vìtelárium; 2. vìteléəriəm]. See **vitellus** & **-ary**. Part of the ovary in certain lowly organisms producing yolk-filled cells, distinct from the true eggs.

vitelligenous, adj. [1. vìtelíjenus; 2. vìtelídʒinəs]. See **vitellus** & **-genous**. Yolk-producing, of certain cells in the ovaries of insects.

vitellin, n. [1. vitélin; 2. vitélin]. **vitellus** & **-in**. A protein found in the yolk of an egg.

vitelline, adj. [1. vitélīn; 2. vitélain]. **vitellus** & **-ine**. (embryology) Pertaining to the yolk of an egg.

vitello-, vitel-, pref. Forms of **vitellus** used in compounds.

vitellus, n. [1. vitélus; 2. vitéləs]. Lat., 'a little calf; the yolk of an egg', dimin. of *vitulus*, 'a calf'; see **vitular**. Yolk of an egg; (archaic) entire contents of an egg-shell.

viti-, pref. denoting connexion w. the vine, or w. vines; fr. Lat. *vitis*, 'grape-vine, vine branch'; cogn. w. O. Slav. *viti*, 'something twisted'; O.H.G. *wīda*, 'willow', & O.E. *wiðiġ*, 'a willow; a band', see **withy**; fr. base seen in Lat. *viēre*, 'to twist, twine'. See **vine**.

vitiate, vb. trans. [1. víshiāt; 2. víʃieit], fr. Lat. *vitiāt-(um)*, P.P. of *vitiāre*, 'to make faulty, to mar; to taint, corrupt' &c., fr. *vitium*, 'defect, blemish, vice'. See **vice (I.)**. 1. To render faulty, to detract from, destroy force or merit of: *to vitiate an argument by exaggeration of statement*. 2. To sully, make impure; to taint, contaminate, pollute: *gas may vitiate the air of a room*. 3. To destroy validity of, render ineffective, to deprive of force as a legal instrument: *to vitiate a will, a contract &c.*

vitiated, adj. [1. víshiāted; 2. víʃieitid], fr. P.P. of prec. Made defective; contaminated, impure.

vitiation, n. [1. vìshiáshun; 2. vìʃiéiʃən]. **vitiate** & **-ion**. Act or process of vitiating; state of being vitiated; a contamination, pollution; **b** invalidation.

viticultural, adj. [1. vìti-, vìtikúlchural; 2. váiti-, vìtikáltʃərəl]. Next word & **-al**. Pertaining to the culture of the vine or to grape-growing.

viticulture, n. [1. víti-, vítikùlchur; 2. váiti-, vítikàltʃə]. **viti-** & **culture**. Cultivation of the vine; grape-growing.

viticulturist, n. [1. vìti-, vìtikúlchurist; 2. vàiti-, vìtikáltʃərist]. Prec. & **-ist**. A grape-grower.

vitiosity, n. [1. vìshiósiti; 2. víʃiósiti]. Lat. *vitiōsitāt-(em)*, 'faultiness, corruption', fr. *vitiōsus*, see **vicious**, & **-ity**. Corruption, viciousness.

vitreo-, pref. Form of Lat. *vitreus*, 'glass, glassy', fr. *vitrum*, 'glass', used in compounds. The origin of this rather late word is doubtful; Walde suggests that it may be either a loan fr. Gmc. representing some such type as **hwītra*, comparative meaning 'whitish', see **white**, or may be orig. identical w. *vitium*, 'woad', on account of the blue colour of much early glass. See **woad**.

vitreous, adj. [1. vítreus; 2. vítriəs]. Lat. *vitreus*. See prec. & **-ous**. 1. Resembling glass; transparent, glassy: *vitreous rocks*; *vitreous humour*, transparent, jelly-like substance which fills the hinder portion of the eye-ball. 2. Pertaining to, made of, glass.

vitrescence, n. [1. vitrésens; 2. vitrésəns]. Next word & **-ce**. Tendency to become glass.

vitrescent, adj. [1. vitrésent; 2. vitrésənt]. Lat. *vitrum*, 'glass'. See **vitreo-** & **-escent**. Tending to become glass.

vitrescible, adj. [1. vitrésibl; 2. vitrésibl]. Fr., *vitresc-*, as in prec., & **-ible**. Capable of becoming glass or glassy.

vitri-, pref. Form of Lat. *vitrum*, 'glass', used in compounds. See **vitreo-**.

vitric, adj. [1. vítrik; 2. vítrik]. Lat. *vitrum*, 'glass'. See **vitreo-** & **-ic**. Having the character of glass; glass-like.

vitrics, n. pl. [1. vítriks; 2. vítriks]. See prec. Art of glass working and manufacture; study of this.

vitrifaction, n. [1. vìtrifákshun; 2. vìtrifǽkʃən]. **vitri-** & **-faction**. Vitrification.

vitrifacture, n. [1. vítrifàkchur; 2. vítrifǽktʃə]. **vitri-** & **-facture**. Glassmaking; manufacture of glassware.

vitrifiability, n. [1. vìtrifìabíliti; 2. vìtrifàiəbíliti]. Next word & **-ity**. Capacity of being, liability to be, vitrified.

vitrifiable, adj. [1. vítrifìabl; 2. vítrifàiəbl]. **vitrify** & **-able**. Capable of being vitrified.

vitrification, n. [1. vìtrifikáshun; 2. vìtrifikéiʃən]. **vitri-** & **-fication**. Act, process, of vitrifying; state of being vitrified.

vitriform, adj. [1. vítriform; 2. vítrifɔm]. **vitri-** & **-form**. Having the appearance and consistency of glass; glass-like.

vitrify, vb. trans. & intrans. [1. vítrifì; 2. vítrifai]. **vitri-** & **-fy**. 1. trans. To convert into glass; to cause to become vitriform, esp. by heat. 2. intrans. To become converted into glass; to become vitriform.

vitriol, n. [1. vítriol; 2. vítriəl]. In M.E., fr. Fr.; fr. Lat. *vitreolus*, 'made of, resembling, glass', dimin. form of *vitreus*. See **vitreo-**. The name is due to the glassy lustre exhibited by some of the sulphuric acid salts. 1. (chem.) A sulphate of any of various metals —copper, iron, zinc, known respectively as blue, green, and white vitriol; *oil of vitriol*, also merely *vitriol*, an oily, highly corrosive liquid distilled from blue vitriol; this substance is sometimes used by criminals, esp. women, to blind and disfigure the faces of those against whom they have a grudge: *to throw vitriol over, at*. 2. Corrosive, biting, caustic mode of expression: *to put plenty of vitriol in a speech, a review*.

vitriolate, vb. trans. [1. vítriōlāt; 2. vítriouleit]. Prec. & **-ate**. **a** To convert into vitriol; to subject to the effects of vitriol; **b** to throw vitriol at or over.

vitriolation, n. [1. vìtriōláshun; 2. vìtriouléiʃən]. Prec. & **-ion**. Act, process, of vitriolating.

vitriolic, adj. [1. vìtriólik; 2. vìtriólik]. vitriol & **-ic**. 1. Connected with, consisting of, resembling, vitriol. 2. (fig.) Biting, corrosive; heated, fiery, vehement: *vitriolic temper*; *vitriolic invective, eloquence &c*.

vitriolizable, adj. [1. vítriolìzabl; 2. vítriəlàizəbl]. **vitriolize** & **-able**. Capable of being converted into vitriol.

vitriolization, n. [1. vìtriolizáshun; 2. vìtriəlaizéiʃən]. **vitriolize** & **-ation**. Act, process, of vitriolizing; state of being vitriolized.

vitriolize, vb. trans. [1. vítrioliz; 2. vítriəlaiz]. vitriol & **-ize**. **a** To attack, injure (a person), by throwing vitriol at or over; also **b** to convert into vitriol.

Vitruvian, adj. [1. vitrōōvian; 2. vitrúviən], fr. name of Vitruvius Pollio, a Roman architect in the age of Augustus. Pertaining to, connected with, Vitruvius or his work. *Vitruvian scroll*, undulating decoration used in friezes.

vitta, n., pl. **vittae** [1. víta, -ē; 2. vítə, -i]. Lat., 'a band, fillet, chaplet; a sacerdotal fillet'; perh. fr. **vĭtwa*, fr. base of *vīta*, 'life', see **vital**, w. *-wa* suff., doubling of *-t-* before *-w-*, & shortening of preceding vowel. (bot.) Oil-bearing tube in the fruit of certain umbelliferous plants.

vittate, adj. [1. vítāt; 2. víteit]. Prec. & **-ate**. Having vittae.

vitular, adj. [1. víchoolar; 2. vítʃulə], fr. Lat. *vitulus*, 'calf', & **-ar**. Orig. meaning of *vitulus* is 'a yearling animal'; cp. Lat. *vetus*, 'old, having lived, or lasted, many years', see **veteran**; cogn. w. Gk. *étos*, 'year', for **wetos*, whence Gk. *éteion*, 'yearling animal'; cp. w. different derivative suff. Scrt. *vatsás*, 'yearling calf, lamb'; Goth. *wiþrus*, 'a lamb'; O.E. *weþer*; cp. further **veal, veterinary**. Pertaining to, connected with, a calf or calves; *vitular apoplexy*, that to which cows are liable when calving.

vitulary, adj. [1. víchoolari; 2. vítʃuləri]. Prec. & **-y**. Vitular.

vituline, adj. [1. víchoolin; 2. vítʃulain]. Lat. *vitulīnus*, fr. *vitulus*, 'calf', see **vitular**, & **-ine**. Pertaining to a calf, or to veal.

vituperable, adj. [1. vītúperabl; 2. vaitjúpərəbl]. Lat. *vituperābilis*, 'blameworthy'. See next word & **able**. Deserving vituperation.

vituperate, vb. trans. [1. vītúperāt; 2. vaitjúpəreit]. Lat. *vituperāt-(um)*, P.P. of *vituperāre*, 'to censure, blame, disparage'; fr. Lat. *vitium*, 'fault, defect', see **vice (I.)**, & *parāre*, 'to prepare, provide'. See **parade, pare**. To rate, scold, soundly; to abuse loudly and forcibly; to dress down, trounce.

vituperation, n. [1. vìtūperáshun; 2. vàitjūpəréiʃən]. Prec. & **-ion**. Act of vituperating; loud, vehement, abuse; verbal castigation.

vituperative, adj. [1. vītúperativ; 2. vaitjúpərətiv]. See prec. & **-ive**. **a** Uttering abuse; given to rating and scolding; **b** abusive, denunciatory: *a vituperative speech*.

viva (I.), interj. & n. [1. vēva; 2. vívə]. Ital., 'let him live, long live ...' 1. interj. Long (may he) live, uttered as a greeting, welcome &c. 2. n. The cry *viva*; hence (*vivas*), shouts of greeting, applause &c.: *the hall resounded with the vivas of the crowd*.

viva (II.), n. & vb. trans. & intrans. [1. víva; 2. váivə]. Lat., for **viva voce**. 1. n. Examination conducted viva voce. 2. vb. **a** trans. To submit (person) to a viva; to examine (person) orally; **b** intrans., to conduct a viva voce examination.

vivace, adv. [1. viváhchā; 2. vivátʃe]. Ital., 'vivaciously'. See **vivacious**. (musical direction) Vivaciously, with spirit and liveliness.

vivacious, adj. [1. vīváshus; 2. vaivéiʃəs]. Lat. *vivāci-*, stem of *vivax*, 'tenacious of life'; lively, vigorous', fr. *vivere*, 'to live'. See **vital** & **vivid** & **-ous**. Full of life and spirit; lively, sprightly, animated, gay.

vivaciously, adv. Prec. & **-ly**. In a vivacious manner.

vivaciousness, n. See prec. & **-ness**. Quality of being vivacious.

vivacity, n. [1. vīvásiti; 2. vaivǽsiti]. Lat. *vivācitāt-(em)*, 'tenacity of life'. See **vivacious** & **-ity**. Liveliness, sprightliness, gaiety, playfulness.

vivandière, n. [1. vèvandiár; 2. vīvādiér]. L. Lat. *vivanda*, 'provisions', see **viand**, & *-ière*, Fr. fem. of *-ier*. Female who formerly accompanied a French army and sold provisions and liquor to the troops.

vivarium, n. [1. vīvárium; 2. vaivéəriəm]. Lat., 'enclosure in which game and fish are kept alive; a preserve'; fr. base *vīv-*, as in *vivere*, 'to live', see **vital**; for suff. see **-ary**. An enclosure or preserve in which (terrestrial) animals live, as far as possible, under natural conditions.

viva voce, adv., adj., & n. [1. vīva vōsi; 2. váivə vóusi]. Lat., 'with the living voice', abl. fem. of *vivus*, 'living', see **vivacious** & **vital**, & abl. of *vox*, 'voice', see **vox, vocal**, & **voice**. 1. adv. **a** Out loud: *to speak viva voce*; **b** by means of the voice, by word of mouth, orally; contrasted with *in writing*. 2. adj. Uttered with the voice, oral; *viva-voce examination*, one conducted by word of mouth, instead of by written questions and answers. 3. n. A viva-voce examination.

vive, interj. [1. vēv; 2. vīv]. Fr., 'let him live, long live ...', 3rd pers. pres. subj. of *vivre*, 'to live', fr. Lat. *vivere*, see **vivacious** & **vital**. *Vive le roi, la reine, le Président, la France &c.*, long live the King, Queen, President, France &c. See also **qui vive**.

vives, n. [1. vīvz; 2. vaivz]. O. Fr. *avives*, fr. Span. *advivas*, fr. Arab. *al-dhiba*. Disease of the ear in young horses.

vivi-, pref. Form of Lat. *vivus*, 'living', used in compounds; the etymological relations of this base are discussed under **vital**.

vivid, adj. [1. vívid; 2. vívid]. Lat. *vividus*, 'full of life, living, animated; full of vigour', fr. base *vīv-*, 'life, live', see prec. & **vital**. Full of life, vigour, liveliness &c. (in various senses). 1. Vigorous, abounding in force, animated, lively: *a vivid imagination*; *a vivid personality*. 2. **a** (of colour and visual images) Clear, bright, intense, brilliant; reverse of *dull, subdued, indistinct*: *vivid colouring*; *the vivid green of leaves in spring*; *a vivid reflection in water*; *a vivid flash of lightning*; **b** bringing a clear and life-like image before the mind: *a vivid description*; *a vivid picture of life in the fields*.

vividly, adv. Prec. & -ly. In a vivid manner; with vividness.

vividness, n. See prec. & -ness. Quality of being vivid.

vivificate, vb. trans. [1. vĭ-, vivíficāt; 2. vai-, vivífikeit]. vivi- & -fic & -ate. (rare) To put life into, to vivify; to revive.

vivification, n. [1. vìvifikắshun; 2. vìvifikéiʃən]. Prec. & -ion. Act, process, of vivifying; condition of being vivified.

vivify, vb. trans. [1. vívifī; 2. vívifài]. vivi- & -fy. To give life or liveliness to; to animate, quicken, revive.

viviparity, n. [1. vìvipáriti; 2. vàivipǽriti]. See viviparous & -ity. State, quality, of being viviparous.

viviparous, adj. [1. vīvíparus; 2. vaivíparǝs]. vivi- & par-, fr. base in Lat. *parere*, 'to bear, bring forth (young)', see parent, & -ous. Bringing forth young alive and fully formed and immediately capable of independent life; contrasted with *oviparous*.

viviparously, adv. Prec. & -ly. In a viviparous manner.

viviparousness, n. See prec. & -ness. Quality of being viviparous.

vivisect, vb. trans. & intrans. [1. vìvisékt; 2. vìvisékt]. vivi- & base *sec-*, 'to cut', see secant & sect. 1. trans. To dissect (animal) while alive, to practise vivisection upon. 2. intrans. To practise vivisection.

vivisection, n. [1. vìvisékshun; 2. vìvisékʃən]. Prec. & -ion. The practice of performing operations upon living animals, of inoculating them with the germs of disease &c., in order to observe their behaviour and symptoms, to test remedies and, generally, to enlarge medical, pathological, or biological knowledge.

vivisectional, adj. [1. vìvisékshunal; 2. vìvisékʃənǝl]. Prec. & -al. Connected with, arising from, of the nature of, vivisection.

vivisectionist, n. [1. vìvisékshunist; 2. vìvisékʃənist]. vivisection & -ist. 1. One who practises vivisection. 2. One who approves of and advocates the practice of vivisection.

vivisector, n. [1. vívisektor; 2. vívisektǝ]. vivisect & -or. One who practises vivisection.

vixen, n. [1. víksn; 2. víksn]. O.E. *fyxen*, 'female fox', fr. *fuhs-in-*, see fox. 1. A female fox. 2. An ill-tempered, vinegary, shrewish, spiteful woman.

vixenish, adj. [1. víksenish; 2. víksəniʃ]. Prec. & -ish. Like a vixen in character; spiteful, malicious.

viz. See videlicet.

vizier, n. [1. vizér; 2. vizíǝ]. Turk. *vezīr*, 'counsellor', fr. Arab. *wezīr*, *wazīr*, lit. 'one who bears burdens'. High State official in Mohammedan countries, esp. in the old Ottoman Empire. *Grand Vizier*, chief minister of state.

vizierate, vizirate, n. [1. vizérāt; 2. vizíǝreit]. Prec. & -ate. The office, status, of a vizier; term of this.

Vlach. See Wallach.

vocable, n. [1. vókabl; 2. vóukǝbl]. Fr., fr. Lat. *vocābulum*, 'that by which anything is called, designation, name'; fr. base *vŏc-*, as in *vōc-em*, fr. *vox*, 'voice', & *vocāre*, 'to call', see vocation, & vox. A word, esp. one regarded as composed of certain sounds without reference to meaning.

vocabulary, n. [1. vokábulari; 2. voukǽbjulǝri]. Lat. *vocābulum*, see prec. & -ary. 1. The stock of words employed by an individual speaker, author, class of persons &c.; range, scope, of language: *an ordinary labourer is said to have a vocabulary of only a few hundred words*; *Shakespeare's rich vocabulary*. 2. Alphabetical list of the principal words as found in a particular work or language, or used in some special branch of study, together with a translation of each into another language, or explanations in elucidation of the meaning.

vocal, adj. [1. vókl; 2. vóukl], fr. Lat. *vocālis*, 'uttering a voice or sound'; sounding, sonorous, vocal', fr. *vōc-(em), vox*, 'voice', & -al; for an account of the base *vōc-* &c. see vox. 1. Pertaining to the voice or to voice production: *the vocal organs*; *vocal chords*, vibrating membranes in the glottis which produce voice. 2. Uttered, produced, by the voice; spoken or sung: *vocal music*, that intended for singing; contrasted with *instrumental*. 3. Filled with the sound of voices; endowed with a voice: '*hill or valley, fountain, or fresh shade, Made vocal by my song*' (Milton, 'P. L.', v. 203-4). 4. Expressing oneself or itself in words; giving vent in speech or language: *public opinion has at last become vocal*; *this class may be very vocal and noisy, but carries little weight*.

vocalic, adj. [1. vokálik; 2. voukǽlik]. Prec. & -ic. Pertaining to, consisting of, of the nature of, a vowel sound or sounds.

vocalism, n. [1. vókalizm; 2. vóukəlizəm]. vocal & -ism. a Use of the voice and vocal organs in speech, song &c.; b (rare) system of vowel sounds used in a given language.

vocalist, n. [1. vókalist; 2. vóukǝlist]. vocal & -ist. A singer.

vocality, n. [1. vokáliti; 2. voukǽliti]. vocal & -ity. Quality of being vocal; resonance.

vocalization, n. [1. vòkalizắshun; 2. vòukəlaizéiʃən]. vocalize & -ation. a Act of vocalizing; method of utterance, esp. of the singing voice; b the use of vowel signs in writing certain languages, where they are usually omitted, as in Hebrew, Arabic &c.

vocalize, vb. trans. & intrans. [1. vókaliz; 2. vóukəlaiz]. See vocal & -ize. A. trans. 1. (phon.) a To make vocal; to utter with voice; b to make vocalic or syllabic. 2. To point or supply vowel signs to (written form of a language such as Hebrew which commonly omits these). B. intrans. To use the voice, to sing.

vocally, adv. [1. vókali; 2. vóukəli]. vocal & -ly. In a vocal manner; by voice or speech, in words.

vocation, n. [1. vokắshun; 2. voukéiʃən]. Fr., fr. Lat. *vocātiōn-(em)*, 'a summons; invitation', fr. *vocāt-(um)*, P.P. type of *vocāre*, 'to call'. See vocal & vox & -ion. 1. (theol.) a God's calling or invitation to an individual or nation to a life of salvation by grace; specif., a call to a religious life, as to the ministry; the divine guidance towards a spiritual or religious life; b that form of spiritual life to which one has been called by God. 2. A special fitness, aptitude, talent, for a particular occupation or profession; a calling: *to have little or no vocation for business life*; *to find one's vocation in life*. 3. Habitual occupation, followed as a means of livelihood; profession, business, walk in life, calling.

vocational, adj. [1. vokắshunal; 2. voukéiʃənǝl]. Prec. & -al. Relating, adapted, preparatory, to a vocation, profession, or occupation: *vocational education, school* &c.

vocationally, adv. Prec. & -ly. In a vocational manner; from the point of view of a vocation.

vocative, adj. & n. [1. vókativ; 2. vókətiv], fr. O. Fr. *vocatif, -ive*, fr. Lat. *vocātīvus*, sc. *casus*, fr. *vocāt-(um)*, P.P. type of *vocāre*, 'to call', see vocation & vox & -ive. 1. adj. Used in addressing or calling a person or object: *vocative case*. 2. n. The vocative case.

vociferance, n. [1. vosíferans; 2. vousífərəns]. See next word & -ce. Shouting, noise, clamour.

vociferant, adj. [1. vosíferant; 2. vousífərənt]. fr. Lat. *vōciferant-(em)*, Pres. Part. of *vōciferāri*, see next word. Vociferating, shouting, clamorous.

vociferate, vb. trans. & intrans. [1. vosíferāt; 2. vousífəreit], fr. Lat. *vōciferāt-(um)*, P.P. type of *vōciferāri*, 'to cry, call out, to shout'; fr. *vōci-*, stem of *vox*, & *-fer*, see under -ferous, & -ate. 1. trans. To shout, utter with a loud voice; to bawl out: *to vociferate oaths*; *the crowd vociferated* '*Sit down!*' 2. intrans. To bawl, shout, utter loud cries.

vociferation, n. [1. vosìferắshun; 2. vousìfəréiʃən], fr. Lat. *vōciferātiōn-(em)*; see prec. & -ion. Shouting, bawling; clamour.

vociferator, n. [1. vosíferātor; 2. vousífəreitə]. Lat., see vociferate & -or. One who vociferates; shouter, bawler.

vociferous, adj. [1. vosíferus; 2. vousífərəs]. Lat. *vōci-*, stem of *vox*, see vox, & -ferous. 1. Having plenty of voice; using the voice with energy, making a loud outcry, clamorous: *a vociferous mob*; *birds were so vociferous that I woke up*. 2. Uttered with a loud voice; noisy, loud: *vociferous cheers*.

vociferously, adv. Prec. & -ly. In a vociferous manner; noisily.

vociferousness, n. See prec. & -ness. Quality of being vociferous.

vodka, n. [1. vódka; 2. vódkǝ]. Russ., dimin. of O. Slav. & Russ. *vodá*, 'water'; cogn. w. Gk. *húdōr*, 'water'; Goth. *watō*; O.E. *wæter*, water, wash, & wet; Lat. *unda*, 'wave', see undulate. A Russian spirituous drink, distilled formerly from rye, maize, or potatoes.

voe, n. [1. vō; 2. vou], fr. O.N. *vágr*, Mod. Icel. *vógr*. A creek, inlet, or small bay in the Orkney and Shetland Islands.

vogue, n. [1. vōg; 2. voug]. Fr., 'swaying motion, as of boat, sway, drift, course', fr. *voguer*, 'to sway, set sail', as in Phr. *vogue la galère*, lit. 'let the galley set sail', hence 'let things take their course whatever happens'; the word is found in Ital. as *vogare*, & in Span. as *bogare*, 'to row', & is of Gmc. origin; cp. O.H.G. *wāg*, later *wōg*, 'wave', O.E. *wǣg*, 'wave', a form of the Gmc. base *weʒ-*, 'to carry, bear', see weigh. 1. The prevailing fashion; popular mode, custom, practice at the time: *the vogue of very short skirts* &c.; *a mere passing vogue*; *what will the next vogue be?* 2. Popularity, popular acceptance or favour: *to have a short vogue*. Phr. *in vogue*, in fashion, fashionable; *all the vogue*, the latest thing, the dernier cri.

voice (I.), n. [1. vois; 2. vɔis]. M.E. & O. Fr. *vois* &c., fr. Lat. *vōci-*, stem of *vōx*, 'voice', see vox. 1. Sound produced, uttered, through the mouth by the human organs of speech, in speaking, singing, laughing; also used of the vocal sounds produced by birds, and, more rarely, of those made by other animals. 2. Specif. (phon.) that kind of sound produced by the organs of speech when the air-stream sets up vibrations in the vocal chords; contrasted with *breath*. 3. The sound or sounds produced by the human organs of speech considered in relation to their quality, individual character, peculiar characteristic timbre and so on: *his master's voice*; *a good, poor, strong, loud, sweet, harsh, voice*. Phr. *to lift up one's voice*, to speak. 4. Faculty, power, of using the voice; desire and capacity to speak: *indignation gave me voice*. 5. a Any sound regarded as resembling, or as comparable to, that of the human voice: '*Earth with her thousand voices praises God*' (Coleridge, 'Vale of Chamouni'); *the voice of the stream, of the waves* &c.; b anything regarded as resembling the human voice as a means of expression, as delivering a message &c.: '*E'en from the tomb the voice of Nature cries*' (Gray's 'Elegy'); *the voice of the law*; *the voice of conscience*. 6. Wish, desire, opinion, choice, esp. as expressed in a vote or less formally indicated: *to give one's voice for war*. Phr. *to have a voice in*, have a choice, have the right to express an opinion or wish, to have some influence in a decision. 7. (gram.) Form of a verb which shows the relation of the subject to the action. See active, passive.

voice (II.), vb. trans., fr. prec. 1. To give utterance to, to express: *to voice the feelings of a meeting*. 2. (phon.) To utter (a speech, sound) with voice, that is, pronounce it with vibration of the vocal chords.

voiced, adj. [1. voist; 2. vɔist]. P.P. of prec. (phon.) Uttered with voice, i.e. with vibration of the vocal chords: *voiced sounds, consonants* &c.; contrasted with *voiceless*.

-voiced, adj. Having a specified kind of voice: *sweet-voiced, loud-voiced* &c.

voiceful, adj. [1. vóisfl; 2. vóisfl]. **voice** (I.) & **-ful**. Having a voice; sonorous, sounding.

voiceless, adj. [1. vóisles; 2. vóislis]. **voice** & **-less**. **1. a** Having no voice; **b** having lost (temporarily) the power of speech. **2.** (phon.) Uttered without voice, uttered with breath alone; unvoiced.

voicelessly, adv. Prec. & **-ly**. In a voiceless manner; without voice.

voicelessness, n. See prec. & **-ness**. The quality of being voiceless.

voicing, n. [1. vóising; 2. vóisiŋ]. **voice** (II.) & **-ing**. (phon.) Act or process of producing voice; act of uttering speech sounds with vibration of the vocal chords.

void (I.), adj. [1. void; 2. void]. In M.E., fr. O. Fr. *vuit, vuide, voide,* fr. L. Lat. *vocitum,* 'empty', dialectal for Lat. *vacāt-(um),* P.P. of *vacāre,* 'to be empty, to be void of, free from', see **vacate** & **vacant**. **1.** Empty, vacant: '*without form, and void*' (Gen. i. 2). **2.** Having no occupant, holder, or tenant: *a void benefice, farm, dwelling-house* &c. **3.** Lacking, wanting, deficient in, devoid of: *a landscape void of all beauty*; *a person quite void of common honesty*. **4.** Legally invalid, of no effect: *the contract was declared void on account of the insanity of one of the parties*; also *null and void.*

void (II.), n., fr. prec. **1. a** An empty space, a vacuum; *the void,* space, infinity; **b** an unoccupied house, esp. rated as such. **2.** (fig.) A sense of emptiness, vacancy, loss: *his death has left a void in our lives which can never be filled*; (commonly) *an aching void* (*in one's heart*), deep sense of irreparable loss.

void (III.), vb. trans., fr. **void** (I.). **1.** To discharge, evacuate: *to void excrement, a stone from the bladder*. **2.** To make null and void; to make invalid, of no effect; to nullify.

voidable, adj. [1. vóidabl; 2. vóidəbl]. **void** (III.) & **-able**. Capable of being made, or judged, as of no effect; capable of being nullified.

voidance, n. [1. vóidans; 2. vóidəns]. **void** (III.) & **-ance**. **1.** Act of voiding; evacuation; casting away, removal. **2.** (eccles.) **a** Act of ejecting from a benefice; **b** state of being void; vacancy (of a benefice).

voided, adj. [1. vóided; 2. vóidid], fr. P.P. of **void** (III.). (her., of an ordinary) Having central part removed or cut away, and showing the tincture of the field in the vacant space.

voider, n. [1. vóider; 2. vóidə]. **void** (III.) & **-er**. (her.) An ordinary, consisting of a figure with two concave sides, occupying the greater part of the field.

voile, n. [1. vwahl; 2. vwāl]. Fr., 'a veil', fr. Lat. *vēlum,* see **velum** & cp. **veil**. A thin cotton, woollen, or silken material used for women's dresses.

voivode, n. [1. vóivōd; 2. vóivoud]. Russ. *voevoda,* 'leader in war'. Title formerly borne by the reigning princes of Moldavia and Wallachia.

volant, adj. [1. vŏlant; 2. vóulənt]. Fr., fr. Lat. *volant-(em),* Pres. Part. of *volāre,* for *$g^w ol$-,* 'to fly'; cogn. w. Scrt. *garút,* 'wing', fr. *$g^w ol$-*; further relations doubtful, but perh. fr. same base as Lat. *volvere,* 'to roll, turn, tumble', see **volute** & second element in **devolve, revolve**. **1. a** (zool.) Flying, capable of flying; **b** (her.) represented as flying. **2.** Passing rapidly through the air as though flying on wings.

Volapük, n. [1. vólapōōk, -pook; 2. vólapūk, -puk]. 'World's speech'. Artificial language invented by J. M. Schleyer in 1879 with the object of providing a means of intercourse between all nations of the world; superseded long since in public estimation by Esperanto, Ido, and similar inventions.

volar, adj. [1. vŏlar; 2. vóulə]. Lat. *vola,* 'palm of hand; sole of foot'; for *$gwela$* or *$gwola$,* conn. w. base *$geu(l)$-*; cogn. w. Gk. *gúalon,* 'a hollow, cave'; Scrt. *gōlaś,* 'ball'; O.N. *kjŏlr,* O.E. *čēol,* 'keel, ship', see **keel** (I.). Pertaining to the palm or the sole.

volatile, adj. [1. vólatīl; 2. vŏlətail]. Fr., fr. Lat. *volātilis,* 'flying, winged; rapid; fleeting, transitory', fr. *volāt-(um),* P.P. type of *volāre,* 'to fly', see **volant**. **1.** Tending to waste, to be carried off by evaporation, vaporization &c.; easily vaporizable (of spirituous liquids). **2.** (fig.) Tossed hither and thither by the caprice of the moment, lacking concentration of purpose; changeable, wayward, fickle.

volatileness, n. Prec. & **-ness**. Volatility.

volatility, n. [1. vòlatíliti; 2. vòlətíliti]. See prec. & **-ity**. Quality, mental characteristic, of being volatile.

volatilizable, adj. [1. vòlatilízabl; 2. vòlətil-áizəbl]. **volatilize** & **-able**. Capable of being volatilized.

volatilization, n. [1. volátilizáshun; 2. vəlǽ-tilaizéiʃən]. **volatilize** & **-ation**. Process of volatilizing; state of being volatilized.

volatilize, vb. trans. & intrans. [1. vólatilíz; 2. vòlətílaiz]. **volatile** & **-ize**. **1.** trans. To render volatile, cause to evaporate. **2.** intrans. To evaporate, pass off in vapour.

vol-au-vent, n. [1. vól ō vòn; 2. vól ou vã]. Fr. Kind of raised pie made of puff paste, filled with chicken, game, fish &c.

volcanic, adj. [1. volkánik; 2. vɔlkǽnik]. **volcano** & **-ic**. **1.** Pertaining to, of the nature of, produced by, due to action of, a volcano or of volcanoes: *volcanic activity; volcanic eruption* &c.; *volcanic bomb,* a round, hollow mass of lava; *volcanic glass,* glass-like substance formed by the rapid cooling of lava; *obsidian*. **2.** (fig.) Resembling a volcano in violence; ebullient, violent, intense: *a volcanic character; volcanic energy.*

volcanicity, n. [1. vòlkanísiti; 2. vɔlkənísiti]. Prec. & **-ity**. State, quality, of being volcanic.

volcanism, n. [1. vólkanizm; 2. vɔlkənizəm]. **volcano** & **-ism**. **a** Volcanic action; **b** combination of natural forces which produces volcanic action.

volcanist, n. [1. vólkanist; 2. vɔlkənist]. **volcano** & **-ist**. Student of volcanoes and volcanic action.

volcanization, n. [1. vòlkanizáshun; 2. vɔlkən-aizéiʃən]. Next word & **-ation**. Process of subjecting or of being subjected to volcanic heat.

volcanize, vb. trans. [1. vólkanīz; 2. vólkənaiz]. **volcano** & **-ize**. To subject to the action of volcanic heat.

volcano, n. [1. volkánō; 2. vɔlkéinou]. Ital., fr. Lat. *Vulcānus,* see **Vulcan**. Hill or mountain having a deep vent in the summit from which lava, ashes, gases &c., coming from the interior of the earth, are ejected continuously or periodically. Phr. *extinct volcano,* (i.) one which has ceased to be active; (ii.) a person who is no longer productive, one who has lost his vigour, spirit, enthusiasm, creative energy, and capacity for thought and action.

volcanological, adj. [1. vòlkanōlójikl; 2. vòl-kənouló̌dʒikl]. **volcano** & **-logy** & **-ic** & **-al**. Pertaining to volcanology or volcanologists.

volcanologist, n. [1. vòlkanólojist; 2. vòlkənól-ədʒist]. **volcanology** & **-ist**. Student of volcanology.

volcanology, n. [1. vòlkanóloji; 2. vòlkənól-ədʒi]. **volcano** & **-logy**. The science which deals with volcanoes, their causes, and attendant phenomena.

vole (I.), n. & vb. intrans. [1. vōl; 2. voul], fr. Fr. *voler,* 'to fly', fr. Lat. *volāre,* see **volant**. **a** n. The winning of all the tricks in a deal in certain card games; **b** vb., to make a vole.

vole (II.), n. For *vole mouse,* fr. O.N. *vollr,* 'field', cogn. w. O.E. *wēald, wăld,* see **wold**. One of various kinds of rat-like rodent mammals, genus *Microtus,* with blunt noses, short tails, and thickish bodies: *field vole,* field-mouse; *water-vole,* water-rat.

volet, n. [1. vólā; 2. vólei]. Fr., 'shutter'. **vole** (I.) & **-et**. One of the panels of a triptych.

volitant, adj. [1. vólitant; 2. vólitənt]. Lat. *volitāre,* 'to fly', freq. of *volāre,* see **volant**. (zool.) Flying.

volitation, n. [1. vòlitáshun; 2. vòlitéiʃən]. Lat. *volitāt-(um),* P.P. type of *volitāre,* 'to fly', see prec., & **-ion**. Act of flying; capacity to fly.

volition, n. [1. vōlíshun; 2. voulíʃən]. Med. Lat. *volitiōn-(em),* formed fr. base **vol-**, 'to wish, will', cp. Lat. *volo,* 'I wish' &c., infin. *velle;* cogn. w. Scrt. *vṛnāti* &c., 'he chooses, desires, prefers', for *vl̥-; văranam* for *val-,* 'act of choosing, wishing'; Goth. *wiljan,* 'to will', O.E. *willan,* see **will** (II.); O. Slav. *volitĭ,* 'to will, desire', *volja,* 'the will, desire' &c.; Gk. *elpís,* 'hope', for *wel-*. **1.** Act of willing or choosing; exercise of the will. **2.** Power of exercising a choice, of forming an intention or a determination; will.

volitional, adj. [1. vōlíshunal; 2. voulíʃənəl]. Prec. & **-al**. Connected, having to do, with volition or the will; of the nature of volition; arising from, due to, volition.

volitionally, adv. Prec. & **-ly**. By volition.

volitionary, adj. [1. vōlíshunari; 2. voulí-ʃənəri]. **volition** & **-ary**. Volitional.

volitionless, adj. [1. vōlíshunles; 2. voulíʃən-lis]. **volition** & **-less**. Lacking volition; having no power of will.

volitive, adj. [1. vólitiv; 2. vólitiv]. See **volition** & **-ive**. Pertaining to, arising from, the will.

Volkslied, n. [1. fólkslēd; 2. fólkslīd]. Mod. Germ. Folk-song, national song or air.

Volksraad, n. [1. fólksrahd; 2. fólksrād]. Du., see **folk**, & *raad,* 'counsel' &c., cogn. w. O.E. *rǣd,* 'advice, counsel', see under **read**. National legislative body in the old Orange Free State.

volley (I.), n. [1. vóli; 2. vóli], fr. Fr. *volée,* 'a flight; discharge of a number of guns', fr. Lat. *volātum,* P.P. of *volāre,* 'to fly', see **volant**. **1.** A number of missiles discharged at the same time against a common objective: *a volley of arrows, of stones*; if not specified, *a volley* implies at the present time, a number of shots fired simultaneously from fire-arms or from cannon. **2.** (fig.) A rapid, continuous, noisy utterance, a torrent (of oaths, imprecations, abuse &c.), esp. when directed against a particular person, party, set of circumstances &c. **3.** In various ball games, a as tennis &c., the striking and return of the ball before it touches the ground; **b** as cricket &c., the delivery of ball full pitch at batsman or wicket; *half-volley,* ball pitched and struck just after it touches the ground.

volley (II.), vb. trans. & intrans., fr. prec. **1.** trans. **a** (i.) (rare) To direct, fire, (missiles) in a volley; (ii.) in ball games, to deliver or strike by a volley; **b** to utter (abuse &c.) in a volley. **2.** intrans. **a** To fire a volley; **b** to deliver or hit a volley.

volplane, vb. intrans. & n. [1. vólplān; 2. vól-plein], fr. Fr. *vol planer,* see **volant** & **plane** (V.). **a** vb. (of aeroplane or pilot) To descend by a long and somewhat steep glide after shutting off the engine; **b** n., such a descent.

volt (I.), n. [1. volt; 2. vɔlt]. Fr., see **vault** (I.). **1.** (fencing) Rapid step to escape a thrust. **2.** Pace of a horse in which it steps with high springy movements of the legs.

volt (II.), n., fr. name of the Italian, A. Volta, d. 1827. Unit of electromotive force or potential difference; defined as the electromotive force which, steadily applied to a resistance of 1 ohm, will produce a current of 1 ampère.

volta, n., pl. **volte** [1. vólta, -ā; 2. vólta, -e]. Ital., 'time'. (mus.) *Una volta,* 'once'; *due volte,* 'twice'.

voltage, n. [1. vóltij; 2. vóltidʒ]. **volt** (II.) & **-age**. Amount of electromotive current measured in volts.

voltaic, adj. [1. voltáik; 2. vɔltéi-ik]. *Volta,* see **volt** (II.), & **-ic**. Designating electricity produced by, apparatus producing electricity by, chemical action.

Voltairian, adj. & n. [1. voltárian; 2. vɔltéəriən], fr. name of French philosopher Voltaire & -ian. **1.** adj. Pertaining to Voltaire and his mode of thought. **2.** n. Adherent of the doctrines and principles of Voltaire.

Voltair(ian)ism, n. [1. voltár(ian)izm; 2. vɔltéər(iən)izəm]. See prec. & -ism. Philosophical doctrines of Voltaire; specif., religious scepticism.

voltameter, n. [1. voltámeter; 2. vɔltǽmitə], fr. *Volta*, see **volt** (II.), & -meter. (obs.) Instrument for measuring electrical force.

volte-face, n. [1. vòlt fáhs; 2. vòlt fǎ́s]. Fr. A complete turn round, so as to face the opposite way; **a** reversal of physical, bodily, position; **b** a change of front, complete reversal of opinions, mental attitude &c.

voltite, n. [1. vóltīt; 2. vɔ́ltait], fr. **volt** (II.) & -ite. A kind of insulating material for covering electric wires.

voltmeter, n. [1. vóltmēter; 2. vóltmītə]. **volt** (II.) & -meter. (elect.) Instrument for measuring potential difference in volts.

volubility, n. [1. vòlubíliti; 2. vɔ̀ljubíliti]. See next word & -ity. Habit, quality, of being voluble; extreme fullness, fluency, of utterance and expression; talkativeness.

voluble, adj. [1. vólūbl; 2. vɔ́ljubl]. Lat. *volūbilis*, fr. base of *volvere*, 'to roll', see **volute**. Having, speaking with, a great flow of words; fluent in speech; talkative.

volume, n. [1. vólūm; 2. vɔ́ljəm, -jum]. Fr., fr. Lat. *volūmen*, 'a roll; book written on parchment and rolled up'; fr. base of *volvere*, 'to turn, roll', see **volute**. **1.** A book, a tome; collection of printed or written sheets bound up together and forming a unity, whether forming a complete literary work or a portion of one: *a library of many thousand volumes*; *a work in six volumes*; *Volume I. has just appeared* (abbr. as *vol.*). Phr. *to speak volumes for*, to afford strong, favourable, or confirmatory testimony. **2.** A considerable mass, body, amount: *a great volume of water*; *volume of smoke, vapour*, large, dense cloud; (fig.) *a great volume of sound*, a powerful gust, blast. **3. a** Solid content, bulk, mass, amount: *the total volume of masonry, débris, earth, covering the ruins is enormous*; **b** space occupied by a liquid, gas &c. measured in cubic units, as feet, inches &c.; **c** (special use) *a voice of great, little, volume*, resonant quality, capacity for filling a large space.

-volumed, adj. [1. vólūmd; 2. vɔ́ljəmd, -jūmd]. Consisting of so many volumes: *many-volumed, three-volumed*.

volumenometer, n. [1. volùmenómeter; 2. vɔljùmínɔ́mitə]. Lat., see **volume** & -meter. Instrument for measuring the volume of a solid body.

volumetric(al), adj. [1. vòlūmétrik(l); 2. vɔ̀ljumétrik(əl)]. **volume** & -metric (& -al). Pertaining to the measurement of volume.

voluminal, adj. [1. volúminal; 2. vɔljúminəl]. Lat. *volūmin-*, stem of *volūmen*, see **volume**, & -al. Pertaining to volume.

voluminosity, n. [1. volùminósiti; 2. vɔljùminɔ́siti]. Lat. *volūminōsus*, see **voluminous**, & -ity. Quality, condition, of being voluminous.

voluminous, adj. [1. volúminus; 2. vɔljúminəs], fr. Lat. *volūmin-*, stem of *volūmen*, see **volume**, & -ous. Having considerable volume; occupying much space; bulky, abundant; extensive: *voluminous robes*; *voluminous correspondence*.

voluminously, adv. Prec. & -ly. To a voluminous extent or degree.

voluminousness, n. See prec. & -ness. Quality, condition, of being voluminous.

voluntarily, adv. [1. vóluntarili; 2. vɔ́ləntərili]. See **voluntary** & -ly. In a voluntary manner; freely, of one's own accord, without compulsion.

voluntariness, n. [1. vóluntarines; 2. vɔ́ləntərinis]. See prec. & -ness. Quality of being voluntary.

voluntarism, n. [1. vóluntarizm; 2. vɔ́ləntərizəm]. **voluntary** & -ism. System, as of religious education, military enlistment &c., which depends entirely on voluntary action.

voluntary (I.), adj. [1. vóluntari; 2. vɔ́ləntəri]. Lat. *voluntārius*, cp. *voluntāt-(em)*, 'free will', fr. base in *volo*, 'I wish, desire' &c., see **volition**, & -ary. **1.** Acting of one's own free will, by one's own desire, without compulsion, constraint, or necessity: *a voluntary worker, helper*. **2.** Done, performed, rendered, freely and at one's own choice; not compulsory; unconstrained: *voluntary services, work, tasks*; *a voluntary confession*; *voluntary contributions*. **3.** Brought about, carried on, supported, by voluntary effort, expenditure &c.: *a voluntary hospital*; *voluntary school*, one supported by a religious body; as distinguished from a state or Council school. **4.** Deliberate: *voluntary waste* (of owner's property by tenant's act or order). **5.** Specif. (physiol.) affected by, depending on, the action of the will: *voluntary muscles*, those under the control of the will; *voluntary movements*; contrasted with *involuntary*.

voluntary (II.), n., fr. prec. An organ solo played in a church, esp. before or after a service.

volunteer (I.), n. [1. vòluntér; 2. vɔ̀ləntíə]. Formed fr. *volunt-*, as in **voluntary** &c., & -eer. **1.** Person who voluntarily offers to perform specific services, esp. such as involve danger or arduous effort; one not compulsorily enrolled for such service, but coming forward of his own free will, and primarily from a sense of duty rather than from hope of reward: *volunteers were called for to act as special constables, as engine-drivers* &c. Phr. *one volunteer is worth two pressed men* (orig. of service in the Navy), service given freely and willingly is more effective than that exacted under compulsion. **2.** Specif., a member of a voluntary military organization for defensive purposes, with branches all over England, officially recognized in 1859 as the *National Rifle Association*. This force was later reorganized and known as the *Territorial Army*.

volunteer (II.), vb. trans. & intrans., fr. prec. **1.** trans. To offer freely and voluntarily: *to volunteer one's services, help, a subscription* &c. Phr. *to volunteer a remark, an opinion*, to speak, intervene in a discussion, offer an opinion, without being directly invited or consulted. **2.** intrans. **a** To offer voluntarily to perform certain services: *I asked if anyone present would undertake to collect money for the hospital, but no one volunteered*; specif. **b** to offer oneself for military service: *during the first few days of the Great War many thousands volunteered*.

voluptuary, n. [1. vòlúptuari; 2. vouláptjuəri]. Lat. *voluptu-*, as in next word, & -ary. A voluptuous person; one fond of, addicted to, sensual pleasure.

voluptuous, adj. [1. vòlúptūus; 2. vouláptjuəs]. Formed fr. Lat. type *volupt-*, as in *voluptas*, 'pleasure', w. addition of -*u-*, on the model of *sensu-ous, virtu-ous*, & -ous. The base of *voluptas* is that of *volo*, 'I desire, wish' &c., see **volition**. **a** Fond of, addicted to, sensual pleasure; sensual: *a voluptuous person*; **b** tending to promote sensual or sensuous delight; tending to excite sensual desire: *a voluptuous atmosphere, book, picture*; **c** expressing desire: *a voluptuous glance*.

voluptuously, adv. Prec. & -ly. In a voluptuous manner.

voluptuousness, n. See prec. & -ness. State, quality, of being voluptuous; voluptuous cast of mind; voluptuous habits.

volute, n. [1. volút; 2. vɔljút]. Fr., fr. Lat. *volūta*, P.P. fem. of *volvere*, 'to roll, turn', fr. the Aryan base *wolw-, *welw-*, whence also Gk. *elúein*, 'to roll', for *welw-*, see **helix**; Scrt. *valaya*, 'circle'; Lith. *welti*, 'to roll'; Goth. *walwjan*, 'to roll', O.E. *wealwian*, 'to roll round', see **wallow**, & cp. **walk, wallop**, & **gallop**; also -*volve* in **devolve, evolve** &c. **1.** (archit.) The spiral scroll forming the principal feature in Ionic and Corinthian capitals. **2.** (zool.) Any of various kinds of tropical snail (gasteropod) with beautiful shells.

voluted, adj. [1. volúted; 2. vɔljútid]. Prec. & -ed. (archit.) Decorated with volutes.

volution, n. [1. volúshun; 2. vɔljúʃən]. **volute** & -ion. **a** Spiral, whorls, of a shell; **b** (anat.) a convolution.

volutoid, adj. & n. [1. vólūtòid; 2. vɔ́ljutɔid]. **volute** & -oid. **a** adj. Shaped like a volute; **b** n., volutoid shell &c.

vomit (I.), vb. intrans. & trans. [1. vómit; 2. vɔ́mit], fr. Lat. *vomit-(um)*, P.P. type of *vomere*, 'to vomit'; cogn. w. Gk. *emeīn*, 'to vomit', *emetikós*, 'provoking sickness', for *wem-*, see **emetic**. **A**. intrans. **1.** To discharge the contents of the stomach through the mouth, to be sick. **2.** (of volcano) To discharge lava, ashes &c. through the crater. **B**. trans. **1. a** To discharge from the stomach through the mouth: *to vomit one's dinner*; **b** (fr. n., archaic) to cause to vomit by administering an emetic: *in the 17th and 18th centuries people were periodically vomited, purged, and bled*. **2.** (fig.) To pour forth vehemently in speech, to utter with violence and volubility: *to vomit insults, abuse, curses* &c.; also to give forth in printed or written form: *the reptile Press vomited its libels*; *every scribbler vomited filthy lampoons*. **3.** To emit, pour out, belch forth suddenly or impetuously, copiously, and more or less continuously: *a chimney vomits forth smoke*; *the guns vomited fire, shells*; *dragons were said to vomit fire and smoke*; *excursion trains hourly vomited crowds of trippers into quiet country districts*.

vomit (II.), n. M.E. *vomite*, fr. Lat. *vomitus*, 'a vomiting', see prec. **1. a** Matter vomited from the stomach; **b** (fig.) something of an abusive or disreputable character, uttered by word of mouth or written &c.: *the foul vomit of lampoonists*. **2.** Act of vomiting. **3.** Drug which causes vomiting; an emetic.

vomiting, n. [1. vómiting; 2. vɔ́mitiŋ]. **vomit** & -ing (II.). Act of one who vomits; retching, sickness.

vomitive, adj. & n. [1. vómitiv; 2. vɔ́mitiv]. **vomit** (I.) & -ive. **a** adj. Tending to cause vomiting; **b** n., drug which causes vomiting; an emetic.

vomitory, adj. & n. [1. vómituri; 2. vɔ́mitəri]. **vomit** (I.) & -ory. **a** adj. Causing vomiting, vomitive; **b** n., drug which does this; an emetic.

vomiturition, n. [1. vòmitūríshun; 2. vɔ̀mitjuríʃən], fr. Lat. *vomitus*, 'act of vomiting'; see **vomit** (II.). **a** Strong but abortive desire to vomit, violent retching; **b** frequent vomiting.

voodoo, n. & vb. trans. [1. vōōdōō; 2. vúdú]. Creole Fr., not fr. Fr. *Vaudois*, Waldensian, but fr. a native Dahomey word, *vodu*. **1.** n. Witchcraft, kind of black magic, practised among negroes in W. Indies and United States. **2.** vb. To bewitch, affect, with voodoo.

voodooism, n. [1. vōōdōōizm; 2. vúdúizəm]. Prec. & -ism. Practice of, belief in, voodoo.

voodooist, n. [1. vōōdōōist; 2. vúdúist]. **voodoo** & -ist. Believer in, practitioner of, voodoo.

-vora, suff. fr. neut. pl. of Lat. *-vorus*, 'eating', used to form ns. designating animals classified according to the kind of food they eat: *carnivora*, 'flesh-eating animals'; see **-vorous**, & etymol. under **voracious**.

voracious, adj. [1. voráshus; 2. vɔréiʃəs]. Lat. *vorāci-*, stem of *vorax*, 'hungry, greedy', fr. base *$g^w er-$, *$g^w or-$*, seen in *vorāre*, 'to devour'; & also in Gk. *borá*, 'food'; *brōma*, 'food'; Scrt. *garás*, 'drink'; *gargaraš*, 'gulf'. Eager to consume food; at once greedy and hungry; ravenous; urgently requiring food; (fig.) *a voracious reader*.

voraciously, adv. Prec. & -ly. In a voracious manner.

voraciousness, n. See prec. & -ness. State, quality, of being voracious; voracity.

voracity, n. [1. vorásiti; 2. vɔræsiti]. Fr. *voracité*, 'greed' &c., fr. Lat. *vorāci-*, **voracious**, & -ity. State, quality, of being voracious; eagerness, capacity, to devour; greed springing from hunger; also figurative.

-vore, suff. Fr., fr. Lat. *-vorus*, see **-vorous** & **voracious.** Suffix forming name of an animal designated from the character of its food: *carnivore*, a flesh-eating animal.

-vorous, suff. fr. Lat. *-vorus*, see prec. & **voracious** & **-ous**, forming adjectives meaning 'eating such and such food': *carnivorous*, flesh-eating &c.

vortex, n. [1. vórteks; 2. vǭtɛks], pl. **vortexes**, **vortices** [1. vórtisēz; 2. vǭtisīz]. Lat., 'whirlpool, eddy'; gradational variant fr. base **vert-*, 'to turn', see **version. 1. a** Fluid in rotational motion; a whirlpool, powerful eddy; **b** whirling motion or mass. **2.** (fig.) Any social or intellectual movement, system &c., a set of social or other conditions possessing such liveliness and intensity that they are considered as absorbing and engulfing completely those who approach them: *the vortex of war, revolution, religious controversy* &c.

vortical, adj. [1. vórtikl; 2. vǭtikl], fr. Lat. *vortic-*, stem of **vortex**, & **-al.** Resembling, of the nature of, a vortex.

vortically, adv. Prec. & **-ly.** So as to form a vortex.

vorticism, n. [1. vórtisizm; 2. vǭtisizəm], fr. **vortex** & **-ism.** An artistic movement on futurist lines, in which nature is imaginatively reconstructed in formal designs, its practitioners using vortices much as the cubists use cubes.

vorticist, n. [1. vórtisist; 2. vǭtisist]. See prec. & **-ist.** One who practises or advocates vorticism.

vorticose, adj. [1. vórtikōs; 2. vǭtikous]. *vortic-*, as in **vortical**, & **-ose.** Having a vortex; abounding in vortices.

vortiginous, adj. [1. vortíjinus; 2. vǭtídžinəs]. Cp. **vortex** & **vertiginous.** Whirling, eddying, resembling a vortex; vortical.

votable, adj. [1. vṓtabl; 2. vóutəbl]. **vote (II.)** & **-able. a** Entitled, competent, to vote; **b** able to be voted for.

votaress, n. [1. vṓtarès; 2. vóutərès]. See **votary** & **-ess.** A female votary.

votary, n. [1. vṓtari; 2. vóutəri], fr. Lat. *vōtum*, 'a vow, a wish', see next word, & **-ary. 1.** Person vowed, devoted, to the service of a god: *the ancient gods sometimes destroyed their votaries.* **2. a** Ardent adherent, supporter, advocate of a cause, ideal, system &c.: *a votary of celibacy, of total abstinence, of vegetarianism* &c.; **b** one who is much addicted to a certain pursuit: *a votary of pleasure*; *a votary of athletic sports, of hunting* &c.

vote (I.), n. [1. vōt; 2. vout]. Fr., fr. Lat. *vōtum*, 'wish; vow', for **vovetum*, fr. P.P. of *vovēre*, 'to vow; to wish for'; cogn. w. Scrt. *vāghát-*, 'one who offers a sacrifice'; Aryan base **(e)wĕgʷh-*, **(e)wōgʷh-*, 'to offer sacrifice, pray, vow', whence also Gk. *eúkhomai* 'to pray'; *eukhḗ*, 'vow; wish'. **1.** Formal expression, by ballot or show of hands &c., of one's wish, choice, opinion, esp. in regard (i.) to the election of a candidate for a post, or as a member of Parliament or other legislative or administrative body; or (ii.) to the passing of a resolution, law, measure, sanctioning or prohibiting some specific form of action. Phr. *to cast a vote*, express one's opinion by voting. **2.** The choice, will, opinion of an individual, or of a party, thus formally expressed: *I gave my vote to X*, voted for him; *the Conservative vote was unanimously given against the measure*; *one man one vote.* **3.** The right to vote, at parliamentary elections, or on other occasions when matters are decided by votes: *at what age should women have a vote?*; *he was present at the committee, but without a vote.*

vote (II.), vb. intrans. & trans., fr. prec. **A.** intrans. To exercise the right to express one's wishes, opinion &c. by casting a vote; to give a vote: *you may attend the meeting but you may not vote*; *shall you vote for or against the resolution?*; *vote for Brown and cheap bread*; *my mind is not made up, so I would rather not vote.* **B.** trans. **1.** In such Phrs. as: *to vote a measure through*, get it passed by voting; *to vote a person into Parliament*, elect him by votes; *to vote down a measure*, defeat it by voting. **2.** To assign, allot, bestow, by vote: *Parliament often votes considerable sums of money to successful generals.* **3.** To regard as, feel to be and designate as: *he was generally voted a public nuisance*; *the public voted the new play a distinct success.* **4.** (colloq.) *I vote (that) we go to the theatre to-night* &c., I suggest, propose that &c.; let us (go &c.).

voteless, adj. [1. vṓtles; 2. vóutlis]. **vote (I.)** & **-less.** Lacking a vote or the right to vote.

voter, n. [1. vṓter; 2. vóutə]. **vote (II.)** & **-er.** One who votes; specif. **a** one entitled to vote at parliamentary elections; **b** person actually casting a vote on a specific occasion.

voting, n. [1. vṓting; 2. vóutiŋ]. **vote (II.)** & **-ing.** Act of one who votes; the exercise of the right to vote: *voting paper*, official form on which votes are recorded at a ballot.

votive, adj. [1. vṓtiv; 2. vóutiv]. Lat. *vōtīvus*, 'belonging to a vow; given in consequence of a vow'; see **vote (I.)** & **-ive.** Dedicated, devoted, consecrated, to a particular purpose, in fulfilment of a vow: *a votive offering, sacrifice.*

vouch, vb. intrans. & trans. [1. vouch; 2. vautʃ], fr. O. Fr. *voucher*, 'to cite, or call in aid, in a suit', fr. Lat. *vocāre*, 'to call', see **vocal** & **vox. 1.** intrans. Chiefly *vouch for*, to guarantee, answer for (a person's honesty &c.); assert, confirm (statement or assertion), undertake: *he is a perfectly honest man for whom I can vouch*; *I can't vouch for it that the house is not already sold*; (also more rarely) *vouch that* &c. **2.** trans. (very rare) To declare, guarantee to be: *will you vouch him honest?*

voucher, n. [1. vóucher; 2. váutʃə]. Prec. & **-er.** He who, that which, vouches for something; specif., a document which establishes some fact or the authenticity of something, esp. that money has been paid.

vouchsafe, vb. trans. [1. vouchsā́f; 2. vautʃséif]. M.E. *vouchen sāfe*, 'to undertake that it is safe'; see **vouch** & **safe.** To condescend to grant; to give as an act of grace: *can you vouchsafe me a few minutes' conversation*; *I think he might at least have vouchsafed an answer.*

voussoir, n. [1. vo͞oswar; 2. vū́swā]. Fr., cogn. w. *voute*, **vault.** Any of the wedge-shaped stones forming an arch, as of a bridge or vault.

vow (I.), n. [1. vou; 2. vau]. O. Fr. *vou, veu*, fr. Lat. *vōtum*, see **vote (I.). 1.** A solemn and, under ordinary circumstances, an inviolable promise, pledge, or undertaking, made under an oath, to God, or taking God to witness, to do, or to abstain from doing, something: *a vow of celibacy*; *marriage vows*; *to be under a vow, to be bound by a vow*; *to take, make a vow*, to bind oneself by vow. **2.** Content, implication, of a vow; action &c. to which one is pledged by a vow.

vow (II.), vb. trans., fr. prec. **1.** To make a solemn promise or vow; to promise faithfully: *to vow that one will be loyal to the king.* **2.** To make vow, promise under oath, to do or make: *to vow a pilgrimage to the Holy Land.* **3.** To promise solemnly to give: *the king vowed an abbey to God for his victory.* **4.** To devote, dedicate, consecrate, esp. under a vow: *to vow oneself to a life of self-sacrifice*; *vowed to poverty and obedience.* **5.** Archaic, in colloquial Phr. *to vow and declare*, often merely emphatic for to assert; archaic and colloquial as in *I vow you are in a pretty mess*, I must say . . . **6.** To state emphatically, to assert as an intention, resolution &c.: *he vowed he would never return to such an unpleasant place.*

vowel, n. [1. vóuil, -el; 2. váuil, -ɛl, -əl], fr. O. Fr. *vouel*, cp. Mod. Fr. *voyelle*, fr. Lat. *vocālis (littera)*, 'vocal letter'; see **vocal. 1.** (phon.) A speech sound, usually voiced, formed by the tongue, and sometimes with the participation of the lips, in the utterance of which the air-passage in the mouth is never sufficiently constricted to produce audible friction; contrasted with *consonant. Vowel gradation*, see **gradation**; *vowel mutation*, see **mutation. 2.** Graphic symbol representing a vowel sound.

vowel harmony, n. Phonological principle observable in the Finno-Ugric languages, whereby the vowel sounds in the second and subsequent syllables of words are assimilated in phonetic character to that in the first syllable—a front vowel being followed by front vowels, back by back.

vowelize, vb. trans. [1. vóuilīz; 2. váuilaiz]. **vowel** & **-ize.** (rare) **1.** To change a consonantal sound into a vowel sound: *final -j in Gothic is vowelized to -i.* **2.** To add the vowel symbols or points in a Hebrew or Arabic text.

vowelless, adj. [1. vóuilles; 2. váuillis]. **vowel** & **-less.** Lacking vowels; pronounced without a vowel or vowels.

vowel-like, adj. **vowel** & **-like.** Resembling a vowel in phonetic or acoustic properties; esp. having the power of forming a syllable; syllabic; e.g. the *l* in *bottle* [bɔ́tl].

vox, n. [1. voks; 2. vɔks]. Lat., 'voice, sound, tone, cry, call'; genit. *vōc-is*; fr. same base as Lat *vocāre*, 'to call' &c., see **vocal** & **vocation**, & vbs. ending in *-voke.* This base, wh. appears in Lat. as *vŏc-, vōc-*, represents Aryan **wokʷ-, wōkʷ-, wekʷ-*, & occurs in Scrt. *vačiti*, 'he speaks', *vakaš*, 'sound', & in Gk. *épos*, 'word, song, narrative', see **epic.** Cp. also **voice.** *Vox barbara*, a linguistic barbarism, i.e. a hybrid formation or concoction; *vox humāna*, one of the stops in an organ, the quality and tone of which resemble those of the human voice; *vox populi*, the voice of the people; public opinion.

voyage (I.), n. [1. vói-ij; 2. vói-idž, vɔidž], fr. O. Fr. *veiage, voiage*, 'journey', fr. Lat. **viaticum.** A journey by sea or on another large sheet of water; used especially of a long sea journey: *a voyage to Australia, round the world*; but also, occasionally, of short journeys by sea: *one has a brief but often a rough voyage from Dover to Calais*; *crossing* would be the more usual word here.

voyage (II.), vb. intrans. & trans., fr. prec. **1.** intrans. To make a voyage, to travel by sea, to undertake a long sea journey. **2.** trans. (very rare and poet.) To journey upon, or through, to traverse: '*Long were to tell What I have done, what suffered, with what pain Voyaged the unreal, vast, unbounded deep*' (Milton, 'P. L.', x. 469–71).

voyager, n. [1. vóiajer; 2. vɔ́idžə]. Prec. & **-er.** A traveller by water; specif., an adventurous explorer of the ocean.

vraisemblable, adj. [1. vresomblā́hbl; 2. vrɛsãblā́bl]. Fr., 'having the appearance of truth'. Seeming true; having plausibility, within the bounds of probability.

vraisemblance, n. [1. vresomblā́hns; 2. vrɛsãblā́s]. Fr., 'verisimilitude'. The quality of being vraisemblable; verisimilitude.

Vulcan, n. [1. vúlkan; 2. válkən]. Lat. *Vol-, Vulcānus*, name of the Roman god of fire & metal-working; cogn. w. Scrt. *ulká*, 'a firebrand', for **wḷká-*. *Vulcan powder*, a high explosive.

Vulcanist, n. [1. vúlkanist; 2. válkənist]. Prec. & **-ist.** (geol.) One who held the Plutonic theory, namely, that most geological phenomena have been caused by the action of fire in the interior of the earth.

vulcanite, n. [1. vúlkanīt; 2. válkənait]. **vulcan** & **-ite.** Form of india-rubber produced by an admixture of sulphur; ebonite.

vulcanization, n. [1. vùlkanīzā́shun; 2. vàlkənaizéiʃən]. Next word & **-ation.** Process of vulcanizing rubber.

vulcanize, vb. trans. [1. vúlkanīz; 2. válkənaiz]. **Vulcan** & **-ize.** To treat (rubber) by mixing with sulphur to increase its elasticity.

vulgar, adj. [1. vúlgar; 2. válgə]. Lat. *vulgāris*, 'belonging to the multitude; general, usual, common, commonplace, vulgar'; fr. *vulgus*, 'the multitude', see **vulgus**, & **-ar.**

vulgarian, n. [1. vulgárian; 2. valgéəriən]. Lat. vulgāri-, stem of vulgāris, see prec., & -an. A vulgar, flamboyant, person; esp. a pretentious person, often one newly enriched, without good breeding, decent manners, or delicacy of feeling; a bounder.

1. Pertaining to the multitude, hence common, in common or ordinary use, having currency among the mass of the people, usual; obs. except in Phr. *the vulgar tongue*, the vernacular. 2. Pertaining to the common people as contrasted with the upper and more civilized classes: *vulgar life, circles* &c. 3. a Characteristic of the people, as contrasted with the upper and more refined or polite classes of society; not current in refined circles; low, base, unrefined; indelicate; ill-bred: *vulgar manners, language; a vulgar accent, way of speaking*; b not conforming to, unfamiliar with, the manners and customs of good society; lacking delicacy of feeling; bad, coarse, indecorous: *a vulgar fellow*; as n., *the vulgar*, vulgar people.

vulgarism, n. [1. vúlgarizm; 2. válgərizəm]. vulgar & -ism. 1. Vulgar behaviour; vulgarity. 2. A vulgar, unrefined mode of speech; a mode of pronunciation, choice of words, grammatical form, not current among the well-bred and refined classes of society; a solecism.

vulgarity, n. [1. vulgáriti; 2. valgǽriti]. See vulgar & -ity. Quality of being vulgar; vulgar behaviour; coarseness, commonness of moral fibre, lack of refinement and delicacy in feeling; rudeness, ill-breeding; pretentious, offensive arrogance and display, coupled with bad taste and bad manners; indecorum.

vulgarization, n. [1. vùlgarizǽshun; 2. vàlgəraizéiʃən]. vulgarize & -ation. 1. Act, process, of rendering vulgar; state of having become vulgar. 2. (rare) Act of rendering more widely known and current; popularization.

vulgarize, vb. trans. [1. vúlgariz; 2. válgəraiz]. vulgar & -ize. 1. To make vulgar, common, unrefined, commonplace: *the tripper has vulgarized many of the loveliest spots in England*. 2. (rare) To render better known; to popularize.

vulgarly, adv. [1. vúlgarli; 2. válgəli]. vulgar & -ly. 1. Commonly, generally, popularly: *vulgarly supposed to be a cure* &c. 2. In a vulgar manner; with vulgarity: *to behave, speak, vulgarly*.

Vulgate, n. [1. vúlgat; 2. válgit]. Lat. *vulgāta ēditio*, lit. 'popular edition', fr. fem. of *vulgātus*, P.P. of *vulgāre*, 'to make general, common, or universal', formed fr. *vulgus*, 'the multitude' &c., see vulgus & vulgar. Latin translation of the Scriptures made towards the end of the 4th cent., recognized by the Roman Church as authentic and authoritative.

vulgus, n. [1. vúlgus; 2. válgəs]. Lat., 'the great mass of the people; the masses, the multitude, the people, the common run'; cogn. w. Scrt. *várgaś*, 'division, section, group'; not connected with folk. 1. The common people, the multitude. 2. (archaic or obs.) A collection of exercises in Latin or Greek verse used in schools.

vulnerability, n. [1. vùlnerabíliti; 2. vàlnərəbíliti]. Next word & -ity. Quality, condition, of being vulnerable.

vulnerable, adj. [1. vúlnerabl; 2. válnərəbl]. Lat. *vulnerābilis*, fr. vulner-, stem of *vulnus*, earlier *volnus*, 'wound'; cogn. w. Gk. *oulḗ*, fr. *wolnā*, 'a scar'; prob. fr. same base as that in Lat. *vellere*, 'to pluck, pull, tear', see villus, vellicate. Capable of being, liable to be, wounded; open to, susceptible of, not protected against, attack, injury, criticism.

vulnerably, adv. Prec. & -ly. So as to be vulnerable.

vulnerary, adj. & n. [1. vúlnerari; 2. válnərəri]. Lat. *vulner-*, see vulnerable, & -ary. 1. adj. Used, useful, for healing wounds. 2. n. A remedy for wounds.

vulpicide, n. [1. vúlpisīd; 2. válpisaid]. Lat. *vulpi-*, stem of *vulpes*, 'fox', see vulpine, & -cide. 1. Person who shoots or traps foxes. 2. The killing of foxes otherwise than by the normal method of hunting them.

vulpine, adj. [1. vúlpīn; 2. válpain], fr. Lat. *vulpīnus*, 'pertaining to, like, a fox; crafty', fr. *vulpēs*, 'a fox', earlier volp-, & -ine. The Lat. name for fox may either be fr. Aryan base *kʷelpi-*, *kʷolpi-*, whence also, fr. variant *kʷelb-*, O.E. *hwelp*, 'young dog', see whelp (I.), or, as seems more probable, fr. Aryan *wulkʷi-*, *wulpi-*, fr. a different grade of wh. comes Lith. *wilpiszis*, 'wild cat'; fr. another variant, *wl̥kʷos*, comes Lat. *lŭpus*, 'wolf', see lupine & cp. wolf (I.). Pertaining to, resembling, a fox; a having the appearance of a fox: *vulpine countenance*; b like a fox in character; sly, crafty.

vulpinism, n. [1. vúlpinizm; 2. válpinizəm]. Prec. & -ism. (rare) Guile, craftiness, slyness.

vulture, n. [1. vúlchur; 2. váltʃə]. M.E. *vultur*, fr. O. Fr. *voltur*, fr. Lat. *vultur, voltur*, name of the bird, connected w. *vellere*, 'to pluck', see vellicate & words there referred to. 1. Large bird of prey, allied to the hawks and eagles, which lives chiefly on carrion. 2. (fig.) An unscrupulous, rapacious rogue and extortioner who preys upon his fellow-creatures.

vulturine, adj. [1. vúlchurīn; 2. váltʃərain]. Prec. & -ine. Pertaining to, resembling, a vulture in appearance or habits: *vulturine eagle*.

vulturous, adj. [1. vúlchurus; 2. váltʃərəs]. vulture & -ous. Having the characteristics of the vulture; rapacious.

vulva, n. [1. vúlva; 2. válvə]. Lat., also *volva*, 'wrapper, covering; the womb', connected w. *volvere*, 'to turn, roll, fold' &c., see volute. External orifice of female genital organs.

vulvar, adj. [1. vúlvar; 2. válvə]. Prec. & -ar. Pertaining to the vulva.

vulvitis, n. [1. vulvítis; 2. valváitis]. vulva & -itis. Inflammation of the vulva.

vulvo-, pref. Form of vulva used in compounds: *vulvo-uterine*, pertaining to, affecting, the vulva and the uterus.

W

W, w [1. dúbl-ū; 2. dábl-ju]. The twenty-third letter of the alphabet. For abbreviations &c. see list at end of Dictionary.

wabble. See wobble.

wacke, n. [1. wáke; 2. wǽkə], fr. Mod. Germ. *wacke*; M.H.G. *wacke*, O.H.G. *wacko*, 'gravel'. Soft, greyish or brownish rock developed from decomposed trap-rock.

wad (I.), n. [1. wod; 2. wɔd]. Prob. fr. Swed. *vadd*, 'wadding'; cp. Mod. Germ. *watte*, fr. Du. *watje*. According to Kluge, the word first appears in 1380, as Med. Lat. *wadda*. 1. a Small mass or lump of soft, fibrous material packed round or between objects to prevent shifting and rattling, concussion &c.; or used to stop up an opening; specif. b disk of leather, felt &c. to hold charge in position in gun &c. 2. Collection of sheets, esp. of bank-notes, pressed or folded together so as to form a compact bundle.

wad (II.), vb. trans., fr. prec. 1. To pack, press (soft material), into a wad. 2. a To pack, pad, stuff, with a wad; b to stop up (opening) with a wad. 3. To line (garment &c.) with wadding, to give warmth, softness &c.

wadable, adj. [1. wádabl; 2. wéidəbl]. wade (I.) & -able. Capable of being waded.

wadding, n. [1. wóding; 2. wɔ́diŋ]. wad & -ing. 1. Soft, fluffy material used for stuffing, packing, lining garments &c.; esp. cotton-wool in sheets. 2. Felt or other material used for gun-wads.

waddle, vb. intrans. & n. [1. wódl; 2. wɔ́dl]. wade & -le. 1. vb. To walk with short steps and a rolling gait, as of a stout, short-legged person, or a heavy short-legged bird, esp. a duck &c. 2. n. Act of waddling; a heavy, ungraceful gait accompanied by a roll from side to side as each foot is placed on the ground.

waddling, adj. [1. wódling; 2. wɔ́dliŋ], fr. Pres. Part. of prec. Inclined to waddle; characterized by a waddle.

waddlingly, adv. Prec. & -ly. In a waddling manner.

waddy, n. [1. wódi; 2. wɔ́di]. Australian. Wooden war-club of Australian aborigines.

wade (I.), vb. intrans. & trans. [1. wād; 2. weid]. O.E. *wadan*; M.E. *wāden*, 'to go'; cp. O. Fris. *wada*; O.H.G. *watan* & O.N. *vaða*, 'to go, walk'; cogn. w. Lat. *vādere*, 'to go', seen in vade-mecum, *vadum*, 'ford'; *vadāre*, 'to wade'. A. intrans. 1. a To walk through water, liquid mud, wet snow &c., or other penetrable substance: *to wade across a stream*; *to wade through the mud*; also b (fig.) 'to wade through slaughter to a throne' (Gray's 'Elegy'). 2. Specif., to walk in the water of a river while fly-fishing. 3. (fig.) To peruse, go through laboriously, with effort: *to wade through a book*. 4. *Wade in*, a to enter, advance into shallow water, on foot, not swimming: *he waded in and rescued the drowning child*; b (fig.) to enter, take part in, intervene, in a fight, piece of business, discussion &c.: *he must needs wade in and delay the business with petty objections*. B. trans. To cross, traverse (piece of water) by wading, ford: *to wade a stream*.

wade (II.), n., fr. prec. Act, spell, of wading.

wader, n. [1. wáder; 2. wéidə]. Prec. & -er. 1. One who, that which, wades; specif., a wading bird. 2. (pl.) *Waders*, long waterproof garments covering feet and legs and coming up above the waist, worn by fly-fishermen &c.

wadi, wady, n. [1. wódi; 2. wɔ́di]. Arab. *wādī*. (in Arabia &c.) a Watercourse, river-bed, which is dry except in rainy season; b an oasis.

wading, adj. [1. wáding; 2. wéidiŋ]. Pres. Part. of wade (I.). *Wading bird*, one which has long legs enabling it to walk in shallow water to obtain food, such as a crane, a heron &c.

Wafd, n. [1. wahft, waft; 2. waft, wæft]. Arab. Name of the extreme Nationalist party in Egypt.

wafer (I.), n. [1. wáfer; 2. wéifə]. M.E. *wāfre*, 'thin cake', fr. O. Fr. *waufre*, of Gmc. origin; cp. O.H.G. *waba*, 'honeycomb'; cogn. w. weave (I.), web. 1. A very thin sheet or disk of flour, used for various purposes: a small disk formerly used for sealing letters &c.; b small disk used in Holy Communion. 2. A small disk of red paper affixed to a document in place of a seal. 3. A thin sweet, cake, or biscuit, esp. one eaten with ices. Phr. *as thin as a wafer*, very thin.

wafer (II.), vb. trans., fr. prec. To fasten with a wafer.

wafery, adj. [1. wáferi; 2. wéifəri]. wafer & -y. Resembling a wafer in thinness and consistency.

waffle, n. [1. wófl; 2. wɔ́fl], fr. Du. *wafel*, cogn. w. wafer. Thin, crisp cake of batter cooked over the fire in a waffle-iron.

waffle-iron, n. Iron cooking utensil, consisting of two shallow pans hinged together and reversible.

waft (I.), vb. trans. [1. wahft; 2. wăft]. Prob. a variant of **wave**; or possibly a back-formation fr. obs. *wafter*, 'convoying ship', the latter perh. fr. Du. *wachter*, 'guard', cogn. w. **watch** (I.) & **wake** (I.). To carry lightly and buoyantly through the air or water; to bear smoothly along: *the leaves were wafted along by the breeze*; *a distant song was wafted to our ears*.

waft (II.), n., fr. prec. 1. Smooth movement, sweep, of flying or floating body. 2. Hint of fragrance; faint odour, whiff.

wag (I.), vb. trans. & intrans. [1. wag; 2. wæg]. M.E. *waggen*, prob. fr. M. Swed. *wagga*, 'to oscillate, fluctuate'; cogn. w. O.E. *wagian*, M.E. *wāwien*, 'to move'; O.H.G. *wagōn*; Goth. *wagjan*, 'to move'; cogn. w. O.E. *wegan*, 'to carry'; see **weigh** (I.), & cp. also **wag(g)on, wain. A.** trans. 1. To cause to oscillate, shake (object fastened at one end) lightly up and down or from side to side: *to wag one's forefinger*. 2. Specif. (of a dog) *to wag the tail*, to move it rapidly to and fro as expression of pleasure &c. **B.** intrans. (of object fastened at one end) To move quickly and lightly up and down or from side to side: *the dog's tail wags when his master appears*; *their heads wagged in time to the music*. Phrs. *to set tongues, chins, wagging*, cause people to talk, esp. to provoke mild scandal; *so the world wags*, thus human affairs go on.

wag (II.), n., fr. prec. Motion of wagging; single movement forming part of oscillation: *the dog replied with a wag of its tail*.

wag (III.), n. Earlier *wag-halter*, a person likely to swing at the end of a rope, i.e. to be hanged; hence a rascal; commonly used playfully. A jester; a merry, roguish person; one fond of quips and jokes; a humorous person, one full of comical, laughable sayings.

wage (I.), n. [1. wāj; 2. weidž]. M.E. *wāge*, fr. O. Fr. *wage*; fr. Low Lat. *wadium*, 'a pledge'; of Gmc. origin; cp. Goth. *wadi*, 'a pledge', & (*ga*)*wadjōn*, 'to pledge'; cp. O.E. *wedd*, 'pledge, agreement', see **wed**. **gage** (I.) is fr. a Fr. variant. 1. (archaic) Recompense, reward; often in plural treated as singular: '*the wages of sin is death*'; '*Thou thy worldly task hast done, Home art gone, and ta'en thy wages*' (Shakespeare, '*Cymbeline*', iv., song). 2. a Payment made at regular intervals in return for services; now chiefly used of payment made for manual labour, the contract between the parties being terminable at short notice; contrasted with *stipend* and *salary*: *I pay my man a good weekly wage*; Phr. *a living wage*, one adequate for the support of recipient; **b** more usually in plural, *wages*, the periodical payment earned by, and made to, domestic servants and manual labourers generally: *a reliable workman can earn good wages*; *take your month's wages and go at once*; *when wages are high, prices are high*.

wage (II.), vb. trans. M.E. *wāgen*, O. Fr. *wagier*, 'to pledge, promise, engage', fr. *wage*, 'a pledge', see prec. To carry on, conduct, prosecute (war, a campaign).

wage-earner, n. [1. wāj ẽrner; 2. weidž ånə]. Person working for wages.

wageless, adj. [1. wājles; 2. weidžlis]. **wage** (I.) & **-less**. Receiving no wages.

wager (I.), n. [1. wājer; 2. weidžə]. M.E. *wāgeoure*, fr. O. Fr. *wageure*, fr. L. Lat. *wadiatūra*, fr. *wadiāre*, 'to pledge', fr. *wadium*, 'a pledge', see **wage** (I.). 1. Engagement between two persons to risk money on the outcome of an event; bet. 2. (hist.) *Wager of battle*, mode of trial by personal combat; *wager of law*, mode of defence in which defendant, together with a number of witnesses, swears to his innocence, absence of liability &c.

wager (II.), vb. trans., fr. prec. 1. a To bet, risk, offer as stake: *to wager half a crown on a race*; **b** to pledge: *to wager one's reputation on*. 2. To bet (that): *I would not wager that I shall succeed*.

wage(s)-fund, n. [1. wāj(ez) fúnd; 2. weidž(iz) fånd]. (polit. econ.) That part of the capital of a community which is to be expended on wages and salaries.

waggery, n. [1. wágeri; 2. wǽgəri]. **wag** (III.) & **-ery**. Waggish behaviour or sayings; drollery, comicality.

waggish, adj. [1. wágish; 2. wǽgiʃ]. **wag** (III.) & **-ish**. Inclined to, of the nature of, waggery; comical, droll: *a waggish fellow*; *a waggish look, speech* &c.

waggishly, adv. Prec. & **-ly**. In a waggish manner.

waggishness, n. See prec. & **-ness**. Quality of being waggish; waggery.

waggle (I.), vb. intrans. & trans. [1. wágl; 2. wǽgl]. Freq. of **wag** (I.); see **-le**. (colloq.) To move slightly backwards and forwards, to oscillate.

waggle (II.), n., fr. prec. (colloq.) A slight backward and forward movement.

wag(g)on, n. [1. wágun; 2. wǽgən], fr. Du. *wagen*; cogn. w. **wain**. 1. Strong, four-wheeled vehicle used for carrying heavy loads, often drawn by two or more horses, and sometimes with removable top or cover. 2. Railway truck.

wag(g)on-boiler, n. Steam-boiler of semi-cylindrical shape, like that of cover of waggon.

wag(g)oner, n. [1. wáguner; 2. wǽgənə]. **wag(g)on** & **-er**. Driver of waggon; man in charge of waggon(s) and horses &c.

wag(g)on-roof, n. Roof of semi-cylindrical shape.

wag(g)on-vault, n. Semicircular vault.

wagonette, n. [1. wàgunét; 2. wæ̀gənét]. **wag(g)on** & **-ette**. Four-wheeled open carriage, with two seats facing each other behind the coachman's box.

wagon-lit, n. [1. vàgon lē; 2. væ̀gɔ̃ lí]. Fr. Railway carriage fitted with beds.

wagtail, n. [1. wágtāl; 2. wǽgteil]. **wag** (I.) & **tail**. One of a genus, *Motacilla*, of small birds with long wings, and tail feathers which move constantly up and down as the bird runs along the ground.

Wahabi, -ee, n. [1. wahhábi; 2. wahɑ́bi]. Member of Puritanical Mohammedan sect founded in the 18th cent. in Central Arabia by Abd-el-Wahhab, who died about 1792.

waif, n. [1. wāf; 2. weif]. In M.E., fr. O.N. *veif*, 'something flapping or waving'; meaning influenced by O. Fr. *waif*, fr. L. Lat. *waivium*, 'goods thrown away by a thief in flight', also fr. O.N. See **waive**. 1. a A homeless, straying, wandering person or animal; Phr. *waifs and strays*, homeless, abandoned children; **b** a person or animal of miserable, poverty-stricken, neglected appearance. 2. Object without an owner, esp. something which drifts in water or is blown by the wind, or brought by unknown agency.

wail (I.), vb. intrans. & trans. [1. wāl; 2. weil]. M.E. *wailen*, fr. O.N. *vǽla*, 'to lament', fr. *væ*, 'woe'; cogn. w. **woe. A.** intrans. 1. (of living creatures and of the wind) To utter or produce a long, shrill, lugubrious or plaintive cry or sound; to shriek, howl. 2. To express sorrow or regret; to lament: *to wail over one's misfortunes*. **B.** trans. To bewail; to lament, grieve over: *to wail one's sorrows*.

wail (II.), n. See prec. a Wailing sound; prolonged, plaintive sound produced by a living creature or by the wind &c.; **b** a complaint, expression of regret, grief, annoyance &c.

wailful, adj. [1. wālfool; 2. weilful]. Prec. & **-ful**. In the nature of a wail; plaintive: *a wailful cry*.

wailing (I.), adj. [1. wāling; 2. weiliŋ]. Pres. Part. of **wail** (I.). Of the nature of, resembling, a wail.

wailing (II.), vbl. n. **wail** & **-ing**. The sound of a wail.

wailingly, adv. **wailing** (I.) & **-ly**. In a wailing manner.

wain, n. [1. wān; 2. wein]. O.E. *wægn*, M.E. *wain*, 'waggon'; cp. O. Fris. *wain*; O.N. *vagn*; O.H.G. *wagan*; in gradational relation to O.E. *wegan*, 'to carry', see **weigh** (I.); cp. also **vehicle**. (chiefly poet.) A waggon; *Charles's Wain*, the constellation also called the Plough, the Great Bear, and Ursa Major.

wainscot, n. & vb. trans. [1. wénskut, wǎnskōt; 2. wénskət, wéinskout, -kət], fr. Du. *wagenschot*; the first element is doubtful; perh. cogn. w. O.E. *wǎg*, 'wall', but by some referred to Du. *wage*, 'a wave', in reference to the grain of wood; the second element means 'board'; etymol. doubtful; cp. **camp-shot**. 1. n. a Originally applied to a fine oak used for panelling imported from Holland; now, any wooden panelling on a wall, but esp. the wooden panel at the base of, and running round, the wall of a room just above the floor; **b** name of various moths of the sub-family Orthosiidae, with streaked wing markings. 2. vb. To affix wainscot to (wall).

wainscoting, n. [1. wénskuting; 2. wénskətiŋ]. Prec. & **-ing**. a Material for wainscot; **b** wooden panelling on a wall.

waist, n. [1. wāst; 2. weist]. M.E. *wǎst*, 'stature; waist'; cp. O.H.G. *wahst*; Goth. *wahstus*, 'growth'; cogn. w. O.E. *wæstm*, 'growth', fr. base of *weahsan*, *weaxan*, 'to grow', see **wax** (III.). 1. a Narrowest part of human trunk, between ribs and hip-bones: *to have a sash round one's waist*; *a large, small, waist*, one of large, small, circumference; **b** well-marked narrowing and slimness of the figure at the waist: *waists have gone out of fashion*. 2. Part of woman's garment corresponding to the waist. Specif. U.S.A., a woman's blouse or bodice; also *shirt-waist*. 3. Part of an object resembling the human waist in shape and position; central, narrowed portion, e.g. of a violin. 4. (naut.) Middle part of ship, between quarter-deck and forecastle.

waist-band, n. Band, part of garment, fitting round the waist.

waist-belt, n. Belt worn round the waist.

waist-cloth, n. Loin-cloth.

waistcoat, n. [1. wéskut, wǎs(t)kōt; 2. wéskət, wéis(t)kout]. Close-fitting, usually sleeveless garment worn under a coat and reaching to the waist.

waist-deep, adj. & adv. 1. adj. a Reaching up to the waist: *the water was waist-deep*; **b** covered up to the waist: *to be waist-deep in bracken*. 2. adv. So as to reach the waist.

waisted, adj. [1. wǎsted; 2. wéistid]. **waist** & **-ed**. Having a waist; shaped to form a waist; also in compounds: *long-, short-, small-waisted* &c.

waist-high, adj. & adv. High enough to reach to the waist.

wait (I.), vb. intrans. & trans. [1. wāt; 2. weit]. M.E. *waiten*, fr. O. Fr. *waitier* (also *gaitier*), 'to watch, wait', fr. *waite*, 'watcher', fr. O.H.G. *wahta*, 'watcher', fr. *wahhēn*, 'to be awake'; see further under **wake** (I.). **A.** intrans. 1. To remain in expectation of something happening; to delay action &c., until a particular time, until an event has taken place: *the train is due, so we shall not have long to wait*; *don't wait if I am late*; *let us wait in the shade*; *you mustn't keep him waiting*; *wait until you are asked*; *please wait a minute*; *we have waited for hours*. 2. To act as waiter, serve and hand round dishes at table &c.: *to wait at table*; *she will never learn to wait*. **B.** trans. 1. To wait for, remain in expectation of, on the watch for: *to wait one's chance*; *to wait a person's return*; *to wait one's convenience, pleasure* &c. Phr. *to wait dinner, tea, luncheon &c. for* (a person), to put off having (dinner &c.) until he arrives. **C.** Followed by adverbs and prepositions with special meanings. *Wait for*, intrans., to remain in expectation of, await; delay action, resumption of action, departure &c., until specified time, person's arrival &c.: *I will wait for you at the gate*; *we have been waiting for the clock to strike*; *to wait for a person's reply*; *to wait for* *a signal. Wait (up)on*, **1.** (archaic) to call upon, pay one's respects to; **2.** (archaic) **a** to escort; **b** (fig.) to accompany, attend: *may good luck wait upon you*; **3.** to serve, attend upon, act as attendant on, fetch and carry for: *to be waited on hand and foot*; **4.** to follow as result, be a consequence of: '*Now good digestion wait on appetite*' (Shakespeare, 'Macbeth', iii. 4).

wait (II.), n., fr. prec. **a** Act of waiting; Phrs. *to lie in wait (for)*, remain hidden and waiting to waylay or attack; *to lay wait for*, prepare an ambush for; **b** time during which one waits: *a long, tedious wait*.

wait (III.), n., fr. O. Fr. *waite*, 'watcher'; see **wait (I.)**. (chiefly in pl.) *The waits*, a band of persons who go from house to house and sing Christmas carols.

waiter, n. [1. wăter; 2. wéitə]. **wait (I.) & -er. 1.** A male servant who serves guests at meals in public restaurants and hotels. **2.** Tray, salver, for handing dishes &c.

waiting, n. [1. wăting; 2. wéitiŋ]. **wait & -ing.** Act or occupation of one who waits. Phr. *in waiting*, in attendance, esp. on royalty: *lady-in-waiting*; *lords, grooms, in waiting*.

waiting-maid, n. Female personal attendant.

waiting-room, n. Room at railway station for the use of persons waiting for trains; sitting-room in a house for person awaiting an interview with a medical man &c.

waitress, n. [1. wătres; 2. wéitris]. **waiter & -ess.** Female waiter at a hotel or restaurant.

waive, vb. trans. [1. wāv; 2. weiv]. M.E. *waiven*, fr. A.-Fr. *wayver*; of Gmc. origin; cp. O.N. *veifa*, 'to fluctuate, vibrate'; cogn. w. O.E. *wāfian*, 'to be astonished at, to hesitate'; O.H.G. *weibōn*, 'to be unsteady'; cogn. w. Lat. *vibrāre*. See **vibrate** & cp. **waif.** To relinquish, esp. temporarily, refrain from insisting on or pressing: *to waive one's rights, a claim* &c.

waiver, n. [1. wăver; 2. wéivə]. A.-Fr. *wayver*, infin. as n.; see prec. Legal renunciation, relinquishing of claim &c.

wake (I.), vb. intrans. & trans. [1. wāk; 2. weik]. There are two closely related vbs. in O.E., *wacian*, 'to be awake, watch', & *wacan*, 'to originate, rise, be born'; M.E. *wāken*, 'to be awake, watch, keep vigil'; O.H.G. *wahhēn*; O.N. *vaka*, 'to be awake'; Goth. *wakan*; cp. further O.E. *wacor*, 'watchful'; O.H.G. *wahhar*, 'lively'; O.N. *vakr*, 'vigilant'; cogn. w. Lat. *vegēre*, 'to be active; to arouse', see **vegetable**; cp. **watch (I.). A.** intrans. **1.** To be, remain, awake: '*He wakes or sleeps with the enduring dead*' (Shelley, 'Adonais', xxxviii. 3). Phr. *in our waking hours*, those during which we are awake. **2. a** Also *wake up*, to return to consciousness from sleep: *I wake (up) early*; *to wake up with a start*; **b** to return to consciousness from a state resembling sleep: *to wake from a stupor, hypnotic trance* &c.; **c** to become mentally alert following condition of dullness and torpor: *it is time for you to wake up and attend to your business*. Phr. *to wake to* (a realization of danger &c.), become conscious of, realize. **3.** To come to life, become active; to emerge from a state of inactivity and quiescence: *his conscience woke and smote him*; *many fierce and angry passions wake during controversy*. **B.** trans. Also *wake up*, **1.** To cause to wake, rouse: *the noise woke me* (*up*); *wake me at seven*. Phr. *to wake the echoes*, make a loud noise. **2.** To rouse, provoke mental alertness in, to stimulate into activity of mind: *the shock seemed to wake him up and make him less lethargic*. **3.** To excite, rouse, recall to activity, render lively; to stir: *to wake memories of the past*; *to wake passions*.

wake (II.), n., fr. prec. **1.** (hist.) **a** Festival of dedication of church, preceded by all-night vigil; **b** festivity, merrymaking, in celebration of this. **2. a** Vigil beside a corpse, kept up throughout the night preceding the funeral; **b** festivities accompanying a wake; (frequent among the poorer classes in Ireland). **3.** Annual holiday taken by workers in the industrial towns of Lancashire, Yorkshire &c.

wake (III.), vb. trans., fr. prec. To hold a wake over (dead person).

wake (IV.), n., fr. O.N. *vök*, 'hole in ice'; cp. O.N. *vökr*, 'damp'; cogn. w. Gk. *hugrós*, 'moist'; Scrt. *uksáti*, 'sprinkles'; Lat. *ūvidus*, 'wet'; (h)*umor*, 'moisture', see **humour (I.)**. Long streak of smooth water behind moving vessel. Phr. *in the wake of*, (i.) (of vessel) following in the track of; (ii.) (fig.) following as consequence of; *wars bring misery in their wake*.

wakeful, adj. [1. wăkfool; 2. wéikful]. **wake (I.) & -ful. 1.** Watchful, vigilant, alert. **2. a** Remaining awake, unable to sleep; **b** *a wakeful night*, one passed with little or no sleep.

wakefully, adv. Prec. & -ly. In a wakeful manner.

wakefulness, n. See prec. & -ness. State of being wakeful.

waken, vb. intrans. & trans. [1. wăken; 2. wéikən]. O.E. *wæcnan*, 'to be born, have origin'; M.E. *waknen*, 'to be awakened', fr. *wacan*, 'to have origin, arise', see **wake (I.). 1.** intrans. **a** To wake up, be awakened; **b** to recover consciousness, be roused. **2.** trans. **a** To cause to wake, rouse up; **b** to rouse to activity, stir up.

wake-robin, n. Wild arum.

Walach(ian). See **Wallach, Wallachian**.

Waldenses, n. pl. [1. wòldénsēz; 2. wòldénsīz], fr. Peter Waldo, of Lyons, founder of the sect. Sect of Puritan reformers in Western Church, still persisting in the region of the Cottian Alps, founded about 1170, and much persecuted in 16th and 17th cents.

Waldensian, adj. [1. wòldénsian; 2. wòldénsiən]. Prec. & -ian. Pertaining to the Waldenses.

wald-horn, n. [1. váhlt horn; 2. vált hōn], fr. Germ. *wald*, 'forest', see under **wold**, & **horn**. Hunting-horn.

wale, n. & vb. trans. [1. wăl; 2. weil]. O.E. *walu*, 'weal, stripe; bar, gunwale'; M.E. *wāle*; cp. O.N. *völr*; O. Fris. *walu*; Goth. *walus*, 'rod'; cogn. w. Lith. (*ap*)*valùs*, 'round'; Lat. *vallus*, 'pillar'; *vallēs*, 'valley'; see **vallum, valley, wall**. **weal (II.)** is a variant. **1.** n. Raised streak formed on the flesh by a blow from a whip, stick &c. **2.** vb. To raise wales on, mark with wales.

wale-knot, n. Also *wall-knot*, mode of interweaving strands at end of rope to prevent unravelling.

Waler, n. [1. wăler; 2. wéilə], fr. New South Wales. One of a breed of horses imported into India from Australia.

Walhalla. See **Valhalla**.

walk (I.), vb. intrans. & trans. [1. wawk; 2. wōk]. O.E. *walcan*, 'to roll, fluctuate, whirl, twist'; M.E. *walken*, 'to move, go, roll, walk'; O.H.G. *walkan*, 'to strike, beat'; cp. O.N. *valka*, 'to roll'; Du. *walken*, 'to press'; Mod. Germ. *walken*, 'to full (cloth)'; cogn. w. Scrt. *valgati*, '(he) hops'. **A.** intrans. **1. a** To move along by putting alternately each foot in front of the other, and advancing at a moderate pace; contrasted with *sit*, or *stand still*; to pace along: *to walk slowly, steadily, up and down*; *children learn to walk at 13 months or so*; *it is too cold to stand about, you had better walk a bit*; Phr. *walking lady, gentleman*, actor who appears on the stage, but has no spoken part; **b** specif. (of a ghost) to be seen moving, stirring, in a specific place, to be visible, to haunt a place: *the ghost walks at midnight*. **2. a** (of persons) To move along at a comparatively slow or walking pace; contrasted with *to run*: *I'm quite out of breath with running, I must walk for a bit*; **b** (of a horse &c.) to move along at the slowest pace; contrasted with *to trot, canter, gallop*. **3.** To go on foot, as opposed to riding, or being conveyed in a vehicle: *let us stop the carriage and get down and walk*; *shall we go by car or walk?* **4.** (archaic) To conduct oneself, to behave, order one's conduct, mode of life &c.: '*to walk humbly with one's God*'. **B.** trans. **1. a** To cause to go at a walk: *to walk one's horse down hill*; **b** to lead, accompany, at a walk: *to walk a horse up and down*; *to walk a man all over the town*; Phr. *to walk a person off his legs*, tire him out by making him walk too far; **c** specif., *to walk a puppy*, to train and exercise him. **2.** To traverse on foot: *I have walked this country for miles round*. Phrs. (archaic) *to walk the hospitals*, attend cases, watch operations, in hospital, as part of practical training for medical profession; *to walk the boards*, to act on the stage; *to walk the plank*, be murdered by pirates by being compelled to walk up a plank which tips up and precipitates one into the sea; *to walk the chalk*, to demonstrate that one is sober by walking along a narrow chalk line. **3.** To traverse a specified distance on foot: *to walk a mile*. **4.** To contend with, pit oneself against, in walking: *I'll walk you ten miles any day you like*. **C.** Followed by adverbs and prepositions with special meanings. *Walk about*, intrans., to walk here and there, stroll up and down &c. *Walk away*, **1.** intrans., to depart at a walk; **2.** trans., to lead away at a walk. *Walk away from*, intrans., (lit. and fig.) to outstrip with ease in a contest. *Walk away with*, intrans., to carry off. *Walk in*, intrans., to enter, come, go in. *Walk into*, intrans., (slang) **a** to eat heartily of, devour; **b** to abuse, rail at, pitch into. *Walk off*, **1.** intrans., to depart at a walk; **2.** trans., to cause to walk off. *Walk off with*, intrans., to carry off; to steal: *the page-boy has walked off with the spoons*. *Walk out with*, intrans., (of lower classes) to be in initial stages of courtship with, prior to formal engagement. *Walk over*, trans., (in contest, race &c.) **a** to pass over (course) at walking pace in absence of other competitors; **b** to have an easy victory over.

walk (II.), n., fr. prec. **1.** Action of walking, **a** (of person) pace in which the feet are moved forward successively, without taking both off the ground simultaneously; **b** (of quadruped) slowest pace, two feet at least being always on the ground: *to go at a walk*; *to drop into a walk*. **2.** Manner of walking, characteristic gait, carriage: *one can often recognize a person by his walk*; *a dignified, a shambling, walk*. **3.** Spell of walking, journey, excursion, on foot, esp. for exercise or recreation: *to go for a walk*; *to take a walk*; *we had a long, tiring walk*. **4. a** Route traversed on foot: *this is my favourite walk*; **b** specif., regular route, beat, of hawker &c. Phr. *walk of*, or *in*, *life*, (i.) station, position, rank in society: *persons in the humbler walks of life*; (ii.) habitual occupation, profession: *he chose the Bar as his walk in life*. **5.** (archaic) Mode of ordering one's life and behaviour; general conduct. **6.** Place, strip of ground, set apart for walking; path, promenade: *a grass, gravel, walk*; *a walk bordered with a yew-hedge*. **7.** District, enclosure, piece of ground, for exercising animals, pasturing sheep &c.; also in compounds, *sheep-walk* &c.

walkable, adj. [1. wăwkabl; 2. wŏkəbl]. **walk (I.) & -able.** Capable of being walked: *a walkable distance*.

walker, n. [1. wăwker; 2. wŏkə]. **walk (I.) & -er. 1. a** One who walks, a pedestrian; **b** person who habitually practises and enjoys walking as an exercise: *not much of a walker*. **2.** Bird which moves along the ground by successive steps instead of hopping.

walking, vbl. n. [1. wăwking; 2. wŏkiŋ]. **walk (I.) & -ing.** The act or motion of one who walks: *to be fond of, to dislike, walking*.

walking-dress, n. Dress suitable for wearing out of doors.

walking-fern, n. North American evergreen fern whose fronds bend backwards and take root at the tip.

walking-gentleman, -lady, n. Actor, actress, who takes a part needing little skill but a good appearance.

walking-leaf, n. Leaf-insect.

walking-papers, n. (slang) Dismissal from employment.

walking-stick, n. 1. Stick carried in the hand while walking. 2. Insect with long, slender body and legs; stick-insect.

walking-ticket, n. Walking-papers.

walking-tour, n. Extended excursion, journey for pleasure, on foot.

walk-over, n. [1. wàwk óvər; 2. wɔ̀k óuvə]. (sporting) Easy or unopposed victory.

Walkyrie. See **Valkyrie.**

wall (I.), n. [1. wawl; 2. wɔ̃l]. O.E., M.E. *wall*; cp. O. Fris., O.S. *wal*; M.H.G. *wall*; early loan-word fr. Lat. *vallum*, 'wall, rampart', fr. *vallus*, 'stake, palisade; pillar'; see **vallum.** 1. a Solid structure of stones, bricks, timbers, sods &c., usually relatively thin in proportion to its height and length, and erected as barrier, partition, means of defence, enclosure &c.: *to build the walls of a house*; *the garden is surrounded by a wall*; Phrs. *wall of partition, party wall*, wall dividing rooms, gardens &c.; *retaining wall*, one supporting bank of earth &c.; *blank wall*, unbroken by doors, windows &c.; *walls have ears*, one is liable to be overheard; *to be able to see through a brick wall*, have remarkable perceptive power; *to run one's head against a wall*, attempt obvious impossibilities; *with one's back to the wall*, at bay; *wooden walls*, the old wooden men-of-war, considered as the true protection of England against her enemies; b specif., defensive wall of town &c. 2. Extended, densely packed group of objects resembling a wall in appearance or function: *a wall of bayonets*. 3. Side of, partition in, a cavity, organ, vessel &c. of animals or plants: *the walls of the heart* &c. 4. (min.) One of the rock-surfaces enclosing the lode. 5. That side of the pavement in a street nearest to the walls of the houses &c., and therefore farthest from the gutter or kennel; hence various Phrs.: *to give a person the wall*, allow him to pass on the inside; *to take the wall of*, refuse to yield the inner side of the pavement and cause another pedestrian to pass on the outside near the edge of the pavement; *to push, drive, thrust (a person) to the wall*, thrust him aside, treat with contempt; *to go to the wall*, to be thrust aside as useless and ineffective.

wall (II.), vb. trans., fr. prec. 1. To surround, protect, defend, with a wall; often P.P., *walled towns*. 2. Usually *wall up*, to block up (space, opening &c.) with a wall.

walla(h), n. [1. wóla; 2. wɔ́lə], fr. Hind., agent-suff. *-wālā*. (Anglo-Indian) Person engaged in specified occupation or employed in specific business; equivalent to man, fellow: *punkah walla(h)*, the servant whose job it is to keep the punkah going. Phr. *competition walla(h)*, term applied in contempt by the now extinct generation of British military officers, or civilian officials, in India, who owed their entry into the East India Company's service to interest and nomination, to those who passed in by examination.

wallaby, n. [1. wólabi; 2. wɔ́ləbi]. Native Australian. Species of small kangaroo.

Wallach, n. [1. wólak; 2. wɔ́læk]. Slav., ultimately fr. O.H.G. *walh*, 'foreigner', q.v. under **Welsh.** Member of one of the Romance-speaking peoples of Roumania.

Wallachian, adj. & n. [1. woiákian; 2. wɔléi-kiən]. Prec. & -ian. 1. adj. Pertaining to the Wallachs or their language. 2. n. a A Wallach; b language of the Wallachs.

wallaroo, n. [1. wòlaròo; 2. wɔ̀lərú]. Native Australian. One of the larger varieties of kangaroo.

wall-creeper, n. Small insectivorous bird.

wall-cress, n. Kind of arabis.

wallet, n. [1. wólet; 2. wɔ́lit]. Etymol. doubtful; possibly a variant of M.E. *watel*, 'hurdle, basket, bag'; see **wattle.** 1. (archaic) Bag or scrip carried by traveller, pilgrim &c. and containing food and other necessaries. 2. Flat leather case or pocket-book for carrying banknotes, papers &c. 3. Small leather bag or case for tools &c.

wall-eye, n. Back-formation fr. next word. 1. a Opacity of the cornea of the eye; b white appearance of eye affected in this way. 2. Eye showing large proportion of cornea on account of squint &c.

wall-eyed, adj. M.E. *wawl-ēʒed*, fr. O.N. *vagl eygðr*, fr. *vagl*, 'beam in the eye', *eygðr*, 'eyed, having eyes', fr. *auga*, 'eye', q.v. under **eye.** The etymol. of the first element is unknown. Affected with wall-eye.

wall-fern, n. Small evergreen fern; polypody.

wallflower, n. [1. wáwflòur; 2. wɔ́lflàuə]. 1. Garden perennial of the mustard family, genus *Cheiranthus*, with clusters of fragrant, yellow, red, or brown flowers. 2. Woman at a ball who, from lack of partners, cannot dance and occupies a seat against the wall of the ball-room.

wall-fruit, n. Fruit produced by trees trained on a garden wall.

wall-game, n. A variety of football played at Eton.

wall-knot, n. Variant of **wale-knot.**

wall-less, adj. [1. wáwlles; 2. wɔ́llis]. **wall** (I.) & -less. Having no wall.

wall-moss, n. Stonecrop.

Walloon, n. & adj. [1. wolŏon; 2. wɔlún], fr. O. Fr. *Wallon*, fr. Gmc. *walh, O.H.G. *walh*, 'foreigner', see **Welsh.** 1. n. a One of a people of mixed descent living in Belgium and the adjoining part of France; b French dialect spoken by Walloons. 2. adj. Of, pertaining to, the Walloons or their dialect.

wallop, vb. intrans. & trans. [1. wólup; 2. wɔ́ləp]. Origin somewhat obscure; certainly of Gmc. origin, but perh. derived through O. Fr.; a variant of **gallop**, & formerly used in English in that sense; possibly connected w. O.E. *weallan*, 'to boil, to be agitated'. See **well** (I.) & cp. **potwalloper.** 1. intrans. (archaic or provinc.) To move along rapidly but heavily; esp. *to wallop along*. 2. trans. To beat severely, to thrash.

walloping, adj. [1. wóluping; 2. wɔ́ləpiŋ]. Pres. Part. of prec. (slang) Of large size; big, strapping, whacking: *a walloping great hare*.

wallow (I.), vb. intrans. [1. wóloˉ; 2. wɔ́lou]. O.E. *wealwian*; M.E. *walwen*, 'to turn, roll'; cp. Goth. *walwjan*, 'to roll'; *waltan*, 'to turn round'; cogn. w. Lat. *volvere*, 'to turn, roll', see **volute;** Gk. *eluein*, 'to wind'; *élutron*, 'sheath', see **elytron;** Scrt. *varútram*, 'outer garment'; *ulūtaś*, 'python'; O. Slav. *valiti*, 'to revolve'; cp. also **waltz** & **welter** (I.). 1. To roll about, flounder, in liquid or semi-liquid substance: *to wallow in the mire, mud, water* &c. Phr. *wallowing in money*, very rich. 2. (fig.) To indulge in to excess, plunge into, revel in: *to wallow in sensuality* &c.

wallow (II.), n., fr. prec. Hollow, pool, mud-hole, in which an animal habitually wallows.

wallowing, n. [1. wólŏing; 2. wɔ́louiŋ]. **wallow & -ing.** The floundering, rolling, movement of an animal that wallows.

wall-painting, n. Decorative painting, picture, on the wall of room &c.

wall-paper, n. Paper, often highly decorated in colours, used for covering interior walls and ceilings of rooms.

wall-pepper, n. Stonecrop.

wall-plate, n. Timber in or on top of a wall to take the pressure of beam, girder &c.

wall-rue, n. Small evergreen fern, *Asplenium Ruta-muraria*, growing on cliffs &c.

Wallsend, n. [1. wáwlzend; 2. wɔ́lzend], fr. Wallsend in Northumberland. Fine grade of household coal.

Wall Street, n. Street in New York City. American money-market.

walnut, n. [1. wáwlnut; 2. wɔ́lnət]. O.E. *w(e)alhhnutu*, fr. *w(e)alh*, 'foreign', see **Welsh, & nut.** 1. Edible nut of oily consistency, and rough irregular surface, contained between two very hard, easily separable shells, outside which is a thick pulpy husk. 2. a The tree (*Juglans*) producing these nuts; b hard, finely grained timber of this tree, used in cabinet-making and for gunstocks.

walnut-tree, n. Same as **walnut,** 2, a.

Walpurgis-night, n., semi-Germ. [1. vàhlpérgis nìt; 2. vàlpʎgis nàit], fr. Germ. *Walpurgis (nacht)*, fr. St. Walpurga, abbess of Heidenheim, died c. 779. Witches' festival on the Brocken, on the eve of May 1st.

walrus, n. [1. wól-, wáwlrus; 2. wól-, wɔ́lrəs], fr. Du., fr. Swed. *vallross*, transposed fr. Icel. *hrosshvalr*, fr. *hross*, 'horse', & *hvalr*, 'whale'; cp. O.E. *horshwæl*, 'walrus'; see **whale & horse.** Large, amphibious, seal-like mammal with long, drooping tusks, found in Arctic seas.

waltz (I.), n. [1. wawls; 2. wɔ̃ls]. Mod. Germ. fr. *walzen*, 'to revolve'; cp. O.E. *waltan*, 'to turn round'. See **welter** (I.). 1. Dance for couples, with smooth, even step, to music in 3 or 2 time. 2. Musical composition to which this is danced.

waltz (II.), vb. intrans. & trans., fr. prec. 1. intrans. a To dance a waltz; b to dance, twirl, skip about rapidly, with joy, excitement &c. 2. trans. To cause to waltz; to lay hold of (person) and dance about with (him or her): *waltz me round again*.

wampee, n. [1. wompḗ; 2. wɔmpí], fr. Chinese, fr. *hwang*, 'yellow', & *pī*, 'skin'. 1. Berry with tough, yellow rind and edible pulp. 2. Tropical tree, growing in China, East Indies &c., producing this fruit.

wampum, n. [1. wómpum; 2. wɔ́mpam], fr. N. American Ind. *wampum(peag)*, fr. *wompi*, 'white', & *ompumpeag*, 'string of beads or money'. Beads made of shells, worn in strings by N. American Indians as money or ornament.

wan, adj. [1. won; 2. wɔn]. O.E. *wann*, 'livid, dark'; M.E. *wan*, 'faint, pale'; perh. connected w. **wane.** Pallid, pale, colourless (esp. through illness, anxiety &c.), sickly; (also poet. of sky, atmosphere &c.) neither dark nor light; livid; palish, colourless.

wand, n. [1. wond; 2. wɔnd]. M.E. *wand*, fr. O.N. *vɔndr*, 'rod'; cp. Goth. *wandus*, 'rod'; Goth. *wandjan*, 'to turn round'; O.E. *windan*, 'to wind', see **wind (IV.).** The primitive meaning seems to be 'something pliable'. Long, slender rod, esp. a one carried in the hand as symbol of office &c.; b conductor's baton; c conjuror's light rod: *the wand of the magician*.

wander, vb. intrans. & trans. [1. wónder; 2. wɔ́ndə]. O.E. *wandrian*; M.E. *wandrien*, 'to wander'; cp. M. Du. *wanderen*; M.H.G. *wandern*, 'to wander'; fr. same base, w. i-mutation, O.E. *wenden*, 'to turn', see **wend (I.);** *windan*, 'to wind', see **wind (IV.).** A. intrans. 1. a To move from place to place, or from one object to another, without a specific route or purpose; to roam, ramble, rove: *to wander through the woods*; *to wander from flower to flower*; *to wander about the world*; b (of the eyes, glance &c.) to shift from point to point, stray. 2. a To deviate from the proper course, go out of one's way, to stray, go astray: *to wander out of one's way*; *to wander off the track*; b to depart from a clear and logical line of thought; to go aside from a subject of thought or discussion, become diffuse or confused: *to wander from the point*. 3. a To become incoherent in thought and expression; to ramble in one's mind, be delirious, and unconscious of what one is saying: *he is wandering, is wandering in his mind, as the result of high fever*; b (of the mind, thoughts, attention) to lack concentration, go wool-gathering, to be preoccupied, distrait, absent-minded. B. trans. To traverse, roam over, journey through at random, without settled course.

wanderer, n. [1. wónderer; 2. wɔ́ndərə]. Prec. & -er. One who wanders; person given to wandering.

wandering (I.), n. [1. wóndering; 2. wɔ́ndəriŋ]. **wander** & -ing. 1. (gen. in pl.) a An aimless ramble; b widely extended journeyings; travels from place to place: *to return from one's wanderings*. 2. (gen. in pl.) Incoherent or delirious speech: *the vapid wanderings of insanity*.

wandering (II.), adj. fr. Pres. Part. of **wander**. 1. Moving about in a rambling, purposeless manner; roving, strolling. Phr. *wandering Jew*, (i.) legendary character condemned to perpetual wandering on account of an insult offered to Christ on the road to the Crucifixion; (ii.) person addicted to wandering from country to country; (iii.) kind of trailing plant. 2. Moving about within the body, not attached, floating: *wandering cell* &c.

wanderingly, adv. Prec. & -ly. In a wandering manner.

wanderoo, n. [1. wònderōō; 2. wɔ̀ndərū́], fr. Cingalese *wanderu*. a Large, black, langur monkey of Ceylon and Malabar, with light-coloured or grey mane and ruffs; b the lion-tailed Indian macaque.

wane (I.), vb. intrans. [1. wān; 2. wein]. O.E. *wanian*, 'to diminish, decline, fade, wane'; M.E. *wanien* & *wānen*, 'to lessen, wane, grow pale'; cp. O.H.G. *wanōn*; O.N. *vana*; O. Fris. *wania*, 'to decline'; cp. further O.E., O.H.G. *wan*, Goth. *wans*, O.N. *vanr*, 'wanting'; cogn. w. Lat. *vānus*, 'empty, useless', see **vain**; Gk. *eũnis*, 'bereaved of', for *ewnis*; see also **want**. 1. To grow less, to diminish; to become less in amount, intensity, power &c.: a *our supply of ammunition steadily wanes*; b chiefly used of non-material things and of qualities: *waning influence, popularity; his strength is slowly waning*. 2. Specif. (of the moon and certain other heavenly bodies) to expose an ever smaller part of the illuminated surface to the earth; contrasted with **wax**.

wane (II.), n., fr. prec. Act or process of waning; decline; esp. in Phr. *on the wane*.

wanghee. See **whanghee**.

wangle, vb. trans. [1. wánggl; 2. wǽŋgl]. Weekley derives tentatively fr. provinc. *wangle*, 'to shake, totter', & compares M.E. *wankel*, 'unstable', O.E. *wancol*; this is cogn. w. O.H.G. *wankōn*, 'to totter', Mod. Germ. *wanken*. **wink** is perh. in gradational relation to these. On the other hand, the word is quite recent, though since the War in widespread use, so that an obscure provinc. origin seems improbable. Further, the present usage is very remote fr. the idea of 'tottering'. May the word not rather be a humorous concoction fr. a combination of 'wily' & 'to angle' in fig. sense, or something of the kind? (recent slang) To obtain by diplomacy or artifice: *to wangle a few days' extra leave; to wangle five pounds out of a person*.

wanion, n. [1. wónyun; 2. wónjən], fr. *waniand*, M.E. Nthn. Pres. Part. of **wane**, w. reference to waning moon as unpropitious. Archaic Phr. *with a wanion on, to*, ill-luck to (as imprecation).

wanly, adv. [1. wónli; 2. wónli]. **wan** & -ly. With a wan appearance; (also fig.) dismally, bleakly: *to smile wanly*.

wanness, n. [1. wónnes; 2. wónnis]. See prec. & -ness. State or quality of being wan.

want (I.), n. [1. wont; 2. wɔnt]. M.E. *want*, fr. O.N. *vant*, 'deficiency', fr. neut. form of *vanr*, 'lacking', see **wane**; for another example of this neut. suff. *-t* see **scant**. 1. State of being absent; lack, deficiency: *to suffer from want of food, air; want of common sense, tact* &c. 2. State of being without; a need; absence of something felt to be necessary: *to be in want of food; the building seems to be in want of repair; I feel the want of a real friend*; b specif., destitution, indigence, penury; insufficiency, lack, of means of livelihood: *to live in want; to know the bitterness of want*. 3. (chiefly pl.) Thing or things desired and felt to be necessary; requirements: *my wants are few; you should try to reduce your wants; I will supply all your essential wants*. Phr. *a long-felt want*, something for which the necessity has long been felt, but which is not available.

want (II.), vb. trans. & intrans. M.E. *wanten*, fr. O.N. *vanta*, 'to be lacking', fr. *want*, 'deficiency'; see prec. A. trans. 1. To lack, be deficient in; to fall, or be, short of; to require addition of in order to reach specified or desired standard or quality: *the house only wants a few more rooms to be perfect; the book wants a page at the end; he certainly does not want intelligence, or is not wanting in* &c.; *your coat wants an inch or so of the proper length, is an inch or so short of*... 2. a To need, have need of, to require; feel the necessity for: *children want plenty of sleep; we shan't want a fire today; I shall want dinner for four; you badly want a new hat* = you ought to have; *what do you want?; shall you want anything more tonight, sir?*; (colloq.) *what you want is a good thrashing*, i.e. what would do you good is &c.; b to desire to obtain, procure, get hold of, buy &c.: *I want some evening ties, please; I want some hot water at once*. 3. To desire to have, wish for, have a longing for: a *I want many things that I can't have; he wants everything he sees*; b (followed by infin.) (i.) *I want to see what is going on; I want you to be happy*; (ii.) (with neg.) *I don't want you to be hurt* = want you to avoid being; *he doesn't want to go* = wants not to go. 4. (i.) To be so circumstanced that it is desirable to do (something specified); to be obliged to do; ought, must: *you want to have your teeth seen to; one wants to be very careful in handling poisons*; (ii.) (with neg.) *you don't want to be rude* = you needn't, oughtn't, to be; *you don't want to overdo it for a bit* = mustn't overdo it; *he doesn't want to be treated too severely* = does not require &c. 5. Specif. a to desire to see or to speak to, to require presence of: *tell the boy I want him; you won't be wanted this afternoon; I want you for a minute or two*; b P.P. in special Phr. *wanted by the police, wanted for (murder* &c.), being sought for as a suspicious person, as being suspected to be guilty of (murder). B. intrans. 1. a To lack, be lacking or absent; (impers.) *it wanted only this last outrage, that alone was lacking; it wants but one word more and I shall turn you out, if you utter one more word* &c.; *it wants half an hour to the appointed time; it wants just a minute to the hour*; b (in Pres. Part.) *nothing is wanting to make the party a success; style and dignity are quite wanting from the play*; c specif. (colloq.) lacking normal intelligence, defective in mind: *such a strange boy, he seemed to me to be slightly wanting* (see also **wanting** (I.)). 2. a To be destitute, to lack the necessities of life: *he must not be allowed to want in his old age*; b want for, to be without, be unable to obtain: *he shall want for nothing that care and affection can bestow*.

wanting (I.), adj. [1. wónting; 2. wɔ́ntiŋ], fr. Pres. Part. of **want** (II.). (pred.) 1. a Deficient, defective; lacking some essential and necessary quality: *wanting in some respects, in initiative* &c.; *weighed and found wanting*; b specif., (absol.) deficient in intelligence, partly imbecile (see prec., B. 1, c). 2. Lacking, absent, missing: *there is a volume wanting to complete the set*.

wanting (II.), Pres. Part. as prep. Without, less, in the absence of: *wanting a leader, nothing could be done*.

wantless, adj. [1. wóntles; 2. wɔ́ntlis]. **want** (I.) & -less. Without a want.

wanton (I.), adj. [1. wóntun; 2. wɔ́ntən]. M.E. *wantowen, wantoun*, fr. pref. *wan-*, 'without, lacking', cogn. w. **want**, & M.E. *towen*, O.E. *togen*, P.P. of *tēon*, 'to draw, pull; to bring up, educate', q.v. under **tow** (I.). 1. Unrestrained, not under control; specif. a frolicsome, capricious, irresponsible: *a wanton kid, child; wanton play, tricks* &c.; b wild, wayward in growth or arrangement; luxuriant, unchecked or uncontrolled: *'golden tresses... Dishevelled, but in wanton ringlets waved'* (Milton, 'P. L.', iv. 305-6); c without motive, purposeless; irresponsible, arbitrary: *wanton destruction*. 2. Unchaste, loose, licentious.

wanton (II.), n., fr. prec. Wanton person, esp. an unchaste woman.

wanton (III.), vb. intrans. a To frolic, sport, without restraint: *'The birds that wanton in the air'* (Lovelace, 'To Althea'); b to luxuriate, flourish, run riot, produce, in limitless abundance and prodigality: *'Nature here Wantoned as in her prime'* (Milton, 'P.L.', v. 394-5).

wantonly, adv. [1. wóntunli; 2. wóntənli]. **wanton** (I.) & -ly. In a wanton manner; esp. without motive; unnecessarily, gratuitously: *wantonly cruel*.

wantonness, n. [1. wóntunnes; 2. wóntənnis]. See prec. & -ness. State or quality of being wanton; a light-heartedness, irresponsibility; b dissolute conduct, unchastity.

wapentake, n. [1. wápentāk; 2. wǽpənteik]. L.O.E. *wǣpentæc*, 'expression of consent or loyalty by touching weapon; district governed by leader thus appointed', fr. O.N. *vāpntak*, fr. *vāpn*, 'weapon', q.v. under **weapon**, & *taka*, 'to touch', see **take**. An old division of one of the counties of Yorks., Lincs., Derby, Leics., Rutland, Notts., corresponding to a hundred elsewhere.

wapiti, n. [1. wópiti; 2. wɔ́piti], fr. N. Am. Ind. *wapitik*. Large N. American antlered deer, *Cervus canadensis*, related to red deer; called 'elk' in popular usage.

war (I.), n. [1. wōr; 2. wɔ̄]. M.E., fr. O. Fr. *werre*, of Gmc. origin; cp. O.H.G. & O.S. *werran*, 'to confuse, hinder, injure'; cp. O.N. *vorr*, 'stroke of oar'; cogn. w. Lat. *verrere*, 'to sweep; to draggle, trail', see **verricule**; Gk. *érrein* for *wer-* 'to move painfully'; O. Slav. *vrešti*, 'to thresh'. 1. a Open conflict between nations, active international hostility carried on by force of arms; *civil war*, between two parties in the same nation; *holy war*, in support or defence of religious cause; *private war*, between individuals or families. Phrs. *to make, wage, war (on); to declare war (on)*, make formal announcement (to government of another nation) of intention to make war; hence (fig.) proclaim one's hostility to; *to go to the wars*, see active service in army; *to have been in the wars*, show signs of physical injuries &c.; *at war*, engaged in war; *on a war footing*, (of army &c.) at full strength, prepared for war; *war to the knife*, irreconcilable hostility; *war of elements*, storm, tempest; *art of war*, strategy; *council of war; declaration of war*, formal announcement of intention to make war; *seat of war*, district in which war is being carried on, scene of campaign; *sinews of war*, (fig.) money necessary for carrying on war; *to carry the war into the enemy's camp*, (fig.) to attack, or make complaint against, a hostile person or body alleging the same grounds as those alleged against oneself; b armaments, instruments, engines, of war: *'bring forth all my war, My bow and thunder'* (Milton, 'P. L.', vi. 712-13). 2. Hostility, bitterness of spirit: *to have war in one's heart*.

war (II.), vb. intrans., fr. prec. To contend, strive, compete: *war with, against*. Phr. *warring elements*, opposed, irreconcilable.

waratah, n. [1. wáhratah; 2. wǎ́rətǎ]. Native. Australian shrub bearing clusters of crimson or scarlet flowers.

warble (I.), vb. intrans. & trans. [1. wórbl; 2. wɔ̄bl]. M.E. *werblen*, 'to blow' (of the wind), 'to sound', fr. O. Fr. *werbler*, of Gmc. origin; cp. O.H.G. *wirbil*, 'whirl'; Mod. Germ. *wirbeln*, 'to whirl', cogn. w. **whirl**. 1. intrans. a (of bird) To sing with trills and vibrations; b (of person) (i.) to sing with trills and tremolo effect, suggestive of birds' song; (ii.) to sing generally. 2. trans. a (of bird or person) To utter, produce (a song, notes), with a series of roulades and trills; cp. Milton's *'the warbled string'* ('Arcades', 87), one made vibrant, trilled; **b** to sing (a song). (N.B. The earlier usage seems always to imply 'trilling' and the like, and not merely 'singing' in a general sense; Milton has '*Warble his native wood-notes wild*' (of Shakespeare, 'L'Allegro', 134); of the notes of Orpheus which were '*warbled to the string*' ('Il Penseroso', 106); and '*Fountains, and ye that warble as ye flow, Melodious murmurs*' ('P. L.', v. 195).)

warble (II.) n., fr. prec. Act, sound, of warbling.

warble (III.), n. Etymol. doubtful; cp. M. Swed. *varbulde*, 'boil'. **a** Larva of the botfly; **b** small hard tumour on horses or cattle caused by this.

warbler, n. [1. wórbler; 2. wǒblə]. **warble (I.) & -er.** Person who, bird which, warbles; specif., the popular name of a genus *Sylvia* and sub-family *Sylviinae* of singing birds, usually small, including the sedge- and reed-warbler, the white-throat, willow-wrens &c.

warbling, n. [1. wórbling; 2. wǒblɪŋ]. **warble (I.) & -ing.** **a** A trill, a roulade; **b** (poet.) a song : *plaintive warblings of the birds*.

war-bonnet, n. Feather-trimmed, ceremonial head-dress of N. American Indian.

war-cloud, n. Signs, circumstances, indicating imminence of war.

war-cry, n. Word, name &c. shouted as a signal or rallying-cry in battle.

ward (I.), n. [1. word; 2. wǒd]. (1) O.E. *weard*, masc., 'watchman, guardian'; (2) O.E. *weard*, fem., 'guard, protection'; M.E. *ward*; cp. O.H.G. *wart*, O.N. *voðr*, 'warden, keeper'; O.H.G. *warta*, 'guardianship'; Goth. *wardja*, 'guard'; see **ware (II.)**, & cp. **guard**. **1.** Now only in Phr. *watch and ward*, act of guarding, protection. **2.** State of being under control, esp. **a** (of minor) control of guardian, esp. in Phr. *in ward*; **b** (archaic) custody, confinement : *to put a person in ward*; **c** (archaic) warder, guard, now esp. in compounds : *hayward* &c. **3.** A minor under control of guardian; *ward in Chancery*, under guardianship of Court of Chancery. **4.** Division of a city, or (archaic) of a forest, for administrative purposes. **5.** Section, specific room, of building; specif. **a** (of hospital) *fever, isolation, ward*; **b** (of prison) *condemned ward* &c.; **c** (of workhouse) *casual ward* &c. **6.** Projection, ridge, notch, in a lock, or in a key, intended to prevent insertion and turning of any but a particular key in a given lock. **7.** (fencing) a Guard; **b** parry.

ward (II.), vb. trans. O.E. *weardian*, 'to guard', fr. *weard*, 'guard', see prec. **1.** (archaic) To defend, protect, act as guardian to. **2.** *Ward off*, to avert, turn aside, repel; to take measures to guard oneself against : *to ward off a blow, an attack* ; *to ward off sleep, a cold* &c.

-ward, -wards, suff. O.E. *-weard*, M.E. *-ward- (es)*; cp. O.H.G. *-wert*, Goth. *-wairþs*, 'having specified direction'; cogn. w. O.E. *weorðan*, 'to become', see **worth** (I.); Lat. *vertere*, 'to turn', see **version, vertex**. With meaning, 'in specified direction', & forming **a** *-ward*, adj., e.g. *forward, inward* &c.; **b** *-ward(s)*, adv., e.g. *backwards, afterwards, westwards, homeward(s)* ; **c** *-ward(s)*, prep., e.g. *toward(s)*. Also as living suff., esp. in facetious compounds, *bedward* &c.; '*When the young Augustus Edward Most reluctantly goes bedward*' (Calverley).

war-dance, n. Savages' ceremonial dance before battle, or to celebrate a victory.

warden (I.), n. [1. wórdn; 2. wǒdn]. M.E., fr. O. Fr. *wardein*, fr. Gmc. **ward-*, 'guard', see **ward (I.)**, & *-ian*, & cp. **guardian**. **1.** (archaic) Watchman, guard. **2.** (in official titles) **a** Person having control, jurisdiction, authority, over specific district &c.; governor: *Warden of the Marches, of the Cinque Ports* &c.; **b** the title of the head of five colleges in Oxford University, and of some schools; one of two principal officers in Freemasons' lodge, *Senior and Junior Warden*. **3.** Church-warden : *Vicar's warden, people's warden*.

warden (II.) also **wardon**, n. Weekley suggests connexion w. **ward (I.)** & interprets as 'keeping pear'; he cites Cotgrave, who gives *poire de garde*, 'a warden, or winter peare, a peare which may be kept verie long'. Variety of cooking pear.

wardenship, n. [1. wórdnship; 2. wǒdnʃip]. **warden (I.) & -ship.** Office or jurisdiction of warden.

warder, n. [1. wórder; 2. wǒdə]. **ward (II.) & -er. 1.** (archaic) Watchman, guard, still surviving in the name *Tower Warders*, of the guards of the Tower of London, wrongly called Yeomen of the Guard. **2.** Prison guard, gaoler. **3.** Staff symbolic of authority carried by sovereign, commander &c.

ward-mote, n. **ward (I.) & moot (I.)** Meeting of inhabitants of city ward.

Wardour Street, n. [1. wórder strēt; 2. wǒdə strīt]. London street formerly containing many antique furniture shops &c. *Wardour-street English*, a style pervaded with bogus archaism.

wardress, n. [1. wórdres; 2. wǒdris]. **warder & -ess.** Female gaoler.

wardrobe, n. [1. wórdrōb; 2. wǒdroub]. M.E.; cp. O. Fr. *garderobe*; see **ward (I.) & robe. 1.** A large piece of furniture including divisions for hanging clothes, and often also with drawers. **2.** Person's stock of clothes : *to renew one's wardrobe*.

ward-room, n. Common room on warship for commissioned naval officers below the rank of commanding officer and above that of sub-lieutenant.

wardship, n. [1. wórdship; 2. wǒdʃip]. **ward (I.) & -ship.** State of being a guardian; office of guardian, tutelage : *to be under the wardship of*.

ware (I.), n. [1. wǎr; 2. weə]. O.E. *waru*; M.E. *wāre*, 'goods, wares'; cp. Mod. Germ. *ware*; M. Du. *ware*, 'goods'; O.N. *vara*, 'skin, fleece; merchandise'; cogn. w. Scrt. *ūrā*; Gk. *arnós*, 'lamb' (genit.), fr. **arén* for **war-*; Lat. *vervex*, 'wether'. **1. a** (in compounds) Manufactured articles of commerce : *ironware, hardware* &c.; **b** specif., pottery, often preceded by qualifying word : *stoneware*; *Staffordshire wares*. **2.** (pl.) *Wares*, things offered for sale, goods, merchandise.

ware (II.), adj. O.E. *wær*, 'cautious, aware'; M.E. *war*, 'wary'; cp. O.S. *war*; O.H.G. *(gi)war*; O.N. *var*; Goth. *wars*, 'watchful'; O.E. *bewarian*; O.H.G. *biwarōn*, 'to guard, defend'; cogn. w. Lat. *verēri*, 'to observe anxiously, revere, fear', see **revere**; Gk. *oûros* for **wor-wos*, 'watchman'; *horáein* for **wor-*, 'to see'; cp. w. extensional suff., Goth. *wardja*; O.H.G. *warto*; O.E. *weard*, 'watchman', cp. **ward**. (poet.) Alert, vigilant : '*You'll find me ware and waking, As you found me long ago*' (Newbolt, 'Drake's Drum').

ware (III.), vb. trans. [1. wǎr, wōr; 2. weə, wō]. O.E. *warian*, 'to guard, guard against', fr. *war*, 'heedful', see prec. **1.** (esp. hunting, imperat.) Beware, look out for : *ware hounds!* ; *ware wire!* **2.** (colloq.) To guard against, avoid.

warehouse (I.), n. [1. wǎrhous; 2. weəhaus]. **ware (I.) & house (I.). 1.** Storehouse for goods before distribution to retailers &c.; store for furniture &c. temporarily unwanted; repository. **2.** Large retail shop, store.

warehouse (II.), vb. trans. [1. wǎrhouz; 2. weəhauz]. **ware (I.) & house (II.).** To store (esp. furniture) temporarily in a warehouse.

warehouseman, n. [1. wǎrhousman; 2. weəhausmən]. **1.** Man employed in warehouse. **2.** Keeper, owner, of a warehouse; specif., one who keeps or owns a wholesale establishment, for Manchester or cotton goods or for woollen and other textiles &c.

warfare, n. [1. wórfǎr; 2. wǒfeə]. **war (I.) & fare (III.). a** Act or process of waging war : *the science of warfare*; **b** state of being at war; active hostility, strife.

war-game, n. Kriegspiel.

war-god, n. Deity presiding over, and invoked in, war.

war-head, n. Explosive cap on torpedo as used in time of war.

war-horse, n. **a** (archaic) A horse used in battle, a charger; **b** *a seasoned old war-horse*, a person with long experience in political struggle, and affairs generally; a veteran.

warily, adv. [1. wǎrili; 2. weərili]. **wary & -ly.** In a wary manner.

wariness, n. [1. wǎrines; 2. weərinis]. See prec. & **-ness.** State or quality of being wary.

warlike, adj. [1. wórlīk; 2. wǒlaik]. **war (I.) & -like. 1.** Of, pertaining to, characteristic of, war; martial. **2.** Inclined for, tending to, war; bellicose.

warlock, n. [1. wórlok; 2. wǒlɔk]. O.E. *wǣrloga*, 'traitor'; M.E. *warloghe*, 'traitor, sorcerer', fr. O.E. *wǣr*, 'truth'; cogn. w. Lat. *vērax*, 'truthful', q.v. under **veracious**, & O.E. *loga*, 'liar', fr. base seen in O.E. (*ġe)logen*, P.P. of *lēogan*, 'to lie', see **lie (I.)**. (archaic) A sorcerer, wizard, magician.

war-lord, n. Military leader, general, chiefly as translating German *Kriegsherr*, in reference to the Kaiser, as such.

warm (I.), adj. [1. worm; 2. wǒm]. O.E. *wearm*, M.E. *warm*, 'warm'; O.S., O.H.G. *warm*; O.N. *varmr*, 'warm'; fr. base **gʷhor-m-, *gʷher-m-* &c., 'warm'; whence also Lat. *formus*, 'warm'; Gk. *thermós*, 'warm', see **thermo-**; Scrt. *gharmáṣ*, 'glow'; O. Prussian *gorme*, 'heat'. **1. a** Giving sensation of mild, pleasant heat; implying lower temperature than *hot* : *warm water* ; *this water is barely warm* ; *a warm iron* ; **b** often used as equivalent of *hot*, and to imply a considerable degree of temperature : *I find the day, the room, rather warm*. The context must determine whether **a** or **b** is intended; then *to get warm* may mean either (i.) an agreeable, comfortable, temperature, as : *come and get warm by the fire*, or (ii.) to put oneself in a state of excessive heat : *I got warm playing in the sun* ; *warm weather, climate* ; *a warm room* ; specif., *warm blood*, that of mammals and birds, having a normal temperature ranging between 98° and 112°; imparting or promoting heat : *a warm fire* ; *warm clothes*. Phrs. *warm work*, (i.) work which makes one hot; (ii.) a strenuous, arduous, dangerous occupation ; *a warm corner, to make things warm for a person*, harass him by attacks or annoyances. **2.** Ardent, enthusiastic, devoted : *warm support(er)* ; *a warm welcome*. **3.** Affectionate, sympathetic, responsive : *a warm heart*. **4.** (fig.) Heated, excited, vehement : *the disputants grew warm*. Phr. *in warm blood*, in passion. **5.** (of colour) Deep, intense, in shade, giving suggestion of warmth, esp. having red or yellow as basis. **6. a** (hunting, of scent) Fresh, recently made, strongly marked; **b** (of seeker in children's hiding games) close to the object sought. Phr. *you are getting warm*, you are on the right track of what you are seeking ; *you are getting near the truth*. **7.** (colloq.) Well-to-do, comfortably off.

warm (II.), vb. trans. & intrans., fr. prec. **A.** trans. **1.** To make warm, raise temperature of : *to warm one's hands, oneself, at the fire* ; *the sun has warmed the air* ; also *warm up : kindly warm up the mutton*, make it hot again. **2.** To animate, excite, cause to glow with feeling or enthusiasm : *to warm one's heart*. **B.** intrans. To become warm or warmer : *the pudding is warming in the oven* ; also *warm up : the room will soon warm up*. Phr. *to warm to one's work*, become keenly interested in it, intent upon it.

warm (III.), n., fr. prec. Act or process of warming, process of being warmed : *to have a warm by the fire*.

warm-blooded, adj. [1. wórm blʌded ; 2. wǒm blʌdid]. **1.** Having warm blood ; specif. (of mammals and birds) having a normal temperature above that of the surrounding medium; contrasted with *cold-blooded*. **2.** Having an ardent temperament; having the passions and emotions easily roused.

warmer, n. [1. wórmer; 2. wǒmə]. **warm (I.)** & **-er**. That which warms, device for warming; esp. in compounds: *foot-warmer* &c.

warm-hearted, adj. Having a warm heart; kind, sympathetic.

warm-heartedly, adv. Prec. & **-ly**. In a warm-hearted manner.

warm-heartedness, n. See prec. & **-ness**. State of being warm-hearted.

warming, n. [1. wórming; 2. wǒmiŋ]. **warm (II.)** & **-ing**. a Act of warming; process of being warmed; b (slang) a thrashing: *to give a boy's jacket a good warming*.

warming-pan, n. Round, flat, covered metal vessel with long handle, formerly filled with live coals and used for airing or heating a bed.

warmish, adj. [1. wórmish; 2. wǒmiʃ]. **warm (I.)** & **-ish**. Fairly warm.

warmly, adv. [1. wórmli; 2. wǒmli]. **warm (I.)** & **-ly**. In a warm manner.

warmth, n. [1. wormth; 2. wǒmþ]. **warm (I.)** & **-th**. 1. A moderately high temperature; contrasted with *cold*. 2. Enthusiasm, ardour, cordiality: *the warmth of one's welcome*. 3. Emotional excitement, vigour, vehemence; anger: *to reply with some warmth*.

warn, vb. trans. [1. worn; 2. wɔ̄n]. O.E. *wearnian*, *war(e)nian*, 'to beware of'; M.E. *warnen*, 'to warn, admonish'; influenced by O.N. *varna*, 'to warn'; cp. O.H.G. *warnōn*; fr. stem *war-, 'heedful', see **ware (II.)**. 1. To advise (a person) to be careful, put on his guard against possible risk, danger &c.; to admonish: *to warn a person of danger, of the consequences of an action* &c.; *to warn a person against another*; *I warn you that you will be punished*. 2. To intimate, be a signal to: *the gong warned us that it was time to dress for dinner*.

warning (I.), n. [1. wórning; 2. wǒniŋ]. Prec. & **-ing**. 1. Act of one who, that which, warns; notice, hint, of, caution against, possible danger, consequences of action &c.; admonition: *the General received a warning of the coming attack*; *to take warning by another's example*. 2. Something which warns; indication of something about to happen; premonition: *the branch fell without the slightest warning*. 3. Specif., notice given by employer to servant, or by servant to employer, of intention to terminate engagement: *I have given the cook warning*; *a month's warning*, notice to quit situation, or of intention to leave, at the end of a month.

warning (II.), adj., fr. Pres. Part. of **warn**. Serving, intended, to warn; admonitory, cautionary: *a warning signal, look* &c. Phr. *warning colours*, (zool., entom. &c.) conspicuous marks or colourings on poisonous insects &c. supposed to give warning to other creatures.

warningly, adv. Prec. & **-ly**. In a warning manner; so as to convey a warning.

War Office, n. Government department controlling the army and all matters connected with war, under the Secretary of State for War.

warp (I.), vb. trans. & intrans. [1. worp; 2. wɔ̄p]. M.E. *warpen*, fr. O.N. *varpa*, 'to throw, bend'; cp. O.E. *weorpan*, 'to throw'; *wearp*, 'warp'; O.H.G. *werfen*; Goth. *wairpan*, 'to throw'. A. trans. 1. a To alter shape of, bend, twist, distort: *the heat has warped the timber*; b (in moral sense) to bias, distort, pervert: *to warp the mind, judgement*; *his whole character was warped*. 2. (naut.) To bring (vessel) into specific place or position by hauling on ropes attached to fixed object: *to warp a boat out into the channel*. 3. To fertilize (land) by spreading it with alluvial deposit. B. intrans. 1. To become distorted, bent, twisted, by shrinkage, contraction &c.: *the table-top has warped*. 2. (naut.) of ship) To be moved, change position, by means of warps.

warp (II.), n., fr. O.E. *wearp*; M.E. *warp*, see prec. 1. Threads running lengthwise in a fabric and crossed by woof. 2. Rope, fastened to a fixed point, as buoy, anchor &c., used in warping vessel. 3. Distortion in timber, wooden object &c., caused by contraction &c. 4. Alluvial deposit, silt.

war-paint, n. a Paint applied to the face and other exposed parts of the body by savages before battle; b (fig.) full dress, complete ceremonial uniform &c.

war-path, n. Route of Red Indians on military expedition. Phr. *on the war-path*, (also fig.) planning an attack, preparing to launch an attack, to embark on hostile action of any kind; in fighting mood.

warplane, n. Military aeroplane.

warrant (I.), n. [1. wórant; 2. wǒrənt]. M.E. *warant*, fr. O. Fr. *warant, guarant*, 'safeguard, guarantee'; of Gmc. origin; cp. O.H.G. *werēnto*, 'guarantor', fr. *werēn*, 'to guarantee, vouch'; cp. O. Fris. *wera*, 'to vouch for'. Cp. variant **guarantee**. 1. Justification, authority, reasonable grounds: *you have no warrant for such a statement*. 2. That which authorizes, gives sanction for, an action; esp. a document authorizing a specified course of action; (in various special senses); a a writ issued by a competent legal authority, authorizing an arrest, a search &c.; b document authorizing payment of money: *a dividend warrant*; c certificate of appointment of a naval or military officer below commissioned rank (see **warrant officer**); d similar certificate issued to certain tradesmen supplying the Royal household, styled *royal warrant-holders*.

warrant (II.), vb. trans., fr. prec. 1. To justify, constitute sufficient ground for: *nothing can warrant this intrusion*. 2. To vouch for, guarantee, certify as: *I'll warrant him a perfectly honest man*; trade Phr. *warranted real silk*. To declare, assert confidently: *he never was so handsomely treated before, I'll warrant*, i.e. I would wager that my statement is true.

warrantable, adj. [1. wórantabl; 2. wǒrəntəbl]. Prec. & **-able**. 1. Capable of being justified. 2. (of deer) In sixth year, old enough to be hunted.

warrantee, n. [1. wòrantḗ; 2. wòrəntī]. **warrant** & **-ee**. Person to whom warrant is given.

warranter, n. [1. wóranter; 2. wǒrəntə]. **warrant** & **-er**. Warrantor.

warrant officer, n. Highest rank of non-commissioned officer.

warrantor, n. [1. wóranter; 2. wǒrəntə]. **warrant** & **-or**. One who gives a warranty to another.

warranty, n. [1. wóranti; 2. wǒrənti]. M.E., O. Fr. *warantie*, fr. fem. P.P. of *warantir*, 'to warrant', fr. *warant*, n., see **warrant (I.)**. 1. Sufficient reason, justification, or authority: *you have no warranty for that statement*. 2. (law) Assurance, undertaking, expressed or implied on part of vendor that property sold is his, that it fulfils the requirements specified, and is in accordance with his description of it.

warren, n. [1. wóren; 2. wǒrən]. M.E., fr. O. Fr. *varene*, fr. *warir*, 'to preserve', of Gmc. origin; cp. O.S. & O.H.G. *warōn*, 'to take care of', cogn. w. **ware (III.)**. 1. (law) a A tract of ground the right to enclose which, for the purpose of keeping or preserving hares, rabbits, partridges, pheasants, has been granted by the king: *beasts of warren*; b also *free warren*, the right or privilege to keep a warren: *rights of warren*; a warren ranks next in dignity to a *park*. 2. Tract of land, usually honeycombed with burrows, in which rabbits breed and abound. Phr. *packed like, as thick as, rabbits in a warren*, of a densely crowded population.

warrigal, n. [1. wórigal; 2. wǒrigəl]. Native. Australian dingo.

warrior, n. [1. wórier; 2. wǒriə]. M.E. *werreour*, fr. O. Fr.; see **war** & **-iour, -ior**. (now chiefly poetical) Soldier, fighter; esp. an experienced fighting-man, veteran.

war-ship, n. Man-of-war, battleship.

war-song, n. Song sung before, or in celebration of, a battle.

wart, n. [1. wort; 2. wɔ̄t]. O.E. *wearte*; M.E. *wart*; cp. O.H.G. *warza*; M. Du. *warte*; O.N. *varta*, 'wart'; cp. further O.E. *wearr*, 'wart'; cogn. w. Lat. *verrūca*, 'wart', see **verruca**; Scrt. *vársman-*, 'height, point'; Lith. *virszùs*, 'the upper'. 1. Small, hard growth on surface of skin. 2. Small, hard excrescence on bark of tree &c.

wart disease, n. Fungoid growth to which potatoes are liable.

warted, adj. [1. wórted; 2. wɔ̄tid]. **wart** & **-ed**. Having warts on the surface, skin &c.

wart-grass, -weed, n. Kind of spurge the juice of which is used to remove warts.

wart-hog, n. African wild hog, *Phacochoerus*, with hard excrescence on either side of face, and tusks curving upwards.

warty, adj. [1. wórti; 2. wɔ̄ti]. **wart** & **-y**. Resembling, of the nature of, covered with, warts.

war-wearied, adj. [1. wɔ̄r wèrid; 2. wɔ̄ wìərid]. War-worn.

war-whoop, n. Red Indians' war-cry.

war-worn, adj. Injured in, wearied by, war.

wary, adj. [1. wấri; 2. wéəri]. **ware (II.)** & **-y**. Cautious; on the look-out for danger &c.; circumspect.

was, vb. [1. woz; 2. wɒz]. O.E. *wæs*, 1st & 3rd pers. sing. Pret. of *wesan*, 'to be'; cp. O.S. & Goth. *was*; cp. O.S. & O.H.G. infin. *wesan*, Goth. *wisan*; cp. further Goth. *wizōn*, 'to live'; Scrt. *vásati*, '(he) dwells, remains, stays', & *vastu-*, 'seat, place'; Gk. *ástu* for *wastu*, 'a city'; cp. also **were**. Past tense sing. 1st and 2nd person of **be**.

wash (I.), vb. trans. & intrans. [1. wosh; 2. wɒʃ]. O.E. *wascan*, M.E. *wasshen*, 'to wash'; cp. O.S., O.H.G. *wascan*; prob. fr. earlier *wat-ska-*, fr. base *wat-*, 'water', see **water**, & cp. **wet**. A. trans. 1. a To cleanse by application of, immersion in, water or other liquid: *to wash one's hands, oneself, one's clothes, the dishes* &c.; Phr. *to wash one's hands of*, disclaim further responsibility for; b (in moral sense) to purify, render guiltless. 2. Usually *wash away, off, out* &c.; a (in physical sense) to remove by application of water &c.: *to wash the dust off*; *to wash a stain out*; also b (in moral sense) to purge, do away: *to wash away one's guilt, sin*. 3. To serve as a cleansing agent for: *the soap that won't wash clothes*. 4. (of water of the sea, a lake, river) To come into contact with; to flow past, lap, bathe, lave: *the sea washes the cliffs*; *the castle walls are washed by the waters of the river*. 5. To hollow out, produce, by flowing over and removing substance: *the rain washes channels in the ground*. 6. To carry along, transport, by the movement or drift of water: *washed ashore by the tide, waves*. 7. To separate, sift, heavier parts of (ore &c.) by shaking in water. 8. To cover with a thin coat of metal or of paint &c. B. intrans. 1. To wash oneself, one's hands &c., perform one's ablutions: *unpleasant to wash in cold water*. 2. To wash clothes, household linen &c.: *to wash once a week*. 3. (of fabric, colour, paint &c.) To be able to stand washing without deterioration: *will this material wash?* Phr. *that theory &c. won't wash*, will not bear investigation, won't go down, is unconvincing, cannot be accepted. 4. To reach and plash or lap against or over: *the waters of the lake wash upon the shore*. C. Followed by adverbs or prepositions with special meanings. *Wash against*, intrans., to come up to and splash or lap against: *the waves wash against the houses at high tide*. *Wash down*, trans., 1. to cleanse by washing, apply a stream of water to: *to wash down the walls*; 2. a to drive down by flow or rush of water: '*It may be that the gulfs will wash us down*' (Tennyson, 'Ulysses', 62); b in such Phr. as *a meal washed down by a draught of ale*, accompanied by, taken immediately before. *Wash out*, 1. trans., to remove by washing: *to wash out a blood-stain*; also fig. colloq., to give up, abandon as futile, as a plan, suggestion, &c., cp. **wash-**

44

out, below; 2. intrans., to be removed by washing: *the stain won't wash out*; Phr. (colloq.) *to be, look, feel, washed out*, be, look, pale and worn; to feel exhausted. *Wash up*, trans., & intrans. (absol.), to wash (dishes, cutlery &c.) after use at meals &c.

wash (II.), n., fr. prec. **1. a** Act of washing: *to have a wash*; *to give a thing a wash*; **b** process of being washed. Phrs. *to send clothes to the wash*, send them to the laundry to be washed; *at the wash*, at the laundry, in process of being washed. **2.** (familiar) Clothes, household linen &c., ready to be sent to the laundry, in the process of being washed, or just returned from the laundry: *the wash goes on Monday and comes back on Saturday*; *to hang out the wash to dry*. **3. a** Movement to and fro, outward flow, of water: *the wash of the waves*; **b** sound produced by this; **c** backward movement or current in water caused by steamer's screw or by oars. **4. a** Liquid or semi-liquid refuse from kitchen &c., esp. as food for pigs; **b** weak, thin liquid intended for consumption: *I don't like tea, soup &c. that is only wash*; **c** the fermented wort in the distillation of spirits. **5.** Medicinal lotion: *a wash for the eyes, hair &c.*; also in compounds: *mouth-wash, hair-wash &c.* **6. a** Thin, flat application of water-colour, distemper &c. put on in liquid state; **b** thin coating of metal. **7.** Alluvial deposit, sediment, silt.

washable, adj. [1. wóshabl; 2. wóʃəbl]. **wash (I.) & -able**. Capable of being washed without deterioration.

wash-basin, n. Basin for washing in.

wash-board, n. Corrugated board on which clothes &c. may be scrubbed.

wash-boiler, n. Vessel for boiling clothes &c. after washing.

wash-bottle, n. Apparatus for purifying gases &c.

wash-bowl, n. [1. wósh bōl; 2. wóʃ boul]. Large basin for washing dishes &c.

wash-cloth, n. Piece of material used in washing dishes &c.

wash-day, n. Washing-day.

washer, n. [1. wósher; 2. wóʃə]. **wash (I.) & -er**. **1. a** Person who, that which, washes; specif. **b** washing-machine. **2.** Small perforated disk of metal, rubber &c. used to tighten joint, nut &c.

washerwoman, n. [1. wósherwòoman; 2. wóʃəwùmən]. Woman employed to do household washing &c.

wash-hand-basin, n. [1. wósh (h)and bāsn; 2. wóʃ (h)ænd bèisn]. Wash-basin.

wash-hand-stand, n. [1. wósh (h)and stànd; 2. wóʃ (h)ænd stænd]. Wash-stand.

wash-house, n. Room or building in which clothes &c. are washed.

washily, adv. [1. wóshili; 2. wóʃili]. **washy & -ly**. In a washy manner.

washiness, n. [1. wóshines; 2. wóʃinis]. See prec. & **-ness**. State or quality of being washy.

washing, n. [1. wóshing; 2. wóʃiŋ]. **wash (I.) & -ing**. **1. a** Act of one who washes, process of cleansing: *engaged in washing*; **b** process of being washed: *children sometimes dislike, though they frequently need, washing*. **2. a** Collection of articles ready to be sent to, or just returned from, the laundry; **b** clothes and other articles in process of being washed: *to hang out the washing to dry*. **3.** Liquid, substance, washed off in process of cleaning anything: *the washings of plates and dishes*.

washing-day, n. Day on which household washing is done, or clothes &c. are sent to the laundry.

washing-machine, n. Mechanical apparatus for washing clothes &c.

washing-stand, n. Wash-stand.

Washington, n. [1. wóshingtun; 2. wóʃiŋtən]. Town in N. America, seat of government of U.S.A. Government of U.S.A.

washingtonia, n. [1. wòshingtōnia; 2. wòʃiŋtóuniə]. Named after George Washington. Genus of palms of Southern California, with white flowers and fan-shaped leaves.

washing-up, n. Process of washing dishes &c. used at meals.

wash-leather, n. Chamois leather, or substitute for this.

wash-out, n. [1. wósh out; 2. wóʃ aut]. **1.** Erosion of earth by flood &c. **2.** (slang) Ineffective, disappointing, unsuccessful, person or enterprise &c.; a failure: *he was a wash-out as a lecturer*; *the attempt was a complete wash-out*.

wash-pot, n. **a** Vessel containing liquid tin for coating tin-plate; **b** (archaic, Bib.) any vessel in which something is washed: '*Moab is my wash-pot*'.

wash-stand, n. Flat-topped piece of furniture for holding basin and other requisites for personal ablutions.

wash-tub, n. Large wooden tub in which clothes &c. are washed.

washy, adj. [1. wóshi; 2. wóʃi]. **wash (II.) & -y**. **1.** (of drink or liquid food) Thin, weak, highly diluted. **2.** (of colour) Pale, without intensity or depth. **3.** (fig., of style &c.) Feeble, insipid, lacking in force or character.

wasp, n. [1. wosp; 2. wɔsp]. O.E. *wæfs, wæps, wæsp*; M.E. *waspe*; cp. O.H.G. *wafsa, wefsa*; cogn. w. Lat. *vespa*; O. Prussian *wobse*; O. Slav. *vosa*, 'wasp', Lith. *vapsà*, 'horsefly'; fr. stem *webh-, *wobh- &c., 'to weave', w. reference to appearance of nest. See **weave**. **a** Family of hymenopterous insects with slender waist and powerful sting; specif. **b** the common variety, *Vespa vulgaris*, with alternate yellow and black stripes.

wasp-bee, n. Bee with colouring like that of wasp.

wasp-fly, n. Fly with black and yellow stripes.

waspish, adj. [1. wóspish; 2. wɔspiʃ]. **wasp & -ish**. Ill-tempered, spiteful, sour, shrewish: *a waspish person*; expressing ill-temper and malignity; biting: *a waspish nature, speech &c.*

waspishly, adv. Prec. & **-ly**. In a waspish manner.

waspishness, n. See prec. & **-ness**. State or quality of being waspish.

wasp-waisted, adj. Having a very slender or much-compressed waist.

wassail (I.), n. [1. wósl, wásl, wásāl; 2. wósl, wǽsl, wǽseil &c.]. M.E. *wesseil*, for *wes*, 'be', & O.N. *heil*, 'whole'; the O.E. formula of greeting, *wes þū hāl*, 'be thou whole, or sound'; see **was** & **whole**. (obs. or lit.) **1.** Carousal, merry drinking-bout; feasting. **2.** Ale &c. drunk at such festivity.

wassail (II.), vb. intrans. M.E. *wesseilen*; fr. prec. To take part in a wassail, drink healths; to carouse.

wassail-bowl, -cup, -horn, n. Drinking vessel used at a wassail; festive potations, junketing.

wast, vb. [1. wost; 2. wɔst]. 2nd person Pret. sing. of **be**. See **was**.

wastage, n. [1. wástij; 2. wéistidʒ]. **waste (II.) & -age**. **a** Process of wasting; **b** a wasteful loss; **c** amount wasted.

waste (I.), adj. [1. wāst; 2. weist]. M.E. *wāst*, fr. O. Fr. *wast*, fr. M.H.G. *wast*, fr. Lat. *vastus*, 'empty; waste, desert'. See **vast**. **1.** Not cultivated or occupied by man; desolate, unproductive, either from natural causes or through destructive effect of war &c.: *waste land, a waste space*. Phrs. *to lie waste*, remain uncultivated; *to lay waste*, destroy, ravage. **2.** Not wanted; useless, superfluous; thrown aside as worthless; left over after an action or process: *waste matter, scraps*; *waste effort*; *waste products*.

waste (II.), vb. trans. & intrans., fr. O. Fr. *waster*, fr. Lat. *vastāre*, 'to lay waste, devastate', fr. *vastus*, 'empty, waste'. See **vast**. A. trans. **1.** To expend or use extravagantly or uselessly; squander, be prodigal of: *to waste one's time, money, energy &c.* **2.** To lay waste, devastate. **3.** To cause to shrink and diminish; cause to lose vigour, strength, substance &c.; to sap, blight: *a frame wasted by disease*. Phr. *a wasting disease*, causing emaciation and lack of strength. **4.** (law) To allow (property &c.) to be impaired through neglect &c. B. intrans. **1. a** Also *waste away*, to lose substance or strength, become emaciated; **b** (of time) to pass gradually, be consumed. **2.** To be wasted, run to waste.

waste (III.), n., fr. **waste (I.)**. **1.** Desolate expanse of land or water; desert, uncultivated region; barren or devastated tract. **2.** Gradual diminution, reduction, in amount, substance, vigour &c. **3.** Act of wasting; state of being wasted; extravagant, unprofitable, or ineffective use or expenditure. **4.** Something wasted; waste material; useless, superfluous, or rejected matter; refuse. **5.** (law) Damage, impairment, of property &c. through neglect &c.

waste-basket, n. Waste-paper-basket.

waste-book, n. Book in which commercial transactions are entered temporarily.

wasteful, adj. [1. wǻstfool; 2. wéistful]. **waste (III.) & -ful**. **1. a** Extravagant; given to unprofitable, reckless, expenditure: *a wasteful man*; **b** tending to cause, involving, waste and extravagance: *a wasteful process, wasteful habits &c.*; **c** liable to waste or to be wasted: *a wasteful substance*. **2.** (poet.) Resembling, having the character of, a desolate waste (cp. **waste (III.), 1**): '*the vast immeasurable abyss, Outrageous as a sea, dark, wasteful, wild*' (Milton, 'P. L.' vii. 211-12).

wastefully, adv. Prec. & **-ly**. In a wasteful manner.

wastefulness, n. See prec. & **-ness**. Quality of being wasteful.

wasteless, adj. [1. wǻstles; 2. wéistlis]. **waste (III.) & -less**. Not liable to waste.

waste-paper-basket, n. Basket kept in a room, for holding waste scraps of paper, old letters and envelopes.

waste-pipe, n. Pipe for carrying off waste or surplus water.

waster, n. [1. wǻster; 2. wéistə]. **waste (II.) & -er**. **1.** A wasteful, extravagant, useless person. **2.** Thing spoilt in manufacture.

wastrel, n. [1. wǻstrel; 2. wéistrəl]. **waste (II.) & dimin. suff.** *-rel*. Idle, extravagant, good-for-nothing fellow; a waster.

watch (I.), n. [1. woch; 2. wɔtʃ]. O.E. *wæcce*; M.E. *wacche*, 'vigil; watch'; cp. O.H.G. *wacha*; fr. stem seen in O.E. *wacian*, 'to be awake', see **wake (I.)**. **1.** (archaic) Vigil, wakefulness; forbearance, abstention, from sleep: *in the night watches*; *passed like a watch in the night*. **2.** Act of watching; alertness, vigilance; constant observation, look-out: *to keep watch*; *to be on the watch for a person or expected event &c.*; *to keep watch and ward*. **3.** (archaic) **a** Person employed to watch or guard; a watchman; **b** party of persons employed for this purpose. **4.** One of the periods of three or four hours into which the night was formerly divided: *the evening, morning, watch &c.* **5.** (naut.) **a** Spell of duty on board ship, four hours except in the case of the *dog-watch*, q.v.; **b** one of the two divisions of a ship's crew taking alternate watches: *starboard, port, watch*. **6.** Small timepiece worked by a coiled spring, usually enclosed in a flat, round case suitable for carrying on the person; cp. **clock**.

watch (II.), vb. intrans. & trans. O.E. *wæccan*, formed fr. base of *wacian*, 'to be awake, to keep watch'; see prec. A. intrans. **1. a** To remain awake and alert; to be vigilant: '*watch and pray*'; **b** to keep vigil: *to watch beside a sick-bed*. **2. a** To play the part of a spectator; to observe, look on at events: *he remained silent during the whole scene and merely watched*; **b** *watch for*, to be on the look-out for; await with vigilance the arrival or occurrence of something: *to watch for the procession to go by*; *to watch for an opportunity to speak, for a chance to pounce*. **3. a** To be on guard, act as sentinel or lookout; **b** *watch over*, to guard, protect, have in one's care; keep an observant eye on: *to watch* over flocks; *to watch over the destinies of a nation.* **B.** trans. **1. a** To look at, observe, as a spectator; to direct the attention upon; esp. to consider attentively a series of actions or of moving objects: *to watch a procession pass; to watch the crowd from a window; to watch a person's face;* **b** to direct the mind upon, keep oneself acquainted with (a series of events): *to watch the development of affairs.* **2.** To keep under observation: *spies and suspicious persons are carefully watched; a good nurse watches her patient continuously.* **3. a** To guard; to observe for the purpose of protecting: *David as a boy watched his father's sheep;* **b** (specif. of a barrister) *to watch a case for an interested party,* to be present in court during the hearing, and ensure as far as possible that nothing is said or done to the prejudice of his client. **4.** To be on the lookout for: *to watch a favourable opportunity.*

watch-box, n. Sentry-box.

watch-case, n. Metal outer case containing mechanism of watch.

watch-chain, n. Chain for securing watch to clothing &c.

watch-dog, n. **a** Dog guarding property &c., giving warning of approach of strangers &c.; **b** person who keeps a vigilant look-out against possible infringement of, or injury attempted to, some particular group of interests, rights &c.

watcher, n. [1. wócher; 2. wɔ́tʃə]. **watch (II.)** & **-er.** One who watches.

watch-fire, n. Fire kept burning at night by camp-guards, or as signal &c.

watchful, adj. [1. wóchfool; 2. wɔ́tʃful]. **watch (I.)** & **-ful.** Vigilant, on the watch, alert, observant.

watchfully, adv. Prec. & **-ly.** In a watchful manner.

watchfulness, n. See prec. & **-ness.** State or quality of being watchful.

watch-glass, n. Thin, round piece of glass fixed over the face of a watch.

watch-guard, n. Chain, strap, cord &c. for fastening watch to clothing &c.

watch-gun, n. Gun fired at changing of watch.

watch-house, n. Building occupied by guard.

watch-key, n. Key for winding up a watch.

watchmaker, n. [1. wóchmāker; 2. wɔ́tʃmèikə]. Person whose trade is to make and repair watches.

watchman, n. [1. wóchman; 2. wɔ́tʃmən]. **1.** (hist.) Member of guard formerly patrolling streets at night. **2.** Man employed to guard buildings &c. at night.

watch-night, n. New Year's Eve, esp. as celebrated by religious services.

watch-oil, n. Fine oil for lubricating mechanism of watch.

watch-pocket, n. Small pocket, usually in a waistcoat, for holding a watch.

watch-spring, n. Spring which actuates the movement in mechanism of a watch.

watch-stand, n. Small stand which supports a watch in such a way that its face can be seen.

watch-tower, n. Lofty tower from which a wide view can be obtained of the surrounding country, upon which sentinels were placed formerly to give warning of approach of an enemy.

watchword, n. [1. wóchwërd; 2. wɔ́tʃwɪ̄d]. **1.** Password, countersign. **2.** Word or phrase intended to embody the principles of a party, cause &c.

water (I.), n. [1. wáwter; 2. wɔ́tə]. O.E. *wæter;* M.E. *wāter;* cp. O.H.G. *wassar;* O.S. *watar;* O.N. *vatu,* 'water'; cogn. w. Gk. *húdōr,* 'water', see **hydro-;** Scrt. *udán-,* 'wave'; O. Slav. *voda,* see **vodka;** Lith. *vandŭ;* O. Prussian *unds,* 'water'; the base is **wed-, *wod-, *ud-,* 'water'; cp. also **wash, wet.** **1.** A widely distributed, nearly colourless, transparent, liquid, composed of hydrogen and oxygen, either pure or containing mineral or other matter in solution: *fresh, salt, hot, cold water* &c.; *hard, soft, water* (see **hard, soft**); sometimes in compounds, indicating source &c.; *rain-, spring-, river-, sea-, ground-water*

&c.; *mineral waters,* characterized by specific mineral ingredient; *strong waters,* (archaic) spirits; *table waters,* bottled for use at meals; *holy water,* water which has been blessed and is used for various religious purposes; Phrs. *water bewitched,* (colloq.) very weak tea &c.; *water of life* (Bib.), spiritual refreshment; *waters of forgetfulness,* oblivion, death; *in deep water(s),* in difficulties, tribulation; struggling; *in smooth water(s),* prosperous, having an easy progress; (*like*) *a fish out of water,* out of one's element, in unaccustomed and uncongenial surroundings; *written in water* (of name, fame &c.), soon forgotten, transient; *to back water,* to go backwards in rowing-boat by reversing motion of oars; *to fish in troubled waters,* endeavour to profit by discords &c.; *to get into hot water,* get into trouble; *to drink the waters,* take prescribed quantity of medicine-water treatment at a spa; *to go through fire and water,* undergo great hardships; *to hold water,* (of theory, statement &c.) admit of proof, investigation &c.; *to keep one's head above water,* contrive to avoid succumbing to financial embarrassments; manage to hold one's own, in various senses; *to pour oil on the waters,* to induce calm, serenity; (*to spend money &c.*) *like water,* extravagantly, lavishly; *to throw cold water on* (*a plan* &c.), discourage. **2.** (often pl.) Body of water: *the waters of the lake; the head-waters of the Amazon.* **3.** Tide, state of tide, at specific moment: *high, low, water;* Phr. *in low water,* in want of money &c. **4.** (in compounds) Solution of vegetable or mineral substance in water: *rose-water, soda-water* &c. **5.** Liquid secretion of animal body, e.g. tears, perspiration, urine &c.: *water on the brain, knee,* accumulation of serous fluid. Phr. *to make, pass, water,* discharge urine. **6.** Quality, lustre, brilliance, of precious stone, esp. diamond; Phrs. *of the first water,* of the finest quality; (also fig.) embodying in a high degree the characteristic qualities of a type or class.

water (II.), vb. trans. & intrans., fr. prec. **A.** trans. **1.** To sprinkle with water, moisten, irrigate: *to water the garden, plants* &c. Phr. *to water one's pillow with tears.* **2.** To provide (animals &c.) with water for drinking. **3.** To supply with moisture, streams &c.: *the country is watered by large rivers.* **4.** To dilute with water: *to water the whisky, milk* &c.; also *water down,* (i.) to dilute (milk &c.) with water; (ii.) to weaken force, pungency, cogency, expressiveness, of (a statement &c.) by alterations and omissions, in order to make it more generally acceptable to the timid or half-hearted. **5.** (chiefly in P.P.) To give a wavy pattern to surface of (textile fabric): *watered silk.* **6.** (finance) To increase number of shares in (stock &c.) without increasing actual capital. **B.** intrans. **1. a** (of animal &c.) To drink water, go to watering-place; **b** (of engine, ship &c.) to take in a supply of water. **2.** To have increased secretion, become filled with water: *the light makes one's eyes water; one's mouth waters,* through anticipation of food &c. Phr. *to make one's mouth water,* to fill one with longing to possess or enjoy.

water-anchor, n. Floating, wooden framework used to check leeway of ship.

water-bailiff, n. Custom-house official inspecting ships entering port.

water-bed, n. Rubber mattress filled with water.

water-beetle, n. General name for various aquatic beetles (*Dytiscus*) which live habitually under the surface of water.

water-bellows, n. Apparatus by means of which air for a forge is forced into, and expelled from, a wooden tube through sloping holes by the pressure of falling water; also called a *trompe.*

water-bird, n. Bird frequenting water; aquatic bird.

water-biscuit, n. Thin, hard biscuit made of flour and water.

water-blink, n. In arctic regions, cloud-like appearance on the horizon indicating the presence of open water.

water-blister, n. Blister on the skin, containing serous fluid.

water-boatman, n. Aquatic insect, *Notonecta,* with boat-shaped body and long legs.

water-borne, adj. (of mail, goods &c.) Transported by water.

water-bottle, n. **1.** Glass bottle holding drinking-water for table or bedroom use. **2.** Metal flask for water, as part of military equipment &c.

water-brash, n. Form of indigestion with vomiting of bitter, watery liquid.

water-buck, n. Large S. African antelope, with white stripe on buttocks, genus *Cobus.*

water-buffalo, n. Indian buffalo.

water-butt, n. Large cask for collecting rain-water.

water-carriage, n. Transportation of goods by water.

water-carrier, n. **a** Person employed to carry water; **b** (cap.) the constellation of Aquarius.

water-cart, n. Cart for carrying water, esp. one with device for watering roads.

water-chute, n. Boarded slope down which toboggans rush into a pool of water, as a form of amusement.

water-clock, n. Clock regulated by flow of water.

water-closet, n. Privy with pan flushed out by water.

water-colour, n. **1.** Pigment diluted with water instead of oil. **2.** Picture painted with such pigments. **3.** (also pl.) Art of painting with such pigments.

water-colourist, n. [1. wáwter kùlurist; 2. wɔ́tə kàlərist]. Painter in water-colour.

water-cooled, adj. [1. wáwter kōōld; 2. wɔ́tə kŭld]. *Water-cooled engine,* one in which the cylinders are kept from overheating by the circulation of water round them; contrasted with *air-cooled.*

watercourse, n. [1. wáwterkòrs; 2. wɔ́təkɔ̀s]. **1.** Body of running water, stream. **2.** Channel for stream &c.

watercress, n. [1. wáwterkrès; 2. wɔ́təkrès]. Creeping herb *Nasturtium officinale,* growing in water and used in salads.

water-cure, n. Medical treatment by application of water; hydropathy.

water-drinker, n. One who drinks water; specif., one who abstains from alcohol.

water-dropwort, n. [1. wáwter drópwërt; 2. wɔ́tə drópwɪ̄t]. Poisonous plant, genus *Oenanthe,* resembling celery.

watered, adj. [1. wáwterd; 2. wɔ́təd], fr. P.P. of **water (II.).** **1.** Supplied with streams &c.; irriguous: '*a quiet water'd land, a land of roses*' (Rolleston, 'Clonmacnois'). **2.** (of silk &c.) Having a pattern of wavy lines.

waterfall, n. [1. wáwterfàwl; 2. wɔ́təfɔ̀l]. Body of water descending perpendicularly or nearly so; cascade.

water-finder, n. Person who is able to find a spring of water in the ground by means of divining-rod; a dowser.

water-flag, n. Yellow iris.

water-flea, n. Small fresh-water crustacean.

waterfowl, n. [1. wáwterfòul; 2. wɔ́təfàul]. (usually coll.) Aquatic birds.

water-gas, n. Illuminating or power-gas derived, produced, by passing steam through red-hot coke or anthracite and decomposing it.

water-gate, n. **1.** Gate for checking or releasing flow of water. **2.** Gate opening from building on to river, lake &c.

water-gauge, n. Gauge indicating level of water in tank, boiler &c.

water-glass, n. **1.** Tube with glass bottom for observing objects under water. **2.** Transparent solution of silica &c. sprayed over fresco painting to preserve it; also used for preserving eggs.

water-hammer, n. Concussion of water when its flow through pipe &c. is suddenly checked.

water-hen, n. Moorhen.

water-hyacinth, n. Tropical plant with spikes of blue flowers and thick, tangled leaf-stalks.

water-ice, n. Confection of frozen water, fruit-juice, and sugar &c.

water-inch, n. Amount of water flowing in twenty-four hours through a hole one inch in diameter.

wateriness, n. [1. wáwterines; 2. wɔ́tərinis]. watery & -ness. Quality of being watery.

watering-can, n. [1. wáwtering kàn; 2. wɔ́tər-iŋ kæ̀n]. Vessel with long spout, often fitted with perforated nozzle, for watering plants.

watering-cart, n. Cart carrying a supply of water and fitted with a device for watering roads.

watering-place, n. 1. Pool to which animals resort to drink. 2. a Health resort with medicinal springs; b seaside resort.

watering-pot, n. Watering-can.

water-jacket, n. Casing containing water and surrounding cylinder &c. for cooling purposes.

water-joint, n. Water-tight joint.

water-junket, n. Sandpiper.

water-lens, n. Magnifying lens consisting of water enclosed in a brass cell with a glass bottom.

waterless, adj. [1. wáwterles; 2. wɔ́təlis]. water & -less. Without water.

water-level, n. 1. Surface of body of water, esp. as datum for measurement. 2. (geol.) Irregular upper surface of ground-water; upward limit of saturation. 3. Levelling instrument in which the position of a drop of water indicates horizontality.

water-lily, n. Plant, *Nymphaea*, with flat, heart-shaped leaves, and large, white, yellow, pink, or blue flowers, which float on the surface of water.

water-line, n. 1. Line along ship's side corresponding to water-level; *load-, light-water-line*, level reached by water when ship is loaded, empty. 2. Line forming part of watermark.

water-logged, adj. a (of wood or wooden objects) Saturated or filled with water and having lost buoyancy; b (of the ground) soaked with water beyond saturation-point, so that it remains swampy; c (of a ship) rendered almost unmanageable, through water leaking excessively into hold.

water-main, n. Chief pipe in system of water-supply.

waterman, n. [1. wáwterman; 2. wɔ́təmən]. 1. Boatman, ferryman &c. plying for hire. 2. Oarsman: *a good, bad, waterman &c.*

watermanship, n. [1. wáwtermanshìp; 2. wɔ́tə-mənʃìp]. Prec. & -ship. Skill in management of oars.

watermark, n. & vb. trans. [1. wáwtermàrk; 2. wɔ́təmàk]. 1. n. a Design imprinted on surface of paper, showing quality, date or place of manufacture &c., and faintly visible when the paper is held against the light; b (i.) mark or line showing the height to which water has risen, as *high-watermark*, on a beach &c.; (ii.) fig. *high-watermark*, the highest attainable point or degree of excellence; *low-watermark*, lowest attainable degree of demerit. 2. vb. To imprint a watermark on (paper) in process of manufacture.

water-meadow, n. Low-lying meadow periodically inundated by river &c.

water-melon, n. Large, edible, sweet, pulpy fruit of a trailing plant of the gourd family.

water-mill, n. Mill worked by water-power.

water-mocassin, n. Poisonous N. American snake.

water-monkey, n. Long-necked, earthenware water-jar of eastern countries.

water-motor, n. Motor driven by water pressure.

water-nymph, n. Spirit haunting river, lake &c.; naiad.

water-pillar, n. Pillar with swinging spout for supplying steam-engines with water.

water-pipe, n. Pipe for conveying water.

water-plane, n. 1. Plane in which water-line lies, level with surface of water. 2. Seaplane.

water-plate, n. Plate with double bottom enclosing space for hot water.

water-platter, n. Variety of water-lily.

water-polo, n. Ball-game played by swimmers, the object being to throw the ball into the goal of the opposing side.

water-power, n. Power generated by pressure, fall &c. of water.

waterproof, adj., n., & vb. trans. [1. wáwter-pròof; 2. wɔ́təprùːf]. 1. adj. Proof against water, capable of excluding or resisting water, not permitting water to pass through. 2. n. Waterproof coat &c. 3. vb. To make waterproof by coating with rubber &c.

water-rail, n. Long-legged, short-winged wading bird; the common rail.

water-ram, n. Hydraulic ram.

water-rat, n. Popular name for the water-vole.

water-rate, n. Official charge made for public water-supply.

water-sail, n. (naut.) Sail below lower studding-sail.

water-seal, n. Body of water held in a trap &c. to prevent passage of gas &c.

watershed, n. [1. wáwtershèd; 2. wɔ́təʃèd]. fr. **water (I.)** & **shed (I.)**, in earlier sense to divide, separate. a Elevation dividing two river valleys or basins; line of division between two river-systems; b (a loose incorrect usage) river-basin; catchment area.

water-shoot, n. Pipe, trough, gutter, for discharging water from roof &c.

water-side, n. Edge, margin, of body of water.

water-skin, n. Bag of skin for carrying water.

water-soldier, n. Water plant, *Stratiotes*, rooted at bottom of water and having sword-like leaves and flowers above the surface.

water-spider, n. Kind of spider which lives in a bell-shaped nest under water.

waterspout, n. [1. wáwterspòut; 2. wɔ́tə-spàut]. Pillar of water drawn upward by a funnel-shaped mass of whirling cloud which descends vertically to meet it.

water-sprite, n. Supernatural being haunting river, lake &c.

water-supply, n. 1. System of procuring and storing water to supply house, town &c. 2. Water used or supplied by such a system.

water-table, n. 1. Water-level. 2. (archit.) Moulding, projecting ledge &c. designed to throw off water from building.

water-tiger, n. Destructive larva of a kind of water-beetle.

watertight, adj. [1. wáwtertìt; 2. wɔ́tətàit]. a Capable of resisting passage of water; fixed or fitted tightly enough to prevent water passing through; b (fig., of argument &c.) perfectly sound, unassailable.

water-tower, n. Structure containing raised tank designed to furnish pressure necessary to system of water-supply.

water-vole, n. Kind of aquatic rodent, *Microtus amphibius*, often called the water-rat.

water-wagtail, n. Wagtail.

water-way, n. 1. Navigable channel. 2. Channel round edge of ship's deck to carry off water.

water-wheel, n. Wheel turned by flow of water.

water-witch, n. 1. Water-finder. 2. Any one of several kinds of diving bird.

water-withe, n. West Indian vine with branches full of watery juice.

waterworks, n. [1. wáwterwèrks; 2. wɔ́tə-wàks]. a System of buildings, machinery, reservoirs, pipes &c. for supplying water to town &c. Slang Phr. *to turn on the waterworks*, shed tears; b (colloq.) the bladder and urinary organs generally.

water-worn, adj. (of rock, pebble &c.) Rounded, smoothed, polished, by action of water.

watery, adj. [1. wáwteri; 2. wɔ́təri]. **water (I.)** & **-y**. 1. Consisting of water; cp. such poet. Phr. as *watery waste, wilderness*, the sea; '*He must not float upon his watery bier Unwept*', the sea, in which Lycidas had perished (Milton). 2. Containing, full of, saturated with, water; specif. a (of eyes) having a weak, moist appearance, as though they were watering; b (of boiled food) containing too much water, sodden. 3. a (of liquid) Over-diluted with water; thin, weak, insipid: *watery tea, soup* &c.; b hence, (fig.) insipid, without force or character. 4. (of moon or sky) Indicating approach of rain.

watt, n. [1. wot; 2. wɔt], fr. James Watt, inventor, d. 1819. Unit of electrical power, the equivalent to work at the rate of one joule per second, 746 watts = 1 h.p.

Watteau, n. [1. wótō; 2. wɔ́tou], fr. name of Antoine Watteau, French painter (1684–1721); with reference to costumes &c. shown in his paintings. *Watteau back*, back of woman's dress, arranged to form a long pleat from neck to hem; *Watteau bodice*, with square neck-opening.

wattle (I.), n. [1. wótl; 2. wɔ́tl]. O.E. *watol*, 'hurdle'; M.E. *watel*, 'hurdle'; basket, bag'. Origin uncertain; cp. O.E. *wætla*, 'bandage'. 1. Structure of wickerwork on a framework of stiffer rods, used in form of hurdles. 2. Fleshy excrescence hanging from neck of bird, esp. turkey. 3. Barbel of fish. 4. Kind of acacia of Australia and S. Africa.

wattle (II.), vb. trans. To make of, construct with, wattle-work.

wattle-and-daub, n. [1. wótl an(d) dáwb; 2. wɔ́tl ən(d) dɔ́b]. Wattle-work daubed with clay, mud &c.; used for the walls of rough huts.

wattle-bird, n. Australian bird with wattle below each ear.

wattled, adj. [1. wótld; 2. wɔ́tld]. **wattle (I.)** & **-ed**. 1. Made of, covered with, wattle-work. 2. (of birds and fish) Having wattles.

wattle-work, n. Hurdle &c. made of wattles.

wattling, n. [1. wótling; 2. wɔ́tliŋ]. **wattle (II.)** & **-ing**. Wattle-work.

watt-meter, n. **watt** & **-meter**. Instrument measuring electrical power in terms of watts.

waul, vb. intrans. [1. wawl; 2. wɔl]. Imitative. To cry, howl, squall, like a cat.

wave (I.), vb. intrans. & trans. [1. wāv; 2. weiv]. O.E. *wafian*, 'to wave, brandish', M.E. *wāven*; cp. O.N. *vafa*; M.H.G. *waben*, 'to wave, fluctuate'; cp. **waver**. A. intrans. 1. (of flexible object) To move to and fro in air or water with curving, sinuous, motion; to sway, sweep to and fro; to stream, fluctuate: *flags, branches, wave in the breeze; waving corn; seaweed waves below the surface of the water*. 2. (of line or surface) To be arranged, lie, in a series of curves; to have alternate curving elevations and depressions, undulate: *one's hair waves*. 3. To signal by waving hand &c.: *to wave in farewell &c*. B. trans. 1. To cause to move to and fro with a sweeping motion; to brandish, flourish: *to wave one's hand; to wave a wand*; also (of flags) to allow to stream in the wind, to flaunt: '*Wave, Munich, all thy banners wave!*' (Campbell, 'Hohenlinden'). 2. To signal to by waving: *the leader waved his men on with his sword; to wave a person away*; to *wave away a proposal* &c., signify disapproval of by a waving gesture, to brush it aside. 3. To express by a wave of the hand &c.: *to wave a farewell*. 4. To give an undulating surface, edge, appearance, to: *to wave one's hair*.

wave (II.), n., prob. fr. or due to association w. prec. The O.E. word was *wǣg*, M.E. *wawe*, wh. was ousted by *wave* in 16th cent. 1. a A swelling, curving ridge on the surface of the sea or other large sheet of water in motion; a billow; b specif. (poet.) *the waves*, the sea. 2. An undulation, or undulating movement, in any surface, resembling in appearance that caused by wind on the surface of water: '*Waves of shadow went over the wheat*' (Tennyson, 'Poet's Song'). 3. (phys.) Any disturbance which is periodic in both space and time. The interval between its repetition in space is its *wave-length*, the interval of time is its *period*, and the reciprocal of its period is its *frequency*. 4. An undulating mark or streak on a surface, e.g. in a silk fabric, reflecting light differently from the rest of the surface. 5. One of a series of wide curves or curls in a substance such as the hair. 6. A waving movement, a shaking to and fro: *a wave of the hand*. 7. An emotional or intellectual impulse, movement, tendency, a gust of feeling &c.: *a wave of religious passion, of enthusiasm, of indignation*, &c.

wave-length, n. a The distance between the crests of two adjacent waves in water; b (phys.) regular interval of space between each recurrence of a periodic disturbance.

waveless, adj. [1. wāvles; 2. wéivlis]. **wave** (II.) & **-less**. Without waves.

wavelet, n. [1. wāvlet; 2. wéivlit]. **wave** (II.) & **-let**. A small wave, a ripple.

waver, vb. intrans. [1. wāver; 2. wéivə]. M.E. *wāveren*, 'to waver'; cp. M.H.G. *waberen*, O.N. *vafra*; 'to waver'; **wave** (I.) & **-er**. 1. To move unsteadily, to shift with irregular movements from place to place, or to and fro; to fluctuate; to tremble, to flicker, to come and go: *a wavering shadow, mist, light, cloud of smoke*. 2. To totter, recede and show signs of breaking or giving way: *the line wavered and finally broke before the shock of the cavalry*. 3. a To halt between two opinions, to vacillate, to shilly-shally; b to remain undecided between two courses of action; to be irresolute, to lack fixity of purpose; to yield, give way: *inflexible in his resolve, he never wavered in spite of abuse and denunciation*.

waverer, n. [1. wāverer; 2. wéivərə]. Prec. & **-er**. One who wavers; an irresolute, vacillating person.

wavering, adj. [1. wāvering; 2. wéivəriŋ], fr. Pres. Part. of **waver**. a Flickering, quivering; b hesitating, vacillating.

waveringly, adv. Prec. & **-ly**. In a wavering manner.

wavily, adv. [1. wāvili; 2. wéivili]. **wavy** & **-ly**. In a wavy manner; with undulations.

waviness, n. [1. wāvines; 2. wéivinis]. Next word & **-ness**. State or quality of being wavy.

wavy (I.), adj. [1. wāvi; 2. wéivi]. **wave** (II.) & **-y**. 1. Inclined to wave, waving, e.g. as grass, plumes &c. in the wind. 2. (of surface or line) Having, showing, undulating curves, alternately convex and concave: *a wavy line*; *wavy hair*.

wavy (II.), **wavey**, n., fr. Am. Ind. *wawa*. North American Arctic goose; snow-goose.

wawl. Variant of **waul**.

wax (I.), n. [1. waks; 2. wæks]. O.E. *weax*; M.E. *wax*; cp. O. Fris. *wax*; O.H.G. *wahs*; O.N. *vax*, 'wax'; prob. cogn. w. O.H.G. *waba*, 'honeycomb', & w. **weave, web, wick** (I.). 1. a Plastic, yellow, fatty substance secreted by bees and used by them in construction of cells; b prepared wax, bleached and purified, used for manufacture of candles, for modelling &c. Phr. *like wax (in one's hands* &c.), easily influenced. 2. Substance resembling wax in appearance, consistency &c.; specif. a also *vegetable wax*, waxy substance exuded by some plants; b also *ear-wax*, substance secreted by ear; cerumen; c also *mineral wax*, ozocerite; d *cobbler's wax*, kind of resin used by shoemakers to coat thread.

wax (II.), vb. trans., fr. prec. To cover, coat, impregnate, treat, with wax.

wax (III.), vb. intrans. O.E. *weaxan*; M.E. *waxan*, 'to grow'; cp. O.H.G. *wahsan*; O. Fris. *waxa*; O.N. *vaxa*, 'to grow'; Goth. *wahsjan*, 'to grow'; cogn. w. Sert. *vakšaṇam*, 'growth, increase'; *úkṣati*, 'he strengthens'; Gk. *aéxein*, 'to increase', earlier *awex-; cp. also Lat. *augēre*, 'to cause to grow', see **augment, auction**. 1. To increase, grow larger; now used chiefly of the moon, to present the appearance of growing in size in passing towards the phase of full moon; contrasted with *wane*. 2. To pass into a specified state; to become: *to wax merry*; *their mirth waxed loud*; (archaic) *to wax old and feeble*.

wax (IV.), n. Etymol. unknown. (school slang) Fit of anger, rage, esp. in Phr. *to be in, get into, a wax*.

wax-berry, n. The candle-berry,

waxbill, n. [1. wáksbil; 2. wǽksbil]. Small kind of weaver-bird with beak having appearance of sealing-wax.

wax candle, n. Candle made of wax.

wax-chandler, n. Maker of, dealer in, wax candles.

wax-cloth, n. Cloth coated or treated with wax for polishing floor, furniture &c.

wax doll, n. Doll with head and extremities made of prepared beeswax &c.

waxen, adj. [1. wáksen; wǽksən]. **wax** (I.) & **-en**. 1. a (archaic) Made of wax; b resembling wax in appearance; esp. (i.) smooth, unwrinkled; also (ii.) colourless: *a waxen complexion*. 2. (archaic) Impressionable, easily melted or influenced; yielding: '*the waxen hearts of men*' (Tennyson, 'In Mem.' xxi. 8).

wax-end, n. Shoemaker's waxed thread.

wax-flower, n. Tropical Asiatic plant with thick, glossy leaves and waxy flowers, *Hoya carnosa*.

waxiness, n. [1. wáksines; 2. wǽksinis]. **waxy** & **-ness**. State or quality of being waxy.

wax-insect, n. Insect secreting wax.

wax-light, n. Wax candle, taper &c.

wax-moth, n. Moth liable to infest bee hives and lay its eggs on the combs.

wax-myrtle, n. American shrub producing nuts coated with white wax from which candles are made; the candle-berry.

wax-painting, n. Encaustic painting.

wax-palm, n. South American palm producing vegetable wax.

wax-paper, n. Paper made waterproof by coating with wax.

wax-plant, n. Plant producing waxy flowers; the wax-flower.

wax-pocket, n. One of the cavities of the under side of bee's abdomen in which wax is secreted.

wax tree, n. Tree yielding vegetable wax.

waxwing, n. [1. wákswing; 2. wǽkswiŋ]. Small bird, *Ampelis*, with feathers tipped with red, horny appendages.

waxwork, n. [1. wákswërk; 2. wǽkswāk]. Figure modelled in wax; esp. wax effigy of the human figure dressed for exhibition &c.; *waxworks*, an exhibition of such figures.

waxy (I.), adj. [1. wáksi; 2. wǽksi]. **wax** (I.) & **-y**. 1. Pertaining to, resembling, treated with, having the consistency of, wax. 2. (specif. of complexion, skin &c.) Having a pallid, translucent appearance. 3. (of organ of body, tissue &c.) Affected by a morbid change towards a structure of waxy appearance.

waxy (II.), adj. **wax** (IV.) & **-y**. (school slang) Angry, annoyed.

way, n. [1. wā; 2. wei]. O.E. *weġ*; M.E. *wei*, 'way'; cp. O.S., O.H.G. *weg*; O. Fris. *wei*; O.N. *vegr*; Goth. *wigs*, 'way'; cp. also O.E. *weġan*, 'to carry, move', see **weigh**; *wæġn*, 'cart', see **wain**; cogn. w. Lat. *vehere*, 'to drive, carry', see **vehicle**; Gk. *ókhos* for *wokhos*, 'waggon'; Lith. *vežimas*, 'cart'. 1. a Road, track, path, trail, leading from one place to another: *a rough, winding way*; Phrs. *covered way*, roofed-in passage, path &c.; *Appian, Icknield, Fosse, Way* &c., names of Roman roads; *permanent way*, railway track; *six-foot way*, space between two sets of rails on railway track; *Milky Way*, see **milky**; *the Way of the Cross*, (i.) series of representations of the stages on the road to Calvary; (ii.) set of devotions referring to these stages; Phr. *to pave the way for*, prepare for, facilitate approach or introduction of: *to pave the way for reform* &c.; b also in compounds, *highway, byway* &c. 2. Route followed, or to be followed, in going from place to place: *do you know the way?*; *this is the way home*; *to find, lose, one's way*; *to ask, point out, the way*; *which is the way out?* Phrs. *the longest way round is the shortest way home*, short cuts are often not reliable (lit. and fig.); *to take one's way*, go; *to go one's way*, depart; *to lead the way*, (lit. and fig.) go in front, act as leader; *to see one's way to*, feel that one is able to (do something); *to go out of one's way to*, make special effort to; *to put oneself out of the way*, take trouble; *to go the way of all flesh, of all the earth*, die; *the parting of the ways*, (fig.) moment for decisive action along one of two opposed lines; *by way of*, by a route passing through; *by the way*, (i.) during journey; (ii.) (fig., introducing an irrelevancy) in passing, incidentally; *on the way*, travelling, passing from one place to another; going or approaching; *out of the way*, unusual, unfamiliar: *he has done nothing out of the way*; *out-of-the-way* (attrib. adj.), remote, inaccessible: *an out-of-the-way place*. 3. Direction, point towards which motion takes place: *he went that way*; *which way were you looking?* 4. Distance traversed, or to be traversed; distance between two points: *it is only a little way to the town*; *we have still some way to go*; *England is a long way from Australia*; *the roots go a long way down*. 5. a Passage from point to point; progress, advance: *to make one's way*; *to make the best of one's way*, go as fast as possible; b (lit. and fig.) forward movement, tendency or power to advance; momentum: *to make, gather, lose, way*. Phrs. *to be under way*, *to have way on*, (esp. of ship) be moving forward; (also fig.) *preparations are now under way* &c. 6. (lit. and fig.) Freedom to advance, opportunity for progress; space for unimpeded forward movement: *to make way (for)*; *to be in one's way*; *to get out of one's way*; *to clear the way*. Phrs. *to put (person) out of the way*, kill him &c.; *to put one in the way of*, give an opportunity to; *to give way*, yield, cease to resist. 7. Method, mode of procedure, manner of achieving an object or performing an action; course of action: *the right or wrong way of doing something*; *to try new ways of working*; *to speak in a careless way*; *do it your own way*. Phrs. *to have one's own way*, get what one wants; *to my* &c. *way of thinking*, in my opinion; *by way of*, (i.) with intention of, with a view to; (ii.) as substitute for: *to say a few words by way of introduction*; *in the way of (business* &c.), in the ordinary course of. 8. a Characteristic method, customary procedure, habit: *it's not his way to be generous*; *the way of the world*; b specific manner of life, habits: *to like old-fashioned ways*; *to live* &c. *in a small way*, unpretentiously, on a small scale. 9. Scope, sphere of attention, occupation, action &c.: *such things have never come (in) my way*. Phr. *to be in the drapery* &c. *way*, trade as draper &c. 10. a State, condition; (colloq.) *to be in a bad way*; Phr. *in the family way*, pregnant; b specif. (slang) state of agitation: *she is in a terrible way*. 11. Respect, regard, particular: *they are in no way similar*; *it is good in some ways*; *bad in every way*. 12. (pl.) Lines of framework of timber down which ship slides when launched.

way-bill, n. List of passengers or goods carried by public conveyance.

way-board, n. Thin seam of rock lying between two thicker strata.

wayfarer, n. [1. wáfārer; 2. wéifɛərə]. **way** & **fare** (III.) & **-er**. Person passing from one place to another, traveller.

wayfaring, adj. [1. wáfāriŋ; 2. wéifɛəriŋ]. **way** & **fare** (III.) & **-ing**. Passing from place to place; travelling, itinerant.

wayfaring tree, n. European shrub with white flowers and black berries, common in hedgerows; viburnum.

waylay, vb. trans. [1. wālá; 2. weiléi]. **way** & **lay** (III.). To lie in wait for in order to attack &c.; to ambush.

way-leave, n. Right of way; specif., right to carry minerals, goods &c. over another's property.

way-mark, n. Milestone or other indication on public way.

way-post, n. Sign-post.

-ways, adv. suff. representing O.E. *weģes*, genit. of *weģ*, 'way'; **way** & **-es**. Used to form advs. indicating position, direction &c. : *sideways, always, lengthways* &c.

way-shaft, n. For *weigh-*. Rocking shaft in steam-engine.

wayside, n. & adj. **1**. n. Side, margin, of path or road. **2**. adj. Found, situated, at the side of the road : *wayside flowers*.

wayward, adj. [1. wǎward ; 2. wéiwəd]. Earlier *awayward* ; **away** & **-ward**. Not yielding to control ; perverse, capricious, wilful.

waywardly, adv. Prec. & **-ly**. In a wayward manner.

waywardness, n. See prec. & **-ness**. State or quality of being wayward.

way-worn, adj. Wearied by travel, esp. on foot.

wayzgoose, n. [1. wǎzgoōs ; 2. wéizgūs]. 17th cent. *waygoose* ; etymol. unknown. Annual entertainment held by printing-house employees.

we, pron., 1st pers. pl. [1. wē ; 2. wī]. O.E., M.E. *wē* ; O.S. *wī* ; Du. *wij* ; O.H.G. *wir* ; Goth. *weis* ; cogn. w. Scrt. *vayám*, 'we'.

weak, adj. [1. wēk ; 2. wīk]. M.E. *wēke*, fr. O.N. *veikr*, wh. is cogn. w. O.E. *wāc*, 'weak ; slender', M.E. *wōk*, now obs. ; cp. O.S. *wēc* ; O.H.G. *weich*, 'weak' ; cp. w. Gk. *eíkein*, 'to yield, draw back' ; Lat. *vicis*, 'change' ; *vicissim*, 'in turn', see **vice (IV.)** & **vicissitude**. **1**. **a** Not strong ; lacking in vigour, strength, firmness, solidity, durability &c. ; easily disturbed, shaken, broken down &c. ; not able to resist force, pressure &c. : *weak supports, foundations* ; *weak wrists* ; *weak defences* ; **b** (of person or group of persons &c.) easily overcome, unable to attack or resist : *a weak side, team* &c. ; Phr. *the weaker sex*, women ; **c** liable to attack, offering little resistance : *the weak points, spots, of a fortification* &c. Phr. *the weak point* (of a person, scheme, argument &c.), quality &c. most open to attack. **2**. **a** Enfeebled by illness, injury, age &c. ; frail, lacking in strength and vigour : *to be too weak to walk* ; **b** of delicate constitution, not robust ; **c** (of organ of body) not functioning with normal force or efficiency : *a weak heart*. **3**. (of senses or organs of sense) Lacking in perceptive power, not normal in action : *weak hearing* ; *weak eyes, sight* &c. ; *a weak voice*, one that is feeble and lacking in resonance. **4**. (of mind &c.) Not reaching normal standard of intelligence ; lacking in mental power ; feeble, deficient. **5**. (of person or character) Lacking in moral force, tending to irresolution, wanting in decision, stability &c. ; vacillating. **6**. (of action) Not forcible, decisive, firm ; showing lack of firmness, resolution, courage &c. : *weak refusal, argument, resistance, defence* &c. **7**. Inadequately supplied with something necessary for particular purpose : *a weak hand at cards*. **8**. (of statement, argument &c.) Insufficiently supported by facts &c. ; lacking cogency ; unconvincing, illogical. **9**. Not efficient in, not good at ; below required standard : *weak in spelling, in Latin*. **10**. Much diluted, watery, insipid : *weak tea*. **11**. (of style) Lacking in force, vigour, conciseness &c. **12**. (commerc., of trade &c.) Not active, lacking in briskness. **13**. (gram.) **a** *Weak verb*, in English and other Germanic languages, one forming past tense & past participle by addition of *-d* or *-t* ; **b** *weak declension* (of nouns and adjectives), belonging originally to the so-called *-n-* stems, that is, having stems ending in *-n-* to which the case-endings are added ; in Old English, except in genitive plural, the case suffixes are lost, leaving only *-n*, which takes the place of these ; the dative plural of weak declensions is identical with that of the strong.

weaken, vb. trans. & intrans. [1. wēkn ; 2. wīkən]. Prec. & **-en**. **1**. trans. **a** (of material action) (i.) To render bodily weak or weaker ; to reduce power of resistance, cause to lose strength and vigour, intensity : *his illness has permanently weakened him* ; (ii.) to reduce stability of, diminish capacity of bearing strains, weights, pressure &c. : *you will weaken the bridge if you reduce the number of arches* ; *the sea-wall has been weakened by the force of the storm* ; **b** (of non-material action) to reduce, detract from, intellectual force, cogency, convincingness of : *to weaken an argument by exaggerated statement, one's case by claiming too much* &c. **2**. intrans. **a** (rare, in material sense) To become bodily weaker, lose force and vigour : *he seems to be weakening daily* ; **b** (in non-material sense) to become less assured and determined ; to be shaken in one's opinion ; to offer less resistance, be inclined to give way : *I was afraid he would weaken when he heard the plausible arguments on the other side* ; *he still makes a show of opposition, but he is obviously weakening*.

weak-eyed, adj. Having weak eyes.

weak-headed, adj. Weak-minded.

weakish, adj. [1. wēkish ; 2. wīkiʃ]. **weak** & **-ish**. Somewhat weak.

weak-kneed, adj. [1. wēk nēd ; 2. wīk nīd]. (chiefly fig.) Weak in resolution, lacking determination and firmness of character.

weakling, n. [1. wēkling ; 2. wīkliŋ]. **weak** & **-ling**. Person &c. lacking in physical or moral strength.

weakly (I.), adj. [1. wēkli ; 2. wīkli]. **weak** & **-ly**. Not robust, feeble, sickly.

weakly (II.), adv. **weak** & **-ly**. In a weak manner.

weak-minded, adj. Lacking in intelligence, feeble-minded.

weakness, n. [1. wēknes ; 2. wīknis]. **weak** & **-ness**. **1**. State or quality of being weak ; specif. a bodily infirmity, debility, feebleness : *the weakness and helplessness of old age* ; **b** intellectual feebleness, imbecility : *weakness of mind, brain-power* ; **c** feebleness of character, irresolution, instability of will ; **d** (rare) lack of strength in material objects ; insecurity, liability to be upset, broken down &c. : *the weakness of a lock, of a hedge, a wall* &c. **2**. Characteristic defect, failing, weak point in character &c. : *his chief weakness is being too easily amenable to flattery, a fondness for the bottle*. **3**. (colloq.) **a** Predilection, particular taste, fondness : *a weakness for apple-dumplings* ; **b** thing for which one has a weakness : *detective novels are a weakness of many hard-working students*. **4**. Lack of cogency, unconvincingness, illogicality, absence of ground : *the weakness of an argument, of a case* &c. **5**. Imperfection, defectiveness, inadequacy : *the weakness of a man's classical knowledge* ; *weakness in scholarship*. **6**. Feebleness in action, effort &c. : *the weakness in resistance shown by the enemy*.

weak-sighted, adj. Lacking in strength of vision.

weal (I.), n. [1. wēl ; 2. wīəl]. O.E. *wela*, 'prosperity' ; M.E. *wēle* ; cp. O.E. *wel*, 'well', see **well (III.)**. Prosperity, welfare, state of well-being ; now only in Phr. *in weal and woe* ; *the public weal* &c.

weal (II.), n. See **wale**. A mark or ridge on living flesh, raised by a blow from a rod or lash.

weald, n. [1. wēld ; 2. wīəld]. O.E. (Saxon) *wēald*, M.E. *weeld*, 'forest, wold' ; cp. O.E. *wǎld*, see **wold**, wh. is an Anglian variant. *The Weald*, district of southern England comprising parts of Kent, Sussex, Surrey, Hampshire.

weald-clay, n. (geol.) Clay, limestone, and sandstone beds forming part of the Wealden series.

Wealden, adj. & n. [1. wēldn ; 2. wīəldn]. **weald** & **-en**. **1**. adj. Pertaining to, resembling, the Weald, esp. in its characteristic geological formation. **2**. n. (geol.) Series of sandstone and clay strata forming the lower part of the Lower Cretaceous system.

wealth, n. [1. welth ; 2. welþ]. M.E. *welþe*, 'pleasure, happiness, wealth' ; **weal (I.)** & **-th**. **1**. Plentiful supply, abundance, profusion : *a wealth of flowers, words, affection* &c. **2**. Abundance of material resources, riches, accumulation of property : *a man of considerable wealth* ; *to possess wealth is not always to be happy*. **3**. (archaic) Well-being, prosperity : 'Grant him in health and wealth long to live' (Prayer for King's Majesty).

wealthily, adv. [1. wélthili ; 2. wélþili].

wealthy & **-ly**. In a wealthy manner.

wealthiness, n. [1. wélthines ; 2. wélþinis]. Next word & **-ness**. State of being wealthy.

wealthy, adj. [1. wélthi ; 2. wélþi]. **wealth** & **-y**. Possessing, characterized by, wealth.

wean (I.), vb. trans. [1. wēn ; 2. wīn]. O.E. *wenian*, 'to accustom, train, make familiar ; to wean' ; M.E. *wēnen*, 'to wean' ; cp. O.H.G. *wennan* ; M. Du. *wennen* ; O.N. *venja*, 'to accustom', cp. O.N. *vanr* ; cp. further, with different vowel grade, O.H.G. *(gi)won* ; O.E. *wuna*, 'accustomed', see **wont (I.)** ; O.E. *wunian*, 'to dwell' ; ultimately all fr. base **wen-* &c., 'to love' ; see also **wish, Venus**. **1**. To accustom (child or other young mammal) to food other than its mother's milk. **2**. (also *wean away*) To withdraw (person &c.) gradually from former habit, occupation, object of affection &c. ; to estrange, distract, draw away, alienate, esp. by substitution of fresh interests, associations &c.

wean (II.), n. Apparently fr. Scots *wee ane*, 'little one'. (Scots) Child.

weanling, n. [1. wēnling ; 2. wīnliŋ]. **wean (I.)** & **-ling**. Newly weaned child or other mammal.

weapon, n. [1. wépun ; 2. wépən]. O.E. *wæpen* ; M.E. *wēpen*, 'weapon' ; cp. O.H.G. *wāfen* ; O. Fris. *wēpen* ; O.N. *vāpn*, 'weapon' ; Goth. *wēpna*, pl. The short vowel in present form is due to M.E. shortening before two consonants in inflected forms : *wēpnes* &c. **1**. **a** Material object, instrument, tool, designed, or used, as means of attack or defence ; **b** organ of animal or plant used for similar purpose. **2**. Intellectual or moral means of attack or defence : *the strike as a political weapon* ; *tariffs as a weapon for bargaining*.

weaponless, adj. [1. wépunles ; 2. wépənlis]. Prec. & **-less**. Without a weapon.

wear (I.), vb. trans. & intrans. [1. wār ; 2. weə]. O.E. *werian*, 'to wear (clothes) ; to clothe', M.E. *wěr(i)en*, 'to wear (clothes)' ; apparently a specialized use of *werian*, 'to protect, defend' ; cp. O.E. *waru*, 'defence' ; cp., however, in special sense Goth. *wasjan*, 'to clothe', & *wasti*, 'garment', cogn. w. Lat. *vestis*, 'garment' ; see **vest (I.)** & cognates there given. It looks as if some of the present meanings, such as 'to fatigue, exhaust, wear out' &c., were due to association w. an entirely different word—O.E. *wōrian*, 'to crumble, wear away', wh. is connected w. O.E. *wēriġ*, 'weary', & *wēriġean*, 'to weary, exhaust', see **weary**. **A**. trans. **1**. **a** To be covered, clothed, with, have upon the person as a garment, or as an ornament : *to wear a frock-coat, a white waistcoat, wool next the skin, a pair of top-boots, a clean collar* &c. ; *to wear mourning* ; *to wear a wreath of flowers* ; *to wear diamonds* ; Phr. *to wear one's heart on one's sleeve*, to show one's feelings readily ; **b** to have emotions which are easily roused ; **b** to have as a characteristic of one's personal appearance, to have as an appendage to one's person : *to wear one's hair waved, parted in the middle* ; *to wear side-whiskers*. **2**. **a** To bear, exhibit, as a characteristic expression of face, cast of features &c. : *to wear a troubled look, a harassed expression* ; *her features wore a pleasant smile* ; **b** (of external nature or other objects) to give an impression of, to exhibit, to be clad in : '*This city now doth like a garment wear The beauty of the morning*' (Wordsworth, 'On Westminster Bridge'). **3**. To sustain, carry, bear, as closely associated with one : *to wear one's honours* *with modesty and grace.* **4.** To remove part of, cause wastage of substance from, as by attrition; to produce a furrow, depression, in surface of by frequent passage, friction &c.: *the constant flow of water has worn the stone; steps worn by the feet of thousands; to wear one's shoes into holes.* **5.** To produce injury to, diminution of substance, attrition in; to beat, smooth, down, as by constant use, frequent passage over, rough handling and usage, friction &c.: *to wear ruts on a road; to wear a track across a field; a rope at last wears a groove in a stout stanchion.* **6.** To cause bodily or mental fatigue to; to exhaust, waste: *sorrow and anxiety wear one more than hard work; a constitution worn by years of hardship;* also *wear out.* **B.** intrans. **1.** To last, remain unimpaired, withstand the stress of hard usage: *this material will wear for ever; you will find that this colour won't wear.* **2.** To offer specified kind or amount of resistance to usage, severe treatment &c.: *shoddy clothes never wear well; these clothes have worn splendidly.* Phr. (of persons) *to wear well,* bear one's years lightly, show few signs of age. **3.** To pass, traverse a period of time, advance: *the day, one's life, wears towards its close;* 'never morning wore To evening, but some heart did break' (Tennyson, 'In Mem.' vi.). **C.** Followed by adverbs with special meanings. *Wear away,* **1.** trans., to remove, efface, as by friction, to rub out: *time has worn away the inscription; the feet of many generations have worn away the steps.* **2.** intrans., (of time) to pass, esp. tediously, to drag out: *the long day wore away. Wear down,* trans., **a** to reduce, lessen height of, by friction: *to wear one's heels down; the steps have been worn down;* **b** (fig.) to break down, reduce, as by constant attack or importunity: *to wear down opposition. Wear off,* **1.** trans., to rub off, remove, reduce, by constant friction; **2.** intrans., **a** to be removed, lessened, by friction: *the nap will wear off;* **b** (fig.) to pass away, become less: *the strangeness, his roughness &c., will wear off in time. Wear out,* **1.** trans., **a** to render shabby, threadbare, dilapidated; to reduce value or usefulness of by usage: *to wear out one's clothes, a machine* &c.; **b** to exhaust: *his temper, patience &c., is worn out;* **c** to exhaust in body or mind, to tire out by excessive bodily or mental strain: *hardship and penury wore him out before his time;* **2.** intrans., to become worn out: *the clothes will soon wear out.*

wear (II.), n., fr. prec. **1. a** Wearing of, act of wearing (clothes &c.): *a suit for Sunday wear;* **b** act of using; usage: *a carpet which has been many years in wear; it shows signs of wear,* i.e. of having been used. **2.** Amount of diminution in usefulness, effectiveness, value, which an article undergoes in the process of normal use: *in fixing the rent of a furnished house one must allow for wear.* Phrs. *wear and tear,* natural dilapidation caused by time and usage; specif., *fair wear and tear,* such as is considered permissible for a person hiring an article to cause by normal usage, without being called upon to compensate owner.

wear (III.), vb. trans. & intrans. Variant of **veer.** (naut.) **1.** trans. To bring (ship) about by putting the helm up. **2.** intrans. (of ship) To go about before the wind.

wear (IV.), n. [1. wĕr; 2. wiə]. See **weir.**

wearable, adj. [1. wăr*ă*bl; 2. wéər*ə*bl]. **wear (I.) & -able.** Capable of being worn; fit to be worn.

weariless, adj. [1. wĕrilĕs; 2. wiərilis]. **weary (I.) & -less.** (rare) Incapable of being wearied.

wearily, adv. [1. wĕrili; 2. wiərili]. **weary (I.) & -ly.** In a weary manner.

weariness, n. [1. wĕrinĕs; 2. wiərinis]. See prec. & **-ness.** State or quality of being weary; fatigue, tiredness.

wearing, adj. [1. wăring; 2. wéəriŋ], fr. Pres. Part. of **wear (I.)** Exhausting; tending to fatigue body or mind: *a wearing task; children are often very wearing.*

wearing-apparel, n. Clothes, garments.
wearing-iron, n. Wearing-plate.
wearing-plate, n. Plate designed to guard part of a machine &c. from friction.
wearisome, adj. [1. wĕrisum; 2. wiərisəm]. **weary (I.) & -some.** Tending to cause weariness; tiresome, tiring, tedious.
wearisomely, adv. Prec. & **-ly.** In a wearisome manner.
wearisomeness, n. See prec. & **-ness.** State or quality of being wearisome.
weary (I.), adj. [1. wĕri; 2. wiəri]. O.E. *wērig;* M.E. *wēri,* 'weary'; fr. **wōr-ig,* cp. O.E. *wōrian,* 'to crumble', & O.S. *wōrig, -ag,* 'weary'; O.H.G. *wuorag,* 'drunk'; cogn. w. Gk. *hōrākiān,* 'to be giddy, faint'; cp. further O.N. *órar,* 'fits of madness'; Gk. *ōros* for **wōr-,* 'sleep'. **1.** Tired, fatigued, exhausted, by effort. **2.** *Weary of,* tired of, bored by, impatient of: *to be weary of life; to be weary of a person's chatter, nonsense* &c. **3.** Causing weariness; tedious, irksome: *a weary world, life.*
weary (II.), vb. trans. & intrans., fr. prec. **A.** trans. **1.** To make weary; to tire, fatigue, exhaust. **2.** To bore, wear out patience of, harass: *to weary a person with idle talk.* **B.** intrans. **1.** To grow weary, become fatigued. **2.** *Weary of,* to become bored by, lose patience with: *to weary of too much gaiety.* **3.** *Weary for,* to long for, yearn after; to miss greatly, long for presence of: *she wearies for her absent children.*
weasand, n. [1. wĕzand, wĭzand; 2. wĭzənd, wĭzənd]. O.E. *wǣsend, wǣsand;* M.E. *wēsand;* cp. O.H.G. *weisunt;* O. Fris. *wāsende.* (archaic) Trachea, windpipe; esp. in Phr. *to cut, slit, his weasand.*
weasel, n. [1. wĕzl; 2. wĭzl]. O.E. *wesle;* M.E. *wēsele;* cp. O.H.G. *wisela,* 'weasel'; Du. *wezel;* Dan. *väsel.* Small, carnivorous, reddish-brown quadruped, *Putorius nivalis,* of the polecat family, with long body and short legs; related to stoat, ferret &c. Phr. *to catch a weasel asleep,* catch an habitually alert person off his guard.
weasel-faced, adj. [1. wĕzl făst; 2. wĭzl fèist]. Having a thin, sharp-featured, mean face.
weather (I.), n. [1. wĕdher; 2. wéðə]. O.E., M.E. *weder,* 'storm'; cp. O.S. *wedar;* O.H.G. *wetar;* O.N. *veðr,* 'storm'; cogn. w. O. Slav. *vedro,* 'good weather'; cp. also O. Slav. *větrŭ,* 'storm'; *vějati,* 'to blow'; Lith. *vĕtra,* 'storm'; O. Prussian *wetro,* 'wind'; connected w. Lat. *ventus;* Scrt. *vātaś;* O.E. *wind,* 'wind', see **wind (I.).** General atmospheric conditions prevailing at a specific time and place, as regards temperature, amount of moisture in the air, direction &c. of wind, clouds &c.: *bad, good, fine, wet, hot, windy, weather* &c. Phrs. (naut.) *to make good, bad, weather,* experience such weather; *April weather,* sunshine and showers alternately; *under the weather,* depressed, indisposed, not up to the mark; *under stress of weather,* affected by, under compulsion of, bad weather.
weather (II.), vb. trans. & intrans., fr. prec. **A.** trans. **1.** (esp. geol.) To affect surface of, to disintegrate (rock &c.), by action of rain, wind &c. **2.** To expose to action of weather; to season. **3.** To slope (roof-slates, boards &c.) downwards, in order that rain may drain off. **4.** (naut.) To pass, sail, to windward of: *to weather a point.* **5.** To come through successfully, survive: *to weather a storm;* also fig.: *to weather a financial crisis* &c. **B.** intrans. To be affected, disintegrated, by atmospheric action, as stones &c.
weather (III.), adj., fr. **weather (I.).** (naut.) Windward; facing, turned towards, direction of wind: *the weather bow, beam* &c. Phrs. *to have the weather ga(u)ge of,* to be to windward of; (fig.) to gain an advantage over; *to keep one's weather eye open,* be on the alert.
weather-beaten, adj. Showing effects of exposure to sun, wind, rain; hence, having a rough, hearty, sunburnt, reddened complexion.

weather-board, vb. trans. To supply with weather-boarding.
weather-boarding, -boards, n. Series of overlapping boards designed to throw off rain from house &c.
weather-bound, adj. Detained by bad weather.
weather-bureau, n. Meteorological office.
weather-chart, n. Map showing distribution of atmospheric characteristics.
weather-cloth, n. Canvas screen fixed to ship's bridge to give protection from rain, wind &c.
weathercock, n. [1. wédherkòk; 2. wéðəkòk]. **1.** Revolving plate or bar, often in shape of a cock, fixed on vertical rod and indicating direction of wind. **2.** (fig.) Fickle, capricious person; a flibbertigibbet.
weather-contact, n. Leakage of electricity from one telegraph-wire to another caused by damp.
weather-cross, n. Weather-contact.
weather-forecast, n. Forecast of weather to be expected during an ensuing period of 12, 24, hours &c.
weather ga(u)ge. See **weather (III.).**
weather-glass, n. Barometer.
weathering, n. [1. wédhering; 2. wéðəriŋ]. **weather (II.) & -ing.** **1.** (archit.) Slight slope given to surface in order that rain &c. may drain off. **2.** Atmospheric action on rock &c.
weatherliness, n. [1. wédherlines; 2. wéðəlìnis]. Next word & **-ness.** State or quality of being weatherly.
weatherly, adj. [1. wédherli; 2. wéðəli]. **weather & -ly.** (naut.) Capable of sailing close to the wind without making much leeway.
weather-map, n. Weather-chart.
weathermost, adj. [1. wédhermòst; 2. wéðəmòust]. Farthest to windward.
weather-moulding, n. Projecting moulding on wall &c. designed to throw off rain.
weather-proof, adj. Capable of resisting rough weather.
weather-prophet, n. Person making forecast of weather.
weather-service, n. Institution for collecting and distributing meteorological information.
weather-stain, n. Discolouration through exposure.
weather-station, n. Meteorological observation-post.
weather-strip, n. Strip of leather, wood &c. for keeping out draughts, rain &c.
weather-tiles, n. pl. Overlapping tiles as substitute for weather-boarding.
weather-vane, n. Weathercock.
weather-wise, adj. Able to foretell the weather.
weather-worn, adj. Affected by exposure to rough weather.
weave (I.), vb. trans. & intrans. [1. wĕv; 2. wĭv]. O.E. *wefan,* M.E. *wēven;* cp. O.H.G. *weban;* O.N. *vefa,* 'to weave'; M. Du. *weven,* 'to move to and fro; to weave'; M.H.G. *webelen,* 'to fluctuate'; O.N. *vafra,* 'to move to and fro'; *(kongur)vāfa,* 'spider'; cogn. w. Scrt. *(ūrṇa)vābhis,* 'spider', lit. 'woolweaver'; fr. base **webh-* &c., 'to weave'; see also **web.** **A.** trans. **1. a** To form (threads) into a web, tissue, fabric, by intertwining on a loom; **b** to make (fabric &c.) out of threads, on a loom. **2. a** To form (a wreath, garland) by twisting and intertwining stalks of leaves and flowers &c.; **b** to twist (leaves, flowers &c.) into a wreath. **3.** To pass, twist, in and out among: *to weave ribbons through one's hair.* **4.** (fig.) **a** To construct by an act of the mind and imagination: *to weave a romance, story, round a person or incident;* **b** to weave facts, incidents &c. into a continuous narrative, to arrange, treat, display (facts &c.) so as to form (them) into a narrative &c. **B.** intrans. To practise weaving.
weave (II.), n., fr. prec. Style of weaving, manner in which threads &c. are interlaced to form a fabric.

weaver, n. [1. wĕ́ver; 2. wīvə]. **weave** (I.) & -er. 1. Person habitually engaged in weaving on a loom. 2. Member of an ancient Company of the City of London—*the Weavers*—founded 1130. 3. Weaver-bird.

weaver-bird, n. Small finch-like bird constructing a pouch-shaped woven nest.

weazand. See **weasand**.

weazen(ed). See **wizen(ed)**.

web, n. [1. web; 2. wɛb]. O.E., M.E. *webb*; fr. *wŏ̄bja*; gradational variant of base of **weave**; cp. O.H.G. *weppi*; Du. *web*; O.N. *wefr*, 'web'. 1. a Woven fabric; textile formed by interlacing threads on a loom; Phr. (fig.) *a web of intrigue* &c., an intricate system; **b** piece of fabric woven in a single length. 2. Network of threads spun by spider &c.; cobweb. 3. Membrane between the digits of aquatic bird, flying animal &c. 4. Set of barbs on either side of the shaft of a feather; vane. 5. Roll of printing-paper. 6. Thin plate of metal, sometimes perforated, connecting heavier parts of machinery &c.

webbed, adj. [1. webd; 2. wɛbd]. Prec. & -ed. United, having the digits united, by a web : *water-birds have webbed feet*.

webbing, n. [1. wĕ́bing; 2. wɛ́biŋ]. **web** & -ing. 1. a Narrow strip of strong, woven material used in upholstery, saddlery &c.; **b** edging of a fine fabric made in stronger material. 2. Tapes used to guide web in printing-machine.

web-eye, n. Ophthalmic disease in which the eye becomes covered with a film.

web-eyed, adj. Prec. & -ed. Affected with web-eye.

web-fingered, adj. Having the fingers connected by membranes.

web-foot, n. Foot the toes of which are joined together by membranes, as those of aquatic birds.

web-footed, adj. Prec. & -ed. Having web-feet.

web-toed, adj. Having the toes joined by membranes.

web-wheel, n. Wheel with disk or plate instead of spokes.

web-worm, n. Larva which spins itself a web as shelter.

wed, vb. trans. & intrans. [1. wed; 2. wɛd]. O.E. *weddian*, 'to promise, pledge', M.E. *wedden*, 'to pledge; to wed'; fr. O.E. *wedd*, 'pledge, agreement'; cp. M.H.G. *wetten*; O.N. *veðja*; Goth. *-wadjōn*, 'to pledge'; O. Fris. *wed*; O.H.G. *wetti*; Goth. *wadi*, 'pledge, compact'; cogn. w. Lat. *vas*, stem *vad-*, 'pledge'; Lith. *vadúti*, 'to redeem a pledge'; cp. **gage** (I.) & **wager** (I.). A. trans. 1. To take as husband or wife; to marry. 2. To join in marriage; perform marriage ceremony over, or for. 3. To give in marriage, cause to marry : *to wed one's daughter to a soldier*. In senses 1, 2, 3 the word is archaic or rhetorical, though the P.P. as adjective is in common use; see **wedded**. 4. (fig.) To unite, join, combine : *to wed simplicity with art*. B. intrans. To take a husband or wife; to be married.

wedded, adj. [1. wéded; 2. wɛ́did], fr. P.P. of prec. 1. a Married, in the state of matrimony : *the wedded pair*; **b** pertaining to, derived from, matrimony : *wedded bliss*. 2. (fig.) Devoted, firmly attached (to): *wedded to one's profession*; *I am not wedded to that particular plan* &c., am not committed to it, do not insist on it.

wedding, n. [1. wéding; 2. wɛ́diŋ]. **wed** & -ing. **a** Marriage ceremony; **b** this together with the festivities connected with it; *silver wedding*, 25th, *golden wedding*, 50th, *diamond wedding*, 60th, anniversary of a marriage.

wedding-breakfast, n. Festivity accompanied by a banquet, attended by the principal parties and the guests after a wedding.

wedding-cake, n. Rich cake covered with almond paste and highly ornamented with white sugar and silvered decorations, usually cut by the bride at a wedding-breakfast, and afterwards distributed in small pieces to friends.

wedding-day, n. **a** Day upon which a particular wedding is celebrated; **b** anniversary of this.

wedding-favour, n. White rosette worn in honour of wedding.

wedding-ring, n. Ring placed by the bridegroom upon the bride's finger at the time of marriage, and ever afterwards worn by her.

wedge (I.), n. [1. wej; 2. wɛdʒ]. O.E. *wecg*, M.E. *wegge*; cp. O.H.G. *weggi*; M. Du. *wegghe*; O.N. *veggr*, 'wedge'; cp. further O.H.G. *waganso*; O.N. *vangnsi*, 'ploughshare'; cogn. w. Lat. *vōmer*; O. Prussian *wagnis*, 'ploughshare'; Lith. *vágis*, 'wedge'. 1. A piece of wood or metal relatively thick at one end, and gradually tapering to a thin edge at the other, used for splitting wood, or for rendering immovable separate parts or objects between which there is too much space, &c.; one of the elementary mechanical powers. Phr. *the thin end of the wedge*, a slight, unimportant action or event which may have considerable results later; esp. an incipient attempt to achieve important results by means which at first are hardly noticeable. 2. A wedge-shaped object, e.g. **a** a hunch of cheese, bread &c. in this form; **b** *a wedge of troops*, *population* &c., body of troops &c. disposed in such a form.

wedge (II.), vb. trans., fr. prec. 1. To fix, make firm, compress, with a wedge : *to wedge a door to keep it open* (or *shut*), *a window to prevent it from rattling*. 2. To split, cleave, by means of a wedge. 3. Usually *wedge oneself in*, to squeeze oneself in forcibly through or into narrow space.

wedge-shaped, adj. Having the shape of a wedge.

wedge-tailed, adj. (of bird &c.) Having the tail in the shape of a wedge.

wedgewise, adv. [1. wéjwiz; 2. wɛ́dʒwaiz]. **wedge** (I.) & -wise. In the manner of a wedge.

Wedgwood, n. [1. wéjwood; 2. wɛ́dʒwud], fr. name of inventor, Josiah Wedgwood (1730–1795). Fine earthenware made at the Wedgwood works in Staffordshire.

Wedgwood-blue, n. Shade of blue typical of some varieties of Wedgwood ware.

wedlock, n. [1. wédlok; 2. wɛ́dlɔk]. O.E. *wedlāc*, 'wedlock', M.E. *wedlŏc*; fr. O.E. *wedd*, 'pledge', see **wed**, & *lāc*, 'sport, game; movement; gift (to bride &c.)'; cp. O.N. *leikr*; O.H.G. *leich*; Goth. *laiks*, 'sport'; Goth. *laikan*, 'to spring, hop, fly'; cogn. w. Gk. *elelízein*, 'to shake'; Lith. *láigyti*, 'to run about wildly'; the form of second element may be due to association w. O.E. *loc*, 'enclosure; settlement' &c. The married state, matrimony. Phr. *born in wedlock*, of legally married parents.

Wednesday, n. [1. wénzdi; 2. wɛ́nzdi]. O.E. *Wōdnesdæg*; M.E. *Wodenes-, Wednesdai*; fr. O.E. *Wōden*, Gmc. god, & **day**; cp. O.H.G. *Wuotan*; O.S. *Wōden*; O.N. *Ōðinn*; the name is connected w. Goth. *wōds*, O.E. *wōd*, 'raging, possessed'; cp. O.E. *wōþ*, 'voice, song'; O.N. *ōðr*, 'poetry, song'; cogn. w. Lat. *vātēs*, 'prophet, seer', see **vaticinate**. Fourth day of the week. Phr. *Ash Wednesday*, first day of Lent.

wee, adj. [1. wē; 2. wī], fr. M.E. *wei*, M. Scots *wē*, 'bit', fr. O.E. *wǣge*, 'weight, balance', see **wey**. (Scots and provinc.) Very small, tiny; in England chiefly in *a wee bit* (as adv.): *a wee bit tedious*, i.e. rather, slightly.

weed (I.), n. [1. wēd; 2. wīd]. O.E. *wēod*, M.E. *wēd*, 'weed'; cp. O.S. *wiod*. Etymol. unknown. 1. **a** Any plant which grows where it is not wanted, in a garden among cultivated plants, or in a field among crops; esp. applied to hardy, rank-growing plants which tend to choke those which it is desired to cultivate; Phrs. *to grow like a weed*, to grow rampantly; *the soothing weed*, tobacco; **b** (slang) a cigar. 2. A thin, lanky, badly grown person or animal, one in poor condition.

weed (II.), vb. trans. & intrans. O.E. *wēodian*, 'to weed'; see prec. A. trans. 1. To clear (ground) of weeds; to remove weeds from (ground). 2. *Weed out*, to remove, eliminate (esp. weak, undesirable, elements &c.) by selective process : *to weed out useless books from one's library*, *undesirable persons from a community* &c. B. intrans. To perform the act of weeding.

weeder, n. [1. wéder; 2. wīdə]. Prec. & -er. **a** Person employed to pull up weeds; **b** mechanical device for removing weeds.

weed-grown, adj. Overgrown with weeds.

weediness, n. [1. wédines; 2. wīdinis]. **weedy** & -ness. State of being weedy.

weeding-fork, n. [1. wéding fòrk; 2. wīdiŋ fɔk]. Fork used in removing weeds.

weedless, adj. [1. wédles; 2. wīdlis]. **weed** (I.) & -less. Without, free from, weeds.

weeds, n. [1. wēdz; 2. wīdz]. Pl. form, fr. O.E. (*ge*)*wǣde*, M.E. *wēde*, 'garment'; cp. O.S. *wādi*; O.H.G. *wāt*; O.N. *vāð*, 'garment'; cogn. w. Gk. *othónē* (fr. *wothónē*), 'linen, fine cloth'; Lith. *áudmi*, 'to weave'. Only in Phr. *widow's weeds*, widow's mourning dress.

weedy, adj. [1. wédi; 2. wīdi]. **weed** (I.) & -y. 1. Containing, overgrown with, weeds. 2. (of persons and animals) Thin, lanky, and weak; badly grown, in poor condition, weakly.

week, n. [1. wēk; 2. wīk]. O.E. *wice*, M.E. *wēke*, 'week'; O.H.G. *wehha*; O.N. *vika*; Goth. *wikō*, 'week'; connected w. the base in O.H.G. *wehsal*, 'exchange; change'; O.N. *vixla*, 'to exchange'; O.E. *wice*, 'exchange'; cogn. w. Lat. *vicis*, 'change, alternation, turn'; *vicissim*, 'in turn', see **vicissitude**; & cp. further **weak**. 1. **a** A period of any seven successive days : *he came for a week and stayed a month*; Phr. *today week*, a week counting backwards or forwards from today; *Saturday* &c. *week*, a week backwards or forwards from Saturday; **b** specif., a period extending from any Sunday to the following Saturday inclusive : *this week, next week*; *Easter Week*, that beginning on Easter Sunday; *Holy Week*, the one immediately preceding Easter. 2. (colloq.) Period embracing all the working days of the week, that is, the whole week with the exception of Sunday : *he spends the week in town, but is at home on Sundays*.

week-day, n. 1. Any day of the week with the exception of Sunday. 2. (attrib.) Occurring on, pertaining to, a week-day : *week-day services*.

week-end, n. & vb. intrans. 1. n. Period usually from part of Friday, or from Saturday, to Monday morning : *to have one's week-ends free*. 2. vb. To spend a week-end (usually in specified place).

weekly (I.), adj. & n. [1. wékli; 2. wīkli]. **week** & -ly. 1. adj. **a** Performed, due, occurring, appearing, regularly every week : *weekly wages*; *weekly publication*; **b** performed during the week: *weekly work*. 2. n. Weekly newspaper or other periodical.

weekly (II.), adv. **week** & -ly. Once a week, every week: *wages paid, a room cleaned, weekly*.

ween, vb. trans. [1. wēn; 2. wīn]. O.E. *wēnan*, 'to hope, expect'; M.E. *wēnen*, 'to hope, suppose; to think, have an opinion'; M.E. *wēnen*, 'to hope, suppose'; cp. O. Fris. *wēna*; cp. O.H.G. *wānan*; O.S. *wānian*; O.N. *vǣna*; Goth. *wēnjan*, 'to expect, suppose'; cp. also the ns. O.E. *wēn*, 'hope, expectation, belief'; Goth. *wēns*; O.H.G. *wān*; cogn. w. Lat. *venus*, 'charm, love', see **Venus**; Scrt. *vaníś*, 'desire, wish'; cp. also **winsome, wish**. (archaic) **a** To think, believe, be of opinion; to trow: '*they ween'd she was escaped away*' (Spenser, 'F. Q.' v 2. 25); **b** to hope, expect: '*by force or fraud Weening to prosper*' (Milton, 'P. L.' vi. 794-5).

weep, vb. intrans. & trans. [1. wēp; 2. wīp]. O.E. *wēpan*; M.E. *wēpen*, 'to weep, bewail'; O.H.G. *wuofan*; O. Fris. *wēpa*; O.N. *ǣpa*; Goth. *wōpjan*, 'to weep, cry out'; fr. *wōpjan, cp. O.E., O.S. *wōp*; O.N. *ōp*, 'lamentation'; cogn. w. O. Slav. *vabiti*, 'to summon, call up'; cp., w. different formative suff., Lat. *vāgīre*, 'to cry, squeal'; Gk. *iakhé*, 'a cry', for *wi-wagh-; ēkhéein, 'sound, echo', for *wēgh-; see echo. A. intrans. 1. a To shed tears, cry; b weep for, to lament, bewail: *to weep for one's sins*. 2. To exude moisture &c.; to be covered with condensed moisture. 3. (of trees) To droop gracefully, to have pendent boughs. B. trans. 1. To shed: *to weep bitter tears*. 2. To show, exude, drip (moisture), give out (moisture) in drops. 3. To shed tears for, to lament, bewail: *to weep one's sad fate*.

weeper, n. [1. wḗper; 2. wípə]. weep & -er. 1. One who weeps or mourns; esp. a hired mourner, or undertaker's assistant, at a funeral. 2. Garment &c. as symbol of mourning; specif. a hat-band or scarf of black crape; b widow's crape veil; c (pl.) widow's white cuffs.

weeping (I.), adj. [1. wḗping; 2. wípiŋ], fr. Pres. Part. of weep. 1. Dripping, exuding, or giving off moisture: *weeping eczema*, characterized by moist exudation; *weeping pipe*, designed to drip slowly. 2. (of trees) Having the branches bent downwards, curving, drooping towards the ground: *weeping ash, willow* &c.

weeping (II.), vbl. n., fr. weep & -ing. Act of one who weeps; lamentation, wailing.

weeping-gas, n. Tear-gas.

weepingly, adv. [1. wḗpingli; 2. wípiŋli]. weeping (I.) & -ly. Tearfully.

weet, vb. trans. & intrans. [1. wēt; 2. wīt]. M.E. *wēten*, 'to know'; variant of **wit (I.)**. (archaic) To know, perceive, recognize: '*he kist her wearie feet, And lickt her lilly hands with fawning tong, As he her wronged innocence did weet*' (Spenser, 'F. Q.' i. 3. 6).

weever, n. [1. wḗver; 2. wívə]. O. Fr. *wivre*, 'wyvern, weever'; see wivern. Genus of fishes with very sharp, poisonous dorsal spines.

weevil, n. [1. wḗv(i)l; 2. wív(i)l]. O.E. *wifol, -il*; M.E. *wēvel*, 'weevil'; cp. O.S. *-wivil*; O.H.G. *wibil*, 'weevil'; fr. base of weave. One of various small beetles with elongated snouts which feed upon plants, grain, fruit, cork &c.; often in compounds, boll-, corn-, rice-weevil &c.

weevilled, adj. [1. wḗv(i)ld; 2. wív(i)ld]. Prec. & -ed. Damaged, infested, by weevils.

weevil(l)y, adj. [1. wḗvili; 2. wívili]. weevil & -y. Infested by weevils.

weft, n. [1. weft; 2. wɛft]. O.E. *weft*, fr. base of *wefan*, 'to weave', see weave, & n. suff. -t. a Threads interwoven with warp, q.v.; b (loosely) thing woven, web.

weigh (I.), vb. trans. & intrans. [1. wā; 2. wei]. O.E. *wegan*, 'to carry, move'; M.E. *weien*, 'to bear; to weigh'; cp. O.H.G. *wegan*; O.N. *vega*; Goth. *(ga)wigan*, 'to move, carry'; cogn. w. Lat. *vehere*, 'to carry, bring, drive', see vehicle; Gk. *ókhos*, 'cart'; Scrt. *váhati*, 'drives, carries'; cp. also wain, way. A. trans. 1. To test, ascertain, weight of by means of scales or balances. 2. To turn over in the mind, to ponder, consider critically; to form an estimate of; to compare and contrast so as to ascertain relative value of: *to weigh a proposal*; *to weigh the advantages and disadvantages*. Phr. *to weigh one's words*, choose them carefully. 3. *Weigh anchor*, (i.) raise it from water; hence, (ii.) to start on a voyage. B. intrans. 1. To have a specified weight: *it weighs little, heavily* &c.; *how much do you weigh?*; *it weighs a ton*. 2. To have moral or logical weight and importance; to count for something; to exert moral or intellectual influence: *personal considerations ought not to weigh at all in the matter*. C. Followed by adverb or preposition with special meanings. *Weigh down*, trans., a to press down, bend down: *the fruit is so thick that it weighs down the branches*; b to cause depression of mind, to oppress: *weighed down by grief*. *Weigh in*, intrans., (specif. of jockey) to be weighed, in order to prove that weight is up to stipulated amount; Phr. *to weigh in with*, to bring (fact, argument &c.) to bear on discussion. *Weigh out*, 1. trans., to measure out, divide, take portions of, by weight: *to weigh out rations, materials for a cake* &c.; 2. intrans., (of jockey) to be weighed after a race. *Weigh upon*, trans., to be burdensome to, to afflict, be oppressive: *the matter weighed upon his conscience*. *Weigh with*, trans., to affect the judgement of, have moral or intellectual influence upon: *what weighs with me most in deciding to oppose the measure is the impossibility of carrying out its provisions*; *selfish interests don't weigh with him at all*.

weigh (II.), n., fr. prec. Act or process of weighing. Phr. *under weigh*, variant of *under way*, see way.

weighable, adj. [1. wā́abl; 2. wéiəbl]. weigh (I.) & -able. Capable of being weighed.

weighage, n. [1. wāij; 2. wéiidʒ]. weigh (I.) & -age. Fee paid for weighing of goods.

weigh-beam, n. Steelyard hung in a frame.

weigh-bridge, n. Instrument for weighing carts &c. and their loads.

weigh-house, n. Building for official weighing of goods.

weighing-machine, n. [1. wā́ing mashēn; 2. wéiiŋ məʃīn]. Instrument for determining weight of person, heavy objects &c.

weigh-lock, n. Canal lock with apparatus for weighing vessels.

weight (I.), n. [1. wāt; 2. weit]. M.E. *weiht*, new formation fr. weigh. The O.E. form was *(ge)wiht*, M.E. *wiht*. 1. The property which makes bodies tend to move towards the centre of the earth by virtue of gravity, the degree of this tendency being in proportion to the mass of the body; the property of being heavy: *vapours and gases appear to have hardly any weight*. 2. a Specific amount of heaviness, actual relative amount which body weighs as shown by a balance: *a full-grown man has a weight of ten stone upwards*; b weight considered as a burden; an oppressive degree of heaviness: *in ancient times horses often sank beneath the weight of a rider in full armour*. 3. Event, circumstances, material or non-material conditions which are burdensome and oppressive; something which weighs upon and oppresses the mind, or cripples action &c.; a burden: *the weight of public responsibility*; *a weight of care, sorrow* &c. Phr. *that is a great weight off my mind*, a relief from anxiety, responsibility, and the like. 4. a Intellectual or moral influence and importance; value, significance: *a man of weight in council*; *an argument of great weight*; b preponderating fact, circumstance, argument, which exerts influence, supplies a motive for action, determines a decision, and so forth: *considerations of self-interest had no weight with him*. 5. Mode of weighing, particular system or standard by which weight is ascertained: *avoirdupois, apothecary's, weight*. 6. A heavy mass; name of various objects; a one of a series of lumps or disks of metal used as standards in ascertaining the weight of a body on a balance; b (i.) mass of metal, or other heavy substance, used to press down, and keep in place, light objects, esp. *paper-weight*; (ii.) heavy mass of metal suspended from a wheel in a large clock, which serves gradually to unwind a spring and keep the machinery in motion.

weight (II.), vb. trans. fr. prec. 1. a To add weight to, make heavy; to load: *a stick weighted with lead*; *weight down*, to fasten down with a weight; b to burden, overload, oppress: *weighted with a rifle and heavy uniform*. 2. To adulterate, load (fabric &c.), with a foreign, esp. a mineral, substance.

weightily, adv. [1. wā́tili; 2. wéitili]. weighty & -ly. In a weighty manner; (esp. fig.) with moral weight and importance.

weightiness, n. [1. wā́tines; 2. wéitinis]. See prec. & -ness. Quality of being weighty (in material and non-material senses).

weightless, adj. [1. wā́tles; 2. wéitlis]. weight (I.) & -less. With little or no weight; light.

weighty, adj. [1. wā́ti; 2. wéiti]. weight (I.) & -y. 1. Heavy, of considerable weight: *a package too weighty for the post*. 2. a (of persons) Exhibiting moral or intellectual power; wielding influence: *a weighty speaker*; b cogent, convincing: *a weighty argument, utterance, reason*. 3. Important, full of significance, momentous: *weighty matters of state*.

weir, wear, n. [1. wēr; 2. wiə]. O.E. *wer*; M.E. *wēre*, 'weir, dam, pond'; cp. O.E. *werian*, 'to defend; to dam up (a pool)'; cp. Mod. Germ. *wehr*, 'defence'; Goth. *warjan*, 'to defend'; cogn. w. Scrt. *varūtár*, 'protector'; Gk. *érusthai* for *wer-*, 'to save, preserve'. 1. Dam constructed to raise level of part of stream or to hinder or divert flow of water. 2. Structure of stakes or wattles erected in a stream as fish-trap.

weird (I.), n. [1. wērd; 2. wiəd]. O.E. *wierd*, M.E. *werd, wird*, 'fate'; cp. O.H.G. *w(u)rt*; O.S. *wurd*, 'fate', fr. stem seen in O.E. *weorðan*, 'to become', see worth (III.). (archaic or provinc.) Fate, destiny; cp. Scots Phr. *to dree one's weird*, work out, undergo, one's destiny.

weird (II.), adj., fr. prec. 1. Connected with, pertaining to, fate; esp. *the weird sisters*, the Fates. 2. Supernatural, uncanny, eerie. 3. (slang) Strange, odd, queer: *ultra-fashionable dress sometimes gives people rather a weird appearance*.

weirdly, adv. Prec. & -ly. In a weird manner.

weirdness, n. See prec. & -ness. State or quality of being weird.

Weismannism, n. [1. vísmanizm; 2. váismanizm], fr. its propounder, August Weismann (1834-1914). A theory of heredity in which the germ-plasm is regarded as the basis, the possibility of the transmission of acquired characters being denied.

Welch (I.), adj. & n. [1. welsh; 2. welʃ]. Variant of Welsh (I.), used in name of the *Welch Regiment*, and the *Royal Welch Fusiliers*.

welch (II.), vb. Variant of welsh (II.).

welcome (I.), adj. [1. wélkum; 2. wélkəm], fr. O.N. *velkominn*, 'welcome'; see well (III.). The O.E. is *wilcuma*, 'welcome guest', lit. 'one who comes in accordance with one's will or desire', see will (I.); M.E. has both the Engl. *wilcume* & the Scand. *welcume*. 1. (of person) Received with pleasure into one's presence, society &c.; giving pleasure by one's presence, visit, companionship &c.: *a welcome guest* &c. Phr. *to make (a person) welcome*, exhibit, express, satisfaction at his arrival, presence &c. 2. *Welcome to*, a free, having full permission, to the use or enjoyment of: *you are welcome to any book in my library*; also b (followed by infin.) free, having permission to do something, go somewhere &c.: *you are quite welcome to come and go as you please*; c (iron.) *you are welcome to your own opinion, to any opinion you like, to go to the devil your own way*=it is a matter of indifference to me. 3. (of events, circumstances &c.) Affording pleasure by occurrence, greeted with satisfaction; opportune: *a welcome relief from pain*; *a holiday is very welcome after a long spell of work*; *financial help would be very welcome*. 4. In elliptical construction: *welcome, little stranger!*; *welcome home again!*; i.e. you are welcome.

welcome (II.), n., fr. prec. Act of welcoming; expression, by word or deed, of satisfaction and pleasure at a person's arrival, presence, companionship &c.: *to receive a hearty, a cold, welcome*.

welcome (III.), vb. trans., fr. welcome (I.). 1. To give a welcome to; to express gratification at arrival or presence of: *I welcome you to my house*; *the king was enthusiastically welcomed by the large crowds*. 2. a To feel and express satisfaction at an action, utterance, event &c.: *I shall welcome the coming of warm weather*; *we welcome the Prime Minister's assurances*; b to accept, receive, with satisfaction: *I welcome your help, your criticism, the suggestion* &c.

welcomeness, n. [1. wélkumnes; 2. wélkəmnis]. welcome (I.) & -ness. (rare) Quality of being welcome.

weld (I.), n. [1. weld; 2. wɛld]. M.E. *welde*; perh. connected w. O.E. *wald*, 'forest', see **wold**, & cp. **luteous**. Annual herb yielding a yellow dye; dyer's weed.

weld (II.), vb. trans. & intrans., fr. M.E. *wellen*, 'to boil, bubble up; to melt, weld'; see **well** (II.). **A.** trans. **1.** To unite (pieces or masses of metal heated to a plastic condition) by hammering or pressure. **2.** (of non-material action) To unite; to join into a compact whole: *the incidents are welded into an interesting narrative*; *to weld the different elements of a party together*. **B.** intrans. (of metal) To undergo, be in a suitable condition for, welding: *different metals weld at different temperatures*.

weld (III.), n., fr. prec. Joint formed by welding.

weldability, n. [1. wèldəbíliti; 2. wèldəbíliti]. See next word & -ity. State or quality of being weldable.

weldable, adj. [1. wéldabl; 2. wɛ́ldəbl]. **weld** (I.) & -**able**. Capable of being welded.

welfare, n. [1. wélfār; 2. wélfɛə]. **well** (III.) & **fare** (III.). Well-being, prosperity; state of bodily or spiritual health, of satisfactory progress &c. Phr. *welfare work*, organized effort to improve or preserve the physical and general well-being of shop employees, factory workers &c.

welk, vb. trans. & intrans. [1. welk; 2. wɛlk]. M.E. *welken*, cp. M. Du. *welken*; O.H.G. *welchen*, 'to fade, decay, rot'; O.H.G. *welc(h)*, 'moist'; cogn. w. O. Slav. *vlaga*, 'moisture'; *vlŭgŭku*, 'moist'; Lett. *wélgans*, 'damp'; cp. **gauche**. (archaic) To wither, fade, shrivel, shrink. Used by Spenser both trans.: '*But now sad Winter welked hath the day*' ('Shep. Cal.', Nov.); and intrans.: '*By that, the welked Phoebus gan availe, His weary waine*' ('Shep. Cal.', Jan.).

welkin, n. [1. wélkin; 2. wɛ́lkin]. O.E. *wolcen*, M.E. *wolken, welken*, 'cloud'; cp. O.S., O.H.G. *wolcan*, 'cloud'; perh. fr. the same base as **welk**. (poet.) Sky, vault of heaven; otherwise now current chiefly in Phr. *to make the welkin ring* (with shouting &c.).

well (I.), n. [1. wel; 2. wɛl]. O.E., M.E. *welle*, 'spring, fountain', cp. O.H.G. *wella*, 'wave'; O.N. *vella*, 'torrent'; cp. further O.E. *wellen*, 'to boil, bubble up, well up, flow'; *weallan*, 'to boil'; O. Fris. *walla*, O.H.G. *wallan*, 'to boil'; cogn. w. Goth. *walwjan, waltjan*; O.H.G. *walzan*, 'to revolve'; Lat. *volvere*, 'to turn, roll, revolve', see **volute** & words there referred to. **1. a** Shaft, usually cylindrical and lined with brick, stone &c., sunk in the ground to collect water from a subterranean source; **b** a boring from which oil gushes. **2.** Natural spring; (in Place-Names &c.) e.g. *Chadwell* (Essex), i.e. O.E. *cealde well*. **3.** (fig.) Source of supply; fount: '*that renowned Poet . . . Dan Chaucer, well of English undefyled, On Fames eternall beadroll worthie to be fyled*' (Spenser, 'F. Q.' iv. 2. 32). **4.** Any of various enclosed spaces, more or less deep, and supposed to resemble a well; **a** a relatively narrow shaft in a building formed by enclosing an area or court by the walls of surrounding buildings; **b** open space from ground-floor to the top of a house in which a staircase is placed; **c** enclosed chamber in the hold of a ship or fishing-boat; **d** hollowed-out depression in a desk made to contain an ink-pot. **5.** Specif., *the well of the court*, space in front of the judge's seat in law court, usually occupied by solicitors.

well (II.), vb. intrans. O.E. *wellan*, 'to boil, bubble up', see prec. To spring, gush, start, from, or as from, a spring or well: *streams well from the ground*; *blood wells from a wound*; *tears well from the eyes* &c.; also *well up, forth*.

well (III.), adv. O.E. & M.E. *wel*, 'well; in a great degree; very; fully'; O.S. *wel*; O.H.G. *wela*; Goth. *waila*; O.N. *vel*; fr. same base as **will** (II.), orig. sense being 'according to one's desire'. **1.** In a pleasing, desirable, satisfactory manner: *to dine well*; *to sleep well*. Phr. *to live well, do oneself well*, to fare sumptuously; *to stand well with*, be in good graces of. **2.** Skilfully, in a proper manner: *to play and sing well*; *to speak well*; *to do a thing well*. **3. a** In a becoming, seemly manner; suitably, with propriety: *to behave well*; *to treat a person well*; *his modesty became him well*; **b** in a manner suitable to the occasion; in a way suitable under the circumstances: *you may quite well plead illness as an excuse*; *you can't very well pretend you didn't hear*. **4. a** (i.) To the full extent; fully, thoroughly: *a stone well and truly laid*; *he had to abandon his journey before it was well begun*; *he ought to be well beaten*; *shake the bottle well*; (ii.) (archaic, before numbers) fully, quite: '*At night was come into that hostelrye Wel nyne and twenty in a companye*' (Chaucer, Prol. of 'C. T.' 24); **b** to a considerable degree, extent: *well on in years*; *lean well back*; *I am well forward with my work*; *I should like very well to come*. **5.** *As well*, in addition, besides: *I'll have some meat and some pudding as well*. **6.** In various idiomatic Phrs., sometimes with force of an interjection: **a** *it's all very well*, expressing ironic disagreement with, protest against, doubt concerning, something which has been said or done: *it's all very well to say that you are sorry, but . . .*; **b** expressing expectation: *well, what next? tell me all about it*; **c** expressing acquiescence, submission to the inevitable: *well, well, I suppose there's nothing more to be said!*; **d** (*just*) *as well*, with equal advantage, reason, justification &c.; without prejudice or injury, harm &c.: *you might just as well make a clean breast of it*; *one might as well throw money away as spend it in betting*; *as well be hung for a sheep as a lamb*; **e** in beginning or resuming a narrative: *well, it was like this*; *well, as I was saying* &c.; **f** expressing comprehension of, or agreement with, what has been, and indicating that a stage or phase has been disposed of, and that it is time for the next: *very well (then), now go on*; *very well, in that case I shall refuse absolutely*.

well (IV.), adj., fr. prec. (only in pred. use). **1.** In good health, physically strong; contrasted with *ill*: *to be, to look, to feel, well*; *I hope you are pretty well*; *I'm not very well today*; *you can't work when you are not well*. **2.** Suitable, advisable, satisfactory: *it were, would have been, well for him if* &c.; *it would be as well to ask permission*. **3.** In a satisfactory state; favourable, propitious; comfortable: *all is not well with him*; *we are very well where we are*; *past midnight and all well!* Phr. *well enough*, tolerable, fairly good or satisfactory: *the rooms are well enough, but we don't like the landlady*.

well (V.), n., fr. prec. That which is good, satisfactory, or to be desired: *let well alone, don't interfere with a satisfactory state of affairs*.

welladay, interj. [1. wèladá; 2. wèlədéi]. Variant of **wellaway**.

well-advised, adj. Prudent, judicious, considered: *a well-advised step, action* &c.

well-appointed, adj. [1. wèl apóinted; 2. wèl əpóintid]. Having good, adequate, well-chosen appointments, equipment &c.: *a well-appointed house, expedition* &c.

wellaway, interj. [1. wèlawá; 2. wèləwéi]. O.E. *wālā wā*, see **woe**, **lo**. (archaic) Exclamation of grief, lamentation; equivalent to *alack-a-day*.

well-balanced, adj. [1. wél bálanst; 2. wél bǽlənst]. (chiefly used of the mind) Sane, steady, judicious.

well-behaved, adj. [1. wèl behǽvd; 2. wèl bihéivd]. Having good manners; behaving well.

well-being, n. **a** Bodily comfort: *a sense of physical well-being*; **b** prosperity, progress; sound moral or social conditions: *the well-being of the community at large*.

well-born, adj. Of good, noble, or distinguished family.

well-bred, adj. Having, exhibiting, good breeding; of good family and polite manners.

well-chosen, adj. Chosen with judgement; apt, suitable to the occasion, appropriate: *well-chosen words* &c.

well-conditioned, adj. **a** In sound bodily condition; **b** having good manners and behaviour.

well-conducted, adj. [1. wèl kundúkted; 2. wèl kəndáktid]. Of good, orderly, behaviour; behaving in a moral manner.

well-connected, adj. [1. wél kunékted; 2. wél kənéktid]. Having high family connexions; related to people of distinction and good standing.

well-cooked, adj. [1. wèl kóokt; 2. wèl kúkt]. **a** Skilfully cooked and served; **b** thoroughly cooked, well-done.

well-deck, n. Space on deck surrounded by upper decks.

well-directed, adj. [1. wél dirékted; 2. wél diréktid]. Accurately or skilfully placed or aimed: *a well-directed blow*; carefully prepared, and applied in a suitable direction: *well-directed effort*.

well-dish, n. Meat dish with depression at one end to catch gravy.

well-disposed, adj. [1. wèl dispṓzd; 2. wèl dispóuzd]. **a** Having friendly and kindly disposition and feelings towards one's fellowmen; **b** favourably inclined towards specific persons, ideas, schemes &c.

well-doer, n. Person who performs moral obligations.

well-doing, n. Virtuous conduct; good actions.

well-done, adj. Thoroughly cooked; contrasted with *underdone*.

well-favoured, adj. Having a good, prepossessing appearance; comely, handsome.

well-found, adj. Adequately and suitably equipped.

well-founded, adj. [1. wèl fóunded; 2. wèl fáundid]. Based on facts: *well-founded suspicions* &c.

well-graced, adj. [1. wèl grā́st; 2. wèl gréist]. Attractive, having many good qualities.

well-grounded, adj. **1.** Adequately trained in the elements of a subject. **2.** Well-founded.

well-head, n. **a** Source of a spring or fountain; **b** a coping of stone, lead &c., sometimes of ornamental form, surrounding the head of a well.

well-hole, n. Central, well-like shaft in building, surrounded by walls, stairs &c.

well-informed, adj. Having extensive knowledge.

Wellingtonia, n. [1. wèlingtṓnia; 2. wèliŋtóuniə]. Named after 1st Duke of Wellington & -ia. Genus of large Californian pines; sequoia.

Wellingtons, n. pl. [1. wélingtunz; 2. wéliŋtənz], fr. 1st Duke of Wellington. Also *Wellington boots*, boots reaching up to the knee.

well-intentioned, adj. Well-meaning; desiring to do the right thing; well-meant; springing from good motives.

well-judged, adj. [1. wél jujd; 2. wél dʒadʒd]. Judicious; appropriate, timely: *a well-judged reply, action, blow* &c.

well-knit, adj. Firmly jointed, compact, powerful, sinewy: *a well-knit frame, figure* &c.

well-liking, adj. In good condition, having prosperous appearance.

well-looking, adj. Handsome, comely.

well-made, adj. **a** Specif. (of body &c.) well-proportioned, strongly knit; **b** (of handiwork) skilfully shaped, fitted, put together.

well-mannered, adj. Possessing good manners; polite, well-bred.

well-marked, adj. Possessing characteristic features; distinct, definite, unmistakable: *well-marked differences*.

well-meaning, adj. Having good intentions.

well-meant, adj. [1. wèl mént; 2. wèl mént]. Done, said &c. with good intention.
well-nigh, adv. Very nearly.
well-off, adj. [1. wél áwf; 2. wél ɔ́f]. (chiefly pred.) a Possessing ample financial resources; wealthy, well-to-do; b fortunate, advantageously situated; c *well-off for*, well supplied with, possessing abundance of.
well-oiled, adj. [1. wél oild; 2. wél ɔild]. (fig.) a Flattering, intended to cajole; b (slang) having drunk quite as much as is good for one; mellow, slightly tipsy.
well-ordered, adj. [1. wèl órderd; 2. wèl ɔ́dəd]. Well arranged or organized.
well-padded, adj. a (of furniture &c.) Thoroughly provided with padding, cushions &c.; b (of persons, facet.) plump, stoutish, cushiony.
well-pleasing, adj. (archaic) Highly agreeable.
well-proportioned, adj. Exhibiting due, symmetrical, proportions.
well-read, adj. a Possessing extensive reading and information; well acquainted with literature : *a well-read person*; b *well-read in*, possessing deep knowledge of, well trained and instructed in (some specific branch of learning).
well-reputed, adj. Of good repute.
well-room, n. Building where water from mineral spring is served out.
well-rounded, adj. [1. wèl róunded; 2. wèl ráundid]. a (of the person) Plump; portly, chubby; b (of style, sentence &c.) well and elegantly proportioned, gracefully balanced and finished off.
well-seeming, adj. Apparently satisfactory.
well-seen, adj. (slightly archaic) Versed, accomplished, in some specified branch of learning: *well-seen in Latin*.
well-set, adj. (esp. of body) Firmly knit, strong, and sinewy.
well-sinker, n. Person employed in making wells.
well-spoken, adj. Having a pleasing address and manner of speech; specif. a having a cultivated pronunciation; speaking like an educated person; b speaking with courtesy and urbanity.
well-spring, n. Source of a spring; well-head.
well-timed, adj. [1. wèl tímd; 2. wèl táimd]. Performed, executed, said &c. at an appropriate or opportune moment.
well-to-do, adj. [1. wèl tə dóo; 2. wèl tə dú]. In prosperous financial circumstances; wealthy, well-off; also as collective n., *the well-to-do*, the richer classes; contrasted with *the poor*, *the needy*.
well-trodden, adj. a Often traversed, beaten down by the feet of many passers-by; b (fig.) often explored, worked at, elaborated, before; therefore hackneyed, lacking freshness.
well-turned, adj. (of compliment, phrase &c.) Turned, expressed, with grace.
well-wisher, n. [1. wél wisher; 2. wél wiʃə]. Person who is kindly disposed to another or to a cause &c.
well-worn, adj. (fig.) Hackneyed, commonplace, stale.
Welsh (I.), adj. & n. [1. welsh; 2. wɛlʃ]. O.E. *welisċ*, 'foreign', M.E. *wel(i)sh*, fr. *w(e)alh*, 'foreigner', esp. applied to a Celt. inhabitant of Britain, & *-ish*; cp. O.N. *Valskr*; O.H.G. *Walhisc*. 1. adj. Of, pertaining to, Wales, its people or its language; *Welsh mutton*, meat of small, Welsh breed of sheep. 2. n. a *The Welsh*, the people of Wales; b *Welsh*, language of Wales.
welsh, welch (II.), vb. intrans. & trans. Etymol. unknown. 1. intrans. (of bookmaker &c.) To abscond with stake-money without paying winners of bets. 2. trans. To cheat (winner of bet) by absconding with money staked.
Welshman, Welshwoman, ns. [1. wélshman, -wooman; 2. wélʃmən, -wumən]. **Welsh** (I.) **& man, woman**. Male, female, native of Wales.

welsh rabbit, incorrectly **rarebit**, n. Toasted cheese.
welt (I.), n. [1. welt; 2. wɛlt]. M.E. *welte*; cp. O.E. *w(i)eltan*, *wæltan*, 'to roll', see **welter** (I.). 1. Leather strip stitched into shoe to strengthen join between sole and upper. 2. Piece of ribbed knitting finishing top of sock &c. 3. Inflamed stripe raised on skin by blow; wale, weal.
welt (II.), vb. trans., fr. prec. 1. To furnish (shoe &c.) with a welt. 2. a To raise welts on (skin); b (colloq.) to strike, thrash.
welter (I.), vb. intrans. & n. [1. wélter; 2. wéltə], fr. O.E. *w(i)eltan*, 'to roll, turn, overturn', M.E. *welten*, 'to overturn', & *-er*. Cp. O.N. *velta*; M.H.G. *welzen*, 'to turn, revolve', see **waltz**; Goth. *waltjan*, 'to roll'; cogn. w. Lat. *volvere*, 'to turn, roll', see **volute**; cp. also **well** (I.), **wallow** (I.). 1. vb. To wallow, roll, tumble, about, be rolled in : *weltering in gore*. 2. n. Surging, tumult, confusion; disorderly mass: (in material and non-material senses) *the welter of the waves, of a crowd*; *a welter of confused ideas*.
welter (II.), n. Etymol. doubtful; perh. fr. **welt** (II.), 2, & *-er*. (boxing, racing &c.) Heavy weight; chiefly in compounds : *welter-race, welter-weight* &c.
wen (I.), n. [1. wen; 2. wen]. O.E., M.E. *wenn*; cp. Du. *wen*; M.L.G. *wene*, 'wen'; etymol. doubtful. Indolent tumour on surface of body; esp. one on the scalp or neck. Phr. *The Great Wen*, London, so called by Cobbett.
wen (II.), n. O.E. *wenn*, S.E. variant of *wynn*, 'joy', see **winsome**, used on account of its initial letter; this letter was also called *wēn*, 'hope, expectation'; cp. **thorn**. The old English letter *Þ = w*.
wench, n. [1. wench; 2. wentʃ]. M.E. *wenche(l)*, 'child'; fr. O.E. *wencel*, n. 'child', adj. 'weak'; cp. O.E. *wancol*, 'feeble'; O.H.G. *wanchal*, 'tottering'; *wankōn*, 'to totter'; O.N. *vakka*, 'to be unsteady'; cogn. w. Scrt. *vaṅgati*, 'limps'; Lat. *vagāri*, 'to wander', see **vagary**. Prob. cogn. w. **wince**. 1. (archaic or facetious) A girl, young woman, esp. servant, country girl. 2. (archaic) Prostitute.
wend (I.), vb. trans. & intrans. [1. wend; 2. wɛnd]. O.E. *wendan*, M.E. *wenden*, 'to turn, go'; fr. gradational type *wand-*, as seen in Pret. of O.E. *windan*, see **wind** (IV.), *went*. 1. trans. To turn, direct, proceed on; only in Phr. *to wend one's way*. 2. intrans. (archaic) To go, betake oneself.
Wend (II.), n., fr. Germ. *Wende*. Member of a Slavonic race living in parts of Northern and Eastern Germany.
Wendic, adj. [1. wéndik; 2. wéndik]. Prec. & *-ic*. Of, pertaining to, the Wends or their language.
Wendish, adj. & n. [1. wéndish; 2. wéndiʃ]. See prec. & *-ish*. 1. adj. Of, pertaining to, the Wends. 2. n. The language of the Wends.
Wenlock, adj. [1. wénlok; 2. wénlɔk]. Shropshire Place-Name. (geol.) Pertaining to the middle division of the Silurian system of rock.
Wensleydale, n. [1. wénzlidāl; 2. wénzlideil]. Yorkshire Place-Name. Kind of cheese.
went, vb. [1. went; 2. wɛnt]. Pret. of **wend** (I.), now used as Pret. of **go**.
wentletrap, n. [1. wéntltrap; 2. wéntltræp], fr. Du. *wenteltrap*, earlier 'spiral staircase', fr. *wentel*, 'turning', fr. stem of *winden*, 'to turn', q.v. under **wind** (III.), & *trap*, 'stair, step'. Univalve shellfish with spiral shell.
wept, vb. [1. wept; 2. wɛpt]. Pret. & P.P. of **weep**.
were, vb. [1. wăr, wer; 2. wɛə, wə]. Pret. pl. of **be**. O.E. *wæron*; M.E. *wēren*; cp. O.H.G. *wārun*; fr. earlier **wæz*-, fr. a gradational variant of the base **wes-*, seen in **was**.
werewolf, werwolf, n. [1. wérwoolf; 2. wíəwulf]. O.E. *werewulf*, fr. *wer*, 'man'; cp. Goth. *wair*; O.H.G. *wer*; O.N. *verr*, 'man'; cogn. w. Lat. *vir*, 'man', see **virile**, & *wulf*, see **wolf**. (folklore) Person who assumed voluntarily or involuntarily the shape of a wolf, either permanently or periodically.
wert, vb. [1. wĕrt; 2. wāt]. (archaic) 2nd pers. sing. Pret. of **be**; cp. **were** & **wast**.
Wertherism, n. [1. wérterizm; 2. wátərizəm], fr. *Werther*, hero of Goethe's novel, 'Die Leiden des jungen Werthers', 1774. Extravagant, morbid, and sickly sentimentality.
Wesleyan, adj. & n. [1. wézlian, wèzléan; 2. wézliən, wèzlíən] (pronounced [1. wes-; 2. wes-] by members of the body), fr. name of founder, John Wesley, d. 1791. 1. adj. Of, pertaining to, John Wesley, or the body of Methodist dissenters named after him. 2. n. Member of this body.
Wesleyanism, n. [1. wezléanizm; 2. wezlíənizəm]. Prec. & *-ism*. Method, doctrine, of the Wesleyans, or of their founder, John Wesley.
west (I.), adv. [1. west; 2. wɛst]. O.E., M.E. *west*; cp. Du., Germ. *west*, 'west'; prob. orig., 'of the setting sun', & fr. stem **we-*, 'down'; cp. Scrt. *aváś*, 'down'; *avástād*, 'below'; cp. also Lat. *vesper*, 'evening', see **vesper**; Gk. *hésperos*, 'evening', see **Hesperian**. Towards, in the direction of, the setting sun; in or towards the region faced by person observing the setting sun at the equinox from the line of the equator : *to look, face, go, sail, west*; Phr. *to go west*, to die; *to sail due west*, exactly towards W. point of compass. Phr. *west of*, farther west than.
west (II.), adj., fr. prec. 1. Of, pertaining to, situated in, facing the west : *a west window, room*, &c.; *west end* (of church), end, part, opposite to the altar; *west-country*, southwestern and south-west midland part of England. 2. (of wind) Blowing from the west.
west (III.), n., fr. prec. 1. a One of the cardinal points of the compass, opposite to east; b region of earth, sky &c. lying in this direction. 2. Western part of continent, country, county &c.; specif. a Western Europe, Occident; Phr. *the Empire of the West*, Western Empire (see **western**); b West of England; c Western United States, west of Alleghany mountains, or including prairie and Pacific states.
west-country, n. & adj. 1. n. South-western and south-west midland England. 2. adj. Of, pertaining to, the west-country.
west-countryman, -woman, n. Native of west-country.
West End, n. A somewhat loose term applied to the district of London in which are the residences of fashionable society, higher-class shops, hotels, theatres &c., roughly including the area from Trafalgar Square to Hyde Park; also, by transf., the society living in this district.
West-end, adj. Of, pertaining to, the West End of London.
westering, adj. [1. wéstering; 2. wéstəriŋ], fr. obs. *wester*, fr. M.E. *westren*, 'to go west', fr. **west** (I.). Turning, tending, towards the west.
westerly, adj. & adv. [1. wésterli; 2. wéstəli], fr. **west** on anal. of **easterly**. 1. adj. a Of, pertaining to, the west; western; b directed, proceeding, towards the west : *a westerly course*; c (of wind) coming from the west. 2. adv. Towards the west.
western (I.), adj. [1. wéstern; 2. wéstən]. **west & -ern**. 1. Of, pertaining to, situated in, coming from, characteristic of, the west. Phrs. *Western Church*, Papal branch of the Catholic Church; *Western Empire*, western part, including Rome, of the Roman Empire as divided by Theodosius in 395. 2. (of wind) Blowing from the west; westerly.
western (II.), n., fr. prec. Native of the west; westerner.
westerner, n. [1. wésterner; 2. wéstənə]. **western** (I.) & *-er*. Native of the west, esp. of the Western United States.
westernize, vb. trans. [1. wésterniz; 2. wéstənaiz]. **western** (I.) & *-ize*. To introduce western civilization into (esp. Oriental countries, races &c.).

westernmost, adj. [1. wéstərnmòst ; 2. wéstənmòust]. western (I.) & -most. Farthest towards the west.

West Indian, adj. West Indies & -ian. Of, pertaining to, coming from, the West Indies.

westing, n. [1. wésting ; 2. wéstiŋ]. west (I.) & -ing. Distance traversed by, movement of, ship in westerly direction.

Westminster, n. [1. wéstmìnster ; 2. wéstmìnstə]. 1. District of London. 2. Westminster Abbey. 3. The Houses of Parliament ; (also fig.) parliamentary politics &c. 4. a Westminster School ; b member of this school ; old Westminster, former pupil of the school.

west-north-west, adj., adv., & n. [1. wést nòr(th) wést ; 2. wést nò(þ) wést]. (In or towards) direction or point midway between W. & N.W.

west-south-west, adj., adv., & n. [1. wést sòu(th) wést ; 2. wést sàu(þ) wést]. (In or towards) direction or point midway between W. & S.W.

westward, adj., adv., & n. [1. wéstward ; 2. wéstwəd]. west (I.) & -ward. 1. adj. Tending towards, lying towards, the west. 2. adv. Towards the west. 3. n. Westward region or direction.

westwards, adv. [1. wéstwardz ; 2. wéstwədz]. west (I.) & -wards. Towards the west.

wet (I.), adj. [1. wet ; 2. wɛt]. O.E. wǣte ; M.E. wēte, 'wet' ; cp. O. Fris. wēt ; O.N. vātr, 'wet' ; cogn. w. water. 1. Covered, saturated, dripping, or moistened with liquid : wet clothes, cheeks, umbrellas, wood, leaves &c. ; the grass is wet with dew. Phrs. a wet bargain, one clinched and celebrated by drinks ; wet blanket, see blanket ; wet bob (Eton slang), see bob (VI.) ; wet pack, medical treatment of patient by wrapping him in wet sheets covered with dry blankets ; wet through, wet to the skin, with one's clothes soaked. 2. Characterized by constant or abundant rain : a wet day, season, month ; wet weather. 3. (Am. slang) Not prohibiting the sale of alcoholic liquor : a wet state, one in which such liquor is obtainable ; contrasted with dry.

wet (II.), n., fr. prec. 1. Liquid, wet substance, moisture. 2. (vulg. slang) A drink. 3. (U.S.A.) An anti-Prohibitionist.

wet (III.), vb. trans. O.E. wǣtan ; M.E. wēten, 'to wet, moisten' ; fr. wet (I.). To apply liquid to, sprinkle, cover, saturate, with liquid. Phr. to wet one's whistle, drink.

wet-bulb thermometer, n. Thermometer with bulb kept moist and used in conjunction with a dry-bulb thermometer in a hygrometer.

wet dock, n. Dock filled with water.

wether, n. [1. wédher ; 2. wéðə]. O.E., M.E. weðer, 'sheep, lamb' ; cp. Germ. widder ; O.N. veðr ; Goth. wiþrus, 'lamb' ; cogn. w. Scrt. vatsá- 'calf, yearling' ; vatsará, 'year' ; Lith. vetuszas, 'old' ; Lat. vitulus, 'calf', orig., 'yearling' ; vetus, 'old' ; see veteran, vitular. Castrated ram.

wetness, n. [1. wétnes ; 2. wétnis]. wet (I.) & -ness. State or condition of being wet.

wet-nurse, n. & vb. trans. 1. n. Woman who suckles another's child. 2. vb. To act as wet-nurse to.

wet-plate, n. Photographic plate treated with collodion and exposed while still wet from sensitizing bath.

wetting, n. [1. wéting ; 2. wétiŋ]. wet (III.) & -ing. State of being, process of becoming or being made, wet.

wettish, adj. [1. wétish ; 2. wétiʃ]. wet (I.) & -ish. Fairly wet.

wey, n. [1. wā ; 2. wei]. O.E. wǣġe ; M.E. wēȝe, 'weight, weighing-machine, wey' ; cp. O.N. vāg ; O.H.G. wāga, 'scales' ; cp. further O.E. weġan, 'to carry, move', & see weigh. Unit of weight varying in amount with different substances, usually 182 lb. (of wool).

whack (I.), vb. trans. & intrans. [1. wak ; 2. wæk]. Imitative. 1. trans. To strike, slap, sharply and with audible sound. 2. intrans. To give sharp, resounding blows.

whack (II.), n., fr. prec. 1. Sharp, audible blow with stick &c. 2. (slang) Allotted, suitable, or adequate portion ; due share.

whacker, n. [1. wáker ; 2. wǽkə]. whack (I.) & -er. (slang) a Unusually large person or thing ; b a lie.

whacking (I.), n. [1. wáking ; 2. wǽkiŋ]. whack (I.) & -ing. Act of striking with stick &c. ; a beating.

whacking (II.), adj., fr. Pres. Part. of whack (I.). (slang) Tremendous, thundering : a whacking lie ; as adv., a whacking big horse.

whale (I.), n. [1. wāl ; 2. weil]. O.E. hwæl ; M.E. whal, whāle ; cp. O.N. hvalr ; O.H.G. wal, 'whale' ; cogn. w. Lat. squalus, 'large fish' ; perh. cogn. w. Gk. áspalos, 'fish' ; Gk. skúlion, 'dog-fish'. Large, fish-like, warm-blooded aquatic mammal, order Cetacea, with short, broad, flattened fore-limbs ; hunted for its oil, whalebone, spermaceti &c. Phrs. (colloq.) very like a whale, expressing ironical agreement with an incredible statement or promise ; he's a regular whale for work &c., a very diligent, laborious worker ; a whale at tennis, very good at it.

whale (II.), vb. intrans. To engage in whaling.

whale-back, n. Type of boat with rounded covering on deck, for use in rough seas.

whale-boat, n. a Boat employed in whaling ; b ship's boat resembling this.

whalebone, n. [1. wálbōn ; 2. wéilboun]. Thin, horny, flexible substance found in a series of plates in the upper jaw of some varieties of whale ; used for light framework, for stiffening fabric &c.

whale-calf, n. Young whale.

whale-fin, n. (commerc.) Whalebone.

whale-fishery, n. 1. Business of catching whales ; whaling. 2. Part of sea or coast where whaling is carried on.

whale-head, n. Central African bird of heron family with broad, hooked beak.

whale-line, n. Stout rope used for harpoons in whaling.

whaleman, n. [1. wálman ; 2. wéilmən]. Man employed in whaling.

whale-oil, n. Oil obtained from whale's blubber.

whaler, n. [1. wáler ; 2. wéilə]. whale (II.) & -er. 1. Ship engaged in whale-fishery. 2. Man employed in whaling.

whaling, n. [1. wáling ; 2. wéiliŋ]. whale (II.) & -ing. The pursuit and killing of whales.

whaling-gun, n. Apparatus for discharging harpoon &c. at whale.

whaling-master, n. Captain of whaler.

whang (I.), vb. trans. & intrans. [1. wang ; 2. wæŋ]. Imitative. 1. trans. To strike with a clanging, resounding blow. 2. intrans. To clang, resound as result of a blow.

whang (II.), n. See prec. Clanging, resounding blow, bang.

whanghee, wangee, n. [1. wangġḗ ; 2. wæŋġí], fr. Chinese hwang. A Chinese variety of bamboo, used for walking-sticks.

wharf (I.), n. [1. worf ; 2. wōf]. O.E. hwerf, 'dam' ; M.E. wherfe, 'wharf' ; cp. M.L.G., M. Du. werf, 'wharf' ; cp. further O.N. hvarf, 'act of turning' ; fr. the base in O.E. hweorfan, 'to turn' ; O.N. hverfa ; O.H.G. hwerfan, 'to turn round' ; Goth. hwairban, 'to go round' ; cogn. w. Gk. karpós, 'wrist', see carpus. Structure of timber or stone, alongside which ships may be moored for receiving and discharging goods &c.

wharf (II.), vb. trans., fr. prec. 1. To moor (vessel) to a wharf. 2. To unload, store (goods), on a wharf.

wharfage, n. [1. wórfij ; 2. wōfidʒ]. Prec. & -age. Dues paid for use of a wharf for mooring, loading, or unloading a ship.

wharfinger, n. [1. wórfinjer ; 2. wōfindʒə]. Earlier wharfager ; see wharfage & -er. Owner of wharf where vessels are unloaded, cargoes shipped and unshipped &c.

what (I.), adj. [1. wot ; 2. wɔt]. O.E. hwæt ; M.E. w(h)at ; neut. form of interrog. pron. hwā, 'who' ; O.H.G. hwaz ; cogn. w. Lat. quod, 'that, in that' ; see who. 1. (interrog.) Asking for specification of quality, kind, amount, identity &c. of person or thing referred to : what kind of food do they eat? ; what supplies have they? ; what places did you go to? ; what weather did you have? ; what man are you speaking of? ; what ship is that? ; (also in indirect questions) do you know what ship that is? 2. (rel.) That, those, which ; as much, as many as, of the kind that &c. : bring what parcels you can carry ; wear what clothes you please. Phr. what time, see time (I.). 3. (exclamatory) How great &c., implying surprise, disapproval &c. of the quality, amount &c. of something : what fools they are! ; what waste! ; what a miserable day! ; what strange people!

what (II.), pron., fr. prec. 1. (interrog.) Asking for specification of identity, quality, quantity, amount, &c. ; what thing : what did he do, say &c.? ; what do you know about it? ; what has happened? ; what is his name? Phrs. (often elliptical) what about it? = what do you know, shall we do &c. about . . . ? ; what next? = what will happen &c. next?, expressing surprise at event, conduct &c. ; what though the skies may fall &c. = what does it matter? ; what if we should fail &c.? = what will be the result? ; what? = what did you say &c.? ; what for?, for what reason? ; what is he?, what is his occupation? ; what of it?, what does it matter? ; what-d'you-call-him, it &c., used as substitute for forgotten name &c. 2. (rel.) The thing(s) which, that which : what I say is true ; he told me what to say ; I will do what I can ; what happened was quite an accident ; that is what I heard ; what I always say is . . . Phrs. I know what! = I know what we will, or ought to, do &c., introducing new plan &c. ; to know what's what, know the real, proper, or genuine thing &c. 3. (exclamatory) What a large amount, how much &c. ; what things &c. : what these ancient walls could tell us!

whate'er, adj. & pron. [1. wòtâr ; 2. wòtéə]. Contracted fr. next word. (poet.) Whatever.

whatever (I.), adj. [1. wòtéver ; 2. wòtévə]. what (I.) & ever. 1. What (with additional emphasis) ; of any kind, degree &c. : whatever orders he gives are obeyed ; whatever excuses he may make, we will not believe him. 2. (in negative clause, emphasizing negation) Of any kind, at all : I can see nothing whatever ; no motive whatever can excuse his conduct.

whatever (II.), pron. what (II.) & ever. (rel., emphatic form of what (II.)) Anything, everything that, all that ; no matter what : whatever happens, he is safe ; I am right, whatever you may think ; take whatever you like ; whatever I do I'm always wrong ; whatever you do, don't drink too much = on no account are you to . . .

what-not, n. [1. wót not ; 2. wót nɔt]. Piece of furniture usually consisting of slender uprights supporting a set of shelves for holding odds & ends, ornaments, books &c.

what's-his-name, pron. [1. wótsiznām ; 2. wótsizneim]. Discourteous, contemptuous mode of referring to a person whose name one cannot, or which one affects not to, remember : not a soul there except old what's-his-name.

whatso, adj. & pron. [1. wótsō ; 2. wótsou]. what & so. (archaic) Same as whatsoever.

whatsoe'er, adj. & pron. [1. wòtsōâr ; 2. wòtsouéə]. Contracted from next word. (poet.) Whatsoever.

whatsoever, adj. & pron. [1. wòtsōéver ; 2. wòtsouévə]. what & so & ever. Emphatic and rhetorical form of whatever.

whaup, n. [1. wawp ; 2. wōp]. Imitative. (chiefly Scots) Curlew.

wheal (I.), n. [1. wēl ; 2. wiəl]. M.E. whēle, 'pustule' ; cp. O.E. hwelian, 'to suppurate' ; hwyle, 'boil, tumour' ; perh. cogn. w. Lett. kwēle, 'inflammation of a wound'. Small, inflamed tumour, a pustule.

wheal (II.), n., fr. Corn. hwel. Mine ; specif., tin-mine.

wheat, n. [1. wēt; 2. wīt]. O.E. *hwǣte*; M.E. *whēte*; cp. O.S. *hwēti*; O.H.G. *hweiti*; O.N. *hveiti*; Goth. *hwaiteis*, 'wheat'; cogn. w. **white** (I.). **1.** Annual, or biennial, cereal plant, *Triticum*, esp. *T. sativum*, bearing a spike of edible seeds. **2.** Edible grain produced by this plant, usually ground and made into bread &c., and forming a staple food.

wheatear, n. [1. wētĕr; 2. wītiə]. Earlier *white-ears* (cp. Fr. *cul-blanc*); **white** (I.) & **arse**. Small, grey and white, thrush-like migratory bird, *Saxicola oenanthe*.

wheaten, adj. [1. wētn; 2. wītn]. **wheat** & **-en**. Of, composed of, containing, of the colour of, wheat.

wheat-fly, n. Insect whose larvae are injurious to wheat.

wheat-grass, n. Couch-grass.

Wheatstone bridge, n. [1. wētstun brĭj; 2. wītstən brĭdž]. An electrical device for measuring an unknown by a known resistance. It was invented by S. H. Christie (d. 1865), but was named after Sir C. Wheatstone (d. 1875).

wheedle, vb. trans. [1. wēdl; 2. wīdl]. Prob. fr. O.E. *wǣdlian*, M.E. *wēdlien*, 'to beg'; fr. O.E. *wǣdl*, 'poverty'; the latter is perh. connected w. O.H.G. *weisso*, Mod. Germ. *waise*, 'an orphan'; cp. also O.E. (*wudu*)*wāsa*, 'faun, satyr', lit. 'waif of the woods'. **1. a** To influence by crafty flattery, bring artful persuasion to bear upon; to coax, cajole: *to wheedle a person into doing something*; **b** to beguile, deceive (person) by flattery and cajolery. **2.** To obtain (thing from person &c.) by coaxing or flattery: *to wheedle something out of a person*.

wheedling, adj. [1. wēdling; 2. wīdliŋ], fr. Pres. Part. of prec. Insinuatingly persuasive; using, characterized by, seductive flattery and blandishments.

wheedlingly, adv. Prec. & -ly. In a wheedling manner.

wheel (I.), n. [1. wēl; 2. wīəl]. O.E. *hwēol*, *hweogol*; M.E. *whēle*; cp. M. Du. *weel, wiel*; Dan. *hiul*; O.N. *hjōl*, 'wheel'; all fr. reduplicated type *hwehwlo-* &c.; cogn. w. Gk. *kúklos*, 'circle, wheel', fr. *k^wek^wlo-*, see **cycle**; Scrt. *čakráš*, 'wheel'; Lith. *kãklas*, 'neck'; cp. further, without reduplication, O.N. *hvel*, 'wheel'; O. Prussian *kelan*; O. Slav. *kolo*, 'wheel'; Gk. *pélein*, 'to turn'; *pólos*, 'pivot, axis', see **pole** (III.); Lat. *colere*, 'to engage in, occupy oneself with, cultivate, inhabit'; see **colony**. **1.** Disk, or circular rim and concentric disk connected by radiating bars (spokes), having, or capable of, rotatory motion, and used to facilitate movement of body, esp. vehicle, or to transmit or modify motion in machine &c.; (often in compounds) *Catherine-wheel, cogwheel, spinning-wheel, steering-wheel* &c., q.v. Phrs. *Fortune's wheel*, symbolic representation of vicissitudes of life; *to break (person) on the wheel*, kill or injure by binding on revolving wheel and striking with iron bar, as mediaeval form of torture: *to put a spoke in one's wheel*, hinder, prevent progress; *to put one's shoulder to the wheel*, make an effort to assist progress of undertaking, cause &c.; *wheels within wheels*, referring to a complicated and involved combination of motives or influences, acting and reacting on each other. **2.** Specif. **a** a bicycle; **b** steering-wheel; **c** spinning-wheel; **d** round, horizontal disk revolving on a spindle, on which a potter shapes his clay: *potter's wheel*. **3. a** Wheeling, sweeping or revolving motion: *the wheel of birds* &c.; **b** specif., movement of line of troops &c. as on a pivot.

wheel (II.), vb. trans. & intrans., fr. prec. **A.** trans. **1. a** To cause (wheeled vehicle &c.) to move; to propel, pull, on wheels: *to wheel a truck, barrow* &c.; **b** to propel (person, load &c.) in a wheeled vehicle or barrow. **2.** To cause (line of men &c.) to turn as on a pivot. **B.** intrans. **1. a** Often *wheel round*, to move, swing, round so as to face another direction; **b** (of line of troops &c.) to swing round as on a pivot. Phr. *right, left, wheel*, words of command to carry out this movement. **2.** (of bird &c.) To move in a sweeping, circular course. **3.** To ride a bicycle &c.

wheel-and-axle, n. A wheel fixed to and revolving on an axle, one of the elementary mechanical powers.

wheelbarrow, n. [1. wēlbarō; 2. wīəlbærou]. Strong, usually oblong, receptacle of wood or thin iron sheets, having a single low wheel in front, and short stout legs, with shafts or handles for pushing, set at right angles to the legs behind; used for transporting small loads by hand.

wheel-chair, n. Chair mounted, and moving, on wheels.

wheeled, adj. [1. wēld; 2. wīəld]. **wheel** (I.) & **-ed**. Provided with a wheel or wheels; often in compounds, *two-, four-wheeled* &c.

wheeler, n. [1. wēlər; 2. wīlə]. **wheel** (II.) & **-er**. **1.** One who, that which, wheels. **2.** Wheel-horse. **3.** In compounds, *four-wheeler* &c., vehicle with specified number of wheels. **4.** Wheelwright.

wheel-horse, n. Horse, or one of two horses, harnessed to the pole or shafts of a vehicle and preceded by leader(s).

wheel-house, n. Shelter erected round ship's helm; pilot-house.

wheelless, adj. [1. wēlles; 2. wīəllis]. **wheel** (I.) & **-less**. Without wheels.

wheel-lock, n. **1.** Ancient form of gun-lock, with steel wheel whirling round and striking flint when released by trigger. **2.** Obsolete type of pistol &c., with wheel-lock.

wheelman, n. [1. wēlman; 2. wīəlmən]. Cyclist.

wheel-seat, n. End of axle, fitting on to hub.

wheel-tread, n. Part of tire or rim that touches road &c.

wheel-window, n. Circular window with tracery radiating from centre.

wheelwright, n. [1. wēlrīt; 2. wīəlrait]. **wheel** (I.) & **wright**. Person engaged in making or repairing wheels or wheeled vehicles.

wheeze (I.), vb. intrans. & trans. [1. wēz; 2. wīz]. O.E. *hwēsan*; M.E. *whēsen*, fr. *hwōsjan*; cp. O.E. *hwōsta*, 'a cough'; O.H.G. *huosto*; cogn. w. Lith. *koseti*, 'to cough'. **1.** intrans. To breathe with a rattling, grating, rasping, whistling sound due to phlegm in the throat or bronchial tubes. **2.** trans. To utter with a wheezing sound.

wheeze (II.), n., fr. prec. **1.** Wheezing sound, noisy breathing. **2.** (slang) Actor's interpolated remark, joke &c.; gag; a joke in general: *a good wheeze*, an amusing anecdote.

wheezily, adv. [1. wēzili; 2. wīzili]. See **wheezy** & **-ly**. In a wheezy manner.

wheeziness, n. [1. wēzines; 2. wīzinis]. See next word & **-ness**. State or quality of being wheezy.

wheezy, adj. [1. wēzi; 2. wīzi]. **wheeze** (I.) & **-y**. **a** Speaking, breathing, with a wheeze; **b** performed, uttered, with wheezing: *wheezy breathing; a wheezy laugh*.

whelk (I.), n. [1. welk; 2. wɛlk]. O.E. *wiluc*, M.E. *wilk, welk*; prob. cogn. w. Gk. *hélix*, 'spiral'; *helikē*, 'spiral shell' &c., see **helix**; fr. stem *wel-*, *wol-* &c., 'to turn, revolve', seen in **volute**, **wallow**, **well** (I.) &c. Marine, edible, gastropod mollusc with univalve spiral shell having few whorls.

whelk (II.), n. M.E. *whelke*; cp. **wheal** (I.) & dimin. suff. **-ock**. Pimple, small inflamed swelling.

whelked, adj. [1. welkt; 2. wɛlkt]. Prec. & **-ed**. Marked or covered with pustules, pimply.

whelm, vb. trans. [1. welm; 2. wɛlm]. M.E. *whelmen*, 'to turn over'; the word seems, in form & later meaning, to be the result of association between O.E. *helmian*, 'to cover over', see **helm**(et), & (*ā*)*hwelfan*, 'to cover to overwhelm'; the latter is cogn. w. O.S. *bihwelbian*, 'to cover over, to arch over', O.H.G. *welben*, Mod. Germ. *wōlbe*; further cognates are Gk. *kólpos*, 'bosom, gulf'; Lat. *culcita*, 'pillow'. It is possible that the O.E. poetical word *welman, wielman*, 'to boil, surge, rage' &c., used of the sea, wh. survives in its old sense in M.E. *welmen*, may also have influenced the form. (poet.) To flow over, overwhelm, engulf, submerge &c. (in material and non-material senses): '*Where thou perhaps, under the whelming tide, Visit'st the bottom of the monstrous world*' (Milton, 'Lycidas', 157-8); *whelmed in ruin, in sorrow* &c.

whelp (I.), n. [1. welp; 2. wɛlp]. O.E. *hwelp*, M.E. *whelp*, 'puppy'; cp. O.S. *hwelp*; O.H.G. *welf*; O.N. *hvelpr*; connexion w. Lat. *vulpes*, 'fox', see **vulpine**, is doubtful. **1. a** Puppy; **b** cub of lion, tiger, seal &c. **2.** Ill-bred, mannerless boy or youth.

whelp (II.), vb. intrans. & trans., fr. prec. **1.** intrans. (of animal) To bring forth young: '*sea-monsters whelped And stabled*' (Milton, 'P. L.' xi. 751-2); (also contemptuously of woman). **2.** trans. To bring forth (whelps).

when (I.), adv. [1. wen; 2. wɛn]. O.E. *hwænne*, M.E. *whan(ne)*, 'when', cp. O.S., Goth. *hwan*, 'when'; O.H.G. *wanne*; fr. pronominal base seen in **who**. **1.** (interrog.) At what time or period, on what occasion: *when will you come?; when did it begin to rain?; when did you see him last?* **2. a** At the moment, during the time that: *it was raining when we started, when we were out; I will see you when I return*; in elliptical Phr. *a dog wags his tail when pleased; say when*=tell me when you have enough, used when pouring drink into another's glass; **b** on any occasion that, whenever: *it is cold when it snows*; **c** after the time that: *he will go when he has had his dinner*; **d** just then, at that moment: *we were about to start when it began to rain*; **e** in spite of the fact that, although: *he keeps on talking when he knows it annoys us*; **f** considering the fact that: *how can I explain when you won't listen?* **3.** (as n., rare) The time at which: *the when and the where*.

when (II.), pron., fr. prec. **1.** (rel.) At or during which: *during the time when you were away; at a moment when we were busy*. **2.** (interrog. or rel. after prep.) What or which time or moment: *till when shall you be here?; since when have you been here?; we came a week ago, since when the weather has been bad*.

whence, adv. & rel. pron. [1. wens; 2. wɛns], M.E. *whennes*, formed fr. **when** & advbl. suff. *-es*. (archaic) **1.** (interrog.) From what place, from what source: *whence did you come?; whence comes this great river, all this uproar?* The usual construction would be, *where did you come from?* &c. Phr. *whence comes it that . . . ?*, how is it that? **2. a** The place or source from which: *tell me whence you come*; also *from whence*; **b** to the place from which: *go back whence you came*.

whencesoever, adv. [1. wensōĕvər; 2. wɛnssouévə]. Prec. & **so** & **ever**. From whatever place, source &c.

whene'er, adv. [1. wenār; 2. wɛnéə]. Contracted fr. next word. (poet.) Whenever.

whenever, adv. [1. wenévər; 2. wɛnévə]. **1.** At whatever time; as soon as; at the moment that, no matter when: *I'll see him whenever he likes to come*. **2.** On whatever occasion, as often as: *I hope you'll come and play whenever you feel inclined*.

whensoever, adv. [1. wensōĕvər; 2. wɛnsouévə]. **when** & **so** & **ever**. Whenever (emphatic).

where (I.), adv. [1. wār; 2. wεə]. O.E. *hwǣr*; M.E. *whēre*; cp. O.S. *hwār*; O.H.G. *wār*; O.N. *hvār*; Goth. *hwar*; orig. locative of pronominal base seen in **who**, **when** &c. cp. Lat. *cūr*, 'why'; fr. *k^wō-r*, old locative of pron. *k^woi*, Lat. *quī*, 'who'; Scrt. *kar-hi*, 'when'; Lith. *kùr*, 'where'. **1.** (interrog.) **a** (implying motion) To or towards what place, in what direction, whither: *where are you going?*; **b** (implying rest) at or in what place, situation, position, or part: *where are you going to stay?; where is my hat?; where does the river rise?; where did you hear that tale?*; **c** in what respect or condition: *where does it* *concern us?*; *where will you be if you offend him?*; *where is the use of being obstinate?* 2. (introducing dependent clause) **a** (implying motion) To what place, in what direction : *let him go where he likes*; **b** (implying rest) in or at what place or part : *we must camp where we can get water*; *he knows where they are*; *things are never where one wants them*; **c** in what respect, at what point, in which circumstances : *one never knows where to have him*, at what point he is vulnerable.

where (II.), pron., fr. prec. 1. (interrog.) **a** (followed by *from*) From what place &c. : *where have you come from?*; (followed by *to*) to what place : *where are you going to?* 2. (rel.) **a** At, to, or in which : *that is the place where he lives*; *this is the point where we stuck*; also **b** *this is where I live*, the place in or at which; *this is where we get out*; **c** *from where*, from the place which; *to where*, to the place which; **d** the respect, the circumstances, conditions in which : *that's just where you're wrong*.

where-, pref., compounded with preps., **a** denoting in what place, part, respect &c.; e.g. *whereas, wherever* &c.; **b** see **whereby, wherein, wherewith**.

whereabouts, adv. & n. [1. wărabòuts; 2. wèərəbàuts]. 1. adv. **a** (interrog.) In what place, where approximately : *whereabouts did you put it?*; **b** (rel.) the place where &c. : *I like to know whereabouts you are*. 2. n. Approximate place or position, locality, situation : *his present whereabouts is unknown*.

whereas, conj. [1. wăráz; 2. wèəréz]. 1. Formula in opening legal documents, in consideration of the fact that, since, in view of specified circumstances : *whereas it hath seemed good to the King's Majesty*. 2. When on the other hand, while; used in contrasting two statements : *whereas in her youth she was slim and beautiful, in later years she became fat and hideously ugly*.

whereat, adv. [1. wărát; 2. wèərét]. 1. (interrog., archaic and rare) At, about, what : *whereat was he annoyed?* 2. (rel.) **a** At, about, which : *the things whereat you are displeased*; **b** upon which : '. . . They vote : *whereat his speech he thus renews'* (Milton, 'P. L.' ii. 389).

whereby, adv. [1. wărbí; 2. wèəbái]. 1. (interrog.) By what, by what means, how : *whereby may we be saved?* 2. (rel.) By means of which : *a plan whereby we may escape*.

where'er, adv. [1. wărár; 2. wèəréə]. Contracted fr. **wherever**. (poet.) Wherever.

wherefore, adv. & n. [1. wărfór; 2. wèəfó]. 1. adv. **a** (interrog.) For what reason, why : *wherefore do you weep?*; **b** (rel.) for which reason : *he was angry, wherefore I was afraid*. 2. n. Reason, cause; in Phr. *the why and the wherefore*.

wherefrom, adv. [1. wărfróm; 2. wèəfróm]. (rare) From which, whence.

wherein, adv. [1. wărín; 2. wèərín]. 1. (interrog.) In what point, respect, particular : *wherein do they differ?* 2. (rel.) In which; in which place, respect, circumstance : *points wherein we differ*.

whereinsoever, adv. [1. wărìnsöéver; 2. wèərìnsouévə]. Prec. & **so** & **ever**. In whatever respect, part &c.

whereinto, adv. [1. wărintöö; 2. wèərìntú]. 1. (interrog.) Into what. 2. (rel.) Into which : *the shelter whereinto he crept*.

whereof, adv. [1. wăróf; 2. wèəróf]. Of which, of what : *the matter whereof we spoke*.

whereon, adv. [1. wărón; 2. wèərón]. 1. (interrog.) Upon what : *whereon is your trust?* 2. (rel.) On, upon, which : *the rock whereon the house is built*.

whereout, adv. [1. wărǒut; 2. wèəráut]. (rare) Out of which.

wheresoever, adv. [1. wărsöéver; 2. wèərsouévə]. **where** & **so** & **ever**. Emphatic for **wherever**.

wherethrough, adv. [1. wărthröö; 2. wèəþrú]. Through which.

whereto, adv. [1. wărtöö; 2. wèətú]. 1. (interrog.) For what, for what purpose? 2. (rel.) **a** To which (place &c.) : *the point whereto they hasten*; **b** to which (question, remark &c.) : *he asked them their business, whereto they replied* &c.

whereunder, adv. [1. wărúnder; 2. wèəründə]. (rare) Under which : *the trees whereunder they rested*.

whereunto, adv. [1. wăruntöö; 2. wèərúntú]. Whereto.

whereupon, adv. [1. wărupón; 2. wèərəpón]. 1. (interrog.) Whereon, on what. 2. (rel.) Upon which, after, in consequence of, following upon which : *they showed signs of yielding, whereupon we renewed the attack*.

wherever, adv. [1. wărévər; 2. wèəréva]. In, to, at, whatever place, in any place : *sit wherever you like*; *he will get lost wherever he goes*.

wherewith, adv. [1. wărwídh; 2. wèəwíð]. 1. (interrog., archaic) With what : *wherewith shall they be fed?* 2. (rel., archaic) With which : *we have nothing wherewith to feed them*.

wherewithal, adv. & n. [1. wărwidhàwl; 2. wèəwìðôl]. 1. adv. (archaic) Wherewith. 2. n. Resources, esp. necessary money : *he lacked the wherewithal to bring up and educate his family*.

wherry, n. [1. wéri; 2. wéri]. Etymol. unknown. 1. Light row-boat used for passengers on river, lake &c. 2. Broad, heavy barge used on Norfolk Broads.

wherryman, n. [1. wériman; 2. wériman]. Man in charge of a wherry.

whet (I.), vb. trans. [1. wet; 2. wet]. O.E. *hwettan*, 'to sharpen, make keen'; M.E. *whetten*; cp. O.H.G. *wezzan*; Goth. (*ga-*)*hwatjan*, 'to sharpen'; O.N. *hvetja*; fr. *hwatjan, cp. O.E. *hwæt*, 'sharp, keen, active, brave'; O.S. *hwat*; O.H.G. *hwaz*; cogn. w. Lat. (*tri*)*quetrus*, 'three-cornered'. 1. To sharpen, put an edge on (a knife, scythe &c.), esp. with a hone. 2. To stimulate, excite (appetite, curiosity).

whet (II.), n., fr. prec. Act of whetting, **a** a knife &c.; **b** appetite &c.

whether (I.), pron. [1. wédher; 2. wéðə]. O.E. *hwæðer*; M.E. *w*(*h*)*eper*; O.H.G. *hwedar*; O.N. *hvárr*; Goth. *hwaþar*; fr. pronominal base seen in **who**, & **-ther**. Cp. Gk. *kóteros, póteros*, 'which of two'; Scrt. *kataráš*; Lith. *katràs*; O. Slav. *kotorŭ*, 'which'. (archaic or obs.) Which of the two.

whether (II.), conj., fr. prec. Expresses doubt, alternative possibility; correlative *or*, *or or whether*; in various constructions : *I don't know whether to go away or stay where I am*; *I wonder whether he will go himself or whether he will send you*; *I don't know whether it is raining or not*; *he asked whether he could help*; *whether we help or not, the enterprise will fail*. Phr. *whether or no*, in either case.

whetstone, n. [1. wétstōn; 2. wétstoun]. O.E. *hwetstān*; **whet** & **stone**. **a** Stone used for whetting, and putting sharp edge to knives, scythes &c.; **b** person who, problem, subject &c. which, provokes and stimulates mental action.

whey, n. [1. wā; 2. wei]. O.E. *hwæg*; M.E. *whei*. Clear watery liquid left when the curd is separated from milk, as by the action of rennet.

whey-faced, adj. [1. wá fåst; 2. wéi fèist]. Of sallow or pallid complexion through ill-health, fear &c.

which (I.), adj. [1. wich; 2. witʃ]. O.E. *hwelč* &c., 'which of what sort? what kind of?' fr. *hwa-līč*, 'what like'; cp. O.S. *hwilic*; O.H.G. *hwelīh*; Goth. *hwileiks*; see **who** & **like (I.)**. 1. (interrog.) What individual person or thing?, what group of persons or things?; used to demand selection, specification, identification, of one or more things from a number, class &c. : *which books did you choose?*; *which piece of cake will you have?*; *which teacher of all those you were under did you like best?* 2. (rel., rare) The specific thing referred to : *he told me all he had suffered, which things were well-nigh incredible*.

which (II.), pron., fr. prec. 1. (interrog.) In demanding selection, identification, specification, choice between two or more alternative persons, things &c. : *which of the members were present?*; *which is the right road?*; *which would you like?* Phr. *which is which?*, asking for more explicit distinction between two persons or things. 2. (rel.) **a** (not used now in reference to persons) The thing, circumstance &c. referred to in an antecedent sentence or clause; that individual thing or group of things : *all the documents which I have examined are forgeries*; *this is the book which I chose*; *this fact, which I think you have forgotten, proves the contrary*; *I lost my way, which delayed me considerably*; Phr. (archaic) *the which*, which; **b** (archaic) referring to person(s), (chiefly Bib. and liturgical) *our Father, which art in heaven*.

whichever, adj. & pron. [1. wichéver; 2. witʃévə]. **which** & **ever**. (indef. rel.) Any individual from several persons or things specified : *I will take whichever piece you reject*; *pray take whichever suits you best*.

whichsoever, adj. & pron. [1. wìchsōéver; 2. witʃsouévə]. **which** & **so** & **ever**. (rare) Whichever (emphatic).

whidah-bird, n. [1. wída bĕrd; 2. wídə bə̀d]. Apparently orig. *widow-bird*, later influenced by Place-Name *Whidah*, on W. African coast. West African weaver-bird, with black plumage, the male of which has tail-feathers twice its own length.

whiff (I.), n. [1. wif; 2. wif]. Imitative of sound of sniffing, inhaling, or the like. 1. **a** A puff, a breath, slight gust : *a whiff of air, of sea-air*; **b** a light puff or breath of air having a characteristic odour; a slight odour : *I got a whiff of a good cigar as he passed*; *I thought I noticed a slight whiff of the stable about him*. Phr. *to take a whiff or two* (of a pipe &c.), to have a brief smoke. 2. (colloq.) A small cigar.

whiff (II.), vb. intrans., fr. prec. To emit a slight, light, odour.

whiff (III.), n. Etymol. unknown. Light, outrigged sculling boat.

whiff (IV.), n. Etymol. unknown. A flat-fish, esp. a dab.

whiff (V.), vb. intrans. Etymol. unknown. To fish with hand-line from a moving boat, drawing the bait along near surface of water.

whiffle, vb. intrans. & trans. [1. wifl; 2. wífl]. **whiff (I.)** & **-le**. **a** intrans. (of wind &c.) To veer, blow lightly; **b** trans., to disperse, scatter, as with a puff of wind.

whiffy, adj. [1. wifi; 2. wífi]. **whiff (I.)** & **-y**. Emitting a slight, fitful, but unpleasant odour; smelly.

Whig, n. [1. wig; 2. wig], fr. obs. *Whiggamore*, nickname of Presbyterians in Scotland in 17th cent.; etymol. doubtful, possibly fr. Scot. *whig*, 'drive', & **mare (II.)**. 1. Member of the party, earlier called Roundheads, which during the 17th and early 18th cents. opposed the Royal prerogative and Episcopacy, upheld the supremacy of Parliament, and favoured toleration for Dissenters; later in the 18th cent. the Whigs were the party who opposed the Stuarts and supported the Hanoverian and Protestant succession. The Whigs developed in the 19th cent. into the Liberal party. The word expresses the antithesis of everything expressed by *Tory*. 2. (chiefly derisive) A straight-laced, narrow-minded person who is, or is believed to be, a prey to trifling moral scruples, to be opposed to mirth and conviviality.

Whiggery, n. [1. wígeri; 2. wígəri]. Prec. & **-ery**. (contemptuous) The political principles, moral attitude, of Whigs.

Whiggish, adj. [1. wígish; 2. wìgiʃ]. **Whig** & **-ish**. Pertaining to, characteristic of, a Whig; savouring of Whiggery.

Whiggishly, adv. Prec. & **-ly**. After the manner of a Whig.

Whiggishness, n. See prec. &- ness. Whiggish state of mind, principles, practice.

Whiggism, n. [1. wígizm; 2. wígizəm]. **Whig** & -ism. Doctrine, principles, of the Whigs.

while (I.), n. [1. wīl; 2. wail]. O.E. *hwīl*, 'space of time', M.E. *whīl*; O.H.G. *hwīla*; Goth. *hweila*; O.N. *hvīla*, 'space of time'; cogn. w. Lat. *quiēs*, 'rest', see **quiet**; (*tran*)*quillus*, 'quiet', see **tranquil**. Space of time, period : *to stay for a while* ; *to rest a while* ; *it took a long while to do* ; *a while ago* ; *in a little while*, soon ; *once in a while*, occasionally. Phrs. *the while*, during that time, at the same time : *he went about his work and sang the while* ; *worth one's while*, repaying one for time and trouble bestowed ; *to make it worth one's while*, to reward, pay one adequately ; (also in pejorative sense) to bribe.

while (II.), vb. trans., fr. prec., but prob. confused or associated w. **wile**. *While away* (*time*), to spend, cause to pass in such a way as to reduce the tedium.

while (III.), conj., fr. **while** (I.). 1. During the time that ; as long as : *sit down while you are waiting* ; *it was raining while we were out* ; *the lark sings while on the wing* ; at a moment in the space of time that : *he had an accident while on the way here*. 2. Though, at the same time (implying a contrast) : *he became an earl, while his brother was only made a knight*.

whiles, conj. [1. wīlz; 2. wailz]. O.E. *hwīles*, genit. of *hwīl*; see **while**. (archaic) While.

whilom, adv. & adj. [1. wīlum ; 2. wáiləm]. O.E. *hwīlum*, 'in the times, at times', dat. pl. of *hwīl*, 'time', used as adv. ; see **while** (I.). (archaic) 1. adv. At one time, formerly. 2. attrib. adj. Former, quondam.

whilst, conj. [1. wīlst; 2. wailst]. Earlier *whiles*, advbl. genit. of **while** (I.), & -*t*, for addition of wh. cp. **amongst**. While.

whim, n. [1. wim ; 2. wim], fr. O.N. *hvīma*, 'to let the eyes wander' ; connected w. Norw. *kvīma*, 'to flutter', cp. **whimsy**. 1. A passing fancy ; a trifling desire, an irresponsible caprice ; a fad, a crotchet. 2. Winch for use in a vertical mine-shaft.

whimbrel, n. [1. wímbrel; 2. wímbrəl]. Earlier *whimrel*, fr. imitation of bird's cry, & dimin. suff. -*rel*. Species of small curlew, the jack curlew.

whimper (I.), vb. intrans. & trans. [1. wímper ; 2. wímpə]. Prob. imitative ; cp. Mod. Germ. *wimmern*, 'to whimper'. 1. intrans. To cry weakly, fretfully, plaintively ; to utter feeble cries, as of a frightened child or young animal. 2. trans. (rare) To utter in a whimpering voice.

whimper (II.), n., fr. prec. Feeble, fretful cry, wail, whine.

whimpering, adj. [1. wímpering ; 2. wímpəriŋ]. **whimper** (I.) & -ing. Inclined to whimper ; resembling, of the nature of, a whimper.

whimperingly, adv. Prec. & -ly. With, in, a whimper.

whimsical, adj. [1. wímzikl ; 2. wímzikl]. **whimsy** & -ic & -al. 1. Given to whimsies, capricious, fanciful. 2. Quaint, fantastic.

whimsicality, n. [1. wìmzikáliti ; 2. wìmzikǽliti]. Prec. & -ity. 1. Quality of being whimsical (in both senses of adj.). 2. a Caprice, fad, crotchet ; b a quaint, original fancy.

whimsically, adv. [1. wímzikali ; 2. wímzikəli]. **whimsical** & -ly. In a whimsical manner.

whimsy, n. [1. wímzi ; 2. wímzi]. Connected w. Norw. *kvimsa*, 'to skip', fr. *kvima*, 'to flutter', cp. also **whim**. Capricious idea, freak, whim.

whimwham, n. [1. wímwam ; 2. wímwæm]. Redupl. form of **whim**. (archaic) 1. Whimsical idea ; a whimsy, a fad, a crotchet. 2. Toy, trifle, plaything.

whin (I.), n. [1. win ; 2. win]. Cp. Norw. *hvin*, a kind of grass. Gorse ; gorse bushes.

whin (II.), n. Etymol. unknown. One of several varieties of hard basaltic rock, also called greenstone, trap, &c. ; diabase, used for roadmaking.

whinberry, n. [1. wínberi ; 2. wínbəri], fr. O.E. *winberiġ*, 'grape'. **wine** & **berry**, influenced by **whin** (I.). Whortleberry.

whin-chat, whinchat, n. [1. wínchat ; 2. wíntʃæt]. Small brown and reddish bird, allied to the wheatear.

whine (I.), vb. intrans. & trans. [1. wīn ; 2. wain]. O.E. *hwīnan*, 'to shriek', esp. of an arrow &c. flying through the air ; M.E. *whīnen* ; cp. O.N. *hvīna*, 'to whirr' ; Dan. *hvine*, 'to shriek'. 1. intrans. a (of animal, esp. dog, or of child) To utter prolonged wailing cry ; b (of person) to complain, esp. about trifles ; to utter constant, fretful, childish complaints. 2. trans. To utter in whining tone.

whine (II.), n., fr. prec. 1. Prolonged, wailing, plaintive cry of dog, child &c. 2. Fretful, childish complaint.

whinger, n. [1. wínger ; 2. wíŋə]. Origin doubtful ; perh. connected w. **whine**, & imitative of sound of stroke. Dagger or short sword.

whining, adj. [1. wíning ; 2. wáiniŋ], fr. Pres. Part. of **whine**. Habitually complaining ; snivelling: *a whining rascal* ; uttered with or in a whine.

whiningly, adv. Prec. & -ly. In a whining manner.

whinny, vb. intrans. & n. [1. wíni ; 2. wíni], fr. **whine** (I.). 1. vb. (of horse) To neigh gently and playfully. 2. n. A gentle neigh of a horse, expressive of pleasure, friendly greeting &c.

whinsill, n. [1. wínsil ; 2. wínsil]. **whin** (II.) & **sill**. (geol.) Sheet of intrusive basalt.

whinstone, n. [1. wínstōn ; 2. wínstoun]. Same as **whin** (II.).

whinyard, n. [1. wínyard ; 2. wínjəd]. (obs.) Variant of **whinger**, with ending suggested by *poniard*.

whip (I.), vb. trans. & intrans. [1. wip ; 2. wip]. M.E. *whippen* ; cp. M. Du. *wippe*, 'to skip' ; Mod. Germ. *wippen*, fr. L.G. source, 'to move up & down' ; O.H.G. *wipf*, 'swing' ; M.H.G. *wifen*, 'to swing' ; cogn. w. Lith. *wȳbur-iu*, 'to oscillate' ; Lat. *vibrāre*, 'to swing, shake', see **vibrate**; see also **wimple**. A. trans. 1. a To apply a whip to, to strike with a lash : *to whip a horse* ; Phr. *to whip up one's horse*, cause to start or to increase pace by whipping ; b to strike with a pliable stick ; to flog in any way, as incitement or punishment &c. : *to whip a naughty child* &c. ; Phrs. *to whip eggs*, whisk them into a froth ; *to whip a stream*, to fish with a fly, continually throwing the line over a piece of water ; c to effect, remove &c. by whipping ; *to whip sense into, the nonsense out of, a child* &c. ; d (hunting) to control (hounds) by means of whip &c., esp. in Phr. *to whip in, off* &c. ; hence transferred to control of members of political party in House of Commons &c. 2. (colloq.) To defeat, overcome, beat. 3. To bind, lash (rope, rope-end &c.), by wrapping in repeated coils of twine &c. 4. To join, fasten (seam, frill &c.) by oversewing rolled edges. B. intrans. 1. To use a whip &c. for beating, flogging &c. 2. To move with great rapidity and suddenness : *he whipped upstairs in a flash*. C. Followed by preposition or adverb. *Whip out*, 1. trans., a to draw, pull, snatch, out with a sudden swift action : *to whip out a knife* ; b to utter suddenly and violently, rap out : *to whip out an oath, a reply* &c. ; 2. intrans., to make a hasty exit : *to whip out of a door*. *Whip off*, 1. trans., a to snatch suddenly away : *to whip a cloth off the table* ; b to carry away, cause to accompany one in a sudden swift departure : *he whipped me off to play bridge* ; c to drive away by whipping ; 2. intrans., to depart hastily, or with sudden, rapid motion : *to whip off to the continent*. *Whip round*, intrans., to turn round suddenly and swiftly : *he had his back to me but whipped round in a second when I shouted*. *Whip up*, trans., a to make (horse) start, or increase speed, by whipping ; b to seize with a sudden grab, to snatch up : *to whip up a pistol and shoot an intruder* ; c to gather, collect : *to whip up an audience, subscriptions*.

whip (II.), n., fr. prec. 1. Object consisting of lash attached either to a long, pliant, or to a short, stiff, handle, for delivering blows as punishment or to incite (animal &c.) to increased effort. 2. Driver (of horses), esp. in Phr. *a good, an accomplished, whip*. 3. Hunt servant controlling hounds in hunting-field. 4. (Parliament) a Person appointed by a party to enforce discipline among, ensure attendance of, members at voting time, meetings of committees &c. ; the chief whip of the Government is the Patronage Secretary of the Treasury ; b message, appeal, issued by a party whip to members to attend sessions, divisions &c. of Parliament : *a three-line whip*, underlined three times, as sign of urgency ; also any urgent appeal to action to supporters of a cause &c. 5. Whip-and-derry.

whip-and-derry, n. [1. wíp an(d) déri ; 2. wíp ən(d) déri]. See **derrick**. Hoisting apparatus consisting of rope and pulley.

whip-cord, n. 1. Hard, tightly twisted cord made of hemp and used for whip-lashes. 2. A strong, tough woven fabric with ribs resembling whip-cord.

whip-fish, n. Fish having a dorsal spine elongated into a long filament.

whip-gin, n. Block for use in whip-and-derry apparatus.

whip-hand, n. Hand used to hold whip. Phr. *to have the whip-hand of*, have control of, mastery over, the upper hand of.

whipper-in, n. [1. wíper ín ; 2. wípər ín]. Hunt official managing hounds ; whip.

whipper-snapper, n. [1. wíper snáper ; 2. wípə snǽpə]. Small, insignificant but uppish person ; one who is negligible in mind, person, and standing, but yet is inclined to be impudent and presuming.

whippet, n. [1. wípet ; 2. wípit]. Etymol. doubtful. 1. Small, cross-bred, greyhound-like dog used for racing. 2. Light, small, armoured army tank capable of rapid movement.

whipping, n. [1. wíping ; 2. wípiŋ]. **whip** (I.) & -ing. 1. a Punishment inflicted with a whip or stick ; a thrashing ; b a defeat inflicted in a contest or match of any kind ; a beating. 2. Lashing of twine securing end of rope &c.

whipping-boy, n. (hist.) Boy formerly educated with, and taking chastisement in place of, a prince or child of exalted birth.

whipping-post, n. Stake &c. to which a malefactor is bound to receive a flogging.

whipping-top, n. Child's top kept spinning by lashing with whip.

whipple-tree, n. [1. wípl trē ; 2. wípl trī], fr. **whip** (I.), 'to move up and down, to and fro'. The movable bar of a cart, plough &c. to which the traces of a horse are hitched ; swingle-tree.

whip-poor-will, n. [1. wíporwíl ; 2. wípəwíl]. Imitative of bird's cry. Small, American nocturnal bird allied to goatsucker or nightjar.

whippy, adj. [1. wípi ; 2. wípi]. **whip** (II.) & -y. Resembling a long-handled whip in slenderness and pliancy ; hence, slender, inclined to bend along the whole length ; reverse of *stiff* or *stocky*.

whipster, n. [1. wípster ; 2. wípstə]. **whip** & -ster. Insignificant person.

whir(r), vb. intrans. & n. [1. wër ; 2. wə̄]. Prob. imitative ; but cp. Dan. *hvirre*, 'to whirl', cogn. w. **whirl**. 1. vb. a To revolve, vibrate, move, with great rapidity ; b to produce a buzzing sound by such movement. 2. n. a Rapid rotating or vibratory motion ; b sound produced by this.

whirl (I.), vb. intrans. & trans. [1. wërl ; 2. wə̄l]. M.E. *whirlen*, fr. O.N. *hvirfla*, 'to whirl' ; cp. M. Du. *wervelen* ; M.H.G. *wirbelen*, 'to whirl, rotate' ; O.N. *hvirfill*, 'circle' ; O.H.G. *wirbel*, 'whirlwind' ; cp. further O.E. *hweorfan*, 'to turn', see **wharf**; cp. also, w. different formative element, Lat.

vertere, 'to turn'; see **version** & words there referred to. **A.** intrans. **1.** To rotate, spin, gyrate, rapidly, on an axis: *a whirling top*; *the sails of the windmill whirl round and round.* **2.** To pass quickly along a circular course, move swiftly in an orbit: *the horses whirled round the circus-ring*; *dancers whirl round a ballroom.* **3.** (of vehicle or person in vehicle) To move swiftly, spin, dash: *the carriage whirled out of sight.* **4. a** (of brain) To be giddy, confused, bewildered; to reel; **b** (of thoughts &c.) to be in confusion, throng swiftly and disconnectedly. **B.** trans. **1.** To cause to revolve, rotate, move swiftly about a centre or point, or in a more or less circular course: *he whirled his stick about his head*; *he whirled his partner off round the room*; *the wind whirled the snowflakes in eddies.* **2.** To convey rapidly (implying revolving or eddying motion, of wheeled vehicle &c.): *the cart whirled him down the hill.*

whirl (II.), n., fr. prec. **a** Whirling motion, rapid revolution; **b** (fig.) confusion of mind, bewilderment: *my thoughts are, brain is, in a whirl.*

whirl-bone, n. Ball-and-socket joint.

whirligig, n. [1. wěrligig; 2. wǽligig]. **whirl** (I.) & **gig**. **1. a** Mechanical device, toy &c. designed to rotate rapidly on an axis; specif. **b** a merry-go-round. **2.** (fig.) That which passes with rapid changes or revolutions: *the whirligig of time* &c. **3.** Water-beetle, of bright, metallic appearance, moving in swift circles to catch its prey.

whirling-table, n. [1. wěrling tàbl; 2. wǽliŋ tèibl]. Apparatus for demonstrating effects of centrifugal force.

whirlpool, n. [1. wěrlpōōl; 2. wǽlpūl]. Violent, rapid, movement of water in a circular sweep; rapid, circular eddy.

whirlwind, n. [1. wěrlwind; 2. wǽlwind]. Swift, circular movement of cylindrical or funnel-shaped column of air.

whirr. See **whir(r)**.

whisk (I.), n. [1. wisk; 2. wisk]. Cp. Dan. *viske*; cp. Mod. Germ. *wischen*, 'to wipe'; O.H.G. *wisk*, 'wisp'; & further, O.E. *weoxian*, 'to wipe down a horse'; cogn. w. Lat. *virga*, 'rod', see **virgate**. **1.** Small bunch of light twigs, bristles, straw, feathers &c. for use as brush; sometimes in compounds: *fly-whisk* &c. **2.** Light, metal instrument for beating eggs, cream &c. to a froth.

whisk (II.), vb. trans. & intrans., fr. prec. **A.** trans. **1.** Usually *whisk off, away*, **a** to remove, flick off, with light, brushing movement, sweep lightly and briskly: *to whisk flies away*; *whisk crumbs off one's coat*; **b** to carry off, cause to accompany one, with impetuous, rapid action: *they whisked him off to see the sights.* **2.** To wave, sweep, twitch lightly and quickly through the air: *the cow whisked her tail.* **3.** To beat, agitate, lightly, whip: *to whisk eggs, cream* &c. **B.** intrans. To move, esp. depart, disappear, with rapid, abrupt, motion: *to whisk round, out of sight, out of the room* &c.

whisk (III.), n., fr. prec. Sudden, light, sweeping movement: *with a whisk of the tail.*

whisker, n. [1. wísker; 2. wískə]. **whisk** (I.) & **-er.** **1.** Usually pl., *whiskers*, hair growing on the sides of a man's face. **2.** (usually pl.) The long bristles growing at side of mouth of cat, tiger &c.

whiskered, adj. [1. wískerd; 2. wískəd]. Prec. & **-ed.** Having, wearing, whiskers.

whiskey, n. See whisky.

whiskified, adj. [1. wískifīd; 2. wískifaid]. Next word & **-fy** & **-ed.** (colloq.) Under the influence of, affected by, whisky.

whisky (I.), also **whiskey**, n. [1. wíski; 2. wíski], fr. Gael. *uisge-(beatha)*, see **usquebaugh.** Alcoholic liquor obtained by the distillation of malted grain, esp. barley.

whisky (II.), n., fr. **whisk** (I.). Light, two-wheeled vehicle; gig.

whisky-jack, n. Canadian jay.

whisky-liver, n. Alcoholic disease of liver; cirrhosis.

whisky-toddy, n. Hot whisky and water; usually flavoured with lemon and sugar.

whisper (I.), vb. intrans. & trans. [1. wísper; 2. wíspə]. O.E. *hwisprian*; M.E. *whispren*; cp. M. Du. *wisperen*; cp. Mod. Germ. *wispern*; O.H.G. *wispalōn*, 'to whisper'; also w. different formative element, O.N. *hvīsta*, 'to whisper'; *hvissa*, 'to buzz'; cogn. w. O. Slav. *svistati*, 'to whisper'. **A.** intrans. **1. a** To speak in a low voice, without the resonance produced by vibration of the vocal chords; **b** (specif. phon.) to utter speech-sounds with a definite contraction of the glottis, differing from the condition in *voice* on the one hand, and in *breath* on the other. **2.** (poet., of breeze, leaves &c.) To make a faint sound, suggestive of whispering, by gentle motion; to murmur, rustle. **B.** trans. **1. a** To utter (words, sounds) in a whisper; **b** (fig.) to tell as a secret, or as something not to be revealed. **2.** To put about furtively, circulate as a rumour: *the strangest things were whispered concerning him.*

whisper (II.), n., fr. prec. **1. a** Act of whispering; subdued speech, uttered without vibration of vocal chords: *to speak in a whisper*; **b** (specif. phon.) articulation produced with a slight but definite contraction of the glottis. **2. a** That which is whispered; remark &c. made in a whisper; **b** rumour, secret communication. **3.** Gentle rustling, murmuring sound, of leaves, wind &c.

whisperer, n. [1. wísperer; 2. wíspərə]. **whisper** (I.) & **-er.** **a** One who whispers; **b** a tale-bearer, a privy gossip.

whispering (I.), n. [1. wíspering; 2. wíspəriŋ]. **whisper** (I.) & **-ing.** Whispered speech.

whispering (II.), adj., fr. Pres. Part. of **whisper** (I.). Speaking in, producing, a whisper.

whispering-gallery, n. Gallery, usually in a dome, where, owing to the construction, a sound uttered without any great resonance travels a considerable distance; there is a well-known example of this in the dome of St. Paul's Cathedral.

whisperingly, adv. [1. wísperingli; 2. wíspəriŋli]. **whispering** (II.) & **-ly.** In a whisper; in a manner resembling a whisper.

whist, whisht (I.), interj. & vb. intrans. [1. wist, wisht; 2. wist, wiʃt]. Conventionalized imitation of natural sound. **1.** interj. Exclamation of warning, to demand silence. **2.** vb. To be silent; to cease speaking.

whist (II.), n. [1. wist; 2. wist]. Earlier **whisk**, fr. quick movements of players in taking cards fr. table. Game of cards played by two pairs of players with pack of 52 cards, in which ten, five, points are required for game; *progressive whist*, a number of games of whist played simultaneously at different tables, one or more players from each passing at intervals to the next.

whist-drive, n. Social function at which progressive whist is played.

whistle (I.), vb. intrans. & trans. [1. wísl; 2. wísl]. O.E. *hwistlian*; M.E. *whistlen*, 'to whistle'; imitative; cp. O.N. *hvīsla*, *hvīsta*, 'to whisper'; perh. connected w. **whisper.** **A.** intrans. **1.** To produce a shrill, clear, piping note, or sound, or a series of such notes; **a** (of human beings) by pursing up the lips and forcing the air through them, altering the note by changing position of the tongue; **b** (of birds) by forcing air through the beak; **c** (of mechanical device) by forcing air or steam through a narrow aperture. **2.** Specif. (of human beings) to produce a series of characteristic musical notes, or a tune, by whistling. **3.** (of moving body) To produce a clear, shrill sound by rapid passage through the air: *the bullets whistled round our ears.* **4.** (of wind) To produce a shrill, clear, continuous sound by blowing through a narrow chink or aperture. **B.** trans. **1.** To utter, produce (an air), by whistling: *to whistle a tune.* **2.** To summon by whistling: *to whistle a dog back.*

whistle (II.), n., fr. prec. **1.** Shrill, clear, piping sound produced by whistling. **2.** Device, instrument, for producing such a sound: *penny whistle*, small *tin whistle*; *steam whistle*, with sound produced by jet of steam. Phr. *to pay for one's whistle*, pay dearly for insignificant action or object. **3.** Throat, esp. in slang Phr. *to wet one's whistle*, to drink.

whistler, n. [1. wísler; 2. wíslə]. **whistle** (I.) & **-er.** One who, that which, whistles; specif. **a** broken-winded horse, producing a whistling sound in breathing; **b** one of several species of birds.

whistling, adj. & vbl. n. [1. wísling; 2. wísliŋ], fr. Pres. Part. of **whistle** (I.). **1.** adj. Producing a sound resembling a whistle; esp. as descriptive epithet for bird or animal, e.g. *whistling duck, eagle, marmot, thrush* &c. **2.** n., fr. **whistle** (I.) & **-ing.** The sound produced by person who, or thing which, whistles: *the whistling of the wind.*

whit (I.), n. [1. wit; 2. wit]. O.E. *wiht*, 'thing, creature'; M.E. *wight*; cp. O.S., O.H.G. *wiht*; Goth. *waihts*, O.N. *vætt*, 'thing'; cogn. w. O. Slav. *vešti*, 'thing'; cp. **wight.** Smallest amount, minute particle, jot; chiefly in Phrs. *not a whit, no whit.*

Whit (II.), **Whitsun**, adj. [1. wít(sun); 2. wít(sən)], fr. M.E. *hwīte (sunnedei)*, lit. 'white Sunday', fr. the white robes worn by persons to be baptized, christenings being most numerous on this day. Of, pertaining to, following, Whitsunday; only in Phrs. *Whit Monday, Tuesday*; *Whit week*; *Whitsun week.*

white (I.), adj. [1. wīt; 2. wait]. O.E. *hwīt*; M.E. *whīt*; cp. O.S. *hwīt*; O.H.G. *hwīz*; O.N. *hvītr*; Goth. *hweits*, 'white'; cogn. w. Scrt. *çvitrá*, *çvētáš*, 'white, light'; O. Slav. *světŭ*, 'light'; Lith. *szvaitýti*, 'to brighten'. **1.** Having the colour of unstained snow; or the luminous appearance of sunlight reflected from a surface without the absorption of any of the visible rays of the spectrum; colourless; opposed to *black*; largely, partly, or nearly white: *as white as snow*; *white clouds*; *white hair*, having lost its colour and become silvery, esp. through age; *white meat*, poultry, rabbit, veal. **2.** (of animal, bird, plant &c.) Entirely or partly white, or with characteristic white markings: *white crab, goat, poplar, owl, wagtail* &c. Phr. *a white crow*, a rarity. **3. a** Of fair complexion, of the colouring of the Caucasian race as distinct from the yellow, brown, red, and black races: *the white races*; *a white man*, (also fig., colloq.) honourable, sincere, man; **b** pale, pallid, through illness, fatigue, fear &c. **4.** (of wine) Of clear, amber or golden colour, contrasted with *red.* **5.** Beneficent, working or used for good purpose: *white magic*; *a white witch*; contrasted with *black.*

white (II.), n., fr. prec. **1.** White or whitish colour. **2.** White pigment, often with qualifying epithet, *flake-, zinc-white*; *Chinese, Dutch, white* &c. **3.** White object, substance, matter; specif. **a** white fabric: *to dress in white*; **b** also *white of egg*, colourless, albuminous liquid surrounding yolk of egg; **c** white part of cornea surrounding iris of eye; **d** white butterfly, esp. the cabbage butterfly. **4.** Member of fair-skinned, Caucasian race; white man. **5.** (pl.) *Whites*, leucorrhoea.

white (III.), vb. trans., fr. **white** (I.). (archaic) To whiten, make white.

white-, pref. representing **white** (I.), forming adjectival compounds descriptive of bird, animal, insect &c.; e.g. *white-crested, -necked, -tailed* &c., having a white crest, neck, tail &c.

white alloy, n. White metal.

white ant, n. Termite.

whitebait, n. [1. wítbāt; 2. wáitbeit]. Fry of several varieties of edible fish, sprat, herring &c., eaten as a delicacy.

whitebeam, n. [1. wítbēm; 2. wáitbīm]. Flowering shrub or small tree, *Sorbus aria*, with whitish down on lower surface of leaves.

white bear, n. Polar bear.

whiteboy, n. [1. wítboi; 2. wáitbɔi]. Member of white-robed gang of Irish agricultural agitators of 18th cent.

white-cap, n. The redstart.

white-caps, n. pl. Foam-crested waves.

Whitechapel cart, n. [1. wítchapl kárt; 2. wáitʃæpl kǽt], fr. Whitechapel in East End of London. Tradesman's light, two-wheeled cart.

white corpuscle, n. Leucocyte.

white currant, n. Variety of *Ribes*, with glistening, whitish berries.

white elephant, n. **a** Light grey variety of elephant venerated in Burma and Siam; **b** unwanted, burdensome possession.

white ensign, n. St. George's red cross on a white ground, the flag of Royal Navy; cp. *red ensign*.

white feather, n. Symbol of cowardice.

white fish, n. Fish which have white flesh and are not oily; i.e. excluding salmon, mackerel &c.

white flag, n. Symbol of surrender or truce.

White Friar, n. Carmelite.

white-gum, n. Infant's white rash.

Whitehall, n. [1. wít-hawl; 2. wáithɔ̄l]. Street in London where many Government offices are situated. **a** British Government; **b** (fig.) departmental government.

white-handed, adj. Having white hands; (fig.) innocent, unspotted, blameless.

white-heart (-cherry), n. Large yellowish-white variety of cherry.

white heat, n. Temperature at which metals become white; also fig. of passion, enthusiasm &c.

white-horses, n. pl. Foam-crested waves, white-caps.

white-hot, adj. (of metal &c.) Raised to white heat; also fig. of enthusiasm &c.

White House, n. Official residence of President of U.S.A. at Washington.

white-iron, n. **1.** Thin sheets of iron coated with tin. **2.** A brittle variety of cast-iron.

white-land, n. Soil consisting of whitish clay.

white lead, n. Pigment made of lead carbonate and hydrated lead oxide.

white light, n. Natural, colourless sunlight.

white-lipped, adj. Having pallid lips, through fear, illness &c.

white-livered, adj. [1. wít liverd; 2. wáit livəd]. Cowardly.

whitely, adv. [1. wítli; 2. wáitli]. **white** (I.) & -ly. With a white appearance.

white metal, n. Pewter, or any other alloy of silvery appearance.

whiten, vb. trans. & intrans. [1. wítn; 2. wáitn]. **white** (I.) & -en. **1.** trans. To make, cause to grow, give white colour to. **2.** intrans. To become, grow, turn, white, assume white appearance.

whiteness, n. [1. wítnes; 2. wáitnis]. **white** (I.) & -ness. State or quality of being white.

whitening, n. [1. wítning; 2. wáitniŋ]. **whiten** & -ing. Dried and prepared chalk for use in whitewash, for polishing &c.; also *whiting*.

white paper, n. Government report giving information on specific subject.

white rent, n. Annual tax on tinners in Devon and Cornwall, payable to the Prince of Wales as lord of the Duchy of Cornwall.

white sheet, n. Garb of penitent, esp. in Phr. *to stand in a white sheet*, make confession.

white slave, n. Girl entrapped, and usually exported, as prostitute; also attrib., *white-slave traffic*.

whitesmith, n. [1. wítsmith; 2. wáitsmiþ]. Tradesman working in tin, silver &c.

white squall, n. Sudden squall at sea, arising in fine weather, without clouds.

white-thorn, n. Hawthorn.

white-throat, n. Small European warbler.

whitewash (I.), n. [1. wítwosh; 2. wáitwɔʃ]. **1.** Solution of lime, white when dry, used to coat walls &c. of rooms, outhouses &c. **2.** (fig.) Mode of description, report &c. designed to clear, justify, person's name, actions &c.

whitewash (II.), vb. trans., fr. prec. **1.** To coat, daub, with whitewash. **2.** (fig.) To attempt to rehabilitate (person or his character) by explaining away, or putting favourable interpretation upon, bad actions, concealing defects, setting good qualities in high relief &c. **3.** To free from debt by passing through bankruptcy court.

whither (I.), adv. [1. wídher; 2. wíðə]. O.E. *hwider*, M.E. *whider*; fr. pronominal base seen in **who**, & -ther; cp. **whether**. **1.** (interrog.) To or towards what place, in what direction: *whither did they go?* **2.** (introducing dependent clause) To the place which, to any place that: *let him go whither he will*.

whither (II.), pron., fr. prec. (rel.) To or towards which: *the place whither they went*.

whither (III.), n., fr. prec. Place to which one goes, is going; destination: *we know not the whence nor the whither of our destinies*.

whithersoever, adv. [1. wídhersōèver; 2. wíðəsouèvə]. **whither** & **so** & **ever**. (archaic) To whatever place, in any direction whatever.

whitherward, adv. [1. wídherward; 2. wíðəwəd]. **whither** & -ward. (archaic) In which or what direction, towards what point.

whiting (I.), n. [1. wíting; 2. wáitiŋ]. **white** (III.) & -ing. Dried, purified, and powdered chalk for polishing, making colour-wash &c.

whiting (II.), n. **white** (I.) & -ing. Small, edible, European sea-fish, *Gadus merlangus*, of the cod family.

whiting-pout, n. Fish with inflatable membrane over the eyes.

whitish, adj. [1. wítish; 2. wáitiʃ]. **white** (I.) & -ish. Fairly white.

whitleather, n. [1. wítledher; 2. wítleðə]. **white** (I.) & **leather**. Leather whitened by dressing with alum.

whitlow, n. [1. wítlō; 2. wítlou]. M.E. *whit(f)lawe*, influenced by **white**, O.N. *kwika*, 'quick below the nail', see **quick** (III.), & **flaw** (I.). Earlier *quick-(f)lawe*. Small, inflamed tumour, usually below the skin, on the end-joint of a finger.

whitlow-grass, n. Small, white-flowered cruciferous plant.

Whit Monday, n. Day after Whitsunday, an English Bank Holiday.

Whitsun. See **Whit** (II.).

Whitsunday, n. [1. wítsúndi; 2. wítsándi]. O.E. *on hwītan Sunnan dæg*, M.E. *hwīte sunnedei*, see **Whit** (II.) & **Sunday**. Seventh Sunday after Easter, commemorating the descent of the Holy Spirit on the Day of Pentecost.

Whitsuntide, n. [1. wítsuntīd; 2. wítsəntàid]. **Whitsun** & **tide**. Week-end or week including Whitsunday.

Whitsun week, n. Week beginning with Whitsunday.

whittle (I.), n. [1. wítl; 2. wítl]. M.E. *þwitel*, 'whittle, jack-knife', fr. O.E. *þwītan*, 'to cut up', & -le. Cp. O.N. *þveitr*, 'enclosed piece of land', see **thwaite**. Large sheath-knife or butcher's knife.

whittle (II.), vb. trans. & intrans., fr. prec. A. trans. **1.** To pare, slice thin shavings off (piece of wood), with a knife. **2.** To construct (object) by carving and trimming piece of wood &c. **3.** (fig.) To reduce gradually in amount: *to whittle down a person's salary*; *to whittle down a statement*, to weaken, destroy force of; also *whittle away* (a doctrine), to minimize its significance, explain it away. B. intrans. To shape, trim, carve, a piece of wood into desired shape by slicing shavings with a knife.

whity, whitey, adj. [1. wíti; 2. wáiti]. **white** (I.) & -y. Fairly white; whitish; sometimes in compounds: *whity-brown* &c., white tinged with brown.

whiz(z), n. & vb. intrans. [1. wiz; 2. wiz]. Imitative. **1.** n. Humming and hissing sound produced by body flying rapidly through the air. **2.** vb. To rush through the air at great speed, producing a hissing or buzzing sound in the passing.

whizzbang, n. [1. wízbang; 2. wízbæŋ]. Prec. & **bang** (I.); imitative. (mil. slang) A light, high velocity shell, the sound of approach and explosion being almost simultaneous.

who, pron. [1. hōō; 2. hū]. O.E. *hwā*, M.E. *hwō, hō;* cp. Goth. *hwa*; O. Swed. *hvar;* O.H.G. *hwer*, 'who'; fr. Aryan *k^wo-* &c., & cogn. w. Gk. *pê, pôs*, 'how'; *póthi*, 'where', fr. *k^wo-*; Scrt. *kaś*, 'who'; O. Slav. *kúto;* Lith. *kàs*, 'who'; Lat. *quod*, 'that'; cp. also Lat. *quis*, 'who'; Scrt. *kím;* O. Slav. *čito*, 'what'; Gk. *tis*, 'who?'; all fr. stem *k^wo-*, *k^wi-*, *k^woi-* &c., 'who? what', in many pronominal & advbl. forms, see **what, when, whether, where, why**. **1.** (interrog.) What or which person: *who is there?*; *who(m) did you see?*; *who do you think you are?*; *who was he speaking to?*; *whose ugly face is that?*; *whose is it?* **2.** (rel.) **a** That person, the one mentioned in preceding clause or sentence: *the man who was here is an artist*; *I don't know the people who live next door*; *is there anyone who can be trusted?*; *I know the man whom you mean*; *that is the boy whose head was punched*; *he struck his opponent, who promptly returned the blow*; **b** (in elliptical constructions) the person(s) that, any person(s) that, he that: *who delays, pays*; *whom the gods would destroy, they first make mad*.

whoa. See **wo**.

whoe'er, pron. [1. hōōár; 2. hūéə]. Contracted form of next word. (poet.) Whoever.

whoever, pron. [1. hōōéver; 2. hūévə]. **who** & **ever**. (rel., indef., without antecedent expressed) Who, the person, any person, anybody, be he who he may, that: *whoever comes first may have it*; *give it to who(m)ever you like*; *whose-ever it is, you must return it*.

whole (I.), adj. [1. hōl; 2. houl]. O.E. *hāl*, M.E. *hōl*; cp. O.S., O. Fris. *hēl*; O.H.G. *heil*; O.N. *heill*; Goth. *hails*, 'complete, whole, sound'; cogn. w. O. Prussian *kailūstikan*, 'health'; O. Slav. *cělŭ*, 'complete'. The spelling *w-, wh-,* wh. is fairly common in scattered examples in the 16th cent., seems to express a variant dialectal pronunciation long since extinct except in certain provinc. forms. See also **hale** (I.), **heal, health, holy**. **1.** In a sound condition of health; intact; not injured or diseased: '*the multitude wondered, when they saw . . . the maimed to be whole*' (Matt. xv. 31); *lucky to get off with a whole skin*. **2.** Complete in all its parts, unbroken, unimpaired; intact, entire: *not a single whole cup or saucer in the house*. **3.** All of anything, including every part, complete, undivided, without subtraction of any element or aspect: *whole cities were destroyed*; *the whole country was swept by a violent storm*; *I can't deal now with the whole question, but must select one or two points*; *one's whole mind, energies* &c.; *to eat a whole sheep at a sitting*; *to roast an ox whole*, without cutting it up. Phr. *to go the whole hog*, to do a thing thoroughly, hold an opinion with complete conviction; *to be whole-hearted*, go all lengths.

whole (II.), n., fr. prec. **1.** All there is; every part, member, aspect; the complete sum, amount, quantity, of anything; the entirety: *the whole is greater than its parts*; *the whole of one's property, family* &c.; *the whole of the affairs of state devolve upon him*; *the whole of the Christian religion*. **2.** A unity, an undivided, unbroken individual entity with all parts duly proportioned, adjusted, and interrelated; a complete system: *the Catholic faith is a whole, and cannot be divided into a number of separate and distinct tenets*. Phr. *on the whole*, all things considered.

whole-bound, adj. (of book) Bound entirely in leather.

whole-coloured, adj. Entirely of one colour.

whole-hearted, adj. Acting, done, felt, with the whole heart; devoted, sincere, single-minded: *whole-hearted enthusiasm, support* &c.

whole-heartedly, adv. Prec. & -ly. In a whole-hearted manner.

whole-heartedness, n. See prec. & -ness. Quality of being whole-hearted.

whole-hogger, n. [1. hōl hóger; 2. hóul hógə]. One who does a thing, supports a cause &c. to the utmost limit, and without reservations or misgivings; see Phr. *to go the whole hog*, under **whole** (I.), 3.

whole-hoofed, adj. Not having cloven hoofs.
whole-length, adj. & n. **1.** adj. *Whole-length portrait* &c., one representing person's whole figure. **2.** n. A whole-length portrait &c.
wholemeal, n. & adj. [1. hŏlmēl ; 2. hóulmēl]. **1.** n. Flour containing all the constituents of the grain. **2.** adj. Made of wholemeal: *wholemeal bread* &c.
wholeness, n. [1. hŏlnes ; 2. hóulnis]. **whole** (I.) & **-ness.** State of being whole; completeness.
whole number, n. Number involving no fractions ; integer.
wholesale, n., adj., & adv. [1. hŏlsāl ; 2. hóulseil]. **1.** n. Sale of goods in bulk or quantity; contrasted with *retail*; chiefly in Phr. *by wholesale*. **2.** adj. **a** Pertaining to, carried on by, sale of goods in bulk : *wholesale prices* ; *wholesale trade* ; **b** selling by wholesale: *wholesale trader* ; **c** (fig.) involving large amounts, on a large scale : *wholesale destruction* ; *a wholesale liar.* **3.** adv. **a** By wholesale, in bulk or quantity : *to buy goods wholesale* ; **b** hence (fig.) on a large scale, indiscriminately : *to incur debts, waste one's money, wholesale.*
wholesaler, n. [1. hŏlsāler ; 2. hóulseilə]. A wholesale trader.
wholesome, adj. [1. hŏlsum ; 2. hóulsəm]. **whole** (I.) & **-some. 1.** Favourable to, promoting, health; salubrious, good for one, healthful : *wholesome food, surroundings* &c. **2.** Conducive to moral well-being; salutary : *a little wholesome punishment* ; *a clean, wholesome story.*
wholesomely, adv. Prec. & **-ly.** In a wholesome manner.
wholesomeness, n. See prec. & **-ness.** State or quality of being wholesome.
whole-souled, adj. Acting, feeling, experienced, with one's whole soul; whole-hearted; *a whole-souled supporter* ; *whole-souled devotion.*
wholly, adv. [1. hŏlli, hŏli ; 2. hóulli, hóuli]. **whole** (I.) & **-ly. 1.** Completely, in all parts or respects, entirely : *few men are wholly bad.* **2.** Altogether, without qualification : *I don't wholly agree.*
whom, pron. [1. hōōm ; 2. hūm]. Objective case of **who** ; O.E. *hwām* (dat.), M.E. *whōm* ; now often replaced colloquially by *who* : *I don't know who(m) you mean.*
whoop, vb. intrans. & n. [1. hōōp ; 2. hūp], fr. Fr. *houper*, imitative. **1.** vb. To utter a whoop, esp. that heard in whooping-cough. **2.** n. Loud cry or shout : *whoops of joy.*
whooper swan, n. [1. hōōper swŏn ; 2. hūpə swŏn]. Whooping swan.
whooping-cough, n. [1. hōōping kàwf ; 2. hūpiŋ, hūpiŋ, kŏf, kɔ̌f]. Also **hooping-cough,** infectious disease of children, characterized by paroxysms of coughing which end in loud whoops, *Pertussis.*
whooping swan, n. The wild swan, *Cygnus musicus.*
whop, vb. trans. [1. wop ; 2. wɔp]. Etymol. doubtful. **1.** To beat, thrash. **2.** (fig.) To overcome, vanquish, defeat.
whopper, n. [1. wóper ; 2. wɔ́pə]. Prec. & **-er.** (slang) Anything especially large or fine ; specif., a lie of remarkable magnitude and shamelessness.
whopping (I.), n. [1. wóping ; 2. wɔ́piŋ]. **whop** & **-ing. 1.** Thrashing, beating. **2.** Defeat.
whopping (II.), adj. & adv., fr. Pres. Part. of **whop.** (slang) **a** adj. Especially large or fine of its kind ; **b** adv., very, extremely ; chiefly *whopping great (fish* &c.).
whore, n. & vb. intrans. [1. hōr ; 2. hō]. O.E., M.E. *hōre* ; cp. O.H.G. *huora* ; O.N. *hōrr* ; M. Du. *hoere*, 'fornicator'; Goth. *hōrs*, 'adulterous' ; cogn. w. Lat. *cārus*, 'dear', see **caress**; Lett. *kārs*, 'covetous'; Scrt. *cārus*, 'beloved'. **1.** n. **a** A woman who is guilty of sexual immorality ; **b** a prostitute. **2.** vb. To indulge in fornication.
whoredom, n. [1. hórdum ; 2. hɔ́dəm]. Prec. & **-dom.** (obs.) Fornication.

whoremonger, n. [1. hórmùngger ; 2. hɔ́màŋgə]. (archaic) A fornicator.
whorl, n. [1. wěrl ; 2. wǎl]. M.E. *whorvil*, fr. stem of O.E. *hweorfan*, 'to turn', see **wharf,** & **-le**; cp. M. Du. *worvel*, 'spindle-whorl'. **1.** Disk used to balance or steady a spindle. **2.** (bot.) Group of petals, leaves, stamens &c. arranged in a circle about a point. **3.** (esp. zool.) Single turn of spiral (in shell &c.).
whorled, adj. [1. wěrld ; 2. wǎld]. Prec. & **-ed.** Having, arranged in, whorls.
whortleberry, n. [1. wěrtlberi ; 2. wǎtlbəri]. Earlier *hurtleberry*, possibly connected w. O.E. *horta*, 'bilberry'. Bilberry, whinberry.
whose, pron. [1. hōōz ; 2. hūz]. Possessive case of **who.**
whoso, pron. [1. hōōsō ; 2. hūsou]. **who** & **so.** (archaic) The person(s) that ; whoever.
whosoever, pron. [1. hōōsōéver ; 2. hùsouévə]. **who** & **so** & **ever.** (archaic) Whoso.
why (I.), adv. [1. wī ; 2. wai]. O.E. *hwī, hwȳ,* instrumental case of *hwā, hwæt*, 'who, what' ; see **who. 1.** (interrog.) For what reason ?, with what intent ?, on what grounds ?, wherefore ? : *why are you here?* ; *why do you think so?* ; *do you know why he was late?* ; *you say you are unhappy* ; *why?* Phr. *why so?*, for what reason, on what grounds ? **2.** (introducing dependent clause, with or without antecedent expressed) Because of which, by reason of which ; the reason for which : *tell us the reason why you came* ; *this is why I came.*
why (II.), n., fr. prec. The reason, cause, purpose, ground ; esp. in Phr. *the why and wherefore (of an action, situation* &c.).
why (III.), interj., fr. **why** (I.). Expressing surprise, protestation &c., or merely introducing a new idea : *what, going out? why, it's quite dark* ; *why, he told me he was only fifty* ; *why, it's nearly five o'clock.*
whydah. See **whidah-bird.**
wick (I.), n. [1. wik ; 2. wik]. O.E. *wice*, 'wick of lamp' &c., M.E. *wicke*, *wicke*, &c. ; cp. O.H.G. *wieche,* M. Du. *wieke*, 'wick' ; cogn. w. O.E. *wōciġ*, 'net, snare', & w. **wax** (I.). **a** Twisted strands of thread forming the centre of a wax candle or taper, and projecting beyond one end, which when lighted burn with a small flame until the wax is consumed ; **b** piece of woven material, flat, or in form of a tube, having one end immersed in the oil of a lamp, and the other end left in suitable position for lighting ; the incandescent and illuminating properties of such a wick are derived from the oil which it sucks up.
wick (II.), n. Prob. fr. O.N. *vīk*, 'creek, bay', w. sense fr. O.E. *wīc,* 'dwelling, village'. The word is prob. an early loan fr. Lat. *vīcus*, 'village, hamlet ', wh. is cogn. w. Gk. *oîkos*, 'house', see under **economy.** Village, place &c. Now obsolete except in compounds such as **bailiwick,** and in Place-Names ; *-wich,* in *Greenwich* &c., is from the O.E. word.
wicked, adj. [1. wíkid ; 2. wíkid]. M.E. *wikked*, fr. *wikke*, 'evil', & **-ed.** Cp. O.E. *wicće*, 'witch', see **witch** ; cogn. w. O.E. *wīcan*, 'to fall, grow feeble ' ; *wāc*, 'weak, pliant', see **weak. 1.** Evil, morally reprehensible ; sinful ; reverse of *good, virtuous, pious* ; **a** (of persons) deliberately thinking or practising what is evil ; habitually opposed to virtue, piety, justice ; vicious, depraved ; **b** (of thoughts and actions) springing from, inspired by, of the nature of, sin, depravity, vice. **2.** Mischievous ; playfully naughty, roguish.
wickedly, adv. Prec. & **-ly.** In a wicked manner.
wickedness, n. See prec. & **-ness. 1.** State of being wicked: *the wickedness of our hearts.* **2. a** Wicked thought or action : *to practise wickedness* ; **b** specific wicked act.
wicker, n. & adj. [1. wíker ; 2. wíkə]. Orig. sense, 'pliant rod, osier', fr. Scand. ; cp. Swed. dial. *vikker*, 'willow ', M. Swed. *wika*, 'to bend', cogn. w. O.E. *wīcan*, 'to grow feeble, fall', *wāc*, 'weak, pliant', see **wicked, weak. 1.** n. Fabric made of interwoven osiers, or other pliant stems ; used for baskets,

light furniture &c. **2.** adj. Made of wicker: *wicker tables* &c.
wickered, adj. [1. wíkerd ; 2. wíkəd]. Prec. & **-ed.** Made of or covered with wicker-work.
wicker-work, n. & adj. **1.** n. **a** Wickers wrought into a fabric ; **b** things made of this ; **c** act, art, of making such objects. **2.** adj. Made of wicker.
wicket, n. [1. wíkit ; 2. wíkit]. M.E. *wiket*, fr. A.-Fr. *wiket* ; of Gmc. origin, & prob. connected w. O.N. *vikja*, 'to move, turn'. **1.** Small door or gate, esp. one at side, or forming part of, larger one. **2.** Small opening, hatch, in wall, door &c. closed by sliding panel, grating &c. **3.** Half-door, barring lower half of doorway, as in stable &c. **4.** (cricket) **a** Group of three upright stumps with two bails, defended by batsman ; Phrs. *to take a wicket,* (of bowler) get batsman out ; *to keep wicket,* act as wicket-keeper, q.v. ; *two* &c. *wickets down,* two &c. batsmen out ; *to win by two* &c. *wickets,* with three batsmen still to be got out ; **b** state of pitch, chiefly in Phr. *a good, hard, dry, wicket* &c.
wicket-door, -gate, n. Same as **wicket, 1.**
wicket-keeper, n. Fieldsman standing immediately behind wicket for catching, stumping, and saving byes.
widdershins. Variant of **withershins.**
wide (I.), adj. [1. wid ; 2. waid]. O.E. *wīd* ; M.E. *wīde* ; O.S. *wīd* ; O.H.G. *wīt* ; O.N. *vīðr* ; prob. cogn. w. Lat. *(dī)videre*, 'to separate', see **divide. 1.** Of great or comparatively great extent from side to side ; broad : *a wide road, river, ribbon, ditch, skirt* &c. ; *wide margins* ; *a wide forehead* ; *the gate is not wide enough.* Phr. *to give a wide berth to,* avoid, keep out of the way of. **2.** Having specified measurement from side to side : *how wide is it?* ; *a foot wide.* **3. a** Of great extent; spacious, vast : *a wide expanse of desert* ; *the wide sea* ; *wide dominions* ; *the wide world,* whole world ; *wide intervals* ; **b** (i.) covering, occurring over, a wide area : *a wide distribution* ; (ii.) affecting a large circle of persons: *a wide appeal.* **4.** Striking, falling, being, at some distance from a specific point or object : *the bullet was wide of the mark, target* &c. ; *a wide ball,* at cricket ; (also fig.) *a remark, reply* &c. *wide of the mark,* irrelevant, not to the point ; *wide of the truth,* deviating from it. **5.** (in non-material sense) **a** Of extensive scope, range, and grasp : *wide knowledge* ; *scholarship* ; **b** (i.) not narrow or restricted ; catholic, liberal, comprehending many and different objects : *a man of wide interests, sympathies* &c. ; (ii.) far-seeing, taking large views : *wide vision* ; (iii.) broad, general ; reverse of *minute* and *specialized* : *education at the school stage should be wide and humane.*
wide (II.), adv., fr. prec. **1.** Widely, to a considerable extent, to a distance ; esp. in Phr. (*to search* &c.) *far and wide.* **2.** Extensively ; to full extent : *with eyes wide open* ; *open your mouth wide.* Phr. *to have one's eyes wide open,* (i.) to be alert, shrewd ; (ii.) to be fully alive to what is happening ; *to open one's mouth too wide,* (i.) to be greedy and grasping ; (ii.) to be too ambitious, undertake more than one can perform. **3.** Remotely, to a considerable distance from specific point : *to fall, shoot, wide of the mark* ; also, *to speak wide of the mark,* not to the point.
wide (III.), n., fr. **wide** (I.). (cricket) Also *wide ball,* one bowled so as to pass wicket out of reach of batsman, adding one run to score of latter's side.
wide-awake (I.), adj. [1. wíd awǎk ; 2. wáid əwéik]. **a** Thoroughly awake ; **b** alert, vigilant, wary.
wide-awake (II.), n. [1. wíd awǎk ; 2. wáid əwéik]. A soft felt hat with a broad, floppy brim and a low crown ; the name is now as obsolete as the hat to which it was applied.
widely, adv. [1. wídli ; 2. wáidli]. **wide** (I.) & **-ly. 1.** (referring to spatial conditions) **a** At wide intervals, so as to occur over a wide area : *widely scattered, distributed, over Europe* ; *widely separated* ; **b** so as to affect persons in

different parts of a wide area: *to appeal widely for support*; *widely known*. **2.** (referring to degree, extent, of diversity &c.): *widely unlike, different*; *to differ widely*, (i.) to have little or no resemblance; (ii.) to disagree considerably, hold quite different opinions.

widen, vb. trans. & intrans. [1. wídn; 2. wáidn]. **wide (I.) & -en. 1.** trans. To make wider, increase width, extent, scope, of; to broaden: **a** (in material sense) *to widen a ditch*; **b** (in non-material sense) *to widen one's outlook, one's intellectual horizon*. **2.** intrans. (in material and non-material senses) To become, grow, wider; to extend, expand.

widespread, adj. [1. wídspred; 2. wáidspred]. Having a wide distribution, extending over large area: *a widespread tendency, superstition* &c.; *to become less widespread*.

widgeon, n. [1. wíjun; 2. wídʒən], fr. O. Fr. *vigeon*, fr. Lat. *vipiōnem*, nom. *vipio*, 'kind of small crane', according to Pliny a Balearic word. A short-billed, short-legged migratory wild duck, *Mareca penelope*, the drake having a chestnut head and neck and light patch on forehead.

widish, adj. [1. wídish; 2. wáidiʃ]. **wide (I.) & -ish.** Somewhat wide.

widow (I.), n. [1. wídō; 2. wídou]. O.E. *widwe*; M.E. *wídewe*; cp. Mod. Germ. *witwe*; O.S. *widowa*; Goth. *widuwō*; cogn. w. Lat. *vidua*; Scrt. *vidhávā*; O. Slav. *vidova*; O. Prussian *widdewū*, 'widow'; cp. further Gk. (ē)ítheos, 'unmarried'; Lat. (di)videre; see **divide** & words there referred to. Woman whose husband has died, and who remains unmarried. Phrs. *grass widow*, woman temporarily separated from her husband; *widow's peak*, hair growing downwards in a point, at centre of forehead; *widow's weeds*, see **weeds**; *widow's cruse, mite*, see **cruse, mite (I.)**; *widow's cap*, one made of lawn and with long streamers behind.

widow (II.), vb. trans., fr. prec. **1.** To make a widow or widower, bereave of husband or wife; esp. in P.P.: *widowed by war*; *thrice-widowed*. **2.** (fig., chiefly poet.) To deprive, bereave, esp. by death or disaster: '*a dying king, Laid widow'd of the power in his eye*' (Tennyson, 'Passing of Arthur').

widow-bird. See **whidah-bird.**

widower, n. [1. wídōer; 2. wídouə]. **widow (I.) & -er.** Man whose wife has died, and who has remained unmarried.

widowhood, n. [1. wídōhòod; 2. wídouhùd]. **widow (I.) & -hood.** Condition of being a widow.

widow woman, n. (Bib., colloq. and facet.) A widow.

width, n. [1. width; 2. widþ]. **wide (I.) & -th**; not in O.E.; new formation on anal. of **length. 1.** (material and non-material senses) State or quality of being wide: *a river of considerable width; width of mind*. **2.** Measurement from side to side: *to have a width of four feet*. **3.** Piece of material of full width as manufactured: *to join two widths*.

wield, vb. trans. [1. wēld; 2. wiəld]. Formally, most prob. fr. O.E. (ġe-)wěldan, 'to subdue, dominate', but the meaning is derived fr. the cogn. O.E. *wealdan*, 'to have control over'; to wield (a weapon), to rule, govern'; (the Mod. form can be explained, however, as derived either fr. a Sthn. variant of this, or on the anal. of the mutated 3rd pers. sing. pres.). Both vbs. are formed fr. O.E. *weald*, 'power'; cp. O.S. *waldan*; O.H.G. *waltan*, 'to govern'; Goth. *waldan*; cogn. w. Lat. *valēre*, 'to be strong' &c., q.v. under **valiant. 1. a** To have control or power over; chiefly in Phr. *to wield the sceptre, to rule as king*; **b** to have at one's command: *to wield influence*. **2.** To handle, make use of (some implement or weapon grasped by the hands): *to wield a sword, an axe, a flail* &c.; Phr. *to wield the pen*, to write.

wife, n. [1. wíf; 2. waif]. O.E., M.E. *wíf*, 'woman, wife'; cp. O.S. *wīf*; O.H.G. *wīb*; O.N. *víf*. Etymol. unknown. **1.** Married woman, spouse: *husband and wife*; *a man and his wife*; *his lawful, wedded, wife*; *she has been a good wife to him*. Phrs. *to have a wife*, be married; *to take (a woman) to wife*, to marry her. **2.** (archaic) A woman; esp. *an old wife*, a feeble old woman of humble rank. Phr. *old wives' tale*, a foolish, fantastic story, told and believed by the credulous.

wifehood, n. [1. wífhood; 2. wáifhud]. Prec. **& -hood.** Condition of being a wife.

wifeless, adj. [1. wífles; 2. wáiflis]. **wife & -less.** Without a wife.

wifelike, adj. [1. wífīk; 2. wáiflaik]. **wife & -like.** a Like a wife; **b** suitable, appropriate, for a wife; **c** appertaining to a wife.

wifely, adj. [1. wífli; 2. wáifli]. **wife & -ly.** Wifelike.

wig (I.), n. [1. wig; 2. wig]. Abbr. fr. **periwig. 1.** A covering for the head, made of hair; **a** head-dress of human hair, worn by the bald, or by actors &c., made to imitate naturally-growing hair; **b** head-dress of horse hair, made in various forms, worn in 17th and 18th cents. as a fashionable ornament; similar head-dress still worn in court &c. by judges and counsel. Phr. *wigs on the green*, (i.) a rough, hand-to-hand fight; (ii.) a heated public altercation or dispute. **2.** (facet. and colloq.) A natural head of hair: *you had better brush your untidy wig*.

wig (II.), vb. trans. Perh. orig. in physical sense, fr. idea of striking person on the head, knocking his wig off &c.; cp. somewhat similar transference of meaning in such vbs. as *to jacket, dress down,* & Phrs. *comb his hair, dust his jacket for him* &c. (slang) To blame severely, take to task; to rate, scold.

wigan, n. [1. wígan; 2. wígən], fr. name of town in S. Lancashire. Kind of stiff canvas used for stiffening hems of garments, collars &c.

wig-block, n. Round block, shaped more or less like a human head, used to hold wigs while being combed &c.

wigged, adj. [1. wigd; 2. wigd]. **wig (I.) & -ed.** Having, wearing, a wig.

wigging, n. [1. wíging; 2. wígin]. **wig (II.) & -ing.** (slang) **a** Severe scolding, a rating; a dressing-down.

wiggle, vb. trans. & intrans. [1. wigl; 2. wigl]. Variant of **waggle**, or blend of this & **wriggle**. (colloq.) **1.** trans. To cause to move with a slight but rapid movement: *to wiggle one's little finger*. **2.** intrans. To make slight, jerky, nervous movements; to wriggle.

wight, n. [1. wīt; 2. wait]. O.E. *wiht*, 'creature, thing'; see **whit (I.)**. (archaic or facet.) Creature, person, human being: *a luckless wight*.

wigless, adj. [1. wígles; 2. wíglis]. **wig (I.) & -less.** Without a wig.

wig-maker, n. Tradesman who makes and sells wigs and deals in human hair.

wigwam, n. [1. wígwam, -wom; 2. wígwæm, -wom] fr. N. Am. Indian *weekuwom*. N. American Indian's roughly made, conical tent of poles hung with bark, hides &c.

wild (I.), adj. [1. wild; 2. waild]. O.E. *wilde*, M.E. *wilde*, 'wild, savage, uncultivated'; cp. O.S. *wilde*; O.H.G. *wildi*; O.N. *villr*; Goth. *wilþeis*, 'wild'. Further etymol. doubtful. **1. a** (of birds, beasts &c.) Living in original, natural state; not domesticated, not in subjection to man; contrasted with *tame*: *wild animals*; Phr. *to be drawn by wild horses*, form of torture; **b** easily startled, shy: *the deer are very wild*. **2.** (of plants &c.) Uncultivated, not planted or tended by man; growing naturally: *wild roses, cherries* &c. Phrs. *to run wild*, (i.) grow without training or cultivation; (ii.) (fig. of persons) to grow up without due control; *to sow one's wild oats*, to indulge in those follies and dissipations supposed to be natural to youth. **3.** (of man) Uncivilized, savage, in a primitive state of culture. **4.** (of land) Left in, or having reverted to, natural, uncultivated and uninhabited state: *wild mountain regions*; *a wild and desolate country*. **5.** Disarranged, disturbed, disordered: *wild hair, attire* &c.; *in a state of wild confusion*. **6.** Dissipated; fond of riotous, extravagant, wanton pleasure and excitement; reverse of *steady, sedate*: *rather wild as a young man*. **7.** Disturbed, violently agitated, tumultuous, turbulent, stormy, boisterous: *a wild sea*; *a wild night*; *wild cheers*. **8.** In a condition of mental excitement or disturbance, roused to a state of enthusiasm or frenzy, distracted; **a** excited by joy, desire &c.: *they are wild to go*; *wild with delight*; *wild excitement*; Phr. *to be wild about* (person, cause &c.), intensely devoted to; **b** mentally deranged, crazy, frantic: *he has a wild look*; *wild laughter*; Phr. *to drive wild*, to render, distracted; **c** (colloq.) very angry: *it made me wild to listen to such nonsense*. **9.** Rash, ill-advised; reckless; ill-aimed; done or said at random: *wild talk, accusation, shooting*; *wild schemes*.

wild (II.), adv., fr. prec. Wildly, esp. without care, consideration, or proper aim: *to shoot wild*.

wild (III.), n., fr. **wild (I.)**. **a** Land in natural, uncultivated state; wilderness: '*Till from the garden and the wild A fresh association blow*' (Tennyson, 'In Mem.' ci. 5); **b** remote, savage, uncivilized country: *the wilds of Africa*; *the call of the wild*.

wild-boar, n. Kind of pig, *Sus scrofa*, still found wild in parts of Europe, from which domesticated swine have descended.

wild-cat, n. **1.** Large, very fierce, undomesticated cat found in N. Scotland and other parts of Europe &c. **2.** (attrib.) In Phr. *wild-cat schemes*, fantastic, visionary, impracticable schemes.

wild-duck, n. One of various kinds of wild, freshwater ducks.

wildebeest, n. [1. wéldebàst; 2. wíldəbèist]. S. Afr. Du.; see **wild (I.) & beast.** Variety of large antelope; gnu.

wilder, vb. trans. [1. wílder; 2. wíldə]. Prob. abbr. fr. **bewilder**. (poet.) To mislead, bewilder, perplex.

wilderness, n. [1. wíldernes; 2. wíldənis], fr. M.E. *wildern*, 'desert', fr. O.E. *wildēor*, *wilder*, 'wild beast', fr. *wilde*, 'wild', see **wild (I.)**, & *dēor*, 'animal', see **deer**, & **-ness**. **1.** Uncultivated, sometimes barren, region, wholly or for the most part uninhabited; desert; specif., that region in which the children of Israel wandered forty years before reaching the Promised Land. **2.** Vast, desolate expanse of land or water: *a wilderness of waters*. Phr. *a wilderness of streets, houses*, long, monotonous series of dull, squalid streets or houses. **3.** Part of garden allowed to grow naturally, without cultivation.

wildfire, n. [1. wíldfīr; 2. wáildfàiə]. **1.** Combustible, highly inflammable compound, formerly used to set fire to hostile ships &c.; Greek fire. Chiefly in Phr. *to spread like wildfire*, very rapidly. **2.** Phosphorescent light, e.g. St. Elmo's fire.

wild-fowl, n. Wild birds hunted as game.

wild-goose, n. Undomesticated goose. Phr. *a wild-goose chase*, a futile enterprise; search for something which can never be found, or which has no existence.

wilding, n. [1. wílding; 2. wáildiŋ]. **wild (I.) & -ing. 1.** Uncultivated plant, esp. among cultivated plants, or one that has sprung naturally from originally cultivated stock. **2.** Fruit of such a plant.

wildish, adj. [1. wíldish; 2. wáildiʃ]. **wild (I.) & -ish.** Somewhat, inclined to be, wild.

wildly, adv. [1. wíldli; 2. wáildli]. **wild (I.) & -ly.** In a wild manner.

wildness, n. [1. wíldnes; 2. wáildnis]. **wild (I.) & -ness. a** State or quality of being wild (in various senses of adj.); **b** wild, dissipated conduct or habits: *wildnesses of youth*.

wild-wood, n. Natural forest-land.

wile, n. & vb. trans. [1. wīl; 2. wail]. O.E. *wīl*; M.E. *wíle*, 'trick'; etymol. doubtful. **1.** n. (usually pl.) Means of enticing, persuading, or cajoling; cunning stratagem, ruse, craft: *to* *defeat the wiles of the devil.* **2.** vb. **a** To entice, lure, mislead; **b** in Phr. *to wile away the time,* to spend it pleasantly; confused with **while (II.)**.

wilful, adj. [1. wílfool; 2. wílful]. **will (I.)** & **-ful.** **1.** (of person or character) Obstinately and perversely determined to have one's own way; headstrong, stubborn, wayward; capricious. **2.** (of action) Springing from deliberate intention; premeditated; not the result of sudden passion or of accident: *wilful waste, destruction*; specif., *wilful murder.*

wilfully, adv. Prec. & **-ly.** In a wilful manner.

wilfulness, n. See prec. & **-ness.** **a** Quality of being wilful; **b** wilful conduct.

wilily, adv. [1. wílili; 2. wáilili]. **wily** & **-ly.** In a wily manner.

wiliness, n. [1. wílines; 2. wáilinis]. **wily** & **-ness.** State or quality of being wily; craft, cunning.

will (I.), n. [1. wil; 2. wil]. O.E. *willa,* 'will', see **will (II.)**. **1.** Faculty of controlling one's thoughts and actions, of determining and directing the activities of mind or body; cp. *volition*: *freedom of the will.* **2.** Power of imposing one's influence and controlling force on oneself or others; strength of will: *a strong will; he has no will of his own.* **3.** Energy directed to a particular end; enthusiasm in action: *to work with a will.* **4.** Definite intention, determined course of action: *where there's a will there's a way; against one's will; to take the will for the deed.* **5.** Disposition, feelings towards others; now chiefly in compounds: *good-, ill-will.* **6.** That which one wills; purpose, intention: *God's will be done; to work one's will, have one's will.* **7.** Personal right of action; discretion; esp. in Phr. *at will,* when and how one pleases; *tenant at will,* liable to be dispossessed without notice. **8.** Legal document by which a person makes disposition of his property, taking effect after his death: *one's last will and testament; to make, draw up, a will.*

will (II.), vb. trans. & intrans. O.E. *willan*; M.E. *willen,* 'to desire, wish'; cp. O.S. *willian*; O.H.G. *wellan*; O.N. *vilja*; Goth. *wiljan,* 'will'; cogn. w. Goth. *waljan*; O.H.G. *wellan,* 'to choose'; Goth. *wilja,* O.E. *willa,* 'will', n.; O.H.G. *wala,* 'choice'; cogn. w. Lat. *velle,* 'to wish'; *voluptas,* 'pleasure', see **voluptuous** & **volition**; Gk. *elpís,* 'hope'; Scrt. *varaṇam,* 'choice'; *vṛṇīté,* 'chooses, prefers'; Lith. *vēlyju,* 'to wish'; *viltis,* 'hope'; O. Slav. *volją,* 'will', vb. **A.** trans. **1.** To be desirous of, wish, be anxious or eager for: (archaic) *what would you? let him do what he will; would that he were come; I would to heaven I had stayed.* **2.** To resolve, decide, upon (action &c.) by exercise of the will; make choice of: *whatever he wills he may accomplish.* **3.** To control (person &c.) by means of the will, exercise power over: *to will oneself to fall asleep; to will a person to look at one.* **B.** intrans. To be desirous, anxious, or eager; to exercise the will: *it must be as God wills; they had to obey, whether they would or not.*

will (III.), auxil. vb., fr. prec. The auxil. is usually unstressed & is then, in ordinary speech, reduced to [l], written *'ll.* When it follows a personal pron. *will* ceases to be syllabic, & is attached as a final consonant to the preceding syll., *i.e.* the pron.: *I'll, he'll, she'll, we'll, you'll, they'll* = [ail, hīl, jūl, ðeil] &c. After words ending in voiceless consonants *'ll,* [l] has force of a syll.: *this'll, what'll* &c. After words ending in voiced consonants *'ll* is sounded [əl]: *Jones'll come* = [džóunzəl kàm], *the king'll be pleased* = [ðə kiŋəl bi plīzd]. *Will* only retains its full form in natural, rapid speech (1) when strongly stressed, & this only happens when the idea, or function, expressed by the *will* is emphasized: *if he says that he'll come, he will* = [*if* (h)i séz ðət hīl kám, hi wíl], *boys will be boys* = [bóiz wíl bi bóiz], & so on; (2) initially, in interrog. sentences, even when the stress is weak: *will he come, do you think?* **1.** (expressing future pure and simple) *You never know what he'll do next; we'll be there in good time; you'll hurt yourself if you're not careful; what'll be the end of it all?* **2.** (i.) (expressing a certain degree of purpose and intention alongside of futurity) *I'll certainly go and see him if you like; I'll be a good boy for the future*; (ii.) (expressing firm resolution; strongly stressed) *I will be obeyed; he will have his joke.* **3.** (expressing habitual or repeated action) *There he'll sit hour after hour without saying a word.* **4.** (expressing natural process or action, inevitability) *Boys will be boys; accidents will happen.* **5.** (expressing inference, expectation that the facts will turn out to be as stated) *This'll be our train, I fancy; I suppose she would be about 40 when she died.* (For negative constructions with **will**, see **won't.**)

will (IV.), vb. trans., fr. **will (I.)**, 8. **a** To devise, bequeath, by means of a will, leave as legacy: *to will one's property away from one's natural heirs*; **b** to bequeath property &c. to.

-willed, adj. [1. wild; 2. wild]. **will (I.)** & **-ed.** Having a will of specific quality: *strong-, weak-willed* &c.

willet, n. [1. wílet; 2. wílit]. Imitative. Large N. American sandpiper.

willing, adj. [1. wíling; 2. wíliŋ]. **will (II.)** & **-ing.** **1.** Favourably disposed, inclined (for action); desirous, eager (to do something): '*Willing to wound, and yet afraid to strike*' (Pope, 'Epist. to Arbuthnot', 203); *if you would like me to intervene, I'm quite willing.* **2. a** (of living beings) Ready and eager to help, or to perform tasks proposed or allotted; serviceable: *a willing guide, heart; a willing horse; he doesn't know his job very well, but he's willing and obliging*; **b** (of services, actions) rendered, performed, offered, willingly.

willingly, adv. Prec. & **-ly.** In a willing manner; gladly, readily.

willingness, n. See prec. & **-ness.** Quality of being willing.

will-less, adj. [1. willes; 2. wíllis]. **will (I.)** & **-less.** Without will-power, wanting in volition.

will-o'-the-wisp, n. [1. wíl o dhe wísp; 2. wíl ə ðə wísp], fr. personal name *Will,* & **wisp** in sense of 'bundle of tow, straw &c., used as torch'. Ignis fatuus.

willow (I.), n. [1. wílō; 2. wílou]. O.E. *wiliġ, weliġ*; M.E. *wilghe, wilwe*; cp. M. Du. *wilghe*; cogn. w. Gk. *helikē,* 'willow', for **welik-*; Scrt. *válšaš,* 'shoot, pliant twig'; fr. base **wel-, *wol-,* 'to turn'; see **well (I.)**, **wallow**, **volute** &c. **1.** Any tree or shrub of the genus *Salix,* many species of which are found in the Northern hemisphere, esp. in watery ground; most species have slender, pliant branches, and some yield strong timber, used for cricket-bats &c.; *weeping willow,* kind with long, drooping branches. Phr. *to wear the willow,* as symbol of mourning. **2.** A cricket-bat, as made of willow wood: *to wield the willow,* to bat.

willow (II.), vb. trans. & n., fr. prec., fr. use of willow branches for beating fibre. **1.** vb. To clean (fibres) by beating in a machine. **2.** n. Also *willowing-machine,* machine with revolving spikes for cleaning fibre.

willow-herb, n. Any of many species of herb, *Epilobium,* some tall, with pale, pinkish-purple flowers and long leaves like those of willow.

willow-pattern, n. **a** Chinese design for china, with pagodas, a river, willow trees, a bridge upon which are three persons, and two birds flying overhead, usually printed or painted in blue on white ground; **b** china bearing this design.

willow-warbler, n. Bird resembling chiff-chaff.

willow-wren, n. Small bird belonging to the warblers.

willowy, adj. [1. wílōi; 2. wíloui]. **willow (I.)** & **-y.** **1.** Abounding in willows. **2.** Slender, supple, and graceful: *a willowy figure.*

will-power, n. Strength of will, ability to control, endure, determine course of events &c.

will-worship, n. (archaic) Self-invented, arbitrary, form of religion.

willy nilly, adv. [1. wíli níli; 2. wíli níli]. Variant of *will I* or *he, nill I* or *he*; see **will (II.)** & **nill.** Whether one will or not; inevitably, of necessity.

wilt (I.), vb. [1. wilt; 2. wilt]. 2nd pers. sing. pres. of **will (II.)**.

wilt (II.), vb. intrans. & trans. Etymol. doubtful; possibly connected w. **welk.** **1.** intrans. (of plant &c.) To lose freshness and strength; to fade, droop. **2.** trans. To cause to fade, droop; to wither.

Wilton, n. [1. wíltun; 2. wíltən], fr. town in Wiltshire. Also *Wilton carpet,* kind of Brussels carpet with cut pile, made at, or similar to those made at, Wilton, formerly made at Axminster.

wily, adj. [1. wíli; 2. wáili]. **wile** & **-y.** Full of, characterized by, wiles; artful, crafty, cunning.

wimple, n. [1. wímpl; 2. wímpl]. O.E., M.E. *wimpel,* 'neck-covering, cloak'; cp. M. Du. *wimpel,* 'streamer'; O.N. *vimpill*; O.H.G. *wimpal,* 'veil'; cp. further M.H.G. *wīfen,* 'to swing'; O.H.G. *wipf,* 'swing'; cogn. w. Lat. *vibrāre,* 'to swing, vibrate'; Lith. *wỹburiu,* 'to wave'; see **vibrate**; cp. **whip (II.)**. Cloth of linen, silk &c. folded about head so as to expose the face; now worn in W. Europe only by nuns.

wimpled, adj. [1. wímpld; 2. wímpld]. Prec. & **-ed.** Wearing a wimple.

win (I.), vb. trans. & intrans. [1. win; 2. win]. O.E. *winnan,* 'to toil, suffer, fight'; *ġewinnan,* 'to gain, conquer'; M.E. *winnen,* 'to strive; to win'; cp. O.S., O.H.G. *winnan*; O.N. *vinna*; O.H.G. *giwinnan,* 'to strive after'; cogn. w. Scrt. *vánati,* 'wishes, desires; fights for, wins'; *vánaš,* 'desire'; Lat. *venus,* 'love', see **Venus**; fr. base **wen-,* 'to wish'; see also **wont, winsome, wish.** **A.** trans. **1. a** To gain, obtain, acquire, by effort, esp. in competition, against opposition &c.: *to win a prize, the victory, a laurel wreath, honour, a lady's hand, golden opinions* &c.; Phrs. *to win one's spurs,* (i.) (hist.) achieve knighthood by valiant service; hence (ii.) to do something which proves one's real value; *to win ore,* extract it from mine; **b** to reach, arrive at, with effort: *to win the shore, the mountain-top* &c. Phr. *to win one's way,* (chiefly fig.) to succeed in life, a career &c. by dint of effort. **2.** To achieve victory in: *to win a race, battle, game* &c. Phr. *to win the day, field,* be victorious. **3.** To gain: *to win all hearts; he won the jury over to his side.* **B.** intrans. **1.** To win a contest, fight, game, race &c.; be victorious, prevail: *he is sure to win; may the best man win; to win by a length, a head, a neck.* Phrs. *to win hands down,* (colloq.) to be easily successful. **2.** *Win clear, win out, win through,* to come, get, through or out, to escape, with difficulty.

win (II.), n., fr. prec. Act of winning; victory, success in a contest: *to celebrate a win; another win for Lancashire.*

wince, vb. intrans. & n. [1. wins; 2. wins]. M.E. *winc(h)en,* 'to kick out; to start; to draw back'; cp. O. Fr. *guenchir, guincir,* fr. O.S. *wenkien*; cogn. w. O.H.G. *wanchōn,* 'to draw back'; O.H.G. *wanchal*; O.E. *wancol,* 'unstable', see **wench**; O.H.G. *winkan,* 'to move sideways, start; wink'; O.E. *wincian,* 'to wink, nod', see **wink**; cogn. w. Lat. *vagāri,* 'to wander', see **vagary.** **1.** vb. To start or draw back suddenly, to shrink away; to show sensitiveness to sudden bodily or moral pain or shock; to flinch: *to wince under the blows; to bear pain without wincing; brutal, vulgar jests make her wince.* Phr. *let the galled jade wince,* let him who considers that an insult &c. is levelled at him resent it. **2.** n. Involuntary movement, recoil, shrinking, caused by mental or physical pain.

wincey, n. [1. wínsi; 2. wínsi]. Perh. coined fr. *woolsey and linsey.* Strong cotton and wool fabric.

winch, n. [1. winch; 2. wintʃ]. O.E. *wince*, 'pulley'; M.E. *winche*, 'winch, windlass'; cogn. w. Lith. *vingis*, 'bow, curve'; Scrt. *vángati*, 'limps'; Lat. *vagāri*, 'to wander', see **vagary**; cp. further O.E. *wincian*, 'to nod, wink', see **wink**; *wancol*, 'unstable', see **wench**. 1. Windlass, esp. with revolving drum worked by a crank. 2. Crank for use as a handle.

Winchester, n. [1. wínchester; 2. wíntʃistə], fr. place-name in U.S.A. Kind of repeating rifle.

wind (I.), n. [1. wind; 2. waind]. Pronounced [wind; waind] to end of 18th cent., & still often so rhymed by poets. Cp. **wind** (III.). O.E., M.E. *wīnd*; cp. Goth. *winds*; O.S. *wind*; O.H.G. *wint*; O.N. *vindr*, 'wind'; cogn. w. Lat. *ventus*, see **ventilate**; W. *gwynt*; cp. further O.E. *wedar*, see **weather**; O. Prussian *wetro*, 'wind'; O. Slav. *vedro*, 'good weather'; Scrt. *vāti*, 'blows'; *vāyúš*, 'wind, air'; O. Slav. *vějati*; O.H.G. *wājan*; O.E. *wāwan*, 'to blow'; Gk. *áēmi*, 'I blow'; *aētēs*, 'wind'; *āēr*, 'air', fr. *awē-, see **air**. 1. Air set in motion by natural causes, esp. when moving rapidly enough to be perceptible: *a gentle, strong, hot, cold, wind*; *favourable, variable, winds*; *a wet wind*, one bringing rain; *contrary, fair, winds*, unfavourable, favourable, to navigation &c.; *constant winds*, blowing always in same direction over specific area; *periodical winds*, those changing their direction at specific periods; *north, west, S.E., wind* &c., blowing from specified direction; *the wind rises, falls*, becomes stronger, weaker; *(to) the four winds*, to all points of the compass, broadcast; *a capful of wind*, small gust; *against the wind, in the wind's eye, in the teeth of the wind*, towards the direction from which the wind is blowing; *between wind and water*, (i.) line where surface of water meets vessel's hull; (ii.) (fig.) part of human body between the thorax and the abdomen: *hit between wind and water*; *by the wind*, (naut.) close-hauled; *down wind, before the wind*, in the direction of, carried along by, the wind; *(to know, find out, see) how the wind blows, lies*, what direction affairs are taking, tendency of public opinion &c.; *in the wind*, in process of development, discussion &c., esp. secretly: *what's in the wind?, there's something in the wind*; *to cast (prudence, one's reputation &c.) to the winds*, act without consideration for it; *to get, have, the wind of*, have advantage over, be in more favourable position; *to go, run &c. like the wind*, very fast; *to raise the wind* (slang), raise funds; *to sail close to the wind*, (fig.) to verge on dishonesty, illegality, impropriety &c.; *to take the wind out of one's sails*, render action of abortive by anticipating and counteracting it. Phrs. *To put the wind up* (person), to frighten; *get the wind up*, be frightened (army slang). 2. Air set in motion by artificial, mechanical, means &c.: *the wind from the bellows*; *the wind of the passing train*. 3. a Scent borne by the wind; (hence fig.) b rumour, hint: *to get wind of*, hear as rumour &c. 4. Gas produced in stomach or bowels by acidity, indigestion &c.; flatulence. 5. a Breath; regularity or force of breathing, lung power: *to lose, get, one's wind*; *sound in wind and limb*; *broken wind*, impaired breathing (esp. of horse); *second wind*, regularity of breathing regained during violent exercise after first breathlessness; b part of body below diaphragm, blow on which temporarily checks breathing: *to hit one in the wind*. 6. Empty talk, purposeless or extravagant use of words. 7. (mus.) Wind-instruments in an orchestra; contrasted with strings: *brass wind*, trumpets &c.; *wood-wind*, flutes &c.

wind (II.), vb. trans., fr. prec. 1. To scent, detect by scent: *the hounds winded the quarry*. 2. To exhaust the breath of, cause to breathe with an effort: *to be winded by running*. 3. To recover the wind of, give opportunity of getting breath to: *to stop in order to wind the horses*.

wind (III.), vb. trans. [1. wīnd; 2. waind], fr. **wind** (I.). 1. To sound a call or signal on (horn, bugle &c.). 2. To sound, produce, on wind-instrument: *to wind a call &c.*

wind (IV.), vb. intrans. & trans. [1. wīnd; 2. waind]. O.E. *wīndan*; M.E. *wīnden*, 'to wind; to go, circle round'; cp. O.S. *wīndan*; O.H.G. *wintan*; O.N. *vinda*; Goth. *windan*, 'to wind, turn, twist'; cp. further Goth. *wandjan*; O.E. *wenden*, 'to turn', see **wend** (I.); Goth. *wandus*; O.N. *vǫndr*, 'supple rod', see **wand**. A. intrans. 1. a (of series or line of moving beings) To go, pass along: 'The lowing herd winds slowly o'er the lea' (Gray's 'Elegy'); b to pass by a curving, tortuous course: 'And as the boat-head wound along The willowy hills and fields among' (Tennyson, 'Lady of Shalott'). 2. a (of road, stream, course) To run, flow, lead, in bends and twistings; b (of stairway) to pass upwards or downwards in spirals round a central structure. 3. *Wind round*, (of a serpent, climbing plant &c.) to coil, twine, round. B. trans. 1. a (i.) To turn, cause to revolve: *to wind a handle*; (ii.) to raise, draw up, by winding: *to wind a bucket, water, from a well*; b to start mechanism of by winding; (i.) to tighten spring of (watch or clock) by turning a key; (ii.) to raise weights of (certain kinds of clock) by turning a handle. 2. To form into a ball by a series of circular movements, by coiling up evenly on itself, or round something as a basis: *to wind wool*; *to wind thread on to a reel, a line on to a stick &c*. Phr. *to (be able to) wind a person round one's little finger*, bend him to one's will, make him do what one pleases. 3. To enfold with, wrap round, twine round: *to wind one's arms round a person's neck*; *wind a shawl round a baby, a baby in a shawl &c*. 4. To wind one's way, to pursue one's course, esp. deliberately, cautiously. C. Followed by adverbs & preps. *Wind off*, trans., to remove by unwinding, uncoiling: *to wind cotton off a reel*. *Wind up*, 1. trans., a to coil round and round, form into a ball: *to wind up wool, string &c.*; b to recoil, or increase tightness of spring to fullest extent, in order to set, or keep, going: *to wind up a watch*; c to increase intensity of feeling of: *wound up to a high pitch of excitement*; d to bring to an end, terminate, conclude: *to wind up a speech by a quotation*; *the Chancellor wound up the debate*; *to wind up a company, dissolve it*; 2. intrans., (of person) to stop, conclude: *I hope this tedious speaker will soon wind up*; (of trading company) to go into liquidation.

wind (V.), n., fr. prec. 1. Act of winding; turn of handle, crank &c.; single turn in winding wool &c. 2. Bend, curve, turn, twist; winding: *the winds of a path, stream &c*.

windage, n. [1. wíndij; 2. wíndidʒ]. **wind** (I.) & -age. 1. a Amount of deviation of projectile from its normal course owing to wind; b allowance for such deflection made in aiming. 2. Difference between diameter of projectile and that of bore of gun from which it is discharged.

windbag, n. [1. wíndbag; 2. wíndbæg]. (slang) A person who talks much but says little; one who utters platitudes in a high-flown, verbose style.

wind-bound, adj. Delayed by contrary winds.

wind-break, n. Fence, hedge &c. breaking force of wind.

wind-chest, n. Box in organ from which compressed air is supplied to the pipes.

wind-colic, n. Pain due to flatulence.

wind-cutter, n. Upper lip of mouth of organ pipe.

wind-egg, n. a Imperfect egg with very thin shell; b unfertilized egg.

winder, n. [1. wínder; 2. wáində]. **wind** (II.) & -er. One who, that which, winds; esp. a mechanical apparatus for winding thread &c.

windfall, n. [1. wíndfawl; 2. wíndfɔl]. 1. Fruit blown down by wind. 2. Unexpected piece of good luck; specif., unanticipated legacy or sum of money received.

wind-fanner, n. Windhover.

windflower, n. [1. wíndflòuer; 2. wíndflàuə]. Wood anemone.

wind-gall, n. Soft swelling on horse's fetlock.

wind-gauge, n. 1. Instrument for measuring force of wind. 2. Indicator showing amount of air in wind-chest of organ. 3. Device fixed on gun indicating force of wind and allowance to be made for windage.

windhover, n. [1. wínd-hòver; 2. wíndhòvə]. Kestrel.

windily, adv. [1. wíndili; 2. wíndili]. **windy** & -ly. In a windy manner.

windiness, n. [1. wíndines; 2. wíndinis]. **windy** & -ness. State or quality of being windy.

winding (I.), adj. [1. wínding; 2. wáindiŋ], fr. Pres. Part. of **wind** (IV.). Tending to wind; having numerous turns and twists, constantly curving in a different direction: *a winding stream, path, passage &c.*; *a winding staircase*, one built in a spiral.

winding (II.), n. **wind** (IV.) & -ing. a Twist, turn, curve, bend, of winding course; coil, spiral, of coiled object; esp. b (pl.) *windings*, series of bends or curves of stream, road &c.

windingly, adv. [1. wíndingli; 2. wáindiŋli]. **winding** (I.) & -ly. With many windings.

winding-sheet, n. Sheet used to wrap a corpse; a shroud.

winding-up, n. a Act or process of concluding; state of being concluded; termination; specif. b liquidation of a company.

wind-instrument, n. Musical instrument, the notes of which are produced by air, esp. by breath.

wind-jammer, n. [1. wínd jàmer; 2. wínd dʒæmə]. Large, swift sailing ship.

windlass, n. & vb. trans. [1. wíndlas; 2. wíndləs]. M.E. *windelas*, prob. fr. A.-Fr. *windas*, fr. O.N. *vindáss*, fr. *vinda*, 'to wind', fr. base in **wind** (IV.), & *áss*, 'beam, pillar'; cp. Goth. *ans*, 'beam'; cogn. w. Gk. *ánios*, 'burdensome'; *anía*, 'trouble'; & prob. w. Lat. *onus*, 'burden', see **onus**. 1. n. Apparatus for hoisting or hauling by means of a rope or wire wound on to a horizontal drum &c. 2. vb. To hoist by means of a windlass.

windless, adj. [1. wíndles; 2. wíndlis]. **wind** (I.) & -less. Without wind; still, calm: *a windless day*.

windlestraw, n. [1. wíndlstraw; 2. wíndlstrɔ]. O.E. *windelstrēaw*, fr. *windel*, 'twisting', fr. **wind** (IV.) & **straw** (I.). Dry, withered grass-stalk.

windmill, n. [1. wín(d)mil; 2. wín(d)mil]. 1. Mill for grinding corn turned by the pressure of the wind upon the sails. 2. Any apparatus resembling the sails of a windmill which, when made to revolve by wind pressure, performs certain work, esp. that of pumping water.

window, n. [1. wíndō; 2. wíndou]. M.E. *windohe, windowe*, fr. O.N. *vindauga*; see **wind** (I.) & **eye**. Opening in the wall or roof of a building to admit light, usually filled with panes of glass fixed in a movable frame; similar glazed opening in a closed vehicle; *to break a window*, break one or more panes of glass in a window.

window-box, n. 1. Hollow recess in a window-frame in which the sash-weight moves. 2. Box on window-sill for growing plants.

window-dressing, n. Art of arranging goods in shop-window.

windowed, adj. [1. wíndōd; 2. wíndoud]. **window** & -ed. Having, furnished with, windows.

windowless, adj. [1. wíndōles; 2. wíndoulis]. **window** & -less. Without windows.

window-pane, n. Pane of glass in a window.

window-seat, n. Broad seat fitted below a window, so adapted that a person using it can see out.

windpipe, n. [1. wíndpīp; 2. wíndpaip]. Air-passage between mouth and lungs; trachea.

windrow, n. [1. wíndrō; 2. wíndrou]. Line of hay raked into a low ridge after cutting, and left to dry before putting into cocks.

wind-sail, n. Canvas funnel or tube for ventilating ship's hold &c.

2 E

wind-screen, n. Transparent plate of glass &c. to shelter driver of motor &c. from wind.

Windsor, n. [1. wíndzer; 2. wíndzə], fr. Windsor in Berkshire, where is the royal palace of Windsor Castle. *The House and Family of Windsor*, the style, adopted 1917, of the reigning dynasty of Great Britain and Ireland; *Windsor chair*, wooden chair with curving back and sides; *Windsor soap*, also *brown Windsor*, kind of cheap brown, scented toilet soap; *Windsor uniform*, uniform worn, at Windsor Castle only, by members of the royal family and certain officers of the Household, consisting of a dark blue evening-dress coat with scarlet collar, facings, and cuffs, white waistcoat, and black breeches or trousers.

wind-spout, n. Revolving column of air; tornado, whirlwind.

wind-stick, n. (slang) Propeller of aeroplane.

wind-swept, adj. Exposed to winds.

wind-tight, adj. Not permitting the passage of, impervious to, wind.

windward, adj. & n. [1. wíndward; 2. wíndwəd]. **wind**(I.) & **-ward**. 1. adj. Facing, exposed to, the direction from which the wind is blowing: *the windward side*. 2. n. Windward side or region: *the boat passed to windward*. Phr. *to get to windward of*, to get an advantage over.

windy, adj. [1. wíndi; 2. wíndi]. **wind**(I.) & **-y**. 1. Abounding in, exposed to, wind: *a windy day*; *windy weather*; *a windy spot*; *the windy side of the house*. 2. Addicted to, characterized by, empty verbosity: *a windy speaker*; *windy rhetoric*. 3. (slang) Having the wind up; nervous, frightened.

wine(I.), n. [1. wīn; 2. wain]. O.E.; M.E. *win*; O.H.G. *wīn*; O.N. *vīn*; Goth. *wein*; very ancient loan-word fr. Lat. *vīnum*, 'wine', see **vine**. 1. Fermented grape-juice. Phr. *Adam's wine*, water; *in wine*, intoxicated; *to take wine with (a person)*, to raise one's glass ceremoniously, bow to the person, and drink to his health. 2. Fermented juice of other fruit or flowers, the kind being usually specified: *currant, cowslip, elderberry, dandelion, wine* &c. 3. (univ.) A friendly evening party, usually of limited size, at which wine is drunk: *to have a wine in one's rooms*. 4. (med.) Medicinal solution of drug in wine. 5. Also *wine-colour*, colour of red wine.

wine(II.), vb. intrans., fr. prec. To drink wine, esp. to indulge to excess in wine-drinking.

winebag, n. [1. wínbæg; 2. wáinbæg]. 1. Wineskin. 2. (slang) Winebibber.

winebibber, n. [1. wínbìber; 2. wáinbìbə]. Person given to excessive drinking of wine.

winebibbing, n. [1. wínbibing; 2. wáinbibiŋ]. Excessive indulgence in wine.

winebottle, n. [1. wínbòtl; 2. wáinbòtl]. 1. Glass bottle for wine. 2. Wineskin.

winebowl, n. [1. wínbōl; 2. wáinboul]. Bowl used for drinking wine.

wine-carriage, n. Wheeled vessel for passing a decanter or bottle of wine round table.

wine-cellar, n. Cellar in which wine is stored.

wine-cooler, n. Vessel for holding ice in which bottle of wine is placed to cool.

winecup, n. [1. wínkup; 2. wáinkap]. Cup from which wine is drunk.

winefat, n. [1. wínfat; 2. wáinfæt]. The second element is an old, Nthn. or Midland, form of **vat**. (Bib. and archaic) Wine-press; cp. Lev. lxiii. 2.

wineglass, n. [1. wínglahs; 2. wáinglȧs]. 1. Drinking-glass, varying in size and shape, used for wine. 2. (as measure) Usually, sherry glass.

wineglassful, n. [1. wínglahsfòol; 2. wáinglȧsfùl]. Prec. & **-ful**. Amount contained in a wineglass, about two fluid ounces.

wineless, adj. [1. wínles; 2. wáinlis]. **wine** & **-less**. Without wine.

wine-marc, n. Refuse left after juice has been crushed from grapes.

wine-palm, n. Variety from which palm wine is made.

wine-press, n. Apparatus for pressing juice from grapes for making wine.

winery, n. [1. wíneri; 2. wáinəri]. **wine** & **-ry**. Establishment where wine is made.

wineskin, n. [1. wínskin; 2. wáinskin]. Animal's skin made into a bag for holding wine.

wine-stone, n. Tartar deposited by wine.

wine-vault, n. 1. Cellar for storing wine. 2. Cellar, shop, bar, where wine is sold and consumed.

wine-whey, n. Drink made of wine, whey, and sugar.

wing(I.), n. [1. wing; 2. wiŋ]. M.E. *weng*, *wing*, fr. O.N. *vengja*, 'wing'; cp. change (in pronunciation) of *e* to *i* before *-ng* in England &c.; cogn. w. Swed. *vinge* 'wing'; further etymol. doubtful. 1. One of the fore-limbs, including bones, feathers &c., by means of which a bird flies. Phrs. *grey-goose wing*, *arrow*; *on the wings of the wind*, very swiftly; *fear &c. lent him wings*, made him go extra fast; *to clip the wings of*, limit activities of; *to take to itself wings*, depart, vanish, quickly; *under the wing of*, under the protection of; *on the wing*, (i.) in flight; (ii.) (fig.) in the act or process of departing; *to take wing*, to fly away; to depart. 2. Organ, usually membranous, by means of which an insect, bat, flying-fish &c. propels itself through the air. 3. One of the broad, flat surfaces by means of which an aeroplane is supported in the air. 4. **a** Structure resembling a wing in position, appearance &c.; specif. **b** projection at side or end of building, at right angles to main part; **c** (pl.) sides of stage; scenery placed in this position. 5. Appendage resembling a wing in shape or position; specif. **a** thin, flat membrane attached to some kinds of seed, by means of which it is carried through the air; **b** one of the two side petals of a flower of the bean family. 6. **a** Division of army, member of team &c. working on one side of main body: *right, left, wing*; **b** a division, consisting of three squadrons, of the Royal Air Force.

wing(II.), vb. trans. & intrans., fr. prec. A. trans. 1. To give wings to, furnish (arrow &c.) with wings. 2. (lit. and fig.) To set in motion, start in flight; impel rapidly, increase speed of: *to wing an arrow at its mark*; *horror winged his steps*; *jealousy winged his shafts*. 3. (of birds) To fly over, traverse on the wing: '*Part loosely wing the region*' (Milton, 'P. L.' vii. 425); also *to wing the air*; *wing its way through the air*; *wings its flight*, flies. 4. To wound (bird) in the wing, or (person) in the arm. B. intrans. To fly through the air on wings: *the angel wings heavenwards*.

wing-beat, n. Single complete movement of bird's wing in flying.

wing-case, n. Thickened horny development of fore-wing of some insects, forming a protective cover for posterior wing.

wing-commander, n. Officer in Royal Air Force corresponding in rank to a commander in navy, or a lieutenant-colonel in the army.

wing-covert, n. One of the small feathers at joint of wing, covering base of flying feathers.

winged, adj. [1. wingd; 2. wiŋd]. **wing**(I.) & **-ed**. Having, furnished with, wings; *the winged god*, Mercury; *the winged horse*, Pegasus.

wing-footed, adj. (poet.) Flying as on wings; swift.

wingless, adj. [1. wíngles; 2. wíŋlis]. **wing**(I.) & **-less**. Without wings.

winglet, n. [1. wínglet; 2. wíŋlit]. **wing**(I.) & **-let**. Small wing.

wing-sheath, n. Wing-case.

wing-spread, n. Width across extended wings from tip to tip.

wing-stroke, n. Wing-beat.

wink(I.), vb. intrans. & trans. [1. wingk; 2. wiŋk]. O.E. *wincian*, 'to nod, wink'; M.E. *winken*; cp. M.H.G. *winken*; see **wince**. A. intrans. 1. (of person) **a** To open and close eyelids quickly, blink; **b** to lower and raise one eyelid, esp. as signal or hint to another person; see *wink at*. 2. (of eye) To close and open rapidly. Phr. (slang) *like winking*, very swiftly. 3. (of light, star &c.) To shine, flash, intermittently or fitfully; twinkle. B. trans. To close and open (eye) rapidly. C. Followed by preposition. *Wink at*, 1. to give a hint or signal to a person by lowering and raising one eyelid quickly; 2. to connive at, ignore deliberately (misconduct, an abuse &c.).

wink(II.), n., fr. prec. Act of winking; a momentary closing of eyes: *I have not slept a wink, did not get a wink of sleep*; Phr. *forty winks*, short nap; **b** rapid closing and opening of one eye to convey a signal, hint &c. Phr. (slang) *to tip (a person) the wink*, give him a hint.

winkle, n. [1. wíngkl; 2. wíŋkl]. O.E. *-wincla*, 'shell-fish' (with spiral shell); cogn. w. O.E. *wincian*, 'to nod, wink'; see **wink**; O.H.G. *wanchōn*, 'to draw back, start, move sideways'; Lat. *vagari*, 'to wander'; see **vagary** & words there referred to. Edible shell-fish, sea-snail, periwinkle.

winner, n. [1. wíner; 2. wínə]. **win**(I.) & **-er**. 1. One who, that which, wins; specif., a horse that wins a race: *the evening papers will give all the winners*. 2. *-winner*, earner, see **bread-winner**.

winning, adj. [1. wíning; 2. wíniŋ], fr. Pres. Part. of **win**(I.). 1. Victorious in contest &c.: *the winning horse, team, side* &c. 2. Giving, leading to, victory in contest, game &c.: *the winning hit, stroke, shot, move* &c. 3. Charming, attractive, engaging: *winning manners, smile, personality* &c.

winningly, adv. Prec. & **-ly**. In a winning manner; engagingly.

winning-post, n. Post marking end of race-course.

winnings, n. [1. wíningz; 2. wíniŋz]. **win**(I.) & **-ing**. Amount won, esp. money won in betting.

winnow, vb. trans. [1. wínō; 2. wínou]. O.E. *windwian*; M.E. *wind(e)wen, winewen*, 'to winnow'; cp. Goth. *(dis)winþjan*, 'to throw apart'; O.H.G. *wintōn*, 'to winnow'; cogn. w. Lat. *vannus*, 'winnowing fan', see **van**(III.) & **fan**(I.); *ventilāre*, 'to blow, winnow', see **ventilate**; Gk. *ainein* (fr. **wanj-*), 'to separate grain from chaff'; Lith. *vėtau*, 'to winnow'; cogn. also w. **wind**(I.). 1. **a** To separate (grain &c.) from husks, chaff &c. by allowing a current of air to play upon it; **b** to separate, remove, clear off (chaff &c.) from grain by means of a current of air. 2. (fig.) **a** To separate, sort out, discern, sift, what is good, true, reliable &c., from what is bad, worthless, doubtful &c.: *to winnow the facts from a mass of words*; **b** to separate (what is false, inferior &c.) from what is good or reliable. 3. (poet.) **a** To beat with or as with wings; to agitate, stir, (of Satan) '*with quick fan Winnows the buxom air*' (Milton, 'P. L.' v. 269-70); **b** (of air) to pass through and stir.

winsome, adj. [1. wínsum; 2. wínsəm]. O.E. *wynsum*, 'pleasant', M.E. *winsome*; fr. *wynn*, 'joy, pleasure', q.v. under **wish**, & **-some**. Engaging, attractive; sweet and charming: *a winsome maiden, smile, face* &c.; *winsome manners*.

winsomely, adv. Prec. & **-ly**. In a winsome manner.

winsomeness, n. See prec. & **-ness**. Quality of being winsome.

winter(I.), n. [1. wínter; 2. wíntə]. O.E., M.E. *winter*; cp. O.S., O.H.G. *winter*; Goth. *wintrus*, 'winter'; prob. orig., 'the white or snowy season', cp. O. Gaul. *vindo-*, 'white', W. *gwynn*. 1. Coldest season of the year, between autumn and spring, usually considered to include, in Northern hemisphere, the months of December, January, February; (astron.) from autumn solstice (Dec. 22nd) to vernal equinox (Mar. 20th). Phr. *hard winter*, a very cold one. 2. (poet.) Year, esp. in reckoning age of old person: *a man of eighty winters*.

winter (II.), vb. intrans. & trans., fr. prec. **1.** intrans. To spend, live during, the winter : *to winter in Italy, on the Riviera* &c. **2.** trans. To keep, graze (cattle &c.) during the winter.

winter (III.), adj., fr. winter (I.). Occurring in, characteristic of, used or occupied in, carried on during, the winter : *winter frosts, clothes, quarters, sports, apples* &c. ; *winter sleep*, hibernation.

winter-apple, n. One which ripens during the winter.

winterberry, n. [1. wínterbèri ; 2. wíntəbèri]. Red-berried N. American shrub ; black alder.

winter garden, n. Large conservatory, warmed, stocked with semi-tropical trees and shrubs, and used as a smoking and sitting room.

winter-green, n. Genus of low-growing, evergreen plants, *Gaultheria*, the leaves of which yield an aromatic oil, used for flavouring and scenting.

winterless, adj. [1. wínterles ; 2. wíntəlis]. winter (I.) & -less. Without cold season.

winter-lodge, n. (bot.) Bulb &c. enclosing embryo during winter.

winterly, adj. [1. wínterli ; 2. wíntəli]. winter & -ly. Wintry.

winter sports, n. Open-air sports, skiing, skating &c. indulged in, esp. in Switzerland, Norway &c., in winter.

wintertide, n. [1. wíntertìd ; 2. wíntətàid]. Season of winter.

wintriness, n. [1. wíntrines ; 2. wíntrinis]. Next word & -ness. Quality of being wintry.

wintry, adj. [1. wíntri ; 2. wíntri]. winter & -y. **1.** Characteristic of winter ; cold, stormy, snowy &c. **2.** (fig.) Cold, unfriendly, frigid, in manner, expression &c. : *a wintry smile, greeting* &c.

winy, adj. [1. wíni ; 2. wáini]. wine & -y. Resembling, having colour or taste of, wine.

winze, n. [1. winz ; 2. winz]. Perh. connected w. wind (I.). Small mine-shaft for ventilation or communication between two levels.

wipe (I.), vb. trans. [1. wīp ; 2. waip]. O.E. *wipian* ; M.E. *wipen*, ' to wipe ' ; cp. O.H.G. *wipf*, ' impulse, movement ' ; *wipfil*, ' the top of a tree ', lit. ' the swaying part ' ; also O.H.G. *weif*, ' a band ' ; Goth. *waips*, ' a crown ' ; *weipan*, ' to crown ' ; O.N. *veipr*, ' cloth for binding the head ' ; cogn. w. Lat. *vibrāre*, ' to move rapidly, brandish, shake ' &c., see **vibrate**. **A.** trans. **1.** To pass a cloth or other material over surface of, in order to clean or dry, rub gently, esp. with absorbent material : *to wipe the dishes after they have been washed* ; *wipe the floor with a damp cloth* ; Phr. *to wipe the floor with* (person), (slang) to defeat utterly in debate or controversy ; *to wipe one's eyes*, dry tears ; Phr. *to wipe a person's eye (for him)*, (slang) to rebuff, humiliate, check, by harsh action or speech. **2.** To remove, clean off, by rubbing with cloth or other absorbent material : *to wipe the mud off with a handful of grass* ; *to wipe one's tears away*. **B.** Followed by adverb. *Wipe off*, trans., **a** to remove by wiping, rub off, erase. *Wipe out*, trans., **1.** to clean (vessel &c.) by rubbing round interior ; **2. a** to remove, erase, by wiping : *to wipe out a mark, stain* &c. ; **b** (fig.) to erase, obliterate, cancel effects of : *to wipe out an insult, debt* &c. ; **c** to destroy utterly, exterminate (a military force, a race, family &c.). *Wipe up*, trans., to take up by mopping or rubbing with a cloth &c. : *to wipe up spilt milk*.

wipe (II.), n., fr. prec. **1.** Act of wiping, state of being wiped : *to give the floor a wipe*. **2.** (slang) A blow, a clip, a biff. Phr. *a wipe in the eye*, (also fig.) a rebuff, snub. **3.** (vulg. slang) Handkerchief.

wiper, n. [1. wíper ; 2. wáipə]. wipe (I.) & -er. One who, that which, wipes ; device, material for wiping ; esp. in compounds, e.g. *pen-wiper*, q.v.

wire (I.), n. [1. wīr ; 2. waiə]. O.E., M.E. *wīr* ; cp. O.H.G. *wiara*, ' wire ' ; O.N. *virr*, ' spiral ' ; Swed. *vira*, ' to twist ' ; cogn. w. Lat. *viriae*, ' armlet ' ; of Celt. origin, cp. O. Ir. *fiar*, ' bent ' ; fr. base *wei-, *wi-, ' to bend ', seen also in Lat. *viēre*, ' to twist, weave ' ; Scrt. *vyájati*, ' winds ' ; Gk. *itus*, ' rim of shield ' ; O.E. *widiġ*, ' band ; willow ', see **withy**. **1.** Fine-drawn, slender, flexible thread, rod &c. of metal : *copper, iron, steel, wire* &c. ; *telegraph, telephone, wires* ; *barbed wire*, see **barb (I.)**. Phr. *to pull the wires*, (i.) to move puppets by means of wires &c., hence, (ii.) to control affairs through secret influence ; *a live wire*, (i.) one charged with electricity, hence (ii.) a vigorous, pushing, vital person. **2. a** Telegraphy as means of communication : *to send a message by wire* ; **b** (colloq.) a telegram : *to send, receive, a wire*.

wire (II.), vb. trans. & intrans., fr. prec. **A.** trans. **1. a** To secure, fasten, stiffen, connect &c. with wire : *to wire the stems of flowers* ; *to wire beads together* ; **b** to snare, catch (birds, rabbits &c.), with wires. **2.** To provide with wire ; to lay wire or wires in, for any purpose : *to wire a house for electric light*. **3.** To communicate by telegraph : *to wire the news to a person*. **B.** intrans. To send a telegram : *please wire as soon as you hear*. **C.** Followed by adverb. *Wire in*, intrans., (slang) to engage energetically in some enterprise ; to set to work vigorously : *you had better wire in and finish the job*.

wire-cloth, n. Fabric woven of wire.

wire-cutter(s), n. Instrument for cutting wire.

wire-dancer, n. Acrobat who performs on a taut wire.

wiredraw, vb. trans. [1. wírdràw ; 2. wáiədrɔ̀]. **1.** To draw out (metal) into wire by passing it through holes of required diameter. **2.** To treat (argument &c.) with excessive subtlety or over-refinement.

wire-edge, n. Very thin edge formed on a cutting instrument by over-grinding or honing, which turns over or peels off when the instrument is used.

wire-entanglement, n. Form of military defence consisting of barbed wire stretched and twisted in and out between and round stout stakes firmly planted in the ground.

wire-gauge, n. Gauge for measuring size of round wire.

wire-gauze, n. Thin fabric woven of wire.

wire-gun, n. Cannon made of an iron tube with wire wound round it.

wire-haired, adj. Having short, rough, stiff hair ; esp. describing a breed of fox-terrier.

wire-heel, n. Disease affecting horse's foot.

wireless, adj. & n. [1. wírles ; 2. wáiəlis]. wire & -less. **1.** adj. Without wire(s) ; specif. **a** connected with, pertaining to, a system of telegraphy or telephony in which sounds or signals are conveyed from a transmitting station to various receiving stations, through the ether direct, by means of radiating electric waves ; **b** (of message &c.) transmitted by wireless. **2.** n. **a** Wireless telegraphy or telephony ; **b** a message sent by this means.

wireless-cabin, n. Wireless-room.

wireless operator, n. Ship's wireless telegrapher.

wireless-room, n. Room on a ship containing wireless installation.

wireless station, n. Place equipped for transmitting and receiving wireless messages &c.

wire-netting, n. Network of thin wire, made with various sizes of mesh, used for fencing &c.

wire-puller, n. Person who pulls the wires ; specif., one who brings secret influence to bear to effect a purpose.

wire-rope, n. Rope of twisted wire.

wire-worm, n. Stiff, worm-like larva which attacks the roots of plants.

wire-wove, adj. (of paper) Smooth and unlined, made in a frame of wire-gauze.

wirily, adv. [1. wírili ; 2. wáiərili]. wiry & -ly. In a wiry manner.

wiriness, n. [1. wírines ; 2. wáiərinis]. wiry & -ness. Quality of being wiry.

wiring, n. [1. wíring ; 2. wáiəriŋ]. wire & -ing. System of wires for conveying electric current &c.

wiry, adj. [1. wfri ; 2. wáiəri]. wire (I.) & -y. **1.** Resembling wire in being thin, stiffish, but flexible. **2.** (of persons &c.) Strong and tough, capable of physical endurance ; sinewy without being especially large or muscular.

wis, vb. [1. wis ; 2. wis]. Bogus vb. used in sham archaism (used by Spenser) in *I wis*, supposed to mean ' I know, ween ' ; due to misinterpretation of M.E. *y-wis, i-wis*, ' certainly ', fr. O.E. *ġewis*. This sham Pres. was no doubt partly a back-formation fr. the genuine Pret. *wiste*, ' knew ' ; see **wist**. Browning actually has *you wis*!

wisdom, n. [1. wízdum ; 2. wízdəm]. O.E. *wīsdōm* ; M.E. *wisdom* ; wise & -dom. **1.** The quality of being wise ; sound judgement, sagacity. **2.** (archaic) Learning, knowledge, science : *the wisdom of the ancients*. **3.** (cap.) Name of two books of the Apocrypha, *Wisdom (of Solomon)*, and *Wisdom of Jesus, the son of Sirach*, usually known as *Ecclesiasticus*.

wisdom-tooth, n. Third molar of human being, usually cut about the twentieth year. Phr. *to cut one's wisdom-teeth*, acquire a mature judgement by age and experience.

wise (I.), adj. [1. wīz ; 2. waiz]. O.E., M.E. *wīs* ; cp. O.S., O.H.G. *wīs* ; O.N. *vīss* ; Goth. *weis*, ' wise ' ; fr. earlier *wīss-, fr. Aryan *wĭd-tō, fr. base *wid-, *weid-, ' to see ; to know ' ; see further under **wit (I.)**, **vide**, **idea**. **1. a** (of persons) Having sound judgement ; sagacious, prudent, shrewd ; **b** (of thought or action) informed with, springing from, based on, wisdom, sagacity, prudence ; **c** (of utterance, sayings, writings) embodying, expressing, wisdom. **2.** Having knowledge of, information upon, some subject : *I was none the wiser for his explanation*. Phr.(Am.) *to put a person wise to, on* (a matter, a situation &c.), give him full information, explanation &c. concerning it ; *wise woman*, (archaic) one supposed to be versed in some branch of occult science, having mysterious powers, (i.) a witch ; (ii.) a midwife.

wise (II.), n. O.E., M.E. *wīse*, ' way, manner ' ; cp. O.S., O.H.G. *wīsa*, ' manner ' ; O.E. *wīsian*, ' to show, guide ', lit. ' to put wise ' ; cogn. w. wise (I.), & cp. **guise**. (archaic) Way, manner, fashion : *in any wise* ; *in no wise* ; *on this wise* ; *in stately wise*.

-wise, suff. representing prec., used w. ns. & advs. to form advs. of manner, e.g. *lengthwise, likewise, crosswise* &c.

wiseacre, n. [1. wízăker ; 2. wáizèikə], fr. M. Du. *wijs-segger*, fr. Germ. *weissager*, wh. was formed by popular etymol., as though *weis*, ' wise ', see **wise**, & *sager*, ' sayer ', see **say**, really fr. M.H.G. *wīzago* ; O.H.G. *wīz(z)ago*, ' sage, prophet ' ; cp. O.E. *wītiga* ; O.N. *vitki*, ' sage ' ; fr. base of wise & wit. Person who assumes an air of wisdom.

wish (I.), vb. trans. & intrans. [1. wish ; 2. wiʃ]. O.E. *wȳscan* ; M.E. *wischen*, ' to wish ' ; cp. O.H.G. *wunskan* ; M. Du. *wunschen*, ' to wish ' ; O.H.G. *wunsc* ; cogn. w. O.E. *wynn*, ' joy ', see **winsome** ; *wunian*, ' to remain, live ', see **wont** ; O.E. *(gi)winnan*, ' to obtain ', see **win** ; cogn. w. Lat. *venus*, ' love, charm ' ; see **Venus** ; Scrt. *vánaš*, ' desire '. **A.** trans. **1.** To desire, crave, want, feel a longing for : *I will do what you wish* ; *you may have whichever you wish*. **2. a** To feel and express a desire that oneself or another should have something, obtain a benefit, be in a specified condition &c. ; to invoke (good or evil) upon : *to wish oneself at home, anywhere but where one is* ; *won't you wish me good luck?* ; *I wish you a happy life, a good journey, good health* &c. ; *I don't wish you any harm* ; Phr. (colloq.) *to wish a person further*, to feel annoyance or boredom at his presence and wish he were gone ; **b** (in weakened sense) to bid : *I wish you good-bye, good morning, farewell* &c. Phr. *I'll wish you good morning*, formula for abrupt dismissal, or of sudden, happy departure. **3.** (followed by *that* and dependent clause, often with *that* suppressed) To desire, be anxious and desirous that : *I wish (that) you wouldn't make such a noise* ; *don't you* *wish (that) we were at home?; I wish I could see him now.* **B.** intrans. *Wish for,* to desire; to desire to possess, long for; to desire coming of &c.: *We are apt to wish for what we can't have; it is no good wishing for rain with the glass so high.*

wish (II.), n., fr. prec. **1.** Desire, longing, craving: *a wish for better times; he has no wish to live.* **2.** Expression of desire, specif. **a** request, order: *to obey one's slightest wish;* **b** expressed hope for another's success &c.: *you have our good wishes; with every good wish.* **3.** That which one wishes, object of desire: *you shall have your wish; you must carry out your father's last wish(es); my dearest wish is to see you prosperous and happy.*

-wisher, n. [1. wísher; 2. wíʃə]. **wish (I.)** & **-er.** One who wishes, as in *well-wisher.*

wishful, adj. [1. wíshfool; 2. wíʃful]. **wish (II.)** & **-ful.** (followed by infin.) Having a specified wish, desirous; anxious, willing: *wishful to depart; wishful to please.*

wishing-bone, n. [1. wíshing bōn; 2. wíʃiŋ bōun]. Forked bone in front of breast of bird; when this is pulled apart by two persons, the one subsequently holding the longer part is supposed to be entitled to the fulfilment of a wish; also *wish-bone.*

wishing-cap, n. Fabulous magic cap, supposed to accomplish the wishes of the wearer.

wish-wash, n. [1. wísh wosh; 2. wíʃ wɔʃ]. Redupl. form of **wash.** (colloq.) Insipid, watery drink; wash.

wishy-washy, adj. [1. wíshi wòshi; 2. wíʃi wɔ̀ʃi]. Redupl. form of **washy.** (colloq.) **a** Thin, tasteless, weak, sloppy: *wishy-washy tea* &c.; **b** (fig.) insipid, without force, sloppy: *wishy-washy talk, sentiment* &c.

wisp, n. [1. wisp; 2. wisp]. M.E. *wisp, wips;* cp. L.G. *wiep;* Swed. dial. *vipp;* O.N. *vippa,* 'wisp'; perh. cogn. w. **wipe.** Small bunch, tuft, handful of straw, hay &c.; thin, straggly lock of hair.

wispy, adj. [1. wíspi; 2. wíspi]. Prec. & **-y.** Like, forming, a wisp: *wispy hair,* thin and straggly.

wist, vb. [1. wist; 2. wist]. O.E. & M.E. *wiste,* Pret. of *witan,* 'to know', a Pret. Pres. vb., see **wit (I.).** O.E. *wiste* was itself a new formation, the orig. form, also preserved in O.E., being *wisse.* This being an isolated type of Pret. in O.E., a form w. the normal suff. *-te* was made on the anal. of *cyste,* 'kissed' &c. (archaic, Bib.) Knew: *wist ye not* &c.

wistaria, n. [1. wistária; 2. wistéəriə], fr. name of Caspar Wistar, American professor of anatomy, d. 1818. Genus of climbing plants of the bean family, with long clusters of pale purplish flowers.

wistful, adj. [1. wístfool; 2. wístful]. Prob. fr. *wishful,* w. differentiation of meaning, influenced by obs. *wistly,* fr. *wisly,* 'prudently', fr. O.E. *wīsliče,* 'wisely' &c., w. M.E. shortening of long vowel before *-sl-.* **1.** Indicating, expressing, unfulfilled longing; pathetically eager, esp. for something unobtained or unobtainable; yearning: *wistful eyes, look, voice* &c. **2.** Pensive, musing: *he grew silent and wistful.*

wistfully, adv. Prec. & **-ly.** In a wistful manner.

wistfulness, n. See prec. & **-ness.** State or quality of being wistful.

wit (I.), vb. trans. & intrans. [1. wit; 2. wit]. O.E. *witan,* 'to know' (Pret. Pres. vb.); M.E. *witen,* also *wěten,* cp. **weet;** cp. O.S., Goth. *witan;* O.H.G. *wizzan;* O.N. *vita,* 'to know'; cogn. w. Lat. *vidēre,* 'to see', see **vide;** Gk. *oida,* 'know'; *eîdon,* 'saw'; *idéa,* 'appearance', see **idea;** Scrt. *vēda,* 'I know', see **Veda;** O. Slav. *viděti,* 'to see'; *vědě,* 'I know'; cp. further O.E. *wīs,* 'wise', see **wise (I.);** also other forms of the vb. under **wot** & **wist.** (archaic and defective) This type only survives now in Phr. *to wit,* namely, that is to say.

wit (II.), n. O.E., M.E. *witt,* 'mind, intelligence'; cp. O. Fris. *wit;* O.S. *(gi)wit;* M. Du. *wite;* O.H.G. *wizzi;* O.N. *vit;* Goth. *-witi,* 'wit'; cogn. w. prec. **1.** (sing. or pl.) Mind, understanding, mental power or perception; activity, alertness, of mind: *to exercise one's wit; a man of quick, little, wit* &c.; *to depend on one's mother wit,* natural intelligence. Phrs. *the five wits,* (archaic) (i.) the senses; (ii.) the mind; mental faculties; *out of one's wits,* insane, demented; *to have, keep, one's wits about one,* be alert and resourceful; *to be at one's wits' end,* (i.) not know what to do or say; (ii.) be without financial resources: *to live by one's wits,* earn one's living by haphazard, unscrupulous methods, without settled occupation or work. **2. a** Defined by Dryden in relation to poetry as being in the wider sense 'propriety of language', and in narrower sense 'sharpness of conceit'; **b** in present-day usage the word means, (i.) a faculty or quality of mind which perceives unexpected relations between ideas not usually associated, and the power of clothing such perceptions in a happy, neat, epigrammatic form; (ii.) the expression of such perception of relations between ideas in a felicitous, striking way.

wit (III.), n., fr. prec. Person possessing wit in sense 2.

witch (I.), n. [1. wich; 2. witʃ]. O.E. *wiċċe,* '(female) witch'; cp. O.E. *wicca,* 'wizard'; fr. O.E. *wiccian,* 'to bewitch'; cp. M.L.G. *wicken;* connected w. **wicked. 1.** Woman in league with, or under the influence of, evil spirits and in possession of occult powers; female follower of the black art, female sorcerer. Phrs. *white witch,* one using her powers for beneficent purposes; *witches' Sabbath,* see **Sabbath. 2.** Ugly, malevolent old woman; a hag, a crone. **3.** Fascinating, bewitching woman, who uses her beauty and charm to influence people.

witch (II.), vb. trans., fr. prec. To bewitch, enchant, cast a magic spell over.

witch-, pref. See **wych-.**

witchcraft, n. [1. wíchkrahft; 2. wítʃkrāft]. Power and practices of a witch; sorcery.

witch-doctor, n. Magician, medicine man among savage tribes.

witchery, n. [1. wícheri; 2. wítʃəri]. **witch** & **-ery. 1.** Powers of a witch; witchcraft. **2.** (fig.) Bewitching effect, fascination, magic.

witch-hazel, wych-hazel, n. [1. wích hāzl; 2. wítʃ heizl]. See **wych-;** the twigs were, & are, used as divining rods, to wh. cause the more usual spelling is due. **a** A N. American shrub, *Hamamelis virginica,* with yellow late-flowering blossoms; also formerly in England name of the hornbeam and the wych-elm; **b** astringent medicinal substance extracted from *Hamamelis.*

witching, adj. [1. wíching; 2. wítʃiŋ]. **witch (II.)** & **-ing.** Capable of bewitching; captivating, fascinating.

witchingly, adv. Prec. & **-ly.** In a witching manner.

witch-knots, n. Small tangled clumps of twigs on branch of oak &c., caused by fungi.

witch-meal, n. The pollen of the club-moss.

witenagemot, n., formerly ignorantly pronounced [1. wìtenágemōt; 2. wìtinǽgimout], now more correctly [1. wítena yemōt; 2. wítɛna jɛmóut], O.E. *witena ġemōt,* fr. *witena,* genit. pl. of *wita,* 'wise man, counsellor', see **wit,** & *(ġe)mōt,* 'meeting', see **moot.** (hist.) Public national assembly of the Anglo-Saxons.

with, prep. [1. widh; 2. wið]. O.E. *wiþ* expresses opposition, hostility to; protection against; rest near, or opposite to; separation from; association with; in later M.E. the word has the senses of 'together with; among; by means of', replacing O.E. *mid* in these senses; cp. O.S., O. Fris. *wið;* O.N. *við;* cogn. w. O.E. *wiðer;* O.H.G. *widar;* Goth. *wiþra,* 'against'; fr. base *wi-, 'two', cp. second element of **divide,** & **widow. 1.** Against, in opposition to; only after verbs and nouns expressing struggle, hostility &c.: *to fight, struggle, contend, with;* also *a fight, battle &c. with savages.* **2.** Expressing association; **a** in action: in the company of: *to ride, walk, dine, shoot, drink &c. with one's friends;* **b** association by physical propinquity: alongside of: *to live, sleep, sit, stay &c. with;* **c** expressing community and reciprocity of action: *to play cricket with; to discuss politics with.* **3.** Expressing association in aims and interests; assistance, alliance; on the side of, side by side with: *in the Great War we fought with the French against the Germans.* **4.** Expressing agreement in, harmony of, opinions, ideals &c.: '*Burns, Shelley, were with us*' (Browning, 'Lost Leader'); *I am entirely with you in this;* '*he that is not with me is against me*' (Matt. xii. 30). **5. a** Indicating the object of thought, attention, preoccupation: *the lecture was concerned with early English poetry;* **b** denoting the object of an action: *to deal with each piece of business as it arises.* **6.** Indicating contrast and comparison: *compare Pope's treatment of Nature with that of Wordsworth.* **7. a** Expressing an attribute or possession: *a lady with golden hair; a man with ten thousand a year;* **b** expressing temporary association or possession: '*Methinks I see her now, With the wreath of orange blossoms, Upon her snowy brow*' (T. Haynes Bayly); *the man with the frock-coat and bowler hat;* **c** expressing manner in adverbial phrases: *standing with his hands in his pockets; with an ugly smile on his face; he came home with a black eye.* **8. a** Expressing a cause; on account of: *I am dying with hunger; roses wet with dew; eyes dim with tears;* **b** indicating the instrument; by means of: *he struck me with a stick; to light a house with electricity; to amuse oneself with a book;* **c** indicating material or content: *stuffed with straw; a hole filled with rubbish.* **9.** Expressing coincidence in time, simultaneity of two actions or occurrences; at the same time as: *to rise with the lark; to come home with the milk; with the death of Queen Victoria a great epoch ended.* **10.** Expressing correspondence; **a** in proportion to, in the same degree as: *to move with the age; it grew colder with the approach of sunset;* **b** in the same direction as: *the shadow moves with the sun.* **11.** After certain verbs expressing **a** physical separation: *I parted with him at the door;* **b** separation, division, in opinion; disagreement: *to quarrel with, differ with* (a person) &c. **12.** Notwithstanding, in spite of: *with all his wealth he is unhappy.* **13.** To the accompaniment of; indicating manner: *he greeted me with smiles;* '*come before his presence with a song*' (Ps. c. 1).

with-, pref. Same as prec. **1.** Expresses departure, removal, see **withdraw. 2.** Expresses refusal, see **withhold.**

withal, adv. & prep. [1. widháwl; 2. wiðɔ́l]. Prec. & **all.** (archaic) **1.** adv. In addition, besides, moreover: *a man of breeding and a very honest fellow withal.* **2.** prep. = with, esp. when expressing the instrument, at the end of a sentence: *the sword he used to defend himself withal.*

withdraw, vb. trans. & intrans. [1. widhdráw; 2. wiðdrɔ́]. **with-** & **draw. A.** trans. **1.** To draw back, pull aside, move backwards from position: *she put out her hand and then withdrew it; to withdraw one's head from the window.* **2.** To take away, recall, remove: *to withdraw troops from a country; to withdraw a book, coins &c. from circulation.* **3.** To recall, retract, contradict (one's statement, remark, promise &c.). **B.** intrans. **a** To move, draw, back; to retire, recede: *the troops withdrew; to withdraw from one's presence;* **b** to go back on one's word, back out of an undertaking: *after all your promises you can't withdraw now.*

withdrawal, n. [1. widhdráwal; 2. wiðdrɔ́əl]. Prec. & **-al.** Act or process of withdrawing.

withdrawing-room, n. [1. widhdráwing room; 2. wiðdrɔ́iŋ rum]. (archaic) Drawing-room.

withe, n. [1. widh, with; 2. wið, wiþ]. O.E. *wiððe;* M.E. *wiþþe,* 'withy; fetter; chaplet'; cp. O. Fris. *withthe;* O.H.G. *wīda;* O.N. *við(ja);* M. Du. *wiede,* 'willow, withy'; O.H.G. *wid,* 'cord of twisted branches';

cogn. w. Gk. *itéa*, 'willow'; Scrt. *vītáś*, 'twisted'; *vītikā*, 'band'; Lith. *výtis*, 'willow branch'; Lett. *vītols*; Lat. *viēre*, 'to bind, twist', *vīnum*, 'vine'; see **viti- & vine**, & cp. **withy**. Flexible band of twisted osier or other tough pliant shoots, used for tying up faggots &c.

wither, vb. intrans. & trans. [1. wídher; 2. wíðə]. Prob. fr. O.N. *viðra*, 'to wither'; cp. M.E. *wideren*, *wederen*, 'to expose to the weather', fr. O.E. *weder*, see **weather**. **A.** intrans. **1.** (of plants and flowers) To dry up, shrivel, shrink, wilt, fade, whether as a natural process or as result of exposure to excessive heat or drought. **2.** (of affections, hopes &c.) To grow weaker, die away, be blighted. **B.** trans. **1.** To cause (flowers &c.) to wither. **2.** To blight (affections, hopes &c.), cause to die down and diminish in intensity. **3.** To disconcert, rebuff, snub, reduce to confusion and silence : *she withered him with a scornful glance*.

withered, adj. [1. wídherd; 2. wíðəd], fr. P.P. of prec. **1.** (of plants &c.) **a** Faded, shrivelled, parched from lack of water; **b** having attained maturity and died down. **2.** (of persons) Having a dried-up, faded, wrinkled appearance. **3.** (of hopes &c.) Diminished, blighted.

withering, adj. [1. wídhering; 2. wíðəriŋ], fr. Pres. Part. of prec. Tending to, having power to, wither; **a** (lit.) *a withering drought, sun*; **b** (fig.) *a withering glance, sarcasm* &c.

witheringly, adv. Prec. & -ly. In a withering manner.

withers, n. [1. wídherz; 2. wíðəz], fr. O.E., M.E. *wider*, 'against', see **with**, as part on wh. collar presses. Part of a horse's shoulder at the base of the neck. Phr. *my, his &c. withers are unwrung*, that does not affect me, him &c.

withershins, adv. [1. wídhershinz; 2. wíðəʃinz]. Scots, fr. M.L.G. *weddersins*, fr. *wider*, 'against', cp. prec., & *sin*, 'way, direction'. In a direction contrary to the apparent course of the sun; counter-clockwise.

withhold, vb. trans. [1. with-, widhhóld; 2. wiþ-, wiðhóuld]. O.E. *wiðhāldan*; **with- & hold**. **1.** To hold, keep back, refrain from using or allowing to act, restrain from action : *to withhold one's hand*; *the sun withheld his light*. **2.** To refrain from granting, refuse to bestow: *to withhold one's consent, help, favour* &c.

within (I.), adv. [1. widhín; 2. wiðín]. O.E. *wiðinnan*; M.E. *wiþinnen*, 'on the inside'; **with- & in**. (archaic) On the inside, in the interior, internally : *the banana is yellow outside and cream-coloured within*; specif. **a** in the house, indoors : *to stay within*; *is Mrs. Smith within?*; '*the king's daughter is all glorious within*' (Ps. xlv. 14); **b** in the heart or mind, inwardly : *to be pure within*.

within (II.), n., fr. prec. The interior, inner part, inside : *seen from within, the cave looks larger*.

within (III.), prep. See **within (I.)**. **1. a** Inside, in the interior of, in the inner part of : *within the building*; *to call from within the house*; *within doors, indoors*; Phr. *wheels within wheels*, secret agencies at work; **b** in the inward, mental part of : *hope sprang up within him*. **2. a** Inside the limit, scope, range, compass, power, of : *within hearing, earshot*; *within call*; *within sight of home*; *within one's powers*; *within the meaning of the Act*; *within the law*, not transgressing it ; Phr. (of athlete &c.) *to be running, fighting &c. well within himself*, keeping a reserve of effort; **b** so as to be limited by, and not to exceed, amount of : *to live within one's income*. **3.** Inside of, not exceeding the limits of a specified time or distance : *to return within two hours (of one's departure &c.)*; *within a few miles of London*; *within an easy walk of*, at a distance easily covered in a walk; *within an ace of death*, barely escaping.

without (I.), adv. [1. widhóut; 2. wiðáut]. O.E. *wiþūtan*; M.E. *wiþūten*, 'without, beyond'; **with- & out**. **a** On the exterior, outside, externally : *fair without and foul within*; specif. **b** outside the house, building &c. : *the messenger stands without*.

without (II.), n., fr. prec. The exterior, outside : *to look at a thing from without*.

without (III.), prep. See **without (I.)**. **1.** (archaic) On the outside of, external to : *without the gate, house &c.* ; '*a green hill ... Without a city wall*' (Mrs. Alexander); *without doors*, out of doors. **2.** Not having, using, unaccompanied by; destitute, in want, of; free from, lacking : *without money, home, or friends*; *he cannot walk without a stick*; *to be without servants*; *the child came without its nurse*; *without hope of reward*; *without stint*; *without ceremony*; *all without exception*; *without rhyme or reason*; *without fear and without reproach*; *without doubt*, doubtless, certainly; *without fail*, for certain; *without end*, interminable, everlasting; *without number*, innumerable; *without prejudice* (see **prejudice**); *without regard for*, having no consideration for. Phr. *that goes without saying*, is too obvious to be mentioned. **3.** (before Pres. Part. or vbl. n. in -*ing*) Having neglected to; in such a way as to avoid: *to travel without taking a ticket*; *go in without waking him*; *without shedding of blood*.

without (IV.), conj., fr. prec. (archaic or vulg.) Unless, except, but : *you will never succeed without you work hard*; *he never goes out without he loses his umbrella*.

withstand, vb. trans. & intrans. [1. widhstánd; 2. wiðstǽnd]. O.E. *wiðstandan*, 'to resist'; **with- & stand**. **1.** trans. To oppose, resist, endure force or attack of, esp. resist successfully : *to withstand the enemy, temptation* &c. **2.** intrans. (chiefly poet.) To offer resistance, endure.

withy, n. [1. wídhi; 2. wíði]. O.E. *wiðiġ*, variant of *wiððe*, 'withe', see **withe**. A young willow or osier plant.

withy-bed, n. Plantation of osiers or willows.

witless, adj. [1. wítles; 2. wítlis]. **wit (II.) & -less**. Lacking in, destitute of, wit; dull, foolish.

witlessly, adv. Prec. & -ly. In a witless way.

witlessness, n. See prec. & -ness. State or quality of being witless.

witling, n. [1. wítling; 2. wítliŋ]. **wit (II.) & -ling**. Person of little intelligence.

witness (I.), n. [1. wítnes; 2. wítnis]. O.E., M.E. *witnes(s)*; cp. O.H.G. *(gi)wiznessi*; **wit (I.) & -ness**. **1.** Evidence in support of theory, statement &c.; testimony, corroboration : *to give witness on behalf of*; *bear witness to, of*; *to support another's witness*. **2.** Person who is able to give a first-hand account of an incident, state of affairs &c.; one who has personal knowledge of an event; eye-witness. **3.** Person or thing furnishing proof : *the empty cupboard was a witness of his poverty*; *he is a living witness to the success of the scheme*. **4.** (law) **a** Person giving evidence under oath in a court of law; **b** person who appends his signature by the side of that of the person who executes a document &c., in testimony of having seen the latter sign.

witness (II.), vb. trans. & intrans., fr. prec. **A.** trans. **1. a** (archaic) To give or furnish evidence of, testify to : *none could witness that he was present*; **b** to show, give, evidence of : *his expression witnessed his discomfiture*. **2.** To be present as an eye-witness of, to see personally : *many people witnessed the incident*. **3.** Specif., *to witness a person's signature*, to write one's own signature by the side of his, in testimony of having seen him sign; also *to witness a document*, act as witness to the signing of it. **B.** intrans. To give evidence, bear witness, testify : *to witness against one*; *to witness to a person's conduct*; *witness Heaven!*

witness-box, n. Enclosure in law-court in which a witness stands to give evidence.

-witted, adj. [1. wíted; 2. wítid]. **wit (II.) & -ed**. Having wits of specified quality : *quick-, slow-witted* &c. ; *half-witted*, imbecile.

witticism, n. [1. wítisizm; 2. wítisizəm], fr. **witty**, on anal. of **solecism** &c. Witty remark, phrase &c.

wittily, adv. [1. wítili; 2. wítili]. **witty & -ly**. In a witty manner.

wittiness, n. [1. wítines; 2. wítinis]. **witty & -ness**. Quality of being witty.

wittingly, adv. [1. wítingli; 2. wítiŋli]. Pres. Part. of **wit (I.) & -ly**. Consciously, intentionally, by design.

wittol, n. [1. wítol; 2. wítəl], fr. M.E. *wodewale*, 'green woodpecker'; cp. M.H.G. *witewal*; M. Du. *wedewal*. (archaic) Husband who condones his wife's unfaithfulness; a compliant, accommodating cuckold.

witty, adj. [1. wíti; 2. wíti]. O.E. *witiġ*; M.E. *witi*, 'witty, skilful'; **wit (II.) & -y**. Possessed of, displaying, wit: *a witty speaker, speech* &c.

wive, vb. trans. & intrans. [1. wīv; 2. waiv]. O.E. *wīfian*; M.E. *wiven*, 'to marry', fr. *wīf*, 'woman, wife', see **wife**. (archaic) **1.** trans. To take as wife, marry. **2.** intrans. To take a wife, get married.

wivern, wyvern, n. [1. wívern; 2. wáivən]. M.E. *wivere*, 'serpent', fr. O. Fr. *wivre*, fr. Lat. *vīpera*, 'viper'; see **viper**. (her.) Fabulous monster, depicted with the head and tail of a dragon, wings, and two legs.

wizard, n. [1. wízard; 2. wízəd]. M.E. *wisard*; prob. fr. *wīs*, 'wise', & -*ard*. **1.** Magician, sorcerer. **2.** Person possessing apparently magical powers, one who works wonders; a fascinating, charming person, able to influence others.

wizardry, n. [1. wízardri; 2. wízədri]. Prec. & -ry. **a** Powers or practices of a wizard; sorcery; **b** charm, fascination.

wizen(ed), weazen(ed), adj. [1. wízen(d), wézen(d); 2. wízən(d), wízən(d)]. M.E. *wisenen*, 'to dry up'; cp. O.H.G. *wesenēn*; O.N. *visna*, 'to shrivel'; cogn. w. Lat. *viescere*, 'to fade, shrivel'; Lith. *výstu*, 'wither'; perh. cogn. w. Lat. *vīrus*, 'moisture, slime, sap, poison', see **virus**. Dried up, shrivelled, shrunken : *a wizen(ed) old man*; *a wizen(ed) complexion*; *wizened apples*.

wizier. See **vizier**.

wo, whoa, interj. [1. wō; 2. wou]. Cry uttered to a horse; stop!

woad, n. [1. wōd; 2. woud]. O.E. *wād*; M.E. *wōd*; cp. O.H.G. *weit*; O. Fris., M. Du. *weed*; Goth. *wizdila*, 'woad'; cogn. w. Lat. *vitrum*, 'woad', perh. also w. Gk. *isátis*, 'woad' (fr. *wis-). **1.** Herbaceous plant, *Isatis tinctoria*, of the mustard family, with clusters of yellow flowers and leaves yielding a blue dye. **2.** Blue dye obtained from this plant.

wobble, wabble (I.), vb. intrans. [1. wóbl; 2. wóbl], fr. M.E. *wappen*, 'to beat', & -**le**. **1. a** To sway unsteadily from side to side; to oscillate, be shaky and unsteady : *the bridge does not feel safe, it wobbles*; *the jelly wobbles*; **b** specif. (of wheels) to rock while rotating, revolve unsteadily. **2.** (fig.) To waver in purpose; to vacillate, hesitate, be inconstant in principles and opinions.

wobble (II.), n., fr. prec. **1.** Unsteady, rocking, swaying, motion; oscillation. **2.** (fig.) Vacillation in principles; instability in opinions; weakness of purpose.

woe, n. [1. wō; 2. wou]. O.E. *wā*; M.E. *wō*, 'calamity, sorrow'; cp. O.S., O.H.G. *wē*; O.N. *væ, vei*; Goth. *wai*, 'sorrow'; cogn. w. Lat. *vae*, 'cry of pain'; Lett. *wai*, 'alas'; *waidi*, 'lament, need'. **1.** (archaic and poet.) Sorrow, grief, trouble, misery. Phrs. *weal and woe* (see **weal (I.)**); *woe is me!*, alas!; *woe be to ...*, *woe betide ...*, a curse be upon : *a face of woe*, a lugubrious countenance; *a tale of woe*, recitation of sorrows and grievances. **2.** Cause of sorrow; affliction, calamity : *to tell all one's woes*.

woebegone, adj. [1. wóbegàwn, -gòn; 2. wóubigòn, -gɔ̀n]. **woe** & O.E. *begān*, M.E. *begoon*, P.P. of O.E. *begān*, 'to possess, occupy, surround'; **by & go**. Of sorrowful appearance, doleful, mournful.

woeful, adj. [1. wǒfool; 2. wóuful]. **woe** & **-ful**. Causing, characterized by, expressive of, woe; mournful: *a woeful day, spectacle, cry* &c.

woefully, adv. Prec. & **-ly**. In a woeful manner.

woke, vb. [1. wŏk; 2. wouk]. O.E. *wōc*; M.E. *wook*; Pret. of **wake** (I.). The Mod. Engl. pronunciation, where one wd. have expected [1. wook; 2. wuk], cp. **took**, has been explained by Zachrisson as due to the influence of *spoke, spoken*; the infins. **wake** (I.) & **speak** were pronounced w. the same vowel [1. ā; 2. ē] by many speakers in the 17th & 18th cents.

woken, vb. [1. wŏken; 2. wóukən]. P.P. of **wake** (I.). The vowel is perh. due to the influence of that of **spoken**, see prec. Cp. O.E. (*ġe)wacen*, M.E. *wāken*.

wold, n. [1. wōld; 2. would]. O.E. *wāld*, 'forest, woodland'; M.E. *wōld*; cp. O.S., O.H.G. *wald*, Du. *woud*, 'forest'; O.N. *vollr*, 'uncultivated land'; prob. cogn. w. Gk. *lásios*, 'tufted, wooded', earlier *wlát-jo-*; Russ. *vóloti*, 'fibre'; Lith. *váltis*, 'ear of corn'. Cp. variant **weald**. Tract of elevated, uncultivated, open country.

wolf (I.), n. [1. woolf; 2. wulf]. O.E. *wulf*; M.E. *wulf, wolf*; cp. O.H.G. *wolf*; Goth. *wulfs*; O.N. (fem.) *ylgr*; cogn. w. Scrt. *vŕkas*; Gk. *lúkos*, see **lycanthropy**; Lat. *lūpus*, see **lupine**; O. Prussian *vilkis*; Lett. *wilks*; O. Slav. *vlŭkŭ*, 'wolf'; fr. base *wlkʷ-os*, 'wolf'. Cp. **vulpine**. **1**. One of several species of savage, carnivorous, gregarious quadrupeds of the dog family, esp. *Canis lupus* of northern latitudes, often preying on sheep and cattle. Phrs. *a wolf in sheep's clothing*, person of mild appearance and manners, but of a sinister and malevolent nature; *to cry wolf*, raise a false alarm; *to keep the wolf from the door*, stave off want or destitution; *to have a wolf by the ears*, be in a dangerous dilemma. **2**. Rapacious, greedy, person. **3**. (mus.) Discords heard from keyboard instrument when tuned according to a system of unequal temperament.

wolf (II.), vb. trans., fr. prec. To devour ravenously and rapidly, as from hunger or greed: *to wolf one's dinner*, also *wolf down*, gulp down, swallow hungrily.

wolf-cub, n. **1**. Young wolf. **2**. Member of the junior branch of the Boy Scouts.

wolf-dog, n. **1**. Dog for hunting or guarding sheep &c. against wolves. **2**. Hybrid between dog and wolf.

wolf-fish, n. Large voracious fish of Atlantic coasts.

wolf-hound, n. *Irish, Russian, wolf-hound*, breeds of large dogs originally kept for hunting wolves.

wolfish, adj. [1. woolfish; 2. wulfiʃ]. **wolf** (I.) & **-ish**. Resembling a wolf, esp. in nature; cruel, fierce, rapacious.

wolfishly, adv. Prec. & **-ly**. In a wolfish manner.

wolfishness, n. See prec. & **-ness**. Quality of being wolfish.

wolfram, n. [1. woolfrəm; 2. wulfrəm]. Mod. Germ., fr. *wolf*, see **wolf**, *rahm*, 'cream'; for the second element, cp. O.E. *rēam*; Du. *room*; O.N. *rjómi*, 'cream'. **1**. Mineral ore yielding tungsten. **2**. (now rare) Tungsten.

wolframite, n. [1. woolframīt; 2. wulfrəmait]. Prec. & **-ite**. Wolfram.

wolf's-bane, n. Aconite, esp. species found in the Alps &c., with yellowish flowers.

wolf's-claws, n. Also *wolf's-foot*, club-moss.

wolf's-fist, n. Puff-ball.

wolf's-foot, n. Wolf's-claws.

wolfskin, n. [1. woolfskin; 2. wulfskin]. **a** Skin of wolf; **b** rug, cloak &c. made of this.

wolf's-milk, n. Kind of spurge, with sticky, milky sap.

wolf-spider, n. **a** Tarantula; **b** spider that chases its prey instead of entrapping it in a web.

wolf-tooth, n. Small extra tooth sometimes developing in horse in front of molar.

wolverene, -ine, n. [1. woolverēn; 2. wulvərīn]. Formed as dimin. of **wolf** (I.). **1**. Carnivorous mammal, *Gulo luscus*, of N. American forests, with strong limbs and bushy tail; skunk-bear or glutton. **2**. The skin of this animal as fur.

woman (I.), n. [1. wooman; 2. wumən]. O.E. *wīfman*; M.E. *wimman, wumman*; **wife** & **man**. **1**. Human being of female sex; **a** as contrasted with *man*; Phrs. *woman of the world*, one who is sophisticated, accustomed to society &c.; *single woman*, spinster; *to play the woman*, give way to unmanly weakness, weep &c.; *women's rights*, legal equality with men; *my good woman*, patronizing mode of address; **b** adult human female, as contrasted with *child, girl*: *my daughter will soon be a woman*. **2**. Women in general, female part of human race, womankind: *woman is weaker than man*. Phr. *born of woman*, mortal. **3**. Lady-in-waiting: *one of the queen's women*. **4**. Feminine character, emotions, qualities &c.: *there is little of the woman in her*. **5**. Man with feminine or effeminate qualities: *the governors are a set of old women*. **6**. (attrib.) Female: *woman-doctor* &c.

woman (II.), vb. trans., fr. prec. (rare) **1**. To cause to act like a woman, make effeminate or weak. **2**. To address as, refer to as a 'woman', instead of using the supposedly more dignified term 'lady'.

-woman, as suff., denoting woman connected with, occupied with, some specified object or profession &c.; or of specified nationality &c., e.g. *churchwoman, dairywoman, Englishwoman, horsewoman, needlewoman* &c.

woman-hater, n. [1. wooman hātər; 2. wumən hèitə]. Man with habitual aversion to women; a misogynist.

womanhood, n. [1. woomanhood; 2. wumənhud]. **woman** (I.) & **-hood**. Condition of being a woman; character or qualities of women in general.

womanish, adj. [1. woomanish; 2. wuməniʃ]. **woman** (I.) & **-ish**. (usually in disparaging sense) Characteristic of or resembling a woman; weak, effeminate: *womanish sentiment*.

womanishly, adv. Prec. & **-ly**. In a womanish manner.

womanishness, n. See prec. & **-ness**. State or quality of being womanish.

womanize, vb. trans. & intrans. [1. woomanīz; 2. wumənaiz]. **woman** (I.) & **-ize**. **1**. trans. To make womanish, effeminate. **2**. intrans. (colloq.) To practise sexual intercourse with women outside wedlock.

womankind, n. [1. woomankīnd; 2. wumənkaind]. **woman** (I.) & **-kind**. Women collectively. Phr. *one's womankind*, women of one's family or household.

womanless, adj. [1. woomanles; 2. wumənlis]. **woman** (I.) & **-less**. Without women.

womanlike, adj. [1. woomanlīk; 2. wumənlaik]. **woman** (I.) & **-like**. Resembling or characteristic of a woman.

womanliness, n. [1. woomanlines; 2. wumənlinis]. Next word & **-ness**. Quality of being womanly.

womanly, adj. [1. woomanli; 2. wumənli]. **woman** (I.) & **-ly**. **a** Having the good qualities of a woman; tender, sympathetic, kind &c.; **b** suited, natural to, a woman: *womanly feelings, intuition, modesty* &c.

womb, n. [1. wōōm; 2. wūm]. O.E. *wāmb*, M.E. *wōmb*, 'belly, womb'; cp. O.H.G., Goth. *wamba*; O.N. *vǫmb*; Dan. *vom*. Organ in female mammal in which the offspring are developed until the time of birth; uterus. Phrs. *falling of the womb*, downward displacement, prolapsus uteri; *fruit of the womb*, children (Isaiah xiii. 18); *in the womb of time*, in the unknown future.

wombat, n. [1. wōmbat; 2. wǒmbæt], fr. Australian native *womback, wombar*. Marsupial, nocturnal, herbivorous mammal of Australia and Tasmania, genus *Phascolomys*, of several species.

womenfolk, n. [1. wiminfōk; 2. wiminfòuk].

a Women in general, womankind; **b** *the, one's, womenfolk*, women of a family or household &c.

won(n) (I.), vb. trans. [1. wun; 2. wan]. O.E. *wunian*, 'be accustomed; to dwell, inhabit'; M.E. *wun(i)en, wonen*; cp. O.H.G. *wonēn*, 'to inhabit'; *ġiwonēn*, 'to be accustomed'; cogn. w. Goth. *wunan*, 'to take pleasure'; cp. further O.E. *wynn*, 'joy', see **wish**, **winsome**; Lat. *venus*, 'love', see **Venus**; Scrt. *vánaš*, 'desire'. See also **win**. Cp. **wont** (I.) & (II.). Obs. vb. still used by Spenser: '*the noblest knight alive Prince Arthur is, that wonnes in Faerie lond*' ('F. Q.' ii. 3. 18).

won (II.), vb. [1. wun; 2. wan]. O.E. (*ġe)wunnen*; M.E. *wunne(n), wonne(n)*; P.P. of **win**, now used also as Pret.; cp. O.E., M.E. Pret. sing. *wann*.

wonder (I.), n. [1. wunder; 2. wandə]. O.E. *wundor*, M.E. *wonder*; cp. O.H.G. *wuntar*; M. Du. *wonder*; O.N. *undr*, 'miracle, wonder'; perh. cogn. w. O.E. *wandian*, 'to flee from, to fear; to revere'; O.E. *wenden*, 'to turn, go', see **wend**; *windan*, 'to turn, twist', see **wind** (IV.). **1**. Object, person, incident &c. that excites a feeling of surprised admiration; a prodigy, miracle, marvel: *the seven wonders of the world*; *it is a wonder that he is still alive*. Phrs. *to do, work, wonders*, work with marvellous results; *signs and wonders*, miracles, portents; *a nine days' wonder*, event creating temporary sensation; (*it is*) *no wonder* (*that*), it is not surprising that: *no wonder you are late after such a night*; *for a wonder*, it is a surprising thing: *he is punctual today for a wonder*; *he's a perfect wonder*, a remarkable person. **2**. Feeling, emotion, of awe, astonishment, surprise, and admiration, excited by marvellous object, person, incident &c., feeling of awe aroused by something unexpected, apparently impossible &c.: *to be filled with wonder*; *to stare in wonder*; *their wonder increased*.

wonder (II.), vb. intrans. & trans. O.E. *wundrian*, M.E. *wundrien*, 'to wonder'; fr. O.E. *wundor*, 'miracle', see prec. **A**. intrans. To experience wonder, feel amazement, to marvel: *I wondered to see you there*; *I don't wonder at his anxiety*; *I wonder at you*, expressing disapproval. **B**. trans. **1**. *Wonder that*, to be amazed, marvel, feel astonishment at: *I wonder* (*that*) *you were able to escape*; *can you wonder that he refused?* **2**. To be desirous of knowing, feel curiosity about, be anxious to learn: *I wonder who he is*; *I can't help wondering if we were wise to do it*. Also as polite formula introducing a request: *I wonder whether I might ask you* &c., *whether I might trouble you to*...

wonderberry, n. [1. wunderberi; 2. wandəberi]. A cross between the raspberry and the dewberry.

wonderful, adj. [1. wunderfool; 2. wandəful]. **wonder** (I.) & **-ful**. **1**. Surpassing what was known or expected, arousing wonder, amazing, marvellous: *wonderful courage*; *a wonderful wealth of flowers*; *a wonderful sight*; *wonderful scenery*; *a wonderful escape*. **2**. (slang, often used as more or less meaningless intens.) Very good, splendid: *a wonderful dinner, sermon, frock* &c.

wonderfully, adv. Prec. & **-ly**. In a wonderful manner.

wondering, adj. [1. wundering; 2. wandəriŋ]. Pres. Part. of **wonder** (II.). Feeling or expressing wonder; marvelling, amazed.

wonderingly, adv. Prec. & **-ly**. In a wondering manner.

wonderland, n. [1. wunderlānd; 2. wandəlænd]. Real or imaginary country of marvels, surprising beauty or fertility &c.; fairyland.

wonderment, n. [1. wunderment; 2. wandəmənt]. **wonder** & **-ment**. Wonder, astonishment, amazement.

wonder-struck, adj. Deeply affected by some marvellous sight or event &c.; overcome with wonder.

wonder-worker, n. Person who works miracles.

wondrous, adj. & adv. [1. wúndrus; 2. wándrəs], fr. obs. *wonders*, genit. of **wonder (I.)** used as adv. & adj., see **-es**; now altered on the anal. of adjs. in **-ous**. (chiefly poet.) **1.** adj. Exciting wonder; wonderful. **2.** adv. Extraordinarily, wonderfully: *wondrous kind, beautiful* &c.

wondrously, adv. Prec. & **-ly**. In a wondrous manner, to a wondrous degree.

wondrousness, n. See prec. & **-ness**. State or quality of being wondrous.

wonky, adj. [1. wóngki; 2. wóŋki]. Apparently a new word, but formed fr. an old base; cp. O.E. *wancol*, 'wavering', & Mod. Germ. *wanken*, 'to totter' &c. From another gradational form of the base comes **wink**. (slang) **a** Shaky, tottery, unsteady; groggy, dicky: *wonky on one's legs; the wall, this tooth, is a bit wonky; the Company seems rather wonky*; **b** frail, in uncertain health; **c** wavering, unreliable, shilly-shallying.

wont (I.), adj. [1. wŏnt; 2. wount]; archaic [1. wunt; 2. want]. M.E. *wuned*, P.P. of *wunien, wunen*, O.E. *wunian*, 'to be accustomed', see next word; cp. O.H.G. *giwon*; O.N. *vanr*, 'accustomed'. (pred.) Accustomed, habituated: *as he was wont to do*.

wont (II.), vb., new formation fr. prec.; M.E. *wuned*, infin. *wunien*; O.E. *wunian*, 'to dwell; to be accustomed'; see **won (I.)**. (poet. or archaic) Only in Pres. 2nd and 3rd pers. (pl. rare); chiefly in the construction *as he wonts, as thou wontest*, (to do), as he is, as thou art, accustomed, used, (to do). The past tense is also *wont*.

wont (III.), n., fr. P.P. of prec. Usual practice, habit, custom. Prob. fr. impers. construction *her &c. was wont*, wh. became *her wont was, it was his, her, wont*: *it was her wont to rise at six*. Phr. *use and wont*, custom.

won't, vb. [1. wŏnt; 2. wount], fr. M.E. *wol not*, 'will not'. (colloq.) Will not.

wonted, adj. [1. wŏnted, wúnted; 2. wóuntid, wántid], fr. **wont (I.)** & **-ed**. (attrib.) Accustomed, customary, usual: *to return at one's wonted hour*.

wonyer, n. [1. wúnyer; 2. wánjə], fr. **won**, 'dwell, inhabit', & **-yer**. This word appears in Shakespeare, '1 Henry IV.' II. i. 73 (Cambr. Shakesp.), in the form *oneyers*, '*burgomasters and great oneyers*'. Various conjectures have been made by the Editors, but by far the most convincing is that of Mr. J. M. Robertson, who takes it to be for *wonyer*, the origin of wh. is as above. The meaning wd. thus be 'inhabitants, dwellers', & in this passage, prob. 'citizens'. The spelling is easily accounted for. The word *one* was pronounced by a large number of speakers in the 16th cent. pretty much as at present, & is often spelt *wone, won* (e.g. by Henry VIII. & Queen Elizabeth among others). Thus *won*, 'dwell', & *one* were pronounced alike, & just as *wone* was written for the latter, so, in the Shakespeare passage, *one* is written, or printed, for the former. This is known as an 'inverted spelling'.

woo, vb. trans. [1. woō; 2. wū]. O.E. *wōgian*; M.E. *wōwen*, 'to woo'; lit. 'to bend, incline, in a certain direction'; fr. stem seen in O.E. *wōh, wōg*, 'bent'; hence 'crooked, perverse'; cp. O.S. *wāh*, 'perverse'; Goth. *unwāhs*, 'blameless'; cogn. w. Scrt. *vakráś*, 'bent'. **a** To seek in marriage, try to gain the affections of; to court, make love to; **b** (hence fig.) to try to win, attempt to obtain: *to woo fame, fortune, slumber; to woo the muses*, cultivate, practise, the arts.

woobut, oubit, n. [1. ōōbit; 2. úbit]. M.E. *wolbude*, fr. **wool**, & O.E. *budda*, M.E. *bude*, 'weevil, beetle'. Hairy caterpillar, esp. woolly-bear.

wood, n. [1. wood; 2. wud]. O.E. *wudu*, 'forest; timber', earlier **widu*; M.E. *wōde*; cp. O.H.G. *vitu*; M. Du. *wede*; O.N. *viðr*, 'wood'; cogn. w. W. *gwydd*; Gael. *fiodh*, 'wood'. **1.** Tract of tree-covered land; number of trees growing in a group and covering a comparatively large space; forest: *a wood of larches; to ride through the wood(s); a house in the middle of the wood*. Phrs. *to be out of the wood*, out of danger or difficulty; *don't halloo till you are out of the wood*, don't congratulate yourself on success too soon; *to be unable to see the wood for the trees*, have one's mental vision obscured by details. **2.** Solid fibrous substance of which the hard part of a tree or shrub is composed, esp. as cut for manufacturing or other use; timber. Phrs. *in the wood*, (of wine) in cask; *from the wood*, straight from the cask, not bottled. **3.** (mus.) *The wood*, part of orchestra including wind-instruments made of wood.

wood-agate, n. Petrified wood.

wood-anemone, n. Wild anemone, having white flowers tinged with purple.

woodbine, -bind, n. [1. wóodbīn(d); 2. wúdbain(d)]. Honeysuckle.

wood-block, n. Block of fine-grained wood engraved with design for printing.

Woodbury-type, n. [1. wóodburi tīp; 2. wúdbəri taip], fr. name of inventor. **1.** Method of engraving in which a print is transferred from gelatine to a metal plate, from which further prints are made. **2.** Print produced by this method.

wood-carving, n. **1.** Act or method of carving designs or figures in wood. **2.** Piece of carving, sculpture, in wood.

woodchuck, n. [1. wóodchuk; 2. wúdtʃak]. Formed by popular etymol. fr. N. Am. Indian *wejack*. Small, brown, burrowing rodent of N.E. America, variety of marmot.

woodcock, n. [1. wóodkok; 2. wúdkɔk]. A migratory game-bird, *Scolopax rusticula*, of the same family as the snipe and sandpiper.

wood-craft, n. Knowledge of, skill in, adapting oneself to conditions of life, hunting &c. in the forest.

wood-cut, n. **1.** Engraving on block of wood used for printing. **2.** Picture, design &c. produced by printing from wood-block.

wood-cutter, n. **1.** Person engaged in cutting wood, felling trees &c. **2.** Wood-engraver.

wooded, adj. [1. wóoded; 2. wúdid]. **wood** & **-ed**. Covered with, abounding in, woods: *wooded hills, a well-wooded country*.

wooden, adj. [1. wóod(e)n; 2. wúd(ə)n]. **wood** & **-en**. **1.** Made of wood: *wooden steps, spoons*. Phrs. *wooden walls*, ships; *wooden-head*, stupid person, blockhead. **2. a** Stiff, motionless, inexpressive &c. as though carved from wood: *a wooden smile, stare, expression* &c.; **b** (of action) stiff, clumsy, ungraceful. **3.** (of character, type of intelligence &c.) Rigid, unyielding, unadaptable.

wood-engraver, n. **1.** Person who makes wood-cuts. **2.** Beetle boring beneath bark of tree.

wooden-headed, adj. Dull, stupid, unintelligent.

wooden-headedness, n. Dullness, stupidity.

woodenly, adv. [1. wóodenli; 2. wúdənli]. **wooden** & **-ly**. In a wooden manner.

woodenness, n. [1. wóodennes; 2. wúdənnis]. See prec. & **-ness**. State or quality of being wooden.

wood-fibre, n. Fibre obtained from wood and used for making paper &c.

wood-gas, n. Kind of illuminating-gas, obtained from wood.

wood-house, n. Building for storing wood.

wood-ibis, n. N. American stork, white, with black wings and tail.

woodiness, n. [1. wóodines; 2. wúdinis]. **woody** & **-ness**. State or quality of being woody.

woodland, n. [1. wóodland; 2. wúdlənd]. **1.** Land covered with forest; woods. **2.** (attrib.) Characteristic of, belonging to, growing, living, in, the woods: *woodland scenery; woodland flowers*.

woodlark, n. [1. wóodlark; 2. wúdlāk]. Small lark with spotted breast.

wood-leopard, n. Leopard moth.

woodless, adj. [1. wóodles; 2. wúdlis]. **wood** & **-less**. Destitute of woods.

wood-louse, n. Small land crustacean found in or under logs &c.

woodman, n. [1. wóodman; 2. wúdmən]. Person engaged in the care of woods, and in felling of trees.

wood-note, n. (usually pl.) **a** Song of bird; **b** (fig.) natural, artless verse.

wood-nymph, n. **1.** Nymph inhabiting woodland; dryad. **2.** Kind of moth. **3.** Kind of humming-bird.

wood-opal, n. Silicified fossil wood.

wood-paper, n. Paper made from wood-pulp.

wood-pavement, n. Pavement composed of wooden blocks.

woodpecker, n. [1. wóodpèker; 2. wúdpèkə]. Any one of a large number of species of birds, family *Picidae*, with parti-coloured plumage and strong, sharp beak, with which they extract insects from the bark of trees.

wood-pie, n. Spotted woodpecker.

wood-pigeon, n. Kind of wild pigeon, ringdove.

wood-pulp, n. Wood-fibre reduced to pulp and treated chemically for making paper.

wood-reeve, n. Official superintending woods and forests.

woodruff, n. [1. wóodruf; 2. wúdraf]. O.E. *wudurōfe*, M.E. *woderōve*. Woodland herb, *Asperula odorata*, with clusters of white scented flowers.

woodshed, n. [1. wóodshed; 2. wúdʃed]. Shed where firewood is cut and stacked.

woodsman, n. [1. wóodzman; 2. wúdzmən]. Person living in or employed in the woods; one skilled in wood-craft.

wood-sorrel, n. Genus of herbs, esp. *common wood-sorrel*, small, white-flowered herb with creeping rhizome, the wild oxalis.

wood-tar, n. Tar obtained from wood by distillation.

wood-warbler, n. Variety of American warbler.

wood-wasp, n. **a** Wasp making its nest in rotten wood; **b** wasp that hangs its nest from a branch.

wood-wind, n. Wooden wind-instruments as a section of an orchestra.

wood-wool, n. Fine shavings of pine &c. used for dressing wounds &c.

woodwork, n. [1. wóodwerk; 2. wúdwāk]. Wooden structure, esp. wooden parts of building, doors, wainscots, window-frames &c.; contrasted with *plaster work, stone-work* &c.

woody, adj. [1. wóodi; 2. wúdi]. **wood** & **-y**. **1.** Resembling, of the nature of, consisting of, wood: *woody stems*. **2.** Covered with, abounding in, woods; wooded.

woody nightshade, n. Bitter sweet.

wooer, n. [1. wōōer; 2. wūə]. **woo** & **-er**. One who woos; suitor.

woof, n. [1. wōōf; 2. wūf]. O.E. *āwef, ōwef*; M.E. *oof*, 'woof'; fr. *a-*, & *wef*, 'web', fr. *wefan*, 'to weave', see **weave**. Cross-threads in woven fabric; weft; contrasted with *warp*.

wooing, n. [1. wōōing; 2. wúiŋ]. **woo** & **-ing**. Act of one who woos; courtship.

wool (I.), n. [1. wool; 2. wul]. O.E. *wull*; M.E. *wulle, wolle*; cp. O.H.G. *wolla*; Goth. *wulla*, 'wool'; cogn. w. Lett. *wilna*; Lith. *vílna*, 'wool'; O. Prussian *wilna*, 'coat'; Lat. *lāna*; Scrt. *ū́rnā*; Gk. *lênos*, 'wool'; fr. base **wlănă-* &c., 'wool'. Cp. **avulsion** & **vellicate**. **1.** Soft, elastic hair, with scaly fibres, forming the fleece of the sheep; applied also to the coat of some varieties of goat, llama, alpaca &c.; used in the manufacture of many textile fabrics. Phrs. *dyed in the wool*, dyed before spinning; *much cry and little wool*, a fuss about nothing. **2.** Thread spun from wool; woollen yarn. **3.** Fabric woven or knitted of wool. **4.** Short, soft downy fur forming under-coat of fur-bearing animal. **5. a** Negro's crisp, curly hair; **b** (slang) person's hair; Phr. *to lose one's wool*, get excited and angry. **6.** Fibrous substance resembling wool in appearance, texture &c.; often in compounds, *cotton-, wood-wool* &c. Phr. *to pull the wool over a person's eyes*,

WOOL (II.)

deceive, hoodwink, him; *mineral wool*, mass of fine thread-like substance obtained by exposing molten slag to a strong blast. **7.** As adj.: *wool merchant*; *wool sales* &c.

wool (II.), vb. trans., fr. prec. To pull tufts or wisps of wool out of a sheep's fleece; said of a dog which chases and snaps at sheep.

wool-ball, n. Ball of matted wool sometimes found in sheep's stomach.

wool-carding, n. [1. wóol kàhrding; 2. wúl kådiŋ]. Preparation of wool-fibres by carding.

wool-combing, n. Method of preparing wool for spinning by combing and straightening fibres.

wool-dyed, adj. [1. wóol dīd; 2. wúl daid]. Dyed in the wool before spinning.

-wooled, adj. [1. woold; 2. wuld]. **wool** (I.) & -ed. Having wool of specified kind: *long-wooled* &c.

wool-fat, n. Natural oil found in sheep's wool; lanolin.

wool-fell, n. Sheep's skin and fleece.

wool-gathering, n. & adj. **1.** n. Absent-mindedness, preoccupation of mind, state of inattention to what goes on around one. **2.** adj. In a condition of absent-mindedness. Phr. *one's wits have gone wool-gathering*.

wool-grower, n. Person raising sheep for the wool.

wool-hall, n. Wool merchant's place of business.

woollen, adj. & n. [1. wóolen; 2. wúlən]. **wool** (I.) & -en. **1.** adj. Made of wool: *woollen cloth, stockings* &c. **2.** n. Woollen fabric or garment: *dressed in woollen*; (also in pl.) *woollens must be washed carefully*.

woollen-draper, n. Retail dealer in woollen garments and fabrics.

woollenette, n. [1. wòolenét; 2. wùlənét]. **woollen** & -ette. Light woollen fabric.

woolliness, n. [1. wóolines; 2. wúlinis]. Next word & -ness. State or quality of being woolly.

woolly, adj. & n. [1. wóoli; 2. wúli]. **wool** (I.) & -y. **1.** adj. **a** Pertaining to, resembling, of the nature of, made of, covered with, wool or wool-like down: *woolly sheep*; *a woolly fibre*; *woolly hair*; *woolly clothes*. **b** (fig.) indistinct, vague, blurred; lacking clearness, definiteness, precision; reverse of clear-cut, precise &c.; with various applications: *woolly painting, thinking*; *a woolly mind*; *a woolly voice* &c. **2.** n. Sweater or other woollen garment.

woolly-bear, n. Caterpillar of the tiger-moth.

wool-oil, n. Wool-fat.

wool-pack, n. Bale of wool containing 240 lb.

woolsack, n. [1. wóolsak; 2. wúlsæk]. **1.** Wool-stuffed cushion on which the Lord Chancellor sits as presiding officer of House of Lords. **2.** (fig.) Office of Lord Chancellor: *many a young lawyer has dreams of the woolsack*.

woolsey, n. [1. wóolzi; 2. wúlzi], fr. **linsey-woolsey**. Linsey-woolsey.

wool-staple, n. Quality of wool, considered specially as regards the length of the fibre.

wool-stapler, n. (archaic) Wool merchant.

wool-work, n. Embroidery in wool.

woorali, woorara, n. [1. wōōráhli, wōōráhra; 2. wūŕdli, wūŕdrə], fr. S. Am. Indian *wurali*. South American poisonous herb, curare, q.v.

wootz, n. [1. wōōts; 2. wūts], fr. native word. A variety of steel made in India.

wop (I.). See **whop**.

Wop (II.), n. Origin doubtful. (Am. slang) Name given to any immigrant into the United States from the south of Europe, esp. from Italy.

word (I.), n. [1. wěrd; 2. wǎd]. O.E. *word*, 'word; what is said; speech; sentence', M.E. *wōrd*; O.H.G. *wort*; O.S. *word*; Goth. *waurd*; cogn. w. Lat. *verbum*; O. Prussian *wirds*, 'word'; Lith. *var̃das*, 'name'; fr. base *wer-dh-*, 'word', expanded fr. *were-* &c., 'to speak', seen in Gk. *eirein*, 'to say' (fr. *werjō-*); *rhēsis*, 'speech'; *rhētōr*, 'orator', see **verb** & cp. **rhetor**; Scrt. *vratám*, 'order'; O. Slav. *rota*, 'oath'; possibly also, w. -k-

extension, Goth. *wrōhs*, 'accusation'; O.E. *wrēgan*, 'to accuse'. **1.** The simplest element of speech; a group of speech-sounds, or even a single sound, serving as the name of an object, representing an idea, or indicating the relation between ideas: *words are classified as parts of speech*; *a word of two syllables*; *an English word*; *to use long words*; *I can't hear a word (of what) you say*; *to say a few words*, make a few remarks, a short speech; *words without actions are of little use*; *to put one's thoughts into words*. Phrs. *(a man) of few words*, habitually taciturn; *in a word*, in short, to sum up; *to have no words for*, be unable to describe; *play upon words*, pun; *a word and a blow*, impetuous action; *the last word*, (i.) latest authoritative pronouncement; (ii.) *last word in*, of something embodying the most recent discoveries and improvements: *the last word in wireless, in comfort* &c.; *to have the last word*, make a crushing, unanswerable, final remark in a dispute; *the last word has not yet been said on (a subject)*, there are further arguments to be considered, fresh facts still to be discovered; *word for word*, literally; verbatim; *word of command*, direction indicating specific movement to soldiers drilling &c. **2.** Written or printed word, group of graphic symbols representing a word: *to write a few words*; *to cross out a word*. **3.** (often pl.) Thing said, speech, remark: *to listen to one's concluding words*. Phrs. *warm, hot, words*, angry speech; *fair words*, flattering, conciliatory, speech; *big words*, boasting; *by word of mouth*, orally; *on, with, the word*, immediately after specific word has been uttered; *a word in, out of, season*, advice offered seasonably, inopportunely; *a word in one's ear*, confidential remark, hint &c.; *to have words (with)*, quarrel (with); *can I have a word with you?*, a private conversation with; *to suit the action to the word*, carry out an action mentioned; *to eat one's words*, to retract what one has said, apologize for insult &c.; *to bandy words with*, argue, dispute, with; *to put in a word for*, speak in defence or recommendation of; *to waste one's words*, speak in vain; *no good wasting words on*, (i.) useless to argue with (a person); (ii.) useless to discuss (a subject); *to hang on one's words*, listen eagerly to. **4.** Command, order, direction, spoken signal: *his word is law*; *to give the word to fire*. Phrs. *mum's the word*, the matter is not to be mentioned; *sharp's the word*, hurry up. **5.** Password: *to give the word*. **6.** Message, communication; tidings: *to send word to a person*; *to receive word of one's coming*; *I have had no word from him since he left*. **7.** Promise, assurance: *to give, pledge, keep, break, one's word*; *a man of his word*; *to be as good as one's word*, live up to one's promises; *word of honour*, statement made, promise given, upon one's honour; *upon, or 'pon, my word!*, exclamation of surprise; *upon my word (I don't know what to make of it* &c.), I assure you that I really don't &c. **8.** (theol.) **a** *The Word*, translating Gk. *Lógos*; the second person of the Trinity before the Incarnation; **b** (i.) the Holy Scriptures; (ii.) specif., the Gospel message: *to preach the Word to the heathen*; also *God's Word, Word of God*; *ministers of the Word*, the clergy.

word (II.), vb. trans., fr. prec. To put into, express in, words; to phrase, turn: *I should word it rather differently*; *a beautifully worded address* &c.

word-blind, adj. Unable, through mental defect, to understand written or printed words.

word-book, n. A recent Germanizing affectation based on Mod. Germ. *wörterbuch*; cp. also Du. *woordenbock* & Swed. *ordbok*. Lexicon, dictionary.

word-deaf, adj. Unable, through mental defect, to understand spoken words.

word-formation, n. Mode of forming words by inflexion, or by other suffixes, or by composition.

WORK (I.)

wordily, adv. [1. wěrdili; 2. wǎdili]. **wordy** & -ly. In a wordy manner; verbosely.

wordiness, n. [1. wěrdines; 2. wǎdinis]. **wordy** & -ness. Quality of being wordy.

wording, n. [1. wěrding; 2. wǎdiŋ]. **word** (II.) & -ing. The way in which anything is said; choice and arrangement of words in expressing specific ideas, esp. in writing; phrasing.

wordless, adj. [1. wěrdles; 2. wǎdlis]. **word** (I.) & -less. Without words; incapable of speech.

word-painter, n. Person skilled in word-painting.

word-painting, n. The act of calling up an image, a scene, an action, or an event before the mind by verbal description; vivid description of actions, events &c.

word-perfect, adj. Knowing, and able to repeat, a passage, a part in play &c., word for word, by heart.

word-picture, n. A description of an object, scene, event &c. which is so vivid as to call up before the mind that which is described.

word-play, n. **1.** Subtle discussion or exchange of repartee, verbal fencing. **2.** Play on words.

word-splitting, n. [1. wěrd splitiŋ; 2. wǎd splitiŋ]. Over-subtle argument, sophistry.

word-square, n. Arrangement, one below another, of a set of selected words of equal length so that each may be read from top to bottom or from side to side.

wordy, adj. [1. wěrdi; 2. wǎdi]. **word** (I.) & -y. **1.** Consisting of, expressed in, words: *wordy warfare*. **2. a** Given to using too many words; prolix, verbose: *a wordy speaker*; **b** expressed in an unnecessary number of words; verbose, diffuse: *his style is too wordy*.

wore, vb. [1. wōr; 2. wō]. Pret. of **wear**.

work (I.), n. [1. wěrk; 2. wǎk]. O.E. *weorc*, 'work (act and result); action; a building; a fortification'; M.E. *werk, worc*; O.S. *werk*; O.H.G. *werach*; cogn. w. Gk. *érgon*, 'action, work', for *wergon*, see **erg**; also Gk. *órganon*, 'instrument', for *worg-* see **organ**. Generally, any form of physical or intellectual activity engaged in for the purpose of accomplishing a desired end. **1.** Bodily or intellectual labour deliberately performed and directed to some specific object; purposeful activity: *he does the work of two men*; *the work of building a house, of writing a dictionary, is exacting*; *many men, rich and poor, appear to do no work*. Phrs. *to set to work*, start doing something; *at work upon*, engaged in, occupied with. **2.** Labour of specific kind performed as a person's regular occupation and employment, esp. **a** as a means of livelihood; handicraft, trade, profession &c.: *the work of a stone-mason, of a miner, an agricultural labourer* &c.; *a clerk does his work at a desk, a surgeon does his at an operating table*; *the man had been out of work for many weeks*; *father has gone to (his) work*; Phr. *at work*, specif., engaged in one's regular business; **b** special study, scientific investigation, research &c. **3.** Particular task, duty, undertaking, which one is morally or legally bound to perform, or which one has set oneself to accomplish: *I have a lot of work I must do tonight*. Phr. *to have one's work cut out (for one)*, to have a difficult task before one. **4.** Object, stuff, materials, instruments, of any kind at, or with which, one is working: *bring your work out into the garden*; specif., embroidery, needlework. **5.** Something produced by manual or intellectual work; **a** artistic creations of the craftsman: *the work of silversmiths, sculptors, and other artificers*; **b** creations of imagination; writings, paintings, musical compositions &c.: *a work, the works, of Scott, Keats, Beethoven, Velazquez*; specif., *the works of* ——, usually the complete set of works, musical compositions, pictures, of a writer, composer, painter &c.; **c** (sing.) the product of the intellectual or imaginative activity of the artist, craftsman,

author &c., considered from the point of view of form, structure, style: *one can hardly fail to recognize the work of Milton, of Velazquez, of Grinling Gibbons, when one sees it*. **6.** (in pl.) Various kinds of engineering structures, such as bridges, docks, embankments &c. **7.** Any of various structures wrought by hand or by machinery; usually preceded by a qualifying word, or as the second element of a compound: *iron-work, basket-work, earthwork* &c. (See each word.) **8.** (in pl., often with sing. construction) Establishment where industry or manufacturing is carried on: *brick works, iron works* &c.; *many owners of factories spend most of their lives at the works*. **9. a** Those essential parts of a machine which move, and either themselves perform the functions for which the machine was designed, or set up the necessary movements in other parts: *the works of a watch, a piano*; **b** (colloq., facet.) the internal organs of the body, esp. of the thorax and abdomen. **10. a** Activity, or action generally: *the devil and all his works*; *it was the work of a moment to cut off the light*; **b** the result of some specific process, operation, action: *this is the work of an enemy*. **11.** (theol.) Good deeds performed by religious persons, which if springing from a true and lively faith are pleasing to God and an element, through the merits of Christ, in effecting the salvation of the soul; contrasted from the latter point of view with *Faith*; *works of supererogation*, such works performed over and above what is necessary for the individual's salvation. **12.** (phys.) The result of a transference of one kind of energy into another.

work (II.), vb. intrans. & trans. O.E. *wyrċan*, M.E. *virchen* wd. have become Mod. Eng. [wɅtʃ]; the present vb. is a new formation fr. the n., q.v. See also **wrought**. **A.** intrans. **1. a** To expend effort, engage in mental or physical activity, to some specific end; to toil, labour, exert oneself: *to work hard*; *to work with a will*; *to work for a good master*; *to work for the public good*; *you have worked too long*; Phrs. *to work against*, to oppose, use one's influence &c. against; *to work against time*, strive to finish a task within limited time; **b** specif., to do needlework &c., sew, embroider. **2. a** (of mechanism, an organ of the body &c.) To perform its normal function, operate, have some form of activity, be in action: *his heart is working badly*; *the saw-mill is not working*; *the electric bell won't work*; *the door works on a spring*; *to work smoothly, freely, stiffly*; **b** (fig.) to be successful, effective; achieve desired result: *the charm worked, failed to work*; *the plan worked well*. **3. a** (usually followed by adv.) To make, wear, a way, a passage; to pass in a specific direction, esp. gradually, encountering opposition: *his elbow has worked through the sleeve*; *the root worked down between the stones*; *we worked south through the forest*; also *to work through a list*; *to work round to the point from which the discussion started*; **b** (followed by adj.) to come gradually, as result of repeated movement, into a specified condition: *to work loose, free* &c. **4.** To be employed, have regular occupation: *he is not working just now*; *he works in a jam factory, for a farmer*. **5.** (lit. and fig.) To be in a state of agitated activity; to twitch: *his features worked with excitement*. **6. a** To ferment; **b** (fig.) to permeate by slow degrees and produce results: *just drop a judicious hint and leave it to work in his mind*. **7.** (hort., of dormant bud) To become active, to shoot. **B.** trans. **1. a** To control or supply motion of, operate, cause to function: *to work a machine*; *to work a treadle with one's foot*; *the mill-wheel is worked by the stream*; **b** to compel to work: *to work one's servants unmercifully*; **c** to move, bring into action: *to work one's jaws*. **2. a** To expend effort upon, labour in, do or direct work of, operate in: *to work a farm*; *the silver-mines are no longer worked*; *to work a house with one servant*; *the fisherman works the stream*; **b** to solve (a sum, problem &c.). **3. a** To prepare, treat, by applying intermittent pressure, kneading, hammering &c.: *to work dough to the right consistency*; *to work iron* (see **wrought**); **b** to prepare, cultivate (soil &c.) by digging, ploughing &c. **4.** To bring about, effect, accomplish: *to work a miracle*; *time works many changes*; *to work one's will*; *to work wonders*. **5. a** To achieve a passage, penetrate, by exertion: *to work one's way upwards, through the jungle* &c.; **b** to obtain by labour: *to work one's passage* (on a ship), pay for it in work. **6. a** (reflex.) To pass into specified condition, as result of repeated movements: *the rope has worked itself loose*; **b** to bring oneself into specified frame of mind, or bodily condition: *to work oneself into a temper, a fever* &c. **7. a** To embroider, produce (design &c.), in needlework: *to work a design on a banner*; **b** to make a design on, in needlework &c.: *to work a robe with lilies in silver thread*. **C.** Followed by adverb or preposition. *Work at*, intrans., to elaborate, apply oneself to: *he is working at a new invention*; to study, apply one's energies to learning: *to work at history and literature*. *Work for*, intrans., to strive, work, with specified object in view: *to work for peace, for a prize* &c. *Work in*, **1.** trans., to introduce, put in, mingle: *the lecture would be improved if you could work in a few jokes*; **2.** intrans., to combine well, fit in: *his plans will not work in with ours*. *Work off*, trans., **1.** to dispose of, get rid of, palm off: *he worked off all his oldest goods*; *to work off a stale joke on a victim*; **2.** to get rid of by expending: *to work off superfluous energy*. *Work on, upon*, intrans., to influence, have an effect on, act upon. *Work out*, **1.** trans., **a** to discover by study and application; to reckon, calculate, compute (amount, solution &c.): **b** to exhaust: *the mine was worked out long ago*; *the subject was soon worked out as a topic of conversation*; **c** to develop, elaborate, amplify, plan out (a scheme &c.); **2.** intrans., **a** (of problem &c.) to admit of solution; **b** (of amount) to be calculated, appear as result of reckoning: *it works out at £5 each*. *Work up*, trans., **1.** to build up gradually, by effort, industry &c.: *to work up one's custom, reputation* &c.; **2. a** to promote, instigate, foment: *to work up a rebellion, a friendly feeling* &c.; **b** to arouse, excite, strong emotion in: *to work up an audience to a state of frenzy*; also *to work up the feelings* &c. *of an audience*; **3. a** to combine and manipulate (raw materials) into a finished work: *to work up a lump of clay into a bust*; **b** to elaborate and develop (a piece of work) into something more highly wrought: *to work up a sketch into a picture* &c.

workability, n. [1. wĕrkabíliti; 2. wɅkəbíliti]. See next word & -ity. State of being workable.

workable, adj. [1. wĕrkabl; 2. wɅkəbl]. **work** (II.) & **-able**. **a** Capable of being worked, cultivated, worked upon: *the ground is too wet to be workable*; **b** capable of being executed, carried out; practicable: *a workable plan*.

workableness, n. Prec. & **-ness**. State or quality of being workable; practicability.

workably, adv. See prec. & **-ly**. In a workable manner.

workaday, adj. [1. wĕrkadā; 2. wɅkədei]. Characteristic of, suitable for, ordinary working days; hence ordinary, dull, commonplace: *this workaday world, life* &c.

work-bag, n. Bag for holding materials for needlework &c.

work-basket, n. Basket for holding materials necessary for needlework &c.

work-box, n. Box for holding materials for sewing &c.

workday, n. [1. wĕrkdā; 2. wɅkdei]. Day on which ordinary work is carried on; contrasted with *Sunday*, or *holiday*.

worker, n. [1. wĕrker; 2. wɅkə]. **work** (II.) & **-er**. **a** One who, that which, works; specif. **b** worker-ant, -bee &c.

worker-ant, n. One of the main body of ants (undeveloped females) which carry on the work of the community.

worker-bee, n. One of the main body of bees in a hive (contrasted with *drones*, or *queens*) which collect honey.

workhouse, n. [1. wĕrkhous; 2. wɅkhaus]. Institution, supported by public funds, in which the paupers of a parish or larger area are maintained.

working (I.), adj. [1. wĕrking; 2. wɅkiŋ], fr. Pres. Part. of **work** (II.). **1.** Occupied by, spent in, work: *working hours*. **2.** Required for actual financial needs of commercial enterprise, firm &c.: *working capital, expenses*. **3.** Adapted to requirements of constructor or person elaborating a scheme, theory &c.: *a working drawing, plan* &c.; *a working hypothesis*. **4.** Engaged actively in work, not merely supervising: *a working builder*.

working (II.), n. **work** (II.) & **-ing**. **1.** Act, operation, activity, process: *the working of conscience*; *the workings of nature*. **2.** Mode, manner, according to which an action or process takes place: *the exact working of wireless telephony cannot be understood without a training in physics*. **3.** (usually pl.) That part of a mine or quarry which is being worked.

working-class, n. Manual workers collectively.

working-day, n. **1.** [1. wĕrking dā; 2. wɅkiŋ dei]. One on which ordinary work is carried on, workday; contrasted with a holiday. **2.** [1. wĕrking dā; 2. wɅkiŋ déi]. Number of hours recognized as normal day's work.

working-man, n. Member of working-class; man employed in manual work.

working-out, n. Development of detail, elaboration of drafted scheme &c.

workless, adj. [1. wĕrkles; 2. wɅklis]. **work** (I.) & **-less**. Having no work, without employment.

workman, n. [1. wĕrkman; 2. wɅkmən]. **1.** Man employed in manual work; labourer, artisan, mechanic &c. **2.** One who does, or makes, something, considered from the point of view of the quality of his work; a craftsman: *a very decent fellow but a poor workman*. Phr. *a bad workman finds fault with his tools*, inefficient people always find excuses for their failures.

workmanlike, adj. [1. wĕrkmanlīk; 2. wɅkmənlǎik]. Prec. & **-like**. Like, suitable for, characteristic of, a skilled workman.

workmanship, n. [1. wĕrkmanship; 2. wɅkmənʃip]. **workman** & **-ship**. **1. a** The special skill of a craftsman; **b** this thought of in relation to its quality: *the exquisite workmanship of Cellini*. **2.** Something produced as the result of work, skill &c.: *this box is my workmanship*.

work-people, n. Manual workers collectively; persons employed by a master to do manual labour.

work-room, n. Room in which work is done.

workshop, n. [1. wĕrkshop; 2. wɅkʃɔp]. Room or building in which work, esp. a handicraft, is carried on.

work-shy, adj. Unwilling to work.

work-table, n. Table with furnished fittings and accessories for needlework.

workwoman, n. [1. wĕrkwooman; 2. wɅkwumən]. Woman employed in manual work; specif., one employed in needlework.

world, n. [1. wĕrld; 2. wɅld]. O.E. *weorold*. M.E. *wer(e)ld, wor(e)ld*; cp. O.S. *werold*. O.H.G. *weralt*, 'world'; a very old compound fr. stem *wer-*, 'man', see first element of **werewolf**, & **ald-**, 'age, generation of men'; see **old, eld. 1.** The earth and the heavens; the universe. Phrs. *not for the world*, not on any account; *for all the world like*, exactly like; *to be all the world to*, be everything to. **2.** The earth and its inhabitants; the human race; mankind as a whole: *great reformers* *generally have the world against them at first; Athanasius against the world; the whole world suffered in the Great War.* **3.** Mode, form, of life or existence : *this world and the next; too good for this world; the world to come,* the future state ; '*He ... Allur'd to brighter worlds, and led the way*' (Goldsmith, 'Deserted Village', 170); *the other world,* existence after this present life, heaven. **4.** Human life on earth ; specif. **a** individual life and experience in the world : *how is the world using you ?, the world goes very well with me;* **b** individual outlook on life; range of thought, and emotional experience &c. : *his world was a very narrow one ;* **c** habits, customs, way of life, mode of thought &c., of mankind in general : *to see much of the world in every part of the globe.* **5. a** The purely material concerns of human life as contrasted with the spiritual : *the world, the flesh, and the devil; he forsook the world and turned his thoughts to heaven;* **b** the part of mankind chiefly occupied with material concerns, worldly persons. **6. a** Humanity considered in its social aspect ; organized society : *he retired to the country and shut out the world;* '*The world forgetting, by the world forgot*' (Pope, 'Eloisa to Abelard', 208); **b** some particular phase or section of society: *the ancient world; the fashionable world; I do not move in his world.* Phr. *man of the world,* one versed and experienced in life and society. **7.** A particular sphere, or range, of organized activities, occupations, interests ; persons identified with any of these : *the world of commerce ; the dog world ; the sporting, racing, world ; the scientific world.* **8.** One of the great primary divisions of natural objects; kingdom: *the animal, vegetable, mineral, world.* **9.** One of the hemispheres of the globe and its inhabitants ; *the New World,* America ; *the Old World,* Europe, Asia, Africa, as known before the discovery of America. **10.** One of the heavenly bodies thought of as having inhabitants and as constituted like our earth : *we are surrounded in space by innumerable worlds which may resemble our own.* **11.** As a symbol of vast size, amount, number ; a host, a sea : *a world of troubles, of sin* &c.

world - language, n. **a** Language used throughout the world ; **b** an artificial language intended for universal use.

worldliness, n. [1. wĕrldlines ; 2. wǎldlinis]. **worldly & -ness.** State or quality of being worldly.

worldling, n. [1. wŏrldling ; 2. wǎldliŋ]. **world & -ling.** Worldly person.

worldly, adj. [1. wĕrldli ; 2. wǎldli]. **world & -ly. 1.** Pertaining to the present world; earthly, mundane: *worldly interests, pleasures, ambitions, affairs ; worldly goods, property, possessions ; worldly wisdom,* experience in the ways of men, shrewdness in dealing with human affairs, esp. in advancing one's own interests. **2.** Devoted to, concerned chiefly with, the material affairs of life ; having the mind mainly bent on success in life, material riches, glory, prosperity &c.

worldly - minded, adj. Concerned mainly with, interested in, mundane matters.

worldly - mindedness, n. State of being worldly-minded.

worldly - wise, adj. Possessed of worldly wisdom.

world-old, adj. As old as the world, hence, of extreme antiquity.

world-power, n. Political state whose policy affects the world.

world-weary, adj. Generally discontented with life and earthly conditions.

world-wide, adj. Extending over the whole world : *world-wide fame.*

worm (I.), n. [1. wĕrm ; 2. wǎm]. O.E. *wyrm ;* M.E. *wurm,* 'serpent, worm, dragon '; cp. O.H.G. *wurm ;* M. Du. *worm ;* O.N. *ormr ;* Goth. *waurms,* 'worm, serpent'; cogn. w. Lat. *vermis,* earlier **vormis,* 'worm'; see **vermi-. 1. a** One of several varieties of legless, invertebrate animals, including earth-worms, tapeworms &c. Phrs. *food for worms,* of dead person ; *even a worm will turn,* the most oppressed, humblest or meekest person will retaliate under sufficient pressure ; *the worm of conscience,* remorse ; **b** a mean-spirited, abject, contemptible person. **2.** Spiral grooving on a screw. **3.** Spiral arrangement of pipes in a still. **4.** Worm-like organ in human or animal body, specif., membrane under tongue of dog.

worm (II.), vb. trans. & intrans., fr. prec. A. trans. **1. a** *Worm one's way,* to make one's way along cautiously and gradually, in spite of obstacles and difficulties ; also (fig.) *to worm one's way into society, into a person's confidence* &c., to wriggle in, insinuate oneself by stealth, cunning, and persistence ; **b** also *worm oneself in,* same as **a. 2.** To remove worms from, esp. *to worm a dog,* purge him of intestinal worms. **3.** To extract (information &c.) by cajolery, insistent questioning &c. : *to worm secrets out of a person.* B. intrans. (rare) To crawl, wriggle, along like a worm.

worm-cast, n. Cylindrical mass of earth excreted by earth-worm, left on surface of the ground.

worm-eaten, adj. [1. wĕrm ĕtn ; 2. wǎm ĭtn]. **1.** Gnawed, bored into, perforated, by weevils &c. : *worm - eaten wood* &c. **2.** (fig.) Old, worn, out-of-date: *worm-eaten regulations, customs* &c.

worm-fishing, n. Angling with worm as bait.

worm-gear, n. Gear-wheel with teeth arranged to engage with a worm of a screw.

worm-hole, n. Hole bored by worm in earth, or by a weevil in wood &c.

worm-holed, adj. [1. wĕrm hōld ; 2. wǎm hould]. Riddled with worm-holes.

worminess, n. [1. wĕrmines ; 2. wǎminis]. **wormy & -ness.** State of being wormy.

worm-seed, n. **a** Seed of certain plants used as a vermifuge ; **b** plant yielding this seed, esp. a herb of the Levant.

worm-wheel, n. Wheel in worm-gear.

wormwood, n. [1. wĕrmwood ; 2. wǎmwud]. Not connected w. **worm** (I.). O.E., M.E. *wermōd;* cp. O.H.G. *werimuote;* etymol. doubtful ; cp. **vermouth ;** Du. *wermoet.* Aromatic, bitter perennial herb, *Artemisia absinthium,* wild and cultivated, with downy, segmented leaves and yellow flowers, used in the manufacture of absinth, vermouth &c. Phr. (fig.) *gall and wormwood,* bitter humiliation and mortification ; circumstance causing these.

wormy, adj. [1. wĕrmi ; 2. wǎmi]. **worm** (I.) **& -y.** Infested with, abounding in, bored through by, worms.

worn, adj. [1. worn ; 2. wŏn]. P.P. of **wear.** O.E. *(ge)woren.* M.E. *wōr(e)n.* **1.** Injured, impaired, made thin &c. by use, wear &c. : *worn garments.* **2.** Pinched, showing signs of exhausting toil, care &c. : *a worn and haggard face.*

worriless, adj. [1. wúriles ; 2. wárilis]. **worry** (II.) **& -less.** Without worries.

worriment, n. [1. wúriment ; 2. wárimənt]. **worry** (I.) **& -ment. 1.** Vexation, anxiety, worry. **2.** Cause of uneasiness, anxiety, or vexation.

worry (I.), vb. trans. & intrans. [1. wúri ; 2. wári]. O.E. *wyrgan ;* M.E. *wurȝen,* 'to choke, strangle, tear, worry'; cp. O.H.G. *wurgan ;* O. Fris. *werga ;* M. Du. *worghen,* 'to choke'; cp. further O.S. *wurgil,* 'band, cord '; cogn. w. Lith. *veržiu,* 'to bind, compress'; Lett. *werst,* 'to turn, twist '; O. Slav. *vrěsti,* 'to bind'; Gk. *erkhatáein,* 'to hedge in'; Lat. *vergere,* 'to bend, bow', see **verge** (II.) ; fr. base **wer(e)g-, *wṛg-* &c., 'to bend, curve, turn' ; cp. further forms w. nasal under **wring, wrong.** A. trans. **1.** (of dog &c.) To seize (quarry), shake and lacerate with the teeth : *the dog worried the rat.* Phr. *to worry the sword,* to make a quick succession of feints in fencing, in an attempt to distract opponent. **2. a** To cause annoyance to, to pester, harass, by constant importunity &c. : *to worry a person with perpetual questions, demands ;* **b** to annoy with persistent, importunate demands : *he was always worrying her to marry him.* **3. a** To cause uneasiness and anxiety to : *his prolonged absence worries me; don't let that worry you;* **b** to cause wearing bodily pain or discomfort to : *his old wound, toothache* &c. *worries him a good deal.* B. intrans. To be anxious, troubled, uneasy: *don't worry if you are late.* Phr. *to worry along,* manage to get on in spite of difficulties.

worry (II.), n., fr. prec. **1.** (of dog &c.) Act of worrying. **2.** Feeling of wearing anxiety and uneasiness : *to show signs of worry.* **3.** That which worries, cause of anxiety or annoyance : *to have many worries.*

worrying, adj. [1. wúriing ; 2. wáriiŋ], fr. Pres. Part. of **worry** (I.). Causing worry, anxiety, irritation ; annoying, vexatious : *to have a worrying time.*

worryingly, adv. Prec. **& -ly.** So as to cause worry.

worse (I.), compar. adj. [1. wĕrs ; 2. wǎs]. O.E. *wyrsa,* M.E. *wurs ;* cp. O.S. *wirs(a) ;* O.H.G. *wirs ;* Goth. *wairs,* 'worse'; cogn. w. O.S., O.H.G. *werran,* 'to confuse, mix up '; further w. Lat. *verrere,* 'to sweep, brush'; see **verricule. 1.** Bad in a higher degree: *there could be no worse misfortune ; this road is even worse than the other ; the worse for wear.* **2.** (pred.) **a** In a less satisfactory physical condition, more ill : *the patient is worse this morning ; he grew rapidly worse ; he is none the worse for the accident ;* **b** more badly situated, in less satisfactory condition or circumstances: *he will not be the worse for the change.*

worse (II.), compar. adv. O.E. *wyrs,* see prec. **1. a** In a worse manner, to a worse extent : *he sings worse than ever ;* **b** none the worse, no less ; all the better : *to like* (a person) *none the worse for being outspoken* &c. ; *to think none the worse of,* to esteem more highly. **2.** To a greater degree, with more severity : *it is blowing worse than before.*

worse (III.), n., fr. **worse** (I.). Worse thing, something more unsatisfactory or evil : *worse remains to tell.* Phr. *to go from bad to worse,* deteriorate steadily.

worsen, vb. trans. & intrans. [1. wĕrsen ; 2. wǎsən]. **worse** (I.) **& -en. 1.** trans. To make worse. **2.** intrans. To become worse.

worship (I.), n. [1. wĕrship ; 2. wǎʃip]. O.E. *weorðscipe;* M.E. *wur(ð)shipe,* 'dignity, honour, worship'; **worth** (I.) **& -ship. 1.** (archaic and obs.) Honour, dignity ; status, character, which commands the highest respect: *a man of great worship.* **2.** *Your, his, Worship,* conventional formula of respect used in addressing, or referring to, a magistrate on the bench ; also as title of a mayor : *his Worship the Mayor of B.* **3. a** The highest form of veneration and adoration, accorded only to a deity ; **b** religious observances : *divine worship, public worship.* **4.** Intense love and admiration; respect, veneration, felt for anything : *the worship of beauty, money, intellect, success* &c.

worship (II.), vb. trans. & intrans., fr. prec. A. trans. **1.** To accord worship to, to revere and adore as God. **2. a** To regard with great or excessive admiration or reverence; idolize, adore : *to worship one's wife, money ;* **b** to honour, show respect for : '*with my body I thee worship*' (Marriage Service). Phr. *to worship the ground a person treads on,* entertain the intensest affection for him (her). B. intrans. **1.** To take part in religious observances : *many people have worshipped in this church.* **2.** To feel deep reverence, adoration : *to worship at the shrine of beauty.*

worshipful, adj. [1. wĕrshipfŏol ; 2. wǎʃipfŭl]. **worship** (I.) **& -ful.** (archaic, except in titles of respect) Worthy of honour, respected : *the Worshipful Company of Fishmongers ; the Worshipful the Master* (masonic).

worshipfully, adv. Prec. **& -ly.** In a worshipful manner.

worshipfulness, n. See prec. **& -ness.** Quality of being worshipful.

worshipper, n. [1. wĕrshiper ; 2. wǎʃipə]. **worship** (II.) **& -er.** One who worships.

worst (I.), adj. [1. wĕrst; 2. wɑ̄st]. O.E. *wyrsta*; M.E. *wurst*; **worse (I.)** & **-est**. **a** Bad, severe, harmful, to the highest possible degree; exhibiting bad qualities to a more intense degree than any other or others of the same kind: *the worst dinner I ever ate*; **b** most intense: *the worst frost for a hundred years*.

worst (II.), adv. O.E. *wyrst*; see prec. In the worst manner, most badly: *there were many who played badly, but he played worst*.

worst (III.), n., fr. **worst (I.)**. That which is worst; worst person or thing; worst part, circumstance, event, result &c.: *of all bad kings, John was probably the worst*; *to prepare for the worst*; *to keep the worst for the last*; *tell me the worst*; *the worst of the winter must be past*; *the storms are at their worst in February*; *he always makes the worst of his troubles*. Phrs. *at worst*, under the most unfavourable circumstances; *to see somebody, something, at his, its, worst*, under the worst aspects; *do your worst, let him do his worst*, formula of defiance; *to get the worst of it*, be defeated; *if the worst comes to the worst*, if the most disastrous thing should happen, should it turn out as badly as possible; *the worst of it is that ...*, the most unfortunate, unfavourable, circumstance is, it happens most unfortunately that.

worst (IV.), vb. trans., fr. prec. To defeat, gain a victory over, vanquish in a contest, overthrow.

worsted, n. & adj. [1. wŏosted; 2. wŭstid], fr. Worste(a)d, in Norfolk, orig. place of manufacture. **1.** n. Twisted woollen yarn of long staple. **2.** adj. Made of worsted: *worsted socks* &c.

wort (I.), n. [1. wĕrt; 2. wɑ̄t]. O.E. *wyrt*; M.E. *wurt*, 'root, herb'; cp. O.S. *wurt*; O.H.G. *wurz*; O.N. *urt*; Goth. *waurts*, 'root, plant, herb'; cogn. w. Lat. *rādix*, 'root', see **radix**; Gk. *rhādix*, 'branch, rod'; *rhiza*, 'root', see **rhizo-**; cp. further O.N. *rōt*, 'root', see **root**. (chiefly in compounds) Herb, plant, e.g. *milkwort, ragwort*.

wort (II.), n. M.E. *wurte*; O.E. *-wyrte*; cp. M.H.G. *würze*; M. Du. *worte*, 'wort in brewing'; prob. fr. same stem as prec. Infusion of malt before fermentation.

worth (I.), adj. [1. wĕrth; 2. wɑ̄þ]. O.E. *wyrðe*; M.E. *wurþe*, 'worthy'; cp. O.S. *werth*; O.H.G. *wert*; O.N. *verðr*; Goth. *wairþs*, 'worthy'. (pred.) **1.** Having a specified value: *you can have it for sixpence, but it is worth more*; *it is worth little, much*; *it is not worth a penny*; (poet.) *it is little, nothing, worth*. **2.** Deserving of, meriting, giving adequate return for: *it is worth seeing*; *worth the trouble*. Phrs. *the game isn't worth the candle*, see **candle**; *to be worth one's salt*, see **salt**; *worth while*, (colloq.) *worth it*, worth the time, trouble, spent on it, worth the difficulty, danger &c. incurred; *not worth a damn*, quite worthless. **3.** Having property to the value of, possessions amounting to: *what is he worth?* *he is worth several millions*. Phr. *run &c. for all you are, one is, worth*, exerting the utmost strength, making every effort.

worth (II.), n. O.E. *weorð, wurð, wyrð*, 'worth, price; ransom; honour, dignity', see prec. **1. a** Material value or price of anything: *a jewel of great worth*; **b** spiritual qualities of mind and character, moral excellence: *few knew his true worth*. **2.** Amount of anything purchasable for a given sum; number of specified coins equivalent to one of higher value: *half a crown's worth of oranges*; *a shilling's worth of bird-seed*; *two shillings' worth of coppers*; also in the compounds, *pennyworth, ha'porth* &c.

worth (III.), vb. intrans. O.E. *weorðan*, M.E. *worthen*, 'to become'; cp. O.S. *werthan*; O.H.G. *werdan*; O.N. *verða*; Goth. *wairþan*, 'to become'; cp. Goth. *-wairþs*; O.E. *-weard*, 'in specified direction', see **-ward**; cogn. w. Lat. *vertere*, 'to turn', see **version**; Scrt. *vártatē*, 'turns, rolls, goes'. To betide, befall; poet., in Phr. *woe worth*, ill betide; cp. M.E. *wo mote worpen*: '*Woe worth the chase, woe worth the day!*' (Scott, 'Lady of the Lake', I. ix.).

worthily, adv. [1. wĕrdhili; 2. wɑ̄ðili]. **worthy** & **-ly**. In a worthy manner.

worthiness, n. [1. wĕrdhines; 2. wɑ̄ðinis]. See prec. & **-ness**. Quality of being worthy.

worthless, adj. [1. wĕrthles; 2. wɑ̄þlis]. **worth (II.)** & **-less**. **a** Of no worth; valueless; useless; **b** (specif. of persons) unprincipled, unreliable, of no character.

worthlessly, adv. Prec. & **-ly**. In a worthless manner.

worthlessness, n. See prec. & **-ness**. Quality of being worthless.

worthy (I.), adj. [1. wĕrdhi; 2. wɑ̄ði]. **worth (II.)** & **-y**. **1. a** Meriting honour or respect; virtuous, estimable, of good character: *a worthy man*; **b** deserving approval and support: *a worthy cause*. **2.** Fitted by character or quality for, suited to; deserving: *courage worthy of a better cause*; *a worthy adversary*; *worthy to be considered*; *worthy of death, reward* &c.

worthy (II.), n., fr. prec. **a** Person of importance and of estimable character; eminent person; a notable; *the Worthies of England*; *the Nine Worthies*; **b** (ironic) equivalent to *person, merchant*: *who is the worthy with the bald head and a beard?*

wot, vb. [1. wot; 2. wɔt], fr. O.E. *wāt*, 'I know', M.E. *wōt*; a Pret. Pres. fr. O.E. *witan*, 'to know', see **wit (I.)**. (archaic) I know; the 3rd sing. now usually *wots*, on anal. of other vbs.; but note archaic form in Phr. *God wot*, in M.E. *Godot*, 'God knows'.

would, vb. [1. wood; 2. wud]. O.E., M.E. *wolde*, Pret. of **will (III.)**.

would-be, adj. & adv. [1. wŏod bē; 2. wŭd bī]. (attrib.) Expressing a quality or state desired or intended: *a would-be poet*; *would-be poetical phrases*.

wound (I.), n. [1. wŏond; 2. wŭnd]. O.E., M.E. *wund*, 'wound'; cp. O.E. *wund*, 'wounded'; O.S. *wunda*; O.H.G. *wunda*; Du. *wond*, 'wound'; prob. cogn. w. O.E. *winnan*, 'to fight' &c.; see **win**. **1. a** Injury to any part of the body in which the skin, and often the muscular tissue, is penetrated, cut, torn &c.: *wounds received in battle*; *a fatal, mortal, wound*; *an open, contused, wound*; **b** in obs. Phr. *God's wounds*; as oath; see **zounds**. **c** injury to plant &c., involving cutting or tearing of bark &c. **2.** Injury to the feelings, self-respect, honour, affections &c.; an insult, affront.

wound (II.), vb. trans., fr. prec. To inflict a wound upon; to hurt, injure, the body or the feelings: *the shell wounded him in the head*; *he was profoundly wounded in his deepest affections*.

wound (III.), vb. [1. wound; 2. waund]. O.E. *(ge)wunden*, M.E. *wunde(n)*, P.P. of **wind (IV.)**; now used also as Pret.; cp. O.E. Pret. *wand*.

woundily, adv. Obs., fr. **woundy**, q.v.

woundless, adj. [1. wŏondles; 2. wŭndlis]. **wound (I.)** & **-less**. Free from wounds, uninjured.

wound-wort, n. Plant formerly used as remedy for wounds.

woundy, adj.[1. wŏondi; 2. wŭndi]. **wound (I.)**, **1 b**, & **-y**. Profane but rather mild and meaningless epithet, used colloquially as intensive in 17th or first half of 18th cent.; apparently more or less equivalent to *confounded*; cp. '*There was a neighbour's daughter I had a woundy kindness for*' (Farquhar, 'Twin Rivals', 1702).

wourali. See **woorali**.

wove(n), adj. [1. wŏv(en); 2. wóuv(ən)], fr. P.P. of **weave**; M.E. *(i)wōve(n)*, on the anal. of **stolen** &c.; cp. O.E. P.P. *(ge)wefen*. Made by weaving: *woven fabrics*; *wove paper*, smooth paper made on wire-gauze frame.

wow, n. [1. wou; 2. wau]. (slang, U.S.A.) A great success; something wonderful, extraordinary.

wrack, n. [1. rak; 2. ræk]. M.E. *wrac*, 'wreck', prob. fr. O.N. *wrak*, 'a wreck; refuse, trash'; cp. the O.E. cogn. *wræcu*, 'vengeance; misery'; also the cognates *wræcca, wrecca*, 'an exile'; lit. 'one driven out', see **wretch**, & cp. *wrecan*, 'to drive, expel', see **wreak** & **wreck (I.)**. The fundamental meaning is 'what is driven about, or away'. **1.** (archaic or poet.) Ruin, destruction: *everything is gone to wrack*; cp. Phr. *wrack*, now usually *rack*, *and ruin*, see **rack (III.)**. **2.** Marine vegetation cast up on the shore.

wraith, n. [1. rāth; 2. reiþ]. Etymol. doubtful; perh. a variant of **wreath**. **a** Apparition of a living person, or of one who has recently died, foretelling or announcing his death; **b** a spectre, ghost, disembodied spirit generally.

wrangle, vb. intrans. & n. [1. rănggl; 2. ræŋgl]. M.E. *wranglen*, 'to wrangle'; prob. a gradational variant of **wring (I.)** & **-le**. **1.** vb. To take part in a heated or noisy discussion or quarrel, dispute angrily, brawl. **2.** n. Noisy altercation, quarrel.

wrangler, n. [1. rănggler; 2. ræŋglə]. Prec. & **-er**. **1.** Person who wrangles, brawler. **2.** (Cambridge University) Person placed in first class of mathematical tripos; (the name has reference to the public disputation in which candidates formerly took part); *senior wrangler*, person heading the list of wranglers in any year when the order of merit was published, now obsolete.

wranglership, n. [1. rănglership; 2. ræŋgləʃip]. Prec. & **-ship**. Position of wrangler.

wrap (I.), vb. trans. & intrans. [1. rap; 2. ræp]. M.E. *wrappen*; etymol. doubtful. Cp. obs. *wlappen*, 'to wrap', & see **lap (II.)**. **A.** trans. **1.** To fold round, enfold, cover, roll up, envelop, (a person or thing) in (a folding material or garment): *to wrap a parcel in paper*; *to wrap a child in a shawl*; also *wrap up (a parcel in paper)* or *wrap a parcel up in paper*; *to wrap oneself, or another, up in a cloak*; specif., *to wrap oneself up (well)*, put on warm clothes. **2.** (in non-material sense) **a** To enshroud in, surround with, envelop (oneself): *he wraps himself in an impenetrable reserve*; Phr. *wrapped up in*, devoted to, entirely absorbed by, preoccupied with: *wrapped up in his children, in his work*; **b** to disguise, conceal: *he wraps up a sensitive diffidence of nature in a rather boisterous manner*; *to wrap up a censure in a polite formula*. **3.** To place, arrange, fold (of flexible material) so as to cover: *wrap paper round it*; *to wrap one's cloak round one*. **B.** intrans. **1.** Usually *wrap up*, to cover, enfold oneself, in wraps; specif., to put on a number of warm clothes: *mind you wrap up well*. **2.** Wrap over, to overlap.

wrap (II.), n., fr. prec. **1.** Material used for wrapping: *to take a mummy out of its wraps*. **2.** Specif., a garment, cloak &c., or a rug or other piece of fabric used for wrapping up and protecting the person from cold: *take plenty of wraps with you in the car*.

wrappage, n. [1. rápij; 2. ræpidʒ]. **wrap (I.)** & **-age**. Material used for wrapping.

wrapper, n. [1. ráper; 2. ræpə]. **wrap (I.)** & **-er**. One who, that which, wraps; material used for wrapping; specif. **a** slip of paper used to wrap up newspaper &c. for posting; **b** loose paper cover for book; **c** light dressing-gown; **d** tobacco-leaf of good quality used for outer layer of cigar.

wrapping, n. [1. ráping; 2. ræpiŋ]. **wrap (I.)** & **-ing**. Material, piece(s) of fabric &c., in which a thing is wrapped: *put plenty of wrapping round it*; *a mummy is enclosed in many wrappings*.

wrapt. See **rapt**.

wrasse, n. [1. ras; 2. ræs], fr. W. *gwrachen*. Family of brightly coloured, European sea-fish, often with very thick lips, found inshore near rocky coasts.

wrath, n. [1. rawth; 2. rɔþ]. The O.E. n. is *wrǣþþo, wrǣþu*, 'anger', w. mutation; the unmutated form *wrāþ* occurs in the adj.

meaning 'angry' &c.; cp. O.S. *wrēð*, O.H.G. (*w*)*reidi*, O.N. *reiðr*, 'angry'. Perh. cogn. w. Lat. *irrītāre*, 'to provoke, enrage', if this is fr. **in-wrīt-āre*; see **irritate**; cp. **writhe** & **wroth.** Deep, intense, anger and indignation.

wrathful, adj. [1. ráwthfool; 2. rɔ́þful]. Prec. & **-ful.** **a** Feeling or expressing wrath; angry, deeply indignant, incensed; **b** animated by wrath: *wrathful indignation.*

wrathfully, adv. Prec. & **-ly.** In a wrathful manner.

wreak, vb. trans. [1. rēk; 2. rīk]. O.E. *wrecan*, 'to drive, push; to avenge'; M.E. *wrēken*, 'to avenge'; cp. O.S. *wrekan*; O.H.G. *rehhan*, 'to punish, avenge'; O.N. *reca*; O. Fris. *wreka*, 'to drive, oppress, revenge'; Goth. *wrikan*, 'to pursue'; cogn. w. Lat. *urgēre*, 'to push, force, drive', see **urge**; O. Slav. *vragŭ*, 'enemy'; Lith. *vargas*, 'oppression'. See **wrack** & **wreck.** **1.** (archaic) To avenge. **2.** To carry out, inflict, put into operation: *to wreak vengeance, one's wrath, malice &c., upon a person.*

wreath, n. [1. rēth; 2. rīþ]. O.E. *wrǣþ*, 'band, wreath', fr. **wrāþi-*; cp. O.E. *wrīðan*, 'to twist', Pret. sing. *wrāþ*; see **writhe** & **wraith.** **1. a** A circle made of twisted branches, sprays &c., often adorned with leaves and flowers, used as decoration for tombs and other monuments, in commemorations and celebrations, as a crown for a poet; a garland; **b** (fig.) as symbol of the honour and veneration paid to a poet or conqueror; **c** carved or other representation of a wreath. **2.** A curling, eddying, drifting spiral, streak, wisp &c., esp. of smoke, vapour, mist &c.; also a light, drifting mass of sand, snow &c.

wreathe, vb. trans. & intrans. [1. rēdh; 2. rīð]. Formed fr. prec. The final consonant of the vb. is voiced because orig. followed by a suff.; cp. *breathe*, contrasted w. *breath.* **A.** trans. **1.** To twist, wind, weave, into a wreath: '*From his slack hand the garland wreathed for Eve Down dropt*' (Milton, 'P. L.' ix. 892-3). **2.** To adorn, hang, encircle, with, or as with, a wreath: *the bays that wreathe the poet's brow.* Phr. *wreathed in smiles*, smiling. **3.** To wind round, clasp, entwine: *to wreathe one's arms about a person.* **B.** intrans. (of smoke, mist, plants, &c.). To move, coil, in, or as in, wreaths.

wreck (I.), n. [1. rek; 2. rɛk]. Variant of **wrack**; O.E. *wræc*, 'exile, misery', M.E. *wrac, wrec*; cp. O.E. *wrecan*, 'to drive, expel', see **wreak.** **1.** Destruction, esp. **a** such disablement of a ship by winds and waves that she has to be abandoned; **b** destruction of other objects, esp. the demolition of houses and buildings generally, by fire, storm &c. **2.** Ruin, the bringing to nought, upsetting, annihilation (of one's fortunes, plans, hopes &c.). **3. a** A ship that has been wrecked and abandoned at sea; a ship cast on a reef, or the shore, and broken up by the force of the waves &c.; **b** a ruined building demolished by fire, storm &c.; Phr. *a* (*mere*) *wreck of his former self*, said of a person who is emaciated and weakened by ill-health or the ravages of some disease; **c** ruined hopes, plans &c.

wreck (II.), vb. trans. & intrans., fr. prec. **A.** trans. **1.** To cause wreck, **a** to a ship; **b** to a train, building &c. **2.** To ruin, destroy, bring to nought (plans, hopes &c.). **B.** intrans. **1.** (rare, chiefly fig.) To be destroyed, come to grief: *our plans will wreck, if at all, on our own lack of conviction.* **2.** To be concerned with a wreck, either as a rescuer or as a plunderer.

wreckage, n. [1. rékij; 2. rékidž]. **wreck** & **-age.** **1.** Material from a ship, building &c. that has been wrecked; remnants, dilapidated fragments left from a wreck. **2.** (fig.) Act or process of wrecking: *to witness the wreckage of one's hopes.*

wrecked, adj. [1. rekt; 2. rɛkt], fr. P.P. of **wreck.** Involved in a wreck; having suffered from, having been damaged by, wreck: *wrecked ship, sailors.*

wrecker, n. [1. réker; 2. rékə]. **wreck** & **-er.** **1. a** One who, that which, wrecks; specif. **b** person who attempts to lead ship to destruction on a coast in order that he may plunder the wreckage. **2.** Person employed in recovering cargo &c. from wrecked ship.

wrecking, adj., fr. Pres. Part. of **wreck (II.).** Causing ruin, tending to destroy; esp. *a wrecking amendment, motion*, one designed to frustrate a previous motion, or a bill.

wreck-master, n. Official appointed to take charge of cargo &c. from wrecked vessel.

wren, n. [1. ren; 2. rɛn]. O.E. *wrǣnna*, name of the bird; M.E. *wrenne*; prob. fr. O.E. *wrǣne*, 'lecherous'; etymol. unknown. Name of a genus, *Troglodytes*, of small passerine song-birds with rounded wings and short, erect tail; also name of certain warblers, esp. the *willow-wren*, and of the kinglet or *golden-crested wren.*

wrench (I.), n. [1. rench; 2. rɛntʃ]. O.E. *wrenċ*, 'trick, artifice'; M.E. *wrench*, 'guile'; cp. M.H.G. *ranc*, 'deceit'; cp. further O.E. *wrincle*, see **wrinkle**; *wringan*, 'to twist', also **wring, wrong** & words there referred to. **1. a** Sudden violent twist, jerk, pull, strain: *to pull out a tooth with one wrench*; **b** injury inflicted on a joint, tendon, muscle by a wrench: *to give one's knee a wrench.* **2.** (fig.) Painful emotion comparable to a physical wrench in its intensity, esp. such an emotion felt at separation, abrupt discontinuance of old habits and occupations &c.: *it was a terrible wrench to leave the old home*; *the wrench of parting with one's children.* **3.** Tool for grasping and turning nuts &c.

wrench (II.), vb. trans. O.E. *wrenċan*, 'to twist, turn'; fr. prec. **1.** To pull with a sudden, sharp, violent, jerk: *to wrench a plant out of the ground*; *to wrench a box open*; *cows wrench the grass.* **2. a** To twist, jerk, and tear from normal position (a tendon, ligament &c. of the body); **b** (fig.) to distort, pervert, give a twist to (meaning of what is said, facts, words).

wrest (I.), vb. trans. [1. rest; 2. rɛst]. O.E. *wrǣstan*; M.E. *wrasten, wresten*, 'to twist, wrest'; cp. Du. *vriste*; O.N. *reista*, 'to twist'; fr. stem **wrei-*, **wri-* &c., 'to turn, twist'; see **writhe.** **1. a** To pull away forcibly, tear, wrench away: *to wrest a weapon from one's grasp*; **b** (also fig.) to extract by toil and pains; to extort: *to wrest a living from the barren ground*; *to wrest her secrets from Nature.* **2.** To distort, pervert, turn away from its true meaning, intent &c.: *you must not wrest my words from their obvious meaning in that way.*

wrest (II.), n., fr. prec. Key for tuning a stringed instrument, esp. a harp.

wrest-block, n. Part of piano-frame to which wrest-pins are fastened.

wrestle (I.), vb. intrans. & trans. [1. résl; 2. résl]. O.E. *wrǣstlian*; M.E. *wrestlen*; cp. M. Du. *wrastelen.* **wrest (I.)** & **-le.** **1.** To struggle with opponent by grappling with and endeavouring to throw him, by lifting and levering, esp. in a contest of strength and skill; constructions: (i.) (absol.) *I saw the champions wrestle*; (ii.) *to wrestle with*; (iii.) (trans. use) *to wrestle a man for a prize, I'll wrestle you for it.* **2.** (fig.) *Wrestle with*, to strive, contend with, struggle against, make an effort to deal with or overcome: *to wrestle with a task, difficulty, temptation* &c. Phr. *to wrestle with God*, pray with great earnestness.

wrestle (II.), n., fr. prec. **1.** Act of wrestling, specif., wrestling-bout. **2.** (fig.) A struggle, tussle, strenuous effort to deal with a difficult task.

wrestler, n. [1. résler; 2. réslə]. **wrestle (I.)** & **-er.** One who wrestles; specif., a trained person who regularly engages in wrestling matches.

wrestling, n. [1. résling; 2. résliŋ]. **wrestle (I.)** & **-ing.** Act of person who wrestles; specif., the art of overpowering and throwing, pulling down an opponent by various grapples, locks, modes of lifting and tripping &c.

wrest-pin, n. Steel pin in a piano to which one end of each string is fixed, by turning which the instrument is tuned.

wretch, n. [1. rech; 2. rɛtʃ]. O.E. *wrǣċċa*, 'exile; wretch'; M.E. *wrecche*; fr. stem seen in O.E. *wrecan*, 'to drive; to expel', see **wreak**; cp. O.H.G. *reccho*; O.S. *wrekkio*, 'exile, wretch'. **1.** Person involved in utter distress; miserable, thoroughly unhappy or unfortunate person; *poor wretch*, often pityingly contemptuous. **2. a** Base, contemptible scoundrel; an abandoned ruffian: *the servants of a revolution are often wretches devoid of mercy or conscience*; **b** (i) (playful and affectionate) as in *the little wretch did all she could to tease him* = little rogue; (ii) (archaic) *the pretty wretch.*

wretched, adj. [1. réched; 2. rétʃid]. Prec. & **-ed.** **1. a** (i.) Miserable, unhappy, deeply depressed in mind: *boys are often wretched when they first go to school*; (ii.) (implying some degree of censure) unfortunate: *the wretched man had lost all his money*; **b** suffering extreme bodily discomfort: *to feel thoroughly wretched with influenza*; **c** causing wretchedness and discomfort of mind or body: *a wretched business, state of things* &c.; *a wretched cold, toothache, pain in the side.* **2.** (of external surroundings) squalid, mean, poverty-stricken; full of discomfort; dismal, depressing: *a wretched hovel*; *what a wretched place to live in.* **3.** Of poor quality, inferior; thoroughly bad: *the play was wretched stuff*; *the food at this hotel is wretched*; *wretched accommodation*; *his voice and delivery are wretched.*

wretchedly, adv. Prec. & **-ly.** In a wretched manner.

wretchedness, n. See prec. & **-ness.** State or quality of being wretched.

wretchlessness, n., variant of **recklessness.** The *w-* is due to association with *wretch*: '*the Devil doth thrust them*' (i.e. '*curious and carnal persons*') '*either into desperation, or into wretchlessness of most unclean living*' (No. xvii., Articles of Religion, Prayer Book).

wrick, rick, vb. trans. & n. [1. rik; 2. rik]. M.E. *wricken*, 'to move, jerk, twist'; cp. Dan. *vrikke*; Swed. *vricka*; Du. *wrikken*, 'to move to and fro'; cogn. w. **wring (I.).** **1.** vb. To twist, sprain slightly: *to wrick one's neck, back* &c. **2.** n. Slight sprain, twist, of a joint.

wriggle (I.), vb. intrans. & trans. [1. rígl; 2. rígl]. Freq. of **wrig-*, fr. same base as **wry**; cp. L.G. *wriggeln.* **A.** intrans. **1. a** To twist and turn (the body) this way and that, with rapid, jerky motions; to squirm, to fidget about: *keep still, and don't wriggle*; *to wriggle about*; **b** *wriggle along*, move along, proceed, with wriggling motions; **c** *wriggle out* (of a hole, tight place &c.), (i.) manage to escape by wriggling; also (ii.) (fig.) to escape from an awkward situation by cunning; *to wriggle out of a bargain, undertaking*, find a pretext for not sticking to it. **2.** (fig.) To give evasive answers to questions, to dodge, to equivocate. **3.** To betray uneasiness of mind, to show embarrassment: *the implied criticism made him wriggle.* **B.** trans. **a** (reflex.) *To wriggle oneself along, into, free* &c., move along, penetrate, extricate oneself by means of wriggling; (also fig.); **b** *wriggle one's way*, to make one's way by wriggling.

wriggle (II.), n., fr. prec. Wriggling motion; twist, squirm.

wriggler, n. [1. rígler; 2. ríglə]. **wriggle (I.)** & **-er.** **1.** Person or animal that wriggles; specif., a worm or wriggling insect; *red wriggler*, worm used for fishing. **2.** One who equivocates; one who evades his promises.

wright, n. [1. rīt; 2. rait]. O.E. *wyrhta*; M.E. *wirhte, wrihte*, 'carpenter, workman, wright', fr. base **wurk-*, gradational variant of **werk-* &c., 'work', seen in O.E. *weorc*, 'work', see **work**; O.E. *wyrċan*, 'to work'. **a** (archaic) A worker, a constructive workman, artificer; **b** now chiefly in compounds, *ship-, wheelwright* &c.; also *playwright.*

wring (I.), vb. trans. [1. ring; 2. riŋ]. O.E. *wringan*; M.E. *wringen*, 'to wring, twist';

cp. M. Du. *wringhen*; O.H.G. *ringan*, 'to twist'; Goth. *wruggō*, 'noose, snare'; O.N. *rangr*; Swed. *vrång*, 'twisted; wrong', see **wrong**, & **wrangle**. **1.** To twist and press, twist strongly; to strain, squeeze, compress by twisting: *to wring clothes (out)*, squeeze and twist them to remove moisture. Phrs. *to wring the neck of* (chicken &c.), kill by twisting neck of; *wringing wet*, wet enough to wring water out of; *to wring one's hands*, (fig.) to feel and express sorrow and despair; *to wring the hand of* (another person), to clasp it warmly, expressing cordiality; *it wrings my heart*, causes anguish, pity, sorrow &c. **2. a** To extract, press out by wringing: *to wring moisture out of clothes*; **b** (fig.) to extort by persistent persuasion, by compulsion &c.: *to wring money out of a stingy person*; *to wring a reluctant promise, answer &c., from a person.*

wring (II.), n., fr. prec. Action of wringing; squeeze.

wringer, n. [1. rínger; 2. ríŋə]. **wring (I.)** & **-er.** One who, that which, wrings; specif., machine with rollers for pressing water out of clothes.

wrinkle (I.), n. [1. ríngkl; 2. ríŋkl]. O.E. *wrincle*; M.E. *wrinkel*; cp. M. Du. *wrinkel*; cogn. w. O.E. *wrenċan*, 'to twist', see **wrench. a** Small depression, furrow, or ridge caused by crumpling or puckering a flexible surface; specif. **b** crease or pucker produced by contraction of skin through old age &c.: '*Time writes no wrinkle on thine azure brow*' (Byron, 'Childe Harold', iv. 182).

wrinkle (II.), vb. trans. & intrans., fr. prec. **1.** trans. To form wrinkles in, to pucker, crease: *to wrinkle (up) one's forehead*, as in perplexity. **2.** intrans. To become wrinkled, to pucker.

wrinkle (III.), n. O.E. *wrenċ*, 'an artifice, a trick', w. dimin. suff.; cp. O.E. *wrenċan*, 'to twist'; & see **wrench.** Ingenious hint, suggestion or device; dodge; useful piece of advice.

wrinkly, adj. [1. ríngkli; 2. ríŋkli]. **wrinkle (I.)** & **-y.** Full of wrinkles.

wrist, n. [1. rist; 2. rist]. O.E., M.E. *wrist*; cp. O.N., M.H.G. *rist*, 'instep'; O. Fris. *(hond)-wirst*, 'wrist'; fr. base seen in O.E. *wrīðan*, 'to turn', see **writhe**; ultimate meaning, 'the turning joint'. **1.** Joint between fore-arm and hand; the carpus. **2.** Method of using, skill in using, wrist in art, craft, sport &c. **3.** Wrist-pin.

wristband, n. [1. rízband; 2. rízbənd]. (archaic) The band at the lower part of a shirt sleeve.

wrist-drop, n. Paralysis of the muscles controlling the hand, which prevents the straightening of the hand and interferes with its active use.

wristlet, n. [1. rístlet; 2. rístlit]. **wrist** & **-let.** Band worn round the wrist for support, warmth, ornament, for holding a watch &c.; also attrib.: *a wristlet watch.*

wrist-pin, n. (mechan.) Pin, peg, shaft, on which a connecting-rod turns.

writ, n. [1. rit; 2. rit]. O.E. *(ġe)writ*, 'something written'; M.E. *writ*; see **write. 1.** (archaic) That which is written; document, writing; now only in *holy, sacred, writ*, the Bible. **2.** (law) An instrument or document issued in the king's name to a particular person, enjoining specific action or instructing him to abstain from action.

write, vb. intrans. & trans. [1. rīt; 2. rait]. O.E. *wrītan*, 'to engrave, draw, write'; M.E. *wrīten*, 'to write'; cp. O.S. *wrītan*, 'to tear, scratch; to write'; O.H.G. *rīzan*, Mod. Germ. *reissen*, 'to tear'; O.N. *rīta*, to write'; O.E. *ġewrit*, 'writing'; Goth. *writs*, 'stroke, line, point'. No cognates known outside Gmc. **A.** intrans. **1.** To trace on a surface symbols representing letter(s) or word(s), esp. on paper, parchment &c.: *to learn to write*; *to write well, illegibly* &c. **2.** To communicate in writing, send letter or written message: *he promised to write*; *I write every week to my family when absent.* **3.** To engage in literary composition, compose book(s), article(s) &c.; to practise the trade of author: *to write for a living*; *to write amusingly, well* &c. Phr. *to write oneself out*, write so much that one's vein is exhausted. **B.** trans. **1.** To put down, trace (symbols representing letters, words), on paper, parchment, or other surface: *to write one's name*; *to write notes in the margin*; *to write shorthand*; *to write Chinese characters.* Phrs. *to write a good, legible, hand*, produce good, legible writing; *writ(ten) in water*, leaving no permanent mark or record; *writ large*, widely proclaimed, clearly visible and recognizable: *the character and spiritual outlook of Milton are writ large in every page of 'Paradise Lost'.* **2. a** To express, state, put down, in writing (as an opinion or fact): *it is written that . . .*; *a great scholar has written that . . .*; **b** to communicate in writing, tell by means of a letter: *be sure to write me all your news.* **3. a** Specif., to produce, create, as a literary or artistic composition: *to write a book, article, poem, review* &c.; **b** to draw up, put down, in writing: *to write a letter.* **4. a** To fill up, cover, with writing: *to write several pages*; **b** to fill in, insert necessary writing in: *to write a cheque, certificate* &c. **5.** To designate, describe as, in writing: *he writes himself 'Colonel'.* **6.** (fig.) To show clearly, give clear signs of, imprint indelibly: *his selfishness, fear &c. is written on, all over, his face*; *the tendencies of the times are written in current events.* **C.** Followed by adverb. *Write down*, trans., **1.** To put down, record, in writing: *to write down an address*; *write it down before you forget it*; **2.** to depreciate in writing; **3.** to describe as, put down for: *I should write him down a fool.* *Write off*, trans., **1.** to compose quickly and easily; **2. a** to cancel, write a statement annulling (debt &c.); **b** to regard as cancelled. *Write out*, trans., to write in full, put whole of into writing; Phr. *to write out fair*, make fair copy of. *Write up*, trans., **1.** to praise in writing, compose a eulogy of; **2.** to elaborate, exaggerate, details of (event), in writing; **3.** to fill up, complete, bring up to date &c., in writing: *to write up a report, one's diary.*

writer, n. [1. ríter; 2. ráitə]. **write** & **-er. 1.** One who writes; specif. **a** person who practises literary composition; an author; **b** a clerk, esp. in a government office; **c** *writer to the signet*, Scottish solicitor. **2.** Book giving instructions for writing, esp. foreign language.

writer's cramp, n. Muscular affection of the hand and fingers, due to excessive and prolonged use of the pen.

writership, n. [1. rítership; 2. ráitəʃip]. **writer** & **-ship.** Position, rank, of writer in an office &c.

writhe (I.), vb. intrans. & trans. [1. rīdh; 2. raið]. O.E. *wrīðan*, M.E. *wrīðen*, 'to twist, turn, writhe'; cp. O.H.G. *rīdan*; O.N. *rīða*, 'to turn'; O.H.G. *(w)reid*, 'crinkled'; cogn. w. O.E. *wrāð*, 'angry'; see **wrath** & **wreath**, & cp. **wrist. A.** intrans. **1.** To twist, contort, the body about; to squirm: *to writhe in agony.* **2.** (fig.) To undergo acute mental discomfort, to wince in spirit: *to writhe under a person's taunts.* **B.** trans. (rare) To cause to writhe, to twist; (chiefly reflex.) *to writhe oneself.*

writhe (II.), n., fr. prec. Act, motion, of writhing.

writhen, adj. [1. rídhen; 2. ríðən]. O.E. *wriðen*, P.P. of *wrīðan*, see **writhe (I.)**. (archaic or poet.) Twisted, distorted.

writing, n. [1. ríting; 2. ráitiŋ]. **write** & **-ing. 1.** Act of one who writes. Phr. *to put a thing in writing*, record it in written form. **2.** Lettering, an inscription, written by hand; written document; contrasted with something printed or engraved. **3. a** Act of literary composition: *fond of, busy with one's, writing*; **b** (pl.) the literary works of an author: *the writings of Pope*; *hitherto unpublished writings of X.* **4.** Method, style, of writing, handwriting; penmanship.

writing-case, n. Case for holding writing-materials.

writing-desk, n. **1.** Folding case or box containing writing materials, with hinged cover, part of which when opened forms a sloping slab on which paper can be placed for writing. **2.** Piece of furniture in various forms, having a receptacle for papers &c., and a table convenient for writing.

writing-ink, n. Ink prepared for writing; contrasted with *printer's ink.*

writing-paper, n. Paper prepared for writing, esp. for letters &c.

writing-table, n. Table used, or specially made, for writing at.

written, adj. [1. rítn; 2. rítn], fr. P.P. of **write**; O.E. *(ġe)writen*; M.E. *writen.* **a** Expressed, set down, in writing; specif., *written language*, that type used in writing and literature, distinguished from the colloquial by certain features of dialect, construction, and vocabulary; contrasted with *spoken language*; **b** in writing, inscribed; contrasted with *verbal*: *written orders* &c.

wrong (I.), adj. [1. rong; 2. rɔŋ], fr. O.E. *wrang*, n., fr. Scand.; cp. O.N. *rangr*; Swed. *vrång*, 'crooked, wrong'; cogn. w. Goth. *wruggō*, 'snare, noose'; O.H.G. *ringan*, 'to twist'; O.E. *wringan*, 'to turn, twist', Pret. *wrang*, see **wring**; also w. different final consonant, O.E. *wrenċ*, 'trick, guile', see **wrench**; O.H.G. *renken*, 'to twist'; cogn. w. Lat. *vergere*, 'to bend, be inclined, turn, lean', see **verge (II.)**; Scrt. *vr̥jinás*, 'crooked; false'; Lith. *veržiù*, 'to snare'; Lett. *werst*, 'to turn'; Gk. *erkhatáein*, 'to hedge in'. Orig. sense 'twisted; morally distorted'. **1.** Not in accordance with what is morally right or just; reprehensible, wicked, sinful: *it is wrong to tell lies*; *how very wrong of him to mislead you in this way.* **2. a** (of statements, opinions, calculations, beliefs) Not in accordance with ascertained fact, with the truth, or with reason; erroneous, based on ignorance; misleading, inaccurate, incorrect: *we know now that many of the old scientific teachings were wrong*; *certain doctrines have been ruled out by the Church as definitely wrong and heretical*; *you have got all your sums wrong*; **b** (i.) not in accordance with what has been fixed or decided: *the wrong day, the wrong station*; (ii.) not what is asked for or desired: *you've brought the wrong book.* **3.** (of persons) Mistaken in opinions, having been misled; having misunderstood, been ignorant of, or misstated facts: *you were quite wrong in what you said*; *the ancients thought the sun went round the earth, but they were wrong.* **4.** Unsuited for particular purpose, not adapted to produce desired result: *the wrong way to do it, to set about it.* **5.** Unsuited to a particular time; unseasonable, inopportune; unsuitable for particular circumstances, or for a given company: *quite the wrong clothes for the evening, for the hot weather*; *he always says and does the wrong thing in society*; *just the wrong story to tell a bishop.* Phrs. *to go wrong*, (of persons) (i.) to lapse from the strict path of rectitude; (ii.) to come to grief, go to the bad; (iii.) (of actions, plans, affairs) to fail, end disastrously: *in the wrong box*, in an awkward or disconcerting position; *to get hold of the wrong end of the stick*, to misconceive, have mistaken impression of, a fact, statement, intention &c.; *wrong fount* (usually abbr., *w.f.*), direction to printer that type is from a different fount from that required; *wrong side out*, inside out; *on the wrong side of* (30 &c.), older than.

wrong (II.), adv., fr. prec. In a wrong manner; **a** incorrectly, erroneously, inaccurately, mistakenly: *you have done it wrong*; *to guess, answer, wrong*; Phr. *to get it wrong*, (i.) to miscalculate, reckon (a sum) incorrectly; (ii.) to misunderstand, misconceive; **b** unsuitably, in a manner not adapted to secure desired result: *you are treating him all wrong.*

wrong (III.), n. O.E. *wrang*, 'wrong', see **wrong (I.)**. **1. a** Wrongful act; action at variance with what is right, with justice, duty &c.; sin, wickedness, evil-doing: *to distinguish between right and wrong*; *to do wrong*; **b** injustice, injury: *to suffer wrong*; *you do him wrong*, have an unjust, or too low an, opinion of him. **2.** (law, pl.) **a** Infringement of the rights of persons; *a private wrongs*, privation of the private or civil rights of an individual as such; also termed *civil injuries*; **b** *public wrongs*, a breach or violation of public rights and duties, which affect the whole community considered as such; these are distinguished as *crimes* and *misdemeanours*. **3.** State in which responsibility attaches for wrongful action, mistake &c.: *to be in the wrong*. Phr. *to put one in the wrong*, make him appear responsible for mistake &c.

wrong (IV.), vb. trans., fr. prec. **1.** To do wrong to, injure, treat wrongfully, unjustly: *an honest man will not knowingly wrong another*. **2.** To have an unjust opinion of, impute evil to undeservedly: *I wronged you in believing you unfaithful*.

wrongdoer, n. [1. róngdōoer; 2. róŋdùə]. Person who does wrong; sinner, evildoer.

wrongdoing, n. [1. róngdōoing; 2. róŋdùiŋ]. Commission of a wrongful act; evil-doing, offence, crime; sin.

wrongful, adj. [1. róngfool; 2. róŋful]. **wrong (III.)** & **-ful**. Wrong; unjust; criminal.

wrongfully, adv. Prec. & **-ly**. In a wrongful manner; unjustly; illegally.

wrongfulness, n. See prec. & **-ness**. Quality of being wrongful.

wrong-headed, adj. Persevering in a wrong course; perverse, stubbornly mistaken.

wrongly, adv. [1. róngli; 2. róŋli]. **wrong (I.)** & **-ly**. In a wrong manner; erroneously; wickedly.

wrongous, adj. [1. rónggus; 2. róŋgəs]. **wrong (I.)** & **-ous**. (Scots law) Illegal, unjust, inequitable.

wrote, vb. [1. rōt; 2. rout]. O.E. *wrāt*, M.E. *wroot*, Pret. of **write**.

wroth, adj. [1. rŏth, roth; 2. rouþ, rɔþ]. O.E. *wrāþ*, M.E. *wrōþ*, 'angry'; cp. O.S. *wrēþ*; O.N. *reiðr*, 'angry, hostile'; O.H.G. (*w*)*reid*, 'crooked, crumpled'; see **wrath** & **writhe**. (archaic, Bib., and poet.) Angry, incensed.

wrought (I.), vb. intrans. & trans. Pret. & P.P. [1. rawt; 2. rɔt]. O.E. *worhte*, 'worked', Pret. of *wyrcan*, 'to work', M.E. *wrohte*; P.P. O.E. (*ge*)*worht*, M.E. *worht*, *wroht*. Now replaced by new Pret. *worked* in ordinary English. **A.** intrans. (archaic, poet., or provinc.) Worked, laboured, toiled: *he wrought very hard at his task*. Phr. *he wrought upon me to . . .*, persuaded me. **B.** trans. **1. a** Effected, produced, brought about; (i.) Pret.: *he wrought a great change in the spirit of his age*; (ii.) P.P.: *what evil he has wrought!*; **b** (Pret. & P.P.) made, constructed. **2.** Used as Pret. of **work** in sense of to treat metal by hammering &c.

wrought (II.), adj. O.E. (*ge*)*worht*; M.E. *wroht*, *wrouht*; P.P. of O.E. *wyrcan*, 'to work', q.v. under **work**. Specif., *wrought iron*, worked by hammering; contrasted with *cast iron*.

wrung, vb. [1. rung; 2. raŋ]. Pret. & P.P. of **wring**; O.E. (*ge*)*wrungen*, P.P.; M.E. *wrung*(*en*); now used also as Pret. Cp. O.E. Pret. *wrang*.

wry, adj. [1. rī; 2. rai]. M.E. *wrīe*, 'twisted', fr. *wrīen*, 'to turn, twist'; cp. O.E. *wrīgian*, 'to turn; go forward'. Cp. **wriggle**. Crooked, distorted, pulled or bent aside, twisted; rare except in *to make a wry face*, to pull a grimace expressing disgust.

wrybill, n. [1. rībil; 2. ráibil]. Species of plover.

wryly, adv. [1. rīli; 2. ráili]. **wry** & **-ly**. In a wry manner.

wrymouth, n. [1. rīmouth; 2. ráimauþ]. Seafish with vertical mouth-opening.

wry-mouthed, adj. Having a crooked mouth.

wryneck, n. [1. rīnek; 2. ráinɛk]. Bird related to woodpecker, able to twist its neck to a considerable angle.

wryness, n. [1. rīnes; 2. ráinis]. **wry** & **-ness**. State of being wry; distortion, crookedness.

Wyandotte, n. [1. wīandot; 2. wáiəndɔt], name of tribe of N. American Indians. Breed of domestic fowls.

wych-, wich-, witch-, pref. [1. wich; 2. witʃ]. O.E. *wiċe*, M.E. *wiche*, 'wych-elm'; cogn. w. **wicker**. (in names of trees) *Wych-elm*, *Ulmus montana*, with drooping branches and pointed leaves; *wych-hazel*, see **witch-hazel**.

wye, n. [1. wī; 2. wai]. **a** Letter Y; **b** Y-shaped object.

Wykehamist, n. [1. wíkamist; 2. wíkəmist], fr. William of Wykeham, d. 1404, founder of school, & **-ist**. Member of Winchester College; *Old Wykehamist*, former member.

wynd, n. [1. wind; 2. waind]. Spelling variant of **wind (IV.)**. (Scots) Alley, narrow lane between walls &c.

wyvern. See **wivern**.

X

X, x [1. eks; 2. ɛks]. **a** Twenty-fourth letter of alphabet; for use in abbreviations &c. see end of Dictionary; **b** the Roman symbol for the numeral 10; **c** (alg.) principal unknown quantity; hence **d** an unknown or mysterious factor or influence; **e** *double-*, *triple-x*, ale of specific strength, marked xx or xxx on cask.

xanth(o)-, pref., fr. Gk. *xanthós*, 'fair, yellow', for **k(ə)san-*; cogn. w. Lat. *cascus*, 'hoary, old'; *cānus*, 'grey, ashen'; fr. earlier **kasno-*; cogn. w. O.E. *hasu*; O.N. *hoss*, 'greyish brown'; O.E. *hara*, 'hare', see **hare**; O. Prussian *sasins*, 'hare'. Yellow.

xanthein(e), n. [1. zánthiin; 2. zænþiin]. Prec. & **-in**. Soluble yellow colouring-matter in flowers.

Xanthian, adj. [1. zánthian; 2. zænþiən], fr. Xanthus, in Lycia, Asia Minor, & **-ian**. Pertaining to Xanthus; *Xanthian marbles*, sculptures discovered on this site and now in the British Museum.

xanthic, adj. [1. zánthik; 2. zænþik]. **xanth(o)-** & **-ic**. Yellow, yellowish; *xanthic flowers*, having yellow as typical colour and varying to white or red.

xanthin, n. [1. zánthin; 2. zænþin]. **xanth(o)-** & **-in**. **1.** Insoluble yellow colouring-matter in flowers. **2.** Crystalline compound contained in animal secretions.

Xanthippe, n. [1. zantípi, -thípi; 2. zæntípi, -þípi]. Gk., name of the wife of Socrates. An ill-tempered, shrewish woman or wife.

xanthite, n. [1. zánthīt; 2. zænþait]. **xanth(o)-** & **-ite**. Kind of yellowish-brown rock.

xantho-, pref. See **xanth(o)-**.

xanthochroi, n. pl. [1. zànthókroī; 2. zænþókrouài]. **xanth(o)-** & Gk. *khrōá*, 'skin, complexion', cp. Gk. *khrōma*, 'skin, colour', see **chromo-**. Blond, blue-eyed races.

xanthomelanous, adj. [1. zànthomélanus; 2. zænþomélənəs]. **xanth(o)-** & Gk. *melān-*, stem of *mélās*, 'black', see **melanism**, & **-ous**. Black-haired and dark- or olive-skinned.

xanthophyll, n. [1. zánthofil; 2. zænþofil]. **xanth(o)-** & Gk. *phúllon*, 'leaf', see **phyllo-**. Yellow pigment colouring autumn leaves.

xanthous, adj. [1. zánthus; 2. zænþəs]. **xanth(o)-** & **-ous**. Of yellow or Mongolian type.

xebec, zebec(k), n. [1. zébek; 2. zíbɛk]. Cp. Ital. *sciabecco*, Fr. *chebec*, prob. of Eastern origin. Small three-masted vessel used on the Mediterranean.

xenelasia, n. [1. (g)zenelásia; 2. (g)zènīléisiə]. Gk. *xenēlasía*, 'expulsion of foreigners', fr. *xénos*, 'stranger, guest', fr. **ghsenwo-*; cogn. w. Lat. *hostis*, 'stranger, enemy', see **host (I.)**; & *élasis*, 'a driving away', fr. *elaúnein*, 'to drive, drive out'; cogn. w. Lat. *alacer*, 'quick, active', see **alacrity**; Goth. *aljan*, 'zeal'; O.E. *ellen*, 'courage'. Constitutional custom in ancient Sparta of preventing aliens from settling in the country.

xen(o)-, pref., fr. Gk. *xénos*, 'stranger, guest', see prec. **a** Relating to hospitality; **b** external.

xenial, adj. [1. (g)zénial; 2. (g)zéniəl]. Prec. & **-ial**. Of, pertaining to, denoting, relations between guest and host.

xenogamy, n. [1. zenógami; 2. zenógəmi]. **xen(o)-** & **-gamy**. Cross-fertilization.

xenogenous, adj. [1. zenójenus; 2. zenódžinəs]. **xen(o)-** & **-genous**. Produced by external agency.

xenon, n. [1. zénon; 2. zénɔn]. Gk., neut. form of *xénos*, 'strange', see **xen(o)-**. Heavy, inert gas present in the air, first isolated in 1898.

xer(o)-, pref. Representing Gk. *xērós*, 'dry'; cogn. w. Scrt. *kṣārás*, 'burning'; Lat. *serēnus*, 'dry, clear, calm', see **serene**. Dry; dryness.

xeransis, n. [1. zēránsis; 2. ziəreńnsis]. Gk. *xēransis*, 'drying up', fr. *xērainein*, 'to dry', fr. *xērós*, 'dry', see prec. Drying up, desiccation.

xeranthemum, n. [1. zēránthemum; 2. ziəræńþiməm], fr. **xer(o)-** & Gk. *ánthemon*, 'flower', q.v. under **anther**, **anthology**. The everlasting flower.

xerasia, n. [1. zērázia; 2. ziəréiziə]. Gk. *xērasía*, 'dryness', fr. *xērainein*, 'to dry', fr. *xērós*, 'dry', see **xer(o)-**. Morbid dryness of the hair.

xerophilous, adj. [1. zērófilus; 2. ziərófiləs]. **xer(o)-** & **-philous**. (of plant) Drought-loving, living in dry climate.

xerophthalmia, n. [1. zĕrofthálmia; 2. zìərɔfþælmiə]. **xer(o)-** & **ophthalmia**. Variety of conjunctivitis.

xerophyte, n. [1. zérofit; 2. ziərɔfait]. **xer(o)-** & **-phyte**. Xerophilous plant.

xiph(i)-, xipho-, pref. Representing Gk. *xíphos*, 'sword'; etymol. doubtful. Sword-shaped; e.g. *Xiphidae*, swordfishes; *xiphisternum*, xiphoid appendage.

xiphoid, adj. [1. zífoid; 2. zífɔid]. Prec. & **-oid**. Sword-shaped; *xiphoid appendage*, *process*, sword-shaped, cartilaginous process at the lower extremity of the sternum.

xoanon, n. [1. (g)zŏanòn; 2. (g)zóuənɔ̀n]. Gk. *xóanon*, 'piece of sculpture in wood; statue of a deity'; cp. Gk. *xúein*, 'to scrape, scratch, polish'; *xustón*, 'polished spear-shaft'; *xustḗr*, 'graving-tool'; *xuréein*, 'to shave'; cogn. w. Scrt. *kṣuráś*, 'razor'; cp. also, w. infixed nasal, Scrt. *kṣṇáuti*, 'he rubs, whets'; O.N. *snǫggr*, 'shorn'. Primitive wooden statue of a deity.

x-rays, n. pl. [1. éks ráz; 2. éks réiz]. Pref. implies that their precise nature was unknown. Röntgen rays.

xyl(o)-, pref. Representing Gk. *xúlon*, 'wood, timber', fr. **kʷsulom*; cogn. w. O.N. *súla*; Goth. *sauls*; O.H.G. *sūl*, 'column'; see also **sill**. Wood.

xylem, n. [1. zīlem; 2. záilɛm]. See prec. & **-m**. Woody tissue forming part of a vegetable body.

xylobalsamum, n. [1. zīlobáwlsamum; 2. záilobɔ́lsəməm]. **xyl(o)-** & see **balsam**. Dried twigs of the balm-of-Gilead tree.

xylocarp, n. [1. zílokàrp; 2. záilɔkåp]. **xyl(o)-** & Gk. *karpós*, 'fruit', see **carpel**. a Hard woody fruit; b tree bearing such fruit.

xylograph, n. [1. zílogràhf; 2. záilɔgrȧf]. **xyl(o)-** & **-graph**. a Wood-engraving, esp. of early type; b representation of, or impression from, grain of wood as decoration.

xylographer, n. [1. zílografer; 2. zailógrəfə]. Prec. & **-er**. Wood-engraver.

xylographic, adj. [1. zílográfik; 2. zàilɔgrǽfik]. **xyl(o)-** & **-graphic**. Pertaining to, produced by means of, xylography.

xylography, n. [1. zílógrafi; 2. zailógrəfi]. **xyl(o)-** & **-graphy**. The art of wood-engraving.

xylonite, n. [1. zílonīt; 2. záilənait], fr. Gk. *xúlon*, 'wood', see **xyl(o)-**, & **-ite**. Celluloid.

xylophagous, adj. [1. zilófagus; 2. zailófəgəs]. **xyl(o)-** & **-phagous**. (of insect) Feeding on, boring into, wood.

xylophone, n. [1. zílofōn; 2. záilɔfoun]. **xyl(o)-** & **-phone**. Musical instrument of percussion, consisting of a series of wooden bars, graduated in length.

xyster, n. [1. zíster; 2. zístə]. Gk. *xustér*, 'graving-tool'; fr. base of *xúein*, 'to scratch, scrape'; for **ksū-*, cp. Scrt. *kṣuráṣ*, 'razor'. See also **xoanon**. Instrument for scraping membrane from bones.

xystus, n. [1. (g)zístus; 2. (g)zístəs]. Lat. *xystus*, fr. Gk. *xustós*, 'covered colonnade, with polished floor, in gymnasium', fr. *xustós*, 'polished', as prec. **1.** (class. antiq.) Covered portico used for athletic exercises. **2.** Garden walk.

Y

Y, y [1. wī; 2. wai]. a Twenty-fifth letter of alphabet; for use in abbreviations see end of Dictionary; b (alg.) second unknown quantity; c Y-shaped object, arrangement &c.

Y- (I.), pref. [1. wī; 2. wai]. Representing prec. Y-shaped; e.g. *Y-cartilage*, *Y-ligament* &c.; *Y-branch*, forked pipe &c.; *Y-level*, spirit-level with Y-shaped supports; *Y-moth*, with Y-shaped mark on upper wings; *Y-track*, short, Y-shaped railway track at right angles from a main line, used to enable engine to reverse direction.

y- (II.), pref. [1. i; 2. i]. O.E. *ge-*, M.E. *i-*, *y-*; pref. used in O.E. to form trans. fr. intrans. vbs., also, gen., before P.P.'s of vbs.; to form coll. ns. &c.; cp. O.H.G. *gi-*, Goth. *ga-*. Now used only in archaic P.P. **yclept**. Mistaken for pers. pron. in *iwis*, written *I wis*, see **wis**.

-y (I.), suff. representing a Fr. *-ie*, Lat. *-ius*, *-ia*, *-ium*, in abstract ns. & adjs., e.g. *augury*, *century*, *family*, *fury*; *necessary*, *contrary*; or b Fr. *-ie*, Lat. *-ia*, fr. Gk. *-iā*, e.g. *history*, *-logy*, *homily*.

-y (II.), suff. representing O. Fr. n. suff. *-e*, *-ee*, fr. Lat. P.P.'s in *-ātus*, *-a*, *-um*, e.g. *army*, *city*, *entry*, *treaty*. The suff. is also used to form ns. fr. vbs. on anal. of these, e.g. *expiry*.

-y (III.), suff. forming ns., w. dimin. sense, a fr. other ns., e.g. *baby*, *dolly*, *pussy*; b fr. adjs., e.g. *darky*. Sometimes appears as *-ie*, e.g. *laddie*, *lassie*.

-y (IV.), suff. forming adjs., a fr. O.E. *-iġ*, M.E. *-y* (cogn. Lat. *-ic-*), e.g. *many*, *holy*; & by anal., fr. mod. ns., *lumpy*, *horsy*, *stony*, *shiny* &c.; b fr. adjs. of colour, e.g. *yellowy*, esp. in compounds, *bluey-grey* &c.; c chiefly poet., fr. other adjs., e.g. *stilly*.

-y (V.), n. suff. representing O.E. *-iġ*, M.E. *-i(e)*, e.g. *body*, *lady*.

yacht (I.), n. [1. yot; 2. jɔt], fr. Du. *jacht*, fr. stem of *jagen*, 'to hunt', w. reference to speed of vessel; cp. O.H.G. *jagōn*, 'to hunt'; etymol. doubtful. a Vessel, whether propelled by sails or by mechanical power, designed for pleasure-cruising; specif. b small, light sailing-vessel used for racing &c.

yacht (II.), vb. intrans., fr. prec. To sail, race &c. in a yacht.

yacht-club, n. Club for yachtsmen, esp. for yacht-racing.

yachting, n. [1. yóting; 2. jótiŋ]. **yacht** (II.) & **-ing**. Art or practice of sailing in, or managing, a yacht.

yachtsman, n. [1. yótsman; 2. jótsmən]. One who habitually sails a yacht.

yaffle, yaffil, n. [1. yáfl; 2. jǽfl]. Imitative of cry. (provinc.) The green woodpecker.

yager, n. [1. yåger; 2. jéigə], fr. Germ. *jäger*, 'hunter', fr. *jagen*, O.H.G. *jagōn*, 'to hunt', q.v. under **yacht**. Member of one of various German infantry or cavalry corps, usually riflemen.

yahoo, n. [1. yàhhōō; 2. jȧhú]. Coined by Swift in *Gulliver's Travels* (Voyage to the Houyhnhnms). **1.** One of a fictitious race of loathsome and vicious creatures, described by Swift, having the forms of men but the habits of lower animals; intended as a satire on the human race. **2.** An ungainly, coarse, rude, mannerless person.

Yahveh, n. [1. yahvǎ; 2. jȧvéi], fr. Heb. *yahaveh*, see **Jehovah**. Jehovah.

Yahvist, n. [1. yáhvist; 2. jȧ́vist], fr. prec. & **-ist**. Jehovist.

Yahvistic, adj. [1. yàhvístik; 2. jȧvístik]. Prec. & **-ic**. Jehovistic.

yak, n. [1. yak; 2. jæk]. Tibetan *gyak*. Wild and domesticated, long-haired, bovine quadruped of Central Asiatic mountains, used as a beast of burden.

yam, n. [1. yam; 2. jæm], fr. Port. *inhame*, S. African. **1.** Fleshy, edible root of a tropical, climbing plant, *Dioscorea Batatas*. **2.** Any plant of the *Dioscorea* family, producing edible tubers.

Yama, n. [1. yáhma; 2. jɑ́mə]. Scrt. *Yama*. Hindu god and judge of the dead.

yamen, -un, n. [1. yáhmen; 2. jɑ́mɛn]. Chinese. Mandarin's official residence; office of public department.

yank (I.), vb. trans. & n. [1. yangk; 2. jæŋk]. Etymol. unknown. a vb. (slang) To pull sharply, with a jerk; b n., a sudden hard pull.

Yank (II.), n. Abbr. fr. next word. (slang) Yankee.

Yankee, n. [1. yángki, -ē; 2. jǽŋki, -ī]. Possibly fr. *Jankin*, dimin. of *Jan* = John, applied by Dutch settlers of New York to the English colonists of Connecticut. **1.** Specif., an inhabitant of New England, U.S.A., esp. a descendant of the original settlers. **2.** (colloq. in England) Any inhabitant of the United States, esp. one of British descent; an American.

Yankeedom, n. [1. yángkidom; 2. jǽŋkidəm]. Prec. & **-dom**. Yankees collectively.

yankeefied, adj. [1. yángkifīd; 2. jǽŋkifȧid]. **Yankee** & **-fy**. Imbued with, exhibiting, Yankee characteristics or ideas; Americanized.

Yankeeism, n. [1. yángkiizm; 2. jǽŋkiizəm]. **Yankee** & **-ism**. Yankee characteristic(s).

yap, vb. intrans. & n. [1. yap; 2. jæp]. Imitative. **1.** vb. (of a dog) To utter a sharp, shrill bark or series of barks; to yelp. **2.** n. Sharp, excited yelp or bark.

yapon, n. [1. yápon; 2. jǽpɔn]. Prob. Am. Indian. An evergreen shrub of the southern United States of America.

yapp, n. [1. yap; 2. jæp]. Name of inventor. Style of bookbinding, with limp cover projecting beyond the edges.

Yarborough, n. [1. yárburo; 2. jɑ́bərə], fr. an Earl of Yarborough who betted against the possibility of such a hand. A hand at bridge or whist containing no card higher than a nine.

yard (I.), n. [1. yard; 2. jȧd]. O.E. *ġerd*, M.E. ȝerde, yerde, 'rod, staff; yard'; O.S. *gerda*; O.H.G. *gerta*; Du. *garde*; O.N. *gaddr*, 'rod'; Goth. *gazds*, 'point, sting'; cogn. w. Lat. *hasta*, 'staff, shaft, spear'; see **hastate**. **1.** a Unit of length, 36 inches, 3 feet; b piece of material a yard in length. **2.** (naut.) Long, nearly cylindrical spar, tapering towards the ends, fastened to mast and used to support sails; *square, lateen, yard*, forming a right, oblique, angle with the mast; (in compounds, indicating mast or sail to which the yard is attached) *lower-*, *topsail-yard* &c. Phr. *to man the yards*, to station sailors, be stationed, on the yards, esp. as form of salute. **3.** (archaic) Male organ of generation.

yard (II.), n. & vb. trans. O.E. *ġeard*; M.E. ȝard, 'piece of land, garden, yard'; cp. O.S. *gard*, 'enclosure, dwelling'; O.H.G. *gart*, 'circle'; O.N. *garðr*, 'hedge, enclosure'; Goth. *gards*, 'house'; cogn. w. Lat. *hortus*, 'garden'; (co)-*hors*, 'yard, enclosure; company, cohort; crowd', see **cohort, court** (I.), **garden**, & **garth**; cp. further Goth. *gairdan*, O.S. *gyrdan*, 'to gird', see **gird** (I.). **1.** n. a Enclosed, or partially enclosed, space, often paved, used for various purposes, near or adjoining a house, stable, or other building; often particularized in compounds: *farm-yard*, *rick-yard*, *stable-yard* &c.; b piece of open ground fenced off, in which some particular occupation is carried on: *a builder's*, *stone-mason's yard*; *railway yard*, open space near a station where trucks &c. are kept; specif., *the Yard*, *Scotland Yard*, as headquarters of the Criminal Investigation Department. **2.** vb. To put (cattle) into stock-yard.

yardage, n. [1. yárdij; 2. jȧ́dɪdʒ]. Prec. & **-age**. **1.** Right of enclosing cattle &c. in stock-yard. **2.** Sum payable for this right.

yard-arm, n. (naut.) Either half of yard.

yard-man, n. Man employed in railway yard.

yard-master, n. Manager of railway yard.

yard-measure, n. Tape, wooden or steel rod, measuring one yard and marked in feet, inches &c.

yard-stick, n. Wooden or metal yard-measure.

yard-wand, n. Yard-stick.

yare, adj. [1. yȧr; 2. jɛə]. O.E. *ġearu*, 'ready, prepared'; M.E. ȝare, yȧre. Cogn. w. O.S. *garu*, O.H.G. *garo*; cp. also **gear** (I.). (archaic) a Ready, prepared; b moving quickly, active.

yarn (I.), n. [1. yarn; 2. jȧn]. O.E. *ġearn*; M.E. ȝarn, 'yarn'; O.N. *garnar*, 'entrails'; Gk. *khordḗ*, 'intestines; catgut; cord', see **cord**; Scrt. *hirā*, 'vein'; Lat. *haru-(spex)*, 'diviner inspecting entrails'; cp. **hernia**. **1.** a Fibrous material spun for weaving, knitting &c.; b specif., thread composed of two or more twisted strands of yarn; c twisted fibres prepared for rope-making. **2.** (colloq., orig. naut.) a A tale, narrative; Phr. *spin a yarn*, tell a story; also to exaggerate, tell a traveller's tale; b a false, exaggerated report or statement; an ill-founded rumour; c a friendly conversation, a chat.

yarn (II.), vb. intrans., fr. prec. (colloq., orig. naut.) a To tell a yarn; b to talk at length, to chatter; to hold a long conversation.

yarn-beam, n. Roller on which warp-threads are wound in a loom.

yarrow, n. [1. yárō; 2. jǽrou]. O.E. *ġearwe*; M.E. ȝar(o)we, 'yarrow'; cp. O.H.G. *gar(a)wa*; Du. *gerw*, 'yarrow'. Highly astringent perennial herb, *Achillea millefolium*, with clusters of small white flowers, milfoil.

yashmak, n. [1. yáshmak; 2. jǽʃmæk], fr. Arab. Veil worn by Mohammedan women.

yataghan, n. [1. yátagàn; 2. jǽtəgæ̀n], Turkish. Turkish sword with double-curved blade and no cross-piece.

yaw, vb. intrans. & n. [1. yaw; 2. jɔ̄], fr. O.N. *jaga*, 'to curve back', orig. 'to hunt', cp. O.H.G. *jagōn*, 'to hunt'; see **yager**, **yacht**. (naut.) **1.** vb. (of ship or aircraft) To fall away from the course, move or steer unsteadily. **2.** n. Act of yawing; unsteady motion in, falling away from, ship's or aircraft's course.

yawl (I.), vb. intrans. & n. [1. yawl; 2. jɔ̄l]. Variant of **yowl**. Perh. influenced by **bawl**.

yawl (II.), n., fr. Du. *jol*; cp. Dan. *jolle*. **1.** Small, cutter-rigged sailing-vessel. **2.** Small ship's boat, jolly-boat.

yawn (I.), vb. intrans. & trans. [1. yawn; 2. jɔ̄n]. O.E. forms are *gānian* & *ġīnan*, 'to yawn'; also *ġinian*, *ġeonian*; M.E. *gōnen*, *yōnen*, *ȝeonien* &c. Cogn. w. Lat. *hiāre*, see **hiatus**. The Mod. form owes its initial to O.E. *ġeonian* &c., & the vowel is perh. imitative. **A.** intrans. **1.** To open the mouth owing to an involuntary muscular contraction, the tendency to which often arises from drowsiness. Phr. *to make a person yawn*, cause him to become sleepy; hence, to bore him. **2.** To open wide, be wide open, to gape: *a gulf, abyss, chasm &c., yawned in front of us.* **B.** trans. To utter with a yawn.

yawn (II.), n., fr. prec. The act of yawning, involuntary opening of the mouth.

yawning, adj. [1. yáwning; 2. jɔ̄́niŋ], fr. Pres. Part. of **yawn (I.)**. Wide open, gaping: *a yawning pit, cavern* &c.

yawningly, adv. Prec. & **-ly**. With a yawn.

yaws, n. [1. yawz; 2. jɔ̄z]. Prob. fr. African. Skin disease prevalent among negroes in the tropics, characterized by blains on various parts of the body; called also framboesia.

yclept, adj. [1. iklépt; 2. iklépt]. O.E. *ġecleopod*; M.E. *icleped*; P.P. of *clipian*, *cleopian*, 'to call'. Used by Spenser, & cp. Milton: '*Come thou Goddess fair and free, In heaven yclept Euphrosyne*' ('L'Allegro', 11-12). (archaic or facet.) Called, having the name of, known as.

ye (I.), pron. [1. yē; 2. jī], unstressed [1. (y)i; 2. (j)i]. O.E. *ġē*; M.E. *ȝē*; cp. Du. *gij*; Mod. Germ. *ihr*; Goth. *jus*. Cogn. w. Lith. *jūs*; Scrt. *yūyám*, 'you'. (archaic and poet.) Old nom. pl. of pron. of 2nd pers. *Ye* began to be superseded by *you* in nom. by the middle of 16th cent., but many writers keep the forms distinct much later. The Authorized Version always does so. As nom. the form survives in *how d'ye do?* = [haudidú], in the now obs. or provinc. *hark ye, look ye* [hā́ki, lúki]. On the other hand, *ye* is used not infrequently instead of *you*, in the acc. & dat., in colloq. style in 16th & 17th cents., & still survives in the old-fashioned *thank ye* [þǽŋki]. This usage is prob. due orig. to the anal. of *thee*. See also **you**.

ye (II.), def. art. [1. dhē; 2. ðī], archaic method of printing *the*, due to 15th-cent. confusion of þ (see **thorn**) & *y*; sometimes ignorantly pronounced [1. yē; 2. jī], as a pseudo-archaism: *ye olde shoppe* &c.

yea, interj. & n. [1. yā; 2. jei]. O.E. *ġēa*, *ġǣ*; M.E. *ȝē*, *ȝā*, 'yes'; cp. O.S., O.H.G., O.N. *jā*; O. Fris. *jē*; Goth. *jā*, 'yes'; *jai*, 'certainly'; fr. the pronominal stem **i-*, **ei-*, wh. occurs also in **it**. (archaic) **1.** interj. **a** Yes, expressing affirmation; **b** moreover, not only that but: '*Nature's whole wealth, yea, more, 'A Heav'n on Earth*, (Milton, 'P. L.', iv. 407-8). **2.** n. Affirmative statement, expression of affirmation or agreement; Phr. '*Let your yea be yea*'.

yean, vb. trans. & intrans. [1. yēn; 2. jīn]. O.E. *ēanian*; M.E. *ēnen*, 'to yean'; cp. Du. *oonen*, 'to yean'; prob. formed fr. Gmc. base **agʷna-*, 'lamb'; cogn. w. Lat. *agnus*, 'lamb'; Gk. *amnós*, earlier *abnos*; O. Slav. *(j)agne*, 'lamb'. **1.** trans. To bring forth (lamb or kid). **2.** intrans. (of sheep or goat) To bring forth a lamb or kid.

yeanling, n. [1. yḗnling; 2. jínliŋ]. Prec. & **-ling**. Young lamb or kid.

year, n. [1. yēr, yĕr; 2. jiə, jɅ̄]. O.E. *ġēr*; M.E. *ȝēr*; cp. O.S. & O.H.G. *jār*; O.N. *ār*; Goth. *jēr*, 'year'; cogn. w. Gk. *hōrā*, 'period, season'; *hôros*, 'year', see **hour**; O. Slav. *jara*, 'spring'; prob. also Lat. *hornus*, 'of this year', earlier **hōjōrīnos*, fr. Instrumental **hō jōro-*, 'in this year'. **1.** **a** Period of time taken by the earth to revolve once round the sun; called specifically *astronomical, natural, equinoctial, solar, tropical year*; *common year*, this period reckoned as 365 days; *leap year, bissextile year*, of 366 days; **b** time taken by the sun to return to the same apparent position among the fixed stars; also called *astral, sidereal year*; **c** *lunar year*, period of twelve lunar months. **2.** Unit of time, period of 365 days (in leap-year, 366 days) reckoned from Jan. 1st to Dec. 31st next following, also *calendar, civil, legal year*: *this year*; *next year* &c.; *new, old, year*, year just beginning, ending; *this year of grace, year of our Lord*, of the Christian era. Phrs. *year in, year out*, continuously through the years; *from year to year*, every year; *in the year one*, very long ago. **3.** Period of 365 days reckoned from any or from a specific date: *it is just a year since I saw him*; *just a year ago*; *in a year's time*; *academic, school, year*, one reckoned from beginning of session in the autumn; *Christian, Church, year*, from Advent; *a year and a day*, period designated to ensure lapse of full year. **4.** (pl.) Age: *young, old, for one's years*; *a man of his years*; *to reach years of discretion.*

year-book, n. **1.** Annual publication giving statistics, reports &c., up to date. **2.** (hist.) One of a series of annual reports of courts of justice from Edward III. to Henry VIII.

yearling, n. & adj. [1. yḗr-, yĕ̀rling; 2. jíə-, jɅ́liŋ]. **year** & **-ling**. **1.** n. **a** Animal in its second year; **b** (racing) colt one year old from January 1st of year of foaling. **2.** adj. A year old.

year-long, adj. Lasting, persisting, throughout the year, for a whole year.

yearly, adj. & adv. [1. yḗr-, yĕ̀rli; 2. jíə-, jɅ́li]. **year** & **-ly**. **1.** adj. Occurring **a** once a year; **b** every year. **2.** adv. Every year, annually.

yearn, vb. intrans. [1. yĕrn; 2. jɅ̄n]. O.E. *ġeornan*; M.E. *ȝernen*; cp. O.S. *gernean*; O.H.G. *gernen*; O.N. *gìrna*; Goth. *gairnjan*, 'desire, long'; O.H.G. *gern*, 'eager, desirous'; cogn. w. Lat. *hori, hortāri*, 'to incite, exhort', see **hortation**; Scrt. *háryati*, 'desires'; Gk. *khairein*, 'to rejoice'; *kháris*, 'grace; joy; favour', cp. **eucharist**. **a** (followed by *for* or *after*) To desire earnestly and tenderly; to feel a tender longing towards: *to yearn for home*; *to yearn after one's absent friends*; **b** to desire, long: *I am yearning to make myself useful.*

yearning (I.), adj. [1. yĕ̀rning; 2. jɅ́niŋ], fr. Pres. Part. of prec. Animated by, expressing, desire; longing: *a yearning look.*

yearning (II.), n. **yearn** & **-ing**. Strong desire for something; wistful longing.

yearningly, adv. [1. yĕ̀rningli; 2. jɅ́niŋli]. **yearning (I.)** & **-ly**. In a yearning manner.

yeast, n. [1. yēst; 2. jīst]. O.E. *ġest*; M.E. *ȝēste*, 'yeast'; cp. M.H.G., *jest*, 'foam'; O.H.G. *iesan*, 'to ferment'; cogn. w. Gk. *zéein*, 'to boil'; *zóē*, 'foam', see second element of **eczema**; Scrt. *yásati*, 'to boil'; cp. also **enzyme** & **zymosis**. **1.** Fungoid growth consisting of a yellowish, frothy substance, with cells germinating in contact with saccharine liquid and producing alcoholic fermentation; used in brewing, distilling, bread-making &c. **2.** Mass of dried yeast compressed into a cake for keeping &c.

yeastiness, n. [1. yḗstines; 2. jístinis]. **yeasty** & **-ness**. State or quality of being yeasty.

yeast-powder, n. Baking-powder used as substitute for yeast.

yeasty, adj. [1. yḗsti; 2. jísti]. **yeast** & **-y**. **1.** Consisting of, or covered with, froth. **2.** (fig.) **a** In a state of ferment; restless, unsettled: *yeasty thoughts* &c.; **b** unsubstantial, trifling, frivolous: *yeasty words* &c.

yelk, n. [1. yelk; 2. jɛlk]. See **yolk**.

yell (I.), vb. intrans. & trans. [1. yel; 2. jɛl]. O.E. *ġellan*; M.E. *ȝellen*, 'to yell, shout'; cp. O.H.G. *gellan*, 'to yell, shriek'; *galm*, 'sound'; prob. cogn. w. Gk. *khelīdṓn*, 'swallow'. Cp. also O.E. *galan*, 'to sing, scream', see last syll. of **nightingale**. **1.** intrans. **a** To utter a yell, cry loudly and sharply: *to yell with pain* &c.; **b** specif., to laugh loudly and suddenly, indulge in a prolonged burst of laughter. **2.** trans. To utter, express, with a yell: *to yell an order.*

yell (II.), n., fr. prec. **1.** Loud, sharp outcry, scream; vocal expression, often involuntary, of sudden strong emotion, pain &c.: *a yell of pain, fear, defiance* &c. **2.** (U.S.A.) Specific cry, phrase, series of vocal sounds, used by college students as an organized cheer of encouragement, salute &c.

yellow (I.), adj. [1. yélō; 2. jélou]. O.E. *ġeolo*; M.E. *ȝelowe*; cp. O.H.G. *gelo*, 'yellow'; cogn. w. Lat. *helvus*, 'tawny'; Lith. *želvas*, 'greenish'; cp. further Scrt. *hári*, 'yellow, greenish'; O. Slav. *zelenu*, 'green'; Gk. *khlōrós*, 'green', see also **chloral**, & **gold**. **1.** Of the colour found between green and orange in the spectrum, similar to the colour of gold, daffodils, buttercups &c.; Phrs. *yellow boy*, (slang) gold coin; *yellow looks*, sour, suspicious glances. **2.** (of race or person) Yellow-skinned, Mongolian; Phr. *yellow peril*, supposed danger of the yellow races obtaining world-power. **3.** (low slang) Cowardly, lacking spirit and pluck.

yellow (II.), n., fr. prec. **1.** **a** Yellow colour; **b** yellow pigment. **2.** (archaic) *Yellows*, jaundice.

yellow (III.), vb. trans. & intrans., fr. **yellow (I.)**. **1.** trans. To give a yellow colour to, turn yellow. **2.** intrans. To grow yellow.

yellow-, pref. representing **yellow (I.)**. **1.** (in names of animals, insects, plants &c.) Of a yellow colour. **2.** (with name of part of body, forming names of plants, animals &c.) Of a yellow colour in specified part, e.g., *yellow-bill*; *yellow-tail*; *yellow-jacket* &c. **3.** (in names of animals, plants &c., compounded w. adjs. formed fr. parts of body) e.g. *yellow-backed, yellow-legged* &c.

yellowback, n. [1. yélōbàk; 2. jéloubæ̀k]. (archaic) A cheap novel, esp. of an exciting, sensational character, formerly issued bound in boards covered with shiny yellow paper, with a picture on the front.

yellow-bird, n. N. American goldfinch.

yellow-book, n. Official report of French or Chinese government, issued with a yellow paper cover.

yellow box, n. Australian box-tree.

yellow cartilage, n. Elastic wall of artery.

yellow earth, n. Yellow ochre.

yellow fever, n. Acute, infectious, malignant, tropical fever, marked by jaundice, black vomit, and bleeding &c., caused by a micro-organism conveyed by the bite of a mosquito.

yellow-gum, n. Infants' black jaundice.

yellow-hammer, n. Earlier *yellow ammer*, fr. **yellow (I.)** & O.E. *amore*, a kind of bird; cp. O.H.G. *amer*, 'yellow-hammer'. Small, European bunting, *Emberiza citrinella*, with yellow head, neck, and breast.

yellowish, adj. [1. yélōish; 2. jélouiʃ]. **yellow (I.)** & **-ish**. Somewhat yellow.

yellow jack, n. Yellow fever.

yellowly, adv. [1. yélōli; 2. jélouli]. **yellow (I.)** & **-ly**. In a yellow manner; so as to give an impression of yellowness.

yellow metal, n. Alloy of 60 parts copper and 40 parts zinc.

yellowness, n. [1. yélōnes; 2. jélounis]. **yellow (I.)** & **-ness**. Quality of being yellow.

yellow ochre, n. Kind of clay coloured with oxide of iron, used as pigment.

yellow press, n. Sensational newspapers.

yellow-rattle, n. Yellow-flowered herb.

yellow spot, n. Point of most acute vision in the retina.

yellow wood, n. Tree yielding yellow timber.

yellow wort, n. A plant of the gentian family, the flowers of which are used medicinally.

yellowy, adj. [1. yéloi; 2. jélouɪ]. **yellow** (I.) & -y. Yellow, yellowish.

yelp, vb. intrans. & n. [1. yelp; 2. jɛlp]. O.E. *ġelpan*, 'to boast'; M.E. *ȝelpen*, cp. M.H.G. *gelfen*; O.N. *gjalpa*, 'to yelp'. 1. vb. To utter a yelp, to yap. 2. n. Short, sharp cry or bark, a yap, of rage or pain, esp. of a dog.

yen, n. [1. yen; 2. jɛn]. Jap., fr. Chinese *yüan*, 'round; a dollar'. Unit of Japanese coinage, worth about 2s. 1d.

yeoman, n. [1. yŏman; 2. jóumən]. M.E. *ȝēman, ȝōman*, 'manservant, steward'; cp. O. Fris. *gāman*, 'villager'. The origin of the first element is rather doubtful, & it is uncertain fr. what source the word got into M.E. O.E. *ġeā* is not found, but it has been suspected to lurk in the Pl.-N. *Ely*, O.E. *Eli-ge, -ga*. The meaning was presumably 'village, district', & its cognates must be sought in O. Fris. *gā, gō*, 'village', O.H.G. *kawi, goui* &c., Mod. Germ. *gau*, 'village, township' &c.; Goth. *gawi*. On the other hand, O.E.D. suggests not entirely without some plausibility that the word stands for *yongman*, w. the sense of 'page, retainer' &c., & adduces early forms *yemman, yomman*. 1. (hist.) Owner of free land to the value of forty shillings yearly, thereby entitled to certain rights. Phr. *yeoman('s) service*, effective assistance. 2. Farmer cultivating his own land, a small landowner. 3. Member of yeomanry force of cavalry. 4. *Yeoman of the Guard*, in full, *His Majesty's Body Guard of the Yeomen of the Guard*, member of a royal bodyguard founded in 1485, and now employed solely in ceremonial duties.

yeomanly, adj. [1. yŏmanli; 2. jóumənli]. Prec. & -ly. Of, resembling, characteristic of, a yeoman.

yeomanry, n. [1. yŏmanri; 2. jóumənri]. yeoman & -ry. 1. Yeomen collectively. 2. Territorial, formerly volunteer, cavalry force recruited chiefly from country districts.

-yer, suff. expressing an agent. Now used only in a few words—*lawyer, bowyer, sawyer*. From earlier *-ier*; cp. *-eer*; or formed as fr. *-ien* vbs., & *-er*; cp. M.E. *luvien*, 'to love', whence earlier *luvier, loveyer* instead of *lover*; cp. **wonyer**.

yerba, n. [1. yĕrba; 2. jə́bə]. Span. *yerba* (*maté*), 'the herb maté'. Paraguay tea, maté.

yercum, n. [1. yĕrkum; 2. jə́kəm], fr. Tamil *erukku*. Fibre of an E. Indian plant called mudar, which resembles flax.

yes, interj. or advbl. particle [1. yes; 2. jɛs]. O.E. *ġiese, gese*, fr. *ġea swā*, **yea** & **so**. 1. Expressing affirmation, consent, **a** esp. in answer to a question : *are you ready ? yes*; **b** expressing acquiescence in what has been said : *this is an excellent book; yes, it is*. 2. (uttered with rising tone) **a** Expressing interrogation; is it so ? &c. in reply to another's statement: *he is a very unscrupulous fellow. Yes ?*; **b** also following a statement of one's own, with sense do you understand ?, do you agree ?, is that clear ? &c. : *we first go two miles west, then bear to the north and continue in a straight line for several miles—yes ?* 3. As emphasising or amplifying a statement; moreover, in addition: *he will insult you, yes, and cheat you as well*.

yester-, pref. representing O.E. *ġeostran-*, M.E. *ȝestren-*, 'yester-'; cp. O.H.G. *gestaron*, 'yesterday'; Goth. *gistra(dagis)*, 'tomorrow'; cogn. w. Lat. *here*, earlier **hezi*, 'yesterday', fr. **ghes-*; *hesternus*, 'of yesterday'; Scrt. *hyáś*; Gk. *khthés*, 'yesterday'. (chiefly poet.) Forming nouns and adverbs, **a** with the sense 'of yesterday', e.g. *yester-night, -eve* &c.; **b** with the sense 'last, preceding', e.g. *yester-year*, (poet.) past times.

yesterday, n. & adv. [1. yésterdi; 2. jéstədɪ]. O.E. *ġeostran dæġ*, 'yesterday'; see prec. & **day**. 1. n. **a** The day before today, the day just past. Phr. (*a thing*) *of yesterday*, something of but recent growth, appearance &c.; **b** (pl.) past times, former days: '*A man of cheerful yesterdays*' (Wordsworth, 'Excursion', vii. 536); **c** (attrib.) *yesterday morning, evening, night*. 2. adv. On the day before today : *he went away yesterday*.

yestreen, n. & adv. [1. yestrēn; 2. jɛstrín]. Contracted fr. *yester-even*; see **yester-**. (Scots) **a** n. Yester-even, the evening of yesterday; **b** adv., on the evening of yesterday.

yet (I.), adv. [1. yet; 2. jɛt]. O.E. *ġet*; M.E. *ȝet*; cp. O. Fris. (*j*)*eta*; M.H.G. *ieze*, 'yet, now'. 1. (usually with neg.) **a** Up to this time, until now, heretofore : *he has not come yet*; *I know nothing yet*; **b** up to a specified point of time in the past : *when dawn broke the reinforcements had not yet arrived*. 2. At this present time, now : *need you go yet ?*; *I can't come just yet*. 3. Still, up to and including the present time, even now : *he is yet alive; while there is yet time; he loves her yet; the work is yet unfinished*. Phr. *as yet*, up to now, so far. 4. In addition, besides : *he has yet much to say; there is work yet to be done; we have yet more to ask*. 5. Before a future time, some day : *he will yet be victorious; he may surprise you yet*. 6. Even, as much as : *he will not accept help nor yet advice*. 7. (with compar.) Still, even, additionally, even more: *travelling is yet more rapid today than it was ten years ago*. 8. Nevertheless, in spite of that : *the house was humble, yet clean; poor, yet honest*.

yet (II.), conj., fr. prec. Nevertheless, but still : *appearances are against him, yet I cannot think him guilty*.

yew, n. [1. ū; 2. jū]. O.E. *ēow, īw*; M.E. *eu*, 'yew'; cp. O.H.G. *īwa*, Mod. Germ. *eibe*; Du. *ijf*; O.N. *ȳr*; cp. also O.E. *eoh*; O.H.G. *iche*, 'yew'. 1. Evergreen coniferous tree, *Taxus baccata*, with small, slender, densely growing, dark-green leaves and rough bark. 2. Close-grained, durable wood obtained from the yew, used formerly for making bows.

yew tree, n. Same as **yew**, 1.

Yg(g)drasil, n. [1. ígdrasɪl; 2. ígdrəsɪl]. O.N. (*askr*) *Yggdrasils*, perh. 'ash of the horse of Yggr' or Odin. (Norse mythol.) Great tree of the universe, whose roots and branches bind together heaven, earth, and hell.

Yiddish, n. & adj. [1. yídish; 2. jídɪʃ], fr. Jewish pronunciation of Germ. *jüdisch*, 'Jewish', fr. *Jude*, 'Jew', O.H.G. *judeo*, fr. Lat. *judaeus*, 'Jew'; see **Judaic**. 1. n. Mixed dialect with German, Hebrew, and Slavonic elements, used by German Jews, largely spoken in the East End of London. 2. adj. Spoken, written &c., in Yiddish.

yield (I.), vb. trans. & intrans. [1. yēld; 2. jīəld]. O.E. *ġelden*; M.E. *ȝeelden*, 'to pay'; cp. O.H.G. *geltan*, 'to pay; to be worth'; O.N. *gjalda*, 'to pay'; Goth. *-gildan*, 'to requite'; Du. *gelden*, 'to cost'. A. trans. 1. **a** To produce, give, as result of a natural process: *the land yields heavy crops; cows yield milk*; **b** to produce in return for effort, trouble &c.: *my labours, researches, yielded but a poor result*; **c** to produce as financial return: *investments yield a profit*. 2. To give up, relinquish under pressure, compulsion &c., surrender : *to yield a fortress to the enemy*. 3. To concede, grant: *to yield precedence to another ; to yield a point in argument*. B. intrans. 1. To produce, give a return for effort &c. : *the land yields abundantly*. 2. (often with *to*) **a** To give way, submit, cease resistance : *he will never yield; to yield to pressure, to force*. Phr. *I yield to none* (*in my admiration for him* &c.), I do not admit that anyone (admires him &c.) more than I do; **b** (of material object) to give way to, or before, physical pressure: *the door yielded to a strong push*; '*Oft did the harvest to their sickle yield*' (Gray's 'Elegy'); **c** (of diseases) *to yield to treatment*, be amenable to, become less acute, be cured, as result of.

yield (II.), n., fr. prec. Amount produced; result, profit, return.

yielding, adj. [1. yélding; 2. jíəldɪŋ], fr. Pres. Part. of **yield** (I.). **a** Tending to bend; capable of being bent or altered in shape; flexible, not rigid ; **b** easily influenced, liable to yield to persuasion; compliant ; reverse of *stubborn*.

yieldingly, adv. Prec. & -ly. In a yielding manner.

-yl, suff. representing Gk. *hūlē*, 'wood, forest; timber ; material; matter'; etymol. doubtful. Used to form chemical terms denoting a radical, q.v., e.g. *methyl*.

ylang-ylang, n. [1. ɪláng ɪláng; 2. ɪlǽŋ ɪlǽŋ]. Philippine. Malayan tree with fragrant flowers.

yodel, vb. intrans. & trans., & n. [1. yŏdl; 2. jóudl], fr. Germ. *jodeln*, prob. imitative. 1. vb. **a** intrans. To produce a yodel; **b** trans., to sing (a song) by yodelling. 2. n. Series of musical notes uttered by the voice, in form of a kind of warble or run, passing alternatively from chest voice to falsetto, and vice versa.

yoga, n. [1. yŏga; 2. jóugə]. Hind. System of philosophy and practice of esoteric meditation, having as object the union of the individual human spirit with that of the universe.

yogh, n. [1. yogh; 2. jɔχ]. Prob. fr. M.E. *ȝoc*, 'yoke', see **yoke**, wh. begins w. this letter. The Middle English letter ȝ.

yogi, n. [1. yŏgi; 2. jóugi]. Hind. Devotee of yogism.

yogism, n. [1. yŏgizm; 2. jóugizəm]. Prec. & -ism. Doctrines of the yoga.

yo-heave-ho, interj. [1. yō hēv hō; 2. jou hɪv hou]. (naut.) Cry used in heaving the anchor &c.

yoho, interj. [1. yŏhō; 2. jòuhóu]. Yo-heave-ho.

yoick, vb. intrans. & trans. [1. yoik; 2. jɔɪk]. fr. next word. 1. intrans. To cry yoicks. 2. trans. To encourage, urge on (hounds), with the cry of 'Yoicks'.

yoicks, interj. [1. yoiks; 2. jɔɪks]. Etymol. unknown. Huntsman's cry to hounds.

yoke (I.), n. [1. yōk; 2. jouk]. O.E. *ġeoc*; M.E. *ȝoc, ȝōke*; cp. O.H.G. *joh*; Goth. *juk*; cogn. w. Lat. *jugum*, 'yoke', see **jugate**; Gk. *zugón*, 'yoke', see **zyg(o)-**; Scrt. *yugám*, 'yoke, pair'; conn. w. Lat. *jungere*, 'to join', see **join**. 1. Cross-piece forming part of harness of, and shaped to fit necks of, draught-animals, oxen &c. Phr. *to pass, come, under the yoke*, to submit to defeat; from ancient Roman custom of causing conquered enemy to pass beneath an uplifted yoke, or an arch of spears, as a symbol of servitude. 2. Object resembling a yoke in shape ; specif. **a** wooden bar or frame shaped to fit person's shoulders and used for carrying milkpails &c. ; **b** cross-bar from which a bell is hung ; **c** cross-bar on rudder, to which steering-lines are fastened; **d** coupling for pipes ; **e** part of garment cut or designed to fit shoulders. 3. **a** Pair of oxen, for ploughing &c. ; **b** *yoke of land*, amount of land ploughed by a pair of oxen in a day. 4. (fig.) Sway, domination, authority : *the yoke of an oppressor*. 5. (rare) Moral or legal bond.

yoke (II.), vb. trans. & intrans. ; see prec. A. trans. 1. To put a yoke upon, harness with a yoke. 2. To join together, to unite : (chiefly fig.) *yoked in marriage*. B. intrans. (rare) *Yoke together*, to be joined.

yoke-bone, n. Cheek-bone, malar, joining bones of head and face.

yoke-fellow, n. Person joined or associated with one in work &c. or in marriage.

yokel, n. [1. yŏkl; 2. jóukl]. Prob. **yoke** & **-el**. Countryman, rustic.

yoke-lines, n. Pair of lines attached to yoke of rudder for steering small boat.

yokemate, n. [1. yŏkmāt; 2. jóukmeɪt]. Yoke-fellow.

yolk, n. [1. yōk; 2. jouk]. O.E. *ġeolca*, 'yolk'; M.E. *ȝolke*; connected w. O.E. *ġeolu*, 'yellow', see **yellow**. 1. Yellow central mass of egg. 2. Fatty secretion in sheep's wool.

yolk-bag, n. Yolk-sac.

yolked, adj. [1. yōkt; 2. joukt]. **yolk** & **-ed**. Having a yolk ; sometimes in compounds, e.g. *double-yolked*, with two yolks.

yolk-sac, n. Membranous sac attached to an embryo from which nutrition is derived.

yolky, adj. [1. yŏki; 2. jóuki]. yolk & -y. Containing or resembling yolk.

yon, adj., adv., & pron. [1. yon; 2. jɔn]. O.E. *ġeon*; M.E. *ȝon*, 'yon'; cp. O. Fris. *jene*; O.H.G. *jener*; O.N. *enn*; Goth. *jains*, 'that'; cogn. w. Scrt. *yáś*, 'which, who'; Gk. *hós*, 'that'; fr. pronominal stem **i-* &c., seen in *it* &c. (archaic or provinc.) **1.** adj. That one yonder. **2.** adv. Yonder, over there. **3.** pron. Yonder person or thing: *did you ever see the like of yon?*

yonder, adj. & adv. [1. yónder; 2. jóndə]. M.E. *ȝonder*; **yon** & **-ther**. **1.** adj. In that (more or less remote) place, over there. **2.** adv. Over there: *yonder stands an oak.*

yore, n. [1. yōr; 2. jɔ̄]. O.E. *ġēara*, *ġ(e)āra*, M.E. *ȝōre*, 'formerly', adv. fr. n. *ġēar*, 'year', see **year**. Only in *of yore*, formerly, long ago; *days of yore*, in ancient times.

York (I.), n. [1. york; 2. jɔ̄k]. fr. Place-Name York; O.E. *Eoforwīc*, adaptation of Brito-Lat. *Eboracum*. *York-and-Lancaster rose*, red-and-white variety, named from respective badges of Lancastrians and Yorkists in Wars of the Roses.

york (II.), vb. trans., fr. next word. To bowl (person) out with a yorker.

yorker, n. [1. yórker; 2. jɔ́kə]. Prob. fr. York, Pl.-N. (cricket) Ball which pitches immediately in front of batsman's block.

Yorkist, adj. & n. [1. yórkist; 2. jɔ́kist]. York & **-ist**. **1.** adj. Of, pertaining to, the house of York, family descended from Edmund, son of Edward III. **2.** n. Adherent of House of York in Wars of the Roses.

Yorkshire, adj. [1. yórksher; 2. jɔ́kʃə]. fr. name of county. Of, pertaining to, originating in Yorkshire; *Yorkshire flannel*, made of undyed wool; *Yorkshire grit*, grit used for polishing; *Yorkshire pudding*, baked batter eaten with meat; *Yorkshire terrier*, small, long-haired variety.

you, pron. [1. ū; 2. jū]; unstressed [ju]. O.E. *ēow*, dat. of *ȝē*, pl. pron. of 2nd pers., see **ye**; M.E. *ȝou*, which was already used in respectful address to a single person. **1.** Used as nominative and objective case of pronoun of 2nd person, singular and plural. By the middle of 16th cent., while *you* is still often kept distinct from nominative *ye*, the two forms are used indifferently by many, and some writers (e.g. Queen Elizabeth) appear to use *you* only, as at present. **2.** indef. pron. One, anyone: *you never can tell; you often find that just when you want something you haven't got it by you.* **3.** (reflex., archaic) Yourself: *stay and rest you on this bank.*

young (I.), adj. [1. yung; 2. jaŋ]. O.E. *ġeong*; M.E. *ȝung*; cp. O.S., O. Fris., O.H.G. *jung*; Goth. *juggs*, 'young'; cogn. w. Lat. *juvenis*, 'young', see **juvenile**; *juvencus*, 'bullock'; Scrt. *yuvaśáś*, 'youthful'; *yúvā*, 'young'; Lith. *jáunas*; O. Slav. *junŭ*, 'young'. **1.** **a** (of men and other living creatures) In the early stages of life, in a period of life not long after birth; contrasted with *old* or *middle-aged*: *a young man, animal, plant* &c.; *a young tree*, one planted only a short time, not fully grown; Phrs. *a young family*, one consisting of small children; *the young person*, inexperienced, unsophisticated youth collectively; (*look here*), *young man*, familiar, slightly condescending form of address; **b** applied to the younger of two persons of same name or family, to distinguish a son from his father, or a man from his elder brother &c.: *young Jones, the young Mrs. Brown* &c.; *younger branch of family*, descended from a younger son. **2.** Characteristic of youth; **a** having the appearance, habits &c. of youth; fresh, vigorous, not decrepit: *a man is as young as his arteries; young for his age, years;* **b** enjoyed, possessed, by young persons: *young love; young ambitions*; Phr. *young blood*, fresh, vigorous, triumphant youth; **c** embodying new ideas, tendencies &c., esp. in names of progressive political parties, movements &c.: *Young England; Young Turks.* **3.** Having had a comparatively short historical existence. **4.** (of periods of time, seasons &c.) Not far advanced, having begun but a short time before: *the night, the century, is still young.* **5.** Inexperienced; not inured: *young in crime.*

young (II.), n., fr. prec. (coll.) The offspring of animals: *every animal will defend its young to the utmost of its powers.* Phr. (of female animals) *with young*, pregnant.

youngish, adj. [1. yúngish; 2. jáŋiʃ]. young & **-ish**. Fairly young; barely middle-aged.

youngling, n. [1. yúngling; 2. jáŋliŋ]. young & **-ling**. (poet.) Young child, animal &c.

youngster, n. [1. yúngster; 2. jáŋstə]. young & **-ster**. A young man; a child, esp. a boy.

younker, n. [1. yúngker; 2. jáŋkə], fr. Du. *jonker*, fr. *jong*, 'young', cogn. w. **young**, & *heer*, 'sir'; cp. Germ. *Herr*, O.H.G. *hērro*, *hēriro*, 'lord, master', fr. compar. of *hēr*, 'distinguished, respected', orig. 'old' (Mod. Germ. *hehr*); cp. O.E. *hār*, 'grey, hoary', see **hoar**. (archaic) Young man, youngster.

your, adj. [1. yōr, ūr; 2. jɔ̄, juə]. O.E. *ēower*; genit. pl. of *ġē*, 'you', see **ye**; M.E. *eour, ower*, & *ȝour, your*, w. *y-* on anal. of nom.; cp. O.S. *iuwar*; O.H.G. *iuwer*; Goth. *izwara*, 'of you'. **1.** Pertaining or belonging to you. **2.** (archaic and colloq.) Used to give indefinite, general sense to following noun: *your true savage can never be thoroughly civilized.*

yours, pron. & predic. adj. [1. yorz, ūrz; 2. jɔ̄z, juəz]. M.E. *youres*. your & **-es**. **1.** pron. Possessive of *you*, **a** the thing or things belonging to you; used absolutely: *this seat is yours;* **b** also preceded by *of: a little whim of yours; I saw a friend of yours.* **2.** adj. **a** Belonging to you: *the credit is much more yours than mine;* **b** at your service, devoted to you: in formulae at close of letters: *yours truly, faithfully, affectionately; yours to command.* **3.** As n. Those (persons) belonging to you, your nearest and dearest: *all good wishes to you and yours.*

yourself, pron. [1. yor-, ūrself; 2. jɔ̄-, juəsélf]. your & **-self**. **1.** Emphatic form of *you*: *you told me so yourself; do it yourself*, implying you rather than someone else; (*all*) *by yourself*, (i.) alone, without company; (ii.) by your own efforts, without help from others. **2.** (reflex.) *Don't hurt yourself; you will wear yourself out.*

youth, n. [1. yōoth; 2. jūþ]. O.E. *ġeoguþ*, fr. **juguñþ*; M.E. *ȝuweþe, youhþe* &c.; O.S. *juguth*; O.H.G. *jugund*, 'youth'; cogn. w. Lat. *juventa, -tus*, 'youth'; see **young, -th**. **1.** Early life; **a** specif., period of life between childhood and physical maturity; adolescence; contrasted with *childhood* on one hand and *manhood* on the other; **b** young manhood or young womanhood; period of life before middle age; contrasted with *middle age* or *old age: the wife of his youth; after thirty we feel that youth is slipping away;* (fig.) *the youth of nations*, early period in their history or development. **2.** Physical and mental characteristics of youth; buoyancy, vigour: *the way to keep one's youth is to exercise both mind and body regularly.* **3.** A young man: *a most agreeable youth; a bevy of youths and maidens.* **4.** Young persons of both sexes collectively: *the youth of the place.*

youthful, adj. [1. yōothfool; 2. júpfəl]. Prec. & **-ful**. **1.** Possessing youth; young, not old: *a youthful bride, mother.* **2.** Pertaining to, characteristic of, suitable for, youth: *youthful ambitions* &c.; *a youthful appearance, smile; her clothes were too youthful for her face and figure.*

youthfully, adv. Prec. & **-ly**. In a youthful manner.

youthfulness, n. See prec. & **-ness**. State or quality of being youthful.

yowl, vb. intrans. & n. [1. youl; 2. jaul]. Cp. Du. *jolen*; O.N. *gaula*, 'to yell'. Imitative. **a** vb. To howl dismally; **b** n., a dismal howl.

ytterbic, adj. [1. itérbik; 2. itʌ́bik]. See next word & **-ic**. Connected with, pertaining to, ytterbium.

ytterbium, n. [1. itérbium; 2. itʌ́biəm], fr. Place-Name Ytterby, in Sweden, place of discovery. Rare element, forming colourless salts.

yttric, adj. [1. itrik; 2. itrík]. See **yttrium** & **-ic**. Pertaining to yttrium.

yttriferous, adj. [1. itríferus; 2. itrífərəs]. yttro- & **-ferous**. Containing yttrium.

yttrious, adj. [1. ítrius; 2. ítriəs]. See **yttrium** & **-ous**. Derived from yttrium.

yttrium, n. [1. ítrium; 2. ítriəm], fr. Place-Name Ytterby, in Sweden, place of discovery. Rare metal, found as a greyish powder.

yttro-, pref. representing prec. Forming names of minerals containing yttrium, e.g. *yttrocerite*, a violet-coloured mineral sometimes found in quartz.

yucca, n. [1. yúka, yooka; 2. jákə, júkə]. Span., fr. Am. Indian. Genus of plants of the lily family, indigenous to Central America, Mexico &c., having a dense crown of stiff, thick, sword-shaped leaves and large white flowers.

yuga, n. [1. yōoga; 2. júgə]. Hind., fr. Scrt. *yugá-*, 'era, age'. Any one of the four cycles into which the duration of the world is divided in the Hindu religious writings.

yule, n. [1. yōol; 2. jūl]. O.E. *ġeōl*, M.E. *ȝōl*; cp. O.N. *jōl*. Etymol. unknown. Christmas season or festival.

yule-log, n. Log burnt as part of Christmas celebrations.

yule-tide, n. Christmas.

Z

Z, z [1. zed; 2. zɛd]. **a** The twenty-sixth letter of the alphabet; for use in abbreviations &c. see list at end of Dictionary; **b** (alg.) third unknown quantity.

zaffre, zaffer, n. [1. záfer; 2. zǽfə], fr. Fr. *zafre*, perh. fr. Arab. Blue pigment made from cobalt ore and silica, used in enamelling, glass-painting &c.

zamindar, n. [1. zámindar; 2. zǽmindɑ̄]. See **zemindar**.

zany, n. [1. záni; 2. zéini], fr. Fr. *zani*, fr. Ital. *zanni*, abbr. fr. *Giovanni*, John. **1.** (hist.) Buffoon who mimics the chief clown and other actors in a theatrical performance. **2.** A fantastic, foolish person; a buffoon, a merry-andrew.

Zanzibari, n. & adj. [1. zànzibáhri; 2. zænzibɑ́ri]. fr. Place-Name Zanzibar. **1.** n. Native of Zanzibar. **2.** adj. Of, coming from, Zanzibar.

zaptieh, n. [1. záptiā; 2. zǽptiei]. Turkish. Turkish policeman.

Zarathustrian. See **Zoroastrian**.

zareba, zariba, n. [1. zarḗba; 2. zərī́bə], fr. Arab. *zariba*, 'pen, enclosure'. (in the Soudan &c.) Camp or village enclosed for protection by hedge or stockade.

zeal, n. [1. zēl; 2. ziəl], fr. O. Fr. *zele*, fr. L. Lat. *zēlus*, 'zeal', fr. Gk. *zêlos*, 'emulation; zeal', possibly cogn. w. Slovene *jal*, 'envy'; O. Slav. *jaru*, 'furious'; Scrt. *yávan*, 'persecutor'. Intense enthusiasm for person, cause, enterprise &c.; ardour, fervour.

zealot, n. [1. zélot; 2. zélət], fr. O. Fr. zelote, fr. Lat. zēlōtes, fr. Gk. zēlōtés, 'zealous follower', fr. zêlos, 'emulation', see prec., & -ot. Person with excessive enthusiasm for an object, cause &c.; a fanatic.

zealotry, n. [1. zélotri; 2. zélətri]. Prec. & -ry. Practice or feeling of a zealot.

zealous, adj. [1. zélus; 2. zéləs]. zeal & -ous. Acting with, characterized by, expressing, zeal.

zealously, adv. Prec. & -ly. In a zealous manner; with zeal.

zebec(k), n. See xebec.

zebra, n. [1. zébra; 2. zíbrə]. Port., fr. Afr. Genus of African quadrupeds related to the horse and ass, with light-coloured body, marked with dark brown or black stripes.

zebra-, pref. implying stripiness: zebra-antelope, -fish &c.

zebra-wood, n. Striped wood obtained from a tree found in Guiana.

zebrine, adj. [1. zébrīn; 2. zíbrain]. zebra & -ine. Resembling, allied to, the zebra.

zebu, n. [1. zēbū; 2. zíbjū], fr. Fr. zébu, fr. Tibetan mdzopo. Large animal of the bovine family, with a hump; domesticated in India and China.

zed, n. [1. zed; 2. zed], fr. Fr. zède, fr. Lat., fr. Gk. zêta, sixth letter of alphabet; according to Boisacq, prob. formed fr. Heb. zajin, on anal. of êta, thêta. Name of the letter z.

zedoary, n. [1. zédōari; 2. zédouəri], fr. O. Fr. zedoaire, fr. Med. Lat., fr. Pers. zadwar. Cp. setwall. An aromatic drug used in India as a medicine and stimulant.

zeitgeist, n. [1. tsītgīst; 2. tsáitgaist]. Germ., fr. zeit, 'time', q.v. under tide, & geist, 'spirit', q.v. under ghost. Spirit of the times; general body of opinions and intellectual tendencies prevalent at a particular period.

Zelanian, adj. [1. zilānian; 2. ziléiniən], fr. Latinized form (Nova) Zelania, 'New Zealand', & -an. Connected with, belonging to, New Zealand.

zeloso, adv. [1. zelōsō; 2. zelóusou]. Ital., fr. Lat. zēlōsus, 'emulous', see jealous. (direction in mus.) Fervently, energetically.

zemindar, n. [1. zémindàr; 2. zémindà], fr. Pers. zemīndār, 'landholder', zamīn, 'land', & -dar, suff. indicating the agent. (in India, esp. Bengal) a A person holding land for which he pays revenue to the Government; b a landholder generally.

zemstvo, n. [1. zémstvō; 2. zémstvou]. Russ., fr. zemlya, 'land', cogn. w. Lith. žéme; Scrt. kšắš; Lat. humus, 'earth'; see humus. Provincial, elective, economic assembly in the old Russian Empire.

zenana, n. [1. zenáhna; 2. zinánə]. Pers. zenāna, 'of women', fr. zan, 'woman'; cp. Scrt. jániš, 'woman'; cogn. w. Gk. gunḗ, 'woman', see gyno-; O.E. cwene, 'woman', see quean; cwēn, 'wife, queen', see queen. Apartments in an Indian native house in which the women are secluded; zenana mission, one for religious, medical, and educational reform among Indian women.

Zend, n. [1. zend; 2. zend], fr. O. Pers. zend, 'commentary'; named fr. that upon the Parsee scriptures. Ancient form of Old Persian, called also Old Bactrian, in which the Avesta is written; a language belonging, together with Sanscrit and the modern Indian languages, to the Aryan branch of Aryan speech.

Zend-Avesta, n. [1. zénd avésta; 2. zénd avéstə], fr. Pers. Avistāk va Zand, 'text and commentary'. The sacred writings of the Zoroastrians; also applied to the interpretation of these in Pehlevi.

zenith, n. [1. zénith; 2. zéniþ], fr. O. Fr. zenith, fr. O. Span. zenit, fr. Arab. semt, 'way, path', abbr. fr. semt-er-ras, 'way of the head'. 1. Point of the heavens directly above the observer. 2. (fig.) Culminating point, highest degree of intensity, strength, success &c.: at the zenith of one's fame, powers &c.

zenithal, adj. [1. zénithal; 2. zéniþəl]. Prec. & -al. Of, pertaining to, the zenith.

zenith-distance, n. Angular distance of a heavenly body from the zenith.

zeolite, n. [1. zéolīt; 2. zíəlait], fr. Gk. zé-(ein), 'to boil', see second element of eczema, & -lite. Hydrous silicate found in the cavities of lava.

zephyr, n. [1. zéfer; 2. zéfə], fr. Fr. zéphire, fr. Lat. zephyrus, fr. Gk. zéphuros, 'west wind'; perh. cogn. w. zóphos, 'darkness'. 1. a (cap.) West wind; b (poet.) soft wind, gentle breeze. 2. a Fine, very thin, woollen material; b under-garment made from such material.

Zeppelin, n. [1. zépelin; 2. zépəlin], fr. name of inventor, Count von Zeppelin, d. 1917. Large dirigible airship.

zero, n. [1. zērō; 2. zíərou], fr. Fr., fr. Ital. contracted fr. zefiro, fr. Arab. çifr, see cipher. 1. Arabic numeral 0, a cipher, a nought; symbol of nothingness. 2. a Central point in a scale from which positive and negative quantities are reckoned; specif. b central point of scale of temperature; in centigrade thermometer, freezing-point of water; c zero hour, (mil.) precise time from which the times of the various operations in an offensive are calculated. 3. (fig.) Lowest point in scale of comparison or reckoning; nothingness: our hopes were reduced to zero.

zest, n. [1. zest; 2. zest], fr. O. Fr. zeste, 'lemon-peel used for flavouring; skin of walnut kernel', fr. Lat. schistos, 'split', fr. Gk. skhistós, 'divided', fr. skhizein, 'to cleave', see schism. 1. Piquant addition, flavouring, relish; (chiefly fig.) piquancy, stimulating quality, esp. in Phr. to give a zest to (pleasure &c.). 2. Keenness, enjoyment, gusto, ardour: to enter into a game, a piece of work &c. with zest.

zeta, n. [1. zēta; 2. zítə]. Gk. name of symbol ζ, the sixth letter in Greek alphabet, which expressed either [dz] or [zd]. See zed.

zetetic, adj. [1. zētétik; 2. zītétik], fr. Gk. zētētikós, 'searching, inquiring', fr. zētētés, 'seeker', fr. zēteein, 'to search after, inquire into', fr. earlier *djatej-, pr. stem *djā-, *dja-, 'to hasten towards, strive after'; cp. Gk. (dí)zēmai, 'strive to reach'; zálē, 'storm at sea'. (rare) Proceeding by inquiry: zetetic method.

zeugma, n. [1. zūgma; 2. zjúgmə]. Gk. zeúgma, 'band, bond, yoke', fr. zeúgnūmi, 'I yoke, bind'; cp. Gk. zeûgos, 'harness'; zugón, 'yoke', see zyg(o)- & yoke. Figure of grammar in which a verb or adjective is applied to two nouns, to only one of which it is strictly applicable either grammatically or logically; see also syllepsis.

zeugmatic, adj. [1. zūgmátik; 2. zjūgmǽtik], fr. Gk. zeúgmatos, genit. of zeúgma, 'yoke', see prec., & -ic. Characterized by zeugma.

Zeus, n. [1. zūs; 2. zjūs]. Gk. Zeús; cp. Scrt. dyáúš, 'heaven'; Lat. deus, 'god', see deity, & words there referred to. Supreme Olympian deity of ancient Greeks.

zeuxite, n. [1. zūksīt; 2. zjúksait], fr. Gk. zeûxis, 'joining', fr. zeúgnūmi, 'I join, yoke, bind', see zeugma, & -ite. Kind of pale brown tourmaline.

zibet, n. [1. zíbet; 2. zíbet], fr. Ital. zibetto, fr. Arab. zabad. Asiatic or Indian civet-cat.

zigzag, n., adj., adv., & vb. intrans. [1. zígzag; 2. zígzæg], fr. Fr., fr. Germ. zickzack, re-dupl. fr. zacke, 'tooth', cogn. w. tack. 1. n. A line having a series of short angular deviations from the straight, turning or winding now in one direction, now in another; anything having such a form or course. 2. adj. Having, forming, describing, a zigzag. 3. adv. So as to follow or describe a zigzag line: the road ran zigzag across the hills. 4. vb. a To move in, follow, a zigzag course: he zigzagged slowly homewards after dinner; b (of road, river) to run, be shaped, in zigzags.

zillah, n. [1. zíla; 2. zílə], fr. Hind. dilah. District in British India under the control of a deputy-commissioner or collector.

zinc, n. & vb. trans. [1. zingk; 2. ziŋk]. Germ. zink; etymol. doubtful. 1. n. Bluish-white metallic element, used in the industrial arts; zinc oxide, white pigment used as substitute for oxide of lead. 2. vb. To treat, coat, with zinc.

zincic, adj. [1. zíngkik; 2. zíŋkik]. Prec. & -ic. Of, pertaining to, derived from, zinc.

zinciferous, adj. [1. zingkíferus; 2. ziŋkífərəs]. zinc & -i- & -ferous. Yielding, producing, zinc.

zincification, n. [1. zìngkifikáshun; 2. zìŋkifikéiʃən]. See zincify & -fication. Act of zincifying; state of being zincified.

zincify, vb. trans. [1. zíngkifī; 2. zíŋkifai]. zinc & -i- & -fy. To coat or impregnate with zinc.

zinco, n. [1. zíngkō; 2. zíŋkou]. Abbr. fr. zincograph. Zincograph.

zinco-, pref. representing zinc & -o-. Zinc, e.g. zincograph, zincotype &c.

zincograph (I.), n. [1. zìngkogràhf; 2. zíŋkəgràf]. zinco- & -graph. a Design in relief on zinc plate; b picture produced by printing from such a plate.

zincograph (II.), vb. intrans. & trans., fr. prec. 1. intrans. To produce pictures by zincographic process. 2. trans. To print, produce (design, picture), from a zincograph.

zincographer, n. [1. zingkógrafer; 2. ziŋkógrəfə]. Prec. & -er. Person employed or skilled in zincographing.

zincographic, adj. [1. zìngkográfik; 2. zìŋkəgrǽfik]. zincograph (I.) & -ic. Of, pertaining to, of the nature of, a zincograph.

zincography, n. [1. zingkógrafi; 2. ziŋkógrəfi]. zinco- & -graphy. Process of producing design in relief on zinc plates for printing.

zincoid, adj. [1. zíngkoid; 2. zíŋkɔid]. zinco- & -oid. Resembling zinc.

zincotype, n. [1. zíngkotīp; 2. zíŋkətàip]. zinco- & type. Zincograph.

zincous, adj. [1. zíngkus; 2. zíŋkəs]. zinc & -ous. Of, pertaining to, derived from, zinc.

zingaro, n., pl. **zingari** [1. zíngarō, -i; 2. zíŋgərou, -i]. Ital. Ultimately fr. Pers. or Indian word meaning 'blacksmith'; cp. Pehlevi asinkār, 'blacksmith'. Gipsy.

zinke, n. [1. tsíngke; 2. tsíŋkə]. Mod. Germ. Old form of musical wind-instrument with leather-covered, slightly tapering tube.

zinky, adj. [1. zíngki; 2. zíŋki]. zinc & -y. Made of, containing, or resembling, zinc.

zinnia, n. [1. zínia; 2. zíniə], fr. J. G. Zinn, German botanist, d. 1759. Genus of annual herbs of the aster family, with bright-coloured, composite flowers.

Zion, n. [1. zíon; 2. záiən]. Eccles. Lat. Síon, fr. Heb. Tsīyōn, 'hill'. 1. a Hill in Jerusalem; b the city of Jerusalem. 2. (fig.) a Ancient Hebrew theocracy; b the Christian Church; c heaven, the Heavenly Jerusalem.

Zionism, n. [1. zíonizm; 2. záiənizəm]. Prec. & -ism. Movement with the object of re-settlement of the Jews in Palestine and the establishment of a national home there.

Zionist, n. [1. zíonist; 2. záiənist]. Zion & -ist. Adherent of Zionism.

Zionwards, adv. [1. zíonwardz; 2. záiənwədz]. Zion & -wards. Heavenwards.

zip, n. [1. zip; 2. zip]. Imitative. Light, whizzing sound, as of bullet passing through the air.

zircon, n. [1. zérkon; 2. zákən], fr. Arab. zarkun, 'cinnabar', fr. Pers. zargūn, 'gold-coloured'. Silicate of zirconium, variously coloured; varieties are the hyacinth and the jargoon.

zirconate, n. [1. zérkonāt; 2. zákəneit]. Prec. & -ate. Salt of zirconic acid.

zirconic, adj. [1. zērkónik; 2. zəkónik]. zircon & -ic. Of, derived from, zirconium.

zirconium, n. [1. zērkónium; 2. zəkóuniəm]. zircon & -ium. Blackish or greyish metallic element found in combination with silica.

zither, n. [1. zíther; 2. zíþə], fr. Germ., fr. Lat. cithara, see cither(n). Musical instrument with flat sounding-board and strings plucked with a plectrum.

zitherist, n. [1. zítherist; 2. zíp*ə*rist]. Prec. & -ist. Player on the zither.

zloty, n. [1. zlóti; 2. zlóti]. Pol. Polish coin = 10d.

-zoa suff. [1. zóa; 2. zóu*ə*], representing pl. of Gk. *zôon*, 'animal', see **zoo-**.

Zoar, n. [1. zŏar; 2. zóu*ə*]. With reference to story of Lot, Genesis xix. 22. Place of refuge.

zodiac, n. [1. zŏdiàk; 2. zóudìæk], fr. Fr. *zodiaque*, fr. Lat. *zōdiacus*, fr. Gk. *zōdiakós*, 'containing animals', fr. *zōdion*, 'small figure'; pl., 'signs of zodiac', dimin. of *zôon*, 'animal, living creature'; fr. *zōós*, 'living', see **zoo-**. **1. a** An imaginary belt in the heavens, having the ecliptic in the centre, within which the moon and all the principal planets have their paths; divided into twelve sections or signs; **b** the region in the heavens enclosed by the zodiac. **2. A** figure representing the zodiac and its divisions, each with its appropriate symbol.

zodiacal, adj. [1. zŏdíakl; 2. zòudáiəkl]. Prec. & **-al**. Of, pertaining to, situated within, the zodiac : *zodiacal light*, faintly luminous, apparently triangular tract of sky sometimes seen in the west after dusk or in the east before dawn, chiefly in the tropics.

zoetrope, n. [1. zŏetrŏp; 2. zóuìtròup], fr. Gk. *zōē̆*, 'life', fr. *zōós*, 'living', see **zoo-**, & *trópos*, 'a turn', see **-trope**, & **trepidation**. Toy with revolving cylinder showing series of pictures in apparent motion; wheel of life.

zoic, adj. [1. zŏik; 2. zóuik], fr. Gk. *zōikós*, fr. *zôon*, 'animal', see **zoo-**, & **-ic**. **a** Of, pertaining to, characterized by, animal life; specif. **b** (geol., of rock) containing fossils of plants or animals.

Zolaesque, adj. [1. zŏlaésk; 2. zòulə́ésk], fr. *Zola*, see next word, & **-esque**. Resembling, characteristic of, the style and manner of Zola.

Zolaism, n. [1. zŏlaìzm; 2. zóulə̀izəm], fr. Emile Zola, French novelist, d. 1902, & **-ism**. Literary style and method characteristic of Zola; vigorous but coarse naturalism.

Zolaist, n. [1. zŏlaìst; 2. zóulə̀ist], fr. *Zola*, see prec. Writer in the style of Zola.

Zolaistic, adj. [1. zŏlaístik; 2. zòuləístik]. Prec. & **-ic**. Of, resembling, the style of Zola.

zollverein, n. [1. tsól-, zólferìn; 2. tsŏl-, zólfəràin]. Germ., fr. *zoll*, 'tax', see **toll** (III.), & *verein*, 'union', fr. pref. *ver-*, cogn. w. **for-**, & *ein*, 'one', see **one**. Union of states having a common tariff of duties on imports from other countries, and free trade among themselves.

zonal, adj. [1. zŏnal; 2. zóunəl]. **zone** & **-al**. Of, pertaining to, arranged or marked out in, zones.

zonally, adv. Prec. & **-ly**. In a zonal manner.

zonary, adj. [1. zŏnari; 2. zóunəri]. **zone** & **-ary**. Resembling a belt in form or appearance.

zonate, adj. [1. zŏnāt; 2. zóuneit]. **zone** & **-ate**. (bot., zool.) Marked with bands.

zone (I.), n. [1. zōn; 2. zoun], fr. Fr., fr. Lat. *zōna*, fr. Gk. *zṓnē*, 'belt, girdle'; cp. Gk. *zṓnnūmi*, 'I gird'; Zend *yāsta-*, 'girded'; Lith. *jùsta*, 'belt'; O. Slav. (*po-*)*jasŭ*, 'girdle'. **1.** (archaic or poet.) Girdle, belt : '*that milky way, Which nightly, as a circling zone, thou seest Powdered with stars*' (Milton, P.L., vii. 579-81). **2.** Belt, band, stripe, area, distinguished from surface &c. on either side by appearance, colour, characteristics, formation &c. **3.** (geog.) One of the five regions into which the surface of the earth is divided by imaginary lines parallel to the equator ; *frigid zones*, within Arctic and Antarctic circles ; *torrid zone*, between tropics of Cancer and Capricorn ; *temperate zones*, between torrid and frigid zones. **4.** (math.) Portion of surface of sphere, cone, cylinder, &c. enclosed between two parallel planes at right angles to its axis.

zone (II.), vb. trans., fr. prec. To mark, encircle, with a zone.

zonular, adj. [1. zŏnūlar; 2. zóunjulə]. **zone** & **-ule** & **-ar**. Of, pertaining to, in the shape of, a small belt or band.

Zoo, n. [1. zōō; 2. zū]. Abbr. fr. **zoological**. Zoological garden, esp. the Zoological Gardens in London.

zoo-, pref. representing Gk. *zōós*, 'living'; *zôon*, 'animal'; cp. Gk. *záō*, *zēn*, 'to live'; earlier **gʷjōjō-* &c. ; cp. Gk. *bios*, 'life', fr. stem **gʷej-* &c., 'to live', see **bio-** & words there referred to. Of animals or animal life.

zooblast, n. [1. zŏoblahst; 2. zóuəblāst]. **zoo-** & Gk. *blastós*, 'sprout', see **blastoderm**. Animal cell.

zoochemistry, n. [1. zŏokémistri; 2. zòuəkémistri]. Chemistry of solid and fluid constituents of animal body.

zoodynamics, n. [1. zŏodīnámiks; 2. zòuədainǽmiks]. Animal physiology.

zoogamy, n. [1. zōógami; 2. zouógəmi]. **zoo-** & **-gamy**. Sexual reproduction.

zoogeny, n. [1. zōójeni; 2. zouódžini]. **zoo-** & **-geny**. Doctrine of the origin of living beings.

zoogeography, n. [1. zŏojiógrafi; 2. zóuədžiógrəfi]. Science of geographical distribution of animals.

zoography, n. [1. zōógrafi; 2. zouógrəfi]. **zoo-** & **-graphy**. Descriptive zoology.

zooid (I.), adj. [1. zŏoid; 2. zóuɔid]. **zoo-** & **-oid**. Resembling, but not completely being, an animal organism.

zooid (II.), n., fr. prec. **1.** An organic body or cell possessing independent locomotion. **2.** An animal organism produced by fission, or some similar process, and not by direct sexual reproduction, and having an imperfect individuality.

zoolatrous, adj. [1. zōólatrus; 2. zouólətrəs]. See next word & **-ous**. Pertaining to, characterized by, zoolatry.

zoolatry, n. [1. zōólatri; 2. zouólətri]. **zoo-** & **-latry**. Worship of animals.

zoolite, n. [1. zŏolīt; 2. zóuəlait]. **zoo-** & **-lite**. Fossil animal.

zoological, adj. [1. zŏolójikl; 2. zòuəlódžikl]. **zoo-** & **-logy** & **-ic** & **-al**. **a** Connected with, pertaining to, zoology; **b** connected with animal life and structure.

zoological garden(s), n. Large garden or park in which wild animals of all kinds are kept for exhibition.

zoology, n. [1. zŏóloji; 2. zòuə́lədži]. **zoo-** & **-logy**. Branch of biology dealing with the structure, physiology, classification of animals.

zoom, vb. intrans. [1. zōōm; 2. zūm]. Etymol. doubtful. (aeron.) To compel an aeroplane to ascend rapidly and at a steep angle.

zoomagnetism, n. [1. zŏomágnetizm; 2. zòuəmǽgnitìzəm]. Animal magnetism.

zoomancy, n. [1. zŏomànsi; 2. zóuəmænsi]. **zoo-** & **-mancy**. Divination by observing the behaviour of animals.

zoomorphic, adj. [1. zŏomórfik; 2. zòuəmɔ́fik]. **zoo-** & Gk. *morphḗ*, 'form, shape', see **morphology**, & **-ic**. Pertaining to, represented by, animal forms; having the forms of animals.

zoomorphism, n. [1. zŏomórfizm; 2. zòuəmɔ́fizəm]. See prec. & **-ism**. The conception and representation of gods in the form of animals.

zoophysics, n. [1. zŏofíziks; 2. zóuəfíziks]. Science of the physical structure of animal bodies.

zoophyte, n. [1. zŏofīt; 2. zóuəfàit]. **zoo-** & **-phyte**. Invertebrate animal of plant-like form, including sea-anemones, sponges &c.

zoophytic, adj. [1. zŏofítik; 2. zóuəfítik]. Prec. & **-ic**. Pertaining to, of the nature of, zoophytes.

zoophytology, n. [1. zŏofītóloji; 2. zòuəfaitólədži]. See prec. & **-logy**. The study of zoophytes.

zooplastic, adj. [1. zŏoplástik; 2. zòuəplǽstik]. Pertaining to that form of surgery in which living tissue from an animal is grafted on to a human body.

zoopsychology, n. [1. zŏosīkóloji; 2. zòuɔsaikólədži]. Psychology of animals other than man.

zoosperm, n. [1. zŏospĕrm; 2. zóuəspə̀m]. **1.** Spermatozoon. **2.** Zoospore.

zoospore, n. [1. zŏospŏr; 2. zóuəspɔ̀]. Spore capable of independent motion.

zootaxy, n. [1. zŏotàksi; 2. zóuətæ̀ksi], fr. **zoo-** & Gk. *táxis*, 'arrangement', see **taxis**, & **-y**. The classification of animals.

zootheism, n. [1. zŏothĕizm; 2. zóuəþìizəm]. Religious system based on the worship of animals.

zootomy, n. [1. zŏótomi; 2. zòuótəmi]. **zoo-** & **-tomy**. **1.** Dissection of animals. **2.** Animal anatomy.

zoril, n. [1. zóril; 2. zóril], fr. Fr. *zorille*, fr. Span. *zorrilla*, dimin. of *zorra*, 'fox'. Small African carnivorous quadruped resembling skunk.

Zoroastrian, Zarathustrian, adj. & n. [1. zòroástrian, zàrathōōstrian; 2. zòrɔǽstriən, zæ̀rəpū́striən], fr. Lat. *Zōroastres*, 'Zarathustra', fr. O. Pers. *Zarathustra*, founder of Pers. religion. **1.** adj. Pertaining to Zoroaster and his religion. **2.** n. An adherent, worshipper, of Zoroaster.

Zoroastrianism, n. [1. zòroástrianizm; 2. zòrɔǽstriənizəm]. Prec. & **-ism**. Religious system of ancient Persia and of the Parsees, based on the recognition of the dual principle of good and evil or light and darkness.

zouave, n. [1. zŏōahv; 2. zŭǎv]. Fr., fr. name of Kabyle tribe. Member of French, light-armed corps of infantry, originally recruited from Algerians and wearing Eastern uniform.

zounds, interj. [1. zoundz; 2. zaundz]. Contracted fr. *God's wounds*. Archaic exclamatory expression.

zucchetta, zucchetto, n. [1. tsukéta, -étŏ; 2. tsukétə, -étou]. Ital., dimin. of *zucca*, 'gourd'. Skull-cap worn by ecclesiastics.

zuffolo, n. [1. tsúfolŏ; 2. tsúfolou]. Ital. *zufolo*, 'whistle'. A small flageolet.

Zulu, n. [1. zŏōlōō; 2. zúlū]. Native. **1.** Member of a people of the Bantu or Kaffir family of S. Africa. **2.** Language of this people.

zwieback, n., Anglicized to [1. zwébahk; 2. zwíbāk]. Germ. *zwie*, 'twice', & *backen*, 'bake'. Cp. etymol. of **biscuit**. Kind of thin rusk; consisting of a slice cut from a lightly baked loaf, baked again till crisp.

Zwinglian, adj. & n. [1. zwíngglian; 2. zwíŋgliən], fr. name of Zwingli, Swiss Protestant reformer, d. 1531, & **-an**. **1.** adj. Pertaining to the doctrines of Zwingli. **2.** n. Follower of Zwingli, one of whose characteristic doctrines was that in the Eucharist the presence of Christ in the elements is not an objective fact, but depends upon the faith of the recipient, and that the service is merely commemorative and has no sacrificial character.

zyg(o)-, pref. representing Gk. *zugón*, 'yoke', cogn. w. Scrt. *yugám*; Lat. *jugum*, see **jugate**; Goth. *juk*; O.E. *ģeoc*, 'yoke', see **yoke**; cp. also Gk. *zeûgos*, 'harness'; *zeûgma*, 'bond, yoke', see **zeugma**. Existing in pairs; shaped like a yoke.

zygal, adj. [1. zígal; 2. záigəl]. **zyg(o)-** & **-al**. Having the shape of a yoke; H-shaped; esp. of brain fissures.

zygapophysis, n. [1. zìgapófizis; 2. zàigəpófizis]. **zyg(o)-** & Gk. *apóphusis*, 'offshoot; process of a bone', see **apo-** & **physic**. Articulating portion of vertebra.

zygodactyl, n. [1. zìgodáktil; 2. zàigɔdǽktil]. See **zyg(o)-** & **dactyl**. Bird with toes arranged in pairs, two pointing forward and two backward.

zygodactylous, adj. [1. zìgodáktilus; 2. zàigɔdǽktiləs]. Prec. & **-ous**. Of the nature of a zygodactyl.

zygoma, n. [1. zī-, zìgŏma; 2. zài-, zìgóumə], fr. Gk. *zúgōma*, 'yoke', fr. *zugóein*, 'to yoke together', fr. *zugón*, 'yoke', see **zyg(o)-**, & **-m**. The cheek-bone.

zygomatic, adj. [1. zī-, zìgomátik; 2. zài-, zìgɔmǽtik], fr. Gk. *zugṓmatos*, genit. of *zúgōma*, see prec., & **-ic**. Pertaining to, situated near, the zygoma; *zygomatic arch*, bony ridge

zygophyte, n. [1. zígofĭt; 2. záigəfàit]. zyg(o)- & -phyte. Plant in which reproduction is effected by means of zygospores.

zygosis, n. [1. zĭ-, zigōsis; 2. zài-, zigóusis], fr. Gk. *zugôsis*, 'joining', see **zyg(o)-** & **-osis**. (biol.) Coalescence of two cells; conjugation.

zygospore, n. [1. zígospōr; 2. záigəspō]. zyg(o)- & spore. Zygote.

zygote, n. [1. zígōt; 2. záigout], fr. Gk. *zugōtos*, 'yoked', fr. *zugóein*, 'to yoke together', see **zygoma**. Product of coalescence of two sexual cells or gametes; a zygospore.

zymosis, n. [1. zĭ-, zìmōsis; 2. zài-, zìmóusis], fr. Gk. *zúmōsis*, 'fermentation', fr. *zūmoûn*, 'to ferment', fr. *zūmē*, 'leaven', fr. *zéein*, 'to boil'; cp. Gk. *zóē*, 'foam'; cogn. w. Scrt. *yásati*, 'to boil'; O.H.G. *iesan*, 'to ferment'; O.E. *gest*, 'yeast', see **yeast**, & **eczema**, & cp. **enzyme**. 1. Fermentation. 2. Zymotic disease.

zymotic, adj. [1. zĭ-, zìmótik; 2. zài-, zìmótik], fr. Gk. *zúmōsis*, 'fermentation', see prec., & **-otic**. Pertaining to, produced by, fermentation; *zymotic diseases*, epidemic, endemic or sporadic diseases produced by propagation of living germs introduced from without.

zymurgy, n. [1. zímĕrji; 2. záimʌdži], fr. Gk. *zūmē*, 'leaven', see **zymosis**, & *-ourg-(os)*, fr. *érg-(on)*, 'work', see **ergon**. Branch of applied chemistry dealing with the science of wine-making, brewing, and distilling.

Addenda and Corrigenda

HERE are printed corrections of a few errors in the text which came to the Editor's notice while the Dictionary was passing through the press, together with definitions of certain words inadvertently omitted from their alphabetical positions in the body of the work.

P. 5. **abstention**, n. [1. absténshun; 2. əbsténʃən]. Fr., fr. Lat. *abstention-(em)*, fr. *abstent-(um)*, P.P. type of *abstinere*, see **abstain**. The act of abstaining from any action; specif. **a** act of abstaining from any form of enjoyment, e.g. from food &c.; abstinence; **b** refusal to record one's vote.

P. 5. **abstraction**, n. [1. abstrákshun; 2. əbstrǽkʃən]. Fr., fr. Lat.; see **abstract** (I.) & **-ion**. 1. **a** (i.) Act of abstracting; (ii.) condition of being abstracted; withdrawal, removal; **b** (euphemistic) unlawful removal; theft, stealing. 2. **a** Mental act of regarding things from an abstract point of view; **b** something so considered. 3. Preoccupied state of mind; absent-mindedness, abstractedness.

P. 15. **adscititious**, adj. [1. àdsitíshus; 2. ædsitíʃəs], fr. Lat. *adscit-(um)*, P.P. type of *adsciscere*, 'to approve, adopt; to receive, admit (person)'; inceptive fr. *adscire*, 'to take, associate with oneself', fr. ad- & *scire*, 'to know', see **science**, & **-itious**. Additional, supplemental; adventitious.

P. 34. **anaglyph**. After 'cameo', add 'Picture obtained by printing a pair of prints one above the other in red and green inks, producing a stereoscopic effect when viewed through spectacles having one green and one red lens'.

P. 77. **bank** (IV.), vb. 2. After *Barclay's*, add '3. Bank on, to depend with confidence upon, rely, count on, make arrangements on the assumption that this or that will happen, or be done: *I'm banking on the fine weather lasting till I get my hay in*; *I shouldn't bank on his sticking to his promise if I were you*'.

P. 84. **bat** (IV.), vb., cp. Fr. *battre*, 'to beat' &c. Only in Phr. *he didn't bat an eyelid, eyelash*, didn't blink, never turned a hair.

P. 85. **batty**, adj. [bǽti], fr. **bat** (III.) & **-y**. **a** Infested by bats; **b** (slang) having strange ideas; cracked, dotty (cp. *bats in the belfry*, under **belfry, b**).

P. 90. **Bedfordshire**, n. [bédfədʃə], fr. name of county with punning ref. to *bed*. (colloq. and facetious) Bed; in Phr. *to go to Bedfordshire*.

P. 94. **belfry, b**. After words 'where bells hang', add 'Phr. (slang) *to have bats in the belfry*, to have strange notions, be queer in the head, to be cracked &c'.

P. 108. **blimy**, interjec. [bldími] for (*God*) *blind me*, see **gorblimy**. (vulg.) Mild expletive expressing surprise or annoyance.

P. 108. **blind** (III.). After *Asylum*, at end of entry, add '4. (slang, cp. **blind** (I.) 3). **a** A rollicking, noisy party, esp. one at which a large amount of liquor is consumed; **b** (by extension) a merry social gathering generally, without implication of excessive drinking; a jolly party, a beano'.

P. 108. **blind** (IV.), vb. intrans., fr. **blind** (I.) (slang) generally *blind along*. To run, ride or drive along recklessly, and heedlessly, at excessive speed.

P. 110. **blow-out**, n. [bloùdut]. (colloq.) A copious or elaborate meal; a feast, a hearty feed. Used already by Scott, 'St. Ronan's Well', Ch. 33, at end.

P. 115. Under **book** (I.) **1. a** after words 'or paper &c', add 'or in paper alone'.

P. 143. **calabar bean**. For 'by oculists for dilating', read 'for contracting the pupil of'.

P. 154. **carline** (III.), n., also *carling* [1. kárlin; 2. kɑ́lin]. Etymol. doubtful; cp. Fr. *carlingue*. A wooden beam, generally fitted at right angles to and below the main deck timbers of a wooden ship, to strengthen the deck in way of openings.

P. 161. **cathode**. For 'Negative electrode ... current leaves', read 'Negative pole of a cell, Crookes tube, or other current-passing apparatus'.

P. 200. **cock-and-bull story**, n. [kɔ̀kənbúl stɔ̀ri]. A fantastic, inaccurate account of what has happened; a rambling, inconsequent, confused tale, containing untrue and unconvincing statements.

P. 266. **cup-o'-tea**, n. [kàpətí]. (facet. and rather vulgar) To and of a person; in such Phrs. as *you're a nice cup-o'-tea, a funny old cup-o'-tea* &c.

P. 280. **debag**, vb. trans. [dībǽg], fr. de- & see **bag** (I. 1. b). To remove (person's) trousers and inflict corporal punishment.

P. 297. **derrick**. For 'early 18th', read '17th or even (?) late 16th'.

P. 301. **devastating**, adj., fr. Pres. Part. of prec. [1. dévəstāting; 2. dévəstèitiŋ]. 1. Causing devastation. 2. (colloq. expressing dislike, disgust, disapproval &c.), very bad, insufferable: *a devastating bore*.

P. 306. **diehard**, n. [dáihād]. Person of brave and resolute character who fights to the death for a cause or a principle; specif. 1. *the Die-hards*, name given to Middlesex Regiment after battle of Albuera. 2. Member of the extreme Right of the Conservative party which adheres consistently to Tory principles, and refuses to compromise on these.

P. 311. **dippy**, adj. [dípi]. (slang) Queer in the head; cracked, dotty, barmy.

P. 323. **dither**, vb. intrans. [díðə] Provinc. origin. **a** To talk in an excited, rapid, inconsequent manner; to talk nonsense; **b** to be temporarily in an excited, unbalanced state of mind.

P. 324. **dives**, n. [dáivīz], fr. Lat. *dives*, 'rich, splendid'; name popularly given to the former in the parable of the rich man and the beggar Lazarus in Lk. xvi. A callous, selfish rich man, who lives in great luxury while showing indifference to the sufferings of the poor.

P. 328. **dolichocephalic**. Indication of pronunciation—Add after 1., dòlikoséfalik—and after 2. dòlikouséfalik.

P. 329. Under **dope** (I.). At end, after 'conscience', add '**c** *the dope*, the facts of the case; *give me the dope*, tell me the full facts, put me *au courant*'.

dope (II.). At end, after 'hoodwink', add '**c** *dope (it) out*, puzzle out, find explanation of'.

P. 340. **drunk** (II.), n. 2. read 'a drinking party; a social gathering; **b** by extension, a meeting for any purpose: *a political drunk, a bible drunk*; *pi drunk*, prayer-meeting'.

P. 345. After **Dutch**, add—(I.).

P. 345. 2. **a**—after *the Dutch*, add 'Phr. *that beats the Dutch*, beats everything'.

P. 345. **Dutch** (II.), n., abbrev. of *duchess*, in Phr. *my, his, old dutch*, wife, missis. Fr. name of Albert Chevalier's song.

P. 345. **Dutch comfort**, n. Strong drink, grog.

P. 345. **Dutch uncle**, n. A stern, strict guardian, or mentor; *he talked to me like a Dutch uncle*.

P. 345. **Dutchman**. After 'Phr.' and before '*Flying Dutchman*', insert—*(if that isn't so) I'm a Dutchman*, emphasizing a statement.

P. 348. **east-north-east**, n., adj., & adv. (In or towards) direction or point midway between east and north-east.

P. 348. **east-south-east**, n., adj., & adv. (In or towards) direction or point midway between east and south-east.

P. 350. **economist**, n. [1. ĕkónomist; 2. ĭkónəmist]. See **economy** & **-ist**. 1. (rare) One who manages domestic or other affairs. 2. One given to economizing; a thrifty person. 3. A student of, authority on, the science of political economy.

P. 362. **emulsion**. For 'An oily liquid ... consistency', read 'A mixture of two liquids, one in the form of minute globules produced by a third substance, often in the form of a white liquid'. For 'curative purposes', read 'for preventive and curative purposes'.

P. 380. **etymology**. After -logy, line 4 of entry, insert—1. (older use) Milton says 'Etymologie, or right-wording, teacheth what belongs to every single word or part of speech'.

Re-number sections so that the present **1**. becomes **2**, and present **2—3**.

FIGWORT

P. 418. **figwort**, n. Any one of a large and widely spread genus of herbs, natural order Scrophulariaceae, with greenish-purple or yellow flowers, and usually an unpleasant smell.

P. 455. **Free Church.** For 'part of the Presbyterian Church ... 1929)', read 'Part of the Presbyterian Church, the minority of the former Free Church which failed to enter the Union with the United Presbyterian Church in 1900'.

P. 464. **funny-bone.** Delete 'sensitive'. Add 'The sensitiveness of this part of the arm is due to the ulnar nerve which passes between the end of the bone of the upper arm (humerus) and that of the larger bone (ulna) of the forearm. The name *funny-bone* is a popular joke based on the anatomical term *humerus* (q.v.).'

P. 467. **gaga**, adj. [gága]. Imitative of stammering. (slang) a Reduced to state of gibbering bewilderment and incapacity, as by fright, nervous shock &c.; b affected by permanent weakening of the mind; cracked, dotty; Phr. *to go gaga*.

P. 474. Under **gay.** After **1. a** insert '(i.)'. After words '*laugh* &c.' in this section insert '(*in spite of ill health he is always gay*); Phr. *the gayest of the gay*; (ii.) (of persons and their social life) enjoying, filled with, frequent social gatherings, engagements and amusements: *we were very gay in town this season*'.

P. 483. Under **girl** indication of pronunciation should read—[1. garl, gə̄əl] (this is now rather old-fashioned; the more usual pronunciation, even among good speakers, is now— [1. gërl; 2. gāl]). After **3. a** add 'Phr. *one's best girl*, she who for the moment is the object of special admiration and devotion'.

P. 494. **goof**, n. [gūf] origin unknown. A silly fellow; a clumsy, awkward, oafish person.

P. 494. **gorblimy**, interjec. & n. [góblai*mi*], fr. *Gaud* (=God) *blind me*. **a** interjec. Low expletive of surprise or annoyance; **b** n. military hat with the round flat crown unstiffened by a wire frame, so that it flops rather like that of a tam-o'-shanter.

P. 528. **hare**, vb. intrans. (slang) To run like a hare, run very fast, hurry: *you had better hare down to the post*; also *hare away*, to run away, esp. to fly in order to escape pursuit.

P. 531. **hat** (I.). Last line but one, just before '*my hat!*' insert '*to keep something under one's hat*, keep it to oneself, not divulge it; *a good deal under his hat*, a powerful mind, learning &c.; *lame under the hat*, of weak mind; foolish, lacking intelligence'.

P. 536. **hearing**, n. Add '3. Something heard, news; esp. in Phr. *that's a good hearing*, something that it is pleasing to hear.'

P. 564. **hot** (III.) vb. trans. & n., fr. **hot** (I.). (colloq.) **1.** vb. **a** Also *hot up*, to warm up food already cooked which has become cold; **b** (fig.) to revive, put new life into, stimulate (a cause, business, enterprise &c.) which is declining. **2.** n. A stimulus, re-animation, re-vivification.

P. 573. After **hydro**, n., insert—[1. hídrō; 2. hái*drou*].

P. 631. **jim-jams**, n. pl. [džímdžæmz] (slang) *The jim-jams*, a delirium tremens; **b** a highly nervous, over-wrought state of mind; jumpiness, fussy excitability; the willies.

P. 660. **lewdsby**, n. [ljúdzb*i*], facet. formation fr. lewd w. *by*, Pl. N. ending. A lewd, loose, immoral person.

P. 686. **loony bin**, n. (slang) Lunatic asylum, madhouse.

P. 686. **loopy**, adj. [lúp*i*]. (slang) Weak in the intellect, slightly mad; dippy, batty.

P. 687. **Lord-Lieutenant.** For 'Governor-General of the Free State of N. Ireland' read 'Governor of Northern Ireland'.

P. 799. Under **omnibus. 2.**—after words 'number of persons', add '; *omnibus volume*, one containing several complete novels, or short stories by the same author, or by several authors'.

P. 800. After **oneyer**—add (I.).

P. 800. **oneyer** (II.), n. See **wonyer**.

WOBBLER

P. 861. **pi** (II.). For '(school slang)' read '(school and Univ. slang).' Definition should read—a Pious; religious; **b** connected w., expressing, setting forth, religious or moral ideas and principles.

P. 864. **pi-jaw**, n. [1. pī́jaw; 2. pái*dž*5]. See **pi** (II.) & **jaw** (I.) 5. **b**. (school slang) Religious or moral address; a sermon.

P. 1017. **ride** (II.). After **1. b** ... *carriage*, add '; Phr. (Amer. gangster slang) *to take* (person) *for a ride*, take him out into the country in a motor car and murder him'.

P. 1126. Under **sixpence**, in **b** Phrs. after words 'of no consequence' add '; *the same old sixpence*, of person, implying that he is unchanged either for better or for worse'.

P. 1185. Under **step** (II.), in A. 2. after word 'intervene', insert '; *step on the gas, step on it*, to accelerate in a motor car; hence to drive at high speed; to hurry'.

P. 1232. For '**tab**' read '**tab** (I.)'.

P. 1232. **tab** (II.), n. abbrev. of **Cantab**, q.v. Same sense as Cantab, but not a polite mode of reference.

P. 1387. **wench**, at end, after 'Prostitute', add '**3.** vb. To frequent company of prostitutes'.

P. 1387. **wenching**, vbl. n., fr. prec. (archaic) Practice of sexual intercourse outside wedlock.

P. 1396. **willies**, n. pl. [w*í*liz] adapted fr. *bewilder*? (slang) *the willies*. State of nervous excitement caused by fear or shock; temporary mental incapacity, jumpiness, and so on: *a fit of the willies, it gave me the willies*.

P. 1399. **w(e)isenheim**, n. Facet. use of Germ.-Jewish name. (American slang) A knowing, sharp-witted person; applied ironically to one who prides himself on possessing the latest information, and an infallible judgement, and on being cleverer than other people.

P. 1401. **wobbler**, n., fr. **wobble** (I.) & -er. One who wobbles; specif. one who is unstable and vacillating in opinions, principles &c.

Familiar Abbreviations

In these pages we give a reasonably full list of the abbreviations commonly used in speech and in writing. We have included also a number which, though no longer current, are still to be met with in standard works of reference.

A, argon (chem.).
a., aged (of racehorse over six years old).
A1, at Lloyd's, first-class ship on the register; also first-class in physique, health &c.
A.A., Automobile Association; Associate in Arts.
A.A.A., Amateur Athletic Association.
A.A.C., Lat. *anno ante Christum*, in the year before Christ.
A.A.G., Assistant Adjutant-General.
A.A.I., Associate of the Auctioneers' Institute.
A. and M., Ancient and Modern (hymn-book).
A.A. of A., Automobile Association of America.
A.A.Q.M.G., Acting Assistant Quartermaster-General.
A.A.U., Amateur Athletic Union (of U.S.A.).
A.B., able-bodied seaman; Lat. *Artium Baccalaureus*, Bachelor of Arts, usually B.A.
A.B.A., Amateur Boxing Association.
abbr., **abbrev.**, abbreviation, abbreviated.
ABC, the alphabet; alphabetical railway guide.
A.B.C., Aerated Bread Co.
abd., abdicated.
ab init., Lat. *ab initio*, from the beginning.
abl., ablative.
abp., archbishop.
A.B.S., American Bible Society.
abs., absolute; abstract.
absol., absolute(ly).
abt., about.
A.C., Appeal Court; Appeal Cases in this court (in law reports); Alpine Club; Aero Club; Athletic Club; Lat. *anno Christi*, in the year of Christ, A.D.; Lat. *ante Christum*, before Christ, B.C.
a/c, account.
A.C.A., Associate of the Institute of Chartered Accountants.
acc., account; accusative.
accel., accelerando (mus.).
acct., account; accountant.
accus., accusative.
A.C.G.I., Associate of the City & Guilds of London Institute.
A.C.I.S., Associate of the Chartered Institute of Secretaries.
A.C.P., Associate of the College of Preceptors.
A.C.S., Additional Curates Society.
A.C.U., Auto-cycle Union.
A.D., Lat. *anno Domini*, in the year of our Lord.
a.d., after date.
ad., adapted; advertisement.
adag., adagio (mus.).
A.D.C., Aide-de-camp; Amateur Dramatic Club (esp. of Cambridge University).
ad eund., Lat. *ad eundem (gradum)*, admitted to the same degree (at another university).
ad fin., Lat. *ad finem*, at, to, the end.
ad inf., Lat. *ad infinitum*, to infinity.
ad int., Lat. *ad interim*, meanwhile.
Adj., Adjutant.
adj., adjective.
Adjt., Adjutant.
ad lib., Lat. *ad libitum*, at pleasure.
ad loc., Lat. *ad locum*, at the place.
Adm., Admiral, Admiralty; Administrator.
Adml., Admiral.
admor., administrator.
A.D.O.S., Assistant Director of Ordnance Stores.
Adv., Advent; Advocate.
adv., adverb.
adv., Lat. *adversus*, against.
ad val., Lat. *ad valorem*, according to the value.
advbl., adverbial.
advt., advertisement.

Æ, third-class ship at Lloyd's.
aeg., Lat. *aeger*, ill.
aegrot., Lat. *aegrotat*, he is ill, in Engl. univs., certificate that student is too ill to take examination.
A.E.L.T.C., All England Lawn Tennis Club.
aeron., aeronautics.
aet., *aetat.*, Lat. *aetatis*, aged (so many years).
A.E.U., Amalgamated Engineering Union.
A.F., Admiral of the Fleet.
A.F.A., Amateur Football Association.
A.F.B.S., American & Foreign Bible Society.
A.F.C., Air Force Cross.
A.F.M., Air Force Medal.
A.-Fr., Anglo-French (Anglo-Norman).
Afr., African.
A.F.R.Ae.S., Associate Fellow of the Royal Aeronautical Society.
A.G., Adjutant-General; Attorney-General; Accountant-General; Agent-General; German, *Aktiengesellschaft*, joint-stock company.
Ag, Lat. *argentum*, silver (chem.).
agric., agriculture.
A.G.S.M., Associate of the Guildhall School of Music.
Agt., Agent.
Agt.-Gen., Agent-General.
A.H., Lat. *anno Hegirae*, in the year of the Hegira.
A.H.S., Lat. *anno humanae salutis*, in the year of human salvation.
A.I., American Institute.
A.I.A., Associate of the Institute of Actuaries.
A.I.C., Associate of the Institute of Chemistry.
A.I.C.E., Associate of the Institution of Civil Engineers.
A.I.D., Army Intelligence Department.
A.I.F., Australian Imperial Force.
A.I.Mech.E., Associate of the Institution of Mechanical Engineers.
A.I.S.A., Associate of the Incorporated Secretaries' Association.
A.K.C., Associate of King's College, London.
Al, aluminium (chem.).
Ala., Alabama (U.S.A.).
Alas., Alaska.
Alban., St. Albans, in signature of Bishop.
A.L.C.M., Associate of the London College of Music.
Ald., Alderman; Aldine.
Alex., Alexander.
alg., algebra.
A.L.S., Associate of the Linnean Society.
alt., alternate; altitude.
Alta., Alberta, Canada.
A.M., Lat. *Artium Magister*, Master of Arts, usually M.A.; Albert Medal; Lat. *anno mundi*, in the year of the world.
a.m., Lat. *ante meridiem*, before noon.
Am., American.
A.M.C., Army Medical Corps (since 1898, R.A.M.C.).
A.M.D.G., Lat. *ad majorem Dei gloriam*, to the greater glory of God.
A.M.I.C.E., Associate Member of the Institution of Civil Engineers.
A.M.I.E.E., Associate Member of the Institution of Electrical Engineers.
A.M.I.Mech.E., Associate Member of the Institution of Mechanical Engineers.
amp., ampère.
A.M.S., Army Medical Staff.
amt., amount.
anal., analogy; analysis.
anat., anatomy.

anct., ancient.
Angl., Lat. *Anglice*, in English.
Angl., Anglican.
anon., anonymous.
anr., another.
anthropol., anthropology.
antiq., antiquity.
A.N.Z.A.C. (Anzac), Australian and New Zealand Army Corps, in Great War.
A.O., Army Order.
a/o, account of.
A.O.C., Army Ordnance Corps (since 1918, R.A.O.C.).
A.O.D., Ancient Order of Druids; Army Ordnance Department.
A.O.F., Ancient Order of Foresters.
A.O.H., Ancient Order of Hibernians.
aor., aorist.
ap., Lat. *apud*, according to, in the works of, in literary references.
A.P.D., Army Pay Department.
Apl., April.
A.P.M., Assistant Provost-Marshal.
Apoc., Apocalypse; Apocrypha.
app., appendix; appointed; apprentice.
appro., approval, approbation.
approx., approximate(ly).
Apr., April.
A.P.S., Aborigines Protection Society.
A.Q.M.G., Assistant Quartermaster-General.
A.R., Lat. *anno regni*, in the year of the reign; annual return.
A.R.A., Associate of the Royal Academy.
Arab., Arabic.
A.R.A.M., Associate of the Royal Academy of Music.
A.R.B.A., Associate of the Royal Society of British Artists.
arbor., arboriculture.
A.R.C., Automobile Racing Club.
A.R.C.A., Associate of the Royal College of Art; Associate of the Royal Cambrian Academy.
archaeol., archaeology.
archit., architecture.
A.R.C.I., Associate of the Royal Colonial Institute.
A.R.C.M., Associate of the Royal College of Music.
A.R.C.O., Associate of the Royal College of Organists.
A.R.C.S., Associate of the Royal College of Science.
A.R.E., Associate of the Royal Society of Painter-Etchers and Engravers.
Argyl., Argyllshire.
A.R.H.A., Associate of the Royal Hibernian Academy.
A.R.I.B.A., Associate of the Royal Institute of British Architects.
arith., arithmetic.
Ariz., Arizona (U.S.A.).
Ark., Arkansas (U.S.A.).
A.R.M.S., Associate of the Royal Society of Miniature Painters.
A.R.P.S., Associate of the Royal Photographic Society.
A.R.R., Lat. *anno regni regis (reginae)*, in the year of the king's (queen's) reign.
arr., arrives (of train &c.).
A.R.S.A., Associate of the Royal Scottish Academy; Associate of the Royal Society of Arts.
A.R.S.L., Associate of the Royal Society of Literature.
A.R.S.M., Associate of the Royal School of Mines (now Royal College of Science).

A.R.S.W., Associate of the Royal Scottish Society of Painters in Water Colours.
art., article.
A.R.W.A., Associate of the Royal West of England Academy.
A.R.W.S., Associate of the Royal Society of Painters in Water Colours.
A.-S., Anglo-Saxon.
As, arsenic (chem.).
A.S.A., Amateur Swimming Association.
A.S.A.A., Associate of the Society of Incorporated Accountants and Auditors.
Asaph., St. Asaph, in signature of Bishop.
A.S.C., Army Service Corps (since 1918, R.A.S.C.
A.Sc., Associate in Science.
A.S.E., Amalgamated Society of Engineers.
A.S.L.E. & F., Associated Society of Locomotive Engineers and Firemen.
A.S.R.S., Amalgamated Society of Railway Servants.
Assn., association.
Assoc., associate, association.
Asst., assistant.
astrol., astrology.
astron., astronomy.
A.T.C.L., Associate of Trinity College (of Music), London.
At(t).-Gen., Attorney-General.
attrib., attributive(ly).
at. wt., atomic weight.
A.U., Ångström unit (physics).
Au, Lat. *aurum*, gold (chem.).
A.U.C., Lat. *anno urbis conditae* or *ab urbe condita*, in the year of, or from the foundation of the city (Rome).
Aug., August.
Aus., Austria; Austrian.
auxil., auxiliary.
A.V., Authorized Version.
av., average.
avdp., avoirdupois.

B, boron (chem.); black (of pencil-lead).
B., Bay.
b., born; (cricket) bowled, bye.
B.A., Lat. *Baccalaureus Artium*, Bachelor of Arts; British Academy; British Association.
Ba, barium (chem.).
bacter., bacteriology.
B. Agr(ic)., Bachelor of Agriculture.
Balto-Slav., Balto-Slavic.
B. & S., brandy and soda.
B. & W., Bath and Wells, in signature of Bishop.
Bart., Baronet.
Bart's, St. Bartholomew's Hospital.
Bath. & Well., Bath and Wells, in signature of Bishop.
Batt., Battery; Battalion.
Battn., Battalion.
BB, double black (of pencil-lead).
B.B., Blue Book.
BBB, treble black (of pencil-lead).
B.B.C., British Broadcasting Corporation.
B.C., Before Christ; British Columbia.
B.Ch., Lat. *Baccalaureus Chirurgiae*, Bachelor of Surgery.
B.Ch.D., Bachelor of Dental Surgery.
B.C.L., Bachelor of Civil Law.
B.Com., Bachelor of Commerce.
B.C.S., Bengal Civil Service.
B.D., Bachelor of Divinity.
Bde., Brigade.
Bde. Maj., Brigade Major.
B.D.S., Bachelor of Dental Surgery.
B.E., Bachelor of Engineering; (Order of the) British Empire; Board of Education.
b.e., bill of exchange.
Be, beryllium (chem.).
B.E.A., British East Africa.
Beds, Bedfordshire.
B.E.F., British Expeditionary Force, in Great War.
Belg., Belgium; Belgian.
B.Eng., Bachelor of Engineering.
Berks, Berkshire.
B.E.S.A., British Engineering Standards Association.

B. ès L., Fr. *Bachelier ès Lettres*, Bachelor of Letters.
B. ès S., Fr. *Bachelier ès Sciences*, Bachelor of Science.
B.F.B.S., British and Foreign Bible Society.
B.G.G.S., Brigadier-General, General Staff.
B'ham, Birmingham.
B'head, Birkenhead.
b.h.p., brake horse-power.
B.I., British India.
Bi, bismuth (chem.).
Bib., Biblical.
bibliog., bibliography; bibliographical.
biog., biography; biographical.
biol., biology; biological.
bk., book, bank.
bkg., banking.
bkrpt., bankrupt.
bkt., basket.
B.L., Bachelor of Law; black letter; breech-loading.
b.l., bill of lading.
bl., barrel; bale.
B.Litt., Bachelor of Letters (Literature).
B.LL., Bachelor of Laws, more commonly LL.B.
B.M., Bachelor of Medicine, more commonly M.B.; Lat. *Beata Maria*, Blessed Mary, the Virgin, more commonly B.V.M.; Lat. *beatae memoriae*, of blessed memory; Brigade Major; British Museum.
B.M.A., British Medical Association.
B.M.E., Bachelor of Mining Engineering.
B.M.J., British Medical Journal.
B.Mus., Bachelor of Music, more commonly Mus. Bac.; British Museum.
B.N.C., Brasenose College, Oxford.
B.N.O.C., British National Opera Company.
b.o., branch office; buyer's option.
B.O.A., British Olympic Association; British Optical Association.
B.O.A.F.G., British Order of Ancient Free Gardeners.
B. of E., Bank of England; Board of Education.
B. of H., Band of Hope; Board of Health.
B. of T., Board of Trade.
bomb., bombardier.
Bom. C.S., Bombay Civil Service.
Bom. S.C., Bombay Staff Corps.
B.O.P., Boys' Own Paper.
bor., borough.
bos'n, boatswain.
bot., botany; botanical.
B.P., British Pharmacopoeia; the British public (humorous).
b.p., below proof (of spirits); bills payable; birthplace; boiling-point.
B.-P., Baden-Powell.
bp., bishop.
B.P.B., bank post bills.
Bp. Suff., Bishop Suffragan.
B.Q., Lat. *bene quiescat*, may he (she) rest well.
Br, bromine (chem.).
Br., Brother; Brigade; Brig; Bombardier; Bugler.
b.r., bills receivable.
Brazil., Brazilian.
B.R.C.S., British Red Cross Society.
b. rec., bills receivable.
Brecon, Brecknockshire.
Bret., Breton.
brev., brevet; brevier.
Brig., Brigade; Brigadier.
Brig.-Gen., Brigadier-General.
Brit., Britain; British; Britannia.
Brit. Mus., British Museum.
Brit. Pharm., British Pharmacopoeia.
Britt., Lat. *Brit(t)an(n)iarum*, of (all) the Britains, on coins.
bro., brother.
Bros., Brothers (commercial).
bryol., bryology.
B.S., Bachelor of Surgery; Bachelor of Science (U.S.A.).
b.s., balance sheet; bill of sale.
B.S.A., British South Africa; Birmingham Small Arms Co.; British School at Athens.
B.S.C., Bengal Staff Corps.

B.Sc., Bachelor of Science.
B.S.L., Botanical Society of London.
B.S.R., British School at Rome.
Bt., Baronet.
bt., bought.
B.Th., Bachelor of Theology.
B.Th.U., British thermal unit.
B.T.U., (elect.) Board of Trade unit.
Bty., Battery.
bu., bushel.
Bucks, Buckinghamshire.
Bulg., Bulgaria; Bulgarian.
B.V., Bible Version (of the Psalms).
B.V.M., Lat. *Beata Virgo Maria*, the Blessed Virgin Mary.
B.W., Board of Works; bonded warehouse; Black Watch.
B.W.G., Birmingham wire gauge.
B.W.I., British West Indies.
B.W.T.A., British Women's Temperance Association.

C, Roman numeral, *centum*, 100; carbon (chem.).
C., Cape; Catholic; Centigrade; Conservative.
c., Lat. *circa, circum, circiter*, about; cent; centime; chapter; child; (cricket) caught.
C3, lowest in physique, state of health, efficiency, &c.
C.A., Chartered Accountant; Chief Accountant; Commercial Agent; County Alderman; Court of Appeal; Church Association; Church Army.
Ca, calcium (chem.).
ca., cathode (elect.).
ca., Lat. *circa*, about.
cad., cadenza (mus.).
caet. par., see cet. par.
C.A.F., Curates' Augmentation Fund.
Cal., California (U.S.A.).
C. Am., Central America(n).
Cambs., Cambridgeshire.
Can., Canada; Canon; Canto; *Cantoris* (of choir).
c. & b., caught and bowled (cricket).
Cant., Canticles (O.T.); Canterbury.
Cantab., Cambridge University; member of Cambridge University.
cantab., cantabile (music).
Cantuar., Lat. *Cantuariensis*, of Canterbury, in signature of Archbishop.
cap., Lat. *capitulum*, chapter; capital letter; number of statute in year of reign of sovereign; captain.
caps., capital letters.
Capt., Captain.
Car., Lat. *Carolus*, Charles.
Card., Cardinal.
Cardig., Cardiganshire.
Carib., Caribbean.
Carliol., Carlisle, in signature of Bishop.
Carmarths., Carmarthenshire.
cat., catalogue; catechism.
Cath., Catholic; Cathedral.
cath., cathode (elect.).
Cathol., Catholic; Catholikos.
cav., cavalry; caveat (law).
C.B., Companion of the Bath (civil or military); confined to barracks, as punishment in army; Cape Breton (Canada); County Borough.
Cb, columbium (chem.).
C.B.E., Commander of the British Empire.
C.B.S., Confraternity of the Blessed Sacrament; Church Building Society.
C.C., Caius College (Cambridge); Cape Colony; Chamber of Commerce; Circuit Court; Common Council(man), City of London; County Council(lor); County Court; Cricket Club; Cycling Club.
c.c., cubic centimetre.
C.C.C., Corpus Christi College, Oxford and Cambridge; Central Criminal Court.
C.C.P., Court of Common Pleas; Code of Civil Procedure.
C.C.S., Ceylon Civil Service; Casualty Clearing Station.
C.D., Chancery Division.
Cd, cadmium (chem.).
Cd., Command Paper, up to 1918 (see **Cmd.**).

cd., could.
C.D. (Acts), Contagious Diseases (Acts).
c.d.v., carte-de-visite (photograph).
C.E., Civil Engineer; Chief Engineer; Church of England.
Ce, cerium (chem.).
Cels., Celsius (thermometer).
Celt., Celtic.
C.E.M.S., Church of England Men's Society.
Cent., Centigrade.
cent., Lat. *centum*, 100; central; century.
Cent. Am., Central America(n).
cert., certif., certificate; certified.
C.E.S.S.I., Church of England Sunday School Institution.
Cestr., Chester, in signature of Bishop.
cet. par., Lat. *ceteris paribus*, other things being equal.
C.E.T.S., Church of England Temperance Society.
C.E.U., Christian Endeavour Union.
C.E.W.M.S., Church of England Working Men's Society.
C.F., Chaplain to the Forces.
cf., Lat. *confer*, compare.
C.F.G., Fr. *Confédération Générale de Travail*, General Confederation of Labour.
c.f.i., cost, freight, and insurance.
C.G., Captain-General; Captain of the Guard; Coast Guard; Coldstream Guards; Commissary-General; Consul-General.
cg., centigramme.
C.G.H., Cape of Good Hope.
C.G.M., Conspicuous Gallantry Medal.
C.G.S., Chief of the General Staff; centimetre-gramme-second system of scientific measurement.
C.H., Companion of Honour; Custom House; Court House.
Ch., Church; Chancery.
Chap., Chaplain; Chapter.
Chap.-Gen., Chaplain-General.
Chas., Charles.
Ch.B., Lat. *Chirurgiae Baccalaureus*, Bachelor of Surgery.
Ch.Ch., Christ Church, Oxford University.
chem., chemistry; chemical.
Ches., Cheshire.
Chev., Fr. *Chevalier*, knight.
Chin., China; Chinese.
Ch.J., Chief Justice.
Ch.M., Lat. *Chirurgiae Magister*, Master of Surgery.
Chmn., Chairman.
chq., cheque.
Chron., Chronicles (O.T.).
chron., chronology; chronological.
chrs., chambers.
C.I., (Imperial Order of the) Crown of India (for ladies); Channel Islands.
Cicestr., Chichester, in signature of Bishop.
C.I.D., Criminal Investigation Department, Scotland Yard.
C.I.E., Companion of the Indian Empire.
c.i.f.c., cost, insurance, freight, and commission.
C.I.G.S., Chief of the Imperial General Staff.
C.I.Mech.E., Companion of the Institution of Mechanical Engineers.
C.-in-C., Commander-in-Chief.
circ., Lat. *circa, circiter, circum*, about.
cit., citation; cited.
C.I.V., City Imperial Volunteers.
C.J., Chief Justice.
C.L., Commander of the Order of Leopold (Belgium).
Cl, chlorine (chem.).
cl., centilitre.
Clar., Clarendon (printing type).
class., classics; classical; classification.
C.L.B., Church Lads' Brigade.
cld., cleared (goods, shipping); coloured.
C.M., Lat. *Chirurgiae Magister*, Master of Surgery; Church Missionary; Certificated Master; Corresponding Member; common metre (of hymns).
c.m., Lat. *causa mortis*, by reason of death.
cm., centimetre.
C.M.A.S., Clergy Mutual Assurance Society.

Cmd., Command Paper, from 1919 (see **Cd.**).
cmdg., commanding.
C.M.G., Companion of St. Michael and St. George.
C.M.R., Cape Mounted Rifles.
C.M.S., Church Missionary Society.
C.O., Commanding Officer; Colonial Office; Crown Office; Criminal Office.
Co, cobalt (chem.).
Co., Company; County.
c/o, care of.
C.O.D., cash on delivery.
C. of E., Church of England.
C. of G.H., Cape of Good Hope.
C. of S., Chief of Staff.
cogn., cognate.
Col., Colossians (N.T.); Colonel.
col., colony; colonial; colour(ed); college; column.
Coll., College.
coll., collective(ly).
collat., collateral.
colloq., colloquial.
Colo., Colorado (U.S.A.).
Coloss., Colossians (N.T.).
Col.-Sergt., Colour-Sergeant.
Com., Commander; Commissioner; Committee; Commodore; Commonwealth; Communist.
com., common; commune; commerce; communications; comedy; commentary; commission.
Comdg., Commanding.
Comdr., Commander.
Comdt., Commandant.
Com.-in-C., Commander-in-Chief.
commerc., commercial.
Commn., Commission.
Commr., Commissioner.
comp., company; comparative; compare; compositor; compound.
compar., comparative.
Com. Serj., Common Serjeant (City of London).
Comy.-Gen., Commissary-General.
Con., Consul.
con., Lat. *contra*, against; conics.
conch., conchology.
conf., Lat. *confer*, compare.
Cong., Congress; Congregation.
conj., conjunction; conjunctive; conjugation.
Conn., Connecticut (U.S.A.).
conn., connected.
Cons., Consul; Conservative.
cons., consonant.
Conserv., Conservative.
Consols, Consolidated Stock.
constr., construction.
contr., contracted; contraction; contrary.
Co-op., Co-operative (Stores).
Cop., Copernican.
C.O.P.E.C. (Copec), Conference on Politics, Economics, and Citizenship (Ch. of Eng.).
Copt., Coptic.
Cor., Corinthians (N.T.); Coroner.
Corn., Cornwall; Cornish.
corol., corollary.
Corp., Corporal; Corporation.
correl., correlative.
Corr. Mem. or Fell., Corresponding Member or Fellow (of a foreign learned society or academy).
corrupt., corruption.
C.O.S., Charity Organisation Society.
cos, cosine.
cosec, cosecant.
cosmog., cosmogony; cosmography.
coss., Lat. *consules*, consuls.
cot, cotangent.
cox, coxswain.
Coy., Company.
C.P., Carriage Paid; Carter Paterson; Clerk of the Peace; Common Pleas; Central Provinces (India); Court of Probate.
c.p., candle-power.
cp., compare.
C.P.C., Clerk of the Privy Council.
Cpl., Corporal.
C.P.R., Canadian Pacific Railway.

C.P.R.E., Council for the Preservation of Rural England.
C.P.S., Lat. *Custos Privati Sigilli*, Keeper of the Privy Seal.
C.R., Lat. *Carolus Rex*, Charles, King; Caledonian Railway.
Cr, chromium (chem.).
Cr., Crown; credit(or).
cr., created.
cresc., crescendo (mus.).
crim. con., criminal conversation, i.e. adultery in old divorce law.
crystal., crystallography.
C.S., Chemical Society; Civil Service; Clerk to the Signet; Common Serjeant; Court of Session; *Custos Sigilli*, Keeper of the Seal.
Cs, caesium (chem.).
C.S.A., Confederate States of America, Confederate States Army.
C.S.C., Conspicuous Service Cross.
C.S.I., Companion of the Star of India.
C.S.M., Company Sergeant-Major.
C.S.S.A., Civil Service Supply Association.
C.T., Certificated Teacher; Commercial Traveller.
Ct., Count; Court.
ct., caught (cricket); cent.
C.T.C., Cyclists' Touring Club.
Cte., Fr. *Comte*, Count.
Ctesse., Fr. *Comtesse*, Countess.
Cu, Lat. *cuprum*, copper (chem.).
C.U.A.C., Cambridge University Athletic Club.
C.U.A.F.C., Cambridge University Association Football Club.
cub., cubic.
C.U.B.C., Cambridge University Boat Club.
C.U.C.C., Cambridge University Cricket Club.
C.U.G.C., Cambridge University Golf Club.
C.U.H.C., Cambridge University Hockey Club.
cum., cumulative.
Cumb., Cumberland.
cum div., with dividend.
Cum. Pref., Cumulative Preference (shares).
C.U.M.S., Cambridge University Musical Society.
cur., current; currency.
C.U.R.F.C., Cambridge University Rugby Football Club.
C.V.O., Commander of the Royal Victorian Order.
c.w.o., cash with order.
C.W.S., Co-operative Wholesale Society.
cwt., hundredweight.
cyl, cylinder.
Cym., Cymric.

D, Roman numeral, 500.
D., Don; Dom; Lat. *Deus*, God.
d., date; daughter; delete; Lat. *denarius*, penny, pence; died; dollar.
d——, damn.
D.(A.)A.G., Deputy (Assistant) Adjutant-General.
dag., decagramme.
D.A.H., disordered action of the heart.
Dak., Dakota (U.S.A.).
dal., decalitre.
dam., decametre.
Dan., Daniel (O.T.); Danish.
D.A.Q.M.G., Deputy Assistant Quartermaster-General.
dat., dative.
dau., daughter.
d.b., day-book.
D.B.E., Dame Commander of the British Empire.
dbk., drawback.
D.C., District of Columbia (U.S.A.); direct current (elect.).
D.C., Ital. *da capo* (mus.), repeat from the beginning.
D.C.L., Doctor of Civil Law.
D.C.L.I., Duke of Cornwall's Light Infantry.
D.C.M. Distinguished Conduct Medal.
D.C.S., Deputy Clerk of Session.

D.D., Doctor of Divinity.
D.D.; d.d., Lat. *dono dedit,* gave as a gift.
d—d, damned.
D.D.D., Lat. *dat, dicat, dedicat,* gives, devotes, and dedicates.
D.D.S., Doctor of Dental Surgery.
deb., debenture.
Dec., December; Decorated (archit.); *Decani* (of choir).
dec., deceased.
dec(l.), declension.
Def., Deferred (stocks or shares); Defendant.
def., definite; definition.
deg., degree.
Del., Delaware (U.S.A.).
del(e)., delete.
del(t)., Lat. *delineavit,* he (she) drew (it).
Dem., Democrat.
demon(s)., demonstrative.
D.Eng., Doctor of Engineering.
Dent., dental; dentistry; dentist.
dep., departs (of train &c.); deputy; department.
dep(t)., department.
deriv., derivation.
Deut., Deuteronomy.
D.F., Lat. *defensor fidei,* Defender of the Faith, usually F.D.; Dean of the Faculty; direction finding.
D.F.C., Distinguished Flying Cross.
D.F.M., Distinguished Flying Medal.
dft., defendant; draft.
D.G., Lat. *Dei gratia,* by the grace of God; Lat. *Deo gratias,* thanks to God; Director-General; Dragoon Guards.
dg., decigramme.
dial., dialect.
diam., diameter.
D.I.C., Diploma of the Imperial College.
dict., dictionary.
diff., differ; difference; different.
dim., diminuendo (mus.).
dimin., diminutive.
Dioc., Diocese; Diocesan.
Dir., Director.
dis., disc(t)., discount.
Dist., District.
dist., distinguish(ed).
Div., Division (army).
div., dividend; division.
D.L., Deputy-Lieutenant.
dl., decilitre.
D.L.I., Durham Light Infantry.
D.Lit., Doctor of Literature.
D.Litt., (at Aberdeen) Doctor of Letters.
D.L.O., Dead Letter Office (now R.L.O., Returned Letter Office).
D.M., Doctor of Medicine, now usually M.D.; Deputy Master.
dm., decimetre.
D.M.R.E., Diploma in Medical Radiology and Electrology.
D.Mus., Doctor of Music, now Mus.D(oc.).
D.N.B., Dictionary of National Biography.
do., ditto, the same.
doc., document.
D.O.M., Lat. *Deo optimo maximo,* to God the best and greatest.
Dom., Lat. *Dominus,* Lord, Master; Dominion.
D.O.M.S., Diploma in Ophthalmic Medicine and Surgery.
Dor., Doric.
D.O.R.A., Defence of the Realm Act(s).
doz., dozen(s).
D.P., double pole.
D.P.H., Diploma in, Department of, Public Health.
D.Ph., Doctor of Philosophy, usually Ph.D.
D.Phil., Doctor of Philosophy.
D.P.I., Director of Public Instruction.
D.P.O., Distributing Post Office.
dpt., department.
D.Q.M.G., Deputy Quartermaster-General.
D.R., dead reckoning.
Dr., Doctor; debtor.
dr., drachm; drawer (banking).
dram. pers., Lat. *dramatis personae,* characters of the play.

D.S., Ital. *dal segno* (mus.), from the sign.
d.s., days after sight (on bills of exchange).
D.S.C., Distinguished Service Cross.
D.Sc., Doctor of Science.
D.S.M., Distinguished Service Medal.
D.S.O., Distinguished Service Order.
d.s.p., Lat. *decessit sine prole,* died without issue.
D.T., (colloq.) delirium tremens.
D.Theol., Doctor of Theology.
D.T.M., Diploma in Tropical Medicine.
Du., Dutch.
Dunelm., Durham, in signature of Bishop.
D.V., Lat. *Deo volente,* God willing.
D.V.M., Doctor of Veterinary Medicine.
d.v.p., Lat. *decessit vita patris,* died during lifetime of father.
D.V.S., Doctor of Veterinary Science or Surgery.
dwt., pennyweight.
dyn., dynamics.
D.Z., Doctor of Zoology.

E, erbium (chem.).
E., earth; east; eastern (London postal district); second-class ship at Lloyd's; Egyptian, in £E.
ea., each.
E. & O.E., errors and omissions excepted (mercantile).
E.B., Encyclopædia Britannica.
Ebor., fr. Lat. *Eboracensis,* of *Eboracum,* York, in signature of Archbishop.
E.C., east central (London postal district).
Eccl(es)., Ecclesiastes (O.T.).
eccl(es)., ecclesiastical.
Ecclus., Ecclesiasticus (O.T., Apoc.).
econ., economics.
E.C.U., English Church Union.
ed., edited; edition; editor.
Edin., Edinburgh.
edit., edited; edition; editor.
E.D.S., English Dialect Society.
eds., editors.
educ., education.
Edw., Edward.
E.E., Envoy Extraordinary; errors excepted (mercantile).
E.E.T.S., Early English Text Society.
e.g., Lat. *exempli gratia,* for example.
Egyptol., Egyptology.
E.I., East Indian; East Indies; East India.
E.I.C., East India Company.
ejusd., Lat. *ejusdem,* of the same.
el., elected.
eld., eldest.
elect., electricity.
Eliz., Elizabeth; Elizabethan.
Elz., Elzevir.
E.M.D.P., electromotive difference of potential.
E.M.F., electromotive force.
Emp., Emperor, Empress.
E.M.U., electromagnetic units.
Ency., Encyclop(a)edia.
E.N.E., east-north-east.
Eng., England; English.
eng., engineer, engineering; engraver, engraving.
engin., engineering.
Engl., English.
ent(om)., entomology; entomological.
Ent. Sta. Hall, Entered at Stationers' Hall.
Env. Extr., Envoy Extraordinary.
Ep., Epistle.
E.P.D., Excess Profits Duty.
Eph., Ephesians (N.T.).
Epiph., Epiphany.
episc., episcopal.
eq., equal, equivalent.
equiv., equivalent.
E.R., East Riding, Yorkshire.
E.R. (et I.), Lat. *Edwardus Rex (et Imperator),* Edward King (and Emperor).
eschat., eschatology.
E.S.E., east-south-east.
esp(ec)., especially.
Esq(re)., Esquire.

est(ab)., established.
Esth., Esther (O.T.).
E.S.U., electrostatic units.
et al., Lat. *et alibi,* and elsewhere; *et alia,* and other things; *et alii,* and other people.
E.T.C., Eastern Telegraph Co.
etc., Lat. *et cetera,* and (the) other things.
eth., ethics, ethical.
ethnol., ethnology, ethnological.
et seq., et sqq., Lat. *et sequens, et sequentia,* and the following.
E.T.U., Electrical Trades Union.
etymol., etymology, etymological.
euphem., euphemism, euphemistically.
Ex., Exodus (O.T.).
ex., examined; example; except.
exam., examination.
Exc., Excellency.
exc., except.
exc., Lat. *excudit,* he (she) engraved (it).
ex div., ex dividend.
Exod., Exodus (O.T.).
ex off., Lat. *ex officio,* by virtue of office.
Exon., Exeter, in signature of Bishop.
exor., executor.
exp., export, exporter.
Ez., Ezra (O.T.).
Ezek., Ezekiel (O.T.).

F, firm (of pencils).
F., Fahrenheit; French.
f., farthing; fathom; foot; filly; folio; franc.
f, Ital. *forte,* loud (mus.).
F.A., Football Association.
f.a.a., free of all average.
facet., facetious.
F.A.C.S., Fellow of the American College of Surgeons.
fac(s)., facsimile.
F.A.G.S., Fellow of the American Geographical Society.
Fahr., Fahrenheit.
F.A.I., Fellow of the Auctioneers' Institute.
F.A.L.P.A., Fellow of the Incorporated Society of Auctioneers and Landed Property Agents.
F.A.S., Fellow of the Society of Arts; do. of the Antiquarian Society (Edinburgh); do. of the Anthropological Society.
f.a.s., free alongside ship.
F.B., Fire Brigade; Fenian Brotherhood; Free Baptist.
F.B.A., Fellow of the British Academy.
F.B.H., fire brigade hydrant.
F.B.I., Federation of British Industries.
F.B.S., Fellow of the Botanical Society;
F.B.S.E., do. of the Botanical Society of Edinburgh.
F.C., Football Club; Free Church (Scotland).
F.C.A., Fellow of the Institute of Chartered Accountants.
fcap., foolscap.
F.C.G.I., Fellow of the City and Guilds of London Institute.
F.C.I.I., Fellow of the Chartered Insurance Institute.
F.C.I.S., Fellow of the Chartered Institute of Secretaries.
F.C.O., Fellow of the College of Organists, now F.R.C.O.
F.C.P., Fellow of the College of Preceptors.
fcp., foolscap.
F.C.S., Fellow of the Chemical Society.
F.D., Lat. *fidei defensor,* Defender of the Faith; also D.F.
Fe, Lat. *ferrum,* iron (chem.).
Feb(y)., February.
fec., Lat. *fecit,* he (she) did, made (it).
fed., federal; federated.
F.E.I.S., Fellow of the Educational Institute of Scotland.
fem., feminine.
F.E.S., Fellow of the Entomological Society; Fellow of the Ethnological Society.
feud., feudal(ism).
ff., folios; following pages.
ff, Ital. *fortissimo,* very loud (mus.).
F.F.A., Fellow of the Faculty of Actuaries.

ffy., faithfully.
F.G., Foot Guards.
f.g.a., free of general average.
F.G.S., Fellow of the Geological Society.
F.H., fire hydrant.
F.I.A., Fellow of the Institute of Actuaries.
F.I.A.A., Fellow Architect Member of the Incorporated Association of Architects and Surveyors.
F.I.A.S., Fellow Surveyor Member of the Incorporated Association of Architects and Surveyors.
F.I.A.T., Ital. *Fabrica Italiana Automobile Torino*, make of motor-car.
F.I.C., Fellow of the Institute of Chemistry.
F.I.C.A., Fellow of the Institute of Chartered Accountants.
F.I.C.S., Fellow of the Institute of Chartered Shipbrokers.
F.I.D., Fellow of the Institute of Directors.
Fid. Def., Lat. *fidei defensor*, Defender of the Faith.
fi. fa., Lat. *fieri facias* (law).
fig., figure (illustration); figurative(ly).
F.I.Inst., Fellow of the Imperial Institute.
F.I.J., Fellow of the Institute of Journalists.
fin., financial; finis; finished.
Finn., Finnish.
F.Inst.P., Fellow of the Institute of Physics.
F.I.O., Fellow of the Institute of Ophthalmic Opticians.
F.I.P.I., Fellow of the Institute of Patentees (Inc.).
F.I.S.A., Fellow of the Incorporated Secretaries Association.
F.I.S.E., Fellow of the Institution of Structural Engineers.
F.J.I., Fellow of the Institute of Journalists.
F.K.C.(L.), Fellow of King's College (London).
Fl, fluorine (chem.).
fl., florin.
fl., Lat. *floruit*, he (she) flourished, lived.
f.l., Lat. *falsa lectio*, false reading (of MS. &c.).
F.L.A., Fellow of the Library Association.
Fla., Florida (U.S.A.).
F.L.A.A., Fellow of the London Association of Accountants.
F.L.A.S., Fellow of the Land Agents' Society.
Flem., Flemish.
flor., Lat. *floruit*, he (she) flourished, lived.
F.L.S., Fellow of the Linnean Society.
F.M., Field-Marshal.
fm., fathom.
F.M.S., Federated Malay States.
F.O., Foreign Office; Field Officer; full organ (mus.).
fo., folio.
f.o.b., free on board.
fol., folio; following.
foll., following.
f.o.r., free on rail.
fort., fortification.
F.P., fire-plug; field punishment.
fp., foot-pound; foolscap.
fp, Ital. *forte piano*, loud and soft (mus.).
f.p.a., free of particular average.
F.Phys.S., Fellow of the Physical Society.
F.P.S., Fellow of the Philosophical Society; Fellow of the Philharmonic Society; Fellow of the Philological Society.
Fr., Father; France, French; Friar.
fr., franc; from.
F.R.A.I., Fellow of the Royal Anthropological Institute.
F.R.A.M., Fellow of the Royal Academy of Music.
F.R.Ae.S., Fellow of the Royal Aeronautical Society.
F.R.A.S., Fellow of the Royal Astronomical Society; Fellow of the Royal Asiatic Society.
F.R.B.S., Fellow of the Royal Botanic Society.
F.R.C.I., Fellow of the Royal Colonial Institute.
F.R.C.M., Fellow of the Royal College of Music.
F.R.C.O., Fellow of the Royal College of Organists.
F.R.C.P., Fellow of the Royal College of Physicians; **F.R.C.P.E.**, do. of Edinburgh; **F.R.C.P.I.**, do. of Ireland.
F.R.C.S., Fellow of the Royal College of Surgeons; **F.R.C.S.E.**, do. of Edinburgh; **F.R.C.S.I.**, do. of Ireland.
F.R.C.V.S., Fellow of the Royal College of Veterinary Surgeons.
F.R.Econ.Soc., Fellow of the Royal Economic Society.
freq., frequentative; frequently.
F.R.F.P.S., Fellow of the Royal Faculty of Physicians and Surgeons.
F.R.G.S., Fellow of the Royal Geographical Society.
F.R.Hist.S., Fellow of the Royal Historical Society.
F.R.Hort.S., Fellow of the Royal Horticultural Society.
Fri., Friday.
F.R.I.B.A., Fellow of the Royal Institute of British Architects.
Fris., Frisian.
Frisco, San Francisco, California.
Frl., Fräulein.
F.R.Met.S., Fellow of the Royal Meteorological Society.
F.R.M.S., Fellow of the Royal Microscopical Society.
F.R.N.S.A., Fellow of the Royal Naval School of Architects.
F.R.P.S., Fellow of the Royal Photographic Society.
F.R.P.S.L., Fellow of the Royal Philatelic Society, London.
F.R.S., Fellow of the Royal Society.
F.R.S.A., Fellow of the Royal Society of Arts.
F.R.S.A.I., Fellow of the Royal Society of Antiquaries of Ireland.
F.R.San.I., Fellow of the Royal Sanitary Institute.
F.R.S.E., Fellow of the Royal Society of Edinburgh.
F.R.S.G.S., Fellow of the Royal Scottish Geographical Society.
F.R.S.L., Fellow of the Royal Society of Literature.
F.R.S.S., Fellow of the Royal Statistical Society.
F.R.S.S.A., Fellow of the Royal Scottish Society of Arts.
F.R.U.I., Fellow of the Royal University of Ireland.
F.S., Fleet Surgeon.
fs., foot-second.
F.S.A., Fellow of the Society of Antiquaries; Fellow of the Society of Arts.
F.S.A.A., Fellow of the Society of Incorporated Accountants and Auditors.
F.S.I., Fellow of the Surveyors' Institute.
F.S.R., Field Service Regulations.
F.S.S., Fellow of the Statistical Society, now F.R.S.S.
ft., foot, feet.
F.T.C.D., Fellow of Trinity College, Dublin.
F.T.C.L., Fellow of Trinity College (of Music), London.
fur., furlong.
fut., future.
F.W.B., four wheel brake; Free Will Baptist.
F.W.D., four wheel drive.
F.Z.S., Fellow of the Zoological Society of London; **F.Z.S.Scot.**, do. of Scotland.

g., guinea; gramme.
G.A., General Assembly.
Ga., Georgia (U.S.A.).
Ga, gallium (chem.).
Gael., Gaelic.
Gal., Galatians (N.T.).
gal., gallon.
Gaul., Gaulish.
gaz., gazette; gazetteer.
G.B., Great Britain.
G.B. & I., Great Britain and Ireland.
G.B.E., Knight (or Dame) Grand Cross of the British Empire.
G.C., Grand Chaplain, Grand Chapter (freemasonry).
G.C.B., Knight Grand Cross of the Bath.
G.C.C., Gonville and Caius College, Cambridge.
G.C.F., greatest common factor.
G.C.H., Knight Grand Cross of Hanover.
G.C.I.E., Knight Grand Commander of the Indian Empire.
G.C.L.H., Knight Grand Cross of the Legion of Honour.
G.C.M., greatest common measure.
G.C.M.G., Knight Grand Cross of St. Michael and St. George.
G.C.R., Great Central Railway, now part of L.N.E.(R.).
G.C.S.I., Knight Grand Commander of the Star of India.
G.C.V.O., Knight Grand Cross of the Royal Victorian Order.
Gdns., Gardens.
Gds., Guards.
Ge, germanium (chem.).
Gen., General; Genesis (O.T.).
gen., gender; genus; general(ly); generic.
geneal., genealogy.
genit., genitive.
Genl., General.
Geo., George.
geod., geodesy.
geog., geography.
geol., geology.
geom., geometry.
G.E.R., Great Eastern Railway, now part of L.N.E.(R.).
ger., gerund.
Germ., German; Germany.
G.F.S., Girls' Friendly Society.
G.F.T.U., General Federation of Trade Unions.
G.G., Grenadier Guards.
g.gr., great gross, 144 dozens.
G.H.Q., General Headquarters.
Gib., (colloq.), Gibraltar.
G.J.C., Grand Junction Canal.
Gk., Greek.
G.L., Grand Lodge (freemasonry).
Gl, glucinum (chem.).
Glam., Glamorganshire.
Glos., Gloucestershire.
gloss., glossary.
Glo'ster, Gloucester.
Gloucs., Gloucestershire.
G.M., Grand Master (orders of knighthood and freemasonry); Gold Medallist (Bisley).
gm., gramme.
G.M.B., Great Master of the Bath; good merchantable brand (of metals).
Gmc., Germanic.
G.M.I.E., Grand Master of the Indian Empire.
G.M.M.G., Grand Master of St. Michael and St. George.
G.M.S.I., Grand Master of the Star of India.
G.M.T., Greenwich Mean Time.
G.N.R., Great Northern Railway.
G.O., General Order.
G.O.C., General Officer Commanding; **G.O.C. in C.**, do. in Chief.
G.O.M., Grand Old Man (originally of W. E. Gladstone).
G.O.P., Girls' Own Paper.
Goth., Gothic.
Gov., Governor.
Gov.-Gen., Governor-General.
Govt., Government.
G.P., general practitioner (doctor); general paralysis of the insane (also G.P.I.); Lat. *Gloria Patri*, Glory to the Father.
G.P.D.S.T., Girls' Public Day School Trust.
G.P.I., general paralysis of the insane.
G.P.M., Grand Past Master (freemasonry).
G.P.O., General Post Office.
G.R., General Reserve.
G.R. (et I.), Lat. *Georgius Rex (et Imperator)*, George, King (and Emperor).
Gr., Greek.
gr., gramme; grain.
gram., grammar.
Gr. Gds., Grenadier Guards.
grm., gramme.
G.S., General Staff; General Service.
g.s., grandson.

G.S.N.C., General Steam Navigation Co.
G.S.O., General Staff Officer.
G.T., Good Templar.
Gt. Br., Great Britain.
guar., guarantee(d).
G.W.R., Great Western Railway.
gym., gymnasium; gymnastics.

H, hydrogen (chem.); hard (of pencil-lead).
H., hydrant.
h., hour.
H.A., heavy artillery.
H.A. & M., Hymns Ancient and Modern.
Hab., Habakkuk (O.T.).
hab., Lat. *habitat*, he lives.
Hab. Corp., Habeas Corpus (writ).
H.A.C., Honourable Artillery Company.
Hag., Haggai (O.T.).
H.A.L., *Hamburg-Amerika Linie* (German steamship company).
h. and c., hot and cold (water supply).
Hants, Hampshire.
HB, hard black (of pencil-lead).
H.B.C., Hudson's Bay Company.
H.B.M., His (Her) Britannic Majesty.
H.C., House of Commons; Heralds' College.
hcap., handicap.
H.C.F., highest common factor.
H.C.M., His (Her) Catholic Majesty.
H.C.S., Home Civil Service.
hd., hogshead.
hdbk., handbook.
hdqrs., headquarters.
H.E., His Excellency; His Eminence; high explosive.
He, helium (chem.).
Heb., Hebrew; Hebrews (N.T.).
hectog., hectogramme.
hectol., hectolitre.
hectom., hectometre.
H.E.I.C., Honourable East India Company.
Hellen., Hellenic; Hellenistic.
her., heraldry.
Herts, Hertfordshire.
HF, hard firm (of pencil-lead).
H.F., high frequency.
hf., half.
hf.-bd., half-bound.
H.F.R.A., Honorary Fellow of the Royal Academy.
H.G., High German; Horse Guards; His (Her) Grace.
Hg, Lat. *hydrargyrum*, mercury (chem.).
hg., hectogramme; heliogramme.
H.G.D.H., His (Her) Grand Ducal Highness.
H.H., His (Her) Highness; His Holiness (the Pope).
HH, double hard (of pencil-lead).
hhd., hogshead.
HHH, trebly hard (of pencil-lead).
H.I.H., His (Her) Imperial Highness.
H.I.M., His (Her) Imperial Majesty.
Hind., Hindustani; Hindi.
hist., history; historical.
H.J.(S.), Lat. *hic jacet (sepultus)*, here lies (buried).
H.K., House of Keys (Isle of Man).
H.L., House of Lords.
hl., hectolitre.
H.L.I., Highland Light Infantry.
H.M., His (Her) Majesty.
hm., hectometre.
H.M.A., His Majesty's Airship; Head Masters' Association.
H.M.C., His Majesty's Customs.
H.M.I.(S.), His Majesty's Inspector (of Schools).
H.M.P., Lat. *hoc monumentum posuit*, erected this monument.
H.M.S., His Majesty's Ship; His Majesty's Service.
H.M.S.O., His Majesty's Stationery Office.
H.O., Home Office.
Hon., Honourable; Honorary.
Honble., Honourable.
Hon. Sec., Honorary Secretary.
hor., horizon.
horol., horology.
hort., horticulture; horticultural.

Hos., Hosea (O.T.).
H.P., House Physician.
h.p., horse-power; half-pay; high pressure.
h.p.n., horse-power nominal.
H.Q., Headquarters.
H.R., House of Representatives; Highland Railway.
hr., hour.
H.R.C.A., Honorary Member of the Royal Cambrian Academy.
H.R.E., Holy Roman Empire, Emperor.
H.R.H., His (Her) Royal Highness.
H.R.H.A., Honorary Member of the Royal Hibernian Academy.
H.R.I.P., Lat. *hic requiescit in pace*, here rests in peace.
Hrs., Hussars.
H.R.S.A., Honorary Member of the Royal Scottish Academy.
H.S., House Surgeon.
H.S.E., Lat. *hic situs (sepultus) est*, here is laid (buried).
H.S.H., His (Her) Serene Highness.
h.t., high tension (elect.).
Hung., Hungary; Hungarian.
Hunts, Huntingdonshire.
H.W., high water.
h.w., hit wicket (cricket).
Hy., Henry.
hydr., hydraulics.
hydro, hydropathic establishment.
hydrostat., hydrostatics.

I, Roman numeral; iodine (chem.).
I., Idaho (U.S.A.); Island.
I.A., Indian Army; Incorporated Accountant.
Ia., Iowa (U.S.A.).
I.A.A.M., Incorporated Association of Assistant Masters.
I.A.O.S., Irish Agricultural Organization Society.
I.A.R.O., Indian Army Reserve of Officers.
ib., ibid., Lat. *ibidem*, in the same place.
i/c, in charge of.
I.C.E., Institution of Civil Engineers.
Icel., Icelandic; Iceland.
ichth., ichthyology.
icon., iconography.
I.C.S., Indian Civil Service.
I.D., Intelligence Department.
id., Lat. *idem*, the same.
Ida., Idaho (U.S.A.).
I.D.B., illicit diamond buyer, buying (South Africa).
I.D.N., Lat. *in Dei nomine*, in the name of God.
i.e., Lat. *id est*, that is.
I.E.E., Institution of Electrical Engineers.
I.F.S., Irish Free State.
I.F.T.U., International Federation of Trade Unions.
I.G., Inspector-General.
ign., Lat. *ignotus*, unknown, of painter &c.
i.h.p., indicated horse-power.
IHS, Lat. *Jesus Hominum Salvator*, Jesus, Saviour of Mankind; properly IHΣ, in Greek, the first three letters of IHΣOYΣ, Jesus.
Ill., Illinois (U.S.A.).
ill., illustration; illustrated.
illit., illiterate.
I.L.O., International Labour Office, Geneva (League of Nations).
I.L.P., Independent Labour Party.
imit., imitative.
Imp., Imperial; Lat. *Imperator*, Emperor, *Imperatrix*, Empress.
imp., Lat. *imprimatur*, let it be printed; imported.
imperat., imperative.
imperf., imperfect; imperforated (stamps).
impers., impersonal.
I.M.S., Indian Medical Service.
In, indium (chem.).
in., inch.
I.N.A., Institution of Naval Architects.
I.N.C., Lat. *in nomine Christi*, in the name of Christ.
inc., incorporated.

incl., including; inclusive.
incog., Ital. *incognito*, unknown.
incorp., incorporated.
I.N.D., Lat. *in nomine Dei*, in the name of God.
Ind., Indian, India; Indiana (U.S.A.).
ind., independent; indicated; index.
indecl., indeclinable.
indef., indefinite.
indic., indicative.
Ind.T., Ind. Terr., Indian Territory (U.S.A.).
inf., infantry.
inf., Lat. *infra*, below.
infin., infinitive.
infra dig., Lat. *infra dignitatem*, beneath one's dignity.
init., Lat. *initio*, at, from, the beginning.
I.N.J., Lat. *in nomine Jesu*, in the name of Jesus.
in lim., Lat. *in limine*, on the threshold, at the outset.
in pr., Lat. *in principio*, in the beginning.
I.N.R.I., Lat. *Jesus Nazarenus Rex Judaeorum*, Jesus of Nazareth, King of the Jews.
insc., inscribed (stock).
insep., inseparable.
Insp., Inspector.
Insp.-Gen., Inspector-General.
I.N.S.T., Lat. *in nomine Sanctae Trinitatis*, in the name of the Holy Trinity.
inst., instant (the present month); institute; institution, instrument(al).
Inst. Act., Institute of Actuaries.
Inst. C.E., Institution of Civil Engineers.
Inst. E.E., Institution of Electrical Engineers.
Inst. M.E., Institution of Mechanical Engineers.
Inst. N.A., Institution of Naval Architects.
instr., instrument(al).
int., interest; internal; interior; interpreter; international.
int. al., Lat. *inter alia*, among other things.
intens., intensive.
inter., interrogation, interrogative; intermediate.
interj., interjection.
internat., international.
interrog., interrogative.
intrans., intransitive.
intro(d)., introduction.
inv., invented, inventor; invoice.
inv(en)., Lat. *invenit*, he (she) invented, discovered (it).
I.O.F., Independent Order of Foresters.
I. of M., Isle of Man.
I. of W., Inspector of Works.
I.O.G.T., International Order of Good Templars.
I.O.O.F., Independent Order of Oddfellows.
I.O.P., Institute of Painters in Oil Colours.
IOU., I owe you (loose form of promissory note).
I.P.D., Lat. *in praesentia Dominorum*, in the presence of the Lords of Session.
ipecac., ipecacuanha.
I.P.L., Lat. *In partibus infidelium*, in the regions of unbelievers.
i.q., Lat. *idem quod*, the same as.
I.R., Inland Revenue.
Ir, iridium (chem.).
Ir., Irish; Ireland.
I.R.A., Irish Republican Army.
I.R.B., Irish Republican Brotherhood.
I.R.O., Inland Revenue Office.
iron., ironical(ly).
irreg., irregular.
I.S., Irish Society.
Is., Isaiah (O.T.); Island.
I.S.C., Indian Staff Corps.
Isl., Island.
I.S.M., Incorporated Society of Musicians.
I.S.O., Imperial Service Order.
isth., isthmus.
I.T., Indian Territory (U.S.A.); Inner Temple (Inn of Court).
Ital., Italian; Italy.
ital., italics.
I.W., Isle of Wight.
I.W.T.D., Inland Water Transport Department.

I.W.W., Industrial Workers of the World.
I.Y., Imperial Yeomanry.
I.Z., I Zingari (Cricket Club).

J, broad-pointed pen marked J.
J., Judge, Justice; joule (elect.).
J.A., Judge-Advocate.
J.A.G., Judge Advocate-General.
Jam., James (N.T.); Jamaica.
Jan., January.
Jap., Japanese.
Jas., James.
Jav., Javanese.
J.C., Lat. *jurisconsultus*, jurisconsult; Justice Clerk.
J.C.D., Lat. *Juris Civilis Doctor*, Doctor of Civil Law.
J.C.R., Junior Common Room (Oxford University).
J.D., Lat. *Jurum Doctor*, Doctor of Laws.
Jer., Jeremiah (O.T.).
JHS, see **IHS**.
J.I.C., Joint Industrial Council.
jn., junction.
Jno., John.
jnr., junior.
Jo., Joel (O.T.).
Jos., Joseph; Josiah.
Josh., Joshua (O.T.).
J.P., Justice of the Peace.
jr., junior.
J.U.D., Lat. *Juris utriusque Doctor*, Doctor of both (Civil and Canon) Laws.
Jud., Judith (O.T., Apoc.).
Jud(g)., Judges (O.T.).
Jul., July.
Jun., June.
jun., junior.
junc., junction.
Jun. Opt., Junior Optime (Camb. Univ. Math. Tripos).
junr., junior.

K, Lat. *kalium*, potassium (chem.).
Kal., Lat. *kalendae*, Calends.
Kan., Kansas (U.S.A.).
K.B., Knight Bachelor; King's Bench.
K.B.E., Knight Commander of the British Empire.
K.C., King's Counsel; King's College.
kc., kilocycle.
K.C.B., Knight Commander of the Bath.
K.C.H., Knight Commander of Hanover.
K.C.I.E., Knight Commander of the Indian Empire.
K.C.M.G., Knight Commander of St. Michael and St. George.
K.C.S.I., Knight Commander of the Star of India.
K.C.V.O., Knight Commander of the Royal Victorian Order.
K.G., Knight of the Garter.
kg., kilogramme.
K.G.C.B., Knight Grand Cross of the Bath, more usually G.C.B.
K.G.F., Knight of the Golden Fleece.
K.H., Knight of Hanover.
K.H.C., Honorary Chaplain to the King.
K.H.P., Honorary Physician to the King.
K.H.S., Honorary Surgeon to the King.
K.-i-H., Kaisar-i-Hind.
kilo(g)., kilogramme.
kilo(l)., kilolitre.
kilo(m)., kilometre.
K.K., Germ. *Kaiserlich, Königlich*, Imperial, Royal, i.e. of German Empire and Kingdom of Prussia.
K.K.K., Ku Klux Klan (U.S.A.).
kl., kilolitre(s).
K.L.H., Knight of the Legion of Honour.
K.L.I., King's Light Infantry.
K.M., Knight of Malta.
km., kilometre(s).
Knt., Knight.
Knt. Bach., Knight Bachelor.
K.O.S.B., King's Own Scottish Borderers.
K.O.Y.L.I., King's Own Yorkshire Light Infantry.
K.P., Knight of St. Patrick.

K.R., King's Regulations.
Kr, krypton (chem.).
K.R.R., King's Royal Rifles.
K.S., King's Scholar.
K.S.I., Knight of the Star of India.
K.T., Knight of the Thistle; Knight Templar.
Kt., Knight.
Kt. Bach., Knight Bachelor.
kv., kilovolt.
kw., kilowatt.
Ky., Kentucky (U.S.A.).

L, Roman numeral, 50.
L., Lake; Liberal; Late; left.
£, Lat. *libra*, pound sterling.
l., left; lira; litre.
L.A., Literate in Arts; Law Agent; Legislative Assembly.
La, lanthanum (chem.).
La., Louisiana (U.S.A.).
Lab., Labrador.
L.A.C., London Athletic Club; Licentiate of the Apothecaries' Company.
L.A.H., Licentiate of Apothecaries' Hall, Dublin.
L.A.M., London Academy of Music.
Lam., Lamentations (O.T.).
Lancs., Lancashire.
L. & N.E.R., see **L.N.E.(R.)**.
L. & S.W.R., London and South-Western Railway, now part of S.R.
L. & Y.R., Lancashire and Yorkshire Railway, now part of L.M.S.(R.).
lang., language.
L.A.S., Lord Advocate of Scotland.
Lat., Latin.
lat., latitude.
lb., Lat. *libra*, pound(s).
l.b., (cricket) leg-bye.
L.B. & S.C.R., London, Brighton and South Coast Railway, now part of S.R.
l.b.w., (cricket) leg before wicket.
L.C., Lord Chancellor; Lord Chamberlain; left centre (of stage).
l.c., (print.) lower case; Lat. *loco citato*, in place cited; letter of credit.
L.C. & D.R., London, Chatham and Dover Railway, now part of S.R.
L.C.B., Lord Chief Baron (obs.).
L.C.C., London County Council(lor).
L.Ch., L.Chir., Licentiate in Surgery.
L.C.J., Lord Chief Justice.
L.C.M., least common multiple.
L.-Corp., Lance-Corporal.
L.C.P., Licentiate of the College of Preceptors.
L.-Cpl., Lance-Corporal.
L.D., Doctor of Letters (U.S.A.); Lady Day; Lat. *laus Deo*, praise be to God.
Ld., Lord; Limited.
L.Div., Licentiate in Divinity.
L.D.S., Licentiate in Dental Surgery; Lat. *laus Deo semper*, praise be to God for ever.
£E., Egyptian pound.
Leics., Leicestershire.
L. ès L., Fr. *Licencié ès Lettres*, Licentiate of Letters.
Lett., Lettish.
Lev., Leviticus (O.T.).
L.F., low frequency.
L.F.P.S., Licentiate of the Faculty of Physicians and Surgeons (Glasgow).
L.G., Low German; Life Guards.
L.G.B., Local Government Board.
L.G.O.C., London General Omnibus Co.
l.h., left hand.
L.I., Light Infantry; Long Island (U.S.A.).
Li, lithium (chem.).
Lib., Library, Librarian; Liberal.
Lic. Med., Licentiate in Medicine.
Lieut., Lieutenant.
Lieut.-Col., -Gen., -Gov., Lieutenant-Colonel, -General, -Governor.
Lincs., Lincolnshire.
Linn., Linn(a)ean; Linnaeus.
lit., literal(ly); litre.
Lit.D. See **Litt.D**.
liter., literature; literary.
Lith., Lithuania; Lithuanian.
litho(g)., lithograph; lithography.

Lit. Hum., Lat. *Literae Humaniores*, Final Classical Honour School, Oxford University, usually known as 'greats'.
Litt.D., Lat. *Literarum Doctor*, Doctor of Letters (Literature).
liturg., liturgy; liturgical.
L.J., Lord Justice (of Appeal).
L.L., Lord-Lieutenant.
ll., lines.
L.L.A., Lady Literate in Arts.
LL.B., *Legum Baccalaureus*, Bachelor of Laws.
LL.D., *Legum Doctor*, Doctor of Laws.
LL.JJ., Lords Justices of Appeal.
LL.M., *Legum Magister*, Master of Laws.
L.M., Licentiate in Midwifery; Lord Mayor.
L.M.B.C., Lady Margaret Boat Club (St. John's College, Cambridge).
L.M.S., London Missionary Society.
L.M.S.(R.), London, Midland and Scottish (Railway).
L.M.S.S.A., Licentiate in Medicine and Surgery of the Society of Apothecaries.
L.M.T., length, mass, time (physics).
L.N.E.(R.), London and North-Eastern (Rly.).
L.N.W.R., London and North-Western Railway, now part of L.M.S.(R.).
loc. cit., Lat. *loco citato*, in the place cited.
log., logarithm; logic.
Lond., London.
Londin., also **London.**, London, in signature of Bishop.
long., longitude.
loq., Lat. *loquitur*, (he) speaks.
L.P., Lord Provost; Labour Party.
l.p., large paper (edition); long primer (type); low pressure.
L'pool, Liverpool.
L.P.S., Lord Privy Seal.
L.R.A.M., Licentiate of the Royal Academy of Music.
L.R.C., Leander Rowing Club; London Rowing Club.
L.R.C.P., Licentiate of the Royal College of Physicians; **L.R.C.P.E.**, do. Edinburgh; **L.R.C.P.I.**, do. Ireland.
L.R.C.S., Licentiate of the Royal College of Surgeons; **L.R.C.S.E.**, do. Edinburgh; **L.R.C.S.I.**, do. Ireland.
L.R.C.V.S., Licentiate of the Royal College of Veterinary Surgeons.
L.R.F.P.S.G., Licentiate of the Royal Faculty of Physicians and Surgeons, Glasgow.
Lrs., Lancers.
L.S., Linnean Society; Lat. *loco sigilli*, in the place of the seal (legal documents).
L.S.A., Licentiate of the Society of Apothecaries.
L.S.B., London School Board (obs.).
L.S.D., Lightermen, Stevedores and Dockers.
£.s.d., Lat. *librae, solidi, denarii*, pounds, shillings, pence.
Lt., Lieutenant.
l.t., (electricity) low tension.
£T., pound Turkish.
L.T.A., Lawn Tennis Association; London Teachers' Association.
L.T.C., Lawn Tennis Club.
L.T.C.L., Licentiate of Trinity College of Music (London).
Lt.-Col., Lieutenant-Colonel.
Lt.-Comm., Lieutenant-Commander (R.N.).
Ltd., Limited.
Lt.-Gen., -Gov., Lieutenant-General, -Governor.
Lt. Inf., Light Infantry.
L.T.M., Licentiate of Tropical Medicine.
L.U., Liberal Unionist.
L.V., Licensed Victuallers.
L.W.L., load water line.
LXX, Roman numeral, 70; the Septuagint.

M, Lat. *mille*, 1000, Roman numeral.
M., maiden (over, cricket); Fr. *Monsieur*.
m., mark (coin); married; metre; mile; minute.
M.A., Master of Arts; Military Academy.
M.A.B., Metropolitan Asylums Board.
Macc., Maccabees (O.T., Apoc.).
mach., machinery.

2 F

mag., magazine.
mag(n)., magnetism; magneto.
M.Agr(ic)., Master of Agriculture (U.S.A.).
Maj., Major.
Maj.-Gen., Major-General.
Mal., Malachi (O.T.).
Malay., Malayan.
Mancun., Lat. *Mancunium*, Manchester, in signature of Bishop.
Man(it)., Manitoba (Canada).
manuf., manufactured; manufacturer; manufacturing; manufactory.
Mar., March.
mar., married.
March., Marchioness.
Marq., Marquess.
masc., masculine.
Mass., Massachusetts (U.S.A.).
math(s)., mathematics.
matric., matriculation.
Matt., Matthew (N.T.).
M.B., Lat. *Medicinae Baccalaureus*, Bachelor of Medicine.
M.B.E., Member of the British Empire.
M.B.W., Metropolitan Board of Works (obs., now L.C.C.).
M.C., Master of Ceremonies; Member of Congress; Member of Council; Military Cross.
M.C.C., Marylebone Cricket Club.
M.Ch., Lat. *Magister Chirurgiae*, Master of Surgery.
Mch., March.
M.Ch.D., Master of Dental Surgery.
M.Ch.Orth., Master of Orthopaedic Surgery.
M.Com., Master of Commerce (Birmingham).
M.Comm., Master of Commerce and Administration (Manchester).
M.C.P., Member of the College of Preceptors.
M.C.S., Madras Civil Service; Malay Civil Service.
M.D., Lat. *Medicinae Doctor*, Doctor of Medicine.
Md., Maryland (U.S.A.).
Mddx., Middlesex.
Mdlle. See **Mlle**.
Mdme. See **Mme**.
M.D.S., Master in Dental Surgery.
M.Du., Middle Dutch.
Mdx., Middlesex.
M.E., Methodist Episcopal; Middle English; Mining (Mechanical) Engineer.
Me., Maine (U.S.A.).
M^e., Fr. *maitre*, title applied to barristers, etc.
meas., measure.
M.E.C., Member of Executive Council.
mech(an)., mechanical; mechanics.
Med., Mediaeval.
med., medical; medicine.
Medit., Mediterranean (Sea).
M.E.F., Mediterranean Expeditionary Force (Great War).
mem., Lat. *memento*, remember; memorandum.
memo., Lat. *memorandum*, to be remembered.
M.Eng., Master of Engineering.
M. ès A., Fr. *Maitre ès Arts*, Master of Arts.
Messrs., Fr. *Messieurs*, Gentlemen; also as pl. of Mr.
Met., Metropolitan.
metal(l)., metallurgy.
metaph., metaphorical; metaphysical, metaphysics.
meteor., meteorology.
Meth(od)., Methodist.
meton., metonymy.
Met. R., Metropolitan Railway.
m^f, Ital. *mezzo forte* (mus.), moderately loud.
M.F.B., Metropolitan Fire Brigade (obs., now L.C.C.).
mfd., manufactured.
mfg., manufacturing.
M.F.H., Master of Fox Hounds.
M.F.N., Most Favoured Nation.
M.Fr., Middle French.
m.g., machine-gun.
mg., milligramme.
M.G.C., Machine-Gun Corps.
M.G.G.S., Major-General, General Staff.
Mgr., Ital. *Monsignor*, of Papal dignitaries.

M.H.A., Member of House of Assembly.
M.H.G., Middle High German.
M.H.K., Member of the House of Keys (Isle of Man).
mho, unit of conductivity, reciprocal of the ohm (elect.).
M.H.R., Member of the House of Representatives.
M.Hy., Master of Hygiene.
M.I., Mounted Infantry.
Mic., Micah (O.T.).
M.I.C.E., Member of the Institution of Civil Engineers.
Mich., Michaelmas; Michigan (U.S.A.).
M.I.E.E., Member of the Institution of Electrical Engineers.
M.I.J., Member of the Institute of Journalists.
mil., military; militia.
Mil. Att., Military Attaché.
M.I.Mar.E., Member of the Institute of Marine Engineers.
M.I.M.E., Member of the Institution of Mechanical Engineers; Member of the Institution of Mining Engineers.
M.I.Mech.E., Member of the Institution of Mechanical Engineers.
M.I.Min.E., Member of the Institution of Mining Engineers.
M.I.M.M., Member of the Institution of Mining and Metallurgy.
Min., Minister; Ministry.
min., mineralogy; mining; minute.
M.I.N.A., Member of the Institution of Naval Architects.
mineral., mineralogy.
Minn., Minnesota (U.S.A.).
Min. Plen., Minister Plenipotentiary.
M.Inst.C.E., Member of the Institution of Civil Engineers.
M.Inst.E.E., Member of the Institution of Electrical Engineers.
M.Inst.Mar.E., Member of the Institute of Marine Engineers.
M.Inst.Mech.E., Member of the Institution of Mechanical Engineers.
M.Inst.Met., Member of the Institute of Metals.
M.Inst.Min.E., Member of the Institution of Mining Engineers.
M.Inst.M.M., Member of the Institution of Mining and Metallurgy.
misc., miscellaneous; miscellany.
Miss., Mississippi (U.S.A.).
M.J.I., Member of the Institute of Journalists; now commonly M.I.J.
M.J.S., Member of the Japan Society.
mk., mark (coin).
mkt., market.
ml., millilitre.
M.L.A., Member of the Legislative Assembly; Modern Language Association.
M.L.C., Member of the Legislative Council.
M.L.G., Middle Low German.
Mlle., Fr. *Mademoiselle*.
M.L.S.B., Member of the London School Board (obs.).
M.M., Master Mason; Military Medal.
MM., Majesties; Fr. *Messieurs*.
mm., millimetre.
Mme., Fr. *Madame*.
Mn, manganese (chem.).
M.O., Medical Officer; Money Order.
Mo, molybdenum (chem.).
Mo., Missouri (U.S.A.).
mo., month.
Mod., Modern.
Mods., Moderations (Oxford University).
M.O.H., Master of Otter Hounds; Medical Officer of Health; Ministry of Health.
mol. wt., molecular weight.
Mon., Monday; Monmouthshire.
Mons., Fr. *Monsieur*.
Mont., Montana (U.S.A.).
M.O.O., Money Order Office.
morph(ol)., morphology.
M.P., Member of Parliament; Metropolitan Police; Military Police.
m.p., melting-point.

mp, Ital. *mezzo piano* (mus.), moderately soft.
M.Ph., Master of Philosophy (U.S.A.).
m.p.h., miles per hour.
M.P.S., Member of the Pharmaceutical Society; do. of the Philological Society; do. of the Physical Society.
M.R., Master of the Rolls; Midland Railway, now part of L.M.S.(R.); Municipal Reform Party, L.C.C.
Mr., Mister.
M.R.A.S., Member of the Royal Academy of Science; Member of the Royal Asiatic Society.
M.R.C.C., Member of the Royal College of Chemistry.
M.R.C.P., Member of the Royal College of Physicians; **M.R.C.P.E.**, do. of Edinburgh; **M.R.C.P.I.**, do. of Ireland.
M.R.C.S., Member of the Royal College of Surgeons; **M.R.C.S.E.**, do. of Edinburgh; **M.R.C.S.I.**, do. of Ireland.
M.R.C.V.S., Member of the Royal College of Veterinary Surgeons.
M.R.G.S., Member of the Royal Geographical Society.
M.R.I., Member of the Royal Institution.
M.R.I.A., Member of the Royal Irish Academy.
Mrs., Mistress.
M.R.S.L., Member of the Royal Society of Literature.
M.R.U.S.I., Member of the Royal United Service Institution.
M.S., Master in Surgery; Military Secretary.
m.s., month's sight.
MS., manuscript.
M.S.A., Master of Science and Art (U.S.A.); Member of the Society of Arts.
M.S.C., Madras Staff Corps; Medical Staff Corps.
M.Sc., Master of Science.
M.S.H., Master of Stag Hounds.
M.S.I., Member of the Sanitary Institute; Member of the Surveyors' Institution.
M.S.L., mean sea-level.
MSS., manuscripts.
M.T., mechanical transport.
Mt., mount(ain).
M'ter, Manchester.
mth., month.
Mt. Rev., Most Reverend.
mus., music; museum.
Mus.B(ac)., Bachelor of Music.
Mus.D(oc)., Doctor of Music.
Mus.M., Master of Music.
M.V., motor vessel.
M.V.O., Member of the Royal Victorian Order.
M.W., Most Worshipful; Most Worthy.
M.W.B., Metropolitan Water Board.
M.W.G.M., Most Worshipful (Worthy) Grand Master (freemasonry).
Mx., Middlesex.
myth(ol)., mythological; mythology.

N, nitrogen (chem.).
N., Nationalist; New; north.
n., neuter; nominative; noon; noun.
N.A., Nautical Almanac; North America(n).
Na, Lat. *natrium*, sodium (chem.).
n/a, no account (on cheques).
Nah., Nahum (O.T.).
N.A.S., National Academy of Science, U.S.A.
Nat., National; Nationalist; Natal.
nat. hist., natural history.
Nat. Ord., Natural Order.
nat. phil., natural philosophy.
nat. sc., natural science.
naut., nautical.
nav., naval; navigating; navigation; navy.
N.B., New Brunswick; North Britain; North British; Lat. *nota bene*, note well.
n.b., no ball (cricket).
Nb, niobium (chem.).
N.B.A., North British Academy.
N.B.R., North British Railway, now part of L.N.E.(R.).
N.C., North Carolina (U.S.A.).
n.c., nitro-cellulose.

N.C.C.V.D., National Council for Combating Venereal Diseases.
N.C.O., non-commissioned officer.
N.C.U., National Cyclists' Union.
n.d., no date, not dated (on cheques &c.).
N. Dak., North Dakota (U.S.A.).
N.D.L., *Norddeutscher Lloyd* (German steamship company).
N.E., New England; no effects (banking, on cheque); north-east; north-eastern (London postal district).
Ne, neon (chem.).
Neb(r)., Nebraska (U.S.A.).
N.E.D., New English Dictionary; see **O.E.D.**
neg., negative.
Neh., Nehemiah (O.T.).
nem. con., Lat. *nemine contradicente*, no one contradicting.
nem. dis., Lat. *nemine dissentiente*, nobody dissenting.
N.E.R., North-Eastern Railway, now part of L.N.E.(R.).
Neth., Netherlands.
neut., neuter; neutral.
Nev., Nevada (U.S.A.).
N.F., Newfoundland; Norman French.
Nfd., Nfld., Newfoundland.
N.H., New Hampshire (U.S.A.).
N. Heb., New Hebrides.
n.h.p., nominal horse-power.
N.H.R.U., National Home Reading Union.
N.H.R(ules), National Hunt Rules.
N.I., Native Infantry; Northern Ireland.
Ni, nickel (chem.).
N.I.D., Naval Intelligence Department.
ni. pr., Lat. *nisi prius* (law).
N.J., New Jersey (U.S.A.).
N.L., National Liberal; Navy League.
N.L.C., National Liberal Club.
N.L.F., National Liberal Federation.
N.L.I., National Lifeboat Institution.
n.m., nautical mile(s).
N. Mex., New Mexico (U.S.A.).
N.N.E., north-north-east.
N.N.W., north-north-west.
N.O., Natural Order (bot. and zool.); New Orleans (U.S.A.).
n.o., not out (cricket).
No., *numero*, number.
N.O.D., Naval Ordnance Department.
nol. pros., Lat. *nolle prosequi* (law).
nom(in)., nominative; nominal.
Non-Coll., Non-Collegiate.
non. com., non-commissioned (officer).
Noncon., Nonconformist.
non obst., Lat. *non obstante*, notwithstanding.
non pros., Lat. *non prosequitur*, he does not prosecute.
non seq., Lat. *non sequitur*, it does not follow.
n.o.p., not otherwise provided.
Norm., Norman.
Northants, Northamptonshire.
Northumb., Northumberland.
Norvic., Norwich, in signature of Bishop.
Norw., Norway; Norwegian.
Nos., numbers.
Notts, Nottinghamshire.
Nov., November.
N.P., Notary Public.
n.p., new paragraph.
N.P.D., North Polar distance.
N.P.L., National Physical Laboratory.
N.R., North Riding (Yorkshire).
nr., near.
N.R.A., National Rifle Association.
N.S., New Style, of Gregorian Calendar; Nova Scotia; Lat. *non satis*, not sufficient (funds) on cheques, do. (in excellence) on examination papers &c.
N.S.A., National Skating Association.
N.S.I.C., *Noster Salvator Jesus Christus* (Our Saviour Jesus Christ).
N.S.L., National Service League; National Sunday League.
N.S.P.C.C., National Society for Prevention of Cruelty to Children.
N.S.Trip., Natural Science Tripos (Cambridge University).
N.S.W., New South Wales (Australia).

N.T., New Testament; Northern Territory (Australia).
Nthn., northern.
N.U., Northern Union (Rugby football).
n.u., name unknown.
N.U.J., National Union of Journalists.
Num., Numbers (O.T.).
num., numerals; number.
numis., numismatics.
N.U.R., National Union of Railwaymen.
N.U.S.E.C., National Union of Societies for Equal Citizenship.
N.U.T., National Union of Teachers.
N.U.W.S.S., National Union of Women's Suffrage Societies.
N.U.W.T., National Union of Women Teachers.
N.V., New Version.
N.V.M., Nativity of the Virgin Mary.
N.W., north-west; north-western (London postal district).
N.W.M.P., North-West Mounted Police (Canada), now R.C.M.P.
N.W.P(rov)., North-West Provinces (India).
N.W.T., North-Western Territories (Canada).
N.Y., New York (state, U.S.A.).
N.Y.C., New York City (U.S.A.).
N.Y.K., Jap. *Nippon Yusen Kaisha*, Japan Mail Steamship Company.
N.Z., New Zealand.

O, oxygen (chem.).
O., Ohio (U.S.A.); Old.
o., over(s) (cricket).
o/a, on account of.
O.B., outside broadcast.
ob., Lat. *obiit*, (he) died.
Obad., Obadiah (O.T.).
obb., obbligato (mus.).
obdt., obedient.
O.B.E., Officer of the British Empire.
obj., object; objection; objective.
obs., observation; obsolete.
obsol(esc)., obsolescent.
ob.s.p., Lat. *obiit sine prole*, died without issue.
obstet., obstetrics.
O.C., Officer Commanding; Old Catholic.
o'c., o'clock.
Oct., October.
oct., octavo.
O.D., Old Dutch; Ordnance Data.
O. Dan., Old Danish.
O.E., Old English; Old Etonian.
O.E.D., Oxford English Dictionary.
O.F., Odd Fellows; Old French.
off., offered; office; official; officinal.
offg., officiating.
offic., official.
O.F.M., Order of Friars Minor.
O. Fr., Old French.
O. Fris., Old Frisian.
O.F.S., Orange Free State.
O.H.B.M.S., On His (Her) Britannic Majesty's Service.
O.H.G., Old High German.
O.H.L., Oxford Higher Local (examinations).
O.H.M.S., On His (Her) Majesty's Service.
O. Ir., Old Irish.
O.K., All Correct (orl k'rect).
Okla., Oklahoma (U.S.A.).
O.L., Officer of the Order of Leopold, Belgium.
Ol., Olympiad.
O.L.G., Old Low German.
Olym., Olympiad.
O.M., Order of Merit.
O.M.I., Oblate of Mary Immaculate.
O.N., Old Norse.
onomat., onomatopoeia.
Ont., Ontario.
O.P., Old Playgoers (club); Old Prices (theatr. hist.); opposite prompt (side, in theatre); Order of Preachers; out of print (of books).
o.p., over proof (spirits).
op., Lat., *opus*, a work.
op. cit., Lat. *opere citato*, in the work cited.
o. pip., (signallers' slang) observation post.
o.p.n., Lat. *ora pro nobis*, pray for us.
opp., opposes; opposite.

opt., Lat. *optimus*, best, *optime* (adv.); optative; optics; optical; optional.
O.R., Official Receiver; Official Referee.
Or., Orient(al).
orat., oratorical; oratory.
O.R.C., Orange River Colony (now O.F.S.); Order of the Red Cross.
ord., ordained; order; ordinary; ordnance.
Ore(g)., Oregon (U.S.A.).
orig., original(ly).
ornith., ornithology.
ors., others.
Os, osmium (chem.).
O.S., Old Saxon; Old Style (Julian Calendar); Order of Servites; ordinary seaman; Ordnance Survey.
o.s., only son.
O.S.A., Order of St. Augustine.
O.S.B., Order of St. Benedict.
O.S.D., Order of St. Dominic.
O.S.F., Order of St. Francis.
O. Slav., Old Slavonic.
O.S.N.C., Orient Steam Navigation Company.
o.s.p., Lat. *obiit sine prole*, died without issue.
O. Swed., Old Swedish.
O.T., Old Testament.
O.T.C., Officers' Training Corps.
O.U.A.C., Oxford University Athletic Club.
O.U.A.F.C., Oxford University Association Football Club.
O.U.B.C., Oxford University Boat Club.
O.U.C.C., Oxford University Cricket Club.
O.U.D.S., Oxford University Dramatic Society.
O.U.G.C., Oxford University Golf Club.
O.U.H.C., Oxford University Hockey Club.
O.U.R.F.C., Oxford University Rugby Football Club.
Oxon., Oxfordshire; Oxford University; Oxford, in signature of Bishop.
oz., ounce(s).

P, phosphorus (chem.).
P., Pawn (chess); Progressive (party, L.C.C.); President.
p., page; participle; past; perch; pint; population.
p, Ital. *piano*, soft (mus.).
Pa., Pennsylvania (U.S.A.).
P.A., Press Association.
p.a., per annum.
paint., painting.
Pal., Palestine.
pal., palaeography; palaeontology.
palaeog., palaeography.
palaeont., palaeontology.
P. & O., Peninsular and Oriental (steamship line).
par., paragraph; parallel; parenthesis; parish.
parl., parliament; parliamentary.
pars., paragraphs.
part. participle; particular.
P.A.S.I., Professional Associate of the Surveyors' Institution.
pass., passive.
P.A.T.A., Proprietary Articles Trade Association.
path(ol)., pathology.
Pat. Off., Patent Office.
Paym., Paymaster.
Paym.-Gen., Paymaster-General.
payt., payment.
P.B., Lat. *Pharmacopoeia Britannica*, British Pharmacopoeia; Plymouth Brother, Brethren; Prayer Book; Primitive Baptist(s).
Pb, Lat. *plumbum*, lead (chem.).
P.C., Privy Council(lor); Police Constable; Perpetual Curate.
p.c., Lat. *per centum*, by the hundred; post card.
P.C.R.C., Poor Clergy Relief Corporation.
P.C.S., Principal Clerk of Session.
P.D., potential difference.
Pd, palladium (chem.).
pd., paid.
P.D.A.D., Probate, Divorce, and Admiralty Division.

pdr., pounder (of gun, fish &c.).
P.E., Protestant Episcopal; Presiding Elder.
ped., pedal (mus.); pedestrian.
P.E.F., Palestine Exploration Fund.
P.E.I., Prince Edward Island.
pen(in)., peninsula.
Penn., Pennsylvania (U.S.A.).
Pent., Pentateuch.
per an., Lat. *per annum*, per year, yearly.
per cent, Lat. *per centum*, per hundred.
perf., perfect; perforated (stamps).
perh., perhaps.
per pro(c)., Lat. *per procurationem*, by proxy, as agent &c.
Pers., Persia; Persian.
pers., person.
Peruv., Peruvian.
Pet., Peter (N.T.).
Petriburg., Peterborough, in signature of Bishop.
petrol., petrology.
P.F., Procurator Fiscal.
pf, Ital. *piano-forte*, soft, then loud (mus.).
pfd., preferred.
P.G., paying guest.
P.G.A., Professional Golfers' Association.
P.G.D., Past Grand Deacon (freemasonry).
P.G.M., Past Grand Master (freemasonry).
phar(m)., pharmaceutical; pharmacist; pharmacology; pharmacy.
Ph.B., Bachelor of Philosophy.
Ph.D., Doctor of Philosophy.
Phil., Philippians (N.T.).
phil., philosophy; philology.
Philem., Philemon (N.T.).
philol., philology.
phil(os)., philosophy; philosophical.
phon(et)., phonetics.
phonog., phonography.
phot(og)., photography.
Phr., phrase.
phren., phrenology.
phys., physics; physical; physician; physicist; physiology.
physiol., physiology.
pinx., Lat. *pinxit*, he (she) painted (it).
pk., peck.
P.L., Primrose League; Poet Laureate; Lat. *Pharmacopoeia Londinensis*, London Pharmacopoeia.
pl., place; plural; plate.
P.L.A., Port of London Authority.
P.L.C., Poor Law Commissioners.
Plen., Plenipotentiary.
P.-L.-M., Paris-Lyon-Mediterranée (railway).
Pl.-N., Place-Name.
plup(f)., pluperfect.
P.M., Past Master (freemasonry); Prime Minister; Police Magistrate; Postmaster; Provost Marshal.
p.m., Lat. *post meridiem*, after noon; Lat. *post mortem*, autopsy (colloq.).
pm., premium.
P.M.G., Postmaster-General; Paymaster-General.
P.M.O., Principal Medical Officer.
p.n., promissory note.
pnxt., Lat. *pinxit*, he (she) painted (it).
P.O., Petty Officer (nav.); Postal Order; Post Office.
p.o.d., pay on delivery.
poet., poetry; poetical.
Pol., Poland; Polish.
pol., political.
pol. econ., political economy.
polit., political; politics.
P.O.O., Post Office Order.
P.O.P., (photog.) printing out paper.
pop., popular; population.
Port., Portugal; Portuguese.
pos., position; positive.
P.O.S.B., Post Office Savings Bank.
posit., position; positive.
poss(ess)., possessive.
P.P., Parish Priest (R.C.); past participle; Lat. *Pastor Pastorum*, Shepherd of the Shepherds, as title of the Pope; Past President; Lat. *Pater patriae*, father of his country.

p.p., per pro(c).
pp., pages.
pp, Ital. *pianissimo*, very soft (mus.).
P.P.C., Fr., *pour prendre congé*, to take leave.
p.p.i., policy proof of interest (insurance).
ppp, Ital. *pianississimo*, as softly as possible (mus.).
P.P.S., additional postscript.
P.R., Prize Ring (obs.); Lat. *Populus Romanus*, the Roman people; Proportional Representation.
Pr., Priest; Primitive; Prince; Provençal.
pr., pair; per; present; price; printer; pronoun.
P.R.A., President of the Royal Academy.
P.R.B., Pre-Raphaelite Brotherhood.
P.R.C., Lat. *post Romam conditam*, after the foundation of Rome.
P.R.C.A., President of the Royal Cambrian Academy.
Preb., Prebendary; prebend.
prec., preceding.
pred., predicate, predicatively.
Pref., Preface; Preference; preferred (stock and shares).
pref., prefix.
prelim., preliminary (examination).
prem., premium.
prep., preparation; preparatory (school &c.); preposition.
Pres., President.
pres., present; presumptive.
Presb., Presbyter; Presbyterian.
Pres. Part., present participle.
pret., preterite.
prev., previously.
Pri., Private (mil.).
Prim., Primary; Primate; Primitive.
Prin., Principal.
print., printer; printing.
priv., private; privative.
prem., premium.
P.R.H.A., President of the Royal Hibernian Academy.
pro., professional (cricketer, footballer &c.).
Prob., Probate (Division and Law Reports).
prob., probably.
Proc., Proceedings; Proctor.
Prof., Professor.
Prom., promenade (concert); promontory.
pron., pronominal; pronoun; pronounced; pronunciation.
prop., properly; property; proprietary; proposition.
propr., proprietary; proprietor.
pros., prosody.
Prot., Protestant.
pro tem., Lat. *pro tempore*, for the time being.
Prov., Provençal; Proverbs (O.T.); Province; Provost.
Provenç., Provençal.
Prov. G.M., Provincial Grand Master (freemasonry).
provinc., provincial.
prox., Lat. *proximo*, next month.
prox. acc., Lat. *proxime accessit*, he came next, as in examination for prize &c.
P.R.S., President of the Royal Society.
prs., pairs.
P.R.S.A., President of the Royal Scottish Academy.
P.R.S.E., President of the Royal Society of Edinburgh.
Prus(s)., Prussia; Prussian.
P.S., Permanent Secretary; Police Sergeant; Lat. *post scriptum*, postscript; Privy Seal; prompt side (in theatre).
p.s., (mil.) passed School (of Instruction).
Ps., Psalms (O.T.).
P.S.A., Pleasant Sunday Afternoons (movement).
p.s.a., Graduate of the Royal Air Force Staff College.
p.s.c., Graduate of the Military (or Naval) Staff College.
pseud., pseudonym, pseudonymous.
P.S.N.C., Pacific Steam Navigation Co.
psych., psychic, psychical.

psychol., psychological, psychology.
P.T., Physical Training; Pupil Teacher; post town.
Pt, platinum (chem.).
pt., part; payment; pint(s).
Pte., Private.
P.T.O., please turn over.
pub., publisher; published; publication; public; public house.
P.U.C., Lat. *post urbem conditam*, after the foundation of the city (Rome).
punct., punctuation.
P.V., Priest Vicar.
P.W.D., Public Works Department.
pwt., (usually dwt.) pennyweight.
pxt., Lat. *pinxit*, he (she) painted (it).

Q., queen; question; coulomb (elect.).
q., quasi; query; quintal.
Q.A.B., Queen Anne's Bounty.
Q.B., Queen's Bench; Queen's Bays (2nd Dragoon Guards).
Q.B.D., Queen's Bench Division (law reports).
Q.C., Queen's Counsel.
q.d., Lat. *quasi dicat*, as if one should say; Lat. *quasi dictum*, as if said.
q.e., Lat. *quod est*, which is.
Q.E.D., Lat. *quod erat demonstrandum*, which was to be proved (applied to a geometrical or other theorem).
Q.E.F., Lat. *quod erat faciendum*, which was to be done (applied to a geometrical or other problem).
Q.E.I., Lat. *quod erat inveniendum*, which was to be found.
Q.F., quick-firing (gun).
Q.M., Quartermaster.
qm., Lat. *quomodo*, by what means.
Q.M.A.A.C., Queen Mary's Army Auxiliary Corps (W.A.A.C.).
Q.M.G., Quartermaster-General.
Qmr., Quartermaster.
Q.M.S., Quartermaster-Sergeant.
qn., question.
qq.v., Lat. *quae vide*, which (things) see.
qr(s)., quarter(s); quire(s).
Q.S., Quarter Sessions.
Q.T., (slang) on the quiet, in Phr. *on the strict Q.T.*, privately, in secret.
qt., quantity; quart(s).
qto., quarto.
qu., Lat. *quasi*, as if; *quaere*, query.
quad., quadrangle; quadrant; quadrat; quadruple.
quart., quarterly.
Q.U.B., Queen's University, Belfast.
Que., Quebec.
Queensl., Queensland.
quor., quorum.
quot., quotation; quoted.
q.v., Lat. *quod vide*, which see (in references); Lat. *quantum vis*, as much as you wish.
qy., query.

R., Railway; Réaumur (therm.); Republican; Lat. *rex*, king, *regina*, queen, in criminal action at law; right; river; rook or castle (chess); ohm, unit of electrical resistance.
r., right; rod; rood; run(s) (cricket); rupee.
℞, Lat. *recipe* (in medical prescriptions).
₨, rupee(s).
R.A., Royal Academician; Royal Academy; Rear-Admiral; Road Association; Royal Arch (freemasonry); Royal Artillery.
Ra, radium (chem.).
R.A.A., Royal Academy of Arts.
R.A.C., Royal Agricultural College; Royal Automobile Club; Royal Arch Chapter (freemasonry).
rad., Lat. *radix*, root (math.); radical.
R.-Adm., Rear-Admiral.
R.A.E., Royal Air Force Establishment.
R.Ae.S., Royal Aeronautical Society.
R.A.F., Royal Air Force; Royal Aircraft Factory.
R.A.G.C., Royal and Ancient Golf Club, St. Andrews.

rall., Ital. *rallentando*, gradually slower (mus.).
R.A.M., Royal Academy of Music.
R.A.M.C., Royal Army Medical Corps.
R.A.N., Royal Australian Navy.
R.A.O.B., Royal Antediluvian Order of Buffaloes.
R.A.O.C., Royal Army Ordnance Corps.
R.A.P.C., Royal Army Pay Corps.
R.A.S., Royal Agricultural Society; Royal Asiatic Society; Royal Astronomical Society.
R.A.S.C., Royal Army Service Corps.
R.A.V.C., Royal Army Veterinary Corps.
R.B., Rifle Brigade.
Rb, rubidium (chem.).
R.B.A., Royal Society of British Artists.
R.B.S., Royal Society of British Sculptors.
R.C., Red Cross; Roman Catholic; right centre (of stage).
R.C.A., Royal Cambrian Academy, Academician; Royal Canadian Academy; Royal College of Art; Railway Clerks' Association.
R.C.I., Royal Colonial Institute (now R.E.S.).
R.C.M., Royal College of Music (London).
R.C.M.P., Royal Canadian Mounted Police, formerly N.W.M.P.
R.C.N., Royal Canadian Navy.
R.C.O., Royal College of Organists.
R.C.P., Royal College of Physicians.
R.C.S., Royal College of Surgeons; Royal Corps of Signals.
R.C.V.S., Royal College of Veterinary Surgeons.
R.D., Refer to drawer (on cheques); Royal Dragoons; Royal Naval Reserve (and Volunteer Reserve) Decoration; Rural Dean.
Rd., Road.
R.D.C., Royal Defence Corps; Rural District Council.
R.D.S., Royal Drawing Society; Royal Dublin Society.
R.D.Y., Royal Dockyard.
R.E., Royal Engineers; Royal Society of Painter-Etchers and Engravers; Royal Exchange.
Rear-Adm., Rear-Admiral.
Rec., Recorder.
rec., recipe.
recd., received.
recit., recitative (mus.).
recogns., recognizances (law).
rect., rectified.
red., reduced.
redupl., reduplicated.
Ref., Referee; Reformation.
ref., referred; reference; reformed.
Ref. Ch., Reformed Church.
refd., referred.
refl(ex)., reflexive.
Reg., Lat. *regina*, queen; Registrar; Register.
reg., registered; regular(ly).
regd., registered.
Reg.-Gen., Registrar-General.
Reg. Prof., Regius Professor.
Regt., Regent; regiment.
rel., religion; religious; relative.
relig., religion.
Reliq., Lat. *reliquiae*, remains.
Rep., Representative; Republic; Report; Reporter.
repr., reprinted.
Repub., Republic; Republican.
R.E.S., Royal Empire Society (formerly R.C.I.).
res., reserve; resigned; resident; residence.
ret(d)., retired; returned; retained.
R. et I., Lat. *Rex (Regina) et Imperator (Imperatrix)*, King (Queen) and Emperor (Empress), in British Royal signature.
retnr., retainer (law).
Rev., Reverend; Revelation (N.T.).; Review.
rev., revolution (mechan.); reverse(d); revised; revision; revenue.
Rev. Ver., Revised Version (Bible).
R.F., Fr. *République française*, French Republic; Royal Fusiliers.
R.F.A., Royal Field Artillery.
R.F.C., Royal Flying Corps (now R.A.F.).
R.Fus., Royal Fusiliers.
R.G.A., Royal Garrison Artillery.

R.G.G., Royal Grenadier Guards.
R.G.S., Royal Geographical Society.
Rgt., regiment.
R.H., Royal Highlanders; Royal Highness.
Rh, rhodium (chem.).
r.h., right hand.
R.H.A., Royal Horse Artillery; Royal Hibernian Academy, Academician.
rhet., rhetoric; rhetorical.
R.H.G., Royal Horse Guards.
R.Hist.S., Royal Historical Society.
R.H.S., Royal Humane Society; Royal Horticultural Society; Royal Historical Society.
R.I., Rhode Island (U.S.A.); Royal Institute (of Painters in Water Colours); Royal Institution.
R.I.A., Royal Irish Academy.
R.I.B.A., Royal Institute of British Architects.
R.I.C., Royal Irish Constabulary.
R.I.M., Royal Indian Marine.
R.I.P., Lat. *requiescat in pace*, may he (she) rest in peace.
rit(ard)., Ital. *ritardando*, gradually slower (mus.).
R.L.O., Returned Letter Office.
R.L.S., Robert Louis Stevenson.
Rly., Railway.
R.M., Royal Marines; Resident Magistrate (Ireland); Royal Mail.
rm., ream.
R.M.A., Royal Military Academy (Woolwich); Royal Marine Artillery; Royal Military Asylum.
R.M.C., Royal Military College (Sandhurst).
R.Met.S., Royal Meteorological Society.
R.M.L.I., Royal Marine Light Infantry.
R.M.S., Royal Mail Service; Royal Mail Steamer; Royal Microscopical Society; Royal Society of Miniature Painters.
R.M.S.P., Royal Mail Steam Packet (Co.).
R.N., Royal Navy.
R.N.A.F., Royal Naval Air Force (now R.A.F.).
R.N.A.S., Royal Naval Air Service (now R.A.F.).
R.N.A.V., Royal Naval Artillery Volunteers.
R.N.D., Royal Naval Division.
R.N.L.I., Royal National Lifeboat Institution.
R.N.R., Royal Naval Reserve.
R.N.V.R., Royal Naval Volunteer Reserve.
R.O., Receiving Office, Order; Receiving Officer; Relieving Officer; Recruiting Officer; Returning Officer.
Ro., Lat. *recto*, on the right-hand page.
Robt., Robert.
Roffen., Rochester, in signature of Bishop.
R. of O., Reserve of Officers.
R.O.I., Royal Institute of Oil Painters.
Rom., Romans (N.T.); Rome; Roman; Romance (lang.).
rom., roman type.
Rom. Cath., Roman Catholic.
Roy., Royal.
R.P., Royal Society of Portrait Painters.
R.P.D., Regius Professor of Divinity; Lat. *Rerum Politicarum Doctor*, Doctor of Political Science.
r.p.m., revolutions per minute.
R.P.S., Royal Photographic Society.
rpt., report.
R.R., Right Reverend.
Rr., Rear.
R.R.C., (Lady of) the Royal Red Cross.
R.S., Royal Society.
Rs., rupees.
R.S.A., Royal Scottish Academy, Academician; Royal Society of Antiquaries.
R.S.D., Royal Society of Dublin.
R.S.E., Royal Society of Edinburgh.
R.S.F.S.R., Russian Socialist Federal Soviet Republic (Russia proper).
R.S.Fus., Royal Scots Fusiliers.
R.S.L., Royal Society of Literature; Royal Society of London.
R.S.M., Regimental Sergeant-Major; Royal School of Mines; Royal Society of Medicine.

R.S.O., Railway Sub-Office; Railway Sorting Office.
R.S.P.C.A., Royal Society for the Prevention of Cruelty to Animals.
R.S.S., Lat. *Regiae Societatis Socius*, Fellow of the Royal Society.
R.S.V.P., Fr. *répondez s'il vous plaît*, please reply.
R.S.W., Royal Scottish Society of Painters in Water Colours.
R/T, radio-telegraphy.
R.T.C., Royal Tank Corps.
Rt. Hon., Right Honourable.
R.T.O., Railway Transport Officer.
Rt. Rev., Right Reverend.
R.T.S., Religious Tract Society; Royal Toxophilite Society.
R.U., Rugby Union (football).
Ru, ruthenium (chem.).
R.U.I., Royal University of Ireland.
R.U.Rif., Royal Ulster Rifles.
R.U.S.I., Royal United Service Institution.
R.U.S.Mus., Royal United Service Museum.
Russ., Russia; Russian.
R.V., Revised Version; Rifle Volunteers.
R.V.C., Rifle Volunteer Corps.
R.V.O., Royal Victorian Order.
R.W., Right Worshipful, Worthy.
R.W.A., Royal West of England Academy.
R.W.D.G.M., Right Worshipful Deputy Grand Master (freemasonry).
R.W.G.M., Right Worshipful Grand Master.
R.W.G.S., Right Worthy Grand Secretary.
R.W.G.T., Right Worthy Grand Templar; Right Worthy Grand Treasurer.
R.W.G.W., Right Worthy Grand Warden.
R.W.S., Royal Society of Painters in Water Colours.
R.W.S.G.W., Right Worshipful Senior Grand Warden.
Rx, tens of rupees.
Ry., Railway.
R.Y.S., Royal Yacht Squadron.

S, sulphur (chem.).
S., Saint; Signor; Señor; Socialist; soprano; south.
s., second; shilling; singular; son; substantive.
S.A., Salvation Army; South Africa; South America; South Australia.
s.a., Lat. *sine anno*, without date.
S.A.C., Scottish Automobile Club.
S.A.E., Society of Automobile Engineers.
Salop, Shropshire.
Sam., Samuel (O.T.).
S. and M., Sodor and Man, in signature of Bishop.
Sarum., Salisbury, in signature of Bishop.
S.A.S., Lat. *Societatis Antiquariorum Socius*, Fellow of the Society of Antiquaries.
Sask., Saskatchewan.
Sat., Saturday.
S.A.T.B., soprano, alto, tenor, bass.
S.B., simultaneous broadcast.
Sb, Lat. *stibium*, antimony (chem.).
S.C., Lat. *senatus consultum*, decree of the senate; South Carolina (U.S.A.).
s.c., small capital letters.
Sc, scandium (chem.).
sc., scene (play); scruple (weight).
sc., Lat. *scilicet*, namely, being understood; Lat. *sculpsit*, he (she) engraved (it).
Scand., Scandinavian.
S.C.A.P.A. (Scapa), Society for Checking the Abuses of Public Advertising.
s.caps., small capital letters.
Sc.B., Lat. *Scientiae Baccalaureus*, Bachelor of Science.
Sc.D., Lat. *Scientiae Doctor*, Doctor of Science.
sch., scholar; school; schooner.
sched., schedule.
sci., science; scientific.
sci. fa., Lat. *scire facias*, do you cause to know (law).
scil., Lat. *scilicet*, namely, being understood.
S.C.L., Student of Civil Law.
S.C.M., Student Christian Movement.
Scot., Scotland; Scottish.

scr., scruple (weight).
Script., Scripture.
Scrt., Sanskrit.
sculp., sculptor; sculpture.
sculps., Lat. *sculpsit*, he (she) engraved (it).
sculpt., sculptor; sculpture.
S.D., Senior Deacon (freemasonry).
s.d., several dates.
s.d, Lat. *sine die*, without day (appointed), indefinitely.
sd., said.
S. Dak., South Dakota (U.S.A.).
S.D.F., Social Democratic Federation.
S.D.P., Social Democratic Party.
S.E., south-east; south-eastern (London postal district).
Se, selenium (chem.).
S.E. & C.R., South-Eastern and Chatham Railway, now part of S.R.
Sec., Secretary.
sec., second.
Sec. Leg., Secretary of Legation.
S.E.C.R., South-Eastern and Chatham Railway, now part of S.R.
sect., section.
secy., secretary.
sel., selected; selection.
Sem., Seminary; Semitic.
Sen., Senator; Senate; Senior.
Sen. Opt., Senior Optime.
senr., senior.
Sep(t)., September; Septuagint, usually LXX.
seq., *seqq.*, Lat. *sequens*, *sequentia*, the following.
S.E.R., South-Eastern Railway, now part of S.R.
ser., series.
Serb., Serbia; Serbian.
Serg(t)., Sergeant.
Serj(t)., Serjeant.
servt., servant.
S.F., Sinn Fein.
s.f., Lat. *sub finem*, towards the end.
sf, Ital. *sforzando*, with sudden emphasis (mus.).
S.F.A., Scottish Football Association.
sfz, Ital. *sforzando*, with sudden emphasis (music).
S.G., Solicitor-General; specific gravity.
S.G.W., Senior Grand Warden (freemasonry).
S.H., School House.
sh., shilling.
shd., should.
s.h.p., shaft horse-power.
s.h.v., Lat. *sub hac voce*, or *hoc verbo*, under this word.
Si, silicon (chem.).
S.I.C., specific inductive capacity.
sig., signature.
S.I.M., Sergeant Instructor of Musketry.
sim., similar(ly); simile.
sin, sine (trigonometry).
sing., singular; single.
S.J., Society of Jesus (Jesuits).
S.J.C., Supreme Judicial Court (U.S.A.).
Skr(t)., Sanskrit.
S.L., Serjeant-at-Law.
Slav., Slavonic; Slavic.
s.l.p., Lat. *sine legitima prole*, without legitimate offspring.
S.M., Sergeant-Major; short metre; silver medallist (Bisley).
S.M.Lond.Soc., Lat. *Societatis Medicae Londoniensis Socius*, Member of the London Medical Society.
S.M.M., Lat. *Sancta Mater Maria*, Holy Mother Mary.
S.M.O., Senior Medical Officer.
s.m.p., Lat. *sine mascula prole*, without male issue.
S.M.T.O., Senior Mechanical Transport Officer.
Sn, Lat. *stannum*, tin (chem.).
S.O., Staff Officer; Sub-Office; Stationery Office.
s.o., seller's option.
Soc., Society; Socialist.
sociol., sociology; sociological.
sol., solicitor; solution.
Sol.-Gen., Solicitor-General.

Som., Somerset.
Song of Sol., Song of Solomon (O.T.).
sop., soprano.
SOS, wireless code signal for ships &c. in extreme distress.
sost(en)., Ital. *sostenuto*, sustained (mus.).
sov., sovereign.
S.P., small paper (edition); small pica (typography); starting price (betting).
s.p., Lat. *sine prole*, without issue.
Sp., Spain; Spanish.
Span., Spanish.
S.P.C.A., Society for the Prevention of Cruelty to Animals, now R.S.P.C.A.
S.P.C.C., Society for the Prevention of Cruelty to Children, now N.S.P.C.C.
S.P.C.K., Society for the Promotion of Christian Knowledge.
S.P.E., Society for Pure English.
spec., special; specification.
specif., specific(ally).
S.P.G., Society for the Propagation of the Gospel.
sp. gr., specific gravity.
spirit., spiritualism.
S.P.Q.R., Lat. *Senatus Populusque Romanus*, the Senate and People of Rome; small profits and quick returns.
S.P.R., Society for Psychical Research.
s.p.s., Lat. *sine prole superstite*, without surviving issue.
S.P.S.P., St. Peter and St. Paul (papal seal).
spt., seaport.
S.P.V.D., Society for the Prevention of Venereal Diseases.
sq., square.
sq., Lat. *sequens*, the following.
Sqd. Ldr., Squadron Leader (R.A.F.).
sqn., squadron.
sqq., Lat. *sequentia*, the following.
S.R., Southern Railway.
Sr, strontium (chem.).
Sr., Senior; Señor.
S.R.I., Lat. *Sacrum Romanum Imperium*, Holy Roman Empire.
S.R.S., Lat. *Societatis Regiae Socius*, Fellow of the Royal Society.
S.S., screw steamer; Secretary of State; steamship; Straits Settlements; Sunday School.
SS, Saints; (Collar of) Esses; Lat. *Sanctissimus*, Most Holy.
S.S.C., Solicitor of the Supreme Court, Scotland; Lat. *Societas Sanctae Crucis*, Society of the Holy Cross.
SS.D., Lat. *Sanctissimus Dominus*, Most Holy Lord (the Pope).
S.S.E., south-south-east.
S.S.F.A., Soldiers' and Sailors' Families Association.
S.S.J.E., Society of St. John the Evangelist.
S.S.U., Sunday School Union.
S.S.W., south-south-west.
St., Saint; Street; Strait.
st., stone (weight); stumped (cricket); stanza stet.
stacc., staccato (mus.).
Staffs., Staffordshire.
stat., statics; stationary; statistics; statute.
S.T.B., Lat. *Sacrae Theologiae Baccalaureus*, Bachelor of Sacred Theology.
S.T.D., Lat. *Sacrae Theologiae Doctor*, Doctor of Theology.
Ste., Fr. *Sainte*, feminine of Saint.
stereo, stereotype.
ster(l)., sterling.
St. Ex., Stock Exchange.
stg., sterling.
Sthn., southern.
Stip., Stipendiary (magistrate).
S.T.L., Lat. *Sacrae Theologiae Lector*, Reader in Sacred Theology.
S.T.M., Lat. *Sacrae Theologiae Magister*, Master of Sacred Theology.
stn., station.
S'ton, Southampton.
S.T.P., Lat. *Sacrae Theologiae Professor*, Professor of Sacred Theology.
str., steamer; stroke oar.

S.T.S., Scottish Text Society.
sub., subaltern; subject; submarine boat; subscription; substitute; suburb.
subj., subject; subjective; subjectively; subjunctive.
subst., substantive; substitute.
suc(c)., succeeded; successor.
suff., sufficient; suffix.
Suff(r)., Suffragan.
sug(g)., suggested; suggestion.
Sun., Sunday.
sup., superior; supreme; supplement.
sup., Lat. *supra*, above.
super., superintendent; supernumerary.
superl., superlative.
supp(l)., supplement; supplementary.
supr., supreme.
supt., superintendent.
surg., surgeon; surgery; surgical.
Surg.-Gen., Surgeon-General.
Surr., Surrogate.
surv., surveying; surveyor; surviving.
Surv.-Gen., Surveyor-General.
sus. per. col(l)., Lat. *suspensio per collum*, hanging by the neck (as capital punishment).
S.V., Lat. *Sancta Virgo*, Holy Virgin; Lat. *Sanctitas Vestra*, Your Holiness.
s.v., Lat. *sub voce*, under the word, heading &c.
S.W., Senior Warden (freemasonry); south-west; south-western (London postal district).
Sw., Swed., Sweden; Swedish.
S.W.G., standard wire gauge.
Swit., Switzerland.
S.Y., steam yacht.
syll., syllable.
sym., symbol; symphony.
syn., synonym; synonymous.
syst., system.

T., tenor; Turkish, in £T.
t., taken (betting); tempo (mus.); ton.
t., Lat. *tempore*, in the time of.
T.A., telegraphic address; Territorial Army.
Ta, tantalum (chem.).
tal. qual., Lat. *talis qualis*, just as they come.
tan., tangent (math.).
t. and o., taken and offered (betting).
tar-mac., tar-macadam.
Tasm., Tasmania.
Tb, terbium (chem.).
T.B., torpedo boat; tuberculosis.
T.B.D., torpedo boat destroyer.
T.C., Tank Corps; temporary constable; Town Councillor.
T.C.D., Trinity College, Dublin.
T.C.F., Touring Club de France.
T.D., Telegraph, Telephone, Department; Territorial Officers' Decoration.
Te, tellurium (chem.).
tech(n)., technical(ly); technology.
technol., technology.
t.e.g., top edges gilt.
tel., telegram; telegraph; telephone.
teleg., telegram; telegraph; telegraphy.
teleph., telephone; telephony.
telg., telegram.
temp., temperature; temporary.
temp., Lat. *tempore*, in the time of.
ten., tenor.
ten., Ital. *tenuto* (mus.), held, sustained.
Tenn., Tennessee (U.S.A.).
term., termination; terminology.
Ter(r)., Terrace; Territory.
Test., Testament; testamentary; testator.
Teut., Teutonic.
Tex., Texas (U.S.A.).
text. rec., Lat. *textus receptus*, the received, accepted text.
T.F., Territorial Force.
Th, thorium (chem.).
Th., Thomas.
theat(r)., theatre; theatrical.
theol., theological; theology.
theor., theorem.
theos., theosophy.
therap., therapeutics.
therm., thermometer.
Thess., Thessalonians (N.T.).

Tho(s)., Thomas.
Thurs., Thursday.
T.H.W.M., Trinity high-water mark.
Ti, titanium (chem.).
T.I.H., Their Imperial Highnesses.
Tim., Timothy (N.T.).
tinct., tincture.
Tit., Titus (N.T.).
tit., title.
Tl, thallium (chem.).
T.M., trench mortar.
T.M.O., telegraph money order.
tn., ton.
T.N.T., trinitrotoluene (high explosive).
T.O., Telegraph, Telephone, Office; Transport Officer; turn over.
Tob., Tobit (O.T., Apoc.).
Toc H., Talbot House.
tonn., tonnage.
topog., topographical; topography.
tp., township; troop.
tpr., trooper.
Tr., Treasurer; Trustee.
tr., transactions; translate; translator; transport; transpose.
trans., transactions; transitive; translation; transport.
transf., transference; transferred.
transl., translated; translation.
T.R.C., Thames Rowing Club; tithe rent charge.
Treas., Treasurer; Treasury.
T.R.H., Their Royal Highnesses.
trig., trigonometry.
trop., tropic(s); tropical.
Trs., trustees.
trs., transpose.
Truron., Truro, in signature of Bishop.
T.S.H., Their Serene Highnesses.
T.S.O., Town Sub-Office.
T.T., torpedo tubes.
T.U., Trades Union.
T.U.C., Trades Union Congress; Trades Union Council.
Tues., Tuesday.
Turk., Turkey; Turkish.
2LO, London (broadcasting).
T.W.U., Transport Workers' Union.
T.Y.C., Thames Yacht Club.
typ(og)., typographical; typography.

U, uranium (chem.).
U., Unionist.
u., uncle.
U.C., Upper Canada.
u.c., upper case (printing).
U.C.L., University College, London.
U.D.C., Union of Democratic Control; Urban District Council.
U.F.(C.), United Free (Church of Scotland).
U.G.S.S.S., Union of Girls' Schools for Social Service.
u.i., Lat. *ut infra*, as below.
U.J.D., Lat. *Utriusque Juris Doctor*, Doctor of both (Civil and Canon) Laws.
U.K., United Kingdom.
U.K.A., United Kingdom Alliance.
ult., Lat. *ultimo*, in the last preceding month.
U.M.F.C., United Methodist Free Churches.
unabr., unabridged.
Unit., Unitarian.
univ., university; universal(ly).
unm., unmarried.
U.P., United Presbyterian (Church).
u.p., under proof.
up., upper.
U.P.C., United Presbyterian Church.
U.S., United Services; United States.
u.s., Lat. *ut supra*, as above.
U.S.A., United States of America; United States Army.
U.S.M., United States Mail; United States Marine.
U.S.M.A., United States Military Academy.
U.S.N., United States Navy.
U.S.N.A., United States Naval Academy.
U.S.P., United States Pharmacopoeia.
U.S.S., United States Senate; United States ship or steamer.

U.S.S.C., United States Supreme Court.
U.S.S.R., Union of Socialist Soviet Republics (Russia).
usu., usually.
U.S.V., United States Volunteers.
Ut., Utah (U.S.A.).
ut dict., Lat. *ut dictum*, as said.
ut inf., Lat. *ut infra*, as below.
ut sup., Lat. *ut supra*, as above.

V, Roman numeral, 5; vanadium (chem.).
V., volt (elect.).
v., verb; verse; versus.
v., Lat. *vice*, in the place of; Lat. *vide*, see; Ital. *voce*, voice.
V.A., Victoria and Albert (Order); Vicar Apostolic; Vice-Admiral; Volunteer Artillery.
Va., Virginia (U.S.A.).
v.a., Lat. *vixit annos*, lived (so many) years.
V.A.D., Voluntary Aid Detachment (nursing service, Territorial Force).
V.-Adm., Vice-Admiral.
val., value.
V. and M., Virgin and Martyr.
var., variant; variation; variety.
var. lect., Lat. *varia lectio*, variant reading (of MS. &c.).
Vat., Vatican.
vb., verb.
vbl., verbal.
V.C., Vice-Chancellor; Vice-Chairman; Vice-Consul; Victoria Cross.
V.D., Volunteer (Officers') Decoration; venereal disease.
v.d., various dates.
V.D.H., valvular disease of the heart.
Ven., Venerable.
verb. (sat) sap., Lat. *verbum sat sapienti*, a word is enough to the wise.
Vert., Vertebrata.
vet, veterinary surgeon.
veter., veterinary.
v.f., very fair.
V.G., Vicar-General.
v.g., very good.
v.i., verb intransitive.
Vic., Victoria (queen).
Vice-Adm., Vice-Admiral.
Vice-Pres., Vice-President.
Vict., Victoria (Australia).
vid., Lat. *vide*, see.
Vigorn., see **Wigorn.**
vil., village.
Vis(ct)., Viscount.
viz., Lat. *videlicet*, namely.
v.l., Lat. *varia lectio*, variant reading (of MS. &c.).
v/m, volts per metre.
V.O., (Royal) Victorian Order.
Vo., Lat. *verso*, on the left-hand page.
voc., vocative.
vocab., vocabulary.
Vol., Volunteer; Volume.
V.P., Vice-President.
V.R.C., Volunteer Rifle Corps.
V.R. (et I.), *Victoria Regina (et Imperatrix)*, Victoria, Queen (and Empress).
V.Rev., Very Reverend.
V.S., veterinary surgeon.
v.s., Lat. *vide supra*, see above; Ital. *volti subito* (mus.), turn over quickly.
vs., Lat. *versus*, against.
V.S.C., Volunteer Staff Corps.
v.t., verb transitive.
Vt., Vermont (U.S.A.).
V.T.C., Volunteer Training Corps.
Vulg., Vulgate.
vulg., vulgar(ly).
vv., verses.
vv.ll., Lat. *variae lectiones*, variant readings (of MS. &c.).
vy., very.

W, (chem.) tungsten (wolfram).
W., west; Welsh; western (London postal district).
w., wicket, wide (cricket); with; wife.
W.A., Western Australia; West Africa.

W.A.A.C., Women's Army Auxiliary Corps (Q.M.A.A.C.).
w.a.f., with all faults.
W.A.F.F., West African Frontier Force.
W.Afr.R., West African Regiment.
War., Warwickshire.
Wash., Washington (U.S.A.).
W. Aust., Western Australia.
W.B., Water Board; way bill.
W.C., west central (London postal district); Wesleyan Chapel.
w.c., water closet; without charge.
W.D., War Department; Works Department.
wd., would.
W.E.A., Workers' Educational Association.
Wed., Wednesday.
w.f., wrong fount (printing).
W.F.L., Women's Freedom League.
W. Gmc., West Germanic.
wh., which.
W'hampton, Wolverhampton.
whf., wharf.
W.I., West Indies; West India; West Indian.
Wigorn., Worcester, in signature of Bishop.
Wilts., Wiltshire.
Winton., Winchester, in signature of Bishop.
W.I.R., West India Regiment.
Wis(c)., Wisconsin (U.S.A.).
Wisd., Wisdom (of Solomon) (O.T., Apoc.).
wk., week; weak.
W/L, wave length.
Wm., William.
W.M.S., Wesleyan Missionary Society.
W.N.L.F., Women's National Liberal Federation.
W.N.W., west-north-west.
W.O., War Office; warrant officer.
Wor., Worshipful.
Worcs., Worcestershire.
W.P., weather permitting.
W.P.B., waste-paper basket.
W.R., West Riding, Yorkshire.
W.R.A.F., Women's Royal Air Force.
W.R.N.S., Women's Royal Naval Service.
W.S., West Saxon; Writer to the Signet.
W.S.P.U., Women's Social and Political Union.
W.S.W., west-south-west.
W.T., wireless telegraphy, telephony.
wt., weight.
W.U.S.L., Women's United Service League.
W. Va., West Virginia (U.S.A.).
Wyo., Wyoming (U.S.A.).

X, Roman numeral, 10.
x-cp., ex coupon.
xd, x-d., x-div., ex dividend.
Xe, xenon (chem.).
x-i., ex interest.
Xmas, Christmas.
x-n., ex new shares.
Xt(ian)., Christ(ian).
XX, XXX, double-X, triple-X, indicating strength of ales.

Yb, ytterbium (chem.).
yd., yard.
yday., yesterday.
Yeo(m)., Yeomanry.
Y.L.I., Yorkshire Light Infantry.
Y.M.C.A., Young Men's Christian Association.
Yorks., Yorkshire.
Y.P.S.C.E., Young People's Society for Christian Endeavour.
yr., year; your; younger.
Y.R.A., Yacht Racing Association.
yrs., years; yours.
Yt, yttrium (chem.).
Y.W.C.A., Young Women's Christian Association.

Zech., Zechariah (O.T.).
Zeph., Zephaniah (O.T.).
Zn, zinc (chem.).
zool., zoology; zoological.
Zr, zirconium (chem.).
Z.S., Zoological Society.

Appendix
By HUGH BUSS, M.A.

The following entries have, whenever possible, been made to read as continuations of entries that will be found in the body of the Dictionary. The word 'Add:' means 'Add, at the end of the entry in the Dictionary, or of the division of it just mentioned.' The absence of any word 'Add:' in an entry shows that it is not such a continuation but has been newly added.

Two additional abbreviations have been used: Dict.=(in) the body of the Dictionary. Suppl.=(in) this Supplement.

Unless otherwise stated, references are to the body of the Dictionary.

aerobatic, adj. [1. àrobátik; 2. èərəbǽtik]. See **aero-** & **acrobat** & **-ic**. Of, pertaining to, performing, aerobatics.

aerobatics, n., fr. prec. (The performance of) feats of skill or of daring, in piloting aircraft through spectacular motions in the air; stunt flying.

age (I.), n. 2. Add: Phr. *to be* (or *act*) *one's age*, (slang, orig. U.S.), to behave in a reasonable manner, as befits one's years.

aide mémoire, n. [1. ád mǟmwàhr; 2. éd memwâr]. Fr., 'memorandum.' A note sent by a government through its Foreign Office to another Power, stating clearly its attitude on a point at issue.

air (I.), n. 1. c Add: *to be on the air*, (i.) be broadcasted, (ii.) to be broadcasted from time to time.

aircraftman, n. [1. árkrahftman; 2. éərkräftmən]. **aircraft** & **man**. Man in the ranks of the Royal Air Force.

airworthiness, n. [1.árwërdhines; 2.éəwȫðinis] See next word & **-ness**. State, quality, of being airworthy.

airworthy, adj. [1. árwërdhi; 2. éəwȫði]. **air** & **-worthy**. (of aircraft) Fit to undertake a flight; sound in all parts, construction, &c.

allelomorph, n. [1. alélomorf; 2. ælílouməːf]. Gk. *allelōn*, 'of each other', & Gk. *morphé*, 'shape', see **morphology**. (biol.) One of any pair of organisms related, in respect of a particular feature, as dominant to recessive.

all-in, adj. 1. attrib. (of cost, insurance, arbitration, &c.) All-inclusive, including every possible item, contingency or dispute. 2. (colloq.) *All-in wrestling, an all-in contest*, a type of wrestling match in which only very few kinds of foul are recognized. 3. pred. (slang, orig. U.S.) (of persons) Tired out, exhausted.

all-out, adv., fig., prob. from motoring 'with all throttles out'. (slang) Using all one's strength and resources unreservedly: *to go all-out*, strive with all one's might.

altitude, n. 1. b Phr. *grabbing for altitude*, (slang) (i.) trying to climb above an enemy in aerial combat; (ii.) (fig.) becoming furiously angry.

analysis, n. Add: 3. Psycho-analysis (of a person): *under analysis*.

angle (I.), n. Add: 3. (slang, orig. U.S.) *to get, use a new angle on something*, find a new way of thinking about it.

A + B theorem, n. Major C. H. Douglas's contention that, if A denotes every firm's payments to individuals (wages, salaries, dividends) and B denotes its payments to other firms (for raw materials, plant, bank charges, &c.), consumers, while their total incomes=A, must be charged in prices at the rate of A + B, if not more. See **Social Credit**, Suppl.

apneusis, n. [1. apnúsis; 2. æpnjúsis], fr. a- (priv.) & Gk. *pneûsis*, 'a breathing', fr. *pneûsai*, 'to breathe'; see **pneuma**. (med.) Suspension of breathing; apnoea.

Arcos, n. (1. árkos; 2. ákɔs], abbr. fr. *All-Russian Co-operative Society* (U.S.S.R.). Anglo-Russian Trade Delegation.

arrive, vb. intrans. Add: 4. (fr. mod. Fr. *arriver*) To achieve success and recognition.

astronomic(al), adj. Add: 2. (colloq., of figures, &c.) Not unlike the inconceivably large figures used in measuring astronomical distances; astoundingly big, immense.

autarchy, n. [1. áwtarki; 2. ȫtāki], fr. Germ. *autarchie*, fr. Gk. *autárkeia*, 'self-sufficiency' (Gk. *árkein*, 'to suffice'), but perh. influenced by Gk. *autarkhía*, 'absolute power' (Gk. *árkhein*, 'to rule'); see **auto-** & **arch-**. Economic self-sufficiency of a political unit.

authoritarian, b adj. Add: specif., of, pertaining to, a dictatorship; anti-democratic, non-parliamentary & oppressive towards civil liberties.

auto-radio-gram, n. Radio-gramophone fitted with a device for changing records automatically several times.

axe, vb. trans., fr. Phr. *the axe*. (See **axe**, Dict.). (Colloq. & chiefly in P.P.). To dismiss, dispense with, as a measure of drastic economy.

Babbitt, n. [1. bábit; 2. bǽbit], fr. George F. Babbitt, central figure of a novel by Sinclair Lewis. A business man, or the like, typical of the low cultural and ethical standards associated with 20th century commercialism.

baby, n. 1. Add: Phr. *to be left holding the baby* (colloq., fig.) to be left with all the trouble, responsibility, &c., on one's hands; Add: 4. (slang, orig. U.S.) Man's girl friend.

bakelite, n. [1. bákelīt; 2. béikəlait], fr. Baeyer, the inventor. A synthetic resin of the phenol-aldehyde type very widely used instead of wood, pottery, &c.

balletomania, n. [1. báletománia; 2. bǽlitəméiniə]. ballet & -mania. Extravagant enthusiasm for witnessing performances of ballet.

band-pass, adj. (wireless) Constructed on a special principle so that the receiving set will pass a predetermined width of frequencies: *band-pass tuning*.

bang-up, adj. [1. báng úp; 2. bǽŋ áp]. (U.S. slang) Very high class, excellent. Cp. **slap-up**.

bankocracy, n. [1. bangkókrasi; 2. bæŋkókrəsi]. bank & -cracy, 'government'. 1. Dictation or control of state policy by a bank or banks. 2. Bank directors, as dictators or controllers of state policy.

bankster, n. [1. bángkster; 2. bǽŋkstə]. bank & -ster. (Colloq.) Derogatory term for a partisan of bankocracy.

barometer, n. Add: 2. (fig. & gen.) Any readily ascertainable factor that can be consulted as a safe indicator of more elusive fluctuations: *by-elections as a barometer of public opinion*.

barysphere, n. [1. bárisfër; 2. bǽrisfiər]. See **baro-** & **sphere**. (geol.) Internal substance of the earth, enclosed by the lithosphere.

Basic, Basic English, n. & attrib. n. 1. n. The English Language systematically restricted to a vocabulary of 850 words (together with compounds and combinations of these), not counting words that may be considered as technical or of international currency: *Lamb's Stories from Shakespeare in Basic*. 2. attrib. n. Of, or belonging to, rendered in, Basic English: *the Basic Rules of Reason*, principles of logic expounded in Basic English.

bathysphere, n. [1. báthisfër; 2. bǽþisfiə]. See **bathos** & **sphere**. Hollow sphere constructed so that it can be let down to a considerable depth in the sea (and e.g. bring up sample of water).

bawl (I.), vb. trans. 3. Add: c *to bawl (a person) out*, (U.S. slang), to reprove, reprimand him.

beacon (I.), n. 2. Add: b (*Belisha*) *beacon*, a sign, consisting of a yellow globe on a metal post, indicating where pedestrians may safely cross the street.

bean, n. Add: 2. (slang, orig. U.S.) Head: *to bat someone on the bean*, hit him on the head.

beat (I.), vb. trans. Add: 6. *Beat up* (slang, orig. U.S.), to maltreat cruelly, treat with brutal violence.

beauty parlour, n. (colloq.) Shop fitted out for women's hairdressing, massage, &c.

beetle (IV.), vb. intrans., facet. fr. **beetle** (I.). (slang) a To hurry, esp. *to beetle off, beetle along*; b to go, depart.

bell, n. 1. Phrs. Add: *to ring the bell* (slang, orig. U.S.), to be successful, get good results (fig., from a strength-testing mechanism which rings when heavily punched).

bellyache, vb. intrans. [1. béliăk; 2. bélieik]. See **belly**, 2. (Am. slang) to complain, whine.

besbozhnik, n. pl. -niki. [1. besbózhnik; 2. bəsbóžnik], Russ., *bes*, 'without', *bog*, 'god', -nik (suff.). (U.S.S.R.). Member of the League of the Godless, for anti-religious propaganda.

bibful, n. [1. bíbfool; 2. bíbfúl], fr. **bib** (I.) & -ful, 2. Enough to cover a bib. *To slobber a bibful* (of words), (U.S. slang) to talk freely, have much to say; sometimes iron.; cp. **spit** (III.). **B**. 1. b.

big end, n., abbr. of *big end bearing*. (motor-cars) The bearing or joint where the piston rod joins the crank shaft.

bird, n. 3. Phr. Add: *to give someone the bird*, (slang) orig. theatr., give him a rough house, now gen., get rid of, snub him, curtly, rudely; *to get the bird*, be given it.

bit (I.), n. Add: 4. Slang for *piece of flesh*, a girl or woman. See **piece** (I.), 6.

black out, black-out, vb. intrans. & n. 1. vb. (theatr.) To switch off all lights during a performance, purposely leaving the stage in complete darkness. 2. n. a (theatr.) Instance, period, of blacking out; b (transf.) a temporary failure of the electric light anywhere; c (fig.) a temporary loss of memory.

Blackshirt, n. [1. blákshërt; 2. blǽkʃȧt], fr. the black shirt worn as uniform. A member of the Fascist party. See **Fascist**.

Blimp, n. [blímp]. Imitative word. *Colonel Blimp*, figure in cartoons by Low caricaturing an extreme diehard type of outlook.

bloc, n., Fr., 'block'; see next entry.

block (I.), n. Add: 8. Group of countries, political parties, &c., with some common policy.

blood group, n. (med.) All persons having the same type of blood, as recognised for purposes of transfusion; there are four such types and only certain combinations of them are safe.

body-line, adj. (cricket) *body-line bowling*, fast bowling aimed at the body of the batsman with the object of defeating him by intimidation, if he does not previously retire hurt.

boko, n. [1. bókō; 2. bóukou]. (slang) The human head.

boloney, baloney, n. [1. bolóni; 2. bəlóuni]. **a** Insincere talk; **b** nonsensical talk.

bone (I.), n. **1.** Add: *to cut* (costs, &c.) *to the bone*, reduce them to the minimum.

bonehead, n. [1. bónhed; 2. bóunhɛd]. (Am. slang.) **a** a blockhead; **b** fool's mistake.

boob, n. [1. bōōb; 2. būb]. Slang, abbr. of **booby**.

bottled, adj. Add: **2.** (slang) Intoxicated.

bottle-neck, n. Short strip of narrow road through which considerable traffic has to pass.

bounce (I.), B. vb. trans. Add: **3.** (slang. orig. U.S.) To dismiss from a post.

bounce (II.), n. Add: **3.** (slang, orig. U.S.) *The (grand) bounce*, dismissal from a post.

box up, vb. trans. (slang) To bungle and mess up, make chaotic.

box-up, n. (slang). **a** Instance of causing utter confusion by bungling; **b** confusion so caused.

brain trust, n. **a** A group of advisers called in by President Franklin D. Roosevelt; **b** (by extension) any group of 'experts'.

break (II.), n. Add: **6.** (Am. slang) A run of luck (usu. qualified by an adj.): *a bad break*; *a lucky break*. **7.** (Am. slang) A breach of good manners or of social discretion.

bromide, n. Add: **2.** (Am. slang) **a** A dull, utterly conventional and uninventive person; **b** a remark characteristic of such a person; a cliché.

Brownian movement, n. (phys.) Erratic movement imposed on suspended particles by bombardment from molecules of the suspending medium.

Brownshirt, n. [1. brónshërt; 2. bráunʃāt], fr. the brown shirt worn as uniform. A member of the Nazi party. See **Nazi**.

Buchmanism, n. [1. bóokmunizm; 2. búkmənizm], fr. Rev. Frank Buchman, its originator. The so-called 'Oxford Groups', an undenominational Protestant movement of the 1930's, emphasising individual divine guidance and the method of evangelistic 'team-work'.

Buchmanite, n. & adj. [1. bóokmunīt; 2. búkmənait]. prec. & **-ite**. **a** n. An adherent of Buchmanism; **b** adj. of, pertaining to, Buchmanism.

bum, n., adj. & vb. intrans. **1.** n. **a** Buttocks; **b** (Am. slang) vagabond, tramp. **2.** adj. (slang, orig. U.S.) Worthless, rotten. **3.** vb. intrans. (slang) To tramp about, hike.

bumper, n. Add: **2.** Metal projection on the front or back of a motor vehicle to take the first shock of a collision. **3.** (attrib., cp. **1.**) *Bumper book*, book containing little matter, but deceptively large in appearance.

burg, n. [1. bërg; 2. bāg], fr. Germ. *burg*, 'stronghold, &c.', formerly 'walled town'. (Colloq. & facet., orig. U.S.) A town.

burp, vb. intrans. [1. bërp; 2. bāp]. Imitative. (U.S. slang) To belch, eructate.

business, n. **2. b** Phr. Add: *out of business*, bankrupt.

butt (IV.), vb. Add: **B.** intrans. *Butt in*, (colloq.) to intrude, to break in upon proceedings, conversation, &c.

camera man, n. (films) Man responsible for the lighting and, in conjunction with the director, for the angles from which shots are taken.

can (III.), vb. trans. Add: **2.** (fig., Am. slang) To cease, stop, put a stop to (anything).

canned, adj. Add: **b** (slang) intoxicated.

cash, vb. Add: **B.** intrans. Phr. *to cash in*, (colloq., lit. & fig.) realize one's assets, 'make hay while the sun shines'.

cat (I.), n. **1. a** Phr. Add: *the cat's whiskers*, (slang, orig. U.S., with many variants) something quite out of the ordinary, remarkable, excellent, esp. iron., i.e. in person's own estimation.

cat burglar, n. (colloq.) Burglar who enters a building by climbing in, e.g., through a skylight.

cellophane, n. [1. sélofăn; 2. séloufein], fr. *cell(ulose)* & Gk. *phănós*, 'bright', fr. *phan-stem of phaínein*, 'to show'. A glossy, transparent substance made from wood pulp in the form of cellulose xanthate, and used commercially for thin wrappings to resist air and damp. Phr. *wrapped in cellophane*, (colloq.) unapproachable, stand-offish.

cert, n. Slang abbr. of *certainty*, sense 2, Dict.

chamber (I.), n. **4.** Add: **c** the coiled horn enclosed in a gramophone.

change (I.), vb. **B.** intrans. Add: **5.** (in motor driving) *To change up, change down*, change to a higher, lower, gear.

chipper, adj. [1. chíper; 2. tʃípə]. (U.S. slang) Lively, in good form, in good spirits.

chisel (II.), vb. Add: **B.** intrans. *Chisel in*, (colloq.) to intrude, interfere.

choke (II.), n. Add: **2.** Device for closing the air inlet in a petrol engine. **3.** (wireless) Coil for reducing the strength of an electric current by self-induction.

clam, n. Add: **2.** (fig., Am. slang) A silent, uncommunicative person. **3.** vb. intrans. (Am. slang) To be, or become, silent, uncommunicative.

clean (I), adj. **1.** Phr. Add: *come clean*, (gangster slang) make a clean breast of it. Add: **7. a** Free from dishonesty; **b** free from obscenity; cp. **dirty (I. 3.,** Dict.).

clean-up, n. Add: **c** (slang, orig. U.S.) organized action to eradicate crime or corruption in a certain sphere or locality.

cobber, n. [1. kóber; 2. kɔ́bə]. (Australian slang) A chum, pal.

cold-storage, n. **a** Add: also fig.

collective, adj. **2.** *collective (farm)*, see **kolkhos**, Suppl.; *collective security*, (League of Nations) security for nations, obtained not by arming independently but by trusting in the united strength of the League as sufficient to restrain or resist an aggressor.

collectivize, vb. trans. [1. kuléktiviz; 2. kəléktivaiz], fr. prec. & **-ize**. To reorganize on collective lines.

Comintern, n. [1. kómintërn; 2. kɔ́mintān], abbr. for 'Communist International'. Committee elected by the Communist parties of all countries to co-ordinate and direct the activities of those parties.

compensation, n. Add: **3.** (psycho-analysis) Cultivation of some trait or accomplishment as an offset to a feeling of inferiority that may be due to some physical or other disability.

concentration camp, n. Place converted into, improvised as, a prison e.g. for political prisoners or prisoners of war.

condition (II.), vb. trans. **2.** Add: **b** to adopt measures for keeping (e.g., merchandise, air) in a state of freshness; **c** (psychol.) to induce by association of stimuli to behave in a predetermined way in given circumstances; *conditioned reflex*, capacity to act in a familiar way to a new stimulus.

conditioning, n. prec. & **-ing**. Process, effect, of being conditioned (as in prec.).

conk (II.), vb. intrans. Imitative word. (slang) To cease functioning; to become suddenly exhausted and inert; also *conk out*.

-conscious, suff. used to form adjs. expressing persons' full awareness of their connexion with (something): *class-conscious*.

-consciousness, suff. forming ns. from prec.

consumer credit, n. A proposed kind of money credit, non-repayable, to be issued to the public in part claim for their share of the potential output of commodities. See **Social Credit**.

continuity, n. Add: **e** special captions inserted between sections of a film to bridge over and explain, e.g. an imaginary interval of time; also attrib.: *continuity writer, clerk*.

co-op, n. Slang abbr. of (consumers') **co-operative society**.

co-operator, n. [1. kōóperăter; 2. kouópəreitə], **co-operate** & **-or**. One who co-operates; specif., member of a consumers' co-operative society.

core (I.), n. **4.** Add: **b** *the hard core* (esp. of unemployment), irreducible residuum.

corporation, n. **1.** Add: **d** (Fascist Italy) body representing employers and employees of an industry and responsible, under the State, for its direction, &c.

corporative, adj. Add: **b** of, pertaining to, having under it, corporations, as in prec.: *the corporative State*.

crack (II.), n. Add: **4.** (slang, orig. U.S.) A witticism, a sententious, often a sarcastic, remark: *a wise crack*; (cp. **crack (I.) A. 2.**)

crackers, adj. [1. krákerz; 2. krǽkəz]. (slang) Mentally unbalanced; insane, dotty.

cramp (III.), n., vb. trans. **3.** (fig.) Add: Phr. (of persons or things, colloq.) *to cramp one's style*, put one ill at ease.

crash (I.), vb. **A.** intrans. Add: **4.** *Crash in (on)*, (slang) to intrude (on). **B.** trans. (slang) To intrude into (a party, &c.) as a gate-crasher, q.v. Suppl.

crush (II.), n. Add: **3.** Drink made of the juice of crushed fruit; squash; chiefly in compounds: *orange crush*, &c. **4.** (slang) *To have (got) a crush on* (a person or thing), be very fond of.

cut (I.), vb. **C.** *Cut in* (intrans.); Add: specif.; **a** While driving a motor vehicle, to overtake and get in front of another motor vehicle, in circumstances which make it dangerous or inconsiderate to do so; **b** (in ball-room dancing, of a man) to claim another man's partner from him while he is dancing with her.

cut (III.), n. Insert as **7.** (films) An abrupt, instantaneous change from one shot to the next. (Re-number 7 as 8, 8 as 9.)

cutey, cutie, n. [1. kúti; 2. kiúti], fr. **cute** & **-y (III.)**. (U.S. slang) A bright, rather smart young girl.

day, n. **3.** Add: **c** Phr. (slang) *call it a day*, reckon the day's work or main occupation finished, i.e., leave off anything.

dead (I.), adj. **5. a**; Add: Phr. *dead from the neck up*, (slang, orig. U.S.) brainless, devoid of intelligence.

deal (III.), n. **1.** Add: *a raw deal*, (grossly) unfair treatment; cp. **raw (II.)**, Dict. Add: **3. a** *The New Deal*, President Franklin D. Roosevelt's attempted liberal reconstruction of the administrative and economic system in the U.S.A.; **b** (by extension) any similar or comparable attempt at reconstruction.

debunk, vb. trans. [1. dĕbúnk; 2. dĭbánk]. fr. **de-** & **bunk (III)**. (slang) To unmask, to divest of humbug.

decontaminate, vb. trans. [1. dĕkuntáminăt; 2. dĭkəntǽmineit], fr. **de-** & **contaminate**. To rid of, purify from, contamination; specif., to rid of poison gas used in warfare.

deep (I.), adj. **1. a** Phr. Add: *to go (in) off the deep end*, (colloq. & fig.) (i.) to make the plunge; (ii.) to give vent to anger, vituperation.

definitely, adv. Add: **b** (colloq.) yes indeed.

dendrite, n. Add: **2.** (anat.) Branching twig of a nerve cell.

deposit (II.), n. Add: **2.** An overdraft.

depress, vb. trans. **2.** Add: **b** (chiefly P.P. pass.) to deprive of trade and prosperity; *depressed areas*, regions so affected.

dilution, n. **1. b**; Add: specif., the introduction of some semi-skilled workers into a body of skilled workers.

dipper, n. Add: **e** contrivance for dipping and raising the headlights of a motor-car while driving it.

director, n. Add: **c** (films) person having supreme control of the actual production of a film; cp. **producer**, Suppl.; *assistant director*, person responsible for assembling actors at the right time and for all details connected with the floor.

dispersion, n. Add: **3.** (chem.) A system in which one component consists of discrete particles (usually of colloidal dimensions) dispersed in the other component, which is a continuous medium called the vehicle.

dissociated, adj. P.P. of *dissociate*. (psychoanalysis) Suffering from loss of, failure to develop, some normal type(s) of association : *dissociated personality*; cp. **integrated**, Suppl.

dissociation, n. Add: specif., (psychoanalysis) fact, instance, of being dissociated, as in prec.

dissolve (II.) n. (films) (The device, effect, of) making one shot dissolve into the next, growing less and less, while the new shot grows more and more, distinct.

distributism, n. [1. distríbūtizm; 2. distríbjūtizm]. **distribute** & **-ism**. Doctrine that the solution of economic problems lies, not in transferring ownership of land and capital to the state, but in distributing it from the few to all adult citizens.

distributist, n. & adj.[1. distríbūtist; 2. distríbjūtist]. prec. & **-ist**. **a** n. Advocate, adherent of distributism; **b** adj. of, pertaining to, distributism.

distributive, adj. Add: **3.** Distributist.

distributor, n. [1. distríbūter; 2. distríbjūtə]. **distribute** & **-or**. Person or thing that distributes; specif., (motor-cars) device which determines the order in which the plugs shall spark.

dog (I.), n. **1. a**; Add: *the dogs*, (slang) greyhound races or racing : *he's lost money at the dogs*; Add : **d** (Am. colloq., facet. for sausage-meat) *hot dog*, hot sausage sandwiched in bread. **2.**; Add: **c** (Canadian slang) side, swagger : *black sheep putting on dog*, swaggering Englishman who has had to leave England in disgrace.

doggone, attrib. adj. [1. dógon; 2. dógɔn], fr. the phr. *to go to the dogs*. (Am. slang) Accursed, miserable, confounded.

doing, n., in pl. Add : **2.** (slang) Casual and facet. substitute word for a thing the name of which one cannot, or affects not to, remember; what-d'you-call-it : *pass the doings to me*.

doll (II.), vb. trans. & intrans. from **doll (I.)**. *Doll up*, (slang) dress up in best clothes.

dome (I.), n. **2**. Add: **c** (slang, orig. U.S.) the human head.

dominant, adj. & n. Add: **3.** adj. & n. (biol.) (A Mendelian character) that prevails over a recessive and wholly or partially determines some feature of the organism.

dope (I.), n. See p. 1417. To **c** Add : *inside dope*, a tip from racing-stables or the like; Phr. *to spill the dope*, give inside information; *to upset the dope*, turn out widely, disconcertingly otherwise than as forecasted. Add : **3.** (U.S. slang) A senseless, idiotic person. **4.** (slang) Motor spirit.

double (III.), n. Add : **6.** A linked bet on two separate events, receiving heavier odds because of the greater risk to the backer.

Douglasism, n. [1. dúglasizm; 2. dáglǝsizm]. See **Social Credit**.

Douglasite, n. & adj. [1. dúglasīt; 2. dáglǝsait]. **1.** n. Social Crediter, q.v. Suppl. **2.** adj. Of, or connected with, the doctrine of Social Credit or with the Social Credit movement.

drain (II.), n. **1.** Add : Phr. *to go down the drain*, (slang) go from bad to worse.

draught (I.), n. **2. d** Add : Phr. *to feel the draught*, (colloq. & fig.) be in financial straits.

drophead coupé, n. (motor-cars) Coupé such that the roof folds down.

dust-up, n. [1. dúst úp; 2. dást áp]. See **dust (I. 2.)**. (colloq.) A commotion, disturbance, row, free fight.

Dutch treat, n. (U.S. colloq.) An occasion to which each of the party brings his own refreshments; *to go Dutch*, to adopt this arrangement.

easy (I.), adj. **2. a** Add : Phr. (slang) *easy on the eye*, pleasant to look at. **4.** Add : *on Easy Street* (slang, orig. U.S.).

eat (I.), **C. b** *eat up*; Add : also fig., to cover (distance or ground) rapidly: *to eat up the road*.

eats, n. [1. ēts; 2. īts]. (slang) Eatables.

ectogenesis, n. [1. èktojénesis; 2. èktoudžénisis]. **ecto-** & **genesis**. (biol.) A predicted method of generating and developing human embryos, not in the uterus, but in the laboratory.

ectogenetic, adj. [1. èktojenétik; 2. èktoudžənétik]. prec. & **genetic**. Of, pertaining to, produced by, ectogenesis.

edit, vb. trans. **2.** Add : **b** *to edit a film*, piece it together, cutting out superfluous strips and revising montage.

eidetic, adj. [1. idétik; 2. aidétik], fr. Gk. *eidētikós*, adj. fr. *eîdos* 'form, appearance', cogn. w. Gk. *ideîn* 'to see'. (psychol.) (of images) Reviving an optical impression with hallucinatory clearness.

elevenses, n. [1. elévnziz; 2. ilévnziz], facet. double pl. of eleven. (slang) Mid-morning refreshment, e.g. coffee and biscuits.

emmetropia, n. [1. èmetrōpia; 2. èmetróupiə]. Gk. *émmetros*, adj. '(being) in due measure', & Gk. *ōps*, 'eye'. Normal sight.

emulsion, n. Add : **3.** (chem.) Colloidal dispersion of a liquid in a liquid.

endocrinology, n. [1. èndōkrinóloji; 2. èndoukrinólǝdži]. See **endocrine** & **-ology**. (physiol.) The theory and experimental study of the internal secretions of the ductless glands.

engram, n. [1. éngram; 2. éngræm], fr. Gk. *en*, 'in', & **-gram**, fr. Gk. *eggráphein*, 'to inscribe, incise, engrave'. (psychol.) Presumed pattern of nerve-paths, due partly to heredity and partly to previous experience of the individual, and tending to cause specific behaviour; the physiological basis of a habit.

epicritic, adj. [1. èpikrítik; 2. èpikrítik]. See **epi-** & **critic**. (physiol.) (of sensations) Accurately localized and estimated; opposed to **protopathic**, Suppl.

epidiascope, n. [1. èpidíaskōp; 2. èpidáiəkoup]. See **epi-** & **dia-** & **-scope**. Instrument for projecting a magnified image of a small picture on to a white screen.

erg, n. Add : **2.** (technocracy) A proposed unit for measuring the value of commodities according to the amount of mechanical energy consumed in the production of them.

ergolatry, n. [1. ëgólatri; 2. ā̄gólǝtri]. See **ergon** & **-latry**. Idolization of work as a thing good in itself, whether directed towards a good purpose or not.

ergosophy, n. [1. ërgósofi; 2. āgósǝfi], fr. **ergon** & Gk. *sophía*, 'wisdom'. Wisdom in the systematic utilization of physical sources of energy.

escapism, n. [1. eskápizm; 2. ɛskéipizm]. **escape** & **-ism**. Escaping, tendency to escape, from unpleasant or intractable realities into fantasy.

escapist, n. & adj. [1. eskápist; 2. ɛskéipist]. **escape** & **-ist**. **a** n. One who has a tendency to escapism; **b** adj. having this characteristic or tendency.

exchange (II.), n. **2. b**; Add : *Exchange Equalization Fund* or *Account*, a reserve fund set aside and used by the Bank of England on behalf of the Treasury for stabilizing the foreign exchange value of the pound sterling, since the abandonment of the gold standard.

exhibitionism, n. [1. èksibíshunizm; 2. èksibíʃənizm]. **exhibition** & **-ism**. **1.** (psycho-analysis) Morbid eagerness to display one's naked body. **2.** Excessive propensity for focussing the attention of others on oneself.

exhibitionist, n. & adj. [1. èksibíshunist; 2. èksibíʃənist]. prec. & **-ist**. **a** n. One who is given to exhibitionism; **b** of, pertaining to, manifesting, exhibitionism.

eye (I.), n. **1. c** Phr. Add: *easy on the eye*, (slang) good-looking, of pleasing appearance.

face-lifting, n. See **lift (I.)**, Suppl.

fade, vb. intrans. **A. 1. b** Add : specif. (wireless) to become weaker through fading.

fade-in, n. (films) The gradual appearance of a new shot on the screen out of darkness into full intensity.

fade-out, n. **a** (films) The gradual disappearance of a shot on the screen from full intensity into darkness; **b** (colloq. & fig.) gradual withdrawal from publicity.

fading, n., fr. **fade**, Suppl. (wireless) The periodical weakening of tone experienced in reception, esp. on medium wave-lengths.

fall (I.), vb intrans. **B.** Add: *Fall for*, (slang, orig. U.S.) to fall a victim to, be captivated by, the charm, &c., of (a person or thing).

Fascism, n. Add : **2.** Any similar or comparable movement or tendency elsewhere than in Italy: *boiled-shirt Fascism*.

Fascist, n. & adj. Add : **3.** (Person) having convictions, sympathies or tendencies similar or comparable to those of the Italian Fascists.

favouring, vbl. n. (films) Regulating the volume of sound recorded, by movement of the sound-boom, e.g. towards the actor who is speaking.

finger-tip control, n. Arrangement of controls in a motor-car, such that they can be operated without removing the hand from the steering-wheel.

fit (I.), n. **1.** Add : *to throw a fit*, to be, to behave as one, shocked, infuriated, outraged.

Five Year Plan, n. (U.S.S.R.) Comprehensive scheme for industrial and general development of resources, to cover a period of five years; the first such scheme was begun in 1928.

flame (I.), n. **1.** Add : as interj., (slang) euphemism for 'hell'.

flash-back, n. (films) Episode beginning with a sudden change to an earlier point of time.

flat (II.), adv. **2.** Add : Phr. *to go flat out*, cp. **all-out**, Suppl.; *flat spin*, see **spin**, Suppl.

flick (II.), n. fr. *flicker*. (slang) A motion picture, film, cinema show; also pl.

flood-light, vb. trans. To illuminate (a building) with powerful electric lamps directed upwards and away from the spectator's eye.

flood lighting, n. The kind of illumination described in prec.

floor (I), n. **2.** Add : **b** the part of a film studio where the actors perform.

flop (I.), vb. intrans. **1.** Add : **c** (fig. & slang) to be a failure, a fiasco.

flop (III.), n. Add : *to go flop*, (fig. & slang) to be a failure, a fiasco.

fly (I.), n. **1.** Phr. Add : (slang) *there are no flies on* (a person), he is very active (and efficient).

for (I.), prep. **2.** Add : Phr. (colloq.) *to be in for trouble*, &c., *to be in for it*, (slang) *to be for it* [fór it], have trouble, punishment, a reprimand, in store for one; *to be out for trouble, for a row, &c.*, (colloq.) be intending to cause it; *to be out for* (anything), (colloq.) have it as one's aim.

free-for-all, n. Cp. Phr. *a free fight*, under **free (I. 9. a.)**. (Am. colloq.) A rough and tumble, a row.

Free Money, n. Money which, as advocated by Silvio Gesell, automatically depreciates in value at a rate approximately equal to the average rate of depreciation in the value of commodities.

frig, n. [1. frij; 2. fridž], slang abbr. for **refrigerator**.

front (I.), n. 2. Add: e (fig.) any sphere of conflict; f a coalition of political forces, united front: popular front (fr. Fr. *front populaire*).
fundamentalism, n. Add: c (colloq.) naïve adherence to traditional beliefs of any kind, e.g. to Free Trade.
futilitarian, n. & adj. [1. fūtĭlĭtárĭən; 2. fjŭtĭlĭtéərĭən]. Formed facet. fr. **futile** & **utilitarian**. (facet.) a (one who is) made arid by narrowly utilitarian aims; b (one who is) pessimistic in outlook.

gain control, n. (wireless) Volume control increasing and decreasing the amplification of a wireless receiver.
gangsterism, n. [1. gángsterizm; 2. gǽŋstərizm]. **gangster** & **-ism**. Gangster-like behaviour.
gat, n. [1. gat; 2. gæt]. Am. slang abbr. of Gatling-gun.
gate-crash, vb. intrans. (slang) To effect entrance to a dance, party or entertainment without invitation or ticket of admission.
gate-crasher, n. fr. prec. (slang) One who gate-crashes.
gee, interj. [1. jē; 2. dži]. Abbr. for **God** or for **Jesus**. (slang, orig. U.S.)
gel, n. [1. jel; 2. džel], abbr. fr. **gelatine**. (chem.) A colloid which, under suitable conditions, has set or formed a jelly.
genotype, n. [1. jénotĭp; 2. džénoutaip]. Gk. *génos*, ' birth, breed, &c.', see **genus** & **type**. (biol.) Hereditary genetic constitution of an organism.
gentleman, n. 4. Add: Phr. *gentleman's agreement*, a mutual understanding (i.) with no guarantee but the honour of those entering into it; (ii.) (euphemistically) with a more or less dishonest aim.
G-man, n. [1. jémàn; 2. džímæn], abbr. of **government man**. (U.S.) One of the American secret police.
Gesellite, n. & adj. 1. n. Follower of Silvio Gesell. 2. adj. Of, pertaining to, the doctrine of Free Money, q.v. Suppl.
gestalt, n. [1. geshtált; 2. gəʃtǽlt], Germ. ' form '. (psychol.) An organized whole in experience; chiefly used attrib.: *gestalt psychology*, a theory which explains psychological phenomena by their relation to organized wholes, at least some of which are immediately given in experience.
Gestapo, n. [1. geshtáhpo; 2. geʃtápou], abbr. fr. Germ. *geheime Staatspolizei*, ' secret state police '. The secret police organization of the Nazi régime in Germany.
get (I.), vb. trans. & intrans. A. 1. Phr. Add: *to get religion, socialism, films, &c.*, (colloq.) become preoccupied with. B. intrans. Add: 5. *Get!* (imperat., slang), abbr. for ' get along!' C. Add: *Get* (an idea, &c.) *across*, trans. (colloq., orig. U.S.) get the public to accept it. *Get away with;* b Add: *to get away with it*, (colloq.) perpetrate something impudent, forbidden or risky without being punished, prevented, reprimanded, hurt, &c. *Get off;* Add: d (slang, orig. U.S.) to go wrong, make a mistake; esp. *to tell someone where he gets off*. *Get off with*, (slang) to establish amorous relations with (someone); *get off* (of two persons), to get off with each other. *Get over*, Add: f *to get* (a thing) *over:* (i.) finish and have done with it; (ii.) get it across (as above, Suppl.).
getaway, n. [1. gétawā; 2. gétəweɪ]. **get (I.C.)**. (slang) Escape: *to make a getaway*.
gigolo, n. [1. jígolō; 2. džígəlou], Fr., formed fr. *gigole*, 'loose woman'. Male dancing partner, &c.
ginger (I.), n. 2 a Add: also attrib.: *ginger group*, a minority acting as a spur to a more passive majority.
give (I.), vb. A. trans. 1. Phr. Add: *not to give a damn* (*for*), (slang) not to care at all; cp. **care (II. 1. b.)**.

give-away, n., fr. **give (I.) C.** & **away**. (slang) a A betrayal (usu. unintentional) of something intended to be kept hidden from observation or knowledge; b an act of giving, or throwing, away an opportunity or something which should have been retained.
glacine, n. [1. glásēn; 2. glǽsīn]. See **glacial** & **-ine (VI.)**. a A substance similar in nature and use to cellophane, but semi-opaque and less glossy.
godbooster, n. [1. gódbōoster; 2. gódbūstə], fr. **god** & **boost** & **-er**. (U.S. slang) A minister of religion, a preacher.
godbox, n. fr. **god** & **box, 5**. (U.S. slang) A church or chapel.
gold bloc(k), n. Since 1931, the group of countries still on the gold standard, after Great Britain and many other countries went off it.
gold bullion standard, n. A modified gold standard whereby a central bank is obliged to exchange its notes only for bar gold (value about £1,560 each bar).
gold currency standard, n. The gold standard, in the strict sense.
gold-digger, n. Add: 2. (slang, orig. U.S.) (fig.) An adventuress who deliberately cultivates admirers for the sake of what money she can extract from them.
gold exchange standard, n. A modified gold standard whereby a central bank is permitted to base part of its note issue, not on its own gold reserves, but on foreign exchange of a country that is on the gold standard.
gold standard, n. a The monetary system by which a unit of currency is based strictly on gold, and a central bank is obliged to exchange its notes for gold on demand, and there is no restriction on the flow of gold into and out of a country; b loosely for *gold bullion standard* or *gold exchange standard*, q.v.
gong (II.), vb. trans. (slang, orig. U.S., of motor police) To notify (the driver of a motor vehicle) by signal that he must stop.
gongster, n. [1. góngster; 2. góŋstə]. prec. & **-ster**. (slang, orig. U.S.) Motor police officer who gongs people.
goo, n. [1. gōō; 2. gū]. (Am. slang) a Any sticky substance; b (fig.) sickly sentiment.
good (I.), adj. 1. Add: d *to be feeling good*, (slang, orig. U.S.) to be in good health and spirits. 2. b Phr. Add: *not so good!* (colloq. iron.) what a bad mistake, what a failure, &c.!
good looker, n. (slang) A handsome person.
good (II.), n. 4. (pl.) b Add: *the goods* (fig., slang) a The requisite qualities: *he has the goods*, is thoroughly well qualified and competent; b exactly what is wanted: *I tell you, it's the goods, he's the goods.*
gooey, adj. [1. gōōi; 2. gūi]. **goo** & **-y (IV.)**. (Am. slang) a Sticky, gummy; b sentimental.
goofer, n. [1. gōōfer; 2. gúfə]. **goof**, p. 1418, & **-er**. (Am. slang) Dupe; victim.
goofy, adj. [1. gōōfi; 2. gúfi], **goof**, p. 1418, & **-y (IV.)**. (Am. slang) Daft, stupid.
goo-goo eyes, n. (slang, orig. U.S.) Ogling.
goosey (II.), **goosy**, adj. [1. gōōsi; 2. gúsi]. **goose** & **-y (IV.)**. a. (colloq.) a (of persons) Scared, &c.; see **goose-flesh**, Dict.; b (of things) such as to make one scared, &c.
Gosplan, n. [1. gósplan; 2. gósplæn]. Russ., *gosudarstvo*, ' state '. (U.S.S.R.) State planning committee of the Soviet Union.
Gostorg, n. [1. góstorg; 2. góstɔg]. Russ., *gos*, abbr. of *gosudarstvo*, ' state ', & *torg*, ' trade '. State trading department of the U.S.S.R.
gracing, n., abbr. of **greyhound-racing**. (vulg. slang) Participating in, witnessing, greyhound races.
Greenshirt, n. One belonging to that section of the Douglasite movement which parades in green for the purpose of advertising the doctrine of Social Credit. Also attrib.

grid, n. Add: c specif., *the grid*, the system of overhead wires supported by iron pylons that distributes electric current from main generating stations to towns and intervening villages.
grill (II.), vb. A. trans. 1. Add: d (slang) to subject to intimidation and harshness, e.g. in examination of suspects.
grilling, n., fr. prec. & **-ing**. Process of being ' grilled ', as in prec.
grim, adj. Add: c (slang, usu. pred.) Rather trying, mildly distressing.
gripe (I.), vb. Add: 2. intrans. (fig., Am. slang) To complain, whine. Cp. **bellyache**, Suppl.
gripe (II.), n. 2. Add: b (fig., sing., Am. slang) a cause of annoyance.
gump, n. [1. gump; 2. gamp], fr. Mr. Gump, name of a butt in the comic papers. (U.S. slang) A fool, blockhead, noodle.
gut (I.), n. 2. Add: c pl. (Am. slang) Impudence, insolence. Cp. **nerve (I. 3. a)**.

hang-over, n. (slang) Unpleasant after-effects of alcoholic indulgence.
hard-boiled, adj. Add: 2. a (of persons) Shrewd, hard-headed, exacting; b (of schemes, &c,) practical, esp. in a financial sense.
have, vb. trans. A. (end of). Various Phrs. & idioms. Add: *to have a person on*, (slang) to deceive him.
have-on, n. [1. hǽvɒn; 2. hævɔ́n], fr. prec. (slang) An instance of having a person, or people, on.
hay (I.), n. a Phr. Add: *to hit the hay*, (slang) retire to bed.
hay-wire, adj. (U.S. slang) Crazy, mad.
headliner, n. [hédlainə]. **headline** & **-er**. (slang, orig. U.S.) A principal performer, e.g. in a variety entertainment.
Heaviside layer, n. [1. hévisīd; 2. hévĭsaid], fr. name of discoverer. See **ionosphere**, Suppl.
heeby-jeebies, n. pl. [1. hěbijěbiz; 2. hībĭdžībiz]. (slang, orig. U.S.) State of alarm and trepidation.
he-man, n. [1. hē mán; 2. hī mǽn]. **he** & **man** (pleonastic emphasis). (slang, orig. U.S.) A sturdy and virile man, attractive to most women.
het up, adj. [het áp], P.P. of **heat (II.)** & **up**. (slang, orig U.S.) Emotionally disturbed, agitated; esp., annoyed: *all het up*, thoroughly so.
high-hat, n. & vb. trans. (slang, orig. U.S.) 1. n. Supercilious person. 2. vb. trans. To talk (patronizingly) down to.
high-pressure, adj. b Add: intensive: *high-pressure salesmanship, methods* (of business).
high-stepper, n. Add: c supercilious, presumptuous person; social climber.
hiker, n. [1. hĭker; 2. háikə]. **hike** & **-er**. (colloq.) One who hikes, or is hiking.
hitch-hike, vb. intrans. To travel about with the help of lifts from motor vehicles.
Hitlerism, n. [1. hítlerizm; 2. hítlərizm]. fr. *Hitler* & **-ism**. See **Nazism**.
hock, vb. trans. [1. hok; 2. hɔk]. (U.S. slang) 2. Add: b To pawn, put in pledge.
hock shop, n. (U.S. slang) Pawn-shop.
-hog, element of abuse in slang compounds: *road-hog*, *speed-hog*. a n. one who selfishly and regardlessly drives a car at high speed; b vb. intrans. *to road-hog*, &c., to behave in such a way.
hokum, hocum, n. [1. hŏkum; 2. hóukəm]. ? fr. **hocus-pocus** & **bunkum**. (U.S. slang) Stale, outworn conventional situations and recipes for a plot, &c., in plays, novels and the like; esp. Phr.: *the same old hokum*.
homo, adj. & n. [1. hŏmō; 2. hóumou], abbr. of **homosexual**. (U.S. slang) a adj. homosexual; b n., a homosexual person.
hooey, n. [1. hōoi; 2. húi]. (slang, orig. U.S.) a **hokum** (Suppl.); b **boloney** (Suppl.)
hooky (II.), n. (slang, orig. U.S.) *To play hooky*, play truant.

hoot (I.), vb. intrans. **1. a** Add: Phr. *to hoot with laughter*, (slang) to laugh uproariously.

hoot (II.), n. Add: Phr. (slang) *not to care a hoot* (or *two hoots*), not at all; Add: **b** (slang) a reason for uproarious laughter, a great joke: *What a hoot!*

horn (II.), vb. Add: **B.** intrans. *Horn in*, (colloq. orig. U.S.) to intrude, interfere, butt in.

hot (I.), adj. Add: **7.** (mus.) Having an elaborate and stimulating jazz rhythm. **8.** (financ.) (of Treasury Bonds) Just issued. **9.** *Hot money*, (slang, orig. U.S.) dangerous, because connected with some crime or illegality.

hot-gospeler, n. [1. hótgóspelər; 2. hɒ́tgóspələ], fr. **hot** (5.) & **gospel** & **-er**. (U.S. slang) A revivalist preacher.

hound (I.), 3. Add: **b** In compounds, (U.S. slang) an uncomplimentary term for one who habitually hunts after a certain thing: *news-hound*, hunter after newspaper 'copy'; *publicity hound*, one who is always trying to get himself into the news; *smut-hound*, self-appointed investigator and censor of public morals; *sin-hound*, prison chaplain.

how, 4. b Add: also absol., (U.S. slang) *and how*, (yes) in the extreme, to a remarkable extent, on a big scale: *it was a swell party, and how.*

human, adj. Add: **3.** n. (colloq. & usu. in pl.) A human being.

(a) hundred-per-cent, adj. & adv. (U.S. colloq.) Complete(ly): *a hundred-per-cent he-man.*

hundred-per-center, n. prec. & **-er**. (U.S. slang) **a** Fervent American patriot; **b** whole-hogger.

hunky-dory, pred. adj. [1. húŋki dóri; 2. háŋki dɔ́ri]. (slang, orig. U.S.) Quite all right, fine, excellent.

hush-hush, adj., fr. **hush (IV.)**. (colloq.) Kept secret and so (sometimes intentionally) rather mysterious.

hypoplasia, n. [1. hĭpŏplázia; 2. hàipoupléiziə. See **hypo-** & **plasma** & **-ia** (anat.) Under-developed condition of any part of an organism.

immunology, n. [1. imūnóloji; 2. imjŭnɒ́ləʤi]. See **immune** & **-logy**. The study of immunity from disease, infection, &c., and the conditions governing it.

indicator, n. Add: **b** (chem.) A compound which by means of a change in colour indicates a chemical change.

integrated, adj., P.P. of **integrate**. (psychol.) Successfully combined, co-ordinated, into a whole; cp. **dissociated**, Suppl.

intelligence, n. **1. a** Add: *intelligence test*, (psychol.) supposedly scientific method of classifying persons according to their mental powers.

ionosphere, n. [1. ĭŏnosfēr; 2. aiɒ́unəsfiə]. **ion** & **sphere**. The ionized region high up in the stratosphere from which wireless waves are reflected.

iron (III.), vb. trans. **1.** Add: *to iron out*, (fig.) keep (e.g. prices) from fluctuating.

-ish (I.), Add: & adv. (of time, colloq.) round about: *4.30-ish*.

isolationism, n. [1. ìsoláshunizm; 2. àisəléiʃənizm]. **isolation** & **-ism**. A policy aiming at the greatest possible freedom for a nation from dependence on other nations, whether politically or economically.

isolationist, n. & adj. [1. ìsoláshunist; 2. àisəléiʃənist]. **isolation** & **-ist. a** n. One who advocates or adopts a policy of isolationism; **b** adj. of, pertaining to, isolationism.

isostasy, n. [1. ìsóstasi; 2. aisɒ́stəsi]. See **iso-** & **stasis**. (geol.) The hypothesis that between the land or water surface and the centre of the earth there is the same amount of matter under every unit of surface area.

isostatic, adj. [1. ìsostátik; 2. aisoustǽtik]. See prec. & **static**. Of, pertaining to, isostasy.

jerk (I.), n. **1.** Add: **b** (slang) *to get a jerk on* (*with* something), to hurry up, be quick (doing it).

jigger (I.), n. Add: **3.** (slang, orig. U.S.) Any appliance or mechanical device; a contraption.

jitters, n. pl. [1. jíterz; 2. ʤítəz]. *The jitters*, (Am. slang) 'the creeps', nervous fluster, trepidation.

job (I.), n. **1.** Phr. Add: *on the job*, busily at work.

kick (II.), n. **d** Add: Phr. *to get a kick out of something*, to find it stimulating, amusing, enjoyable.

knee-action spring, n. A type of independent motor-car spring.

knock-out, n. & adj. Add: **3.** adj. (in competitions) Such that a competitor or team defeated in any round does not compete again: *knock-out competition, knock-out system*.

kolkhos, n. [1. kólkos; 2. kɔ́lkɔs], Russ., abbr. of *kollektivii*, 'collective' & *khos*, base of *khozyaistvo*, 'household', &c. (U.S.S.R.) Collective farm organized, esp. under Five Year Plan, by pooling of peasant holdings. cp. **sovkhos**, Suppl.

Komintern, n. See **Comintern**.

Komsomol, n. [1. kómsomol; 2. kɔ́msɔmɔl], Russ., abbr. of *kommunisticheskii soyus*, 'union', & *molodyozhi*, 'youth'. (U.S.S.R.) Communist League of Youth.

kulak, n. [1. kŏolak; 2. kúlæk], Russ., 'fist, grasper'. (U.S.S.R.) Independent well-to-do peasant: a class 'liquidated' under the system of 'collectives'.

lattice, n. Add: **4.** The regular and more or less reticulate arrangement of atoms in a crystal.

Laurentian, n. & adj. [1. lōrénshian; 2. lɔrénʃiən]. **1.** n. A follower or ardent admirer of D. H. Lawrence. **2.** adj. Of, pertaining to, a Laurentian; tending to make a religion of primitiveness and sex.

lay (III.), vb. **C.** *Lay off*, trans., to dismiss (an employee) temporarily through slackness of trade, &c.

left-wing, adj. Of, pertaining to, the political Left; progressive.

lemon, n. **1.** Add: Phr. (slang) *the answer's a lemon*, the question is problematic; *to hand someone a lemon*, swindle him in a transaction.

libido, n. [1. libído, libédo; 2. libáidou, libídou]. Lat., see **libidinous**. (psycho-analysis) Psychic urge, vital impetus, total life energy.

lift (I.), vb. trans. **A. 5.** Add: **c** *to lift a person's face*, when the muscles of it have sagged, to restore it by surgical treatment to a more normal shape.

line (II.), n. Add: **17.** (slang, orig. U.S.) Information, special or inside information: *to get a line on*, obtain information about.

line-up, n. See **line (III. B.)**. (colloq.) Alignment.

liquidate, vb. trans. **1.** Add: **c** (colloq., orig. U.S.S.R.) to put an end to, suppress, stamp out (anything regarded as a public nuisance).

Locarno (agreement, pact), n. [1. lōkáhnō; 2. loukánou]. fr. the Locarno treaty of 1925. Any international treaty binding each of three or more nations to give full military assistance against the aggressor, in the event of one nation signatory to the treaty being attacked by any of the others; a regional pact: *an Eastern Locarno*, a treaty of this kind between nations in Eastern Europe.

location scene, n. (films) Scene produced not in the studio but at some chosen spot elsewhere.

logorrhoea, n. [1. lògōréa; 2. lɔ̀gouríə]. **logo-** & Gk. *rhoia*, 'a flow, flowing'. (facet. allusion to *diarrhoea*) Excessive flow of words; wordiness, verbosity, prolixity.

lorry-hop, vb. intrans. To travel by getting lifts on lorries and other motor vehicles.

lousy, adj.: Add: **c** (slang) *lousy with*, very well provided with; esp., *lousy with money*.

lowdown, n. fr. criminals' slang usage. (slang. orig. U.S.) True facts, correct information: *I'm giving you the lowdown*.

magneto-, pref. Add: *magnetometer*, instrument for measuring the strength of the earth's magnetic field.

make-up, n. Add: **d** components: *elements in one's make-up*, fundamental qualities of one's nature.

-making, adjectival suffix in compound with other adjectives. (Colloq.) Such as to make one this or that: *sick-making, shy-making*.

manage (I.), A. vb. trans. **2.** Add: **c** (financ.) *a managed currency*, one that is off the gold standard and for whose stability the central bank is responsible.

man-sized, adj. (Am. slang) Large, difficult enough to occupy or tax a man's energies: *a man-sized job*.

Marxian, n. & adj. [1. máhksian; 2. mǽksiən]. Next word & **-ian**. **1.** n. Follower of Karl Marx; adherent of Marxism. **2.** adj. Of, pertaining to, Marxism or Karl Marx.

Marxism, n. [1. máhksizm; 2. mǽksizm]. fr. Karl Marx (1818–1883) & **-ism**. The doctrine of Karl Marx concerning the materialistic (i.e. economic) interpretation of history, the class struggle caused by capitalistic appropriation of 'surplus-value', and the ultimate triumph of the proletariat, leading to a system of Communism.

Marxist, n. & adj. [1. máhksist; 2. mǽksist]. fr. prec. & **-ist**. Marxian.

matey, adj. [1. máti; 2. méiti]. **mate (II.) 1.** & **-y (IV.) a** (colloq.) Sociable, companionable, friendly.

mean (I.), n. **4. a** Add: Phr. *means test*, official inquiry as to what means of subsistence an applicant for unemployment benefit can already obtain from members of the family and household where he lives: *family means test, household means test*.

mechanization, n. [1. mèkanizáshun; 2. mèkənaizéiʃən]. **mechanize** & **-ation. a** Technical transformation, for the sake of increased efficiency, by substituting machinery for direct human effort; **b** (specif. the transformation of military units, re-designing them for mobility and resistance to gun-fire.

mental (I.), adj. **1.** Add: **c** (slang, pred. & often by hyperbole) mentally deficient, feeble-minded; stupid.

mezzo-brow, n. & adj. [1. métsōbrou; 2. métsoubrau]. (Person) intermediate between highbrow and low-brow (colloq.)

micro-waves, n. Radio-waves of wave-length less than 1 metre.

mike, n. [1. mĭk; 2. maik]. Slang abbr. of *microphone*.

mill (I.), n. **1. a** Add: Phr. (colloq.) *to go through the mill*, to be severely disciplined, to get a gruelling.

milling, vbl. n. **1. b** (colloq.) (The act of) being 'put through the mill', severely disciplined; a gruelling experience.

mind, vb. **B.** intrans. **1.** Add: *mind out*, (slang) look out, (and) keep (or get) out of the way.

-minded, adjectival suffix. **1.** (preceded by an adj. or adv.) Having such-and-such a turn of mind: *politically-minded*. **2. a** (colloq.) Alive to the importance of such-and-such: *air-minded*, keenly interested in civil aviation, &c.; **b** (commerc. slang) willing to pay money for such-and-such: *telephone-minded, refrigerator-minded*.

mitt, n. abbr. of **mitten**. (slang, orig. U.S.) Hand: *he gave me the frozen mitt*, shook my hand very coldly, shewed marked unfriendliness to me; *I tipped his mitt*, (i.) shook him by the hand; (ii.) (fig.)

mixing, vbl. n. (films) Re-recording such as to mix in, e.g., music with the actors' voices.

money, n. 5. Phrs. Add: *it's money for jam*, (slang) good remuneration or profit for little or no trouble; *to be in the money*, hobnobbing with the rich.

Mongolian, 1. adj. Add: **b** *Mongolian idiocy*, Mongolism.

Mongolism, n. [1. mónggolizm; 2. mɔ́ŋgəlizm]. **mongol** & **-ism**. A form of mental deficiency accompanied by physical resemblance to the Mongolian race.

monomark, n. [1. mónōmark; 2. mónəmāk], (trade name) fr. **mono-** & **mark**. Mark, consisting chiefly of letters of the alphabet, which an individual person can use in the place of a permanent address and for the identification of his belongings.

montage, n. Add: **b** (more strictly) cut, cuts, designed to elicit an emotional response not registered in the shots themselves.

motorize, vb. trans. [1. mótorīz; 2. móutəraiz], fr. **motor (I.)** 2. & **-ize** (esp., military units) To transform by substituting motor for horse transport.

mouthful, 3. (fig. & sometimes iron., colloq.) *To say a mouthful*, say something striking, important.

mud, n. Phr. Add: (person's) *name is mud*, (colloq.) he has lost any prestige, good name, credit, he once had.

museum-piece, n. **a** Valuable object in, suitable for, a museum; **b** (fig.) person or thing of special interest or value, esp. if not up-to-date.

nance, n. [1. nans; 2. næns], abbr. of next word. An effeminate male person.

nancy, adj. & n. [1. nánsi; 2. nǽnsi]. fr. the girl's name, Nancy. **a** n. An effeminate male person; **b** adj. of this nature; Phr. *a nancy boy*.

Nazi, n. & adj. [1. náhtsē; 2. nátsī], Germ. abbr. of *Nazionalsozialist(ische)*. **1. n. a** A member of the National Socialist party, formed by Adolf Hitler at Munich in 1925 with the aim of making Germany united and powerful after ridding it of Communism, Social Democracy, &c. Success in the election of Jan. & March, 1933, enabled this party to establish itself, ruthlessly sweeping away all opposition. Cp. **Fascist**. **b** A member of the actively pro-German party since formed in one of several other states, such as Austria. **2.** adj. Of, or pertaining to, the Nazis or their system, aims or methods.

Nazism, Naziism, n. [1. náhtsizm, náhtsēizm; 2. nátsizm, nátsīizm]. The political system, the aims or the methods of the Nazis.

necking, vbl. n. (slang) Hugging, petting (demonstratively).

neon, n. Add: *neon sign*, lettering, &c., usually forming an advertisement, lit up by means of neon light.

Nep, n. [1. nep; 2. nɛp], Russ., abbr. of *novaya ekonomicheskaya politika*. (U.S.S.R.) The New Economic Policy, permitting a controlled capitalism in certain trades, from 1921 till the first Five Year Plan; *Nep man*, private entrepreneur or trader under Nep.

nerts, interj. & n. [1. nërts; 2. nɜ̄ts]. Imitative (vulg. slang). See **pshaw**. **a** interj. **b** n. *nerts to you!* I (deliberately) say to you 'Nerts!'

neutrino, n. [1. nūtrēnō; 2. njūtrīnou]. **neutron** & **-ine (VI.)**; **b** (phys.) Electrically neutral particle having the same mass as an electron.

neutron, n. [1. nūtron; 2. njūtron]. **neuter** & ending on the anal. of **electron**. (phys.) Particle having about the same mass as a proton, but without electrical charge. It is thought to consist of a proton combined with an electron.

news, n. pl. Add: **c** anything that the public can be induced to read about in newspapers: *cats are news now; news value* (degree of) salability as news.

news reel, n. A talking-film giving items of current or recent news.

nitwit, n. [1. nítwit; 2. nítwit], fr. **nit negative** & **wit**. (U.S. slang) A dolt, blockhead.

no man, n. (Am. slang) An unobliging and contrary man, who refuses to join in. Cp. **yes man**, Suppl.

Non-co-operation, n. The Indian movement, led by Mahatma Gandhi, of non-violent civil disobedience to British rule.

non-skid, adj. Designed so as not to skid.

non-starter, n. [1. nòn stárter; 2. nɔ́n stắtə]. (colloq.) A person, or horse, that fails to start as a competitor in a race. Also fig.

nose-dive, nosedive, n. & vb. intrans. Add: **2. a** n. A débâcle, precipitate downward trend in fortune, &c.; **b** vb. to take such a downward trend.

nucleus, n. Add: **4.** (phys.) The positively charged central core of an atom.

nut, n. Add: **6.** (Am. slang) An idiot, dolt.

nuts, adj. See prec. & **nut**, 2., Dict. (slang) Cracked, crazy, dotty.

okay, adv. & adj. [1. ō kǎ; 2. ou kéi], = O.K.

oke, adv. & adj. [1. ōk; 2. ouk], abbr. fr. prec. (slang) Quite all right.

okey doke, adv. & adj. [1. ŏki dŏk; 2. óuki dóuk], fr. prec. & *doke*, meaningless rhyming syllable. (slang) Quite all right.

on (I.), prep. Add: **9.** At the expense of, **a** (financially): *have this one on me*; **b** (generally): *the joke's on him*; **c** *that's a new one on me*, is news to me (i.e. shows up my ignorance).

once-over, n. (slang, orig. U.S.) Cursory survey, hasty examination: *to give* (person or thing) *the once-over*.

one (II.), n. 2. Add: **b** *a one*, (colloq. & vulg.) an odd, strange, eccentric, person: *you are a one!*

one-track, adj. **a** (of railways, &c.) Having only a single line of rails; **b** (fig.) one-idea'd: *a one-track mind*.

one way, one-way, adj. Restricted to one direction: *one way traffic*, lit. & fig.

out for, to be. See **for**, Suppl.

outsize(d), adj. [áutsàiz(d)]. (of ready-made clothes; & gen., colloq.) Exceptionally large.

overcall, vb. trans. & intrans. [òuvə kɔ́l]. (in bridge) **A.** trans. **a** To outbid; **b** *to overcall one's hand*, bid higher than it justifies; also fig. **B.** intrans. **a** To outbid one's partner or opponent; **b** to overcall one's hand.

over-compensation, n. (psycho-analysis) Excess of compensation, often taking the form of an overbearing manner; see **compensation**, Suppl.

Oxford group, n. See **Buchmanism**.

Oxford-grouper, n. (colloq.) An adherent of the 'Oxford groups'.

panatrope, n. [1. pánatrōp; 2. pǽnətroup]. See **pan-** & **trope**. Electrical contrivance, consisting of pick-up, amplifier and loud-speaker, for making audible the sounds recorded on a gramophone record.

panning, vbl. n., abbr. fr. **panorama**. (films) **a** Sweeping horizontally with the camera to get a panoramic effect; **b** the visual effect so produced.

pansy, n. Add: adj. & vb. trans. & intrans. Also add: (slang) **2.** n. (fig.) An effeminate male person given to self-adornment. **3.** adj. **a** (of persons) Effeminate and given to self-adornment; **b** (of things) of, pertaining to, or in any way reminiscent of, such persons; chic. **4.** vb. **a** trans., also *pansy up*, to render (oneself or one's intimate belongings) pansy or chic; **b** intrans., with reflexive meaning.

pants, n. Add: **c** (slang, U.S. orig.) Phr. *a kick in the pants*, i.e. on the buttocks; but chiefly fig., (the administering of) a sharp check or rebuff.

park, vb. trans. Add: **3.** (slang) **a** To place a thing on one side or in some spot chosen for safety or convenience; **b** (facet., pretending that a person is an inanimate object) (i.) to leave (e.g. a child) in someone's charge; (ii.) to place in position, plant: *park yourself here*.

part-time, adj., Employed for, taking up, only part of the working day: *a part-time worker, a part-time job*.

part-timer, n. (colloq.) Part-time worker.

party (I.), n. **2. a** Add: *hen party, stag party*, party consisting entirely of females, of males; *petting party*, see below.

pass (I.), vb. **B.** trans. **5. a** Add: Phr. *to pass the buck*, hand on something embarrassing. **C.** Add: *Pass out*, (colloq.) (i.) to faint, become unconscious; (ii.) to become dead drunk; (iii.) to die.

peak year, n. A year for which statistics recording some selected data reach a maximum point as compared with surrounding years.

perishing, adj. Add: **2.** (colloq., in place of an expletive) Confounded, infernal.

perm, n., slang abbr. of **permanent wave** (colloq., hairdressing).

petting, vbl. n., fr. **pet (II.).** Caressing; *a petting party*, bout of caressing.

phase, n. Add: **4.** (physical chem.) One component of a heterogeneous mixture.

phenomenology, n. [1. fenòmenoloji; 2. finɔ̀minɔ́lədʒi]. **phenomenon** & **-logy**. A recent school of philosophical thought originating from Husserl, which claims to reject rational concepts and judgments and to start from reality as it appears in pure intuition.

phenotype, n. [1. fénotīp; 2. fínoutaip]. See (first element in) **phenomenon** & **type**. (biol.) The part of its hereditary constitution that an organism actually displays.

phoney, adj. [1. fóni; 2. fóuni], fr. **phone & -y (IV.).** (slang) Fishy, suggestive of foul play: *a phoney message*.

phut, adv. [1. fut; 2. fʌt], fr. Hind. *phaṭna*, 'to split, burst'. *To go phut*, become suddenly broken; collapse, end in nothing.

phylogeny, n. [1. fīlójeni; 2. failɔ́dʒeni]. See **phylogenesis** & **-y**. Phylogenesis.

physical chemistry, n. Chemistry interpreted in terms of physics.

pick (II.), vb. trans. **c** *Pick up*, 3. Add: **d** (slang) to take into custody, arrest. Add: *Pick on*, to single (someone) out and pester, badger (him).

pick-up, n. Device by which the sound-track on a gramophone record causes corresponding variation in an electric current in a loud speaker.

piezo-electric effect, n. [1. pīĕzō; 2. paiézou], fr. Gk. *piezein*, 'to press'. The production of an electro-motive force in certain crystals by means of pressure.

pink (VI.), vb. intrans. Imitative word. (of petrol engines) To make a metallic sound, caused by premature explosion; to knock (**B. b**).

pipe (II.), vb. **A.** intrans. **2.** Add: **d** Phr. (colloq.) *to pipe down*, become less cock-sure, less exorbitant.

plane table, n. **plane (IV.)** & **table**. Drawing board mounted on a tripod and used, e.g., by surveyors.

plate (I.), n. **7. a** Add: (iii.) Phr. *to hand someone something on a plate*, (fig.) surrender something gratuitously.

pointer, n. Add: **3.** *pointer* (*ad.*), (commerc. slang) Small advertisement indicating where a larger one is to be found.

pop-shop, n. (slang) Pawn-shop.

positron, n. [1. pózitron; 2. pózitrɔn]. *positive* & ending on the anal. of *electron*. (phys.) Positively charged particle having mass equal to that of the electron.

pot-bound, adj. a (of a plant) Suffering from insufficiency of space for its roots in a pot; b (fig.) suffering from lack of room to expand.

preselector gear, n. (motor-cars) Gearing device such that the gear about to be engaged is previously selected.

producer, n. 1. Add: c person who takes the initiative and financial responsibility in producing a film; cp. **director**, Suppl.

prom, n. abbr. of **Promenade Concert**.

protopathic, adj. [1. prōtōpáthik; 2. pròutoupǽpik]. See **proto-** & **pathos** & **-ic**. (physiol.) (of sensations) Not accurately localized nor accurately estimated; opposed to **epicritic**, Suppl.

pseudo, adj., fr. **pseudo-**. (colloq., of things material & immaterial) Not genuine, not real; sham, counterfeit: *all this panelling is pseudo*. Sometimes of persons; see **bogus**, Suppl.

punk (I.), n. Add: c adj. (slang, orig. U.S.) Rotten, worthless, no good at all.

put (I.), vb. A. trans. 1. Add: *to stay put*, (colloq., of a thing) to stay where, or as, it is put. C. *Put over*, Add: b trans., (colloq., orig. U.S.) to get the public to accept (an idea, &c.).

radio- pref. Add: b to wireless: *radiogramophone*.

radio, n. Add: c a wireless receiving set.

radio-gram, n. Colloq. abbr. for next word.

radio-gramophone, n. Combined wireless receiving set and gramophone with pick-up. (See **pick-up**, Suppl.)

rake-off, n. (colloq.) Pecuniary profit made illegitimately by one or more persons concerned in a transaction; also, middle-man's profit.

raspberry, n. Add: Phr. (slang, orig. U.S.) *to give, hand, (a person) a raspberry*, insult by a gesture of contempt.

ray (II.), n. 2. Add: *cosmic rays*, a penetrating radiation producing ionization and coming from an extra-terrestrial source.

reaction control, n. Device for increasing the receptivity of a wireless receiving set.

recordist, n. [1. rekórdist; 2. rikáudist]. **record (I.)** & **-ist**. Person responsible for everything connected with the audible part of a film during its production.

rectification, n. Add: 4. (elect.) The process of converting an alternating into a direct current.

reducing, n. See **slimming**, Suppl.

reflate, vb. trans. & intrans. [1. rēflā́t; 2. rīflḗit]. See **re-** & **inflate**. 1. trans. To increase (the amount of money in circulation) towards what it was before a period of deflation began. See **inflate**. 2. intrans. To increase the amount of money in circulation, as in **1**.

reflation, n. [1. rēflā́shun; 2. rīflḗiʃən]. **reflate** & **-ion**. Act or process of reflating; state of being reflated.

register (II.), vb. A. trans. 1. Add: c (i.) (of a film) To depict, express (usu. some emotion); (ii.) (by extension, gen.; colloq.) To express, represent.

relativistic, adj. [1. rèlətivístik; 2. rèlətivístik], fr. **relativist** & **-ic**. In accordance with the principles of, accepting the postulates of, relativity: *relativistic, as opposed to Newtonian, mechanics*.

re-recording, vbl. n. (film-producing) Changing the sound-track by mixing or by adding a voice or voices to it.

retread, n. & vb. trans. [1. rètréd; 2. rītréd], fr. **re-** & **tread (II. 2. c.)**. a n. Motor-tire the original tread of which has been removed and replaced by new rubber; b vb. trans. to furnish with new treads.

revisionism, n. [1. revízhunizm; 2. rivíʒənizm]. **revision** & **-ism**. Policy, advocacy, of revising something; specif., of revising (i.) the Versailles and associated treaties; (ii.) Marxism.

revisionist, n. & adj. prec. & **-ist**. (One who works, or is) in favour of revisionism.

rexine, n. [1. réksēn; 2. réksīn]. A type of imitation cloth used for bookbinding, &c.

rheology, n. [1. rēóloji; 2. rīólədʒi]. **rheo-** & **-logy**. The scientific study of the flow of liquids, gases and plastic substances.

ribbon development, n. The uncontrolled building of houses and shops along main roads, esp. those leading out of towns.

road-hog, n. & vb. intrans. See **-hog**, Suppl.

rod, n. 1. Add: e (Am. slang) revolver, gun.

roll (II.), vb. intrans. C. *Roll in;* Add: (slang) to pay a casual or unexpected visit, to arrive. *Roll up;* Add: 3. To keep a rendezvous, put in an appearance; to arrive (in large numbers).

rough-house, vb. intrans., fr. Phr. *a rough house*, see under **rough (I. 4. a.)**. To behave rowdily; to brawl.

roundabout, adj. & n. Add: 3. n. Arrangement of the roadways at a junction, such that traffic circulates in one direction round a central object or space.

routineer, n. [1. rōōtinér; 2. rūtíniə]. **routine** & **-eer**. One who is efficient in routine work, but, through lack of imagination and originality, is unable to deal with wide issues and great changes, and expects others to be like himself.

rubber (III.), vb. abbr. of next word.

rubber-neck, n. & vb. intrans. [1. rúbernek; 2. rábənek]. (slang, U.S. origin) a n. One who peers and pries about inquisitively; b vb. to pry, peer about inquisitively.

rubber stamp, rubber-stamp, n. & vb. trans. 1. n. a Ill-considered and quasi-mechanical approval or authorization; b a person who gives such authorization or approval. 2. vb. trans. To authorize, as if mechanically, without consideration.

rube, n. [1. rōōb; 2. rūb]. (U.S. slang) A rustic, country bumpkin.

sadist, n. [1. sáhdist; 2. sádist], fr. **sadism** & **-ist**. Person who displays sadism.

sadistic, adj. [1. sadístik; 2. sədístik], fr. prec. & **-ic**. (Characteristic) of, pertaining to, a sadist.

salariat(e), n. [1. saláriat; 2. sələériət], fr. **salary (I.)** & **-ate**. Salaried workers as a class.

sales-resistance, n. (commerc. slang, orig. U.S.) Resistance to salesmanship, refusal to buy or order goods, &c.

sanction (I.), n. 2. Insert: b (League of Nations) chiefly pl., measures concerted by League members against an aggressor nation, in order to coerce it into acceptance of arbitration: *financial sanctions*, restriction or cessation of loan credits; *economic sanctions*, restriction or cessation of trade with it; *military sanctions*, force, e.g. a naval blockade.

sanctionist, adj. & n. [1. sángkshunist; 2. sǽŋkʃənist]. prec. & **-ist**. (Person) advocating, supporting, sanctions as in prec.

sap, n. Abbr. of **saphead**.

scene, n. 4. a Add: in films, a shot, see **shot**, Suppl.

schadenfreude, n. [1. sháhdenfroider; 2. ʃádənfrɔ̀idə]. Germ. fr. *schaden*, 'injury', & *freude*, 'joy'. Malicious joy at the misfortunes of others.

schizoid, adj. & n. [1. skízoid; 2. skáizoid]. See next word & **-oid**. Mildly schizophrenic (person).

schizophrenia, n. [1. skìzōfrénia; 2. skàizoufrínia]. See **schizo-** & **phrenic**. Dementia praecox.

schizophrenic, adj. [1. skìzōfrénik; 2. skàizoufrénik]. prec. & **-ic**. Suffering from, liable to, dementia praecox.

scram, n. & vb. intrans. [1. skram; 2. skræm], fr. **scramble**. (U.S. slang) 1. n. A hasty departure. 2. vb. intrans. To depart hastily, esp. imperat.: *Scram!* off with you!

screwy, adj. Add: 3. (U.S. slang) Not quite right in the head, slightly mad. See Phr. *to have a screw loose*, under **screw (I.) 1**.

scrip (II.), n. Add: c Paper or token money issued not by a bank or by a state treasury, but by a municipality or by some organization for production and exchange, and backed not by gold but by goods. Also attrib.: *scrip money; scrip group*, group of persons using this medium of exchange.

sedimented, adj. [1 sédimèntid; 2. sédimèntid], fr. **sediment**. (chem.) Having formed a sediment.

seersucker, n. [1. sérsuker; 2. síəsəkə]. (orig. U.S.) A cotton material with rough surface.

send (I.), vb. C. Add: *Send over*, to broadcast, trans.

sense (I.), n. Add: B. In combination with another noun, intuitive understanding and good judgment in a particular sphere: *road sense*; but, for **horse-sense**, see Dict.

sensum, n., pl. *sensa*. [1. sénsum, -a; 2. sénsəm, -ə], Lat. (P.P. neut. of *sentire*, 'to feel'), 'a thing felt'; see **sense**. (philos.) (Term used for) the immediate content of sensation (to avoid pre-judging whether this content is mental or physical).

sequence, n. 3. Add: d (films) succession of shots together forming a main division of a film.

servo (-assisted) break, n. (motor-cars) Some form of break such that the motion of the car reinforces the breaking which the driver applies to the shoes.

set (III.), adj., 3. Add: b (slang, orig. U.S.) ready to begin; ready to start away: esp., *all set*, quite ready.

sez you, adverbial phr. [1. sèz yōō; 2. sèz yū], for *says* (i.e. say) *you*. (slang, U.S. orig.) (iron.) As you say, (but I doubt it, or I don't believe it); sometimes interrog.

shemmozzle, n. [1. shemózl; 2. ʃimózl]. (U.S. orig., slang) A rough and tumble, a row, an uproar.

shock-absorber, n. (motor-cars) A device for damping out excessive road vibration and counteracting the effects of axle movement.

shoot (I.), vb. A. trans. 4. Phr. Add: *to shoot down* (person or crowd), suppress, dispose of by shooting and killing or wounding; *to shoot down* (aircraft), bring down by gunfire; *shot down*, (slang, fig.) decisively defeated in an argument.

short time, n. Employment cut down to some fraction of full time, with a corresponding curtailment of wages.

shot (III.), n. 7. Add: c An example, short continuous piece, of cinema photography: *an unusually interesting shot*. *Long shot*, shot taken from long distance; *mid-shot*, shot taken from medium distance; *crane shot, zoom shot*, shot taken while the camera is moved by a crane; *model shot*, shot taken, not of the subject represented, but of a (small-scale) model of it. Add: 8. Phr. (colloq., U.S.) *big shot*, an important person.

show (II.), n. 2. a Add: (ii.) (colloq.) stage performance: *leg show*, revue, &c., in which the legs of the chorus are a prominent feature.

show-down, n., fr. the 'showing down' (i.e. showing face-upwards on the table) of the cards after bidding, &c., in certain card games. (slang) a Any test of real strength and backing in a struggle, e.g. between political parties. Phr. *if it comes to a show-down;* b a frank avowal of, or exchange of confidences about, personal motives.

snip (II.), n. Add: 4. (slang) A cert; see **certainty (2.)**, Dict.

siblings, n. pl. [1. síblingz; 2. síblɪŋz], fr. **sib** & **-ling (I.)**. (biol.) Offspring of the same parents.

sign, vb. B. intrans. 3. Add: b *sign in, out, off*, &c., sign one's name as being, going to be, in, out, away from, &c.

simp, n. (U.S. slang) Abbr. of **simpleton**.

sissy, n. & adj. [1. sísi; 2. sísi]. **a** n. An effeminate (male) person; **b** adj. of this nature.

skin game, n. Cp. **skin** (II.) 1. 2. (slang) Fraud, deception, swindling.

slam (I.), vb. trans. 1. Add: **d** (fig.) (Am. slang) To criticize, censure.

slant (II.), n. Add: 2. (slang. orig. U.S.) A view, opinion; cp. **angle**, Suppl.

slick, adj. 1. Add: **c** (of persons or things, slang) smart but unsound, specious.

slim (II.), vb. intrans. (colloq.) To practise slimming.

slimming, n. & adj. [1. slíming; 2. slímiŋ], fr. prec. (colloq.) 1. n. Measures, treatment adopted by a person, esp. through diet or drugs, with the object of making her, or his, figure slimmer. adj. 2. Of, pertaining to, slimming: *slimming diet*, &c.

slip (I.), vb. A. intrans. 2. *slip up;* Add: also fig., colloq.) to make a mistake.

slosh, n. Add: 2. (slang) A heavy resounding blow.

slosh (II.), vb. trans. Cp. **slop** (II.) & **slap** (I.). 1. *To slosh* (paint, &c.) *on*, (colloq.) spread it thickly, audibly (and clumsily). 2. (slang) To hit with a resounding blow.

smoke-screen, n. Add: 2. (fig.) Anything done or put forward as a blind, to conceal one's real aims and activities.

snack-bar, n. (Shop with a) bar or counter at which light refreshments are sold.

snap (I.), vb. B. intrans. Add: 6. Phr. *snap into it,* (slang, orig. U.S.) to make a vigorous start, act with decision, enthusiasm.

Social Credit, n. The mainly financial doctrine of Major C. H. Douglas. It claims that the potential abundance which industrial technique can now produce (with less and less labour) is 'the unearned increment of association', belongs to the whole community and ought to be made available to all as consumers, by certain changes in monetary policy, including the issue of National Dividends of Consumer Credit. See also **A + B theorem**, Suppl.

Social Crediter, n. Advocate, adherent of Social Credit; see prec.

sol (III.), n. abbr. fr. **solution**. (chem.) A colloidal solution.

solute, n. [1. sólūt; 2. sóljūt], see **solution**, (chem.) The dissolved substance in a solution.

sound (VI.), vb. A. trans. 1. Add: **b** transf., To explore (the upper air, esp. the stratosphere and tropopause; *e.g.* by means of a balloon fitted with automatic recording instruments, and ascertain its temperature, density, movement, &c., at different heights, latitudes, &c.

sound-boom, n., fr. **sound** (I.) & **boom** (I. 1.). (films) Apparatus for moving a microphone about as required during a shot.

sound-box, n. The part of a gramophone which contains the diaphragm.

sound camera, n. Camera which records the sounds on the sound-track of a film.

sound-head, n. That part of a film-projector which emits audible sound picked up from the sound-track.

sound-track, n. That part of a sound-film on which accompanying sounds are recorded.

sour (I.), adj. 2. Add: Phr. *to be sour on*, (U.S. slang) To hate, detest.

sour (III.), vb. 2. intrans. Add: **b** (fig.) *to sour on*, (U.S. slang) to change from liking to disliking (a person or thing).

sourtop, n. [1. sóuertop; 2. sáuətop], fr. **sour** (I.) 2. & **top**, 'head'. (U.S. slang) Morose, disagreeable person.

Sovnarkom, n. [1. sóvnarkom; 2. sɔ́vnākɔm], Russ., abbr. of *soviet, narod,* 'people', & *komissar*. (U.S.S.R.) Soviet of people's commissaries.

sovkhos, n. [1. sóvkos; 2. sɔ́vkɔs], Russ., abbr. of **soviet** & **khos**, see **kolkhos** 'farm'. (U.S.S.R.) State farm instituted on rationalized methods, esp. under Five Year Plan. Cp. **kolkhos**, Suppl.

so what? Phr. (slang, orig. U.S.) What of that? What has it to do with the matter in hand? What is the bearing of your remark? Has it any?

sozzled, adj. [1. sozld; 2. sózld]. Probably imitative word; cp. **soak** (I. B. 2.) & **muzzy** & **fuddle**. (slang) Intoxicated.

special, adj. 3. Add: *special areas,* industrial regions in a condition of chronic depression.

speed-cop, n. (slang, orig. U.S.) Policeman on the watch for offences against the speed-limit.

spigotty, adj. [1. spígoti; 2. spígəti], ? origin. (U.S. slang) Strangely interesting, romantic.

spin (II.), n. Add: 3. Phr. *to get into a flat spin*, (i.) (aeron.) to spin round horizontally without hope of recovery; (ii.) (fig. & colloq.) to get into inextricable difficulties.

stab (II.), n. Add: **c** an attempt: *to have a stab at* (something).

stag (II.), vb. intr. (Stock Exchange) To act in the manner of a stag; see **stag** (4., Dict.)

stag party, n. See **party**, Suppl.

stakhanovite, n. & adj. [1. stakáhnofīt; 2. stækánɔfait], fr. Stakhanov, a Russian miner who, in 1935, succeeded in increasing his individual output prodigiously. **a** n. One of those Russian workers belonging to a rank-and-file movement for the increase of industrial output through rationalization and individual initiative; **b** adj. of, pertaining to, that movement.

stamped scrip, n. Scrip money that has to be stamped at stated intervals (e.g. monthly) at a cost to the holder equalling its automatic depreciation in value; see **Free Money** & **scrip**, Suppl.

stand (I.), vb. C. *Stand off;* Add: trans., to discharge (an employee) temporarily, owing to slackness of trade, &c.

stay-in, attrib. adj. *Stay-in strike,* a strike in which the employees remain on the premises of the employers; *stay-in tactics.*

stick (I.), vb. A. trans. 2. Add: **d** (slang) to put; (gangster slang) *stick 'em up!* put up your hands!

stiff (II.), n. 2. Add: **b** A stupid or clumsy person; esp. *big stiff,* an utter fool or bungler.

still (II.), n. Add: 2. A single snapshot abstracted from a motion film and, in many cases, displayed as a photograph.

sting (I.), vb. A. intrans. 3. (fig.); Add: **c** (slang) to make (a person) pay an exorbitant price, to fleece.

stooge, n. [1. stōōj; 2. stūdž]. (slang, orig. U.S.) **a** (theatr.) Butt in slapstick comedy; **b** scapegoat.

storm trooper, n. Member of the semi-military nucleus of the Nazi party.

storm troops, n. 1. Military units reserved for arduous offensive engagements. 2. Body of storm troopers.

stratosphere, n. [1. strátōsfēr; 2. strǽtousfiə]. See **stratum** & **sphere**. The upper and more rarefied part of the atmosphere above the tropopause; see **troposphere** & **tropopause**, Suppl.

stroboscope, n. [1. stróboskōp; 2. stróbəskoup]. See **strophe** & **-scope**. A device for studying periodic motion by means of intermittent glimpses.

stuff (I.), n. Add: 4. (slang) In the phr. *to do one's stuff*, special accomplishment or subject; prearranged performance or harangue: *Now then, do your stuff!*

stylus bar, n. [1. stílus bàr; 2. stáiləs bà]. See **style** & **bar**. Rod conveying vibrations from the point of a gramophone needle to the centre of the diaphragm.

subotnik, n. [1. soobótnik; 2. subɔ́tnik], Russ., fr. *subota,* 'Saturday', & *-nik* (suff.). (U.S.S.R.) Labour freely given to the State on off days.

sucker, n. Add: 6. (Am. slang) **a** Ill-informed and gullible stock market speculator; *sucker list,* list of such people for the use of dishonest company promoters; **b** any gullible and easily exploitable person.

sugar daddy, n. (slang, orig. U.S.) An elderly man who takes about, or keeps as his mistress, a young woman and, consciously or unconsciously, allows himself to be exploited by her as a liberal source of revenue and luxuries.

sunk, adj. Add: 2. pred. (slang) Utterly frustrated, in a desperate situation or fix; *now we're sunk,* that finishes our chances.

super (II.), adj., fr. the prefix **super-**, (g & h). (slang) Excellent; unusually good, useful, clever, &c.

superhet, adj. [1. súperhet; 2. sjūpəhet], abbr. of *superheterodyne*, **super-**, (**h**), & **heterodyne**. (colloq.) Excellently heterodyne.

supraconductivity, n. Increased electrical conductivity at exceptionally low temperatures.

surrealism, n. [1. surēalizm; 2. sùriəlizm], fr. Fr. *surréalisme;* see **sur-** (II.) & **realism**. A recent movement in literature and art which originated in France. Its subject-matter is derived chiefly from 'the unconscious', even from dreams, and its emphasis on immediacy and spontaneity, with a minimum of conscious elaboration, makes it an exaggerated antithesis of academic art.

surrealist, n. & adj. [1. sùrēalist; 2. sùriəlist]. See prec. & **-ist**. 1. n. An exponent or adherent of surrealism. 2. adj. Of, pertaining to, or exemplifying, surrealism.

suspension, n. Add: specif., (phys. chem.) a liquid containing finely divided & stably suspended solid particles.

suspensoid, n. [1. suspénsoid; 2. səspénsoid], fr. **suspension** & **-oid**. (chem.) The disperse phase in a suspension.

swill (II.), n. Add: 4. (U.S. slang) *Swell swill:* (i.) Garbage the inspection of which suggests a luxurious standard of living; (ii.) excellent food and drink.

swish (III.), adj. (slang) Strikingly smart or stylish.

swop, **swap** (II.), n. Add: Phr. *to take a swop*, (commerc. slang) meet with a rebuff in salesmanship.

synchro-mesh, n., abbr. of *synchronized mesh*. (motor-cars) A device in the gearbox for making the gears engage automatically at their correct speed.

tabloid press, n. Contemptuous collective term for illustrated newspapers that give only scanty and compressed news.

Tass (II.), n., Russ., abbr. fr. *Telegraphnoye Agentstvo Sovyetskovo Soyuza.* (U.S.S.R.) Telegraphic Agency of the Soviet Union.

teaser, n. Add: 3. *teaser* (*ad.*), (commerc. slang) advertisement designed to stimulate curiosity by holding out hopes of a startling future announcement.

technocracy, n. [1. tĕknókrasi; 2. tèknókrəsi]. See **technic** & **-cracy**. A type of social organization, imagined and advocated by a group of Americans, in which engineers and technicians would exercise a decisive control of industry, maintaining output at the maximum in the interests of the public as consumers. See also **erg**, Suppl.

technocrat, n. [1. téknokràt; 2. tékn ɔkræt]. See **technic** & **-crat**. 1. An advocate of technocracy. 2. An engineer or technician, as controller of production in such a régime.

technocratic, adj. [1. tèknokrátik; 2. tèknokrǽtik]. prec. & **-ic**. Having the characteristics of a technocrat, or of a technocracy.

televisor, n. [1. télevīsor; 2. télivaisə]. See **television** & **-or** (2). Instrument for receiving audio-signals and converting them into visual signals.

tell, vb. **A.** trans. **3. b**; Add: Phr. *you're telling* me! (slang) don't, or there's no need to, tell me that!

thixotropy, n. [1. thiksótropi; 2. þiksɔ́trəpi], fr. Gk. *thíxis*, 'a touching', fr. base *thig-* in *thigánein*, 'to touch', cogn. w. *touch*, &c., & *-trope*. (chem.) Property of a substance, apparently a liquid, whereby it can pass from gel to sol on agitation, and back to gel on standing.

thrombin, n. [1. thrómbin; 2. þrɔ́mbin], fr. Gk. *thrómbos* 'a clot' & *-in*. (physiol.) The substance in the blood which causes clotting.

thrombopenia, n. [1. thrȯmbōpḗnia; 2. þrɔmboupī́niə], fr. prec. & Gk. *penía*, 'poverty'. (physiol.) Deficiency of thrombine in the blood.

throw, (I.) vb. **A.** trans. Add: **9.** (slang) To give (as a social gesture, e.g. a dinner, a cocktail party). Phr. *to throw a fit*, (slang) see **fit** (**I. 1.**, Suppl.).

throwaway, n. (slang) An advertising circular, leaflet.

throw-out, n. Article thrown aside, esp. in the factory where it is made, as defective or useless.

tiddly, adj. [1. tídli; 2. tídli]. (slang) Intoxicated.

tie (I.), n. **2.** Add: Phr. *the old school tie*, (fig. & colloq.) (i.) snobbishness of, (ii.) solidarity, freemasonry among, members of certain Public Schools, &c.

tie (II.), vb. **C.** *Tie up*, **3.** Add: Phr. *to tie* (person) *up* (*in knots*), (colloq.) put into (great) difficulties.

tie-up, n. (commerc. slang) Arrangement for the display of advertised goods simultaneously with advertisement of them in the press.

tightwad, n. [1. títwod; 2. táitwɔd]. **tight** (**6. b**) & **wad** (**I. 2.**). (Am. slang) A miser.

time-lag, n. Interval of time between one phenomenon and another which is associated with it or caused by it.

tone-arm, n. The part of a gramophone connecting the sound-box to the horn.

topliner, n. See **headliner**, Suppl.

totalitarian, adj. [1. tȯtalitárian; 2. tɔutælitɛ́əriən]. **totality** & **-arian**. **a** (concerned with) Arrogating (to the State & the ruling party) all rights and every liberty of choice, including those normally belonging to individuals and various corporate bodies: *the totalitarian State;* **b** conscripting a country's entire resources in population and material.

tracking, vbl. n., fr. **track (I.)**. (films) **a** Moving the camera nearer and nearer to, or further away from, the subject; **b** the visual effect so produced.

trafficator, n., abbr. of **traffic-indicator**. (motor-cars) Automatic red pointer for warning traffic whenever the driver intends to change direction.

trailer, n. Add: **4.** Parts of a forthcoming film shown on the screen at a public performance, to advertise the film.

tropopause, n. [1. trópōpawz; 2. trɔ́poupɔ̄z], fr. **troposphere** & **pause**. A belt of atmosphere, about two miles thick, between the troposphere and the stratosphere., i.e. from seven to twelve miles above sea-level.

troposphere, n. [1. trópōsfēr; 2. trɔ́pousfīə], see **trope** & **sphere**. That part of the atmosphere, which immediately surrounds the earth reaching up as far as the tropopause, and in which increase of height is associated with decrease of temperature; cp. **stratosphere**, Suppl.

turn (I.), vb. **A.** trans. Add: **11.** *To turn a film*, be responsible for the action of the camera in the production of a film.

trust (I.), n. **3.** Add: **c** *investment trust*, a joint stock company whose profits are drawn from investments distributed among a number of other companies and from the judicious buying and selling of investments; *fixed trust*, investment trust whose capital is permanently invested in a few securities.

try (I.), vb. **A.** trans. **6.** Add: **b** *to try* (a thing) *out*, (colloq.) (i.) test it thoroughly, (ii.) give it a trial.

try-on, n. [tráiɔn]. See **try, A. 4. b.** (ii.) (slang) An instance of 'trying it on', seeing how far one will be allowed to go in some piece of audacity.

try-out, n. [tráiaut]. See **try**, Suppl. (slang) **a** An instance of trying something out; **b** something that is being tried out.

turn-out, n. Add: **3.** (colloq.) Way in which, degree of smartness with which, a person is dressed and groomed.

twin, 2. n. **a** Add: *identical twins*, twins developed from the same fertilized ovum and therefore of identically the same genotype; *fraternal twins*, twins developed from different ova and spermatozoa and therefore of different genotypes, though from the same pregnancy.

udarnik, n., pl. *-niki*. [1. ōōdárnik; 2 ūdáník], Russ., *udar*, 'a blow', & *-nik* (suff.). (U.S.S.R.) Shock-brigader, usu. in an industrial sense.

ultra-short, adj. & n. See **wave-length**, Suppl.

unc, n. [1. ungk; 2. aŋk], slang abbr. of **unconscious** (q.v., 4., Dict.).

underworld, n. **3.** Add: **b** social circles in which obscure and possibly sinister moves, bargains, &c., are made: *political underworld*.

unstick, vb. trans. Add: Phr. *to come unstuck*, (slang) to get into difficulties.

up-and-up, n. Phr. (slang) *to be on the up-and-up*, to be succeeding, making progress, having a run of prosperity.

up-stage, adj. [1. úp stăj; 2. áp stèidž]. **up** & **stage**. (colloq.) Supercilious, standoffish, apt to give oneself airs.

vehicle, n. **2.** Add: specif., (chem.) medium in which a substance is dispersed to form a suspension or an emulsion.

virtual wealth, n. The aggregate of goods and services that a community theoretically could at any time exchange for the aggregate of its money.

Voks, n. [1. voks; 2. vɔks]. Russ., fr. *Vsesoynznoye Obschestvo Kulturnoy Svyazi*, 'All-Union Society for Cultural Relations'. (U.S.S.R.) Soviet-Union Society for Cultural Relations with foreign countries.

wad, (I.) n. **2.** Add: **b** (gen., slang) money.

waffle (II.), vb. intrans. Imitative word. (slang) To talk nonsense, blether.

walk (I.), vb. **C.** Add: *Walk out* (of an assembly), walk out ostentatiously to show strong disapproval or contempt. *Walk out on*, (slang, orig. U.S.) decamp, clear off, leaving (person) in the lurch. Cp. **on** (9., Suppl.)

water-waggon, n. Wheeled vehicle for carrying water; Phr. *gone on the water-waggon*, (slang, orig. U.S.) having forsworn all alcoholic drinks; for *on*, see **diet**, Dict.

-wave, suff., abbr. for **wave-length**, in the adjs., *short-wave, medium-wave* and *long-wave;* see next word.

wave-length, n. **b** Add: *long*, 600–30,000 metres; *medium*, 100–600 metres; *short*, 10–100 metres; *ultra-short*, 1–10 metres.

wave mechanics, n. A development of quantum mechanics in which matter is treated as a wave motion.

wet (I.), adj. Add: **4.** (slang) (of persons or things) Unacceptable, distasteful; foolish; sloppy, sentimental; *you're all wet*, quite off the track. **5.** n. (slang) One who is wet, as in 4.

whale (I.), n. Add: *a whale of a*, (slang, orig. U.S.) a very big: *a whale of a lot*.

whoopee, interj. & n. [1. wóopē; 2. wúpī]. (slang) **a** interj., expressing gaiety and exhilaration; **b** n. riotous gaiety; Phrs. *to make whoopee; whoopee period*, (U.S.) period of prosperity.

wide (I.), adj. **3. a** Add: (slang) *to the wide* (sc. world), utterly: *done to the wide*, utterly exhausted, done-for.

win (I.), vb. **B.** intrans. *Win back*, (colloq.) to recover lost ground by strenuous efforts.

window-shopping, vbl. n. & adj. (colloq.) Gazing at what is displayed in shop windows.

wipe, n. **1.** Add: **b** (films) (the device, effect, of) making one shot appear to be peeled off revealing another as if it had been underneath it.

wipe-out, n. & attrib. n. (wireless) **1.** n. **a** The effect which a wireless transmitting station has of rendering all messages on its own wave-length inaudible within a certain radius; **b** the zone thus affected. **2.** n. attrib.: *wipe-out zone* or *area*.

wise (IV.), 2. Add: (U.S. slang) *wise guy*, a disconcertingly, irritatingly well-informed or conceited person, one who 'knows it all'; a would-be-smart exposer of frauds; an iconoclast.

wise crack, wise-crack, n. & vb. intrans. **1.** n. **a** A witticism, a sententious, esp. a sarcastic, remark; **b** one who makes such remarks. **2.** vb. To make such remarks.

wish, n. Add: **4.** (psycho-analysis) An unconscious desire which is tending to translate itself into action through some bodily mechanism, but which may be diverted or inhibited.

wish-fulfilment, n. (psycho-analysis) Fulfilment of a desire, either in a dream or in phantasy as expressed, e.g., in some inadvertent gesture or verbal error.

wiz, whiz, n., prob. punning on **whiz(z)** & **wizard**. (U.S. slang) An expert.

wizard, adj., fr. **wizard (2.)**. (slang) **a** (of persons or things) Clever, ingenious; **b** (chiefly of things) fascinating, attractive.

wog, n. [1. wog; 2. wɔg], fr. **golliwog**. (slang) A negro.

wolf (I.), n. **1.** Add: Phr. (colloq. & facet.) *Who's afraid of the big bad wolf?* such-and-such villain or bug-bear is not so formidable as may appear.

work (I.), n. **5.** Add: **c** *a nasty piece of work*, (slang) an objectionable person. **9.** Add: **c** (gangster slang) *give him the works*, fire every cartridge in the revolver or gun at him.

worry (I.), vb. **B.** intrans. Phr. Add: *I should worry*, (colloq., iron.) should not mind, should be glad.

wuzzy, n. [1. wúzi; 2. wázi]. Muzzy.

X-unit, n. The unit, $10^{-11} \times 1$ cm., used for wave-lengths of X- and gamma-rays.

yen (II.), n. (Am. slang) A yearning, ambition: *a yen for knowledge, a yen to write*.

yes man, n. (slang, orig. U.S.) A man who lacks initiative and obsequiously assents to the opinions of others.

zip, n. Add: *zip fastener*, ingenious metallic attachment to clothing, &c., enabling it to be undone or done up with a single pull; Add: **b** (fig., slang) brisk energy or vigour.

zip (II.), vb. trans. & intrans. (slang) **A.** intrans. To dart, shoot; also fig.; Phr. *to zip across the horizon*, (Am. slang) come suddenly into fame, prominence, notoriety. **B.** trans. *zip up*, to put (more) briskness and vigour into (something).

zoom, vb. intrans. & trans. [1. zōōm; 2. zūm]. Imitative. (slang). **A.** vb. intrans. **1.** To climb vertically in an aeroplane. **2.** (fig.) To boom, make a great hit. **B.** trans. To boost, advertise by high-pressure methods.

zoom, n., fr. prec. Vertical climb in flying.